Worldwide Tax Summaries

Corporate Taxes 2012/13

Foreword

Welcome to the latest edition of *Worldwide Tax Summaries* (WWTS), one of the most comprehensive tax guides available. This year's edition provides detailed information on corporate tax rates and rules in 152 countries worldwide.

The country summaries, written by our local PwC tax specialists, include information on changes in legislation, residency, gross income, deductions, tax credits and incentives, tax administration, other taxes and tax rates. All information in this book, unless otherwise stated, is up to date as of 1 June 2012.

Our online version of the summaries is available at www.pwc.com/taxsummaries. The WWTS site is updated continuously and provides quick access to the latest information and changes. Some of the enhanced features available online include Quick Charts to compare rates across jurisdictions, and reference materials on OECD, EU, and WTO member countries, amongst other valuable information.

If you have any questions, or need more detailed advice on any aspect of tax, please get in touch with us. The PwC tax network has member firms throughout the world, and our specialist networks can provide both domestic and cross-border perspectives on today's critical tax challenges. A list of some of our key network and industry specialists is located at the back of this book.

I hope you will find these summaries useful, and please don't hesitate to contact any PwC specialist with comments or feedback on WWTS.

Rick

Rick Stamm
Global Vice Chairman, Tax
+1 646 471 1035
rick.stamm@us.pwc.com

Contents

Country chapters

Albania

PwC contact

Loreta Peci
PricewaterhouseCoopers Audit sh.p.k.
Blvd. Deshmoret e Kombit, Twin Towers, Tower 1, 10th floor,
Tirana, Albania
Tel: +355 4 2242 254
Email: loreta.peci@al.pwc.com

Significant developments

The double tax treaty (DTT) between the Republic of Albania and the Federal Republic of Germany has come into force from 1 January 2012, and a DTT has been signed with the Republic of Singapore.

Based on a recent change, non-resident taxable persons who are providing services related to immovable property located in Albania are liable to pay value-added tax (VAT) in Albania, regardless of the value of the services supplied, by appointing a tax representative in Albania.

Starting from 15 July 2011, taxpayers involved in business activities such as driving school services, city cleaning services, and fishing are allowed to credit VAT on the purchase of fuel used wholly and exclusively for their business activities, up to a limit represented by a certain percentage of the annual total turnover of the taxpayer.

Starting from 1 July 2011, the minimum and maximum monthly salaries for social and health contributions changed, respectively, from 16,820 Albanian lek (ALL) and ALL 84,100 to ALL 17,540 and ALL 87,700.

Starting from 24 August 2011, excise taxes on beer made from malt, either from local or foreign producers, changed. Details are included in the table below:

Amount (in hectolitres per year)	Previous excise tax (ALL/litre)	New excise tax (ALL/litre)
Up to 70,000	30	10
70,001 to 200,000	30	12
200,001 to 300,000	40	15
More than 300,000	40	30

Excise duty on heavy oil used as fuel (such as solar and mazut) rose from 20 ALL/kg to 37 ALL/kg, while excise duty on petroleum coke rose from 1 ALL/kg to 2 ALL/kg.

Starting from 24 August 2011, no custom duties are applicable on products such as leather used for clothes, cotton, viscose, velvet, sewing accessories, etc.

Starting from 6 December 2011, the minimum share capital required for joint stock companies increased from ALL 2 million to ALL 3.5 million. Joint stock companies established before the change are required to have completed the capital increase procedures by 6 December 2011. If the share capital drops below the minimum threshold set, the company should be dissolved.

Albania

Taxes on corporate income

Albanian law applies the principle of worldwide taxation. Resident entities are taxed on all sources of income in and outside the territory of Albania, while non-resident entities are taxed on income generated only in the territory of Albania.

The corporate income tax (CIT) rate in Albania is 10%. CIT is assessed on the taxable profits calculated as taxable income less deductible expenses.

Local income taxes
Entities with total annual turnover of lower than ALL 8 million are subject to local taxes on income.

Corporate residence

Based on Albanian legislation, a legal entity is deemed to be resident in Albania if it has its head office or its place of effective management in Albania.

Permanent establishment (PE)
PE in Albania means a fixed place of business where an entity carries out, wholly or partly, its business activities, including, but not limited to, an administration office, a branch, a factory, a workshop, a mine, and a construction or installation site.

The determination of a PE, where applicable, is based on the provisions of the double tax treaties (DTTs) that Albania has entered into with a number of countries. When dealing with DTT provisions, the Albanian tax authorities refer to the Organisation for Economic Co-operation and Development (OECD) commentaries.

Other taxes

Value-added tax (VAT)
The standard VAT rate is 20%, and the standard VAT period is the calendar month.

Taxable transactions include goods and services supplied domestically as well as goods imported into Albania by a taxable person. The following transactions are also taxable:

- Transactions performed for no consideration or for a consideration less than market value.
- Barter transactions.
- The private use of taxable goods by a taxable person (self-supply).

Determination of VAT taxpayers
Taxable persons are all physical persons and legal entities registered, or required to be registered, for VAT purposes.

The VAT registration threshold in Albania is annual turnover over of ALL 5 million (37,000 euros [EUR]). Any person providing taxable supplies and whose annual turnover does not exceed ALL 5 million (EUR 37,000) is not required to register, although voluntary registration is possible.

Albania

Taxpayers who, in the course of their business activities, provide services in any of the following listed professions are required to register for VAT purposes in Albania, regardless of their annual turnover:

- Lawyer
- Engineer
- Attorney (notary)
- Laboratory technician
- Specialist doctor
- Designer
- Dentist
- Economist
- Specialist dentist
- Agronomist
- Pharmacist
- Certified Public Accountant
- Nurse
- Approved Accountant
- Midwife
- Property evaluator
- Veterinarian
- Hotelier business
- Architect

VAT obligations for non-resident entities
Foreign entities not registered with the Albanian tax authorities, carrying out business activities in Albania, are subject to 20% VAT in Albania when services rendered are related to immovable property located in Albania. This is applicable regardless of the value of the services supplied.

In this case, the foreign entity is obligated to register and pay VAT in Albania by nominating a VAT representative.

In cases where the foreign entity is in non-compliance with the above requirement, the tax liabilities and respective penalties derived from such non-compliance should be paid by the local beneficiary of the services.

Reduced-rate goods and services
The supply of drugs and health services provided by private or public institutions are subject to a reduced VAT rate of 10%.

Zero-rated goods and services
The following goods and services are subject to 0% VAT in Albania:

- Export of goods.
- The supply of goods related to the international transport of goods or passengers.
- The supply of goods and services in relation to trading and industrial activities at sea.
- Services related to transport of goods and passengers.
- Services related to international telecommunications.

VAT-exempt goods and services
The following are considered VAT exempt:

Albania

- The lease of land.
- The lease of buildings (only if the rental period is limited to two months), except in cases where there is a contract between parties in which the supply is deemed as taxable.
- Provision of services performed by Albanian subcontractors relevant to the processing of semi-finished goods intended for export.
- Financial services.
- Postal services (only if the post does not import or carry out other postal services and its annual turnover doesn't exceed ALL 5 million).
- Gambling, casino, and ractrack services.
- Written media and books.
- Advertising in electronic and written media.
- Interest payments on leasing transactions.
- Export of services.
- The sale of land and buildings, although the construction process itself is subject to VAT.
- The supplies made against a reduced payment by religious or philosophical organisations for the purpose of spiritual welfare.
- The supplies of packages and materials used for the manufacture and confection of drugs.
- Educational services.
- Hydrocarbon operations.
- Supply of free goods distributed for emergencies.

VAT calculation

The amount of VAT to be paid is calculated as the difference between the VAT applied to purchases (input VAT) and the VAT applied to sales (output VAT). If the input is higher than the output, then the difference is a VAT credit which can be carried forward to subsequent months. Otherwise, if the output VAT is higher than the input VAT, the difference represents VAT payable to the state.

Taxpayers who carry out taxable VAT activities, as well as VAT exempt activities, can credit only that portion of their input VAT that corresponds to the VAT-able activities. To determine the amount of input VAT that can be claimed from the state, the taxpayer should estimate a VAT credit coefficient, being the rate of the taxable VAT activities over total activities.

Items of machinery and equipment imported by Albanian registered entities for their own use in the business activity (i.e. not for resale) are subject to a VAT deferral scheme under which the payment of VAT is postponed up to 12 months with a possibility of extension for an additional 12-month period.

VAT reimbursement

Taxable entities have the right to claim VAT reimbursement if the period in which VAT credits are carried forward exceeds three consecutive months and the total amount of accumulated VAT credit is equal to or above ALL 400,000 (EUR 2,965).

Following the request for VAT reimbursement, taxable entities have the right to obtain the reimbursement of VAT credit within 30 days after the request is submitted.

VAT returns

The submission of VAT returns and sales and purchase books must be done electronically by all taxpayers.

Electronic submission deadlines fall on the dates below:

- For VAT books, the deadline is the fifth day of the following month.
- For VAT returns and for the payment of the related VAT liability, the deadline is the 14th day of the following month.

VAT representatives are not subject to electronic submission of VAT books and returns. Instead, they are required to submit (by sending to the tax authorities through courier) only the VAT books and make the related VAT liability payment by the 14th day of the following month.

Customs duties

Albania uses the Harmonized Code System for tariff classification.

The custom duty rates range from 0% to 15%, depending on the type of goods.

Import of machineries and equipment for use in the taxpayer's business activity are generally subject to custom duties at the zero rate.

Custom duties on imports of vehicles are 0%.

Excise duties

Any individual, or legal entity (including their fiscal representatives), that either produces or imports into the territory of the Republic of Albania any commercial goods defined to be subject to excise tax, is subject to excise tax in Albania.

Albania levies excise tax on the following products:

- Beer: ALL 10/litre to ALL 30/litre, depending on the annual quantity in hectolitre (*see the Significant developments section*).
- Wine: ALL 20/litre to ALL 35/litre, depending on the annual amount in hectolitre.
- Other alcoholic drinks: ALL 100/litre to ALL 400/litre.
- Tobacco and its by-products: ALL 1,500/kg to ALL 2,500/kg, and ALL 70/pack.
- Liquid by-products of petroleum: ALL 20/litre to ALL 50/litre.
- Solid by-products of petroleum: ALL 5/kg to ALL 40/kg.
- Fireworks: ALL 200/kg.
- Pneumatic tyres: ALL 20/kg to ALL 40/kg for new purchased tyres and ALL 100/kg for used tyres.
- Incandescent lamps: ALL 100/unit.
- Plastic, glass, and mixed packages: ALL 100/litre, ALL 10/litre, and ALL 20/litre respectively.

Reimbursement of excise tax can be obtained on:

- The excise tax paid on fuel used by entities engaged in the constitution of energy resources with installed capacities of not less than 5 MW for both its own needs and for sale.
- The excise tax paid on fuel used in green houses as well as in production of industrial and agricultural products.
- Plastic, glass, and mixed packaging used as input in the local recycling industries of these materials are reimbursed 50% of the excise paid for the packaging.

Real estate tax

Entities that own real estate property in Albania are subject to real estate tax.

Albania

Real estate tax on buildings

Real estate tax on buildings is calculated based on the type of activity the business entity owning the building carries out.

Type of activity	Tax rate (ALL/sq m/year)
Buildings used for commercial purposes and the rendering of services	
Health, handicraft, social, cultural, educational, and scientific services	140
Production activities	140
Commercial and administrative services	200
Other buildings used for commercial purposes and the rendering of services	200
Other buildings not used for commercial purposes and the rendering of services (e.g. buildings owned by non-governmental organisation [NGOs] or foundations; damaged, amortised, non-functional buildings that are state-owned properties or privatised ex-state-owned properties in which no activity is performed)	50

Real estate tax on agricultural land

Real estate tax on agricultural land is levied on each hectare and varies depending on the district where the agricultural land is located and on the land productivity categorisation.

Stamp duties and notary taxes

There are no stamp duties on the sale contract of land or other properties. There are, however, notary taxes which are, in nature, similar to stamp duties. The notary tax on sales contracts that relate to change in ownership of immovable properties is ALL 1,000. The notary tax on sales contracts that relate to change in ownership of movable properties is ALL 700.

Depending on the agreement reached between the seller and the buyer, the notary tax can be paid either by the seller, or by the buyer, or shared between both of them.

Registration taxes

The fee for the registration of a business entity is ALL 100.

Branch income

Branch offices in Albania are subject to the same taxes as all other forms of legal entities.

Income determination

Inventory valuation

Inventory is valued at the end of each tax period using the methods stipulated in the Accounting Law, which should be applied systematically. The methods stipulated in the National Accounting Standards for the valuation of inventory at year-end are the average cost and first in first out (FIFO) methods.

Capital gains

Capital gains are taxed at the same rate as the company's ordinary business income.

Dividend income

Dividends and other profit distributions received by a resident entity from another resident entity or from a non-resident entity are not subject to CIT for the resident beneficiary of such income. This applies despite the participation quote (in amounts or number of shares) of the entity distributing profits in the shareholder capital, voting rights, or its participation in initial capital of the beneficiary.

Interest income

Interest income is taxed at the same rate as the company's ordinary business income.

Foreign income

Albanian resident corporations are taxed on their worldwide income. If a DTT is in force, double taxation is avoided either through an exemption or by a granting tax credit up to the amount of the applicable Albanian CIT rate.

Albanian legislation does not contain any provisions under which income earned abroad may be tax deferred.

Deductions

Depreciation and amortisation

Allowed tax depreciation and amortisation rates and methods for each category of fixed assets are shown below:

Asset category	Method	Rate (%)
Buildings and machinery and other fixed structures installed in the building.	Reducing-balance basis	5
Computers, software products, and information systems.	Reducing-balance basis	25
Other assets	Reducing-balance basis	20
Intangible assets (including goodwill and start-up expenses).	Straight-line basis	15

Land, fine art, antiques, and jewelleries are non-depreciable assets.

Depreciation and amortisation of fixed assets at amounts higher than those allowed for tax purposes is considered a non-deductible expense.

Interest expenses

Interest paid in excess of the average 12-month credit interest rate applied in the banking system, as determined by the Bank of Albania, is a non-deductible expense. The amount of deductible interest expense may also be limited by thin capitalisation rules (see Thin capitalisation in the Group taxation section).

Bad debt

Bad debts are only deductible if the following conditions are met simultaneously:

- An amount corresponding with the bad debt was included earlier in income.
- The bad debt is removed from the taxpayer's accounting books.
- All possible legal action to recover the debt has been taken.

This applies to all entities except those operating in the financial sector.

Albania

Fines and penalties

Fines and other tax-related sanctions are non-deductible expenses.

Taxes

Income taxes, VAT, and excise duties are non-deductible expenses.

Other significant items

The Albanian legislation also defines the following specific costs as non-deductible:

- Expenses not supported with fiscal invoices.
- Expenses paid in cash of amounts exceeding ALL 300,000.
- Benefits in kind and gifts.
- Wages, bonuses, and any other form of income deriving from an employment relationship and paid to the employees in cash.
- Provisions and reserves (with some exemptions applicable to the financial sector).
- Expenses for technical services, consultancy, and management received from foreign entities that are not registered for tax purposes in Albania and for which no withholding tax (WHT) has been paid by 31 December, at the latest.
- Losses, damages, wastage incurred during production, transiting, or warehousing, exceeding the norms defined by laws and related instructions.
- Impairment losses on fixed assets.
- Representation and reception expenses exceeding 0.3% of annual turnover.
- Sponsorship expenses exceeding 3% of profit before tax and sponsorships of press and publications exceeding 5% of profit before tax.

The amounts allocated to special reserve accounts in banks and insurance companies are deductible, provided that they do not exceed the limits stated in the Bank of Albania regulations.

Employers' contributions towards the life and health insurance of employees are deductible.

Net operating fiscal losses

Fiscal losses may be carried forward up to three consecutive years. However, losses may not be carried forward if more than 25% of direct or indirect ownership of the share capital or voting rights of the company is transferred during the tax year.

Albanian legislation does not allow losses to be carried back.

Group taxation

There is no group taxation in Albania.

Transfer pricing

Transfer pricing adjustments may be made if the conditions set in a transaction between related parties differ from those that would have been set if the parties were independent. In particular, the following are regarded as related parties:

- A legal entity and any person who owns, directly or indirectly, at least 50% of the shares or voting rights in that entity.
- Two or more legal entities if a third person owns, directly or indirectly, at least 50% of the shares or voting rights in each entity.

Thin capitalisation

The interest paid on outstanding loans and prepayments exceeding four times the amount of net assets are not deductible. This rule does not apply to banks and insurance companies.

Controlled foreign companies (CFCs)

There is no CFC regime in Albania.

Tax credits and incentives

The following entities are exempt from CIT:

- Legal entities that conduct religious, humanitarian, charitable, scientific, or educational activities.
- Trade unions or chambers of commerce, industry, or agriculture.
- International organisations, agencies for technical cooperation, and their representatives, the tax exemptions of which are established by specific agreements.
- Foundations or non-banking financial institutions established to support development policies of the government through credit activities.
- Film studios and cinematographic productions (among other types of entity/ activity) that are licensed and funded by the National Cinematographic Centre.

Foreign tax credit

Albania does not apply foreign tax credits except in the case of DTTs (*see Foreign income in the Income determination section*).

Withholding taxes

The gross amount of interest, royalties, dividends, and shares of partnerships' profits paid to non-resident companies is subject to a 10% WHT, unless a DTT provides for a lower rate.

The 10% WHT is levied on the gross amount of payments for technical, management, installation, assembly, or supervisory work, as well as payments to management and board members.

If a non-resident company does not create a PE in Albania, and a DTT exists between Albania and the home country of the non-resident company, the payment of WHT can be avoided.

Double tax treaties (DTTs)

Albania has signed 36 DTTs, of which 32 are in force.

WHT rates envisaged by applicable DTTs are provided in the following table:

Recipient	WHT (%)			Applicable from
	Dividends	Interest	Royalties	
Austria	5/15	5	5	1/1/2009
Belgium	5/15	5	5	1/1/2005
Bosnia and Herzegovina	5/10	10	10	N/A
Bulgaria	5/15	10	10	1/1/2000

Albania

Recipient	WHT (%) Dividends	Interest	Royalties	Applicable from
China	10	10	10	1/1/2006
Croatia	10	10	10	1/1/1999
Czech Republic	5/15	5	10	1/1/1997
Egypt	10	10	10	1/1/2006
Estonia	5/10	5	5	N/A
France	5/15	10	5	1/1/2006
Germany	5/15	5	10	1/1/2012
Greece	5	5	5	1/1/2001
Hungary	5/10	N/A	5	1/1/1996
Ireland	5/10 (5)	7	7	N/A
Italy	10	5	5	1/1/2000
Korea	5/10	10	10	1/1/2009
Kosovo	10	10	10	1/1/2006
Kuwait	0/5/10 (3)	10	10	N/A
Latvia	5/10	5/10 (2)	5	1/1/2009
Luxemburg	5/10	5	5	N/A
Macedonia	10	10	10	1/1/1999
Malaysia	5/15 (6)	10	10	1/1/1995
Malta	5/15	5	5	1/1/2001
Moldova	5/10	5	10	1/1/2004
Netherlands	0/5/15 (1)	5/10 (2)	10	1/1/2006
Norway	5/15	10	10	1/1/2000
Poland	5/10	10	5	1/1/1995
Romania	10/15	10	15	1/1/1995
Russia	10	10	10	1/1/1998
Serbia and Montenegro	5/15	10	10	1/1/2006
Singapore	5	5	5	1/1/2012
Slovenia	5/10	7	7	1/1/2010
Spain	0/5/10 (4)	6	10 (7)	4/5/2011
Sweden	5/15	5	5	1/1/2000
Switzerland	5/15	5	5	1/1/2001
Turkey	5/15	10	10	1/1/1997

Notes

1. If the recipient company owns directly or indirectly 50% of the capital of the paying company, 0% rate of the gross amount of the dividends applies. If the recipient company owns directly or indirectly 25% of the capital of the paying company, 5% rate of the gross amount of the dividends applies. A tax rate of 15% of the gross amount of the dividends applies in all other cases.
2. A tax rate of 5% of the gross amount of the interests applies in case of interests in a contracting state, which are paid to a loan granted by a bank or any other financial institution of the other contracting state, including investment banks and savings banks and insurance. A tax rate of 10% of the gross amount of the interests applies in all other cases.
3. If the recipient company or any other governmental body is resident of other contracting state, 0% rate of the gross amount of the dividend applies. If the recipient company (other than a partnership) owns directly or indirectly at least 10% of the capital of the paying company, 5% rate of the gross amount of the dividends applies. A tax rate of 10% of the gross amount of the dividends applies in all other cases.
4. If the recipient company (other than a partnership) owns directly or indirectly at least 75% of the capital of the paying company, 0% rate of the gross amount of the dividends applies. If the recipient company (other than a partnership) owns directly or indirectly at least 10% of the capital of the paying

company, 5% rate of the gross amount of the dividends applies. A tax rate of 10% of the gross amount of the dividends applies in all other cases.

5. If the recipient company (other than a partnership) owns directly or indirectly at least 25% of the capital of the paying company, 5% rate of the gross amount of the dividends applies. A tax rate of 10% of the gross amount of the dividends applies in all other cases.

6. If the recipient company (other than a partnership) owns directly or indirectly at least 25% of the capital of the paying company, 5% rate of the gross amount of the dividends applies. A tax rate of 15% of the gross amount of the dividends applies in all other cases.

7. A tax rate of 10% of the gross amount of the royalties applies, unless it can be avoided.

Tax administration

Taxable period
The tax year is the calendar year.

Tax returns
The final CIT return is due by 31 March of the year following the tax year.

Payment of tax
Predetermined advance payments of CIT are due by the 15th day of each month. Advance payments of CIT payable by the small business category are payable on a quarterly basis.

According to the tax laws, CIT is paid during the year on a prepayment basis. The amount of monthly CIT prepayments is determined as follows:

Years of activities	Period from January to April	Period from May to December
Year 1	Taxpayer's estimation	Taxpayer's estimation
Year 2	Taxpayer's estimation	CIT of Year 1 divided by months of activity in Year 1
Year 3	CIT of Year 1 divided by months of activity in Year 1	CIT of Year 2 less CIT prepaid during January to April in Year 2 divided by 8 months

Companies should decide on the use of their prior fiscal year after-tax profit within six months of the subsequent year and submit the decision to the tax authorities no later than 31 July. The decision should state the amount allocated as statutory reserve, the amount to be used for investments and/or for increase in share capital, and the amount to be distributed as dividends.

The final due date for the payment of the final CIT for a fiscal year is 31 March of the following year. Note that this payment is calculated as the total amount of CIT self-assessed from the taxpayer for that particular fiscal year less total CIT instalments paid related to that year.

Companies have the obligation to pay the tax on dividends to the tax authorities no later than 30 July of the year the financial results are approved, regardless of the fact of whether the dividend has been distributed or not to the shareholders.

Statute of limitations
With regard to Albania's tax administration practices, the statute of limitations of a tax audit is five years. However, the statute of limitations can be extended by 30 calendar days in cases where:

Albania

- a new assessment is made as a result of an appeal against a previous tax assessment
- a tax assessment is made as a result of a tax audit or investigation of the taxpayer by the tax administration, or
- the taxpayer is subject to a penal case related to one's tax liabilities.

Angola

PwC contact

Pedro Calixto
PricewaterhouseCoopers
Presidente Business Center
Largo 4 de Fevereiro n.º 3 , 1º andar - Sala
137. Luanda - República de Angola
Tel: +244 222 311 166
Email: pedro.calixto@ao.pwc.com

Significant developments

Under the ongoing Angolan Tax Reform, the following legislation was published in the Official Gazette:

- Amended Investment Income Tax (Presidential Decree Law nr 5/11): *See the Taxes on corporate income section.*
- New Stamp Tax Code (Presidential Decree Law nr 6/11): *See the Other taxes section.*
- Amendments to the Consumption Tax Regulation (Presidential Decree Law 7/11): *See the Other taxes section.*

Although only released at the end of February 2012, the Official Gazette dates back from 30 December 2011, and the changes now introduced are in force since 1 January 2012. Due to this time gap, the informal understanding of the authorities is that the changes are effectively in force since March 2012.

Some other very relevant tax changes are expected at the end of 2012, namely concerning corporate income tax (CIT) and employment income tax.

Taxes on corporate income

The standard CIT rate of 35% is levied on the taxable income of the following corporate income taxpayer groups (although, in practice, the last two are not applicable in actual Angolan economic reality):

- Group A - Tax is levied on actual profits as shown in taxpayers' accounting records (e.g. public and private companies, permanent establishments [PE] of foreign entities), adjusted accordingly with the provisions of the CIT Code.
- Group B - Tax is levied on taxpayers' presumable profit (taxpayers not included in groups A or C).
- Group C - Taxation is based on profits that taxpayers could normally earn/obtain (e.g. small family companies).

Resident entities are subject to CIT on worldwide income. Non-resident entities deemed to have a PE in Angola are subject to CIT on Angola-source income.

Special regimes, rules, and tax rates are provided for the oil and gas industry and the mining industry.

Exemptions from CIT are provided for:

- Agricultural companies (for up to ten years).

Angola

- Cooperatives.
- Culture associations.
- Non-resident shipping operators (as long as reciprocity exists).

Investment income tax (IAC)

Investment income tax (*Imposto sobre a Aplicação de Capitais* or IAC) is due on interest, dividends, royalties, and other income of a similar nature. In Angola, the IAC code divides such income into two taxable sections as follows:

Section A

Section A investment income includes the following:

- Interest on credit facilities.
- Interest on loans.
- Income derived from deferred payments.

Tax is due at the moment that the interest or income is earned or at the moment when it is presumed to have been earned.

Note that a minimum annual interest rate of 6% is deemed on loan agreements and credit facilities, except if another rate is proven through a written contract.

Section B

Section B investment income includes the following:

- Dividends.
- Capital remunerations of members of 'cooperatives'.
- Bond interest.
- Treasury bond interest.
- Interest on shareholders' loans.
- Income derived from profits of non public interest entities not collected until the end of the year.
- Gambling income.
- Royalties.

For the purposes of this group of income, note that:

- The concept of royalties includes the remuneration of any kind attributed to the use of or consent to use copyrighted literature; arts or science works, including movies and films or recordings for radio or television transmissions; patents; brands; drawings or models of a plan; formulas; or secret processes. The concept of royalties also applies to the use of or the consent to use industrial, commercial, or scientific equipment and information related to an experience acquired on the industrial, commercial, or scientific sector.
- A minimum annual interest rate equal to the rate used by commercial banks on credit operations is deemed interest for shareholders' loans.

Tax is due at the moment the effective attribution of income (dividends) is earned (interest) or paid (other income).

Exemptions
The following income is exempt from IAC:

- Interest on deferred payment of commercial transactions.
- Payment of dividends to Angolan CIT-payers that hold a share higher than 25% for more than one year.
- Interest from financial products approved by the Ministry of Finance that intend to encourage savings, capped to capital invested of 500,000 Angola kwanza (AOA) for each person.
- Interest from housing saving accounts intended to encourage savings for main permanent dwelling.

IAC rate
The IAC rate is 15%, except for the following income for which the rate is 10%:

- Dividends.
- Capital remuneration of members of 'cooperatives'.
- Bond interest.
- Interest from treasury bonds (or 5% for interest of bonds with a maturity equal to or greater than three years).
- Royalties.

Tax is withheld by the payer on Section B income.

For Section A income, tax is assessed by the taxpayer through a tax return to be filed in January of the following year. When the payment of that income is made to a non-resident entity, Angolan law provides that the tax payment obligation shifts to the Angolan resident entity paying the income.

Any IAC paid is regarded as a tax deductible cost and, in addition, 65% of that tax paid is deducted up to the CIT liability. The only exception will be any investment income tax paid on dividends exempted.

Corporate residence

Business entities with a head office or effective management in Angola are considered resident entities and are taxed on worldwide income.

Permanent establishment (PE)
Angola has not signed any double tax treaties, therefore its domestic tax provisions apply with regards to PE.

The Angolan concept of tax PE is inspired in the United Nations (UN) Double Tax Treaty Model. A foreign entity is deemed to create a PE in Angola if it:

- has a branch, an office, or place of management in Angola
- has a construction or installation site, or provides supervision over such site, only when such site or activities exceed a period of 90 days in any given 12-month period, or
- carries out services in Angola, including consulting, acting through employees or other personnel contracted for that end, when such services are provided for a period of at least 90 days in any given period of 12 months.

Angola

Other taxes

Consumption tax

There is no value-added tax (VAT) or sales tax in Angola. However, a consumption tax exists, which is similar to that of an excise duty. For goods imported or produced locally, the rates vary from 2% to 30%. For services, the following rates apply:

Type of service	Consumption tax rate (%)
Lease of areas designated for collection and parking of motor vehicles	5
Leasing of machinery and other equipment, as well as work carried out in tangible assets	10
Leasing of areas used for conferences, colloquiums, seminars, exhibitions, showrooms, advertising, or other events	10
Consultancy services, namely legal, tax, financial, accounting, IT, engineering, architecture, economics, real estate, audit services, and legal services	5
Photographic services, film processing and imaging, IT services, and construction of web sites	5
Port, airport, and custom agent services	5
Private security services	5
Tourism and travel services promoted by travel agencies or equivalent tour operators	10
Canteen, cafeteria, dormitory, real estate, and condominium management services	5
Access to cultural, artistic, and sporting events	5
Road, sea, train, and air transportation of cargo and containers, including the management of warehouses related to this transport, and passenger transportation, if provided in Angolan territory	5

For all the services mentioned above, the tax compliance obligations are the responsibility of the Angolan service providers, who can then add the tax to the amount charged to the acquirers. However, if the service providers are non-resident entities in Angola, the obligation will revert to the resident entities acquiring the services, if they are liable to pay CIT.

Customs duties

Duties are levied on imports at *ad valorem* rates varying from 2% up to 30%. The range of taxation for both consumption tax and import duties varies according to the type of goods. The rates are set out in the tariff book.

Listed equipment may be imported temporarily, if a bank guarantee is provided.

A 0.1% statistical fee and a 1% stamp duty is also due on importation plus custom fees (from 1% to 3%).

A special exemption regime applies for the oil industry for some listed equipment.

Stamp tax

Stamp tax is payable on a wide variety of transactions and documents, at specific amounts or at a percentage based on value.

Important examples include:

Type of operations	Stamp tax rates
On receipts	
Stamp tax on receipts (in cash or in kind) is still applicable.	The rate of stamp tax for receipts is of 1%.
Financial operations	
Stamp tax is applicable to financial operations, such as credit utilisation (and not only open credit accounts) and bond guarantees, interest and commission charged by financial institution, as well as foreign withdrawals, foreigner public debt bonds, foreign notes, and coins.	Credit facilities are subject to stamp tax on the utilisation of such funds, and, depending on the period, the rates of stamp tax will vary from 0.3% to 0.5%.
As a general rule, stamp tax is due for the entity that provides the credit and charge for the interest and commissions being then charged to the borrower or the interest/commissions debtor.	For regular credit, bank overdrafts, or credit where the period is not determined, stamp tax applies at a rate of 0.001%. Housing credits are subject to stamp tax at a rate 0.001%. Financial leasing on real estate and financial and operational leasing of tangible assets (maintenance and technical assistance included) are now subject to stamp tax at a rate of 0.3% and 0.4%, respectively.
Real estate operations	
Stamp tax is due on a paid acquisition of real estate by the acquirer.	Stamp tax applies on the acquisition of real estate at a rate of 0.3%.
Stamp tax is also due on letting and sub-letting, as well as on financial leasing of real estate, except when the leasing is for a permanent dwelling, which is exempt from stamp tax.	Stamp tax applies on the registration of letting and sub-letting contracts at a rate of 0.4%.
It is now clear in the law that tenants and sub-tenants are liable to stamp tax on letting and sub-letting.	
Corporate operations	
Stamp tax is due on the initial or increase of share capital, whether made in cash or in kind.	On share capital and increase of share capital stamp tax applies at a rate of 0.1%.
Insurance	
Insurance provided by national companies is subject to stamp tax, being the tax settled by the insurance company cost of insured person.	The stamp tax applies on the amount of premium paid, and rates may vary from 0.1% to 0.3%, depending on the policy's nature.
The commissions generated in the insurance mediation business will also be subject to stamp tax.	Commissions for mediation are subject to stamp tax at a rate of 0.4%.
Premiums and commission related to life insurance products, insurance against accidents at work, health insurance, and agricultural processing and livestock insurance are exempt from stamp tax.	

Angola

Type of operations	Stamp tax rates
Other operations	
In addition to the operations referred to above, the new table also refers the stamp tax applicable to written agreements, financial and operation leasing in tangible assets, custom operations, cheques, lending, civil deposits, gambling, licences, traders' books, deeds, report, credit bonds, and transfer of business, among other acts.	The following other stamp taxes are applicable: • Transfer of industrial or agricultural business: Stamp tax applies at a rate of 0.2%. • Stamp tax of 1% on the import value.

The following exemptions apply:

- Credit granted for a period of up to a maximum of five days, micro-credit, credit related to young accounts and old age accounts, and others of a similar nature that does not exceed the amount of AOA 17,600 each month.
- Credit derived from credit card utilisation, when the reimbursement is made free of interest, according to the terms of the contract.
- Credits related with exportation, when duly documented with the respective custom clearance.
- Amounts due on the mortgage for the acquisition of a permanent dwelling.
- On interest and commissions charged on financial operations, such as young accounts, old age accounts, and credits related to export under the terms mentioned above.
- Interest from Treasury Bonds and Angolan Central Bank notes.
- Commissions charged for subscriptions, deposit and withdrawal from units of investment funds, as well as the charges from pension funds.
- Commission charged on the opening and utilisation of saving accounts.
- Credit operations (including interest) for periods not exceeding one year, provided these are obtained exclusively to cover treasury needs, when realised between shareholders and entities in which a direct capital shareholding not lower than 10% is held and which has remained in their ownership for a year (consecutively), or since the incorporation of the respective entity.
- Loans bearing the characteristics of shareholder loans, including the respective interest, made by shareholders to the company in respect of which an initial period not shorter than one year is stated and no reimbursement is occurred before the end of that period.
- Treasury management operations, carried out between companies within the same group.
- Insurance premiums and commissions related to life insurance, work accidents, health, and agriculture and livestock insurance products.

Real estate income tax (IPU)
IPU is levied on rental income earned by individuals or companies owning real estate assets. It is based on actual rental income when the assets are leased and on the assets' registered value when the assets are not leased.

Leased assets
IPU is levied on rental income at a 25% rate.

The rental income is automatically reduced by 40% of its value, as it is presumed to finance all real estate related expenses.

Therefore, in practice, IPU applies at an effective 15% rate on rental income (i.e. 25% multiplied by 60% of rental income), with a minimum amount of 1% of the asset registered value.

A real estate asset is registered at the higher of (i) its valuation (based on criteria and tables to be published which will take into account the area (square metres) and the characteristics of the property) or (ii) the value of its latest transfer.

Assets that are not leased

IPU is levied as follows for assets that are not leased:

Patrimonial value (AOA)	IPU rate (%)
Up to 5 million	0
Over 5 million (on the excess) (1)	0.5

Notes

1. An asset registered at AOA 35 million will pay IPU only on AOA 30 million, resulting in an IPU payable of AOA 150,000.

Exemptions

The only accepted exemptions of IPU will be the following:

- State public institutions and associations that are granted with the public utility statute.
- Property of Embassies or Consulates of foreign countries, provided there is reciprocity.
- Religious temples.

Payment

Rents paid by Angolan entities (individuals or companies) that carry out commercial activity must withhold the 15% IPU from rents paid. The IPU so withheld must be paid over to the tax authorities by the end of the following month.

For any other cases, owners of real estate assets must pay the IPU in January and July of the following year. At the request (by July each year) of the IPU taxpayer, if approved, the IPU is payable over four instalments in January, April, July, and October of the following year.

Filing requirements

IPU Model 1 must be filed by IPU taxpayers each January, disclosing the rents effectively received in the preceding year, distinguishing the leases agreed and received.

Real estate transfer tax (SISA)

SISA is levied at a 2% rate for all acts that involve onerous permanent or temporary transmission of real estate. The value liable to tax is the higher of (i) the sale value or (2) the registered value.

Exemptions of SISA are only applicable to the following entities:

- State public institutions and associations that are granted with the public utility statute.

Angola

- Property of Embassies or Consulates of foreign countries, provided there is reciprocity.
- Religious temples.
- Real estate transferred for less than UCF 78,000 (currently UCF 1 = AOA 88) only when (i) at the first sale and (ii) for residential purposes.

Branch income

Branch taxable income is taxed on the same basis as separate legal entities. Income remitted by a branch to the head office is not subject to IAC.

Income determination

Inventory valuation
Inventory is valued at the historic acquisition cost. Any other method of valuation needs to be approved by the tax authorities.

Capital gains
Capital gains arising from the disposal of fixed assets are taxed as part of normal income.

Capital gains are determined by the difference between the sales proceeds and the acquisition value, deducted from tax deductible depreciation, adjusted by a devaluation coefficient.

Dividend income
Dividends received are exempt from CIT, provided that the share participation is owned for two consecutive years (or since the incorporation of the entity where the participation is held) and the share participation is not less than 25%.

Dividends from Angolan participations owned by insurance companies to fund their technical reserves are also exempt from CIT.

Interest income
Interest from public bonds is exempt from CIT.

Rental income
Rental income, as being liable to real estate income tax, is not liable to CIT. *See the Other taxes section for more information.*

Royalty income
Royalty income is taxed as normal income. Any IAC paid is regarded as a tax deductible cost and, in addition, 65% of that tax paid is deducted, up to the CIT liability.

Foreign income
An Angolan resident corporate income taxpayer is taxed on all its foreign income. Any income tax proved to be paid outside the country for activity carried on out outside the country will be credited against the CIT liability.

No tax deferral provisions exist in Angola.

Deductions

Depreciation

Depreciation should be computed using the straight-line method; any other method must be approved by the tax authorities.

The tax depreciation rates should respect the limits imposed by Government Ruling 755/72, and, in absence in this Ruling, the tax authorities interpretation, as follows:

Type of asset	Rate (%)
Office building	2
Industrial building	4
Computers	33.33
Office equipment	10
Furniture	10
Software	33.33
Light passenger vehicles	33.33
Start-up expenses	33.33

Depreciation not accounted for at cost is not permitted as a deduction in the following years.

Further, depreciation of land and goodwill is not accepted for tax purposes.

30% of the increase on depreciation resulting from a legal revaluation of fixed assets is not accepted for tax purposes, as well as the total increase in depreciation resulting from free revaluation of the fixed assets.

Interest expenses

Interest costs are accepted as deductible for tax purposes.

Bad debt

Write-off of debts is considered as deductible only if the write-off resulted from a bankruptcy court process.

Provisions

The only provisions accepted as deductible for tax purposes are:

- Doubtful debts within an annual limit of 2% of the client's current total account value and provided that a 6% accumulated provision limit is not exceeded.
- Inventory depreciation within limits that vary from 1% and 8% (annual and accumulated) depending on the nature of the company's activity.
- Those respecting the limits and rules imposed by the Insurance Supervision Institute for insurance companies, as well as the Central Bank for Financial Institutions.
- Provisions for possible losses resulting from a court process.

Charitable contributions

Donations are accepted as deductible up to a limit of 2% of the taxable income if the donations are granted to Angolan education, science, charity, and cultural institutes. If granted to Angolan government, central and local administration bodies, the donations are fully deductible.

Angola

Fines and penalties
Fines and penalties are not accepted for tax purposes.

Net operating losses
Tax losses are deductible from the taxable income of the following three years. Carryback of losses is not allowed.

Payments to foreign affiliates
Payments to foreign affiliates are accepted for tax purposes, although the arm's-length principle should be respected.

Group taxation

There are no special rules for group taxation in Angola.

Transfer pricing
Despite the existence of the arm's-length principle in Angolan corporate tax law, there are no detailed regulations on transfer pricing. Taxpayers should be aware that, in light of existing generic rules included in the corporate tax code, the tax authorities do have means to adjust inter-company charges.

Thin capitalisation
There are no thin capitalisation rules in Angola.

Tax credits and incentives

Foreign tax credit
Any income tax proved to be paid outside the country for activity carried out outside the country will be credit against the CIT liability.

Investment incentives
Profits retained and then reinvested by the company in new installations or equipment during the following three financial years may be deductible from taxable income during the following three years after the investment is finalised. Note that this benefit is not yet regulated.

Special regulations also provide tax and customs incentives for investment projects in strategic economic development areas and sectors. One such incentive can provide up to 15 years of CIT exemption.

Withholding taxes

Withholding tax (WHT) is applicable on payments for services provided to Angolan entities. For Angolan taxpayers, this is regarded as an advance payment of the CIT due at the year-end. For non-resident companies, this is a final tax.

The payments subject to this WHT are those related to:

- Construction, improvement, repair, or conservation of immovable property withheld at a rate of 3.5% on the gross payments (CIT rate of 35% applicable on a 10% deemed margin).

A

- Other services, namely technical assistance and management fees, withheld at a rate of 5.25% on the gross payments (CIT rate of 35% applicable on a 15% deemed margin).

Due to the IAC, Angola does not have a separate WHT for dividends, interest, and royalties (*see the Taxes on corporate income section for more information*).

Tax administration

Taxable period
The tax year follows the calendar year.

Tax returns
The annual corporate tax return must be submitted by the last business day of May of the year following the year to which the income relates.

Payment of tax
Tax is paid in four instalments. The first three correspond to advance payments based on the expected tax to be paid or, if unknown at that date, 75% of the taxable income computed on the previous year multiplied by the tax rate (35%). The instalments are paid in January, February, and March, and the final instalment is paid with the submission of the annual tax return on the last business day of May.

Audit cycle
There are no specific provisions related to the audit process in Angola.

Statute of limitations
The statute of limitations in Angola is five years.

Antigua and Barbuda

PwC contact

Charles Walwyn
PricewaterhouseCoopers
11 Old Parham Road
St. John's, Antigua
Tel: +1 268 462 3000 ext. 121
Email: charles.walwyn@ag.pwc.com

Significant developments

On 1 January 2012, the Antigua and Barbuda Sales Tax (ABST) rate on hotel accommodation increased from the transitional rate of 10.5% to 12.5%. ABST is a value-added tax (VAT).

Taxes on corporate income

Companies incorporated in Antigua and Barbuda pay corporate income tax (CIT) on their worldwide income, with relief available under existing double taxation agreements (DTAs). Non-resident companies deriving income from Antigua and Barbuda are liable for CIT and should be registered if they have a physical presence in Antigua and Barbuda.

Antigua and Barbuda imposes a flat CIT rate of 25%.

Taxable income or chargeable income is ascertained by deducting from income all expenses that are wholly and exclusively incurred during the year in the production of the income. Chargeable income is normally arrived at by adjusting the net profit per the financial statements for non-taxable income, non-deductible expenses, and prior period losses up to 50% of chargeable income.

Where a person resident in Antigua and Barbuda makes to another person not resident in Antigua and Barbuda a payment which the payor is entitled to deduct in arriving at chargeable income, then a withholding tax (WHT) must be deducted. In addition, if the income received by the non-resident person would have been subject to tax under the Income Tax Act, then WHT must be deducted by the payor.

Reduced CIT rate for certain financial institutions
Financial institutions licensed under the Banking Act that maintain, throughout the tax year, residential mortgage rates at or below 7% are subject to a reduced CIT rate of 22.5%.

Corporate residence

A corporation is deemed to be a resident if it is incorporated in Antigua, if it is registered as an external company doing business in Antigua, or if the central management and control of its business are exercised in Antigua.

Permanent establishment (PE)
A PE is not defined in the Income Tax Act; however, any company which would meet the general definition of a PE must be registered.

Other taxes

Value-added tax (VAT)

Antigua and Barbuda Sales Tax (ABST) is a VAT applicable to a wide range of goods and services. The standard rate is 15%, and hotel accommodation carries a transitional rate of 12.5% (10.5% prior to 1 January 2012).

A number of services, including financial services, local transportation, sale of residential land, education, long-term accommodation (greater than 45 days), and medical and veterinary services, are exempt from ABST. Certain supplies are zero-rated, including exports, basic food items, water, electricity for residential use, sale of new residential property, construction of new residential premises, and fuel. Intergroup transactions are taxable.

A period in the ABST Act represent one month. The threshold for registration is 300,000 East Caribbean dollars (XCD) in taxable activity per 12-month period.

Customs duties

All imports are subject to customs duties, ABST, Antigua and Barbuda Revenue Recovery Charge, and an environmental levy. In all instances, certain exemptions will apply.

Customs duty is levied on a wide range of imported goods at rates from 0% to 70% as specified in the Custom Duties Act. Customs duty is levied on goods based on the cost, insurance, and freight (CIF) values and rates determined by the Caribbean Community (CARICOM) Common External Tariff.

Antigua and Barbuda Revenue Recovery Charge

Antigua and Barbuda Revenue Recovery Charge is applied at a flat rate of 10% on the CIF value on all goods imported into or produced in Antigua and Barbuda. Exemptions will include entities with which the government has International Assistance Agreements, certain government entities, and most supplies or imports of fuel.

Property taxes

Property tax is levied annually at graduated rates on the basis of the market value of real property (as assessed by the Property Valuation Department) and its use (residential or commercial).

Property tax rates are as follows:

- Agricultural land 0.10%.
- Residential land 0.20%.
- Residential building 0.30%.
- Buildings classified as other property 0.50%.
- Land classified as other property 0.40%.

Allowances and tax rebates are available as follows:

- 5% rebate for payment of tax on or before the due date.
- Between 25% and 100% tax rebate available for special development property and property for public use; 25% for hotels.

Antigua and Barbuda

Non-citizens undeveloped land tax

Undeveloped land tax is levied on the basis of the value of land owned by non-citizens which has not been developed.

Rates of tax are as follows:

- Second year of ownership: 5%
- Third year of ownership: 15%
- Fourth and subsequent years of ownership: 20%

Stamp tax

Stamp tax applies to a very wide range of transactions (e.g. bill of sale, leases, mortgages, contract, bill of lading). Stamp tax on transfer of real property and shares are specifically covered below.

Transfer of real property

Stamp tax is imposed on both the buyer and the seller and is levied on the consideration for the sale or the value of property as assessed by the Chief Valuation Officer, whichever is higher. The stamp tax for vendors is 7.5%, and the stamp tax for purchasers is 2.5%.

Non-citizens vendors are required to pay a land value appreciation tax at the rate of 5%, which is assessed on the difference between the value of property when purchased, plus improvements, and the value of property at the time of sale.

Non-citizens purchasers are also required to pay 5% of the value of property with reference to a non-citizens license required to hold property in Antigua and Barbuda.

Transfer of shares

Stamp tax is imposed on both the buyer and the seller and is levied on the market value of the shares or book value of the shares, whichever is higher. The stamp tax for vendors is 5%, and the stamp tax for purchasers is 2.5%.

A non-citizen must obtain a licence (at a cost of XCD 400) to hold shares or be a director in a company that owns land or has a lease on land in excess of five acres for a period greater than five years.

Environmental levy

Environmental levy is calculated based on dollar value rates from XCD 0.25 to XCD 2,000 and is used to finance the cost of protecting and preserving the environment.

Life insurance premium tax

A premium tax of 3% is levied on the premium income (net of agent's commission) of all life insurance companies, whether resident or non-resident.

General insurance premium tax

A premium tax of 3% is levied on the premium income, excluding motor business (net of agent's commission), of all general insurance companies, whether resident or non-resident.

Branch income

Branch income is taxed on the same basis and at the same rate as that of corporations. A resident branch of a foreign company shall be regarded as a separate company and shall be taxed on the same basis as that of a locally registered corporation.

Recharges of expenses from head office to the branch are subject to WHT at a rate of 25%. The recharges have to be justifiable, consistent, and cannot just be based on a percentage allocation.

Income determination

Inventory valuation

Inventories are generally stated at the lower of cost or net realisable value. First in first out (FIFO) and average cost methods of valuation are generally used for book and tax purposes. However, the Commissioner of Inland Revenue will normally accept a method of valuation that conforms to standard accounting practice in the trade concerned. Last in first out (LIFO) is not permitted for tax or book purposes.

Capital gains

Capital gains are not subject to tax in Antigua and Barbuda.

Dividend income

Dividends received by a company resident in Antigua from another company resident in Antigua are taxed at the CIT rate of 25%. Credit is given to the recipient for the tax already paid on the dividend in computing the tax liability.

Stock dividends

An Antiguan corporation may distribute a tax-free stock dividend proportionately to all shareholders.

Interest income

Interest income received by a company registered in Antigua is taxed at the CIT rate of 25%. Interest earned on local and other CARICOM government securities are normally exempt from the payment of CIT.

Foreign income

An Antiguan corporation is taxed on foreign branch income as earned and on foreign dividends as received. Double taxation is avoided by means of foreign tax credits where active tax treaties exist and through deduction of foreign income taxes in other cases (the United Kingdom [UK] and CARICOM). There is also relief from British Commonwealth taxes. *See Foreign tax credit in the Tax credits and incentives section for more information.*

Deductions

Depreciation

Depreciation allowed for tax purposes is computed by the diminishing-balance method at prescribed rates (*see table below*). Initial allowances are granted on industrial buildings and on capital expenditures incurred on plant and machinery by a person carrying on a trade or undertaking, as defined. In addition, an annual allowance of

Antigua and Barbuda

2% is granted on all buildings. Conformity between book and tax depreciation is not required.

Any gain on the sale of depreciated assets is taxable as ordinary income up to the amount of tax depreciation recaptured.

Assets	Depreciation rate (%)
Building, roads, fencing, and pavements	2
Plant and machinery, generators	10
Furniture, fixtures, fittings, and equipment	10
Air conditioning units	12.5
Motor vehicles	20
Computer hardware, accessories, and software	33.33

Goodwill
Goodwill and trademarks are not depreciating assets, and amortisation is not allowed.

Start-up expenses
There are no specific provisions in relation to deductions for start-up expenses. However, certain start-up expenses, such as costs of incorporation and other initial start-up costs, may qualify for a five year straight-line write-off.

Interest expenses
No deduction is allowed for interest on loans owing to shareholders, directors, their spouses, children or relatives, or to any related parties. Only interest paid to banks and financial institutions licensed under the Financial Institutions (Non-Banking) Act on loans borrowed at commercial rates and terms is deductible.

Bad debt
General allowances made for bad debts are not deductible. For a bad debt claim to be deductible, it must be specific and the taxpayer must prove to the Inland Revenue Department (IRD) that the debt became bad during the year.

Cultural and social contributions
A deduction of 50% of all substantial contributions made by any person with respect to sport, education, or culture in Antigua and Barbuda is allowed against a person's assessable income from trade, business, or profession. Contributions must be in excess of XCD 10,000 in any assessment year, and deductions during any assessment year will be limited to XCD 250,000.

Restriction on rents paid
Rents paid by a company to shareholders, directors, their spouses, children or relatives, or to any related parties in excess of 5% of the otherwise chargeable profits of the company may not be deducted.

Restriction on compensation
Salaries, wages, directors' fees and other payments made for services rendered by the shareholders, directors, their spouses, children, or relatives in excess of 25% of otherwise chargeable profits may not be deducted.

Fines and penalties
Fines and penalties imposed under Antiguan tax law are not deductible expenses.

Taxes

There are no provisions in the Income Tax Act in relation to the deductibility of taxes paid by a company. However, in general, ABST, ABST input tax credits, and adjustments under the ABST Act are disregarded for income tax purposes. Other taxes, including property tax, transfer taxes, payroll taxes, insurance, except income tax and share transfer tax, are deductible to the extent they are incurred in producing chargeable income.

Net operating losses

Income tax losses may be carried forward for six years following the year in which the loss was incurred. However, the chargeable income of a company in any one income year may not be reduced by more than one half by losses brought forward. No carryback of losses is permitted.

Payments to foreign affiliates

An Antiguan corporation may claim a deduction for royalties, management fees, and interest charges paid to foreign affiliates, provided the payments are equal to or less than what the corporation would pay to an unrelated entity. The deductibility of any payments to a foreign affiliate will be subject to an arm's-length test.

Group taxation

Group taxation is not permitted in Antigua and Barbuda.

Transfer pricing

There are no provisions for transfer pricing in the tax laws of Antigua and Barbuda.

Thin capitalisation

There are no provisions for thin capitalisation in the tax laws of Antigua and Barbuda.

Tax credits and incentives

Tax incentives are currently available under the following legislation.

Fiscal Incentives Ordinance (1975)

The Fiscal Incentive Ordinance provides manufacturers of an 'approved product' with an exemption from taxes for varying periods, up to a maximum of 15 years. After the period of exemption, relief by way of tax credits of up to 50% of CIT paid on profits derived from certain export sales may be obtained. The net losses arising during the tax holiday period (i.e. the excess of accumulated tax losses over total profits) may be carried forward and relieved against profits following the expiration of the tax holiday in accordance with the normal rules for set-off of losses.

International Business Corporations (IBC) Act (1982)

An IBC is an entity incorporated under the IBC Act for the purpose of carrying on international trade or business. The IBC structure allows for a comprehensive range of business opportunities including international banking, trust business, insurance, manufacturing, and other international trade activities to persons outside of Antigua and Barbuda within a tax-free environment. An IBC is exempt from the payment of CIT, ABST, and WHT.

Antigua and Barbuda

The Investment Authority Act (2006)

The Investment Authority Act provides the framework for the promotion of investment opportunities in Antigua and Barbuda by introducing a system of registration of businesses, an investment code, and a range of incentives that are available to both resident and non-resident investors. The available incentives and concessions to which an investor may be entitled for consideration are as follows:

- Exemption from the payment of customs duty.
- Reduction of property tax.
- Exemption from CIT.
- Reduction of stamp duty.
- Exemption from WHT.

The amount of the incentives and concessions depend on the amount of the investment and the number of employees in the proposed business.

The investment categories are as follows:

- Capital investment of up to XCD 1 million or employs up to 26 persons: This investor may qualify for exemption from the payment of customs duty on certain imports, reduction in property tax by up to 10%, exemption from the payment of CIT and WHT for up to three years, and a reduction of stamp duty by up to 10% on the sale of land and buildings used in the business operation.
- Capital investment of over XCD 1 million, employs over 26 persons, and has at least one director or owner who is a resident of Antigua and Barbuda: This investor could qualify for exemption from the payment of customs duty on certain imports, reduction in property tax by up to 20%, exemption from the payment of CIT and WHT for up to five years, and a reduction of stamp duty by up to 20% on the sale of land and buildings used in the business operation.
- Capital investment of over XCD 10 million, employs over 51 persons, and has at least one director or owner who is a resident of Antigua and Barbuda: This investor could qualify for exemption from the payment of customs duty on certain imports, reduction in property tax by up to 30%, exemption from the payment of CIT and WHT for up to ten years, and a reduction of stamp duty by up to 30% on the sale of land and buildings used in the business operation.
- Capital investment of over XCD 25 million, employs over 75 persons, and has at least one director or owner who is a resident of Antigua and Barbuda: This investor could qualify for exemption from the payment of customs duty on certain imports, reduction in property tax by up to 40%, exemption from the payment of CIT and WHT for up to 12 years, and a reduction of stamp duty by up to 40% on the sale of land and buildings used in the business operation.
- Capital investment of over XCD 75 million, employs over 100 persons, and has at least one director or owner who is a resident of Antigua and Barbuda: This investor could qualify for exemption from the payment of customs duty on certain imports, reduction in property tax by up to 50%, exemption from the payment of CIT and WHT for up to 15 years, and a reduction of stamp duty by up to 50% on the sale of land and buildings used in the business operation.
- Capital investment of over XCD 100 million, employs over 150 persons, and has at least one director or owner who is a resident of Antigua and Barbuda: This investor could qualify for exemption from the payment of customs duty on certain imports, reduction in property tax by up to 75%, exemption from the payment of CIT and WHT for up to 20 years, and a reduction of stamp duty by up to 75% on the sale of land and buildings used in the business operation.

Antigua and Barbuda

The Small Business Development Act (2007)

The Small Business Development Act provides the framework for the growth of the small business sector in Antigua and Barbuda by introducing a system of registration of small businesses and a range of concessions which are available to the business. The available concessions to any small business that would be entitled for consideration are as follows:

- Concession on customs duty of up to 100% (includes raw material, building material, equipment, vehicles, furniture, furnishings, appliances, fixtures and fittings, tools, spare parts, and machinery and equipment used in the construction and operation of the business).
- Property tax reduction of up to 75%.
- CIT exemption for a period not exceeding five years.
- CIT exemption after the initial five year period of up to 10%.
- WHT exemption for a period of up to three years.
- Stamp duty exemption on the registration of a mortgage.
- Stamp duty exemption on the transfer of property and any applicable non-citizen land holding licence.

A small business to which this Act applies must meet all of the following criteria:

- No more than 25 employees.
- Not a wholly owned or majority owned business or subsidiary of a larger company.
- Capital investment not exceeding XCD 3 million.
- Annual sales that do not exceed XCD 2 million.
- Majority owned by citizens of Antigua and Barbuda, or majority owned by non-citizens with all of the following restrictions:
  - Over 50% of the products must be exported.
  - Minimum investment of XCD 500,000.
  - At least 50% of the employees must be citizens of Antigua and Barbuda.
  - At least 40% of the goods and services used in production must be acquired from businesses in Antigua.

Foreign tax credit

Double taxation is avoided by means of foreign tax credits where active tax treaties exist and through deduction of foreign income taxes in other cases (the United Kingdom and CARICOM). A foreign tax credit is also available to persons in Antigua and Barbuda who have paid or are liable to pay British Commonwealth income tax.

Residents

The relief available from tax in Antigua and Barbuda for a person resident in Antigua from tax paid in Antigua and Barbuda is the British Commonwealth income tax rate if that rate does not exceed one-half the tax rate in Antigua and Barbuda. If the British Commonwealth income tax rate exceeds the Antigua and Barbuda tax rate, then the relief will be limited to one-half the tax rate in Antigua and Barbuda.

Non-residents

The relief available from tax in Antigua and Barbuda for a person not resident in Antigua from tax paid in Antigua and Barbuda is one-half the British Commonwealth income tax rate if that rate does not exceed one-half the tax rate in Antigua and Barbuda. If the British Commonwealth income tax rate exceeds the Antigua and Barbuda tax rate, then the relief will be limited to the amount by which it exceeded one-half the rate of British Commonwealth income tax.

Antigua and Barbuda

No relief is available unless similar provisions exist in the laws of the relevant British Commonwealth country.

Withholding taxes

Tax is currently withheld from income as follows:

Recipient	Dividends	Dividends (preferred shares)	Interest and rentals	Management fees, royalties, and other payments to a non-resident	Interest on bank deposits
			WHT (%)		
Resident corporations and individuals	0	0	0	0	0
Non-resident corporations	25	25	25	25	25
Non-resident individuals	25	25	20	25	0
Residents of a CARICOM member state:					
Corporations	0	15	15	15	15
Individuals	0	15	15	15	0

Note that interest payments on bank deposits made to non-resident individuals are not subject to WHT. Interest payments on bank deposits made to non-resident corporations are taxed at the rate of 25%.

Where a non-resident lends money at arm's length for the purpose of promoting industrial, commercial, scientific, housing, or other development, the rate of WHT is 10%. Prior approval must be sought from the Commissioner of Inland Revenue, and it is recommended that Cabinet approval also be obtained.

WHT becomes due at the time of payment or accrual and must be paid within seven days thereof.

Tax treaties

There is a tax treaty with the United Kingdom and a DTA between member states of CARICOM.

The UK tax treaty provides that persons in either the United Kingdom or Antigua and Barbuda are entitled to relief from CIT and WHT. The treaty allows for the following relief:

- Where a UK resident is liable to pay income tax in the United Kingdom in respect of the same income which is taxable in Antigua and Barbuda, one will be entitled to relief at a rate that is equal to the amount by which the tax rate in Antigua and Barbuda exceeds one half the UK rate.
- If the tax rate in Antigua exceeds the UK tax rate, then one will be entitled only to relief at a rate equal to the half the UK tax rate.

Tax administration

Taxable period
Taxes are assessed on a fiscal-year basis.

Tax returns
The taxpayer must file a CIT return, which includes audited financial statements, within three months of the fiscal-year end. The authorities will subsequently raise an assessment.

If a return is not filed on a timely basis, the authorities have the power to issue estimated assessments. There is a 5% penalty for late filing (minimum of XCD 500). The taxpayer can object to assessments raised within 30 days and ask the Commissioner of Inland Revenue to review and revise. In the event that the objection is unsuccessful, the taxpayer may appeal to the Tax Appeal Board. The Commissioner of Inland Revenue has the power to enforce the collection of tax prior to the determination of any objection or appeal. The Commissioner also has the discretion to order a stay on the collection and payment of all or part of any assessed tax until such time as the objection or appeal is finalised if it would be unjust not to do so.

Payment of tax
Advance tax is payable in monthly instalments and is ordinarily based on the tax chargeable and assessed in the previous fiscal-year. The standard amount of each instalment is determined as one-twelfth of the tax chargeable in the previous fiscal-year. If the assessment for the prior year has not been finalised, the Commissioner of Inland Revenue can raise an assessment based on best judgment.

The balance of tax due after deduction of advance tax, as notified in the assessment, is payable at the time of submitting the annual CIT return, which must not be later than three months after the financial year-end or one-month after service of the final assessment.

Tax is deemed to be in default if not paid within 30 days of the date on which it becomes due and payable. A penalty of 20% and interest of 1% per month is charged on unpaid taxes in default.

Audit cycle
The Antiguan tax system for companies is based on self-assessment; however, the IRD undertakes ongoing compliance activities to ensure that corporations are meeting their tax obligation. There is no specific approach used by the IRD in relation to compliance and audit activities. Compliance activities generally take the form of reviews of specific issues and audits.

Statute of limitations
The IRD can reassess CIT returns within a six year period. In addition, the IRD can make additional assessments of tax, interest, or penalties.

Topics of focus for tax authorities
The IRD does not have any specific compliance program; however, when an audit is done, the focus is mainly on the detection of basic non-compliance, such as omission of income, inclusion of non-deductible expenses, and classification of item between expenses and capital items.

Argentina

PwC contact

Jorge A.San Martin
PricewaterhouseCoopers
Edificio Bouchard Plaza
Bouchard 557
C1106ABG Ciudad de Buenos Aires
Argentina
Tel: +54 11 4850 6722
Email: jorge.a.san.martin@ar.pwc.com

Significant developments

Tax Penalty Amendments were introduced at the end of 2011, which became effective on 6 January 2012. The Criminal Tax Law now provides for up to nine years of imprisonment for tax and social security fraud and stipulates objective thresholds (a fixed amount of Argentine pesos [ARS]) for determining the amount of unpaid taxes that constitute a criminal offense. Those amounts had become outdated because of inflationary pressures in Argentina since the devaluation of the peso in early 2002. Because of the outdated amounts, almost every tax dispute before the amendments triggered a criminal tax issue because the previous thresholds were too low. The mentioned amendment quadruples the old thresholds, for example: increasing the amount that constitutes 'simple evasion' from ARS 100,000 to ARS 400,000 (from approximately 23,146 United States dollars [USD] to approximately USD 92,586), and the amount that constitutes 'aggravated evasion' from ARS 1 million to ARS 4 million (from approximately USD 231,465 to approximately USD 925,862).

An information system was established by the fiscal authorities on transfers of equity holdings in Argentine companies and, according to the case, also in foreign entities. It applies for transactions as of 1 January 2012, and, depending on the transaction, it should be completed by the seller, acquirer, transferred entity, or public notary intervener.

As of 1 April 2012, residents in Argentina who provide or receive services to or from overseas must complete, electronically, a tax return reporting information of these services so as to request approval from the tax authority (legal requirement in order to make the payment).

Fiscal authorities (AFIP) broadened the scope of the registration and reporting obligations (previously limited to domestic trusts) to target foreign trusts and other equivalent foreign structures that have a substantial nexus with an Argentine party (that is, when the settler, trustee, or any beneficiary is located in Argentina).

Since October 2011, there are new exchange controls that introduced restrictions on the exchange markets. The Argentine government imposed a requirement for mining companies and hydrocarbon to repatriate 100% of foreign exchange arising in their exports (it is worth reminding that previously they were only required to enter 30% of such amounts). Also, a control system was implemented through which the AFIP will approve the purchase of foreign currency.

The Argentine government has formally notified the Swiss authorities that it has terminated the provisional application of the double tax treaty (DTT) signed by both countries in 1997. The notification was sent on 16 January 2012 but was not published in the Official Gazette until 31 January 2012.

On 23 April 2012, Argentina authorities signed an agreement with Uruguay for tax information exchange purposes and a clause related to avoid double taxation between the countries.

During 2011/12, Argentina has signed several tax information exchange agreements (TIEAs) based on Organisation for Economic Co-operation and Development (OECD) regulations with China, Ecuador, Guernsey, Bermuda, India, and Jersey. The TIEAs signed with China and Guernsey have entered into force.

Taxes on corporate income

Profits tax
The rate of profits tax on net taxable business profits is 35%. Legal entities resident in Argentina are subject to tax on Argentine and foreign-source income. Resident legal entities are able to claim any similar taxes actually paid abroad on foreign-source income as a tax credit. The tax rate applies on net income determined on a worldwide basis.

Corporations, limited liability partnerships (LLPs), and branches, as well as other entities, are required to make a flat and final income tax withholding of 35% from dividend payments to resident or non-residents beneficiaries, to the extent that the amount of such dividends exceeds the net taxable income determined at a corporate level in accordance with the general tax rules.

Argentine-source income (e.g. royalties, interests) received by foreign entities is subject to withholding tax (WHT) in full and final settlement at source (*see the Withholding taxes section*).

Tax on minimum notional income
In addition to the profits tax, there is a tax on minimum notional income. The rate is 1% on the value of fixed and current assets. The presumed tax, imposed annually, is applied only in excess of the profits tax of the same fiscal year. In addition, payment of this presumed tax, not offset by the profits tax, will be treated as payment on account of profits tax chargeable during a maximum period of ten years.

Banking and insurance entities are only subject to this tax on 20% of the corresponding taxable assets.

Corporate residence

Corporate residence is determined on the basis of centres of activity, which may be the location of a company's economic activity or management activity.

Permanent establishment (PE)
Centres of activity in Argentina of non-Argentine corporations are treated as PEs.

Argentina

....

Other taxes

Value-added tax (VAT)

VAT is assessable on the sales value of products (e.g. raw materials, produce, finished, or partly finished merchandise) with few exemptions, most services (e.g. construction, utilities, professional and personal services not derived from employment, rental), and on import of goods and services. The VAT rate is 21%, although certain specific items are subject to a 10.5% and 27% rate. It is payable by filing monthly tax returns.

The increased rate of 27% applies to 'utilities services' (e.g. telecommunications, household gas, running water, sewerage, and energy) not rendered to dwelling-purposes real estate.

A reduced rate of 10.5% applies to certain transactions, including (but not limited to) the following:

- Construction of housing.
- Interest and other costs on personal loans granted to final consumers by financial institutions.
- Sales and imports of living bovine animals, supply of publicity and advertising in some specific cases.
- Any passenger transportation operating inside the country when the distance does not exceed 100 km.
- Medical assistance in some specific cases.
- Certain capital goods depending on the Custom Duty Code.

VAT paid on purchases, final imports, and rental of automobiles not considered as inventory, cannot be computed by the purchaser as a VAT credit. The same tax treatment applies to other services, such as those provided by restaurants, hotels, and garages.

VAT exemptions

Among others, the following transactions are exempt from VAT:

- Sales of books, ordinary natural water, common bread, milk, medicine, postage stamps, aircraft used in commercial activities and for defence or internal safety, and ships or boats acquired by the national government.
- Supply of services such as: services rendered by the government (national, provincial, or local) or by public institutions, school or university education provided by private institutions subject to public educational programmes; cultural services supplied by religious institutions; hospital and medical care and related activities, transportation services for sick or injured persons in vehicles specially designed for the purpose; tickets for theatre, cinema, musical shows, and sport events, the production and distribution of motion picture films; local transport of passengers (e.g. taxis, buses) up to 100 km, international transportation.
- Rental of real estate for housing purposes.

VAT exemption on importation

The following transactions shall be exempted from VAT:

- Final importation of goods qualifying for exemption from customs duties under special regimes for tourists, scientists and technicians, diplomatic agents, etc.
- Final importation of samples and parcels exempted from customs duties.

A

VAT export reimbursement regime

Exports of goods and services are treated as a zero-rated transaction. Nevertheless, input VAT related to these transactions can either be used as a credit against output VAT or refunded pursuant to a special procedure.

Services rendered within the country shall be deemed to be exports if they are effectively applied or economically utilised outside the country.

Exporters must file an export return with the tax authorities, reporting the VAT receivables related to their exports to be reimbursed on VAT paid in relation to the export operations. This return has to be filed within the following tax period in which the export took place. A report certified by a public accountant with respect to the value, registrations, and other characteristics related to the refund must be attached to the export return.

The tax credit related to exports and other taxable activities can only be refunded in proportion to the exports, and can be fully refunded to a cap of 21% of the freight on board (FOB) value of the exported products.

There is no specific method stated in the legislation for allocating the tax credit related to exports, but taxpayers are able to use any methods of calculation that would be suitable to their business model. This calculation has to be approved by the tax authorities.

Finally, it is important to highlight that the tax authorities have to approve the tax credit to be refunded.

Electronic invoicing

The electronic invoicing regime is mandatory only for specific businesses according to Appendix I of R.G. 2485 (i.e. software development, consulting, accounting and audit services, exporters, advertising, mobile telecommunications, supplied services to government, etc.), and it is optional for the rest of the taxpayers. In order to opt for applying this regime, an authorisation must be obtained from the tax authorities. As a result, the tax authorities will assign an Electronic Authorization Code (*Código de Autorización Electrónico* or CAE).

The fiscal authorities are also allowed to nominate taxpayers to apply this regime, even though their activities are not included in Appendix I of R.G. 2485. This notification will be duly made to such taxpayers.

It is important to highlight that the fiscal authorities are expecting to make this regime mandatory for all the taxpayers in 2012.

Import and export duties

The levels of import duty currently range between 0% and 35%, except in cases where a specific minimum duty is applied or which involves merchandise with a specific treatment. These percentages were established considering the individual competitive conditions prevailing in different production sectors and the relative advantages of contributing to the introduction of equipment and technology for local industry. In general, merchandise originating from LAIA (Latin America Integration Association - ALADI) countries is entitled to preferential duty.

Argentina

In the case of export transactions, goods are valued based on the FOB clause, and the approach is based on their theoretical value, rather than a positive basis as in the case of imports.

Definitive exports of all goods are subject to export duties. The rates vary from 5% to 45%, depending on the tariff code of the merchandise (while 5% is typical, higher rates are considered for exports of agricultural products or hydrocarbons).

Excise taxes

Excise tax is assessable on a wide variety of items sold in Argentina (not on exports), principally on tobacco, wines, soft drinks, spirits, gasoline, lubricants, insurance premiums, automobile tires, mobiles services, perfumes, jewellery, and precious stones. The bases of the assessment and tax rate of some items are as follows:

Products	Rates (%)	
	Nominal	Effective
Tobacco	16/20/60	19.05 to 25
Alcoholic drinks	20	25
Beers	8	8.70
Soft drinks	4 to 8	4.17 to 8.70
Jewellery and precious stones	20	25

Stamp tax

Stamp tax is levied by each of the 24 jurisdictions, and applies principally to contracts and agreements, deeds, mortgages, and other obligations, agreements and discharges of a civil, financial, or commercial nature of which there is written evidence or, in certain instances, that are the subject of entries in books of account. The average tax rate is 1% applicable on the economic value of the contract.

In the city of Buenos Aires, the standard tax rate is 0.8% of the aggregate amount of the transactions, contracts, and deeds that are subject to the stamp tax. Special rates of 0.5%, 1%, and 2.5% are also established; and, in the case of transactions involving uncertain consideration, a fixed tax of ARS 1,000 is applicable (on the fulfilment of certain conditions).

Turnover tax (gross income tax)

Each of the 24 jurisdictions into which Argentina is divided imposes a tax on gross revenues from the sale of goods and services. Exports of goods are exempt, and certain industries are subject to a reduced tax rate. Rates, rules, and assessment procedures are determined locally.

Information on tax rates of the economically largest jurisdictions is provided as follows:

Jurisdiction	General rate (%)	Commerce (%)	Services (%)	Industry (%)
Province of Buenos Aires	4.5	3 to 4.5	3.5 to 4.5	1 to 3
City of Buenos Aires	3/3.75 to 4	3.75 to 4	3.75 to 4	1
Córdoba	4	2 to 7.5	2 to 10.5	0.25 to 1.5
Mendoza	4	4 to 4.5	4 to 4.5	1.5/3 to 4
Santa Cruz	3	3	3	1.5
Santa Fe	3.5/3.8 to 4.2	1 to 4.5	1 to 4.5	0

Tax on financial transactions - on credits and debits on bank accounts

Bank account movements (deposits and withdrawals) are subject to this national tax at the following rates:

- 0.6% of deposits and withdrawals in bank accounts opened in local financial entities.
- 1.2% of any transactions made in a bank without using a bank account.

The 34% or 17% of the tax on financial transactions effectively paid on bank account deposit transactions (0.6%) and movement of funds (1.2%), respectively, is creditable against income tax and minimum notional income tax and/or respective tax advances.

Wealth tax

An annual wealth tax is levied on the shares or holding in the capital of local companies owned by individuals or undivided estates domiciled in Argentina or abroad, and/or companies and/or any other type of legal person domiciled abroad. It shall be assessed and paid directly by the local company, as a full and final payment on behalf of the shareholders (the issuing company has the right to recover from the shareholder the tax paid).

The applicable tax rate is 0.5% on the value of the participation, which is generally calculated on the difference between assets and liabilities arising from the financial statements closed at 31 December or during the respective fiscal year.

Payroll taxes

Foreign and local nationals working for a local company must be included on the local payroll and will be considered as local employees for local labour, tax, and social security purposes. Both the local company and the employees will be subject to the corresponding regulations.

All the compensation paid in Argentina or abroad for work performed for the local company will be considered as local compensation and should be reported to the tax and social security authorities, as the case may be, and included in the salary slips and recorded in the local labour books.

The local employer must withhold income tax on an actual and monthly basis and make the corresponding payments to the tax authorities through monthly WHT returns. Individual tax rates range from 9% to 35%, and personal deductions are available.

The local entity must issue salary slips every month for each employee included on its payroll, considering the total compensation mentioned above.

Employer social security contributions add between 23% and 27% to payroll costs. There is a compulsory 13th-month salary. There is no restriction regarding the employment of foreigners, provided they hold working visas.

Workers' (Employees') Compensation: Argentine labour regulations determine different forms of compensation for employees. These include, but are not limited to, the following:

- Vacation compensation.
- Compensation in a case of termination of employment contract with employee (prior notice of dismissal and to a severance payment, both based on seniority).

Main social taxes and contributions assessable on salaries are as follows:

Argentina

Social taxes and contributions	Percentage of gross monthly earnings (%) (including 13th month salary)	
	Employer (2, 3)	Employee (1)
Pension fund	17/21	11
National unemployment fund	-	-
Family allowances fund	-	-
Social services institute for pensioner	-	3
Social health care plan	6	3
Total	23/27	17

Notes

1. Social security charges borne by employees are applicable up to a monthly salary cap which currently amounts to ARS 19,070.55 (updated as of March 2012).
2. Contributions made by employers are applicable to total compensation without application of any cap.
3. Employers' contributions to the national unemployment fund, family allowances fund, and social services institute for pensioners is paid at a unified rate of 17%. The rate is increased to 21% for companies whose main activity consists of rendering services or commerce, provided the amount of their average total annual sales for the last three years exceeds USD 11.56 million (at the current exchange rate of USD 1.00 = ARS 4.45, equivalent to ARS 51.5 million).

Branch income

The rate of profits tax on net taxable profits from Argentine sources and from activities performed abroad by the branch is 35%. Branches are also subject to minimum notional income tax.

Income determination

Inventory valuation
Inventory valuation is based on the latest purchase. Thus, the last in first out (LIFO) method may not be elected for tax purposes. Conformity between book and tax reporting is not required.

Capital gains/losses
Capital gains and losses attract normal profits tax treatment, except that losses from the sale of shares and other equity interests may be offset only against the same type of income.

Capital gains on equity
Capital gains derived by foreign shareholders from the disposal of shares (either publicly or privately held) of Argentine companies (SAs) are currently tax exempt. Although, with certain risk, it may be argued that capital gains derived from the sale of quotas of the capital of Argentine limited liability companies (SRLs), or when the shares are sold by foreign 'offshore' entities, may also benefit from this tax exemption. Moreover, it´s important to highlight that there is no mechanism to pay the tax when the transaction is between foreign parties.

Capital gains on debt
Capital gains derived by foreign beneficiaries from the sale of either public or privately held securities (*títulos valores*), such as *'obligaciones negociables'* (to the extent it is

accepted that they are equivalent to securities), notes issued by financial trusts (*títulos de deuda*), or public bonds (i.e. government bonds) should be exempt from income tax.

Any other capital gain derived from the sale of debt, not covered by the above exemption, should be subject to normal tax treatment (i.e. withholding of 17.5% of gross proceeds or withholding of 35% on the actual gain).

Dividend income
Dividends, including stock dividends, are not included in the tax base by the recipient if distributed by an Argentine company (*see the Withholding taxes section for additional information*). However, tax is levied if the dividends are distributed by a foreign company.

Foreign exchange gains/losses
The general rule is that foreign exchange results (gain or losses) have to be recognised on an accrual basis. However, in some cases, cash basis is applicable.

Foreign exchange losses can only be offset against foreign source taxable income.

Foreign income
Foreign income received or held undistributed abroad (in case of investments in non-stock companies) by resident corporations is subject to tax. Argentina does not have a controlled foreign company (CFC) regime. Tax losses from a foreign source can only be offset against income from a foreign source.

....

Deductions

Expenses necessary to generate, maintain, and preserve taxable income, and related to the company activity, are usually tax deductible, with a few exceptions, to the extent they are fair and reasonable.

Depreciation and depletion
Depreciation is generally computed on a straight-line basis over the technically estimated useful life of the assets or, alternatively, over the standard useful life (e.g. machinery and equipment: 10 years; furniture: 10 years). Depreciation of buildings and other construction of real estate is 2% per annum on cost (on a straight-line basis), unless it can be proved that useful life is less than 50 years.

Depreciation of automobiles whose original cost exceeds ARS 20,000 is not deductible. Related expenses (gasoline vouchers, insurance, rentals, repairs and maintenance, etc.) are deductible up to an amount of ARS 7,200 per automobile per year.

Conformity between book and tax depreciation is not required.

Profit or loss on the sale of depreciated property is determined with reference to cost less depreciation, restated for inflation as at March 1992, and is included in ordinary taxable income.

Percentage depletion is available for natural resources (mines, quarries, woods).

Argentina

Goodwill

The amortisation of goodwill cannot be deducted for income tax purposes. At the moment of sale, the taxable gain will be calculated deducting the cost expenses (purchase price).

With regards to self-developed goodwill, at the moment of sale the cost will be the amount of expenses incurred in obtaining it, if not deducted for income tax purposes before.

Research and development (R&D)

R&D expenditures (for the development of intangible assets) may be deducted when they are incurred or amortised over not more than five years, at the option of the taxpayer. Expenditures for R&D in connection with the creation of fixed assets form part of the assets' cost and are amortised over their useful lives.

The amortisation of brands and licences acquired can be deducted if they have a limited term of duration.

Start-up expenses

Start-up expenses may be deducted when incurred or amortised over not more than five years, at the option of the taxpayer.

Interest expenses

Tax law establishes a restriction on the deductibility of interest arising from debts of a financial nature, contracted by taxpayers with controlling/related non-resident entities, for income tax purposes (*see Thin capitalisation in the Group taxation section*).

Bad debt

The deduction of accounting bad debts is not allowed for tax purposes. However, if the debts fulfil certain characteristics (i.e. bankruptcy, prescription, among others), and with the corresponding supporting documentation, they can be deducted.

Charitable contributions

When made to societies and associations expressly exempt from assessment to profits tax, donations are admissible deductions up to a maximum of 5% of the donor's net taxable profits, provided certain requirements are fulfilled.

Representation expenses

If adequately documented, representation expenses are permissible deductions at up to 1.5% of the amount of salaries accrued during the fiscal year. According to the Regulatory Decree, representation expenses are payments made in order to represent the company in the market, to improve and maintain its relationship with suppliers and clients, etc.

Directors' fees

Amounts up to the greater of 25% of after-tax profit or ARS 12,500 per individual are deductible in the financial year to which they apply, provided they are approved and available for the director before the due date of the tax return, or in a later year of payment.

Taxes

Except for profits tax and the tax on minimum notional income, all taxes are deductible.

Net operating losses

Net operating losses may be carried forward for five years. Loss carrybacks are not permitted. Furthermore, foreign source losses must be offset by income from similar sources.

Losses on derivatives and hedging transactions can only be offset against income from the same transaction.

Payments to foreign affiliates

Transactions between related parties should be at arm's length (*see Transfer pricing in the Group taxation section for more information*). This principle is extended to transactions with companies located in low or no tax jurisdictions. Payments to foreign affiliates or related parties and companies located in low or no tax jurisdictions that represent income of Argentine source are tax deductible, provided they are paid before the due date for filing the tax return and the corresponding withholding is paid to the tax authorities. Otherwise they would be deducted in the fiscal year in which they are paid.

Technical assistance and services that involve transfer of technology should be covered by agreements duly registered with the National Institute of Intellectual Property for information purposes. These transactions are governed by the Transfer of Technology Law.

Group taxation

Group taxation is not permitted in Argentina.

Transfer pricing

The transfer pricing regulations governing inter-company transactions, adopt principles similar to those of the OECD pursuant to which companies must comply with the arm's-length principle in order to determine the value of goods and services in their transactions with foreign related companies.

The following taxpayers, among others, must generally file, together with their annual income tax return, a supplementary return (transactions encompassed by regulations governing transfer prices) and transfer pricing study:

- Taxpayers carrying out transactions with related individuals or legal entities set up, domiciled, or located abroad. Two or more persons are considered to be related parties when one of them takes part, either directly or indirectly, in the administration, control, or capital of the other, or when a person or group of persons takes part, either directly or indirectly, in the administration, control, or capital of those persons.
- Taxpayers carrying out transactions with related individuals or legal entities set up, domiciled, or located in countries with low or no taxation, whether related or not.
- Argentine residents carrying out transactions with PEs located abroad and owned by them.
- Argentine residents, owners of PEs located abroad, for transactions carried out by the latter with persons or other type of related entities domiciled, set up, or located abroad.

Argentina

The Regulatory Decree provides specific rules to determine the fairness of the transfer pricing methodology. These rules are similar to those set by the OECD and contemplate six methods, including the following:

- Comparable Uncontrolled Price (CUP).
- Resale Price Method (RPM).
- Cost Plus.
- Profit Split Method (PSM).
- Transactional Net Margin Method (TNMM).
- Special Method for Export of goods with prices quoted in transparent markets.

There is no specific hierarchy, as each particular transaction must be analysed based on the assets, functions, and risks involved and on information available. Regulations establish that the most appropriate method is that which reflects the economic reality of the transactions.

Thin capitalisation
Thin capitalisation rules apply as a restriction on the deductibility of interest arising from debts of a financial nature that are contracted by taxpayers with controlling non-resident entities and can be summarised as follows:

- For interest subject to a 15.05% withholding (i.e. paid on loans granted by certain banking institutions), the portion of interest stemming from financial liabilities exceeding two times the shareholders' equity is not deductible for tax purposes and is treated as dividends.
- Interest subject to a 35% WHT is fully deductible.

According to the Regulatory Decree of the Income Tax Law, the thin capitalisation rules are also applicable to any case where a lower withholding rate of 35% is applicable (for instance, interest payments to a controlling company resident of certain tax treaty countries).

Controlled foreign companies (CFCs)
Argentina does not have a CFC regime.

Tax credits and incentives

Foreign tax credit
National taxpayers are entitled to recognise a tax credit for any taxes actually paid in the countries where they have obtained foreign-source income, in respect of similar national taxes, up to a cap which is the increase in their Argentine tax liability due to the inclusion of the foreign income. Any excess not offset in a given fiscal year may be carried forward to the next five fiscal years.

Province of Tierra del Fuego Regime
Companies set up in the province of Tierra del Fuego enjoy a general tax exemption and important benefits in customs matters. Tax exemption includes income tax, tax on minimum notional income, tax on personal wealth, and excise tax. The VAT benefit consists of the release from payment of the technical balance of the tax (VAT debits less VAT credits). Also, a reduction of the prevailing rate for tax on financial transactions and the exemption from taxation on the transfer of fuels is contemplated.

Mining activity

An investment regime for mining activity is applicable to natural and legal persons. Mining ventures included within this regime enjoy fiscal stability (i.e. tax rates will remain basically the same) for a term of 30 years, except for VAT, which will adjust to the general regime. Furthermore, the regime grants incentives for profits tax, tax on assets, import duties, and any other tax for introduction of certain assets. Additionally, this mining investment law established an exploration recovery regime for the mining investors, which allows the reimbursement of the VAT credit balances originated in the mining exploration activity.

This regime allows the reimbursement of such VAT credits after a 12-month period since the expenditure was incurred, and only if it has been paid.

Through specifics regulations, the authorities established the requirements (e.g. filing a tax return, filing a report certified by a public accountant with respect to the VAT, a presentation to the Mining Secretary) to be followed by the taxpayers in order to apply for this benefit.

Forestry

There is an investment regime for plantation, protection, and maintenance of forests. It contains rules similar to those for mining activity tax incentives:

- Fiscal stability for a period of 30 years. The period may be extended to 50 years.
- Refund of VAT resulting from the purchase or final importation of goods, leases, or services effectively for forestry investment project in a period of less than 365 days.

Export incentives

Exports of goods and services are exempt from VAT and excise taxes. The temporary importation of raw materials and intermediate and packaging goods for the manufacture of products for export is free from duties with the obligation of offering sufficient guarantees for the import. A reimbursement regime is in place for VAT credits paid to suppliers in relation to the export activity.

Oil and gas industry

The Argentine government has granted attractive benefits to the oil and gas sector to encourage the exploration of the nation's hydrocarbons reserves.

This legislation grants special incentives to investments in underdeveloped regions, speeding reimbursement of VAT (after a three-month period, inputs will be credited against other federal taxes or returned to the taxpayer), exemption from import duties, and offering an accelerated depreciation (over three years) for income tax purposes.

In addition, a three-year relief from minimum notional income tax, which is levied at 1% rate on the company assets, is provided by the law.

The incentive package will be in effect for 15, 12, or ten years, depending on whether the activities are performed in areas identified as (i) continental platform, (ii) within the country other than continental platform, and (iii) currently in production, respectively.

The benefits noted above will apply to the exploration permits granted as of the enactment of the law (1 November 2006) and up to five years, for the cases mentioned in (i), four years, for those described in (ii), and three years in the latter cases.

Argentina

There also exists a Promotion Regime, which grants similar benefits for the exploration of alternative sources of energy (e.g. wind energy).

Biotechnology industry
A promotional tax regime for development and production of modern biotechnology has been introduced. Pursuant to this law, the beneficiaries of the projects that qualify for this regime are entitled to the following benefits:

- Income tax: accelerated depreciation of capital goods, special equipment, parts, or components of newly acquired goods destined for the promoted project.
- VAT: Early refund of the tax applicable to the assets acquired for the project.
- Social security contributions: the amount representing 50% of social security contributions actually paid on the payroll salaries involved in the project shall be converted into a tax credit bond that may be applied to payment of national taxes.

Software industry
Under a software promotion regime, taxpayers carrying out software related activities as their main purpose may qualify for the following benefits:

- Fiscal stability for a ten-year period covering national taxes.
- Reduction of social security charges (70% of these charges may be credited against certain national taxes).
- Income tax relief (up to 60% of the applicable tax).

While most of the software related activities qualify for the fiscal stability benefit, the remaining incentives only apply to software R&D, quality control procedures, and software exports.

Some changes were introduced in 2011, and the period of application was extended until 31 December 2019. The possibility of using a bond tax credit, given by an amount equal to 70% of contributions to the social security system paid by the employer, as an 'advance payment' of the income tax was provided. There is also an increase in the control mechanisms.

Province incentives on local taxes
Most of the provinces have legislation establishing incentives for the development of industries within their boundaries, especially industries that utilise or develop their natural resources and provide work for their residents. The incentives, in general, consist of exemptions from provincial and municipal taxes.

Various provinces have investment promotion regimes. Even when there are certain differences among these regimes, generally they include the following incentives:

- Exemption from provincial taxes such as turnover tax, stamp duty, real estate tax.
- Reduced public utility rates.
- Support for infrastructure and equipment projects.
- Facilities for purchase, rental, or lease without charge of public property.

These regimes are not automatically applied, and a special procedure should be followed to be entitled to the respective benefits.

Free trade zones
The free trade zones offer exporters the possibility to import free from customs duties, statistics rate, and VAT all the necessary equipment for construction of a 'turnkey plant'

within the zones. Furthermore, exporters manufacturing within the zones enjoy the benefit of buying supplies and raw materials from third countries, without having to pay duties or taxes that lead to increased prices.

Customs authority regulating these goods considers them as stored in a third country; therefore, incoming products are subject to inspection with the sole purpose of classifying quantity and type. In other words, goods enjoy a duty-free status until they enter the Argentine customs territory. Goods may remain in the free zone for a maximum period of five years.

Withholding taxes

Equalisation corporate tax
Corporations, LLPs, and certain other entities are required to make a flat and final income tax withholding of 35% from dividend payments or profit distributions to resident or non-resident payees, to the extent that the amount of such dividends or profit distributions exceeds the taxable income of the distributing company, determined by applying the general tax rules (i.e. without considering any exemptions, abatements, and other adjustments arising from special promotional laws) included in their retained earnings at the end of the fiscal year, immediately preceding the date of payment or distribution.

Other payments
Other payments to residents and to non-residents are subject to WHT rates as follows:

Recipient	Interest (%) (1)	Royalties (%) (1, 2)
Resident corporations	6/28 (3)	6 (4)
Resident individuals	6/28 (3)	6 (4)
Non-resident corporations and individuals:		
Non-treaty:	15.05/35	21/28
Treaty:		
Australia	12	10/15
Belgium	0/12 (5)	3/5/10/15
Bolivia	15.05/35	21/28
Brazil	15.05/35	21/28
Canada	12.5	3/5/10/15
Chile	15.05/35	21/28
Denmark	12 (5)	3/5/10/15
Finland	15	3/5/10/15
France	15.05/20 (6)	18
Germany	10/15 (7)	15
Italy	15.05/20 (5)	10/18
Netherlands	12	3/5/10/15
Norway	12.5 (8)	3/5/10/15
Spain	12.5	3/5/10/15
Sweden	12.5	3/5/10/15
Switzerland (9)	12	3/5/10/15
United Kingdom	12 (5)	3/5/10/15

Argentina

Notes

1. Withholding from payments of interest and royalties to non-residents is based on a flat rate of 35% applied to an assumed percentage gross profit margin. This margin is not contestable, but the resultant rate may be limited by bilateral treaty. Under the 1998 tax reform, the general margin for interest paid for credits obtained abroad is 100%. However, a margin of 43% is applicable (i) if the debtor is a local bank, (ii) if the creditor is a foreign financial institution located in a country not considered as a low or no tax jurisdiction, or in countries that have signed an agreement with Argentina for exchange of information and have no bank secrecy laws, which are under the supervision of the respective central bank, (iii) if the interest is paid on a loan dedicated to the purchase of tangible assets other than cars, (iv) if the interest is paid on debt certificates (private bonds) issued by local companies and registered in certain countries that have signed an agreement with Argentina for the protection of investments, and (v) on interest paid on time deposits with local banks. 'Royalties' covers a variety of concepts. The rates given in this column relate specifically to services derived from agreements ruled by the Foreign Technology Law, as follows:
   a. Technical assistance, technology, and engineering not obtainable in Argentina: 21% (35% on assumed profit of 60%).
   b. Cessation of rights or licenses for invention patents exploitation and technical assistance obtainable in Argentina: 28% (35% on assumed profit of 80%). On non-registered agreements the rate is 31.5% (profit of 90% is assumed) or 35% (profit of 100% is assumed), depending on the case.
   Several other concepts of 'royalties' are subject to rates that, in turn, may be limited by treaty. A broad sample of these concepts and the non-treaty effective rates are set forth in Note 2.
2. Payments to non-residents (only) for 'royalties', rentals, fees, commissions, and so on, in respect of the following are subject to withholding at the rates given below on the basis of assumed gross profit margins (Note 1) unless limited by treaty. The treaty concerned should be consulted to determine any limitation in each case.

Payment	WHT (%)
Freight and passenger bookings (other than those covered by special treaties), news and feature services, insurance underwriting	3.5
Containers	7.0
Copyright	12.25
Rental of movable assets	14.0
Motion picture, video, and sound tape rentals and royalties; radio, television, telex and telefax transmissions; any other means for projection, reproduction, transmission, or diffusion of image or sound; sale of assets located in Argentina (10, 11)	17.5
Rental of real estate (10)	21.0
Any other Argentine-source income (unless the non-resident is or was temporarily resident)	31.5

3. The higher tax rate is applicable on non-registered taxpayers. On interest paid to corporations by financial entities or stock exchange/open market brokers, income tax must be withheld at 3% (10% if not registered); individuals are tax exempt.
4. Resident corporations and individuals who are registered for tax purposes are subject to 6% withholding (28% if not registered).
5. Interest is exempt if paid on credit sales of machinery or other equipment, specific bank loans at preferential rate or loans by public entities.
6. The treaty limits taxation of interest to 20% (registered).
7. The 10% rate is applicable to interest on credit sales of capital equipment, any bank loan, or any financing of public works; otherwise 15%.
8. Interest paid on loans with guarantee of the Norwegian Institute for Credit Guarantees or paid in relation to imports of industrial equipment is tax exempt.
9. On 16 January 2012, the DTT with Switzerland was terminated.
10. Deduction of actual costs and expenses may be optionally exercised.
11. Gains on the sale of shares are exempt, except for companies, PEs, or other entities residing abroad whose main activity based on their statutes consists of investments to be made outside of their country of formation. These entities are subject to income tax withholding at the definite flat rate of 17.5%.

Tax administration

Taxable period
Tax is assessed on a fiscal-year, self-assessment basis.

Tax returns
The due date for filing the profits and the minimum notional income tax return is during the second week of the fifth month after the fiscal year end. Tax returns are filed electronically.

Payment of tax
Instalment payments on account of both profits tax and minimum notional income tax must be made in the course of the tax year. The instalment payments must be made on a monthly basis, beginning in the first month after the due date of filing of the tax returns.

Penalties
Penalties derived from tax infractions may be applied by tax authorities, as follows:

- Failing to file the tax return: Fines range between ARS 200 and ARS 400 (approximately USD 45 and USD 88).
- Tax omission or incorrect tax determination: Fines range from 50% to 100% of unpaid taxes or incorrect tax calculation.
- Tax avoidance: Fines range between two and ten times the avoided tax.
- Certain tax infractions may be penalised by closing the business premises for three to ten days. In addition, fines ranging between ARS 300 and ARS 30,000 (approximately USD 66 and USD 6,600) may be imposed.
- Simple evasion: Entities or individuals evading payment of social security contributions or withholdings, or both, payable to the Tax Authorities under the social security regime, through deceitful declarations, malicious concealment, or any fraudulent or deceitful procedure, either through action or omission, in excess of ARS 80,000 per fiscal period, shall be punished with two to six years' imprisonment. Such amount will be ARS 400,000 in the case of taxes, it being applied by tax and by fiscal year.
- If the infringement qualifies as aggravated evasion: Imprisonment could be extended from three years and six months to nine years in certain situations.

Interest on late payments
Late payment of taxes is subject to a monthly 3% interest rate. Interest will start accruing on the day after the filing due date.

Statute of limitations
The actions and powers of the tax authorities to determine and require payment of federal taxes, and to implement and enforce fines and closures planned, prescribe:

- five years in the case of registered taxpayers, as well as in the case of unregistered taxpayers who are not legally required to register in AFIP; or that, having that obligation, had not fulfilled them and, spontaneously, regularise their situation, and
- ten years in the case of unregistered taxpayers.

Audit cycle
The tax authorities are entitled to audit taxpayers within the statute of limitations period. Audits consist of revising the calculation of any national or provincial tax based on formal requirements. Where any assessment is issued by the tax authorities, the

Argentina

taxpayer is entitled to either accept it or file a claim. Assessments can be done under a real or estimated basis, depending on the specific case and the information that the taxpayers have on their transactions. In the case that the taxpayers do not accept the assessment during the administrative period, they can claim against Tax Courts before any judicial process.

There are no specific provisions about e-auditing.

Topics of focus for tax authorities
Topics of focus for tax authorities include the following:

- Increasing cooperation: tax information exchange.
- Tax treaty network under review (Chile and Spain).
- Tax treaty benefits: substance over form principle.
- High penalties and tax criminal law.
- Transfer pricing (inter-company charges and export of commodities to international intermediaries).
- Wealth tax: applicability on branches and the use of Montevideo Agreement.
- Possible tax modifications under analysis: the initiative seeks to make substantial changes in the income tax, with focus on financial income (taxability on securities sales), limitation of payments to tax havens, and the computation of tax losses.

Other issues

Convertibility Law
Although the Convertibility Law (which by Argentina's currency board established a fixed pegging of one-to-one parity between the peso and the US dollar during the 1990's and up to 2002 and inflation adjustment was not allowed) is no longer in place, the adjustment of inflation for tax purposes is not yet in force. There is a strong debate regarding the reinforcement of this procedure for fiscal years ended up to December 2002. However, a final decision has not yet been reached. The wholesale price index from 2004 to 2010 fluctuated in the range of 8% to 12% (reaching a peak of 15% in 2007) according to government statistics that seem to differ from those estimated by private consultants (2 or 2.5 times higher).

Exchange control regime
As a result of the devaluation of the Argentine peso at the beginning of 2002, several regulations were issued to limit the transfer of money abroad. They have been made more flexible up to date.

Regulations referring to the entrance of funds to the country, the obligation of liquidation of foreign currency in the Exchange Market of payments of exports of goods and services, remain in force. The terms to comply with the liquidation obligation vary between 60 and 360 days.

There are no restrictions for the payment abroad of interest, dividends, profits, royalties, and other commercial payments duly supported by the corresponding documentation. Payment abroad for other concepts may be subject to further filing requirements.

In addition, it should be particularly highlighted that a rule issued by the central bank in mid-2005 requires a compulsory one-year temporary deposit equivalent to 30% of funds brought by non-residents to Argentina, which must be kept in a reserve (*encaje*) for the term of one year. This deposit is made in foreign currency and does not earn interest.

There are some exceptions, for instance, direct investments such as interest in Argentine companies (minimum 10%) or real estate are not subject to this rule, or if the funds were borrowed for the acquisition of fixed assets and the re-payment term is longer than two years.

Legal entities

Foreign companies in Argentina, carrying out their business or activity in Argentina, must have a local legal vehicle, of which the most common legal entity types are the following:

* Branch.
* Corporation (*Sociedad Anónima* or SA).
* Local Limited Liability Company (*Sociedad de Responsabilidad Limitada* or SRL).

Argentine corporations and LLPs, as Argentine residents, are subject to the Argentine tax system. Branches of foreign companies, whatever the nature of their activities, are taxed under the same rules as those applicable to corporations and LLPs.

Several documents are required to register an entity with the relevant authorities. Some of said documentation must be filed in the original language, duly translated and certified with the Apostille issued pursuant to The Hague Convention or legalised by the Argentine Consulate of the company's place of origin.

At present, the minimum capital requirement to incorporate an SA is ARS 12,000 (approximately USD 2,800). There are no special requirements regarding the minimum amount of capital for SRLs.

A branch does not require capital contributions unless it is engaged in certain specific activities (e.g. banking and financing). The branch must carry its financial statements separately from those of the foreign company.

The three legal types are subject to the same legal, tax, and accounting regulations.

Armenia

PwC contact

Davit Harutyunyan
PricewaterhouseCoopers Armenia
1 Northern Avenue
Business Center Nord, 5th floor
Yerevan 0001, Armenia
Tel: +374 10 59 21 66
Email: davit.harutyunyan@am.pwc.com

Significant developments

The following amendments generally became effective in January 2012:

- In addition to the existing cap (twice of the Armenian Central Bank's settlement rate), the deductible interest expense payable within the tax year should not exceed:
  - nine times the value of net assets of a taxpayer, if borrowings received from banks and credit organisations, or
  - twice the value of net assets of a taxpayer, if borrowing received from other entities.

  The net assets are a positive difference between the taxpayer's assets and liabilities. The value of net assets should be considered based on results of the reporting year.

  The restriction does not apply to the banks and credit organisations and to the funds borrowed from international organisations specified by the government. The restriction also does not apply to the interest payable on funds attracted from publicly placed debt instruments (securities).

- If prepayments for goods and fixed assets are made to a non-resident offshore entity and those assets are not received within one year, then corporate income tax (CIT) at the 20% rate will apply on the amount of the prepayment.
- The deductibility of management service expenses has also been limited by the law. However, the limits and definition of 'management services' is still to be established by the government.
- Excise tax on alcoholic beverages is now the same for both local producers and importers.
- Customs duty on cars that cost more than 25 million Armenian drams (AMD) has been raised by 20% (luxury tax).
- Presumptive tax for the organisation of casinos, games with winnings, games with winnings by internet, and lottery has been raised (*see new rates under Presumptive tax system in the Taxes on corporate income section*).
- Some activities became subject to license payments, shifting from the presumptive tax system (*see the types of activities and rates under License payments in the Taxes on corporate income section*).

Double tax treaties (DTTs) with Cyprus, Hungary, Kazakhstan, Spain, and the United Kingdom and Northern Ireland have become effective in 2012.

A

Taxes on corporate income

Armenian resident entities, and non-resident entities doing business in Armenia through a branch or a representative office, are liable for CIT. Armenia taxes residents on their worldwide income; non-residents are subject to CIT only on their Armenian-source income.

The standard CIT rate is 20%.

Taxable income is defined to be the difference between a taxpayer's gross income and deductible expenses:

- Gross income encompasses all revenues received by a taxpayer from all economic activities, unless the revenues are expressly exempted under the law.
- Deductible expenses encompass all necessary and documented expenses that are directly related to conducting business or earning profit, unless a specific provision in the law restricts the deduction.

Taxpayers engaged in agricultural production are exempt from CIT on that income.

Note that resident entities, branches and representative offices of foreign entities, and individual entrepreneurs are required to withhold income tax at source on payments to non-residents not having a permanent establishment (PE) in Armenia (*see the Withholding taxes section*).

Investment funds pay CIT based on 0.01% of net assets.

Presumptive tax system

Taxpayers engaged in certain activities must use the presumptive tax system. Under this system, the taxpayer pays a fixed tax based on the location and area occupied by the business and will not be required to pay CIT or value-added tax (VAT). The rate of tax depends on the activity undertaken, as follows:

Type of business	Base data	Adjustment ratio	Monthly presumptive payment (AMD)
Activity related to vehicles	Transportation of passengers by cars: 1.0	In Yerevan: 3.4; Depends on region: 3.1 or 2.8	2,000 times the product of the base data and the adjustment ratio(s)
	For activities carried out by trucks: the lading in terms of tons	Depends on region: 1.1 to 1.9	
	For activities carried out by buses: the number of seats	Depends on region: 0.5 to 1.2	
Gambling house (casinos) organisers	Number of game tables		5 million times the base data
Gambling machine exploiters	Area in square metres		18,750 times the base data
	Number of machines		156,250 times the base data

Armenia

Type of business	Base data	Adjustment ratio	Monthly presumptive payment (AMD)
Lottery games organisers	Total value of lotteries sold during a month		25% of base data
	Number of computers for totalisators		75,000 times the base data in case of totalisators
	Number of websites provisioned for organising internet totalisator		1 million times the base data if connected to the global internet network

Activities connected with gambling house, gambling machine exploitation, and lottery games will be invalid from 1 January 2013.

License payments

Individuals (individual entrepreneurs) and legal entities engaged in certain activities should make license payments, which replace CIT and/or VAT. Under this system, the taxpayer pays a fixed tax based on the location and the business activity base data.

Type of activities	Base	Quarterly rate of license payment for 1 unit (thousand AMD)				
		Yerevan	Regions	In other cities and communities within 20 km from the Yerevan city's administrative borders	Other bordering location	Remote and Other bordering locations
Commercial trade activity outside of locations designed for implementation of trade, through the use of kiosks with the area of 7 m2 (in Yerevan) or 10 m2 in other regions	Total area of kiosk, m2	5.0	2.5	2.0	2.0	1.0
Transportation of passengers with passenger cars		20.5	18.75	17.5	17.5	17.5
Organisation of billiard game	Game table	120.0	60.0	60.0	60.0	60.0
Organisation of table tennis	Game table	40.0	20.0	20.0	20.0	20.0
Barber's shops		45.0	36.25	36.25	27.0	27.0
Technical maintenance and repairs of vehicles		45.0	36.25	36.25	36.25	36.25
Organisation of computer games	Monitor	62.5	60.0	45.0	30.0	25.0

Local income taxes

Armenia does not have any local government taxes on income.

Corporate residence

Resident entities are legal and business entities whose existence is established under Armenian law. Non-resident entities are those whose existence is established under foreign law.

Permanent establishment (PE)

The domestic definition for a PE essentially adopts the definition for PE found in the Organisation for Economic Co-operation and Development (OECD) Model Tax Convention.

Other taxes

Value-added tax (VAT)

Armenia's current VAT law is based loosely on the principles of the European Union (EU) VAT Directive. Armenia operates the input-output model of VAT. VAT-registered persons may deduct the VAT paid on their inputs from the VAT charged on their sales and account for the difference to the tax authorities.

The standard rate of VAT on domestic sales of goods and services and the importation of goods is 20%. Exported goods and related services are zero-rated. Advertising, consulting, engineering, legal, accounting, translation, data processing, banking, financial, and insurance services provided to non-residents are zero-rated if the non-resident's place of business is outside Armenia. Various supplies, including most financial and education services, are VAT-exempt.

Services supplied in Armenia by non-residents that are not registered in Armenia are subject to application of a VAT reverse charge.

The liability to account for VAT is based on taxable turnover for transactions implemented in the previous calendar year. If those revenues exceed AMD 58.35 million, the taxpayer must account for VAT on all sales. If the previous year's revenues were less than AMD 58.35 million (e.g. the taxpayer is in the first year of operations), the taxpayer is obliged to account for VAT only on sales in the current year that exceed AMD 58.35 million. Taxpayers whose revenues are below the AMD 58.35 million threshold may voluntarily elect to account for VAT.

Businesses that require a license costing more than AMD 100,000 to operate and businesses producing/importing excisable goods are required to account for VAT on their sales.

Generally, VAT payers should file VAT returns on a quarterly basis. However, taxpayers with sales (excluding VAT) in the previous calendar year exceeding AMD 100 million are required to file VAT returns monthly. VAT payments must be made and VAT returns filed within 20 days following the end of the reporting period.

As of 1 January 2012, VAT payers must be registered at tax authorities based on VAT payer registration numbers.

Also starting from 1 January 2012, those VAT payers whose monthly turnover exceeds AMD 100 million are required to increase their VAT tax base by 20% (effectively pay 24% VAT on their supplies) if 10% or more of their transactions are implemented without issuing proper VAT invoices or specified accompanying documents. This rule

Armenia

only applies to those VAT payers who directly import goods into the country or produce them locally.

Customs duties

The Customs Code of Armenia regulates customs procedures in Armenia. The most frequently used customs regimes are import for free circulation, temporary import, temporary export, and export for free circulation.

Customs levies are payable by persons whose goods cross the customs border of Armenia. Customs levies consist of customs duties, taxes, duties, and other mandatory charges.

Generally, customs duty is imposed as an *ad valorem* duty, which means that the tax is calculated as a percentage of the customs value of the goods. Armenia uses only two *ad valorem* rates: 0% and 10%.

Customs duty is collected on the customs value of the imported goods. Importers must take into account specific rules (based on World Trade Organization [WTO] rules) to determine the customs value on which the import tax will be applied. The general rule is that the customs value will be the price actually paid or payable for the goods when sold for export to Armenia.

Customs fees are payable within three days from the provision of customs services, but not later than the release of goods from customs.

Excise tax

Excise tax is payable on alcoholic beverages and tobacco products, whether imported or produced domestically, as follows:

Goods	Unit of measure	Tax rate
Beer	1 litre	30%, but not less than AMD 105 for 1 litre
Grape and other wines, wine ingredients	1 litre	10% of factory price, but not less than AMD 100 for 1 litre
Vermouth and other types of wine that contain vegetarian and other aromatic extracts	1 litre	50%, but not less than AMD 750 for 1 litre
Other brewed drinks (apple cider, pear cider, honey-drinks)	1 litre	25%, but not less than AMD 270 for 1 litre
Ethyl spirit	1 litre (by recalculation of 100% spirit)	50%, but not less than AMD 900 for 1 litre
Alcoholic drinks	1 litre	50%, but not less than AMD 500 for 1 litre
Tobacco substitutes	1 kilogram	AMD 1,500
Raw oil and oil materials	1 ton	AMD 27,000
Gases produced from oil and other hydro-carbons (except natural gas)	1 ton	AMD 1,000
Petrol	1 ton	AMD 25,000
Diesel fuel	Customs value or 1 ton	10%, but not less than AMD 32,500 for 1 ton

Goods	Unit of measure	Tax rate
Motor oil	1 kilogram	10%, but not less than AMD 400 for 1 kg
Cars having more than AMD 25 million customs value	Customs value of importation	20%

Taxpayers producing excisable goods in Armenia should submit a quarterly excise tax return and pay the tax liability by the 20th day of the month following the quarter.

Land tax

Land tax is assessed and collected at the municipal level and is paid bi-annually by landowners and the permanent users of state-owned land. Tax on rented land is levied on the lessor. The land cadastre (valuation system) is used to determine the value of the land. Land tax for agricultural land is calculated at 15% of the net income determined by the cadastral evaluation. For non-agricultural land, the rate is 0.5% to 1.0% of the cadastral value of the land.

Property tax

Property tax is assessed and collected at the municipal level on buildings, motor vehicles, and means of water transport. The tax rate on buildings is 0.3%, which is paid on the cadastral value.

Property tax for motor vehicles with up to ten seats is calculated as follows:

Capacity (horsepower)	Tax rate (per horsepower)
Up to 120	AMD 200
121 to 150	AMD 300
151 to 250	AMD 300 + AMD 1,000 per horsepower in excess of 150
251 and over	AMD 500 + AMD 1,000 per horsepower in excess of 150

Property tax for motor vehicles with more than ten seats is calculated as follows:

Capacity (horsepower)	Tax rate (per horsepower)
Up to 200	AMD 100
201 and over	AMD 200

The annual property tax on motorcycles is calculated at the rate of AMD 40 for each horsepower of tax base. The annual rate of property tax on watercraft is calculated at AMD 150 for each horsepower of tax base.

Beginning from the fourth year after the year of production, the tax base for motor vehicles and means of water transport is reduced by 10% per year, up to a maximum reduction of 50%.

Legal entities should calculate property tax and pay this to the municipal budget on a semi-annual basis. The semi-annual property tax calculations should be submitted to the local tax inspectorates not later than the 20th day following the reporting half-year.

Transfer taxes

Armenia does not have any transfer taxes.

Armenia

Stamp taxes
Armenia does not have any stamp taxes.

Branch income

When a non-resident company conducts business in Armenia through a subdivision (i.e. a branch or a representative office) and maintains separate accounting records for that subdivision, taxable income generally should be determined on the same basis as for resident entities. Note that a subdivision is taxable on dividends received from Armenian companies and may not carry forward losses, which differs from the treatment of resident entities (*see the Deductions section for more information*). However, the subdivision may be able to overcome these restrictions under a relevant tax treaty.

If it is not possible to determine taxable profit based on the direct method (i.e. taxable income less deductible expenses) for the subdivision of the foreign entity in Armenia, income is determined based on a method agreed upon between the taxpayer and the tax authorities. The law explicitly recognises the allocation method (the taxpayer allocates a portion of its worldwide income and expenses to Armenia) as a possible approach.

Armenia has no special tax rules for non-commercial representative offices established to engage in liaison-type activities. Such offices are subject to the normal CIT, but an exemption from CIT may be available under a relevant tax treaty if the activities of the representative office are not sufficient to constitute a PE for the foreign entity.

See the Withholding taxes section for a list of countries with which Armenia has a tax treaty.

Income determination

Taxable profits are defined as a positive difference between a taxpayer's gross income and deductible expenses. Gross income encompasses all revenues received by a taxpayer from all economic activities, unless the revenues are expressly exempt from inclusion under the law. Deductible expenses encompass all necessary and documented expenses that are directly related to conducting business or earning profit, unless a specific provision in the law restricts the deduction.

Inventory valuation
Inventories are generally stated at the lower of cost and net realisable value. First in first out (FIFO) and average cost methods of valuation are generally used for tax purposes.

Capital gains
Capital gains are included in taxable income. Non-residents are taxable on the realised capital gains from the increase of the value of the assets (including shares) located in Armenia.

Dividend income
Dividends derived by an Armenian entity from another Armenian entity are exempt from tax. Dividends derived by non-residents from Armenian entities are subject to 10% withholding tax (WHT), unless relief is available under a relevant tax treaty (*see the Withholding taxes section*).

Interest income

Interest income attracts normal CIT treatment.

Foreign income

Resident entities are liable to Armenian tax on their worldwide income. Foreign taxes should be available for credit against Armenian tax liabilities, up to the amount of Armenian tax payable on the foreign income.

There are no provisions in Armenian tax law allowing any tax deferral on income earned abroad.

Deductions

Expenses incurred in the furtherance of a taxpayer's business activities generally are deductible, unless a specific provision in the law provides otherwise. Expenses that are not supported by relevant documentation are not deductible.

The deductibility of following common items is limited for CIT purposes:

- Expenses incurred for advertising outside Armenia are limited to the greater of 3% of gross income or 20% of the value of services or goods exported from Armenia.
- Expenses for training of staff outside Armenia is limited to the lesser of 4% of the gross income of the reporting year or AMD 3 million per employee.
- Expenses for foreign trips are limited to 5% of the gross income of the reporting year.
- Representative expenses are limited to the lesser of 0.5% of the gross income of the reporting year or AMD 5 million.

Depreciation and amortisation

Fixed assets are required to be depreciated using the straight-line method.

The maximum rates per annum for depreciating fixed assets are:

Asset	Maximum depreciation rate per annum (%)
Other industrial and commercial buildings, constructions and transmission devices	5
Hotels, resorts, rest houses, educational institutions	10
Robot equipment and assembly lines	33.3
Calculating devices and computers	100
Fixed assets with the value up to AMD 50,000	100
Industrial and commercial buildings, constructions and transmission devices located in a designated disaster area (currently Gyumri)	100
Other fixed assets	20

Land may not be depreciated.

Intangible assets may be amortised using the straight-line method over the lesser of the asset's useful economic life or ten years.

Armenia

Goodwill
Payments with respect to goodwill and amortisation of goodwill are not deductible in Armenia.

Start-up expenses
Start-up expenses are fully deductible, provided they are properly documented.

Interest expenses
As a general rule, interest is deductible if the related debt is used to fund business activities of the taxpayer and the interest rate is not more than double the Central Bank of Armenia rate (currently, the deductible interest rate is capped at 24%).

In addition to the existing cap (twice of the Armenian Central Bank's settlement rate), from January 2012 the deductible interest expense payable within the tax year should not exceed:

* nine times the value of net assets of a taxpayer, if borrowings received from banks and credit organisations, or
* twice the value of net assets of a taxpayer, if borrowing received from other entities.

The net assets are a positive difference between the taxpayer's assets and liabilities. The value of net assets should be considered based on results of the reporting year.

The restriction does not apply to the banks and credit organisations and to the funds borrowed from international organisations specified by the government. The restriction also does not apply to the interest payable on funds attracted from publicly placed debt instruments (securities).

Bad debt
A taxpayer is entitled to deduct bad debts if the taxpayer creates a reserve and allocates the amount of bad debt in the following proportions:

* Up to 90 days from the due date: 0%.
* From 91 to 180 days from the due date: 25%.
* From 181 to 270 days from the due date: 50%.
* From 271 to 365 days from the due date: 75%.

Beyond 365 days, bad debts of less than AMD 100,000 may be deducted. For larger debts, the company would need to have pursued the debt through the courts before a deduction may be taken.

Charitable contributions
Charitable donations and contributions to non-profit organisations are deductible in amounts of up to 0.25% of gross income.

Lease payments
Lease payments on operating leases are deductible. The lessor claims a deduction for depreciation of the leased assets. Financial leasing is treated for tax purposes as if a sale had been made. The lessee includes the value of the property in the relevant group of fixed assets and claims depreciation charges. The lessee also deducts the interest and commission elements of the lease payments in the period in which they are payable. Similarly, the lessor recognises taxable income for the total principal amount of the lease at the time when the asset is transferred and recognises the interest and commission element of the payments over the term of the lease.

Fines and penalties

Commercial fines and penalty expenses are deductible for CIT purposes. Fines and penalties paid to the state or municipal budgets are not deductible.

Taxes

Non-refundable (non-credited) taxes (e.g. property tax, land tax, expensed VAT), duties, and other obligatory payments are deductible for CIT purposes.

Net operating losses

Companies are entitled to carry forward losses to the five subsequent income years. Armenian law does not allow the carryback of losses.

Payments to foreign affiliates

Payments to foreign affiliates are deductible, if they meet the normal tests for deductibility.

Group taxation

There are no group taxation provisions available in Armenia.

Transfer pricing

Armenia does not have formal transfer pricing rules. The tax authorities may apply market prices in limited cases, but this does not happen very often.

Thin capitalisation

Armenia does not have thin capitalisation rules. However, there are certain limitations on deductibility of interest expenses (*see Interest expenses in the Deductions section*).

Tax credits and incentives

Taxpayers engaged in agricultural production are exempt from tax on that income.

Resident companies listed on the Armenian Stock Exchange, as well as companies that list on the Exchange by 31 December 2012, with at least 20% of their shares publicly held by 100 or more shareholders, are entitled to a reduction in CIT.

Provided such companies prepare and publish their financial statements under International Financial Reporting Standards (IFRS), they are entitled to a 50% reduction in their CIT (up to a maximum of AMD 300 million per year). The incentive applies to the 2009 to 2012 income years. The incentive will be repayable (plus penalties) if the company delists, liquidates (other than for bankruptcy), or reduces the public issue below 20% before 31 December 2015.

Foreign tax credit

Tax residents are allowed to credit foreign taxes paid on income received abroad against their Armenian tax liabilities. The amount of foreign tax credit is limited to the amount of Armenian tax that would arise from the equivalent income in Armenia.

Armenia

Withholding taxes

Payments to non-residents are subject to the following WHT rates:

* Payments for insurance, reinsurance, and transportation are subject to WHT at the rate of 5%.
* Other income received from Armenian sources is subject to WHT at the rate of 10%.

WHT is required to be transferred to the budget not later than the 20th day of the month following the payment of income. A WHT return should be submitted by 20 February following the reporting year.

WHT rates for non-residents may be reduced under a relevant tax treaty.

Recipient	Dividends (%) Non-portfolio	Portfolio	Interest (%) (1)	Royalties (%)
Non-treaty	10	10	10	10
Austria	5 (2)	10	0/10 (3)	5
Belarus	10 (4)	10	10	10
Belgium	5 (2)	10	0/10 (3)	8
Bulgaria	5 (5)	10	10	10
Canada	5 (6)	10	10	10
China (P.R.C.)	5 (7)	10	10	10
Croatia	0 (8)	10	10	5
Cyprus	0/5 (9)	10	5	5
Czech Republic	10	10	0/5/10 (10)	5/10 (11)
Estonia	5 (7)	10	10	10
Finland	5 (7)	10	5	5/10 (12)
France	5 (2)	15	0/10 (13)	5/10 (14)
Georgia	5 (7)	10	10	5
Greece	10	10	10	5
India	10	10	10	10
Iran	10 (7)	10	10	5
Italy	5 (15)	10	0/10 (16)	7
Kazakhstan	10	10	10	10
Latvia	5 (7)	10	10	10
Lebanon	5 (7)	10	8	5
Lithuania	5 (7)	10	10	10
Luxembourg	5 (2)	10	10 (16)	5
Moldova	5 (7)	10	10	10
Netherlands	0/5 (17)	10	0/5 (13)	5
Poland	10	10	5	10
Qatar	5 (18)	10	5	5
Romania	5 (7)	10	10	10
Russia	5 (5)	10	0	0
Spain (22)	0 (20)	10	5	5/10 (11)
Switzerland	5 (19)	10	0/10 (3)	5
Syria	10	10	10	12
Thailand	10	10	10	10

Recipient	Dividends (%)		Interest (%) (1)	Royalties (%)
	Non-portfolio	Portfolio		
Turkmenistan	5 (7)	10	10	5
Ukraine	5 (7)	10	10	0
United Arab Emirates	3	3	0	5
United Kingdom and Northern Ireland (23)	5/15 (21)	10	5	5

Notes

1. Several treaties contain a 0% rate on interest paid to or guaranteed by a government or one of its agencies. The table does not analyse such provisions.
2. The ownership threshold for the non-portfolio rate is 10%.
3. The 0% rate applies to the sale on credit of industrial, commercial, or scientific equipment, and capital goods, and interest on loans granted by banking enterprises. The 10% rate applies in other cases.
4. The ownership threshold for the non-portfolio rate is 30%.
5. The ownership threshold for the non-portfolio rate is direct investment of 40,000 United States dollars (USD).
6. The ownership threshold for the non-portfolio rate is 25%, and the direct investment must exceed USD 100,000.
7. The ownership threshold for the non-portfolio rate is 25%.
8. The 0% rate applies if the dividends are paid to a foreign company that has owned more than 25% of the Armenian company for at least two calendar years preceding the distribution and the dividends are not subject to profit tax in the foreign company's country of residence.
9. The 0% rate applies if the beneficial owner has invested at least 150,000 euros (EUR) in equity.
10. The 0% rate applies to government debt and government-assisted debt; the 5% rate applies to interest on loans or credit granted by banks; and the 10% rate applies in other cases.
11. The 5% rate applies to literary, artistic, or scientific work copyright royalties and to film and broadcasting royalties. The 10% rate applies in other cases.
12. The lower rate applies to consideration for the use of, or the right to use, any computer software, patent, trademark, design or model or plan, secret formula or process, or information concerning industrial, commercial, or scientific experience (know-how).
13. The 0% rate applies to the credit sale of industrial, commercial, or scientific equipment, to the credit sale of merchandise or services, and to loans granted by a bank. Higher rate applies in other cases.
14. The 5% rate applies to copyright royalties, and the 10% rate applies in other cases.
15. The ownership threshold for the non-portfolio rate is 10%, and the direct investment must exceed USD 100,000.
16. The 0% rate applies to interest on a loan granted by a banking enterprise. The 10% rate applies in other cases.
17. The ownership threshold for the 5% non-portfolio rate is 10%. The 0% rate applies if the dividends out of which the profits are paid have been effectively taxed at the normal rate for CIT and the dividends are exempt income to the Dutch recipient.
18. The ownership threshold for the non-portfolio rate is direct investment of USD 100,000.
19. The ownership threshold for the non-portfolio rate is 25%, and the direct investment must exceed 200,000 Swiss francs (CHF).
20. The 0% rates applies if the beneficiary owner is resident of the other contracting state, the beneficiary owners owns at least 25% of shares at least two years prior to the payment, and dividends are exempted for CIT purposes in the other contracting state.
21. Lower rate applies when the actual owner owns at least 25% of the capital and has made at least a 1 million British pound (GBP) investment prior to the payment. Higher rate applies when dividends are paid form an investment in real estate.
22. Provisions of the treaty generally apply from 22 March 2012.
23. Treaty provisions will apply in Armenia from 1 January 2013. In the United Kingdom, the provisions for income subject to WHT will apply from 1 January 2013. For income tax and capital gain tax, from 6 April 2012, and for corporation tax from 1 April 2012.

Tax administration

Taxable period

In Armenia, the taxable period is the calendar year.

Tax returns

The annual CIT return for resident entities must be filed by 15 April.

Armenia

Presumptive payment payers should submit application on base data and adjustment ratios twice a year or by the 15th day of the following month (depending on the type of activities).

Payment of taxes

The tax corresponding to the CIT return for resident entities is payable by 25 April.

Taxpayers are also required to make advance CIT payments by the 15th day of the last month of each quarter. Each advance payment is equal to 18.75% of the CIT paid for the previous year. For payments before the previous year's tax is calculated (e.g. January to March), tax is paid based on the last filed tax return, and an adjustment is made in the first advance tax payment made after the previous year's tax is calculated to correct the amount paid. If advance payments exceed the CIT liability for the year, the excess may be refunded.

Advance payments are not required if a taxpayer's profit for the proceeding year was less than AMD 500,000. Thus, newly established companies do not need to make advance payments until 25 April of the year following the start of operations.

Armenia also has a quarterly minimum CIT. If the advance CIT payable is less than 1% of revenues for the previous quarter less depreciation charges (up to a maximum of 50% of revenues), the excess is paid as a minimum CIT. The minimum CIT is applied against CIT payable for the year. Any excess is applied against the CIT liability for the subsequent year.

Taxpayers are required to make either advance payments or minimum CIT, whichever is higher.

Branches of foreign companies pay advance CIT biannually, but only if their CIT for the proceeding year exceeded AMD 2 million. Each advance payment is equal to ¼ of the CIT paid for the previous year. Branches are not subject to the minimum CIT. The annual tax return for branches is filed by 15 April. The corresponding tax is payable by 25 April.

Taxpayers are required to make presumptive payments within 15 days after the end of each month.

Audit cycle

Risk based audits

For the purposes of planning audits, the authorities develop risk criteria that are approved by the Armenian government. Based on the risk criteria, entities are classified into the following three categories:

- High risk entities.
- Medium risk entities.
- Low risk entities.

The authorities should approve the audit plan (list of audit targets) for the following year before 1 December of the preceding year.

Tax audits

The tax authorities may carry out scheduled audits a maximum of once each year for high risk taxpayers, once each three years for medium risk taxpayers, and once each five years for low risk taxpayers.

Business entities must be notified of the audit in writing at least three days before the scheduled audit.

For normal business entities, the scheduled audit should be carried out within 15 business days, although the period may be extended by up to ten days. For companies whose annual revenue exceeds AMD 3 billion (approximately USD 8.3 million), the period may be extended by up to 75 business days.

The actual period of the inspection for normal business entities should not exceed 30 business days and 90 business days for large companies.

Before starting an audit, the tax inspector must present a written order to the taxpayer outlining the scope and period of the tax audit. The written order specifies the names of the officials who may participate in the audit.

Statute of limitations

The statue of limitations is three years.

Topics of focus for tax authorities

There are no specific topics of focus for the tax authorities. In practice, the tax authorities perform a comprehensive audit of the taxpayer's books, covering all taxes and mandatory payments.

Aruba

PwC contact

Hans Ruiter
PricewaterhouseCoopers
L.G. Smith Boulevard 62
Oranjestad, Aruba
Tel: +1 297 522 1647
Email: hans.ruiter@an.pwc.com

Significant developments

The free zone company

As of 1 January 2012, service companies are no longer required to be established in one of the current designated free zones. As per the abovementioned date, service companies may have an office elsewhere in Aruba other than the designated free zones. However, these service companies should have the approval from Free Zone Aruba N.V. and the Aruba tax authorities and should further comply with specific rules. The prohibition to provide services to the local market remains effective.

Previously, the free zone company was allowed to generate a maximum of 25% of its turnover with local consumers. The percentage of the turnover allowed with local consumers had to be reduced annually, for seven years from 25% to 5%. As a result, after seven years, only 5% of the turnover was allowed to be generated with local consumers. As of 1 January 2012, this is no longer the case. The free zone company is allowed to generate a maximum of 25% of its turnover with local consumers and no longer has to reduce this percentage to 5%. However, all activities performed for residents will remain subject to the regular corporate income tax (CIT) rate of 28%. Furthermore, import duties and excise tax are due on goods sold to local consumers.

Tax reform

The government of Aruba instituted a tax reform commission. The tax reform commission is in charge of the review and optimisation of the current Aruba tax system, taking into consideration:

* fair social income distribution
* increased tax base
* attracting new investors
* better tax collection
* improvement of the competitive position of Aruba, and
* transparence and substance in accordance international trends and rules.

The current corporate taxes that are subject to review by the tax reform commission are CIT, social security premiums, wage tax, dividend withholding tax (WHT), land tax, transfer tax, import duties and excise tax, turnover tax, and foreign exchange commission (FEC).

Taxes on corporate income

Resident companies are taxed on their worldwide income. Non-resident companies are taxed on the following Aruba-source income:

- Profits allocated to a permanent establishment (PE) or permanent representative in Aruba.
- Profits from real estate located in Aruba.
- Profits on loans secured by a mortgage on real estate located in Aruba.

Aruba has a flat CIT rate of 28%. Aruba also has special tax regimes (e.g. the imputation payment company, the Aruba exempt company, the fiscal transparent company, the free zone company, the so-called oil refinery or oil terminal regime), which are ultimately taxed at a lower tax rate. *For a full discussion of these special tax regimes, see the Tax credits and incentives section.*

CIT is levied on the income as reflected in the profit and loss statement less any allowable deductions based on Aruba tax and case law.

Corporate residence

The place of residency of a corporation, association, society, foundation, or body is determined based on the circumstances. If the aforementioned entities are managed and controlled in Aruba, they will, in principle, be deemed to be resident in Aruba. If the legal form of an entity is governed by the Aruban law, then its place of residency will be considered continuously to be in Aruba.

Permanent establishment (PE)
If a foreign entity carries on a business through a PE or a permanent representative in Aruba, it will be subject to CIT in Aruba. While Aruba does not have rules and regulation as to the definition and interpretation of the term 'permanent establishment', a PE is deemed to exist if the place of execution of a building site or construction, excavation, maintenance, cleaning, assembly, or installation activities surpasses a period of 30 days. The memorandum of explanation refers to the commentary on Article 5 of the Organisation for Economic Co-operation and Development (OECD) model convention for the definition and interpretation of the term 'permanent establishment'.

Other taxes

Turnover tax
Aruba does not have a value-added tax (VAT) or sales tax, but it does have a business turnover tax. Turnover tax is levied at the rate of 1.5% on the delivery of goods or services rendered in Aruba. Goods that are imported into Aruba are not subject to turnover tax. A turnover tax exemption is applicable on exports. The exemption is applicable if the entrepreneur has asserted that the turnover is realised in connection with the delivery of goods to customers located outside of Aruba, where the goods in connection with the delivery are sent or transported to a destination outside Aruba.

Goods are all physical objects as well as electricity, gas, heating, cooling, and such. Services are all performances rendered against payment. A payment is defined as all proceeds in connection with the delivery of goods or services rendered. If a payment is not completely made via money, the fair market value of the compensation should be taken into account.

In the case of goods, the place of the taxable event is either where the transportation starts (if sold abroad) or at the physical location of the goods at the moment it is

Aruba

delivered. The place of the taxable event with regard to services is generally the place where the entrepreneur is established or from where one has a PE from which the service is rendered. As an exception to the aforementioned general rule, the place of the taxable event for certain services (e.g. services related to a real property) is the place where the actual services are rendered (e.g. the place where the real property is situated).

Some exemptions apply. For example, no turnover tax is levied on the sale of immovable property if it is also subject to transfer tax. Furthermore, exemptions also apply to interest received or payments for hotel rooms or leasing of apartments (insofar as room tax has been paid on the proceeds) and casino revenues (insofar as gambling duties are due on these revenues).

The turnover tax is due within 15 days of the calendar month following the calendar month over which the turnover tax is due. A turnover tax return must be submitted to the tax authorities together with payment of the amount due.

Import duties
Import duties are imposed by a tariff, which is set as a percentage of the cost, insurance, and freight (CIF) value of the product. A classification rule has been published that categorises various imported products into groups. A tariff ranging from 0% to 50% is levied on the various groups of products.

Excise duties
Excise duties are imposed on products such as spirits, cigarettes, mineral oil, and distillery. The taxable base of the excise duties is based on either the weight, volume, and/or the amount of the aforementioned products.

Ground tax
A person or entity that, as of 1 January of each year, owns real estate in Aruba or uses real estate based on property rights is subject to ground tax. The ground tax is levied on the registered value, which is determined once every five years by the tax authorities, and can only be protested in the first year of the aforementioned period (taking into account the two month objection period as of the date of the assessment). The rate amounts to 0.4% of the registered value of the real estate minus a general exemption of 60,000 Aruban florins (AWG). If the real estate is not used or is empty for more than six months in a year, a reduction in the ground tax due can be requested from the tax authorities.

Real estate transfer tax
If real estate situated in Aruba is transferred, the buyer of the real estate must pay transfer tax on the sales price of the real estate (unless the value registered at the tax authorities is higher, in which case the registered value is the basis for the levy). The rate for the transfer of the legal ownership of real estate with a value not exceeding AWG 250,000 is 3%. The rate for the transfer of the legal ownership of real estate with a value exceeding AWG 250,000 is 6% (due on the total amount).

If shares in a real estate company are sold, no transfer tax is due.

Stamp taxes
Stamp taxes are, in principle, due on all documents as indicated in the Stamp State Ordinance. In practice, it is usually only levied on the documents used in the course of a legal suit.

Registration taxes
Aruba does not impose registration taxes.

Foreign exchange commission (FEC)
An FEC is due when residents make a payment abroad in connection with certain legal transactions. The FEC is calculated as 1.3% of the payment abroad. Based on the State Ordinance, a payment abroad is considered:

- a payment with local currency or a payment from a florin account, whether or not by electronic transfer
- a payment with foreign currency or a payment from a foreign currency account, whether or not by electronic transfer, or
- a payment from a foreign currency account held abroad or from an inter-company account held by a person or entity abroad, whether or not by electronic transfer.

FEC is due to the extent the abovementioned payment is a result of one or more of the following legal transactions:

- the purchase of foreign instruments of payments or foreign monetary instruments
- obtaining control over receivables in one or more foreign currencies, or
- the crediting of an account in name of a non-resident of Aruba held at a foreign exchange bank or an institution abroad.

An exemption of the FEC was applicable for certain inter-island bank transactions. However, in connection with the dissolution of the Dutch Antilles as of 10 October 2010 and due to the fact that the United States dollar (USD) is the official currency of the islands of Bonaire, St. Eustatius, and Saba (BES islands), the general exemption of the FEC from Aruba to the BES islands for inter-island transactions in florins is no longer applicable as of 1 January 2011.

As a result, the FEC of 1.3% is applicable on all transactions from Aruba to Curaçao, St. Maarten, and the BES islands.

Furthermore, FEC will be levied on the purchase of foreign currencies with Aruban florins.

According to the policy of the Central Bank of Aruba, another exemption for the FEC applies when cash is transferred to a foreign bank account of an Aruban resident. In order to apply for this exemption, certain formalities must be met. First, the foreign bank account of the Aruba resident must be registered at the Central Bank of Aruba. Secondly, the Central Bank of Aruba must grant a so-called exemption for requirements. In addition, certain overviews of transactions regarding the foreign bank account must be filed with the Central Bank of Aruba on a quarterly basis.

Tourist levy
The tourist levy rate is 9.5% of the compensation (including charges) that the tourist pays for the use of lodging or a hotel room.

Also, the fixed fees for timeshare units have been increased. The taxable base for the tourist levy on timeshare units is set on:

- AWG 179 per day for studio units.
- AWG 193.95 per day for one bedroom units.
- AWG 223.75 per day for other than the abovementioned units.

Aruba

Abovementioned fixed fees are not applicable in the event the time-share unit is made available to other guests that are not time-share guests. In that case, 9.5% tourist levy is due per day on the compensation paid by other guests for the use of the unit.

With regard to all-inclusive packages, the taxable base is set on 40% of the price of the all-inclusive package with a minimum of AWG 162 per day, increased with charges (e.g. service charges and energy charges).

Local citizens registered in the Aruban municipal register are not subject to the tourist levy. The owner of a condominium is also exempted from the tourist levy.

Branch income

Branch income is, in principle, determined according to the separate entity approach. Branches of foreign insurance companies apply a specific profit determination method. Furthermore, the transfer of profits to the head office is not subject to taxation.

Branch profits are subject to the normal CIT rate of 28%.

Income determination

Inventory valuation
Inventories may generally be stated on a last in first out (LIFO) or first in first out (FIFO) basis, provided the method chosen conforms to sound business practices. Conformity of book and tax reporting is not required.

Capital gains
Capital gains are taxed as ordinary income. However, capital gains realised on the disposal of a shareholding qualifying for the participation exemption are tax exempt.

The participation exemption applies, in general, if an Aruban company holds shares or participation certificates in companies, associations, or foundations that carry on a business. If shares or participation certificates are held in a foreign entity, the participation exemption only applies if they are not held as an investment and the foreign entity is subject to a tax on profits.

The capital gain realised on the disposal of assets may be carried over to a special tax deferral reinvestment reserve but must be deducted from the acquisition costs of the new asset. In principle, this reinvestment reserve cannot be maintained for more than four consecutive years. If the reserve has not been used after four years, the remainder will be subject to taxation.

Capital losses are tax-deductible unless these losses are incurred on shares to which the participation exemption is applicable.

Dividend income
Provided the conditions of the participation exemption are met (*see the Capital gains section above*), an Aruban company is exempt from taxation on all benefits from the participation, including inter-company (cash) dividends.

Costs made in connection with the ownership of the participation (i.e. administration costs, interest, management expenses) are not deductible from the taxable result of the Aruba parent company.

Stock dividends

Stock dividends are allowed and treated as regular dividend income. The stocks will be valued at market value for tax purposes.

Foreign income

A resident taxpayer is subject to CIT on its worldwide income. Double taxation of certain foreign source income is avoided by means of the exemption method. If there is no legal possibility to exempt income and prevent double taxation, the foreign tax paid can be claimed as a deduction.

An Aruba corporation is taxed on foreign interest and other income as earned, and on foreign dividends when received. Undistributed income of foreign subsidiaries is not taxable.

The profits of a PE in Curaçao, St. Maarten, or the Netherlands, including the Caribbean Netherlands, are tax exempt on Aruba based on the tax arrangement with the Kingdom of the Netherlands. In the case of a PE outside the Kingdom of the Netherlands (i.e. other than the Netherlands, Aruba, Curaçao, and St. Maarten), the income realised through the PE, after deduction of foreign taxes, is tax exempt.

Deductions

Depreciation

Depreciation of tangible fixed assets, excluding land, is taken over the estimated useful life of the asset. The tax department has issued the following estimated depreciation table:

Assets	Depreciation rate (%)	Residual value (%)
Buildings	2/2.5	10
Renovation	10	0
Inventory	10 /20	10
Computer		
Hardware	33/50	0
Mainframe	10/12.5	0
Machinery and installations	10	10
Transportation		
Cars	20	10
Rental cars	33	15
Trucks and buses	10	15
Start-up costs	20	0
Goodwill	20	0

The basis for the depreciation includes all costs incurred with the purchase of this asset less the residual value. The straight-line method is customary; however, the declining-balance method is also acceptable.

Aruba

As of 1 June 2010, accelerated depreciation has been introduced on assets which are used in the course of an industrial business and whose acquisition or production costs are above AWG 90 million. Aforementioned assets may be depreciated in ten equal annual parts. Note that imputation payment companies (IPCs) can not apply this facility.

Charitable contributions

The allowable gift deduction is AWG 50,000. The institution must be established in Aruba and serve one of the following interests:

- Religious.
- Charity.
- Cultural.
- Sportive.
- Scientific.
- Public interest.

Taxes

Taxes paid by the company, with the exception of CIT, are tax-deductible. Taxes paid by the company with respect to the purchase of an asset (e.g. real estate transfer tax paid while obtaining real estate) should be capitalised in the cost of the asset.

Net operating losses

A net operating loss may be carried forward to the five years following the tax year in which the loss was incurred. If the net operating loss has not been offset against profits within this period, the remaining net operating losses will expire. Net operating losses incurred by an IPC and companies operating an oil refinery or oil terminal as of 1 January 2010 may be carried forward indefinitely. Carrybacks of net operating losses are not permitted.

Payments to foreign affiliates

If interest or other payments (e.g. remunerations paid for the use of material and/or immaterial goods or services rendered) are made to entities, these payments should be made at arm's length. If the transaction is not at arm's length, only the arm's-length payment may be deducted from the taxable income.

Even if the transaction is at arm's length, the interest or other payments may still not be deductible from the taxable result of the Aruban company unless the Aruban company asserts that one of the following circumstances is applicable:

- The receiving company is not affiliated (*see below*) to the Aruban company.
- The receiving company is subject to an effective tax rate of at least 15%.
- The shares in the receiving company are all held directly or indirectly by a company whose shares (for at least 50% of the outstanding shares and representing at least 50% of the voting rights) are listed at a qualified stock exchange.

An affiliation with the taxpayer is deemed to exist in each of the following cases:

- The taxpayer has an interest of at least one third in another entity.
- An individual or entity has an interest of at least one third in the taxpayer.
- A third party has an interest of at least one third in another entity, while this third party also has an interest of at least one third in the taxpayer.

If an arm's-length payment is made to an affiliated company that is subject to taxation but pays an effective tax rate of less than 15%, only 75% of the payment made is allowed as a deduction.

Group taxation

Fiscal unity
Based on a policy of the Aruban tax authorities, Aruban resident public limited companies (*naamloze vennootschap* or NV) with at least 99% of the shares in other Aruban resident NVs can file a consolidated tax return (i.e. fiscal unity). In order to apply for this facility, a request must be filed with the Aruban tax authorities. Certain conditions must be met for the application of this regime, for instance the companies in the fiscal unity must be of the same tax regime. Advantages of this facility are that the recognition of inter-company profits may be deferred and losses may be offset with profits of other companies within the fiscal unity.

Transfer pricing
The arm's-length principle (ALP) rule is codified in the Aruban State Ordinance Profit Tax (SOPT). If a corporate entity or individual participates, directly or indirectly, in the management, supervision, or the capital of two or more corporate entities, the conditions related to all transactions between these affiliated parties should be at arm's length. The ALP is applicable on all transfer pricing between affiliated companies with regard to all mutual legal relations (e.g. purchase prices, management fees, remunerations for services provided, royalty payments). The conditions should be business like, whereas the same conditions should apply as they would have been if the same transaction would take place with a third party.

A documentation obligation is applicable in the SOPT. The explanatory notes on the bill state that for the meaning and application of the ALP and the documentation obligation, the OECD guidelines for Multinational Enterprises and Tax Administration should be considered. The documentation obligation is applicable at the moment that a transaction takes place.

Non-compliance to the documentation obligation leads to a reversed burden of proof to the taxpayer. From the explanatory notes of the profit tax return forms, it seems that the tax authorities require, as a minimum amount of documentation about the transfer pricing method used, the reason why the method was chosen and a substantiation of the manner of how the price was determined.

In light of the extensive OECD guidelines and considering the small-scale economy of Aruba, it is unclear to what extent the aforementioned requirements and the OECD guidelines should be followed. Up to this moment, the legislature has not provided detailed implementation guidelines on the documentation obligation.

Thin capitalisation
Aruba does not have thin capitalisation rules.

Controlled foreign companies (CFCs)
Aruba does not have CFC legislation.

Aruba

Tax credits and incentives

Aruban CIT legislation no longer provides tax incentives. The legislation does, however, provide incentives for certain special tax regimes that can be used to reduce the overall tax liability, such as the IPC, the Aruba exempt company, the fiscal transparent company, the free zone company, and the so-called oil refinery and oil terminal regime.

Temporary investment allowance

A temporary investment allowance applies for the year 2011 and 2012. The investment allowance amounts to 6% of the investment. The investment allowance is a deduction on the taxable profit of a company and is applicable on investments greater then AWG 5,000 that are made in a financial year. One of the conditions is that the investment must take place with an Aruban company or entrepreneur. An Aruban company or entrepreneur includes an individual or legal entity that is respectively established and carries out business in Aruba. PEs of foreign legal entities are also included in the definition of an Aruban company for investment allowance purposes. Legal entities that are incorporated for the sole purpose of making investments in the context of the investment allowance do not qualify as an Aruban company or entrepreneur for investment allowance purposes.

Certain investments do not qualify for the investment allowance (e.g. land, houses, and cars for personal use; stocks and shares; goodwill; animals; investments designated for the use by third parties or as part of the exploitation of an oil refinery or an oil terminal). Furthermore, there are also certain transactions that do not qualify for the investment allowance (e.g. certain inter-company transactions).

The investment allowance does not apply to investments by oil refineries, free zone companies, and IPCs.

If an investment, on which the investment allowance was claimed, is sold within six years after the start of the calendar year in which the investment took place, a capital disposal charge of 6% of the sales price is due.

The imputation payment company (IPC)

The IPC is, in principle, an NV or a limited liability company (*vennootschap met beperkte aansprakelijkheid* or VBA) that pays the regular CIT rate of 28%. However, when certain stringent conditions are met, the shareholder of the IPC can request an imputation payment of 26/72 of the (formal) dividend distributed. Provided that the 0% dividend WHT is applicable, the effective tax rate can be lowered to 2%.

In order to qualify for the IPC status, the following requirements must be met:

* The IPC must perform qualifying activities (*see below*) in Aruba.
* An Aruba-resident individual must be a member of the board of managing directors of the IPC.
* The articles of association state that the shares of the IPC are registered and that the directors keep a shareholders registry in which all shareholders are registered.
* The articles of association state that the financial statements are drawn up according to internationally accepted principles (like IAS or GAAP) and an audit by a qualified (group of) independent certified public accountant(s) is necessary.
* The board of managing directors must notify the tax authorities within a restricted period, and after the dividend has been distributed, that the shareholder will claim the imputation payment.

A

An independent certified public accountant must provide a yearly opinion regarding the compliance of the abovementioned first three requirements for the IPC status.

The shareholder must also meet certain requirements before the imputation payment can be granted, including:

- The shareholder must hold the (economic and legal ownership of the) shares for an uninterrupted period of at least 12 months to be eligible for the imputation payment.
- The shareholder must file a request (with several enclosures) with the tax authorities to receive the imputation payment.

The activities of the IPC are limited. The IPC company is not allowed to conduct non-qualified activities, no matter how small. The following activities are regarded as qualified activities:

- Exploitation of quality hotels. A quality hotel exists when the average revenue per available room (RevPar) amounts at least AWG 354 (USD 200), the hotel has a hotel licence, and is operated at its own risk and account. Note that the RevPar can be changed annually.
- Exploitation of shipping enterprises.
- Exploitation of aviation enterprises.
- Developing, acquiring, holding, maintaining, and licensing of intellectual and industrial ownership rights.
- Insuring special entrepreneurial risks (captive insurance).
- Holding of shares or other participation certificates. The IPC may not hold more than 5% of low taxed shares or other participation certificates in foreign companies. The aforementioned are low taxed if they are subject to a 'profit' tax rate of at least 14%.
- Active financing (not being a credit institution) of other enterprises or companies, whether or not intra-group.
- Investing of funds, except in real estate and funds that are put at the disposal of group companies.
- Exploitation of a company aimed on generating sustainable energy.

The Aruba exempt company (AVV)

The Aruba exempt company (*Aruba Vrijgestelde Vennootschap* or AVV) is a particular form of a NV and is often used for international tax planning purposes. The AVV is, in principle, subject to CIT against the normal CIT rate and the dividend WHT. However, the profit of the AVV may be exempted completely from CIT and dividend WHT if its activities are limited to one or more of the following qualified activities:

- Holding of shares or other participation certificates. The IPC may not hold more than 5% of low taxed shares or other participation certificates in foreign companies. The aforementioned are low taxed if they are subject to a 'profit' tax rate of at least 14%.
- Financing (not being a credit institution) of other enterprises or companies, whether or not intra-group.
- Investing of funds, except in real estate.
- Licensing of intellectual and industrial ownership rights.

As mentioned below, the AVV may, if certain conditions are met, also opt for the fiscal transparency regime for which it will not be subject to CIT and dividend WHT. In this case, the AVV is not required to perform the abovementioned qualified activities in order to enjoy the fiscal transparency status.

Aruba

Fiscal transparent company

An NV, VBA, or AVV may opt, if certain conditions are met, to be treated as a partnership (fiscal transparent company). The fiscal transparent company is not subject to CIT, unless the fiscal transparent company carries on a business on Aruba. In that case, the shareholder would be subject to CIT with regard to the business it carries through a PE.

Dividends distributed by the fiscal transparent company to its shareholder are not subject to dividend WHT, since due to its transparency, all income and asset and liabilities are deemed to be attributed to its shareholder. The main requirements for this status is that all the company's shares must be registered, and a notification for the application for this status must be filed with the tax authorities within one month after the company has been incorporated.

The free zone company

The free zone is a specially designated area in Aruba where goods can be stored, processed, adapted, assembled, packaged, displayed, spread out, or subject to other treatments or where services can be provided.

Services include activities consisting of maintenance or repairs of goods of a non-Aruba enterprise, maintenance or repairs abroad of goods of a non-Aruba enterprise, or providing advice to or research on behalf of a non-Aruba enterprise/institution/private person. Financial services, however, are not allowed.

Conditions

A free zone company has to be a limited liability company that is incorporated according to the laws of Aruba. The free zone company is also only allowed to perform qualifying activities in the free zone (a designated area on Aruba). If activities are performed that are not allowed, the company may be banned from the free zone.

Taxation

- All profits generated from activities abroad are subject to 2% CIT. The free zone company must have a licence to perform activities for residents. All activities performed for residents are subject to the regular CIT rate of 28%. The free zone company is allowed to generate a maximum of 25% of its turnover with local consumers.
- No import duties are due if the products are imported, used in the activities in the free zone on Aruba, and exported abroad.
- No turnover tax is due by the free zone company on cross border supply of goods and/or the rendering of services.
- The free zone company is subject to the dividend WHT, which implies an effective tax rate of the free zone company of 11.8% or 6.9% (equal to the IPC).
- On request, the free zone company can be exempted from 1.3% foreign exchange commission (subject to approval of the Central Bank of Aruba). Normally this approval is a formality and no foreign exchange commission is due by the free zone company.

Other characteristics

The free zone company does not have to apply for a business licence or an establishment licence. Furthermore, a free zone company is subject to a so-called free zone facility charge of 1.1% of the sales over its turnover.

Oil refinery or oil terminal regime

In connection with the aim of the Aruba government to improve the investment climate for the exploitation of oil refineries or oil terminals, a so-called oil refinery or oil terminal regime was introduced as of 1 June 2010. The regime regards application, under certain conditions, of a lower CIT rate. Oil refineries or terminals whose shares are all held directly or indirectly by a company listed on a stock exchange recognised by the Minister are subject to a 7% CIT rate, while all other oil refineries or oil terminals are subject to a rate of 12%.

As of 1 January 2010, an unlimited carryforward loss compensation applies for companies operating an oil refinery or oil terminal.

Moreover, a 0% dividend tax rate applies as of 1 June 2010 for distributions from profits from the operation of an oil refinery and oil terminal.

Foreign tax credit
A tax credit applies to income from abroad that has been subject to tax at source or to another tax on income. The tax credit is allowed for the income tax levied abroad, but shall not exceed the Aruba profit tax that is attributable to that foreign income.

Withholding taxes

Dividend WHT
A dividend WHT is levied on all (formal and non-formal) dividend distributions of Aruba-resident entities. The tax rate is:

* 10% of the dividend distribution.
* 5% of the dividend distribution, if the shares (at least 50% of the outstanding shares and representing at least 50% of the voting rights) of the distributing company are listed at a qualified stock exchange. The same tax rate applies if all the shares of the distributing entity are held directly or indirectly by a company whom shares are (at least 50% of the outstanding shares and representing at least 50% of the voting rights) listed at a qualified stock exchange.
* 0% if the participation exemption (*see Capital gains in the Income determination section*) is applicable on the receiving company.

Dividends distributed from Aruba to countries within the Dutch Kingdom are subject to the Regulation for the Dutch Kingdom (the Regulation).

In certain situations, the Regulation reduces the rate of the dividend WHT from 10% to 7.5% or even 5%. The dividend WHT can be reduced to:

* 7.5% if the parent company owns at least 25% of the paid in capital of the distributing company.
* 5% if the parent company owns at least 25% of the paid in capital of the distributing company and the dividend at the parent company level is subject to a profit tax of at least 5.5%.

If a company is incorporated under Aruba law and transfers its factual place of management to another country, all dividend distributions by this relocated company will remain subject to the Aruba dividend WHT.

Dividend distributions include, among others:

* Formal dividend distributions.
* Liquidation payment.

Aruba

- Bonus shares.
- Paying back of share capital, unless strict conditions are met.
- Imputation payment.

Formal requirements

Within 15 days (based on the tax return: within one month) after a dividend becomes payable, a dividend WHT return must be filed together with payment of the amount due. A dividend is payable if it is at the disposal of the shareholder (i.e. the board of directors of the distributing company does not have to take any more action in order for the shareholder to claim the dividend). A dividend is also payable if the debt becomes interest bearing because of the distribution.

A statement of approval of the Central Bank of Aruba is required if dividends are distributed to a foreign shareholder. If the dividend exceeds AWG 750,000, a licence from the Central Bank of Aruba is required.

Tax administration

Tax returns

Once a CIT return is issued by the tax authorities, the taxpayer is obligated to file the tax return within two months after date of issuance. If, within six months after the tax year has ended, no tax return has been issued, the taxpayer is obligated to request a return within 15 days after the six months period. It may be argued that this obligation does not exist if a taxpayer is not subject to taxation.

If the final CIT return cannot be filed within the required two-month period, a request for an extension may be filed. The tax inspector may grant an extension for a maximum period of 12 months.

Payment of tax

CIT is due upon receipt of an assessment. The amount of tax due should be paid within two months after the date of the assessment.

The dividend WHT is due within 15 days after the dividend has become payable. A dividend WHT return must be submitted to the tax authorities together with payment of the amount due.

Audit cycle

There is no specific cycle for audits. Depending on a desk review of the tax returns of the last couple of years, an audit may follow.

Statute of limitations

An additional assessment can be imposed, in general, until five years after the tax year. In cases where the taxpayer is considered to be in bad faith, this period can be extended up to ten years or, in some cases, up to 12 years (e.g. if the tax differences relate to a component that is being held in a foreign country) after the tax year.

Topics of focus for tax authorities

There are no specific topics of focus. In case an audit is started, each aspect may be investigated. Often, the audit will not only focus on the profit tax, but also the other tax obligations, such as turnover tax, wage tax, and social security premiums.

Australia

PwC contact

Tom Seymour
PricewaterhouseCoopers
Riverside Centre
123 Eagle Street
Brisbane, Queensland 4000
Australia
Tel: +61 7 3257 8623
Email: tom.seymour@au.pwc.com

Significant developments

Legislation was enacted in early September 2011 to change the tax treatment of expenditure on research and development (R&D). The concessional deductions have been replaced with an R&D tax credit with effect from 1 July 2011. For companies with an annual turnover of less than 20 million Australian dollars (AUD), there will be a 45% refundable tax credit, equivalent to a 150% tax concession, and for companies with a turnover of greater than AUD 20 million, they will have access to a non-refundable 40% tax credit, equivalent to a 133% tax concession. *See the Tax credits and incentives section for more information.*

A 'carbon pricing mechanism' is now legislated to apply with effect from 1 July 2012. There are a number of income tax and indirect tax impacts of the measure, both for those directly liable under the carbon emissions regime and for those impacted by associated measures, such as changes to the fuel tax and excise rates, and for small business impacted by the tax-related compensation measures.

Since the release in May 2010 of the government's interim response to the recommendations made following the comprehensive review of Australia's tax system (Henry Review), one of the key changes implemented by the government has been the new Minerals Resource Rent Tax (MRRT) applicable to iron ore and coal projects in Australia and an extension of the existing Petroleum Resource Rent Tax (PRRT) to apply to all Australian onshore and offshore oil and gas projects, including the North West Shelf. The MRRT and extended PRRT apply from 1 July 2012. *See Minerals Resource Rent Tax and Petroleum Resource Rent Tax in the Other taxes section for more information.*

To further develop the Australian tax reform landscape, the government hosted a Tax Forum on 4 and 5 October 2011 to continue the debate of the Henry Review with a focus on business tax, state taxes, environmental and social taxes, personal tax, and system governance and to assist the government in prioritising its agenda for further tax reforms. One of the key outcomes of the Tax Forum was the establishment of a Business Tax Working Group that will look at reforms that can increase productivity and deliver tax relief to businesses. The Working Group initially considered reforms to the treatment of business tax losses, and recommended a loss carryback regime, which was subsequently accepted by the government. The loss carryback regime is proposed to apply to all companies for tax losses incurred from 1 July 2012. *See Net operating losses in the Deductions section for more information.*

Australia

The Working Group is now considering longer term options for business tax reform, such as reducing the corporate tax rate or moving to a business expenditure tax system (such as an allowance for corporate equity).

In February 2011, the Assistant Treasurer released exposure draft legislation setting out the proposed legislative details of the taxation laws to modernise the controlled foreign company (CFC) rules and to implement new foreign accumulation fund (FAF) rules. The government announced the modernisation of the CFC rules in May 2009 as part of wider reforms to Australia's foreign source income anti-tax-deferral (attribution) rules. The foreign investment fund (FIF) rules were repealed with effect from the 2010/11 income year and are proposed to be replaced with the proposed FAF regime which, in broad terms, is directed at investments in non-CFCs or fixed trusts which fail 'bright line' investment and accumulation tests. The changes are yet to be finalised and given legislative effect. The commencement date for the new rules is currently unknown. *See Foreign income in the Income determination section for more information.*

Taxes on corporate income

Companies are subject to federal tax on their income at a flat rate of 30%.

Companies that are resident of Australia are subject to Australian income tax on their worldwide income. Generally, non-residents are subject to Australian income tax on Australian-sourced income only. However, where a company is resident in a country with which Australia has concluded a double tax agreement (DTA), generally Australia's right to tax business profits is limited to profits attributable to a permanent establishment (PE) in Australia.

Local income taxes

There are no state or municipal taxes on income.

Corporate residence

A company is a resident of Australia for income tax purposes if it is incorporated in Australia or, if not incorporated in Australia, it carries on business in Australia and either (i) its central management and control are in Australia or (ii) its voting power is controlled by shareholders who are residents of Australia.

Permanent establishment (PE)

The concept of a PE is established in both domestic law and various DTAs that have been concluded with Australia. Where a company is resident in a country with which Australia has a DTA, it is important to have regard to the definition of PE contained therein as this will generally apply in priority to the domestic law.

Broadly, under Australia's domestic law, a PE is a place at or through which a person carries on any business, and includes:

* A place where the person is carrying on business through an agent (except where the agent does not have, or does not habitually exercise, a general authority to negotiate and conclude contracts on behalf of the person).
* A place where the person has, is using, or is installing substantial equipment or substantial machinery.
* A place where the person is engaged in a construction contract.

- Where the person is engaged in selling goods manufactured, assembled, processed, packed, or distributed by another person for, or at or to the order of, the first-mentioned person and either of those persons participates in the management, control, or capital of the other person or another person participates in the management, control, or capital of both of those persons, the place where the goods are manufactured, assembled, processed, packed, or distributed.

Most DTAs contain a definition of PE which is similar, though not identical to, the definition under domestic law.

Other taxes

Goods and services tax (GST)

The federal government levies GST at a rate of 10%, and distributes the revenue to state governments. The GST is a value-added tax (VAT) applied at each level in the manufacturing and marketing chain and applies to most goods and services, with registered suppliers getting credits for GST on inputs acquired to make taxable supplies.

Food with some significant exceptions; exports; most health, medical, and educational supplies; and some other supplies are 'GST-free' (the equivalent of 'zero-rated' in other VAT jurisdictions) and so not subject to GST. A registered supplier of a GST-free supply can recover relevant input tax credits, although the supply is not taxable.

Residential rents, the second or later supply of residential premises, most financial supplies, and some other supplies are 'input-taxed' ('exempt' in other VAT jurisdictions) and are not subject to GST. However, the supplier cannot recover relevant input tax credits, except that financial suppliers may obtain a reduced input tax credit of 75% of the GST on the acquisition of certain services.

Health insurance is GST-free. Life insurance is input-taxed. General insurance is taxed. Reverse charges may apply to services or rights supplied from offshore, where the recipient is registered or required to be registered, and uses the supply solely or partly for a non-creditable supply.

Wine equalisation tax (WET)

The federal government levies WET at the wholesale level at a rate of 29%, in addition to 10% GST, which is calculated on the price including the WET, and it applies to wine from grapes, fruit and certain vegetables, mead, and sake. Retailers do not receive an input tax credit for WET. A rebate is available to a wine producer of 29% of the wholesale price (excluding WET or GST) for wholesale sales, and of 29% of the notional wholesale selling price for retail sales and applications for own use (up to a maximum of AUD 500,000).

Luxury car tax

The luxury car tax is levied by the federal government at the rate of 33% of the value of the car that exceeds the luxury car tax threshold (AUD 57,466 for both the 2010/11 and 2011/12 financial years) and is payable on the GST-exclusive value above the threshold. No input tax credit is available for luxury car tax, regardless of whether the car is used for business or private purposes.

Customs duties

Imports into Australia are subject to duties under the Australian Customs Tariff. The top duty rate is 5%, other than for clothing and finished textiles which are currently taxed

Australia

at 10% (to be reduced to 5% in 2015). A textile, clothing, and footwear (TCF) strategic investment program will operate until 2015.

Australia currently has comprehensive free trade agreements with Chile, New Zealand, Singapore, Thailand, and the United States. In addition, a regional free trade agreement between Australia, New Zealand, and Southeast Asian nations commenced on 1 January 2010, which progressively eliminates all barriers to trade in goods, services, and investments.

Excise taxes
Excise duties are imposed at high levels on beer, spirits, liqueurs, tobacco, cigarettes, and petroleum products. These excise rates are indexed bi-annually in February and August based on movements in the consumer price index (CPI). Some examples of current excise rates include:

- Beer not exceeding 3% by volume of alcohol packaged in an individual container not exceeding 48 litres: AUD 37.86 per litre of alcohol calculated on that alcohol content by which the percentage by volume of alcohol of the goods exceeds 1.15.
- Tobacco in stick form not exceeding in weight 0.8 grams per stick actual tobacco content: AUD 0.34681 per stick.
- Petroleum condensate, crude petroleum oil, and diesel: AUD 0.38143 per litre.
- Liquefied petroleum gas, other than liquefied petroleum gas exempted from excise duty: AUD 0.025 per litre.

A fuel tax credit system provides a credit for fuel tax (excise or customs duty) that is included in the price of taxable fuel. Broadly, credits are available to entities using fuel in their business and to households using fuel for domestic electricity generation and heating.

Land tax
All states and territories (except the Northern Territory) impose a tax based on the unimproved capital value of land. In general, the principal place of residence and land used for primary production is exempt from land tax.

Stamp duty
All states and territories impose a stamp duty on a wide variety of transactions at different rates. All jurisdictions impose a stamp duty on real estate conveyances, but most exempt conveyances of goods (not associated with other property) from stamp duty. The imposition of duty on share transfers involving unlisted entities differs from state to state. Corporate reconstruction exemptions are available. Advice from a stamp duty specialist should usually be obtained where substantial stamp duty may be imposed because the amount of duty may depend on the form of the transaction.

Fringe benefits tax (FBT)
The federal government levies FBT on employers at the rate of 46.5% on the 'grossed-up value' of non-salary and wages fringe benefits provided to employees (and/or the employee's associates) by the employer or associates. The grossing-up of the value ensures tax neutrality between providing benefits and cash remuneration. FBT generally is deductible for income tax purposes. There are some exemptions from FBT, including some minor benefits, remote area housing in certain circumstances, and specified relocation costs. In addition, there are some concessional valuation rules, in particular for living-away-from-home benefits (although the government is proposing to remove the concessions for living-away-from-home allowances from 1 July 2012, subject to certain transitional rules).

In relation to car fringe benefits, a new 'statutory formula' method applies to new cars acquired under contracts entered into after 7.30pm (AEST) on 10 May 2011. The new statutory formula is a flat 20% (phased in over four years) applied to the FBT base of the car, regardless of the annual kilometres travelled, and replaces the previous four-tiered statutory rate system.

Payroll tax

States and territories impose a tax on employers' payroll (broadly defined). The various jurisdictions have harmonised their payroll tax legislation, but some differences remain, particularly tax rates and the thresholds for exempting employers whose annual payroll is below a certain level, after taking into account grouping rules. For example, in New South Wales from 1 July 2011 the rate is 5.45% per annum with an annual exemption threshold of AUD 678,000. In Victoria, the rate is 4.9% from 1 July 2010, and the annual exemption threshold is AUD 550,000. A variety of rates and thresholds apply in other state and territory jurisdictions.

Superannuation guarantee levy

The federal government effectively requires employers to contribute 9% of an employee's earnings base, subject to limited exceptions, to a registered superannuation fund or retirement savings account on behalf of the employee. Failure to make these contributions will result in the employer being liable for a non-deductible superannuation guarantee charge.

The superannuation guarantee percentage is currently 9% but will gradually increase up to 12% starting from 1 July 2013.

No level of Australian government imposes a social security levy.

Insurance tax

States impose taxes on insurance premiums, which may be substantial.

Minerals Resource Rent Tax (MRRT)

MRRT is a new tax effective from 1 July 2012 applied to the mining profit made from extracting iron ore, coal, anything produced from a process that results in iron ore or coal being consumed or destroyed without extraction, or coal seam gas extracted as a necessary incident of mining coal from the ground before it undergoes any significant processing or value add.

The MRRT liability for each mining project interest in a MRRT year is calculated as follows:

MRRT liability = (Mining profit – MRRT allowances) x MRRT rate

The effective MRRT rate is 22.5%, being the headline rate of 30% reduced by a 25% extraction allowance to recognise the miner's employment of specialist skills.

MRRT allowances reduce the mining profit and include appropriate recognition for mining royalties paid under a Commonwealth, State or Territory law, mining losses, and recognition for the investment in assets relating to upstream mining operations from a mining project interest that exists at 1 July 2012.

Australia

A miner's MRRT payable for a MRRT year is then calculated as follows:

MRRT payable = Sum of MRRT liabilities for each mining project interest – Low-profit offset (if applicable) – Rehabilitation tax offset

Small miners are subject to the MRRT but may be entitled to compliance concessions, including a low-profit offset that will ensure that a miner who (together with certain connected entities) has total mining profits for a MRRT year of AUD 75 million or less has no liability for MRRT. The offset is phased-out for profits between AUD 75 million and AUD 125 million.

Similar to income tax, MRRT is self assessed by the miner. The miner is, in most cases, required to give the Commissioner of Taxation a MRRT return for each MRRT year in which it has a mining project interest or pre-mining project interest. MRRT is generally payable by quarterly instalments.

MRRT applies in addition to normal income tax. MRRT payments (including quarterly instalments) are, however, deductible for income tax purposes.

Petroleum Resource Rent Tax (PRRT)
PRRT applies from 1 July 1986 to all petroleum projects in Australian offshore areas (or Commonwealth adjacent areas) other than production licences derived from the North West Shelf project and the Joint Petroleum Development Area in the Timor Sea. From 1 July 2012, PRRT applies to all Australian onshore and offshore oil and gas projects, including the North West Shelf.

PRRT is applied to a 'project' or 'production licence area' at a rate of 40% of the taxable profits derived from the recovery of all petroleum in the project, including:

- crude oil
- condensate
- sales gas
- natural gas
- liquefied petroleum gas (LPG), and
- ethane.

The taxable profit of a project is calculated as follows:

Taxable profit = Assessable receipts – Deductible expenditure

Deductible expenditure broadly includes exploration expenditure, all project development, and operating expenditures.

PRRT is self assessed by the relevant taxpayer. The taxpayer is, in most cases, required to give the Commissioner of Taxation a PRRT return for each PRRT year. PRRT is generally payable by quarterly instalments.

PRRT applies in addition to normal income tax. PRRT payments (including instalments) are, however, deductible for income tax purposes.

Local municipal taxes
Local taxes, including water, sewerage, and drainage charges, are levied based on the unimproved capital value of land and include a charge for usage (for example water usage).

Branch income

Branch profits are subject to ordinary corporate rates of taxation, and there is no withholding on repatriated profits.

Income determination

Inventory valuation

Inventory generally may be valued at cost (full absorption cost), market selling value, or replacement price. Where, because of obsolescence or other special circumstances, inventory should be valued at a lower amount, the lower valuation generally may be chosen, provided it is a reasonable valuation. Special rules apply, however, regarding the valuation of trading stock for certain companies joining a consolidated group. Last in first out (LIFO) is not an acceptable basis of determining cost, nor is direct costing in respect of manufactured goods and work-in-progress.

Conformity is not required between book and tax reporting. For tax purposes, inventory may be valued at cost, market selling value, or replacement price, regardless of how inventory is valued for book purposes. Those who choose to come within the small-business entity measures (broadly defined as taxpayers who carry on business and who, together with certain 'connected' entities, have an aggregated turnover of less than AUD 2 million for the year) may ignore the difference between the opening and closing value of inventory, if on a reasonable estimate this is not more than AUD 5,000.

Capital gains

A capital gains tax (CGT) applies to assets acquired on or after 20 September 1985. Capital gains realised on the disposal of such assets are included in assessable income and are subject to tax at the company's corporate tax rate, if the disposal is by a company. In order to determine the quantum of any gain for any assets acquired before 21 September 1999, the cost base is indexed according to price movements since acquisition, as measured by the official CPI until 30 September 1999. There is no indexation of the cost base for price movements from 1 October 1999. Disposals of plant and equipment are subject to general rules rather than the CGT rules. Capital losses are allowable as deductions only against capital gains and cannot be offset against other income. In calculating capital losses, there is no indexation of the cost base.

Residents of Australia generally are liable for the tax on gains on the disposal of assets wherever situated, subject to relief from double taxation if the gain is derived and taxed in another country. However, the capital gain or capital loss incurred by a company from a CGT event in relation to shares in a foreign company is reduced by a percentage reflecting the degree to which the foreign company's assets are used in an active business, if the company holds a direct voting percentage of 10% or more in the foreign company for a certain period before the CGT event. Attributable income from CGT events happening to shares owned by a CFC are reduced in the same way. Capital gains and capital losses made by a resident company in respect of CGT events happening in respect of 'non-tainted' assets used to produce foreign income in carrying on business through a PE in a foreign country are disregarded in certain circumstances.

For CGT events occurring on or after 12 December 2006, non-residents are subject to Australian CGT only where the assets are taxable Australian property (i.e. Australian real property, or the business assets of Australian branches of a non-resident). Australian CGT also applies to indirect Australian real property interests, being non-portfolio interests in interposed entities (including foreign interposed entities), where

Australia

the value of such an interest is wholly or principally attributable to Australian real property. 'Real property' for all these purposes is consistent with Australian treaty practice, extending to other Australian assets with a physical connection with Australia, such as mining rights and other interests related to Australian real property. A 'non-portfolio interest' is an interest held alone or with associates of 10% or more in the interposed entity.

Dividend income

A 'gross-up and credit' mechanism applies to franked dividends (dividends paid out of profits which have been subject to Australian tax) received by Australian companies. The corporate shareholder grosses up the dividend received for tax paid by the paying company (i.e. franking credits attaching to the dividend) and is then entitled to a tax offset (i.e. a reduction of tax) equal to the gross-up amount. A company with an excess tax offset entitlement converts the excess into a carryforward tax loss using a special formula.

Dividends paid to another resident company that are unfranked (because they are paid out of profits not subject to Australian tax) are taxable, unless they are paid within a group that has chosen to be consolidated for tax purposes. Dividends paid between companies within a tax consolidated group are ignored for the purposes of determining the taxable income of the group.

Franked dividends paid to non-residents are exempt from dividend withholding tax (WHT).

An exemption from WHT is also available for dividends that are 'unfranked' under the dividend imputation rules and are declared to be conduit foreign income (CFI) received by non-resident shareholders (or unitholders) in an Australian corporate tax entity (CTE). These rules may also treat the CFI component of an unfranked dividend received by an Australian CTE from another Australian CTE as not taxable to the recipient, provided it is on-paid within a specified timeframe. Broadly, income will qualify as CFI if it is foreign income, including certain dividends, or foreign gains, which are not assessable for Australian income tax purposes or for which a foreign income tax offset has been claimed in Australia.

Foreign dividends are not assessable and are not eligible for a tax offset if received by an Australian resident company from a foreign affiliate where the recipient company has a voting power of at least 10% in the foreign affiliate. Income of a non-resident entity in which Australian residents hold interests is not assessable when repatriated to Australia where the income has been previously attributed to those residents and taxed in Australia (see below).

Stock dividends

Stock dividends, or the issue of bonus shares, as they are known under Australian law, are, in general, not taxed as a dividend, and the tax treatment is the spreading of the cost base of the original shares across the original shares and the bonus shares. However, if a company credits its share capital account with profits when issuing bonus shares, this will taint the share capital account (if it is not already a tainted share capital account), causing the bonus share issue to be a dividend. Certain other rules may apply to bonus share issues, depending on the facts.

Financial arrangements

Special rules apply to the taxation of financial arrangements (TOFA). 'Financial arrangement' is widely defined to cover arrangements that involve a cash settlable legal or equitable right to receive, or obligation to provide, something of economic value in the future.

These measures provide six tax-timing methods for determining gains or losses in respect of financial arrangements, along with revenue account treatment of the resulting gains or losses to the extent that the gain or loss is made in earning assessable income or carrying on a business for that purpose. The default methods are the accruals method and the realisation method, one or other of which will apply depending on the relevant facts and circumstances of a particular financial arrangement. The accruals method will apply to spread an overall gain or loss over the life of the financial arrangement where there is sufficient certainty that the expected gain or loss will actually occur. A gain or loss that is not sufficiently certain is dealt with under the realisation method.

Alternatively, a taxpayer may irrevocably choose one of four elective methods (i.e. fair value, retranslation, financial reports, and hedging) to determine the tax treatment of financial arrangements covered by the legislation. Qualification criteria must be met before the elective methods may be used. Generally, these criteria require that the taxpayer prepare a financial report in accordance with Australian (or comparable) accounting standards and be audited in accordance with Australian (or comparable) auditing standards.

Exemptions from this regime may be available having regard to the duration of the arrangement or the nature of the relevant taxpayer and the annual turnover or value of assets of that taxpayer. Certain types of financial arrangements are excluded from these rules, including leasing and hire purchase arrangements. Foreign residents are taxable on gains from financial arrangements under these measures to the extent that the gains have an Australian source.

Foreign exchange gains and losses
Foreign currency gains and losses are recognised when realised, regardless of whether there is a conversion into Australian dollars, and are included in or deducted from assessable income, subject to limited exceptions. There are exceptions to the timing and characterisation aspects of the realisation approach where the foreign currency gain or loss is closely linked to a capital asset. To reduce compliance costs with foreign currency denominated bank accounts, taxpayers may elect to disregard gains or losses on low balance transaction accounts that satisfy a *de minimis* exemption or may elect for retranslation by annually restating the balance of the account by reference to deposits, withdrawals, and the exchange rates at the beginning and end of each year (or by reference to amounts reported in accordance with applicable accounting standards).

For foreign exchange gains and losses associated with financial arrangements as defined, the compliance impact of the foreign exchange rules will be reduced for those taxpayers eligible to elect the retranslation or financial reports tax-timing methods under the TOFA measures (*as discussed above*).

Entities or parts of entities, satisfying certain requirements, are able to choose to account for their activities in a currency other than Australian dollars for income tax purposes as an intermediate step to translating the result into Australian dollars.

Foreign income
On 17 February 2011, the government released exposure draft legislation for public comment setting out the legislative design of reforms to modernise the CFC rules and to implement new foreign accumulation fund (FAF) rules, which broadly, are aimed at

Australia

investments in non-CFCs and fixed trusts. The commencement date for the new CFC and FAF rules has not been announced.

The current basis upon which the foreign income of corporations resident in Australia is taxed is set out below.

- Non-active income of foreign companies controlled by Australian residents (determined by reference to voting rights and dividend and capital entitlements) may be attributed to those residents under rules which distinguish between companies resident in 'listed countries' (e.g. Canada, France, Germany, Japan, New Zealand, the United Kingdom, and the United States) and in other 'unlisted' countries. In general, if the CFC is resident in an unlisted country and it fails the active income test (typically because it earns 5% or more of its income from passive or tainted sources), the CFC's tainted income (very broadly, passive income and gains, and sales and services income which has a connection with Australia) is attributable. If a CFC is resident in a listed country, a narrower range of tainted income is attributed even if the CFC fails the active income test.
- When income previously taxed on attribution is repatriated, it is not assessable for tax.
- Dividends received directly by a resident company from a foreign company are not assessable for tax where the resident company has a (non-portfolio) voting interest of at least 10% in the foreign affiliate and does not receive the dividend in its capacity as a trustee. The basis upon which distributions may qualify for such relief (i.e. where the payee has a voting interest of at least 10% in the payer) is currently under consideration as part of the redesign of the CFC rules.
- Active foreign branch profits of a resident company from carrying on business through a PE in a foreign country and capital gains made by a resident company from the disposal of non-tainted assets used in deriving foreign branch income (except income and capital gains from the operation of ships or aircraft in international traffic) are not assessable for tax.
- Foreign income of Australian resident corporations, and income of such taxpayers which is subject to foreign income taxes that is not effectively exempt, is subject to tax; however, in most cases, an offset for foreign income tax paid is allowed to the extent of Australian tax payable on such income.
- Generally, limited partnerships are treated as companies for Australian tax purposes. In certain circumstances, foreign limited partnerships, foreign limited liability partnerships, United States (US) limited liability companies, and United Kingdom (UK) limited liability partnerships will be treated as partnerships (i.e. as a flow-through entity) rather than as a company for the purposes of Australia's income tax laws.

Deductions

Depreciation and depletion

A capital allowances regime allows a deduction for the decline in value of depreciating assets held by a taxpayer. The holder of the asset is entitled to the deduction and may be the economic, rather than the legal, owner. A 'depreciating asset' is an asset that has a limited effective life and can reasonably be expected to decline in value over the time it is used, but does not include land, trading stock, or, subject to certain exceptions, intangible assets. Deductions are available for certain other capital expenditure.

A

Intangible assets that are depreciating assets (if they are not trading stock) are:

* Certain mining, quarrying, or prospecting rights and information.
* Items of intellectual property.
* In-house software.
* Indefeasible rights to use an international telecommunications submarine cable system.
* Spectrum licences under radio communications legislation.
* Datacasting transmitter licences.
* Telecommunications site access rights.

Taxpayers that do not qualify as a small business must depreciate the asset over its useful life (known as 'effective life') using either straight-line (known as the 'prime cost' method) or diminishing-value method (straight-line rate multiplied by 200% for depreciating assets acquired on or after 10 May 2006).

Taxpayers may self-determine the effective life of a unit or plant or may choose the effective life contained in a published determination of the Commissioner of Taxation.

Non-small-business taxpayers are able to choose to write-off all items costing less than AUD 1,000 through a low-value pool at a diminishing-value rate of 37.5% per annum.

For those who satisfy the small business entity threshold (broadly defined as taxpayers who are carrying on business and who, together with certain connected entities, have an aggregated turnover of less than AUD 2 million for the year), a simplified depreciation system applies with more attractive depreciation rates, including (with effect from 1 July 2012) an immediate write off for depreciating assets with a cost of less than AUD 6,500.

'Project pool' rules allow expenditures that do not form part of a depreciating asset to be deductible over the life of a project that is carried on for a taxable purpose. Amongst other things, items that fall within the rules include the following:

* Amounts paid to create or upgrade community infrastructure for a community associated with the project.
* Site preparation costs for depreciating assets (except horticultural plants in certain circumstances).
* Amounts incurred for feasibility studies for a project.
* Environmental assessment costs applicable to the project.
* Amounts incurred to obtain information associated with the project.
* Amounts incurred in seeking to obtain a right to intellectual property.
* Costs of ornamental trees or shrubs.

The so-called 'blackhole' expenditure provisions allow a five-year straight-line write-off for capital expenditure in relation to a past, present, or prospective business, to the extent that the business is, was, or is proposed to be carried on for a taxable purpose. The expenditure is deductible to the extent that it is not elsewhere taken into account (e.g. by inclusion in the cost base of an asset for capital gains tax purposes) and that it is not denied deductibility for the purposes of the income tax law (e.g. by the rules against deducting entertainment expenditure).

Special rules apply for primary producer assets, such as horticultural plants, water and land care assets, and the treatment of expenditure on R&D (*see the Tax credits and incentives section for more information*) and expenditure on certain Australian films.

Australia

A luxury car cost limit applies for depreciating the cost of certain passenger motor vehicles (AUD 57,466 cost limit for both the 2010/11 and 2011/12 income years).

Expenditure on the development of in-house software may be allocated to a 'software development pool' and written off over three years, starting in the year after the expenditure was incurred (40% in year two, 40% in year three, and 20% in year four). Amounts spent on acquiring computer software or the right to use it (except where the acquisition is for developing in-house software) generally is treated as incurred on acquiring a depreciating asset, deductible over its effective life (taken to be four years) commencing in the first year it is first used or installed ready for use. 'Shrink-wrapped' software acquired or manufactured for sale generally will be treated as trading stock.

A loss arising on the sale of a depreciating asset (depreciated value of the asset less sale consideration) is generally an allowable deduction. A gain on the sale of a depreciating asset, to the extent of depreciation recaptured, generally is taxed as ordinary income. Gains exceeding the amount of depreciation recaptured are also taxed as ordinary income.

Subject to exceptions referred to below, capital expenditure incurred after 15 September 1987 in the construction or improvement of non-residential buildings used for producing assessable income is amortised over 40 years at an annual 2.5% rate. Capital expenditure on the construction of buildings used for short-term traveller accommodation (e.g. hotels, motels) and industrial buildings (typically factories) is amortised over 25 years at an annual 4% rate where construction commenced after 26 February 1992. The cost of eligible building construction that commenced after 21 August 1984 and before 16 September 1987 (or construction contracted before 16 September 1987) is amortised over 25 years at an annual 4% rate. There is no recapture of the amortised amount upon disposal of the building, except where the expenditure is incurred after 13 May 1997, in which case recapture will apply, subject to certain transitional rules.

Similar provisions apply in relation to income-producing residential buildings on which construction commenced after 17 July 1985.

The cost of income-producing structural improvements, the construction of which started after 26 February 1992 is eligible for write-off for tax purposes on the same basis as that of income-producing buildings, that is, at a rate of 2.5% per annum.

The cost of consumables may be either written off immediately, or as used.

The following expenditure attracts an immediate 100% deduction: environmental protection activities, dealing with pollution and waste; landcare operations; exploring or prospecting for minerals (and from 1 July 2012 for exploration of geothermal energy sources); mine site rehabilitation; and certain expenditure in respect of the establishment of carbon sink forests.

Tax depreciation is not required to conform to book depreciation.

Percentage depletion based on gross income or other non-cost criteria is not available.

Goodwill
Goodwill and trademarks are not depreciating assets, and tax amortisation is not available.

Start-up expenses

There are no specific provisions in relation to deductions for start-up expenses. However, certain start-up expenses, such as costs of company incorporation or costs to raise equity, may qualify for a five-year straight-line write-off to the extent that it is capital expenditure in relation to a current or prospective business that is, or is proposed to be, carried on for a taxable purpose.

Interest expenses

Special rules classify financial arrangements as either debt or equity interests. These rules focus on economic substance rather than legal form and take into account related schemes, and extend beyond shares. In this situation, interest expense on non-share equity would be treated as a dividend, which is potentially frankable, and would be non-deductible for the paying company/group.

Thin capitalisation measures apply to the total debt of the Australian operations of multinational groups (including branches of those groups). *See Thin capitalisation in the Group taxation section for more information.*

Bad debts

A deduction may be available for bad debts written off as bad before the end of an income year. Generally, a deduction will only be available where the amount of the debt was previously included in assessable income, or the debt is in respect of money lent in the ordinary course of a money lending business. The ability to claim a deduction for a bad debt is also subject to other integrity measures.

The amount of a commercial debt forgiven (other than an intra-group debt within a tax consolidated group) that is not otherwise assessable or does not otherwise reduce an allowable deduction is applied to reduce the debtor's carryforward tax deductions for revenue tax losses, non-deducted capital losses, non-deducted capital expenditure, and other capital cost bases in a certain order. Any amount not so applied generally is not assessable to the debtor. Forgiveness includes the release, waiver, or extinguishment of a debt (other than by full payment in cash) and the lapsing of the creditor's recovery right by reason of a statute of limitations.

Charitable contributions

Charitable contributions are generally deductible where they are made to entities that are specifically named in the tax law or endorsed by the Commissioner of Taxation as 'deductible gift recipients'. However, deductions for such gifts cannot generate tax losses. That is, generally the deduction is limited to the amount of assessable income remaining after deducting from the assessable income for the year all other deductions.

Entertainment

Subject to limited exceptions, deductions are denied for expenditure on 'entertainment', which broadly is defined as entertainment by way of food, drink, or recreation, and accommodation or travel to do with providing such entertainment.

Fines and penalties

Fines and penalties imposed under any Australian and foreign law are generally not deductible. This includes fines and penalties imposed in relation to both civil and criminal matters.

Australia

The General Interest Charge (GIC) and Shortfall Interest Charge (SIC), which are imposed for failure to pay an outstanding tax debt within the required timeframe, or where a tax shortfall arises under an amended assessment, are deductible for Australian tax purposes.

Taxes
In general, GST input tax credits, GST, and adjustments under the GST law are disregarded for income tax purposes. Other taxes, including property, payroll, MRRT, PRRT, and fringe benefits tax, as well as other business taxes, excluding income tax, are deductible to the extent they are incurred in producing assessable income or necessarily incurred in carrying on a business for this purpose, and are not of a capital or private nature.

Other significant items
Where expenditure for services is incurred in advance, deductibility of that expenditure generally will be prorated over the period during which the services will be provided, up to a maximum of ten years.

General value shifting rules apply to shifts of value, direct or indirect, in respect of loan and equity interests in companies or trusts. Circumstances in which these rules may apply include where there is a direct value shift under a scheme involving equity or loan interests, or where value is shifted out of an asset by the creation of rights in respect of the asset, or where there is a transfer of assets or the provision of services for a consideration other than at market value. The value shifting rules may apply to the head company of a tax consolidated group or multiple entry consolidated (MEC) group for value shifts also involving entities outside the group, but not to value shifting between group members, which the tax consolidation rules address (*see the Group taxation section for more information*).

Net operating losses
Losses may be carried forward indefinitely, subject to compliance with tests of continuity of more than 50% of ultimate stock ownership or compliance with a same business test. For consolidated group companies, the ability to utilise these losses is determined by a modified version of these tests (*see the Group taxation section for more information*).

In May 2012, the government announced that a loss carryback regime will apply to companies from 1 July 2012. Under this regime, companies will be able to 'carryback' tax losses to offset prior year profits, and obtain a refund of tax previously paid on those prior year profits. While the specific details of the regime are still to come, key features of the proposal include:

- an initial one year carryback period from the 2012/13 income year (i.e. 2012/13 tax losses can be carried back and offset against tax paid in 2011/12)
- a two year loss carryback period to apply from the 2013/14 income year
- an AUD 1 million cap on the amount of losses able to be carried back, and
- refunds will be limited to the balance of a company's franking account.

Payments to foreign affiliates
A corporation can deduct royalties, management service fees, and interest charges paid to non-residents, provided the amounts are commercially realistic and referable to activities aimed at producing assessable income.

Group taxation

A tax consolidation regime applies for income tax and capital gains tax purposes for companies, partnerships and trusts ultimately 100% owned by a single head company (or certain entities taxed like a company) resident in Australia. Australian resident companies that are 100% owned (either directly or indirectly) by the same foreign company and have no common Australian head company between them and the non-resident parent are also allowed to consolidate as a multiple entry consolidated (MEC) group. The group that is consolidated for income tax purposes may differ from the group that is consolidated for accounts or for GST purposes. Groups that choose to consolidate must include all 100%-owned entities under an all-in rule, and the choice to consolidate is irrevocable. However, eligible tier-1 companies (being Australian resident companies that have a non-resident shareholder) that are members of a potential MEC group are not all required to join an MEC group, when it forms, but may form two or more separate MEC groups, if they so choose, of which the same foreign top company is the 100% owner. If an eligible tier-1 company joins a particular MEC group, all 100% subsidiaries of the company must also join the group. While the rules for forming and joining MEC groups allow more flexibility than with consolidated groups, the ongoing rules for MEC groups are more complex, particularly for tax losses and on the disposal of interests in eligible tier-1 companies, which are subject to cost pooling rules, although for practical purposes these rules are relevant only if the non-resident is holding or disposing of an indirect Australian real property interest (*see Capital gains in the Income determination section for more information*).

A single entity rule applies to members of a consolidated or MEC group so that for income tax purposes the subsidiary members are taken to be part of the head company, while they continue to be members of the group and intra-group transactions are not recognised. In general, no group relief is available where related companies are not members of the same consolidated or MEC group. Rollover relief from CGT is available on the transfer of unrealised gains on assets, which are taxable Australian property between companies sharing 100% common ownership where the transfer is between non-resident companies, or between a non-resident company and a member of a consolidated group or MEC group, or between a non-resident company and a resident company that is not able to be a member of a consolidated group.

Consolidated groups file a single tax return and calculate their taxable income or loss ignoring all intra-group transactions.

When a consolidated group acquires 100% of an Australian resident entity, so that it becomes a subsidiary member, the cost base of certain assets (in general, those that are non-monetary) of the joining member are reset for all tax purposes, based on the purchase price plus the entity's liabilities, subject to certain adjustments. In this way, an acquisition of 100% of an Australian resident entity by a consolidated group is broadly the tax equivalent of acquiring its assets. Subject to certain tests being passed, tax losses of the joining member may be transferred to the head company and may be utilised subject to a loss factor, which is broadly the market value of the joining member divided by the market value of the group (including the joining member). The value of the loss factor (referred to as 'the available fraction') that applies for transferred losses may be reduced by capital injections (or the equivalent) into the member before it joined, or into the group after the loss is transferred.

Australia

Franking credits and tax losses remain with the group when a member exits, and the cost base of shares in the exiting member is calculated based on the tax value of its assets at the time of exit, less liabilities subject to certain adjustments.

Generally, members of the group are jointly and severally liable for group income tax debts on the default of the head company, unless the group liability is covered by a tax sharing agreement (TSA) that satisfies certain legislative requirements. A member who enters into a TSA generally can achieve a clean exit from the group where a payment is made to the head company in accordance with the TSA.

Transfer pricing

Australia has a comprehensive transfer pricing regime aimed at protecting the tax base by ensuring that dealings between related, international parties are conducted at arm's length. The arm's-length principle, which underpins the transfer pricing regime, uses the behaviour of independent parties as a benchmark for determining the allocation of income and expenses between international related parties.

Where the Commissioner of Taxation is satisfied that the arm's-length principle has not been maintained, the Commissioner has the power to make transfer pricing adjustments.

Legislation is currently proposed (with retrospective effect from 1 July 2004) to allow the Commissioner of Taxation to issue transfer pricing assessments under the Associated Enterprises or Business Profits Articles of Australia's DTAs in addition to the Commissioner's existing ability to raise transfer pricing assessments under domestic law.

Thin capitalisation

Thin capitalisation measures apply to the total debt of the Australian operations of multinational groups (including branches of those groups). The measures cover investment into Australia of foreign multinationals and outward investment of Australian-based multinationals, and include a safe-harbour debt-to-equity ratio of 3:1. Interest deductions are denied to the extent that borrowing exceeds the safe-harbour ratio. Where borrowing exceeds the safe-harbour ratio, multinationals are not affected by the rules if they can satisfy the arm's-length test (that the borrowing could have been borne by an independent entity). A further alternative test is available for outward investing entities based on 120% of their worldwide gearing.

As mentioned above, the thin capitalisation rules apply to inward investment into Australia. In particular, they will apply where a foreign entity carries on business through an Australian PE or to an Australian entity in which five or fewer non-residents have at least a 50% control interest, or a single non-resident has at least a 40% control interest, or the Australian entity is controlled by no more than five foreign entities. Separate rules apply to financial institutions. To facilitate their inclusion in the rules, branches are required to prepare financial accounts.

International Financial Reporting Standards (IFRS), equivalents of which currently apply in Australia, make it more difficult for some entities to satisfy thin capitalisation rules because of the removal of internally generated intangible assets from the balance sheets. Accordingly, thin capitalisation law allows departure from the Australian equivalents to IFRS in relation to certain intangible assets and excludes deferred tax assets and liabilities and surpluses and deficits in defined benefit superannuation funds from applicable calculations.

....

Tax credits and incentives

Foreign income tax offsets

Foreign income tax offsets (FITOs) are available to avoid double taxation in respect of foreign tax paid on income which is assessable in Australia. Generally, a corporation will be entitled to claim a FITO where it has paid, or is deemed to have paid, an amount of foreign income tax, and the income or gain on which the foreign income tax was paid is included in assessable income for Australian tax purposes.

The amount of the FITO available is limited to the greater of AUD 1,000 and the amount of the 'FITO limit'. The FITO limit is broadly calculated as the difference between the corporation's actual tax liability and its tax liability if certain foreign taxed and foreign-sourced income and related deductions were disregarded. Excess FITOs are not able to be carried forward and claimed in later income years.

Inward investment incentives

Depending on the nature and size of the investment project, state governments may give rebates from payroll, stamp, and land taxes on an *ad hoc* basis and for limited periods.

Capital investment incentives

Incentives for capital investment are as follows:

*   Accelerated deductions are available for capital expenditures on the exploration for and extraction of petroleum and other minerals (and, from 1 July 2012, for exploration of geothermal energy sources), the rehabilitation of former mineral extraction sites, certain environmental protection activities, the establishment of certain 'carbon sink' forests, certain expenditure of primary producers, and for certain low cost depreciating assets held by small business entities.
*   There are a number of tax concessions aimed at encouraging investments in the venture capital sector. Non-resident pension funds that are tax-exempt in their home jurisdiction, are residents of Canada, France, Germany, Japan, the United Kingdom, the United States, or another country prescribed by regulation, and satisfy certain Australian registration requirements, are exempt from income tax on the disposal of investments in certain Australian venture capital equity held at risk for at least 12 months. A similar exemption is extended to other tax-exempt non-resident investors, including managed funds and venture capital fund-of-funds vehicles and taxable non-residents holding less than 10% of a venture capital limited partnership. These investors are able to invest in eligible venture capital investments through an Australian resident venture capital limited partnership or through a non-resident venture capital limited partnership. Eligible venture capital investments are limited to specified interests in companies and trusts. Detailed rules in the legislation prescribe the nature of such investments and the characteristics, which such companies and trusts, and their investments, must possess.
*   There is a venture capital tax concession applicable to an 'early stage venture capital limited partnership' (ESVCLP). The thresholds for qualification include requirements that, amongst other things, the committed capital of the ESVCLP must be at least AUD 10 million but not exceed AUD 100 million, the investments made must fall within prescribed parameters as to size and proportion of total capital, and the ESVCLP must have an investment plan approved by Innovation Australia. Where the thresholds for their application are met, the ESVCLP provisions provide flow-through tax treatment to domestic and foreign partners, with the income and capital received by the partners being exempt from taxation. As the income will be tax exempt, the investor will not be able to deduct investment losses.

Australia

- The taxable income derived from pure offshore banking transactions by an authorised offshore banking unit in Australia is taxed at the rate of 10%.
- Refundable tax offsets are available to companies for certain expenditure incurred in Australia in producing specified classes of film or undertaking specified post, digital, or special effects production activities in respect of specified classes of films. The concessions are only available to a company that is either an Australian resident or a non-resident carrying on business through an Australian PE and which has been issued with an Australian Business Number (ABN). The availability of the offsets is subject to a number of conditions, including meeting registration and minimum spend requirements. The rate of the offset varies from 15% to 40% depending upon the nature of the relevant film and activities undertaken.
- Up until the 2011/12 income year, there was an Entrepreneurs' Tax Offset (ETO) of up to 25% for businesses run by small business entities, which can include companies with an annual turnover of up to AUD 75,000.

Research & development (R&D) tax credit

The tax treatment of expenditure on R&D was changed for income years commencing on or after 1 July 2011, such that the previously applicable concessional deduction is replaced with an R&D tax credit. For companies with an annual turnover of less than AUD 20 million, there is a 45% refundable tax credit, equivalent to a 150% tax concession. This equates to a cash savings of 15% on every dollar of R&D spend and will be refundable where the company is in a tax loss position. Companies with a turnover of greater than AUD 20 million have access to a non-refundable 40% tax credit, equivalent to a 133% tax concession. This equates to a cash savings of 10% on every dollar of R&D spend.

Generally, only R&D activities undertaken in Australia qualify for the new R&D tax incentive. However, R&D activities conducted overseas also qualify in limited circumstances where the activities cannot be undertaken in Australia. The 175% premium concession and international premium concession have been abolished. Eligibility criteria have been tightened to support 'only genuine R&D'. Special grant programmes also may be available to assist corporations in the conduct of certain R&D in Australia. These grants are awarded on a discretionary basis.

Other incentives

Cash grants for export-market development expenditure are available to eligible businesses seeking to export Australian-source goods and services.

Withholding taxes

Withholding tax (WHT) rates are shown in the following table.

Recipient	Dividends (%) (1)	Interest (%) (2)	Royalties (%) (3)
Resident corporations or individuals	0	0	0
Non-resident corporations or individuals:			
Non-treaty	30	10	30
Treaty:			
Argentina	10/15 (4)	12	10/15 (5)
Austria (46)	15	10	10 (6)
Belgium	15	10	10 (6)

Recipient	Dividends (%) (1)	Interest (%) (2)	Royalties (%) (3)
Canada	5/15 (7)	10 (7)	10 (6, 7)
Chile (47)	5/15	5/10/15	5/10 (6)
China, P.R. (8)	15	10	10 (6)
Czech Republic	5/15 (9)	10	10 (6)
Denmark	15	10	10 (6)
East Timor (Timor Sea Treaty) (10)	15 (11)	10 (11)	10 (11)
Fiji	20	10	15 (6)
Finland (12)	0/5/15 (37)	0/10 (38)	5 (6, 39)
France (13)	0/5/15 (13)	0/10 (13)	5 (6, 13)
Germany	15	10	10 (6)
Hungary	15	10	10 (6)
India	15	15	10/15 (14)
Indonesia	15	10	10/15 (15)
Ireland, Rep. Of	15	10	10 (6)
Italy	15	10	10 (6)
Japan (40)	0/5/10/15 (40)	0/10 (40)	5 (6, 40)
Kiribati	20	10	15 (6)
Korea, Rep. Of	15	15	15 (6)
Malaysia	0/15 (16)	15	15 (6)
Malta	15 (17)	15	10 (6)
Mexico	0/15 (18)	10/15 (19)	10 (6)
Netherlands	15	10	10 (6)
New Zealand (45)	0/5/15 (45)	0/10 (45)	5 (6) (45)
Norway	0/5/15 (35)	0/10 (41)	5 (6) (42)
Papua New Guinea	15/20 (20)	10	10 (6)
Philippines	15/25 (21)	15	15/25 (22)
Poland	15	10	10 (6)
Romania	5/15 (23)	10	10 (6)
Russian Federation	5/15 (24)	10	10 (25)
Singapore	0/15	10	10 (6)
Slovak Republic	15	10	10 (6)
South Africa (43)	5/15 (43, 36)	0/10(43)	5 (6, 43)
Spain	15	10	10 (6)
Sri Lanka	15	10	10 (6)
Sweden	15	10	10 (6)
Switzerland	15	10	10 (6)
Taipei/Taiwan	10/15 (26)	10	12.5 (6)
Thailand	15/20 (27)	10/25 (28)	15 (6)
Turkey (48)	5/15 (49)	0/10 (50)	10 (6)
United Kingdom (44)	0/5/15 (29)	0/10 (30)	5 (6)
United States	0/5/15/30 (31)	0/10/15 (32)	5 (6, 33)
Vietnam	10/15 (34)	10	10 (6)

Notes

1. Dividends paid to non-residents are exempt from dividend WHT except when paid out of a company that has not borne Australian tax (i.e. unfranked dividends). Dividends include those stock dividends that are taxable. The rates shown apply to dividends on both portfolio investments and substantial holdings other than dividends paid in connection with an Australian PE of the non-resident. Unfranked

Australia

dividends paid to non-residents are exempt from dividend WHT to the extent that the dividends are declared by the company to be conduit foreign income. There is also a deduction from 1 July 2000 in certain cases to compensate for the company tax on inter-entity distributions where these are on-paid by holding companies to a 100% parent that is a non-resident *(see Dividend income in the Income determination section)*. Dividends paid to a non-resident in connection with an Australian PE are taxable to the non-resident on a net assessment basis (i.e. the dividend and associated deductions will need to be included in the determination of the non-resident's taxable income, the dividend is not subject to dividend WHT), and a franking tax offset is allowable to the non-resident company for franked dividends received.

2. Australia's interest WHT rate is limited to 10% of gross interest, although the treaty may allow for a higher maximum limit. An exemption from Australian WHT can be obtained for interest on certain public issues or widely held issues of debentures. Provisions exist to ensure that discounts and other pecuniary benefits derived by non-residents on various forms of financings are subject to interest WHT. Interest paid to non-residents by offshore banking units is exempt from interest WHT where offshore borrowings are used in offshore banking activities (including lending to non-residents). An offshore borrowing is defined as a borrowing from (i) an unrelated non-resident in any currency or (ii) a resident or a related person in a currency other than Australian currency.

3. Royalties paid to non-residents (except in respect of a PE in Australia of a resident of a treaty country) are subject to 30% WHT (on the gross amount of the royalty), unless a DTA provides for a lesser rate.

4. For Australian-sourced dividends which are franked under Australia's dividend imputation provisions and paid to a person who directly holds at least 10% of the voting power of the company, the limit is 10% (although note that Australia does not impose WHT on franked dividends). For Argentinean-sourced dividends paid to a person who holds at least 25% of the capital in the company, the limit is 10%. A 15% limit applies to other dividends.

5. Source-country tax is limited to 10% of the gross amount of royalties in relation to copyright of literary, dramatic, musical, or other artistic work; the use of industrial or scientific equipment; the supply of scientific, technical, or industrial knowledge; assistance ancillary to the above; or certain forbearances in respect of the above. Source-country tax is limited to 10% of the net amount of royalties for certain technical assistance. In all other cases, it is limited to 15% of the gross amount of royalties.

6. Tax is limited to the indicated percentage of gross royalty.

7. Under a protocol signed on 23 January 2002, the maximum WHT rate on interest is 10%. The Protocol adopts a 5% dividend WHT rate to franked dividends paid by an Australian resident company and, in the case of dividends paid by a Canadian resident company (other than a non-resident owned investment corporation), to a company that holds directly at least 10% of the voting power in the dividend company (although note that Australia does not impose WHT on franked dividends). Otherwise, the maximum WHT rate on dividends will continue to be 15%. The protocol has effect in Australia in relation to dividends, interest, and royalties derived on or after 1 January 2003.

8. Except Hong Kong and Macau.

9. The treaty between Australia and the Czech Republic allows Australia to impose a 5% WHT on the franked part of a dividend in certain circumstances (although note that Australia does not impose WHT on franked dividends). In the Czech Republic, a rate of 15% applies to the gross amount of dividends if the dividends are paid to a company which holds directly at least 20% of the capital of the company paying the dividend.

10. East Timor does not have a comprehensive DTA with Australia. However, the Timor Sea Treaty governs the taxation rights between the two countries for petroleum-related activities conducted in the Joint Petroleum Development Area of the Timor Sea by any person or entity, irrespective of the residency status of that person or entity.

11. Where the Timor Sea Treaty applies to third-country resident payees, only 10% of the total gross interest, dividend, or royalty payment is subject to Australian WHT, as follows:
    * Interest: 10% of total gross interest paid is subject to WHT at a rate of 10%.
    * Dividends: 10% of total gross unfranked dividends paid are subject to WHT at a rate of 15%, or at the relevant DTA rate of the recipient.
    * Royalties: 10% of total gross royalties paid is subject to WHT at a rate of 10%, or at the relevant DTA rate of the recipient. However, the other 90% of each such amount is subject to East Timorese WHT at the same rates.

12. The current agreement came into force on 10 November 2007 and has effect in Australia in respect of WHT for income derived on or after 1 January 2008 and in respect of other income, profit, or gains derived on or after 1 July 2008.

13. On 20 June 2006, Australia and France signed a new agreement. The new agreement has effect in Australia in respect of WHT on income derived on or after 1 January 2010, being the calendar year next following 1 June 2009, which was the date on which the new agreement entered into force. The source country will exempt inter-corporate non-portfolio (i.e. minimum 10% shareholding) dividends paid out of profits that have borne the normal rate of company tax. There is a 5% rate limit for all other non-portfolio dividends. A rate limit of 15% will continue, otherwise, to apply for dividends. A rate limit of 10% applies to interest, except no tax will be chargeable in the source country on interest derived by a financial institution resident in the other country or a government or political or administrative subdivision or local authority or central bank of the other country. The rate limit for royalties reduced to 5% from 1 January 2010. Amounts derived from equipment leasing (including certain container leasing) are excluded from the royalty definition and treated either as international transport operations or business profits.

14. The source-country limit under the Indian agreement is 10% for royalties paid in respect of the use of or rights to use industrial, commercial, or scientific equipment or for the provision of consulting services related to such equipment. In other cases the limit is 15%.
15. The source-country limit under the Indonesian agreement is 10% for royalties paid in respect of the use of or the right to use any industrial, commercial, or scientific equipment or for the supply of scientific, technical, industrial, or commercial knowledge or information, and it is 15% in other cases.
16. A zero dividend WHT rate applies to franked dividends paid by an Australian resident company to an entity that holds directly at least 10% of the voting power in the dividend paying company, otherwise a 15% WHT rate applies. In relation to dividends paid by a company resident of Malaysia, no WHT applies.
17. Source-country tax in Malta is limited to the tax chargeable on the profits out of which the dividends are paid.
18. A zero dividend WHT rate applies to franked dividends paid (in Mexico, those dividends that have been paid from the net profit account) to a company that holds directly at least 10% of the voting power in the dividend paying company. In all other cases, a 15% WHT rate will apply to dividends.
19. Source-country tax is limited to 10% when interest is paid to a bank or an insurance company, derived from bonds and securities that are regularly and substantially traded on a recognised securities market, paid by banks (except where the prior two criteria apply), or paid by the purchaser to the seller of machinery and equipment in connection with a sale on credit. It is 15% in all other cases.
20. For Australian-source dividends, the limit is 15%. Where dividends are sourced in Papua New Guinea, the limit is 20%.
21. Source-country tax is limited to 15% where relief by way of rebate or credit is given to the beneficial owner of the dividend. In any other case, source-country tax is limited to 25%.
22. Source-country tax generally is limited to 15% of gross royalties if paid by an approved Philippines enterprise. In all other cases, the rate is limited to 25% of the gross royalties.
23. Source-country tax (Australia) is limited to 5% where a dividend is paid to a Romanian resident company that holds directly at least 10% of the capital of the Australian company paying the dividend to the extent that the dividend is fully franked. Source-country tax (Romania) is limited to 5% where a dividend is paid to an Australian resident company that holds directly at least 10% of the capital of the Romanian company paying the dividend if the dividend is paid out of profits that have been subject to Romanian profits tax. In other cases, it is limited to 15%.
24. Source-country tax generally is limited to 15%. However, a rate of 5% applies where the dividends have been fully taxed at the corporate level, the recipient is a company which has a minimum direct holding in the paying company, and the recipient has invested a minimum of AUD 700,000 or the Russian ruble equivalent in the paying company. Where the dividends are paid by a company that is a resident in Russia, the dividends are exempt from Australian tax.
25. The agreement with the Russian Federation is the first of Australia's new treaties to include spectrum licences in the definition of royalties.
26. Source-country tax (Taiwan) is limited to 10% of the gross amount of the dividends paid to a company which holds at least 25% of the capital of the company paying the dividends. A rate of 15% applies in all other cases. To the extent that dividends are franked because they are paid out of profits that have borne Australian tax, they are exempt from dividend WHT (See Note 1 above). The treaty allows Australia to impose a 10% WHT on the franked part of a dividend.
27. The source-country limit where the recipient has a minimum 25% direct holding in the paying company is 15% if the paying company engages in an industrial undertaking; 20% in other cases.
28. The source-country limit is 10% when interest is paid to a financial institution. It is 25% in all other cases.
29. Source-country tax is generally limited to 15%. However, an exemption applies for dividends paid to a listed company which satisfies certain public listing requirements and which controls 80% or more of the voting power in the company paying the dividend, and a 5% limit applies to dividends paid to other companies with voting power of 10% or greater in the dividend paying company.
30. Source-country tax is generally limited to 10%. However, generally zero interest WHT is payable where interest is paid to a financial institution or a government body exercising governmental functions.
31. Source-country tax is generally limited to 15%. No source country tax is chargeable on dividends to a beneficially entitled company which satisfies certain public listing requirements and holds 80% or more of the voting power in the company paying the dividend. A 5% limit applies to dividends paid to other companies with voting power of 10% or greater in the dividend paying company. No limit applies to US tax on dividends paid on certain substantial holdings of Australian residents in US real estate investment trusts (REITs). In practical terms, US tax on these dividends is increased from 15% to the current US domestic law rate of 30%. The 15% rate applies to REIT investments made by certain listed Australian property trusts subject to the underlying ownership requirements not exceeding certain levels. Investments in REITs by listed Australian property trusts acquired before 26 March 2001 are protected from the increased rate.
32. Source-country tax generally is limited to 10%. However, generally zero interest WHT is payable where interest is paid to a financial institution or a government body exercising governmental functions. Rules consistent with US tax treaty policy and practice will allow interest to be taxed at a higher 15% rate (the rate that generally applies to dividends) and for tax to be charged on intra-entity interest payments between a branch and its head office.
33. Amounts derived from equipment leasing (including container leasing) are excluded from the royalty definition.

Australia

34. Source-country tax is limited to 15% (Australia) and 10% (Vietnam).
35. A zero WHT rate will apply in certain cases to inter-corporate dividends where the recipient holds directly at least 80% of the voting power in the dividend paying company for the 12-month period prior to payment. A rate of 5% applies to all other inter-corporate dividends where the recipient holds directly 10% or more of the voting power of the company paying the dividend. A general limit of 15% applies to all other dividends.
36. Prior to 1 January 2009, a zero WHT rate applied to dividends paid out of profits that have borne the normal rate of company tax and are paid to a company which holds directly at least 10% of the capital of the dividend paying company. A 15% rate applied in all other cases.
37. For dividend income derived on or after 1 January 2008, a zero WHT rate applies to inter-corporate dividends where the recipient holds directly 80% or more of the voting power of the company paying the dividend. A 5% rate limit applies on all other inter-corporate dividends where the recipient holds directly 10% or more of the voting power of the company paying the dividend. A 15% rate applies in all other cases.
38. A rate limit of 10% will apply to interest, except no tax will be chargeable in the source country on interest derived by a financial institution resident in the other country or a government or political or administrative subdivision or local authority or central bank of the other country.
39. Amounts derived from equipment leasing (including certain container leasing) are excluded from the royalty definition and treated either as international transport operations or business profits. The rate of 5% applies to royalties derived on or after 1 January 2008. Before that date, a 10% rate applied.
40. On 31 January 2008, Australia and Japan signed a new agreement. The new agreement has effect in Australia in respect of WHTs on income derived on or after 1 January 2009. The source country will exempt inter-corporate dividends where the recipient holds directly 80% or more of the voting power of the company paying the dividend and certain limitation of benefit thresholds are met. A 5% rate limit will apply on all other inter-corporate dividends where the recipient beneficially holds directly 10% or more of the voting power of the company paying the dividend. A rate limit of 10% will otherwise apply for dividends. However, where the dividends are paid by a company that is a resident of Japan, which is entitled to a deduction for the dividends in Japan, the rate limit is 15% where more than 50% of the assets of the paying company consist, directly or indirectly, of real property situated in Japan and 10% in all other cases. Special rules apply to distributions to Japanese residents by REITs. A rate limit of 10% applies to interest, except no tax will be chargeable in the source country on interest derived by a financial institution resident in the other country or a government or political subdivision or local authority or central bank or other specified entity of the other country. As of 1 January 2009, a 5% WHT rate on royalties applies. Before 1 January 2009, a general limit of 10% WHT on royalties applied. Under the new agreement, amounts derived from equipment leasing (including certain container leasing) will be excluded from the royalty definition and treated either as international transport operations or business profits.
41. A general rate limit of 10% applies to interest. However, in respect of interest derived on or after 1 January 2008, no tax will be chargeable in the source country on interest derived by a government of the other country (including its money institutions or a bank performing central banking functions) from the investment of official reserve assets and on interest derived by a financial institution resident in the other country (excluding interest paid as part of a back-to-back loan arrangement).
42. The rate limit for royalties of 5% applies to royalties derived on or after 1 January 2008. Before that date, a 10% rate applied.
43. On 31 March 2008, Australia and South Africa signed a protocol amending the agreement. The provisions of the new Protocol relating to Australian WHTs have effect in respect of income derived by a non-resident on or after 1 January 2009. A 5% rate limit will apply on all inter-corporate dividends where the recipient beneficially holds directly 10% or more of the voting power of the company paying the dividend. A rate limit of 15% will otherwise apply for dividends. As of 1 January 2009, a general rate limit of 10% applies to interest. However no tax will be chargeable in the source country on interest derived by a government of the other country (including a bank performing central banking functions) and on interest derived by a financial institution resident in the other country (excluding interest paid as part of a back-to-back loan arrangement). As of 1 January 2009, a 5% rate on royalties applies. Before 1 January 2009, a general limit of 10% WHT on royalties applied.
44. On 28 October 2008, it was announced that the Australian and the United Kingdom governments would commence negotiations on a revised tax treaty. No further announcements have been made in relation to the progress of treaty negotiations.
45. On 26 June 2009, a new double tax agreement was signed between Australia and New Zealand. The new treaty took effect for WHT purposes on 1 May 2010. As of 1 May 2010, a zero WHT rate applies in certain cases to inter-corporate dividends where the recipient holds directly at least 80% of the voting power in the dividend paying company. A rate of 5% applies on all other inter-corporate dividends where the recipient holds directly 10% or more of the voting power of the company paying the dividend. A general limit of 15% applies for all other dividends, including those paid prior to 1 May 2010. As of 1 May 2010, source-country tax on interest continues to be limited to 10%. However, no tax is chargeable in the source country on interest derived by a government or a political subdivision or local authority of the other country (including a government investment fund or a bank performing central banking functions) or on interest derived by a financial institution which is unrelated to and dealing wholly independently of the payer (excluding interest paid as part of a back-to-back loan arrangement and, for New Zealand payers, where that person has not paid approved issuer levy). As of 1 May 2010, the royalty WHT rate reduced from 10% to 5%.

46. The government announced on 4 February 2010 that negotiations to update Australia's tax treaty with Austria would take place in March 2010. No further announcements have been made in relation to the progress of treaty negotiations.
47. Australia and Chile signed a new DTA on 10 March 2010. The new agreement has not yet entered into force.
48. On 29 April 2010, the Australian and Turkish Governments signed a DTA. The DTA will enter into force when both countries advise that they have completed their domestic requirements.
49. Once in force, the DTA will apply a 5% WHT rate to inter-corporate dividends where the recipient owns directly 10% of the voting power of an Australian resident company or directly owns 25% of the capital of a Turkish resident company where the profits out of which the dividend is paid has been subject to the full rate of corporation tax in Turkey. In all other cases, a 15% WHT rate will apply.
50. Once in force, the DTA will apply a general limit of 10% WHT on interest. However, interest derived from the investment of official reserve assets by the either the Australian or Turkish Government, the Australian or Turkish central bank, or a bank performing central banking functions in either Australia or Turkey shall be exempt from interest WHT.

Other payments

A Pay-As-You-Go (PAYG) withholding regime applies to require the deduction and remittance of taxes on behalf of foreign resident individuals and entities that are in receipt of the following types of payments:

Type of payment	Rate of withholding (%)
Payments for promoting or organising casino gaming junket arrangements	3
Payments for performing artists and sportspersons, including payments to support staff such as art directors, bodyguards, coaches, hairdressers, and personal trainers:	
if recipient is a company	30
if recipient is an individual	the applicable non-resident marginal tax rate
Payments under contracts entered into after 30 June 2004 for the construction, installation, and upgrading of buildings, plant, and fixtures, and for associated activities	5

Managed investment trust distributions

For managed investment trust fund payments to a non-resident investor, a WHT regime applies, with divergent outcomes, depending upon whether or not the recipient of such fund payments is resident of a country identified as being one with which Australia has an effective exchange of information (EEOI) arrangement and which is regulated as such for purposes of these rules. For a resident of a regulated EEOI country, a final WHT at a 7.5% rate applies for distributions relating to income years starting before 1 July 2012 (a final WHT at a 15% rate is proposed to apply to distributions relating to subsequent income years).

EEOI countries that have been identified by regulation are Anguilla, Antigua & Barbuda, Aruba, the Bahamas, Belize, Bermuda, the British Virgin Islands, the Cayman Islands, Gibraltar, Guernsey, Isle of Man, Jersey, Monaco, the Netherlands Antilles, San Marino, St. Christopher and Nevis, St. Vincent and the Grenadines, and the Turks and Caicos Islands, as well as countries with which Australia has concluded DTAs, other than Austria, Greece, Korea, the Philippines, and Switzerland. Australia has entered into EEOI agreements with Andorra, Bahrain, the Cook Islands, Costa Rica, Dominica, Grenada, Liberia, Liechtenstein, Macao, the Marshall Islands, Mauritius, Montserrat, Saint Lucia, Samoa, and Vanuatu; however, these countries have not yet been identified in regulations to be EEOI countries.

Australia

....

Tax administration

Taxable period

The Australian tax year runs from 1 July to 30 June. However, a corporation may apply to adopt a substitute year of income, for example, 1 January to 31 December.

Tax returns

A corporation (including the head company of a tax consolidated group) lodges/files a tax return under a self-assessment system that allows the Australian Taxation Office (ATO) to rely on the information stated on the return. Where a corporation is in doubt as to its tax liability regarding a specific item, it can ask the ATO to consider the matter and obtain a binding private ruling.

Generally the tax return for a corporation is due to be lodged/filed with the ATO by the 15th day of the seventh month following the end of the relevant income year or such later date as the Commissioner of Taxation allows. Additional time may apply where the tax return is lodged/filed by a registered tax agent.

Payment of tax

A PAYG instalment system applies to companies other than those whose annual tax is less than AUD 8,000 that are not registered for GST. Most companies are obliged to pay instalments of tax for their current income year by the 21st day of the fourth, seventh, and tenth months of that year and by the 21st day of the month immediately following that year. Instalments are calculated on a quarterly basis by applying an instalment rate to the amount of the company's actual ordinary income (ignoring deduction) for the previous quarter. The instalment rate is notified to the taxpayer by the ATO and determined by reference to the tax payable for the most recent assessment. The ATO may notify a new rate during the year on which subsequent instalments must be based. Taxpayers can determine their own instalment rate, but there may be penalty tax if the taxpayer's rate is less than 85% of the rate that should have been selected.

Final assessed tax is payable on the first day of the sixth month following the end of that income year or such later date as the Commissioner of Taxation allows by a published notice.

Audit cycle

The Australian tax system for companies is based on self-assessment; however, the ATO undertakes ongoing compliance activity to ensure corporations are meeting their tax obligations. The ATO takes a risk-based approach to compliance and audit activities, with efforts generally focused on taxpayers with a higher likelihood of non-compliance and/or higher consequences (generally in dollar terms) of non-compliance. Compliance activities take various forms, including general risk reviews, questionnaires, reviews of specific issues, and audits.

Statute of limitations

Generally, the Commissioner of Taxation may amend an assessment within four years after the day of which an assessment is given to a company. Under the self-assessment system, an assessment is deemed to have been given to the company on the day on which it lodges its tax return. The four year time limit does not apply where the Commissioner is of the opinion there has been fraud or evasion, or to give effect to a decision on a review or appeal, or as a result of an objection made by the company, or pending a review or appeal.

Topics of focus for tax authorities

The ATO annually releases its compliance program that identifies issues that are attracting its attention, what it sees as risks for the upcoming year, and how it plans to respond to these risks. The following areas were identified in the *2011/12 Compliance Program*:

- For large businesses, a focus on good tax corporate governance, corporate restructures, mergers and acquisitions, capital gains of foreign residents, stapled group financing, blackhole expenditure, tax and capital losses, R&D claims, and implementation of the TOFA provisions.
- For small to medium enterprises, a focus on detection of basic non-compliance, such as omission of income and inappropriate access to small business concessions. Other risks subject to ongoing compliance activity include classification of items between revenue and capital account, access to company profits other than via dividends, overseas interests and international dealings, and arrangements involving trusts.

Austria

PwC contact

Herbert Greinecker
PwC Österreich GmbH
Erdbergstraße 200
1030 Vienna
Austria
Tel: +43 1 501 88 3300
Email: herbert.greinecker@at.pwc.com

Significant developments

On 15 November 2011, the 'Budgetbegleitgesetz 2012' passed the Austrian parliament. This act includes numerous amendments having significant impact on the Austrian Income Tax Act and the Austrian Corporate Income Tax Act, such as the following:

- Further to a European Court of Justice (ECJ) decision, the deductibility of donations to organisations performing research and education activities was expanded to donations to foreign institutions with residence in the European Union/European Economic Area (EU/EEA) or third countries with which Austria has concluded an agreement on mutual assistance and collection of taxes. The requirement for deductibility is that the activities of the organisation are carried out mainly for the benefit of Austrian science or the Austrian economy. *See the Deductions section for more information.*

On 29 March 2012, the 'Stabilitätsgesetz 2012' was enacted, which resulted in several changes to the Austrian Income Tax Act and the Austrian Corporate Income Tax Act.

- One change relevant for corporations is the introduction of additional requirements for receiving a research and development (R&D) premium. *See the Deductions section for more information.*

In April 2012, the draft of a tax reform ('Abgabenänderungsgesetz 2012') was published. This draft is still subject to examination; however, it seems that there will not be any significant changes to the Austrian corporate tax system.

Taxes on corporate income

Basis of corporate income tax (Körperschaftsteuer)
Corporations (i.e. GmbH, AG) are subject to unlimited taxation in Austria of their entire (domestic and foreign) income if they have their legal seat or place of effective management in Austria. A non-Austrian corporate tax resident (with neither a legal seat nor place of effective management in Austria) is subject to limited taxation on certain sources of income in Austria.

Rates of corporate income tax (Körperschaftsteuer)
Due to the qualification of corporations as independent tax subjects, a distinction must always be made between tax ramifications at the level of the company and those at shareholder level. At the level of the company, profits are taxed at the standard corporate income tax (CIT) rate of 25%, regardless of whether profits are retained or distributed. At the shareholder level, the profit distributions are usually subject to withholding tax (WHT) of 25%.

There is also a minimum CIT, payable by companies in a tax-loss position. The minimum CIT amounts to 437.50 euros (EUR) for limited liability companies (GmbH) and EUR 875 for stock corporations (AG) for each full quarter of a year. To promote the formation of new companies, the minimum CIT is reduced to EUR 273 for the first four quarters. The minimum CIT can be carried forward without time limitation and be credited against future CIT burdens of the company.

Local income taxes
There is no additional local income tax levied at the company level.

Corporate residence

A corporation is resident in Austria for tax purposes if either it is registered in Austria (legal seat) or its place of effective management is located in Austria. The 'place of effective management' is located where the day-to-day management of the company is actually carried out and not where singular board decisions are formally made.

However, the definition of place of effective management under Austrian tax law does not significantly deviate from its definition under the Organisation for Economic Co-operation and Development (OECD) guidelines.

Permanent establishment (PE)
An Austrian PE is defined under Austrian tax law as a fixed establishment where a business is carried out, in particular:

- the place where the management is carried out
- plants, warehouses, purchase and sales establishments, and other establishments where an entrepreneur or one's permanent representative carries out one's business, or
- construction sites, which last for more than six months.

However, the definition of PE is different in some tax treaties. The Austrian tax authorities generally follow the commentary to the OECD model convention regarding the PE concept.

Other taxes

Value-added tax (VAT) (Mehrwertsteuer)
Generally, the Austrian VAT law is based on the 6th European Union (EU) VAT Directive. Under the Austrian VAT law, companies and individuals carrying out an active business on a permanent basis are qualified as entrepreneurs for VAT purposes. As entrepreneurs, they have to charge the supply of goods or services provided to their customers with Austrian VAT at a rate of 20%. A certain limited range of goods and services (such as food, books, passenger transportation, cultural events) is taxed at the reduced rate of 10%. Certain other transactions are exempted from Austrian VAT (e.g. export transactions).

Input VAT
Entrepreneurs are entitled to deduct Austrian input VAT insofar as the input VAT does not result from goods/services purchased which are directly linked to certain VAT exempt sales (e.g. interest income, insurance premium). However, certain transactions are exempt from Austrian VAT (e.g. export transactions) without limiting the ability of

Austria

the entrepreneur to deduct the related input VAT. To be entitled to deduct input VAT, the entrepreneur must obtain an invoice from one's supplier which fulfils certain formal requirements.

VAT filing and payment

Entrepreneurs have to file monthly or quarterly VAT returns by the 15th day of the second month following the month concerned or by the 15th day of the second month following the quarter concerned. The balance of the VAT due and the input VAT deducted has to be paid to the tax office (if VAT burden) or is refunded by the tax office (if in a net input VAT position) to the electronic tax account of the entrepreneur. A separate report has to be filed by the entrepreneur at the tax office showing the cross-border intra EU-transactions made.

Customs duties

Certain cross-border inbound movements of goods from non-EU countries trigger Austrian customs duty. The duty is levied according to the Austrian customs duty scheme, which is based on the EU-customs duty scheme. It defines the customs duty tariffs, dependent on the nature of the good.

Excise taxes

Excise taxes are imposed on certain products including petroleum (approximately EUR 40 to EUR 600 per 1,000 litres), tobacco products (13% to 47% of price), and alcoholic beverages (tax rate depends on type of alcohol).

Real estate tax

Local authorities annually levy real estate tax on all Austrian real estate property whether developed or not. The tax is levied on the assessed standard ratable value (*Einheitswert*) of immovable property. The assessed value is usually substantially lower than the market value. The effective tax rate depends on the intended use of the real estate and is calculated using a special multiplier.

Tax rates:

- Agricultural area and forestry
  - 1.6‰ for the first EUR 3,650 of the assessed standard ratable value.
  - 2‰ for the amount of the assessed standard ratable value exceeding EUR 3,650.
- Buildings and property are taxed at 2‰ of the assessed standard ratable value. This multiplier is reduced for:
  - Single family houses
    - to 0.5‰ for the first EUR 3,650 of the assessed standard ratable value and
    - to 1‰ for the next EUR 7,300.
  - Leasehold and shared property
    - to 1‰ for the first EUR 3,650 of the assessed standard ratable value and
    - to 1.5‰ for the next EUR 3,650.
  - All other property
    - to 1‰ for the first EUR 3,650 of the assessed standard ratable value.

After the assessed standard ratable value is multiplied by the relevant multiplier, the real estate tax is calculated by using a special municipal rate fixed by each municipality (maximum 500%). Finally, the tax amount is reduced by a general reduction of 25% as stated by law and increased by a 35% inflation adjustment.

Real estate transfer tax

Tax is levied at 3.5% on any transaction which causes a change in the ownership of Austrian real estate or in the person empowered to dispose of such property (e.g. direct owner). Real estate transfer tax is generally calculated on the basis of the acquisition price. However, in the case of corporate restructuring under the Reorganisation Tax Act and in case of real estate transfers free of consideration, the two-fold (in the case of the former) and the threefold (in the case of the latter) assessed standard ratable value for tax purposes is taken as the tax base.

Real estate transactions with a tax base of EUR 1,100 or below are exempt.

Note that an additional 1.1% registration fee (same tax base as real estate transfer tax) becomes due upon incorporation to the land register.

Capital transfer tax (Gesellschaftsteuer)

Capital transfer tax is imposed at a rate of 1% on the initial contribution of capital, other contractual or voluntary contributions in cash or in kind, and certain hybrid financing instruments to Austrian corporations. However, in many cases a taxable event for capital transfer tax purposes can be eliminated by careful structuring (e.g. contributions made by the indirect shareholder of an Austrian company (so called 'grandparent contributions') do not trigger capital transfer tax).

Stamp duty

Stamp duty is imposed in connection with certain legally predefined transactions for which a written contract has been established (e.g. lease contracts, bills of exchange, assignments of receivables). The Austrian administration's understanding of a 'written contract' is very broad and covers not only paper contracts but also contracts concluded by electronic means (e.g. electronically signed emails).

The stamp duty is triggered upon the establishment of a legal relationship if at least one Austrian party is contractually involved or, even if a contract is concluded between non-Austrian parties only, if the subject of the contract relates to Austria (e.g. lease contract on Austrian real estate). However, various possibilities are available for most legal transactions subject to stamp duty to structure them in a way without triggering stamp duties (e.g. setting up of contracts abroad, offer-acceptance procedure, usage of audio-tapes).

Loan and credit agreements are not subject to stamp duty.

The stamp duty rates for the most common legal transactions are as follows:

Legal transactions	Stamp duty (%)
Lease agreements	1.00
Certificates of bonds	1.00
Bill of exchange	0.13
Assignment of receivables	0.80

Payroll taxes

Payroll taxes are income taxes levied on employment income, withheld by the employer. A progressive tax rate is applied to the tax base, being the salary after deduction of allowances and various expenditures (e.g. social security contribution). The employer is legally obligated to withhold the payroll tax and liable to do so vis-a-vis the Austrian tax

Austria

authority. *For more information, see Other taxes in Austria's Individual summary at www. pwc.com/taxsummaries.*

....

Branch income

Austrian branches of foreign corporations are taxed in the same way as Austrian corporations, except that inter-company dividends received by Austrian branches of non-EU corporations are not tax exempt (*see the Income determination section*) and Austrian tax losses can be carried forward only if they exceed non-Austrian profits. Books and records generally can be kept abroad but must be brought to Austria in case of a tax audit (upon official request).

....

Income determination

Taxable income is determined based on statutory accounts under Austrian generally accepted accounting principles (GAAP) adjusted for certain deductions and additions prescribed by the tax law.

Inventory valuation
In general, inventories are valued at the lower of cost or market. If specific identification during stock movements is not possible, other methods, such as last in first out (LIFO) and first in first out (FIFO) are permitted when shown to be appropriate. Conformity between financial book keeping and tax reporting is required.

Capital gains/exit taxation/inbound transfer
Generally, capital gains (short and long-term) are part of the normal annual result of a corporation and therefore are taxed at the ordinary CIT rate (25%).

A special tax treatment applies to capital gains with respect to the exit of taxable assets. In the case of a transfer of assets which formed part of a business from Austria to a foreign country (e.g. allocation of assets to foreign branch), latent capital gains generally are taxed at the time of the transfer. However, if these assets are transferred to an EU member state, capital gains taxation can be postponed upon request until the assets are sold or transferred outside the European Union.

In case of an inbound transfer, generally, the fair market value of the assets is considered for Austrian income tax purposes (step up). Therefore, any hidden reserves accumulated abroad are not taxed in Austria.

Dividend income
Dividends received from an Austrian company at the corporate shareholder level are generally excluded from the tax base (no minimum stake, no minimum holding period). This tax exemption refers to domestic dividends only, not to capital gains or losses.

Additionally, dividends received from companies located within the European Union or from countries within the European Economy Area with which Austria has concluded a comprehensive agreement on mutual assistance regarding the exchange of information are also tax exempt if the foreign company is subject to a tax similar to the Austrian CIT and if the foreign CIT rate is not below 15%.

In cases where the dividends from foreign investments are taxable, foreign CIT can be credited against the Austrian CIT.

Portfolio dividends

Portfolio dividends (i.e. dividends from an investment below 10%) received from corporations located in member states of the European Union, as well as dividends from corporations which are located in those EEA countries with which Austria has concluded a comprehensive agreement on mutual assistance regarding the exchange of information, are generally exempt from CIT. However, under special circumstances, a switch-over to the credit method, as outlined under *International participation exemption for dividends and capital gains below*, has to be considered.

In the past, the exemption of portfolio dividends applied to dividends from EU/EEA countries only, but not to those from third countries. According to a decision of the ECJ of February 2011 (C-436/08 and C-437/08, Haribo/Salinen), the limitation of the exemption to portfolio dividends received from countries within the EU/EEA is contrary to EU law. Therefore, an extension of the exemption to portfolio dividends from third countries with which Austria has concluded a comprehensive agreement on mutual assistance regarding the exchange of information was implemented for the fiscal years from 2011 onwards in the course of the 'AbgÄG 2011'. For fiscal years before 2011, the credit method has to be applied.

Stock dividends

A conversion from revenue reserves (retained earnings) to capital by a company does not lead to taxable income for the shareholder (but triggers 1% capital transfer tax). However, capital reductions are treated as taxable income if within ten years prior to the capital reduction the above-mentioned increase in capital was repaid to the shareholder. Otherwise, they are tax exempt.

International participation exemption for dividends and capital gains

Dividends received from a foreign company are also tax exempt at the corporate shareholder level if the Austrian company holds at least 10% of the issued share capital for a minimum holding period of one year (international participation exemption). Furthermore, both capital gains and capital losses derived from shares qualifying for the international participation exemption are tax neutral. This means a deduction of capital losses is no longer available. However, the parent company can exercise an (irrevocable) option for each single participation acquired to treat both capital gains and capital losses as taxable (spread of losses and depreciations over a period of seven years). The option refers to capital gains (losses) only and does not affect the tax treatment of ongoing dividend distributions.

In the case of presumed tax abuse, the participation exemption for dividends and capital gains is replaced by a tax credit (switch-over-clause). The credit system is applied if the foreign subsidiary does not meet an active-trade-or-business test (i.e. passive income from royalties, interest, etc. is greater than 50% of total income of subsidiary) and is not subject to an effective foreign minimum CIT rate of more than 15%. The domestic and foreign participation exemptions are available to Austrian resident corporations and to Austrian branches of EU corporations only, but not to Austrian branches of non-EU corporations.

Interest income

Interest income is taxed at the general CIT rate of 25%.

Rental income

Rental income is treated as normal business income.

Austria

Foreign income

Austrian resident corporations are taxed on their worldwide income. If a double taxation treaty (DTT) is in force, double taxation is mitigated either through an exemption or by granting a tax credit equal to the foreign WHT at the maximum (capped with the Austrian CIT incurred on the foreign source income). If foreign WHT cannot be credited at the level of the Austrian corporation (e.g. due to a loss position), Austrian tax law does not allow to carry forward the foreign WHT to future assessment periods. However, if the source of the income is a non-treaty country, exemption or a tax credit shall be available based on unilateral relief (representing a discretionary decision of the Austrian Ministry of Finance only but no legal entitlement for the applicant). Austrian tax law does not provide for a deferral of taxes on foreign income. Special rules for taxing undistributed income of foreign subsidiaries are applicable only to foreign investment funds.

Please note that Austrian Tax Law does not define special controlled foreign company (CFC) rules. However, under certain circumstances, the Austrian tax administration, under a substance over form approach, taxes passive income of foreign subsidiaries of Austrian companies located in low tax jurisdictions (*see switch-over-clause under International participation exemption for dividends and capital gains above*).

Deductions

Depreciation and amortisation

Only the straightline method is accepted for tax purposes, whereby the cost is evenly spread over the useful life of an asset. For certain assets, depreciation rates relevant for tax purposes are prescribed by the tax law and shown in the following chart:

Assets	Depreciation rate (%)
Buildings (industrial use)	3.0
Buildings (banking, insurance)	2.5
Other buildings	2.0
Automobiles	12.5

Tax depreciation is not required to conform to financial depreciation under Austrian GAAP. If depreciated property is sold, the difference between tax value and sale proceeds is taxed as a profit or loss in the year of sale.

Trademarks are usually amortised over 15 years. Other intangibles have to be amortised over their useful lives.

Goodwill

Goodwill arising in the course of an asset deal for tax purposes must be amortised over 15 years. Goodwill arising in the course of a share deal can be amortised only if the acquired company is included in a tax group (*see the Group taxation section*). Goodwill arising as a result of a corporate merger cannot be amortised.

Organisational and start-up expenses

Generally, organisational and start-up expenses are tax deductible.

A

Interest expenses
Interest payments (also inter-company) are generally tax deductible if they meet the general arm's-length requirements. *See Thin capitalisation in the Group taxation section for more information.*

Financing costs
According to current tax law, interest expenses resulting from the debt financed acquisition of shares are usually tax deductible. This is so even if the Austrian participation exemption regime applies (*see the Income determination section*).

As of 2011, interest expenses relating to the debt-financed acquisition of shares from related parties or (directly or indirectly) controlling shareholders are generally non-deductible. This disallowance of interest also applies in circumstances where the shareholder acquiring the shares has been funded by a debt-financed equity contribution (insofar as the equity contribution was made in direct connection with the share acquisition). Interest expenses resulting from intra-group share acquisitions conducted prior to 1 January 2011 are also covered by the new regulation. The deductibility of interest expenses incurred in connection with the debt-financed acquisition of shares from a third party is not impacted.

Other financing costs (e.g. fees, legal advice) directly related to tax exempt dividend income are not deductible. However, foreign exchange expenses or profits accumulated in connection with the financing of tax exempted international participations are treated as a deductible or taxable (respectively) item.

Accrued expenses
Certain accruals (such as provisions for liabilities and impending losses) running for more than 12 months as of the closing date of the accounts are accepted for tax purposes at 80% of their value only. Exempted from this reduction are provisions for personnel benefits (severance payments, pensions, vacations, and anniversary awards) for which specific reduction and computation methods have been provided and provisions that were already calculated by discounting a future obligation.

In general, lump-sum accruals and accruals for deferred repairs and maintenance are not allowed for tax purposes.

Bad debt
Valuation allowances for bad debts are, in principle, deductible for tax purposes, unless they are calculated on a lump-sum basis. In case of intercompany receivables, appropriate documentation regarding the compliance with the arm's-length principle is required.

Charitable contributions
Donations to certain charitable institutions are generally tax deductible, up to a limit of 10% of the prior year's profit.

Furthermore, donations to certain public Austrian institutions, such as universities, art colleges, or the academy of science, and to non-profit organisations performing research and educational activities mainly for the benefit of the Austrian science or economy may also be deducted as operating expenses, up to the limit of 10% of the prior year's profit. Further to a decision of the ECJ (C-10/10, issued in June 2011), the limitation of the privilege to Austrian institutions is contrary to EU law. As a result, in the course of the 'Budgetbegleitgesetz 2012', the deductibility of donations was expanded to donations granted to foreign institutions with residence in the EU/EEA or

Austria

third countries with which Austria has concluded an agreement on mutual assistance regarding the exchange of information. The requirement for deductibility is that the activities of the organisation are carried out mainly for the benefit of Austrian science or the Austrian economy.

Meals and entertainment

The deductibility of costs for business lunches generally is limited to 50% of actual expenses incurred (provided the business lunch had the purpose of acquiring new business).

The deductibility of entertainment expenses is restricted to advertising expenses.

Payment to directors

Payments to a member of the supervisory board (*Aufsichtsrat*) are tax deductible up to a limit of 50%. Payments to members of the executive (managing) board are tax deductible without special limitation.

Fines and penalties

Fines and penalties are generally not tax deductible.

Taxes

Austrian and foreign taxes on income and other personal taxes, as well as VAT insofar as it relates to non-deductible expenditures, are non-deductible. Other taxes, such as payroll or capital transfer taxes, are deductible.

Net operating losses

Tax losses can be carried forward without any time limit. However, tax loss carryforwards generally can be offset against taxable income only up to a maximum of 75% of the taxable income for any given year. Some exceptions apply (e.g. in connection with tax groups or in the case of liquidations), allowing a company to charge tax loss carryforwards available against 100% of annual taxable income.

The Austrian tax law does not provide for a carryback of tax losses.

Loss-trafficking (Mantelkauf)

Tax loss carryforwards may be lost in the case of a share deal being classified as loss-trafficking (so called '*Mantelkauf*') or in the course of a legal restructuring leading to similar results.

Under Austrian tax law, a share deal against compensation is classified as a *Mantelkauf*, if, from a substance over form perspective, the 'economic identity' of a company is changed due to the transaction. The change of economic identity of a company is realised if all of the following structural changes are made to the acquired Austrian company having the tax loss carryforwards available:

* Change of shareholder structure.
* Change of the organisational structure.
* Change of the business structure.

All three conditions cumulatively have to be met. There is no exact time period defined within which they have to be met; however, meeting them within one year after the share transfer usually is regarded as a strong indication for a *Mantelkauf*.

Payments to foreign affiliates

Generally, there are no restrictions on the deductibility of royalties, interest, and service fees paid to foreign affiliates, provided they are at arm's length (which should be appropriately documented by agreements, contracts, calculation sheets, etc.). Payments to affiliated companies not meeting arm's-length standards are treated as a hidden distribution of earnings (i.e. they are not tax deductible, and WHT is usually triggered at source). *See Transfer pricing in the Group taxation section for more information.*

Note that the domestic implementation of the EU Interest Royalty Directive which abolishes WHT on cross-border payments of interest and license fees (regardless of whether taken out by deduction or by assessment) between affiliated companies in the member states should be considered.

Group taxation

Two or more companies can form a tax group, provided the parent company directly or indirectly owns more than 50% of the shares in the subsidiaries. The tax group also can include foreign group members. If a group member withdraws from the group within a minimum commitment-period of three years, all tax effects derived from its group membership must be reversed.

Within a tax group, all of the taxable results (profit and loss) of the domestic group members are attributed to their respective group parent. From foreign tax group members, tax losses in the proportion of the shareholding quota are attributed to the tax group parent. The foreign tax loss has to be calculated in accordance with Austrian tax law. However, it is capped with the amount actually suffered based on foreign tax law. Foreign tax losses utilised by the Austrian tax group parent are subject to recapture taxation at the time they are utilised by the tax group member in the source state, or in the moment the group member withdraws from the Austrian tax group. Under the recapture taxation scheme, the Austrian tax group has to increase its Austrian tax base by the amount of foreign tax losses used in prior periods.

For the purpose of the application of the recapture taxation scheme, a withdrawal from the tax group is also assumed if the foreign group member significantly reduces the size of its business (compared to the size of the business at the time the losses arose). Reduction of size is measured on the basis of business parameters such as turnover, assets, balance sheet totals, and employees, while the importance of the respective criteria depends on the nature of the particular business.

Goodwill arising in the course of a share deal (acquisition of an active business company from a third party contractor) must be amortised over 15 years, provided that the acquired company is included in a tax group.

Write-downs of participations in tax group members are not tax deductible.

Transfer pricing

Under Austrian Tax Law, there are no explicit transfer pricing regulations available defining in detail the local requirements with regards to arm's length, the documentation standards required, penalties, etc. In general, Austria applies the OECD transfer pricing guidelines referring to the OECD model tax convention. Furthermore, Austrian transfer pricing guidelines were recently issued by Austrian tax authorities. The guidelines represent the Austrian authority's understanding of

Austria

intercompany business relationships with regards to their arm's-length classification and are based on the OECD transfer pricing guidelines.

According to these guidelines, all business transactions between affiliated companies must be carried out under consideration of the arm's-length principle. Where a legal transaction is deemed not to correspond to arm's-length principles, the transaction price is adjusted for CIT purposes. Such an adjustment constitutes either a constructive dividend or a capital contribution. Currently, there is the option of applying for a non-binding ruling of the tax authorities. Additionally, a reform of the Austrian CIT Act was recently enacted, which contains the introduction of an advanced ruling opportunity. With the implementation of this new regulation, binding information in the fields of transfer pricing, group taxation, and mergers and acquisitions (M&A) can be requested from the Austrian tax authorities against payment of an administrative fee (the fee rate depends on the size of the applicant's business). The advanced ruling opportunity is applicable as of the 2011 fiscal year.

Thin capitalisation

There are no explicit tax regulations available under Austrian tax law stipulating the minimum equity required by a company ('thin capitalisation rules'). Basically, group financing has to comply with general arm's length requirements. Therefore, an Austrian group entity being financed by an affiliated entity must be able to document that it would have been able to obtain funds from third party creditors under the same conditions as from an affiliated financing entity. Therefore, the appropriate ratio between an Austrian company's equity and debt will mainly depend on the individual situation of the company (profit expectations, market conditions, etc.) and its industry. Nonetheless, the fiscal authorities in administrative practice (i.e. no 'safe-harbour' rule) tend to accept a debt-equity ratio of approximately 3:1 to 4:1. However, the debt-equity ratio accepted by tax authorities also strongly depends on the average ratio relevant for the respective industry sector. If in intercompany loan for tax purposes is not accepted as debt, it is reclassified into hidden equity and related interest payments into (non-deductible) dividend distributions.

Furthermore, under Austrian commercial law (for companies subject to statutory audits), a minimum equity ratio of 8% is claimed. If the equity ratio of the company falls below 8% and its earning power (virtual period for debt redemption) at the same time does not meet certain requirements, a formal and public reorganisation process will have to be initiated.

Tax credits and incentives

Foreign tax credit (matching credit)

Generally, foreign WHT can be credited against Austrian CIT (*see Foreign income in the Income determination section*). In special cases (e.g. Brazil, China, Korea), the DTT provides for a matching credit, which allows the credit of a pre-defined amount which exceeds the actually paid foreign WHT.

Research and development (R&D) incentives

R&D costs are fully deductible at the time they accrue. An R&D premium of 10% (i.e. R&D expenses x 10% = tax refund) may be claimed for R&D activities performed in Austria.

As a result of the '*Stabilitätsgesetz 2012*', an expert report (issued by an Austrian research promotion organisation) is required in order to receive the R&D premium of 10%.

The R&D premium is also available in case of contract R&D; however, R&D incentives cannot be claimed by both principal and agent. In case of contract R&D, the privileged R&D costs are capped at EUR 1 million per year.

Employment incentives
A tax bonus payment of 6% or, alternatively, an allowance of 20% can be claimed for expenditures in connection with the training of employees. These incentives can be claimed for external training expenditures and for in-house training expenditures, provided that there is a dedicated in-house training department (for in-house training expenditures, only the allowance can be applied for).

A premium scheme for apprenticeships is available and based on the amount of actual wage as set out in the applicable collective contract. It provides tax free subsidies, depending on the duration of the apprentice's employment.

Investment incentives
For investment in certain regions, government grants and subsidies are available and are generally individually negotiated.

Withholding taxes

Dividend WHT
Under Austrian domestic law, there is generally a 25% WHT on dividends (profit distributions) paid to a foreign parent company. The WHT has to be deducted and forwarded by the Austrian subsidiary to the tax office.

To end up with the reduced WHT rate as defined under the DTT applicable, Austrian tax law provides for the following alternative methods of WHT relief: refund method or exemption at source method.

Refund method
The Austrian subsidiary generally has to withhold 25% WHT on profit distributions to the foreign parent company, and the parent company has to apply for a refund (of the difference between 25% WHT and the lower DTT rate). In the course of the refund process, the Austrian tax administration analyses whether the foreign shareholder can be qualified as beneficial owner of the dividends paid. If the refund is approved by the Austrian tax authority, dividend distributions within the following three years can be done without deduction of WHT (for distributions of a comparable size and provided the foreign holding structure did not change in the meantime).

Exemption at source method
Relief at the source is available only if the direct parent company issues a written declaration confirming that it is an 'active' company carrying out an active business that goes beyond the level of pure asset management (holding activities, group financing, etc.) and has its own employees and office space at its disposal (substance requirements).

Austria

WHT on dividends paid to EU companies

With regard to dividends paid to EU resident corporate shareholders, Austria has implemented the EU Parent/Subsidiary Directive according to which domestic WHT is reduced to zero. The requirements for the reduction are that the EU resident parent company, which also has to meet the substance requirements mentioned above (*see Exemption at source method*) at the moment of the dividend distribution, must directly own at least 10% of the share capital of the Austrian subsidiary for a period of at least one year. In case of foreign EU shareholders being qualified as pure holding companies, the Austrian tax administration does not allow an exemption at source but claims the application of the refund method.

Provided the requirements according to the EU Parent/Subsidiary Directive are not met, Austrian WHT has to be deducted. If an EU parent company cannot credit the Austrian WHT deducted against the CIT of its resident state (e.g. because the foreign dividend income is exempted from the CIT or due to a loss position of the shareholder), it is entitled to apply for a refund of the Austrian WHT. This application has to include a confirmation/documentation that the Austrian WHT could (fully or partly) not be credited at the level of the parent company.

Repayment of equity

The tax wise equity of a company has to be annually reported to the Austrian tax authority as part of the CIT return (so called '*Evidenzkonto*'). This equity can be repaid to the domestic or foreign shareholders without triggering Austrian WHT. However, the tax wise classification of a dividend as 'capital repayment' has to be shown in the shareholder resolution about the distribution.

Interest WHT

Interest payments to non-resident companies are not subject to WHT (provided no Austrian real estate property is used as security).

Royalties WHT

On royalties paid to a non-resident company, Austrian WHT at a rate of 20% has to be deducted. This tax rate can be reduced under an applicable DTT or under the application of the EU Interest Royalty Directive which was implemented in Austrian Tax Law.

Tax treaties

The following table lists the countries with which Austria has signed a DTT and provides details of the amount of Austrian WHT.

	WHT (%)		
Recipient	Dividends (1, 2)	Interest (3)	Royalties, licences (4)
Resident corporations	0/25 (5)	0/25	0
Resident individuals	25 (6)	0/25	0
Non-residents:			
Non-treaty:			
Corporations and business enterprises	25	0	20
Individuals	25	0	20

Recipient	WHT (%)		
	Dividends (1, 2)	Interest (3)	Royalties, licences (4)
Treaty:			
Albania (7)	5*/15	0	5
Algeria	5+/15	0	10
Argentina (8) (DTT was recalled by Argentina in 2008)			
Armenia	5+/15	0	5
Australia	15	0	10
Azerbaijan	5/10/15 (9)	0	5/10 (10)
Bahrain (11)	0	0	0
Barbados (12)	5+/15	0	0
Belarus (White Russia)	5*/15	0	5
Belgium	15	0	0/10**
Belize	5*/15	0	0
Bosnia and Herzegovina (13)	5*/10	0	5
Brazil	15	0	10/15/25 (14)
Bulgaria (15)	0	0	5
Canada	5+/15	0	10
China	7*/10	0	6/10 (16)
Croatia	0+/15	0	0
Cuba	5*/15	0	0/5 (19)
Cyprus	10	0	0
Czech Republic (17)	0+/10	0	5 (18)
Denmark (20)	0+/15	0	0
Egypt	10	0	0/20 (21)
Estonia	5*/15	0	5/10 (22)
Finland	0+/10	0	5
France	0+/15	0	0
Georgia	0**/5+/10 (23)	0	0
Germany	5+/15	0	0
Greece (24)	5*/15	0	7
Hong Kong (25)	0+/10	0	3
Hungary	10	0	0
India	10	0	10
Indonesia	15/10*	0	10
Iran	5*/10	0	5
Ireland	10	0	0/10**
Israel	25	0	10
Italy	15	0	0/10**
Japan	10**/20	0	10
Kazakhstan	5+/15	0	10
Korea	5*/15	0	2/10 (26)
Kuwait	0	0	10
Kyrgyzstan	5*/15	0	10
Latvia (27)	10/15*	0	5/10 (28)
Libya (29)			
Liechtenstein	15	0	5/10 (30)

Austria

Recipient	WHT (%)		
	Dividends (1, 2)	Interest (3)	Royalties, licences (4)
Lithuania	5*/15	0	5/10 (31)
Luxemburg	5*/15	0	0/10**
Macedonia (34)	0+/15	0	0
Malaysia	5*/10	0	10/15 (32)
Malta	15	0	0/10 (33)
Mexico	5+/10	0	10
Moldova	5*/15	0	5
Mongolia	5+/10	0	5/10 (35)
Morocco (36)	5*/10	0	10
Nepal	5*/10+/15	0	15
Netherlands	5*/15	0	0/10**
New Zealand (37)	15	0	10
Norway	5*/15	0	0
Pakistan (38)	10+++/15	0	10
Philippines	10+/25	0	15
Poland	5+/15	0	5
Portugal	15	0	5/10 (39)
Qatar (54)	0	0	5
Romania	0*/5	0	3
Russia	5*/15 (40)	0	
Russian Federation (41)	0	0	0
San Marino	0+/15	0	0
Saudi Arabia (42)	5	0	10
Serbia (43)	5*/15	0	5/10 (44)
Singapore	0+/10	0	5
Slovakia (45)	10	0	5
Slovenia	5*/15	0	5
South Africa	5*/15	0	0
Spain	10**/15	0	5
Sweden	5*/10	0	0/10**
Switzerland	0+++/15 (46)	0	0
Syria (47)	5*/10	0	12
Tajikistan (55)	5++/10	0	8
Thailand	10*/25	0	15
Tunisia	10*/20	0	10/15 (48)
Turkey (49)	5*/15	0	10
Ukraine	5+/10	0	5
United Arab Emirates	0	0	0
United Kingdom	5*/15	0	0/10**
United States	5+/15	0	0/10 (50)
Uzbekistan	5+/15	0	5
Venezuela (51)	5++/15	0	5
Vietnam (52)	5***/10*/15	0	7.5/10 (53)

Notes

1. Dividend distributions attributable to a prior release of paid-in surplus or other shareholder contributions (classified as capital reserves) are deemed to be a repayment of capital, i.e. no WHT is incurred. At the shareholder's level, dividends received and those classified as contribution refund will reduce the tax basis assessment for investments. To the extent to which the tax basis would become negative, such dividends are treated as taxable income (unless taxation is eliminated by a tax treaty).
2. Under certain treaties, the amount of the WHT is dependent on the extent of the proportion of issued share capital held by the recipient. Where this is the case, all rates are given. Those marked with + refer to an investment of 10%, ++ to 15%, those marked with +++ refer to an investment of 20%, those marked with * refer to an investment of 25%, those marked with ** refer to an investment of 50%, and those marked with *** refer to an investment of 70%.
3. Interest on cash deposits in euro or foreign currency in bank accounts and fixed interest bearing securities in foreign currency (issued after 31 December 1988) and on fixed interest bearing securities denominated in Austrian Schillings or EUR (issued after 31 December 1983) are subject to a 25% WHT. If the recipient is an individual, this WHT is final (no further income taxation and inheritance taxation). Companies receiving interest payments may obtain an exemption from WHT if they provide the bank or other custodial agent with a written confirmation from the recipient that such interest payments constitute a part of the recipient's operating revenues (exemption statement). Interest payments to non-residents without a PE in Austria are generally not subject to WHT. At interest payments between affiliated companies, the regulations stipulated by the EU interest directive have to be taken into consideration.
4. In case of payments to countries marked with **, the rate is 0% unless more than 50% of the issued share capital of the company paying the royalties is held by the recipient, in which case the rate given applies. At royalty payments between affiliated companies, the regulations stipulated by the EU interest directive have to be taken into consideration
5. If the recipient holds a participation of less than 10% in the distributing company, the dividends are subject to a 25% WHT. Since dividends distributed by an Austrian corporation to another Austrian corporation are generally not subject to taxation, the WHT is credited against CIT upon assessment of the recipient corporation for the respective tax year.
6. WHT on dividends from Austrian companies is final, i.e. no further income tax is collected from the recipient (provided it is an individual).
7. The treaty was signed on 14 December 2007 and entered into force on 1 September 2008. It is applicable as of the beginning of fiscal year 2009.
8. The treaty was recalled by Argentina in 2009. Austrian tax citizens are protected by section (§) 48 BAO (*Bundesabgabenordnung* (Austrian Fiscal Federal Code)) against double taxation. Austria will try to enter into new negotiations with Argentina.
9. 5% for shares of at least 25% and worth at a minimum of 250,000 United States dollars (USD); 10% for shares of at least 25% and worth at least USD 100,000; 15% in all other cases.
10. 5% for industrial licences and know-how not more than three years old; 10% in all other cases.
11. The treaty entered into force on 17 February 2011 and is applicable as of the beginning of fiscal year 2011.
12. The treaty entered into force on 1 April 2007 and is applicable as of the beginning of fiscal year 2008.
13. The treaty entered into force on 1 January 2012 and is applicable as of the beginning of fiscal year 2012.
14. 10% for copyright licence fees in connection with literature, science, and art; 25% for trademarks licence fees; 15% in all other cases.
15. The new treaty has entered into force on 3 February 2011 and is applicable as of the beginning of fiscal year 2011.
16. 6% for industrial, commercial, or scientific equipment; 10% in all other cases.
17. The treaty entered into force on 22 March 2007 and is applicable as of the beginning of fiscal year 2008.
18. 5% for licence income from copyrights, brands, plans, secret formulas or procedures, computer software, industrial, commercial or scientific use of equipment, and information.
19. 0% for copyright royalties in connection with the production of literary, dramatic, musical, or artistic work; 5% in all other cases.
20. The new treaty was signed on 25 May 2007 and entered into force on 27 March 2008. It is applicable as of the beginning of fiscal year 2009.
21. 20% for films.
22. 5% for leasing of mobile goods, and 10% for other licences.
23. 0% for shares of at least 50% and worth at a minimum of EUR 2,000,000; 5% for shares of at least 10% and worth at least EUR 100,000; 10% for shares in all other cases.
24. The treaty entered into force on 1 April 2009 and is applicable as of the beginning of fiscal year 2010.
25. The treaty entered into force on 1 January 2011 and will be applicable as of the beginning of fiscal year 2012 (Austria: 1 January 2012, Hong Kong: 1 April 2012).
26. 2% for licence income from industrial, commercial, or scientific use, and 10% for other licenses.
27. The treaty entered into force on 16 May 2007 and is applicable as of the beginning of fiscal year of 2008.
28. 5% for the use of commercial or scientific equipment; 10% in all other cases.
29. The treaty was signed on 16 September 2010. It has not yet been decided when it will enter into force.

Austria

30. 5% in case of direct (or indirect over a patent-realisation-company) payments of royalties by companies of the other member state (with an industrial establishment in the other member state), and 10% for other licences.
31. 5% in case of licence income from industrial, commercial, or scientific use, and 10% for other licences.
32. 15% for films.
33. 0% for copyright licence fees in connection with literature, art, and scientific use, and 10% for other licences.
34. The treaty was signed on 7 September 2007 and entered into force on 20 January 2008. It is applicable as of the beginning of fiscal year 2008.
35. 10% for the right of use of copyrights to artistic, scientific, or literary as well as cinematographic works, and 5% for other licences.
36. The new treaty was signed on 13 September 2006 and entered into force on 13 November 2006. It was applicable as of the beginning of fiscal year 2007.
37. The treaty was signed on 21 September 2006 and entered into force on 1 December 2007. It is applicable as of the beginning of fiscal year 2008.
38. The treaty entered into force on 1 June 2007 and is applicable as of the beginning of fiscal year 2008.
39. For Portugal, the rate of WHT is 5%, but 10% if more than 50% of the issued share capital is owned by the recipient.
40. 5% if capital share amounts to at least 10% and worth at least USD 100,000; 15% in all other cases.
41. The treaty applies to Tajikistan and Turkmenistan. With Russia, a new treaty has been ratified.
42. The treaty entered into force on 1 June 2007 and is applicable as of the beginning of fiscal year 2008.
43. The treaty entered into force on 17 December 2010 and is applicable as of the beginning of fiscal year 2011.
44. 5% for copyright licence fees; 10% for other licences.
45. Until a new treaty will be established, the treaty with Czechoslovakia remains applicable.
46. For dividend distributions retroactive as of 1 January 2000.
47. The treaty was signed on 3 March 2009. It has not yet been decided when it will enter into force.
48. 15% for films.
49. The new treaty was signed on 28 March 2008 and entered into force on 1 October 2009. It is applicable as of the beginning of fiscal year 2010.
50. 10% for films.
51. The treaty entered into force on 17 March 2007 and is applicable as of the beginning of fiscal year of 2008.
52. The new treaty was signed on 2 June 2008 and entered into force on 1 January 2010. It is applicable as of the beginning of fiscal year 2011.
53. 7.5% for fees for technical services; 10% for royalties.
54. The treaty entered into force on 7 March 2012 and is applicable as of the beginning of fiscal year of 2013.
55. The treaty was signed on 7 June 2011 and will not enter into force before 1 January 2013.

Tax administration

Taxable period
The standard tax assessment period in Austria is the calendar year. However, a company's financial year may deviate. When the tax and financial years deviate, the tax assessments for a year are based on the profits derived in the financial year(s) ending in the respective calendar year (e.g. if tax year is 1 June 2012 to 31 May 2013, then assessment is financial year 2013).

Tax returns
Generally, the CIT return has to be submitted electronically by 30 June of the calendar year following the year in which the fiscal year of the company ends. However, if the company is represented by an Austrian certified tax advisor, the tax return can be submitted by 31 March of the second following year at the latest (if the company will not be formally requested by the tax office to file it earlier). If the end of a tax year is 31 May 2012 for example, filing deadline is 30 June 2013 (without tax advisor) or 31 March 2014 (with tax advisor).

Electronic filing of annual CIT returns
The annual CIT return (as well as the annual VAT return) has to be filed by electronic means. In the case of a company that cannot reasonably be expected to file tax returns

electronically due to the lack of technical prerequisites, filing of the tax return is allowed to be done via pre-printed forms.

Payment of tax

CIT is prepaid in quarterly instalments during the calendar year, with a final settlement subsequent to the annual assessment. Prepayments of CIT generally are based on the most recently assessed tax year's tax burden (unless the taxpayer can show that its tax charge for the current year will be lower).

The difference between CIT as per the final assessment and the prepayments made is interest bearing from 1 October of the year subsequent to the year when the tax claim arose up to the date when the assessment is released (late payment interest). Interest at a rate of currently 2.38% is applied to underpayments (as well as overpayments) of tax.

Tax audits

Tax audits usually cover CIT, VAT and WHT. Separate audits are carried out in connection with payroll taxes and social security contributions.

In general, companies are audited every three to four years. The audit period usually covers three to four fiscal years, so generally each fiscal year is audited.

The duration of a tax audit depends on the number of years covered and on the complexity of topics (usually between 0.5 and 1.5 years). These topics usually cover ongoing compliance such as tax returns. Specific topics vary from company to company and can involve, for instance,:

- Business restructurings (applicability of Austrian reorganisation tax act, transfer of intangibles, etc.).
- Tax groups (all group members are audited together).
- WHT on dividends, licences, etc.
- Compliance with arm's-length principle in case of group transactions (tax auditors recently tend to focus on transfer pricing issues).

Statute of limitations

The right to assess CIT is subject to a general limitation period of five years after the end of the calendar year in which the fiscal year ends. Additionally, the limitation period can be extended for another two years in cases where certain interruptive events (e.g. tax audit, tax assessment) take place within the general limitation period.

The maximum limitation period in the case of tax evasion is ten years.

In certain cases, the maximum limitation period can be extended to 15 years.

Other issues

Choice of business entity

The most important types of companies in Austria are the limited liability corporation (GmbH), and the joint stock corporation (AG). Foreign investors generally choose the GmbH since it provides a higher degree of corporate law control and allows for lower equity provision.

Austria

As a legal entity, the GmbH exists upon registration with the Companies' Register. The application for registration must contain the notarised signatures of all managing directors. The articles of association must be drawn up in the form of a notarial deed (written document executed by a public notary) and must, as minimum requirements, include the name of the company as well as its seat, the business purpose, the amount of registered capital, and the capital contribution of each of the various owners.

A GmbH's minimum registered capital amount is EUR 35,000. Generally, one half of the registered capital must be raised in cash while the remainder may be contributed in the form of assets (contributions in kind). Of the original capital contribution, 25%, or at least EUR 17,500, must actually be paid in upon incorporation. Under certain conditions, the capital can be provided exclusively in the form of assets (incorporation in kind, in this case the contribution is subject to an audit verifying the market value of the assets contributed). The articles of association may provide for additional capital contributions payable by the owners on the basis of a resolution adopted by the shareholder meeting.

The minimum share capital of an AG is EUR 70,000. For an AG, the same payment regulations apply as for a GmbH, but the owners can agree upon a further capital contribution going beyond the nominal value of the shares (premium). The premium is shown on the company's balance sheet as a capital reserve.

Since 2004, the company type *Societas Europaea* (SE) can be chosen in Austria. The SE is a stock corporation based on community law. The advantages of this legal form are the simplification of organisational structures (in particular for international groups) and the possibility of cross-border transfers of corporation seats without loss of the legal identity. The SE allows the choice of a business location under an economic point of view as well as the choice of the most favourable legislation. The minimum share capital required for the incorporation of a SE is EUR 120,000 while the statutory seat of the corporation must be located in the same country where the place of management is located in.

Restructuring measures (M&A from a business perspective)

Transfers of assets and undertakings can be realised with retroactive effect and be tax neutral within the framework of the Austrian Reorganisation Tax Act.

The legislation administers the following areas (Article I-VI):

- Mergers (within EU also cross border) of corporations.
- Special conversion (from corporations to partnerships).
- Contribution of businesses and exchange of shares.
- Merger of partnerships.
- Demerger of partnerships.
- Demerger of corporations.

If the reorganisation qualifies for the application of the Austrian Reorganisation Tax Act, the reorganisation steps are realised tax neutrally and with a retroactive effect as of the reorganisation due date. Existing tax loss carryforwards can be transferred under certain conditions as well. Furthermore, several other tax privileges are granted under the Reorganisation Tax Act for stamp duties, capital transfer tax, etc.

Azerbaijan

PwC contact

Movlan Pashayev
PricewaterhouseCoopers
The Landmark Office Plaza III
12th floor, 96A Nizami Street
Baku AZ1010, Azerbaijan
Tel: +994 12 497 25 15
Email: movlan.pashayev@az.pwc.com

A

Significant developments

There have been no significant corporate tax developments in Azerbaijan during the
past year.

Taxes on corporate income

In Azerbaijan, resident taxpayers are subject to a profit tax on their worldwide income.
A non-resident enterprise operating in Azerbaijan through a permanent establishment
(PE) must pay tax on the gross income generated from Azerbaijan sources, less any
related deductions attributable to the PE. Gross income of a non-resident enterprise
generated from Azerbaijan sources and not connected with a PE will be taxed at the
source of payment without any deductions allowed for expenses.

Taxable profits are defined to be the difference between a taxpayer's gross income and
deductible expenses.

Gross income encompasses all revenues received by a taxpayer from all economic
activities, unless the revenues are expressly exempted under the law.

Deductible expenses encompass all properly documented expenses that are incurred in
the furtherance of a taxpayer's business activities.

Domestic enterprises and PEs of non-residents are subject to profit tax at the flat rate
of 20%.

Simplified tax system
The Tax Code stipulates payment of taxes based on a simplified system for enterprises
not registered as value-added tax (VAT) payers and whose annual gross revenue is less
than 150,000 Azerbaijani manats (AZN), except for enterprises producing excisable
goods, credit and insurance organisations, and investment funds and professional
participants in the securities market. The simplified tax is imposed on gross revenue at
a rate of 4% in Baku and at a rate of 2% in other regions of Azerbaijan. A special rate
of simplified tax is set for enterprises involved in residential construction at a fixed
amount of AZN 10 per square metre plus an applied co-efficient, which is determined by
regional executive authorities.

Other special corporate tax regimes
There are other tax regimes applicable under special agreements concluded between
the Azerbaijan government and foreign oil companies: production sharing agreements
(PSAs) and host government agreements (HGAs). The PSA and HGA regimes apply
to all enterprises involved in these agreements, including foreign oil companies

Azerbaijan

functioning as contractors and foreign service companies providing services to the contractor or the operating company.

Currently, there are 31 signed and ratified PSAs and two HGAs, each with its own separate tax regime. Each PSA and HGA contains a tax article that outlines the tax regime for that particular agreement. While there are several similarities with respect to tax terms in the various PSAs, there are some differences, other than merely differing tax rates (e.g. taxation of foreign subcontractors) or reporting requirements. Additionally, tax protocols for each PSA and HGA, which provide specific guidance regarding the procedures for payment of taxes and filing of reports, are negotiated with the Ministry of Taxes and other executive authorities.

Local income taxes
Local income taxes are paid only by companies and organisations that are in the property of municipalities. Tax rates do not exceed 20% for profit taxpayers and 4% for simplified taxpayers.

Corporate residence

A resident enterprise is any legal entity established in accordance with the legislation of Azerbaijan and performing entrepreneurial activity or any entity that is managed in Azerbaijan.

Permanent establishment (PE)
A PE of a foreign legal entity is subject to taxation with respect to the income attributable to such PE. A PE is an establishment of a foreign legal entity, through which it fully or partially performs commercial activities (for these purposes, a PE may be considered a management unit, office bureau, agency, construction site, etc.) for more than 90 cumulative days within any 12-month period. Activities of auxiliary or preparatory nature (e.g. exclusively storing or exhibiting goods or products belonging to a non-resident, purchasing goods, collecting data by a non-resident enterprise for its own purposes) do not create a PE.

Other taxes

Value-added tax (VAT)
VAT is levied on the supply of goods and services, and on the import of goods.

VAT rates
The standard rate of VAT is 18%.

Zero rating applies to the following:

- Exportation of goods and services.
- Importation under the PSA and HGA regimes.
- Importation of goods, the supply of goods, and the implementation of works and provision of services to grant recipients on the expense of financial aid (grants) received from abroad.
- International and transit cargo and passenger transportation, as well as the supply of works and services directly connected with international and transit flights.
- The supply of gold and other valuables to the National Bank of Azerbaijan.

Azerbaijan

Taxable persons

Any person who is, or is to be, registered as a VAT payer is regarded as a taxable person.

A

Companies are required to register for VAT if their taxable income exceeds AZN 150,000 for the previous 12 months.

Taxable amount

The taxable base is established by starting with the value of the goods and services without adding the VAT amount, but including any customs duty and excise duty, if applicable.

The value of taxable imports consists of the value of the goods determined in accordance with the customs legislation and taxes and duties (other than VAT) to be paid upon importation to Azerbaijan.

The amount of VAT to be paid is the difference between the amount of VAT received on taxable supplies of goods and services and VAT paid on the purchase of goods and services necessary to generate taxable supplies of goods and services.

The Cabinet of Ministers can grant exemptions for the import of goods and equipment used for production purposes or to provide advanced technology know-how. Such exemptions are granted for a specific period and in a specific area, and can only be granted if it is impossible to satisfy the respective needs from local resources.

Customs duties

In 2011, a new Customs Code was adopted effective from 1 January 2012.

The Customs Code sets out the rules governing all aspects of the regime, including:

- The establishment of bonded warehouses and duty-free zones.
- Temporary imports and the processing of foreign goods in Azerbaijan.
- The procedures for the re-import and re-export of goods.

Azerbaijan has adopted the internationally accepted classification system for goods. The valuation procedures for customs purposes are to be determined in line with the general principles of the World Trade Organization (WTO).

The rates of customs duties are contained in the list of customs duties for the goods to be imported to Azerbaijan. These rates vary between 0% and 15%, depending on the type of goods.

Full or partial relief from the duty on temporary imports (generally, for a period of up to one year) is also available.

Under the PSA regime, contractors, their agents, and subcontractors are entitled to import and re-export from Azerbaijan, free from any import duties and restrictions, goods used for hydrocarbon activities.

Excise duty

Excise duties are imposed on tobacco products, alcoholic beverages, light vehicles, leisure and sports yachts, petroleum, and lubricants.

Azerbaijan

Taxable persons

Excise duties are paid by companies and organisations, including companies with foreign investment, as well as branches, divisions, and other independent subdivisions of companies in Azerbaijan that render services and sell self-produced goods.

Taxable operations

The following operations are subject to excise duties:

- Release of excise goods produced in Azerbaijan outside the premises of the building in which they were produced.
- Import of excise goods pursuant to the customs legislation of Azerbaijan.

Tax rates

The relevant executive authority shall determine rates of excise tax for excise goods imported into Azerbaijan (with exception of light vehicles, leisure and sports yachts, and other floating transports stipulated for these purposes).

The following excise rates apply for the following items:

- Food alcohol (including ethyl alcohol non-denatured with alcohol content of not less than 80%; ethyl alcohol non-denatured with alcohol content of less than 80%): AZN 0.8 per litre.
- Vodka, strong drinks and strong beverage materials, liqueurs, and liqueur products: AZN 0.5 per litre.
- Cognac and cognac products: AZN 0.2 per litre.
- Sparkling wines: AZN 0.2 per litre.
- Wine and vineyard materials: AZN 0.1 per litre.
- Beer (with the exception of non-alcoholic beer) and other beverages containing beer: AZN 0.08 per litre.
- All types of tobacco products: 12.5%.

Excise rates on petroleum materials, light vehicles, leisure and sports yachts and other floating transports stipulated for these purposes produced in the Azerbaijan Republic shall be established by the relevant executive authority.

Property tax

Property tax is levied on both movable and immovable tangible assets owned by individuals and companies.

Property tax rates

Property tax is imposed on the average annual book value of the taxable property at the rate of 1%.

Taxable persons

Taxable persons are comprised of the following:

- Resident companies, including companies with foreign investment that are treated as residents under Azerbaijani law; international organisations engaged in economic activities; and other enterprise.
- Branches and affiliated companies of such taxpayers.
- Agencies and representative offices of foreign legal entities located in Azerbaijan.
- Non-resident companies performing activities through a PE in the territory of Azerbaijan.

Azerbaijan

Enterprises can combine their assets and cooperate as joint owners. Joint owners are liable to pay tax according to their interest in the property concerned.

Tax base

The property tax base varies according to the residency status of the taxpayer. Resident companies are subject to property tax on their tangible assets recorded on their balance sheet. Non-resident companies carrying out a business activity through a PE in Azerbaijan are only subject to property tax on their tangible assets connected with the PE.

The following assets are exempt:

- Facilities used for the purposes of the environment, fire protection, and civil defence.
- Product lines, railways and motorways, communication and power lines, and melioration and watering facilities.
- Automobile transport taxed for the road tax.
- Facilities of companies involved in education, health, culture, and sports that are used only for the purposes of such areas of activity.

Administration

Companies are required to report the average annual value of taxable property and pay property tax on a quarterly basis, subject to any necessary recalculations at the end of the year. Tax payments are due within 15 days of the second month of each quarter. The payment should be 20% of the previous year property tax amount.

The tax on water and air transport means is estimated on 1 January each year by the tax offices based on data provided by the organisations responsible for registration of means of transport. The tax is assessed on the person named in the registration document.

When an asset changes ownership during the tax year, the tax liability is defined as the liability of the new owner.

Land tax

Land tax is levied on Azerbaijan's land resources that are in the possession of or used by individuals or companies.

Land tax rates

The rate of land tax for agricultural land is AZN 0.06 per unit. The units are determined by the relevant authority on the basis of the purpose, geographical location, and the quality of agricultural land in the administrative regions.

The rate of land tax for industrial, construction, transport, telecommunications, trade and housing servicing, and other dedicated land varies from AZN 0.1 to AZN 10 per 100 square metres, depending on the city or region.

Taxable base

Land plots that are in ownership or used are subject to land tax. Exemptions apply to various types of land owned or used for public purposes by the state or other public authorities. The government may grant further tax exemptions and reliefs.

Assessment and procedure of payment

Companies must compute the exact amount of the land tax each year on the basis of documents evidencing the title of ownership, possession, and use. The computation

Azerbaijan

must be submitted to the tax authorities by 15 May of each year. The tax must be paid by 15 August and 15 November in equal amounts.

Transfer taxes

No specific transfer taxes are levied upon the transfer of immovable property. However, certain notary fees and other sale duties applicable to transfer of property may apply.

Stamp duties

There are no stamp duties. State notary fees are payable upon notarisation of certain transactions.

Road tax

Legal entities and foreign nationals are subject to road tax. The road tax rate varies depending on vehicle engine volume, number of axles, weight carried, and how long the vehicle will be in Azerbaijan (for foreign vehicles). The tax rate may be assessed at a maximum of AZN 2,800 per year.

Mining tax

Legal entities and individuals involved in the recovery of minerals in Azerbaijan are obligated to pay the mining tax. The rate depends on the type of mineral extracted and varies from 3% to 26% of its total wholesale price.

Branch income

In addition to profit tax paid by a PE of a non-resident, the amount transferred from the net profit of such PE to the non-resident is taxed at the source of payment at a rate of 10%.

Income determination

Profit tax is levied on an enterprise's taxable profits. Profits are defined as the difference between the gross income and deductions defined by law.

Inventory valuation

Inventory valuation is determined according to national accounting standards.

No inventory valuation method is stipulated for tax purposes.

Capital gains

There is no separate capital gains taxation in Azerbaijan. Proceeds from the disposal of capital assets are included in ordinary taxable income.

Dividend income

Dividends distributed to residents and non-residents are subject to withholding tax (WHT) (taxable at source upon payment). Therefore, the received dividend amounts of legal entities and physical persons are not taxable for profit (income) tax purposes.

Interest income

If income is received from an Azerbaijani source, interests paid by a resident or a non-resident's PE, or on behalf of such establishment, with the exception of interests paid on credits (loans), deposits (accounts) of resident-banks, including from loan interests

A

paid on financial leasing operations, to resident persons carrying out financial leasing or non-resident banks, or PE of a non-resident carrying out financial leasing, shall be taxed at the source of payment at a rate of 10%.

Foreign income
If a resident of Azerbaijan directly or indirectly holds more than 20% of shareholders' equity or possesses more than 20% of the voting shares of a foreign legal entity that, in turn, received income from a state with favourable taxation, then such income shall be included in the resident's taxable income.

A state with favourable taxation is considered a country in which the tax rate is two or more times lower than that determined under the Tax Code of Azerbaijan, or a country in which the laws on confidentiality of information about companies exist (which allow secrecy to be maintained concerning financial information, as well as the actual owner of property or receiver of income).

Anti-deferral measures
In order to avoid shifting of income from a taxpayer to a foreign subsidiary that may result in deferral or elimination of tax, the following limited anti-deferral measures are provided in the Tax Code:

The Tax Code provides that if a resident of Azerbaijan holds directly or indirectly more than 20% of share capital or voting rights in a foreign legal entity that derives income from a low-tax jurisdiction, then the proportionate share in income of the foreign entity must be included in the taxable income of the resident taxpayer.

A low-tax jurisdiction is considered to be (i) a country in which the tax rate is at least two times lower than the tax rate in Azerbaijan, or (ii) a country which has laws on confidentiality allowing secrecy of financial information, as well as information on the actual owner of property or recipient of income.

Deductions

All expenses connected with generating income, except for non-deductible expenses and expenses with limited deductibility, specifically defined by the law, are deductible from income.

Depreciation
Depreciation may be calculated at the following rates:

* Buildings and premises: up to 7%.
* Machines, equipment, and calculation appliances: up to 25%.
* Means of transportation: up to 25%.
* Working cattle: up to 20%.
* Expenses incurred for geological and exploration works, as well as for preparatory works for the production of natural resources: 25%.
* Intangible assets with an undetermined period of use: up to 10%. For those with a determined period of use, pro-rata amount as per the useful life, in years.
* Other fixed assets: up to 20%.

Goodwill
Azerbaijani tax legislation does not specify the definition of goodwill.

Azerbaijan

Start-up expenses
The cost of assets shall include expenses for their acquisition, production, construction, assembly, and installation as well as other expenses that increase their value with the exception of expenses for which the taxpayer is entitled to a deduction.

Interest expenses
Interest on loans received from overseas and/or from related parties may be deducted, limited to the interest rate on loans with similar currency and maturity at the interbank credit auction. In absence of such an auction, deductions for interest may not exceed rates of 125% of the interbank auction credit rates published by the Central Bank of Azerbaijan.

Bad debt
A taxpayer shall be entitled to a deduction for doubtful debts connected with goods, work, and services that have been realised where income from them was previously included in the gross income received from entrepreneurial activity. Doubtful debt deduction shall be allowed only if the debt is written off as worthless in the taxpayer's books.

Charitable contributions
Charitable contributions are non-deductible expenses in Azerbaijan.

Fines and penalties
No deduction is allowed for financial sanctions or interest calculated for delayed payment of taxes.

Taxes
Road, property, land, and mining taxes are deductible.

Other expenses deductible within certain limits
* The amount of repair expenses deductible each year is limited to the amount of the tax written down value of each category of fixed assets as of the end of the previous year. For buildings and premises, the limit is 2%; for machinery and equipment, the limit is 5%; and for other fixed assets, the limit is 3%. An amount exceeding these limits shall be taken as an increase of the residual balance value of the fixed assets in the appropriate category.
* Actual business trip expenses are deductible from income within the standards established by the Cabinet of Ministers.
* A legal entity engaged in insurance activities is entitled to deduct allocations to reserve insurance funds within the standards established by the legislation of Azerbaijan.
* Banks and credit entities engaged in certain types of banking activities shall be entitled to deduct from income the amounts assigned for establishment of special reserve funds, depending on the classification of assets in compliance with legislation and in accordance with procedures established by the relevant executive authority.

Non-deductible expenses
The following expenses are non-deductible:

* Capital expenses.
* Expenses connected with non-commercial activity.
* Entertainment and meal expenses, accommodation, and other expenses of a social nature incurred for employees.

Net operating losses

Taxable losses incurred by legal entities may be carried forward for five years to offset future taxable profit, without limitations.

Payment to foreign affiliates

Payment to charter capital in order to create an affiliate in a foreign country is not tax deductible and is instead treated as investment to subsidiary on the balance sheet.

Under local transfer pricing rules, payment for goods and services supplied by foreign affiliates is deductible up to the fair market price of such supplies.

Group taxation

Each taxpayer is liable to fulfil one's own tax liabilities. Azeri tax legislation does not have the concept of 'group taxation'.

Transfer pricing

The Tax Code provides that relations between associated (interrelated) entities must be based on the arm's-length principle.

Interrelated persons for the purposes of taxation are natural and/or legal persons, relations between which might have direct effect on economic results of their activities or the activities of persons they represent.

Thin capitalisation

There is no concept of thin capitalisation in Azerbaijani tax law. However, the Tax Code provides that interest on loans received from overseas and/or from related parties may be deducted, limited to the interest rate on loans with similar currency and maturity at the interbank credit auction. In absence of such an auction, deductions for interest may not exceed rates of 125% of the interbank auction credit rates published by the Central Bank of Azerbaijan.

Tax credits and incentives

Foreign tax credit

Azeri legal entities are taxed on worldwide profit; however, any tax paid overseas, up to the tax amount that would be calculated under Azeri law, will be allowed to offset the Azeri profits tax. The tax credit may not exceed the tax that would be imposed on such income in Azerbaijan. This credit applies only to residents of Azerbaijan.

Incentive for agricultural producers

Taxpayers producing agriculture products are exempt from profit tax, VAT, and property tax until 2013.

Incentive for increasing nominal equity of banks and insurance companies

Banks, insurance, and re-insurance companies were exempt from profit tax on profit distributed for increasing their nominal equity (so called, charter capital) during the three years prior to 1 January 2012.

Azerbaijan

The Law on the Special Economic Regime for Export-Oriented Oil and Gas Activities

The Law on the Special Economic Regime for Export-Oriented Oil and Gas Activities was adopted in April 2009 and will remain effective for 15 years. This law avails the following tax incentives to contractors and subcontractors (excluding foreign subcontractors without PE in Azerbaijan):

- Local companies are permitted to choose between (i) profit tax at a rate of 20% or (ii) 5% WHT on gross revenues.
- Foreign subcontractors are taxable only by a 5% WHT.
- A 0% VAT rate.
- Exemption from dividend WHT and taxation on branch's net profits.
- Exemption from customs duties and taxes.
- Exemptions from property tax and land tax.

In order to derive these benefits, the relevant taxpayer should obtain a special confirmation certificate from the Ministry of Industry and Energy.

The Law on Special Economic Zones (SEZs)

The Law on Special Economic Zones (SEZ) became effective in June 2009. The companies operating in SEZs shall have the following tax benefits:

- A 0.5% tax levied on profits from supplied goods, performed services, or works.
- A 0% VAT rate.
- Customs exemptions.

In order to operate in a SEZ, a special residency certificate is necessary. However, the following companies may not apply for this certificate:

- Companies producing or processing oil and gas.
- Companies producing alcoholic beverages and tobacco.
- Television or radio broadcasting companies.

As of January 2012, no SEZs have yet been established in Azerbaijan.

Incentive for the employment of disabled persons

The rate of profit tax levied on production enterprises belonging to community organisations for disabled persons, and involving at least 50% of disabled persons, shall be reduced by 50%.

In determining eligibility for these privileges, disabled persons substituting permanent employees, contractors (i.e. who work under contractor agreements, civil legal contracts), or disabled persons till the age of 18 are not included into the average number of employees.

Withholding taxes

Income received from Azerbaijan sources not attributable to a PE of a non-resident in Azerbaijan is subject to WHT at the following rates:

- Dividends paid by resident enterprises: 10%.
- Interest paid by residents, PEs of non-residents, or on behalf of such PEs (except for interest paid to resident banks or to PEs of non-resident banks): 10%.

- Rental fees for movable and immovable property: 14%.
- Royalties: 14%.
- Leasing, risk insurance, or reinsurance payments: 4%.
- Telecommunications or international transport services: 6%.
- Other Azeri-source income: 10%.

If a resident enterprise or a PE of a non-resident receives interest, royalties, or rental fees taxable at the source of payment in Azerbaijan, it is entitled to consider the tax deducted from the source of payment, providing the documents supporting the tax deduction are in place.

Tax treaties
The following chart contains the WHT rates that are applicable to dividend, interest, and royalty payments by Azerbaijan residents to non-residents under the tax treaties in force as of 1 January 2012. If the treaty rate is higher than the domestic rate, the latter is applicable.

| | WHT (%) | | | |
| | Dividends | | | |
Recipient	Individual companies	Qualifying companies	Interest	Royalties
Austria	15	5/10	10	5/10
Belarus	15	15	10	10
Belgium	15	5/10	10	5/10
Bulgaria	8	8	0/7	5/10
Canada	15	10	0/10	5/10
China (People's Rep.)	10	10	10	10
Czech Republic	8	8	5/10	10
Estonia	10	5	10	10
Finland	10	5	0/10	5/10
France	10	10	10	5/10
Georgia	10	10	10	10
Germany	15	5	10	5/10
Greece	8	8	8	8
Hungary	8	8	0/8	8
Iran	10	10	10	10
Italy	10	10	10	5/10
Kazakhstan	10	10	10	10
Korea	7	7	10	5/10
Latvia	10	5	10	5/10
Lithuania	10	5	10	10
Luxembourg	10	5	10	5/10
Moldova	15	8	10	10
Netherlands	10	5	0/10	5/10
Norway	15	10	10	10
Poland	10	10	10	10
Qatar	7	7	7	5
Romania	10	5	8	10
Russia	10	10	10	10
Serbia	10	10	10	10

Azerbaijan

Recipient	WHT (%)			
	Dividends			
	Individual companies	Qualifying companies	Interest	Royalties
Switzerland	15	5	5/10	5/10
Tajikistan	10	10	10	10
Turkey	12	12	10	10
Ukraine	10	10	10	10
United Arab Emirates	10	10	7	5/10
United Kingdom	15	10	10	5/10
Uzbekistan	10	10	10	10

Tax administration

Taxable period
The tax year in Azerbaijan is the calendar year.

Tax returns
Resident enterprises and PEs of non-residents must file profit tax returns for a calendar year by 31 March of the following year. During liquidation of a legal entity or a PE of a non-resident, the tax return should be submitted within 30 days after the adoption of a decree on liquidation.

A non-resident that has no PE in Azerbaijan and receives income subject to WHT (except for dividends and interest) may file a tax return with respect to such income and expenses, connected with the generation of the income, for purposes of reassessment of profit tax at the rate of 20%.

If a taxpayer applies for an extension of time to file the profit tax return prior to the expiration of the filing deadline and at the same time settle the full tax amount due, the filing deadline may be prolonged for up to three months. The prolongation of the terms for filing the return will not modify the terms of tax payment.

Legal entities and entrepreneurs that withhold tax at the source of payment are obliged to file the WHT report with the tax authority within 20 days following the end of the quarter.

Payment of tax
Taxpayers must make advance quarterly tax payments of profit tax by the 15th day of the month following the end of the calendar quarter. Payments are determined either (i) as 25% of tax for the past fiscal year or (ii) by multiplying the amount of actual income through the quarter by a ratio of tax to gross income for the previous year.

The final payment of profit tax coincides with submission of the declaration of profit tax, i.e. 31 March.

Audit cycle
The on-site tax audit shall be conducted not more than once in a year. A tax audit may be performed at any time under the following conditions:

- If tax return documents that are necessary for tax calculation and payment are not submitted in time or not submitted at all upon the warning of tax authority.
- If incorrect information is found in the report made on the results of tax inspection.
- When exceedingly paid amount of VAT, interest and financial sanction is assigned for the payment of other taxes, interests, and financial sanctions or assigned as payments on future liabilities. In such cases, the out of turn tax audit can be conducted only on taxable VAT operations of the taxpayer.
- When application is submitted by the taxpayer to return exceedingly paid amounts of tax, interests, and financial sanctions.
- When tax authority obtained information from known source on hiding (decreasing) of incomes or object of taxation by the taxpayer.
- When, in accordance with criminal legislation, there is a decision of the court or law-enforcement agency on implementation of tax audit.
- In case of failure to provide the documents specified in the Tax Code.
- In the event of application for liquidation, reorganisation of the taxpayer legal entity, or seizure of business operations of the natural person operating without formation of legal entity.

Statute of limitations
Tax authorities are entitled to calculate and recalculate taxes, penalties, and financial sanctions of the taxpayer within three years after termination of the taxable reporting period and to impose calculated (recalculated) sums of taxes, penalties, and financial sanctions within five years after termination of taxable reporting period.

Topics of focus for tax authorities
The main issues challenged by tax authorities during a tax audit include, but are not limited to, the following:

- Application of the 20% profit tax on 'deemed profit'.
- Application of benchmarking principle for income of foreign employees subject to tax in Azerbaijan.
- Correctness of claim of input VAT from budget and identification of operations taxable to VAT.
- Taxes withheld on payments to non-resident suppliers in cases where income of non-residents is considered as Azerbaijani-source income.
- Application of VAT on market price of assets that were written off, disposed free of charge, or at discount rate.
- Challenging the transfer price.
- Grossed-up WHT paid at cost of the buyer disallowed for deduction.
- Deductibility of the head office costs.

Bahrain

PwC contact

Ebrahim B Karolia
PricewaterhouseCoopers
13th Floor, TJ Tower
Building no: 683, Road no: 2811,
Block no: 428, Seef District
PO Box 21144
Kingdom of Bahrain
Tel: +973 1711 8800 (ext. 8884)
Email: ebrahim.karolia@bh.pwc.com

Significant developments

There have been no significant corporate tax developments in Bahrain during the past year.

Taxes on corporate income

There are no taxes in Bahrain on income, sales, capital gains, or estates, with the exception, in limited circumstances, to businesses (local and foreign) that operate in the oil and gas sector or derive profits from the extraction or refinement of fossil fuels (defined as hydrocarbons) in Bahrain. For such companies, a tax rate of 46% is levied on net profits for each tax accounting period irrespective of the residence of the taxpayer.

Corporate residence

Income Tax Law No. 22 of 1979 (which only applies to oil and gas businesses) does not define residence.

Other taxes

Companies are subject to social insurance in respect of their employees, stamp duties, customs duties, as well as a series of corporate registration fees, licence fees, and certain municipal taxes (e.g. taxes on leases of property and registration of land title). There are currently no VAT or excise duties in Bahrain.

Branch income

Profit from branch income is taxable in Bahrain at 46% if it is derived from activities in the oil and gas sector.

Income determination

There are no specific rules in Bahrain with respect to the calculation of specific items of income, such as inventory valuation, capital gains, dividend income, interest income, or foreign income. However, the income tax law requires that taxable profits be calculated using generally accepted accounting principles (GAAP).

Deductions

The law generally allows deductions for all costs associated with taxable activities in Bahrain, such as the cost of production, refinement, remuneration of employees associated with these taxable activities (including social insurance and pensions paid for the benefit of these employees), and other operational losses.

All reasonable and justifiable costs of production and exploration of products sold during the current taxable year are deductible for tax purposes, provided that these expenses have not been deducted elsewhere in calculating net taxable income.

Depreciation and depletion
Tax deductions may be claimed with respect to reasonable amounts for depreciation, obsolescence, exhaustion, and depletion incurred during the taxable year for properties used by the taxpayer in a trade or businesses from which income, taxable under the income tax law, is derived. Generally, such amounts may be claimed on a straight-line basis over the estimated remaining useful life of the properties, unless otherwise approved by the Minister of Finance.

Taxes
All taxes and duties not imposed by the Bahrain income tax law, including customs duties, may be deducted from taxable income as stipulated in Bahrain's income tax law.

Net operating losses
Unutilised losses may be carried forward and deducted up to an amount equivalent to the net income in future years as defined by the Bahrain income tax law. Carryback of losses is not permitted.

Payments to foreign affiliates
There are no specific restrictions in the income tax law pertaining to payments made to foreign affiliates.

Group taxation

There is no legislation or mechanism for group relief or the taxation of group activities in Bahrain. Additionally, there is currently no specific legislation regarding transfer pricing and thin capitalisation in Bahrain.

Tax credits and incentives

There are no tax incentives in Bahrain. There is also currently no legislation regarding foreign tax relief in Bahrain.

Withholding taxes

There are no withholding taxes (WHTs) on the payment of dividends, interest, or royalties in Bahrain.

Bahrain

Tax treaties

Bahrain has double tax treaties (DTTs) in force with various countries, including Algeria, Austria, Belarus, Brunei, Bulgaria, China, Egypt, France, Iran, Ireland, Isle of Man, Jordan, Lebanon, Luxembourg, Malaysia, Malta, Mexico, Morocco, the Netherlands, Pakistan, Philippines, Singapore, Sudan, Syria, Thailand, Turkey, the United States, Uzbekistan, and Yemen.

Tax administration

Taxable period

A company's accounting period should normally follow the (Gregorian) calendar year (i.e. 1 January to 31 December).

Tax returns

The law is silent on the due date for the filing of the final income tax statement. However, an estimated income tax statement must be submitted on or before the 15th day of the third month of the taxable year. Where applicable, a taxpayer may also be required to file an amended estimated income tax statement quarterly thereafter, unless a final income tax statement has been provided.

Approved accountants must prepare a certified tax return for the return to be acceptable to the authorities.

Payment of tax

Taxes (based on the initial estimated tax statement filed) are payable in 12 equal monthly instalments. Payments are due starting on the 15th day of the fourth month of the taxable year. Income tax as per the subsequent amended estimated income tax statements or the final income tax statement will form the basis of tax payments for the remainder of the 12 monthly instalments that are yet to be paid. The final payment is due on the 15th day of the third month after the end of the taxable year or the date the final income tax statement is filed, whichever is later.

Any excess income tax paid will be credited and used in the first invoice for income tax following the establishment of the credit by the Minister.

Statute of limitations

The Income Tax Law No. 22 of 1979 does not specify any statute of limitations.

Barbados

PwC contact

Gloria Eduardo
PricewaterhouseCoopers SRL
The Financial Services Centre
Bishop's Court Hill
PO Box 111
St. Michael, BB14004
Barbados, West Indies
Tel: +1 246 626 6700
Email: gloria.eduardo@bb.pwc.com

Significant developments

Barbados currently has 21 double taxation agreements (DTAs) in force. In addition, three signed DTAs with the Czech Republic, Portugal, and the Republic of Ghana and five signed protocols to the existing DTAs with Canada, Finland, Norway, Sweden, and the United Kingdom (UK) are awaiting ratification. Treaties with Bahrain, Belgium, Italy, and Vietnam have been initialled, along with a new treaty with the United Kingdom, and await signature and subsequent ratification.

Tax information exchange agreements (TIEAs) with Denmark, Greenland, and the Faroe Islands are also awaiting ratification, and TIEAs with France and Germany have been initialled and are awaiting signature.

Effective 1 June 2012, the value-added tax (VAT) rates of 17.5% for standard rated supplies and 8.75% for short-term accommodation will remain in effect until further notice.

As of income year 2011, the offsetting of tax losses from business income against employment income is no longer permitted.

As of tax year 2011/12, the land tax bands have been adjusted upwards. Effective from tax year 2012/13, land tax rebates have also been extended to approved manufacturers and to companies engaged in the production of solar energy. A number of tax concessions have also been enacted with respect to the conservation of energy.

As of income year 2011, the penalty for the late filing of corporation income tax (CIT) returns has been increased from 100 Barbados dollars (BBD) to BBD 500.

Please note this information is current as of 1 June 2012. Please visit the Worldwide Tax Summaries website at www.pwc.com/taxsummaries to see any significant corporate tax developments that occurred after 1 June 2012.

Taxes on corporate income

Companies resident in Barbados are taxed on income earned from all sources, whether generated within or outside of Barbados, less expenses incurred for the purpose of producing assessable income in a fiscal period not to exceed 53 weeks. Non-resident companies are generally only taxed on income derived from sources and operations conducted within Barbados.

Barbados

Corporate income tax (CIT) rates

The following rates apply to taxes on corporate income:

Type of entity	CIT rate (%)
Regular companies	25
Small companies (1)	15
Manufacturing companies (2)	15
Approved developers in special development areas	15
International business companies, international banks, and international societies with restricted liability	2.5 to 1
Life insurance companies (computed on gross investment income)	5
Companies engaged in the construction of houses (3)	15
Exempt insurance companies (4)	0

Notes

1. This concessionary tax rate is available to any small company as defined in the Small Business Development Act.
2. This concessionary tax rate is available only to companies registered as manufacturers with the Barbados Customs & Excise Department.
3. Selling price of the houses must be less than BBD 400,000, including the house and land.
4. The exemption is available for a period of 15 years.

Corporate residence

A corporation is deemed to be resident in Barbados if its management and control is exercised in Barbados.

Other taxes

Value-added tax (VAT)

VAT is levied at the rate of 17.5% on the value of a wide range of goods and services imported or supplied in Barbados by VAT registered persons.

A number of services, including financial services, real estate, medical services, and education are exempt. Intergroup transactions are taxable.

Persons operating under Barbados' VAT regime must be registered for VAT. The threshold for VAT registration is BBD 80,000, but voluntary registration is permitted for persons whose annual turnover is less than BBD 80,000.

Certain supplies are zero-rated, including exports, basic food items, prescription drugs, crude oil, and the supply of certain items to the international financial services sector, e.g. legal and accounting fees. There is a concessionary rate of 8.75% as of 1 May 2011 applicable to the supply of accommodation by guest houses, hotels, inns, or any similar place, including a dwelling house normally let or rented for use as a vacation or holiday home.

Registered persons may deduct input tax from their output tax in calculating the tax payable for that VAT accounting period. Where input tax exceeds output tax, the registrant will be entitled to a refund of VAT.

Customs duties

Customs duty is levied on a wide range of imported goods at rates specified in Part 1 of the First Schedule of the Customs Act. Barbados' Customs Tariff is based on the Common External Tariff of the Caribbean Common Market (CARICOM) with special derogations for certain items, e.g. spirituous beverages. Customs duty is calculated on either an *ad valorem* basis or at specific quantitative rates. The *ad valorem* rates for most items vary between 0% and 20%, but certain goods regarded as luxury items are subject to higher rates (e.g. jewellery 60%). In addition, a select group of items that are produced within Barbados and CARICOM (including some agricultural products) are subject to a duty rate of 60% when imported from outside the region.

Manufacturers and agriculturists, including persons involved in fishing and horticulture, are exempt from the payment of duty on inputs (including packaging materials, machinery, equipment, and spares) imported for use in their businesses.

The various departments and institutions, international bodies, and organisations listed in Part II-B of the Customs Tariff are exempt from the payment of customs duty. Specific goods (e.g. computers), also mentioned in Part II-B, are exempt from customs duty.

Excise taxes

Four categories of goods (both locally manufactured, as well as imported) are subject to excise taxes. These are motor vehicles, spirituous beverages, tobacco products, and petroleum products. Most excisable goods are subject to the tax at a specific rate, with the exception of motor vehicles, which are subject to *ad valorem* rates.

A few persons and goods are exempt from excise taxes. These include motor vehicles imported by the diplomatic corps, and other organisations exempt from customs duty under Part II-B of the Customs Tariff, goods imported for temporary use or for a temporary purpose that will be re-exported within three months, and goods (other than spirits) intended to be used as raw materials for the manufacture or production in Barbados of other taxable goods.

Land tax

The following land tax rates are in effect as of tax year 2011/12:

Land	Land tax rate
On the improved value of each parcel of land on which there is a dwelling house that is used exclusively for residential purposes:	
On first BBD 190,000	0
On amounts between BBD 190,000 and BBD 500,000	0.10% of the improved value
On amounts between BBD 500,000 and BBD 1,250,000	0.45% of the improved value
On amounts exceeding BBD 1,250,000	0.75% of the improved value
On the improved value of each parcel of land on which there is a building other than a residence	0.65% of the improved value
On the site value of each parcel of unimproved land	0.60% of the site value

The following concessions have been granted for land taxes:

• For villas, as defined by the Tourism Development Act, land tax is calculated and payable on only 75% of the improved value of the property. It is proposed that the rebate be calculated on the land tax demanded.

Barbados

- For hotels, as defined by the Tourism Development Act, land tax is calculated and payable on only 50% of the improved value of the property. It is proposed that the rebate be calculated on the land tax demanded.
- For pensioners occupying their own homes, land tax is calculated and payable on only 50% of the improved value of the property in excess of BBD 150,000.

A 10% discount is granted if the land tax is paid within 30 days from the date of the tax demand notice or 5% if paid within 60 days. It is proposed that, as of tax year 2011/12, hotels and restaurants will be allowed to pay their land tax bills during January to March without losing access to the discount granted.

The following rebates have been proposed:

- Land tax rebates for income year 2012/13 will now be extended to approved manufacturers who can certify exports to a value of BBD 100,000 or more in any one calendar year.
- Any company certified by the Division of Energy to be engaged in the production of solar energy and/or the manufacturing sector of solar energy equipment will be entitled to the rebate of no more than 50% on the land tax demanded for that year.
- It is further proposed that the Department of Inland Revenue and/or VAT Division will be required to access rebates.

Property transfer taxes
Property transfer taxes are levied as set out in the following table:

Property	Transfer tax rate
Shares of companies listed on the Barbados Stock Exchange	Exempt
Shares of private companies*	2.5% of value or amount of gross consideration above BBD 50,000
Land with a building	2.5% of value or amount of gross consideration above BBD 150,000
Land with no building	2.5% of value or amount of gross consideration
Leases of 25 years or more or short-term leases that are continuously renewed for a period equal to 25 years or more	2.5% of value or amount of gross consideration

* Any transfer of shares to a person who is resident outside of Barbados, whether or not the transferor is resident in Barbados, where the assets of the company concerned consists of foreign assets and its income is derived solely from sources outside Barbados, will not be subject to transfer taxes in Barbados.

Land development duty
Where a person disposes of property situated in a specially designated development area within 15 years of the date specified by statute, duty may be charged. This may be at rates of up to 50% on the excess of the value of the consideration over the improved value at the specified base date, plus certain other expenses and an amount representing capital appreciation of the property.

Stamp duty
Barbados imposes a stamp duty tax on various instruments, including written documents. The rates imposed vary depending on the document. Stamp duties applicable to documents for the transfer of shares, real estate, and for mortgages are set out below:

Instruments	Stamp duty rate
On sale of shares of companies listed on the Barbados Stock Exchange	Exempt
On sale of real estate, leases, and shares in public companies*	BBD 10 per BBD 1,000 or part thereof
On mortgages	BBD 3 on each BBD 500 or part thereof

* Any transfer of shares to a person who is resident outside of Barbados, whether or not the transferor is resident in Barbados, where the assets of the company concerned consists of foreign assets and its income is derived solely from sources outside Barbados, will not be subject to transfer taxes in Barbados.

Life insurance premium tax
In addition to the CIT computed on the gross investment income of life insurance companies, a life insurance premium tax is levied on gross direct premium income earned by resident and foreign life insurance companies as set out in the following table:

	Resident life insurance companies (%)	Foreign life insurance companies (%)
New business written for the income year	6	6
Renewal business	3	5

As of income year 2012, the 20% withholding tax (WHT) on the remittance of payments of insurance premiums to foreign persons will no longer apply.

General insurance premium tax
In addition to the CIT computed on the taxable profits of general insurance companies, a general insurance premium tax is levied on gross direct premium income at a rate of 4.75% in respect of property insurance business and 4% for other general insurance business.

Branch income

Branches are taxed on the same basis as corporations. In addition, a 10% tax is assessed on the transfer or deemed transfer of the after-tax profits to the head office that are not reinvested in Barbados, unless a DTA overrides this.

Income determination

Inventory valuation
Inventory is generally stated at the lower of cost and net realisable value. First in first out (FIFO) or average values are generally used for book and tax purposes. Last in first out (LIFO) is not acceptable for tax purposes. The Inland Revenue will normally accept a method of valuation that conforms to standard accounting practice in the trade. Conformity between book and tax values is expected.

Capital gains
Capital gains are not taxed in Barbados.

Barbados

Dividend income
Dividends between two companies resident in Barbados are not taxed in the hands of the recipient. Dividends received by a resident Barbados company from a non-resident entity where the equity interest owned is at least 10% of the non-resident company and the shareholding is not held solely for the purpose of portfolio investments are not subject to tax.

Interest income
Amounts received on account of, in lieu of, or in satisfaction of interest are included in the calculation of assessable income. In certain instances (to the extent specified by regulation) certain types of interest may be exempt from inclusion into the calculation of assessable income, including interest on bonds, debentures, or stock of the government of Barbados that is beneficially owned by a non-resident; interest on tax reserve and tax refund certificates; and interest on holdings (within certain limits) of National Development Bonds, National Housing Bonds, Savings Bonds, and Sugar Industry Bonds classified as non-taxable bonds, as well as interest income from some CARICOM countries.

Partnership income
Amounts received from a partnership or syndicate for the income year, regardless of whether or not these amounts were withdrawn during the income year, are included in the calculation of assessable income.

Foreign income
A Barbados corporation is taxed on foreign branch income as earned. Double taxation is avoided by means of foreign tax credits or an exemption where double taxation treaties exist.

Deductions

Business expenses that are reasonable and incurred for the purpose of producing assessable income are deductible for tax purposes unless disallowed by a specific provision of the Income Tax Act. Deduction of capital expenditures is specifically prohibited, but special provisions may allow tax depreciation on these expenditures.

Depreciation
Depreciation for tax purposes is computed on a straight-line basis at prescribed rates. The process is accelerated by additional initial allowances in the year of acquisition. Conformity between book and tax depreciation is not required. Gains on sales of depreciable assets are taxable as ordinary income up to the amount of tax depreciation recaptured, and losses on sales below depreciated value are deductible.

Capital allowance

Capital allowance	Rate
Initial allowance:	
Plant and machinery	20%
Industrial buildings	40%
Annual allowance:	
Plant and machinery	Various rates
Industrial buildings	4%
Intellectual property	10% of 50% of the amount expended

Barbados

Capital allowance	Rate
Investment allowance (an incentive allowance limited by statute to entities operating in certain industries, claimed in lieu of initial allowances):	
Basic industry*	20%
Businesses or persons entitled to export allowance for exports outside of CARICOM countries	40%
Business engaged in the manufacture and refining of sugar	40%
Business engaged in the manufacture of clay and limestone products	40%

* as prescribed by the regulations to the Barbados Income Tax Act.

Note: This allowance is not deducted from the cost of the asset in calculating tax written down value.

Manufacturing allowance

Companies involved in the manufacturing sector are granted an additional 50% of the annual allowance claimed in an income year. Such companies are also often able to claim investment allowances.

Commercial building allowance

A deduction is available in respect of a commercial building. For each income year, the available allowance is calculated at 1% of the land tax improved value, or 10% of the land tax improved value if the building is registered with the National Trust.

Depletion

For oil and gas companies, depending on certain circumstances, a depletion allowance of 20% or 10% is given in addition to annual depreciation on prescribed types of capital expenditure.

Goodwill

Goodwill is not a depreciating asset, and tax amortisation is not available.

Start-up expenses

There are no specific provisions in relation to deductions for start-up expenses. However, some of these are treated as costs incurred on account of capital expenditure. Such costs are therefore not allowable deductions for tax purposes.

Interest expenses

A Barbados corporation can claim a deduction for interest expenses. However, where interest claimed as a deduction has not been paid within two years of being accrued (one year for related parties), it should be added back to assessable income.

Charitable contributions

Charitable contributions are generally deductible where they are made to entities that are specifically registered as charities or not-for-profit organisations with the Corporate Affairs and Intellectual Property Office.

Bad debt

Amounts representing debts owed that have been established as bad debts during the income year and have been previously included in calculating assessable income for that income year or a previous income year are deductible in calculating assessable income.

Barbados

Pension expenses
Contributions made by companies under registered pension schemes are deductible in calculating assessable income.

Fines and penalties
Fines and penalties imposed are generally not deductible.

Taxes
Taxes on income are not deductible.

Net operating losses
No carryback is allowed for CIT losses. Losses can generally be carried forward for nine years after the income year in which they are incurred and may be applied in full against future taxable profits. Notwithstanding this, a tax loss incurred by a person in respect of residential property can only be deducted against assessable income earned by that person in respect of residential property.

Losses of general insurance companies can only be carried forward for five years, and losses of life insurance companies cannot be carried forward at all.

Payments to foreign affiliates
A Barbados corporation can claim a deduction for royalties, management fees, and interest charges paid to foreign affiliates, provided that payments are no greater than what it would pay to an unrelated party.

Group taxation

Trading losses (i.e. the tax loss for the year, excluding capital allowances) incurred during an income year of a surrendering company may be set off wholly or partially against the profits of a claimant company, where both are members of the same group (defined as where one company is a 75% subsidiary of another, or both companies are 75% subsidiaries of a third company).

Group relief is not available to companies operating in the international business and financial services sector or any other company which is operating under concessionary legislation.

Transfer pricing
Although Barbados has no specific transfer pricing legislation or regulations in place, the Income Tax Act contains a section dealing with artificial transactions. This enables the revenue authorities to amend the assessable income of a person where they believe the main purpose of a non-arm's-length transaction is to artificially reduce that person's assessable income.

In such circumstances, the transaction is disregarded or modified to achieve the effect that it no longer results in the artificial reduction of that person's assessable income.

Thin capitalisation
Barbados does not have tax provisions relevant to thin capitalisation.

Controlled foreign companies (CFCs)
Barbados does not have tax provisions relevant to CFCs.

Tax credits and incentives

Foreign tax credit
Barbados allows a credit for foreign taxes (taxes paid in jurisdictions outside Barbados). The credit should not exceed the Barbados tax attributable to the income derived outside Barbados.

Agricultural cash rebate
The following rebates may be claimed on agricultural or agro-processing machinery or plant that is new or imported into the island for the first time:

- Sugar cane harvesters: 10% or 15%
- Other: 18%

Export allowance
There is a rebate of tax under the Income Tax Act in respect of income from export sales outside CARICOM. The maximum tax credit on eligible sales is 93%, which is available where eligible sales exceed 81% of total sales.

Exempt Insurance Act
The Exempt Insurance Act is applicable to companies in Barbados that insure risks and earn premiums outside the island and for companies that own or manage the former. Under the Act, all three types of companies are exempt from exchange control regulations. In lieu of standard CIT rates, exempt insurance companies are subject to tax at the rate of 0% for the first 15 years; thereafter, the rate is 8% on the first BBD 250,000 of taxable income and 0% on taxable income in excess of BBD 250,000. No WHT is levied on remittances of dividends or interest.

Exempt insurance companies are subject to an annual license fee of BBD 20,000.

Fiscal Incentives Act
The Fiscal Incentives Act provides to manufacturers of an 'approved product' a full exemption from taxes and duties for varying periods, up to a maximum of 15 years.

Foreign currency earnings credit
Persons carrying on business in Barbados may claim a tax credit of up to 93% of CIT on net profits from foreign currency earnings derived from construction projects or professional services undertaken outside of CARICOM international insurance business or services provided to the international business sector.

Employment tax credit
As of income year 2011, a tax credit of 10% of the actual amount of the expenditure incurred in respect of wages for the increase in employees is available where:

- there is an increase in profits directly attributable to the business
- there is an increase in the number of employees who are employed directly in the operations of the business by the amount of at least 10% of the total workforce employed during the previous year, and
- the increase in the number of employees referred to is maintained for a period of three years.

The credit is applied in the year in which persons meet the above mentioned criteria. Any unused credit can be carried forward for three years from the end of the income year in which the credit was obtained, and no cash refund shall be allowed.

Barbados

Productivity and innovation tax credit

As of income year 2011, entities incurring expenditure that is innovative in nature and leading to the development of a new manufacturing process, product, service, or organisation procedure will be granted a tax credit of 25% of the amount expended in that income year. The credit will only be granted if the innovation was successfully introduced to the market as evidenced by increases in sales, productivity, or organisational efficiency.

Any unused tax credit shall be carried forward for a maximum of three years from the end of the income year in which the credit was obtained, but no cash refund will be allowed. Certification from the Executive Director of the National Productivity Council is required.

Renewable Energy

As of income year 2011, a number of tax concessions have been enacted with respect to the conservation of energy. These measures include a 150% deduction of actual expenditure, not exceeding BBD 25,000, for each year for five years in respect of the following:

- energy audits and
- 50% of the cost of retrofitting premises or installing systems to produce electricity from sources other than fossil fuels.

The business must be current in the payments of its corporation tax, VAT, land tax, and national insurance contributions, or where not current, has entered into an agreement with the respective authorities to settle outstanding arrears.

Housing Incentives Act

The Housing Incentives Act provides CIT, import duty, WHT, and other concessions to developers who implement low income housing projects. Approved developers are subject to CIT at a rate of 15%.

International Business Companies (IBCs) Act

IBCs resident in Barbados but deriving income solely from sources outside Barbados are taxed at the following rates:

Taxable income (BBD)	Rate (%)
Up to 10 million	2.5
10 million to 20 million	2
20 million to 30 million	1.5
In excess of 30 million	1

Freedom from exchange controls is granted to IBCs, as well as duty-free concessions on certain imports. No WHT is levied on remittances of dividends, royalties, interest, management fees, fees, or other income paid by IBCs to persons outside Barbados. IBCs may also claim a credit for taxes paid outside Barbados, provided that this does not reduce the company's rate of CIT in Barbados to less than 1%.

IBCs are subject to an annual license fee of BBD 850.

International Financial Services Act (IFSA)

The IFSA provides for the establishment of international banking, trust administration, and other related or ancillary services by eligible companies incorporated in Barbados or branches of qualified foreign banks. An annual licence fee of BBD 100,000 is payable by IFSA licensees who are in the business of receiving foreign money deposits, while IFSA licensees who are not involved in deposit taking financial services are required to pay BBD 50,000.

International financial service entities are exempt from exchange controls and are granted duty-free concessions on certain imports. Profits and gains are taxed at the same rates as for IBCs. No WHTs are levied on remittances of dividends, interest, or fees. International financial service entities may also claim a credit for taxes paid outside Barbados, provided that this does not reduce the entity's rate of CIT in Barbados to less than 1%.

International Trust Act

The International Trust Act is aimed at facilitating the use of Barbados trusts for purposes previously made possible in many tax free financial centres. An international trust is taxed in Barbados as an individual that is resident but not domiciled in Barbados. This allows the trust to take advantage of a network of tax treaties while not subjecting its foreign earnings to Barbados tax unless they are remitted there. The Act exempts trusts from exchange control and WHT requirements. No registration is required.

Market development allowance for export sales or the tourist industry

150% of certain expenditure on research and development for export sales outside of CARICOM or on tourism development is deductible.

Shipping (Incentives) Act

The Shipping (Incentives) Act was enacted to encourage the development of Barbados' shipping activities by granting CIT, import duty, WHT and other concessions to approved shipping companies for a period of ten years.

Small Business Development Areas Act

Companies incorporated under the Companies Act with at least 75% of their shares owned locally and having share capital of not more than BBD 1 million, annual sales not in excess of BBD 2 million, and not more than 25 employees may obtain approval as a small business. Such companies pay CIT at a reduced rate of 15% and are exempt from the payment of import duties on equipment imported for use in the business and from stamp duty in some instances. In addition, 120% of certain expenditures directly related to the development of the business are deductible for tax purposes. Investors in such businesses are exempt from WHT on interest and dividends earned on their investment.

Societies with Restricted Liability (SRL) Act

An SRL is a hybrid entity that can be recognised as a corporation or partnership in certain jurisdictions depending on the nature of its organisational documents. The entity has limited liability, and membership units are known as quotas. Societies qualifying under this Act may apply for a license to operate as international SRLs and as such are taxed at the same rates as IBCs. No WHT is levied on any distributions, interest, or other income paid by an international SRL to non-residents. International SRLs are granted duty-free concessions on certain imports, and no exchange control requirements are applicable. Entity mobility is also a prominent feature of this legislation. Qualifying societies organised overseas can be continued into Barbados under the Act.

Barbados

Special Development Areas Act

The Special Development Areas Act provides relief for approved developers constructing or improving a building or structure in certain defined locations in Barbados and to persons financing such work (other than a commercial bank). Persons financing such work are exempt from income tax on interest received. Approved developers are exempt from import duties and VAT on inputs for the construction or renovation of buildings, WHTs on repatriation of interest (for a period of 15 years), land tax, and property transfer tax payable by vendors on the initial purchase of the company. An approved developer pays CIT at the rate of 15% and is granted initial and annual allowances on industrial buildings of 40% and 6%, respectively, and on commercial buildings of 20% and 4%, respectively.

Qualifying insurance companies

Companies registered under the Insurance Act that derive at least 90% of their premiums from sources outside of CARICOM and at least 90% of whose risks originate outside of CARICOM may obtain a certificate of qualification. Such companies are entitled to the same exemptions from WHTs and exchange controls as exempt insurance companies. They are also entitled to the foreign currency earnings credit, which may reduce their CIT rate from 25% to 1.75% for general insurance business. The rate of tax on gross investment income applicable to life insurers may fall from 5% to 0.35%.

Tourism Development Act

The Tourism Development Act provides that a qualifying owner of a tourism project or of a completed tourism product may offset expenditures on construction or the provision of certain amenities against its profits.

A tourism project includes the following:

- The construction of a new hotel.
- The alteration or renovation of an existing hotel.
- The conversion of an existing building or buildings into a hotel by reconstruction, extension, alteration, renovation, or remodelling.
- The furnishing and equipping of a building to be utilised as a hotel.
- The provision of tourist recreational facilities and tourism related services.
- The construction and equipping of a new restaurant.
- The alteration or renovation of an existing restaurant.
- The construction of a new attraction or the alteration or renovation of an existing attraction.
- The restoration, preservation, and conservation of natural sites.
- The establishment, restoration, preservation, and conservation of monuments, museums, and other historical structures and sites.
- The construction and furnishing of villas.
- The construction and furnishing of timeshare properties.
- The addition to a tourism product of any facilities or services intended to increase or improve the amenities that the tourism product provides.

Concessions extend to the following:

- The importation of building materials and supplies without payment of customs duty and an exemption from the payment of customs duties on specified supplies to be used for equipping the project.
- A refund of customs duty (including VAT) where the holder of a permit can satisfy the Comptroller of Customs that the building materials and supplies purchased for a

tourism product have been purchased in Barbados, or in the case of importation that the customs duty was paid by the holder of the permit.
* Income tax concessions with respect to the write-off of interest, accelerated deduction of expenditure, interest rate subsidy, equity financing, training, and marketing.
* The set off of approved capital expenditures against revenues for a period of 15 years where the owner of a qualifying tourism project (except restaurants), which has a project with a value of up to BBD 200 million. Hotels with capital expenditure over BBD 200 million are allowed one additional year to write off expenditure for each additional BBD 20 million expended, up to a maximum of 20 years.

Withholding taxes

WHTs are levied as follows:

Recipient	WHT (%)				Entry into force
	Dividends	Interest	Royalties	Management fees	
Non-treaty countries	15	15	15	15	
Austria	5/15 (1)	0 (2)	0 (2)	0	1 April 2007
Botswana	5/12 (3)	10	10	0	12 August 2005
Canada	15	15 (4)	10 (5)	5	22 December 1980 (27)
CARICOM	0	15	15	15	7 July 1995
China P.R.C.	5/10 (6)	10	10	0	27 October 2000 (28)
Cuba	5/15 (7)	10	5	0	16 March 2000
Czech Republic *	5/15 (7)	5	5/10 (8)	0	
Finland	5/15 (1)	5	5	5	20 August 1992 (27)
Ghana *	5/15 (1)	0 (9)	0 (10)	0	
Iceland	5/15 (1)	10	5		24 February 2012
Luxembourg	0/15 (11)	0 (2)	0 (2)	0	8 August 2011
Malta	5/15 (12)	5	5	0	19 June 2002
Mauritius	5	5	5	0	28 January 2005
Mexico	5/10 (13)	10	10	0	16 January 2009
Netherlands	0/15 (14)	5	5	0	12 July 2007 (29)
Norway	5/15 (1)	5	5	5	3 July 1991 (27)
Panama	5 (15)	5/7.5 (16)	7.5	0	18 February 2011
Portugal *	5/15 (17)	10	5	0	
Seychelles	5	5	5	0	21 April 2008
Spain	0/5 (18)	0 (2)	0 (2)	0	14 October 2011
Sweden	5/15 (1)	5	5	5	1 December 1991 (27)
Switzerland	0 (19)	0 (19)	0 (19)	0	26 August 1963
United Kingdom	0 (20)	15 (21)	15 (22)	0	26 November 1970 (30)
United States	5/15 (23)	5	5	0	28 February 1986 (31)
Venezuela	5/10 (24)	5/15 (25)	10	0	1 January 2001
IBCs, ISRLs, QICs, & EICs	(26)	(26)	(26)	(26)	

* Treaty/protocol not yet in force; awaiting ratification.

Barbados

Notes

1. The rate is 15% for portfolio dividends and 5% for holdings of at least 10%.
2. Interest and royalties are only taxable in the country in which the beneficial owner of the dividends or interest is resident.
3. The rate is 12% for portfolio dividends and 5% for holdings of at least 25%.
4. This rate applies, provided that the interest is subject to tax in the other country.
5. This rate applies, provided that the royalties are subject to tax in the other country.
6. The rate is 10% for portfolio dividends and 5% for holdings of at least 25%.
7. The rate is 15% for portfolio dividends and 5% for holdings of at least 25%.
8. 5% of the gross royalties on any literary, artistic, or scientific work, including films or television broadcasting, and 10% on any patent, trademark, commercial, or scientific equipment, among others.
9. Interest is only taxable in the country in which the beneficial owner of the interest is resident.
10. Royalties are only taxable in the country in which the beneficial owner is resident.
11. The rate is 15% for portfolio dividends and 0% for holdings of at least 10% held for at least 12 uninterrupted months prior to dividend distribution.
12. The rate is 15% for portfolio dividends and 5% for holdings of at least 5%.
13. The rate is 10% for portfolio dividends and 5% for holdings of at least 10%.
14. The rate is 15% for portfolio dividends and 0% for holdings of at least 10%.
15. The rate is 75% of the statutory nominal rate at the time of distribution; 5% for companies with holdings of at least 25%.
16. The rate is 7.5% of the gross amount; 5% if the beneficial owner is a bank.
17. The rate is 15% for portfolio dividends and 5% for holdings of at least 25%.
18. The rate is 5% for portfolio dividends and 0% for holdings of at least 25%.
19. Agreement extended to Barbados by virtue of the agreement between Switzerland and the United Kingdom, on payments to non-residents from Barbados.
20. Dividends are exempt from WHT if they are subject to tax in the other country.
21. This rate applies, provided that the interest is subject to tax in the other country.
22. WHT applies only to royalties in respect of cinematographic or television films. All other royalties are exempt from WHT, provided that they are subject to tax in the other country.
23. The rate is 15% for portfolio dividends, 5% for holdings of at least 10%. Dividends paid by a regulated investment company will bear WHT at a rate of 15%, regardless of the percentage of shares held by the recipient. Dividends paid by a real estate investment trust (REIT) will qualify for the 5% WHT rate only if the beneficial owner is an individual holding less than 10% of the shares in the REIT, otherwise, a 30% WHT rate will apply.
24. The rate is 10% for portfolio dividends, 5% for holdings of at least 5%.
25. The rate is 5% if the recipient is a bank, 15% in all other cases.
26. International business companies (IBSs), international societies with restricted liability (ISRLs), exempt insurance companies (EICs), and qualifying insurance companies (QICs) are exempt from WHTs on payments to non-resident persons or international business entities. Specific legislation applies.
27. Protocol signed November 2011, awaiting ratification.
28. Protocol in force 9 June 2010.
29. Protocol in force 23 December 2010.
30. New treaty initialed.
31. General effective date 1 January 1984. First protocol in force 29 December 1993. Second protocol in force 20 December 2004.

Tax administration

Taxable period
CIT returns are prepared on a fiscal year basis.

Tax returns
Companies with fiscal years ending between 1 January and 30 September (both dates inclusive) are required to file a CIT return on or before 15 March in the year following the end of the fiscal period. Companies with fiscal years ending any time between 1 October and 31 December (both dates inclusive) are required to file a CIT return on or before 15 June in the year following the end of the fiscal period.

The Department of Inland Revenue has instituted an online filing system, which is optional.

Payment of tax

Companies with fiscal years ending between 1 January and 30 September (both dates inclusive) are required to make an instalment of CIT for the income year in which the fiscal period ends on or before 15 September of that year. The instalment is 50% of the net CIT payable for the preceding income year. The remainder of CIT due (if any) must be paid on filing of the CIT return by 15 March of the following year.

Companies with fiscal years ending between 1 October and 31 December (both dates inclusive) are required to make two instalments of CIT for the income year in which the fiscal period ends on or before 15 December of that year and 15 March of the following year. The instalments are each 50% of the net CIT payable for the preceding income year. The remainder of CIT due (if any) must be paid on filing of the CIT return by 15 June of the following year.

It is possible to apply for a reduction or waiver in the instalments if lower profits are anticipated in the current year when compared with those of the preceding year.

Audit cycle

A person authorised by the Commissioner may, at any reasonable time, audit the books and records, or other documents that may relate to the information that should be in the books or records, examine property, request reasonable assistance from the owner, or, as necessary, seize or retain any documents that may be relevant.

Statute of limitations

Every person required to deliver a return of one's assessable income for an income year shall keep adequate records and shall retain every such record or voucher for a period of up to five years after the end of the relevant income year, unless the Commissioner otherwise directs, before the disposal of such records.

Penalties

The penalties and interest for failing to file a return on time and pay the CIT due are as follows:

- Penalty for failing to file a CIT return by the due date is BBD 500 plus 5% of the tax assessed at the due date.
- Penalty for failing to pay CIT by the due date is 5% of the tax assessed and unpaid at the due date.
- Interest charge of 1% per month on the tax and penalties calculated for each month during which any amount of tax and penalties remain unpaid on the largest amount of tax and penalties that were due and unpaid at any time during that month.

The penalty for failing to make an instalment of CIT by the due date is 10% of the CIT instalment due, plus interest at 0.5% per month on the CIT instalment and penalty outstanding.

Belarus

PwC contact

Oleg Gvozd
PricewaterhouseCoopers FLLC
40 Orlovskaya Street
Office 39
220053 Minsk, Belarus
Tel: +375 17 335 4000
Email: oleg.gvozd@by.pwc.com

Significant developments

Effective 1 January 2012, the standard corporate income tax (CIT) rate has been reduced from 24% to 18%; consequently, a reduced 9% CIT is levied on capital gains from disposal of shares or stocks in a Belarusian entity.

As of 1 January 2012, amendments to the Tax Code introduced new rules related to:

*   Transfer pricing (*see the Group taxation section for a description of the general rules*).
*   Tax loss carryforward (*see the Deductions section for a description of the general rules*).
*   Thin capitalisation (*see the Group taxation section for a description of the rules, which are effective from 1 January 2013*).

Also as of 1 January 2012, taxpayers are entitled to apply the so-called 'depreciation premium'. This benefit allows taxpayers to classify/record part of the initial value of fixed assets and intangible assets as deductible costs for CIT purposes as of the date when such assets were initially accounted for. The amount of a premium is limited to 10% of the initial value with regard to buildings and constructions and to 20% of the initial value with regard to machines, equipment, vehicles, and intangible assets.

As of 13 March 2012, the last in first out (LIFO) and weighted-average cost methods are no longer applicable in Belarus.

Taxes on corporate income

As of 1 January 2012, the standard CIT, also known as profits tax, rate is 18%. Prior to 1 January 2012, the CIT rate was 24%.

CIT is charged on taxable income (net profits). Taxable income is generally determined as revenues from sales of goods, works, and services, excluding value-added tax (VAT), less production and business related costs, less other deductible expenses, plus net results of non-operating income and expenses.

Resident companies are taxed on their worldwide income.

Non-resident companies are taxed on Belarus-sourced income derived through a permanent establishment (PE) with CIT (at the rate of 18%). Income of non-resident companies sourced in Belarus that is not related to the activities of a PE is subject to withholding tax (WHT) (at rates varying from 6% to 15%).

Local income taxes

There are no local taxes due on net profits. As of 1 January 2011, the 3% local area development tax on net profits has been repealed.

Corporate residence

A company is resident in Belarus if it is incorporated in Belarus.

Permanent establishment (PE)

According to local legislation, a non-resident company is deemed to have a PE in Belarus in cases where:

- it permanently carries out commercial activities in Belarus in whole or in part
- it carries out its activities through a dependent agent
- it uses a building site or construction, assembly, or equipment objects, or
- it provides services or performs works within a period of 90 days continuously or in the aggregate during a calendar year.

Double taxation treaties (DTTs) may establish different rules of PE recognition. According to domestic law: where there is a DTT, the provisions of the treaty shall prevail.

Notwithstanding the activities which create a PE in Belarus, a non-resident company must be registered with the local tax authorities controlling the territory where activities are carried out before starting a business in Belarus.

Any profits derived by a non-resident company via a PE in Belarus are subject to 18% CIT. Expenses incurred by a non-resident company either in Belarus or abroad that relate to a PE can be deducted, subject to local deductibility restrictions.

Other taxes

Value-added tax (VAT)

The standard VAT rate is 20%, whereas the preferential rate is 10%.

The 10% preferential rate applies on:

- local supplies of crop products (excluding floriculture, cultivation of ornamental plants), beekeeping, livestock (except for fur production), and fisheries locally produced and
- import and/or local supplies of certain food products and goods for children.

In general, local supplies of goods, works, and services made by a taxpayer performing its economic activities in Belarus, as well as the importation of goods, are subject to VAT.

Place of supply rules established by the Tax Code of Belarus should be followed to determine whether goods, works, and services are supplied locally, and therefore subject to tax in Belarus.

When a non-resident company, which does not have a PE registered in Belarus, sells goods or provides works and services that are considered local supplies according to the

Belarus

place of supply rules, the VAT due on such supplies is paid by the purchaser registered with the local tax authorities from its own funds. This VAT could be deducted against output VAT, if any, or refunded from the budget in the established order.

Some exceptions apply to provision of construction and other similar works.

Exemptions with credit (zero-rated) include, but are not limited to, the following:

- Supply of goods exported outside of Belarus.
- Provision of works and services involving maintenance, loading, reloading, and any other similar works and services related to supply of exported goods.
- Transportation and any directly linked ancillary services related to the export or import of goods, including transit forwarding, as well as exported works for goods processing.
- Works and services related to repair (modernisation, conversion) of aircrafts (including engines and railway vehicles) and provided to non-resident companies or individuals.

In order to apply zero-rated VAT on goods carried out from Belarus, VAT payers must hold supporting documents as evidence that these goods were actually exported from Belarus to another country. Application of zero-rated VAT on respective works and services must be supported by the appropriate documents, which have to be provided to the local tax authorities where the taxpayer is registered for tax purposes.

Exemptions without credit include, but are not limited to, the following:

- Disposal of shares in resident legal entities.
- Supply of material rights for industrial property objects (e.g. inventions, utility models, industrial designs, breeding achievements, integrated circuits, know-how, trade names, trademarks, and service marks).
- Supply of securities, derivatives, and other similar financial instruments, certain limitations apply.
- Fiduciary management services related to funds and assets owned by an individual or an entity.
- Provision of all types of insurance and re-insurance (co-insurance) services rendered by insurance and re-insurance agents.
- Supply of medicines, medical equipment, instruments, medical products, as well as drugs, devices, equipment, veterinary products, under certain conditions.
- Personal or public health care services, under certain conditions.
- Social services supplied by institutions for children and young people care, nursing homes for the elderly and/or by care/guardianship institutions for disabled or by other non-profit entities.
- Supply of services in the field of culture and art, under certain conditions.
- Public services (services of barbers, baths, and showers; laundry and dry cleaning services; watch repairing; manufacturing and repair of clothing and footwear; repair and maintenance of household appliances; repair of personal and household goods).
- Services provided by religious organisations, if these services correspond to the purposes set out in their canons, statutes, and other documents.
- Funeral services, maintenance of the graves, tombstones, fences, and other objects associated with burial, as well as works on their production, under certain conditions.
- Supply of postage stamps, postcards, and envelopes marked, excise and control (identification) stamps for marking of goods at their nominal value, stamps which

can be used as a confirmation of fees and charges payable in accordance with the legislation.
- Supplies of jewels as well as related services, under certain conditions.
- Retail trade of goods in duty-free shops, under certain conditions.
- Communication services rendered to individuals.
- Legal services supplied by certified lawyers.
- Research and development, design, and technological works and services, under certain conditions.
- Education and training services.
- Lotteries and gambling, under certain conditions.
- Financial services supplied by the banks, under certain conditions.
- Goods and equipment imported into Belarus, under certain conditions.
- Transactions related to provision of loans.

In order to apply exemptions, taxpayers should ensure that the services and goods supplied meet the appropriate VAT exemption requirements.

VAT returns shall be submitted on either a monthly or quarterly basis, by the 20th day of the month following the reporting period. VAT shall be paid on either a monthly or quarterly basis, no later than the 22nd day of the month following the reporting period.

Customs payments

The Customs Union between Russia, Kazakhstan, and Belarus, with its unified trade regulations and customs code, has significantly affected administering, customs clearance, and payment procedures followed by Belarus in regards to exports and imports.

Indirect taxation issues within the Customs Union shall be administered in compliance with the International Agreement on Indirect Taxation and two Protocols signed by the Customs Union Member States.

The following charges are considered customs payments:

- Import duties.
- Export duties.
- Special anti-dumping and countervailing duties.
- VAT and excise taxes due upon importation of goods.
- Fees for customs processing/services.

Rates of import duties as well as description of goods subject to them are established by the Single Nomenclature of Goods of the Customs Union (HS Nomenclature) and Single Customs Tariff of the Customs Union.

However, for certain goods specified in Appendix 5 of HS Nomenclature, Belarus is allowed to apply specific rates of import duties different from the rates set in HS Nomenclature.

Export duties are not levied on exported goods, with the following exceptions: certain soft oil; light distillates; fuels and gasoline; wasted petroleum products; propane, butane, ethylene, propylene, and other liquefied gases; petroleum coke; petroleum bitumen, benzol, toluene, xylenes, potash fertilisers; etc. According to the Customs Union regulations, rates of export duties in regards to mentioned goods shall be established by Belarusian Government and shall be equal to the rates applied in Russia.

Belarus

Import and export duties are calculated on the customs value of the goods, which is defined pursuant to the price of transaction method established by the Customs Union regulations. Generally, the following components are considered when calculating the customs value of imported goods:

- Contract price of the goods.
- Rebates and discounts provided by a supplier, under certain conditions.
- Transportation related expenses to the border of the Customs Union (i.e. Belarusian border).
- Insurance premiums.
- Cost of containers and other packaging.
- Part of direct or indirect income to be derived by the seller from future resale, transfer, or other use of imported goods.

Special, anti-dumping, and countervailing duties could be imposed as a measure to protect economic interests of Belarus.

Tax base for VAT calculation due on imported goods includes the total amount of customs value, import duty, and excise tax paid, if any.

Generally, the taxpayer is required to pay customs duties before the customs clearance of the appropriate goods; however, under certain conditions, a taxpayer may be provided with an extension of payment deadlines or allowed to pay only part of customs duties. It is also possible to pay customs duties in advance.

In 2011, electronic customs filing was introduced. Electronic customs declaration is currently available for customs clearance of the goods declared in customs procedures of temporary exports, re-exports (exports) as well as re-imports, free circulation (imports), and free customs zones.

Excise taxes

Excise taxes are imposed on the following goods produced and sold in or imported to Belarus:

- Rectified ethyl alcohol and alcoholic drinks, including beer and wine.
- Alcohol-containing food products in the form of solutions, emulsions, suspensions, produced with the use of ethanol from all types of raw materials, other alcohol-containing products.
- Tobacco (excluding raw tobacco), including cigarettes, cigars, cigarillos, and smoking tobacco.
- Energetic products, including petrol, kerosene, diesel, and bio diesel, gasoline, fuel, marine fuel, oils for diesel engines, and engines with a carburettor and an injector.
- Liquefied hydro carbonated gas and compressed natural gas used as motor fuel.
- Vans and passenger cars, including those converted to cargo.

The tax rate depends on the type and quantity of goods. Rates of excise taxes are stipulated by the Appendix to the Tax Code of Belarus. Compared to the rates applicable in 2011, rates of excise taxes effective in 2012 have increased considerably. The Tax Code provides for a gradual increase of rates of excise taxes over the course of the year by establishing different rates effective during each following quarter.

As of 2012, the excise tax rate for cigarettes with filters is defined on the basis of (i) maximum retail price per pack of cigarettes of certain brands declared by a taxpayer and (ii) reference of certain brands of cigarettes to one of three price groups defined in the Tax Code.

Generally, the following tax rates are applied (2Q 2012):

Description of tax object	Taxable item	Tax rate in BYR* per taxable item
Rectified ethyl alcohol and alcoholic drinks, including beer and wine	1 litre of 100% alcohol, or 1 litre of complete product	From 110 to 65,460
Tobacco (excluding raw tobacco), including cigarettes, cigars, cigarillos, and smoking tobacco	1 kg of raw tobacco, or 1 cigar or 1,000 cigarettes, cigarillos	From 5,500 to 114,540
Energetic products (petrol, kerosene, diesel, and biodiesel, gasoline, fuel, marine fuel, oils for diesel engines and engines with a carburettor and an injector)	1 ton	From 250,900 to 1,700,000
Liquefied hydro carbonated gas and compressed natural gas used as motor fuel	1,000 litres and 1,000 cbm	141,840 and 267,620
Vans and passenger cars, including those converted to cargo	1 hp (0.75 kw.)	From 1,820 to 18,120

* Belarusian rubles (BYR)

Excise taxes paid on the purchasing/importation of excisable goods to be used in manufacturing of goods or provision of works and services in Belarus are considered as deductible for CIT purposes, with certain exceptions.

The tax is reported and paid on a monthly basis, no later than the 20th day of the month following the reporting period.

Real estate tax (immovable property tax)
Real estate tax is levied at the annual rate of 1% on the residual value of buildings, including separated premises, and constructions, late construction in progress (if construction works take longer than the deadline established in technical documentation), owned by legal entities.

The tax base of buildings and constructions located in the territory of Belarus and leased by individuals to legal entities will be the contract value of the leased real estate not less than its value established by the evaluation. Evaluation can be made in the order approved by the President of Belarus as well as by a certified appraiser or local authority responsible for state registration of real estate.

When the real estate subject to taxation is located in Belarus and leased by a resident company to a lessee, the lessee is considered a real estate taxpayer provided that the leased real estate is accounted for in its balance sheet. The lessee is also obliged to pay the tax due on real estate leased from foreign companies that are not considered as having a PE in Belarus.

Belarus

The amount of tax, except the tax due on late construction in progress (if construction works take longer than the deadline established in technical documentation), is deductible for CIT purposes.

The tax reporting obligation must be fulfilled by a taxpayer before 20 March of the reporting year. The tax is paid on a quarterly basis by equal parts, no later than the 22nd day of the third month of each quarter.

Land tax

Belarusian and foreign entities are subject to land tax collected by the local tax authorities with respect to land that they own or use in Belarus.

The tax base depends on plot location and purpose and is normally determined pursuant to cadastral value of a land plot.

The Tax Code provides for a number of land plot categories that are exempt from, or not subject to, land tax in Belarus.

The tax is payable on an annual basis at the rates established by the Appendixes to the Tax Code of Belarus. Tax rates for agricultural plots vary from BYR 208 to BYR 56,661 per hectare. Tax rates on the land plots located in towns and rural areas range from 0.025% to 3% payable on the cadastral value.

Land tax is deductible, with some exceptions, for CIT purposes.

Land tax is reported annually, no later than 20 February of the current reporting year. Generally, the tax is paid quarterly by equal parts, before the 22nd of the second month of each quarter. Concerning payment terms for land tax due on agricultural plots, some exceptions can be applied.

State dues

State dues are payable by legal entities that apply to the state institutions for the issuance of documents having legal force or other deeds, bring the cases before the courts for consideration, use bills of exchange in their activities, etc.

State dues include the following payments and duties:

- State fees (payable on suits, applications, appeals, and other documents that are submitted to or claimed from the courts or prosecution authorities, payable on applications for state registration of a legal entity, notary public services, real estate registration services, etc.).
- Patent fees (payable for registration and use of intellectual property).
- Stamp fees (payable on activities with bills of exchange).
- Consular fees (payable on the activities of state consular and diplomatic departments performed under the request of any applicant).

Offshore charge

An offshore charge is levied upon the following activities of domestic entities:

- Any transfer of funds to an entity registered in an 'offshore jurisdiction', to a third party who is a creditor of that entity, or to the bank account of an offshore jurisdiction.
- In kind performance of obligation to an offshore entity, with some exceptions.

- Any transfer of material rights and obligations as a result of changes in commitment (cession or transfer of debt) between a domestic entity and an offshore entity.

According to Belarusian laws, an offshore jurisdiction is a territory which is included in the list of offshore territories established by the President, has a preferential tax treatment, and/or does not disclose the information related to financial transactions made by resident entities.

A list of 51 offshore territories has been published. With certain exceptions specified in the law, all payments to offshore companies or their branches for any kind of work or services, commodities, interest on loans, insurance premiums, guarantees, etc. are subject to an offshore charge, which is deductible for CIT purposes.

Tax relief is granted to: (i) repayment of loans including interests on them, borrowed from entities located in offshore territories, (ii) payments due under international marine cargoes and forwarding services, and (iii) payments for bank operations under certain conditions.

An offshore charge is paid at a 15% rate and is deductible for CIT purposes.

The tax is reported and paid on a monthly basis, no later than the 20th day of the month following the reporting period.

Capital gains tax
Capital gains from disposal of shares/stocks in a Belarusian entity are taxed as part of the taxpayer's profits and are subject to a 9% tax (12% prior to 1 January 2012). No tax exemptions are provided by the Tax Code for the capital gains taxation.

Ecological (environmental) tax
Ecological (environmental) tax is imposed on pollutants discharged into the environment, storage and disposal of industrial wastes, wastewater discharges, and on importation of ozone-depleting substances, including those contained in the products.

The following are excluded from taxation, including but not limited to:

- Pollutants discharged into the air by mobile sources (e.g. cars, vehicles).
- Transit of ozone-depleting substances, including those contained in the products through the territory of Belarus.

The tax base of environmental tax is the actual quantity of respective pollutants used/discharged. Tax rates of environmental tax are stipulated by the Tax Code of Belarus.

Environmental tax paid, with certain exceptions, is treated as deductible for CIT purposes.

The tax is reported and paid on a quarterly basis, by the 20th and 22nd day of the month following the reporting quarter, accordingly. Certain exemptions are provided to legal entities effecting tax payments on the basis of established annual limits. These taxpayers will have to file an annual tax return and provide it to a tax authority no later than 20 April of the calendar year.

Tax on natural resources
A tax on natural resources is payable on the actual value of extracted natural resources. It depends on the kind and quantity of extracted resources.

Belarus

Tax rates are established by the Tax Code of Belarus and are applied on natural resources that have been extracted by a taxpayer within established limits. Natural resources extracted over established limits are taxed by a standard tax rate multiplied by ten.

Tax paid on resources extracted within established limits, or if the limits are not established (for certain type of resources), is treated as deductible for CIT purposes.

The tax is reported and paid on a quarterly basis. Those taxpayers who calculate the tax on the basis of annual limits for extraction fulfil tax reporting and payment liability on an annual basis.

Local tax on providers (suppliers)
The local tax on providers is levied on legal entities engaged in gathering/purchasing of wild plants (or parts thereof), mushrooms, and technical and medical raw materials of floral origin for their further industrial processing or resale.

Tax base is the cost of gathered items defined on the basis of procurement (purchasing) prices.

Tax rates do not exceed 5%. Tax on providers is treated as deductible for CIT purposes.

The tax is reported and paid on a quarterly basis.

Branch income

Non-resident legal entities pay tax on profits attributable to a PE. A PE is broadly defined as "a branch, division, office, bureau, agency, or any other place through which a foreign legal entity regularly carries out its business activities in Belarus". Belarus's various DTTs may define a PE differently, which could in some cases result in tax relief. Conducting business through an agent may also create a taxable PE in Belarus.

Taxation of a PE
A PE's profits are computed on substantially the same basis as Belarusian legal entities, including the composition of tax deductible expenses. The Tax Code provides for the deductibility of expenses incurred abroad by a head office with respect to its PE in Belarus (including a reasonable allocation of administration costs).

To calculate a PE's taxable income, a non-resident company is required to provide a tax authority with financial documents (i.e. accounting records, income statement, general ledger accounts, invoices, statements of services/works fulfilment, etc.) supporting the amount of revenue earned and expenses incurred. Generally, a PE's taxable income is defined on a revenue less costs basis. Documentary support of each revenue and/or costs item is required.

When it is not possible to calculate a profit attributable to a PE, this profit can be calculated by the tax authority using one of the following methods:

- A profit sharing method (i.e. gross foreign profit is allocated to PE by using one of the following coefficients related to a PE: working time costs, expenses incurred, services/works performed).
- Benchmarking method (tax authority performs benchmarking study by collecting the respective ratios/indexes of other entities engaged in similar activities).

Head office expenses related to a PE are considered for calculation of taxable income in Belarus and require confirmation of an independent foreign auditor. Splitting of expenses is highly recommended in the audited financial statements of the parent company (head office).

If a non-resident company is deemed to have a PE in Belarus, it will have to register with a local tax authority and declare related profit. Profit related to a PE will be taxed by CIT at a rate of 18%.

Non-resident legal entities operating in Belarus through a PE are required to follow the filing and payment schedules established for Belarusian legal entities.

Representative office
Non-resident legal entities are also allowed to operate in Belarus via a representative office or to set up a resident legal entity.

A representative office of a non-resident company is defined as the structural subunit registered with the Ministry of Foreign Affairs, which is entitled either to engage in commercial activities in Belarus or not, conclude contracts, and undertake obligations according to the power of attorney issued to the management official of the branch by its head company (founder).

The representative office is not considered a legal person.

A representative office conducting commercial activities is taxed in the same manner as a PE or as a local resident company, with some exceptions.

A non-commercial representative office pays taxes due on its primary and auxiliary activities, such as real estate tax (with some exceptions), customs duties, input VAT, personal income tax, social security contributions due on employment of individuals, etc.

Income determination

Inventory valuation
Under domestic accounting legislation, stock used in the production and included in the cost of produced goods may be generally valued by the following methods:

* Cost of each unit.
* Average cost.
* First in first out (FIFO).

As of 13 March 2012, the LIFO and weighted-average cost methods are no longer applicable.

The inventory valuation method used for CIT purposes must be the same method established by the taxpayer's accounting policy.

Capital gains
Capital gains are subject to WHT. *See Capital gains tax in the Other taxes section for more information.*

Belarus

Dividend income

Dividends distributed by a resident company to another resident company are subject to 12% CIT, which is withheld by a paying company.

Dividends distributed by a foreign entity represent non-operating income of a receiving Belarus entity and are subject to 12% CIT payable by the receiving entity in Belarus, irrespective of the fact that the foreign entity has paid the WHT on dividends distributed.

Dividends received by venture companies are exempt from CIT.

Dividends received by taxpayers from Belarusian companies are exempt from CIT in hands of such taxpayers, since CIT on dividend income is withheld by a respective dividend-distributing entity.

Inter-company dividends

The Tax Code provides no exemptions for taxation of inter-company dividends.

Interest income

Interest on most types of bonds, including state, municipal, bank, and corporate bonds, is exempt from Belarusian CIT under certain conditions provided for in the Tax Code.

CIT at the standard rate of 18% is charged on interest income derived by a Belarus entity from another resident company.

Interest income derived by a Belarus entity from a foreign entity represents non-operating income of a receiving Belarus entity and is subject to 18% CIT payable by the receiving entity in Belarus, irrespective of the fact that the foreign entity has paid the WHT on interest income.

Other significant items

The following types of income are, *inter alia*, exempt from CIT:

- 'Target financing' received from the state or municipal budget. The taxpayer is required to hold separate accounting records of income and expenses derived and incurred within 'target financing'.
- Amounts payable to a shareholder, whether in cash or in kind, not in excess of its contribution to the statutory capital of a legal entity in case of:
  - its liquidation
  - a shareholder's withdrawal from a legal entity, or
  - if the shares are purchased by a legal entity from its shareholder.
- Payments to a shareholder in the value of its shares or as a result of an increase in their nominal value made by the legal entity's sources, as long as such payments do not change the percentage of participation of either shareholder or change the percentage for less than 0.01%.
- Goods (works, services), material rights, and monetary means granted:
  - to the successors by a legal entity in case of its restructuring
  - as an inter-company transfer pursuant to corporate decision
  - to taxpayers engaged in crop production, animal husbandry, fish farming, and beekeeping, provided that this income is spent for the appropriate activities, or
  - as a foreign gratuitous help on conditions stipulated by the President.

- Monetary means or assets received by a taxpayer from its shareholders as their contributions to the statutory capital, not in excess of amounts provided by the statutory documents.

Foreign income

Foreign income of Belarusian resident legal entities is taxed, except for dividends, as ordinary business income at the standard 18% CIT rate.

There are no provisions in tax legislation that allow tax deferral with regard to foreign income.

Deductions

Deductible expenses include all the usual costs that an entity actually incurs for the purpose of earning income or receiving economic benefit, unless the Tax Code of Belarus or presidential regulations provide otherwise.

Depreciation

Assets may be depreciated using the directly proportional (straight-line) depreciation method, indirect disproportionate depreciation method, production depreciation method, or a declining-balance depreciation method. Depreciation may not exceed maximum rates established by the law.

Almost all types of fixed assets (buildings, premises, equipment, vehicles) are depreciated for tax purposes in accordance with the established procedures. Land plots are not depreciated. There are many different depreciation rates established for different types of fixed assets. Generally, fixed assets may be divided into five basic groups as follows:

Group of assets	Description of the assets	Annual depreciation rate (%)
1	Buildings and constructions, premises	1 and 2
2	Vehicles and equipment	10
3	Cars and vehicles	12.5
4	Inventories (furniture, tools, etc.)	10
5	Computers and other related devices	20

Application of depreciation premium is possible, i.e. taxpayers are entitled to classify/record part of the initial value of fixed assets and intangible assets as costs of production and supply of goods (works, services) for CIT purposes as of the date when such assets were initially accounted for. The amount of a premium is limited to 10% of the initial value with regard to buildings and constructions and to 20% of the initial value with regard to machines, equipment, vehicles, and intangible assets.

Fixed assets recorded on accounts of state-owned companies are obligatorily re-valued one time per year because of BYR inflation.

Starting from 1 January 2012, annual re-evaluation of fixed assets for companies other than state-owned is required only with regard to buildings, constructions, and transfer units. A particular company is entitled to re-evaluate fixed assets on its own initiative as of 1 January of the year following the reporting one.

Belarus

Goodwill

Goodwill and personnel experience cannot be recognised as intangible assets for CIT purposes.

Start-up expenses

Deduction of start-up expenses is possible only after registration of a business presence (i.e. respective resident entity) and starting from the first year of its operations, provided respective provisions for deductions of such expenses are outlined in the accounting policy of that resident entity.

Interest expenses

Interest expenses are generally deducted for CIT purposes unless interest is accrued on past-due loans. Moreover, from January 2013, thin capitalisation restrictions have to be considered (*see Thin capitalisation in the Group taxation section*).

Bad debt

Bad debts are deductible only if proved and specific criteria are met.

Charitable contributions

Amounts not exceeding 10% of an entity's gross profit granted to health, education, social welfare, culture, and sports state institutions; religious organisations; and public associations (i.e. 'Belarusian Society of Disabled Persons', 'Belarusian Society of Deaf Persons', 'Belarusian Fellowship of Visually Impaired Persons'), or spent for acquisition of goods, works, or services for the benefit of the named institutions, are deductible.

Taxes

Generally, the following taxes, dues, and other compulsory charges to the budget are deductible for CIT purposes:

- Excise taxes paid at purchasing/importation of excisable goods to be used in manufacturing of goods or provision of works and services in Belarus, with some exceptions.
- Environmental tax, with certain exceptions.
- Real estate tax, except the tax due on late construction in progress.
- Land tax, with some exceptions.
- Tax on natural resources, with some exceptions.
- State dues.
- Offshore charge.
- Tax on providers.
- Payments for social and other mandatory security.

The following taxes shall not be deducted for CIT purposes:

- VAT paid, with certain exceptions (*see below*).
- CIT.

VAT can be treated as deductible for CIT purposes only if acquired goods, works, or services are used for production or sale of goods, works, or services that are VAT exempt.

Other significant items

Limited deductible expenses also include the following:

- Modernisation and reconstruction of fixed assets. The value of modernisation or reconstruction is included in the acquisition costs.
- Business trips.
- Representation.
- Management fees payable to outsourcing companies, with restrictions.
- Natural losses, with certain exceptions.
- Cost of fuel and energy resources, with restrictions established for certain entities.
- Membership fees, contributions, and premiums, with restrictions.
- Premiums on certain types of voluntary insurance, with restrictions.
- Amounts of financial rebates granted by a supplier to a customer.

Non-deductible expenses also include the following:

- Expenses on provision or acquisition of works and services not related to the taxpayer's business activities.
- Construction, maintenance, and other works, including all types of repair of assets that are not used for the purpose of earning income or receiving economic benefit.
- Default interest (forfeit), fines, and other sanctions paid to the budget.
- Dividends paid and similar type of payments.
- Contributions made to the authorised share capital.
- Expenses incurred on purchase and/or creation of depreciable assets.
- Depreciation for tangible and intangible assets not used in business, as well as for tangible assets that are not in operation.
- Cost of assets or material rights transferred as advance or a pledge to a third party.
- Expenses covered by reserves for future expenses created by a taxpayer in the prescribed manner.
- Interest on overdue loans, as well as on loans related to the acquisition of tangible and intangible assets, other long-term assets.
- Other expenses not related to the deriving of income and not attributed to operating activities of the entity as well as expenses that are not considered as allowable deductions under the Tax Code of Belarus.

Net operating losses
As of 1 January 2012, procedures for carrying forward tax losses have been introduced in the Tax Code.

Belarusian companies are given the possibility to recognise in the current tax period the tax losses incurred in the previous tax periods. Taxpayers are entitled to carry forward losses incurred in 2011 and subsequent tax periods. Losses can be carried forward only for ten years after the tax period when the losses have occurred.

However, tax loss carry forward is not applied to losses:

- incurred as a result of the activities outside Belarus, if a company is registered as a taxpayer in a foreign state with regard to such activities, or
- incurred in a tax period when a company was entitled to apply CIT relief (tax exemption) established for several tax periods.

Tax losses may not be carried back in Belarus.

Payments to foreign affiliates
Payments to foreign affiliates of a Belarusian resident legal entity in amounts of financing aimed to cover ongoing costs thereof are deductible for CIT purposes in Belarus.

Belarus

Group taxation

Currently, group taxation legislation and regimes are not available in Belarus. Each Belarusian entity is regarded as a separate taxpayer and may not deduct tax losses of any other group entity. The Belarus Tax Code does not allow the deduction of foreign losses from domestic taxable income, or domestic losses from foreign taxable income.

Transfer pricing

Amendments to the Tax Code, effective from 1 January 2012, empower tax authorities to carry out transfer pricing control. Though Belarusian transfer pricing legislation is not as thorough as it is in the European Union (EU) member states, taxpayers should be aware of the following:

- In the course of the tax audit, tax authorities are entitled to check whether prices set by particular taxpayers are in line with market prices.
- Tax authorities can apply the market price of a transaction for taxation purposes in the following cases:
  - Selling of immovable property/real estate when the transaction price is 20% lower than the market price.
  - Entering into a foreign-trade transaction, including one with a related party, when the transaction price (price of a number of transactions with one person per year) is simultaneously higher than BYR 20 billion and 20% lower than the market price.
- The tax base for CIT purposes can be adjusted by the tax authorities on the basis of a market price only if the amount of CIT to be paid to the budget of Belarus goes up as a result of such adjustment.
- To determine the CIT base on the basis of a market price, the tax authorities are entitled to apply the following methods:
  - Comparable uncontrolled price method (CUP).
  - Resale price method.
  - Cost plus method.
- Before the tax audit has been carried out, a taxpayer who applied transaction prices not corresponding to market prices is entitled to independently adjust the CIT base according to market prices and pay the remaining CIT.

Moreover, there is a mechanism to control transfer pricing provided by the DTTs applicable for Belarus. When interests under the loan agreement between related parties exceeds the arm's-length rate/basis (the amount which will be agreed upon between independent parties under normal business circumstances), a 5% rate of WHT (provided by the DTT) will be charged on the arm's-length interest charge. Excess amounts, if any, will be taxed by WHT at a 10% rate.

Thin capitalisation

Starting from 1 January 2013, the amount of interest accrued on a loan granted to a taxpayer by a foreign company that can be deducted for CIT purposes will be limited if, in aggregate:

- a foreign company holds over 20% of shares in a statutory capital of a taxpayer or a foreign company and a taxpayer are treated related parties, and
- the amount of loan exceeds the value of a foreign company's share in a statutory capital of a taxpayer by more than three times.

Tax credits and incentives

Foreign tax credit
If a Belarusian legal entity derives income subject to taxation abroad, the tax paid abroad may be deducted from the calculated CIT.

In accordance with the Tax Code, the amount deducted from CIT may not exceed that part of the tax calculated in Belarus that is attributed to the income received in a foreign jurisdiction. If there is a valid DTT with the country in question, the provisions of the treaty regarding avoidance of double taxation shall apply.

Special tax treatments
The Belarusian Tax Code provides a more favourable tax environment for particular resident legal entities. Special tax treatments are available for certain taxpayers depending on their location, amount of revenue, number of individuals employed, types of business, etc. Special tax treatments include, but are not limited to, the following:

* Simplified taxation.
* Tax on farmers and other producers of agricultural products.
* Tax on gambling business.
* Tax on lotteries.
* Tax on electronic interactive games.
* Free economic zones.

In cases where activities fulfil the criteria of a special tax treatment, the taxpayer is not permitted to use the general taxation regime with regard to income deriving from those activities, with certain exceptions. Concerning simplified taxation and tax on farmers, the taxpayer is entitled to determine whether to apply such treatment or not.

Incentive for employing disabled persons
Entities employing disabled persons, if their number exceeds 50% of the average number of employees for the reporting period, are exempt from CIT due on taxable profit derived from production activity.

Exemption of CIT on profits derived from various activities
* Profit of entities engaged in baby food production is exempt from CIT.
* Profit derived by insurance companies from investments of insurance reserves under the contracts of voluntary life insurance is exempt from CIT.
* Entities engaged in manufacturing of prosthetic and orthopaedic devices (including dental prostheses), provision of rehabilitation, and disability services are exempt from CIT due on profit derived from sales of these items.
* Entities deriving profit from sales of plants (except for flowers, ornamental plants), livestock (except for farming), fish farming, and beekeeping, provided the entities raise them, are exempt from CIT.

Tax holidays
Profit from the services provided by hotels, sport complexes, ski complexes, touristic complexes, motels, campgrounds, etc. located at tourist sites established by the President of Belarus is exempt from CIT for three years starting from the commencement of its activities, with certain exceptions.

Profit derived by motels, hotels, campgrounds, maintenance stations, objects of trade and catering, cleaning, located on the roadsides of national highways is exempt from CIT for five years starting from the day when the permission for such activities

Belarus

was received. This privilege does not cover roadside objects located on land plots granted for construction of gasoline stations.

Scientific and Technological Association incentive

Entities that are members of the Scientific and Technological Association established by Belarusian State University, in accordance with legislation, are entitled to apply a 5% CIT rate on their profit derived from sales of information technology and provision of information technology development services.

Incentives for the production of innovative, high-technology goods and laser-optical equipment

Income derived from selling goods of one's own production included in the list of innovative goods approved by the Council of Ministers is exempt from CIT.

Income from selling goods of one's own production that are included in the list of high-technology goods approved by the Council of Ministers is exempt from CIT, provided revenue from selling of such goods comprises at least 50% of total revenue of a taxpayer. If revenue from selling high-technology goods is less than 50% of total revenue, such income is taxable at a reduced CIT rate of 10%.

Entities engaged in production of laser-optical equipment, accounting for at least 50% of the entity's total production, can benefit from a reduced CIT rate of 10% under certain conditions.

Free economic zones

Entities that are registered in Belarusian free economic zones are exempt from CIT for five years, starting from the date when the profits were declared, in relation to goods, works, and services of their own production that are either exported or included in the list of import-substituting goods and supplied in Belarus. After expiration of this term, the CIT rate is 9%.

Land plots within the borders of free economic zones, provided to free economic zone residents registered after 1 January 2012 for the purpose of objects construction, are exempt from land tax for the period of such objects' design and construction, but not more than for five years from the registration date. Free economic zone residents registered before 1 January 2012 can take advantage of this land tax exemption only during the period from 1 January 2017 till 1 January 2022, as long as design and/or construction works are performed.

Moreover, residents of free economic zones are granted, under certain conditions, a partial VAT relief and a relief for real estate tax on buildings and constructions located in free economic zones.

High Technologies Park (HTP)

The following tax privileges are granted to residents of the HTP:

- Full exemption from CIT.
- Full exemption from VAT when selling goods, works, or services in the territory of Belarus.
- Full exemption from VAT and customs duties when importing certain goods for the purpose of using them in activities connected with high technology.
- No land tax is applicable to land plots situated in the HTP on which a construction project is being carried out; however, this exemption will last no longer than three years.

- Full exemption from real estate tax on buildings and installations, including above-standard incomplete constructions that are situated in the territory of the HTP.
- 9% personal income tax (PIT) for employees of residents of the HTP.
- No social security contributions on the part of employees' income exceeding the average salary in Belarus.

Taxation of holding companies

A holding company is a group of companies where one company of the group is considered to be a management company by virtue of influence over decisions passed by other group companies (i.e. the subsidiaries) as a result of holding 25% and more of their ordinary stock (shares).

A management company is entitled to create a centralised fund by means of contributions of subsidiaries from net income thereof. Subject to certain conditions, monetary means received by a management company (Belarusian tax resident) from subsidiaries (Belarusian tax residents) for the purpose of a centralised fund formation as well as monetary means transferred from a centralised fund to subsidiaries are not considered taxable income for CIT purposes.

Free of charge transfer of assets within a qualifying holding group is exempted from CIT in Belarus, conditional on certain terms, in particular:

- A management company possesses more than 50% of shares (stock) of its subsidiaries receiving or transferring assets.
- Participants of a holding group receiving or transferring assets are not under special tax treatment and are not registered in any free economic zone.
- Participants of a holding group receiving or transferring assets do not participate in securities market and do not manufacture alcoholic and tobacco products; they are not banks, non-bank financial intermediaries, or insurance companies.
- Received assets are used to manufacture products, to perform works, and to render services.

Withholding taxes

The following income of a non-resident entity in Belarus that is not derived through a PE is deemed to be Belarusian-source income and is subject to WHT at the rates provided:

Income	WHT (%)
Freight charges, (including demurrage) and freight-forwarding services (excluding freight charges for marine transportation and forwarding services)	6
Interest on any type of debt obligations including securities	10
Royalties	15
Dividends and other similar income	12
Penalties, fines, and other sanctions received for breach of contractual liabilities	15
Income derived from sports, entertainment activities, or performers' activities	15
Income derived from innovative, design, research and development activities, design of technological documentation engineering design, and other similar works and services	15
Income from provision of guarantees	15
Income from provision of disk space and/or communication channel for placing information on the server and services for its maintenance	15

Belarus

Income	WHT (%)
Proceeds from the sale, transfer (with title), or lease of immovable property located in Belarus	15
Income derived by a foreign entity from the sale of an enterprise as a complex of assets located in Belarus	15
Capital gains (income from the sale of shares/stocks) in local companies	12
Income from the sale of securities (except shares)	15
Income derived from provision of works and services	15

In calculation of WHT due on certain types of income, a taxpayer is permitted to deduct related expenses following the rules specified by the Tax Code.

Generally, the tax is withheld and paid to the budget by a local entity, an individual entrepreneur, a branch, or a PE of a foreign company. When certain types of Belarusian-source income is received (e.g. capital gains, sale, transfer of title of ownership or lease of immovable property, provision of licenses for software, and other copyright objects), a WHT shall be paid directly by a foreign entity.

Currently, Belarus has over 60 DTTs with foreign countries. Where a treaty for the avoidance of double taxation with the country in question contradicts the local tax regulations, the treaty provisions prevail.

Reduction of or an exemption from WHT under a DTT may be obtained if a special residence certificate is completed and provided to the tax authorities before the payment is made.

If the payment that is covered by the DTT has already been made and WHT at the local rate was withheld, it is possible to obtain an appropriate refund (reduction) by completing a special claim for a refund. The claim for a refund must be filed with additional documents, such as a residence certificate, copies of the contract, and other documents related to the payment.

The following table indicates WHT rates stipulated in DTTs Belarus is a party to:

Recipient	WHT (%) Dividends	Interest	Royalties	Construction site duration before creation of a PE (months)	Treaty benefits available from
Armenia	10/15	0*/5	10	12	19 November 2001
Austria	5/15	0*/5	5	12	24 March 2002
Azerbaijan	15	0*/5	10	12	29 April 2002
Bahrain	5	0*/5	5	12	16 April 2008
Belgium	5/15	0/10	5	12	13 October 1998
Bulgaria	10	0*/10	10	12	17 February 1998
China	10	0*/10	10	18	3 October 1996
Croatia	5/15	10	10	12	4 June 2004
Cyprus	10/15	5	5	12	12 February 1999
Czech Republic	5/10	0/5	5	12	15 January 1998

Recipient	WHT (%)			Construction site duration before creation of a PE (months)	Treaty benefits available from
	Dividends	Interest	Royalties		
Democratic People's Republic of Korea	10	10	10	12	20 November 2007
Denmark **	15	0	0	24	28 September 1987
Egypt, Arab Republic of	15	10	10	12	27 May 1999
Estonia	10	10	10	6	22 July 1998
Finland	5/15	0/5	5	12	13 July 2008
France **	15	10	0	24	28 March 1987
Germany	5/15	0/5	3/5	12	31 December 2006
Hungary	5/15	5	5	12	24 June 2004
India	10/15	10	15	6	17 July 1998
Iran, Islamic Republic of	10/15	0*/5	5	12	15 November 2001
Ireland	5/10	5	5	12	9 July 2010
Israel	10	5/10	5/10	12	29 December 2003
Italy	5/15	0*/8	6	12	30 November 2009
Japan **	15	10	10	12	27 November 1986
Kazakhstan	15	0*/10	15	12	10 December 1997
Korea, Republic of	5/15	0*/10	5	12	17 June 2003
Kuwait	0*/5	0*/5	10	6	27 March 2002
Kyrgyz Republic	15	0*/10	15	12	12 May 1998
Latvia	10	0*/10	10	6	31 October 1996
Lebanon	7.5	0*/5	5	an aggregated period of more than 9 months in any 12-month period	29 December 2002
Libya	5/15	0*/5	5	an aggregated period of more than 3 months in any 12-month period in a tax year	Has not entered into force
Lithuania	10	0*/10	10	12	26 June 1996
Macedonia, Former Yugoslav Republic of	5/15	10	10	12	26 January 2006
Malaysia **	15	0*/15	10/15	6	4 July 1988
Moldova	15	10	15	12	28 May 1996
Mongolia	10	0*/10	10	12	27 January 2002
Netherlands	5/15	5	5/10	12	31 December 1997
Oman	0*/5	0*/5	10	6	9 January 2008

Belarus

Recipient	WHT (%) Dividends	Interest	Royalties	Construction site duration before creation of a PE (months)	Treaty benefits available from
Pakistan	10/15	0*/5	15	6	5 October 2006
Poland	10/15	10	0	12	1 January 1994
Qatar	5	0*/5	5	an aggregated period of more than 3 months in any 12-month period commencing or ending in a relevant tax year	24 November 2007
Romania	10	0*/10	15	12	14 July 1998
Russia	15	0*/10	10	no special provisions in the relevant DTT, local tax legislation provisions should apply	21 January 1997
Saudi Arabia	5	5	10	6	1 August 2010
Serbia **	5/15	8	10	12	24 November 1998
Slovakia	10/15	0*/10	5/10	12	5 July 2000
Slovenia	5	5	5	12	31 May 2011
South Africa Republic	5/15	5/10	5/10	an aggregated period of more than 120 days in any 12-month period commencing or ending in a relevant tax year	29 December 2003
Spain **	18	0	5	12	7 August 1986
Sweden	5/10	0*/5	3/5/10	12	27 December 1994
Switzerland	5/15	0*/5/8	3/5/10	12	28 December 1999
Syria	15	10	18	6	3 April 2002
Tajikistan	15	0*/10	15	12	16 December 1999
Thailand	10	0*/10	15	6	2 September 2006
Turkey	10/15	0*/10	10	12	29 April 1998
Turkmenistan	15	0*/10	15	6	29 December 2004
Ukraine	15	10	15	12	30 January 1995
United Arab Emirates	5/10	0*/5	5/10	12	1 February 2001
United Kingdom of Great Britain and Northern Ireland **	0	0	0	24	30 January 1986

Belarus

Recipient	WHT (%) Dividends	Interest	Royalties	Construction site duration before creation of a PE (months)	Treaty benefits available from
United States of America **	0	0*	0	36	28 January 1976
Uzbekistan	15	0*/10	15	12	11 January 1997
Venezuela	5/15	0*/5	5/10	9	20 January 2009
Vietnam	15	0*/10	15	6	26 December 1997

* In general, a 0% tax rate applies to interest payments to the governments of contracting states and to payments guaranteed by the governments of contracting states.

** DTT with this country is in force since Belarus is a successor of the former USSR.

Tax administration

Taxable period
The taxable period for CIT is a calendar year. The taxable period for CIT withheld on dividends accrued by Belarusian companies is a month.

Tax returns
A CIT return shall be submitted on an annual basis, whether a company has taxable income or not, by the 20th day of March following the reporting year.

The above CIT reporting rule is also applicable on PEs of foreign companies as well as non-commercial representative offices. Since 2011, an annual CIT return filed by non-commercial representative offices does not have to be audited by a Belarusian certified auditor.

CIT withheld on inter-company dividends must be reported by a tax withholding entity no later than the 20th day of the month following the month in which the dividends were accrued.

A tax-withholding entity must submit a WHT return to the tax authorities no later than the 20th day of the month following the month when the payment was made.

Payment of tax
CIT must be paid via equal instalments, on a quarterly basis, before 22 March, 22 June, 22 September, and 22 December of a current tax period.

Remaining CIT, if any, shall be paid not later than 22 March following the expired tax period. The above deadlines shall also be followed by PEs of foreign entities.

CIT on inter-company dividends shall be paid no later than the 22nd day of the month following the month when dividends were paid.

WHT is to be calculated, withheld, and paid by a Belarusian company or a PE of a non-resident company no later than the 22nd day of the month following the month when the payment was made.

Belarus

Audit cycle

Subject to certain exceptions, tax authorities are not permitted to carry out scheduled audits within two years after the company's incorporation or representative office's (of a foreign company) registration. Subsequently, scheduled audits can be performed every one, three, or five years depending on whether a company is referred to as high-risk, middle-risk, or low-risk.

Tax authorities can perform off-schedule audits only on the grounds defined in legislation (e.g. reorganisation or liquidation of a taxpayer, information about tax violations).

Statute of limitations

Generally, a statute of limitations for tax liability is either three years after the date when violation was committed or six months after the date when violation was exposed by tax authorities.

Belgium

PwC contact

Frank Dierckx
PwC
Woluwe Garden
Woluwedal 18
B-1932 Sint-Stevens-Woluwe
Belgium
Tel: +32 2 710 43 24
Email: frank.dierckx@pwc.be

Significant developments

At the end of November 2011, various new Belgian tax measures were proposed under the 2012 budget agreement. Some were enacted in the Miscellaneous Provisions Act of 28 December 2011. Parts of the other measures were adopted in the Program Act of 29 March 2012. Note that other proposed tax measures will, in principle, take statutory form later in 2012, e.g. carryforward restriction of excess notional interest deduction (NID).

Please note this information is current as of 1 June 2012. Typically, pending legislation is announced in June or July. Please visit the Worldwide Tax Summaries website at www.pwc.com/taxsummaries to see any significant corporate tax developments that occurred after 1 June 2012.

Notional interest deduction (NID)
Belgian corporate income taxpayers can claim an NID, reflecting the economic cost of the use of capital (based on the cost of long-term, risk-free financing). The NID rate for a given tax year is, in principle, based on the ten-year government bond interest rate. The NID rate is 3.425% (3.925% for small and medium-sized enterprises [SMEs], *see the Tax credits and incentives section for the definition*) for tax year 2012 (financial year 2011). As of tax year 2013, the rate of the NID is capped at 3% (3.5% for SMEs). The effective NID rate for tax year 2013 (accounting years ending between 31 December 2012 and 30 December 2013, both dates inclusive) is 3% (3.5% for SMEs).

Note that the 2012 Belgian budget agreement provides that new excess NID (i.e. NID that exceeds the taxable basis to set-off) can no longer be carried forward (still to be enacted by the Belgian parliament), whereas, under the current rules, 'excess NID' (i.e. NID that cannot be claimed owing to the taxpayer having insufficient taxable income) can be carried forward for a maximum of seven years.

However, the 'stock' of excess NID (stemming from previous years, i.e. tax years 2012 and before) can, under the proposed rules, still be carried forward for a maximum of seven years (as is currently the case), though the excess NID that can be applied in a given year will, in principle, be limited according to the proposal (not yet enacted).

Anti-abuse rule
According to the old section 344 (1) of the Belgian Income Tax Code (BITC), the Belgian tax authorities could (under certain conditions) reclassify a legal deed (transaction) into a different transaction (with generally a higher tax burden), provided both transactions had the same or similar legal consequences. A similar provision existed for registration duties and inheritance tax purposes.

Belgium

Under the new anti-abuse section 344 (1) of the BITC (Act of 29 March 2012), a legal deed (or a whole of legal deeds) is not opposable towards the tax authorities if the tax authorities can demonstrate that there is tax abuse. For the purpose of the anti-abuse rule, 'tax abuse' is defined as:

- A transaction in which the taxpayer places oneself, in violation with the purposes of a provision of the BITC or related royal decree, outside the scope of this provision of the BITC or related royal decree, or
- a transaction that gives rise to a tax advantage provided by a provision of the BITC or related royal decree whereby getting this tax advantage would be in violation with the purposes of this provision of the BITC or related royal decree and whereby getting the tax advantage is the essential goal of the transaction.

In case the tax authorities uphold that a legal deed or a whole of legal deeds can be considered as tax abuse, it is up to the taxpayer to prove the choice for the legal deed or the whole of legal deeds is motivated by other reasons than tax avoidance (reversal of burden of proof). In case the taxpayer cannot prove this, the transaction will be subject to a taxation in line with the purposes of the income tax law, as if the tax abuse did not take place.

Entry into force: The new rule is applicable as of tax year 2013 and on legal deeds performed during a taxable period closing on or after 6 April 2012. Any change made as of 28 November 2011 to the closing date of the annual accounts will be disregarded. For inheritance and registration duties purposes, the new rule is applicable to legal deeds performed as of 1 June 2012.

Capital gains on shares
Capital gains realised by a Belgian company (or Belgian branch) on shares are 100% tax exempt (if certain conditions are met). Under the new rule (Act of 29 March 2012), an extra condition is introduced, being a minimum holding period of an uninterrupted period of one year in full ownership. If the capital gain is realised before the minimum holding period of one year is reached, the capital gain is taxed at a rate of 25.75% (25% plus a 3% crisis tax plus tax increase in case of insufficient prepayments). There are some exceptions (e.g. for financial institutions).

Capital losses on shares continue to be non-deductible.

Entry into force: The new rule is applicable as of tax year 2013 and on capital gains realised as of 28 November 2011 during a taxable period closing on or after 6 April 2012. Any change made as of 28 November 2011 to the closing date of the annual accounts will be disregarded.

Thin capitalisation rules
Before the Act of 29 March 2012, Belgian tax law did not have general thin capitalisation rules. A specific thin capitalisation rule existed for interest payments or attributions to (real) beneficiaries taxed at low rates on that interest. This was the so-called 7:1 debt-to-equity ratio.

The new thin capitalisation rule according to the Program Act of 29 March 2012 replaces the 7:1 rule with a new rule introducing a 5:1 debt-to-equity ratio. Note that the entry into force will be determined by a Royal Decree, no later than 1 July 2012.

For the purposes of the thin capitalisation rule, equity is defined as the sum of the taxed reserves at the beginning of the taxable period and the paid-up capital at the end of the taxable period. For the purposes of this new rule, certain non-taxed reserves are deemed to be taxed reserves. It regards certain tax-free reserves created upon a merger/ de-merger (e.g. as a result of merger goodwill).

For the purposes of the thin capitalisation rule, debt is defined as:

- all loans, whereby the beneficial owner is not subject to income taxes, or, with regard to the interest income, is subject to a tax regime that is substantially more advantageous than the Belgian tax regime, and
- all intra-group loans (whereby 'group' should be interpreted in accordance with section 11 of the Companies Code).

Bonds and other publicly issued securities are excluded, as well as loans granted by financial institutions.

Interest payments or attributions in excess of the 5:1 ratio are not tax deductible. The new thin capitalisation rule is not applicable to loans contracted by (movable) leasing companies (as defined by article 2 of the Royale Decree n° 55 of 10 November 1967) and companies whose main activity consists of factoring or immovable leasing and this within the financial sector and to the extent the funds are effectively used for leasing and factoring activities.

An anti-abuse rule is introduced stating that in case the loans are guaranteed by a third party or in case loans are funded by a third party that partly or wholly bears the risk related to the loans, the third party is deemed to be the beneficial owner of the interest, if the guarantee or the funding has tax avoidance as main purpose.

According to the draft program law of 15 May 2012, the proposed thin capitalisation rules will modify in order to safeguard companies having a centralised treasury function in Belgium. The amendment will introduce a netting for thin capitalisation purposes at the level of the interest payments and interest income related to the centralised financing function/cash pool function.

Company cars

Disallowed expenses
The Act of 28 December 2011 introduces an additional disallowed expense in relation to company cars.

The new disallowed expense is 17% of the new benefit in kind. This new disallowed expense cannot be offset against the NID, tax losses, or other tax deductions. Thus, the new disallowed expense results in a minimum tax base.

Entry into force: Benefits in kind attributed as of 1 January 2012.

Withholding tax (WHT) measures

Dividend WHT
- The current general WHT rate of 25% does not change.
- The current 15% rate (applicable in certain cases) becomes 21%.
- The WHT rate applicable to liquidation surpluses remains at 10%.
- The WHT rate on redemptions of own shares increases from 10% to 21%.
- The numerous WHT exemptions (specifically for payments to companies) are not affected.

Belgium

Entry into force: Income attributed or made payable as of 1 January 2012.

Interest WHT
The WHT on interest increases from (generally) 15% to 21%.

The numerous WHT exemptions (especially for payments to companies) are not affected.

Entry into force: Income attributed or made payable as of 1 January 2012.

Royalty WHT
The standard 15% WHT rate on royalties does not change. The numerous WHT exemptions are also not affected.

Taxes on corporate income

Corporate income tax (CIT)
In general, the tax base for CIT purposes is determined on an accrual basis and consists of worldwide income less allowed deductions. The rules are equally applicable to companies and permanent establishments (PEs). It is assumed that all income received by a company is, in principle, business income. The income tax base is based on the Belgian Generally Accepted Accounting Principles (GAAP) financial statements of the company.

General rate
CIT is levied at a rate of 33% plus a 3% crisis tax, which is a surtax, implying an effective rate of 33.99%. This rate applies to both Belgian companies (subject to Belgian CIT) and Belgian branches of foreign companies (subject to Belgian non-resident CIT). Capital gains on shares realised without meeting the one year holding requirement are taxed at 25.75% (25% plus a 3% crisis tax).

Reduced rates
A progressive scale of reduced rates applies to taxpayers with lower amounts of taxable income. If the taxable income is lower than 322,500 euros (EUR), the following rates apply (including the 3% crisis tax):

Taxable income (EUR)	CIT rate (%)
0 to 25,000	24.98
25,001 to 90,000	31.93
90,001 to 322,500	35.54

Even if their taxable income does not exceed the aforesaid ceilings, certain companies are excluded from the reduced rate and always subject to the normal CIT rate. These companies include, amongst others, companies that are owned 50% or more by one or more companies.

Surcharge

A surcharge is due on the final CIT amount upon assessment (including the crisis surtax). The surcharge can be avoided if sufficient advance tax payments are made (*see Payment of tax in the Tax administration section for more information*). For tax year 2012 (i.e. financial years ending between 31 December 2011 inclusive and 30 December 2012 inclusive), the surcharge is 2.25%.

Secret commissions tax

A special assessment of 309% (300% plus 3% crisis tax) is applicable to so called 'secret commissions', which are any expense of which the beneficiary is not identified properly by means of proper forms timely filed with the Belgian tax authorities. These expenses consist of:

* Commission, brokerage, trade, or other rebates, occasional or non-occasional fees, bonuses, or benefits in-kind forming professional income for the beneficiaries.
* Remuneration or similar indemnities paid to personnel members or former personnel members of the paying company.
* Lump-sum allowances granted to personnel members in order to cover costs proper to the paying company.

The secret commissions tax is not applicable if the payer demonstrates that the payments have been reported in the beneficiary's Belgian tax return. The 309% rate is also applicable to hidden profits that are not part of the property of the company, with the exception of certain specific hidden reserves. The special assessment of 309% and the expenses themselves are, however, fully deductible for CIT purposes.

Local income taxes

No tax is levied on income at the regional or local level. Note that immovable assets (land, building, and possibly machinery and equipment) situated within the Belgian territory are, in principle, subject to an immovable WHT that is levied locally.

....

Corporate residence

A company is considered to be a resident of Belgium for tax purposes if it has its registered office, its principal place of business, or its seat of management in Belgium. The seat of management has been defined by Belgian case law as the place from where directing impulses emanate or the place where the company's effective management and central administration abide, meaning the place where the corporate decision-making process actually takes place.

Permanent establishment (PE)

The definition of a Belgian establishment under Belgian domestic tax law corresponds, but is broader than, the definition of a PE under both either the Organisation for Economic Co-operation and Development (OECD) Model Tax Convention (OECD MC) or Belgium's double tax treaties (DTTs). Since the latter prevail over domestic law, Belgium cannot levy tax if a non-resident has a Belgian establishment that does not constitute a PE under the relevant DTT. Although Belgium would not be entitled to tax the profit attributable to the Belgian establishment in such a case, the foreign company should still abide by certain formal tax requirements (e.g. filing a non-resident tax return, responding to requests for information).

Belgium

Other taxes

Value-added tax (VAT)

Scope of VAT
The following transactions are subject to VAT in Belgium:

- The supply of goods effected for consideration by a taxable person acting as such.
- The supply of services effected for consideration by a taxable person acting as such.
- The importation of goods.
- Intra-Community acquisition of goods for consideration by a taxable person acting as such or by a non-taxable legal person.

Intra-Community supply and intra-Community acquisitions
An intra-Community supply of goods is a supply of goods whereby the goods are moving from one European Union (EU) member state to another EU member state. In the member state of departure of the goods, the goods can be, under certain conditions, VAT exempt. As a result, the intra-Community acquisition of the goods (i.e. the arrival of the goods in the other member state) will be taxable.

Standard and other VAT rates
The standard VAT rate is 21%. This rate applies to all goods and services not qualifying for one of the reduced VAT rates.

The following supplies of goods and services have a 12% VAT rate:

- Restaurant and catering services, excluding beverages.
- Phytopharmaceutical products.
- (Inner) tubes.
- Certain combustible material.

The following supplies of goods and services have a 6% VAT rate:

- Works on immovable property (limited in time and with strict conditions).
- Basic necessities, such as food and pharmaceuticals.
- Some printed materials.
- Transport services of persons.
- Hotels and camping.
- Admission to cultural, sporting, and entertainment venues.

The following supplies of goods and services are VAT exempt with credit ('zero-rated'):

- Exports and certain related services.
- Intra-Community supplies of goods.
- Certain transactions on goods placed in a Customs or VAT warehouse.
- Cross-border passenger transportation by ship or aircraft.
- Supplies to diplomats and international organisations.
- Certain supplies of goods and services to certain vessels and aircrafts mainly involved in international passenger transport.

The following supplies of goods and services are VAT exempt without credit:

- Healthcare services.
- Social services.

- Education services.
- Sport services.
- Cultural services.
- Services of lawyers.
- Banking services.
- Interest charges.
- Financial services.
- Insurance services.
- Land and real estate sales.
- Property leasing and letting.

It should be noted that specific conditions may apply to the above two categories.

VAT grouping
VAT grouping came into effect in Belgium on 1 April 2007. Under a VAT group, independent legal persons are treated as one single taxable person for VAT purposes if they are closely linked financially, economically, and organisationally. Hence, for VAT purposes, all supplies of goods and services to or by the group members are deemed to be made to or by the group itself.

The application of a VAT group has, amongst other, the following consequences:

- No issuance of 'inter-company' invoices between companies in the VAT group.
- No charging of VAT between companies in the VAT group.
- Filing of one VAT return for all companies in the VAT group.
- No risks of incorrect VAT treatment of transactions between companies in the VAT group.
- No cascade of the limitation of the right to deduct VAT when on charging costs to companies in the VAT group.

Import duties
Goods coming from outside the European Union and imported into Belgium are subject to import duties. Import duties are calculated based on three main elements:

Classification
All products are classified based on the rules laid down in the Combined Nomenclature (CN). A single commodity code (CN-code) applies for every product. An import duty rate is linked to every CN-code.

Origin
Based on international trade agreements, a preferential import duty rate (read: a lower import duty rate) may apply to products imported in the European Union meeting the origin criteria in the country participating in the agreement.

Valuation
The customs value is determined based on one of the six rules laid down in the Community Customs Code. These valuation rules are harmonised on a global level through the General Agreement on Tariffs and Trade (GATT) valuation agreement.

Various economic customs regimes are available allowing optimisation schemes throughout the supply chain.

Excise duties
Excise products are divided into the following two groups:

Belgium

- Community excise products: These are defined as excise products at the EU-level, and the same procedures should apply in all EU member states. Products in scope are (i) alcohol, (ii) alcoholic beverages, (iii) energy products, and (iv) manufactured tobacco.
- National excise products: These are defined by the individual countries. Specific Belgian legislation applies to the national excise products, which are (i) non-alcoholic beverages and (ii) coffee.

The excise duty rates for community and national excise products are fixed at the national level and vary and change regularly. Excise legislation includes compliance.

Registration duties
Purchases and transfers of real estate located in Belgium, including buildings (except new buildings, which are subject to VAT as described above), are subject to registration duty at the rate of 12.5% of the higher of transfer price or fair market value (except in the Flemish Region, where the applicable rate is 10%).

In cases where the purchase or transfer of land is subject to VAT, no registration duties will be charged on the purchase or transfer.

In principle, no registration duty is due upon a capital contribution; only a fixed fee of EUR 25 is due.

Stamp duties
Stamp duties are due on transactions relating to public funds that are concluded or executed in Belgium, irrespective of their (Belgian or foreign) origin, to the extent that a professional intermediary intervenes in these transactions. Exemptions for non-residents and others are available.

Branch income

Branch profits are subject to the normal tax rate for Belgian corporations of 33.99% (or 25.75% for certain capital gains on shares not meeting the one-year holding period) plus the possible surcharge for absence/insufficiency of advance payments (*see the Taxes on corporate income section*). Transfers of branch profits to the head office abroad do not give rise to further taxation in Belgium. Branches can benefit from the reduced CIT rates under specific conditions (*see the Taxes on corporate income section*).

Capital gains realised on real estate located in Belgium by non-resident companies are subject to a professional withholding tax (WHT) at the normal CIT rate of 33.99%. The professional WHT is in fact an advance payment of the final Belgian non-resident CIT and can be offset against it. Any balance is refundable.

In general, taxable basis is the difference between the profits actually realised and the tax-deductible costs actually incurred in the hands of the Belgian branch as determined from the separate set of accounts of the Belgian branch. Please note, however, that no legal requirement exists to keep a separate set of accounts in the hands of the PE, in case no legal branch is deemed to exist in Belgium.

Should no separate set of accounts be kept, the taxable basis in the hands of the Belgian branch, in principle, will be determined on the basis of the Royal Decree implementing the BITC. As a result, the yearly taxable basis will be determined on 10% of the gross turnover realised in Belgium with a minimum of EUR 7,000 per employee and an

Belgium

absolute minimum of EUR 19,000. Note that such determination of the taxable basis is often formalised in a written agreement with the local Belgian tax inspector without deviating from the tax law criteria as mentioned.

Income determination

Inventory valuation
Belgian accounting law provides for the following four methods of inventory valuation: the method based on the individualisation of the price of each item, the method of the weighted average prices, the last in first out (LIFO) method, and the first in first out (FIFO) method. All of these methods are accepted for tax purposes.

Capital gains
Capital gains are subject to the normal CIT rate. For tax purposes, a capital gain is defined as the positive difference between the sale price less the costs related to the disposal of the asset and the original cost of the acquisition or investment less the depreciations and write-offs which have been deducted for tax purposes.

Capital gains realised on tangible fixed assets and intangible assets can be subject to a deferred and spread taxation regime, provided that the following conditions are cumulatively met:

* The assets realised have been held by the company for more than five years, and depreciations have been claimed on them for tax purposes.
* The proceeds of the transfer are reinvested fully in tangible or intangible assets subject to depreciation in Belgium within three years (or five years in the case of reinvestments in buildings, vessels, or aircrafts).

If the above conditions are met, the taxation of the net capital gain is spread over the depreciation period allowed for tax purposes of the asset that is acquired to fulfil the reinvestment obligation. Deferred and spread taxation occurs at the normal CIT rate.

Net capital gains realised on shares are 100% tax exempt if dividends from such shares would meet the 'taxation conditions' under the dividends-received deduction regime (*see the Deductions section for more information*). The 'minimum participation condition' provided under that regime needs not be satisfied for capital gain exemption.

Recently, a minimum holding period of an uninterrupted period of one year in full ownership was introduced in order to qualify for the capital gain exemption on shares.

The minimum holding requirement is applicable as of tax year 2013 and on capital gains on shares realised as of 28 November 2011 during a taxable period closing on or after 6 April 2012. Any change made as of 28 November 2011 to the closing date of the annual accounts will be disregarded.

If the capital gain is realised before the minimum holding period of one year is reached, the capital gain is taxed at a rate of 25.75% (25% plus a 3% crisis tax plus tax increase in case of insufficient prepayments). There are some exceptions (e.g. for financial institutions).

Dividend income
Dividends received by a Belgian company are first included in its taxable basis on a gross basis when the dividends are received from a Belgian company or on a

Belgium

net basis (i.e. after deduction of the foreign WHT) when they are received from a foreign company.

Provided certain conditions are met, 95% of the dividend income can be offset by a dividends-received deduction (DRD).

Dividends-received deduction (DRD)

A DRD of 95% of dividend income can be applied under certain conditions (*see below*). Any unused portion of the DRD from dividends received from a European Economic Area (EEA) subsidiary or a subsidiary from a country with which Belgium has concluded a DTT with a non-discrimination clause on dividends can be carried forward to future tax years. The possibility of carrying forward the unused portion of DRD from qualifying non-EEA dividends has not been codified, but should continue to apply based on an October 2009 practice note. The same also applies for dividends from Belgian subsidiaries.

The DRD is subject to a (i) minimum participation condition and (ii) a taxation condition.

Minimum participation condition

According to the minimum participation condition, the recipient company must have, at the moment of attribution, a participation of at least 10% or an acquisition value of at least EUR 2,500,000 in the distributing company. However, that condition neither applies to dividends received or attributed by investment companies nor to dividends attributed by intra-municipal organisations. The beneficiary of the dividend must have been holding the full legal ownership of the underlying shares for at least one year prior to the dividend distribution or commit to hold it for a minimum of one year.

Taxation condition

The taxation condition, in summary, means that the dividend income received must have been subject to tax at the level of the distributing company and its subsidiaries if the former redistributes dividends received.

The taxation condition is based on five 'exclusion' rules and certain exceptions to these rules. Basically, the exclusion rules apply to the following:

- Tax haven companies, which are companies that are not subject to Belgian CIT (or to a similar foreign tax) or that are established in a country where the common taxation system is notably more advantageous than in Belgium. Countries in which the minimum level of (nominal or effective) taxation is below 15% qualify as tax havens for the application of the regime (a list of tainted countries has been published). The common tax regimes applicable to companies residing in the European Union are, however, deemed not to be notably more advantageous than in Belgium.
- Finance, treasury, or investment companies that, although are subject in their country of tax residency to a taxation system similar to that of Belgium as mentioned in the item above, nevertheless benefit from a taxation system that deviates from the one commonly applicable.
- Offshore companies, which are companies receiving income (other than dividend income) that originates outside their country of tax residency and in these countries such income is subject to a separate taxation system that deviates substantially from the common taxation system.

- Companies having branches that benefit globally from a taxation system notably more advantageous than the Belgian non-resident corporate taxation system. This exclusion is deemed not applicable to EU companies with an EU branch.
- Intermediary holding companies, which are companies (with the exception of investment companies) that redistribute dividend-received income, which on the basis of regulations mentioned under the items above would not qualify for the DRD for at least 90% of its amount in case of direct holding.

While this is a summary of the major exceptions, numerous exceptions to these exclusion rules exist and need to be analysed on a case-by-case basis.

Bonus shares (stock dividends)
Distribution of bonus shares to shareholders in compensation for an increase of the share capital by incorporation of existing reserves is, in principle, tax free. The situation may be different if the shareholder has the choice between a cash or stock dividend.

Interest, rents, and royalties
Interest that accrued, became receivable by, or was received by a company, and rents and royalties received by a company, are characterised as business profits and taxed at the general CIT rate of 33.99%. The income can be offset against available tax assets.

Foreign income
A Belgian resident company is subject to CIT on its worldwide income, and foreign source profits not exempt from taxation by virtue of a DTT (*see the treaty list in the Withholding taxes section*) are taxable at the normal CIT rate in Belgium (i.e. 33.99%, or 25.75% for certain capital gains).

A foreign tax credit may be available for foreign royalty income and foreign interest income. *See the Tax credits and incentives section for more information.*

Undistributed income of subsidiaries, whether or not they are foreign, is not subject to any Belgian income tax (i.e. no controlled foreign company [CFC] rules).

Deductions

As a general rule, expenses are tax deductible in Belgium provided that they are incurred in order to maintain or to increase taxable income, they relate to the taxpayer's business activity, they are incurred or have accrued during the taxable period concerned, and that evidence of the reality and the amount of such expenses is provided by the taxpayer.

Depreciation and amortisation
Depreciation of an asset is tax deductible to the extent that it results from a devaluation of the asset, and the devaluation effectively occurred during the taxable period concerned. The depreciation methods that are accepted by Belgian tax law are the straight-line method (linear method) and the double-declining balance method. In the latter case, the annual depreciation may not exceed 40% of the acquisition value. The double-declining method may not be used for intangible fixed assets, automobiles, minibuses and automobiles used for mixed purposes, and for assets, the use of which has been transferred to a third party (e.g. in the case of operational leasing).

Belgium

Depreciation rates are based on the estimated lifetime of the assets concerned, which are normally agreed upon by the taxpayer with the tax authorities. However, for certain assets, rates are set by administrative instructions as follows:

Assets	Depreciation rate (%)
Commercial buildings	3
Industrial buildings	5
Machinery and equipment (depending on the type)	20 or 33
Rolling stock	20

Intangible fixed assets have to be amortised over a period of at least five years for tax purposes (except research and development [R&D] expenses, for which the minimum amortisation period is three years).

For the year of acquisition of an asset, only the proportionate share of an annual depreciation calculation can be accepted as depreciation for income tax purposes (in principle to be computed on a daily basis). This provision, however, applies only to companies that cannot be considered as SMEs (*see the Tax credits and incentives section for the definition*). In contrast, SMEs can deduct a full year of depreciation in the year of acquisition.

Ancillary expenses incurred at the time of acquisition must be depreciated in the same way as the asset to which they relate (i.e. no full deduction in the year of acquisition, except for SMEs). Alternatively, ancillary expenses relating to the acquisition of land can be written down and such write-downs, if they are justified, may constitute a deductible expense.

Goodwill
Belgian accounting and tax laws allow amortisation of goodwill arising at the occasion of an asset deal. For Belgian tax purposes, the amortisation period, which depends on the elements included in the goodwill, is a minimum of five years, and the straight-line method must be applied. According to the Minister of Finance, '*clientele*' (client lists) should be amortised over a period of ten to 12 years. The aforesaid accounting and tax amortisation for goodwill is not available in the case of mergers or de-mergers that occur tax free (i.e. they, among other things, follow the continuity principle from an accounting perspective).

Start-up expenses
Incorporation costs, at the election of the taxpayer, may be deducted fully in the year of incorporation or can be depreciated over a maximum period of five years.

Interest expenses
Interest paid is not tax deductible to the extent that it exceeds an amount corresponding to the market rate, taking into account factual circumstances proper to the appraisal of the risk linked to the operation and particularly the financial situation of the debtor and the duration of the loan. The latter test, however, is not applied with respect to interest paid to a Belgian-based financial institution.

Provisions and bad debt reserves
Provisions and bad debt reserves are tax deductible provided that:

- they are set up to cover clearly identified losses and charges (i.e. not to cover 'general' risks that have been rendered probable by events) which took place during the taxable period concerned
- they are booked at the end of the financial year in one or more separate accounts on the balance sheet
- they are reported on a specific form enclosed with the tax return, and
- they relate to losses and charges that are deductible for Belgian tax purposes.

Charitable contributions
Charitable contributions may not be less than EUR 40 and may not exceed 5% of the total net income of the taxable period, with a maximum of EUR 500,000 to be tax deductible. The law includes an exhaustive list of gifts that are deductible, including gifts in cash to certain social, cultural, or scientific organisations. Gifts to other organisations are deductible if approved by a Royal Decree or by (mediation of) the Minister of the Federal Public Service of Finance.

Automobile costs
As of 1 January 2010, the deductibility rate of automobile costs in the hands of Belgian companies (and Belgian branches) varies in a range between 50% and 120% of the automobile costs, depending on the CO_2 emission of the automobile.

Moreover, the deduction for fuel costs has been limited to 75% as of 1 January 2010.

An additional disallowed expense in relation to company cars entered into force as of 1 January 2012. The new disallowed expense is 17% of the benefit in kind. This new disallowed expense cannot be offset against the NID, tax losses, or other tax deductions. Thus, the new disallowed expense results in a minimum tax base.

Taxes, fines, and penalties
Belgian resident and non-resident CIT, including advance tax payments, any surcharge imposed in case of insufficient advance tax payments, any interest for late payment of the CIT, and any Belgian movable WHT, is not tax deductible in Belgium. Immovable WHT (i.e. real estate tax), secret commissions tax and foreign taxes, however, are considered as tax deductible.

Regional taxes and contributions, including penalties, increases, ancillary expenses, and interest for late payment, are not tax deductible in Belgium (certain exceptions apply).

Any administrative and judicial fines or penalties (except for VAT proportionate fines) are not tax deductible in Belgium.

Disallowed expenses
The following expenses are not tax deductible in Belgium (this list is not exhaustive):

- 31% of restaurant expenses.
- 50% of representation expenses and business gifts (there are exceptions).
- Advantages granted to employees for social reasons with certain exceptions (e.g. hospitalisation insurance premiums, gifts of a small value).
- Capital losses on shares (except in the case of liquidation, up to the amount of paid-up capital of the liquidated company).
- Brokerage, commissions, commercial discounts, or other payments allocated directly or indirectly to a person in the form of a Belgian public bribery.
- 17% of the benefit in kind of company cars.

Belgium

Net operating losses

Principle: carryforward without limitation in time
Tax losses can, in principle, be carried forward without any limitation in time.

Change of control
In case of change in control of a Belgian company (e.g. if the shares of the company are transferred and along with them the majority of the voting rights), the amount of tax losses and notional interest deduction carried forward available in that company (before the change of control) can no longer be offset against future profits unless the change can be justified by legitimate needs of a financial or economic nature in the hands of the loss realising company (i.e. evidence must be brought that the change is not purely tax driven).

The condition of legitimate needs of a financial or economic nature is considered to be fulfilled when the employees and activities of the company are maintained by the new shareholder or when the company's control is acquired by a company belonging to the same consolidated group of companies as the former controlling company.

A ruling can be obtained from the Belgian tax authorities to obtain upfront certainty on the Belgian tax treatment of the contemplated operation, so as to ensure the losses are not forfeited as a result of a change of control.

Tax-free merger or (partial) de-merger
In the case of a taxfree merger or (partial) de-merger, Belgian tax law provides for a partial transfer/maintenance of the rollover tax losses of the absorbed/absorbing company. The carried forward tax losses of the companies involved are then reduced based on the proportionate net fiscal value of the company (before the restructuring) compared to the sum of the net fiscal values of both the merging entities (before the restructuring).

No carryback
There is no tax loss carryback provision under Belgian tax law.

Payments to foreign affiliates
A Belgian corporation can claim a deduction for royalties, management service fees, and interest charges paid to foreign affiliates, provided such amounts are at arm's length. However, when such payments are made, either directly or indirectly, to a foreign person, entity, or branch which is not subject to tax or is subject to a tax regime that is notably more advantageous than the Belgian tax regime on such income, there is a reversal of the burden of proof. Such charges will be disallowed unless the Belgian enterprise can prove that the payments are reasonable and that they correspond to genuine and real transactions.

Fees, commissions, etc. paid to beneficiaries located in foreign countries, which are not properly reported on Form 281.50 and Summary Form 325.50, will, in principle, be subject to the secret commissions tax (of 309%), unless the taxpayer can prove that the beneficiaries have declared this income in their Belgian tax return.

Payments to tax havens
Companies subject to Belgian CIT or Belgian non-resident CIT that make direct or indirect payments to recipients established in tax havens are obligated to declare them if they are equal to or exceed EUR 100,000 during the tax year. The reporting has to be made on a special form to be attached to the (non-resident) CIT return.

In the event of nonreporting, the payments will be disallowed expenses for CIT purposes. Where the payments have been reported duly and timely, their tax deductibility will be subject to the ability of the taxpayer to prove that (i) said payments were made as part of genuine, proper transactions and (ii) they were not made to an entity under an artificial construction.

A tax haven is defined as: (i) a jurisdiction regarded by the OECD as not being cooperative concerning transparency and international exchange of information or (ii) a jurisdiction where the nominal corporate tax rate is less than 10%. A royal decree containing the list of countries where the nominal corporate tax rate is lower than 10% is published. The countries which are mentioned in the royal decree are the following:

- Abu Dhabi
- Ajman
- Andorra
- Anguilla
- the Bahamas
- Bahrain
- Bermuda
- British Virgin Islands
- Cayman Islands
- Dubai
- Fujairah
- Guernsey
- Jersey
- Jethou
- Maldives Islands
- Isle of Man
- Micronesia (Federation of)
- Moldavia
- Monaco
- Montenegro
- Nauru
- Palau
- Ras el Khaimah
- Saint-Barthelemy
- Sark
- Sharjah
- Turks and Caicos Islands
- Umm al Qaiwain
- Vanuatu
- Wallis-and-Futuna

Group taxation

Belgium does not apply any tax consolidation mechanism with respect to corporate tax.

Transfer pricing

The arm's-length principle is formally codified in the BITC. In addition, the authorities can make use of other, more general, provisions in the BITC to challenge transfer prices (e.g. the general rules on the deductibility of business expenses). The BITC contains provisions that tackle artificial inbound or outbound profit shifting. These are the so-called provisions on abnormal or gratuitous benefits.

If a Belgian tax resident company grants an abnormal or benevolent benefit, the benefit should be added back to the taxable income as a disallowed expense unless the benefit was taken into account to determine the taxable basis of the beneficiary. Even if the abnormal or gratuitous benefit is taken into account for determining the taxable basis of the beneficiary, the tax deductibility of the related expenses can still be denied in the hands of the grantor. Notwithstanding the above exception, the abnormal or benevolent benefit should be added back to the taxable income when the benefit is being granted to a non-resident affiliated company. Such granted abnormal or benevolent benefits can be offset against any tax deductible items (e.g. tax losses carried forward, notional interest deduction).

If a Belgian tax resident company receives an abnormal or benevolent benefit, and to the extent that such benefit is received from a related company, the benefit received cannot be offset by the Belgian company against its current year or carryforward tax losses or other tax deductions (e.g. dividends-received deduction, patent income deduction, notional interest deduction, and investment deduction). According to the position of the tax authorities, the taxable basis of a Belgian company equals at least the amount of the benefit received.

Belgium

There are no specific transfer pricing documentation requirements or rules on the selection of transfer pricing methods included in the Belgian tax legislation. Nevertheless, the Belgian tax authorities adhere to the OECD Transfer Pricing Guidelines for Multinational Enterprises and Tax Administrations and the EU Code of Conduct. In the administrative guidelines that were issued, taxpayers are urged to proactively compile a coherent and consistent documentation set, although there is no legal obligation to do so.

Belgium has a special transfer pricing investigation unit with a mission to (i) build up and share transfer pricing expertise and (ii) carry out transfer pricing audits of multinationals present in Belgium through a subsidiary or branch.

Thin capitalisation
Before the Act of 29 March 2012, Belgian tax law did not have general thin capitalisation rules. A specific thin capitalisation rule existed for interest payments or attributions to (real) beneficiaries taxed at low rates on that interest. This was the so-called 7:1 debt-to-equity ratio.

The new thin capitalisation rule according to the Program Act of 29 March 2012 replaces the 7:1 rule with a new rule introducing a 5:1 debt-to-equity ratio. Note that the entry into force will be determined by a Royal Decree, no later than 1 July 2012.

For the purposes of the thin capitalisation rule, equity is defined as the sum of the taxed reserves at the beginning of the taxable period and the paid-up capital at the end of the taxable period. For the purposes of this new rule, certain non-taxed reserves are deemed to be taxed reserves. It regards certain tax-free reserves created upon a merger/de-merger (as a result of merger goodwill).

For the purposes of the thin capitalisation rule, debt is defined as:

- all loans, whereby the beneficial owner is not subject to income taxes, or, with regard to the interest income, is subject to a tax regime that is substantially more advantageous than the Belgian tax regime, and
- all intra-group loans (whereby 'group' should be interpreted in accordance with section 11 of the Companies Code).

Bonds and other publicly issued securities are excluded, as well as loans granted by financial institutions.

Interest payments or attributions in excess of the 5:1 ratio are not tax deductible. The new thin capitalisation rule is not applicable to loans contracted by (movable) leasing companies (as defined by article 2 of the Royale Decree n° 55 of 10 November 1967) and companies whose main activity consists of factoring or immovable leasing and this within the financial sector and to the extent the funds effectively are effectively used for leasing and factoring activities.

An anti-abuse rule is introduced stating that in case the loans are guaranteed by a third party or in case loans are funded by a third party that partly or wholly bears the risk related to the loans, the third party is deemed to be the beneficial owner of the interest, if the guarantee or the funding has tax avoidance as main purpose.

According to the draft program law of 15 May 2012, the proposed thin capitalisation rules will modify in order to safeguard companies having a centralised treasury function in Belgium. The amendment will introduce a netting for thin capitalisation purposes at the level of the interest payments and interest income related to the centralised financing function/cash pool function.

Excess profit rulings

The Belgian tax authorities have at their disposal instruments to make both upward and downward adjustments to a taxpayer's Belgian taxable basis in case of non-arm's-length dealings. Belgium will refrain from taxing profits that a Belgian tax resident company would not have realised if it had not been party to related-party dealings.

As the cost structure (or the profit potential) of a member of a multinational group of companies will normally differ from that of a stand-alone entity, its profit will normally also be higher. Applying the arm's-length principle, this profit differential, which does not result from the functions performed and risks assumed by the respective entities, should not be allotted to the Belgian group member. As such, Belgian tax law allows for unilateral adjustments of the Belgian tax base similar to the corresponding adjustments in Article 9 of the OECD Model Convention. The underlying assumption is that the 'excess profit' forms part of the profits of the foreign related party.

The part of profit that is deemed to derive from related-party dealings and that is exempted from taxation in Belgium and how the 'part-of-the-profits-of-the-foreign-related-party' condition should be interpreted will need to be submitted to the Belgian Ruling Office to obtain a ruling in advance. Such rulings are granted for renewable periods of five years and are based on a detailed functional, economic analysis of the relevant Belgian activities with a view to determining a profit level commensurate with the company's functional and risk profile.

Tax credits and incentives

Foreign tax credits (FTCs)

Unilateral relief from double taxation of foreign-source income may be provided in the form of an exemption, credit, or tax reduction, depending on the type of income. Where taxable, foreign income is subject to tax only on its net amount (i.e. after deduction of expenses and foreign taxes).

Dividend income FTC

Generally, no FTC is available for foreign dividends.

Royalty income FTC

Unless a more advantageous provision (e.g. a tax sparing provision) would apply based on a DTT concluded by Belgium (*see the treaty list in the Withholding taxes section*), a FTC is granted under Belgian tax law with respect to foreign royalty income, provided that this income has effectively been subject to taxation in its source country. This FTC is equal to 15/85 of the net frontier amount (i.e. after deduction of foreign WHT) of the royalty. The FTC is included in the taxable basis of the recipient company and is only creditable against Belgian income tax to the extent that said foreign income is included in the taxable basis of the Belgian company. Excess FTC, if any, is not refundable.

Interest income FTC

Unless a more advantageous provision (e.g. a tax sparing provision) would apply based on a DTT concluded by Belgium (*see the treaty list in the Withholding taxes section*), the Belgian beneficiary of foreign interest income is entitled to a FTC under Belgian tax law, provided that this income effectively has been subject to taxation in its source country. The computation of the FTC is based on the net frontier interest income (i.e. after

Belgium

deduction of foreign WHT) and adjusted with a ratio taking into account the financial cost. The FTC is included in the taxable base of the Belgian lender. It is creditable against the CIT due but is not refundable in case of excess.

Notional interest deduction (NID)

Belgian corporate income taxpayers can claim NID for tax purposes, reflecting the economic cost of the use of capital, equal to the cost of long-term, risk-free financing. The NID rate for a given tax year is, in principle, based on the ten-year government bond interest rate for the calendar year two years prior to the tax year (e.g. for tax year 2012, reference is made to 2010 government bonds). The NID rate is 3.425% (3.925% for SMEs) for tax year 2012 (financial year 2011). The NID rate for tax year 2013 is 3% (3.5% for SMEs).

An SME is a company that does not exceed more than one of the following criteria during the two foregoing financial years when evaluated on a consolidated level: a yearly average number of employees of 50, a turnover of EUR 7.3 million (excluding VAT), or total asset value of EUR 3.65 million.

A company that employs more than 100 employees on the basis of an annual average workforce is automatically considered to be a 'large' company.

As of tax year 2013, (accounting years ending between 31 December 2012 and 30 December 2013, both dates inclusive) the NID rate is capped at 3%.

Note that the 2012 Belgian budget agreement provides that new excess NID can no longer be carried forward (to be enacted by the Belgian parliament), whereas, under the current rules, 'excess NID' (i.e. NID that cannot be claimed owing to the taxpayer having insufficient taxable income) can be carried forward for a maximum of seven years.

However, under the proposed rules, the 'stock' of excess NID (stemming from previous years, i.e. tax years 2012 and before) can still be carried forward for seven years (as is currently the case), though the excess NID that can be applied in a given year will be limited to 60% of the taxable profit (i.e. the profit remaining after setting off carried-forward tax losses and other tax deductions). The 60% limit will only be applicable to the part of taxable profit exceeding EUR 1 million. The portion of excess NID that cannot be used due to the '60% rule' (i.e. 40% of taxable profit minus EUR 1 million) can be carried forward indefinitely.

As for determining the basis on which this deduction is calculated, the company's share capital plus its retained earnings, as determined for Belgian generally accepted accounting principles purposes and as per the last year-end date, will have to be taken into account.

Certain adjustments to the equity should be made in order to avoid double use. The accounting equity as per the last year-end date has to be reduced by, amongst others, (i) the fiscal net value of financial fixed assets qualifying as participations and other shares, and (ii) in case of a company that has a foreign PE, located in a jurisdiction with which Belgium has concluded a tax treaty, the positive difference between the net book value of assets attributable to the foreign PE and the liabilities (other than equity). Whether or not the latter adjustment is in violation with the EU freedom of establishment is currently being investigated by the European Court of Justice.

In addition, various adjustments should be made in order to avoid abuse.

Belgium

Investment deductions

The investment deduction is a deduction from the tax base in addition to the normal tax depreciation on, amongst others, qualifying patents, environmentally friendly R&D investments, and energy-saving investments.

A company can benefit from a one-shot investment deduction of 15.5% (for tax year 2013, i.e. financial years ending between 31 December 2012 inclusive and 30 December 2013 inclusive) of the acquisition value of qualifying investments. With respect to environmentally friendly R&D investments, a company can also opt for a spread investment deduction of 22.5% (for tax year 2013) of the depreciation on qualifying environmentally friendly R&D investments.

In case of insufficiency or absence of taxable profits, the investment deduction can be carried forward without any limitation in time or in amount. Certain restrictions apply as to the maximum amount of investment deduction carried forward that is tax deductible in a given year.

Under certain conditions, the investment deduction carried forward can be lost after a change of ownership (see Net operating losses in the Deductions section).

Note that the investment deduction for patents and R&D cannot be combined with the tax credit for patents and R&D.

Patents and R&D tax credit

As an alternative for the above investment deduction for patents and R&D, a company may opt for a tax credit for which the advantage corresponds to the advantage of the investment deduction (i.e. 15.5% one-time and 22.5% for a spread investment deduction), multiplied by the normal CIT rate of 33.99%. The investment deduction implies a deduction of the taxable basis, while the tax credit is a reduction of the tax due. A key advantage of the tax credit for patents and R&D is that it is refundable if it has not been deducted for five subsequent tax years.

Note that the amount of the tax credit should be deducted from the basis of the notional interest deduction.

Reduced payroll tax for qualifying researchers

75% of the payroll tax withheld from wages of qualifying researchers by a Belgian company or establishment does not need to be remitted to the Belgian Tax Revenue provided that the researchers are employed in research and development programmes and have a qualifying degree (such as a degree in (applied) sciences, veterinary medicines, bio-technology, etc.). For the employee's personal tax liability, the Belgian Tax Revenue considers that the payroll WHT amount entirely was withheld.

Patent income deduction (PID)

The PID allows a taxpayer to deduct, as an extra tax deduction in the tax return, 80% of qualifying gross patent income. Therefore, only 20% of gross patent income will be taxable at the normal CIT rate (33.99%), resulting in a maximum effective tax rate of 6.8%.

Qualifying taxpayers are corporate taxpayers in Belgium that are involved in the development or further improvement of patents through an in-house R&D centre. They include both Belgian companies and Belgian PEs of foreign companies. The company must be the owner, licencee, or usufruct holder of the patents for which they claim the benefits of the PID.

Belgium

To benefit from the PID, the R&D centre should qualify as a 'branch of activity' or 'line of business', which means that it should be a division of an entity that is capable of operating autonomously. The Belgian company or PE should have relevant substance to perform and supervise research and development activities, but may use subcontractors, related or unrelated, in its development of the patents or extended patent certificates. The R&D centre can be located outside Belgium but must belong to a Belgian legal entity.

Belgian companies or PE's acting as 'contract R&D' service providers on behalf of another company cannot qualify for PID because they are not the owners, holder of beneficial rights to, or licencee of the patent.

Qualifying patents

The PID applies where patents or supplementary protection certificates are owned by a Belgian company or establishment as a result of its own patent-development activities (partly or fully) in an R&D centre in Belgium or abroad. The PID also applies where patents or supplementary protection certificates are acquired by a Belgian company or establishment from a related or unrelated party, in full ownership, joint ownership, usufruct, or via license agreement, provided it has further improved the patented products or processes in the company's R&D centre in Belgium or abroad.

Other intellectual property (IP), such as copyrights, know-how, designs, trade or marketing intangibles, are as such not eligible for the Belgian PID.

The Belgian company or establishment can license the patents to other parties. Alternatively, it can use the patents, which are owned by it or licensed to it, to manufacture and supply patented products or services.

For patents licensed by the Belgian company or establishment to any party, whether related or unrelated, the tax deduction amounts to 80% of the relevant patent income to the extent the income does not exceed an arm's-length price.

For patents used by the Belgian company or establishment for the manufacture of patented products, manufactured by itself or by a contract manufacturer on its behalf, the tax deduction is 80% of the license fee (known as 'embedded royalties') that the Belgian company would have received had it licensed the patents used in the manufacturing process to an unrelated party.

No advance ruling is required to benefit from this deduction since it is applicable generally and automatically. Only minor compliance formalities apply. The taxpayer should submit a special application form together with the CIT return.

Withholding taxes

Domestic corporations and branches of foreign corporations paying dividends, interest, royalties, and/or certain rentals are required to withhold tax. The standard rates applicable under Belgian tax law are fixed at 25% for dividends, 21% for interest, and 15% for royalties and certain rentals. However, some WHT reductions/exemptions are foreseen under Belgian domestic tax law.

- A reduced Belgian WHT of 21% applies to dividend distributions relating to non-preference shares subscribed in cash, issued as of 1 January 1994 and which, upon issuance, are nominative or have been deposited with a financial institution in

B

Belgium, on condition that the distributing company does not irrevocably renounce its right to benefit from the reduced rate of WHT.

- A reduced Belgian WHT of 21% is possible for dividend distributions relating to non-preference shares issued as of 1 January 1994 in the context of a public offering (i.e. shares quoted on the stock exchange) on condition that the distributing company does not irrevocably renounce its right to benefit from the reduced rate of WHT.
- Under certain conditions, a reduced WHT of 21% applies to dividend distributions made by companies (located in the EEA) quoted on a stock market or by companies whose capital has been (partly) contributed by a PRIVAK/PRICAF (located in the EEA), which must also be quoted on a stock market. A PRIVAK/PRICAF is a company with the sole objective of collective investment in non-quoted companies and in growth companies.
- A WHT exemption is foreseen for the distribution of profits made by a Belgian subsidiary to an EU parent company, if both the parent and subsidiary have a legal form that is mentioned in the Annex to the EU Parent-Subsidiary directive, if both are subject to CIT, and if the parent company holds during an uninterrupted period of at least one year a shareholding of at least 10% in the capital of the distributing company (implementation of the Parent-Subsidiary directive). If the one-year holding requirement is not fulfilled at the time of distribution, the distributing company provisionally should withhold the amount of WHT due (but it does not have to pay the tax authorities). Once the one-year holding requirement is met, the provisionally withheld tax amount can be paid out to the parent company. If the one year holding requirement eventually is not complied with (e.g. because the Belgian participation is disposed of by the parent company before the one year holding requirement is met) then the Belgian company has to pay the amount provisionally withheld increased by interest for late payment (at an annual rate of 7%) to the competent services of the Belgian tax authorities.
- The application of the Parent-Subsidiary directive to dividend payments has been extended towards non-EU-resident companies. Dividends distributed towards a country that has concluded a tax treaty with Belgium containing a qualifying exchange of information clause can be exempt from WHT, subject to the same conditions as laid down in the Parent-Subsidiary directive.
- A 21% tax is applicable to the redemption of its own shares by a company.
- A 10% tax is applicable to profits that are attributed or made payable as a result of the full or partial liquidation of a company. However, the exemption of Belgian WHT is maintained for liquidation proceeds distributed by a BEVEK (*Beleggingsvennootschap met veranderlijk kapitaal*)/SICAV (*Société d'investissment à capital variable*), for dividends resulting from tax-free mergers, and for liquidation proceeds resulting from the redemption of own shares by a company listed on a regulated stock exchange. If the conditions described above apply, an exemption is also available.
- There is a WHT exemption on interest on loans granted by professional investors to banks established in the EEA or in a country which has concluded a DTT with Belgium. For example, banks situated in France, the United Kingdom, or the United States should be able to benefit from this exemption.
- No Belgium interest WHT arises where two related companies with tax residence outside Belgium are involved in a financial transaction with the intervention of a Belgium based intra-group financial enterprise. Under these circumstances, the Belgium intra-group financial enterprise is not required to retain Belgium interest WHT if the entity merely intervenes as 'paying agent intermediary'.
- Belgian domestic tax law also provides for a WHT exemption on the following movable income sourced in Belgium (this list is not exhaustive):

Belgium

- Income from deposits allocated or attributed to non-resident savers by Belgian banks.
- Income from bonds, treasury bonds, or other similar instruments of which the beneficiaries are identified as financial institutions.
- Income from receivables (this includes income from commercial receivables) or loans of which the beneficiaries are identified as financial institutions or professional investors. Professional investors are defined as any Belgian resident company or branch not being a financial institution or any equivalent. As a result, interest payments between two Belgian companies are exempt from WHT. The applicability of this exemption has been extended. As a result, on transactions with banks situated in a country with which Belgium has concluded a DTT, no withholding will be due. In practice this means that on transactions with inter alia French, UK, and US banks no withholding will be due.
- Income from bonds paid by a Belgian resident financial institution or by a Belgian resident company to non-resident savers, provided that such bonds are registered on a nominal basis with the debtor of the income during the entire period to which the interest relates and that the foreign beneficiaries of the interest are not located in a tax haven country or held by more than 50% by Belgian residents.
- Income from bonds and loans granted to 'eligible quoted companies' and 'eligible intra muros financial companies' to non-residents (under certain conditions).
- Interest payments between a Belgian company and an EU tax resident company in case of direct or indirect shareholding of at least 25% for an uninterrupted period of at least one year (i.e. transposition of EU Interest & Royalty directive in Belgian tax law).

With respect to payments made to non-resident corporations or individuals, WHT exemptions and/or reductions can also be found in the double taxation treaties concluded by Belgium.

Recipient	WHT (%)		
	Dividends	Interest (6)	Royalties, certain rentals (6)
Non-resident corporations and individuals			
Non-treaty:	25	21	15
Treaty:			
Albania	5/15 (4)	5	5
Algeria	15 (4)	15	5/15
Argentina	10/15 (4)	12	3/5/10/15
Armenia	5/15 (4)	10	8
Australia	15 (4)	10	10
Austria	15 (4)	15	10
Azerbaijan	5/10/15 (4)	10	5/10
Bangladesh	15 (4)	15	10
Belarus	5/15 (4)	10	5
Bosnia-Herzegovina (1)	10/15 (4)	15	10
Brazil	10/15 (4)	10/15	10/15/20 (7)
Bulgaria	10 (4)	10	5
Canada	5/15 (4)	10	0/10
Chile	0/15 (4)	5/15	5/10
China, P.R. (2)	10 (4)	10	10

Belgium

Recipient	WHT (%)		
	Dividends	Interest (6)	Royalties, certain rentals (6)
Congo	5/10 (4)	10	10
Croatia	5/15 (4)	10	0
Cyprus	10/15 (4)	10	0
Czech Republic	5/15 (4)	10	5/10
Denmark	15 (4)	10	0
Ecuador	15 (4)	10	10
Egypt	15/20 (4)	15	15/25
Estonia	5/15 (4)	10	5/10
Finland	5/15 (4)	10	5
France	10/15 (4)	15	0
Gabon	15 (4)	15	10
Georgia	5/15 (4)	10	5/10
Germany	15/25 (4)	0/15	0
Ghana	5/15 (4)	10	10
Greece	5/15 (4)	5/10	5
Hong Kong	0/5/15 (4)	10	5
Hungary	10 (4)	15	0
Iceland	5/15 (4)	10	0
India	15 (4)	10/15	20 (7)
Indonesia	10/15 (4)	10	10
Ireland, Republic of	15 (4)	15	0
Israel	15 (4)	15	10
Italy	15 (4)	15	5
Ivory Coast	15 (4)	16 (4, 7)	10
Japan	5/15 (4)	10	10
Kazakhstan	5/15 (4)	10	10
Korea, Republic of	15 (4)	10	10
Kuwait	0/10 (4)	0	10
Kyrgyzstan (3)	15	15	0
Latvia	5/15 (4)	10	5/10
Lithuania	5/15 (4)	10	5/10
Luxembourg	10/15 (4)	0/15	0
Macedonia (1)	10/15 (4)	15	10
Malaysia	0/15 (4)	10	10
Malta	15 (4)	10	0/10
Mauritius	5/10 (4)	10	0
Mexico	5/15 (4)	10/15	10
Moldova (3)	15	15	0
Mongolia	5/15 (4)	10	5
Montenegro (1)	10/15 (4)	15	10
Morocco	6.5/10 (4)	10	10
Netherlands	5/15 (4)	0/10	0
New Zealand	15 (4)	10	10
Nigeria	12.5/15 (4)	12.5	12.5
Norway	5/15 (4)	15	0

Belgium

	WHT (%)		
Recipient	Dividends	Interest (6)	Royalties, certain rentals (6)
Pakistan	10/15 (4)	15	15/20 (7)
Philippines	10/15 (4)	10	15
Poland	5/15 (4)	5	5
Portugal	15 (4)	15	10
Romania	5/15 (4)	10	5
Russia	10 (4)	10	0
Rwanda	0/15 (4)	0/10	10
San Marino	0/5/15 (4)	10	5
Senegal	15/16 (4)	15/16	10
Serbia (1)	10/15 (4)	15	10
Singapore	0/5/15 (4)	5	5
Slovakia	5/15 (4)	10	5
Slovenia	5/15 (4)	10	5
South Africa	5/15 (4)	10	0
Spain	15 (4)	10	5
Sri Lanka	15 (4)	10	10
Sweden	5/15 (4)	10	0
Switzerland	10/15 (5)	10 (5)	0
Taiwan	10 (4)	10	10
Tajikistan (3)	15	15	10
Thailand	15/20 (4)	10/25	5/15
Tunisia	5/15 (4)	5/10	11
Turkey	15/20 (4)	15	10
Turkmenistan (3)	15	15	0
Ukraine	5/15 (4)	2/10	0/10
United Arab Emirates	5/10 (4)	5	0/5
United Kingdom	5/10 (4)	15	0
United States	0/5/15 (4)	0/15	0
Uzbekistan	5/15 (4)	10	5
Venezuela	5/15 (4)	0/10	5
Vietnam	5/10/15 (4)	10	5/10/15

Notes

1. The treaty concluded with ex-Yugoslavia is still applicable to Bosnia-Herzegovina, Macedonia, Serbia, and Montenegro.
2. Not applicable to Hong Kong. Note that a new treaty with China has been signed (but not yet into force). The rates under the new treaty are 5% and 10% for dividends, 10% for interest, and 7% for royalties.
3. The treaty concluded with the former USSR is still applicable to Kyrgyzstan, Moldova, Tajikistan, and Turkmenistan.
4. It concerns an EU country or the treaty contains a qualifying exchange of information clause. Hence, the rate of 0% is applicable subject to the same conditions as invoked by the Parent-Subsidiary directive (see above). Where multiple rates apply, the difference is generally based on the percentage of participation the recipient holds (directly) in the capital of the company paying the dividends.
5. Under the Bilateral II agreement concluded between Belgium and Switzerland, a rate of 0% is applicable under certain conditions.
6. With respect to EU countries, a WHT exemption is applicable provided that the conditions laid down in the Interest & Royalty directive are met (see above).
7. Since the Belgian domestic rate for interest is maximum 21% and for royalties is maximum 15%, the higher treaty rate will in principle not be applicable on interest and royalties arising from Belgium.

The treaties which are currently in force are listed above. The following tax treaties are signed, modified, or under renegotiation but have not yet entered into force (including some for the exchange of information clause): Andorra, Anguilla, Antigua & Barbuda, Australia, Bahamas, Bahrain, Belize, China, Czech Republic, Denmark, Dominica, Isle of Man, Finland, France, Germany, Gibraltar, Greece, Grenada, Iceland, Italy, Japan, Korea, Luxembourg, Macao, Macedonia, Malaysia, Malta, Moldova, Monaco, Montserrat, the Netherlands, New Zealand, Norway, Oman, Qatar, Saint Kitts & Nevis, Saint Lucia, Saint Vincent & the Grenadines, San Marino, Seychelles, Singapore, Spain, Tajikistan, Uganda, and the United Kingdom.

Tax administration

Taxable period
The assessment is based on the taxable income of a financial year. For the application of the rules on statutory limitations and of new laws, an assessment year is related to each taxable period. If the financial year corresponds with the calendar year, the assessment year is the following calendar year (e.g. financial year closing 31 December 2012 corresponds with assessment year 2013). If the financial year does not correspond with the calendar year, the assessment year equals the calendar year during which the financial year ends (e.g. financial year closing 30 June 2012 corresponds with assessment year 2012).

Tax returns
As a general rule, the annual resident or non-resident CIT return cannot be filed less than one month from the date when the annual accounts have been approved and not later than six months after the end of the period to which the tax return refers. For instance, assuming that the accounting year has been closed on 31 December 2012, the corporate tax return needs to be filed, in principle, by 30 June 2013 at the latest (this deadline is often postponed).

Payment of tax
CIT is payable within two months following the issue of the tax assessment. Interest for late payment is charted at the (non-cumulative) rate of 7% per year.

The advance tax payments needed to avoid the CIT surcharge (*see the Taxes on corporate income section*) can be made in quarterly instalments. In the situation where the company's financial year ends on 31 December 2011, the due dates for the advance tax payments are 10 April 2012, 10 July 2012, 10 October 2012, and 20 December 2012. Advance tax payments give rise to a tax credit. The tax credit amounts to 3%, 2.5%, 2%, or 1.5% of the advance tax payment made, depending on whether such payment has been made respectively in the first, second, third, or fourth quarter (percentages applicable for tax year 2012). If the total amount of credits exceeds the surcharge, no surcharge is due, but the excess is not further taken into account for the final tax computation. The taxpayer can choose to either have the excess reimbursed by the tax authorities as the excess can be used as an advance tax payment for the next year.

Audit cycle
A tax audit normally begins with a written request for information from the tax inspector. The taxpayer must provide the data requested within (in principle) one month. Any documentary evidence considered relevant to the audit can be requested and reviewed by the authorities. Once the tax inspector has completed the analysis, any adjustment is proposed in a notification of amendment outlining the reasons for the proposed amendment. The taxpayer has 30 days to agree or to express disagreement.

Belgium

The tax inspector then makes an assessment for the amount of tax that the tax inspector believes is due (taking into account any relevant comments of the taxpayer with which the inspector agrees). Thereafter, the taxpayer has six months within which to lodge an appeal with the Regional Director of Taxes. The decision of the Regional Director of Taxes may be appealed and litigated. In a number of circumstances, the intervention of the courts can be sought prior to receiving the decision of the Regional Director of Taxes.

Statute of limitations

Based on the Belgian income tax statute of limitations, the period during which the tax authorities are authorised to perform a tax audit and adjust the taxable basis is three years (except in cause of fraud, where the statute of limitations is extended to seven years) starting from the first day of the assessment year, unless the company's financial year does not correspond to the calendar year. Note that with respect to payroll tax or movable WHT, the statute of limitations period is five years.

Belgian ruling practice

Belgium has a long tradition of providing formal and informal rulings. Currently, a taxpayer may request an advance tax ruling on a wide range of subjects including but not limited to: CIT, individual tax, non-resident income tax, legal entity income tax, VAT, customs, and registration duties. The request should cover a 'specific and concrete' operation, which effectively is envisaged to be realised in a foreseeable future. The ruling should be filed before the transaction takes place. In practice, the ruling decision should be granted prior to the filing of the CIT return of the year of the transaction. A ruling is binding upon the Belgian tax authorities for a renewable period of a maximum of five years. Delivery of a requested ruling takes, on average, three months.

The Ruling Office is autonomous from the Belgian tax authorities and has the legal authority to issue decisions, which are binding upon the Belgian tax authorities. The Ruling Office increasingly has adopted a constructive approach towards the taxpayer and is seen in the Belgian tax practice as a powerful insurance instrument ascertaining the Belgian tax treatment of contemplated operations.

Topics of focus for tax authorities

Topics of interest to Belgian tax authorities include:

- Significant increase in transfer pricing audits by the special transfer pricing investigation unit.
- Payments of management fees or technical support fees.
- The deductibility of interest payments (e.g. to tax haven companies).
- Transactions with entities based in tax havens.
- Lump-sum allowances.
- Substance.

Bermuda

PwC contact

Richard (Rick) Irvine
PricewaterhouseCoopers
Dorchester House
7 Church Street West
Hamilton HM 11, Bermuda
Tel: +1 441 299 7136
Email: richard.e.irvine@bm.pwc.com

Significant developments

The Bermuda government has extended the tax exemption granted to Bermuda companies under the Exempt Undertakings Act of 1976 from 28 March 2016 until 2035. The extended Undertaking provides protection to companies from any newly enacted taxes on income or capital gains until 2035. Existing companies are required to apply for the tax exemption extension.

Taxes on corporate income

Income tax and taxes on capital gains are not imposed on corporations in Bermuda.

Corporate residence

Entities that are incorporated in Bermuda are considered to be resident in the country.

Other taxes

Value-added tax (VAT)
There is no VAT or sales tax in Bermuda.

Customs duties
Customs duties are imposed on almost all goods arriving on the island at varying rates.

Excise taxes
There are no excise taxes imposed in Bermuda.

Property taxes
A land tax is imposed on all developed land throughout Bermuda, with certain exceptions. The tax is assessed on the annual rental value of each valuation unit, depending on whether such unit is a private dwelling or any other dwelling. The owner of the valuation unit is liable for the land tax.

Private dwellings are taxed on a progressive scale of tax rates that ranges between 0.6% and 19% based on the annual rental value of the unit, while commercial properties are taxed on a single rate of tax of 4.4%.

Transfer taxes
There is no transfer tax imposed in Bermuda.

Bermuda

Stamp taxes
Bermuda does impose a stamp duty on certain types of legal instruments; however, exempt companies are not subject to stamp duty.

Social insurance
If an employer has employees in Bermuda for 26 or more weeks in a calendar year, the employer will have to register and obtain an account number from the Department of Social Insurance (DSI) (unless previously registered) and pay social insurance tax for its employees. At the same time, the employer must also apply for and obtain from the DSI a social insurance number for each employee, which is required to pay social insurance. Once the employer has registered for a social insurance account number and the employees have obtained social insurance numbers, the DSI will automatically send an electronic print-out to the employer with an itemised list of employees as well as the amount of social insurance tax due for the month. Under certain facts and circumstances, the employer may also file an Employee Amendment Form, which shows any change in status (i.e. termination or unpaid leave) of employees that could affect the amount of social insurance tax due.

The amount of social insurance tax due is calculated as 60.80 Bermudian dollars (BMD) per employee per week (effective 1 April 2010), with the employer and employee each paying half of the liability (or BMD 30.40). The employer must pay and remit monthly (for all employees), to the DSI, the total social insurance tax due per employee. The amount of social insurance tax due per month is based on the number of Mondays in the month and must be paid by the end of the following month. Employed persons over the age of 65 are not required to pay their half (BMD 30.40). The employer continues to pay their half (BMD 30.40).

Payroll tax
Under Section 3 of the Payroll Taxes Act 1995, an employer (viewed as the entity that has control over an individual's remuneration) is required to remit payroll taxes (currently 14% on all remuneration paid or given, up to a maximum compensation of BMD 750,000) for each of its employees whose employment in Bermuda exceeds four consecutive weeks in a calendar year (whether or not with one or more employers). If an employee's stay in Bermuda is for a period of less than four consecutive weeks, the employer is not obligated to remit the payroll taxes.

Once an employee's service period in Bermuda has exceeded four consecutive weeks, the employer must register the employee with the Office of the Tax Commissioner (OTC). The employer must obtain a payroll tax account number by filing an application with the OTC, if no previous account exists for such employee. The application must be filed within seven days after the end of the quarterly tax period (the four quarters end on 1 January, 1 April, 1 July, and 1 October) in which the employee's stay exceeded four consecutive weeks. A payroll tax return and remittance of tax must be filed with the OTC 15 days after the end of each quarterly period (i.e. 15 January, 15 April, 15 July, and 15 October). A return is due only when an employee's stay exceeds four consecutive weeks in a tax period. The employer may recover from the employee a maximum of 5.25% of the 14% payroll tax, and the employer is allowed an exemption of BMD 600 (of remuneration paid) per employee for each quarterly tax period. Penalties for tax returns filed late are 5% of the payroll tax due for each month (or part thereof) that the tax return is late (with a maximum of 30%).

Compensation subject to the payroll tax under the Payroll Taxes Act includes all remuneration paid or given to the employee. Remuneration includes:

- Wages, salary, leave pay, commission, gratuity, fee, bonus, perquisite, or allowance.
- Money paid under a profit-sharing scheme.
- Money or anything of value paid or given to an employee or ex-employee in connection with the permanent termination of employment.
- Any amount paid with respect to a retirement or provident fund, scheme, or society, or under a hospital or health insurance scheme.
- The value of meals, boarding, lodging, or other benefit of any kind, whether provided in cash or otherwise.
- The rental value of any place of residence provided rent-free, or the difference between the rent paid and the rental value if the rent paid is lower than the rental value.
- Any gain on the exercise or right to acquire company stock based on services rendered.

All employers or self-employed persons are required to report remunerations up to a maximum of BMD 750,000 per annum per employee, deemed employee, or self-employed person. There is no payroll tax on remunerations above BMD 750,000.

Please note that the Payroll Taxes Act is extremely broad in its definition of remuneration. Therefore, a Bermuda employer should take caution when calculating the amount of remuneration paid to an employee.

Annual company fee
Every exempted company shall, in the month of January, forward to the Registrar of Companies a declaration, signed on behalf of the company, as to the company's principal business and its assessable capital together with the appropriate fee payable. For the purposes of the Companies Act 1981, an exempted company means a local company which does not comply with the requirements of the Companies Act 1981. Exempt companies are generally owned by non-Bermudans.

Assessable capital of the exempted company (BMD)	Annual company fee (BMD)
0 to 12,000	1,870
12,001 to 120,000	3,820
120,001 to 1,200,000	5,890
1,200,001 to 12,000,000	7,850
12,000,001 to 100,000,000	9,815
100,000,001 to 500,000,000	17,530
500,000,001 or more	29,220

Corporate services tax
A 4% corporate service tax is imposed on a provider of corporate services in respect of gross earned revenue derived from an exempted undertaking for taxable corporate services provided during a tax period. Corporate services include corporate administrative services, corporate management services, corporate secretarial services, the provision of a registered office, the performance of functions in the capacity of director or resident representative, and the provision of accounting and/or financial services.

Hotel occupancy tax
A 7.25% tax is imposed on revenue received from hotels and other forms of accommodation.

Bermuda

Betting duty
There is a betting duty charge of 20% imposed on all bets made, received, or negotiated by a person licensed under the Betting Act of 1975.

Branch income

Branches are treated the same as other corporations doing business in Bermuda.

Income determination

Since income taxes are not imposed on corporations in Bermuda, income determination is not relevant in the context of Bermuda taxation.

Deductions

Since income taxes are not imposed on corporations in Bermuda, deductions from income are not relevant in the context of Bermuda taxation.

Group taxation

Since income taxes are not imposed on corporations in Bermuda, group taxation is not relevant in the context of Bermuda taxation.

Tax credits and incentives

Bermuda offers no specific tax incentives.

Withholding taxes

There are no withholding taxes in Bermuda.

Tax administration

Since income taxes are not imposed on corporations in Bermuda, tax returns are not required to be completed for corporate income tax compliance purposes. *For information regarding tax returns, due dates, and the payment of tax for non-income taxes imposed in Bermuda (e.g. Social insurance and Payroll tax), please see the Other taxes section.*

Other issues

Foreign exchange controls
Exempt companies and permit partnerships are considered as non-residents for exchange control purposes. This allows these entities to make dividend payments, distribute capital, open and maintain foreign bank accounts, maintain bank accounts in any currency, and purchase securities.

Bermuda

There is a Foreign Currency Purchase Tax imposed at the rate of 1% on foreign currency purchased by a resident from a local bank.

Tax treaties

There are no tax treaties between Bermuda and other nations due to the fact that Bermuda does not impose direct taxes. However, Bermuda has a double taxation agreement (DTA) with the Kingdom of Bahrain and a limited tax treaty with the United States which only applies to 'enterprises of insurance'. Bermuda also has tax information exchange agreements (TIEAs) with the following 24 countries: Aruba, Australia, Canada, China, Denmark, Faroe Islands, Finland, Germany, France, Greenland, Iceland, India, Ireland, Italy, Japan, Mexico, Netherlands, Netherlands Antilles, New Zealand, Norway, Portugal, Sweden, the United Kingdom, and the United States.

Under certain circumstances, the United States-Bermuda Tax Treaty provides for relief from taxation of insurance business profits. The business profits of a Bermudian insurance company will not be taxed in the United States unless a company has a permanent establishment (PE) in the United States. The United States-Bermuda Tax Treaty also provides for mutual assistance on tax matters. The purpose of a mutual assistance provision is to prevent or decrease tax avoidance. The United States also believed that having a tax treaty with Bermuda would be beneficial for the United States-Bermuda diplomatic relations.

Bermuda's DTA with the Kingdom of Bahrain includes a provision for the full exchange of information on criminal and civil tax matters, consistent with the internationally agreed standard for transparency and the exchange of information for tax purposes set by the Organisation for Economic Co-operation and Development (OECD).

Bolivia

PwC contact

César O Lora Moretto
PricewaterhouseCoopers
Avenida Mariscal Santa Cruz y Yanacocha
Edificio Hansa, 19th floor
La Paz
Bolivia
Tel: +591 2 240 8181
Email: cesar.lora@bo.pwc.com

Significant developments

Law 154, passed July 2011, established that compliance of taxes is mandatory and that it is not subject to a 'statute of limitation' period. This is in line with the provisions set forth under the tax policy included in the Bolivian Constitution approved in February 2009. Note that the current Bolivia Tax Code does still establish a period of four years (five in practice) in which the tax authorities have the right to review and recalculate taxes determined by taxpayers. Further regulations are expected to understand how provisions of Law 154 will be applied.

The Bolivian government, through Law 169, passed in September 2011, has restricted the utilisation of accumulated tax losses to the following three fiscal years. Note that financial institutions cannot utilise tax losses accumulated through December 2010; however, tax losses generated starting from fiscal year 2011 can be utilised over the following three fiscal years, as stated above. In addition, Law 169 establishes that new entrepreneurial productive projects with a minimum capital of 1 million bolivianos (BOB) can utilise tax losses over the five fiscal years following the start-up of operations. Finally, tax losses cannot be restated due to inflation in any case.

In late 2011, the Bolivian government, through Law 211, approved an additional income tax for financial institutions (except for development banks) with a return on equity index higher than 13%. This additional income tax rate is 12.5% and is applicable as of fiscal year 2012. Its calculation procedure has not yet been regulated.

In late 2011, the Bolivian government, through Law 212, introduced the 'solve et repete' instrument applicable to tax enquires above 15,000 *Unidad de Foremnto a la Vivienda* (UFV, which is a sort of local currency adjusted by inflation) (approximately 3,650 United States dollars [USD]) which will be appealed by taxpayers through a litigation process before a judicial court. This instrument states that taxpayers must first pay the tax enquiry (including restatement of the omitted tax by inflation, interest, and penalties) before starting the tax litigation process. If the result of the tax litigation process is in favour of the taxpayer, the Bolivian tax authorities will refund the taxpayer the wrongfully paid tax, including restatement by inflation calculated from the date of payment up to the date of the refund.

Taxes on corporate income

All companies in Bolivia are subject to CIT at a rate of 25%. The taxable base is the profit arising from financial statements prepared in accordance with Bolivian generally accepted accounting principles (GAAP), adjusted for tax purposes (i.e. by non-deductible and non-taxable items) as per the requirements established in the tax law and regulations.

Bolivia taxes the income generated by corporations following the 'income source' principle (i.e. on a territorial basis). Therefore, income arising from goods and assets located or utilised economically within Bolivian territory and from any activity carried out within the country is considered Bolivian income source. Hence, such income is subject to CIT, regardless of the nationality/residence of the parties involved in generating such income or the place where the contracts were subscribed.

Additional income tax on certain financial institutions
Note that as of fiscal year 2012, financial institutions (except for development banks) with a return on equity index higher than 13% must pay an additional income tax of 12.5%. The procedure to calculate this additional tax has not yet been regulated.

Surtax on extractive activities
There is an additional CIT at a rate of 25%, which affects only extractive activities of non-renewable natural resources (mining and oil/gas). This additional tax is calculated on the same basis as the normal CIT, except that two additional deductions are allowed: (i) up to 33% of the accumulated investment as from 1991; and (ii) 45% of the gross revenue of each extractive operation (e.g. a field or a mining site) with a threshold of BOB 250 million for each extractive operation.

Special taxes on mining companies
In addition to the general CIT of 25% and the 25% surtax on extractive activities, all mining companies are also subject to an additional tax, calculated on the taxable net profits, at the following rates:

- 12.5%, if the mining company carries out exploitation activities.
- 7.5%, if the mining company carries out manufacturing activities with raw minerals that add value.

Mining companies are also subject to mining royalties at a rate of between 1% and 7% (depending on the kind of mineral), calculated on the total sales price. Note that there is a 60% discount on the rates of mining royalties if minerals are sold within the Bolivian market. Mining royalties can be offset against CIT if official mineral prices are lower than the prices established by the tax law; however, in this case, mining royalties paid will not be deductible for CIT purposes. On the contrary, if official mineral prices are higher than the prices established by the tax law, then mining royalties will be considered a deductible expense for CIT purposes.

Tax on gross income
The tax on gross income (also known as transaction tax) generally taxes gross income arising from the performance of any economic or commercial activity (including non-profitable activities) at a rate of 3% on a monthly basis. However, exceptions exist for the sale of investments (as defined by the Stock Exchange Law) and the sale of minerals, oil and gas within the local market, as long as such sales will ultimately be exported.

Corporations pay either CIT or transaction tax, whichever is higher. From an administrative perspective, CIT is due and paid at the end of each tax year and is considered an advanced payment of transaction tax, while transaction tax is due monthly. If during the year the cumulative monthly transaction tax due exceeds the CIT prepayment, the taxpayer will be subject to transaction tax on a monthly basis until the

Bolivia

end of the tax year. For example, a corporation pays CIT for the 2012 fiscal year in April 2013. This payment is considered a prepayment for the transaction tax due between May 2013 and April 2014.

Local income taxes
There are no local taxes on income in Bolivia.

Corporate residence

A corporation is considered resident in Bolivia if it has been incorporated in Bolivia.

Permanent establishment (PE)
Note that Bolivian commercial laws allow foreign corporations to carry out isolated commercial acts in Bolivia without the obligation to constitute a permanent representation in Bolivia; however, such corporations cannot carry out habitual commercial acts without fulfilling the requirements established to constitute a company in Bolivia (e.g. through either a subsidiary or a branch). Unfortunately, Bolivian legislation does not include provisions to regulate situations that could trigger PE nor does it define what should be understood by 'carrying out habitual commercial acts'.

Other taxes

Value-added tax (VAT)
VAT is levied on the sale of movable goods and provision of services carried out within Bolivian territory at a rate of 13%, including definitive importations. Since this tax is included in the final price, the effective tax rate amounts to 14.94% (13%/87%).

Customs duties
Definitive importations are also subject to customs duties at a rate of 10% and 5% for consumption goods and capital assets, respectively. Customs duties are calculated over the 'transaction value' of the merchandise valued as per Bolivian customs legislation, plus transportation and insurance costs.

Taxes on specific goods for consumption (excise tax)
Specific goods are taxed at the following rates:

Product	Tax rate (%)
Cigarettes and tobacco for pipes	50 to 55
Vehicles (except those of high capacity and weight, which will pay a 10% rate of excise tax)	18

Other specific products taxed by specific measure:

Product	Tax rate (BOB)
Soft drinks (except natural water and fruit juices)	0.31/litre
Energising drinks	3.50/litre
Maize liquor	0.62/litre
Alcohol	1.18/litre
Beers with 0.5% or more volumetric degrees	2.60/litre + 1%

Product	Tax rate (BOB)
Wines	2.40/litre + 5%
Ciders and sparkling wines (except maize liquor)	2.40/litre + 5%
Liquors and creams in general	2.40/litre + 5%
Rum and vodka	2.40/litre + 10%
Other brandies/liquors	2.40/litre + 10%
Whiskey	10.01/litre + 10%

Special tax on hydrocarbons and derived products

A tax is charged on the commercialisation of the following products within the local market, regardless of whether they are produced in Bolivia or imported:

Product	Tax rate (BOB)
Gasoline	1.23/litre
Premium gasoline	2.18/litre
Aviation gasoline	1.85/litre
Kerosene	0.29/litre
National jet fuel	0.32/litre
International jet fuel	4.28/litre
National diesel oil	0.00/litre
Agro fuel	0.00/litre
Fuel oil	1.25/litre

Direct tax on hydrocarbons

A direct tax on hydrocarbons (IDH) is applied on the production of hydrocarbons, measured at the wellhead point, at a rate of 32%. To determine the taxable base for this tax, production of hydrocarbons must be valued taking into account the average sales price and considering the market (internal/external) where such hydrocarbons were sold.

Property tax on real estate and vehicles

Real estate and vehicles are subject to a property tax calculated at different rates based on a scale value determined by the municipal government as follows:

Property value (BOB)		Property tax liability		
From	Up to	BOB	Plus (%)	over excess of (BOB)
0	200,000	0	0.35	0
200,001	400,000	700	0.50	200,000
400,001	600,000	1,700	1.00	400,000
600,001	Onwards	3,700	1.50	600,000

Vehicle value (BOB)		Vehicle tax liability		
From	Up to	BOB	Plus (%)	over excess of (BOB)
0	24,606	0	1.50	0
24,607	73,817	492	2.00	24,607
73,818	147,634	1,722	3.00	73,818
147,635	295,268	4,306	4.00	147,635
295,269	Onwards	10,949	5.00	295,269

Bolivia

Stamp taxes
There are no stamp taxes in Bolivia.

Financial transaction tax
A financial transaction tax is levied on bank transactions (deposit or transfer of funds), carried out within the domestic financial system, at a rate of 0.15%.

Special tax on lottery and gambling games
A specific tax on lottery and gambling games is applied in Bolivia. The tax is also applicable to business promotions that involve a raffle or random activities in providing awards in order to increase sales or attract clients. The tax rate for lottery and gambling games is 30%, whereas the tax rate for business promotions is 10%.

Social contributions
The Pension Law establishes employer social contribution obligations. Social tax charges for employers are equal to 16.71% of gross salary in general and 18.71% for the mining sector.

Branch income

Branch income is subject to the same tax applicable to other types of Bolivian corporations (i.e. CIT of 25%). However, note that net profits of Bolivian branches are deemed to be distributed to the head office at the annual filing due date for CIT (i.e. 120 days after the fiscal year end); hence, a Bolivian branch must withhold 12.5% on such deemed distributed profits. Note that this can be avoided as long as the head office decides to reinvest Bolivian branch's net profits.

Income determination

Taxable income is determined based on the financial statements prepared under Bolivian GAAP; then the income is adjusted for tax purposes in accordance with guidelines provided with respect to non-deductible and non-taxable items.

Inventory valuation
Inventories must be valued at replacement cost or market value for tax purposes, whichever is lower. Replacement cost is defined as the necessary costs incurred in acquiring or producing the assets as of the year-end, whereas market value is defined as the net value that the company would have obtained for the sale of assets in normal conditions as of the year-end, less commercialisation direct expenses.

Capital gains
Bolivian legislation does not include specific regulations for capital gains. Capital gains must be included in annual CIT if they are considered Bolivian-source income and hence will be taxed at a rate of 25%.

Dividend income
Dividend income obtained from domestic corporations subject to CIT must be excluded from the net taxable profits of the investor. Dividend income obtained from foreign corporations is not subject to CIT due to the fact that is not considered Bolivian-source income.

Interest income

Interest income is subject to annual CIT if loans have been economically utilised within Bolivian territory and hence associated interest is considered Bolivian-source income.

Rent/royalty income

Rent/royalty income is subject to annual CIT as long as the income comes from an asset situated or economically utilised in Bolivian territory.

Foreign income

Bolivian corporations are taxed only on income generated within Bolivian territory.

Deductions

As a general principle, expenses may be deducted for CIT purposes as long as they are necessary to generate Bolivian-sourced income and are properly documented.

Apart from the above, the Bolivian Tax Code (BTC) has established minimum amounts (BOB 50,000) for which taxpayers must document their economic transactions through documents of payments recognised by the Bolivian financial system and regulated by the *Autoridad de Supervisión del Sistema Financiero* (ASFI) (i.e. the bank regulator), including the possibility to document economic transactions through payments made via foreign financial institutions. Non-compliance with these requirements implies the lack of the possibility to compute input VAT and to deduct the associated expenses for CIT purposes.

Depreciation

Depreciation of fixed assets is permitted for CIT purposes if fixed assets contribute to generate taxable income. Depreciation must be calculated based on a straight-line method and considering useful lives included in tax law. Fixed assets which are not included in the tax law must be depreciated under a straight-line method in accordance with their useful lives, and this need to be communicated before the tax authorities within ten working days following the incorporation of the affected fixed assets.

Some of the assets included in the tax law are as follows:

Asset	Useful life (years)	Depreciation rate (%)
Building	40	2.5
Fixture and furniture	10	10.0
Machinery	8	12.5
Equipments and facilities	8	12.5
Vehicles	5	20.0
Computer equipment	4	25.0
Tools	4	25.0
Processing plants for the oil/gas industry	10	10.0
Pipeline	10	10.0
Aircraft	5	20.0
Ships and motorboats	10	10.0

Bolivia

Goodwill
Intangible assets (including goodwill) with a true cost can be deductible for tax purposes within a five-year period as long as taxpayers have paid a price for their acquisition.

Start-up expenses
Taxpayers may choose to deduct start-up expenses within the first fiscal period or distribute proportionally their amortisation within a four-year period, commencing the first year of operation. Note that start-up expenses cannot exceed 10% of paid-in capital.

Interest expense
Interest paid to owners or shareholders is not deductible to the extent the interest rate exceeds the London Interbank Offered Rate (LIBOR) plus 3% in the case of foreign owners/shareholders and to the extent the interest rate exceeds the official interest rate on loans published by the Central Bank of Bolivia for national owners/shareholders. Interest deductible on shareholder loans may not exceed 30% of the total interest paid to third parties.

Bad debt
Allowances for bad debt provisions are permitted if determined as required by law, which establishes an average method based on uncollectable receivables of the last three years. Uncollectable receivables are defined by current legislation as those which come from trade receivables and either: (i) remain unpaid for more than one year and have been sued without obtaining a seizure or (ii) when the receivables do not justify being sued due to the quantity of the receivables, remain unpaid for more than three years.

Charitable contributions
Donations are not deductible unless made to non-profit organisations that are not subject to CIT. These donations are deductible up to a maximum of 10% of the donor's net taxable profit.

Compensation expenses
Salaries, as well as associated compensations, paid to employees without the application of withholding taxes (WHT) (i.e. RC-IVA) are not deductible. Employees are subject to RC-IVA at a rate of 13%, which is calculated on the gross salary (including any other compensation in kind/cash) less social contributions and four minimum national salaries (approximately BOB 48,950). RC-IVA must be withheld and paid to the tax authorities by the employer on a monthly basis.

Provisions for employees' severance payments are deductible. Provisions of other bonuses (e.g. holiday, productivity bonuses) accrued on behalf of employees are tax deductible as long as they are paid prior to the annual CIT filing due date and the company demonstrates it has withheld taxes (if applicable).

Fines and penalties
Fines and penalties arising from late tax payments are not tax deductible (except interest and restatement by inflation associated with tax obligations).

Taxes
Taxes effectively paid by the corporation as a direct taxpayer, other than CIT, are deductible for tax purposes. Any transaction tax (tax on gross income) that has been offset against CIT paid is not deductible for CIT purposes.

Taxes paid in the acquisition of fixed assets are not deductible. These taxes must be included in the cost of the asset and depreciated accordingly.

Other significant items

In broad terms, the following additional items are not deductible for tax purposes, according to current legislation:

- Owners' or shareholders' personal withdrawals and living expenses.
- Fees paid to individuals (i.e. acquisition of goods and services) for which no WHT have been withheld.
- Amortisation of trademarks and other intangible assets, unless a price has been paid to acquire them.
- Provisions that are not specifically authorised by the tax law and regulations.
- Depreciation of fixed assets that include a revaluation reserve.
- Losses arising from illegal acts.

Net operating losses

Tax losses can be utilised over the following three fiscal years. New entrepreneurial productive projects with a minimum capital of BOB 1 million can utilise tax losses over the five fiscal years following the start-up of operations (including hydrocarbons and the mining sector).

Financial institutions cannot utilise tax losses accumulated through December 2010; however, tax losses generated starting from fiscal year 2011 can be utilised over the following three fiscal years, as stated above.

Tax losses cannot be restated due to inflation in any case.

Bolivian legislation does not envisage carryback provision for tax losses.

Payments to foreign affiliates

Payments to foreign affiliates are subject to a 12.5% WHT with no restriction if the Bolivian company is remitting Bolivian-sourced income (e.g. interest on loans, provision of any kind of services, royalties).

Group taxation

Bolivia does not include group taxation rules within its legislation.

Transfer pricing

Bolivian legislation does not include provisions for transfer pricing; however, transactions carried out between related companies must be performed at market value or as they were carried between third parties (i.e. sort of arm's-length principle) and any excess must be considered non-deductible for tax purposes. Note that there are not further regulations as regards to how taxpayers must demonstrate that transactions carried out between related parties were carried out at market value.

Thin capitalisation

Bolivian legislation does not include provisions for thin capitalisation apart from establishing restrictions on deductibility of interest when funding is provided by shareholders (*see Interest expense in the Deductions section*).

Bolivia

Tax credits and incentives

Investment incentives
No incentives are granted in Bolivia for domestic or foreign investment.

Export incentives
Export activities benefit from reimbursement of VAT and customs duties paid in the process of producing goods to be exported (with some limitations for oil/gas companies).

Other incentives
Foreign exchange transactions are legal in Bolivia, and a system of free-floating exchange rates exists.

Tourist and lodging services by hotels to foreign tourists without a residence or address in the country are exempt from VAT.

Regional manufacturing tax incentives
New investments in manufacturing in the states of Oruro and Potosi are entitled to the following tax exemptions:

Exemption	Conditions of exemption
Import tariffs and VAT on imported machinery	Machinery imported exclusively for the new industry until start-up of operations.
Import tariffs on imported inputs	They do not replace domestic inputs of the same kind and are destined to a transformation process. The exemption is granted for the first ten years of operation.
Transaction tax	For ten years from the start-up of operations.
CIT	For ten years from the start-up of operations if the amount exempt is reinvested in fixed assets in the following fiscal year.

Withholding taxes

Payments made to Bolivian residents
Dividends paid to Bolivian residents, either individuals or corporations, are not taxable.

Payments made by corporations to individuals with respect to the acquisition of goods or provision of services that are not supported with an invoice or fiscal receipt are subject to a WHT of 8% on goods and 15.5% on services.

Payments to non-residents
Dividend payments, distributions of profits to the head office by Bolivian branches, interest payments, royalty payments, and fees paid for any type of services made to non-residents are subject to a WHT of 12.5%.

Tax treaties
Bolivia currently has in force double tax treaties (DTTs) with the Andean Community (i.e. Colombia, Ecuador, and Peru), Argentina, France, Germany, Spain, Sweden, and the United Kingdom.

Beneficial WHT rates on dividend distributions are provided by DTT with Spain and Sweden at 10% and 0%, respectively, provided the Spanish or Swedish holding company demonstrates it is the ultimate beneficial owner and holds more than a 25% interest in the Bolivian company.

Tax administration

Taxable period
The taxable year is the fiscal year. The fiscal year varies according to the activity of the corporation. Banks and commercial and other service activities have a fiscal year end as of 31 December; industrial, oil, and gas companies as of 31 March; agribusiness and forestry companies as of 30 June; and mining companies as of 30 September.

Tax returns
CIT is assessed on a self-assessment basis every fiscal year, and the due date for submission is 120 days after the fiscal year-end. Tax returns must be accompanied by audited financial statements (if applicable) and ancillary tax information as requested by the tax authorities.

Payment of tax
CIT is payable in one annual payment 120 days after the fiscal year-end, except for mining companies which are obliged to make advance payments on a monthly basis with respect to the additional tax (i.e. 12.5% and 7.5% for exploitation and manufacturing mining companies, respectively).

Audit cycle
The tax audit process starts by a formal notification from the tax authorities where they indicate fiscal periods and taxes to be reviewed, together with a requirement of information. Tax inspection may generally take a 12-month period. Shortly after the provision of the finalisation of the tax inspection, a preliminary report of the tax audit's results is provided to the taxpayer in which the total tax debt is described (i.e. tax due, restatement, interests and penalties), together with the legal arguments supporting the tax enquires.

Taxpayers do have 30 days after receiving the preliminary report to present all supporting documentation and technical arguments if consider that the tax enquires do not have grounds to be claimed. Tax authorities do have 60 days to review all documentation/arguments provided by the taxpayer and then issue the final report, which is the formal document that could be subject to tax litigation, either via administrative process of by a judicial court.

Statute of limitations
According to the current Bolivian Tax Code, tax authorities do have a four year period (five in practice) to review and recalculate taxes determined by taxpayers. However, note that Law 154, approved in July 2011, establishes that compliance of taxes is mandatory and is not subject to a 'statute of limitation' period. This is in line with the provisions set forth under the tax policy included in the Bolivian Constitution approved in February 2009. Further regulations are expected to understand how provisions of Law 154 will be applied.

Bolivia

Topics of focus for tax authorities

There are not specific topics/taxes of focus in which the tax authorities address their review. This will generally depend on the nature of the taxpayer and the industry where they belong, e.g. a mining company could be more likely to be subject to tax inspections than an industrial company. There are no formal statistics to provide information in this regard.

Bosnia and Herzegovina

PwC contact

Krzysztof Lipka
PricewaterhouseCoopers d.o.o.
Fra Anđela Zvizdovića 1
71000 Sarajevo
Bosnia and Herzegovina
Tel: +387 33 295 234
Email: krzysztof.lipka@rs.pwc.com

Significant developments

Obligatory electronic filing of tax returns for companies in Republika Srpska (RS)

Companies operating in Republika Srpska that employ more than 15 employees
are obligated to file electronic personal income tax and social security
contributions returns.

The new Rulebook on submission of tax returns is published and applicable as from
April 2012.

Tax incentive expected to be re-introduced in Republika Srpska

Taxpayers who invest in equipment used in their own production activity in the
territory of Republika Srpska will be able to deduct the value of such investment from
the tax base under a tax incentive expected to be adopted by the RS government.
Only companies registered for production activity in accordance with the RS standard
classification code will be allowed to use this tax incentive, and the tax incentive will
need to be used in the tax period when the equipment is put to use.

Taxes on corporate income

Bosnia and Herzegovina consists of two entities: Federation of Bosnia and Herzegovina
(FBiH) and Republika Srpska (RS), with a third region, the Brčko District (BD), being
administered by both. Direct taxes are imposed at the entity/district level, while
indirect tax regulations are imposed at the state level. Corporate income tax (CIT)
systems in Bosnia and Herzegovina have been partially harmonised in the past few
years, but significant differences remain.

The Federation of Bosnia and Herzegovina, Republika Srpska, and the Brčko District tax
resident corporations on a worldwide basis. Non-residents are taxed on income realised
in the FBiH, RS, and BD territories.

FBiH CIT

A CIT payer in the Federation of Bosnia and Herzegovina is a resident business
association or other legal entity performing independent and permanent business
activity through the sales of products and providing services on the market for the
purpose of generating profit.

A CIT payer in the Federation of Bosnia and Herzegovina is also a non-resident who
generates profits through business activity from a business unit in the territory of the
Federation of Bosnia and Herzegovina.

Bosnia and Herzegovina

A non-resident whose registered seat or management is not in the Federation of Bosnia and Herzegovina and who does not have a business unit in the Federation of Bosnia and Herzegovina is subject to withholding tax (WHT) for income generated in the Federation of Bosnia and Herzegovina.

The CIT rate in the Federation of Bosnia and Herzegovina is 10%.

RS CIT

A CIT payer in Republika Srpska is:

- A legal entity from Republika Srpska that generates income from any source in Republika Srpska or abroad.
- A business unit of a legal entity that generates income in the territory of Republika Srpska.
- A non-resident legal entity that conducts business activity and has a permanent establishment (PE) in Republika Srpska, for income that is related to that PE.
- A non-resident legal entity that generates income from immovable property in Republika Srpska, for the income generated in Republika Srpska.
- A non-resident legal entity that generates income in Republika Srpska, not mentioned above, and is subject to WHT in accordance with the CIT law of Republika Srpska.

The CIT rate in Republika Srpska is 10%.

BD CIT

A CIT payer in Brčko District is:

- A legal entity from Brčko District that generates income from any source in Bosnia and Herzegovina or abroad.
- A business unit of a legal entity with headquarters in the Federation of Bosnia and Herzegovina or Republika Srpska, for income generated in Brčko District.
- A non-resident legal entity that conducts business activity and has a PE in Brčko District, for income that is related to that PE.
- A non-resident legal entity that generates income from immovable property in Brčko District, for the income generated in Brčko District.
- A non-resident legal entity that generates income in Brčko District, not mentioned above, and is subject to WHT in accordance with the CIT law of Brčko District.

The CIT rate in Brčko District is 10%.

Corporate residence

FBiH residency

Under FBiH CIT law, a resident is a legal entity whose headquarters (registration) is entered into a court registry or whose management and supervision over the business activities is located in the Federation of Bosnia and Herzegovina.

FBiH permanent establishment

A PE of a non-resident is a permanent place of business through which the non-resident performs activity in whole or partially throughout the territory of the Federation of Bosnia and Herzegovina.

A PE under FBiH CIT law is considered to be one of the following:

Bosnia and Herzegovina

- Management headquarters.
- Branch office.
- Business office.
- Factory.
- Workshop.
- Location of natural resources extraction.
- Construction site (construction or mounting project) when the work is performed during a period exceeding six months.
- Providing consulting or business services lasting for a period exceeding three months consecutively over a 12-month period.
- A representative acting independently on behalf of a non-resident related to the activities of signing a contract or keeping supplies of products delivered on behalf of a non-resident.

RS residency
Under RS CIT law, a resident is a legal entity registered in Republika Srpska.

RS permanent establishment
A PE is considered to be a place of business of a non-resident in Republika Srpska (i.e. construction works, installation and assembly works, infrastructure used for research or exploitation of natural resources or supervisory of the same). A PE shall also be considered to be a place of business where an individual or legal person has the authorisation to conclude contracts for a foreign legal entity.

BD residency
The BD CIT law prescribes that a resident is a legal entity registered in Brčko District.

BD permanent establishment
A PE of a non-resident in Brčko District is considered to be:

- construction works, installation and assembly works, infrastructure used for research or exploitation of natural resources, or supervisory of the same, or
- a place of business where an individual or legal person has the authorisation to conclude contracts for a foreign legal entity.

Other taxes

Value-added tax (VAT)
The standard VAT rate is 17%, and the VAT regime applies equally throughout the country of Bosnia and Herzegovina. There is no reduced VAT rate in Bosnia and Herzegovina.

Taxable persons are all individuals and legal entities registered, or required to be registered, for VAT. Any person making taxable supplies of goods and services that exceeds or is likely to exceed a threshold of 50,000 konvertibilna marka (convertible mark or BAM) (25,000 euros [EUR]) is required to register as a VAT payer.

The export of goods is zero-rated.

Taxable transactions include the supply of goods and services in Bosnia and Herzegovina by a taxable person, as well as the importation of goods to Bosnia and Herzegovina by any person. The following transactions are also taxable:

Bosnia and Herzegovina

- Transactions for no consideration or for a consideration less than the market value.
- The private use of taxable goods by a taxable person (self-supply).

The following services are exempt from VAT in Bosnia and Herzegovina:

- The leasing and subletting of residential houses, apartments, and residential premises for a period of longer than 60 days.
- The supply of immovable property, except for the first transfer of the ownership rights or the rights to dispose of newly constructed immovable property.
- Financial services.
- Insurance and reinsurance services.
- Educational services provided by private or public educational institutions.
- Postal services.

The VAT period is one calendar month.

Any tax credit that has not been used after a period of six months shall be refunded. Registered exporters are to be refunded within 30 days.

Customs duties
The customs policy law and the rates of customs tariffs to be applied exist and are largely based on European Union (EU) standards. Bosnia and Herzegovina has signed the Stabilisation and Association Agreement (SAA) and the Central European Free Trade Agreement (CEFTA).

Excise duties
There is a single excise regime throughout Bosnia and Herzegovina which levies excise tax on the following products:

- Petroleum products: BAM 0.3 to BAM 0.4 per litre.
- Tobacco products: 42% on retail price and an additional BAM 0.15 per pack of 20 cigarettes.
- Non-alcoholic drinks: BAM 0.1 per litre.
- Alcohol and alcoholic drinks: BAM 8 to BAM 15 per litre of absolute alcohol.
- Beer and wine: BAM 0.2 to BAM 0.25 per litre.
- Coffee (unroasted, roasted, and ground coffee and coffee extracts): BAM 1.5 to BAM 3.5 per kilogram.

Property taxes (real estate)

FBiH property taxes
FBiH property taxes are imposed at the cantonal level (ten cantons in total), and the rates as well as the taxpayers are different between the cantons. The taxes are paid in the range of BAM 0.5 to BAM 3 per square metre.

RS property taxes
RS property taxes are imposed at the entity level. The annual tax rate is between 0.05% and 0.5% of the market value of the property. The applicable tax rate is determined every year by the municipalities.

BD property taxes
BD property taxes are imposed by the BD assembly. The annual tax rate is between 0.05% and 1% of the market value of the property. The rate is adopted by the assembly for every year based on the proposed annual budget.

Bosnia and Herzegovina

Tax on transfer of land and real estate

FBiH transfer taxes
The FBIH tax on transfer of land and real estate is imposed at the cantonal level. The rate differs by canton; however, it cannot be higher than 5%.

RS transfer taxes
The RS tax on transfer of land and real estate is imposed at the entity level. The rate is 3%.

BD transfer taxes
There is no tax on transfer of land and real estate in Brčko District.

Other taxes
There are several other taxes introduced at the entity, cantonal, and municipality level. The duties differentiate based on company location, business size, and type of business.

FBiH other taxes
FBiH other taxes include the communal tax, fire prevention contribution, tourist community contribution, forestry contribution fee, Foreign Trade Chamber of Bosnia and Herzegovina duty, Chamber of Commerce FBiH duty, and administrative stamp duties.

RS other taxes
RS other taxes include the special republic tax, communal tax, forestry contribution fee, fire prevention contribution, Foreign Trade Chamber of Bosnia and Herzegovina duty, Chamber of Commerce FBiH duty, and administrative stamp duties.

BD other taxes
BD other taxes include the communal tax, fire prevention contribution, forestry contribution fee, Foreign Trade Chamber of Bosnia and Herzegovina duty, and administrative stamp duties.

Branch income

Representative offices of foreign companies are permitted, although the concept of an international branch has not been recognised in Bosnia and Herzegovina.

Income determination

Taxable profit is profit determined by adjusting the accounting profit as stated in the profit and loss statement and determined in accordance with International Financial Reporting Standards/International Accounting Standards (IFRS/IAS) and accounting legislation, in accordance with the provisions of the CIT law.

FBiH income
Income for assessment of taxable profit in the Federation of Bosnia and Herzegovina is income from the sales of products, services, goods, and materials, as well as financial, extraordinary and other income calculated in the profit and loss balance in accordance with accounting regulations and IFRS/IAS.

Bosnia and Herzegovina

Income on the basis of collected written-off debt, in the event that it was included in income in a previous period and was not subject to tax allowable or recognised expenditure, shall not be included in the tax base.

FBiH inventory valuation

Expenses of production in accordance with accounting regulations and IFRS/IAS shall be recognised in the value of stocks of unfinished production, semi products, and finished products for the calculation of taxable profit.

The inventory is valued by using the average price method.

FBiH capital gains

The taxable base shall include profit from liquidation and capital gain from the balance sheet.

FBiH dividend income

Dividends realised based on participation in the capital of other taxpayers shall not be included in the tax base. Shares in the profit of a business association will be considered dividends.

FBiH interest income

Interest income is generally included in the taxable base. The exception, as per FBiH government decision, is for interest income realised from state bonds issued for war claims, which should not be included in the taxable base (the CIT law does not explicitly allow for this, which may be lead to discussion with the tax authority).

FBiH foreign income

The Federation of Bosnia and Herzegovina taxes resident corporations on a worldwide basis. There are no deferral or anti-deferral provisions in the Federation of Bosnia and Herzegovina.

RS income

Taxable revenue for the purpose of computing the tax base in Republika Srpska includes all revenue (domestic and foreign) from whatever source derived whether in cash or in kind or whether related or unrelated to the legal person's economic activity.

In the event of revenue received in the form of property (other than cash) or services, the amount of revenue is equal to the market price of the property or services received.

RS inventory valuation

Inventory includes goods used for resale, final goods produced by the taxpayer, semi-final goods used for further production, as well as main and auxiliary materials for production.

Purchase value of inventories at the beginning and end of a fiscal year has to be expressed using the same method for determination of purchase value of inventories.

The purchase value of inventories can be determined by using the first in first out (FIFO) method or the weighted average cost method.

RS capital gains

Capital gain is realised through the sale or other type of transfer of capital or investment assets and represents a difference between the sales price and adjusted base of an asset. The sales price is the contracted price (i.e. the market price established by the competent tax authority in case it finds the contracted price to be lower than the market price).

Capital gains or losses realised during the fiscal year can be offset, and the realised net gain or loss is added or subtracted from the taxable base, if they are not already included in the income or expense.

RS dividend income

Income from dividends is not included in the taxable base.

RS interest income

Interest income is generally included in the taxable base.

Income from securities issued by or guaranteed by the state authority, Central Bank BiH, or local authority, as well as interest income from bank deposits, is excluded from the taxable base.

RS foreign income

Republika Srpska taxes resident corporations on a worldwide basis. There are no deferral or anti-deferral provisions in Republika Srpska.

BD income

Taxable income in Brčko District includes all income from any source (domestic or foreign), whether in cash or in kind, independently of the fact of whether the income is related to the business activity of the legal person.

BD inventory valuation

The purchase value of inventories can be determined by using the first in first out (FIFO) method or the average cost method.

BD capital gains

Capital gain is realised by sale or transfer of capital and investment goods and represents positive difference between the sales price and adjusted property base.

Capital gains or losses realised during the fiscal year can be offset, and the realised net gain or loss added or subtracted from the taxable base, if they are not already included in the income or expense.

BD dividend income

Income from dividends is not included in the taxable base.

BD interest income

Income from securities issued by or guaranteed by the state authority, Central Bank BiH, or local authority is excluded from the taxable base.

BD foreign income

Brčko District taxes resident corporations on a worldwide basis. There are no deferral or anti-deferral provisions in Brčko District.

Bosnia and Herzegovina

Deductions

FBiH deductions

Expenditures are deductible from revenue in computing the FBiH tax base if the expenditures directly relate to the realised revenue.

FBiH depreciation

Depreciation cost is deductible only if it relates to the property subject to depreciation and being used.

Depreciation of fixed assets is deductible up to the amount established by proportionate application of the highest annual depreciation rates using the linear method, prescribed by the FBiH government, as follows:

Assets	Rate (%)
Buildings, except	10
Management, administration, office, and other buildings for providing service activities	3
Apartment houses, hotels, restaurants	14.3
Roads, communal objects, upper railway rails machine	14.3
Equipment, vehicles, mechanicals except	20
Equipment for water management, water-supply, and canalisation	14.3
Computers and equipment for environment protection	33.3
Crops	14.4
Livestock units	40
Intangible non-current assets	20

Property being depreciated with a value of less than BAM 1,000 may be fully deducted in the purchase year, on condition that that the property was put in service.

The purchase value of computer hardware and software may be deducted fully in the year the purchase was made.

Depreciated assets, once depreciated, shall not be re-included in the depreciation calculation for the purposes of the tax balance.

Depreciation is allowed for increases in the value of fixed assets due to revalorisation in accordance with IFRS/IAS, up to the amount of calculated depreciation on the revalorisation base and by using the proportion method prescribed by law.

FBiH goodwill

Amortisation of goodwill is not tax deductible.

FBiH start-up expenses

Start-up expenses are tax deductible if the expenses occurred were necessary and related to the registered company and if original documentation in regard to those expenses are available for inspection.

FBiH interest expenses

Interest expense is generally tax deductible, except for interest that is not calculated at arm's length and interest on taxes, social security contributions, and other public revenue.

FBiH bad debt

The expenses occurring based on the write-off of doubtful debts are deductible. Debts are considered doubtful if one of the following is fulfilled:

- The debts have not been collected within 12 months from due date.
- The taxpayer has started court procedures in regard to the receivable or started the enforced collection procedure.
- The receivable is registered in the bankruptcy procedure.
- Agreement has been reached with the debtor in the bankruptcy or liquidation procedure.

FBiH charitable contributions

Costs of humanitarian, cultural, educational, scientific, and sports purposes (except professional sports) are deductible in the amount of up to 3% of total income.

FBiH tax reserves

Tax-deductible expenditures include expenditures to set up reserves for the following:

- Severance pay paid up to the prescribed amount.
- Expenditures of natural resources renewal.
- Expenditures in guaranteed time frames.
- Initiated court procedures.
- Potential credit losses of banks and microcredit organisations.

FBiH fines and penalties

Fines and penalties are not tax deductible.

FBiH taxes

Taxes are generally tax deductible expenses, except for paid CIT.

FBiH other significant items

Representation costs pertaining to business activity are deductible in the amount of 30% of representation costs.

Expenses of membership fees to the chambers are deductible in the amount not exceeding 0.1% of total income, with the exception of membership fees regulated by the law.

Expenses based on sponsorship are deductible in the amount of 2% of total income.

FBiH net operating losses

Tax losses may be offset against profits in a future tax period, not exceeding five years. Tax losses are utilised on a first in first out (FIFO) basis.

Tax losses cannot be carried back.

FBiH payments to foreign affiliates

Payments to foreign affiliates are generally allowed if they relate to realised revenue.

Bosnia and Herzegovina

RS deductions
Expenditures are deductible from revenue in computing the RS tax base if the expenditures directly relate to the realised revenue.

RS depreciation
Depreciation deductions are allowed only with respect to depreciable assets that are being used.

A depreciable asset is any tangible or intangible asset that is held for use in the production or supply of goods and services, for rental to others, or for administrative purposes. Land or any other asset that does not decrease in value through wear and tear or obsolescence is not considered a depreciable asset.

The assets are depreciated using the linear method of depreciation except for machines and equipment which can be depreciated with acceleration (first year at 40%, second year at 30%, and third year at 30%). The CIT Rulebook prescribes a wide range of accepted depreciation rates, depending on type of assets, ranging from 1% to 50% annually.

RS goodwill
Amortisation of goodwill is not tax deductible.

RS start-up expenses
Start-up expenses are tax deductible if the expenses occurred were necessary and related to the registered company and if original documentation in regard to those expenses are available for inspection.

RS interest expenses
Interest on loans used for business purposes are tax deductible. The exceptions are interest that is not at arm's length, interest on loans for private use, and interest on overdue tax payments.

RS bad debts and tax reserves
A legal person using the accrual form of accounting is allowed a deduction with respect to bad debts and reserves.

Legal persons, other than banks, authorised credit institutions, or insurance companies, are entitled to a bad debt deduction that arose in connection with a sale of goods or services but only if the revenue from the sale was previously included in the tax base of the legal person.

A loan or trade receivable is considered to be a bad debt only if the receivable has not been collected within 12 months from the due date and

- the taxpayer has started court litigation for the receivables or if enforced collection procedure is initiated
- the receivables are registered in the bankruptcy procedure of the debtor, or
- an agreement has been reached with the debtor who is not a physical or related person in the bankruptcy or liquidation procedure.

In the case of a bank or other authorised credit institution, a deduction is allowed for increases in the reserve account for customary losses due to unpaid loans, and the amount may not exceed 20% of the tax base.

In the case of an insurance or reinsurance company, a deduction is allowed for increases in reserves as registered in accounting documents and as authorised according to applicable law. For insurance contracts pertaining to reinsurance, reserves are to be reduced so that they cover only part of the risk remaining with the insurer, and the amount may not exceed 20% of the tax base.

The tax savings resulting from a reduction or cancellation of any reserve that is collected later on will be included in taxable revenue at the moment of collection in accordance with this law.

RS charitable contributions
Contributions to public institutions and humanitarian, cultural, and educational organisations are deductible in an amount not exceeding 3% of the fiscal year's total revenue. Any excess contribution may be carried forward three years.

RS fines and penalties
Fines and penalties are not tax deductible.

RS taxes
Taxes are generally tax deductible expenses, except for paid CIT.

RS other significant items
Expenditures that are recognised and deductible from revenue also include the following:

- 30% of the cost of entertainment, meals, and amusements related to the legal person's economic activity.
- Sponsorship expenses in an amount not exceeding 2% of the fiscal year's total revenue.
- Scholarships to students in an amount of up to 75% of average monthly net salary per employee in Republika Srpska in accordance with the latest published data from the body in charge of statistics.

RS net operating losses
Losses may be carried forward and offset against income in the following five years. Tax losses are utilised on a FIFO basis.

Tax losses cannot be carried back.

RS payments to foreign affiliates
Payments to foreign affiliates are generally allowed if they relate to realised revenue.

BD deductions
Expenditures are deductible from revenue in computing the BD tax base if the expenditures directly relate to the realised revenue.

BD depreciation
Depreciation deductions are allowed only with respect to depreciable assets that are being used.

A depreciable asset is any tangible or intangible asset that is held for use in the production or supply of goods and services, for rental to others, or for administrative purposes. Land or any other asset that does not decrease in value through wear and tear or obsolescence is not considered a depreciable asset.

Bosnia and Herzegovina

The assets are depreciated using the linear method of depreciation except for machines and equipment which can be depreciated with acceleration (first year at 40%, second year at 30%, and third year at 30%). The CIT Rulebook prescribes a wide range of accepted depreciation rates, depending on type of assets.

The calculation of depreciation for newly purchased property starts the following month on the day when it was put to use. The calculation of depreciation for newly constructed buildings starts from the first day of the following year in which it was put to use.

BD goodwill
Amortisation of goodwill is not tax deductible.

BD start-up expenses
Start-up expenses are tax deductible if the expenses occurred were necessary and related to the registered company and if original documentation in regard to those expenses are available for inspection.

BD interest expense
Interest on loans used for business purposes are tax deductible. The exceptions are interest that is not at arm's length, interest on loans for private use, and interest on overdue tax payments.

BD bad debts and tax reserves
Legal persons, other than banks, authorised credit institutions, or insurance companies, shall be entitled to a bad debt deduction that arose in connection with a sale of goods or services but only if the revenue from the sale was previously included in the tax base of the legal person. For this purpose, a credit or trade receivable is considered a bad debt only if one of the following is true:

- It is more than 12 months past the due date for payment of the invoiced receivable and the creditor has sued for the receivables or an enforced collection procedure is initiated due to receivables.
- The receivables are registered in the bankruptcy procedure of the debtor or an agreement has been reached with the debtor who is not a physical or related person in the bankruptcy or liquidation procedure.

In the case of a bank or other authorised credit institution, a deduction is allowed for increases in the reserve account for customary losses due to unpaid loans, and the amount may not exceed 20% of the tax base.

In the case of an insurance or reinsurance company, a deduction is allowed for increases in reserves as registered in accounting documents and as authorised according to applicable law. For insurance contracts pertaining to reinsurance, reserves are to be reduced so that they cover only part of the risk remaining with the insurer, and the amount may not exceed 20% of the tax base.

BD charitable contributions
Contributions to public institutions and humanitarian, cultural, and educational organisations are deductible in an amount not exceeding 3% of the fiscal year's total revenue.

BD fines and penalties
Fines and penalties are not tax deductible.

BD taxes
Taxes are generally tax deductible expenses, except for paid CIT.

BD other significant items
Expenditures that are recognised and deductible from revenue also include the following:

- 30% of the cost of entertainment related to the legal person's economic activity.
- Awards to employees, up to the prescribed amount.
- Costs of business trips, meal allowance, transportation, and holiday allowance, up to the prescribed amount.
- Sponsorship expenses in an amount not exceeding 2% of the fiscal year's total revenue.
- Scholarships to students in an amount up to 75% of average monthly net salary in Brčko District.
- Committee membership fees, up to 0.2% of total revenue in the tax year.
- Expenses for research and development (R&D) in accordance with the Rulebook.

BD net operating losses
Losses may be carried forward and offset against income in the following five years. Tax losses are utilised on a FIFO basis.

Tax losses cannot be carried back.

BD payments to foreign affiliates
Payment to foreign affiliates is generally allowed if it relates to realised revenue.

Group taxation

FBiH group taxation
A business association has the right to request tax consolidation on the condition that all businesses in the group are residents of the Federation of Bosnia and Herzegovina.

A headquarters company and its branches may form a business association when there is direct or indirect control between them with no less than 90% share.

A request for tax consolidation must be filed to the authorised branch office of the tax authorities by a headquarters company.

Each group member is required to file its tax balance, and the headquarters of the business association may file a consolidated tax balance for the group.

The consolidated tax balance may offset losses of one or more businesses against the profit of other businesses in the association.

Individual group members are liable for the tax calculated on the consolidated balance proportionately to the profit from the individual tax balance, and the headquarters is the payer of the tax calculated on the consolidated balance.

Once approved, tax consolidation shall be applied for the consecutive period of no less than five years.

Bosnia and Herzegovina

When one, several, or all the businesses in the association later opt for individual taxation, all group members shall be obliged to pay the difference proportionately on behalf of the tax privilege they have used.

RS group taxation
An affiliated group of legal persons located within Republika Srpska may elect to file a consolidated annual tax declaration.

An affiliated group of legal persons is a group of one or more legal entities from Republika Srpska that are connected through the ownership of stock with a common parent, provided that the common parent owns at least 80% of the stock in a legal person that is included in the affiliated group. If the common parent does not own at least 80% of the stock in a legal person that is included in the affiliated group, then the parent may file a consolidated tax declaration if one or more other legal persons in the affiliated group own at least 80% of the stock in such legal person.

BD group taxation
An affiliated group of legal persons located within Brčko District may elect to file a consolidated annual tax declaration.

An affiliated group of legal persons is a group of one or more legal entities from Brčko District that are connected through the ownership of stock with a common parent provided that the common parent owns at least 80% of the stock in a legal person that is included in the affiliated group.

Transfer pricing
Transfer pricing requirements are imposed at the entity level. The Federation of Bosnia and Herzegovina, Republika Srpska, and Brčko District have different regulations in place, including different rules in regard to applicable methods, related parties, and documentation. The regulations in place do not differ if the transactions are within one entity, cross-border, or international. Basically, this means that all transactions can fall under the transfer pricing scope.

With Bosnia and Herzegovina not being an EU or an Organisation for Economic Co-operation and Development (OECD) member, the local legislation does not have the same requirements with respect to transfer pricing documentation as in EU countries nor does the legislation refer to the OECD guidelines.

FBiH related parties
In the Federation of Bosnia and Herzegovina, a related party is considered to be an individual or legal person who has the possibility of control or significant influence on the business decisions of the taxpayer. Owning more than half or individually the most stocks or shares in a company is considered to be enabled control.

Significant influence is considered to be mutually high sales turnover, technical dependence, or otherwise gained control over the management.

FBiH prescribed methods
The FBiH CIT law recognises only two methods:

*   Comparable price method (primary method).
*   Cost plus method.

RS and BD related parties

As per the applicable RS and BD legislation, related parties of a legal person are considered to be physical or legal persons if those persons possess more than 10% of active shares with voting rights.

A legal person can be a related party if it possesses more than 10% active shares in the other person indirectly or directly. Indirect ownership is considered to be:

- If a legal person possesses more than 10% of a dependant company, and that dependant company possesses more than 10% in the other legal person.
- If both legal persons have a common shareholder who possesses more than 10% active shares with voting rights in both legal persons.

RS and BD prescribed methods

The RS and BD regulations prescribe the following five methods that can be used in order to establish whether the prices are in accordance with the arm's-length principle:

- Comparable price method (primary method).
- Cost plus method.
- Resale price method.
- Profit split method.
- Transactional net margin method.

Thin capitalisation

There are no thin capitalisation rules in Bosnia and Herzegovina.

Tax credits and incentives

FBiH tax incentives

FBiH foreign tax credit

When a taxpayer generates income or profit through business activities outside of the Federation of Bosnia and Herzegovina (directly or through a business unit) and pays the profit tax on such activities, the tax paid abroad shall be credited up to the amount of the profit tax that would have been paid for the income or profit generated by the same activities in the Federation of Bosnia and Herzegovina.

FBiH investment incentive

A taxpayer who invested in production within the territory of the Federation of Bosnia and Herzegovina for five consecutive years for a minimum fee of BAM 20 million will be relieved from taxation for a period of five years, starting with the first year in which it has invested at least BAM 4 million.

FBiH special needs employment incentive

A taxpayer who employs more than 50% of handicap or special needs individuals within its company for a period of time longer than one year is relieved from CIT for the year in which more than 50% of handicap or special needs individuals are employed within the company.

FBiH export incentive

A taxpayer who realises more than 30% of annual income by export will be relieved from CIT for that year.

Bosnia and Herzegovina

RS tax incentives

RS foreign tax credit
If a legal entity from Republika Srpska obtains revenue from a foreign state and the revenue is taxed both in Republika Srpska and in the foreign state, then the tax paid to the foreign state, whether paid directly or withheld and remitted by another person, is to be credited from RS CIT, unless such legal entity from Republika Srpska elects to treat the foreign tax as a deductible expenditure in determining the fiscal year tax base.

There are no other tax incentives available in Republika Srpska.

BD tax incentives

BD foreign tax credit
If a legal entity from Brčko District obtains revenue from a foreign state and the revenue is taxed both in Brčko District and in the foreign state, then the tax paid to the foreign state, whether paid directly or withheld and remitted by another person, is to be credited from the BD CIT, unless such legal entity from Brčko District elects to treat the foreign tax as a deductible expenditure in determining the fiscal year tax base.

BD investment incentive
For a taxpayer who invests in machines and equipment for performing its own registered business activity on the territory of Brčko District, a deduction is allowed for the amount of the investment.

BD employment incentive
For a taxpayer who employs new employees for an indefinite period of time during the tax period, a second deduction is allowed for the total amount of paid gross salaries for the new employees.

Withholding taxes

FBiH WHT
WHT in the Federation of Bosnia and Herzegovina is calculated on non-resident income generated throughout the territory of the Federation of Bosnia and Herzegovina.

The base for calculation of WHT is the gross amount paid by a resident of the Federation of Bosnia and Herzegovina to a non-resident for dividends, interest, royalties and other intellectual property rights, compensations for market research, tax consulting services, auditors' services, fun and sports events, premium insurance for insurance or reinsurance of risk in the Federation of Bosnia and Herzegovina, telecommunication services between the Federation of Bosnia and Herzegovina and other countries, as well as all other services performed on the territory of the Federation of Bosnia and Herzegovina.

WHT shall be paid at the rate of 5% on dividend payments and 10% for interest, royalties, and other, if not reduced under a tax treaty.

RS WHT
Any legal or physical person from Republika Srpska, as well as any non-resident legal or physical person with PE in Republika Srpska, who pays revenue to a non-resident legal person is to withhold tax from the total payment of revenue and is to remit the withheld tax to the Public Revenues Account of Republika Srpska.

The WHT applies to the following revenue payments, regardless of whether the revenue is received in Republika Srpska or abroad:

- Payment of interest or its functional equivalent under financial instruments and arrangements from a resident.
- Payment for entertainment or sporting activities carried out in Republika Srpska, regardless of whether the revenue is received by the entertainer or sportsman or by another person.
- Payment for the performance of management, consulting, financial, technical, or administrative services, if the revenue is from a resident or if the revenue is paid by or included in the books and records of a PE in Republika Srpska or if such payment is deducted for the purpose of determining the tax base.
- Payment in the form of insurance premiums for the insuring or reinsuring of risks in Republika Srpska.
- Payment for telecommunication services between Republika Srpska and a foreign state.
- Payment of royalties.
- Payment of lease for movable property.
- Payment for the performance of other services in Republika Srpska.

WHT is not due on dividend payments.

The WHT rate in Republika Srpska is 10%.

BD WHT
Any legal or physical person from Brčko District, as well as any non-resident legal or physical person with PE in Brčko District, who pays revenue to a non-resident legal person is to withhold tax from the total payment of revenue and is to remit the withheld tax to the Public Revenues Account of Brčko District.

The WHT applies to the following revenue payments, regardless of whether the revenue is received in Brčko District or abroad:

- Payment of interest or its functional equivalent under financial instruments and arrangements from a resident.
- Payment for entertainment or sporting activities carried out in Brčko District, regardless of whether the revenue is received by the entertainer or sportsman or by another person.
- Payment for the performance of management, consulting, financial, technical, or administrative services, if the revenue is from a resident or if the revenue is paid by or included in the books and records of a PE in Brčko District or if such payment is deducted for the purpose of determining the tax base.
- Payment in the form of insurance premiums for the insuring or reinsuring of risks in Brčko District.
- Payment for telecommunication services between Brčko District and a foreign state.
- Payment of royalties.
- Payment of lease for movable property.
- Payment for the performance of other services in Brčko District.

WHT is not due on dividend payments.

The WHT rate in Brčko District is 10%.

Bosnia and Herzegovina

WHT rates based on available double taxation treaties (DTTs)

Recipient	Dividends (%)	Interest (%)	Royalties (%)
Albania	5/10	10	10
Algeria	10	10	12
Austria	5/10	5	5
Belgium	10/15	15	10
China	10	10	10
Croatia	5/10	10	10
Cyprus	10	10	10
Czech Republic	5	0	10
Denmark	5/15	0	10
Egypt	5/15	15	15
Finland	5/15	0	10
France	5/15	0	0
Germany	15	0	10
Hungary	10	0	10
Iran	10	10	15
Ireland	0	0	0
Italy	10	10	10
Jordan	5/10	10	10
Kuwait	5	5	10
Malaysia	5/10	10	8
Moldova	5/10	10	10
Netherlands	5/15	0	10
Norway	15	0	10
Pakistan	10	20	15
Poland	5/15	10	10
Qatar	5/10	7	7
Romania	5	7.5	10
Serbia and Montenegro	5/10	10	10
Slovakia	5/15	0	10
Slovenia	5/10	7	5
Spain	5/10	7	7
Sri Lanka	12.5	10	10
Sweden	5/15	0	0
Turkey	5/15	10	10
United Arab Emirates	5/15	10	10
United Kingdom	5/15	10	10

Tax administration

FBiH tax administration

FBiH taxable period
The taxable period is considered to be the calendar month.

FBiH tax returns
An FBiH taxpayer is obliged to file correctly and accurately a completed tax return (declaration) with the tax balance to the authorised branch office of the tax administration by 31 March of the following year.

The deadline for submission of annual calculation of business results is 28 February of the following year.

FBiH payment of tax
A taxpayer shall pay FBiH CIT pursuant to the final tax declaration. CIT prepayments are determined based on the tax return from the prior year and have to be paid monthly until the last day of the month for the previous month.

FBiH audit cycle
The tax system is generally based on self-assessment; however, many large and mid-size businesses are under continuous audit by the tax authority and the indirect tax authorities. The audits may include the entire list of taxes for which the business is liable. Smaller businesses with lower incomes are generally subject to audit on a random basis.

FBiH statute of limitations
The statute of limitations is five years.

RS tax administration

RS taxable period
The taxable period is considered to be the calendar month.

RS tax returns
The RS tax declaration for a tax year shall be filed no later than 90 days upon the end of the tax year, and in case of a calendar year, no later than 31 March of the current year for the previous year.

RS payment of tax
A taxpayer shall pay RS CIT pursuant to the final tax declaration. CIT prepayments are determined based on the tax return from the prior year and have to be paid monthly until the tenth day of the month for the previous month.

RS audit cycle
The tax system is generally based on self-assessment; however, many large and mid-size businesses are under continuous audit by the tax authority and the indirect tax authorities. The audits may include the entire list of taxes for which the business is liable. Smaller businesses with lower incomes are generally subject to audit on a random basis.

RS statute of limitations
The statute of limitations is five years.

Bosnia and Herzegovina

BD tax administration

BD taxable period
The taxable period is considered to be the calendar month.

BD tax returns
The BD tax declaration for a tax year shall be filed no later than 90 days upon the end of the tax year, and in case of a calendar year, no later than 31 March of the current year for the previous year.

BD payment of tax
A taxpayer shall pay BD CIT pursuant to the final tax declaration. CIT prepayments are determined based on the tax return from the prior year and have to be paid monthly until the tenth day of the month for the previous month.

BD audit cycle
The tax system is generally based on self-assessment; however, many large and mid-size businesses are under continuous audit by the tax authority and the indirect tax authorities. The audits may include the entire list of taxes for which the business is liable. Smaller businesses with lower incomes are generally subject to audit on a random basis.

BD statute of limitations
The statute of limitations is five years.

Botswana

PwC contact

Suren Perera
PricewaterhouseCoopers
Plot 50371
Fairground Office Park
Gaborone
Botswana
Tel: +267 395 2011
Email: suren.perera@bw.pwc.com

Significant developments

Botswana implemented the following changes to its tax regime with effect as of 1 July 2011:

Corporate income tax (CIT)
- The two tier CIT system was replaced by a single CIT rate of 22% for resident companies.
- The CIT rate for non-resident companies (i.e. branch income) was increased to 30%.
- The tax rate for manufacturing companies and International Financial Services Centre (IFSC) companies remained at 15% in respect of approved activities for such businesses.
- Companies ceased generating Additional Company Tax (ACT) for the tax year ending 30 June 2012 and subsequent tax years.
- Utilisation of accumulated ACT ended on 30 June 2011, after which date all unutilised ACT fell away.
- Withholding tax (WHT) may no longer be offset against CIT.

Withholding tax (WHT)
The WHT on dividends was reduced to 7.5%.

All rent and commission payments to residents or non-residents are subject to WHT at 5% where the total payment is 36,000 Botswana pulas (BWP) per annum or more or the monthly payment is BWP 3,000 or more.

Capital gains
The exemption from tax on capital gains on the sale of certain shares, units, or debentures of a public resident company now only apply if the shares, units, or debentures were held by the taxpayer for a period of at least one year prior to the date of disposal.

Mines and minerals
The mining tax rate for non-diamond mining companies (derived in terms of the existing formula) shall not be less than the CIT rate of 22%.

Taxes on corporate income

Botswana has a source-based taxation system.

As of 1 July 2011 (i.e. during the 2012 tax year), CIT is charged at a single flat rate of 22%.

Botswana

Prior to 1 July 2011, CIT was imposed at a rate of 15% for non-manufacturing companies and 5% for manufacturing companies. ACT was also imposed at a rate of 10%, and the ACT amount could be carried forward up to five years to be offset against WHT payable on dividends paid. As of 1 July 2011, there is no ACT component. Any accumulated ACT not utilised before 1 July 2011 fell away.

International Financial Services Centre (IFSC) profits
IFSC companies are currently taxed at a flat rate of 15% and will continue to be taxed at that rate going forward. Companies must apply for a certificate to be classified as IFSC companies, which deal only in specified services and only with non-residents.

Mining profits
Mining profits, other than profits from diamond mining, are taxed according to the following formula:

Annual tax rate = 70 minus (1,500/x), where x is taxable income as a percentage of gross income.

As of 1 July 2011, the tax rate shall not be less than the flat CIT rate of 22%. Prior to 1 July 2011, the tax rate was not less than the combined CIT and ACT rate of 25%.

Diamond mining
Diamond mining is usually taxed in terms of an agreement with the government of Botswana.

Corporate residence

If a company's registered office or place of incorporation is in Botswana or if the company is managed and controlled in Botswana, then the company is considered a resident of Botswana.

Permanent establishment (PE)
PE has been defined in the Income Tax Act only in the limited context of interest, commercial royalty, and management or consultancy fee. However, the PE is defined in all the double taxation agreements (DTAs) that Botswana has entered into with other contracting states. The definition of PE in the DTA follows the definition in the Organisation for Economic Co-operation and Development (OECD) Model Tax Convention on Income and Capital.

Other taxes

Value-added tax (VAT)
VAT is imposed on taxable supplies and the importation of goods into Botswana. The standard VAT rate of 12% applies to all supplies that do not qualify for an exemption or are not zero-rated.

Vocational training levy (VTL)
VTL is payable when submitting the VAT return, by every taxpayer who is registered for VAT. It is calculated as a percentage of turnover ranging from 0.2% to 0.05%, depending on the turnover of the company.

Capital transfer tax (CTT)

CTT is levied on the donee upon the transfer (by way of inheritance or gratuitous disposal of property) of tangible or intangible, movable or immovable, property, at 12.5%.

Transfer duties on immovable property

Transfer duty is levied at 5% of the value of immovable freehold and leasehold property. The first BWP 200,000 of such value is exempt from transfer duty in case of transfer to a Botswana citizen.

In the case of agricultural property, transfer duty is levied at the rate of 30% for a non-citizen. This duty is 5% in the case of a Botswana citizen.

Property taxes

There are no property taxes in Botswana.

Stamp taxes

There is no stamp duty in Botswana.

Branch income

As of 1 July 2011, CIT payable on branch profits was increased to 30% from 25%.

Income determination

Inventory valuation

Inventories are valued at cost less such amounts, if any, that the Commissioner General believes are reasonable as representing the amount by which the value of such stock has been diminished because of damage, deterioration, obsolescence, or other cause. Although not expressly excluded by legislation, last in first out (LIFO) has not been accepted in practice by the tax authorities.

Capital gains

Gains from disposal of specified capital assets (immovable property and marketable securities, including shares in private companies) are included in taxable income in the hands of the corporate taxpayer. Acquisition costs of immovable property are subject to a 10% compound annual addition for inflation for the period from acquisition to 30 June 1982, and thereafter to an inflation addition based on the increase in the consumer price index to the date of sale. For other gains, no inflation allowances are granted, but the taxable gain is set at 75% of the total gain.

Currently, the sale of any shares, units, or debentures of a resident company is exempt from tax under any of the following circumstances:

- The resident company whose shares are being sold is a public company.
- The shares, units, or debentures are traded on the Botswana Stock Exchange.
- The company has released for trading 49% or more of its equity on the Botswana Stock Exchange.

As of 1 July 2011, this exemption only applies if the shares, units, or debentures were held by the taxpayer for a period of at least one year prior to the date of disposal.

Botswana

The aggregate amount of capital losses is offset against the aggregate amount of capital gains in the same tax year. Any excess of loss is deducted from aggregate gains over losses accruing in the succeeding tax year only. Capital losses cannot, in any circumstances, be deducted against other income.

Dividend income
Dividend income from local sources is not subject to tax.

Interest income
In case of a resident company, interest income is included in gross income and taxed at the CIT rate. In case of a non-resident company, interest income will be subject to WHT, which will constitute a final tax.

Royalty income
Royalty income is included in gross income and taxed at the CIT rate. In case of a non-resident company, royalty income will be subject to WHT, which will constitute a final tax.

Partnership income
Partnership income is taxed in the hands of the partners, in proportion to their share in the partnership.

Foreign income
Resident corporations are not generally taxed on a worldwide income basis. However, interest and dividend income from a foreign source is taxed in the hands of the resident company on an accrual basis. Prior to 1 July 2011, relief was given for any WHT imposed on such income. As of 1 July 2011, however, WHT may not be offset against CIT.

Deductions

Depreciation and depletion
Annual and capital allowances available are as follows.

Companies other than mining companies
Annual taxation allowances for expenditures incurred on machinery and equipment before 30 June 1982 can be claimed up to 100%. This allowance may be for any proportion of previously unclaimed expenditures. For expenditures incurred on machinery and equipment after 30 June 1982, annual allowances are granted, calculated on cost by the straight-line method on the basis of the expected useful lives of the individual assets. Guidelines are provided for expected useful lives of different categories of assets, which vary from four to ten years. Book depreciation is not required to conform to tax depreciation. The capital allowance claimable on a company motorcar is restricted to a maximum of BWP 175,000.

An initial allowance of 25% of cost is granted on certain industrial buildings. All industrial and commercial buildings (excluding residential properties) are granted a 2.5% annual allowance based on cost or, in the case of an industrial building on which an initial allowance has been claimed, the original cost less the initial allowance.

Balancing allowances and charges are brought to account on the disposal of assets on which allowances have been claimed. Where disposal value of an item of machinery or equipment exceeds the difference between expenditures incurred on the asset and allowances granted, the whole amount is taxable as corporate income or the balancing charge can be offset against further additions of new equipment, thus providing rollover relief. However, there is no rollover relief on motorcars except where the cars are used in a car rental or taxi service business.

Mining companies

In ascertaining the business income for any tax year from a business of mining, there shall be deducted from business income an allowance, to be known as a mining capital allowance, computed in accordance with 100% of the mining capital expenditure made in the year in which such expenditure was incurred, with unlimited carryforward of losses.

Taxes

Any taxes paid are specifically disallowed in computing a company's taxable income.

Other significant items

An allowance is granted for dwelling houses erected for employees by a business other than a mining business. The amount of the allowance is the lower of cost or BWP 25,000 for each dwelling house constructed.

A deduction of 200% of the cost of an approved training expenditure is allowed.

Companies with shareholders having 5% or more of equity, either directly or indirectly, are classified as close companies, and there are additional tax regulations in respect of these shareholders.

Small companies, that is resident private companies whose gross income does not exceed BWP 300,000, may elect that the company be taxed as a partnership.

Expenses incurred by the company for having its shares listed on the Botswana Stock Exchange are deductible in determining the chargeable income of the company.

Net operating losses

Losses may be carried forward for five years, with the exception of farming, mining, and prospecting operations, for which there is no time limit. There is no allowance for carrybacks.

Payments to foreign affiliates

Royalties, interest, and service fees paid to foreign affiliates are generally deductible, provided such amounts are at arm's length and WHT is paid.

In the case of a mining company, head office expenses allowed as a deduction in ascertaining gross revenue from mineral licence shall be limited to 1.5% of gross income for the year of assessment, and any excess of such expense above the limit shall be treated and taxed as a dividend.

Where the interest rate on a loan made by a foreign-based mining company to an affiliate mining company resident in Botswana is considered by the commissioner to be in excess of the market rate, such excess will be disallowed as a deduction and taxed as a dividend.

Botswana

....

Group taxation

There are no concessions for group taxation, other than for wholly-owned subsidiary companies of the Botswana Development Corporation Limited (BDC).

BDC was established in 1970 to be the country's main agency for commercial and industrial development. The Government of Botswana owns 100% of the issued share capital of the Corporation.

Where in any tax year a wholly owned subsidiary of BDC has incurred any assessed loss, such member may, during the current tax year, by notice in writing to the Commissioner General, elect that the whole or part of such assessed loss shall be deducted in ascertaining the chargeable income of one or more of the other wholly owned subsidiaries.

Transfer pricing

Botswana currently does not have any transfer pricing regulations, so transfer pricing is currently monitored through the anti-avoidance provisions contained in Section 36 of the Income Tax Act.

The arm's-length principle should always be followed in transactions between related parties. If such transactions have created rights or obligations that would not normally be created between independent persons dealing at arm's length, the Commissioner General may determine the liability in such manner as deemed appropriate. However, related party balances arising out of normal trading transactions (e.g. credit purchases with 30 days credit period) would not be subjected to these provisions.

Interest (at prime rate) should be charged/provided on loans from shareholders/amounts due to related parties. If no interest has been charged/provided, in terms of the close company legislation, the Botswana Unified Revenue Service (BURS) may deem interest at the prime rate prevailing at the beginning of the tax year, as income in the hands of the lender without allowing the corresponding interest as a charge against the profits of the borrower. The borrower is obliged to deduct WHT at the prevailing rate on the deemed interest.

Amounts due from shareholders/directors may be deemed as dividend income and shall form part of the taxable income of the borrower, in which event these will be taxed at the prevailing dividend WHT rate in the hands of the borrower.

Thin capitalisation

Thin capitalisation rules can be found in the Income Tax Act, but only in relation to mining companies and IFSC companies.

Where a foreign controlled resident mining company has a foreign debt-to-equity ratio in excess of 3:1 at any time during the year of assessment, the amount of interest paid by the resident company during that year on that part of the debt that exceeds the ratio shall be disallowed as a deduction, and the amount so disallowed shall be treated and taxed as a dividend.

In case of an IFSC company, where an amount of foreign debt interest is allowable as a deduction in a particular tax year and, at any time during that tax year, the total foreign debt exceeds the foreign equity product for that year, then the amount of foreign debt interest ascertained in accordance with the following formula will be disallowed:

I x (A/B) x (C/365)

A = amount of the excess of the total foreign debt over the foreign equity product.

B = the total foreign debt.

C = the number of days in that tax year during which the total foreign debt exceeded the foreign equity product by that amount.

I = the foreign debt interest.

Tax credits and incentives

To encourage investment in Botswana, extra tax relief on revenue or capital accounts will be granted for specific business development projects if the government is satisfied that such projects are beneficial to Botswana.

Withholding taxes

WHT, at the following rates, must be deducted from payments to residents and non-residents unless a DTA exists.

Residents	WHT rate (%)
Interest	10
Dividends (15% prior to 1 July 2011)	7.5
Payments due under certain construction contracts	3
Non-residents	WHT rate (%)
Interest	15
Dividends (15% prior to 1 July 2011)	7.5
Payments due under certain construction contracts	3
Payments for royalties, management, or consultancy fees	15
Payments for entertainment fees	10

With effect from 1 July 2011 (tax year 2012), all rent and commission payments to residents or non-residents are subject to WHT at 5% where the total payment is BWP 36,000 per annum or more or the monthly payment is BWP 3,000 or more.

Botswana has tax agreements with the following countries, which provide for WHT at the rates shown.

Recipient	Dividends (%) (1)	Interest (%)	Royalties (%)	Management and consultancy fees (%)
Barbados	5/7.5 (2)	10	10	10
France	5/7.5 (2)	10	10	7.5
India	7.5	10	10	10
Mauritius	5/7.5 (2)	12	12.5	15
Namibia	7.5	10	10	15
Russia	5/7.5 (2)	10	10	10
Seychelles	5/7.5 (2)	7.5	10	10

Botswana

Recipient	Dividends (%) (1)	Interest (%)	Royalties (%)	Management and consultancy fees (%)
South Africa	7.5	10	10	10
Sweden	7.5	15	15	15
United Kingdom	5/7.5 (2)	10	10	7.5
Zimbabwe	5/7.5 (2)	10	10	10

Notes

1. The rate of WHT was reduced from 15% to 7.5% on 1 July 2011.
2. 5% rate of WHT is applicable if the beneficial shareholder is a company resident in the DTA country and holds at least 25% of the share capital in the company paying dividends. Otherwise, the other rate applies.

Tax administration

Taxable period
Botswana has a fiscal year ending on 30 June. However, a business may select its own accounting year, which may end on a date other than 30 June. This accounting year is accepted for the computation of the company's taxable income.

Tax returns
Botswana requires self-assessment, which means that the return submitted constitutes the assessment. The system is one that requires all taxpayers to file tax returns in standard format (providing information relating to taxable income earned) within four months after the financial year end of the company.

Payment of tax
Under the self-assessment tax procedures, if the tax payable for a tax year exceeds BWP 50,000, then estimated tax is required to be paid in equal quarterly instalments over the period of 12 months ending on the company's financial year-end date. Accordingly, the first quarterly payment should be made within three months of the beginning of the financial year and the balance quarterly payments at three monthly intervals thereafter. The final (balance) payment, if any, is to be made within four months from the end of the financial year, when submitting the return.

Where the tax is less than BWP 50,000, then the tax is payable within four months from the company's financial year-end date.

Brazil

PwC contact

Carlos Iacia
PricewaterhouseCoopers
Centro Empresarial Agua Branca
Avenida Francisco Matarazzo 1400
Torre Torino
05001-903 São Paulo, SP
Brazil
Tel: +55 11 3674 3544
Email: carlos.iacia@br.pwc.com

Significant developments

New incentives to boost competitiveness of national goods

In early August 2011, the Brazilian government announced several measures with the aim of benefitting local manufacturers and exporters of goods and services. Referred to as 'Brasil Maior' (Greater Brazil), and the subject of much media attention, the government's plan was to augment national competitiveness through incentives for technical innovation, research, and added value in production, as well as provide clear advantages for exporters who were suffering from the continued appreciation of the Brazilian real (BRL).

The measures include incentives to increase financing lines; reduction of payroll costs in some industry sectors, which foresees the substitution of the 20% social security contribution with a 1.5% tax on gross revenue; cash refunds for exporters based on export revenue, potentially up to 4%; cash refunds of PIS/Cofins (federal contribution taxes) credits and their payment within 60 days; incentives for the automotive industry; and excise tax reductions, among others. Some of the benefits include the following:

- PIS/Cofins credits on the value of new capital assets may be offset at gradually reduced rates, allowing for a 1/11 offset for goods acquired in August 2011 to a full offset for goods acquired from July 2012. This applies to new assets bought or received as of 3 August 2011.
- Companies that qualify for the government's digital inclusion programme are exempted from income tax and surtax calculated based on the exploitation profit (i.e. the profit of activities relating to sectors and enterprises that benefit from special tax incentives). Further, costs incurred in scientific research conducted in private, non-profit, qualifying institutions are now deductible for calculating the profit and social contribution tax base.
- From December 2011 to December 2012, payroll costs are to be reduced in certain industries, including information technology, clothing, leather, footwear, and furniture manufacturers. In place of existing employer contributions to social security (20% on payroll), a fixed rate of 1.5% (2.5% for information technology services) applies to the companies' gross revenue.
- As a disincentive to imports of the aforementioned goods, the rate of Cofins on import has been increased from 7.6% to 9.1%.

Brazil

6% IOF tax rate is now applicable to foreign loans of less than five years

The Brazilian government has once again changed the tax on financial transactions (*Imposto sobre operações de crédito, câmbio, seguro e sobre operações relativas a títulos e valores mobiliários* or IOF) legislation applicable to foreign exchange transactions regarding foreign loans, within a period of less than two weeks.

As per Decree number 7,698, published on 12 March 2012, the applicable IOF tax rate of 6% applies to foreign currency exchange transactions (inflow of funds into the country only) related to cross-border loans (e.g. intercompany loans) subject to registration at the Brazilian Central Bank, with an average payment term of up to 1,800 days (five years). Conversely, if the average maturity date is longer than 1,800 days, the rate is reduced to 0%.

This new measure is applicable solely to loans signed on or after 12 March 2012.

Important changes to Brazilian transfer pricing rules

The Brazilian government published, on 4 April 2012, new legislation providing for important changes to Brazilian transfer pricing rules.

The following are worth mentioning:

- The resale minus method (PRL) shall be calculated based on a specific mark-up determined for some industries, and a mark-up of 20% for the industries/sectors that are not specified in the legislation.
- Taxpayers are no longer required to include custom duty and other customs expenses in the tested price, nor include freight and insurance contracted with third parties, provided they are not located in low tax jurisdictions/jurisdictions with privileged tax regimes.
- The use of the taxpayer's own transactions with third parties for purposes of the use of the PIC method (equivalent of the comparable uncontrolled price method) will be acceptable only to the extent the comparable transactions are equivalent to 5% of the tested transactions.
- Interest on related party loans, even if duly registered with the Brazilian Central Bank, will be deductible only up to an interest rate equal to the LIBOR dollar rate for six-month loans plus a spread to be annually determined by the Ministry of Finance, based on average market rate.
- Imports and exports of commodities, quoted in commodities exchange markets, must be tested through the use of the newly introduced methods PCI and PECEX, respectively; based on these methods, taxpayers shall compare the transaction amounts with the daily average quote for each product; the Federal Revenue Service shall issue instructions on how these methods shall be applied.

The changes above are included in a Provisional Measure (PM 563) and shall be effective for transactions to be carried out as of 2013.

As a general rule, a PM is issued by the executive branch of the federal government and has the effect of law while it is analysed by the Brazilian Congress, that can approve (with amendments or not) or reject it. This process should take place within a 60-day period, a term that may be extended for an additional 60-day period. If Congress does not act within this 120-day period, the PM expires and loses effectiveness.

Taxes on corporate income

Brazilian resident companies are taxed on worldwide income. Non-resident companies are generally taxed in Brazil through a registered subsidiary, branch, or permanent establishment (PE), based on income generated locally. Other than that, non-resident companies can be subject to withholding income tax on income derived from a Brazilian source.

Corporate income tax (*Imposto de Renda de Pessoa Jurídica* or IRPJ) is assessed at the fixed rate of 15% on annual taxable income, using either the 'actual profits' method or the 'presumed profits' method (*see the Income determination section*).

Surcharge
Corporate taxpayers are also subject to a surcharge of 10% on the annual taxable income in excess of BRL 240,000.

Social contribution on net income
All legal entities are subject to a social contribution to the federal government (*Contribuição Social sobre o Lucro Líquido* or CSLL) at the rate of 9% (except for financial and insurance institutions, which are taxed at the rate of 15%), which is not deductible for IRPJ purposes. The tax basis is the profit before income tax, after some adjustments.

Local income taxes
Corporate income taxes are levied only at federal level (i.e. there are no state or municipal income taxes).

Corporate residence

A corporation is considered resident in Brazil if it has been incorporated in Brazil, and its tax domicile is where its head office is located.

Permanent establishment (PE)
Brazilian tax law has yet to develop rules similar to those existing in other countries, which treat a non-resident as having a PE under various factual circumstances.

Currently, there are few rules to determine whether a foreign business constitutes a taxable presence in Brazil and the concept of 'permanent establishment' only appears in Brazil's treaties.

In general, a non-resident company may be treated as having a taxable presence if it operates in Brazil either through: (i) a fixed place of business or (ii) an agent who has the power to enter into contracts in Brazil in the name of or on behalf of the non-resident.

Other taxes

Value-added tax (VAT)
VAT is payable on imports, sales, and transfers of goods and products in the form of (i) a federal excise tax (*Imposto sobre Produtos Industrializados* or IPI) at various rates in accordance with the nature of the product (normally around 10% to 15%, but in certain cases ranging to over 300%) and (ii) a state sales and service tax (*Imposto sobre*

Brazil

as operações relativas à Circulação de Mercadorias, e sobre a prestação de Serviços de transporte interestadual e intermunicipal e de comunicação or ICMS) with rates ranging from 7% to 25%.

Except for services related to freight and transportation, communications, and electric energy, which are subject to ICMS, income from services rendered is normally subject to a municipal service tax (*Imposto Sobre Serviços de qualquer natureza* or ISS), which is not a VAT, with rates ranging from 2% to 5%.

Import tax

Import tax (*Imposto de Importação* or II) is levied on the cost, insurance, and freight (CIF) price of the imported good. The rates depend on the degree of necessity and are defined in accordance with the product's tariff code contained in the Mercosur Harmonised System (NCM/SH). The rates tend to be in the range of 10% to 20%, although there are many exceptions which are subject to higher or lower rates.

Property taxes

Imposto Predial e Territorial Urbano (IPTU) is a property tax levied annually based on the fair market value of property in urban areas at rates that generally vary according to the municipality and location of the property. In the municipality of São Paulo, the basic IPTU rate is 1% for residential properties or 1.5% for commercial properties (both rates may be increased or decreased according to the market value of the property).

Transfer taxes

Imposto de Transmissão de Bens Imóveis Inter Vivos (ITBI) is a property tax levied at the transfer of immovable property, with rates also varying based on the municipality where the property is located. The ITBI rate in the municipality of São Paulo is currently 2%, applied over the market value of the property.

Imposto sobre Transmissão Causa Mortis e Doações (ITCMD) is a state property transfer tax normally payable at rates varying from state to state on inheritances and donations of goods and rights. In the State of São Paulo, ITCMD is charged at the rate of 4%.

Tax on financial transactions (IOF)

IOF is a tax levied primarily on certain financial transactions, such as loans, foreign exchange operations, insurance, and securities, as well as transactions with gold (as a financial asset) and foreign exchange instruments. The applicable rate will vary depending on the transaction. The IOF rate may be reduced to 0% in some cases, such as: (i) exchange transactions relating to the inflow of revenues in Brazil deriving from the export of goods and services; (ii) exchange transactions relating to the inflow and outflow of resources in and from Brazil, stemming from foreign loans with average term exceeding 1,800 days; and (iii) remittances of interest on net equity and dividends relating to foreign investment.

Cross-border loans signed on or after 12 March 2012, with average payment terms of up to 1,800 days (five years), are subject to IOF tax at the rate of 6%, applicable on the foreign currency exchange transactions (inflow of funds into the country only).

Social assistance contribution (*Contribuição para o Financiamento da Seguridade social or Cofins*)

Cofins, a monthly federal social assistance contribution calculated as a percentage of revenue, is levied at the rate of 7.6%. A Cofins credit system is meant to ensure the tax is applied only once on the final value of each transaction. However, some taxpayers (such as financial institutions, telecommunication companies, cooperatives, and companies which opt to calculate IRPJ and CSLL using a 'presumed profits' method) are still subject to the previous Cofins system, which applies a rate of 3% with no credit system.

Federal social contribution (Programa de Integração Social or PIS)

PIS, which is also a federal social contribution calculated as a percentage of revenue, is levied at the rate of 1.65%. A PIS credit system is meant to ensure the tax is applied only once on the final value of each transaction. However, some taxpayers (such as financial institutions, telecommunication companies, cooperatives, and companies that opt to calculate IRPJ and CSLL using a 'presumed profits' method) are still subject to the previous PIS system, which applies a rate of 0.65% with no credit system.

PIS and Cofins on imports

Importation of goods and services are also subject to PIS and Cofins (in addition to all other taxes imposed on import transactions). PIS and Cofins are imposed on the Brazilian entity or individual (the importer of goods or services) and applied at the rates of 1.65% and 7.6%, respectively. The contributions paid upon import transactions may, in some instances, be creditable.

Contribution for the Intervention in the Economic Domain (Contribuição de Intervenção no Domínio Econômico or CIDE)

CIDE is a contribution levied at the rate of 10% on remittances made by corporate taxpayers for royalties and for administrative and technical services provided by non-residents. CIDE is payable by the local entity, and therefore, not creditable to the non-resident. CIDE does not represent a liability to the foreign recipient. CIDE is not applied on the payments relating to the license to use, market, or sublicense software, provided that it does not involve transfer of technology.

Branch income

Profits of branches of foreign corporations are taxable at the normal rates applicable to Brazilian resident corporations.

Income determination

Brazilian taxpayers have the option (subject to some restrictions) to calculate IRPJ and CSLL using an 'actual profits' method ('*Lucro Real*'), which is based on total taxable income (book results before taxes), adjusted by certain additions and deductions as determined in the legislation.

Brazilian taxpayers also have the option to calculate IRPJ and CSLL using a 'presumed profits' method ('*Lucro Presumido*'). Under the 'presumed profits' method, the income is calculated on a quarterly basis on an amount equal to different percentages of gross revenue (based on the entity's activities) and adjusted as determined by the prevailing legislation.

Inventory valuation

Brazilian income tax regulations require that inventory may be valued at the actual average cost or by the cost of the most recently acquired or produced goods. Rulings to the effect that last in first out (LIFO) is not acceptable have been given.

Brazil

Capital gains

Capital gains derived from the sale of assets and rights, including shares/quotas, are taxed as ordinary income. However, profits on certain long-term sales of permanent assets may be computed for tax purposes on a cash basis. Profits on long-term contracts may be computed on a percentage-of-completion basis. When these contracts are entered into with the government or government-owned companies, the profit may be recognised on a cash basis for tax purposes.

Except during the year when incurred, capital losses may be offset only against capital gains. Unused capital losses are treated similarly to income tax losses with regard to limits on use and carryforward period.

Capital gains derived by non-residents (including transactions carried out abroad between two non-resident investors, involving assets or rights located in Brazil) are taxed in Brazil. The Brazilian source performing the remittance of capital gains to the non-resident (whether a Brazilian acquirer or the local solicitor of a foreign acquiring entity) must withhold the applicable income tax on such amounts on behalf of the latter at the rate of 15% (or 25% if the beneficiary is located in a tax haven jurisdiction).

Dividend income

No withholding tax (WHT) is payable on cash dividends or profits paid or credited to either corporate or individual local shareholders. Brazilian resident beneficiaries are not subject to further income tax.

Foreign-source dividend income is subject to Brazilian income tax.

Financial income

Fixed-rate interest income from short, medium, or long-term financial market transactions, including swap transactions, is subject to WHT at rates ranging from 15% to 22.5%. Non-fixed financial gains related to stock/commodities exchange and/or futures market transactions are taxed at the rates of 20% (day-trade) and 15% (all other cases). The total income or gain is considered taxable income, and the tax withheld may be offset against the total tax due by the corporate taxpayer.

Foreign currency exchange gain/loss

With respect to foreign currency exchange gain/loss, which may arise from receivables or liabilities denominated in foreign currency, Brazilian tax legislation allows the local company to elect to consider the related effect, for tax computation purposes, either upon accrual or cash basis (i.e. actual receipt/payment of funds).

Foreign income

Brazilian resident companies are taxed on worldwide income. Profits of foreign subsidiaries, affiliates, and controlled companies are taxed at the date of the financial statements in which the profits are calculated, regardless of remittance. Double taxation may be avoided by means of foreign tax credits.

Deductions

Depreciation and depletion

Depreciation is allowable on a straight-line basis over the useful life of the asset. The annual rates normally allowable are 10% for machinery, equipment, furniture, and installations; 20% for vehicles; and 4% for buildings. Accelerated depreciation is allowed for companies with a two or three working shift operation by increasing normal rates by 50% and 100%, respectively.

Depletion allowances are allowed for natural resources on a useful-life basis. Special incentive depletion allowances are granted for mining operations.

The new Brazilian accounting rules determine that companies must obtain a useful life study for fixed assets in order to determine the acceptable depreciation rates. However, for tax purposes, depreciation rates established by the Brazilian tax authorities are still being accepted under the so called 'Transitional Tax Regime' (*Regime Tributário de Transição* or RTT).

Goodwill

Amortisation of goodwill that arises as a result of accounting for investments in subsidiary and associated entities by the equity pick-up method is deferred for taxation purposes until the related investment has been realised (e.g. sold, disposed). However, under certain requirements, goodwill paid upon the acquisition of the shares or quotas of a permanent investment may be amortised before this realisation occurs (e.g. after a merger or a spin-off). It is important to note that, although still applicable for tax purposes (under the RTT, and until further regulation is issued), the amortisation of goodwill is no longer accepted under Brazil's new accounting practices.

Amortisation of patents, trademarks, and copyrights, based on their legal limited life, is a deductible expense within approved limits.

Start-up expenses

As a general rule, and under the RTT, for tax purposes start-up expenses may be deferred and amortised on the straight-line basis over a period of not less than five years, beginning the month in which the business starts operating.

Research and development (R&D) expenditures

At the option of the company, R&D expenditures may be deducted when incurred or deferred until termination of the project and then amortised over a period of not less than five years.

Interest on net equity

Companies can pay interest (calculated on a pro rata basis and up to a given rate known as the 'long-term interest rate' (*Taxa de Juros de Longo Prazo* or TJLP), which is currently set at 6% in 2012) to partners and/or share/quotaholders, based on the company's net equity. Such interest, which may not exceed the highest of 50% of the annual profits or 50% of the accumulated earnings and profits, is deductible for both IRPJ and CSLL purposes and is subject to 15% WHT at the source (or 25% if the beneficiary is located in a tax haven jurisdiction). Whenever the beneficiary is a legal entity subject to normal income tax in Brazil, the tax withheld at the source may be taken by the recipient as a tax credit against the normal corporate income tax due or the tax due at the source on distributions of interest. If the beneficiary is a Brazilian resident individual, such interest will not become subject to any further taxation.

Interest and other payments to entities in a tax haven or under a privileged tax regime

Provisions similar to those for thin capitalisation (see the Group taxation section) are also applicable to interest paid or credited by a Brazilian entity to an individual or legal entity (whether or not a related party) resident or domiciled in a tax haven or

Brazil

in a jurisdiction under a privileged tax regime. In these cases, the interest expense is only deductible for Brazilian income tax purposes if it is viewed as necessary to the company's activities and the total amount of the Brazilian entity's debt with any foreign party resident or domiciled in a tax haven or in a jurisdiction under a privileged tax regime does not exceed 30% of the Brazilian entity's net equity.

The Law also provides that amounts paid, credited, delivered, used, or remitted under any title, directly or indirectly, to related or unrelated individuals or legal entities which are resident or domiciled in a tax haven or in a jurisdiction under a privileged tax regime will only be viewed as deductible for Brazilian income tax purposes if all of the following conditions are met: (i) the effective beneficiary of the payment is identified; (ii) there is evidence that the payment beneficiary has operational capacity (i.e. substance); and (iii) there is adequate documentation to support the relevant payments and the corresponding supply of goods, rights, or utilisation of services.

Tax havens and privileged tax regime lists

Normative Instruction (NI) n. 1,037/2010, issued by the Brazilian tax authorities, lists several jurisdictions that are considered not to tax income or to tax it at a rate lower than 20% or that deny access to information regarding shareholding and ownership of assets and rights.

The NI also enumerates jurisdictions that are considered to have 'privileged tax regimes', as set forth in Brazilian legislation. The following types of entities are included in the updated list:

- Holding Companies incorporated under the law of Denmark, which do not carry out substantial economic activity.
- Holding Companies incorporated under the law of the Netherlands, which do not carry out substantial economic activity. Note that inclusion has been temporarily suspended pending a review requested by the Dutch government.
- International Trading Companies (ITC) incorporated under the law of Iceland.
- Offshore Companies (KFT) incorporated under the law of Hungary.
- Limited Liability Companies incorporated under the state law of the United States, owned by non-residents and not subject to US federal income tax.
- Holding Companies (ETVE) incorporated under the law of Spain. Note that inclusion has been temporarily suspended pending a review requested by the Spanish government.
- International Trading Companies (ITC) and International Holding Companies (IHC) incorporated under the law of Malta.

It is generally understood that the concept of a privileged tax regime is subject to stricter transfer pricing, thin capitalisation, and tax deduction rules. As for the jurisdictions considered as tax havens, besides the tax consequences applicable for privileged tax regimes, the withholding income tax rate due on capital gains and cross-border payments such as services fees, royalties, and interest is increased from 15% to 25%.

Bad debt

Losses on bad debts are tax deductible, depending on the amounts, time overdue, and administrative and/or legal actions taken to recover losses. Losses arising from inter-company transactions are not tax deductible.

Charitable contributions
Donations are deductible up to certain limits if recipients are registered as charitable institutions.

Travel expenses
Travel expenses may only be considered deductible if they are duly documented and substantiated.

Medical and pension expenses
Expenses of group medical care and health insurance programmes for employees and contributions to private supplementary pension schemes are considered deductible if supplied to all employees indistinctly.

Fines and penalties
Punitive tax/contribution penalties are not deductible for tax purposes.

Taxes/contributions
Taxes, contributions, and related costs, such as late-payment interest, are deductible for tax purposes on the accrual basis. This rule does not apply to taxes/contributions being or to be challenged by the taxpayer at any level of litigation, which are deductible for tax purposes only on a cash basis.

Net operating losses
Tax losses may be carried forward without any time limitation. However, the tax loss may not reduce taxable income by more than 30% of its amount prior to the compensation of the tax loss itself. Tax loss is defined as the accounting loss adjusted for tax purposes.

There is no carryback of tax losses.

Payments to foreign affiliates and related companies
Royalties and technical service fees payable to foreign companies with a direct or indirect controlling interest in the Brazilian company are deductible for tax purposes (observing applicable deduction limits), provided the contract has been duly registered with the National Institute of Industrial Property (*Instituto Nacional da Propriedade Industrial* or INPI) and approved by the Brazilian Central Bank.

In addition to the thin capitalisation rules, which restrict the deductibility of interest expenses in Brazil, deductibility of interest is also conditioned to approval of the respective contract by the Brazilian Central Bank. However, on unregistered related-party loans, the deductible interest may not exceed interest calculated using the six-month US dollar deposit LIBOR (London Interbank Offered Rate) rate plus 3%. It is important to note that, based on Provisional Measure n. 563/2012, interest on related party loans, even if duly registered with the Brazilian Central Bank, will be deductible only up to an interest rate equal to the LIBOR dollar rate for six-month loans plus a spread to be annually determined by the Ministry of Finance, based on average market rate. This change shall be effective for transactions to be carried out as of 2013.

Group taxation

Consolidated tax returns are not permitted in Brazil.

Brazil

Transfer pricing

The Brazilian transfer pricing rules apply to import and export transactions of goods, services, and rights between related parties (the legislation provides a broad list of the parties considered as 'related' for transfer pricing purposes). Under such rules, the transfer price determined between related parties will be acceptable, for Brazilian tax purposes, if it is determined that such price is at arm's length according to one of the traditional methods established by the legislation (no profit methods available). Moreover, all operations with jurisdictions considered as tax havens will also be subject to transfer pricing rules whether involving related parties or not.

The statutory rules provide that interest on related party loans that are duly registered with the Brazilian Central Bank will not be subject to transfer pricing adjustments. However, interest paid on a loan contracted with a related party, not registered with the Brazilian Central Bank, will be deductible only to the extent that the interest rate equals the LIBOR dollar rate for six-month loans plus 3% per year (adjusted to the contract's period).

Notwithstanding the above, it is important to note that Provisional Measure n. 563/12 set forth new transfer pricing rules applicable to inter-company loans, as mentioned before. Accordingly to such rules, interest on related party loans, even if duly registered with the Brazilian Central Bank, will be deductible only up to an interest rate equal to the LIBOR dollar rate for six-month loans plus a spread to be annually determined by the Ministry of Finance, based on average market rate. This change shall be effective for transactions to be carried out as of 2013.

Operations involving royalty agreements will not be subject to the rules below if the related contract is registered with the Banco Central do Brasil (BACEN) and INPI.

Therefore, the adequacy of the price practiced between the related parties in any operations involving goods, services, and rights may be supported through the application of one of the following methods, as determined under the Brazilian transfer pricing regulations (the company may choose the most convenient method).

Methods used on import transactions:

- Comparable Independent Price Method (PIC).
- Resale Price Less Profit Method (PRL).
- Production Cost Plus Profit Method (CPL).

Methods used in export transactions:

- Export Sales Price Method (PVEx).
- Resale Price Method.
- Acquisition or Production Cost Plus Taxes and Profit Method (CAP).

Please note that imports and exports of commodities, quoted in commodities exchange markets, must be tested through the use of the newly introduced methods PCI and PECEX, respectively. Based on these methods, taxpayers shall compare the transaction amounts with the daily average quote for each product; the Federal Revenue Service shall issue instructions on how these methods shall be applied.

Relief of proof rules for inter-company export transactions are available.

The referred Provisional Measure also introduced other relevant changes to Brazilian transfer pricing rules, such as:

- The resale minus method (PRL) shall be calculated based on a specific mark-up determined for some industries, and a mark-up of 20% for the industries/sectors that are not specified in the legislation.
- Taxpayers are no longer required to include custom duty and other customs expenses in the tested price, nor include freight and insurance contracted with third parties, provided they are not located in low tax jurisdictions/jurisdictions with privileged tax regimes.
- The use of the taxpayer's own transactions with third parties for purposes of the use of the PIC method (equivalent of the comparable uncontrolled price method) will be acceptable only to the extent the comparable transactions are equivalent to 5% of the tested transactions.

Thin capitalisation

The Brazilian thin capitalisation rules establish that interest paid or credited by a Brazilian entity to a related party (individual or legal entity), resident or domiciled abroad, not constituted in a tax haven or in a jurisdiction with a privileged tax regime, may only be deducted for income tax purposes if the interest expense is viewed as necessary for the activities of the local entity and the following requirements are met: (i) the amount of debt granted by the foreign related party (which has participation in the Brazilian entity) does not exceed twice the amount of its participation in the net equity of the Brazilian entity; (ii) the amount of debt granted by a foreign related party (which does not have participation in the Brazilian entity) does not exceed twice the amount of the net equity of the Brazilian entity; (iii) the total amount of debt granted by foreign related parties as per (i) and (ii) does not exceed twice the sum of participation of all related parties in the net equity of the Brazilian entity; and (iv) in case debt is only granted by related parties that do not have a participation in the Brazilian entity, the total amount of debt granted by all of these related parties does not exceed twice the amount of the Brazilian entity's net equity. If one of the mentioned 2:1 ratios is exceeded, the portion of interest related to the excess debt amount will not be deductible for Brazilian income tax purposes.

Normative Instruction 1,154, issued by the Brazilian Revenue Service on 13 May 2011, further regulated the concept of related party and the calculation procedures in connection with the thin capitalisation tests.

Tax credits and incentives

Foreign tax credit

Brazilian resident companies are taxed on worldwide income, but they may compensate the income tax paid in the country of domicile of the branch, controlled, or associated company, and the tax paid on earnings and capital gains, against the corporate income tax due in Brazil. The amount of tax effectively paid abroad, to be compensated, may not exceed the amount of income tax and surtax due in Brazil on the amount of profits, earnings, and capital gains included in the calculation of taxable income.

Investment project incentives

Total or partial exemption from duty, excise tax, and social contributions on imported equipment is granted on certain approved investment projects.

Brazil

Approved investment projects are also granted accelerated depreciation on nationally produced equipment and access to low-cost financing. Sales of some capital equipment are exempt from state sales tax.

Brazilian corporate taxpayers can apply a percentage of their income tax liability on deposit for reinvestment and investment in their own approved investment projects. These approved investment projects are normally granted total or partial income tax exemption.

The Brazilian legislation also provides tax incentives for projects focusing on technological innovation.

Greater Brazil Plan (Plano Brasil Maior)
In August 2011, the Brazilian government announced several measures with the aim to benefit local manufacturers and exporters of goods and services. Referred to as 'Brasil Maior' (Greater Brazil), the government's plan focuses on increasing national competitiveness through incentives for technical innovation, research, added value in production, as well as providing clear advantages for exporters.

RECOPA
RECOPA is a special tax regime for the construction, expansion, reform, or modernisation of football stadiums, which will host the official matches of the 2013 Confederations Cup and the 2014 World Cup, to take place in Brazil. A specific licence is required prior to fruition of the associated benefits.

Legal entities that hold construction/reform projects approved by the Ministry of Sports may be entitled to the following benefits:

- Suspension of II, IPI and PIS/Cofins-import on the import of machinery, working instruments, equipments, and construction material to be used or incorporated in the construction of football stadiums.
- Suspension of PIS/Cofins and IPI on local acquisition of the abovementioned goods.
- Suspension of PIS/Cofins-import on import of services by the RECOPA beneficiary.
- Suspension of PIS and Cofins on local provision of services to RECOPA's beneficiaries.

These suspensions may be converted to a 0% tax rate (exemption) after the incorporation of such goods in the construction/reform process.

The Brazilian government also grants tax benefits to those involved with the organisation of FIFA's 2013 and 2014 Football Cups in Brazil, provided that such entities and events are previously licensed by the Brazilian tax authorities based on a list provided by FIFA.

These benefits include tax exemptions on import of several perishable goods or merchandise for use and consumption in the organisation of the events promoted by FIFA and its related entities.

Regional incentives
Income tax exemptions or reductions are also available for companies set up in specified regions within Brazil, primarily the north and northeast regions. These incentives are designed to accelerate the development of certain less-developed regions and industries considered to be of importance to the economy.

Brazil

Other incentives
Excise and sales tax exemptions are granted to exporters of manufactured goods.

B

Withholding taxes

Profits/dividends distributed to resident or non-resident beneficiaries (individuals and/or legal entities) are not subject to WHT. This provision is also applicable to dividends paid to non-resident companies located in a tax haven jurisdiction.

The WHT rate applicable to payments for services rendered by non-resident companies or individuals is generally 15% but can be increased to 25% in certain cases.

Payments for services, royalties, and interest to non-resident companies located in a tax haven jurisdiction are subject to WHT at the rate of 25%.

Certain types of income paid by Brazilian companies to non-resident recipients are subject to WHT as follows:

Recipient	WHT (%) (3) Dividends (1)	Interest	Royalties
Non-resident companies and individuals:			
Non-treaty:	0	15	15
Tax haven	0	25	25
Treaty (2):			
Argentina	0	15	15
Austria	15	15	10/15/25
Belgium	10/15	10/15	10/15/20
Canada	15	10/15	15/25
Chile	10/15	15	15
China, P.R.	15	15	15/25
Czech Republic	15	10/15	15/25
Denmark	25	15	15/25
Ecuador	15	15	15/25
Finland	10	15	10/15/25
France	15	10/15	10/15/25
Hungary	15	10/15	15/25
India	15	15	15/25
Israel	10/15	15	10/15
Italy	15	15	15/25
Japan	12.5	12.5	12.5/15/25
Korea, Republic of	10/15	10/15	10/15/25
Luxembourg	15/25	10/15	15/25
Mexico	10/15	15	10/15
Netherlands	15	10/15	15/25
Norway	15	15	15/25
Peru	10/15	15	15
Philippines	15/25	10/15	15/25
Portugal	10/15	15	15

Brazil

Recipient	WHT (%) (3)		
	Dividends (1)	Interest	Royalties
Slovak Republic	15	10/15	15/25
South Africa	10/15	15	10/15
Spain	10/15	10/15	10/15
Sweden	25	25	25
Ukraine	10/15	15	15

Notes

1. Note that the remittance of dividends is not subject to taxation in Brazil.
2. Treaty rates in excess of those in force for non-treaty countries are automatically reduced. The treaty concerned should be consulted to confirm that the tax reduction is applicable in each case.
3. For treaties with multiple WHT rates, the following rules generally apply:
   - Dividends: if there was WHT on dividends, which is not the case according to Brazilian legislation, the 10% (or 15%) rate would generally apply if the beneficial owner is a company which holds directly a certain minimum participation in the capital of the company paying the dividends; the 15% (or 25%) rate is considered for all other cases.
   - Interest: the 10% rate generally applies to loans with a certain minimum term granted for specific purposes (e.g. acquisition of capital goods); the 15% rate is considered for all other cases.
   - Royalties: the 10% rate generally applies to royalties arising from the use of, or the right to use, cinematograph films, and films or tapes for television or radio broadcasting, and any copyright of literary, artistic, or scientific work produced by a resident of a contracting state; the 25% (or 15%) rate generally applies to royalties arising from the use of, or the right to use, trademarks; and the 15% (or 10%) rate is considered for all other cases.

Tax administration

Taxable period
For tax purposes, a company's year-end is 31 December. A different year-end for corporate purposes is irrelevant.

Tax returns
With few exceptions, corporate entities, including those that are foreign-controlled, must file an annual adjusting tax return consolidating the monthly results of the previous calendar year. This tax return must normally be filed by the end of June following the tax year ending on 31 December.

Supporting documentation must be retained for at least five years.

Payment of tax
In the case of income tax, it is calculated monthly, and prepayments must be paid by the last working day of the subsequent month. Any amounts of income tax due for the year (exceeding the prepayments performed) must be paid by the last working day of March of the subsequent year.

There is an option to pay the tax due at the end of each quarter in three installments, the first one starting from the subsequent month to the end of the quarter. When income tax is calculated quarterly, the taxpayer must perform the applicable payment by the last working day of the month subsequent to the end of the quarter.

Statute of limitations

For corporate income tax purposes, the tax authorities may generally audit taxpayers up to five years after the close of the tax year (31 December). However, in case of alleged fraud or simulation, and if the taxpayer did not perform the payment of the corporate income tax for the relevant fiscal year, the statute of limitations of five years will begin as from the first day of the following year to the one in which the tax authorities could have assessed the taxpayer for the alleged fraud/simulation or unpaid tax.

As for other taxes, such as VAT (ICMS), excise tax (IPI) and import duty (II), the statute of limitations of five years begins as from the date of the taxable event.

Public digital bookkeeping system (SPED)

Brazil is currently implementing a new public system of digital bookkeeping known as SPED, which aims at gradually replacing paper copies of invoices and tax records for electronic files. SPED can be defined as an instrument that unifies the activities of reception, validation, storage, and legalisation of records and documents that are part of the commercial and tax bookkeeping of companies, through a single, computerised flow of data.

Comprised of three pillars (electronic invoice, digital fiscal bookkeeping, and digital accounting bookkeeping), the implementation of SPED requires adjustments to the relationship with tax authorities, clients, suppliers and, mainly, on the internal operational processes, which will demand an integrated action from different areas (tax, accounting, information technology, supplies, production, commercial, and others). On the other hand, occasional inconsistencies from databases, as well as operational errors related to tax and accounting information to be generated, usually unknown to the companies' administration, will be subject to an increased visibility and monitoring by the Brazilian tax authorities.

Topic of focus for tax authorities

It should be noted that, over the years, Brazil has applied a 'form over substance' approach. Nonetheless, as of 10 January 2001, Complementary Law 104/2001 has introduced a substantial modification in the Brazilian tax code (the so-called anti-avoidance rule). This law establishes a substance over form approach that, once regulated, may allow the Brazilian tax authorities to disregard tax-driven transactions.

In our local practice, we have seen that tax authorities are more and more keen on assessing taxpayers in relation to the economic substance of their operations (e.g. the use of special purpose entities to enable the amortisation of goodwill for tax purposes in Brazil).

Bulgaria

PwC contact

Irina Tsvetkova
PricewaterhouseCoopers Bulgaria EOOD
9-11 Maria Louisa Blvd., 8th Floor
1000 Sofia, Bulgaria
Tel: +359 2 91 003
Email: irina.tsvetkova@bg.pwc.com

Significant developments

There have been no significant corporate tax developments in Bulgaria during the past year.

Taxes on corporate income

Bulgarian tax residents are taxed on their worldwide income. Non-residents are taxed on their income from Bulgarian sources only, through a permanent establishment (PE) and/or via withholding tax (WHT), depending on the case (*see the Branch income section*).

In general, corporate income is subject to corporate income tax (CIT) at a flat rate of 10%.

Alternative tax
Income earned by organisers of games of chance is subject to 12% or 15% alternative tax, applied on a specific tax basis (e.g. the total value of the stakes made). A fixed-sum tax is applied to the operation of gaming machines.

Tonnage tax regime
A special alternative tax regime applies to the operation of commercial maritime vessels, as per their net tonnage, at a rate of 10%.

Local income taxes
There are no local government corporate income taxes in Bulgaria.

Corporate residence

A corporation is resident in Bulgaria for tax purposes if it is incorporated in Bulgaria.

Permanent establishment (PE)
PEs of foreign tax residents (e.g. branches) are treated as separate entities similar to Bulgarian residents for tax and accounting purposes.

The definition of a PE in the Bulgarian legislation follows, in general, the Organisation for Economic Co-operation and Development (OECD) model; however, it covers a broader scope of activities leading to a tax presence in Bulgaria. A PE is generally defined as a fixed place (own, rented, or otherwise used) through which a foreign entity partly or wholly carries out business activities in the country.

Other taxes

Value-added tax (VAT)

The standard VAT rate is 20%. A reduced VAT rate of 9% applies to certain tourist services. Some activities are zero-rated, including intracommunity supplies, exports of goods to countries outside the European Union (EU), and international transport of goods (i.e. transport to or from countries outside of the European Union).

Some supplies are VAT exempt without the right to a VAT credit, including (but not limited to) certain land transactions; leasing of residential property to individuals; and financial, insurance, gambling, educational, and health services. Options to charge VAT exist for certain land transactions, leasing of residential property to individuals, and finance lease contracts.

The following statutory periods for VAT refunds apply:

* 30 days for persons that have performed supplies subject to zero-rate (e.g. exports) within the last 12 months exceeding 30% of the total value of all taxable supplies performed by them in the same period, as well as by large investors meeting certain specific conditions.
* Two months and 30 days in all other cases.

The following mechanism for VAT recovery applies to VAT-registered companies: the positive or negative difference between the output VAT charged by the company and the input VAT for the respective month for which recovery is claimed results, respectively, in VAT payable or refundable. The VAT payable should be remitted to the state budget not later than the 14th day of the month following the respective month. VAT refundable is offset against any VAT payable in the following two months, and any remainder is effectively recovered within 30 days thereafter.

It is possible to claim a refund for VAT paid with respect to assets acquired not earlier than five years prior to the VAT registration, under certain conditions. In the case of real estate, the term is 20 years.

Customs duties

Customs duties are calculated in accordance with the EU customs tariff and regulations.

Excise duties

Excise duties are charged as a percentage of the sales price or customs value or as a flat amount in Bulgarian lev (BGN) per unit, unless a suspension regime applies. For 2012, excisable products include petrol and diesel fuel, liquefied petroleum gas (LPG), heavy oil, kerosene, beer and spirits, tobacco products, and electricity.

The applicable rates are as follows:

* Unleaded petrol: BGN 710 per 1,000 litres.
* Diesel: BGN 630 per 1,000 litres.
* LPG: BGN 340 per 1,000 kg.
* Kerosene: BGN 630 per 1,000 litres.
* Natural gas: BGN 0 per gigajoule (as of 1 June 2012 the rate is BGN 0.85 per gigajoule if used as motor fuel and BGN 0.10 if used for production purposes).
* Heavy oil: BGN 600 per 1,000 litres.
* Electricity: BGN 2 per MWh (zero rate if used by households).
* Beer: BGN 1.50/hl/°Plato.

Bulgaria

- Wine: zero rate.
- Ethyl alcohol: BGN 1,100 per hectolitre.
- Cigarettes: 23% *ad valorem* + 101/1,000 pieces (min. BGN 148).

Lower rates may apply in certain cases (e.g. energy products used for heating purposes or mixed with bio fuels, beer produced by independent small breweries, etc.).

The Excise Duties and Tax Warehouse Act introduced the tax warehousing regime and regulates the production, storage, and movement of excisable products.

Property tax

The annual property tax rate is determined by each municipality and currently ranges from 0.01% to 0.45% of the tax value of property. Individuals and legal entities that are owners of immovable property (i.e. land and buildings) are liable for property tax. For individuals and residential properties of enterprises, the taxable base is the tax value as determined by the municipal authorities based on certain statutory criteria. The taxable base for properties of enterprises is the higher of the property's gross book value and its tax value determined by the respective municipal authorities.

A garbage collection fee is payable for immovable property at a rate determined by the local municipal council annually.

Transfer tax

A transfer tax is due on the value of transferred real estate or motor vehicles, subject to certain exemptions (e.g. contributions in-kind, acquisitions under the Law on Privatisation and Post-privatisation Control). The rate of the transfer tax ranges from 0.1% to 3% and is determined by each municipality.

Stamp taxes

There are no stamp duties in Bulgaria.

Insurance premium tax

A tax of 2% is levied on all insurance premiums paid after 1 January 2011 under insurance agreements covering risks insured in Bulgaria. Life insurance, reinsurance, aircraft, vehicle, and international transport insurance agreements are exempted from this tax. The taxable base is the insurance premium received by an insurance company under an insurance agreement.

Insurance companies and their tax representatives are liable to collect the tax and remit it to the budget monthly by the end of the month following the month when the insurance premium was collected.

Tourist tax

The tourist tax is levied with respect to the number of nights spent in hotels and other places for accommodation. The municipalities may determine the tax within a range of BGN 0.20 to BGN 3 per night depending on the type of accommodation facility.

The tax is payable on a monthly basis by the 15th day of the following month.

One-off taxes

The following corporate expenses are subject to a one-off tax:

- Representative expenses related to a company's business.

- Social expenses provided to employees in kind (monetary social expenses are subject to personal income tax).
- Expenses related to the exploitation and maintenance of cars where they are used for management activities (as distinguished from administrative activities).

The rate of the one-off tax with respect to the above expenses is 10%. Both the expenses and the related one-off taxes are deductible for CIT purposes.

Branch income

Although branches are not deemed to be separate legal persons, branches of non-resident companies have separate balance sheets and profit and loss accounts and are subject to CIT at the standard rate of 10% as well as other general taxes (e.g. VAT, property tax).

Representative offices of foreign entities are not allowed to carry out business activities and are not subject to CIT. A representative office registered under the Encouragement of Investments Act may perform only those activities that are not regarded as 'economic activities' (e.g. marketing activities normally carried out by a representative office and auxiliary to the activities of its head office). Representative offices do not constitute PEs of the non-resident entities, unless they engage in business activities in breach of the law.

Profits repatriated by a branch to its head office abroad are not subject to withholding tax (WHT). However, certain income payable by a Bulgarian branch or a PE to other parts of the enterprise abroad may trigger WHT (e.g. income from technical services, interest, royalties), unless the respective expenses are not deductible to the branch or the PE, or are recharged at cost.

Income determination

The taxable result is based on the statutory accounting principles relating to profit/loss and adjusted for tax purposes. Statutory accounting is maintained on an accrual basis in line with the applicable accounting standards.

Small and medium-sized companies may apply specific national standards for the financial statements of small and medium-sized companies, or optionally, International Financial Reporting Standards (IFRS). The principles provided by the Standards for the Financial Statements of Small and Medium-sized Companies are similar to those provided by IFRS. Certain types of companies, including banks and insurance companies, are obliged to apply IFRS.

Inventory valuation
The tax legislation follows the accounting rules for inventory valuation methods. The accounting rules may restrict the application of certain methods (e.g. last in first out [LIFO] is not allowed under IFRS).

Inventory valuation and revaluation methods applicable under accounting standards may be used for tax purposes. Companies may choose the method of inventory valuation but must apply the chosen method consistently throughout the accounting period. An inventory of assets and liabilities is carried out in each accounting period. Accounting gains and losses realised upon revaluation of inventory will not be

Bulgaria

recognised for tax purposes and will form a temporary tax difference. These gains and losses will be recognised for tax purposes in the period in which the inventory is disposed of.

Capital gains
Realised capital gains are included in corporate income and are taxed at the full CIT rate.

Note that capital gains from securities will not be subject to taxation if resulting from shares in listed companies and tradable rights in such shares on a regulated securities market in the EU/European Economic Area (EEA). Assets distributed as dividends are deemed realised at market value, and any capital gains arising from this will be subject to tax.

Dividend income
Dividends distributed by Bulgarian companies to foreign shareholders and resident individuals are subject to 5% WHT under the domestic legislation (*see the Withholding taxes section for exceptions for payments to EU/EEA tax residents and under double tax treaties [DTTs]*).

Inter-company dividends
Inter-company dividend payments between Bulgarian companies and dividends distributed by EU/EEA residents to Bulgarian companies (except for dividends from special purpose investment companies or in case of 'hidden distribution of profits') are not included in the tax base of the recipient company.

Stock dividends
No explicit regulation with respect to stock dividends exists in the Bulgarian CIT act. Rather, the tax treatment of stock dividends follows the accounting treatment.

Exchange rate gains/losses
Exchange rate gains and losses are reported in the profit and loss account and reflected in the assessment of taxable profit.

Foreign income
Income derived outside Bulgaria by resident legal entities and income derived in Bulgaria by Bulgarian branches of non-residents is included in the taxable base for the purpose of CIT, regardless of whether such income is subject to taxation abroad.

In instances where the provisions of a DTT are applicable, a tax credit or exemption for the foreign tax paid may be allowed. There is also a unilateral tax credit which may not exceed the amount of the tax that would be payable in Bulgaria for the same type of income.

Undistributed income of foreign subsidiaries of a Bulgarian resident company is not taxed.

Deductions

Depreciation and depletion
For accounting purposes, depreciation is calculated in accordance with the straight-line, progressive, or declining-balance methods of depreciation. Accounting regulations

permit Bulgarian companies to establish a depreciation schedule for each tangible and intangible fixed asset on the basis of the method chosen by the company.

For tax purposes, only the straight-line method is permitted. For machines and equipment that are part of the initial investment, accelerated depreciation may also apply, subject to certain conditions.

For tax purposes, fixed assets are divided into the following seven categories:

Category	Assets	Maximum rates (%)
I	Massive buildings, industrial constructions/equipment, transmission facilities/lines (including electricity)	4
II	Machinery, production facilities, apparatuses	30/50
III	Vehicles (except cars), coverage of roads and runways	10
IV	Computers, peripherals to computers, software and rights to use software, mobile phones	50
V	Cars	25
VI	Long-term intangibles with legal or contractual limitations on the period of use	33 1/3
VII	Other assets	15

Under certain conditions, assets classified in Category II that are new may be depreciated at a maximum rate of 50% for tax purposes.

The depreciation rate for Category VI is determined by the period of limitations, but not more than 33 1/3%.

Depletion is not specifically regulated for tax purposes.

Goodwill
Goodwill is not amortisable under Bulgarian tax law.

Start-up expenses
Start-up expenses may be recognised as deductible in the year of establishment of the company.

Interest expenses
Interest expenses are recognised as deductible expenses, subject to the thin capitalisation rules applicable in Bulgaria (*see Thin capitalisation in the Group taxation section*).

Bad debt
Bad debt impairment costs can be deducted upon expiration of the statute of limitation period. Also, the impairment costs can be recognised for tax purposes upon transferring the receivables. Such impairment costs are tax deductible for financial institutions in the year of recognition.

Charitable contributions
Generally, charitable contributions to certain organisations or persons, specified by law, can be deductible at up to 10% of a company's accounting profit.

Bulgaria

Fines and penalties
Expenses for fines and penalties for violation of the legislation are not deductible.

Taxes
CIT is not deductible for tax purposes. However, other taxes, such as one-off taxes on certain expenses (e.g. representative expenses, certain types of fringe benefits) or local taxes and fees may be recognised as deductible for CIT purposes.

Net operating losses
The taxpayer has the right to carry forward tax losses incurred in a given year over the following five years. The loss subject to carryforward is the negative amount of the financial result adjusted for tax purposes, with certain add-backs and deductions specified in the tax legislation.

Tax losses may be reversed up to the amount of the positive financial result after tax adjustments (without the effect of the loss subject to be carried forward itself).

Carryforwards of foreign-source losses may only offset income from the same source. However, EU/EEA-source losses may offset income from other sources, including Bulgarian sources.

Loss carryback is permitted in very specific cases.

Payments to foreign affiliates
Payments to foreign affiliates may be subject to recalculation by the tax authorities if such payments are not made at arm's length.

Group taxation

No group consolidation is permitted for tax purposes in Bulgaria. All companies must pay tax on the basis of individually assessable profits and losses.

Transfer pricing
Bulgarian law requires that taxpayers determine their taxable profits and incomes applying the arm's-length principle to prices at which they exchange goods, services, and intangibles with related parties (transfer prices). Bulgarian transfer pricing rules generally follow OECD Transfer Pricing Guidelines.

Transfer prices are not set in compliance with the arm's-length principle where:

* prices of the supply of goods or services differ from the market prices or
* loans are received or granted against an interest rate that differs from the market interest rate effective at the time the loan agreement is concluded.

The market interest rate is defined as the interest payable under the same conditions for a loan provided or received, notwithstanding the form of the loan, between non-related parties. The market interest is determined according to the market conditions.

The taxable person should be able to evidence that its relations with related parties are in line with the arm's-length principle.

For the purposes of transfer pricing rules, market prices are determined by the following methods:

- Comparable uncontrolled price method.
- Resale price method.
- Cost plus method.
- Transactional net margin method.
- Profit split method.

Preparation of transfer pricing documentation is not mandatory but is recommendable for material related party transactions. Recently, the revenue authorities tend to focus more on the transfer pricing area.

Currently, there is no possibility to obtain an Advance Pricing Agreement (APA). However, it is possible to obtain an opinion from the revenue authorities on a case-by-case basis. Such opinions are not binding, but they may provide protection from assessment of interest for late payment and penalties.

Thin capitalisation

Interest payable by local companies to local or foreign persons may be restricted by the thin capitalisation rules (which also apply to interest due to non-affiliated companies).

The tax deductibility for interest expenses that exceed interest income is restricted to 75% of the accounting result of the company, exclusive of interest income and expense. If the accounting result of the company before including the effect of the interest income and expenses is a loss, none of the net interest expense will be deductible for tax purposes. Interest on bank loans and interest under financial lease agreements are subject to thin capitalisation regulations only when the agreements are between related parties or guaranteed by or extended at the order of a related party.

The thin capitalisation rules do not apply if the debt-to-equity ratio does not exceed 3:1 for the respective tax period.

Interest expenses restricted in a given year under the thin capitalisation rules may be deducted from the financial result for tax purposes during the following five consecutive years. This reversal may be made up to the tax allowed interest expenses, as per the above formula.

Tax credits and incentives

Tax incentives may apply in certain circumstances, including:

- Partial granting of the CIT due for performance of agricultural activities.
- Additional tax deductions for hiring of long-term unemployed, handicapped, or elderly persons.
- Full granting back of the CIT due for investment in regions with high unemployment.

Foreign tax credit

See Foreign income in the Income determination section for a description of the foreign tax credit regime.

Withholding taxes

Bulgarian companies are required to withhold tax on payments of dividends and liquidation proceeds; interest (including that incurred under finance lease agreements

Bulgaria

and on bank deposits); royalties; fees for technical services; payments for the use of properties; payments made under operating leasing, franchising, and factoring agreements; and management fees payable to non-residents.

Capital gains from the transfer of shares in a Bulgarian company or immovable property located in Bulgaria realised by a non-resident are also subject to domestic WHT; however, the tax is payable by the non-resident. Capital gains from securities are not subject to WHT if they result from shares in listed companies and tradable rights in such shares on a regulated securities market in the EU/EEA.

Dividends and liquidation proceeds are also taxed where payments are made to resident individuals and non-profit organisations (*for details on dividend payments between domestic companies, see Dividend income in the Income determination section*). Dividends capitalised into shares (stock dividends) are not subject to WHT.

Interest and royalty payments payable to EU-based associated companies are subject to a reduced 5% WHT rate in Bulgaria. Associated company criteria are identical to those in the Interest and Royalty Directive and require holding of at least 25% for at least two years. Exemption from WHT on interest and royalties payable to associated companies will be introduced as of 1 January 2015.

Any fees for services and use of rights (in addition to technical services fees and royalties) accrued to entities in low-tax jurisdictions will attract 10% Bulgarian WHT unless there is proof of the effective provision of the supply. Subject to 10% WHT would also be any accruals for penalties or damages payments to entities in low-tax jurisdictions, except for insurance compensations. The tax legislation introduces a list of low-tax jurisdictions. These are certain off-shore territories which are explicitly listed, as well as countries with which Bulgaria has not signed a DTT and in which the applicable corporate tax rates are more than 60% lower than the applicable rate in Bulgaria.

Certain types of income (other than dividends) accrued by a PE of a foreign person to other parts of its enterprise located outside the country are subject to WHT (*except for that mentioned in the Branch income section*).

Dividends
When a dividend is accrued to a non-resident company or an individual (both resident and foreign), it is subject to WHT at a rate of 5%, unless the rate is reduced by an applicable DTT. No differentiation is made between portfolio and substantial holdings for purposes of this WHT on dividends.

Dividends distributed by a Bulgarian resident company to an entity that is a tax resident in an EU/EEA member state are not subject to Bulgarian WHT.

Interest
A 10% rate applies to interest (including interest from bank deposits) payable to a non-resident, unless the rate is reduced by an applicable DTT.

Interest on borrowings by the government or the Bulgarian National Bank from international financial institutions is not taxable if the respective loan agreements contain relevant exemption arrangements (international treaties override domestic legislation).

Bulgaria

Interest paid to an associated EU-based related company is subject to a 5% WHT unless reduced by a DTT (require at least 25% holding for at least two years).

Royalties
Royalties payable to foreign persons are taxed at a rate of 10% at source, unless the rate is reduced by an applicable DTT.

Royalty payments to an associated EU-based related company are subject to a 5% WHT unless reduced by a DTT (require at least 25% holding for at least two years).

Capital gains and technical services
Capital gains and technical service fees payable to foreign residents are subject to 10% WHT, unless the rate is reduced by an applicable DTT. As per the domestic legislation, technical services include installation and assembly of tangible assets as well as consultancy services and marketing research.

Application of DTT relief
Applying DTT relief is generally possible only after completing an advance clearance procedure with the Bulgarian tax authorities. Companies have to evidence that they satisfy the requirements for applying the DTT (e.g. tax residence, beneficial ownership, existence of contractual relationship, actual accrual/payment of the income). The procedure usually takes 60 days to complete.

The above procedure has to be followed only if the annual income payable by a Bulgarian resident exceeds BGN 500,000 (approximately 250,000 euros [EUR]). In all other cases, DTT relief can be applied directly, through submitting a tax residence certificate and a beneficial ownership declaration with the payer of the income.

Beneficial ownership is explicitly defined in Bulgarian legislation. A company is considered a beneficial owner of the income if it has the right to dispose of the income, has discretion over its use, bears the whole or a significant part of the risk of the activity from which the income is realised, and does not qualify as a conduit company.

A conduit company is a company which is controlled by persons who would not benefit from the same type and amount exemption if the income was realised directly by them, does not carry out any economic activity except for owning and/or administering the rights or the assets from which the income was realised, and does not own assets, capital, or personnel relevant to its economic activity or does not control the use of the rights or assets from which the income was realised.

The conduit company restriction does not apply to companies which have more than a half of their voting shares traded on a registered stock exchange.

The following is a summary of the main parameters of the Bulgarian DTTs as of 1 January 2012:

Recipient	WHT (%)			
	Dividends*	Interest**	Royalties**	Capital gains
Albania (3, 6, 9, 28)	5/15	0/10	10	0/10
Algeria (24)	10	0/10	10	0
Armenia (1, 2, 6, 28, 36)	5/10	0/5/10	5/10	0/10
Austria (6, 10, 35)	0/5	0/5	0/5	0/10

Bulgaria

Recipient	WHT (%)			
	Dividends*	Interest**	Royalties**	Capital gains
Azerbaijan (6, 28, 34)	8	7	5/10	0
Bahrain (6)	5	0/5	5	0
Belarus (6)	10	0/10	10	0
Belgium (6, 10, 27)	10	0/10	5	0
Canada (9, 16, 28)	10/15	10	10	0/10
China (2, 6, 9, 28)	10	0/10	7/10	0/10
Croatia	5	5	0	0
Cyprus (3, 26, 27)	5/10	7	10	0/10
Czech Republic (11, 27)	10	10/0	10	0
Denmark (3, 27)	5/15	0	0	0
Egypt (6)	10	0/12.5	12.5	10
Estonia (9, 16)	0/5	5	5	0/10
Finland (4, 9, 12, 27)	10	0	0/5	0/10
France (5, 27)	5/15	0	5	0
Georgia (6)	10	0/10	10	0
Germany (11, 16, 26, 27, 36)	5/15	0/5	5	0/10
Greece (27)	10	10	10	0
Hungary (6, 27)	10	0/10	10	0
India (6)	15	0/15	15/20	10
Indonesia (6)	15	0/10	10	0
Iran (6, 9, 28)	7.5	0/5	5	0/10
Ireland (3, 6, 9, 27, 28)	5/10	0/5	10	0/10
Israel (18, 19, 20, 21)	10/7.5 to 12.5	0/5/10	7.5 to 12.5	7.5 to 12.5
Italy (27)	10	0	5	0
Japan (3, 6)	10/15	0/10	10	10
Jordan (6, 28)	10	0/10	10	0
Kazakhstan (8, 9, 28)	10	0/10	10	0/10
Kuwait (3, 22)	0/5	0/5	10	0
Latvia (3, 9, 24, 25, 27, 28)	5/10	0/5	5/7	0/10
Lebanon (6)	5	7/0	5	0
Lithuania (16, 28, 29)	0/10	0/10	10	0/10
Luxembourg (3, 10, 27)	5/15	10	5	0
Macedonia (3, 6)	5/15	0/10	10	0
Malta (12, 17, 27)	0/30	0	10	0
Moldova (3, 6, 9, 28)	5/15	0/10	10	0/10
Mongolia (6)	10	0/10	10	0
Morocco (5, 9, 28)	7/10	10	10	0/10
The Netherlands (3, 7, 9, 27)	5/15	0	0/5	0/10
North Korea (6)	10	0/10	10	0
Norway	15	0	0	0
Poland (6, 27)	10	0/10	5	0
Portugal (3, 6, 27)	10/15	0/10	10	0
Qatar (6, 36)	0	0/3	5	0
Romania (3, 6)	10/15	0/15	15	0
Russian Federation (6)	15	0/15	15	0
Serbia (3)	5/15	10	10	0

	WHT (%)			
Recipient	Dividends*	Interest**	Royalties**	Capital gains
Singapore (6)	5	0/5	5	0
Slovak Republic (27)	10	10	10	0
Slovenia (3, 23, 27, 28)	5/10	0/5	5/10	0/10
South Africa (3, 6, 23, 24)	5/15	0/5	5/10	0/10
South Korea (5, 6)	5/10	0/10	5	0
Spain (3, 27)	5/15	0	0	0
Sweden (9, 27, 28)	10	0	5	0/10
Switzerland (3, 10, 13)	5/15	0/10	0/5	0
Syria	10	0/10	18	0
Thailand (14, 15)	10	10/15	5/15	10
Turkey (3, 6, 9)	10/15	0/10	10	0/10
Ukraine (3, 6, 9, 28)	5/15	0/10	10	0/10
United Arab Emirates (6, 22, 34)	0/5	0/2	0/5	0
United Kingdom (27)	10	0	0	0
United States (16, 24, 28, 30, 31, 32, 33)	5/10	5/10	5	0
Uzbekistan (6, 28)	10	0/10	10	0/10
Vietnam (6, 9)	15	0/10	15	0/15
Zimbabwe (3, 6, 9, 28)	10/20	0/10	10	0/10

Notes

* Under Bulgarian domestic legislation, dividends distributed to non-residents are subject to 5% WHT, unless the recipient is a resident of an EU/EEA member state.

** Under Bulgarian domestic legislation, interest and royalty payments to EU-resident companies satisfying the Interest and Royalty Directive requirements are subject to a reduced 5% WHT rate.

1. The lower rate applies to dividends paid out to a non-resident that is the direct owner of at least the equivalent of 100,000 United States dollars (USD) forming part of the capital of the company making the payment.
2. The reduced rate for royalties is available for the use of (or right to use) industrial, commercial, or scientific equipment.
3. The lower rate applies to dividends paid out to a foreign company that controls directly at least 25% of the share capital of the payer of the dividends. In the specific cases of the different countries, more requirements may be in place.
4. There is no WHT on royalties for the use of (or the right to use) scientific or cultural works.
5. The lower rate applies to dividends paid out to a foreign company that controls directly at least 15% of the share capital of the payer of the dividends.
6. There is no WHT on interest when paid to public bodies (government, the central bank, and, in several cases, certain governmental bodies).
7. 5% royalties are applicable if the Netherlands applies WHT under its domestic law.
8. Up to 10% branch tax may be imposed on PE profits.
9. The 10% rate on capital gains from securities applies in specific cases that are described in the respective treaty.
10. The zero rate on interest applies if the loan is extended by a bank and also for industrial, trade, and scientific equipment on credit.
11. The zero rate on interest applies if the interest is paid to public bodies (government, municipality, the central bank, or any financial institution owned entirely by the government), to residents of the other country when the loan or the credit is guaranteed by its government, or if the loan is extended by a company for any equipment or goods.
12. The Council of Ministers has stated its intention to renegotiate the DTTs with Austria, Malta, and Finland.
13. A 5% rate on royalties applies if the Swiss Confederation introduces in its domestic law WHT on royalties paid to non-residents.
14. The 10% rate on interest applies if the interest is received from a financial institution, including an insurance company.

Bulgaria

15. The 5% rate on royalties applies if the royalties are paid for the use of copyright for literary, art, or scientific work.
16. The lower rate applies to dividends paid out to a foreign company that controls directly at least 10% of the share capital of the payer of the dividends.
17. The zero rate applies to dividends payable by a Bulgarian resident entity to an entity resident in Malta. The 30% rate applies to dividends payable by a Maltese entity to a Bulgarian entity.
18. The 10% rate applies to dividends distributed by companies that enjoy a reduced or zero CIT by virtue of a tax incentive for investments. In all other cases, the rate is equal to one half of the applicable rate as per the national legislations of Bulgaria and Israel. Nevertheless, the WHT rate may not be less than 7.5% or more than 12.5%.
19. The 5% rate applies to interest payable to banks or other financial institutions. The zero rate applies to interest payable to certain public bodies (governments, municipalities, central banks) or to residents of the other country when the loan or credit is guaranteed, insured, or financed by a public body of that country or by the Israeli International Trade Insurance Company.
20. The rate on royalties is equal to one half of the applicable rate as per the national legislations of Bulgaria and Israel. Nevertheless, the WHT rate may not be less than 7.5% or more than 12.5%.
21. The rate on capital gains from securities is equal to one half of the applicable rate as per the national legislations of Bulgaria and Israel. Nevertheless, the WHT rate may not be less than 7.5% or more than 12.5%. However, capital gains from transfers of shares in entities whose real estate properties exceed 50% of their assets are taxed in the country in which the real estate is located.
22. The zero rate applies to dividends and interest paid to certain public governmental and local bodies as well as entities fully owned by the state.
23. The 5% rate on royalties applies if the royalties are paid for the use of copyright for literary, art, or scientific work as well as for the use of industrial, commercial, or scientific equipment.
24. There is no WHT on interest when paid to and beneficially owned by public bodies (government, local public authorities, the central bank, or any financial institution wholly owned by the government), as well as on interest derived on loans guaranteed by the foreign government or based on an agreement between the governments of the states.
25. The 7% rate on royalties applies if the royalties are paid for the use of, or the right to use, cinematograph films and films or tapes for radio or television broadcasting, any patent, trademark, design or model, plan, secret formula, or process.
26. The zero rate applies for capital gains from shares in a Bulgarian resident company that are traded on the Bulgarian Stock Exchange.
27. In accordance with the EU Parent-Subsidiary Directive implemented in the Bulgarian legislation, dividends distributed by a Bulgarian resident company to an entity that is a tax resident in an EU member state may not be subject to Bulgarian WHT.
28. Full WHT at source may be levied on capital gains from the sale of shares in companies, the main assets of which are directly or indirectly holdings in real estate situated in Bulgaria, and in some other cases (subject to the specifics stipulated in the respective treaty).
29. There is no WHT on interest when paid to public bodies (government, the central bank, governmental institutions) or any financial institution wholly owned by the government.
30. Pension funds and charities are considered resident persons.
31. The zero rate does not apply to dividends distributed to real estate investment trusts (REITs).
32. The zero rate does not apply to interest paid under a back-to-back loan.
33. The benefits of the treaty are limited to entities that satisfy certain criteria (Limitation of Benefits clause).
34. The 5% rate on royalties applies if the royalties are paid for the use of, or the right to use, any patent, design, model, plan, secret formula, process, or know-how.
35. The treaty provides for 10% WHT on capital gains unless shares were sold on a recognised stock exchange or seller owned at least 20% of the issuing company's capital.
36. The reduced rate for interest is available for bank loans (subject to specifics in the treaty).

Under some DTTs, technical service payments fall within the definition of royalty payments and are taxed accordingly.

Tax administration

Taxable period
The financial and tax years coincide with the calendar year.

Tax returns
Annual profit must be declared no later than 31 March of the year following the financial (tax) year. Along with their annual CIT returns, companies are required to file financial information for their business activities during the year in a standard statistical form not subject to a financial audit. The self-assessment principle is applied.

Payment of tax

If a company ended the preceding financial year with a taxable profit, it is liable for advance CIT payments each month in the current year at the rate of 10%. The monthly taxable base for the second, third, and fourth quarters is one-twelfth of the annual taxable profit for the preceding year multiplied by a coefficient determined in the State Budget Act for the current year. However, the taxable base for the advance payments during the first quarter is one-twelfth of the taxable profit of the company for the year before the preceding year multiplied by a coefficient defined in the State Budget Act for the current year.

Corporate taxpayers having a tax loss or zero taxable result in the previous year and companies established during the current year make quarterly advance payments during the current fiscal year. The base of the quarterly advance payments is the profit for the corresponding period accumulated from the beginning of the current year.

Companies with a net sales revenue below BGN 200,000 for the preceding year and newly incorporated companies (if not established as a result of a transformation of another entity) are not required to make advance payments of CIT.

Overpayment of CIT may be offset against advance and annual payments of the respective taxes due for the next period. The difference between the annual tax declared in the CIT return and the advance tax paid for the corresponding year must be paid by the deadline for submitting the tax return on 31 March of the following year.

Statute of limitations

The statute of limitations, i.e. the period within which the state authorities are entitled to collect the tax liabilities and other related mandatory payments, is five years from the beginning of the year following the year in which the tax liabilities became payable. The above periods can be extended in certain cases. However, the maximum period of the statute of limitations is ten years.

Audit cycle

Tax audits are usually performed every four to five years, corresponding to the period of the statute of limitations.

Topics of focus for tax authorities

Transfer pricing is likely to become an area of focus for the tax authorities.

Cambodia

PwC contact

Sira Intarakumthornchai
PricewaterhouseCoopers (Cambodia) Limited
35 Sihanouk Boulevard, Sangkat Tonle Bassac, Khan Chamkarmon
Phnom Penh, Cambodia
Tel: +855 23 218 086
Email: sira.intarakumthornchai@th.pwc.com

Significant developments

Tax on immovable property (ToIP)
Further to the 2010 Law on Financial Management and Prakas No. 493 MEF/PrK on the
ToIP, the Ministry of Economy and Finance has issued Prakas No. 371 MEF/PrK on the
tax base of ToIP. The Prakas determines that the ToIP is effectively collected from year
2011 on immovable properties located in Phnom Penh and other cities of the provinces.

The ToIP base is 80% of the total value of immovable property (both land and
buildings) stated in Appendix 1 of the Prakas less the threshold of 100 million
Cambodian riels (KHR) (approximately 25,000 United States dollars [USD]).

Subsequent Notifications were issued that extended the deadline for the 2011 property
tax payment to 31 December 2011.

Sub-Decree on tax incentives in securities sector
The Royal Government of Cambodia has issued Sub-Decree No.70 to provide tax
incentives to companies listed on the Cambodian Stock Exchange (CSX) and public
investors who hold and/or trade government, equity, and debt securities on the
securities market. *See the Tax credits and incentives section for more information.*

Prakas on additional tax incentives for rice farming, paddy rice purchase, and export of milled rice
The Ministry of Economy and Finance has issued a Prakas to provide additional tax
incentives to any enterprises in the business of rice farming, paddy rice purchase, and
export of milled rice. *See the Tax credits and incentives section for more information.*

Prakas on charitable distribution
Under Prakas No. 656 SHV/KRB, dated 19 September 2011, the Ministry of Economy
and Finance confirmed that donations made during the financial years 2010 and 2011
to support victims of the border dispute or the incident at Koh Pich through the CTN
and Bayon Foundations can be deducted from taxable profit in the 2010 and 2011
tax on profit (ToP) returns. The taxpayers must have proper evidence supporting the
payments.

Taxes on corporate income

Cambodia's taxation rules vary according to the taxpayer's regime, the classification
of taxpayers under different tax collection and control procedures of the General
Department of Taxation (GDT). Real-regime taxpayers include large or incorporated
taxpayers duly registered with the Ministry of Commerce and the GDT. The majority of
foreign investors will fall into the real regime. Unless otherwise stated, the focus of this
summary is on real-regime taxpayers.

Resident taxpayers are subject to tax on worldwide income while non-residents are taxed on Cambodian-sourced income only. A permanent establishment (PE) is taxable on its Cambodian-source income only.

Corporate tax rate

The standard rate of corporate income tax, known as tax on profit (ToP), for companies and PEs is 20%.

Industry-specific tax rates

Oil and gas and certain mineral exploitation activities are subject to ToP at the rate of 30%.

Insurance companies are taxable at a rate of 5% on the gross premium income and at the rate of 20% on other income derived from non-insurance/reinsurance activities. Net interest income of insurance companies received after 4% or 6% withholding tax (WHT) is not taxable income.

Minimum tax

Real-regime taxpayers are subject to a separate minimum tax. The minimum tax is an annual tax with a liability equal to 1% of annual turnover inclusive of all taxes except value-added tax (VAT). However, an exemption has been provided for Qualified Investment Projects (QIPs) (*see the Tax credits and incentives section for more information*).

As a separate tax to the ToP, the minimum tax is due irrespective of the taxpayer's profit or loss position (i.e. the minimum tax will be liable if the 1% of total annual turnover exceeds the 20% ToP liability).

Additional ToP on dividend distribution

A dividend-paying taxpayer is required to pay an additional ToP at the time of dividend distribution if the profit was previously subject to a 9% or 0% ToP.

A shareholder is entitled to establish a special dividend account from which the relevant dividend that was already subject to 20% ToP may be on-paid without further additional ToP obligations.

A dividend will be exempt from tax in the hands of the shareholder if additional ToP and WHT for non-resident shareholders has been paid.

Local income taxes

Local income taxes are not applicable in Cambodia.

Corporate residence

Resident taxpayers include companies organised, managed, or having their principal place of business in Cambodia.

Permanent establishment (PE)

A PE may be determined if there is a permanent place or entity through which the non-resident persons carry on their business or if there is an exercise of the authority to conclude a contract on behalf of a foreign entity or if business activities exceed certain time periods in Cambodia.

Cambodia

Factors to be considered in determining a PE include a place of management, an agent or office, a warehouse or factory, a workshop, any place of extraction of natural resources, a plantation, etc. Carrying out projects (e.g. supervisory activities of construction project, provision of services) exceeding a time period of six months in any 12-month period may also be considered as having a PE.

Other taxes

Value-added tax (VAT)

VAT is applicable to real-regime entities and is charged at 10% on the value of the supply of most goods and services.

Exported goods and services rendered outside Cambodia are zero-rated. In addition, 0% VAT applies to the supporting industries or contractors who directly supply goods or services to the export-oriented garment manufacturers, textile, footwear industries, and domestic supplies of paddy rice.

Some supplies are VAT exempt, the main categories being public postal services, medical and dental services, electricity, transportation of passengers by wholly state-owned public transport systems, insurance services, and primary financial services.

VAT returns and payments are due within 20 days of the following month. Note that strict record-keeping requirements do exist.

Import and export duties

Import duties are levied on a wide range of products. Rates vary from 0% to 35%. Following Cambodia's entry into the Association of South-East Asia Nations (ASEAN) during 1999, the government is required to reduce import duties in accordance with the Common Effective Preferential Tariffs program.

Export duties are levied on a limited number of items, such as timber and certain animal products (including most seafood).

Specific tax on certain merchandise and services (SPT)

SPT is a form of excise tax that applies to the importation or domestic production and supply of certain goods and services. SPT on domestically produced goods is generally applied to the 'ex-factory selling price', which is defined as 65% of the selling price before VAT and any discount. For imported goods, SPT is due on the CIF (cost, insurance, and freight) value inclusive of customs duty. For hotel and telecommunication services, SPT is payable based on the invoice prices.

For local and international air transportation of passengers, SPT is 10%, payable based on the air ticket value issued in Cambodia for travel within and outside Cambodia. The SPT base is inclusive of all taxes other than SPT and VAT. For example, for return air tickets from Phnom Penh to Singapore costing USD 500, exclusive of airport tax, the SPT payable is USD 45.45 (USD 500/1.1 x 10%).

Accommodation tax

Accommodation tax is calculated at 2% of the accommodation fee inclusive of all taxes and other services except accommodation tax and VAT.

Cambodia

Tax for public lighting (TPL)

TPL is imposed on the distribution in Cambodia of both foreign made and locally produced alcoholic and tobacco products. TPL is levied at 3% of the value of such products at the time of each in-country sale. Value for these purposes includes all taxes other than TPL and VAT.

Tax on immovable property (ToIP)

ToIP is levied at 0.1% per annum of the ToIP base. The tax base is 80% of the market value of the immovable properties stated in Appendix 1 of Prakas No. 371 less the threshold of KHR 100 million (approximately USD 25,000). The immovable property valued below the threshold is not subject to ToIP. The Prakas also determines that ToIP is effectively collected, at the first phase, from year 2011 on immovable properties located in Phnom Penh and other cities of the provinces.

Immovable property is defined to include land, buildings, and other constructions on land (e.g. infrastructures built on land, regardless of having a wall or roof). Certain exemptions exist for government-owned property, agricultural land, property owned and used for cultural and religious purposes, property of foreign embassies and non-governmental organisations (NGOs), and property in the special economic zones.

The owners, possessors, and final beneficiaries of immovable property are required to register and obtain a Tax Identification Number for each immovable property valued above the threshold from the tax administration where the immovable property is located. Any changes in relation to the registered immovable property (e.g. a change of title) are also required to be reported.

The owners, possessors, and final beneficiaries hold responsibility for calculating ToIP, preparing and filing ToIP return, as well as remitting the ToIP liability to the tax administration once per year by 30 September. A ToIP return is required for every single immovable property and must be completed and filed separately. Since this is a self-assessment tax, the tax administration will perform tax audit on ToIP in the subsequent years.

Note that subsequent Notifications were issued that extended the deadline for the 2011 property tax payment to 31 December 2011.

Tax on unused land

Land in towns and other specified areas without any construction, or with construction that is not in use, and even certain built-upon land, is subject to the tax on unused land. The tax is calculated at 2% of the market value of the land per square metre as determined by the Commission for Valuation of Unused Land on 30 June each year. The owner of the land is required to pay the tax on 30 September each year.

Registration tax (property transfer tax)

Certain documents relating to the establishment, dissolution, or merger of a business, or the transfer of title in certain assets (such as land and vehicles), are subject to registration tax. The tax is imposed at the rate of 4% and is generally levied on the transfer value.

Fiscal stamp tax

Fiscal stamp tax is to be paid on certain official documents and, perhaps more importantly for foreign investors, certain advertising postings and signage. Amounts vary according to such factors as the location of the signage, illumination, and nationality of any scripted words.

Cambodia

Patent tax

Registered businesses must pay a (relatively nominal) patent tax on initial business registration and annually thereafter. Patent tax is levied with reference to turnover or estimated turnover.

In practice, the GDT imposes patent tax at the top band regardless of the level of turnover.

The annual patent tax return and payment are to be filed annually, within three months of calendar year-end.

Tax on means of transportation

The tax on means of transportation imposes a number of statutory fees on the registration of certain vehicles, including trucks, buses, motor vehicles, and ships.

Tax stamp

Domestic producers or importers of cigarettes have the obligation to buy and affix tax stamps on packets of cigarettes. No person is allowed to sell or display packaged cigarettes for sale without a tax stamp.

Tax on salary (ToS)/fringe benefits (ToFB)

Cambodia's ToS rules follow internationally familiar residency and source principles. A Cambodian resident taxpayer's worldwide salary will be subject to Cambodian ToS. For non-residents, only the Cambodian sourced salary will be subject to ToS. The place of salary payment is not considered relevant in determining source.

A distinction is made between cash and fringe benefit salary components. Different tax scales also apply.

ToS or ToFB is a tax on employees' income, but employers are held liable to these taxes if the employers fail to withhold.

Branch income

Income of a branch is taxable in the same way as those for corporate profits.

Income determination

Inventory valuation

Inventory can be valued at weighted-average cost, first in first out (FIFO), or current value at the close of the period, where this value is lower than the purchase price or production cost. Work-in-progress should be valued at production costs.

Capital gain

There is no specific provision on capital gain tax in Cambodia. However, capital gains form part of taxable profit.

Dividend income

Dividend means any distribution of money or property that a legal person distributes to a shareholder with respect to the shareholder's equity interest in such legal person, with the exception of stock dividends and distributions in complete liquidation of the company. Whether or not a distribution is a dividend shall be determined under the

Cambodia

preceding condition without regard to whether or not the legal person has current or accumulated income or profit or earnings.

Inter-company dividend
Inter-company dividends between residents are exempt from ToP (*see the Withholding taxes section for more information*).

Passive income
Designated passive income (such as interest, royalties, and rent) forms part of the taxable profit.

Foreign income
Resident entities are taxed on their worldwide income, and tax credits are available for foreign taxes incurred. Foreign income is taxable in the period it is earned; there is no provision allowing tax to be deferred on the income earned overseas.

Deductions

Depreciation and amortisation
Property should be depreciated at rates according to four classes of assets as specified in the tax legislation. Land is not considered a depreciable asset. The straight-line or the declining-balance method is specifically required to be used for each class of assets.

Assets	Method	Rate (%)
Building and structures	Straight line	5
Computers, electronic information systems, software, and data handling equipment	Declining balance	50
Automobiles, trucks, office furniture, and equipment	Declining balance	25
All other tangible property	Declining balance	20

Expenditures on intangible property are amortisable over the life of the property or at 10% per annum.

Special depreciation
A QIP will be entitled to a 40% special depreciation in the first year of purchase or, if later, the first year the assets are used. However, the special depreciation will only apply to assets used in 'manufacturing and processing' (still to be defined) and only if the taxpayer has elected not to use a tax holiday. A clawback provision exists for assets held for less than four years.

Goodwill
Purchased goodwill is a depreciable intangible fixed asset for ToP purposes. If the useful life of the intangible fixed assets can be determined, the annual depreciation charges shall be calculated on the useful life by using the straight-line method. If the useful life cannot be determined, the annual depreciation rate of 10% shall be used.

Start-up expenses
Preliminary and formation expenses are allowed to be fully deducted in the period in which the expenses arise, or they can be amortised over two years.

Cambodia

Interest expenses
Interest deductibility in any year is limited to the amount of interest income plus 50% of the net profits excluding interest income and interest expense. The excess non-deductible interest expense can be carried forward to the following tax years indefinitely.

Bad debt
A loss on a claim (i.e. bad debt) is deductible where the impossibility to recover the loss can be clearly shown and that claim has been written off from the accounting books, except where the giving up of the claim is an abnormal act of the management (still to be defined).

Charitable contributions
The charitable contribution expense is deductible to the extent the amount does not exceed 5% of taxable profit. Donations made during the financial year 2010 and 2011 to support victims in the border dispute or the Koh Pich incident through Cambodian Television Network (CTN) and Bayon Foundations are fully deductible on the 2010 and 2011 ToP returns. The taxpayer must have proper evidence supporting the payments.

Fines and penalties
Additional tax, late tax payment interest, and fines of all types incurred for the violation of various legal provisions are not deductible.

Taxes
Taxes that are not a charge to the enterprise (e.g. WHT, ToS, ToFB, ToP, and additional ToP on dividend distribution) are not deductible.

Loss between related parties
No deduction is available for certain losses incurred on dealings between 51% commonly owned parties.

Net operating losses
Taxpayers may carry forward their losses for five years. The carryback of losses is not permitted. There is no provision for any form of consolidated filing or group loss relief.

To be eligible to carry forward tax losses a taxpayer must not change its activities or ownership.

If a taxpayer received a unilateral tax reassessment from the GDT, a taxpayer will not be able to utilise the tax losses brought forward in the year of reassessment.

Payments to foreign affiliates
An expense payable to a related party that is not paid within 180 days of year end will not be deductible. A deduction can be claimed in the year in which the payments are made. This rule is not applicable for an outlay or expense for inventory, capital property, and depreciable property.

Group taxation

There is no specific provision for group taxation in Cambodia.

Transfer pricing

The GDT has wide powers to redistribute income and deductions between parties under common ownership in order to prevent the avoidance or evasion of taxes. Common ownership exists at a relatively low level of 20%.

Thin capitalisation

There is no provision for thin capitalisation in Cambodia.

Tax credits and incentives

Foreign tax credit

Residents earning foreign-sourced income can receive credits for foreign taxes paid.

Inbound investment

The Council for the Development of Cambodia (CDC) may be approached for a one-stop service to register a project and obtain approval for a QIP status. CDC licensing is, however, not mandatory (except for certain large, politically sensitive projects) and is applicable to those projects that do not fall within the 'negative list'. Some of the projects in the 'negative list' include the following:

- All kinds of commercial activities, import and export activities, and transportation services (except the railway sector).
- Currency and financial services.
- Activities that relate to newspapers and media.
- Production of tobacco products.
- Provision of value-added services of all kinds of telecommunication services.
- Real estate development.

The current investment incentives which are applicable to the QIP registered with the CDC include a ToP exemption period of up to six years or special depreciation (*see Special depreciation in the Deductions section*), import duty exemptions, and exemption from minimum tax. Not all QIP will be entitled to all incentives.

Annually, a QIP is required to obtain a Certificate of Compliance (CoC) from the CDC to guarantee its investment incentives. The CoC is intended to provide confirmation that the QIP has acted in compliance with the relevant tax regulations.

Tax incentives in securities sector

The Royal Government of Cambodia has issued Sub-Decree No.70 to provide tax incentives to companies listed on the Cambodian Stock Exchange (CSX) and public investors who hold and/or trade government, equity, and debt securities on the securities market.

The listed companies are entitled to a 10% reduction on the annual ToP payable for three years, starting from the beginning of the current financial year if the share is issued within the first half of the fiscal year or the following financial year if the share is issued within the second half of the fiscal year. A QIP is not entitled to the tax reduction during the tax holiday period. Public investors are entitled to a 50% reduction on the WHT payable on interest and/or dividends received from the above securities for three years, starting from the launch of the securities market. However, there are various conditions under which the Ministry of Economy and Finance can forfeit the tax incentives granted to the listed companies.

Cambodia

Additional tax incentives for rice farming, paddy rice purchase, and export of milled rice

The Ministry of Economy and Finance has issued a Prakas to provide additional tax incentives to any enterprises in the business of rice farming, paddy rice purchase, and export of milled rice, as follows:

VAT:

- Domestic supplies of paddy rice: 0%.
- Domestic supplies of milled rice: 10%.
- Export of milled rice: 0%.
- Input VAT related to rice farming, paddy rice purchase, and export of milled rice is creditable or refundable.

ToP and minimum tax:

- Exempt from 1% minimum tax.
- Entitled to tax holiday period (i.e. trigger period plus three years plus three year priority period).
- Exempt from 1% prepayment of ToP during the tax holiday period.

Withholding taxes

WHT needs to be withheld on payments made by residents (and it seems only to those who fall under the real regime). The withheld tax constitutes a final tax when withheld in respect of resident and non-residents.

The types of payments caught are as follows.

WHT on payment to residents
- Rental: 10%.
- Interest: 15% (except payment to a Cambodian bank).
- Services: 15% (except payment to a registered taxpayer and supported by a valid VAT invoice).
- Royalties: 15%.

WHT on payment to non-residents
- Interest: 14%.
- Rent or right for use of property: 14%.
- Management or technical fees (not defined): 14%.
- Dividends: 14%.

Public investors invested on the Cambodia Stock Exchange (CSX) are entitled to a 50% reduction on the WHT payable on interest and/or dividends received from the government, equity, and debt securities for three years, starting from the launch of the securities market.

WHT is due when the amount is paid. An expense is considered 'paid' when it is recorded in the accounting records.

Tax administration

Taxable period
The standard tax year is the calendar year, although different accounting year-ends may be granted upon application.

Tax returns
The return for annual tax (i.e. ToP/minimum tax) is to be filed annually, within three months of tax year-end.

Returns for monthly taxes (e.g. 1% Prepayments of ToP, WHT, ToS or ToFB, SPT, PLT, and accommodation tax) are to be filed monthly, within 15 days of the following month.

Payment of tax
ToP or minimum tax is due for payment three months after tax year-end. The ToP or minimum tax liability can be reduced by prepayment of ToP payments.

Monthly taxes are due for payment by the 15th day of the succeeding month.

Prepayment of ToP
A prepayment of ToP equal to 1% of monthly turnover inclusive of all taxes, except VAT, is required to be paid on a monthly basis. The prepayment can be offset against the annual ToP liability and the minimum tax.

Where a taxpayer is in the period of ToP holiday, the taxpayer is also exempted from the prepayment obligations. However, a nil monthly return will need to be lodged.

Where a taxpayer is not subject to minimum tax, a monthly prepayment of ToP must still be made. However, unutilised prepayments from a prior year can be used to offset the current amount due, and no physical payment may be required.

Statute of limitations
The tax audit period (i.e. the limitation of within which period the tax authorities can perform tax audits) is as follows:

- Within three years of the date of submission of the tax returns.
- Within ten years of the date of submission of the tax returns if there is any evidence of 'obstruction of the implementation of laws'.
- Any time with the written consent of the taxpayers.

In practice, the GDT regularly extends the time limit for tax audit up to ten years.

Topics of focus for tax authorities
In practice, the tax authorities focus the tax reassessment on various matters ranging from payment to third parties overseas and fringe benefits provided employees to related party transactions (e.g. payment of management fee to head office, loans from shareholder).

Cambodia

....

Other issues

Statutory audit requirement

All enterprises (physical or legal persons) that meet two of the following criteria are required to have their financial statements audited by an independent external auditor registered with the Kampuchea Institute of Certified Public Accountants and Auditors (KICPAA):

- Annual turnover above KHR 3 billion (approximately USD 750,000).
- Total assets above KHR 2 billion (approximately USD 500,000).
- More than 100 employees.

QIPs registered with the CDC are required to have their financial statements audited by independent external auditors registered with the KICPAA.

The law does not state the deadline for the enterprises to submit their audited financial statements. However, the deadline for audited financial statements to be completed is six months after accounting year-end (i.e. for the financial year ended 31 December 2011, the deadline is 30 June 2012).

Cameroon, Republic of

PwC contact

Nadine Tinen Tchangoum
PricewaterhouseCoopers Tax and Legal
Immeuble PwC, Rue Christian Tobie Kouoh BP: 5689
Douala Bonanjo
Republic of Cameroon
Tel: +237 33 43 24 43/44/45
Email: nadine.tinen@cm.pwc.com

Significant developments

The following significant tax developments were part of the 2012 Finance Law that went into effect from 1 January 2012:

- Non-deduction of remunerations paid to individuals or entities located in tax havens.
- Application of 15% withholding tax (WHT) on capital gain resulting from transfer of shares. Shareholders located abroad are particularly targeted by this new provision.
- Application of WHT on software. It has been clearly highlighted that software acquired overseas shall be subject to 15% WHT.
- Obligation of presenting transfer pricing documentation at the beginning of tax audits.
- Expenses relating to remunerations of all kinds paid to liberal professionals exercising in violation of the regulations in force governing their respective professions shall not be deductible.
- Reduction of the number of tax regimes from four to three, and modification of the rates of corporate income tax (CIT) instalments.
- The value-added tax (VAT) shall be invoiced only by natural and legal persons who are assessed on the basis of actual earnings (i.e. whose turnover [taxes excluded] is equal to or above 50 million *Communauté Financière Africaine francs* (XAF).

Taxes on corporate income

Resident corporations in Cameroon are taxed on their worldwide income; non-resident corporations are taxed only on Cameroon-source income.

The profits subject to the company tax are determined with sole regard to profits earned by entities located in Cameroon (for residents) or transactions effected in Cameroon (for non-residents having a permanent establishment [PE] in Cameroon).

The net taxable profits are established after deduction of all charges directly entailed by the exercise of activities subject to assessment in Cameroon.

The total Cameroon CIT rate is 38.5%.

Reduced CIT rate for newly listed companies
The basic CIT rate of 38.5% is reduced to 33% for companies during their first three years of listing on the national stock exchange of Cameroon.

Cameroon, Republic of

Minimum tax

There is a 1.1%, 3.3%, or 5.5% minimum tax in Cameroon that is based on turnover. This minimum tax is an instalment of CIT. As such, it shall be offset against CIT. It is the sole tax payable if it is greater than CIT.

Local income taxes

A local tax of 10%, called Additional Council Tax, generally applies to the following taxes:

- CIT
- Personal income tax
- WHT on income from stock and shares
- VAT

The rate of each tax above is therefore made up of a basic rate plus 10% surcharge.

Corporate residence

An entity is deemed resident if its registered office, centre of activity, or management is located in Cameroon, if it has resident employees in Cameroon that provide services to customers, or if it has a PE in Cameroon.

Permanent establishment (PE)

In Cameroon, the internal regulations do not provide for any definition of the concept of PE. For this reason, the tax authorities may refer to the definitions provided by the models of United Nations (UN) and that of Organisation for Economic Co-operation and Development (OECD) Tax Conventions, which constitute the basis of the double tax treaties concluded between Cameroon and France, Canada, and Tunisia.

According to these conventions, a PE is a fixed place of business through which an enterprise wholly or partly performs its activities.

Other taxes

Value-added tax (VAT)

VAT shall be levied on natural persons or corporate bodies which automatically, habitually, or occasionally carry out taxable transactions consisting of provisions of services or sales of goods.

The total VAT in Cameroon is 19.25%. Exports are zero rated. The VAT paid upstream is recoverable, except where otherwise stated.

As of 1 January 2012, VAT shall be invoiced only by natural and legal persons who are assessed on the basis of actual earnings (i.e. whose turnover [taxes excluded] is equal to or above XAF 50 million).

Custom duties

Customs duties of between 5% and 30%, depending on the nature of the goods imported, are levied based of the customs value.

Excise taxes

An excise duty of 25% is applicable to cigarettes, drinks, cosmetics, or luxury (e.g. jewels, precious stones). A reduced rate of excise duty (12.5%) shall apply to soft drinks and private vehicles with engine capacities of 2,000 cm³.

Real property tax

Cameroon property tax is payable annually on real estate with or without an ownership certificate or an administrative or judicial order issued. Tax is charged at 0.11% of the assessed property value.

Transfer tax

The sale of a business in Cameroon is subject to a transfer tax rate of 15%.

Registration duty

The registration duty applies to certain deeds listed by the General Tax Code. The assessment basis depends on the nature of transactions, and the rate varies from 1% to 15%.

The formation of a company and subsequent capital increases in Cameroon are not subject to registration duties.

Business licence tax

Any natural person or corporate body carrying on trade, industry, or profession in Cameroon shall be liable to a business licence tax. The business licence tax is paid annually according to a graduated scale and is assessed on turnover.

New enterprises shall be exempt from the payment of the business licence tax during the first two years of operation.

Social security contributions

Employer and employee must contribute on a monthly basis to Cameroon's National Social Insurance Fund at 11.2% and 2.8%, respectively. The basis of contribution is capped at XAF 300,000 per month. Employers in Cameroon must also contribute 1.75%, 2.5%, or 5% of total salaries to the National Social Insurance Fund for Industrial Accidents, depending on the risk category of activities performed by employees. The calculation basis in this category is the gross salary including the benefits in kind assessed for their actual amount.

Payroll tax

Employers in Cameroon are required to make monthly contributions of 2.5% of the total amount of salaries and fringe benefits of their employees to the Housing Loan and Employment Fund of Cameroon.

Branch income

The local branch of any foreign company is taxed at the same rate as a company. The net profits (after CIT) of entities having their residence or head office outside Cameroon (such as the branch of a foreign company) are assumed to be distributed each fiscal year to companies not located in Cameroon. Their net profits (after CIT) shall therefore be subject to the WHT on distributions at 16.5%.

Cameroon, Republic of

Income determination

Inventory valuation
For valuation purpose, the general tax code (GTC) only provides that stocks shall be valued at cost price; however, if the market price is lower than the cost price, the undertaking shall make provisions for depreciation of inventory. No reference is made to the accounting method that shall be used (e.g. first in first out [FIFO], last in first out [LIFO]). Only FIFO and weighted average methods are allowed under the Organisation for the Harmonisation of Business Law in Africa (OHADA) Accounting Principles. Where there is any difference between the valuation method permitted by the GTC and the book valuation, the accounting result shall be modified accordingly.

Capital gains
Capital gains are normally taxed at full CIT rates.

As of January 2012, the net overall capital gains arising from the transfer of stocks, bonds, and other capital shares made by natural and legal persons, occasionally or habitually, either directly or through a financial establishment, shall be subject to the 16.5% WHT.

Dividend income
Dividends are subject to the WHT of 16.5%. However, dividends shall be treated as proceeds for the purpose of CIT, and the tax withheld at source is used as instalment for the payment of CIT.

Interest income
Interests are subject to the WHT of 16.5%. However, interests shall be treated as proceeds for the purpose of CIT, and the tax withheld at source shall be used as instalment for the payment of CIT.

Foreign income
As matter of both fact and law, revenue from abroad earned by corporate bodies situated in Cameroon shall be subject to CIT in Cameroon. There is no provision on tax deferral in Cameroon.

Deductions

Depreciation
Depreciation is generally computed on a straight-line basis over the useful life according to the rates provided for by the Tax Code, including those which might have already been deferred in times of deficit.

The following depreciation rates are generally accepted for tax purposes:

Assets	Depreciation rates (%)
Construction	5 to 20
Stationary equipment and tools	5 to 20
Portable equipment	10 to 100
Transport equipment	10 to 33.33
Railway lines	1 to 10
Engines	5

Assets	Depreciation rates (%)
Rehabilitation	5 to 25
Furniture fittings and other equipment	10 to 33.33
Fishing equipment and fishing vessels	15

The deduction of depreciation can be carried forward indefinitely.

Goodwill

With regards to rules governing the deduction of provision and depreciations, impairment of goodwill shall not be allowable for CIT purpose.

Start-up expenses

There is no specific provision in the GTC relating to start-up expenses.

However, the OHADA Accounting Principles effectively state that start-up expenses shall be capitalised and must be completely depreciated as early as possible: 2 to 5 years, except bond premiums, which are depreciated throughout the life of the loan.

No distribution of profit should be carried out before the complete depreciation of start-up expenses.

Interest expenses

Interest expenses are fully deductible.

However, interest paid to partners/shareholders in respect of the sums they leave with or place at the disposal of the company over and above their capital, irrespective of the type of company, shall be acceptable within the limits of those calculated at the rate of the central bank discount rate, raised by 2 points.

Bad debt

The deductibility of provisions for bad debts is subject to the following conditions:

- The debt must be specified (i.e. clarification is needed on the nature, amount, and the debtor).
- The company must show that it has unsuccessfully carried out actions for debt recovery (e.g. reminder letters, notice to pay, complaints).

For losses related to bad debts to be deductible, they shall have been subjected to all amicable or forced collection methods and means provided for by the OHADA Uniform Act on the Organization of Simplified Procedures for Collection and Enforcement Procedures. Otherwise, they shall not be deductible.

In this regard, the impossibility of recovering the debt must be evidenced by:

- a deficiency report prepared by a bailiff
- a bankruptcy decision duly passed by the judge, if necessary, or
- a decision passed by a judge, bearing out the debtor who disputed the debt.

Cameroon, Republic of

Charitable contributions

Acts of liberality, gifts, and subsidies shall not represent the charges deductible from profits.

However, payments made to research and development (R&D) bodies and to collective philanthropic, educational, sports, scientific, social, and family institutions and bodies, on condition that the latter are situated in Cameroon, shall be deductible as soon as there is proof of payment and as long as they do not exceed 0.5% of the turnover for the fiscal year. Similarly, gifts made on the occasion of a disaster shall be deducted in the form and conditions determined by order of the Minister of Economy and Finance.

Fines and penalties

Compounding fees, fines, confiscations, and any penalty concerning persons who violate the legal, economic, and fiscal provisions shall not be deducted from the profits subject to taxation.

Taxes

Only the professional taxes issued for collection during the fiscal year and which are to be borne by the firm in relation to the operations carried out in Cameroon shall be subject to deduction.

CIT, WHT, and personal income tax shall not be considered as deductible expenses for the levying of taxes.

Net operating losses

Any loss sustained in a given year can be carried forward up to the fourth year following the recording of the loss. The carryback of losses is not permitted in Cameroon.

Payments to foreign entities

Head office overhead expenses for operations carried out in Cameroon and the remuneration of certain effective services (studies, technical, financial, or accounting assistance) provided to Cameroonian firms by foreign natural persons or corporate bodies are not totally deductible. Fees paid are deductible up to a maximum of 10% of the taxable profit before deducting the expenses concerned.

According to the 2012 Finance Law, expenses linked to transactions with natural persons or legal entities resident or established in a territory or state considered to be a tax haven shall not be deductible. This rule shall not apply to imports of goods made in those countries. A tax haven is any state wherein the tax on the income of natural person or legal entity is less than a third of that paid in Cameroon, or any state or territory considered not to be co-operative in matters of transparency or of exchange of information required for fiscal purpose by international or financial organisations. The rate of the Cameroonian CIT to be considered for that purpose is 35%.

Group taxation

There is specific taxation of groups within the Economic and Monetary Community of Central Africa (CEMAC) area.

Where a joint stock company and a private limited company own either registered stock in a joint stock company or shares in a private limited company, the net proceeds of the share in the second company paid to the first during the financial year shall be deducted from the total net profit of the latter, less a percentage for costs and charges. This percentage is fixed at 10% of the total amount of the proceeds. This system shall apply when all of the following conditions are met:

- The stocks or shares owned by the parent establishment represent at least 25% of the capital of the subsidiary firm.
- The parent and subsidiary firms have their registered office in a CEMAC state (Cameroon, Central African Republic, Chad, Gabon, Equatorial Guinea, and Republic of Congo).
- The stocks or shares allotted at the time of issue are still registered in the name of the participating company which undertakes to retain them for at least two consecutive years in registered form.

Transfer pricing
There are provisions in the General Tax Code that relate to transfer pricing, but audits from the Tax Administration are not yet aggressive.

According the 2012 Finance Law, within the framework of a tax audit, the documents required for the justification of transfer pricing shall be presented to the tax inspectors at the start of the procedure. Items such as business transactions, payments in consideration for intangible rights, allocations of costs and expenses (head office costs, agreements to share costs, disbursements, etc.), financial transactions, etc. are particularly targeted for close scrutiny.

Thin capitalisation
There is no specific thin capitalisation rule in Cameroon.

Tax credits and incentives

Three major tax incentives are granted in Cameroon under the tax systems.

The system of reinvestment relief
Any corporate body reinvesting in Cameroon may be granted, under certain conditions, a reduction in CIT.

The reinvestment must take a form described by the General Tax Code as construction or extension of permanent buildings for industrial, agricultural, forestry, tourism, or mining purposes, including technical offices, housing salaried workers free of charges, etc.

Note that total investment less than XAF 25 million are not eligible for reinvestment relief.

The reinvestment relief consists of a deduction from the taxable basis in an amount equal to 50% of the investment effected by the undertaking and approved by the tax authorities. The rate is 25% for telecommunication companies.

The special fiscal regime for structuring projects
The special fiscal regime for structuring projects applies to major enterprises with annual turnover not less than XAF 1 billion and small and medium-sized enterprises with annual turnover of less than XAF 1 billion.

Cameroon, Republic of

The tax incentives consist of:

- Exemption from payment of the business licence tax for the first two years of operation.
- Fixed registration fee of XAF 50,000 for transfers of real estate which directly concern the establishment of the project.
- Exemption from payment of VAT on local purchases of building materials and on imports related to the establishment of the project.
- Extension of the carryover period for deficits from four to five years.

A taxpayer must apply, required conditions must be met, and authorisation must be issued for this tax incentive to be granted.

Incentives applicable to listed companies

Companies whose ordinary shares are listed on the Cameroon Stock Exchange shall be entitled to the following CIT reduced rates:

- 22% for a period of three years for capital increases that represent at least 20% of the share capital.
- 27.5% for a period of three years for transfers of shares that represent at least 20% of the share capital.
- 30.8% for a period of three years from the date of listing for capital increases or transfers of shares that represent less than 20% of the share capital.

Companies whose ordinary shares are listed on the bond market in Cameroon shall be entitled to pay basic CIT at a reduced rate of 33% for three years, effective from the date of listing.

Foreign tax credit

Taxes paid abroad are not considered as tax credits unless provided as such by international tax treaties.

....

Withholding taxes

A special tax is levied at an overall discharging rate of 15% on income paid to natural persons and corporate bodies domiciled outside of Cameroon by enterprises or establishments based in Cameroon for various services provided or used in Cameroon. The tax is withheld at source by the Cameroonian entity that pays the remuneration.

Within the 2012 Finances Law, it has been clearly highlighted that software acquired overseas shall be subject to the 15% WHT.

Dividends

A total WHT of 16.5% applies to dividends paid to both Cameroon residents and non-residents. The WHT rate may be reduced under an applicable tax treaty.

Interest

As of 1 January 2011, the interest from foreign loans is subject to 16.5% WHT. Prior to 1 January 2011, the payment of 16.5% WHT on interest from foreign loans had been suspended.

Royalties

Royalties paid to non-residents are subject to a 15% WHT (the 10% surcharge is not applicable). The tax rate may be reduced under an applicable tax treaty.

Tax treaties

Cameroon has tax treaties with Canada, France, Tunisia, and members of CEMAC (Cameroon, Gabon, Equatorial Guinea, Congo, Chad, and Central African Republic).

Recipient	Dividends (%)	Interest (%)	Royalties (%)	Head office expenses and technical assistance (%)
CEMAC	16.5	16.5	N/A	N/A
Canada	16.5	16.5	16.5	15
France	15	15	N/A	7.5
Tunisia	12	15	15	15

Tax administration

Taxable period

The tax year in Cameroon is the calendar year.

Tax returns

On or before 15 March, taxpayers are expected to submit to the tax administration the annual return of revenue derived from their business venture during the period serving as tax base.

This return must be presented in conformity with the OHADA accounting system.

Payment of tax

An instalment representing the 1.1%, 3.3%, or 5.5% minimum tax of turnover realised during each month shall be paid to the tax authorities not later than the 15th day of the following month.

Advance payment of 5% on imports or purchases of goods for resale is withheld at source by the supplier.

The balance of CIT is paid, at the latest, on 15 March following the fiscal year-end, when submitting the CIT return.

Surplus tax payments

A surplus tax payment can be offset against future taxes of the same nature to be paid. For the specific case of VAT, a reimbursement process is provided for by the General Tax Code under certain conditions.

Audit cycle

There is no audit cycle in Cameroon.

Statute of limitations

The statute of limitations is four years.

Cameroon, Republic of

Topics of focus for tax authorities

The topics of focus for tax authorities include the following:

* Remunerations paid for services provided to local entities by providers located overseas.
* Transfer pricing.

Canada

PwC contact

Christopher P. Kong
PricewaterhouseCoopers LLP
PwC Tower
18 York Street, Suite 2600
Toronto, Ontario, M5J 0B2, Canada
Tel: +1 416 869 8739
Email: christopher.p.kong@ca.pwc.com

Significant developments

Canada's corporate summary reflects all 2012 federal, provincial, and territorial budgets. Many of the tax changes continue what was started a year ago, tightening perceived loopholes or inequities in various aspects of the tax system. Notably, tax rules were proposed as part of the 2012 federal budget to curtail certain transactions seen as eroding the Canadian corporate tax base. Other proposals in the federal budget relate to secondary adjustments associated with international transfer pricing assessments and target the scientific research and experimental development (SR&ED) program, the first of many to come aimed at enhancing the effectiveness and efficiency of research and innovation in Canada. The summary is based on enacted and proposed legislation and assumes that the proposed legislation will become law.

Corporate income tax (CIT) rates
Federal general (and manufacturing and processing) CIT rates decreased from 16.5% to 15% on 1 January 2012.

Capital taxes
All provincial general capital taxes have been eliminated, except for Nova Scotia's, which will be eliminated by 1 July 2012.

Scientific research and experimental development (SR&ED)
Stemming from a 2010 federal budget proposal, an independent panel released a report, *Innovation Canada: A Call to Action*, that provides "advice in respect of the effectiveness of federal programs to support business and commercially oriented research and development (R&D), the appropriateness of the current mix and design of these programs, as well as possible gaps in the current suite of programs and what might be done to fill them". As a result, significant changes are expected to Canada's SR&ED program in the coming years. *For changes that were announced in the 29 March 2012 federal budget, see Scientific research and experimental development (SR&ED) credit in the Tax credits and incentives section.*

Tax avoidance
Draft legislation makes an 'avoidance transaction' meeting certain conditions a 'reportable transaction' that must be reported to the Canada Revenue Agency (CRA), generally for transactions entered into after 2010, and those that are part of a series of transactions completed after 2010. Quebec already has a provincial reporting regime for certain aggressive tax planning transactions, generally carried out after 14 October 2009.

Cross-border tax evasion
To facilitate and improve the exchange of tax information and combat cross-border tax evasion, Canada has signed a Protocol amending the Convention on Mutual

Canada

Administrative Assistance in Tax Matters. The member States of the Council of Europe and the member countries of the Organisation for Economic Co-operation and Development (OECD) are signatories.

Thin capitalisation

Proposed rules that modify the Canadian thin capitalisation rules reduce the debt-to-equity ratio from 2:1 to 1.5:1 and broaden the scope of these rules. *See Thin capitalisation in the Group taxation section for more information.*

Transfer pricing adjustments

The 29 March 2012 federal budget confirmed that all upward transfer pricing adjustments to a taxpayer's income will be treated as deemed dividends subject to withholding tax (WHT). The WHT can be eliminated, at the discretion of the Minister of Revenue, if the amount of the primary transfer pricing adjustment is repatriated to the Canadian corporation. *See Transfer pricing adjustments in the Group taxation section for more information.*

Foreign affiliate amendments

On 19 August 2011, the federal government released a significant package of proposed amendments to Canada's international tax rules applicable to Canadian corporations with foreign affiliates. The proposals significantly revise proposed amendments that were released at different times over the past decade and introduce new measures. *See Foreign affiliate amendments in the Income determination section for more information.*

'Foreign affiliate dumping' proposals

The 29 March 2012 federal budget introduced sweeping rules to curtail a variety of transactions it describes as 'foreign affiliate dumping' transactions. These transactions involve an investment in a foreign affiliate by a corporation that is (i) resident in Canada and (ii) controlled by a non-resident of Canada. When certain conditions are met, a dividend will be deemed to have been paid by the corporation to its foreign parent to the extent of any non-share consideration given by the corporation for the 'investment' in the foreign affiliate. The proposals generally apply to transactions occurring after 28 March 2012. *See 'Foreign affiliate dumping' proposals in the Income determination section for more information.*

Non-resident trusts (NRTs)

Draft legislation refines the NRT rules that generally apply to taxation years ending after 2006; trusts subject to these rules will be deemed resident for Canadian income tax purposes. A trust will be allowed to elect to be deemed resident for 2001 and subsequent years.

Offshore investment funds

Draft legislation maintains the enacted provision for investments in offshore investment funds, but increases the prescribed income percentage by 2%, and extends the statute-barred period for taxpayers that have invested in offshore investment funds by three years, for taxation years ending after 4 March 2010.

Specified investment flow-throughs (SIFTs), real estate investment trusts (REITs), and publicly traded corporations

Draft proposals that apply to SIFTs, REITs, and publicly traded corporations in respect of transactions involving certain stapled securities limit the deductibility of amounts paid or payable after 19 July 2011, in respect of those stapled securities, subject to a transitional period.

Partnership deferral

For corporate partners with taxation years ending after 22 March 2011, certain corporate partners with a significant interest in a partnership will be unable to defer taxation on the partnership income. Instead, they must accrue partnership income up to the end of the corporation's taxation year. An election may be available to change the partnership's fiscal period. Partnerships in multi-tier structures must adopt the same fiscal period (31 December, unless otherwise elected by the partnerships). Certain transitional reserves may be available for up to five years. The CRA has modified its administrative policy for joint venture fiscal periods to reflect similar rules (*see Joint venture deferral below*).

Joint venture deferral

Consistent with the new partnership anti-deferral rules (*see Partnership deferral above*), the CRA announced on 29 November 2011 that joint venture arrangements can no longer report income using a separate fiscal period. As a result, corporate participants must report their actual share of joint venture income or loss up to the end of their own year-end, for tax years ending after 22 March 2011. A transitional reserve, similar to that allowed under the partnership deferral changes, may be available for the additional income included in that year by a corporate participant.

New CRA risk assessment audit approach

The CRA has implemented a new 'risk assessment' model to select corporations, partnerships, income trusts, and private equity funds for audit. Large corporations and their affiliated entities are classified as high, medium, or low risk and are subject to either a full, restricted, or compliance audit depending on the entity's determined category. Factors that determine the risk category include the taxpayer's history with the CRA, the type of industry, and the internal controls in place. *See Audit cycle in the Tax administration section*.

Group taxation

The federal government has issued a consultation paper, *The Taxation of Corporate Groups*, which explores possible approaches for taxing corporate groups in Canada, and subsequently reaffirmed its commitment to consider this issue.

Provincial sales tax harmonisation

Although British Columbia's provincial sales tax (PST) was harmonised with the federal goods and services tax (GST) on 1 July 2010, a referendum in 2011 determined that the harmonised sales tax (HST) will be cancelled and replaced with a PST and GST regime on 1 April 2013.

Prince Edward Island will enter into formal negotiations with the federal government to implement an HST, effective 1 April 2013. The HST rate will be 14% (i.e. 9% provincial component plus the 5% GST), and will replace the current combined PST/GST rate of 15.5% (i.e. 10% PST, which applies on the 5% GST).

Quebec has agreed in principle to harmonise the Quebec sales tax (QST) with the 5% GST on 1 January 2013, at which time the harmonised rate will be 14.975%.

Taxes on corporate income

As a general rule, corporations resident in Canada are subject to Canadian CIT on worldwide income. Non-resident corporations are subject to CIT on income derived from carrying on a business in Canada and on capital gains arising upon the disposition

Canada

of taxable Canadian property (*See Capital gains in the Income determination section for more information*). The purchaser of the taxable Canadian property is generally required to withhold tax from the amount paid unless the non-resident vendor has obtained a clearance certificate.

Canadian CIT and WHT can be reduced or eliminated if Canada has a treaty with the non-resident's country of residence. *A list of treaties that Canada has negotiated and applicable WHT rates is provided in the Withholding taxes section.*

Federal income tax

The following rates apply for 31 December 2012 year-ends. For non-resident corporations, the rates apply to business income attributable to a permanent establishment (PE) in Canada. Different rates may apply to non-resident corporations in other circumstances. Non-resident corporations may also be subject to branch tax (*see the Branch income section*).

	Federal rate (%)
Basic rate	38.0
Less - Provincial abatement (1)	(10.0)
Federal rate	28.0
Less - General rate reduction or manufacturing and processing (M&P) deduction (2)	(13.0)
Net federal tax rate (3, 4)	15.0

Notes

1. The basic rate of federal tax is reduced by a 10% abatement to give the provinces and territories room to impose CITs. The abatement is available in respect of taxable income allocated to Canadian provinces and territories. Taxable income allocable to a foreign jurisdiction is not eligible for the abatement and normally is not subject to provincial or territorial taxes.
2. The general rate reduction and M&P deduction do not apply to the first 500,000 Canadian dollars (CAD) of active business income earned in Canada by Canadian-controlled private corporations (CCPCs), investment income of CCPCs, and income from certain other corporations (e.g. mutual fund corporations, mortgage investment corporations, and investment corporations), which may benefit from preferential tax treatment. The general rate reduction and M&P deduction increased from 11.5% to 13% on 1 January 2012.
3. Provincial or territorial taxes apply in addition to federal taxes. Provincial and territorial tax rates are noted below.
4. For small CCPCs, the net federal tax rate is levied on active business income above CAD 500,000; a federal rate of 11% applies to the first CAD 500,000 of active business income. Investment income (other than most dividends) of CCPCs is subject to the federal rate of 28%, in addition to a refundable federal tax of 6 2/3%, for a total federal rate of 34.7%.

Provincial/territorial income tax

All provinces and territories impose income tax on income allocable to a PE in the province or territory. Generally, income is allocated to a province or territory by using a two-factor formula based on gross revenue and on salaries and wages. Provincial and territorial income taxes are not deductible for federal income tax purposes. The rates given apply to 31 December 2012 year-ends and do not take into account provincial tax holidays, which reduce or eliminate tax in limited cases.

Province/territory	Income tax rate (%) (1, 2)
Alberta	10.0
British Columbia (3)	10.0
Manitoba (4)	12.0
New Brunswick (5)	10.0

Province/territory	Income tax rate (%) (1, 2)
Newfoundland and Labrador	14.0 or 5.0
Northwest Territories	11.5
Nova Scotia	16.0
Nunavut	12.0
Ontario (6)	11.5 or 10.0
Prince Edward Island	16.0
Quebec	11.9
Saskatchewan (7)	12.0 or 10.0
Yukon territory	15.0 or 2.5

Notes

1. When two rates are indicated, the lower rate applies to M&P income.
2. In all provinces and territories, the first CAD 500,000 (CAD 400,000 in Manitoba and Nova Scotia) of active business income of a small CCPC is subject to reduced rates that range from 0% to 8.0%, depending on the jurisdiction.
3. British Columbia's rate will increase from 10% to 11% on 1 April 2014. The increase is a temporary measure to be triggered only if the province's fiscal situation worsens.
4. Manitoba's rate will decrease from 12% to 11% at a date to be determined, subject to balanced budget requirements.
5. New Brunswick's rate decreased from 11% to 10% on 1 July 2011. New Brunswick's 2011 budget maintains the rate at 10%. The rate was to decline to 8% on 1 July 2012.
6. The lower Ontario rate applies to profits from M&P, and from farming, mining, logging, and fishing operations, carried on in Canada and allocated to Ontario.

   Ontario's non-M&P rate decreased from 12% to 11.5% on 1 July 2011. Ontario's 2012 budget freezes the rate at 11.5% until the province returns to a balanced budget (scheduled for 2017/18). The rate was to drop to 11% on 1 July 2012 and to 10% on 1 July 2013. If this proposal is not enacted, the rate in the table will be 11.2%.

   Corporations subject to Ontario income tax may also be liable for corporate minimum tax (CMT) based on adjusted book income. The CMT is payable only to the extent that it exceeds the regular Ontario income tax liability. The CMT rate is 2.7% and applies when total assets are at least CAD 50 million and annual gross revenue is at least CAD 100 million on an associated basis.
7. Saskatchewan's M&P rate is as low as 10% (reduced from the 12% non-M&P rate), depending on the extent to which the corporation's income is allocated to the province.

Corporate residence

Under the Income Tax Act, a corporation incorporated in Canada (federally or provincially/territorially) will be deemed to be resident in Canada. A corporation not incorporated in Canada will be considered to be resident in Canada under Canadian common law if its central management and control is exercised in Canada. Where a corporation's central management and control is exercised is a question of fact but typically is where the Board of Directors meets and makes decisions, provided the Board takes action.

A corporation incorporated in Canada or a corporation incorporated outside of Canada but with its central management and control situated in Canada will be deemed to be a non-resident of Canada if it qualifies as a non-resident of Canada under treaty tie-breaker rules.

A corporation incorporated in Canada will cease to be a Canadian resident if it is granted articles of continuance in a foreign jurisdiction or if it is a predecessor corporation in a cross-border amalgamation. Similarly, a foreign corporation will

Canada

become resident in Canada if it is continued in Canada or is a predecessor corporation of an amalgamated corporation that is resident in Canada.

Permanent establishment (PE)

Canada's tax treaties generally provide that the business profits of a non-resident corporation are not subject to Canadian tax unless the non-resident corporation carries on business in Canada through a PE situated in Canada and the business profits are attributed to that PE. Canada's tax treaties may also restrict the imposition of branch tax to situations when the non-resident corporation carries on business in Canada through a PE situated in Canada and/or limit the applicable branch tax rate. While the wording of tax treaties varies, a PE generally is defined as:

- a fixed place of business through which the business of the non-resident corporation is wholly or partly carried on
- a place of management, a branch, an office, a factory, and a workshop; a mine, an oil or gas well, a quarry, or any other place of extraction of natural resources; a building site, construction, or assembly project that exists for a specified period of time, and
- a dependent agent or employee who has and habitually exercises an authority to conclude contracts in the name of the non-resident corporation.

The Canadian domestic definition of PE (federal and provincial/territorial) generally mirrors the above.

Other taxes

Consumption taxes

Federal goods and services tax (GST)

The federal GST is levied at a rate of 5%. It is a value-added tax (VAT) applied at each level in the manufacturing and marketing chain and applies to most goods and services. However, the tax does not apply to sales of zero-rated goods, such as exports and basic groceries, or to tax-exempt supplies, such as health care, educational services, and certain services provided by financial institutions.

Generally, businesses pay GST on their purchases and charge GST on their sales, and remit the net amount (i.e. the difference between the GST collected and the input tax credit for the tax paid on purchases). Suppliers are entitled to claim input tax credits on zero-rated goods and services, but not on tax-exempt supplies.

Harmonised sales tax (HST)

Five provinces have harmonised their sales tax systems with the GST and impose a single HST. The HST includes the 5% GST and a provincial sales tax component. It is imposed on essentially the same base as the GST. HST rates follow.

Province	HST rate (%)
British Columbia (1)	12
New Brunswick	13
Newfoundland and Labrador	13
Nova Scotia (2)	15
Ontario	13

Notes

1. British Columbia harmonised its 7% PST with the 5% GST on 1 July 2010. However, as a result of a provincial referendum that was held in 2011, the 12% HST will be cancelled and replaced with a 7% PST and 5% federal GST on 1 April 2013.
2. Nova Scotia will reduce its HST rate from 15% to14% by 1 July 2014, and to 13% by 1 July 2015 (i.e. the provincial portion of the HST will decrease from 10% to 9% and 8%, respectively).

Prince Edward Island will enter into formal negotiations with the federal government to implement an HST, effective 1 April 2013. The HST rate will be 14% (i.e. 9% provincial component plus the 5% GST), and will replace the current combined PST/GST rate of 15.5% (i.e. 10% PST, which applies on the 5% GST).

In addition, Quebec has agreed in principle to harmonise the Quebec sales tax (QST) with the 5% GST on 1 January 2013. The harmonised rate on 1 January 2013 will be 14.975%.

Retail sales tax
Manitoba, Prince Edward Island, and Saskatchewan levy a retail sales tax at 7%, 10%, and 5%, respectively, on most purchases of tangible personal property for consumption or use in the province and on the purchase of specific services. As mentioned above, British Columbia will reinstate a retail sales tax on 1 April 2013, while Prince Edward Island intends to replace its retail sales tax regime with the HST on 1 April 2013.

Quebec's sales tax is structured in the same manner as the GST and applies to most goods and services that are subject to the GST. The general QST rate is 9.5% (8.5% in 2011). Quebec administers the GST in that province. However, as noted above, Quebec has agreed in principle to harmonise its QST with the GST on 1 January 2013; the effective harmonised rate will be 14.975%.

Only Prince Edward Island and Quebec levy sales tax on prices that include the GST.

Neither Alberta nor the three territories (the Northwest Territories, Nunavut, and the Yukon) impose a retail sales tax. However, the GST applies in those jurisdictions.

Customs duties
Customs duties generally are intended to protect Canadian industry from foreign competition and not as a source of revenue. The majority of most-favoured-nation (MFN) duty rates are below 10%; notable exceptions are footwear, textiles and apparel, and certain food products (the last may be subject to 'tariff rate quotas'). Goods imported from developed countries with which Canada does not have free trade agreements will attract the MFN duty rate. Many products, however, are duty-free regardless of their country of origin.

Qualifying goods that originate in the North American Free Trade Agreement (NAFTA) territory (Canada, the United States, and Mexico) can enter Canada duty-free. Canada has implemented free trade agreements (FTAs) with Chile, Colombia, Costa Rica, the European Free Trade Association countries, Israel, and Peru, and has signed or is negotiating agreements with several other countries. Like the NAFTA, these agreements set out rules of origin for determining whether the goods are eligible for preferential duty rates under the particular FTA.

Canada extends preferential duty rates to most (but not all) products imported from developing countries (the General Preferential Tariff) and has granted further concessions to goods originating in 'Least Developed Countries'. In either case, goods

Canada

must satisfy rules of origin and be shipped directly to Canada from the beneficiary countries to qualify for these rates.

Excise taxes and duties

Excise duties are levied at various rates on alcohol, alcoholic beverages, and tobacco products manufactured in Canada, while imports are subject to customs duties (*see above*).

Excise tax is imposed on petroleum products and automobiles. In addition, a 10% federal excise tax is imposed on insurance against a risk in Canada if it is placed by insurers through brokers or agents outside Canada or with an insurer that is not authorised under Canadian or provincial/territorial law to transact the business of insurance. Certain premiums are exempt, including those for life, personal accident, marine, and sickness insurance.

Property taxes

Property taxes are levied by municipalities in Canada on the estimated market value of real property within their boundaries and by provinces and territories on land not in a municipality. In most provinces and territories, a general property tax is levied on the owner of the property. Some municipalities levy a separate business tax, which is payable by the occupant if the premises are used for business purposes. These taxes are based on the rental value of the property at tax rates that are set each year by the various municipalities. School taxes, also generally based on the value of real property, are levied by local and regional school boards or the province or territory.

Land transfer tax

All provinces and territories levy a land transfer tax or registration fee on the purchaser of real property within their boundaries. These levies are expressed as a percentage, in most cases on a sliding scale, of the sale price or the assessed value of the property sold, and are generally payable at the time title to the property is registered. Rates generally range from 0.02% to 2%, depending on the province or territory, but may be higher if the purchaser is a non-resident. Some exemptions (or refunds) are available. Additional land transfer taxes apply for properties purchased in the municipalities of Montreal or Toronto. Other municipalities may also impose these taxes and fees.

Federal capital taxes

The federal government does not levy a general capital tax. It imposes the Financial Institutions Capital Tax (Part VI Tax) on banks, trust and loan corporations, and life insurance companies at a rate of 1.25% when taxable capital employed in Canada exceeds CAD 1 billion. The tax is not deductible in computing income for tax purposes. It is reduced by the corporation's federal income tax liability. Any unused federal income tax liability can be applied to reduce Part VI Tax for the previous three and the next seven years. The thresholds are shared among related financial institutions. In effect, the tax constitutes a minimum tax on financial institutions.

Provincial capital taxes

All provincial general capital taxes have been eliminated, except for Nova Scotia's, which will be eliminated by 1 July 2012. However, most provinces still impose a capital tax on financial institutions. Capital taxes are deductible for federal income tax purposes. The federal government had proposed to limit the deductibility of capital taxes, but has delayed implementing this proposal indefinitely. However, a proposed interim measure disallows a deduction for any increase in these taxes, with certain exceptions. The territories do not impose capital taxes.

Provincial capital taxes are imposed at the following rates for 31 December 2012 year-ends. Certain exemptions and reduced rates apply.

Province	General (%)	Banks, trust and loan corporations (%)
Alberta	-	-
British Columbia	-	-
Manitoba (1)	-	4
New Brunswick (2)	-	3.75
Newfoundland and Labrador	-	4
Nova Scotia (3)	0.025	4
Ontario	-	-
Prince Edward Island	-	5
Quebec (4)	-	0.25
Saskatchewan (5)	-	3.25

Notes

1. Manitoba's financial institutions capital tax was eliminated for financial institutions with taxable paid up capital under CAD 4 billion for taxation years ending after 12 April 2011. Manitoba's 2012 budget increases the financial institutions capital tax rate from 3% to 4% for taxation years ending after 17 April 2012.
2. New Brunswick's 2012 budget increased the financial institutions capital tax rate from 3% to 4% on 1 April 2012.
3. Nova Scotia's general rate decreased from 0.1% to 0.05% on 1 July 2011 and will decrease to 0% on 1 July 2012. The rate is doubled for corporations with taxable capital under CAD 10 million.
4. Quebec's 0.25% financial institution rate is the 0.25% compensation tax on paid-up capital. A compensation tax of 3.9% (2% for taxation years ending before 31 March 2010 or beginning after 31 March 2014) on payroll also applies.
5. Saskatchewan's rate for financial institutions that have taxable paid-up capital of CAD 1.5 billion or less is 0.7%. Financial institutions that qualified for the 0.7% capital tax rate in taxation years ending after 31 October 2008 and before 1 November 2009, will be subject to a 0.7% capital tax rate on their first CAD 1.5 billion of taxable capital, and a 3.25% capital tax rate on taxable capital exceeding CAD 1.5 billion.

Additional taxes on insurers
All provinces and territories impose a premium tax ranging from 2% to 4.4% on insurance companies (both life and non-life). In addition, Nova Scotia imposes a capital tax on all insurance companies (which will be eliminated on 1 July 2012), while Ontario and Quebec impose a capital tax on life insurance companies only. Quebec also levies a compensation tax on insurance premiums at a rate of 0.55% (0.35% for taxation years ending before 31 March 2010, or beginning after 31 March 2014).

Part III.1 tax on excess designations
Federal Part III.1 tax applies at a 20% or 30% rate if, during the year, a CCPC designated as eligible dividends an amount that exceeds its general rate income pool (GRIP), or a non-CCPC pays an eligible dividend when it has a positive balance in its low rate income pool (LRIP). A corporation subject to Part III.1 tax at the 20% rate (i.e. the excess designation was inadvertent) can elect, with shareholder concurrence, to treat all or part of the excess designation as a separate non-eligible dividend, in which case Part III.1 tax will not apply to the amount that is the subject of the election.

Eligible dividends are designated as such by the payor and include dividends paid by:

• public corporations, or other corporations that are not CCPCs, that are resident in Canada and are subject to the federal general CIT rate (i.e. 15% in 2012), or
• CCPCs, to the extent that the CCPC's income is:

Canada

- not investment income (other than eligible dividends from public corporations), and
- subject to the general federal CIT rate (i.e. the income is active business income not subject to the federal small business rate).

Non-eligible dividends include dividends paid out of either income eligible for the federal small business rate or a CCPC's investment income (other than eligible dividends received from public companies).

Social security taxes

For 2012, employers are required to pay, for each employee, government pension plan contributions up to CAD 2,306.70 and employment insurance premiums up to CAD 1,175.96. However, Quebec employers contribute, per employee, a maximum of CAD 2,341.65 in Quebec government pension plan contributions, CAD 944.62 in employment insurance premiums, and CAD 516.12 to a Quebec parental insurance plan.

Provincial/territorial payroll taxes

Employers in Manitoba, Newfoundland and Labrador, Ontario, and Quebec are subject to payroll tax. Maximum rates range from 1.95% to 4.3%. In addition, Quebec employers with payroll of at least CAD 1 million must allot 1% of payroll to training or to a provincial fund. Employers in the Northwest Territories and Nunavut must deduct from employees' salaries a payroll tax equal to 2% of employment earnings.

Branch income

A non-resident corporation will be subject to income tax at normal corporate rates on profits derived from carrying on a business in Canada. However, Canada's tax treaties generally restrict taxation of a non-resident's business income to the portion allocable to a PE located in Canada.

In addition, a special 25% 'branch tax' applies to a non-resident's after-tax profits that are not invested in qualifying property in Canada. The branch tax essentially is equivalent to a non-resident WHT on funds repatriated to the foreign head office. In the case of a company resident in a treaty country, the rate at which the branch tax is levied may be reduced to the WHT rate on dividends prescribed in the relevant tax treaty (generally 5%, 10%, or 15%). Some of Canada's treaties prohibit the imposition of branch tax or provide that branch tax is payable only on earnings in excess of a threshold amount. The branch tax does not apply to transportation, communications, and iron-ore mining companies. Nor does it apply to non-resident insurers, except in special circumstances.

Whether or not a treaty applies, a non-resident corporation that has a PE in Canada may be subject to federal and provincial capital taxes (i.e. financial institutions only). *See the Other taxes section.*

Income determination

Inventory valuation

In most cases, all property included in inventory can be valued at fair market value, or each item can be valued at its cost or fair market value, whichever is lower. Most well-established and reasonable approaches to inventory costing can be used for tax purposes, except for the last in first out (LIFO) method. Conformity between methods used for book and tax reporting is not mandatory, but the method chosen should be used consistently for tax purposes. Inventory must be valued at the commencement of the year at the same amount as at the end of the immediately preceding year.

Capital gains

Half of a capital gain constitutes a taxable capital gain, which is included in the corporation's income and taxed at ordinary rates. Capital losses are deductible, but generally only against capital gains. Any excess of allowable capital losses over taxable capital gains in the current year can be carried back three years and carried forward indefinitely, to be applied against net taxable capital gains from those years, except in the case of an acquisition of control. No holding period is required. Intent is a major factor in determining whether the gain or loss is income or capital in nature.

Non-resident corporations are subject to CIT on taxable capital gains (50% of capital gains less 50% of capital losses) arising on the disposition of taxable Canadian property. Taxable Canadian property of a taxpayer includes, among other things:

- Real estate situated in Canada.
- Both capital and non-capital property used in carrying on a business in Canada.
- In general, shares in a Canadian-resident corporation that are listed on a stock exchange if, at any time in the preceding 60 months:
  - 25% of the shares of the corporation are owned by the taxpayer or persons related to the taxpayer, and
  - more than 50% of the fair market value of the shares are derived from real property situated in Canada, Canadian resource properties, and timber resource properties.
- In general, shares in a Canadian-resident corporation that are not listed on a stock exchange if, at any time in the preceding 60 months, more than 50% of the fair market value of the shares is derived directly from property similar to that described above for shares of a public corporation.

However, in specific situations, the disposition by a non-resident of a share or other interest that is not described above may be subject to Canadian tax (e.g. when a share is deemed to be taxable Canadian property).

The general requirement is that a non-resident vendor of taxable Canadian property must report the disposition to the CRA and obtain a clearance certificate in respect of the disposition. If no certificate is obtained, the purchaser is required to withhold and remit to the CRA 25% of the sales proceeds.

Relief from the reporting and 25% withholding requirements may be available if specified conditions are met (e.g. if the gain from the disposition is not taxable in Canada by virtue of a tax treaty Canada has with another country). However, if the parties to the transaction are related, the CRA must be notified to be exempt from these requirements.

Dividend income

Dividends received by one Canadian corporation from another Canadian corporation generally can be deducted in full when determining taxable income. However, dividends on certain preferred shares are an important exception and are taxed at full corporate rates. The intent is to allow preferred share investors to transfer benefits of accumulated deductions or losses from the entity that incurred the expense.

Canada

Dividends on most preferred shares are subject to a 10% tax in the hands of the recipient, unless the payer elects to pay a 40% tax (instead of a 25% tax) on the dividends paid. The payer can offset the tax against its income tax liability. The tax is not imposed on the first CAD 500,000 of taxable preferred-share dividends paid in a taxation year. Nor does it apply to dividends paid to a shareholder with a 'substantial interest' in the payer (i.e. at least 25% of the votes and value).

Dividends received by private corporations (or public corporations controlled by one or more individuals) from Canadian corporations are subject to a special refundable tax of 33 1/3%. The tax is not imposed if the recipient is connected to the payer (i.e. the recipient owns more than a 10% interest in the payer) unless the payer was entitled to a refund of tax in respect of the dividend. When the recipient pays dividends to its shareholders, the tax is refundable at CAD 1 for every CAD 3 of dividends paid.

Stock dividends
If the payer is resident in Canada, stock dividends are treated for tax purposes in the same manner as cash dividends. The taxable amount of a stock dividend is the increase in the paid-up capital of the payer corporation because of the payment of the dividend. Stock dividends received from a non-resident are exempt from this treatment. Instead, the shares received have a cost base of zero.

Interest income
Interest that accrued, became receivable by, or was received by a corporation is taxable as income from a business or property, as the case may be.

Rental income
Rents received by a corporation are taxable as income from a business or property, as the case may be.

Royalty income
Royalties received by a corporation are taxable as income from a business or property, as the case may be.

Foreign exchange gains and losses
The foreign exchange gains and losses of a Canadian taxpayer that arise from business transactions (i.e. on income account), including the activities of a branch operation, are generally fully includable in income or fully deductible, as the case may be. Any method that is in accordance with generally accepted accounting principles (GAAP) may be used to determine foreign exchange gains or losses on income transactions, provided that the treatment is consistent with previous years and conforms to the accrual method of accounting.

A foreign exchange gain or loss that is on capital account is treated the same as any other capital gain or loss. The accrual method of accounting cannot be used for purposes of reporting gains or losses on capital account. This follows from the CRA's view that a taxpayer has not made a capital gain or sustained a capital loss in a foreign currency until a transaction has taken place. Therefore, paper gains and losses are disregarded.

Partnership income
For Canadian tax purposes, a partnership is treated as a conduit, and the partners are taxed on their share of the partnership income, whether or not distributed. A corporation is not restricted from being a member of a partnership. Income is determined at the partnership level and is then allocated among the partners according

to the terms of the partnership agreement. However, certain deductions, such as depletion allowances, exploration and development expenses, and donations, will flow through to be deducted by the various partners directly, as will any foreign tax credits, dividend tax credits, or investment tax credits. Partners generally may deduct expenses incurred directly, such as interest on borrowings to acquire partnership interests, in computing income from the partnership.

C

For corporate partners with taxation years ending before 23 March 2011, income earned by a corporation as a member of a partnership was included in the corporation's income for the corporate taxation year in which the fiscal period of the partnership ended. Therefore, if the fiscal year of a partnership differed from the taxation year of a corporate partner, income and tax could be deferred by up to one year (or longer, potentially, in the case of multiple 'tiers' of partnerships with different fiscal periods). Newly enacted legislation that applies to corporate partners with taxation years ending after 22 March 2011 generally prevents these partners from deferring taxation on partnership income in respect of partnerships in which they (together with related parties) hold a greater than 10% interest (share of income or entitlement to assets); income from these partnerships must be accrued up to the end of the corporation's taxation year.

The accrual is based on partnership income for the fiscal period ending in the corporation's taxation year (the 'formulaic amount'), unless a lower amount is designated by the partner. Penalties can apply if the designated amount reported is less than both the formulaic amount and the actual prorated income of the subsequent partnership fiscal period. An election may be available to change the partnership's fiscal period. Partnerships in multi-tier structures must adopt the same fiscal period (31 December unless otherwise elected by the partnerships). Certain transitional reserves may be available for up to five years.

Joint venture income

An unincorporated joint venture is not recognised as a separate legal entity, and no specific statutory rules govern the taxation of a joint venture in Canada. However, many business arrangements that are set up as a joint venture may be considered partnerships, and treated as such for Canadian tax purposes. Whether a partnership exists in a particular situation is a legal question based on the specific facts and circumstances.

Consistent with the new partnership anti-deferral rules (*discussed in Partnership income above*), the CRA announced on 29 November 2011 the cancellation of a pervious administrative position allowing joint venture arrangements to report income using a separate fiscal period. As a result, corporate participants must report their actual share of joint venture income or loss up to the end of their own year-end for tax years ending after 22 March 2011. A transitional reserve will be allowed, in respect of the additional income included in that year by a corporate participant (i.e. any actual income of the participant for the stub period), using the same rules as for the partnership transitional reserve. However, to claim a reserve, the corporation must file an election with its tax return for that first year.

Non-resident trusts (NRTs) and offshore investment funds

Draft legislation changes Canada's approach to taxing NRTs and will affect NRTs that have (i) Canadian resident contributors or (ii) Canadian resident beneficiaries if certain current or former Canadian residents have contributed property to the NRT. The legislation deems these NRTs to be resident for Canadian income tax purposes. However, Canadian tax generally applies only to income or gains from the properties

Canada

contributed by Canadian residents. Many direct or indirect transfers or loans of property or services can be deemed to be contributions to the NRT. The NRT rules will apply commencing 2007. A trust can elect to be deemed resident for the 2001 and subsequent years if it was created from 2001 to 2006.

The offshore investment fund rules affect Canadian residents that have an interest as a beneficiary in these funds. The current legislation that applies to these funds is to be maintained with some modifications. For taxation years ending after 4 March 2010, draft legislation increases the prescribed income percentage by 2% and extends the statute-barred period for taxpayers who have invested in offshore investment funds by three years. Also, for certain non-discretionary trust funds in which a Canadian-resident person, and persons that do not deal at arm's length with the person, have interests in aggregate of 10% or more of the total fair market value of the total interests in the trusts, the trust is deemed to be a controlled foreign affiliate of the Canadian beneficiary and is thereby subject to the Canadian foreign accrual property income (FAPI) rules.

Earnings of specified investment flow-throughs (SIFTs)

Certain earnings of SIFTs (i.e. publicly traded income trusts and partnerships) are subject to a SIFT tax and are deemed to be a dividend when distributed, starting with the 2007 taxation year for SIFTs first publicly traded after 31 October 2006, and starting with the 2011 taxation year for other SIFTs. These rules are intended to discourage corporations from converting to income trusts and effectively force existing trusts to consider either restructuring or abandoning the income trust model. The rules do not apply to Real Estate Investment Trusts (REITs) that meet certain conditions.

Foreign income

Corporations resident in Canada are subject to Canadian federal income taxes on worldwide income, including income derived directly from carrying on business in a foreign country, as earned. In addition, resident corporations may be taxable currently on certain passive and active income earned by foreign subsidiaries and other foreign entities. Relief from double taxation is provided through Canada's international tax treaties, as well as foreign tax credits and deductions for foreign taxes paid on income derived from non-Canadian sources.

14 Tax Information Exchange Agreements (TIEAs) have already entered into force (one on behalf of five jurisdictions). Canada is currently negotiating 14 other TIEAs and has signed two that have not yet entered into force. Canada intends to sign more TIEAs with other non-treaty countries. To encourage non-treaty countries to enter into TIEAs:

- an exemption will be available for dividends received out of active business income earned by foreign affiliates resident in non-treaty countries that have agreed to a TIEA with Canada, and
- active business income earned by foreign affiliates in non-TIEA, non-treaty countries will be treated as FAPI, which is taxable in Canada on an accrual basis, if a TIEA with Canada is not concluded within a specified time period.

Foreign investment income earned directly, other than dividends, is taxed as earned, with foreign tax credits available in respect of foreign WHTs. Dividends received by private corporations from non-connected foreign corporations are subject to the special refundable tax of 33 1/3% (see above), to the extent that the dividends are deductible in determining taxable income.

The tax treatment of foreign dividends depends on whether the payer corporation is a foreign affiliate of the recipient. Dividends received from foreign corporations that are not foreign affiliates are taxed when received, with foreign tax credits available in respect of foreign WHTs. Dividends received from foreign affiliates are permitted to flow tax-free between corporations, subject to certain limitations. These limitations pertain to the nature of the earnings from which the dividends were paid, the underlying foreign taxes paid and WHTs paid.

See Controlled foreign affiliates and foreign accrual property income (FAPI) in the Group taxation section for a discussion on foreign affiliates, controlled foreign affiliates, and FAPI.

Foreign affiliate amendments

On 19 August 2011, the federal government released a significant package of proposed amendments to Canada's international tax rules applicable to Canadian corporations with foreign affiliates. The proposals substantially revise proposed amendments that were released at different times over the past decade and introduce new measures. Some of the proposals have retroactive effect. Key proposed amendments include:

- New income inclusion rules for upstream loans made by foreign affiliates.
- The creation of a 'hybrid surplus' regime to track certain capital gains realised by a foreign affiliate on the disposition of certain shares or partnership interests.
- New rules dealing with distributions made by foreign affiliates (generally deemed to be dividends).
- New stop loss rules applicable to dispositions of foreign affiliate shares or partnership interests.
- New rules for the streaming of passive capital losses realised by foreign affiliates.
- New foreign affiliate reorganisation rules applicable to liquidations, dissolutions, and foreign mergers (including absorptive mergers) involving foreign affiliates.
- A new anti-avoidance rule targeting increases in the exempt earnings of a foreign affiliate that are considered abusive.

'Foreign affiliate dumping' proposals

The 2012 federal budget introduced sweeping rules to curtail a variety of transactions it describes as 'foreign affiliate dumping' transactions. These transactions involve an investment in a foreign affiliate by a corporation that is (i) resident in Canada and (ii) controlled by a non-resident of Canada. When certain conditions are met, a dividend will be deemed to have been paid by the corporation to its foreign parent to the extent of any non-share consideration given by the corporation for the 'investment' in the foreign affiliate. The proposals define 'investment' broadly to include:

- an acquisition of shares or contribution of capital
- transactions where the foreign affiliate becomes indebted to the corporation (or a related Canadian company), and
- an acquisition of certain options in shares or debt of the foreign affiliate.

Any deemed dividend will be subject to Canadian WHT (as reduced by the applicable treaty). As currently worded, the proposals do not provide for relief from additional WHT when funds invested in a foreign affiliate are actually repatriated to its foreign parent. In addition, the paid-up capital of any shares of the corporation that are given as consideration for the 'investment' is disregarded (including for purposes of the thin capitalisation rules). The proposals generally apply to transactions occurring after 28 March 2012.

Canada

Deductions

Business expenses that are reasonable and paid out to earn income are deductible for income tax purposes unless disallowed by a specific provision in the Income Tax Act. Some expenses are deductible subject to limitation, e.g. charitable donations, entertainment expenses, and the cost of providing an automobile to employees. Deduction of capital expenditures is specifically prohibited, but special provisions may allow depreciation or amortisation of these expenditures.

Because Canadian corporations are taxable on worldwide income, there are basically no territorial limits on the deductibility of related expenses. Payments to affiliates are deductible if they reflect arm's-length charges. Transfers of losses and other deductions between unrelated corporate taxpayers are severely limited after an acquisition of control.

Depreciation and amortisation

Generally, depreciation for tax purposes (capital cost allowance) is computed on a pool basis, with only a few separate classes (pools) of property. Annual allowances are generally determined by applying a prescribed rate to each class on the declining-balance basis. For example, the prescribed annual rate is 20% on most furniture and fixtures, 30% on automotive equipment, and 4% to 10% on most buildings. In the year of acquisition, only half of the amount otherwise allowable may be claimed on most classes of property. Generally, capital cost allowance may not be claimed until the taxation year the property is available for use. The taxpayer can claim any amount of capital cost allowance up to the maximum. Capital cost allowance previously claimed may be recaptured if assets are sold for proceeds that exceed the undepreciated cost of the class. Temporary incentives to accelerate depreciation for eligible manufacturing and processing machinery and equipment acquired after 18 March 2007, and before 2014, revise the rate and method from 30% declining-balance to 50% straight-line.

Three-quarters of capital expenditures for goodwill and certain other intangible properties can be amortised at a maximum annual rate of 7%, on a declining-balance basis. A portion of proceeds may be taxable as recapture or as a gain on disposition.

Mining and oil and gas activity

Generally, mining and oil and gas companies are allowed a 100% deduction for exploration costs and certain preproduction development costs. Other development costs are deductible at the rate of 30% on a declining-balance basis. Capital property costs are subject to the depreciation rules *noted above under Depreciation*. In addition, in certain cases, significant asset acquisitions and assets acquired for a new mine or major expansion benefit from accelerated depreciation of up to 100% of the income from the mine. For certain oil sands assets acquired after 18 March 2007, accelerated depreciation will be reduced gradually starting in 2011 and will be eliminated by 2015.

Provinces levy mining taxes on mineral extraction and royalties on oil and gas production. These provincial levies are mostly deductible.

Newly enacted legislation that brings the taxation of oil sands properties more in line with that of the conventional oil and gas sector, generally for acquisitions after 21 March 2011, reduces the deduction rate per year:

- for the cost of acquiring oil sands leases and other oil sands resource or oil shale property from 30% to 10% on a declining-balance basis, and

- for preproduction development expenses from 100% to 30% on a declining-balance basis (transitional relief is available).

Investment tax credits (ITCs) are available federally (and in some provinces) to individuals who invest in shares to fund prescribed mineral exploration expenditures. The federal credit in 2012 for qualified 'flow-through' share investments is 15% of qualifying mining grassroots exploration expenditures. Certain mining exploration and preproduction expenditures that are incurred by a Canadian corporation and not used for flow-through are eligible for a 10% ITC. These credits can be used to offset current taxes payable or carried over to certain previous or subsequent taxation years. The 10% corporate credit is phased out:

- for pre-production mining exploration expenses from 10% to 5% in 2013 and nil after 2013 and
- for pre-production development expenses from 10% to 7% in 2014, 4% in 2015, and nil after 2015 (transitional relief may be available).

Scientific research and experimental development (SR&ED)
Canada provides a generous combination of deductions and tax credits for SR&ED. Until 2013, current and capital expenditures on R&D can be deducted in the year incurred or carried forward indefinitely to be used at the taxpayer's discretion to minimise tax payable. *See Scientific research and experimental development (SR&ED) credit in the Tax credits and incentives section for information on the tax credits currently available and for changes to SR&ED incentives that were announced in the 29 March 2012 federal budget.*

Interest expenses
Interest on borrowed money used for earning business or property income, or interest in respect of an amount payable for property acquired to earn income, is deductible, provided the interest is paid pursuant to a legal obligation and is reasonable in the circumstances.

Doubtful accounts and bad debts
A reasonable reserve for doubtful accounts may be deducted for tax purposes. The reserve calculation should be based on the taxpayer's past history of bad debts, industry experience, general and local economic conditions, etc. Special rules apply for determining reserves for financial institutions. A taxpayer can deduct the amount of debts owing that are established to have become bad debts during the year, provided the amount has previously been included in the taxpayer's income or relates to loans made in the ordinary course of business. Recoveries of bad debts previously written off must be included in income in the year of recovery.

Business meals and entertainment
Deductions by a corporation for business meals and entertainment expenses are limited to 50% of their cost. This includes meals while traveling or attending a seminar, conference, or convention, overtime meal allowances, and room rentals and service charges, etc. incurred for entertainment purposes. If the business meal and entertainment costs are billed to a client or customer and itemised as such, the disallowance (i.e. the 50% not deductible) is shifted to the client or customer.

Insurance premiums
Insurance premiums relating to property of a business are generally deductible, but life insurance premiums are generally not deductible if the company is the named beneficiary. However, if a financial institution lender requires collateral security in the

Canada

form of life insurance, a deduction is allowed for the associated net cost of any pure insurance for the period.

Charitable contributions
Charitable donations made to registered Canadian charitable organisations are deductible in computing taxable income, generally to the extent of 75% of net income. A five-year carryforward is provided.

Fines and penalties
Most government-imposed fines and penalties are not deductible. Fines and penalties that are not government-imposed are generally deductible, if they were made or incurred by the taxpayer for the purpose of gaining or producing income from the business or property.

Taxes
Federal, provincial, and territorial income taxes are not deductible in determining income subject to tax. The tax treatment of federal capital taxes and provincial payroll and capital taxes is discussed in the *Other taxes section*.

Net operating losses
Net operating losses generally may be carried back three tax years and forward 20 (ten years if the loss was incurred in taxation years ending before 2006 and after 22 March 2004, seven years if before 23 March 2004). Special rules may prohibit the use of losses from other years when there has been an acquisition of control of the corporation.

Payments to foreign affiliates
Royalties, management fees, and similar payments to related non-residents are deductible expenses to the extent that they are incurred to earn income of the Canadian company and do not exceed a reasonable amount (fair market value in most cases). The receipt of these payments by a foreign affiliate of the Canadian taxpayer will, in certain cases, give rise to foreign accrual property income, which is taxable on an accrual basis in Canada.

Group taxation

Group taxation is not permitted. However, the federal government issued a consultation paper, *The Taxation of Corporate Groups*, which explores possible approaches for taxing corporate groups, and subsequently reaffirmed its commitment to consider this issue.

Transfer pricing
Canadian transfer pricing legislation and administrative guidelines are generally consistent with the OECD Guidelines. Statutory rules require that transactions between related parties be carried out under arm's-length terms and conditions.

Penalties may be imposed when contemporaneous documentation requirements are not met. A taxpayer will be deemed not to have made reasonable efforts if the taxpayer does not maintain complete and accurate documentation to evidence that it has determined and used arm's-length prices for its related-party transactions. The documentation must be prepared on or before the taxpayer's documentation due date, which is six months after the end of the taxation year.

The transfer pricing penalty is 10% of the transfer pricing adjustment, if the adjustment exceeds the lesser of CAD 5 million and 10% of the taxpayer's gross revenue for the year. The penalty is not deductible in computing income, applies regardless of whether the taxpayer is taxable in the year, and is in addition to any additional tax and related interest penalties.

Canada has an Advance Pricing Agreement (APA) program that is intended to help taxpayers determine transfer prices acceptable to the local tax authorities and, when negotiated as bilateral or multilateral APAs, with tax authorities in other jurisdictions. Under this program, 253 APAs have been completed or are in progress.

Many of Canada's international tax agreements contain provisions concerning income allocation in accordance with the arm's-length principle. These include a Mutual Agreement Procedure, which is a treaty-based mechanism through which taxpayers can petition competent authorities for relief from double taxation resulting from transfer pricing adjustments.

Transfer pricing adjustments

When the Canadian transfer pricing rules have applied to adjust, for tax purposes, amounts related to transactions between a Canadian corporation and one or more non-arm's length non-residents (a 'primary adjustment'), the related benefit to the non-residents is generally treated by the CRA as a deemed dividend (a 'secondary adjustment'), subject to WHT. The 29 March 2012 federal budget confirms that the tax treatment of a secondary transfer pricing adjustment with a foreign affiliate will be a deemed dividend, subject to WHT, which can be eliminated, at the discretion of the Minister of Revenue, if the amount of the primary transfer pricing adjustment is repatriated to the Canadian corporation.

Thin capitalisation

Thin capitalisation rules can limit interest deductions when interest-bearing debt owing to certain non-residents (or persons not dealing at arm's length with certain non-residents) exceeds two times the corporation's equity.

Proposed rules have been announced that will modify the Canadian thin capitalisation rules as follows:

* Reduce the debt-to-equity ratio from 2:1 to 1.5:1, for taxation years beginning after 2012.
* Extend the rules to apply to debts of a partnership in which a Canadian-resident corporation is a member, for taxation years beginning after 28 March 2012.
* Treat disallowed interest as a dividend for WHT purposes, for taxation years ending after 28 March 2012.
* Prevent double taxation when a controlled foreign affiliate of a Canadian-resident corporation lends funds to the corporation and the interest would otherwise be both disallowed as a deduction in Canada and included in the foreign accrual property income of the affiliate, for taxation years ending after 28 March 2012.

Controlled foreign affiliates and foreign accrual property income (FAPI)

Under Canada's FAPI rules, Canadian corporations are taxed on certain income of controlled foreign affiliates (typically, certain income from property, income from a non-active business, and taxable capital gains) as earned, whether or not distributed. A grossed-up deduction is available for foreign income and WHTs paid in respect thereof. In general, a foreign corporation is a foreign affiliate of a Canadian corporation if:

Canada

- the Canadian corporation owns, directly or indirectly, at least 1% of any class of the outstanding shares of the foreign corporation, and
- the Canadian corporation and related persons (together) own, directly or indirectly, at least 10% of any class of the outstanding shares of that foreign corporation.

The foreign affiliate will be a controlled foreign affiliate of the Canadian corporation if certain conditions are met (e.g. more than 50% of the voting shares are owned, directly or indirectly, by a combination of the Canadian corporation, persons at non-arm's length with the Canadian corporation, a limited number of Canadian resident shareholders, and persons at non-arm's length with such Canadian resident shareholders).

Tax credits and incentives

Foreign tax credits

Taxpayers that have foreign-source income and are resident in Canada at any time in the year are eligible for foreign tax credit relief. Separate foreign tax credit calculations are prescribed for business and non-business income on a country-by-country basis. All provinces and territories also allow a foreign tax credit, but only in respect of foreign non-business income taxes.

Foreign business income or loss is computed for each foreign country in which a branch is located. Income or profit taxes paid to foreign governments generally are eligible for credit against a taxpayer's Canadian income taxes payable. The credit in respect of taxes paid on foreign income is restricted to the amount of Canadian taxes otherwise payable on this income. Excess foreign business income tax credits may be carried back three years or forward ten. Generally, foreign tax credits are available only to reduce Canadian tax on foreign-source income that is subject to tax in the foreign country.

The foreign non-business income tax credit applies to all foreign taxes other than those classified as business income tax. The credit is the lesser of:

- the foreign non-business income tax paid for the year on foreign non-business income, and
- Canadian federal tax otherwise payable for the year on the foreign non-business income.

The foreign non-business tax credit is available only to reduce Canadian income tax otherwise payable on foreign non-business income that is subject to income tax in the foreign country. No carryover is allowed with respect to the non-business income foreign tax credit. Unused foreign non-business income tax may be deducted in computing income.

Regional incentives

In specified regions of Canada (i.e. Atlantic provinces, the Gaspé region, and Atlantic offshore region), a 10% federal investment tax credit (ITC) is available for various forms of capital investment (generally, new buildings and/or machinery and equipment to be used primarily in manufacturing or processing, logging, farming, or fishing). The ITC is fully claimed against a taxpayer's federal tax liability in a given year. Unused ITCs reduce federal taxes payable for the previous three years and the next 20, or may be 40% refundable to CCPCs. Changes to the 10% federal ITC that generally apply to assets acquired after 28 March 2012:

- Phase out (subject to possible transitional relief) the ITC for certain oil and gas and mining activities, from 10% to 5% in 2014 and 2015, and nil after 2015.
- Ensure that 'qualified property' includes certain electricity generation equipment and clean energy generation equipment used primarily in an eligible activity (except oil and gas or mining activities).

The provinces and territories may also offer incentives to encourage corporations to locate in a specific region. Income tax holidays are available in Newfoundland and Labrador, Nova Scotia, Ontario, Prince Edward Island, and Quebec for certain corporations operating in specific industries (e.g. in Ontario and Quebec, commercialisation of intellectual property; in Prince Edward Island, bioscience or aviation) or meeting certain conditions (e.g. job creation for Newfoundland and Labrador).

Industry incentives
Canada offers many tax incentives at the federal, provincial, and territorial levels, for various industries and activities, including those related to:

- Research and development (*see below*).
- Film, media, computer animation and special effects, and multi-media productions.
- Manufacturing and processing.
- Environmental sustainability.

Scientific research and experimental development (SR&ED) credit
In addition to the R&D deduction, a taxpayer can benefit from an ITC, which is generally a 20% non-refundable credit on SR&ED expenditures that can be applied against taxes payable. Alternatively, this tax credit can be carried back three years or forward 20 to be applied against taxes owing.

A qualifying CCPC can qualify for a 35% refundable tax credit annually on its first CAD 3 million in expenditures. This enhanced credit is subject to certain income and capital limitations.

SR&ED ITCs have been extended to certain salary and wages (limited to 10% of salary and wages directly attributable to SR&ED carried on in Canada) incurred in respect of SR&ED carried on outside Canada.

In addition to the federal research and development incentives, all provinces (except Prince Edward Island) and the Yukon provide tax incentives to taxpayers that carry on R&D activities.

The Independent Panel on Federal Support to Research and Development released the report, *Innovation Canada: A Call to Action*, that provides "advice in respect of the effectiveness of federal programs to support business and commercially oriented R&D, the appropriateness of the current mix and design of these programs, as well as possible gaps in the current suite of programs and what might be done to fill them". As a result, significant changes are expected to Canada's SR&ED program in the coming years. Changes that were announced in the 29 March 2012 federal budget:

- Reduce the 20% SR&ED ITC rate to 15% for taxation years ending after 2013 (pro-rated for taxation years straddling 1 January 2014).
- Provide that capital property acquired generally after 2013 is not deductible as an SR&ED expenditure nor eligible for ITCs.
- Reduce the overhead proxy rate from 65% to 60% for 2013 and to 55% after 2013.

Canada

* Allow only 80% of SR&ED contract payments (net of SR&ED capital expenditures) to an arm's-length contractor incurred after 2012 to be eligible for ITCs.

In addition, the government will conduct a study to understand why taxpayers hire SR&ED consultants on a contingency-fee basis and determine actions needed to reduce taxpayer compliance costs to adhere to the SR&ED program.

Withholding taxes

Withholding tax at a rate of 25% is imposed on interest (other than most interest paid to arm's length non-residents), dividends, rents, royalties, certain management and technical service fees, and similar payments, made by a Canadian resident to a non-resident of Canada.

Canada is continually renegotiating and extending its network of treaties, some with retroactive effect. This table summarises WHT rates on payments arising in Canada. The applicable treaty should be consulted to determine the WHT rate that applies in a particular circumstance.

Recipient	Dividends (%)	Related-party interest (%) (1)	Royalties (%) (2)
Resident corporations and individuals	0	0	0
Non-resident corporations and individuals:			
Non-treaty	25	25	25
Treaty:			
Algeria	15	15	0/15
Argentina	10/15 (4)	12.5	3/5/10/15
Armenia	5/15 (4)	10	10
Australia	5/15 (4)	10	10
Austria	5/15 (4)	10	0/10
Azerbaijan (7)	10/15 (4)	10	5/10
Bangladesh	15	15	10
Barbados	15	15	0/10
Belgium	5/15 (4)	10	0/10
Brazil	15/25 (4)	15	15/25
Bulgaria	10/15 (4, 5)	10	0/10 (5)
Cameroon	15	15	15
Chile (5)	10/15 (4)	15	15
China, P.R. (6)	10/15 (4)	10	10
Colombia (3)	5/15 (4)	10	10 (5)
Croatia	5/15 (4)	10	10
Cyprus	15	15	0/10
Czech Republic	5/15 (4)	10	10
Denmark	5/15 (4)	10	0/10
Dominican Republic	18	18	0/18
Ecuador	5/15 (4)	15	10/15 (5)
Egypt	15	15	15

Recipient	Dividends (%)	Related-party interest (%) (1)	Royalties (%) (2)
Estonia (7)	5/15 (4)	10	10 (5)
Finland	5/15 (4)	10	0/10
France	5/15 (4)	10	0/10
Gabon	15	10	10
Germany	5/15 (4)	10	0/10
Greece	5/15 (4)	10	0/10
Guyana	15	15	10
Hungary	5/15 (4)	10	0/10
Iceland	5/15 (4)	10	0/10
India	15/25 (4)	15	10/15/20
Indonesia	10/15 (4)	10	10
Ireland, Republic of	5/15 (4)	10	0/10
Israel	15	15	0/15
Italy (8)	5/15 (4)	10	0/5/10
Ivory Coast	15	15	10
Jamaica	15	15	10
Japan	5/15 (4)	10	10
Jordan	10/15 (4)	10	10
Kazakhstan (7)	5/15 (4)	10	10 (5)
Kenya	15/25 (4, 5)	15	15
Korea, Republic of	5/15 (4)	10	10
Kuwait	5/15 (4)	10	10
Kyrgyzstan (7)	15 (5)	15 (5)	0/10
Latvia (7)	5/15 (4)	10	10 (5)
Lebanon (3)	5/15 (4)	10	5/10
Lithuania (7)	5/15 (4)	10	10 (5)
Luxembourg	5/15 (4)	10	0/10
Malaysia	15	15	15
Malta	15	15	0/10
Mexico	5/15 (4)	10	0/10
Moldova	5/15 (4)	10	10
Mongolia	5/15 (4)	10	5/10
Morocco	15	15	5/10
Namibia (3)	5/15 (4)	10	0/10
Netherlands	5/15 (4)	10	0/10
New Zealand (9)	5/15 (4)	10	5/10
Nigeria	12.5/15 (4)	12.5	12.5
Norway	5/15 (4)	10	0/10
Oman	5/15 (4)	10 (5)	0/10
Pakistan	15	15	0/15
Papua New Guinea	15	10	10
Peru (5)	10/15 (4)	15	15
Philippines	15	15	10
Poland (10)	5/15 (4)	10	5/10
Portugal	10/15 (4)	10	10
Romania	5/15 (4)	10	5/10

Canada

Recipient	Dividends (%)	Related-party interest (%) (1)	Royalties (%) (2)
Russia (7)	10/15 (4)	10	0/10
Senegal	15	15	15
Serbia (3)	5/15 (4)	10	10
Singapore	15	15	15
Slovak Republic	5/15 (4)	10	0/10
Slovenia	5/15 (4)	10	10
South Africa	5/15 (4)	10	6/10
Spain	15	15	0/10
Sri Lanka	15	15	0/10
Sweden	5/15 (4)	10	0/10
Switzerland	5/15 (4)	10	0/10
Tanzania	20/25 (4)	15	20
Thailand	15	15	5/15
Trinidad and Tobago	5/15 (4)	10	0/10
Tunisia	15	15	0/15/20
Turkey (11)	15/20 (4)	15	10
Ukraine (7)	5/15 (4)	10	0/10
United Arab Emirates	5/15 (4)	10	0/10
United Kingdom	5/15 (4)	10	0/10
United States	5/15 (4)	0 (12)	0/10
Uzbekistan (7)	5/15 (4)	10	5/10
Venezuela	10/15 (4, 5)	10	5/10
Vietnam	5/10/15 (4)	10	7.5/10
Zambia	15	15	15
Zimbabwe	10/15 (4)	15	10

Notes

1. Interest: Canada does not impose WHT on interest (except for 'participating debt interest') paid to arm's-length non-residents. Most treaties have an explicit provision for higher WHT on interest in excess of fair market value in non-arm's-length circumstances.
2. Royalties: A zero royalty rate generally applies to:
   - copyright royalties and payments for a literary, dramatic, musical, or other artistic work (but not royalties for motion picture films, work on film or videotape, or other means of reproduction for use in television), and/or
   - royalties for computer software, a patent, or for information concerning industrial, commercial, or scientific experience (but not royalties for a rental or franchise agreement).

   Different rates may apply in the case of immovable property (e.g. payments that relate to Canadian natural resources). Most treaties explicitly provide for higher WHT on royalties in excess of fair market value in non-arm's-length circumstances. A zero rate of tax may apply in certain circumstances.
3. The treaty has been signed, but is not yet in force. In the absence of a treaty, Canada imposes a maximum WHT rate of 25% on dividends, interest, and royalties.
4. The lower (lowest two for Vietnam) rate applies if or when the beneficial owner of the dividend is a company that owns/controls a specified interest in the paying company. The nature of the ownership requirement, the necessary percentage (10%, 20%, 25%, or higher), and the relevant interest (e.g. capital, shares, voting power, equity percentage) vary by treaty.
5. If the other state (Canada for the treaty with Oman) concludes a treaty with another country providing for a lower WHT rate (higher rate for Kenya), the lower rate (higher rate for Kenya) will apply in respect of specific payments within limits, in some cases.
6. Canada's treaty with China does not apply to Hong Kong.
7. The treaty status of the republics that comprise the former USSR is as follows:
   - Azerbaijan, Estonia, Kazakhstan, Kyrgyzstan, Latvia, Lithuania, Russia, Ukraine, and Uzbekistan: new treaties entered into force (*see table for rates*).
   - Other republics: no negotiations are underway.

Belarus, Tajikistan, and Turkmenistan will not honour the treaty with the former USSR. As a result, Canada will impose a maximum WHT rate of 25% on dividends, interest, and royalties until a new treaty enters into force. For other republics that comprise the former USSR, the status of the former treaty with the USSR is uncertain. Because the situation is subject to change, Canadian taxpayers are advised to consult with the CRA as transactions are carried out.

8. The Canada-Italy treaty entered into force on 25 November 2011. Its provisions apply in Canada:
   * for purposes of non-resident WHT, to amounts paid or credited after 31 December 2010, and
   * for other taxes, for taxation years beginning after 2010.
9. A new treaty and Protocol with New Zealand was signed on 3 May 2012. Upon ratification, its provisions will apply in Canada:
   * for purposes of non-resident WHT, to amounts paid or credited after the end of the first month after they enter into force, and
   * for other taxes, for taxation years beginning after the calendar year they enter into force.
   The rates in the table are from the new treaty and Protocol. Under the new treaty and Protocol, the WHT rate will be reduced from 15% to:
   * 5% on dividends paid to a company that owns at least 10% of the payor's voting stock (the rate will remain 15% on other dividends)
   * 10% on interest, but certain interest payments will be exempt, and
   * 10% on royalties, but certain royalties for the use of computer software, patents, and know-how, and certain copyright royalties, will be subject to a rate of 5%.
10. A new treaty and Protocol with Poland was signed on 14 May 2012. Upon ratification, its provisions will apply in Canada:
   * for purposes of non-resident WHT, to amounts paid or credited after the calendar year they enter into force, and
   * for other taxes, for taxation years beginning after the calendar year they enter into force.
   The rates in the table are from the new treaty and Protocol. Under the new treaty and Protocol, the WHT rate will:
   * be reduced from 15% to 5% on dividends paid to a company that owns directly at least 10% of the payor's capital (the rate will remain 15% on other dividends)
   * be reduced from 15% to 10% on interest, but certain interest payments will be exempt, and
   * remain 10% on royalties, but certain royalties for the use of computer software, patents, and know-how will be subject to a rate of 5%, and certain copyright royalties will no longer be exempt and will be subject to a rate of 5%.
11. The Canada/Republic of Turkey treaty entered into force on 4 May 2011. Its provisions apply in Canada:
   * for purposes of non-resident WHT, to amounts paid or credited after 31 December 2011, and
   * for other taxes, to taxable years beginning after 2011.
   Before that, the rates were 25%.
12. For the United States, the zero rate applies, subject to the Limitation of Benefits article.

Tax administration

Taxable period

The tax year of a corporation, which is normally the fiscal period it has adopted for accounting purposes, cannot exceed 53 weeks. The tax year need not be the calendar year. Once selected, the tax year cannot be changed without approval from the tax authorities.

Tax returns

Both the federal and the provincial/territorial corporation tax systems operate on an essentially self-assessing basis. All corporations must file federal income tax returns. Alberta and Quebec tax returns must also be filed by corporations that have PEs in those provinces, regardless of whether any tax is payable. Corporations with PEs in other provinces that levy capital tax must also file capital tax returns. Tax returns must be filed within six months of the corporation's tax year-end. No extensions are available.

Certain corporations with annual gross revenues exceeding CAD 1 million are required to electronically file (e-file) their federal CIT returns via the internet. Also, information return filers that submit more than 50 information returns annually must e-file via the internet. Penalties are assessed for failure to e-file.

Canada

Payment of tax

Corporate tax instalments are generally due on the last day of each month (although some CCPCs can remit quarterly instalments, if certain conditions are met). Any balance payable is generally due on the last day of the second month following the end of the tax year.

Functional currency

The amount of income, taxable income, and taxes payable by a taxpayer is determined in Canadian dollars. However, certain corporations resident in Canada can elect to determine their Canadian tax amounts in the corporation's 'functional currency'.

Audit cycle

The tax authorities are required to issue an assessment notice within a reasonable time following the filing of a tax return. These original assessments usually are based on a limited review, if any, of the corporation's income tax return. However, the notice of assessment will identify any changes made (i.e. correcting discrepancies on any balances carried forward).

Traditionally, all corporations with gross income over CAD 250 million and their affiliates are assigned a large case file team and audited annually. Medium-sized corporations (gross income between CAD 20 million and CAD 250 million) generally are selected based on a screening process and identified risks. Smaller corporations, which are usually CCPCs with gross income under CAD 20 million, have been subject to compliance or restricted audits, selected based on statistical data and a screening process. Audits of CCPCs are generally restricted to covering the current and one previous taxation year.

However, the CRA announced in the fall of 2010 that, over the next five years, it will implement a new 'risk assessment' model to select corporations, partnerships, income trusts, and private equity funds for audit. Large corporations and their affiliated entities are to be classified as high, medium, or low risk, and their categorisation will dictate the scope of the audit undertaken. Factors that determine the risk category include the taxpayer's history with the CRA, the type of industry, and the internal controls in place. The CRA is implementing this new risk assessment approach in 2012 by subjecting 50 of approximately 1,100 large corporations to it.

In 2010, the CRA issued a policy paper describing the powers that CRA officials have to obtain information and supporting documentation from taxpayers, registrants, and third parties. It also discusses the CRA's policies and procedures for obtaining information, and how concerns with any specific information gathering process can be addressed by taxpayers or their representatives. The paper confirms that auditors determine what information is relevant for the review being conducted. It lists the compliance tools that can be used to obtain the information and the consequences for non-compliance. The CRA expects transparency and cooperation from the taxpayer, registrant, or third party to benefit the compliance process.

Statute of limitations

A reassessment of the tax payable by a corporation that is not a CCPC may be made within four years from the date of mailing of the original notice of assessment, usually following a detailed field audit of the return and supporting information. The limitation period is three years for CCPCs. The three-year and four-year limits are extended a further three years to permit reassessment of transactions with non-arm's-length non-residents. Reassessments generally are not permitted beyond these limits unless there has been misrepresentation or fraud. Different time limits may apply for provincial reassessments.

Appeals

A taxpayer that disagrees with a tax assessment or reassessment may appeal. The first step is to file a formal notice of objection within 90 days from the date of mailing of the notice of assessment or reassessment, setting out the reasons for the objection and other relevant information. Different time limits may apply for provincial reassessments. Corporations that qualify as 'large corporations' must file more detailed notices of objection. The CRA will review the notice of objection and vacate (cancel), amend, or confirm it. A taxpayer that still disagrees has 90 days to appeal the CRA's decision to the Tax Court of Canada, and if necessary, to the Federal Court of Appeal and the Supreme Court of Canada. However, the Supreme Court hears few income tax appeals.

Topics of focus for tax authorities

Topics of interest to Canadian tax authorities include:

- The deductibility of:
  - royalty payments made by Canadian corporations to non-arm's-length non-residents
  - business restructuring expenses incurred by a group of corporations located in more than one country
  - interest paid on loans if the funds derived from the loans are used offshore, and
  - guarantee fees paid by Canadian corporations to related non-resident corporations.
- The offshoring of Canadian-source income by factoring the accounts receivable of Canadian corporations.
- Treaty shopping to reduce Canadian WHT and capital gains tax.
- Surplus stripping to reduce Canadian WHT by artificially increasing a Canadian corporation's paid-up capital and subsequently distributing the surplus as a return of capital.
- The generation of foreign tax credits by a corporation for foreign income taxes that have not been borne by the corporation.

Foreign reporting

Reporting requirements apply to taxpayers with offshore investments. The rules impose a significant compliance burden for taxpayers with foreign affiliates. Failure to comply could result in substantial penalties.

Tax avoidance

Draft legislation makes an 'avoidance transaction' meeting certain conditions a 'reportable transaction' that must be reported to the CRA, generally for transactions entered into after 2010, and those that are part of a series of transactions completed after 2010. Quebec already has a provincial reporting regime for certain aggressive tax planning transactions, generally carried out after 14 October 2009.

Cross-border tax evasion

To facilitate and improve the exchange of tax information and combat cross-border tax evasion, Canada has signed a Protocol amending the Convention on Mutual Administrative Assistance in Tax Matters. The member states of the Council of Europe and the member countries of the OECD are signatories.

Canada

....

Other issues

Forms of business enterprise

Canadian law is based on the British common-law system, except in Quebec where a civil-law system prevails. The principal forms of business enterprise available in Canada are the following.

- Corporation: A legal entity distinct from its shareholders, whether public or private, incorporated federally, provincially, or territorially.
- Partnership: A business relationship between two or more 'persons' (i.e. individuals, corporations, trusts, or other partnerships) formed for the purpose of carrying on business in common. Not treated as a legal entity distinct from its partners.
- Sole proprietorship: An unincorporated business operated by an individual that is carried on under the individual's own name or a trade name.
- Trust: A relationship whereby property (including real, tangible, and intangible) is managed by one person (or persons, or organisations) for the benefit of another. May hold commercial enterprises.
- Joint venture: Generally, the pursuit of a specific business objective by two or more parties whose association will end once the objective is achieved or abandoned. Not treated as a legal entity distinct from the participants.

Foreign investors usually conduct business in Canada through one or more separate Canadian corporations, although operation as a branch of a profitable foreign corporation may be preferable during the start-up period. In addition, foreign investors may participate as partners in partnerships carrying on business in Canada or as joint venturers.

Financial statement reporting

For fiscal years beginning after 31 December 2010:

- Most 'publicly accountable enterprises' must adopt International Financial Reporting Standards (IFRS).
- Private enterprises must adopt either IFRS or Accounting Standards for Private Enterprises (ASPE).

As a result, IFRS and ASPE have become Canadian GAAP. This could affect the measurement and reporting of income taxes for financial statement purposes and the calculation of Canadian taxes payable.

Cape Verde

PwC contact

Leendert Verschoor
PricewaterhouseCoopers & Associados - SROC, Lda.
Palácio Sottomayor
Rua Sousa Martins 1 - 3º
1069-316 Lisboa
Portugal
Tel: +351 213 599 642
Email: leendert.verschoor@pt.pwc.com

Significant developments

2012 State Budget Law
Cape Verde's 2012 State Budget Law (2012 State Budget) was published in the Official
Gazette of 30 December 2011. Law Number 10/VIII/2011 entered into force on 1
January 2012. The main changes introduced to Cape Verdean tax law are the following.

Excise duties
The 2012 State Budget increased the excise duties rates to 40% in the case of beers,
wines, vermouths, and other alcoholic drinks, and to 20% in the case of tobacco.

Vehicles used for transportation, up to 5 tons, will be subject to rates of up to 150%,
according to their age.

Exemptions from Imposto *Único sobre os Rendimentos* (IUR)
Exemption applicable to small and medium-sized companies set up by young entrepreneurs
The exemption from IUR applicable for a three-year period will apply to more than one
company owned by the same entrepreneur, provided that cumulatively the exemption
does not exceed six years.

Tax benefits revoked
Incentives to pharmaceutical industry
The import of packaging materials of products produced by the national
pharmaceutical industry will no longer be exempt from custom duties.

Taxes on corporate income

Cape Verde has a single tax on income, called *Imposto Único sobre os Rendimentos* (IUR),
which is levied on profits arising from business activities carried out in Cape Verde
by resident companies or individual entrepreneurs and by Cape Verdean permanent
establishments (PEs) of non-resident entities.

Taxable profit is computed according to the local accounting rules and adjusted for tax
purposes. The taxation system in Cape Verde is based on a territorial principle; if the
source of the income is located abroad, no Cape Verde taxation is imposed on it.

Income tax rates
The following IUR rates are applicable:

- Companies are subject to a tax rate of 25%, where taxable income corresponds to the
  profit less any tax benefits and any losses carried forward, as stated in the tax return.

Cape Verde

- Non-residents without a PE in Cape Verde are subject to a 20% withholding tax (WHT) on the amount of the invoice.

Surcharge
The IUR rate is increased by a fire brigade surcharge, called *Taxa de Incêndio*, of 2% on the tax due. This surcharge is levied in the municipalities of Praia (Island of Santiago) and Mindelo (Island of São Vicente).

Corporate residence

A company or entity is deemed to be resident in Cape Verde if its registered head office or its place of effective management is in the Cape Verde territory.

Permanent establishment (PE)
Non-resident companies deemed to have a PE in Cape Verde are also subject to tax in Cape Verde. Under Cape Verdean tax law, a non-resident company is deemed to have a PE if the non-resident company:

- has any fixed installation or permanent representation located in Cape Verde through which, among others, activities of commercial, industrial, or agricultural nature, or fishing and rendering of services are carried out (including agricultural, fishing, and cattle raising explorations, or other quarries or any other places of natural resources extraction) or
- carries out its activity in Cape Verde through employees, or any other personnel hired for that purpose, for a period (continuous or not) of not less than 90 days within a 12-month period.

Other taxes

Value-added tax (VAT)
The VAT system in Cape Verde closely follows the European Union (EU) VAT system, and it is assessed at the standard rate of 15% and at a reduced rate of 6%.

The standard VAT rate of 15% is a general tax on consumption, applicable to the import and sale of goods and services in Cape Verde territory.

The 6% reduced VAT rate applies to lodging and restaurants, due to the important role they assume in the Cape Verde economy.

The VAT regulations establish two types of exempt transactions: exempt transactions without credit and exempt transactions with credit (i.e. zero-rated transactions). VAT incurred is recoverable in as far as the goods and services are used for the purposes of the taxed transactions of a taxable person or for zero-rated transactions.

Exempt transactions without credit include the following:

- Hospital and medical care and closely related activities undertaken by bodies governed by public law, or comparable activities undertaken by other hospitals and centres for medical treatment.

C

- The provision of medical care through the exercise of the medical and paramedical professions, as well as the supply of transport services for sick or injured persons, and the supply of human organs, blood, and milk.
- The supply of services and goods closely linked to welfare and social security work.
- The supply of services and goods closely linked to the protection of children and young people by bodies governed by public law.
- The provision of children's or young people's education, school or university education, including the supply of services and goods closely related thereto.
- The supply of services, and goods closely linked thereto, by non-profit-making organisations.
- The supply of copyright and art objects by the original creators or their heirs.
- The supply by the public postal services of stamps and stamped paper.
- The supply of certain cultural, educational, technical, and recreational services.
- Garbage removal.
- Burial and cremation supplies.
- Banking, financial, insurance, and reinsurance transactions, including related services performed by insurance brokers and insurance agents.
- Immovable property transactions (excluding the provision of accommodation in the hotel sector or in sectors with a similar function, the granting of facilities for collective parking of vehicles, the leasing of permanently installed machinery and equipment, and the granting of facilities for exhibitions and advertising).
- Specified basic foodstuffs and pharmaceutical products.
- Goods used in agriculture, stockbreeding, forestry, and fisheries.

Exempt transactions with credit (i.e. zero-rated transaction) on imports include the following:

- Import of goods whose supply qualifies for exemption.
- Re-import of goods by the person who exported them, in the state in which they were exported, where they qualify for exemption from customs duties.
- Services in connection with the import of goods where the value of such services is included in the taxable amount.
- Import of gold by the central bank.
- Import into ports by sea fishing undertakings of their catches, unprocessed or after undergoing preservation for marketing but before being supplied.
- Import of goods under diplomatic and consular arrangements that qualify for exemption from customs duties.
- Import of goods for the fuelling and provisioning of sea-going vessels and aircraft.

The most important exemptions with credit (i.e. zero-rated) for exports and connected transactions include the following:

- Supply, modification, repair, maintenance, chartering, and hiring of aircraft used by airlines operating both on domestic and international routes, and the supply, hiring, repair, and maintenance of equipment incorporated or used therein.
- The supply of goods for the fuelling and provisioning of such aircraft.
- Services meeting the direct needs of such aircraft or their cargoes.

Customs duties/Import tariffs

Customs duties are levied at rates ranging from 0% to 50% on the customs value of most imported goods. Since Cape Verde imports the majority of the goods it consumes, a 50% tariff protection applies for certain domestically produced goods.

Cape Verde

Raw materials or capital goods can be imported with an exemption from custom duties or at a low rate.

Special consumption tax

A special consumption tax is imposed at rates ranging from 10% to 150% on goods which are deemed superfluous, luxurious, or undesirable for economic, social, or environmental policy reasons.

The 2012 State Budget increased the excise duties rates to 40% in the case of beers, wines, vermouths, and other alcoholic drinks, and to 20% in the case of tobacco.

Vehicles used for transportation, up to 5 tons, will be subject to rates of up to 150%, according to their age:

- Up to four years: not applicable.
- More than four and up to six years: 40%.
- More than six and up to ten years: 80%.
- More than ten years: 150%.

Property taxes

A property tax, called *Imposto Único sobre o Património* (IUP), is levied at the rate of 3% in Cape Verde.

IUP is due on the ownership of immovable property on an annual basis by the owner of the real estate, registered as such on 31 December of the relevant year. The taxable basis corresponds to 25% of the value attributed by the Evaluation Commission.

IUP is also due on the transfer (gratuitously or for a consideration) of real estate, based on the value of the contract declared by the transferee.

Exemption of IUP due on the acquisition is granted to:

- Cape Verdean emigrants who own saving bank accounts.
- Retired individuals.
- Projects with Touristic Utility Status (*see the Tax credits and incentives section for more information*).

In taxable transfers (not exempt), IUP is payable by the transferee.

IUP is also due on the capital gains arising from the sale of:

- plots of land for construction, if the sales price is more than double the purchase price, and
- buildings or other real estate, if the sale price exceeds the purchase price by more than 30%.

IUP on capital gains is normally paid by the transferor, on the highest of the declared price and the official value of the property concerned.

Capital gains obtained by companies that are in the business of buying real estate for resale are not subject to IUP.

Cape Verde

Stamp duty

Stamp duty is payable on a wide variety of transactions and documents, at rates that may be set in specific amounts or on a percentage basis.

Stamp duty rates:

Item	Stamp duty rate
Loans	
With determined term, over one year	0.5%
With undetermined term or under one year (for each month)	0.05%
Bank interest and fees/commissions	3.5%
Guarantees	0.5%
Insurance	3.5%
Promissory notes, securities	0.5%
Corporate structuring operations	0.5%
Real estate purchases and sales	1%
Sale of a business as a going concern	5%
Letting of immovable property	10%
Property leasing	1%
Emoluments, registrations acts	15%
Contracts	CVE 1,000 *

* Fixed exchange rate 1 euro (EUR) = 100.265 Cape Verdean escudos (CVE) under an exchange agreement between Cape Verde and Portugal.

Ecologic charge

Cape Verde's ecologic charge, in force since August 2010, is applied to packing material, whether empty or full, imported or produced internally, non-biodegradable or made out of metal, glass, or plastic.

The ecologic charge varies from CVE 2 to CVE 100 per item, depending on the quantity or weight of the goods.

This fee is due by the local producer or the importer.

Exemptions are available in the case of packing material used in medicine, essential food (e.g. corn, rice, sugar, flour, and milk), and construction (e.g. cement). Packing material that is exported, reutilised, or recycled is also exempt.

Branch income

A branch is not considered a separate legal entity distinct from the foreign head office. It is governed by the domestic law of Cape Verde.

From a tax perspective, branches are subject to corporate income tax, if considered a PE under Cape Verde law.

Cape Verde

Income determination

Taxable income is computed on the basis of the accounting income, adjusted by deducting from taxable profits the prior years' losses and any deductions under the tax (incentive) legislation.

Inventory valuation

The tax law does not foresee any mandatory inventory valuation method that should be adopted by Cape Verdean taxpayers. For tax purposes, accepted inventory methods should be consistent with the accounting rules in force and with local business practice generally accepted, if and when such methods are applied in a consistent way during the financial years and were also based on the prices effectively paid or under regulated prices established by official documents.

Capital gains

Capital gains are not subject to a separate capital gains tax and are treated and taxed as ordinary business income.

The gain corresponds to the amount by which proceeds from disposal exceeds the cost of asset acquisition.

Capital gains realised from the sale of shares and part of the capital of companies with a registered head office or place of effective management in Cape Verde, if owned for at least one year, are not subject to taxation.

Dividend income

Dividend income is currently fully exempt from taxation in Cape Verde.

Interest income

There is no special tax provision regarding interest income. Interest income is treated and taxed as ordinary business income.

Foreign income

Resident companies and PEs of non-resident companies are taxable on a territorial base principle, meaning that income obtained outside Cape Verde is not subject to taxation therein.

Deductions

Depreciation

Depreciation is considered a deductible cost with respect to all fixed assets (except land), up to the limits determined by the applicable tax law.

As a general rule, depreciation must be computed by using the straight-line method. Tax authorities may allow other depreciation methods on the basis that the actual depreciation is higher than the one calculated at regular rates or according to the taxpayer's accounting practice.

Under the straight-line method, the maximum depreciation that is deductible is calculated by applying the general depreciation rates set out in a Ministerial Decree of 28 January 1984 to the adjusted purchase cost or production cost.

Cape Verde

Land is not depreciable.

Main depreciation rates:

Group	Asset	Depreciation rate (%)
1	Plantations, land for exploration, other land and natural resources	To be determined on a case-by-case basis
2	Buildings and other constructions	
	Residential, commercial, and industrial buildings	4
	Light structures (fibreglass wood, wood, metal) and other constructions	10
	Quays, docks, and similar harbour infrastructure	2
	Walls, silos, parks, roads, adornments, runways	5
3	Basic equipment, machines, and other installations	
	Fishing gear	25
	Electronic, sound, laboratory, telephone, and radar equipment	20
	Telecommunication stations and installations	12.5
	Water installations	6.66
	Machines	16.66
	Oil pipelines, fuel and gas reservoirs	8.33
	Transformation stations, air networks, equipment, and underground cables for communications and transport of energies	5
	Other equipment and machines	10
4	Tools (for industries / others)	20/25
5	Cargo and transport material	
	Animals and lightweight motor vehicles	12.5
	Aircrafts	14.28
	Ships and boats	10
	Cranes, barges, etc.	7.14
	Trucks	20
	Other cargo and transport material	16.66
6	Administrative and social equipment and furniture	
	Furnishings and decorative items	16.16
	Calculating machine, typewriter, and accounting machine	20
	Metallic furniture	8.33
	Non-metallic furniture	12.5
	Clothes, tableware, and glasses	50
	Others administrative and social equipment and furniture	25
7	Packing material (wood/metal/other)	14.28/20/33.33
8	Other tangible fixed assets	10
9	Intangibles	
	Patents, trademarks, licences, concessions and other rights	10
	Formation and organisation of the company	33.33
	Other intangibles	33.33

Goodwill

Goodwill is an asset subject to impairment tests. The goodwill's impairment is not a deductible cost for tax purposes.

Cape Verde

Start-up expenses
Start-up expenses include, among others, cost incurred with set-up and organisation of companies, projects, and increase of capital. Start-up expenses are considered a deductible cost up to the limits derived from the applicable tax law, 33.33% per year being deductible over a period of three years.

Interest expenses
Interest expenses are deductible if considered indispensable for the realisation of taxable profits/gains.

There are no thin capitalisation rules.

Bad debt
Provision regarding bad debts is accepted as a deductible cost within the following limits: 4% of accounts receivable per year with a cumulative maximum of 5%.

Charitable contributions
Charitable contributions granted to certain entities whose main activity consists in the execution of initiatives in the social, cultural, environmental, scientific or technologic, sports, and educational areas are considered as cost for tax purposes (within certain limits, and in certain circumstances, with an additional deduction).

Fines and penalties
Tax (and fines) penalties are not deductible for tax purposes.

Taxes
Taxes paid in connection with the activity of the company are tax deductible, excluding IUR and the IUP due on an annual basis. However, under the current tax law, the annual IUP can be deducted from the IUR assessed.

Net operating losses
Income tax losses can be offset against taxable profit and can be carried forward for three years. Carryback of tax losses is not allowed in Cape Verde.

The tax losses incurred by a company are not transferable to another company unless previously accepted by the tax authorities.

Payments to foreign affiliates
Currently, there are no special restrictions on the deductibility of royalties, interest, and service fees paid to foreign affiliates, provided that the payments are regarded as indispensable to generate taxable profits and gains and to maintain the business of the company.

Group taxation

There is no special tax regime for groups of companies in Cape Verde.

Transfer pricing
There is no special tax regime regarding transfer pricing in Cape Verde.

Thin capitalisation
There is no special tax regime regarding thin capitalisation in Cape Verde.

Tax credits and incentives

Foreign Investor Status (Estatuto do Investidor Externo)

Direct foreign investments in Cape Verde made in any business sector by entities with the Foreign Investor Status benefit from an exemption from WHT on distribution of profits, as well as interest derived from the financing of the investment, paid to foreign investors. Currently, dividends are not taxed in Cape Verde under a domestic exemption. The benefit applies for the first five years of the investment or whenever the profits are reinvested in Cape Verde, in the same or another economic activity. This benefit is granted following a request filed with the Cape Verdean Agency for Foreign Investment.

Industrial Activity Law

The following tax and custom benefits are provided for industrial activity:

IUR benefits

Industrial Entrepreneurs benefit from a five-year exemption from IUR on the income generated by each industrial establishment. Under this regime, 'Industrial Entrepreneurs' are individuals and/or companies that solely or jointly declare the intention to develop an industrial project.

This exemption is renewable for the same period in the case of reinvestment, via a tax deduction corresponding to the total sum of the profits reinvested in the same or in other industrial unit.

The exemption period is increased to seven years in the case of industrial projects set up in less-developed areas (yet to be defined), which contribute to job creation or to diversify the production of goods and services.

IUP benefits

Industrial Entrepreneurs benefit from a ten-year exemption from IUP on the ownership of real estate used exclusively for industrial purposes. There is also an exemption on the acquisition of real estate for the same purpose and on cargo and passenger transport vehicles used exclusively for the purposes of the industrial activity.

VAT benefits

Industrial Entrepreneurs benefit from a VAT exemption on the acquisition of equipment and vehicles (not more than five years old) for the transport of goods and workers of the industrial establishment.

Custom duty benefits

Industrial Entrepreneurs benefit from an exemption from custom duties on the import of construction material, machines, utensils, semi and finished materials, and products used exclusively in the production of goods within a new industrial product.

The law also provides for an exemption from custom duties on the acquisition of fuel and lubricants (except gasoline) used in the production of energy and desalinised water for consumption by the industrial establishment.

International Business Centre (IBC) of Cape Verde

The IBC regime is in force as of 2 March 2011. The Cape Verdean Agency for Foreign Investment is the entity responsible for granting the licences to operate within the IBC,

Cape Verde

upon previous proposal of the Zona Franca Comercial S.A.. The following tax benefits are applicable to entities licensed to operate in the IBC on income from industrial or business activities and services in respect of operations carried out with other IBC licensed entities or with non-residents entities (without a PE in Cape Verde).

Note that these tax benefits are not applicable to entities engaged in tourism, banking and insurance, real estate, or construction.

IUR benefits
From 1 January 2011 through 31 December 2018, the IUR rate is reduced by 90% to an effective rate of 2.5%.

From 1 January 2019 through 31 December 2025, the IUR rate is reduced by 85% to an effective rate of 3.75%.

Under current IUR law, foreign-sourced income is not subject to taxation in Cape Verde.

VAT and custom duty benefits
All the exemptions foreseen in the VAT Regulation apply.

An exemption from custom duties applies with respect to certain goods used within the scope of the activity developed and licensed under the IBC.

WHT benefits to shareholders of entities licensed to operate in the IBC
An exemption from WHT applies with respect to distributed profits which have been taxed at the reduced IUR rates applicable within the IBC. Currently, besides the foreign income not being subject to taxation in Cape Verde, distributed dividends are not subject to taxation.

An exemption from WHT applies with respect to interest, and other income, from shareholders loans or other capital entries.

Tax and financial incentives for internationalisation of Cape Verdean companies
A regime that provides for tax and financial incentives for investment projects in order to promote the internationalisation of Cape Verdean companies is in force as of 23 March 2011.

The following incentives, to be granted under a contract of not more than three years, apply to internationalisation projects of companies with head office and place of effective management in Cape Verde, which are undertaken before 31 December 2020.

IUR benefits
The IUR rate is reduced by 50% to an effective rate of 12.5% throughout the duration of the investment contract.

An additional deduction of 30% of costs incurred in training young (i.e. not older than 30 years of age) people is available, as is an additional deduction of 30% of costs incurred in hiring young people or long-term unemployed people.

An additional deduction of 50% or 80% of the costs of non-fixed term labour agreements is available, provided there is creation of net employment (respectively more than ten or more than 50 jobs).

IUP benefits
An exemption from IUP is available on the acquisition of real estate for the establishment or expansion of the activity of the investor.

VAT and custom duty benefits
Exemptions provided for in the VAT Code apply, as well as custom duties incentives as provided for in the applicable legislation.

C

Stamp duty and other benefits
An exemption from stamp tax is available on the incorporation of companies and increase of share capital of existing companies. An exemption from stamp duty is also available on financing transactions.

An exemption from notary and registration fees is available on the incorporation and registration of companies.

Tax benefits for social housing
Entities responsible for the construction of social housing, duly authorised by the competent regulatory authority (*Comissão de Coordenação e Credenciação do Sistema Nacional de Habitação de Interesse Social* or CCC-SNHIS), may benefit from the following:

* Only 30% of the income derived from the activity carried out within the scope of the social housing project is subject to IUR, under certain conditions.
* A refund of 80% of the VAT incurred in the Cape Verdean market is available in cases where those entities carry exclusively exempt operations without the right to deduct input VAT.
* A reduction of 75% of custom duties levied on construction material listed in an annex to the diploma is available.

Development promotion entities, provided they are also authorised by CCC-SNHIS, are also eligible for VAT benefits.

Touristic Utility Status (Estatuto de Utilidade Turística)
Cape Verde may grant Touristic Utility Status to certain touristic projects. Touristic Utility Status is granted to the following types of touristic projects:

* Installation: Granted to new touristic projects.
* Functioning: Granted to touristic projects starting to operate.
* Refurbishment: Granted to touristic projects in case of refurbishment projects with a value of at least 25% of the initial investment.

Touristic Utility Status generally allows for the following tax incentives and benefits:

* Exemption from IUR: 100% in the first five years of activity, 50% in the following ten years.
* Exemption from IUP on the acquisition of real estate used for construction and installation of touristic projects.
* Exemption from custom duties on the importation of materials and equipment used in the touristic project, capped at 15% of the total amount of the investment.

Cape Verde

Tax incentives for renewable energies
A regime for promotion, encouragement and access, licensing, and exploitation inherent to the exercise of independent production and self-production of electricity based on renewable energy sources is in force as of 1 January 2011.

Water, wind, solar, biomass, biogas or industrial, agricultural or urban waste, oceans and tides, and geothermal are to be consider sources of renewable energy. Under the regime, renewable energy producers may benefit from the following.

IUR benefits
The IUR rate is reduced by 100% during the first five years of production of energy (per project) and by 50% during the next five years production of energy (per project). The IUR rate is reduced by 25% during another five years (years 11 through 15) of production of energy (per project), provided the reinvestment accumulated in the last three years exceeds 50% of the initial investment.

Custom duty benefits
An exemption from custom duties and other custom charges (except stamp duty, charges, and fees due for the provision of services) applies on the importation of capital goods, raw materials and supplies, finished and semi-finished products, and other materials which are incorporated or used in the production of goods or services involved in the production of electrical energy from renewable sources.

Shipping transport industry incentive
A five-year income tax exemption, beginning in the year of activity, is available to Cape Verde individual entrepreneurs and domestic companies engaged in shipping transport as well as to shipping transport companies which are owned at least 25% by Cape Verde citizens and/or companies.

Job creation incentives
Companies are entitled to an increased payroll expense deduction with respect to the net permanent job increase related to newly hired workers who are not older than 30 years of age or have been unemployed for one year or more. The total deduction allowed corresponds to 130% or 150% of the payroll costs, depending on whether the net job increase that year is between five and ten or more than ten, respectively.

A deduction equal to 180% of the payroll cost is available to companies that hire, for six months or more, workers with a disability between 50% and 66%. The deduction is 130% in case of workers with a disability of less than 50%. In case of disabled workers hired for less than six months, the deduction is reduced to 140% and 115%, respectively.

Companies are entitled to a deduction equal to 130% of expenses incurred for scholarships granted to students who are not older than 25 years of age.

Employers are entitled to a deduction equal to 150% of expenses incurred for training workers who are not older than 35 years of age in official training centres.

Industries of production and importation of sand
Exemption of custom duties and other custom charges are granted to companies on the importation of machines, equipments, accessories, and other materials that are incorporated or used in the production of sand, as well as materials related to the transportation and shipping of goods exclusively for the production and importation of

sand. Companies that perform activities related to extraction of sand in Cape Verde are not entitled to benefit of such incentives.

Transportation of passengers companies
Exemption on custom duties on the importation of new vehicles (bus) with the purpose of transportation of passengers is granted to companies engaged in the activity regarding the urban transportation of passengers.

C

Cargo transportation companies
The import of vehicles aged until five years is exempt from custom duties.

Healthcare and pharmaceuticals
The importation of raw materials, goods, and semi-finished goods to be incorporated in the production or sale of the national pharmaceutical industry are exempt from custom duties.

Media, telecommunications, and internet
Importation of good, materials, equipment, vehicles, and other equipment exclusively for the purpose of telecommunications and media are exempt from custom duties.

Bonds
Bonds listed on the stock market, which do not represent public debt, are taxed under a reduction IUR rate of 5%.

Withholding taxes

WHT of 15% is due on payments of interest and royalties made between resident companies.

Payments of services between resident companies are generally not subject to WHT.

Rental payments due by resident companies are, however, subject to WHT of 10%.

For a Cape Verde-based recipient, tax withheld is a payment on account against the final single income tax due.

Any non-Cape Verdean resident entity carrying out an economic activity in Cape Verde is subject to a final 20% WHT, applied on interest, royalties, rents, services, and fees. Note that the inclusion of payments for services to non-residents was explicitly added to the Cape Verdean tax law as part of the 2011 State Budget Law, retroactive to 1 January 2011. Prior to this, the Cape Verdean Tax Authorities considered that the payment for services to non-residents was subject to WHT even though this understanding did not fully adhere to the wording of the Cape Verdean tax law at the time.

Dividends are not subject to WHT, irrespective of the residence status of the recipient.

Tax treaties
The only tax treaty that Cape Verde has in force is with Portugal. Under the Cape Verde/Portugal tax treaty, WHT is limited as follows:

- Royalties: 10%.
- Interest: 10% (0% applies to interest paid by public bodies).

Cape Verde

Note that WHT on dividends under the Cape Verde/Portugal tax treaty is limited to 10%. However, dividends are currently not taxed in Cape Verde.

A new tax treaty was signed between Cape Verde and Macao, which is not yet in force.

Tax administration

Taxable period
As a general rule, the tax year is the calendar year. A different tax year may be applied, subject to authorisation from the Ministry of Finance, in the case of non-resident companies with a PE in Cape Verde and in other situations duly justified by economical reasons.

Tax returns
Taxpayers are required to file a tax return by 31 May of the year following the end of the tax year.

Payment of tax
Corporate taxpayers must make a prepayment of their income tax liability for the current tax year. The prepayment is calculated as 30% of the preceding tax year's income tax liability and should be paid by 20 January of the following year.

Taxpayers are required to self-assess the tax due by 31 May of the year following the end of the tax year.

The tax authorities will verify the tax return and raise a final assessment of tax liability by 20 July of the same year. The taxpayer must then pay the remaining tax due by 31 July.

Audit cycle
There are no specific rules regarding the tax audit cycle in Cape Verde.

Statute of limitations
The statute of limitations period in Cape Verde is for five years.

Topics of focus for tax authorities
The main topics of focus for Cape Verdean tax authorities regard cost incurred for assets considered of mixed use (e.g. vehicles, communications), personnel costs, management fees, and payments to non-residents.

Caribbean Netherlands

PwC contact

Steve Vanenburg
PricewaterhouseCoopers
Julianaplein 38
Willemstad, Curaçao
Tel: +599 9 4300 000
Email: steve.r.vanenburg@an.pwc.com

C

Significant developments

Since the introduction on 1 January 2011 of the new tax system that replaced the corporate profit tax with a new real estate tax and a revenue tax, no further changes have been made.

Taxes on corporate income

Income from immovable property is subject to real estate tax. The real estate tax is levied based on the value of real estate. As is the case at present, the value is established for five years each time. The income is deemed to be 4% of the value of the real estate and the tax rate is 25%. Therefore, effectively 1% of the value is taxed.

Exemptions apply for the dwelling that serves as the principal residence, real estate with a value not exceeding 50,000 United States dollars (USD) (the 'kunuku' house), and land that is being commercially operated for agricultural or forestry purposes.

A revenue tax is levied on the revenues from shares and profit-sharing certificates, as well as on distributions from foundations, special purpose funds, or a closed-end common fund. The rate of the revenue tax is 5%.

There are no other taxes on income or capital gains.

The revenue tax and the real estate tax only apply if certain requirements of residency have been met. A corporation that is established in the Caribbean Netherlands that does not meet certain criteria will, for the purpose of the revenue tax and the real estate tax, be deemed to be established in the Netherlands and will be taxed accordingly. That means that instead of revenue tax and real estate tax, the Dutch corporate income tax of 25.5% will apply, as well as the Dutch dividend tax of 15% (*see the Corporate residence section for more information*).

Corporate residence

Corporate residence is, in principle, determined by the place of incorporation. However, other factors may also determine residence. For example, a foreign company with effective management in the Caribbean Netherlands is considered to be a resident.

For the purposes of the revenue tax and the real estate tax, however, a resident corporation is deemed to be established in the Netherlands unless specific criteria have been met, the purpose of which is to guarantee commercial ties with the Caribbean Netherlands.

Caribbean Netherlands

An entity is deemed to be established in the Caribbean Netherlands, not the Netherlands, based on the following criteria:

- It has been admitted to a bonded warehouse for commerce and services, or
- It obtained a declaration from the Inspector of Taxes that one of the following conditions applies:
    - It is not active in financial services or insurance, turnover is not more than USD 80,000, and assets are not more than USD 200,000.
    - The assets usually consist of less than 50% of investments, participations, liquidities, and assets that are made available for use to persons outside the Caribbean Netherlands, as well as assets, directly or indirectly, used for financing persons outside the Caribbean Netherlands.
    - It usually provides permanent work to at least three persons living in the Caribbean Netherlands who engage independently in activities relating to the assets mentioned above and whose responsibility is in line with their job position, and it has, at its disposal, real estate situated in the Caribbean Netherlands for a period of at least 24 months with a value of at least USD 50,000 for the activities, and this real estate is used as an office with facilities that are customary in the financial sector.
    - It holds, at a minimum, 95% of the shares of an entity as mentioned above.

Resident corporations that do not meet these criteria are deemed to be established in the Netherlands, which causes them to be subject to the Dutch corporate income and dividend withholding taxes (WHT). This does not apply to foundations, special purpose funds, or a closed-end common fund.

Other taxes

Sales tax

A general expenditure tax (*Algemene Bestedings Belasting* or ABB) has replaced the levy of import duties, as well as the former sales tax (*Omzetbelasting* or OB and *Belasting op Bedrijfsomzetten* or BBO), of the former Netherlands Antilles. The rate is 8% in Bonaire and 6% in Saba and St. Eustatius. The rate for insurances is 9% and 7%, respectively.

As of 1 October 2011, the rate for restaurants and bars is 6% and 4% respectively.

A rate of 25% applies to cars, unless it concerns a very low energy car, in which case the rate is 0%.

ABB is levied in respect of:

- Sale of goods by manufacturers.
- Delivery of services within the levy area.
- Import of goods.

Therefore, the sale of goods will only be subject to tax once, at the manufacturer or at the time of import. The sale of bread has been exempt. In addition, the supply of grain, potatoes, and rice will also be exempt. Other exemptions that apply, similar to the former OB and BBO legislation, are:

- Public transportation.
- Medical services and hospitals.
- Water and electricity.

- Fuels and other products, including supplies, for international transportation.
- Renting of houses.

Excise taxes

Excise tax is due on gasoline. On Bonaire, excise tax is also due on alcohol, with different tariffs for liquor, wine, and beer, as well as for tobacco. This does not apply to Saba and St. Eustatius.

C

The excise rates are:

- USD 41.86 per hectolitre of gasoline or approximately USD 1.60 per gallon on Bonaire (USD 1.30 on Saba and St. Eustatius).

Only on Bonaire:

- USD 67.04 per hectolitre of beer.
- USD 128.50 per hectolitre of wine.
- USD 12.85 per volume percent of alcohol per hectolitre of distilled products.
- USD 5.34 per 100 cigarettes.
- USD 9.78 per 100 cigars.
- USD 4.89 per 100 cigarillo's.
- USD 30 per kilogram of smoking tobacco.

Property taxes

There is an annual property tax of 0.3% on the value of real estate.

Transfer taxes

The transfer of immovable property on the islands of the Caribbean Netherlands is subject to a 5% transfer duty.

Stamp tax

No stamp tax is levied in the Caribbean Netherlands.

Branch income

Entities not established in the Caribbean Netherlands are only taxed on the fixed income of local real estate (i.e. 25% real estate tax on 4% of the value of the property the corporation owns in the Caribbean Netherlands). The revenue tax does not apply to the remittance of profits from the permanent establishment (PE) to the head office of the corporation. No other taxes are levied.

The criteria for deemed residency in the Caribbean Netherlands do not apply to PEs, except for a PE of a corporation that is a resident of Aruba, Curaçao, or St. Maarten. In cases where the activities of such a PE would not qualify for deemed residency in the Caribbean Netherlands if it had been a corporation, this PE is liable to taxation in the Netherlands.

Income determination

In the Caribbean Netherlands, there is a tax on the fixed income of local real estate (real estate tax) and on profits distributed to the shareholders (revenue tax). As long

Caribbean Netherlands

as income is not distributed, profits other than from real estate are not subjected to tax. Therefore, there are no regulations with regard to income determination.

Deductions

No deductions are allowed on the fixed income with regard to real estate tax or the distributions of profit for revenue tax purposes.

Group taxation

Distribution of profits to another corporation on one of the islands of the Caribbean Netherlands is exempt from revenue tax if the other corporation holds, at minimum, a 5% interest in the corporation that is making the distribution.

Tax credits and incentives

A corporation that has been designated as a bonded warehouse for commerce and services is exempt from ABB and excise tax. As a result, goods in transhipment remain tax free. However, if goods that have been admitted to a bonded warehouse are sold within the Caribbean Netherlands, this will be considered importing these goods and ABB and excise tax will be due.

Withholding taxes

A revenue tax of 5% is levied on distributions from corporations as well as distributions from foundations, special purpose funds, or a closed-end common fund.

Tax treaties
The Caribbean Netherlands currently has a tax treaty in effect with Norway. A double tax agreement (DTA) has been negotiated with Jamaica, but this has not entered into force yet. Furthermore, tax information exchange agreements (TIEAs) have been signed with several countries, including Australia, Canada, Denmark, Mexico, New Zealand, Spain, Sweden, and the United States. As a result, the Caribbean Netherlands, as part of the former Netherlands Antilles, has been moved to the white list of the Organisation for Economic Co-operation and Development (OECD) Global Forum.

Tax arrangement for the Kingdom of the Netherlands (TAK)
As part of the Kingdom of the Netherlands (TAK), the Caribbean Netherlands is party to a federal tax agreement with Aruba, Curaçao, and St. Maarten as well as a tax agreement for the Netherlands (TAN) with regard to the attribution of tax between the Netherlands and the Caribbean Netherlands. Subject to the TAK and the TAN, dividends, interest, and royalties paid to a company resident in the Caribbean Netherlands may qualify for reduced rates of WHTs in the subject countries or in the Netherlands.

Dutch dividend WHTs are 15% if the Caribbean Netherlands company owns less than 10% of the Dutch company. If the Caribbean Netherlands company's interest is 10% or more, Dutch WHT can be reduced to 0%. Aruban dividend tax will be reduced from the statutory rate of 10% to 5%. In the Caribbean Netherlands, the dividends will not be taxed when they are received. However, at the time the dividends are distributed to the shareholder, they will be subject to the 5% revenue tax.

The TAN came into force on 1 January 2011. The TAK is to be revised. Negotiations have already started between Aruba and Curaçao each with the Netherlands. In the end, the existing TAK will then be replaced by separate tax agreements between two countries (e.g. between Aruba, Curaçao, and St. Maarten each with the Netherlands [and including the Caribbean Netherlands]). The aim is to have the new agreements in place in 2013.

Tax administration

Tax returns
Revenue tax returns must be filed and the amount due must be paid at the end of the quarter of the year in which the distribution has been made.

The real estate tax is levied by way of a tax assessment.

Payment of tax
Revenue tax must be paid at the time of filing and in a lump sum on the basis of the self-assessment.

The real estate tax must be paid within two months of the date of the tax assessment.

Statute of limitations
A reassessment can be imposed until five years after the tax year.

Cayman Islands

PwC contact

Frazer Lindsay
PricewaterhouseCoopers
Strathvale House
90 North Church Street
PO Box 258
George Town, Grand Cayman
Cayman Islands
KY1-1104
Tel: +1 345 914 8606
Email: frazer.lindsay@ky.pwc.com

Significant developments

There have been no significant corporate tax developments in the Cayman Islands during the past year.

Taxes on corporate income

Corporate income, capital gains, payroll, or other direct taxes are not imposed on corporations in the Cayman Islands.

Corporate residence

Since no corporate income, capital gains, payroll, or other direct taxes are currently imposed on corporations in the Cayman Islands, corporate residency is not relevant in the context of Cayman Islands taxation.

Entities engaged in 'scheduled' trade and business in the Cayman Islands (as defined in the Trade & Business Licensing Law) are required to have a trade and business licence. Effecting and concluding contracts in the Cayman Islands and exercising, in the Cayman Islands, powers necessary for the carrying on of a business outside the Cayman Islands is generally not considered to be engaging in trade and business in the Cayman Islands.

Other taxes

Value-added tax (VAT)
There is no VAT imposed in the Cayman Islands.

Import duties
Import duty is paid, at various rates, on importation of most goods.

Excise taxes
There are no excise taxes in the Cayman Islands.

Property taxes
There are no property taxes in the Cayman Islands.

Stamp taxes

Stamp duty is paid, at various rates, on transfers of land/property and execution of certain documents.

Branch income

Branches are treated the same as other corporations doing business in the Cayman Islands.

Income determination

Since no corporate income, capital gains, or other taxes are imposed on corporations in the Cayman Islands, income determination is not relevant in the context of Cayman Islands taxation.

Deductions

Since no corporate income, capital gains, or other taxes are imposed on corporations in the Cayman Islands, deductions from income are not relevant in the context of Cayman Islands taxation.

Group taxation

Since no corporate income, capital gains, or other taxes are imposed on corporations in the Cayman Islands, group taxation is not relevant in the context of Cayman Islands taxation.

Tax credits and incentives

Since no corporate income, capital gains, or other taxes are imposed on corporations in the Cayman Islands, tax incentives are not relevant in the context of Cayman Islands taxation. However, Cayman entities carrying on business outside the Cayman Islands can register as 'exempted companies' (i.e. a company formed primarily to do business outside of the Cayman Islands and subject to certain requirements) and can apply under the Tax Concessions Law for an undertaking to be issued by the Governor-in-Council (i.e. the Cayman Islands government) exempting such company from any tax on profits, income, gains, or appreciation which might be introduced in the period of 20 years following the grant of such concessions. The concession is extendable for a further ten years after expiry. 'Exempted limited liability partnerships' (i.e. certain partnerships formed primarily to do business outside of the Cayman Islands) can apply under the Exempted Limited Partnership Law for a similar concession which is for 50 years (rather than 20 years).

Withholding taxes

Currently, no withholding taxes are imposed on dividends or payments of principal or interest.

Cayman Islands

Tax administration

No tax returns, forms, or procedures are required to be completed for tax compliance purposes in the Cayman Islands.

While there are no tax treaties, there are tax information exchange agreements (TIEAs) between the Cayman Islands and a number of countries. Please refer to the Cayman Islands Tax Information Authority's website (http://www.tia.gov.ky/html/assistance.htm) for the latest list.

The Cayman Islands agreed with the United Kingdom government to implement the Savings Directive, and so the Reporting of Savings Income Information (European Union or EU) Law (2007 Revision) came into force, setting out a reporting regime whereby Cayman paying agents making interest payments to individuals who are tax resident in a EU member state may have to report interest paid. The Cayman Tax Information Authority receives or facilitates submission of such information reporting.

Chad

PwC contact

Dominique Taty
Fidafrica SA
Immeuble Alpha 2000
20th Floor
Rue Gourgas - Plateau
Abidjan 01
Côte d'Ivoire
Tel: +225 20 31 54 60
Email: d.taty@ci.pwc.com

Significant developments

There have been no significant corporate tax developments in Chad during the past year.

Taxes on corporate income

The profits subject to the company tax are determined with sole regard to profits earned by businesses carried out or transactions conducted in Chad.

The net taxable profits are established after deduction of all charges directly entailed by the exercise of activities subject to assessment in Chad. As income from other countries is not liable to tax, foreign charges and losses are not deductible either.

The corporate tax rate in Chad is 40%.

Minimum tax

There is a minimum tax of 1.5% based on the turnover and an additional 1 million Central African CFA francs (XAF) as the minimum/floor rate.

Corporate residence

Registered entities (i.e. companies, branches, and subsidiaries) conducting economic activities in Chad are liable to pay corporate tax. Specifically:

- Limited companies.
- Limited partnership with shares.
- Limited liability companies.
- Cooperative societies and their unions.
- Public institutions.
- Agencies of the state with financial autonomy.
- Municipal bodies and any other legal entity engaged in an operation for gain.
- Real estate companies, regardless of their form.
- Civil companies, other than real estate companies, involved in industrial, commercial, or agricultural activities.
- The limited partnerships, on the share of profits relating to the rights of sponsors.
- Associations in participation, including financial syndicates, on the share of profits relating to the rights of sponsors.

Chad

- Co-owners of ships companies, on the share of profits relating to the rights of sponsors of associated co-owners other than those with unlimited liability or whose names and addresses are not listed with the administration.

Other taxes

Valued-added tax (VAT)

The standard VAT in Chad is 18%.

An operation performed in Chad which constitutes an economic activity and for which payment is made, unless included in the list of exemptions in the law governing VAT, is liable for VAT, even if the residence of the natural person or the registered office of the legal entity is located outside Chad.

The VAT law provides a list of transactions exempted from VAT that includes the following:

- Sales of products that are directly made by farmers, cattle farmers, or fishermen to consumers, farming, and fishing operations.
- Imports, operations, and sales of newspapers and periodicals, other than the advertising revenues.
- Exports and related international transportation.

There are no specific rules relating to refunds to non-residents.

There are no refunds of the excess in practice. If the amount paid exceeds the VAT payable, the credit can be offset against the VAT payable until the end of the second financial year following the birth of this credit. After that, it becomes a loss, which is deductible under corporate tax.

Customs duties

The tax base of customs duties corresponds with the customs valuation, namely the selling price of the goods plus cost of delivery to Chad (costs of insurance, transportation, etc.).

The rates of customs duties depend on the nature of the goods and range from 5% to 30%. These rates can be summarised as follows:

- Goods of first need (basic necessities): 5%.
- Raw materials and goods of equipment: 10%.
- Intermediate and miscellaneous goods: 20%.
- Consumer goods: 30%.

Excise duty

Excise duty applies to goods of great consumption: cigarettes, drinks (water, beers and wines), cosmetics, and luxury products. Excise duty rates depend on the nature of the goods and range from 5% to 25% of the value of the good.

This value differs depending on the origin of the good. If the good has been manufactured in the Economic and Monetary Community of Central Africa (CEMAC) zone, the value corresponds with the selling price charged by the manufacturer. If the good is imported into the CEMAC zone, the value is the sum of the freight value plus insurance costs and custom duties.

The rates are as follows:

- Water: 5%.
- Beer under 6.5% alcohol: 15%.
- Tobacco, perfume, jewelry, electronic devices (except computers and telephones etc.), private vehicle with an engine capacity above 1600 cm³, and weapons: 20%.
- Other alcoholic drinks: 25%.

Real property tax
The annual real property tax differs according to whether it is a built or an unbuilt property and whether it is located in N'Djamena or elsewhere.

The tax rate on built property is 10% in N'Djamena and 8% elsewhere.

The tax rate on unbuilt property is 21% in N'Djamena and 20% elsewhere.

The calculation base is the potential revenue of that property. The potential revenues correspond to 4/5 of the rental value, the rental value being 10% of the market value. For rural unbuilt property, the market value is fixed to XAF 50,000 per hectare.

Accommodation tax
The person occupying a building (owner or tenant) has to pay the following amount as accommodation tax annually:

Type of construction	N'Djamena (XAF)	Elsewhere (XAF)
For constructions in local material	3,000	1,500
For hard or semi-hard constructions	10,000	5,000
For R+ hard constructions	10,000 and a supplement of 10,000 per level	5,000 and a supplement of 5,000 per level

Transfer tax
Fixed or proportional transfer duties must be paid on the transfer of ownership of estates, personal property, and real property. Transfer duties are also due on contributions to companies and divisions of property.

Stamp duties
Stamp duties must be paid on each civil or judicial document intended to be used as evidence. Stamp duty is generally XAF 1,000 per page.

There is no stamp duty greater than XAF 2,000 or less than XAF 900, whatever the size of the paper.

Registration duty
The registration duty applies to certain deeds listed by the general tax code. The assessment basis depends on the nature of transactions, and the rate varies from 1% to 15%.

Business licence tax
Any natural person or corporate body carrying on a trade, industry, or profession in Chad shall be liable to a business licence tax. The business licence tax is paid annually and is assessed as follows:

Chad

- A determined duty based on 0.1% of the first XAF 2 billion of turnover; above that, only 1/10 of the turnover is taxed.
- 10% of the rental value of the premises.
- 10% of the determined duty for the Social Security Fund.
- 7% of the determined duty for the consular commercial chamber.
- XAF 480 per year for the rural intervention fund.
- 10% of the annual rental value of business premises.

For a new company, the determined duty is calculated based on the projected turnover estimated by the taxpayer as compared to similar activities or those achieved during the first 12 months of activity.

The business licence tax is due 31 December of the tax year.

Capital gains and dividends tax
Capital gains and dividends are taxed at 20%.

Social security contributions
The monthly contribution to Chad's Social Security Fund is 16.5% of total salaries for the employer (upper limit: XAF 82,500 per month) and 3.5% for the employee (upper limit: XAF 17,500 per month), withheld by the employer.

Payroll tax
Employers in Chad are required to make monthly contributions of 7.5% of the total amount of salaries and fringe benefits paid to permanent employees.

Apprenticeship tax
Employers in Chad are required to make monthly contributions of 1.2% of the total amount of salaries and fringe benefits of their employees (permanent and temporary) to the National Professional Training Fund (FONAP).

Branch income

In Chad, there is a presumption of distribution of profits realised by branches. These profits are deemed distributed to their headquarters and are therefore subject to tax on income from capital gains at the rate of 20%.

However, this presumption of distribution is simple. Branches can provide evidence that the profits they have made have not actually been transferred but remained in the accounts of the branch.

Income determination

Inventory valuation
Stocks shall be valued at cost price; however, if the market price is lower than the cost price, the undertaking shall make provisions for depreciation of inventory.

Capital gains
Capital gains are taxed at 20%.

Dividend income
Dividends are taxed at 20%.

Interest income
The interest paid to associates or shareholders in respect of sums paid by them in the social fund in addition to their share of capital are taxable within the limit of those calculated at the advance rate of the bank of emission and increased by two points.

Foreign income
Income from other countries is not liable to tax in Chad.

Deductions

Expenses are deductible under the following conditions:

- They must lead to a reduction of the assets.
- They must be incurred in the interest of the enterprise.
- They must be regularly included in the accounts of the entity and justified by receipts.
- They must be related to the present fiscal year or a former fiscal year.
- They must not be considered as non-deductible by the law.

Depreciation
According to accountancy principles, depreciation is calculated based on the probable length of use of the asset. The straight-line system of depreciation is applicable, and rates vary according to the nature of the business activity concerned and the normal useful life of the assets involved.

From an accountancy point of view, it is possible to depreciate whatever amount seems corresponding to the above mentioned principles. However, from a tax point of view, depreciation (i.e. enabling a deduction of the depreciated amount from the taxable income) is only possible under one condition and within certain limits.

Deduction of depreciation is only possible under the condition that the depreciation has been entered into the statement of accounts. Therefore, only a legal entity in Chad owning the assets is able to depreciate its assets.

In addition, a 1997 order sets a yearly limit of depreciation. As a consequence, if depreciation in the statement of accounts is higher than the depreciation authorized, the difference is not deductible and has to be reinstated in the taxable income.

The starting point for depreciation is the day of first use. If this date is not the first day of the financial year, the first year's depreciation is reduced pro-rata.

It should be noted that, despite the above, goods that are leased are depreciated at the rate that they are paid for.

Depreciation of goods that are made available for free to managers and supervisors of the business are deductible if the corresponding benefit in kind is declared.

The sum of depreciation applied to the acquisition or creation of an asset cannot, at the end of each financial year, be less than the amount of depreciation calculated on the linear system and spread out over the normal usage period.

Depreciation in loss-making years may be carried forward to the first profitable financial year, and to subsequent years if necessary.

Chad

Goodwill
There are no provisions for goodwill.

Start-up expenses
There are no provisions for start-up expenses.

Interest expenses
Interests paid for the depositing of funds by a shareholder are deductible within the base rate of the Central Bank plus two points, calculated on the basis of the share capital.

Bad debt
Provisions for credit customers are deductible once they meet the conditions for deductible expenses mentioned above.

Charitable contributions
Donations and liberalities are deductible within a 0.5% limit of the annual turnover, net of tax, when they are duly justified. However, a decision from the Minister of Finances is required.

Fines and penalties
Tax and customs penalties are not deductible.

Taxes
Income taxes are not deductible.

Other significant items
The following expenses are not deductible:

- Provisions for laying off employees.
- Provisions for self insurance.
- Insurance premiums paid for a third-party.

The following expenses are not fully deductible:

- Foreign social security contributions are deductible only within 15% of the base salary of the expatriates when related to a compulsory retirement plan. Nonetheless, Chad's social security contributions are fully deductible.
- Restaurants, hotels, receptions, and related costs are deductible within a 0.5% limit of the turnover, net of tax.
- Travel expenses for expatriates and their families for vacation are deductible, limited to one trip per year.

Net operating losses
Losses arising from normal business activities of the company are deductible and may be carried forward for up to three years.

Carryback of losses is not permitted.

Payments to foreign affiliates
There is a specific regulation relating to head office and foreign technical assistance costs that are subject to a 10% limitation of deductibility.

The scope of the 10% limitation covers study expenses, technical assistance, and other expenses, including commercial and industrial royalties, paid to the head office of an enterprise established outside Chad and outside the CEMAC zone.

Duly justified, these costs are only deductible within 10% of the intermediary fiscal profit (accounting profits plus non-allowable charges/costs) prior to their deduction.

C

Group taxation

There is a specific taxation of groups within the CEMAC area.

Where a joint stock company and a private limited company own either registered stock in a joint stock company or shares in a private limited company, the net proceeds of the share in the second company paid to the first during the financial year shall be deducted from the total net profit of the latter, less a percentage for costs and charges. This percentage is fixed at 10% of the total amount of the proceeds. This system shall apply when all of the following conditions are met:

- The stocks or shares owned by the parent establishment represent at least 25% of the capital of the subsidiary firm.
- The parent and subsidiary firms have their registered office in a CEMAC state (Cameroon, Central African Republic, Chad, Gabon, Equatorial Guinea, and Republic of Congo).
- The stocks or shares allotted at the time of issue are still registered in the name of the participating company that undertakes to retain them for at least two consecutive years in registered form.

Transfer pricing

The Tax Code acknowledges that dependant or controlled companies may transfer benefits indirectly to their company abroad it is dependant of or to the company abroad it is controlled by.

In order to calculate the real benefit, the indirectly transferred benefits (by means of increase of purchase price or decrease of sales price to the controlling company or by any other means) are incorporated into the result established by the accounts.

If the tax administration does not have enough precise elements to determine the benefit, it will establish the taxable benefit by way of comparison to companies normally operated in Chad.

The Tax Code provides further, in accordance with CEMAC regulation, that interest paid to shareholders on sums that they lend over and above their share capital is deductible at the rate for loans allowed by the central bank increased by two percentage points. This deduction is only possible if the amounts lent do not exceed 50% of the share capital.

Thin capitalisation

Chad applies Organisation for the Harmonization of Business Law in Africa (OHADA) regulations with regards to thin capitalisation rules.

In cases where the equity capital gets, due to the recorded losses in the summarising financial statement, below 50% of the share capital, a shareholder consultation has to

Chad

be organised within four months to decide upon a potential anticipated dissolution of the company.

If the dissolution is excluded, the company has to reconstitute its equity capital up until it equals 50% of the share capital within the two years following the date of the end of the loss-making financial year.

Otherwise, provided it stays above the legally required share capital minimum, the company has to reduce its share capital of an amount at least equal to the losses that it has not been able to charge against reserves.

In cases where no decision has been taken regarding dissolution, any interested person may claim dissolution of the company in front of a court. Any interested person is allowed to bring a legal action if the reconstitution of the equity capital has not taken place within the legal timeline.

This action ceases to exist the day the cause for dissolution ceases to exist or if the court has ruled on the grounds.

Tax credits and incentives

Chad does not offer any tax incentives.

Withholding taxes

Withholding tax (WHT) on commerce of retail goods
A 4% WHT rate applies to natural persons and legal entities that purchase or sell wholesale or retail goods. This WHT also applies to imports.

According to the 2004 Finance Act, companies with more than one shareholder that regularly pay their taxes may apply for a suspension of payment of WHT (renewable every three months).

WHT on capital gains
WHT on capital gains is 20% and applies to residents and non-residents.

WHT on income of non-residents
WHT on income of non-residents is 25%. It applies to income of any legal or natural person that is not resident in Chad.

WHT on personal income
The employer withholds tax on personal income every month.

WHT on income from public procurement contracts financed from outside of the country and income from petroleum projects.
Chad's lowest WHT rate on income is of 12.5%. It applies in either of the following two cases:

- On income of agents, consultancy firms, and corporations executing a contract within the framework of public procurement contracts financed from outside of the country.
- On income of companies working within the petroleum projects.

Chad

WHT on interests of bonds, certificates, and notes
Bonds and notes are subject to a WHT of 20% of the interests for registered bonds and 30% of the interests for bearer participation certificates.

WHT on rent
WHT on rent is 15% for residents and 20% for non-residents.

Tax treaties
Chad has one tax treaty with the member states of CEMAC (Cameroon, Gabon, Equatorial Guinea, Congo, Chad, and Central African Republic).

Tax administration

Tax returns
Corporate tax returns are due on 15 April.

Payment of tax
Certain taxes are considered instalment payments of corporate tax. Once the amount of corporate tax is known, these payments are deductible from the amount and only the balance has to be paid. These taxes include the minimum corporate tax, the quarterly instalment payments, and the 4% discharge for retail goods, if applicable.

Minimum corporate tax (monthly)
The minimum corporate tax payment must be made prior to the 15th day of the month following the month of achievement of the turnover. However, for the payment of the floor rate, payment may be made in four installments of XAF 250,000 each, 15 days after the end of the quarter.

If this instalment payment exceeds the annual corporate tax, the remainder is lost.

One third instalment payments (paid three times quarterly)
Corporations which fulfil the following conditions are subject to quarterly instalment payments:

* Liable to corporate tax.
* Made a profit during the prior fiscal year.
* The amount of the corporate tax of the prior fiscal year is superior to at least XAF 100,000.

The quarterly instalment payments are equal to one-third of the difference between the corporate tax due during the prior fiscal year and the minimum income tax paid during the same period.

The payment must take place before the 10th day of April, July, and October.

Audit cycle
The tax audit exercise of the *Direction Générale des Impôts* (Directorate General of Taxes), Chad is completed in the following manner:

Tax officials having at least the rank of an inspector and with their professional card and a copy of the audit notice perform spot checks on the accounting documents that taxpayers are required to submit.

Chad

Accounts are audited at the head office of the enterprise or at the place of its main establishment. Where this is not possible in either of these two places, the taxpayer must expressly request that it be conducted either in the accountant's office or in the offices of the tax authority.

The operations include confronting the accounts presented with certain facts or material to control the accuracy of returns filed and to proceed, where necessary, to the establishment of the taxes and the taxes evaded.

At least eight days before the date of the first intervention, the taxation administration shall send to the taxpayer a verification notice by personally delivered registered mail with acknowledgement of receipt or discharge slip to inform the taxpayer of the date of the first intervention and the possibility of getting a tax consultant of the taxpayer's choice to assist the taxpayer. It must, under pain of rejection, be mentioned in the verification notice.

In case of postponement of the original date of the first intervention, on the initiative of the administration, the tax authorities must imperatively send the taxpayer a notice of correction.

The taxpayer may also request a postponement of control by writing, giving reasons for his request within 48 hours of receipt of the notice. This report must be expressly accepted by the administration.

The administration may conduct unannounced inspections; it then sends an audit notice personally to the taxpayer, who acknowledges receipt, at the first intervention.

Where the notice bears no indication as to the taxes, duties, or years or periods of assessment, the items to be audited shall be all the taxes owed by the taxpayer for the period still due for payment. In such case, the audit is called a 'general audit'.

However, where it is specified in the audit notice, the administration may limit the scope of the audit to one or more taxes due on all or part of the period still due for payment or on a group of operations over a period less than one fiscal year, in which case a spot check is done.

The verification can, nevertheless, go up to one or more years beyond the prescribed period when these exercises are in deficit, as long as the deficits made under a year are carried forward and are deducted from the profits of the non-specified first year which constitute charges.

The verification can also go up to one or more years beyond the prescribed period when these exercises show a tax credit of a VAT carried over the first statement of the non-barred period.

Where the tax service intends to extend the audit to a period or a tax that is not indicated on the initial audit notice, it shall forward another notice following the same manner and deadline laid down in Article R. 13 et seq. of this Book, indicating the new period or new tax to be audited.

Where the accounts auditing or adjustment procedure require special technical knowledge, the tax authority may hire the consultants appearing on a list drawn up by Order of the Minister of Economic and Finance. Such consultants shall be professionally liable in case of damage resulting from their work.

When the accounts are kept using computerised systems, the tax administration is empowered to require, in accordance with Article L 18 above, the technical advice from experts for carrying out tests on the hardware that hosts the operation and to check:

- the accounting operating system
- all information, data, and processes that contribute directly or indirectly in the formation of accounting or tax results and the elaboration of documents mandated by the General Tax Code, and
- the documentation, relating to analysis, programming, and the execution of processing.

The civil and military authorities lend support and assistance to Tax Officers for the exercise of their functions, whenever they are needed.

Statute of limitations

According to Article R. 33 of the General Tax Code of Chad:

"The total or partial omissions found in the tax base, the inadequacies and inaccuracies, or the taxation errors, can be repaired by the tax administration until the end of the third year following that in which the tax or fee is payable.

Furthermore, any omission or insufficiency of tax revealed by a proceeding before the criminal courts or by a contentious claim may, without prejudice to the general period of repetitions established above, be repaired until the end of the third year following the revelation of the facts."

Topics of focus for tax authorities

Topics of focus for tax authorities include the following:

- Obligation to file a return.
- The verification of the return filed.
- Taxation of office/Arbitrary Assessment.
- The right of access to taxpayers' documents.
- Obligation to pay tax.
- Procedure for the abuse of control.
- Limiting the right of control.
- Tax collection procedure.
- Prosecution measures.

Chile

PwC contact

Francisco Selame
PricewaterhouseCoopers
Avenida Andrés Bello 2711
Torre de la Costanera, Cuarto Piso
Santiago, Chile
Tel: +56 2 940 0460
Email: francisco.selame@cl.pwc.com

Significant developments

First Category tax

For income received or accrued during calendar year 2012, the First Category tax (i.e. corporate income tax) rate decreased from 20% to 18.5%. Income received or accrued during calendar year 2013 and subsequent years will be subject to a 17% tax. The monthly income tax prepayments must be adjusted accordingly.

Derivative instruments

On 22 October 2011, the tax treatment of derivatives instruments was published in the Official Gazette Law N°20.544. Among others, the most significant amendments include:

* Income borne by derivatives instruments is treated as Chilean-sourced income when perceived or accrued by a Chilean resident or when they settled by the delivery of shares or quotas of a Chilean company.
* The distinction between derivative instruments agreed for hedging and speculation purposes is eliminated. This was relevant for withholding tax (WHT) and also for deductibility purposes.
* As a general rule, profits and losses should be recognised on a cash basis. The taxpayers carrying full accounting records should recognise them on an accrual basis considering the difference between the fair value of the underlying at the moment of the acquisition of the derivative and the fair value at year end.

Mine closure plans

On 11 November 2011, a special tax treatment regarding Mine Closure Plans was published in the Official Gazette Law N°20.551. In this regard, the Law makes reference to the tax treatment of the disbursements incurred during the closure process. This Law provides that they can be deducted from taxable income as an expense but only in the last third of the mine's useful life and limited only to the amount of the compliance guarantee (required of any mining project, in order to guarantee the compliance of the mine closure obligations).

Regarding the value-added tax (VAT) borne in the acquisition of goods or provision of services in order to execute the Mine Closure Plan, the Law establishes that the mining companies that have ceased on their activities and thus are not able to offset the VAT credit borne on the execution of the Mine Closure Plan against VAT debit or to obtain its refund through the exporter's VAT refund mechanism are able to obtain a refund of this VAT credit.

Finally, it is necessary to point out that these new regulations are not in force until 11 November 2012.

Research and development (R&D) improvement
Among other modifications, the most significant R&D improvements include:

- Extension of the benefit to intramural tax incentives, encouraging the investment on R&D performed by companies through internal capacities. The former Law only allowed tax benefits on contributions to extramural R&D contributions.
- The maximum cap on the amount of the tax credit was increased from UTM 5,000 to UTM 15,000 (approximately 1,200,000 United States dollars [USD]), and also removing the threshold with respect to the taxpayer's gross taxable income.
- The restriction of the tax benefits regarding related parties was eliminated.
- As established in the former Law, CORFO is the public authority in charge of the R&D projects certification. This certification is needed in order to use the tax benefits settled in this Law. However, Law N°20.570 introduces an important modification, allowing contributors to use part of the tax benefits even before they applied for CORFO's certification. In this case, 65% of the expenses incurred by the R&D project can be deduced immediately. Moreover, once the CORFO's certificate is issued, the contributor is allowed to use the complete tax benefit, even for the period prior to the certificate's issue, amending its previous tax returns.
- The tax benefits of R&D investments are extended from the original 31 December 2017 deadline to 31 December 2025.

Finally, it is necessary to point out that this new regulation will become enforceable six months after its publication in the Official Gazette.

Taxes on corporate income

First Category tax
The basic tax on income of a Chilean legal entity domiciled or resident in Chile and engaged in commerce, mining, fishing, or industry is the First Category tax, which is assessed at a rate of 18.5% on the entity's worldwide income during calendar year 2012. Prior to 2012, the rate was 20%. Income received or accrued during calendar year 2013 and subsequent years will be subject to a 17% tax.

Non-domiciled and non-resident shareholders and partners are subject to an 'additional' WHT of 35% on their Chilean-source distributions or remittances, with a credit granted for the First Category tax paid on the underlying profits. This results in an effective tax rate of 35%.

Local income taxes
Chilean legislation does not establish any local income taxes.

Corporate residence

Companies incorporated in Chile are considered to be domiciled in the country.

Permanent establishment (PE)
An entity may be considered as a PE under double taxation treaty (DTT) terms but not under the local legislation. In this case, in principle, the correspondent WHT should apply over the gross basis of the remittance.

However, Chilean Internal Revenue Service (IRS) rulings have interpreted the relation between the two different PE concepts in the sense that, notwithstanding the local

Chile

requirements are not met, the taxpayer can choose to be treated as a local PE in order to be allowed to deduct the expenses that are incurred for the purpose of the PE.

Other taxes

Value-added tax (VAT)
VAT is payable on transfers and services at a rate of 19%. In general terms, this tax is levied over the price of the following goods and services:

- Sales and other contracts used to transfer ownership of tangible goods, or real estate owned by a construction company, provided that said operations are customary. The law assumes that all sales made within the ordinary course of business are customary.
- Services that are commercial, industrial, or financial, or that are connected to mining, construction, insurance, advertising, data processing, and other commercial operations.
- Imports, customary or not.

Normally, the sale of fixed assets is not subject to VAT, unless the assets are sold before the end of their useful lives or within four years from the date of acquisition. The sale of immovable property as fixed assets is subject to VAT only when the sale takes place within 12 months from the date of acquisition.

VAT works on a credit-debit system. The tax borne by a company or business in the acquisition of goods or services is called the 'VAT credit'. The VAT charged on the goods and services sold to customers is called the 'VAT debit'. As a general rule, the seller or service provider is obligated to withhold and pay the VAT. The tax amount is added to the invoice for goods or services, as the final consumer is the economic taxpayer.

Exceptionally, when a seller or service provider is not domiciled in Chile or when, for other reasons, it is difficult for the IRS to supervise the correct payment of VAT, the responsibility to withhold and pay the tax is transferred to the buyer or beneficiary of the service.

The tax is paid every month by deducting the VAT credit from the VAT debit. The balance due to tax authorities (when the debit is larger than the credit) must be paid no later than the 12th of the following month.

If on a given month the VAT credit is larger than the VAT debit, the balance may be kept and carried forward in the following months.

Custom duties
The rate of custom duty is, in general, 6%.

Chile has an extended network of Free Trade Agreements (e.g. with China, United States, Mexico, Japan, European Union, Canada, Panama, Central America, and South Korea). Therefore, reduced or non-existing customs duties rates are available.

Duties on goods are imposed on the cost, insurance, and freight (CIF) price, without deducting special discounts.

In general, Chile has a very open economy and there are no significant barriers to foreign trade.

C

Excise taxes

Alcoholic and non-alcoholic beverages and certain luxury items, such as jewels, are subject to additional sales taxes ranging from 13% to 50%.

A variable gasoline tax is also levied on the difference between a fixed amount and the sales price of gasoline and diesel oil.

Real Estate Tax

Real Estate Tax is levied over an official valuation of real estate at an annual rate of 1.2% in case of non-farming real estate, and 1% for farming real estate. Some real estate is exempt from this tax.

For purposes of financing the plan for reconstruction of the country after the 2010 earthquake, a temporary increase in the Real Estate Tax rate of 0.275% per year was enacted for non-farming real estate with an official valuation equal to or superior to 96 million Chilean pesos (CLP) (approximately USD 205,000) during 2011 and 2012.

Transfer taxes

Currently, Chilean regulations do not state that there are any transfer taxes.

Stamp tax

Stamp tax is payable mainly on documents that evidence money lending operations, and its rate varies depending on the document being executed.

The maximum stamp tax rate is 0.6%.

Branch income

Branches of foreign corporations that are operating in Chile are taxed on their Chilean-source income. Branches are subject to the First Category tax, which is assessed at a rate of 18.5%.

Branches are also subject to a 35% 'additional' tax on amounts remitted or withdrawn during a given calendar year, less a credit for the First Category tax paid, which is payable in April of the year following the distribution. Thus, the tax burden for a branch is 35%.

Income determination

For purposes of the First Category tax, as a general rule, corporate revenue must be determined on an accrual basis.

Inventory valuation

Inventories must be valued in accordance with monetary correction provisions, basically by adjusting raw material content and direct labour to replacement cost (which is generally the most recent cost), but excluding indirect costs. No conformity is required between book and tax reporting for income determination. Last in first out (LIFO) is not allowed.

Chile

Capital gains

Capital gains are subject to normal taxation unless special provisions, such as those pertaining to gains on the sale of shares or monetary correction on capital repayments, establish exemptions.

Under domestic laws, in certain circumstances, the capital gains derived from the following securities will be subject to a preferential tax treatment:

* Stock of listed local companies.
* Investment fund quotas, listed on an authorised stock exchange.
* Mutual funds quotas, if the fund invests in stock trade values.
* Investment funds quotas with no stock exchange participation or mutual funds, where at least a 90% of the investment portfolio is in a stock market.

Dividend income

Dividends received from Chilean corporations are exempt from the First Category tax.

Stock dividends

Stock dividends are not taxed.

Foreign income

Resident corporations are subject to taxes on their worldwide income. In general, foreign income and dividends received by a domestic corporation are subject to Chilean taxation in the financial year when received (i.e. on a cash basis). A tax credit for taxes paid abroad is granted, subject to the regulations of the Income Tax Law.

Branches of foreign corporations are taxed on their income without regard to the results of the head office.

Deductions

Net taxable income of a taxpayer is arrived at by deducting from gross income the expenses incurred to generate the income that have not been already deducted from gross revenue as costs.

As a general rule, expenses are not deductible for income tax purpose if they are not incurred to generate taxable income.

Depreciation and depletion

Depreciation rates are calculated based on the estimated useful life of the assets. The normal periods of depreciation for new assets under normal conditions are as follows: heavy machinery, 15 years; trucks, seven years; factory buildings, in general, 20 years to 40 years. At the request of the Foreign Investment Committee or the taxpayer, the IRS may reduce the normal useful life.

Annual depreciation is taken by the straight-line method. However, taxpayers may recover capitalised costs by using the accelerated depreciation method for up to one third of the normal useful life with respect to new or imported fixed assets, provided that the normal period of depreciation is at least three years.

Accelerated depreciation may be used only to reduce the taxable basis of the First Category tax. For the purpose of the tax applicable to distributions of dividends, accelerated depreciation is not considered.

No conformity is required between book and tax depreciation.

For tax purposes, depletion for natural mineral resources is allowed on a unit-of-production basis.

Goodwill
The amortisation of tax goodwill is not regulated by Law but only in the context of IRS interpretations. In this sense, goodwill should be allocated proportionately among the non-monetary assets of the absorbed entity.

Keep in mind that under current Chilean IRS interpretations, there is no threshold with respect to the goodwill amount to be allocated among the absorbed entity non-monetary assets.

Provided there are no non-monetary assets in the absorbed entity, goodwill will be considered as an intangible that can be amortised as a necessary expense in a period of up to six years.

Start-up expenses
Start-up expenses must be capitalised and be considered as an asset for tax purposes. They can be amortised over a six year period counted from the year when they were incurred or starting from commercial exploitation.

Furthermore, they are usually deducted when the income is generated.

Interest expenses
As long as the interest paid complies with the general requirements set forth by the Law, interest expenses can be deducted.

Bad debt
In general, bad debts are deductible only if they are a consequence of operations related to the business purpose, if they have been opportunely written off into accounting, and the company has prudentially exhausted all reasonable means to collect them.

Determination of whether the company has prudentially exhausted all reasonable means to collect the bad debts varies according to the total amount of the debts. Therefore, a simple estimation or general provision for bad debts is not allowable.

Charitable contributions
Charitable contributions may be deducted provided they are made to the institutions named by varied Laws (i.e. primary and secondary educational institutions; universities, professional or technical educational institutions, National Fire Brigade, National Solidarity Fund, etc.).

In case of charitable contribution, the total annual tax deduction for this purpose is limited. The deductible amount for this purpose may not exceed 5% of the company's net taxable income.

Fines and penalties
Fines and penalties imposed for breaking the law or a contract are not deductible, although a deduction is usually available for legal cost incurred in defending such an action.

Chile

Taxes

Taxes imposed by Chilean laws are deductible, provided they are related to the normal activities of the company. However, income taxes and special contributions for promotion or improvement are not deductible.

Net operating losses

An indefinite carryforward of losses is allowed. Consistent with monetary correction, losses are carried forward, adjusted by a cost-of-living increase. No carrybacks are allowed, except in a case where a taxpayer has retained tax profits and has a subsequent tax loss.

Payments to foreign affiliates

The deductibility of payments made abroad for the use of trademarks, patents, formulas, and consulting and similar services is limited to a maximum of 4% of the income derived from sales and services in the corresponding year, unless the royalty is subject to income tax of greater than 30% in the country of the beneficiary.

Transfer pricing regulations are in line with general Organisation for Economic Co-operation and Development (OECD) principles.

Group taxation

Consolidated returns are not allowed in Chile.

Transfer pricing

Special provisions of the Income Tax Law regulate the prices charged between related companies located in Chile and companies located in other jurisdictions.

The rules contained in the Income Tax Law on transfer pricing matters apply to both operations between a branch and its head office, and operations between a foreign company and a Chilean company in which the former participates (directly or indirectly) in the conduction, control, or capital.

These rules allow the IRS to challenge the prices paid by the Chilean company branch to its head office or to a foreign related company when the prices agreed are not adjusted to those applicable in operations between unrelated parties.

In order to contest the prices, the IRS may take into account a reasonable profit, bearing in mind the characteristics of the operation, or else the production costs plus a reasonable profit margin.

The same rules will apply with regard to prices paid or owed for goods or services provided by the head office, or by any of its branches or related companies, when those prices are not adjusted to the normal market prices charged in operations between non-related parties.

If the branch (or the local company) only has operations with related companies, the IRS will be allowed to challenge those prices taking into consideration the values of the respective goods or services in the international market.

Although domestic legislation regulating transfer pricing aspects of related-party transactions is broad and general, the fact that Chile became an OECD member in 2010 has been of great relevance from a tax perspective in the Chilean local market.

The IRS has made public its intention to ensure its assessment policies and general practices are adequate and consistent with international OECD approaches to corporate restructuring, general tax planning, and in particular transfer pricing.

To date, new transfer pricing legislation has not been approved in Chile. However, based on public communications made by key tax officials in the local media, a new tax bill is due to be tabled before the parliament, and it is expected that this bill will introduce the main principles and pricing methodologies established by the OECD Guidelines.

Thin capitalisation

Thin capitalisation rules apply in case of related party loans at a 3:1 debt-to-equity ratio. In this regard, the total annual amount of such loans is deemed to exceed the 3:1 ratio if the monthly average value of the sum of all related party loans and financial liabilities that the debtor has at the end of the taxable year in which the loan was granted exceeds three times the debtor's adjusted tax equity.

Tax credits and incentives

Foreign tax credit

In order to avoid double taxation, the Chilean Tax Law recognises a tax credit mechanism in which the tax effectively paid abroad may be deducted from the taxes to be paid in Chile.

In order to regulate this matter, the Chilean Tax Law distinguishes between those countries with which there is a DTT in force with Chile and those that do not have a DTT in force with Chile.

Investment incentives

The principal investment incentives are the following:

- Tax benefits and other incentives for companies operating in the northernmost and southernmost parts of the country.
- Tax benefits to forestry companies, contracts for oil operation, and nuclear material operations.

Inbound investment incentives

The principal incentives to encourage foreign capital contributions are statutory guarantees covering the repatriation of capital, remittance of profits, non-discrimination toward foreign investment, and access to the foreign exchange market for remittance purposes. In general, foreign investors are subject to the same legislation as national investors. A guaranteed income tax rate of 42% may be granted for ten years or, provided the capital investment project exceeds USD 50 million, 20 years for the development of industrial or extractive projects.

The overall rate is comprised of the corporate tax on profits and WHT on dividend or branch profit distributions. The tax rate on dividend or profit distributions is the difference between 42% and the underlying tax paid at a corporate level. The option to be subject to an overall effective tax rate of 42% without change for ten or 20 years is usually not exercised by foreign investors, because the current combined effective tax rate on profits and dividend distribution is 35% under the general tax regime.

Chile

Under the Foreign Investment Contract, a foreign investor may petition for tax stability with respect to VAT and customs duty regimes. With respect to customs duties, however, stability is granted only for the importation of certain machinery and equipment not available in Chile.

Export incentives
The principal incentives for exports can be summarised as follows:

- Taxes paid in the importation or acquisitions of goods required in the export activity are reimbursed.
- VAT on exports is zero-rated.
- Chile has signed free-trade agreements with Australia, Bolivia, Canada, Central America (i.e. Costa Rica, El Salvador, Guatemala, Honduras, Nicaragua), China, Colombia, the European Union (EU), Mexico, Panama, Peru, Republic of South Korea, Turkey, and the United States. All these agreements provide for reduced customs duties.

Withholding taxes

Dividends paid to a non-resident recipient are subject to a 35% withholding of 'additional' tax, with a credit available that is equivalent to the income tax effectively paid at the corporate level, corresponding with the First Category tax paid by the corporation. This credit is added to the amount that is distributed to form the taxable base for the 'additional' tax. Consequently, the tax burden for a non-resident recipient of dividends, including taxes at the company level, is 35%. Branches are subject to a 35% 'additional' tax on amounts remitted or withdrawn, less the First Category tax credit. *See the Branch income section for more information.*

In the case of a foreign investor that has applied for the 42% tax invariability, the effective tax burden is also 42%.

Interest paid to non-residents is subject to additional WHT at a general 35% rate. Interest on loans granted by foreign banking or financial institutions is subject to a sole 4% additional WHT. Thin capitalisation rules requesting a 3:1 debt-to-equity ratio become applicable when the debt generating interest subject to the 4% rate is secured by related entities.

Royalties paid to non-residents are subject to additional WHT at a 30% rate. Royalty payments in connection to software are subject to additional WHT at a 15% rate. Such rate is increased in case the beneficiary of the payment is resident in a tax haven or in case the payment is made to a related entity.

Tax treaties
Chile has in force DTTs with the following countries: Argentina, Belgium, Brazil, Canada, Colombia, Croatia, Denmark, Ecuador, France, Ireland, Malaysia, Mexico, New Zealand, Norway, Paraguay, Peru, Poland, Portugal, Republic of South Korea, Spain, Sweden, Switzerland, Thailand, and the United Kingdom.

Please note that Chile has signed DTTs with Australia, Russia, and the United States that are not yet in force.

The following table shows the higher and lower rates on WHT applicable by Chile and the countries with which DTTs exist. The application of one or the other rate will depend on the specific provisions of each treaty.

Recipient	Dividends (%)	Interest (%)	Royalties (%)
Belgium	15	5/15 (1)	5/10 (2)
Brazil	10/15 (3)	15	15
Canada	5/15 (4)	10/15 (5)	10
Colombia	0/7 (6)	5/15 (7)	10
Croatia	5/15 (8)	5/15 (7)	5/10 (2)
Denmark	5/15 (4)	5/15 (9)	5/10 (10)
Ecuador	5/15 (4)	5/15 (10)	10
France	15	5/15 (1)	5/10 (2)
Ireland	5/15 (4)	5/15 (1)	5/10 (2)
Malaysia	5/15 (8)	15	10
Mexico	5/10 (11)	5/10/15 (12)	10
New Zealand	15	10/15 (13)	10
Norway	5/15 (4)	5/15 (9)	5/10 (2)
Paraguay	10	10/15 (14)	15
Peru	10/15 (3)	15	15
Poland	5/15 (8)	5/15 (9)	5/10 (2)
Portugal	10/15 (3)	5/10/15 (15)	5/10 (2)
South Korea	5/10 (16)	5/15 (9)	5/10 (2)
Spain	5/10 (11)	5/15 (1)	5/10 (2)
Switzerland	15	5/15 (1)	5/10 (2)
Sweden	5/10 (11)	5/15 (7)	5/10 (2)
Thailand	10	10/15 (14)	10/15 (17)
United Kingdom	5/15 (11)	5/15 (1)	5/10 (2)

Notes

1. 15% as a general rule. Interest arising from bank or insurance company loans, bonds, some securities that are regularly negotiated on stock markets, and credit sales of industrial equipments are taxed at a 5% tax rate.
2. 10% as a general rule. 5% is applicable for the use or the right to use some equipment.
3. 10% if the beneficiary owns at least 25% of the company's shares. 15% in all other cases.
4. 5% if the beneficiary owns at least 25% of the company's shares. 15% in all other cases.
5. 15% as a general rule. 10% if the most favoured nation clause applies.
6. 0% if the beneficiary owns at least 25% of the company's shares. 7% in all other cases.
7. 5% if the beneficiary is a bank or an insurance company. 15% in all other cases.
8. 5% if the beneficiary owns at least 20% of the company's shares. 15% in all other cases.
9. 15% as a general rule. It could be 5% by the application of the most favoured nation clause.
10. 5% for the use of, or the right to use, some equipment. 10% by the application of the most favoured nation clause.
11. 5% if the beneficiary owns at least 20% of the company's shares. 10% in all other cases.
12. 15% as a general rule. If the most favoured nation clause applies, 10% as a general rule, 5% if interest are paid to a bank.
13. 15% as a general rule. 10% if interest are paid to banks or insurance companies, or if the most favoured nation clause applies.
14. 10% if the beneficiary is a bank or an insurance company. 15% in all other cases.
15. 15% as a general rule. 10% or 15% depending on the interest source.
16. 5% if the beneficiary owns at least 25% of the company's shares. 10% in all other cases.
17. 15% as general rule. 10%.for the use of, or the right to use, any copyright of literary, artistic, or scientific work, or for the use of, or the right to use, industrial, commercial, or scientific equipment.

Chile

Tax administration

Taxable period
The tax year coincides with the calendar year.

Tax returns
The tax system is one of self-assessment by the taxpayer, with occasional auditing by the tax authorities. Tax returns must be filed with the IRS before 30 April of each year with respect to the income of the previous calendar year.

Note that there are many other sworn statements with different deadlines, from March until June of each year.

Payment of tax
Taxes are payable when the annual tax return is submitted in April of each year. Taxpayers, in general, are subject to monthly advance payments on account of their yearly income taxes. The difference between the advance payments and the final tax bill is payable in cash at the time the tax return is filed. If prepayments exceed the final tax bill, the excess is reimbursed by the Treasury.

Statute of limitations
As a general rule, the statute of limitations is three years. However, it can be extended to six years if no tax return was filed or if the tax return was maliciously false.

China, People's Republic of

PwC contact

Cassie Wong
PricewaterhouseCoopers Zhong Tian CPAs Limited Company
26/F Office Tower A, Beijing Fortune Plaza
7 Dongsanhuan Zhong Road
Chaoyang District
Beijing 100020
People's Republic of China
Tel: +86 10 6533 2222
Email: cassie.wong@cn.pwc.com

Significant developments

Pilot Program of indirect tax reform in Shanghai

In order to mitigate the multiple taxation issue associated with goods and services and to support the development of 'modern service industries' in China, the State Council resolved in early 2011 to introduce a Pilot Program in the city of Shanghai to expand the scope of value-added tax (VAT) to cover selected industries that were originally subject to business tax (BT).

The Pilot Program in Shanghai started from 1 January 2012. This earmarks the official kick off of the long-awaited transformation of BT to VAT for service industries in China. The industries selected for the Pilot Program and the applicable VAT rates (for general VAT-payers) are set out in the following table.

Pilot industries	Applicable VAT rate (%)
Transportation service industry	11
Certain modern service industries:	
Research, development, and technical services	6
Information technology services	6
Cultural creative services	6
Logistic auxiliary services	6
Certification and consulting services	6
Tangible movable property leasing services	17

Small-scale VAT-payers in the above Pilot Industries are subject to the VAT rate of 3%.

Enterprises (including foreign enterprises) providing Pilot Services in Shanghai are subject to VAT instead of BT from 1 January 2012.

There are some other cities, including but not limited to Beijing, expressing interest to run similar Pilot Programs in the near future. It is possible that after the Pilot Programs in different localities, the Chinese authorities will collect the experience and modify the Pilot Programs before the transformation is implemented nationwide. It is generally contemplated that the transformation will need to be completed within China's 12th Five Year Plan (2011 to 2015).

China, People's Republic of

Taxes on corporate income

Tax resident enterprises (TREs) are subject to corporate income tax (CIT) on their worldwide income. A non-TRE that has no establishment or place in China is taxed only on its China-source income. A non-TRE with an establishment or place in China shall pay CIT on income derived by such establishment or place from sources in China as well as income derived from outside China that effectively is connected with such establishment or place.

Under the CIT law, the standard tax rate is 25%.

A lower CIT rate is available for the following sectors/industries:

* Qualified new/high tech enterprises are eligible for a reduced CIT rate of 15%. An enterprise has to fulfil a set of prescribed criteria and be subject to an assessment in order to qualify as a new/high tech enterprise.
* Integrated circuit (IC) production enterprises with a total investment exceeding 8 billion renminbi (CNY), or which produce integrated circuits with a line-width of less than 0.25 micrometre, are eligible for a reduced CIT rate of 15%.
* Key software production enterprises are eligible for a reduced CIT rate of 10%. An enterprise has to fulfil a set of prescribed criteria and be subject to an assessment in order to qualify as a key software production enterprise.
* From 1 January 2009 to 31 December 2013, qualified technology-advanced service enterprises in 21 cities (e.g. Beijing, Shanghai, Tianjian, Guangzhou, and Shenzhen) are eligible for a reduced CIT rate of 15%. This incentive is only available to certain technology-advanced service sector members, and an enterprise has to fulfil a set of prescribed criteria and be subject to an assessment in order to qualify as a technology-advanced service enterprise.
* Qualified small and thin-profit enterprises are eligible for a reduced CIT rate of 20%. An enterprise has to fulfil certain conditions in order to qualify as a small and thin-profit enterprise.
* From 1 January 2011 to 31 December 2020, encouraged enterprises in the Western Regions are eligible for a reduced preferential CIT rate of 15%.

Local income taxes
There is no local or provincial income tax in China.

Corporate residence

Enterprises established in China are always TREs. A foreign enterprise with a place of effective management in China is also regarded as a TRE.

Permanent establishment (PE)
An 'establishment or place' is defined in the CIT regulations as an establishment or place in China engaging in production and business operations, including the following:

* Management organisations, business organisations, and representative offices.
* Factories, farms, and places where natural resources are exploited.
* Places where labour services are provided.
* Places where contractor projects, such as construction, installation, assembly, repair, and exploration are undertaken.
* Other establishments or places where production and business activities are undertaken.

- Business agents who regularly sign contracts, store and deliver goods, etc. on behalf of the non-TRE.

Other taxes

China has a turnover tax system consisting of the following three taxes: value-added tax (VAT), business tax (BT), and consumption tax.

Value-added tax (VAT)

The sales or importation of goods and the provision of repairs, replacement, and processing services are subject to VAT. VAT is charged at a standard rate of 17%, and the rate for small-scale taxpayer is 3%. The sales of certain necessity goods may be subject to VAT at a reduced rate of 13%, as specified in the VAT regulations.

The VAT system is a consumption-based VAT system, which means that input VAT on fixed assets is fully recoverable except for situations specified in the VAT regulations.

Export of goods from China may be entitled to a refund of VAT incurred on materials purchased domestically. The refund rates range from 0% to 17%. There is a prescribed formula for determining the amount of refund, under which many products do not obtain the full refund of input VAT credit and suffer different degree of export VAT costs.

In order to mitigate the multiple taxation issue associated with goods and services and to support the development of 'modern service industries' in China, the State Council resolved in early 2011 to introduce a Pilot Program in the city of Shanghai to expand the scope of VAT to cover selected industries that were originally subject to BT.

The Pilot Program in Shanghai started from 1 January 2012. This earmarks the official kick off of the long-awaited transformation of BT to VAT for service industries in China. The industries selected for the Pilot Program and the applicable VAT rates (for general VAT-payers) are set out in the following table.

Pilot industries	Applicable VAT rate (%)
Transportation service industry	11
Certain modern service industries:	
Research, development, and technical services	6
Information technology services	6
Cultural creative services	6
Logistic auxiliary services	6
Certification and consulting services	6
Tangible movable property leasing services	17

Small-scale VAT-payers in the above Pilot Industries are subject to the VAT rate of 3%.

Enterprises (including foreign enterprises) providing Pilot Services in Shanghai are subject to VAT instead of BT from 1 January 2012.

China, People's Republic of

Business tax (BT)

A BT is imposed on services, transfer of intangible assets, and immovable property taking place within China. Services taking place within China refers to situations where the service provider, the service recipient, or both are in China. This may make services even being rendered outside China subject to BT in China. BT rates are 3% or 5%, except for the leisure and entertainment industry, which may be subject to a rate of up to 20%. BT is not recoverable but is deductible for CIT purposes.

As indicated above, under the Pilot Program of the indirect tax reform in Shanghai, enterprises providing Pilot Services in Shanghai will be subject to VAT instead of BT from 1 January 2012.

Customs duties

In general, a customs duty is charged in either specific or *ad valorem* terms. For specific duty, a lump sum amount is charged based on a quantitative amount of the goods (e.g. CNY 100 per unit or per kg). For *ad valorem* duty, the customs value of the goods is multiplied by an *ad valorem* duty rate to arrive at the amount of duty payable. The applicable duty rate generally is determined based on the origin of the goods.

An exemption from customs duty applies to machinery and equipment imported by a foreign investment enterprise within the amount of its total investment, for its own use if the project falls within the encouraged category of the 'Catalogue for the Guidance of Foreign Investment Industries', and the imported machinery or equipment is not within the list of commodities that are not exempted from customs duty.

A customs duty and VAT exemption may be allowed on importation of raw materials for contract processing or import manufacturing. Goods may be imported into, and exported out of, designated Free Trade Zones and Bonded Logistics Zones without liability to customs duty or VAT.

Consumption tax

A consumption tax is imposed on 14 categories of goods, including cigarettes, alcoholic beverages, and certain luxury and environmental unfriendly items. The tax liability is computed based on the sales amount and/or the sales volume depending on the goods concerned. It is not recoverable but is deductible as an expense for CIT purposes.

Real estate tax

A real estate tax, which is based on the value of the property or rental received, is assessed annually on land and buildings used for business purpose or leased. The tax rate is 1.2% of the original value of buildings. A tax reduction of 10% to 30% is commonly offered by local governments. Alternatively, tax may be assessed at 12% of the rental value. Real estate tax is deductible for CIT purposes.

Urban and township land-use tax

An urban and township land-use tax is levied on taxpayers who utilise land within the area of city, country, township, and mining districts. It is computed annually based on the space of area actually occupied by a taxpayer multiplied by a fixed amount per square metre that is determined by the local governments.

Arable land occupation tax

Arable land occupation tax is levied on companies and individuals who build houses or carry out non-agricultural construction on arable lands. It is computed based on the space of area actually occupied by a taxpayer multiplied by a fixed amount per square that is determined by the local governments and is settled in a lump sum.

China, People's Republic of

Land appreciation tax
A land appreciation tax is levied on the gain from the disposal of properties at progressive rates from 30% to 60%. Land appreciation tax is deductible for CIT purposes.

Stamp tax
All enterprises and individuals who execute or receive 'specified documentation', including 11 types of contracts and a few specified documents, are subject to stamp tax. The stamp duty rates vary between 0.005% on loan contracts to 0.1% for property leasing and property insurance contracts. A flat amount of CNY 5 applies to certification evidencing business licences and patents, trademarks, or similar rights.

Deed tax
A deed tax, generally at rates from 3% to 5%, may be levied on the purchase or sale, gift or exchange of ownership of land use rights or real properties. The transferee/assignee is the taxpayer.

Urban construction and maintenance tax
Urban construction and maintenance tax is imposed at a certain rate on the amount of China's indirect taxes (i.e. business tax, VAT, and consumption tax) payable by the taxpayer. Effectively, the taxpayers of indirect taxes are also the taxpayers of urban construction and maintenance tax. It is charged at three different rates depending on the taxpayer's location, 7% for urban areas, 5% for county areas, and 1% for other areas.

Educational surcharge
Educational surcharge is imposed at 3% on the amount of China's indirect taxes (i.e. business tax, VAT, and consumption tax) payable by the taxpayer. Effectively, the taxpayers of indirect taxes are also the taxpayers of educational surcharge.

Local educational surcharge
Local educational surcharge is levied at 2% on the amount of China's indirect taxes (i.e. business tax, VAT, and consumption tax) payable by the taxpayer. Effectively, the taxpayers of indirect taxes are also the taxpayers of local educational surcharge.

Note that the local educational surcharge is not levied in many places in China. On 7 November 2010, the Ministry of Finance (MOF) released a circular requesting all the local governments to unify/resume the collection of local educational surcharge. However, as the circular does not specify the effective date, the current local practice varies.

Motor vehicle acquisition tax
A motor vehicle acquisition tax at a rate of 10% of the taxable consideration will be levied on any purchase and importation of cars, motorcycles, trams, trailers, carts, and certain types of trucks.

Vehicle and vessel tax
A vehicle and vessel tax is a tax that is levied on all vehicles and vessels within China. A fixed amount is levied on a yearly basis. Transport vehicles generally are taxed on a fixed amount according to their own weight, with passenger cars, buses, and motorcycles being taxed on a fixed unit amount. Vessels are taxed on a fixed amount, according to the deadweight tonnage.

China, People's Republic of

Vessel tonnage tax

Vessel tonnage tax is levied on any vessel entering into a port inside the territory of China from overseas and is collected by the General Customs. The tax payable is computed based on the net tonnage multiplied by the applicable tax rate that is determined depending on the net tonnage and the term of tonnage tax license.

Resource tax

The exploitation of crude oil and natural gas is subject to resource tax on a sales turnover basis. The exploitation of other natural resources, including coal, other raw non-metallic metals, raw ferrous metals, non-ferrous metallic minerals, and salt (including solid and liquid salt), is subject to resource tax on a tonnage or volume basis. The range of tax rates are specified by the State Council.

For Sino-foreign joint ventures exploiting crude oil or natural gas established before 1 November 2011, mine area usage fees are levied in lieu of resource tax.

Tobacco tax

Tobacco tax is levied on taxpayers who purchase tobacco leaves within the territory of China. The tax is assessed at the rate of 20% on the purchasing value and shall be settled with the local tax bureau at the place of the purchase.

Branch income

Under the CIT law, a branch of a non-TRE in China is taxed at the branch level. If there is more than one branch, they may elect to file their tax at the main office in China on a consolidated basis. There is no further tax upon remittance of branch profits.

Income determination

Taxable income is defined as "gross income in a tax year after deduction of non-taxable income, tax exempt income, various deductions, and allowable losses brought forward from previous years". The accrual method of accounting should be used.

Gross income refers to monetary and non-monetary income derived by an enterprise from various sources, including, but not limited to, the sales of goods, provision of services, transfer of property, dividends, interest, rentals, royalties, and donations.

Non-taxable income refers to fiscal appropriation, governmental administration charges, governmental funds, and other income specified by the central government.

Inventory valuation

Inventory must be valued according to costs. In computing the cost of inventories, the enterprise may choose one of the following methods: first in first out (FIFO), weighted average, or specific identification.

Unrealised gain or loss due to changes in fair value

An unrealised gain or loss due to changes in the fair value of financial assets, financial liabilities, and investment properties held by an enterprise is not taxable/deductible for CIT purpose. The gain/loss is taxable/deductible only when the asset/liability actually is disposed or realised.

China, People's Republic of

C

Capital gains
Capital gains are treated in the same way as ordinary income of a revenue-nature for a TRE.

Dividend income
An exemption exists for CIT on dividend derived by a TRE from the direct investment into another TRE except for where the dividend is from stocks publicly traded on the stock exchanges and the holding period is less than 12 months.

Interest income
Interest income is treated as ordinary income.

Rental income
Rental income is treated as ordinary income.

Royalty income
Royalty income is treated as ordinary income.

Partnership income
Partnerships registered in China are not subject to CIT. The income of a partnership is taxable at the partners' level.

Unrealised exchange gains
Unrealised exchange gain (loss) from the year-end translation of assets (liabilities) denominated in foreign currency generally is taxable (deductible).

Foreign income
The worldwide income of a TRE and its branches both within and outside China is taxable. There are no provisions in the CIT law that allow foreign income directly earned by the TRE to be deferred for tax purposes. The CIT law contains a controlled foreign company (CFC) rule under which the unremitted earning of a foreign company controlled by Chinese enterprises may be taxable in China (*see the Group taxation section for more information*). A foreign tax credit is allowed for foreign income taxes paid on foreign-source income.

Deductions

Generally, an enterprise is allowed to deduct reasonable expenditures which actually have been incurred and are related to the generation of income.

Depreciation of fixed assets
Fixed assets with useful lives of more than 12 months must be capitalised and depreciated in accordance with the CIT regulations. Generally, depreciation is calculated by the straight-line method. Shorter tax depreciation life or accelerated depreciation may be allowed due to advancement of technology or suffering from constant vibration or severe corrosion. Production-nature biological assets, such as livestock held for breeding and commercial timber, also have to be capitalised and depreciated using the straight-line method.

Under the straight-line method, the cost of an item, less its residual value, is depreciated over the useful life of the asset. Residual value should be reasonably determined based on the nature and usage of the asset. The CIT law provides minimum useful lives for the following assets:

China, People's Republic of

Assets	Years
Buildings and structures	20
Aircrafts, trains, vessels, machinery, mechanisms, and other production equipment	10
Appliances, tools, and furniture etc. related to production and business operations	5
Means of transport other than aircrafts, trains, and vessels	4
Electronic equipment	3
Production-nature biological assets in the nature of forestry	10
Production-nature biological assets in the nature of livestock	3

Amortisation of intangibles and goodwill

A deduction is allowed for amortisation of intangible assets, such as, but not limited to, patents, trademarks, copyrights, and land use rights. Generally, intangible assets have to be amortised over a period of not less than ten years. For an intangible asset obtained through capital contribution or assignment, it can be amortised according to the useful life prescribed in the laws or agreed in the contracts, if any. However, acquired goodwill is not deductible until the invested enterprise is entirely transferred or liquidated.

Organisational and start-up expenses

Organisational and start-up expenses are tax deductible fully in the first year of operation.

Research and development (R&D) expense

For R&D expenses incurred for new technology, new products, or new craftsmanship, an extra 50% of the actual expenses incurred are also tax-deductible as an incentive.

Asset loss

Asset loss (including bad debt loss) may be deductible in the tax year during which such loss is incurred, provided that supporting documents are submitted to and accepted by the in-charge tax bureau before annual income tax reconciliation filing.

Interest expenses

Interest on loans generally is tax-deductible. For interest expenses on borrowings from non-financial institutions by a non-financial institution, the portion that does not exceed the commercial rate is deductible. The tax deduction of interest paid to related parties is subject to the thin capitalisation rule under the CIT law (*see the Group taxation section for more information*).

Reserves and provisions

Provisions for asset impairment reserves (e.g. bad debt provisions) and risk reserves generally are not tax-deductible unless otherwise prescribed in the tax rules. Financial institutions and insurance companies may deduct certain provisions and reserves subject to the caps specified in the relevant tax circulars.

Contingent liabilities

The CIT law does not specifically address the deductibility of contingent liabilities. According to the general principle of the CIT law, contingent liabilities are liabilities that an enterprise has not actually incurred and thus shall not be tax-deductible.

Charitable donations

Charitable donations are tax-deductible at up to 12% of the annual accounting profit. Non-charitable donations, as well as sponsorship expenditures that are non-advertising and non-charitable in nature, are not deductible.

Wages and staff welfare expenses

Reasonable wages and salaries of employees incurred by an enterprise are tax-deductible. Directors' fees are also tax-deductible.

Basic social security contributions, including basic pension insurance, basic medical insurance, unemployment insurance, injury insurance, maternity insurance, and housing funds, that are made by an enterprise in accordance with the scope and criteria as prescribed by the state or provincial governments are deductible.

Commercial insurance premiums paid for investors or employees shall not be tax-deductible unless it is paid for safety insurance for workers conducting special types of work.

Staff welfare expenses, labour union fees, and staff education expenses are tax-deductible up to 14%, 2%, and 2.5% of the total salary expenses, respectively.

Entertainment expenses

Entertainment expenses are tax-deductible to the lesser of 60% of the costs actually incurred and 0.5% of the sales or business income of that year. The excess amount must not be carried forward to and deducted in the following tax years.

Advertising expenses and business promotion expenses

Advertising expenses and business promotion expenses are deductible up to 15% of the sales (business) income of that year unless otherwise prescribed in the tax regulations. Any excess amount is allowed to be carried forward and deductible in the following tax years. Advertising expenses and business promotion expenses incurred by the tobacco industry are entirely not tax-deductible.

Fines and penalties

Fines, penalties, and losses arising from confiscation of property are not deductible for CIT purposes.

Taxes

CIT payments and tax surcharges are not deductible for CIT purposes.

Net operating losses

Tax losses can be carried forward for no longer than five years starting from the year subsequent to the year in which the loss was incurred. Carryback of losses is not permitted.

Payments to affiliates

Management fees for stewardship are not deductible, but services fees paid for genuine services provided by affiliates in China or overseas and charged at arm's length should be deductible. Other payments to affiliates, such as royalties, are also tax-deductible provided that the charges are at arm's length.

Group taxation

Group taxation is not permitted under the CIT law unless otherwise prescribed by the State Council.

China, People's Republic of

Transfer pricing

All enterprises are required to conduct transactions with related parties on an arm's-length basis. The Chinese tax authorities are empowered to make adjustments to transactions between related parties which are not conducted at arm's length and resulting in the reduction of taxable income of the enterprise or its related parties using the following appropriate methods: comparable uncontrolled price method, resale price method, cost plus method, transactional net margin method, profit split method, and other methods which are consistent with the arm's-length principle. China also adopts stringent requirements on the disclosure of related party transactions in the filing of the annual tax return. In addition, there is also a requirement to prepare contemporaneous transfer pricing documentation if the amount of related parties' transactions with an enterprise exceeds a certain prescribed threshold.

The CIT law also contains transfer pricing provisions relating to cost sharing arrangements and advance pricing arrangements. In addition, it also contains a few tax avoidance rules such as a CFC rule, a thin capitalisation rule, and general anti-avoidance rules.

Thin capitalisation

The CIT law has a thin capitalisation rule disallowing interest expense arising from excessive related party loans. The safe harbour debt/equity ratio for enterprises in the financial industry is 5:1 and for enterprises in other industries is 2:1. However, if there is sufficient evidence to show that the financing arrangement is at arm's length, these interests may still be fully deductible even if the ratios are exceeded.

Controlled foreign companies (CFCs)

Under the CFC rule, the undistributed profits of CFCs located in low-tax jurisdictions with an effective income tax rate of less than 12.5% may be taxed as a deemed distribution to the TRE shareholders. The Chinese tax authorities have published a list of countries (i.e. a 'white list') that they do not regard to be low-tax jurisdictions.

Tax credits and incentives

The CIT law adopts the 'Predominantly Industry-oriented, Limited Geography-based' tax incentive policy. Key emphasis is placed on 'industry-oriented' incentives aiming at directing investments into those industry sectors and projects encouraged and supported by the state. The tax incentive policies mainly include the following and are applicable to both domestic and foreign investments.

Tax reduction and exemption

CIT may be reduced or exempted on income derived from the following projects:

Projects/industries	CIT incentive	Valid period
Agriculture, forestry, animal-husbandry, and fishery projects	Exemption or 50% reduction	All years, as long as it is engaged in these projects
Specified basic infrastructure projects	3 + 3 years tax holiday (2)	Starting from the first income-generating year
Environment protection projects and energy/water conservative projects	3 + 3 years tax holiday (2)	Starting from the first income-generating year

Projects/industries	CIT incentive	Valid period
Qualified new/high tech enterprises established in Shenzhen, Zhuhai, Shantou, Xiamen, Hainan, and Pudong New Area of Shanghai after 1 January 2008	2 + 3 years tax holiday (1)	Starting from the first income-generating year
Newly established software production enterprises	2 + 3 years tax holiday (1)	Starting from the first profit-making year
Integrated circuits design enterprises	2 + 3 years tax holiday (1)	Starting from the first profit-making year
Integrated circuits production enterprises with a total investment exceeding CNY 8 billion or which produce integrated circuits with a line-width of less than 0.25um, provided that its operation period exceeds 15 years	5 + 5 years tax holiday (3)	Starting from the first profit-making year
Integrated circuits production enterprises which produce integrated circuits with a line-width of less than 0.8um	2 + 3 years tax holiday (1)	Starting from the first profit-making year
Qualified energy-saving service enterprises	3 + 3 years tax holiday (2)	Starting from the first income-generating year
Encouraged enterprises in underprivileged areas of Xinjiang	2 + 3 years tax holiday (1)	Starting from the first income-generating year

Notes

1. '2 + 3 years tax holiday' refers to two years of exemption from CIT followed by three years of 50% reduction of CIT.
2. '3 + 3 years tax holiday' refers to three years of exemption plus three years of 50% reduction of CIT.
3. '5 + 5 years tax holiday' refers to five years of exemption plus five years of 50% reduction of CIT.

For income derived from the transfer of technology in a tax year, the portion that does not exceed CNY 5 million shall be exempted from CIT; and the portion that exceeds CNY 5 million shall be allowed a 50% reduction of CIT.

A CIT exemption applies to the dividend derived by a TRE from the direct investment into another TRE except where the dividend is from stocks publicly traded on the stock exchanges and the holding period is less than 12 months.

A CIT exemption also applies to the income derived by recognised non-profit-making organisations engaging in non-profit-making activities.

Reduced tax rate
The CIT rate may be reduced under certain conditions for different industries (*see the Taxes on corporate income section for more information*).

Reduction of revenue
Where an enterprise uses resources specified by the state as its major raw materials to produce non-restricted and non-prohibited products, only 90% of the income derived is taxable.

China, People's Republic of

Offset of certain venture capital investment

For a venture capital enterprise that makes an equity investment in a non-listed small to medium-sized new/high tech enterprise for more than two years, 70% of its investment amount may be used to offset against the taxable income of the venture capital enterprise in the year after the holding period has reached two years. Any portion that is not utilised in that year can be carried forward and deducted in the following years.

Investment tax credit

Enterprises purchasing and using equipment specified by the state for environmental protection, energy and water conservation, or production safety purposes are eligible for a tax credit of 10% of the investment in such equipment. Any unutilised amount can be carried forward and creditable in the following five years.

Other incentives

There are also tax incentives in relation to the deduction of expenses and cost (e.g. 50% additional R&D deduction, shorter tax depreciation period, and accelerated depreciation). *See the Deductions section for more information.*

Foreign tax credit

A TRE is allowed to claim foreign tax credit in relation to foreign income tax already paid overseas in respect of income derived from sources outside China based on a country-basket principle. The creditable foreign tax also includes foreign income tax paid by qualified CFCs. However, the creditable amount may not exceed the amount of income tax otherwise payable in China in respect of the foreign sourced income. In addition, there is a five-year carryforward period for any unutilised foreign tax.

Withholding taxes

Foreign enterprises without establishments or places of business in China shall be subject to a unilaterally concessionary rate of withholding tax (WHT) at 10% on gross income from dividends, interest, lease of property, royalties, and other China-source passive income unless reduced under a tax treaty. Nevertheless, dividends distributed by a foreign investment enterprise out of its pre-2008 profit are still exempted from WHT.

WHT rates under China's tax treaties with other countries/nations are as follows (as of 1 June 2012):

Recipient	Dividends (%)	Interest (%) (1)	Royalties (%) (2)
Albania	10	10	10
Algeria	5/10 (3a)	7	10
Armenia	5/10 (3a)	10	10
Australia	15	10	10
Austria	7/10 (3b)	7/10 (4a)	6/10
Azerbaijan	10	10	10
Bahrain	5	10	10
Bangladesh	10	10	10
Barbados	5/10 (3a)	10	10
Belarus	10	10	10
Belgium	10	10	6/10
Brazil	15	15	15/25 (5a)

China, People's Republic of

Recipient	Dividends (%)	Interest (%) (1)	Royalties (%) (2)
Brunei	5	10	10
Bulgaria	10	10	7/10
Canada	10/15 (3f)	10	10
Croatia	5	10	10
Cuba	5/10 (3a)	7.5	5
Cyprus	10	10	10
Czech Republic	10	10	10
Denmark	10	10	7/10
Egypt	8	10	8
Estonia	5/10 (3a)	10	10
Ethiopia (6)	5	7	5
Finland	5/10 (3a)	10	7/10
France	10	10	6/10
Georgia	0/5/10 (3c)	10	5
Germany	10	10	7/10
Greece	5/10 (3a)	10	10
Hong Kong Special Administrative Region	5/10 (3d)	7	7
Hungary	10	10	10
Iceland	5/10 (3a)	10	7/10
India	10	10	10
Indonesia	10	10	10
Iran	10	10	10
Ireland, Republic of	5/10 (3b)	10	6/10
Israel	10	7/10 (4a)	7/10
Italy	10	10	7/10
Jamaica	5	7.5	10
Japan	10	10	10
Kazakhstan	10	10	10
Korea, Republic of	5/10 (3a)	10	10
Kuwait	5	5	10
Kyrgyzstan	10	10	10
Laos	5	5 (in Laos) 10 (in Mainland China)	5 (in Laos) 10 (in Mainland China)
Latvia	5/10 (3a)	10	10
Lithuania	5/10 (3a)	10	10
Luxembourg	5/10 (3a)	10	6/10
Macao Special Administrative Region	5/10 (3a)	7	7
Macedonia	5	10	10
Malaysia	10	10	10/15 (5b)
Malta	10	10	10
Mauritius	5	10	10
Mexico	5	10	10
Moldova	5/10 (3a)	10	10
Mongolia	5	10	10
Morocco	10	10	10
Nepal	10	10	15

China, People's Republic of

Recipient	Dividends (%)	Interest (%) (1)	Royalties (%) (2)
Netherlands	10	10	6/10
New Zealand	15	10	10
Nigeria	7.5	7.5	7.5
Norway	15	10	10
Oman	5	10	10
Pakistan	10	10	12.5
Papua New Guinea	15	10	10
Philippines	10/15 (3g)	10	10/15 (5b)
Poland	10	10	7/10
Portugal	10	10	10
Qatar	10	10	10
Romania	10	10	7
Russia	10	10	10
Saudi Arabia	5	10	10
Seychelles	5	10	10
Singapore	5/10 (3a)	7/10 (4a)	6/10
Slovak Republic	10	10	10
Slovenia	5	10	10
South Africa	5	10	7/10
Spain	10	10	6/10
Sri Lanka	10	10	10
Sudan	5	10	10
Sweden	5/10 (3a)	10	7/10
Switzerland	10	10	6/10
Syria (6)	5/10 (3a)	10	10
Tajikistan	5/10 (3a)	8	8
Thailand	15/20 (3a)	10	15
Trinidad and Tobago	5/10 (3e)	10	10
Tunisia	8	10	5/10 (5c)
Turkey	10	10	10
Turkmenistan	5/10 (3a)	10	10
Ukraine	5/10 (3a)	10	10
United Arab Emirates	7	7	10
United Kingdom	10	10	7/10
United States	10	10	7/10
Uzbekistan	10	10	10
Venezuela	5/10 (3h)	5/10 (4a)	10
Vietnam	10	10	10
Yugoslavia	5	10	10
Zambia	5	10	5

Source: State Administration of Taxation, China

Notes

- This table is a summary only and does not reproduce all the provisions relevant in determining the application of WHT in each tax treaty/arrangement.
- The former Czechoslovak Socialist Republic is divided into Czech Republic and Slovak Republic.
- The former Yugoslavia is divided into Bosnia, Croatia, Macedonia, Serbia, Slovenia, and Yugoslavia.

- There is no tax treaty signed between China and Bosnia and Serbia.

1. 0% is due on interest paid to government bodies except for Australia, Brunei, Cyprus, Israel, Slovenia, and Spain. Reference should be made to the individual tax treaties.
2. The lower rate on royalties applies for the use of or right to use any industrial, commercial, or scientific equipment.
3. The following notes apply to dividend WHT:
   a. The lower rate applies where the beneficial owner of the dividend is a company (not a partnership) that directly owns at least 25% of the capital of the paying company.
   b. The lower rate applies where the beneficial owner of the dividend is a company that directly owns at least 25% of the voting shares of the paying company.
   c. The lowest rate (i.e. 0%) applies where the beneficial owner is a company that owns directly or indirectly at least 50% of the capital of the paying company and the investment exceeding 2 million euros (EUR). The lower rate (i.e. 5%) applies where the beneficial owner is a company that directly or indirectly owns at least 10% of the capital of the paying company and the investment exceeding EUR 100,000.
   d. The lower rate applies where the beneficial owner of the dividend is a company that directly owns at least 25% of the capital of the paying company.
   e. The lower rate applies where the beneficial owner of the dividend is a company that directly or indirectly owns at least 25% of the capital of the paying company.
   f. The lower rate applies where the beneficial owner of the dividend is a company that owns at least 10% of the voting stock of the paying company.
   g. The lower rate applies where the beneficial owner of the dividend is a company that directly owns at least 10% of the capital of the paying company.
   h. The lower rate applies where the beneficial owner is a company (other than a partnership) which directly owns at least 10% of the capital of the paying company.
4. The following notes apply to interest WHT:
   a. The lower rate applies to interest payable to banks or financial institutions.
5. The following notes apply to royalties WHT:
   a. The higher rate applies to trademarks.
   b. The higher rate applies to copyright of literary, artistic, or scientific work, including cinematograph films or tapes for television or broadcasting.
   c. The lower rate applies to royalties paid for technical or economic studies or for technical assistance.
6. These tax treaties have not yet entered into force as of 1 June 2012.

In addition to the above tax treaties, China has also entered into tax information exchange agreements (TIEAs) with the following countries:

- Argentina.
- Bahamas.
- Bermuda.
- British Virgin Islands (BVI).
- Cayman Islands.
- Guensey.
- Jersey.
- Isle of Man.

Tax administration

Taxable period
The tax year commences on 1 January and ends on 31 December.

Tax returns
Enterprises are required to file their annual income tax return within five months after the end of the tax year, together with an audit certificate of a registered public accountant in China. Information on related party transactions must be filed with the annual income tax return.

China, People's Republic of

Payment of tax

Enterprises are required to file and pay provisional income taxes on a quarterly or monthly basis within 15 days following the end of each month/quarter. Three options are available to the taxpayer in computing the provisional tax: (i) actual profits of the month/quarter, (ii) average monthly or quarterly taxable income of the preceding year, or (iii) other formulas approved by the local tax authorities.

Settlement of tax payment is due, in conjunction with the annual income tax return, within five months after the end of the tax year.

Statute of limitations

For unintentional errors (e.g. calculation errors) committed by the taxpayer in its tax filing, the statute of limitation is three years and extended to five years if the amount of tax underpaid is CNY 100,000 or more. For transfer pricing adjustments, the statute of limitation is ten years. There is no statute of limitation for tax evasion, refusal to pay tax, or defrauding of tax payment.

Audit cycle

There is no fixed audit cycle in China. Tax audit targets are selected pursuant to certain criteria.

Recent focus of Chinese tax authorities

Since 2009, the Chinese tax authorities have strengthened their tax administration on transfer pricing and income derived by non-TREs. The State Administration of Taxation (SAT) has released a number of tax circulars addressing the tax administration of transfer pricing, foreign contractors and service providers, WHT on passive income, etc.

In particular, the Chinese tax authorities have geared up their efforts in recent years to scrutinise investment structures involving intermediate holding companies incorporated in low tax jurisdictions. One of their focuses is on the indirect equity transfer of Chinese companies by non-TRE. The income derived by a non-TRE from the disposal of a non-Chinese company is not taxable under China's domestic income tax law. However, if the Chinese tax authorities are of the view that the non-TRE transferor has used an abusive arrangement to indirectly transfer the equity of the Chinese company (i.e. interposing and disposing of the special purpose vehicle for no reasonable commercial purpose, but just for avoidance of China withholding income tax), it may re-characterise the equity transfer based on the 'substance over form' principle and disregard the existence of the special purpose vehicle. Once the special purpose vehicle is disregarded, the transfer would be effectively a transfer of the underlying Chinese company's equity, and the transfer gain would be China source and subject to China withholding income tax.

In addition, the SAT has also released circulars relating to the claiming of treaty benefits by non-TREs and interpretation of certain articles and terms in the tax treaties, such as dividends, royalties, beneficial ownership, etc. Aggressive tax planning (including, but not limited to, tax-avoidance and treaty-abusive arrangements) not supported by reasonable commercial purposes and substance will be subject to scrutiny by the Chinese tax authorities.

On 26 July 2010, the SAT issued a Departmental Interpretation Note (DIN) for the tax treaty concluded between China and Singapore. It is the first time the SAT has introduced a set of technical views, interpretation, and practice guidelines for the implementation of a tax treaty in such a comprehensive manner. More importantly, this set of interpretation is also applicable to other tax treaties concluded by China if the provisions of the relevant articles in those tax treaties are the same as those in the China/Singapore tax treaty. Thus, it is likely to have a wide impact to tax residents of other countries/regions which have entered into tax treaties with China.

General anti-avoidance rules (GAAR)

There is a GAAR provision in the CIT law allowing the Chinese tax authorities to make adjustments to taxable revenue or taxable income where business arrangements, structures, or transactions are entered into without reasonable commercial purpose and result in a reduction, exemption, or deferral of tax payment. The Chinese tax authorities may initiate GAAR investigation if they suspect that an enterprise undertakes any of the following arrangements: abuse of preferential tax treatments, abuse of tax treaties, abuse of corporate structure, use of tax havens for tax avoidance purposes, or other arrangements that do not have a reasonable commercial purpose.

Other issues

Choice of business entity

Foreign companies, enterprises, or individuals may, subject to approval from the Ministry of Commerce or other relevant ministries, establish equity joint ventures, contractual joint ventures, wholly foreign-owned enterprises, or representative offices in China. Certain foreign financial institutions, including banks and insurance companies, may, subject to approval, set up branches in China. Foreign investors are allowed to establish foreign invested partnerships in China.

Exchange controls

Foreign exchange transactions are administered by the State Administration of Foreign Exchange (SAFE) and its branches. The regulatory administration on foreign exchange transactions of an enterprise depends on whether the transaction is a current account item or a capital account item. Current account items refer to ordinary transactions within the context of international receipts and payments, including, but not limited to, balance of payments from trade, labour services, and unilateral transfers. Capital account items refer to items of increase or decrease in debt and equity due to inflow or outflow of capital within the context of international receipts and payments, including, but not limited to, direct investment, all forms of loans, and investment in securities. If a transaction falls under the category of capital account items, generally prior approval from the SAFE should be obtained. Generally, a payment that falls under the category of a current account may be remitted to overseas if supported with proper contracts, invoices, and tax payment/exemption certificates.

Intellectual properties

Patents, trademarks, and copyrights are governed by separate laws and administered by separate governmental bodies. The government encourages the development and transfer of intellectual properties. The transfer of technology and technical services are currently exempted from business tax.

Mergers and acquisitions (M&A) activities

Both Chinese domestic and foreign investors increasingly are using M&A transactions to establish or expand their Chinese operations.

The MOF and the SAT jointly released a tax circular that addresses the CIT treatments for six forms of restructuring transactions, namely, change in legal form, debt restructuring, equity acquisition, assets acquisition, merger, and spin-off. The general principle is that enterprises undergoing corporate restructuring should recognise the

China, People's Republic of

gain/loss from the transfer of relevant assets/equity at fair value when the transaction takes place. However, if certain prescribed conditions are satisfied, the parties involved could opt for special tax treatments, which are essentially tax deferral tax treatment. In other words, recognition of gain/loss of the transferor from transfer of assets/equity can be deferred with respect to the equity-payment portion; and the transferee may take over the transferor's tax basis of the acquired assets/equity. Such special tax treatments are only available to a very few specific types of cross-border transactions.

Colombia

PwC contact

Carlos Chaparro
PricewaterhouseCoopers Servicios Legales y Tributarios
Calle 100 #11A-35 Piso 3
Bogotá, Cudinamarca
Colombia
Tel: +57 1 634 0555
Email: carlos.chaparro@co.pwc.com

Significant developments

Colombia has signed double taxation treaties (DTTs) with Spain, Chile, Switzerland, Canada, and Mexico, the first three are in force, while the others are still being finalised or awaiting ratification. In addition, negotiations for DTTs with China, Korea, and Germany have recently commenced.

No tax reform occurred in 2011; only formal changes to the tax regulation (Decrees 4907, 4908, 4919, and 4963).

We expect an important tax reform in 2013.

Taxes on corporate income

National companies (i.e. incorporated in Colombia under Colombian law) are taxed on worldwide income. Foreign non-resident companies and local branches of foreign companies are taxed on their Colombian-source income only. The current general corporate income tax (CIT) rate is 33%, which is applied on taxable income, with taxable income being generally defined as the excess of all operating and non-operating revenue over deductible costs and expenses. The current general capital gains tax rate is also 33%. However, qualifying businesses located in free trade zones (FTZs) enjoy a reduced rate of 15% (while subject to capital gain tax at 33%)

The customary costs and expenses of a business are generally acceptable as deductible expenditure for CIT purposes provided they are necessary, reasonable and have been realised during the relevant tax year under the accrual or cash method of accounting, as the case may be.

In Colombia, as a general rule, there are no industry-specific income tax rates, dual income tax rates, or hybrid tax systems relating to corporate income or tax consolidation. The only material deviation from the statutory CIT rate that is worth mentioning is the special income tax rate that applies for certain FTZ users, which is 15% (as opposed to the statutory 33% CIT rate).

Minimum presumptive tax

Corporate income taxpayers are required to pay a minimum amount of income tax, which is determined based on the so-called presumptive income method. Under this method, presumptive taxable income is measured as 3% of net assets (or tax equity) as of 31 December of the prior tax year as reported by the taxpayer on the corresponding CIT return. The CIT rate is then applied to the greater of regular taxable income (revenue less allowable costs and expenses) or presumptive taxable income (exempting certain business activities).

Colombia

In order to determine the taxable base for presumptive income purposes, it is necessary to subtract from the total amount of net assets, which is the base to calculate presumptive income, the following amounts:

- The net asset value of the shares owned in national companies.
- The net asset value of the assets affected by *force majeure*.
- The net asset value of assets associated with operations in unproductive periods.

Each year, taxpayers must compare the value resulting from the application of the foregoing two systems. The income tax for the taxable year will be calculated on the higher value resulting from this comparison. If presumptive income is higher than the ordinary net income, the difference constitutes an excess of presumptive income, which can be carried forward (adjusted for inflation) to any of the following five taxable years and offset against the net income determined by the taxpayer.

Stability Agreement Regime
In an effort to continue to attract local and foreign investments, a 2005 law created a Stability Agreement Regime whereby taxpayers can, upon satisfaction of several requirements, agree with the government on a contract that any future adverse tax changes may (direct taxes only) not apply. However, to the extent changes are for the benefit of the taxpayer (i.e. CIT rate reduction), they will apply. In order to obtain a legal stability contract, an investor has to satisfy certain requirements, which include the payment of a premium of 0.5% or 1% on the investment commitment, the definition of which is a new investment or enhancement of an existing investment that is worth over 3,907,350,000 Colombian pesos (COP) (150,000 Tax Value Units [TVU]).

Note that the Tax Office, by means of ruling 98797 of 28 December 2010, interpreted that: "The Legal Stability, applied in connection with tax regulations, is primarily directed to maintain incentives (such as the special deduction for investment in real productive fixed assets), subject to the possibility of stabilising other general provisions as those related to taxable rates and tax bases that are being applied at the moment of executing the agreement (...) In this regards this office considers that there is a legal impossibility to stabilise rules that are non-existent at the moment of executing the agreement".

Corporate residence

Corporate residence is determined by the place of incorporation of any given company.

For CIT purposes, companies incorporated under foreign laws and which have their main domicile abroad are considered 'foreign companies', whereas any company incorporated in Colombia under Colombian law qualifies as a 'national company' even if fully owned by foreign shareholders.

Permanent establishment (PE)
The concept of PE is not included under Colombian internal legislation for CIT laws. This concept is only relevant in the context of DTTs, and therefore, its applicability varies between one DTT to another one.

The concept of PE, in the case of the DTTs, follows the Organisation for Economic Co-operation and Development (OECD) criteria. In the case of Spain, Chile, and Switzerland, the concept of PE therefore means a fixed place of business throughout which an entity carries out its activity, whether partially or in its whole.

Regarding the above, each DTT has exemptions for the incorporation of a PE.

Other taxes

Value-added tax (VAT)

The Colombian VAT taxes the sale in the country of any items of tangible personal property that are not fixed assets and are not covered by an exemption, the provision of services within the national territory (certain services supplied outside Colombia but imported also attract VAT), and the importation of tangible personal property that is not covered by an exemption.

The Colombian VAT is based on a credit-debit system throughout the entire chain of a business. However, certain products are only taxed at the manufacturer level (one-phase VAT). For purposes of VAT calculation, the VAT taxpayer may credit the VAT (input) paid to vendors (certain limitations apply) against any VAT (output) collected from customers.

The general VAT rate is 16%. However, certain services and goods are taxed at 10% (i.e. coffee, rice) and 20% (i.e. mobile phone services). Luxury goods attract higher rates within the range between 20% and 35%. Wines and other alcoholic beverages are not considered as luxury goods, but the applicable VAT rate is higher (ranging between 20% and 25%) than the general rate.

Under current law, there are VAT exemptions available for the following items, among others:

- Equipment and materials for the construction, installation, assembly, and operation of environmental monitoring and control systems.
- Imports of raw materials and supplies made under the so-called Vallejo Plan for further processing and incorporation into products that are to be subsequently exported (*see the Tax credits and incentives section for more information on the Vallejo Plan*).
- Temporary importation of heavy machinery and equipment for basic industries (mining, hydrocarbons, heavy chemistry, the iron and steel industry, metallurgy, power generation and transmission, and the water industry).
- Importation of machinery and equipment, which is not produced in the country, for recycling and processing of waste and refuse.
- Regular imports by major exporters of industrial equipment, which is not produced in the country, for the transformation of raw material.
- Freight transportation.
- Public transportation of passengers in the national territory by water or land.
- Transportation of gas and hydrocarbons.
- Interest and other financial income from credit operations.
- Financial leasing.
- Medical care services.
- Public utilities.
- Internet services for low to mid-income residential customers.

A non-resident supplier of VAT-subject services does not require VAT registration. Rather, it is the locally-based recipient that must apply a reverse-charge. No VAT fiscal representation is allowed.

As of 2011, no VAT filings are required for periods where no inputs or outputs exist.

Colombia

Customs duties

Imports, according to customs rules, consist of the entry of goods to the 'national customs territory' from the rest of the world, or from an FTZ, with the purpose of remaining permanently or temporarily in it for the achievement of a specific purpose.

The importation processes before the Colombian Internal Revenue and Customs Service (DIAN) can only be carried out by users registered in the Customs Information System, either Customs Agencies (previously called Customs Intermediation Companies) or Permanent Customs Users (UAPs). The latter may file their own customs declarations, as long as the value of the imported goods exceeds the sum of 1,000 United States dollars (USD); otherwise, they must do it through the Customs Agencies.

According to the Harmonized System of Designation and Coding of Goods approved by the World Trade Organization (WTO), imported goods are classified into subentries composed of six digits. Also, two digits are added, which are for exclusive use of the Andean Community (CAN), and two final digits, which correspond to the digits for use of Colombia. The custom subentry, which is the ten-digit result, is exposed in the Colombian Customs Tariff, which is governed by Decree 4589 of 2006, which also reflects the applicable tariff of each duty. VAT, which is also part of the customs duties, is regulated in the Colombian Tax Code.

The general VAT rate for the importation of goods is 16% and the general rate for custom duties is 5%.

Excise taxes

There are some excise taxes for the consumption of beer and its derivates, wine, liquor and its derivates, and cigarettes and similar products.

The excise taxes are of municipal in nature. Therefore, the tax rates and applicable laws vary from one municipality to another.

Property tax

The property tax is a municipal tax that is imposed annually on real estate property located in urban, suburban, or rural areas. It is levied on both improved and unimproved real estate. Therefore, the taxpayers of this tax are the owners or holders of the real estate property.

The taxable base of this tax is the current cadastral value of the property, as adjusted for inflation. In some cities, such as Bogotá, the taxable base is the value of the property as appraised by the taxpayer directly.

Property tax rates depend upon the nature and usage of the property, and generally range between 0.4% and 1.2%.

This tax is fully deductible for CIT purposes, provided the same has a causal nexus with the income producing activity of the taxpayer (for example, where the tax is paid on rental property).

Stamp tax

The stamp tax rate was reduced to 0% for documents executed as of 1 January 2010.

Capital gains tax

The general capital gains tax rate is 33%.

Equity tax

The life of the former equity tax (2007 through 2010) was extended to 2011 for those taxpayers who held an amount of tax equity that was equal to or greater than COP 3 billion but less than COP 5 billion as of 1 January 2011, with the tax rate being 2.4% of the entire tax equity amount. Where the tax equity was equal to or greater than COP 5 billion, a 4.8% rate applied to the entire tax equity amount.

The 2011 equity tax is payable in eight equal instalments, starting in 2011 and ending in 2014. The 2011 equity tax is not deductible for CIT purposes and cannot be offset against any tax receivables. However, the law authorises taxpayers to charge this tax against the asset revaluation account, without affecting the income statement for the year.

The third and fourth instalments are to be paid in 2012.

Financial transactions tax

The financial transactions tax is a permanent tax on financial transactions, the collection of which is the responsibility of regulated financial institutions and the Central Bank (*Banco de la República*).

The tax rate is 0.4%, and the taxable event is the carrying out of financial transactions that involve the disposal of resources deposited in checking or savings accounts as well as in deposit accounts with *Banco de la República*, and the issuance of cashier's checks.

25% of the total tax paid is deductible for CIT purposes, regardless of whether or not the transactions have a causal nexus with the income producing activity of the taxpayer.

The law establishes a series of operations and transactions that are exempted from this tax.

The 2010 tax bill established that the financial transactions tax will be reduced to 0.2% for year 2014 and 2015, to 0.1% for years 2016 and 2017, and to 0% for year 2018 and onwards. Currently, 25% of this tax is deductible for CIT purposes; however, 50% of this tax will be deductible from 2013 onwards. Planning strategies such as payment to third parties using overdrafts, repos, buy/sell back transactions, or portfolio investments that did not trigger this tax, are not permitted.

Industry and trade tax

The industry and trade tax is a municipal tax that is imposed on revenue obtained from the exercise of industrial, commercial, or service activities in any Colombian municipal jurisdiction. It can be viewed as a special form of a turnover tax.

The industry and trade tax rates are determined by each municipality, and as a rule they range between 0.2% and 1%. All of this tax can be deducted for CIT purposes when effectively paid.

Branch income

Branch income is taxed at the same rate as corporate income, which is 33%. A 7% remittance tax on branch profits was eliminated in 2007 but still applies to retained profits incurred prior to 2007.

Colombia

Income determination

Inventory valuation
The value of inventories, which includes all expenses and direct and indirect charges necessary to put an item in a position to use or sell, must be determined using one of the following methods: first in first out (FIFO), last in first out (LIFO), specific identification, or weighted average. Special rules may authorise the use of other methods of recognised technical value.

Capital gains
Capital gains are taxed separately from income. *See Capital gains tax in the Other taxes section for more information.*

Dividend income
The so-called double income taxation on corporate earnings was eliminated from the Colombian tax system many years ago. This means that shareholders of Colombian companies are, as a rule, not required to pay any income taxes on dividend distributions, but only to the extent that dividends are paid out from earnings that were taxed at corporate level prior to distribution. When the dividends are paid out from earnings that went untaxed at the corporate level, a foreign shareholder is required to pay income taxes on the dividends at 33% via a withholding tax (WHT) collected by the distriburing company. Certain DTTs offer limited or full relief for the 33% CIT on dividends.

Interest income
Interest income derived from activities in Colombia is considered part of the CIT base for Colombian entities; however, if interest is paid to a non-resident that is not compelled to file CIT in Colombia, a WHT is accrued over the payment or deposit at a rate of 33%, if the loan term does not exceed of one year, or 14%, if the loan term does exceed of one year.

Note that there are some special conditions derived from DTTs that decrease the WHT rate.

Royalties
Royalties paid in favour of a Colombian entity are subject to taxes in Colombia; consequently, such royalty payments are part of the CIT base. If royalties are paid in favour of a non-resident (i.e. in favour of an entity that is not compelled to file CIT in Colombia), WHT is accrued over the payment or deposit at a rate of 33%.

Foreign income
The following cases, among others, qualify as foreign-source income:

- Income obtained from external debt, if it complies with some requirements provided by law. Interest produced by this external debt is not taxed via CIT, and there is no WHT liability. Additionally, the expense derived from this concept will be 100% deductible.
- Income derived from technical services of repair and maintenance of equipment carried out abroad.

There are no tax deferral provisions in Colombia.

Deductions

In Colombia, the customary costs and expenses of a business are generally acceptable as deductible expenditure for CIT purposes, provided they are necessary, reasonable, and have been realised during the relevant tax year under the accrual method of accounting. Examples of common (and not so common) deductions include the items below.

Depreciation
As a general rule, the acquisition cost of tangible fixed assets is fully depreciable for CIT purposes. The normal estimated useful lives are as follows:

Asset	Useful life (years)
Buildings and pipelines	20
Machinery and equipment, office furniture, and fixtures	10
Vehicles and computer equipment	5

The acceptable methods for the depreciation are:

- Straight-line: The straight-line method is the easiest and most commonly used method of depreciation by companies; it is calculated by dividing the value of the asset by the asset's useful life.
- Declining-balance: The reducing-balance method allows one to consider a certain depreciation percentage to depreciate the alignment machine rate annually. This method takes into consideration an accelerated rate of depreciation. This is useful for those assets in which a higher value is lost during the beginning years of usage.
- Any other method of recognised value in accordance with the opinion of the tax authorities.

Depreciation rates can be increased by 25% for each additional eight-hour shift of asset use (and pro rata for fractions thereof). When tax depreciation exceeds book depreciation, the taxpayer is required to establish a reserve equivalent to 70% of the difference. Recapture of depreciation on the sale of depreciated property is taxed at 33%.

Depletion
Depletion is available under certain specific circumstances.

Amortisation of intangible assets
Taxpayers can amortise, for CIT purposes, the cost of any acquired intangible asset over a period of five years, at a minimum, unless the taxpayer is able to prove that the amortisation period should be less because of the specific nature or conditions of the business.

Goodwill
Goodwill is deductible for CIT purposes, provided it is related to the business purpose or income producing activity. In order for such goodwill to be deductible, the intangible (goodwill) must fit the definition of an asset subject to be amortised. Amortisable investments are ones that, under the normal accounting rules, are subject to demerit and should be recorded as assets subject to be amortised in a period exceeding one year.

Goodwill cannot be amortised in a period of less than five years.

Colombia

Start-up expenses
Start-up expenses are deductible for CIT purposes, provided they are necessary, reasonable, and have been realised during the relevant tax year under the accrual method of accounting.

Interest expenses
Taxpayers are generally entitled to deduct any interest paid to financial institutions or to third parties.

Bad debt
Bad debt is deductible for CIT purposes, provided the company keeps it accounting books under the accrual method, the debt is originated as a result of the development of an income producing activity, and the following requirements are met:

- The debt is due for over a year.
- The company is able to prove that the debt has a nature of bad debt.
- The company has registered the provision, related to the bad debt, within the same fiscal period.
- The debt does exist at the moment of the registration of the provision.
- The company has included the debt in the calculation of its CIT of previous fiscal periods.

Charitable contributions
Some specific charitable contributions are allowed as deductions, provided they are made to certain institutions dedicated to development of health, education, culture, religion, sports, scientific and technological research, ecology and the protection of the environment, or to social development programs of general interest. Most of these charitable contributions are limited with respect to their deduction.

Expenses incurred abroad
As a general rule, the deduction of expenses incurred abroad that are not subject to WHT are limited to 15% of the taxpayer's net income.

Fines and penalties
Fines and penalties are not deductible for CIT purposes.

Taxes
It is important to mention that the current tax regulations state the following as the only taxes that can be claimed as a deductible expense:

- 100% of the industry and trade tax.
- 50% of the financial transactions tax.
- 100% of the property tax.
- The VAT that cannot be treated as output.
- Some local stamp taxes.

Special deductible items
Colombian income tax laws have established certain special deductible items, which include the following:

- 100% of the industry and trade tax and real property tax actual payments and 50% of the financial transactions tax actual payments are deductible.
- 100% of acquisition costs are available as a tax amortisation or depreciation base.

- 125% of the investments made in certain scientific and/or technological projects or in professional training projects of governmental, public, or private institutions of higher education are deductible. This deduction cannot exceed 20% of the taxpayer's net income as determined before subtracting the amount of the investment.
- 100% of the investments made for the control and improvement of the environment are deductible. This deduction cannot exceed 20% of the taxpayer's net income as determined before subtracting the amount of the investment.

Net operating losses

Net tax losses (adjusted for inflation) incurred in 2007 or thereafter may be carried forward without limitation. There is no loss carryback provision. Certain limitations apply to the offset of losses transferred on merger reorganisations.

Payments to foreign related parties

Royalties and similar charges

Royalties and the costs of exploitation or acquisition of all kinds of intangible property that are charged by foreign related parties are allowable as CIT deductions, provided that the corresponding WHT is collected at generally 33% (10% in the case of most DTTs). Other types of payments are subject to the general rules for expenses incurred abroad.

Management overhead expenses

Management overhead expenses paid to a foreign related party (e.g. the parent company) are deductible provided they meet the arm's-length test under transfer pricing regulations and provided the management services are real and are specifically related to the income producing activity of the local subsidiary that pays them. These expenses must also be carefully documented such that the local subsidiary can provide evidence to the authority of the fact that they are specifically related to its Colombian operations: to the planning and direction of the operations, the setting and implementation of management controls, the measurement of progress made toward specific business goals, the related financial results, etc. Where these services are supplied inside Colombia, a 33% WHT is also required to ensure deductibility.

Interest

Interest and related financial costs (including foreign exchange losses) paid to foreign related parties are deductible provided they meet the arm's-length test under transfer pricing regulations. Furthermore, interest and the related financial costs paid on short-term financing relating to imports of merchandise and raw materials directly supplied by foreign related parties are also deductible for CIT purposes. Interest paid to non-resident triggers WHT over the payment or deposit at a rate of 33%, if the loan term does not exceed of one year, or 14%, if the loan term does exceed of one year.

Financial and non-financial institutions registered with the Colombian Central Bank are permitted to extend loans into Colombia.

Group taxation

Group taxation or group consolidation is not allowed for CIT purposes in Colombia.

Transfer pricing

In Colombia, transfer pricing rules are applicable to the transactions performed by local taxpayers with foreign related parties. Thus, for CIT purposes, Colombian taxpayers

Colombia

must determine their income, costs, expenses, assets, and liabilities on the basis of prices and profit margins used in comparable transactions entered into with or between independent or unrelated parties.

In general terms, the rules related to comparability criteria, supporting documents, and advanced pricing agreements (APAs) follow international transfer pricing standards. However, they introduce a wide definition of 'related companies' for transfer pricing purposes, including subordination and individual or joint control exercised by a foreign parent company or by individuals located in Colombia or abroad.

The law presumes that transactions with foreign non-domiciled entities located in the so-called 'tax havens' are transactions performed with related parties and are subject to transfer pricing rules. However, the Colombian government has not yet issued the list of tax havens for these purposes, nor further regulations applicable to the payments made to such jurisdictions. Therefore, the Colombian tax rules related to tax havens are not yet applicable.

If (i) the gross equity (assets) of the local taxpayer on 31 December of each year is equal to, or higher than, the equivalent to TVU 100,000 (COP 2,604,900,000 or approximately USD 1,450,000) or (ii) the gross income obtained by the local taxpayer in a given year is equal to, or higher than, the equivalent to TVU 61,000 (COP 1,588,989,000 or approximately USD 883,000), it shall be required to prepare transfer pricing supporting documents (i.e. a transfer pricing study) and to file with the tax authority an informative return in connection with the transactions performed, during the corresponding year, with the foreign related parties.

If the local taxpayer does not file the supporting documents, it may be subject to fines equivalent to 1% of the total value of the transactions performed with related parties. This fine would not exceed the equivalent to TVU 39,000 (COP 1,015,911,000 or approximately USD 565,000).

Thin capitalisation
There are no thin capitalisation rules applicable in Colombia.

....

Tax credits and incentives

Foreign tax credit
Foreign income taxes are creditable, subject to certain limitations. Generally, the amount of the credit cannot exceed the Colombian CIT rate. DTT's provide for more comprehensive credit systems as well.

The foreign tax credit on dividend income is enhanced to include a third-tier of credit availability subject to specific ownership requirements. A third-tier of credit means that Colombian entities can claim a tax credit not only for taxes paid by a company in which it has a direct investment, but also for taxes paid by a company in which it has an indirect investment.

CIT exemptions
As items of exempt income, the law has established the following:

* Income obtained by publishing companies from the publication of scientific and cultural books, until year 2013.

- The principal and interest (as well as related commissions and fees) paid pursuant to public foreign debt operations.
- Income from the sale of electric power generated from wind, biomass, or agricultural waste, for a period of 15 years, provided the seller issues and negotiates Greenhouse Gas Reduction Certificates.
- Income obtained from slow yield crops and plantations, including cocoa, rubber, palm oil, citrus, and other fruits.
- Income obtained from river transportation services with shallow draft vessels and barges, for a period of 15 years, starting in 2003.
- Income obtained from hotel services offered in new hotels that are built within 15 years counted from 2003, for a term of 30 years, until 2032.
- Income obtained from hotel services offered in refurbished or enlarged hotel facilities, where the related work is started within 15 years counted from 2003, for a term of 30 years.
- Income obtained from ecotourism services, for 20 years starting in 2003.
- Income obtained from investment in new forestry plantations, sawmills, and plantations of timber-yielding trees.
- Income obtained from new medicinal and software products developed in Colombia and protected under new patents registered with the authorities, with a high content of national research and technology, until 2013.
- As of 2011, the gain in trading derivatives that are qualified as securities will not be subject to CIT, provided that the underlying asset is stock traded in the Colombian stock exchange, indexes, or participations in funds tracking such stock.

Special CIT rate for free trade zones (FTZs)
FTZ industrial users enjoy a special CIT rate. The so-called FTZ industrial goods users and industrial service users pay CIT at a reduced rate of 15% on income earned from their FTZ operations.

Note that capital gains are still taxed at the standard CIT rate of 33%.

Reduction to the statutory CIT rate for small companies
Small companies (not exceeding USD 1,575,000 in total assets or 50 employees) initiating activities after 1 January 2011 are subject to CIT at the following reduced rates: 0% of the statutory CIT rate for the first two years, 25% of the statutory CIT rate for the third year, 50% of the statutory CIT rate for the fourth year, and 75% of the statutory CIT rate for the fifth year.

Reduction of payroll fees for small companies
Small companies (not exceeding USD 1,575,000 in total assets or 50 employees) initiating activities after 1 January 2011 are subject to payroll fees at the following reduced rates: 0% of the payroll fees for the first two years, 25% of the payroll fees for the third year, 50% of the payroll fees for the fourth year, and 75% of the payroll fees for the fifth year.

Tax credit on payroll fees paid
A tax credit is granted to employers hiring employees under 28 years old; women above 40 years old that have not been legally employed in the previous year; low-income workers earning less than 1.5 times the minimum monthly wage (approximately USD 475); and disabled, reintegrated (from armed conflict), or displaced (as victims of armed conflict) workers, subject to certain requisites and time limitations (two to three years).

Colombia

Vallejo Plan for raw materials

The Vallejo Plan allows for the total or partial suspension of customs duties upon receipt, within the national customs territory, of specific goods destined to be totally or partially exported within a certain period of time, after having undergone transformation, manufacture, or repair, including the materials needed for these operations. Under the Vallejo Plan, machinery, equipment, and spare parts may also be imported, to be used partially or entirely in the production and sale of goods and services destined for export. The goods so imported remain under restrictions of sale.

Withholding taxes

The Colombian tax system provides for WHT as a general mechanism of advance tax collection. Under the law, as a general rule, all corporate entities are required to collect or withhold taxes from payments made to third parties. The WHT collection agents must collect the applicable WHT amounts, deposit the withheld amounts with the authority, file monthly WHT returns, and issue WHT certificates to the payees. The payees who are also CIT return filers credit the withheld taxes against the annual CIT liability computed on their returns.

As noted above, foreign non-resident persons are taxed on their Colombian-source income only. Generally, the full tax liability accruing on payments made to foreign non-resident persons is satisfied via the collection of the applicable WHT. The WHT rate on payments made to foreign non-resident persons for taxable dividends, royalties, and taxable interest is 33%. On payments made for consulting, technical assistance, and technical services, the WHT rate is 10% (whether supplied inside or outside Colombia). On payments made for software licences, the WHT rate is 26.4%.

On other types of payments that give rise to Colombian-source income, the general WHT rate is 14%, with the foreign non-resident payee being required to file a CIT return in Colombia to report the final CIT liability, at 33% of net income (and being entitled to a refund where the final liability is less than the amount withheld at the 14% rate or being required to pay the deficit should the case be the opposite).

As of 2011, WHT returns do not need to be filed where there are no taxes to declare or pay. An amnesty is granted for taxpayers who failed to file such returns in the past, such that they will not be subject to late failing penalties if making the delinquent filings within six months following the enactment of the law.

Offsetting of WHT

WHT returns filed on a non-payment basis will be treated as not filed, except if the filer has a refundable tax credit balance over USD 1,185,000 to offset the outstanding payment. A six-month deadline applies for the taxpayer to apply the offsetting of the credit balance. Otherwise, late filing penalties will apply.

Self-withholding on some exports

The tax reform granted an authorisation to the government to establish up to a 10% self-WHT on exports for the mining, oil, and gas industry. The self-withholding would be creditable against the CIT liability.

Exempt interest

As of 2011, the interest payments abroad on loans or cross-border leasing agreements, formerly not subject to WHT if the debtor's activities were deemed of interest for the economic and social development of the country, are now subject to a 14% WHT, if the loan term exceeds one year. If the loan or cross-border agreement has a term not exceeding one year, a 33% WHT is triggered.

A grandfather rule was provided for loans and leasing agreements executed before 31 December 2010.

Summary WHT chart

Type of payment	WHT rate (%)
Dividends	33
Taxable interest	14 or 33
Royalties	33
Royalties on software licences	26.4
Technical assistance, consulting, and technical services	10
Other types of payments	14

DTT rates

Recipient	Dividends (%)	Taxable interest (%)	Royalties (%)
Non-treaty	33	14/33	33
Treaty:			
Chile	0/7	0/15	0/10
Spain	0/5	0/10	0/10
Switzerland	0/15	0/10	0/10

Tax administration

Taxable period
For CIT purposes, the taxable period is the calendar year, with no exceptions being admissible.

Tax returns
Income tax return filing due dates are set by the government every year. Usually, they fall in the month of April; but in the case of large taxpayers, the filing due dates are usually in February.

Payment of tax
For CIT purposes, corporate taxpayers are divided into 'large taxpayers' and 'other taxpayers'. Large taxpayers pay their estimated outstanding CIT liability (outstanding after deducting applicable WHT from the estimated final liability) in five instalments over the year in which they file their annual CIT return. The due date varies according to the last digits of its NIT (Number of Tax Identification).

Other taxpayers pay their estimated outstanding CIT liability in two instalments over the year in which they file their annual CIT return. The due date varies according to the last digit of its NIT (Number of Tax Identification).

Please be aware that the final CIT due dates for fiscal year 2011 were between 11 April 2012 and 24 April 2012.

The specific CIT due dates for fiscal year 2012 will be determined by a Decree issued by the government at the end of 2012.

Colombia

Audit cycle
The audit cycle corresponds to the taxable period, which for the case of CIT is one year.

Statute of limitations
The statute of limitations is generally two years following the actual filing of the return (a longer or shorter statute of limitations applies in certain cases).

A method to reduce the statute of limitations was due to expire in 2010 but was rolled over into years 2011 and 2012. This benefit enables one to reduce the statute of limitations of a CIT return if the CIT liability increases by a given number of times inflation with respect to the former year. The ordinary two years statute of limitations may be reduced to: 18 months if the CIT liability increases by five times inflation, 12 months if the CIT liability increases by seven times inflation, and 6 months if the CIT liability increases by 12 times inflation.

Topics of focus for tax authorities
While there are no specific topics to be observed by the tax authorities when performing an audit, usually they look at the formal compliance requirements and the correct application and deductibility of cost and expenses.

Other issues

Choice of business entity
The most common type of company used in Colombia is the so-called simplified stock company or simplified corporation, known as a SAS (*sociedad por acciones simplificada*). Besides SAS, foreign investors also use branch offices of an offshore entity as their investment vehicles in Colombia.

As a general rule, from a high-level perspective, there are no mayor differences between a branch office and a subsidiary (such as a SAS), as far as Colombian taxation is concerned, other than the taxation regarding dividends or profits.

However, the following is a chart explaining the main differences between a branch and a subsidiary in Colombia.

Colombia

Tax	Subsidiary in Colombia	Branch of a foreign entity
CIT	Colombian companies are subject to CIT on their worldwide income at a rate of 33%. The CIT base applicable to Colombian companies is, as a general rule, the ordinary net taxable income determined by subtracting from the gross income of the corresponding taxpayer the cost and expenses allowed by the tax laws; however, Colombian law establishes a minimum taxable base called 'presumptive income' which is equivalent to 3% of the net equity (i.e. the result of subtracting the liabilities from assets) of the taxpayer on 31 December of the previous taxable year. The CIT of a taxpayer must be determined based on the presumptive income if the ordinary taxable income of the corresponding year, determined according to the ordinary or normal rules, is lower than the presumptive income. In addition, please bear in mind that related party liability is not allowed, except when a DTT applies.	Branches of foreign companies are taxed only on their Colombian-source income. The rate at which branches pay income taxes is the general CIT rate of 33%. The presumptive income rule applicable to Colombian companies is applicable to the branches of foreign entities as well.
Income tax on dividends or profits	Dividends received by foreign non-domiciled entities (which would be the case of the foreign shareholders of the local company) are not subject to income tax withholding, provided that such dividends correspond to profits subject to income tax at a corporate level. If such dividends correspond to profits that would have been subject to taxation if distributed to a Colombian resident (profits not taxed at the corporate level), they shall be subject to a 33% income tax withholding on the amount paid. In addition, please bear in mind that Colombia has DTTs with Spain and Chile that are currently in application. Under these treaties, the dividends or profits shall not be levied in Colombia or will be levied with a lower WHT rate. The taxes applicable to dividends received by foreign non-domiciled entities must be withheld on the basis of the total amounts distributed or accrued. Please be advised that foreign non-domiciled entities are not required to file income tax returns in Colombia if their entire income was subject to the withholdings provided in articles 407 to 411 of the Colombia Tax Code (which refer to dividends, among other concepts). Therefore, if the entire income obtained by the foreign shareholders of the local company corresponds to dividends remitted by the company, and the applicable withholdings are duly performed, they would not be required to file income tax returns for the relevant periods.	In the case of profits obtained through a branch, please note that such profits are not considered as dividends and Colombian law does not provide for an income or remittance tax applicable to the transfer of profits from a branch to its main office. Therefore, if the profit obtained by a branch is not subject to income tax in Colombia at the branch level, the profit may be remitted abroad to the home office without the payment of any additional tax in Colombia.

Colombia

Tax	Subsidiary in Colombia	Branch of a foreign entity
WHT	As a means to collect income taxes in advance, the Colombian law establishes a system of tax withholdings that requires every person making payments to a taxpayer to withhold a certain percentage depending on the concept being paid. For those who must file an income tax return, all amounts withheld are a prepayment of the final tax liability and, as such, are credited on their return. The withholding agent must file every month a WHT return. Please bear in mind that technical services, technical assistance services, and consultant services rendered by a foreign non-domiciled entity are subject to 10% income tax withholding, regardless of the place in which the service is rendered, in Colombia or abroad.	Applies exactly the same WHT described for a subsidiary as for the branch of a foreign entity.

In conclusion, as per Colombian law, there are no substantial differences between the fiscal treatment of a subsidiary or a branch, apart from the tax implications for the payment of dividends and territorial source of taxation.

All the taxes discussed in this summary would apply equally to a branch operation or a subsidiary operation. However, from a commercial perspective, and specifically from the perspective of corporate liability, operating through a branch office means that the head office is exposed to direct liability for all the obligations of the branch, tax obligations included. Operating through a subsidiary means that only the subsidiary is liable for its obligations as a general rule, that is to say that the shareholders are not liable for company obligations. Of corporations, the advisable choice would be a SAS, which is very flexible in nature, easy to incorporate, and can be held by one single shareholder (regular corporations require a minimum of five shareholders).

Congo, Democratic Republic of the

PwC contact

Emmanuel Le Bras
PricewaterhouseCoopers Tax & Legal
88 Avenue du Général de Gaulle
Pointe Noire, Republic of Congo
Tel: +242 05 534 09 07
Email: emmanuel.lebras@cg.pwc.com

Significant developments

On 25 August 2010, the Value Added Tax (VAT) Ordinance Law No 01-001 was promulgated in the Democratic Republic of the Congo (DRC) Official Gazette, indicating that the VAT would become effective within 18 months from its date of signature. Some implementing regulations were passed in November and December 2011 that confirm that VAT has become effective as of 1 January 2012. The standard rate of VAT is 16%, with a 0% rate on exports. VAT replaces ICA (sales tax) that was levied on supply of taxable goods and services manufactured or provided in the Democratic Republic of the Congo by a taxable person in the course or furtherance of a business carried out by that person, and on the importation of goods and services in the Democratic Republic of the Congo. A deduction mechanism existed under the ICA regime, but it was limited and exclusively applicable to industrial businesses.

Taxes on corporate income

Corporate income tax (CIT), known as *impôt sur les bénéfices et profits* (IBP) in the Democratic Republic of the Congo, is paid on profits realised by a company which carries out any operational activity in the country.

The Democratic Republic of the Congo taxes resident corporations on a territorial basis or source basis of taxation. Foreign-sourced profits (e.g. dividends received from a foreign subsidiary, for instance) are thus exempt from CIT.

Non-resident companies that carry out an activity in the Democratic Republic of the Congo are taxable on profits they realise through permanent establishments (PEs) or fixed establishments located in the Democratic Republic of the Congo.

The CIT rate is currently 40% (30% for mining companies).

Minimum income tax

There is a minimum tax of 0.1% of the yearly turnover. Note that the minimum tax cannot be less than 2,500 United States dollars (USD). Also note that turnover includes all profits and interest received, as well as exception profits, in essence any credits on the income statement that have the nature of income or gain.

Tax on rental income

Rental income related to buildings, houses, offices, premises, warehouses, etc. is taxed in the Democratic Republic of the Congo at the rate of 22%.

In order to secure the payment of this tax, the tax code has put into practice a withholding tax (WHT) system. The tenant is liable to withhold 20% of the rentals paid

Congo, Democratic Republic of the

and to remit this tax to the authority. The tax authority may challenge rentals that are not at arm's length by referring to similar houses rented.

Corporate residence

Permanent establishment (PE)

A non-resident company is deemed as having a PE in the Democratic Republic of the Congo in either of the following cases:

- It has a material place of business (e.g. head office, branch) or any other fixed or permanent installations producing revenues in the Democratic Republic of the Congo.
- Without having a material place of business, it carries out a professional activity under its own name during a period of at least six months, insofar as such an activity cannot be considered as a technical assistance rendered to a local company.

Other taxes

Value-added tax (VAT)

Mechanisms of VAT

An entrepreneur is entitled to offset VAT paid on purchase of goods and services used for business purposes against VAT charged on sales of goods and/or services. Businesses exempted from VAT on part of their sales are, in principle, entitled to deduct VAT paid either on a *pro rata* basis or by splitting their activity into taxable and exempted sections.

No VAT credit is allowed for expenditures not necessary for business purposes, nor on some specific expenditure (i.e. accommodation or entertainment for directors and employees, gifts, company cars).

VAT returns must be filed by the 15th day of each month in respect of transactions made the previous month. The net amount of VAT payable must be remitted to the tax authorities together with the return. If VAT paid exceeds VAT charged, the resulting VAT credit can be carried forward.

VAT rates

VAT is calculated on the net invoice price of the goods or services concerned, excluding the tax itself. For imports, VAT is normally charged on the customs value of the goods concerned, plus the customs duty and import-related expenses. There are two rates:

- A standard rate of 16%.
- A rate of 0% on exports and assimilated transactions.

VAT exemptions

The main exempted activities include some banking and financial services, education, medical services, charitable and social activities, and transactions that are subject to a specific taxation.

Application to non-residents

A non-resident having no PE in the Democratic Republic of the Congo must appoint a representative in the Democratic Republic of the Congo who will be responsible for

Congo, Democratic Republic of the

the non-resident's VAT payments and collections. If no representative is appointed, the authorities will require the DRC customer to pay VAT due.

Customs duties

Customs duty on imports
Customs duty on imports is calculated on the CFA franc value of the goods. The customs tariff on imports is the following:

Example of goods	Customs tariff rate (%)
Chemical products	
Machine tools	5
Material for transport of merchandise	
Flour	
Aggregate	10
Petrol, diesel, kerosene	
Clothing	
Furniture	20
Cigarettes	

Imported goods are also subject to the following levies at the time of border crossing:

- VAT on imports.
- For certain goods, consumption and excise duties.
- Various para-fiscal levies.

Customs regulation also allows for certain suspensive rates, such as temporary admission.

Customs duty on exports
Customs duty on exports applies to certain categories of products produced locally, which are:

- Green coffee.
- Electric current.
- Mineral products and their concentrates.
- Mineral oils.
- Logs.
- Scrap metal.

The bond value on exports of the said goods is fixed either by ministerial decree upon suggestion of the customs administration, or in the absence of a decree, by reference to the value of the goods when they leave the Democratic Republic of the Congo.

The rates of customs duties on exports are the following:

Example of goods	Customs duty rate (%)
Coffee	1.0
Electrical energy	
Diamond (small-scale mining)	1.5
Gold (small-scale mining)	

Congo, Democratic Republic of the

Example of goods	Customs duty rate (%)
Diamond (industrial mining)	3.0
Gold (industrial mining)	
Minerals (copper, nickel, lead, etc.)	5.0
Timber	6.0
Silver	10.0
Platinum	

Consumption and excise duties

Scope
The following goods are affected by consumption and excise duties:

- Alcohol and alcoholic drinks.
- Carbonated drinks.
- Mineral oils (petrol, oil, jet A1, diesel, etc.).
- Tobacco.
- Sugar.
- Hydraulic cement.
- Matches.
- Alcohol-based liquid perfume.

Reason for existence and tax base
The reason for the existence of consumption and excise duty is:

- the production in the Democratic Republic of the Congo of consumer goods subject to duty and
- the import of these products to the Democratic Republic of the Congo.

Consumption and excise duties accrue on imports, as well as customs duties and ICA.

On imports, the tax base on consumption and excise duties is the raised CFA franc value of the customs duties, except for mineral oils for which the tax base is the average fiscal threshold price.

Rates
The rates of consumption and excise duties vary from 5% to 40% according to the products concerned.

Para-fiscal taxes
Various para-fiscal taxes shall be received at the time of the import and/or export of goods in the Democratic Republic of the Congo.

The main applicable levies include the following:

- Administrative payment: 5% of the cost, insurance, and freight (CIF) value.
- Congolese Audit Office (OCC) payments: 1.5% of the CIF value, plus various other administrative charges (De Tally charge: 5 United States dollars (USD)/tonne; Laboratory and analysis charges: USD 30 maximum per test).
- *Office de Gestion du Fret Maritime* (OGEFREM) payment: 0.59% of the CIF value.
- Funds for the Promotion of Industry (FPI) charge: 2% of the CIF value.

Property tax (IF)

Scope
IF is applicable to constructions and land located in the Democratic Republic of the Congo.

Construction means villas, apartments, and other buildings.

The person owing this tax is the owner (bearer of title deed, holding, long leasehold, mining) of the construction on 1 January of the tax year.

The following are exempt from IF:

- The state, regions, towns, and public businesses disposing of no other resources than those coming from budgetary grants.
- Recognised religious, scientific, or philanthropic institutions.
- Private non-profit making organisations involved in religious, scientific, or philanthropic works and having obtained civil personality.
- Foreign states as far as embassy offices, consulates, or lodgings of diplomats or consuls are concerned (upon condition of reciprocity).

Certain constructions and land are, notwithstanding, exempt from IF, notably depending on the status of their owner. In this way, the following are exempt from the property tax on goods:

- Constructions and land allocated by the owner exclusively for agriculture or farming, including constructions serving to prepare agricultural or farming products, on the condition that at least 80% of these derive from the farming of the property owner concerned.
- Constructions and land allocated by the owner for non-profit purposes:
  - for the execution of a public service, teaching, scientific research, the setting up of hospitals, hospices, clinics, free clinics, or other similar charitable institutions
  - for chambers of commerce having obtained civil personality, or
  - for social activity of mutual companies and professional unions (syndicates) having obtained civil personality, with the exception of locales providing accommodation, a public house, or any business.

Tax determination
The tax rates vary according to the nature of the goods (villas, buildings of more than one floor, flats, and other buildings) and locality ranks.

For villas, rates are fixed per square metre of area (between USD 0.3 and 1.5), while for other taxable items the contribution is determined on an inclusive basis (by floor, by flat, by unused land - in Kinshasa, the rate for one floor is USD 75).

Transfer tax
The transfer of a building in the Democratic Republic of the Congo gives rise to the payment, by the purchaser, of a registration duty amounting to 3% of the building's value.

Stamp taxes
There are no stamp taxes in the Democratic Republic of the Congo.

Congo, Democratic Republic of the

Branch income

Tax rates on branch profits are the same as on corporate profits. However, the costs incurred abroad by the head office of the branch are not deductible in the Democratic Republic of the Congo, and the branch is liable for taxation of deemed distributed profits on top of the CIT. On profits realised, a branch will pay both the 40% CIT and a 20% tax based on 50% of the net profits after deduction of CIT.

Income determination

Taxable income consists of profits from any industrial, commercial, agricultural, or real estate operations entered into by the taxpayer in the Democratic Republic of the Congo, as well as any increases of assets invested as a result of such activities and any increases derived from capital gains either realised or not, of any nature and origin.

Inventory valuation
The following three inventory valuation methods are permitted under DRC law:

- Average cost of goods in stock at time of issuance, multiplied by the number of object or quantity output (i.e. weighted average cost method).
- Last in first out (LIFO).
- First in first out (FIFO).

Deductions

To arrive at taxable income, a taxpayer may deduct all costs actually incurred and which have served in the production of income of the company during the year.

Depreciation
Depreciation of fixed assets used in the company's operations may be deducted. Depreciation rates are as follows:

Nature of the good	Depreciation rate (%)
Buildings	2 to 5 (depending on the materials used)
Machinery and equipment	10
Vehicles	20 to 25 (depending on its use)
Fixtures, facilities	10

Item's nature	Useful lives adopted (years)
Building - general purpose or heavy equipment	20 to 25
Building - specific purpose	8
Computer equipment	3 to 5
Software	3 to 5
Motor vehicles	4 or 5
Furniture and fittings	8 or 10
Office equipment	10

C

Interest expenses
Interest costs on funds borrowed from third parties and invested in the company's operations are deductible.

Please note that if the borrower is a private limited company (*Société Privée à Responsabilité Limitée* or SPRL) and if the lender is one of its shareholders, the interest on loans paid are not deductible from the CIT basis.

Fines and penalties
Legal or administrative fines of any nature are not deductible.

Taxes
Income taxes are not deductible.

Other significant items
The following are examples of other expenses that may be deducted to arrive at taxable income:

- Rents actually paid and rental expenses linked to buildings or parts of buildings used in the exercise of the activity and any overheads derived from their maintenance, lighting, etc.
- Overheads costs, from maintenance of furniture and equipment used in connection with the company's activities.
- Wages, salaries, bonuses, and allowances of employees and workers used in the operation, as well as benefits in kind if these have been added to remunerations paid.
- Professional expenses directly related to the acquisition of income.

The following are examples of other expenses which may not be deducted to arrive at taxable income:

- Expenses of a personal nature, such as accommodation, school fees, leave indemnities, and any other expenses not necessarily incurred in the business.
- Expenses linked to rental properties as a landlord as well as related depreciation expenses.
- Any kind of provisions (e.g. for taxes, for bad debts).

Net operating losses
Tax losses can be carried forward for the next five years following the tax loss year; however, the losses must be deducted from the first year of tax profits of the company.

There is no carryback loss regime in the Democratic Republic of the Congo.

Payments to foreign affiliates
In respect of payments made by a local company to a foreign company for services (e.g. management services, technical assistance services), such expenses are deductible provided that:

- the services rendered can be clearly identified
- the services cannot be rendered by a local company, and
- the amount paid for the service is not overstated and is commensurate to the nature of the service itself.

Technical assistance/management services must be clearly formalised in an agreement, including the modalities of calculation of the corresponding fees payable.

Congo, Democratic Republic of the

Group taxation

There is no group taxation regime per the DRC tax legislation.

Transfer pricing

Transfer pricing rules are limited to the following provisions:

- Interests on loans are not considered as deductible expenses for the borrower, provided that it is an SPRL (private limited company) and that the lender is a shareholder.
- Where a local company is directly or indirectly controlled by a foreign company, any abnormal advantage given to the latter is considered as an indirect distribution of profits and is then added back to the profits of the local company.
- In respect of payments made by a local company to a foreign company, for services (management services, technical assistance services), the Tax Code provides that such expenses may be deductible if (i) the services rendered can be clearly identified, (ii) the services cannot be rendered by a local company, and (iii) the amount paid for the service is not overstated and is commensurate to the nature of the service itself.

Thin capitalisation

There are no thin capitalisation rules in the DRC tax legislation. However, mining companies are required to observe a capital-to-equity ratio of 75:25 (i.e. 3:1).

Tax credits and incentives

The Investments Code allows for a certain number of tax, customs, and general order measures designed to favour direct investments. The preferential tax treatment measures of the Investments Code apply to direct investments and/or to entities that carry them out.

The regime of the Investments Code does not apply to numerous sectors, notably:

- Mining and hydrocarbon.
- Banking and insurance.
- Trade.

In order to take advantage of the provisions of the Investments Code, the following conditions must be fulfilled by the investor:

- The investor must be a Congolese legal entity.
- The investment must be at least USD 200,000.
- The investing company must comply with the rules and regulations relating to environment.
- The investing company must undertake to train local personnel in technical and executive duties.
- The investing company must undertake to create an added value of 35% of its initial investment (within a stipulated time period to be agreed).

The application file is examined by the National Agency for the Promotion of Investments in the Democratic Republic of the Congo (ANAPI) and then sent to the Minister of Finance, who decides on the grant of the advantages foreseen in the Investments Code to the applicant, by the way of a Ministerial Order.

Congo, Democratic Republic of the

Tax holiday
The Investments Code grants appointed investors an exemption from CIT during the investment period, depending on the location of the investments: three years in Kinshasa, four years in Lubumbashi or Kolwezi, and five years in Katanga.

Withholding taxes

The following payments are subject to a WHT in the Democratic Republic of the Congo:

• Dividends paid by a local company to its shareholders.
• Royalties.
• Interest on funds borrowed for business purposes. Note that if the interest is paid to a local company, the WHT does not apply since the interest is included in the taxable income of the company charging such interest.

The Democratic Republic of the Congo has not entered into a double tax treaty with any other nation, so it is impossible to get any WHT reimbursed.

WHT rate and payments
The rate of WHT is 20%, which is based on the gross amount of sums paid.

If the payee does not withhold the tax from the amount invoiced and pays the tax of 20% directly, then the tax authorities consider that the basis of the 20% tax is composed of the amount invoiced plus the amount of the tax.

Consequently, in the case that the DRC company takes in charge the corresponding WHT, the WHT rate will be 25% (20/80) and the amount of tax will not be tax-deductible.

For royalties, the WHT is charged on the net amount of the royalties paid. The tax authorities consider that the net amount of royalties is calculated by deducting 30% from the royalties invoiced (i.e. the taxable basis will be 70% of the royalties invoiced).

Mining companies are, under certain conditions, exempt from WHT on interest paid and are subject to just a 10% WHT on dividends paid to their shareholders.

Tax administration

Taxable period
The taxable period is 1 January to 31 December.

Tax returns
The yearly CIT return is due by 31 March of the following year.

Payment of tax
Final payment of CIT is required when submitting the yearly tax return, which is due by 31 March of the following year.

CIT is payable in local currency through a DRC bank account by a wire transfer to the bank account of the Public Treasury. Consequently, in order to operate in the Democratic Republic of the Congo, the opening of a bank account in a DRC bank is

Congo, Democratic Republic of the

mandatory. Moreover, the tax authorities require the bank account number of the applicant in order to grant a taxpayer number.

The collection of CIT is on an instalment basis or by way of prepayments (depending on taxpayer type).

Instalments of corporate tax

Instalments, in respect of CIT, apply to taxpayers who come under the supervision of two specific kinds of tax departments: the Directorate General (DGE), the department of the tax authorities in charge of the most important taxpayers, and the *Centre des Impôts* (CDI), tax centres.

These taxpayers have to pay two instalments each representing 40% of the CIT paid during the previous fiscal year (including the amounts assessed by the tax authorities). This, therefore, totals 80% of the CIT actually paid in the previous year. The first instalment must be paid before 1 August, and the second instalment before 1 December. Both payments are offset against the final CIT due for the fiscal year. The balance is paid when the tax return is submitted.

Prepayments of corporate tax (Précompte BIC)

Prepayments of CIT are to be paid by taxpayers (excluding those under the supervision of DGE and the CDI) in respect of import and export activities by wholesalers and on the settlement of invoices relating to provisions of services or for building works.

Prepayments of CIT are withheld at source and collected by:

- the customs authorities, *L'Office des Douanes et Accises* (OFIDA), for imported and exported goods
- local manufacturers, wholesalers or semi-wholesalers, and beneficiaries for services rendered, and
- customers or contracting authority for building works on the settlement of the invoices.

Amounts withheld at source must be remitted monthly to the tax authorities and are creditable against the final CIT to be paid at the end of the fiscal year by the importer, exporter, service provider, etc.

The prepayment rate is 1%, which is based on the invoice value.

Audit cycle

In practice, there is a tax audit every year.

Statute of limitations

A company may get audited up to five years after submission of a tax return.

Topics of focus for tax authorities

The tax authorities shall discuss any relevant topic.

Congo, Republic of

PwC contact

Prosper Bizitou
PricewaterhouseCoopers Tax & Legal
88 Avenue du Général de Gaulle
Pointe Noire, Republic of Congo
Tel: +242 05 534 09 07
Email: prosper.bizitou@cg.pwc.com

Significant developments

Further to the promulgation of the 2012 Finance Act on 29 December 2011, the following new tax measures for companies have been introduced and are effective as of 1 January 2012.

- The corporate income tax (CIT) rate is now at 34% (previously 35%).
- The act constituting liability for the simplified tax regime for CIT purposes is now the execution of services or delivery of goods (previously the issuance of invoice).
- The request for deferment of the payment of the lump sum tax between the legal deadline and the end of the current month where the tax is due is now subject to the payment of a fine of 500,000 Central African CFA francs (XAF) (previously XAF 100,000 for a longer period).
- A fixed fee of XAF 1 million is now charged for the obligatory registration of every oil contract with foreign companies and their subcontractors before the execution of the contract (previously free of charge).
- Transfer pricing rules have been reinforced, and companies can now agree on a transfer pricing method with the tax administration before execution of this method.
- A new tax for pollution has been implemented at the rate of 0.2% on the annual turnover of hydrocarbon and mining companies in the production phase and not deductible for CIT purposes (its application is subject to a Tax Circular yet to be published).
- The withholding tax (WHT) for persons carrying out activities at the unitization zone is now at 5.75% (previous 7.7%).
- The deduction to be made on the taxation basis for real estate contributions of built-on property has been increased to 75% (previously 25%).
- The tax on rental value of commercial buildings has been reduced from 15% to 10%.
- All petroleum fittings are now subject to tax on rental value of commercial buildings at a fixed tax of XAF 5 million per exploration permit.
- Companies benefiting from special tax exemptions may now lose their tax exemptions in a financial year if they fail to file their summary financial statements.
- All tax claims are now subject to a prior deposit of 10% of the sum contested (previously 20%).
- The treatment of all tax litigation files are now subject to the payment of 5 per thousand of the sum contested (previously 2 per thousand).
- For purposes of incorporation of companies, the registration of all deeds is free of charge.
- All insurance policies carried out by oil, mining, and telephone companies are subject to registration free of charge; failure to register will result in penalties at the rate of 25%.
- Reduction of registration fee on lease of movables and immovables used for habitation or commercial purposes at the rate of 3% (previously 5%).
- Reduction of the registration fee on the transfer of rights in a lease from 15% to 10%.

Congo, Republic of

- 70% of the net profits made by branch offices and foreign companies carrying out business are automatically considered as distributed profits and subject to tax on dividends.
- No value-added tax (VAT) deduction of VAT resulting from a tax audit.
- Funds resulting from exportation activities not repatriated to Congo are now subject to tax on transfer of funds at the rate of 1%.
- Pre-existing laws have been codified. This relates to the tax regime of the code on state property, the mining code, forestry code, and hydrocarbons code.
- A unique tax on salaries has been implemented at the rate of 7.5% on the gross salary to replace the lump sum tax on salaries, apprenticeship tax, National Housing Fund contribution, and National Employment Office contribution.

Taxes on corporate income

Congolese registered companies are taxed on the territoriality principle. As a result, Congolese companies engaged in business outside of the Republic of Congo are not taxed in the Republic of Congo on the related profits.

In the absence of a tax treaty stating otherwise, a non-resident company is liable for CIT on income realised in the Republic of Congo or derived from or resulting from work/ services of any nature supplied or used in the Republic of Congo.

Corporate income tax (CIT) rates
The standard CIT rate in the Republic of Congo is 34%, with certain exceptions.

The minimum tax payable is 1% of the annual turnover and cannot be less than 1,524.49 euros (EUR) (EUR 762.25 if annual turnover is less than EUR 15,244.90).

A 2% minimum tax is payable by companies showing losses during two consecutive fiscal years. The 2% rate is applied to the sum of gross turnovers and products and benefits realised by the company in the most recent year in which it earned a profit. The 2% tax is not deductible for CIT purposes. However, in a company's first profit-making year after incurring the losses, half of the 2% tax is deductible.

A 20% WHT is imposed on income sourced in the Republic of Congo that is derived by foreign companies not necessarily engaged in activities in the Republic of Congo.

Industry specific rates
A CIT rate of 25% applies for:

- agricultural companies
- microfinance companies, and
- private schools organised as a company.

A CIT rate of 30% applies for:

- mining companies and
- real estate companies.

The minimum CIT rate for oil companies is 34%.

Congo, Republic of

A CIT rate of 35% is applied on a deemed profit equal to 22% of the total gross remuneration (i.e. an effective tax rate of 7.70% of the taxable turnover made in the Republic of Congo) derived from services rendered by:

* foreign companies that qualify for this simplified tax regime and
* local companies and branches that realise more than 70% of their annual turnover with oil companies and oil services companies (in this case, the deemed profit tax is regarded as an advance payment of CIT levied at the rate of 35% on net profits).

Note that these companies would revert to the general taxation regime the year after which the turnover realised with oil and gas sector companies became less than 70%.

Headquarters operations of foreign companies
The headquarters operations of foreign enterprises taxation regime is subject to prior approval by the tax authorities.

If enacted, headquarters operations of foreign enterprises and international groups will be granted a favourable tax status in the Republic of Congo. For those that qualify, CIT is charged on a deemed profit equivalent to a prescribed percentage of headquarters expenses. The percentage of which is currently unknown.

To qualify, the headquarters must be registered under the form of a public limited company or branch and must act solely for the benefit of the group in the area of management, control, or coordination.

Global flat taxation
The global flat tax is at 10%. It is calculated on the annual turnover of small and medium-size enterprises taxable under the flat rate regime, whose turnover does not exceed EUR 60,980.

Corporate residence

A company is considered resident in the Republic of Congo if it has its registered office or principal office for all its activities in the Republic of Congo.

Permanent establishment (PE)
There is no general definition for a PE. However, a PE has been defined by the double tax treaties (DTTs) signed between Congo and France, the Common Organisation for Africa and Madagascar (OCAM), and the Customs and Economic Union of Central Africa (UDEAC) to include a place of management, a branch, an office, a factory, a workshop, and a mine, oil or gas well, quarry, or other place of extraction of natural resources.

Other taxes

Value-added tax (VAT)
The Congolese VAT rate is 18%. In addition to VAT, there is a sales tax (surtax) calculated at the rate of 5%, applied to the amount of VAT, which must be invoiced and paid at the same time as the VAT. Therefore, the VAT rate is globally 18.9%. The surtax is not deductible (final cost).

Congo, Republic of

Under the provisions of the VAT law, all economic activities conducted in the Republic of Congo are subject to VAT, regardless of their purpose, profitability, or the legal status of the business performing them, and irrespective of whether these activities are habitual, occasional, or originate in the Republic of Congo or from a foreign country. Therefore, any person, natural or legal, engaged in an industrial, commercial, or professional activity is subject to VAT unless specifically exempt by law.

Section 8 of the VAT law states a service is considered as provided in the Republic of Congo when the service is used or exploited in the Republic of Congo.

In principle, an entrepreneur is entitled to credit the VAT paid on purchases of goods, equipment, and services for use in business (input VAT) against the total of the tax charges to one's customers for deliveries made and services rendered (output VAT).

Taxpayers not exclusively carrying out transactions giving rise to a VAT deduction shall deduct VAT proportionally on the portion of the income pertaining to taxable transactions and not a flat rate, as was previously the case.

VAT resulting from tax assessment is not deductible.

A VAT return must be filed on a monthly basis before the 15th day of every month.

Customs duties
When applicable, import duties are payable at rates ranging from 5% to 30% on the customs value of imported goods. Customs value is calculated on the cost, insurance, and freight level (CIF).

Customs duties rates

Group	Rates (%)
Basic necessities	5
Raw materials and capital goods	10
Intermediate and miscellaneous goods	20
Consumer goods	30

Additional entry taxes
Additional entry taxes apply on the importation of goods, such as:

- Economic and Monetary Community of Central Africa (CEMAC) integration tax: 1% on CIF value.
- Statistic tax: 0.20% on CIF value.
- Organisation for the Harmonisation of Business Law in Africa (OHADA) contribution: 0.05% on CIF value.
- Economic Community of Central African States (CEEAC) contribution: 0.04% on CIF value.

Computer royalty
The 2003 Finances Act instituted a 2% computer royalty, to cover expenses incurred by the Customs Administration on computer data processing, applicable without exception or exemption to all importation and exportation of goods. The royalty applies on the customs taxable value of any imported or exported goods in the Republic of Congo.

Congo, Republic of

Excise taxes

Excise duties on locally made products are at the rate of 10% while imported goods are subject to excise duty at the rate of 25%.

Land tax on built properties

Land tax is payable annually on built properties and is due from the owner. However, properties built for the purpose of accommodation are exempt for ten years, and properties built for business purposes are exempt for five years. The effective rate is determined every year by the local council.

The land tax is levied on the rental value after a deduction of 75% (decline, maintenance, and repair expenses) for properties built for business purposes. The land tax is levied on the cadastral value after a deduction of 75% (decline, maintenance, and repair expenses) for properties built for accommodation purposes.

Land tax on non-built properties

Land tax is payable annually on non-built properties and is due from the owner. However, properties intended for plantations and breeding are temporarily exempt for a three to ten year range. The effective rate is determined every year by the local council.

The land tax is levied on 50% of the cadastral value, determined every year by the Ministry of Finances. The land tax is arbitrarily assessed by hectares in rural areas according to the nature of the plantations.

Rent tax

Rent tax is payable annually on the rental of built property. It also applies on non-built property for business purposes. The rent tax is imposed on the occupant of the premises (whether the occupant is the owner, a tenant, or a subtenant).

The rent tax, which is equal to one-twelfth of the rents due within a year, is due annually on or before 28 February. For new lease agreements, the rent tax is due within three months of the effective date of the lease agreement and is calculated as a proportion of the rents due until the end of the year.

The rent tax is paid by the tenant on behalf of the owner, or by the subtenant on behalf of the tenant. The tenant/subtenant has the legal obligation to pay this tax on behalf of the lessor. Tenant and subtenants make a once-a-year deduction between 1 January and 30 April of the same year from all the rents due to the owner.

A 50% fine, assessed on the amount of the tax, is due for any late payment of the rent tax.

Registration fees and stamp duties

Lease agreement registration fees amount to 3% of the value of the annual rent paid during the tax year, including premises charges if any. 'Additional centimes' also apply at a 5% rate of the registration fees. Stamp duties and registration fees should be paid for the total duration of the lease agreement. In the case where the lease agreement is renewed, stamp duties and registration fees should be paid for the renewable period.

Stamp duty ranges from XAF 200 to XAF 20,000 on certain documents.

Examples of documents that are subject to stamp duty include:

Congo, Republic of

- Letters of agreement and other letters, which are prepared for use as evidence of act, fact, or condition of civil nature.
- Notarial deeds and their copies.
- Visas and flight tickets.

The following fees for the registration of contracts are due within three months from date of signature:

- Private commercial contracts (as opposed to public commercial contracts) at the rate of 1% on the estimated amount of the transaction.
- Purchase orders for public contracts at the rate of 2% for contracts with a value exceeding EUR 15,240.
- Subcontracts in building construction and public work sector at a fixed fee of EUR 155.44.
- Insurance contracts are registered free of charge.

Insurance contracts shall be registered and tax on insurance paid on the 15th day of the month following the insurance subscription.

Transfer of company shares are subject to a 5% registration fee.

Oil and gas
Specific rules and caps apply for the upstream (production) oil and gas industry.

Tax on pollution
The tax on pollution is payable by petroleum and mining extracting companies in the production phase, at the rate of 0.2% on the annual turnover.

This tax constitutes a non-deductible expense for the extracting mining/hydrocarbon company in the production phase.

This tax is due in the course of the year and payable quarterly by instalment, proportionally to the production realised during the just ended quarter and not later than the 20th day of the month following the end of the quarter.

Business tax and accessory taxes
The business tax ('*patente*', in French) is a tax collected by local communities. This tax, paid during the first three months of every year, includes both a fixed and variable fee depending on the specifications of the profession. The principal amount of the tax is increased with 'additional centimes', 'communal centimes', and 'contributions to the National Investment Fund' (accessory taxes).

Business tax is paid by traders and professionals. It is imposed on most commercial, industrial, and professional enterprises (including branches of foreign enterprises), although some traders are exempt. The business tax is charged on the actual or deemed annual rental value of the tangible assets of the enterprise, on the power of the machines, and on the average number of employees.

Any new taxpayer undertaking an activity requiring a trading licence must declare it in writing to the tax administration within 15 days following the start of the business. For the first tax year, the business tax is paid based on the date on which the business started (i.e. the tax is due from the first day of the quarter during which the business started).

Oil sub-contracting companies are now subject to business tax and accessory taxes under a specific nomenclature. The business tax and accessory taxes are made up of a fixed tax of EUR 422.89 and variable taxes of EUR 1.83 and EUR 3.05 following the power of the equipment and the number of employees.

Tax on company-owned cars
The tax on company-owned cars applies to the previous fiscal year company-owned cars and is due on 1 March at the latest.

With the exception of estate cars, private cars of companies falling into the category of own use cars for the issuance of vehicle registration documents are subject to tax.

The tax rates vary from EUR 304.89 for engine ratings not over 9 horsepower, to EUR 762.24 for the rest.

Cars registered more than ten years ago are exempt from tax.

Branch income

Tax rates on branch profits are the same as for domestic corporations. No tax is withheld on transfers of profits to the head office.

Income determination

Taxable income is based on financial statements prepared according standard statements of the OHADA treaty.

Business expenses are generally deductible, unless specifically excluded by law.

Inventory valuation
Stocks are valued at cost price. However, if the market price is lower than the cost price, the undertaking shall make provisions for depreciation of inventory.

Capital gains
Capital gains are treated as ordinary business income and are taxed at the standard CIT rate of 34%. However, a capital gain realised on the disposal of a fixed asset in the course of trading is excluded from income for a period of three years if the taxpayer reinvests the gain in new fixed assets for the business.

If the business is totally or partially transferred or discontinued, only half of the net capital gain is taxed if the event occurs less than five years after the start-up or purchase of the business and only one-third of the gain is taxed if the event occurs five years or more after the business is started or purchased. However, the total gain is taxed if the business is not carried-on in any form.

Dividend income
Dividends are treated as ordinary business income and are taxed at the standard CIT rate of 34% for resident corporations.

After three years, profits credited to the non-compulsory reserve are considered to be dividends and are accordingly subject to the 20% WHT on dividends.

Congo, Republic of

Inter-company dividends

Dividends received from a Congolese company (DivCo) by a commercial company incorporated in the Republic of Congo (HoldCo) are exempt from CIT and subject to a final 20% WHT if the following conditions are met:

- HoldCo and DivCo are incorporated in the CEMAC.
- HoldCo holds 25% of the capital of DivCo.
- HoldCo holds the shares for at least two years from the date of purchase.

However, 10% of dividends that are deemed to represent the share of cost and expenses are included in the taxable profits of HoldCo and liable for the CIT.

If the above conditions are not met, dividends received from a Congolese company by another Congolese company are subject to a 20% WHT, which is an advance payment of the recipient's CIT.

Deductions

Generally, a deduction is allowed for all expenditures incurred to obtain, collect, and maintain business profits. To be deductible, expenses should be incurred necessarily for the normal purposes of the business and be supported by suitable evidence.

Depreciation and depletion

In general, all types of fixed assets, except land, are depreciable for tax purposes as long as they can be shown to have been acquired for business purposes of the corporation. Depreciation must be calculated on the original purchase price. The straight-line method is used, and the Congolese General Tax Code sets forth maximum rates of depreciation. Goods costing less than EUR 152.44 per item may be written-off at purchase as expenses.

Depreciation recorded when the company is in a loss position may be carried forward without limitation and deducted from the first available taxable profits, provided it was appropriately disclosed in the annual CIT return.

Recoverable and identifiable packaging are regarded as fixed assets. They are recorded in a fixed asset account at the time of purchase. This packaging is regarded as returnable packaging when the supplier intends to act as the sole owner of the packaging.

Unrecoverable packaging is recorded as an expense and is deductible for tax purposes.

Exceptional accelerated depreciation may be authorised in certain circumstances for heavy equipment with a value of more than EUR 60,979.60. This special accelerated depreciation does not apply to private vehicles owned by the enterprises.

The following list contains maximum rates of depreciation as set forth in the General Tax Code:

Assets	Rates per year (%)
Construction	5 to 20

Assets	Rates per year (%)
Fixed devices and equipment	5 to 25
Movable equipment	10 to 100
Transport materials	5 to 33.33
Furniture, fittings, and other equipment	10 to 33.33
Fishing equipment	10 to 20
Hotels, bars, and restaurants	10 to 50
Plastic equipment (moulding)	10 to 33.33
Equipments subject to chemical action	20

Exceptional depreciation method

The exceptional depreciation method is an accelerated depreciation method.

Companies may elect the accelerated depreciation method for heavy materials and equipments that:

- are purchased new for a value higher than EUR 60,979.60
- have a useful life of at least three years
- are used for manufacturing, processing, transport, and handling, and
- are bound to an intensive use.

The application for the accelerated depreciation must be submitted to the head office of taxes within three months of the purchase of the assets to be depreciated. The option is granted upon approval of the ministry in charge of finances. If the administration fails to respond to the application for accelerated depreciation within three months, the application is tacitly granted.

Under the exceptional depreciation method, a 40% deduction may be taken in the year of acquisition of the previously mentioned assets, increased with the normal rate calculated on the residual value after application of the accelerated depreciation. These assets are depreciated on a straight-line basis thereafter.

Start-up expenses

There is no specific provision in the Congolese General Tax Code on the deduction of start-up expenses. Start-up expenses that occurred in the first year of incorporation (N) are deductible in the second year of operation (N+1).

According to the OHADA Uniform Act relating to Accounting Systems and Accountancy, start-up expenses can be amortised either in one year (in such case, they are booked in the deductible expenses during the first fiscal year) or in two years (50% during the first fiscal year and 50% during the second fiscal year).

Interest expenses

Interests are deductible subject to the following conditions:

- General limit: Regardless of the form under which a legal entity is registered, the deduction is allowed with an interest rate limited to the rate of the advances in current accounts on states funds of the Bank of the States of Central Africa (BEAC) raised by two points. Currently, the ceiling for the deduction of interests is 7.25%.
- For private limited companies and public limited companies, the deduction is allowed according to the status of control over the management of the enterprise, as follows:

Congo, Republic of

- For shareholders who have control over the company *de facto* or *de jure*, the deduction is allowed only to the extent that the sums paid do not exceed, for the shareholders as a whole, half of the paid-up capital and are within the limit sets forth in the 'general limit'.
- For other shareholders, the 'general limit' applies.

Charitable contributions

The maximum amount of deductible donations is limited to 0.5 per thousand of the net turnover when these charitable contributions are made to beneficiaries situated in Congo and are justifiable.

Fines and penalties

Penalties relating to violation of regulations are not deductible.

Taxes

Taxes, other than income taxes, are usually deductible. Examples of deductible taxes include customs duties, excise duties, payroll taxes, business tax and accessory taxes, registration taxes, and unrecoverable VAT.

CIT itself is not deductible, nor is the special tax on company-owned cars.

Taxes withheld on remuneration, paid to third parties (third parties taxes), and remitted to the tax office by a Congolese enterprise are not deductible.

Net operating losses

For tax purposes, losses may be carried forward to offset profits earned in the three succeeding fiscal years. Carry back losses are not permissible.

As mentioned above, depreciation recorded when the company is in a loss position may be carried forward without limitation.

Payments to foreign affiliates

Allowable deductions include sums paid abroad to foreign companies for:

- actual services, notably overhead for the operations made for the benefit of a company based in the Republic of Congo, including costs of studies; technical, financial, and accounting assistance; commissions and fees; and interests, and
- use of patents, licences, trademarks, drawings, manufacturing processes, patterns, and similar rights to the extent the payer proves they correspond to actual operations, and they are neither abnormal nor excessive.

Subject to the provisions of tax treaties (France, CEMAC, OCAM), the deduction is allowed within a limit of 20% of taxable profits before deduction of the expenses in question.

In the event of losses, the rate is applied on the results of the last profit period, which is not statutory limited. In the absence of profits during the period out of statutory limitation, the sums paid are not allowed as tax deductions.

When the sums are not allowed, as a whole or in part, in the deductible expenses, they are deemed to be paid benefits and are subject to tax on the dividends at the rate of 20%.

Royalties for the transfer or concession of patents, trademarks, drawings, and other similar titles are deductible to the extent the payer proves they are still valid. When these royalties benefit an enterprise contributing in the management or share capital of an enterprise in the Republic of Congo, they are deemed to be paid benefits and are subject to tax on the dividends at the rate of 20%.

Commission or brokerages, relating to goods purchased on behalf of enterprises based in Congo, are allowable tax deductions up to 5% of the purchase amount made by the central purchasing office, the head office, or the intermediaries. The reductions shall benefit enterprises based in the Republic of Congo. An original supplier's invoice must be attached to the intermediary's invoice.

The payer shall prove that:

- the purchases necessitated the interventions of a broker or intermediary
- the commissions provided better supply conditions compared with the actual situations on the market, and
- the commissions are not excessive compared with the nature of the services.

Group taxation

There is specific group taxation within the CEMAC area.

Where a joint stock company and a private limited company own either registered stock in a joint stock company or shares in a private limited company, the net proceeds of the share in the second company paid to the first during the financial year shall be deducted from the total net profit of the latter, less a percentage for costs and charges. This percentage is fixed at 10% of the total amount of the proceeds. This system shall apply when all of all the following conditions are met:

- The stocks or shares owned by the parent company represent at least 25%of the capital of the subsidiary company.
- The parent company and subsidiary companies have registered office in the CEMAC state (Cameroon, Central Africa Republic, Chad, Gabon, Equatorial Guinea, and Republic of Congo).
- The stocks or shares allotted at the time of issue are still registered in the name of the participating company, which undertakes to retain them for at least two consecutive years in registered form.

Transfer pricing
For companies under the control, *de facto* or *de jure*, of companies or groups situated outside the Republic of Congo, payments made by whatever means are considered as transfer of profits and subject to CIT and tax on income from securities if the transfer includes:

- Increase in the purchase price or decrease in the sale price.
- Payment of excessive royalty or without a consideration.
- Loans without interest or at an unjustifiable rate.
- Reduction of debts.
- Benefits that are out of proportion in relation to the service rendered.

Thin capitalisation
There are no specific thin capitalisation rules in the Republic of Congo.

Congo, Republic of

....

Tax credits and incentives

The current investment regime in the Republic of Congo was set out by Law No. 6-2003 of 18 January 2003, which established the investment charter. The charter's application, Decree No. 2004-30 of 18 February 2004 established modes of business registration.

- Scope: The following may be registered under the investment charter:
  - Businesses wishing to pursue an activity in the Republic of Congo, except for activities such as brokerage, trade, import and production of arms, and import or processing of toxic waste and by products.
  - Under certain conditions, commercial activities linked to collection, storage, distribution, and export of locally produced products, except alcoholic beverages and tobacco.
  - New activities (as opposed to pre-existing activities).
  - Forestry businesses benefiting from a forestry permit called the forestry development unit.
  - New companies coming from the redemption of a registered company.
- Conditions of eligibility for the investment charter: To be eligible, a company must satisfy the following conditions:
  - Be registered with the Trade and Personal Credit Registry in the Republic of Congo.
  - Create permanent employment, to be carried out over a minimum of 280 days per year.
  - Maintain company share capital equal to or greater than 20% of investments.
  - Primarily use local principal materials necessary for the production of the finished or semi-finished product, when available, with equal conditions concerning price, quality, and time of delivery to outside, in the case of industry.
  - Primarily use local business services, when available, with equal conditions concerning quality, price, and time of realisation regarding payments to external businesses, for the case of service businesses.
  - Be registered at the Congolese National Welfare Fund.
  - Open an account at a local bank or any other financial, savings, or credit establishment.
  - Primarily use a local workforce, when available, with the same expertise as the foreign workforce.
- Registration procedure: Entitlement to the benefits prescribed by the charter is subject to obtaining a registration agreement, provided by the National Investment Commission.
- Fiscal and customs benefits set out by the Investment Charter: These benefits vary according to privileged regimes, motivation measures, and in a general manner.

Privileged regimes
The charter sets out three privileged regimes:

- General regime (G).
- Special regime (S).
- Preferential development zone regime.

General regime (G)
The general regime applies to businesses that fulfil the aforementioned general requirements, and carry out investments greater than or equal to EUR 152,450.

Special advantages are conferred according to the period of activity of the registered business.

During the set-up period and the first three exploitation tax years, the company receives several benefits, as follows:

- In customs matters, the company benefits from the provisions of the CEMAC customs code relative to asset improvement mechanisms for export activity and from the suspension of customs duty in the form of temporary admission or franchise for natural resource research activities.
- In fiscal matters, the company benefits from the 50% reduction of registration fees for business foundation, increases in capital, company mergers, and transfer of company stocks and shares.

For the three first exploitation tax years and until the first year of sale or first service, the following fiscal benefits are added with the aforementioned reduction of registration duties:

- Total exemption from the tax on company earnings.
  - Companies that are subject to CIT because of their size or activity will be exempt from CIT.
  - Businesses that are subject to personal income tax because of their size or activity will be exempt from personal income tax.
- The authorisation to proceed to accelerated depreciation.
- The authorisation to carry forward losses for the first three tax years.
- The application of zero-rate VAT on exported products.

Special regime (S)
The special regime applies to businesses that fulfil the aforementioned general requirements and carry out investments between EUR 45,734 and EUR 152,450.

In addition to the advantages of the aforementioned (G) regime, businesses registered under the (S) regime benefit during the set-up period and the first three exploitation tax years from the moderation of registration duties for the incorporation of the business, increases in capital, company mergers, and transfer of company stocks and shares.

This moderation of registration duties is granted exclusively by decree of the Minister in charge of the Economy and Finances upon a decision of the National Investment Commission.

Preferential development zone regime
All exporting businesses registered under the investment charter are eligible for the preferential development zone system, including free-trade zones.

The institution, organisation, and function of the preferential development zone are fixed by a specific text.

Incentives to set up in remote areas
All new businesses registered under (G) or (S) regimes, which are located in a remote area, benefit from a reduction of 50% on the tax on company earnings in the fourth and fifth year following the first three tax years for which the business benefited from total exemption from the tax on earnings or personal income tax.

Congo, Republic of

The business is considered as belonging to a remote area from the moment its production units are set-up and 90% of the production unit workforce is working in the remote location.

The appraisal of a zone's location results from the exclusive competency of the National Investment Commission.

Incentives for social and cultural investment

All new businesses registered under (G) or (S) regimes, carrying out investments of a social and cultural character, may benefit from a fiscal reduction by ministerial decree of the Minister in charge of Finance and the Economy, upon the decision of the National Investment Commission.

These benefits may not, however, be added to those mentioned above and allocated to remote areas, even if the business concerned is set-up in such a location.

General measures

For the duration of the privileged regime, and subject to current texts, the company shall enjoy fiscal stability in terms of local and state taxes.

Privileged regimes (G) and (S) are allocated only once and are not renewable. The business may receive fiscal and customs advantages pertaining to the set-up period.

Fiscal advantages concerning the exploitation period are applicable only after the set-up period.

The end of the set-up period is certified by decision of the Minister in charge of Economy and Finance after the adoption of the verification report by the National Investment Commission.

Respect of the aforementioned general requirements set out by the charter is a prerequisite for benefiting from these motivation measures.

Export incentives

This measure is reserved for businesses that export at least 20% of their production.

The benefits are as follows:

- The provisions of the CEMAC customs code, relating to asset improvement mechanisms.
- Exemption from customs duties and taxes on manufactured products, except computing fees and statistic tax.
- Application of a zero-rate VAT on exported products.

Non-manufactured goods remain subject to the common law export system.

Incentive to reinvest earnings

This measure is reserved for businesses that carry out new investments of at least one-third of existing assets.

The benefit conferred consists of a 50% reduction of the tax on company earnings for the three years following the realisation of the investment.

Notwithstanding, this benefit is granted upon the following conditions:

- The business declares to the permanent secretary of the National Investment Commission its investments, planned investment, and the state of existing capital assets.
- The National Investment Commission, on the report of checking teams, verifies if the new investments correspond to one-third of the preceding capital assets.
- All investments are realised within one year.
- Investments generate new employment.
- Investments increase capacity of production by at least 10%.
- The business has sound ethical concerns.

Withholding taxes

Services, dividends, and attendance fees

Services
The tax regime set forth for foreign suppliers is defined in Section 185 of the Congolese General Tax Code. According to the provisions of Section 185, as well as the wide interpretation made by the Congolese Tax Authorities, the services rendered by the foreign suppliers should be subject to a 20% WHT.

In addition, Section 185 provides that companies which have no tax residence in the Republic of Congo are subject to a 20% WHT if they earn revenues realised in the Republic of Congo or coming from the Republic of Congo, and which come from works or services of any nature performed or used in the Republic of Congo.

The provisions of the Section 185 do not apply to resident suppliers of a country that has signed an international tax treaty with the Republic of Congo, provided certain conditions are met.

Dividends
Dividends distributed by a Congolese company are subject to a 20% WHT unless a different rate applies under an international tax treaty (e.g. France, CEMAC, OCAM). The same rate applies for dividends distributed to a resident shareholder.

Under the tax treaty between France and Congo, the applicable WHT rate is 15%. There is no specific rate defined in the CEMAC and OCAM tax treaties.

Attendance fees
Attendance fees are subject to a 22% WHT unless a different rate applies under an international tax treaty (e.g. France, CEMAC, OCAM).

Payments to local independent contractors
Payments to local independent contractors (self-employed contractors, i.e. those not registered with the Congolese Trade Registry) are subject to a WHT at the rate of 5% from such payments, to be remitted to the Public Treasury.

Late remittance of the WHT is subject to a late payment penalty of 50% within the first two months and 100% if the late payment exceeds two months.

Congo, Republic of

WHT rates summary

Recipient	Dividends (%)	Interest (%)	Royalties (%)
Resident corporations	20	0	0
Resident individuals	20	0	0
Non-resident corporations and individuals (Non-treaty)	20	20	20
Treaty with:			
France	15	0	15
OCAM	0	0	0
CEMAC	0	0	0

Tax treaties

The Republic of Congo is a member of CEMAC, which unites the following six states: Cameroon, Central African Republic, Republic of Congo, Gabon, Equatorial Guinea, and Chad.

The Republic of Congo has signed the following tax treaties.

The tax treaty of the Common Organisation for Africa and Madagascar (OCAM)

The member states of this organisation adopted a tax cooperation agreement 29 January 1971, which was ratified by the Republic of Congo on 3 September 1971. The OCAM, which initially had 14 members, had 17 members when it was dissolved by the Conference of Heads of State in 1985. Those members were Cameroon, Central African Republic, Chad, Congo, Ivory Coast, Dahomey, Gabon, High Volta, Madagascar, Mauritius, Niger, Rwanda, Senegal, Togo, and the Democratic Republic of Congo. The Republic of Congo has not denounced the application of this tax treaty.

The tax treaty of the CEMAC Convention

The Republic of Congo signed the UDEAC Convention of 13 December 1966, which was designed to avoid or to limit double taxation among the member states: Cameroon, Central African Republic, Congo, Gabon, Equatorial Guinea and Chad. This tax treaty remains significant to companies interested in affiliate creation in Central Africa countries.

The tax treaty between the Republic of Congo and the French Republic

This tax treaty, which concluded on 27 November 1987, was designed to avoid double taxation and to prevent tax evasion related to income tax, inheritance tax, registration law, and stamp duty.

Tax administration

Taxable period

The taxable period is the calendar year.

Tax returns

Taxable business profits are computed on the basis of normal accounting principles as modified by certain tax adjustments.

The annual CIT return is a specific form (*Document Statistique et Fiscal* or DSF) which should be prepared in accordance with OHADA accounting principles. The form cannot be completed electronically.

The books must be maintained in French and in XAF. This accounting system must follow the OHADA chart of account. All entries have to be booked under OHADA standard throughout the year.

The annual CIT return must be filed within four months following the end of the fiscal year of the company (i.e. before 30 April).

Payment of tax

Resident companies are required to pay quarterly instalments of tax (15 February, 15 May, 15 August, and 15 November), and these quarterly instalments are generally calculated with reference to the most recent CIT return. Special calculations of instalments apply to new taxpayers.

Based on the self-assessment system, when submitting annual tax returns due by 30 April every year, taxpayers must pay the amount of tax calculated in the annual tax return to the extent this amount exceeds tax instalments paid during the year.

Non-resident companies and individuals shall appoint tax representatives in the Republic of Congo. The Congolese resident shall be considered as tax representative if the non-resident person fails to appoint a tax representative.

Statute of limitations

Generally, the statute of limitations period for CIT is four years following the year in which the tax was due. However, this rule does not apply in the case of fraudulent acts reported by the tax administration.

Costa Rica

PwC contact

Ramon Ortega
PricewaterhouseCoopers
Scotiabank Building
3rd floor
Santo Domingo
Dominican Republic
Tel: +1 809 567 7741
Email: ramon.ortega@do.pwc.com

Significant developments

In December 2011, a law was published that enforced a new registration tax on every corporation/company that is registered in the Costa Rican Mercantile Registry and every new corporation that is formed after the creation of this law. *See Registration tax in the Other taxes section for more information.*

Taxes on corporate income

The Costa Rican tax system is based on the principle of territoriality, according to which all incomes earned by the taxpayer in virtue of lucrative activities carried out in the national territory, as well as those produced from the use of assets, goods, or rights used or invested in the country and those arising from civil, commercial, banking, financial, industrial, agricultural, forestry, fishing, mining or other exploitations of natural deposits, those originating in the rendering of public services, the exercise of professions, offices, arts, and all sorts of remunerated labour, the rendering of personal services, or the performance of functions of any kind, carried out or negotiated within the territory of Costa Rica, will be considered to be Costa Rican-source income and subject to Costa Rican income tax.

Under the Costa Rican income tax law, income from transactions carried out abroad may be regarded as non-Costa Rican-source income and is not subject to income taxes.

In addition, it is important to bear in mind that Costa Rican income tax applies specifically to those incomes that directly originate in the lucrative activities carried out by the taxpayer within the country's territory.

Corporate income is taxed at a 30% rate. However, the law establishes special regulations for small companies whose gross income does not exceed 91,573,000 Costa Rican colones (CRC). For this category, the following rates apply:

* 10% for companies with gross income up to CRC 45,525,000.
* 20% for companies with gross income of more than CRC 45,525,000, but not more than CRC 91,573,000.
* 30% for companies with gross income over CRC 91,573,000.

Please note that these corporate income tax (CIT) brackets are adjusted yearly, effective 1 October to 30 September of the following year. The tax brackets listed are for the 2012 fiscal year.

Corporate residence

In most cases, the place where a company is incorporated is regarded by Costa Rican authorities as the corporate residence.

Permanent establishment (PE)

According to Costa Rica's tax system, a PE of non-domiciled persons in the country is every office, factory, building, or any other real estate; plantation, mining, forest, agricultural, and farming development; warehouse or any other permanent business center, included the temporary use of warehouse facilities as well as the ones destined to the purchase and sell of merchandise and products inside the country; and any other company property of non-domiciled persons that develops commercial and lucrative activities in Costa Rica.

The Costa Rican Tax Administration has manifested that the essential characteristic of a PE is given by a territorial criteria, according to which are taxable the income and earnings generated in Costa Rica as well as the assets located in it, not taking into consideration the nationality or domicile of its owner.

The Tax Administration also applies the criteria of the Organisation for Economic Co-operation and Development (OECD) to determine when a person can be considered a PE of a company in determined state. Accordingly, the Tax Administration takes into consideration the following conditions to determine the existence of a PE:

- The existence of a business center (i.e. facilities such as an office or business center or, in certain cases, machinery).
- Said business center must be permanent (i.e. must be established in a determined place with a significant level of permanence).
- The company has to develop its essential activity through this permanent center (i.e. the persons who depend in a way or another on the company (the staff) must develop the company's business inside the country on which the permanent center is located).

Note that the Costa Rican Tax Administration uses these OECD criteria to support and base its administrative resolutions; therefore, they hold a significant importance for the Costa Rican tax system. Regarding these criteria, the OECD has established as a generally accepted principle that a company will be treated as the owner of a PE in a determined state if a person acts on behalf of that company under certain circumstances, even if they are not in the presence of a permanent business centre in said state. These circumstances are as follows:

- The person has to be an agent on account of the non-domiciled company: A dependent agent, individual, or company, under an employment regime or outside of this, that, due to the nature of its activities or to the scope of is faculties, involves the non-domiciled company in commercial activities of certain significance.
- The person or local company has to be a dependent agent with enough faculties to celebrate and subscribe agreements on behalf of the non-domiciled company. The faculties of the person or local company have to be sufficient to involve the non-domiciled company in business activities inside the country on which the person or local company are situated.
- The agent has to be authorised to negotiate all elements and details of agreements on which the non-domiciled company is involved and obligated, even if said agreement is signed by another person in the country on which the non-domiciled

Costa Rica

company is located. In other words, it isn't simply a mere authorisation to sign the agreement.
- The faculty to subscribe agreements must include those agreements that are part of the main commercial activity of the company. It is irrelevant the fact that the person has the faculty to celebrate agreements exclusively related to internal operations of the company.
- The agent has to take risks on behalf of the abroad domiciled company.
- The agent has to act accordingly to detailed instructions or general control of the abroad domiciled company.
- The concept of PE under this context implies that this agent uses its authority on a repeatedly basis and not only on isolated cases. The faculties must be exercised regularly in the country on which the agent is located, a characteristic that is determined according to the real commercial situation.

A person or company whose activities are limited to the following conditions and circumstances is not considered a PE:
- Its activities consist only in storage, expose, or delivery of goods and merchandise that belong to the company domiciled in another country.
- Its activity consists only in purchase of goods or merchandise or compiling information for the abroad domiciled company.
- Its activity consists only in developing any other auxiliary or preparatory activity for the company.
- To consider a person as a PE of a company in a state, it has to be determined if the activities that this person develops are, by themselves, an essential and significant part of the activities of the company as a whole, which is why every case must be studied and analysed according to its own particular circumstances.

Other taxes

Sales tax
A fixed sales tax rate of 13% is applied at all stages of the sale of merchandise or the invoicing of certain limited services. The tax is levied on (i) sales of merchandise within the national territory (except sales of land, buildings, exports, and certain basic necessity items, such as basic foodstuffs, certain medicines, and veterinary products); (ii) the value of services performed by restaurants, bars, motels, printing companies, social and recreational clubs, painting and repair shops, and others; and (iii) imports consisting of merchandise for personal use or consumption or to satisfy commercial needs.

Selective consumption tax
The selective consumption tax may be applied at a rate of up to 100% and is levied on goods that are considered non-essential. The tax base is the cost, insurance, and freight (CIF) price plus import duties for imported items or the sales value for items produced in Costa Rica. The tax is levied at only one stage in the sale of merchandise. Payment of the tax is required at the time of importation or, for articles produced in Costa Rica, within 15 days of the month of the sale.

Customs duties/import tariffs
In Costa Rica, all importation of goods and merchandise, with certain exemptions, are liable for corresponding import tariffs and customs duties. Other taxes (e.g. sales tax, selective consumption tax) are also levied on the importation of said goods and merchandise.

The most important legal instruments for customs regulations are the Central American Uniformed Customs Code, the Customs Law and its rulings, and other administrative rulings that are periodically issued by the Customs Authority.

Property tax
Each local municipal government is in charge of real estate appraisal. The annual property tax to be applied throughout the Costa Rican territory is 0.25% of the appraised value, registered in the respective municipality where the tax liability originates.

Real estate transfer tax
Real estate transfer tax is calculated as 1.5% of the selling price of the real estate or its property tax value, whichever is greater.

Stamp duties
Stamp duties in Costa Rica are determined according to the transaction that is carried out (e.g. property transactions, service contracts, movable assets transactions).

Registration tax
In December 2011, a law was published that enforced a new registration tax on every corporation/company that is registered in the Costa Rican Mercantile Registry and every new corporation that is formed after the creation of this law.

The rate of this new tax is approximately 300 United States dollars (USD) for commercially active companies and USD 150 for inactive ones (commonly known as shelf companies). The taxable event happens every 1 January and affects all companies, corporations, and branches that are registered in the Mercantile Registry to that date. For existing companies, the tax will be paid during the 30 calendar days following 1 January; for new companies, the tax will be paid at the moment of their registration.

Franchise tax
The payments realised abroad for the use of a franchise will be subject to remittances abroad, with a 25% withholding tax (WHT).

Branch income

Branch income is subject to tax at the same rates as corporate income. There is a WHT of 15% on dividends distributed within the country and a 15% tax, in lieu of a dividend WHT, on profits transferred abroad.

Income determination

Inventory valuation
Inventories are generally stated at cost and can be valued using the compound average-cost method, first in first out (FIFO), last in first out (LIFO), retailer method, or specific identification method. Since all entities must keep legal records, any adjustment resulting from different methods of inventory valuation for tax and financial purposes should be recorded.

Costa Rica

Capital gains

Capital gains and losses on the disposition of non-depreciable fixed assets or shares of other companies are excluded for income tax purposes if such dispositions are not a habitual activity.

Capital gains are taxed, at the regular CIT rate, on the sale of depreciable assets when their sale price is higher than their adjusted basis (book value).

Dividend income

Dividends between domestic subsidiaries and other domestic corporations are not subject to taxes. There are no ownership requirements to qualify for this exclusion.

Stock dividends

Stock dividends are subject to CIT at 15% if the stock is not listed in an officially recognised stock exchange or 5% if the stock is registered in a stock exchange officially recognised by the Costa Rican government.

Dividends paid in the form of stock of the distributing company are allowed and are exempt from taxes.

Interest income

Interest income coming from sources related to normal business activities is taxable. Interest income coming from investments on financial entities included in the National Banking System is subject to an 8% withholding on the source as definitive tax.

Interest coming from investments abroad is considered non-Costa Rican-source income and is not taxable.

Foreign income

Foreign-source income is not taxable in Costa Rica.

Deductions

In general, any costs and expenses that are useful, necessary, and pertinent for the production of actual or potentially taxable income will be deductible from the company's gross income, as long as they are duly supported by documentation authorised by the law and they comply with the following requirements:

- That they are necessary expenses to obtain actual or potential income, taxed under the law.
- That any withholding obligations, as stated in other sections of the law, have been carried out.
- That the supporting documentation has been authorised by the Tax Administration.

However, the Tax Administration may reject or disregard, in whole or in part, any expenses that it considers excessive, inadmissible, or not indispensable to obtain taxable income.

Depreciation

The straight-line and sum-of-the-years-digits methods of depreciation are allowed over the following useful lives:

Costa Rica

Assets	Useful life (years)
Buildings	50
Machinery and equipment	10
Furniture and fixtures	10
Vehicles	10
Agricultural plantations	3 to 20

The Tax Administration, at the request of the taxpayer, can adopt technically acceptable special depreciation methods in cases duly justified by the taxpayer. In addition, the Tax Administration can authorise, through general resolution, accelerated depreciation methods on new assets acquired by corporations with monetary activities requiring constant technological updates, higher installed production capacity, and productive reconversion processes in order to maintain and strengthen their competitive advantage.

Start-up expenses
Companies organisational expenses may be deducted in the tax year in which they are paid or credited, or, if they accumulate, in five consecutive tax years, starting from the date of start of productive operations, until the balance is exhausted. Organisational expenses will be considered to be those costs and expenses that are necessary to initiate the production of taxable income, that, in accordance with the law, are deducted from gross income.

Interest expenses
Interest and other financial expenses paid or incurred by the taxpayer during the fiscal year directly related to the management of their business and the creation of taxable income are deductible from gross income, as long as those interest expenses are not capitalised.

Note that those interest expenses with rates that exceed the usual market rates will not be considered deductible expenses by the Tax Administration.

Bad debt
Manifestly uncollectible unpaid debt will be deductible as long as this debt is originated in habitual operations from the taxpayer's business and all legal actions towards its collection have been exercised.

Charitable contributions
All donations duly supported by documentation that are given to the government, public institutions, municipal corporations, public universities, to the Social Protection Board, to the Educational Boards, to the Costa Rican Red Cross, and other institutions, such as those foundations and associations with non-charitable, goodwill, scientific, and cultural ends that are authorised by the Tax Administration to receive deductible donations, among other entities, will be deductible from gross income.

Taxes
With the exception of sales tax, selective consumption tax, specific taxes over consumption and special duties established by law, penalties and interest paid over any tax obligation, and the income tax itself, all other taxes that affect the goods, services, and negotiations of the company's habitual commercial activity will be considered deductible.

Costa Rica

Net operating losses

Losses incurred by industrial and agricultural enterprises may be carried forward and deducted from the taxable profits for the following three years for industrial enterprises and five years for agricultural enterprises. Loss carrybacks are not allowed.

Payments to foreign affiliates

Corporations may claim deductions for royalties, technical and management service fees, and interest charges paid to foreign affiliates, provided that a tax of 25% for royalties, franchises, and other services, and a tax of 15% for interest is withheld. However, the deductions for technical, management service fees, and royalties may not exceed 10% of gross sales in the aggregate if paid to the parent company.

Group taxation

There is no group taxation in Costa Rica.

Transfer pricing

Costa Rican legislation makes no mention of transfer pricing as such, and any attempt to govern transfer pricing is the product of interpretation and precedents and not strictly the product of the law or its rules and regulations. Although the law and its regulations do not specifically mention the phenomenon of transfer prices in its texts, the Tax Administration has attempted to approach the subject by means of an official interpretation of the law, as regards its application to transfer pricing among related companies.

By means of Interpretive Guideline No. 20-03 of 10 June 2003, the Tax Administration has applied the Principle of Economic Reality, regulated in Articles 8 and 12 of the Costa Rican Code of Tax Rules and Procedures, to transfer pricing.

The Tax Administration's argument basically states that the tax laws must be interpreted in accordance with their objectives, their economic meaning, and the facts, as they actually occurred. The Tax Administration will therefore apply the arm's-length principle, as understood by the OECD, which compares the conditions of a transaction between related parties with transactions that are carried out by independent companies; in other words, said prices must be equivalent to prices corresponding to those of transactions that are similar to operations carried out by independent entities, in order to grant them the appropriate fiscal treatment, particularly in light of the fact that the norm between related entities is the application of transfer prices.

Thin capitalisation

In Costa Rican legislation, there is no mention of thin capitalisation rules. However, as with transfer pricing, the Tax Administration applies general rules and principles for the treatment of these types of situations. For instance, the Income Tax Law gives the Tax Administration the faculty of reviewing and rejecting all expenses that it may consider excessive, not proportional, or unreasonable. Additionally by means of Interpretive Guideline No. 20-03 of 10 June 2003, the Tax Administration has applied the Principle of Economic Reality, regulated in Articles 8 and 12 of the Costa Rican Code of Tax Rules and Procedures, to thin capitalisation, limiting related companies to market value prices for their transactions.

Tax credits and incentives

Free zones

Entities established in free zones may enjoy exemption from import duties on goods, income tax, sales tax, export tax, selective consumption tax, real estate transfer tax, and WHT on payments abroad, as well as the discretionary use of foreign currency generated abroad. However, these incentives will be affected by the rules established by the World Trade Organization (WTO) in force in the year 2015.

Drawback industries

Special benefits exist for industries that import semi-manufactured materials for assembly in Costa Rica and export finished products. Benefits consist of duty-free imports of raw materials for subsequent export as manufactured products. Machinery for these industries may also be imported duty-free.

Tourism development

The Incentive Law for Tourism Development grants several tax benefits, such as exemption from import duties on certain tourism service-related goods and from property tax for companies dedicated to tourism, but only for those with a signed tourism agreement.

Withholding taxes

Payments to non-domiciled foreign corporations or individuals

Regarding payments to non-domiciled foreign corporations or individuals, taxes are withheld as follows:

Payment	WHT rate (%)
Dividends (1)	15
Interest and other financial expenses (2, 3)	15
Royalties, patents, trademarks, franchises, and formulas	25
Technical service and management fees	25
Personal services from a Costa Rican source:	
Employees	10
Directors	15
Others	30
Transportation and communication services	8.5

Notes

1. Withholding depends on the origin or source of the retained earnings. Total or partial exemption will be authorised by the Tax Administration to the extent that a foreign tax credit is totally or partially disallowed to the taxpayer in the taxpayer's country of residence. This exemption will not be allowed, however, if this type of income is not taxable to the taxpayer in the country of residence.
2. No tax is withheld if the recipient is a bank or a financial institution recognised as a first-class bank by the Central Bank of Costa Rica or a supplier of merchandise. Interest or financial expenses paid to parties other than those aforementioned are subject to a 15% WHT. An 8% WHT applies to interest on bearer documents issued by financial entities registered at the Central Bank's General Auditor's Office or stock exchange. No WHT applies to interest paid on securities issued by the Workmen's Bank or the Mortgage Housing Bank and its authorised institutions or on foreign currency securities issued by the state banks.
3. Banks or non-resident financial entities that are part of a local financial group are payers of a special tax. The taxpayers mentioned in Note 2 must pay, in lieu of tax on remittances abroad, a local currency tax equivalent to USD 125,000 per annum. The tax period will run from 1 January to 31 December of each year.

Costa Rica

Tax treaties

Free-trade bilateral treaties
Costa Rica is a full member of the Central American Common Market, which guarantees free trade among the countries of the area. It also has a free-trade bilateral treaty in force with Mexico (1994), the Dominican Republic (1998), Chile (1998), Canada, and Panama. The US-Central American-Dominican Republic Free Trade Agreement (CAFTA-DR) entered into force on 1 January 2009. These agreements aim to provide favourable conditions for the exchange of merchandise between contracting parties.

Tax information exchange agreements (TIEAs)
The only tax treaty in force between Costa Rica and the United States, effective since 12 February 1991, is a TIEA, whereby both countries agree to exchange information, from and/or in relation to public and private entities and individuals, at the request of the party's corresponding authority, in relation to any tax relevant issue.

Double taxation treaties (DTTs)
Law No. 8888, regarding the DTT between Costa Rica and Spain, was published in the Official Gazette on 6 December 2010. This treaty entered into force on 1 January 2011 with the purpose of avoiding double taxation and tax evasion between the two countries.

Tax administration

Taxable period
The tax year in Costa Rica is a 12-month period from 1 October to 30 September. Current legislation contemplates that other fiscal year-ends may be adopted with the prior approval of the Tax Administration.

Tax returns
With certain exceptions, all corporations must file a tax return by 15 December on the basis of a fiscal year-end of 30 September. Entities with an operating period of less than four months may present a return together with the following year's tax return.

The tax system is one of self-assessment with occasional auditing by the Tax Administration.

Payment of tax
In March, June, and September, all corporations and taxpayers must prepay instalments that total 75% of the average income taxes paid in the past three fiscal years, or the amount paid in the prior year, whichever is greater. Failure to pay on these dates results in the accrual of interest unless the taxpayer has requested, on a timely basis, that the Tax Administration eliminate the corresponding payments. Any amount owed in excess of the instalments should be paid by 15 December.

Audit cycle
For a tax audit to begin, it is necessary that the Tax Administration send a notification to the taxpayer to be audited. The taxpayer is selected according to one of the selection criteria previously established, and this should be indicated in the communication at the beginning of the tax audit. The Tax Administration must start the audit within two months of the communication to the taxpayer.

Once the audit is completed, the auditors hold a meeting with the company and invite them to correct the issues found.

If the company does not accept the correction, then the Tax Administration will present a tax assessment with the issues and tax adjustment. The taxpayer has 30 days to respond to the assessment as well as to pay it. An appeal may be requested to the Tax Administrative Court, where the administrative section finishes. Further appeals are handled by the judicial court.

Statute of limitations
The statute of limitations is three years starting from 1 January of the year following the income tax return filing. For taxpayers with an ordinary tax period with a due date to file their 2011 period return on 15 December 2011, the statute of limitations starts counting on 1 January 2012; however, for taxpayers with a special period of January to December with a due date to file their 2011 period return on 15 March 2012, the statute of limitations starts counting on 1 January 2013.

Topics of focus for tax authorities
Important topics for tax audits are sales tax credits, gross margin on sales, employee benefits, and income tax.

Croatia

PwC contact

Cherie Ford
PricewaterhouseCoopers d.o.o.
Alexandera von Humboldta 4
10000 Zagreb, Croatia
Tel: +385 1 6328 880
Email: cherie.ford@hr.pwc.com

Significant developments

Croatia introduced some changes in tax regulations starting from 1 March 2012.

Corporate taxation

A tax deduction is introduced for the amount of realised profit used to increase the founding capital of the company. After submitting the annual tax return, taxpayers have six months to obtain proof of registering the increase of their share capital, as per the Companies Act. This provision shall apply to submissions of the annual tax return for the year 2012.

The impairment arising from adjustments in customer's receivables is a tax deductible expense, if the maturity of debts by the end of the tax period is more than 60 days (before 120 days). This decision applies to receivables created from 1 March 2012 onwards.

Taxation of dividends and profit shares

Changes to the legislation introduced taxation of dividends and shares in profit at the rate of 12%. The withholding tax (WHT) will apply on payments of dividends and profit shares when they are made to:

- a foreign shareholder or
- an individual (natural person).

Changes in the Value-added Tax (VAT) Act

The general VAT rate has increased from 23% to 25%.

The following goods are taxed at a preferential 10% VAT rate:

- Eatable oils and fat of animal and vegetable origin.
- Children's food and processed cereal based foods for infants and small children.
- Water delivery, except for water in bottles and other packaging on the market.
- White sugar from cane or beet.

Input VAT is not deductible for:

- the purchase of goods and services for entertainment purposes or
- purchase and rental of cars and other means of personal transport, vessels for leisure, and airplanes, including purchase of all goods and services related to those goods. However, this provision does not apply if the cars, vessels, and aircrafts are used for performing business activity of transportation of goods and passengers, rent, or further sales.

Fines imposed for the responsible person of the taxpayer are increased up to the amount of 50,000 Croatian kuna (HRK), depending on the type of breach.

Taxes on corporate income

Profit tax is paid at a flat 20% rate by enterprises engaged in independent activities on a long-term basis for the purpose of deriving profit, branches of foreign enterprises, enterprises that control shares in capital (unless the object of investment itself pays profit tax), and natural persons who choose to pay profit tax instead of personal income tax.

The profit tax base is the accounting profit adjusted for deductions and disallowed items. Croatian residents pay profit tax on profit derived in Croatia and abroad, and non-residents (e.g. branches) pay profit tax only on profits derived in Croatia. The tax base also includes gains arising from liquidation, sale, change of legal form, and division of the taxpayer where it is determined at the market rates.

Payments into voluntarily pension funds paid by an employer for an employee under certain conditions prescribed by Corporate Income Tax Act are also considered expenditures.

Expenditures are not considered to be expenditures if they are not related to the taxpayer's business activity.

The profit tax base is reduced by the following items:

- Income from dividends and profit sharing.
- Unrealised profits from value adjustments of shares (increase of financial asset value), if these were included as profit in the profit and loss (P&L) account.
- Income from collected written-off claims that were included in the tax base in the previous tax periods, but not excluded from the tax base as recognised expenditure.
- The amount of depreciation not recognised in previous tax periods, up to the amount prescribed by the Corporate Income Tax Act.
- The amount of tax relief or tax exemption in line with special regulations (i.e. costs of education, costs of research and development (R&D), costs of a new employee's salary).
- For reinvested profit, other than that earned in the banking or the financial non-banking sector.

The profit tax base is increased by the following items:

- Unrealised losses from value adjustments of shares (decrease of financial asset value), if these were included as expenses in the P&L account.
- The amount of depreciation in excess of the amounts prescribed by the Corporate Income Tax Act.
- 70% of entertainment costs (food and drink, gifts with or without the printed firm logo or product brand, and expenses for vacation, sport, recreation and leisure-time, renting cars, vessels, airplanes, and holiday cottages). Entertainment costs do not include the costs of goods and merchandise adapted by a taxpayer for business entertainment purposes, labelled 'not for sale', and other promotional objects with the name of the firm or merchandise or other advertising objects (e.g. glasses, ashtrays, table cloths, mats, pencils, business diaries, cigarette lighters, tags) put to

Croatia

use in the selling area of the purchaser and given to consumers, provided that their value does not exceed HRK 80 per item.

- 30% of the costs, except insurance and interest costs, incurred in connection with owned or rented motor vehicles or other means of personal transportation (e.g. personal car, vessel, helicopter, airplane) used by managerial, supervisory, and other employees, provided that the use of means of personal transportation is not defined as salary.
- Asset shortfalls exceeding the amount prescribed by the Croatian Chamber of Economy or Croatian Chamber of Trades and Crafts, in accordance with the VAT Act and on the basis of which no personal income tax was paid.
- The costs of forced collection of tax and other levies.
- Fines imposed by competent bodies.
- Late payment interest charged between associated persons.
- Privileges and other economic benefits granted to natural or legal persons for the purpose of causing or preventing a certain event in favour of the company (generally related to commissions paid to parties acting on behalf of the taxpayer).
- Donations in excess of the amounts prescribed by the Corporate Income Tax Act.
- Expenditures identified during tax authority's audit, including VAT and contributions related to hidden profit payments and withdrawals from shareholders, company members, and physical persons performing independent activities taxable by profit tax.
- Any other expenditure not directly related to profit earning, as well as other increases in the tax base, which were not included in the tax base.

Local income taxes

A legal entity that is liable to pay profit tax and is registered for the performance of the business activity may be subject to tax on trade name at the amount of up to HRK 2,000, depending on the decision of the municipality or city.

Corporate residence

In terms of Corporate Income Tax Act, residents are legal or natural persons whose seat is recorded in the Register of Companies or other register in Croatia, or whose place of effective management and control of business is in Croatia. Residents are also entrepreneurs/natural persons with domicile or habitual residence in Croatia, whose business activity is recorded in a register or other records.

A non-resident is any person who does not satisfy one of the requirements referred to above.

Permanent establishment (PE)

Definition of a business unit of a non-resident is based on the Organisation for Economic Co-operation and Development (OECD) guidelines, which provides that a non-resident's business unit is a place of management, a branch, an office, a factory, a workshop, a mine, an oil or gas well, a quarry, or any other place of extraction of natural resources or construction site or project for a period longer than six months, including agents acting in its name, having the right to conclude contracts or hold stock of products which it distributes on the Croatian market in the name of a foreign entrepreneur. The business unit of a non-resident also includes the performance of services (i.e. advisory and business consulting services) for the same or a related project, which lasts for more than three months in a 12-month period.

Other taxes

Value-added tax (VAT)
The general VAT rate is 25%.

VAT is a consumption tax and has a neutral effect on enterprises by operation of the input and output mechanism. Accordingly, the tax burden is borne by the final consumer.

VAT returns and payments
A VAT-registered entity must calculate its VAT liability or refund and submit a monthly (by the end of the following month) VAT return to the relevant Tax Authority Office or a quarterly VAT return (by the end of month following the quarter) if the taxpayer is classified as small (annual turnover below HRK 300,000). An annual VAT return must be submitted by 30 April of the following year.

Where the amount of input tax credits exceeds the entity's VAT liability, a taxpayer is entitled to a refund of the difference or may choose to use the difference as a VAT prepayment.

VAT paid to the customs office at the time of import can be credited to the taxpayer's VAT account and offset against any domestic VAT liability. A VAT entity must self-assess VAT on imported services provided by a foreign entity. This VAT can be reclaimed through the VAT return as described above.

Determination of VAT taxpayers
VAT taxpayers are defined as entrepreneurs that deliver goods or perform services in Croatia. An 'entrepreneur' is a legal entity or a natural person that continuously and independently performs an activity for the purpose of deriving profit. In addition to those that may be regarded as 'normal' taxpayers, domestic enterprises receiving imported services from foreign enterprises and legal entities and individuals that issue invoices or receipts including VAT without authorisation are also liable to pay VAT.

A taxpayer is required to register for VAT where turnover in the previous year exceeded HRK 85,000. Voluntary registration is also possible.

Foreign entrepreneurs may also become VAT registered in Croatia through a tax representative. This will entitle them to reclaim input VAT incurred in Croatia.

In addition to foreign individuals, foreign legal entities are now also entitled to claim a VAT refund under reciprocity agreement terms.

Determination of VAT base
The VAT base for goods and services supplied domestically is the consideration received. Where no consideration is provided, for instance where goods are exchanged, the VAT base is the market value of the good or service. The VAT base of imports is the customs value as prescribed by customs regulations, increased by customs duties, import duties, special taxes, and other fees paid during customs clearing.

VAT-exempt supplies
VAT-exempt supplies are similar to those contained in the European Union's (EU's) Sixth Directive and include rental of residential property (with some exceptions); granting of credits and credit guarantees; transactions related to bank accounts, interest, winnings from special games of chance in casinos, slot machine clubs, and

Croatia

other forms of gambling; supplies of domestic and foreign legal tender, securities and shares, and supplies of gold by the central bank.

Other exemptions include the following:

- Services and deliveries of goods by public institutions in the field of culture, such as museums, galleries, archives, libraries, theatres, religious communities and institutions, primary and secondary schools, universities, and student catering and boarding institutions.
- Medical services, including services conducted by doctors, dentists, nurses, physiotherapists, and biochemistry laboratories engaged in private practices; services of medical care performed in healthcare institutions; and services performed by social care institutions and child and adolescent care institutions.
- Supplies (transfers) of real estate (land, buildings, parts of buildings, housing premises, and other structures) with the exception of newly built buildings.
- Temporary imports of goods which are exempt from customs duty.

Zero-rated supplies
The following supplies are zero-rated or 'VAT free' under the Croatian VAT legislation:

- Bread and milk, including baby food used as a substitute for mother's milk.
- Books of a scholarly, scientific, artistic, cultural, and educational character as well as school textbooks (primary, secondary, and tertiary education, including materials printed on paper and other media, such as CD-ROMs, video cassettes, and audio tapes).
- Certain medicines and surgical implants.
- Scientific journals.
- Services rendered by cinemas.

Reduced-rate services
There is a reduced rate of 10% for services related to the following:

- Organised stays (accommodation or accommodation with breakfast, full or half board, in all kinds of commercial hospitality facilities) and agency fees with respect to the above mentioned services.
- Daily and periodic newspapers and magazines (with the exception of those that consist entirely of advertisements or are used mainly for advertising purposes).
- Eatable oils and fat of animal and vegetable origin.
- Children's food and processed cereal based foods for infants and small children.
- Water delivery, except for water in bottles and other packaging on the market.
- White sugar from cane or beet.

Electronic invoices
An electronic invoice is defined as an invoice issued in a form of electronic document, provided that there is consent from the receiver to accept such invoice. An electronic invoice is also deemed to be the electronically issued document signed with the electronic signature.

An electronic invoice is also an invoice issued by one of the following methods:

- Via electronic data exchange, if the contract on exchange enables the use of procedures guaranteeing the authenticity of invoices and integrity of data content on the invoice.

- Using any method of business control that enables a link of invoice with deliveries of goods and services and with other business documents; and authentication of origin and integrity of the contents by an agreed process of issuing and receipt of an invoice.

The above mentioned methods have to meet the following conditions:

- Ensured authenticity of origin of the invoice so that the recipient can unambiguously determine who it was sent by.
- Ensured integrity of the contents of the invoice in a way that applied technologies and processes that make it impossible to change the data.
- Ensured authenticity of origin and integrity of the invoice contents during the transfer of accounts electronically from the issuer to the recipient.
- Ensured readability and visual accounts and user-friendly display of issued invoice on a computer screen or other electronic devices as well as on paper.
- Visible timing and the address of dispatch and receipt of such invoice.

Issuance, receipt, or any other action related to an electronic invoice can be performed through an information agent/intermediary.

Electronic invoices have to be stored in a genuine electronic form as they have been issued; they should not be modified, and the taxpayer has to provide insight into them upon the Tax Authorities' request.

Provisions of VAT legislation relating to physical invoices also apply to electronic invoices.

Custom duties
The general customs duty rate is 10%. However, it varies depending on the type and the origin of imported goods, as prescribed by the Customs Tariff. The Customs Tariff is based on the Harmonized Commodity Description and Coding System (HS Nomenclature).

Excise duties
There are a number of excise duties levied on specific products. They are levied at a fixed amount and are payable by the producer or importer. VAT is applied first, after which the fixed amounts are added.

- Oil derivatives: Tax ranging from HRK 110 to HRK 3,600 per 1,000 litres.
- Tobacco products: Tax on cigarettes may reach up to HRK 180 per 1,000 pieces plus 30% proportional special (excise) tax from retail price; for cigars HRK 1,100 per 1,000 pieces; for cigarillos HRK 220 per 1,000 pieces; and HRK 234 per kilogram for tobacco (HRK 136 prior to 1 January 2011).
- Beer: HRK 40 per 1% volume fraction of the actual alcohol contained in one hectolitre of finished product.
- Soft drinks: HRK 40 per hectolitre for domestically produced brands and imported soft drinks. Some soft drinks, including mineral water and natural fruit juices, are exempt.
- Alcohol:
  - Excise duty on products with the volume of actual alcohol content at 15% and higher is paid in the amount of HRK 800 per hectolitre of finished product.
  - Excise duty on products with the volume of actual alcohol content of less than 15% is paid in the amount of HRK 500 per hectolitre of finished product.

Croatia

- Excise duty on ethyl alcohol is to be paid in the amount HRK 5,300 per hectolitre of pure alcohol.
- Imported coffee: HRK 5 to HRK 20 per kilogram.
- Passenger cars and motor cycles: from 13% to HRK 177,500 plus 63% of the amount exceeding HRK 500,000.
- Imported boats and aircrafts: from 5% to HRK 445,000 plus 16% of the amount exceeding HRK 4 million.
- Luxury products: 30% of the sales value of the product without VAT.
- Liability and comprehensive road vehicle insurance premiums: for obligatory motor vehicle insurance premium, 15% of the contractual amount; and for comprehensive motor vehicle insurance premium, 10% of the contractual amount.

Property taxes
There are no property taxes in Croatia.

Real estate tax
The acquisition of real estate is subject to taxation. 'Real estate' includes agricultural, construction, and other land as well as residential, commercial, and other buildings. Transactions include the sale, exchange, and any other means of acquiring real estate for consideration.

Tax is charged at 5% of the market value of the real estate on the contract date and is paid by the acquirer.

Stamp tax
There are no stamp taxation provisions in Croatia.

Chamber of Commerce contribution
Employers pay a mandatory contribution to the Croatian Chamber of Commerce. The amount varies between HRK 55 to HRK 5,500 depending on company size and 0.0056% of total income.

Branch income

Foreign corporations carrying on business in Croatia are taxed on their Croatian-source income at a 20% rate.

Income determination

Inventory valuation
Inventories are generally valued at the lower of their acquisition cost or net realisable value. Taking into consideration the accounting principles set out in the Accounting Act and the International Accounting Standards (IAS), a company can choose to adopt the most favourable method.

Capital gains
Capital gains or losses are covered by the profit tax regime. They are either an increasing or decreasing item to the profit tax base.

Dividend income
Dividends and profit shares are taxed at the WHT rate of 12%. This applies to all non-residents until Croatia becomes a part of the European Union.

Dividend and profit shares payments made to resident companies are not taxable.

Interest income

Interest income is taxable at the rate of 20% as a part of total income stated in the P&L account.

Deductions

Depreciation

Most companies depreciate assets on a straight-line basis; this is because depreciation calculated this way, at the prescribed rates, is recognised for tax purposes. Companies are, however, free to use any depreciation method defined in the IAS and to estimate the useful lives of all fixed assets in accordance with their accounting policies.

Prescribed annual depreciation rates are as follows:

Assets	Depreciation period (years)	Depreciation rate (%)
Buildings and ships of over 1,000 gross registered tonnage (GRT)	20	5
Basic herd and personal cars	5	20
Intangible assets, equipment, vehicles (except personal cars), and machinery	4	25
Computers, computer hardware and software, mobile telephones, and computer network accessories	2	50
Other non-mentioned assets	10	10

However, depreciation expenses in excess of the amount allowed for tax purposes are taxable. The value adjustment of tangible fixed assets rarely occurs in practice, except in the case of financial assets and claims.

The Corporate Income Tax Act no longer allows taxpayers to wholly write off plant and equipment acquired or built during the tax period. The cost of depreciation of assets which are not used for business purposes is not deductible.

Plant and equipment are taken to be acquired in the period in which it is installed or ready for use. Plant and equipment includes: tools of trade, information technology infrastructure including software, furniture and fittings, and motor vehicles (excluding vehicles for personal use).

If the taxpayer writes off a portion of a depreciable asset, the remaining undepreciated portion will be depreciated at the rate prescribed by law. According to the Corporate Income Tax Act, the taxpayer can double the depreciation rates.

Land and forests (renewable resources) are not depreciated.

Financial assets, cultural monuments, and art work are not depreciated.

Depreciation of vessels, aircrafts, condominiums, and vacation houses can be tax deductible only if certain conditions are met.

Croatia

Goodwill
Goodwill paid on the acquisition of a business must be amortised over five years. It is usually the difference between the estimated statistical value of assets and liabilities and their book value.

However, the amortisation of goodwill arising from mergers and acquisitions is not recognised for taxation purposes.

Start-up expenses
When establishing a business in Croatia, start-up expenses consist of minimum of share capital of EUR 2,500 and other administrative and lawyer's costs up to EUR 1,500. The start-up expenses depend on the amount of share capital. Start-up expenses are included in operating costs for profit tax purposes.

Interest expenses
According to the Corporate Income Tax Act, late payment interests are tax deductible, unless those interests are due to related companies transactions, no matter if the late payment interests are charged by resident of non-resident related parties.

Interest on loans is also deductible, up to the amount prescribed by the Ministry of Finance or Croatian National Bank (prescribed interest rate in Croatia is 7%) and if compliant with thin capitalisation rules (4:1).

Bad debt
Value adjustments arising from the adjustment of the value of claims against customers for goods delivered and services rendered are recognised as deductible expenditures if more than 60 days elapsed between the maturity of the claim and the end of the tax period, and if the claims were not paid up to 15 days before filing the tax return. The claim needs to be recorded in the business books as revenue, and all measures for debt collection have to be taken (legal actions) in accordance with best management practices.

Charitable contributions
Donations in a form of gifts in kind or cash for cultural, scientific, educational, health, humanitarian, sports, religious, environmental, or other socially beneficial purposes are tax deductible by 2% of the revenues generated in the previous year. Exceptionally, the amount may exceed 2% of the revenues generated in the previous year, provided that it is granted pursuant to the decisions of competent ministries on the financing of special programs and activities.

Fines and penalties
Fines and penalties prescribed by Croatian administrative and judicial authorities are considered to be non-deductible expenses.

Net operating losses
Tax losses may be carried forward and utilised within five years following the year in which the losses were incurred and must be utilised in the order in which they occurred. The losses may not be transferred to any third entity except in the case of merger, de-merger, or acquisition. Tax losses cannot be carried back.

Utilisation of tax losses from previous years in case of statutory changes of legal entities is prescribed in detail in the Corporate Income Tax Act, limiting the entitlement where the legal predecessor is inactive and in case of a significant change in business activity or ownerships structure.

Croatia

Payments to foreign affiliates
The treatment of payments made to foreign affiliates is dealt with through the mechanism of the profit tax base. The profit tax base is increased for any concealed profit payments made. The Tax Administration may audit the expenditure of non-resident taxpayers, examining expenditure on goods and services abroad as well as management, intellectual property, and other fees and payments that may have the character of a profit transfer. If the Tax Administration discovers that transactions have been used to conceal profit transfers, the difference between the declared price/fee and the average market price/fee will be added back into the taxpayer's tax base.

Group taxation

There are no group taxation provisions in Croatia.

Transfer pricing
Prices between a Croatian entity and its foreign related parties must be set at fair market value (the arm's-length principle). Provisions on transfer pricing and interests are also introduced in transactions between resident related parties if one of the parties has:

- beneficial tax status (i.e. reduced tax rates) or
- entitlement to carry forward tax losses from previous years.

If the prices between related entities are different than those between non-related resident and non-resident entities, the tax base must be calculated with prices that would be charged between unrelated companies. In order to determine the market value of the related party's transaction, the following methods can be used:

- Comparable uncontrolled price.
- Resale price.
- Cost plus.
- Profit split.
- Net-profit.

Thin capitalisation
Interest on loans from a shareholder or a member of a company holding at least 25% of shares or voting power of the taxpayer will not be recognised for tax purposes, if the amount of the loan exceeds four times the amount of the shareholder's share in the capital or their voting power. Interest on loans obtained from financial institutions is exempt from this provision. A third-party loan will be considered to be given by a shareholder if it is guaranteed by the shareholder.

Tax credits and incentives

The Investment Incentive Act provides the following relief and incentives for taxpayers.

Investment incentives
Investment incentives are usually organised as corporate tax credits applicable for up to ten years upon completion of various conditions.

General incentives apply for investors profit earned as a result of an investment under the following conditions:

Croatia

Investment amount (EUR*)	Tax benefit rate (%)	Period (years)	Necessary to employ (employees)
From 300,000 to 1.5 million	50	10	10
More than 1.5 million	65	10	30
More than 4 million	85	10	50
More than 8 million	100	10	75

* euros

Tax benefits cannot exceed investment amount.

Incentives for investments in technological development and innovation activities and strategic business support activities

A non-refundable money subsidy in the amount of up to 5% of justified costs related to investment in technological development and innovation activities and strategic business support activities (maximum amount of up to EUR 500,000) can be granted to a company, provided that equipment bought is high technology equipment.

Also, for opening new work places as part of investments in technological development, there is an increase of the subsidy in the amount of 50% related to costs for opening new work places, or 25% concerning investments in strategic business support activities (maximum amount of EUR 3,000 per employee).

Incentive for investment in significant projects

A non-refundable money subsidy in an amount of up to 5% of justified costs related to investment in significant projects (maximum amount of up to EUR 1 million) may be granted to a company, providing that certain conditions are met.

A significant project investment consists of high economic activity, such as the construction of a new plant or industrial facility, initiation of a new economic activity, or new technology development, with investment in assets greater than EUR 15 million. At least 100 workplaces must be opened upon expiration of one year of investment.

Custom free zones

Taxpayers in custom free zones can take advantage of incentives prescribed in the Investment Incentives Act. Taxpayers that were engaged in or participating in the building of infrastructure within a zone, in projects with a value exceeding HRK 1 million before July 2008, and that did not fully utilise the incentive prescribed by the Investment Incentive Act, are exempt from paying profit tax until the full amount has been used, but no later than 31 December 2016.

Employment incentives

Employment benefits occur in a form of non-refundable money subsidy in relation to justified costs according to the unemployment rate of the county as follows:

Unemployment rate	Non-refundable cash subsidy (%)	Maximum costs per employee (EUR)
Up to 10%	10	1,500
10% to 20%	15	2,000
More than 20%	20	3,000

Croatia

Research and development (R&D) incentives

Registered scientific organisations, centres of scientific excellence, individual scientists, and groups of scientists are entitled to apply for the state subsidies and tax incentives for scientific research, basic research, applied R&D research.

Depending on the type of research (e.g. scientific, basic, applied research, or technical feasibility) and size of entrepreneur (i.e. small, medium, or large entrepreneur, according to the Accounting Act), the percentage of the costs covered by state subsidy can vary between 25% and 100%. Additionally, the profit tax base can be decreased (depending on the same criteria) by up to 150% of the amount of the costs covered by the state subsidy, where the profit tax liability decrease is granted up to the amount of the percentage of the costs covered by state subsidy.

Foreign tax credit

If a domestic taxpayer has paid tax abroad on profit derived abroad, the tax paid can be included in its profit tax return, up to the profit tax rate in Croatia. The amount of paid tax abroad, which can be offset with the domestic tax, is calculated in the following way:

• The domestic tax rate is charged on the revenues/profit derived from abroad, and the result represents the highest amount of tax which can be offset with the domestic tax.

If the amount of paid tax abroad was charged at the rate lower than 20%, the actual amount of foreign tax paid can be offset with the domestic tax.

Withholding taxes

Taxpayers who pay fees for the use of intellectual property rights (the right to reproduction, patents, licenses, copyrights, designs or models, manufacturing procedures, production formulas, blueprints, plans, industrial or scientific experience, and such other rights); fees for market research services, tax consulting services, legal, auditing, or such other services; or interest to foreign legal entities, natural persons excluded, shall, when making the payment, calculate and withhold tax at a rate of 15%. Exceptionally, WHT on dividends and shares in profit are taxed at the rate of 12%

If a country has a double tax treaty (DTT) signed with Croatia, WHT rate are lowered. There is specific application that needs to be fulfilled in order to benefit from a DTT between countries.

The following countries have a DTT with Croatia:

Recipient	Royalties (%)	Interest (%)	Dividends and shares in profit	
			% of shares	Tax rate (%)
Albania	10	10	Regardless of the share	10
Armenia	5	10	up to 25	10
			25 and more	0
Austria	0	5	up to 10	15
			10 and more	0

Croatia

Recipient	Royalties (%)	Interest (%)	Dividends and shares in profit	
			% of shares	Tax rate (%)
Belarus	10	10	up to 25	15
			25 and more	5
Belgium	0	10	up to 10	15
			10 and more	5
Bosnia and Herzegovina	10	10	up to 25	10
			25 and more	5
Bulgaria	0	5	Regardless of the share	5
Canada	10	10	up to 25	15
			25 and more	5
Chile	51	53	up to 20	5
	102	154	20 and more	15
China	10	10	Regardless of the share	5
Czech Republic	10	0	Regardless of the share	5
Denmark	10	5	up to 25	10
			25 and more	5
Estonia	10	10	up to 10	15
			10 and more	5
Finland	10	0	up to 25	15
			25 and more	5
France	0	0	up to 10	15
			10 and more	0
Germany	0	0	up to 10	15
			10 and more	5
Greece	10	10	up to 25	10
			25 and more	5
Hungary	0	0	up to 25	10
			25 and more	5
Iran	5	5	up to 25	10
			25 and more	5
Ireland	10	0	up to 10	10
			10 and more	5
Israel	5	55	up to 25	15
			10 and more	10
		104	25 and more	5
Italy	5	10	Regardless of the share	15
Jordan	10	10	up to 25	10
			25 and more	5
Korea	0	5	up to 25	10
			25 and more	5
Kuwait	10	0	Regardless of the share	0

Croatia

Recipient	Royalties (%)	Interest (%)	Dividends and shares in profit	
			% of shares	Tax rate (%)
Latvia	10	10	up to 25	10
			25 and more	5
Lithuania	10	10	up to 10	15
			10 and more	5
Macedonia	10	10	up to 25	15
			25 and more	5
Malezija	10	10	up to 10	10
			10 and more	5
Malta	0	0	Regardless of the share	5
Mauricius	0	0	Regardless of the share	0
Moldova	5	10	up to 25	10
			25 and more	5
Montenegro	10	10	up to 25	10
			25 and more	5
Netherlands	0	0	up to 10	15
			10 and more	0
Norway	10	0	Regardless of the share	15
Oman	10	5	Regardless of the share	0
Poland	10	10	up to 25	15
			25 and more	5
Qatar	10	0	Regardless of the share	0
Romania	10	10	Regardless of the share	5
Russia	10	10	up to 25	10
			25 and more	5
San Marino	5	10	up to 25	10
			25 and more	5
Serbia	10	10	up to 25	10
			25 and more	5
Slovakia	10	10	up to 25	10
			25 and more	5
Slovenia	5	5	Regardless of the share	5
Spain	0	0	up to 25	15
			25 and more	0
Sweden	0	0	up to 25	15
			25 and more	5
Switzerland	0	5	up to 25	15
			25 and more	5
Syria	12	10	up to 10	10
			10 and more	5
Turkey	10	10	Regardless of the share	10

Croatia

Recipient	Royalties (%)	Interest (%)	Dividends and shares in profit	
			% of shares	Tax rate (%)
Ukraine	10	10	up to 25	10
			25 and more	5
United Kingdom	10	10	up to 25	15
			25 and more	5

In addition to the current WHT rates of 15% and 12%, an increased rate of 20% applies to all services paid to foreign entities whose place of seat or management is in a country with a profit tax rate below 12.5%. This provision does not apply to EU member countries.

The following countries have a profit tax below 12.5%:

- Andorra
- Anguilla
- Antigua and Barbuda
- Aruba
- Bahamas
- Bahrain
- Belize
- Bermuda
- British Virgin Islands
- Cayman Islands
- Cook Islands
- Dominica
- Gibraltar
- Grenada
- Guernsey
- Isle of Man
- Jersey
- Liberia
- Liechtenstein
- Marshall Islands
- Monaco
- Montserrat
- Nauru
- Netherlands Antilles
- Niue
- Panama
- Saint Kitts and Nevis
- Saint Lucia
- Saint Vincent and the Grenadines
- Samoa
- Seychelles
- Turks and Caicos Islands
- US Virgin Islands
- Vanuatu

Note that tax is not withheld from interest payments on the following:

- Commodity loans for the purchase of goods used for carrying out a taxpayer's business activity.
- Loans granted by a non-resident bank or other financial institution.
- To holders of government or corporate bonds who are non-resident legal persons.

Tax administration

Taxable period
The profit tax shall be assessed for a period which is normally a calendar year. The tax administration may agree, at the request of a taxpayer, that the tax period should not correspond with the calendar year, where the tax period may not exceed 12 months. The chosen tax period cannot be changed for five years.

Tax returns
All profit tax taxpayers are obliged to submit an annual profit tax return to the tax authorities no later than four months after the end of the tax period for which profit tax is assessed.

The Ministry of Finance administers taxation matters through the Tax Administration and the Financial Police. These organisations have responsibilities and powers defined by law.

Payment of tax

Every taxpayer is required to make monthly profit tax instalments (on the last day of each month) on the basis of the previous year's tax return.

In the first year of operation, taxpayers are not obliged to pay any profit tax advances.

Profit tax is assessed at the end of the calendar year, and the assessed amount, less any instalments made, is payable by the day of submission of the tax return.

Statute of limitations

The Croatian tax authority is entitled to review the tax returns of a company within three years following the end of the year in which the tax return is submitted. This period may be extended to a maximum of six years where the three-year period has been interrupted by actions taken by the tax authority, such as a tax audit. Where the tax authority considers that there may be a significant impact from the results of the investigation, earlier years may be examined. This means that, in theory, even the closed years can be reopened and additional taxes can be imposed.

Topic of focus for tax authorities

Tax authorities are focusing on business relations with related parties.

Curaçao

PwC contact

Steve Vanenburg
PricewaterhouseCoopers
Julianaplein 38
Willemstad, Curaçao
Tel: +599 9 4300 000
Email: steve.r.vanenburg@an.pwc.com

Significant developments

Recent tax developments

On 1 January 2012, the corporate profit tax rate was reduced from 34.5% to 27.5%.

The rate of the turnover tax increased from 5% to 6% on 1 January 2012.

It is now also possible for corporations established according to Curaçao law to opt for a transparent status. A transparent company will be treated as a partnership for tax purposes, and the shareholders will be treated as partners in that partnership.

These changes are part of an overall plan to reduce the corporate profit tax rate in a shift from direct to indirect tax and to broaden the tax base in general. Further changes are expected to enter into force in 2013, which may simplify the requirements to apply for certain investment incentives and incentives that comply with international fiscal standards and will improve the competitiveness of the financial services sector of Curaçao.

Transitional legislation

While the offshore tax regime was abolished in 2001, qualifying offshore companies incorporated before 1 January 2002 may continue to apply the old regime until 2019, provided that certain conditions are met under transitional legislation.

Taxes on corporate income

Resident corporations are taxed on worldwide income. Non-resident companies are taxed on the following Curaçao-source income:

- Income attributable to a permanent establishment (PE).
- Income from real property situated on Curaçao.
- Interest on loans secured by a mortgage on property situated on Curaçao.

Capital gains are not differentiated from operating income and are subject to the same applicable rates. Corporations are taxed on their income as reflected in their profit and loss account, less certain deductible items.

Companies are generally taxed at a flat rate of 27.5%. The tax rate for the years prior to 2012 was 34.5%.

Special minimum rates apply to the taxable income of certain companies:

Type of company	Rate (%)
E-zone companies	2
New industries and hotels	2
Land development companies	2

Shipping business

Shipping companies are subject to the general profit tax rate of 27.5% but may apply for the tonnage regime. If applicable, their profit is calculated based on the rates provided in the table below. If a shipping company applies the tonnage regime, the actual profits or losses are not taken into account, regardless of whether they are regular profits or capital gains.

The calculated profit based on the table below is subject to the general profit tax rate of 27.5%.

Over (tons)	Not over (tons)	Profit per net ton (ANG*)
0	10,000	2.00
10,000	25,000	1.35
25,000		0.60

* Antilles guilders

Exempt companies

Please see the Tax credits and incentives section for information on tax exempt companies.

Companies under transitional offshore rules

The transitional rules distinguish three types of offshore companies.

- Offshore companies which, on the last day of the financial year that ended before 1 January 2002, had all (or almost all) investments in or revenues from portfolio investments, royalties, holding companies, finance companies, or technical support subject to tax rates of 2.4% to 3% (while capital gains and losses were not taken into account) will be grandfathered through the last day of the financial year of the company that starts before 1 July 2019.
- Offshore companies which, on the last day of the financial year that ended before 1 January 2002, had all (or almost all) their profit subject to tax rates of 4.8% to 6% or, under certain circumstances, 2.4% to 3% and which had a valid ruling with the tax inspector (e.g. trading companies, banks, captives commissions, and fee-earning companies) on the aforementioned date or for which a request for (extension of) such a ruling had been filed on that date will be grandfathered through the last day of the financial year of the company that starts before 1 July 2019.
- Offshore companies that, on the last day of the financial year that ended before 1 January 2002, had invested all (or almost all) investments in or revenues from real estate property or rights connected thereto, located outside the Netherlands Antilles. These revenues were, under the old offshore regime, exempt from tax. For profit tax purposes, these companies will be grandfathered through the last day of the financial year of the company that starts before 1 July 2019.

Specific rules are applicable to companies that were incorporated after 30 June 1999 but before 31 December 2001. These companies may also qualify for the aforementioned transitional rules provided that these companies have been active in a meaningful way. In principle, a company will not be considered to have been active in

Curaçao

a meaningful way if the assets of the companies consist predominantly of deposits or receivables on shareholders or affiliated parties.

The grandfathering period continues until 2019.

Corporate residence

Corporate residence is, in principle, determined by the place of incorporation. However, other factors may also determine residence. For example, a foreign company with effective management on Curaçao is considered to be a resident. A company that has been established on Curaçao will always be considered a resident of Curaçao.

Offshore entities on Curaçao must have a local managing director. This function is easily provided by one of the many trust companies established on Curaçao.

Permanent establishment (PE)
The definition of a PE on Curaçao is generally in line with the Organisation for Economic Co-operation and Development (OECD) model.

Transfer of legal seat
Legislation has been enacted under which a Curaçao company is allowed to transfer its legal seat to another jurisdiction (if permitted under the laws of the outside jurisdiction), and a foreign company is allowed to migrate to Curaçao.

Other taxes

Turnover tax
A 6% turnover/sales tax is levied on the revenue derived from services and deliveries rendered by an entrepreneur or company on Curaçao. Prior to 1 January 2012, the turnover tax rate was 5%.

On 1 January 2012, two amendments were made to the turnover tax:

- In addition to services rendered on Curaçao, if a foreign entrepreneur performs a service from abroad to a customer on Curaçao, this service will now also be subject to turnover tax.
- The business concept has been extended. Non-commercial rental of property will now also be subject to turnover tax. Rental of a dwelling that is the principal residence of the tenant is exempt from tax.

A limited number of services and deliveries are exempt, such as:

- Exports.
- Electricity and water.
- Certain services to non-residents.
- Medical services.
- Services at the airport or in the harbour regarding imported or exported goods or goods in transit.
- Advisory and management services provided to or by offshore companies and offshore banks.

An entrepreneur liable to turnover/sales tax must file a declaration, with the Tax Inspectorate before the 16th day of the month following the month concerned, at the Tax Collector's office.

Customs duties/import tariffs

Import tariffs vary in general between 5% and 27%. There is also a range of products that may be imported without import duties. Below, we provide some examples, but we note that in each category there may be specific exemptions to the general tariff.

- Basic food products are tax exempt.
- Other food products are generally taxed at a rate of 5.5% up to 13%.
- Books, computers: 0%
- Furniture: 22%
- Cars: 27%

Excise taxes

Excise tax is due on gasoline; alcohol, with different tariffs for liquor and beer; and tobacco.

Some examples include:

- ANG 0.4725 per litre of gasoline.
- ANG 23 per volume percent of alcohol per hectolitre of distilled products.
- ANG 14.55 per 100 cigarettes (imported).

Land tax

A land tax is levied on real estate located on Curaçao at an annual rate of 0.3% on the value of the land.

Transfer taxes

The transfer of immovable property located on Curaçao is subject to a 4% transfer duty.

Stamp taxes

A stamp tax is levied in two ways, in the form of stamps and as stamped paper.

Stamp tax applies to documents such as government licences, leases, agreements, and court documents. The rate depends on the type of document. As an example, the stamp tax for bank checks is ANG 0.25. The general rate for each page of a legal document is ANG 5.

Branch income

Tax rates on the profits of PEs are the same as for resident corporations.

There are specific rules for the PE of an insurance company. In that case, the company may elect to declare profit based on a percentage of premiums received by the PE, as well as premiums the company has received from insured residents and from insured risks on Curaçao. The insurance company may also elect to declare a profit that is in the same proportion to total profit of the company as the aforementioned premiums to total premiums.

No tax is withheld on transfers of profits to the head office.

Curaçao

Income determination

Inventory valuation
Both the last in first out (LIFO) and first in first out (FIFO) methods of inventory valuation are permitted, provided the chosen method conforms to sound commercial practice. Conformity of book and tax reporting is not required. However, occasions or situations for differences are very rare.

Capital gains
Capital gains or losses are, in principle, considered ordinary income and subject to standard corporate rates. An exemption from profit tax is granted for advantages (dividends and capital gains) from a qualifying participation (*see Dividend income below*).

The gain on disposal of depreciable assets may be carried over to a special tax deferral reinvestment reserve but must then be deducted from the acquisition cost of the later acquired asset. The reserve may be maintained for a maximum of four years. If the reserve has not been fully applied, the remainder will be liable to taxation in the fourth year.

Under the transitional regime for offshore companies (investment, holding, finance, and patent holding companies), capital gains and losses are tax exempt.

Dividend income
In general, a full participation exemption applies to all local as well as foreign participations for dividends as well as for capital gains. However, it is now required that dividends be derived from an active participation (non-portfolio investment) or a participation that is subject to tax.

Expenses incurred in connection with a qualifying participation (including capital losses) are not deductible, unless it can be demonstrated that these are indirectly incurred to realise profits that are subject to tax on Curaçao.

Non-portfolio investment clause
A participation is deemed to be active if the gross income of that participation consists of not more than 50% of dividends, interest, or royalties received other than from an enterprise of that participation.

Subject-to-tax clause
A participation is deemed to be subject to tax if it is subject to a tax rate of at least 10%.

If at least one of these clauses has been met, the 100% participation exemption will apply. If none of these clauses are met, the participation exemption is limited to 63% of dividends. Consequently, the dividends would be subject to an effective tax rate of 10.17% (37% x 27.5% regular tax rate).

The 100% exemption also applies to income other than dividends, such as capital gains derived from qualifying participations.

Immovable property
The aforementioned clauses do not apply to dividends from a participation that (almost) exclusively (directly or indirectly) holds immovable property. The 100% participation exemption applies to these dividends.

Curaçao

Definition of dividend
A dividend is defined as a distribution of profits on shares or profit-sharing notes, paid from statutory profits or profit reserves. Dividends shall not be considered payments for the purchase of own shares or profit-sharing notes, distributions on shares upon liquidation, repayment of paid-up capital, or the distribution of bonus shares.

Minimum cost-price threshold for participations
The minimum cost-price threshold for shareholdings, profit-sharing notes, or voting rights of less than 5% is ANG 890,000.

Interest income
There is no specific regime for interest received. Interest income is therefore taxed at the same rate as other income.

Foreign income
A Curaçao corporation is taxed on foreign interest and other income as earned, and on foreign dividends when received. Undistributed income of foreign subsidiaries is not taxable.

Curaçao has adopted a definition of a branch (permanent establishment/permanent representatives) that is in line with the definition in the OECD Model Double Taxation Convention on Income and Capital.

The profits of a PE in Aruba, St. Maarten, or the Netherlands, including the Caribbean Netherlands, are tax exempt on Curaçao based on the tax arrangement with the Kingdom of the Netherlands. In the case of a PE outside the Kingdom of the Netherlands (i.e. the Netherlands, Aruba, Curaçao, and St. Maarten), the income realised through the PE, after deduction of foreign taxes, is tax exempt. In the case of a foreign loss, this is not deductible.

The profits of a branch with more than 50% low-taxed passive investment income will only be 63% exempt. In case of a loss, 63% of the loss will not be deductible. The branch profit is in line with the treatment of participation profits and losses.

Foreign real estate is always deemed to be part of a PE and, as such, is fully tax exempt.

Deductions

Depreciation and amortisation
Depreciation of tangible fixed assets, excluding land, is taken over the estimated useful life of the asset. The depreciable base includes purchase price, customs duties, shipping costs, and installation costs, less residual value, if any. The straight-line method is customary, but the declining-balance method is also acceptable. In addition, an accelerated deduction of one-third of the assets' depreciable basis may be taken. The assets' remaining cost basis (two-thirds) is depreciated using one of the acceptable methods.

The cost basis of certain intangible assets, such as patents, trademarks, and copyrights, can be amortised over their expected useful lives. Goodwill and other intangibles resulting from the excess of purchase price over the cost basis of assets purchased are amortised over three to five years.

The tax department has issued the following estimated depreciation table.

Curaçao

Assets	Rate (%)	Residual value (%)
Buildings	2-2.5	10
Renovation	10	0
Inventory	10-20	10
Computer		
Hardware	33-50	0
Mainframe	10-12.5	0
Machinery and installations	10	10
Transportation		
Cars	20	10
Rental cars	33	15
Trucks and buses	10	15
Start-up costs	20	0
Goodwill	20	0

Start-up expenses

Start-up expenses should be capitalised and may be depreciated, comparable to goodwill, over five years.

Anti-abuse rules regarding interest and loans

Due to existing anti-abuse rules, the deduction for interest paid on intra-group debts relating to certain transactions is disallowed. However, if the taxpayer provides credible evidence of overriding commercial reasons for the transaction, or in case the interest in the hands of the recipient is taxed at an effective tax rate that is considered adequate by Curaçao standards, the interest may be deductible.

In case of intra-group financing, for profit tax purposes the amount of interest paid or received should be based on arm's-length principles.

In case of profit participating loans, the interest will be qualified as dividend and will not be deductible. Interest received on such loans may meet the definitions of the participation exemption if the creditor also holds a qualifying participation in the debtor.

A write-down of an intra-group loan may be denied in case of a profit-participating loan, or if at the time of issuance it was foreseeable that the loan would never be repaid fully.

Charitable contributions

Charitable donations to qualifying entities within the Kingdom of the Netherlands may be deducted to the extent that they exceed 1% of net income and ANG 100 after utilisation of tax loss carryforwards. The maximum deduction is 3% of net income.

Fines and penalties

Fines and penalties are not deductible in cases where they have been imposed by a criminal court in Curaçao, or have been paid to avoid prosecution, and in cases of administrative fines imposed by a Government agency in Curaçao.

Taxes

Taxes, other than the corporate profit tax itself, incurred in the course of doing business are deductible.

Curaçao

Bribes, kickbacks, and illegal payments
Expenses that are connected to a criminal offence for which a taxpayer has been convicted are not deductible. Bribes paid to public servants and politicians are not deductible.

Net operating losses
Losses may be carried forward for a period of ten years. Start-up losses during the first four years for companies having tax holidays may be carried forward indefinitely. Carrybacks are not permitted.

Payments to foreign affiliates
The Corporate Tax Act provides for specific limitations for deduction of interest in certain cases of restructuring and refinancing involving the creation of artificial flows of interest payments to persons who are tax exempt or subject to lower taxes in their jurisdiction.

Group taxation

Fiscal unity
The Corporate Tax Act provides for fiscal unity treatment for corporate profit tax purposes. Resident companies with wholly owned resident subsidiaries could qualify for this regime. The parent company is entitled to submit one consolidated income tax return on behalf of the entire fiscal unity group. As a result, only the parent company is assessed.

Within certain limitations, losses of one company can be offset against the profits made by another company in the fiscal unity group. No profits need to be recognised on inter-company transactions, as these are disregarded for tax purposes. The fiscal unity applies for profit tax purposes only; the participating entities remain separate and identifiable under civil law.

Fiscal unity relief is confined to companies organised under the laws of Curaçao, the Netherlands, Aruba, or St. Maarten. The companies which invoke this relief must have their place of management on Curaçao.

On the basis of the non-discrimination provision of a relevant tax treaty, entities established under the laws of a tax treaty party may also be admitted to the fiscal unity regime provided that they are resident on Curaçao.

Transfer pricing
There are no specific regulations with regard to transfer pricing. However, based on case law, businesses can be required to show that in case of intra-company transactions, these transactions have been made at arm's length.

Thin capitalisation
In cases where a company receives a loan from an associated exempt private limited liability company (*Besloten Vennootschap* or BV), and the amount of the loan is more than three times the net equity of the company, the interest on the loan is not deductible for the part that is more than three times the net equity.

Curaçao

Tax credits and incentives

Foreign tax credit
A tax credit applies to income from abroad that has been subject to tax at source or to another tax on income. The tax credit is allowed for the income tax levied abroad, but shall not exceed the Curaçao profit tax that is attributable to that foreign income.

Inward investment and capital investment
There are tax incentives or holidays for the establishment of new economic enterprises and hotels with a predetermined minimum employment and capital investment. Special provisions relate to the taxation of shipping and insurance companies.

Investment allowance
For a minimum investment of ANG 5,000, an 8% investment allowance on acquisitions and improvements (for new buildings, 12%) is permitted as a deduction from taxable profit in the year of investment and in the subsequent year, for businesses operating on Curaçao.

Accelerated depreciation and tax rollover reserve
An accelerated deduction of one-third of the assets' depreciable basis may be taken. If a profit results at the time of sale of capital assets with the intention to replace that asset, the profit may be placed in a tax rollover account.

Tax exempt company
It is possible to elect tax-exempt status for a BV. To qualify for the exemption, a number of conditions must be met, including (but not limited to) the disclosure of beneficiaries, management, financials, and the activities (only investment and financing activities) of the company. Recently, the licensing of intellectual and industrial property rights and other comparable property and usage rights have been added to the list of allowed activities.

Another condition has been added that requires that no more than 5% of the revenues of the exempt company consist of dividends from subsidiaries that are not subject to a tax regime comparable to that of Curaçao. A profit tax regime is comparable to that of Curaçao if the foreign tax regime provides for a profit tax rate of at least 13.75% (50% of the Curaçao tax rate).

The subject-to-tax requirement is also met if the foreign tax regime appears on a list of comparable tax regimes. The list that has been issued includes all EU and OECD member states and all jurisdictions with which Curaçao has a tax treaty. According to the list, the subject-to-tax requirement is also met in the case of a jurisdiction that is included in the white list issued by the OECD, provided that no special tax regime is applicable.

Independent expert
Currently, an independent expert is required to certify that the exempt company meets the requirements for exempt status. If more than 5% of the revenues of the exempt company consist of dividends from subsidiaries that are not subject to a tax comparable to that of Curaçao, the independent expert must inform the Inspectorate of Taxes. The inspector notifies the company that it no longer meets the requirements for exempt status. The exempt status is then terminated starting the first day of the year following the year in which the notification becomes final.

Ocean shipping companies

Ocean shipping companies are taxed on a fixed profit per net ton of ANG 0.60 up to ANG 2.00 (or per 10 net ton in case of management and control). International aviation companies may apply a reduced tax rate against 80% of their profit, as their profits are deemed to be gained outside of Curaçao. As a result, the overall effective tax rate is 9.66%.

E-zone companies

An e-zone is an area designated for international trade and services. The activities of companies established in an e-zone must be focused on trading or providing services to companies located outside of Curaçao. There are two types of e-zones:

- Designated areas where, amongst others, goods can be stored, processed, machined, assembled, packaged, displayed, and released or handled in any other way. On Curaçao, there are two of this type of e-zone that are dedicated to goods, one located at the harbour, and the other at the airport.
- E-zones where international trade and trade supportive services may be performed, supported by electronic communication and information equipment (e-commerce). There are several e-commerce zones on Curaçao.

E-zone companies are subject to a minimum 2% corporate profit tax until 1 January 2026. They will be granted special facilities regarding turnover tax.

New industries and hotels

New industries and hotels are granted partial exemption from profit tax and a minimum 2% tax rate for a period of five to 11 years. A minimum investment is required. Losses incurred during the first four years of operations may be used to offset taxable income for an indefinite period of time.

Land development companies

Land development companies are granted a tax holiday. They are exempt from tax on profits realised on the sale of the developed land. A minimum investment of ANG 1 million is required. Activities should be expected to enhance the economic development of Curaçao.

Private foundations

Private foundations are exempt from Curaçao profit tax, and their distributions are exempt from Curaçao gift tax, as are contributions of assets to the foundation by a non-resident. Gift tax in the contributor's country may be applicable.

The 'private' foundation is a variant of the long-existing 'common' foundation. The most important difference is that the purposes of a common foundation may not include making distributions (other than distributions of an idealistic or social nature). This restriction does not apply to private foundations, whose purpose may include making distributions to the founders and others. A private foundation may not run a business or enterprise for profit. If, however, a private foundation does realise profits from a business or enterprise, that profit will be taxed at the normal tax rate of 27.5% (as of 1 January 2012). Acting as a holding company or investment company is not considered running a business. The private foundation is intended to be an alternative to the Anglo-Saxon trust, especially in civil law jurisdictions.

It is possible to opt for a taxable status for a private foundation. In that case, its profits, other than those arising from active business activities, will be taxed at a rate of 10%.

Curaçao

Transparent companies

As of 1 January 2012, it is now possible to opt for a transparent status. This option is only available to a BV or a limited liability company (*Naamloze Vennootschap* or NV) established according to Curaçao law. It is, however, possible to convert a corporation that has been established elsewhere to a BV or NV, at which time the transparent status can be requested. Newly established companies can request the status from the start, if the request is filed with the Inspectorate within three months. Existing companies can request the status as of the next following year.

A transparent company will be treated as a partnership for tax purposes, and the shareholders will be treated as the partners in that partnership.

Withholding taxes

Although a dividend withholding tax (WHT) was approved in 1999, it has been decided that for the foreseeable future this tax will not enter into force. If it is decided that the tax will enter into force, there is a mandatory transitional period during which the tax will not be applicable to legal entities resident at that time on Curaçao.

Tax treaties

Curaçao currently has tax treaties in effect with Aruba, the Netherlands, Norway, and St. Maarten. A double tax agreement (DTA) has been negotiated with Jamaica, but this has not entered into force yet. Furthermore, tax information exchange agreements (TIEAs) have been signed with several countries, including Australia, Canada, Denmark, Mexico, New Zealand, Spain, Sweden, and the United States. As a result, Curaçao, as part of the former Netherlands Antilles, has been moved to the white list of the OECD Global Forum.

Tax arrangement for the Kingdom of the Netherlands (TAK)

As part of the Kingdom of the Netherlands (TAK), Curaçao is party to a federal tax agreement with the Netherlands, Aruba, and St. Maarten. Subject to this treaty, dividends, interest, and royalties paid out to a Curaçao company may qualify for reduced rates of WHT in the subject countries.

Dutch dividend WHT is 15% if the Curaçao company owns less than 25% of the Dutch company. On Curaçao, only 5% of these dividends are taxed, at a rate of 34.5%, which results in an effective profit tax rate of 1.725%.

If the Curaçao company's interest is 25% or more, Dutch WHT can be reduced to 8.3%. This tax is then paid, under a special procedure, to the Curaçao tax authorities. These dividends are fully exempt from profit tax on Curaçao.

Capital gains derived from shareholdings in Netherlands' corporations are fully exempt from profit tax on Curaçao, provided that the shareholding amounts to at least 25% interest in the corporation. If the shareholding amounts to less than 25%, the capital gain is tax exempt for 95%.

The WHT regime in the TAK also applies to the old Curaçao offshore companies.

The TAK is to be revised. Negotiations have already started between Aruba and Curaçao each with the Netherlands. In the end, the existing TAK will then be replaced by separate tax agreements between two countries (e.g. between Aruba, Curaçao, and St. Maarten each with the Netherlands), as well as separate agreements between the three islands Aruba, Curaçao, and St. Maarten. The aim is to have the new agreements in place in 2013.

Tax administration

Taxable period
Profit tax is levied by way of a self-assessment system. Returns are to be filed on a calendar-year basis. Non-resident corporations may file their returns based on a calendar year basis or on a different book-year. On request, this may also apply, for example, when a resident company is the subsidiary of a foreign parent company (i.e. only a local company must request for a different tax year-end).

Tax returns
A provisional return must be filed within three months after the end of the book-year. A final return must be filed within six months after the end of the book-year.

For the provisional return, no extensions are granted. For the final return, an extension may be requested. In general, no extensions will be granted for more than 12 months after the book-year.

Payment of tax
Payment is to be made at the time of filing and in a lump sum on the basis of the self-assessment. This means that if the book-year equals the calendar year, the provisional return is due before 1 April of the following year, and the final return before 1 July of the following year.

In general, at the time of filing the provisional return, an amount equal to the profit tax of the previous year must be paid; the remaining balance due for the year for which the return is filed must be paid at the time of filing the final return.

For example, if the tax due for the year 2011 was 100, then at the time of filing the provisional return for 2012, which is due before 1 April 2013, that same amount must be declared and paid. If there is reason to believe that the amount for the year 2012 will be lower than for 2011, upon request, the estimated lower amount may be paid at the time of filing the provisional return.

At the time of filing the final return for the year 2012, which is due before 1 July 2013, the balance due must be paid, or if the total amount is less than the amount already paid up, a repayment will follow.

Audit cycle
As the profit tax is levied based on self-assessment, the tax department does not issue a final tax assessment. There is no specific cycle for audits. Depending on a desk review of the tax returns of the last couple of years, an audit may follow.

Statute of limitations
A reassessment can be imposed until five years after the tax year. In cases where the tax payer is considered to be in bad faith, a reassessment can be imposed until ten years after the tax year.

Curaçao

Topics of focus for tax authorities

There are no specific topics of focus. In case an audit is started, each aspect may be investigated. Often the audit will not only focus on the profit tax, but also the other tax obligations, such as sales tax, wage tax, and social security premiums.

....

Other issues

Exchange controls

In general, exchange control regulations are very liberal for offshore companies. Offshore companies established on Curaçao can obtain non-resident status for exchange control purposes, which basically provides for total exemption from exchange controls. Onshore companies are subject to slightly stricter rules. These companies are subject to a licence fee of 1%.

Business combinations

The Corporate Tax Act provides for a tax facility for business mergers. In a business merger, a company acquires all or a substantial part of the trade or business of another company with a view towards combining the business operations of the two companies into a permanent financial and economic organisation. If the business is transferred as part of a business merger, the gains realised by the transferor are not subject to profit tax if certain conditions are met.

Although there is no specific provision in the Corporate Tax Act with regard to legal mergers, legal split-ups, and re-incorporations, the Tax Inspectorate has announced that when certain conditions are met, a tax facility also applies in these cases.

Cyprus

PwC contact

Nicos Chimarides
PricewaterhouseCoopers
Julia House
3 Themistocles Dervis Street
CY-1066 Nicosia, Cyprus
Tel: +357 22 555270
Email: nicos.chimarides@cy.pwc.com

Significant developments

The Cyprus income tax office has recently given clarity on the minimum acceptable spreads of interest on related-party, back-to-back financing transactions involving Cyprus companies. *See The Cyprus financing company in the Tax credits and incentives section for a table of acceptable spreads.*

Further, the income tax law itself has been amended to provide generous exemptions from tax on income related to intellectual property (IP) (*see the Intellectual property [IP] regime in the Tax credits and incentives section for more information*), as well as accelerated tax depreciation on certain assets (*see Depreciation and amortisation in the Deductions section for more information*).

Arm's-length rules have also been relaxed (*see Transfer pricing in the Group taxation section for more information*).

As of 1 March 2012, the standard VAT rate in Cyprus increased from 15% to 17%.

Taxes on corporate income

All companies that are tax residents of Cyprus are taxed on their income accrued or derived from all sources in Cyprus and abroad. A non-Cyprus tax resident company is taxed on income accrued or derived from business activity which is carried out through a permanent establishment (PE) in Cyprus and on certain other income arising from sources in Cyprus.

The corporate income tax (CIT) rate in Cyprus is 10% on taxable income.

However, the Cyprus income tax law provides explicitly for a number of exemptions for many and varied types of incomes, profits, and gains of Cyprus-based corporations (*see the Income determination section for more information*).

Special contribution for defence

Special contribution for defence is imposed on certain income earned by Cyprus tax residents. Non-tax residents of Cyprus are exempt from this special contribution for defence.

Dividends generally are exempt from special contribution for defence, subject to certain rarely applicable limitations (*see Dividend income in the Income determination section*).

Cyprus

Interest received by close-ended or open-ended collective investment schemes (CIS) is never subject to special contribution for defence. Such interest is only taxed under CIT after deducting expenses at the standard CIT rate of 10%.

Interest received by other companies in the ordinary course of business, including interest closely connected to the ordinary course of business, is also only taxed under CIT after deducting expenses at the standard CIT rate of 10%.

When companies receive interest that does not satisfy the conditions prescribed immediately above, the interest is subject to special contribution for defence without expense deduction at the rate of 15%. Such 'passive' nature interest would, however, be exempt from CIT.

In addition to CIT of 10%, gross rental income reduced by 25% is subject to special contribution for defence at the rate of 3%.

Companies, partnerships, the government, or any local authorities that pay rents to Cyprus tax resident landowners should withhold special contribution for defence at source.

Tonnage tax
For ship-owning companies, the profits derived by the owner of a ship registered in the European Union (EU) or European Economic Area (EEA) (as well as other foreign jurisdictions, subject to conditions) from its operation are fully exempt from all direct taxes. The term 'owner' includes a bareboat charterer of a non-Cyprus flag vessel parallel registered in Cyprus. A similar exemption applies to charterers and ship managers.

Instead of CIT, ship owners, charterers, and managers pay tonnage tax on the net tonnage of the ships they own, charter, or manage. In addition, there is no tax on dividends paid at all levels of distribution by the above persons out of profits subject to tonnage tax and related capital gains on the sale of the ship and no capital gains tax on the sale or transfer of a ship, share in a ship, or shares in a ship-owning company. The same legislation also provides for income tax exemption of the salaries and benefits of the captain, the officers, and the crew aboard a Cyprus flag vessel.

This treatment applies until 2020 and is compulsory for Cyprus flag ship owners, but optional for other ship owners, charterers, and ship managers.

Local income taxes
There are no local government taxes on income in Cyprus.

Corporate residence

Only companies managed and controlled in Cyprus are treated as tax resident of Cyprus.

Permanent establishment (PE)
Cyprus domestic income tax legislation also explicitly provides for the determination of a taxable PE of a non-Cyprus tax resident company in Cyprus. These specific legislative provisions are in line with the relevant article of the Organisation for Economic Co-operation and Development (OECD) model treaty.

Other taxes

Value-added tax (VAT)

VAT is imposed on the provision of goods and services in Cyprus as well as on the acquisition of goods from the European Union and the importation of goods into Cyprus. Taxable persons charge VAT on their taxable supplies (output tax) and are charged with VAT on goods or services which they received (input tax).

C

As of 1 March 2012, the standard VAT rate in Cyprus is 17% (15% through 29 February 2012). Two reduced VAT rates, an 8% rate and a 5% rate, apply in Cyprus:

- The reduced VAT rate of 8% applies on accommodation, restaurant and catering services, as well as on certain local passenger transport services. As of 10 January 2011, the term 'restaurant and catering services' includes the supplies of prepared and unprepared foodstuffs and beverages that are accompanied by sufficient support services that enable the immediate consumption of the foodstuffs and beverages supplied.
- The reduced rate of 5% applies on foodstuffs, pharmaceutical products, books and newspapers, as well as on a variety of other goods and services which are beyond the scope of this summary. The reduced rate of 5% also applies, subject to conditions, on the sale of new buildings/houses to individuals/eligible persons, who will use them as their primary and main residences, provided the contract has been signed after 1 October 2011.

Exports from Cyprus are zero-rated (i.e. no VAT must be charged on the export, and the company is entitled to recover the relevant input VAT suffered). The services for the international transport of passengers as well as the transportation of goods either from or to countries outside the European Union are also zero-rated.

Supplies of goods to businesses resident in other EU member states are outside the scope of Cyprus VAT.

Certain education services, as well as the majority of financial, insurance, and medical services, are exempt from Cyprus VAT. Supplies of land and buildings also are exempt from VAT, unless the supply relates to new buildings before first use.

VAT registration

VAT registration is compulsory for business with:

- turnover in excess of 15,600 euros (EUR) during the 12 preceding months or
- an expected turnover in excess of EUR 15,600 within the next 30 days.

Business with turnover of less than EUR 15,600, or with supplies that are outside the scope of VAT but for which the right to claim the amount of the related input VAT is granted, have the option to register on a voluntary basis.

An obligation for registration also arises for businesses which make acquisition of goods from other EU member states in excess of EUR 10,251.61 during any calendar year.

In addition, as of 1 January 2010, an obligation for VAT registration arises for businesses engaged in the supply of intra-Community services for which the recipient must account for VAT under the reverse charge provisions. Furthermore, an obligation for VAT registration arises for businesses carrying out economic activities from the receipt of services from abroad for which an obligation to account for Cyprus VAT under

Cyprus

the reverse charge provision exists, subject to the registration threshold of EUR 15,600 per any consecutive 12-month period.

No registration threshold exists for the provision of intra-Community supplies of services.

Exempted products and services, and disposals of items of capital nature, are not taken into account for determining annual turnover for registration purposes.

Registration is effected by completing the appropriate application form.

VAT declaration and payment/return of VAT

VAT returns must be submitted quarterly, and the payment of VAT must be made by the tenth day of the second month that follows the month in which the tax period ends.

VAT registered persons have the right to request for a different filing period. Approval of the VAT authorities is required. The VAT Commissioner also has the right to request for a taxable person to file one's VAT returns for a different period.

Where in a quarter input VAT is higher than output VAT, the difference is refunded or is transferred to the next VAT quarters.

Immovable property tax

Immovable property is subject to property tax, which is levied on the market value of the property as of 1 January 1980, and is payable by the end of September each year.

The 2012 tax rates and bands vary as follows:

Property value as of 1 January 1980 (EUR)	Tax rate (%)
Up to 120,000	0
120,001 to 170,000	0.4
170,001 to 300,000	0.5
300,001 to 500,000	0.6
500,001 to 800,000	0.7
Over 800,000	0.8

Public property, buildings under preservation order, buildings of charitable organisations, and agricultural property are generally exempt.

Stamp duty

The general rule is that Cyprus stamp duty is imposed only on written contracts relating to assets located in Cyprus or to matters that will take place in Cyprus. The applicable rates are based on the value of each document and are 0.15% for the first EUR 170,860 and 0.20% thereafter, subject to an overall maximum of EUR 17,086 per contract.

Capital duty

Upon incorporation of the company

Upon incorporation of the company, capital duty is due on the authorised share capital at EUR 102.52 plus 0.6% of the authorised share capital.

As for the issued share capital, there is no stamp duty payable if the shares are issued at their nominal value. There is a flat duty of EUR 17.09 if the shares are issued at a premium.

Upon subsequent increases

Upon subsequent increases, capital duty is due on the authorised share capital at 0.6% of the nominal value of the additional share capital.

As for the issued share capital, EUR 17.09 is due on every issue batch, whether the shares are issued at a premium or not and irrespective of the number of shares issued every time.

Capital gains tax

Capital gains tax is imposed at the rate of 20% on gains arising from the disposal of immovable property situated in Cyprus and of shares in companies (other than companies whose shares are listed in any recognised stock exchange) that own immovable property situated in Cyprus. Liability is confined to gains accruing since 1 January 1980. The costs deducted from gross proceeds on the disposal of immovable property are its market value at 1 January 1980, or the costs of acquisition and improvements of the property, if made after 1 January 1980, as adjusted for inflation up to the date of disposal on the basis of the consumer price index in Cyprus.

Other expenses which are related to the acquisition and disposal of immovable property also are deducted, subject to certain conditions (e.g. interest costs on related loans, transfer fees, legal expenses).

Social security contributions

Employed persons are compulsorily insured under a state-administered social insurance fund. Contributions to the fund are borne by both employer and employee. The employer's contributions are made as a percentage of earnings to the following funds:

Funds	Employer contribution (%)
Social insurance fund	6.8
Redundancy fund	1.2
Training development fund	0.5
Social cohesion fund	2.0
Holiday fund (option for exception)	8.0

With the exception of the social cohesion fund, the maximum amount of monthly earnings on which the contributions are made is EUR 4,442 as of 1 January 2012. This maximum is usually adjusted for inflation annually at the beginning of each calendar year.

Special Contribution

As of 2012, the following Special Contributions are payable on the gross monthly incomes of individuals working within Cyprus:

Gross monthly emoluments from employment/pension (EUR)	Contribution (%) (1)
0 to 1,500	0
1,501 to 2,500	0

Cyprus

Gross monthly emoluments from employment/pension (EUR)	Contribution (%) (1)
2,501 to 3,500	2.5
	(minimum EUR 10)
3,501 to 4,500	3.0
Over 4,500	3.5

Notes

1. In the case of employed individuals, the recipient of the remuneration is liable for half the Special Contribution and the employer for the other half.

Branch income

The rate of tax on Cyprus branch profits is the same as on corporate profits. No further tax is withheld on transfers of profits on funds to a foreign head office.

Income determination

Inventory valuation

Inventories generally are stated at the lower of cost and net realisable value. Last in first out (LIFO) is not permitted for taxation purposes. First in first out (FIFO) is permitted. Conformity between book and tax reporting is not required.

Capital gains

Profits from disposals of corporate titles are unconditionally exempt from CIT. 'Titles' is defined as shares, bonds, debentures, founders' shares, and other titles of companies or other legal persons incorporated in Cyprus or abroad, and options thereon, as well as futures/forwards on titles, short positions on titles, swaps on titles, depositary receipts, repos, units in close-ended or open-ended CIS, international collective investment schemes (ICIS), undertakings for collective investments of transferable securities (UCITS), investment trusts and funds, mutual funds, real estate investment trusts (REITS), and units in stock exchange indices.

Capital gains on immovable property are taxed at a separate rate in Cyprus. *See Capital gains tax in the Other taxes section for more information.*

Dividend income

All dividends received from other Cyprus companies are excluded from all taxes at all times, unless they are declared after the lapse of four years from the end of the year in which profits generated.

Dividends earned from foreign investments are exempt from income tax in Cyprus. Such dividend income is also exempt from special contribution for defence unless:

- more than 50% of the foreign paying company's activities result directly or indirectly in investment income and
- the foreign tax is significantly lower than the tax burden in Cyprus (i.e. less than 5%).

Note that where the Cyprus participation exemption on foreign dividend income is not available, then any foreign withholding tax (WHT) imposition on dividends paid to the

Cyprus

Cyprus company will be credited against the Cyprus flat special contribution for defence rate of 20% on such dividends. Furthermore, in some cases, an underlying tax credit will also be granted.

Stock dividends
A Cyprus corporation can distribute tax-free dividends of common stock (bonus shares) proportionately to all common stock shareholders.

Interest income
See Special contribution for defence in the Taxes on corporate income section for a description of the tax treatment of interest income.

Rental income
See Special contribution for defence in the Taxes on corporate income section for a description of the tax treatment of rental income.

Foreign income
Resident corporations are subject to tax on their worldwide income. However, foreign-branch income, as well as dividend income from abroad (*see above*), is exempt from taxation in Cyprus.

Where foreign income is taxed in Cyprus, double taxation is avoided through unilateral relief, by giving credit for foreign taxation, or by treaty relief. This credit may not exceed the Cyprus taxes imposed on the same income.

Profits from a PE abroad are exempt from CIT. This exemption is always applicable, unless:

- more than 50% of the foreign PE's activities result directly or indirectly in investment income and
- the foreign tax on the income of the foreign PE is significantly lower than the tax burden in Cyprus (i.e. less than 5%).

Deductions

All expenditure wholly and exclusively incurred for the generation of taxable income is deductible against the company's taxable income. All such expenditure should be supported by invoices and relevant receipts or other supporting documents.

Depreciation and amortisation
Depreciation is computed on a straight-line basis at rates that vary, depending on the life and type of asset. Tax depreciation is not required to conform to book depreciation. Gains on the sale of depreciated property are taxable as ordinary income to the extent of depreciation allowed.

Property and equipment acquired during the tax years 2012, 2013, and 2014 will be eligible to claim accelerated tax depreciation at the rate of 20% (excluding assets that are already eligible for a higher annual rate of tax depreciation).

In case of industrial and hotel buildings that are acquired during the tax years 2012, 2013, and 2014, tax depreciation at the rate of 7% per annum may be claimed.

Cyprus

Any expenditure of a capital nature for the acquisition or development of IP will be claimed as a deduction in the tax year in which it was incurred and the immediate four following years on a straight-line basis (*see Intellectual property [IP] regime in the Tax credits and incentives section*).

Goodwill
Any amounts paid for the acquisition of trading goodwill should be deductible upon the subsequent sale of such trading goodwill.

Research and development (R&D) expenses
Any expenditure on scientific research of a capital nature for which no capital allowance is granted is deductible from taxable income and spread equally over the year in which it has been incurred and the five subsequent years. Scientific expenditure of a revenue nature is deducted in the year incurred.

Interest expenses
Any interest expenses incurred by the company for the generation of its taxable income should be deductible in the company's tax computation.

Bad debt
Bad debts of any business should be deductible, provided they are provided against specific trading receivables and the taxpayer can evidently prove that all necessary steps were taken beforehand to recover them.

Charitable contributions
Charitable donations or contributions made for educational, cultural, or other charitable purposes to Cyprus, or to approved charitable institutions, are wholly deductible, provided that these expenses are supported with relevant vouchers.

Taxes
Taxes that are deducted in computing profits for CIT purposes include VAT not recovered and the employer's share of contributions to the social insurance and other funds.

Net operating losses
Tax losses can be carried forward indefinitely and set-off against taxable profits of future years. Carrybacks are not permitted.

Payments to foreign affiliates
A Cyprus corporation can claim a deduction for royalties and interest charges paid to foreign affiliates, and a reasonable amount of head office expenses of an overseas company, provided such expenditures can be justified as having been incurred in the production of the income.

In the case of insurance companies, the amount of head office expenses should not exceed 3% of the net premiums in Cyprus for the general insurance business and 2% for the life insurance business.

Group taxation

Group relief provisions allow, subject to certain conditions, companies of the same group to transfer losses from the loss-making companies to profitable companies. A group includes only Cyprus resident companies with at least a 75% direct or indirect holding relationship.

Transfer pricing

Cyprus tax law does not contain any transfer pricing provisions. However, transactions between related parties should be carried out at pure commercial terms (i.e. at arm's length).

Arm's-length rules may not apply to transactions between a Cyprus tax resident parent company and its 100% direct Cyprus tax resident subsidiary company in certain circumstances.

Tax credits and incentives

Foreign tax credit

See Foreign income in the Income determination section for a description of the foreign tax credit regime.

The Cyprus holding company

The exemptions for dividends received from abroad, foreign PE trading profits, and profits from transactions in titles (see Capital gains in the Income determination section for a description of titles), together with the fact that Cyprus does not withhold taxes on dividend, interest, and royalty (unless right is used in Cyprus) payments made abroad, and its extensive double tax treaty (DTT) network as well as full adoption and access to all EU Directives, makes Cyprus an ideal 'holding company' EU jurisdiction.

The Cyprus financing company

The low CIT rate of 10% imposed on interest incomes coupled with acceptable thin spreads on related-party, back-to-back financing arrangements make Cyprus a very competitive 'financing company' EU jurisdiction.

The minimum acceptable spreads are as follows:

Amount of loan (EUR)	Spread (%)
Less than 50 million	0.35
50 to 200 million	0.25
Greater than 200 million	0.125

Intellectual property (IP) regime

As of 1 January 2012, the income tax law provides for generous exemptions from tax of income related to IP.

More specifically:

* 80% of any income generated from IP owned by Cypriot tax resident companies (net of any direct expenses) is exempt from income tax
* 80% of profit generated from the disposal of IP by Cypriot tax resident companies (net of any direct expenses) is exempt from income tax
* the definition of IP includes all intangible assets, including copyrights, patents, and trademarks, and

Cyprus

- any expenditure of a capital nature for the acquisition or development of IP can be claimed as a deduction in the tax year in which it was incurred and the immediate four following years on a straight-line basis.

The Cyprus international collective investment schemes (ICIS)
The ICIS law, enacted in 1999, provides the required legal framework for the registration, regulation of operations, and supervision of ICIS. The sole objective of ICIS is the collective investment of funds of the unit-holders.

ICIS can take the following legal forms:

- International fixed capital company.
- International variable capital company.
- International unit trust scheme.
- International investment limited partnership.

ICIS are exempt from tax on profits arising on disposal of titles. Dividend income also is exempt (with minor limitations), whereas interest income is taxed at the rate of 10%.

ICIS set-up in Cyprus can utilise the DTT network of Cyprus.

Withholding taxes

The following tables give a summary of the WHT provided under the DTTs entered into by Cyprus.

Paid from Cyprus

Recipient	WHT (%) (1)		
	Dividends	Interest	Royalties
Non-treaty countries	0	0	0/10 (2)
Treaty countries:			
Armenia	0 (30)	5	5
Austria	10	0	0
Belarus	5 (17)	5	5
Belgium	10 (8)	10 (6, 18)	0
Bulgaria	5 (22)	7 (6)	10
Canada	15	15 (4)	10 (5)
China, P.R.	10	10	10
Czech Republic	0 (28)	0	0 (29)
Denmark	0 (6, 32)	0	0
Egypt	15	15	10
France	10 (9)	10 (10)	0 (3)
Germany	5 (8)	0	0
Greece	25	10	0 (11)
Hungary	0	10 (6)	0
India	10 (9)	10 (10)	10 (15)
Ireland, Republic of	0	0	0 (11)
Italy	0	10	0
Kuwait	10	10 (6)	5 (7)
Kyrgyzstan (19)	0	0	0

Recipient	WHT (%) (1)		
	Dividends	Interest	Royalties
Lebanon	5	5	0
Malta	15	10	10
Mauritius	0	0	0
Moldova	5 (26)	5	5
Montenegro (25)	10	10	10
Norway	0	0	0
Poland	10	10 (6)	5
Qatar	0	0	5 (27)
Romania	10	10 (6)	5 (7)
Russia (33)	5 (16)	0	0
San Marino	0	0	0
Serbia (26)	10	10	10
Singapore	0	10 (6, 24)	10
Slovak Republic	10	10 (6)	5 (7)
Slovenia	5 (31)	5	5
South Africa	0	0	0
Seychelles	0	0	5
Sweden	5 (8)	10 (6)	0
Syria	0 (8)	10	10
Tajikistan (19)	0	0	0
Thailand	10	15 (20)	5 (21)
Ukraine (19)	0	0	0
United Kingdom	0	10	0 (3)
United States	0	10 (10)	0

Received in Cyprus

Payer	WHT (%)		
	Dividends	Interest	Royalties
Treaty countries:			
Armenia	0 (30)	5	5
Austria	10	0	0
Belarus	5 (17)	5	5
Belgium	10 (8)	10 (6, 18)	0
Bulgaria	5 (22)	7 (6, 23)	10 (23)
Canada	15	15 (4)	10 (5)
China, P.R.	10	10	10
Czech Republic	0 (28)	0	0 (29)
Denmark	0 (6, 32)	0	0
Egypt	15	15	10
France	10 (9)	10 (10)	0 (3)
Germany	5 (8)	0	0
Greece	25	10	0 (11)
Hungary	5 (8)	10 (6)	0
India	10 (9)	10 (10)	15 (14)
Ireland, Republic of	0	0	0 (11)
Italy	15	10	0

Cyprus

Payer	WHT (%) Dividends	Interest	Royalties
Kuwait	10	10 (6)	5 (7)
Kyrgyzstan (19)	0	0	0
Lebanon	5	5	0
Malta	0	10	10
Mauritius	0	0	0
Moldova	5 (26)	5	5
Montenegro (25)	10	10	10
Norway	0 (12)	0	0
Poland	10	10 (6)	5
Qatar	0	0	5 (27)
Romania	10	10 (6)	5 (7)
Russia (33)	5 (16)	0	0
San Marino	0	0	0
Singapore	0	10 (6, 24)	10
Slovak Republic	10	10 (6)	5 (7)
Slovenia	5 (31)	5	5
South Africa	0	0	0
Serbia (25)	10	10	10
Seychelles	0	0	5
Sweden	5 (8)	10 (6)	0
Syria	0 (8)	10 (4)	10
Tajikistan (19)	0	0	0
Thailand	10	15 (20)	5 (21)
Ukraine (19)	0	0	0
United Kingdom	15 (13)	10	0 (3)
United States	5 (9)	10 (10)	0

Notes

1. Under Cyprus legislation there is no WHT on dividends, interests, and royalties paid to non-residents of Cyprus.
2. Royalties earned on rights used within Cyprus are subject to WHT of 10%.
3. A WHT rate of 5% is applicable on film and TV royalties.
4. 0% if paid to a government or for export guarantee.
5. 0% on literary, dramatic, musical, or artistic work.
6. 0% if paid to the government of the other state.
7. This rate applies for patents, trademarks, designs or models, plans, secret formulas, or processes, or any industrial, commercial, or scientific equipment, or for information concerning industrial, commercial, or scientific experience.
8. A rate of 15% if received by a company controlling less than 10% of the voting power.
9. A rate of 15% if received by a person controlling less than 10% of the voting power.
10. 0% if paid to a government, bank, or financial institution.
11. A WHT rate of 5% is applicable on film royalties.
12. A WHT rate of 5% is applicable if received by a person controlling less than 50% of the voting power.
13. This rate applies to individual shareholders regardless of their percentage of shareholding. Companies controlling less than 10% of the voting shares are also entitled to this rate.
14. A WHT rate of 10% is applicable for payments of a technical, managerial, or consulting nature.
15. Treaty rate is 15%, therefore restricted to Cyprus legislation rate.
16. A rate of 10% if a dividend is paid by a company in which the beneficial owner has invested less than 100,000 United States dollars (USD)/EUR 100,000 as of 1 January 2013.

17. If investment is less than EUR 200,000, dividends are subject to 15% WHT, which is reduced to 10% if the recipient company controls 25% or more of the paying company.
18. No WHT is applicable for interest on deposits with banking institutions.
19. Kyrgyzstan, Tajikistan, and Ukraine apply the USSR/Cyprus treaty.
20. A WHT rate of 10% is applicable on interest received by a financial institution or when it relates to sale on credit of any industrial, commercial, or scientific equipment or of merchandise.
21. This rate applies for any copyright of literary, dramatic, musical, artistic, or scientific work. A 10% rate applies for industrial, commercial, or scientific equipment. A 15% rate applies for patents, trademarks, designs or models, plans, secret formulas, or processes.
22. This rate applies to companies holding directly at least 25% of the share capital of the company paying the dividend. In all other cases the WHT is 10%.
23. This rate does not apply if the payment is made to a Cyprus international business entity by a resident of Bulgaria owning directly or indirectly at least 25% of the share capital of the Cyprus entity.
24. A WHT rate of 7% is applicable if paid to a bank or financial institution.
25. Serbia and Montenegro apply the Yugoslavia/Cyprus treaty.
26. This rate applies if received by a company (excluding partnerships) that holds directly 25% of the shares. A rate of 10% applies in all other cases.
27. Applies to any consideration for the use of, or the right to use, any copyright of literary, artistic or scientific work (including cinematograph films and films, tapes or discs for radio or television broadcasting), computer software, any patent, trademark, design or model, plan, secret formula or process, or for information concerning industrial, commercial, or scientific experience.
28. This rate applies if received by a company (excluding partnership) which holds directly at least 10% of the shares for an uninterrupted period of no less than one year. 5% applies in all other cases.
29. 10% for patent, trademark, design or model, plan, secret formula or process, computer software or industrial, commercial, or scientific equipment, or for information concerning industrial, commercial, or scientific experience.
30. A WHT rate of 5% is applicable if a dividend is paid by a company in which the beneficial owner has invested less than EUR 150,000.
31. The provisions of the Parent-Subsidiary EU directive are applicable.
32. A WHT rate of 15% is applicable if received by a company controlling less than 10% of the share capital of the paying company or the duration of any holding is less than one uninterrupted year.
33. The new treaty between Russia and Cyprus will come into effect as of 1 January 2013. There will be no change to the rates appearing on the tables above.

....

Tax administration

Taxable period
In Cyprus, the tax year is the calendar year.

Tax returns
Business organisations are required to prepare audited accounts based on International Financial Reporting Standards (IFRS). Tax returns are completed based on these accounts on a calendar-year basis. The tax return normally needs to be submitted to the tax authorities by 31 December of the year following the relevant tax year.

Electronic submission
Companies should be registered online and submit their tax returns for the tax years 2011 onwards electronically. In this respect, the submission deadline of the corporate tax returns has moved to three months later, i.e. 31 March 2013.

Payment of tax
Corporate entities must pay provisional tax on the current year's income in three equal instalments on 1 August, 30 September, and 31 December. A final payment must be made on or before 1 August of the following year on a self-assessment basis to bring the total payments of tax to the total actually due according to the tax return.

Statute of limitations
The Cyprus tax authorities have six years from the end of the relevant tax year to enquire and examine the tax affairs of the taxpayer. However, if fraud has been established, the statute of limitations extends to 12 years.

Cyprus

Other issues

Business combinations

Transfers of assets and liabilities between companies can occur without tax consequences within the framework of a tax-exempt qualified reorganisation. Reorganisations include mergers, demergers, partial divisions, transfers of divisions of activities, and exchanges of shares.

Czech Republic

PwC contact

Paul Stewart
PricewaterhouseCoopers Česká republika, s.r.o.
PricewaterhouseCoopers Legal s.r.o., advokátní kancelář
Business Community Center
Kateřinská 40/466
120 00 Praha 2, Czech Republic
Tel: +420 251 151 111
Email: paul.stewart@cz.pwc.com

Significant developments

The 2012 year brought the following significant changes to the value-added tax (VAT):

- The reduced rate of 10% has been raised to 14%.
- The reverse charge mechanism has been extended for construction or assembly work (under the product classification code number of CZ-CPA 41 to 43). The application of the reverse charge mechanism is mandatory for this work when provided between taxable persons (i.e. between businesses).

There are a few changes in the corporate income tax (CIT) effective from 2012. These changes include the following:

- Income from lotteries and similar game business is now fully taxable (previous tax exemption was abolished together with previous obligatory contribution paid by the lottery administrators instead of the CIT).
- The remuneration of members of statutory bodies (i.e. board of directors of joint stock companies and cooperatives) is now tax deductible.
- Possibility to utilise tax loss carried forward is extended even to cross-border mergers (subject to certain limitations).
- Deadlines for filing a tax return in the course of mergers (both cross-border and domestic) have been slightly amended.
- Minor changes in taxation of investment companies.

Substantial changes are planned from 2014 or 2015, when a one-stop-shop system for collection of taxes and social security contributions will be introduced (amendment to the tax legislation has been approved, but changes are expected even prior to the law becoming effective).

Hand in hand, exemption of dividend income and liquidation surplus will be introduced. However, the exemption should not apply to profit shares from collective investment vehicles (both Czech and foreign).

Collective investment vehicles are planned to be subject to 0% taxation; however, 19% withholding tax (WHT) should be introduced on profits from these vehicles flowing to corporations. The new rules on taxation of profit shares should apply only to profits generated after the effective date of the change.

Czech Republic

Taxes on corporate income

CIT applies to the profits generated by all companies, including branches of foreign companies. Corporate partners in general partnerships (i.e. unlimited) and corporate general partners (i.e. unlimited) in a limited partnership are subject to CIT on their share of the profits in the partnership.

Czech resident companies are required to pay CIT on income derived from worldwide sources. Non-resident companies are required to pay CIT on income sourced in the Czech Republic.

The 19% CIT rate applies to all business profits, including capital gains from the sale of shares (if not exempt under the participation exemption regime).

There is a special tax rate of 15% levied on dividend income of Czech tax resident entities from non-resident entities (unless subject to participation exemption).

Local income taxes
There are no local income taxes in the Czech Republic.

Corporate residence

A company is resident in the Czech Republic for CIT purposes if it is registered in, or has a place of management located in, the Czech Republic.

Permanent establishment (PE)
Under domestic law, the creation of a PE of a foreign tax resident in the Czech Republic is triggered by a fixed place available for carrying out business activities, long-term provision of services (for more than six months in any 12 consecutive months), or presence of a dependent agent unless an applicable double tax treaty (DTT) stipulates otherwise. For interpretation purposes, the Organisation for Economic Co-operation and Development (OECD) Model Tax Commentary is followed. The Czech Republic tends to have a service PE clause included in its DTTs.

Other taxes

Value-added tax (VAT)
VAT is charged at 20% on the supply of goods and services within the Czech Republic, but certain supplies (such as groceries) are taxed at a rate of 14%. While only one unified VAT rate of 17.5% should apply from 2013 onwards, the possibility of increasing the unified rate is being discussed due to the state budget deficit.

Exports are generally exempt from VAT with a credit. Some supplies are exempt without a credit, including the lease of real estate (with certain exceptions), financial and insurance services, radio and TV broadcasting, education, health, and welfare.

VAT registration
A company must be registered for VAT if its taxable supplies exceed CZK 1 million for a period of 12 consecutive months or purchases of goods from other European Union (EU) countries exceeds CZK 326,000 per calendar year. A company can register voluntarily even if its turnover fails to reach the threshold if it renders taxable supplies

Czech Republic

in the Czech Republic. These are general rules applicable to entities established in the Czech Republic. Different rules apply to non-Czech entities.

VAT returns and payments
The VAT return must be filed and tax paid within 25 days after the end of the taxable period. The taxable period is a calendar month or calendar quarter depending on taxpayer turnover. Tax overpayment should be returned to the taxpayer by the tax office within 30 days after the request for the tax overpayment refund.

Customs duties
The Czech Republic is an EU member state, therefore the EU customs code applies.

Excise taxes
Excise tax is charged on the production or import of tobacco and tobacco products, wines, semiproducts, spirits and pure ethanol beer, fuel, and mineral oils.

Excise tax on cigarettes amounts to 28% of the price for final consumer plus CZK 1.12 per piece; however, the duty cannot be less than CZK 2.10 per piece. Excise duty on cigars and cigarillos is CZK 1.25 per piece and on tobacco for smoking is CZK 1,400 per kilogram.

Excise tax on still wine is CZK 0 and CZK 2,340 per hectolitre in case of sparkling wine and semiproducts. Excise tax on spirits and pure ethanol amounts to CZK 28,500 per hectolitre of pure ethanol. The basic rate of excise tax on beer is CZK 32 per hectolitre for each whole percentage of the original primary brew; however, lower rates for small independent breweries apply. The rates of excise duty on fuels and other mineral oils vary from CZK 0 and CZK 3.933 per ton in case of liquefied petroleum gases and their mixtures and from CZK 10.950 to CZK 13.710 per thousand litres in case of motor and other petrols, aviation petrol-type fuels, and their mixtures.

Energy taxes
Energy tax is charged on natural gas and certain other gases, solid fuels, and on electricity sold to final customers in the Czech Republic.

The tax rates applied on gases vary from CZK 30,60 per MWh of gross energy (combustion heat) to CZK 264,80 per MWh of gross energy (combustion heat).The tax rates amounts to CZK 8.50 per GJ according to the original sample in case of solid fuels. The tax rate on electricity amounts to CZK 28.30 per MWh.

Real estate tax
Real estate tax is payable annually by the owner of land or buildings. The amount of the tax is dependent on area, location, and usage of the land or buildings. As of 2012, paved areas used for business purposes (such as concrete areas in logistics centres) are taxable, with taxpayers obliged to self-assess the tax. However, some areas (e.g. publicly accessible parking lands in shopping malls) are not taxable.

Real estate transfer tax
Real estate transfer tax is levied on the transferor of real estate at a rate of 3% on the greater of the transaction price or the officially appraised value. The taxpayer is the transferor; transferee acts as tax guarantee.

Stamp duties
There are no stamp duties in the Czech Republic. Certain business operations in which a notary has to be involved by operation of law are subject to notarial fee.

Czech Republic

Road tax
Road tax is payable annually with respect to vehicles (including private vehicles) used for commercial purposes. Foreign vehicles are also liable to road tax while in the Czech Republic. Rates vary depending on engine capacity and vehicle size.

Environmental taxes
Environmental taxes are imposed on electricity and natural gas, and on certain solid fuels. The environmental taxes have a character similar to excise taxes.

Social security and health insurance contributions
Employers contribute 34% of the employee's gross salary to the state health and social security funds. A cap on the premium is available.

Branch income

A foreign company can trade in the Czech Republic through a Czech branch. A branch usually creates a Czech permanent establishment (PE) of the foreign entity for CIT purposes (depending on the character of the activities carried out through the branch). The basis of taxation is the same as for corporations (i.e. tax base is calculated as taxable revenues less tax-deductible costs). In some cases, it may be possible for taxpayers to negotiate with the tax authorities regarding the basis on which profits are attributed to the branch.

A branch is liable for tax on its attributable profits at the standard CIT rate.

Income determination

Inventory valuation
Stock (i.e. inventory) is valued at cost. Czech legislation specifically provides for the use of the arithmetical average cost and first in first out (FIFO) methods to value stock. Last in first out (LIFO) and the replacement-cost methods (except for livestock) may not be used.

Capital gains
No separate capital gains tax is levied in the Czech Republic. Capital gains are included in the CIT base and taxed as ordinary income in the year in which they arise.

Capital gains from the sale of shares may be exempt from Czech taxation if all of the following conditions are met:

* The Czech or EU parent holds at least 10% of the shares of the subsidiary for at least 12 months.
* The subsidiary is a tax resident of the Czech Republic or another EU member state.
* Both the parent and the subsidiary have one of the legal forms listed in the Annex to the EU P/S directive.

If the subsidiary is not a tax resident of the Czech Republic or another EU member state, the exemption may be applied, provided that the subsidiary is a tax resident of a country where there is a DTT in place with the Czech Republic, it has a legal form similar to a limited liability company or a joint stock company, it is subject to CIT at the nominal rate of at least 12% in a year when dividends are paid, and the time test of 10%

for at least 12 calendar months is met. The time test may be met both prospectively and retrospectively.

Dividend income
Dividends received by Czech tax resident corporations from non-resident entities are subject to a special tax rate of 15%, unless exempt under the participation exemption regime *described below*.

C

Dividends paid by Czech tax resident corporations to Czech resident entities are subject to 15% final WHT, unless exempt under the participation exemption regime.

Dividends paid by Czech tax resident corporations to Czech non-resident entities are subject to 15% final WHT, unless exempt under the participation exemption regime or decreased under the relevant DTT.

Participation exemption regime
Dividend income may be exempt from Czech taxation (i.e. WHT, when a Czech company is paying dividends and CIT, when a Czech company is receiving dividends) if all of the following conditions are met:

- The Czech or EU parent holds at least 10% of the shares of the subsidiary for at least 12 months.
- The subsidiary is a tax resident of the Czech Republic or another EU member state.
- Both the parent and the subsidiary have one of the legal forms listed in the Annex to the EU P/S directive.

Regarding dividends paid, provided that conditions above are met, the exemption also applies when dividends are paid by a Czech subsidiary to Switzerland, Norway, or Iceland.

Regarding dividends received, if the subsidiary is not a tax resident of the Czech Republic or another EU member state, exemption on dividends received by a Czech resident may be applied, provided that the subsidiary is a tax resident of a country where a DTT with the Czech Republic is in place, it has a legal form similar to a limited liability company or a joint stock company, it is subject to CIT at the nominal rate of at least 12% in a year when dividends are paid, and the time test of at least 10% for at least 12 consecutive calendar months is met.

Interest income
Interest received by Czech tax residents is included in the standard tax base subject to the 19% CIT rate.

Czech source interest income received by Czech tax non-residents is subject to 15% WHT unless subject to domestic exemption or a DTT stipulates otherwise.

Under domestic law, interest income is exempt if it is paid by a Czech payer or a Czech PE to an EU resident recipient who is a beneficial owner of the interest income, provided that for at least 24 months before the payment:

- the payer is in at least a 25% parent-subsidiary or at least a 25% sister relation to the recipient of the income and
- the interest is not attributable to a Czech PE of the recipient.

The exemption is applicable subject to approval by the tax authorities.

Czech Republic

Exchange gains and losses

Realised foreign exchange gains and losses are accounted for in profit and loss accounts and represent taxable revenues or tax-deductible costs, respectively. The same treatment applied to unrealised foreign exchange differences. However, recently, the Supreme Administrative Court concluded in a particular case that unrealised foreign exchange gains do not represent taxable income. Therefore, the treatment of unrealised foreign exchange differences may change in the future.

The default functional currency is the Czech koruna. A Czech company cannot opt for any foreign currency to be the functional currency for tax purposes.

Foreign income

Companies resident in the Czech Republic are taxed on their worldwide income. A Czech corporation is taxed on its foreign branch income when earned (accrual basis) and on foreign dividends when approved by general meeting.

The participation exemption regime *described above* may be applicable.

There is no controlled foreign company (CFC) legislation in the Czech Republic.

Deductions

Depreciation and amortisation

Methods of tax depreciation are prescribed by tax legislation and are independent from depreciation methods for accounting purposes. Tax depreciation is calculated on an asset-by-asset basis, applying the straight-line or accelerated basis methods of depreciation at statutory rates. Under both methods, depreciation expense in the first year is lower than for subsequent years. The company may choose which method to apply to a new asset, but once the choice is made, it cannot be altered. All assets are classified into six groups, which determine the number of years over which the asset will be written off, as follows:

Assets	Depreciation group	Minimum depreciation period (years)
Office machines and computers, tools	1	3
Engines, motor vehicles, machines, audio-visual equipment	2	5
Elevators, escalators, turbines, air conditioning equipment, electric motors, and generators	3	10
Buildings made of wood and plastic, long-distance lines, and pipes	4	20
Buildings (except for those listed in groups 4 and 6), roads, bridges, tunnels	5	30
Administrative buildings, department stores, historical buildings, and hotels	6	50

'Tangible assets' (i.e. assets which are subject to tax depreciation) are defined by tax legislation generally as assets with economic useful lives of greater than one year and acquisition prices higher than CZK 40,000. Certain assets, such as buildings, are always considered tangible assets.

Czech Republic

Taxpayers are generally not obliged to depreciate a tangible asset for tax purposes every year. Depreciation may be interrupted in any year and continued in a later year without a loss of depreciation potential.

Tangible assets are generally depreciated by the taxpayer with ownership title. Certain exceptions apply, for instance, technical appreciation of a rented asset carried out by a tenant may be depreciated by that tenant, subject to certain conditions.

Depreciation can start only once the assets are put into use and comply with the requirements of specific laws.

Certain assets have special depreciation methods (e.g. moulds are depreciated based on expected life or number of products).

The value to be used as the basis for tax depreciation depends on how the asset is acquired, for example:

- Acquisition cost (construction and equipment costs, architect fees, legal fees, notary's fees, etc.), if the asset is acquired for consideration.
- Internal costs incurred, if the asset is acquired or produced internally.

'Intangible assets' are defined by tax legislation as software, valuable rights, intangible results of research and development (R&D), and other assets regarded as assets for accounting purposes, provided that they:

- were acquired from a third party or developed internally for the purpose of trading with them
- have an acquisition price of more than CZK 60,000, and
- have a useful life of greater than one year.

Intangible assets are amortised for tax purposes based on the number of years that the taxpayer has a licence for the assets, if the licence is for a limited number of years. Otherwise, amortisation for tax purposes will vary depending on the asset (e.g. software is amortised over 18 months, results of R&D is amortised over 36 months).

Goodwill
Goodwill arisen as result of purchase of business (or its part) as a going concern may be evenly amortised for 180 months. Any other goodwill (e.g. arisen within a merger) is disregarded for tax purposes.

Start-up expenses
Start-up expenses exceeding CZK 60,000 with a useful life of more than one year accounted in line with Czech generally accepted accounting principles (GAAP) should be amortised evenly for a period of 60 calendar months.

Interest expenses
Interest as accrued and duly accounted for under Czech GAAP is generally tax deductible, with the following exceptions:

- Interest disallowed based on the thin capitalisation restriction (*please refer to Thin capitalisation in the Group taxation section*).
- Interest disallowed for its relation to income that is tax exempt or taxed outside the standard tax base.
- Interest disallowed due to its relation to holding a subsidiary.

Czech Republic

Bad debt
Doubtful or bad receivables may be provisioned for under special rules. Generally, provisions may be created for trade receivables overdue for more than six months. Provisions of 100% may be created to debts duly registered in bankruptcy proceedings. For receivables, banks, insurance companies, and defined financial institutions have their specific system for provisioning.

Charitable contributions
Certain charitable donations are deductible. The minimum deductible donation is CZK 2,000 and the maximum deductible donation is 5% of the tax base (a maximum of up to 10% of the tax base is possible if gifts are granted to universities or R&D centres).

Travel expenses and meal allowances
Payments for travel expenses and meal allowances that are made to employees are tax-deductible, but only within the statutory limits.

Fines and penalties
Contractual fines and penalties are generally tax deductible on a cash basis.

Taxes
Road tax, real estate tax, and most other taxes, with the exception of income taxes, are deductible, as are social security contributions paid by an employer with respect to employees.

Other significant items
As of 2012, fees paid to members of other statutory bodies of companies (i.e. board of directors of joint stock companies and cooperatives) for their services are deductible for tax purposes.

Net operating losses
Losses incurred in a tax year may be carried forward to offset taxable profits generated in the following five tax years. Losses may not be carried back. From 2012, the possibility to utilise tax loss carried forward is extended even to cross-border mergers (subject to certain limitations).

Payments to foreign affiliates
Generally, deductions may be claimed for royalties, management service fees, and interest charges paid to foreign affiliates, provided such amounts are at arm's length.

Group taxation

Currently, the Czech Republic does not permit group taxation. Each company in a group is taxed individually. Consolidated tax base applies only for the general partners and their shares in profit of their general partnership.

Transfer pricing
For tax purposes, prices agreed between related parties have to meet the definition of the arm's-length principle, and these prices are often subject to tax audits by tax authorities. The consequences of incorrect transfer pricing adjustments are tax exposure and penalties. In the case of companies receiving investment incentives, incorrect transfer pricing can cause a loss of the investment incentives. Generally, pricing methods as described in OECD guidelines should be followed.

Czech Republic

Although there is no legal requirement to keep transfer pricing documentation, in practice it is strongly recommended to keep it as the taxpayer bears the burden of proof upon challenge of prices by tax authorities.

Taxpayers may request the tax administrators to issue an advance pricing agreement (APA) regarding progressing or future transactions between related parties.

C

Thin capitalisation
Thin capitalisation rules apply in the Czech Republic and may limit the tax deductibility of interest payments on debt financing from related parties as well as from third parties.

Below is a brief summary of the thin capitalisation rules:

* The tax-deductibility test applies not only to interest but also to all so-called 'financial costs' on loans (e.g. interest plus other related costs, such as bank fees).
* Thin capitalisation applies only to related-party loans.
* The debt-to-equity ratio for related-party loans is 4:1.
* Unrelated-party loans (e.g. bank loans) guaranteed by a related party are not considered related-party loans for thin capitalisation purposes. If, however, a bank provides a back-to-back loan to a Czech entity where the loan is provided to the bank by a related party, such a bank loan to the Czech entity is considered a related party loan.
* Interest on profit-participating loans is not deductible for tax purposes.

Controlled foreign companies (CFCs)
There is no CFC legislation in the Czech Republic.

Tax credits and incentives

Foreign tax credit
Foreign tax credits are available only under tax treaties. If credit is not available under a treaty, CIT paid abroad may be deducted as an expense in the following year provided it is imposed on the income included in Czech taxable income.

Investment incentives
Investment incentives are available only to Czech entities (including Czech subsidiaries of foreign companies) engaged in the manufacturing industry. Incentives include income tax relief, financial support for the creation of new jobs, financial support for training or retraining of employees, and a transfer of land at a specially reduced price.

The former programmes for the support of business support service centres and for the development of technology centres, which were focused primarily on investments in human capital as well as the training or retraining of skilled staff, were abolished based on the decision of the Ministry of Industry and Trade in July 2008. However, these activities currently are supported by the EU structural funds, especially under the operational programmes Enterprise and Innovation.

Research and development (R&D) allowance
Up to 100% of specific R&D expenses (or costs) incurred in a given tax year may be deducted from the tax base as a special tax allowance. These costs are deducted twice for tax purposes: once as a normal tax-deductible cost and then again as a special tax allowance.

Czech Republic

The following costs can be included in the R&D tax allowance:

- Direct costs (e.g. personnel costs of R&D engineers, consumed materials).
- Tax depreciation of fixed assets used for R&D activities.
- Other operational expenses directly related to the realisation of R&D activities (e.g. telecommunications fees, electricity, water, gas).

Only qualifying expenses are deductible for tax purposes and must be separately identified from other expenses (or costs). This allowance does not apply to costs of purchased services or intangible results of R&D acquired from other entities, except for expenses (or costs) incurred in connection with the certification of the results of R&D projects. In addition, expenses that were supported from public sources are also excluded.

Any non-utilised R&D allowance may be carried forward for three subsequent years.

A taxpayer may request a binding ruling with respect to R&D costs from the respective Tax Office in the event that the taxpayer is unsure of whether certain R&D costs are eligible for the allowance.

Withholding taxes

Czech corporations are required to withhold tax on payments of dividends, interest, and royalties as follows:

Recipient	Dividend (%) (1)	Interest (%) (2)	Royalties (%) (3)
Resident corporations	15	0	0
Resident individuals	15	0	0
Non-resident corporations and individuals:			
Non-treaty	15	15	15
Treaty:			
Albania	5/15	0/5	10
Armenia	10	5/10	5/10
Australia	5/15	10	10
Austria	0/10	0	0/5
Azerbaijan	8	5/10	10
Belarus	10	0/5	10
Belgium	5/15	10	0/10
Bosnia	5	0	0/10
Brazil	15	10/15	15/25
Bulgaria	10	0/10	10
Canada	5/15	0/10	0/10
China, P.R.	10	0/10	10
Croatia	5	0	10
Cyprus	0/5	0	0/10
Denmark	15	0	0/5
Egypt	5/15	0/15	15
Estonia	5/15	0/10	10
Ethiopia	10	0/10	10

Recipient	Dividend (%) (1)	Interest (%) (2)	Royalties (%) (3)
Finland	5/15	0	0/1/5/10
France	10	0	0/5
Georgia	5/10	0/8	5/10
Germany	5/15	0	5
Greece	Local rates	0/10	0/10
Hungary	5/15	0	10
Iceland	5/15	0	10
India	10	0/10	10
Indonesia	10/15	0/12.5	12.5
Ireland, Republic of	5/15	0	10
Israel	5/15	0/10	5
Italy	15	0	0/5
Japan	10/15	0/10	0/10
Jordan	10	0/10	10
Kazakhstan	10	0/10	10
Korea, Republic of	5/10	0/10	0/10
Latvia	5/15	0/10	10
Lebanon	5	0	5/10
Lithuania	5/15	0/10	10
Luxembourg	5/15	0	0/10
Malaysia	0/10	0/12	12
Malta	5	0	5
Mexico	10	0/10	10
Moldova	5/15	5	10
Mongolia	10	0/10	10
Netherlands	0/10	0	5
New Zealand	15	0/10	10
Nigeria	12.5/15	0/15	15
Norway	5/15	0	0/5
Philippines	10/15	0/10	10/15
Poland	5/10	0/10	5
Portugal	10/15	0/10	10
Romania	10	0/7	10
Russia	10	0	10
Singapore	5	0	10
Slovak Republic	5/15	0	0/10
Slovenia	5/15	0/5	10
South Africa	5/15	0	10
Spain	5/15	0	0/5
Sri Lanka	15	0/10	0/10
Sweden	0/10	0	0/5
Switzerland	5/15	0	10/5
Syria	10	10	12
Tajikistan	5	0/7	10
Thailand	10	0/10	5/10/15
Tunisia	10/15	0/12	5/15
Ukraine	5/15	5	10

Czech Republic

Recipient	Dividend (%) (1)	Interest (%) (2)	Royalties (%) (3)
United Arab Emirates	0/5	0	10
United Kingdom	5/15	0	0/10
United States	5/15	0	0/10
Uzbekistan	10	0/5	10
Venezuela	5/10	0/10	12
Vietnam	10	0/10	10
Yugoslavia (former)	5/15	0	10

Notes

1. The lower rate applies if the recipient is a company that owns at least a certain amount of the capital or a certain amount of the voting shares of the company paying the dividend directly.
2. The lower rate applies mostly in situations when the interest is received by the government or a state-owned institution or is paid by the government.
3. The lower rate applies mostly to cultural royalties.

Tax administration

Taxable period
A corporation may choose between the calendar year or an accounting year as its tax year.

Tax returns
Returns must be filed within three months of the end of the tax period.

A three-month extension of the filing deadline is available if a taxpayer is represented by a registered tax advisor or if the taxpayer is subject to a statutory accounting audit.

In some special cases, a filing deadline of less than three months may apply (e.g. upon merger or liquidation). This shorter deadline may, however, be extended if approved by the tax office.

Payment of tax
Tax payments are due on the same day as the filing deadline.

A company is obliged to make CIT advances based on its last known tax liability. The tax advances are paid semi-annually or quarterly, depending on the amount of the last known tax liability.

Upon filing a tax return, tax advances paid during the year for which the tax return is filed will offset the tax liability declared in the tax return. Any outstanding amount must be paid on the date the tax return is due. Any overpayment will be refunded upon request or may be credited against future tax liabilities.

Audit cycle
There is no statutory tax audit cycle. Entities are picked by the tax authorities based on selected criteria (e.g. tax loss position, huge marketing costs) or randomly.

Statute of limitations

The tax may be assessed within three years after the deadline for regular tax return filing. In certain cases (e.g. filing of supplementary tax return), such assessment period may be prolonged by one year, maximally up to ten years. Tax liability arisen as result of criminal action may be assessed any time within two years after the year of the relevant penal court decision becoming effective.

Topics of focus for tax authorities

The tax authorities seem to focus on marketing costs, intra-group relations, entities in tax loss position, and entities with tax investment incentives. In 2012, the Czech Republic introduced a so-called specialised tax authority for large businesses with turnover of over CZK 2 billion and financial institutions. It is expected that the specialised tax authority will be responsible for about 1,000 entities.

Denmark

PwC contact

Jan Huusmann Christensen
PricewaterhouseCoopers
Strandvejen 44
DK 2900 Hellerup, Denmark
Tel: +45 3945 9405
Email: jhc@pwc.dk

....

Significant developments

Taxation of dividends and interest paid by Danish entities to foreign group companies
has been a hot topic in Danish taxation in the last few years. One of the main issues
seems to be whether holding companies incorporated in the European Union (EU)
can qualify as the beneficial owner of dividends and interest payments received from
Danish group entities and, consequently, whether these payments can be remitted from
Denmark without source taxation (withholding taxes).

Five cases have been publicly disclosed, of which the Danish tax authorities have
prevailed in two. The remaining three, of which one was decided by the Danish High
Court in December 2011, were won by the taxpayer.

The Danish tax authorities brought up these issues when they started to enquire into
the tax implications related to intercompany payments and, more specifically, whether
Danish entities have complied with the withholding tax (WHT) requirements regarding
dividends and interest. After these enquiries, numerous Danish entities belonging to
international groups have been asked to pay substantial amounts of non-withheld taxes
to the Danish tax authorities. Many of the Danish companies involved in these cases
have disputed the claims.

The main focus of the Danish tax authorities seems to be private-equity-owned Danish
groups, a number of which have been subject to the enquiries by the Danish tax
authorities. However, industrial groups have also been subject to enquiries from the
Danish tax authorities.

Several cases are currently being appealed through both the administrative and court
system, and a final position regarding both interest and dividend therefore remains
unclarified.

In addition to the cases involving WHT, the Danish tax authorities have increased their
focus on tax deductions for costs related to the creation of tax exempt income, such as
dividend from and capital gains on certain shares.

In November 2011, a landmark case regarding tax deductions for management fees was
decided by the Danish Supreme Court. The taxpayer, a venture company, was allowed
a deduction only because the fees generated income that, in great majority, was taxable
in the hands of the venture company.

Laying down a condition that costs must be connected to taxable income in order to be
deductible for tax purposes seems to be a novelty in Danish tax law, which may have a
severe impact on venture funds etc. and even 'ordinary' holding companies. However,
the exact fallout from this case depends on how liberal an interpretation the Danish tax
authorities put on the ruling over the next year or two.

Taxes on corporate income

According to Danish tax law, a territoriality principle prevails. Hence, a Danish company is not taxed on its worldwide income. Instead, income from a permanent establishment (PE) outside Denmark or from real estate located abroad is excluded from taxable income. Non-resident companies are taxed only on profits distributed from income sourced in Denmark.

The corporate income tax (CIT) rate is 25%.

D

Hydrocarbon income tax
A special CIT is levied on profits from the exploration and extraction of oil and gas on the Danish continental shelf at a rate of 52% under the new system applicable for licences granted after 1 January 2004. CIT (25%) is deductible in computing the hydrocarbon tax.

Tonnage Tax Scheme
Danish tax law provides for a special tax scheme for shipping entities.

The main principle of the Tonnage Tax Scheme is that qualifying shipping entities are not taxed on the basis of their actual income derived from their business but on a fictitious income based on the net tons carrying capability of their fleet used for purposes covered by the Tonnage Tax Act.

The Tonnage Tax Scheme is available to Danish shipping entities organised as limited liability companies (*Aktieselskab* [A/S] or *Anpartsselskab* [ApS]), foreign shipping companies with the place of management and control in Denmark, and European Union (EU) shipping companies with a PE in Denmark.

The scheme is available upon application to the Danish tax authorities. A decision to enter into the scheme is binding for a period of ten years.

As a general rule, group related shipping companies based in Denmark must make the same choice regarding the Tonnage Tax Scheme. However, shipping companies that do not have the same management or operating organisation and do not conduct business in related fields may be exempt from the joint decision provision.

The Tonnage Tax Scheme is restricted to certain types of business activities. The entity must carry out commercial transportation of passengers or cargo between different destinations. The ships must be owned or chartered on a 'bareboat' or time-charter with a call/buy option by the company' basis and have a minimum gross tonnage of 20 tons. Certain restrictions apply for ships chartered on a time charter basis without a call/buy option. The ships must be strategically and commercially run from Denmark.

Income from activities that are carried out in close connection with this business, such as the usage of containers and loading facilities, etc. may also be included in the Tonnage Tax Scheme. Ships used for exploration, diving, fishing, towing, sand dredging, etc. are specifically exempt from the scheme. The same applies for certain types of ships, such as barges, floating docks, etc. However, EU or European Economic Community (EEC) registered ships used for towage activities at sea (i.e. not in and around ports) during at least 50% of its operating time during the income year may be included in the tonnage tax system.

Denmark

Ship operating companies may also use the Danish Tonnage Tax Scheme. A ship operator is defined as a company doing business with crew management and technical management of ships qualified for use in the tonnage tax system. It is a requirement that the ship operator has taken over the full operating responsibility and all obligations and responsibilities according to the International Safety Management codex.

Taxable income

The taxable income for the part of the business that qualifies for the Tonnage Tax Scheme is determined for each ship as a fixed amount of Danish kroner (DKK) per 100 net tons (NT) per day according to the following:

Ship net ton	Fixed amount per day (DKK per 100 NT)
0 to 1,000 NT	7.80
1,001 to 10,000 NT	5.60
10,001 to 25,000 NT	3.35
Over 25,000 NT	2.20

The income is taxed at the ordinary corporate tax rate (25%). No deductions relating to shipping income will be allowed. Special rules apply for financial income and financial expenses, and in relation to so called 'thin capitalisation'. Income that does not qualify for the tonnage tax scheme is taxed according to the general tax provisions in Denmark.

Depreciation

Shipping entities that apply the Tonnage Tax Scheme from the time of their establishment may not deduct depreciation for tax purposes. Special rules apply for shipping entities that were already in existence when they elected to become subject to the scheme and for entities that elect to include certain other assets at a later point in time that were not previously subject to the scheme.

Gains on the sale of ships

Gains on the sale of ships that have not been used in the scheme prior to 1 January 2007 are tax exempt. The same applies to gains on the sale of contracts on the delivery of ships, provided that the ship was destined to be delivered after 1 January 2007. Gains on the sale of ships used in the scheme in prior years are taxable. The taxable gain is calculated as the sale price minus the purchase price plus improvements. Any losses on ships acquired and sold within the same income year as the income year in which a gain is realised may be offset against the gain.

Local income taxes

There is no local CIT or similar surcharge.

Corporate residence

A corporation is resident in Denmark for tax purposes if it is incorporated in Denmark and registered in the Companies Register as having a Danish place of business. Further, foreign companies having their actual place of management in Denmark are also tax resident in Denmark. The actual place of management is typically the place where the management decisions concerning the company's day-to-day operations are made.

Denmark

Permanent establishment (PE)
Non-resident companies are only liable to tax in Denmark on business profit if derived trough a PE in Denmark. The existence of a PE is determined according to Danish tax law, which makes either a reference to a specific double taxation treaty (DTT) or to text similar to Article 5 of the Organisation for Economic Co-operation and Development (OECD) Model Convention.

D

Other taxes

Value-added tax (VAT)
The general VAT rate is 25% of the price charged (exclusive of VAT).

Exemption or a special reduced rate of 0% applies to a limited range of supplies (e.g. newspapers; hospital treatment; insurance and reinsurance services; most financial activities, including deposits of money, loans, and provision of loans).

Denmark was one of the first countries to introduce a VAT system. Since the first VAT Act came into force on 3 July 1967, the VAT legislation in Denmark has undergone several changes. The most important changes have been modifications to bring the legislation in line with the Council Directive 2006/112/EC on the common system of Value Added Tax.

Compared to the Directive, the Danish VAT legislation includes minor deviations and the use of various discretionary provisions.

All supplies of goods and services by so-called 'taxable persons' (entrepreneurs who independently carry out economic activity) are subject to VAT, unless specifically exempted. The VAT exemptions are restricted to a limited range of services and goods but are nonetheless subject to discussions and complications in the Danish VAT jurisprudence. Transactions are subject to Danish VAT only when they are deemed to take place in Denmark. For the sake of tax neutrality, VAT is also levied on (i) imports (i.e. receipt of goods from non-EU territories), (ii) intra-Community acquisitions (i.e. receipt of goods from EU member states), and (iii) purchase of most types of services from abroad.

In order to avoid VAT being borne by any other than the final consumer, those who qualify as taxable persons can, with some exceptions, recover VAT charged by their suppliers according to the invoice/credit method, provided that the purchases relate to VAT taxable transactions. VAT is recovered either via the periodical VAT return (as a deduction in VAT payable) or by filing a special application.

In general, it is the supplier's responsibility to collect and report VAT on supply of goods or services.

Customs duties
Denmark is a member state of the European Union, and, according to EU's Common Customs Tariff, many goods imported into Denmark from outside the European Union are subject to customs duties. The rates of duty vary widely between goods.

Excise duties
According to Danish tax law, several excise duties are levied. Some of the excise duties are enacted based on EU regulations while others are enacted according to domestic law only.

Denmark

Excise duties are chargeable on a long list of goods, including hydrocarbon oil products, packaging, alcoholic drinks and tobacco, chocolate and products containing sucker, coffee/tea, etc.

The excise duty rates depend on the type of goods (e.g. chocolate, packaging) as well as, in some cases, the category of the goods (e.g. plastic bags, paper bags).

Only goods sold in Denmark (or taken into Denmark) are liable to the Danish excise duties. Companies importing goods into Denmark or companies producing goods in Denmark must be registered with the Danish tax authorities to settle the excise duties. This also applies even though the goods are taken out of Denmark again. If goods are taken from Denmark to another country, difficulties may appear regarding the reimbursement of excise duties paid.

Property taxes
Owners of non-residential property must pay land tax annually. The land tax rate is set by the municipalities and must be between 1.6% and 3.4% of the value of the land. Municipalities may also levy a special coverage charge on certain properties at a maximum of 1% of the value minus the value of the land. Land tax and coverage charge are deductible from CIT.

Stamp tax
Stamp tax is payable on a few documents, such as a deed of transfer of real estate (0.6% of the transfer sum). There is no stamp duty on transfer of shares.

Employer's tax (social security charges)
The employer's contribution to *Arbejdsmarkedets Tillægspension* (ATP) (i.e. old-age pension) charges is DKK 2,160 per annum for a full-time employee.

Companies that provide VAT-exempt services are liable to pay the employer's tax, which is calculated on the total annual salary cost. The rate can be as high as 9.13%, which is the rate for banks and other financial institutions, the most significant sector paying the employer's tax. This tax is deductible for income tax purposes.

Other than these taxes, an employer's obligation for social security taxes is minimal. The main social security charge is an additional income tax of 8% on salaries and wages, which is borne by employees.

Environmental taxes
Danish companies must pay environmental taxes, which were introduced to reduce companies' energy consumption, discharges of fluids with an environmental impact, and emission. The tax is paid to the company that provides the energy, who pays the tax to the Danish tax authorities.

In general, almost all VAT registered companies in Denmark can receive a reimbursement of some of the environmental taxes. From 2010, the environmental taxes have increased, the possibilities to get a reimbursement have decreased, and the majority of companies will likely suffer a significant increase in tax costs.

Branch income

Danish branches and PEs of foreign companies are taxed under the same rules and rates as Danish resident companies. There is no branch remittance tax or other similar tax on branch profits.

Income determination

Taxable income generally is calculated as income determined for accounting purposes that is adjusted and modified for several items, as prescribed by the tax laws. Typical timing differences include reserves, work in progress, and depreciation.

Inventory valuation

Inventory is valued at either acquisition costs, current market value, or manufacturing costs (if manufactured by the company itself) according to a first in first out (FIFO) principle. The company may opt for different principles for each category of goods and may furthermore change principle from income year to income year, provided certain conditions are met.

Capital gains

Gains and losses realised on the sale of tangible and intangible assets, including goodwill, are generally included in taxable income. However, gains realised on the sale of shares are tax-exempt if the shares qualify as either 'subsidiary shares' or 'group shares'.

'Subsidiary shares' are shares held by a corporate shareholder that holds a minimum of 10% of the share capital in a subsidiary that is located in the European Union, European Economic Area (EEA), or a country with which Denmark has a DTT. A special anti-avoidance rule applies, which is targeted at Danish shareholders joining their shareholdings in order to reach the 10% threshold.

'Group shares' are defined as shares in companies with which the shareholder is jointly taxed or might be jointly taxed. The definition of a group is therefore the same as in the joint taxation rules and generally corresponds to the definition of a group for accounting purposes. The location where the companies are registered is irrelevant, as long as the companies are affiliated.

If the shares do not constitute group shares, subsidiary shares, or treasury shares, they constitute portfolio shares. Gains on portfolio shares are fully taxable regardless of holding period. Losses on the sale of portfolio shares generally are tax-deductible. However, special rules may apply for losses on unlisted shares.

Gains realised on the sale of real estate property are taxable whereas losses are not tax-deductible unless the property is a building qualifying for tax depreciation. A loss realised on the sale of land and other buildings may be utilised only against taxable profits on the sale of real estate properties in the same year or may be carried forward infinitely.

A capital gain may, under certain conditions, be deferred if the capital gain is reinvested in properties. Reinvestment must be made no later than the income years following the income year of disposal.

Denmark

Gains and losses on financial instruments generally are included in taxable income, according to the mark-to-market principle, which is required. There are special rules for losses on certain share-based contracts.

Dividend income
Dividends received on 'subsidiary shares' or 'group shares' are tax exempt regardless of the length of the ownership period, whereas dividends received on portfolio shares are fully included in taxable income.

Regardless of whether the shares qualify as 'subsidiary shares' or 'group shares', dividends are fully taxable if received from a foreign company that can deduct the dividends paid, unless a tax exemption is provided for in the EU parent/subsidiary directive.

Stock dividends
Stock dividends may be distributed to shareholders free of tax, provided that the dividends are in proportion to the existing shareholdings (i.e. bonus shares).

Interest income
Interest income is generally included in the determination of taxable income.

Foreign income
As a general rule, foreign-source income, such as interest, is included in taxable income. However, income from a PE or real estate outside Denmark is excluded from taxable income.

The income of a foreign subsidiary may be taxed in the hands of its Danish parent company if the subsidiary constitutes a controlled foreign company (CFC). *See the Group taxation section for more information.*

....

Deductions

Depreciation, amortisation, and depletion
Tax depreciation need not be in conformity with book depreciation.

Annual depreciation allowances on machinery and equipment may be claimed under the diminishing-balance method at up to 25%. The depreciation base is the cost of fixed assets less sales proceeds from disposals and depreciation allowances previously claimed.

For ships, the depreciation rate is 20% in the year of construction and a 12% declining-balance basis in subsequent years.

Depreciation allowances on buildings (other than residential buildings and office buildings not adjoining an industrial building) may be claimed at up to 4% on the straight-line basis.

Airplanes, trains, and utility plants can be depreciated only at a 15% declining balance (presently subject to phasing-in rates).

Rails, telecommunications facilities, and certain other long-life plant and equipment can be depreciated only at a 7% declining balance.

Depreciation allowances that are recaptured as part of a capital gain on the sale of an asset generally are fully taxable.

Acquired goodwill and other intangible property rights can be amortised at up to one-seventh per year on a straight-line basis. Costs related to the purchase of patents or know-how (including rights/licences to utilise patents or know-how) can either be fully expensed in the year of acquisition or amortised over a seven-year period on a straight-line basis.

Certain restrictions regarding the depreciable value of goodwill apply in the case of group transactions. Goodwill on the purchase of shares cannot be amortised for tax purposes.

Depletion of the cost of acquisition or exploitation of natural resources is subject to special rules.

Starts-up expenses
No specific rules in Danish tax law govern the treatment of start-up expenses. Instead, these expenses are treated according to general tax law.

As per 1 January 2012, companies may, under certain conditions, benefit from a new scheme allowing for a cash payment equal to the tax value (25%) of negative taxable income, provided the negative income is created from research and development (R&D) costs (*see the Tax credits and incentives section*).

Interest expenses
See Thin capitalisation and interest relief limitations in the Group taxation section.

Bad debt
Companies may deduct loss on bad debt.

The main rule for calculation and taxation of companies' gains and losses on receivables for tax purposes will be the inventory principle (i.e. taxation based on the difference in value at the beginning and end of the assessment year). Use of the inventory principle means that recognition of losses on these types of receivables for tax purposes is not conditional on a final loss having been ascertained.

Special rules apply to gains and losses on trade and inter-company receivables, as these, as a main rule, should be calculated according to realisation principles. Companies may, however, opt for the inventory principle for each category of receivables.

Charitable contributions
Companies may deduct a small amount in gifts to certain organisation approved by the Danish tax authorities and mentioned in the Danish tax authorities' guidelines. The deduction cannot exceed DKK 14,500 per year.

Furthermore, companies may deduct gifts to cultural organisations that receive a maintenance grant for operating expenses from either the government or the municipality. According to these rules, there is no limitation in terms of value, but certain restrictions regarding the use of the gift are applicable.

Finally, gifts to certain charitable organisation within Denmark or the European Union may be deducted, provided the recipient uses the funds for research. Deductibility is

Denmark

conditioned upon the organisation being approved by the Danish tax authorities. No limitation in regards to amount is applicable.

Fines and penalties
Fines and penalties are, in general, not deductible, as these are not considered operational expenses.

Bribes, kickbacks, and illegal payments
Even if considered economically reasoned and custom in certain jurisdictions, amounts used for bribery are not deductible.

Taxes
Taxes are non-deductible for CIT purposes, except for employer's tax, non-recoverable VAT, land tax, and coverage charge (*see the Other taxes section*).

Net operating losses
Tax losses may be carried forward indefinitely.

Certain restrictions on the right to carry tax losses forward apply when more than 50% of the share capital or 50% of the voting rights at the end of the financial year are owned by shareholders different from those that held control at the beginning of the income year in which the tax loss was incurred.

Similarly, under certain circumstances, tax losses are cancelled if a Danish company receives a debt forgiveness or comparable transaction. However, there are numerous exceptions (e.g. inter-company transactions).

Tax losses may not be carried back and utilised in previous income years.

Payments to foreign affiliates
A Danish corporation can claim a deduction for royalties, management fees, and similar payments made to foreign affiliates, provided that such amounts are made on an arm's-length basis and reflect services received. Interest at normal commercial rates paid to foreign affiliates generally will be allowed as a deduction but is subject to very complex thin capitalisation and interest relief limitation rules.

Group taxation

Mandatory Danish tax consolidation
A mandatory tax consolidation regime obliges all Danish resident companies and Danish branches that are members of the same domestic or international group to file a joint group tax return. The definition of a group generally corresponds with the definition of a group for accounting purposes. The tax consolidated income is equal to the sum of the taxable income of each individual Danish company and branch that are a member of the consolidated group.

The top parent company participating in the Danish tax consolidation group will be appointed the role of a so-called management company; this company is responsible for settling advance and final corporate tax payments of all group members.

Elective cross-border tax consolidation
A non-Danish subsidiary may be included as a member to a Danish tax grouping, provided that the group includes all of its foreign companies and branches in the Danish

tax grouping. In effect, this all-or-nothing provision rules out the possibility for major international groups to have their Danish subgroup file a Danish group tax return that includes only certain hand-picked (typically loss-making) foreign group members.

If a general cross-border tax consolidation is established, it will be binding for ten years; however, there are certain possibilities of 'breaking' the ten-year period (e.g. in connection with takeovers).

The comments under Mandatory Danish tax consolidation with respect to the calculation of the tax consolidation income, 'management' company, etc. generally also apply to international tax consolidation.

Transfer pricing
Danish transfer pricing rules apply to transactions between related parties (e.g. intergroup transactions) whether the transactions are made between residents or non-residents. The rules apply when a company or person directly or indirectly owns at least 50% of the share capital or 50% of the voting rights in another company.

Companies are obliged to disclose in the annual tax return certain information regarding type and volume of intra-group transactions. Companies also are obliged to maintain detailed and extensive transfer pricing documentation to substantiate that intra-group transactions are conducted in accordance with arm's-length principles. A company is subject to fines for failure to comply with the documentation rules.

Thin capitalisation and interest relief limitations
Danish resident companies and Danish branches of foreign companies are subject to three sets of restrictions, each of which may seriously limit or disallow Danish tax relief for financing costs. There is no recharacterisation of interest as dividends.

Firstly, there is the thin capitalisation rule. This rule works to disallow gross interest costs and capital losses on related party debt to the extent the overall debt to equity ratio exceeds 4:1. Related party debt is defined so as to include external bank debt if group member companies or shareholders have provided guarantees to the bank. This rule does not apply if the controlled debt is less than DKK 10 million. When calculating the 4:1 ratio, a special consolidation rules applies if two or more companies are considered affiliated (note that the definition of affiliated companies differs from the definition under the Danish rules on joint taxation).

Secondly, there is an asset-based rule. To the extent a Danish company on a stand-alone basis or, if part of a joint tax group, together with group companies has net financing costs in excess of DKK 21.3 million, tax relief may be obtained only within an amount equal to 4.5% (rate applicable for 2011) of the tax basis of certain assets of the group (rate applicable for 2012 is 3.5%). Net financing costs consist of, among other things, interest income/expenses, taxable gains/losses on debt, receivables and financial contracts, taxable gains/losses on shares, and taxable dividend.

Thirdly, there is an earnings before interest and tax (EBIT) based rule that works to limit interest relief to an amount equal to 80% of the Danish company's/tax group's taxable EBIT income. This rule applies the same definition of net financing costs as the asset-based rule, and it also allows for a minimum deduction of DKK 21.3 million in cases where EBIT is too low or negative.

Denmark

Controlled foreign companies (CFCs)

According to the Danish CFC rules, a Danish company has to include in its taxable income the total income of a subsidiary, foreign or Danish, if such subsidiary qualifies as a CFC. A subsidiary qualifies as a CFC if all of the following criteria are met:

- The Danish company, together with other group member companies, directly or indirectly owns more than 50% of the capital or controls more than 50% of the voting rights in the subsidiary.
- More than half of the subsidiary's taxable profits, as hypothetically assessed under Danish tax laws, are predefined CFC income types (mainly interest, royalty, capital gains, etc.).
- During the income year, the subsidiary's CFC assets (assets, where the return is characterised as a CFC income type) make up more than 10% of the subsidiary's total assets.

There is no black or white list that exempts subsidiaries resident in certain countries.

Tax credits and incentives

Foreign tax credit

According to Danish tax law, relief is generally available to credit foreign tax paid on non-Danish source profits against the Danish tax on the same profits. As Danish companies are not taxed on income from foreign PEs or properties, the rules have limited application.

For share holdings of 10% or more of the share capital in foreign companies, Denmark has further rules allowing 'underlying' tax relief in respect of foreign dividends, so that tax suffered at lower levels can be relieved where dividends flow to Denmark via a chain of companies. As Danish tax law, as a main rule, exempts dividends from companies resident in countries with which Denmark has a tax treaty in which the Danish recipient company holds 10% or more, this rule, as well, has a limited application.

Capital expenditure incentives

A small variety of tax incentives are available in the form of deductions for capital expenditures.

Danish tax law allows for an immediate write-off of capital expenditures for R&D. Alternatively, the taxpayer may choose to take tax depreciation in the same year and the following four years on a straight-line basis. Costs incurred in connection with the exploration for raw materials may also be fully deducted in the same year.

Companies in a loss making situation may not benefit from an immediate write-off of capital expenditures. As of 1 January 2012, companies have been granted the opportunity to apply to the Danish tax authorities for a payment equal to the tax value (25%) of negative taxable income. It is a condition that the negative taxable income relates to R&D costs. The rule does not cover costs incurred in connection with exploration for raw materials.

Tax payment according to this rule cannot exceed an amount of DKK 1.25 million (tax value of DKK 5 million). For companies participating in joint taxation, the limit of DKK 1.25 million applies for all companies in total.

Denmark

Costs related to purchase of patents and know-how (including rights/licences to utilise patents or know-how) may either be fully expensed in the year of acquisition or amortised over a seven-year period on a straight-line basis.

Withholding taxes

WHTs on payments to foreign corporations and non-resident aliens

D

Dividends

Dividends paid to a parent company in another EU member state or a state with which Denmark has a DTT are exempt from WHT provided that the shares qualify as subsidiary shares. The same applies for dividends paid on group shares (that are not also subsidiary shares, i.e. holdings below 10%), provided that the recipient company is resident within the EU/EEA.

Dividends paid on portfolio shares to a foreign shareholder are levied WHT of 27% (28% prior to 2012). If the portfolio shareholder is situated in a country with which Denmark has a Tax Information Exchange Agreement (TIEA), the tax rate on the dividend is reduced to 15% and the difference between the higher WHT rate and the lower WHT rate may be reclaimed. However, the reduced rate does not apply if the shareholder is resident outside the European Union and together with related entities owns more than 10% of the capital in the Danish distributing company.

Interest

Interest generally is not subject to WHT unless paid to a foreign group member company that is tax resident outside the European Union and outside any of the states with which Denmark has concluded a tax treaty. In this situation, interest WHT is levied at 25%. Certain other exemptions apply, mainly relating to CFC taxation.

Royalties

Royalties are subject to a 25% WHT. In most cases, the payer may reduce its withholding in accordance with the tax treaty applicable to the payee. Also, the EU Interest/Royalty Directive may provide an exemption from WHT if the payee is an immediate parent, sister, or subsidiary company resident in the European Union.

Recipient	WHT (%)			
	Dividend			
	Qualifying companies (1a+b)	Others	Interest (2)	Royalty
Resident corporations	0	27	0	25 (5)
Resident individuals		27	0	25
Non-treaty (4):				
Non-resident corporations	27	27	25 (3, 5)	25 (5)
Non-resident individuals		27	0	25
Treaty:				
Argentina	0 (1a)	15	0	3/5/10/15 (7)
Australia	0 (1a)	15	0	10
Austria	0 (1a+b)	15	0	0
Bangladesh	0 (1a)	15	0	10
Belgium	0 (1a+b)	15	0	0
Brazil	0 (1a)	25	0	15/25 (7)

Denmark

	WHT (%)			
	Dividend			
Recipient	**Qualifying companies (1a+b)**	**Others**	**Interest (2)**	**Royalty**
Bulgaria	0 (1a+b)	15	0	0
Canada	0 (1a)	15	0	0/10 (7)
Chile	0 (1a)	15	0	5/15 (7)
China, P.R.	0 (1a)	10	0	10
Croatia	0 (1a)	10	0	10
Cyprus	0 (1a+b)	15	0	0
Czech Republic	0 (1a+b)	15	0	5
Egypt	0 (1a)	20	0	20
Estonia	0 (1a+b)	15	0	5/10 (7)
Faroe Islands	0 (1a)	15	0	0
Finland	0 (1a+b)	15	0	0
Georgia	0 (1a)	10	0	0
Germany	0 (1a+b)	15	0	0
Greece	0 (1a+b)	18	0	5
Greenland	0 (1a)	15	0	10
Hungary	0 (1a+b)	15	0	0
Iceland	0 (1a+b)	15	0	0
India	0 (1a)	25	0	20
Indonesia	0 (1a)	25	0	15
Ireland, Republic of	0 (1a+b)	15	0	0
Israel	0 (1a)	15	0	10
Italy	0 (1a+b)	15	0	5
Jamaica	0 (1a)	15	0	10
Japan	0 (1a)	15	0	10
Kenya	0 (1a)	28	0	20
Korea, Republic of	0 (1a)	15	0	10/15 (7)
Kuwait	0 (1a)	15	0	10
Kyrgyzstan	0 (1a)	15	0	0
Latvia	0 (1a+b)	15	0	5/10 (7)
Lithuania	0 (1a+b)	15	0	5/10 (7)
Luxembourg	0 (1a+b)	15	0	0
Macedonia	0 (1a)	15	0	10
Malaysia	0 (1a)	0	0	0
Malta	0 (1a+b)	15	0	0
Mexico	0 (1a)	15	0	10
Morocco	0 (1a)	25	0	10
Netherlands	0 (1a+b)	15	0	0
New Zealand	0 (1a)	15	0	10
Norway	0 (1a+b)	15	0	0
Pakistan	0 (1a)	15	0	12
Philippines	0 (1a)	15	0	15
Poland	0 (1a+b)	15	0	5
Portugal	0 (1a+b)	10	0	10
Romania	0 (1a+b)	15	0	4
Russia	0 (1a)	10	0	0

Denmark

Recipient	WHT (%) Dividend Qualifying companies (1a+b)	Others	Interest (2)	Royalty
Serbia (6)	0 (1a)	15	0	10
Singapore	0 (1a)	10	0	10
Slovak Republic	0 (1a+b)	15	0	5
Slovenia	0 (1a+b)	15	0	5
South Africa	0 (1a)	15	0	0
Sri Lanka	0 (1a)	15	0	10
Sweden	0 (1a+b)	15	0	0
Switzerland	0 (1+a)	15	0	0
Taiwan	0 (1a)	10	0	10
Tanzania	0 (1a)	15	0	20
Thailand	0 (1a)	10	0	5/15 (7)
Trinidad and Tobago	0 (1a)	20	0	15
Tunisia	0 (1a)	15	0	15
Turkey	0 (1a)	20	0	10
Uganda	0 (1a)	15	0	10
Ukraine	0 (1a)	15	0	10
United Kingdom	0 (1a+b)	25	0	0
United States	0 (1a)	15	0	0
Venezuela	0 (1a)	15	0	5/10 (8)
Vietnam	0 (1a)	15	0	15
Zambia	0 (1a)	15	0	15

D

Notes

1. Denmark does not operate a system of WHT on dividends when the parent company holds:
   a. at least 10% of the share capital of the distributing Danish company, provided the receiving company is resident in a EU/EEA member state or a state with which Denmark has entered a double tax treaty (subsidiary shares) or
   b. less than 10% of the share capital in the distributing company, provided that the receiving company is an EU/EEA-resident and the distributing and the receiving company are affiliated companies (group shares).
2. Interest generally is not subject to WHT unless paid to a foreign group member company that is tax resident outside of the European Union and outside of any of the states with which Denmark has concluded a tax treaty. In this situation, interest WHT is levied at 25%.
3. Exemptions apply if the receiving company is directly or indirectly controlled by a Danish parent company or if the receiving company is controlled by a company resident in a state with which Denmark has a double tax convention and that company may be subject to CFC taxation. Finally, an exemption applies if the receiving company establishes that the foreign taxation of interest is not less than three-quarters of the Danish corporate taxation and that the interest is not paid to another foreign company subject to taxation less than three-quarters of the Danish corporate taxation.
4. Denmark has terminated its treaty with Spain and France with effect from 1 January 2009. The termination means that each country will tax the relevant income according to its domestic tax rules. New treaties are not expected to be agreed in the near future. Companies in Spain and France receiving dividends from a Danish company may, however, qualify for tax exempt dividends since they are EU member states.
5. The EU Interest/Royalty Directive may provide an exemption from WHT if the payee is an immediate parent, sister, or subsidiary company resident in the European Union.
6. Serbia has succeeded in the treaty between Denmark and Yugoslavia.
7. Different rates apply depending on the characteristics of the assets on which royalty is paid.
8. The 10% rate is applicable for royalties, whereas the 5% rate is applicable to fees for technical support.

Denmark

....

Tax administration

Taxable period
Danish corporate taxpayers are taxed on an annual basis. Corporate taxpayers may choose a tax year that is different from the calendar year.

Tax returns
Tax returns are completed on the basis of audited financial accounts with adjustments for tax. Tax returns should be filed no later than six months following the end of the accounting year. Corporations with an accounting year-end that falls in the period from 1 January to 31 March must file a tax return no later than 1 August in the same calendar year.

The tax system, in practice, is based on self-assessment. Tax assessments are made automatically by the tax authorities on the basis of the tax return. However, the tax authorities may subsequently audit the tax return.

Payment of tax
CIT must be paid on a current year basis in two equal instalments due on 20 March and 20 November. The authorities request payments of 50% of the average of the last three years' final income tax. In addition, voluntary additional payments may be made at the same dates; such voluntary payments are adjusted by 0.7% when set against the final tax bill.

The final tax bill is settled by 20 November in the following year. Underpaid tax is then payable by 20 November with a surtax of 4.8% of the tax amount (for the 2011 tax year). Overpaid tax is refunded by November of the following year with interest of 1.3% (for the 2011 tax year).

Audit cycle
The Danish tax system is based on self-assessment. Companies are, in general, subject to audit on a random basis, but some large companies/groups are subject to annual audit by the Danish tax authorities.

Statute of limitations
The general statute of limitations is 1 May in the fourth calendar year after that of the end of the relevant accounting period. This limitation is extended for another two years with respect to inter-company (transfer pricing) issues.

Topics of focus for tax authorities
Once a year, the Danish tax authorities publish a list of topics subject to increased focus by the tax administration during their audit. Transfer pricing issues figures on top of this list.

In general, all aspects of transfer pricing are in focus. However, specific topics certainly seem to have caught the tax authorities' attention. These are mainly transactions with group companies resident in countries with which Denmark does not have a tax convention, use and transfer of intangible assets, restructurings, and companies making continuous losses.

As described in the Significant developments section, attention has also been drawn to whether Danish entities have complied with the WHT requirements regarding dividends and interest.

Last but not least, the tax authorities have increased their focus on tax deductions for costs related to the creation of tax exempt income, such as dividend from and capital gains on certain shares.

Other issues

Tax-free restructuring

Restructuring (e.g. mergers, demergers, share exchanges, drop-down of assets) can, in many cases, be carried out tax-free under the provisions of the EU Mergers Directive as implemented into Danish law. These types of restructuring can be carried out in a tax-exempt manner without prior approval from the tax authorities. However, several objective conditions must be fulfilled. Formation, merger, reorganisation, and liquidation expenses are mostly non-deductible.

D

Dominica, Commonwealth of

PwC contact

Richard Peterkin
PricewaterhouseCoopers
Pointe Seraphine
Castries, St. Lucia
Tel: +1 758 456 2600 Ext. 2626
Email: richard.n.peterkin@lc.pwc.com

Significant developments

There are no significant developments during the past year, other than the reduction of stamp duty on land transfer between parent and child, which is now reduced from 4% to 2%, and the removal of transferor's fees.

Taxes on corporate income

Resident companies are taxed on gains or profits accrued directly or indirectly from all sources, whether in and out of Dominica, and are subject to tax at a flat rate of 30%.

Non-resident companies are taxed on Dominican-source income. The gross amount of such income is liable to 15% withholding tax (WHT).

Associations of underwriters are taxed at 30% on 10% of the gross premium arising in Dominica, and life insurance companies are taxed at 30% on 20% of the gross investment income arising in Dominica.

Corporate residence

Companies are regarded as resident if they are incorporated in Dominica or managed and controlled through a permanent establishment (PE) in Dominica.

Permanent establishment (PE)

A PE is defined in Dominica as a fixed place or premises through which the business is wholly or partly carried on. A PE includes:

- A place of management.
- A branch or office.
- A factory or workshop.
- Premises used as a sales outlet.
- A building site or construction or assembly project.
- The maintenance of plant and machinery for rental.

Other taxes

Valued-added tax (VAT)

VAT came into effect on 1 March 2006. VAT replaced the Consumption Tax, Sales Tax, Hotel Occupancy Tax, and Entertainment Tax.

VAT applies to practically all supply of services and import of goods or import of services, other than an exempt import. The tax is imposed at a rate of 15% of the value of every taxable supply by a taxable person in Dominica, except if the supply is classified as accommodations and diving activity, which carries a rate of 10%.

Certain transactions are zero-rated or exempt from VAT. Export sales by VAT-registered persons are zero-exempt.

Certain supply of services is exempt from VAT, including services provided by financial intermediaries, schools, and medical practitioners. Exempt imports include goods imported by Dominicans returning home for permanent residence, motor vehicles imported by natural persons on change of permanent residence, unconditional gift of goods to an approved charitable organisation, other than for purposes of re-sale, etc.

Every registered person is required to file a tax return for each tax period with the Inland Revenue Division (IRD) within 20 calendar days after the end of the period, whether or not tax is payable in respect of that period. This return should be in the form prescribed by the IRD and should state the information necessary to calculate the tax.

Customs duties

Custom duties are charged on a wide range of imported goods. Exemptions are granted for raw materials and plant and machinery used in manufacturing and for certain items imported by hotels under construction, extension, or refurbishing projects.

Excise taxes

Excise tax is imposed on taxable goods (other than taxable goods previously imported into Dominica) removed for consumption in Dominica from a warehouse of a manufacturer registered or required to be registered and taxable goods imported into Dominica.

For both importers and local manufacturers, the due date for payment is the 20th day of each calendar month.

Taxable goods include alcohol, cigarettes, petrol, and vehicles.

Stamp taxes

Stamp tax is charged on any document that evidences a legal or contractual relationship between two or more parties. Additionally, many types of commercial and legal documents must be stamped, denoting the payment of taxes, which may be either at a fixed rate or at an *ad valorem* rate, depending, for example, on the value of the property transferred.

For a conveyance or transfer on sale of any property (except stock and debentures), a stamp duty of 6.5% on the value of the property, real or personal, transferred shall be paid of which 2.5% shall be paid by the transferor and 4% by the transferred. Provided that on any stock or shares of a company or corporation whose assets to the extent of 50% or more consists of real property, stamp duty as set out above shall be paid.

Branch income

The tax rate on branch income is the same as that on income earned by resident companies. Every non-resident company carrying on business in Dominica is liable to

Dominica, Commonwealth of

WHT of 15% on such part of the profits of the business for any year of assessment as is remitted out of Dominica.

Where a controlled company fails to make a sufficient distribution in relation to any year of assessment, it is liable to pay tax on the undistributed profits of that year of assessment at the rate of 15%. A 'controlled company' means a resident company that is owned by not more than five shareholders, excluding the government and any company that is not itself a controlled company.

In determining the amount of a sufficient distribution, the Comptroller of the IRD shall have regard to the nature of the sources of its income and the financial resources available to it and may, where satisfied that it would be detrimental to the business of the company to regard the whole of its chargeable income after deduction of the tax payable thereon as a sufficient distribution, direct that such proportion thereof as the Comptroller may specify (hereinafter referred to as 'a retention allowance') may be retained for the purpose of the business without liability to tax.

Income determination

Inventory valuation
Stocks generally are valued at the lower of cost or market value. Obsolescence is permitted where it occurs, but there are no provisions to account for monetary inflation on inventory valuation.

Capital gains
There is no tax on capital gains except in instances where such gains comprise a portion of the income-earning activities of the business. In such instances, the corporate tax rate applies.

Dividend income
Dividends are subject to tax at a rate of 30%. However, there is a tax credit given that is equal to the amount by which the tax payable of a company has been increased by the inclusion of such dividend in its taxable income.

Interest income
The corporate tax rate applies to interest income. However, income earned on securities issued by member governments of the Easter Caribbean Central Bank and any income accruing to the buyer, seller, or issuer from any transfer of securities which are listed on the Eastern Caribbean Securities Exchange through the facilities of that Exchange is tax exempt.

Any expenditure incurred for the purpose of producing exempt income is not deductible.

Deductions

Depreciation and amortisation
Capital allowance is available in Dominica.

Annual allowances for wear and tear, ranging from 3% to 20%, are granted on the acquisition of industrial and commercial buildings; on plant and machinery, including motor vehicles and furniture; and on fixtures and equipment.

The Comptroller of the IRD may also grant, on application, a higher rate for annual allowance for assets that have higher or abnormal wear and tear.

Goodwill

Neither the amortisation of impaired goodwill nor the related write-off of it is an allowable deduction.

Start-up expenses

All expenditures incurred in connection with incorporation costs for the establishment of a company are deductible unless considered as capital expenditure.

Interest expenses

Interest on any loan, including interest payable on debentures, is an allowable deduction to the extent that the amount of such loan was used for the purpose of producing assessable income.

Bad debt

Bad debt expense is deductible provided it has been brought to account in generating the company's assessable income for any income year.

Charitable contributions

Charitable contributions are an allowable deduction when the contributions are made by way of subscription or donation to a business or professional organisation approved by the Comptroller of the IRD where the Comptroller is satisfied that the organisation is a non-profit body established with the object of maintaining and advancing the standards of the business or profession.

Fines and penalties

Fines and penalties are not allowable deductions.

Taxes

Taxes are not allowable deductions except taxes imposed on any immovable property used for the purpose of producing assessable income.

Net operating losses

Net operating losses may be carried forward up to a maximum five years. In carrying losses forward, the amount that can be claimed in any subsequent year is the full amount of the available loss.

Payments to foreign affiliates

There are no restrictions on the deductibility of interest paid to foreign affiliates if the transaction is carried out at arm's length and at commercial rates. However, deduction for management charges, which is subject to 15% WHT, is restricted to the lesser of such charges or 5% of all allowable deductions, excluding such charges and capital allowances.

Group taxation

Group tax filing is not allowed in Dominica.

Dominica, Commonwealth of

Transfer pricing

Related party transactions are accepted if they are made on an arm's-length basis. The Comptroller of the IRD has the power under the Income Tax Act to make any adjustment deemed necessary to place such transaction at arm's length.

Thin capitalisation

No provision exists for thin capitalisation in Dominica.

Tax credits and incentives

Foreign tax credit

Where income has accrued to a resident and has been taxed in a foreign country with which there is no double tax agreement (DTA), or is income to which a DTA, if there is one, does not relate, credit for tax on such income is allowed for the lesser of the tax payable in the foreign country or the tax charged under Dominican tax law.

Tax holidays

Tax holidays are available for manufacturing companies. The incentives are aimed at increasing the manufacturing base of Dominica, the level of exports, and the use of local materials and labour in production. An approved manufacturing enterprise will be granted a tax holiday up to a maximum of 15 years. In determining the length of the tax holiday, the extent of the local value added to approved products is taken into account.

Investment incentives

Income tax incentives and other fiscal concessions are provided under the Fiscal Incentives Act, and other concessions granted by the Cabinet of Ministers. The extent of the incentives and concessions granted are specific to the legislation or Cabinet conclusions and depend on the impact that the investment would have on local employment, exports, and the generation of foreign exchange earnings. The incentives granted include the following:

- Duty free importation of raw materials, machinery, components, and spare parts and other inputs used in manufacturing, and the duty-free importation of construction materials, equipment, and other inputs used in the construction and operation of hotels and other hospitality products.
- Income tax waivers of up to 100% of the taxable income of companies engaged in manufacturing, tourism, and agriculture and other employment generating activities, for periods of up to 15 years.
- Whole or partial waivers of stamp duties, Alien Landholding License fees, and WHT with respect to investments in specific areas, or in specific industries and activities.
- Export allowances for goods manufactured in Dominica and exported. Companies who engage in such activity are given tax exemption on the export of such goods up to a maximum of 10 to 15 years.

Withholding taxes

Resident corporations and persons that make certain payments of an income nature to residents or non-residents are required to withhold tax on these payments:

Payment	WHT (%)
Dividend	15

Payment	WHT (%)
Interest or discounts	15
Rental, lease, premium, or licence in relation to immovable property	15
Rental of plant, machinery, equipment, or other movable property	15
Royalty	15
Management charge	15
Commission or fee, not being in respect of employment	15
Annuities or other periodic payments	15
Distribution of income of a trust	15
Any other payment of an income nature	15
Profits of a non-resident company from carrying on business in Dominica that is remitted out of Dominica	15

Tax administration

Tax returns

Tax returns must be filed within three months of the company's fiscal year-end. An extension of the filing date may be obtained. Returns must cover a 12-month period, which may be changed only with the Comptroller's permission.

Financial statements must be submitted with the returns, together with a schedule reconciling taxable income with book income and various other schedules of additional information.

The system is one of self-assessment. Upon receipt of the returns, the IRD examines the information provided and issues a notice of assessment at any time, subject to the statute of limitations. The IRD may also issue assessments in the absence of returns.

Payment of tax

Tax is payable in instalments on 31 March, 30 June, and 30 September in each income year, based on the preceding income year. Any remainder is payable on or before 31 March of the subsequent year.

Audit cycle

The IRD carries out audits of a selection of tax returns, usually at the taxpayer's place of business. Audits may be carried out at any time prior to the expiration of the statute of limitations, whether or not notices of assessment have been issued. The IRD has wide powers in determining the information it requires for these audits.

Appeals

Within 30 days after the date of service of a notice of assessment or reassessment, the taxpayer may submit a written objection to the IRD on any matters in such assessment or reassessment. If the IRD confirms its assessment, the taxpayer may file an appeal with the Appeal Commission, which comprises four persons appointed by the Cabinet. A decision by that body may be further appealed to the High Court. An appeal against on an order from this Court may be made to the Court of Appeal.

Statute of limitations

Assessments are not final until six years after the end of the income year, within which period assessments may be made at any time. In cases of misrepresentation or failure to disclose any material fact, a reassessment can be made at any time.

Dominican Republic

PwC contact

Ramon Ortega
PricewaterhouseCoopers
Scotiabank Building
3rd floor
Santo Domingo
Dominican Republic
Tel: +1 809 567 7741
Email: ramon.ortega@do.pwc.com

Significant developments

General Norm 04-11 of 2 June 2011

General Norm 04-11 of 2 June 2011 established the rules for transfer pricing determination on transactions between related parties. It applies to any transaction between local entities of foreign equity and:

- related parties abroad
- residents or persons domiciled in tax havens or in jurisdictions of low tax rates, and
- related parties classified as a Free Trade Zone (FTZ) entity.

This rule established the obligation of taxpayers to file an annual Informative Tax Return of transactions between related parties, which shall contain detailed information of each transaction and the related party's identification. Furthermore, tax authorities have the faculty to challenge these transactions if the price or amount stated by the taxpayer differs from those established in the market.

Law No. 139-11 of 29 June 2011 on income tax increase to allocate funds to education

Law No. 139-11, effective on 29 June 2011, introduced the following important modifications:

- The corporate income tax (CIT) rate increased from 25% to 29% for a two-year period.
- The following withholding tax (WHT) rates increased for a two-year period:
  - Payments abroad: from 25% to 29%.
  - Interest paid to non-financial institutions abroad: from 25% to 29%.
  - Dividends paid or credited in cash: from 25% to 29%.
  - Fringe benefits tax: from 25% to 29%.
- An additional tax of 1% (.083% monthly) was introduced on net financial assets, which will constitute a deductible expense for CIT purposes. The annual tax amount should not exceed the net taxable income (before the deduction of this tax), determined for the CIT return. The base of this tax is the total average interest-earning financial assets for the year, and the tax applies to the amount of assets exceeding 700 million Dominican pesos [DOP]). The application of this tax was established for a 24-month period and affects for multiple banks, savings and loans associations, savings and credit banks, and credit corporations.

  Companies under the financial assets tax must make a monthly advance payment equivalent to one-twelfth the rate of 1% (.083%) over the productive assets of the month.

- A 2.5% tax was created on the gross sales of goods and services by companies in Dominican FTZs to individuals and legal entities in the local market.

General Norm 07-11 of 1 July 2011

General Norm 07-11 of 1 July 2011 establishes a 1% WHT on the value of the transfer of shares paid to the seller. Foreign entities are not exempt from this obligation.

Such WHT is a payment on account against capital gain tax, payable by the seller through the Form IR-2 (legal entities) or Form IR-1 (individuals), as applicable. However, if they can substantiate that the transaction will generate a capital loss, they may request from the tax authorities, no later than 30 days prior to withholding filing/payment's due date, to be exempt from this obligation.

General Norm 13-11 of 5 September 2011

General Norm 13-11 of 5 September 2011 appoints financial institutions as 1% WHT agents on the value paid or credited on account for interest payments of any nature to legal entities.

The interests paid by financial institutions will constitute a deductible expense for tax purposes, provided the WHT was made.

In addition, this rule obliges financial institutions to provide a monthly electronic file, directly to the tax authorities or through the Banks Superintendency, containing all the information related to the interest payment, including the date, value, and identity of the beneficiary.

Taxes on corporate income

The Dominican Republic follows a territorial concept (i.e. resident companies, branches, and permanent establishments [PEs] are generally subject to taxation on Dominican-source income only); therefore, the tax treatment for corporations, partnerships, and limited liability companies is similar in most aspects.

As of 29 June 2011, the current CIT rate is a flat rate of 29%. Prior to 29 June 2011, the CIT rate was 25%. After 29 June 2013, the CIT rate will return to 25%. Please note that the asset tax is an alternative minimum tax that is payable when it is higher than a company's CIT liability (see Asset tax in the Other taxes section).

Dividends remitted abroad or paid locally by Dominican entities (not applicable to branches or PEs) are subject to a WHT of 29% (25% prior to 29 June 2011 and after 29 June 2013). This WHT may be used as a credit against the company's CIT of the same tax year as long as the dividends were paid out of profits which had already been subject to CIT.

Local income taxes

In the Dominican Republic, local government income taxes do not apply.

Corporate residence

A company is resident when it is registered or incorporated under the laws of the Dominican Republic. Foreign entities are considered as domiciled when they

Dominican Republic

are registered in the Dominican Republic as a branch or PE, and they are subject to local tax in the same manner.

Permanent establishment (PE)

According to local tax legislation, which follows the Organisation for Economic Co-operation and Development (OECD) Model Tax Convention on Income and on Capital, a PE is defined as a fixed place of business where a foreign entity or individual performs all or part of its activities, such as:

- An address in the Dominican Republic.
- Office.
- Branches.
- Workshop.
- Mine.
- Petroleum or gas well.
- Quarry or any other natural resource extraction place.
- Assembly projects, including supervision activities of such projects.
- Construction/supervision activities derived from the sale of machinery and equipment when its cost exceeds 10% of the sale price of such equipment.
- Consulting services, provided these exceed six months within the same fiscal period.
- Representatives or dependent or independent agents, when these act on behalf of the entity.

Other taxes

Tax on the Transfer of Industrialised Goods and Services (ITBIS)

ITBIS is a value-added tax (VAT) applied to industrialised goods (movable) and services at a rate of 16%, with exemptions established by law to certain goods and services.

Exempt goods include a wide variety of goods, among which are basic products (eggs, milk, grains, live animals, frozen meats), seeds for planting, fruits and vegetables, sausages and canned sardines, chocolate/cacao, infant foods, medicine, insecticide and pesticides, books/magazines, educational material, wheelchairs, and prosthesis.

Exempt services include educational, health, financial (including insurance), pensions, ground transportation of people and cargo, electricity, water and waste pick-up, housing rental and personal care, and exported services.

A 0% rate applies to exports, including sales to FTZs.

Tax on gross sales made by FTZs to local market

A 2.5% tax was created on the gross sales of goods and services made by companies in Dominican FTZs to individuals and legal entities in the local market.

Customs duties

Customs duties are assessed at various rates depending on the nature of the goods and their country of origin. Free trade agreements exist (e.g. Central America-Dominican Republic-US Free Trade Agreement [DR-CAFTA]) which decrease the custom duty rates for goods imported from the member countries.

Selective consumption taxes (Impuesto Selectivo al Consumo or ISCs)

ISC is applied to the acquisition or import of certain goods and services.

There is an ISC for alcoholic goods and cigarettes, adjusted by inflation annually:

* Alcohol: ranges from DOP 356.84 to DOP 437.56 for every litre of pure alcohol.
* Cigarettes: DOP 33.24 for a 20 pack and DOP 16.62 for a 10 pack.

There are ISCs that vary based on the product, which range from:

D

* 7.5% on the transfer of alcoholic beverages, applied on the retail price. Imports and transfers made by local manufacturers are accountable for this tax.
* 20% on the transfer of tobacco products, applied on the retail price. Imports and transfers by local manufacturers are accountable for this tax.
* 19.5% to 130% on the consumption of certain imported goods (listed in the law) that are considered to be non-essential.
* 10% on telecommunications services.
* 16% on insurance services.
* 0.0015% on the value of cheques or wire transfers made through financial entities (this tax does not apply to cash withdrawals or credit card use).

Asset tax

Asset tax/Law No. 557-05 imposes a 1% tax on total assets, net of depreciation, amortisation, and bad debt reserves. Share investments in other companies, land in rural areas, immovable property pertaining to livestock and agriculture, asset revaluations, and tax advance payments are excluded from this tax base.

The asset tax is a minimum tax filed and liquidated through the annual CIT return (Form IR-2) and paid applying the following rules:

* CIT is allowed as a credit against the asset tax.
* If CIT is greater than the asset tax, the obligation to pay the asset tax is cancelled and CIT is paid instead.
* If CIT is less than the asset tax, the difference (in order to complete the asset tax value) shall be paid in two equal instalments as follows:
  * First instalment shall be paid during 120 days subsequent to closing date.
  * Second instalment shall be paid within six months after first quote's due date.

Entities may request a temporary exemption from the asset tax. Entities that require large capital (among other requirements established by General Ruling 3-06) may make such a request, which should be submitted at least 90 days before the filing due date. The local internal revenue service shall evaluate the merits of the request and approve or deny, as appropriate.

If the entity has an income tax credit arising from excess advance payments, it may request the refund of such balance be applied against the asset tax.

In the case of financial institutions, power generation and distribution companies, pension fund entities, and stock brokerage companies, the tax is calculated based on the fixed assets book value.

According to Rule 07-2007, construction companies may seek exemption from the asset tax, provided that such entities meet the requirements established in this rule.

Real Property Transfer Tax

The Real Property Transfer Tax is assessed at a basic rate of 3% on any transfer of ownership of real estate.

Dominican Republic

Stamp taxes
Stamp taxes have been abolished in the Dominican Republic.

Financial assets tax
A 1% tax per year on net financial assets (which should not exceed net taxable income before expenses generated by this tax, calculated on the total average interest-earning financial assets for the year, and applies to the net financial assets over DOP 700 million) was established on 29 June 2011 for a two-year period (until 29 June 2013) for multiple banks, savings and loans associations, savings and credit banks, and credit corporations. The amount paid for this tax will constitute a deductible expense for tax purposes if the tax is paid in the fiscal year.

Companies under the financial assets tax must pay a monthly payment equivalent to one-twelfth the rate of 1% over the productive assets of the month.

Branch income

Branch profits are taxed at the same rate as corporate profits (29% as of 29 June 2011; 25% prior to 29 June 2011 and after 29 June 2013). There is no WHT on branch profit remittances to the company's headquarters, provided that the corresponding annual CIT has been paid.

Income determination

Inventory valuation
The last in first out (LIFO) method of inventory valuation is established for tax purposes. Other methods may be authorised upon request.

Conformity between book and tax reporting is not required.

Capital gains
Capital gains are added to ordinary taxable income and subject to the CIT rate. Capital gains are defined as the difference between the sale price of an asset and the acquisition or production price, adjusted for inflation.

Dividend income
Dividend distributions in cash are subject to a 29% WHT, which should constitute a tax credit for the distributing entity against the annual CIT corresponding to the same taxable year in which the distribution was made. Dividends are tax exempt, provided they were subject to WHT.

Stock dividends
Stock dividends are not subject to taxation.

Interest income
Interest income is considered as part of taxable income; in the case of non-resident non-domiciled taxpayers, the tax should be paid through WHT.

Foreign income
Dominican-resident companies, branches, and PEs are subject to taxation on income from Dominican sources and on income from foreign sources arising from investments and financial gains. Tax determined on income from foreign source is subject to a credit

mechanism. Taxes paid in the country where the income is originated can be credited up to the amount of the tax payable in the Dominican Republic on the same income.

Deductions

Depreciation and amortisation

Depreciation allowances on fixed assets are determined by the declining-balance method at the following rates:

Assets	Depreciation rate (%)
Buildings	5
Office furniture, fixtures, computers, light vehicles, etc.	25
Other assets not specified	15

The fiscal book value is adjusted by the annual inflation rate.

Amortisation of intangible assets (e.g. patents, author's rights, drawings, franchises, and contracts without set expiration date) is not deductible.

Goodwill

Goodwill is not deductible.

Start-up expenses

The Dominican tax legislation does not establish specific provisions regarding the deduction of start-up expenses. The general deductions rule is the accrual method.

Interest expenses

Interest expenses are deductible, provided they are associated with the acquisition, maintenance, and/or exploitation of taxable income-generating assets.

Bad debt

Bad debts are deductible only in the year the loss is suffered. Authorisation may be obtained to use an alternative method, which consists of creating a provision allowing the deduction only in the year the bad debts qualify as doubtful, up to 4% of the balance of the accounts receivable at year-end.

Charitable contributions

Donations made are not tax deductible in the Dominican Republic.

Fines and penalties

Fines and penalties are considered non-deductible expenses.

Taxes

Income taxes are not deductible. Other taxes can be deductible; however, interest and surcharges imposed on taxes are not deductible in general.

Other significant items

For tax purposes, the following significant items should be considered:

* Changes in methods are not allowed without prior approval.

Dominican Republic

- Bonuses paid to employees within 120 days after the end of the taxable year are deductible for the year just ended.

Net operating losses
The carryforward of losses of legal entities can be used to offset profits up to the fifth year following the year in which the losses were generated, with a maximum amortisation of 20% in each year. For the fourth year, the deduction allowed should not exceed 80% of the net taxable income. In the fifth year, the percentage is 70%.

There is no carryback loss mechanism in the Dominican Republic.

Payments to foreign affiliates
Payments to foreign affiliates for royalties, interest, or service fees are deductible, provided that the 29% WHT was paid.

Payments of interest on loans abroad to foreign financial institutions are subject to a WHT of 10%.

Group taxation

Group taxation is not permitted in the Dominican Republic.

Transfer pricing
General Norm 04-11 of 2 June 2011 established the rules for transfer pricing determination on transactions between related parties. It applies to any transaction between local entities of foreign equity and:

- related parties abroad
- residents or persons domiciled in tax havens or in jurisdictions of low tax rates, and
- related parties classified as a Free Trade Zone (FTZ) entity.

This rule established the obligation of taxpayers to file an annual Informative Tax Return of transactions between related parties, which shall contain detailed information of each transaction and the related party's identification. Furthermore, tax authorities have the faculty to challenge these transactions if the price or amount stated by the taxpayer differs from those established in the market.

Thin capitalisation
Thin capitalisation rules do not exist in the Dominican Republic.

Tax credits and incentives

In the Dominican Republic, tax incentive laws exist for the following.

Tourism incentives
Law 158-01 on the Promotion of Tourist Development for New or Low Development Locations in Provinces and Areas with Great Tourist Potential, and for the Creation of the Tourist Promotion Official Fund, enacted on 9 October 2011, establishes special incentives and benefits to individuals or companies, residing in the Dominican Republic, that promote or invest capital in any tourist activity described in said Law. In order to benefit from said Law, a special Resolution shall be obtained from the Council for the Promotion of Tourism.

Dominican Republic

Alternative energy incentives
Law 57-07 provides significant incentives for the use and development of renewable sources of energy. The renewable energy sources subject to this law include bio-fuel, bio-diesel, ethanol, and wind, solar, and other renewable energy.

Industrial renovation and modernisation incentives
The main objective of Law 392-07 about competitive development and local industrial manufacture is to promote policies and support programs for industrial renovation and innovation so to diversify local production, create industrial parks, and link the country to international markets. Main benefits include VAT exemption on import of machinery and materials, priority on imports granted at customs, and accelerated depreciation.

D

Industrial FTZ operations
Law 8-90 about Export Free Trade Zones was created to promote employment, production, and economic growth. Entities that would like to benefit from said Law shall be engaged in manufacture/service within a confined space (FTZ park). Call centre activities are allowed to be provided outside the FTZ parks. Benefits include 100% exemption on CIT and VAT, custom duties, construction taxes, transfer taxes, etc.

Border development incentives
Law No. 28-01, dated 1 February 2001, creates a special development frontier zone for industrial, agro-industrial, agriculture/livestock, metalmechanic, free zone, tourism, metallurgical, and energy companies that exist at the time of promulgation of said law, and those that may be installed in the future within the border of the Dominican Republic and Haiti. Main incentives include 100% exemption on CIT and VAT, as well as custom duties.

Foreign tax credit
Taxes paid abroad on foreign income taxed in the Dominican Republic may be credited up to the amount of the Dominican tax liability generated by such income. The credits should be determined on a case-by-case basis.

Withholding taxes

WHT on dividends
Dividends paid in cash to resident and non-resident individuals or corporations are subject to a WHT of 29% (25% prior to 29 June 2011 and after 29 June 2013).

The WHT on payments to foreign corporations, which are not permanently established in the Dominican Republic, are as follows:

Recipient	WHT (%)			
	Dividends and interest	Royalties	Technical assistance	Other services
Non-treaty, basic	29 (1, 2)	29 (2)	29 (2)	29 (2)
Treaty (Canada)	18	18	29 (2)	29 (2)

Notes

1. Payments on interest (loans) to foreign financial institutions are subject to a WHT of 10%.
2. 29% WHT rate to be reduced to 25% on 29 June 2013.

Dominican Republic

WHT on transfers of shares

General Norm 07-11 of 1 July 2011 establishes a 1% WHT on the value of the transfer of shares received by the seller. Foreign entities are not exempt from this obligation. In this case, WHT may be made by a person appointed as WHT agent by the tax authorities.

Such WHT is a payment on account against capital gain tax, payable by the seller through the Form IR-2 (legal entities) or Form IR-1 (individuals), as applicable. However, if they can substantiate that the transaction will not generate a capital gain or that the 1% WHT would generate a capital loss, they may request the tax authorities, no later than 30 days prior to withholding filing/payment's due date, to be exempt from this obligation.

This 1% WHT should be filed and paid to the tax authorities through the monthly WHT return (IR-17 Form) within the first ten days of the month following the payment to the seller. In case the purchaser is an individual, the 1% WHT is not applicable.

WHT on interest payments

General Norm 13-11 of 5 September 2011 appoints financial institutions as 1% WHT agents on the value paid or credited on account for interest payments of any nature to legal entities.

The interests paid by financial institutions will constitute a deductible expense for tax purposes, provided the WHT was made.

In addition, this rule obliges financial institutions to provide a monthly electronic file, directly to the tax authorities or through the Banks Superintendency, containing all the information related to the interest payment, including the date, value, and identity of the beneficiary.

Tax administration

Taxable period

Corporate bylaws should establish as year-end one of the following: 31 December, 31 March, 30 June, or 30 September. Once the year-end is selected, any change should be authorised by the tax authorities.

Tax returns

The Corporate Annual Tax Return (Form IR-2) must be filed within 120 days after year-end. Tax authorities may allow extensions of up to 60 days, upon request.

Tax returns are based on self-assessment and must be filed on electronic forms supplied by the internal tax department.

Payment of tax

The balance of any tax due must be paid no later than the due date for filing the return. Corporations domiciled in the country and PEs of foreign enterprises shall be obliged to make advance payments on the 15th day of every month for tax related to the period in progress.

Audit cycle

The audit cycle is not established by law or practice. During the statute of limitations, tax authorities select the taxpayers subject to audit based on internal criterion.

Dominican Republic

Statute of limitations
The statute of limitations is three years, and five years if the entity has been notified of a tax audit, counting from the filing due date.

Topics of focus for tax authorities
Among the topics of focus are: non-deductible expenses, withholdings, VAT, and proportionality of VAT credits.

D

Ecuador

PwC contact

Pablo Aguirre
PricewaterhouseCoopers
Diego de Almagro N 32-48 & Whymper 1st. Floor
Quito, Pichincha
Ecuador
Tel: +593 2 382 9351
Email: pablo.aguirre@ec.pwc.com

Significant developments

According to the tax reform introduced in the Production Code at the end of 2010, corporate income tax (CIT) rates will be reduced from 23% in 2012 to 22% in 2013.

As of 24 November 2011, the Law of Environmental Development and Optimization of State Revenues is in force. This Law intends to promote environmental-friendly behaviour from taxpayers and levies taxes on the acquisition and maintenance of certain vehicles and on goods contained in plastic bottles. Additionally, a new increase of the remittance tax was introduced (from 2% to 5%) including the taxation on transfer of funds located in foreign bank accounts.

International Financial Reporting Standards (IFRS) are in force for all entities. Local tax authorities have established that, for CIT purposes and its corresponding pre-payments, companies are obligated to follow these accounting principles.

Taxes on corporate income

Resident entities are taxed on their worldwide income. Non-resident entities are subject to tax on Ecuadorian-source income only.

Taxes on corporate income are levied at the following rates for fiscal year 2012:

Type of income	CIT rate (%)
Distributed or undistributed profits of local corporations and branches	23
Reinvested profits of local corporations and branches	13

Note that these rates will be reduced by 1% in 2013 in order to reach 22% and 12%, respectively.

Local income taxes
No other government taxes on income are imposed on companies.

Corporate residence

Corporate residence is determined by the place of incorporation. For foreign branches, it is the place stated in the domiciliary deed.

Permanent establishment (PE)

According to the tax legislation, a company can be deemed to have a PE in Ecuador if it maintains any place or fixed centre within the country, in which a foreign company develops all or part of its activities.

The corresponding regulations point out that a PE also exists when a foreign company maintains, within the country, a person or an entity that acts on its behalf and habitually exercises an economic activity. It contemplates several instances where this is applicable, among them:

- A person with legal representation, which is normally granted through a power of attorney or through a legalised decision by the company and includes the capacity to legally act on behalf of the company.
- A person working under a contractual relationship for a foreign company to carry out economic activities on behalf of that company.
- A centre for the direction of the activities of the foreign company.
- A branch, agency, or office that acts on behalf of the foreign company.
- An office for the provision of technical consultancy services related to contracts that are executed in the country.

Other taxes

Value-added tax (VAT)

VAT is levied at the rates of either 12% or 0% on the transfer of goods, import of goods, and the rendering of services, as well as on services rendered within the country or imported. Royalties and intangible property imported or locally paid are also levied with a 12% VAT.

The following are transactions exempt from VAT:

- In-kind contributions to capital of companies.
- Inheritance and assets obtained from liquidation of companies.
- Transfer of business as a whole, amalgamations, mergers, takeovers, and spin-offs.
- Donations to public entities and non-profit organisations.
- Transfers of shares and securities.

Goods and services which are subject to 0% rate are explicitly listed in the law.

Among others, the following goods are taxed at a 0% rate upon either importation or local transfer of ownership:

- Most agricultural goods and foodstuff, when these remain in their natural state; this includes refrigerated or packaged goods that have not undergone further processing. Also included in this category are milk, meats, sugar, salt, bread, butter and margarine, flour, and cooking oil.
- Drugs, medicines, and other pharmaceutical products, including raw materials for their production.
- Fertilisers, insecticides, animal foods, and similar products, including the raw materials required for processing such goods.
- Agricultural machinery and equipment.
- Goods that are exported.
- Paper, books, magazines, and newspapers.

Ecuador

Among others, the following services are taxed at a 0% rate:

- Transportation of persons and cargo, except air transportation of persons and local air transportation of cargo.
- Book printing services.
- Housing rental.
- Water, electric, sewage, and other public services, including garbage collection.
- Financial services.
- Exported services.

The 12% VAT paid on imports and local purchases can be deducted from the 12% VAT charged on sales or services rendered. VAT paid on raw materials, fixed assets, or components required for the production of goods or rendering of services is also creditable when the final product is considered taxable at 12%. On the other hand, VAT paid on raw materials, services, components, or fixed assets necessary for production of export goods is recoverable.

The 12% VAT paid in the acquisition of goods and services utilised for the production or rendering of services levied at 0% VAT is not creditable. Therefore, it will be considered as part of the cost.

Companies designated as 'special taxpayers' (qualified as such by the tax authorities, which, in recognition of its economic importance defined in special parameters, contributes to the effective collection of taxes, subject to special regulations regarding the compliance of their formal duties and payment of taxes) are required to withhold 30% of VAT applicable on their purchases of goods taxed at 12%, and 70% of VAT applicable on their purchase of services taxed at 12%, except with respect to services rendered by professionals, in which case 100% of VAT charged must be withheld.

In the importation of services, VAT at 12% must be self-determined and withheld at 100% by the local entity. This VAT is creditable.

Customs duties

Since Ecuador is a member of the Andean Community, goods to be imported are classified under the Common Nomenclature of the Andean Countries participating in the Cartagena's Agreement (NANDINA) Pact, which is based on the Customs Cooperation Council Nomenclature (also known as the Brussels tariff nomenclature). Most consumer good imports pay 25%, while intermediate goods are usually imported at a 10% or 15% rate. Raw materials and capital goods generally pay 0% to 5%. Ecuador has negotiated exceptions under the Andean common tariff that allow lower duties on certain capital goods and industrial inputs. There is duty-free import of agricultural goods and equipment.

The price listed on the commercial bill or invoice is the basis for the assessment of duties, except when the Central Bank of Ecuador (CBE) considers the listed price unreasonable, in which case market prices in arm's-length transactions will be used. The burden of proof lies with the importer.

In addition to import duties, all imports are subject to 12% VAT and other minor taxes that do not exceed 1%. Charges are based on the cost, insurance, and freight (CIF) value of the merchandise.

All Ecuadorian imports and exports are subject to inspection by authorised international verification companies operating in the country (there are some imports exempt from verification). Goods are appraised for value, quantity, quality, and weight at the port of origin.

Special consumption tax (Impuesto a los Consumos Especiales or ICE)
ICE is imposed on domestic and imported goods which are explicitly listed in the law. This tax is levied at a progressive rate from 5% to 35% on certain automobiles and 15% on airplanes, helicopters, and boats. The taxable basis on cigarettes and alcoholic beverages is obtained by the number of produced or imported cigarettes or degrees of alcohol, respectively. It must be paid monthly and is collected upon sales. The ICE tax base for imported goods is the *ad valorem* value.

Foreign assets tax (Impuesto a los Activos en el Exterior)
The tax base for the foreign assets tax is the average monthly balance of cash deposits held in foreign entities by private entities registered in the stock market and regulated by the Superintendent of Banks and Companies. The monthly tax rate is 0.084%.

Remittance tax (Impuesto a la Salida de Divisas)
Remittance tax is imposed on the transfer of money abroad in cash or through cheques, transfers, or courier of any nature carried out with or without the mediation of the Ecuadorian financial system. As of 24 November 2011, the applicable rate is 5%. Dividends are exempt from this tax, under certain considerations.

Stamp taxes
No stamp taxes are levied in Ecuador.

Redeemable Tax on Non-Returnable Plastic Bottles
A tax is levied on the bottling of beverages in non-returnable plastic bottles utilised for containing alcoholic and non-alcoholic drinks, beverages, soft drinks, and water. In the case of imported beverages, this tax is levied upon their customs clearance for home use.

For each plastic bottle levied with this tax, the rate is up to two cents of a United States dollar (USD 0.02). This amount is fully reimbursed to whoever collects, delivers, and returns the bottles.

Taxpayers of this tax will be the bottlers of drinks contained in plastic bottles and importers of drinks in plastic bottles.

Milk products and medicines filled in plastic bottles are exempt from this tax.

This tax will not be considered as a deductible expense for CIT purposes.

Environmental Tax on Vehicle Pollution (ETVP)
ETVP is levied to offset environmental pollution caused by the use of ground transportation motor vehicles.

Taxpayers of ETVP are individuals, undivided inheritances, and national or foreign corporations who are proprietors of ground transportation motor vehicles.

There are several vehicles exempt from this tax, including government vehicles, public transportation of passengers, school buses, taxis, ambulances, moving hospitals, vehicles regarded as 'classical', electric vehicles, and those destined for the use and transportation of handicapped individuals.

Ecuador

The taxable base of the ETVP corresponds to the cylinder capacity of the vehicle motor, expressed in cubic centimetres, and a percentage related to the potential level of environmental pollution provoked by motorised vehicles in connection with the vehicle´s motor´s years of antiquity.

Social Security contributions
Employers and employees pay contributions to the Social Security at the rates of 11.15% and 9.35%, respectively, on the minimum monthly taxable wages as established for the different contributing categories by the Social Security. Such categories are revised annually.

Labour profit sharing
Although it is not considered a tax, companies are obligated to pay 15% of their pre-tax earnings to their employees. This payment is considered a deductible expense for CIT computation purposes.

Municipal taxes

Municipal asset tax
The municipal asset tax is levied on all individuals and companies required to keep accounting records in accordance with Ecuadorian tax legislation. This tax is levied annually at a rate of 1.5 per thousand (or 0.15%) of total assets less current and contingent liabilities, as shown on the balance sheet.

Municipal real estate tax
The city governments assess an annual municipal property tax , which ranges between 0.25 per thousand and 5 per thousand (0.025% to 0.5%) of the commercial value of the property, as determined by valuation carried out by the city government, for both urban and rural properties (rural property is taxed at a maximum of 0.3%).

Municipal tax on capital gain in the transfer of real estate (Plusvalía)
The real estate transfer tax applies to the transfer of real estate. It is taxed at 10% of profits.

Branch income

Distributed or retained branch profits are taxed at a 23% rate. No further taxes are payable when profits are remitted to headquarters, except if located in a tax haven country. Re-invested profits are levied at a 13% CIT rate. Companies must increase their share capital within the following fiscal year to be beneficiaries of the CIT rate reduction. There is not a branch remittance tax in Ecuador, except for payments to tax haven countries, which are subject to a withholding tax (WHT) of 12%.

Ecuador

Countries and territories considered as tax havens by tax authorities

- Albania
- Andorra
- Angola
- Anguilla
- Antigua and Barbuda
- Aruba
- Ascension Island
- Azores Islands
- Bahamas
- Bahrain
- Barbados
- Belice
- Bermudas
- Brunei Darussalam
- Cabo Verde
- Cayman Islands
- Campione D´italia
- Canaria
- Chipre
- Christmas Islands
- Cocos Island or Keeling
- Commonwealth of Dominica
- Cook Island

- Djibouti
- Emirates of Saudi Arabia
- French Polinesia
- Gibraltar
- Granada
- Greenland
- Guam
- Guernsey, Jersey, Alderney, Great Stark Islands, Herm, Little Sark, Brechou, Jethou Lihou
- Guyana
- Hong Kong
- Kingdom of Jordania
- Kingdom of Swaziland
- Kingdom of Tonga
- Kiribati
- Kuwait
- Labuan
- Liberia
- Liechtenstein
- Luxembourg
- Macao

- Madeira (Portugal)
- Maldivas
- Malta
- Man Islands
- Marshall Islands
- Mauricio
- Mónaco
- Montserrat (UK)
- Myanmar
- Nauru
- Netherlands Antilles
- Nigeria
- Niue
- Norfolk Islands
- Oman
- Ostrava
- Pacific Islands
- Palau
- Panama
- Pitcairn
- Puerto Rico
- Qatar
- Qeshm Islands
- Saint Elena
- Saint Kitts and Nevis Islands
- Saint Lucia

- Saint Marino
- Saint Peter Islands and Miguelon
- Saint Vincent and the Grenadines
- Salomon Islands
- Samoa
- Seychelles
- Sri Lanka
- Svalbard Islands
- Tokelau
- Triesta (Italy)
- Trinidad and Tobago
- Tristan Da Cunha
- Tunisia
- Turks and Caicos Islands
- Tuvalu
- Vanuatu
- Virgin Islands (British)
- Virgin Islands of the United States
- Yemen

Income determination

Inventory valuation
The valuation of inventories is not specifically treated in the tax law, IFRS must be applied.

Capital gains
Occasional gains from stock sales are tax exempt, and gains from investment funds and investment trusts are CIT exempt, as long as the income has been taxed at source. Gains on the sale of fixed assets are added to the taxable base and levied at regular CIT rates, except gains derived from occasional sales of real estate, which are tax exempt.

Dividend income
Dividends received by a resident company or foreign company, not domiciled in a tax haven, from a resident company are tax exempt.

Interest income
In general terms, interest income is considered as part of the CIT base for Ecuadorian entities.

Ecuador

Foreign income

Foreign-source income is considered exempt for tax purposes if the company demonstrates that the income tax was paid abroad. Income generated in tax haven jurisdictions is not considered to be part of this exemption and should be added to regular income.

Deductions

As a general rule, payments on operations that exceed USD 5,000 should be made through an institution of the financial system; otherwise, such operations will become non-deductible.

Depreciation and amortisation

Straight-line depreciation applies, at rates specified by law. The director of the Internal Revenue Service of Ecuador can authorise higher rates of depreciation in cases such as obsolescence, excessive use, and faster than expected wear-out of assets.

Annual depreciation rates are as follows:

Asset	Depreciation rate (%)
Real estate (except land), aircraft, naval crafts, and similar property	5
Facilities, machinery, equipment, and furniture	10
Vehicles, trucks, and tractors used for construction	20
Computer equipment and software	33.33

Depreciation rates apply to the cost of assets.

In the case of vehicles, if at the time of purchase of the vehicle its appraisal exceeds USD 35,000, the deductibility on the excess will not apply, unless it is an armoured car or a vehicle exempt from the tax on vehicles. The limitation on the deductibility will also not apply in the cases of taxpayers that have as their only activity the car rental business.

Intangible assets are amortised either within the terms specified in the contract or over a 20-year period.

Goodwill

There are no specific rules in Ecuador about goodwill. However, it can be amortised as an intangible asset.

Organisational and start-up expenses

Organisation, experimentation, and preoperational expenses are to be amortised over five years at the rate of 20% per year.

Interest expenses

Interest on debts incurred for business purposes are deductible.

In general, foreign loan interests are deductible for CIT purposes, to the extent that the credits are registered before the CBE, and the interest rates do not exceed the referential rates established by the CBE.

Interest paid for loans granted by a related party are subject to WHT at 23%.

Thin capitalisation rules apply: Interest payments for foreign loans granted by a related party are deductible only if the foreign debt does not exceed 300% of the entity´s equity. In case of branches, the ratio applies considering the total of the assigned equity. Credits granted by the head office to its branch are not considered as loans; therefore, any financial cost related to it is non-deductible.

If the above mentioned criteria are not met at the moment of the registration of the loan before the CBE, the excess will not be deductible for CIT purposes. This does not eliminate the obligation of the WHT on the total amount of the interests.

Interest paid on loans obtained from non-resident financial institutions is deductible and not subject to WHT unless the interest rate is higher than the referential interest rate established by the CBE. In such cases, any excess is subject to a 23% WHT. The above mentioned rules do not apply for financial entities domiciled in tax haven countries; in such cases, interest expense is non-deductible.

E

Bad debt
If the bad debt provision is less than 1% of the portfolio granted in the year, it will be deductible. Any excess will be non-deductible.

Charitable contributions
Payments for charitable contributions are non-deductible for CIT purposes.

Fines and penalties
Interest and fines paid as penalties imposed on late payments of tax obligations and on CIT payments are not deductible for CIT calculation purposes.

Taxes
Taxes, rates, and levies related to the generation of taxable income, as well as contributions to the social security system, are deductible.

Net operating losses
The carryforward of losses is allowed to a maximum of five years, with an amortisation limit of 25% per year over the taxable base. There is no loss carryback.

Payments to foreign affiliates
In most cases, payments made abroad are deductible, as long as income taxes have been withheld (at the rate of 23% over the taxable base). Professional fees, royalties, commissions, or any payment made abroad is subject to WHT at a rate of 23% over the taxable base. Payments on imports are deductible and are not subject to WHT.

Group taxation

Group taxation is not permitted in Ecuador.

Transfer pricing
The transfer pricing regime in Ecuador is based on the Organisation for Economic Co-operation and Development (OECD) guidelines. Related party transactions must be carried out at arm's length. Formal documentation requirements exist.

Ecuador

Thin capitalisation

A thin capitalisation rule on foreign loans granted by related parties at a 3:1 ratio over equity must be considered. For branches of a foreign corporation, only capital must be taken into account.

Tax credits and incentives

Foreign tax credit

There are no provisions in Ecuador for a foreign tax credit. In general terms, income taxed abroad is considered as exempt income, with some special exceptions.

Handicapped employee and new employee increases

An amount equivalent to 150% and 100% remunerations of handicapped and new employees, respectively, can be considered an additional deduction for income tax calculation purposes. New employees must be working with the company for at least six months.

CIT exemptions

Investments made by new companies located outside the cities of Quito and Guayaquil, in specific sectors determined by law, will have a five year CIT exemption.

Tax credit on remittance tax paid

5% remittance tax paid on imports of raw material and goods with a 0% custom duty rate and used for the production of other goods and services can be considered as a tax credit for CIT computation purposes.

Withholding taxes

Prepaid dividends are subject to a 23% WHT.

Dividends paid to non-resident entities generally are not subject to WHT. However, dividends paid to non-resident entities in tax haven countries are subject to 12% WHT at source.

Interest paid on loans obtained from non-residents is subject to a 23% WHT unless reduced by tax treaty. Royalties paid to a non-resident are subject to 23% WHT unless reduced by tax treaty.

Revenues from occasional services provided by non-resident individuals are levied at 23% WHT. Payments made abroad to non-resident individuals and companies are subject to a 23% WHT. Other payments made abroad, other than dividends or profits, are subject to a 23% WHT.

Periodically, the Internal Revenue Service of Ecuador establishes WHT percentages on local payments, which are not greater than 10%. Current rates are 1%, 2%, 8%, and 10% withholding.

Tax treaties

As a member of the Andean Community, Ecuador has adopted Decision 578, which provides relief from double taxation for individual or company members. Furthermore, Ecuador has similar tax treaties with Belgium, Brazil, Canada, Chile, France, Germany, Italy, Mexico, Romania, Spain, Switzerland, and Uruguay.

WHT rates may vary from 0% to 15%, depending on the nature of the payment.

Tax administration

Taxable period
The fiscal year is the calendar year.

Tax returns
The tax system operates on the basis of self-assessment, with subsequent inspection by the tax authorities.

Tax filing deadlines begin on 10 April and continue up to 28 April. The tax return due dates are determined by the ninth digit of the company's Tax Identification Number (TIN).

Payment of tax
Local tax authorities have established that for CIT purposes and its corresponding pre-payments companies are obligated to follow IFRS accounting principles.

Corporations are required to keep accounting records and must make CIT prepayments, in two equal instalments in July and September, based on the following calculation:

The sum of 0.4% of the taxable income, 0.4% of total assets, 0.2% of total equity, and 0.2% of deductible expenses from the last fiscal year.

The final CIT obligation cannot be lower than the total amount of the tax prepayment calculated; there are minimum exceptions to this rule. The final CIT payment is due between 10 April and 28 April.

Statute of limitations
Fiscal authorities have three years from the date of filing to start proceedings for tax audits or assessment and collection of taxes.

The statute of limitations is extended from three to six years if the corresponding tax returns have not been filed or are incompletely filed. A tax audit can be reopened, verified, or amended within one year from the date of completion.

Egypt

PwC contact

Amr El Monayer
PricewaterhouseCoopers
Plot No 211
Second Sector
City Centre
New Cairo 11835, Egypt
Tel: +20 2 27597879
Email: amr.elmonayer@eg.pwc.com

Significant developments

Law no. 51 of 2011 was issued by the Supreme Council of the Armed Forces (SCAF) in July 2011 as a part of the 2011/12 Budget (effective 1 July 2011 and thus affecting all fiscal periods ending after that date), imposing a new corporate tax bracket of 25% on annual net income equaling or exceeding 10 million Egyptian pounds (EGP). Accordingly, the 20% corporate tax applies to the first EGP 10 million of annual net income only, with any income exceeding this threshold subject to the 25% rate.

On 16 January 2012, SCAF issued Law no. (11) for the year 2012, regarding the provision of tax incentives for settling taxes due. In addition, Ministerial Decree no. (38) for the same year was issued by the Finance Minister, detailing the procedures of the implementation.

According to the above-mentioned Law and Decrees, a taxpayer is entitled to obtain an incentive, which is a discount on corporate tax due balances as well as the associated delay fines and additional dues, as follows:

- 25% on the amounts to be paid from 17 January 2012 (the effective date of this law) till 31 March 2012.
- 15% on the amounts to be paid from 1 April 2012 till 30 June 2012.
- 10% on the amounts to be paid from 1 July 2012 till 31 December 2012.

Regarding the application of the withholding tax (WHT) on payments to non-residents and the refund of the differences of the rates between the Egyptian Income Tax rate and the rate of the double tax treaty (DTT), a special unit responsible for interest and royalty WHT refunds was established in January 2012. This unit is tasked with reviewing each refund case and with issuing refund letters (subject to compliance with the requirements of the 2009 Ministerial Decree). A refund letter is required to be able to get a refund of excess WHT from the tax office to which the taxes were actually paid.

The monthly social insurance thresholds have increased from EGP 900 to EGP 912 for basic salaries and to EGP 1,050 for variable salaries. This is effective as of 1 July 2012.

Taxes on corporate income

Resident companies are taxed on worldwide income. Non-resident corporations and partnerships pay tax on income derived from their permanent establishments (PE) in Egypt.

The corporate tax rates in Egypt are 20% for annual net income that does not exceed EGP 10 million, and 25% for any income that equals or exceeds the EGP 10 million threshold. The tax is calculated at two brackets rather than a lump sum amount subject to the 25% rate. The 25% rate is applicable as of 1 July 2011.

The above rates apply to all types of business activities except for oil exploration companies, whose profits are taxed at 40.55%. In addition, the profits of the Suez Canal Authority, the Egyptian Petroleum Authority, and the Central Bank of Egypt are taxable at a rate of 40%.

E

Local income taxes
In Egypt, there are no other local income taxes for corporate income other than those mentioned throughout this summary.

Corporate residence

Foreign corporations and partnerships are classified as residents of Egypt if they meet one of the following conditions:

- The entity is established according to the Egyptian law.
- The government or a public authority owns more than 50% of the capital of the entity.
- The effective place of management is in Egypt.

The executive regulations of the law indicate that Egypt is considered as the effective place of management if the entity meets any two of the following conditions:

- Daily managerial decisions take place in Egypt.
- Members of the board of directors hold their meetings in Egypt.
- At least 50% of the board members or managers reside in Egypt.
- The major shareholders (owners of more than 50% of the shares or voting rights) reside in Egypt.

Permanent establishment (PE)
The PE concept is defined in the income tax law as follows:

- Headquarters.
- Branch.
- Building used as sale outlet.
- Office.
- Factory.
- Workshop.
- Places of extraction of natural resources.
- Farms.
- Building site, construction or assembly point, installations, supervisory activities of the same.
- An agent who has the power to ratify contracts on behalf of a foreign company.
- An independent broker or agent who is proved to have dedicated most of one's time during the year in the interest of a foreign company.

A foreign company that is deemed to have a PE risk, according to the Egyptian Companies Law, should incorporate a legal entity in Egypt.

Egypt

There are several legal forms existing under the Egyptian Companies Law from which a foreign company can choose to incorporate, and these are: joint-stock company, limited liability company, branch, or a representative office.

Other taxes

Sales tax

The standard sales tax rate is 10% of the value of commodities (except for those referred to in special schedules of the law) and 5% to 10% for specific services. Some examples of the commodities subject to sales tax rates other than the standard 10% rate are as follows:

- Cement: 5%.
- Specific types of televisions and fridges: 25%.
- Air conditioners: 25%.

The Sales Tax Department is responsible for assessing the tax on the sales of locally produced goods and imported goods, except for those exempted by a special decree.

Consequently, all natural persons and legal entities are required to collect general sales tax and remit it to the Sales Tax Department. This includes manufacturers and providers of taxable services and every importer of commodities or taxable services.

The Ministry of Finance (MOF) has previously announced its intention to introduce a full-fledged Value Added Tax (VAT) Law to be applicable starting January 2013.

Customs duties

The liability for customs duty rests with the person who is importing the goods from abroad.

Customs duty rates on imported goods range from 5% to 40%, with the exception of vehicles for which different rates apply.

Where entities import machines and equipment as capital assets, and to establish the company's project, the machines and equipment will be charged customs duty at 5%.

Component parts, which are imported to be assembled in Egypt, are assessed customs duty based on the complete product. Then, it is reduced by a percentage ranging from 10% (if the local content of the final product is less than 30%) to a maximum of 90% (if the local content exceeds 60%).

Machines, equipment, and similar capital assets (with the exception of private motor cars) imported on a temporary basis, are subject to fees at 20% of the original customs duty for each year or fraction of a year during which they remain in Egypt until they are exported.

There is also a proposed new law regarding this issue, which is currently at the draft stage.

Excise taxes

There are no excise taxes in Egypt.

Real estate taxes

The real estate tax law takes into consideration the different variables that can affect the value of a property, such as location, value of similar buildings, and the economic situation of the district in which the property is located. This is to be updated every five years.

Real estate tax is levied annually on all constructed real estate units. This covers land and building, excluding plant and machinery.

Such tax is assessed based on the rental value of the land and building, and these value assessments are set by the committees, after approval of the Minister or whomever the Minister delegates, and published in the Official Journal. Based on the announcement, any taxpayer can appeal the rental value assessment.

The real estate tax rate is 10% of the rental value, and the calculation of the rental value differs for residential units and non-residential units. Specific percentages of deductions are provided by the law to account for all the expenses incurred by the taxpayer, including maintenance costs.

Law no. 118 of 2011 was issued by the SCAF amending the Real Estate Tax Law no. 196 of 2008, whereby the implementation of the 2008 Law should be effective starting from 1 January 2012. So starting from that date, taxpayers should start remitting the real estate taxes due. However, the MOF has recently confirmed that it intends to revisit such Law to amend the following and to be effective January 2013 instead:

- Increase the threshold for Real Estate Tax application.
- Exempt owner occupied houses from this tax.

It is worth noting though that the above amendments are still being considered and therefore cannot be guaranteed.

Stamp tax

There are two distinct types of stamp tax, which are imposed on legal documents, deeds, banking transactions, company formation, insurance premiums, and other transactions, as follows:

- The nominal stamp tax is imposed on documents, regardless of their value. The tax rate for items such as contracts is EGP 1 for each paper.
- Percentage or proportionate stamp tax is levied based on the value of transactions.

A proportional tax at the rate of 0.4% is imposed on the balances of credit facilities and loans and advances provided by Egyptian banks or branches of foreign banks during the financial year, with the bank paying 0.1% on the balance at the end of each quarter of the year. The bank and the customer each bear half of the tax.

Loans from other establishments are not subject to this tax.

Social insurance (employer's contribution)

The contribution of the employer is 26% of the basic salary (up to EGP 912) and 24% of the variable salary (up to EGP 1,050).

Egypt

Branch income

Branches of foreign corporations operating in Egypt receive tax treatment identical to that of corporate entities for the results of their activities in Egypt.

A branch, but not a subsidiary, may deduct a 'head office charge' of an amount up to 7% of its taxable income.

Income determination

Inventory valuation

Egyptian generally accepted accounting principles (GAAP) should be applied to inventory valuation, and all methods that are acceptable by Egyptian GAAP can be used.

Capital gains

A foreign company is taxed on all capital gains realised in Egypt. However, capital gains on the sale of Egyptian securities listed on the Egyptian Stock Exchange are not taxable.

Capital gains are not taxed separately; they are considered as part of the company's income and taxed accordingly (i.e. at the 25% corporate tax rate) after deducting all tax deductible expenses.

Dividend income

Dividends distributed by a company residing in Egypt are not subject to corporate taxes. Conversely, dividends that non-resident companies distribute are subject to the Egyptian corporate tax, after deducting foreign taxes paid abroad.

Stock dividends

Stock dividends receive the same treatment as ordinary dividends.

Interest income

Interest expenses are deducted from interest income when calculating the interest income to be included in taxable income.

Rent/royalties income

Rent/royalties income are not taxed separately; they are considered as part of the company's income and taxed accordingly (i.e. at the 25% corporate tax rate).

Foreign income

Income from any source, domestic or foreign, received by a corporation within Egypt is subject to corporate tax. The scope of tax covers the activities carried out inside and outside Egypt, which are administered or managed within Egypt.

There is no provision for deferring income earned abroad.

Deductions

In order for expenses to be acceptable for tax deduction, such expenses must be:

- actual and supported by documents
- business related, and
- necessary for performing the company's activity.

Depreciation and amortisation

The tax law set the depreciation and amortisation rates for tax purposes to the following:

* 5% of the cost of purchasing, establishing, developing, and renovating buildings and establishments is deductible based on the straight-line method.
* 10% of the cost of purchasing, developing, and improving intangible assets is deductible based on the straight-line method.
* Computers, information systems, software, and data storage sets are depreciated at a 50% rate on a declining-balance method.
* All others assets are depreciated at a rate of 25% of the depreciation basis for each fiscal year, on a declining-balance method.

E

Accelerated depreciation

A company may deduct 30% accelerated depreciation from the cost of new or used machines and equipment used in industries during the first fiscal year of their employment.

Goodwill

According to Article 25 of the Egyptian Income Tax Law, goodwill is amortised at the rate of 10% using the straight-line method.

Start-up expenses

Start-up expenses are tax deductable, and the whole amount can be amortised for the first year.

Interest expenses

Interest expenses are deductible for tax purposes after offsetting any tax-exempt interest income.

Interest expense deductions are only allowed if the following conditions are fully met:

* The interest rate does not exceed twice the discount rate as determined by the Central Bank of Egypt at the beginning of the calendar year in which the tax year ends.
* The interest expense is in return for loans complying with the local thin capitalisation rule: 4:1 debt-to-equity ratio.
* The Egyptian transfer pricing rules (i.e. arm's-length principle) must be followed (*see Transfer pricing in the Group taxation section for more information*). In case of a tax audit, if the interest rate wasn't proven to be at arm's length, the Tax Authority would have the right to adjust this price to arrive at a 'neutral price' and re-calculate the taxes due accordingly.
* The loan is business related.

Bad debt

According to Article 28 of the Egyptian Income Tax Law, deduction of bad debts shall be allowed, subject to submitting a report from the external auditor indicating the fulfillment of the following conditions:

* The company is maintaining regular books and records.
* The debt is related to the company activities.
* That debt value should have been previously included within the company accounts and records.

Egypt

- The company shall have taken serious procedures for settlement of such debt and has been unable to collect it after 18 months from its due date.

Charitable contributions

Donations to the government are tax deductible. Donations to Egyptian charities are also deductible, but only up to 10% of taxable income.

Fines and penalties

Financial fines and penalties paid by the taxpayer because they or one of their subordinates has committed a deliberate felony or misdemeanor are not deductible.

Taxes

Income tax payable according to the income tax law is not deductible.

Other significant items

The following other items are not deductible:

- Reserves and appropriations of all different types.
- Profit shares, distributed dividends, and the attendance fees paid to shareholders for attending the general assembly's meetings.
- Compensation and allowances obtained by the chairmen and board members.
- Workers profit share to be distributed according to the law.

Net operating losses

A company may carry losses forward for a period not to exceed five years. Nevertheless, if a change occurs in the ownership of its capital exceeding 50% of the shares, stocks, or the voting rights, if the company is either a Joint Stock Company or a Company Limited by Shares whose shares are not listed on the Egyptian Stock of Exchange, and if the company changes its activity, the company cannot carry the losses forward.

In general, companies cannot carry losses back, except for contracting companies, which are allowed a loss carryback period of five years.

Payments to head office

A branch may deduct head-office charges up to 7% of its taxable income. Moreover, the branch or subsidiary should withhold taxes before the payment of interest, royalties, and service fees to non-resident foreign corporations or affiliates.

Group taxation

The Egyptian tax law treats every company in a group of companies as a separate legal entity. Thus, affiliated companies or subsidiaries cannot shift the profits/ losses within the group.

Transfer pricing

Transfer pricing rules follow the arm's-length principle, specifying that any transaction between related parties should be at arm's length (i.e. market value).

The law does not specify penalties with regard to transfer pricing. However, the law states that the Egyptian tax authorities may adjust the pricing of transactions between related parties if the transaction involves elements that would not be included in transactions between non-related parties, and whose purpose is to shift the tax burden to tax exempt or non-taxable entities. Where this is the case, the tax authorities may determine the taxable profit on the basis of the neutral price. The acceptable methods for determining such neutral price, according to the rule of the law, are as follows:

- Comparative free price same as Comparable Uncontrolled Price method (CUP).
- Total cost with an added margin of profit (same as Cost Plus method).
- Resale price.

On 29 November 2010, the Egyptian Tax Authority launched the Transfer Pricing Guidelines ('TP Guidelines'). The TP Guidelines are being issued as a series of parts, the first part of which was issued in final version to the public and provides guidance on the arm's-length principle, how to establish comparability, choosing the most appropriate transfer pricing method(s), and documentation requirements. The coming parts should cover more complex transfer pricing topics, specifically transactions involving intellectual property, intra-group services, cost contribution arrangements, and advanced pricing agreements.

Taxpayers are required to prepare contemporaneous documentation studies to support the arm's-length nature of their controlled transactions. The Egyptian Tax Authority does not require the submission of transfer pricing documentation studies with the tax return; rather, they are required to be available upon request in a tax audit. Studies are acceptable in English, but a translation may be requested from the taxpayer.

The Egyptian Tax Authority explained that TP Guidelines will be utilised as a practical guide to assist taxpayers and tax inspectors in understanding how to implement and examine transfer pricing transactions. Egyptian TP Guidelines were compared to the Organisation for Economic Co-operation and Development (OECD) by an OECD representative and were found to be similar.

Thin capitalisation
The Egyptian thin capitalisation rule provided by the Egyptian income tax law dictates that the debt-to-equity ratio is 4:1. Accordingly, the law disallows the deductibility of debit interests of Egyptian companies on loans and advances if such loans and advances are in excess of fourfold the equity average (which is calculated according to the financial statements prepared pursuant to the Egyptian accounting standards).

The debit interest includes all amounts chargeable by the company in return for the loans; advances of any kind obtained thereby, bonds and bills. The loans and advances include, for purposes of this item, bonds and any form of financing by debts through securities with fixed or variable interest.

For determining the equity, the following items represent the basis for the calculation: the paid up capital in addition to all reserves and dividends reduced by retained losses, provided that the differences of the adjusted account is not included in the reserves account and is determined to be non-taxable. In case of retained or carry-forward losses, they must be used to reduce retained profits and reserves solely; the percentage is calculated on basis of total loans and advances in proportion to the remaining equity amount, after deducting the retained losses with a minimum of the paid up capital.

Tax credits and incentives

Egypt offers no specific tax incentives.

Egypt

Foreign tax credit
The foreign tax paid by a resident company on its profits earned abroad is deductible from the tax payable in Egypt; however, losses incurred abroad are not deductible.

Withholding taxes

A corporation paying invoices must withhold 0.5% to 5% of payments, depending on the services and commodities, to local taxpayers and remit them quarterly to the Tax Department.

Payments of interest, royalties, and services by a domestic corporation to foreign or non-resident bodies are subject to WHT as follows.

Interest
Interest on loans with a three-year term or more entered into by private sector companies are exempt from WHT, while loans of less than three years are subject to 20% WHT on interest. However, an applicable DTT between Egypt and the foreign country may result in the reduction of such tax rate. *Please see below for the ministerial decree affecting the treatment of interest and royalty payments.*

Royalties
Royalty payments are subject to the 20% WHT. However, an applicable DTT signed between Egypt and the foreign country may result in a reduction in this rate. *Please see below for the ministerial decree affecting the treatment of interest and royalty payments.*

Service payments
Service payments are subject to the 20% WHT. However, an applicable DTT signed between Egypt and the foreign country may result in the exemption of these payments if the services are performed abroad and not through PE in Egypt.

Tax treaties
Egypt has concluded DTTs with about 50 countries, which could change the tax treatment of transactions carried out between Egyptian entities and residents of a treaty country.

Recipient	Interest (%)	Royalties (%)
Non-treaty	20	20
Treaty:		
Algeria	5	10
Austria	15	-
Bahrain	-	-
Belarus	10	15
Belgium	15	15
Bulgaria	15	15
Canada	15	15
China	10	8
Cyprus	15	10
Czech Republic	15	15
Denmark	15	20
Finland	15	20

Recipient	Interest (%)	Royalties (%)
France	15	15% franchise
		15% for other royalties
Germany	15	15
Holland	12	12
Hungary	15	15
India	20	20
Indonesia	15	15
Iraq	20	16
Italy	20	15
Japan	20	15
Jordan	15	20
Korea	15	15
Lebanon	10	5
Libya	-	-
Malaysia	15	15
Malta	10	12
Morocco	20	10
Norway	20	15
Oman	12.50	15
Pakistan	15	15
Palestinian Territories	15	15
Poland	12	12
Romania	15	15
Russia	10	15
Serbia & Montenegro	15	15
Singapore	15	15
South Africa	12	15
Sudan	20	10
Sweden	15	14
Switzerland	15	12.50
Syria	15	20
Tunisia	10	15
Turkey	10	10
Ukraine	12	12
United Arab Emirates	10	10
United Kingdom	15	15
United States	15	15
Yemen	10	10

Procedures for applying the WHT on payments to non-residents

A ministerial decree declared that the reduced rate of WHT on interest or royalties provided by an applicable DTT should be ignored when withholding the tax. However, under certain conditions, the foreign recipient of payments would be able to get a refund for the amount resulting from the variance between the normal rate of 20% and the reduced treaty rate.

A special unit responsible for interest and royalty WHT refunds was established in January 2012. This unit is tasked with reviewing each refund case and with issuing

Egypt

refund letters (subject to compliance with the requirements of the 2009 Ministerial Decree). A refund letter is required to be able to get a refund of excess WHT from the tax office to which the taxes were actually paid.

Tax administration

Taxable period
The tax year is the financial year of the taxpayer.

Tax returns
The taxpayer is required to assess taxes due for every financial year and settle them with the tax return.

The corporate tax return is due within four months from the end of the financial year; so if a company's financial year ends 31 December, then the tax return has to be filed before the end of April of the following year.

Payment of tax
Advance payments are deducted from taxes assessed per the tax return, and the balance is payable in a lump sum at the date of submitting the tax return.

The advance payment (i.e. WHT) is submitted on a quarterly basis.

Audit cycle
The audit cycle proceeds as follows.

Inspection
The tax authority inspects the company based on its documents and records in order to assess the total tax dues on the company and determines the difference in tax dues as per the company declaration and the tax authority assessment. The authority issues an assessment including the total tax due on the company. If the company objects the inspection result, the dispute is transferred to the Internal Committee.

Internal Committee
The dispute is transferred to the Internal Committee to discuss the dispute points that arose from the inspection further to issue a modified assessment based on its opinion. If the company objects to the Internal Committee result, the dispute is transferred to the Appeal Committee to review the dispute points arising from the Internal Committee.

Appeal Committee
The Appeal Committee's decision is final and binding on the company and the tax department, unless a case is appealed by either of them at the court within 30 days of receiving the decision. Based on the fact that the total taxes due on the assessment as per the Appeal Committee are considered final, if they are not paid within the appropriate period, there will be penalties for the late payment.

Court
If the decision of the Appeal Committee is not satisfactory for either party, the case will be transferred to the court system, which is considered the final stage of the disputes. Normally, the court will appoint an expert witness to investigate the case and prepare a report. The court process usually takes a long period of time.

Statute of limitations

The statute of limitations is five years according to the Egyptian Income Tax Law and is extended to be six years in case of tax evasion.

Topics of focus for tax authorities

The most important topic for tax authorities is transfer pricing.

E

El Salvador

PwC contact

Ramon Ortega
PricewaterhouseCoopers
Scotiabank Building
3rd Floor
Corner of John F. Kennedy and Lope de Vega Avenues
Santo Domingo, Dominican Republic
Tel: +809 567 7741
Email: ramon.ortega@do.pwc.com

Significant developments

The following amendments were made to the Income Tax Law and Tax Code, effective 1 January 2012:

* The corporate income tax (CIT) rate was increased to 30% for entities with revenues of 150,000 United States dollars (USD) or above.
* The income tax advance payment monthly rate was increased to 1.75%.
* Profits distributed to shareholders, partners, trustees, participants, investors, or beneficiaries are subject to withholdings of 5%. This withholding also applies to headquarter (HQ) representatives, affiliates, branches, subsidiaries, agencies, and others who pay or credit dividends to subjects not domiciled in El Salvador.
* A definite minimum payment is established at 1% of gross income, with the following specific exceptions:
  * Subjects that are exempt of the obligation of payment of CIT.
  * Taxpayer companies during their three first years of operation, proving that the related operations are new investments and that there are not acquisitions, assets, or rights related to investments that previously existing.
  * Subjects that had losses in only one fiscal year.
  * Taxpayers that in a determined sector of the economy have been affected in their operations for exceptional situations generated by natural disasters duly declared as that by the Legal Assembly or the President of the Republic.
  * Taxpayers that in the fiscal year have a gross profit margin below 2%.
  * Taxpayers that have incomes of USD 150,000 or less.

Taxes on corporate income

As of 1 January 2012, the CIT rate is 30% for entities with revenues above USD 150,000, and this rate is applicable on the total amount of the mentioned revenues. For those companies that have revenues of USD 150,000 or less, the applicable rate is 25%. The 25% rate was the rate that applied to all companies prior to 1 January 2012.

CIT is based on the principle of territoriality, and, by general rule, taxes are paid on goods located, activities realised, and capital invested in El Salvador as well as on services rendered or utilised in the country. Nevertheless, there is a special rule regarding securities and financial instruments, since income is considered to be obtained in El Salvador if the issuing entity is domiciled in El Salvador.

Taxable income is equal to gross income net of costs and expenses considered necessary for generating and maintaining the related source of income and other deductions allowed by law. Gross income is comprised of income or profits collected or accrued, either in cash or in kind, from any sources in El Salvador.

Corporations are required to follow the accrual method of accounting, and income is computed for 12-month periods beginning on 1 January and ending on 31 December of each year.

Income tax advance payment
As of 1 January 2012, a 1.75% tax is applied to gross revenues accrued. This tax is paid monthly as an advance payment which is applied against the CIT at the end of the year. Prior to 1 January 2012, the advance payment rate was 1.5%.

Local income taxes
There is a municipal tax related to taxpayers' income. This tax depends on the location of the operations where the taxpayer performs its activity.

Corporate residence

A company incorporated in El Salvador is a resident entity in the country for tax purposes and subject to CIT on Salvadorian source income. Also, branches from foreign companies authorised in El Salvador and entities operating as a permanent establishment (PE) are considered resident entities for tax purposes and subject to CIT on Salvadorian source income.

The general rule for the determination of the corporate domicile is that it will be the one established on the incorporation document.

Permanent establishment (PE)
The PE for a company is determined by a fixed place of business with installed infrastructure owned or leased by the company, with employees hired in the country, and where the taxpayer performs its activity.

Other taxes

Value-added tax (VAT)
VAT (i.e. *Impuesto al Valor Agregado* or IVA) is levied at a rate of 13% over the taxable amount. As a general rule, the taxable amount is the price or remuneration agreed upon by the parties. For imports, the taxable amount is the customs value.

The following transactions are subject to VAT when performed within the Salvadoran territory:

- Transfer/sale of tangible movable goods.
- Withdrawal of tangible movable goods from the inventory made by the company for self-consumption by its partners, directors, or personnel.
- Import of goods and services.

El Salvador

- The supply of services of any type whether permanent, regular, continuous, or periodic, including technical advice and project designs; lease and sublease agreements over tangible goods; lease and sublease agreements over real estate for commercial purposes; lease of services in general; construction of real estate properties or building contracts; auctions; freight, whether inland, air, or maritime; and lease, sublease, and any form of use regarding trademarks.

The following imports are exempt from VAT:

- Imports made by diplomats and consulate representatives of foreign nations with presence in the country according to international agreements adopted by El Salvador.
- Imports made by international organisations to which El Salvador is a party.
- Traveller's luggage according to customs regulations.
- Donations to non-profit organisations.
- Imports made by municipalities, if the goods imported are for the public benefit of the community.
- Imports of machinery by taxpayers duly registered for this purpose, which will be part of the taxpayer's fixed assets.
- Vehicles for public transportation, which can only be transferred after five years.

The following services are exempt from VAT:

- Health services rendered by public institutions.
- Lease and sublease of real estate properties for housing.
- Services rendered under a labour relationship, as well as those rendered by public and municipal employees.
- Cultural public performances authorised by competent authorities.
- Educational services rendered by authorised entities, i.e. *Ministerio de Educación* (the Ministry of Education).
- Interest on deposits and loans provided by local financial institutions or entities registered at the Salvadoran Central Bank (BCR).
- Interest on securities issued by the government and/or private entities traded through a stock exchange.
- Water supply by public institutions.
- Public transportation.
- Insurance premiums covering individuals, and reinsurance in general.

VAT is levied on exports at a rate of 0%. Foreign-source income is not subject to VAT.

VAT paid by a registered taxpayer company on its purchases (tax credits) is credited against VAT charged to its customers (tax debits) on a monthly basis.

VAT returns are filed on a monthly basis within the first ten working days of each month following the period under taxation.

Customs duties

In El Salvador, the *Arancel Centroamericano de Importación* (Central America Import Duty) is applied, which is constituted in the *Sistema Arancelario Centroamericano* (SAC) (Duty Central American System) and its correspondent duties for import.

All duties for import are *ad valorem* and are applied at the cost, insurance, and freight (CIF) value of the merchandise. The duty is common for all the countries in Central America.

Excise taxes

Tax on simple or sweetened soft drinks
An *ad valorem* tax on simple or sweetened soft drinks is levied at the rate of 10% over the selling price to the public as suggested by the manufacturer, importer, or distributor, excluding VAT and returnable bottle taxes.

Tax on the production and importation of alcohol and spirits
A tax is levied on domestically produced or imported alcohol and spirits at rates ranging from USD 0.0825 to USD 0.15 for each 1% of alcohol volume per litre or in proportion thereof. Spirits and alcohol also have an *ad valorem* tax levied at the rate of 5% over the suggested selling price to the public, excluding VAT.

Tax on tobacco products
A tax is levied at USD 0.005 per cigarette, cigar, little cigarette, or other tobacco product. Also, an *ad valorem* tax is levied at the rate of 39% over the suggested consumer selling price to the public, excluding VAT.

Tax on transfer of real estate property
A 3% tax is applied to transfers of real estate property. This tax is applied to the amount by which the value of the real estate exceeds USD 28,571.43.

Stamp taxes
No stamp taxes are assessed as the pertinent law was abrogated in 1992.

Capital gains tax
Capital gains are taxed at a flat rate of 10% of net profits, except when gains are realised within 12 months following the purchase date, in which case they are taxed as ordinary income. Capital losses can only be offset against capital gains. Whenever capital losses exceed capital gains, the remaining balance may be carried forward to future capital gains within a five-year period.

Annual business tax
Companies are required to register themselves with the Registry of Commerce and pay an annual business licence fee assessed on the company's assets, as follows:

Assets (USD)	Fee (USD)
2,000 to 57,150	91.43
57,151 to 114,286	137.14
114,287 to 228,572	228.57
An additional charge for each office, branch, or agency property of a company	34.29

If the assets exceed the amount of USD 228,572, there is an additional duty of USD 11.43 for each additional USD 100,000 in assets or fraction thereof. In any case, the relevant duties are limited to USD 11,428.57.

Social security contributions
Social security contributions (ISSS) are mandatory for both employee and employer and are destined to public health services. The employee's contributions are withheld from the employee's monthly salary and are transferred by the employer to the Salvadorian Institute of Social Security through monthly payrolls. The contribution amounts are summarised in the table below:

El Salvador

Monthly employee's salary (USD)	Employee's rate (%)	Employer's rate (%)
0 to 685.71	3	7.50

Note: For individuals who have salaries above USD 685.71, the social security contribution applicable is USD 20.57 for the employee, and USD 51.49 for the employer.

Contributions to pension fund (AFP) are mandatory for both employee and employer. The employee's contributions are withheld from the employee's monthly salary and are transferred by the employer. The employer's contributions are paid to the AFP. Both contributions are reported to the Pension Fund Administrator through a monthly payroll. The percentages are summarised below:

Monthly employee's salary (USD)	Employee's rate (%)	Employer's rate (%)
0 to 5,311.52	6.25	6.75

Note: For individuals who have salaries above USD 5,311.52, the pension fund contribution applicable is USD 331.97 for the employee, and USD 358.53 for the employer.

Entities with more than ten employees must also pay a payroll tax which is destined to the National Institute of Professional Development (INSAFORP), which promotes professional development through courses and complementary studies. The percentages are summarised below:

Monthly employee's salary (USD)	Employer's rate (%)
0 to 685.71	1
Over 685.71	0

Municipal taxes

Municipal taxes are assessed according to a progressive tariff list issued by each municipality. The taxes are applicable to the company's assets located in each municipality, and are paid on a monthly basis. The tariff lists are applied separately to commercial, industrial, and financial sectors.

Branch income

In El Salvador, tax rates on branch profits are the same as for domestic corporations. Dividends and profits paid or credited by HQ representatives, affiliates, branches, subsidiaries, agencies, and others not domiciled in El Salvador are subject to 5% WHT.

The law does not provide separate treatment for administrative offices located in El Salvador.

The general regulations indicate that branches, agencies, and/or establishments permanently operating in the country, with owned or leased installed infrastructure, employing domestic staff, and performing their economic activities in a material and perceptible manner in the country, are subject to the same taxes as companies duly incorporated.

El Salvador

Income determination

In El Salvador, income is considered taxable if it is obtained from goods located in the country, activities undertaken within the national territory, or services rendered or utilised in the country.

Inventory valuation

For tax purposes, taxpayers are authorised to use any one of the following inventory methods, provided they are technically appropriate for the particular business, consistently applied, and easily audited:

- Purchase or manufacturing costs.
- Last purchase costs.
- Direct average allocation costs.
- Average costs.
- Last in first out (LIFO).
- First in first out (FIFO).
- Specific methods for fruits and farm products.
- Specific method for cattle.

Other than the methods enumerated above, taxpayers are not permitted to use other methods for valuing their inventories except with prior authorisation of the tax office, provided that in the latter's judgement the method in question contains clear determination and *bona fide* elements available to the office. Once an inventory valuation method is adopted, the taxpayer may not change it without the tax office's prior authorisation.

Capital gains

Capital gains are subject to capital gains tax, except when gains are realised within 12 months following the purchase date, in which case they are taxed as ordinary income. *See Capital gains tax in the Other taxes section for more information.*

Dividend income

Cash profits or dividends remitted or credited to shareholders are subject to a 5% WHT.

Stock dividends

Stock dividends (different from the ones generated from shares) for companies are treated as ordinary income obtained for these companies in the correspondent fiscal year. These revenues are taxable according to the 30% rate on gross income.

Interest income

Interest income is taxable in El Salvador when the entity paying the interest is resident in El Salvador, when the capital is invested in the country, and when the risk is assumed in El Salvador.

Partnership income

Partnership income is taxable if it is Salvadorian-source income; nevertheless, no specific provisions exist in El Salvador regarding partnership income.

Rent/royalties income

Rent and royalties income is taxable if it is Salvadorian-source income; nevertheless, no specific provisions exist in El Salvador regarding rent and royalties income.

El Salvador

Condoned debts
Condoned debts are considered taxable income and must be included as part of the income generated in that fiscal period.

Foreign income
Under the territoriality source of income principle, extraterritorial income is not taxable in El Salvador, with the exception of income and other benefits from securities and other financing operations. In this case, interest arising from loans granted to a resident of El Salvador is considered as taxable income, and the person or entity paying the loan must withhold 10% of the interest. If financial services are rendered between related parties, the withholding must be at 20%.

Deductions

All business expenses considered necessary to produce taxable income and/or maintain income sources (e.g. freight, marketing, power, telecommunications, water, salaries, lease contracts, merchandise and transport insurance, fuel, and interest paid on loans used by income generating sources) are deductible for income tax purposes.

Depreciation and amortisation
Depreciation is calculated using the straight-line method, which results in the following maximum annual rates for determining depreciation deductions.

Assets	Rate (%)
Buildings	5
Machinery	20
Vehicles	25
Other movable assets	50

Depreciation of new software is permitted at a rate of 25% of purchase or production costs.

Amortisation of goodwill, trademarks, and other similar intangible assets are not deductible for income tax purposes.

Start-up expenses
In El Salvador, there is not a special regulation for expenses related to the starting up of a company.

Interest expenses
Interest expenses are deductible if the amount of the loan is invested in a source that generates taxable income.

Bad debt
In El Salvador, bad debt is deductible if the following requirements are presented:

* The debt is generated from the business activity.
* The debt had been registered as taxable income.
* The debt is registered in the accounting system.
* The debt has been expired for 12 months.

Charitable contributions
The deductibility of charitable donations is limited to 20% of the donor's net income after deducting the donation amount.

Fines and penalties
In general, penalties, late payment charges, and fines of that type are not deductible.

Taxes
Taxes paid are not deductible.

Net operating losses
Operating losses cannot be carried forward to future years or carried back. Capital losses, however, may be carried forward to offset capital gains for five years.

Payments to foreign affiliates
Remittance of royalties, interest income, and service fees to foreign affiliates are deductible provided proper contracts are in place, a 20% WHT is applied, and these services have actually been received. Note that payments to entities located in tax haven regimes are subject to a 25% WHT.

Group taxation

There are no grouping rules in El Salvador between independent entities. Each entity, even if related, is treated separately and must report and pay their taxes independently.

Transfer pricing
In El Salvador, it is mandatory for entities that have operations with related parties or with entities resident in tax havens to undertake these operations according to the rules of market prices.

Local tax authorities can establish the value of the operations according to market prices rules if, according to their point of view, these operations have not been undertaken according to the arm's-length principle.

Thin capitalisation
No specific provision for thin capitalisation exists in El Salvador.

Tax credits and incentives

El Salvador offers a wide range of incentives to attract foreign investment and drive new commercial and industrial developments. There are also no restrictions on foreign ownership or on mergers, acquisitions, or joint ventures.

There are three specific laws in El Salvador that seek to encourage foreign investment by improving the country's competitiveness in all areas involving the granting of tax incentives. These laws are the Industrial and Commercial Free Zone Law, the Law of International Services, and the Export Reactivation Law.

The Industrial and Commercial Free Zone Law No. 405, dated 3 September 1998, grants companies the following incentives:

- CIT exemption.

El Salvador

- VAT exemption.
- Municipal tax exemption.
- Exemption from real estate transfer taxes when land is intended to be used for productive activities.
- Exemption from duties for imports on machinery, raw materials, equipment, and intermediate goods used for production.
- An option to sell merchandise or services linked to international trade produced in the free zone in the Salvadoran market as long as the corresponding import taxes, CIT, VAT, and municipal taxes are paid on the final goods or services.

Any foreign company may establish and function in a free zone or bonded warehouse and benefit from these incentives if they are engaged in production, assembly, manufacturing, processing, transformation, or commercialisation of goods and services and/or rendering of services linked to international or regional trade, such as gathering, packaging and repackaging, cargo consolidation, distribution of merchandise, and other activities connected or complementary to them.

The Law of International Services No. 431, dated 11 October 2007, grants the same benefits as the Free Zone Law, but the beneficiaries are companies operating in Service Centres specially created according to this law and dedicated to international services as defined therein.

The Export Reactivation Law No. 460 (i.e. *Ley de Reactivación de las Exportaciones*), dated 15 March 1990, grants reimbursement of 6% free on board (FOB) value of exports destined outside the region.

Withholding taxes

Payments or amounts credited to non-residents arising from income obtained in El Salvador are subject to a 20% WHT. Income earned in El Salvador covers income from assets located in the country, from any activities performed or capital invested in the land, and from services rendered or used in the national territory, regardless of whether they are provided or paid outside the country. Income from services used in the country is income earned in El Salvador by the service provider, irrespective of whether the relevant income generating activities are performed abroad. Note that payments to foreign entities located in tax haven regimes are subject to a 25% WHT.

Payments to resident individuals with respect to services rendered, other than under a labour relationship, are subject to a 10% WHT.

The acquisition of intangible goods among resident entities in the country is subject to a 10% WHT.

Certain transactions are subject to a reduced WHT rate of 5%, such as the following:

- International transport services paid to non-residents.
- Insurance services, re-insurances, and bondings paid to non-residents.
- Payments for transfer of intangible assets or use of the rights to intangibles and tangible assets related to films, movies, music records, cable TV, satellite, etc.

Moreover, a treaty to avoid double taxation exists between El Salvador and Spain, this treaty established reduced WHT, such as the following:

- 12% WHT made to dividend payments.
- 10% WHT made to interest payments.
- 10% WHT made to rent and royalties payments.
- 10% WHT made to payments for services.

Tax administration

National taxes, fees, and other contributions on all types of goods, services, and income in El Salvador are levied by the National Congress. Local governments (municipalities) may suggest contribution rates and propose their approval to the National Congress by way of a specific law.

The Ministry of Finance (*Ministerio de Hacienda*) controls the State's finances and defines and guides the government's financial policy. It also harmonises, directs, and implements its policies on taxation through its agencies.

Taxable period

In El Salvador, the fiscal year is from 1 January to 31 December.

Tax returns

CIT annual returns must be filed each year no later than 30 April, following the end of the year under taxation.

Payment of tax

Taxes are due on the date established for filing the tax returns. In El Salvador, tax payments are made together with the filing of tax returns, and payments must be made at the banks of the local financial system.

In addition, public and private legal entities resident in the country for tax purposes, other than farm and cattle concerns, are required to make advance income tax payments at 1.75% of gross revenues. These advance payments are due, together with the corresponding return, within ten working days following the corresponding calendar month and are ultimately applied against the CIT at the end of the year.

Audit cycle

In El Salvador, the audit cycle is constituted by the following steps:

- Tax administration issues a resolution of an auditor designation.
- The requirement of financial information of the company.
- The requirement of complimentary documentation to verify possible issues.
- The tax administration issues an audit report where the issues are expressed.
- A resolution hearing is issued by the tax administration, which gives the taxpayer the right to provide evidence to refute the issues made by the mentioned authority.
- Final resolution is determined regarding the complimentary tax or the penalties to be paid.

Statute of limitations

In El Salvador, the statute of limitations for the compliance of the payment of tax debts is ten years.

El Salvador

The tax administration's power to perform a tax audit is for three years in the case of tax returns presented on time by the taxpayer; three years in the case of tax returns presented in a delay way, but this time is going to start from the day after the extemporary presentation; and five years in cases where the taxpayer has not presented the tax return.

Topic of focus for tax authorities
In El Salvador, when the tax administration performs a tax audit, it focuses on the following topics:

* Compliance of the transfer pricing rules, this can be considered as the main element for the tax authorities.
* Compliance of the obligations held with non-domiciled subjects, especially those domiciled in tax havens.

Equatorial Guinea

PwC contact

Sébastien Lechêne
Main Road Malabo 2 EGICO Tower, 3rd and 4th Floor, PO Box 431
Equatorial Guinea
Tel: +240 333 09 14 34
Email: sebastien.lechene@ga.pwc.com

Significant developments

There have been no significant tax regulatory developments regarding corporate taxation in the past year in Equatorial Guinea.

Taxes on corporate income

The corporate income tax (CIT) must be paid by any resident entity.

Taxable profit is determined by deducting from gross income all expenses tied to the performance of taxable activities in Equatorial Guinea. In principle, all expenses are deductible, but the Tax Code provides rules of deductibility for some of them.

Resident companies are subject to CIT on their worldwide income. Non-resident entities are subject to a 10% withholding tax (WHT) on gross income derived from sources in Equatorial Guinea.

The CIT rate is 35% on taxable profits.

Minimum income tax
Minimum income tax is 1% of the turnover of the company for the previous year.

This amount cannot be lower than 800,000 Central African CFA francs (XAF) (even if the company does not have revenues). The minimum income tax can be totally or partially deducted from the CIT to be paid.

Local income taxes
There are no local income taxes in Equatorial Guinea.

Corporate residence

A legal entity present in Equatorial Guinea more than three months within a calendar year, or more than six months within two consecutive calendar years, and performing an economic activity or providing paid services in the country is considered as a resident for taxation purposes.

The notion of residence applies equally to any kind of activity (even if there is some specificity in the oil and gas sector).

Permanent establishment (PE)
The notion of 'permanent establishment' is not defined in the Tax Code. The authorities mainly refer to the notion of residence as defined above.

Equatorial Guinea

Other taxes

Value-added tax (VAT)
VAT is an indirect tax on consumption based on turnover.

All operations performed in Equatorial Guinea are subject to VAT, unless they are included in the list of exemptions provided by the Equatorial Guinea Tax Code or a specific tax regime.

VAT is generally chargeable on the following:

- Goods sold or assigned for valuable consideration.
- Services provided.
- Self-consumed goods and services.
- Imports.
- Other operations carried on by individuals or legal entities in their sphere of business, professional, and individual activities, including extraction activities.

The standard VAT rate is 15%.

A rate of 0% is applicable to a specific list of products and equipment provided in the Tax Code (e.g. certain medical products, some equipment for construction).

A reduced rate of 6% is applicable to a limited list of basic consumables and books.

Custom duties
The customs duties are based on the categories of goods as follows:

- Category I: Primary necessity goods: 5%.
- Category II: Raw material and materials: 10%.
- Category III: Intermediary goods and miscellaneous: 20%.
- Category IV: Current consumption goods: 30%.

Excise taxes
Excise taxes are applicable on specific goods, such as alcoholic drinks and tobacco. The rates are from 20% to 50% plus a special Economic and Monetary Community of Central Africa (CEMAC) contribution from 0% to 35%.

Real property tax
A 1% urban property tax applies annually to 40% of the value of the land and the buildings on such land. Urban property is defined by the Tax Code as "any land with or without buildings and the buildings built thereon, whenever located in urban areas".

Transfer tax
For the transfer of goods between residents and non-residents, and between non-residents, there is a 3% tax on the value of the goods.

Real estate transfers between residents are taxed at the rate of 5% on the value of the real estate. The rate increases to 25% on real estate transfers between residents and non-residents, and between non-residents.

Stamp duties
Stamp duties are payable on a variety of instruments and transactions and vary depending on the concerned legal act.

Social security contributions

Employers contribute 1% of gross salary to the Work Protection Fund (*Fondo de Protección al Trabajo*) and 21.5% to the National Social Security Fund (INSESO) on a monthly basis.

Employees contribute 0.5% of net salary to the Work Protection Fund and 4.5% to the INSESO on a monthly basis.

Branch income

Branch income is subject to CIT. We understand that there is no branch remittance tax, even if the tax authorities sometimes try to apply this tax.

Income determination

Inventory valuation

Inventory is evaluated at cost price for tax purposes. The tax method generally matches the book method.

Capital gains

Capital gains are, in principle, subject to CIT.

Some exemptions and specific tax regimes can apply, as follows:

- The capital gains that come from the assignment, in the ongoing operation, of the components of the fixed assets will not be included in the taxable profit of the fiscal year in the course of which they have been obtained if the taxpayer puts them in a special account named 'capital gains to be reused' and is committed to reinvesting in new fixed assets in the company before the expiration of a period of time of three years, starting from the close of this fiscal year, an amount equal to the amount of these capital gains plus the cost of the assigned components.
- The capital gains different from those obtained on goods, resulting from free assignment of stock, corporate portions, or liabilities, as a consequence of the merger of corporations, limited partnerships by shares, or limited companies, will be exempt from the tax regarding the profits made by those corporations, on condition that the take-over company or the new company has its corporate headquarters in Equatorial Guinea.

Dividend income

All dividends received by a resident company are subject to CIT.

A personal income WHT of 25% is applicable on dividends paid to individuals or companies not having their usual domicile or headquarters in Equatorial Guinea. This tax is a final tax for those taxpayers.

The net products of the shares owned and earned by the parent company from its subsidiary can be deducted from the total net profits of the parent company after offsetting from this amount 25% (expenses and charges lump sum amount) if the:

- shareholder holds at least 25% of shares of the subsidiary and

Equatorial Guinea

- shareholder guarantees the shares have always been registered in the name of the participating company and commits it will hold these shares for at least two consecutive years.

This proportional part is established at 10% of the amount of these products and represents the management expenses already deducted from overhead costs.

Interest income
Interest earned by companies is subject to CIT at a 25% rate.

Foreign income
Resident companies are subject to CIT on their worldwide income.

There is no tax deferral in Equatorial Guinea.

Deductions

Depreciation
A straight-line method of computation of depreciation should be applied to fixed assets according to the normal useful lives of the assets involved, as provided by the Tax Code.

Goodwill
Goodwill is, in principle, not deductible.

Start-up expenses
Start-up expenses can be amortised.

Interest expenses
Interest expenses are deductible if they do not exceed the limit for loans set up by the Central Bank.

Bad debt
Bad debts are deductible, given they are supported.

Charitable contributions
Charitable contributions are deductible, given they are for philanthropic, sport, educative, scientific, social, or family purposes and do not exceed 0.5% of the turnover for the fiscal year of the company.

Fines and penalties
Fines and penalties are not deductible.

Taxes
Only professional taxes are deductible.

Net operating losses
Net operating losses can be carried forward for three years. Losses cannot be carried back. Losses of one entity cannot be transferred to another entity in a reorganisation.

In theory, when the results of a company, no matter the kind of the company, are negative during a maximum period of three consecutive years, this company will immediately be removed from the register by the Tax Administration for the practice of the activity for which it was registered, except when the company is newly created.

Equatorial Guinea

Payment to foreign affiliates
The deductibility of the technical assistance made by the parent company to its subsidiary is limited to 50% of the intermediary tax result (accounting result plus potential fiscal reintegration).

In case of a deficit, the relevant basis for the evaluation of the foreign technical assistance amount to be reintegrated will be the intermediary result of the last beneficiary fiscal year.

E

Group taxation
Equatorial Guinea law does not provide specific provisions for taxation of groups.

Transfer pricing
There are no specific rules regarding transfer pricing, even if there are indirect references in the Tax Code.

Thin capitalisation
According to the Tax Code:

"Interest paid to the partners for amounts made available to the company, in addition to their capital contributions, no matter the form of the company, will be admitted within the limits established for the advances of the Central Bank.

In the incorporated or limited companies, the deduction of interest will not be allowed for partners or shareholders that have the right to hold, or actually hold, the company management except to the extent that the amounts deposited do not exceed the combination of the contributions of these partners or shareholders."

Tax credits and incentives
Some tax and customs exemptions can be granted by the government for some specific economic sectors (e.g. oil and gas sector, public work sector). These exemptions shall be negotiated in the contract signed between the company and the administration (e.g. Production Sharing Contract, Public Work Contract).

Foreign tax credit
There is no foreign tax credit in Equatorial Guinea.

Withholding taxes

WHT in the non-oil and gas sector
There is a 10% tax withheld on the gross incomes obtained in Equatorial Guinea by non-residents.

There is a 25% WHT on royalties for non-CEMAC residents.

Dividends and interests paid to non-residents are subject to 25% WHT.

Equatorial Guinea

WHT on the oil and gas sector
In Equatorial Guinea:

- a 6.25% WHT is imposed on payments made to a resident entity within the oil and gas sector and
- a 10% WHT is imposed on payments made to a non-resident entity within the oil and gas sector.

In practice, the tax authorities consider this tax only applies to sales of services.

The tax basis is composed of the gross amount paid to the provider.

Tax administration

Taxable period
The taxable period is from 1 January to 31 December for CIT purposes.

Tax returns
CIT returns must be filed within the first four months of the year following the taxable fiscal year.

Payment of tax
Payment of CIT must be made within 15 days from the day following the date of receipt of the tax liquidation issued by the Ministry of Finance and Budget.

The minimum company tax of 1% of the previous year's turnover is payable by 31 March.

Penalties
Penalties of XAF 200,000 per month late, up to 75% of the tax owed, apply for late filing of CIT returns.

A penalty of 50% to 100% of the undeclared amount applies in case of shortfall in the return and in case of arbitrary settlement, 50% of the total amount if the good faith of the taxpayer is established or assumed and 100% wherever the taxpayer does not prove good faith.

Audit cycle
There is no specific provision related to the tax audit cycle in Equatorial Guinea.

Statute of limitations
The statute of limitations is generally five years from the date the tax is due.

Estonia

PwC contact

Villi Tõntson
PricewaterhouseCoopers AS
Pärnu mnt 15
10141 Tallinn
Estonia
Tel: +372 614 1970
Email: villi.tontson@ee.pwc.com

Significant developments

Estonia is regarded as offering a relatively favourable income tax regime, as all undistributed corporate profits are tax exempt. Estonia levies a corporate income tax (CIT) only on profits that are distributed as dividends, share buy-backs, capital reductions, liquidation proceeds, or deemed profit distributions. Distributed profits are generally subject to 21% corporate tax (21/79 on the net amount of the profit distribution). According to the law amendment passed by the Parliament on 16 June 2011, the CIT rate will be reduced to 20% in 2015.

On 1 January 2012, the tax treaty with Jersey became effective. During 2011, tax treaties with India, Turkmenistan, and the United Arab Emirates were signed, but these treaties are not yet effective.

Local sales and boat tax were abolished effective from 2012.

As of 1 April 2012, the value-added tax (VAT) reverse charge mechanism has also been extended to gold.

Taxes on corporate income

All undistributed corporate profits are tax exempt. This exemption covers both active (e.g. trading) and passive (e.g. dividends, interest, royalties) types of income. It also covers capital gains from the sale of all types of assets, including shares, securities, and immovable property. This tax regime is available to Estonian resident companies and permanent establishments (PE) of non-resident companies that are registered in Estonia.

The taxation of corporate profits is postponed until the profits are distributed as dividends or deemed to be distributed, such as in the case of transfer pricing adjustments, expenses and payments that do not have a business purpose, fringe benefits, gifts, donations, and representation expenses.

Distributed profits are generally subject to the 21% CIT at 21/79 of the net amount of profit distribution. For example, a company that has profits of 100 euros (EUR) available for distribution can distribute dividends of EUR 79, on which it must pay CIT of EUR 21.

According to the law amendment passed by the Parliament on 16 June 2011, the CIT rate will be reduced to 20% in 2015.

Estonia

From the Estonian perspective, this tax is considered a CIT and not a withholding tax (WHT), so the tax rate is not affected by an applicable tax treaty. Certain distributions are exempt from such tax (*see the Income determination section*).

In Estonia, resident companies are taxed on profits distributed from their worldwide income, while PEs of non-residents are taxed only on profits distributed from income derived from Estonian sources. Other Estonian-source income derived by non-residents may be subject to final WHT or CIT by way of assessment.

Local income taxes
There are no local income taxes in Estonia.

Corporate residence

A legal entity is considered resident in Estonia for tax purposes if it is established under Estonian law. There is no management and control test for the purpose of determining corporate residency. Most tax treaty tie-breakers for legal entities are based on competent authority procedures.

Permanent establishment (PE)
A PE (including a branch registered in the Commercial Register) of a foreign entity is deemed to be a non-resident taxpayer. Under the domestic law, which deviates from the Organisation for Economic Co-operation and Development (OECD) Model Tax Convention, a PE is defined as an enterprise through which the permanent business activities of the non-resident are conducted in Estonia. A PE is deemed to be created as a result of the business activities conducted in Estonia which are geographically linked or having movable character or as a result of the business activities of an agent which is authorised to conclude contracts in the name of the non-resident.

Other taxes

Value-added tax (VAT)
The following transactions are subject to Estonian VAT:

* Taxable supplies of goods and services (the place of supply of which is Estonia).
* Taxable imports of goods.
* Taxable intra-community acquisitions of goods.

The standard VAT rate is 20%. A reduced rate of 9% is applied to books, periodicals with few exceptions, hotel accommodation services, and listed pharmaceuticals.

The VAT rate on the export of goods and certain services is 0% (i.e. exempt with credit). Some services, such as health care, insurance, certain financial, and transactions with securities, are exempt (i.e. exempt without credit).

Transactions in real estate are generally exempt from VAT, but there are certain significant exceptions (e.g. transactions in new and significantly renovated buildings). Taxpayers can elect to add VAT to real estate transactions if certain conditions are met.

As of 2011, the reverse charge mechanism has been extended to the supply of waste metal and real estate, under which VAT is accounted for by the VAT liable purchaser and not by the supplier. For real estate, the reverse charge applies only when the seller has

Estonia

opted for taxation of real estate. As of 1 April 2012, the reverse charge mechanism is also extended to gold.

If the taxable supplies of Estonian resident businesses or a PE of a non-resident business in Estonia exceed EUR 16,000 in a calendar year, VAT registration is required. Voluntary registration is also possible. Certain transactions of non-resident businesses require Estonian VAT registration without any threshold.

The VAT accounting period is generally a calendar month, and VAT should be declared and paid on or before the 20th day of the following month.

Under certain conditions, a European Union (EU) taxable person that is not registered for VAT in Estonia will be entitled to a refund of input VAT paid in Estonia. Non-EU taxable persons are entitled to claim VAT refunds based on reciprocity.

Estonia has implemented a system that allows, under certain conditions, a company to account for VAT on imports on the VAT return without paying VAT to the customs authority.

Customs duties

After becoming a member of the European Union, Estonia also became a member of the Customs Union. The Community Customs Code and related implementation regulations apply, meaning that:

- trade between Estonia and other EU countries is customs-free
- imports from non-EU countries are subject to EU customs tariffs, and
- numerous free trade agreements concluded between EU and non-EU countries apply to Estonia.

Excise duties

Excise taxes are levied on tobacco, alcohol, electricity, some packaging materials, and motor fuel.

Land and property taxes

Land is subject to an annual land tax, which is calculated on the assessed value of land at rates between 0.1% and 2.5%, depending on the municipality. The tax is paid by the owners of land, or sometimes by the users of land, in two instalments, by 31 March and 1 October (amounts not exceeding EUR 64 are paid in one instalment by 31 March).

There is no property tax (i.e. tax on the value of buildings).

Property transfers are generally subject to state and notary fees.

Transfer taxes

There are no transfer taxes in Estonia.

Stamp taxes

Certain transactions may be subject to insignificant stamp taxes (i.e. state fees).

Social security and unemployment insurance

Employers operating in Estonia (including non-residents with a PE or employees in Estonia) must pay social tax on certain payments to individuals at the rate of 33% (where 20% is used for financing public pension insurance and 13% is used for financing public health insurance). Social tax paid by employers is not capped and

Estonia

mainly applies to salaries, directors' fees, and service fees paid and fringe benefits granted to individuals. According to the new program of the coalition government, it is expected that the monthly social tax (except its public health insurance component) will be capped at EUR 4,000 per individual from the year 2014.

In addition to social tax, employers are also required to pay and withhold unemployment insurance contributions. Employers must pay 1.4% and employees must pay 2.8% (collected by employers through payroll withholding). The contributions mainly apply to salaries and service fees paid to individuals.

Compulsory accumulative pension scheme
Employers' payroll withholding includes 2% contributions to the compulsory accumulative pension scheme, if the employee has joined that pension scheme.

Heavy goods vehicle tax
The heavy goods vehicle tax is paid for the following classes of vehicles that are registered with the Estonian National Motor Vehicle Register and are intended for the carriage of goods:

- Lorries with a maximum authorised weight or gross laden weight of not less than 12 tons.
- Road trains composed of trucks and trailers with a maximum authorised weight or gross laden weight of not less than 12 tons.

The tax is paid by the owners or users of the vehicles. The quarterly tax rates range from EUR 0 to EUR 232.60 per heavy goods vehicle.

Gambling tax
Gambling tax is imposed on amounts received from operating games of skill, totalisator, betting, lotteries, and promotional lotteries. Tax is also charged on gambling tables and machines used for games of chance located in licensed premises. The tax is paid monthly by authorised operators.

Local taxes
Local taxes can be imposed by rural municipalities or city councils; however, the fiscal significance of local taxes is almost nonexistent. Local taxes include advertisement tax, road and street closure tax, motor vehicle tax, tax on keeping animals, entertainment tax, and parking charges. Note that the sales tax and boat tax were abolished from the list of local taxes effective from year 2012.

Branch income

Registered PEs of non-residents, much as with resident companies, are subject to CIT only in respect of profit distributions, both actual and deemed, as defined in domestic law.

Transactions and dealings between a head office and its PE(s) should be conducted on arm's-length terms. Thus, such profits should be attributed to a PE of a non-resident taxpayer that the PE would be expected to make if it were a distinct and separate taxpayer engaged in the same or similar activities, and under the same or similar conditions, and dealing in a wholly independent manner with its head office.

Income determination

Distributable profits are determined based on financial statements drawn up in accordance with Estonian Generally Accepted Accounting Principles (GAAP) or International Accounting Standards (IAS)/International Financial Reporting Standards (IFRS), and there are no adjustments to accounting profits for tax purposes (e.g. tax depreciation, tax loss carryforward or carryback).

The CIT liability associated with the distribution of dividends is accounted for as an expense at the time the dividends are declared, regardless of when the profits were generated or distributed.

E

Dividends paid by Estonian companies are generally subject to 21/79 CIT at the level of the distributing company. However, dividends distributed by Estonian companies are exempt from CIT if the distributions are paid out of:

* dividends received from Estonian, EU, European Economic Area (EEA), and Swiss tax resident companies (except tax haven companies) in which the Estonian company has at least a 10% shareholding
* profits attributable to a PE in the EU, EEA, or Switzerland
* dividends received from all other foreign companies in which the Estonian company (except tax haven companies) has at least a 10% shareholding, provided that either the underlying profits have been subject to foreign tax or if foreign income tax was withheld from dividends received, or
* profits attributable to a foreign PE in all other countries provided that such profits have been subject to tax in the country of the PE.

In addition, stock dividends (bonus shares) distributed to stockholders are exempt from 21/79 CIT charge.

Certain domestic and foreign taxes can also be credited against the 21/79 CIT charge under domestic law or tax treaties.

Deductions

Distributable profits are determined based on financial statements drawn up in accordance with Estonian GAAP or IAS/IFRS, and there are no adjustments to accounting profits for tax purposes (e.g. tax depreciation, tax loss carryforward or carryback).

Fringe benefits

Employers operating in Estonia (including non-resident companies that have a PE or employees in Estonia) are liable to Estonian taxation on any fringe benefits granted to their employees (including directors).

Fringe benefits are subject to an exceptional tax treatment in Estonia, as only the employer is obliged to pay taxes on the fringe benefits furnished to the employee. Taxable fringe benefits received by a resident employee are generally not included in the taxable income of the employee for Estonian tax purposes. Fringe benefits are subject to 21/79 CIT and 33% social tax. For example, where the amount of the benefit is EUR 100, the CIT due by the employer would be EUR 26.58 (21/79 x 100) and the social tax due EUR 41.77 (0.33 x 126.58), for a total fringe benefit tax charge of EUR 68.35.

Estonia

Gifts, donations, and representation expenses

The 21/79 CIT is generally due on gifts and donations. Gifts and donations made to certain qualifying recipients are only subject to 21/79 CIT if such expenses exceed one of two limitations:

- 3% of the calculated social tax base for the existing calendar year or
- 10% of the profit of the last financial year according to statutory financial statements.

Representation expenses, those expenditures whose character and primary purpose is for representational or entertainment related activities, are generally subject to 21/79 CIT only if they exceed the threshold of EUR 32 per month plus 2% of the calculated social tax base of the calendar month in which the expenses are paid.

Taxes

All taxes paid are deductible for CIT purposes. In certain circumstances, domestic or foreign taxes may be creditable against the 21/79 CIT charge under domestic law or an applicable tax treaty.

Other significant items

The 21/79 CIT is generally due on expenses and payments that do not have a business purpose and that are regarded as deemed profit distributions. These may include, for example, late payment interest on tax arrears, penalties imposed by law, bribes, purchase of services, or settlement of obligations not related to taxpayer's business and acquisition of assets not related to taxpayer's business.

Furthermore, there are specific anti-tax haven rules treating certain transactions and dealings with tax haven companies as deemed profit distributions, which are therefore subject to 21/79 CIT. These include the following:

- Acquisition of securities issued by a tax haven entity (exception for certain listed securities).
- Acquisition of an ownership interest in a tax haven entity.
- Payment of fines or penalties to a tax haven entity, unless settled by court or arbitrage.
- Granting loans or making prepayments to a tax haven entity or otherwise acquiring a claim against a tax haven entity.

Payments to foreign affiliates

Payments to foreign affiliates are deductible for tax purposes (i.e. not subject to 21/79 CIT as deemed profit distributions) if the payment serves a business purpose, provides a benefit to the payer, is at arm's length, and is substantiated by sufficient documentation.

Payments to foreign affiliates may also be subject to various WHT. Certain payments to affiliates located in tax haven countries are always subject to 21/79 CIT or a 21% WHT rate.

Group taxation

There is no form of consolidation or group taxation for CIT purposes in Estonia.

Transfer pricing

Transfer pricing rules are applicable to all types of transactions between related parties. Both domestic and cross-border transactions with related parties must be conducted at arm's length. Estonian tax legislation includes a relatively broad definition of related parties. Under the present corporate tax system, if the transactions between related parties do not follow the arm's-length principle, then the subsequent transfer pricing adjustments are treated as hidden profit distributions subject to 21/79 monthly CIT.

As a general rule, Estonian group companies and PEs of foreign companies are obliged to prepare transfer pricing documentation to prove the arm's-length nature of the inter-company transactions with all related parties.

However, this documentation requirement does not apply to small and medium-size enterprises (SME), unless they have conducted transactions with entities located in low-tax territories. A company or PE is deemed to be an SME provided that the consolidated results of the previous financial year of an Estonian company or a PE together with its associated enterprises or head office (i.e. at the group level) are below all of the following criteria:

* Annual sales below EUR 50 million.
* Balance sheet below EUR 43 million.
* The number of employees below 250.

Apart from the formal transfer pricing documentation and general requirement to disclose the transactions with the related parties in the annual reports, there are no additional reporting requirements related to transfer pricing in relation to inter-company transactions.

Thin capitalisation

There are no thin capitalisation rules in the Estonian tax legislation.

Controlled foreign companies (CFCs)

Estonia has no CFC rules for corporate taxpayers.

Tax credits and incentives

There are no special tax incentives in Estonia. However, the entire Estonian corporate tax system, which provides for an indefinite deferral for taxing corporate profits, may be viewed as a tax incentive that promotes reinvestment of profits and thus stimulates economic growth.

Foreign tax credit

In certain circumstances, domestic or foreign taxes may be creditable against the 21/79 CIT charge under domestic law or an applicable tax treaty. *See the Income determination section for more information.*

Withholding taxes

Withholding agents must withhold CIT from certain payments. Withholding agents include resident legal entities, resident individuals registered as sole proprietorships or acting as employers, and non-residents having a PE or acting as employers in Estonia. The tax must be reported and paid by the tenth day of the month following

Estonia

the payment. CIT is not withheld from payments to resident companies, registered sole proprietorships, and registered PEs of non-resident companies. The following rules are in place with respect to payments that are subject to WHT:

- There is no WHT on dividends.
- There is no WHT on interest payments to non-residents on the condition that the interest charged does not significantly exceed the arm's-length rate at the time the debt is incurred and the interest payments are made. A 21% Estonian WHT rate will thus apply only to the part of interest that significantly exceeds the arm's-length amount.
- Royalties (including payments for the use of industrial, commercial, or scientific equipment) paid to non-residents are generally subject to a 10% WHT rate under domestic law, but reduced rates may be available under double tax treaties (DTT). Certain royalty payments to associated EU and Swiss companies that meet certain conditions are exempt from WHT.
- Rental payments to non-residents for the use of immovable property located in Estonia and movable property subject to registration in Estonia (excluding payments for the use of industrial, commercial, or scientific equipment) are subject to a 21% WHT rate under domestic law, but DTTs may exempt payments for the use of movable property from WHT.
- Royalties and rental payments to resident individuals are subject to a 21% WHT rate.
- Payments to non-resident companies for services provided in Estonia, including management and consultancy fees, are subject to a 10% WHT rate under domestic law, but may be exempt under DTTs. Service fee payments to tax haven entities are always subject to a 21% WHT rate.
- Salaries, directors' fees, and service fees paid to individuals are subject to a 21% WHT rate under domestic law, but DTTs may exempt service fee payments to non-resident individuals from WHT.
- Payments for the activities of non-resident artistes or sportsmen carried out in Estonia are subject to a 10% WHT rate.
- Certain pensions, insurance benefits, scholarships, prizes, lottery winnings etc. paid to non-residents and resident individuals are subject to a 21% WHT rate under domestic law.

For non-residents without a PE in Estonia, the tax withheld from these payments at domestic or treaty rates constitutes final tax in terms of their Estonian-source income and they do not have any tax reporting requirements in Estonia.

For certain types of Estonian-source income, non-residents are liable under Estonian domestic law to self assess their Estonian tax and submit a tax return to the Estonian tax authorities. These types of income include:

- Taxable capital gains.
- Profits derived from business conducted in Estonia without a registered PE.
- Other items of income from which tax was not withheld but should have been withheld.

Estonia has effective tax treaties with: Albania, Armenia, Austria, Azerbaijan, Belarus, Belgium, Bulgaria, Canada, the People's Republic of China, Croatia, the Czech Republic, Denmark, Finland, France, Germany, Georgia, Greece, Hungary, Iceland, Ireland, Isle of Man, Israel, Italy, Jersey, Kazakhstan, the Republic of Korea, Latvia, Lithuania, Luxembourg, Macedonia, Malta, Moldova, the Netherlands, Norway, Poland, Portugal, Romania, Serbia, Singapore, Slovakia, Slovenia, Spain, Sweden, Switzerland, Turkey, Ukraine, the United Kingdom, and the United States. Treaties have also been concluded

Estonia

with India, Russia, Turkmenistan, and the United Arab Emirates, but these are not yet effective.

The following WHT rates apply to dividends, interest, and royalties paid to a recipient or beneficial owner resident in a tax treaty country. The lower of the domestic or the treaty rate is given.

Recipient	Dividends (%) (1)	Interest (%) (2)	Royalties (%) (3)
Non-treaty	0	0/21	0/10
Treaty:			
Albania	0	0/21	5
Armenia	0	0/21	10
Austria	0	0/21	0/5/10 (4)
Azerbaijan	0	0/21	10
Belarus	0	0/21	10
Belgium	0	0/21	0/5/10 (4)
Bulgaria	0	0/21	0/5
Canada	0	0/21	10
China, People's Rep. of	0	0/21	10
Croatia	0	0/21	10
Czech Republic	0	0/21	0/10
Denmark	0	0/21	0/5/10 (4)
Finland	0	0/21	0/5/10 (4)
France	0	0/21	0/5/10 (4)
Georgia	0	0/21	10
Germany	0	0/21	0/5/10 (4)
Greece	0	0/21	0/5/10 (4)
Hungary	0	0/21	0/5/10 (4)
Iceland	0	0/21	5/10 (4)
Ireland, Rep. of	0	0/21	0/5/10 (4)
Isle of Man	0	0/21	0
Israel	0	0/21	0
Italy	0	0/21	0/5/10 (4)
Jersey	0	0/21	0
Kazakhstan	0	0/21	15
Korea, Rep. of	0	0/21	5/10 (4)
Latvia	0	0/21	0/5/10 (4)
Lithuania	0	0/21	0/10
Luxembourg	0	0/21	0/5/10
Macedonia	0	0/21	5
Malta	0	0/21	0/10
Moldova	0	0/21	10
Netherlands	0	0/21	0/5/10 (4)
Norway	0	0/21	5/10 (4)
Poland	0	0/21	0/10
Portugal	0	0/21	0/10
Romania	0	0/21	0/10
Serbia	0	0/21	5/10 (5)
Singapore	0	0/21	7.5

Estonia

Recipient	Dividends (%) (1)	Interest (%) (2)	Royalties (%) (3)
Slovakia	0	0/21	0/10
Slovenia	0	0/21	0/10
Spain	0	0/21	0/5/10 (4)
Sweden	0	0/21	0/5/10 (4)
Switzerland	0	0/21	0/5/10 (4)
Turkey	0	0/21	5/10 (4)
Ukraine	0	0/21	10
United Kingdom	0	0/21	0/5/10 (4)
United States	0	0/21	5/10 (4)

Notes

1. Under the domestic law, the rate is nil for all non-resident individual and corporate shareholders.
2. The rate is nil on the condition that the interest paid to a non-resident does not significantly exceed the arm's-length rate at the time the debt is incurred and the interest payments are made. Estonian WHT at the domestic rate of 21% will thus apply only to the part of interest that significantly exceeds the arm's-length amount. This WHT could be reduced under tax treaties.
3. The rate is nil for arm's-length royalties paid to an associated EU or Swiss company if certain conditions are met.
4. The lower 5% rate applies to royalties paid for the use of industrial, commercial, or scientific equipment.
5. The lower 5% rate applies to royalties paid for the use of copyright royalties, excluding software royalties.

Tax administration

Taxable period
The tax period is a calendar month.

Tax returns
The combined CIT and payroll tax return (form TSD with appendices) must be submitted to the local tax authorities by the tenth day of the month following a taxable distribution or payment. Tax returns may be filed electronically via the Internet.

Payment of tax
CIT and payroll taxes must be remitted to the local tax authorities by the tenth day of the month following a taxable distribution or payment. No advance CIT payments are required.

Advance rulings
An advance ruling system became available in Estonia on 1 January 2008. The aim of the procedure is to provide certainty on the tax consequences of specific transactions or combination of transactions taking place in the future. The ruling is binding on the authorities (and not on the taxpayer) if the transaction was made within the deadline and the description provided in the ruling and the underlying legislation has not been substantially changed in the meantime. Estonian legislation specifically excludes obtaining rulings when the interpretation of the legislation is objectively clear, the situation is hypothetical, or the main purpose of the planned transaction is tax avoidance. In addition, transfer pricing valuation issues are excluded from the scope of the binding ruling system.

Audit cycle
There is no statutory tax audit cycle in Estonia.

Statute of limitations
As a general rule, the statute of limitations is three years. In case of intentional tax evasion, it is six years.

Topics of focus for tax authorities
The main topics of focus for tax authorities are 'envelope wages', VAT fraud, and transfer pricing.

E

Other issues

Company restructurings
In accordance with the EC Directive 2009/133/EC on mergers, divisions, partial divisions, transfers of assets, and exchanges of shares concerning companies of different member states, the mergers, divisions, and re-organisations of companies are generally tax-neutral in Estonia. The principle of going concern is applied in taxation of referred restructuring transactions.

Fiji Islands

PwC contact

Jerome Kado
PricewaterhouseCoopers
Level 8
Civic Tower
272 Victoria Parade
Suva
Fiji
Tel: +679 331 3955
Email: jerome.kado@fj.pwc.com

Significant developments

The following changes to the Fiji Income Tax Act became effective for tax years commencing on 1 January 2012:

- The corporate income tax (CIT) rate has been reduced from 28% to 20%.
- Telecommunication levy of 1% is imposed on all voice call charges.
- Credit card levy of 2% is imposed on the monthly credit card balance, including interest and other bank charges.
- Third party insurance levy of 20% is imposed on the total third party insurance premium collected in a month.
- Only 50% of the employer's statutory Fiji National Provident Fund (FNPF) contribution paid by the employer shall be allowed as a deduction for tax purposes in the year the contribution was paid.
- 40% of capital expenditure of not less than 50,000 Fijian dollars (FJD) incurred by any existing business located in Vanua Levu shall be allowed as a deduction for tax purposes, subject to certain conditions.
- Tax losses for all business activities will only be allowed to be carried forward for four consecutive years, except for tax losses in relation to certain hotel business, which will be allowed to be carried forward for eight years.
- Transfer pricing provisions of the Fiji Income Tax Act have been amended.
- Company advance tax payment requirements have been changed, with 90% of the income tax due being payable on or before year-end.

The following changes became effective from 1 January 2012:

- Fringe benefit tax (FBT) of 20% on the grossed-up value of fringe benefits provided has been introduced (effective rate of 25%).
- Hotel turnover tax of 5% has been replaced by the service turnover tax (STT) of 5%. The STT is applicable on certain services in addition to hotel services.
- The value-added tax (VAT) threshold has been increased from FJD 50,000 to FJD 100,000.
- The Tax Administration Decree (TAD) is now applicable to FBT and STT.
- The penalties for tax offences have been increased substantially (*see Penalties in the Tax administration section for more information*).

Taxes on corporate income

Resident corporations are taxed on their worldwide income. Non-resident corporations may only be taxed on their Fiji-sourced income.

Normal tax is payable and assessed on the chargeable income of the business calculated by subtracting deductible expenses from all assessable income specified under Section 11 of the Fiji Income Tax Act.

Normal tax is payable on taxable income at the following rates:

Type of company	Rate (%)
Non-resident shipping companies in respect of outgoing business from Fiji	2
All other companies, including non-resident companies carrying on business in Fiji (e.g. branch profits)	20 (effective for tax years commencing on 1 January 2012; previously 28)

Corporate residence

A company incorporated in Fiji is considered a 'resident' in Fiji. A company not incorporated in Fiji is resident in Fiji if it carries on business in Fiji and either its practical management and control are in Fiji or its voting powers are controlled by shareholders who are residents of Fiji.

Permanent establishment (PE)

PE is determined based on the applicable tax treaty. There is no specific definition of 'permanent establishment' under the Fiji Income Tax Act. However, generally a PE may be defined as a fixed place of business and would include the following:

- A place of management, branch, office, factory, warehouse, or workshop, but does not include a liaison office.
- A mine, oil or gas well, quarry, or other place of extraction of natural resources.
- A building site, or a construction, assembly, or installation project, or supervisory activities connected with such site or project, but only if the site, project, or activities continue for more than six months.
- The furnishing of services by the person, including consultancy services, through employees or other personnel engaged by the person for such purpose, but only if activities of that nature continue for the same or a connected project for a period or periods aggregating more than six months in any 12-month period.
- A person, referred to as an 'agent', acting on behalf of another person, referred to as the 'principal', if the agent:
  - has and habitually exercises an authority to conclude contracts on behalf of the principal or
  - habitually maintains a stock of trading stock from which the agent regularly delivers trading stock on behalf of the principal but does not include an agent of independent status.

Other taxes

Value-added tax (VAT)

VAT of 15% generally applies on the supply of goods and services in Fiji by a registered person in the course or furtherance of a taxable activity carried on by that person. Effective 1 January 2012, the threshold amount for VAT registration is FJD 100,000 (previously FJD 50,000) for the supply of goods and/or services.

Fiji Islands

The supply of financial services (except for certain insurance services), residential accommodation, and education by an approved institution is exempt.

The sale of edible oil, tin fish, rice, flour, tea, powdered milk, and kerosene are zero-rated. Exports of goods and services and international transportation are also zero-rated. The export of services, however, is zero-rated only under certain conditions.

The due date for lodgement of VAT returns and payment of any VAT payable is the end of the month following the taxable period. Where an entity's supplies do not exceed FJD 300,000, it may opt to lodge VAT returns and pay any VAT payable on an annual basis.

VAT refunds can no longer be transferred or assigned to another registered entity.

Under certain conditions, directors of companies with insufficient funds may be held liable for any outstanding VAT or CIT liability of the company and may be sued in their personal capacity.

Customs duties/import excise taxes
Import excise tax (from 5% to 15%) applies to selected goods (in addition to the fiscal duties imposed on importation), including:

* Alcohol and tobacco.
* Used or second hand liquefied petroleum gas (LPG) powered motor vehicles.
* New or used licensed mini buses.
* Some goods that are also locally manufactured.
* Certain white goods and luxury items.

Excise taxes
Excise tax is payable on tobacco, alcohol products, and carbonated soft drinks manufactured in Fiji based on quantities produced.

Property taxes
There are no property taxes at the national level. However, the municipalities may charge property rates in their respective area.

Stamp duties
Under the Fiji Stamp Duties Act, stamp duty is payable in respect of instruments, including, but not limited to, declaration of trusts, leases, mortgages, transfer of property (or interest therein), and shares.

Capital gains tax (CGT)
Effective 1 May 2011, the capital gains made from the following assets may be subject to CGT of 10%:

* Land or an interest therein.
* Vessel of over 100 tonnage.
* Yacht.
* Share, security, equity or other financial asset (except shares listed in the South Pacific Stock Exchange).
* Intangible asset.
* Interest in a partnership or trust.
* Aircraft.
* Option, right, or other interest in an asset referred to above.

A capital gain made on disposal of an asset that is used solely to derive income exempt from tax under the Income Tax Act shall be exempt from CGT.

Foreign tax paid in respect of the disposal of a capital asset may be allowed as a tax credit against the CGT payable.

There is no carryforward of capital losses in calculating CGT.

Service turnover tax (STT) (formerly hotel turnover tax)
Effective 1 January 2012, STT at the rate of 5% is imposed on turnover of a person conducting a business involving the provision of a prescribed service, which includes the following:

- Provision of accommodation, refreshments, and other services by a hotel.
- Any services provided in a vessel that is principally or wholly engaged in the carriage of tourists in Fiji.
- Provision of meals and drinks in a bar.
- Provision of services in a nightclub.
- Provision of in-bound tour services.
- Live entertainment provided by artists for a fee.
- Provision of services for recreational activity for gain.
- Provision of services relating to exhibition of films to the public or section thereof by an exhibitor where a charge is made for admission, including services provided by cinema operators.
- Provision of services by rental car operators.
- Provision of meals and beverages by bistros or coffee shops with an annual gross turnover over FJD 1.5 million.
- Provision of meals on sale by restaurants with annual gross turnover over FJD 1.5 million.
- Provision of charter flight services by an aircraft or helicopter with an annual gross turnover over FJD 300,000.
- Provision of all water sports, including underwater activities and river safaris, with an annual gross turnover in excess of FJD 300,000.
- Provision of accommodation in a private residence or property that accommodates tourists, international students, or overseas visitors who are paying guests.

The due date for payment is aligned with the VAT Decree requirements (i.e. end of the month following the taxable period).

Fringe benefit tax (FBT)
Effective 1 January 2012, FBT of 20% is payable on the grossed-up value of certain fringe benefits provided (the effective tax rate is 25%).

Telecommunication levy
Telecommunication levy of 1% is imposed on all voice call charges.

Credit card levy
Credit card levy of 2% is imposed on the monthly credit card balance, including interest and other bank charges.

Third party insurance levy
Third party insurance levy of 20% is imposed on the total third party insurance premium collected in a month.

F

Fiji Islands

Gambling turnover tax (GTT)
Under the Gambling Turnover Tax Decree of 1991, GTT is imposed on the value of consideration paid or payable in respect of the provision of prescribed gambling services (i.e. acceptance of bets and provision of tickets for any lottery) at the rate of 15%.

Branch income

The profits of a foreign company's branch operating in Fiji are subject to the same tax rate as the tax rate levied on profits of a resident corporation (i.e. 20% for tax years commencing on 1 January 2012; previously 28%).

Income determination

Normal tax is payable and assessed on taxable income of the business. Taxable income is calculated by subtracting allowable deductions from all assessable income (i.e. all sources of income).

Inventory valuation
Inventories are normally valued at the lower of cost and net realisable value. While the first in first out (FIFO) method is acceptable, the last in first out (LIFO) method is not, for either book or tax purposes. Conformity between book and tax reporting is not required, and there are no special provisions for valuing inventories or determining inventory flows.

Capital gains
Any profit or gain accrued or derived from the sale or disposal of real or personal property, or any interest therein, shall be subject to income tax when:

* the business of the company comprises dealing in such property
* the property is acquired for the purpose of selling or otherwise disposing thereof, or
* any profit or gain is derived from the carrying on or carrying out of any undertaking or scheme entered into or devised for the purpose of making a profit.

Notwithstanding the above, the profit or gain derived from a transaction that does not form part of a series of transactions and that is not itself in the nature of trade or business shall not be included.

In such a case, the capital gain may be subject to CGT of 10% (*see Capital gains tax [CGT] in the Other taxes section for more information*).

Dividend income
Transfers of property by private companies to shareholders and associates may be deemed to be a dividend paid by that company.

Dividends received from a company incorporated in Fiji by resident corporations are exempt from tax.

Interest income
Interest income over FJD 200 derived by a resident from a financial institution shall be subject to resident interest withholding tax (WHT) of 31%, which may be claimed as a tax credit against income tax payable on income.

Fiji Islands

Partnership income

The income of the partners from a partnership for any income year is equal to each partners' respective share of income from that partnership. Each partner declares income separately and is individually liable for filing a tax return for each applicable year.

Liability of directors/shareholders

Directors/shareholders of companies in liquidation or with insufficient assets to satisfy tax liabilities may be held liable for any outstanding tax liability of the company, under certain conditions.

Other significant items

Where a foreign-controlled business in Fiji produces less income than might be expected, the revenue authorities may determine the income for tax purposes.

An entity normally residing outside Fiji, which disposes of an interest in land in Fiji held directly or through a shareholding in a company, may be assessed for income tax on the profit on that disposal.

Foreign income

Resident corporations are taxed on their worldwide income. Foreign income derived from a treaty country is taxed according to the treaty. Foreign income sourced from a non-treaty country is subject to income tax in Fiji. A credit is allowed in Fiji for foreign tax paid on foreign income. The tax credit is limited to the lesser of the Fiji tax payable or the foreign tax paid on such income. There are no special provisions for taxing undistributed income of foreign subsidiaries.

Deductions

Generally, expenses wholly and exclusively incurred in deriving assessable income are allowable deductions. Expenditures that are capital or domestic in nature are generally not deductible.

Depreciation and depletion

Depreciation is calculated on the cost of an asset on a straight-line basis. The prescribed rates of depreciation are based on the estimated life of the asset. Upon disposal of an asset, either recoupment of depreciation claimed is taxable or the excess of tax written-down value over sale proceeds is deductible. The taxpayer has an option to set-off recoupment of depreciation against the cost of replacement assets. Conformity between book and tax depreciation is not required.

There are seven broad bands of depreciation rates for assets acquired after 1 January 1998, and the prescribed effective life of the asset is used to determine the relevant depreciation rate. The seven broad bands and the depreciation rates are as follows:

Band	Effective life (years)	Standard rate (%)	Maximum rate (%)
1	2 to less than 3	50	60
2	3 to less than 5	$33^{1}/_{3}$	40
3	5 to less than 6 $^{2}/_{3}$	20	24
4	6 $^{2}/_{3}$ to less than 10	15	18
5	10 to less than 20	10	12

Fiji Islands

Band	Effective life (years)	Standard rate (%)	Maximum rate (%)
6	20 to less than 40	5	6
7	40 and over	2.5	3

An optional 20% loading, which applies on the broadband rate, may be claimed. Assets acquired before 1 January 1998 continue to be depreciated at the former rates.

Subject to certain conditions, accelerated depreciation is available for (i) buildings constructed between 1999 and 2014 that are to be used for agricultural, commercial, or industrial purposes; (ii) multi-storey, multi-unit residential buildings; and (iii) other capital expenditure considered of benefit for the economic development of Fiji. Up to one-fifth of the expenditure may be claimed in each of any five years of an eight-year period.

Certain renewable energy plant and water storage facilities also qualify for a 100% write-off.

Capital expenditure aimed at economising on the consumption of fuel, electricity, or its derivatives, or on an asset using energy sources indigenous to Fiji, may be eligible for accelerated depreciation at varying rates.

The cost of the acquisition of a mining lease or tenement and the cost of development of mines may be written off in equal instalments in any five of the first or last eight years of a nine-year period, commencing with the year in which the expenditure was incurred.

A deduction for depletion of other natural resources is not available.

Goodwill
Goodwill, and the amortisation thereof, is generally not deductible for income tax purposes.

Start-up expenses
Start-up expenses are generally not deductible for income tax purposes.

Interest expenses
Interest expenses that are revenue expenditure wholly and exclusively incurred in deriving taxable income are deductible in calculating taxable income.

Provisions
Provisions for expenses not yet incurred (e.g. bad debts) are not tax-deductible. Deductions are generally permitted in respect to amounts that are actually paid or written off.

Charitable contributions
Contributions to approved charitable organisations of up to FJD 100,000 are deductible.

There are certain other specific donations that qualify for varying levels of deductions, including:

- Donations to the Fiji Heritage Foundation, which qualify for a deduction of 150%.
- Cash donations exceeding FJD 50,000 to the Poverty Relief Fund for education, which qualify for a deduction of 200%.

- Cash donations exceeding FJD 100,000 to a Sports Fund (as approved by the Commissioner of Inland Revenue) for purposes of sports development in Fiji, which qualify for a deduction of 150%.

Fines and penalties
Generally, fines and penalties are not deductible for income tax purposes.

Taxes
Taxes levied on income are not deductible. Effective 1 January 2012, only 50% of the employer's statutory FNPF contribution paid by the employer shall be allowed as a deduction for tax purposes in the year the contribution was paid.

F

Net operating losses
From 2012, losses may be carried forward for four consecutive years (previously eight years), provided the company can demonstrate a minimum 51% continuity of shareholding between the year of loss and the year of claim. Notwithstanding the change in ownership, losses may also be carried forward where a company carries on the same business in the carried forward year as it did in the loss year.

In relation to certain hotel business, tax losses may be carried forward for eight years (previously 13 years). *Please refer to the Hotel industry incentives in the Tax credits and incentives section.*

Loss carrybacks are not permitted.

Payments to foreign affiliates
Subject to the normal rules of deductibility, a deduction may be claimed for royalties, management service fees, and interest charges paid to foreign affiliates. However, any deductions claimed by any company carrying on business in Fiji (whether incorporated in Fiji or not) in respect of head office charges or any other like payments shall not exceed 3% of total gross Fiji income.

Group taxation

Group taxation is not available in Fiji.

Transfer pricing
Effective 1 January 2012, the Income Tax Act has been amended to include new transfer pricing provisions. The provisions state that the tax authority may allocate income and expenses between associates (related entities) to reflect income and expenses on an arm's-length basis.

The Income Tax (Transfer Pricing) Regulations have also been issued. The Regulations provide that the Organisation for Economic Co-operation and Development (OECD) Transfer Pricing guidelines may be used in interpreting the provisions of the Regulations in determining income or expenses on an arm's-length basis.

Thin capitalisation
There are no thin capitalisation rules in Fiji.

Fiji Islands

Tax credits and incentives

The tax incentives in Fiji are designed primarily to promote export sales and to encourage the development of industries that are considered of benefit to the economic development of Fiji.

Export income deduction

A deduction for export income is allowed in accordance with the following:

Year of assessment	Percentage of export income to be deducted (%)
2011	50
2012	40
2013	30
2014	20
2015	10

'Export income' means net profit derived by a taxpayer from the business of exporting goods and services; and the Commissioner of Inland Revenue may, where separate records for export income are not maintained, determine such income on the basis of a formula as set out in the legislation.

The 5th Schedule of the Fiji Income Tax Act, 'Export Incentives', has been repealed. However, the existing beneficiaries are expected to continue to enjoy the incentives under this schedule until the expiry of the incentives granted.

Information communication technology (ICT) tax incentives

The income of an information communication technology operator may be exempt from CIT, provided that the business employs 50 employees or more for six months within the income year and 60% or more of the total value of its services in that income year is exported, if it is:

- operating on or before 1 January 2009 in the declared Kalabu Tax Free Zone (exempt from 1 January 2007 to 31 December 2016) or
- granted a licence after 1 January 2009 (exempt for a period of 13 years from the date of issue of the licence).

The following tax incentives are available to taxpayers engaged in new ICT business and for existing taxpayers so engaged who are able to show a significant increase in capacity and number of employees:

- 80% tax exemption for businesses employing more than 101 employees.
- 60% tax exemption for those that employ between 60 and 100 employees.
- 40% tax exemption for those employing 10 to 59 employees.

A 150% deduction is available for costs incurred for the development of an ICT business by any taxpayer employing 500 or more employees. This deduction is available until 31 December 2012.

'Information communication technology business' means an entity engaged in software development, call centres, or internet service provision. It does not include an internet café, any retail or wholesale of information technology products, or the repair, sale, or service of any such products.

Employment incentives

Salary and wages paid to first-time employees for the first 12 months of employment qualify for a 150% deduction. This deduction is available until 31 December 2012.

Hotel industry incentives

Approved capital expenditure incurred in building, renovating, or expanding a hotel is subject to an investment allowance of 55% of the approved expenditure, in addition to normal depreciation.

Under the Short Life Investment Package (SLIP) the following concessions are available to a company:

- Exemption from CIT for a period of ten years, provided that the capital investment in the hotel is more than FJD 7 million.
- Duty-free entry of certain capital equipment, plant, and machinery upon receiving provisional approval from the Minister.
- Permission to generate own electricity, the excess to be sold to the Fiji Electricity Authority.

Any tax losses incurred by an entity granted approval for the investment allowance or SLIP may be carried forward for eight years, but may only be set off against income of the hotel business or from the hotel premises.

The recipients of provisional approval for hotel investment tax incentives are required to commence implementation of the hotel projects within one year from the date provisional approval is granted.

Filmmaking and audiovisual incentives

A tax exemption or reduced tax rate is available on the income of non-resident employees of an approved non-resident company engaged or intending to be engaged in making a film in Fiji.

A resident entity (excluding an entity holding a broadcast license in television or radio in Fiji or with substantial shareholdings in the same) may deduct of up to 150% of expenditure on audio-visual production in respect of income in the year of the expenditure. 'Audio-visual productions' include production for exhibition or sale of theatrical films, broadcast television, direct-to-video and video disk programme, audio recording, computer software, and interactive websites.

A tax exemption is available on the income derived by a taxpayer from the commercial exploitation of a copyright until the taxpayer has received from the commercial exploitation a return of up to 60% of the expenditure. The expenditure must be of capital nature and in relation to the audio-visual production costs in respect of a qualifying audio-visual production.

Tax concessions are also available for residents of areas declared as studio city zones by the appropriate government minister.

Other tax incentives

An investment allowance of 55% is available for the construction or refurbishment and renovation of a vessel, in addition to normal depreciation, subject to certain conditions.

Fiji Islands

An approved mining company may, for a specified period, be exempt from CIT or taxed at a lower rate. The holder of a valid prospecting licence may write off approved expenditure on prospecting for minerals against income from all sources.

A 150% deduction is available for direct capital expenditure incurred by commercial banks in rural banking programmes.

Investors engaged in value adding processes in the food processing, agricultural processing, fisheries, or forestry business may be able to claim a 100% deduction with respect to amounts invested or re-invested (for expansion), provided that the businesses meet the 50% local content rule.

A CIT exemption may be available to a taxpayer engaged in the following commercial agricultural farming and agro-processing activities, subject to certain conditions:

* Any new activity approved and established between 1 January 2009 and 31 December 2009, for a period of four to ten consecutive fiscal years, depending on the level of capital investment.
* Any new activity with a capital investment of at least FJD 2 million approved and established between 1 January 2010 and 31 December 2014, for a period of ten consecutive fiscal years.

Income derived by a taxpayer from a new activity in processing agricultural commodities into bio-fuels may be exempt from CIT for a period of ten years under certain conditions.

An exemption from CIT for a period of five years may be available to a taxpayer engaging in renewable energy projects and power cogeneration.

Entities in the agriculture, fisheries, and tourism industries, with a maximum turnover threshold of FJD 300,000, may also be exempt from CIT.

An investment allowance equal to 60% of the qualifying expenditure is available as a deduction for investment in Fixed Line Next Generation Networks. A qualifying expenditure means an expenditure of FJD 50,000 or more incurred for the purpose of acquiring a capital asset in any of the years from the 2009 year of assessment to the 2012 year of assessment.

A 150% deduction is available on expenses incurred in reorganising a company for the purpose of listing on the South Pacific Stock Exchange.

Effective for tax years commencing on 1 January 2012, 40% of capital expenditure of not less than FJD 50,000 incurred by any existing business located in Vanua Levu is allowed as a deduction for tax purposes, subject to certain conditions.

Foreign tax credit
A credit is allowed in Fiji for foreign tax paid on foreign income, limited to the lesser of the Fiji tax payable or the foreign tax paid on such income.

Withholding taxes

WHTs are levied as follows:

Fiji Islands

Recipient	Dividends	Interest	Royalties	Know-how, management fees	Professional fees
Resident corporations	0	31 (1)	0	0	0
Non-resident corporations:					
Non-treaty	15	10	15	15	15
Treaty:					
Australia	15	10	15	15	0 to 15 (4)
Japan	0 to 15 (4)	10	10	10	0 to 15 (4)
Korea, Republic of	10/15 (2)	10	10	10	0 to 15 (4)
Malaysia	15	15	15	15	0 to 15 (4)
New Zealand	15	10	15	15	0 to 15 (4)
Papua New Guinea	15	10	15	15	0 to 15 (4)
Singapore	5/15 (3)	10	10	10	0 to 15 (4)
United Kingdom	15	10	15	15	0 to 15 (4)

The table is headed **WHT (%)**.

F

Notes

1. Applies to interest (over FJD 200) on savings and deposits with commercial banks and other financial institutions.
2. 10% of gross amount of dividends if beneficial owner is a company (other than a partnership) that holds directly at least 25% of the capital of the company paying the dividends; 15% in all other cases.
3. 5% of gross amount of dividends if beneficial owner is a company (other than a partnership) that holds directly at least 10% of the capital of the company paying the dividends; 15% in all other cases.
4. Depending on the provisions of the applicable double taxation agreement.

Tax administration

The Tax Administration Decree (TAD) was promulgated with the stated intention of harmonising the administration of the various tax laws, including CIT and VAT. FBT and STT are now also covered by the provisions of the TAD.

If a due date falls on a Saturday, Sunday, or holiday, the due date is the last working day before the due date.

Taxable period

Tax is assessed on income derived during the calendar year preceding the year of assessment. Returns are therefore generally accepted on a calendar-year basis, although approval is also given to use an alternative fiscal-year basis. For purposes of assessment of returns completed on a fiscal-year basis, the calendar year in which more than one-half of the fiscal year falls is deemed to be the calendar year in which the income is derived.

Tax returns

The Fiji tax system is not based on self-assessment. Returns of income contain information on the basis of which assessments are raised by the tax authorities.

The due date for lodgement of CIT returns is three months after the end of the income year. However, under the Tax Agent Lodgement Programme, an extension of time may be granted to lodge the CIT returns.

Fiji Islands

Payment of tax

Effective for tax years commencing on 1 January 2012, advance tax payments are required in four instalments, as follows:

- First advance: Due on the last day of the sixth month of the current fiscal year (30% of the estimated tax payable).
- Second advance: Due on the last day of the ninth month of the current fiscal year (30% of the estimated tax payable).
- Third advance: Due on the last day of the fiscal year (30% of the estimated tax payable).
- Fourth advance: Due two months after the fiscal year-end (10% of the estimated tax payable).

The TAD provides for various ways to ensure the collection of taxes including, but not limited to, the following:

- Departure prohibition order: A departure prohibition order may be used by the tax office to prevent taxpayers from leaving the country without settling outstanding taxes.
- Garnishee orders: The tax office may garnish bank accounts for outstanding taxes.
- Registration of charges on personal and real properties of the taxpayer.
- Distress and sale of personal property.
- Temporary closure of business.

Penalties

Administrative penalty provisions have been amended and increased under the TAD. Some of the penalties are as follows:

- Failure to register: Every person who fails to apply for registration as required pursuant to the Decree, commits an offence against the Decree, and will, on conviction, be liable to a fine not exceeding 50% of the tax payable, where the delay does not exceed six months; or a fine not exceeding the tax payable, where the delay exceeds six months.
- Late filing of a return: A registered person who fails to lodge a tax return is liable for a penalty of 20% of the tax payable in the case where tax is payable and, effective 1 January 2012, a penalty of 5% of the tax payable for every month of default.
- Late payment of tax payable: Where any tax remains unpaid on the expiry of the due date, a penalty of 25% of the tax payable in respect of that taxable period will apply.
- Failure to comply with the late payment penalty: Every person who fails to comply with the late payment penalty is liable for penalty of 5% of the unpaid tax for each month of default.
- Failure to maintain proper records: A registered person who fails to keep, retain, or maintain account, documents, or records is liable for a penalty of 75% (knowingly or recklessly made) or 20% (in other cases).
- Insufficient payment of advance taxes: Effective 1 January 2012, a taxpayer who makes insufficient advance payment of taxes on the third and fourth instalments is liable for a penalty of 40% (previously 10%).

Topics of focus for tax authorities

The TAD has introduced a binding ruling system. However, the provisions will only apply after the Minister of Finance has appointed a date by notice in the Gazette.

The tax authorities may void any transaction, agreement, or arrangement made or entered into for the purpose of altering the incidence of tax; relieving any person from tax liability; or defeating, evading, or avoiding any tax imposed.

Finland

PwC contact

Petri Seppälä
PricewaterhouseCoopers Oy
Itämerentori 2
FI-00180 Helsinki, Finland
Tel: +358 9 2280 1909
Email: petri.seppala@fi.pwc.com

Significant developments

As of 1 January 2012, the corporate income tax (CIT) rate decreased from 26% to 24.5%. The new tax rate applies to tax years ending on 1 January 2012 or later (i.e. tax year ended 31 December 2012 for calendar year end companies).

In addition, there have been some changes with respect to withholding taxation. The domestic withholding tax (WHT) on dividends, royalties, and interest paid to foreign entities has been reduced to 24.5%, and the special WHT on certain dividends has decreased to 18.38%.

At the moment, there is no thin capitalisation legislation. However, in April 2012, the Ministry of Finance sent the draft Government Bill concerning intra-group interest deduction limitations out for comments. According to the draft, the rules would be effective from the beginning of 2013.

The Ministry of Finance has also nominated a work group mentioned in the government programme to evaluate the current CIT system and the possibilities to reform it in order to ensure Finland's competitiveness and tax base. The targets of the group's work include e.g. the following:

- Group taxation reform.
- Possibilities to remove the separation of different income sources.
- Expanding possibilities to carry forward net operating losses.

The transfer tax on shares may also be partly increased in 2013.

Taxes on corporate income

Finnish resident companies are subject to Finnish CIT on their worldwide income (i.e. unlimited tax liability). Also, Finnish permanent establishments (PE) of non-resident companies are subject to Finnish CIT on their worldwide income attributable to the PE.

The CIT rate is 24.5%.

Local income taxes
No local income taxes are levied in Finland on the income of a company.

Corporate residence

A company is deemed to be resident on the basis of incorporation. Consequently, a company is deemed to be resident in Finland if it is incorporated (registered) in Finland.

Finland

Permanent establishment (PE)
A PE is, in general, formed in line with the Organisation for Economic Co-operation and Development (OECD) Model Convention.

Other taxes

Value-added tax (VAT)
The general VAT rate is 23%. A reduced rate of 13% is applied to food and animal feed. The reduced VAT rate of 13% also applies to restaurant and catering services. A reduced VAT rate of 9% is applied to books, subscriptions of newspapers and magazines lasting one month or longer, accommodation, and passenger transport.

A zero rate applies in certain instances (e.g. intra-Community supplies of goods and exports of goods). Additionally, certain services (e.g. financial services, insurance services, and certain educational services) are exempted from VAT.

Customs duties
Many goods imported into Finland from outside the European Union (EU) are subject to customs duties. The rates of duty are provided by the EU's Common Customs Tariff and vary widely.

Excise duties
Alcohol and alcoholic beverages, tobacco products, liquid fuels, electricity, natural gas, and coal are subject to EU harmonised excise duties. National excise duties are levied in Finland on waste delivered to landfill sites, lubricating oil, oil imported into or through Finland, ice cream, sweets, soft drinks, beverage containers, and tall oil.

Real estate tax
Municipalities impose an annual real estate tax. The tax is levied on the taxable value of buildings and land. The municipal council determines the applicable tax rates, although the minimum and maximum tax rates are set by tax legislation (e.g. 0.32% to 0.75% for permanent dwellings, 0.6% to 1.35% for other real estate). The tax is deductible from taxable business income if the real estate is used for business purposes. The tax is deductible from taxable income of the so-called other source of income if the real estate is used to acquire other taxable income than business income.

Transfer tax
A transfer tax of 4% of the sales price is payable on the transfer of real estate situated in Finland. The transfer of shares in Finnish companies and other domestic securities is subject to a transfer tax of 1.6% (*see the Significant developments section*). Generally, the transfer tax is payable by the transferee.

No transfer tax is payable on the transfer of securities made through the stock exchange. Similarly, no transfer tax is payable if both the seller and the transferee are non-residents. Transfer tax is, however, always payable on transfers between non-residents if the transferred shares are shares in a Finnish housing or real estate company.

Stamp tax
No stamp taxes are levied in Finland.

Social security contributions

According to the Finnish social security legislation, both Finnish and foreign employers have a liability to pay several social security payments in Finland in cases where an employee performs one's tasks partly or wholly in Finland. The liability concerns all employers, regardless of the form of the company and whether the foreign company has a PE in Finland. The percentage rates for the employer's (and employee's) social security contributions are revised on an annual basis.

Compulsory social security contributions payable by the employer in 2012, according to the paid salaries, are as follows:

*   Employer's social security charge: 2.12% (no cap).
*   Employer's pension insurance contribution: 17.35% (on average, no cap).
*   Employer's unemployment insurance contribution: 0.80% for the first 1,936,500 euros (EUR) of gross salaries and 3.20% for the portion of the gross salaries exceeding EUR 1,936,500 (no cap).
*   Group life insurance premium: 0.07% (on average, no cap).
*   Accident insurance premium: 1.00% (on average, no cap).

The new rates for employer's social security charge are applicable to salaries paid as of 1 January 2012. The employer's social security charge is paid to the regional tax office, and the other contributions are paid to the insurance company. All of these contributions are tax deductible as salary cost.

Compulsory social security contributions payable by the employee in 2012 are as follows:

*   Employee's pension insurance contribution: 5.15% or 6.50% used for employees of age 53 or over (no cap).
*   Employee's unemployment insurance contribution: 0.60% (no cap).

Abovementioned contributions are tax deductible for the employee. These contributions are withheld from the gross salary at the time of salary payment and remitted by the employer to the appropriate insurance company together with the employer's pension and unemployment contributions.

*   Employee's sickness insurance contribution: 2.04% (no cap)

The sickness insurance consists of two payments, daily allowance contribution 0.82% and medicare contribution 1.22%. From these two contributions, only the daily allowance contribution is tax deductible for the employee. The medicare contribution is not tax deductible. Unlike other employee's social security contributions, the sickness insurance contribution is included in the WHT rate of the employee's personal WHT card and, thus, withheld and remitted to the tax authorities together with the withheld income taxes and is finally settled in the final assessment.

If an employee is regarded as a foreign-posted employee and has an A1 certificate or a certificate of coverage from one's home country, neither the aforementioned employer's social security contributions nor the employee's social security charges are payable in Finland.

Finland

Branch income

As a general rule, a branch is taxed like a corporation (tax rate 24.5%) on the profits attributable to it, provided the branch constitutes a PE in Finland. No tax is withheld on transfers of (taxed) profits to the head office.

Income determination

Companies and other legal entities may have income from three different sources: income from business activities, agricultural income, and personal source income. The net taxable income is calculated separately for each source. The expenses of one source of income cannot be deducted from the taxable income of another source, and a loss from one source of income cannot offset taxable income from another source. All taxable income received by a company is taxed at the CIT rate of 24.5% irrespective of the source to which it is attributable.

Income from business and professional activities falls into 'business source' income (taxed in accordance with Business Income Tax Act or BITA), while income from non-business activity is 'personal income'. Typically, personal income is passive income derived, for example, from investments. As an example, rental income from real estate let to non-related companies is usually regarded as 'personal source' income. The same can apply to a dividend received from stock exchange quoted companies, where the recipient of the dividend is a passive holding company. Farming and forestry income are, as a main rule, treated as agricultural source income.

In general, Finland has a very broad income concept, and taxable income includes all income derived from a company's activities, though there are some significant exceptions, including (among others):

- Capital contributions by shareholders.
- In most cases, dividends from unlisted companies (*see Dividend income below*).
- Liquidation gains and capital gains qualifying for the participation exemption (*see Capital gains below*).
- Proceeds from disposal of company's own shares.
- Merger gain.

There is no general distinction between capital gains and other income; capital gains of a company are taxed as part of its general income either in the 'business income' basket or the 'other income' basket. No rates other than the general CIT rate of 24.5% are applied to any part of taxable income of a company.

Taxable income of a company generally is computed on an accrual basis (i.e. income is taxable in the year it is earned). However, exemptions to this main rule do exist, including unrealised exchange gains and losses, which are taxable/deductible in the year of the rate change.

Inventory valuation
Inventories may be written down to the lower of direct first in first out (FIFO) cost, replacement cost, or net realisable value. Conformity between book and tax reporting is required.

Capital gains

Capital gains and losses are generally included in the taxable business income (i.e. sales proceeds are included in the taxable income, and the undepreciated balance of the asset sold is deducted in the sales year) and treated as ordinary income. However, the entire stock of machinery and equipment is treated as a single item, and the capital gain on machinery and equipment is entered as income indirectly by deducting the selling price from the remaining value of the stock of machinery and equipment.

Capital gains arising from the sale of shares are tax exempt via a participation exemption, under certain circumstances. Specifically, capital gains arising from the sale of shares are tax exempt if:

* the seller is not a company carrying out private equity activities (as defined by BITA)
* the seller has owned continuously, for a period of at least one year, at least 10% of the share capital of the target company, and
* the shares are part of the seller's fixed assets and the shareholding is included in the seller's business income source for tax purposes.

For the participation exemption to apply, the target company cannot be a real estate company, a housing company, or a company the activities of which mainly include owning of real estates. The target company must also be a Finnish company, a company referred to in the European Commission (EC) Parent-Subsidiary Directive, or a company resident in a country with which Finland has concluded a tax treaty that applies to the target company's dividend distribution.

Note that a capital gain is taxable to the extent that the gain corresponds with a previous tax-deductible write-down or provision made in connection with the acquisition cost of shares, subsidies received for acquiring shares, or previous capital losses deducted for Finnish tax purposes from intra-group transfer of the shares.

Capital losses are non-deductible in situations where capital gains are exempt from tax.

Dividend income

Dividends received by a Finnish company are tax exempt in most cases. However, dividends received are partly (75%) taxable if:

* the dividend is received on shares belonging to 'investment assets' and the receiving company does not own at least 10% of the equity of the distributing company that is resident in another EU member state and covered by the EC Parent-Subsidiary Directive (note that only financial, pension, and insurance institutions may have assets which are considered as 'investment assets')
* the dividend is received from a company other than a Finnish or EU resident, and
* the dividend is received from a publicly quoted company, the receiving company is not a publicly quoted company, and the shareholding is less than 10% of the equity of the distributing company.

Dividends that a Finnish company receives from other than a company resident in Finland or another EU member state are, however, fully taxable (100%) if there is no applicable tax treaty. Note that most of the Finnish tax treaties include provision enabling tax-exempt dividends from the tax treaty country in case of at least a 10% shareholding.

Finland

Stock dividends
Stock dividends (bonus shares) may be distributed to stockholders, which are corporations and other legal entities with some exceptions, free of tax on the shareholder (*see Dividend income above*).

Interest income
Interest income of a company is taxed as part of its general income, thus the regular CIT rate of 24.5% is applied.

Foreign income
A Finnish corporation is taxed on foreign dividends when the decision to distribute dividends is made and on foreign branch income and other foreign income (e.g. interest and royalties) as earned. The principal method of avoiding double taxation is the credit method, although the exemption method is still applied in a few older treaties (*see the Tax credits and incentives section for more information*).

Deductions

As with taxable income, the concept of deductible costs is wide and covers, in general, all costs incurred in the pursuance of taxable income. Significant exceptions to this rule include (among others):

- Income taxes (*see below*), tax late payment interests, and punitive tax increases.
- Fines and other punitive payments.
- 50% of entertainment costs.
- Capital losses and liquidation losses if capital gains from the sale of shares of a target company would qualify for the participation exemption (*see Capital gains in the Income determination section*).
- Losses from the disposal of a company's own shares.
- Merger losses.

As the accrual method is applied to calculation of taxable income, expenses are usually deductible in the year they are realised (i.e. the year the obligation to pay has arisen).

Depreciation, amortisation, and depletion
Maximum annual rates of depreciation calculated on net book value (declining-balance method) are 25% for machinery and equipment and from 4% to 20% for buildings and other constructions, depending on the type and estimated life of the asset. Net book value is defined as cost less accumulated depreciation and, in the case of machinery and equipment, proceeds on disposal of the assets. The straight-line method is applied to certain intangible assets and capitalised expenditures and to assets with long economic use, such as dams. Tax depreciation is limited to the cumulative charges made in the books.

Costs related to qualifying intangible property are usually amortisable over a period of ten years or a shorter period if the economic life is proven to be less than ten years.

The capital cost of mines, sandpits, quarries, and peat bogs is written off in proportion to the quantities extracted. Short-lived items (the economic life of which is three years or less) may be written off immediately.

Land is not a depreciable asset.

Finland

Goodwill
Acquired goodwill is amortisable for tax purposes over its economic life, up to a maximum of ten years.

Start-up expenses
Start-up expenses are generally deductible expenses when determining taxable income.

Interest expenses
As a general rule, interest expenses are fully deductible. However, the Ministry of Finance has sent the draft Government Bill concerning intra-group interest deduction limitations out for comments (*see the Significant developments section*).

Bad debt
In general, bad debts incurred from sales receivables, etc. are tax deductible. It is also required that the debt is deducted for accounting purposes. Also, loan receivables may be tax deductible in cases where external loans or ownership of less than 10% is in question.

Charitable contributions
Donations are deductible for CIT purposes in certain cases.

In order to be tax deductible, the amount of a donation should be at least:

- EUR 850, but not more than EUR 250,000. In addition, it is required that the donation is made to a European Economic Area (EEA) member state or to a publicly financed university or other higher educational institution of Finland or any other EEA country, to benefit the sciences, the arts, or the Finnish cultural heritage.
- EUR 850, but not more than EUR 50,000. In addition, it is required that the donation is made to an association, foundation, or other institution in the EEA nominated by the Tax Administration and to benefit the sciences, the arts, or the Finnish cultural heritage.

Donations of not more than EUR 850 (e.g. to charitable purposes) are, in general, tax deductible.

Taxes
No income taxes are deductible when determining taxable income. However, the real estate tax is deductible.

Net operating losses
Losses may be carried forward for ten subsequent years. However, the right to carryforward may be forfeited in certain instances, such as in cases where there is a direct or indirect change in the ownership of the company operating at a loss. Loss carrybacks are not allowed.

Payments to foreign affiliates
A Finnish corporation may claim a deduction for royalties, service fees, and interest charges paid to foreign affiliates, provided the underlying transaction is beneficial to it and the amounts paid are at arm's length.

Finland

Group taxation

Companies within a group are not consolidated for CIT purposes. However, via group contributions (i.e. lump sum payments of cash based on annual taxable profits), group companies may even out their taxable profits and losses, which leads effectively to the same result as consolidation would. A group contribution is a deductible cost for the granting company and taxable income for the receiving company, provided that all of the following are true:

* Both companies belong to a structure where there is a direct or indirect common ownership of at least 90%, and the structure has existed for the entire tax year.
* Both companies are Finnish resident for tax purposes.
* Both companies are limited liability companies or co-operatives with business activities (i.e. have a source of income from business activities, *see the Income determination section*) and are not financial, insurance, or pension institutions.
* The contribution is recorded in the annual statutory accounts of both companies involved and must affect their annual net income.
* The accounting period for both companies ends at the same date.
* The amount of contribution does not exceed the taxable business income of the granting company.
* The contribution is not considered a capital investment.

Based on case law, the ownership chain may also be traced via foreign entities, provided there is a tax treaty between Finland and the country wherein the ultimate parent for the group is resident.

Transfer pricing
All transactions between related parties must happen at arm's length. The requirement is imperative even in relation to purely domestic transactions. If the arm's-length requirement is not followed, income or deductions of a company may be adjusted for tax purposes, in addition to which a risk for substantial penalties exists.

A Finnish company is obliged to prepare transfer pricing documentation to support transactions between its non-Finnish related parties. Documentation is subject to statutory requirements regarding content, which vary depending on the volume of related party transactions. The documentation requirement does not concern small and medium-sized companies that have less than 250 employees and feature a turnover of no larger than EUR 50 million or a balance sheet of no more than EUR 43 million.

Thresholds are calculated at the group level. Failure to present appropriate documentation may lead to a punitive tax increase.

Thin capitalisation
There is no special legislation governing thin capitalisation. A Finnish company may deduct interest payments to affiliates provided that the amount of debt and rate of interest are at arm's length. If not, a possibility for application of the general anti-avoidance provision may exist.

Note that the Ministry of Finance has sent the draft Government Bill concerning intra-group interest deduction limitations out for comments (*see the Significant developments section*).

Finland

Controlled foreign companies (CFCs)

The Finnish CFC regime was amended in 2009 for the purpose of bringing the regime into compliance with European Community law.

The CFC rules are applicable with respect to foreign entities in low tax jurisdictions controlled by Finnish residents. The undistributed profits of such foreign entities may be taxed as profit of the Finnish resident direct or indirect shareholders. The entity is deemed to be controlled by Finnish residents if at least 50% of the capital or total voting rights are directly or indirectly held by Finnish residents or if Finnish residents have the right to at least 50% of the profits of the entity. The taxable person in such a case is the Finnish resident shareholder who owns directly or indirectly at least 25% of the capital of the corporate body or have right to at least 25% of the profits of the entity. A foreign entity is considered to be low taxed if the actual income tax burden of the foreign corporation in its country of residence is lower than three-fifths of the tax burden of a comparable Finnish corporation (i.e. an effective rate of less than 14.7%, which is three-fifths of the Finnish tax rate of 24.5%).

Foreign PEs of non-resident companies can be regarded as equal to foreign companies provided that the PE's profits are not taxed in the head office state. Due to the transitional period, the PE provision would be applicable to PEs of foreign entities only as of 1 January 2015.

Certain types of businesses are excluded from the scope of the CFC rules (e.g. income principally from industrial, manufacturing, or shipping activities, as well as sales or marketing activities related to such activities, if they are directed principally to the country of residence of the sales or marketing company). Also, companies resident in a country with which Finland has a double tax treaty (DTT) generally are outside the scope of the CFC rules if the company does not benefit from any special tax incentives in that treaty country. Tax treaty countries that are not covered by this rule are exhaustively mentioned in a specific 'black list' provided by the Ministry of Finance. These countries are Barbados, Bosnia-Herzegovina, Georgia, Macedonia, Malaysia, Moldova, Montenegro, Serbia, Singapore, Switzerland, United Arab Emirates, and Uzbekistan.

In addition to these two mentioned exclusions, the Finnish CFC rules are not applicable in cases of genuine economical establishment in a foreign country, which is either an EU/EEA member state or a tax treaty state not on the 'black list'. The genuine economical establishment is evaluated in light of the requirements of the business in question and paying special attention to capable personnel and office space located in the low tax jurisdiction.

Tax credits and incentives

Foreign tax credit

The principal method of avoiding double taxation is the credit method, although the exemption method is still applied in a few older treaties. Foreign tax can be credited against taxes payable in Finland on the same income over the same period on a pro-rata basis. The credit is given for taxes paid to a foreign state and covered by the relevant double tax treaty. The maximum credit is the lesser of either the amount of the foreign tax or an amount equal to the Finnish tax payable on the income from a foreign state. This maximum is calculated on a source-by-source basis. Unused credit of foreign tax paid may be carried forward for five years on an income basket basis.

Finland

Research and development (R&D) activities

Qualifying R&D related costs may be deducted annually under certain circumstances, despite the fact that they should be capitalised under general rules.

Withholding taxes

Finnish corporations paying certain types of income are required to apply a 24.5% or 18.38% WHT on payments to foreign corporations and a 30% WHT on payments to non-resident individuals or other than corporate entities.

According to domestic legislation, interest paid to a non-resident is usually tax exempt in Finland.

Dividends paid to a company referred to in the EC Parent-Subsidiary Directive, owning at least 10% of the capital of the dividend distributing company, are also tax exempt.

No WHT is levied on dividend payments received by companies resident in the EU/EEA area (other than in Liechtenstein), which would have been tax-free if paid to a Finnish corporate body, if the WHT cannot be credited in the company's country of residence.

The domestic WHT rate is 18.38% if the requirements for WHT exemption listed above are not met and

- the non-resident recipient is a financial, insurance, or pension institution resident in the EU/EEA area (other than Lichtenstein)
- the shares belong to its investment assets, or
- the non-resident recipient is a non-listed company or a private company resident in the EU/EEA area (other than Lichtenstein) receiving dividends from a resident listed company in which it holds less than 10%.

See the table below for WHT rates on dividends and other payments from Finland to non-residents.

For countries not included in table, the WHT rate is 24.5% (corporate entity) and 30% (individual or other than corporate entity).

Note that each tax treaty should be studied carefully because there are often exceptions to general rules.

Recipient	WHT (%)			
	Dividend (portfolio)/interest on cooperative capital	Dividend (direct investment) *	Investment fund profit share	Royalties
Argentina	15	10 [25%]	24.5/30	15 (18)
Armenia	15	5 [25%]	0	10 (6)
Australia	15	5 [10%] (6, 14)	24.5/30	5 (8)
Austria	10 (2)	0 [10%] (2, 14)	0	5 (24)
Azerbaijan	10	5 [25%] (8)	24.5/30	5 (4)
Barbados	15 (5)	5 [10%] (14)	24.5/30	5 (1, 5)
Belarus	15	5 [25%]	0	5

Recipient	WHT (%) Dividend (portfolio)/interest on cooperative capital	Dividend (direct investment) *	Investment fund profit share	Royalties
Belgium	15 (2)	5 [25%] (2)	0	5 (1, 24)
Bosnia-Herzegovina	15	5 [25%]	0	10
Brazil (see protocol)	24.5/30	24.5/30	24.5/30	24.5/30
Bulgaria	10 (2)	10 (2)	0	5 (1, 24)
Canada	15	5 [10%] (14)	24.5/30	10 (1)
China, P.R. of	10	5 [25%]	24.5/30	10 (9)
Croatia	15	5 [25%]	0	10
Cyprus	24.5/30 (2, 23)	24.5/30 (2, 23)	24.5/30 (15)	24.5/30 (24)
Czech Republic	15 (2)	5 [25%] (2)	0	10 (1, 16, 24)
Denmark (including the Faroe Islands)	15 (2)	0 [10%]	0	0
Egypt	10	10	24.5/30	24.5/25
Estonia	15 (2)	5 [25%] (2)	24.5/30 (15)	10 (12, 24)
France	0	0	0	0
Georgia	10	0 [50%]/5 [10%] (8)	0	0
Germany	15 (2)	10 [25%] (2)	See dividend (15)	5 (1, 24)
Great Britain	0 (5)	0	0 (5, 15)	0 (5)
Greece	13 (2)	13 (2)	0	10 (1, 24)
Hungary	15 (2)	5 [25%] (2)	0	5 (1, 24)
Iceland	15 (2)	0 [10%]	0	0
India	10	10	24.5/30	10
Indonesia	15	10 [25%]	24.5/30	15 (4)
Ireland, Rep. of	0 (5)	0	0 (5, 15)	0 (5)
Israel	15	5 [10%]	0	10
Italy	15 (2)	10 [50%] (2)	0	5 (1, 24)
Japan	15	10 [25%] (8)	0	10
Kazakhstan	15	5 [10%]	0	10
Korea, Rep. of	15	10 [25%]	0	10
Kyrgyzstan	15	5 [25%]	0	5
Latvia	15 (2)	5 [25%] (2)	24.5/30 (15)	10 (12, 24)
Lithuania	15 (2)	5 [25%] (2)	24.5/30 (15)	10 (12, 24)
Luxembourg	15 (2)	5 [25%] (2)	0	5 (1, 24)
Macedonia	15	0 [10%] (14)	0	0
Malaysia	15	5 [10%]	24.5/30	5
Malta	15	5 [10%] (2, 14)	0	0
Mexico	0	0	24.5/30	10
Moldova	15	5 [25%]	0	7 (6)
Morocco	15	15	0	10
Netherlands	15 (2)	0 [5%]	0	0
New Zealand	15	15	24.5/30	10
Norway	15 (2)	0 [10%]	0	0
Pakistan	20 (20)	12 [25%]	24.5/30	10
Philippines	24.5/30	15 [10%] (14)	24.5/30	24.5/25 (3)
Poland	15 (2)	5 [25%]	0	5 (24)

Finland

	WHT (%)			
Recipient	Dividend (portfolio)/interest on cooperative capital	Dividend (direct investment) *	Investment fund profit share	Royalties
Portugal	15 (2)	10 [25%] (2)	0	10 (24)
Romania	5 (2)	5 (2)	0	5 (19, 24)
Russia	12	5 [30%] (7)	0	0
Serbia and Montenegro	15	5 [25%]	0	10
Singapore	10	5 [10%] (14)	24.5/30	5
Slovak Republic	15 (2)	5 [25%] (2)	0	10(1,16,24)
Slovenia	15 (2)	5 [25%] (2)	0	5 (24)
South Africa	15	5 [10%]	0	0
Spain	15 (2)	10 [25%] (2)	0	5 (24)
Sri Lanka	15	15	0	10
Sweden	15 (2)	0 [10%]	0	0
Switzerland	10	0 [10%]	0	0
Tanzania	20	20	0	20
Thailand	24.5/30	20 [25%] (13)	24.5/30	15
Turkey	20	15 [25%]	24.5/30	10
Ukraine	15	5 [20%]	0	10 (17)
United Arab Emirates	24.5/30 (22)	24.5/30 (22)	24.5/30 (22)	24.5/30 (22)
United States	15 (21)	5 [10%] (14, 21)	0	0
Uzbekistan	15	5 [10%] (14)	0	10 (6)
Vietnam	15	5 [70%]/10 [25%]	24.5/30	10
Zambia	15	5 [25%]	24.5/30	15 (1, 11)

Notes

* The recipient is a company whose share in the company making the payment is at least the percentage indicated in brackets.

1. Tax is not levied on literary, scientific, or artistic royalties (for film royalties see text of treaty).
2. If corporate entity, then:
   • no tax if these dividends were tax free under Business Tax Act and if the recipient does not receive a full credit for the Finnish tax in the country of residence, and
   • no tax on dividend paid to a company meant in the EC Parent-Subsidiary Directive owning at least 10% of the capital of the paying company.
3. The tax rate is 15% on films, tapes used in television or radio broadcasts, use of copyright of literary, artistic, or scientific works, or royalty paid for usufruct.
4. The tax rate is 10% on literary, scientific, artistic, and film royalties.
5. The tax rate for an individual is 30% if income is tax-exempt in the country of residence.
6. A lower tax in certain cases.
7. Foreign capital greater than 100,000 United States dollars (USD) when dividend becomes due and payable.
8. See the treaty for additional requirements.
9. The tax rate is 7% on industrial, scientific, and commercial royalties.
10. The tax agreement does not apply if the recipient is a special holding company.
11. The tax rate is 5% on royalties from films and tapes.
12. The tax rate is 5% on royalties paid for the use of industrial, commercial, or scientific equipment.
13. The tax rate is 15% if the payer is also an industrial enterprise.
14. The 10% is calculated on the total voting stock.
15. There is no tax on profit shares meant in EC Directive 2003/48/EC.
16. The tax rate is 1% for finance lease of equipment, 5% for operating lease of equipment and computer software.
17. The tax rate is 5% for the use of secret process or for know-how, no tax for computer software, or patent.

Finland

18. The tax rate is 10% on industrial royalty, 3% on royalties to news agency, and 5% on artistic royalty to the author or the author's *mortis causa* successor.
19. The tax rate is 2.5% on royalties paid for the use of industrial, commercial, or scientific equipment or computer software.
20. The tax rate is 15% if the recipient is a company.
21. No tax on dividends to qualified parents-subsidiaries and pension funds.
22. No tax, if the recipient proves that one has domicile (individual) or is incorporated in the United Arab Emirates.
23. If corporate entity tax is 18.38% or 24.5%.
24. No tax on royalties between associated companies meant in EC Directive 2003/49/EC.

Non-treaty areas include Andorra, Antigua and Barbuda, Bahama Islands, Bahrain, Belize, Cayman Islands, Channel-Islands, Cyprus, Gibraltar, Grenada, Greenland, Hong Kong, the Spitsbergen, Jan Mayen, Liberia, Macao, Mauritius, Monaco, Panama, Samoa, San Marino, Vanuatu, and Virgin Islands.

F

Tax administration

Taxable period

The tax year is generally the calendar year. A company having an accounting period other than the calendar year is taxed for the accounting period or the accounting periods ending during the calendar year.

Tax returns

A company must file a CIT return within four months from the end of the accounting period.

Payment of tax

Income taxes are levied as prepayments during the tax year. Advance tax payments for companies are collected in two or 12 instalments during the tax year. If the total amount to be paid is not more than EUR 1,700, the instalments are due in the third and the ninth month of the accounting period. If the total amount to be paid exceeds EUR 1,700, the instalments are due monthly (due date is the 23rd day of each month).

If the final taxes exceed the advance payments, the difference is payable in the form of a supplementary payment due on the 25th day of the month following the month during which the final assessment is completed (ten months after the end of accounting period). Interest is payable on the supplementary amount if paid after the filing deadline of the CIT return (*see above*).

After the assessment of the taxes, any excess prepayments are refunded without application.

Audit cycle

Tax audits are performed at irregular intervals by tax auditors who are entitled to examine the accounts of a company and to request additional information necessary to the examination. Generally, the taxpayer receives an advance notice of an audit from the tax authorities.

Statute of limitations

Tax assessment must be completed within ten months from the end of the last month of the accounting year. After the assessment, a tax office can change an incorrect assessment. A correction for the benefit of the taxpayer has to be made in five years, calculated from the beginning of the year following the assessment year.

Any correction disadvantageous for the taxpayer must be made within the following time limits, calculated from the beginning of the year following the assessment year:

Finland

- One year: All errors.
- Two years: Writing errors made by the administration, calculation errors, and other comparable errors, as well as errors caused by erroneous or inadequate information given by third parties.
- Five years: If the taxpayer has failed to file one's return or e.g. has filed an incomplete, false, or misleading return.

Topics of focus for tax authorities
Current issues in special focus of tax audits are transfer pricing and permanent establishments.

The Tax Account system
As of the beginning of 2010, a new system for reporting and paying unprompted taxes (e.g. VAT and employer's social charges) was introduced. The Tax Account system is a taxpayer-specific information system under which unprompted taxes are declared on a monthly basis. There are changes in the existing system of monthly returns, due dates, payments, and refunds. Payments are made through regular payment channels.

Tax types not covered by the Tax Account system are income tax, real estate tax, inheritance tax, gift tax, forestry fees, and transfer tax. It is important to note that WHTs are henceforth declared through the Tax Account system.

Other issues

Company restructurings
In accordance with the EC directive 2009/133/EC on mergers, divisions, partial divisions, transfers of assets, and exchanges of shares concerning companies of different EU member states, it is possible to carry out the said restructurings tax neutral, if statutory conditions are met. In cross-border situations, both parties should be resident in the European Union. The principal of going concern is applied in taxation (i.e. the receiving company receives the assets with the values the transferring company had for those assets in its taxation).

France

PwC contact

Michel Combe
Landwell & Associés
Crystal Park
61 rue de Villiers
92208 Neuilly-sur-Seine Cedex
France
Tel: +33 1 56 57 45 86
Email: michel.combe@fr.landwellglobal.com

Significant developments

New French Financial Transaction Tax
The first amended Finance Act for 2012 introduced a financial transaction tax (FTT).
The FTT applies to transactions consisting of acquiring equity securities or similar
securities. This also includes instruments giving access to capital or voting rights in the
company and includes securities issued under foreign law.

These transactions will be in the scope of the FTT if the following criteria are met:

* foresaid securities are issued by listed companies that have their head office in
  France and whose market capitalisation exceeds 1 billion euros (EUR) on 1 January
  of the year during which the transfer occurs
* foresaid securities are listed on a regulated market
* the acquisition of the above specified French listed equity securities arises from a
  direct sale, the exercise of a physically settled option, a forward sale with physical
  delivery, an exchange, or an acquisition of said securities as consideration for a
  capital contribution, and
* the transactions result in a transfer of ownership of said securities for consideration.

The FTT does not apply, in particular, in the following situations: primary market,
clearing house/central depositary, market making activities, intra-group transaction,
and temporary transfers.

The FTT applies to securities issued by entities that have their registered head office in
France, regardless of whether the transaction is executed inside or outside France.

The tax amounts to 0.1% of the acquisition price of the shares and is due by the
financial intermediary that has executed the purchase order or the custodian,
irrespective of its place of establishment.

Date of implementation: acquisitions made as from 1 August 2012 will be subject to
the FTT.

Transfer taxes on the disposal of listed shares

Finance Act for 2012
Article 3 of the Finance Act for 2012 has introduced new provisions regarding transfer
taxes. Amongst others, the new Finance Act has amended the provisions regarding the
disposal of listed shares. The new provisions are applicable to transfers realised as of 1
January 2012.

France

This Article removed the transfer duties cap (EUR 5,000) applicable to the sale of shares of French companies and introduced the following new rates:

- 3% for the portion of the value below EUR 200,000.
- 0.5% for the portion of the value between EUR 200,000 and EUR 500 million.
- 0.25% for the portion of the value above EUR 500 million.

The Finance Act extended the territorial scope of this tax to all sales of listed shares issued by listed companies having their head office in France and that are documented by a written deed, irrespective of whether that deed is executed in France or outside of France.

The Finance Act introduced specific tax exemptions to existing ones, notably share buy-backs by the issuing company, transfer of shares in companies placed under a safeguard or receivership procedure, sale of shares between companies that are members of the same tax consolidated group, and share-for-share exchanges that fall within the scope of roll-over relief under the EU Merger Directive, as implemented in France.

Amended Finance Act for 2012
The French Parliament finally decided to maintain the regime amended in December 2011 but has reduced the rate applicable to listed shares to 0.1% and let the cap of EUR 5,000 be removed.

The territorial scope of the transfer duties is unchanged.

Several exemptions were added to the list of transactions that are not subject to transfer duties:

- Transactions subject to the FTT.
- Repurchase by companies of their own shares intended to be sold to the subscribers of a company employee saving plan.
- Transactions between companies in the same group within the meaning of article L233-3 of the French Commercial Code.
- Transfer of ownership resulting from a merger, a contribution, or a spin-off made under the provisions of article 210 A and 210 B of the French Tax Code and acquisition shares of a company by its employees.

Conversely, some share-buy-back operations will no longer benefit from the exemption provided by the Finance Act for 2012.

The changes introduced by the Amended Finance Act for 2012 will be applicable to sales realised as of 1 August 2012.

The text as amended by Finance Act for 2012 is applicable until then.

Temporary corporate income tax (CIT) surcharge
Article 30 of the fourth amended Finance Act for 2011 introduced a new CIT surcharge of 5%.

This tax is applicable to companies that (i) are liable to CIT and (ii) have a turnover higher than EUR 250 million.

Regarding French tax groups, the turnover to be used corresponds to the aggregate of the turnover of each company member of the tax group.

The amount of the contribution is determined by applying a rate of 5% to the foresaid tax base.

The global CIT rate is therefore raised to 36.10%.

This temporary tax is applicable to fiscal years ending on or after 31 December 2011 until 30 December 2013.

Corporate tax losses
The second amended Finance Act for 2011 has restricted the mechanism to use corporate tax losses.

The new rules regarding tax losses are applicable starting from fiscal years ending on 21 September 2011.

Carryforward of tax losses
The new provisions set out that tax losses carried forward are available to offset the first EUR 1 million of taxable profits arising in future periods and 60% of taxable profits in excess of this.

Carryback of tax losses
Tax losses will now only be available for carryback to the fiscal year immediately preceding that in which the losses arise and up to a maximum of EUR 1 million. Any unused surplus will be carried forward and used as set out above. In addition, the election to carry back tax losses must be filed prior to the deadline for submission of the tax return for the loss-making period.

Tax groups
The overall tax losses of a French tax group, as well as pre-election tax losses of the individual members of the group will be attributed, whether carried forward or carried back, in the same manner and within the same limits as those set out above.

New limitation on interest expense deductibility
In accordance with Article 40 of the fourth amended Finance Act for 2011 (i.e. '*Carrez Amendment*'), interest expenses incurred by a French company for the acquisition of participation or shareholding acquisitions will not be deductible for CIT purposes if the French acquiring company is not in a position to demonstrate that it actually:

- makes decisions relating to the acquired participation and
- exercises an actual control or influence over the participations.

The purpose of the legislation is to prevent the interest deduction for the participation acquisition by a French entity when the acquired participation is effectively managed outside of France.

This new rule will not apply where:

- the total fair market value of the participations owned by the French acquiring company does not exceed EUR 1 million
- the participation acquisition has not been financed by debt at the level of the French acquiring company or at the level of a company of the same group, or
- the debt-to-equity ratio of the group is equal to or higher than the acquiring company's debt-to-equity ratio.

France

Transfer taxes on the disposal of shares in real estate companies
According to the Article 5 of the Finance Act for 2012, in case of disposal of shares held in real estate companies, the taxable basis for transfer tax purposes is equal to the fair market value of the real estate assets or rights reduced by the debt contracted for the acquisition of such assets or rights.

Other kinds of debts are not taken into account to compute the taxable basis of the transfer tax.

Capital gains and losses on shares sold to a related company
In accordance with the Article 41 of the amended Finance Act for 2011, capital gains deriving from the disposal of shares held in subsidiaries for less than two years are immediately taxable at the common rate of CIT.

Capital losses deriving from such disposal are not immediately deductible. In such a case, the loss will be deducted if, before a period of two years (as from the date of acquisition by the purchaser):

* the vendor stops being subject to CIT
* the shares are, after a restructuring of the transferee company, held by a company that is not related to the vendor, or
* the shares stop being held by the related company (notably further to a new sale).

If no event mentioned above arises within a period of two years starting from the acquisition by the vendor, the capital loss that has not been immediately deducted is treated in accordance with the long-term regime (i.e. the capital loss is therefore not deductible).

Otherwise, the vendor has to join to its corporate tax return a specific form mentioning capital losses that are not immediately deducted.

These new rules apply to fiscal years that open starting from 1 January 2012.

Limitation on royalty deductions
Article 11 of the Finance Act for 2012 restricts the conditions for deducting licensing royalties where the licensor and the licensee are related parties. A full deduction for the royalty expense may only be allowed if the licensee can demonstrate, and properly document, that:

* the use of the licence results in added value for the licensee over the entire licensing period and
* such use is real (i.e. does not consist in an artificial scheme).

Turnover taxes

Increase of the common rate of 19.6% to 21.2%
As of 1 October 2012, the common rate of 19.6% will be increased to 21.2%.

Introduction of a second reduced rate of 7%
According to Article 13 of the amended Finance Act for 2011, a second reduced rate of 7% is applicable, as of 1 January 2012, to most products formerly subject to a turnover tax rate of 5.5% (i.e. transport of persons, sales of certain kinds of medicines, book sales, etc.).

The following products remain subject to the rate of 5.5%:

- Alimentary products.
- Subscription to gas and electricity (under certain circumstances).
- Products and services provided to disabled persons.

Contributions on certain beverages containing added sugar or synthetic sweeteners

Articles 26 and 27 of the Finance Act for 2012 introduced new contributions on (i) beverages containing added sugar and (ii) drinks containing artificial sweeteners.

The amount of each of these contributions is EUR 7.16 per hectolitre.

Taxes on corporate income

France levies CIT at a rate of 33.33%.

A resident company is subject to CIT in France on its French-source income. In that respect, income attributable to foreign business activity (if there is no treaty in force between France and the relevant foreign country) or to a foreign permanent establishment (PE) (if a tax treaty applies) is excluded from French tax basis.

A non-resident company is subject to CIT in France on income attributable to French business activity or to a French permanent establishment (PE), as well as on income from real estate located in France.

Social contribution tax

Concerning large size companies, a social contribution tax amounting to 3.3% is assessed on the CIT amount from which a EUR 763,000 allowance is withdrawn.

Temporary CIT surcharge

A CIT surcharge of 5% assessed on the CIT amount is due by companies whose turnover exceeds EUR 250 million.

This temporary surcharge is applicable to fiscal years ending on or after 31 December 2011 until 30 December 2013.

Patent box regime

Under certain conditions, income derived from the sale or license of patents or patentable inventions is taxed at a reduced 15% rate.

Capital gains

A reduced tax rate of 15% applies to certain capital gains. *See Capital gains in the Income determination section for more information.*

Local income taxes

No tax is levied on income at the regional or local level.

France

Corporate residence

France is defined as metropolitan France (excluding Monaco, but including the continental shelf), Corsica, and the overseas departments (French Guyana, Guadeloupe, Martinique, Reunion).

As a general rule, a resident company is a company that is incorporated under French commercial laws.

Permanent establishment (PE)

The notion of PE is not defined by the French Tax Code and has been specified by a case law of the French Administrative Supreme Court (i.e. *'Conseil d'Etat'*). The notion of PE refers to an enterprise exploited in France that can be materialised in one of the three following situations:

- Business activity conducted through an establishment, that is, a fixed business installation operating with some degree of autonomy (e.g. a branch, sales office, etc.).
- Business conducted in France by a dependant agent.
- Existence of a complete commercial cycle in France.

Other taxes

Turnover taxes

Turnover taxes are assessed on goods sold and services rendered in France, and operate much like a value-added tax (VAT). The normal rate is 19.6% (increased to 21.2% as of 1 October 2012). Sales of certain kinds of medicines, transports of persons, and sales of books are taxable at a 7% reduced rate. Food products, subscription to gas and electricity (under certain circumstances), and products and services provided to disabled persons are taxable at a 5.5% rates. Other specific sales and services are taxable at a 2.1% reduced rate. Exports and certain specific services invoiced to non-French residents are zero-rated.

Business-to-business (B2B) suppliers of services are taxable at the location of the customer and not at the location of the supplier. For business-to-consumer (B2C) suppliers of services, the place of taxation is where the supplier is established.

Turnover taxation applies only to taxable persons, partly taxable persons, and non-taxable legal persons that are registered for turnover taxes.

Specific turnover taxation rules apply to leases of transportation equipment; cultural, arts and sports services; electronic and telecommunication services; and transportations of goods.

Real estate tax

All properties located in France are subject to a 3% real estate tax. The tax is assessed annually on the fair market value of the real estate, in proportion to the direct or indirect interest held. All entities in the chain of ownership are jointly liable for the payment of the tax.

Automatic exemptions apply in three situations. First, to entities whose French real estate assets represent less than 50% of their total French assets. Second, to entities listed on a regulated market whose shares, units, or rights are significantly traded on a regular basis. Third, to entities having their registered office in France, in a European Union (EU) member state, or in a country that has concluded a double tax treaty (DTT) with France providing for an administrative assistance or a non-discrimination clause, where:

- their direct or indirect interest in the French real estate is less than either EUR 100,000 or 5% of the fair market value of the French real estate
- they are pension funds or public charities recognised as fulfilling a national interest whose activities justify the need to own French real estate, or
- they are non-listed French real estate funds (*société de placement à prépondérance immobilière à capital variable* [SPPICAV] or *fonds de placement immobilier* [FPI]) or foreign funds subject to equivalent regulations.

Where an automatic exemption does not apply, a claim may be submitted for conditional exemption.

Territorial economic contribution

The territorial economic contribution (*Contribution Economique Territoriale* or CET) is comprised of two different taxes: the companies' land contribution (*Cotisation Foncière des Entreprises* or CFE) and the companies' added value contribution (*Cotisation sur la valeur ajoutée des entreprises* or CVAE). Although they have a similar scope, the taxes are subject to very different rules.

The CFE tax is based on the rental value of assets that are subject to the real estate tax, excluding movable goods and equipment. For industrial plants, the taxable base is reduced by 30%. There is a specific rental value for each town and an upgrading ratio is set forth at the national level each year.

The CVAE is based on a company's added value. Only taxpayers which are not exempt from the CFE and whose turnover is greater than EUR 152,500 are subject to CVAE. However, tax relief equal to the amount of the tax is provided for companies whose turnover is below EUR 500,000. The tax rate for companies whose turnover ranges from EUR 500,000 to EUR 50 million is assessed according to a progressive scale, which ranges from 0% to 1.5%.

There is an upper ceiling on the added value that applies to the CET. As a consequence, tax relief applies and is equal to the excess of the sum of CFE and CVAE over 3% of the added value of the company.

Registration duties

Registrations duties mentioned hereafter are imposed on the purchaser. However, the seller may be liable for these duties in case of non-settlement by the purchaser.

Transfer of goodwill

The transfer of goodwill is subject to a registration duty at a rate of 3% on the part of the transfer price amounting from EUR 23,000 to EUR 200,000 and at a rate of 5% on the part exceeding EUR 200,000.

Transfers of shares

Regime applicable until 31 December 2011
Until 31 December 2011, the transfer of shares of *Société anonyme* (SAs, which are corporations) and *Société par Actions Simplifiées* (SASs, which are simplified

France

corporations) was subject to registration duty at a rate of 3%, with a maximum of EUR 5,000 per transfer.

Regime applicable as of 1 January 2012 until 1 August 2012
The transfer duties cap (EUR 5,000) applicable to the sale of shares of French companies is removed, and the following new rates are introduced:

* 3% for the portion of the value below EUR 200,000.
* 0.5% for the portion of the value between EUR 200,000 and EUR 500 million.
* 0.25% for the portion of the value above EUR 500 million.

The territorial scope of this tax is extended to all sales of listed shares issued by listed companies having their head office in France and that are documented by a written deed, irrespective of whether that deed is executed in France or outside of France.

Specific tax exemptions are introduced, notably share buy-backs by the issuing company, transfer of shares in companies placed under a safeguard or receivership procedure, sale of shares between companies that are members of the same tax consolidated group, and share-for-share exchanges that fall within the scope of roll-over relief under the EU Merger Directive, as implemented in France.

Regime applicable as of 1 August 2012
As of 1 August 2012, the transfer of shares will be subject to registration duty at a rate of 3% with no cap.

The transfer of listed shares recorded by a deed will be subject to registration duty at a rate of 0.1%.

Several exemptions are added to the list of the transactions that are not subject to transfer duties:

* Transactions subject to the FTT.
* Repurchase by companies of their own shares intended to be sold to the subscribers of a company employee saving plan.
* Transactions between companies in the same group within the meaning of article L233-3 of the French Commercial Code.
* Transfer of ownership resulting from a merger, a contribution, or a spin-off made under the provisions of article 210 A and 210 B of the French Tax Code and acquisition shares of a company by its employees.

Conversely, some share-buy-back operations will no longer benefit from the above mentioned exemption applicable as of 1 January 2012.

Transfer of interest or quotas in legal entities whose capital is not divided into shares
The transfer of interests or quotas in legal entities whose capital is not divided into shares (e.g. *Société à responsabilité limitée* or SARLs, which are a form of private limited liability corporate entity) is subject to a registration duty of 3%.

Transfer of shares in non-quoted real estate companies
The transfer of shares in non-quoted companies whose assets consist principally of immovable property is subject to a registration duty of 5%. According to Article 5 of the Finance Act for 2012, in case of disposal of shares held in real estate companies, the taxable basis for transfer tax purposes is equal to the fair market value of the real estate assets or rights reduced by the debt contracted for the acquisition of such assets

or rights. Other kinds of debts are not taken into account to compute the taxable basis of the transfer tax.

Transfer of real estate
The sale of land and buildings is subject to registration duty at a rate of 5.09% on the transfer price, including expenses.

Systemic risk tax
As of 2011, a bank tax known as a systemic risk tax has been implemented to prevent excessive risk behaviour by banks. The new tax is payable by certain financial institutions (including credit institutions).

It should be noted that 'fund' entities (e.g. hedge funds or securitisation vehicles) are outside the scope of the tax.

French banks are subject to the bank tax on their worldwide business activities. The equity requirements that are used as the taxable basis for the calculation of the bank tax are calculated on a consolidated basis. Therefore, institutions that fall within the scope of the tax and that belong to a consolidated group are not subject to the tax on an individual basis. Where they are not part of such a group, institutions pay a contribution calculated on their individual position. The taxable basis is made up of the minimum equity required of the institution, as set out by the Prudential Control Authority to meet reserve ratio requirements in accordance with Basel II standards and specified during the previous calendar year.

The rate of the bank tax amounts to 0.25% of the taxable basis, and any amounts paid in that respect will be deductible for CIT purposes.

A tax return must be filed by 30 June every year, and the tax due must be settled at the same time.

Subject to the principle of reciprocity, it should be noted that taxpayers, for which the registered office or the group parent company is located in a country that has enforced a similar tax on systemic risk, can benefit from a tax credit. This tax credit can be used to settle the tax due or can be reimbursed.

Contributions on certain beverages containing added sugar or synthetic sweeteners
Articles 26 and 27 of the Finance Act for 2012 introduced new contributions on (i) beverages containing added sugar and (ii) drinks containing artificial sweeteners.

The amount of each of these contributions is EUR 7.16 per hectolitre.

Branch income

Tax rates on branch profits are the same as on corporate profits. As a principle, branch profits are deemed to be distributed to the head office. A withholding tax (WHT) is levied on French branches of non-resident non-EU corporations at the rate of 30%, or a reduced tax treaty rate (e.g. for the United States, 5%) on net profits. Refund (limited or full) of tax may be claimed to the extent that the taxable amount exceeds the dividend(s) actually distributed by the foreign corporation during the 12 months following the close of the fiscal year concerned, or to the extent the dividends are distributed to residents of France.

France

Profits realised in France by non-resident corporations whose head offices are located in an EU country are not subject to branch WHT, provided that certain conditions are met (e.g. effective head office in an EU country or non-resident corporation subject to corporate taxation).

Income determination

Inventory valuation
Inventories must be valued at the lower of cost or market. Cost must be determined in accordance with the first in first out (FIFO) or the average-cost method. The last in first out (LIFO) method is prohibited.

Capital gains
Capital gains generally are taxable as ordinary income and subject to CIT at the standard rate of 33.33%, regardless of the duration of ownership of the assets sold.

However, a reduced rate of 15%, increased by the social contribution tax, is applied to capital gains on the disposal of patents or patentable inventions, as well as on income from the licensing of patents or patentable inventions.

Gains on the sale of shares in subsidiaries held for at least two years benefit from significant relief (90% of such capital gains are excluded from CIT, with the remaining 10% portion being taxed at the standard 33.33% rate).

Capital gains and losses on shares sold to a related company
In accordance with the Article 41 of the amended Finance Act for 2011, capital gains deriving from the disposal of shares held in subsidiaries for less than two years are immediately taxable at the common rate of CIT.

Capital losses deriving from such disposal are not immediately deductible. In such a case, the loss will be deducted if, before a period of two years (as from the date of acquisition by the purchaser):

- the vendor stops being subject to CIT
- the shares are, after a restructuring of the transferee company, held by a company that is not related to the vendor, or
- the shares stop being held by the related company (notably further to a new sale).

If no event mentioned above arises within a period of two years starting from the acquisition by the vendor, the capital loss that has not been immediately deducted is treated in accordance with the long-term regime (i.e. the capital loss is therefore not deductible).

Otherwise, the vendor has to join to its corporate tax return a specific form mentioning capital losses that are not immediately deducted.

These rules apply to fiscal years that open starting from 1 January 2012.

Capital gains of non-residents
As a general rule, non-resident companies are not taxable in France regarding capital gains which derive from the disposal of French assets unless these are part of a PE.

There are two main exceptions to this principle:

- Capital gains derived from the disposal of real estate assets located in France or derived from the disposal of French real estate non-listed companies are subject in France to WHT at a 33.33% rate.
- Capital gains deriving from the disposal of shares held in a French company subject to CIT are subject in France to WHT at a 19% rate in the specific case where the seller has owned, at any point in time during the five years preceding the sale, at least 25% of the rights in the profits of the French company.

Note that in the specific case where the non-resident company is located in a non-cooperative state or territory (NCST), all capital gains deriving from the disposal of French assets are subject to WHT in France at a specific rate of 50%.

F

Dividend income
Dividends generally are taxable as ordinary income and subject to CIT at the standard rate of 33.33%.

Inter-company dividends
For information on the taxation of inter-company dividends, see Participation exemption regime in the Group taxation section.

Interest income
Interest income generally is taxable as ordinary income and subject to CIT at the standard rate of 33.33%.

Foreign income
Resident corporations are not taxed on foreign-source income derived from activities carried out abroad through foreign branches and foreign PEs. Other foreign income is not taxable until actually repatriated to French resident corporations. As a result, undistributed income of foreign subsidiaries is not taxable. The only exception to the territoriality principle is provided by Article 209 B of the Tax Code, known as the Controlled Foreign Company (CFC) rules (*see the Group taxation section for more information*).

Deductions

Depreciation
The depreciation of fixed assets has to be carried out component by component. The components of a fixed asset have to be depreciated separately according to their own lifetime.

Declining-balance depreciation is allowed for certain new and renovated assets whose useful life is in excess of than three years.

For assets bought or manufactured between 4 December 2008 and 31 December 2009, the rate is computed by multiplying the rate of straight-line depreciation by:

- 1.75, if the useful life of the asset is three or four years,
- 2.25, if the useful life of the asset is five or six years, or
- 2.75, if the useful life of the asset is more than six years.

For assets bought or manufactured after 31 December 2009, the rate is computed by multiplying the rate of straight-line depreciation by:

France

- 1.25, if the useful life of the asset is three or four years
- 1.75, if the useful life of the asset is five or six years, or
- 2.25, if the useful life of the asset is more than six years.

Goodwill
Under French tax rules, goodwill (e.g. *clientele*, trademarks) cannot be amortised.

Research and development (R&D) and software expenses
Concerning R&D and software expenses, a business may elect to immediately deduct costs incurred in R&D of software or to amortise their cost straight-line over a maximum period of five years.

The cost of acquiring software may be written off straight-line over 12 months.

The cost of patents acquired can be amortised over a five years period.

Interest expenses
In principle, interest expenses are tax deductible.

Thin capitalisation
Please see comments regarding thin capitalisation in the Group taxation section.

Carrez Amendment
In accordance with Article 40 of the fourth amended Finance Act for 2011 (i.e. 'Carrez Amendment'), interest expenses incurred by a French company for the acquisition of participation or shareholding acquisitions will not be deductible for CIT purposes if the French acquiring company is not in a position to demonstrate that it actually:

- makes decisions relating to the acquired participation and
- exercises an actual control or influence over the participations.

The purpose of the legislation is to prevent the interest deduction for the participation acquisition by a French entity when the acquired participation is effectively managed outside of France.

This new rule will not apply where:

- the total fair market value of the participations owned by the French acquiring company does not exceed EUR 1 million
- the participation acquisition has not been financed by debt at the level of the French acquiring company or at the level of a company of the same group, or
- the debt-to-equity ratio of the group is equal to or higher than the acquiring company's debt-to-equity ratio.

Bad debt
Bad debts that are definitively non-recoverable are treated, from a tax point of view, as losses.

Under certain conditions, a tax-deductible reserve can be established for debts whose collection is uncertain.

Charitable donations

Charitable donations made by companies to certain foundations or societies are deductible up to 60% of their amount (limited to EUR 5,000 of the turnover before taxes).

Taxes

Most taxes, including unrecoverable turnover taxes, registration duties, and CET, are deductible. The major exceptions are CIT and tax penalties.

Corporate tax losses

Carryforward of tax losses

Tax losses carried forward are available to offset the first EUR 1 million of taxable profits and 60% of taxable profits in excess of this.

Carryback of tax losses

Tax losses are available for carryback to the fiscal year immediately preceding that in which the losses arise and up to a maximum of EUR 1 million. Any unused surplus will be carried forward and used as set out above. In addition, the election to carry back tax losses must be filed prior to the deadline for submission of the tax return for the loss-making period.

Tax groups

The overall tax losses of a French tax group, as well as pre-election tax losses of the individual members of the group will be attributed, whether carried forward or carried back, in the same manner and within the same limits as those set out above.

Payments to foreign related parties

Payments to foreign affiliates are allowed, as long as they meet the arm's-length test. If they do not, Article 57 of the French Tax Code provides that income directly or indirectly transferred to the foreign related parties, through either the increase or the reduction of the purchase or sales price of goods and services, or through any other means, must be added back to taxable income. For the purpose of this provision, foreign related parties are defined as parent subsidiaries or sister companies.

Where the payments are made to companies located in a country with a privilege tax regime, the French taxpayer must prove that the transaction is bona fide and that the amount due is not exaggerated (*see the Group taxation section for more information on countries with a privilege tax regime*).

Royalties

Article 11 of the Finance Act for 2012 restricts the conditions for deducting licensing royalties where the licensor and the licensee are related parties. A full deduction for the royalty expense may only be allowed if the licensee can demonstrate, and properly document, that:

- the use of the licence results in added value for the licensee over the entire licensing period and
- such use is real (i.e. does not consist of an artificial scheme).

France

Group taxation

Tax consolidation regime

French corporations and their 95% owned domestic subsidiaries may elect to file one single tax return, thus allowing offset of losses of one group corporation against the profits of a related corporation. CIT is then levied on the aggregate income after certain adjustments for intra-group provisions (e.g. debt waivers, dividend distributions) have been made.

When shares in a company that will be integrated into the group are acquired by a group company from individuals or legal entities that control this group, either directly or indirectly, a portion of the group's overall financial expense incurred by the members of the group is progressively added back to the group's taxable income on a straight-line basis over a nine year period.

A French subsidiary can be included in a tax consolidated group even if its parent company is not located in France. However, at least 95% of the share capital of the foreign company must be held, directly or indirectly, by the French company that is head of the tax consolidated group. In addition, the foreign company must be subject to CIT, be located in the European Union or in a member state of the European Economic Area (EEA) whose tax treaty with France includes a mutual administrative assistance clause to fight tax fraud and tax evasion, and hold 95% of the lower-tier subsidiary's shares.

A PE of a foreign company subject to French CIT can be a member of a French tax consolidated group if the shares of the foreign company are held by other French companies, which are members of the consolidated group.

Provisions on the tax neutrality of intra-group transaction flows (e.g. dividends, provisions, waivers of debts, interest, and capital gains on the sales of shares) have been modified to treat tax consolidated groups with an intermediate foreign company the same as other tax consolidated groups.

Allocation of the tax charge within a tax consolidated group

In an important decision dated 12 March 2010 ('Wolseley Centers France'), the French Supreme Court disagreed with the French Tax Authorities by ruling that the tax charge of the group can be freely allocated between members of the consolidated tax group.

Following this decision, group companies are free to enter into a tax consolidation agreement stating the conditions for the allocation of the group tax charge or, where applicable, the tax savings arising from the group arrangement.

The Supreme Court concludes that since the terms of an agreement to allow a re-allocation taking into account the specific results of each of the group companies, the terms of this re-allocation cannot be regarded as an indirect subsidy. However, this allocation should not undermine the corporate benefit of each group member nor the minority shareholders rights otherwise this will result in an abnormal act of management.

Underpriced sale of asset between two entities of a same tax consolidated group

In a decision dated 10 November 2010 ('*Société Corbfi*'), the French Supreme Court has specified that an underpriced sale of an asset between two members of the same tax group must be neutralised at the group level only after the computation of the entities results on a standalone basis.

First, on a standalone basis, the seller has to add back the advantage given to the buyer (i.e. the difference between the fair market value and the amount paid) and the buyer adds back this advantage as if it was a dividend. Second, when reprocessing the different entities results, the advantage added back by the buyer has to be neutralised at the group level.

Other group consolidation systems
Other group consolidation systems were available with the prior authorisation of the Ministry of Finance, as follows:

* *Bénéfice consolidé*: The 50% owned subsidiary consolidation system allows the combined reporting of profits and losses of all controlled branches, subsidiaries, and partnerships, whether French or foreign.
* *Bénéfice mondial*: Worldwide tax consolidation allows French corporations to include in their French tax return the results of their foreign activities carried out by branches.

Those regimes no longer apply regarding fiscal years that end as of 6 September 2011.

Participation exemption regime
French parent companies (i.e. companies incorporated in France and holding qualifying shares that represent at least 5% of the issued capital of subsidiaries, French or foreign) have the option of excluding 95% of the subsidiaries' net dividends from CIT (5% of charges and expenses must be added back to the parent company's taxable results). The French parent-subsidiary regime extends to certain shares without voting rights. There is no formal commitment to hold the shares for at least two years, and companies can benefit from this regime from the acquisition date of the shares. However, the obligation remains to hold the shares over this period of time. Certain shares of listed real estate companies are not eligible to the French parent-subsidiary regime.

Regarding fiscal years ending on or after 31 December 2010, the taxation of dividends received by a parent company from its subsidiary cannot be capped at the amount of the expenses actually incurred by the parent company. Thus, the tax liability will be equal to 5% of the dividends received, tax credits included.

As of 1 January 2011, the French parent-subsidiary regime is no longer applicable to dividends paid from entities located in an NCST.

Distribution followed by absorption or sale of subsidiary
The rules abolish the possibility for a company to accumulate the exemption of dividends received from its subsidiaries (under the participation exemption regime or the tax consolidation regime) and the deduction of a loss in value resulting from the dividends' distribution due to previous distributions at the time of the securities exchange or sale of shares.

In principle, the subsidiary's shares must be kept by the parent company for at least two years in order to benefit from the participation exemption regime. However, some operations lead to a break of the two-year holding period. In that case, the exchanged shares are deemed withheld until the sale of the securities received in exchange.

France

For fiscal years ending after 31 December 2010, the exchanged shares will be deemed kept for the application of the participation exemption regime only if the gain or loss is not taken into account in the result of that exchange. If the gain or loss is included in the result, the dividends received may not benefit from the participation exemption regime and will be taxed.

Transfer pricing

Transfer pricing documentation
Large corporations located in France (i.e. with annual turnover or amount of gross assets in excess of EUR 400 million) are required to provide documentation containing general information regarding the relevant group of companies, including main activities, operational and legal structures of the related companies, functions performed and risks borne, main intangible assets, and group transfer pricing policy, amongst others.

Individual advanced pricing agreements (APAs)
APAs are available for taxpayers only on the basis of international agreements entered into in accordance with Article 25 of the Organisation for Economic Co-operation and Development (OECD) Model Tax Convention. Currently, taxpayers are allowed to enter into APAs with the French tax authorities on a unilateral basis. In practice, taxpayers are entitled to submit their transfer pricing policy to the French tax authorities. Agreement of the tax authorities to the APA precludes a later challenge.

Thin capitalisation
Under current rules, the tax deduction of interest paid by a French company to its foreign controlling shareholders is subject to the following three restrictions:

Interest rate limitation
Under the amended Article 212 of the French Tax Code, tax deduction of interest paid to related parties is limited to the higher of (i) the average annual interest rate applied by credit institutions to companies for medium-term variable rate loans or (ii) the interest that the borrowing company could have obtained from independent banks under similar circumstances. This rate is 3.99% for financial years ending on 31 December 2011. Having passed this interest rate test, French indebted companies have to pass a second test: the debt ratio.

Debt ratio
That part of interest paid to related parties which is deductible under the rate limitation test is disqualified if it exceeds all of the three following limitations during the same financial year:

- Interest relating to financing of any kind granted by related parties, within the limit of 1.5 times the net equity of the borrower.
- 25% of adjusted net income before tax ('*résultat courant avant impôt*', defined as the operating income, increased by certain items).
- Interest income received from related parties (i.e. there is no limitation on thin capitalisation grounds when the borrowing company is in a net lending position vis-a-vis related entities).

The portion of the interest which exceeds the three above limits is not deductible, except if it is lower than EUR 150,000.

Carryforward of excess interest

That part of the interest which is not deductible immediately by the borrowing company can be carried forward, without time limit, for relief in subsequent years, provided there is an excess capacity during such years. The amount in excess is, however, reduced by 5% each year, from the second financial year following the financial year in which the interest expense has been incurred.

Exceptions

The thin capitalisation rules do not apply to interest payable by banks and credit institutions, and also to certain specific situations such as interest in connection with intra-group cash pools or with certain leasing operations.

The thin capitalisation rules do not apply if the French indebted company can demonstrate that the debt-to-equity ratio of the worldwide group to whom it belongs exceeds its own debt-to-equity ratio.

Deductibility is also facilitated within a French tax consolidated group. The thin capitalisation rules apply to each company member of the group taken on a stand-alone basis. Any excess interest incurred by such company is, however, not carried forward by it. Instead, it is appropriated at group level.

Extension of the thin capitalisation mechanism to loans granted by related parties

In the specific case where the repayment of a loan granted by a third party (including banks) is guaranteed by a related party or by a third party whose commitment is itself secured by a related one, then the proportion of interest that is payable on that part of the loan that is secured in this way is potentially subject to thin capitalisation rules.

The provisions will not apply where the loan:

- takes the form of a bond issued by way of a public offering or under equivalent foreign regulations, although this excludes private placements
- is guaranteed by a related party solely by way of a pledge of shares in the debtor, security over the debtor's receivables, or shares in a company directly or indirectly owning the debtor so long as the holder of such shares and the debtor are members of the same tax group; as a result, this exception will not apply where a foreign company grants a pledge of shares in its French subsidiary to guarantee the bank loan granted to it
- is obtained in the context of a refinancing to allow the debtor to complete the mandatory repayment of a pre-existing debt, which is required as a result of a direct or indirect takeover of the debtor (allowed up to the amount of the loan principal repaid and accrued interest to that date), or
- has been obtained prior to 1 January 2011 in connection with an acquisition of securities or the refinancing of such acquisition debt.

Controlled foreign companies (CFCs)

The CFC rules provide that:

- French corporations are required to include in their taxable income profits made by their more than 50% owned foreign subsidiaries and branches. The 50% holding is determined by direct and indirect control of shares and voting rights.
- The minimum holding threshold has to be reduced to 5%, if over 50% of the share capital of the foreign entity is indirectly held through French or foreign companies controlled by the French parent company. However, if the shares in the foreign entity

France

are listed on a regulated market, the French tax authorities will have to demonstrate that the French parent company, together with other entities holding shares in such foreign entity, is acting in concert.

- The CFC rules are only applicable if the foreign legal entity or PE in which the French company owns the requisite percentage of shares is in a country with a privileged tax regime. A privileged tax regime is defined by the French tax code as a tax regime in which a foreign jurisdiction subjects taxable income of a foreign entity to at least 50% or lower of the income tax liability which would been incurred in France, had the activity of the foreign entity been performed in France.

- Profits of the foreign entity which fall under the CFC rules are no longer taxed separately. They are now aggregated with the other taxable profits of the French parent company. Consequently, any tax losses incurred by the French parent company may be offset against the foreign entity's profits.

- The French parent company can avoid the application of the CFC rules if it demonstrates that the foreign entity carries an effective trading or manufacturing activity, conducted from its country of establishment or registered office. Furthermore, the CFC rules, in principle, are not applicable with respect of foreign branches or subsidiaries located in another EU country. However, this exception is not applicable if the French tax authorities can demonstrate that the foreign entity located in another EU country constitutes an artificial arrangement, set up to circumvent French tax legislation. This concept is similar to the 'abuse of law' concept, although it does not have all the same characteristics.

Tax credits and incentives

R&D tax credit
The R&D tax credit is determined on the basis of the eligible R&D expenses incurred during the calendar year.

Currently, the R&D credit equals 30% of the R&D eligible expenses incurred during the year, up to EUR 100 million in eligible R&D expenses, and 5% beyond this amount. In addition, eligible R&D expenses incurred by the company can be included in the basis for computation of the tax credit at up to 100% of that amount.

Moreover, the 30% 'standard' rate is increased to 40% and 35% for the first and the second year, respectively, during which the company incurs eligible R&D expenses, or after the expiration of a period of five consecutive years during which the company did not benefit from the tax credit, provided, in both cases, that the concerned company is not affiliated with another company which benefited from the R&D tax credit within the same time period.

The tax code classifies eligible technical and scientific research operations in three areas: fundamental research, applied research, and experimental development.

The eligible expenditures include the following:

- Tax deductible depreciation expenses relating to fixed assets, created or acquired newly, assigned to eligible R&D works/projects, including patents acquired.
- Costs relating to staff qualifying as scientists and/or engineers (staff costs relating to 'young graduate doctors' are retained at up to 200% during the 24 months following their hiring by the company).
- Expenses resulting from outsourced R&D works/projects.

- Expenses incurred for patent registration and/or in connection with the defence of patents.
- Expenses relating to the monitoring of technical developments.
- Premiums paid in connection with insurance contracts relating to the legal defence of patents.

Operating costs are now taken into account by retaining 50% of the R&D staff costs plus 75% of the depreciation on the assets allocated to the research. Also, spending on outsourcing to private research organisations now is included in the limit of three times the total amount of other research expenses qualifying for the tax credit.

The use of patented or patentable technologies in manufacturing

Companies that are involved in the manufacturing of products in France containing patented or patentable technologies, or companies that incorporate such technologies into goods that are manufactured in France, benefit from a reduced effective rate of tax.

In the case of a licensing arrangement between connected French companies, the licensor will benefit from a reduced 15% tax rate on royalty income, whereas the licensee company will benefit from a tax deduction at 33.33%.

In order for a licensee company to benefit from full deductibility for royalties paid, the rules require that the licensee company 'effectively exploits' the rights available to it.

Inbound investment incentives

No particular incentives are available to foreign investors in France. However, the government offers a comprehensive programme of tax incentives and development subsidies to encourage investment in underdeveloped areas.

Capital investment is encouraged through the declining-balance method of depreciation as well as through exceptional depreciation for certain capital expenditures.

Withholding taxes

Payments to resident corporations and individuals are not subject to WHT.

Payments to non-resident corporations and individuals are subject to WHT, as shown below.

	Dividend WHT (%)		
Column 1	**Column 2**	**Column 3**	**Column 4**
Country of residence	**Individuals and non-parent companies**	**Parent companies**	**Shareholding required to be a parent**
Non-treaty:	21/30 (39)	30	-
Treaty:			
Algeria	15	5	10
Argentina	15	15	-
Armenia	15	5	10
Australia	15	0	10
Austria	15	0	10
Bahrain	0	0	-
Bangladesh	15	10	10

France

	Dividend WHT (%)		
Column 1	**Column 2**	**Column 3**	**Column 4**
Country of residence	**Individuals and non-parent companies**	**Parent companies**	**Shareholding required to be a parent**
Belgium	15	0 (1)	10
Benin	30	30	-
Bolivia	15	15	-
Botswana	12	5	25
Brazil	15	15 (2)	-
Bulgaria	15	0/5 (1)	10/15
Burkina Faso	15 (20)	30 (2)	-
Cameroon	15	15	-
Canada	15	5	10
Central African Republic	15	5	10
China	30	30	0
Comoro Islands	15/25	15/25	-
Congo, Republic of	30	15	10
Croatia	15	0	10
Cyprus	15	0/10 (1)	10
Czech Republic	10	0 (1)	10
Denmark	21/30 (39)	0 (1)	-
Ecuador	15	15	-
Egypt	0	0	-
Estonia	15	0/5 (1)	10
Finland	0/15	0/5 (1)	10
Gabon	15	15	-
Georgia	10	0/5/10	10/50
Germany	15	0 (3)	10
Ghana	15	5	10
Greece	21/30 (39)	0/30 (1)	10
Hungary	15	0/5 (1)	10
Iceland	15	5	10
India	10	10	-
Indonesia	15	10	25
Iran	20	15	25
Ireland, Republic of	15	0/10 (1)	10/50
Israel	15	5	10
Italy	15	0/5/15 (1)	10
Ivory Coast	15	15	-
Jamaica	15	15	10
Japan	10	5	10
Jordan	15	5	10
Kazakhstan	15	5	10
Korea, Republic of	15	10	10
Kuwait	0	0	-
Latvia	15	0/5 (1)	10
Lebanon	0	0	-
Lithuania	15	0/5 (1)	10

	Dividend WHT (%)		
Column 1	Column 2	Column 3	Column 4
Country of residence	Individuals and non-parent companies	Parent companies	Shareholding required to be a parent
Luxembourg	15	0/5 (1)	10/25
Holding company (5)	30	30	-
Macedonia	15	0	10
Madagascar	25	15	25
Malawi	30	30	-
Malaysia	15	5	10
Mali	15/30	30 (2)	-
Malta	15	0 (1)	10
Mauritania	30	30	-
Mauritius	15	5	10
Mayotte	30	25 (2, 6)	-
Mexico	15	0/5	5/10
Monaco	25	25	10
Mongolia	15	5	10
Morocco	0/15	0/15 (7)	-
Namibia	15	5	10
Netherlands	15	0/5 (1)	10/25
New Caledonia	15	5 (37)	-
New Zealand	15	15	-
Niger	25	-	-
Nigeria	15	12.5 (37)	10
Norway	15	0	10
Oman	0	0	-
Pakistan	15	10	10
Philippines	15	10 (37)	10 (38)
Poland	15	5	10
Polynesia, French	30	30	25
Portugal	15	0/5 (1)	10
Qatar	0	0	-
Romania	10	0 (1)	10
Russia	15	5/10/15 (8)	-
Russian Federation	15	5	10
St. Pierre & Miquelon	15	5	-
Saudi Arabia	0	0	-
Senegal	15	15 (5)	-
Singapore	15	10	10
Slovakia	10	0/10 (1)	20
South Africa	15	5	10
Spain	15	0	10
Sri Lanka	30	30	-
Sweden	15	0/15 (1)	10
Switzerland (9)			
A (10)	15	0 (9)	10 (9)
B (11)	15 (9)	0/15 (9)	10 (9)

France

	Dividend WHT (%)		
Column 1	Column 2	Column 3	Column 4
Country of residence	Individuals and non-parent companies	Parent companies	Shareholding required to be a parent
C (12)	30	30	-
Thailand	25	15	25
Togo	15/30	25 (2)	-
Trinidad and Tobago	15	10	10
Tunisia	30	30	-
Turkey	20	15	-
Ukraine (13)	15	5/0	10/50
United Arab Emirates	0	0	-
United Kingdom	15	0/5 (1)	10
United States	15	0/5	10/80
Uzbekistan	10	5	10
Venezuela	15	0/5	10
Vietnam	15	5	10
Zambia	30	30	50
Zimbabwe	15	10	25

	WHT (%)		
	Interest	Royalties	Distributions
Column 1	Column 5	Column 6	Column 7
Country of residence	For instruments other than borrowings		Automatically levied on after-tax profits of PEs
Non-treaty: (14, 15, 16)	0 (17)	33.33	25
Treaty:			
Algeria	0	5/10 (35)	0
Argentina	0	18	5
Armenia	0	5/10 (35)	5
Australia	0	5	15
Austria	0	0	0
Bahrain	0	0	25
Bangladesh	0	10	15
Belgium	0	0	0/10 (23)
Benin	0	0	25 (18)
Bolivia	0	15	0
Botswana	0	10	5
Brazil	0	10/15/25 (19)	15
Bulgaria	0	0/5 (40)	0/5 (23)
Burkina Faso	0	0	25 (18)
Cameroon	0	15 (20)	15
Canada	0	10 (20)	5
Quebec	0	10	5
Central African Republic	0	0	25 (18)
China	0	6/10 (21)	0
Comoro Islands	0	33.33	25 (18)

France

	WHT (%)		
	Interest	Royalties	Distributions
Column 1	Column 5	Column 6	Column 7
Country of residence	For instruments other than borrowings		Automatically levied on after-tax profits of PEs
Congo, Republic of	0	15	15
Croatia	0	0	0
Cyprus	0	0 (22, 40)	0/10 (23)
Czech Republic	0	0/5/10 (24, 36, 40)	0 (23)
Denmark	0	0/33.33 (40)	0/25 (23)
Ecuador	0	15	15
Egypt	0	10/15 (25)	0
Estonia	0	0/5/10 (36, 40)	0
Finland	0	0	0/15 (23)
Gabon	0	10	0
Georgia	0	0	0
Germany	0	0	0
Ghana	0	10	0
Greece	0	0/5 (40)	0/25 (23)
Hungary	0	0	0/5 (23)
Iceland	0	0	5
India	0	0	0
Indonesia	0	10	10
Iran	0	10	15
Ireland, Republic of	0	0	0/25 (23)
Israel	0	0/10 (22, 20)	5/10
Italy	0	0/5 (24, 40)	0
Ivory Coast	0	0/10 (26)	0
Jamaica	0	10	10
Japan	0	0	0
Jordan	0	5/15/25 (19)	5
Kazakhstan	0	10	5
Korea, Republic of	0	10	5
Kuwait	0	0	25
Latvia	0	0/5/10 (36, 40)	0
Lebanon	0	33.33	25
Lithuania	0	0/5/10 (36, 40)	0
Luxembourg	0	0	0/5 (23)
Holding company (5)	10 to 15	33.33	25
Macedonia	0	0	0
Madagascar	0	10/15 (27, 28)	25
Malawi	0	0/33.33 (20)	10
Malaysia	0	10 (28)	15
Mali	0	0	25 (18)
Malta	0	0/10 (24, 40)	0/10 (23)
Mauritania	0	0	25 (18)
Mauritius	0	0/15 (24)	15

F

France

	WHT (%)		
	Interest	Royalties	Distributions
Column 1	Column 5	Column 6	Column 7
Country of residence	For instruments other than borrowings		Automatically levied on after-tax profits of PEs
Mayotte	0	0	25 (18)
Mexico	0	10 (21, 24)	0
Monaco	0	33.33	25
Mongolia	0	5 (24)	0
Morocco	0	5/10 (29)	0
Namibia	0	10 (24)	0
Netherlands	0	0	0
New Caledonia	0	10 (24)	10
New Zealand	0	10	15
Niger	0	0	25 (18)
Nigeria	0	12.5	25
Norway (5)	0	0	0
Oman	0	0	25
Pakistan	0	10	0
Philippines	0/15/50	15	10
Poland	0	0/10 (24)	25
Polynesia, French	0	33.33	25 (18)
Portugal	0	0/5 (40)	0/15 (23)
Qatar	0	0	25
Romania	0	0/10 (40)	0/10 (23)
Russia	0	0	0
Russian Federation	0	0	25
St. Pierre & Miquelon	0	10 (24)	10
Saudi Arabia	0	0	25
Senegal	0	0	0
Singapore	0	0/33.33 (30)	15
Slovakia	0	0/5 (24)	10
South Africa	0	0	0
Spain	0	0/5 (31, 40)	0
Sri Lanka	0	0/10 (32)	25
Sweden	0	0	0 (23,24)
Switzerland (9)			
A (10)	0	0/5 (9, 33)	0 (9)
B (11)	0	0/5 (9, 33)	0 (9)
C (12)	0	33.33	0 (9)
Thailand	0	5/15 (29)	25
Togo	0	0	25 (18)
Trinidad and Tobago	0	0/10 (21)	10
Tunisia	0	5/15/20 (34)	25 (18)
Turkey	0	10	7.5
Ukraine	0	0/10	25
United Arab Emirates	0	0	0
United Kingdom	0	0	0 (23)

	WHT (%)		
	Interest	Royalties	Distributions
Column 1	Column 5	Column 6	Column 7
Country of residence	For instruments other than borrowings		Automatically levied on after-tax profits of PEs
United States	0	0	5
Uzbekistan	0	0	0
Venezuela	0	5	0
Vietnam	0	10	0
Zambia	0	0/33.33 (20)	10
Zimbabwe	0	10	0

Explanation of columns

Column 2: Individuals and companies not qualifying as parents are subject to the WHT rates for dividends as indicated in this column.

Columns 3 and 4: Column 3 indicates the WHT rate for dividends paid to a foreign 'parent' company. To be considered as a parent company, the foreign company must hold a specified percentage of the French company's share capital or voting rights. These minimum percentages range from 0% to 50%, as indicated in Column 4, and certain other conditions must be met (*see each treaty*). If no percentage is indicated, either no minimum shareholding is required, or the tax treaty does not reduce the WHT rate of 30%.

No WHT is levied on dividends paid to an EU parent company by a French company that is subject to CIT, provided all the following conditions are met:

- The EU parent company has held a minimum percentage of the share capital of the distributing company, directly and continuously, for at least two years. As of 1 January 2009, the participation required is 10%.
- The EU parent company is the effective beneficiary of the dividends.
- The EU parent company has its effective seat of management in an EU State and is not deemed to be domiciled outside the EU under an applicable tax treaty.
- The EU parent company is one of the legal forms enumerated by the relevant Directive.
- The EU parent company is subject to CIT in the member state where it has its effective seat of management.
- There is an anti-avoidance rule.

Column 5: The tax mechanism has been changed so as to exempt the interest from WHT in France except where the interest is paid to a financial institution established in a non-cooperative state or territory (WHT at a rate of 50% applicable). The payer can, however, be exempt if one proves that the main purpose and effect of such a payment is not to take advantage of locating the income in such a jurisdiction.

These provisions apply to income paid as of 1 March 2010. A special provision applies to loans entered into outside of France by French companies and some investments funds prior to this date. Interest paid on these loans and on related loans after 1 March 2010 will continue to be exempt.

France

Column 6: There is no requirement to withhold income tax on royalties paid to EU companies if all the following conditions are met:

- The taxpayer is a French resident company or a French PE of a company resident in another EU member state.
- The recipient of the income is an EU resident company.
- The taxpayer and the recipient are at least 25% associates, which means that either one holds directly 25% or more of the share capital or voting rights in the other, or a third party holds directly 25% or more of the capital or voting rights in them both.

Column 7: WHT is automatically imposed on after-tax profits of a PE unless certain conditions are met. The rate is 25% or the reduced tax treaty rate.

Notes

1. *See explanation of Columns 3 and 4.*
2. Exceptions where the dividends are excluded from the taxable income of the company which has received the dividends.
3. A rate of 15% is applicable for dividends distributed by certain companies. The dividend WHT rate can be eliminated if the recipient owns 15% or more of the share capital.
4. The 1929-type Luxembourg holding companies are not entitled to any of the benefits of the France-Luxembourg tax treaty.
5. A 25% rate applies if dividends are not included in the income taxed to either corporate or income tax.
6. No WHT applies if dividends are taxable in Morocco.
7. The 5% rate applies to dividends when three conditions are fulfilled, as follows: (1) the effective recipient of the dividends must have invested at least EUR 76,224.51 in the company that pays these dividends; (2) the recipient must be a company liable for corporate tax; and (3) the latter company must be exempt from corporate tax. The rate is 10% when only condition (1) or conditions (2 and 3) are fulfilled. In all other cases, the rate is 15%.
8. An addendum signed on 22 July 1997 modifies the provisions of the French-Swiss tax treaty relating to dividends, interest, and royalties, and provides for the removal of the 5% WHT on profits realised by French PE of Swiss resident companies.
9. The rate indicated applies to Swiss resident companies controlled by Swiss residents.
10. The rate indicated applies to Swiss resident companies that are controlled by non-Swiss residents (non-UE) (Article 11.2.b ii) and meet the conditions of Article 14 of the tax treaty. In the case of column 3, the 15% rate applies to these companies, provided both the recipient and the distributing company are not quoted on a stock exchange. If these conditions are not met, the tax exemption applies.
11. The rate indicated applies to Swiss resident companies controlled by non-Swiss residents but not complying with Article 14 of the tax treaty.
12. The 5% rate applies to gross dividends if the effective recipient is a Ukrainian company that holds directly or indirectly at least 10% of the French company's capital. The rate is 0% if the participation exceeds 50% and EUR 762,245. It is 15% in all other cases.
13. Non-treaty recipients of royalties and management fees are subject to a 33.33% withholding rate. Where a treaty exists, management fees are exempt from WHT unless they are included in the definition of royalties subject to WHT.
14. In France, the WHT is levied on a provisional basis at 25% of the net profit. This amount is reduced to the extent it exceeds the dividends actually paid by the company during the previous 12 months, and the amount of dividends paid to residents of France. Consequently, if the foreign head office undertakes not to distribute dividends in a given year, the after-tax profits of its French branch are not subject to WHT, even when they are transferred abroad.
15. WHT on interest on loans with a contract is 0%, while withholding on other interest is in a range from 15% to 50%. For treaty rates, consult the individual entry in the table.
16. The WHT rate can be 60% for certain securities if the investor's identity is not disclosed.
17. The WHT is levied on the following amount: French net profit divided by the total foreign company net profit, multiplied by the amount of the distribution.
18. The rate of 10% is applicable on royalties for the use of literary, artistic, or scientific works, including films, 25% on royalties for the use of trademarks, and 15% otherwise.
19. No WHT is applicable on a royalty arising from the use of or the right to use literary, artistic, or scientific works (excluding film).
20. WHT is reduced to 6% for royalties paid for the lease of industrial, commercial, or scientific equipment.
21. A rate of 5% (Cyprus) and 10% (Israel) is applicable on royalties paid for the use or the right of the use of films.
22. Profits realised in France by foreign corporations whose head offices are located in a European country are not subject to WHT if certain conditions concerning the foreign corporation are met (effective head office in a European country; foreign corporation subject to corporate taxation).

23. No WHT is applicable on a royalty arising from the use or the right to use literary, artistic, or scientific works.
24. The rate of 25% is applicable on royalties paid for the use of trademarks.
25. No WHT is levied on certain royalties paid in the field of audiovisual techniques.
26. The rate of 15% is applicable on royalties paid for the use of industrial property and trademarks.
27. A rate of 33.33% is applicable on royalties paid for the use of or the right to use films.
28. The rate of 5% is applicable on royalties paid for the use of literary, artistic, or scientific works, excluding films.
29. The rate of 33.33% is applicable on royalties paid for the use of literary and artistic works, including films, and for information concerning commercial experience.
30. No WHT is levied on royalties paid for the use of or the right to use literary or artistic works, excluding films and recordings.
31. No WHT is levied on royalties paid for the use of or the right to use copyrights or films.
32. No WHT is levied on royalties paid for the use of or the right to use industrial, commercial, or scientific equipment.
33. The rate of 20% is applicable on royalties paid for the use of trademarks, 15% for the use of industrial property, and 5% for the use of literary, artistic, or scientific works.
34. The rate of 5% is applicable on royalties for the use of literary, artistic, or scientific works, not including films.
35. The rate of 5% is applicable on royalties for the use or the right to use industrial, commercial, or scientific equipment.
36. The reduced rate is applicable if the beneficial owner is a company (other than a partnership).
37. Voting shares solely.
38. French domestic law decreases the WHT rate from 30% to 21% concerning individuals who are resident in another EU member state, in Iceland and in Norway.
39. *See explanation of Column 6.*

Anti-avoidance rules applicable to Non-Cooperative States or Territories (NCST)

The French parent-subsidiary regime is not applicable to dividends paid from entities located in an NCST.

WHT on passive income is 55% for transactions with an NCST person or entity. This rate was 50% prior to 1 January 2012.

For French tax purposes, a state or territory is considered non-cooperative if it meets at least one of the following criteria:

- It is not a member of the European Community.
- It has been reviewed and monitored by the OECD Global Forum on Transparency and Exchange of Information.
- It has not concluded at least 12 administrative assistance agreements/treaties that allow a complete exchange of information for tax purposes.
- It has not concluded an administrative assistance agreement/treaty with France.

Payments (e.g. interests, royalties, payments for services) made to an NCST person or entity are, as a general rule, not tax deductible. In addition, it is not possible to offset WHT in France with any foreign WHT borne by the entity located in a NCST.

Moreover, concerning shareholders (individuals and companies) located in a NCST, a tax amounting to 55% is levied on capital gains derived from the disposal of shares in French companies whatever the level of shareholding.

France

Tax administration

Tax returns
Regarding fiscal years that end on 31 December, CIT returns are due by the end of April of the following year.

Payment of tax
Payment of tax is made during the fiscal year by way of four instalments totalling 33.33% of the taxable income of the preceding year. Regarding fiscal years that end on 31 December, final CIT payment is due on 15 April of the following year.

Currently, for companies that have gross income in excess of EUR 500 million, the last down-payment is now assessed on the basis of the estimated taxable income of the present year (in case of significant increase of the taxable profits in comparison with the previous fiscal year). This modification leads to an anticipated payment of CIT.

Late payment interest
For a reassessment after a tax audit, late-payment interest is currently 4.8% per year or 0.4% per month.

Statute of limitation
Regarding CIT, the general statute of limitation expires at the end of the third year following the one that has triggered the tax liability.

Under certain circumstances, the statute of limitation can be extended (e.g. fraud, undisclosed/hidden activity); statute of limitation can also be interrupted (e.g. notification of a notice of reassessment).

The ruling system
To secure the tax status of a situation, foreign companies and individuals can request a private ruling from the French tax authorities as to whether their activities constitute a PE or fixed base.

The French tax authorities have to provide an answer within three months after the receipt of the request. In the absence of response from the French tax authorities within this period of time, the foreign company or individual will be deemed not to have a PE in France.

APAs are also provided by the French tax authorities for transfer pricing purposes.

Other issues

The recent election of a new President is likely to lead to new tax regulations impacting companies operating in France, including changes to existing legislations.

Gabon

PwC contact

Christophe Relongoue
PricewaterhouseCoopers Tax and Legal
366 Rue Alfred-Marche
Libreville
Republic of Gabon
Tel: +241 74 59 11
Email: christophe.relongoue@ga.pwc.com

Significant developments

Further to the promulgation of the 2012 Financial Act on 2 January 2012, the following
new tax measures have been introduced:

* Possibility for companies investing in the tourism sector to be exempted from
  corporate income tax (CIT) during the first three years of existence, provided that
  the amount of the investment equals or exceeds 800 million Central African CFA
  francs (XAF).
* Possibility to benefit from a 5% tax credit for companies investing in the tourism
  sector for an amount inferior to XAF 800 million.
* Possibility for companies benefiting from the specific regime applicable to small and
  medium-sized companies and manufactures to be exempted from CIT during the five
  first years of existence.

The Financial Act for 2012 also provides new provisions pertaining to the accounting
obligations applicable to oil subcontractors as well as some amendments on the
provisions of the Gabonese Tax Code, notably the provisions dealing with value-added
tax (VAT) rates, VAT deductibility, registration duties, and penalties for late payment
of taxes.

Finally, the Financial Act for 2012 provides tax and customs incentive measures for
wood and cement industries.

Taxes on corporate income

Subject to the provisions of double tax treaties (DTTs), profits subject to CIT in Gabon
are those obtained by companies exploited in Gabon or those relating to operations
carried out in this country.

The CIT rate is fixed at 35%.

CIT is assessed on profits minus deductible expenses and charges. Profits are composed
of all operations carried out in Gabon by companies during the period of taxation,
including notably fixed assets capital gains.

Non-resident companies shall be taxed via withholding tax (WHT) at the rate of 10% for
income raised in Gabon if they have no permanent establishment (PE) in Gabon.

In cases where non-resident companies have PE in Gabon, they shall be subject to CIT
on the income raised in Gabon via the Gabonese PE.

Gabon

Impôt Minimum Forfaitaire (IMF)

The IMF is a lower limit to the CIT and is calculated as 1% of the global turnover carried out during the fiscal year of taxation. Note that the IMF cannot be less than XAF 1 million, even in the case of a negative turnover.

New companies are exempt from this minimum tax during the first two fiscal years of their existence.

Local income taxes

There are no local government taxes on income in Gabon.

Corporate residence

As a general rule, a resident company is a company that is incorporated under commercial laws in force in Gabon.

Permanent establishment (PE)

From a general treaty perspective, PE designates a permanent business installation through which a company carries out the whole or part of its activity.

The expression 'permanent establishment' notably includes the following:

- Head office.
- Branch.
- Office.
- Plant.
- Workshop.
- Mine, oil or gas shaft, quarry or other place of natural resources extraction.
- Building site or assembly line.

Other taxes

Value-added tax (VAT)

VAT is a cumulative tax levied on the sale of goods and the provision of services rendered or used in Gabon.

There are four rates of VAT:

- Standard rate: 18%, which applies to all transactions unless otherwise provided for by the law.
- Reduced rates:
    - 10%, which applies to manufacturing operations and sales of products mentioned in a limitative list provided by Article 221 of the new Gabonese Tax Code, including mineral water, chicken, and sugar.
    - 5%, which applies to sales and services relating to cement.
- Zero-rate: 0%, which applies to exports and international transports.

Customs duties

Gabon is member of the Central African Economic and Monetary Community (CEMAC), a customs union that comprises countries from Central Africa.

Merchandise entering into the CEMAC customs territory is subject to importation duties registered into the Customs Tariff.

Four customs regimes are available in Gabon, notably one standard regime and three specific regimes (an exemption regime, a temporary admission regime, and a reduced tax regime).

Apart from customs duties, the importation of merchandise in Gabon is subject to the community tax of integration (CCI) at rate of 0.4% and to the Organisation for the Harmonisation of Business Law in Africa (OHADA) withholding (duty) at rate 0.05% of the customs value of the imported merchandise.

Excise duty

Excise duty principally applies to luxury goods, such as alcoholic drinks, perfume and cosmetic products, caviar, salmon, cigars, and cigarettes.

The rates of the excise duty are comprised between 20% and 32%.

Tax on property

Tax on buildings (*Contributions Foncières des Propriétés Bâties* or CFPB) is levied annually at the rate of 15% of the rental value of the building after deduction of 25% for deterioration and maintenance. Tax on non-built property is levied annually at the rate of 25% of the taxable revenue corresponding to 4% to 5% of the rental value or 10% of the purchase value.

Transfer tax

The tax on funds transfer is due on remote transfer operations carried out in Gabon at destination of countries outside the Central Africa Monetary Union (UMAC) countries.

The tax is calculated on the amount of the funds to be transferred except related fees and commissions paid by the giver.

The rate of the transfer tax is 1.5%.

Stamp duty

A stamp duty is levied on all paperwork relating to civil and judicial actions and to documents that could be produced in court as evidence.

All signatories for mutually binding contracts, lenders and borrowers for loans, and ministerial officials who receive or modify deeds announcing unstamped deeds or books are jointly responsible for the payment of stamp duties and fines.

Business licence tax

The business licence tax applies to both individuals and entities, Gabonese and foreign, engaged in a profession, business, or industry in Gabon.

Business license tax corresponds to a professional tax borne annually. It is deductible from the taxable income for CIT purposes.

The rates of this tax vary according to the profession, business, and location within Gabon territory (this tax may vary between XAF 15,000 and XAF 540,000).

The head of the group of companies is exempted from the payment of the business licence tax.

Gabon

Franchise tax

The franchise tax is a fixed annual duty varying from XAF 10,000 to XAF 500,000, according to the size, nature, and location of the company. Each company that carries on a trade, business, or activity that is not expressly exempted is liable for franchise tax.

Activities that are expressly exempted from franchise tax are those carried out by companies of provident, craftsmen, teachers and professors, lyrical and dramatic artists, farmers, cattle-breeders, fishers, etc.

Registration duties

Registration duties in Gabon are fixed, proportional, or progressive, depending on the nature of the acts and transfers in question.

Tax on insurance premiums

Insurance or annuity agreements made with insurance companies or any other Gabonese or foreign insurer are subject to an annual obligatory tax.

The tax is levied on the sums charged by the insurer and on any accessory payments made to this party by the insured party according to the following rates:

Nature of the policies	Rate (%)
Marine policies	5
Life policies	Exempt
Fire policies	30
Other (e.g. personal liability, transportation)	8
Reinsurance	Exempt

Social security contributions

Employers must contribute to the social security system (National Social Security Fund or CNSS).

The taxable basis for social security contributions is made up of gross salaries including indemnities having the function of a salary and any benefits in kind. However, there is an annual ceiling of XAF 18 million (or XAF 1.5 million per month).

The social security contributions are determined according to the following rates:

Contribution	Rate (%)
Family allowances	8
Industrial accidents (work injuries)	3
Retirement pensions	5
Health evacuation funds	0.6
Medication distribution	2
Hospitalisations	1.5
Total	20.1

Branch income

Taxation of branch income is the same as for corporate income. However, a 10% WHT on profit is due at the time the profit is taken by the head office of the branch located abroad.

Simplified tax regime for oil subcontractors

There is a simplified tax regime specific to the oil sector which is a lump-sum tax regime granted for a triennial period. The rates for the 2012, 2013, and 2014 fiscal years is 8.75%, corresponding to CIT (5.95%) and personal income tax for expatriate employees (2.80%). Features of this specific regime are as follows:

- The option for this regime is irrevocable.
- The option is granted by the Director of the General Tax Office to foreign companies.
- The subcontractor must have signed, with an oil company, a temporary agreement for the provisions of services to this company.
- The option is no longer granted to companies that have been in Gabon for more than nine years. The duration of nine years is calculated from the year during which the company started its activities in Gabon.
- The subcontractor must constitute a Gabonese branch office.

Specific regime for regional offices (quartiers généraux)

A regional office is a company or a branch that renders various administrative services such as management or accounting exclusively to other companies of the same group based in a given geographical area (usually a group of countries).

Taxation is based on the expenses of the regional office. A rate, between 5% and 12%, is applied to operating expenditures to determine the tax basis. The CIT rate is then applied to that basis.

Income determination

Capital gains

Capital gains arising from the transfer of assets must be used for the calculation of taxable profits. However, the tax on capital gains can be deferred if a company reinvests an amount equal to the capital gain and the sale price of the transferred asset back into its fixed assets within three years.

Dividend income

The rate of transferable securities income tax (IRCM) is 15% on distributed dividends when the beneficiary is a company and 20% when the beneficiary is an individual.

IRCM, charged on the beneficiaries of the earnings, is withheld at source by the distributing company. It is paid over to the Registration Officer within 30 days from the payment of the dividends.

Inter-company dividends

Inter-company dividends are taxed at a reduced rate in full discharge of the 10% WHT if paid and received by or from companies with their registered office in a CEMAC country, shares were allotted at the time of issue or kept for two years, and the Gabonese company owns more than 25% of the share capital of the subsidiary.

Gabon

Foreign income

Foreign interest, royalties, and dividends are included in taxable income, subject to international tax treaties. Note that tax treaties provide that certain/all types of income are not includable in Gabon taxable income. Gabon has tax treaties with France, Belgium, the other countries of CEMAC, and the African and Malagasy Common Organisation (OCAM).

The concept of deferred tax is not applicable in Gabon.

Deductions

Depreciation

The straight-line method and an accelerated depreciation method are permitted in Gabon. Tax and book conformity is obligatory (i.e. annual depreciation must be booked to preserve tax deductibility).

The main depreciation rates provided by the Gabonese tax code are the following:

Asset	Rate (%)
Buildings	8
Machinery, equipment	8 to 20
Office furniture	15
Office equipment	20
Vehicles	20 to 33.3
Computing equipment	25 to 33.3

Interest expenses

Interests paid to shareholders with respect to the sums made available by them to the company are only deductible within the global limit amounting to half of the share capital and within the limit of the intervention rate on invitation to tender (TIAO) of the Bank of the Central African States raised by 2%, provided that the share capital is fully paid up.

Bad debt

Bad debt can be deducted from the result of the fiscal year during which the debt became completely unrecoverable, subject to the irrecoverable character of the compromised debt being justified due to the situation of the debtor.

Provisions

To be tax deductible, provisions must relate to existing liability or loss. General provisions are not deductible.

Charitable contributions

Charitable contributions do not, in principle, constitute expenses deductible from the taxable result. However, contributions for charity can be deducted, provided that the donation is made to the profit of organisms of public interest located in Gabon and that the donation is justified.

The deduction is limited to 1/1,000 of the company's turnover for the considered fiscal year.

Fines and penalties
Fines and third-party taxes borne by companies are not tax deductible.

Taxes
Only professional taxes for which the recovery proceeding has started in the current fiscal year and for which the company is effectively liable due to operation carried out in Gabon can be deducted.

Net operating losses
The Gabonese Tax Code does not provide the possibility to carry back losses. It does, however, provide for a three-year carryforward for net operating losses.

Regarding depreciation deferred in the accounts, they can be carried forward indefinitely.

G

Payments to foreign affiliates
Management fees paid to a foreign parent company are deductible if they meet all of the following conditions:

- They reflect real transactions.
- They do not present an abnormal characteristic.
- They are not exaggerated.

Management fees determined in a lump sum basis are not deductible.

Interests paid to shareholders are deductible only within the limit of the Central Bank's (BEAC) normal rate for advances plus two percentage points, on the condition that the registered capital is entirely paid. The portion exceeding the ceiling is not deductible and is thus subject to taxation.

Group taxation

Specific group tax regime
The Financial Act of 2011 has instituted a specific tax regime derogatory to the common law tax regime that is applicable, under conditions, to groups of companies.

According to the provisions of Article 11 b. of the Law No. 44/2010, groups of companies are those that are organised around a head of the group of companies having its head office located in Gabon and having the control of companies located in Gabon and/or abroad.

To be eligible for this specific tax regime, and without any prejudice of other activities performed to the profit of third parties, the head of the group of companies must perform to the profit of other companies of the group an activity relating exclusively to the following fields:

- Provisions of services of any kind notably technical, accounting, financial, administrative, data processing, legal, human resources, and commercial corresponding to functions of management, coordination, and control of the group's companies.
- Research and development (R&D) to the sole profit of the group.
- Management of the finance intra-group.

Gabon

Each company subject to CIT that is a member of the group and fulfils the conditions provided by the law will be subject to a separate taxation of its results according to the rules of common law and subject to amendments expressly provided by the law for the determination of the taxable result.

The express amendments provided in the scope of the specific tax regime applicable to groups of companies are the following:

Capital gains
Net capital gains are taxed at a reduced rate of 20% when they are realised in the scope of intra-group operations.

Expenses deductible from the taxable result subject to CIT
The following expenses are deductible within the group:

- Head office fees and management fees determined in a lump sum basis, according to the conditions of allocation of the expense between the companies members of the group defined in a previous ruling with the Tax Authorities.
- The whole of the interests on partners' current accounts (i.e. on the sums put, by the partners, at the disposal of a company of the group) within the sole limit of the intervention rate on invitation to tender (TIAO) of the Bank of the Central African States (equivalent to 4%) raised by 2%.
- Rentings of movables carried out within the group by the mother company or between companies of the same group.

10% WHT
Sums subject to CIT according to the provisions of Article 206 of the Gabonese Tax Code paid by a Gabonese debtor member of a group of companies to a foreign company member of the same group are exempted from the 10% WHT even though no DTT aiming to avoid double taxation has been concluded between Gabon and the country of residence of the beneficiary of the remunerations.

Transferable securities income tax (IRCM)
Companies of the group which benefit from transferable securities income originating from Gabon are exempted from IRCM when the said revenues are paid by a company member of the group.

In return, payments carried out by the head of the group of companies to the profit of its partners (individuals or legal entities) are subject to IRCM at a unique and at source rate of 10% (instead of 20% for individuals and 15% for legal entities).

It is to be noted that the transferable securities incomes having their source abroad and which gave rise to taxation in their country of origin give the right in Gabon to a tax credit of the amount of the taxation which is deductible from the CIT of the fiscal year of perception of the incomes. The aforesaid tax credit applies even though no DTT aiming to avoid double taxation has been concluded between Gabon and the country of origin of the incomes.

VAT
The head of the group of companies is liable for VAT.

Members of a group of companies could, however, on option, consider the following provisions of services performed within the group as being out of the scope of application of VAT.

- Provisions of services of any kind, notably technical, accounting, financial, administrative, data processing, legal, human resources, and commercial.
- Fees relating to studies.
- Putting at disposal of personal.
- Management of finance.

The option for the subjection of the abovementioned operations must be formulated by the concerned taxpayers on express request addressed to the General Tax Manager.

Registration duties
Deeds relating to incorporation, increase or reduction of share capital, breaking up with or without clearance, merger, scission, partial contribution of assets, and transfer of shares of a company member of a tax group, are subject to a fixed duty of XAF 20,000.

In the absence of a more favourable duty provided by the common law of registration, the changes of ownership and use which are not provided at Article 6 of the Gabonese Tax Code are subject to a proportional rate of 1% when carried out by members of the same tax group.

Requirements relating to declaratory obligations
The adherence to the group tax regime must be notified in writing by the head of the group of companies to the General Tax Manager accompanied by the list of the companies included in the tax perimeter of the group.

Each company remains liable for the periodical returns applicable to its activity.

For the purpose of calculation and verification of the returns, each tax return relating to the CIT of each company of the group will be gathered and filed at the same time by the head of the group of companies before the Tax Office.

Transfer pricing
The Gabonese Tax Code provides rules regarding transfer pricing issues.

According to these rules, any payment considered to be a result of mismanagement will be subject to the CIT rate at 35% plus penalties.

Indeed, Article 12 of the Code provides that "By virtue of law or in fact, for companies which are dependent of companies or groups of companies located outside the CEMAC area, or for those which possess the control of companies located outside the CEMAC area, payments or expenses realised by any mean whatsoever, comparable to abnormal act of management, constitute transfer of profits subject to corporate income tax".

It is applicable for the following:

- Payments constituting increase or decrease of purchases or sales.
- Payments of excessive royalties or royalties without compensation.
- Relinquishment of revenues (underestimated sale price, free of charge service provision, granting of a free loan or a loan with low interests).

The abnormal act of management is not limited to expenses; it also includes any form of advantages or allowances granted to third parties without any equivalent compensation for the company.

Gabon

Article 13 of the Gabonese Tax Code provides that "The advantages or assistance granted by companies belonging to the same group can only be considered as resulting from a normal management if the company which grants these advantages or assistance demonstrates the existence of its own interest in acting as such. The general interest of the group is not sufficient to justify such practices".

Thin capitalisation

There is no specific tax rule under Gabon legislation related to thin capitalisation.

Tax credits and incentives

Foreign tax credit

DTTs include provisions relating to the attribution of foreign tax credits. Such tax credits aim to limit the double taxation of profits that are subject to taxation in both Member States of the treaty.

Tax credits for job creation

There is a mechanism in place for granting corporate tax credits for any salaried appointments of Gabonese personnel.

This tax credit is equal to 20% of the gross salary paid to new employees and is subject to the creation of a minimum number of jobs, according to the size of the company as follows:

* Two jobs, for companies with less than 20 employees.
* Three jobs, for companies with 20 to 50 employees.
* Five jobs, for companies with more than 50 employees.

Note that the tax credit is granted only on newly created jobs since the preceding fiscal year. Contracts concluded with the employees must also be for an undetermined duration, and the new jobs must not result from the diminution of existing jobs.

Inbound investment incentives

Due to the provisions of the Investments Law, any private investment in Gabon can benefit from:

* A common law framework.
* Privileged frameworks.
* Specifically agreed frameworks.

Depending on the frameworks it is eligible for, a company can benefit from customs privileges and tax breaks.

Industrial companies already set up in Gabon and wishing to increase their production capacity can be admitted to a preferential tariff framework. This entails the application of a global reduced rate of 5% for duties and taxes paid on imports of equipment (excluding materials, furniture, and spare parts) provided that these correspond to an investment schedule and their value is in excess of XAF 100 million.

New industrial companies can also benefit from this framework, if they are not subject to any of the other privileged frameworks outlined by current legislation.

The granting of this privileged tariff framework occurs on the basis of a decision by the Minister of Finances, following a proposal from the Director of Customs and Indirect Taxes.

Capital investment incentive
New companies are exempt from the IMF, the minimum taxation of CIT, during the first two years of operations.

Social housing incentive
The Financial Act of 2011 provides some exemptions of taxes applicable exclusively to authorised companies during the performance of a social housing investment project.

The concerned companies are those authorised for the planning of urban lands intended for social habitat and the building of housings of a socio-economic nature and industrial units of manufacturing of materials and other inputs used for the building of social housings. The above mentioned tax exemptions relate to CIT, VAT, and business licence tax.

G

Withholding taxes

10% WHT
When they are paid by a debtor established in Gabon to individuals or companies subject to CIT or personal income tax (PIT) that do not have a permanent professional base in Gabon, the following amounts are subject to a 10% WHT:

- All amounts paid pursuant to the practice of an 'independent profession' in Gabon.
- Payments received by inventors, payments relating to copyrights, and all payments relating to intellectual and commercial property as well as assimilated rights.
- All amounts paid for services materially rendered or effectively used in Gabon.
- Interest, arrears, and all others fixed-income investment-products, pertaining to income declared as professional revenue of the beneficiary.

Net profits carried out by branches of foreign companies having their head offices abroad are also subject to a 10% WHT in Gabon before they are taken into account by the foreign companies.

Transferable securities income tax (IRCM) at rate 15%
IRCM is due on revenues from stocks and shares paid to legal entities. It is due by beneficiaries of these revenues and must be withheld by the distributing company.

Tax administration

Taxable period
Companies are required by law to have a 31 December closing of any fiscal year.

Tax returns
Returns for the previous calendar year are to be filed before 30 April of each year.

Payment of tax
Tax is payable to the General Tax Office in two instalments on 30 November and 30 January. The balance of the tax due must be paid by 30 April. The first instalment must

Gabon

equal one-quarter of the tax assessed in the previous year and the second instalment must equal one-third of this tax.

Audit cycle
There is no a specific audit cycle in Gabon.

Statute of limitations
The tax administration can proceed to tax audit until the fourth year following the year for which the tax is due.

Topics of focus for tax authorities
The tax administration shall particularly focus on the following aspects:

- Compliance of deductibility of management fees.
- Compliance of deductibility of corporate expenses.
- Compliance of WHT on payments made to foreign services providers.
- Payment of VAT on behalf of third parties.

Other issues

Legal reserve
According to the provisions of the OHADA Uniform Act relating to commercial companies and economic interest groups, one-tenth of the year's profits, reduced, if applicable, by any previous losses, must be put into a reserve account named 'Legal Reserve'.

The endowment of this reserve ceases to be obligatory when its value reaches one-fifth (20%) of the company share capital.

Georgia

PwC contact

Robin McCone
PricewaterhouseCoopers Central Asia and Caucasus B.V.
#7 Bambis Rigi Street
Business Center Mantashevi
Tbilisi 0105, Georgia
Tel: +995 32 50 80 50
Email: robin.mccone@ge.pwc.com

Significant developments

To attract foreign investment, the Georgian government is gradually reducing withholding tax (WHT) rates on passive income as follows:

- The 5% WHT rate on dividends paid to non-residents will be reduced to 3% on 1 January 2013 and to 0% on 1 January 2014.
- The 5% WHT rate on interest paid to non-residents will be reduced to 0% on 1 January 2014.
- The WHT rate on all other types of income received by non-residents was changed to 15% in 2011 but has since decreased to 10%.

Taxes on corporate income

Corporate income tax (CIT) in Georgia is applied to taxable profit at a rate of 15%. Taxable profit is defined as gross income minus deductible expenses.

Resident enterprises are subject to CIT on worldwide income.

Non-resident enterprises carrying out economic activities in Georgia through a permanent establishment (PE) are subject to CIT with respect to gross income earned from Georgian sources, which can be reduced by deductions attributable to such income.

Non-resident enterprises earning income from Georgian sources, other than through a PE, are subject to WHT (*see the Withholding taxes section for more information*).

Local income taxes
There are no local income taxes imposed on the profit of legal entities.

Corporate residence

A resident enterprise is any legal entity that is established under the laws of Georgia or has its place of effective management in Georgia.

Permanent establishment (PE)
The domestic definition for a PE essentially adopts the definition for PE found in the Organisation for Economic Co-operation and Development (OECD) Model Tax Convention.

Georgia

Local legislation provides the definition for economic activity to be any activity undertaken with the intent to gain profit, income, or compensation, regardless of the results of such activity, unless otherwise provided by the tax code.

Other taxes

Value-added tax (VAT)
The standard VAT rate is 18% and applies to the sale of all goods and services supplied in Georgia. Goods are considered to be supplied in Georgia if they are transferred in or their shipment originates in Georgia. Services generally are considered to be supplied in Georgia if they are performed in Georgia. However, special rules apply for services relating to immovable property and certain services provided to non-residents.

The export and re-export of goods is exempt from VAT with the right to credit input tax (formerly referred to as zero-rated). VAT-exempt supplies include financial services, goods and services required for oil and gas operations, and medical services.

Reverse-charge VAT applies to services provided to Georgian taxpayers by a non-resident entity.

A VAT payer is a person who is registered or required to be registered as a VAT payer. Any person whose annual taxable turnover exceeds 100,000 Georgian lari (GEL) in any continuous period up to 12 months or who produces or imports excisable goods must register as a VAT payer. In addition, an enterprise that expects to perform one-off taxable transaction of more than GEL 100,000 must also register as a VAT payer before effecting the transaction.

Customs duties
Import tax is levied on the goods that crossed the economical borders of Georgia (except export). Depending on the types of products, general rates on imported goods are: 0%, 5%, and 12%. Imported cars (listed in the section # 8703 of warehouse nomenclature) are taxed at GEL 0.05 * by volume of engine, plus 5% of import tax on each additional year of ownership.

Excise tax
Excise tax is levied on specified goods that are produced in Georgia or imported into Georgia. Excise tax generally is calculated with reference to the quantity of goods (e.g. volume, weight), or in the case of automobiles, on the basis of the engine capacity and vehicle age. Excise tax rate varies from GEL 0.15 to 400 for one unit.

Excise tax applies to the following goods:

- Alcoholic drinks (i.e. GEL 5 per litre of whiskey).
- Condensed natural gas, except for pipeline.
- Oil distillates.
- Goods produced from crude oil.
- Tobacco products.
- Automobiles.

The export of excisable goods is exempt from excise tax with the right to credit.

Georgia

Property tax

Property tax is payable at the rate of 1% on the annual average residual value of fixed assets (except for land) on the balance sheet as well as on leased out property of Georgian entities or foreign entities with taxable property in Georgia. For property acquired before 2005, the average residual value must be multiplied by a coefficient of between 1.5 and 3, depending on the acquisition date.

Land tax

The annual land tax rate for agricultural land varies according to the administrative unit and the land quality.

The base tax rate per 1 hectare of agricultural land varies from GEL 1.50 to GEL 100. The tax is further adjusted by a territorial coefficient of up to 150%, depending on the location.

The base tax rate payable on non-agricultural land is GEL 0.24 per square metre, which is further adjusted by a territorial coefficient not exceeding 150%.

Transfer taxes

There are no transfer taxes in Georgia.

Stamp taxes

There are no stamp taxes in Georgia.

Branch income

Branch income is taxed at the general rate of 15%. There is no tax on branch profit remittances.

Income determination

Taxable income is determined as the difference between the gross income of a taxpayer and the relevant deductions granted under the Georgian tax code.

Inventory valuation

A taxpayer is required to record the value of goods produced or acquired as the outlays (except for depreciation charges) or the purchase price in tax accounting. Furthermore, the taxpayer shall include the storage and transportation expenses into the value of such goods.

A taxpayer is entitled to record the cost of inventory using the individual accounting method, the average weighted cost method, or first in first out (FIFO).

Capital gains

The Georgian tax code does not define any separate tax for capital gains. Capital gains are taxable as normal business income at the general CIT rate.

Dividend income

Dividends received by local legal entities (except for the sole enterprises and entrepreneur partnership) are not subject to taxation at the source and shall not be included in gross income.

Georgia

Dividends received by non-resident enterprises from resident enterprises are subject to WHT at source (*see the Withholding taxes section for more information*).

Interest income
Resident legal entities and PEs of non-residents that received interest income that was taxed as source in Georgia are entitled to a credit tax paid to the state budget.

Interest income received from a licensed financial institution is not subject to WHT at source, and it should not be included in the gross income of a recipient unless the recipient is another licensed financial institution.

Rent/royalty income
Rent and royalty income received by resident companies and/or PEs of non-resident enterprises should be included in the gross income of the enterprise and taxed at the CIT rate of 15%.

Foreign income
Resident legal entities are subject to CIT on their worldwide income. Foreign income is subject to CIT at 15%.

Deductions

Expenses connected with the receipt of income generally are deductible from income, provided sufficient primary documentation is available.

Depreciation
The declining-balance method of depreciation applies to fixed assets for tax purposes. The maximum rate of depreciation is 20% for most fixed assets, though buildings and construction are subject to depreciation at the rate of 5% (please contact us for additional information regarding other groups and rates).

A taxpayer is entitled to fully deduct costs of fixed assets (excluding those contributed to capital) in the year when the fixed assets are put into operation (a form of capital allowance). In case the taxpayer employs the right of full deduction in this manner, this method may not be changed for five years.

Amortisation of intangible assets
Intangible assets (e.g. goodwill) are amortisable in proportion with the period of beneficial use. However, intangible assets of value less then GEL 1,000 are fully deductable from gross income.

If the period of beneficial use of an intangible asset cannot be defined, it is amortisable at the rate of 15%.

Start-up expenses
Expenses incurred before registration of an entity as a taxpayer (e.g. public registry fee) are not deductible under Georgian tax legislation.

Interest expenses
Interest paid on loans is deductible within the limits established by the Finance Minister. The annual deductible interest rate limitation established by the Minister of Finance of Georgia for the year 2012 is 24%.

Bad debts

A taxpayer is entitled to deduct bad debts only if all of the following conditions are met:

- The bad debt is related to the taxpayer's goods or services sold.
- Income receivable from the sale of goods or services was previously included in taxable gross income.
- The bad debt has been written off and recorded as such in the taxpayer's accounting records.

Charitable contributions

Charitable contributions are deductible, up to 10% of taxable profit.

Fines and penalties

Fine and penalties paid to the state budget are not deductible.

G

Taxes

CIT is disallowed for deduction.

Other significant items

The following other expenses are not deductible:

- Expenses not related to the generation of income.
- Expenses related to the receipt of income exempted from CIT.

The deduction of certain expenses is subject to limitations, including:

- Representation expenses, up to 1% of gross income.
- Repair expenses, up to 5% of the book value of the relevant asset at the end of the year. Any excess must be capitalised and deducted through depreciation.

Net operating losses

Losses may be carried forward for five years but may not be carried back.

A taxpayer may elect to extend the carryforward period to ten years. However, this also results in the statute of limitations period being extended from six to 11 years.

International financial companies, international enterprises, and Special Trading Companies are not entitled to carry forward losses.

An international financial company is a financial institution that, on behalf of the application of plenipotentiary representative, gets state registered, is granted as 'international financial company', and is given a status confirming certificate. These are resident companies that, after application, were granted the status of international financial company.

An international enterprise is an enterprise operating in the free industrial zone, which, for the purposes of tax exemption, is granted the status of international enterprise.

Group taxation

Georgian law does not provide for taxation of groups.

Georgia

Transfer pricing

The transfer pricing rules introduced in the tax code are broadly based on the OECD arm's-length principle adopted in tax treaties and by most countries when they implement domestic transfer pricing rules.

The law recognises the five OECD transfer pricing methods for evaluating whether prices are at arm's length:

- Comparable uncontrolled price method.
- Resale price method.
- Cost plus method.
- Net profit margin method.
- Profit split method.

The tax code stipulates that in accordance with the Ministry of Finance instructions, the tax authority may recalculate the taxes if they can prove that the prices applied by related parties of transactions differ from the market prices.

The following general penalties, determined by tax legislation, apply for non-compliance with the arm's-length principle or failing to prepare or submit transfer pricing documentation:

- An understated tax liability (e.g. VAT, CIT) is subject to a penalty of 50% of the understated tax.
- Late payment of taxes is subject to interest at a rate of 0.07% per overdue day.
- Failing to submit a required document is generally subject to a penalty of GEL 400 (approximately 220 United States dollars [USD]).

Thin capitalisation

With the introduction of the tax code, thin capitalisation rules became effective on 1 January 2011. Interest expense may be disallowed if a company's debt-to-equity ratio exceeds 5:1. The thin capitalisation rules will not apply to financial institutions, entities that have gross income of less than GEL 200,000, and entities with interest expense that is less than 20% of their taxable income before deducting such interest expense.

Tax credits and incentives

Foreign tax credit

Income tax or profit tax paid on income earned from outside Georgia may be credited against CIT payable in Georgia. The amount of credited taxes may not exceed the Georgian tax payable on the foreign income.

CIT exemptions

The following are exempt from CIT (the list is not exhaustive):

- Income of budgetary, international, and charitable organisations (including grants, membership fees, and donations), except for the profit from commercial activity.
- Profit received from financial services conducted by international financial companies.
- Gains on sales of securities issued by international financial companies.

Free industrial zone (FIZ)

The following rules apply for enterprises located in a FIZ:

- Income received by an international enterprise from its permitted activities conducted in a FIZ is exempt from CIT.
- The importation of foreign goods into FIZ is free of customs duties and VAT-exempt.
- Operations carried out in FIZ are VAT-exempt without the right to credit.
- Property located in FIZ is exempt from property tax.
- The personal income tax of employees is paid by those individuals through self-reporting.

Withholding taxes

Non-resident enterprises earning income from Georgian sources, other than through a PE, are subject to WHT at the following rates:

Income	WHT (%)
Dividends (reducing to 3% on 1 January 2013)	5
Royalties	10
Interest (reducing to 0% on 1 January 2014)	5
Oil and gas subcontractor income	4
International transportation/communication	10
Income from services rendered in Georgia	10
Other Georgian-source income	10
Insurance and re-insurance	0

Tax administration

The tax departments under the Ministry of Finance are responsible for tax administrative matters in Georgia.

Taxable period
The tax year is the calendar year in Georgia.

Tax returns
A CIT return should be submitted before 1 April of the year following the reporting period.

Payment of tax
CIT is paid in advance in four equal instalments, before 15 May, 15 July, 15 September, and 15 December. The advance instalments are estimated according to the previous year's annual tax. A taxpayer with no prior-year CIT obligation is not required to make advance payments.

Final payment is due by 1 April of the year following the reporting period. Excess CIT payments may be offset against other tax liabilities.

Statute of limitations
The statute of limitations is six years in Georgia. For those taxpayers who decide to increase the loss carryforward to ten years, the statute of limitations is 11 years.

Germany

PwC contact

Dieter Endres
PricewaterhouseCoopers AG
Wirtschaftsprüfungsgesellschaft
Friedrich-Ebert-Anlage 35-37
60327 Frankfurt am Main
Germany
Tel: +49 69 9585 6459
Email: dieter.endres@de.pwc.com

Significant developments

At the start of the year, the political intention was to proceed through to the end of 2013 without substantial changes to the corporate tax system. This was still the intention at the end of 2011. Tax revenue collection has, however, been better than expected, but the government's first priority is to relieve individuals, rather than corporations. The current thinking is a modest reform of the progression scale of income tax rates in two stages, in 2013 and 2014.

The 2013 Annual Tax Bill has recently been published. Noteworthy is a radical change in approach to the taxation of permanent establishments (PEs). Henceforth, these are to be treated as though they are separate entities dealing with their own head office and other parts of the company on arm's-length terms. This conforms to the approach as authorised by the Organisation for Economic Co-operation and Development (OECD).

The European Court of Justice has recently rejected the withholding tax (WHT) on dividends to foreign companies as an unacceptable hindrance on the free movement of capital. The case concerned a portfolio dividend to a corporate recipient in another European Union (EU) member state. The Supreme Tax Court has followed the ruling in another case on a dividend to a sole-shareholder French corporation, but the impact on inter-corporate dividends paid outside the EU/European Economic Area (EEA) is not yet clear. The finance ministry has not yet announced its position.

Taxes on corporate income

Germany taxes its corporate residents on their worldwide income. However, most double tax treaties (DTTs) exempt income attributable to a foreign PE. Non-residents with PE or property income are taxed by assessment on German-source income; those earning royalties and dividends are taxed by withholding at source. Interest paid abroad is, in most cases, free of German tax altogether.

German business profits are subject to two taxes, corporation tax and trade tax.

Corporation tax (Körperschaftsteuer)
Corporation tax is levied at a uniform rate of 15% and is then subject to a surcharge of 5.5% (solidarity levy).

Trade tax (Gewerbesteuer)
The effective rate of trade tax varies by location from a minimum of 7%, which is the legal minimum and applies in a few small villages in depressed areas, to the Munich rate of 17.1%. The local rates in most cities range between 14% and 16%, whilst those

in small towns can be as low as 12%. The basis for this tax is the adjusted accounting profit: in particular, 25% of all financing costs over 100,000 euros (EUR), including the implicit financing costs in leasing, rental, and royalty payments, are added back to taxable income.

If the basis for the two taxes is identical (unlikely in practice), the overall burden on corporate profits earned in Munich would be 33%. In Frankfurt, the burden would be 31.9%. In Berlin, the burden would be 30.2%.

Corporate residence

A corporation is resident in Germany for tax purposes if either its place of incorporation or its main place of management is in Germany. A corporation meeting neither of these criteria will be regarded as non-resident with tax obligations limited to its income from German sources. These include active business activities through a PE or the letting of property, as well as investment income, royalties, and equipment rental (leasing). Income of the first two categories is generally taxed by assessment on the actual net earnings. That of the last three is usually taxed at source by withholding from the gross amount payable. Interest paid abroad is generally tax-free. However, interest on convertible or profit-sharing bonds is taxed as a dividend; interest on a German property or ship mortgage is seen as property or shipping income respectively.

Permanent establishment (PE)
Domestic law defines a PE as any fixed business facility serving the corporate purpose. 'Fixed' is not defined further, but is generally taken to imply a duration of at least six months. A permanent representative is someone who 'habitually' deals on behalf of the instructions of the principal, again without any specific time limit. Germany consistently follows the OECD model in her tax treaty PE definitions; thus purchasing activities, delivery stores, and independent agents acting in the ordinary course of their business are regularly excluded from the PE concept.

Other taxes

Value-added tax (VAT)
Proceeds of sales and services effected in Germany are subject to VAT under the common system of the EU at the standard rate of 19% (7% on certain items, such as food and books). The taxpayer generally is entitled to deduct the VAT charged on inputs from that payable on outputs.

VAT is administered by the tax office responsible for the corporation tax assessment of a company. It is based on returns filed monthly or quarterly by the tenth of the following month (monthly where the output tax in the previous year was more than EUR 7,500) drawn up on the basis of the actual transactions during the filing period as shown in the books of account. A permanent filing extension of one month is available against an advance payment of one-eleventh of the total net tax due during the previous year. Otherwise, payment is due when the return is filed.

Legally, VAT is an annual tax. Each taxpayer must file an annual return for each calendar year, regardless of the actual accounting date for the business. The VAT return is filed together with the corporation and trade tax returns. If the annual return does not agree with the total of the monthly or quarterly returns, the tax office can be expected to ask for a detailed explanation and to penalise any irregularity.

Germany

Customs duties

Customs duties are levied under a common system on imports into the European Union. The rate is set at zero on most imports from EU candidate countries and on many imports from countries with which the European Union has an association agreement.

For manufactured products from other countries, the rates generally lie within the range of 0% to 10%. The basis is the import value of the goods and thus includes uplifts for royalty or other payments associated with their use but not apparent from the transit documents.

The European Commission also sets 'countervailing' duties from time to time on specific imports from specific countries in order to counter dumping attempts. The countervailing duty rate is set to fully absorb the dumping margin and is therefore usually much higher than 10%.

Excise taxes

Excise taxes on fuel, electric power, insurance, and some other products are not a compliance issue for businesses other than dealers in bonded goods and insurance companies, although they can be a significant additional cost factor for business users. These excise taxes also have an environmental element in as much as the rates are set to discourage excessive use of pollutants. However, an air passenger duty is the only tax on pollution as such. Energy producers (such as power stations) can claim a refund of the excise tax borne in the cost of the energy products used in the production process.

Property taxes

There are no taxes on wealth or capital employed. There is a minor local authority tax on property, but the effect of this is largely offset by an additional trade tax deduction.

Stamp taxes

The only significant German stamp tax is the real estate transfer tax of, in most parts of the country, 3.5% of the consideration on conveyances of German property.

This tax is also levied on indirect transfers from the acquisition of at least 95% of the shares in property owning companies. This applies to shares in the shareholder throughout the corporate chain. If the transfer is indirect, and therefore without its own specific consideration, the basis for the tax is 12.5 times the annual rentable value. This value is derived from rents actually achieved over the past three years or estimated from statistics maintained by the local authority.

The tax is not levied on direct or indirect transfers without consideration in the course of a corporate reorganisation under the laws of a member state of the European Economic Area, provided at least 95% of the ultimate interest in the property remains unchanged for five years before and after the transaction.

Real estate transfer tax is currently under attack before the Constitutional Court.

Social security contributions

All employers are required to account for social security contributions on wages and salaries paid, up to set monthly limits. There are four separate types of insurance: for old-age pensions, unemployment benefits, health care, and invalidity care. Employees regularly earning more than EUR 4,125 per month can opt out of the health and invalidity insurances provided they take out appropriate coverage with a private insurance company. The pension and unemployment insurances are compulsory for all employees. The upper monthly salary limits are EUR 5,500 (EUR 4,800 in the eastern part of Germany) for the pension and unemployment insurances and EUR 3,712.50 for the health and invalidity insurances. The rates are as follows:

- Pension insurance: 19.6%, of which the employee's share is one half.
- Unemployment insurance: 3.0%, of which the employee's share is one half.
- Health insurance: 15.5%, of which the employee's share is 8.2%.
- Invalidity insurance: 1.95%, of which the employee's share is one half.

Branch income

Both corporation tax and trade tax are imposed on the taxable income of a foreign company's German branch. The rates are the same for branches as for resident German companies, although the WHT on dividend distributions by German companies is not deducted from profits transferred by a German branch to its foreign head office.

Income determination

Strict conformity between book and tax reporting is no longer required. Rather, a company must draw up its financial statements according to the dictates of fair presentation, but may exercise all valuation and other options in the tax acts in its own best tax interest without regard to the accounting treatment for the item concerned. It must keep a register of all variances between the financial statements and the tax computation showing the basis on which each arose and its reversal. IFRS financial statements are not accepted as a basis for computing taxable income.

Inventory valuation
Inventories normally are valued at the lower of actual cost, replacement cost, and net realisable value. However, any write-downs below actual cost must be for specific reasons. If specific identification of the inventories is not possible, valuation at either standard or average cost is acceptable. The last in first out (LIFO) method is accepted as an option. First in first out (FIFO) is not accepted unless its assumption accords with the facts, although this condition is often fulfilled in practice.

Long-term liabilities and accruals
Non-interest bearing long-term liabilities, other than advance payments received, must be discounted at 5.5% per year. A similar provision applies to refurbishment (to restore an asset to its original condition) and other accruals which accumulate over time.

Capital gains
Generally, capital gains realised by a corporate entity from a disposal of business assets are treated as ordinary income. It is possible to postpone the taxation of part or all of the gain on real estate by offsetting the gain against the cost of a replacement property.

Capital gains from the sale of investments in other companies are exempt from corporation and trade taxes. Corresponding losses are not deductible. However, 5% of the capital gains are added back to taxable income as non-deductible directly related expenses.

Dividend income
Dividends received are exempt from corporation and trade taxes, regardless of the level of shareholding and the length of time it has been held. However, portfolio dividends

Germany

(on holdings of less than 15%) are subject to trade tax. 5% of the tax-free gross dividend is added back to taxable income as non-deductible business expenses.

Note that banks do not enjoy this exemption on dividends from securities held for trading.

Stock dividends

In principle, a declaration of stock dividends (by converting reserves to capital stock) by a company will not lead to taxable income for the shareholder or to other tax effects. Subsequent capital reductions, however, will be treated as cash dividends in most circumstances. There is no German tax reason for distributing a stock dividend as opposed to merely leaving accumulated profits on the books to be carried forward. The decision, therefore, depends upon the situation in the investor's home country.

Interest income

Interest received is taxed as part of a company's ordinary trading income. There is no exemption corresponding to the trade tax disallowance of 25% of the interest expense or to the general tax disallowance of net interest expense in excess of 30% of EBITDA under the interest limitation rule. However, since the interest limitation is based on the net interest margin, a company can benefit from earning income as interest as opposed to an interest substitute.

Foreign income

Foreign income, except dividends, received by a German corporation from foreign sources is included in taxable income for corporation tax unless a tax treaty provides for an exemption. Foreign PE income, in most cases, is exempt from corporation and trade taxes, while double taxation on most items of passive income (e.g. interest and royalties) is avoided by foreign tax credit or, at the taxpayer's option, by a deduction of the foreign taxes as an expense.

Irrespective of any tax treaty, income from a foreign branch or partnership is not charged to trade tax.

A Foreign Tax Act sets anti-avoidance (including controlled foreign company [CFC]) rules with respect to subsidiaries in certain lines of business subject to a low-tax regime. A low tax regime is one in which the rate applicable to the income in question is less than 25%. Most forms of passive income fall under the CFC rules, which essentially attribute the income to the German shareholder as though it had been earned directly. Active business income is not generally caught where the business operates from properly established facilities.

Investment income held in an EU/EEA subsidiary (except Liechtenstein) is also exempt from attribution, provided the subsidiary is commercially active in its country of operation and maintains at least a minimum establishment.

Other provisions give the tax office the right to insist on full disclosure of all the facts and circumstances surrounding a transaction as a condition for the deduction of a business expense incurred within an essentially tax-free environment for the supplier. This rule operates independently of ownership or shareholding considerations.

Deductions

Depreciation and amortisation
Depreciation on movable fixed assets is calculated on the straight-line method over the asset's anticipated useful life. The declining-balance method was available for assets capitalised in 2009 and 2010 at a maximum of two and a half times the straight-line rate, but in no case to exceed 25%. If this option was taken, it may be continued within subsequent years. On the other hand, a taxpayer is free to change from declining-balance to straight-line at any time. This election is by individual asset and cannot be reversed later. Depreciation takes the residual value of the asset into account only if it is material, with any gains on a sale being treated as normal business income.

Buildings are depreciated on a variety of straight-line or reducing rate systems designed to reach a full write-down between 25 and 50 years, depending on the age of the building and on whether the taxpayer was its first owner.

In addition to normal depreciation, special depreciation is deductible for tax purposes in certain limited circumstances (e.g. small businesses, ancient monuments, buildings in designated renovated city zones).

Intangibles are amortised straight-line over their estimated useful lives with goodwill amortised over 15 years.

Start-up expenses
Start-up and formation expenses are deductible as incurred.

Interest limitation
Annual net interest expense (the excess of interest paid over that received) of group companies is only deductible up to 30% of 'earnings before interest, tax, depreciation, and amortisation' (EBITDA) for corporation and trade tax purposes. The 30% limitation applies to all interest, whether the debt is granted by a shareholder, related party, or a third party.

This limitation does not apply where the total net interest expense for the year is less than EUR 3 million or where the net amount paid to any one shareholder of more than 25% (or a related party) is no more than 10% of the total. However, this latter concession is dependent on the demonstration that the equity to gross assets ratio of the company is no more than two percentage points below that of the group as a whole. Unused EBITDA potential may be carried forward for up to five years to cover future excess interest cost. This carryforward is otherwise subject to the same principles as the loss carryforward, including curtailment on change of shareholder(s).

It is emphasised that the interest limitation is additional to, and not a substitute for, the transfer pricing requirement that related party finance be at arm's length.

Bad debts
Bad debts incurred on trading with unrelated parties are deductible once irrecoverability is apparent and all attempts to pursue the debt have failed or been abandoned. Provision for future bad debts may be made; general provisions must reflect the past experience of the business; specific provisions require specific justification based on the actual circumstances. Loans to shareholders of more than 25% or to their related parties may not be written down or off with tax effect, unless a third party creditor would have granted the loan or allowed it to remain outstanding in otherwise similar circumstances.

Germany

Charitable contributions
Donations to recognised charities in cash or in kind are deductible, up to the higher of 20% of otherwise net taxable income or 0.4% of the total of sales revenue and wages and salaries paid during the year. Donations to charities registered in other EU/EEA member states also qualify for deduction if the recipient charity meets the German requirements for recognition.

Fines and penalties
Fines and other penalty payments levied by a court, or by an authority, with an intent to punish are not deductible. By contrast, those levied to confiscate ill-gotten gains or income, or to relieve damage to the victims or to the public good, are. Penalty payments levied for attempted tax evasion are not deductible, but late payment surcharges are, if the tax itself is, for example VAT.

Taxes
All taxes borne are deductible except for corporation tax, trade tax, and VAT on non-deductible expenses.

Net operating losses
Net operating losses are carried forward without time limit. For corporation tax (but not trade tax), there is an optional carryback to the previous year of up to EUR 511,500.

The loss relief brought forward claimable in any one year is limited to EUR 1 million plus 60% of current income exceeding that amount. The remaining 40% of income over EUR 1 million is charged to trade and corporation taxes at current rates. This is referred to as 'minimum taxation'.

The loss carryforward ceases if a single (immediate or ultimate) shareholder acquires more than 50% of the issued capital (voting rights) within a five year period. An acquisition of between 25% and 50% leads to a corresponding reduction in the loss carryforward.

Under the statute, these forfeiture rules do not apply to share acquisitions in connection with the recovery of a troubled business, where the change is part of a group internal reorganisation without effect on the single ultimate shareholder, or inasmuch as the loss carryforward is covered by hidden reserves in the company's assets that, on realisation, will lead to German taxation. This excludes the appreciation in value of shareholdings in other companies as well as business assets held in foreign PEs. However, the European Commission has recently decided to view the exemption from the forfeiture rules for share acquisitions within the context of a corporate recovery bid as unlawful state aid. Application of the provision has been suspended since April 2010; the government is contesting the Commission's finding before the European Court of Justice.

Payments to foreign affiliates
A German corporation can claim a deduction for royalties, management service fees, and, subject to the interest limitation, interest charges paid to foreign affiliates, provided the amounts are at arm's length. Detailed provisions covering both form and substance define this. In particular, all services must be covered by prior written agreement, and it is also necessary to conclude agreements for the purchase and sale of goods in writing where this would be usual between third parties (e.g. for quantity rebates on sales). The substance tests must be satisfied, both as to value for money and as to business relevance. Thus, the manager of a German subsidiary must be able to show both an adequate business benefit from a related party transaction and that

the company could not have obtained a better deal on the open market. These and all other aspects of inter-company (related-party) trading fall under strict and extensive documentation requirements, breach of which can lead to serious penalties.

Special features for trade tax
There are a number of differences between the income subject to trade tax and to corporation tax.

The most significant is the trade tax disallowance of one-quarter of the interest costs, including interest included implicitly in leasing, rental, and royalty charges. Banks have an exemption from this interest disallowance.

Group taxation

If a German parent holds more than 50% of the voting rights in a domestic subsidiary, the two may conclude a formal, five-year, court-registered profit pooling agreement. The ensuing relationship is then referred to as an *Organschaft*. Effectively, the annual results of an *Organschaft* are pooled in the accounts and tax returns of the parent. Profits and losses within a group can therefore be offset, but there is no provision for the elimination of intra-group profits from the total tax base.

Transfer pricing
Extensive rules on transfer pricing in respect of all transactions with foreign related parties are in force. The basic principle is that all trading should be at arm's length, but the documentation requirements go far beyond the level of documentation normally found sufficient to demonstrate a conscientious approach to true third party business. Failure to meet these rules exposes the company to serious risk of penalties as well as unfavourable estimates by the authorities with the right to exercise every possible leeway or margin to the taxpayer's disadvantage.

Thin capitalisation
There are no thin capitalisation rules as such; their substitute is the 'interest limitation' to, basically, 30% of EBITDA discussed in the *Deductions* section.

Controlled foreign companies (CFCs)
Germany operates a CFC regime aimed at passive income sheltered abroad and taxed at less than 25%. Essentially, the income is added to that taxable in Germany in the regular manner against a credit for the foreign tax actually paid and not recoverable by either the foreign entity or its shareholder. Active business income, except from tourism and the arms trade, is generally exempt from the CFC net, provided it is earned through a properly established facility of a scale appropriate to the activity concerned and treaty (or EU directive) rules exempting foreign income from German taxation are respected. However, taxpayers will have to demonstrate their treaty entitlement.

Tax credits and incentives

Germany does not offer tax incentives except in very limited circumstances, not usually of direct business relevance (e.g. special depreciation for buildings under a conservation order). Partly, this is a question of the state budget, and partly, it reflects the constitutional requirement for equal treatment of all taxpayers.

Germany

Other incentives

Investment grants of 5% or 10% are available on capital investment in new manufacturing facilities or hotels in the eastern part of Germany. The system is to be phased out by 2013.

Local authorities may offer facilities on favourable terms, such as the provision of cheap land on industrial estates.

Foreign tax credit

If foreign-source income is not exempt from German taxation, a credit will be given for the foreign tax actually paid and not otherwise recoverable. However, the credit is limited to the corporation tax (including the solidarity levy) on the net income after deducting the related expense. Unused credit is lost, as there are no provisions for carryforward or for offset against other taxes, such as trade tax. There are still a few cases of fictitious foreign tax credits under tax treaties with developing countries (to protect the treaty partner's investment incentives), but German treaty policy is to abandon such provisions at the first opportunity.

Withholding taxes

Resident corporations paying certain types of income are required to withhold tax as shown in the following tables. There is also a solidarity levy of 5.5% on the tax due.

General

Recipient of German-source income	WHT (%)			
	Dividends (1)	Interest (1, 2, 3)	Royalties	Movable asset rentals (4)
Resident corporations and individuals	25	25	0	0
Non-resident corporations and individuals (1):				
EU corporations (5, 6)	0	0	0	0
Non-treaty corporations	25	25	15	15
Non-treaty individuals	25	25	15	varies

Notes

1. Corporate recipients of dividend and interest income (interest on convertible and profit-sharing bonds) can apply for refund of the tax withheld over the corporation tax rate of 15% regardless of any further relief available under a treaty.
2. Generally, only interest paid by banks to a resident is subject to a WHT. A 25% tax is also withheld from income on convertible or profit-sharing bonds.
3. Interest paid to non-residents other than on convertible or profit-sharing bonds is generally free of WHT. Tax on loans secured on German property is not imposed by withholding, but by assessment to corporation tax at 15% (plus solidarity levy) of the interest income net of attributable expenses. The tax authorities can order a WHT of 15.825% (including solidarity levy) if ultimate collection of the tax due is in doubt. Both forms of tax are reduced by treaty relief.
4. Movable asset rentals are taxed by assessment rather than by withholding. For corporations, the rate is the standard 15% corporation tax rate (plus solidarity levy) unless reduced by treaty.
5. Where the European Commission (EC) Parent/Subsidiary Directive applies, dividends paid by a German company to a qualifying parent company resident in another EU member state are exempted from German WHT. The minimum shareholding is 10%, to be held continuously for at least one year.
6. The EC Interest and Royalties Directive exempts payments from WHT if made to an associated company in another EU member state. The association must be through a common shareholding of at least 10%, to be held continuously for at least one year.

Treaty rates

Recipient of German-source income	WHT (%)			Movable asset rentals (4)
	Dividends (1)	Interest (1, 2, 3)	Royalties	
Albania	5/15	5	5	0
Algeria	5/15	10	10	0
Argentina (5)	15	10/15	15	15
Armenia (5, 6)	15	5	0	0
Australia (5)	15	25	10	10
Austria (5)	5/15	0	0	0
Azerbaijan (7)	5/15	0/10	5/10	0
Bangladesh (5)	15	25	10	10
Belarus (7)	5/15	0/5	3/5	5
Belgium (5, 8)	15	0/25	0	0
Bolivia (5)	10	25	15	15
Bosnia-Herzegovina (5, 9)	15	25	10	10
Bulgaria (5)	5/15	5	5	5
Canada (10)	5/15	0/10	0/10	10
China, P.R. (5)	10	25	10	7
Croatia (5)	5/15	25	0	0
Cyprus	10/15	0	0	0
Czech Republic (11)	5/15	0	5	5
Denmark (5)	5/15	25	0	0
Ecuador	15	10/15	15	15
Egypt (5, 12)	15	15	15	15
Estonia (5)	5/15	25	10	5
Finland (13)	10/15	0	0/5	5
France	5/15	0	0	0
Georgia (5)	0/5/10	25	0	0
Ghana (5)	5/15	25	8	0
Greece	25	10	0	0
Hungary (5)	5/15	0	0	0
Iceland	5/15	0	0	0
India (5)	10	10	10	10
Indonesia (5, 25)	10/15	25	10/15	10
Iran	15/20	15	10	10
Ireland, Republic of	10	0	0	0
Israel (24)	25	15	0/5	5
Italy (5, 15)	15	25	0/5	5
Ivory Coast (5)	15	25	10	10
Jamaica (21)	10/15	10/12.5	10	10
Japan	15	10	10	10
Kazakhstan (5)	5/15	25	10	10
Kenya	15	15	15	15
Korea, Republic of (5)	5/15	25	10	2
Kosovo (5, 9)	15	25	10	10
Kuwait (5)	5/15	25	10	10
Kyrgyzstan (5)	5/15	25	10	0

Germany

Recipient of German-source income	WHT (%)			
	Dividends (1)	Interest (1, 2, 3)	Royalties	Movable asset rentals (4)
Latvia (5)	5/15	25	10	5
Liberia (14)	10/15	10/ 20	10/15	10
Lithuania (5)	5/15	25	10	5
Luxembourg	10/15	0	5	5
Macedonia (5)	5/15	5	5	0
Malaysia (21)	5/15	10	7	7
Malta (5)	5/15	25	0	0
Mauritius (5, 14)	5/15	0/25	15	15
Mexico (5)	5/15	5	10	10
Moldova (5, 6)	15	25	0	0
Mongolia (5)	5/10	2	10	10
Montenegro (5, 9)	15	25	10	10
Morocco	5	10	10	10
Namibia (5)	10/15	25	10	10
Netherlands (16)	10/15	0	0	0
New Zealand (5)	15	25	10	10
Norway (5)	0/15	25	0	0
Pakistan (5)	10/15	5	10	10
Philippines (5, 17)	10/15	25	10/15	10
Poland (5)	5/15	25	5	5
Portugal (5)	15	25	10	10
Romania (5)	5/15	25	3	0
Russia (5)	5/15	0	0	0
Serbia (5, 9)	15	25	10	10
Singapore (5)	5/15	8	8	8
Slovakia (11)	5/15	0	5	5
Slovenia (5)	5/15	25	5	0
South Africa (18)	7.5/15	10	0	0
Spain	10/15	10	5	5
Sri Lanka (5)	15	25	10	10
Sweden (5)	0/15	25	0	0
Switzerland (5)	0/15	25	0	0
Syria	5/10	10	12	0
Tajikistan (5)	5/15	25	5	0
Thailand (19, 21)	15/20	0/10/25	5/15	0
Trinidad and Tobago (20, 21)	10/20	10/15	0/10	10
Tunisia (22)	10/15	10	10/15	0
Turkey (26)	5/15	10	10	10
Turkmenistan (5, 6)	15	25	0	0
Ukraine (5, 19)	5/10	25	0/5	0
USSR (5, 6)	15	0	0	0
United Arab Emirates (5)	5/10	0	10	10
United Kingdom (5, 18)	5/10/15	0	0	0
United States (5, 23)	0/5/15	25	0	0
Uruguay (5)	5/15	10	10	0

Recipient of German-source income	WHT (%)			Movable asset rentals (4)
	Dividends (1)	Interest (1, 2, 3)	Royalties	
Uzbekistan (5, 19)	5/15	25	3/5	0
Venezuela (5)	5/15	25	5	5
Vietnam (5)	5/10/15	25	10	10
Yugoslavia (5, 9)	15	25	10	10
Zambia	5/15	10	10	10
Zimbabwe (5)	10/20	25	7.5	7.5

Notes

1. Corporate recipients of dividend and interest income (interest on convertible and profit-sharing bonds) can apply for refund of the tax withheld over the corporation tax rate of 15% regardless of any further relief available under a treaty.
2. Generally, only interest paid by banks to a resident is subject to a WHT. A 25% tax is also withheld from income on convertible or profit-sharing bonds.
3. Interest paid to non-residents other than on convertible or profit-sharing bonds is generally free of WHT. Tax on loans secured on German property is not imposed by withholding, but by assessment to corporation tax at 15% (plus solidarity levy) of the interest income net of attributable expenses. The tax authorities can order a WHT of 15.825% (including solidarity levy) if ultimate collection of the tax due is in doubt. Both forms of tax are reduced by treaty relief.
4. Movable asset rentals are taxed by assessment rather than by withholding. For corporations, the rate is the standard 15% corporation tax rate (plus solidarity levy) unless reduced by treaty.
5. The treaty does not (effectively) limit the taxation of profit-based interest income; thus, the domestic rate (plus solidarity levy) applies.
6. The USSR treaty continues in force with Armenia, Moldova, and Turkmenistan.
7. The lower royalty rate applies to commercial and industrial royalties, as opposed to cultural royalties.
8. Mortgage interest to a Belgian business is exempt unless the recipient holds at least 25% of the voting rights in the payer.
9. The Yugoslav treaty continues in force with Bosnia-Herzegovina, Kosovo, Montenegro, and Serbia. Croatia, Macedonia, and Slovenia have their own treaties.
10. The higher royalty rate applies to film and television (TV) royalties, licences to use trademarks and names, and to franchises.
11. The Czechoslovak treaty continues to apply to the Czech Republic and to Slovakia. Interest on profit-sharing bonds is taxed as a dividend.
12. 25% on trademark royalties.
13. The higher royalty rate of 5% applies to commercial, industrial, and scientific royalties.
14. Interest to banks is exempt. Otherwise, tax is levied at the domestic rate (including solidarity levy) without treaty relief.
15. Cultural royalties are exempt.
16. Interest on convertible and profit-sharing bonds is taxed as a dividend; mortgage interest is exempt.
17. The 15% royalty rate applies to copyrights.
18. Treaty relief on interest, royalties, and rentals is conditional on taxation in country of receipt.
19. The 5% royalty rate applies to copyrights.
20. Royalties for copyrights, except for films and TV, are exempt.
21. The 10% interest rate applies in certain circumstances where the recipient is a bank.
22. The 15% royalty rate applies to patents, trademarks, films, and TV.
23. The dividend exemption applies to corporate shareholders with at least 80% throughout the previous 12 months.
24. The 5% royalty rate applies to industrial, commercial, film, and TV royalties.
25. The 10% royalty rate applies to access to industrial, commercial, or scientific experience.
26. This treaty is not yet in force pending ratification. If ratified, it will have retroactive effect from 1 January 2011.

Treaties signed, but awaiting ratification: Ireland, Luxembourg, Mauritius, South Africa, Spain, Taiwan, and Turkey.

Tax administration

Taxable period
The tax year in Germany is the calendar year.

Germany

Tax returns

Returns are filed for each calendar year and reflect the financial statements for the business year ending in that calendar year. Assessments are issued once the tax office has reviewed the return.

In principle, returns are due by 31 May of the following year. However, there is a virtually automatic extension to 31 December for those filing with professional assistance. A further extension to 28/29 February is possible, if justified under the circumstances. Known late-filers and those with a record of other irregularities can be asked to submit their returns before these extension dates, though not before 31 May.

Electronic returns

Monthly or quarterly returns for WHT from employee salaries, dividends, interest, royalties, and other payments, and for VAT must be submitted electronically. Electronic filing of the annual returns for trade tax and VAT is encouraged, but is not yet required. For corporation tax, electronic filing was not available in 2011 but is required in 2012 for 2011 returns. There is also an electronic filing requirement for the financial statements supporting the return. In principle, this applies to business years beginning in 2012, although the finance ministry has announced that no objection will be taken to paper filings of financial statements for the first year of the new system.

Payment of tax

Taxes are payable in quarterly instalments during the year, with a final settlement when the assessment is issued (usually five to six weeks afterwards). The quarterly instalments are based on the estimated ultimate liability. Usually, this is the total tax due shown by the last assessment issued, as adjusted by any rate changes. The corporation tax instalments are due on the tenth day of March, June, September, and December. For trade tax, the due dates are the 15th day of February, May, August, and November. Failure to pay by the due date followed by a three day grace period leads to a penalty of 0.5% per month.

Corporation and trade tax assessments bear interest on the net amount payable after deduction of all credits and previous payments. The rate is 0.5% per month simple interest, and the period runs from 1 April of the second year following the year of assessment. The interest period is independent of the actual date of assessment. It thus runs in retrospect on assessments issued later, for example following a tax audit.

Rulings

Tax offices are able to issue binding rulings in respect of planned transactions, provided the taxpayer can show a particular interest in the tax consequences of the intended action. The fee varies between EUR 121 and EUR 91,456, depending upon the amount of tax involved.

Advance pricing agreements (APAs)

A taxpayer can request the Central Tax Office to negotiate an APA on related-party transactions with a foreign tax authority on one's behalf. The vehicle is the mutual agreement procedure under the treaty, and the fee is a lump sum EUR 20,000 for each new agreement.

Audit cycle

Germany relies heavily on tax audits as a means of ensuring taxpayer discipline. Audits of small businesses are carried out at random, although those for larger operations and for the local subsidiaries of foreign groups tend to be regular. With some district variations, audits are usually conducted at four to five yearly intervals, though not always with equal intensity for the entire period since the auditors' previous visit.

Statute of limitations

The statutory limitation period for the issue or correction of assessments is four years from the end of the year in which the return was filed. If no return was filed, the period runs from the end of the third year following the end of the year of assessment. The four-year period is extended to five in cases of taxpayer negligence and to ten in the event of evasion.

The statutory limitation period for the collection of tax debts is five years from the end of the year in which payment became due.

Topics of focus for the tax authorities

Tax office reviews of tax returns prior to issuing the assessment notice and payment demand are often rather superficial. Audits, though, are intense, being field reviews on site often lasting for several weeks or even months. Companies with an international focus can expect significant audit emphasis on all aspects of their dealings with their foreign business partners. If the company is a member of an international group, its most important audit component will usually be its transfer pricing on its dealings with foreign related parties and the relevant documentation. It is emphasised that these two topics are separate fields, as documentation deficiencies can lead to unfavourable estimates on the taxpayer, even if the taxpayer is able to justify the taxpayer's group company pricing in terms of overall result.

G

Ghana

PwC contact

Darcy White
PricewaterhouseCoopers
No. 12 Airport City
Una Home, 3rd Floor
Accra
Ghana
Tel: +233 302 761 576
Email: darcy.white@gh.pwc.com

Significant developments

2012 budget proposals

In keeping with its commitment to improve tax administration, the government made the following proposals in the 2012 budget, which have been assented to by the President. The purpose of these amendments, amongst others, includes strengthening the Ghana Revenue Authority (GRA) by harmonising and organising the administrative procedures and processes for effective revenue mobilisation.

- Tax Administration Bill, which seeks to consolidate the common procedures of all the tax laws.
- The Internal Revenue Bill, which is expected to include the following provisions:
  - Increase the tax holiday for the Ghana Stock Exchange (GSE) for a further five years and extend the capital gains tax (CGT) exemption for five years on capital gains of shares traded on the GSE.
  - Reduce the corporate income tax (CIT) rate for the hotel industry.
  - Raise the CIT rate for mining companies to 35%.
  - Provide a uniform regime for capital allowances for plant and machinery used in the mining sector at 25% per annum.

Expiration of National Fiscal Stabilisation Levy (NFSL)

Originally set at a rate of 5% for two years from 2009 to 2010, the NFSL was extended to the end of 2011. We are not aware of any current proposed amendment to extend the NFSL to 2012.

NFSL was chargeable on the profit before tax of businesses and was applicable only to banks (excluding rural and community banks), non-bank financial institutions, insurance companies, communications companies, mining companies, and breweries.

Taxes on corporate income

A resident is taxed on income accruing in, derived from, brought into, or received in Ghana. The income of a resident is treated as accruing in or derived from Ghana unless attributable to a permanent establishment (PE) of the resident outside Ghana.

A non-resident is taxed on income accruing in or derived from Ghana. The income of a non-resident is treated as accruing in or derived from Ghana if the income is attributable to a PE of the non-resident in Ghana.

National CIT is payable on the following:

- Income accruing in, derived from, brought into, or received in Ghana in respect of gains or profits from a trade, business, profession, or vocation.
- Dividends, interest, or discounts.
- Any charge or annuity.
- Royalties, premiums, and any other profits arising from property, including rents.
- Receipts, including royalties and deferred payments of any kind.

The general CIT rate is 25%. Companies listed on the GSE are subject to a reduced CIT rate of 22% (this rate is applicable for only a three year period for companies that listed on the GSE after 1 January 2004).

The CIT rate for companies engaged in non-traditional export is 8%, while bank lendings to the agricultural and leasing sectors pay a CIT rate of 20%.

Corporate residence

Corporate residence is determined by the place where the trade, business, profession, or vocation is carried on. A company is resident if it is incorporated under the laws of Ghana or has its management and control exercised in Ghana at any time during a year of assessment.

Where a non-resident corporate body carries on any trade, business, profession, or vocation in Ghana (part of the operations of which may be carried on outside Ghana), the full gains or profits of the trade, business, profession, or vocation are deemed to be derived from Ghana.

Permanent establishment (PE)

A PE is determined under the tax law as the place where a person carries on business, as well as a place where a person:

- carries on business through an agent, other than a general agent of independent status acting in the ordinary course of business as such
- has, is using, or is installing substantial equipment or machinery, or
- is engaged in a construction, assembly, or installation project for 90 days or more, including a place where a person is conducting supervisory activities in relation to such project.

A non-resident carrying on business in Ghana through a PE is subject to tax in Ghana only on that income attributable to the PE in Ghana.

Other taxes

Value-added tax (VAT)

Other than exempt goods and services, VAT of 12.5% and the National Health Insurance Levy (NHIL) of 2.5% are charged on the following:

- Every supply of goods and services made in Ghana.
- Every importation of goods.
- Supply of any imported service.

The VAT and NHIL is charged on the supply of goods and services where the supply is a taxable supply and made by a taxable person in the course of business.

Ghana

VAT and NHIL are payable:

* in the case of taxable supply, by the taxable person making the supply.
* in the case of imported goods, by the importer, and
* in the case of imported services, by the receiver of the service.

Most professional services are also subject to the same VAT and NHIL rates, including the following:

* Management services.
* Insurance brokerage and other services.
* Financial, tax, and economic consulting.
* Engineering and technical services.
* Accounting services.
* Courier services.
* Legal services.
* Provision of satellite television.
* Architectural services.
* Mobile cellular phone services.
* Services rendered by surveyors.

Exports of goods and services are zero-rated. Unless specifically exempt, supplies of all goods and services are subject to VAT.

There is a VAT Flat Rate Scheme (VFRS) under which traders who meet certain thresholds are expected to pay 3% of their annual turnover as VAT without recourse to input VAT.

All businesses with an annual turnover between 10,000 Ghana cedi (GHS) and GHS 90,000 are currently obligated to operate the VFRS charging a rate of 3%. All businesses whose annual turnover exceeds the GHS 90,000 threshold are obligated to charge and account for charged VAT at 15%. Businesses whose designation has changed due to the amendment are to convert to the appropriate system which they now qualify for.

Customs and excise duties

Customs and excise duties are imposed on the importation of goods at the port of entry and certain manufactured goods produced or imported into Ghana.

The current rates of excise duties range from 150% on tobacco products, to 22.5% on wines, to 17.5% on water.

Some significant changes made in 2011 to excise duties included a 2.5% reduction in *ad valorem* excise duty rates on all excisable goods, except spirits and cigarettes, and a revocation of the concessionary duty rate for the inputs of the tourism industry. In addition to these, the government imposed a 20% environmental excise duty on polythene bags and other plastic packaging materials covered under the harmonised system and customs tariff schedules, effective from 1 February 2011. This excludes the plastic packaging materials for water and mineral water.

Capital gains tax (CGT)

CGT is payable by every person, including a corporate body, on any capital gain accruing or derived from the realisation of any chargeable asset situated in Ghana. These chargeable assets include buildings of a permanent or temporary nature;

Ghana

business and business assets, including goodwill; land other than agricultural land; and any assets declared as chargeable by legislative instrument made under the law.

Capital gains in excess of GHS 50 are subject to tax at 15%. However, gains resulting from a merger, amalgamation, reorganisation, or reconstruction are exempt from CGT under certain conditions, as are gains accruing to or derived from a venture capital financing company.

A 20-year exemption that was granted on gains from the sale of securities of companies listed on the GSE and that ended in January 2011 has been proposed to be extended for five additional years to encourage transactions on the stock exchange and, in the long term, to make the securities market more vibrant and fluid.

Details of further exemptions can be found in the income tax laws of Ghana.

G

Communications service tax (CST)

CST of 6% is levied on charges payable by both individual and corporate consumers for the use of communication services provided by Communications Class 1 licensees as defined in the National Communications Authority Act. This essentially covers national fixed and mobile cellular network operators and internet service providers (ISPs). CST has also been proposed to be extended to cover the following:

- Public/corporate data operators.
- Providers of radio (FM) broadcasting services.
- Providers of free-to-air and pay-per-view television service.

Airport taxes

Ghana's airport taxes, as of 1 January 2011, are as follows:

Type of travel	Airport tax rate
Domestic travel (DT)	GHS 5
International travel (IT): Within West Africa (WA)	USD 60
IT: Outside WA (Economy class)	USD 100
IT: Outside WA (Business class)	USD 150
IT: Outside WA (First class)	USD 200

There are indications that an additional levy may be introduced to fund the government's planned expansion aimed at reducing the congestion and pressure on existing infrastructure and facilities at the airport.

Branch income

The tax rate on branch profits is the same as on corporate profits.

Branch profit tax at a rate of 10% will be triggered when profits are repatriated or are deemed to have been repatriated by the permanent establishment (PE). Repatriated profits, or deemed repatriated profits, is determined by a formula under the tax law that computes the movements of the accumulated profits and net assets.

Note that the profits for the period deemed to arise in connection with the operations of the branch may, at the discretion of the tax authorities, be computed by reference to the

Ghana

total consolidated profits of the entire group, taking into account the proportion that the turnover of that branch bears to the total consolidated turnover of the group.

Income determination

Inventory valuation
The Internal Revenue Act 2000 (Act 592), under Section 31, provides general guidance on the principles of stock (inventory) valuation for income tax purposes. A company that accounts for tax on an accrual basis is required to account for inventory using the absorption-cost method. A company accounting for tax purposes on a cash basis may calculate the cost of stock using a prime-cost method or absorption-cost method. The closing value of inventory is valued for tax purposes at the lower of cost or market value.

Capital gains
Capital gains are taxed at a separate rate in Ghana. *See Capital gains tax in the Other taxes section for more information.*

Dividend income
A dividend paid to a resident company by another resident company is exempt from tax where the company receiving the dividend controls, directly or indirectly, 25% or more of the voting power in the company paying the dividend.

Stock dividends
The issue of stock dividends is permitted under Section 74 (1) of the Ghana Companies Code 1963, Act 179. It is, however, subject to income tax at the dividend withholding tax (WHT) rate of 8%.

Interest income
Interest received by a resident company from another resident company is subject to WHT at a rate of 8%.

However, no WHT applies on any interest paid by an individual person, on government of Ghana bonds, or on interest received by a resident financial institution.

In addition, interest of an approved unit trust scheme or mutual fund is exempt from tax.

Exempt income
Specific exemptions from tax include the following:

*   Income of a local authority.
*   Income of a statutory or registered building society.
*   Income of a charitable or an educational institution.
*   Income of organisations formed for the purpose of promoting social or sporting amenities.
*   Income accruing from a farming enterprise, for a limited period.
*   Income of a registered trade union.
*   Income of rural banks, for the first ten years of operations.
*   Gain or profit from the business of operating ships or aircraft by non-resident persons if an equivalent exemption is granted by the person's country of residence to persons resident in Ghana.
*   Investment income of a pension or provident society.

- Income or profit of any registered cooperative society.

Foreign income

Resident corporations are taxed on their foreign income as and when it is brought into or received in Ghana. Foreign income is taxed together with other income derived in Ghana, and double taxation is avoided through treaties or foreign tax credits. No special rules exist for taxing undistributed income of foreign subsidiaries.

Deductions

Depreciation and depletion

Depreciation of depreciable assets in the accounts of a business is not an allowable deduction in computing taxable profits. It is replaced by capital allowances at statutorily prescribed rates, as follows:

Class	Comments	Rate
1	Assets pooled (allowance calculated on a reducing-balance basis). Mainly computers and data handling equipment.	40%
2	Assets pooled (allowance calculated on a reducing-balance basis). Mainly automobiles, buses, mini buses, construction and earth-moving equipment, trailers and trailer-mounted containers, plant and machinery used in manufacturing.	30%
3	Assets not pooled (allowance calculated on a straight-line basis). Mainly mining and petroleum rights assets, such as exploration and development costs, buildings, structures and works of a permanent nature related and plant and machinery.	20%
4	Assets pooled (allowance calculated on a reducing-balance basis). Mainly railroad cars, locomotives and equipment, vessels and similar water transportation equipment, aircraft, public utility plant, equipment, office equipment and fixtures, and any other depreciable asset not elsewhere classified.	20%
5	Assets not pooled (allowance calculated on a straight-line basis). Mainly other building structures and works of a permanent nature.	10%
6	Assets not pooled (allowance calculated over the useful life of the asset). For other intangible assets.	Useful life

Allowances are granted only on the following conditions:

- The taxpayer must own the asset.
- Capital expenditure must be incurred.
- The asset must be used in the trade.
- The asset must be in use up to the end of the basis period.

Capital allowances are granted for every year in which the asset is in use. Balancing allowances and charges are made, as the case may be, on disposal of the asset.

For intangibles, such as goodwill, patents, trademarks, and copyrights, the law allows for capital allowance deduction over the useful life of the asset.

Start-up expenses and pre-operating costs

Although the tax law does not specifically mention start-up expenses or pre-operating costs, generally a deduction is allowed for start-up and pre-operating costs incurred by

Ghana

a business, provided such expenses are wholly, exclusively, and necessarily incurred in the production of income of the taxpayer.

Interest expenses
Any sum payable by way of mortgage or debenture interest by any company to a non-resident, except where tax has been deducted and accounted for, is considered non-deductible.

Bad debt
A deduction is allowed for bad debt incurred in the normal course of business, other than advances made on capital accounts. A bad debt will be allowed as a deduction if the taxpayer has taken all reasonable steps to pursue payment and the person reasonably believes payment will not be made.

Any amounts recovered in respect to a bad debt previously written off should be included in income and subject to tax accordingly.

An existing debt that becomes a bad debt after a 50% or more change in underlying ownership is not allowed as a bad debt deduction after the change in ownership has taken place.

Charitable contributions
The following contributions/donations are allowable as deductions in ascertaining the taxable income of a person:

- Contributions made to a charitable institution or fund approved by the government.
- Payments towards a scholarship scheme approved by the government for a technical, professional, or other course of study.
- Donations made for the purpose of any rural or urban area and approved by the government.
- Donations for the purpose of sports development approved by the government.
- Donations to the government for worthwhile government causes approved by the Commissioner.

Fines and penalties
Fines and penalties arising as a result of non-compliance with the provisions of the tax law are generally not allowable deductions.

Taxes
Taxes are not deductible in determining taxable income.

Other significant items
No other special deductions are allowed. Principal non-deductible items include the following:

- Domestic or private expenses, including cost of travel between residence and place of business or employment.
- Any disbursement or expense not being wholly and exclusively paid or expended for the purpose of acquiring income.
- Capital withdrawn or any sum employed or intended to be employed as capital.
- Capital employed in improvement.
- Any sum recoverable under an insurance contract of indemnity.
- Rent of or any expense in connection with premises or a part of premises not occupied or used for the purpose of producing business income.

- Any payment to a provident, savings, or other society or fund unless specifically allowed by the tax Commissioner General (CG); this may change under tiers 2 and 3 under the new Pensions Act.

Net operating losses

Tax losses can be carried forward and deducted from assessable income for the five years immediately following the year in which the loss was incurred. This provision covers the following industries: farming and agro-processing, mining, manufacturing (mainly for export), tourism, and information communications technology (ICT) (i.e. software development) industries.

Carryback of losses is permitted for persons deriving income relating to a long-term contract, except this is not allowed where there has been a change in ownership of 50% or more compared with the prior year. A long-term contract of a business includes a contract for manufacture, installation, or construction that is not completed within the company's accounting year in which it is commenced.

Payments to foreign affiliates

No special restrictions are imposed on the deductibility of royalties, interest, and service fees paid to foreign affiliates, provided they are expenses incurred wholly, exclusively, and necessarily in the production of the income. However, the CG may disallow certain transactions if they are deemed artificial or fictitious.

Group taxation

No form of combined reporting of results of operations by a group or affiliates is permitted.

Transfer pricing

Currently, there is a transfer pricing regulation yet to be passed into law in Ghana. The transfer pricing regulation is currently under review by the Parliament of Ghana and is expected to be released before the end of June 2012.

The draft transfer pricing regulation is expected to follow the internationally accepted guidelines published by the Organisation for Economic Co-operation and Development (OECD) but with a much broader perspective on the nature of entities and transactions that would be governed under the transfer pricing rules of Ghana.

Until the detailed transfer pricing regulations are passed, the general anti-avoidance provisions under the Internal Revenue Act shall continue to apply.

Thin capitalisation

Interest expenses and foreign exchange currency losses incurred by an exempt-controlled resident entity are not allowed as a deduction in arriving at the chargeable income of the entity if the entity is thinly capitalised. An exempt-controlled entity is deemed to be thinly capitalised if its exempt debt to exempt equity ratio exceeds the ratio 2:1.

A resident entity is deemed to be exempt-controlled if at least 50% of the underlying ownership or control is held by a non-resident person, either alone or together with an associate or associates.

Thin capitalisation provisions do not apply to resident financial institutions.

Ghana

There are currently no thin capitalisation provisions in the Petroleum Income Tax Laws, and, as such, the provisions are deemed not to apply to petroleum licence holders.

Tax credits and incentives

Foreign tax credit
A resident is entitled to a credit in respect to any foreign income tax paid to the extent to which the tax paid is in respect to the resident's foreign taxable income. The foreign tax credit available on specific income type should not exceed the average rate of Ghanaian income tax of the resident for a year.

Inward investment
Under the Ghana Investments Promotion Centre Act 1994, various incentives are available to encourage investments in the country, particularly in the areas of agriculture; manufacturing industries engaged in export trade or using predominantly local raw materials or producing agricultural equipment, etc.; construction and building industries; mining; and tourism.

Incentives generally include exemption from customs import duties on plant and machinery; reduced CIT rates; more favourable investment and capital allowances on plant and machinery; reduction in the actual CIT payable, where appropriate; retention of foreign exchange earnings, where necessary; guaranteed free transfer of dividends or net profits, foreign capital, loan servicing, and fees and charges in respect of technology transfer; and guarantees against expropriation by the government.

Capital investments
Venture capital tax incentives include the following:

* Relief from stamp duty in each year on subscriptions for new equity shares in venture capital funds.
* Full tax exemption from CIT, dividend WHT, and CGT for five years.
* Carryforward of losses from disposal of shares during the tax-exempt period to the post-exempt period, up to five years.
* Chargeable income tax deduction equal to 100% of their investment, for financial institutions which invest in venture capital subsidiaries.

Tax holidays
Until January 2011, the income of a company engaged in the construction and sale or letting of residential premises was exempt from tax for a period of five years. This was abolished in the 2011 national budget. The tax holiday is now limited to companies that partner with the Minister responsible for Works and Housing in the construction and sale or letting of low cost affordable residential premises and are certified as such by the Minister responsible for Works and Housing.

Tax holidays are also extended to entities in agro-processing, farming business, and for venture capital financing entities.

Withholding taxes

Income	WHT rate (%)
Resident persons:	
Interest (excluding individual & resident financial institutions)	8
Dividend *	8
Rent (for individuals and as investment income) *	8
Fees to part-time teachers, lecturers, and examiners, and endorsement fees *	10
Commissions to insurance agents, sales persons, and fees to directors, board members, etc.	10
Commissions of lottery agents	5
Supply of goods and services exceeding GHS 500	5
Non-resident persons:	
Dividend *	8
Royalties, natural, resources payments, and rents *	10
Management, consulting, and technical service fees, and endorsement fees *	15
Interest income *	8
Short-term insurance premium *	5

* Final tax.

Tax administration

Taxable period
The tax year runs from 1 January to 31 December. Corporations with financial periods other than the calendar year are taxed on their financial period ending during the calendar year.

Tax returns
Companies are expected to submit a tax return not later than four months after the end of the financial year. They may file an application for extension of filing time for not more than two months.

Assessments
The CG publishes in the Gazette or print media a list of persons who are under the Large Taxpayer Office and are under the self assessment scheme. Companies under the self assessment scheme are required to make an estimate of their annual chargeable income to be derived for the year and the tax to be payable thereon. The annual tax estimated by the taxpayer is paid in quarterly instalments on or before the last day of the third, sixth, ninth and 12th months of the period. These tax instalments are an advance payment deductible against the actual tax payable at the end of the year.

The CG may also serve a provisional assessment on a taxpayer's chargeable income and estimated tax payable. Taxpayers are required to proceed to make advance quarterly tax instalment based on the provisional assessment.

Payment of tax
Where an assessment has been finalised, the tax is payable within 30 days after service of the notice. At the discretion of the CG, the time for payment may be extended.

Ghana

In instances where the CG does not issue a notice or demand, a taxpayer is required to pay not less than the total of the tax paid or payable in respect of the preceding year of assessment. This may be paid by equal quarterly instalments at the end of March, June, September, and December in each year of assessment, but such payments are not deemed to be the actual tax payable.

Where tax is not paid by the due date, a penalty is assessed at 10% of the tax payable in addition to the tax unpaid up to three months after the due date; thereafter, the penalty is 20%.

Tax amnesty
The government has proposed to offer a tax amnesty to individuals and companies that have may not be up to date on their tax compliance. This exercise is intended to run for nine months from 1 January 2012 to 30 September 2012.

During this period, the GRA also intends to conduct a registration and re-registration of taxpayers as part of its efforts to increase the tax base. This exercise will be done in conjunction with the upcoming e-registration of taxpayers. This is not only expected to offer a good opportunity for businesses to reassess and regularise their tax affairs to ensure compliance but also to increase the GRA's revenue prospects.

Other issues

Double tax treaties (DTTs)
Ghana has, for the relief from double taxation on income arising in Ghana, double tax treaties with Belgium, France, Germany, Italy, the Netherlands, South Africa, Switzerland, and the United Kingdom.

Gibraltar

PwC contact

Edgar Lavarello
PricewaterhouseCoopers Limited
International Commercial Centre
Casemates Square
Gibraltar
Tel: +350 200 73520
Email: edgar.c.lavarello@gi.pwc.com

Significant developments

Budget summary

Below is a summary of the taxation changes to existing legislation as a result of the Chief Minister's budget speech on 4 July 2011. These changes are effective as of 1 July 2011.

Changes in import duty rates

The import duty rate for the following goods has been halved to 6%:

- Televisions.
- Hi-fi and other electrical audio or visual equipment.
- Tableware and kitchenware.
- Other household goods.
- Sunglasses or spectacles.
- Lamps and lighting.
- Paints and varnishes.
- Tools.
- Toys.
- Porcelain goods, statues, and ornamental pieces.
- Glassware objects (excluding sheet glass).

The duty on cigarettes increased to 1.20 British pounds (GBP) per carton of 200, and the duty on rolling tobacco increased to GBP 2.50 per 250 gram pouch.

Commercial property rate incentives

The early payment discount on property tax rates for the wholesale and retail sector (including bars and restaurants) increased to 20%.

Bars or restaurants implementing and enforcing a 'no smoking policy' are entitled to a 10% refund of the property tax rate paid.

Pending legislation

Please note this information is current as of 1 June 2012. Proposed amendments to tax legislation are announced by the Chief Minister in his budget speech, which is annual and is usually during the month of June. These amendments are usually effective as of 1 July. Please visit the Worldwide Tax Summaries website at www.pwc.com/taxsummaries to see any significant corporate tax developments that occurred after this date.

Gibraltar

Taxes on corporate income

Companies are subject to Gibraltar taxation on income accrued in and derived from Gibraltar.

The standard rate of corporate income tax (CIT) is 10%, with utility and energy providers and companies that abuse a dominant position paying a higher rate of 20%.

Corporate residence

A company will be considered resident in Gibraltar if the management and control of its business is exercised from Gibraltar.

The location of central management and control will be established under legal principles laid down in the United Kingdom and is the place of the highest form of control and direction over a company's affairs, as opposed to decisions on the day-to-day running of the business.

Permanent establishment (PE)
Gibraltar has not entered into any double tax treaties (DTTs); consequently, there are no provisions on PE from a general treaty perspective.

Other taxes

Value-added tax (VAT)
There is no VAT in Gibraltar.

Customs duties
Goods imported into Gibraltar from outside are, with some exceptions, generally subject to import duty at the applicable rate of 6% or 12%.

The duty on cigarettes is GBP 1.20 per carton of 200, and the duty on rolling tobacco is GBP 2.50 per 250 gram pouch.

Property tax
A general business property rate is levied annually on all businesses in Gibraltar. The amount varies depending on the property and is subject to an annual review.

Stamp duty
Stamp duty is payable on the transfer or sale of any Gibraltar real estate or shares in a company owning Gibraltar real estate (on an amount based on the market value of said real estate) at the following rates:

- GBP 200,000 or less: 0%.
- Between GBP 200,001 and GBP 350,000: 2% on the first GBP 250,000 and 5.5% on the balance.
- Over GBP 350,000: 3% on the first GBP 350,000 and 3.5% on the balance.

Stamp duty is also payable on mortgages secured on Gibraltar real estate at the rate of 0.13% for mortgages less than GBP 200,000 and 0.20% for mortgages over GBP 200,000.

Gibraltar

Gaming tax

Gaming tax is levied at 1% of the gaming income. The tax paid is subject to a minimum of GBP 85,000 and maximum of GBP 425,000.

Capital duty

Capital duty of GBP 10 is payable on the initial authorisation of share capital or any subsequent increase thereto.

Social insurance

Employers are obliged to pay social insurance for every person in their employment.

Employers' social insurance contribution for employees paid weekly is calculated as 20% of gross earnings, subject to a minimum of GBP 15.00 and a maximum of GBP 32.97 per week.

Employers' social insurance contribution for employees paid monthly is calculated as 20% of gross earnings, subject to a minimum of GBP 65.00 and a maximum of GBP 142.87 per month.

Branch income

The basis for taxation of branches of foreign enterprises is the same as for corporations.

Allowable head office charges or expenses incurred by a Gibraltar branch for the common purpose of the company and its branches, or for the purpose of the head office or another branch exclusively, are limited to 5% of turnover of the Gibraltar branch.

Income determination

Generally, companies are subject to Gibraltar taxation on income accrued in and derived from Gibraltar.

Inventory valuation

Inventory is valued at the lower of historical cost or net realisable value. The last in first out (LIFO) method is not permitted. Generally, there are no material differences between accounts prepared on a normal accounting basis and those prepared on a tax basis.

Capital gains

Capital gains are not subject to tax in Gibraltar.

Dividend income

There is no charge to tax on the receipt by a Gibraltar company of dividends from any other company.

Interest income

Except in the case of companies with a banking or money lending licence, interest receivable is not taxable in Gibraltar.

For companies where interest is taxable, no tax shall be charged on the net interest receivable from deposits received from related parties to the extent that these funds do not themselves generate interest income from money lending activities to third parties.

Gibraltar

Royalty income
Income from royalties is not taxed in Gibraltar.

Foreign income
Where a taxpayer seeks to reduce their liability to tax by creating an artificial split between activities in Gibraltar and outside of Gibraltar, the Commissioner shall use anti-avoidance provisions to defeat such an attempt.

Deductions

For the purpose of ascertaining the assessable income, all expenses wholly and exclusively incurred in the production of the income shall be deducted.

Capital allowances
The first GBP 30,000 of qualifying expenditure on plant and machinery (including fixtures and fittings) and the first GBP 50,000 of qualifying expenditure on computer equipment is fully deductible in the first year as a 'first year allowance'.

Thereafter, qualifying assets are pooled and are subject to an annual capital, or wear and tear, allowance. Allowances are available for plant and machinery (including fixtures and fittings), computer equipment, and motor vehicles at the rate of 15% (20% for companies that are obliged to pay the higher CIT rate - *see the Taxes on corporate income section*) and are calculated on a reducing balance basis. Capital allowances for industrial buildings are deductible at the rate of 4% per annum on a straight-line basis.

Capital payments for leases which are for periods of less than 12 years qualify for capital allowances on a straight-line basis over the remaining period of the lease.

Goodwill
Amortisation of goodwill is not a deductible expense.

Start-up expenses
Expenditure incurred with a view to carrying on a trade is treated as incurred on the first day on which the trade is carried on for the purposes of computing the profits or gains of the trade.

Interest expenses
Full deduction is available in respect of interest expenses, subject to anti-avoidance rules (*see the Group taxation section for more information*).

Bad debt
Only specific bad debts or specific bad debt provisions are deductible to the extent that they are respectively estimated to be bad during the said period, notwithstanding that such bad debts were payable prior to the commencement of the period. General doubtful debt provisions are not an allowable expense.

Charitable contributions
A charitable donation is not considered as having been wholly and exclusively expended for the purposes of the production of the income of the trade and is therefore not allowable as a deduction for tax purposes.

Fines and penalties

Fines and penalties, including those resulting from late payment of taxation or from failure to make the necessary tax submissions, are deemed to be a tax and therefore are not a deductible expense.

Taxes

No deduction is allowed for any tax charges under the Income Tax Act.

Other significant items

Additionally, no deduction is allowed in respect of the following:

* Domestic or private expenses.
* Expenses not incurred wholly and exclusively in the generation of income.
* Any expenses of a capital nature.
* Any sum recoverable under an insurance contract or contract of indemnity.
* Property expenses not incurred for the purposes of producing income.
* Depreciation of assets (although capital allowances are available, *see above*).
* Employee remuneration not accompanied by a certified statement of name, address, and amount of remuneration.
* Certain business entertainment expenditure falling within guidelines published by the Commissioner.
* Interest paid to a non-Gibraltar resident that is more than a reasonable commercial rate.

In the case of a company that has income, some of which is chargeable to tax and some of which is not, the deductions allowed shall be apportioned on a pro-rata basis between the chargeable and non-chargeable income.

Net operating losses

A trading loss incurred in an accounting period may be offset against trading income arising in the same period or subsequent period, provided that within a period of three years there has not been both a change in the ownership of the company and a major change in the nature or conduct of the trade.

There is no provision for the carrying back of losses.

Payments to foreign affiliates

In the case of branches, the amount of general head office expenses incurred that would be deductible would be limited to 5% of its turnover.

The Income Tax Act 2010 includes anti-avoidance provisions. These provisions state that if the amount charged for goods or services by a connected person is not at 'arm's length', then the expenses that would be allowed would be subject to a maximum of:

* the expense
* 5% of the gross turnover of the company, or
* 75% of the pre-expenses profit of the company.

Group taxation

Companies are assessed on an individual basis, and trading losses of group members may not be offset against profits of other members of the group.

Gibraltar

The Income Tax Act contains a generic anti-avoidance clause which allows the Commissioner to disregard an arrangement which the Commissioner believes is fictitious or artificial. In addition, it includes the following specific anti-avoidance measures.

Transfer pricing
The amount of interest payments to connected persons which is in excess of that payable at arm's length will be deemed to be a dividend. Where the amount charged for goods and services by connected persons is not at arm's length, this will be disallowed as a taxable expense. Any expenses allowed will be subject to the lesser of (i) the expense, (ii) 5% of the gross turnover of the company, and (iii) 75% of the pre-expense profit of the company.

Thin capitalisation
Interest paid on a loan to related parties which are not companies (or loans where security is provided by related parties) where the ratio of the value of the loan capital to the equity of the company exceeds five to one will be considered as dividend payments and thus not a deductible expense for tax purposes. This provision is not applicable to Gibraltar banks or money lenders.

Back-to-back loans
Since interest income is not taxable on back-to-back loans, the interest expense is not deductible.

Dual employment
Income from dual employment contracts is taxed in Gibraltar if both employers are connected persons.

Transfer of assets abroad
Where assets are transferred abroad with the purpose of avoiding tax and the taxpayer has the power to enjoy these assets either now or in the future, then any income or benefits received from these assets will be deemed to be income chargeable to tax.

Tax credits and incentives

Development aid
In order to encourage private development in Gibraltar, promoters and developers of approved projects are offered certain incentives such as tax relief, import duty relief, and rates relief.

In order to qualify for the above reliefs, the project needs to be a new project which is for the economic benefit of Gibraltar and the aim of which is:

* to create a tangible immovable asset in Gibraltar that will remain in existence after the applicant has ceased to derive the benefits under the licence
* to provide more than two additional units of housing accommodation in Gibraltar
* to contribute materially to the development of the tourist industry in Gibraltar
* to afford any new employment opportunities or career prospects in Gibraltar, or
* to improve materially the economic or financial infrastructure of Gibraltar.

The project needs to be completed within a specified time (dependent on the type of project) following the issue of the licence, and the applicant must not expend less than the prescribed amount for the project.

Applications for development aid must be made to the Minister for Trade.

Deduction of approved expenditure on premises

For taxpayers with an interest in a building situated in Gibraltar, an allowance is available for approved expenditure on the painting, decorating, repair, or enhancement of the frontage of that building.

The approved amount will be available as a deduction against the taxpayer's income. This deduction is in addition to any deduction, relief, or allowance given in accordance with any other provision of the Income Tax Act in respect of the same expenditure.

The claim for the deduction must be made within two years after the end of the year of assessment with respect to which the deduction is claimed.

Commercial property rate incentives

There is an early payment discount of 20% available on property tax rates payable by the wholesale and retail sector (including bars and restaurants).

In addition, any bar or restaurant implementing and enforcing a 'no smoking policy' is entitled to a 10% refund of property tax rates paid.

G

Withholding taxes

There are no WHTs in Gibraltar, except in the following cases:

- Payments to subcontractors in the construction industry. Unless the subcontractor is in possession of an exemption certificate, tax is withheld at the rate of 25% of the amount which relates to the labour and profit element of the contract.
- Payments to employees under the Pay As You Earn (PAYE) system. Under the PAYE regulations, employers are obliged to deduct an amount of tax in accordance with the employee's tax code.

Tax administration

Taxable period

The taxable period is the accounting period of the company, which begins on the later of the beginning of the accounting period and the date when the company first receives a source of taxable income and ends on the earlier of the end of the accounting period, 12 months from the beginning of the accounting period, or the date on which trade ceased.

Tax returns

Companies are required to file returns and calculate their tax liability for the year. The return, together with the estimated liability, needs to be accompanied by payment of the tax due six months after the date of the company's financial year end.

Companies with turnover of less than GBP 500,000 are obliged to file accounts accompanied by an Independent Accountant's Report together with the tax return within six months of the company's financial year end.

Gibraltar

Companies with turnover of GBP 500,000 or more may submit unaudited accounts together with the tax return but are required to file audited accounts within nine months of the company's financial year end.

Payment of tax

Companies are required to make payments on account of future liabilities on 28 February and 31 August in each calendar year. Each payment should be equal to 50% of the tax based on the previous year's tax liability.

The balance of tax due (i.e. the actual liability less payments on account) is due on the date of filing of the return.

Audit cycle

The Gibraltar tax system is based on self assessment. However, the Income Tax Office has powers to make an enquiry into the tax return of a company within a period of 12 months from the date when the return is due to be filed or, if filed later than the deadline, 12 months from the date it was filed. If the Commissioner of Income Tax believes a return to be fraudulent, the above time limits will not apply.

Statute of limitations

The Commissioner has up to six years following the date of assessment to revise any incorrect assessments. There is no limit where the incorrect assessment is as a result of fraud, willful default, or neglect.

Appeals

A taxpayer may appeal against a disputed assessment by notice in writing addressed to the Commissioner within 28 days of the date of service of the notice of the assessment.

Fines and penalties

The following penalties and fines are applicable:

- For the late payment of tax, there is a penalty of 10% of the amount of tax due on the day immediately after such payment was due. If unpaid for 90 days, a further amount of 20% of the tax due is charged; and if still unpaid after this period, then a 10% per annum surcharge will be added which is compounded on a daily basis until the amount of the tax and penalties are fully paid.
- Failure to file a return by the due date will result in a penalty of GBP 50 with a further penalty of GBP 300 if the return is not submitted within three months after the due date.
- Failure to respond to a notice or request to submit information or documentation will result in a fine of GBP 200 on the day the failure occurs and a penalty of up to GBP 500 per day thereafter. Failure to comply beyond a three month period, if convicted, can result in imprisonment.
- For fraudulently, recklessly, or negligently delivering to the Commissioner an incorrect return, accounts, or information, there is a fine of up to 150% of the difference between the actual tax due and the tax due as per the original declaration. The amount of the penalty will depend on:
  - the amount of the tax lost and/or delayed
  - the gravity of the offence (i.e. if deliberate or an honest mistake), and
  - the level of cooperation in the investigation.
- Failure to pay to the Commissioner PAYE or social insurance which has been withheld or should have been withheld will become a criminal offence leading to imprisonment and/or a fine.

- If an amount of PAYE and/or social insurance exceeding GBP 5,000 is outstanding for over three months, the Commissioner will, after giving 14 days notice, publish in the Gibraltar Gazette the name of the person whom the Commissioner has reason to believe has failed to comply with the PAYE regulations.
- Failure to notify the Commissioner of an arrangement, the main benefit of which is to avoid the payment of tax, will result in a fine of GBP 100 on the day the failure occurs and a penalty of GBP 200 per day thereafter.

G

Greece

PwC contact

Mary Psylla
PricewaterhouseCoopers
268 Kifissias Avenue
GR-152 32 Athens
Greece
Tel: +30 210 6874 543
Email: mary.psylla@gr.pwc.com

Significant developments

Tax law 4072/2012, adopted by the Greek Parliament, amended the Greek tax and legal regime by introducing new provisions. The most significant amendments are the following:

- Capital gains derived by legal entities maintaining double entry accounting books from the sale of shares listed on the Athens Stock Exchange, which are acquired from 1 January 2013 onwards, will be taxed based on the general income tax provisions.
- The introduction of a new corporate form, the 'Private Company' (PC).
- Improvement of the investment law using 'fast track' procedures.
- Extension of the possibility of establishment of 'free zones' and customs warehouses (e.g. allowing the commercial and industrial activities therein).

A more radical tax reform is expected, but is being delayed until a new government is formed.

Taxes on corporate income

The corporate income tax (CIT) rate of legal entities is set at 20%.

Resident corporations are taxed on their worldwide income. Non-resident corporations are taxed in Greece on any Greek-source income they derive. Such tax may take the form of a withholding tax (WHT), depending on the nature of the income, or of permanent establishment (PE) taxation, if the criteria for establishment of a PE in Greece are met.

Local/state/provincial tax rates
No local taxes on income are paid at a local level. However, it should be noted that the aforementioned rates are reduced by 40% for profits of companies derived from activities carried out on islands with less than 3,100 inhabitants.

Corporate residence

Corporate residence is determined primarily by place of incorporation. However, based on the effective management criterion under the corporate law rules, the place of legal seat could be relevant.

Permanent establishment (PE)
Subject to related tax treaty provisions, foreign corporations are subject to Greek taxation if they maintain a PE in the country. Such PE may arise in cases of foreign

companies maintaining inventories from which orders are filled; maintaining offices, warehouses, factories, etc.; carrying out any other operations for the purposes of exploiting natural resources; processing raw materials or agricultural products in their own factories or through third parties; or providing services of a technical or scientific nature (surveys, designs, or research).

Note that the local definition of a PE is generally broader than the standard Organisation for Economic Co-operation and Development (OECD) definition; however, where a double tax treaty (DTT) applies, its provision will override the domestic definition.

Other taxes

Value-added tax (VAT)

The standard VAT rate is 23%. The reduced rate on basic necessities is 13%. A super reduced rate of 6.5% for accommodation in hotels or similar establishments (including holiday accommodation and letting of places in camping or caravan sites), medicines of CN3003 and 3004, and vaccines of CN3002 intended for human consumption is applicable. The aforementioned rate is also applicable for children's books, colouring, and drawing books.

Supplies of goods and services to individuals and legal entities subject to VAT and established in European Union (EU) countries (intra-Community supplies) are exempt from VAT (zero rated). Exports of goods and certain services to non-EU countries are also exempt (zero rated).

With the following exceptions, real estate leases are generally exempt from VAT. Lease contracts for shopping centres and logistics centres may also be subject to VAT, on condition that the taxable person opts for the submission to taxation of the leasing right.

Customs duties

Many goods imported into Greece from outside the European Union are subject to customs duties. The rates of duty are provided by the EU's Common Customs Tariff.

Excise taxes

Excise taxes are imposed on energy and electricity products (e.g. petrol, natural gas, electricity), manufactured tobacco, and alcoholic products. The tax rates vary depending on the category of products.

Real estate tax

An annual real estate tax is imposed on real estate located in Greece, which is owned on 1 January of the tax year by individuals or legal entities, regardless of nationality or residence.

The applicable tax rate for legal entities amounts to 0.6%, 0.3%, or 0.1% depending on their profit or non-profit making character and the use of the properties. The tax rate remains reduced at 0.33% for real estate owned by hotel enterprises and used for their business activities.

An exemption from real estate tax is provided for buildings built within three years from the issuance of the initial building permit, unless these have been leased or in any other way used.

Greece

Extraordinary special duty on built surfaces supplied with electricity (special duty on real estate)

An extraordinary special duty, in favour of the Greek state, is imposed on commercial or residential real estate property to which electricity is supplied and which, on the 17th day of September of every year, will fall within the ambit of the real estate duty (in favour of Local Administration). Subject to said special duty is the legal owner or the beneficial owner of the real estate property, whereas the payment liability will be borne by the tenant of the property. In the event that such person is a lessee (i.e. tenant for consideration), that individual can offset payment of the special duty against future or owed leases.

The determination of the payable duty will be calculated as follows: the square metre built surface of the property (as identified by the relevant electricity bills in the context of determining the real estate duty for Local Administration) will be multiplied by the applicable rate of the area where said property is located (designated value zones) and further multiplied by the surcharge rate (deriving from the building age).

Various exceptions from said special duty are provided, in particular, communal areas of apartment blocks and buildings that have been designated as preserved structures.

The special duty on real estate will be collected by the Public Electricity Company (DEH) or alternative suppliers of electricity through the utility bills for electricity sent to consumers.

Special real estate tax

A special real estate tax of 15% is applicable on legal entities owning real estate property in Greece on the objective value of such property. This tax is mainly directed against property held, directly or indirectly, by offshore companies for the purpose of tax avoidance of transfer and inheritance taxes by the real owners. In this context, exemptions apply to listed companies, companies with registered shares up to the individual shareholder (provided such shareholder holds a tax registration number in Greece), companies for which the income derived from the real estate property does not exceed the income from other activities, EU banks, insurance companies, investment funds, etc, on the condition, however, that these are not established in non-cooperatives states (*see the Deductions section for more information on non-cooperative states*).

Real estate transfer tax

Each transfer of real estate, which is not subject to VAT, is subject to real estate transfer tax. The tax rates of the real estate transfer tax amount to 8% for the value up to 20,000 euros (EUR) and 10% for the exceeding value of the real estate.

Exemptions from real estate transfer tax for the acquisition of primary residences are determined according to the value of the property.

Stamp taxes

Rentals of non-residential properties are subject to 3.6% stamp duty (with the exception of shopping centres and logistics centres subject to VAT).

In general, loans and interest may be subject to a 2.4% stamp duty. However, there are a number of exemptions, the main one covering bank loans and bond issues.

Other stamp duties may apply, in certain limited cases.

Greece

Contribution tax on capital accumulation

A 1% tax contribution is imposed on capital accumulation by:

- business companies and joint ventures
- associations of all degrees and any other form of company, legal entity, or union of persons or society aiming to make profits, and
- branches of foreign companies (unless of EU origin).

For *Societe Anonymes* (SA) companies, an additional 0.1% duty is payable on capital to the competition committee.

Branch income

G

Profits of branches of foreign companies are subject to CIT at a rate of 20%.

Note that the equivalent of a dividend WHT is also imposed on profit repatriations from the branch to its head office or other foreign branches of the legal entity.

Income determination

Inventory valuation

Inventories are stated at the lower of cost or market (replacement value). The Greek tax system recognises various valuation methods such as first in first out (FIFO), last in first out (LIFO), weighted average, etc.

Capital gains

In general, capital gains are included in the taxable profits of Greek companies. Certain special rules apply in the case of sales of shares in listed or non-listed entities.

Capital gains tax on sale of listed shares

The sale of listed shares that were acquired up to 31 December 2012, and irrespective of the time of sale of those shares, is subject to a transaction duty at a rate of 0.2%. The capital gains derived from the sale of such listed shares shall be exempt from CIT, on the condition that the capital gain is booked in a special tax-free reserve.

Capital gains derived by legal entities maintaining double entry accounting books from the sale of listed shares, which are acquired from 1 January 2013 onwards, will be taxed based on the general CIT provisions. Any loss, arising within the same year and for the same reason, shall be offset with capital gains. Moreover, if losses arise following the offset, reference is made to the provision on the carrying forward of losses. The law includes details in relation to the specification of profits. Similar provisions are introduced with regard to profits realised by individuals or legal entities keeping income-expenses accounting books. The transaction duty of 0.2% is abolished for such shares.

Transfer tax on sale of non-listed shares

The sale of Greek shares non-listed on the Stock Exchange triggers a 5% tax calculated on the transfer value as either agreed by the parties or determined on the basis of a 'minimum-value' formula set forth by law, whichever is the higher. The aforementioned 5% tax is also due in the case of transfer of foreign non-listed shares by a Greek tax resident, calculated on the consideration agreed. In the case where the seller is a Greek corporation, the payment of the 5% tax does not exhaust the transferor's tax liability.

Greece

Any capital gains arising thereof, are further subject to tax at the standard CIT rate (i.e. they are included in the taxable profits of the company). It should be noted that the 5% tax paid at the time of the transfer may, under certain conditions, be provided as a credit against the company's annual corporate liability.

Moreover, gains arising from the sale of parts of limited liability companies (LLCs) are subject to a 20% tax rate. In cases where the seller is a Greek entity, the tax liability is not exhausted and the respective capital gain is taxed according to the general tax provisions with the 20% tax being credited against the final CIT liability.

Dividend income
Profits distributed from Greek companies are not included in the taxable profits of their shareholders.

A participation exemption is applicable also on dividends received by Greek SAs and LLCs from subsidiaries that have their registered seat in another EU member state, in which they participate, on the condition that these profits are booked in an untaxed reserve account.

Other foreign dividends are included in taxable profits, but a foreign tax credit may be obtained under certain conditions.

Stock dividends
Stock dividends are treated as cash dividends for CIT purposes.

Interest income
Interest income is generally taxable. There are certain special rules that govern the receipt of interest income from bonds by banks and insurance companies.

Partnership income
Both general partnerships (*Omorrythmi Etairia* or OE) and limited partnerships (*Eterrorythmi Etairia* or EE) are not tax transparent. They are generally taxed at a rate of 25%, but there are special rules on income determination or cases where partners are individuals.

Rents/royalties income
Income derived from rents and royalties is taxed as ordinary income.

Foreign income
Resident corporations are taxed on their worldwide income. Foreign income received by a domestic corporation is taxed together with other income. If related income tax is paid or withheld abroad, a tax credit is generally available up to the amount of the applicable Greek income tax. Losses incurred abroad can only be offset against foreign profits.

There are no special anti-deferral regimes or controlled foreign company (CFC) rules in Greece.

Deductions

Depreciation
Depreciation of tangible assets is compulsory for financial years ending after 30 December 1997 (not compulsory for financial years ended within the period from 1

Greece

January 1992 through 30 December 1997). Fixed assets with acquisition value of up to EUR 1,200 each may be written off to profit and loss in the year acquired or when used in operations. Depreciation is computed on the basis of the straight-line method or, in some cases, the declining-balance method on the acquisition value, increased by any additions and improvements. The straight-line method or the declining-balance method must be used consistently. However, new companies, for the three consecutive financial years that follow the financial year in which their productive operation commenced, are permitted to depreciate all their fixed assets either at 0% or at a rate equal to 50% of the applicable rate, provided that the selected rate will not change from year to year. If the declining-balance method is used, the straight-line method rates increase three times.

For each category of assets, maximum and minimum annual depreciation rates are determined by a presidential decree. Companies may select any rate within this range, provided that this is consistently applied.

Goodwill
There are some court cases which support the deductibility of goodwill as a start-up expense, but the specifics of each case must be carefully considered.

Organisational and start-up expenses
The amount of start-up expenses (including costs for acquisition of real estate) is amortised, either as a lump sum during the year of its realisation or in equivalent instalments within a five year period. Specifically, expenses realised by financial leasing companies in relation to the acquisition of real estate, which will constitute the object of an agreement of the same law, may be depreciated in equivalent amounts, in analogy to the years of duration of the agreement.

Interest expenses
Accrued interest from loans or credits of a company is generally deductible, with the exception of interest on arrears due to the debt of taxes, duties, contributions, and fees to the state and other legal entities governed by public law; interest on loans for the purchase of shares in any type of company, to the extent that this participation is transferred within a two-year period; interest on loans used for the purchase of shares in a legal entity established in non-cooperating states or states with preferential tax regime; and interest paid to companies established in such states.

Bad debt
Tax-deductible bad debt provisions are calculated at 0.5% on the stated value of invoices for sale of goods or provision of services, after a reduction for discounts, sales to the state or other entities governed by public law and the special consumption tax imposed in certain cases. Special restrictions and rules apply to certain transactions, while there is a recapture system for provisions which are not realised.

Charitable contributions
Donations and sponsorships paid to charitable institutions, non-profit making foundations, churches and monasteries, and various other welfare institutions may be deductible up to 10% of the total net profits or income arising from the balance sheet of the legal entity.

Pension expenses
Group life insurance premiums, which include pension plans, may be deducted at up to EUR 1,500 per employee.

Greece

Payment for directors
Fees of board members are taxed at source at a rate of 35%. Such amounts are tax-deductible.

Bonuses (benefits in cash, on top of regular remunerations and overtime payments) paid to executives of credit institutions up to financial year 2013 are subject to special increased taxation. Taxation is based on the general progressive tax scale applicable to individuals provided the total annual income of the executive does not exceed EUR 60,000 and the amount of the bonus does not exceed 10% of the total annual regular remuneration. For amounts exceeding the outlined limitations, taxation at source based on a progressive tax scale is provided as follows:

- Up to EUR 20,000: 50%.
- EUR 20,001 to EUR 40,000: 60%.
- EUR 40,001 to EUR 60,000: 70%.
- EUR 60,001 to EUR 80,000: 80%.

Fines and penalties
Fees received from activities constituting a criminal offence, from penal clauses, fines, and penalties are not recognised as deductible expenses.

Taxes
Taxes, other than income tax and real estate tax, are recognised as deductible expenses if supported by related tax returns and payment receipts and borne by the company.

Other significant items
In general, expenses are deductible subject to certain conditions. The following is a list of certain key conditions or restrictions on expense deductibility:

- The deductibility of hotel expenses, expenses for corporate gifts, education of personnel, special clothing of personnel, and mobile telephone expenses are subject to specific conditions.
- Payroll expenses are not deductible when they are not paid through professional bank accounts or cheques paid through the same accounts.
- The value of raw and ancillary materials and other goods (plus processing thereon), which is paid to a legal entity whose role consists exclusively of the invoicing of the transactions, while the delivery of goods or provision of services is conducted by a third party, is not deducted from the gross profits of companies.
- Car expenses are generally deductible up to 70% for motor vehicles up to 1,600 cc and 35% for motor vehicles exceeding 1,600 cc.
- Expenses concerning transactions realised between Greek companies and entities established in preferential tax regimes may be deductible for Greek companies, on the condition that satisfactory evidence is provided that the transactions are real, usual, and do not result in the transfer of profits, income, or capital for the purpose of tax evasion or tax avoidance.

Accrued expenses are, in principle, non-deductible until they become final and settled, supported by respective invoices.

Net operating and capital losses
Losses can be carried forward five years. Carrybacks are not permitted.

Payments to foreign affiliates
Royalties, interest, and service fees paid to foreign affiliates are deductible expenses under certain requirements and conditions.

Special restrictions on transactions with non-cooperative states and states with preferential tax treatment
Greek tax law has established rules in relation to non-cooperating states and states with preferential tax treatment.

Non-cooperating states are defined as states that are not EU member states and which have not concluded agreements of administrative assistance in the tax sector with Greece or with, at least, 12 other states. Non-cooperative states are enumerated in a Ministerial Decision to be issued annually.

Pursuant to the Ministerial Decision for 2012, the non-cooperating states for 2012 are specified as follows:

- Andorra
- Anguilla
- Antigua & Barbuda
- Aruba
- the Bahamas
- Bahrain
- Barbados
- Bermuda
- Belize
- British Virgin Islands
- Brunei
- Cayman Islands
- the Cook Islands
- Costa Rica
- Dominica
- former Yugoslav Republic of Macedonia (FYROM)
- Gibraltar
- Grenada
- Guatemala
- Guernsey
- Hong Kong
- Isle of Man
- Jersey
- Lebanon
- Liberia
- Liechtenstein
- Malaysia
- Marshall Islands
- Mauritius
- Monaco
- Montserrat
- Nauru
- Netherland Antilles
- Niue
- Panama
- Philippines
- St. Lucia
- St. Kitts and Nevis
- St. Vincent and the Grenadines
- Samoa
- Seychelles
- Singapore
- Turks and Caicos
- Uruguay
- US Virgin Islands
- Vanuatu

An individual or legal entity, irrespective of its legal form, is considered located in a preferential tax regime, even if its residence of registered office is located in an EU member state, in cases where it is not subject to taxation in this state or is *de facto* not subject to taxation, or is subject to tax on income or capital at an amount which is lower than 60% of the tax that would have been due, in accordance with Greek tax legislation, if such entity were resident or were maintaining a PE in Greece.

Expenses concerning transactions realised between Greek companies and entities established in non-cooperative states or preferential tax regimes may be deductible for Greek companies, on the condition, however, that satisfactory evidence is provided that transactions are real and usual and do not have as a result the transfer of profits or income or capital with the purpose of tax evasion or tax avoidance.

Group taxation

Group taxation is not permitted in Greece.

Greece

Transfer pricing

Article 26 of L.3728/2008 on 'Monitoring the Markets and other provisions' of the Ministry of Development introduced, for the first time in Greece, rules on the documentation of prices of intergroup transactions with the intention of "detecting possible overpricing of intergroup transactions, expanding artificially the cost of sold products and services, having as a consequence the reduction of the gross profit of enterprises in Greece, picturing the increase of sale prices to the final consumers as necessary and justified".

In accordance with the relevant transfer pricing rules, companies operating in any form in Greece are obliged to apply to their transactions with companies that are connected to them, terms in accordance with the arm's-length principle.

For this purpose, companies must document the prices for all their inter-group transactions with a complete and standardised study of documentation of prices. The study consists of the 'basic documentation file', concerning groups in which the parent company is Greek and the 'Greek documentation file', with regard to Greek subsidiaries of foreign groups and foreign companies operating in any form in Greece.

These files must be made available when requested by the competent authorities of the Ministry of Development within 30 days from the notification of the relevant request. Moreover, companies that have inter-company transactions must submit annually, within four months and 15 days from the end of the accounting period, to the Ministry of Development a catalogue in which the data of their intergroup transactions, and specifically the number and their value, are documented. In case of non-compliance with these obligations, an independent fine is imposed, equal to 10% of the value of the transactions for which the relative documentation was not submitted or the foreseen catalogue was not submitted timely.

If an infringement of the arm's-length principle is established, the competent tax authorities are immediately informed in order for the provisions of tax legislation and the imposition of the relevant tax penalties to apply.

In parallel to the aforementioned regimes, transfer pricing is also regulated by the Income Tax Code (ITC). Specifically, the ITC expanded the frame of application of the provision to leases of movable or immovable property, while the condition of (direct or indirect) tax avoidance taxes for the application of the provision was abolished. Moreover, the provisions provide for a 20% fine on the surplus net profits arising on behalf of enterprises in case of infringement of the arm's-length principle, as well as a fine equal to 20% on the value of the transaction in case of non-compliance, faulty compliance, or overdue filing of the required documentation. With reference to the obligation of documentation, the deadline within which enterprises are obliged to present the file is 30 days and the minimum amount of transactions for which documentation is required is EUR 100,000 annually.

Thin capitalisation

According to the relevant thin capitalisation rules, accrued interest on loans paid to affiliated companies are deductible on the condition that the debt to equity ratio is 3:1.

There are certain exceptions from the application of the thin capitalisation rules, applicable to banks, factoring companies, leasing companies, investment service companies, and securitisation special purpose vehicles (SPVs). Loans assumed by third companies, and for which any kind of guarantee has been issued by the afore mentioned connected companies, are added to the total amount of loans undertaken by the connected companies.

Controlled foreign companies (CFCs)
There are currently no CFC rules in Greece.

Tax credits and incentives

Foreign tax credit
Tax paid abroad for income taxable in Greece is credited but is limited to the amount of Greek tax due.

Incentives for the maintenance of workplaces
Legal entities, which suffer a reduction of turnover for two consecutive accounting periods without reducing their workforce, can enjoy a reduction of the tax rate by three percentage units. However, a revocation of the granted benefit and imposition of further tax in case of reduction of personnel or increase of the turnover within the three-year period is provided.

Other tax incentives
Apart from the aforementioned tax incentives, L. 3908/2011 on 'Bolstering of Private Investments for Economic Growth, Entrepreneurship and Regional Sustainability' (the new Investment Incentive Law) includes the following tax incentives:

* Any investment plan in any sector of the economy may receive benefits under the law. Only certain cases explicitly specified in the law are exempt (e.g. power generation from photovoltaic arrays).
* The types of subsidised expenditures for tangible and intangible assets are indicatively mentioned, whereas the expenses that may not be subsidised are exhaustively enumerated. Especially the subsidy percentage for the expenditure of intangible assets may not exceed 50% of the total eligible expenditure of the investment plan.
* The term of 'new' enterprises is specifically defined for the new law's purposes. An enterprise is considered as 'new', if the establishment procedures have not been completed before the enterprise applies for aid according to the new law or if it has been established within the past 24 months prior to filing the application.
* There are three types of aid: (i) tax exemption, (ii) subsidy, and (iii) leasing subsidy.
* The new law lists three categories of General Investment Plans and specifies the type of aid for each of them: (i) General Entrepreneurship which only the tax exemption may be granted for, whereas for the (ii) Technological Development and the (iii) Regional Sustainability investment plan, the subsidy and/or the leasing subsidy may be granted in principle, with different percentages for the existing and the new enterprises. The remaining percentage may be covered by tax exemption.
* The law also lists four categories of Special Investment Plans: (i) Youth Entrepreneurship, (ii) Major Investment Plans, (iii) Integrated Long-Term Investment Plans, and (iv) Synergy and Networking. The aids granted are further specified by type, volume, and/or percentage for each of them.
* The percentages of aid available are specified in conjunction with the division of the country into three zones (A, B, and C) and are the following:

Greece

	CIT aid available (%)		
Zones	Large enterprises	Medium-sized enterprises	Small and micro enterprises
ZONE A (Prefecture of Attica, Prefecture of Viotia)	15	20	25
ZONE B (Prefectures with GDP per capita > 75% of the average GDP of the country)	30	35	40
ZONE C (Prefectures with GDP per capita < 75% of the average GDP of the country)	40	45	50

In any case, the above percentages should comply with the ceiling set by the Regional State Aid Map (RSAM) approved by the European Commission.

- An additional 5% aid percentage, up to the ceiling set by the RSAM, is granted for investment plans in Industrial Entrepreneurship Zones and Innovation Zones. Benefits are also granted up to the ceiling set by the RSAM, by enterprise size and up to 50% of the eligible expenditure, for investment plans on islands and regional units of islands that belong administratively to the regions of the mainland.
- The new law sets a ceiling for each aid (EUR 10 million to 15 million in principle, but graduated according to various criteria).
- The period for filing the application (April and October, with the exception of large investment projects) and the conditions for approval are further specified.
- The law specifies the conditions and evaluation criteria for each investment project and determines, in general, the procedure for evaluation, approval, and monitoring of implementation of investment projects (further specification by ministerial decisions).
- The mode of payment of each type of aid is further determined. Especially for the aid of tax exemption, the law stipulates that the amount of tax exemption aid is annually formed with the following restrictions:
  - The enterprise is entitled to the use benefit of the incentive from the fiscal year in which the decision on the completion and beginning of the productive operation of the investment has been published. In this fiscal year, the ceiling of tax exemption to be used is set at $^1/_3$ of the approved amount of the tax exemption aid.
  - In the following fiscal year, the ceiling of tax exemption to be used, including the aid for the first fiscal year, is set at $^2/_3$ of the approved amount of the tax exemption aid.
  - The remaining amount of the approved tax exemption aid may be covered within ten fiscal years for new enterprises and within eight fiscal years for existing enterprises following the fiscal year in which the decision on the completion and beginning of the productive operation of the investment has been published.
- The amount of the tax exemption aid shall be shown as a tax-free reserve in a special account in the enterprise's accounting books and shall consist of the income tax on the net profits reported in the initial timely income tax return which shall not be paid based on the tax exemption granted.
- Where the equipment is acquired through leasing, the tax exemption to which the enterprise is entitled in each fiscal year is calculated on the part of the purchase price of the equipment which is included in the rents already paid by the end of this fiscal year.
- The law stipulates that the amounts of subsidies and leasing subsidies as well as of tax exemption shall be shown as tax-free reserves in special accounts. Said reserves may not be distributed or capitalised and shall be returned in case of dissolution

Greece

of the enterprise. In case of distribution or capitalisation, certain penalties shall be imposed.
- The law stipulates that any aid to be paid is exempt from any tax, stamp duty, right, and any other charge in favor of the state or any third party.
- Finally, the new law specifies the obligations of the beneficiary enterprises and penalties in case of non-compliance.

The above rules are very detailed, and analytical and careful advices needs to be sought before making any decision in respect thereof.

Withholding taxes

Profits distributed by Greek SAs or LLCs (and also some associations) in the form of dividends, Board and Directors fees, profits distributed to personnel, as well as interim dividend payments made to individuals or legal entities, Greek or foreign, and independent of whether the payments are made in cash or in kind (shares), are subject to 25% WHT.

Tax is withheld by Greek SAs, LLCs, and associations with exhaustion of tax liability of the beneficiaries. An exception is provided with regard to individuals that are taxed on their total income at a tax rate lower than the WHT rate, in which case, income derived from dividends or the aforementioned participations shall be taxed based on the general provisions with a credit on the tax withheld.

WHT shall not be imposed on dividends paid to a legal entity established in another member state of the European Union, subject to the conditions of L.2578/1998 (Parent-Subsidiary Directive).

25% WHT shall also be applicable on the distribution of profits remitted or credited by a PE of a foreign legal entity in Greece to its registered seat or to another PE located abroad.

The dividend WHT is equally applicable for distributed or capitalised profits of previous fiscal years.

The following table provides a summary of the WHT applicable under the respective DTT entered into by Greece:

Recipient	Dividends (%)	Interest (%)	Royalties (%)
Resident individuals and companies	21/25 (1)	10/20 (2)	0
Non-resident individuals and companies:			
Non-treaty	21/25 (1)	40 (2)	25 (3)
Treaty:			
Albania	5	5	5
Armenia	10	10	5
Austria (4)	5/15 (5)	8	7
Azerbaijan	8	8	8
Belgium	5/15 (9)	5/10 (8)	5
Bulgaria	10	10	10

G

Greece

Recipient	Dividends (%)	Interest (%)	Royalties (%)
Canada	5/15 (9)	10	0/10 (15)
China	5/10 (6)	10	10
Croatia	5/10 (6)	10	10
Cyprus	25	10	0/5 (7)
Czech Republic	Domestic	10	10
Denmark	38	8	5
Egypt	10	15	15
Estonia	5/15 (6)	10	5/10 (13)
Finland	47	10	0/10 (11)
France	Domestic	10	5
Georgia	8	8	5
Germany	25	10	0
Hungary	45	10	10
Iceland	5/15 (6)	8	10
India	Domestic	Domestic	Domestic
Ireland	5/15 (9)	5	5
Israel	Domestic	10	10
Italy	15	10	0/5 (11)
Korea, Republic of	5/15 (6)	8	10
Kuwait	5	5	15
Latvia	5/10 (6)	10	5/10 (13)
Lithuania	5/15 (6)	10	5/10 (13)
Luxembourg	38	8	5/7 (10)
Malta	5/10 (6)	8	8
Mexico	10	10	10
Moldova	5/15 (6)	10	8
Morocco	5/10 (6)	10	10
Netherlands	35	8/10 (14)	5/7 (10)
Norway	40	10	10
Poland	Domestic	10	10
Portugal	15	15	10
Qatar	5	5	5
Romania	45	10	5/7 (10)
Russia	5/10 (6)	7	7
Saudi Arabia	5	5	10
Serbia	5/15 (6)	10	10
Slovakia	Domestic	10	10
Slovenia	10	10	10
South Africa	5/15 (6)	8	5/7 (10)
Spain	5/10 (6)	8	6
Sweden	Domestic	10	5
Switzerland	5/15 (6)	7	5
Tunisia	35	15	12
Turkey	15	12	10
Ukraine	5/10 (6)	10	10
United Kingdom	Domestic	0	0
United States	Domestic	0/Domestic (12)	0

Recipient	Dividends (%)	Interest (%)	Royalties (%)
Uzbekistan	8	10	8

Notes

1. The 21%/25% WHT applies to distribution of dividends by Greek SAs and Greek LLCs. The rate is 21% for distributions within 2011 and 25% from 2012 onwards.
2. Interest earned on deposits with banks operating in Greece, as well as on any kind of bonds, is subject to WHT at the rate of 10% withheld at source. WHT on interest payable to non-Greek residents is 40%.
3. Payments of royalties and service fees to foreign residents are subject to a WHT at the rate of 25%.
4. It should be taken into account that such rates are based on a new DTT applicable as of 1 January 2011, whilst other rates have been applicable in the past.
5. The rate of 5% will apply if the beneficial owner is a company which holds directly at least 25% of the voting power of the company paying the dividends.
6. The rate of 5% applies in case the beneficiary is a company (excluding a partnership) and directly holds at least 25% of the capital of the paying company.
7. The rate of 5% is applicable only for the right to use cinematograph films.
8. Rate of 5% applies to loans not incorporated into negotiable instruments and granted by banks.
9. A rate of 5% is applicable to shareholders of 25% and above.
10. The rate is 5% applies if the royalties consist of payments of any kind received as a consideration for the use of or the right to use any copyright of literary, artistic, or scientific work, including cinematograph films.
11. Exemption ('0' rate) applies to payments of any kind received as a consideration for the use of, or the right to use, any copyright of literary, artistic, or scientific work including cinematograph films and films or tapes for television or radio broadcasting.
12. Interest (on bonds, securities, notes, debentures, or on any other form of indebtedness) received from sources within Greece by a resident or corporation of the United States (US) not engaged in trade or business in Greece through a PE therein, shall be exempt from Greek tax but only to the extent that such interest does not exceed 9% per annum; but such exemption shall not apply to such interest paid by a Greek corporation to a US corporation controlling, directly or indirectly, more than 50% of the entire voting power in the paying corporation.
13. The 5% rate is applicable if the royalties consist of payments of any kind received as a consideration for the use of industrial, commercial, or scientific equipment, and the 10% rate is applicable for all the other cases.
14. The 8% rate is applicable when the beneficiary of the interests is a bank or a financial institution, 10% rate is applicable for all the other cases.
15. Exemption ('0' rate) applies to copyright royalties and other like payments in respect of the production or reproduction of any cultural or artistic work (but not including royalties in respect of motion picture films nor royalties in respect of works on films or videotapes or other means of reproduction for use in connection with television broadcasting).

In general, it should be noted that certain DTTs may include specific clauses in specific cases that are not all captured in the table; therefore, a careful review of each DTT is highly advisable.

Tax administration

Taxable period
The taxable period is the financial year, which can end either on 30 June or 31 December.

Tax returns
CIT returns of Greek SAs, LLCs, and branches of foreign companies are filed on a special form within four months and ten days from the end of their financial year. By a decision of the Minister of Finance, the filing date for SAs may be extended a few days, depending on the last digit (figure) of their tax registration number (known in Greece as the *arithmos phorologikou metroou* or AFM). Branches and subsidiaries (at least 50% participation) of foreign companies may follow the financial year of the parent company. A Greek company that is at least 50% held by another Greek company that is in turn a subsidiary of a foreign company that has participation with the same or higher

Greece

percentage may also follow the financial year of the foreign parent company. The CIT return constitutes the basis for assessment.

Tax returns are required to be submitted electronically from 2011 onwards.

Payment of tax

CIT and tax prepayment (80% [100% for banks operating in Greece] of the current year's CIT less tax withheld at source) based on the tax return are paid in eight equal monthly instalments, the first of which should be paid upon filing. Therefore, for companies whose financial year ends on 31 December, the final instalment is payable in December. For newly established companies, the pre-payment is reduced to 50% for the first three years of their operating. A deduction of 1.5% is granted in case of a lump sum payment of CIT liability.

Audit cycle

Tax audit procedures

The tax audit commences with the issuance of an audit order for tax open years, usually not more than five. The order concerns the audit of all tax issues (CIT, VAT, WHT, capital gain tax, etc.). The duration of the audit may vary from a few weeks to a few months, in certain cases.

A regular or temporary audit may also be conducted from the office of the audit authority. Such audit from the office is based on the data of the file, the sheets of information, the audit reports of the Financial Crime Prosecution Unit and other authorities of the Ministry of Finance, the books and records that the taxpayer may be required to submit, the data and information of the entities stipulated in article 17 of L. 3842/2010, and the data accruing from the electronic data processing at the General Secretariat for Information-Security Systems. The possibility of issuing from the office an act of partial tax determination for one, or more, fiscal years, without auditing all the books and records and without requiring the audit of other taxes, also applies, in case where it is derived from other data at the disposal of the audit authority (i.e. information sheets, reports of the Financial Crime Prosecution Unit, electronically processed data of the General Secretariat for Information-Security Systems) that the liable entity omitted to declare, or inaccurately declared taxable income, or even miscalculated the percentages, or deductions.

However, the ability of conducting an audit at the registered seat of the legal entity, specifically with regard to cases that are explicitly stipulated in the law, is in parallel applicable.

Following the audit and the notification of tax audit findings, the company may in turn:

- Negotiate with the tax authorities with a view to reducing the tax burden and achieve an 'out of court settlement'. The out-of court settlement offers the possibility to reduce additional taxes (not the principal amount of tax) at the rates provided now under the provisions of L.2238/94 (reduction of the additional tax to $^3/_5$ or $^1/_3$ depending on the case). The conclusion of such a settlement presupposes that the company accepts the findings of the audit (e.g. of expenses) for the audited years and is likely to face the same issues in the following years as well.
- Take the case to court (filing of a recourse), which necessitates an advance payment (50% of the taxes and penalties assessed). The first decision normally takes two to three years and another six to eight years until a decision by the Court of Appeal and

Supreme Court is issued. There are several measures being currently implemented in an attempt to reduce this time.

- There is also a possibility to take the case to a Fiscal Arbitration Body, competent to arbitrate over dispute resolution arising from tax assessments exceeding EUR 150,000, by filing an application and subject to the consent by the Minister of Finance. The commencement of operation of the Fiscal Arbitration Body is to be determined by a Presidential Decree to be issued following the suggestion of the Ministers of Finance and Justice; to date (May 2012), such Presidential Decree has not been issued.

Criminal sanctions are also imposed on the company's representative under certain conditions, which are waived in the case of settlement on the amount of taxes assessed.

Tax auditors' practice

The complexity of the Greek tax legislation and the vagueness of its requirements enable the tax auditors to dispute either the company's results reflected in its accounting records or to disallow expenses. This is true in all tax audits and in spite of companies' endeavours to comply with the tax requirements, tax audits always result in assessment of additional taxes and penalties.

The amount of additional taxes depends mainly on the following:

- Company's vulnerability because of nature of business and transactions.
- Taxes already paid on the basis of the company's income tax returns.
- Profits declared by competitors.
- Weaknesses and shortcomings which the tax auditors might reveal, if a full audit is carried out.

The amount of additional taxes is capped and cannot exceed:

- 60% for the submission of a delayed tax return and
- 120% for the submission of an inaccurate submission or non-submission of a tax return.

In respect of deductible expenses, the legislation prescribes, among other requirements, that such expenses must be of a 'business' nature, without defining what a business expense is. Consequently, the tax auditors dispute the deductibility of various items arguing that, in their opinion, they are not contributing to the company's business.

In a worst-case scenario, if serious violations are detected that make the audit verifications impossible, then the validity of the accounting books may be contested, resulting in the deemed (out-of-books) profit calculation and the imposition of heavy penalties and additional taxes.

Specifically, the validity of the books may be contested on the basis of the kind and gravity of infringements, which are divided in two categories:

- Infringements determining the books as 'inadequate'.
- Infringements determining the books as 'inaccurate'.

In the extreme cases, where the accounting books are treated as 'inadequate' or 'inaccurate', the taxable income and the tax due by the company will not be calculated according to book figures; but instead, the out of books determination method is applied, according to which the company's gross income of each financial year will be

Greece

multiplied by the net profit rates defined by the Greek Ministry of Finance. These rates have been defined on the basis of the business activities of each company. In cases where the books are deemed to be 'inaccurate', these rates would be surcharged by 40% to 80%, depending on the kind of infringement from which the inaccuracy of the books has resulted.

Greek SAs and LLCs whose annual financial statements are subject to a statutory audit by individual Certified Auditors and audit firms are required to obtain an 'annual tax certificate' from their certified auditors upon the completion of a tax audit conducted, confirming compliance with Greek tax legislation. The tax audit is conducted on specific tax areas as defined by a special audit program issued by the Ministry of Finance in cooperation with the Committee of Accounting Standardization and Auditing (ELTE). The audit program will be updated annually and is in accordance with the provisions of International Standard on Non-Audit Assurance Engagements 3000.

Statute of limitations
The right of the Greek state to seek to collect unpaid taxes is normally five years starting from the end of the year in which the relevant tax return should be filed. For example for taxes due in 2011, the clearance VAT return should be filed in 2012 and the statute of limitation expires on 31 December 2017. However, in the case where a return is not filed, then the statute of limitation is extended to ten years. Furthermore, it should be noted that the statutes of limitation may be extended by law. This has happened many times in the past.

Other issues

Choice of business entity
The main differences between a subsidiary (i.e. SA or LLC) and a branch of a company from the law/establishment perspective are as follows:

- A subsidiary is a separate legal entity from its parent company, whereas a branch does not form a separate legal entity, does not have its own shareholders, and consequently the funds needed for its operation are transferred from the overseas parent company.
- The parent company of a branch must be either the equivalent of a Greek SA or an LLC, whereas there is no such restriction for subsidiaries.
- The day-to-day management of a branch is exercised by the legal representative, a person appointed by the parent company, whereas an SA is represented by its board of directors (BoD) and an LLC is administered and directed by the administrator(s).
- No minimum capital is required for the establishment of a branch, nevertheless the share capital of the parent company should be at least EUR 60,000 if it is an SA and EUR 4,500 if it is an LLC.
- An SA appears to be a more prestigious type of company than a branch and an LLC. This has a mainly psychological effect. Certain investors still tend to opt for the establishment of an SA company, particularly if they would like to participate in public tenders, etc.

The main legal differences between an SA and an LLC in Greece from a company law/establishment perspective are as follows:

- An SA is managed by a BoD consisting of at least three members, whereas an LLC can be managed by only one individual, the administrator (legal entities are permitted to be appointed as BoD members or administrators). Both BoD members and administrators have to acquire a Greek tax registration number and a Greek residence permit before the establishment of the companies. Obtaining a residence permit for non-EU citizens is a time consuming procedure.

- The shareholders of an SA are not required to be registered with the Greek tax authorities, whereas the partners of an LLC have to be registered with the Greek tax authorities and this may prove to be a time consuming procedure.
- An SA is established by virtue of registration or approval (in case the company's share capital is higher than EUR 3 million as well as in special cases) of the notarial deed which embodies the company's Articles of Association (AoA). The announcement of the Ministry of Development, containing a summary of the AoA, must be published in the 'Bulletin of *Societes Anonymes* and Limited Liability Companies' of the Government Gazette. Generally, the registration of a SA requires approximately one to two working days after submission of relevant documentation. However, the time period may be extended to ten working days, in the case that a special approval by the Ministry of Development is required. Whereas an LLC is established by a notarial deed, which incorporates the company's AoA, filed with the relevant authority (Registry with the Court of First Instance). A summary of the AoA must be published in the 'Bulletin of *Societes Anonymes* and Limited Liability Companies' of the Government Gazette. Such registration usually takes three to five working days after the signature of the notarial deed.
- An SA company is supervised by the Greek Ministry of Development (Prefecture), which necessitates certain filings to be performed (e.g. minutes of BoD, general announcements, financial statements). Whereas, at least at this stage, no supervising authority exists for an LLC and thus its filing requirements are less restrictive.

New corporate form: the 'Private Company' (PC)

- The PC constitutes a legal entity and is commercial in nature, even if its object is not per se commercial. The PC should have a capital of at least EUR 1, whilst its partners participate in the PC by means of capital, non-capital, and guarantee contributions.
- The participation in the PC presupposes the acquisition of one or more capital parts. The capital parts should have a nominal value of at least EUR 1. The PC is not entitled to acquire, either directly or indirectly, its own capital parts.
- The PC has its registered seat in the municipality referred to in its articles of association, whilst the transfer of the registered seat of the PC in another country of the European Economic Area (EEA) does not necessarily result in the dissolution of the PC, provided that the recipient country recognises the transfer and the continuity of legal personality. The PC is not obligated to have its actual seat in Greece, whilst the PC is capable of establishing various types of secondary establishments either in Greece or abroad.
- The term of the PC is definite; if not otherwise stipulated in the articles of association of the PC, the PC has a term of 12 years following its establishment.
- The PC is administered and represented by one or more administrators.
- The administrator represents the PC and conducts in its name all actions pertaining to the administration of the PC, the management of its assets, and, in general, the pursuit of its objects. Actions of the administrator, even if falling outside the corporate objects, bind the PC vis-à-vis third parties, unless the PC proves that the third party knew or ought to have known the violation of the company's objects.
- The provisions of One Stop Shop Authority are accordingly applied to the establishment of the PC. The establishment of the PC is effected by means of registering the PC with the General Electronic Commercial Registry (GEMI).
- The PC drafts: (i) the balance sheet, (ii) the profit and loss account, (iii) the appropriation account and (iv) the appendix incorporating all required information for the comprehension of the financial statements, as well as the report of the administrator in relation to the corporate activity for the ending fiscal year.

G

Greece

- The PC is dissolved: (i) at any time following a resolution of the partners, (ii) when its definite term has expired, unless the term of the PC is extended by virtue of a resolution of the partners , (iii) if the PC defaults, and (iv) in all other circumstances contemplated by the law or the articles of association.
- As the PC was only introduced in April 2012, no practical experience is yet available as to its implementation and use.

Guatemala

PwC contact

Edgar Mendoza
PricewaterhouseCoopers
6a calle 6-38 Z.9
Edif. Tivoli Plaza
4to Nivel
Guatemala City, Guatemala
Tel: +502 2420-7800 ext. 844
Email: edgar.mendoza@gt.pwc.com

Significant developments

In 2012, the Congress of the Republic of Guatemala approved Decree No. 4-2012, which came into effect on 25 February of the same year, and Decree No. 10-2012, which will come into force starting 1 January 2013. These amendments have been incorporated into the appropriate sections of this summary.

Taxes on corporate income

The tax system of Guatemala is a unitary system, whereby income of all kinds, other than capital gains, is lumped together and subject to a single tax. The components of gross income subject to tax are usually business income, interest, dividends, rent, salaries, and services. Companies are subject to income tax only on their Guatemala-source income. Dividends and other income payable abroad are taxed separately by way of withholding taxes (WHTs).

During 2012, there are two income tax regimes in Guatemala: general and optional.

Starting 1 January 2013, the income tax systems shall be the following: the system on earnings from lucrative activities, replacing the optional 31% system, and the simplified optional system on income from lucrative activities, which replaces the general 5% income tax system.

These systems are disclosed below.

General income tax regime
For 2012, a rate of 5% is applicable to a company's gross income from Guatemalan sources (less exempt income).

A rate of 5% is applicable on gross revenue of juridical entities performing mercantile and non-mercantile activities, resident in Guatemala.

The tax is payable under flat tax withholdings (the tax is to be retained by either the customer or the recipient of services) or by direct remittances to the tax office made monthly within the first ten working days of the month following the invoice date.

Starting 1 January 2013, this system will be named the simplified optional system on income from lucrative activities, and the tax rate will be 6% on income.

Guatemala

Optional income tax regime

For 2012, a rate of 31% is applicable to a company's taxable income from Guatemalan sources.

A rate of 31% is applicable on net income of juridical entities and individuals resident in Guatemala.

Under this system, the tax is determined and paid at the end of each quarter, without prejudicing the end-of-period final tax liquidation.

Starting 1 January 2013, the optional income tax system shall be replaced by the income on earnings from lucrative activities system, and the tax rate shall remain at 31%. This shall vary starting from 2014, when the tax rate shall be 28%.

Corporate residence

The place of incorporation determines corporate residence. Entities incorporated under Guatemalan laws are required to have their fiscal and corporate residence in Guatemalan territory.

Permanent establishment (PE)

For 2012, there are no specific provisions that determine PE.

Starting 1 January 2013, Decree No. 10-2012 includes PE, i.e. activities conducted in the country in a continuous manner, either in a fixed business place or facilities conducting work of any kind, except for insurance and refinancing activities, brokers, independent agents, etc. acting in the normal turn of events.

Other taxes

Value-added tax (VAT)

A 12% VAT is levied on the sale or transfer of merchandise and on non-personal services rendered or effected in Guatemala. The tax is payable to the government by way of the invoice method, whereby the tax charged to the customers is offset by the VAT paid over purchases, and the government collects the net resulting amount. The issuance and circulation of credit titles is VAT-exempt.

Sale of goods

The taxable amount on the sale of goods includes the sales price, less any discounts provided under sound commercial practices, plus other charges shown on the invoice.

Services

The taxable amount of services includes the price of the service, less any discounts provided under sound commercial practices, plus financial charges and products used to render the services.

Imports and leases

The tax base for imports is the value declared for import duties computation purposes.

The tax base for leases of movable or immovable property is the value of the lease.

Guatemala

Exempted sales and services
The following items are exempt from VAT:

- Importations made by:
  - cooperatives legally constituted as registered on imported machinery, equipment, and other goods relating to the activity or service of the cooperative
  - individuals and juridical entities under temporary importation regulations, and
  - diplomatic and consular missions accredited before the Guatemalan government.
- Banking institution services and their agents.
- The issuance, circulation, and transfer of credit bonds, value bonds, and stocks of any kind.
- Interest accrued by credit bonds and other obligations issued by mercantile partnerships, negotiated through an authorised stock exchange.
- Exports of goods and services.
- Contributions and donations to educational, cultural, assistance, or security service partnerships, constituted as not-for-profit entities.

VAT return
The amount payable to the *Superintendencia de Administración Tributaria* (SAT), Guatemala's tax authority, is the difference between the debits and credits accrued during the tax period (one month) and is paid monthly by filing a tax return in the following calendar month at the end of each tax period.

Refunds of VAT
The VAT credit can be claimed on monthly, quarterly, or semiannual tax periods. The refund of VAT credit corresponds to exporter taxpayers who cannot offset the VAT credit with VAT debts.

In addition, the VAT credit can be claimed by those taxpayers who have a high percentage of sales to entities exempt from VAT.

Import duties
The Customs Duties on Imports (DAI) are contained in the Central American Tariff System (SAC), which contains the tax rates applicable to goods imported into the Guatemalan Territory, ranging from 0% to 20%.

The import duties apply to the customs value declared by the importer.

Real estate tax
Real estate taxes are assessed annually at 2 Guatemalan quetzales (GTQ) per thousand on declared property values of from GTQ 2,000 to GTQ 20,000, at GTQ 6 per thousand on values from GTQ 20,000 to GTQ 70,000, and at GTQ 9 per thousand on values in excess of GTQ 70,000 (e.g. property valued at GTQ 1 million will pay real estate taxes of GTQ 9,000).

Transfer of property
VAT is payable on each transfer of title to real estate; however, as of 25 February 2012, only the first sale of real estate is taxable under this regime, and the subsequent sales are taxed under the stamp tax regime.

Stamp taxes
Other than sales invoices, contracts, and documents subject to VAT, and other minor exemptions, a stamp tax must be paid on all documents covering commercial and legal

Guatemala

transactions (e.g. collection of dividends), either by preparing the document on *papel sellado*, which is special stamped paper, or by affixing stamps on the documents. This tax is also assessed on documents issued abroad, other than drafts or promissory notes and commercial invoices from foreign suppliers. Letters of credit and acceptances involving international transfers of funds are generally exempt from stamp taxes.

The normal tax rate is 3% and is calculated on the face value of the documents or on the gross value of the related transaction.

It should be noted that as of 1 January 2013, the stamp tax on dividends payment or credits will be repealed, since on that date, book I of Decree No. 10-2012 will enter into force, which states that a 5% income tax should be paid on dividends payments or credited in account equity.

Solidarity tax (Impuesto de Solidaridad or ISO)
The ISO tax rate of 1% is assessed on the net assets of a corporation, or on the gross income of a corporation, whichever is higher, and there is no limit on the amount to be paid. Tax paid may be credited against the corporation's income tax. If the annual business tax exceeds the income tax, no reimbursement is possible.

The tax is to be paid quarterly on the basis of the corporation's opening balance sheet for each fiscal period.

Social security contribution
Corporations contribute 12.67% of their monthly payroll and employees contribute 4.83% of their monthly salary to social security.

Branch income

In Guatemala, branches are taxed as any other legal entity. There are no specific taxes for branches.

Income determination

Inventory valuation
For tax purposes, taxpayers are authorised to use any of the following methods for valuing stocks (i.e. inventory), provided they technically fit the taxpayers' business and are consistently applied through 31 December 2012:

- Industrial, commercial, or service concerns:
  - Cost of production or purchase.
  - Asset value.
  - Sales prices less selling expenses.
  - The lower of cost of production or purchase and market.

- Farm-cattle outfits:
  - Cost of production.
  - Estimated cost at fixed prices.
  - Selling price for the taxpayer.
  - Purchase costs.

Guatemala

Under the provisions of Decree No. 10-2012, the inventory valuation methods to be used from 1 January 2013 are as follows:

- Cost of production.
- First in first out (FIFO).
- Weighted average.
- Historical price of assets.
- Estimated cost at a fixed price (additional for livestock activities).

Capital gains
Capital gains are taxed at 10% in the general income tax regime and at 31% in the optional income tax regime. Capital losses can be netted only against capital gains, up to a maximum of five years. This provision will be in force up to 31 December 2012.

Under the provisions of Decree No. 10-2012, in force as of 1 January 2013, the regime of capital income, capital gains, and capital losses is established with the following tax rates:

- Real estate equity income: 10%
- Income from trading movables: 10%
- Capital gains and losses: 10%
- Incomes from lotteries and raffles: 10%

Dividend income
Dividends from domestic subsidiaries and other domestic corporations are not subject to income tax withholdings if Guatemalan income tax has been paid. This provision is in force up to 31 December 2012.

According to the provisions of Decree No. 10-2012, in force as of 1 January 2013, dividends earnings and profits are subject to a 5% income tax.

Interest income
As of 31 December 2012, interest earned by residents other than banks are subject to a WHT of 10%; such interest shall be treated as exempt income in the annual tax return.

As of 1 January 2013, pursuant to Decree No. 10-2012, all interest income will be subject to a 10% income tax.

Foreign income
Foreign-source income received by a domestic corporation is generally exempt from Guatemalan income tax.

Deductions

Deductions apply only under the optional income tax regime for taxpayers registered under the income tax optional regime (Decree No. 26-92 in force until 31 December 2012).

As of 1 January 2013, taxpayers under the system of earnings of lucrative activities regime may deduct costs and expenses, including the following, from gross income.

G

Guatemala

Depreciation

Depreciation is calculated annually using the straight-line method. The tax authority may authorise a different method on request of the taxpayer. The annual maximum rates allowed as deductible expenses are the following:

Asset	Rate (%)
Building and improvements	5
Machinery and equipment	20
Furniture and fixtures	20
Vehicles	20
Tools	25
Tree and vegetable species	15
Computer equipment and software	33.33
Any other depreciable asset	10

Goodwill

Intangible assets, such as goodwill, trademarks, manufacturing processes, patents, etc., may be deductible under the straight-line method of amortisation over a period that depends on the conditions of the acquisition or creation of the intangible asset concerned, and cannot be less than five years.

Interest expense

The deduction of interest expense is limited to the maximum interest rate used by the National Bank annually (to date approximately 12% to 13%) in excess of the authorised rate for commercial banks.

Uncollectible accounts

Uncollectible accounts arising in normal business operations can be deducted individually or, alternatively, via an allowance for doubtful accounts, which shall not exceed 3% of the debit balances of accounts and notes receivable.

Charitable contributions

Duly proven donations made to the government, the municipalities, and their agencies, as well as to duly authorised not-for-profit welfare, social service, and scientific associations and foundations, universities, political parties, and guild entities are deductible. The maximum deductible amount for income tax purposes of each period shall not exceed 5% of the donor's net income up to a maximum of GTQ 500,000 per year.

Employee pension/retirement funds

The deduction of provisions to establish or increase employee pension and retirement funds or reserves is allowed, provided the government approves the related plans.

Severance compensation payments

Severance compensation payments are allowed as deductible expenses as well as limited allocations (not to exceed 8.33% of total annual salaries and wages) to a reserve for severance compensation. Provisions pertaining to actual liability for severance compensation per year are also allowed, provided the related plans, based on collective bargaining agreements, are approved by the employer and employees.

Fines and penalties
Charges, penalties, and interest charged by any government institutions are not deductible.

Taxes
All taxes other than income tax and VAT are deductible.

Net operating losses
Operating losses may not be carried forward for deduction from otherwise taxable profits. Guatemalan laws also do not permit carryback of losses.

Payments to foreign affiliates
Deduction for royalties will be allowed, up to 5% of gross income. Charges for technical service fees are deductible, up to 1% of gross income or 15% of total salaries paid to Guatemalans, whichever is larger.

Expenses incurred abroad by non-residents in connection with income earned from Guatemalan sources cannot be deducted for income tax purposes by merely having the supporting receipts, as the regulations to the law do not permit such a deduction for these purposes, unless these expenses are related with the Guatemalan company operations and these expenses are needed for generating taxable income.

Effective from 1 January 2013, pursuant to Decree No. 10-2012, the deductible expenses for technical services rendered from abroad shall not exceed 5% of gross income.

Group taxation

No consolidation for tax purposes is permitted as each group entity is treated as an independent taxpayer, which shall file its own tax return.

Transfer pricing
For 2012, there is no specific transfer pricing legislation. Nonetheless, on 1 January 2013, under the provisions of Decree No. 10-2012, rules regarding transfer pricing will be introduced.

From a Guatemalan transfer pricing perspective, the scope of application of the rules of valuation of transactions between related parties reaches any operation that has been carried out between a person living in Guatemala with a resident abroad.

According to the Decree mentioned above, local legislation allows the selection of traditional methods and profit-based methods consistent with the Organisation for Economic Co-operation and Development (OECD) guidelines.

Advance pricing agreements (APAs) are permitted, and it is also stated that the tax authority can reclassify activities according to its true nature in accordance with Tax Code statements.

Thin capitalisation
As of 2012, there is no specific legislation in force regarding thin capitalisation in Guatemala. Notwithstanding, from 2013 and onwards, thin capitalisation applies regarding deductible expenses for interest paid.

Guatemala

On this matter, Decree No. 10-2012 states that without prejudice to other rules on deduction of interest, the deductible amount for such costs may not exceed the value of multiplying the annual maximum simple interest rate determined by the Guatemalan Monetary Board for tax purposes multiplied by three times the amount of average total net assets submitted by the taxpayer in the annual income tax return.

In addition, the Decree mentioned above defines average total net assets as the sum of total net assets of the previous year with total net assets at the end of the year in force, both values must correspond to the amounts filed in the annual income tax return of each period of final settlement, divided by two. Total net assets are defined by law to correspond to the book value of all goods that are actually the property of the taxpayer.

Tax credits and incentives

Drawback industries (Maquila)

The Law of Promotion and Development of Exports Activities and Drawback Industries is known in Guatemala as *maquila*. This law seeks to promote, encourage, and develop the manufacture of products within areas controlled by the Customs Authority for export to countries outside the Central American region, as well as to regulate exporting and drawback activities.

The exporter may apply for authorisation to operate under any of the following three systems provided by the law:

- Export under a temporary admission system.
- Export under the reimbursement of duties system.
- Export under the total added national component system.

Tax incentives and benefits of the law include the following:

- Exemption of taxes, import duties, and other charges on imports of machinery and equipment, including VAT.
- Discontinuance of VAT payments on temporary raw material imports.
- Exemption of income tax for ten years on profits obtained under this law.

Free Trade Zones Law

The Free Trade Zones Law seeks to encourage and regulate the establishment of free trade zones that promote domestic development by activities carried out within certain zones, particularly those that tend to strengthen export activities, generate employment, and transfer technology.

Tax incentives and benefits of the law include the following:

- Import duties exemption.
- Income tax exemption as follows:
  - Ten-year period for the administrative agency.
  - Ten-year period for industrial & service permit holders.
  - Five-year period for commercial permit holders.
- Exemption of real estate taxes for a five-year period.
- Exemption of tax stamps on the conveyance of title over properties.
- Dividends or profits distributed by the administrative agency and permit holders shall also be considered tax-exempted income.

- Exemption of custom duties and any other charges on import and consumption of fuel oil, bunker, butane, and propane gas used exclusively in the free trade zone.
- Foreigners working in the free trade zone are subject to the provisions of the immigration law and the Labour Code.

Withholding taxes

For 2012, the following WHT rates apply on payments to non-resident corporations or individuals:

Payment	WHT (%)
Dividends, profit participations, earnings, and other benefits (1)	10
Commissions, salaries	10
Interest (2)	10
Professional fees, royalties, technical service fees	31

Notes

1. For taxpayers that already paid corporate income tax, there is no WHT regarding dividends.
2. Interests will not be taxed (i.e. no withholding applies) when:
   - These interests are paid to a legal bank or financial institution.
   - The interests are in connection with a loan registered in the Guatemalan banking system.
   - The loan was used in taxable activities.

Decree No. 10-2012, in force from 1 January 2013, introduces the tax residence figure, which states that non-residents can operate in Guatemala with or without PE; accordingly, income tax treatment depends of the circumstance as follows:

- Non-residents with PE will be subject to income tax, choosing one of the two methods of payment established for residents.
- Non-residents without PE will be subject to WHT, applying specific rates according to the nature of the services rendered.

Tax treaties
Guatemala has no tax treaties in force.

Tax administration

Taxable period

General income tax regime
For 2012, under the general income tax regime, taxes are paid on a monthly basis.

From 1 January 2013 and onwards, the general income tax will no longer exist, but taxpayers who are registered under this regime before the tax authority must continue filing and paying income tax on a monthly basis under a new regime called the simplified optional system on income from lucrative activities.

Optional income tax regime
Under the optional income tax regime, the annual final tax liquidation period begins on 1 January and ends on 31 December of each year.

Guatemala

As of 1 January 2013 and onwards, the optional income tax regime will be replaced by the system on earnings from lucrative activities, and taxpayers registered under this regime will continue to be subject to the same taxable period.

Tax returns

General income tax regime
Under the general income tax regime, there is an obligation to file an annual informative tax return, which is due on 31 March of each year.

As of 1 January 2013 and onwards, the general income tax regime will be replaced by the simplified optional system on income from lucrative activities, and taxpayers registered under this regime will be subject to file an informative annual tax return with the same due date.

Optional income tax regime
Under the optional income tax regime, returns are due after the end of the fiscal period (31 December) but no later than 31 March of each year.

The income tax return shall be accompanied by the documents required by the regulations, which might include a:

- balance sheet
- statement of results of operations
- statement of cash flows, and
- statement of cost of production.

Documents must be duly certified by a professional or an independent accounting firm. The financial statements that accompany the return shall agree with both those recorded in the financial statements ledger and those destined for publication.

Both the income tax return and exhibits thereto shall be signed by the taxpayers, their agent, or their legal representative or by any other responsible persons so determined by this law and the tax code.

As of 1 January 2013, the optional income tax regime will be replaced by the system on earnings from lucrative activities, and taxpayers registered under this regime will be subject to file an annual tax return with the same due date.

Payment of tax

General income tax regime
Under the general income tax regime, tax is payable via flat tax withholdings (the tax is to be retained by either the customer or the recipient of services) or by direct remittances to the tax office made monthly within the first ten working days of the month following the invoice date.

Taxes on income are governed by the income tax law, Ley del Impuesto sobre la Renta, and its related regulations. Administration of the law is vested with the SAT.

Under the provisions of Decree No. 10-2012, in force from 1 January 2013, the general income tax regime will be replaced by the simplified optional system on income from lucrative activities, and taxpayers registered under this regime will be subject to file monthly tax returns.

Taxpayers registered before the tax administration under this regime will settle and pay the tax through the withholding system. Persons or entities obligated to withhold are those taxpayers who pay or credit into account for the acquisition of goods and services to the taxpayers registered under this regime.

Optional income tax regime

Under the optional income tax regime, taxpayers are required to prepay their estimated annual income tax liability in quarterly instalments. The balance is due upon filing the return.

Taxpayers may choose one of the following procedures for computing estimated quarterly tax liability:

- Tax on income shown by partial closure of accounts or computation of presumed liquidation of operations at the end of each quarter.
- Tax on 5% of overall gross income earned during the corresponding quarter of the preceding year (5% of the 30% income tax rate equals 1.5%).
- Tax equivalent to one-fourth of the tax paid for the immediately preceding tax year.

Under the provisions of Decree No. 10-2012, in force from 1 January 2013 and onwards, the optional income tax regime will be replaced by the system on earnings from lucrative activities, and taxpayers registered under this regime are required to prepay their estimated annual income tax liability in quarterly instalments. The balance is due upon filing the return. According to the mentioned above Decree, the tax rate in force for years 2013, 2014, and 2015 onwards will be 31%, 28%, and 25%, respectively.

Statute of limitations

The right of the tax administration to checks, adjustments, corrections, or determinations of tax liabilities; settle and enforce interest and penalties; and enforce payment of taxpayers must be brought within four years. In the same period, taxpayers must exercise their right of recourse for overpaid or unduly charged taxes, interest, penalties, and fines.

Other issues

Accurate and current information regarding taxation in Guatemala is often difficult to obtain as the country lacks reporting services such as those available in other countries. It is also difficult to determine how the tax laws will be applied in practice in complex situations. The laws and regulations are limited and ordinarily cover only the most common situations. The system of legal precedent resulting from court decisions is narrowly used, and each issue is resolved by reference to the respective codes. Guatemala has shown little interest in tax planning, but it is possible to have informal consultations with the tax authorities and to obtain authoritative rulings in many cases. Discrepancies between government and management criteria are commonly brought to judgment by the Constitutional Court, whose binding sentences generally abrogate the laws in dispute.

Guernsey, Channel Islands

PwC contact

Mark Watson
PricewaterhouseCoopers CI LLP
Royal Bank Place
1 Glategny Esplanade
St Peter Port, Guernsey GY1 4ND
Channel Islands
Tel: +44 1481 752029
Email: m.watson@gg.pwc.com

Significant developments

The zero/ten income tax regime is currently under review by the European Union (EU) Code of Conduct Group. At present, the key features of any revised Guernsey corporate tax regime have yet to be determined. Implementation of any new tax regime is not anticipated to come into effect prior to 2013 at the earliest.

Taxes on corporate income

Resident corporations are liable to tax on their worldwide income. Non-resident corporations are subject to Guernsey tax on the Guernsey-source income.

Companies pay income tax at the current standard rate of 0% on taxable income.

Income derived from a banking business is taxable at 10%. 'Banking business' is broadly defined as income that arises as a result of the provision of credit facilities by any type of company and the utilisation of customer deposits. Relief is available for eligible expenses that are allocated against different streams of income.

Any income derived from the exploitation of property located in Guernsey or received by a publicly regulated utility company is subject to tax at the higher rate of 20%.

Exempt companies
Some collective investment schemes and unit trusts may qualify for exempt status, which would place them completely outside the Guernsey tax regime. For each year for which exempt status is sought, a charge of 600 pounds sterling (GBP) is levied.

One of the following conditions, among others, must be met for the company to be considered exempt:

- The company is beneficially owned outside of Guernsey.
- No Guernsey resident individual or company has a beneficial interest in the company (with the exception of shareholders, loan creditors, or nominees/trustees).

It is anticipated that the definition under which entities may qualify for exempt tax status will be broadened in the near future.

Loans to participators
If a company makes loans with preferential terms to an individual or entity connected with the company, this will be deemed to be income in the hands of the debtor, and the

creditor company will be required to account for, withhold, and pay the tax. Certain exemptions apply.

Local income taxes
Guernsey does not operate any local government taxes.

Corporate residence

All Guernsey-registered companies are regarded as tax resident in the island unless granted exempt company status. In addition, a company will be treated as a resident in Guernsey (regardless of where it is incorporated) if shareholder control is exercised by persons resident in the island.

Permanent establishment (PE)
The Income Tax (Guernsey) Law, 1975 defines PE as including:

- a branch
- a factory, shop, workshop, quarry or building site, or
- a place of management.

Note that the fact that a body's directors regularly meet at a particular place does not, in itself, make that place a PE of that body.

Other taxes

Value-added tax (VAT)
Guernsey does not operate a VAT or goods and services tax (GST).

Customs and excise duties
In accordance with the European Community (EC) Customs Code and the Implementing Regulation, Customs Import Duty is liable on all goods arriving in the Customs territory of the Community. The rates of duty are set by the European Community and are the same in all countries of the European Community.

The rates vary according to the commodity. Some may be as high as 22% while for other goods the rate may be free.

The Channel Islands are not within the fiscal territory of the European Union, and, as such, the Community Regulations that concern excise duties do not apply. Excise duty is classed as an internal tax.

The rates are reviewed annually by the States of Guernsey and set at budget time, which is usually in November. These cover Guernsey and Alderney, while Sark have their own rates set by the Chief Pleas.

With effect from 1 May 2011, an additional 15% rate of duty is applicable on some goods originating in the United States (US).

Property taxes
Income from Guernsey land and buildings is subject to Guernsey income tax at 20%, no other property taxes apply.

Guernsey, Channel Islands

Transfer taxes
Guernsey does not levy transfer taxes.

Stamp taxes
Guernsey does not levy any stamp duties.

Branch income

Branch income is taxed in the same manner as companies, at the appropriate rate according to the activity being undertaken.

No further tax is withheld on the transfer of profits abroad to group companies, provided no Guernsey resident individual has an interest in the company.

Income determination

Inventory valuation
Inventory is valued at the lower of historical cost or net realisable value. Use of last in first out (LIFO) is not permitted. Generally, there are no material differences between accounts prepared on a normal accounting basis and those prepared on a tax basis.

Capital gains
Capital gains are not subject to tax in Guernsey.

Dividend income
All dividends paid by a standard tax-paying company (0%) are deemed to have been paid from income arising after 31 December 2007 (i.e. after the introduction of the new zero/10 tax regime), unless the company elects to have them treated otherwise.

Stock dividends
Stock dividends may be treated as income.

Foreign income
Resident corporations are liable to tax on their worldwide income. Income tax is levied on foreign branch income when earned, and on investment income from foreign dividends, interest, rents, and royalties. Double taxation is mitigated either through unilateral relief (by giving credit for foreign taxation of up to three-quarters of the effective Guernsey rate) or by treaty relief.

Deductions

Normally, business deductions are allowed if they are incurred wholly and exclusively for the purpose of the trade.

Depreciation
Annual allowances are granted for income tax purposes in respect of the following:

Assets	Basis	Rate (%)
Buildings:		

Assets	Basis	Rate (%)
Stone, brick, concrete or other substantial structures	Reducing-balance	1.25
Buildings of a less substantial construction	Reducing-balance	5
Farm Buildings	Straight-line	5 or 10 (depending on material utilised)
Machinery and plant	Reducing-balance	20
Glasshouses:		
Expenditure in respect of initial allowance*	Straight-line	10
Other expenditure	Straight-line	5

* Section 123 (3) of the Law defines expenditure and circumstances on which initial allowances can be claimed in respect of glasshouses.

Goodwill

The amortisation of goodwill is not a deductible expense in Guernsey.

Start-up expenses

Pre-trading expenditure incurred within the 12 months prior to the commencement of trade, which would have been allowable had it occurred on the first day of trading, may be allowed as a deduction in computing the profits of the first accounting period.

Interest expenses

Interest is a deductible expense where it is incurred wholly and exclusively for the purposes of the trade.

Bad debt

Bad and doubtful debts discovered in the accounting period to have become bad or irrecoverable may be deducted from taxable profits, but the deduction may not exceed the amount written off as such in the books of the business.

Charitable contributions

Charitable donations by companies are not deductible for Guernsey tax purposes.

Fines and penalties

Fines or penalties incurred are not deductible for Guernsey income tax purposes.

Taxes

Local income tax paid is not deductible in computing taxable income.

Net operating losses

Losses from one class of income may be used to offset the profits from another class of income if both classes are subject to tax at the same rate. Unrelieved trading losses may be carried forward to offset future trading income.

Upon cessation of trade, operating losses arising from balancing allowances may be carried back to the previous two years of charge to be relieved against past trading profits.

Guernsey, Channel Islands

Payments to foreign affiliates
Guernsey-source royalties and long-term interest are subject to taxation at source. Relief is obtained by the retention of the tax deducted. Short-term interest, unless owed to an authorised bank, is not deductible, unless the advance in respect of which it is paid is used wholly and exclusively for the purposes of the trade. Other fees must be paid on an arm's-length basis.

Group taxation

Group loss relief may be claimed when both companies are members of the same group and the companies are either carrying on business in Guernsey through a PE or incorporated in Guernsey. Loss relief is available only against income taxed at the same rate.

A claim for group loss relief must be made by the claimant company within two years after the end of the calendar year in which the relevant accounting period ended, and the claim must be accompanied by a declaration by the surrendering company that it consents to the surrender.

Transfer pricing
Guernsey does not currently have specific transfer pricing legislation in place. However, the general anti-avoidance provisions do apply.

Thin capitalisation
Guernsey does not currently have specific thin capitalisation legislation in place. However, the general anti-avoidance provisions do apply.

Tax credits and incentives

In view of the low rate of tax, no special incentives are available to local businesses in Guernsey.

Foreign tax credit
Guernsey has double taxation agreements (DTAs) in place with Guernsey and Jersey and tax information exchange agreements (TIEAs) with 17 other jurisdictions.

If no bilateral agreement exists, relief available to Guernsey resident companies is the lesser of the other territory's effective rate or three-quarters of the Guernsey effective rate.

Withholding taxes

Deemed distributions
A company will be required to withhold tax on any distributions made to or in reference to any Guernsey resident individual shareholders. The rate at which WHT will apply (0%, 10%, or 20%) is dependent upon the rate at which the company is subject to Guernsey tax (i.e. if the company is subject to Guernsey tax at 0%, then tax will be withheld on distributions at 20%; if the company is subject to Guernsey tax at 10%, then tax will be withheld on distributions at 10%; and if the company is subject to Guernsey tax at 20%, then no tax will be withheld on distributions).

Guernsey, Channel Islands

Furthermore, following certain trigger events (e.g. the sale of shares, death of the beneficial member), the company is deemed to have distributed the Guernsey resident shareholder's entire share of the company's undistributed profits accumulated since 1 January 2008. All investment income is deemed to be distributed as it arises.

Although the liability to tax is the shareholder's, the company is obligated to account for, withhold, and pay tax to the Income Tax Office and may then claim this back from the shareholder.

Agency
A company also is required to withhold tax when it is acting as an agent and making payments to a non-resident liable to Guernsey tax.

Guernsey does not levy any other forms of withholding tax (WHT).

G

Tax administration

Taxable period
The tax year runs from 1 January to 31 December, although companies can adopt a year-end of their choice.

Tax returns
Historically, an income tax return was required to be filed one year and 15 days after the end of the calendar year in which the accounting period ends. As of 2012, however, a new filing deadline of 30 November is in place. Should a company meet the conditions below, a simplified return may be filed without either a computation or financial statements.

In order to qualify for a simplified return, a company must have none of the following:

• Guernsey employees (other than directors).
• Guernsey resident individual beneficial owners.
• Income from utilities (e.g. Guernsey water or electricity companies).
• Income from Guernsey properties.
• Income from a banking business.
• Loans to Guernsey participators.
• Distributions made to Guernsey resident individuals.

Should a company have Guernsey resident individual beneficial members and/or make loans to participators, it will be required to submit quarterly returns accounting for distributions, deemed distributions, and loans advanced.

Payment of tax
In Guernsey, tax is payable in two instalments, on 30 June and 31 December in the year of charge (calendar year). If liabilities have not been determined, this may necessitate initially raising estimated assessments based on prior year figures and raising a final assessment when the figures are agreed. Once the Income Tax Office has received the company's income tax return, they will issue an assessment detailing the final balancing income tax payment due. This amount will be due to be paid within 30 days of the issuing of the final assessment.

Guernsey, Channel Islands

Audit cycle

The Guernsey tax system requires companies to file tax returns prior to 30 November each year (with effect from returns relating to the 2011 year of charge onwards). The Income Tax Office will assess each company tax return as and when it is received, and the turnaround time from submission of a return to the issue of a final assessment varies dependent upon the workloads of the Income Tax Office but is generally dealt with in around three months.

Statute of limitations

The Director can raise an assessment in respect of any income that has not been assessed at any time no later than six years after end of the year of charge in which the income arose.

Guyana

PwC contact

Allyson West
PricewaterhouseCoopers
11 - 13 Victoria Avenue, Port of Spain, Trinidad & Tobago
Tel: +1 868 299 0700
Email: allyson.west@tt.pwc.com

Significant developments

Effective 1 January 2012, Guyana changed its corporate tax rates to:

- 40% for a commercial company, other than a telephone company, and
- 30% for all other companies.

The rate of 45% was retained for telephone companies.

Taxes on corporate income

Resident companies are liable to tax on their worldwide income. Non-resident companies that carry on a trade or business in Guyana are subject to tax on the income that is derived from Guyana.

The current rates of corporate tax are as follows:

Type of company	Corporate tax rate (%)
Telephone companies	45
Commercial companies *	40
Other companies (non commercial)	30

* A commercial company is one that derives at least 75% of its gross income from goods not manufactured by it or if it is engaged in telecommunication, banking, or insurance (other than long-term insurance).

Minimum Corporation Tax (MCT)
In addition to the standard corporate tax rates, MCT of 2% of turnover is payable by commercial companies (other than insurance companies).

Corporate residence

Corporate residence is determined by reference to the location of the central management and control of the business of a company. There are no specific provisions within the law, and, as such, common law principles established by the courts are generally applied in determining residence. The place of incorporation is regarded as merely one of the factors to be taken into account in determining where central management and control are located.

Permanent establishment (PE)
There are no specific provisions in the legislation dealing with PE, so common law principles are applied.

Guyana

Other taxes

Valued-added tax (VAT)
VAT is charged at the rates of 16% or 0% on the taxable supply of goods and services within Guyana by a registered person.

Zero-rated supplies include goods for export, electricity supplied by Guyana Power and Light, water supplied by Guyana Water Incorporated, and international travel. Exempt supplies include educational services, residential rent, and financial services.

Customs duties
Customs duty is paid on all goods imported into Guyana. The rates of duty vary between 5% and 150%, depending on the classification of the item in question. Rates of duty are highest on 'luxury items', which include perfumes.

Excise taxes
Excise tax is imposed on specific imported or home produced products. These products include alcoholic beverages, tobacco products, petroleum products, and motor vehicles.

Property taxes
Property tax is an annual tax charged on the net property of a person at the end of each year. 'Property' for the purpose of this tax refers to movable or immovable, rights of any kind, and effects of any kind. Net property is the amount by which the total value of the property exceeds the total value of all debt owned by the person at that time.

The tax is payable on 30 April at the following rates:

Net property of a company (GYD *)	Property tax rate (%)
On the first 1.5 million	0
On every dollar of the next 5 million	½
On every dollar of the remainder	¾

* Guyanese dollars.

Stamp taxes
Stamp duty is levied at various rates on several instruments, including affidavits, statutory declarations, deeds of conveyance, mortgages, share transfers, awards of arbitrator, powers of attorney, agreements, bills of exchange, receipts, and policies of insurance.

Branch income

A branch is subject to tax in Guyana on all income directly or indirectly accruing in or derived from its operations in Guyana. The tax rates applicable on branch profits are the same as on corporate profits. In addition, branch profits, after deduction of corporate tax and reinvestments, are subject to withholding tax (WHT) at the rate of 20%. The position noted may be varied by the provisions of any applicable double tax treaties (DTTs).

Income determination

Inventory valuation
Inventory is valued at the lower of cost and net realisable value. Cost is generally determined using the average cost method for accounting and tax purposes, but the first in first out (FIFO) method is also acceptable.

Capital gains
Capital gains tax is imposed at the rate of 20% on the net chargeable gains derived from the disposal of capital assets. Gains derived from the disposal of an asset within 12 months of its acquisition are treated as ordinary income and subject to corporate tax at the applicable rates. Gains derived from the disposal of assets held for more than 25 years are exempt from tax.

Dividend income
Corporate tax is payable on dividends received by resident companies from non-resident companies. However, dividends paid by resident companies to other resident companies are exempt from tax.

Interest income
Interest income is taxed at the applicable rate of corporate tax.

Foreign income
Income earned by a non-resident company in Guyana is subject to tax in the year the income was earned. There is no deferral regime in Guyana.

Deductions

All revenue expenses wholly and exclusively incurred in the production of income are generally deductible.

Depreciation
Tax depreciation rates (wear and tear allowances) apply to the following classes of assets, as follows:

Class of assets	Depreciation rate (%)
Aircraft	$33\frac{1}{3}$
Boats	10
Buildings (housing and industrial)	5
Furniture and fittings	10
Motor vehicles	20
Office equipment, including computers and computer software	50
Other	15
Plant and machinery	20

Buildings that house machinery are depreciated using the straight-line method. Other assets may be depreciated using the declining-balance or straight-line methods.

Goodwill
Goodwill expense is generally not allowable in arriving at chargeable income.

Guyana

Start-up expenses
No specific rules exist in respect of start-up expenses, but such expenses are generally not deductible.

Interest expenses
Interest expense incurred in the production of income is deductible. There is no restriction to the deductibility of this expense.

Bad debt
A bad debt is deductible where it has been incurred in the trade in which the company is engaged and has been respectively estimated to the satisfaction of the tax authority to have become bad in the year of income when the claim is made.

Charitable contributions
Charitable donations are not deductible unless these are made under a deed of covenant.

Fines and penalties
Fines and penalties are not generally deductible.

Taxes
Taxes are not generally deductible in arriving at taxable profit.

Net operating losses
Companies may carry forward losses for an unlimited number of years, but the losses may not reduce the taxable income in any year by more than 50%. Loss carrybacks are not permitted.

Payments to foreign affiliates
A corporation engaged in business in Guyana may claim a deduction for royalties and interest charges paid to foreign affiliates, provided the appropriate WHT is deducted and properly accounted. Deductions for administrative, technical, professional, or other management services fees paid to a non-resident company or branch, referred to as 'head office expenses', are restricted to 1% of the annual turnover.

Group taxation

There is no provision under the legislation for group taxation in Guyana. All companies are taxed separately.

Transfer pricing
There is no transfer pricing legislation or rules in Guyana, although the issue has been discussed and is expected to be more formally considered in the future. However, the current Act contains a general anti-avoidance provision, and the tax authority monitors multinationals to ensure that their transactions are conducted at arm's length and in conformance with the applicable tax legislation.

Thin capitalisation
There are no thin capitalisation rules in Guyana.

Tax credits and incentives

Various tax incentives are available, depending on the nature of the industry that the companies are engaged in, including the following:

- Customs duty and VAT exemption on most plant, machinery, and equipment.
- Customs duty and VAT exemption on raw materials and packaging materials used in the production of goods by manufacturers and small businesses.
- Unlimited carryover of losses from previous years.
- Accelerated depreciation on plant and equipment.
- Full and unrestricted repatriation of capital, profits, and dividends.
- Tax deduction for scientific research expenses.
- Initial and annual allowances.
- Tax holidays.

Tax holidays are granted in respect of pioneering activities, that is, to companies whose trade or business are wholly of a developmental and risk-bearing nature and likely to be instrumental to the development of the resources of and beneficial to Guyana.

This does not include trade or business carried on by a gold or diamond mining company or a company carrying on petroleum operations.

Tax holidays are granted for a period of up to ten years.

Foreign tax credit
Foreign tax relief is available under DTTs with Canada, the United Kingdom, and Caribbean Common Market (CARICOM) countries.

Unilateral relief is also available for foreign taxes paid in non-treaty countries with tax systems and legislation similar to those in Guyana. For British Commonwealth countries, the relief is 50% of the relief that would be available if the foreign country were a treaty country. For other countries, the relief is 25% of such available relief. The available relief is the lower of the tax rate in Guyana and the tax rate in the other country.

Withholding taxes

WHT is chargeable on gross payments to non-residents and must be remitted to the tax authority within 30 days of making the payment. In cases where the treaty rate is higher than the statutory rate, the lower statutory rate applies. The rates of WHT for various payments are shown in table below.

Recipient	Dividends (%)	Interest (%)	Royalties (%)
Non Treaty	15	15	10
Treaty:			
Canada	15	15	10
United Kingdom	10	15	10
CARICOM	0	15	15

Guyana

Tax administration

Taxable period
The tax year is the calendar year. Tax is assessed during a tax year on income earned during the year of assessment, which is generally the calendar year preceding the tax year. Companies with an accounting year other than a calendar year may, however, be allowed to account for taxes by adopting their accounting year as their income year.

Tax returns
Tax returns must be filed by 30 April of the tax year.

Payment of tax
Corporate tax is payable in advance quarterly instalments on the preceding year's tax liability. Advance tax payments are due on 15 March, 15 June, 15 September, and 15 December of the calendar year prior to the tax year. However, the Commissioner of Inland Revenue may require the company to calculate the payments based on estimated income for the current year.

Any balance of tax due must be paid by 30 April of the tax year.

Penalties
Failure to file a tax return and pay the balance due by 30 April of the tax year incurs a further charge of 45% on the outstanding tax for the first year and 50% thereafter.

Audit cycle
Companies are generally selected randomly for audits, and the frequency is usually every three years. Companies are generally required to provide financial information and supporting documentation to the tax personnel.

The tax authority is the Guyana Revenue Authority.

Statute of limitations
A company carrying on business in Guyana is required to keep proper accounts and records and is required to retain these accounts for a period of at least eight years after the completion of the transactions, acts, or operations to which they relate.

The Commissioner is empowered to raise an assessment for tax or additional tax within seven years after the expiration of the year of assessment.

Other issues

Foreign investment restrictions
There are no restrictions on the repatriation of capital and investment income, and residents and non-residents have unlimited access to foreign exchange markets and to repatriate funds.

Exchange controls
There are no exchange control rules in place in Guyana.

Choice of business entity
Businesses operating in Guyana may establish a local company or register an external company. Additionally, companies may operate through a joint venture.

Honduras

PwC contact

Ramon Ortega
PricewaterhouseCoopers
Scotiabank Building
3rd Floor
Santo Domingo, Dominican Republic
Tel: +809 567 7741
Email: ramon.ortega@do.pwc.com

Significant developments

Effective 1 June 2011:

- Corporate taxpayers were subject to a 1% (i.e. 0.5% for taxpayers subject to regulated prices) tax on gross income if the income tax calculation for the fiscal year was lower than 1% of gross income. This tax was applicable to taxpayers with income over 10 million Honduran lempiras (HNL).

  This reform was declared unconstitutional on 1 February 2012 and is, therefore, no longer applicable.

Effective 1 July 2011:

- The tax authority is empowered to withhold 1% from import operations as an advance payment to income tax, with some exceptions to the rule according to section 7 of the Income Tax Law. This provision was approved in July 2011; however, as of May 2012, its application by the tax authority is in suspense.
- In instances where a transaction is subject to the capital gains tax and a non-resident is involved, the buyer has an obligation to withhold 2% of the transaction amount as an advance payment to this tax and must pay it to the government within ten business days of the date of the transaction.

Effective October 2011:

- Under the Special Temporary Security Contribution on Financial Transactions (*Contribución Especial por Transacciones Financieras Proseguridad Poblicional*), financial transactions are subject to 0.2% withholding tax (WHT), with some exceptions.
- Companies providing mobile communication services will pay a Special Temporary Contribution of 1% on gross monthly income.
- Under the Special Temporary Contribution for the protection of the environment from the Mining Sector, there is a 2% contribution on the freight on board (FOB) value of the exports filed.
- Special Temporary Contribution from the food and beverages business under special tax regimes is 0.5% on gross monthly income.
- Cooperatives Special Contribution is 3.6% on annual net surplus.

Honduras

Taxes on corporate income

Honduran resident companies are taxed on their worldwide income. Non-resident companies are subject to corporate income tax (CIT) only on income derived from Honduran sources.

The CIT rate for a resident company is 25% of its net taxable income.

Temporary Solidarity Contribution
The Temporary Solidarity Contribution is a non-deductible surcharge levied on all companies on taxable income over HNL 1 million. The Temporary Solidarity Contribution tax rate is 6% for 2012, 5% for 2013, 4% for 2014, and 0% for 2015.

Municipal income taxes

Industry, commerce, and services tax
Companies doing business in Honduras are levied the following municipal tax on annual gross income:

From (HNL)	To (HNL)	Range (HNL)	Tax per '000
1	500,000	500,000	0.3
500,001	10,000,000	9,500,000	0.4
10,000,001	20,000,000	10,000,000	0.3
20,000,001	30,000,000	10,000,000	0.2
30,000,001	And over		0.15

Corporate residence

The place of incorporation is regarded by Honduran authorities as the corporate residence. Non-resident companies are companies incorporated/registered outside of Honduras.

Permanent establishment (PE)
There is a provision in the transfer pricing rules approved on December 2011 that provides the following definition of PE:

"Permanent establishment is a fixed place of business where a natural or juridical person resident or domiciled in another state performs part or all of its activities in Honduras. Likewise, a foreign resident will be considered to have a permanent establishment in Honduras when it acts in the national territory through an independent agent that is not acting under the regular framework of its activity." There are some exceptions to the rule.

There is no treaty definition of PE since, at the present time, Honduras is not a signatory of any double taxation treaty (DTT) with another jurisdiction in the world.

Other taxes

Sales tax

Sales tax is charged on all sale and purchase transactions of goods and services made in Honduran territory.

The general tax rate is 12%. It applies to most goods and services, with the exception of machinery and equipment, basic grains, pharmaceutical products, raw materials for the production of non-taxable goods, petroleum products, school supplies, and insecticides, among others.

The import and sale of beer, other alcoholic beverages, cigarettes, and other tobacco products are subject to 15% sales tax.

There is a 15% sales tax applicable to some PCS, cellular, internet broad band, cable TV, and energy services, depending on the amount of consumption billed by the supplier.

There is an 18% sales tax levied on first class and business class air tickets.

Customs duties

The duty assessed by the Honduran government at the time of customs clearance ranges between 0% and 15% for most items.

Honduras is a member of the Central American Common Market (CACM), which also includes Costa Rica, El Salvador, Guatemala, and Nicaragua. Honduras' rates on most goods from outside CACM are currently within the 0% to 15% range. Under the Dominican Republic-Central America Free Trade Agreement (CAFTA-DR) with the United States (US), about 80% of US industrial and commercial goods can now enter the region duty-free, with the remaining tariffs to be phased out over ten years. Nearly all textile and apparel goods that meet the Agreement's rules of origin are now duty-free and quota-free, promoting new opportunities for US and regional fiber, yarn, fabric, and apparel manufacturing (the Agreement's tariff treatment for textile and apparel goods was made retroactive to 1 January 2004).

It is necessary to first obtain the appropriate Harmonized System (HS) classification number for determining when a particular product can enter the CAFTA-DR region duty-free. With this number, it is then possible to check the country and product-specific tariff elimination schedule.

Ad valorem import taxes can be as high as 20%. In addition, imports are subject to the sales tax of 12% or 15% that applies to the sum of the cost, insurance, and freight (CIF) value; the *ad valorem* duty; and the customs fees.

Excise taxes

There is an excise tax levied on the production and importation of cigarettes, sodas, beer, and alcoholic beverages.

Cigarettes are levied at HNL 350 per unit.

Excise tax on sodas, beer, and alcoholic beverages are levied according to the following table:

Honduras

Description	Tax rate per litre (HNL)
Soda/other prepared drink	0.58
Beer	4.12
Wine	5.17
Brandy, cognac, vermouth	27.92
Whisky	27.92
Rum 40°	17.00
Rum 38°	16.15
Rum 36°	15.30
Gin, vodka, tequila, etc.	27.92

Net assets tax

The net assets tax is an annual 1% tax on the net asset value of the company. It applies to the gross value of assets less reserve for accounts payable and any accumulated depreciation allowed under the income tax law and other deductions allowed by law. The law also allows a special deduction of HNL 3 million.

The net assets tax is in lieu of CIT when CIT is less than the amount due for net asset tax. Resident companies during their preoperative period (i.e. the period in which the company started operations but has not issued its first invoice) and companies operating in free zones, among others, are exempt from the net assets tax.

Non-resident companies are not liable for the net assets tax.

Transfer taxes

Transfer taxes are levied on real estate transactions at HNL 1.5 per every HNL 1,000.

Stamp taxes

There are no provisions for stamp taxes in Honduras.

Capital gains tax

In general, a 10% tax is applied on capital gains, regardless of the person's residence status. Under the Zolitur law territory, a special regime, the tax rate is a 4% flat tax on capital gains.

The payment of capital gains tax must be made within ten business days after the agreed amount of the transaction has been determined.

In instances where a transaction is subject to the capital gains tax and a non-resident is involved, the buyer has an obligation to withhold 2% of the transaction amount as an advance payment to this tax and must pay it to the government within ten business days of the date of the transaction.

Payroll taxes and contributions

Payroll taxes and contributions are paid by employers at the following rates:

- Social security: 7.2%, with a ceiling of HNL 4,800.
- *Instituto Nacional de Formación Profesional* (INFOP): 1%.
- Housing fund ('*Régimen de Aportaciones Privadas*' or RAP/'*Fondo Social para la Vivienda*' or FOSOVI): 1.5%.

Special temporary contributions

For the term of five years:

- Under the Special Temporary Security Contribution on Financial Transactions (*Contribución Especial por Transacciones Financieras Proseguridad Poblicional*), financial transactions are subject to 0.2% WHT, with some exceptions. This contribution started to be applied in April 2012.
- Companies providing mobile communication services will pay a Special Temporary Contribution of 1% on gross monthly income.
- Under the Special Temporary Contribution for the protection of the environment from the Mining Sector, there is a 2% contribution on the FOB value of the exports filed.
- Special Temporary Contribution from the food and beverages business under special tax regimes is 0.5% on gross monthly income.
- Cooperatives Special Contribution is 3.6% on annual net surplus.

Municipal taxes

Companies doing business in Honduras are also subject to the rules and regulations of the respective municipalities. Taxes and obligations are ruled by the '*Plan de Arbitrios*'. Some of these tax obligations include the following:

- Industry, commerce, and service tax, which is based on gross income per year (*see the Taxes on corporate income section*).
- Public services tax, which is paid for services such as waste management.
- Real estate tax, which is a tax on assets and asset gains.
- Sign tax, which is a tax on public advertising.

Branch income

Branch income is subject to income tax at the rates applicable for corporate income.

Income determination

Income is computed in accordance with generally accepted accounting and commercial principles, subject to certain adjustments required by the tax law.

Inventory valuation

Inventories are generally valued using the first in first out (FIFO), last in first out (LIFO), and weighted-average cost methods.

Capital gains

Capital gains are not generally subject to CIT, but may be subject to capital gains tax. *See Capital gains tax in the Other taxes section for more information.*

Dividend income

The income from dividends is considered 'other income', thus non-taxable under the general income tax rates.

Stock dividends

Stock dividends are also not taxable.

Honduras

Interest income
Honduran Bank interests are subject to a 10% WHT at the moment the interest is given, when the sum is over HNL 50,000. Interests from abroad are considered as normal income.

Royalty income
Royalties are taxed in the same manner as general income if the recipient is a local company or branch.

Foreign income
Deferral and anti-deferral of foreign income are not regulated in Honduras.

Deductions

The net taxable income of an enterprise is determined by deducting all the ordinary and necessary expenses incurred in the generation of income, including amortisation and depreciation; municipal taxes; donations made in favour of the state, the central district, the municipalities, and legally recognised educational institutions, charities, and sporting facilities; mandatory employer-employee contributions to the social security system; and 'reasonable' charges for royalties and management services.

In general, all expenses incurred in the generation of taxable income are considered as deductible for income tax purposes. However, there are some 'non-deductible' expenses, even if incurred in the generation of income (e.g. interest paid to owners or shareholders, capital losses).

Depreciation
Depreciation may be computed using the straight-line method. Companies may also obtain authorisation from the tax authorities to use other depreciation methods. However, after a company selects a depreciation method, it must apply the method consistently thereafter. The following are the applicable straight-line method rates for some common assets.

Asset	Rate (%)
Buildings	2.5 to 10
Plant and machinery	10
Vehicles	10 to 33
Furniture and office equipment	10
Tools	25

Goodwill
Goodwill can be amortised over a period of five years.

Start-up expenses
Organisation or reorganisation expenses are deductible for the total amount as long as they do not exceed 10% of the initial capital stock. These expenses can be amortised over five years.

Interest expenses
Interest expenses are deductible as long as they are incurred in order to generate income. Interest paid to stockholders, owners, or spouses are not deductible.

Bad debt

Taxpayers can record a bad debt provision of 1% of the total credit sales, which will not exceed 10% of the accounts receivable balance.

Charitable contributions

Contributions to organisations legally recognised by the government are deductible.

Capital losses

Capital losses are not deductible to determine the net taxable income. Capital losses can only be netted against capital gains, which are subject to a tax rate of 10% (*see Capital gains tax in the Other taxes section*).

Contingent liabilities

Provisions for contingent liabilities, such as severance pay, are not deductible for tax purposes; actual payments during the fiscal period, for those liabilities, are considered to be deductible expenses.

Fines and penalties

Fines and penalties are not deductible.

Taxes

With the exception of the Temporary Solidarity Contribution, net asset taxes, CIT, and sales tax (i.e. if sales tax paid is used as a credit to net the sales tax payable to the government), taxes and contributions paid to district or municipalities are deductible expenses when determining taxable income.

Net operating losses

Companies engaged in agriculture, manufacturing, mining, and tourism may carry forward losses for three years. However, certain restrictions apply. Losses may not be carried back.

Payments to foreign affiliates

Payments to foreign affiliates are deductible as long as the service is effectively received.

Group taxation

No provisions exist for group taxation in Honduras.

Transfer pricing

The new Transfer Pricing Law for Honduras was published in the *Diario Oficial La Gaceta* in December 2011. This law establishes the transfer pricing regulations applicable in Honduras which will become effective January 2014. There is a period of two years to adopt the transfer pricing policies and to negotiate with the tax authority the corresponding advance pricing agreements (APAs).

Thin capitalisation

At the present time, there are no provisions for thin capitalisation in Honduras.

Honduras

Tax credits and incentives

Companies operating under a special tax regime are exempted from CIT, sales tax, customs duties, and some municipal taxes. These special tax regimes are the following:

- Free zone.
- Industrial processing zone ('*Zona Industrial de Procesamiento*' or ZIP).
- Temporary import regime ('*Régimen de Importación Temporal*' or RIT).
- Tourism incentive law.
- Law of the Tourism Free Zone of the Bay Islands ('*Ley de la Zona Libre Turística de las Islas de la Bahía*').
- Law promoting the generation of electric energy with renewable resources ('*Ley de Promoción a la Generación de Energía Eléctrica con Recursos Renovables*'), which provides tax exemptions for projects generating 50MW and over.
- Law for the Promotion and Protection of Invesment (*Ley para la Promoción y Protección de Inversiones*), which provides special tax treatment (i.e. partial CIT rate reduction of up to 50%) for some types of investments.
- In the regulations for the free zone there is a consideration for international service companies (the business processing operations, call centres and contact centres, shared service centres) which will have the same tax exoneration provided by this regime.

Companies must comply with some governmental requirements to operate under one of the above mentioned special regimes.

Drawback industries
Special benefits exist for industries that import semi-manufactured materials for assembly in Honduras and export finished products. Benefits consist of duty-free imports of raw materials for subsequent export as manufactured products. Machinery for these industries may also be imported duty-free.

Withholding taxes

WHT for residents
Distribution or payment of dividends or any other form of distribution of retained earnings or reserves to resident or domiciled individuals is taxed via WHT at 10%.

The tax authority is empowered to withhold 1% from import operations as an advance payment to income tax, with some exceptions to the rule according to Section 7 of the Income Tax Law. This provision was approved in July 2011, but its application by the tax authority is still in suspense as of May 2012.

WHT for non-residents
For non-residents in Honduras, any income derived from Honduran sources is taxable under the following table of the Income Tax Law:

Income source	WHT (%)
Real estate and movable property rent, except dividends and interest	10
Royalties from mining operations and other natural resources	10
Salaries paid for services and other remuneration for rendering of services within national territory or abroad	10
Profit transfers from branch office to head office	10

Honduras

Income source	WHT (%)
Dividends	10
Royalties	10
Interest paid on commercial operations, bonds, securities or negotiable instruments, and other types of obligations	10
Income from operation of airplanes, ships, and vehicles	10
Income from operation of telecommunication companies	10
Insurance premiums	10
Income obtained from public shows	10
Films and video tapes for cinemas, TV, video clubs, and cable TV	10
Any other income not mentioned previously	10

Tax treaties

Honduras has not signed any tax treaties with foreign jurisdictions.

Tax administration

The 'Dirección Ejecutiva de Ingresos' (DEI) is the tax authority in Honduras. It is responsible for the administration of the tax and customs system. Taxpayers may request approval from the DEI regarding direct or indirect taxes (e.g. accelerated depreciation methods on new assets acquired by corporations with monetary activities requiring constant technological update, higher installed production capacity and productive re-conversion processes in order to maintain and strengthen their competitive advantage).

Taxable period

The statutory tax year runs from 1 January through to 31 December. However, taxpayers may apply to use a special tax year by requesting an authorisation from the DEI.

Tax returns

Companies must file a CIT return on 30 April every year.

Payment of tax

Mandatory advance tax payments are payable each quarter, based on the income tax paid for the preceding tax year. Final tax is due with the CIT return on 30 April every year.

Audit cycle

The audit cycle can begin after (i) the date the tax return should have been filed or (ii) sometime after the taxpayer made a request before the tax authority (e.g. tax credit, loss carryforward).

Statute of limitations

The statute of limitations is five years.

Hong Kong

PwC contact

Peter Yu
PricewaterhouseCoopers Limited
21/F Edinburgh Tower, The Landmark
15 Queen's Road Central
Central Hong Kong
Hong Kong, SAR
Tel: +852 2289 3122
Email: peter.sh.yu@hk.pwc.com

Significant developments

Developments in tax treaty network
Hong Kong's treaty network has expanded at an unprecedented pace since March 2010, with 19 comprehensive double tax agreements (CDTAs) signed by Hong Kong with various Asian and European countries during the period from March 2010 to end of April 2012. All these CDTAs adopt the more liberal 2004 Organisation for Economic Co-operation and Development (OECD) version of the Exchange of Information (EoI) article. In addition, the EoI articles of the CDTAs previously signed with Mainland China and Luxembourg were updated to the 2004 OECD version by means of a protocol signed in May and November 2010 respectively. Accordingly, Hong Kong has concluded 21 CDTAs that adopt the latest international standard of EoI as of the end of April 2012.

Of the 19 newly signed CDTAs, the ones concluded with Austria, Brunei, the Czech Republic, France, Hungary, Indonesia, Ireland, Japan, Liechtenstein, the Netherlands, New Zealand, Spain, and the United Kingdom were ratified and entered into force. However, the agreements with the Czech Republic, Indonesia, and Spain will only have effect in Hong Kong from year of assessment 2013/14 (i.e. from 1 April 2013). The CDTAs signed with Jersey, Kuwait, Malaysia, Malta, Portugal, and Switzerland have not yet entered into force, pending completion of the ratification procedures on both sides.

For more information about Hong Kong's existing treaty network, please see the Withholding taxes section.

Developments in profits tax
In December 2011, a piece of tax legislation was enacted to expand the scope of tax deduction for capital expenditure incurred on the purchase of intellectual property (IP) rights. Before the new legislation, tax deduction was available for qualified capital expenditure incurred on purchase of patent or know-how rights only, provided that certain specified conditions are met. The new legislation expands the scope of tax deduction to qualified capital expenditure incurred on the purchase of copyrights, registered trademarks, and registered designs (collectively known as 'specified IP rights'), as far as the conditions specified in the new legislation are satisfied.

However, the new legislation also introduces a number of specific anti-avoidance provisions that guard against possible abuse of tax deduction of both patent/know-how rights and the specified IP rights. In addition, sale proceeds from a subsequent disposal of these IP rights will be deemed as taxable trading receipts to the extent of the amount previously allowed as deduction.

In April 2012, an advance pricing arrangement (APA) program was officially launched in Hong Kong whereby any resident enterprise or non-resident enterprise with a permanent establishment (PE) in Hong Kong may apply for an APA in respect of its transactions with associated enterprises under a CDTA. At the initial stage of the program, only bilateral or multilateral APA applications will be accepted, although a unilateral APA may be considered in some limited exceptional circumstances. The Hong Kong Inland Revenue Department (HKIRD) had issued Departmental Interpretation and Practice Notes No. 48 'Advance Pricing Arrangement' in March 2012 to provide details about the APA program.

Other developments

The capital duty levied on local companies has been abolished, effective as of 1 June 2012.

Taxes on corporate income

H

Hong Kong adopts a territorial basis of taxation. Profits tax is payable by every person (defined to include corporation, partnership, and sole proprietorship) carrying on a trade, profession, or business in Hong Kong on profits arising in or derived from Hong Kong from that trade, profession, or business. However, capital gains and receipts that are capital in nature are not subject to tax. Dividends from local companies chargeable to tax are exempt, whereas dividends from overseas companies are generally offshore in nature and not subject to tax in Hong Kong. The tax residence of a person is generally irrelevant for profits tax purposes. The tax treatments of public and private companies are the same.

Certain income that would not otherwise be subject to Hong Kong profits tax is deemed to arise in or be derived from Hong Kong from a trade, profession, or business carried on in Hong Kong and thus becomes taxable in Hong Kong. This includes royalties received by a non-resident for the use of or right to use a patent, design, trademark, copyright material, secret process or formula, or other property of a similar nature in Hong Kong, or for the use of such intellectual properties outside Hong Kong, but the royalties paid can be claimed as a deduction by a person for profits tax purposes.

The tax rates are 16.5% for corporations and 15% for unincorporated businesses for year of assessment 2012/13.

There are special rules for determining the tax liabilities of certain industries such as shipping, air services, and financial services.

Incomes from certain qualifying debt instruments (QDIs) are either tax exempt or subject to a concessionary tax rate (i.e. 50% of the regular profits tax rate). A specific anti-avoidance provision was recently introduced whereby the concessionary tax rate/ tax exemption does not apply to incomes derived from QDIs by a person who is an associate of the issuer of the QDIs.

Offshore funds having Hong Kong fund managers and investment advisors with full discretionary powers are exempt from Hong Kong profits tax on profits derived in Hong Kong from six types of 'specified transactions' which are carried out or arranged by 'specified persons'. However, there are also specific anti-avoidance provisions in the Inland Revenue Ordinance (IRO) deeming certain resident persons to be subject to profits tax on their share of the non-resident person's tax exempt profits.

Hong Kong

Corporate residence

In general, for Hong Kong profits tax purposes, corporate residency is not important in determining taxability of an entity. The decisive factors for taxability are (i) whether a corporation is carrying on a trade, profession, or business in Hong Kong, and (ii) whether the profits are arising in or derived from Hong Kong.

However, where it is necessary to determine the corporate residence, such as for the purpose of a comprehensive double tax agreement (CDTA), companies incorporated in Hong Kong and companies that are normally managed or controlled/centrally managed and controlled (depending on the provisions of the relevant CDTA) in Hong Kong are generally considered as a Hong Kong tax resident.

Permanent establishment (PE)

For Hong Kong profits tax purposes, whether a foreign corporation is carrying on a trade, profession, or business in Hong Kong and the source of profits, rather than whether there is a PE in Hong Kong, are the decisive factors in determining taxability.

Other taxes

Value-added tax (VAT)

Hong Kong does not have a VAT, goods and services tax, or sales tax.

Customs duties

There is no tariff on general imports in Hong Kong.

Excise tax

Duties are levied on limited categories of dutiable commodities (i.e. tobacco, liquor, methyl alcohol, and hydrocarbons), regardless of whether they are imported or locally manufactured.

Property tax

Property tax is charged annually to the owner of any land or buildings (except government and consular properties) in Hong Kong at the standard rate of 15% on the net assessable value of such land or buildings. Net assessable value of a property is the consideration payable to the owner for the right to use the land or buildings less rates paid by the owner and a 20% notional allowance.

Rental income derived by a company from a Hong Kong property is subject to profits tax. The company that is subject to profits tax may apply for an exemption from property tax in respect of the property. If no exemption is applied, the property tax paid can be used to offset against the profits tax payable by the company.

Transfer tax

Hong Kong does not have a transfer tax.

Stamp duty

Stamp duty is charged on transfer of Hong Kong stock by way of sale and purchase at 0.2% of the consideration (or the market value if it is higher) per transaction. Hong Kong stock is defined as stock the transfer of which must be registered in Hong Kong.

For conveyance on sale of immovable property in Hong Kong, the stamp duty payable depends on the property consideration and ranges from a flat rate of 100 Hong Kong dollars (HKD) (for property consideration of up to HKD 2 million) to the highest rate of 4.25% of the consideration of the property (for property consideration exceeding HKD 20 million), with marginal relief upon entry into each higher rate band.

For lease of immovable property in Hong Kong, stamp duty is calculated at a specified rate of the annual rental that varies with the term of the lease. Currently, the applicable rate ranges from 0.25% (for lease period of not more than one year) to 1% (for lease period of more than three years).

Exemption is available to certain transactions, such as transfer of shares between associated corporate bodies and certain stock borrowing and lending transactions, provided that the specified conditions for exemption are satisfied.

Special Stamp Duty (SSD)

There is an SSD on resale of residential property within 24 months from the date of acquisition. The SSD is imposed on top of the *ad valorem* stamp duty payable on conveyance on sale or agreement for sale of residential property, with a few exemptions. The SSD payable will be calculated based on the stated consideration or the market value (whichever is higher) of the resold property at the regressive rates indicated below.

- 15% for residential properties held for six months or less.
- 10% for residential properties held for more than six months but for 12 months or less.
- 5% for residential properties held for more than 12 months but for 24 months or less.

Business registration fees

Every person who carries on a business in Hong Kong is required to apply for business registration with a fee within one month from the date of commencement of the business. The business registration certificate has to be renewed either on an annual basis or every three years with a payment of a business registration (renewal) fee. Special registration and licence fees are applicable to banks and deposit-taking companies.

Capital duty

The capital duty has been abolished, effective as of 1 June 2012.

Prior to 1 June 2012, a fee of HKD 1 for all or part of HKD 1,000 of the nominal share capital, or increase in nominal share capital, was payable as capital duty by a Hong Kong company at its incorporation or when there was an increase in its nominal share capital. The fee was capped at HKD 30,000 per case, counted on a company (rather than group) basis. When a company allotted shares at a premium, a capital duty of HKD 1 for every, or part of, HKD 1,000 of the aggregate amount of the premiums was payable.

Government rates and rent

Rates are an indirect tax levied on properties in Hong Kong. Rates are charged at 5% of the rateable value, which is the estimated annual rental value of a property at the designated valuation reference date of 1 October.

Privately owned land in Hong Kong is normally held by way of a government lease under which rent is payable to the Hong Kong SAR Government in return for the right to hold and occupy the land for the term (i.e. duration) specified in the lease document.

Hong Kong

Currently, government rent is calculated at 3% of the rateable value of the property and is adjusted in step with any subsequent changes in the rateable value.

Branch income

The tax rate for branches is the same as that for corporations. The Hong Kong profit of a foreign corporation with a branch in Hong Kong is determined according to the accounts maintained for the Hong Kong operation (or business). If the Hong Kong accounts do not disclose the true profits arising in or derived from Hong Kong attributable to the Hong Kong operation, the Hong Kong profit will be computed according to the ratio of turnover in Hong Kong to total turnover (or the proportion of Hong Kong assets over total assets) on the worldwide profits. Alternatively, the HKIRD tax assessor may estimate the profits of the Hong Kong branch. In certain situations, the profits of the Hong Kong branch could be estimated based on a fair percentage of the turnover in Hong Kong.

Income determination

Inventory valuation
Inventory may be stated at the lower of cost or market value. Last in first out (LIFO) may not be used for tax purposes. First in first out (FIFO) must be consistently applied.

The prevailing accounting standards require financial assets and liabilities held for trading purpose (e.g. shares and securities held as trading stock) to be carried at market value, with fluctuations in values of such assets and liabilities taken to the profit and loss accounts, irrespective of whether the profits or losses are realised. The HKIRD requires that this accounting treatment be followed in computing the assessable profits for tax purposes.

There are special tax provisions for valuation upon cessation of a business under which inventory is valued at market value, unless it is sold to a person carrying on business in Hong Kong, who may deduct a corresponding amount as the cost of the inventory in computing the assessable profits.

Capital gains
Gains from realisation of capital assets or receipts that are capital in nature are not taxed.

Dividend income
Dividends from local companies chargeable to tax are exempt, whereas dividends from overseas companies are generally offshore in nature and not subject to Hong Kong profits tax. Hong Kong corporations may declare bonus issues (i.e. stock dividends), which are not taxable in the hands of the recipients.

Interest income
Interest income received by or accrued to a corporation carrying on a trade or business in Hong Kong is subject to profits tax. Exemption is provided to interest income derived from any deposit placed in Hong Kong with a financial institution, unless the deposit secures a borrowing the interest expense of which is deductible. This exemption, however, does not apply to interest accruing to a financial institution.

Interest accruing to a bank or financial institution will be deemed to be sourced and taxable in Hong Kong if the interest arises through or from the carrying on of business in Hong Kong by the bank or financial institution.

Royalties

Royalties paid or accrued to a non-resident for the use of or right to use in Hong Kong or outside Hong Kong (if the royalties are deductible in ascertaining the assessable profits of a person for Hong Kong profits tax purposes) a trademark, patent, design, copyright material, secret process, or other property of a similar nature, or for the use in Hong Kong of cinema or television tape or any sound recording, are deemed to be taxable in Hong Kong.

A total of 30% of the sum receivable is deemed to constitute profits subject to tax in normal situations. Where such royalties are received by or accrued to an associated corporation, however, 100% of the sum is deemed to constitute profits under certain circumstances.

H

Partnership income

Partnership business is taxed as a single entity though an individual partner can use its share of losses incurred by a partnership to offset against the assessable profits of its other business. In general, there is no special registration requirement other than business registration for a partnership. The assessable profits of a partnership are basically determined in the same way as those of a corporation, with certain special rules (e.g. salaries or other remunerations paid to a partner or a partner's spouse are not deductible).

Unrealised exchange gains/losses

In general, unrealised exchange gains/losses are taxable/deductible if they are recognised in the profit and loss accounts in accordance with the generally accepted accounting principles (GAAP), provided that they are revenue in nature and with a Hong Kong source. The nature and source of exchange gains/losses are determined by the nature and source of the underlying transactions. Exchange gains/losses arising from ordinary business transactions (e.g. trade receivables or payables) are taxable/deductible whereas exchange gains/losses arising from capital transactions (e.g. sale of capital assets) are non-taxable/non-deductible.

Foreign income

Hong Kong resident corporations are not taxed on their worldwide income. Foreign-sourced income, whether or not remitted to Hong Kong, is not taxed. As such, there is no specific tax provision dealing with deferral or non-remittance of foreign earnings. Nor does Hong Kong have any controlled foreign company (CFC) legislation.

Deductions

Expenses that are incurred for producing profits chargeable to tax and that are not capital in nature are generally tax deductible. In addition, special tax relief is available for certain capital expenditure. There are special rules for deduction of certain expenses (e.g. interest expenses).

Accounting treatments are usually followed in determining the assessable profits except when there is an explicit rule in the IRO. Accrued expenses recognised in the profit and loss accounts in accordance with the GAAP are usually deductible if they are incurred for producing profits chargeable/subject to tax and are not capital in nature.

Hong Kong

Expense items of which a tax adjustment is necessary in determining the amount of taxable profits from the accounting profits include: tax depreciation allowance vs. accounting depreciation, expenses that are capital in nature, general provisions that are non-deductible, and non-deductible interest expenses on borrowings used to finance non-income producing assets.

Set out below are the Hong Kong profits tax treatments of some common expense items.

Tax depreciation of fixed assets
Tax depreciation allowances/deductions are available for capital expenditure incurred on the construction of buildings or structures and in the provision of machinery and plant for trade or business purposes, as follows:

- Industrial buildings and structures: An initial allowance of 20%, in addition to an annual allowance of 4%, of the cost of construction or cost of purchase from a developer is granted for an industrial building or structure occupied for the purpose of a qualifying trade. Provision is made for balancing allowance or charge in the year of assessment in which the building is disposed of to adjust the written-down value of the building to the disposal price. Balancing charges are restricted to the total of initial and annual allowances previously given.
- Commercial buildings and structures: An annual allowance of 4% of the capital expenditure incurred on the construction is applicable. A balancing allowance or charge applies upon disposal. Balancing charges are restricted to the total annual allowances previously given.
- Plant and machinery: An initial allowance of 60% of the capital expenditure on plant and machinery is given for the year of assessment during the basis period in which the expenditure is incurred. An annual allowance is also given for depreciation at three prescribed rates on the reducing value of each of the three depreciation rate 'pools'. The three prescribed rates are 10%, 20%, and 30%, and the reducing value of each of the three depreciation rate pools is original cost less initial and annual allowances and sales proceeds. Provision is made for balancing charges when plant and machinery within one of the three depreciation rate pools is sold or disposed of and the reducing value of that pool is less than the sale price, which is capped at the original amount incurred in the pool. In addition, balancing allowances or charges may be applicable upon cessation of business. Otherwise, sales proceeds are deducted in calculating the reducing value on which the annual allowance is calculated.

Book depreciation is adjusted for tax purposes in accordance with the above depreciation allowances granted under the IRO.

Goodwill
Cost of acquisition of goodwill/amortisation of goodwill is not deductible as they are capital in nature.

Organisational and start-up expenses
In general, company formation/start-up expenses that are incurred before the commencement of a trade, profession, or business and that are for the establishment of the overall income producing structure are capital in nature and not tax deductible.

Research & development (R&D)
There is a specific provision allowing the deduction of expenditure incurred on R&D (including payments made to an approved research institute and in-house expenditure), provided that certain specified conditions are met.

Hong Kong

Interest expenses
There is no thin capitalisation rule in Hong Kong. However, deduction of interest expense is subject to stringent and complicated rules which are designed to guard against loan arrangements with an intention to avoid Hong Kong profits taxes.

Bad debt
A bad or doubtful debt incurred in any trade, business, or profession, proved to the satisfaction of the HKIRD to have become bad during the basis period for a year of assessment, is deductible. The deduction is limited to debts which were included as a trading receipt in ascertaining the taxpayer's assessable profits or debts in respect of money lent in the ordinary course of a money-lending business in Hong Kong.

If any bad or doubtful debt which has previously been allowed as a deduction is ultimately recovered, it will be treated as taxable profits of the basis period in which it is recovered.

Charitable contributions
A deduction is allowed for cash donations to approved charities made in the basis period for a year of assessment if the aggregate of such donations is not less than HKD100. The deduction is limited to 35% of the assessable profits of the year of assessment.

Pension expenses
A deduction is allowed for regular/ordinary contributions to a mandatory provident fund scheme or recognised occupational retirement scheme made by an employer in respect of an employee to the extent that the contributions do not exceed 15% of the employee's total emoluments for the period to which the contributions relate.

Special payments other than the ordinary contributions to a mandatory provident fund scheme or recognised occupational retirement scheme are capital in nature but can be deducted evenly over a five-year period under a specific provision of the IRO.

There are also specific rules for deduction of provisions for contributions to a mandatory provident fund scheme or recognised occupational retirement scheme.

Payments for directors
Director fees or other remunerations paid by a corporation to its directors are generally deductible under the normal deduction rule. Nevertheless, no deduction is allowed on salaries or other remunerations paid to a sole proprietor or any partners or partners' spouses of a partnership business.

Contingent liabilities
Generally speaking, general provisions for expenses are not deductible whereas specific provisions are deductible if the HKIRD is satisfied that the amount has been incurred (i.e. the taxpayer has a legal/contractual obligation to pay such amount in future) and that the provision represents a reasonably accurate estimate of the future liability.

Special deductions
There are special deduction rules for expenditures incurred (i) for refurbishment of a building or structure, other than a domestic building or structure; (ii) on environmental protection installation and machinery; (iii) on environment-friendly vehicles; (iv) on machinery or plant used specifically and directly for any manufacturing process, computer hardware (other than that which is an integral part of machinery or plant), computer software, and computer systems (collectively known as prescribed fixed

Hong Kong

assets); (v) for registering trademarks, designs, or patents used in the production of taxable profits; and (vi) on the purchase of patent/know-how rights and specified intellectual property (IP) rights (i.e. copyrights, registered trademarks, or registered designs), provided certain specified conditions are met.

Fines and penalties
Fines and penalties are generally not deductible as the HKIRD does not consider them to be expenses incurred for producing profits chargeable/subject to tax.

Taxes paid
Taxes paid on corporate profits are generally not deductible for the purpose of calculating the assessable profits. However, the HKIRD generally accepts that a foreign tax that is an expense that must be borne regardless of whether or not a profit is derived (e.g. a foreign withholding tax levied on the gross amount of interest or royalties received), as opposed to a charge on the profits themselves, is deductible under the general deduction provision. Where interest income or gains from the sale of a certificate of deposit or bill of exchange are deemed to be subject to profits tax, a deduction is allowed for foreign taxes of substantially the same nature of Hong Kong profits tax paid in respect of the same income, provided that the taxpayer is not eligible for double taxation relief under a CDTA.

Net operating and capital losses
Net operating losses incurred in an accounting year can be carried forward indefinitely to offset future profits of the business. A corporation carrying on more than one business may have losses in one business offset profits of the others, with any balance being carried forward. Net operating losses cannot be carried backward.

Capital losses are not tax deductible.

Payments to foreign affiliates
Royalties and service fees paid/payable by a Hong Kong corporation to foreign affiliates are deductible provided they are incurred for the production of profits chargeable/subject to tax. There is no special restriction on the deductibility of these payments. Interest payable to a foreign affiliate is not deductible if the recipient is not chargeable/subject to Hong Kong profits tax on the interest income received.

Group taxation

Hong Kong does not have a consolidated or group taxation regime.

Transfer pricing
Strictly speaking, there is no comprehensive transfer pricing legislation in Hong Kong. While a few existing provisions in the IRO may be employed by the tax authority to tackle non-arm's-length transactions, such provisions are primarily aimed at transactions with closely connected non-residents or tax avoidance transactions rather than specific legislation on transfer pricing.

In 2009, the HKIRD issued two Departmental Interpretation and Practice Notes (DIPNs) to address the transfer pricing issues in Hong Kong. DIPN 45 focuses on the administrative/procedural issues involved in providing double tax relief in a treaty context such as when such relief is available and what are the procedures for claiming such relief. DIPN 46 outlines the HKIRD's view on the legislative framework for transfer pricing in Hong Kong (including the statutory provisions in the IRO and the articles in a CDTA that are relevant to transfer pricing) and provides guidance on numerous transfer pricing related issues such as the application of the arm's-length principle, the acceptable transfer pricing methodologies, which are largely in line with the OECD transfer pricing guidelines. The DIPN also spells out the documentation that taxpayers should consider retaining to support their transfer pricing arrangements and explains the interaction between the transfer pricing and sourcing rules in Hong Kong.

In general, the HKIRD adopts the arm's-length principle and would seek to apply the OECD transfer pricing guidelines except where they are incompatible with the express provisions in the IRO.

An APA program was launched in Hong Kong in April 2012. The objectives of the APA program are to help taxpayers obtain tax certainty on their complex or significant transfer pricing arrangements and reduce the risk of double taxation arising from related-party transactions. Resident enterprises or non-resident enterprises with a PE in Hong Kong may apply for an APA in respect of their transactions with associated enterprises under a CDTA, provided that certain conditions (including the threshold for an APA application) are met.

At the initial stage, the HKIRD is primarily focused on bilateral APA or multilateral APA applications in respect of cross-border related-party transactions involving countries that are CDTA partners with Hong Kong.

Departmental Interpretation and Practice Notes No. 48 - Advance Pricing Arrangement (DIPN 48), which set out the details of the APA program, was issued by the HKIRD in late March 2012. DIPN 48 provides guidance on various aspects of the APA regime, such as the timeframe and threshold for an APA application, the various stages involved in the APA process, an audit involving years covered by a concluded APA, and possible rollback of the transfer pricing methodology agreed under an APA to prior years. The appendices of the DIPN include various sample documents for use in an APA application.

Thin capitalisation
Hong Kong does not have thin capitalisation rules.

Controlled foreign companies (CFCs)
Hong Kong does not have a CFC regime.

Tax credits and incentives

Foreign tax credits
Foreign tax credits are available if foreign taxes are payable/paid on income derived from a jurisdiction which has entered into a CDTA with Hong Kong and the same income is subject to tax in Hong Kong. *See the Withholding taxes section for a list of jurisdictions that have entered into a CDTA with Hong Kong.*

Tax holidays
Hong Kong does not have a tax holiday program.

Foreign investment incentives
Hong Kong does not have any specific incentives for foreign investment except that offshore funds may be exempt from profits tax under certain circumstances.

Hong Kong

Withholding taxes

There is no withholding tax (WHT) on dividends, interest, or royalties. However, the 4.95%/16.5% (for corporations) or 4.5%/15% (for unincorporated businesses) tax on royalties received by non-residents (*see Royalties in the Income determination section*) is in effect similar to a WHT.

Resident consignees are required to furnish quarterly returns to the HKIRD showing the gross proceeds from sales on behalf of their non-resident consignors and to pay to the HKIRD Commissioner a sum equal to 0.5% of such proceeds. The HKIRD normally accepts this as satisfying the Hong Kong tax obligations of the non-resident.

Hong Kong has so far entered into a CDTA with Austria, Belgium, Brunei, the Czech Republic, France, Hungary, Indonesia, Ireland, Japan, Jersey, Kuwait, Liechtenstein, Luxembourg, Malaysia, Malta, the Netherlands, New Zealand, the People's Republic of China (PRC), Portugal, Spain, Switzerland, Thailand, the United Kingdom, and Vietnam.

The CDTAs with Jersey, Kuwait, Malaysia, Malta, Portugal and Switzerland have not yet entered into force, pending the completion of the ratification procedures of the governments concerned. The CDTAs with the Czech Republic, Indonesia, and Spain have been ratified but will only become effective in Hong Kong from year of assessment 2013/14 (i.e. from 1 April 2013).

The following table shows the applicable WHT rates for payments made from Hong Kong payers to non-treaty and treaty country corporate recipients. The rates shown in the table are the lower of the domestic and treaty rates. For WHT rates on payments received by Hong Kong recipients from treaty country payers, please refer to the summaries of the respective treaty countries.

Recipient	Dividends (%) (1)	Interest (%) (1)	Royalties (%)
Non-treaty	0	0	4.95 (2)
Treaty:			
Austria	0	0	3
Belgium	0	0	4.95 (3)
Brunei	0	0	4.95 (3)
China, the People's Republic of (PRC)	0	0	4.95 (3)
Czech Republic	0	0	4.95 (3)
France	0	0	4.95 (3)
Hungary	0	0	4.95 (3)
Indonesia	0	0	4.95 (3)
Ireland	0	0	3
Japan	0	0	4.95 (3)
Jersey	0	0	4
Kuwait	0	0	4.95 (3)
Liechtenstein	0	0	3
Luxembourg	0	0	3
Malaysia	0	0	4.95 (3)
Malta	0	0	3
The Netherlands	0	0	3
New Zealand	0	0	4.95 (3)

Hong Kong

Recipient	Dividends (%) (1)	Interest (%) (1)	Royalties (%)
Portugal	0	0	4.95 (3)
Spain	0	0	4.95 (3)
Switzerland	0	0	3
Thailand	0	0	4.95 (3)
United Kingdom	0	0	3
Vietnam	0	0	4.95 (3)

Notes

1. Hong Kong IRO does not impose WHT on dividends and interest currently. However, the treaties provide for a maximum WHT rate on dividends and interest should Hong Kong IRO impose such WHT in the future. Some of the treaties also provide for a reduced WHT rate on dividends and interest if conditions specified in the treaties are met.
2. Generally, royalties paid to non-resident corporations that are not otherwise chargeable to Hong Kong profits tax are subject to WHT at 4.95%. The 16.5% rate applies if the royalties are received by or accrued to a non-resident from an associate, unless the Commissioner is satisfied that no person carrying on business in Hong Kong has at any time wholly or partly owned the property in respect of which the royalties are paid.
3. Since a higher rate is specified in the treaty, the lower domestic/non-treaty rate of 4.95% will apply.

H

Tax administration

Taxable period

A year of assessment (or tax year) begins on 1 April of a year and ends on 31 March of the following year. The period that is used to compute the taxable profits for a year of assessment is called the basis period, which is normally the financial year ended in the year of assessment.

Tax returns

Tax returns are issued on the first working day of April each year. The filing deadline is usually within a month from the date of issue. However, corporations whose financial year ended after 30 November and are represented by a tax representative are normally granted with an extension for filing their returns. The exact filing due date depends on the accounting year end date of the taxpayer.

The basis of assessment is the accounting profits of the financial year ending within the year of assessment, with appropriate adjustments for tax purposes. A tax return is usually filed together with a tax computation showing the tax adjustments to the accounting profits in arriving at the taxable profits or allowable tax losses for a given year of assessment.

Corporate taxpayers are also required to attach their audited accounts as supporting documents when filing a profits tax return, unless they qualify as a small corporation as defined by the HKIRD (i.e. mainly those with gross income for a basis period of not exceeding HKD 2 million plus a few other conditions). Small corporations are not required to attach supporting documents with their profits tax returns but are still required to keep those documents and submit them upon request. A branch of a foreign corporation doing business in Hong Kong is required to file a profits tax return annually, and the HKIRD may require audited accounts of the foreign corporation to support the Hong Kong branch's profits tax return.

Hong Kong

Notice of assessment will be issued after the tax return has been examined by the HKIRD. Taxpayers may be subject to post-assessment investigation or field audit under the computerised random selection procedures of the HKIRD at a later date.

Payment of tax
The dates of payment of tax are determined by the HKIRD Commissioner and specified in the assessment notice. A system of provisional tax payments applies whereby estimated tax payments are made during the current year. The provisional profits tax payable is normally estimated based on the previous year's profits tax liability. The provisional profits tax already paid is credited against the final profits tax assessed for a year of assessment, which is determined after filing of the return.

Tax audit cycle
There is no specific tax audit cycle in Hong Kong. Tax audit targets are selected with reference to certain criteria determined by the HKIRD.

Statute of limitations
An additional assessment may be made by a HKIRD tax assessor if a taxpayer chargeable to tax has not been assessed to tax or has been assessed at less than the proper amount. The assessment must be made within the relevant year of assessment or within six years after the end of that year of assessment. The time limit for making additional assessments is extended when a taxpayer either has not been assessed, or is under-assessed, due to fraud or wilful evasion. In that case, an additional assessment may be made up to ten years after the end of the relevant assessment year.

A statement of loss is not an assessment, and the above six-year time limit does not apply to issue or revision of a statement of loss. A tax loss year remains technically open until the sixth year after the first year in which the taxpayer has an assessable profit after utilising all the tax losses brought forward.

Topics of focus for tax authorities
Profits tax issues that are often subject to close scrutiny of the tax authority include offshore claim of profits, capital claims of income, transactions with related parties and closely connected non-residents, and deductibility of expenses (e.g. interest expenses, share-based payments, and intra-group management/service fees).

General anti-avoidance rules (GAAR)
The IRO includes a GAAR (i.e. section 61A) allowing the HKIRD to disregard a transaction or counteract the tax benefit conferred by a transaction if the sole or dominant purpose of entering into such a transaction is to obtain a tax benefit. Whether the sole or dominant purpose of entering into a transaction is for obtaining a tax benefit will be assessed according to a set of factors stipulated in section 61A. Another GAAR in the IRO is section 61, which empowers the HKIRD to disregard a transaction that reduces or would reduce the amount of tax payable by any person if that transaction is considered artificial or fictitious. Although both GAARs could be used, in practice, section 61A is more often invoked by the HKIRD in tackling tax avoidance schemes.

Specific anti-avoidance provision for related party transactions
In addition to the general anti-avoidance provisions described above, there is a specific anti-avoidance provision dealing with transactions with closely connected non-residents. Under the specific provision, if a resident person carries on a business with a closely connected non-resident person such that no profits or less than the ordinary profits are derived by the resident person in the course of such business, the non-

resident person can be assessable and chargeable to tax in respect of his profits derived from such business in the name of the resident person.

Other issues

Foreign investment restrictions

In general, Hong Kong does not impose restriction to foreign investors to make investments in Hong Kong; and wholly foreign owned companies are allowed. The only exception is the restriction on foreign ownership of Hong Kong's licensed television/ sound broadcasters, of which the collective foreign ownership ceiling is 49% of the voting power. In addition, an approval from the Broadcasting Authority must be obtained for holding, acquisition, or exercise of voting control by a foreign investor of more than 2% of a licensee.

Exchange controls

Hong Kong does not have any foreign exchange control. There is no restriction on entry or repatriation of capital or remittance of profits from investments. Funds can be freely remitted to persons outside Hong Kong by various means such as dividends, interest, royalties, service fees, and branch profits, etc.

Choice of business entity

The principal forms through which a business can be conducted in Hong Kong are as follows:

- Company incorporated in Hong Kong (either private or public via listing on the Stock Exchange of Hong Kong).
- Branch of a foreign company.
- Representative or liaison office of a foreign company.
- Joint venture (can be set up either as a company or partnership).
- Partnership.
- Sole proprietorship.

Of the above, privately incorporated companies and branches of a foreign companies are most commonly used by foreign investors, as limited liability is usually desirable.

Intellectual property (IP) regulations

The Intellectual Property Department is responsible for monitoring the IP regime and ensuring the protection and enforcement of IP rights in Hong Kong. The Department is also responsible for investigating complaints against infringements and has extensive powers of search and seizure. Registration and protection of patents, copyrights, trademarks, and registered designs are each governed by a separate ordinance.

Merger and acquisition (M&A) activities

There are no specific restrictions on M&A activities in Hong Kong. The following tax considerations are relevant in the M&A context:

- Dividends or other forms of distribution of profits (e.g. distribution of branch profits to the head office) are generally not taxable.
- Capital gains arising from an M&A transaction is not taxable in the hands of the transferor, whereas amortisation of the goodwill in the transferee's accounts is not tax deductible due to its capital nature.

Hong Kong

- For a share deal, stamp duty is payable on the transfer of Hong Kong shares at 0.2% unless an exemption applies; for an asset deal, stamp duty is payable on conveyance of immovable property in Hong Kong at progressive rates of up to 4.25%
- Gains derived from transfer of revenue items (e.g. trade receivables) in an asset deal would be subject to profits tax.
- There is no special tax concession/incentive relating to M&A transactions.
- Tax losses in the acquired company can generally be carried forward indefinitely to set off against future assessable profits. However, there are specific anti-avoidance provisions in the IRO that prevent the transfer of shares of a company with accumulated tax losses to owners of a profitable company for the sole or dominant purpose of utilising the tax losses i.e. offsetting the tax losses against the profits generated from other trade, profession, or business of the transferee.

Hungary

PwC contact

Tamás Lőcsei
PricewaterhouseCoopers Hungary Ltd
Wesselényi utca 16.
H-1077 Budapest
Hungary
Tel: +36 1 461 9358
Email: tamas.locsei@hu.pwc.com

Significant developments

As of 1 January 2012, the following significant changes were introduced to the
Hungarian tax system.

Corporate income tax (CIT)

- The CIT rate is now 10% on the first 500 million Hungarian forint (HUF)
  (approximately 1.58 million euros [EUR]) of a positive CIT base. The tax base above
  this limit is subject to 19% CIT.
- Significant changes to the loss carryforward legislation.
- Introduction of the sport support scheme, which enables companies supporting
  sport organisations to realise up to 119% tax savings on the support provided.
- Introduction of 'registered intangible assets'.
- The thin capitalisation rule now covers non-interest bearing loans as well.

Value-added tax (VAT)

- The general VAT rate increased to 27%.
- The VAT payable on the lease of vehicles for taxable activities is also deductible.
- The opportunity to request a more frequent filing of VAT returns remains available
  for taxpayers who are constantly in a VAT reclaimer's position.
- Changes in the rules on the so-called supply chain transactions: it is possible only for
  the intermediary participant to disprove the legal presumption according to which it
  participated in the transaction as the buyer, and to prove that it took the position of
  the seller.
- The rules on subsequent tax base modification change:
  - The tax base also decreases in cases when the parties have invoiced higher
    amounts than they had agreed on by mistake and when the prepayment given
    before the supply is only partially paid back due to the lack of supply.
  - The number of cases when there is no need for self-revision has increased.
    Therefore, in case in which the amount of taxes due has been decreased due to
    an erroneously used higher tax rate, and not because of a tax rate reduction,
    taxpayers do not need to conduct a self-revision to determine the correct amount
    of tax.
- The rules on the period of limitation has to be applied again to the reclaimable VAT
  carried forward (the deductible VAT can be carried forward only within the period
  of limitation).
- Information in whether a taxpayer has opted for the taxation of the supply of real
  estate will be available on the official website of the Hungarian Tax Authority.
- The VAT treatment of certain transactions during the VAT warehousing procedures
  has changed.
- Extension of the invoicing obligation.
- Refinement of the rules on electronic invoicing.

Hungary

- The market price applicable between related parties has to be taken into account in the apportionment calculations.
- As of 1 February 2012, the deadline for VAT refund increased to 75 days. As an exception, the authorities still have 30 days, or 45 days in the case of a refund that exceeds HUF 1 million, if all the invoices that are affected in the reclaim are cleared.

Excise duty
- Excise duty rates of alcohol and tobacco products increased as of 1 November 2011 and again as of 1 February 2012.
- A new duty rate was introduced for beers, abolishing the distinction between regular beers and flavoured beers.
- Companies with an Authorised Economic Operator (AEO) certificate qualify as a reliable debtor, which may enable the reduction of the amount of excise guarantee.

Public health product tax
Legislation was introduced on 1 September 2011 under which the first domestic distributor of certain products is liable to pay a product tax. The products which fall under this new product tax are beverages, energy drinks, cocoa powder with added sugar, other pre-packed product with sugar, salty snacks, seasonings, flavoured beer and alcoholic beverages, and fruit jam. The rates vary depending on tariff number and salt, sugar, cocoa, methyl-xanthine, or taurin content.

Environmental protection product fee
A new regulation replaced the previous legislation on 1 January 2012.

This new legislation abolished the tax exemption system through coordinating organisations. This will mean that the total tax amount will be payable to the state.

Packaging materials, instead of packaging, will be subject to the product fee. This means that the first distributor of packaging materials (e.g. packaging material producers) or the company that uses packaging materials for its own purposes will have to pay the tax.

Registration taxes
The registration tax rates decreased significantly from 1 January 2012. The applicable rates are as follows:

- Passenger cars: HUF 45,000 to HUF 4.8 million (approximately EUR 143 to EUR 15,225), depending on the technical features of vehicles (cc, engine type) and environmental classification.
- Hybrid or electrical cars: HUF 0 to HUF 76,000 (approximately EUR 241).
- Motorcycles: HUF 20,000 to HUF 230,000 (approximately EUR 70 to EUR 900), depending on technical features of the motorcycles (cc).

The registration tax is also payable by fleet operators.

Food chain supervision fee
Under the amendment to Act XLVI of 2008 on the Food Chain and its Official Supervision adopted at the end of 2011, certain players in the food chain (e.g. food producers and distributors) are required to pay a supervision fee from 2012. The fee is 0.1% of the net sales revenue (excluding excise duty and the public health product tax) derived in the preceding year from activities that fall within the scope of the Act.

Disaster management contribution
The new rules of the 'disaster management contribution' entered into force on 1 January 2012.

The purpose of the contribution is to facilitate the acquisition, upgrading, and renewal of technical equipment and tools used for disaster management; to cover expenses related to disaster prevention, training, and equipment for civil protection organisations; and to provide support to volunteer emergency services.

The following taxpayers will be required to pay the contribution:

- Natural or legal persons and organisations without legal personality engaged in the operation of a plant or other facility dealing with hazardous substances or exercising a controlling influence on the operation of such a facility.
- Economic operators, other than those listed above, that store, manufacture, or process goods subject to the provisions of the European agreement (known as ADR) that regulates the international carriage of hazardous goods by road.

The amount of the contribution will be 0.1% of the annual net sales revenue deriving from the hazardous activity (minus the amount of excise duty and energy tax paid) or the net value of the hazardous goods used.

According to the recent statements of the Hungarian government, it could be possible that the disaster management contribution will be abolished before its first collection in 2012.

Taxes on corporate income

Resident taxpayers are subject to all-inclusive or unlimited CIT liability. Non-residents are subject to CIT on their income from their Hungarian branch's business activities.

The CIT rate is 10% on the first HUF 500 million (approximately EUR 1.58 million) of a positive CIT base without any further preconditions. The tax base above this limit is subject to 19% CIT.

Minimum tax base
If a company's CIT base or the pre-tax profit, whichever is higher, is less than 2% of its total revenues reduced by the cost of goods sold, the value of mediated services, and the income of the foreign permanent establishments (PE) (i.e. the 'minimum tax base'), the company can choose to file a declaration and pay CIT either according to the general provisions or on its minimum tax base.

Special income tax
Companies with the following activities are liable to pay a special 'austerity' tax:

- Retail sales in stores.
- Telecommunications activity.
- Business activity of energy suppliers.

The special 'austerity' tax base is the net sales revenue and not the pre-tax profit. The tax rates are progressive and depend on the company's business activity, as follows:

Hungary

Retail sales in stores
Tax base is the net sales plus revenue on services provided to retail supplier and revenue from discount.

Tax base (HUF)	Rate (%)
0 to 500 million	0
500 million to 30 billion	0.1
30 billion to 100 billion	0.4
above 100 billion	2.5

Telecommunications activity
Tax base is the net sales revenue of the activity of telecommunication.

Tax base (HUF)	Rate (%)
0 to 500 million	0
500 million to 5 billion	4.5
above 5 billion	6.5

Business activity of energy suppliers
Tax base is the net sales revenue of the activity of supplying energy.

Tax base (HUF)	Rate (%)
0 to 5 billion	0.3
500 million to 5 billion	1.05

Financial organisations are also subject to an industry specific special tax, the rate and base of which depend on their scope of activities.

Local taxes/local business tax
All municipalities are entitled to levy local taxes. Local taxes are deductible for Hungarian CIT purposes and are not normally treated as 'income tax' in the application of the tax treaties.

The local business tax base is the net sales revenue reduced by the cost of goods sold, subcontractors' work, the costs of materials, mediated services, and research and development (R&D) costs. General service fees, depreciation, and labour costs are typically not deductible for local business tax purposes. 100% of royalty, interest, or dividend income and the local business tax base of a foreign PE of a Hungarian company are exempt from local business tax. The local business tax rate may differ from municipality to municipality but is capped at 2% by law.

A special tax base allocation method is applicable for companies in the telecommunications sector. The allocation is based on the net revenues a company realises in the municipalities where its clients' billing addresses are located.

Innovation contribution
Companies defined as such in the Accounting Act, except for small and medium-sized enterprises and branches, are also subject to an innovation contribution. The tax base of the innovation contribution is the same as the local business tax base. The tax rate is 0.3%. Additionally, the direct costs of R&D are deductible from the tax payable

(not the tax base). As of 1 January 2012, the definition of R&D is included in the Hungarian domestic legislation as opposed to the earlier practice of referencing the Frascati Manual.

Corporate residence

Corporations are residents for CIT purposes if they are incorporated in Hungary, although foreign corporations may also be deemed to be Hungarian residents for CIT purposes if their place of effective management is in Hungary.

Foreign entities may carry out business through resident corporations or through PEs (branches). Commercial representative offices may be opened for auxiliary activities which do not create a taxable presence.

Permanent establishment (PE)

Hungary treats PEs as separate and distinct entities, and profit is attributed to a PE based on the principles set out in the Organisation for Economic Co-operation and Development (OECD) guidelines.

In the Corporate Income Tax Act a PE is defined as fixed business premises (machinery or equipment) through which the entrepreneurial activity of an enterprise is partly or wholly carried on, regardless of the title of the taxpayer to those premises. A PE may consist of any of the following: a place of management; offices, including representative offices, registered in Hungary; factories and workshops; and mines, crude oil or natural gas wells, quarries, or other places from which natural resources are extracted.

Construction sites (including assembly) and related supervisory activities constitute a PE if they last, in the aggregate, for at least three months in a calendar year. All activities carried out at the same construction site qualify together as a single PE, regardless of whether they are based on separate contracts or were ordered by different persons. Construction sites are defined as sites which represent a unit for economic, business, and geographical purposes.

PEs are also created by the direct utilisation of natural resources by a foreign person. A foreign person is deemed to have a PE in Hungary if it utilises natural resources or immovable property for consideration, including the alienation of any rights related to the immovable property or natural resources.

A non-resident enterprise is considered to have a PE with respect to activities undertaken on its behalf by another person if its agent is authorised to conclude contracts in Hungary on behalf of the non-resident entity and the agent regularly exercises this right or maintains a stock of goods and products from which it regularly makes deliveries in the name of the non-resident entity.

The insurance of risks occurring in Hungary and insured on behalf of the non-resident person by another person constitutes a PE of the foreign insurer, except for reinsurance activities.

Furthermore, as mentioned above, a foreign taxpayer must also be treated as having a PE if it has a Hungarian branch.

The definition of a PE does not include the following:

Hungary

- Establishments used solely for the purpose of storing and presenting the goods or products of a non-resident person.
- The stockpiling of goods and products solely for the purpose of storing, presenting, or processing by another person.
- Establishments used for collecting information, or purchasing goods and products, exclusively for the non-resident person.
- Establishments used for other activities of a preparatory or auxiliary nature.
- Activities of independent agents, provided they are acting in their ordinary course of business.

Note that a different definition of a PE is applicable for local business tax, and no definition is available for special 'austerity' tax.

Other taxes

Value-added tax (VAT)

VAT is payable on sales of goods and the provision of services. VAT is also payable on the importation of intra-Community acquisitions of goods and on the purchase of certain services provided to Hungarian companies by foreign suppliers.

The general VAT rate is 27%.

A reduced VAT rate of 18% is applicable for some products, such as milk, certain dairy products, bread and other bakery products, and hotel and holiday accommodation.

A reduced VAT rate of 5% is available for most medicines and books.

Certain services are exempt from VAT, including, but not limited to, medical, cultural, sporting, and educational services provided as public services; and financial and insurance services. Intra-Community supplies of services and exports are also treated as exempt transactions. For the rental of real estate and for the sale of real estate and land (except building land), VAT exemption is optional. In the case of the sale of residential property, the exemption does not include the sales before it was put into usage and the sales within two years from the date when the usage permit becomes effective.

VAT deduction is available for the business-related element of purchases made partially for non-business purposes.

Under the new general VAT liability regulations, VAT is also chargeable if an invoice is issued but the supply is not carried out.

Place-of-supply rules

The general rule for business to business (B2B) services is that the place of supply is where the customer is established. Some exceptions to this rule have been introduced (e.g. for facilitating entry to cultural, artistic, scientific, educational, entertainment, and sports events and catering services, the place of supply is where the service is physically carried out; for short term hire [not longer than 30 days, 90 days for vessels] of transport, the place of supply is where the asset is put at the disposal of the customer; for services connected to immovable property, the place of supply is where the property is located).

The general rule for business to consumer (B2C) services is that the place of supply is where the supplier is established. Some exceptions to this rule have been introduced (e.g. for passenger transport and non-EU transport of goods, the place of supply is where the transport takes place; for services relating to cultural, artistic, sports, scientific, educational, entertainment, or similar activities, the place of supply is where the activities are physically carried out; for restaurant and catering services, the place of supply is where physically carried out).

Reverse charge mechanism

A domestic reverse charge applies between Hungarian taxable persons for a variety of activities in addition to the sale of waste materials, including construct and install services and services related to real property (repairs, maintenance).

VAT recovery

If a taxpayer has a negative VAT balance in a return period, this amount can be recovered provided that the tax balance reaches or exceeds an absolute value of HUF 1 million for monthly filers, HUF 250,000 for quarterly filers, or HUF 50,000 for annual filers. The condition that only the VAT content of financially settled invoices is reclaimable has been repealed as of 27 November 2011.

Directive for refunds of foreign European Union (EU) taxable persons

EU-registered non-Hungarian taxable persons can recover local VAT. In the new system, refund applications have to be submitted electronically, and the rules governing the time available/deadlines for tax authorities in certain phases of the procedure have changed. Reclaim requests should be submitted to the Tax Authority of the country where the taxable person is established.

Reporting obligations for cross-border transactions

A new requirement is that suppliers of cross-border services must submit full statements for each VAT return period of all the services supplied to taxable and non-taxable legal persons where the latter are liable for VAT in their own country. Please note that purchase lists are required in Hungary in addition to European Community (EC) sales.

Group taxation

The VAT Act allows all companies that have established business presences in Hungary and qualify as related enterprises to form a VAT group. The essence of a VAT group is that its members act under a single VAT number in their transactions (i.e. they issue invoices under a shared VAT number and submit a single, joint tax return), and product and service supplies between the members do not qualify as business transactions from a VAT perspective.

Customs duties

Hungarian customs legislation and policies have been fully harmonised with EU legislation.

The EU customs legislation is comprised of the following main regulations:

* Council Regulation 2913/92/EEC establishing the Community Customs Code.
* Council Regulation 2454/93/EEC laying down provisions for the implementation of Council Regulation 2913/92/EEC establishing the Community Customs Code.
* Council Regulation 1186/2009/EEC setting up a Community system of reliefs from customs duty.
* Council Regulation 2658/87/EEC on the tariff and statistical nomenclature and on the Common Customs Tariff.

Hungary

Excise taxes

The following goods are subject to excise duty:

- Mineral oils.
- Alcohol and alcoholic beverages. Any product with an alcohol content of 1.2% or more by volume qualifies as an alcohol product.
- Beers.
- Wines.
- Sparkling wines.
- Intermediate alcoholic products.
- Tobacco products.

As of 1 January 2012, the excise duty rates are as follows:

- Petroleum products: HUF 110,350 to HUF 124,200 (approximately EUR 350 to EUR 394) per thousand litres or HUF 4,425 to HUF 116,000 (approximately EUR 14 to EUR 368) per thousand kilograms, depending on the type of petroleum product.
- Alcohol products: HUF 289,900 to EUR 414,150 (approximately EUR 920 to EUR 1,313) per hectolitre of pure alcohol.
- Beer: HUF 1,470 (approximately EUR 4.6) per alcohol degree and per hectolitre.
- Wines: HUF 0 for grape wines; HUF 9,870 (approximately EUR 31) per hectolitre for wines made from other types of fruit.
- Sparkling wines: HUF 14,960 (approximately EUR 47) per hectolitre.
- Intermediate alcoholic products: HUF 23,200 (approximately EUR 73) per hectolitre or HUF 735 (approximately EUR 2.3) per alcohol degree and per hectolitre for beer produced in a micro-brewery.
- Cigarettes: HUF 11,500 (approximately EUR 39) per thousand cigarettes plus 30% of the retail sale price, but a minimum of HUF 21,100 per thousand cigarettes. The tax base per cigarette also depends on the length of the cigarette (without filter). It is double if the length of the cigarette is 8 cm to 11 cm, triple if the length is 11 cm to 14 cm, and so on.
- Cigars and cigarillos: 28.5% of the retail price.
- Fine-cut tobacco: 52% of the retail price, but a minimum of HUF 10,150 (approximately EUR 34) per kilogram.
- Other tobacco: 32.5% of the retail price, but a minimum of HUF 10,150 (approximately EUR 34) per kilogram.

The Customs Body of the National Tax and Customs Authority is responsible for excise duty. The European Union's excise duty rules apply in Hungary.

Property and land taxes

Hungarian municipalities can levy property tax and land tax at their own discretion.

Property tax

The owner of a building is subject to property tax liability annually on the first day of the calendar year.

The local government can determine the tax base in either of the following ways:

- The net floor space of the building expressed in square metres, with a maximum tax rate of HUF 1,100/m2.
- The adjusted market value of the building, with a maximum tax rate of 3.6% of the adjusted market value.

Land tax

The owner of the land is subject to land tax liability annually on the first day of the calendar year. Undeveloped plots of land situated within the area of jurisdiction of a local government, including peripheries, are subject to this tax. The local government can determine the tax base in either of the following ways:

- The actual area of the plot expressed in square metres, with a maximum tax rate of HUF 200/m^2.
- The adjusted market value of the plot, with a maximum tax rate of 3% of the adjusted market value.

Stamp duty

Stamp duty has to be paid on the acquisition of a direct or indirect participation of at least 75% in a company that owns real estate (even if the real estate is a minor part of its total assets). Exceptions may be available if certain criteria are met.

There is no transfer tax in Hungary, but transfers of direct or indirect participations in companies that own real estate may be subject to stamp duty.

Transfers of real estate-owning companies' shares between related parties are exempt from real estate transfer tax.

H

CIT

A company and its related parties are defined as real estate holding companies if at least 75% of the market value of their assets is domestic real estate and if they have a foreign shareholder that is not resident in a country that has a double tax treaty (DTT) with Hungary or the treaty allows capital gains to be taxed in Hungary.

The tax base of real estate holding companies in cases of share transfers and share capital decreases is the positive amount of the consideration minus the acquisition price of the shares less the costs of acquisition and of administration. The tax rate is the same as is mentioned in the *Taxes on corporate income* section.

Please note that the definition of the payer for CIT purposes is very different from the definition used for stamp duty purposes.

Stamp duties

The most common types of stamp duty are gift duty and duty on transfers of property for consideration. Stamp duty is levied on movable and immovable property and property rights if they were acquired in Hungary, unless an international agreement rules otherwise.

Gift duty

Gift duty arises on the date when a contract concerning a gift is concluded.

Transfers of movable property, immovable property, and property rights without consideration are subject to gift duty. In these cases, however, gift duty is only incurred if the transaction was formally documented; except for immovable property with a market value of more than HUF 150,000 (approximately EUR 475) , where gift duty must be paid in any event.

The base of gift duty is the net value of the gift, which is the market value minus any liabilities related to the gift. The general duty rates vary, depending on the base, as follows:

Hungary

- 21% for a base of up to HUF 18 million (approximately EUR 58,000).
- 30% on the part of the base exceeding HUF 18 million, up to HUF 35 million (approximately EUR 111,000).
- 40% on the part of the base exceeding HUF 35 million.

Transfers of movable assets without consideration and acquisitions of claims without consideration including waivers of claims and assumptions of debts are exempt from gift duty, provided that the recipient is a company.

Furthermore, if a company is 100% owned by the other company in the transaction, or both companies are 100% owned by a third party, a reduced rate on transfer of assets, including immovable property without consideration, should be applied as follows:

- 11% for a base of up to HUF 18 million (approximately EUR 58,000).
- 15% on the part of the base exceeding HUF 18 million, up to HUF 35 million (approximately EUR 111,000).
- 21% on the part of the base exceeding HUF 35 million.

Duty on transfer of property for consideration

The obligation to pay duty on the transfer of movable and immovable property for consideration arises on the date when the contract is concluded.

For acquisitions of real estate, the stamp duty is 4% of the market value of the property. For acquisitions of direct or indirect participations (stocks, shares, co-operative shares, investor shares, converted investor shares) in a company that owns real estate, the duty base is the part of the market value of the company's properties held that represents the percentage of the participation, except when the transaction is between related parties. The stamp duty for real estate company sales is 4% up to HUF 1 billion and 2% of the amount exceeding HUF 1 billion (approximately EUR 3.2 million) up to a maximum of HUF 200 million (approximately EUR 635,000).

There are special rules for real estate trading companies and credit institutions. Under certain circumstances, exemptions are available more generally.

Stamp duties are also levied on certain court procedures (e.g. Court of Registration) and on submissions to certain authorities (e.g. appeals to the Tax Authority). Stamp duty is, for instance, levied in an amount of:

- HUF 100,000 (approximately EUR 320) on the registration of a private stock company or a limited liability company
- HUF 600,000 (approximately EUR 1,920) on the registration of a public stock company or a European Company
- HUF 100,000 (approximately EUR 320) on the registration of any other entity with legal personality
- HUF 50,000 (approximately EUR 160) on the registration of a branch office, and
- HUF 50,000 (approximately EUR 160) on the registration of a representative office.

Registration taxes

Registration tax is charged on passenger cars, motor homes, and motorcycles before they can be registered and put into service in Hungary. The registration tax is also payable by fleet operators. The duty is payable with the first domestic registration or in the case of a conversion.

The registration tax rate from 1 January 2012 is applied as follows:

Hungary

- Passenger cars: HUF 45,000 to HUF 4.8 million (approximately EUR 143 to EUR 15,225), depending on the technical features of vehicles (cc, engine type) and environmental classification.
- Hybrid or electrical cars: HUF 0 to HUF 76,000 (approximately EUR 241).
- Motorcycles: HUF 20,000 to HUF 230,000 (approximately EUR 70 to EUR 900), depending on technical features of the motorcycles (cc).

The registration tax is levied by the Customs Body of the National Tax and Customs Authority.

Public health product tax

Legislation was introduced on 1 September 2011 under which the first domestic distributor of certain products is liable to pay a product tax. The duty rates from 1 January 2012 are as follows:

- Beverages (depending on sugar content and tariff number): HUF 7 (approximately EUR 0.02) or HUF 200 (approximately EUR 0.63) per litre.
- Energy drink (depending on tariff number, methyl-xanthine and taurin content): HUF 250 (approximately EUR 0.79) per litre.
- Cocoa powder with added sugar (depending on tariff number, sugar and cocoa content): HUF 70 (approximately EUR 0.22) per kilogram.
- Other pre-packed product with sugar (depending on tariff number, sugar and cocoa content): HUF 130 (approximately EUR 0.41) per kilogram.
- Salty snacks (depending on tariff number and salt content): HUF 250 (approximately EUR 0.79) per kilogram.
- Seasonings (depending on tariff number and salt content): HUF 250 (approximately EUR 0.79) per kilogram.
- Flavoured beer and alcoholic beverages (depending on tariff number and sugar content): HUF 20 (approximately EUR 0.06) per litre.
- Fruit jam (depending on tariff number and sugar content): HUF 500 (approximately EUR 1.58) per kilogram.

Environmental protection product fee

The following products are subject to the environmental protection product fee: other crude oil products, tyres, packaging materials, batteries, commercial printing paper, and electrical and electronic products (based on customs tariff numbers applicable on 1 January 2010).

The following entities are liable to pay the product fee:

- The first domestic distributor or user for own purposes.
- In the case of domestically manufactured other crude oil products, the first buyer from the first domestic distributor.
- In the case of toll manufacturing, the party that orders the toll manufacturing.

Product fee rates from 1 January 2012 are as follows:

- Tyres: HUF 52 (approximately EUR 0.16) per kilogram.
- Packaging materials: HUF 17 to HUF 50 (approximately EUR 0.05 to EUR 0.16) per kilogram.
- Commercial packaging materials (packaging of beverages, plastic shopping bags): HUF 17 to HUF 1,800 (approximately EUR 0.05 to EUR 5.7) per kilogram.
- Oil: HUF 112 (approximately EUR 0.35) per kilogram.

Hungary

- Batteries: HUF 60 (approximately EUR 0.19) or HUF 80 (approximately EUR 0.25) per kilogram.
- Paper-based advertisement materials: HUF 64 (approximately EUR 0.20) per kilogram.
- Electrical and electronic products: HUF 50 to HUF 500 (approximately EUR 0.16 to EUR 1.58) per kilogram.

The Customs Body of the National Tax and Customs Authority controls the payment and reporting of the product fee and carries out product fee inspections. The Customs Authority registers taxpayers by customs number. The product fee is self-assessed. The product fee return must be submitted quarterly to the Customs Authority via its electronic system. An advancement payment is payable for the fourth quarter.

The product fee penalty is generally 100% of the product fee shortfall in cases of non-payment or underpayment.

Environmental load charges

Environmental pollution charges were introduced to protect the natural environment, to reduce its impairment, to encourage the users of the environment to engage in activities aimed at the preservation of the natural environment, and to provide funding from the central budget for environmental protection and nature preservation.

Emitting entities liable to pay charges include those who operate point-source emitters subject to registration, pursue activities subject to a water right permit, or who do not use available public drainage systems and dispose of their sewage under a water right permit or a permit from the local water management authorities.

Qualifying materials include sulphur dioxide, nitrogen oxides, mercury, phosphorous, cyanides, and others.

The load charge is calculated on the basis of the quantity of emitted materials multiplied by the fee rate. Basically, the amount of the fee payable depends on the hazard level of the emitted material, e.g. HUF 50 (approximately EUR 0.2) per kilogram for sulphur dioxide and HUF 220,000 (approximately EUR 846) per kilogram for mercury.

Energy tax

Goods are subject to energy tax at the following rates:

- Electricity: HUF 295 (approximately EUR 1) per megawatt hour.
- Coal: HUF 2,390 (approximately EUR 9) per thousand kilograms.
- Natural gas: HUF 88.5 (approximately EUR 0.3) per gigajoule.

The following entities are subject to energy tax:

- Energy traders.
- End-users.
- Producers.

The tax is self-assessed, except in the case of imports, and the Customs Body of the National Tax and Customs Authority is responsible for the related customs administration procedures.

Food chain supervision fee

The purpose of the new food chain supervision fee is to raise revenue for the operation of a regulatory body tasked with the official supervision of the food chain.

The supervision fee is payable by the following natural persons or economic operators:

- Persons who place animals on the market that are kept for food production, breeding, or experimental purposes.
- Persons who place food or fodder crops, seeds, plant products, and planting material on the market.
- Food businesses.
- Registered or authorised feed businesses.
- Persons who manufacture or place on the market veterinary medicines or veterinary medicinal products.
- Persons who manufacture or place on the market 'EEC fertiliser' or other products subject to authorisation.
- Persons involved In the handling, use, further processing, and transport of animal by-products or placing derived products on the market.
- Businesses engaged in the transport of live animals.
- Persons operating facilities for the cleaning and disinfection of vehicles used for transport of live animals, isolation facilities for receiving animals from different stocks, livestock loading ramps, assembly centres, trading sites, feeding and watering stations, rest stations and livestock fairs.
- Persons manufacturing and storing plant propagation material.
- Persons operating a registered or authorised laboratory.
- Persons placing devices on the market that are used for marking animals.

The fee is 0.1% of the net sales revenue (excluding excise duty and the public health product tax) derived in the preceding year from these activities.

The taxpayers concerned will have to comply with their reporting obligation by 31 May. The annual supervision fee is payable in two equal instalments: the first by 31 July, and the second by 31 January. The supervision fee will first have to be paid in full by 31 July 2012.

Branch income

Foreign companies may establish branch offices in Hungary. A branch office is an organisational unit of a foreign company without legal personality, vested with financial autonomy, and registered in the Hungarian companies register as a branch office of the foreign company. The provisions of the Hungarian Accounting Act apply to branch offices, which must prepare reports using double-entry bookkeeping. Statutory audits are obligatory, except for the branches of corporations whose registered office address is in the European Union.

A branch office is regarded as established when it has been entered into the companies register. A branch office may start operating once the application for registering the branch office has been submitted to the Court of registration, provided that it indicates 'under registration' on its corporate correspondence. Until a branch has been registered, it cannot carry out any activities that are subject to official permission. A branch office is considered dissolved upon its removal from the companies register.

Hungary

Branch offices are treated as PEs for taxation purposes. They must determine their tax base according to the general rules applicable to Hungarian companies. The profit for the year (calculated on the basis of the Hungarian accounting system and adjusted by specific provisions of the Corporate Tax and Dividend Tax Act or CDTA) is subject to CIT of 10% on the first HUF 500 million of the positive CIT base. The tax base above this limit is subject to 19% CIT. The definition of PE is similar to that in the tax treaties but somewhat broader. For treaty countries, the respective treaty definition applies.

A foreign company's CIT base is determined for all its domestic PEs (except for branches) collectively and for its branches separately. A branch should account for costs and revenues as if it were independent from its foreign parent company.

For a Hungarian PE, earnings before taxes are reduced by cumulated administrative costs incurred proportionately at the headquarters and any of its PEs, with the maximum proportion defined as the revenues of the PE compared to all revenues of the foreign company.

The increasing items for a Hungarian PE are the administrative costs accounted by the PE plus 5% of the revenue earned by the PE's activities but accounted elsewhere.

However, if there is a treaty between Hungary and the other country, the provisions of the treaty have priority over domestic law. Therefore, the provisions of the treaty have to be followed in the first instance, and all costs related to the activity of the branch have to be allocated to the branch, without the above restrictions in domestic law, and all profit realised with respect to the branch must also be allocated to the branch. The allocation method must be consistent from year to year, unless there is a good reason for changing it.

The foreign parent must continuously provide the assets and funds required for the operation of the branch office and the settlement of its liabilities. The employees of a branch office are in a legal relationship with the foreign company, and the foreign parent exercises employer's rights. A branch is considered to be related to its parent company/headquarters. Therefore, the prices used in inter-company transactions have to be at arm's length, and transfer pricing documentation has to be prepared.

Income determination

The CIT base should be calculated by modifying the accounting pre-tax profit by adjustments and deductions as provided by the CDTA.

Inventory valuation
Inventories are generally valued at their historical cost unless their fair market value is significantly lower than their book value, in which case, the fair market value should be recorded. Cost may be determined on the basis of first in first out (FIFO) or average cost.

Capital gains
Capital gains (losses) are treated as ordinary income (losses) for tax purposes. The gain on the sale of depreciable assets equals the sales revenue reduced by the net value of the asset for CIT purposes.

If a participation (of at least 30%) or an intangible asset is registered within 60 days of acquisition and held continuously for at least one year, capital gains from the sale or contribution in kind of the participation is exempt from CIT in general. Any additional acquisitions in the case of a registered participation may also be registered, provided that the 30% participation was already registered.

Stock transactions
Shareholders of a real estate holding company are also subject to CIT on their income from the sale of the shares in the real estate holding company. Transfers of direct or indirect participations in companies that own real estate may be subject to CIT.

Dividend income
Except in the case of controlled foreign companies (CFCs) (*see the Group taxation section*), dividends received and accounted for as income in the given tax year are tax-free. As of 1 January 2012, a definition of dividend is given in the CDTA.

Interest income
No specific provision exists in Hungary for interest income. Therefore, interest income is taxable for CIT purposes.

Royalty income
50% of royalty income is deductible for CIT purposes, up to 50% of pre-tax profit. Royalties as revenues are derived from (i) permission for the exploitation of patents, from the industrial design of assets under industrial law, and from know-how; (ii) permission to use trademarks, business names, and business secrets; (iii) permission to use copyrights and similar rights attached to protected work; (iv) transfers of the property described above (except for trademarks, business names, and business secrets).

Unrealised exchange gains/losses
Tax deferral may be chosen for unrealised exchange gains/losses.

Foreign income
Taxpayers resident in Hungary and foreign entrepreneurs must calculate their CIT base exclusive of any income that is subject to taxation abroad, if so prescribed by an international treaty. In any other case, a foreign tax credit is available for income taxes paid abroad (*see Foreign tax credit in the Tax credits and incentives section for more information*).

In Hungary, there are no provisions under which income earned abroad may be tax deferred.

Deductions

In general, costs and expenses incurred in relation to the taxpayer's income-generating business activity are deductible for CIT purposes.

Accrued expenses are recognised for taxation purposes in the tax year they affect.

Depreciation and amortisation
Accounting depreciation that is accounted as expenditure, and thus included in the accounting profit, should be added to the CIT base. Tax depreciation calculated according to the CDTA reduces the tax base, even if the tax depreciation is higher than the accounting depreciation. The tax depreciation of tangible assets should be

Hungary

calculated using the straight-line method, on the basis of the historical value from the time when the asset was first used for business purposes.

Examples of tax depreciation rates include the following:

Assets	Depreciation rate (%)
Computers and other high-tech machinery	33 or 50
Vehicles	20
Other tangible assets	14.5
Buildings (long-life structure)	2
Rented buildings	5

Assets newly acquired since 2003 can be depreciated at 50% annually; these instruments include, among other items, machinery and intellectual property (IP).

There is no prescribed amortisation rate for intangibles. The historical value, the residual value, and the useful life should be considered.

Additionally, goodwill cannot be amortised either for accounting or tax purposes if it does not lose its value during its use. However, if extraordinary amortisation is accounted on goodwill, the extraordinary amortisation will also be recognised for CIT purposes. In the case of transformations, specific amortisation rules apply.

Organisational and start-up expenses
Companies are not obliged to capitalise the costs of formation/reorganisation. The capitalisation of these costs is at the company's discretion, but the company should comply with its accounting policy. Furthermore, only the direct costs of formation/ reorganisation that are not classified as investments or renovations and are likely to be recovered ultimately can be capitalised.

Bad debt
Under the Accounting Act, bad debts are only deductible for CIT purposes if they are supported by legally valid third-party documents that the receivable cannot be collected. Expenses claimed that cannot be enforced in court and expired claims are not deductible for CIT purposes.

In addition to the above, 20% of eligible bad debts are deductible from the CIT base if the debt was not settled within 365 days from the due date.

Charitable contributions
Grants made or assets that are transferred without consideration, as well as liabilities assumed or services provided free of charge, will qualify as business expenses if the taxpayer has a declaration from the recipient stating that the recipient's profit will not be negative without the income received.

Grants will always qualify as non-business expenses if they are provided to a foreign person or foreign resident company.

In the case of film and sports (football, basketball, handball, ice-hockey, and water polo) sponsorship grants, the amount of support is deductible both from the CIT base (as an expense) and from the CIT amount, provided that an official sponsorship certificate is available.

Development reserve
50% of pre-tax profit may be assigned as development reserve. The maximum value of the reserve is HUF 500 million (approximately EUR 1.58 million); however, it has increased from four years to six years for development reserves included in the 2008 financial statement. For other development reserves, the period remains four years.

Intellectual property (IP) reserve
Further, there is a possibility to create an IP reserve, from income from sales of intangible assets which generate royalty income, deeming that income non-taxable. The IP reserve should be shown as part of the tied-up reserve in the companies' books. The IP reserve may be used to buy intangible assets which generate royalty income at the company within three years from its creation; otherwise, CIT and late payment penalty should be paid on the amount.

Tax base allowance regarding R&D
A tax base allowance is only applicable for R&D activities if the taxpayer carries out basic research, applied research, or experimental research activities for its own purposes. The direct cost of the basic research, the applied research, and the experimental research, or the amount of depreciation on the research activity (if the cost of R&D activity is capitalised), is deductible from the tax base.

300% of the direct costs of research activity (up to a maximum of HUF 50 million [approximately EUR 158,000]) are deductible from the tax base if the research activity is carried out jointly with a higher education institution, the Hungarian Academy of Sciences, or a research institute established by them.

Employee benefit expenses
Employee benefits and the fringe benefit tax payable on them are tax-deductible.

Bribes, 'kickbacks', other illegal payments
Bribes, 'kickbacks', and illegal payments are not recognised as business costs for CIT purposes and are non-deductible from the tax base.

Fines and penalties
Fines and penalties are not deductible for CIT purposes.

Net operating losses
Losses can be carried forward indefinitely, and the Tax Authority's approval is not required. However, the Tax Authority may later audit whether a company has exercised its rights in accordance with the intended purpose of these rights when carrying losses forward. Furthermore, from 2011, financial institutions can also carry losses forward.

The main changes regarding losses carried forward for 2012 are as follows:

A company's tax losses carried forward cannot be utilised if:

- the majority of the company's shares is directly/indirectly acquired by an independent entity (an entity who was not one of the company's owners in the preceding two financial years)
- the activity of the company changes significantly in the two years following the transformation, or
- the successor company does not generate any revenue from at least one activity of the predecessor.

Hungary

Losses carried forward may only be used to offset up to 50% of the tax base calculated without losses carried forward.

Note that earlier tax losses must be used first (FIFO principle), and the losses of predecessors are also deductible from the successor company's CIT base.

Losses cannot be carried back (except for agricultural companies, who may account deferred losses by self-revision or by correcting the amount of tax paid in the previous two tax years).

Payments to foreign affiliates

There is no general restriction on the deductibility of a consideration due to a foreign entity provided the payment is a justifiable business cost. General anti-avoidance provisions (abuse of law, substance-over-form) may also result in non-deductibility. If the parties are considered to be related parties under the definition of the CDTA, the Hungarian tax office is entitled to adjust the Hungarian party's tax base to reflect the market price (arm's-length price) if the parties did not make the adjustment themselves.

Considerations due for services are only deductible if the actual performance of the services is supported and the Hungarian taxpayer can prove that it benefits from the service.

Thin capitalisation rules may apply to interest on any non-banking debt in excess of three times the equity (*see Thin capitalisation in the Group taxation section*).

The consideration paid to a CFC is not deductible for CIT purposes unless the taxpayer is able to prove and keeps documentation that it serves the purposes of business operations. *For further details on the CFC rules, see the Group taxation section*

Group taxation

Group taxation is not available for CIT purposes in Hungary. *See Value-added tax in the Other taxes section for a description of group taxation for VAT purposes.*

Transfer pricing

If parties qualify as related parties (as defined in the Hungarian CDTA) and the price applied differs from the arm's-length price, the CIT base should be modified by a proper transfer pricing adjustment. In addition, the foreign PEs of a Hungarian company and the Hungarian head office also qualify as related entities and are subject to transfer pricing regulations.

Taxpayers are obliged to prepare transfer pricing documentation on intra-group transactions. The documentation has to be prepared for every contract between related parties (including in-kind contributions made at the time of establishment).

As of 2011, when determining the transfer prices applied between related companies, in addition to the traditional methods (comparable uncontrolled price, resale-minus, and cost-plus methods), it is also possible to use the transactional net margin method and the profit-split method. In addition to these methods, companies may continue to use other methods if the traditional methods are inadequate.

Hungary

Taxpayers are allowed to prepare two types of documentation (as opposed to the previous practice): country-specific documentation or consolidated transfer pricing documentation. Taxpayers may prepare consolidated transfer pricing documentation if this does not jeopardise comparability, and the contracts:

- have the same subject matter and all their terms and conditions are identical or only slightly different or
- closely relate to each other.

Taxpayers are required to make a declaration in their CIT returns as to which type of documentation they choose.

In summary, the requirements of the country-specific documentation have not changed as of 2012 compared to previous documentation requirements. This type of documentation must include, for example, the following:

H

- A functional analysis.
- Industry and company analyses.
- An economic analysis.
- A financial analysis.
- An account of the process of selecting the transfer pricing methodology.

Consolidated transfer pricing documentation must consist of two main parts:

- The core documentation, which includes the standard data for each company within the group which is resident in any EU member state.
- Country-specific documentation, which describes the agreements between the taxpayer and its related parties.

The documentation has to be available no later than the filing deadline for the CIT return in any given year; otherwise, the Tax Authority may assess a default penalty of up to HUF 2 million (approximately EUR 6,300) for each case of missing or deficient documentation. In the case of a repeat offence, it is up to HUF 4 million (approximately EUR 12,600) for each missing or deficient documentation. For the repeat lack or deficiency of the same documentation, the penalty may go up to four times the original penalty levied. Note, however, that this documentation only has to be prepared and kept in the company's files, rather than being filed with the Tax Authority.

Thin capitalisation
Thin capitalisation rules may apply to interest on any non-banking debt in excess of three times the equity.

Where debt means the average daily balance of outstanding loans, outstanding debt securities offered privately and bills payable (with the exception of bills payable on account of suppliers' debts), and any other liability other than loans, debt securities, and bills payable shown in the balance sheet that entails the payment of interest from the taxpayer's profit (with the exception of debts of credit institutions and financial companies incurred in connection with and for the purposes of financial service activities); and equity means the average daily balance of subscribed capital, capital reserve, retained earnings, and tied-up reserves (or own funds of the like). As of 1 January 2012, debt includes non-interest bearing loans as well, with the exception of back-to-back arrangements.

Hungary

Controlled foreign companies (CFCs)

CFCs are foreign persons or entities established abroad and/or foreign resident entities if, among other conditions, they are owned by a resident private individual/entity who is deemed to be the beneficial owner (i.e. has a certain ownership share or voting ratio or dominant influence in the enterprise) or if the majority of their income derives from Hungarian sources and, in both cases, the effective tax rate of the persons/entities is lower than 10%. Certain exceptions may be available (for companies in EU member states, OECD member states, and treaty countries, if a real economic presence can be proved). From 2012 on, it is the taxpayer's obligation to provide proof on the (lack of) CFC status.

Tax credits and incentives

Foreign tax credit

Foreign tax credit is available for income taxes paid abroad, up to the Hungarian tax payable on the creditable income (at a maximum of 90% of income tax paid abroad).

The foreign income has to be classified by country of origin and revenue type. The deducted tax may not exceed the lesser of either the applicable foreign tax or the applicable tax based on the taxation treaty between Hungary and the given country.

If there is no taxation treaty, 90% of the tax payable abroad is credited against the tax liability up to a hypothetical tax liability calculated by using the average Hungarian tax rate. Full tax credit is applicable if so described by a tax treaty. The average tax rate is the CIT rate, reduced by the applicable tax allowances, divided by the tax base. Indirect costs should be allocated in proportion to the revenue of the branch office to the total revenue of the whole company, as per Section 28 (4) of CDTA.

Development tax incentive

Each development tax incentive may be claimed for a ten-year period (beginning on the completion of the development) on the CIT returns over a maximum period of 14 years from the original application for the incentive. In any given tax year, the tax incentive is available for up to 80% of the tax payable but in total up to the state aid intensity ceiling. Applications for the tax incentive only have to be submitted to the Ministry for National Economics if the aggregated eligible costs of the investment exceed EUR 100 million (approximately EUR 320,000). If the investment is below this threshold, taxpayers only need to notify the Ministry for National Economics before starting the investment. Tax incentives are available for investments if:

- the current value of the investment is at least HUF 3 billion (approximately EUR 9.5 million) or
- the current value of the investment is at least HUF 1 billion (approximately EUR 3.2 million) in certain designated areas and provided that:
  - the investment results in the creation of new facilities or the extension of existing facilities, or
  - the investment results in substantially changed products or production processes (excluding investments in basic research, applied research, and experimental development), and
  - in the four years following the year in which the tax incentive is first used against the tax base:
    - the annual average number of employees has increased by at least 150 compared with either the year before the investment was made or the average

Hungary

number of employees for the three years preceding the investment (by 75 in certain designated areas) or

- the annual wage costs have increased by 600 times the minimum wage effective on the first day of the tax year (by a multiple of 300 in certain designated areas) compared with either the annual wage costs of the year before the investment was commenced or the average annual wage cost for the three years preceding the investment.

Provided that the investment results in the creation of new facilities or the extension of existing facilities, or substantially changed products or production processes, the Ministry may also grant incentives to companies that invest:

- at least HUF 100 million (approximately EUR 320,000) in equipment for zoogenic food production
- at least HUF 100 million (approximately EUR 320,000) in environmental protection projects
- at least HUF 100 million (approximately EUR 320,000) in broadband internet services
- at least HUF 100 million (approximately EUR 320,000) in the production of films and videos
- at least HUF 100 million (approximately EUR 320,000) in basic research, applied research, and experimental development projects
- at least HUF 100 million (approximately EUR 320,000) in projects financed by an issue of stock market-quoted shares, if (i) the project is started before the last day of the third calendar year following the date of issue, (ii) the total nominal value of the shares issued by the fifth year following the start of the project continuously reaches 50% of the value of the registered shares, (iii) the total issue price reaches 50% of the eligible costs, and (iv) at the date of the application for the incentive the company has at least 25 shareholders or at least 25% of the issued shares are owned by shareholders where each of them does not have more than 5% of the issued shares' nominal value, and
- at least HUF 500 million (approximately EUR 1.6 million) in projects initiated by small and medium-sized enterprises, if certain criteria are met.

Tax incentives may also be granted for projects that create new jobs. The restrictions prescribed in the CDTA regarding the headcount of staff and the percentage of new entrants to the labour market that may be claimed for such investments have been abolished, although the conditions prescribed in the relevant decree must still be met.

Tax holidays
Tax holidays may be granted in relation to film and theatre subsidies, developments, and small and medium-sized entities (SMEs).

Other tax incentives
Film production companies that receive a state subsidy for their activity may deduct the amount of the subsidy from their CIT base.

A tax incentive is available for small and medium-sized enterprises (basically, those with a maximum of 250 employees; annual net revenue of a maximum of EUR 50 million; or a maximum annual balance sheet total of EUR 43 million). Taxpayers that take a loan from a financial institution for the acquisition or production of tangible assets may deduct 40% of the interest paid on the loan from their tax due, up to a maximum deduction of HUF 6 million (approximately EUR 19,000). However,

Hungary

taxpayers engaged in certain business sectors cannot use this tax incentive (e.g. transportation, agricultural activity).

In order to be eligible for the above tax incentives, the wages and salaries need to be kept at a certain required level, according to relevant regulations.

In addition, a new type of tax allowance may be used in the future to support team sports (football, basketball, handball, ice-hockey, and water polo). The relevant government decree provides detailed rules on the application of this tax incentive.

Withholding taxes

Under the domestic rules, there is no withholding tax (WHT) on dividends, interest, or royalties.

As of 1 January 2011, foreign organisations are no longer subject to 30% WHT on interest, royalties, and service fees received from Hungarian resident companies.

Hungary has an extensive treaty network with maximum WHT rates as follows:

Payer (1)	Dividends (%)	Interest (%)	Royalties (%)
Albania	5/10 (2)	0	5
Armenia	5/10 (2)	0/10 (23)	5
Australia	15	10	10
Austria	10	0	0
Azerbaijan	8	8	8
Belarus	5/15 (2)	5	5
Belgium	10	15 (3)	0
Brazil	15	10/15 (4)	15/25 (5)
Bulgaria	10	10	10
Canada	5/10/15 (6) (7)	10	10
China, P.R (8)	10	10	10
Croatia	5/10 (2)	0	0
Cyprus	5/15	10	0
Czech Republic	5/15 (2)	0	10
Denmark	0/15 (12)	0	0
Egypt	15/20	15	15
Estonia	5/15 (2)	10	5/10 (10)
Finland	5/15 (2)	0	5
France	5/15 (2)	0	0
Georgia	0/5	0	0
Germany	5/15 (12)	0	0
Greece	10/45	10	10
Hong Kong	5/10 (12)	5	5
Iceland	5/10 (2)	0	10
India	10 (19)	10 (12)	10 (11)
Indonesia	15	15	15
Ireland, Republic of	5/15 (2)	0	0
Israel	5/15 (2)	0	0

Payer (1)	Dividends (%)	Interest (%)	Royalties (%)
Italy	10	0	0
Japan	10	10	10 (13)
Kazakhstan	5/15 (2)	10	10
Korea, Republic of	5/10 (2)	0	0
Kuwait	0	0	10
Latvia	5/10 (2)	10	5/10 (20)
Lithuania	5/15 (2)	10	5/10 (20)
Luxembourg	5/15 (2)	0	0
Macedonia	5/15 (14)	0	0
Malaysia	10	15	15
Malta	5/15	10	10
Moldova	5/15 (2)	10	0
Mongolia	5/15 (2)	10	5
Morocco	12	10	10
Netherlands	5/15 (2)	0	0
Norway	10	0	0
Pakistan	15/20 (2)	15	15
Philippines	15/20 (2)	15	15
Poland	10	10	10
Portugal	10/15	10	10
Qatar	0/5	0	5
Romania	5/15 (9)	15	10 (21)
Russia	10	0	0
San Marino	0/5/15 (2)	0	0
Serbia and Montenegro	5/15	10	10
Singapore	5/10 (2)	5	5
Slovakia	5/15 (2)	0	10
Slovenia	5/15 (2)	5	5
South Africa	5/15 (2)	0	0
Spain	5/15 (2)	0	0
Sweden	5/15 (2)	0	0
Switzerland	10	10	0
Taiwan	10	0/10 (22)	10
Taipei	10	10	10
Thailand	15/20 (15)	10/25 (16)	15
Tunisia	12/10 (2)	12 (19)	12
Turkey	10/15 (2)	10	10
Ukraine	5/15 (2)	10	5
United Kingdom	5/15 (2)	0	0
United States	5/15 (17)	15	0
Uruguay	15	15	10/15 (18)
Uzbekistan	10	10	10
Vietnam	10	10	10

Notes

1. List of the DTTs Hungary is a party to and the highest rates of WHT a foreign-source country may charge on (the gross) income paid to Hungarian residents.

Hungary

2. The lower rate applies if the recipient has a stake of at least 25% in the distributing company.
3. Interest is exempt if paid in respect of (i) commercial claims (including claims represented by negotiable instruments) and instalment payments for the delivery or supply of goods and/or services, (ii) current accounts or registered loans placed by a financial institution, and (iii) funds and deposits not represented by bearers' securities placed at any of the financial institutions (including public credit institutions).
4. 10% applies to bank loans used for industrial purposes, R&D, or public works.
5. 25% applies to royalties paid for the use of or the right to use trademarks.
6. The lower rate applies if the recipient has control, directly or indirectly, of 25% of the voting rights in the distributing company.
7. 10% is applicable if a non-resident owned investment corporation pays dividends to a recipient that has control, directly or indirectly, of 25% of the voting rights in the distributing company.
8. The China-Hungary Treaty does not apply to Hong Kong.
9. The lower rate applies if the recipient has a stake of at least 40% in the distributing company.
10. The lower rate applies to royalties for the use of industrial, commercial, or scientific equipment, or for transmission by satellite, cable optic fibre, or similar technology.
11. The same rate applies to technical service fees.
12. The lower rate applies if the recipient has a stake of at least 10% in the distributing company.
13. Cultural royalties are exempt.
14. The lower rate applies if the recipient (other than a partnership) has a stake of at least 25% in the distributing company.
15. The lower rate applies if the recipient has a stake of 25% in the distributing company that carries out industrial activities.
16. 10% applies if the recipient of the interest is a financial institution, including an insurance company.
17. The lower rate applies if the recipient has voting stock of at least 10% in the distributing company.
18. 10% applies to technical service fees.
19. If a lower rate is set in a treaty or agreement or minutes between India and any OECD country (excluding Hungary), then this lower rate should also be applied for India-Hungary.
20. 5% applies for the use of industrial, commercial or scientific facilities or for transmissions by means of satellite, cable, optical fibre, or any similar technology.
21. 5% for commission.
22. 0% on interest paid on inter-bank loans.
23. Interest arising in a contracting state and beneficially owned by a resident of the other contracting state (a) shall be exempted from tax in the state in which interest arises if it is paid (i) to the government of the other contracting state or a local authority thereof, to the central bank of that other state, or to any financial institution owned or controlled by the government of the other state, or (ii) in connection with a loan or a credit guaranteed or insured by the government of the other contracting state, the central bank of that other state, or any financial institution owned or controlled by that government; or (b) shall be taxable in the contracting state in which it arises at a rate not exceeding 5% of the gross amount of the interest if the interest is paid in connection with a loan or a credit of whatever kind granted by a bank.

Tax administration

Taxable period

CIT must be calculated by reference to the accounting year, which is either the calendar year or, for group companies, the group's accounting year.

Tax returns

Returns must be lodged within 150 days following the last day of the accounting year (31 May for a calendar year taxpayer). The tax payable is determined by self-assessment.

Tax returns may be submitted either electronically or in paper format. However, those who are legally obliged to submit monthly tax and contribution returns (e.g. employers and payers) may only submit tax returns electronically.

Payment of tax

CIT instalments must generally be reported and paid quarterly or monthly (above HUF 5 million [approximately EUR 16,000] tax payable). In the case of taxpayers with net sales revenues of over HUF 100 million (approximately EUR 320,000), 100% of the expected final payment is due by the 20th day of the last month of the accounting year (i.e. so-called 'top-up payment'). However, a late payment penalty is only levied if the

Hungary

company fails to pay at least 90% of the expected final payment by the above deadline. The late payment penalty is 20% of the difference between the tax advances paid (including the top-up payment) and 90% of the actual CIT liability.

Statute of limitations
In general, the statute of limitation is five years from the end of the calendar year in which the tax return should be filed. Self-revision interrupts the term of limitation.

Topics of focus for tax authorities
The tax authority will take more stringent measures against 'aggressive tax planning' (tax planning that takes advantage of unintended administrative or legal loopholes) using its international experience and cooperation agreements.

Generally, the following categories of taxpayers may expect to be scheduled for tax audits:

- Taxpayers whose records show frequent changes in registered address or ownership.
- Businesses that have operated for several years with substantial loans from their shareholders.
- Taxpayers that declared significant amounts of payable and deductible VAT during their pre-company period.
- Taxpayers that have been in continuous operation despite continuing losses.
- Taxpayers that spend a significant portion of their sales revenues on services.
- Taxpayers that have significant tax base decreasing items, tax allowances, and subsidies related to investments.
- Taxpayers that deduct R&D expenses.

The tax authority will also pay more attention to the actual content of transactions conducted between related parties and to the methods companies use to determine the arm's-length price.

Other issues

Principal forms of doing business
- Branch.
- Partnership.
- Limited liability company.
- Private company limited by shares.
- Public company limited by shares.

Mergers and acquisitions (M&A) from a business and tax perspective
Mergers in Hungary are tax-free transformations provided that they qualify under the definition of preferential transformation. Preferential transformation means that a company, without going into liquidation, transfers all its assets and liabilities to another company in exchange for the issue to its shareholders of securities representing the capital of that other company, and a cash payment not exceeding 10% of the nominal value, or, in the absence of a nominal value, of the accounting par value of those securities.

In a preferential transformation, the predecessor company does not have to amend its tax base by the difference between the adjusted book value and the book value. The adjusted book value means the historical value of assets less any depreciation deducted from the tax base plus the readjusted amount of extraordinary depreciation.

Hungary

Furthermore, for shareholders, the income accounted in excess of the historical value of the shares they acquire in the preferential transformation is also not taxable for CIT purposes for as long as the shareholder holds its participation.

In any other case, if two companies merge, the difference between the market value and the book value of the assets and liabilities is taxable for the successor company. Furthermore, the predecessor company may decrease its tax base by the amount of the difference between the adjusted book value of its assets and their book value if the adjusted book value is the higher of the two. The company will increase its tax base if the book value is higher than the adjusted book value.

International Financial Reporting Standards (IFRS) adoption

Companies defined in Section 4 of Decision no. 1606/2002/EC (mainly companies listed on the stock exchange) have to prepare their consolidated annual reports according to the IFRS. However, non-listed subsidiaries of EU-listed entities are exempt from the preparation of IFRS consolidated financial statements. If a company chooses IFRS, Hungarian Accounting Rules (HAR) financial statements must also be prepared and filed with the Court of Registration.

Iceland

PwC contact

Fridgeir Sigurdsson
PricewaterhouseCoopers ehf.
Skogarhlid 12
105 Reykjavik, Iceland
Tel: +354 550 5366
Email: fridgeir.sigurdsson@is.pwc.com

Significant developments

Additional bank tax
Financial services permitted to operate as banks and savings banks are subject to 0.041% tax on total debt at year end.

In 2012 and 2013, an additional special 0.0875% tax will be collected from financial services permitted to operate as banks and savings banks.

Financial Activities Tax (FAT)
A new tax on financial institutions, including insurance companies, will be levied on all salary payments. The tax will be collected monthly as of 1 April 2012 (for January, February, and March). *See the Other taxes section for more information.*

A special addition to FAT
In assessment year 2013, an addition of 6% to FAT will be collected on total salary payments that exceed 1 billion Icelandic krónur (ISK). This tax is paid by the same entities that are subject to the general FAT.

Accommodation tax
An accommodation tax was introduced on 1 January 2012. Those who sell accommodation and are subject to value-added tax (VAT) are liable to collect and return a tax of ISK 100 for each sold night.

Tax on pension funds
In 2012 and 2013, a 0.0814% tax will be levied on the net wealth of all pension funds. The tax for 2012 was pre-collected on 31 December 2011, and the next due date is 1 November 2012 for assessment year 2013.

Deduction for dividends and capital gains from sales of shares - ownership requirements and other requirements abolished
Until 1 January 2012, received dividends and gains from sales of shares could only be deducted if the ownership of the company paying dividends or being sold was at least 10%. Also, all operating loss carryforward was required to be offset before any deduction was allowed. Those requirements have been abolished as of 1 January 2012.

Forgiveness of debt
Temporary rules stating that forgiveness of debt is not implicitly to be treated as taxable income were introduced. The rules also include a possibility to distribute a part of forgiven debt over the period of 2015 to 2019.

Iceland

Taxes on corporate income

Resident corporations pay tax on their worldwide income less operating expenses. Deductible operating expenses are comprised of all the expenses and costs needed to provide, insure, and maintain income.

Corporate income tax (CIT) for limited liability companies and limited partnership companies is assessed at a rate of 20%.

CIT for other types of legal entities (e.g. partnerships) is assessed at a rate of 36%.

Non-resident corporations receiving payments for services or business operations carried out in Iceland, as well as corporations operating a permanent establishment (PE) in Iceland or receiving a profit from such establishments, are subject to CIT for their Icelandic income at the same rate as applies to resident corporations.

Corporate residence

In general, all corporations incorporated and registered in Iceland are considered to be tax residents in Iceland. The same applies to corporations which have their home address in Iceland according to their articles of association or if the management of the company is carried out in Iceland.

Foreign corporations are regarded as Icelandic tax residents if the effective management is carried out in Iceland.

The Internal Revenue Directorate can decide with a ruling whether a corporation's residence is in Iceland. The ruling can be appealed to a court of law.

Permanent establishment (PE)
Apart from the above mentioned, when defining whether a business activity in Iceland constitutes a PE, definitions in tax treaties are taken into consideration as well as commentaries to the Organisation for Economic Co-operation and Development (OECD) Model Tax Convention.

Other taxes

Valued-added tax (VAT)
VAT is a consumption tax levied on all stages of domestic business transactions. VAT is levied on all goods and services, as well as on the imports of goods and services, unless specific exemptions apply.

VAT rates
The general VAT rate is 25.5%.

The following goods and services are subject to a reduced VAT rate of 7%:

- Rental of hotel and guest rooms and other accommodation.
- Subscription to radio and television.
- Newspapers, periodicals, and magazines.

- Books, both Icelandic and translated, musical notation as well as their audio recordings. Same applies to compact discs and other similar media as well as electronic media.
- Geothermal hot water, electricity, and fuel oils used for heating houses and swimming pools.
- Food and other consumables for people as detailed in an addendum to the VAT Act.
- Access to roads and other transport related constructions.
- Compact discs, records, audio cassettes, and other equivalent mediums for music only and not videos. Same applies to electronically published music without video.

Certain services and goods are zero-rated, which means that there is, in fact, no VAT charge. All VAT information for zero-rated services and goods must be shown on invoices, and the transactions, as well as input VAT which can be reclaimed, must also be included in VAT returns. Zero-rated VAT mainly applies to exported goods and services provided abroad. As per Article 12 of the VAT Act, the following are zero-rated:

- Export of goods and services. Output tax is not levied on goods exported from the country nor on and services provided abroad.
- Transport of goods between countries. The same applies to domestic transport of goods when the transport is part of a contract for the transport of goods between countries.
- Production of goods at the expense of a foreign party when the production company exports the goods upon completion, as well as the processing and formation of goods at the expense of a foreign party when the production takes place abroad.
- The design, planning, and other comparable services related to construction and other real property abroad.
- Provisions, fuel, instruments, and other equipment delivered for use on board of inter-country vessels, as well as the service provided to such vessels. This exemption does not cover fishing vessels selling their catch abroad, pleasure boats, or private aircraft, only vessels used for the transport of freight.
- The sale and leasing of aircraft and ships. This exemption does not cover boats less than six metres in length, pleasure boats, or private aircraft.
- Shipbuilding and repair and maintenance work on ships and aircraft and their fixed equipment, as well as materials and goods used or provided by the company providing the repair work. This exemption does not cover boats less than six metres in length, pleasure boats, or private aircraft.
- Contractual payments from the Treasury related to the production of milk and sheep farming.
- Services provided to foreign fishing vessels related to the landing or sale of fish catches in Iceland.
- A service of refunding VAT to parties domiciled abroad.
- Sales of services to parties neither domiciled nor having a venue of operations in Iceland, provided that the services are wholly used abroad. A taxable service provided in connection with cultural activity, arts, sports, education, and other similar activity taking place in Iceland, and is tax-exempt cf. Paragraph 3, Article 2 of this Act, is always deemed as being used here. Sales of services to parties neither domiciled nor having a venue of operations in Iceland are, in the same manner, exempt from taxable turnover, even if the service is not wholly used abroad, provided the purchaser could, if its operations were subject to registry in Iceland, count the VAT on the purchase of the services as part of the input tax, cf. Articles 15 and 16. The following services come under this point:
  - The sale or lease of copyright, patent rights, registered trademarks and copyrighted designs, and the sale or lease of other comparable rights.
  - Advertising services.

Iceland

- Services of consultants, engineers, lawyers, accountants, and other similar specialised services as well as data processing and delivery of information, except for labour or services related to liquid assets or real property in Iceland.
- Electronic services; these services are considered used where the buyer is domiciled or having a venue of operations. The same applies to data centres' sale of mixed services to buyers neither domiciled nor having a venue of operations in Iceland.
- Obligations and duties related to business or production activity or the use of rights listed under this point.
- Employment agency services.
- The rental of liquid assets, except for means of transport.
- The services of agents acting on behalf of others and for their account as regards the sale and delivery of services listed under this point.
- Telecommunications services.

VAT-able entities
Businesses engaged in the trade of taxable goods and services for business purposes must register and collect VAT.

Services exempt from VAT
The VAT Act details certain services that are exempt from the tax, such as healthcare services, social services, the operation of schools, various education services, cultural activities, athletic activities, passenger transportation, postal services, sale of real estate (not including the rental of hotel and guest accommodation), rental of car workshops, insurance activity, services of financial banks as well as securities trading, lotteries and betting pools, artistic activities, services of travel agencies, funeral services, and all services of ministers of the church.

Those selling taxable goods and services totalling less than ISK 1 million per year are also exempt from paying VAT.

Agents for non-resident parties
Non-residents who are engaged in taxable transactions in Iceland but are neither domiciled nor have permanent residence in Iceland must appoint VAT agents with residence in Iceland to report on their behalf. Both parties are liable for the VAT payments (responsible for ensuring remittance of VAT). If a non-resident does not appoint a VAT agent, the purchaser of the services/goods is responsible for paying the VAT (reverse charge).

Tax base
Tax base is the price the buyer pays for goods or services before VAT is added and before any costs or service expenses are deducted from the price. VAT is therefore added to the sales price.

VAT accounting periods and due dates
VAT is generally filed and paid on a bi-monthly basis for the following periods: January and February; March and April; May and June; July and August; September and October; November and December. The due date for payment of VAT is one month and five days after the end of the settlement period. For example, the due date for the January and February payments is 5 April.

If the VAT is not paid on the due date, a 1% penalty charge is added for every day up to a total of 10%. Late penalty interests also apply.

Iceland

Should the total input tax exceed the total output tax, the Treasury will refund the difference within 15 days from the due date.

Those selling goods and services totalling less than ISK 3 million during a full calendar year can return the VAT payments on a yearly basis. The due date for filing and paying is 5 February each year.

Parties that do not file a VAT report within the required deadline will have their VAT estimated. The tax authorities are allowed to deregister parties of VAT register if they have had their VAT estimated for two years or longer.

If a VAT report is submitted after the tax authorities have estimated VAT, a penalty of ISK 5,000 is imposed.

VAT reimbursement
Under the provisions of Regulation no 288/1995, issued by the Ministry of Finance, foreign enterprises, which are neither residents of Iceland nor have a PE here, may obtain reimbursement of VAT paid on goods and taxable services which have been purchased or imported for the commercial purposes of such enterprises in Iceland after 1 March 1995.

Such reimbursement can be effected to foreign enterprises that would be subject to registration in Iceland according to Article 5 and Article 6 of the VAT Act if the enterprises in question were engaged in such business in Iceland. This means that such enterprises as travel agencies, insurance companies, banks, and other financial institutions cannot obtain such reimbursement.

Another prerequisite shall be that the enterprise shall have sold neither goods nor taxable services in Iceland during the period to which the application refers.

Any reimbursement of VAT to foreign enterprises shall be only to the same extent as Icelandic enterprises can include the VAT on purchases of a corresponding nature in the tax on purchases according to Article 15 and Article 16 of the VAT Act.

No reimbursement shall thus be granted in respect of VAT on purchases relating to meals for the owners and employees of the enterprises or relating to entertainment expenses and presents.

Parties domiciled abroad can get partial VAT reimbursement on goods they have bought in Iceland if they take them abroad with them within three months from the date of purchase. They then must provide the goods, along with any necessary documents, to the appropriate reimbursement company or to the customs authorities on the date of departure, and the purchase price must amount to at least ISK 4,000.

Customs duties
The Directorate of Customs controls import, transit, and export and also collects duties, taxes, and various state revenue. The general rule is that import duties are to be paid on imported goods (customs, excise duties, VAT, and various other charges), unless otherwise stated in the law. For import of some products, other conditions, such as an import licence, may need to be submitted.

Iceland, Liechtenstein, Norway, and Switzerland are members of the European Free Trade Association (EFTA). The EFTA Convention established a free trade area among its member states. In addition, the EFTA states have jointly concluded free trade

Iceland

agreements with a number of countries in Central and Eastern Europe as well as in the Mediterranean region, Mexico, and Singapore. Also the EFTA states entered into the Agreement on the European Economic Area (EEA) in 1992. The current contracting parties are, in addition to the three EFTA states, the European Community (EC) and the 15 EC member states. Iceland also has a bilateral agreement with its two neighbouring countries, Greenland and Faeroe Islands.

Excise taxes

An excise duty is levied on a variety of goods specified in the Icelandic Excise Tax Act. They include goods, new and second-hand, that are imported from abroad or manufactured, processed, or packed in Iceland. There is no excise duty on exports.

The excise duty is either a quantity-based or a price-based charge. The quantity charge is based on each kilogram or litre of the relevant goods. The price charge is based on the duty-added import price for imported goods or on the factory price of goods produced in Iceland. Several rate brackets apply to each, but the system has been greatly simplified in recent years.

The excise tax based on quantity ranges from ISK 16 to ISK 800 per kg or litre. The excise tax based on manufacturing price is in general 15%, 20%, or 25%.

Property taxes

A municipal property tax is applied annually on the assessed value of real estate in Iceland.

Stamp taxes/transfer taxes

Stamp duty is levied on the execution of various documents at rates ranging from 0.4% to 2%.

A stamp duty of 0.5% is levied on the nominal value of all new share certificates issued to shareholders in a public limited liability company. Private limited companies are not required to issue share certificates and, therefore, are not subject to stamp duty.

The endorsement of documents is generally not subject to stamp duty.

When issuing deeds and purchase agreements of real estate and land, a 0.4% stamp duty is levied on the officially registered value of the real estate. The same applies to the deeds and purchase agreements of ships. Lease agreements are subject to a 2% stamp duty of the rental price.

Turnover taxes

There is an agricultural charge of 1.20% of agricultural turnover.

Taxes on natural resources

Carbon tax

A carbon tax for liquid fossil fuels is paid to the treasury. Liquid fossil fuels are gas and diesel oils, petrol, aircraft and jet fuels, and fuel oils. All importers of fossil fuels are liable for the carbon tax regardless of whether it is for retail or personal use. The tax rate is:

- ISK 5.75 per litre of gas and diesel oils.
- ISK 5 per litre of petrol.
- ISK 4.10 per litre of aircraft and jet fuels.

Iceland

- ISK 7.10 per kilo of fuel oil.

Tax on electricity/hot water
A special tax is collected from parties that sell electricity and/or hot water to end users.

Carbohydrate tax
Corporations licensed for carbohydrate investigations, research, and/or processing, as well as anyone who directly or indirectly participates in the processing or distribution of carbohydrates, must either pay a processing tax, which is independent of processing performance, or a carbohydrate tax, which is collected after the processing starts making a profit.

Bank tax and an additional bank tax
Financial services permitted to operate as banks and savings banks are subject to 0.041% tax on total debt at year end.

In 2012 and 2013, an additional special 0.0875% tax will be collected from financial services permitted to operate as banks and savings banks.

Financial Activities Tax (FAT)
A 5.45% tax will be levied on all salary payments made by financial institutions, including insurance companies. The tax will be collected monthly, on 1 April 2012 for the first time (for January, February, and March).

A temporary addition to FAT
In 2013, an addition of 6% to FAT will be levied and collected on total salary payments that exceed ISK 1 billion. This tax is paid by the same entities that are subject to the general FAT.

Accommodation tax
An accommodation tax was introduced on 1 January 2012. Those who sell accommodation that is subject to VAT are liable to collect and return a tax of ISK 100 for each sold night.

Tax on pension funds
In assessment years 2012 and 2013, a 0.0814% tax will be levied on net wealth of all pension funds. The tax for 2012 was pre-collected on 31 December 2011, and the next due date is 1 November 2012 for assessment year 2013.

Other taxes
There is a National Broadcasting Fee of ISK 18,800 per year.

Branch income

A branch is treated as an extension of a trading activity of the overseas parent company incorporated in another jurisdiction and is not a separate legal entity.

Due to the fact that a branch acts in the name of the overseas parent company, a branch's income is taxable in accordance with the parent company (i.e. if the parent company is a limited liability company, the branch is subject to a CIT rate of 20%).

Tax treaties may allow Icelandic CIT as a credit against foreign income tax imposed on the parent company.

Iceland

There is no branch profits remittance tax on the repatriation of profits to the parent company.

Income determination

Resident corporations pay tax on their worldwide income less operating expenses.

Inventory valuation
The valuation method of raw materials and finished goods is on a first in first out (FIFO) basis or via the average cost method. When computing the value of produced goods, both direct and indirect production cost must be taken into account. For tax purposes, inventories can be further written down at a rate of 5% of calculated value.

Last in first out (LIFO) is not permitted.

Capital gains
Capital gains are treated as taxable income in the year that transfer of ownership occurs and, as such, taxed as part of the general corporate income. Capital gains are generally not subject to withholding tax (WHT). There are rules that allow full deduction of net capital gains from the sale of shares, so, in general, corporations are not subject to taxation on capital gains from sale of shares.

Dividend income
Dividend income is treated as taxable income and taxed as a part of corporate income. There are extensive rules that allow full deduction of the dividend, so, in general, corporations are not subject to taxation on dividends. Dividends are subject to WHT (currently 20%), which is a temporary payment towards the final tax assessment.

Interest income
Interest income derived from bank deposits, mutual and investment funds, bonds, or other financial deeds; any kind of exchange rate profit; and any other income from monetary assets are subject to 20% tax.

Interest income of foreign parties is subject to 10% WHT in Iceland.

Foreign income
Income earned abroad is generally taxed as a part of corporate income since a resident company is subject to CIT on its worldwide income.

Controlled foreign company (CFC) rules stipulate that profits of companies in low-tax jurisdictions must pay income tax of such a profit in direct proportion to shares, regardless of distribution. A low tax jurisdiction is defined as a jurisdiction where the CIT rate is less than two-third of the Iceland´s tax rate (i.e. 13.3%, being two-thirds of 20%). *See Controlled foreign companies (CFCs) in the Group taxation section for more information.*

Double taxation of foreign income is avoided either through tax treaties or domestic tax provisions.

Iceland

Deductions

Deductible operating expenses are comprised of all the expenses and costs needed to provide, insure, and maintain income (e.g. interest expense, employee expense, travel expense, insurance expense).

Depreciation

Assets	Depreciation rate (%)
Ships, ship equipment, and personal vehicles	10 to 20*
Aircraft and accessories	10 to 20*
Heavy machinery, industrial machinery, and equipment	10 to 30*
Rigs, pipeline systems, and more for the use of research and production of hydrocarbons	10 to 30
Office equipment	20 to 35*
Machinery, equipment, and vehicles that are not covered in the above categories	20 to 35*
Residential, commercial, and office accommodation	1 to 3
Factory buildings, garages, warehouses, etc.	3 to 6
Purchased proprietary rights for ideas and trademarks, such as copyrights, publishing rights, information rights, patents, and logos	15 to 20
Purchased goodwill	10 to 20

* The depreciation base for these assets is their purchase value less earlier depreciations (book value).

Goodwill
Purchased goodwill can be written down at 10% to 20% per year.

Start-up expenses
Purchased fishing rights (quotas) cannot be depreciated.

Start-up costs for agricultural production rights can be depreciated without revaluation over five consecutive years. The following assets can be depreciated in full in the year they are initiated or paid with steady payments over five years:

- Start-up costs, such as enterprise registration and obtaining operation licences.
- Cost of research, developments, marketing, obtaining patents and trademarks. If the use of individual assets does not fall into the same depreciation category, the depreciation base will be dependent on how much of it is used, so that if an asset is used for three-quarters or more for the same operation, the whole asset will have the same depreciation percentage.

Interest expenses
Interest expenses are deductible, provided that the loan was taken for business purposes.

Bad debt
As a general rule, 5% of bad debt can be written off. Certain conditions must be met in order to write off a higher percentage of bad debts.

Temporary provisions in Icelandic tax law allow corporations to make a credit entry for only 50% of debt write-off totalling ISK 50 million and 75% of debt write-off for

Iceland

amounts over ISK 50 million in income years 2009 through 2012. The requirement for the provision is that the debt is business-related and operating loss and transferable loss has been offset.

The debt write-off can be carried forward from the income year 2010 to the income year 2014. The transferrable amount that can be carried forward on a yearly basis is the amount that exceeds the transferable operating losses and the possible operating loss, tax depreciation, and write-down each year. All assets that can be depreciated have to be depreciated and all possible write-downs on receivables and stock have to be done to fulfil the requirements of the provisions. No dividend can be distributed for the income years 2010 through 2014, and the company can also not be merged, wound up, or be jointly taxed with another company during the period. At the end of this five year period (i.e. at the end of the income year 2014), it will be possible to transfer any debt write-off that exceeds ISK 500 million as profit with an equal amount each year from the income year 2015 to the income year 2019. If the write-off does not exceed ISK 500 million, the amount will not be subject to taxation.

Charitable contributions
Charitable contributions up to 0.5% of total income are deductible.

Pension expenses
Payments to obligatory pension funds for employees at a minimum of 8% of wages are deductible.

Bribes, kickbacks, and illegal payments
Bribes, kickbacks, and other illegal payments are not deductible.

Fines and penalties
Fines and penalties are not deductible.

Taxes
Taxes levied on business profit are not considered to be deductable. Therefore CIT is not deductible. However, social security contributions and other labour taxes are deductible.

Net operating losses
Operating losses may be deducted from income from business and independent economic activity. Tax losses can be carried forward ten years and utilised over ten years from the year that the loss was incurred.

No carryback of losses is allowed.

Payments to foreign affiliates
An Icelandic corporation can claim a deduction for royalties, management fees, and similar payments made to foreign affiliates, provided that such amounts are made on an arm's-length basis and reflect services received. Interest at normal commercial rates paid to foreign affiliates generally will be allowed as a deduction conditional though that the loan terms are comparable to those that would have been agreed upon by unrelated parties.

Group taxation

Companies may opt for consolidated taxation if a company owns at least 90% share in another company. Consolidated taxation means, among other things, that losses of one company can be offset against profits of other companies. Consolidated taxation cannot be extended to non-resident companies or PEs of foreign companies.

Transfer pricing

The statutory authority for addressing transfer pricing issues is found in the application of general legal concepts, such as the anti-avoidance rule.

Article 57 of the Icelandic Income Tax Act No. 90/2003 (originally included in the tax code in 1971) includes a general anti-avoidance rule that states that business transactions between all parties should be based on the arm's-length principle. With reference to the general concept of this Article, tax authorities can, in cases where transfer prices are not at arm's length, adjust the taxpayer's revenues and expenses in order to reflect market value. These adjustments can be performed only within the domestic statute of limitation period, i.e. six years. Authorities have thus based their transfer pricing conclusions on Article 57.

The Income Tax Act includes several separate rules that can be identified as transfer pricing rules, but those rules generally concern transactions between individuals and not companies, including a rule that obligates employees who receive their wages in kind to account for them on their tax return based on market value.

Thin capitalisation

There are no specific rules regarding thin capitalisation in Iceland, but anti-avoidance principles can be applied (*see Transfer pricing above*).

Controlled foreign companies (CFCs)

Any individual who either directly or indirectly owns a share in any kind of a company, fund, or organisation domiciled in a low-tax jurisdiction must pay income tax on the profit of such corporations in direct proportion to one's own share, regardless of distribution.

The same applies to taxpayers chairing companies, funds, organisations, or associations in a low-tax jurisdiction from which they receive direct or indirect benefits. In order for the above to apply, the foreign party must be domiciled in the low-tax jurisdiction, half the ownership of the foreign party must be directly or indirectly in the hands of Icelandic taxpayers, or they must have effective management and executive control during the income year.

CFC regulations do not apply if a fund or an organisation is protected by a double taxation treaty (DTT) between Iceland and the low-tax country or if such entities are registered in another EEA member country where they have legitimate business operations and the countries have assigned a DTT between them.

Tax credits and incentives

Foreign tax credit

The Income Tax Act offers a foreign tax credit to mitigate the potential for double taxation. The credit applies only to taxes of a nature similar to the tax being reduced

Iceland

by the credit (i.e. taxes based on income). This credit is limited to the amount of tax attributable to foreign-source income.

Temporary Reimbursements in Respect of Filmmaking in Iceland

On account of Act no 43/1999 on Temporary Reimbursement in Respect of Filmmaking in Iceland, it is possible to have 20% of production expenses incurred in the production of films or television material in Iceland reimbursed. When more than 80% of the total production cost of a motion picture or television programme is incurred in Iceland, the reimbursement shall be calculated from the total production cost incurred within the EEA. Production costs refer to all costs incurred in Iceland deductible from the revenues of enterprises pursuant to the provisions of the Act on Income Tax. Payments pertaining to employees and contractors are only to be included in production costs if they are verifiably taxable in Iceland.

Application for reimbursement of production costs shall be submitted to the Ministry of Industry. The application, with supporting documentation, shall be submitted before production commences in Iceland.

In assessing whether a proportion of the production costs of a motion picture or television programme shall be reimbursed, the following conditions must be fulfilled:

* The production shall be suitable for promoting Icelandic culture and the history and nature of Iceland.
* The production shall be suitable for enhancing the experience, knowledge, and artistic ambition of the parties involved. A specific company shall be established in Iceland for the production; an Icelandic branch or agency of a company registered in another member state of the EEA shall be considered a specific company.
* Information about the subject of the production or programme shall be made available.
* An itemised estimate of the production costs and sources of funding shall be made available, together with confirmation by the funding parties and a declaration by the applicant to the effect that the production conforms to the aims of the Act.
* Information about the content of the proposed production of a motion picture or a television programme shall be made available, such as a script and information about filming locations.
* A statement shall be made available to the effect that the material to be produced is intended for general distribution to cinemas or television stations.
* The subject matter of the film or television programming should not violate the provisions of law relating to film inspection and the ban on violent films, nor the provisions of the General Penal Code concerning pornography.
* A confirmation that all taxes and debts in Iceland have been paid.

Act No. 43/1999 on Temporary Reimbursements in Respect of Filmmaking in Iceland expires at year end 2016. All projects approved by that date will be reimbursed in accordance with the law.

Research and development (R&D)

Innovative companies are entitled to a special deduction from CIT amounting to 20% of expenses incurred on the projects, provided certain conditions are met.

The maximum amount on which the deduction is calculated within each company shall not exceed ISK 100 million for each operating year. In the case of purchased R&D services, maximum expenses shall not exceed ISK 150 million.

Withholding taxes

Dividends paid to a resident company are subject to a 20% WHT. Dividends paid to a non-resident company are subject to 18% WHT. The final taxation of dividends paid to a company within the EEA is nil, as WHT will be reimbursed in the year following payment upon filing a tax return.

Interest paid to resident company is subject to a 20% WHT, and interest paid to non-resident company is subject to 10% WHT.

Gross royalties paid to a non-resident are taxable at the standard 20% CIT rate and subject to withholding.

Recipient	Dividends (%)	Interest (%)	Royalties (%)
Non-resident corporations	18	10	20
Non-resident individuals	20	10	37.34 to 46.24
Treaty rates:			
Belgium	5/15 (1)	10	0
Canada	5/15 (1)	10	0/10 (3)
China, P.R.	5/10 (2)	10	10
Czech Republic	5/15 (2)	0	10
Denmark	15	10	0
Estonia	5/15 (2)	10	5/10 (4)
Faroe Islands	0/15 (1)	0	0
Finland	0/15 (1)	0	0
France	0/15 (1)	0	0
Germany	5/15 (2)	0	0
Greece	5/15 (2)	8	10
Greenland	5/15 (2)	0	15
Hungary	5/10 (2)	0	10
India	10	10	10
Ireland, Republic of	5/15 (2)	0	0/10 (5)
Italy	5/15 (6)	0	5
Korea, Republic of	5/15 (2)	10	10
Latvia	5/15 (2)	10	5/10 (4)
Lithuania	5/15 (2)	10	5/10 (4)
Luxembourg	5/15 (2)	0	0
Malta	5/15 (1)	0	5
Mexico	5/15 (1)	10	10
Netherlands	0/15 (1)	0	0
Norway	0/15 (1)	0	0
Poland	5/15 (2)	10	10
Portugal	10/15 (2)	10	10
Romania	5/10 (2)	3	5
Russia	5/15 (7)	0	0
Slovakia	5/10 (2)	0	10
Spain	5/15 (2)	5	5
Sweden	0/15 (1)	0	0
Switzerland	5/15 (2)	0	0

Iceland

Recipient	Dividends (%)	Interest (%)	Royalties (%)
Ukraine	5/15 (2)	10	10
United Kingdom	5/15 (1)	0	0
United States	5/15 (1)	0	0/5 (8)
Vietnam	10/15 (2)	10	10

Notes

1. The lower rate applies to corporate shareholders with a minimum ownership of 10%.
2. The lower rate applies to corporate shareholders with a minimum ownership of 25%.
3. The lower rate applies to copyright royalties (except films, etc.) and royalties for computer software or patent, or for information concerning industrial, commercial, or scientific experience (except information provided in connection with a rental or franchise agreement).
4. The lower rate applies to royalties paid for the use of industrial, commercial, or scientific equipment.
5. The lower rate applies to the right to use computer software or patent concerning industrial, commercial, or scientific experience.
6. The lower rate applies to corporate shareholders with a minimum ownership of 10%, and which has been held for a period of at least 12 months preceding the date the dividends were declared.
7. The lower rate applies to Russian corporate shareholders with a minimum ownership of 25% of capital in the Icelandic company and the foreign capital invested exceeds 100,000 United States dollars (USD).
8. The higher rate applies to royalties for the use of trademarks, know-how in relation to a trademark, and films, etc.

Tax administration

Taxable period

The tax year is the calendar year. However, in certain circumstances, the Internal Revenue Directorate can allow a different fiscal year from the calendar year upon application.

Tax returns

At the beginning of every year, the Internal Revenue Directorate determines the time limit for taxpayers to submit their tax returns and supporting documentation. The deadline for receipt of tax returns from corporations is generally 31 May each year. This deadline is extended upon application. Those who have their tax returns prepared by professional services can generally have the deadline extended until 10 September each year.

The final assessment must be completed no later than ten months after the end of the income year. Tax assessments for corporations will be available at the end of October.

Payment of tax

Advance tax payments are due on the first day of every month, except January and October. Corporations pay income tax in advance, which is in turn deducted from the final tax assessment in October each year. The advance tax is collected in the months of February to September and amounts to 8.5% of the income tax on each due date. In total, the advance tax payments amount to 68% of the income tax. Any deficit remaining when final tax is assessed must be paid in equal instalments in November and December.

Income tax payments on dividends and interest income are due every quarter. Due dates in 2012 are 20 April, 20 July, 20 October, and 20 January (2013), and the final deadline for payment is 15 days later.

Iceland

Statute of limitations

Tax authorities in Iceland have the right to reassess tax returns for CIT six years prior to the year of the assessment (i.e. the statutory period of limitation is six years). The statutory period only reaches a maximum of two years in time if tax returns have been filled out properly and all necessary information presented for tax authorities to establish a correct assessment. This means that in the year 2012, tax authorities can, in theory, reassess the company´s tax back to income year 2006.

Topics of focus for tax authorities

The topic of focus for tax authorities in Iceland is tax avoidance in general.

Other issues

Foreign currency financial statements/Accounting in foreign currencies

Companies can apply to the Registry of Annual Accounts for an authorisation to keep their books and prepare their annual accounts in a foreign currency. An application must be filed no later than two months before the beginning of the company's fiscal year. The authorisation is valid for five years, and the Registry of Annual Accounts is responsible for ensuring that the authorised companies continue to fulfil one or more of the following necessary conditions:

- The company's main business operations take place abroad or the company is a part of a foreign company group.
- The company owns foreign subsidiaries or shares in foreign companies and its main business transactions are with those companies.
- The company's main place of business is Iceland, while a considerable number of their transactions are in foreign currencies.
- A considerable portion of the company's investments and related debts are in foreign currencies.

If the company deems that it no longer fulfils the conditions, it must notify the Registry of Annual Accounts. The Registry can postpone its decision of the authorisation's discontinuance for two fiscal years if the situation that is causing the fact that the company does not continue to fulfil the necessary conditions is deemed to be temporary.

The average exchange rate for the fiscal year must be used when converting income and expenses, depreciations included, into Icelandic króna. The exchange rate at the end of the fiscal year must be used when converting assets, debts, and capital. Exchange rate differences that may arise do not affect income on profit and loss accounts.

Rules on foreign exchange

In 2008, the Central Bank of Iceland issued rules on foreign exchange in order to restrict or temporarily prevent certain types of cross-border capital movements or foreign exchange transactions related thereto, which, according to the Central Bank of Iceland, can cause serious and considerable instabilities in exchange rates and financial matters.

The Act on Foreign Exchange defines capital movements as:

- The issue, sale, or purchase of shares, debt instruments, drafts, unit shares in mutual funds, and other long-term and short-term securities.

I

Iceland

- Deposits in and withdrawals from accounts with depository institutions.
- Lending, borrowing, and the issue of securities not related to international transactions with goods and services.
- The import and export of share certificates and domestic and foreign currencies.
- Forward contracts, options, currency and interest-rate swaps, and other related foreign exchange transactions in which the Icelandic króna is one of the denominated currencies.
- Presents, grants, or other transactions equivalent to the ones detailed above.

Capital movements of foreign currencies

All capital movements of foreign currencies between countries are prohibited, with the exception of payments for the purchase of goods and services or other capital movements specifically exempt from the regulations, according to Rules no. 370/2010 on Foreign Exchange, issued by the Central Bank of Iceland.

Capital movements of domestic currencies

Capital movements between countries in domestic currencies are also prohibited. There are several exceptions to this rule.

Capital movements specifically exempt from the above regulations are as follows:

- Capital movements in relation to the purchase or sale of goods and services (not including lending, borrowing, and the issue of securities not related to international transactions with goods and services) and payments in cash or by withdrawals from an account the buyer has in an Icelandic depositary institution.
- Capital movements in relation to real estate purchases in Iceland or business transactions with securities issued in the domestic currency and payments by withdrawals from an account the buyer has in an Icelandic depositary institution.
- Capital movements in relation to claims from a liquidated company and payments of contractual debts according to composition agreements, according to Act no. 21/1991.

India

PwC contact

Shyamal Mukherjee
PricewaterhouseCoopers Pvt Ltd
Building No. 10, Tower - C
17th & 18th floor,
DLF Cyber City, Gurgaon
Haryana -122002
India
Tel: +91 124 330 6536
Email: shyamal.mukherjee@in.pwc.com

Ketan Dalal
PricewaterhouseCoopers Pvt Ltd
PwC House, Plot No. 18 A
Guru Nanak Road (Station Road), Bandra
Mumbai 400 028, India
Tel: +91 22 6689 1422
Email: ketan.dalal@in.pwc.com

Significant developments

Alternative Minimum Tax (AMT)

Alternative Minimum Tax (AMT) is made applicable to all other persons (other than a company) at the rate of 18.5% (plus applicable surcharge, education cess, and secondary and higher education cess). AMT paid in a year is eligible to be carried forward for set off against normal tax liability for ten years. In the case of an individual, or a hindu undivided family or an association of persons or a body of individuals or an artificial judicial person, AMT is not applicable where the adjusted total income does not exceed 2 million Indian rupees (INR).

General Anti Avoidance Rules (GAAR)

GAAR provisions were introduced by the 2012 Budget empowering the Tax Department to declare an 'arrangement' entered into by an assessee to be an 'Impermissible Avoidance Agreement' (IAA). The consequence would be denial of tax benefit either under the provisions of the Act or under the tax treaty. Any step in, or part of, any arrangement may also be declared as an IAA. The onus to prove that the main purpose of the IAA is to obtain tax benefit is on the Revenue. GAAR provisions are effective from 1 April 2013.

Conversion of a branch of a foreign bank into an Indian subsidiary

Conversion of a branch of a foreign bank into an Indian subsidiary company in accordance with the scheme of Reserve Bank of India will be tax neutral, subject to conditions to be notified. In case of failure to comply with any of the provisions specified in the scheme or the notification, all the provisions of the Act shall then apply to the foreign company and the subsidiary and the tax neutral nature of the conversion will be ignored and capital gains tax will become payable on the conversion.

Tax Residency Certificate (TRC)

For the purpose of obtaining tax treaty benefit, it will now be necessary for a non-resident assessee to furnish a certificate (containing prescribed particulars) of its being resident of that country, obtained by the assessee from the government of that country.

India

Definition of 'royalty'

It is clarified by the Budget 2012 that with retrospective effect from 1 June 1976, the definition of 'royalty' will also include consideration for use of, or right to use, computer software. It is also clarified that transfer of all or any rights in respect of any right, property, or information includes transfer of all or any right for use or right to use a computer software (including granting of a licence), irrespective of the medium through which such a right is transferred. Hence, while applying withholding tax (WHT) on such payments in the nature of royalty, one will need to consider the amended definition.

It is clarified that the term 'process' includes transmission by satellite (including up-linking, amplification, conversion for down-linking of any signal), cable, optic fibre, or by any other similar technology, whether or not such a process is secret.

Taxability of shares issued at premium in excess of fair market value of shares

Where a closely held company (other than a venture capital undertaking receiving from a venture capital fund/company or from any other notified person to be notified by the Central Government) issues shares at premium to a resident for an amount in excess of the fair market value of the shares, then the excess will be deemed to be the income of the company. This is effective from 1 April 2013.

Share premium in excess of fair market value to be treated as income

Any amount received towards share application money, share premium, or share capital by any closely held company will be considered as income, if the explanation offered by such company in relation to the source and nature of the amount so received is not satisfactory in the opinion of the tax officer. This is effective from 1 April 2013.

Domestic transfer pricing

Transfer pricing provisions also apply to specified domestic transactions effective from 1 April 2012, whereby any allowance or expenditure or interest on allocation of any cost or expense or any income in relation to any specified domestic transaction shall be computed having regard to the arm's-length price. The domestic transfer pricing provisions will apply only where the aggregate of the transactions in the previous year exceeds a sum of INR 50 million.

Advance pricing agreement (APA)

The provisions relating to APAs are introduced with effect from 1 July 2012.

The Central Board of Direct Taxes (CBDT), with the approval of the Central Government, can enter into agreement with any assessee for determining the arm's-length price or prescribe methods, adjustments, or variations to the arm's-length price that will be valid for a maximum period of five years. The agreement will be binding (in relation to that transaction) on the assessee, the Commissioner, and the income-tax authorities subordinate to the Commissioner, except where there is a change in law or facts. The CBDT may, with the approval of the Central Government, declare an agreement to be void *ab initio* if it finds that the agreement has been obtained by fraud or misrepresentation of facts.

India

Taxes on corporate income

A resident company is taxed on its worldwide income. A non-resident company is taxed only on income that is received in India, or that accrues or arises, or is deemed to accrue or arise, in India.

The corporate income tax (CIT) rate applicable to an Indian company for the tax year 2012/13 is 30% (plus surcharge, education cess, and secondary and higher education cess). Resident companies are liable to pay surcharge at the rate of 5% on the amount of CIT if the total income exceeds INR 10 million.

Foreign companies operating in India are taxed at 40% (plus surcharge, education cess, and secondary and higher education cess). For tax year 2012/13, surcharge for foreign companies is 2%.

The education cess is 2%, and the secondary and higher education cess is 1%.

Minimum alternative tax (MAT)
Resident companies are liable to pay MAT on their adjusted book profits (not on income from life insurance business) where the tax liability for the year is less than 20.01% of the adjusted book profits for the tax year 2012/13 (19.93% for assessment year 2012/13). In such cases, the tax liability is fixed at 20.01% of the adjusted book profits of the company.

Non-resident companies are liable to pay MAT on their adjusted book profits from India-sourced income where the tax liability for the year is less than 19.44% of the adjusted book profits from India-sourced income for tax year 2012/13 (18.91% for assessment year 2012/13). In such cases, the tax liability is fixed at 19.44% of the adjusted book profits of the company from India-sourced income.

Surcharge is payable only where total taxable income exceeds INR 10 million.

Sick companies (loss companies which have made losses continuously and may or may not be revived to making profits) are not subject to MAT.

From tax year 2010/11, companies are allowed to take the benefit of carrying forward the credit of tax paid under MAT for ten years.

A Special Economic Zone (SEZ) developer and a unit in an SEZ are now liable to pay MAT by virtue of amendment in section 115JB by the Finance Act, 2011 with effect from tax year 2011/12.

Tonnage tax scheme
The tonnage tax scheme can be elected by an Indian company that has a place of effective management in India, owns at least one qualifying ship, and whose main object is to carry on the business of operating qualifying ships. The tonnage tax scheme is in place of CIT and is levied on the basis of tonnage of vessels owned, operated, or chartered by it instead of net income generated by commercial operations.

In relation to non-resident shipping companies that have regular/occasional shipping income, presumptive tax provisions are applicable. Under the tonnage tax scheme, deemed income shall be assessed at a rate of 7.5% of the amount paid or payable (whether in or out of India) for carriage of passengers, livestock, mail, or goods shipped at any port in India and the amount received or deemed to be received in India on account of carriage of passengers, livestock, mail, or goods shipped at any port outside India shall be treated as profits and gains of the business or profession.

Tax rates applicable to a non-resident should take into consideration any treaty provisions.

Under a presumptive tax system, taxpayers can opt to be taxed on their income at a pre-designated tax rate.

A government company, or a public company, formed and registered in India with the main object of operating ships is eligible for a deduction not exceeding 50% of the profits to the extent that it is transferred to a special reserve created for the purpose, which is utilised in accordance with the provisions of the Act.

Direct taxes code
A new direct taxes code replacing the existing Income-tax Act, 1961 is proposed and is expected to be introduced with effect from 1 April 2013.

Corporate residence

A company is treated as a resident of India if:

* it is an Indian company or
* during the tax year, the control or management of its affairs is situated wholly in India.

A company that does not fulfil either of these conditions is treated as a non-resident.

A partnership firm or a limited liability partnership (LLP) is treated as a resident in India if any portion of its control and management is in India. A partnership firm or an LLP is a non-resident if its control and management is situated wholly outside India.

Permanent establishment (PE)
A PE is defined in India as a fixed place of business through which the business of an enterprise is wholly or partly carried on.

Other taxes

Value-added tax (VAT)/Central sales tax (CST)
The sale of movable goods in India is chargeable to tax at the central or state level. The Indian regulatory framework has granted power to state legislatures to levy tax on goods sold within that state. Such sales are, therefore, chargeable to VAT at the rates notified under the VAT laws of the relevant state. All goods sold in the course of interstate trade are subject to CST.

Where goods are bought and sold by registered dealers on an inter-state basis for trading or for use as inputs in the manufacture of other goods or specified activities (such as mining or telecommunication networks), the rate of sales tax is 2%, provided Form 'C' is issued by the purchasing dealer. In the absence of Form 'C', the applicable rate would be the rate of VAT on such goods in the originating state. Interstate procurement, on which CST is charged by the originating state, is not eligible for input tax credit in the destination state and hence is a cost to a buyer.

State level sales tax has been replaced by VAT in all the states. Under the VAT regime, the VAT paid on goods purchased within the state is eligible for VAT credit. The input VAT credit can be utilised against the VAT/CST payable on the sale of goods. It is, thus, ensured that the cascading effect of taxes is avoided and only the value addition is taxed.

Currently, there is no VAT on imports into India. Exports are zero-rated. This means that while exports are not charged to VAT, VAT charged on inputs purchased and used in the manufacture of export good or goods purchased for exports is available to the purchaser as a refund.

The state VAT is charged at tax rates of 1%, 4%, 5%, and 20%. Goods other than those notified to be covered under the above rates are charged in the range of 12.5% to 15%. The rate of VAT depends on the nature of goods involved and varies from state to state.

Turnover threshold is prescribed so as to exclude small traders from the ambit of the VAT. A tax under composition scheme, at a lower rate, may be levied on small traders, within a specified turnover limit, in lieu of VAT.

Customs duty

Customs duty is levied by the Central Government on the import of goods into, and export from, India. The rate of customs duty applicable to a product proposed to be imported or exported depends upon its classification under the Customs Tariff. With regard to exports from India, customs duty is levied only on a very limited list of goods.

The Customs Tariff is aligned with the internationally recognised Harmonised System of Nomenclature (HSN) provided by the World Customs Organization.

Customs duty is levied on the transaction value of the imported or exported goods. According to Section 14 of The Customs Act, 1962 (CA), the concept of transaction value is the sole basis for valuation for the purposes of import and export of goods. While the general principles adopted for valuation of goods in India are in conformity with the World Trade Organization (WTO) agreement on customs valuation, the Central Government has notified independent Customs Valuation Rules applicable to export and import of goods.

India does not have one uniform element of customs duty, and the customs duty applicable to any product is composed of a number of components. The types of customs duty applicable are as follows:

- The Basic Customs Duty (BCD) is the basic component of customs duty levied at the effective rate notified under the First Schedule to the Customs Tariff Act (CTA) and applied to the landed value of the goods (i.e. the cost, insurance, and freight [CIF] value of the goods plus landing charges at 1%). Typically, the rate of BCD is 10%.
- The additional customs duty in lieu of excise duty (CVD) is equivalent to, and is charged in lieu of, the excise duty applicable on like goods manufactured or produced in India. CVD is calculated on the sum of landed value of the goods and the applicable BCD. However, the CVD on specific consumer goods intended for retail sale in India is calculated on the basis of the maximum retail price (MRP) less specified abatement printed on their packs. The general rate of excise duty is currently 12%, and, consequently the rate of CVD is also 12%. In addition, education cess at 2% and secondary and higher education cess at 1% are also levied on the CVD.

India

- Education cess at 2% and secondary and higher education cess at 1% are also levied on the aggregate of the custom duties (except in cases of safeguard duty, countervailing duty, and anti-dumping duty).
- Additional duty of customs (ADC) to countervail state taxes and VAT of 4% is charged in addition to the above duties on imports, subject to exceptions. ADC is calculated on the aggregate of the assessable value of the imported goods, the total customs duties (i.e. BCD and CVD) and the applicable education cess and secondary and higher education cess.

BCD, education cess, and secondary and higher education cess levied on the aggregate of duties of customs are a cost of any import transaction. The duty incidence arising on account of all other components may be set off or refunded subject to prescribed conditions. Where goods are imported for purposes of manufacture, the Indian manufacturer may take a credit of the CVD and ADC paid at the time of import for offset against the output excise duty. In the case of service providers, the credit of only the CVD is available. Similarly, the Central Government provides exemption from payment of ADC on import of certain specified goods. The Central Government also has prescribed a refund mechanism in relation to ADC paid on goods imported for the purpose of trading in India, subject to fulfilment of the conditions prescribed under the governing notifications and circulars issued in this regard.

CENVAT (Excise duty)
Central Value Added Tax (CENVAT) is an excise duty levied by the Central Government on the manufacture or production of movable and marketable goods in India.

The rate at which excise duty is leviable on the goods depends on the classification of the goods under the Excise Tariff. The Excise Tariff is primarily based on the eight digit HSN classification adopted so as to achieve conformity with the Customs Tariff.

The excise duty on most consumer goods, which are intended for retail sale, is chargeable on the basis of the MRP printed on the package of the goods. However, abatements are admissible at rates ranging from 15% to 55% of the MRP. Goods, other than those covered by MRP based assessments, are generally chargeable to duty on the 'transaction value' of the goods sold to an independent buyer. In addition, the Central Government has the power to fix tariff values for charging *ad valorem* duties on the goods.

Typically, the duty rate is 12%. However, notifications granting partial or complete exemption for specified goods from payment of excise duties are also available. Education cess at 2% and secondary and higher education cess at 1% are applicable on the aggregate of excise duties. Thus, the effective rate of excise duty is 12.36%.

The central excise duty is a modified VAT wherein a manufacturer is allowed credit of the excise duty paid on locally sourced goods and the CVD and ADC paid on imported goods. The CENVAT credit can be utilised for payment of excise duty on the clearance of dutiable final products manufactured in India. Manufacturers of dutiable final products are also eligible to avail CENVAT credit of the service taxes paid on input services used in or in relation to the manufacture of final products and clearances of final products from the place of removal, subject to fulfilment of conditions.

Service tax
Service tax is levied on specified taxable services. At present, over 100 services are classified as taxable services. The existing rate of service tax is 12%. In addition, an education cess of 2% and secondary and higher education cess of 1% of the service

tax have also been levied on taxable services. Thus, the effective rate of service tax is 12.36%. There is no service tax on the services which qualify as exports, subject to fulfilment of prescribed conditions.

The onus of payment of service tax lies with the provider of services. However, in the case of specified services, such as transport of goods by road, sponsorship services, and import of services, the service tax liability rests with the recipient of the services as against the service provider.

In light of the integration of goods and services tax, a service provider can avail CENVAT credit of excise duties paid on capital goods and inputs used for providing output services, apart from availing CENVAT credit of the service taxes paid on input services, subject to fulfilment of conditions.

Taxable services provided by service providers located outside India to a recipient in India are subject to service tax. Where the taxable services are provided from outside India and received in India, the service recipient is required to become registered and to pay the tax in accordance with the relevant provisions of law.

I

Further, the Central Government has introduced the Point of Taxation Rules, 2011 which envisages the point in time when a service shall be deemed to have been provided, thereby creating a deeming fiction for imposing the tax even prior to receipt of consideration for the services rendered. These rules prescribe accounting for services tax on an accrual basis as compared to the earlier cash basis system.

Further, the Central Government has proposed to introduce a negative list-based taxation system, which is to be implemented from a date to be notified after the Finance Bill, 2012 is enacted. Pursuant to it, service tax will be levied on all services provided or agreed to be provided in a taxable territory, except the following:

- Services in the negative list.
- Services specifically exempted by notification.

In this regard, the draft Place of Provision of Services Rules, 2012 have also been tabled for public comments.

Advance ruling for customs, excise, and service tax
In order to enable foreign investors to ascertain their indirect tax liabilities arising from proposed business ventures in India, the Central Government has constituted the Authority for Advance Rulings (AAR) as a high level quasi-judicial body. The functions of the AAR comprise of giving advance rulings on a specific set of facts relating to specified matters under customs, central excise, and service tax.

Advance rulings may be sought by any non-resident investor entering into a joint venture in India in collaboration with another non-resident, or a resident of India, or a resident setting up a joint venture in India in collaboration with a non-resident. Through the Finance Act 2005, this facility has also been made available to an existing joint venture in India. The Central Government is also empowered to notify any other class or category of persons as eligible for availing the benefit of an advance ruling.

Dividend distribution tax (DDT)
Indian companies distributing or declaring dividends are liable to pay DDT at 15% (plus surcharge, education cess, and secondary and higher education cess). This tax

India

is payable on declaration, distribution, or payment, whichever is earlier, and it is in addition to the CIT payable on business profits.

SEZ developers and units in a SEZ are liable to pay DDT at 15% (plus applicable surcharge, education cess, and secondary and higher education cess) with effect from 1 June 2011.

As of tax year 2011/2012, a holding company does not have to pay DDT on dividends paid to its shareholders to the extent that it has received dividends from its subsidiary company on which DDT has been paid by the subsidiary. However, the benefit will not be available if the holding company is itself a subsidiary of another company which has a shareholding of more than 50%. The restriction in relation to the holding company not being a subsidiary of any other company has been withdrawn from 1 July 2012, to remove the cascading effect of DDT becoming payable in a multi-tier corporate structure.

Securities transaction tax (STT)

STT is levied at 0.1% (0.25% up to 1 July 2012) and is applicable to transactions involving the purchase or sale of equity shares, derivatives, units of equity-oriented funds through a recognised stock exchange, or the sale of a unit of an equity-oriented fund to any mutual fund. STT paid is eligible to be claimed as a tax-deductible expenditure when computing the tax on income from the sale of securities.

Wealth tax

All companies are liable to pay wealth tax assessed at 1% of the value of specified net assets, if the value of net wealth exceeds INR 3 million. Valuation of assets is in terms of specific rules notified by the government.

Entry tax/Octroi duty

'Entry tax' is a tax on entry of specified goods into the state from outside the state for use, consumption, or sale therein. Entry tax continues to exist under the VAT regime; however, in most states, it has been made VAT-able and can be offset against the output VAT liability in the state. The only exception is where entry taxes have been imposed in lieu of Octroi for which no offset is allowed, and hence it is a cost. It is levied on the purchase value, which is defined to mean the amount of the valuable consideration paid or payable by a person for the purchase of any goods. The value of the specified goods can be ascertained from the original invoice for purchase of such goods. Typically, the rate of entry ranges from 0.5% to 15%, depending upon the respective state.

Further, it is important to note that the levy of entry tax has been considered as unconstitutional by the High Courts of a few of the states. The state governments have filed petitions before the Supreme Court to challenge the decision of the High Courts, and at present, the matter is pending for final adjudication before the Supreme Court.

Octroi is a municipal levy which is levied at the time of entry of specified goods into the limits of the relevant municipal corporation. Thus, Octroi is leviable, if there is movement of goods from one city to another in the same state, in the event the cities fall under the jurisdiction of two different municipal corporations.

Goods and services tax (GST)

The Central Government took a major step towards the transition to a national integrated GST in 2006. In this regard, a Joint Working Group (JWG) was constituted by the Empowered Committee (EC) to study global GST models and identify suitable models for introduction in India. In 2007, the JWG recommended a dual GST model for India which was subsequently studied and approved by the EC and the Ministry of Finance.

The EC released the First Discussion Paper on the proposed GST in India on 10 November 2009. In the discussion paper, the government indicated that GST shall have two components. One levied by the Centre (Central GST or CGST) and the other levied by the states (State GST or SGST). The CGST and the SGST would be applicable on all transactions of goods and services made for a consideration except for exempted goods and services, goods which are outside the purview of GST, and transactions which are below the prescribed threshold limits. The exact date of implementation of GST is not yet decided. Details of taxes which would be subsumed in the dual GST are as follows.

The following taxes will be subsumed in the CGST:

- Excise duty.
- CVD/ADC.
- Service tax.

The following taxes will be subsumed in the SGST:

- VAT.
- Entertainment tax.
- Luxury tax.
- Lottery taxes.
- State cesses and surcharges.
- Entry tax not in lieu of octroi.

It is likely that CST will be phased out in the GST regime.

The input tax credit (ITC) for the CGST and SGST would operate in parallel and would be available for utilisation only against the output payment of CGST and SGST. Both CGST and SGST will be levied on import of goods and services into the country. The incidence of tax will follow the destination principle. Full and complete offset will be available on the GST paid on import of goods and services.

The Union Finance Minister (FM) met the EC on 21 July 2010, and the key highlight of the meeting was a single rate structure with unification of the rate for goods and services proposed to be achieved in a phased manner as below:

	Year one (%)	Year two (%)	Year three (%)
Goods			
Standard rate	10	9	8
Lower rate	6	6	8
Services	8	8	8

The FM has requested that the states adopt similar rates for the SGST.

In the Budget speech, while the FM did not indicate a specific deadline by which the GST would be introduced, he mentioned that there has been considerable progress in the last four years and that the areas of divergence of opinion with the states have been narrowed. He also said that work is underway on drafting of the model legislation for the Central and State GST. Various amendments in the Central Excise, Customs

India

and Service tax law, which include withdrawal of certain exemptions, retaining the present tax/duty rates and structure were done to align the present tax/duty structures consistent with the intended GST rates.

Branch income

Branches of foreign companies are taxed on income that is received in India, or which accrues or arises in India, at the rates applicable to foreign companies. There is no WHT on remittance of profits to the company's head office.

Income determination

Inventory valuation

Inventories are generally valued at cost or net realisable value, whichever is lower. Generally, there is conformity between book and tax reporting. The first in first out (FIFO) and average cost methods are acceptable, provided that they are consistently applied.

Capital gains

Capital gains refer to the gains made on the transfer of a capital asset, including extinguishment of the rights in an asset. Capital assets are classified into short-term capital assets and long-term capital assets. Long-term capital gains are eligible for concessional rate of tax.

Short-term capital assets are capital assets held for a period of less than 36 months. In the case of shares, listed securities, or units of specified mutual funds or zero-coupon bonds, the short-term holding period is less than 12 months. Capital assets that do not qualify as short-term capital assets are considered as long-term capital assets.

Normally, long-term capital gains are determined after increasing the cost by prescribed inflation factors. In the case of foreign companies, capital gains on the transfer of shares or debentures in Indian companies are computed in the foreign currency in which the shares or debentures were acquired, and the capital gains are reconverted into Indian currency.

Capital gains are taxed as follows:

- Long-term capital gains on the transfer of shares in a company, or units of an equity-oriented fund, which are subject to STT are exempt from taxation. However, such gains are taxable under MAT provisions.
- Other long-term capital gains are subject to taxation at 20% (plus the surcharge, education cess, and secondary and higher secondary education cess). However, long-term capital gains arising from the transfer of listed securities, units, or zero-coupon bonds are taxed at 10% (without adjusting the cost for inflation) or at 20% (after adjusting the cost for inflation), whichever is more beneficial to the taxpayer. These rates exclude surcharge, education cess, and secondary and higher education cess.
- Long-term capital gains arising to a non-resident (not being a company) or a foreign company from transfer of unlisted securities, shares, debentures, etc. Are taxable at 10% without any indexation benefit.

- Short-term capital gains on the transfer of shares in a company or units of an equity-oriented fund which are subject to STT are taxed at 15% (plus the surcharge, education cess, and secondary and higher education cess).
- Other short-term capital gains are subject to taxation at the normal corporate rates applicable to a company.

In the case of certain overseas financial organisations (e.g. off-shore funds and foreign institutional investors), long-term capital gains arising on the transfer of units purchased in foreign currency are taxable at 10% (plus the surcharge, education cess, and secondary and higher education cess) on the gross amount.

Long-term capital gains earned by non-residents on the transfer of bonds relating to Indian companies (issued abroad in accordance with government guidelines or approved schemes and acquired in foreign currency) are taxable at 10% (plus surcharge, education cess, and secondary and higher education cess) on the gross amount of gains.

The rules of carryforward and offset of loss for capital gains are as follows:

- Capital losses arising from the transfer of a short-term capital asset can be offset against capital gains arising from any other asset. However, capital losses arising from the transfer of a long-term capital asset can be offset only against capital gains arising from the transfer of any other long-term capital asset.
- Capital losses that cannot be offset can be carried forward and offset against the future capital gains. Losses can be carried forward for offset for a period of eight years after the year of loss.
- Gains and losses arising on the sale of depreciable assets are classified as short-term capital gains or losses, and the gains are taxed at the same rate as business income.

The transfer of unlisted (not tradable and not listed on any stock exchanges) shares of a company to a firm or a company without consideration or for inadequate consideration is taxable as income in the hands of the recipient firm or company.

Taxability of shares issued at premium in excess of fair market value of shares
Where a closely held company (other than a venture capital undertaking receiving from a venture capital fund/company or from any other notified person to be notified by the Central Government) issues shares at premium to a resident for an amount in excess of the fair market value of the shares, then the excess will be deemed to be the income of the company. This is effective from 1 April 2013.

Share premium in excess of fair market value to be treated as income
Any amount received towards share application money, share premium, or share capital by any closely held company will be considered as income, if the explanation offered by such company in relation to the source and nature of the amount so received is not satisfactory in the opinion of the tax officer. This is effective from 1 April 2013.

Dividend income
Dividend income received from Indian companies is not taxable in the hands of all the shareholders. This applies to resident as well as non-resident shareholders.

Income received by overseas financial organisations (offshore funds) from units of specified mutual funds, or from the Unit Trust of India, that is purchased in foreign currency, as well as interest received by non-residents on bonds issued abroad by

India

Indian companies following in terms of government guidelines and acquired in foreign currency, are taxable at 10% on the gross amount of income. Dividends (other than those received from Indian companies) and interest earned by foreign financial institutions from investment in the Indian capital market are taxable at 20% on the gross amount.

Income received from units of specified mutual funds is not taxable in the hands of the recipient. The distributing mutual fund is liable to pay a distribution tax of 25% or 30% (plus surcharge, education cess, and secondary and higher education cess). The above tax is not chargeable in respect of income distributed by an equity oriented fund in respect of distribution under such scheme.

Stock dividends (bonus shares) distributed are not taxed at the time of receipt in the hands of the recipient shareholders, but capital gains provisions are applicable to the sale of these stock dividends.

Interest income

Interest income received by a resident company is taxable at normal CIT rates. Interest income received by a non-resident company is taxed at a concessional rate of withholding at 20%, subject to conditions.

Partnership/LLP income

A partnership firm and an LLP are taxed as a separate legal entity. The share of income of partners from a partnership firm or an LLP is exempt from tax. The partnership and LLP is taxed at the rate of 30% (plus education cess and secondary and higher education cess).

The interest payment to the partner on the capital or current account is allowed as a tax deductible expenditure; however, the maximum interest allowable for tax purposes is 12% per annum. A working partner can be paid salary, bonus, commission, or remuneration. The maximum permissible deduction in respect of remuneration payable collectively to all working partners would be based on the book profit at a specified percentage for different quantum slabs of the book profit.

Unrealised exchange gains/losses

There are no specific rules under the tax law for determining the nature of unrealised foreign exchange gains or losses. However, there are various judicial precedents available which lay down certain principles for classification of foreign exchange gains or losses.

- Profit/loss is considered to be trading profit/loss if foreign currency is held on revenue account or as trading assets or as a part of circulating capital invested in the business.
- Profit/loss is considered to be of a capital nature if a foreign currency loan is taken for capital asset or fixed asset.

Foreign income

A resident company is taxed on its worldwide income. A non-resident company is taxed only on income that is received in India, or that accrues or arises, or is deemed to accrue or arise, in India. This income is subject to any favourable tax treaty provisions.

Double taxation of foreign income for residents is avoided through treaties that generally provide for the deduction of the lower of foreign tax, or Indian tax, on the doubly taxed income from tax payable in India. Similar relief is allowed unilaterally where no treaty exists, in which case a resident would be taxed at the rate which would be the lower of the Indian tax rates or the rate of the other country in which income is already taxed.

Deductions

Expenditures that are revenue in nature are allowed as a deduction if they are:

- incurred wholly and exclusively for the purpose of the business
- not in the nature of a personal expense, and
- not in the nature of a capital expense.

Depreciation

Depreciable assets are grouped in blocks, and each block is eligible for depreciation at a prescribed rate (usually 15% to 100% for machinery, 5% to 100% for buildings, 10% for furniture, 15% for windmills [80% up to 31 March 2012], and 25% for intangible assets) on the opening value (net of depreciation charged in preceding years), plus cost of acquisition, less deletions, during the year. A deletion is the reduction by way of sale, discarding, demolition, or destruction of the assets and the amount realised is reduced.

Depreciation is restricted to 50% of the prescribed rate if the asset acquired is used for less than 180 days during the year of acquisition. If money receivable on the transfer exceeds the opening written-down value plus acquisitions of the block concerned, the excess is taxed as a short-term capital gain at the same tax rates as that applicable to business income.

Additional depreciation of 20% on the cost of new plant and machinery (other than ships or aircrafts) is allowable in the year of commissioning for manufacture. This benefit is extended to power generating and distributing business. Power-generating or power-distributing companies have the option either to apply the reducing balance method provided under the normal schedule or to charge depreciation on a straight-line basis. The straight-line rates are aligned to the power companies' book depreciation rates.

Know-how, patents, licences, franchises, and similar intangible assets form part of the block of depreciable assets, provided that they are owned and put to use in the course of their business and are eligible for depreciation at the prescribed rate, which is 25%.

Tax depreciation is not required to conform to book depreciation.

Start-up expenses

Certain expenses are incurred by taxpayers either before the start-up of a business or after start-up of business, in connection with extension of the industrial undertaking, or in connection with setting-up a new unit. One fifth of such expenditure is allowed as a deduction each year, over a period of five years.

Interest expenses

Any interest paid by an assessee (taxpayer) on capital borrowed for the purposes of their business or profession is a tax-deductible expense. If the capital is borrowed for acquiring a capital asset for the purpose of extension of an existing business or profession, then interest liability pertaining to the period, until the time the asset is put to use, cannot be allowed as a tax deductible expense and will have to be added back to the cost of such asset.

India

Bad debts
The amount of any bad debt, or part thereof, that has been written off as irrecoverable in the accounts of the assessee (taxpayer) for the year is allowed as a tax-deductible write-off.

Charitable contributions
Any charitable contribution made by a company to any charity is allowed as a tax deductible expense. This is subject to certain conditions. The tax deductibility ranges from 50% to 100% of the charitable contribution, depending upon the nature of charity. The tax deductibility of charitable contribution is restricted to 10% of the total taxable income.

Expenses allowable on actual payment basis
Certain expenses, such as, but not limited to, employees' provident fund dues (i.e. retirement benefit funds), bonus to employees, and interest payable to financial institutions and banks are allowed as tax deductible expenses only on actual payment.

Bribes, kickbacks, illegal payments
Expenditures incurred by a taxpayer that are illegal are not deemed to have been incurred for the purpose of the business or profession, and no deduction will be allowed.

Taxes
All taxes (tax, duty, cess, or fees by whatever name called) relating to business (other than income tax and wealth tax) incurred during the tax year are deductible in that year, provided they are paid by the following 30 September. Otherwise, they are deductible in the year of payment.

Net operating losses
Losses can be carried forward and offset against income from subsequent year(s) for periods set out in the following table:

Types of losses	Time limit
Unabsorbed depreciation	Perpetually
Other business losses (other than speculation business losses)	8 years
Speculation business losses	4 years
Capital losses	8 years

There are no provisions in India for carrying losses back.

Payments to foreign affiliates
Indian companies can claim deduction for payment of royalties, and for interest and fees for technical or management service provided by foreign affiliates, as long as they are not capital in nature, are incurred wholly and exclusively for the purpose of the business, and requisite tax is withheld from such payment. However, if the requisite tax is not withheld from such payment, or is not paid into the government treasury after withholding, a tax deduction of the payment is available in the year of payment of tax into the government treasury.

....

Group taxation

Group taxation is not permitted under the Indian tax law.

Transfer pricing

The Indian transfer pricing regulations stipulate that income arising from 'international transactions' between 'associated enterprises' should be computed at 'arm's-length price'. Furthermore, any allowance for expenses or interest arising from any international transaction is also to be determined at arm's-length price.

The expressions 'international transactions' and 'associated enterprises' have been defined in the Indian transfer pricing regulations. Various (presently five) methods for computation of arm's-length price have been specified under the Indian transfer pricing regulations, which are broadly in line with the Organisation for Economic Co-operation and Development (OECD) Guidelines, and taxpayers are required to adopt the most appropriate method. Taxpayers are also required to maintain a comprehensive set of prescribed information and documents relating to international transactions which are undertaken between associated enterprises, on an annual basis, within the prescribed timelines (due date of filing the income tax return). Further, taxpayers are required to obtain an Accountant's Report (in prescribed Form 3CEB) from an independent accountant certifying the nature and amount of international transactions. The certificate needs to be filed along with the Income-tax return. The burden of proving the arm's-length character of the transaction is primarily on the taxpayer.

The Indian transfer pricing regulations adopt an arithmetic mean of comparable prices as the arm's-length price, with a flexibility of the percentage that is notified by the Central Government as +/- 3% of the actual price with effect from FY 2012/13 (+/- 5% up to 31 March 2012).

Where the transfer pricing officer is of the opinion that the arm's-length price was not applied, the officer may re-compute the taxable income after giving the taxpayer an opportunity to be heard. Stringent penalties are prescribed in cases of failure to comply with the provisions of the Indian transfer pricing regulations.

To facilitate quick resolution of disputes, the CBDT has provided for an alternative dispute resolution mechanism and constituted a Dispute Resolution Panel (DRP) comprised of three Commissioners of Income Tax. In cases of foreign companies, the transfer pricing orders passed by the tax officer (TO) on or after 1 October 2009 and which are prejudicial to the taxpayer, the TO shall be required to issue a draft order to the taxpayer. The taxpayer can file objections against the draft order before the DRP. After considering all evidence or objections and further enquiries, the DRP is required to issue binding directions to the TO within a period of nine months. The TO is required to pass an order within one month, in conformity with the directions of the DRP. Orders passed by a TO on the basis of directions of the DRP are appealable directly before the Income Tax Appellate Tribunal (ITAT). The DRP is now empowered to enhance any assessment matter relating to any draft order where it is raised by the assessee or by the revenue.

In order to lessen the litigation under transfer pricing regulations, provisions empowering the issue of safe harbour rules are contained in the tax law which would be separately issued by the CBDT. The safe harbour rules are not yet issued. The rules would provide the circumstances under which the tax authorities would accept the transfer price as declared by the assessee.

India

Taxpayers enjoying a tax holiday in India are also required to comply with the Indian transfer pricing regulations.

Domestic transfer pricing

Transfer pricing provisions also apply to specified domestic transactions effective from 1 April 2012 whereby any allowance or expenditure or interest on allocation of any cost or expense or any income in relation to any specified domestic transaction shall be computed having regard to the arm's-length price.

Only those cases where the aggregate of such transactions entered into by the assessee in the previous year exceeds a sum of INR 50 million are covered.

Advance pricing agreement (APA)

The provisions relating to APAs are introduced with effect from 1 July 2012.

The CBDT, with the approval of the Central Government, can enter into agreement with any assessee for determining its arm's-length price or prescribe methods, adjustments, or variations to the arm's-length price that would be valid for a maximum period of five years. The agreement will be binding (in relation to that transaction) on the assessee, the Commissioner, and the income-tax authorities subordinate to the Commissioner, except where there is a change in law or facts. The CBDT may, with the approval of the Central Government, declare an agreement to be void *ab initio* if it finds that the agreement has been obtained by fraud or misrepresentation of facts.

Thin capitalisation

No prescribed debt-to-equity ratios or thin capitalisation rules exist under India taxation law.

Controlled foreign companies (CFCs)

India currently has no CFC rules, so there will be no India tax on foreign profits that remain unremitted from offshore subsidiaries.

Tax credits and incentives

Tax incentive provisions normally have conditions applicable for the period within which the preferred activity should be undertaken and the period for which the tax incentive is available. It may also be necessary to fulfil certain other conditions such as 'forming' of a 'new' undertaking.

Tax incentives for undertakings other than infrastructure development undertakings

New industrial undertakings located in specified 'backward' states and districts are entitled to full tax exemption of profits for the first three or five years of operation, followed by a partial tax exemption of 30% of profits for the next five years. The list of backward districts has been streamlined into category A and category B districts, depending upon the current level of infrastructure development in those areas. The initial tax holiday period is five years in the case of category A districts and three years in the case of category B districts. A similar incentive is also applicable for hotels satisfying prescribed conditions.

If certain conditions are met, a tax holiday is permitted on the profits of an undertaking engaged in any of the following:

- Integrated business of handling, storage, and transportation of food grains.
- Developing and building of housing project.
- Scientific research.
- Commercial production or refining of mineral oils.
- Setting up and operating a cold chain for agricultural produce.
- Processing, preservation, and packaging of fruits or vegetables.
- Operating and maintaining a hospital in a rural area.

The tax holiday periods range from five to ten years, and the percentage of the rebate is either 30%, 50%, or 100% in initial years and 30% in the later years. The number of years constituting 'initial' and 'later' years varies from sector to sector.

Tax incentives for infrastructure development undertakings

Enterprises engaged in the business of power generation, transmission, or distribution; developing or operating and maintaining a notified infrastructure facility, industrial park, or SEZ; making substantial renovation and modernisation of the existing network of transmission or distribution lines (between specified periods); or laying and operating a cross country natural gas distribution network are eligible to a tax exemption of 100% of profits for any ten consecutive years falling within the first 15 years of operation (20 years in the case of infrastructure projects, except for ports, airports, inland waterways, water supply projects, and navigational channels to the sea).

'Infrastructure facility' means roads, including toll roads, bridges, rail systems, highway projects, water supply projects, water treatment systems, irrigation projects, sanitation and sewerage systems or solid waste management systems, ports, airports, inland waterways, inland ports, or navigational channels to the sea.

Tax incentives for exports

The export profits from a new industrial undertaking satisfying prescribed conditions established in a Free Trade Zone (FTZ), Software Technology Park (STP), or Electronic Hardware Technology Park (EHTP), or a 100% export-oriented undertaking (EOU) or a unit in a SEZ are exempt from income tax for ten years, commencing from the first year of manufacture. However, this exemption was available only if the manufacturing activity commenced before the end of the tax year 2010/11.

The export profits from a new industrial undertaking satisfying the prescribed conditions established in an SEZ is eligible for tax exemption of 100% of profits for the first five years, from the year of commencement of manufacturing, followed by a partial tax exemption of 50% of profits for the next five years. A further tax exemption of 50% of the profits for five years is also available after that, subject to an equal amount of profit being retained and transferred to a special reserve in the books of account.

Tax incentives for units in the North Eastern Region of India

Measures are in place to facilitate the development of the Indian North Eastern Region and of the state of Sikkim. Undertakings located in these states which (i) begin to manufacture or produce any eligible article, (ii) undertake substantial expansion, or (iii) commence an eligible business between 1 April 2007 and 1 April 2017 are eligible for a 100% deduction of profits for ten consecutive years.

A list of eligible businesses has been provided by the Indian government. The eligible businesses include hotels (not below two-star category), adventure and leisure sports including ropeways, the provision of medical and health services in nursing homes with a minimum capacity of 25 beds, operating a vocational training institute for hotel

India

management, catering and food crafts, entrepreneurship development, nursing and para-medical training, civil aviation related training, fashion design and industrial training, running information technology related training centre, manufacturing of information technology hardware, and bio-technology. Businesses other than the above listed eligible businesses are not entitled to claim the tax holiday.

Tax incentives for hotels/convention centres located in specified districts

A tax holiday of five years is provided to hotels (two, three, or four star) and convention centres located in the National Capital Territory of Delhi and the districts of Faridabad, Gurgaon, Gautam Budh Nagar, and Ghaziabad, provided the date of functioning of the hotel or completion of the construction of convention centre was started by 31 July 2010 (the earlier date was 31 March 2010). Hotels located in a specified district having a World Heritage Site, if such a hotel is constructed and has started functioning at any time during the period 1 April 2008 to 31 March 2013, are eligible for a tax holiday for a period of five years.

Tax incentives for certain income relating to offshore banking units and international financial services centre

A scheduled bank, or any bank incorporated by or under the laws of a country outside India, which has an offshore banking unit in an SEZ or an international financial services centre with a specified income which is subject to prescribed conditions, is eligible for a tax exemption of 100% of the specified income for five consecutive years beginning from the year in which the permission under the Indian Banking Regulation Act, 1949 was obtained and for 50% of the specified income for five consecutive years.

Tax incentive of capital expenditure on certain specified businesses

Capital expenditure is allowed at 100% in respect of the following specified businesses:

- Setting up and operating cold chain facilities.
- Setting up and operating warehousing facilities for storage of agriculture produce.
- Setting up and operating an inland container depot, freight station, or warehousing facility for storage of sugar and beekeeping and honey and beeswax produce.
- Laying and operating a cross-country natural gas or crude or petroleum oil pipeline network for distribution, including storage facilities being an integral part of such a network.
- Building and operating a hotel of two-star or above category in India.
- Building and operating a hospital with at least 100 beds.
- Developing and building a housing project under a scheme for slum redevelopment or rehabilitation framed by the government.
- Developing and building specified housing projects under an affordable scheme of the central/state government.
- Investment in a new plant or newly installed capacity in an existing plant for production of fertiliser.

In case of certain specified businesses (commencing operations on or after 1 April 2012), such as cold chain facility, warehousing for agriculture produce, hospital with at least 100 beds, notified affordable housing projects and production of fertilizer, the deduction is 150% of capital expenditure incurred on or after 1 April 2012.

The following characteristics and conditions may be noted:

- Any sum received or receivable in cash or in kind on transfer, etc. of the capital asset shall be considered as business income, if expenditure on such an asset has been allowed as a deduction under this section.
- Any loss computed in respect of the above specified businesses shall be allowed to be offset or carried forward and offset only against the profits and gains of specified businesses.
- The specified business should:
  - not be set up by splitting up or reconstruction of a business already in existence
  - not be set up by transfer of used machinery or plant exceeding 20% of the total value of the machinery or plant used in such business, and
  - have been approved by the prescribed authority (i.e. the government).

Research and development (R&D) expenditure
The weighted deduction available in respect of expenditure incurred on scientific research in an in-house R&D facility approved by the prescribed authority has been increased from 150% to 200% for companies engaged in specified businesses.

A payment made to an approved research association undertaking research in social science or statistical research or to an Indian company to be used by it for scientific research is now eligible for a weighted deduction of 125% of the payment made.

Contributions made to the National Laboratory, approved scientific research associations, universities, and the Indian Institute of Technology are now 200% deductible instead of 175% deductible.

Withholding taxes

There is an obligation on the payer (either resident or non-resident) of income to deduct tax at source (i.e. withhold tax) when certain specified payments are credited and/or paid. Some of the expenses which require tax withholding are as follows.

Payments by resident companies

Nature of payment	Payment threshold for WHT (INR) (1)	WHT rate (%)
Specified type of interest	None	10
Non-specified type of interest	5,000 (2)	20
Professional or technical service	30,000	10
Commission and brokerage	5,000	10
Rent of plant, machinery, or equipment	180,000	2
Rent of land, building, or furniture	180,000	10
Contractual payment (except for individual/Hindu undivided family [HUF])	30,000 (single payment) 75,000 (aggregate payment)	2
Contractual payment to individual/HUF	30,000 (single payment) 75,000 (aggregate payment)	1
Royalty or fees for technical services	30,000	10

Notes

1. Payments have different threshold limits. The payer is only required to withhold tax if the payment is above the limit.
2. The threshold limit for WHT for non-specified type of interest is INR 5,000 except in the case of interest received from a bank, co-operative society, or deposit with post office, for which it is INR 10,000.

India

If the Permanent Account Number (PAN) of the deductee is not quoted, the rate of WHT will be the rate specified in relevant provisions of the Act, the rates in force, or the rate of 20%, whichever is higher.

It is clarified by the Budget 2012, with retrospective effect from 1 June 1976, that the definition of 'royalty' will also include consideration for use or right to use of computer software. It is also clarified that transfer of all or any rights in respect of any right, property, or information includes transfer of all or any right to use computer software (including granting of a licence), irrespective of the medium through which such a right is transferred. Hence, while applying WHT on such payments in the nature of royalty, one will need to consider the amended definition.

Payment to non-resident companies

Nature of payment	WHT rate (%)
Dividend	0
Interest on foreign currency	10
Interest on moneys borrowed in foreign currency under a loan agreement or by way of long-term infrastructure bonds	5
Royalty and technical fees	10
Long-term capital gains other than exempt income	20
Income by way of winning from horse races	30
Other income	40

Notes

- Percentage to be increased by a surcharge, education cess, and secondary and higher education cess to compute the effective rate of tax withholding.
- Income from units of specified mutual funds is exempt from tax in the hands of the unit-holders.
- Dividends received from Indian companies are tax-free in the hands of the shareholder.
- Short-term capital gains on transfer of shares of a company or units of an equity oriented fund would be taxable at 15%, if they have been subjected to STT.
- Long-term capital gains on transfer of shares (through stock exchange) in listed companies or units of an equity oriented fund are exempt from tax if they have been subjected to STT.
- There is no threshold applicable for payment to non-residents companies up to which no tax is required to be withheld.
- If the PAN of the deductee is not quoted, the rate of WHT will be the rate specified in relevant provisions of the Act, the rates in force, or the rate of 20%, whichever is higher.

Treaty rates

Some tax treaties provide for lower WHT rates from certain types of income, as follows:

Recipient	WHT (%)			
	Dividend (1)	Interest	Royalty (12)	Fee for technical services (12)
Albania			Treaty yet to be notified	
Armenia	10	10	10	10
Australia	15	15	10/15 (2)	10/15
Austria	10	10	10	10
Bangladesh	10 (3)/15	10	10	N/A (5)
Belarus	10 (9)/15	10	15	15
Belgium	15	10 (11)/15	10	10
Botswana	7.5 (9)/10	10	10	10
Brazil	15	15	25 (15)/15	N/A (5)

India

	WHT (%)			
Recipient	Dividend (1)	Interest	Royalty (12)	Fee for technical services (12)
Bulgaria	15	15	15 (7)/20	20
Canada	15 (3)/25	15	10 (2)/15	10 (2)/15
China (People's Republic of China)	10	10	10	10
Croatia			Treaty yet to be notified.	
Cyprus	10 (3)/15	10	15	10
Czech Republic	10	10	10	10
Denmark	15 (9)/25	10 (11)/15	20	20
Ethiopia			Treaty yet to be notified.	
Finland	10	10	10	10
France	10	10	10	10
Georgia			Treaty yet to be notified.	
Germany	10	10	10	10
Greece	(14)	(14)	(14)	N/A (5)
Hungary	10 (6)	10 (6)	10 (6)	10 (6)
Iceland	10	10	10	10
Indonesia	10 (9)/15	10	15	N/A (5)
Ireland	10	10	10	10
Israel	10	10	10	10
Italy	15 (3)/25	15	20	20
Japan	10	10	10	10
Jordan	10	10	20	20
Kazakhstan	10	10	10	10
Kenya	15	15	20	17.5
Korea, Republic of	15 (4)/20	10 (13)/15	15	15
Kuwait	10	10	10	10
Kyrgyz Republic	10	10	15	15
Latvia			Treaty yet to be notified.	
Libya	(14)	(14)	(14)	N/A (5)
Luxembourg	10	10	10	10
Malaysia	10	10	10	10
Malta	10 (9)/15	10	15	10
Mauritius	5 (3)/15	(14)	15	N/A (5)
Mexico	10	10	10	10
Mongolia	15	15	15	15
Montenegro	5 (9)/15	10	10	10
Morocco	10	10	10	10
Mozambique	7.5	10	10	N/A (5)
Myanmar	5	10	10	N/A (5)
Namibia	10	10	10	10
Nepal	10 (3)/15	10 (14)/15	15	N/A (5)
Netherlands	10 (6)	10 (6)	10 (6)	10 (6)
New Zealand	15	10	10	10
Norway	15 (9)/25	15	10	10
Oman	10 (3)/12.5	10	15	15

I

India

Recipient	WHT (%) Dividend (1)	Interest	Royalty (12)	Fee for technical services (12)
Philippines	15 (3)/20	10 (13)/15	15	N/A (5)
Poland	15	15	22.5	22.5
Portugal	10 (9)/15	10	10	10
Qatar	5 (3)/10	10	10	10
Romania	15 (9)/20	15	22.5	22.5
Russian Federation	10	10	10	10
Saudi Arabia	5	10	10	N/A (5)
Serbia	5 (9)/15	10	10	10
Singapore	10 (9)/15	10 (11)/15	10	10
Slovenia	5 (3)/15	10	10	10
South Africa	10	10	10	10
Spain	15	15	10 (6)	20 (6)
Sri Lanka	15	10	10	10 (6)
Sudan	10	10	10	10
Sweden	10 (6)	10 (6)	10 (6)	10 (6)
Switzerland	10	10	10	10
Syria	5 (3)/10	7.5	10	N/A (5)
Taipei		Treaty yet to be notified.		
Tajikistan	5 (3)/10	10	10	N/A (5)
Tanzania	10 (3)/15	12.5	20	20
Thailand	15 (3, 8)/20 (9, 8)	10 (13)/25	15	N/A (5)
Trinidad & Tobago	10	10	10	10
Turkey	15	10 (11)/15	15	15
Turkmenistan	10	10	10	10
Uganda	10	10	10	10
Ukraine	10 (9)/15	10	10	10
United Arab Emirates	10	5 (11)/12.5	10	N/A (5)
United Arab Republic (Egypt)	N/A (5)	N/A (5)	N/A (5)	N/A (5)
United Kingdom	15	10 (13)/15	10 (2)/15	10 (2)/15
United States	15 (3)/25	10 (11)/15	10 (2) /15	10 (2)/15
Uruguay		Treaty yet to be notified.		
Uzbekistan	15	15	15	15
Vietnam	10	10	10	10
Zambia	5 (10)/15	10	10	10

Notes

1. The treaty tax rates on dividends are not relevant since under the current Indian tax legislation, most dividend income from Indian companies which is subject to DDT is exempt from income tax in the hands of the recipient.
2. 10% for equipment rental and ancillary services:
    *   for other cases in the first five years: 15% if government or specified organisation is the payer and 20% for other payers.
    *   for subsequent years: 15% in all cases (income of government organisations is exempt from taxation in the country of source).
3. If at least 10% of capital is owned by the beneficial owner (company) of the company paying the dividend or interest.

4. If at least 20% of capital is owned by the beneficial owner (company) of the company paying dividend or interest.
5. In absence of specific provision, it may be treated as business profits or independent personal services under respective treaties, whichever is applicable.
6. The 'most favoured nation' clause is applicable. The protocol to the treaty limits the scope and rate of taxation to that specified in similar articles in treaties signed by India with an OECD or another country.
7. If royalty relates to copyrights of literary, artistic, or scientific work.
8. If the company paying the dividend is engaged in an industrial undertaking.
9. If at least 25% of capital is owned by the beneficial owner (company) of the company paying the dividend
10. If at least 25% of capital is owned by the company during at least six months before date of payment.
11. If paid on a loan granted by a bank/financial institution.
12. The tax rate for royalties and fees for technical services, under the domestic tax laws, is 10%. This rate is to be increased by a surcharge at 2.5% on the income tax and education cess at 2% and secondary and higher secondary education cess at 1% on the income tax including surcharge. As a consequence, the effective tax rate is 10.558%. This rate applies for payments made under an agreement entered into on or after 1 June 2005. Accordingly, a tax resident can either use the Treaty rate or domestic tax rate, whichever is more beneficial.
13. If interest is received by a financial institution.
14. Taxable in the country of source as per domestic tax rates.
15. If royalty payments arise from the use or right to use trademarks.

List of limited agreements between India and other countries

A list of the countries with which India has entered into limited agreements for double taxation relief with respect to income of airlines/merchant shipping, is given here.

Country	Government Notification Reference
Afghanistan	GSR 514(E), dated 30.09.1975
Bulgaria	GSR 184(E), dated 15.04.1977
Ethiopia	GSR 8(E), dated 04.01.1978 as corrected by Notification No. GSR 159(E), dated 02.03.1978
Iran	GSR 284(E), dated 28.05.1973
Kuwait	GSR 302(E), dated 31.03.1983
Lebanon	Nos. GSR 1552 and 1553, dated 28.06.1969
Oman	GSR 313(E), dated 27.03.1985
Pakistan	GSR 792(E), dated 29.08.1989
Peoples Democratic Republic of Yemen	GSR 857(E), dated 12.08.1988
Romania	GSR 2203 dated 20.12.1968
Russian Federation	GSR 943(E), dated 23.12.1976 as modified by GSR 419(E), dated 31.05.1984, dated GSR 952(E), dated 30.12.1992
Saudi Arabia	GSR 950(E), dated 29.12.1992
Switzerland	GSR 761, dated 29.08.1958
United Arab Emirates	GSR 969(E), dated 08.01.1989
Yemen Arab Republic	GSR 2(E), dated 01.12.1987

Tax administration

Taxable period
For India, the tax year ends on 31 March.

Tax returns
Accounts for tax purposes must be made up to 31 March. The electronic return of income is required to be filed by 30 September of the succeeding tax year.

India

Quarterly withholding tax returns

Quarterly statement of taxes withheld are to be filed electronically with the tax authorities on or before 15 July, 15 October, and 15 January for the first three calendar quarters of the tax year and on or before 15 May following the last calendar quarter of the tax year.

Obligation to submit tax return for assets located outside India

A resident taxpayer having any asset (including financial interest in any entity) located outside India or signing authority in any account located outside India is mandatorily required to furnish a tax return. This is effective from 1 April 2011.

In cases where taxpayers have assets outside India, the extant time limits of four and six years for reopening tax assessment (where income has escaped assessment) has been increased to 16 years. In case of a person who is treated as an agent of a non-resident, the time limit for issuing reassessment notice has been extended from two years to six years.

General Anti Avoidance Rule (GAAR)

GAAR provisions were introduced by the 2012 Budget empowering the tax department to declare an 'arrangement' entered into by an assessee to be an 'impermissible avoidance agreement' (IAA). The resulting consequence could be denial of tax benefit either under the provisions of the Act or under the double taxation avoidance agreement (DTAA). Any step in or part of any arrangement can also be declared as an IAA.

An IAA is defined as an arrangement whose main purpose or one of whose main purposes is to obtain a 'tax benefit'. For a transaction to be declared as an IAA, at least one of the following conditions should be satisfied:

- The arrangement creates rights and obligations that are not normally between arm's-length parties.
- It results directly or indirectly in any misuse or abuse of the provisions of the Act.
- It lacks commercial substance.
- The means or manner employed is not ordinary for *bona fide* purposes.

Any arrangement is deemed to lack commercial substance if the substance or effect of the arrangement is inconsistent with the form of its individual steps or parts. The arrangement is deemed to lack commercial substance *inter alia* under the following situations as well:

- It involves round-trip financing.
- It involves an accommodating party.
- It involves elements that set off or cancel each other.
- It involves transaction conducted through one or more persons such that its value, location, source, ownership, or control of funds is disguised.

Once an agreement is declared as an IAA, the consequence could be denial of tax benefit either under the provisions of the Act or under the DTAA. Such a denial could be in any manner, including disregarding, combining, or recharacterising a step, disregarding or treating an accommodating party or any other party as one person, piercing a corporate veil, treating equity as debt, treating capital as revenue and vice-versa, etc.

To take forward the GAAR provisions, the government will be issuing guidelines for proper implementation of GAAR. The guidelines are expected to be released by the end of September 2012. Readers are advised to check the Worldwide Tax Summaries website at www.pwc.com/taxsummaries at that time for this and any other significant developments on GAAR.

Payment of tax
Tax is payable in advance (if tax for the year exceeds INR 10,000) in specified instalments for every quarter, before the 15th day of the succeeding month, during the tax year (April to March) in respect of the income of the tax year ending 31 March. Any balance of tax due on the basis of the return must be paid on a self-assessment basis before the return is filed.

Audit for income tax purposes
Persons carrying on business are required to get their books of account audited for income tax purposes where the turnover is INR 10 million (INR 6 million until 31 March 2012). For persons carrying on a profession, the turnover threshold is INR 2.5 million. The penalty for non-compliance with this audit requirement is INR 0.15 million, subject to 1% of total turnover/gross receipts.

Permanent account number (PAN)
The government/CBDT has released a new PAN form (Form No. 49AA) for persons who are not citizens of India and for LLPs, companies, firms, associations of persons (AOPs), and bodies of individuals (BOIs) formed or registered outside India.

Other issues

Mergers and acquisitions
The expression 'merger' has not been defined in the Act but has been covered as part of the definition of the term 'amalgamation'. Amalgamation is defined as a merger of one or more companies with another, or the merger of two or more companies to form a new company, in such a way that all the assets and liabilities of the amalgamating company or companies become the assets and liabilities of the amalgamated company, and held by the amalgamated company for a mining period of five years, and shareholders holding not less than 75% in value of the shares in the amalgamating company or companies become shareholders of the amalgamated company.

Capital gains
No capital gains tax is levied on the transfer of capital assets by an amalgamating company to the amalgamated company, provided the amalgamated company is an Indian company. Similar is the position in case of a demerger by a demerged company to a resulting company.

In cases where shares of an Indian company are transferred by a foreign company or a demerged foreign company to any another foreign company or resulting foreign company, there is no tax payable, provided it satisfies certain specified conditions. Furthermore, the shareholder of the amalgamating company or demerged company is not liable to pay capital gains tax on the exchange of shares with that of amalgamating company or the resulting company under the scheme of amalgamation.

India

Carryforward of accumulated losses of amalgamating company
The losses and unabsorbed deprecation of the amalgamating company are deemed to be those of the amalgamated company in the year in which the amalgamation takes place, provided it satisfies certain specified conditions.

In the case of amalgamation of a company owning an industrial undertaking, the amalgamated company shall achieve the level of production of at least 50% of the installed capacity of the undertaking before the end of the four years from the date of amalgamation and continue to maintain the minimum level of production till the end of five years from the date of amalgamation. If the above conditions are violated, the benefit claimed will be taxed in the hands of the amalgamated company in the year of default.

In case of demerger of a company, the accumulated losses or unabsorbed depreciation of the demerged company directly relatable to the undertaking or the division transferred is allowed to be carried forward and offset in the hands of the resulting company.

Amalgamation or demerger of co-operative banks
An amalgamated or resulting co-operative bank is eligible for offset and carryforward of the unabsorbed losses or accumulated depreciation of the amalgamating or demerged cooperative bank subject to fulfilment of certain conditions.

The following transactions are not liable for capital gains tax and are tax neutral:

- The transfer of a capital asset in business reorganisation by a predecessor co-operative bank to a successor co-operative bank.
- The transfer by a shareholder, in a business reorganisation of capital assets, of a share or shares held, in the predecessor co-operative bank, if the transfer is made as part of an allotment to the predecessor of any share or shares in the successor co-operative bank.

Indonesia

PwC contact

Ay Tjhing Phan
PT Prima Wahana Caraka (PwC)
JI HR Rasuna Said Kav X-7 No. 6
Jakarta 12940, Indonesia
Tel: +62 21 521 2901
Email: ay.tjhing.phan@id.pwc.com

Significant developments

Several notable regulations have been issued in the past year that provides tax
facilities and clearer guidance on tax administration and relevant value-added tax
(VAT) matters.

A Minister of Finance (MoF) regulation regarding a corporate income tax (CIT)
holiday for certain pioneer industries was released in August 2011. It was followed
by implementing regulations issued at the end of November 2011 by the heads of two
government bodies designated as the gateway for the tax holiday application (i.e. the
Minister of Industry and the Chairman of the Investment Coordinating Board [*Badan
Koordinasi Penanaman Modal* or BKPM]). The latest government regulation pertained
to the Income Tax Facilities, including Investment Allowance, and was issued in
December 2011 (*see the Tax credits and incentives section for more information*).

On the transfer pricing front, despite the continued focus of the Indonesian Tax Office
(ITO) in its ongoing audits, a government regulation, which came into effect on 1
January 2012, provides flexibility for taxpayers to apply for a Mutual Agreement
Procedure (MAP) and to continue local dispute resolution at the same time (*see Transfer
pricing in the Group taxation section*).

Taxes on corporate income

Taxable business profits are calculated on the basis of normal accounting principles
as modified by certain tax adjustments. Generally, a deduction is allowed for all
expenditures incurred to obtain, collect, and maintain taxable business profits. A timing
difference may arise if an expenditure recorded as an expense for accounting, cannot be
immediately claimed as a deduction for tax (*see the Deductions section*).

Resident corporations are taxed based on worldwide income. A foreign company
carrying out business activities through a permanent establishment (PE) in Indonesia
will generally be required to assume the same tax obligations as a resident taxpayer.

Resident taxpayers and Indonesian PEs of foreign companies have to settle their tax
liabilities either by direct payments, third party withholdings, or a combination of both.
Foreign companies without a PE in Indonesia have to settle their tax liabilities for their
Indonesian-sourced income through withholding of the tax by the Indonesian party
paying the income.

CIT rates
A flat CIT rate of 25% applies to net taxable income.

Indonesia

Public company discount

Public companies that satisfy a minimum listing requirement of 40% and certain other conditions are entitled to a tax discount of 5% off the standard rate, providing an effective tax rate of 20%.

Small company discount

Small enterprises (i.e. corporate taxpayers with an annual turnover of not more than 50 billion Indonesian rupiah [IDR]) are entitled to a 50% tax discount of the standard rate, which is imposed proportionally on taxable income on the part of gross turnover up to IDR 4.8 billion.

Final income tax

Certain types of income are subject to a final income tax at a specified percentage of the gross amount of income, without regard to any attributable expenses.

Income	Tax rate (%)
Rental of land and/or building	10
Proceeds from transfers of land and building rights	5
Fees for construction work performance	2/3/4
Fees for construction work planning	4/6
Fees for construction work supervision	4/6
Interest on time or saving deposits and on Bank of Indonesia Certificates (SBIs) other than that payable to banks operating in Indonesia and to government-approved pension funds	20
Interest on bonds other than that payable to banks operating in Indonesia and government-approved pension funds	15
Sale of exchange-traded shares on the Indonesian stock exchange	0.1
Income from lottery prizes	25

Resident companies, PEs, representatives of foreign companies, organisations, and appointed individuals are required to withhold the above final tax from the gross payments to resident taxpayers and PEs.

Special industries and activities

Companies engaged in upstream oil and gas and geothermal industries typically have to calculate CIT in accordance with their production sharing contracts (PSCs). Certain companies engaged in metal, mineral, and coal mining are governed by a contract of work (CoW) for the income tax calculation. Different provisions may apply to them, pertaining to corporate tax rates, deductible expenses, and how to calculate taxable income.

Note that such contractual-based concessions are no longer available to new mining projects since the enactment of the Mining Law in 2009. The Mining Law stipulates that general prevailing tax laws/regulations apply to mining projects; consequently, any tax facilities should be provided accordingly, except as otherwise stated in a particular mining licence.

Local income taxes

There are no local taxes on income in Indonesia. *For a list of other local taxes, see Regional taxes in the Other taxes section.*

Indonesia

Corporate residence

A company is treated as a resident of Indonesia for tax purposes by virtue of having its establishment or its place of management in Indonesia.

Permanent establishment (PE)

Under the Income Tax Law, a non-resident company may be treated as having a taxable presence if it runs a business or conducts activities in Indonesia, which can be in the form of:

- a place of management
- a branch of the company
- a representative office
- an office building
- a factory
- a workshop
- a warehouse
- a room for promotion and selling
- a mining and extraction of natural resources
- a mining working area for oil and natural gas
- a fishery, animal husbandry, agriculture, plantation, or forestry location
- a project of construction, installation, or assembly
- the furnishing of services in whatever form by employees or other person, insofar conducted not more than 60 days within a 12-month period
- a person or corporation acting as a dependent agent
- an agent or employee of an insurance company that is not established and domiciled in Indonesia that receives insurance premiums or insures risk in Indonesia, and
- the computers, electronic agent, or automated equipment owned, leased, or used by an electronic transactions provider to conduct business via the internet.

Where the non-resident company is resident in a country that has a tax treaty with Indonesia, the rules on a PE creation may be changed, usually there is a longer 'time test' for certain activities performed in Indonesia.

Other taxes

Value-added tax (VAT)

With a few exceptions, VAT is applicable on deliveries (sales) of goods and services within Indonesia at a rate of 10%. VAT on export of goods is zero-rated while the import of goods is subject to VAT at a rate of 10%. Zero-rated VAT is also applicable on exported services, but subject to a MoF limitation. Currently, only certain exported services, including toll manufacturing services, are subject to the 0% VAT rate. Services performed within the Customs Area for customers outside of the Customs Area are considered as locally delivered and are therefore subject to the regular VAT rate of 10%. Inbound use or consumption of foreign services or intangible goods, with a few exceptions, is also subject to a self-assessed VAT at a rate of 10%.

The VAT law allows the government to change the VAT rate within the range of 5% to 15%. However, since the enactment of the VAT law in 1984, the government has never changed the VAT rate.

In general, VAT collection is based on the accrual principle, whereby VAT must be collected at the time of delivery of taxable goods or services. The term delivery, in this

Indonesia

case, is defined as the time when risk and ownership of goods have been transferred or when income from a service delivery can be reliably estimated or measured. In the accrual system, income or receivables are acknowledged when a transaction takes place, regardless of whether the transaction has been paid for or not. The recognition of revenue or receivables is indicated by the issue of a commercial invoice, which is a source document for this recognition and a basis for recording it.

VAT filing is done on a monthly basis, with payment and filing being due no later than the last day of the month following the taxable delivery.

Luxury-goods sales tax (LST)
In addition to VAT, some goods are subject to LST upon import or delivery by the manufacturer to another party at rates currently ranging from 10% to 75%.

Import duty
Import duty is payable at rates from 0% to 150% on the customs value of imported goods. Customs value is calculated on cost, insurance, and freight level (CIF).

Group	Good	Rate (%)
Automobiles	Passenger and commercial vehicles	0 to 50
Automobile parts		0 to 10
Vessels	Ships, boats, and floating structures	0 to 5
Electronic goods		0 to 12.5
Footwear		5 to 25
Beverages, ethyl alcohol, and alcoholic drinks	Ethyl alcohol, beer, wine, spirits, and other beverages	5 to 30, IDR 14,000 to IDR 125,000/ltr
Essential oils and resinoids	Odoriferous substances	5 to 150
Agricultural products	Animal and vegetable products	0 to 25
Textile, textile products, and accessories	Bags, harnesses, apparels, and clothing accessories, etc.	5 to 15
Others	Chemicals, pharmaceutical products, plastic, and rubber products, etc.	0 to 25

As a commitment to liberalising trade, the Indonesian government is progressively lowering import duty rates on most products. Higher duty rates remain to protect certain industries and goods regarded as sensitive for security or social and cultural reasons.

Duty relief/exemption/deferral
The Indonesian government offers duty relief, duty exemption, and duty deferral concessions to foreign and domestic investors in order to promote the development of local and export industries. Such concessions include the BKPM Masterlist, Bonded Zone, Bonded Warehouse, import duty exemption and drawback for exports, Free Trade Zone (FTZ) in Batam, Bintan, and Karimun, Association of Southeast Asian Nations (ASEAN) duty rates, Free Trade Area (FTA) agreement duty rates, and MITA (main partners) lanes.

Land and buildings taxes
Land and buildings tax (*Pajak Bumi dan Bangunan* or PBB) is due annually at 5% of the government-determined sales value.

A transfer of land and building will cause income tax on the deemed gain on the transfer/sale to be charged to the tranferor/seller. The tax is set at 5% of the gross transfer value or the government-determined value, whichever is higher (*see Final income tax in the Taxes on corporate income section*).

In a land and building transfer, the acquirer is liable for duty on the acquisition of land and building rights (*Bea Pengalihan Hak atas Tanah dan Bangunan* or BPHTB) at 5% of the greater of the transaction value or the government-determined value.

Stamp duty

Stamp duty is nominal and payable as a fixed amount of either IDR 6,000 or IDR 3,000 on certain documents.

Regional taxes

A corporate taxpayer may be liable for a number of regional taxes and retributions. The rates range from 1.5% to 35% of a wide number of reference values determined by the relevant regional governments. The following are regional taxes that may apply:

- Motor vehicle tax.
- Motor vehicle ownership transfer fee.
- Motor vehicle fuel tax.
- Surface water tax.
- Cigarette tax.
- Hotel tax.
- Restaurant tax.
- Entertainment tax.
- Advertisement tax.
- Road illumination tax.
- Non-metal and rock minerals tax.
- Parking tax.
- Ground water tax.
- Swallow-nest tax.

Jamsostek

Employers are held responsible for ascertaining that their employees are covered by *Jamsostek* (workers social security program) which provides compensation in the event of working accidents, deaths, and old age (55 years) as well as sickness or hospitalisation. The program calls for premium contributions from both the employers and the employees. Employees' contributions are collected through payroll deductions. The premium contributions are calculated as a percentage of regular salaries/wages, ranging from 0.24% to 3%.

Branch income

Branch profits are subject to the ordinary CIT rate of 25%. The after-tax profits are subject to a withholding tax (WHT) (i.e. branch profits tax or BPT) at 20%, regardless of whether the profits are remitted to the home country. However, a concessional WHT rate may be applicable where a tax treaty is in force (*see the Withholding taxes section for more information*). The BPT may be exempt if the profits are entirely reinvested in Indonesia (*see the Tax credits and incentives section for more information*).

Indonesia

Income determination

Inventory valuation
Inventories must be measured at cost by using either the average or first in first out (FIFO) method. Once a costing method is adopted, it must be applied consistently.

Capital gains
Capital gains are generally assessable together with ordinary income and subject to tax at the standard CIT rate. However, gains from the transfer of land and buildings are not subject to regular CIT but rather are subject to final income tax at a rate of 5% of the transaction value or the government-determined value, whichever is higher.

The proceeds from sales of shares listed on the Indonesian stock exchange are not subject to normal CIT. Instead, the proceeds are subject only to a final WHT of 0.1% of the gross sales consideration. An additional tax of 0.5% applies to the share value of founder shares at the time an initial public offering takes place, irrespective of whether the shares are held or sold. Shareholders may elect not to pay this tax, in which case the actual gain will be subject to normal tax at the time the shares are sold.

Dividend income
In principle, dividend income received by a resident taxpayer from a limited liability company (generally referred to as a *Perseroan Terbatas* or PT) is taxable as ordinary income for the taxpayer receiving the dividend. However, if the dividend recipient is a PT with a minimum shareholding of 25% in the company paying the dividend and the dividend is paid out of retained earnings, it is exempt from CIT.

Where the recipient is not resident in Indonesia, a WHT rate of 20% applies, subject to variation by tax treaties (*see the Withholding taxes section for more information*).

The same rules apply to stock dividends (bonus shares), including dividends paid out of share premium (*agio*).

Interest income
Interest income on time or saving deposits and on Bank of Indonesia Certificates (SBIs) received by a resident company or a PE is taxed at a final tax rate of 20%.

Exchange gains and losses
Gains and losses arising from currency fluctuations are generally recognised on an accrual basis in accordance with the prevailing Indonesian Accounting Standards, which resemble International Accounting Standards in most respects.

Foreign income
Foreign branch income of an Indonesian company must be accounted for as Indonesian taxable income under the controlled foreign corporations (CFCs) regulation. These rules apply to Indonesian tax residents owning at least 50% of the paid-up capital (shares) in a CFC. The rules make no reference to such terms as tax avoidance or tax evasion and therefore apply even if the CFC is domiciled in a non-tax haven country. The only situation in which the rules do not apply is when the CFC's shares are listed on a recognised stock exchange. In very broad terms, under the CFC rules, the Indonesian shareholder of the CFC is deemed to receive a dividend with respect to the CFC profits based on a shareholding proportional calculation.

Deductions

In general, expenses incurred in the ordinary course of business (to obtain, collect, and maintain taxable income) are deductible, subject to the requirements for documentary support.

Note that expenses relating to gross income subject to final income tax are not deductible for CIT purposes.

Depreciation, amortisation, and depletion

Depreciable/amortisable assets include both tangible and intangible property or costs, including the cost of extending building use rights, rights for business use, rights for use, and goodwill, with a useful life of more than one year, except land that is owned and used in business. Depreciation and amortisation may be calculated under the straight-line method or the declining-balance method on an individual asset basis. Once a method is chosen, it should be applied consistently. In calculating depreciation, depreciable assets are divided into the following classes:

	Depreciation/amortisation rate (%)	
Class	Straight-line method	Declining-balance method
Property:		
Useful life of four years	25	50
Useful life of eight years	12.5	25
Useful life of 16 years	6.25	12.5
Useful life of 20 years	5	10
Buildings:		
Permanent	5	-
Non-permanent	10	-

Special rules apply for assets used in certain business fields and/or certain areas. Tax depreciation need not conform to book depreciation.

The costs incurred for acquiring rights, with a beneficial life of more than one year, for mining, oil, and natural gas concessions; forest concessions; and other rights to exploit natural resources should be amortised by the production-unit method. Except for the right to acquire oil and natural gas concessions, the depletion rate used should not exceed 20% per annum.

Organisational and start-up expenses

The costs of incorporation and expansion of the capital of an enterprise are claimed in full in the year in which the expenditure is incurred or are amortised using either the declining-balance or straight-line method at the above rates.

Costs incurred before the commencement of commercial operations with a useful life of longer than one year are capitalised and amortised according to the above rates.

Interest expense

Interest incurred in the ordinary course of business is deductible as long as the related loan is used for business purposes.

Interest on loans relating to time deposits (which income is subject to a final tax) is not deductible.

Indonesia

Interest on loans used to buy shares where dividends to be received are not subject to income tax is also not deductible.

Bad debts

Uncollectible debts are deductible for tax purposes, with the following conditions:

- The debtor has recognised the amount of uncollectible receivables as income in the relevant year.
- The taxpayer must submit a list of uncollectible account receivables to the Directorate General of Tax.
- A legal case to enforce collection has been brought to a District Court or government agency that handles state receivables, there is a written agreement on cancellation of receivables/debt release and discharge between the concerned creditor and debtor, it has been publicised in a general or a special publication, or the debtor has otherwise acknowledged that his/her debts have been cancelled.

Charitable contributions

Donations for national disasters, education facilities, sport development, and social infrastructures, with certain conditions, may be deductible in the fiscal year when the donations are provided.

Benefits in kind

Most benefits received in-kind by employees, such as free housing, are not tax-deductible to the entity providing the benefit. Free motor vehicle and telephone expenses, including depreciation, are tax-deductible but only for 50% of the total expenses incurred. Expenses for meals and transportation made available to all staff are tax-deductible. Apart from these, certain benefits in kind (e.g. housing provided in remote areas as designated by the MoF, Integrated Economic Development Areas as designated by Presidential Decree) can also be claimed as tax-deductible expenses.

Fines and penalties

Fines, penalties, and interest on underpayment of taxes are not deductible.

Taxes

Land and buildings tax and regional taxes may be deducted from taxable income. With several exceptions, input VAT is also deductible against taxable income as long as it is not claimed as a credit against output VAT.

Net operating losses

Losses may be carried forward for a maximum period of five years. Carrying back of losses is not permitted. Offsetting losses within a corporate group is not permitted.

Payments to foreign affiliates

WHT is applied as a final tax on the recipient for payments of royalties, interest, and service fees to foreign non-resident companies. Excessive and non-arm's-length payments to related parties are disallowed as deductions. The tax law denies deductions for all payments from a branch to its head office for royalties, interest, and services provided by the head office (exceptions apply for loans between bank branches and their head offices).

Group taxation

Consolidated returns are not allowed in Indonesia.

Transfer pricing

Transactions between related parties must be consistent with the arm's-length principle. If the arm's-length principle is not followed, the Director General of Tax (DGT) is authorised to recalculate the taxable income or deductible costs arising from such transactions applying the arm's-length principle.

Under the General Tax Provisions Law, the government requires specific transfer pricing documentation to prove the arm's-length nature of related-party transactions.

Detailed transfer pricing disclosures are required in the CIT return, which include the following:

- The nature and value of transactions with related parties.
- The transfer pricing methods applied to those transactions and the rationale for selecting the methods.
- Whether the company has prepared transfer pricing documentation.

Transfer pricing disputes may be resolved through the domestic objection and appeal process, or, where the dispute involves a transaction with a related party in a country that is one of Indonesia's tax treaty partners, the parties may request double tax relief under the Mutual Agreement Procedures (MAP) article of the relevant tax treaty. Taxpayers may apply for a MAP and continue the domestic dispute resolution process at the same time. A MAP application shall be discontinued if an appeal decision is declared by the Tax Court prior to the finalisation of the MAP.

The tax law authorises the DGT to enter into Advance Pricing Agreements (APAs) with taxpayers and/or another tax country's tax authority on the future application of the arm's-length principle to transactions between related parties. The process may or may not involve cooperation with foreign tax authorities. Once agreed, an APA will typically be valid for a maximum of three tax years after the tax year in which the APA is agreed. The APA can also be applied to tax years before it was agreed if certain conditions are met, such as the tax year has not been audited and there is no indication of tax crime. However, the rollback of an APA to prior years is not automatic and will be subject to agreement between the taxpayer and the DGT.

Increase in transfer pricing focused investigations

The number of tax audits with transfer pricing as the key focus area has significantly increased following the issuance of new regulations relating to transfer pricing. Transactions under particularly close scrutiny include payments of royalties and technical or management services fees, inter-company services, royalty and financing transactions, and exports to related parties.

Where a taxpayer has no documentation available to substantiate these transactions, there is a high risk that deductions for the payments will be denied in full. In this regard, the 30-day time limit within which a taxpayer must produce any documentation requested by the ITO during an audit is being strictly enforced. Any documentation provided after the 30-day time limit is being disregarded by the ITO in its decision making process.

Indonesia

Several transfer pricing specific audits have been conducted by the ITO for the past year. The ITO will identify high priority targets for transfer pricing specific audits based on:

- profit performance of the company (companies that have incurred consistent losses will be the highest priority but there is also a risk of being selected for companies with profits below industry norms) and
- materiality of the company's related party transactions.

In addition to transfer pricing audit activity, the ITO has also issued questionnaires to several taxpayers who are not under an audit that focus primarily on transfer pricing issues. It is possible that the information gathered by the ITO from these questionnaires will lead to follow-up investigations or audits in some cases.

Thin capitalisation
The MoF is authorised to make a determination on an appropriate ratio of debt to equity. Under the law, debt between related parties may be recharacterised as equity, thus giving rise to the disallowance of a tax deduction for related costs. However, the MoF has not yet issued a ruling on these matters.

Controlled foreign companies (CFCs)
See Foreign income in the Income determination section for a description of the CFC regime.

Tax credits and incentives

Foreign tax credit
Tax paid or payable in foreign countries upon income from abroad received or obtained by a resident taxpayer may be credited against tax payable in Indonesia in the same fiscal year.

The amount of tax credit is in the same amount with income tax paid or payable abroad, but shall not exceed tax payable calculated according to the Indonesian tax law.

Tax holiday
New corporate taxpayers in certain pioneer industries may enjoy a CIT exemption for a period of five to ten years from the start of commercial production. After the end of the CIT exemption, the company will receive a 50% CIT reduction for two years.

To be eligible for the above facilities, taxpayers should be newly incorporated in Indonesia (not earlier than 14 August 2010), should have a legalised new capital investment plan of a minimum IDR 1 trillion, should deposit a minimum of 10% of their planned investment value in banks located in Indonesia, and should not withdraw the deposit prior to the realisation of the investment plan.

An application for the tax holiday must be submitted to the Minister of Industry (MoI) or to the BKPM Chairman. A proposal for approval of the MoF will be made by the MoI or the BKPM Chairman after carrying out research on the applicant. Tax holiday proposals may only be submitted to the MoF until 15 August 2014.

Inbound investment incentives
The DGT, on behalf of the MoF and based on the recommendation of the BKPM Chairman, may provide the following tax concessions to PT companies following their investment in certain designated business areas and/or in certain designated regions with a high priority on the national scale:

- A reduction in net income of up to 30% of the amount invested (generally amount spent on assets), prorated at 5% for six years from commercial production date, provided that the assets invested are not transferred out within six years.
- Acceleration of fiscal depreciation deductions.
- Extension of tax loss carryforwards for up to ten years.
- A reduction of the WHT rate on dividends paid to non-residents to 10%.

A government regulation was issued in December 2011 which lengthened the list of investments eligible for the tax facilities. The list now covers 129 types of investment, which include 52 types of investment in particular sectors and 77 types of investment in particular sectors and regions.

Taxpayers who have enjoyed the income tax facilities above cannot enjoy the tax holiday facility, and vice versa.

The same tax facilities may be granted by the DGT to companies conducting business in an Integrated Economic Development Area (*Kawasan Pengembangan Ekonomi Terpadu* or KAPET). Specific approval must be obtained from the DGT for these tax facilities. If the company has bonded zone (*Kawasan Berikat* or KB) status, the tax facilities will also include those typically enjoyed by a KB company, for example:

- Non-collection of VAT and sales tax on certain luxury goods transactions.
- Exemption from prepaid income tax on the importation of capital goods and other equipment directly relating to production activities.
- Postponement of import duty on capital goods and equipment and goods and materials for processing.
- Exemption from import duty for four years on machinery and certain spare parts.

The designation of an area as a KAPET is set out in a specific presidential decree. Currently, there are approximately 25 areas designated as KAPETs.

Reinvestment of branch profits
PEs that reinvest their after-tax profits in Indonesia within the same year or no later than the following year are exempt from branch profit tax on these profits. The reinvestment should be one of the following forms:

- As a founder or a participant founder in a newly established Indonesian company through capital participation.
- As a shareholder of an established Indonesian company through capital participation.
- Acquisition of a fixed asset used by the PE to conduct its business or activities in Indonesia.
- Investment in the form of an intangible asset used by the PE to conduct its business or activities in Indonesia.

Shares in a newly established company shall not be transferred until, at a minimum, two years from the date that the company commences commercial production. With regard to the investment in an established Indonesian company, acquisition of a fixed asset, or investment of an intangible asset, the investment shall not be transferred until, at a minimum, three years after the investment.

Indonesia

Other incentives

Income earned by venture capital companies in the form of profit-sharing from their investments in Indonesia is exempt from tax, provided that the following conditions are met:

- Entities are small or medium-scale businesses in one of the sectors designated by the Indonesian government.
- Investments are not listed on the Indonesian stock exchange.

Withholding taxes

Indonesian income tax is collected mainly through a system of withholding taxes. Where a particular income item is subject to WHT, the payer is generally held responsible for withholding or collecting the tax. These withholding taxes are commonly referred to using the relevant article of the Income Tax Law, as follows.

Article 23/26 WHT

Article 23/26 WHT is levied on a variety of payments to corporations and individuals, resident and non-resident, at the following rates:

	WHT (%)				
	Dividends				
Recipient	Portfolio	Substantial holdings	Interest (8)	Royalties (9)	Branch profits (10)
Resident corporations (5)	15	0	15	15	N/A
Resident individuals	10	10	15	15	N/A
Non-resident corporations and individuals					
Non-treaty	20	20	20	20	0/20
Treaty:					
Algeria	15	15	0/15	15	10
Australia	15	15	0/10	10/15	15
Austria	15	10	0/10	10	12
Bangladesh	15	10	0/10	10	10
Belgium	15	10	0/10	10	10
Brunei	15	15	0/15	15	10
Bulgaria	15	15	0/10	10	15
Canada	15	10	0/10	10	15
China	10	10	0/10	10	10
Croatia (6)	10	10	0/10	10	10
Czech Republic	15	10	0/12.5	12.5	12.5
Denmark	20	10	0/10	15	15
Egypt	15	15	0/15	15	15
Finland	15	10	0/10	10/15	15
France	15	10	0/10/15	10	10
Germany (1)	15	10	0/10	10/15	10
Hong Kong (7)	10	5	0/10	5	5
Hungary (3)	15	15	0/15	15	20

	WHT (%)				
	Dividends				
Recipient	Portfolio	Substantial holdings	Interest (8)	Royalties (9)	Branch profits (10)
India	15	10	0/10	15	10
Iran	7	7	0/10	12	7
Italy	15	10	0/10	10/15	12
Japan	15	10	0/10	10	10
Jordan (3)	10	10	0/10	10	20
Korea (North)	10	10	0/10	10	10
Korea (South) (2)	15	10	0/10	15	10
Kuwait	10	10	0/5	20	0/10
Luxembourg (1)	15	10	0/10	12.5	10
Malaysia (4)	10	10	0/10	10	12.5
Mexico	10	10	0/10	10	10
Mongolia	10	10	0/10	10	10
Morocco (6)	10	10	0/10	10	10
Netherlands	10	10	0/10	10	10
New Zealand (3)	15	15	0/10	15	20
Norway	15	15	0/10	10/15	15
Pakistan (1)	15	10	0/15	15	10
Papua New Guinea (1, 6)	15	15	0/10	10	15
Philippines	20	15	0/10/15	15	20
Poland	15	10	0/10	15	10
Portugal	10	10	0/10	10	10
Qatar	10	10	0/10	5	10
Romania	15	12.5	0/12.5	12.5/15	12.5
Russia	15	15	0/15	15	12.5
Seychelles (3)	10	10	0/10	10	20
Singapore	15	10	0/10	15	15
Slovakia	10	10	0/10	10/15	10
South Africa (3)	15	10	0/10	10	20
Spain	15	10	0/10	10	10
Sri Lanka	15	15	0/15	15	20
Sudan	10	10	0/15	10	10
Suriname (6)	15	15	0/15	15	15
Sweden	15	10	0/10	10/15	15
Switzerland (1)	15	10	0/10	10	10
Syria	10	10	10	15/20	10
Taiwan	10	10	0/10	10	5
Thailand	20	15	0/15	15	20
Tunisia	12	12	0/12	15	12
Turkey	15	10	0/10	10	10
Ukraine	15	10	0/10	10	10
United Arab Emirates	10	10	0/5	5	5
United Kingdom	15	10	0/10	10/15	10
United States of America	15	10	0/10	10	10
Uzbekistan	10	10	0/10	10	10

Indonesia

| | WHT (%) | | | | |
| | Dividends | | | | |
Recipient	Portfolio	Substantial holdings	Interest (8)	Royalties (9)	Branch profits (10)
Venezuela (1)	15	10	0/10	20	10
Vietnam	15	15	0/15	15	10
Zimbabwe (1, 6)	20	10	0/10	15	10

Domestic Article 23 WHT is also payable at the rate of 2% for most types of services where the recipient of the payment is an Indonesian resident.

Notes

1. Service fees, including for technical, management, and consulting services, rendered in Indonesia are subject to WHT at rates of 5% for Switzerland, 7.5% for Germany, 10% for Luxembourg, Papua New Guinea, Venezuela, and Zimbabwe, and 15% for Pakistan.
2. VAT is reciprocally exempt from the income earned on the operation of ships or aircraft in international lanes.
3. The treaty is silent concerning branch profit tax rate. The ITO interprets this to mean that the tax rate under Indonesian Tax Law (20%) should apply
4. Labuan offshore companies (under the Labuan Offshore Business Activity Tax Act 1990) are not entitled to the tax treaty benefits.
5. In the case of dividends received by a resident shareholder, 'portfolio shareholding' refers to share ownership of less than 25% of the paid-up capital. In this respect, the dividend tax withheld by the payer constitutes a prepayment of the income tax liability of the shareholder. 'Substantial shareholding' refers to the share ownership of 25% of the paid-up capital or more.
6. Ratified but not yet effective, pending the exchange of ratification documents. Expected effective date is 1 January 2013.
7. Entered into force with the effective dates of 1 January 2013 for Indonesia and 1 April 2013 for Hong Kong.
8. Interest:
   - Lower rate or exemption if received by a financial institution.
   - Exempt if paid to the government.
   - Lower rate or exemption if paid by an approved industrial undertaking.
   - Exempt if paid by a bank and received by a bank.
   - Exempt if paid to a bank but linked to a government loan agreement or paid to specific financial institutions/banks.
9. Royalties:
   - Lower rate for payments in connection with literary or artistic copyrights, including film royalties.
   - Lower rate for payments in connection with industrial, commercial, or scientific equipment.
   - Lower rate for payments in connection with patents, designs, secret formulas/processes, or industrial, commercial, or scientific equipment/experience.
10. Branch profits:
    - PEs that reinvest their after-tax profits in Indonesia within the same year or no later than the following year are exempt from branch profit tax on these profits (see the Tax credits and incentives section).

The issue of beneficial ownership has come under tax office scrutiny. For treaty WHT rates to apply to passive income such as interests, dividends, and royalties, the recipient of such income must be the beneficial owner. The recipient must also provide a Certificate of Domicile (CoD) in the form required by the ITO certified by their home country tax authority, certifying that the recipient is a tax resident of that country. The CoD in the form prepared by the other country's tax authority may only be used in limited circumstances. Further, the CoD form also requires a number of declarations to be made by the recipient that acknowledges that the use of the treaty jurisdiction was not merely for obtaining the benefit of the treaty. These declarations place onerous obligations on both the Indonesian payer and the recipient entity. Without a certified CoD, a WHT at a rate of 20% will apply. These aspects need to be considered when paying income of this nature.

Indonesia

Article 22 Income Tax

Article 22 income tax is typically applicable to the following:

Event	Tax rate (%)	Tax base
1. The import of goods (except goods mentioned in number 2 below) using an Importer Identification Number (*Angka Pengenal Impor* or API)	2.5	Import value (i.e. CIF value plus duties payable)
2. The import of soybeans, wheat and flour wheat using an API	0.5	Import value (i.e. CIF value plus duties payable)
3. The import of goods without an API	7.5	Import value (i.e. CIF value plus duties payable)
4. The auctioned imported goods	7.5	Auction prices
5. The sale of goods to the government requiring payment from the State Treasury and Proxy of Budget User (*Kuasa Pengguna Anggaran* or KPA)	1.5	Selling prices
6. The purchasing of oil fuel by state-owned gas stations	0.25	Selling prices
7. The purchasing of oil fuel by private gas stations and non-gas stations	0.3	Selling prices
8. The purchasing of gas fuel	0.3	Selling prices
9. The purchasing of lubricants	0.3	Selling prices
10. The purchasing of steel products	0.3	Selling prices
11. The purchasing of automotive products	0.45	Selling prices
12. The purchasing of paper products	0.1	Selling prices
13. The purchasing of cement	0.25	Selling prices
14. The purchasing of materials by appointed manufacturers or exporters in forestry, plantation, agriculture, and fishery from wholesalers	0.25	Selling prices
15. The purchasing of very luxurious goods	5	Selling prices

Notes

1. The tax does not apply, either automatically or given an Exemption Certificate issued by the DGT, on the following types of imports:
   - Goods exempted from import duties and VAT.
   - Goods that have been temporarily imported (i.e. goods for re-export).
   - Goods for re-importing (i.e. to be repaired or tested for subsequent re-exporting).
2. In event 5, the tax collector (the State Treasury, state-owned company, etc.) must withhold Article 22 income tax from the amount payable to a particular supplier (vendor). In the other events, the importer or the buyer of the designated goods must pay Article 22 income tax in addition to the amounts payable for the goods imported or purchased.
3. Vendors of goods under events 10 through 13 can only collect Article 22 income tax from buyers if they have been appointed by the DGT to undertake this role (i.e. if there has been a specific DGT Appointment Decision).
4. Article 22 income tax constitutes a prepayment of corporate/individual income tax liabilities, except for the purchasing of oil fuel, gas fuel, and lubricants by non-distributors/agents, which is categorised as final tax.
5. Tax exemption applies to certain categories of goods or to the importing/purchasing of goods for non-business purposes.

Tax administration

Payments of tax and tax returns filing

Tax liabilities for a particular period or year must typically be paid to the State Treasury through a designated tax-payment bank (*bank persepsi*) and then accounted for at the DGT office through the filing of the relevant tax returns. The tax payments and tax

Indonesia

return filing for a particular tax must be undertaken monthly or annually, depending upon the tax obligation in question.

Corporate tax liabilities may be settled either by direct payments, third party withholdings, or a combination of both. Monthly tax instalments constitute the first part of tax payments to be made by taxpayers as a prepayment of their current year CIT liability. A monthly tax instalment is generally calculated using the most recent CIT return. The tax withheld by third parties on certain income or tax to be paid in advance on certain transactions (i.e. imports) also constitute prepayments for the current year corporate tax liability of the income recipient or the party conducting the import. If the total amounts of tax paid in advance through the year are less than the total CIT due, the company concerned has to settle the shortfall before filing its CIT return. Returns for transaction taxes such as WHT must be filed on a monthly basis.

A summary of these tax obligations is as follows:

Monthly tax obligations

Type of tax	Tax payment deadline	Tax return filing deadline
Article 21/26 WHT	The 10th of the following month	The 20th of the following month
Article 23/26 WHT	The 10th of the following month	The 20th of the following month
Article 25 Income Tax Instalment	The 15th of the following month	The 20th of the following month
Article 22 Income Tax on imports / Payments to Tax Collectors	The 10th of the following month	The 20th of the following month
Article 4(2) Final Income Tax	The 10th of the following month	The 20th of the following month
VAT and LST	Prior to the tax return filing deadline	The end of the following month

Annual tax obligations

Type of tax	Tax payment deadline	Tax return filing deadline
Corporate Income Tax	The end of the fourth month after the book year end before filing the tax return	The end of the fourth month after the book year end
Land and Building Tax (PBB)	Six months after the receipt of a Tax Due Notification Letter from the ITO	N/A

Penalties

Late payments of the above taxes incur interest penalties at 2% per month, with a maximum of 48%. Part of a month, for example a single day, is considered a full month.

Late filing of a tax return or failure to file a tax return incurs an administrative penalty at the following amounts:

Type of tax return	IDR
VAT return	500,000
Other monthly tax returns	100,000
Corporate income tax return	1,000,000

Tax assessments

Indonesia uses a self-assessment system under which taxpayers are trusted to calculate, pay, and report their own taxes in accordance with prevailing tax laws and regulations. However, the DGT may issue tax assessment letters to a particular taxpayer if it finds that, based on a tax audit or on other information, the taxpayer has not fully paid all tax liabilities. A tax assessment letter may also be issued by the DGT to a taxpayer who ignores a warning letter to file a tax return within a specified period. Failure to maintain books in accordance with the prescribed standards is another condition that may lead the DGT to issue an official tax assessment.

Statute of limitations
Under the current Tax Administration Law, the DGT can issue an underpaid tax assessment letter for the years up to 2007 only within ten years after the incurrence of a tax liability, the end of a tax period (month), or the end of (part of) a tax year, but no later than 2013. For years from 2008 onwards, the time spans for the issuing of underpaid tax assessment letters is reduced to five years.

Tax audits
The tax audit of a company may cover only a particular tax or all taxes for a particular tax period (a tax month) or tax year. It may be conducted at the company's premises, at the DGT offices, or at both.

Conditions triggering a tax audit
A tax refund request will always trigger a tax audit. Due to the requirement for the DGT to decide on a refund request within 12 months, a tax audit will typically begin from a few weeks to several months from the refund request date. A corporate tax refund request will normally trigger a complete tax audit covering all taxes. A refund request of any other tax will normally trigger a tax audit covering only one particular tax. The DGT will likely broaden the tax audit scope to include other taxes.

Other events which may trigger a tax audit include the following:

- A tax return in an overpayment position (not necessarily accompanied by a refund request).
- An annual income tax return presenting/claiming a tax loss.
- A tax return not filed within the prescribed time.
- A tax return meeting certain (undisclosed) DGT criteria.

Industry-based profitability benchmarking
The ITO has introduced profitability benchmarking based on taxpayer industries. The benchmarking is based on analysis conducted internally by the ITO and is intended to be used in assessing the risk profile of Indonesian corporate taxpayers as a tool in its audit selection process. Taxpayers with profitability that falls below the ITO's benchmarks for their industry may be asked for further information, asked to amend a tax return, or possibly be subject to an audit.

The benchmarking contains a range of financial ratios for the industries examined, including gross profit margin, operating profit margin, net profit margin, and corporate tax to turnover. Up to now, the ITO has released benchmarking guidelines of 115 industries. Further benchmarking regulations are likely to be issued in the future which cover additional industries.

Other issues

Business combinations and splits
Transfers of assets in business mergers, consolidations, or business splits must generally be dealt with at market value. Gains resulting from this kind of restructuring are assessable, while losses are generally claimable as a deduction from income.

Indonesia

However, a tax-neutral merger or consolidation, under which assets are transferred at book value, can be conducted but subject to the approval of the DGT. To obtain this approval, the merger or consolidation plan in question must pass a business-purpose test. Tax-driven arrangements are prohibited, and tax losses from the combining companies may not be passed to the surviving company.

Subject to a similar, specific DGT approval, the same concession is also available for business splits that constitute part of an initial public offering (IPO) plan. In this case, within one year of the DGT's approval being given, the company concerned must have made an effective declaration regarding registration for an IPO with the Capital Market Supervisory Board (*Badan Pengawas Pasar Modal* or BAPEPAM). In the event of complications beyond the company's control, the period may be extended by the DGT for up to four years.

Iraq

PwC contact

Stephan Stephan
PricewaterhouseCoopers Jordan
Third Circle, Jabal Amman
14 Hazza' Al-Majali Street
PO Box 5175, Amman 11183
Jordan
Tel: +962 6 500 1300
Email: stephan.stephan@jo.pwc.com

Significant developments

The suppliers of goods and services are subject to withholding tax (WHT) at the rate of 3% to 3.3%.

Foreign oil companies contracting to operate in Iraq in the following activities in Iraq are subject to corporate income tax (CIT) at a rate of 35%:

- Oil and gas fields and exploration areas upstream development contracts.
- Seismic survey.
- Wells excavation.
- Reclamation of wells.
- Technical operations related to wells and including the laying down linings, cementing, wells recovery, electrical boring, and wells completion.
- Surface installations for the operations of producing and extracting oil or gas and the industries related to them.
- Water injection installations.
- Flow pipes.
- Gas treatment coefficient.
- Cathode protection.
- Engineering examination and qualitative control related to oil industries.
- Water wells excavation.
- Activities related to extraction up to the limit at which oil or gas is ready for pumping to exportation outlets.

For the purpose of these instructions, 'foreign company' shall mean the company incorporated in accordance with foreign laws.

The main contractors (operators) are required to deduct 7% of the total payment due for the subcontractor. The amounts deducted shall be transferred to the Public Taxation Authority within 30 days as of the date of payment and shall be entered as trusts to be settled when making the final tax accounting.

Taxes on corporate income

All income derived from Iraq is subject to tax in Iraq regardless of the residence of the recipient.

The effective CIT system presented in Iraq for juristic persons (except partnerships) is based on a statutory CIT rate of 15% at all income levels with no progressive tax rate scale.

Iraq

Foreign oil company income tax
The income realised in Iraq from contracts concluded with foreign oil companies, their branches or offices, and subcontractors working in Iraq in the oil and gas production sector and related industries are taxed at a rate of 35%.

Corporate residence

One of the key issues in determining when a company becomes taxable in Iraq is whether the foreign company is considered to be doing business 'in Iraq' or 'with Iraq'. In 2009, with Instructions No. 2/2008, the Iraqi tax administration provided a clearer distinction between business 'in Iraq' and business 'with Iraq'.

Once the determination has been made that the company is trading 'in Iraq', the company should legally register in Iraq and then register with the General Commission for Taxes (GCT). A company that is registered with the GCT will be subject to CIT and will be required to file a CIT return.

Permanent establishment (PE)
It is important to note that the current Iraq income tax law does not clearly define a PE; therefore, it is important to monitor commercial activity being performed in the country to ensure compliance with the registration requirements and tax law. The company should consult with their internal tax department and external advisers if they have signed a contract to provide any type of services inside Iraq to determine if the company should have a legal registration and begin to file CIT returns.

Other taxes

Sales tax
A sales tax of 10% of the value of services is imposed on services rendered by deluxe and first class restaurants and hotels in Iraq. There are no other sales taxes in Iraq.

Custom duty
The customs duty system and procedures in Iraq are currently evolving. In March 2010, the Iraqi Presidency Counsel issued Law 12 of 2010 (Custom Tariff Law), which is in effect as of 1 June 2012. The law is comprised of 11 articles and primarily addresses custom duties on goods imported into Iraq. The law notes that customs duties shall be levied based on percentages set in the custom tariff and agricultural agenda that is annexed to the Custom Tariff Law. For the purposes of the Custom Tariff Law, the custom tariff and agricultural agenda refers to the schedule comprised of itemised and codified sections and notes based on the international harmonised system adopted by the World Customs Organization (WCO).

Excise taxes
There is no tax provision in the Iraqi Tax Law addressing excise taxes.

Property taxes
A basic tax of 10% is assessed on the annual revenue for all real estate collected from the real estate owner or the long-term lessee (five years). In cases where the owner or long-term lessee cannot be located, the person occupying the real estate will be assessed. Note that the annual revenue for each real estate is discounted by 10% for expenses and maintenance before assessing the tax on that real estate.

Iraq

Transfer taxes

There are no restrictions or taxes on transferring funds into or out of Iraq.

Stamp duty

All direct and indirect contracts related to credit facilities and other bank's activities (e.g. letter of credit contracts) are subject to the stamp fees at a rate of 0.2% of the contract value.

Branch income

The tax treatment for the branch is similar to the local Iraqi corporation. In general, CIT is imposed on corporate entities and foreign branches with respect to taxable profit from all sources arising or deemed to arise in Iraq. However, certain limitations apply to head office expenses.

Income determination

A corporation has to determine its profit/loss according to its income statement for a tax period as established under the Unified Accounting System (Iraqi Generally Accepted Accounting Principles [GAAP]). However, to reach the taxable income, positive or negative adjustments have to be made to the profit/loss as determined according to GAAP.

Inventory valuation
There is no tax provision in the Iraqi Tax Law addressing inventory valuation.

Capital gains
Capital gains on sales of depreciable assets are taxed at the normal CIT rate. To the best of our knowledge and legal practice, gains derived from the sale of shares and bonds not in the course of a trading activity are exempt from tax. Capital gains derived from the sale of shares and bonds in the course of a trading activity are taxable at the normal CIT rate.

Dividend income
Under the tax law, dividends paid out of profits that have been subject to tax are not taxed again in the hands of the shareholder.

Interest income
Interest income deemed to arise in Iraq is taxed at the normal CIT rate.

Rent/royalties income
Rent and royalties income deemed to arise in Iraq are taxed at the normal CIT rate.

Foreign income
There is no tax provision in the Iraqi Tax Law addressing foreign income.

Deductions

In general, all expenses incurred by the taxpayer in order to produce income during the year are deducted from income, provided that such expenses are confirmed by acceptable documents, with some exceptions.

Iraq

Depreciation
The Iraqi Depreciation Committee sets the maximum depreciation rates for various types of fixed assets (please contact us for additional information regarding the specific rates). If the rates used for accounting purposes are greater than the prescribed rates, the excess is disallowed.

The depreciation method is either a straight-line method or declining-balance method.

Goodwill
Iraqi tax law does not contain a provision that covers the deductibility of goodwill.

Start-up expenses
Iraqi tax law does not contain a provision that covers the deductibility of start-up expenses.

Interest expenses
Iraqi tax law does not contain a provision that covers the deductibility of interest expenses.

Bad debt
Bad debt is deductible if it was included in earlier income and there is proof of the unsuccessful steps to collect it.

Charitable contributions
Charitable contributions to the Government and Socialist Sector departments and to scientific, cultural, educational, charitable, and spiritual organisations, which are legally recognised (provided that the Minister of Finance has issued a list containing the names of these organisations), are deductible.

Bribes and illegal payments
Bribes and illegal payments are not allowed or deductible.

Fines and penalties
Broadly speaking, fines and penalties are not deductible items.

Taxes
Broadly speaking, taxes are not deductible items.

Net operating losses
Under the tax law, loss of a taxpayer in some sources of income arising in Iraq, substantiated by legally accepted documents, are generally deducted from profits arising from other sources.

Losses which cannot be settled in this manner shall be carried forward and deducted from the income of the taxpayer over five consecutive years, provided that losses may not offset more than half of the taxable income of each of the five years and the loss is from the same source of income from which it has arisen.

Losses cannot be carried back.

Payments to foreign affiliates
Iraqi tax law does not contain a provision that covers the deductibility of payments to foreign affiliates.

Iraq

Group taxation

Iraqi tax law does not contain any provisions for filing consolidated returns or for relieving losses within a group of companies.

Transfer pricing
The precise meaning of transfer pricing under the effective Iraqi tax system is rather unclear from a tax and legal perspective.

We note that whilst having no specific transfer pricing legislation, Iraq does have a 'third party' arm's-length provision contained within its tax legislation; whereby, if a non-resident taxpayer is engaged in business with a resident and it appears to the tax authority that due to the connection existing between the resident and the non-resident, and the substantial control of one over the other, that the business relationship is arranged in a manner that leaves no profits to the resident, or the profits left are much less than what is normally earned, the tax shall be assessed on the actual profits of the non-resident and charged to the resident as if the resident is the business agent for the non-resident.

Thin capitalisation
Iraqi tax law does not contain a provision that covers thin capitalisation.

Tax credits and incentives

In accordance with the Iraqi Investment Law, approved industrial projects are given certain custom duty and tax incentives; however, oil and gas is not one of the sectors that is normally granted investment promotion exemptions incentives.

The tax incentives may include corporate tax, individual tax, and others; however, the tax incentives vary from one project to another.

The Board of Investment Promotion has the authority to add any sector or specific project to the list of sectors or projects that benefit from the investment promotion law incentives.

Foreign tax credit
Income tax paid to a foreign country on income earned in that country may be credited against tax paid to Iraq. The amount of the credit may not exceed the amount of tax assessed in Iraq.

Withholding taxes

Under the tax law, the amount due from any residing taxpayers to a non-resident, whether the payment is made in cash or credited to the account, is subject to WHT at the rate of 15% if such amounts are related to interest on debentures, mortgages, loans, deposits and advances, as well as annual allowances, pension salaries, or other yearly payments.

Iraq

....

Tax administration

Taxable period
The taxable year in Iraq is the calendar year.

Tax returns
The statutory time line for filing tax returns is the first day of June of the year of assessment. If the self-assessment of tax is not accepted by the tax authorities, tax is assessed on the income of the taxpayer based on the information available to the tax authorities.

Failure to file a tax return may lead to an estimate of income and assessment of tax by the tax authorities; however, such an assessment does not relieve the taxpayer from responsibility for non-submission of the return within the statutory time line stipulated by law.

Payment of taxes
Payment of the tax liability has to be paid within 21 days from the assessment date by the tax authority. There is no requirement of quarterly payments during the taxable year.

Statute of limitations
The statute of limitations is seven years. However, the tax authority has the right to go back beyond seven years in certain instances.

Iraqi GAAP
The Iraqi tax law requires all taxpayers to maintain books and records in accordance with Iraq's local unified accounting system (Iraqi GAAP).

These books shall constitute tax books/accounts. This accounting treatment will determine when income is accrued and costs are incurred for computing taxable profits.

Ireland

PwC contact

Feargal O'Rourke
PricewaterhouseCoopers
One Spencer Dock
North Wall Quay
Dublin 1, Ireland
Tel: +353 1 792 6480
Email: feargal.orourke@ie.pwc.com

Significant developments

Research and development (R&D) tax credit

Tax incentives for companies undertaking in-house R&D activities are at the forefront of Ireland's attempts to establish itself as a knowledge economy. Recent changes introduced in Finance Act 2012 continue to enhance the attraction of Ireland as an R&D location.

In a very innovative policy move, Finance Act 2012 has introduced increased flexibility for companies in terms of utilising the benefit of the R&D tax credit. Companies who are in receipt of an R&D tax credit will now, in certain instances, have the option to reward key employees through an alternative use of that credit. In effect, the company may surrender a portion of their R&D credit that could otherwise have been used to reduce corporation tax against employees' income. Essentially, this new measure can reduce an employee's effective rate of tax to 23% (the average effective tax rate for such employees would typically be in the region of 40% in the absence of such an R&D credit).

Finance Bill 2012 also introduced a limited volume-based approach for the purposes of calculating the tax credit. Going forward, the first 100,000 euros (EUR) of qualifying R&D expenditure will now benefit from the 25% R&D tax credit on a volume basis (thus ignoring the 2003 base year spend), meaning that companies engaging in R&D are guaranteed a credit of EUR 25,000 in respect of their first EUR 100,000 of expenditure.

Cash pooling

The corporate treasury sector sought changes to facilitate international cash pooling operations, and certain relevant changes were brought about in Finance Act 2012. Under a typical cashpool arrangement, interest payments by the Irish cashpool leader typically would constitute 'short' interest for tax purposes because of the overnight/short term nature of these arrangements. Prior to the introduction of Finance Act 2012, an interest payment by an Irish cashpool leader to a 'group' company (75% or more direct or indirect relationship) resident outside the European Union (EU) in a country with which Ireland does not have a double tax treaty (DTT) may have been regarded as a dividend for tax purposes. There were two tax consequences of this. Firstly, this interest was not deductible for corporation tax purposes, giving rise to an Irish tax cost of 12.5%. Secondly, dividend withholding tax (WHT) at a rate of 20% may have applied, although there are a number of exemptions from dividend WHT that may be relevant, depending on the specific circumstances.

Finance Act 2012 has introduced a relieving provision effective for accounting periods ending on or after 1 January 2012 in respect of 'short' interest. Short interest is generally regarded as interest on a loan/deposit where the term is less than a year. Essentially, the Irish company will be entitled to a tax deduction for the interest payable

Ireland

to any group company resident outside the European Union in a non-treaty country, provided the recipient country taxes foreign interest income at a rate equal to or greater than the Irish corporate rate. If the recipient country taxes foreign interest at a rate of less than 12.5%, then relief will be given in Ireland at that effective tax rate. If the recipient country exempts foreign interest, then no relief will be available in Ireland. It should be noted that this will affect not only cash-pooling operations but all forms of short-term lending (i.e. less than one year).

This may create additional borrowing opportunities for Irish treasury companies.

Group relief for Irish loss

Finance Act 2012 contained a positive and very welcome development in relation to the surrender of Irish losses in group situations. It is another significant measure designed to enhance the attractiveness of Ireland to foreign head-quartered groups. Previously, it was the position that a group for Irish loss relief purposes could not exist where it was necessary to trace ownership through a company not resident in an EU member state (or Iceland or Norway) in order to establish a 75% group relationship between the surrendering company and the claimant company. In practice, the most frequent difficulties arose where it was necessary to trace through a parent company resident in Switzerland or the United States (US).

The amendments introduced in the Act now allow Irish losses to be surrendered from the surrendering company to a claimant company where both companies are at least 75% members of the same corporate group, and the difficulties that existed in establishing a 75% group relationship are now relaxed as (in addition to tracing through EU resident companies) it is now possible to trace through companies resident in a country with whom Ireland has a DTT and it is also possible to trace through companies quoted on certain recognised stock exchanges (or 75% subsidiaries of companies so quoted).

Extension of 12.5% tax rate of foreign dividends

An Irish resident company is chargeable to corporation tax at the 12.5% rate on certain foreign dividends that have been paid out of trading profits. This applies to dividends received from:

- a company tax resident in the European Union
- a company tax resident in a country with which Ireland has a DTT, and
- a company tax resident in a non-treaty country, provided the principal class of shares in it or in its parent company are substantially and regularly traded on a recognised stock exchange in the European Union or in a treaty country.

Finance Act 2012 extends the 12.5% corporate tax rate to foreign dividends paid out of trading profits of a company resident in a country that has ratified the Convention on Mutual Assistance in Tax Matters. Such countries include Azerbaijan and Ukraine. Please note that Argentina, Brazil, and Indonesia have signed, but have not yet ratified, the Convention.

Exemption for new start-up companies

Finance Act 2012 extends the exemption for start-up companies from corporation tax and capital gains tax. The relief is now extended to companies that commence a new trade in 2012, 2013, and 2014.

Stamp duty and value-added tax (VAT)

The rate of stamp duty on non-residential property has been reduced from a top rate of 6% to a flat rate of 2%. This new 2% rate not only applies to transfers of commercial and industrial land and buildings but also to transfers of business assets such as goodwill, debtors, contracts, etc.

The main rate of VAT that applies to the supply of the majority goods and services in the course of business has increased from 21% to 23%.

Pooling of foreign tax deductions for royalties

Finance Act 2012 introduced a number of beneficial changes to the computational rules that provide relief for foreign tax on royalties. In effect, the changes provide for a form of pooling of tax deductions in relation to foreign tax on royalties where the royalty income is taken into account in computing the trading income of a trade carried on by the company.

International funds sector

The Finance Act 2012 introduced a number of provisions designed to support and enhance the international funds sector in Ireland, as set out in further detail below:

Funds re-domiciling to Ireland

Finance Act 2012 provides that where the Central Bank has authorised an investment fund that has re-domiciled to Ireland from certain offshore centres, a declaration can be made by the fund stating that the unitholders are non-Irish resident, to ensure that no Irish tax charge arises in respect of such non-residents, thereby clarifying the tax exemption applying to payments made by Irish funds to non-resident investors. To the extent that there are any Irish resident unitholders, these need to be identified in the declaration and tax accounted for, where appropriate, on any payments made to such unitholders.

Cross-border fund mergers involving Irish funds

New measures have been introduced confirming that mergers (both inbound and outbound) involving an Irish fund with a fund located in a member state of the European Union, European Economic Area (EEA), or an Organisation for Economic Co-operation and Development (OECD) country with which Ireland has entered into a DTT will not give rise to a charge to tax in respect of Irish resident investors. Effectively, the charge to tax is deferred until the ultimate disposal of the replacement units. The calculation of any future gain on such units is calculated by reference to the cost of the original units.

Finance Act 2012 also confirms that no charge to Irish tax shall arise on the transfer of units in the formation of certain master/feeder structures.

Finance Act 2012 also includes a number of significant stamp duty exemptions available for collective investment vehicles.

Legislative changes: New Irish corporate structure for investment funds

The Irish funds industry continues to work with the Irish government to explore new products that could enhance the competitiveness of Ireland's fund offering on the global stage.

The Irish Minister of Finance has approved, in principle, legislative proposals for a new form of corporate structure for regulated investment funds.

Ireland

Currently, investment funds in Ireland structured as companies are incorporated as public limited companies ('plc') under the Irish Companies Acts. The new corporate structure will be specifically designed for investment funds and will not be subject to the legislation governing other types of companies, reducing the need to comply with certain inappropriate requirements under the Companies Acts. The legislation will also increase the range of structures open to investment managers and promoters establishing funds in Ireland.

One of the main advantages of new corporate structure will be the ability of this structure to 'check-the-box' (an election to be regarded as tax transparent) for US tax purposes, whereas an Irish plc cannot. This is seen as a very positive development in the funds industry, particularly in the context of investment funds seeking to re-domicile from traditional tax haven jurisdictions to a regulated jurisdiction like Ireland.

It is expected that the proposed new legislation will be enacted by the end of 2012 prior to the entry into force of the EU Alternative Investment Funds Managers Directive in July 2013. It is intended that the new corporate fund would qualify for the tax exemption that applies to Irish regulated funds.

Taxes on corporate income

Corporation tax is chargeable as follows on income and capital gains:

Standard rate on income ('trading rate')	Higher rate on income ('passive rate')	Capital gains rate
12.5%	25%	30%

Resident companies are taxable in Ireland on their worldwide profits (including gains). Non-resident companies are subject to Irish corporation tax only on the trading profits of an Irish branch or agency and to Irish income tax (generally by way of withholding) on certain Irish source income.

Non-trading (passive) income includes dividends from companies resident outside Ireland (with some exceptions), interest, rents, and royalties. Legislation provides that certain dividend income (e.g. income from foreign trades) is taxed at 12.5% (*see the Income determination section*). The higher rate (i.e. 25%) also applies to income from a business carried on wholly outside Ireland and to income from land dealing, mining, and petroleum extraction operations.

An additional 'profit resource rent' tax applies to certain petroleum activities. Depending on the profit yield of a site, the tax rate applicable can range from 25% to 40%.

Close companies (*see the Income determination section*) may be subject to additional corporate taxes on undistributed investment income (including Irish dividends) and on undistributed income from professional services. Examples of professional services include professions such as solicitor, accountant, doctor, and engineer.

Ireland

Corporate residence

A company that is incorporated, or has its place of central management and control, in Ireland will be regarded as resident in Ireland for the purposes of corporation tax and capital gains tax. This is subject to the following two exceptions where a company incorporated in Ireland is not considered a tax resident.

A treaty exception applies if the Irish incorporated company is, by virtue of an Irish DTT, considered to be tax resident in the treaty partner country and not resident in Ireland.

An active trading exception applies if the Irish incorporated company or its 50% affiliate carries on a trade in Ireland and the company has qualifying ownership. A 50% affiliate is essentially a company where:

- one company is a 50% subsidiary of the other or both companies are 50% subsidiaries of a third company
- there is an entitlement to at least 50% of the profits available for distribution, and
- there is an entitlement to at least 50% of the assets available in the case of a winding up of the other company.

Qualifying ownership requires that the Irish incorporated company or a 50% or more affiliate/parent is listed on a stock exchange in a European Union member state or a territory which has a tax treaty with Ireland or, in the absence of such a listing, that the ultimate control (more than 50%) of the Irish incorporated company rests with persons who are tax resident in EU or treaty countries.

Permanent establishment (PE)

Non-resident companies are subject to Irish corporation tax only on the trading profits attributable to an Irish branch or agency, plus Irish income tax (generally by way of withholding, though this is not the case with Irish source rental profits) on certain Irish source income.

For non-resident companies, the liability to corporation tax depends on the existence of any kind of branch or agency through which a trade is carried on. The meaning of branch or agency for Irish tax purposes is set out in statute. The corporation tax liability of a non-resident company will be reduced by a DTT if the company does not have a PE in Ireland.

Subject to the terms of the relevant DTT, a non-resident company will have a PE in Ireland if:

- it has a fixed place of business in Ireland through which the business of the company is wholly or partly carried on or
- an agent acting on behalf of the company has and habitually exercises authority to do business on behalf of the company in Ireland.

A fixed place of business includes (but is not limited to) a place of management, a branch, an office, a factory, a workshop, an installation or structure for the exploration of natural resources, a mine, oil or gas well, quarry, or other place of extraction of natural resources, or a building or construction or installation project. A company is not, however, regarded as having an Irish PE if the activities for which the fixed place of business is maintained or which the agent carries on are only of a preparatory or auxiliary nature (also defined in the statute).

Ireland

Other taxes

Value-added tax (VAT)
VAT is charged at 23% on the supply of most goods and services in the course of business.

There are two lower rates. A 13.5% rate applies to most building services, labour intensive services, domestic fuel and power, and other reduced rate supplies. A 4.8% rate applies to livestock and greyhounds.

As of 1 July 2011, a reduced 9% VAT rate applies to certain services in the tourism sector. These include restaurant and catering services, hotel and holiday accommodation, and various entertainment services, such as admissions to cinemas, theatres, museums, fairgrounds, amusement parks, and sporting facilities. Under current legislation, this rate will apply until 31 December 2013.

Most exports, food, oral medicine, and children's clothing and footwear are zero-rated.

Some supplies are exempt from VAT. The main exempt categories are most banking services, insurance services, medical services, passenger transport, education, and training.

Zero rating is preferable to exemption because most VAT costs incurred in making a zero-rated supply can be recovered, while those incurred in making an exempt supply generally cannot.

Customs duties
Many goods imported into Ireland from outside the European Union are subject to customs duties. The rates of duty are provided by the EU's Common Customs Tariff.

Excise duties
Excise duties are chargeable on most hydrocarbon oil products, electricity supply, alcoholic drinks, and tobacco products imported into or produced in Ireland.

Stamp duty
Stamp duty is a tax on instruments. It is payable on transfers of land and on other assets whose legal title cannot be passed by delivery. It is also chargeable on all instruments of transfer executed in Ireland, and on instruments, wherever executed, which relate to Irish property or activities. The transfer of assets between associated companies may not be liable to stamp duty, provided the following key conditions are met:

- The companies have a 90% relationship (that is, one company is the beneficial owner of at least 90% of the ordinary share capital of the other and is entitled to at least 90% of the profits available for distribution and is entitled to at least 90% of the assets in the case of a winding-up of the other company).
- The companies are in a group 90% relationship as defined above that can be traced as far up the group chain as is necessary to establish the qualifying relationship.
- This relationship is maintained for a period of two years after the transfer of the assets to avoid the relief being clawed back.

There is an exemption for transfers of intellectual property (IP), and the categories of IP qualifying for this exemption are broadly similar to those for which IP capital allowances are available (see Intellectual property [IP] regime in the Tax credits and incentives section).

Ireland

Stamp duty rates are up to 2% of the value transferring. Rates of 1% to 2% apply for residential property. Stamp duty is levied at 1% on transfers of Irish shares.

A EUR 1 stamp duty applies to a policy of insurance, other than life insurance, relating to risks located in Ireland. The stamp duty is normally collected under the terms of a composition agreement, which provides for regular, usually quarterly, payments of duty.

Capital duty on share capital
Ireland does not levy capital duty on share capital of companies.

Capital taxes
Ireland does not levy tax on the net worth of companies.

Social security contributions
Employed persons are compulsorily insured under a state-administered scheme of pay-related social insurance (PRSI). Contributions are made by both the employer and the employee. The employer is responsible for making PRSI contributions up to a rate of 10.75%, and these are an allowable deduction for corporation tax purposes.

Insurance premium tax (IPT)
A levy of 3% of gross premiums received applies in relation to non-life insurance policies relating to risks located in Ireland. This levy is payable four times per annum, within 25 days of the end of each quarter (i.e. within 25 days from quarters ending 31 March, 30 June, 30 September, and 31 December).

A levy of 1% of gross premiums received applies in relation to certain classes of life insurance policies relating to risks located in Ireland. This levy is payable four times per annum, within 25 days of the end of each quarter (i.e. within 25 days from quarters ending 31 March, 30 June, 30 September, and 31 December).

An additional contribution of 2% to the Insurance Compensation Fund applies to premiums received in relation to non-life insurance policies. Similar to the 3% non-life insurance levy, the contribution applies where premiums are received in respect of risks located in Ireland. The contribution is also payable four times per annum in conjunction with the non-life insurance levy on premiums.

Reinsurance business is excluded from the levy.

Emissions allowances
Legislation was introduced in relation to the tax treatment of emission allowances under the EU Emissions Trading Scheme. The legislation distinguishes between allowances acquired free of charge from the Environment Protection Agency under the EU Scheme and those that are purchased.

Environmental taxes
In Ireland, a levy (currently 22 cent per bag) is imposed upon consumers provided with a plastic bag when purchasing goods in supermarkets and other retail outlets. Under the applicable legislation, retailers are obliged to collect 22 cent in respect of every plastic bag or bag containing plastic, regardless of size, unless specifically exempted, that is provided to customers and remit all plastic bag levies collected to Irish Revenue. As a result of the levy, most non-supermarket retailers provide paper carrier bags, and many retailers provide 'bags for life', which are made from non-plastic material and, therefore, not subject to the environmental levy.

Ireland

Carbon tax

A carbon tax has been introduced on mineral oils (e.g. auto fuels, kerosene) which are supplied in Ireland. The rates of carbon tax on oil and gas broadly equate to EUR 20 per tonne of CO_2 emitted. Relief applies where mineral oils are supplied to an Emissions Trading Scheme (ETS) installation or for electricity generation. Pure biofuels are exempt from carbon tax. There is full relief for the biofuel component of the fuel. Where biofuel has been mixed or blended with any other mineral oil, the relief from carbon taxes shall apply to the biofuel content of the mixture or blend, regardless of the percentage.

A carbon tax has also been introduced on natural gas and solid fuel where supplied for combustion. Again, reliefs apply where these fuels are supplied to ETS installations or used in electricity generation, chemical reduction, or in the electrolytical or metallurgical processes.

Local taxes

Local taxes known as 'rates' are not based on income but rather are levied on the occupiers of business property by reference to a deemed rental value of the property concerned. The level of rates levied can depend on the region in which the property is located. Rates are an allowable deduction for corporation tax purposes.

Local authorities are also empowered to levy charges on all occupiers for specific services (e.g. water supply). These charges are also deductible for corporation tax purposes.

Branch income

Irish branches of foreign companies are liable to corporation tax at the rates that apply to Irish resident companies. No tax is withheld on repatriation of branch profits to the head office.

Income determination

Irish trading profits are computed in accordance with Irish Generally Accepted Accounting Principles (GAAP) or International Financial Reporting Standards (IFRS), subject to any adjustment required by law. Prior-year adjustments may arise on the first-time adoption of IFRS, which may result in double counting of income or expenses or of income falling out of the charge to tax. Generally speaking, in order to avoid such an outcome, transitional adjustments exist whereby amounts of income or expenses that could be double-counted or that would fall out of the charge to tax are identified and the amounts concerned are taxed or deducted as appropriate over a five year period.

Inventory valuation

Each item of inventory is valued for tax purposes at cost or market value, whichever is lower, and this will normally accord with the accounting treatment. The method used in arriving at cost or market value of inventory generally must be consistent and must not be in conflict with tax law. The first in first out (FIFO) method is an acceptable method of calculation for tax purposes. The base-stock method has been held to be an inappropriate method for tax purposes, as has the last in first out (LIFO) method.

Capital gains

Companies are subject to capital gains tax in respect of gains arising on the disposal of capital assets. The taxable gain is arrived at by deducting from the sales proceeds the cost incurred on acquiring the asset (as indexed to reflect inflation only up to 31 December 2002). The resulting gain is taxable at 30%. In cases of disposals of interests in offshore funds and foreign life assurance policies, indexation relief does not apply; while, with effect from 1 January 2012, a tax rate of 33% applies to non-corporate shareholders in respect of funds and policies located in EU/ EEA/DTT countries, and a rate of 30% or 40% applies to funds or policies located in all other jurisdictions. Finance Act 2012 reduced the rate of exit tax applying to Irish corporate shareholders investing in Irish funds to 25%, effective 1 January 2012. Special rules apply to gains (and losses) from the disposal of development land in Ireland.

Companies that are tax resident in Ireland (that is managed and controlled in Ireland or incorporated in Ireland and not qualifying for exclusion) are taxable on worldwide gains. Non-resident companies are subject to capital gains tax on capital gains arising on the disposal of Irish land, buildings, mineral rights, and exploration rights on the Irish continental shelf, together with shares in unquoted (unlisted) companies, whose value substantially (greater than 50%) is derived from these assets. Non-resident companies also are subject to capital gains tax from the realisation of assets used for the purposes of a business carried on in Ireland.

Losses arising on the disposal of capital assets may be offset against capital gains in the accounting period or carried forward for offset against future capital gains. No carryback of capital losses is permitted. There is no facility to offset capital losses against business income or to surrender capital losses within a tax group.

Irish capital gains tax legislation facilitates corporate reorganisations on a tax-free basis in situations where there is a share for share exchange. Assets can be transferred within certain company groups without capital gains tax applying (*see the Group taxation section for further information*).

Participation exemption from capital gains

A participation exemption is available to Irish resident companies on the disposal of a shareholding interest if:

- a minimum of 5% of the shares (including the right to profits and assets on winding up) is held for a continuous 12-month period
- the share sale takes place during the period for which the minimum 5% holding is held
- the sale takes place within two years after meeting the holding requirement, to take account of gradual dispositions over time
- the company whose shares are sold is resident in an EU member state (including Ireland) or in a country with which Ireland has a DTT at the time of the disposal (this includes tax treaties that have been signed but not yet ratified), and
- a trading condition is met at the time of the disposal whereby either: (i) the business of the company whose shares are disposed of consists wholly or mainly of the carrying on of one or more trades or (ii) taken together, the businesses of the Irish holding company and all companies in which it has a direct or indirect 5% or more ownership interest consist wholly or mainly of the carrying on of one or more trades.

If the Irish holding company is unable to meet the minimum holding requirement but is a member of a group (that is, a parent company and its 51% worldwide subsidiaries), the gain arising on the disposal still will be exempt if the holding requirement can be

Ireland

met by including holdings of other members of the group. Thus, the Irish company may be exempt from capital gains tax on a disposal of shares even if it does not directly hold a significant shareholding. The exemption also applies to a disposal of assets related to shares, such as options and convertible debt. However, it does not apply to a sale of either shares or related assets that derive the greater part of their value (more than 50%) from Irish real property, minerals, mining rights, and exploration and exploitation rights in a designated area. Shares deriving their value from non-Irish real property, minerals, and mining rights qualify for exemption if the other conditions are met.

Capital losses arising on the disposal of a shareholding where a gain on disposal would be exempt under the participation exemption are not deductible.

Dividend income
Dividends from Irish companies are exempt from corporation tax. Dividends paid out of the trading profits of a company resident in a country with which Ireland has a DTT (or a country with which Ireland has ratified the Convention on Mutual Assistance in Tax Matters) may be taxed at the 12.5% rate, provided a claim is made. The 12.5% corporate tax rate applies to the same type of dividends received from companies resident in non-treaty countries, that is, where the company that paid the dividend is a listed company or is part of a 75% listed group the principal class of the shares of which are substantially and regularly traded on the Irish Stock Exchange, a recognised Stock Exchange in a country with which Ireland has a DTT, or on such other Stock Exchange as is approved by the Minister for Finance for the purposes of this relief from double taxation.

Finance Act 2012 extends the 12.5% corporate tax rate to foreign dividends paid out of trading profits of a company resident in a country that has ratified the Convention on Mutual Assistance in Tax Matters. Such countries include Azerbaijan and Ukraine. Please note that Argentina, Brazil, and Indonesia have signed, but have not yet ratified, the Convention.

Foreign dividends received by an Irish company where it holds 5% or less of the share capital and voting rights in that foreign company are exempt from corporation tax where the Irish company would otherwise be taxed on this dividend income as trading income.

Dividends from Irish resident companies are not liable to further tax, other than a surcharge on close companies if the dividend is not redistributed. Broadly speaking, a close company is a company which is under the control of five or fewer 'participators'. Participators can include individual shareholders, corporate shareholders, loan creditors, any person with a right to receive distributions from the company, etc. Where not less than 35% of the shares of a company (including the voting power) are listed, a company would not be regarded as a close company.

A close company surcharge of 20% is payable on certain non-trading income (for example, rental income, certain dividend income, and interest income) if it is not distributed to shareholders within 18 months of the accounting period in which the income was earned. Since 31 January 2008, a close company making a distribution and the close company receiving a distribution have the option jointly to elect to have the dividend disregarded for surcharge purposes. This can give close companies the option of moving 'trading income' up to a holding company without incurring a surcharge. Generally speaking, close companies avoid the surcharge through the payment of dividends within the prescribed period. Capital gains accruing to a non-resident company that would be close if it were resident can be attributed to Irish resident participants in certain instances.

Stock dividends

Stock dividends taken in lieu of cash are taxed to the shareholder on an amount equivalent to the amount which would have been received if the option to take stock dividends had not been exercised. If the recipient is an Irish resident company and it receives the stock dividend from a quoted (listed) Irish company, then there will be no tax. For a quoted (listed) company paying the stock dividend, dividend WHT with the appropriate exemptions and exclusions applies. Other stock dividends (bonus issues) are generally non-taxable.

Interest income

Interest income earned by Irish companies generally is taxable at the rate of tax for passive income of 25% (interest may be regarded as a trading receipt for certain financial trader companies). It is possible to offset current year trading losses against passive interest income arising in the same year on a 'value basis'. It is not possible to offset prior year trading losses against current year interest income unless that interest constitutes a trading receipt of the particular company.

Foreign income

Resident companies are liable to Irish tax on worldwide income. Accordingly, in the case of an Irish resident company, foreign income and capital gains are, broadly speaking, subject in full to corporation tax. This applies to income of a foreign branch of an Irish company as well as to dividend income arising abroad.

In general, income of foreign subsidiaries of Irish companies is not taxed until remitted to Ireland, although there are special rules that seek to tax certain undistributed capital gains of non-resident close companies (*see Dividend income above for further information in relation to close companies*).

Foreign taxes borne by an Irish resident company (or Irish branch of an EEA resident company), whether imposed directly or by way of withholding, may be creditable in Ireland (*see Foreign tax credit in the Tax credits and incentives section*).

Deductions

In general, expenses incurred wholly and exclusively for the purposes of the trade are tax-deductible.

General accruals and provisions are not tax-deductible.

Depreciation

Book depreciation is not deductible for tax purposes (except in the case of IP assets). Instead, tax depreciation (known as capital allowances) is permitted on a straight-line basis in respect of expenditure incurred on assets which have been put into use by the company. The following rates are applicable:

Asset type	Tax depreciation rate (%)
Plant and machinery	12.5
Industrial buildings used for manufacturing	4
Motor vehicles	12.5

Ireland

Asset type	Tax depreciation rate (%)
IP assets	Book depreciation or 7

The allowances are calculated on the cost after deduction of grants, except for plant and machinery used in the course of the manufacture of processed food for human consumption. In this case, the allowances are calculated on the gross cost. Allowances on cars are restricted to a capital cost of EUR 24,000 and may be restricted further (to 50% or zero) depending on the level of carbon emissions of the vehicle.

Accelerated capital allowances

A 100% first-year capital allowance is available in respect of expenditures incurred on certain approved energy-efficient equipment up to 31 December 2014. The categories of equipment that may be eligible for inclusion are:

* Information and communications technology.
* Heating and electricity provision.
* Electric and alternative fuel vehicles.
* Heating, ventilation, and air conditioning (HVAC) control systems.
* Lighting.
* Motors and drives.
* Building energy management systems.
* Refrigeration and cooling systems.
* Electro-mechanical systems.
* Catering and hospitality equipment.

Leasing

Ireland operates an eight-year tax depreciation life on most assets. A beneficial tax treatment applies to finance leases and operating leases of certain assets. For short life assets (i.e. those with a life of less than eight years), Ireland allows such lessors to follow the accounting treatment of the transaction that provides a faster write-off of the capital cost of an asset rather than relying on tax depreciation over eight years. This effectively allows the lessors to write-off their capital for tax purposes in line with the economic recovery on the asset.

Goodwill

The amortisation of goodwill is generally not allowable as a deduction. However, a tax deduction may be available for capital expenditure on the acquisition of goodwill (*see Intellectual property (IP) regime in the Tax credits and incentives section*).

Start-up expenses

A deduction may be allowed in respect of pre-trading expenses that are incurred for the purposes of a trade and within three years of the commencement of the trade. Such expenses may be offset against the income of that same trade.

Interest expenses

A deduction for interest is allowed only to the extent that borrowings are used for the purpose of a trade or other limited purposes.

R&D expenses

Expenditure on scientific R&D and payments for the acquisition of know-how in general are allowable deductions, as are the costs of obtaining or extending patents and obtaining and renewing trademarks.

Ireland

Bad debts
A deduction is available for bad debts written off in the accounts of a company as irrecoverable. Specific bad debt provisions may also be deductible once they satisfy Irish GAAP or IFRS accounting standards. The creation of a general bad debt provision is not a deductible expense.

Charitable contributions
Companies are entitled to a deduction, as a trading expense, for qualifying donations to approved charities, educational institutions, schools, churches, research foundations, sports bodies, and other approved organisations which satisfy certain conditions. To qualify for a tax deduction, the donation(s) to an organisation in a 12-month accounting period must amount to at least EUR 250.

Meals and entertainment
Costs incurred for third-party entertainment are not tax-deductible. Entertainment includes the provision of accommodation, food, drink, and any other form of hospitality including the provision of gifts. Expenditure on bona fide staff entertainment is allowable as a deduction provided its provision is not incidental to the provision of entertainment to third parties. Certain promotional costs are tax-deductible if they are incurred wholly and exclusively for the purposes of the trade.

Pension expenses
Contributions to certain employee pension schemes and the cost of setting up such schemes are deductible. Pension contributions are allowable as a deduction for employers in the year in which they are paid.

Fines and penalties
Fines and penalties imposed for breaking the law, civil penalties, interest, and late filing surcharges imposed by the Revenue Commissioners are generally not deductible.

Taxes
Taxes that are deductible in computing profits for corporation tax include VAT not recovered, the employer's share of PRSI contributions, and local taxes (i.e. rates levied on commercial property and local authority charges).

Net operating losses
Losses are computed for tax purposes in the same way as business profits. Trading losses can be offset against other income of any nature, either in the current or preceding accounting period (of equal length). The amount of losses required to shelter the income is dependent on the tax rate which would have been applied to the income in the absence of the loss relief. Any excess losses can be carried forward indefinitely against future trading income. Certain changes in ownership may prevent the carryforward of losses to future periods. Terminal losses which arise within 12 months of the date a company ceases to trade may be carried back three years.

Payments to foreign affiliates
Generally, deductions can be claimed for royalties, management service charges, and most interest charges paid to foreign affiliates, provided the amounts do not exceed what would be paid to unrelated entities. Depending on the circumstances, certain elections may be required. Ireland does not have any thin capitalisation rules.

Cash pooling
The corporate treasury sector sought changes to facilitate international cash pooling operations, and certain relevant changes were brought about in Finance Act 2012.

Ireland

Under a typical cashpool arrangement, interest payments by the Irish cashpool leader typically would constitute 'short' interest for tax purposes because of the overnight/short term nature of these arrangements. Prior to the introduction of Finance Act 2012, an interest payment by an Irish cashpool leader to a 'group' company (75% or more direct or indirect relationship) resident outside the European Union in a country with which Ireland does not have a DTT may have been regarded as a dividend for tax purposes. There were two tax consequences of this. Firstly, this interest was not deductible for corporation tax purposes, giving rise to an Irish tax cost of 12.5%. Secondly, dividend WHT at a rate of 20% may have applied, although there are a number of exemptions from dividend WHT that may be relevant, depending on the specific circumstances.

Finance Act 2012 has introduced a relieving provision effective for accounting periods ending on or after 1 January 2012 in respect of 'short' interest. Short interest is generally regarded as interest on a loan/deposit where the term is less than a year. Essentially, the Irish company will be entitled to a tax deduction for the interest payable to any group company resident outside the European Union in a non-treaty country, provided the recipient country taxes foreign interest income at a rate equal to or greater than the Irish corporate rate. If the recipient country taxes foreign interest at a rate of less than 12.5%, then relief will be given in Ireland at that effective tax rate. If the recipient country exempts foreign interest, then no relief will be available in Ireland. It should be noted that this will affect not only cash-pooling operations but all forms of short-term lending (i.e. less than one year).

This may create additional borrowing opportunities for Irish treasury companies.

Group taxation

The concept of 'fiscal unity' or consolidated group tax does not exist in Ireland. However, trading losses as computed for tax purposes may be offset on a current period basis against taxable profits of another group company. As with loss relief in a single company, the amount of losses required to shelter the income is dependent on the tax rate which would have been applied to the income in the absence of the loss relief.

A group consists of a parent company and all of its 75% subsidiaries, with all group members being tax resident in Ireland, in another member state of the EEA or in a country with which Ireland has a DTT. It is also possible to trace through companies quoted on certain recognised stock exchanges (or 75% subsidiaries of companies so quoted). Non-Irish members may only surrender losses from activities which would, if profitable, be subject to Irish tax.

Capital losses cannot be surrendered within a group.

Relief from capital gains tax is available on intra-group transfers of capital assets. Where a capital asset is transferred from a resident company to another resident company in a 75% group, no capital gains tax charge arises. A group, for capital gains tax purposes, consists of a principal company and its 75% subsidiary companies. A 75% subsidiary is defined by reference to the beneficial ownership of ordinary share capital, owned either directly or indirectly. A capital gains tax group can include EEA resident companies for the purpose of analysing the beneficial ownership of a company.

It also is possible for an Irish resident company and an Irish branch of an EEA company in the same group to transfer capital assets without crystallising a capital gains charge, provided the asset transferred remains within the scope of the charge to Irish capital gains tax.

Subsequent to an intra-group transfer, a charge to capital gains tax will arise when either:

- the asset is sold outside the group, in which case the tax is calculated by reference to the original cost and acquisition date of the asset when first acquired within the group or
- a company owns an asset which was transferred by a group company and subsequently leaves the group within a ten year period of the intra-group transfer. The gain on this intra-group transfer crystallises and becomes payable at this point.

Transfer pricing

In April 2010, Ireland enacted broad based transfer pricing legislation. The legislation endorses the OECD Transfer Pricing Guidelines for Multinational Enterprises and Tax Administrations and adopts the arm's-length principle. The introduction of general transfer pricing legislation in Ireland was widely anticipated and brings the Irish tax regime into line with international norms in this area. The new regime applies to domestic as well as international related party arrangements and is effective for accounting periods commencing on or after 1 January 2011 in relation to certain arrangements entered into on or after 1 July 2010.

The new transfer pricing rules apply to arrangements entered into between associated persons, involving the supply or acquisition of goods, services, money, or intangible assets and relating to trading activities within the charge to Irish tax at the trading rate of 12.5%. The rules confer a power on the Irish tax authorities to re-compute the taxable profit or loss of a taxpayer where income has been understated or where expenditure has been overstated as a result of certain non-arm's-length arrangements. The adjustment will be made to the Irish taxable profits to reflect the arrangement had it been entered into by independent parties dealing at arm's length.

The legislation also places an obligation on a taxpayer to provide documentation 'as may reasonably be required' to support the arm's-length nature of the related party arrangements and that documentation will need to be prepared 'on a timely basis'. Guidance notes issued by the Irish tax authorities on transfer pricing documentation support the legislative basis and indicate that a company is required to have transfer pricing documentation available for inspection if requested by the Irish tax authorities. Notably, the guidance notes state that "it is best practice that the documentation is prepared at the time the terms of the transaction are agreed". Additionally, the guidance notes state that in order "for a company to be in a position to make a correct and complete tax return, appropriate transfer pricing documentation should exist at the time the tax return is filed". It is worth noting that the taxpayer can maintain documentation in the form 'of its choosing'. Additionally, where documentation exists in another territory which supports the Irish arrangement, this will also be sufficient from an Irish transfer pricing perspective, provided that the documentation is in English. The Irish tax authorities have also confirmed that they will accept documentation that has been prepared in accordance with either the OECD Transfer Pricing Guidelines or the code of conduct adopted by the EU Council under the title 'EU Transfer Pricing Documentation'.

Note that arrangements entered into between related parties prior to 1 July 2010 are 'grandfathered' and thereby excluded from the scope of the new transfer pricing rules. There is also an exemption from the new rules for small and medium-sized enterprises.

Ireland

Broadly speaking, small and medium-sized enterprises include enterprises employing less than 250 people and that have either a turnover of less than EUR 50 million or assets of less than EUR 43 million.

Thin capitalisation
Ireland does not have any thin capitalisation rules.

Controlled foreign companies (CFCs)
Ireland does not have CFC rules.

Tax credits and incentives

The main tax incentives in Ireland are:

- 12.5% corporation tax rate on active business income.
- A 25% credit on incremental R&D spending over the base year of 2003; total effective tax deduction of 37.5%.
- Ability to exploit IP at favourable tax rates.
- Accelerated tax depreciation allowances for approved energy efficient equipment.
- Ability to carry out investment management activities for non-Irish investment funds without creating a taxable presence in Ireland for such funds.
- An effective legal, regulatory, and tax framework to allow for the efficient redomiciliation of investment funds from traditional offshore centres to Ireland.

R&D credit
Incremental R&D expenditure (over a base year of 2003) qualifies for a tax credit of 25% in addition to a tax deduction. This means that the total tax deduction on qualifying expenditure is 37.5%. A limited volume-based approach applies for the purposes of calculating the tax credit so that the first EUR 100,000 of qualifying R&D expenditure will benefit from the 25% R&D tax credit on a volume basis (thus ignoring the 2003 base year spend). This means that companies engaging in R&D are guaranteed a credit of EUR 25,000 in respect of their first EUR 100,000 of expenditure.

Expenditure on buildings used for R&D now also can qualify for the credit as long as at least 35% of the building is used for R&D activities. This hurdle is measured over the course of four years. This is of particular assistance where R&D is carried on in a manufacturing environment. It should be noted that expenditures incurred on the acquisition of an intangible asset that qualify for capital allowances under the IP regime will not qualify for the R&D credit.

The R&D regime caters for pre-trading expenditures and other specific circumstances. Where a company incurs R&D expenditures but has not yet commenced to trade, all R&D claims in this regard must be made within 12 months from the end of the accounting period in which the company first commences to trade.

Companies who are in receipt of an R&D tax credit will now, in certain instances, have the option to reward key employees through an alternative use of that credit. In effect, the company may surrender a portion of their R&D credit that could otherwise have been used to reduce corporation tax against employees' income. Essentially, this new measure can reduce an employee's effective rate of tax to 23% (the average effective tax rate for such employees would typically be in the region of 40% in the absence of such an R&D credit).

The R&D credit can be used to generate a tax refund through a carryback against prior year profits. In addition, repayment for excess credits is available over the course of a three-year cycle. Repayments are limited to the greater of the corporation tax payable by the company in the preceding ten years or the payroll tax liability for the period in which the relevant R&D expenditure is incurred.

In addition, under Irish GAAP, companies may account for the R&D tax credit through their profit and loss account or income statement in arriving at the pre-tax profit or loss. This immediately impacts on the unit cost of R&D, which is the key measurement used by multi-national corporations (MNCs) when considering the locations of R&D projects.

Intellectual property (IP) regime
Legislation provides for a tax deduction for capital expenditure on the acquisition of qualifying IP assets. The definition of IP assets is widely drafted and includes the acquisition of, or the licence to use, the following:

- Patents and registered designs.
- Trademarks and brand names.
- Know-how (broadly in line with the OECD model tax treaty definition of know-how).
- Domain name, copyrights, service marks, and publishing titles.
- Authorisation to sell medicines, a product of any design, formula, process, or invention (and rights derived from research into same).
- Applications for legal protection (for example, applications for the grant or registration of brands, trademarks, patents, copyright, etc.).
- Expenditure on computer software acquired for commercial exploitation.
- Goodwill, to the extent that it relates directly to the assets outlined above.

Capital allowances will be available at the same rate as the depreciation/amortisation charge for financial accounting purposes. Alternatively, the company may elect to claim allowances over a period of 15 years.

Tax deductions (e.g. financing costs) are available for offset against income generated from exploiting IP assets, up to a maximum deduction of 80% of the relevant IP profits. The remaining 20% is taxable at the 12.5% corporation tax rate. There is no clawback provided the IP is held for ten years (reduced from 15 years in Finance Act 2010).

There is currently an option to elect to stay within the 'old' regime for know-how and patents for IP acquired up until 7 May 2011. A shorter write off period of eight years has also been retained for acquired software rights under the existing capital allowances regime where the rights are not acquired for commercial exploitation (i.e. were acquired for end use by the company).

Exemption for new start-up companies
A corporation tax holiday applies to certain start-up companies that commence to trade during 2012, 2013, and 2014. The relief applies for three years where the total amount of corporation tax payable does not exceed EUR 40,000 in each year. Marginal relief is available where corporation tax payable is between EUR 40,000 and EUR 60,000. The relief available is now linked to the amount of employer's PRSI paid by a company in an accounting period and is intended to target the relief at companies generating employment.

Section 110 company
Ireland has a favourable tax regime for entities known as Section 110 companies. A Section 110 company is an Irish resident special purpose company that holds and/

Ireland

or manages 'qualifying assets' which provides for an onshore investment platform (with access to Ireland's treaty network) in an environment of increased international focus on tax havens and transparency. The Section 110 regime has been in existence since 1991 and with appropriate planning effectively allows for corporation tax neutral treatment, provided that certain conditions are met. The regime is widely used by international banks, asset managers, and investment funds in the context of securitisations, investment platforms, collateralised debt obligations (CDOs), and capital markets bond issuances.

Recent legislative changes, arrived at following extensive industry consultation, have significantly expanded the range of assets that a Section 110 company can invest in, whilst also seeking to restrict the use of Section 110 in specific targeted circumstances.

Prior to 2011, Section 110 companies were limited to investing in financial assets. The term 'financial asset' is widely defined and includes both mainstream financial assets such as shares, loans, leases, lease portfolios, bonds, debt, and derivatives, as well as assets such as greenhouse gas emissions allowance, all types of receivables, etc.

The range of investments in which a Section 110 company can invest has been significantly extended since 2011 to include investments in commodities and plant and machinery. Greenhouse gas emissions allowance has been redefined as a qualifying asset to include 'carbon offsets' and has been broadened significantly. These are very welcome changes, particularly in the context of recent market interest in commodity transactions and the launch of the Irish Government's 'Green International Financial Services Centre (IFSC)' initiative.

In addition, the extension of the Section 110 regime to include plant and machinery will benefit Ireland's position as the preferred destination for aircraft financing and leasing activities and will give an added boost to Ireland's position as the centre of excellence for aircraft financing transactions.

Grants
Cash grants may be available for capital expenditures on machinery and equipment and industrial premises, training of employees, creation of employment, rent subsidies, R&D, manufacturing and exporting products, providing services to customers overseas, etc. The level of grant aid depends on a number of factors and is specific to each project. Rates depend on the location of the new industry.

Foreign tax credit
Foreign taxes borne by an Irish resident company (or Irish branch of an EEA resident company), whether imposed directly or by way of withholding, may be creditable in Ireland. The calculation of the credit depends on the nature of the income item, but for income sources other than dividends and some related party interest, the credit is limited to the Irish tax referable to the particular item of income. A system of onshore pooling of excess foreign tax credits applies to dividends from 5% or greater corporate shareholdings, and excess credits in the dividend pool can be carried forward indefinitely. A similar pooling system applies to some related party interest and also to foreign branch income.

An Irish resident company with a branch or branches outside Ireland is generally taxable in Ireland on the foreign branch profits with a credit for foreign taxes paid on those profits. A unilateral form of credit relief for foreign taxes paid by foreign branches operating in countries with which Ireland does not have a tax treaty is available also. To the extent that there were foreign taxes on branch profits that were not utilised in the relevant period (that is, where credit for foreign tax exceeds the Irish tax payable), these unused credits can be carried forward indefinitely and credited against corporation tax on foreign branch profits in future accounting periods.

Finance Act 2012 introduced a number of beneficial changes to the computational rules that provide relief for foreign tax on royalties. In effect, the changes provide for a form of pooling of tax deductions in relation to foreign tax on royalties where the royalty income is taken into account in computing the trading income of a trade carried on by the company.

Withholding taxes

Irish resident companies are required to withhold tax on certain types of payments as set out below (*see sub-sections below for WHT exemptions and table at end of this section for WHT rate reductions*).

Recipient	WHT (%)		
	Dividends	Interest	Patents, royalties
Resident companies	0	20	20
Resident individuals	20	20	20
Non-resident companies and individuals	20	20	20

Dividend WHT

Dividend WHT applies at 20% to dividends and other distributions. However, an exemption may be available where the recipient of the dividend is either an Irish company or a non-Irish company eligible for the Parent-Subsidiary Directive (which in Ireland requires a 5% or greater shareholding).

Exemptions from dividend WHT also are available where the recipient of the distribution falls into one of the categories listed below and provided an appropriate declaration is made to the company paying the distribution in advance of the distribution. In a move to significantly ease the administrative burden in applying for exemption for dividend WHT, this declaration is now self-assessed and valid for up to six years.

- Irish tax resident companies (a declaration is not required for Irish tax resident companies which hold a 51% or greater shareholding of the company).
- Non-resident companies, which are resident in a country with which Ireland has a tax treaty or in another EU member state, where the company is not controlled by Irish residents.
- Non-resident companies which ultimately are controlled by residents of a tax treaty country or another EU member state.
- Non-resident companies whose principal class of shares is traded on a recognised stock exchange in a treaty country or another EU member state or on any other stock exchange approved by the Minster for Finance (or if recipient of the dividend is a 75% subsidiary of such a listed company).
- Non-resident companies that are wholly owned by two or more companies the principal class of shares of each of which is traded on a recognised stock exchange in a treaty country or another EU member state or on any other stock exchange approved by the Minister for Finance.
- Individuals who are resident in a tax treaty country or in another EU member state.

Ireland

- Certain pension funds, retirement funds, sports bodies, collective investment funds, and employee share ownership trusts.

Companies that make a dividend distribution are required, within 14 days of the end of the month in which the distribution is made, to make a return to the tax authorities containing details of the recipient of the dividend, the reason for any exemption from dividend WHT, and to pay over any tax withheld.

Interest WHT

Financial institutions operating in Ireland are obligated to withhold tax (deposit interest retention tax or DIRT) at 30% out of interest paid or credited on deposit accounts in the beneficial ownership of resident companies, unless the financial institution is authorised to pay the interest gross. There is no DIRT on interest paid to non-residents where a written declaration of non-residence is completed. Certain annual interest payments are subject to WHT at 20%. Interest payments by companies to companies resident in other EU member states or in treaty countries are generally not subject to WHT. The EU Interest and Royalties Directive may also provide an exemption from WHT for payments between associated companies.

Royalties WHT

Royalties, other than patents, are not generally subject to WHT under domestic law. Documentation and reporting may be required to access lower treaty withholding rates in other cases. The EU Interest and Royalties Directive may also provide an exemption from WHT for payments between associated companies. Associated companies, for the purpose of this directive, are companies where one can directly control at least 25% of the voting power of the other or at least 25% of the voting power of both companies is directly controlled by a third company. In all cases, all companies must be resident in a member state of the European Union.

WHT on capital gains

Where any of the following assets is disposed of, the person by whom or through whom the consideration is paid (i.e. the purchaser) must deduct capital gains tax at 15% from the payment:

1. Land or minerals in Ireland or exploration rights in the Irish continental shelf.
2. Unquoted (unlisted) shares deriving their value or the greater part of their value (more than 50%) from assets described in (1).
3. Unquoted (unlisted) shares issued in exchange for shares deriving their value or the greater part of their value from assets as described in (1).
4. Goodwill of a trade carried on in Ireland.

The requirement to withhold tax is not required where the consideration does not exceed EUR 500,000 or where the person disposing of the asset produces a certificate from the Revenue Commissioners authorising payment in full. A clearance certificate may be obtained by making application on Form CG50 to the Revenue Commissioners supported by a copy of the agreement or contract for sale. The certificate may be obtained on the grounds that the vendor is Irish resident or that no capital gains tax is due in respect of the disposal or that the capital gains tax has been paid. WHT is creditable against the capital gains tax liability of the vendor, and any excess is refundable.

To avoid the requirement to withhold, clearance must be obtained before the consideration is paid. There is no exemption from the withholding procedure where the asset is held as trading stock or where the transaction is intra-group and a capital gains

Ireland

tax liability does not arise. Failure to obtain the certificate will lead to the purchaser being assessed to capital gains tax for an amount of 15% of the consideration.

Professional services withholding tax (PSWT)

Individual income tax at the standard rate (currently 20%) is deducted from payments for professional services by government departments, state bodies, and local authorities. Credit is granted for any PSWT withheld against the corporation tax (or income tax for an individual) liability of the accounting period in which tax is withheld.

Relevant contracts tax (RCT)

There are special WHT rules (with exemptions available) relating to payments made by principal contractors to sub-contractors in respect of relevant contracts in the construction, forestry, and meat processing industries. Where relevant operations under a relevant contract are carried out in Ireland, the RCT system applies regardless of whether or not parties to the contract are non-resident in Ireland, parties to the contract are not liable to tax in Ireland in respect of those operations, the contract is executed outside Ireland, or payments under the contract are made outside Ireland. It is important to note that principal contractors, liable to RCT, may not operate in the above industries. In the case of construction in particular, relevant contracts may be entered into by a variety of entity types. For example, electricity generation, oil and gas, and telecommunications undertakings are all classed as principal contractors.

The principal contractor must deduct tax at rates of 20% or 35% from such payments and remit this to the Revenue. The rate that is applied to a subcontractor will principally depend on the sub-contractor's tax compliance record. The 20% rate will apply to sub-contractors who are registered with Revenue and have a good tax compliance record, including foreign tax compliance in the case of foreign companies. A zero rate of RCT applies where the sub-contractor applies for that rate and Revenue authorises the principal subcontractor not to deduct RCT from payments. Principals must notify each payment on Revenue's online system and obtain an authorised rate before making any payment, otherwise penalties may apply. The gross amount receivable under the contract is included in the computation of the profit of the sub-contractor, and the sub-contractor is entitled to credit for, or offset of, the tax suffered.

WHT rate reductions and exemptions

Exemptions and rate reductions apply under domestic law and under tax treaties. Where an exemption from WHT is not available (*please see sections above for domestic law exemptions*), a reduced rate of WHT may apply under an applicable tax treaty. The table below sets out the reduced rates of WHT that may be available to payments of dividends, interest, and royalties under an applicable tax treaty.

Recipient	WHT (%)		
	Dividends (1)	Interest (2)	Patents, royalties (3)
Albania	0/5 (4)/10	0/7	7
Armenia **	0 (4)/5 (7)/15	0/5/10	5
Australia	0	10	10
Austria ***	0	0	0
Bahrain	0	0	0
Belarus	0/5 (4)/10	0/5	5
Belgium *	0	15	0
Bosnia-Herzegovina	0	0	0
Bulgaria	5 (4)/10	0/5	10

Ireland

	WHT (%)		
Recipient	Dividends (1)	Interest (2)	Patents, royalties (3)
Canada	5 (7)/15	0/10	0/10
Chile	5 (6)/15	5 (8)/15	5/10
China	5 (4)/10	0/10	6/10
Croatia	5 (7)/10	0	10
Cyprus *	0	0	0
Czech Republic	5 (4)/15	0	10
Denmark	0	0	0
Egypt **	5 (4)/10	0/10	10
Estonia	5 (4)/15	0/10	5/10
Finland	0	0	0
France *	20	0	0
Georgia	0/5 (9)/10	0	0
Germany *	20	0	0
Greece	5 (4)/15	5	5
Hong Kong	0 (12)	0/10	3
Hungary	5 (7)/15	0	0
Iceland	5 (4)/15	0	0/10
India	10	0/10	10
Israel	0	5 (8)/10	10
Italy *	15	10	0
Japan	20	10	10
Korea, Republic of *	0	0	0
Kuwait **	0	0	5
Latvia	5 (4)/15	0/10	5/10
Lithuania	5 (4)/15	0/10	5/10
Luxembourg	20	0	0
Macedonia	0/5 (6)/10	0	0
Malaysia ***	10	0/10	8
Malta	5 (6)/15	0	5
Mexico	5 (4)/10	0/5 (8)/10	10
Moldova	5 (4)/10	5	0/5
Montenegro	0/5/10	0/10	5/10
Morocco **	6/10	0/10	10
Netherlands	0/15	0	0
New Zealand	0	10	10
Norway	0/5 (7)/15	0	0
Pakistan *	20	(5)	0
Panama **	5	0/5	0
Poland	0/15	0/10	10
Portugal	15	0/15	10
Romania	3	0/3	0/3
Russia	10	0	0
Saudi Arabia **	0 (4)/5	0	5/8
Serbia	5 (4)/10	0/10	5/10
Singapore	0	0/5	5
Slovak Republic	0/10	0	0/10

Ireland

Recipient	WHT (%) Dividends (1)	Interest (2)	Patents, royalties (3)
Slovenia	5 (4)/15	0/5	5
South Africa	0	0	0
Spain	0	0	5/8/10
Sweden	0	0	0
Switzerland ***	0	0	0
Turkey	5/15	10/15	10
United Arab Emirates	0	0	0
United Kingdom	5 (6)/15	0	0
United States	5 (7)/15	0	0
Vietnam	5 (10)/10	0/10	5/10/15 (11)
Zambia	0	0	0

Legislation recently has been amended to allow for favourable treatment in situations where a DTT has been signed but not yet ratified.

* These treaties are currently under renegotiation.

** Awaiting ratification.

*** Protocols to the DTTs with Malaysia, Switzerland, and Austria are awaiting ratification. These protocols do not have any impact upon the exemptions and rate reductions outlined above.

Notes

1. See Dividend WHT sub-section above for domestic WHT exemptions.
2. See Interest WHT sub-section above for domestic WHT exemptions.
3. See Royalties WHT sub-section above for domestic WHT exemptions.
4. Where the beneficial owner of the dividends is a resident of a contracting state and is a company which holds directly at least 25% of the capital of the company paying the dividends.
5. Refer to Ireland/Pakistan DTT.
6. Where the beneficial owner of the dividends is a resident of the contracting state and is a company which controls directly or indirectly 10% or more of the voting power in the company paying the dividends.
7. Where the beneficial owner of the dividends is a resident of the contracting state and is a company which controls directly 10% or more of the voting power in the company paying the dividends.
8. For loans from banks and, in the case of Norway, certain government funds.
9. Where the beneficial owner of the dividends is a resident of the contracting state and controls directly or indirectly at least 10% of the voting power in the company paying the dividend and has invested more than EUR 100,000 in the capital of the company paying the dividend. The above details in general are subject to any special relationship that may exist between the payer and the recipient, and it is assumed that the recipient does not have a permanent establishment (taxable presence) in the other contracting state.
10. Where the beneficial owner of the dividends is a resident of a contracting state and is a company which holds directly at least 70% of the voting power of the company paying the dividends.
11. Refer to Ireland/Vietnam DTT.
12. Treaty came into effect on 1 January 2012.

Ireland is currently negotiating treaties with the following countries

- Argentina
- Azerbaijan
- Qatar
- Thailand
- Tunisia
- Ukraine
- Uzbekistan

Ireland

....

Tax administration

Taxable period
The tax accounting period normally coincides with a company's financial accounting period, except where the latter period exceeds 12 months.

Tax returns
Corporation tax returns must be submitted within nine months (and no later than the 23rd day of the ninth month) after the end of the tax accounting period in order to avoid a surcharge (maximum of EUR 63,485) or a restriction of 50% of losses claimed, to a maximum of EUR 158,715.

Payment of tax
Corporation tax payment dates are different for 'large' and 'small' companies. A small company is one whose corporation tax liability in the preceding period was less than EUR 200,000. Interest on late payments or underpayments is applied at approximately 10% per year.

Large companies
The first instalment of preliminary tax totalling 45% of the expected final tax liability, or 50% of the prior period liability, is due six months from the start of the tax accounting period (but no later than the 23rd day of the month).

The second instalment of preliminary tax is due 31 days before the end of the tax accounting period (but no later than the 23rd day of the month). This payment must bring the total paid up to 90% of the estimated liability for the period.

The balance of tax is due when the corporation tax return for the period is filed (that is, within nine months of the end of the tax accounting period, but no later than the 23rd day of the month in which that period of nine months ends).

Small companies
Small companies only are required to pay one instalment of preliminary tax. This is due 31 days before the end of the tax accounting period (but no later than the 23rd day of the month).

The company can choose to pay an amount of preliminary tax equal to 100% of the corporation tax liability for its immediately preceding period or 90% of the estimated liability for the current period. As is the case for large companies, the final instalment is due when the corporation tax return is filed.

Statute of limitations
A system of self-assessment and Irish Revenue audits is in operation in Ireland. Irish Revenue may undertake an audit of a company's tax return within a period of four years from the end of the accounting period in which the return is submitted.

....

Other issues

Asset management
Irish tax legislation contains provisions aimed at enhancing Ireland as a leading location for the management of both Undertakings for Collective Investment in Transferable Securities (UCITS) and non-UCITS funds. UCITS III and IV brought about fundamental changes to both the management and structuring of UCITS. One of the reforms

introduced permits UCITS management companies located in one EU jurisdiction to manage UCITS domiciled in another EU jurisdiction. One of the areas of concern is whether the activities of the management company could bring a foreign UCITS within the charge to tax in the management company's home jurisdiction (e.g. by creating a branch or agency or causing the fund to be regarded as tax resident there). In the case of an Irish management company managing a non-Irish UCITS, such management company will not be regarded as a branch or agency of the non-Irish UCITS and will not bring the profits of the foreign UCITS within the charge to Irish tax or treat the foreign UCITS as an Irish regulated fund.

Following the US and OECD review of offshore domiciles, which has resulted in increased regulation and tax obligations, fund managers are being forced to consider possible alternative onshore jurisdictions for their investment fund products. Because of its international reputation of its investment funds industry and the favourable corporate tax regime, Ireland is seeing a significant trend in investment managers moving their investment platforms there from the traditional offshore jurisdictions. Recent company law changes also allow corporate funds to migrate to Ireland through a re-registration process, whereby the fund company would benefit from its continued existence, including the ability to retain the fund's performance track record post migration and avoid potential adverse tax consequences and costs that typically arise from a merger of an offshore fund with a new onshore fund. The Irish Financial Regulator has introduced a coordinated authorisation process to facilitate speed to market, which at present is a key advantage in comparison to delays being experienced in other EU domiciles.

International funds sector
The Finance Act 2012 introduced a number of provisions designed to support and enhance the international funds sector in Ireland, as set out in further detail below:

Funds re-domiciling to Ireland
Finance Act 2012 provides that where the Central Bank has authorised an investment fund that has re-domiciled to Ireland from certain offshore centres, a declaration can be made by the fund stating that the unitholders are non-Irish resident, to ensure that no Irish tax charge arises in respect of such non-residents, thereby clarifying the tax exemption applying to payments made by Irish funds to non-resident investors. To the extent that there are any Irish resident unitholders, these need to be identified in the declaration and tax accounted for, where appropriate, on any payments made to such unitholders.

Cross-border fund mergers involving Irish funds
New measures have been introduced confirming that mergers (both inbound and outbound) involving an Irish fund with a fund located in a member state of the European Union, European Economic Area (EEA), or an Organisation for Economic Co-operation and Development (OECD) country with which Ireland has entered into a DTT will not give rise to a charge to tax in respect of Irish resident investors. Effectively, the charge to tax is deferred until the ultimate disposal of the replacement units. The calculation of any future gain on such units is calculated by reference to the cost of the original units.

Finance Act 2012 also confirms that no charge to Irish tax shall arise on the transfer of units in the formation of certain master/feeder structures.

Finance Act 2012 also includes a number of significant stamp duty exemptions available for collective investment vehicles.

Ireland

Legislative changes: New Irish corporate structure for investment funds
The Irish funds industry continues to work with the Irish government to explore new products that could enhance the competitiveness of Ireland's fund offering on the global stage.

The Irish Minister of Finance has approved, in principle, legislative proposals for a new form of corporate structure for regulated investment funds.

Currently, investment funds in Ireland structured as companies are incorporated as public limited companies ('plc') under the Irish Companies Acts. The new corporate structure will be specifically designed for investment funds and will not be subject to the legislation governing other types of companies, reducing the need to comply with certain inappropriate requirements under the Companies Acts. The legislation will also increase the range of structures open to investment managers and promoters establishing funds in Ireland.

One of the main advantages of new corporate structure will be the ability of this structure to 'check-the-box' (an election to be regarded as tax transparent) for US tax purposes, whereas an Irish plc cannot. This is seen as a very positive development in the funds industry, particularly in the context of investment funds seeking to re-domicile from traditional tax haven jurisdictions to a regulated jurisdiction like Ireland.

It is expected that the proposed new legislation will be enacted by the end of 2012 prior to the entry into force of the EU Alternative Investment Funds Managers Directive in July 2013. It is intended that the new corporate fund would qualify for the tax exemption that applies to Irish regulated funds.

Islamic finance
The Irish tax treatment of certain Islamic finance transactions, such as funds, certain *ijara* (leasing), *takaful* (insurance), and *re-takaful* (reinsurance) is accommodated within existing Irish tax legislation. Specific legislation was also introduced to facilitate the issuance of *sukuk* (i.e. Islamic bonds) in Ireland. Overall, the intention of the legislature is to ensure that Islamic finance transactions are treated in the same favourable manner as conventional financing transactions. The legislation also introduced changes in relation to the taxation (and tax impact) of UCITS management companies. The UCITS structure is one of the commonly used structures for many different types of Islamic funds, such as retail Islamic equity funds, Shariah-compliant money market funds, Shariah-compliant exchange traded funds (ETFs), etc. This demonstrates the Irish government and tax authorities desire to enhance the attractiveness of Ireland as a location for Islamic finance transactions by extending to this form of financing the relieving provisions which currently apply to conventional financing.

Islamic insurance
The Irish Revenue has recently provided guidance in respect of the Irish tax treatment of general *takaful* (non-life), *re-takaful* (reinsurance), and family (life) *takaful* arrangements. Legislative changes are not currently required to facilitate Islamic insurance in Ireland.

Exchange control
Ireland does not have exchange control regulations.

Choice of legal entity

Foreign investors tend to operate either through an Irish legal entity or as a branch of a foreign entity. Both are equally valid means of doing business in Ireland, and the choice would normally depend on the commercial fact pattern and individual circumstances of the investor parent company.

Mandatory disclosure

In a move to promote transparency between taxpayers, practitioners, and tax authorities, provisions relating to the disclosure of tax schemes are applicable as of January 2011. These require promoters of such schemes to provide information to the tax authorities within a specified time of having made the scheme available. A transaction which comes within the new law and which therefore must be reported to Revenue is not necessarily a tax avoidance transaction for the purposes of existing legislation. The rules are wide reaching and essentially cover all tax heads including corporation tax, income tax, capital gains tax, stamp duty, VAT, customs duties, and excise duties.

I

Isle of Man

PwC contact

Kevin Cowley
PricewaterhouseCoopers
Sixty Circular Road, 3rd Floor
Douglas IM1 1SA
Isle of Man
Tel: +44 1624 689689
Email: kevin.cowley@iom.pwc.com

....

Significant developments

Tax treaties

The Isle of Man signed a comprehensive double tax agreement (DTA) with Qatar in May 2012, bringing the total number of treaties to five. The DTA with Belgium, signed in July 2009, is still awaiting ratification.

The Isle of Man now has a total of 30 tax information exchange agreements (TIEAs), including those signed during 2011 with Canada, India, Poland, Mexico, Japan, Indonesia, Slovenia and, most recently, the Czech Republic.

Income attributed to shareholders

For accounting periods ending prior to 5 April 2012, legislation existed that attributed the profits of an Isle of Man resident company to any Manx resident shareholders as if that profit had been distributed to them. Although any resulting tax charge fell on the shareholder, the legislation placed reporting and filing obligations on the Isle of Man resident company in respect of profits realised and distributions made.

This legislation was abolished in the 2011 budget and no longer applies for accounting periods commencing after 6 April 2012.

....

Taxes on corporate income

Companies resident in the Isle of Man are taxed on their worldwide income and are required to file an annual income tax return reporting worldwide taxable profits calculated in line with local legislation and practice.

A non-resident company incorporated outside the Isle of Man but having a place of business or a permanent establishment (PE) on the Isle of Man will be taxed on the profit attributable to the Isle of Man establishment.

The majority of companies pay income tax at 0% in the Isle of Man.

A 10% rate of tax applies to income received by a company from any of the following sources:

- Banking business.
- Land and property in the Isle of Man (including property development, residential and commercial rental or property letting, and mining and quarrying, but excluding farming).

The general rules for the calculation of taxable income are the same whether a company is liable to tax at 0%, 10%, or a combination of both rates. Both resident and non-resident companies are taxed on their income at the same rates.

Unilateral relief from double taxation in respect of foreign-source income is given by way of tax credit.

Local income taxes

There are no profit based taxes levied by local government in the Isle of Man. However, commercial business rates are payable. Premises are assessed and given a 'rateable value' that forms the basis of the annual rates charge levied.

Corporate residence

A company incorporated in the Isle of Man is automatically resident for tax purposes and must therefore file an annual income tax return whether it pays tax at 0% or 10%.

A company which is incorporated elsewhere will be considered resident in the Isle of Man if it is 'managed and controlled' in the Isle of Man, and will be taxed on their worldwide income accordingly. 'Managed and controlled' is generally interpreted as being the place where the board of directors meets, although this is not always conclusive.

In cases where a company is resident in a country with which the Isle of Man has a tax treaty, then a tie-breaker may operate to determine residence.

Other taxes

Value-added tax (VAT)

VAT is a transaction based tax applied on the domestic supply of most goods and services and is currently charged at a standard rate of 20%. VAT is designed to be a tax borne by the final consumer, and there is a mechanism for businesses to recover VAT incurred in a supply chain, subject to meeting certain conditions.

For VAT purposes, the Isle of Man forms a single VAT jurisdiction with the United Kingdom (UK), and the VAT rules are broadly identical. This means that VAT is charged on supplies between Isle of Man and UK businesses as if they were domestic supplies. The Isle of Man has its own tax authorities who work in conjunction with the UK tax authorities.

Some supplies are charged at 0%, including food, books and publications, and public transport, and there is also a 5% rate applying to domestic property repairs, amongst others. Finally, some supplies are exempt from VAT, including insurance and financial services, betting and gaming, education, and health.

Customs and excise duties

In addition to VAT, the Isle of Man forms a common jurisdiction for customs and excise duties with the United Kingdom, and, again, the rules are broadly identical. Customs duties are levied on most goods imported from outside the European Union (EU) into the Isle of Man, and there are various rates of duty which apply. Excise duties apply to such things as alcohol, tobacco, and fuels, and there are various rates of duty which apply. There is also a levy on commercial passenger flights known as Air Passenger Duty.

Isle of Man

Property taxes

There are no property related taxes for companies other than income tax payable at a rate of 10% on their profits from the rental or development of land or property situated in the Isle of Man, and business rates *as detailed in the Taxes on corporate income section.*

Transfer taxes

There are no capital transfer taxes in the Isle of Man.

Stamp taxes

There is no stamp duty payable in the Isle of Man.

Betting duty

There are no other transaction taxes in the Isle of Man other than betting duty on gaming transactions, which is levied at differing rates of up to 15%, depending on the nature of the gaming transaction and whether it is online or land based.

Branch income

The income of branches is taxed in the same way as other corporate income in the Isle of Man. Consequently, Isle of Man resident companies with branches overseas are taxable on their worldwide income (although relief may be available for any foreign tax paid). Foreign companies with branches in the Isle of Man will be taxed at the appropriate rate on the profits attributable to the Isle of Man establishment.

Income determination

The general rules for the calculation of taxable income are the same whether a company is liable to tax at 0%, 10%, or a combination of both rates.

Inventory valuation

Inventories are generally stated at the lower of cost or market value. Any method of valuation that accords with sound commercial principles is acceptable for tax purposes, provided it is adopted consistently at the beginning and end of the accounting period and does not conflict with tax law. In practice, inventories are normally valued for tax purposes at the lower of cost or net realisable value. A first in first out (FIFO) basis of determining cost where items cannot be identified is acceptable, but not the base stock method or the last in first out (LIFO) method.

In general, the book and tax methods of inventory valuation must conform.

Capital gains

There is no capital gains tax in the Isle of Man.

Dividend income

Dividends are taxed at the standard rate of 0%. Dividends received from Isle of Man companies will not have suffered WHT.

Banking income

Licensed banks are taxed at 10% on income from deposit taking and any related activities, and interest earned from the investment of regulatory reserves only.

Income earned on capital and reserves in excess of the regulatory capital, group funded lending, fiduciary deposits, assurance, insurance, custody, trust, and corporate services are not banking business and are therefore taxed at 0%.

General expenses are allocated against 0% and 10% income streams on a pro rata basis.

Rental income

Companies with profits arising on rental income in respect of land or property situated in the Isle of Man are charged to income tax at a rate of 10%. This applies whether or not the company is resident in the Isle of Man.

Foreign income

Resident corporations are liable to tax on their worldwide income (albeit the relevant rate of tax is often 0%). UK tax is relieved under the treaty with the United Kingdom by way of tax credits. However, the treaty does not cover dividends or debenture interest. Where a liability to tax at 10% arises, the Isle of Man grants unilateral relief from double taxation in respect of all foreign-source income arising outside the United Kingdom by way of tax credit.

I

Deductions

Relief is given in calculating the taxable profit of a company if the expense is incurred in the normal course of the business and is incurred wholly and exclusively for business purposes. However, certain expenses which are deductible in the computation of profits are not allowable for tax purposes. These include depreciation, unpaid but accrued pension and bonus payments, certain lease payments, and interest paid to non-Manx resident lenders.

Depreciation

Depreciation charged in accounts in not allowable for tax purposes. Instead, relief for depreciation is given using 'capital allowances' based on a reducing-balance method. Plant and machinery, tourist premises, industrial buildings, commercial buildings within a designated area, fish processing buildings, and agricultural buildings and works have an initial allowance of 100%. There are restrictions on allowances for expensive motorcars.

Isle of Man government grants are not taken into account in determining the amount of expenditure on which allowances may be given.

Tax depreciation is not required to conform to book depreciation.

Upon disposal, allowances will be reclaimed on the resale value, restricted to cost.

Goodwill

No relief is given against trading profits for the purchase of goodwill.

Start-up expenses

Start-up expenses incurred in the three years prior to the commencement of trading, which would have been deductible as a trading expense if incurred after the commencement of trading, are treated as a loss arising in the year trading commenced, and relief for these losses can be claimed subject to the normal loss relief rules.

Isle of Man

Interest expenses
Interest paid to lenders subject to Isle of Man tax is allowable in full. Interest paid to lenders not subject to Isle of Man taxation is allowable if it is incurred in the normal course of the business and is wholly and exclusively for business purposes. Only interest charged at a reasonable commercial rate will be allowed as a deduction.

Bad debt
Relief against trading profits is only available in respect of specific bad debts. General provisions are not allowable.

Charitable contributions
Broadly, trading companies are able to claim a deduction for donations made to charities subject to a maximum of 15,000 Isle of Man pounds (IMP) or 1% of their taxable income, whichever is greater.

Fines and penalties
No relief is available for any payments made in respect of fines or penalties, whether related to income tax compliance or otherwise.

Taxes
Local income taxes paid are not deductible when calculating net taxable profit.

Net operating losses
Losses can be carried forward indefinitely against future profits from the same trade.

Trading losses incurred may be carried back against preceding year profits. There are additional rules which apply in the opening years of trade. Terminal losses in the last year of trade can be carried back against profits for the previous three years of trading.

Payments to foreign affiliates
There is no transfer pricing regime in the Isle of Man. If, however, the Assessor of Taxes is of the opinion that the main purpose, or one of the main purposes, of any transaction is the avoidance or reduction of tax liability, assessments may be made to counteract that avoidance or reduction of tax liability.

For details of WHTs, please see the Withholding taxes section.

Group taxation

Trading losses and excess capital allowances may be surrendered (subject to certain restrictions) between 75% affiliates resident in the Isle of Man. Similar concessions are available to members of a consortium, but only a fraction of the loss or excess may be set-off, that fraction being equal to the members' share in the consortium in the relevant year of assessment.

Transfer pricing
There is no transfer pricing regime in the Isle of Man. If, however, the Assessor of Taxes is of the opinion that the main purpose, or one of the main purposes, of any transaction is the avoidance or reduction of tax liability, assessments may be made to counteract that avoidance or reduction of tax liability.

Thin capitalisation
There is no specific thin capitalisation rule in the Isle of Man.

Isle of Man

Controlled foreign companies (CFCs)
There is no CFC regime in the Isle of Man.

Tax credits and incentives

In view of the low rate of income tax in the Isle of Man, there are no special tax incentives available.

Foreign tax credit
See Foreign income in the Income determination section for a description of foreign tax credits.

Withholding taxes

WHT should be deducted from certain payments made to non-residents by Isle of Man resident companies as follows:

- Rent from Manx land and property: 10% if paid to a company, 20% if paid to an individual.
- Dividends: WHT is not required.
- Loan interest and royalties: WHT is generally not required, but there are certain exceptions which may apply.
- Other: The Assessor of Income Tax in the Isle of Man has the power to require WHT, at a rate determined by the Assessor (typically 20%), on payments of taxable income made to a non-resident (e.g. payments made to non-resident sub-contractors).

Tax administration

Taxable period
An accounting period for tax filing purposes can be no more than 12 months.

Tax returns
All companies are required to submit income tax returns on an accounting period basis, whether they are liable to tax at 0% or at 10%. The tax return is due for submission one year and one day following the end of an accounting period. Where the financial statements cover more than 12 months, two (or more) returns may be required.

Fixed rate penalties apply if returns are filed late. The Assessor of Taxes also has the powers to raise a default assessment where a tax return has not been filed.

Payment of tax
Payment of tax is due within one year and one day of an accounting period end. Interest is charged on tax paid late.

Audit cycle
Companies are subject to an audit of their accounts on an annual basis unless they qualify for exemption under the regulatory codes and guidelines issued by the Isle of Man General Registry.

Where a company qualifies for exemption from the audit requirement, it must make an election during the course of the relevant financial period.

Isle of Man

All Isle of Man registered companies are required to file an annual return to the Isle of Man Companies Registry.

Statute of limitations

Generally, the Assessor of Taxes may make an enquiry into a tax return no later than 12 months from the date that the tax return is delivered to the Assessor.

If, however, the Assessor discovers that income tax has not been assessed that should have been assessed, the Assessor is able to make an assessment of that tax within a period of for years from the end of the relevant accounting period.

The Assessor also has powers to require the production of documents.

Topics of focus for tax authorities

The Isle of Man government is focussed on delivering openness and transparency across all areas of Isle of Man taxation. The government and the Tax Authorities work closely with international bodies such as the EU Code of Conduct group and the EU's Economic and Financial Affairs Council to ensure that the Island is fully compliant with international standards in areas such as tax transparency and exchange of information. The Island is already recognised on the Organisation for Economic Co-operation and Development (OECD) White List as being in the top tier of countries for transparency and information exchange.

In addition to maintaining it's international position, the tax authorities are keen to engage taxpayers on important issues through consultation on key areas. It is also striving to maintain and improve its services and levels of efficiency through the continued expansion of its range of services available online.

Other issues

Tax treaties

The Isle of Man signed a comprehensive DTA with Qatar in May 2012, bringing the total number of treaties to five. The DTA with Belgium, signed in July 2009, is still awaiting ratification.

The Isle of Man now has a total of 30 TIEAs, including those signed during 2011 with Canada, India, Poland, Mexico, Japan, Indonesia, Slovenia and, most recently, the Czech Republic.

Choice of business entity

There are several different entities through which businesses may operate in the Isle of Man. These include companies, limited liability companies, partnerships, limited partnerships, and protected cell companies.

Israel

PwC contact

Gerry Seligman
PwC Israel, Kesselman & Kesselman
Trade Tower
25 Hamered Street
Tel-Aviv 68125
Israel
Tel: +972 3 795 4 510
Email: gerry.seligman@il.pwc.com

Significant developments

The Israeli Parliament passed legislation on 6 December 2011 that is based on the tax reform proposals issued by the Committee for Socioeconomic Change (the Committee), a state-appointed committee headed by Professor Manuel Trajtenberg whose proposals were aimed at lowering living costs and economic inequality. The tax amendments are generally effective as of 1 January 2012 and include the following developments:

- As of January 2012, the corporate tax rate has been increased to 25% for 2012 and thereafter.
- During 2011, a 20% tax rate generally applied to interest income, dividend income, and capital gains. A 25% rate applied to dividend income and capital gains generated by shareholders owning 10% or more in a company. As of January 2012, the 20% rate has been increased to 25%, and the rate on dividend income and capital gains for 10% or more shareholders has been increased from 25% to 30%. It should be noted that for foreign residents these taxes may be exempt or reduced in accordance to the provisions of local legislation or an applicable tax treaty.

Taxes on corporate income

Israel incorporated companies and foreign companies that have a branch presence in Israel are both subject to Israeli corporate tax. An Israeli-resident entity is subject to Israeli corporate tax on worldwide income while a non-resident entity is subject to Israeli corporate tax only on income accrued or derived in Israel. Income sourcing rules determine when income is to be considered from an Israeli source.

As of January 2012, the scheduled corporate tax rate reductions have been cancelled and the corporate tax rate has been increased to 25% (from 24%) for 2012 and thereafter.

Approved enterprises are subject to reduced rates of tax depending upon the level of foreign ownership and location (*see the Tax credits and incentives section*).

Local income taxes
Israel does not impose local taxes on corporate income.

Corporate residence

The following are considered to be resident in Israel:

Israel

- A company incorporated in Israel.
- A company whose business is managed and controlled from Israel.

In the absence of a definition of the term 'management and control' either in Israeli legislation or a direct discussion of this term by the Israeli courts, it may be difficult to determine whether a company that is incorporated outside of Israel shall be viewed as managed and controlled from Israel. This is a complex subject that needs to be addressed on a case by case basis. When an entity is both an Israeli tax resident and a resident of a foreign jurisdiction which is party to an income tax treaty with Israel, most treaties provide a tiebreaker test in the determination of an entity's tax residency.

Permanent establishment (PE)
Foreign resident entities might be exempt from corporate tax to the extent that its activities do not constitute a PE under the tax treaty applicable between Israel and the foreign resident's country of residency.

Whether a non-resident has a taxable presence under Israeli domestic tax law is far less clear than the definition of PE under a relevant tax treaty. There is no detailed legislation or Israeli court decisions which directly address this issue.

Other taxes

Value-added tax (VAT)
The current rate of VAT is 16%.

Exports of goods and certain services and various other transactions are zero-rated, and certain transactions are exempt. Banks and other financial institutions pay VAT-equivalent taxes at the rate of 16% based on their total payroll and on profits. Not-for-profit organisations pay VAT (wage tax) at the rate of 8% of their total payroll.

Customs duties
Customs duty is imposed on certain products imported into Israel. The rates of duty depend upon their classification according to the Harmonised Customs Tariff and the country of origin. Israel has concluded free-trade agreements with the United States, Canada, Mexico, the European Union (EU), and the European Free Trade Association (EFTA).

Excise taxes
The government imposes excise taxes on a variety of goods (e.g. fuel, tobacco). The excise taxes are levied item-by-item.

Municipal tax
Municipal tax is levied annually on buildings by local municipalities based on the size, location, and purpose of the property.

Real estate - capital gains
Capital gains on real estate are subject to the Land Appreciation Tax Law. The law relates to any real estate in Israel, including houses, buildings, and anything permanently fixed to land; real estate rights; and leases for 25 years or more. Tax calculations closely follow the calculation of company tax on capital gains (see Capital gains in the Income determination section).

The tax rate on the real gain is the applicable corporate tax rate (25% in 2012).

A special tax rate may apply with respect to real estate acquired prior to 1960.

Transfer tax
The purchaser of real estate is generally subject to acquisition tax at rates of 0.5% up to a maximum of 5%.

Stamp taxes
There are no stamp taxes imposed in Israel.

Employer's national insurance contributions
Employers are obliged to pay national insurance contributions based on a percentage of each employee's income on a monthly basis. Employers are responsible for withholding employees' contributions from wages and remitting these together with the employer's own contributions. The employer's contribution rates (current as of May 2012) for Israeli-resident employees are 3.45% up to monthly income of 5,171 Israeli shekels (ILS) and 5.9% on the difference between ILS 5,171 and the maximum monthly income of ILS 41,850.

For non-resident employees, the employer rates are significantly lower and are 0.49% up to monthly income of ILS 5,171 and 1.17% on the difference between ILS 5,171 and the maximum monthly income of ILS 41,850. The minimal National Insurance payments for non-resident employees do not provide any retirement benefit for the non-resident but generally provides a certain element of work accident coverage.

When an irregular salary payment in excess of one quarter of the usual salary is made, special provisions apply to the computation of social charges by which the application of this payment is equally attributed to the current month and to the past 11 months.

Israel has social security totalisation agreements with 14 countries which may allow for an exemption from Israeli National Insurance throughout the employment period of the employee in Israel.

Branch income

A branch is liable for tax at the standard corporate rate on Israel-source income. No tax is withheld on transfers of profits to the foreign head office unless the branch is an approved enterprise (*see the Tax credits and incentives section*).

Income determination

In general, the annual results (i.e. the excess of income over expenses or vice versa) of an Israeli company or branch, as detailed in the taxpayer's financial statements, form the basis for computing the taxable income of the business.

The base amount is then adjusted pursuant to the provisions of the tax law to arrive at 'taxable income'.

Inventory valuation
Inventories are generally valued at the lower of cost or market value (i.e. net realisable value). Conformity is required between book and tax reporting of inventory. The first in first out (FIFO) or weighted-average basis of valuation is acceptable; the last in first out (LIFO) method is not accepted.

Israel

Capital gains
Capital gains tax is generally payable on capital gains by residents of Israel on the sale of assets (irrespective of the location of the assets) and by non-residents on the sale of the following:

- Assets located in Israel.
- Assets located abroad that are essentially a direct or indirect right to an asset or to inventory, or that are an indirect right to a real estate right or to an asset in a real estate association, located in Israel. Taxation applies only in respect of that part of the consideration that stems from the above property located in Israel.
- Assets that are a share or the right to a share in an Israeli entity.
- Assets that are a right in a foreign resident entity which is essentially a direct or indirect right to property located in Israel. Taxation applies only with respect to that part of the consideration that stems from the property located in Israel.

The cashless transfer of rights and assets arising from certain mergers, spin-offs, and asset transfers may be exempt from tax upon meeting various requirements.

Determination of the capital gain - Computation of real gain and inflationary components
Company tax on capital gains is imposed on the disposal of fixed and intangible assets where the disposal price is in excess of the depreciated cost.

For tax purposes, the capital gain is generally calculated in local currency, and there are provisions for segregating the taxable gain into its real and inflationary components. The inflationary amount is the original cost of the asset, less depreciation (where applicable), multiplied by the percentage increase in the Israeli consumer price index (CPI) from the date of acquisition of the asset to the date of its sale. The inflationary amount component is exempt to the extent it accrued after 1 January 1994 and is generally subject to tax at the rate of 10% if it accrued before that date.

The real gain component, if any, is taxed at the rates set out further below.

A non-resident that invests in capital assets with foreign currency may elect to calculate the inflationary amount in that foreign currency. Under this option, in the event of a sale of shares in an Israeli company, the inflationary amount attributable to exchange differences on the investment is always exempt from Israeli tax.

Sale of assets (including publicly and non-publicly traded shares)
The real gain is generally subject to tax at the corporate tax rate applicable in the year of the gain (25% in 2012). Special exemptions may apply for non-residents (*see further below*).

Special rule for retained profits upon sale of shares
In the case of a disposal by corporations of: (i) non-traded shares and (ii) traded shares when the seller generally directly or indirectly holds at least 10% of the sold Israeli company during the 12-month period preceding the sale, special provisions apply to such part of the real gain which is attributed to the seller's share of retained profits. The share of retained profits is the amount of gain equal to the proportional part of the retained profits of the company that the seller of the shares would have rights to by virtue of those shares. Detailed rules apply in determining this profit component.

Generally, the seller's proportionate part of the company's retained profits is taxed as if this amount had been received as dividends immediately before the sale (i.e. at a tax rate of 0% in the case of an Israeli-resident corporate shareholder or at a tax rate of 30% when the seller is a non-Israeli resident corporate shareholder that generally holds 10% or more in the rights of the Israeli company, subject to a reduced rate in accordance with the provisions of an applicable tax treaty). The part of the retained profits that is attributed to the period ending on 31 December 2002 is subject to tax at the rate of 10%.

Special exemptions for non-residents

Publicly traded Israeli shares
Non-residents corporations not having a PE in Israel are exempt from tax on capital gains from the sale of shares of an Israeli company traded on the Israeli stock exchange or on a foreign stock exchange.

Where the shares were purchased by the non-resident prior to being publicly traded, capital gains tax applies for the portion of the gain that was generated up to the day of the share's public listing but not to exceed the capital gain actually arising upon the sale of the share and provided that the value on the day of public listing was more than their value on the date of purchase and that the proceeds upon sale exceeded the value on the date of purchase.

Non-publicly traded shares
For purchases after 1 January 2009, an exemption exists under domestic law for non-residents, regardless of their percentage holding in an Israeli company, from gains derived from the sale of securities not traded on a stock exchange, provided the following conditions are met:

- The investment is not in a company the majority of whose assets are real estate assets in Israel.
- The capital gains were not derived by the seller's PE in Israel.
- The shares were not purchased from a relative (as defined in the Income Tax Ordinance [ITO]) or by means of a tax-free reorganisation.

For shares purchased between 1 July 2005 and 1 January 2009, more restrictive conditions apply in order to be eligible for the exemption. Detailed rules apply.

Treaty exemption
Non-residents may qualify for a tax treaty capital gain exemption depending upon the particular circumstances and the provisions of the applicable tax treaty (e.g. in some tax treaties, no capital gains exemption is allowed where the holding in the sold Israeli company exceeds a certain percentage).

When assets are attributable to an Israeli PE or are real estate rights (including rights in a real estate association), a treaty exemption will generally not be available.

The Israel Tax Authority (ITA) is very sensitive to treaty shopping, and it will be necessary to demonstrate to the ITA that the foreign holding entity has business substance in its country of residence and that the structuring of the holding through that entity was not implemented for tax treaty benefit purposes.

Capital losses
Capital losses may offset all capital gains (including gains from Israeli or foreign securities) and gains from the sale of property (whether Israeli or foreign source).

Israel

Where the capital loss is from a non-Israeli asset (including when carried forward into future years), the loss must first be offset against foreign source capital gains.

Capital losses derived from the sale of securities may also be offset against interest and dividend income generated from the sold security and also against interest and dividend income received from other securities (where the income was not subject to tax of more than 25%).

Capital losses from the sale of shares are generally reduced by any dividends received by the selling corporation during the 24 months preceding the sale, where tax on the dividends of at least 15% was paid.

Capital losses can generally be carried forward indefinitely and set-off only against capital gains.

Exit tax
When an Israeli tax resident, including a company, ceases to be an Israeli resident for tax purposes, its assets are deemed to have been sold one day before it ceased being an Israeli resident. Although exit tax is primarily applicable to individuals, this might also apply to corporations incorporated outside of Israel whose management and control is transferred from Israel to another jurisdiction at a particular time.

Any gain attributable to the deemed sale of assets may be paid on the day the residency ceased or it may be postponed until the date the assets are actually realised. When the tax event is deferred to the sale date of the assets, the amount of the Israeli capital gain portion is determined by taking the real capital gain at the time of realisation, multiplied by the period of ownership from the day on which it acquired the asset until the day it ceased being an Israeli resident, divided by the entire period from the day of the asset's acquisition until the day of realisation. The Minister of Finance is authorised to prescribe provisions for the implementation of the exit tax including provisions for the prevention of double taxation and the submission of tax reports, but no provisions have yet been issued.

Dividend income

Received by an Israeli-resident company
Dividends received by an Israel-resident company from another Israeli-resident company which originate from income accrued or derived in Israel are exempt from corporate tax, except for dividends paid from income of an approved enterprise (*see the Tax credits and incentives section*). This affords the opportunity to transfer after tax profits within an Israeli group of companies for further investment.

Dividends received by an Israeli-resident company from a non-resident company as well as dividends received from an Israeli company which arise from foreign source income of the distributing company are generally taxable for the receiving company at the rate of 25%. Under certain circumstances, the receiving company may elect to be taxed on such dividends at the corporate tax rate, in which case it would also be entitled to a foreign tax credit with respect to corporate taxes paid by the company distributing the dividend (i.e. an 'underlying' tax credit).

Received by a non-resident shareholder
Dividends received by a non-resident shareholder from an Israeli company are generally subject to tax at the rate of 25% (30% if paid to a 10% or more shareholder), subject to a reduced rate of tax under an applicable tax treaty.

Israel

Several of Israel's tax treaties have very beneficial withholding tax (WHT) rates for dividends being paid from Israel. The ITA is very sensitive to treaty shopping, and it will be necessary to demonstrate to the ITA that the foreign holding entity has business substance in its country of residence and that the structuring of the holding through that entity was not implemented for tax treaty benefit purposes. Furthermore, many of the treaties contain a beneficial ownership clause as a condition to enjoying the treaty WHT rates.

Interest income

Received by an Israeli-resident company
Interest income received by an Israeli-resident company is subject to the regular corporate tax rate (25% in 2012).

Received by a non-resident
Interest income received by a non-resident company is generally subject to tax at the rate of 20% or subject to a reduced rate of tax under an applicable tax treaty.

Interest received by a non-resident from deposits of foreign currency with an Israel bank is exempt from tax, subject to certain conditions.

Rent/royalties income
Rent and royalty income, less allowable deductions for tax purposes, is subject to tax at the regular corporate tax rate (25% in 2012).

Partnership income
From an Israeli tax perspective, a partnership is, in principle, a fiscally transparent vehicle. Accordingly, Israeli tax law does not tax partnerships as such, but generally each partner is taxed in respect of its share of the partnership income, with the taxable income allocated to a corporate partner taxed at the regular company tax rate. Consequently, the actual distribution of partnership income to a partner is a non-taxable event.

Foreign income
An Israeli-resident company is liable for tax on its worldwide income. Double taxation is avoided by way of a foreign tax credit mechanism that also applies unilaterally in the absence of an applicable double taxation treaty (*see the Tax credits and incentives section*).

Under the CFC regime in Israeli tax law, an Israeli company or individual may be taxed on a proportion of the undistributed profits of certain Israeli-controlled non-resident companies in which the Israeli shareholder has a controlling interest (10% or more of any of the CFC's 'means of control'). *See Controlled foreign companies (CFCs) in the Group taxation section for more information.*

Deductions

Costs incurred by a branch or a company are deductible as a business expense for tax purposes where they are incurred 'wholly and exclusively in the production of income'. The amount of the deduction may be limited or disallowed further to other ITO provisions and income tax regulations.

Israel

Depreciation

The ITO and tax regulations prescribe standard annual rates of tax depreciation for assets serving in the production of taxable income. Depreciation is generally on a straight-line basis for industrial and other enterprises based on the specific asset types as set out in the tax regulations.

Accelerated rates of depreciation may be available in regard to certain activities (such as industrial) where there is unusual wear and tear due to additional shifts of equipment use. Detailed rules apply.

Depreciation is not permitted on land.

Goodwill

In general, under Israeli tax regulations, goodwill purchased after 1 July 2003 may be amortisable by the purchaser over a 10-year period (10% annually).

Organisational and start-up expenses

Organisational and start-up expenses are generally not immediately deductible but rather are to be capitalised for tax purposes.

Interest expenses

Interest expenses incurred in the production of taxable income are generally deductible. Since there are no thin capitalisation rules in Israel, there are no specific debt-to-equity ratio requirements and there is no limit to the amount of debt that may be used in establishing a branch or local company operation in Israel. Interest and linkage payments arising from late tax payments are generally not deductible for tax purposes. Interest charges between related parties must be set based on transfer pricing principles. Detailed rules apply.

Bad debt

Provisions for bad debts are deductible in the year in which it is evident that the debt has become irrecoverable. Detailed rules apply for making this determination.

Charitable contributions

Charitable contributions do not constitute a regular business expense. However, a tax credit may be available (see Tax credit for donations in the Tax credits and incentives section).

Research and development (R&D) costs

Special tax relief is provided under the ITO for R&D costs incurred (see the Tax credits and incentives section).

Pension expense

Pension fund contributions made to recognised funds are generally deductible for the employer provided inter alia the contributions do not exceed a prescribed level and are effected on a regular basis.

Directors' fees

Payments for commercially justifiable director fees should generally be deductible.

Accrued expenses

Payments are generally deductible on an accrual basis for commercially justifiable expenses representing arm's-length consideration. However, when payments made to foreign residents attract WHT, the deduction will generally be allowed provided the payment is effected within the tax year. Alternatively, such payments may be deductible in a tax year if the applicable WHT is deducted within three months after the tax year-end and remitted to the tax authorities within seven days of the deduction, together with index linkage differences and interest accrued since the year-end.

However, accrued expenses for severance pay, vacation pay, recreation pay, holiday allowances, and sick pay are not deductible, even if there is an obligation to make these payments. They are only deductible in the year in which they are actually paid to the beneficiary or to a recognised fund.

Contingent liabilities
Based on Israeli court decisions, contingent liabilities may be deductible for tax purposes upon satisfying the following criterion: (i) according to accepted accounting principles, the taxpayer must include in its balance sheet a suitable provision for the potential liability; otherwise, its income will be considered to have been incorrectly reported; (ii) the circumstances of the case and the technical means according to accepted accounting practice must be provided, enabling a determination of the amount of the liability; and (iii) there is a high probability that the potential debt with respect to which the provision was made will become an absolute debt.

Excess (disallowed) expenses
Israeli tax law disallows the partial deduction of certain employee-related expenses incurred by a company doing business in Israel. These include so-called 'excess expenses'. Examples of these are (i) payments for business, travel, and meals which exceed allowable deductions; (ii) expenses incurred in respect of a benefit granted by an employer to its employees but which cannot be attributed to a particular employee; and (iii) certain vehicle maintenance expenses (all expenses relating to a company owned vehicle that was also designated for use of an employee are generally tax deductible).

A company is obliged to pay a monthly advance on excess expenses in the amount of 45% of the excess expense. The amount paid as an advance in respect of excess expenses is deemed a payment on account of the regular tax advances and payments that the company must pay for corporate income tax and is offset against them, but it is not refundable (i.e. when a taxpayer's tax liability in a given year is lower than the excess expense advances paid, the unutilised amount shall be carried forward to future tax years). Detailed rules apply.

Fines and penalties
Payment of fines and penalties are generally not deductible.

Taxes
Municipality taxes incurred in the production of taxable income are generally deductible.

Net operating losses
Business losses can be offset against income from any source in the same year. Loss carrybacks are not allowed. Losses may be carried forward and set-off without time limit against income from any trade or business or capital gains arising in the business, but not against income from any other source.

Payments to foreign affiliates
Payments of interest, royalties, and management fees to foreign affiliates are deductible if based on normal commercial terms and practices and evidenced by an inter-company

Israel

agreement and transfer pricing documentation. Where such payments attract WHT, the deduction will only be allowed where such tax has been withheld and paid in accordance with certain requirements. All cross-border payments to foreign affiliates for goods and services have to comply with arm's-length pricing standards (*see Transfer pricing in the Group taxation section*).

Group taxation

As a general rule, a parent company and its subsidiaries may not submit consolidated tax returns. Only groups of industrial companies in the same line of business, as well as parent companies that control industrial companies in the same line of business and have at least 80% of their assets invested in industrial companies, are eligible to file consolidated tax returns.

Transfer pricing

The ITO and its accompanying regulations contain elaborate transfer pricing provisions, including the arm's-length principle, which apply to any international transaction in which there is a special relationship between the parties to the transaction and for which a price was settled on for property, a right, a service, or credit. In general, the regulations are based upon internationally recognised transfer pricing principles (i.e. United States tax regulations or Organisation for Economic Co-operation and Development [OECD] rules). These regulations generally require the taxpayer to support the pricing of international transactions with a transfer pricing study, inter-company agreements, and other documentation. In accordance to Israeli High Court Rulings, the terms of transaction conducted between related parties should be set in written contracts.

Since transfer pricing is a subject that receives considerable attention from the ITA in its examination of related inter-company transactions, transfer pricing principles and documentation requirements should be carefully adhered to.

A taxpayer is required to include in its annual corporate tax return a special form entitled 'Declaration of International Transactions' providing details for every cross-border transaction conducted with related parties. The taxpayer must sign the form which includes a declaration that the transactions with related parties abroad were in accordance with the arm's-length principle, as defined in the Israeli transfer pricing regulations promulgated under the ITO. As a result of this form and declaration, the importance of appropriate transfer pricing documentation has increased.

Thin capitalisation

Israel has no statutory or regulatory provisions or other rules concerning thin capitalisation for tax purposes as exist in certain other jurisdictions. Since there are no thin capitalisation rules and Israel has no specific debt-equity ratio requirements, a company may be financed with minimum capital and there is no limit to the amount of debt that may be used. Transfer pricing principles shall generally apply with regards to interest charges.

Controlled foreign companies (CFCs)

Under the CFC regime in Israeli tax law, an Israeli company or individual may be taxed on a proportion of certain undistributed profits of certain Israeli-controlled non-resident companies in which the Israeli shareholder has a controlling interest (10% or more of any of the CFC's 'means of control'). A CFC is a company to which a number of cumulative conditions apply including that most of its income or profits in the tax year were derived from passive sources (e.g. capital gains, interest, rental, dividend, royalties) and such passive income has been subject to an effective tax rate that does not exceed 20%.

Tax credits and incentives

Foreign tax credit
Double taxation is avoided by way of a foreign tax credit mechanism that also applies unilaterally in the absence of an applicable double taxation treaty. The foreign tax credit is limited to the Israeli corporate tax payable with respect to the same income. Foreign sourced income is divided into 'baskets' (i.e. categories) on the basis of the income source (e.g. dividends, business income), and a particular credit limitation applies to each basket. Excess uncredited foreign income can be carried forward for the subsequent five tax years.

Approved enterprises (AEs)
AE status, which provides for cash and tax benefits, may be granted under the Law for the Encouragement of Capital Investments (the Law) to enterprises that increase the productive capacity of the economy, improve the balance of payments, or provide new employment opportunities.

The Law differentiates between three geographical regions (A, B, and C). Area A enjoys the most incentives, while Area C (generally the central area of the country) enjoys the least amount of incentives.

New AE programmes and expansion of prior existing AE programmes are governed by the Law, which underwent a major amendment on 29 March 2005 (2005 Amended Law) and also on 29 December 2010 (2011 Amended Law), effective for 2011 and thereafter.

AE programmes which commenced their period of benefits generally prior to 2005 may still be subject to the Law's provisions prior to these amendments.

The 2011 Amended Law is intended to simplify the manner of taxation that applies to income generated from an AE by applying a uniform tax rate for all AE-generated taxable income. Prior to these amendments, as summarised below, the corporate tax rate applicable to an AE depended upon many factors, including the tax route selected, the geographical area in which the industrial site is located, the level of foreign investment ownership, and attribution of taxable income between different tiers of AE plans further to complex formulas.

It should be noted that the 2011 Amended Law shall apply for income generated by an AE during 2011 and thereafter. Transition rules allow AE owners to elect to continue with the AE tax benefits allowed for under the Law prior to these amendments or to choose, in any tax year, to commence to apply the new provisions of the Law and to waive the remaining benefit period those AE benefits provided under the Law prior to its amendment. It should also be noted that once such an election is made by the taxpayer to implement the new provisions, it may not be altered in future tax years. Moreover, as part of the transition rules, an AE owner is generally allowed to elect until 2012 to apply for a new AE status under the terms of the Law in effect prior to its amendment, so long as part of the relating investment was made during 2010. This election can allow the AE owner to further extend the benefits available under the terms of the Law prior to the legislation.

Israel

This general overview will address the Law as applicable prior to the 2011 Amended Law as well as setting forth the material tax law changes under the 2011 Amended Law.

We would caution that our comments in regard to the 2011 Amended Law should be regarded as preliminary in nature and they do not address all of the legislative changes. Further detailed rules apply and certain areas still await further legislation and clarifications as to the Israeli Income Tax Authorities' interpretive positions.

Cash grants (applicable also under the 2011 Amended Law)

Approved enterprises located in development areas A and B are eligible for cash investment grants, which vary according to the geographic location of the enterprise. Under the 2011 Amended Law, only AEs that operate in Area A are eligible for grants. Grant amounts and conditions are subject to governmental change from time to time.

AE tax incentives prior to 2011 Amended Law

Reduced tax rates

In addition to financial incentives for the establishment or expansion of an AE, various tax incentives are available once a new AE or expansion thereof is operational.

The reduced tax rates generally apply for a seven-year benefit period (or a ten-year period in certain cases of local companies established in development area A or in the case of a foreign investor company, see below), commencing with the year in which the AE first generates taxable income.

Generally, this seven or ten-year period of benefits is limited to 12 years from the year of implementation. For AE plans governed prior to the 2005 amendment to the Law, the period of benefits cannot extend beyond 12 years from the year the enterprise commenced its operations or beyond 14 years from the year in which approval of status as an AE was granted, whichever is earlier.

Locally owned companies

Income derived by a company from an AE during the maximum seven-year period of benefits is generally subject to company tax at a rate of 25%.

A WHT rate of 15% (subject to a possible reduction under a tax treaty) applies to dividends paid from profits of an approved enterprise earned during the benefits period, if distributed either during the benefits period or during the subsequent 12 years. Note that dividends from non-approved enterprise profits that are paid to non-residents are generally subject to a maximum 25% WHT rate that may be further reduced under the terms of a relevant tax treaty.

Foreign investors' companies (FIC)

A company that qualifies as a FIC is entitled to enhanced tax benefits on AE income. In general, a FIC is a company having more than 25% of its share capital (in terms of rights to shares, profits, voting, and the appointment of directors) and its combined share capital and investor loan capital owned by foreign residents. To qualify for FIC status, a foreign investor must make an investment in the company of at least ILS 5 million.

A FIC benefits from reduced company tax on the profits of an AE for a period of ten years (instead of seven years) commencing with the first year in which taxable income is generated. The total period of benefits is restricted as discussed above.

A FIC enjoys reduced company tax rates applicable to its AE income as shown below:

Israel

Percentage of foreign ownership	Company tax rate (%)
Over 25% but less than 49%	25
49% or more but less than 74%	20
74% or more but less than 90%	15
90% or more	10

The foreign ownership percentage is annually determined as the lowest level retained during the specific tax year.

Dividends paid by a FIC out of the profits of its AE are subject to tax in the hands of the recipient at the rate of 15%, without limitation as to their distribution date, provided the dividends are distributed out of AE profits derived during the benefits period.

Alternative system of tax benefits for AEs (tax holiday)

Companies with new or expanding AEs may elect to forego all government cash grants and receive instead a total exemption (i.e. tax holiday) from company tax on undistributed profits of the approved enterprise for ten years in development area A, for six years in development area B, and for two years in development area C. The area of incentive being the area in which the company's facilities are located.

The tax holiday provides an Israeli tax exemption so long as the AE profits generated in the exemption period are retained within the company. Should a subsequent distribution of such profits occur, company tax and dividend WHT is imposed on the income distributed, at the rates which would have been applicable if the tax holiday had not been elected (i.e. 25% or at a lower rate if the company is a FIC with a foreign ownership percentage of 49% or more during those years).

Under certain anti-avoidance provisions applicable to tax holidays, amounts paid or credited directly or indirectly by an approved enterprise to a relative, a major shareholder, or to a related entity controlled by either a relative or a major shareholder may be treated as a deemed taxable distribution of profits by the AE.

Ireland track and strategic investment track

For companies having an AE in development area A that seek to distribute dividends while maintaining a low company and dividend tax burden, there is an 'Ireland track' under which the aggregate Israeli corporate and dividend WHT for a foreign resident shareholder is 15% and for an Israeli resident shareholder is 24.8%. This track is in contrast to the standard alternative benefit track discussed above, which provides a tax holiday provided that profits remain undistributed.

Furthermore, a 'strategic investment track' allows for an exemption during the benefit period from company tax and dividend WHT for a company having (depending on its location within Area A of the country) very significant investment and revenue levels. This means that during the benefits period, a company eligible for benefits from income accrued under this track will have no tax liability whatsoever for its productive activity arising from such investment and for the distribution of profits. Detailed rules apply to these tracks.

Israel

Qualifying for AE status

Minimal investment amount
For entitlement of tax benefits under the alternative benefit track, there must be a certain minimal investment amount ('Minimum qualifying investment') towards purchasing productive assets (e.g. machinery and equipment, but not buildings) within three years.

In the case of a new factory, the minimum required investment is ILS 300,000.

For expansion of a factory, the amount of required investment is ILS 300,000 or the amount based on the formula shown below, whichever is higher:

Value of productive assets in the factory in the tax year prior to the year the minimum qualifying investment commences (in ILS million)	Amount of investment required expressed as a percentage of the value of the productive assets (%)
Up to 140	12
140 to 500	7
Above 500	5

Detailed rules apply in determining how to value the assets for purposes of these tests (including in regards to AEs operated by affiliated companies).

For AE plans governed by the Law prior to its amendment, a general condition for approval is that a minimum of 30% of the investment in fixed assets must be equity-financed.

For investors wanting to expand their current AE, a new requirement has been added to the Law that demands at least a two year waiting period before an investor can obtain AE status for its new investments. Upon completion of these investment conditions, the taxpayer must file the election of the investments implementation year. Such election must generally be filed by the filing date of the relevant annual tax return but no later than 12 months from the end of that tax year.

Automatic approval
Where an investment project meets all of the eligibility criterion under one of the alternative tracks (standard alternative track, Ireland track, or strategic investment track) as set out in the Law and in regulations to be issued, a project will automatically qualify for the AE taxation benefits under the Law with no need for prior approval from the ITA (i.e. a 'green lane'). The criteria that confer tax benefits in the alternative track of the Law are handled by the ITA. A mechanism is available which enables a company to apply for a pre-ruling from the ITA, where it desires to obtain certainty as to the taxation status of its investment under the Amended Law. The application to the ITA must be submitted no later than six months following the end of the investment's implementation year (first year of potential benefits for the AE).

For AE plans governed by the Law prior to its 2005 amendment, the certification of a new or expanding approved enterprise status required interaction with the Israeli Investment Centre (IC) which had to approve the application for approved enterprise status and was responsible for issuing a final implementation approval following its determination that all requirements relating to investments in assets and minimum capital have been met.

Israel

Interruption of entitlement to benefits
Unlike the Law prior to its 2005 amendment, where an AE owner was generally required to continue to operate the AE for the entire benefit period, under the Law following its amendment in 2005, the examination as to whether an owner is entitled to enjoy AE benefits for a tax year is determined on a year by year basis. Consequently, if in any tax year during the benefit period a company does not meet any of the conditions required under the Law, then for that tax year it is not entitled to benefits. However, if the company again meets the conditions during the benefit period, the company is entitled to the benefits during the remainder of the benefit period.

Mixed enterprises
Special rules govern the allocation of taxable income of 'mixed enterprises'. These are essentially entities that derive only part of their income from an AE or entities which operate under a number of approvals relating to separate investment projects. The company tax payable in respect of income from each part of a mixed enterprise is separately computed and a composite WHT is applicable to dividends distributed by a mixed enterprise.

Neutralisation of assets
Assets used in the operation of an enterprise that are not part of an AE are regarded as non-approved assets. Consequently, turnover which is deemed to be generated from the non-approved assets will result in non-approved enterprise income that should be taxed at the regular Israeli corporate tax rate applicable for the relevant year.

For plans operating under the Law prior to its 2005 amendment, in some cases, upon request, the Investment Centre granted neutralisation of assets that were not part of the approved investment plan, so that they would have no negative impact on the tax benefits. Neutralised assets have a 'neutral' effect, as they are not considered part of the approved investment plan or part of a non-approved plan. For certain industrial equipment, neutralisation is not available. Assets that are of a non-productive nature may receive neutralisation.

In accordance with the 2005 Amended Law, this issue arises only in connection to assets purchased which had previous use in Israel.

AE 2011 Amended Law overview
Upon the AE owner's election, the various reduced tax routes described above are cancelled and replaced with a new uniform tax rate based on the corporate tax rate applicable during the relevant year, as follows:

Year	Area A (%)	Rest of country (%)	Scheduled regular corporate tax rate (%)
2011 to 2012	10	15	24 (2011), 25 (2012)
2012 to 2014	7	12.5	25
2014 and thereafter	6	12	25

A modified Strategic Investment Track has been introduced, but it appears that its qualifying terms and conditions should make this track not particularly relevant for most investors.

The WHT rate applicable to dividends distributed to foreign shareholders remains 15% (subject to being reduced under the terms of an applicable tax treaty). Distributions to

Israel

Israeli corporations shall not be subject to tax while distributions to Israeli individuals shall be subject to tax at a rate of 15%.

This is a major change in policy from the pre-2011 Amendment FIC route discussed above, which encouraged foreign investment in Israeli companies having AE programs by providing for increasingly reduced rates (e.g. 10% rate where 90% foreign owned). Further to the amendments, there will no longer be available any additional AE tax benefits specifically linked to foreign investment. Notwithstanding the cancellation of the tax holiday route, a distribution or deemed distribution of profits that were tax-exempted under the tax holiday route before the legislative change had taken effect shall continue to be subject to company tax at the applicable AE reduced rates in addition to the dividend WHT that will be imposed on the income distributed.

Although it would appear that the 2011 Amendments may result in an increased Israeli tax liability for many investors, depending on the particular circumstances, some investors may still benefit from the new changes. Consequently, each investor should examine the impact of such changes upon its financial results and prepare its action steps accordingly.

Transition rules

It should be noted that the 2011 Amended Law shall apply for income generated by an AE during 2011 and thereafter. Transition rules allow AE owners to elect to continue with the AE tax benefits allowed for under the Law prior to these amendments or to choose in any tax year to commence to apply the new provisions of the Law and to waive the remaining benefit period those AE benefits provided under the Law prior to its amendment. Once such an election is made by the taxpayer to implement the new provisions, it may not be altered in future tax years. Moreover, as part of the transition rules, an AE owner is generally allowed to elect until 2012 to apply for a new AE status under the terms of the Law in effect prior to its amendment, so long as part of the relating investment was made during 2010. This election can allow the AE owner to further extend the benefits available under the terms of the Law prior to the legislation. According to the approach of the ITA, in order for this election to be applicable for a certain tax year, this election must be filed by 31 May of that year.

Research and development (R&D) incentives

Under special relief provided under the ITO which was enacted for the purpose of encouraging taxpayers to invest in R&D activities, R&D costs can generally be deductible for tax purposes even when they represent capital costs.

The ITO provision generally distinguishes between two types of investors in R&D projects:

- The R&D project is conducted or sponsored by the owner of an enterprise in the fields of industry, agriculture, transportation, and energy, and it is intended to develop this enterprise.
- The R&D costs are borne by a taxpayer that is not the owner of an enterprise in the above mentioned fields or the taxpayer participates in R&D costs of another developer in consideration for a reasonable return, when such R&D projects also enjoy government grants.

In regard to the first group of taxpayers, the R&D expenses shall be deducted in the tax year incurred when such expense has been approved as an R&D expense by the relevant government department (the approval in regard to industrial related projects is generally granted by the Office of the Chief Scientist [OCS]). When such OCS approval is not obtained, the expense shall be deducted over three tax years.

The R&D expenses incurred by the second group of taxpayers shall generally be deducted over two tax years. The deductible expenses allowed to a participant in R&D costs of another developer generally may not exceed 40% of the taxable income of the investor in the year in which the expenses had been incurred.

For acquisitions between 1 January 2011 and 31 December 2015, an Israeli tax resident company that acquires a controlling interest in a private Israeli company that meets certain R&D activity levels shall be entitled to amortise its acquisition amount (i.e. consideration paid for shares less the purchased company's positive equity capital if any) from its taxable income equally over five years beginning with the tax year following the acquisition. Entitlement to this deduction is subject to the fulfillment of detailed qualifying conditions which include *inter alia* that both companies have AE plans in the year of acquisition, meet certain R&D investment levels, employ a certain prescribed percentage of employees having academic degrees in certain qualifying fields, and for the first three years of the amortisation period the R&D expenses of the acquired company are incurred for its own company or that of the purchasing company and at least 75% of such expenses are incurred in Israel. Detailed rules apply.

Tax credit for donations
A tax credit is granted in respect of donations to approved state and charitable institutions aggregating at least ILS 420 (for 2011) in a tax year. The donor is allowed a tax credit equal to the amount of the contribution times the corporate tax rate applicable during the year, provided the donations do not exceed the lower of the following: (i) 30% of the corporation's taxable income in that year or (ii) ILS 4,351,000 (in 2011). The above figures are adjusted each year according to the CPI. Excess unused tax credits may be carried forward for three years subject to detailed rules.

Incentive to promote foreign investment in Israeli corporate bonds
In order to promote foreign investment in the Israeli corporate bonds market, there is an exemption from tax with respect to interest income received by foreign investors on their commercial investments in Israeli corporate bonds traded on the Tel Aviv stock exchange (TASE). The exemption is not granted to a foreign investor that has a PE in Israel or is related to, or holds 10% more of the means of control in, the investee company. In addition, in order for the exemption to apply to a foreign investor that has 'special relations' with the investee company, regularly sells products to or provides services to the investee company, or is employed by the investee company, the investor must prove that the interest rate on the corporate bond was determined in good faith.

Withholding taxes

Under Israeli domestic tax law, a 25% WHT on payments of Israeli-source income is generally deducted by an Israeli paying bank from all income remittances abroad, unless a tax certificate is obtained from the ITA authorising withholding-exempt remittances or a reduced rate of tax pursuant to an applicable tax treaty.

Set out below is a listing of WHT rates for dividends, interest, and royalties under domestic tax law and pursuant to tax treaties in force. Detailed rules apply under certain tax treaties for eligibility to the treaty reduced rates (e.g. beneficial ownership, having no permanent establishment in Israel). The applicable tax treaty should be

Israel

consulted to determine the relevant WHT rate and to examine detailed conditions that may apply for the specific circumstance.

Recipient	Dividends (%)	Interest * (%)	Royalties (%)
Resident corporations	0/25 (1)	25	25
Resident individuals	25/30 (1, 2)	25 (33)	30
Non-resident corporations:			
Non-treaty	25/30 (2)	25	25
Treaty:			
Austria	25	15	0/10 (53)
Belarus	10	5/10 (34)	5/10 (54)
Belgium	15	15	0/10 (55)
Brazil	10/15 (3)	15	10/15 (56)
Bulgaria	10/12.5 (4)	5/10 (35)	12.5 (57)
Canada	15	15	0/15 (58)
China, P.R.	10	7/10 (36)	10 (59)
Croatia	5/10/15 (5)	5/10 (37)	5
Czech Republic	5/15 (6)	10	5
Denmark	25	25	10
Estonia	0/5 (7)	5	0
Ethiopia	5/10/15 (8)	5/10 (38)	5
Finland	5/15 (9)	10	10
France	5/10/15 (10)	5/10 (39)	0/10 (60)
Germany	25	15	0/5 (61)
Greece	20/25 (11)	10	10
Hungary	5/15 (12)	0	0
India	10	10	10
Ireland, Republic of	10	5/10 (40)	10
Italy	10/15 (13)	10	0/10 (62)
Jamaica	15/22.5(14)	15	10
Japan	5/15 (15)	10	10
Korea, Republic of	5/10/15 (16)	7.5/10 (41)	2/5 (63)
Latvia	5/10/15 (17)	5/10 (42)	5
Lithuania	5/10/15 (18)	10	5/10 (64)
Luxembourg	5/10/15 (19)	5/10 (43)	5
Mexico	5/10 (20)	10	10
Moldova	5/10 (21)	5	5
Netherlands	5/10/15 (22)	10/15 (44)	5/10 (65)
Norway	25	25	10
Philippines	10/15 (23)	10	15
Poland	5/10 (24)	5	5/10 (66)
Portugal	5/10/15 (25)	10	10
Romania	15	5/10 (45)	10
Russia	10	10	10
Singapore	5/10 (26)	7	5
Slovakia	5/10 (27)	2/5/10 (46)	5
Slovenia	5/10/15 (28)	5	5
South Africa	25	25	0 (67)

Israel

Recipient	Dividends (%)	Interest * (%)	Royalties (%)
Spain	10	5/10 (47)	5/7 (68)
Sweden	0	25	0 (69)
Switzerland	5/10/15 (29)	5/10 (48)	5
Taiwan (R.O.C.)	10	7/10 (49)	10
Thailand	10/15 (30)	10/15 (50)	5/15 (70)
Turkey	10	10	10
Ukraine	5/10/15 (31)	5/10 (51)	10
United Kingdom	15	15	0 (71)
United States	12.5/25 (32)	10/17.5 (52)	10/15 (72)
Uzbekistan	10	10	5/10 (73)
Vietnam	10	10	5/7.5/15 (74)

Notes

* Some Israeli tax treaties provide for an exemption from WHT on interest involving governmental and quasi-governmental parties. Such exemptions are not separately indicated in the table above.

1. Dividends between Israeli resident companies are generally exempt from Israeli tax. Dividends paid from a foreign resident company received via an Israeli payer (e.g. bank) to an Israeli resident company or individual are subject to WHT at the rate of 25%.
2. 30% rate applies in the case of a 10% or more shareholder (detailed rules apply).
3. 10% where beneficial owner holds directly at least 25% of the capital of the company paying the dividends.
4. At a rate which is 50% of the rate which would have been imposed but for this provision but not to exceed 12.5 % and not less than 7.5%. A 10% rate applies where paid from profits generated by an enterprise entitled to special tax rates under the Encouragement of Investment Law.
5. 5% if the beneficial owner is a company (other than a partnership) which holds directly at least 25% of the capital of the company paying the dividends; 10% rate if the beneficial owner is a company which holds directly at least 10% of the capital of the company paying the dividends where that latter company is a resident of Israel and the dividends are paid out of profits which are subject to tax in Israel at a rate which is lower than the normal rate of Israeli company tax; 15% rate applies in all other cases.
6. 5% if the beneficial owner is a company (other than a partnership) which holds directly at least 15% of the capital of the company paying the dividends; 15% rate in all other cases.
7. 0% if the beneficial owner is a company (other than a partnership) which holds directly at least 10% of the capital of the company paying the dividends; 5% rate in all other cases.
8. 5% if the beneficial owner is a company (other than a partnership) which holds directly at least 10% of the capital of the company paying the dividends; 10% rate if the beneficial owner is a company which holds directly at least 10% of the capital of the company paying the dividends where that latter company is a resident of Israel and the dividends are paid out of profits which are subject to tax in Israel at a rate which is lower than the normal rate of Israeli company tax; 15% rate in all other cases.
9. 5% if the beneficial owner is a company (other than a partnership) which controls directly at least 10% of the voting power in the company paying the dividends; 15% rate in all other cases.
10. 5% if the beneficial owner is a company which holds directly or indirectly at least 10% of the capital of the company paying the dividends; 10% rate if the beneficial owner is a company which holds directly or indirectly at least 10% of the capital of the company paying the dividends and the dividends are paid out of profits which are subject to tax in Israel at a rate which is lower than the normal rate of Israeli company tax; 15% rate in all other cases.
11. At the domestic Israeli tax rate.
12. 5% if the recipient holds directly at least 10% of the capital of the company paying the dividends.
13. 10% if the beneficial owner is a company (other than a partnership) which holds directly at least 25% of the capital of the company paying the dividends.
14. 15% if the beneficial owner is a company (other than a partnership) which holds directly or indirectly at least 10% of the voting power of the company paying the dividends.
15. 5% if the beneficial owner is a company which owns at least 25% of the voting shares of the company paying the dividends during the period of six months immediately before the end of the accounting period for which the distribution of profits takes place.
16. 5% if the beneficial owner is a company which holds directly or indirectly at least 10% of the capital of the company paying the dividends; 10% rate if the beneficial owner is a company which holds 10% of the capital of the company paying the dividends and the dividends are paid out of profits which are subject to tax at a rate which is lower than the normal rate of the corporation tax; 15% rate in all other cases.

Israel

17. 5% if the beneficial owner is a company (other than a partnership) which holds directly at least 10% of the capital of the company paying the dividends; 10% rate if the beneficial owner is a company which holds directly at least 10% of the capital of the company paying the dividends where the dividends are paid out of profits which by virtue of provisions in the Israeli Law of Encouragement of Investments in Israel are exempt from tax or subject to tax at a rate that is lower than the normal rate of Israeli company tax; 15% rate in all other cases.
18. 5% if the beneficial owner is a company (other than a partnership) which holds directly at least 10 % of the capital of the company paying the dividends; 10% rate if the beneficial owner is a company which holds directly at least 10% of the capital of the company paying the dividends where the dividends are paid out of profits which by virtue of provisions in the Israeli Law of Encouragement of Investments in Israel are exempted from tax or subject to tax at a rate that is lower than the normal rate of Israeli company tax; 15% rate in all other cases.
19. 5% if the beneficial owner is a company (other than a partnership) which holds directly at least 10% of the capital of the company paying the dividends; 10% rate if the beneficial owner is a company which holds directly at least 10% of the capital of the company paying the dividends and the dividends are paid out of profits which are subject to tax in Israel at a rate which is lower than the normal rate of Israeli company tax; 15% rate in all other cases.
20. 5% if the beneficial owner is a company which holds directly or indirectly at least 10% of the capital of the company paying the dividends.
21. 5% if the beneficial owner is a company (other than a partnership) which holds directly at least 25% of the capital of the company paying the dividends.
22. With respect to dividends paid to a company which holds directly at least 25%of the capital of the company paying the dividends: (i) 10% where the dividends are paid out of profits which, by virtue of provisions in Israeli law for the encouragement of investment in Israel, are exempted from tax or subject to tax at a rate that is lower than the standard rate levied on the profits of a company resident in Israel; (ii) 5% where paid out of regularly taxed profits. A 15% rate applies in all other cases.
23. 10% if the beneficial owner is a company (excluding partnership) which holds directly at least 10% of the capital of the paying company.
24. 5% if the recipient holds directly at least 15% of the capital of the company paying dividends.
25. 5% if the beneficial owner is a company (other than a partnership) which holds directly at least 25% of the capital of the company paying the dividends; 10% rate if the beneficial owner is a company which holds directly at least 25% of the capital of the company paying the dividends where that latter company is a resident of Israel and the dividends are paid out of profits which are subject to tax in Israel at a rate which is lower than the normal rate of Israeli company tax; 15 % rate in all other cases.
26. 5% if the beneficial owner holds directly at least 10% of the capital of the company paying the dividends.
27. 5% if the recipient holds directly or indirectly at least 10% of the capital of the company paying the dividends.
28. 5% of the gross amount of the dividends if the beneficial owner is a company (other than a partnership) that holds directly at least 10% of the capital of the company paying the dividends; 10% of the gross amount of the dividends if the beneficial owner is a company that holds directly at least 10% of the capital of the company paying the dividends and the dividends are paid out of profits that, by virtue of law of the state in which the payer is a resident, are exempt from company tax or subject to company tax at a rate that is lower than the normal rate in that state; 15% of the gross amount of the dividends in all other cases.
29. 5% if the beneficial owner is a company (other than a partnership) which holds directly at least 10% of the capital of the company paying the dividends; 10% rate if the beneficial owner is a company which holds directly at least 10% of the capital of the company paying the dividends where that latter company is a resident of Israel and the dividends are paid out of profits which are subject to tax in Israel at a rate which is lower than the normal rate of Israeli company tax; 15% rate in all other cases.
30. 10% if the dividends if the recipient holds at least 25% of the capital of the company paying the dividends.
31. 5% if the beneficial owner is a company (other than a partnership) which holds directly at least 25% of the capital of the company paying the dividends; 10% if the beneficial owner is a company which holds directly at least 10% of the capital of the company paying the dividends where that latter company is a resident of Israel and the dividends are paid out of profits which are subject to tax in Israel at a rate which is lower than the normal rate of Israeli company tax.
32. 12.5% but only if (i) during the part of the paying corporation's taxable year which precedes the date of payment of the dividend and during the whole of its prior taxable year (if any), at least 10% of the outstanding shares of the voting stock of the paying corporation was owned by the recipient corporation, and (ii) not more than 25% of the gross income of the paying corporation for such prior taxable year (if any) consists of interest or dividends (other than interest derived from the conduct of a banking, insurance, or financing business and dividends or interest received from subsidiary corporations, 50% or more of the outstanding shares of the voting stock of which is owned by the paying corporation at the time such dividends or interest is received). A 15% rate applies for payments from income derived during any period for which the paying corporation is entitled to the reduced tax rate applicable to an approved enterprise under Israel's Encouragement of Capital Investments Law (1959). A 25% rate applies in all other cases.
33. Different rates ranging from 15% to 35% apply for certain types of instruments. Interest paid to a 10% or more shareholder is subject to tax at the highest marginal tax rate (48% in 2012). Detailed rules apply.

34. 5% for interest in connection with the sale on credit of any industrial, commercial, or scientific equipment or on any loan of whatever kind granted by a bank.
35. 5% for interest in the case of a bank or other financial institution.
36. 7% for interest received by any bank or financial institution.
37. 5% for interest paid on a loan granted by a bank.
38. 5% for interest paid on any loan of whatever kind granted by a bank.
39. 5% where in connection with the sale on credit of any industrial, commercial, or scientific equipment, or sale on credit of any merchandise by one enterprise to another enterprise, or on any loan of whatever kind granted by a bank loans made by banks; 10% in all other cases. An election can be made to be taxed on the net amount of the interest as if such interest were business profits.
40. 5% for interest paid in connection with the sale on credit of any industrial, commercial, or scientific equipment, sale on credit of any merchandise by one enterprise to another enterprise, or on any loan of whatever kind granted by a bank.
41. 7.5% for interest if received by any bank or financial institution.
42. 5% where paid on any loan of whatever kind granted by a bank.
43. 5% where paid on any loan of whatever kind granted by a bank.
44. 10% where paid to a bank or a financial institution.
45. 5% where paid in connection with the sale on credit of any industrial, commercial, or scientific equipment, or sale on credit of any merchandise by one enterprise to another enterprise, or on any loan of whatever kind granted by a bank.
46. 2% rate applies to government debt or government-assisted debt; 5% rate applies when paid to a financial institution; 10% rate applies in all other cases.
47. 5% rate in connection with the sale on credit of any industrial, commercial, or scientific equipment, or in connection with the sale on credit of any merchandise by one enterprise to another enterprise, or on any loan granted by a financial institution.
48. 5% rate for interest paid on any loan of whatever kind granted by a bank.
49. 7% rate for interest paid on any loan of whatever kind granted by a bank.
50. 10% rate for interest received by any financial institution (including an insurance company).
51. 5% rate for interest paid on any loan of whatever kind granted by a bank.
52. 10% for interest derived from a loan of whatever kind granted by a bank, savings institution, or insurance company or the like. 17.5% rate for other interest. An election may be made to be taxed on interest income as if that income were industrial and commercial profits.
53. 0% for literary, dramatic, musical, or artistic work copyright royalties (excluding in respect of motion picture films or films for use in connection with television).
54. 5% for copyright royalties for literary, artistic, or scientific work (excluding cinematograph films) or for the use of, or the right to use, industrial, commercial, or scientific equipment or road-transport vehicles.
55. 0% for copyright royalties for literary, dramatic, musical, artistic, or scientific work (excluding in respect of films for cinema or television).
56. 15% for trademark royalties.
57. The rate is 50% of the rate which would have been imposed but for the treaty provision but not to exceed 12.5% and not to be less than 7.5%.
58. 0% for copyright royalties for the production or reproduction of any literary, dramatic, musical, or artistic work (but not including royalties in respect of motion pictures).
59. For industrial, commercial, and scientific equipment royalties, the 10% rate applies to the adjusted amount of the royalties (70% of the gross amount of the royalties).
60. 0% for copyright royalties for literary, artistic or scientific work (excluding cinematograph films).
61. 0% for copyright royalties for literary, dramatic, musical, or artistic works.
62. 0% for copyright royalties for literary, artistic, or scientific work (excluding cinematograph films or tapes for television or broadcasting).
63. 2% for industrial, commercial, and scientific equipment royalties.
64. 5% for industrial, commercial, and scientific equipment royalties.
65. 10% for royalties for cinematograph films and films or video-tapes for radio or television broadcasting.
66. 5% for industrial, commercial, or scientific equipment royalties.
67. For royalties in respect of cinematograph or television films, the WHT rate shall not exceed tax at the rate applicable to companies on 15% of the gross amount of the royalty.
68. 5% for royalties for copyrights of literary, dramatic, musical, artistic work, or for the use of, or the right to use, industrial, commercial, or scientific equipment.
69. The definition of royalties does not include any royalty or other amount paid in respect of (i) the operation of a mine or quarry or of any other extraction of natural resources or (ii) in respect of cinematograph including television films.
70. 5% for royalties for literary, artistic or scientific work, excluding cinematograph films or films or tapes used for radio, or television broadcasting
71. For royalties in respect of cinematograph or television films, tax may be imposed in Israel, but not to exceed tax at the rate applicable to companies on 15% of the gross amount of the royalty.
72. 10% for copyright or film royalties.
73. 5% of the gross amount of the royalties where such royalties consist of payments of any kind received as a consideration for the use or the right to use any copyright of literary, artistic, or scientific work (excluding cinematograph films).
74. 5% for royalties for any patent, design or model, plan, secret formula or for the use of, or the right to use, industrial, commercial or scientific equipment or for information concerning industrial, commercial or scientific experience; 7.5% for technical fees; 15% for all other royalties.

Israel

Tax administration

Taxable period

The tax year is generally the calendar year. Certain entities may apply to have their tax year-end on different dates, specifically, mutual funds, government companies, quoted companies, and subsidiaries of foreign publicly listed companies.

Tax returns

The Israeli system is based on a combined form of assessment and self-assessment.

The statutory filing date is five months following the end of the tax year, which for a calendar year taxpayer would be 31 May. It is possible, however, to secure extensions of the filing date.

Payment of tax

Generally, 12 monthly advance payments are levied at a fixed ratio of the company's turnover. Alternatively, a company may be required to make ten monthly payments beginning in the second month of its tax year, each payment being a fixed percentage of the previous year's tax assessment.

Penalties are imposed on overdue advance payments and on delays in the submission of tax returns. The balance of any taxes due is payable from the beginning of the following tax year and is linked to the CPI; it bears interest of 4% until paid.

Statute of limitations

The statute of limitation period for corporate tax is three years from the end of the tax year in which the relevant tax return is filed. The Commissioner of the Tax Authorities has the authority to extend this period to four years.

Other issues

Choice of business entities

Investments and business operations in Israel may be structured in a variety of ways. The following are the common types of business entities in Israel: (i) Israeli public or private company; (ii) foreign company in Israel (i.e. a branch); (iii) Israeli general or limited partnership; (iv) foreign general or limited partnership; (v) other entities such as cooperative societies; and (vi) other arrangements (e.g. contractual joint ventures).

Mergers and acquisitions

Israeli tax law allows for non-taxable reorganisations in situations in which the ownership and business enterprise of the original parties is continued after the reorganisation takes place, allowing for the deferral of the tax liability until the shares or assets transferred in such reorganisations are actually sold. Different qualifying requirements and conditions apply (e.g. obtaining a ruling from the ITA in certain cases), depending upon the tax residency of the parties and the type of transfer.

Italy

PwC contact

Fabrizio Acerbis
TLS Associazione Professionale di Avvocati e Commercialisti
Via Monte Rosa 91
20149 Milano, Italy
Tel: +39 02 9160 5001
Email: fabrizio.acerbis@it.pwc.com

Significant developments

The major recent changes in the Italian tax rules that occurred in the last 12 months are as follows:

- Increase of the base withholding tax (WHT) rate on the yields on loans and securities.
- Changes to value-added tax (VAT).
- New shell companies taxation regime.
- Allowance for Corporate Equity (ACE).
- New regime for tax losses to be carried forward for corporate income tax (*Imposta sul Reddito delle Società* or IRES) purposes.
- Taxation on companies operating in the oil, electric, and energy sector.
- Increase of regional production tax (*Imposta Regionale sulle Attività Produttive* or IRAP) rate for certain entities.

Please note that Italy tax updates are generally expected from June to September in connection with the finance bill and approval of related laws. In this respect, we suggest visiting the Worldwide Tax Summaries website after September each year in order to check whether or not relevant changes affect your business.

Increase of the base WHT rate on the yields on loans and securities

Effective from 2012, the base standard WHT rate on the yields on loans and securities (bonds, shares, etc) paid by Italian resident entities to both Italian and non-Italian resident investors has been increased from 12.5% to 20%.

The said increase, however, does not affect the applicability of those rules allowing either the application of reduced WHT rates or full exemption from the said withholdings (e.g. double tax treaties [DTTs], European Union [EU] directives, special domestic tax rules).

VAT changes

For certain supplies of services carried out starting from 17 March 2012, the time of supply has been substantially modified (i.e. time of completion, date of maturity of the consideration).

As of 17 September 2011, the standard rate of VAT increased from 20% to 21%.

Please consider that from 1 October 2012, an additional increase of the standard VAT rate, from 21% to 23%, and the reduced VAT rate, from of 10% to 12%, is expected.

Italy

Changes in shell companies taxation
Starting from fiscal year 2012, companies qualified as shell companies will be subject to an additional corporate tax rate of 10.5% on the deemed taxable income (total IRES rate 38%).

The qualification as a 'non-operating' company is enlarged to companies that declare a tax loss for three consecutive periods.

Allowance for Corporate Equity (ACE)
As of 2011, in order to promote the capitalisation of companies, a new deduction from the IRES tax base has been introduced. The deduction is determined based on the net increase in the equity employed in the entity.

New regime for tax losses to be carried forward for IRES purposes
As of 2011, tax losses to be carried forward for IRES purposes are no longer subject to time limitation. However, the tax loss incurred in a period can only be used to offset taxable income for an amount not exceeding 80% of the taxable income.

Taxation on companies operating in the oil, electric, and energy sector
The additional corporate tax for companies operating in the oil, electric, and energy sector increased from 6.5% to 10.5%. The new tax rate is applicable for three tax periods starting from fiscal year 2011.

Increase of IRAP rate for certain entities
As of 2011, the IRAP rate increased to:

* 4.20% for entities with a determined governmental exclusive right to provide services
* 4.65% for banks and financial entities, and
* 5.90% for insurance corporations.

Taxes on corporate income

Applicable rates
Italian corporate entities are subject to a corporate income tax, known as *Imposta sul Reddito delle Società* (IRES), and to regional production tax, known as *Imposta Regionale sulle Attività Produttive* (IRAP).

The standard rates are as follows:

* 27.5% for corporate income tax (IRES).
* 3.9% for regional production tax (IRAP).

A 6.5% increase (surtax) to the IRES rate is applied to companies operating in the areas of oil, gas (refining, production, or trade), and electrical energy (production or trade) whose turnover exceeded 10 million euros (EUR) and whose net income was EUR 1 million in the prior fiscal year. Limited from 2011 to the 2013 tax period, and additional increase of 4% is applicable (total surtax of 10.5%).

As of 2011, the following increased IRAP rates are applicable for certain entities:

* 4.20% for entities with a determined governmental exclusive right to provide services.

- 4.65% for bank and financial entities.
- 5.90% for insurance corporations.

General rules

IRES
The IRES taxable base is determined according to the worldwide taxation principle, which states that, regardless of the location/jurisdiction where the income is produced, to the extent that the income is legally attributable to an Italian resident entity, the income is taxed in Italy. IRES is charged on the total net income reported in the financial statements of the company as adjusted for specific tax rules. Non-resident companies are taxed only on Italian-source income.

IRAP
There are different methods of computation for the IRAP taxable base, depending on the nature of the business carried out by the taxpayer. Labour costs (with limited exceptions), provisions for liabilities and risks, and extraordinary items cannot be taken into account when determining the IRAP taxable base.

For sales and manufacturing companies, the IRAP taxable base is broadly represented by the company's gross margin in its financial statements. In addition to the non-deductible items mentioned above, interest income and expense and provisions for bad debts are excluded for the purposes of the IRAP taxable base.

For banks, the IRAP taxable base is broadly defined as follows:

- Intermediation margin reduced by 50% of dividends.
- 90% of amortisation costs relating to fixed tangible and intangible assets.
- 90% of other administrative expenses.

Special rules apply to financial institutions, other than banks.

IRAP is levied on a regional basis, and regions are allowed to increase or decrease the standard IRAP rate up to 0.9176%. Companies with facilities in different regions must allocate their overall taxable base to the different regions on the basis of the employment costs of personnel located at the various sites. Facilities become relevant to the calculation of IRAP if they have been established for more than three months. Italian companies with permanent establishments (PEs) abroad, as well as shipping companies qualifying for the tonnage tax regime (*see Tonnage tax below*), are not subject to IRAP on the income earned through these PEs.

For fiscal year 2011, there is a 0.15% increase in the IRAP rates for the regions of Campania, Molise, and Calabria.

Substitutive tax on reorganisations (mergers, demergers, contributions in kind)
Corporate restructurings, such as contributions in kind, (assets versus shares transactions) mergers, and demergers, are, in principle, tax neutral even if, for financial accounting purposes, the transaction results in the recognition of higher values of the assets or of goodwill. Companies may elect to obtain partial or full recognition for tax purposes of the step-up in the financial accounting values of assets or of the goodwill arising from the corporate restructurings, provided they pay a substitutive tax.

Italy

The substitutive tax is calculated on the step-up in tax basis and is based on progressive rates of 12% to 16%. The first EUR 5 million is taxed at 12%, the tranche above EUR 5 million but less than EUR 10 million is taxed at 14%, and the amount in excess of EUR 10 million is taxed at 16%. The substitutive tax may also be paid in three annual instalments of 30% in the year of election, 40% in year two, and 30% in year three plus interest at the rate of 2.5% per year on the deferred amounts. The substitutive tax is not deductible for the purposes of IRES or IRAP.

In addition, stepped-up values of goodwill and trademarks may be depreciated for tax purposes over ten tax years instead of the normally allowed 18 years by paying a substitutive tax of 16%. The higher tax depreciation arising from this election is effective from the tax period subsequent to the one in which the substitutive tax is paid. For example, if a merger transaction occurred in year one and the substitutive tax was paid in year two, the increased tax depreciation would begin in year three.

Tonnage tax

Italian tax resident shipping companies, as well as non-resident shipping companies operating in Italy through a PE, can qualify for and then elect to be subject to the Italian tonnage tax regime. The regime basically allows for the determination of presumptive income based on the net tonnage of the qualifying ships apportioned to the effective shipping days (tonnage income). The tonnage income is subject to IRES only.

To qualify for the tonnage tax, ships must: (i) have a net tonnage of more than 100 net tons (NT); (ii) be used for goods transportation, passenger transportation, salvage, towing, and other services; and (iii) operate in international shipping as defined by the rules disciplining Italian International Registry. Ships chartered out on a bare boat charter are excluded. Chartered ships with crew are included in the tonnage tax regime if their global net tonnage is less than 50% of the total net tonnage.

Tonnage income is calculated on the basis of the ship's net tonnage. The daily income is determined according to the following rate system:

Ship's net tonnage (NT)	Daily income in EUR per NT
0 to 1,000	0.0090
1,001 to 10,000	0.0070
10,001 to 25,000	0.0040
above 25,001	0.0020

No deductions are allowed from tonnage tax income.

Income and expenses from the following activities are all deemed to be covered by the tonnage income determined as previously discussed:

- Transport of goods.
- Transport of passengers.
- Salvage and towing.
- Other services that need to be performed on the high seas.
- Charges related to the above mentioned activities (e.g. administrative and commercial expenses, insurances fees).
- Other operations performed in close connection with the transportation operations (e.g. loading and unloading).
- Other minor activities.

Capital gains or losses arising from the transfer of ships that have been acquired by a company, while under the tonnage tax regime, are also deemed to be included in tonnage tax income. Conversely, for capital gains arising from the transfer of a ship acquired prior to election for the tonnage tax regime, the difference between the sale price and the net tax cost as of the last tax period prior to the election for the tonnage tax regime is subject to the ordinary tax regime. Tax losses, in this latter case, are tax deductible.

An election for the tonnage tax regime should be made for all of a company's or group's qualifying vessels. So called 'cherry picking' is not allowed. Election for the tonnage tax regime is on a voluntary basis, but, once elected, it remains in effect for ten years. The election is renewable.

Corporate residence

Corporate residence of companies

Companies having their legal or administrative headquarters or their principal business activity within the Italian territory are considered to be resident companies and are taxable in Italy on their worldwide income.

A foreign company holding one or more Italian subsidiaries is deemed to be resident of Italy for tax purposes if at least one of the following conditions exists:

- The foreign company is, either directly or indirectly, held by Italian tax resident persons.
- The board of directors of the foreign company is made up mainly of Italian resident individuals.

Non-resident companies are subject to IRES and IRAP only on their Italian-source income. Specifically, Italian non-resident companies having a PE in Italy are subject to IRES and IRAP with respect of the taxable income generated from the PE in Italy.

Permanent establishment (PE)

The domestic definition of PE is substantially aligned with the Organisation for Economic Co-operation and Development (OECD) model.

Corporate residence of a trust

Trusts are considered as persons subject to corporate taxation.

Residence is defined on the basis of the location of the place of management and of the main object of the trust. In the first instance, trusts that operate through an appropriate structure are deemed to be tax resident in Italy, if the said structure is located in Italy. In the absence of any such structure, trusts managed by a trustee will be deemed as tax resident in Italy, if the trustee is tax resident in Italy. In addition, trusts that have the largest part of their assets located in Italy are deemed a tax resident in Italy.

Note that there are anti-avoidance rules for Italian non-resident trusts, setting out the specific conditions on which these trusts can become Italian tax resident.

Italy

....

Other taxes

Value-added tax (VAT)
Italian VAT (*Imposta sul Valore Aggiunto*) applies to the supply of goods and services
carried out in Italy by entrepreneurs, professionals, or artists and on importations
carried out by anyone. Intra-community acquisitions are also subject to VAT taxation
under certain situations.

The Italian standard VAT rate is 21% (20% prior to 17 September 2011). Reduced rates
are provided for specifically listed supplies of goods and services, such as 4% for listed
food, drinks, and agricultural products and 10% for electric power supplies for listed
uses and listed drugs. Intra-community supplies and exports are exempt from VAT.

Specific supplies of goods and services expressly listed in the law are exempt from VAT
(e.g. public postal services, hospital and medical care, education, insurance services,
specific financial services, supply, leasing of particular immovable property). Other
specifically listed transactions are also out of the VAT application scope (e.g. transfer of
money, transfer of business parts).

Input VAT on purchases of goods and services related to business activity generally is
allowed for recovery. Special limitations apply in relation to specific items (e.g. cars,
entertainment expenses).

The filing deadline for VAT returns is 30 September.

Expected modification of VAT rates
In case of deterioration of the financial key performance indicators (KPIs) of the central
government during fiscal year 2012, additional increases of the standard VAT rate, from
21% to 23%, and of the reduced VAT rate, from of 10% to 12%, should be applied. Such
increases would be effective from 1 October 2012. The reduced rate of 4% is expected to
remain, instead, unchanged.

For the same reasons above, a further 0.5% VAT rate increase might occur in 2014.

Service supply rules
Services supplied by a taxable person to another taxable person (business to business
or B2B) are in the scope of the Italian VAT if the services are supplied to Italian taxable
persons or to PEs of an Italian non-resident entity.

The general rules are as follows:

* For services related to immovable property, reference must be made to the place in
  which the immovable property is located.
* For the transportation of passengers, the place in which the transportation takes
  place must be identified including the proportion of the distance covered.
* For catering and restaurant services, the place in which the activity will be physically
  carried out must be identified.
* For short term hiring, leasing, and similar means of obtaining transport services, the
  place in which the vehicle is used must be identified (use and enjoyment rule has
  been implemented on these services).

The general rule for services supplied by a taxable person to a non-taxable person
(business to consumer or B2C) identifies the place of taxation with the country of
residence of the supplier.

Several rules, in addition to the B2B general rules, exist for the following:

- Brokerage services.
- Goods transport services.
- Services related to movable goods and ancillary activities related to transports.
- Long term hiring/leasing of means of transport services.
- Electronic services supplied by extra-European Union (EU) suppliers.
- Telecommunications and television/radio broadcast services.

In addition, special rules are provided for intangible services provided to final customers established outside the European Union.

In relation to the VAT treatment of cultural, artistic, sporting, scientific, educational, recreational, and similar services, VAT is due in the country where the activities were physically carried out for B2C activities and VAT is due in the country of the recipient for B2B activities other than admission. For B2B services in respect of admission, the place of supply is where the events take place.

Time of supply for certain services
For transactions carried out from 17 March 2012, the time of supply is the time of completion in case of:

- supply of services falling under the general rule (i.e. generic supply of services) rendered by EU and non-EU taxable persons to taxable persons established in Italy, and
- supply of services falling under the general rule rendered by taxable persons established in Italy to EU and non-EU taxable persons.

In case of periodic or continuous supply of services, the time of supply is the date of maturity of the consideration.

Moreover, the above supplies of services, if performed/received by taxable persons established in Italy continuously over a period longer than one year and if no payments are carried out, even partially, in the same period, shall be considered carried out at the end of each calendar year up to completion of the same supplies.

Reporting obligation
Transactions carried out with subjects resident in 'black list' countries (i.e. tax haven jurisdictions) must be disclosed in periodical communications to be electronically filed with the tax authorities. The transactions to be reported are those higher than EUR 500.

For transactions carried out from 1 January 2012, a taxable person must also communicate the total amount of the output transactions rendered towards each customer and input transactions received from each supplier. As regards the communication related to transactions for which there is no obligation to issue an invoice, the threshold for this fulfillment is EUR 3,600, VAT inclusive. Specific transactions are excluded from the communication (e.g. importations, exportations, and other transactions that have already been communicated to the tax authorities, such as black list, insurance, electricity supply, and telephone services contracts).

Reverse charge mechanism extension
According to the reverse charge mechanism, the obligations related to supply of goods and provision of services carried out in Italy by non-resident taxable persons towards taxable persons established in Italy are fulfilled by the latter. From a practical point of

Italy

view, the recipient of goods and/or services has to issue a self-invoice and record it in the VAT sales register and VAT purchase register.

The reverse charge mechanism obligation has been extended to the supply of all goods and services in the scope of the Italian VAT carried out by non-resident entities to taxable persons resident in Italy. Non-resident entities (including those having an Italian VAT number through indirect or direct registration) cannot charge Italian VAT to an Italian established VAT person.

Note that sales within the Italian territory of:

- mobile telephones, being devices made or adapted for use in connection with a licensed network and operated on specified frequencies, whether or not they have any other use and
- integrated circuit devices, such as microprocessors and central processing units, in a state prior to integration into end-user products are subject to the reverse charge in case the recipient of the above goods is a taxable person in Italy. This mechanism is not applicable to retail sales and when the supply of the handset is ancillary to the airtime.

VAT credit offset with other taxes
From 1 April 2012, to offset a VAT credit against other taxes for an amount higher than EUR 5,000, it is necessary to wait until the 16th day of the month following the filing of the yearly VAT return on which the credit is shown.

Furthermore, in order to avoid abuse, taxpayers intending to offset a VAT credit for an amount greater than EUR 15,000 are required to ask their tax advisors or auditors to affix their signature to the VAT return, which is known as the 'conformity mark'.

Registration tax
Specific deeds and contracts must be filed with the local registration tax office either upon signature or if specific circumstances occur, and the relevant tax must be paid.

Depending on the nature of the contract and on the assets that are the object of the contract, as well as on the form of the contract, registration tax is levied as a fixed amount or as a percentage of the value of the goods and/or rights that are the object of the contract. As a general rule, no proportional registration tax is due in the case of transactions subject to VAT.

VAT and registration tax on lease of immovable properties
Leases of residential and commercial buildings, or portion thereof, generally are VAT exempt and subject to the registration tax at 2% or 1% rate.

Please refer to the table below for an overview of the tax regime applicable to the leases, including financial leases, of both residential and commercial buildings.

Type of building	Lessor (VAT status)	Lessee (VAT status)	VAT (%)	Registration tax (%)
Residential buildings	Individual or entities not acting in the course of business (not subject to VAT)	Any	Out of scope	2

Type of building	Lessor (VAT status)	Lessee (VAT status)	VAT (%)	Registration tax (%)
Commercial buildings	Individual or entities not acting in the course of business (not subject to VAT)	Any	Out of scope	2
Residential buildings	Taxable persons acting in the course of business	Any	Exempt (with no right to deduction)*	2
Commercial buildings	Taxable persons acting in the course of business	Individual or entities not acting in the course of business (not subject to VAT)	21	1
		VAT taxable persons with a VAT recoverable pro-rata not higher than 25%	21	1
		Other cases	Exempt (with non right to deduction) with the possibility for the lessor to opt for the VAT regime (21% rate)	1

* In some specific cases of subsidised housing, VAT is applicable at a 10% reduced rate.

Specific rules apply in case of financial leases of residential and commercial buildings from a registration tax perspective.

Customs duty

At the moment of the importation of goods into the EU territory, customs duties are applied. The amount of customs duties to pay depends on the value and nature of the goods imported. In particular, for each kind of good, the Common Customs Tariff provides a tax-rate to be applied to the value of the goods imported.

The correct classification of the goods is one of the most important issues to consider when an economic operator introduces goods in Italy. A wrong classification can give rise to the application of higher customs duties, and the operator could face a tax burden not due, or to the application of lower customs duties, and this situation could lead to a Tax Assessment by Italian Customs Authority.

The value of the goods is represented by the transaction value, hence, the price actually paid or payable for the goods when sold for exportation to the customs territory of the EU, provided that:

- there are no restrictions as to the disposal or use of the goods by the buyer
- the sale or price is not subject to some condition or consideration for which a value cannot be determined with respect to the goods being valued
- part of the profits of any subsequent resale, disposal, or use of the goods by the buyer will not be accrued, directly or indirectly, to the seller, and
- the buyer and seller are not related, or, where the buyer and seller are related, that the transaction value is acceptable for customs purposes.

In determining whether the transaction value is acceptable, the fact that the buyer and the seller are related is not, in itself, sufficient for considering the transaction

Italy

value as non acceptable. Where necessary, the circumstances surrounding the sale are examined, and the transaction value is accepted provided that the relationship did not influence the price.

The price actually paid or payable is the total transaction amount paid for the imported goods and includes all payments made as a condition of sale of the imported goods by the buyer to the seller or by the buyer to a third party to satisfy an obligation of the seller.

In determining the customs value, the following items shall be added to the price, to the extent that they are incurred by the buyer and are not included in the price (list not exhaustive):

* Commissions and brokerage.
* Royalties and license fees related to the goods under assessment.
* The cost of transport and insurance of the imported goods.

At the same time, provided that they are shown separately from the price actually paid or payable, the following items shall not be included in to the customs value (list not exhaustive):

* Charges for the transport of goods after their arrival at the place of introduction into the customs territory of the European Community (EC).
* Charges for construction, erection, assembly, maintenance, or technical assistance, undertaken after importation of imported goods such as industrial plant, machinery, or equipment.
* Buying commissions.

A reduced tax-rate at importation can be applied when the goods imported have a preferential origin. The preferential origin depends on the existence of commercial agreements between the European Community and other non-EC states or by facilities provided by European Community to non-EC states unilaterally.

The application of a reduced tax-rate can even depend on the existence of preferential tariff treatment or on the existence of a particular exemption provided by law for some kind of goods.

Any person may appoint a representative in one's dealings with the Customs Authority to perform the activities and formalities laid down by customs rules. Such representation may be direct, in which case the representative shall act in the name and on behalf of another person, or indirect, in which case the representatives shall act in one's own name but on behalf of another person.

For direct representation, a forwarding agent, holder of a particular license, must be appointed.

The representative must be established within the European Community.

Excise duty

The following goods are subject to excise duties:

* Energetic products (e.g. petrol, gas oil, natural gas, coal).
* Alcohol and alcoholic drinks (e.g. wine, beer, ethylic alcohol).

- Processed tobaccos (e.g. cigars, cigarettes, tobacco).
- Electric power.

The subjection of a product to excise duties has to be verified on the basis of its customs combined nomenclature code.

The tax liability, depending on the products, arises:

- at the moment of importation or production (and the excise duties must be paid at the moment in which they are released for consumption in Italy)
- when the excisable goods are used for heating or as fuel, and
- when the excisable goods are released for consumption or used for own use.

As a general rule (with exception from natural gas and coal, coke, and lignite), with reference to excise goods released for consumption during a month, the payment of the relative excise duties has to be done within the 16th day of the following month.

With reference to excise goods imported, customs rules are applied as far as the procedure and terms of payment are concerned.

The production, processing, and holding of 'excise goods', except from natural gas, coal, coke, lignite, and electric power, are subject to a suspensive regime performed through a fiscal warehouse.

In order to manage a fiscal warehouse, it is necessary to acquire a license issued by the Italian Customs Authority, and there are specific obligations for the owner of a fiscal warehouse (e.g. provide for a particular guarantee, keep a particular accounting system for the goods stored, be subject to controls performed by Italian Customs Authority, where requested).

The Italian legislation provides for many exemptions with regards to the use of 'excise goods'.

Furthermore, under certain circumstances, a tax refund is granted to the operator who released for consumption, if, afterwards, the products are not consumed in Italy.

Stamp duty taxes

Stamp duty taxes (*Imposta di Bollo*) apply on a certain list of deeds or documents provided for by the relevant law provision (e.g. checks, bills of exchange, statements of account, certificates, books of account, deeds of transfer of quotas, and, in some cases, invoices).

According to the kind of deed, stamp duty tax is due at the moment of the deeds' origin or in case of use and can be a fixed amount or an amount proportional to the value of the deed or document.

Stamp duty tax can be paid:

- ordinarily, through a physical stamp attached on the document, or
- virtually, through electronic means (in this case, a specific authorisation from the Italian Tax Authorities and a specific process are needed).

Stamp duty tax is usually alternative to VAT; however, in case of considerations partially subject to VAT and partially not subject to VAT, the invoice is subject to stamp duty tax if

Italy

the total amount of the considerations not subject to VAT exceeds EUR 77.47. Moreover, some transactions are stamp duty tax exempted (e.g. intercommunity supply of goods). For transactions which are exempted from VAT (with restriction on VAT credit) and for transactions out of scope of VAT, exceeding EUR 77.47, an amount of EUR 1.81 is due as stamp duty tax for every invoice issued.

Imposta Municipale Unica (IMU)

IMU is the municipal tax on real estate. It is levied annually either on the owner or on the financial lessee of real estate (i.e. buildings, development land, and agricultural land). The standard tax rate is 0.76%. Depending on the municipality, the tax rate can be increased.

The taxable basis generally is determined on the basis of the so called 'cadastral value' (i.e. capitalisation of the income derived from the real estate).

Branch income

The tax regime for PEs is the same as for corporate Italian entities (e.g. joint-stock companies). Accordingly, a branch is subject to IRES as well as IRAP. Both taxes are determined on the basis of the relevant financial statements related to the business activities carried out by the PE.

Transfer pricing principles apply to transactions between a head office and its Italian tax resident PE.

Income determination

In principle, positive and negative components of a company's income statement are, respectively, taxed or deducted on an accruals basis (under the accrual principle) for tax purposes. Additionally, in order to be taxed/deducted, income items have to be certain under a legal standpoint and either objectively determined or capable of objective determination as to their amount (under the certain and objective determination principle). Income statement items accrued in the statutory accounts not meeting the above criteria are not allowed for tax deduction nor taxed as income in the tax period. Deduction or taxation of income is correspondingly deferred to future tax periods when the criteria are met.

Expenses generally are deductible if they relate to activities generating revenues concurring to the company's taxable income (under the inherence to business principle) and provided they are included in the relevant statutory accounts (under the imputation principle). An exception to this general rule is made for those income statement items accrued in the statutory accounts relating to a tax period different from that in which they become relevant for tax purposes in accordance with the principles of certainty and objective determination as described above. These items are taken into account in determining taxable income in the tax period when the latter conditions are met.

For IRAP purposes, relevant income and expense are those reported in the financial statements.

Specific rules have been released for entities which have adopted International Financial Reporting Standards (IFRS) for Italian statutory financial reporting purposes. These provisions are aimed to align income determination rules with IFRS.

Inventory valuation
Italian tax law allows the application of all the most commonly used inventory valuation methods: last in first out (LIFO), first in first out (FIFO), average cost. For IRES only, the reference prices used to calculate the written down value of the inventory items cannot be lower than their market prices during the final month of the tax period.

Companies operating in the oil and gas sector are required to adopt either average cost or FIFO for tax purposes.

Capital gains
Capital gains are taxable in the tax period in which they are realised, as follows:

* Fixed assets: the gain realised on the sale of fixed assets is taxable for both IRES and IRAP purposes. Additionally, for IRES purposes, tax on capital gains can be spread over a maximum of five years. This treatment is allowed provided that the company owns the fixed assets for not less than three years.
* Financial Investments: a specific participation exemption regime (PEX) is applicable. Under this regime, capital gains realised by Italian companies on sales of shareholdings are 95% exempt from IRES.

PEX applies if all of the following conditions are met:

* The shareholding was held uninterruptedly for at least 12 months prior to the sale.
* The investment was classified under financial fixed assets in the financial statements relating to the first tax period of uninterrupted ownership.
* The subsidiary is actually carrying on a commercial activity (e.g. investments in companies mainly performing management of their own real estate are not entitled to the PEX benefits).
* The majority of the subsidiary's income is not generated in a tax haven country or one with a privileged tax regime.

The third and fourth conditions must be met both at the time of the sale of the investment and in the three preceding years. If these conditions are not met, the capital gain realised by the company is ordinarily taxed. Capital losses arising from the sale or write-down of shareholdings meeting PEX conditions are basically not tax deductible. Likewise, the capital losses realised on sales of non-PEX investments are tax deductible. Specific exemptions are provided for those entities adopting IFRS for Italian statutory accounts reporting purposes.

Specific anti-dividend washing rules provide that where capital losses arise from the disposal of shareholdings which are not eligible for PEX, such losses are deductible only for the part exceeding the tax exempt amount of dividends (*see Dividend income discussion below*) received from the shares in question in the 36 months prior to the disposal.

Capital gains on financial investments generally are excluded from the IRAP taxable base.

Italy

Dividend income
Dividends received by Italian resident companies from Italian companies or from companies resident in countries other than tax havens (i.e. not included in the 'black list') are excluded from the IRES taxable base for 95% of their amount. Conversely, no exemption applies to dividends paid by entities that are resident in tax haven jurisdictions (unless those dividends derive from profits that were already taxed under the Italian controlled foreign company [CFC] rules). There are specific rules for entities adopting IFRS for Italian statutory financial reporting purposes. For such entities, dividends from investments in shares and other financial instruments held for trading are fully taxable.

Dividends generally are excluded from the IRAP taxable base.

Interest income
Interest income is generally part of the taxable base.

Foreign income
An Italian resident corporation is taxable on all income whether produced in Italy or abroad. Profits earned by subsidiaries that are resident or located in countries or territories other than tax havens are taxed only on distribution of the relevant profits. Double taxation is, in principle, avoided by means of foreign tax credits.

Shell companies
Resident companies and PEs of non-resident companies can be qualified as non-operating entities if, alternatively, one of the following conditions is met:

- The entity is in a tax loss position for three consecutive tax periods.
- The average revenues recorded in the current fiscal year and in the prior two is lower than the amount resulting by applying certain 'deemed return' percentages to the average balance sheet value of specific assets in the current fiscal year and the two previous years.

  The main assets to be taken into consideration are shares and shareholdings, financial receivables, owned or leased real estate, and owned or leased tangible and intangible assets. The value of any assets that have been acquired or sold during the fiscal year must be adjusted according to the period of ownership.

These conditions must be checked every year. Therefore, it is possible for an entity to be 'non-operative' in one year and operative in the following year.

The shell company is assessed as having a minimum taxable income for both IRES and IRAP purposes.

For IRES purposes, the taxable income of a non-operative entity is determined as the sum of such values emerging from the application of specific percentages to the book values of the above-mentioned assets.

As of 2012, the IRES standard rate for entities qualified as shell companies has increased from 27.5% to 38%.

Tax losses generated in a tax period when the company was deemed to be non-operating cannot be carried forward.

Italy

For IRAP purposes, labour costs and other non-deductible items have to be added back to the deemed minimum IRES income as outlined above.

These rules are not applicable in the first year of a company's incorporation. Exemptions from these rules can be achieved:

* by means of an advance ruling from the Italian tax authorities aimed at assessing the specific circumstances that caused the company not to earn the minimum amount of income or
* by specific objective situations provided for by Italian law (e.g. company directly or indirectly held by quoted companies).

Shell companies are also subject to limitations in their ability to recover VAT credits.

Deductions

The principles outlined in the section on Income determination also apply for deductible costs.

Depreciation and amortisation
All fixed assets that are used in the business of the company, except land, are depreciable for tax purposes (for both IRES and IRAP).

For IRES, the maximum depreciation rates for fixed tangible assets are set forth in a ministerial decree. Such depreciation rates are different, depending on the economic sector in which the company operates. In the event that financial accounting depreciation exceeds the amounts allowed for tax purposes, temporary differences arise. Tax depreciation of fixed tangible assets is allowed from the tax period in which the asset is first used. In the first tax depreciation period, the depreciation rate cannot exceed one-half of the normal rates.

It is worth pointing out that a project aimed at achieving the grouping of the tax amortisation rates has been announced by the government. Timing for the implementation of such a project is still uncertain.

Land is not a depreciable asset. Amortisation of goodwill derived from an acquisition and amortisation of trademarks are deductible for an amount not exceeding one-eighteenth of the cost of the goodwill in any year.

Patents, know-how, and other intellectual property may be amortised over a two-year period.

Concession rights may be depreciated with reference to the utilisation period as determined either by law or in the relevant agreement.

For IRAP purposes only, depreciation and amortisation (other than as related to goodwill and trademarks) are deductible in accordance with the amounts reported in the financial statements, regardless of the limits outlined above.

Interest expense
Generally, interest expense is fully tax deductible up to the amount of interest income. Thereafter, excess interest expense is deductible up to 30% of the gross operating margin (interest deduction capacity) as reported in the financial statements. Gross

Italy

operating margin is defined as the difference between operating revenues and expenses excluding depreciation of tangible and intangible assets and charges for leased assets as stated in the profit and loss account for the year.

Net interest expense in excess of the yearly limitation is carried forward indefinitely. Hence, net interest expense not deducted in previous years can be deducted in any future fiscal year as long as total interest in that year does not exceed 30% of gross operating margin. If net interest expense is lower than the annual limit (i.e. 30% of gross operating margin), this difference can be carried over to increase the company's interest deduction capacity in future years.

Where an election is made for the domestic tax consolidation regime, (*as discussed in the Group taxation section*), the net interest expense limitation applies to the consolidated tax group. As a consequence, if a company participating in a tax group has an excess interest deduction capacity, this excess may be used against the interest deduction deficit in another company belonging to the same tax consolidation group. Under specific conditions, non-resident subsidiaries can also be 'virtually' included in the tax consolidation for the sole purpose of transferring their excess capacity over 30% of gross operating margin in order to increase the overall interest deduction capacity of the Italian group.

The above-mentioned rules are not applicable for financial institutions, such as banks and insurance companies, where the deductibility of interest expense (for both IRES and IRAP purposes) is limited to a fixed amount of 96% of the interest expense shown in the income statement of these entities.

Allowance for Corporate Equity (ACE)
The ACE is a deduction that corresponds to the net increase in the equity employed in the entity, multiplied by an index yearly determined by the Ministry of Finance, currently equal to 3%.

The relevant increase is determined by the equity contributions and by the retained earnings (except profits allocated to a non-disposable reserve) less the following items:

- Reductions of the net equity with assignment to shareholders.
- Investments in controlled companies.
- Business acquisitions.

If the allowance for a year is higher than the net IRES taxable base, the difference will be carried forward to the next periods.

The reference equity is the amount disclosed in the financial statements for the fiscal year as at 31 December 2010, net of the profits for the same year. Fiscal year 2011 is the first period of application for this benefit.

Bad debts
Yearly provision for bad debts not guaranteed by third parties and relating to sales of goods and services is tax deductible at up to 0.5% of the gross value of the receivables. Deduction shall no longer be permitted when the total amount of the bad debts reserve exceeds 5% of the above-mentioned gross value of the receivables as of the end of the fiscal year.

Losses on bad debts exceeding the said provision are allowed for deduction if backed by precise and objective evidence or when the debtor is subjected to bankruptcy proceedings.

Charitable contributions
Deduction of charitable contributions is allowed. The amounts allowed for deductions depend on the specific features of the recipient entity, and specific limitations are set by the law.

Entertainment expenses
For IRES purposes, expenses for gifts and entertainment which meet the requirements (both qualitative and quantitative) contained in the specific Ministerial Decree are fully deductible in the tax period in which they are incurred. Entertainment expenses which do not meet these requirements cannot be deducted.

Expenses related to gifts with a value of EUR 50 or less are entirely deductible.

Travel expenses
For IRES purposes, the deduction for travel expenses incurred within the municipality is limited to 75% of the amount incurred. However, the VAT related to such costs is fully recoverable.

Automobile expenses
For IRES purposes, deduction of the cost of company automobiles is limited to 40% of the total amount of the costs for the automobile. If automobiles are assigned to employees, the company may deduct 90% of the costs associated with the automobile.

Automobile costs may be deducted in their entirety if (i) automobiles are necessary for the company's business or (ii) automobiles are an essential element in the company's activity (i.e. vehicles owned by a car rental company).

Telephone expenses
For IRES purposes, up to 80% of the total expenses related to both mobile and landline telephones are deductible.

Fines and penalties
Fines and penalties are generally not considered inherent costs and are, consequently, not deductible for tax purposes.

Taxes
When calculating the IRES base, 10% of IRAP paid is deductible.

IMU, municipal tax on real estate, is not deductible for either IRES or IRAP.

Purchases from suppliers resident in tax haven jurisdictions
The costs of goods and services purchased from entities which are resident in tax haven jurisdictions are deductible on the condition that the taxpayer can, upon request of the tax authorities, provide evidence that the foreign companies carry out a real business activity or that the transactions were carried out for good and sound economic reasons (e.g. better economic conditions, the foreign supplier is the sole distributor for specific products).

An official list of tax haven jurisdictions (known as the 'black list') has been issued by the Ministry of Finance. A list of countries which are not considered to have a privileged

Italy

tax regime (known as the 'white list') is expected, and countries not on this white list will be deemed tax havens. Specific disclosure is required in a company's income tax return for the expenses arising in tax haven jurisdictions.

Net operating losses
As of 2011, tax losses can be carried forward for IRES purposes and used to offset income in the following tax periods without any time limitation.

Tax losses can only be offset with taxable income for an amount not exceeding 80% of the taxable income. Thus, corporations are required to pay IRES on at least 20% of taxable income.

Note that losses arising in the first three years of activity can be offset with 100% of taxable income.

Tax authorities have clarified that the new regime applies on tax losses generated from 2006 onward.

In the previous regime, the carryforward was limited to the five tax periods following the period in which the tax loss was incurred.

For IRAP purposes, tax losses may not be carried forward.

Specific (tax anti-avoidance) rules limit the carryforward of tax losses in the event of:

- change of control and
- an effective change of the main activity (performed by the company carrying forward the losses).

The aforementioned changes must occur together in order for the limitations to be applicable. The change of the main activity is relevant for these purposes if it takes place in the tax period in which the change of control occurs or in the two subsequent or preceding periods.

Specific anti-abuse provisions are also applicable to net operating losses in cases of merger or demerger.

In Italy, tax losses may not be carried back.

Payments to foreign affiliates
Transactions with foreign affiliated companies should be at 'fair market value' and, generally, as defined by OECD guidelines.

Italian companies transacting business with related non-resident parties may participate in special tax ruling procedures for the transfer pricing procedures used for intra-group transactions. The agreement executed between the tax authorities and the taxpayer is binding for the fiscal year during which the agreement is executed and for the following two fiscal years, unless significant changes in the circumstances relevant for the conclusion of the agreement executed by the taxpayer take place.

Group taxation

Domestic tax consolidation

Companies belonging to the same group can elect domestic tax consolidation. This allows the determination of a single IRES taxable base comprised of the taxable income and losses of each of the participating entities. The tax consolidation does not operate for IRAP purposes.

Where an overall tax loss position arises, this can be carried forward and used against future consolidated taxable income. Conversely, tax losses arising in fiscal years preceding the domestic tax consolidation election can be carried forward and used only by the company to which these losses belong.

The taxable basis determined by each company participating in the tax consolidation arrangement is included in its entirety. No apportionment is made in relation to the percentage of control.

In order to validly elect the Italian domestic tax consolidation regime, the following conditions must be met:

- The consolidating entity must be an Italian tax resident company, and it must hold, directly or indirectly, more than the 50% of the share capital of the consolidated entities (so called 'legal control').
- This control must be in place from the beginning of the tax period for which the tax consolidation is applied for.
- All of the companies participating in the group must have the same year end.

Provided that specific requirements are met, Italian PEs of foreign companies can also participate as controlling entities in a tax consolidation.

The consolidation arrangement operates on an elective basis. Taxpayers may select whether to be included or not, and it is not necessary for all the Italian group/sub-group companies to jointly elect for the tax consolidation.

Once the election is made, it cannot be revoked for three fiscal years.

Worldwide tax consolidation group

A worldwide tax consolidation group is available, allowing the consolidation of foreign subsidiaries.

In addition to the requirements set out for domestic tax group system, the following conditions apply:

- The ultimate parent company must be either owned by individuals who are tax residents of Italy or listed on the Italian Stock Exchange.
- The option must be exercised for all foreign companies (under the 'all in, all out' principle).

Income for each company is apportioned in the tax consolidation based on the actual percentage of control exercised by the ultimate parent company that is an Italian tax resident.

Italy

A number of additional requirements need to be fulfilled in order for a worldwide tax consolidation to be operative, including a mandatory audit of the financial statements of all the foreign subsidiaries.

Once the election is made, it cannot be rescinded for five fiscal years.

Transfer pricing

Income derived from operations with non-resident corporations which directly or indirectly control the Italian entity, are controlled by the Italian entity, or are controlled by the same corporation controlling the Italian entity have to be valued on the basis of the normal value of the goods transferred, services rendered, and services and good received, if an increase in taxable income is derived there from. Possible reductions in taxable income as a result of the normal value rule are allowed only on the basis of mutual agreement procedures or the EU Arbitration Convention.

The normal value is the average price or consideration paid for goods and services of the same or similar type, carried on at free market conditions and at the same level of commerce, at the time and place in which the goods and services were purchased or performed. For the determination of the normal value reference should be made, to the extent possible, to the price list of the provider of goods or services, and, in their absence, to the price lists issued by the chamber of commerce and to professional tariffs, taking into account usual discounts.

Penalty protection regime with transfer pricing documentation support

Transfer pricing rules provide for a penalty protection regime in case of transfer pricing audit, provided that the taxpayer has prepared proper documentation detailing the compliance of intercompany transaction to the arm's-length principle.

The regulation applies to transactions incurred between Italian entities and non-resident entities belonging to the same group (transfer pricing rule are not applicable to domestic transactions). No specific methods have been introduced to test the arm's length of transactions; reference is made to the OECD Guidelines.

On the base of the transfer pricing regulation, taxpayers can obtain penalty protection if they provide the Italian tax authorities with:

* Documentation to support the intercompany transactions drawn up in the specific format detailed in the Regulation issued by the Italian tax authorities and in Italian language. Tax authority confirmed that information in annexes (intercompany contracts and transactions diagram) can be in the English language.
* Notification that documentation has been prepared and available by checking the box in the annual corporate income tax return.

The information required is based on the EU Code of Conduct for Transfer Pricing documentation.

Based on the group structure, Master File and/or Country File have to be prepared.

Italian based groups and Italian sub-groups owning non-Italian subsidiaries must produce both a Master File and a Country File. Italian subsidiaries of multinational groups need to produce a Country File only.

The sub-group provisions are onerous, especially so where they relate to branches. Where a foreign entity has an Italian branch but the company itself is also a holding company, a Master File is required for the foreign entity's subgroup, even if there is no holding directly attributed to the branch.

Sub-holding companies based in Italy with at least one non-Italian subsidiary, which need to produce a Master File, may instead produce the Master File for the entire group in English. If it does not contain all the information in the Italian Regulation, they will need to supplement it.

Documentation must be signed by the legal representative of the company and provided to the authority upon request within ten days. Also, an electronic copy must be provided at authority request.

Small and medium companies (defined as those with an annual turnover of less than EUR 50 million) need to update the economic analysis only every three years, provided that no significant change in the business occurred. Otherwise, it is necessary to update the economic analysis each year.

As the documentation provisions provide a potential benefit for Italian taxpayers (by waiving the automatic tax geared penalties that would otherwise apply to a transfer pricing adjustment), taxpayers have been given the opportunity to take advantage of this penalty protection for all open years if they file a communication that they possess documentation in the required format before they receive notification of any tax audit.

Thin capitalisation
Italy no longer has thin capitalisation rules per se. Instead, net interest expense is deductible only up to an amount equal to 30% of gross operating margin (*see Interest expense in the Deductions section for more information*).

Controlled foreign companies (CFCs)
An Italian company that controls, either directly or indirectly, an entity located in a tax haven jurisdiction is required to consolidate the taxable income arising in proportion to the percentage of shareholding held, irrespective of whether the profits have been distributed or not.

Income from CFCs is taxed separately from the other taxable income of the business at the standard IRES rate (i.e. other tax losses cannot be used to offset CFC income). Foreign taxes paid by the CFCs are recoverable by way of a corresponding tax credit.

Dividends received by an Italian shareholder from a CFC are excluded from taxable income up to the amount of the taxable income attributed under the above CFC provisions. The excess of any dividends over income already included through the CFC regime is fully taxable in the hands of the shareholder.

Where companies are located in a tax haven, the CFC rules also apply for companies holding not less than the 20% of the company's share capital or entitled to not less than 20% share of the company's profits. In such instances, there are specific rules to determine the taxable income attributable to the Italian resident shareholder. The taxable income is determined by applying specific income ratios to the business assets of the CFC as they appear in the relevant accounts.

Exemption from these CFC rules can be achieved by means of an advance ruling from the Italian tax authorities. To obtain such a ruling, adequate evidence must be provided to demonstrate at least one of the following:

Italy

- The foreign company is mainly and effectively engaged in sales and/or industrial activities in the 'market' of the foreign host state or territory. Banks, other financial entities, and insurance companies must demonstrate that most of the financial resources and related proceeds are made in or the result of yields, respectively, from the market of the foreign host state or territory. However, this exemption cannot be requested where more than 50% of the income of the foreign subsidiaries is derived from 'passive income' (e.g. holding or investment in securities, receivables, or other financial assets, transfer or licence of intangible rights) or from intra-group services.
- No less than 75% of all the proceeds of the CFC have been taxed in jurisdictions that are not tax privileged countries (e.g. a company resident in Hong Kong has all of its operations in China mainland and it is subject to ordinary taxation there).

The CFC rules also extend to controlled companies that are located in a jurisdiction with a privileged tax regime that is not a tax haven, if the following conditions exist:

- The effective tax is less than 50% of the tax that would have been charged had the company been resident in Italy.
- More than 50% of revenue is derived from so-called 'passive income' or from intra-group services.

By means of an advance ruling, the Italian parent company is able to obtain an exemption from these rules if it is able to provide proper evidence that the establishment of the company in the privileged tax jurisdiction is not for tax avoidance purposes (unfair tax advantage).

Tax credits and incentives

Foreign tax credit
Where foreign-source income definitively is taxed abroad, a tax credit can be claimed for use against a company's IRES liability. The amount of the tax credit that can be claimed is the lower of the foreign tax incurred and the proportion of the IRES liability related to the foreign-source income. For partially exempt income (e.g. dividends), the foreign tax credit is reduced in proportion to the amount of the income taxable in Italy.

If an Italian company receives foreign income from more than one country, this limitation is applied separately to each country.

Foreign taxes borne by the foreign PE of an Italian resident company are allowed to be offset against the overall consolidated tax liability (IRES).

Any excess of foreign tax credit over the maximum amount allowed for recovery in the same tax period can be carried back or carried forward for eight years and recovered if specific conditions are met (e.g. same source country of the income, occurring because of an excess of the IRES liability related to the foreign-source income).

Inward investment, capital investment, and research and development (R&D) investment incentives
A number of incentives have been established to attract new industry to southern Italy and certain depressed mountain areas in central and northern Italy.

Tax credits are given to companies that increase the number of their employees and that invest in R&D.

The possibility of taking advantage of these rules, however, depends on the taxpayer fulfilling specific conditions and on the actual availability of financial resources by the Italian state. These financial resources generally are set in the annual state budget.

It is worth pointing out that the government is working on an incentive plan. The actual features and contents of such an incentive plan are expected to be out in the next few months.

Tax regime for EU investments in Italy

A special incentive has been introduced for the companies resident in other EU countries starting new economic activities in Italy and for their employees and staff. The possibility is to apply for three years the tax regime of EU countries in alternative to the Italian one.

The new activities need to be effectively performed in Italy.

The possibility to benefit from the new incentive needs to be agreed by means of an international ruling procedure with the Italian tax authorities.

Ministry of Finance is still expected to issue a decree regulating the relevant fulfillments for the practical application of this rule.

Withholding taxes

Effective from 2012, the base standard WHT rate on the yields on loans and securities (bonds, shares, etc.) paid by Italian resident entities to both Italian and non-Italian resident investors has been increased from 12.5% to 20%.

The said increase, however, does not affect the applicability of those rules allowing either the application of reduced WHT rates or the full exemption from the said withholdings (e.g. DTTs, EU directives, special domestic tax rules).

Interest on Treasury bonds will still be subject to a 12.5% domestic WHT.

WHT chart

Domestic corporations paying certain types of income are required to withhold as shown on the following chart. The numbers in parentheses refer to the notes below.

Recipient	Dividends (%)	Interest (%)	Royalties (%)
Resident corporations	0	0/20 (1)	0
Resident individuals	0/20 (2)	0/20 (1)	20 (3)
EU resident corporations	0/1.375 (4, 5)	0 (4)	0 (4)
Swiss resident corporations	0 (6)	0 (6)	0 (6)
Non-resident corporations and individuals:			
Non-treaty countries	20 (7)	20	30 (3)
Treaty countries (8):			
Albania	10	0/5	5
Algeria	15	0/15	5/15
Argentina	15	0/20	10/18

Italy

Recipient	Dividends (%)	Interest (%)	Royalties (%)
Armenia	5/10	0/10	7
Australia	15	0/10	10
Austria	15	0/10	0/10
Azerbaijan (9)	10	10	5/10
Bangladesh	10/15	0/10/15	10
Belgium	15	0/15	5
Bosnia and Herzegovina (Yugoslavia Ex)	10	10	10
Brazil	15	0/15	15/25
Bulgaria	10	0	5
Byelorussia	5/15	0/8	6
Canada	5/15	10	0/5/10
China, People's Republic	10	0/10	10
Croatia	15	10	5
Côte d' Ivoire	15/18	0/15	10
Cyprus	15	10	0
Czech Republic	15	0	0/5
Denmark	0/15	0/10	0/5
Ecuador	15	0/10	5
Egypt	27	0/25	15
Estonia	5/15	0/10	5/10
Ethiopia	10	0/10	20
Finland	10/15	0/15	0/5
France	5/15	0/10	0/5
Georgia	5/10	0	0
Germany	10/15	0/10	0/5
Ghana	5/15	10	10
Greece	15	0/10	0/5
Hungary	10	0	0
Iceland	5/15	0	5
India	15/25	0/15	20
Indonesia	10/15	0/10	10/15
Ireland, Republic of	15	10	0
Israel	10/15	10	0/10
Japan	10/15	10	10
Jordan	10	10	10
Kazakhstan	5/15	0/10	10
Kuwait	0/5	0	10
Latvia	5/15	0/10	5/10
Lebanon	5/15	0	0
Lithuania	5/15	0/10	5/10
Luxembourg	15	0/10	10
Macedonia	5/15	0/10	0
Malaysia	10	0/15	15
Malta	15	0/10	0/10
Mauritius	5/15	27	15
Mexico	15	0/15	0/15

Recipient	Dividends (%)	Interest (%)	Royalties (%)
Moldova	5/15	5	5
Montenegro (Yugoslavia Ex)	10	10	10
Morocco	10/15	0/10	5/10
Mozambique	15	0/10	10
Netherlands	5/10/15	0/10	5
New Zealand	15	0/10	10
Norway	15	0/15	5
Oman	5/10	0/5	10
Pakistan	15/25	0/30	30
Philippines	15	0/10/15	25
Poland	10	0/10	10
Portugal	15	0/15	12
Qatar	5/15	5	5
Romania	10	0/10	10
Russia	5/10	10	0
Saudi Arabia	5/10	5	10
Senegal	15	0/15	15
Serbia (Yugoslavia Ex)	10	10	10
Singapore	10	0/12.5	15/20
Slovak Republic	15	0	0/5
Slovenia	5/15	10	5
South Africa	5/15	0/10	6
South Korea	10/15	0/10	10
Soviet Union Ex	15	0	0
Spain	15	0/12	4/8
Sri Lanka	15	0/10	10/15
Sweden	10/15	0/15	5
Switzerland	15	12.5	5
Syria	5/10	0/10	18
Tanzania	10	15	15
Thailand	15/20	0/10	5/15
Trinidad and Tobago	10/20	10	0/5
Tunisia	15	0/12	5/12/16
Turkey	15	15	10
Uganda	15	0/15	10
Ukraine	5/15	0/10	7
United Arab Emirates	5/15	0	10
United Kingdom	5/15	0/10	8
United States	0/5/15	0/10	0/5/8
Uzbekistan	10	0/5	5
Venezuela	10	0/10	7/10
Vietnam	5/10/15	0/10	7.5/10
Zambia	5/15	0/10	10

I

Italy

Notes

1. The actual applicable rate depends on the features of the recipient. Applicable rates are as follows: 0% applies on loan agreements and ordinary notes when the recipient is a corporation; 20% rate in all other cases.
2. 0% is applicable on dividends received by shareholders holding no less than 20% of the share capital (2% in the case of listed entities), so called 'qualified investments'. The rate applicable to 'non-qualified investments' is 20%.
3. The rate is applicable on 75% of the gross amount of the royalty paid.
4. Pursuant to the EU Directives and provided that the requirements set forth therein are met, payments of dividends, interest, and royalties made by an Italian company to an EU resident group company can be WHT exempt. Specifically for the dividends, the minimum shareholding requirement (to benefit from this exemption) is currently equal to 10%.
5. Should the full WHT exemption not apply, 1.375% is applicable on dividends paid to EU tax residents.
6. Pursuant to the 2004 Swiss EU tax agreement and provided that the requirements contained therein are met, payments of dividends, interest, and royalties made by an Italian company to a Swiss tax resident group company can be WHT exempt.
7. Non-residents persons have the right to obtain reimbursement for up to one-fourth of the withholding effected, upon proof of the actual taxation of the dividends in the foreign country where the recipient is a resident.
8. Provided that all conditions are met, domestic tax legislation is applicable if more favourable for the taxpayer. In a number of circumstances, tax treaties may provide for particular tax rates mainly dependant on the nature of the instruments and on the profile of the recipients/payers. In such cases, the applicable WHT must be verified from an analysis of the relevant tax treaty.
9. The treaty enters into force starting from 1 January 2013.

Tax administration

Taxable period

The ordinary taxable period is equal to 12 months. Conformity with the calendar year is not requested. In particular cases, the duration of the taxable period can be different from 12 months (e.g. newly established companies are allowed to have taxable periods of up to 18 months; companies that are involved in extraordinary transactions [merger, de-mergers, etc.], as well as companies that are liquidated, may have taxable periods shorter than 12 months).

Tax returns

IRES and IRAP returns must be filed by the end of the ninth month following the tax year-end.

The ordinary filing deadline for WHT agent returns is 31 July for both the simplified WHT return and the ordinary WHT return.

Payment of taxes

For IRES and IRAP purposes, the tax law provides for both advance payments and settlement payments. The advance payments are equal to the net tax payable for the previous tax period and are due during the tax period to which they refer. Advance payments are split into two instalments:

- 40% by the 16th day of the sixth month following the tax year-end.
- 60% by the end of the 11th month following the tax year-end.

Settlement payments are due by the 16th day of the sixth month following the tax year-end to which they refer.

Tax payments should be performed through a specific form to be electronically filed to the Tax Authorities (i.e. F24 form).

Offsetting of taxes

Payables and receivables (not claimed for refund) resulting from a return regarding different taxes are allowed for off-setting within a yearly limit of EUR 516,457.90.

Starting as of 1 January 2011, the mentioned offsetting is no longer allowed if taxes definitively assessed by the Tax Authorities and not paid within the deadlines by the taxpayer are higher than EUR 1,500. In case of breach of the above limit, the law provides for a penalty of up to 50% of the undue settled amount.

Administrative penalties

Failure to file a tax return results in a penalty ranging from 120% to 240% of the taxes due. Minimum penalties (ranging from EUR 258 to EUR 1,032) are applicable if no tax liability emerged in the return.

A tax return showing either a taxable income lower than the one assessed or a tax credit higher than those owed to the taxpayer (i.e. an untrue tax return) results in a penalty ranging from 100% to 200% of the higher taxes ultimately due.

Omitted and/or late payments of taxes of whichever kind and nature result in a penalty equal to 30% of the unpaid/late paid tax.

Special rules apply where similar violations are repeated over various years.

Self-curement of tax law breaches are allowed on payment of the higher taxes and of reduced penalties. Such self-curement is allowed on condition that no tax audit is in progress in relation to the tax period in which the breach took place. The reduced penalties are always computed on the floor of the applicable range of penalties. The actual reduction depends on the time elapsed between the occurring of the breach and the self-curement itself. In this respect, reduced penalties may range from 1/8 to 1/10.

Software based tax controls (so-called 'Studi di settore')

The Italian Tax law provides for special tax control procedures for those enterprises whose total turnover does not exceed EUR 7.5 million. The controls, so-called 'Studi di Settore', are based on standardised economic models of the different business fields and are aimed at assessing whether or not a specific subject's taxable income is in line with its own standard model (on statistical basis).

A higher possibility of undergoing tax audit should be considered for entities not meeting such standard model.

Statute of limitations

The Italian tax authorities are entitled to make an assessment in relation to direct taxes (IRES and IRAP), VAT, and WHT returns up to the end of the fourth calendar year following the year in which the tax return was filed. Under certain circumstances (e.g. no return filed or fraud giving rise to criminal law penalties) the above deadlines may be extended.

Audit cycle

For larger companies having a yearly turnover exceeding specific thresholds (that are in the process of being progressively decreased to EUR 100 million), administrative checks on tax returns may be carried out within the year following that in which the tax return has been filed.

Italy

With limited exceptions, corporations that are repeatedly in a tax loss position will be subject to tax audit.

Tax audit can take place at the taxpayer's premises as well as in the tax authorities' offices. The statute of limitations provides that tax auditors can stay at a taxpayer's premises for not longer than 60 working days (30 days ordinary term plus 30 days of extension). At the end of this period, the audit must come to an end unless extraordinary issues arise. Tax auditors must take note of the observations and requests made by the taxpayer. At the end of their audit, the tax auditors must draw up a tax audit report whereby the outcome of the audit activity must be detailed and the findings (if any) must be illustrated and motivated. A copy of the report has to be filed with the tax office.

The tax office receiving the tax audit report examines the findings reported by the tax auditors and starts the assessment procedure, which may lead to the issuing of a tax assessment notice bearing the request for payment of higher taxes and/or penalties.

Topics of focus for tax authorities
Extraordinary transactions (such as mergers, de-mergers, etc.) continue to be a topic of focus for tax authorities due to the potential applicability of tax anti-abuse rules.

As a response to recent cases of carousel-frauds on VAT, cross-border transactions are being more heavily scrutinised.

Over the last few years, we experienced an increasing focus by the tax authorities on transfer pricing related issues. That is, presumably, a result of the introduction in Italy of specific guidelines in relation to infra-group transactions (namely the penalty protection rules).

Tax controversy and dispute resolutions
Should the taxpayer accept all of the challenges raised by the tax authorities, it may take advantage of the application of reduced penalties. The reduced penalties may range from $1/6$ to $1/3$ of the minimum applicable penalties, depending on the status of the controversy.

In case the taxpayer decides not to accept the challenges by the tax authorities, a settlement procedure can be initiated. The favourable outcome of the settlement procedure brings forth (in addition to the agreed-upon reduction of challenged taxes) the reduction of penalties: ordinarily down to $1/3$ of the minimum applicable penalties.

In case no settlement is either achieved or requested for, the taxpayer may start a tax dispute before the Court. The judicial proceedings are structured in three tiers:

- Provincial Tax Commission, in first instance.
- Regional Tax Commission, in second instance.
- Supreme Court of Cassation.

Other issues

Adoption of IFRS and taxation
The Italian tax law provides for two basic principles and some specific rules for taxation of a company adopting International Accounting Standards (IAS)/IFRS in the statutory financial statements:

Italy

- Derivation principle ('*Principio della Derivazione*'): the taxable base of companies is determined starting from the net income arising from the profit and loss, increased or decreased by items directly booked to equity pursuant to the application of IAS/IFRS. To such income, the general tax adjustments set forth by the Corporate Income Tax Law apply. In this respect, as exception to the general tax criteria, the accrual principle, and the qualification and classification criteria stated by the IFRS are relevant for the calculation of the taxable base.
- Neutrality principle ('*Principio della Neutralità*'): such principle aims to neutralise the effects deriving from the movement to IAS/IFRS (First Time Adoption or FTA). Conversely, such principle does not grant an equal treatment for companies adopting or not IAS/IFRS (in fact, specific rules are applicable only to IAS/IFRS adopters, e.g. taxation of dividend on held for trading securities, derivatives).

The following specific rules applicable to IAS adopters must be considered:

- Adjustments or recognitions of transactions made in equity and/or in the 'other comprehensive income (OCI)' are relevant for tax purposes, to the extent that such items are in compliance with general tax principles.
- For equity instruments, the legal classification is prevailing over the accounting one (debt vs. equity classification).
- Under certain conditions, unrealised profits and losses recognised in the profit and loss become taxable and deductible (e.g. fair value on securities other than shareholdings and on derivatives transactions).
- The tax treatment of transactions between IFRS adopters and non-IFRS adopters is based on the accounting principle adopted by each company (e.g. financial leasing transaction).
- Depreciation and amortisation are permitted within the rates provided by the tax rules and limited to the amount booked in the profit and loss statement. In this respect, the abolition of the imperative systematic depreciation of the goodwill and its substitution by the goodwill's review for impairment does not affect the tax deduction of the goodwill amortisation that should be made solely for tax purposes.
- Negative components booked in the income statement as expenses for personnel settled with equity instrument under IFRS 2 are, in principle, deductible for IRES purposes (stock options).
- In order to identify financial instruments with hedging purposes, IFRS adopters are allowed to give relevance to the classification made in the financial statement. In particular, financial instruments designated in the financial statement as hedging instruments in compliance with IFRS principles are considered also as hedging instruments for fiscal purposes (hedging accounting approach including the fair value option [FVO]).
- Given the possibility, under the IAS 39 accounting principle, to reclassify financial securities in a different portfolio from that of the initial booking, the value at which the security is booked in the new portfolio is tax relevant.

Ivory Coast (Côte d'Ivoire)

PwC contact

Dominique Taty
Fidafrica SA
Immeuble Alpha 2000
20th Floor
Rue Gourgas - Plateau
Abidjan 01
Côte d'Ivoire
Tel: +225 20 31 54 60
Email: d.taty@ci.pwc.com

Significant developments

After the political crisis in 2011, the FY11 Financial Law enforced (as of 14 July 2011) some tax reduction and tax holidays for the companies which had suffered losses during the political crisis.

The FY12 Financial Law was enforced on 9 January 2012 and includes some amendments to various tax laws (*see the Other taxes section for more information*).

Taxes on corporate income

Tax on industrial and commercial profits in Côte d'Ivoire is levied at 25%, subject to a minimum tax.

Taxable corporate income in Côte d'Ivoire is based on worldwide income for resident companies. Non-resident entities are subject to withholding tax (WHT) at 20%, subject to existing double taxation agreement (DTA), on their Côte d'Ivoire source income when they do not have a permanent establishment (PE). Non-residents with a PE are taxed in the same way as a resident.

Minimum tax

The minimum tax is based on total turnover and is calculated at the rate of 0.5% (0.15% for banking activities, 0.1% for oil companies), with a minimum tax of 2 million *Communauté financière d'Afrique* (Financial Community of Africa or CFA) francs (XOF) and a maximum tax of XOF 30 million.

Local income taxes

The income tax is levied at the national level. There is no local income tax.

Corporate residence

In Côte d'Ivoire, companies are considered resident in tax jurisdictions where they have a registered fixed establishment (e.g. subsidiaries, branches, representative offices).

Permanent establishment (PE)

A non-resident is considered as having a PE in Côte d'Ivoire when its activities involve a complete commercial cycle in Côte d'Ivoire or when it operates though an dependent agent in Côte d'Ivoire.

According to DTAs, a non-resident is considered as having a PE in Côte d'Ivoire when it has a registered establishment, including a subsidiary, a branch, a representative office, a mine or an oil well, a building site, a manufacture plant, or a trading establishment. Sometimes, a time threshold of six months is considered.

Other taxes

Value-added tax (VAT)

VAT is a non-cumulative tax levied on the sale of goods and services at the rate of 18%. Subject to certain restrictions, VAT is recoverable.

The rate is reduced to 9% for milk, pasta products which contain 100% durum wheat semolina, and the equipment designed for the production of solar energy.

Customs duties

Customs duties rates range from 0% to 20%, depending on the classification of the imported goods according to the customs tariff.

Upon import, goods are also subject to the statistical fee (1%), to community levy (1%), and to VAT (18%).

Special taxes depending on the nature of the imported goods may apply, such as excises duties.

Excise duties

Excise duties apply on cigarette's imports, alcoholic or non-alcoholic beverages, and oil products.

Real estate tax

A real estate tax is imposed at the following rates:

- 1.5% for undeveloped lands.
- 4% on land revenue.
- 11% on developed land or 15% when the built property is used by the company itself. The rate is reduced to 4% for unoccupied buildings.

Property owners are required to withhold 15% of rentals, payable on the 15th day of each month to the tax authorities. This is an advance payment on the annual real estate tax by the owner of the estate property.

Transfer taxes

In the case of the transfer of property through a direct sale, taxes are assessed at the following rates:

- 10% for lease transfers.
- 7.5% or 10% for the sale of real estate. The 7.5% rate applies on estate properties used for business purpose. The 10% rate applies to the other transfers.
- 10% for the sale of businesses.

Stamp duty

A direct tax is paid for any document subject to a registration procedure, for an acknowledgment of a cash payment, and for bills of exchange.

Ivory Coast (Côte d'Ivoire)

Special tax for equipment
This is a tax paid by all taxpayers for the purpose of the equipment of the government. The tax is based on the turnover of the taxpayers.

As of 9 January 2012, tax of 0.1% is calculated on total turnover and is paid monthly. Prior to 9 January 2012, the rate was 0.08%.

Business franchise tax
The business franchise tax includes a turnover tax and a proportional tax. The turnover tax is calculated on turnover at the rate of 0.5%, with a minimum tax of XOF 300,000 and a maximum tax of XOF 3 million. The proportional tax rate is 18.5% and is based on the rental value of the professional office location (based on general office rents).

Tax on banking operations
A cumulative tax of 10% is levied on bank services rendered. Tax on banking operations charged by banks to companies is fully deductible from output VAT.

Registration taxes
Registration of capital contributions is taxed, whether the capital or increase in capital is made in cash or in kind. The rate is 0.6% for contributions up to XOF 5 billion and 0.2% for contributions over XOF 5 billion, with a minimum tax of XOF 18,000. Increases in capital by incorporation of reserves are taxed at 6%.

In the event of a capital increase through a merger, the increase in the share capital of the acquiring company is taxed at half the rate, 0.3% for amounts up to XOF 5 billion and 0.1% for amounts over XOF 5 billion.

Tax on insurance premiums
Insurance premiums are subject to tax as follows:

Policy type	Tax rate (%)
Marine policies	7.0
Life policies	Exempted when contract's duration is more than three years
Fire policies	25.0
Health policies	8.0
Export credit insurance	0.1
Other (e.g. personal liability, transportation)	14.5

Premiums paid under commercial shipping insurance policies for maritime risks are exempt. The tax may be paid by the insurance company, its agent, or the subscriber, in cases where the subscriber had to pay the premium to a foreign insurance company.

Tax on telecommunication services
The FY12 Financial Law has enforced a specific tax of 3% applicable on the turnover of mobile telecommunication companies.

Payroll taxes
Taxes are levied at the rates of 2.8% for local employees and 12% for expatriate employees on the total taxable remuneration, including salaries, benefits, and benefits in kind.

Social security contributions

Employers must contribute to the social security system (CNPS) at the following rates:

Contribution	Contribution rate (%)	Monthly ceiling (XOF)
Family allowance	5.75	70,000
Work injury	2.0 to 5.0	70,000
Retirement pension	6.6	1,647,315

WHT on public contracts for services

Any payment made by government bodies or public institutions to non-resident persons or companies for a contract for goods or services is subject to a 20% WHT, subject to DTA (*see Impôt sur les benefices non commerciaux in the Withholding taxes section*).

Resident persons or companies are not subject to this WHT, except for individual service (or goods) providers registered under the standard tax regime for small companies (*see below*).

WHT on small-size businesses

A 5% or 7.5% WHT is applicable on the remunerations paid to individual service providers registered under the standard tax regime for small companies.

A 10% WHT is applicable on payments made by government bodies or public institutions for a contract for services (or goods).

Branch income

The tax rate for branch income is the same as that for corporate income. After-tax branch earnings are subject to a 12% tax (*Impôt sur le revenu des valeurs mobilières* or IRVM) calculated on 50% of the taxable profit. This is analogous to the WHT on dividends.

Income determination

Inventory valuation

Inventory is generally stated at the lower of cost or market value. Last in first out (LIFO) and first in first out (FIFO) methods are permitted. Book and tax conformity is required.

Capital gains

Capital gains are normally taxed at full corporate rates. However, the tax on capital gains, exclusive of recaptured depreciation, can be deferred if the gain is reinvested within three years.

Dividend income

Dividends are brought into taxable income at 50% of the net amount earned by the company (after 12% WHT).

The exemption is increased to 95% for dividends received from a subsidiary if a parent company domiciled in Côte d'Ivoire owns 10% of the subsidiary.

Ivory Coast (Côte d'Ivoire)

Stock dividends

Stock dividends are unusual, but in the event they are declared, they are not taxable to the recipient.

Interest income

Interest from loans is brought into taxable income at 50% of the net amount earned by the company after 18% WHT.

Foreign income

Resident corporations are taxed on their worldwide income, except for profits derived from business conducted through a PE outside Côte d'Ivoire. Since income derived from business conducted outside Côte d'Ivoire is not taxable, no tax credit is allowed. Interest and dividends from foreign sources are entitled to certain deductions to alleviate instances of double taxation. Subject to provisions of tax treaties, no deductions or tax credits are allowed for revenue from royalties and services.

Deductions

Depreciation and depletion

Depreciation is generally computed on a straight-line basis over the useful life of the asset (e.g. 20 years for buildings, three years for automobiles). Accelerated depreciation is sometimes permitted for machinery. The following depreciation rates are generally accepted for tax purposes:

Assets	Depreciation rate (%)
Buildings	5
Machinery, equipment (rate depending on equipment)	8/10/20
Office furniture	10
Office equipment	20
Vehicles	33.3
Computing equipment	20 to 50

A time coefficient is applied to the rate of depreciation to obtain the declining balance. Depreciation rates may be amended, but only after agreement with the tax authorities.

New plants and equipment may be depreciated at twice the normal rate in the first year of use, provided they are depreciated over at least six years. Under certain circumstances, buildings used for staff housing may be depreciated at 40% of cost in the first year. Annual depreciation must be booked to preserve tax deductibility. The whole or any part of the annual charge can then be deferred in annual accounts for fiscal years showing a tax loss. Recaptured depreciation is taxed at full rates. Tax and book conformity is obligatory.

Depletion allowances, as such, do not exist, but tax incentives are available for exploration to replace depleted natural reserves.

Goodwill

Goodwill (capital gain) deriving from the transfer of assets is included in taxable profit. The gain may be exempted from the income tax basis if the taxpayer commits to reinvest the purchase price of the transferred assets plus the goodwill in the three following years.

Ivory Coast (Côte d'Ivoire)

If the reinvestment is not completed in the three years, the gain will be subject to income taxation.

Interest expenses
Interest paid to shareholders may be deducted. The maximum interest rate allowed is related to the *Banque Central des Etats de l'Afrique de l'Ouest* (BCEAO) rate plus three points. The reimbursement of the loan must take place in the five years following the loan.

Bad debt
Provisions for bad debts are deductible, provided that a minimum set of collection procedures have been engaged.

Bad debts are deductible for income tax purposes, unless the debt results from abnormal business decisions.

Charitable contributions
Charitable contributions to recognised sport and health associations are deductible.

Charitable contributions to individuals or non-recognised beneficiaries are not tax deductible.

Fines and penalties
Fines borne by corporations are not tax deductible.

Taxes
Regular taxes paid by corporations are deductible for income tax purposes.

Third party taxes (such as WHT on non-resident service providers) borne by corporations are not tax deductible.

Other significant items
In respect to legal reserves, 10% of net profit must be transferred to a reserve for legal fees until the reserve equals 5% of the paid-up share capital.

To be tax deductible, provisions must relate to existing liability or loss. General reserves are not deductible.

Net operating losses
Losses may be carried forward five years.

Losses derived from depreciation can be carried forward indefinitely.

Losses cannot be carried back.

Payments to foreign affiliates
Reasonable royalties, interest, and management and service fees paid to foreign parent companies are tax deductible. However, the deductions should not exceed 5% of the turnover and 20% of the overhead. Otherwise, the portion exceeding the ceiling is not tax deductible. The onus is on the taxpayer to prove that expenses are justified and reflect real transactions.

Ivory Coast (Côte d'Ivoire)

Group taxation

Group taxation is not permitted in Côte d'Ivoire.

Transfer pricing
Profits directly or indirectly transferred to related non-resident companies are disallowed from the income tax basis.

The tax administration may inquire on transfer pricing when local subsidiaries having most of their transactions with non-resident group companies record losses.

Transfer price documentation is not generally requested.

Thin capitalisation
The deduction of the interest of loans granted on top of the share capital by related parties is subject to restrictions (*see Interest expenses in the Deductions section*).

When, because of losses, the equity of the company is less than 50% of the share capital, the company must be recapitalised in the two following years, unless the company is dissolved.

Tax credits and incentives

Foreign tax credit
Since income derived from business conducted outside Côte d'Ivoire is not taxable, no tax credit is allowed.

Investment zones
Investment Law No. 95-620 of 3 August 1995 divides the country into two investment zones, offering incentives for up to five or eight years in each area.

The Investment Code provides for 100% tax exemption during the first three or six years (depending on the nature of the activity and the zone), then 50% and 25% progressively for the last two years of exemption. Exemption periods may be extended to complete a scheduled investment program.

Incentives are divided into two programs: 'prior declaration' for investments of less than XOF 500 million that create new activity and 'prior agreement' for investments of XOF 500 million or more that create new activity or develop an existing activity. Both programs are handled by the *Centre de Promotion des Investissements en Côte d'Ivoire* (CEPICI) and are open to all sectors except trade, public works, building construction, transportation, banking, and insurance.

Prior declaration investments may be exempt from tax on corporate income and the business franchise tax. Prior agreement investments benefit from exemptions varying with the size and nature of the project as follows:

*   Creating a new enterprise or a new activity in an existing enterprise:
    *   Investments of XOF 500 million to XOF 2 billion may be exempt from tax on corporate income, business franchise tax, and import duties and taxes (with the exception of a 5% tax on machinery, equipment, and spare parts).
    *   Investments of more than XOF 2 billion may be exempt from real estate tax, in addition to the above.

Ivory Coast (Côte d'Ivoire)

- Developing an existing activity:
  - Investments of at least XOF 500 million may be exempt from import duties and taxes (with the exception of a 5% tax on machinery, equipment, and spare parts).

These incentives may not be combined with sector-specific investment programs, such as those for mining and hydrocarbons.

Capital investment incentives

With prior approval of the tax authorities and varying with geographical location, 35% to 40% of the total investment in fixed assets related to commercial, industrial, or agricultural activity may be deducted from taxable income. The deduction is limited to 50% of taxable profits. The balance of deduction of the first year may be carried forward over the three following years.

Export incentives

No VAT is levied on export sales.

Sales and provisions of services made to export companies, which process certain farm products (i.e. cocoa, coffee, banana, hevea, and palm tree oil) and realise at least 30% of their turnover from exports, are free from VAT. The exemption is granted for the purpose of avoiding new cases of VAT credits in this line of business.

The FY12 Financial Law extended the measure to 31 December 2014.

It is also extended it to the following activities:

- The manufacturing and the sale of natural and synthetic fibres bags.
- The sale of softwood lumber and timber products by enterprises benefiting from the export authorisation granted by the Department of Water and Forestry.

Export incentives for the mining industry

During the exploration phase, investments may be exempt from payroll tax; VAT on goods and services; additional tax (on the sale of goods) on imports and purchases; all import taxes and duties, including VAT on materials, machines, and equipment used in research activities; and half of the registration duties applicable to in-kind or cash share-capital contributions.

During the production phase, mining activities may have a five-year exemption from corporate income tax and relief from all import duties, including VAT on recovered investments required for exploitation. In addition, they may be granted temporary admission of machines and equipment that facilitate research and exploitation. A tax on profit is levied as soon as investment funds are recovered. Mining enterprises may not combine these incentives with those of the Investment Code.

Export incentives for petroleum service contractors

A special and optional tax treatment applies to petroleum service contractors that meet established criteria. Corporate tax, distribution tax, payroll tax, income tax on salaries, and the tax on insurance premiums are calculated on the turnover of the contractor. The total taxes represent 5.636% of turnover. Standard rates apply for business franchise tax and social security contributions for local personnel. The exemption from customs duties and VAT for oil companies is extended to petroleum service contractors.

Ivory Coast (Côte d'Ivoire)

Withholding taxes

WHTs are levied as follows:

- *Impôt sur le revenu des valeurs mobilières* (IRVM): 12% or 18% on dividends and directors' fees.
- *Impôt sur le revenue des créances* (IRC): 18% on interest payments, reduced to 13.5% (individuals) and 16.5% (businesses) on bank deposit interest. Foreign banks are subject to 18% tax on loan interest or 9% on equipment loans with minimum three-year terms.
- *Impôt sur les benefices non commerciaux* (BNC): 25% of 80% of revenues on royalties, license fees, and management and service fees paid by Ivorian companies to foreign companies (effective rate: 20% of net amount paid). Treaties with Belgium, Canada, France, Germany, Italy, Norway, Switzerland, and the United Kingdom provide a maximum BNC rate of 10% on royalties and management fees. The tax treaty between the member states of West African Economic and Monetary Union (UEMOA) provides a maximum BNC rate of 15%.
- Interest on certificates of deposit (*bons de caisse*): 25%.

Tax administration

Taxable period
Companies are required by law to have a 31 December fiscal year-end.

Tax returns
Financial statements are filed annually, according to local generally accepted accounting principles (GAAP). The deadline for the filing is 30 April for entities with more than XOF 1 billion turnover, 30 May for entities with less than XOF 1 billion turnover, and 30 June for entities under the standard tax regime for small companies.

Payment of tax
The corporate income tax due is returned together with the annual financial statements on the dates described above.

Monthly tax returns, including the taxes withheld (on residents or non-residents), must be rendered to the tax authorities by the tenth, 15th, or the 20th day of the following month.

The tenth day of the following month is the due date for industrial companies, oil and mining companies registered with the Department of Large Taxpayers (DGE), and companies under a real tax regime.

The 20th day of the following month is the due date for service providers registered with the DGE.

The 15th day of the following month is the due date for all other taxpayers, mostly for taxpayers under the standard tax regime for small companies.

Statute of limitations
The statute of limitations covers the current year and the three prior years.

Jamaica

PwC contact

Eric Crawford
PricewaterhouseCoopers
Scotiabank Centre
Cnr. of Duke & Port Royal Street
Kingston, Jamaica
Tel: +1 876 932 8323
Email: eric.crawford@jm.pwc.com

Significant developments

Recent tax policy reform measures
The following measures were announced by the Minister of Finance and the Public
Service in the 2011/12 budget speech and became effective in May 2011:

Recovery of general consumption tax (GCT) on capital equipment
GCT registered taxpayers who incur GCT on the acquisition of machinery or equipment
costing more than 100,000 Jamaican dollars (JMD) for the purpose of their taxable
activity are now able to claim this GCT by way of input tax credit over a three-month
period instead of over a 24-month period.

Carryforward of contractors levy
Previously, contractors who suffered the 2% contractors levy on receipts could claim
a credit against their income tax liability only in the year of assessment in which the
levy is deducted. As of the financial year 2011/12, where the levy is deducted from the
contract sum and remitted to the Collector of Taxes, any amount not utilised as a credit
against income tax for that year of assessment may be carried forward to subsequent
years of assessment, not exceeding five years. Previously, there was no provision to
carry forward any levy credit not utilised.

Revision of import duty structure on motor vehicles
The rates of Common External Tariff applicable to several types of motor vehicles were
reduced as of 2 May 2011. This includes sports utility vehicles, vehicles referred to as
pick-ups, certain motor cycles, and all-terrain vehicles.

Tax administration
A series of administrative reforms aimed at enhancing the efficiency and effectiveness
of Jamaica's tax regime have been implemented. As of 1 May 2011, the Inland Revenue
Department, the Taxpayer Audit & Assessment Department, and the Tax Administration
Services Department were merged into a single department called Tax Administration
Jamaica. Jamaica Customs was separated and has been transitioned into an Executive
Agency. Additionally, the Taxpayer Appeals Department has become a Revenue Appeals
Division of the Ministry of Finance, the objective being to ensure that the reporting
structure in relation to assessments and appeals is separated.

During 2011, other administrative reforms were implemented to simplify the
remittance of payroll tax and the associated annual reports required to be filed with the
various payroll tax agencies:

- In January 2011, the remittance of payroll taxes was consolidated by the
  introduction of a single form which replaced the several forms previously required to
  remit payroll taxes on a monthly basis.

Jamaica

- In December 2011, legislation was passed to introduce a Consolidated Employers' Annual Return which is to be used by employers to submit their annual employees' information commencing in 2012. The new form replaces a number of forms, schedules, and deduction cards that were previously required to submit annual payroll returns to the various payroll tax agencies.

Other reform measures
Other reform measures included the removal of transfer tax and stamp duty on securities and a reduction in stamp duty on the refinancing and transfer of mortgages.

Taxes on corporate income

A resident corporation is taxable on its worldwide income. Non-resident companies are subject to tax on Jamaican-sourced income. Tax is imposed on certain sources of income, such as interest, dividends, royalties, and fees by way of withholding at a rate of $33^1/_3$% for corporations. Lower rates of withholding are possible, provided that the recipient is resident in a country that has concluded a double taxation treaty (DTT) with Jamaica.

Income tax at a rate of $33^1/_3$% is payable by most corporations, including Jamaican branches of foreign corporations.

Building societies (similar to Savings and Loans Associations) are taxed at the rate of 30% on their profits.

Life insurance companies are taxed at 15% on their 'investment income' net of 'management expenses', both terms of which are defined by the Income Tax Act. Additionally, 'regionalised' life insurance companies pay income tax on gross premiums (derived from life assurance, pensions, and annuity business) at the rate of 3% while others pay at the rate of 4%.

The income of certain organisations is specifically exempt from income tax. These include pension and superannuation funds and charitable organisations approved by the Commissioner General of Tax Administration Jamaica.

Local income taxes
Income tax is imposed at the national level. Income tax is not separately imposed at the local level.

Corporate residence

A corporation, wherever incorporated, is resident in Jamaica if the central management and control of its business is exercised in Jamaica. Normally, this is the case if meetings of directors and shareholders are held in Jamaica and major policy decisions of the corporation are made in Jamaica.

Permanent establishment (PE)
The term PE is not defined by local law. In the case of a treaty jurisdiction, the relevant treaty will prescribe the meaning of the term. Where a company's activities create a PE, then it must be registered for tax purposes.

Jamaica

Other taxes

General consumption tax (GCT)
The GCT is a value-added tax (VAT), and the standard rate is currently 17.5%. Higher or lower rates of GCT, however, are applicable to certain goods and services. GCT at the rate of 25% applies to the provision of telephone services and handsets, while the tax is imposed on hotels and other businesses in the tourism sector at an effective rate of approximately 10%. Supplies of electricity to residential customers (in excess of 200 KwH per month) and to commercial or industrial consumers are also subject to GCT at the rate of 10%.

GCT is also charged on imported services. Where services are imported from a person who is not resident in Jamaica, the recipient of those services is deemed to be the registered taxpayer and pays the tax chargeable on the service. This may be available as a credit in some cases against the tax payable by the recipient of the service.

The list of items and services exempt from GCT includes a wide range of basic food items, medical supplies, and other items. Certain specified drugs, as well as other items and services, are zero-rated. Supplies of electricity to residential customers up to 200 KwH per month are zero-rated for GCT purposes.

Customs duties
Customs duty is levied on the customs value of goods imported, which is determined in accordance with the World Trade Organization (WTO) rules on customs valuation. The rates are specified by a prescribed Customs Tariff, having regard (where appropriate) to the Common External Tariff agreed between Caribbean Community (CARICOM) member states.

In addition to normal customs duties, a user fee of 2% and an environmental levy of 0.5% are imposed on the value of imports. An additional 5% GCT is levied on the commercial importation of goods subject to GCT. However, certain categories of imports are excluded from this advance GCT charge. Other import duties include additional stamp duty and a standard compliance fee.

Special consumption tax (SCT)
SCT, at various rates, is applicable to some goods, such as tobacco products, liquor, motor vehicles, and petroleum products.

Real estate tax
All land in Jamaica is valued on the 'site value' or 'unimproved value'. Owners of properties valued at JMD 300,000 or less pay a flat rate of JMD 600 annually. Tax is payable at a rate of 0.75% where the property exceeds this value, in addition to the flat rate.

Transfer tax
There is a transfer tax of 4% on the market value of the asset transferred (limited to 37.5% of the capital gain derived, if any) on the transfer of land, buildings, securities, and shares. Transactions on the Jamaica Stock Exchange (JSE) are exempt from transfer tax, as are the transfer of registered corporate bonds, whether or not the company is listed on the JSE.

Stamp duty
There is stamp duty of 1% payable on the transfer/disposal of shares and 3% for real property sold/transferred. Transactions on the JSE are exempt from stamp duty, as are

Jamaica

the transfer of registered corporate bonds, whether or not the company is listed on the JSE. Stamp duty is also imposed at nominal rate of JMD 100 on instruments effecting a refinancing of an existing mortgage. Where, however, the mortgage is increased, the normal stamp duty rates shall apply to the amount by which the mortgage increased.

Annual fee

A fee ranging from JMD 1,000 to JMD 35,000 is payable on or before 1 September, depending on the aggregate value of the company's assets. The minimum fee is payable where the aggregate value of the assets is less than JMD 50,000, and the maximum fee is payable where the aggregate value of the assets is greater than JMD 100 million.

Construction operations levy

A levy of 2% of the gross amount is payable on contracts relating to construction, haulage, and tillage operations. The contractors' levy is in the nature of tax withheld at source and must be deducted by the taxpayer from the gross payment for the construction or tillage operations and paid to the Collector of Taxes within 14 days of the month in which the gross payments are made.

The levy paid is allowable as a credit against the income tax liability of the contractor in the year of assessment in which the levy is deducted, and any amount not utilised as a credit against income tax for that year of assessment may be carried forward to subsequent years of assessment, not exceeding five years.

Branch income

Branch income is taxed at the same rate as that of local corporations and on a similar basis. The transfer of profits to the head office is subject to a withholding tax (WHT) of $33\frac{1}{3}$% or at a lower treaty rate, where applicable.

A branch operation, irrespective of the nature of its business activities, is subject to Jamaican tax on income derived from the island and elsewhere. In computing the income for tax purposes, expenses incurred, wholly and exclusively for the purpose of the branch's trade, are deductible, including a reasonable proportion of head office expenses.

Transactions between the branch, its head office, and affiliates should be at arm's-length values.

Income determination

Inventory valuation

Inventories are valued at the lower of cost or market value. The Commissioner General has made no pronouncement, but last in first out (LIFO) is not generally permitted.

Any method of valuation that accords with standard accounting practice is acceptable for tax purposes, provided it is consistently applied at the beginning and end of the accounting period and it is not in contravention of the Income Tax Act.

Capital gains

There is no tax on capital gains. There is, however, a transfer tax on the market value of certain assets transferred and stamp duty payable on the transfer/disposal of shares or real property. *See the Other taxes section for more information.*

Dividend income

Ordinary dividends and non-deductible preference dividends paid to Jamaican tax residents by resident companies (whether or not they are listed on the JSE) are taxed at a zero rate. However, preference dividends that qualify as tax deductible expenses of the paying company (*see below*) are taxable in the hands of the recipient, whether or not the shares on which they are paid are listed on the JSE.

This tax-free treatment does not extend to non-resident shareholders in receipt of dividends from resident companies, and, accordingly, all dividends paid to non-resident shareholders are subject to income tax thereon at the default rate of $33^{1}/_{3}\%$ in the case of a company and 25% in the case of an individual (subject to any treaty protection or incentive relief available).

Subject to certain conditions being met, a company may claim an income tax deduction in respect of preference dividends paid during the year of assessment. However, to the extent that these preference dividends do not qualify for this income tax deduction, they will be treated in a similar manner to ordinary dividends as indicated above.

Stock dividends

Stocks issued by way of the capitalisation of retained earnings (referred to as 'bonus issues') do not create a taxable distribution in the hands of the shareholders.

J

Interest income

Interest income is included in chargeable income and is subject to tax when received. Where interest is paid by a prescribed person, tax is deducted at source at the rate of 25% (*see the Withholding taxes section for more information*). The interest payable on certain securities issued by the government of Jamaica has been designated as being exempt from tax.

Foreign income

Resident corporations are taxable in Jamaica on their worldwide gains or profits. This includes the income of a foreign branch of a Jamaican company, as well as dividends arising abroad.

Tax deferral is not permitted in Jamaica.

Deductions

Expenses are deductible to the extent that they were incurred wholly and exclusively to earn the income and are claimed in the year in which they were incurred.

Depreciation

Tax depreciation is generally computed on the reducing-balance basis over the anticipated normal working life of the asset at specified rates. An election may be made for machinery and equipment to be depreciated at higher rates on the straight-line basis.

In the year of expenditure, initial allowances are available at the rate of 20% on industrial buildings and structures and machinery and plant. Annual allowances are available as follows:

Jamaica

Assets	Basis	Rate of annual allowance (%)
Industrial buildings	Reducing-balance	5.0
Buildings for rent	Straight-line	2.5
Other buildings	Reducing-balance	2.5
Machinery and equipment (excluding computers)		Various rates
Computers	Straight-line	22.5

Generally, capital gains on depreciable property are not taxed. However, a recharge limited to the extent of the depreciation allowed (balancing charge) is taxable. Tax depreciation may not conform to book depreciation.

Investment allowance
Investment allowances (ranging from 20% to 40%, depending on the type of industry) are available on certain plant, machinery, and buildings used in basic and qualifying industries. As investment allowances are not taken into account in calculating the tax written down value of the assets, the company effectively receives 120% or 140% of the asset's cost as tax depreciation.

Qualifying industries include manufacturing, construction, electricity undertakings, warehousing/cold storage, dock operations, and agriculture.

Accelerated depreciation
New machinery and plant acquired by a 'qualifying business' may be fully depreciated in the year of purchase instead of over the anticipated normal working life of the asset. This allowance is given in lieu of all other capital allowances and is not available for certain business activities. A qualifying business is one so designated by the Minister of Industry, Investment, and Commerce (MIIC).

Provision also exists for increased depreciation on machinery and equipment used for more than one shift in certain qualifying industries.

Goodwill
The amortisation or write-off of goodwill is not an allowable deduction.

Start-up expenses
The costs of incorporation and other expenses incurred in connection with establishing a business are not deductible against income.

Interest expenses
A deduction is available for interest that is paid on capital employed in acquiring the income. Additionally, where interest is paid to a non-resident, tax must be withheld and remitted to the tax authorities in order to secure a deduction.

Bad debts
A deduction is available in respect of specific debts that become bad during the year of assessment.

Charitable contributions
Approved donations (not exceeding 5% of taxable income) to certain qualified charities and educational institutions are deductible.

Foreign exchange gains/losses

Foreign exchange gains and losses arising from trading are included in or deducted from chargeable income when realised, regardless of whether they are converted to Jamaican dollars. Foreign exchange gains and losses arising on capital assets are not taxable or allowable for tax purposes; however, where they pertain to fixed assets, on realisation, they may become part of the underlying acquisition cost and tax depreciation computed thereon.

Fines and penalties

Fines, penalties, and interest arising from tax arrears are not deductible.

Taxes

Taxes on income are not deductible. Additionally, GCT, contractors' levy, transfer tax, and stamp duty incurred on capital assets, as well as input tax credits for GCT purposes, are generally disregarded for income tax purposes. Other taxes, such as property tax, payroll taxes, and other business taxes, are deductible, to the extent that they were incurred to earn the income.

Net operating losses

Losses incurred may be carried forward indefinitely until fully utilised. There are provisions designed to disallow the deduction of such losses where the company that has accumulated them is sold under certain circumstances.

Tax losses are not available for carryback.

Payments to foreign affiliates

Royalties, management fees, and interest charges paid to foreign affiliates are deductible to the extent that these payments are made at arm's-length rates. WHT should be paid in respect of such services, normally at $33^{1}/_{3}\%$ where payment is to a company and 25% in the case of individuals, unless a lower rate is provided for under a DTT. Furthermore, interest paid to non-residents is not deductible until the WHT is remitted.

Group taxation

Group taxation is not permitted in Jamaica.

Transfer pricing

There are no specific transfer pricing rules in Jamaica. Transactions between connected parties are accepted if they are conducted on an arm's-length basis. The Commissioner General, however, has the power to restate the value of such transactions if a view is formed that they are conducted at artificially high/low consideration, for the purpose of avoiding tax.

Thin capitalisation

There are no provisions for thin capitalisation in the tax laws of Jamaica.

Controlled foreign companies (CFCs)

There is no CFC regime in Jamaica.

Jamaica

Tax credits and incentives

A number of incentive laws grant approved persons relief from taxation for a specified number of years.

Specific incentives are set out under the following acts:

- The Export Industry (Encouragement) Act.
- The Industrial Incentives Act.
- The Industrial Incentives (Factory Construction) Act.
- The Jamaica Export Free Zones Act.
- The Hotels (Incentives) Act.
- The Resort Cottages Incentives Act.
- The International Finance Companies (Income Tax Relief) Act.
- The Income Tax Act (Agricultural & Venture Capital Incentives).
- The Urban Renewal (Tax Relief) Act.
- The Motion Picture Encouragement Act.
- The Shipping Act.
- The Factory Construction Act.

The incentives offered under the Industrial Incentives Act, the Export Industry (Encouragement) Act, and those available for the production of goods under the Jamaica Export Free Zones Act are to be phased out, given Jamaica's commitments under the World Trade Organization (WTO) agreement. This was expected to have been phased out by 1 January 2003. An extension of time has been granted for implementation until the end of 2013, with a two year phase-out period.

The Export Industry (Encouragement) Act (EIEA)

The incentives provided under The Export Industry (Encouragement) Act are available to companies incorporated in Jamaica whose products are exclusively for sale outside of Jamaica and CARICOM. The company must be declared an 'approved export manufacturer' in relation to an 'approved export product' by the MIIC. The incentive is also available to companies that are designated as 'partial exporters'.

Benefits available under the EIEA include relief from income tax on export profits and duty exemption on machinery and equipment, consumer goods, raw material, packaging material, and imports for the repair and maintenance of the factory. Although the benefits provided under the EIEA are initially allowed for a specified period, the MIIC has the authority to extend the incentive period by order.

The Jamaica Export Free Zones Act

The Jamaica Export Free Zones Act offers concessions to manufacturers who can operate within a designated free zone area as well as in stand-alone free zones approved by the MIIC. Exporters benefiting from this scheme obtain 100% relief from income tax; duty exemption on capital goods, consumer goods, raw material, or imports for the construction, extension, and repair of free-zone premises.

Companies approved to operate in one of Jamaica's free zones must be registered or incorporated in Jamaica under the Companies Act. They must also obtain approval from the Jamaica Free Zone Council to undertake an approved activity.

The Hotels (Incentives) Act

The Hotels (Incentives) Act provides that an approved hotel enterprise or approved extension is entitled to relief in respect of profits or gains arising from an approved hotel enterprise or extension during the concession period, which is usually ten years. Approved hotel enterprises or extensions also benefit from exemption from customs duty and GCT on building material imported for the construction or repair of the approved hotel enterprise or approved extension, as well as certain equipment and supplies imported to outfit the hotel. An approved hotel enterprise or approved extension is so designated by the Minister of Tourism.

The Act also provides exemption from income tax on dividends to Jamaican-resident shareholders received from an approved hotel enterprise/extension as well as to non-resident shareholders who are not liable to income tax on the dividends in their country of residence.

The Urban Renewal (Tax Relief) Act
The Urban Renewal (Tax Relief) Act provides tax incentives to persons approved under the Act in connection with undertaking programmes of development in areas designated as special development areas, with a view to improving or restoring them. The tax incentive provides certain tax benefits, including relief from income tax on rental income and interest earned by an investor in an Urban Renewal Bond. There is also exemption from stamp duty and transfer tax on the transfers of property.

As of December 2010, an increased tax credit of 33⅓% (up from 25%) of expenditure on capital improvement works in a designated special development area (e.g. Downtown Kingston) is available. In addition, lessees of the improved properties who satisfy certain criteria are now able to claim a tax deduction of double the rental paid.

Non-resident deposits
Non-residents who place deposits with Jamaican banks can earn interest free of Jamaican tax in certain circumstances. The deposits may be designated in foreign currency or Jamaican dollars.

Employee Share Ownership Plan (ESOP)
Certain tax benefits accrue to employees and employers in respect of contributions to an approved ESOP as well as the allocation of shares from such plans.

Foreign tax credit
The avoidance of double taxation is achieved by means of foreign tax credits available under most tax treaties or by means of deduction in the case of the CARICOM treaty. Under the provisions of the Income Tax Act, a foreign tax credit is also available to companies in Jamaica that have paid or are liable to Commonwealth Income Tax. Where recourse cannot be had through either of these methods, by convention, partial relief by way of expense deduction is granted against income for the foreign tax.

Withholding taxes

The Jamaican Income Tax Act refers to deduction at source and not to withholding. The following references are to deduction at source. If it is proved that this exceeds the tax actually payable, refunds are made.

'Prescribed persons', primarily financial institutions, are required to withhold tax at source at a rate of 25% on interest income earned on investment instruments (subject to any lower rate as prescribed in a DTT). The Income Tax Act has been amended to provide a wider definition of the term 'interest'. 'Prescribed persons', as defined, include the Accountant General; banks operating under the Banking Act or the Bank

Jamaica

of Jamaica Act; institutions operating under the Financial Institutions Act; building societies; societies registered under the Industrial and Provident Societies Act, unless certain conditions are met; the Ministry of Finance & the Public Service; life insurance companies; companies registered under the Companies Act in which the government or an agency of the government holds more than 50% of the ordinary shares and which issues interest bearing securities; issuers of commercial paper; unit trust management companies; and any person who is connected with any of the persons mentioned above (with the exception of the Accountant General).

Generally, all WHTs, including taxes withheld from dividend, interest, royalties, and fees must be remitted to the Inland Revenue Department within 14 days of the end of the month in which the payment is made in order to avoid the imposition of interest and penalties.

	WHT (%)				
	Dividends				
Recipient	Portfolio	Substantial holdings	Interest (1)	Royalties	Management fees
Resident corporations	0	0	25 (3)	0	0
Resident individuals	0 (2)	0 (2)	25 (3)	0	0
Non-treaty:					
Non-resident corporations	33⅓	33⅓	33⅓	33⅓	33⅓
Non-resident individuals	25	25	25	25	25
Treaty:					
Canada	15	22.5	15	10	12.5
CARICOM countries	0 (4)	0 (4)	15 (4)	15 (4)	15
China, P.R	5 (5)	5 (5)	7.5 (5)	10	33⅓
Denmark	15	10 (6)	12.5	10	10
France	15	10 (6)	10	10	10
Germany	15	10 (6)	12.5 (7)	10	10
Israel	22.5 (8)	15	15	10	33⅓
Norway	15 (5)	15 (5)	12.5	10	10
Spain	10 (5)	5 (5)	10	10	10
Sweden	22.5 (5, 8)	15 (5)	12.5	10	10
Switzerland	15 (5, 6)	10 (5)	10	10	10
United Kingdom	15 (5, 6)	22.5 (5)	12.5	10	12.5
United States	15 (5, 6)	10 (5)	12.5	10	33⅓ (9)

Notes

1. No WHT is applicable where the interest is paid by a local bank or financial institution to an approved overseas organisation, that is, a foreign bank or financial institution to an approved overseas organisation approved by the Ministry of Finance & the Public Service.
2. Tax is withheld at the rate of 0% as of 1 January 2010 where an ordinary dividend is paid by a company resident in Jamaica to a resident shareholder.
3. Tax is deducted from interest paid to Jamaican residents if payment is made by a prescribed person.
4. Rates apply only to specified member states.
5. The lower treaty rates do not apply if the recipient has a permanent establishment (PE) in the other territory that is 'effectively connected' with the company paying the dividend.
6. A rate of 15% applies to an individual regardless of shareholding.

Jamaica

7. Reduced to 10% if received by a bank recognised as a banking institution under the laws of that state.
8. A rate of 22.5% applies to an individual regardless of the shareholding.
9. Nil in the absence of a PE.

A WHT rate of 25% is required to be applied in respect of interest paid or credited by prescribed persons. However, certain categories of interest income earned on long-term savings accounts (LSAs) were made exempt from tax, including:

- Interest paid or credited in respect of investments or deposits made by individuals with prescribed persons if:
  - the deposit remains a minimum of five years without any withdrawal from the principal sum invested
  - the deposit or investment (other than interest accrued or credited) does not exceed JMD 1 million in any year
  - the account is not transferable, except on the death or bankruptcy of the depositor or investor, and
  - not more than 75% of the interest accrued in any year is withdrawn during the year.
- Benefits derived from investments in certain life insurance policies may also be exempt from income tax if specified criteria are satisfied.

Tax administration

Jamaica has established the following departments to handle tax administration:

- The recently formed Tax Administration Jamaica (TAJ) integrates the functions which were previously undertaken by a number of different departments. These functions include compliance and tax collection, administrative and legal support, audit and assessment of income tax, general consumption tax, stamp duty, and transfer tax. The Commissioner General has responsibility for the direction, supervision, and administration of TAJ and is supported in undertaking this role by several Deputy Commissioners General.
- The former Taxpayer Appeals Department (TAD), which recently became a Revenue Appeals Division of the Ministry of Finance, processes appeals to decisions made by TAJ.
- Jamaica Customs administers taxes at the port of entry.

There is also a Financial Investigations Division in the Ministry of Finance which investigates customs breaches and fraudulent acts in respect of tax legislation.

Taxable period

A corporation is subject to tax on its income for a calendar year. However, where the Commissioner General of TAJ is satisfied that a corporation normally prepares financial statements to a date other than 31 December, the company may be permitted to use the profits of its own financial year rather than the calendar year as the basis of assessment. The basis period should not exceed 12 months; however, a company wishing to file its income tax return for a period exceeding this period must obtain the approval of TAJ.

Tax returns

Income tax returns are due for filing by 15 March in the year following the year of assessment and are based on a system of self-assessment of the tax payable.

Jamaica

Payment of tax

Tax is payable in quarterly instalments on the 15th day of March, June, September, and December of each tax year. Quarterly instalments are based on an estimate of the year's liability or the actual tax payable for the previous year. The balance of income tax payable for a taxation year, after deduction of the instalments of estimated tax, is due on 15 March of the following year. Interest is charged on unpaid tax at a rate of 20% per annum while the amount remains unpaid. A penalty of up to 50% may also be imposed if TAJ issues an assessment.

TAJ has implemented an electronic tax system that taxpayers may use to file various tax returns and remit taxes.

Tax assessments and audits

The Commissioner General is empowered to conducts audits on selected tax returns or to assess a taxpayer for additional tax at any time prior to the expiration of the statute of limitation, which is six years, except in certain cases. Tax audits can be carried out whether or not notices of assessment have been issued. Tax assessments may be raised where the Commissioner General is of the opinion that a taxpayer has been assessed for less tax than the taxpayer ought to have been charged, or where the taxpayer failed to file a tax return.

Other issues

Corporate tax calculation - Calendar year 2012

	JMD	JMD
Net profit before taxation		10,000,000
Add:		
Depreciation charged in the financial statements	500,000	
Interest payable, 2012 - accrued (1)	12,000	
Interest receivable, 2011 - now received (1)	7,000	
Donations not approved	15,000	
Subscriptions disallowable	5,000	
Interest for late payment of income tax	4,000	
Legal fees re increase in share capital	21,000	
Bad debts - increase in general provision (2)	50,000	
Balancing charge (3)	7,500	
Capital expenditure charged in the financial statements	120,500	742,000
Less:		
Interest payable, 2011 - now paid (1)	20,000	
Interest receivable, 2012 - accrued (1)	17,000	
Gain on disposal of fixed assets	18,000	
Losses carried forward from year of assessment 2011	14,000	
Capital allowances (4)	455,000	(524,000)
Taxable income		10,218,000
Income tax payable at 0% (dividends from ordinary shares of Jamaican-resident companies)	2,000,000	(2,000,000)

Jamaica

	JMD	JMD
Net taxable income		8,218,000
Income tax payable at 33⅓%		2,739,333
Less:		
Estimated (advance) tax payments	2,100,000	
Foreign tax credit	11,000	
Tax deducted from local bank interest	3,833	(2,114,833)
Net tax payable by 15 March 2013		624,500

Notes

1. Interest paid/received is dealt with on the cash basis, hence the adjustments for the amount receivable/payable.
2. Reserve for specific bad debts is allowed.
3. Recapture of excess tax depreciation is allowed.
4. Tax depreciation is granted in lieu of book depreciation.

J

Japan

PwC contact

Kazuya Miyakawa
Zeirishi-Hojin PricewaterhouseCoopers
Kasumigaseki Building 15 FL
2-5, Kasumigaseki 3-chome
Chiyoda-ku, Tokyo 100-6015
Japan
Tel: +81 3 5251 2400
Email: kazuya.miyakawa@jp.pwc.com

Significant developments

2012 Tax Reform

The 2012 tax reform bill was passed on 30 March 2012 and became effective as of 1 April 2012. The key changes in the Japanese corporate tax system included in this tax reform were as follows:

- The deductible portion of a corporation's net interest expense to a related party will be restricted to 50% of the adjusted income. The net interest is calculated as interest expense to related parties less corresponding interest income. The adjusted income is defined as taxable income, adding back interest expense, depreciation expense, and exempted dividend income but excluding extraordinary income or loss. This rule will be applicable for tax years beginning on or after 1 April 2013. *See the Income determination section for more information.*
- Prior to the 2012 tax reform, qualifying research and development (R&D) expenses were allowed for taxpayers to claim an R&D tax credit to offset up to 40% of a corporation's tax liability. This preferential tax treatment was amended so that the R&D tax credit may only offset up to 30% of the corporate tax liability, effective for tax years beginning on or after 1 April 2012. *See the Tax credits and incentives section for more information.*

Special Restoration Tax Law

In the Special Restoration Tax Law, a temporary surtax system was introduced to income taxation and corporate taxation. The surtax rate is 10% of corporation tax and 2.1% of income tax. The corporation surtax is applied for three years from the first tax year that begins during the period between 1 April 2012 and 31 March 2015, and the income surtax is applied for 25 years from year 2013. Due to the introduction of the surtax, combined with the decreased corporate tax rate under the 2011 tax reform, the effective corporate tax rate is decreased by approximately 2.6% for the first three years. *See the Taxes on corporate income section for more information.*

Tohoku Earthquake and special tax legislation

On 27 April 2011, special national tax laws to help deal with the Tohoku Earthquake, including associated amendments to the local tax laws, were promulgated and immediately became effective ('Tohoku Legislation'). These tax laws are intended to provide special tax relief for affected individuals or corporations.

Further special tax relief for restoration of the affected area was added to the above Tohoku Legislation, was promulgated, and became effective on 14 December 2011. *See the Tax credits and incentives section for more information.*

Taxes on corporate income

A domestic corporation in Japan is taxed on its worldwide income. A foreign corporation is taxed only on its Japan-source income.

Corporation tax

The corporation tax rates are provided in the table below. While they were reduced, based on the December 2011 Tax Reform, for fiscal years beginning 1 April 2012, a temporary surtax of 10% is being charged, by the enactment of the Special Restoration Tax Law, to the taxpayer of corporation tax for three years from the first tax year that begins during the period between 1 April 2012 and 31 March 2015.

Company size and income	Corporation tax rate (%)		Corporation surtax (2)
	Fiscal years beginning before 1 April 2012	Fiscal years beginning on or after 1 April 2012	
Paid-in capital of over 100 million Japanese yen (JPY).	30.0	25.5	10% of the corporation tax before certain tax credit etc.
Paid-in capital of JPY 100 million or less, except for a company wholly owned by a company which has paid-in capital of JPY 500 million or more:			
First JPY 8 million per annum.	18.0	15.0 (1)	
Over JPY 8 million per annum.	30.0	25.5	

Notes

1. This is a temporary rate, which, if not extended by legislation, will revert to a 19% rate during fiscal years beginning on or after 1 April 2012 but prior to 1 April 2015.
2. The surtax applies to the three year period from the first tax year that begins during the period between 1 April 2012 and 31 March 2015.

Standard enterprise tax (and Special Local Corporate Tax)

Enterprise tax is imposed on a corporation's income allocated to each prefecture. This allocation is generally made on the basis of the number of employees.

The standard rates of enterprise tax, including a Special Local Corporate Tax, are shown below.

Taxable base	Enterprise tax (%)	Special Local Corporate Tax
First JPY 4 million per annum	2.7	81% of the current enterprise tax (see the immediate left column)
Next JPY 4 million per annum	4.0	
Over JPY 8 million per annum	5.3	

If the paid-in capital of a corporation is JPY 10 million or more and the corporation has places of business in more than two prefectures, the graduated rates above are not applicable.

For utilities and insurance companies, the standard tax rate is shown as follows:

Japan

Taxable base	Enterprise tax (%)	Special Local Corporate Tax
Net revenue (net utility charges or net insurance premiums)	0.7	81% of the current enterprise tax (*see the immediate left column*)

Size-based enterprise tax (and Special Local Corporate Tax)

Instead of the above general enterprise tax, a 'size-based' enterprise tax (*Gaikei Hyojun Kazei*) is applied to a company whose paid-in capital is more than JPY 100 million as of the year end.

Factors such as the size of a corporation's personnel costs and its capital (the amount of paid-in capital) will determine the additional amount of tax payable. The existing profit-based enterprise tax will also continue to apply at the tax rates indicated below. Therefore, a loss company in Japan may be required to pay tax based on value-added activities and the corporation's paid-in capital. The applicable standard rates are shown as follows:

Taxable base	Tax rate (%)	Special Local Corporate Tax
Profit-based tax:		148% of the current enterprise tax (*see the immediate left column*)
First JPY 4 million per annum	1.5	
Next JPY 4 million per annum	2.2	
Over JPY 8 million per annum	2.9	
Additional value-based tax	0.48	N/A
Capital-based tax	0.2	N/A

Inhabitant's tax

Inhabitant's tax is imposed on a corporation's income allocated to each prefecture and city (municipal borough). The allocation is generally made on the basis of the number of employees, in the same way as enterprise tax.

The standard tax rate is 5% as prefectural tax and 12.3% as municipal tax. However, the tax rate may be increased up to 6% for prefectural tax and 14.7% for municipal tax, depending upon the determination of each local government.

In addition to the above, inhabitant's tax is imposed on a per capita basis, in the range from JPY 70,000 (in the case that the amount of paid-in capital is JPY 10 million or less, and the number of employees in each prefecture and city is 50 or less) to JPY 3.8 million (in the case that the amount of paid-in capital is over JPY 5 billion and the number of employees in each prefecture and city is over 50). The inhabitant's tax amount is determined by the local government by the factors of paid-in capital and the number of employees.

Effective tax rate

The total corporate income tax burden (i.e. effective tax rate) is in the range of 40.69% to 42.05% (in the case of a corporation located in the Tokyo Metropolitan Area) depending upon the size of a company's paid-in capital. Since enterprise tax is deductible, the effective tax rate is less than the total of the statutory rates of corporation tax, inhabitant's tax, and enterprise tax.

In consequence of the permanent reduction of corporation tax rate and the introduction of temporary surtax mentioned above, the effective tax rate will be altered hereafter. The following is the summary of the effective applicable tax rate in the case of a large corporation operating in Tokyo (taking no thought of an additional-value-based tax and capital-based tax out of the enterprise tax above):

Tax year	Effective corporation tax rate (%)	
	SMEs	Large corporations
Beginning on or before 31 March 2012	42.05	40.69
Beginning between 1 April 2012 and 31 March 2015	39.43	38.01
Beginning on or after 1 April 2015	37.12	35.64

Corporate residence

Domestic and foreign corporation
A company incorporated under the laws of Japan is a domestic corporation. The nationality of its shareholders or place of central management is not relevant.

A corporation other than a domestic corporation is regarded as a foreign corporation.

Permanent establishment (PE)
Under domestic tax law, the scope of Japan-source income in respect of which a foreign corporation is taxable depends upon the type of taxable presence that it has in Japan. The types of taxable presence that a foreign corporation may have in Japan include the following:

- Branch, factory and other fixed places in which business is conducted in Japan, mine, quarry, building for rent, etc. but exclude a specified place used only for the business of purchasing assets and for keeping them (Direct PE).
- Construction, installation, assembly project, or supervisory services related thereto for a period of greater than one year.
- Certain agents (Agent PE), as follows:
  - A person in Japan who has an authority to conclude contracts for a foreign corporation (excluding contracts to purchase assets) and exercises such authority continuously (Contracting Agent).
  - A person in Japan who keeps for a foreign corporation a certain quantity of assets sufficient to meet ordinary demand from the foreign corporation's customers and delivers the said assets to the customers according to their requirements (Fills Order Agent).
  - A person in Japan who, solely or principally for or on behalf one foreign corporation, habitually performs an important part of solicitation of orders, negotiations, or other acts leading up to the conclusion of contracts with respect to the business of the foreign person (Secure Order Agent).

As a matter of law, the articles of Japan's tax treaties have precedence over domestic tax law. In general, there are no significant differences between the definitions of PE under domestic tax law and Japan's tax treaties. However, once a PE has been established for a foreign corporation under domestic law, all Japan-source income is taxable to the PE (as opposed to just income 'attributable to' the PE, as is the case under most treaties).

Japan

Other taxes

Consumption tax

Consumption tax (value-added tax or VAT) is levied when a business enterprise transfers goods, provides services, or imports goods into Japan. The applicable rate is 5%. Exports and certain services to non-residents are taxed at a zero rate. Specified transactions, such as sales or lease of land, sales of securities, and provision of public services, are not subject to taxation.

Consumption tax paid by the business enterprise shall be refundable by filing the consumption tax return to the extent that such transaction is recorded in the accounting book.

Customs duty

A customs duty is levied on imported goods based on the custom tariff table.

Excise taxes

Excise taxes were abolished by introduction of consumption tax.

Fixed assets tax

The annual fixed assets tax is levied by the local tax authorities on real property and depreciable fixed assets used for business purposes. Real property is taxed at 1.7% (standard rate including city planning tax) of the value appraised by the local tax authorities. The depreciable fixed assets tax is assessed at 1.4% of cost after statutory depreciation.

Stamp duty

A stamp duty is levied on certain documents prepared in Japan. The tax amount is generally determined based on the amount stated in the document.

Registration and licence tax

Registration and licence tax is levied where certain property is registered, at a rate from 0.2% to 2% of the taxable basis. The taxable basis depends upon the property being registered (e.g. the amount of paid-in capital registered by a company or the value of real estate as assessed by local tax authorities).

Family corporation tax

If an individual shareholder together with their family members own, either directly or indirectly, more than 50% of the total issued shares or voting rights of a Japanese corporation, the corporation is treated as a family corporation (with the exception of corporations with paid in capital of JPY 100 million or less) and is subject to the family corporation tax in addition to corporation tax.

A family corporation is liable for an additional tax at the rates shown below on its undistributed current earnings in excess of specified limits.

Taxable undistributed current earnings	Family corporation tax rate (%)
First JPY 30 million per annum	10
Next JPY 70 million per annum	15
Over JPY 100 million per annum	20

Business premises tax

Business premises tax is levied and designated by each city in Japan, such as Tokyo, Osaka, Nagoya, Fukuoka, and other cities with a population of more than 300,000. A company that uses business premises in excess of 1,000 square metres and/or has more than 100 employees in a designated city is responsible to pay this tax based on the usage of the business (JPY 600 per square metre) and gross payroll (0.25% of gross payroll).

Branch income

Branch profits are taxed in the same manner as corporate profits. However, the family corporation tax does not apply to a branch of a foreign corporation. In addition, no withholding tax (WHT) is imposed on the repatriation of branch profits to the home office.

Income determination

The taxable income of a corporation is the aggregate income from all sources. There is no specific requirement to differentiate between the types of income. In principle, accounting for tax purposes follows generally accepted accounting principles in Japan, and income of a corporation is determined on an accrual basis.

Inventory valuation

Inventory cost should be determined by applying one of the following methods accepted for corporate tax purposes: actual individual cost, first in first out (FIFO), weighted average, moving average, most recent retail, selling price reduction, and lower of cost or market. However, the method of writing down inventory to market was abolished for accounting periods starting on or after 1 April 2011. The method of adding back the credited reserve amount in full to the income in the following period still remains.

Capital gains

Capital gains and losses are classified as ordinary income and losses respectively.

Under certain circumstances (e.g. qualified reinvestment, exchange property), taxes generally levied on capital gains may be deferred (i.e. provided rollover relief) as long as certain requirements are met. A special relief is available in the case of expropriation of real property by either the national or local government.

The recognition of capital gains or losses from the transfer of certain assets between group companies are to be deferred until the asset is transferred to another group company or a non-group company.

Dividend income

Dividends received from a Japanese corporation are excluded from taxable income for corporate income tax purposes, provided that the recipient corporation owns 25% or more of the shares in the dividend-paying corporation. If a corporation owns less than 25% of the shares in the dividend-paying corporation, 50% of the dividends received from the dividend-paying corporation are excluded from taxable income.

Interest expense which is allocable as an investment cost of the shares that generate the dividend income effectively reduces the amount of dividend income. Note that this rule is not applicable to dividends between 100% group companies.

Japan

95% of dividends received by a company from a foreign company in which it has held at least 25% of the outstanding shares for a continuous period of six months or more, ending on the date on which the dividend is declared, can be excluded from the company's taxable income.

If the foreign company is resident in a country with which Japan has concluded a tax treaty for the avoidance of double taxation, and such treaty provides for the allowance of an indirect foreign tax credit for taxes paid by the foreign company on the profits out of which the dividend is paid where the company holds a certain percentage of the foreign company's outstanding shares (e.g. 10% based on the tax treaty between the United States and Japan), that percentage will apply for the purpose of determining the availability of the above exemption to the extent that it is lower than 25%.

The WHT for dividends is applicable at a rate of 7% (15% on and after 1 January 2014) or 20% depending on the type of stock from which the dividends were received, and a tax credit may also be available for such WHT. The WHT is subject to the income surtax of 2.1%, which is levied for the income earned for the period from 1 January 2013 through 31 December 2037.

Interest income
Interest received is included in taxable income. The WHT for interest is applicable at a rate of 20% (15% national tax and 5% local tax) and a tax credit may be available for such WHT. As with dividend income, the WHT is subject to the income surtax of 2.1%, which is levied for the income earned for the period from 1 January 2013 through 31 December 2037.

Foreign income
A Japanese corporation is subject to Japanese corporate income taxes on its worldwide income. However, to avoid double taxation of foreign-source income, Japanese corporations are allowed to claim a tax credit against corporation and inhabitant's taxes for foreign income taxes paid directly. *See Foreign tax credit in the Tax credits and incentives section for more information.*

Undistributed profits of a foreign subsidiary (i.e. controlled foreign company [CFC]) located in a tax haven are included in the Japanese parent company's taxable income under certain conditions. *See Anti-tax haven (CFC) rules in the Group taxation section for more information.*

Deductions

Depreciation and amortisation
Depreciation is deductible in the calculation of taxable income for corporation tax purposes. Depreciable assets include tangible property (e.g. buildings, attachments to buildings, structures, machinery and equipment). Certain intangible assets are also eligible for amortisation (e.g. goodwill, patents and trademarks).

With regard to depreciation methods, a taxpayer may adopt one of the allowable methods for each of the types of depreciable property. Tangible property is generally depreciated using either the straight-line method or the declining-balance method. Intangible property is generally amortised under the straight-line method.

Useful lives for assets are set forth on the table in detail. For reference, the following is the brief table of useful lives for typical assets.

Types of assets	Useful lives (years)
Concrete buildings	21 to 50 (depending on uses)
Metal building	12 to 38 (depending on uses)
Electrical facilities and lighting	15
Heating and air conditioning	15
Motor vehicles	3 to 6 (depending on uses)
Personal computers	4
Digital telephone equipment	6
Machinery and equipment	3 to 22 (depending on uses)
Patents	8
Software	3 or 5 (depending on uses)

Start-up expenses
Start-up expenses, such as corporation organisation costs and opening costs (costs to begin business after the corporation is established), are treated as deferred assets and allowed to be amortised on a voluntary basis.

Interest expenses
Interest expenses on borrowing are deductible in the calculation of taxable income in principle. However, the interest payment to related parties in the corporate group may be disallowed to be deducted to some extent in certain cases. See 'Thin capitalisation' and 'Interest expense deduction limitation' in the Group taxation section.

Reserves
Reserves recorded in the books of accounts, except for reserves for doubtful receivables and return of goods not sold, are not deductible for corporate tax purposes.

Reserve for doubtful receivables
The deductibility of a reserve for doubtful receivables is limited by the following two components: (i) an estimate of irrecoverable amounts from a debtor and (ii) a calculation of the limit in the aggregate based on either the actual historical bad debt percentage or statutory percentage (reduced for large corporations), excluding the irrecoverable amount of receivable in (i) above.

Per the December 2011 Tax Reform, the reserve for doubtful receivables is abolished, except for SMEs, banks, insurance companies, and other similar financial corporations. The abolishment is phased in over four years, as follows:

Applicable tax years	% of the deductible amount (100% = deductible amount before 2011 tax reform)
Beginning between 1 April 2012 and 31 March 2013	75
Beginning between 1 April 2013 and 31 March 2014	50
Beginning between 1 April 2014 and 31 March 2015	25
Beginning on or after 1 April 2015	0

Reserve for return of goods not sold
A deductible reserve for return of goods not sold is available to corporations such as publishers, wholesalers of books, and others, provided that the corporation sells the merchandise under an unconditional repurchase agreement.

Japan

Charitable contributions

Except for certain designated donations, the tax deduction for charitable contributions is limited to certain amounts (updated for the December 2011 Tax Reform), as follows:

Donation	Tax year beginning before 1 April 2012	Tax year beginning on or after 1 April 2012
General donation	((0.25% of capital plus capital surplus) + (2.5% of income)) x 1/2	((0.25% of capital plus capital surplus) + (2.5% of income)) x 1/4
Donation made to designated public purpose companies	((0.25% of capital plus capital surplus) + (5.0% of income)) x 1/2	((0.375% of capital plus capital surplus) + (6.25% of income)) x 1/2

Donations subject to this limitation include economic benefits considered to be given as a subsidy. Donations to foreign affiliates are not fully deductible.

In the case that a donation occurs between group companies (as defined), there will be no tax implications for either the donor or donee (i.e. no deduction for the donor and no taxation for the donee).

Directors' remuneration

The remuneration paid to directors is deductible only in the following three cases:

- Fixed monthly payments.
- Fixed payments in accordance with an advance notice to the tax office.
- Performance bonuses paid in proportion to the company's earnings to directors who engage in the operation of the company's business, to the extent that certain requirements are met.

If the amount of remuneration is deemed unreasonable by the tax authority, only the reasonable amount is deductible for tax purposes.

Entertainment expenses

In principle, entertainment expenses are not deductible for tax purposes. However, an SME, defined as a company with paid-in capital of JPY 100 million or less (except for a company wholly owned by a company which has paid-in capital of JPY 500 million or more after the group taxation regime is effective) may take a tax deduction up to the smaller of 90% of the actual disbursement for the entertainment expense or JPY 5.4 million (90% of JPY 6 million). With regard to expenses for eating and drinking, a company may deduct such expenses up to JPY 5,000 per person (excluding expenditures for internal purposes) for tax purposes.

Fines and penalties

Fines and penalties are not deductible.

Taxes

Enterprise tax and business premises tax are deductible in the calculation of the taxable income for corporation tax purposes on a cash basis. However, corporation tax and inhabitant's tax are not deductible. Fixed assets tax and other taxes are deductible, when assessed. Foreign income taxes also may be deductible if the Japanese corporation does not elect to claim a foreign tax credit.

Net operating losses

For corporate income tax and enterprise tax purposes (indirectly for inhabitant's tax purposes), a tax loss can be carried forward to offset future income in the case that a taxpayer files a 'blue form' tax return (*see Tax returns in the Tax administration section*) or if the tax loss is incurred as a result of certain disaster events.

Per the December 2011 Tax Reform, the use of carried forward net operating losses is limited to 80% of current taxable income, effective for tax years beginning on or after 1 April 2012. Such limitation does not apply to SMEs and certain 'investment vehicle' corporations. However, the period within which net operating losses can be carried forward is extended from seven years to nine years for the losses incurred in the tax year ending on or after 1 April 2008 on condition that taxpayers maintain their books and records in which net operating losses were recognised.

	Fiscal year beginning before 1 April 2012	Fiscal year beginning on or after 1 April 2012
SMEs and certain 'investment vehicle' corporations		
Deductible losses against taxable income	100%	100%
Carryforward years	7 years	9 years
Corporations other than above		
Deductible losses against taxable income	100%	80%
Carryforward years	7 years	9 years

Where there is a change in ownership of a corporation followed by certain events, such as the cessation of business or a significant change in its business within a five-year period following a business acquisition, the utilisation of its tax loss is restricted.

Carryback of tax losses is generally available for one year for national corporation tax purposes. This carryback rule is suspended until the fiscal year ending 31 March 2014 (except in specified circumstances, e.g. year of liquidation). However, a SME can apply a tax loss recognised in a fiscal year ending on or after 1 February 2009.

No carryback of losses is allowed for enterprise tax and inhabitant's tax.

Payments to foreign affiliates

In order to support a deduction in Japan for expenses incurred by a foreign affiliate and charged to a Japanese corporation, in general, it should be demonstrated that the service arrangement between the foreign affiliate and the Japanese corporation satisfies arm's-length criteria for purposes of Japan's transfer pricing laws and regulations.

Generally, fees that are paid by a Japanese subsidiary to a foreign affiliate should be deductible for Japanese tax purposes if the following conditions are met:

• The services should have the same character as services which take place between non-related companies or such services are essential to Japan's activities.
• There is a written service agreement.
• The services were requested by the Japanese corporation.
• The rendering of services is documented with evidence (e.g. requests for services from the Japanese subsidiary, regular invoices sent by the foreign affiliate).
• The service charges are reasonable.

Japan

....

Group taxation

Consolidated tax regime

Under the consolidated tax regime, a consolidated group can report and pay national corporate income tax on a consolidated basis. A consolidated group may be formed by a Japanese parent company and its 100% owned (directly or indirectly) Japanese subsidiaries. The taxpayer may file an application to elect a consolidated group filing for tax purposes, but the election must include all of the parent's eligible subsidiaries. Once the election is made, the consolidated filing, in principle, cannot be revoked unless there is a specific event, such as an ownership change that causes the qualifying conditions of a consolidated filing to fail, or an application to discontinue the consolidated group has been approved by the Commissioner of the National Tax Agency (NTA).

The taxable income of the consolidated group is computed on a consolidated basis by aggregating the taxable income or losses of each member of the consolidated group followed by the consolidation adjustments. Profits from intra-group transactions, except for transfer of certain assets as defined, should be included in the aggregate taxable income. Gains or losses from the intra-group transfer of certain assets are deferred.

Pre-consolidation tax losses of a subsidiary can be carried forward into a consolidated tax group but may only be offset against taxable income of the subsidiary for the calculation of a consolidation income.

The consolidated national corporate income tax liability is determined by applying the corporate income tax rate to the consolidated taxable income and adjusted for consolidated tax credits. The total tax liabilities are allocated back to each member company. The parent company files the consolidated return and pays the national corporate income tax for the group; however, each member company remains jointly and severally liable for the consolidated group's total national corporate income tax liability.

Local corporate income taxes levied on member companies are paid on a separate company basis, but the amount of local tax payable may be affected because of the consolidated filing.

Group taxation regime

A group taxation regime is applicable to domestic companies that are wholly owned by a domestic company, foreign company, or individual ('group companies'). Unlike the consolidated tax regime, the group taxation regime automatically applies to group companies.

The key points of this regime are summarised as follows:

- The recognition of capital gains or losses from the transfer of certain assets (including the transfer of assets as a result of a non-qualified or taxable merger) between group companies is deferred until the asset is transferred to another group company or a non-group company. The scope of assets is the same as that under the tax consolidation system (i.e. fixed assets, land, securities, monetary receivables, and deferred expenses [excluding securities for trading purposes and assets with a book value of less than JPY 10 million]).
- Where a donation occurs between group companies, there are no tax implications for either the donor or donee (i.e. no deduction for the donor and no taxation for the donee). Note that this treatment is not applied to a group company owned by an

individual. This is consistent with the treatment of a donation between members of a consolidated tax group.

• A dividend received from a group company can be fully excluded from taxable income without any reduction for allocable interest expense. This is consistent with the treatment of dividends between members of a consolidated tax group.

A group company that would otherwise qualify as an SME on a stand-alone basis is not eligible for SME benefits (e.g. reduced corporate tax rate, preferable allowable ratios for deductible portion of bad debt provisions, partial deductibility of entertainment expenses, carry back of tax losses) if the SME is owned by a parent company or two or more parent companies of the group that has paid-in capital of JPY 500 million or more.

As amended in the 2011 tax reform, where a corporation which is a member of a 100% group is in the process of liquidation and is expected to be dissolved, any loss from the impairment or devaluation of the shares of the liquidating corporation cannot be recognised by the parent company as a tax deductible expense, effective on a devaluation on or after 30 June 2011.

Transfer pricing

If a corporation which is subject to corporation tax sells property to or buys property from a foreign-related person, or provides services or conducts other transactions with a foreign-related person, and consideration is received or paid by the corporation, the transaction is required to be carried out at an arm's-length price for corporation tax purposes.

A foreign-related person is a foreign corporation which maintains certain special relationships with the subject corporation, such as parent-subsidiary, brother-sister, or substantial control relationship.

The arm's-length price for the sales or purchase of inventory may be determined using one of the four following methods:

• Comparable uncontrolled price method.
• Resale price method.
• Cost plus method.
• Other method.

For accounting periods starting on or before 30 September 2011, an 'other method' may only be used if the first three methods cannot be applied. After the 2011 tax reform, for accounting periods starting on or after 1 October 2011, the priority between transfer pricing methods has been eliminated, and the 'most appropriate method' should be applied in order to calculate the arm's-length price.

An advanced pricing agreement (APA) system is available to confirm the arm's-length pricing system proposed by a taxpayer. In general, corporations entering into an APA are advised to file a request for mutual agreement procedures (MAP) in order to obtain the agreement of the competent authorities of each country.

Thin capitalisation

Interest paid on debt to controlling foreign shareholders is disallowed to the extent the average balance of debt on which that interest is paid is more than three times the equity of controlling foreign shareholders.

Japan

Interest expense deduction limitation

Under the 2012 tax reform, the new rule regarding the restriction of deductibility of interest expense from a related party was introduced.

The deductible portion of a corporation's net interest expense to a related party will be restricted to 50% of the adjusted income. The net interest is calculated as interest expense to related parties less corresponding interest income. The adjusted income is defined as taxable income, adding back interest expense, depreciation expense, and exempted dividend income but excluding extraordinary income or loss.

This rule will be applicable for tax years beginning on or after 1 April 2013.

Anti-tax haven (controlled foreign company or CFC) rules

Undistributed profits of a foreign subsidiary (i.e. CFC) located in a tax haven are included in the Japanese parent company's taxable income under certain conditions.

Tax havens are defined as certain countries or territories that do not impose corporate income tax or that tax the income of a foreign subsidiary at a rate of 20% or less. A Japanese corporation owning a 10% or more direct or indirect interest in a CFC is required to include its pro-rata share of the taxable retained earnings of the CFC in its gross income under certain circumstances.

A dividend paid by a CFC is not deductible when calculating its undistributed income.

Tax credits and incentives

Foreign tax credit

A Japanese corporation is subject to Japanese corporate income taxes on its worldwide income. However, to avoid double taxation of foreign-source income, Japanese corporations are allowed to claim a tax credit against corporation and inhabitant's taxes for foreign income taxes paid directly.

Creditable foreign taxes are defined as taxes that (i) are incurred directly by the taxpayer; (ii) are levied by foreign governments and local authorities in accordance with local tax laws; (iii) are levied on corporate income; and (iv) have the same characteristics as Japanese income tax, corporation tax, and local income-based taxes. A tax for which refund can be claimed optionally by the taxpayer after the tax payment, or a tax whose payment grace period can be decided by the taxpayer, are not regarded as foreign tax.

In order to prevent the credit from reducing corporation tax on Japan-source income, certain limitations are set on the amount of foreign tax that can actually be credited. Per the December 2011 Tax Reform, the ceiling is lowered from 50% to 35% for the foreign tax paid in the tax year beginning on or after 1 April 2012.

A foreign tax credit is not applicable for enterprise tax purposes, although foreign branch income attributable to a business executed outside Japan is exempt from enterprise tax.

Generally speaking, the foreign tax credit system does not apply to the extent the dividend income from the foreign subsidiary is subject to the dividend exemption system.

Tax credit for research and development (R&D) cost

The tax credit for R&D cost is calculated based on gross R&D cost. Limitation of the credit is determined based on the corporation tax liability as follows:

- For tax years ending on or before 31 March 2012: 30% of the corporation tax liability.
- For tax years beginning 1 April 2012 to 31 March 2014: 20% of the corporation tax liability.

In the case that the amount of the credit exceeds the limitations above, the excess amount can be carried forward for one year.

In addition to the R&D credit, for tax years beginning during the period 1 April 2008 to 31 March 2014, a taxpayer may claim an additional tax credit based on its incremental R&D expenditure or excess R&D cost over sales, as follows:

- 5% of the excess R&D costs over the annual average of R&D costs for the last three years.
- Excess R&D costs over 10% of the average sales amount multiplied by a tax credit ratio equal to ((R&D costs/average sales) - 10%) x 0.2).

The limitation of this additional tax credit is 10% of the corporation tax liability.

Special tax treatment for investment in certain equipment

SMEs filing 'blue form' tax returns may elect, under certain conditions, to claim accelerated depreciation of 30% of the base acquisition cost or a special tax credit equivalent to 7% of the base acquisition cost on designated equipment to the extent that it is acquired by 31 March 2014. The maximum tax credit is limited to 20% of the taxpayers' corporate tax liability.

Special tax treatment for Designated International Strategic Area

Qualifying corporations doing business in certain designated metropolitan areas ('Designated International Strategic Area') will be granted the following tax incentives:

- If qualifying corporations are engaged in specified businesses in the Designated International Strategic Area, certain capital expenditures (JPY 20 million or more for machinery and equipment and JPY 100 million or more for building and construction) incurred for the specified businesses will be eligible for either (i) a deduction equal to 50% of the capital expenditures (building is limited to 25%) or (ii) a tax credit equal to 15% of the capital expenditures (building is limited to 8%), with the maximum credit amount in any given tax year being equal to 20% of the tax liability before the credit, with a one year carryforward.
- If qualifying corporations are engaged primarily in specified businesses in the Designated International Strategic Area, they will be entitled to an income exclusion of up to 20% for five years, provided they are incorporated in the Designated International Strategic Area and incur certain capital expenditures. If qualifying corporations claim the 20% income exclusion, they will not be entitled to the tax credit regime described above.

Qualifying corporations will be eligible for the tax credit regime described above with respect to capital expenditures incurred from the effective date of the law concerning this regime through 31 March 2014. Corporations will be eligible for the 20% income exclusion regime for five years once they are specified as qualifying corporations

Japan

during a period from the effective date of the law concerning this regime through 31 March 2014.

Tax incentives for Asian headquarters
A qualifying corporation filing 'blue form' tax returns that will be primarily engaged in the operational management or R&D activities established by an international foreign corporation will be entitled to claim a 20% income exclusion over five years from the date it is specified (during the period from the effective date of the law concerning this regime through 31 March 2014) as a qualifying corporation pursuant to the relevant law.

Employment promotion taxation
If qualifying corporations increase the number of employees subject to employment insurance by 10% or more and by five people (two in the case of small and medium corporations) or more from the end of the prior tax year, the qualifying corporations will be eligible for the tax credit equal to the increased number of the employees multiplied by JPY 200,000 with the limitation of 10% (20% in the case of small and medium corporations) of the tax liability before the credit, subject to certain conditions for the tax years which commence from 1 April 2011 (excluding years ending before 30 June 2011) to 31 March 2014.

Tohoku Earthquake and special tax legislation

Corporate tax refunds by loss carrybacks
Under the current law, one year tax loss carrybacks are allowed for SMEs. Other corporations are allowed a one year tax loss carryback in the year of liquidation. In the Tohoku Legislation, corporations which incurred a specified disaster loss from the Tohoku Earthquake (the 'Tohoku Earthquake Disaster Loss') may carry back such loss for two years for national tax purposes. Such carryback may be elected either with the annual corporate tax return or an interim tax return based upon a full interim closing of the corporate books. For local tax purposes, the tax loss carryback is not applicable, although carryforward of all losses (including the Tohoku Earthquake Disaster Loss) is allowed over the normal nine year carryforward period.

Applicable tax year and tax return	Carryback years	Refundable tax amount
Final tax return for tax year ending between 11 March 2011 and 10 March 2012	Tax years beginning within two years from the first date of the tax year when the Tohoku Earthquake Disaster Loss is incurred	Tax liability of carryback year X (Tohoku Earthquake Disaster Loss / Taxable income of carryback year)
Closing basis interim tax return for interim period ending between 11 March 2011 and 10 September 2011	Tax years beginning within two years from the first date of the interim period when the Tohoku Earthquake Disaster Loss is incurred	

Special depreciation for newly acquired assets relating to the Tohoku Earthquake
A corporation may claim a special depreciation of certain assets in the year of acquisition in addition to normal depreciation. The qualified assets should be acquired and placed in service between 11 March 2011 and 31 March 2016 and satisfy either (i) or (ii) below:

(i)   Newly acquired assets to replace assets destroyed in the Tohoku Earthquake, including:
  • Buildings, structures, machinery, or equipment.
  • Registered vessels, aircraft, or vehicles.
(ii) Newly acquired assets placed in service in a business carried out at the affected area*, including buildings, structures, machinery, or equipment.

* Areas where destroyed buildings or structures were located and surrounding areas where machinery or equipment were installed.

Assets	Special depreciation rate applicable to the assets acquired and put into service between 11 March 2011 and 31 March 2014 (%)		Special depreciation rate applicable to the assets acquired and put into service between 1 April 2014 and 31 March 2016 (%)	
	SMEs	Other than SMEs	SMEs	Other than SMEs
Buildings, structures	18	15	12	10
Machinery, equipment; registered vessels, aircraft, vehicles	36	30	24	20

J

Rollover relief given to newly acquired assets to replace old assets

Under the current statutes, up to 80% of the capital gain realised when a corporation acquires an asset to replace an old one may be deferred. Under the Tohoku Legislation, for certain assets acquired between 11 March 2011 and 31 March 2016, the entire amount of capital gain may be deferred. Qualified replacement assets include the following:

• Real estate or depreciable assets located in Japan purchased to replace real estate (including buildings or structures fixed to the land) in the affected area that had been acquired prior to 11 March 2011.
• Real estate or depreciable assets purchased in the affected area to replace real estate, buildings, or structures located other than in the affected area.

When applying the rollover relief rules, the due date for acquiring replacement assets is extended for a further two years if it is difficult to acquire the replacement asset by the normal due date as a result of the Tohoku Earthquake.

Applicable transaction	• Acquiring replacement assets due to expropriation. • Acquiring certain other replacement assets.
Cases where the extension will be approved	• Difficulty in acquiring replacement assets by the normal due date which falls within a tax year which ends between 11 March 2011 and 31 March 2012.
Requirements for applying the extension	• A corporation expects to acquire the replacing asset within the designated period (up to two years). • A corporation expects to place the replacing asset in service within one year from the acquisition date (excluding replacement assets due to expropriation). • Extension is approved by the chief of the appropriate tax office.
Filing of the application form	• The application form should be filed within two months from the beginning of the tax year following the transferring year.

Japan

Additional special tax relief for restoration of the affected area

The following additional tax incentives were introduced on 14 December 2011. Please note that a corporate taxpayer must choose one of (i), (ii), or (iii) below, where (ii) can be chosen only where 'employment promotion taxation' (*see above*) is not applied.

i. Tax incentive for a newly established company doing business in designated areas.

A newly established company satisfying certain criterion is not subject to tax on income for the first five years of its existence. However, in effect, the tax holiday is more akin to a deferral since the income is offset by a special reserve that is reversed in later years.

The tax incentive applies to a company that acquires machinery, equipment, and building structures in a specified industrial concentration area which is organised by an approved local government and designated by 31 March 2016 by the local government as a company which contributes to providing opportunities for employment ('Designated Company') and newly established on or after the date when the designated restoration planning is approved.

If a Designated Company set up reserves for reinvestment in each of the tax years (including a day) within a designated period (five years from the date on which a company is designated), the amount of reserve (which may be set up to be 100% of taxable income) is deductible and may essentially defer tax for ten years.

In a tax year where a Designated Company reinvests in machinery or building in a specified industrial concentration area, a corporation is allowed to claim a deduction of the lesser of (i) special depreciation up to the balance of the reserve and (ii) special depreciation equal to the reversed reserve amount.

ii. Special corporation tax credit

Designated Company is allowed to enjoy a tax credit for 10% of salary paid (but limited to 20% of corporation tax due) to employees within a specified industrial concentration area.

iii. Special depreciation and special tax credit

Designated Company is allowed to enjoy special depreciation or a special tax credit for (i) machinery and equipment and (ii) buildings and structures acquired by 31 March 2016 in a specified industrial concentration area.

- Special depreciation: Depreciation rates applicable for machinery and equipment are 100% if acquired and used by 31 March 2014, and 50% if acquired and used on or after 1 April 2014. The depreciation rate applicable for buildings and structures is 25%.
- Special tax credit: The rates of tax credit applicable for (i) machinery and equipment and (ii) building and structures are 15% and 8%, respectively, but limited to 20% of corporation tax due. Any tax credits in excess of this limitation can be carried forward for four years.

Withholding taxes

Tax treaty network

As of 31 March 2012, Japan has entered into 55 tax treaties with 66 countries. Companies making certain payments are required to withhold income taxes using the following rates.

Japan

Recipient	WHT (%) Dividends Portfolio (3)	Substantial holdings (1)	Interest	Royalties (2)
Japanese corporations	7/20 (3)	20	0/20 (4)	0
Resident individuals	10/20 (3)	20	0/20 (4)	0
Foreign corporations, non-resident individuals:				
Non-treaty (5):	7/20 (3)	20	0/15/20	20
Treaty (6):				
Australia	10	0/5	10	5
Austria	20	10	10	10
Bahamas (7)	-	-	-	-
Bangladesh	15	10	10	10
Belgium	15	10	10	10
Bermuda (7)	-	-	-	-
Brazil	12.5	12.5	12.5	12.5/15/25 (8)
Brunei	10	5	10	10
Bulgaria	15	10	10	10
Canada	15	5	10	10
Cayman Islands (7)	-	-	-	-
China, P.R.	10	10	10	10
Czechoslovakia (former) (9)	15	10	10	0/10 (9)
Denmark	15	10	10	10
Egypt (5)	15	15	0/15/20	15/20 (10)
Finland	15	10	10	10
France	10	0/5	10	0
Germany	15	10	10	10
Guernsey (7) (concluded but is not effective)	-	-	-	-
Hong Kong	10	5	10	5
Hungary	10	10	10	0/10 (11)
India	10	10	10	10 (12)
Indonesia	15	10	10	10
Ireland, Republic of	15	10	10	10
Israel	15	5	10	10
Italy	15	10	10	10
Jersey (7) (concluded but is not effective)	-	-	-	-
Kazakhstan	15	5	10	10 (13)
Korea, Republic of	15	5	10	10
Luxembourg	15	5	10	10
Malaysia	15	5	10	10
Man, Isle of (7)	-	-	-	-
Mexico	15	0/5 (14)	10/15	10
Netherlands	10	0/5 (15)	0/10 (15)	0
New Zealand (5)	15	15	0/15/20	20
Norway	15	5	10	10

Japan

Recipient	WHT (%)			
	Dividends			
	Portfolio (3)	Substantial holdings (1)	Interest	Royalties (2)
Pakistan	10	5/7.5 (16)	10	10
Philippines	15	10	10	10/15 (17)
Poland	10	10	10	0/10 (18)
Portuguese Republic (concluded but is not effective)	10	5/10	0/5/10	5
Romania	10	10	10	10/15 (19)
Saudi Arabia	10	5	0/10	5/10 (20)
Singapore	15	5	10	10
South Africa	15	5	10	10
Spain	15	10	10	10
Sri Lanka	20	20	0/15/20 (21)	0/10 (21)
Sweden	15	0/5 (22)	10	10
Switzerland	10	0/5	0/10	0
Thailand	7/20	15/20 (23)	10/25 (23)	15
Turkey	15	10	10/15 (24)	10
USSR (former) (25)	15	15	10	0/10 (25)
United Kingdom	10	0/5	10	0
United States	10	0/5	10	0
Vietnam	10	10	10	10
Zambia	0	0	10	10

Notes

The applicable treaty rates are effective as of 31 March 2012.

1. The tax treaty rates apply only to corporate shareholders. The applicable treaty should be checked for conditions required to claim the reduced rate.
2. The applicable treaty should be reviewed because certain tax treaties exclude film royalties and/or gain from copyright transfer from taxable income.
3. For certain dividends received from 1 January 2004 through 31 December 2013, the reduced rate of 7% (for resident individuals, an additional 3% will be levied) is applied instead of 20%. Thus, the WHT rate for resident individuals is either 10% or 20%, whereas, the rate for corporations or resident individuals in non-treaty countries is 7% or 20%. For residents in treaty countries, 7% or the treaty rate will be applied. As of 1 January 2014, 20% will be applied without exception.
4. Interest on bank deposits and/or certain designated financial instruments is subject to a 15% national WHT and 5% local inhabitants WHT (20% combined). Taxation of such interest is fully realised by tax withholding, so resident individuals are not required to aggregate such interest income with other income. Interest on loans made by resident individuals is not subject to withholding tax; instead, it is taxed in the aggregate with other income. Such WHT is subject to the income surtax of 2.1%, which is levied for the income earned for the period from 1 January 2013 through 31 December 2037.
5. Dividends, interest, and royalties earned by non-resident individuals and/or foreign corporations are subject to a 20% national WHT under Japanese domestic tax laws in principle. An exception rate of 7% is applied to dividends from certain listed companies. An exceptional rate of 15% is applied to interest on bank deposits and certain designated financial instruments. Interest on loans, however, is taxed at a 20% rate. A special exemption from WHT applies to certain long-term corporate bonds issued to non-residents in foreign countries.
6. Tax treaties with many countries provide reduced tax rates, as indicated. Some treaties, however, provide higher tax rates (e.g. Brazil, Thailand) or do not provide rates (e.g. Egypt, New Zealand). In these instances, rates specified under Japanese domestic tax laws apply. Each treaty should be consulted to see if a reduced rate for dividends (in the case of substantial holdings) is applicable.
7. The tax treaty was concluded mainly for the purpose of information exchange.
8. The tax treaty with Brazil provides a 25% tax rate for certain royalties (trademark). However, the WHT rate cannot exceed 20% on any royalties to be received by a non-resident taxpayer of Japan under Japanese income tax law. Film royalties are taxed at 15%. Any other royalties are taxed at 12.5%.

Japan

9. The treaty with the former Czechoslovakia is applied to the Czech Republic and the Slovak Republic. It stipulates that cultural royalties are tax exempt.
10. Film royalties are taxed at 20%, and other royalties are taxed at 15%.
11. Cultural royalties are tax exempt.
12. The rate of 10% for royalties includes consideration for technical services.
13. The rate for royalties is reduced to 5% by Protocol.
14. Dividends received from subsidiaries, by parent companies that have met certain conditions, are exempt from withholding taxes.
15. Dividends received from subsidiaries for which parent company has over 50% shareholding are tax exempt. Interest received by government and other specific entities, or paid as a consequence of sale on credit of any equipment, merchandise, or service, is tax exempt.
16. A 5% rate is applied to a company which has over 50% shares with direct voting rights, and a rate of 7.5% is applied to a company which has over 25% shares with direct voting rights.
17. Film royalties are taxed at 15%. Any other royalties are taxed at 10%.
18. Cultural royalties are tax exempt.
19. Cultural royalties are taxed at 10%.
20. Royalties paid for the use of certain equipment are taxed at 5%.
21. Interest paid to financial institutions is tax exempt, as well as film and copyright royalties. Patent royalties are subject to a 10% rate.
22. If certain conditions for beneficial owners are met, dividends are taxable only in the contracting state of which the beneficial owner is a resident.
23. Dividends paid by a corporation that is engaged in industrial undertakings are taxed at 15%. Interest paid to financial institutions is taxed at 10%.
24. Interest paid to financial institutions is taxed at 10%.
25. The treaty with the former USSR is applied to Armenia, Azerbaijan, Belarus, Georgia, Kyrgyzstan, Moldova, Russia, Tajikistan, Turkmenistan, Ukraine, and Uzbekistan. It stipulates that cultural royalties are tax exempt.

J

Tax administration

Taxable period
The tax year is the corporation's annual accounting period specified in its articles of incorporation. A Japan branch of a foreign corporation must use the same accounting period that is adopted by the corporation in its home country.

Tax returns
Corporate income tax returns (i.e. the national corporation tax return, enterprise tax return, and local inhabitants' tax return) are self-assessment tax returns.

If a corporation meets certain conditions, such as keeping certain accounting books, and makes an application for it in advance, it is allowed to file a 'blue form' tax return. A blue form filing corporation may benefit from loss carryforward and other benefits.

A corporation (including a branch) is required to file the final tax return within two months after the end of its annual accounting period. If a corporation cannot file the final return because of specific reasons, the due date of final return may be extended for one month with the tax authority's approval.

Payment of tax
Income taxes payable on the final corporate income tax return should be paid on or before the filing due date of the final tax returns (usually two months after the end of the corporation's accounting period). If an extension of time for filing is granted, the taxes may be paid on or before the extended due date with interest accrued at a rate of 4.3% (for the year 2012) per annum for the period from the day following the original due date (i.e. two months after the end of an accounting period) to the date of the actual payment.

Provisional tax payments are required for a corporation that has a fiscal period longer than six months. Provisional taxes generally are computed as one-half of the tax

Japan

liabilities for the previous year, but they may be reduced by the filing of interim tax returns that reflect semi-annual results of the operations. The provisional tax payment is required to be made within two months after the end of the sixth month of the corporation's accounting period.

Tax audit
Generally speaking, corporate tax audit is performed in cycles of three to five years' duration. However, this period may be shortened in the case that some significant tax matters were pointed out in the prior audit and so on. If taxpayers request a downward correction, tax audit will be performed to make sure it.

With regard to tax audit procedures, tax laws have not clarified them thus far. Under the December 2011 tax reform, it is clarified that prior to conducting tax audit, in principle, tax agents are required to notify taxpayers and that, upon completion of tax audits, tax agents are required to provide to taxpayers a brief written summary of their findings, etc. It is effective for tax audits commencing on or after 1 January 2013.

Statute of limitations
The statutory limitations to request a downward correction of prior year tax liabilities is five year (six years for transfer pricing) from when the original tax return was filed (with regard to the tax returns due before 2 December 2011, the statutory limitation was one year, as a rule).

The statute of limitations with regard to upward corrections by the tax authorities is also five years (six years for transfer pricing).

Consolidated taxation
The parent company will file the consolidated tax return and pay national corporate income tax for the group. The consolidated tax return and payment due dates are the same as previously discussed; however, the due date of the final return may be extended for two months.

For local corporate income taxes, each member of the consolidated group must separately file the returns and pay the taxes.

Penalties
If the tax return is filed late, a late filing penalty is imposed at 15% to 20% of the tax balance due. In the case that a corporation voluntarily files the tax return after the due date, this penalty may be reduced to 5%.

An under-payment penalty is imposed at 10% to 15% of additional tax due. In the case that a corporation amends a tax return and tax liabilities voluntarily after the due date, this penalty may not be levied.

In addition, interest for the late payment of tax is levied at 4.3% (for the year 2012) per annum for the first two months and increases to 14.6% per annum thereafter.

Jersey, Channel Islands

PwC contact

Wendy Dorman
PricewaterhouseCoopers CI LLP
Twenty Two Colomberie
St Helier, Jersey JE1 4XA
Channel Islands
Tel: +44 1534 838233
Email: wendy.dorman@je.pwc.com

Significant developments

Jersey's business tax regime has recently been reviewed by the European Union (EU) Code of Conduct on Business Taxation Group (Code Group). The Code Group expressed concerns over Jersey's rules for taxing profits of Jersey companies on Jersey shareholders as deemed dividends or attributed profits. To address these concerns, these provisions have been removed as of 31 December 2011. During a meeting held with the Code Group on 13 September 2011, Jersey officials received confirmation that the removal of these provisions means that they will no longer regard Jersey's tax regime as 'harmful'. The formal process of ratification by the Economic and Financial Affairs Council (ECOFIN) was received in December 2011.

Taxes on corporate income

Resident companies are generally taxed on their worldwide income. A permanent establishment (PE), e.g. a branch of a company, is taxed on profits attributable to the PE. Non-resident companies are taxable on Jersey real estate income.

Companies pay income tax at a rate of 0%, 10%, or 20% on taxable income. The general rate applicable is 0%; the 10% and 20% rates apply to certain companies/income streams as explained in this section. The tax rate applies to the company as a whole, the only exception being Jersey-source property income, which is taxed at 20% regardless of the classification of the property holding company.

Certain Collective Investment Funds and Securitisation Vehicles can elect to be exempt from tax on income, other than income from Jersey land or property, for an annual fee of 500 pounds sterling (GBP).

The 20% tax rate applies to Jersey-based utility companies, such as telephone, gas, and electricity companies. Additionally, income from Jersey real estate, including rental income, property development profits, and income from exploiting Jersey land (e.g. quarrying activities) is subject to tax at 20%. From 2012, companies involved in oil importation are taxed at 20%.

The 10% rate applies to financial services companies. A company is defined as a financial services company if:

- it is registered under the 1998 financial services law to carry out investment business, trust company business, or fund services business as an administrator or custodian in relation to an unclassified or an unregulated fund
- it is registered under the 1991 banking business law, or

Jersey, Channel Islands

- it holds a permit under the collective investment funds law of 1988 as an administrator or custodian.

The 0% rate applies to all entities that are not exempt, financial services entities, or utility companies, including fund managers who do not hold any of the permits mentioned above.

Provisions in Jersey tax law under which Jersey-resident beneficial owners of Jersey companies were subject to tax on distributed or undistributed profits were removed as of 31 December 2011.

Local income taxes
There are no local government taxes on income.

Corporate residence

A company is regarded as tax resident in Jersey if it is incorporated in Jersey or if it has its place of central management and control in Jersey. However, a Jersey incorporated company managed and controlled elsewhere will not be regarded as a Jersey resident, provided certain conditions are satisfied.

Permanent establishment (PE)
Under domestic legislation, a PE, in relation to a company, includes a branch of the company, a factory, shop, workshop, quarry or a building site, and a place of management of the company; however, the fact that the directors of a company regularly meet in Jersey shall not, of itself, make their meeting place a PE.

For a definition of PE contained in Jersey's double tax agreements (DTAs), the relevant clause and agreement should be reviewed. In general, it may include a branch, management, or other fixed place of business, but not an agency, unless the agent has, and habitually exercises, a general authority to negotiate and conclude contracts or has a stock of merchandise from which the agent regularly fills orders.

Other taxes

Goods and services tax (GST)
The standard rate of GST is 5%.

Companies with taxable supplies of more than GBP 300,000 per annum are required to register for GST.

International service entity (ISE) status
To address the difficulty of irrecoverable input tax in the financial services sector, and to mitigate the administrative cost of GST for exporters in general, Jersey has introduced the concept of an ISE. Where an entity qualifies for this status:

- it will not be required to register for GST
- services to it will be zero-rated (i.e. treated as an export) where the supply exceeds GBP 1,000, and
- input tax on purchases less than GBP 1,000 may be reclaimed.

ISE status is automatically available to a wide variety of service providers and administered entities based in Jersey, upon application and payment of the relevant fee, including licensed banks, licensed trust service providers, licensed fund administrators, fund managers, and managed managers.

Other entities not automatically eligible under one of the categories above, including companies, partnerships, trusts, unrecognised funds, and special purpose vehicles, may still obtain ISE status if they fulfil certain criteria.

The ISE must be included on a list maintained by the comptroller of income tax. The list will refer either to the entity itself or (e.g. for administered entities) a class of entities as submitted by the administrator.

Customs duties
A common customs tariff is applicable on all goods imported from outside the European Union. The amount is dependent on what the goods are and where they are imported from.

Excise taxes
An excise duty tax is payable on imported alcohol, tobacco, and fuel at varying rates.

Stamp tax
Stamp duty is payable on the purchase or transfer of Jersey real estate, with rates ranging from 0% to 5%. Mortgages secured by a charge over Jersey real estate are subject to stamp duty at rates of up to 0.5% of the amount borrowed. No stamp duty is payable on the transfer of shares.

Transfer tax
A land transaction tax applies when shares in companies are transferred and the ownership of which confers a right of occupation of residential real estate in Jersey. The amount of land transaction tax payable is equal to the stamp duty that would have been suffered if the real estate were held directly.

Branch income

Branch income is taxed at the rate applicable to the company. No further tax is withheld on the transfer of profits abroad.

Income determination

Inventory valuation
Inventory is valued at the lower of historical cost or net realisable value. The last in first out (LIFO) method is not permitted. Generally, there are no material differences between accounts prepared on a normal accounting basis and those prepared on a tax basis.

Capital gains
Capital gains are not subject to tax in Jersey.

Dividend income
There is no requirement to withhold tax at source when paying dividends. If a dividend is paid out of profits that have suffered tax at a 10% or 20% rate, then the net dividend

will be accompanied by a tax credit at the applicable rate. Repayment of the tax credit can be claimed by Jersey investment companies and financial services companies receiving the dividends, subject to certain restrictions. However, trading companies subject to tax at 0% are not entitled to claim a repayment of any of the tax credit.

Stock dividends
Stock dividends are taxed as income.

Interest income
Interest income will form part of taxable income and will be taxed at the rate applicable to the company.

Foreign income
Income tax is levied on foreign branch income when earned and on foreign dividends, interest, rents, and royalties. Double taxation is mitigated by either the granting of unilateral relief to the extent of taxing foreign income net of foreign taxes or by treaty relief, which gives credit for foreign tax. Concessional credit relief might be granted in certain limited circumstances upon application.

In addition to the long standing DTAs with the United Kingdom and Guernsey, Jersey now has DTAs with Australia, Denmark, Estonia, Faroes, Finland, France, Germany, Greenland, Hong Kong, Iceland, Malta, New Zealand, Norway, Qatar, and Sweden. The scope varies from agreement to agreement, but most are of limited scope.

Jersey has also signed tax information exchange agreements (TIEAs) with 23 countries.

Deductions

Normally, business deductions are allowed if they are incurred wholly and exclusively for the purpose of the trade.

Depreciation and depletion
Capital allowances are available using the diminishing-balance method on machinery and equipment, including vehicles, at a rate of 25%. For this purpose, all such assets are pooled, and the allowance is calculated by reference to the value of the pool.

On disposal of an asset, the lower of cost and sale proceeds of the asset is deducted from the pool. A balancing charge is levied if the proceeds exceed the balance of the pool.

Motor vehicles costing more than GBP 21,000 and greenhouses are subject to special rules and are not pooled with other assets.

By concession, an alternative is to claim the full cost of replacement in the year of replacement.

Capital allowances are not applicable to buildings or the depletion of natural resources.

Goodwill
Goodwill expenditure is non-deductible for Jersey income tax purposes.

Start-up expenses
Once a company has commenced its trade, start-up expenditure will be allowable for tax purposes if it is not capital in nature and has been incurred wholly and exclusively for trade purposes.

Interest expenses
Interest expense will be allowable if it is incurred for the purposes of a trade or is paid in connection with a loan taken out for a qualifying purpose.

Bad debts
Trading bad debts are normally allowable for Jersey income tax purposes unless they relate to a general provision.

Charitable contributions
Charitable contributions are generally non-deductible for tax purposes, unless the contribution itself provides a benefit to the trade (i.e. marketing).

Fines and penalties
Fines and penalties are generally non-deductible for tax purposes.

Taxes
Local income tax paid is not deductible in computing taxable income. ISE fees paid are a tax-deductible expense.

Net operating losses
No distinction is drawn between different types of income or losses arising from different trades or sources, apart from Jersey property income which is separately streamed.

Unrelieved losses may be carried forward and used to offset profits in future accounting periods. Alternatively, losses can be group relieved to group companies in the same income tax rate band.

There are now only very limited circumstances where a company can obtain relief for carrying back losses.

Payments to foreign affiliates
There are no withholding taxes (WHTs) on patent royalties paid by Jersey companies to non-residents.

Group taxation

Group taxation is not permitted in Jersey. However, there are provisions for group relief between group companies subject to the same rate of tax. It is not possible to relieve losses between two companies taxed at different rates.

Transfer pricing
There are no specific rules in relation to transfer pricing in Jersey. There is, however, a general anti-avoidance provision in Jersey tax law. It may be applied by the Comptroller of Taxes if a transaction or a combination or series of transactions is entered into for the avoidance or reduction of Jersey income tax.

Thin capitalisation
There are no specific rules in relation to thin capitalisation in Jersey.

Jersey, Channel Islands

Tax credits and incentives

There are generally no special incentives for locally owned businesses in view of the low rate of tax.

Foreign tax credit

There is no local foreign tax credit regime in Jersey. DTAs need to be considered as appropriate. Unilateral relief may be available under very limited specific circumstances.

Withholding taxes

There are no WHTs on dividends or interest paid by Jersey companies.

Tax administration

Taxable period

The tax year is the calendar year. Companies are assessed on income earned in respect of the financial year that ends within the applicable calendar year of assessment.

Tax returns

The system relies on the filing of a return of information with the Jersey tax authority, which then raises an assessment (in the case of companies taxed at 10% or 20% on all or part of their income). Companies taxed at 0% are required to submit a tax return but are not required to submit accounts and tax computations.

As of 1 January 2011, there is a filing deadline for the corporate return of 6pm on the last Friday in July and a late filing penalty of GBP 250.

Payment of tax

For companies, tax is payable in arrears during the calendar year following the year of assessment.

Estimated assessments are issued early during the calendar year following the year of assessment and are broadly based on the tax liability of the previous year of assessment. These assessments are appealed with the tax office, and a payment on account is made based on estimates.

Tax paid after a prescribed date (usually the first Friday in the December following the year of assessment) incurs a 10% surcharge.

Statute of limitations

There is no statutory limitation date, as such. If the Comptroller discovers profits have not been fully assessed, the Comptroller can issue an amended/additional assessment at any time not later than five years after the expiration of the year of assessment. If the error involves fraud, willful default, or neglect, then the assessment can be revised at any time.

Topics of focus for tax authorities

The Jersey tax authorities are committed to being tax transparent, with an increased emphasis on agreeing further DTAs and TIEAs.

Jordan

PwC contact

Stephan Stephan
PricewaterhouseCoopers Jordan
Third Circle, Jabal Amman
14 Hazza' Al-Majali Street PO Box 5175
Amman 11183, Jordan
Tel: +962 6 500 1300
Email: stephan.stephan@jo.pwc.com

Significant developments

The Jordanian tax regime was previously based on the application of the Jordanian Income Tax Law No. 57 of 1985 ('Old' Tax Law). The Old Tax Law was repealed and replaced by a temporary income tax law, which became effective as of 1 January 2010. This temporary income tax law was introduced by the newly appointed Jordanian government in the absence of a Parliament (after a royal edict ordering its dissolution). When the new government was sworn in during December 2009, the introduction of a new income tax law was identified on the agenda of items to be addressed. On this basis, the temporary income tax law was introduced by the new government and will be in force until the elected Parliament enacts the final income tax law; however, an exact date for enactment is not yet known. Part of Parliament's tasks will be to review these temporary laws, make amendments, if appropriate, and then pass the laws as final.

Taxes on corporate income

The corporate tax rates in Jordan are applied based on the industry/business activities from which the taxpayer generates income. The corporate tax rates are as follows:

- 30% for banks.
- 24% for telecommunication, insurance, financial intermediation companies (including exchange and finance leasing companies).
- 14% for other companies.

Jordanian resident corporations are not subjected to income tax on their worldwide income, unless that income is raised from sources that originate and relate to Jordanian deposits and funds. However, for foreign branches of Jordanian resident corporations, 20% of the branch net income after taxes is subject to Jordanian corporate tax.

Non-resident corporations are taxed through withholding tax (WHT) (*see the Withholding taxes section*).

Local income taxes
There are no local income taxes in Jordan.

Corporate residence

An entity will be deemed to be resident in Jordan if it has been established and registered in accordance with the provisions of the Jordanian legislation in force and (i) has an office or branch practicing management and supervision of its work in Jordan,

Jordan

(ii) whose management head office or actual office is located in Jordan, or (iii) which the government or any official or public institutions own more than 50% of its capital.

Permanent establishment (PE)
There are no clear provisions in the Jordan income tax law to define PE.

Other taxes

Sales tax
A general sales tax similar in operation to a value-added tax (VAT) is imposed at the rate of 16% on the following transactions:

* Sales of goods or services, or both.
* Importing any service or goods from outside Jordan or from the free zone areas and markets inside Jordan.

Special tax rates are applied on certain items (*see Excise taxes below*).

A zero rate is applied to the export sales of goods and services outside Jordan or to the free zone areas and markets. A zero rate is also applied to sales inside Jordan of certain food items, books, magazines, manure, farm tractors, other agricultural tools, and salt.

Goods exempt from sales tax include fish, eggs, animals, bread, water packed in less than 5 litres, trees and plants, fruits, vegetable oils, honey, tea, sugar, gold, money, potash, emergency and fire vehicles, electricity, and pharmaceutical products.

Services exempt from sales tax include the following:

* Air transport.
* Education.
* Disposal of sewage and waste.
* Public health and similar activities.
* Activities of religious organisations.
* Activities of social organisations.

Custom duties
Certain goods imported to Jordan are subject to custom duties. Custom duties vary depending on the type and the origin of imported goods, as prescribed by the Customs Tariff. The Customs Tariff is based on the Harmonised Commodity Description and Coding System (HS Nomenclature).

Excise tax
Excise tax is the special sales tax that is imposed on certain goods and services, including cement, iron used in construction, tobacco products, wines, spirits, cars, beer, fuel, and lubricants.

Property taxes
There is a property tax in Jordan that is paid annually, and the tax rate is determined by the municipality depending on the location and size of the property and, in case of buildings, depending on annual rental value.

Jordan

Transfer property taxes
Transfer of property is subject to tax at a rate of 9% (registration fee at a rate of 5% and sale of property tax at a rate of 4%).

Stamp duty
An *ad valorem* stamp duty of 0.3% or 0.6% is levied.

Payroll tax
A company should withhold payroll tax from monthly salaries and benefits at rates ranging from 7% to 14%.

Social security tax
A social security tax is imposed on the employer and the employee by rates of 12.25% and 6.5% respectively on the monthly salaries and certain allowances in kind. The employer should report and withhold these contributions on a monthly basis.

Branch income

Operating branches of non-resident companies registered in Jordan are taxed based on their activities/business being carried out in Jordan at the prevailing corporate income tax rates. Non-operating branches of non-resident companies registered in Jordan are generally prohibited from carrying on any commercial activity in Jordan.

Income determination

Any income incurred in or from Jordan, regardless of the place of payment, shall be subject to tax. This includes, but is not limited to, income from:

- Professional services or activities.
- Interest, commissions, discounts, currency differences, deposit profits, and profits from banks and other legal resident persons.
- Royalties.
- Selling goods produced in Jordan whether sold in Jordan or exported.
- Selling or leasing of movable properties located in Jordan.
- Leasing immovable properties located in Jordan and the income from key money.
- Selling or leasing intangible assets in Jordan, including goodwill.
- Insurance premiums due according to insurance and re-insurance agreements for risk in Jordan.
- All forms of telecommunication services, including international telecommunications.
- Transportation between Jordan and any foreign country.
- Service compensation gained by a non-resident person from Jordan for a service provided to any person if the activity or the work related to this compensation was carried out or the output of this service was used in Jordan.
- Any contract in Jordan, such as construction contracting, commercial agencies profits, and any other similar entities whether their source is inside or outside Jordan.
- Any other employment or business activity, or investment, which has not been exempted according to the provisions of the law.

The following shall be exempted from tax:

Jordan

- The King's allocations.
- Income of public and official institutions and municipalities, excluding its income from rent and key money.
- Income of unions, professional commissions, cooperation societies, and other societies legally registered and licensed from non-profit activities.
- Income of any religious, charity, cultural, educational, sports, or health institutions with a public character, not aiming to achieve profit and the income of charity *awqaf* (public endowment), and income from the Orphans Development Fund investment.
- Income of exempted registered companies according to the companies' law, which is incurred from activities undertaken outside Jordan, except income derived from income sources subject to tax according to the provision of the law.
- Profits from stocks and dividends distributed by a resident to another resident, except profits of mutual investment funds of banks and financial companies.
- Capital gains incurred inside Jordan, other than profits from assets subject to depreciation.
- Income derived from inside Jordan from trading in dividends and stocks, bonds, equity loan, treasury bonds, mutual investment funds, currencies, commodities in addition to futures and options contracts related to any of them, except that incurred by banks, financial companies, financial intermediation and insurance companies, and legal persons who undertake financial lease activities.
- Income from trading in immovable properties located in Jordan except the following:
  - Income incurred from such trade by a legal person.
  - Income incurred from building and selling real-estate.
- Income derived by non-Jordanian resident investors from sources outside Jordan that are initiated from their investments of their foreign capital, returns, profits, and proceeds from their investments' liquidation, returns, or selling of their projects, shares, or stocks after transferring them outside Jordan in accordance to the enacted Investment Law or any other law that will replace it.
- Compensation paid by insurance entities, other than what is paid as reimbursement for the loss of income from business activity or employment.
- Any income generated by banks and financial companies not operating in Jordan from banks operating in Jordan, such as deposit interest, commissions, and deposit profits from investment in interest-free banks and financial companies.
- Profits gained by re-insurance companies from insurance contracts concluded with insurance companies operating in Jordan.
- Income covered by double-taxation agreements (DTA) concluded by the government, to the extent of that which is covered under these agreements.
- The income of public or private pension funds and savings funds and any other funds approved by the Minister shall not be subject to tax if this income is derived from the employees and employers contributions.
- Certain types of local origin goods and services' exports outside Jordan may be totally or partially exempted from tax as set forth in regulations issued for this purpose.

Inventory valuation
Inventory is generally valued in accordance to the International Financial Reporting Standards (IFRS) accounting framework.

Capital gains
Capital gains are not taxable in Jordan except for capital gains that are generated from depreciable assets.

Dividend income
Dividend income received from a resident juristic person is not taxable in Jordan. However, dividend income received from a non-resident juristic person is subject to income tax.

Foreign income
Jordanian resident corporations are not subjected to income tax on their foreign income, except for foreign branches of Jordanian resident corporations, whereby 20% of the branch net income after taxes is subject to Jordanian corporate tax.

Deductions

Depreciation and amortisation
Depreciation and amortisation of fixed assets are determined using the straight-line method, provided that the provisions, procedures, and rates shall be defined by the depreciation regime issued for this purpose. Assets with a cost of less than 100 Jordanian dinars (JOD) shall be totally deducted in the tax period in which they were acquired.

Goodwill
Purchased goodwill can be amortised using the straight-line method, provided that the provisions, procedures, and rates shall be defined by a regulation issued for this purpose.

Start-up expenses
There is no clear provision in the enacted temporary Jordan income tax law to define the treatment of start-up expenses; however, these expenses can be accepted at the establishment year.

Interest expenses
Interest and *Murabaha* (profit-sharing) paid by banks or financial institutions are deductible.

Interest and *Murabaha* that are paid by any taxpayer other than banks and financial institutions and finance leasing companies are deductible, provided that the deduction shall not exceed the rates that are determined in the thin capitalisation rules (*see Thin capitalisation in the Group taxation section*).

Bad debt
Bad debts are deductible.

Charitable contributions
A person may deduct any amount paid during the tax period as a donation to any of the governmental departments, public or official institutions, or municipalities from the gross income in the period in which the payment occurred.

Any person may deduct subscriptions and donations paid in Jordan without any personal benefit, for religious, charitable, humanitarian, scientific, environmental, cultural, sport, and professional purposes if the Council of Ministers approves its character. The deductible amount according to the provisions of this paragraph shall not exceed 25% of the taxable income after deducting what is provided for in the first paragraph above and before making this deduction.

Jordan

Fines and penalties
Fines and penalties are not acceptable expenses for income tax purposes.

Taxes
Taxes and fees paid on taxable activities are deductible.

Foreign income tax paid for income earned from sources outside Jordan that was subject to tax under the provisions of the tax law is deductible.

Other significant items
Approved expenses, including the following, are deductible:

* Insurance premiums.
* Maintenance expenses for assets that were spent within the tax period, provided that such expenses do not exceed 5% of their value.
* Amounts paid as civil compensation under contracts concluded by the taxpayer for the purpose of carrying out taxable activities.
* Amounts paid by the employer for employees to the Social Security Corporation.
* Hospitality and travel expenses incurred by the taxpayer.
* Expenditures for employees' medical treatment, meals during duty, travel, transport, and life insurance against work injuries or death.
* Marketing, scientific research, development, and training expenses.
* Expenses of prior tax periods, which were neither defined nor final.

Net operating losses
Losses may be carried forward indefinitely, but the carryback of losses is not permitted.

Payments to foreign affiliates
A resident generally may claim a deduction for royalties, management service fees, and interest charges paid to foreign affiliates taking into account the transfer pricing regime and the applicable WHT.

Group taxation

Group taxation is not permitted in Jordan.

Transfer pricing
Any disposition transaction which is not based on arm's length, is with parties that have mutual interests, and leads to a decrease in the taxable income is ignored, and the real profits are estimated according to the regular market value of the transactions.

Any illusionary or fake disposition transactions are ignored and the tax due is estimated as if there were no transactions.

Thin capitalisation
Interest and *Murabaha* that are paid by any taxpayer other than banks and financial institutions and finance leasing companies shall be accepted as a deduction, provided that the deduction shall not exceed the following rates of relative value (i.e. total debt to the paid capital or average owners' equity, whichever is higher):

Tax period	Relative value
2011	5:1
2012	4:1
2013 and following years	3:1

Tax credits and incentives

Jordan has had tax reductions for selective sectors categorised by development zones. Generally, these have required pre-approval.

Foreign tax credit
Foreign tax credit treatment is not available in Jordan.

Withholding taxes

Dividends paid
Dividends are not taxable in Jordan.

Non-resident WHT
With respect to services performed by a non-resident juristic or natural person, under the Income Tax Law, "Amounts received or earned by the non-resident person from the Kingdom, which are derived from services provided to any person if the work or service related has been performed in the Kingdom or if the outcome of such services has been used in the Kingdom as well, is subject to tax in Jordan".

The current WHT rate on services performed by a non-resident juristic or natural person is 7% of the payment.

Resident WHT
Resident juristic or natural persons that perform any services in Jordan are subject to a WHT on the services performed. The applicable WHT rate is the rate prevailing at the time the service is performed. The current WHT rate on services performed by a local service provider is 5% of the payment.

Some services are excluded from the 5% WHT regulation, provided that the service provider has an income tax identification number, including the following services:

- Shipping services and related brokerage services.
- Road transport services and related brokerage services.
- Air transport services.
- Financing lease services.
- Hotels and restaurants services.
- Clearance services.
- Programming services provided by the company.
- Hospital services provided by hospitals.
- Advertising services.
- Cleaning services.
- Security services.
- Training services provided by the company.
- Insurance activities services.

Jordan

- Banking services provided by banks.
- Communication activities and services provided by primary telecom companies (defined in the tax law as being communications companies individually licensed in accordance with the provisions of the communications law in effect and regulations and instructions issued pursuant thereto).
- Transportation and distribution of electric power services provided by the Electricity Company Plc.
- Contracting services implemented under contractor certified by the Jordanian Contractors Association.
- Public safety services.
- Maintenance services that include value of materials and goods and labour wages.
- Food processing services, correspondence, and transport and laundry provided to hospitals.
- Loading and unloading services.
- Services that are executed by a juristic person, excluding civil companies, and have a tax number (income and sales).
- Any other service approved by the Minister upon the recommendation of the Director General.

Tax treaties

Jordan has entered into income tax treaties with Algeria, Bahrain, Canada, Croatia, the Czech Republic, Egypt, France, India, Indonesia, Iraq, South Korea, Kuwait, Lebanon, Libya, Malaysia, the Netherlands, Pakistan, Poland, Qatar, Romania, Sudan, Syria, Tunisia, Turkey, the United Kingdom, and Yemen.

Jordan has transportation agreements with many countries and is negotiating treaties with more countries.

Tax administration

Taxable period

A taxpayer's due tax shall be computed on a calendar year basis.

A taxpayer who closes one's accounts on a date other than the end of the calendar year may calculate the due tax according to the fiscal year, provided that prior approval shall be obtained from the General Director of the income tax department.

A taxpayer who commences activity within the first half of the calendar year shall compute the due tax for the period from the establishment date until the end of the calendar year.

A taxpayer who commences activity within the second half of the calendar year may compute the due tax for the period from the establishment date until the end of the next calendar year.

Tax returns

Taxpayers are obliged to file tax returns before the end of the fourth month following the end of the tax period, including details related to income, expenses, exemptions, and tax due. Tax returns are submitted by any of the following means approved by the department according to terms and procedures to be determined by instructions:

- Registered mail.
- Banks.

- Any licensed company to undertake the tasks of public or private mail post approved by the Council of Ministries upon the recommendation of the Minister.
- Electronic means.

The date of filing is considered to be the earlier of the date of receipt by the department, post seal, or deposit receipt at a bank or licensed company. In the case of sending electronic mail, implementation instructions have not yet been introduced to determine the approved date of submitting the same.

Payment of tax
The tax balance is due before the end of the fourth month following the end of the tax period.

A taxpayer who is carrying out business activities and has gross income in the previous tax period exceeding JOD 500,000 from these activities is required to remit two advance payments on the accrued income tax from these activities using the rates determined for each tax period mentioned in the following schedule. The advance payments are calculated according to the income tax in the financial statements presented to the income tax department for the concerned period. In the absence of the financial statements for this period, the income tax included in the immediate preceding tax declaration will be used to calculate the advance payments.

Tax period	Rate on accrued income tax (%)
2011	25
2012 and following years	37.5

The first advance payment is due within a period not exceeding 30 days from the last day of the first half of that income tax period.

The second advance payment is due within a period not exceeding 30 days from the last day of the second half of that income tax period.

Audit cycle
The tax audit is likely to take place within one year from the date of filing the return.

Statute of limitations
The tax auditor may not audit a tax return after four years from the date of filing the return.

Fines and penalties
Failure to pay tax on the assigned dates according to the provisions of the tax law will result in a delay fine at a rate of 0.4% of the value of the tax due or any deductible amounts for each full or partial week of delay.

If a taxpayer submits a tax return and pays the declared tax in a timely manner, but the declared tax is less than the actual amount due, a shortage fee for such differences will be imposed, as follows:

- 15% of the shortage if the difference exceeds 20% but less than 50% of the tax due by law.
- 80% of the shortage if the difference exceeds 50% of the tax due by law.

Kazakhstan

PwC contact

Peter Burnie
PricewaterhouseCoopers Tax & Advisory LLP
34 Al-Farabi Ave
Building A, 4th Floor
050059 Almaty, Kazakhstan
Tel: +7 727 330 3200
Email: peter.burnie@kz.pwc.com

Significant developments

From 1 January 2012, certain amendments were introduced into the Kazakh Tax Code. Some of these amendments relate to such provisions as exemption from taxation of outbound and in-country dividends and capital gains, clarifications regarding permanent establishment (PE) provisions, administration of double tax treaty (DTT) benefits, and provisions on the controlled foreign company (CFC) rules. Another set of amendments introduced a special taxation regime around the project of clearing Kazakhstan banks' toxic assets. In general, the goal of the proposed tax changes is to create a favourable tax environment for the participants in this project.

Also, effective January 2012, the Common Economic Area (CEA) for Kazakhstan, Russia, and Belarus came into effect. The CEA is the next level of cooperation of these countries after the creation of the Customs Union in 2010. Legal framework of the CEA consists of 17 international agreements. The aim of the CEA is to harmonise not only taxation, but also macroeconomic and monetary policies, enabling the free movement of goods and services, capital and labor force, creating shared transport and energy systems, and implementing uniform technical regulations.

It's also worth mentioning that Kazakhstan companies and individuals are currently in the process of transition to new individual identification numbers, which were introduced to replace several existing registration numbers, such as taxpayers' registration number and social security fund identification numbers. The deadline to finalise this transition is set at 1 January 2013.

Taxes on corporate income

The tax rate for corporations is 20% and is based on a calendar year. All Kazakhstan legal entities and branches of foreign legal entities are subject to CIT. Taxable income is determined as the taxpayer's aggregate annual income less allowable deductions.

Resident companies are taxable in Kazakhstan on their worldwide profits, while non-resident companies operating through a PE in Kazakhstan are subject to Kazakhstan CIT only on the profits attributable to that PE.

Non-residents without a PE in Kazakhstan that receive income from sources in Kazakhstan are generally subject to income tax withheld at source of payment on Kazakhstan-source income (*please see the Withholding taxes section for more information*).

Reduced CIT rates

A reduced CIT rate of 6% applies to the qualified agricultural income of legal entities producing agricultural products.

In addition, taxpayers operating in special economic zones may enjoy full exemption from CIT, land tax, and property tax, if certain statutory requirements established for such benefits are met.

Excess profit tax (EPT)

EPT rates are progressive and range from 0% to 60%. The tax base is comprised of the portion of net income of subsurface users exceeding 25% of deductions for EPT purposes. Subsurface users may include asset acquisition costs, capital costs, and losses (with certain limitations) as deductions.

Local income taxes

There are no local income taxes in Kazakhstan.

Corporate residence

Generally, Kazakhstan incorporated companies or other legal entities that have their place of effective management located in Kazakhstan are treated as Kazakhstan tax residents.

Permanent establishment (PE)

Non-resident legal entities having business activities in Kazakhstan may create a PE in the following cases:

- 'Fixed place PE': a non-resident enterprise carries on business activities in Kazakhstan through a fixed place, including, but not limited to, through a place of management.
- 'Services PE': a non-resident enterprise renders services in Kazakhstan through employees or other personnel engaged by the non-resident for such purposes, provided that these activities continue for more than 183 days within any consecutive 12-month period for the same or connected projects.
- 'Construction PE': a construction site, in particular a shop or an assembly facility, performance of projecting work, forms a PE, notwithstanding the timing of performing operations.
- 'Agency PE': a non-resident enterprise carries on business activities in Kazakhstan through a dependent agent. A dependent agent is an individual or legal entity that meets all of the following criteria simultaneously:
  - Has the contractual authority to represent the non-resident's interests in Kazakhstan and makes use of this authority by acting and signing (negotiating) contracts on behalf of the non-resident.
  - The business is carried outside the activity of either a customs broker or professional participant of the securities market or other brokerage type of business (except for activity as an insurance broker).
  - Carries on activities that are not limited to those of preparatory and auxiliary nature.

Kazakhstan

Other taxes

Value-added tax (VAT)

The current VAT rate is 12%. This tax is applicable to the sales value of products, works, and services, as well as imports. Exports of goods are taxed at 0%. There is a list of goods, works, and services exempt from VAT (e.g. financial services provided by financial institutions, financial leasing services, notary and advocacy services, operations with financial securities and investment gold).

Goods and services are subject to VAT if they are deemed to be supplied in Kazakhstan under the place of supply rules.

VAT refunds are generally available with respect to excess input VAT.

The VAT reporting period is the calendar quarter.

Customs duties

Customs duties apply to goods imported to the Customs Union countries from third countries. The customs duties rates are established either based on a percentage (in general ranging between 0% and 30%; higher rates exist for certain goods) of the customs value of goods or in absolute terms in euros.

Goods of the Customs Union countries should be generally exempt from Kazakhstan customs duties.

In addition to membership in the Customs Union, Kazakhstan concluded a number of bilateral and multilateral Free Trade Agreements with the Commonwealth of Independent States (CIS), which provides for exemption of goods circulated between the CIS member states from customs duties, if certain conditions are met.

Kazakhstan is not yet a World Trade Organization (WTO) member.

Customs fees

A customs processing fee is assessed at 60 euros (EUR) for the main page of a customs declaration plus EUR 25 for each supplemental page.

Excise taxes

Excise taxes apply to the sale and import of crude oil, gas condensate, petrol/gasoline (excluding aviation fuel), diesel fuel, spirits and alcoholic beverages, beer, tobacco, and passenger cars.

Type of excisable good	Excise tax rate
Crude oil, gas condensate, petrol/gasoline, diesel	KZT 0 to 450 per tonne
Alcoholic beverages and beer tobacco	KZT 1 to 2,450 per item of measure (pieces or litres)
Passenger cars	KZT 100 per each cm3 of engine capacity

Property tax

Property tax is assessed annually at a general rate of 1.5% of the average net book value of immovable property.

Land tax

Entities and individuals that own land plots (or land share in cases of commonly shared ownership of land plots) must pay land tax annually. Land tax rates vary based on the purpose for which the land is used as well as the size and quality of the land.

Transfer taxes

There are no transfer taxes in Kazakhstan.

Stamp taxes

There are not stamp taxes in Kazakhstan.

Vehicle tax

The vehicle tax rate is based on monthly calculation indices and determined in accordance with the type of vehicle, engine volume, operation period of the vehicle (aircraft only), and other factors.

Social tax

Employers must pay social tax at the rate of 11% of gross remuneration (salaries and certain benefits provided) of all employees (local and expatriate). A deduction is available for obligatory pension contributions.

Mineral extraction tax

The mineral extraction tax applies to the monetary value of extracted volume of crude oil, gas condensate, natural gas, minerals, and groundwater.

The tax is calculated based on the value of the extracted content, which is computed by applying average global prices to the extracted volume (adjusted for content). The determination of average global prices is based on the list of publications that are considered official sources for computation of mineral production tax (Platts Crude Oil Marketwire and Crude Argus).

Currently, the tax rates for crude oil and gas condensate range from 5% to 18%, depending on the accumulated production volume for the calendar year. For hydrocarbons, rates can be reduced by 50% if they are supplied to domestic refineries on the basis of a sale/purchase agreement or tolling agreement.

The tax rate for natural gas is set at 10%. For domestic sales of natural gas, tax rates range from 0.5% to 1.5%.

Tax rates for minerals that have undergone initial processing (except for widespread minerals) and for coal vary between 0% and 22%.

K

Branch income

The net income of branches of foreign legal entities, after CIT at 20%, is subject to a branch profits tax at a rate of 15%, which may be reduced under an applicable DTT. As such, the effective tax rate for the income of branches of foreign legal entities equals 32% if there is no reduction under a DTT.

Kazakhstan

Income determination

Kazakhstan legal entities are taxable on aggregate annual income earned worldwide. Non-resident legal entities, carrying out business activities through a PE in Kazakhstan, are taxable on income attributed to the activities of that PE. All taxpayers must apply the accrual method for recognition of income.

Inventory valuation

For tax purposes, inventory is valued in accordance with International Financial Reporting Standards (IFRS) and Kazakhstan financial accounting legislation. As such, permitted inventory valuation methods include first in first out (FIFO), weighted average, and specific identification methods.

Capital gains

Capital gains are subject to ordinary CIT rates. An exemption is available for capital gains realised from the sale of shares and participation interests in Kazakhstan legal entities or consortiums that are not engaged in subsurface activities.

Dividend income

Dividend income of a Kazakh resident company on inbound dividends is exempt from Kazakh taxation. Dividends from a Kazakhstan resident company to another Kazakhstan resident company are exempt from taxation, except for dividends paid by certain types of investment funds.

Interest income

Interest income should be included in the aggregate annual income of a taxpayer and taxed at the 20% CIT rate.

Foreign exchange gain

Foreign exchange gain should be determined in accordance with the provisions of IFRS and Kazakhstan financial accounting legislation. The excess of foreign exchange gain over foreign exchange loss should be included in the aggregate annual income of a taxpayer.

Foreign income

Foreign income is subject to ordinary CIT.

There are no provisions for tax deferrals in Kazakhstan.

For additional information, please refer to Controlled foreign companies (CFCs) in the Group taxation section.

Deductions

Allowable deductions generally include expenses associated with activities designed to generate income, unless specifically restricted for deduction by tax legislation. All expenses require supporting documentation.

Depreciation and depletion

Tax depreciation is calculated using the declining-balance method at depreciation rates ranging from 10% to 40%, applied to the balances of four basic categories of assets:

* Buildings and facilities: 10%.

- Machinery and equipment: 25%.
- Computers and equipment for information processing: 40%.
- Fixed assets not included into other groups, including oil and gas wells, transmission equipment, oil and gas machinery and equipment: 15%.

Goodwill
There are no special provisions in the Kazakhstan tax Code with respect to deductibility of goodwill expenses.

Start-up expenses
The Kazakhstan Tax Code does not specifically address deductibility of start-up expenses, but, generally, expenses incurred in relation to business activities and aimed at earning revenue occurring at start-up should be deductable.

Interest expenses
Interest paid to unrelated third parties and credit partnerships created in Kazakhstan are deducted in full. *For information about taxation of interest paid to related parties, please refer to Thin capitalisation in the Group taxation section.*

Bad debt
Amounts of receivables that were not paid within three years are to be recognised as bad debt expenses. Such expenses can be deducted in full by a taxpayer, provided that (i) these receivables are reflected in the books of a taxpayer and (ii) proper supporting documents are in place.

K

Charitable contributions
Charitable contributions are entitled to decrease taxable base but are capped at 3% of the company's annual taxable income.

Foreign exchange loss
Foreign exchange loss should be determined in accordance with the provisions of IFRS and Kazakhstan financial accounting legislation. The excess of foreign exchange loss over foreign exchange gain is allowed for deduction.

Fines and penalties
Generally, deductions are available for forfeits, fines, and penalties that are not payable to the state budget.

Taxes
Taxes remitted to the state treasury of Kazakhstan are deductible, except for the following:

- Taxes excluded prior to the calculation of the aggregate annual income.
- Income taxes paid in Kazakhstan and other countries.
- Taxes paid in preferential tax jurisdictions.
- Excess profit tax.

Net operating losses
Net operating losses accumulated prior to 1 January 2009 may be carried forward for up to three years. Net operating losses generated after 1 January 2009 may be carried forward for up to ten years. Loss carryback is not permitted under Kazakhstan tax legislation.

Kazakhstan

Payments to foreign affiliates
Payments to foreign affiliates are deductible for CIT purposes if the payments are intended to generate income, are supported by documentation, and comply with Kazakhstan transfer pricing law.

Group taxation

Kazakhstan tax law does not permit group taxation.

Transfer pricing
Under Kazakhstan transfer pricing law, both customs and tax authorities have the right to monitor and adjust prices used in cross-border and certain domestic transactions when prices are perceived to deviate from market prices, even if such transactions are with unrelated parties. If the authorities adjust prices, the re-assessed liability will include taxes, duties, penalty interest, and fines to the state budget.

Transfer pricing rules impact the following transactions:

- International commercial transactions.
- Domestic transactions that directly relate to international commercial operations where:
  - the sale relates to a subsurface use contract
  - one of the parties has tax preferences, or
  - one of the parties has losses for two years prior the year of the transaction.

Thin capitalisation
Deduction of interest paid to related parties, or to unrelated parties under related parties warranties, or to parties registered in a country with privileged taxation depends on the borrower's capital structure; such that deductible interest will be limited with reference to an 'acceptable' proportion of debt to equity (7:1 for financial institutions, 4:1 for all other entities). The list of jurisdictions with privileged taxation, the so called 'black list' established by the government, includes 62 jurisdictions (*see the Kazakhstan summary at www.pwc.com/taxsummaries for a current list*).

Controlled foreign companies (CFCs)
Under the CFC rules, if a Kazakhstan legal entity has 10% or more of direct or indirect ownership in the share capital or voting rights in a non-resident company, registered or located in a country with privileged taxation (*see above*), the legal entity is subject to Kazakhstan CIT on the portion of the undistributed profits from the non-resident company.

Tax credits and incentives

Foreign tax credit
In general, the Kazakhstan Tax Code allows taxpayers to credit the foreign income taxes paid against the income taxes payable in Kazakhstan provided the documents confirming the payment of such taxes are available. However, a tax credit may not be granted in certain cases (e.g. for taxes paid in countries with privileged taxation).

Investment incentives
Investment incentives are available to certain Kazakhstan legal entities that fit certain criteria and possess objects (e.g. certain fixed assets), for which investment incentives

may be applied. Generally, the investment incentives allow companies to fully deduct, for CIT purposes, the cost of the investment objects and the cost associated with their reconstruction and modernisation either at once or within first three years of their use.

Based on the Investment Law, incentives are granted under an investment contract between the government and companies and focus on priority sectors of the economy, as determined by the government.

Special economic zones
Currently, the following special economic zones have been established in Kazakhstan:

*   'Astana, the New City' in Astana (the expiry date is in 2027).
*   'Aktau Sea Port' in Aktau (the expiry date is on 1 January 2028).
*   'Ontustik' in Sairam district of South-Kazakhstan region (the expiry date is on 1 July 2030).
*   'National Industrial Petrochemical Park' in Atyrau region (the expiry date is on 31 December 2032).
*   'Burabai' in Akmola region (the expiry date is on 1 December 2017).
*   'Park of Innovative Technologies' (the expiry date is 1 January 2028).

In order to enjoy the incentives available in special economic zones, a legal entity must meet the following requirements:

*   It must be registered by the tax authorities in the territories of special economic zones.
*   It must have no structural subdivisions beyond the boundaries of the territories of the special economic zones.
*   90% of aggregate annual income must constitute income earned from activities in the special economic zone consistent with the objectives of the special economic zone's formation.

The general incentives available for legal entities in special economic zones are:

*   CIT: 100% reduction.
*   Land tax: 0% rate.
*   Property tax: 0% rate.

Withholding taxes

Kazakhstan-source income of non-residents and the proceeds from the sale of shares in subsurface users are subject to withholding tax (WHT) at the rates shown in the table below.

A non-resident legal entity is exempt from dividend WHT if:

*   the holding period of shares or participation interest is greater than or equal to three years, and
*   50% or more of the charter capital value of the entity paying the dividends is not the property of a subsurface user.

Types of income at a source of payment	WHT rate (%)
Dividends, capital gains, interest, royalties	15

Kazakhstan

Types of income at a source of payment	WHT rate (%)
Any income of an entity registered in a tax haven jurisdiction	20
Insurance premiums under risk insurance agreements	15
Income from international transportation services; insurance premiums under risk reinsurance agreements	5
Other income	20

Benefits paid by a company to a shareholder, founder, participant, or related party, falling under the definition of constructive dividends, are taxed at a rate of 15%.

The rate of WHT may be reduced under an applicable DTT. A list of DTTs concluded and ratified by Kazakhstan is detailed below:

WHT rates between Kazakhstan and treaty countries as of 1 January 2012

Recipient	Dividends (%)	Interest (%)	Royalties (%)
Non-treaty	15	15	15
Treaty:			
Armenia	10	10	10
Austria	5/15 (4)	10	10
Azerbaijan	10	10	10
Belarus	15	10	15
Belgium	0/5/15 (8, 4)	10	10
Bulgaria	10	10	10
Canada	5/15 (1)	10	10
China	10	10	10
Czech Republic	10	10	10
Estonia	5/15 (2)	10	15
Finland	5/15 (1)	10	10
France	5/15 (4)	10	10
Georgia	15	10	10
Germany	5/15 (2)	10	10
Hungary	5/15 (2)	10	10
India	10	10	10
Iran	5/15 (5)	10	10
Italy	5/15 (4)	10	10
Japan	5/15 (11)	10	10
Korea	5/15 (4)	10	10
Kyrgyzstan	10	10	10
Latvia	5/15 (2)	10	10
Lithuania	5/15 (2)	10	10
Malaysia	10	10	10
Moldova	10/15 (2)	10	10
Mongolia	10	10	10
Netherlands	0/5/15 (9, 10)	10	10
Norway	5/15 (10)	10	10
Pakistan	12.5/15 (10)	12.5	15
Poland	10/15 (3)	10	10

Kazakhstan

Recipient	Dividends (%)	Interest (%)	Royalties (%)
Romania	10	10	10
Russia	10	10	10
Singapore	5/10 (2)	10	10
Slovakia	10/15 (7)	10	10
Spain	5/15 (4)	10	10
Sweden	5/15 (1)	10	10
Switzerland	0/5/15 (9, 10)	10	10
Tajikistan	10/15 (6)	10	10
Turkey	10	10	10
Turkmenistan	10	10	10
Ukraine	5/15 (2)	10	10
United Kingdom	5/15 (1)	10	10
United States	5/15 (1)	10	10
Uzbekistan	10	10	10

Notes

1. 5% if the beneficial owner is a company owning, directly (or indirectly in case of Canada and the United Kingdom), at least 10% of the voting power of the company paying the dividends.
2. 5% (10% in case of Moldova) if the beneficial owner is a company that directly holds at least 25% of the capital of the paying company.
3. 10% if the beneficial owner is a company, directly or indirectly, holding at least 20% of the capital of the paying company.
4. 5% if the beneficial owner is a company (other than partnership), which owns not less than 10% of the capital of paying company.
5. 5% if the recipient is a company (other than partnership), which directly owns not less than 20% of the capital of paying company.
6. 10% if the actual owner is a legal entity, which owns not less than 30% of the authorised capital of the legal entity paying the dividends.
7. 10% if the beneficial owner is a company, which holds directly at least 30% of the capital of the company paying the dividends.
8. 0% if dividends are paid in consideration of an investment of at least 50 million United States dollars (USD) in the paying company.
9. 0% if the company receiving the dividends holds directly or indirectly at least 50% of the capital of the paying company and has made an investment in the company paying the dividends of at least USD 1 million, which investment is guaranteed in full or insured in full by the government of the first contracting state, the central bank of that state or any agency or instrumentality (including a financial institution) owned or controlled by that government, and has been approved by the government of the other contracting state.
10. 5% (or 12.5% in case of Pakistan) if the beneficial owner is a company which directly owns (or indirectly in case of the Netherlands and Pakistan) at least 10% of the capital of paying company.
11. 5% if the beneficial owner is a company owning directly or indirectly, for the period of six months ending on the date on which entitlement to the dividends is determined, at least 10% of the voting power of the company paying the dividends.

Tax administration

Taxable period
The tax year in Kazakhstan is the calendar year.

Tax returns
Annual CIT declarations are due by 31 March of the year following the tax year-end. However, a taxpayer may be granted a 30 calendar-day extension of the deadline upon request.

K

Kazakhstan

Certain taxpayers are required to submit their estimated calculation of monthly advance payments of CIT.

The deadline for other tax returns is the 15th calendar day of the second month following the reporting period. However, a taxpayer may be granted a 30 calendar-day extension of the deadline upon request.

Payment of tax

For CIT, advance payments are due every 25th day of the month. Taxpayers with aggregate annual income during the tax period preceding the previous tax period of less than 325,000 times the amount of the monthly calculation index established for the relevant financial year (approximately USD 3.55 million) are exempt from the obligation to calculate and pay CIT advance payments. Payment of any outstanding CIT liabilities is required within ten calendar days following submission of the annual CIT declaration (i.e. 10 April).

Most other taxes are payable by the 25th day of the second month following the end of reporting period.

Audit cycle

Kazakhstan tax authorities have the right to conduct regular tax audits (at least once a year). Generally, there are two types of audits:

- Planned tax audits. The list of entities that fall under tax audit is published semi-annually on the official web-site of the Kazakh government.
- Unplanned tax audits. Tax authorities may conduct unplanned tax audits. Information about misstatements in tax returns or any other discrepancy may trigger an unplanned tax audit.

Statute of limitations

The statute of limitations for tax purposes in Kazakhstan is five years. For taxpayers operating under subsurface use contracts, the tax authorities maintain the right to assess or revise the assessed amount of excess profit tax and other taxes and obligatory payments to the budget, where a methodology of calculation uses one of the following indices: internal rate of return (IRR) or internal revenue rate or R-factor (earning yield) during the effective period of a subsurface use contract and five years after the end of the effective period of a subsurface use contract.

Topics of focus for tax authorities

Tax audits may be comprehensive or thematic. Comprehensive tax audits cover all applicable taxes, while thematic tax audits may cover only some specific tax liabilities. As a rule, Kazakh tax authorities are form, rather than substance, driven during audits.

Fines and interest penalties

Interest penalties are assessed on late tax payments at 2.5 times the Kazakhstan National Bank refinancing rate. As of 2 April 2012, the National Bank refinancing rate was set at 6.5% per annum.

Substantial fines are imposed for understatement of tax liabilities. Generally, the fines amount to 50% of the understated tax.

For advance CIT payments, an administrative fine of 40% applies to understated advance tax payments compared with the final declared CIT, if the understated amount is greater than 20% of the final declared amount.

If a taxpayer is deemed to have concealed taxable income, a fine of 150% of the concealed amount may be assessed.

Other issues

Accounting system

Kazakhstan legal entities should maintain accounts and produce financial statements in accordance with IFRS or national accounting standards (depending on the size of the company and other factors). In most cases, tax treatment follows accounting treatment.

K

Kenya

PwC contact

Steve Okello
PricewaterhouseCoopers
Rahimtulla Tower
Upper Hill Road
Nairobi, Kenya
Tel: +254 20 2855116
Email: steve.x.okello@ke.pwc.com

Significant developments

Several changes and tax measures have been introduced to Kenya's corporate tax system in the past year aimed at expanding the tax base and capturing more revenue. The overall aim is to increase revenue collection in order to satisfy the government budget requirements. The main areas of reforms include the following:

- Increasing the tax base.
- Realigning policy making.
- Increasing administration and collection.
- Simplification of tax regime.
- Automation of tax administration.

Legislation was enacted to give legal effect to tax information exchange agreements (TIEAs), which the revenue authority intends to enter into with other governments.

The 2012 Finance Act provides clarification in respect of the implementation of deemed interest provisions. The clarifications include the following:

- The Commissioner will now prescribe the rules of calculating deemed interest rather than the 91 day Treasury Bill rate.
- The provisions on withholding tax (WHT) have been enabled to allow the revenue authority to collect WHT on deemed interest.
- The Finance Act has further tightened the rules by providing that deemed interest shall be deemed to be income which accrued in or was derived from Kenya.

The 2012 Act also introduced a 20% WHT on winnings to payments made to both resident and non-resident persons from betting, lotteries, and gaming. These amounts are categorised as income that accrued in or was derived from Kenya. The WHT deducted is a final tax for payments made to both resident and non-resident persons.

Taxes on corporate income

Companies (including a branch of an overseas company) are subject to Kenyan corporate income tax (CIT) at the following rates on all income accrued in or derived from Kenya:

Entity	CIT rate (%)
Resident companies (including subsidiary companies of foreign parent companies)	30
Branches of foreign companies/Permanent establishments (PEs)	37.5

Entity	CIT rate (%)
Export processing zone (EPZ) enterprises:	
First ten years	0
Next ten years	25
Thereafter	30
Registered unit trusts/Collective investment schemes	Exempt (subject to conditions)
Newly listed companies:	
20% of shares listed: first three years after listing	27
30% of shares listed: first five years after listing	25
40% of shares listed: first five years after listing	20
Rates on gross income of non-residents derived in Kenya:	
Transmission of messages	5
Ownership or operation of a ship and aircrafts	2.5

Industry-specific rates

There are special provisions for non-resident shipping companies and airlines; non-residents providing broadcast, internet, and messaging services; and non-resident petroleum industry subcontractors providing exploration and production services in Kenya.

K

Corporate residence

A company is considered resident in Kenya if it meets one of the following criteria:

- It is incorporated under Kenyan laws.
- The management and control of company affairs are exercised in Kenya.
- The company has been declared by the minister, by announcement in the gazette, to be resident in Kenya for any year of income.

Permanent establishment (PE)

A business carried on in Kenya through a fixed place of business gives rise to a PE for branch purposes, as does a building site, or a construction or assembly project, that has existed for six months or more. Note that the definition of a PE may be modified by a double tax agreement (DTA).

Other taxes

Value-added tax (VAT)

VAT is levied on the supply of taxable goods and services in Kenya, as well as on the importation of taxable goods and services into Kenya.

The following VAT rates apply in Kenya:

Activity	VAT rate (%)
Standard rate on all goods and services that are neither exempt nor zero-rated	16
Electricity, diesel oil, and residual fuel oils	12
Export of goods and services, certain other goods and services	0

Kenya

Certain goods and services are designated as exempt from VAT. Exempt supplies do not count towards the registration threshold (*see below*), and the related input VAT is not recoverable.

Zero rating applies to the export of goods or services. The supply of goods or services to certain designated persons and projects are also zero-rated.

The threshold for VAT registration is taxable supplies of 5 million Kenyan shillings (KES) per year. Registered persons must record their turnover using an approved electronic tax register or signature device. Only registered persons may recover input tax. An input tax credit is not available for several items such as non-commercial vehicles, office furniture, and hospitality and entertainment services. An excess input tax credit may be carried forward or refunded, subject to certain conditions.

Import (customs) duty

Import duty is levied under the East African Community Customs Management Act. Imports of goods are generally subject to import duty of 0% for raw materials and capital goods, 10% for intermediate goods, and 25% for finished goods. Enterprises established in an EPZ are exempt from customs duty on machinery and inputs for exported products. Where raw materials that are not subject to 0% import duty are used to manufacture goods for export outside the East African Community, one may apply for remission under the import duty remission scheme. This is subject to a requirement for proof of export and execution of a bond.

Excise duty

Excise duty is imposed on the manufacture or importation of certain commodities and services, such as mobile phone services, bottled water, soft drinks, cigarettes, alcohol, perfumes, fuels, and motor vehicles, at varying rates. There are various classes for each category and commodity where different rates of duty apply.

Category	Goods description	Excise duty rates
Beer	Beer	KES 70 per litre or 40% of RSP (1)
Other alcoholic beverages	Wines (2)	KES 80 per litre or 40% of RSP (1)
	Cider	KES 70 per litre or 40% of RSP (1)
	Spirits, whisky, rum, gin, and vodka	KES 120 per litre or 35% of RSP (1)
	Undentured ethyl alcohol strength by volume of 80% or higher	KES 120 per litre or 65% of the RSP (1)
	Premixed alcoholic beverages of strength not exceed 10% by alcohol content	KES 70 per litre or 40% RSP (1)
Tobacco and tobacco products	Cigarettes	KES 1,200 per mile or 35% of RSP (1)
Soft drinks	Carbonated drinks and juices	7%
	Bottled water	KES 3 per litre or 5% of the RSP (1)
Other excisable products	Plastic bags (3)	50%
	Motor vehicles	20%
	Cosmetic products	5%

Kenya

Category	Goods description	Excise duty rates
	Imported used computers (used computers more than three years from date of manufacture)	25%
Excisable services	Mobile cellular phone services and other wireless telephone services	10%
	Gambling services	5%

Notes

1. Excise value is the higher of the actual value or retail selling price (RSP).
2. This includes a wide range of wines, such as sparkling wine, vermouth, etc.
3. Manufacturers who use plastic bags for packing their products will now be entitled to claim excise duty paid on their plastic bags from the Kenya Revenue Authority (KRA).

Stamp duty

Stamp duty is payable on transfer of properties. In the case of real property, stamp duty is payable at the rate of 4% on the value of the land as assessed by a government valuer. For other properties, other rates of stamp duty apply as specified in the Schedule to the Stamp Duty Act. The rates of stamp duty are shown below:

Activity	Stamp duty rate (%)
Transfer of immovable property:	
Urban	4
Rural	2
Creation or increase of share capital	1
Transfer of unquoted shares or marketable securities	1
Transfer of quoted shares of marketable securities	0*
Registration of a debenture or mortgage	
Primary security	0.1
Auxiliary security	0.1
Transfers	0.05
Lease:	
Period three years and under	1% of annual rent
Period over three years	2% of annual rent

* Transfer of quoted securities is exempt.

Land purchased for expansion and development of schools is exempt from stamp duty, provided the land does not revert to any other use and approval has been obtained from the relevant authorities.

Compensating tax

Where a company pays dividends out of profits that have not been subject to CIT, the company will be liable to pay a compensating tax. The compensating tax rate is 42.8%. The aim of this tax is to ensure that all dividends are paid out of profits that have suffered CIT.

Turnover tax for small business taxpayers

A resident taxpayer whose annual gross turnover does not exceed KES 5 million will be taxed at the rate of 3% per quarter of one's turnover. In such a case, the taxpayer

Kenya

will not be required to register for VAT. Turnover tax does not apply to rental income, management or professional fees, training fees, income subject to WHT as a final tax, and income of incorporated companies. Loss making businesses are allowed to make an election to be exempted from turnover tax. A written application for exemption has to be made to the Commissioner, and there is a procedure to be followed.

Business permit
Every person who carries on a business in Kenya is required to apply for a business permit from the relevant local authority. The business permit is usually based on the size of one's business and is renewable on an annual basis.

Catering levy
This is a levy which is payable to Catering Levy Trustees by hotels and restaurants at a rate of 2% of turnover.

Advance tax on motor vehicles
Advance tax is payable at varying rates per year on commercial vehicles and is creditable against CIT for the year.

Fringe benefit tax (FBT)
The FBT is payable on interest-free or low-interest loans granted to employees. FBT is paid by the employer, whether exempted from tax or not, at the resident CIT rate of 30%. The benefit is the difference between actual interest charged and the interest computed using the Commissioner's prescribed rate published quarterly. The directors and employees are not personally taxed on the benefit.

Employers' national social security contributions
Employees are also obligated to contribute monthly to the National Social Security Fund (NSSF) a standard amount of KES 200, with an equal amount of contribution from the employer.

Local government rent and rates
Rent and rates are levied on properties in Kenya, the rateable value which is payable to the local authority or central government shall vary in each county based on various forms of ratings such as area rate, agricultural rental value, or site value.

Branch income

The profit of a PE is taxed at the branch income tax rate of 37.5%, but there is no further taxation on the distribution of branch profits. However, there are certain restrictions with respect to costs paid to the head office.

Income determination

Inventory valuation
Inventory is stated at the lower of cost or net realisable value, with the exception of biological assets whose value is prescribed by the Commissioner.

Capital gains
Taxation of capital gains was suspended in 1985.

Dividend income

Kenya source dividends are taxable income in Kenya, unless the recipient is a Kenya resident company holding 12.5% or more of voting power of the company paying the dividend. However, for companies holding less than 12.5% of the votes, and other resident taxpayers, the 5% WHT is the final tax. Dividends paid to non-residents and any overseas holding company attract 10% WHT.

Stock dividends

Stock dividends issued in a ratio not proportionate to shareholding of the existing equity are considered as taxable dividends to the extent of the disproportionate increase in the value of the ownership of the company.

Interest income

Interest income is generally included in the determination of taxable income.

Foreign income

Income earned abroad is generally taxed as part of corporate income since a resident company is subject to CIT on its worldwide income.

Deductions

The general principle in Kenya is that expenses are deductible if they are incurred wholly and exclusively to generate taxable income.

K

Depreciation and depletion

No deduction is allowed for accounting depreciation or impairment. However, capital allowances are permitted at varying rates (on a straight-line basis) for certain assets used for business purposes, including buildings and machinery used in manufacturing, industrial buildings and hotels, machinery and plant, agricultural works, and mining.

Capital deductions	Rate (%)
Investment deduction:	
Qualifying investment exceeding KES 200 million (outside Nairobi or the municipalities of Mombasa or Kisumu)	150
Other qualifying investment	100
Industrial building allowance: *	
Hostels and certified education buildings (straight-line)	50
Qualifying rental residential or commercial buildings (straight-line)	25
Other qualifying buildings (including hotels, straight-line)	10
Wear and tear allowance:	
Plant and machinery (reducing-balance)	
Class 1	37.5
Class 2	30
Class 3	25
Class 4	12.5
Telecommunication equipment (straight-line)	20
Other allowances:	
Computer software (straight-line)	20
Capital expenditure under a concessionaire arrangement	Equal proportions over the period of the concession

Kenya

Capital deductions	Rate (%)
Mining specified minerals:	
Year one	40
Year two through seven	10
Farm works (straight-line) **	100

* Different percentages apply for previous years.
** With effect from 1 January 2011.

Goodwill
Cost acquisition of goodwill and amortisation of goodwill are not deductible as they are capital in nature.

Start-up expenses
There is a specific provision allowing the deduction of start-up expenses, provided that the required conditions have been met.

Interest expenses
A deduction for interest is allowed only to the extent that the borrowings are used for the purpose of trade. Where a non-resident person controls a company alone or with four or fewer other persons, interest restriction or 'thin capitalisation' rules apply (*see Thin capitalisation in the Group taxation section*).

Bad debts
Bad debts are deductible in the year in which it is evident that the debt has become irrecoverable. Detailed rules apply for making this determination.

Charitable contributions
Donations to charities and for certain public works are deductible, subject to certain conditions.

Fines and penalties
Generally, fines and penalties are not deductible as they are not considered to be expenses incurred for producing profits chargeable to tax.

Taxes
Kenyan income taxes are not deductible while computing income tax of a person. However, foreign income taxes incurred are generally deductible as an expense if tax credit relief is not available under a DTA.

Net operating losses
Losses calculated under the tax rules may be carried forward against income from the same source for a maximum of five years, including the year in which the losses arise. Losses cannot be carried back, except for petroleum companies, where losses can be carried back for three years from the year of income in which the petroleum company ceased permanently to produce petroleum.

Payments to foreign affiliates
Transfer pricing rules based on Organisation for Economic Co-operation and Development (OECD) principles apply to transactions with foreign affiliates (both companies and branches/PE). Additionally, there are restrictions on the deductibility of expenses incurred outside of Kenya by non-residents with a Kenyan PE. Transfer pricing is not limited to anti-avoidance.

Kenya

Group taxation

Each company in a group is taxed as a separate entity in Kenya.

Transfer pricing
A company that has related party transactions is required to ensure such transactions are at arm's length. The company is therefore required to prepare a transfer pricing policy to justify the pricing arrangements. The Commissioner is allowed to adjust the prices if they do not conform to the arm's-length principle. The policy should be prepared and submitted to the KRA upon request.

Thin capitalisation
In Kenya, a company is thinly capitalised if all of the following occur:

* The company is in control of a non-resident person alone or together with four or fewer persons.
* The company is not a bank or financial institution.
* The highest amount of all loans held by the company at any time exceeds the sum of three times the revenue reserves (including accumulated losses) and the issued and paid up share capital of all classes of shares of the company.

A company that is thinly capitalised cannot claim a deduction on the interest expense incurred by the company on loans in excess of three times the sum of revenue reserves and issued and paid up capital of all classes of shares of the company. The company also cannot claim a deduction for any foreign exchange loss realised by the company with respect to any loans from its shareholders in the period that the company remains thinly capitalised.

K

Tax credits and incentives

Foreign tax credit
For business income, there is no relief for foreign tax paid except as provided for by a DTA (if applicable) between Kenya and the other country.

Investment deduction
Qualifying investments exceeding KES 200 million incurred outside Nairobi or the municipalities of Mombasa or Kisumu are allowed an investment deduction of 150%. All other qualifying investments are allowed a 100% investment deduction in the year the asset is put into service.

Export processing zone (EPZ)
Companies located in an approved EPZ, principally to export goods, are taxed at a 0% CIT rate for ten years from its commencement and at a rate of 25% for the next ten years.

Listed companies
Companies listed on the Nairobi Stock Exchange are entitled to reduced rates of income tax for a period, depending on the proportion of share capital listed (*see the Taxes on corporate income section for the rates*).

Kenya

Withholding taxes

WHT is levied at varying rates (3% to 30%) on a range of payments to residents and non-residents. Resident WHT is either a final tax or creditable against CIT. Non-resident WHT is a final tax.

Payments	Resident WHT rate (%)	Non-Resident WHT rate (%)
Dividend > 12.5% voting power	Exempt	10
Dividend < 12.5% voting power	5	10
Interest:		
Bearer instruments	25	25
Government bearer bonds (maturity ≥ 2 years)	15	15
Bearer bonds (maturity ≥ 10 years)	10	N/A
Other	15	15
Qualifying interest:		
Housing bonds	10	N/A
Bearer instruments	20	N/A
Other	15	N/A
Royalty	5	20
Management or professional fees	5	20
Consultancy fees - Citizen of East Africa Community		15
Training (including incidental costs)	5	20
Rent/leasing:		
Immovable property	N/A	30
Others (other than immovable)	N/A	15
Pension/retirement annuity	Varied *	5
Contractual fees	3	20
Winnings from betting, lotteries, and gaming	20	20

* This will vary depending on the payments paid out.

Double tax agreements (DTAs)

Lower rates may apply to non-residents where there is a DTA in force. The table below shows the maximum rates of tax that recipients in those countries with a DTA with Kenya can be charged on dividends, interest, royalties, and management and professional fees. The table only includes agreements that are currently in force.

Recipient	WHT (%)		
	Dividends	Interest	Royalties and management & professional fees
Canada	15	15	15
Denmark	20	20 (1)	20
France	10	12	10 (5)
Germany	15	15 (1)	15
India	15	15	20 (4)
Norway	15	20 (1)	20
Sweden	15	15	20
United Kingdom	15	15 (1)	15 (2)

Recipient	WHT (%)		
	Dividends	Interest	Royalties and management & professional fees
Zambia	0 (3)	0 (3)	0 (3, 5)

Notes

1. Interest paid by the government and the Central Bank of Kenya is tax-exempt.
2. The rate is 12.5% for management and professional fees.
3. No Kenya tax is due if subject to tax in Zambia.
4. The rate is 17.5% for management and professional fees.
5. Management and professional fees subject to normal WHT rates.

Where the treaty rate is higher than the non-treaty rate, the lower rate applies.

Tax administration

Taxable period
A company has discretion to determine its corporate tax year, provided it is a 12-month period. However, any changes in corporate tax year end must be approved by the Commissioner of the KRA.

Tax returns
Resident companies and PEs of non-resident companies must file a self-assessment tax return accompanied by audited or certified accounts annually. The return is due within six months following a company's year-end.

Payment of tax
Instalment tax payments must be made during the year based on the lower of 110% of the previous year's liability or an estimate of the current year's liability. Agricultural companies are required to pay estimated tax in two instalments of 75% and 25% during the year. Any balance of tax at the end of the year must be paid within four months of the financial year-end.

Payment of agency taxes
The tax withheld from payments must be paid by the 20th day of the month following the month in which the deduction is made.

Penalties for non-compliance
If a self-assessment tax return is not submitted by the due date, a penalty of 5% on the unpaid tax for the year may be imposed, subject to a minimum of KES 10,000. Failure or late submission of an EPZ company return will be subject to a penalty of KES 2,000 per day for as long as the failure continues.

A penalty of 20% and interest at 2% per month are imposed on underestimation and late payment of instalment tax and any balance of tax. Interest is charged only on the principal tax due.

Failure to make a deduction or to remit the WHT deducted attracts a penalty equal to 10% of the amount of tax involved (subject to a maximum of KES 1 million) and accrues interest at 2% per month.

Kenya

Audit cycle

There is no prescribed audit process, as an audit can be triggered by any factor as determined by the revenue authority. Generally, tax audits should be carried out after every two to four years. The audit or inspection will commence with a request from the revenue authority for the taxpayer to make available any such records or information as may be required.

Statute of limitations

The tax authorities must commence an audit before the expiry of seven years after the end of a year of income. The revenue authorities may go back past seven years where fraud is suspected. There is no time limit for completing tax audits. However, they are normally completed within a reasonable time, especially if there are no major disputes.

Topics of focus for tax authorities

The issues that are often subject to close scrutiny by the tax authority include related-party transactions.

Korea, Republic of

PwC contact

Soo-Hwan Park
Samil PricewaterhouseCoopers
LS Yongsan Tower, 14th Floor
191 Hangangno 2-ga
Yongsan-gu
Seoul 140-702, Korea
Tel: +82 2 709 0705
Email: soo-hwan.park@kr.pwc.com

Significant developments

New middle income tax bracket

The basic Korean corporate income tax (CIT) rates for fiscal year (FY) 2011 are 10% on
the first 200 million Korean won (KRW) of the tax base and 22% for the excess. In FY
2012 and thereafter, the top rate of CIT will be maintained while a middle income tax
bracket will be created: 10% on the first KRW 200 million, 20% for the tax base between
KRW 200 million and KRW 20 billion, and 22% for the excess.

New or increased tax credit for job-creating investments

While the 4% to 5% temporary tax credit for facility investments will be terminated
for investments made after 1 January 2012, the existing tax credit for job-creating
investments will be maintained at an increased rate of 5% to 7%, compared with
the current 1% credit. The credit will include a 3% to 4% tax credit for a company
maintaining a status quo employment and an additional 2% to 3% tax credit for new
job-creating investments. The additional tax credit for job creation will not exceed
the ceilings set at KRW 10 million (KRW 15 million per employee between the ages 15
and 29, KRW 20 million per specified occupational high school graduate employee)
multiplied by the number of new employment in net.

Tax law changes upon the adoption of International Financial Reporting Standards (IFRS)

Inventory costing

For inventory costing under IFRS in Korea (K-IFRS), last in first out (LIFO) will no
longer be treated as an acceptable accounting method. Consequently, taxable income
arising from adjusting the inventory balance booked under LIFO using other acceptable
costing methods (e.g. first in first out [FIFO], weighted-average) will be allowed to be
spread in its recognition over a five-year period. This change is applied for the fiscal
year to which 31 December 2011 belongs.

Bad debt allowance

In order to relieve K-IFRS users from any disproportionate burden for tax payment from
book-tax difference due to the adoption of a new accounting method or treatment, the
current tax law allows for deferral of taxable income recognition in various situations.
One such situation is the taxable income created in accounting for bad debt allowance.

This deferral is currently effective to cover a wider scope of entities over an extended
time period. For tax administration purposes, the scope of entities for deferral covers
a domestic place of business of a foreign corporation as well as domestic companies.
Deferral is available through 31 December 2013. The deferred income will be added

Korea, Republic of

back to taxable income of the fiscal year that begins after 1 January 2014. Please note that non-IFRS users will be excluded from the scope of eligible entities.

Taxes on corporate income

The basic Korean CIT rates for FY 2011 are 10% on the first KRW 200 million of the tax base and 22% for the excess. For FY 2012 and thereafter, the rates will be 10% on the first KRW 200 million, 20% for the tax base between KRW 200 million and 20 billion, and 22% for the excess.

Resident corporations are taxed on their worldwide income, whereas non-resident corporations with a permanent establishment (PE) in Korea are taxed only to the extent of their Korean-sourced income. Non-resident corporations without a PE in Korea are generally taxed through a withholding tax (WHT) on each separate item of income.

Agriculture and fishery surtax
When a corporate taxpayer claims certain tax credits or exemptions under the STTCL, a 20% agriculture and fishery surtax is levied on the reduced CIT liability.

Local income taxes (Resident tax surcharges)
A resident tax surcharge of 10% on CIT liability is assessed each year.

Minimum tax
Corporate taxpayers are liable for the minimum tax, which is defined as the greater of 10% (to the tax base of up to KRW 10 billion, 11% on the excess up to KRW 100 billion, 14% on the excess above KRW 100 billion) of the taxable income before various deductions and exemptions pursuant to the Special Tax Treatment Control Law (STTCL) applied to arrive at adjusted taxable income or the actual tax after various deductions and exemptions.

For small and medium enterprises (SMEs), the minimum tax is the greater of 7% of adjusted taxable income or actual tax liability.

Corporate residence

A corporation having its head office or principal office in Korea is a resident corporation. A corporation with a place of effective management in Korea is also treated as a resident corporation.

Permanent establishment (PE)
A non-resident corporation is generally deemed to have a tax presence (i.e. PE) in Korea if one of the following applies:

- It has any fixed place of business in Korea, where the business of the entity is wholly or partly carried on.
- It is represented by a dependent agent in Korea, who has the authority to conclude contracts on its behalf and who has repeatedly exercised that authority.
- Its employee(s) provides services in Korea for more than six months within 12 consecutive months.
- Its employee(s) continuously or repeatedly renders similar services in Korea for two or more years, even if each service visit is for less than six months within 12 consecutive months.

Exceptions to a PE in Korea for a non-resident corporation include fixed places of business used only for purchasing or storage of property at which no sales activities, advertising, publicity, collecting, or furnishing of information, or other activities that are preparatory or auxiliary to the conduct of business, occur.

Other taxes

Value-added tax (VAT)
VAT is levied at a rate of 10% on sales and transfers of goods and services, except zero-rated goods and services (e.g. goods for exportation, services rendered outside Korea, international transportation service by ships and aircraft, other goods and services supplied for foreign exchange earnings) and exempt goods and services (e.g. basic life necessities and services, such as unprocessed foodstuffs and agricultural products; medical and health service; finance and insurance services; duty-exempt goods).

Electronic VAT invoicing is a compulsory requirement. If a taxpayer fails to issue the electronic VAT invoice or report electronically to tax authorities, the relevant penalties shall be imposed.

Customs duties
Customs duties are generally assessed on imported goods. 'Importation' refers to the delivery of goods into Korea (in case of goods passing through a bonded area, delivery of such goods into Korea from such a bonded area) to be consumed or to be used in Korea.

Excise taxes
The individual consumption tax is imposed on specific luxury goods, high-priced durable consumer goods, goods subject to consumption restraints, and certain luxury activities for the purpose of supplementing the VAT single-rate scheme. Tax rates range from 2% to 20%; in certain circumstances, a fixed amount is levied (e.g. KRW 12,000 per person for golf course greens fees).

Property taxes
An annual tax ranging from 0.07% to 5% is charged on the statutory value of land, buildings, houses, vessels, and aircraft. Five times the property tax rate is applied to property that is newly constructed or expanded in the Seoul metropolitan area for five years from its relevant registration date.

Securities transaction tax
A securities transaction tax of 0.5% is imposed on the total value of securities at the time of transfer, but the government is authorised to adjust the tax rate in certain circumstances. The flexible tax rate prescribed by the Presidential Decree is 0.3% on transactions in both the Korea Stock Exchange and Korean Securities Dealers Automated Quotations (KOSDAQ).

Stamp taxes
The stamp tax is levied on a person who prepares a document certifying establishment, transfer, or change of rights to property in Korea. The stamp tax ranges from KRW 100 to KRW 350,000, depending on the type of taxable document.

Registration taxes
Registration tax ranging from 0.1% to 5% is charged upon the registration of title or right and incorporation. Registration tax upon the registration of title or right and

Korea, Republic of

incorporation for corporations located in large cities may be subject to three times the rates otherwise applied.

Acquisition taxes

Acquisition tax is charged on the price of real estate, motor vehicles, construction equipment, golf membership, boats, etc. The minimum rate is 2%. A weighted rate is charged on acquisitions in the Seoul metropolitan area or on acquisition of luxury items, such as villas, golf courses, and yachts.

Branch income

In general, a branch office of a foreign corporation is taxed in the same manner as resident companies.

Remittance of retained earnings from a Korean branch to its head office is subject to reporting to a designated foreign exchange bank in Korea under the Foreign Exchange Transaction Act.

If the tax treaty between Korea and the country in which a foreign corporation is residing allows the imposition of a branch profits tax, the tax is imposed on the adjusted taxable income of the Korean branch.

Where applicable, the branch profit tax is levied in addition to the regular CIT, which is imposed at the rate of 20% (or at a reduced rate as provided in a treaty) of the adjusted taxable income of the Korean branch.

Income determination

Gross income consists of gains, profits, income from trade and commerce, dealings in property, rents, royalties, and income derived from any ordinary transactions carried on for gain or profit.

Inventory valuation

Inventories generally are stated at the lower of cost or market (LCM). Any one of seven inventory valuation methods, including LCM, specific identification, first in first out (FIFO), last in first out (LIFO), weighted-average, moving-average, and retail method can be elected for tax purposes. The method elected should be applied consistently each year unless an application for change has been submitted before three months from the year-end. Different valuation methods may be used for different categories (i.e. products and merchandise, semi-finished goods and goods in process, raw materials, goods in stock) and different business places.

For inventory costing under K-IFRS, LIFO will no longer be treated as an acceptable accounting method. Consequently, taxable income arising from adjusting the inventory balance booked under LIFO using other acceptable costing methods (e.g. FIFO, weighted-average) will be allowed to be spread in its recognition over a five-year period. This change is applied for the fiscal year to which 31 December 2011 belongs.

Stock valuation

The valuation of securities or bonds shall be made using the cost method. For cost method, the weighted-average cost method or moving-average cost method shall be applied for the purpose of valuation of securities and individual cost method may be used for valuation of bonds.

Capital gains

For the purposes of taxation, gross income does not include income derived from gains from capital transactions such as capital surplus; gains on reduction of paid-in capital; or gains from merger, divisions, comprehensive share transfer, or comprehensive share exchange. However, gains from treasury stock transactions are taxed, and losses are deductible from taxable income.

Note that capital gains from the disposal of non-business purpose land or houses may be subject to additional capital gains tax at rates ranging from 10% to 40% after CIT.

Dividend income

All distributions to shareholders are taxed as dividend income, whether paid in cash or in stock.

However, a qualified domestic holding company that owns more than 80% (40% in case of listed subsidiary) share ownership in its domestic subsidiary will receive a 100% deduction for dividends while an 80% deduction is allowed for share ownership of 80% (40% in case of listed subsidiary) or less. A domestic corporation other than a qualified holding company will also receive a 100% deduction for share ownership of 100%, 50% for more than 50% (30% in case of listed subsidiary) share ownership, and 30% for share ownership of 50% (30% in case of listed subsidiary) or less.

K

Interest income

Except for certain cases, all interest income must be included in taxable income. Generally, interest income is included in taxable income as it is received.

Rental income

A company engaged in the business of the rental of real properties is also taxed on the deemed rental income calculated at the financial institutions' interest rate on the lease security money as well as on the recognised rental income.

Royalty income

Royalties are considered to be taxable income when earned.

Gains and losses on foreign currency translation

Companies are allowed to recognise unrealised gains and losses on foreign currency translation of their monetary assets in a foreign currency. This recognition is also allowed with respect to currency forward transactions and swaps to hedge foreign exchange risks of such assets. In this regard, a taxpayer can choose whether to recognise unrealised gains and losses or not for tax purposes. Once elected, the same method must be consistently used.

Foreign income

Resident corporations are taxed on their worldwide income. A Korean company is taxed on its foreign-sourced income as earned at normal CIT rates. To avoid double taxation, taxes imposed by foreign governments on income recognised by a resident company are allowed as a credit against the income taxes to be paid in Korea or as deductible expenses in computing the taxable income. In general, foreign taxes will generally be applied as credit rather than as a deduction.

Korea, Republic of

Income of foreign subsidiaries incorporated outside Korea is not included in the taxable income of a resident company. Income is recognised by a resident company only upon the declaration of dividends from a foreign subsidiary. Therefore, the Korean tax impact may be delayed through deferring the declaration of dividends unless the anti-tax haven rule under the Law for Coordination of International Tax Affairs (LCITA) is triggered.

Korean anti-tax haven rules state that accumulated earnings (distributable retained earnings) of a resident company's subsidiary located in a low tax jurisdiction (i.e. a tax haven where the effective tax rate on the taxable income for the past three years averages 15% or less) are taxed as deemed dividends to the resident company, which has direct and indirect interest of 20% or more in such subsidiary.

The foreign tax paid by a qualifying subsidiary is eligible for foreign tax credit against the dividend income of a resident company regardless of whether there are tax treaties with the relevant foreign countries. Before the amendment, the tax credits were allowed only when an existing tax treaty between Korea and the country of which the foreign subsidiary is a resident allows it. This change is applicable for the fiscal year commencing after 31 December 2011.

In connection with percentage of shareholding for tax credits, a qualifying subsidiary is one in which a resident corporation owns 10% or more of its shares for more than or equal to six consecutive months after the date of dividend declaration. Unused foreign tax credits can be carried forward for five years.

Deductions

In general, expenses incurred in the ordinary course of business are deductible, subject to the requirements for documentary support.

A corporation's disbursements of more than KRW 30,000 for goods or services provided are required to be supported by corroborating documents, such as credit card sales vouchers, cash receipts, tax invoices, and those vouchers and invoices stored in the company's enterprise resource planning (ERP) system. The corporation is required to maintain these documents for five years. If the corporation fails to maintain proper evidences, a 2% penalty shall be levied on the amount of disbursement.

Accrued expenses are not deductible until the expenses are fixed or paid.

Depreciation and amortisation

With the exception of land, depreciation of all property, plant, and equipment (PP&E), which includes buildings, machinery, and auto-vehicles, used to generate income is allowed as a deduction for CIT. Generally, interest on debt acquired to purchase, manufacture, or construct PP&E must be capitalised until the PP&E is operational. This does not apply to the interest associated with the expansion or improvement of existing PP&E. A detailed list of fixed assets, gross values (including capitalised interest), the useful lives of the assets, and the current year's depreciation charge must be submitted to the tax authorities when filing the annual CIT return.

The tax law allows the following methods for calculating depreciation:

* Straight-line or declining-balance method for tangible fixed assets, other than plant and buildings.

- Straight-line method for plant, buildings, and intangible assets.
- Service-output or straight-line method for mining rights.
- Service-output, declining-balance, or straight-line method for tangible fixed assets used in mining.

In determining depreciation using a straight-line method, salvage value of the assets is regarded as zero. However, where the declining-balance method is used, 5% salvage value is required. Changes in the depreciation method must be approved by the tax authorities in advance, and such approval may only be obtained in exceptional cases (i.e. merger between two corporations having different depreciation methods). Although the tax law specifies the useful lives of assets, the useful life of a fixed asset can be increased or decreased by 25% of the specified useful life at the taxpayer's election. The selected depreciation method should be consistently applied.

The standard useful life and the scope of useful life for assets are provided in the following tables:

Tangible fixed assets	Standard useful life (years)	Scope of useful life (years)
Autos and transportation equipment (excluding those used for transportation businesses, leasing service of machinery, equipment, and consumer goods), tools, equipment, and fixtures	5	4 to 6
Ships and aircraft (excluding those used for fishery, transportation, leasing service of machinery, equipment, and consumer goods)	12	9 to 15
All buildings and constructions of brick structure, block structure, concrete structure, mud structure, mud wall structure, wooden structure, wooden frame mortar structure, and other structures	20	15 to 25
All the buildings and constructions of steel-frame/iron bar concrete structures, stone structures, brick/stone structures, steel-frame structures	40	30 to 50

Intangible fixed assets	Useful life (years)
Goodwill, design rights, utility model rights, trademarks	5
Patents, fishery rights, extraction rights under the law of development of mineral resources at the sea bottom (may elect activity method), right of management for toll roads, water rights, right of use for electricity and gas service facilities, right of use for tap water facilities for industrial use, right of use for general tap water facilities, right of use for heating facilities	10
Mining rights (may elect activity method), right of use for exclusive telegraph and telephone facilities, right of use for exclusive sidetracks, right of management for sewage disposal, right of management for tap water facilities	20
Right of use for dams	50

Note that for used fixed assets (including assets acquired through mergers or spin-offs) that have been used for more than half of their useful lives, a new useful life may be

Korea, Republic of

filed with the tax authorities within the range of half of the original useful life and the original useful life filed for the first time of its utilisation.

According to CIT law, depreciation is allowed for tax deduction only when expensed for book purposes. However, in order to alleviate any dramatic increase in tax burden due to decreased depreciation expenses through the adoption of K-IFRS, additional expense deduction through tax adjustment may be allowed on a temporary basis. For tax purposes, depreciable assets acquired on or before 2013 may be depreciated at the rate equivalent to the average of three years before the adoption of K-IFRS. Depreciable assets acquired after 2014 may be depreciated using the tax useful lives.

Goodwill
Goodwill for tax purposes is defined as "value transferred with consideration, apart from transferred assets included in business transfer, valuated by taking into account business premium factors of the transferor such as permission/licence, legal privileges, geographical advantages, business secrets, credit, reputation, transaction partners, etc." Goodwill may be amortised over five years using the straight-line method for tax purposes.

Start-up expenses
Start-up expenses such as incorporation expenses, founders' salary, and registration fees and taxes are deductible when the expenses are actually paid.

Interest expenses
Interest incurred in the ordinary course of business is deductible as long as the related loan is used for business purposes. There are, however, a number of exceptions to the general rule, as follows:

- If borrowings from a foreign shareholder, or from a third party under a payment guarantee by the foreign shareholder, exceed three times the equity of the relevant foreign shareholder, the paid interest and discount fee as to the relevant excessive portion will be treated as a dividend payment and not allowed as a deduction.
- Debenture for which the creditor is unknown.
- Bonds and securities on which recipient of interest is unknown.
- Construction loans and loans for the purchase of land and fixed assets up to the date on which the assets are acquired or completed must be capitalised as a part of the cost of the asset and depreciated over the life of the asset. Interest after the date of completion or acquisition is deductible as incurred.
- Interest on loans related to non-business purpose assets or funds loaned to related parties.

Contingent liabilities
In general, contingent liabilities are not deductible, except for reserves under the following items, which are counted as losses within the tax limit:

- Reserves for retirement allowance.
- Reserves for bad debts.
- Liability reserves and emergency reserves prescribed in the Insurance Business Law.
- Reserves for non-profit organisations.
- Reserves for the write-off of a compensation claim set aside by trust guarantee funds in each business year.

The amounts enumerated below are also counted as losses in calculating income for the business year:

- The amount of gains from insurance claims used to acquire the same kinds of fixed assets as the lost fixed assets, or to improve the damaged fixed assets within two years after the first day of the business year following the business year in which the gains fall.
- The amount of a beneficiary's share of construction costs received by a domestic corporation engaged in the electricity or gas business, etc., used for the acquisition of fixed assets.
- The amount of the national treasury subsidies actually used for acquisition or improvement of fixed assets for business.

Bad debt

A doubtful accounts reserve is allowed for tax purposes of up to 1% (2% for certain financial institutions) or the previous year's ratio of actual loss from bad debts to total balance of account receivables at year-end. Actual losses on bad debts are allowed when certain legal proceedings are satisfied or the statute of limitations has lapsed.

Although companies could set aside bad debt allowances based on reasonable estimates under the old generally accepted accounting principles (K-GAAP), the new GAAP for non-K-IFRS users and K-IFRS users requires objective evidence to recognise the allowance. This stricter rule is expected to create disproportionately higher taxable income on the first year of adoption.

In order to relieve K-IFRS users from any disproportionate burden for tax payment from book-tax difference due to the adoption of a new accounting method or treatment, the current tax law allows for deferral of taxable income recognition in various situations. One such situation is the taxable income created in accounting for bad debt allowance.

This deferral is currently effective to cover a wider scope of entities over an extended time period. For tax administration purposes, the scope of entities for deferral will cover a domestic place of business of a foreign corporation as well as domestic companies, while a domestic place of business of a foreign corporation was not covered in the concerned article before the tax reform of 31 December 2011. Deferral is available through 31 December 2013. The deferred income will be added back to taxable income of the fiscal year that begins after 1 January 2014. Please note that non-IFRS users will be excluded from the scope of eligible entities.

Charitable contributions

Donations to public interest entities, such as government authorities and social welfare organisations, as well as donations for academic research, technical development, etc., are classified as Bub-jung donations. Bub-jung donations are tax-deductible up to 50% of the total taxable income for the concerned fiscal year after deduction of net operating loss (NOL). Ji-jung donations to public entities prescribed by Corporate Income Tax Law (CITL) are also tax-deductible at up to 10% of the total taxable income for the fiscal year after the deduction of deductible Bub-jung donations and NOL.

The amount in excess of such limit may be carried over for three or five years. Donations other than the statutory donations above will not be deductible for tax purposes.

Employee remuneration

There is no statutory limit for employee remuneration, which includes salaries, wages, stipends, bonuses, retirement payments, pensions, and meal and housing allowances as well as all other kinds of subsidies, payments, and compensation. Remuneration of foreign employees is determined according to their engagement contracts.

K

Korea, Republic of

Pension expense

For tax purposes, severance allowance may be deducted at up to 5% of the annual total amount of wages paid. However, the accumulated amount of the severance allowance reserve may not exceed 25% of the actual aggregate liability to employees for FY 2011. This deduction limit will be reduced by 5% every year from 2011 to be entirely eliminated in 2016. If a corporation subscribes to severance insurance with an insurance company to cover future payments of retirement allowances, additional tax deductions beyond the limits described above are available.

Employers hiring five or more employees are required to set aside retirement pensions for their employees. Defined contribution (DC) and defined benefits (DB) are the two available schemes for the retirement pension system. Under the DC scheme, the premiums paid by the employer are deductible upon payment while the reserve under the DB scheme is deductible subject to a limit, similar to the severance insurance.

Payment for directors

Bonuses paid to directors in excess of the amount determined in the articles of incorporation or at a shareholders' meeting, etc. are not deductible. Also, severance benefits paid to directors in excess of the amount prescribed in the tax law are not deductible.

Entertainment expenses

Entertainment expenses of more than KRW 10,000 on an event basis must be supported by corporate credit card vouchers, cash receipts, or tax invoices in order to be deductible. In addition, the entertainment expenses in excess of the tax limit are not deductible.

The deductible limit for entertainment expenses in a business year is computed as:

- an amount calculated by multiplying KRW 12 million (KRW 18 million for a SME) by the number of months in the respective business year divided by 12, plus
- an amount calculated by multiplying the amount of gross receipts for a business year by the rates listed in the following table (in the case of receipts from transactions between related parties, 20% of the amount calculated by multiplying the receipts by following rates shall be applied).

Amount of gross receipts (KRW)	Rate
10 billion or less	0.2%
10 billion to 50 billion	KRW 20 million + 0.1% of the excess over KRW 10 billion
Greater than 50 billion	KRW 60 million + 0.03% of the excess over KRW 50 billion

Insurance premiums

Insurance premiums paid to an insurance company are deductible if the business enterprise is the listed beneficiary. Insurance premiums for which the beneficiary is the employee are also deductible; however, they are treated as salaries for the employees and are subject to WHT on earned income (this excludes the severance insurance premium or social security taxes that are borne by the corporations).

Fines and penalties

Fines, penalties, and interest on underpayment of taxes are not deductible.

Taxes
Income taxes are generally not deductible in determining income subject to CIT.

Net operating losses (NOLs)
In general, an NOL carryover is allowed for ten years for fiscal years commencing after 31 December 2008 (five years for the prior years). Along with the extension of the NOL carryforward period from five years to ten years, when a taxpayer uses the NOL incurred more than five years ago, the statute of limitations shall be one year from the filing due date of the fiscal year when the NOL is utilised.

Generally, loss carrybacks are not allowed. However, SMEs can carry back an NOL for one year.

Payments to foreign affiliates
With sufficient supporting documentation, interest, royalty, and management service fees paid to foreign affiliates are deductible for CIT purposes.

Under the LCITA, the following conditions must be met in order for a management service fee to be deductible:

- The services must be provided based on an agreement entered into by the service provider prior to the service transaction.
- The provision of the service can be verified by a schedule of services, description of services, description of the company providing services and its employees, detailed explanation of expenses incurred, and other supporting documentation.
- A company must be able to anticipate the company's additional profit or reduced expense through the services provided by a foreign affiliate.
- Payment for the provided services should be consistent with arm's-length standards.

K

Group taxation

The consolidated corporate tax filing system can be adopted for a domestic corporation in cases where two or more wholly-owned subsidiaries exist. It is up to the election of the taxpayer, but it cannot be revoked for at least five years after the election of the consolidated tax filing.

Transfer pricing
The LCITA authorises the tax authorities to adjust the transfer price based on an arm's-length price and to determine or recalculate a resident's taxable income when the transfer price of a Korean company and its foreign counterpart is either below or above an arm's-length price.

The LCITA lists the following methods for determining an arm's-length price: the comparable uncontrolled price (CUP) method, the resale price method, and the cost-plus method. Furthermore, the Decree elaborates upon the profit-split method, the transactional net margin method (TNMM), and the Berry Ratio method as methods for determining an arm's-length price based on profits arising from controlled transactions.

The method used and the reason for adopting that particular one for an arm's-length price determination must be disclosed to the tax authorities by a taxpayer in a report submitted along with one's annual tax return.

Korea, Republic of

Thin capitalisation

In cases where a Korean company borrows from its controlling shareholders overseas, an amount greater than three times (six times in the case of financial institutions) its equity interest payable on the excess portion of the borrowing is characterised as dividends to which the article on dividends in tax treaty applies and therefore is treated as non-deductible in computing taxable income.

Anti-tax haven rules

In cases where a Korean company invests in a company located in a tax haven, which unreasonably has reserved profits in the controlled foreign company, the profits reserved therein shall be treated as dividends paid out to that Korean company (individual), despite the fact that the reserved profits are not actually distributed.

Anti-tax haven rules are intended to regulate a company that has made overseas investments of an abnormal nature. Thus, these anti-tax haven rules apply to those Korean companies that have invested in a company incorporated in a foreign country with an average effective tax rate of 15% or less on taxable income for the past three years.

However, if a company incorporated in such a tax haven country actively engages in business operations through an office, shop, or a factory, then the anti-tax haven rules will not apply.

Related party transactions

Under the provision of CITL, the tax authorities may recalculate the corporation's taxable income when CIT is unreasonably reduced due to transactions with related parties. Generally, if the discrepancy between the transaction price and fair market value exceeds 5% of the fair market value or KRW 300 million, the transaction will be subject to this provision.

Tax credits and incentives

Foreign tax credit

Taxes imposed by foreign governments on income recognised by a resident taxpayer are allowed as a credit within the limit against the income taxes to be paid in Korea, or as deductible expenses in computing the taxable income. In general, foreign taxes will be applied as credit rather than as a deduction. The excess foreign tax credit can be carried forward five years.

Investment incentives

Tax credits are generally available for qualified investment in facilities for productivity enhancement, safety, job-creating investments, etc.

Tax credit for investment in facilities for productivity enhancement

If a resident makes an investment in facilities or equipment to increase productivity by no later than 31 December 2012, then 3% (7% in the case of SMEs) of such investment amount shall be deducted from CIT. The unused tax credit can be carried forward five years.

Tax credit for investment in facilities for safety

If a resident or a domestic corporation makes an investment in a facility (excluding any investment in used assets) for safety that is considered necessary for industrial purposes no later than 31 December 2012, then an amount of 3% of such investment shall be deducted from CIT. The unused tax credit can be carried forward five years.

New or increased tax credit for job-creating investments
While the 4% to 5% temporary tax credit for facility investments will be terminated for investments made after 1 January 2012, the existing tax credit for job-creating investments will be maintained at an increased rate of 5% to 7%, compared with the current 1% credit. The credit will include a 3% to 4% tax credit for a company maintaining a status quo employment and an additional 2% to 3% tax credit for new job-creating investments. The additional tax credit for job creation will not exceed the ceilings set at KRW 10 million (KRW 15 million per employee between the ages 15 and 29, KRW 20 million per specified occupational high school graduate employee) multiplied by the number of new employment in net.

Research and development (R&D) tax incentives
The STTCL provides various tax incentives to stimulate R&D activities. These include deduction of R&D reserve, tax credit for research, and manpower development expenses.

Reserves for development of technology and manpower
In cases where a corporation has set aside development of technology and manpower reserves for expenses on development of technology and manpower on or before 31 December 2013, those reserves are considered as deductible expenses up to 3% of annual sales.

Tax credit for development of technology and manpower
Companies presently claim a tax credit in relation to qualifying R&D expenditure to the extent of either (i) 3% to 6% (25% for SMEs) of the current R&D expenses or (ii) 40% (50% for SMEs) of the incremental portion of the current R&D expenses over the average of the previous four years. The tax credit has been extended to include R&D in relation to core technologies as authorised by government ministries as well as pre-designated strategic growth industries until the end of December 2012, and for these industries, the credit rate for the current R&D expenditure is 20% (30% for SMEs).

Tax credit for investment in facilities for technology and human resources development
A corporation purchasing facilities prescribed in the Presidential Decree with the purpose of R&D and job training is eligible for tax credit up to 10% of such investment. The unused tax credit can be carried forward five years.

Energy/environmental incentives

Tax credit for investment in energy-economising facilities
If a resident makes an investment (excluding any investment in used goods) not later than 31 December 2013 in energy-economising facilities, 10% of such investment shall be deducted from CIT. The unused tax credit can be carried forward five years.

Tax credit for investment in facilities for environmental protection
If a resident makes an investment (excluding any investment in used goods) in any facility for the purpose of environmental conservation no later than 31 December 2013, then 10% of the investment amount shall be deducted from CIT. The unused tax credit can be carried forward five years.

K

Korea, Republic of

Inbound investment incentives

The Korean government provides various incentives and benefits for inducing foreign investment under the Foreign Investment Promotion Law.

Foreign invested companies that engage in certain qualified high-technology businesses can apply for 100% exemption from CIT for five years, beginning from the first year of profitable operations (from the fifth year, if not profitable until then) and a 50% reduction for the following two years in proportion to the foreign shareholding ratio. An exemption from WHT on dividends is available for foreign investors in the same manner as above during the same grace period. In addition, the taxpayer can apply for 100% exemption from local taxes, such as acquisition tax, registration tax, and property tax on assets acquired for their business for five years after the business commencement date and 50% reduction for the following two years. For local tax exemption, some local governments grant longer exemption periods (up to 15 years) in accordance with their local ordinances. Qualified foreign investment also can be eligible for exemption from customs duties, VAT, and special excise tax on imported capital goods for the first three years.

In addition, foreign investors satisfying specified criteria are provided with tax incentives and other benefits for investment in specially designated areas, including foreign investment zones (FIZ), free economic zones (FEZ), free trade zones (FTZ), and strategic industrial complexes exclusively developed for foreign invested companies. The tax incentives for qualifying foreign investors in FIZ are similar to those of the above foreign invested high-tech companies. Qualifying investors in FEZ, FTZ, and strategic industrial complexes may receive the 100% exemption from corporate or individual income tax as well as local taxes for the first three years and 50% reduction for the next two years. An exemption from WHT on dividends is granted to qualifying foreign investors in FEZs, FTZs, and such industrial complexes in the same manner as above during the same grace period. They also receive exemption from customs duties on imported goods for the first three years.

Foreign direct investment (FDI) incentive limitations

The FDI credit limits incentives granted to qualified FDIs. The ceiling has been set to encompass both investment amount and job-creation. In terms of investment amount, the level of incentives for FDI has been reduced to 70% of the aggregated FDI amount for companies benefiting from a seven-year incentive period (50% ceiling for companies enjoying a five-year incentive period). In terms of job-creation, the level of incentives for FDI has been reduced to the lower of either 20% of the aggregated FDI amount or KRW 10 million times the company's net increase in employment.

Companies that have enjoyed tax benefits based on job-creation will be subject to tax assessment in cases where there is a net decrease in employment within the subsequent two years in comparison to the year that the relevant tax credit was obtained.

Withholding taxes

Foreign corporations with income derived from sources in Korea are subject to CIT on such income. If the foreign corporation has no 'domestic place of business' in Korea, it will be subject to tax on its Korean-source income on a withholding basis in accordance with the tax laws and the relevant tax treaty, if applicable. Any Korean-source income attributable to a domestic fixed place of business of a foreign corporation will be subject to Korean CIT.

Korea, Republic of

For residents of countries with a tax treaty with Korea, reduced WHT rates may apply. Starting from 1 July 2012, an application form must be submitted to the withholding agents in order to apply the treaty rate. If a beneficiary cannot be identified in the application form, the withholding agents should withhold the tax at the non-treaty rate.

If a foreign company is located in a foreign jurisdiction designated as a tax haven by the Minister of Strategy & Finance, any Korean-source income of such foreign company will be subject to the domestic withholding rate of 20% regardless of whether or not the foreign company is resident of a treaty country. Currently, only Labuan is designated as such a jurisdiction. The foreign company may claim a refund of any excess WHT paid within three years, if it proves to the Korean Tax Office that it is entitled to the reduced treaty rates as the substantive and beneficial owner of the income. Alternatively, a foreign company may attempt to seek a pre-approval in order to have the treaty benefits apply upfront by making an application to the Commissioner of Taxation.

For dividends, interest, and royalties, the WHT rates are limited as follows:

Recipient	Dividends (%)	Interest (%)	Royalties (%)
Resident corporations (1)	0	14/25	0
Resident individuals (1)	14	14/25/30	0
Non-resident corporations and individuals:			
Non-treaty (2)	20	14/20 (36)	20 (39)
Treaty:			
Albania	5/10 (8)	10	10
Algeria	5/15 (8)	10	2/10 (15)
Australia	15	15	15
Austria	5/15 (8)	10	2/10 (15)
Azerbaijan	7	10 (37)	5/10 (22)
Bangladesh	10/15 (3)	10	10
Belarus	5/15 (8)	10	5
Belgium	15	10	10
Brazil	10	10/15 (5)	10/25 (6)
Bulgaria	5/10 (7)	10	5
Canada	5/15 (8)	10	10
Chile	5/10 (8)	10/15 (31)	5/15 (33)
China, P.R.	5/10 (8)	10	10
Croatia	5/15 (8)	5	0
Czech Republic	5/10 (8)	10	10
Denmark	15	15	10/15 (4)
Egypt	10/15 (8)	10/15 (9)	15
Fiji	10/15 (8)	10	10
Finland	10/15 (8)	10	10
France	10/15 (3)	10	10
Germany	5/15 (8)	10	2/10 (15)
Greece	5/15 (8)	8	10
Hungary	5/10 (8)	0	0
Iceland, Republic of	5/15 (8)	10	10
India	15/20 (11)	10/15 (12)	15
Indonesia	10/15 (8)	10	15

Korea, Republic of

Recipient	Dividends (%)	Interest (%)	Royalties (%)
Ireland, Republic of	10/15 (3)	0	0
Israel	5/10/15 (13)	7.5/10 (14)	2/5 (15)
Italy	10/15 (8)	10	10
Japan	5/15 (8)	10	10
Jordan	10	10	10
Kazakhstan	5/15 (3)	10	2/10 (15)
Kuwait	10	10	15
Laos	5/10 (3)	10	5
Lithuania	5/10 (8)	10	5/10 (38)
Luxembourg	10/15 (8)	10	10/15 (16)
Malaysia	10/15 (8)	15	10/15 (17)
Malta	5/15 (8)	10	0
Mexico	0/15 (18)	5/15 (19)	10
Mongolia	5	5	10
Morocco	5/10 (8)	10	5/10 (20)
Nepal	5/10/15 (32)	10	15
Netherlands	10/15 (8)	10/15 (21)	10/15 (22)
New Zealand	15	10	10
Norway	15	15	10/15 (22)
Oman	5/10 (3)	5	8
Pakistan	10/12.5 (11)	12.5	10
Papua New Guinea	15	10	10
Philippines (2)	10/25 (23)	10/15 (24)	10/15 (25)
Poland	5/10 (3)	10	10
Portugal	10/15 (8)	15	10
Qatar	10	10	5
Romania	7/10 (8)	10	7/10 (22)
Russia	5/10 (26)	0	5
Saudi Arabia, Kingdom of	5/10 (8)	5	5/10 (33)
Singapore	10/15 (8)	10	15
Slovak Republic	5/10 (8)	10	0/10 (34)
Slovenia	5/15 (8)	5	5
South Africa (2)	5/15 (8)	10	10
Spain	10/15 (8)	10	10
Sri Lanka	10/15 (8)	10	10
Sweden	10/15 (8)	10/15 (10)	10/15 (22)
Switzerland	10/15 (8)	10	10
Thailand (2)	10	10/15 (27)	5/10/15 (35)
Tunisia	15	12	15
Turkey	15/20 (8)	10/15 (28)	10
Ukraine	5/15 (11)	5	5
Union of Myanmar	10	10	10/15 (4)
United Arab Emirates	5/10 (3)	10	0
United Kingdom	5/15 (8)	10	2/10 (15)
United States (2)	10/15 (30)	12	10/15 (29)
Uzbekistan	5/15 (8)	5	2/15 (15)
Venezuela	5/10 (3)	5/10 (19)	5/10 (33)
Vietnam	10	10	5/15 (22)

Korea, Republic of

Notes

1. Dividends and interest paid to resident individuals by corporations generally are subject to a 14% WHT rate. In addition to this, there is a resident surtax of 10% on the CIT liability.
2. In addition to the indicated tax rate, a resident surtax is charged at a rate of 10% of the respective tax rate.
3. Lower rate applies in case of equity ownership of 10% or more.
4. 10% rate applies to royalties paid for the use of or the right associated with industrial activities.
5. 10% rate applies if the loan period extends to seven years or more, the recipient is a financial institution, and the loan is used for certain designated purposes.
6. 25% rate applies to royalties associated with the use of trademarks or trademark rights.
7. 5% rate applies in case of equity ownership of 15% or more.
8. Lower rate applies in case of equity ownership of 25% or more.
9. 10% rate applies if the term of loans exceeds three years.
10. 10% rate applies when a recipient of interest income is a bank and income is connected with a loan with a term in excess of seven years.
11. Lower rate applies in case of equity ownership of 20% or more.
12. 10% rate applies if a recipient is a bank.
13. 5% rate applies if a recipient holds 10% or more ownership in a paying corporation but, even in case of 10% or more ownership, 10% rate applies if the dividends are paid out of profits subject to tax at a lower rate than the normal corporate tax rate of a country where a payer resides. In other cases, 15% rate applies.
14. 7.5% rate applies when a recipient of interest income is a bank or a financial institution.
15. 2% rate applies to royalties paid for use of or the right to use industrial, commercial, or scientific equipment.
16. 10% rate applies if it is for the use of or the right to use industrial, commercial, and scientific equipment or information.
17. 15% rate applies if royalties are for use of or the right to use cinematography films or tapes for radio or television broadcasting or any copyright of literary or artistic work.
18. 0% rate applies in case of equity ownership of 10% or more.
19. 5% rate applies if a recipient is a bank.
20. 5% rate applies to royalties for use of copyrighted literature and music.
21. 10% rate applies if the term of the loans exceeds seven years.
22. Lower rate applies if it is for the use of or the right to use a patent, trademark, design, or secret formula, or industrial, commercial, and scientific equipment or information.
23. 10% rate applies in cases of equity ownership of 25% or more, or dividend paid by a resident company engaged in a preferred pioneer area and registered with the Board of Investment.
24. 10% rate applies in cases where the interest is paid in respect of public offering of bonds, debentures, or similar obligations or interest paid by a company that is a resident of the Philippines, registered with the Board of Investment, and engaged in preferred pioneer areas of investment under the investment incentive laws.
25. 10% rate applies in case of royalties paid by a company that is a resident of the Philippines, registered with the Board of Investment, and engaged in preferred pioneer areas of investment under the investment incentives laws.
26. 5% rate applies if a recipient holds 30% or more of equity interest in the amount of at least 100,000 United States dollars (USD).
27. 10% rate applies if a beneficial owner of the income is a financial institution (including insurance company) or resident of Thailand who is paid with respect to indebtedness arising as a consequence of a sale on credit by a resident of Thailand of any equipment, merchandise, or services, except where the sale was between persons not dealing with each other at arm's length.
28. 10% rate applies if the term of the loan exceeds two years.
29. 10% rate applies to royalties for use of copyrighted literature, music, films, and television or radio broadcasts. Otherwise, 15% rate applies.
30. 10% rate applies if equity ownership is 10% or more and not more than 25% of the gross income of a paying corporation for a preceding tax year consists of interest or dividends.
31. 10% rate applies when a recipient of interest income is a bank or an insurance company.
32. 5% rate applies when a recipient holds 25% or more of equity interest, and 10%, when a recipient holds 10% or more of equity interest. In other cases, 15% rate applies.
33. 5% rate applies to royalties paid for the use of or the right associated with industrial, commercial, or scientific equipment.
34. 0% rate applies to royalties paid for the use of academic rights.
35. 5% rate applies to royalties paid for the use of or the right associated with any copyright of literary, artistic, or scientific work, including software, and motion pictures and works on film, tape, or other means of reproduction for use in connection with radio or television broadcasting. 10% rate applies to royalties paid for the use of or the right to use a patent, trademark, design or model, plan, secret formula, or process. 15% rate applies to royalties paid for the use of or the right to use industrial, commercial, or scientific equipment, or for information concerning industrial, commercial, or scientific experience.
36. 14% rate applies if interest arises from bonds issued by a Korean company or government bodies.
37. 0% rate applies if a recipient of interest income is government, central bank, etc.
38. 5% rate applies to royalties paid for the use of industrial, commercial, or scientific equipment.

K

Korea, Republic of

39. Fees arising from rental of industrial, commercial, scientific equipment, etc. are classified as rental income subject to 2% WHT.

Tax administration

Taxable period
In Korea, the taxable year is on a fiscal-year basis as elected by the taxpayer. However, it cannot exceed 12 months.

Tax returns
A corporation must file an interim tax return with due payment for the first six months of the fiscal year and the filing/payment must be made within two months after the end of the interim six-month period.

A corporation must file an annual tax return with due payment for the fiscal year and the filing/payment must be made within three months from the end of a fiscal year.

Payment of tax
Where the tax amount to be paid by a resident corporation is in excess of KRW 10 million, part of the tax amount to be paid may be paid in instalments within one month of the date of the expiration of the payment period (two months for SMEs).

Where the tax amount to be paid is less than KRW 20 million, the excess of KRW 10 million shall be paid in instalments; where the tax amount to be paid exceeds KRW 20 million, 50% or less of the tax amount shall be paid in instalments.

Functional currency
In instances where the taxpayer adopts to use a foreign currency as its functional currency, there are three ways to calculate the CIT base: (i) calculate the tax base using the financial statements in functional currency and translate it into Korean won; (ii) prepare the financial statements in Korean won and calculate the tax base; or (iii) translate the financial statements into Korean won and calculate the tax base. Once elected, the same method must be consistently used.

Audit cycle
In January 2012, the National Tax Service (NTS) announced the 'Plan for Tax Audits', which is the criteria for selecting a tax audit target company.

For large companies whose sales revenue is KRW 500 billion or more, the tax audit will be conducted every five years. Other companies are selected by certain standards which were announced by NTS.

Statute of limitations
The statute of limitations is generally five years from the statutory filing due date of the annual CIT return. However, the statute of limitations is extended further in the following cases:

* Ten years if a taxpayer evades taxes by fraud or unjustifiable means.
* Seven years if a taxpayer does not file its tax base by the statutory due date.

Along with the extension of the NOL carryforward period from five years to ten years, when a taxpayer uses the NOL incurred more than five years ago, the statute of limitation shall be one year from the filing due date of the fiscal year when the NOL is utilised.

Topics of focus for tax authorities

The recent topics of focus for tax authorities are as follows:

- Increased scrutiny for the prevention of offshore tax evasion through aggressive tax planning.
- Denial of unfair transactions between related parties.
- Prevention of embezzlement through fictitious expenses or tax evasion using subcontractors.
- Deductibility of management service fees or allocated expenses incurred by foreign affiliates.
- International inter-company transactions and transfer pricing.

Other issues

Exchange controls

Most transactions involving foreign exchange generally do not require approval or reporting under the Foreign Exchange Transaction Act (FETA), with a few exceptions as prescribed by the FETA. Receipt of foreign exchange from outside Korea is freely permitted, and payments to foreign companies are not regulated. Most restrictions on Korean companies' foreign currency transactions with foreigners have been removed. However, the government continues to monitor certain flows of foreign currency in an attempt to minimise incoming speculative currency and outgoing capital flight.

Ever since Korea's currency crisis, most restrictions on short-term as well as mid and long-term borrowings from overseas by corporations have been removed. Most foreign currency loans are allowed and are subject to reporting to a foreign exchange bank. There are no specific regulations, except the reporting requirements, on borrowings from overseas by foreign investment companies in Korea.

Choice of business entity

The following types of commercial entities are permitted in Korea:

- Corporation (*Hoesa*): There are five classes of corporation, outlined as follows:
  - Limited corporation:
    - *Jusik Hoesa* (JH): A corporation incorporated by one or more promoters, with each shareholder's liability limited to the amount of contributed capital. This type of entity is the most commonly used in Korea.
    - *Yuhan Hoesa* (YH): A corporation incorporated by one or more members, with each member's liability limited to the amount of that member's contribution to the corporation.
    - *Yuhan Chegim Hoesa* (a newly adopted form since 2012): A corporation incorporated by one or more members, with each member's liability limited to the amount of that member's capital contribution. With significantly fewer restrictions for establishment and operation, *Yuhan Chegim Hoesa* provides more flexibility and self-control than YH.
  - Unlimited corporation:
    - *Hapmyong Hoesa*: A corporation incorporated jointly by more than two members who are responsible for corporate obligations, if the assets of the corporation are insufficient to fully satisfy those obligations.

Korea, Republic of

- *Hapja Hoesa*: A corporation composed of one or more partners who have unlimited liability and one or more partners with limited liability.
- Partnership: *Hapja Johap* is a legal form of partnership allowed under the Commercial Code.
- Joint venture: A joint venture is generally established as a domestically incorporated corporation whose shareholders have limited liability regarding the obligations of the corporation under the Commercial Code.
- Branch: A foreign corporation can perform its business operation in Korea by setting up a taxable presence in the form of a branch office.
- Liaison office: A foreign corporation can establish a liaison office which is not allowed to execute income-generating business activities in Korea.
- Sole proprietorship: Sole proprietorships are not a legal form of entity in Korea.

Kuwait

PwC contact

Fouad Douglas
PricewaterhouseCoopers Al-Shatti & Co.
Arraya Tower II, 23-24th Floor
Al-Shuhada Street.
Sharq
Kuwait
Tel: +965 2227 5700
Email: fouad.douglas@kwt.pwc.com

Significant developments

Commercial developments

The Ministry of Commerce in Kuwait issued the Ministerial Order No. 237 of 2011, dated 26 May 2011, to regulate the set up of the Gulf Cooperation Council (GCC) companies to operate in Kuwait. As per the order, GCC companies are allowed to operate in Kuwait and are treated as Kuwaiti companies, provided that such companies are 100% owned by GCC nationals.

Tax developments

The tax retention mechanism

The Kuwait Tax Authorities (KTA) have implemented an active approach to ensure the compliance of local companies with the tax retention mechanism, especially those who have franchise operations and agreement with foreign franchisors in Kuwait. In some cases, the KTA has asked the Kuwaiti companies to settle the 5% retention wherein the franchisors have failed to comply with the tax law requirements.

Hence, the tax law now clearly states the following:

"All ministries, authorities, public institutions, companies, any private entities (and the similar) or any natural person that contracted with any incorporated body whether through contracts, agreements or any transactions shall retain 5% of the contract, agreement or transaction value or from each payment to the incorporated body."

The above mentioned authorities have to provide amounts mentioned before and any information required by the tax administration in order to implement the income tax decree; in the violation of this article, the violator is responsible for the payment of the taxpayer's debts.

In the event of breach, the breaching party shall be liable for paying the tax debts payable by the incorporated body.

The KTA is currently adopting a very aggressive attitude for non-compliant taxpayers and franchisors. Tax assessments have been issued on an arbitrary basis by the KTA through the application of an aggressive deemed profit with penalty to the foreign franchisor.

Kuwait

Value Added Tax (VAT) Law

The Ministry of Finance (MOF) in Kuwait is currently studying the implementation of the Value Added Tax Law in Kuwait. Substantial steps, studies, training sessions, and internal meetings within the MOF have been conducted. This Law is estimated to be introduced by the year 2014. However, nothing has been officially issued.

Taxes on corporate income

Kuwait does not impose income tax on companies wholly owned by the nationals of Kuwait or other GCC countries, including Bahrain, Oman, Qatar, Saudi Arabia, and the United Arab Emirates. However, GCC companies with foreign ownership are subject to taxation to the extent of the foreign ownership. Income tax is imposed only on the profits and capital gains of foreign 'corporate bodies' conducting business or trade in Kuwait, directly or through an agent.

Income earned from activities in Kuwait shall be considered subject to tax in Kuwait. In cases where a contract involves the performance of work both inside and outside Kuwait, the entire revenue from the contract must be reported for tax in Kuwait, including the work carried out outside Kuwait. *See the Income determination section for more information on income that is subject to tax in Kuwait.*

The current tax rate in Kuwait is a flat rate of 15%.

Foreign companies carrying on trade or business in the offshore area of the partitioned neutral zone under the control and administration of Saudi Arabia are subject to tax in Kuwait on 50% of taxable profit under the law.

Please refer to the Income determination section for details on taxable income in Kuwait.

Zakat
Zakat is imposed on all publicly traded and closed Kuwaiti shareholding companies at a rate of 1% of the companies' net profits.

Contribution to the Kuwait Foundation for the Advancement of Sciences (KFAS)
All Kuwaiti shareholding companies are required to pay 1% of their net profits as per their financial statements after their transfer to the statutory reserve and the offset of loss carryforwards, to the KFAS, which supports scientific progress.

Corporate residence

A foreign corporate body is any association formed and registered under the law of any country or state other than Kuwait that is registered as having a legal existence entirely separate from that of its individual members. No Kuwait-registered company is subject to income tax. However, any foreign corporate body that is a shareholder in a Kuwait-registered company undertaking business in Kuwait is subject to tax (*see the Taxes on corporate income section*). For the purposes of this law, GCC residents and entities wholly owned by GCC residents are treated in the same manner as Kuwaiti business entities.

Kuwait

Permanent establishment (PE)

The interpretation and application of the tax laws in Kuwait is usually not consistent with internationals standards, and the taxing provisions are usually subjected to the widest possible interpretation by the tax authorities in Kuwait to tax all income from Kuwaiti sources. An insignificant presence of employees or short term visits to Kuwait by the representatives of a company may render the entire revenue from the transactions as taxable in Kuwait. Full value of the contract, including the value of work performed outside Kuwait, is subject to tax in Kuwait.

Other taxes

Value-added tax (VAT)

The Kuwait Tax Law does not currently provide for a VAT. However, we understand that the MOF is considering introducing a VAT in Kuwait by the year 2014.

Customs duties/import tariffs

The GCC states have approved a unified customs tariff of 5% on cost, insurance, and freight (CIF) invoice price, subject to certain exceptions. A higher tariff is imposed on imports of tobacco and its derivatives and other products as notified.

Excise taxes

There are no excise taxes in Kuwait.

Property taxes

There are no property taxes in Kuwait.

Transfer taxes

There are no transfer taxes (e.g. stamp duty, real estate) in Kuwait.

National Labour Support Tax (NLST)

The purpose of the NLST law is to encourage the national labour force to work in the private sector by closing the gap in salaries and benefits between public and private sectors.

As per the law, Kuwaiti companies listed in the Kuwait Stock Exchange (KSE) are required to pay an employment tax of 2.5% of the company's net annual profits.

Social security

There are no social security obligations for expatriate workers. However, for foreign employees, it is generally necessary to make terminal indemnity payments calculated at 15 days' pay-per-year for the first three years of service and 2/3 month's pay-per-year thereafter.

For Kuwaiti employees, contributions are payable monthly by both the employer and employee under the Social Security Law. The employer's contribution is 11% and the employee's is 7.5% of monthly salary, up to a ceiling of 2,500 Kuwaiti dinars (KWD) per month. Benefits provided include pensions on retirement and allowances for disability, sickness, and death.

Kuwait

Branch income

Tax rates on branch profits are the same as on corporate profits.

Income determination

Income tax is imposed on the profit of a business in Kuwait as calculated by the normal commercial criteria, using generally accepted accounting principles (GAAP), including the accrual basis. Note that provisions, as opposed to accruals, are not deductible for tax purposes. In addition, for contract accounting, revenue is recognised by applying the percentage of completion method. Work-in-progress carried forward may not exceed 20% of work executed.

Article 2 of the amended tax law provides that income earned from the following activities in Kuwait shall be considered subject to tax in Kuwait:

- Any activities or business carried out either entirely or partially in Kuwait, whether the contract has been signed inside or outside Kuwait, as well as any income resulting from supply or sale of goods, or from providing services.
- The amounts collected from the sale, rent, or granting of a franchise to utilise any trademarks, design, patents, copyright, or other moral rights, or those related to intellectual property rights for use of rights to publish literary, arts, or scientific works of any form.
- Commission earned or resulting from agreements of representation or commercial mediation, whether such commissions are in cash or in kind.
- Having permanent office in Kuwait where the sale and purchase contracts are signed and/or where business activities are performed.
- Profits resulting from the following:
  - Any industrial or commercial activity in Kuwait.
  - Disposal of assets, either through the sale of the asset, part of the asset, the transfer of the asset's ownership to others, or any other form of disposal, including the disposal of shares in a company whose assets mainly consist of non-movable capital existing in Kuwait.
  - Granting loans in Kuwait.
  - Purchase and sale of property, goods, or related rights in Kuwait, whether such rights are related to monetary assets or moral rights such as mortgage and franchise rights.
  - Lease of property used in Kuwait.
  - Providing services, including profits from management, technical, and consultancy services.
  - Carrying out trading activities in the KSE, whether directly or through portfolios or investment funds.

Inventory valuation
Inventory is normally valued at the lower of cost or net realisable value, on a first in first out (FIFO) or average basis.

Capital gains
Capital gains on the sale of assets and shares by foreign shareholders are treated as normal business profits and are subject to tax at a 15% rate. The tax law provides for a tax exemption for profits generated from dealing in securities on the KSE, whether directly or through investment portfolios.

Dividend income

Treatment of dividends is not specifically addressed in the amended tax law or in its bylaws. The bylaws to the amended tax law, however, require investment companies or banks that manage portfolios, funds, or act as custodians of shares for foreign entities to deduct corporate tax due from payments due to foreign investors. Tax payment should be made within 30 days from the date of the deduction of tax, together with a list showing names of the foreign entities and the amount withheld from each.

Under the original tax law, no tax was imposed on dividends paid to foreign shareholders by Kuwaiti companies.

Interest income

In principle, tax is levied on the foreign company's share of the profits (whether or not distributed by the Kuwaiti company) plus any amounts receivable for any other income in Kuwait (e.g. interest, royalties, technical services, and management fees). However, the Kuwait tax law will still subject the interest received from a Kuwaiti source to tax in Kuwait whether this interest is the only source of income for the foreign entity in Kuwait or the foreign entity has more sources of income in Kuwait than the interest income.

Foreign currency exchange rates and related profits and losses

The tax treatment for realised and unrealised losses and gains related to foreign currency transactions are as follows:

- Unrealised foreign exchange gains are required to be reported in the tax declaration. However, unrealised gains may be excluded from taxable income for calculating the tax due for the fiscal year.
- Realised foreign exchange gains are taxable in Kuwait and therefore added to calculate taxable profits.
- Unrealised losses are not considered as tax deductible costs and therefore excluded for calculating taxable profits.
- Realised losses may be claimed as tax deductible costs, provided such losses are supported by adequate supporting information and documents.

Exempt income

The following sources of income are exempt from tax in Kuwait:

- Kuwaiti merchants purchasing, transporting, and selling goods imported on their own account where the foreign supplier has not been involved in Kuwait operations.
- Profits of a corporate body generated from dealing in securities listed in the KSE, whether such activities are carried out directly or through investment portfolios or funds.

Foreign income

The Kuwait tax law does not clearly state the tax treatment of foreign income. Such income is currently treated on case-by-case basis.

Deductions

For expenses to be deductible, they must be incurred in the generation of income in Kuwait. Such expenses must be supported by adequate documentary evidence.

Kuwait

Depreciation

Depreciation is taken on a straight-line basis at specified rates. However, within 90 days prior to submission of the tax declaration, the taxpayer may request that the tax department calculate the depreciation using a different method than the straight-line method. The tax department shall accept this request provided it is based on a reasonable basis in accordance with the tax accounting principles and rules.

The principal depreciation rates are specified in the law, as follows:

Type of fixed asset	Depreciation rate (%)
Buildings	4
Pre-fabricated buildings, furniture, and office equipment	15
Electronics and electrical equipment	15
Transportation and freight vehicles (trucks)	15
Tools and equipment	20
Cars and buses	20
Drilling equipment	25
Software	25
Computer equipment and accessories	33.3

Goodwill

In accordance with Executive Rule No. 39, amortisation of incorporated body goodwill is not allowed as a tax deductible expense.

Start-up expenses

Expenses incurred prior to signing of the contract are not allowed as tax deductible costs.

Interest expenses

Interest expenses are deductible if they are related to operations in Kuwait and are paid to a local bank.

Bad debt

Bad debt is deductible if related to operations in Kuwait and final resolution from the court is available.

Charitable contributions

Grants, donations, and subsidies paid to licensed Kuwaiti public or private agencies are deductible.

Fines and penalties

Fines and penalties are not tax deductible.

Taxes

Taxes and fees, except income tax, are deductible in Kuwait.

Net operating losses

As per the amended tax law, losses may be carried forward for a maximum of three years, provided that the following situations do not arise in the fiscal period following the period in which the loss was recorded:

- The tax declaration does not include any revenue from the business activities of the taxpayer in Kuwait.
- Change in the legal structure of the taxpayer.
- Merger of the taxpayer with another entity.
- Liquidation or ceasing of the activities of the taxpayer in Kuwait.

Please note that losses cannot be carried back in Kuwait.

Head office expenses/payments to foreign affiliates

The deduction of head office expenses (the overhead or the indirect expenses) is limited to 1.5% of the company's Kuwait revenue after deducting the subcontractors shares (if any).

The direct costs allocated by the head office (e.g. supply of goods, design and consultancy costs) are regulated as follows.

For goods costs incurred outside Kuwait:

Work conducted by	Allowable costs as a percentage of revenue
Head office	85% to 90%
Affiliated companies	90% to 93.5%
Third parties	93.5% to 96.5%

For design costs incurred outside Kuwait:

Work conducted by	Allowable costs as a percentage of revenue
Head office	75% to 80%
Affiliated companies	80% to 85%
Third parties	85% to 90%

For consultancy costs incurred outside Kuwait:

Work conducted by	Allowable costs as a percentage of revenue
Head office	70% to 75%
Affiliated companies	75% to 80%
Third parties	80% to 85%

In case there is no separate revenue for the consultancy, design, or goods work, although the nature of the contract requires the existence of consultancy work, the following formula shall be applied:

Consultancy, design, or goods revenue = (consultancy, design, or goods costs / total direct costs) x contract revenue

Group taxation

If a foreign company conducts more than one business activity in Kuwait, one tax declaration aggregating the income from all activities is required to be submitted in Kuwait. In addition, in the case where two affiliates are involved in similar lines of

Kuwait

business or work on the same project, their taxable results may be aggregated for the assessment of tax by the Kuwait tax authority.

Transfer pricing
Please refer to Head office expenses/payments to foreign affiliates in the Deductions section.

Thin capitalisation
Executive Rule No. 37 deals with the tax treatment of interest and letters of credit. Through this rule, the tax authority will accept the interest paid by a company, provided it is fully supported, paid to a financial institution, and related to the Kuwait operations. However, the tax law provides the Kuwait tax authority the right to determine the proper tax treatment on a case-by-case basis (if required).

Tax credits and incentives

Leasing and Investment Companies Law No. 12 of 1998
Leasing and Investment Companies Law No. 12 of 1998 allows the formation of investment and leasing companies having their principal place of business in Kuwait, with Kuwaiti or foreign shareholders. The law grants a five-year tax holiday to non-Kuwaiti founders and shareholders of such companies, beginning on the date of establishment of the companies.

Direct Foreign Capital Investment Law (DIFCL) No. 8 of 2001
DIFCL aims to encourage foreign investment participation in Kuwait, allowing up to 100% of foreign ownership in Kuwaiti businesses. It also provides a tax holiday of up to ten years with respect to non-Kuwaiti shareholders' shares of the profits from qualifying projects. An additional tax holiday for a similar period is granted for further investment in an already approved project.

Kuwait Free Trade Tone
Businesses set up in the Kuwait Free Trade Zone for carrying on specified operations are exempt from taxes on operations conducted in the zone. Foreign entities can own 100% of such businesses.

Build, operate, and transfer (BOT)
Kuwait has begun to use the BOT method in respect of some large infrastructure projects. Tax and tariff concessions may be built into a BOT contract.

Circular No. 50 of 2002
As per Circular No. 50 of 2002 issued by the Director of Income Taxation (DIT) regarding treatment of exempted companies under tax laws and/or other special laws and/or tax treaty, exempted companies shall comply with the provisions of submission of tax declaration, inspection, and assessment procedures like other companies in order to be eligible for exemption.

Some of the privileges under this law include:

- Exemption from income tax or any other taxes for a period of ten years from the commencing of the actual operations of the enterprise.
- Benefits under double taxation agreements.
- Benefits under investment encouragement and protection agreements.
- Total or partial exemption from custom duties on imports.

- Recruitment of required foreign labour.
- Allotment of land and real estate.

Withholding taxes

Apart from the withholding tax (WHT) on dividends arising from trading in the KSE, there are no other WHTs. However, all government bodies and private entities are required to retain the final payment due to a contractor or subcontractor until presentation of a tax clearance certificate from the MOF, confirming that the respective company has settled all of its tax liabilities. The final payment should not be less than 5% of the total contract value.

Tax treaties

Kuwait has entered into tax treaties with several countries for the avoidance of double taxation. Treaties with several other countries are at various stages of negotiation or ratification.

However, little experience has been gained in Kuwait regarding the application of tax treaties. As a result, disputes about the interpretation of various clauses in tax treaties between taxpayers and the DIT are not uncommon. Disputes with the DIT regarding tax treaties normally arise with respect to the following issues:

- Existence of a PE.
- Income attributable to a PE.
- Tax deductibility of costs incurred outside Kuwait.

The domestic tax law in Kuwait does not provide for WHTs. As a result, it is not yet known how the Kuwaiti government will apply the WHT procedures included in the treaties listed in the table below. The WHT rates listed in the table are for illustrative purposes only.

Recipient	Dividends (%)	Interest (%)	Royalties (%)
Non-treaty countries	0	0	0
Austria	0	0	10
Belarus	0/5 (3)	0/5 (3)	10
Belgium	10	0	10
Bulgaria	0/5 (10)	0/5 (6)	10
Canada	5/15 (13)	10	10
China	0/5 (1)	0/5 (1)	10
Croatia	5/10 (12)	10	10
Cyprus	10	0/10 (2)	5
Czech Republic	0/5 (10)	0	10
Ethiopia	0/5 (3)	0/5 (2)	30
France	0	0	0
Germany	5/15 (5)	0	10
Hungary	0	0	10
India	10 (14)	10 (14)	10
Indonesia	0/10 (3)	0/5 (2)	20
Italy	5	0	10

Kuwait

Recipient	Dividends (%)	Interest (%)	Royalties (%)
Jordan	0/5 (3)	0/5 (2)	30
Korea	10	10	15
Lebanon	0	0	30
Malta	10/15 (4)	0	10
Mauritius	0	0/5 (6)	10
Mongolia	0/5 (8)	0/5 (8)	10
Netherlands	0/10 (9)	0	5
Pakistan	10	0/10 (7)	10
Poland	0/5 (10)	0/5 (10)	15
Romania	1	1	20
Russian Federation	0/5 (3)	0	10
Singapore	0	0/7 (2)	10
South Africa	0	0	0
Sri Lanka	5/10	10	20
Sudan	0/5 (8)	0/5 (8)	10
Switzerland	15	10	10
Syria	0	0/10 (11)	20
Tunisia	0/10 (3)	0/2.5 (2)	5
Turkey	10	10	10
Ukraine	5	0	10
United Kingdom	5/15 (5)	0	10

Notes

1. The rate is 0% for amounts paid to a company of which the government owns at least 20% of the equity.
2. The rate is 0% for interest paid to the government of the other contracting state. Under the Ethiopia treaty, the rate is also 0% for the interest paid to entities in which the government owns a specified percentage of the equity and for interest paid on loans guaranteed by the government.
3. The rate is 0% for dividends and interest paid to the government of the other contracting state. Under the Ethiopia treaty, the rate is also 0% for dividends paid to entities in which the government owns a specified percentage of the equity.
4. The rate is 10% for dividends paid to the government of Kuwait or any of the institutions or any intergovernmental entities. The rate is 15% for other dividends.
5. The 5% rate applies if the recipient of the dividends owns directly or indirectly at least 10% of the payer. The 15% rate applies to other dividends.
6. The rate is increased to 5% if the beneficial owner of the interest carries on business in the other contracting state through a PE and the debt on which the interest is paid is connected to such PE.
7. The rate is 0% for amounts paid to the government of the other contracting state and to entities of which the government owns at least 51% of the paid-up capital.
8. For dividends and interest, the rate is 0% if the payments are made to the government or a governmental institution of the other contracting state, or to a company that is a resident of the other contracting state and is controlled by, or at least 49% of the capital is owned directly or indirectly by, the government or a governmental institution. A 0% rate also applies to interest arising on loans guaranteed by the government of the other contracting state or by a governmental institution or other governmental entity of the other contracting state.
9. A 0% rate applies if the beneficial owner of the dividends is a company that holds directly at least 10% of the capital of the company paying the dividends.
10. The rate is 0% if the payments are made to the government or a governmental institution of the other contracting state, or to a company that is resident of the other contracting state and is controlled by, or at least 25% of the capital is owned directly or indirectly by, the government or a governmental institution of the contracting state.
11. The rate is 0% if the beneficial owner of the interest is a resident in the other contracting state and the loan is secured or financed directly or indirectly by a financial entity or other local body wholly owned by the government of the other contracting state.
12. The 5% rate applies if the recipient of the dividends owns directly or indirectly at least 25% of the payer. The 10% rate applies to other dividends.

13. The rate is 5% if the beneficial owner of the dividends is a company that owns 10% or more of the issued and outstanding voting or 25% or more of the value of all of the issued and outstanding shares. The 15% rate applies to other dividends.
14. Dividends or interest paid by a company that is resident of a contracting state is not taxable in that contracting state if the beneficial owner of the dividends or interest is one of the following:
    * The government.
    * A political subdivision or a local authority of the other contracting state.
    * The Central Bank of the other contracting state.
    * Other governmental agencies or governmental financial institutions as may be specified and agreed to in an exchange of notes between the competent authorities of the contracting state.

In addition to the above existing tax treaties, Kuwait has signed the following tax treaties, but such treaties have not yet been ratified:

Country	Date of signing	Type of agreement	Status of the treaty
Cyprus	7 October 2010	Avoidance of double taxation and income tax evasion	Finally signed
Djibouti	28 March 2010	Avoidance of double taxation and income tax evasion	Finally signed
Egypt	30 December 2010	Avoidance of double taxation and income tax evasion	Initially signed
Goiania	19 July 2010	Avoidance of double taxation and income tax evasion	Finally signed
Indonesia	22 September 2010	Avoidance of double taxation and income tax evasion	Finally signed
Ireland	23 November 2010	Avoidance of double taxation and income tax evasion	Finally signed
Japan	17 February 2010	Avoidance of double taxation and income tax evasion	Finally signed
Kenya	7 January 2010	Avoidance of double taxation and income tax evasion	Initially signed
Myanmar	16 December 2010	Avoidance of double taxation and income tax evasion	Second round discussion
Nigeria	1 May 2010	Avoidance of double taxation and income tax evasion	Initially signed
North Korea	24 March 2010	Avoidance of double taxation and income tax evasion	Initially signed
Syria	1 May 2010	Avoidance of double taxation and income tax evasion	Initially signed

K

Kuwait

Tax administration

Taxable period

Tax is imposed on profits arising in a taxable period, which is defined as the accounting period of the taxpayer and further assumed to be the calendar year. However, the DIT may agree to a written request from the taxpayer to change the year-end to a date other than 31 December. Also, at the taxpayer's request, the DIT may agree to extend the accounting period, provided it does not exceed 18 months.

Tax returns

The taxpayer must submit a tax return, based on the taxpayer's books of account, within three months and 15 days of the end of the taxable period. A foreign entity can request an extension of up to 30 days for filing the tax declaration. Upon application, the DIT may extend the filing period by a maximum of 60 days.

The taxpayer must keep in Kuwait certain accounting records, which are subject to inspection by the tax department's officials. Accounting records may be in English and may be in a computerised system used to prepare financial statements, provided that the system includes the required records and the tax department is previously informed.

The tax return should be supported by the following:

* Audited balance sheet and profit-and-loss account for the period.
* Detailed list of fixed assets (e.g. additions, disposals).
* List of inventory (e.g. quantities and values).
* List of subcontractors and the latest payments to them.
* Copies of current contracts and a statement of income and expenditure for each.
* Trial balance, forming the basis of the accounts.
* Last payment certificate from the client.
* Insurance companies must attach to the Public Budget and the tax declaration a detailed statement with the reinsured documents and the related terms and conditions.

As a general rule, an assessment is finalised only after inspection of records by the tax department. As indicated above, proper documentation must be kept to support expenditure and to avoid disallowances at the time of tax inspection. If support is considered inadequate, the assessment is apt to be made on the basis of deemed profitability. This is computed as a percentage of turnover and is fixed arbitrarily, depending on the nature of the taxpayer's business.

Payment of tax

Tax is payable in four equal instalments on the 15th day of the fourth, sixth, ninth, and 12th months following the end of the tax period. If an extension is approved by the DIT, all of the tax is payable upon the expiration date of the extension. Failure to file or pay the tax on time attracts a penalty of 1% of the tax liability for every 30 days of delay or part thereof.

Objection process

If a company disagrees with an assessment issued by the DIT, the company should submit an objection within 60 days from the date of the assessment. The DIT is required to resolve the objection within 90 days of the filing of the objection, after which a revised tax assessment is issued by the DIT. Upon issuance of a revised tax assessment, any additional tax is payable within 30 days. If the DIT issues no response within 90 days of filing the objection, this implies that the taxpayer's objection has been rejected.

Appeals process

In case the objection is rejected or the taxpayer is still not satisfied with the revised tax assessment, the company may contest the matter further with the Tax Appeals Committee (TAC) by submitting a letter of appeal within 30 days from the date of the objection response or 30 days from the expiry of the 90 days following submission of an objection if no response is provided by the DIT.

The matter is then resolved through appeal hearings, and a final revised assessment is issued based on the decision of the TAC. Tax payable per the revised assessment must then be settled within 30 days from the date of issuance of the revised assessment. Failure to do so results in a delay penalty of 1% of the amount of the tax due per the final assessment for each period of 30 days or part thereof of the delay.

Other issues

Offset program

Kuwait has designed a counter-trade offset program to meet the objectives of its economic development plan. The offset program derives from the government's concern that the long-term benefits from job creation and capital accumulation resulting from government contracts with foreign suppliers unfairly accrue to the suppliers, at the expense of Kuwaiti companies and citizens. The objective of the offset program is to remedy this problem by encouraging collaborative business ventures between foreign contractors and the Kuwaiti private sector. Accordingly, the offset program has been established with the following objectives:

* Promote sustainable economic development in Kuwait, by the assimilation of modern technology and know-how in the local economy.
* Support projects that generate high skilled jobs for Kuwaiti nationals.
* Attract foreign investment capital to facilitate economic development in Kuwait.

The following are significant aspects of the program:

* All civil contracts with a value of KWD 10 million and more, and defence contracts with a value of KWD 3 million and more, attract the offset obligations for contractors. The obligations become effective on the signing date of the contract.
* The contractors covered by the offset obligation are required to invest 35% of the value of the contract with Kuwaiti government bodies.
* Offset obligators have the following options for fulfilling their offset obligation:
  * Implement investment projects suggested by the offset program management.
  * Propose their own investment projects, and seek approval of the offset program management.
  * Participate in any of the funds that the offset program management may establish.
  * Purchase of commodities and services of Kuwaiti origin. The MOF is, however, still finalising detailed regulations in this regard.
* Contractors covered by the offset obligation must provide unconditional, irrevocable bank guarantees issued by Kuwaiti banks to the MOF equal to 6% of the contract price. The value of the bank guarantee submitted will be reduced gradually based on the actual execution of its work by the foreign contractor/supplier. The MOF has the right to cash in the bank guarantee if the offset obligor fails to respect their offset obligation.

K

Kyrgyzstan

PwC contact

Richard Bregonje
PricewaterhouseCoopers Tax & Advisory LLP
34 Al-Farabi Avenue
Building A, 4th Floor
050059 Almaty, Kazakhstan
Tel: +7 727 330 32 01
Email: richard.bregonje@kz.pwc.com

Significant developments

There have been no significant corporate tax developments in Kyrgyzstan during the past year.

Taxes on corporate income

Pursuant to the tax code, resident entities are subject to a corporate income tax, called the 'profit tax', on their aggregate annual income earned worldwide. Non-resident legal entities carrying out business activities through a permanent establishment (PE) in Kyrgyzstan are subject to profit tax on the income attributed to the activities of that PE.

Profit tax is calculated at a rate of 10% of aggregate annual income less allowed deductions.

Corporate residence

There is no concept of corporate residence in the Kyrgyzstan tax legislation.

Legal entities formed under the Kyrgyz law should be taxed in Kyrgyzstan on their worldwide income, whereas foreign legal entities should be taxed only in relation to Kyrgyzstan-sourced income.

Permanent establishment (PE)

Under Kyrgyzstan tax legislation, a PE is a permanent place of business, through which a non-resident carries out business operations, including activities performed through an authorised person. A PE includes the following:

- Any place of management, department, office, factory, workshop, mining, oil and gas wells, land, construction site, or project.
- Any services rendered by non-residents by hiring personnel working in the territory of Kyrgyzstan for a duration of more than 183 calendar days within any consecutive 12-month period.

A PE is not created in Kyrgyzstan if a non-resident is limited to the following activities in Kyrgyzstan:

- Use of warehouses or buildings exclusively for storage or demonstration activities.
- Use of a fixed place of business exclusively for preparatory purposes.
- Performance of activities in Kyrgyzstan through an agent in cases where such agent usually performs such activities in the ordinary course of business.

Creation of a PE may be connected with the establishment of a branch or subsidiary. Both branches and subsidiaries are considered appropriate business vehicles for foreign investors and the choice between them is determined by the business the investor is engaged in, along with various other factors.

Other taxes

Value-added tax (VAT)

In Kyrgyzstan, VAT is assessed on taxable supply and taxable imports. Input VAT assessed on purchases used for business purposes is generally offset against output VAT on taxable supplies. The VAT rate is 12%, except for certain zero-rated supplies and certain exempt turnover (*see below*).

All taxpayers registered for VAT purposes are required to charge VAT on their taxable supply and to calculate and report their VAT liabilities. Taxpayers are required to register for Kyrgyzstan VAT purposes if their taxable supply in the preceding 12 calendar months exceeds 4 million Kyrgyzstani som (KGS) (approximately 86,682 United States dollars [USD]). Even if an entity is not required to register for VAT purposes, it may still do so voluntarily by submitting an application to the appropriate tax committee.

Place of supply of goods

Goods and services are subject to VAT if they are deemed to be supplied in Kyrgyzstan under the place of supply rules. According to these rules, transactions are deemed to be made at the place where transport of the goods begins if the goods are transported by the supplier, and in all other cases, at the place where the goods are transferred to the customer. The rules regarding services are more complicated. Services that are not specifically mentioned are deemed to be supplied at the place where the service provider has established his place of business. Certain other services are deemed to be supplied at the place of the purchaser.

Import of goods

Generally, imports of goods are subject to VAT.

Non-deductible input VAT

The input VAT is not allowed for offset if it is subject to payment in connection with the receipt of goods, works, or services not related to entrepreneurial activity, or if it relates to inputs for VAT exempt supplies.

Zero-rated supplies

Certain supplies are zero-rated for VAT purposes. These include exports (except for certain limited types of export), international transportation, and services connected with the service of transit air flights related with international transportation. Supply of goods, works, or services for official use of diplomatic and consular representations is taxable, but may be refunded provided that certain conditions are met.

Exempt supplies

Certain supplies are VAT-exempt, including supplies and exports of gold and silver alloy and refined gold and silver, supplies of pharmaceuticals, land plots, residual buildings and construction, financial services, and export of works and services. When a taxpayer generates both taxable and exempt supplies, input VAT proportional to the ratio of the exempt supply to the total supply is disallowed for offset.

Kyrgyzstan

VAT incentives

Certain imports are VAT exempt, including imports of technological equipment, if it is used for own production purposes. Recently, a preferential offset method of VAT settlement in respect of certain fixed assets imported to Kyrgyzstan has been introduced, whereby the import VAT does not need to be paid to customs but is reflected simultaneously as input and output VAT in the VAT accounts.

Reverse-charge VAT

The current tax code does not have any provisions on reverse-charge VAT.

VAT liability calculation and VAT offset carryforward

In general, the VAT liability of a taxpayer is calculated as output VAT (i.e. VAT charged by a taxpayer) less input VAT (i.e. VAT paid by a taxpayer to its suppliers) in a reporting period. The excess of input VAT over output VAT may generally be carried forward against future VAT liabilities.

VAT compliance

The tax period for VAT is a calendar month. The submission of the VAT declaration is due by the 25th day of the month following the reporting period (except for major taxpayers, for which it is due by the end of the month following the reporting period). Payment of the VAT liability is due by the 25th day of the month following the reporting period.

Sales tax

Sales tax is assessed on Kyrgyz legal entities or foreign entities operating through a PE in Kyrgyzstan for any sales of goods or rendering of services. The sales tax mechanism differs from VAT, i.e. the sales tax is levied for the whole sales turnover and does not take into account the purchases (input turnover).

Sales tax rates are as follows:

- In case of the sale of goods, works, or services by VAT payers:
  - Trading activities: 1.0%.
  - For other activities: 2.0%.
- In case of the sale of goods, works, or services by non-VAT payers:
  - Trading activities: 2.0%.
  - For other activities: 3.0%.

The Kyrgyz Tax Code further defines trading activities as activities on sale of goods purchased for re-sale purposes.

The tax period of sales tax is a calendar month. Taxpayers have to submit tax returns and make payments of sales tax at the place of tax registration by the 20th day of the month following the reporting month.

Customs duties and regimes

According to the Customs Code, the customs value of goods imported to the customs territory of Kyrgyzstan is determined by applying the following methods:

- Transaction value of imported goods.
- Transaction value of identical goods.
- Transaction value of similar goods.
- Deductive method.
- Computed method.

- Provisional method.

Based on the Kyrgyzstan customs legislation, the rates of customs duties may be:

- *Ad valorem* - charged in percentage to customs value of the taxable goods.
- Specific - charged within established size for unit of the taxable goods.
- Combined - including both above mentioned types.

The rates in percentage range from 0% to 30%; however, the maximum rate of 35% may be charged if the country of origin in unknown.

Import restrictions
Generally, all entities or persons have equal rights to import and export or transfer goods into the Kyrgyzstan territory, including when carrying out foreign trade activity, except in special cases as stipulated by legislation and international treaties.

Import of certain goods (e.g. weapons, nuclear materials) is subject to licensing.

Temporary import relief
There is a temporary import regime under which foreign goods are used in Kyrgyzstan with full or partial conditional exemption from the payment of customs duties and taxes and without application of non-tariff regulatory measures. The term of the 'temporary import' customs regime may not exceed two years.

K

Customs duties incentives
Certain items are exempt from customs payments, including:

- Transportation vehicles used in the international conveyance of passengers and goods and items of material and technical supply in transit.
- Goods imported in the customs territory or imported from the customs territory for official and personal use by official state representatives of foreign states.

Kyrgyzstan provides preferential rates or exemptions on the importation (and export) of certain goods, including goods originating from the states which form free trade zones or a customs union with Kyrgyzstan and goods originating from developing countries, included on a special list provided by the government.

Documentation and procedures
Kyrgyzstan pays close attention to formalities/documentation, so it is necessary to furnish the customs authorities with a set of required documents. For import, such documents usually include cargo customs declaration, invoices, contracts, etc.

Warehousing and storage
There is a bonded warehouse customs regime in Kyrgyzstan. Under this regime, imports entering into Kyrgyzstan may be stored in special facilities or special areas that have the status of a customs warehouse under the customs legislation of Kyrgyzstan. This regime implies exemption from customs duties and taxes.

Generally, most goods (unless otherwise specifically provided for) can be placed under the bonded warehouse customs regime. The period for storage of goods at a bonded warehouse is determined by the person placing the goods into the customs warehouse but cannot exceed three years from the date when the goods were placed under the bonded warehouse customs regime.

Kyrgyzstan

Re-exports

The re-export regime is similar to that used in international practice. It is defined as a customs regime under which goods previously imported into Kyrgyzstan are exported without payment or with a refund of the paid amounts of import customs duties and taxes and without applying the non-tariff regulatory measures with respect to the goods in compliance with Kyrgyz legislation.

There are certain conditions under which goods can be re-exported. Customs duties and taxes are not charged for goods declared as goods intended for re-export. However, if the goods do not meet the re-export criteria, customs duties and taxes are paid in the amount which would be payable if the goods, at their importation, were declared for release for free circulation, as well as interest on them paid at the National Bank rates, as if deferment was provided with respect to the amounts at placement of the goods under the customs regime of re-export.

Excise tax

Certain goods manufactured in Kyrgyzstan or imported to Kyrgyzstan are subject to excise tax. These include certain alcohol and alcoholic drinks, fortified drinks, tobacco goods, and oil products.

The rates of excise tax are adopted annually by the Kyrgyzstan government and range from KGS 10 (approximately USD 0.2) for 1 litre of alcohol drinks to KGS 3,000 for 1 ton of fuel (approximately USD 65). The rate for tobacco goods range from KGS 5 (approximately USD 0.1) to KGS 297 (approximately USD 6.4) based on the type of tobacco.

Stamp taxes

There are no stamp taxes in Kyrgyzstan.

Subsurface use taxes

The subsurface use taxes consist of separate bonus and royalty taxes on subsurface users, both Kyrgyz legal entities and branches of foreign legal entities. Under Kyrgyz legislation, subsurface users are legal entities and individuals who perform exploration and/or extraction of mineral resources.

The government, depending on the type of mineral resources, establishes the bonus rates.

The royalty rates are estimated either as a percentage of sales turnover (1% to 12%) or in absolute terms in Kyrgyzstani som depending on the type of mineral resources.

Local taxes

There are two local taxes in Kyrgyzstan, property tax and land tax.

Property tax

Property tax is a local tax payable quarterly by legal entities owning transport vehicles and immovable property in Kyrgyzstan, including apartment houses, apartments, boarding houses, holiday inns, sanatoria, resorts, production, administrative, industrial, and other buildings or facilities. Certain real estate may not be subject to this tax according to special lists approved by the government.

In respect of immovable property, the tax rate is established by the city or local authorities at a rate not to exceed 0.8% of the estimated value of taxable objects, except for apartment houses and apartments designated solely for residence, for which the rate may not exceed 0.35% of the estimated value. The estimation can be performed by the state competent body and independent appraisers. For transport vehicles, the tax is computed in Kyrgyzstani som depending on engine volume.

Land tax

Land tax is paid quarterly by legal entities on the area of owned land. The basic rates are provided in the tax code, depending on the location and purposes of the land. The basic rates may range from KGS 0.9 to KGS 2.9 per square metre (approximately USD 0.01 to USD 0.06).

Branch income

Branch income is subject to the profit tax. There is no special branch profits tax in addition to profit tax.

Income determination

Aggregate annual income is comprised of all types of income, including, but not limited to, the following, in addition to gross revenue from the sale of goods, works, or services:

- Interest income (except for income already subject to withholding tax [WHT]).
- Dividends.
- Royalties.
- Assets received free of charge.
- Rental income.
- Income from the reduction of liabilities.
- Foreign exchange gain.
- Write-off liability.

The tax code envisages some profit tax privileges aimed at developing certain areas of the business economy. Currently, these include privileges/preferences for:

- Charity organisations.
- Associations of invalids of I and II groups (i.e. persons with disability with different levels of physical disability), associations of blind and deaf persons.
- Agricultural organisations.
- Growing of berries, fruits, and vegetables.
- Credit unions.
- Companies that have been involved in the food industry for less than three years and included in the Kyrgyzstan government's list of exempt companies.

Non-taxable revenues include, *inter alia*, the following:

- Property received as a charter capital contribution and income from realisation of shares of organisations.
- Property donated to special organisations using such property for development purposes under the government's social culture plan. Despite being designated as property used for social culture purposes, such property may still be used for other purposes (i.e. citizen defence projects, mining equipment, water intakes, heat networks, roads, stations).

Kyrgyzstan

Inventory valuation
There are no special provisions on inventory valuation in the Kyrgyzstan Tax Code. Inventory valuation is conducted in accordance with the International Financial Reporting Standards (IFRS).

Capital gains
Capital gains are subject to the ordinary profit tax rate. There is an exemption available for capital gains from selling shares that occur on the date of a given sale in the official lists of the stock exchange in the top two categories of listing.

Dividend income
Dividends from participation in Kyrgyz legal entities are exempt from profit tax. All other dividends are subject to the ordinary profit tax rate.

Partnership income
Simple partnerships are not taxpayers in their own right, and income and expenses flow through to the partners for tax reporting purposes. Kyrgyzstan limited liability partnerships are taxed as corporations.

Foreign income
Generally, Kyrgyz legal entities are taxable on income earned worldwide. Foreign income is subject to the ordinary profit tax rate.

There are no tax deferral provisions in Kyrgyzstan tax legislation.

Deductions

Generally, expenses related to the earning of aggregate annual income are considered deductible for profit tax purposes, including:

- Business trip expenses that were actually incurred and supported by appropriate documentation (*per diems* during business trips are deductible only within the established statutory limits).
- Commissions on payroll expenses for labour.
- Material and social benefits provided to employees.
- Representational expenses connected with earning income (transportation, hotel, and translator services).
- Training and retraining of employees.
- Scientific development and exploration works (deductions are relevant for fixed assets).
- Any other costs related to earning income, which can be supported by appropriate documentation in terms of their nature and amount (e.g. invoices, payment orders, receipts).

The principal categories of expenses that are not deductible include:

- Capital expenses and expenses connected with the purchase, production, and installation of equipment.
- Taxes paid in accordance with the tax code, except for land tax, property tax, VAT that cannot be offset, and subsurface use taxes.
- Any expenses incurred on behalf of any other third persons, except in cases where documentation proves business needs for such expenses.

Kyrgyzstan

- Pricing losses caused by rates, understated below-market prices, and price incentives.
- Expenses connected with purchases of services in entertainment, vacations, and leisure.

Depreciation
The tax code establishes a deduction for depreciation based on the declining-balance method. Depreciable fixed assets are divided into several groups, for which maximum depreciation rates range from 10% to 50%.

Group	Assets	Maximum rate of depreciation (%)
I	Cars, automobile and tractor equipment for use on roads, special instruments, sundries, and accessories; computers, telephone sets, peripherals, and equipment for data processing	30
II	Automotive transport rolling stock: trucks, buses, special automobiles, and trailers; construction equipment; machines and equipment for all sectors of industry, including the foundry; smith-pressing equipment; electronic and simple equipment, agricultural machines. Office furniture, intangible assets	25
III	Depreciable fixed assets not listed in other groups and expenses equated to them	20
IV	Railroad, sea, and river transport vehicles, power machines, and equipment: thermal-engineering equipment, turbine equipment, electric motors and diesel-generators, electricity transmission and communication facilities, pipelines	10
V	Buildings and constructions	10
VI	Taxpayer's costs of geological preparation of deposit reserves, design and engineering-research works, and obtaining the licence for the use of deposits, as well as mining-capital and mining pre-works aimed at further extraction of minerals, as well as the fixed assets of the mining and/or mining-processing enterprises put into operation and actually used in deposit exploration	50

Certain expenses are deductible within specified limits, including expenses on repairs, expenses on procuring and producing capital production assets, and certain other expenses.

Goodwill
Kyrgyzstan domestic tax legislation does not stipulate the allowance of a deduction for goodwill for profit tax purposes.

Start-up expenses
Kyrgyzstan domestic tax legislation does not stipulate the allowance of a deduction for start-up expenses for profit tax purposes.

Interest expenses
Deductions for interest actually paid on debts, where the loan proceeds were used to fund expenses incurred for the taxpayer's business activity, are allowed within limitations provided in the tax code depending on methodology and nature of the debt. For example, interest on loans connected with the purchase of depreciable assets is not deducted, but increases their value.

Kyrgyzstan

Charitable contributions
Deductions for donations of assets to charity and budget organisations are limited to 10% of taxable income.

Fines and penalties
Fines and interest penalties paid to the state budget are not deductible.

Taxes
The following taxes may be deducted:

- Land tax.
- Property tax.
- VAT not allowed for offset.
- Subsurface use taxes.

Net operating losses
Net operating losses can be carried forward for up to five years. There are no provisions in Kyrgyz legislation allowing carryback of losses.

Payments to foreign affiliates
Payments to foreign affiliates are deductible for profit tax purposes if they are aimed at earning income and supported by documentation.

Group taxation

Group taxation is not permitted in Kyrgyzstan.

Transfer pricing
While there is no special law on transfer pricing in Kyrgyzstan, rules on transfer pricing are found in the tax code. The general transfer pricing provisions set in the tax code do not follow Organisation for Economic Co-operation and Development (OECD) guidelines (thus, no advance pricing agreement [APA] mechanism is provided). According to the Kyrgyz transfer pricing regulations, the tax authorities are empowered to determine the value of the following transactions:

- Transfers between related parties.
- Barter transactions.
- Cross-border transactions.

Thin capitalisation
There are no thin capitalisation limitations under the Kyrgyzstan tax code.

Tax credits and incentives

The legislation currently provides the following tax incentives:

Investment incentives
There are no special tax preferences in the Kyrgyzstan Tax Code; however, Kyrgyz Law on Investments envisages that in case of changes in the tax and customs legislation, investors may apply terms which are more beneficial to them.

Kyrgyzstan

Special economic zones

There are four special economic zones in Kyrgyzstan: Naryn, Karakol, Bishkek, and Maimak. The special economic zones generally provide for a tax-neutral regime, exemption from customs duties, and a liberal currency control regime. However, there is a special fee for incentives which varies from 0.1% to 2% of sales (depending on the region).

Park of Innovative Technologies

Activities of residents of the Park of Innovative Technologies are exempt from profits tax, sales tax, and VAT, providing they meet requirements of the Tax Code of Kyrgyzstan. The tax rate for employees of residents of the Park of Innovative Technologies and individual entrepreneurs is 5%.

Foreign tax credits

There is no possibility to offset the amount of tax paid outside Kyrgyzstan against the Kyrgyz tax if there is no double tax treaty (DTT) with this country.

....

Withholding taxes

Passive income from sources in Kyrgyzstan by a non-resident that is not connected with a PE is taxable at the source of payment, without deductions, at the following rates:

- Dividends and interest: 10%.
- Insurance premiums received under risk insurance or re-insurance agreements: 5%.
- Authorship fee and royalty: 10%.

Income obtained by a non-resident from performing activities and services in Kyrgyzstan, not connected with a PE, is taxable at the source of payment, without deductions (with the exception of VAT), at the following rates:

- Income from telecommunication or freight services in international communication and transportation between Kyrgyzstan and other countries: 5%.
- Income from management and consulting services: 10%.
- Other services and activities: 10%.

WHT applies to Kyrgyzstan-source income regardless of whether the payment is made within or outside of Kyrgyzstan.

The application of DTTs often effectively provides a reduction of WHT rates or, in the case of non-passive income, an income tax exemption. Note that the application of treaty privileges is not necessarily automatic, and taxpayers may need to comply with certain administrative procedures to secure relief.

Tax treaties

According to the tax code, the provisions of international tax agreements and other acts to which Kyrgyzstan is a party and ratified by the president or the parliament (as appropriate) take precedence over the provisions of the tax code.

As of 1 April 2012, Kyrgyzstan has concluded DTTs with the countries listed in the following table, which shows the corresponding WHT rates:

Kyrgyzstan

Recipient	Dividends (%)	Interest (%)	Royalties (%)
Non-treaty	10	10	10
Treaty:			
Austria	5/10 (1)	10	10
Belarus	15	10	15
Canada	15	15	10
China	10	10	10
Finland	5/10 (1)	10	5
Germany	5/10 (1)	5	10
India	10	10	15
Iran	5/10 (1)	10	10
Kazakhstan	10	10	10
Latvia	5/10 (1)	10	5
Malaysia	5/10 (2)	10	10
Moldova	5/10 (1)	10	10
Mongolia	10	10	10
Pakistan	10	10	10
Poland	10	10	10
Russia	10	10	10
Switzerland	5/10 (1)	5	5
Tajikistan	5/10 (3)	10	10
Turkey	10	10	10
Ukraine	5/10 (3)	10	10
Uzbekistan	5/10 (3)	10	10

Notes

1. 5% if the beneficial owner is a company (other than a partnership) that directly holds at least 25% of the capital of the paying company.
2. 5% if the beneficial owner is a company (other than a partnership), which owns not less than 10% of the capital of the paying company.
3. 5% if the beneficial recipient is a company, which owns not less than 50% of the capital of the paying company.

Tax administration

Taxable period
The taxable period for profit tax is one calendar year.

Tax returns
The tax code stipulates that the Aggregate Annual Income Tax Declaration must be filed with the tax authorities by 1 March of the year following the reporting year.

Tax authorities may grant an extension for filing a tax return for up to one month upon application by the taxpayer. Such extension does not relieve or prolong the taxpayer's obligation to pay the tax in a timely manner.

Payment of tax
Tax payments should be made as follows:

Kyrgyzstan

- Advance payments on profit tax: quarterly by the 20th day of the second month of the reporting quarter.
- Final payments on profit tax: 1 March of the year following the reporting year.
- Tax withheld at the source of payment by a tax agent: by the 20th day of the month following the month when income was recognised.

Audit cycle
The State Tax Inspectorate of the Ministry of Finance of Kyrgyzstan and its local tax authorities are the only state authorities that have the right to perform tax audits. The Kyrgyzstan tax service consists of relevant subdivisions of the revenue committee of the Ministry of Finance of Kyrgyzstan and its local authorities.

A tax audit is performed based on a written notification from the Head of the State Tax Inspectorate, which specifies the name of the company to audit, the scope of the audit, and the terms of the audit. Tax audits may be performed not more than once a year by one of the tax authorities (district, city, region, or the state tax authorities) and should not last more than 30 days. If necessary, however, a tax audit may be extended for ten additional days with written approval from the State Tax Inspectorate.

Statute of limitations
The period of limitation for tax liability is six years.

K

Lao People's Democratic Republic

PwC contact

Varavudh Meesaiyati
PricewaterhouseCoopers
ANZ Vientiane Commercial Building
33 Lane Xang Avenue, Vientiane, Lao PDR
Tel: +856 21 222 718 9
Email: varavudh.meesaiyati@la.pwc.com

Significant developments

Effective 1 January 2012, the corporate income tax (profits tax or PT) rate has been lowered to 28% from 35%.

Taxes on corporate income

Profits tax (PT)

All companies (including all forms of legal entities) that are registered under Lao People's Democratic Republic (PDR) law are subject to PT on their worldwide income. Companies formed under foreign law, operating a business in Lao PDR, and conducting business in Lao PDR are subject to tax on their income derived in Lao PDR.

Effective 1 January 2012, the standard rate of PT for companies in Lao PDR has been lowered to 28% from 35%. The 28% rate applies to both domestic and foreign investors.

Tax holidays and reduced PT rates are applicable to companies that qualify as promoted investment activities (*see the Tax credits and incentives section for more information*).

Minimum tax (MT)

Companies that operate at a loss or have profits below a certain level are subject to MT. However, if the company's loss or profit is certified by an independent auditing firm recognised by the government and registered with the Ministry of Finance, MT will not be payable.

MT rates are 0.25% of gross receipts for manufacturing companies and 1% of gross receipts for trade and service companies.

Local income taxes

There are no provincial or local income taxes in Lao PDR.

Corporate residence

There is no definition of residence or permanent establishment (PE) for tax purposes under Lao PDR law.

Other taxes

Valued-added tax (VAT)

The standard VAT rate is 10%.

VAT is imposed on the final consumer of goods and services. Goods and services used for production, trading, and consumption in Lao PDR, goods imported into Lao PDR, and services rendered by foreigners to Lao PDR customers are subject to VAT.

Certain goods and services are exempt from VAT. Exempted items include unprocessed agricultural products, seeds, fertilisers, textbooks, education services, medical services, banking services, and insurance.

Exported goods and services are zero rated. The conventional credit method is used to calculate the VAT payable (i.e. output VAT less input VAT). Excess input VAT can be carried forward for six months (extendable). Input VAT for exports is refundable.

Organisations engaged in production or trading of taxable goods and services must register for VAT if their annual revenue is 400 million Lao kip (LAK) or more. Companies below this threshold may voluntarily register. Only registered VAT taxpayers may claim VAT refunds.

One unique feature of Lao PDR VAT is that VAT is charged on withholding taxes (WHTs) (*see the Withholding taxes section for more information*).

Customs duties/Import tariffs
All goods imported into Lao PDR are subject to import duty. Exemptions are available to enterprises operating promoted investment activities (*see the Tax credits and incentives section for more information*).

Lao PDR has adopted the General Agreement on Tariffs and Trade (GATT) valuation principles. Duty rates are based on the Association of Southeast Asian Nations (ASEAN) harmonised tariff nomenclature. Duty rates range between 0% and 40% depending on whether the goods are ASEAN or other source.

L

Excise taxes
Excise tax applies to the import and sale of certain luxury products. Excisable goods include alcohol, beer, cigarettes, perfume, cosmetics, motor vehicles, soft drinks, mineral water, and many types of electrical equipment. Excise tax rates range from 5% to 90%.

Property taxes
Land taxes vary depending on the location and the type of the land (e.g. land for construction, agriculture). The calculation of the land tax is based on both the location and the size of the land and is levied at annual rates per square meter. Land tax is payable in the first quarter of the relevant calendar year.

Transfer taxes
There are no transfer taxes in Lao PDR.

Stamp taxes
There are no stamp taxes in Lao PDR.

Administrative fees
Under the Tax Law, government sectors can collect fees for issuing fiscal licences, business licences, permits, visas, advertisement boards, broadcasting rights, and other services. The charges and service fees are set periodically by Presidential Decree.

Lao People's Democratic Republic

Branch income

Branches of foreign companies are taxable on their income from carrying on business in Lao PDR.

Income determination

The PT calculation is based on an entity's actual accounting profits as adjusted for tax purposes. The Lao PDR Tax Regulations are silent on the treatment of a large number of items. Generally, in such cases, the tax treatment will follow the accounting treatment. Some of the more common differences are depreciation, entertainment expenses, and the non-deductibility of reserves and provisions (until actually paid).

Inventory valuation
Inventory valuation for tax purposes follows the method used for accounting purposes in Lao PDR.

Capital gains
There is no separate tax on capital gains in Lao PDR; however, profits from the sale of shares are subject to tax at a rate of 10%. The buyer of the shares is required to withhold and remit the tax.

Dividend income
Dividends received from another Lao PDR company or a foreign company are taxed at a flat rate of 10%.

Interest income
Interest income is taxable in Lao PDR.

Rents/royalties income
Rents and royalties income are taxable in Lao PDR.

Unrealised exchange gains/losses
Unrealised exchange gains are not taxable and losses are not deductible in Lao PDR.

Foreign income
There is no controlled foreign company (CFC) or similar regime in Lao. Profits of a foreign subsidiary are taxable when remitted as dividends.

Deductions

Accrued expenses are deductible in Lao PDR. Reserves and provisions are not deductible until actually settled.

Depreciation
Depreciation rates are prescribed in the tax law and may differ from financial accounting. Depreciation is on a straight-line basis over prescribed useful lives, as follows:

Assets	Years
Buildings used for industrial purposes:	

Lao People's Democratic Republic

Assets	Years
20 years old or less	20
Over 20 years	40
Buildings used for commercial and residential purposes:	
Permanent structures	20
Semi-permanent structures	10
Machinery, equipment, vehicles	5
Office equipment	10
Ships and passenger aircraft	20

Goodwill
There is no specific guidance on the deductibility of goodwill or amortisation in Lao PDR.

Start-up expenses
Start-up expenses are amortisable over two years in Lao PDR.

Interest expenses
Interest is deductible on an accrual basis following the accounting treatment. All interest payments must be supported by documents showing that the payments are commercially reasonable. Interest paid to a shareholder is not deductible.

Bad debt
Bad debt reserves are not deductible in Lao PDR. However, a deduction is allowed when debt is written off.

Charitable contributions
Charitable contributions in Lao PDR are limited to the smaller of 0.15% of taxable income or LAK 4 million.

Entertainment expenses
Entertainment expenses are capped at 0.4% of annual revenue.

Pension expenses
Pension expenses are deductible when paid in Lao PDR.

Bribes, kickbacks, and illegal payments
Bribes, kickbacks, and illegal payments are not deductible in Lao PDR.

Fines and penalties
Fines and penalties are not deductible in Lao PDR.

Taxes
PT and MT are not deductible.

Net operating and capital losses
Tax losses can be carried forward for three years, but no carryback is allowed. A change in control will not impact a company's loss carryforward. Capital losses are treated as ordinary losses.

Payments to foreign affiliates
Payments to foreign affiliates are deductible if in the ordinary course of business.

Lao People's Democratic Republic

Group taxation

Consolidation or grouping is not permitted, and each entity must file on a separate basis in Lao PDR.

Transfer pricing

There are no specified transfer pricing rules in Lao PDR. However, intercompany transactions should be at arm's length.

Thin capitalisation

There are no thin capitalisation or debt-to-equity rules in Lao PDR.

Tax credits and incentives

Foreign tax credit

There is no foreign tax credit regime in Lao tax law. However, certain tax treaties entered into by Lao PDR do have provisions for either deductibility of foreign tax or a credit.

Promoted investment activities

The following activities are promoted under the Law on the Promotion of Foreign Investment No. 11/NA, dated 22 October 2004 (Existing Foreign Investment Law):

- Production for export.
- Activities relating to agriculture or forestry, and agricultural, forestry, and handicraft processing activities.
- Activities relating to industrial processing, industrial activities using modern techniques and technology, research and development, and activities relating to the protection of the environment and biodiversity.
- Human resource development, skills development, and public health.
- Construction of infrastructure.
- Production of raw materials and equipment to be supplied to key industrial activities.
- Development of the tourism industry and transit services.

The following three zones are promoted under the Existing Foreign Investment Law:

Zone 1:	Mountainous, plain, and plateau zones with no economic infrastructure to facilitate investments.
Zone 2:	Mountainous, plain, and plateau zones with a moderate level of economic infrastructure suitable to accommodate investments to some extent.
Zone 3:	Mountainous, plain, and plateau zones with good infrastructure to support investments.

The tax incentives are as follows:

- Investment in Zone 1 shall be entitled to a PT exemption for seven years and thereafter shall be subject to PT at the rate of 10%.
- Investment in Zone 2 shall be entitled to a PT exemption for five years, then shall be subject to a reduced PT rate of 7.5% for three years, and thereafter a PT rate of 15%.
- Investment in Zone 3 shall be entitled to a PT exemption for two years, then shall be subject to a reduced PT rate of 10% for two years, and thereafter a PT rate of 20%.

Lao People's Democratic Republic

In addition to the incentives as mentioned above, foreign investment enterprises shall be entitled to the following incentives:

- During the tax exemption period and during the tax reduction period, the enterprise shall be entitled to an exemption from MT.
- Profits used for the expansion of licensed business activities shall be exempted from PT during the accounting year.

The Law on the Promotion of Foreign Investment grants incentives to foreign investors investing in activities within the promoted sectors and zones. Raw materials, equipment, machines, and vehicles used directly in production will be exempted from import duties and taxes or will be subject to a combined import duty and VAT rate of 1%. An application/request letter for incentives in respect of the importation of raw materials, equipment, machines, and vehicles used directly in production will be considered within 30 working days from the date of receipt of the application/request letter.

Withholding taxes

WHT is applied to various types of payments made to domestic and foreign recipients.

Payment	WHT rate (%)
Dividends	10
Profit from the sale of shares	10
Interest and guarantee fees	10
Payments for use of trademarks and intellectual property	5

As mentioned in the Other taxes section, VAT of 10% is charged on the above WHT.

In the case of a foreign recipient, the WHT is considered a final tax.

Lao PDR has double tax treaties (DTTs) with the following countries, and WHT rates under the treaties are as follows:

Recipient	Dividends (%)	Interest (%)	Royalties (%)
Brunei (not in force)	-	-	-
China	5	5	5
Kuwait (not in force)	-	-	-
North Korea	5	10	5
Russia	10	10	0
South Korea (not in force)	-	-	-
Thailand	10	10	5
Vietnam	10	10	5

Lao People's Democratic Republic

Foreign contractor withholding tax (FCWT)
A WHT on payments to foreign contractors applies where a Lao PDR contracting party contracts with a foreign party that does not have a licensed presence in Lao PDR regardless of whether the services are provided in Lao PDR or outside Lao PDR. The FCWT comprises both a PT and VAT element and is intended to be a final tax on the foreign company. The FCWT withholding and filing obligation rests with the Lao PDR customer.

For foreign contractors, PT must be withheld at a deemed percentage of taxable turnover. The deemed rates are determined according to the nature of the contract or activity.

Activity	Deemed profit margin (% of business revenue)	Deemed PT rate (%)
Commerce	5	1.75
Production	8	2.8
Transportation and construction	10	3.5
Service	20	7

These PT rates are then added to the VAT at 10% to determine the total FCWT. For example, a foreign service charge of LAK 1,000 would result in LAK 70 of PT and LAK 100 of VAT for a total FCWT of LAK 170.

Tax administration

Taxable period
PT is determined on a calendar year basis.

Tax returns
The tax return is due by 10 March of the subsequent year. Submission of the final tax return will be followed by an audit by the Tax Department.

Payment of tax
PT is payable quarterly in advance, with a final payment after year end. The first three payments are due 10 April, 10 July, and 10 October of the current tax year. The final payment is due with the submission of the final tax return on 10 March of the subsequent year. The quarterly payments are based on the prior year's PT (or expected tax for the current year). Any excess PT payment can be carried forward to the subsequent year.

Audit cycle
Most large companies are audited annually in Lao PDR.

Statute of limitations
The statute of limitations is generally three years in Lao PDR.

Topics of focus for tax authorities
There are no areas of special focus in tax examinations in Lao PDR.

Latvia

PwC contact

Zlata Elksnina-Zascirinska
PricewaterhouseCoopers SIA
Kr. Valdemara iela 19
LV-1010 Riga, Latvia
Tel: +371 6709 4400 / +371 6709 4514
Email: zlata.elksnina@lv.pwc.com

Significant developments

Large investment relief
On 1 January 2011, the government introduced corporate income tax (CIT) relief for investments, at particular investment amounts, in qualifying industries in new, unused fixed assets (buildings and structures classified as industrial buildings and new plant and technological equipment) that can be used for business purposes. As per amendments made to the CIT Act, CIT relief is available for investments over 3 million Latvian lats (LVL). The available tax relief is 25% of the amount of investments made (15% for investments over LVL 35 million). The time in which the investment project has to be completed has been increased from three to five years.

Note that companies have to go through certain procedures in order to receive a Cabinet decision in support of a qualifying investment project. Investments have to enable a company to launch a new line of business or to modernise its existing production, which includes manufacturing new goods, a shift of business activity from producing one type of goods to producing another type of goods, or a complete overhaul of the manufacturing process.

Loss carryforward
Companies will be able to carry forward tax losses accrued since 2008 for an unlimited period of time. Losses accrued before 2008 may be carried forward eight years.

Free-port and enterprise-zone companies
The amendments to the CIT Act make the tax regime in free ports and enterprise zones even more attractive by allowing free-port and enterprise-zone companies to apply 15% CIT (previously 25%) before taking tax relief. The effective tax rate after the relief will be 3% (previously 5%).

Value-added tax (VAT) rate reduction
Effective 1 July 2012, the standard VAT rate will be reduced from 22% to 21%.

CIT Act amendments effective from 2013 and 2014

New withholding tax rules
The amendments to the CIT Act include significant amendments regarding withholding tax (WHT) on dividends, interest, and royalties paid to non-residents, i.e. provide WHT exemption on the following payments:

- Dividends paid to any non-resident company (effective from 1 January 2013).
- Interest payments to any non-resident company that does not reside in an offshore territory (effective from 1 January 2014).
- Royalty payments to any non-resident company that does not reside in an offshore territory (effective from 1 January 2014).

Latvia

Interest and royalties paid to a related European Union (EU)/European Economic Area (EEA) company will not attract WHT from 1 July 2013 based on the transitional period of implementing Interest-Royalty Directive in Latvia.

Capital gains
Starting in 1 January 2013, capital gains from trading in non-public securities (shares), except offshore company shares, are not taxable and losses are not tax deductible. For planning purposes, companies should take into account that the specific regulation on loss carryforward from transactions in non-public securities has been excluded as of 1 January 2013. Therefore, any losses accumulated from trading with non-public securities can be used only in 2012, if certain criteria are met.

Taxation of dividends
Dividends received from companies in other countries, excluding companies registered in low tax jurisdictions or tax havens, should not be included in the taxable income of a Latvian company as of 1 January 2013.

Option to tax introduced in VAT Act
A VAT-registered person will be allowed to use the 'option to tax' regulation in respect to sale of unused real estate as of 1 January 2013, if the real estate is acquired before 27 July 2011.

Taxes on corporate income

The standard rate of CIT is 15%. The tax is assessed on a company's financial profit (loss) that has been adjusted by certain corrections required by law. There are no other taxes on corporate income stated either by the government of Latvia or by local municipalities.

Resident companies are taxed on their worldwide income.

Non-resident companies are taxed on their Latvia-source income through permanent establishment (PE) at the standard CIT rate. If no PE is created, non-residents may be taxed with 2% to 15% withholding tax (WHT) for qualifying payments (e.g. royalties, management fees, interest).

Micro-business tax (MBT)
The Micro-business Tax Act gives existing and newly-formed businesses the opportunity of acquiring micro-business status and registering for MBT if they meet the following criteria:

- The shareholders are individuals who are also concurrently members of the board.
- The turnover does not exceed LVL 70,000 in a calendar year.
- The number of employees does not exceed five at any time. Absent employees or employees suspended from work shall not be included in the number of employees.

The standard MBT rate is 9% of a micro-business's turnover and covers payroll taxes, business risk duties, and CIT. The standard rate may be increased in the following cases:

- If its quarterly staff count exceeds five, then 2% per extra employee will be added to the standard rate.
- If the turnover exceeds LVL 70,000 in a calendar year, the excess will attract a rate of 20%.

- If an employee's net income exceeds LVL 500 a month, the excess will also attract a rate of 20%.

Corporate residence

A company is resident in Latvia if it is incorporated or had to be incorporated in Latvia.

Permanent establishment (PE)

Under the Latvian Taxes and Duties Act, a non-resident has a PE in Latvia if all three of the following conditions are met simultaneously:

- The non-resident uses a fixed place for activities in Latvia.
- The place for activities is permanently used or is established for the purpose of being used permanently.
- The place for activities is used for the performance of commercial activities.

In addition, it is considered that a non-resident has a PE in Latvia if the non-resident performs in Latvia at least one of the following activities:

- Uses a construction site or performs building or installation activities or supervision or consultative activities related to the construction site or aforementioned activities.
- Uses equipment or installations, drilling platforms and special ships intended for the research or extraction of natural resources, or carries out supervisory or consultative work related thereto.
- Within a time period, which together exceeds 30 days in any six-month period, provides services, including consulting, management, and technical services, utilising one's employees or associated personnel.
- Uses the activity of an individual, legal, or other person for the benefit of one's commercial activities, provided that this person is authorised to enter into contracts in the name of the foreign entity and the person regularly (more than once in a taxation period) exercises such an authority.

Note that the PE risk for entities located in treaty countries should be tested in accordance with the relevant double tax treaty (DTT).

Other taxes

Value-added tax (VAT)

The following VAT rates apply in Latvia:

Description of goods	VAT (%)
The standard rate on supplies of goods and services, commodity imports, certain services rendered by non-residents and treated as supplied in Latvia, intra-community acquisitions of goods, and personal consumption.	22 (21 effective 1 July 2012)
A reduced rate on medicines, medical devices, specialised baby food, domestic public transport services, household heating charges, firewood and wooden heating material to households, textbooks, original literature publications, accommodation services, newspapers and other periodical publications, and electronically supplied media information.	12
Exemption with credit on supplies of goods within the European Union to taxable persons registered for VAT in other EU member states.	0

Latvia

Description of goods	VAT (%)
Exemption with credit on commodity exports and imports not released for free circulation in the European Union, supplies of goods and services to diplomats, supplies of goods and services financed by foreign aid, import of gas that is supplied through natural gas system, import of electricity and heat and cooling energy.	0

Please note that the exemption with credit method has been applied on import of gas, import of electricity, and heat and cooling energy only from 1 October 2011.

A number of services are exempt, including education, financial, medical, and insurance services; nursery fees; and the sale of used real estate, including land (except for building land, which is taxable).

Customs duty

Customs duty is levied on goods imported into Latvia. The rate of customs duty generally is between 0% and 20% of the value of imported goods, depending on the type and origin of such goods. Exports are generally exempt from customs tax.

Excise duty

An excise duty is levied on specific categories of goods, mostly as a fixed amount per unit. Excise duties are applied to the following goods, whether made in Latvia or imported:

Product	Excise amount
Oil and oil products	Up to LVL 320 per 1,000 litres, depending on the type of the product.
Alcohol	LVL 45 to 940 per 1,000 litres, depending on the type of alcohol.
Beer	LVL 2.18 for each percent of absolute alcohol, but not less than LVL 4 per 100 litres of beer (LVL 1.09 on the first 10,000 hectolitres for small breweries).
Tobacco products	LVL 32 per 1,000 cigars or cigarillos. LVL 32 per 1,000 cigarettes plus 33% of the maximum retail selling price, but not less than LVL 64 per 1,000 cigarettes. LVL 64 per 1,000 cigarettes plus 33% of the maximum retail selling price for cigarettes 80mm to 110mm in length, but not less than LVL 128 per 1,000 cigarettes. LVL 96 per 1,000 cigarettes plus 33% of the maximum retail selling price for cigarettes 111mm to 140mm in length, but not less than LVL 192 per 1,000 cigarettes. LVL 128 per 1,000 cigarettes plus 33% of the maximum retail selling price for cigarettes exceeding 140mm in length, but not less than LVL 256 per 1,000 cigarettes. LVL 43 per 1,000 grams of fine-cut smoking tobacco intended for the rolling of cigarettes. LVL 43 for other smoking tobacco.
Coffee	LVL 100 per 100 kg.
Certain soft drinks	LVL 5.2 per 100 litres.
Natural gas	LVL 15.6 per 1,000 m3 for use as heating fuel. LVL 70 per 1,000 m3 for use as fuel.

Latvia

Real estate tax

The real estate tax is payable annually for:

- Business properties, such as land and buildings used for economic activities, as well as engineering structures, such as motorways, streets, roads, parking places, bridges, elevated highways, tunnels, pipelines, communication lines, and power lines
- Buildings that form part of a private dwelling house development (also if owned by a company but not used for living purposes).

The following real estate tax rates are applicable:

- The standard rate of 1.5% on the cadastral value of land, buildings, and engineering structures.
- A progressive rate for dwelling houses, their parts, and any parts of a non-residential building that are functionally used for living and not used in trade or business:
  - 0.2% of cadastral values up to LVL 40,000.
  - 0.4% of cadastral values exceeding 40,000 but not exceeding LVL 75,000.
  - 0.6% of cadastral values exceeding LVL 75,000.
- 3% for uncultivated land capable of agricultural use, unless it is up to one hectare in area or subject to statutory restrictions on agricultural activity. By law, uncultivated land capable of agricultural use is agricultural land that is not used for making or growing agricultural products (including harvesting, grazing, and keeping animals for agricultural purposes) or is not kept in good agricultural and environmental condition. A 3% rate can also be applied by municipalities, if buildings may cause a threat to people because of their condition.

Newly constructed or reconstructed buildings are exempt from real estate tax for one year after completion. Other reliefs are available under the Real Estate Tax Act or determined by municipalities.

Stamp duty

Stamp duties are levied on certain legal and other kinds of services, such as court trials, company formation and registration, licences for certain types of business activity, provision of information, notary services, operation of bills of exchange, and registration of real estate at the Land Registry (2% of the higher of deal value or cadastral value capped at LVL 30,000 per property).

Stamp duty is not payable if re-registration of real estate in the Land Registry is necessary due to the reorganisation process. The maximum amount of stamp duty payable for re-registration of the title to immovable property in case of contribution in kind to a company's capital is LVL 1,000.

National social insurance contributions (NSIC)

The company as an employer is liable to pay 24.09% NSIC calculated on employee's gross salary.

Natural resource tax

Any natural resources acquired as a result of economic activities (e.g. surface and underground water, dolomite, and quartz sand), the collection of edible park snails, taking advantage of useful features of the bowels of the earth by pumping natural gas or greenhouse gases into geological structures, pollution (waste, emissions, and pollutants), products harmful to the environment (e.g. lubricating oil, electric batteries, oil filters, and tyres), electrical and electronic equipment and appliances, radioactive substances, packaging, disposable tableware, means of transport, the volume of

Latvia

emitted greenhouse gasses that is not included in the number of emission quotas surrendered, coal, coke and lignite are subject to a natural resource tax in Latvia. The rates are specific for each product and are based on weight, volume, or the amount of the product.

The taxpayer may reduce the natural resource tax by taking part in recycling programs for packaging, products harmful to the environment, electrical and electronic equipment and appliances, and means of transport. Taxpayers do not have an obligation to recycle themselves to be entitled to the relief; instead they can conclude an agreement with the recycling company.

For some of the products, the taxpayer must also pay the disposal tax. The rates differ for a large variety of products.

Vehicle taxes

There are two vehicle taxes in Latvia, a vehicle usage tax and a light corporate vehicle tax. The first is payable for exploitation of trucks, and the second is payable for light vehicles held or owned by a company.

Vehicle usage tax

The vehicle tax on usage (exploitation) for trucks with gross weight up to 12,000 kg is payable in accordance with the gross weight of these trucks in the following amounts:

* Up to 1,500 kg: LVL 1.
* Between 1,501 kg and 1,800 kg: LVL 24.
* Between 1,801 kg and 2,100 kg: LVL 45.
* Between 2,101 kg and 2,600 kg: LVL 64.
* Between 2,601 kg and 3,500 kg: LVL 72.
* Between 3,501 kg and 12,000 kg: LVL 102.

The vehicle usage tax for trucks with gross weight above 12,000 kg shall be payable depending on the number of axles the truck has and the driving axle suspension type.

The vehicle usage tax is payable on a yearly basis and it must be paid in full amount prior to the state technical inspection.

Light corporate vehicle tax

A light corporate vehicle tax (LCVT) was introduced in Latvia on 1 January 2011. LCVT is paid for vehicle(s) owned or held (e.g. rented) by a business person, which is registered for the first time after 1 January 2005, and with information on the engine volume in the registration certificate. There is a fixed rate of LCVT calculated according to the engine volume, as follows:

* Up to 2,000 cc: LVL 19 per month.
* From 2,001 cc to 2,500 cc: LVL 30 per month.
* Over 2,500 cc: LVL 40 per month.

For vehicles not mentioned in the above criteria, the LCVT will be LVL 30 per month.

Car and motorcycle duty

Cars and motorcycles registered for the first time or after modification are subject to a car and motorcycle duty. This duty is payable by any individual or entity registered as the owner of a car or motorcycle.

The applicable tax rates for cars registered in foreign countries are calculated based on the carbon dioxide (CO2) on each kilometre constituted by the car. The rates range from LVL 0.3 to LVL 5 where the CO2 is from 120 grams to 350 grams for each kilometre. The rate for newly registered motorcycles is LVL 0.10 for each cubic-centimetre of the engine's capacity.

For other cars, rates range from LVL 75 to LVL 850, depending on age and capacity. The rate for motorcycles depends on age and is 25% of the rate for cars.

Lottery and gambling tax

A lottery and gambling tax is levied on licensed organisers of games or lotteries. Licence fees range from LVL 3,000 to LVL 300,000. Game organisers, gambling places, and gambling machines are subject to the gambling tax. The tax rates depend on the number and type of gambling machines or percentage of income for several gambling types.

Electricity tax

This electricity tax is levied on electricity supplied to final consumers or consumed by suppliers. The rate is LVL 0.71 per mega-watt-hour. Exemptions are available to producers of electricity and for electricity used by domestic public transport and households.

Local duties

Certain activities are subject to local duties (e.g. construction permits).

Branch income

As a general rule, branches and resident companies are taxed alike, with certain adjustments for payments to the head office. Branch income is subject to a 15% CIT.

Income determination

Inventory valuation

Dictated by the matching and prudence concepts, stock should be valued at the lower of cost or net realisable value. Cost must be computed on a first in first out (FIFO) basis. Cost can mean purchase price or production cost. Any unrealised losses from stock revaluation are non-deductible.

Capital gains

From 1 January 2013, there will not be different treatment of capital gains from the sale of public and non-public securities (including also public securities traded outside the EU/EEA). Profits on trading in securities will not be taxable, provided that income results from the sale of a company not included in the list of low tax jurisdictions stated by the Latvian government, and losses from sale of any securities will not be tax deductible.

A capital gain on the disposal of a capital asset is calculated as the difference between the sale proceeds and cost. This gain is subject to a 15% CIT as ordinary income.

Losses on the sale of non-public securities made in previous years may be carried forward and offset against total taxable income from operating activities in 2012, if a company made a one-off sale of securities that it had held for more than 12

Latvia

months (otherwise losses may be offset against income from the sale of other non-public securities). A possibility to offset the losses will no longer be available as of 1 January 2013.

Profits on trading in securities publicly quoted in the EU/EEA are not taxable, and losses from these securities are not deductible.

Dividend income

From 1 January 2013, dividends received from any companies abroad or in Latvia are exempt from CIT, except dividends from companies registered in blacklisted tax havens (a list of blacklisted tax havens is provided by the Cabinet of Ministers).

In 2012, the following dividends are exempt from CIT:

- Dividends received from Latvian registered companies, except for dividends from companies paying CIT at a reduced rate (e.g. companies operating in free ports or special economic zones [SEZs]).
- Dividends from a company resident in another EU/EAA country.
- Dividends paid by a non-resident company based outside blacklisted tax havens to a Latvian person, directly holding at least 25% of shares in that company at the time the dividends are paid.

Stock dividends

The distribution of new shares to a company's shareholders in proportion to their existing shareholdings (after a share capital increase by conversion of accrued capital) is not a taxable event for the shareholders.

Interest income

Interest income is taxed at the 15% CIT rate.

Foreign income

Resident companies are taxed on their worldwide income. Income is taxed for the given taxation period; there is no possibility to defer taxation until the profit is repatriated to Latvia. Tax paid abroad on income included in the taxable base is allowed as a credit against the CIT charged for the year. However, the credit must not exceed the Latvian tax attributable to the income taxed abroad. Any unused tax credits may not be carried forward.

Deductions

Depreciation and amortisation

Fixed assets may be depreciated for tax purposes according to the reducing-balance method by applying the following rates to tax written-down values:

Types of property	Depreciation rate (%)
Buildings, structures, and perennial plantations	10
Technology and energy installations, fleet, railway	20
Computer hardware and software, information systems, electronic equipment	70
Light passenger cars (except special purpose vehicles), motorcycles, and air transport means	30

Types of property	Depreciation rate (%)
Oil rigs, oil exploration and extraction ships, sea and river transport means	15
Other fixed assets	40

The value of new technological equipment is multiplied by a coefficient (1.5 from 2009 to 2013) before claiming capital allowances. The effect of applying a coefficient is reversed if the new technological equipment is disposed of within five years from acquisition.

Non-business assets are ineligible for capital allowances.

Intangible assets are eligible for capital allowances on a straight-line basis over the following recovery periods:

* Concessions: ten years
* Patents, licences, and trademarks: five years
* Research and development (R&D) expenses: one year

Any intangible assets not fitting into any of these categories (such as goodwill) are ineligible for capital allowances.

The cost of intangible investments is increased by a coefficient of 1.5 if such investments result in a trademark or patent being registered.

Start-up expenses
There is no specific treatment for start-up expenses. Generally, after registration of the company for tax purposes, expenses are deductible. Expenses accrued before registration of company cannot be deducted for CIT purposes due to the lack of supporting documentation with company identifying information. However, input VAT on goods purchased or services received prior to registration for VAT purposes is recoverable if the goods purchased and services received or used will further be used for taxable transactions.

Interest expenses
The CIT Act imposes restrictions on deductibility of interest payable on loans or credits, factoring transactions, and finance leases under two methods. *For further details, please see Thin capitalisation in the Group taxation section.*

Bad debts
Bad debts may only be deducted for CIT purposes if certain conditions are met.

Provision for doubtful debts
Recent amendments allow taxpayers, under certain conditions, to defer payment of CIT on a provision for doubtful debts for three years, without increasing taxable income at the time of making that provision. A special provision for doubtful debts in a tax period that does not increase taxable income must not exceed 20% of taxable income before provisions for bad debts. To take this relief, the following conditions must be met:

* The payment became due more than six months ago.
* The income associated with these debts has been added to taxable income.
* The debtor is a legal entity resident in the EU/EEA or in a country that has an effective DTT with Latvia.

Latvia

- The taxpayer and the debtor are not related companies and neither of them is a person related to the company.
- Dealings with the debtor were stopped at least six months ago and have not been resumed since.
- The taxpayer can prove that steps were taken to recover the doubtful debt.
- The taxpayer has given the debtor written notice by 31 December in the tax year that the debt (with details of the supporting document) is covered by a provision for doubtful debts made in line with this clause.

Unless the provision is reduced within three years by being added to taxable income or through a bad debt being written off, the amount of doubtful debts covered by the special provision will have to be added to taxable income.

The amendments relating to the provision for doubtful debts apply from 2011 to 2013.

Amounts unpaid by a debtor
A taxpayer who has not paid for goods or services within six months after the due date for payment must not deduct the amount of the debt from taxable income if the creditor has notified one that the debt is classified as doubtful and covered by a special provision for doubtful debts. Taxable income can be reduced in the tax period the debt is paid.

The amendments relating to the provision for doubtful debts apply from 2011 to 2013.

Charitable contributions
Donations paid to charitable institutions, non-profit making foundations, churches and monasteries, and various other welfare institutions increase taxable income, but may qualify for a tax relief, if certain criteria are met (*see the Tax credits and incentives section*).

Luxury vehicles
Luxury vehicles (i.e. light passenger cars with a value greater than LVL 25,424, excluding VAT) are not eligible for capital allowances. A tax deduction is denied for expenses incurred in using and maintaining luxury vehicles and for lease or hire purchase payments associated with leasing such vehicles. These rules do not, however, apply to special purpose vehicles (such as emergency vehicles and special passenger vehicles).

Provisions
Any increase in general provisions and reserves for the tax period as compared with the previous tax period is non-deductible. These provisions include accruals for accrued benefits, bonuses and commissions, and other expenses.

Non-business expenses
A tax deduction is not allowed for any expense not directly related to business activities. In fact, non-deductible expenses have to be increased by a coefficient of 1.5 (except donations made to qualifying institutions). Effectively, such expenses are taxed at 22.5% (15% x 1.5).

Non-business expenses include costs that are not directly related to commercial activities; all expenses incurred for the pleasure and recreation of owners and employees; entertainment trips taken by owners and employees in company vehicles; any benefits, gifts, credits, and loans turned into gifts to owners and employees; and any other disbursements in cash or in kind to owners or employees that are not part of remuneration or that are not related to the taxpayer's commercial activities.

Latvia

Representation expenses
Under the Latvian CIT Act, representation expenses are costs that a company incurs in developing and maintaining its prestige at a level acceptable to society. Representation expenses include costs incurred in holding public conferences, receptions, and meals, and the cost of producing items to represent the company (e.g. items bearing its logo). 40% of representation expenses are deductible for CIT purposes.

Fines and penalties
Fines, contractual penalties, and statutory interest on arrears (including increase in principal debt) levied under the Taxes and Duties Act and specific tax laws are not deductible.

Taxes
Excise duties, employer's national social insurance contributions, natural resource taxes, customs duties, and real estate taxes are deductible.

Net operating losses
Tax losses may be carried forward for an unlimited period of time, if accrued since 2008. Tax losses accrued before 2008 may be carried forward eight years (*for more details, please see table below*).

Year losses accrued	Last year losses could be used
2004	2012
2005	2013
2006	2014
2007	2015
2008 and after	Not limited

The carryback of losses is not permitted.

A company in which more than 50% of shares (a controlling interest) have changed hands may utilise its tax losses if it continues for five years the same business that it carried on during the two years prior to the change of control. When companies are reorganised by a merger or spin-off, it may be possible to utilise losses accrued.

Payments to foreign affiliates
In general, a Latvian company may deduct the full amount of royalties, service fees, and interest (subject to statutory limits) made to related parties to the extent that such payments are made at arm's length. Such payments may be subject to a WHT (*see the Withholding taxes section*). However, if a taxpayer fails to deduct the WHT due, the amounts paid cease to be deductible for tax purposes.

Group taxation

Group consolidation is not permitted for tax purposes. However, the members of a group of Latvian companies, whose parent owns directly or indirectly 90% of the capital of its subsidiary or subsidiaries, may surrender their current-year tax losses to one another.

Latvia

Transfer pricing

The Latvian Regulation governing the application of the CIT Act states that for transfer pricing calculation purposes, use may be made of the Transfer Pricing Guidelines for Multinational Enterprises and Tax Administrations, a document issued by the Organisation for Economic Co-operation and Development (OECD).

Latvian law requires that related-party transactions be in compliance with the arm's-length principle. Under the arm's-length principle, the conditions made or imposed between two related enterprises in their commercial or financial relations must not differ from those that would be agreed between independent enterprises engaging in similar transactions under similar circumstances.

A tax audit may examine and adjust the price of a transaction in the following circumstances:

- The transaction is between related parties.
- Barters and set offs.
- A price deviation exceeds 20% of prices that the taxpayer has applied to similar goods or services over a short period.
- Exports and imports.

The transfer pricing requirements for the arm's-length price of a related-party transaction primarily apply to transactions between two or more related companies. Latvian legislation has broadened these requirements, and section 12 of the CIT Act requires the taxpayer to adjust one's taxable income for the difference between the price applied to a transaction and the arm's-length value if the transaction involves:

- individuals related to the company
- related foreign companies
- companies exempt from CIT or enjoying CIT relief pursuant to other Latvian laws, or
- a related company with which it forms a single tax group.

This provision may apply to any transaction, including purchases and sales of fixed assets and goods, supplies of services, loans and borrowings, and intellectual property (IP). It is possible to use corresponding adjustments and adjust taxable income if a related party has made adjustments of its income according to transfer pricing rules. It is possible only if the related party is registered in EU/EEA and documentary evidence from the respective tax authorities is received.

It should also be pointed out that the traditional view that transfer pricing rules only apply to transactions with foreign related companies is no longer consistent with the law because transfer pricing issues are now also important to companies doing business with Latvian-related companies.

There are no obligatory transfer pricing documentation requirements in Latvia yet. According to the proposed amendments, Latvian taxpayers who enter into transactions with any of the parties listed above and whose annual turnover exceeds LVL 1 million will have to prepare transfer pricing documentation for those transactions. Nevertheless, it is highly advisable to prepare the transfer pricing documentation also for companies below the set threshold, as it may be of valuable support during tax audits.

Thin capitalisation
Thin capitalisation rules apply when claiming a tax deduction for interest payments on loans and leasing services.

Taxable income should be adjusted for either:

- interest paid in excess of interest calculated by applying to the liability 1.2 times the average short-term interest rate at Latvian banks as determined by the Central Statistical Office for the last month of the tax period or
- interest in proportion to the excess of the average liability over an amount equal to four times shareholders' equity at the beginning of the tax year less any revaluation reserve.

The higher of these calculations should be added to taxable income.

The following interest payments are fully deductible:

- Interest paid on borrowings from credit institutions resident in Latvia, EEA member states, or countries with which Latvia has an effective DTT.
- Interest paid to the Latvian Treasury, Nordic Investment Bank, European Bank for Reconstruction and Development, European Investment Bank, European Council Development Bank, or the World Bank Group.
- Interest paid on Latvian or EEA debt securities in public trading.
- Interest expenses incurred by credit institutions and insurance institutions, regardless of the lender.

Interest paid on borrowings from a financial institution is deductible up to the amount of interest calculated by applying to the liability 1.2 times the average short-term interest rate at Latvian banks as determined by the Central Statistical Office for the last month of the tax period. The qualifying financial institution must meet the following criteria:

- It is resident in Latvia, the EEA, or a country with which Latvia has an effective DTT.
- It provides lending services or finance lease and is monitored by the controlling institution that supervises credit institutions or the financial sector.

Controlled foreign companies (CFCs)
There is no CFC regime in Latvia.

Tax credits and incentives

Foreign tax credit
Tax paid abroad on income included in the taxable base is allowed as a credit against the CIT charged for the year. However, the credit must not exceed the Latvian tax attributable to the income taxed abroad. Any unused tax credits may not be carried forward.

Donations to public benefit organisations
CIT liability may be reduced by 85% of amounts donated to qualifying state-funded institutions; Latvian-registered societies, establishments, and religious organisations; or to institutions qualifying as public-benefit organisations under the Public Benefit Organisations Act. Such a reduction may not exceed 20% of the total CIT liability. When

Latvia

making a donation, the donor is not permitted to impose an obligation on the recipient of the donation or carry out any acts that may be classified and treated as consideration.

Donation relief is also available for donations to EU/EEA entities that have statuses similar to public-benefit organisations in the country of residence.

Large investment relief

CIT relief is available for investments over LVL 3 million in qualifying industries in new, unused fixed assets (buildings and structures classified as industrial buildings and new plant and technological equipment) which they can use for business purposes. The available tax relief is 25% of the amount of investments made (15% for investments over LVL 35 million). Investment projects must be completed within five years after the tax relief is granted.

Investments have to enable a company to launch a new line of business or to modernise its existing production, which includes manufacturing new goods, a shift of business activity from producing one type of goods to producing another type of goods, or a complete overhaul of the manufacturing process.

Incentives for shareholders to invest profits in companies

Recent changes in CIT law encourage shareholders to invest profits in the development of their company rather than take them out as dividends. Businesses may reduce their taxable income by a notional amount of interest that a taxpayer would have to pay on a loan equal to one's prior-year undistributed profit. This adjustment is calculated by multiplying the annual weighted average rate of interest on loans issued to non-financial Latvian businesses as determined by the Bank of Latvia for the tax period by undistributed profits accrued since 31 December 2008.

Free ports and special economic zones (SEZs)

Companies operating in SEZs are entitled to CIT and real estate tax relief. These areas include the free ports of Ventspils and Riga and the SEZs of Rezekne and Liepaja.

The qualifying companies may apply CIT relief of 80%. Since 2012, the CIT must be calculated at a 15% rate, resulting in an effective CIT rate of 3%. The companies may also apply 80% WHT relief for dividends, management services, and payments for IP made to non-resident companies.

Real estate tax relief amounts to 80%, and the municipality may waive the remaining 20%. Therefore, when meeting certain criteria, qualifying companies may decrease real estate tax to zero.

The amount of total CIT and real estate tax relief that may be claimed by the company depends on the amount of qualifying investments made by the company in the free port or SEZ area. Depending on the size of the company, the total tax relief available ranges from 50% to 70% from the amount of investments made.

Deferred tax on asset replacements

Latvia will allow a deferred payment of tax on profits arising on the sale of a replaced asset in order to encourage manufacturing companies to replace inefficient and outdated plant and machinery.

If a company acquires a functionally similar asset within 12 months before or after the old equipment is disposed of, then any income (profit) on the disposal of the old equipment is ignored in this tax period (i.e. the profit is deductible from taxable income). Tax payment is deferred until the new equipment is sold and may be further postponed if the equipment is replaced.

Withholding taxes

The following types of payments to non-residents and, in some cases according to Latvian transfer pricing rules, to related Latvian companies using CIT reliefs are subject to WHT.

Dividends
Dividends are generally subject to a 10% WHT. DTTs generally reduce the rate to 5%. However, dividends paid after 1 January 2013 to any company will be exempt. Dividends that meet criteria of parent-subsidiary directive and are paid to an EU/EEA resident are already exempt.

Interest
Interest payments to related non-resident parties are generally subject to a 10% WHT. Interest payments to non-related creditors are not subject to WHT. If a bank registered in Latvia pays interest to related companies at the bank's normal interest rate level, then a 5% WHT applies.

Through 30 June 2013, Latvian companies will have to comply with transitional rules of the CIT Act, which provide a 5% WHT on interest payments to a related EU company. From 1 July 2013 onwards, WHT no longer will apply to interest paid by a Latvian company to a related EU member state company that holds at least 25% of the share capital or voting power in that Latvian company and meets certain other statutory criteria.

However, after 1 January 2014, payments to any non-resident company will be tax exempt, excluding payments to tax havens. In certain cases, for payments to tax havens, the company may obtain State Revenue Service confirmation that WHT does not apply, provided that the payment has not been made to reduce the taxable income.

Royalties
Payments for IP (copyright in literary or artistic works, including movies, videos, and sound recordings) are subject to a 15% WHT. A 5% WHT is applied on other intellectual rights, such as patents, royalties, and trademarks. DTTs may reduce the rate.

If the recipient is an EU-related company that holds at least 25% of the share capital or voting power in that Latvian company and meets certain other statutory criteria, the applicable rate for IP is 5% through 30 June 2013 and exempt from 1 July 2013 onwards.

CIT provision states that after 1 January 2014 every payment for IP to any non-resident company will be tax exempt, excluding payments to tax havens. In certain cases, for payments to tax havens, the company may obtain State Revenue Service confirmation that WHT does not apply, provided that the payment has not been made to reduce the taxable income.

Rentals of industrial, commercial, or scientific equipment and real estate
Rental payments for property in Latvia are subject to a 5% WHT.

Latvia

Management fees

Management and consulting fees are subject to a 10% WHT. The term 'management and consulting' means activities carried out by a non-resident directly or by outsourced personnel to ensure the management of a Latvian company or to provide necessary advice. DTTs may reduce the rate to 0%.

Disposal of real estate

A 2% WHT applies to proceeds from real estate disposals. This applies to income from disposed shares or other participation in a Latvian or foreign-registered company or other entity, if real estate in Latvia made up (in the period of disposal or the previous period, whether directly or indirectly, through shareholdings in one or more other entities established in Latvia or abroad) more than 50% of the asset value of the company being disposed of.

Double tax treaties (DTTs)

A Latvian company can rely on a DTT to reduce the rate of WHT on any payments previously mentioned. To this end, the Latvian company must obtain a valid residence certificate for each type of payment to each recipient prior to making the actual payment. A valid residence certificate is one approved by the foreign tax authority and the Latvian tax authority.

Please see the following table for WHT rates applicable to the payments described above:

Recipient	Dividends (1)	Interest (2)	Royalties (2)	WHT (%) Rentals of industrial, commercial, or scientific equipment and real estate	Management fees	Disposal of real estate
Related Latvian companies using certain CIT reliefs	0	5/10	5/15	5	10	2
Companies in tax havens (3)	10	5/15	15	15	15	15
Treaty:						
Albania	5/10 (4)	0/5/10	5/10	5	0	2
Armenia	5/10 (4)	0/5/10	5/10	5	0	2
Austria	5/10 (4)	0/5/10	5/10	5	0	2
Azerbaijan	5/10 (4)	0/5/10	5/10	5	0	2
Belarus	10	0/5/10	5/10	5	0	2
Belgium	5/10 (4)	0/5/10	5/10	5	0	2
Bulgaria	5/10 (4)	0/5	0/5	5/7	0	2
Canada	5/10 (4)	0/5/10	5/10	5	0	2
China	5/10 (4)	0/5/10	5/10	5	0	2
Croatia	5/10 (4)	0/5/10	5/10	5	0	2
Czech Republic	5/10 (4)	0/5/10	5/10	5	0	2

Latvia

Recipient	Dividends (1)	Interest (2)	Royalties (2)	WHT (%) Rentals of industrial, commercial, or scientific equipment and real estate	Management fees	Disposal of real estate
Denmark	5/10 (4)	0/5/10	5/10	5	0	2
Estonia	5/10 (4)	0/5/10	5/10	5	0	2
Finland	5/10 (4)	0/5/10	5/10	5	0	2
France	5/10 (5)	0/5/10	5/10	5	0	2
Georgia	5/10 (7)	0/5/10	5/10	5	0	2
Germany	5/10 (4)	0/5/10	5/10	5	0	2
Greece	5/10 (4)	0/5/10	5/10	5	0	2
Hungary	5/10 (4)	0/5/10	5/10	5	0	2
Iceland	5/10 (4)	0/5/10	5/10	5	0	2
Ireland	5/10 (4)	0/5/10	5/10	5	0	2
Israel	5/10 (6)	0/5/10	5/10	5	0	2
Italy	5/10 (5)	0/5/10	5/10	5	0	2
Kazakhstan	5/10 (4)	0/5/10	5/10	5	0	2
Kirghizia	5/10 (4)	0/5/10	5/10	5	0	2
Korea	5/10 (4)	0/10	5/10	5	0	2
Lithuania	0	0	0	0/5	0	2
Luxembourg	5/10 (4)	0/5/10	5/10	5	0	2
Macedonia	5/10 (5)	0/5/10	5/10	5	0	2
Malta	5/10 (4)	0/5/10	5/10	5	0	2
Moldova	10	0/5/10	5/10	5	0	2
Montenegro	5/10 (4)	0/5/10	5/10	5	0	2
Morocco	6/10 (4)	0/5/10	5/10	5	0	2
Netherlands	5/10 (4)	0/5/10	5/10	5	0	2
Norway	5/10 (4)	0/5/10	5/10	5	0	2
Poland	5/10 (4)	0/5/10	5/10	5	0	2
Portugal	10	0/5/10	5/10	5	0	2
Romania	10	0/5/10	5/10	5	0	2
Serbia	5/10 (4)	0/5/10	5/10	5	0	2
Singapore	5/10 (4)	0/5/10	5/7.5	5	0	2
Slovak Republic	10	0/5/10	5/10	5	0	2
Slovenia	5/10 (4)	0/5/10	5/10	5	0	2
Spain	5/10 (4)	0/5/10	5/10	5	0	2
Sweden	5/10 (4)	0/5/10	5/10	5	0	2
Switzerland	5/10 (7)	0/5/10	5/10	5	0	2
Tajikistan	0/5/10 (8)	0/7	5/10	5	0	2
Turkey	10	0/5/10	5/10	5	0	2
United Kingdom	5/10 (4)	0/5/10	5/10	5	0	2
United States	5/10 (5)	0/5/10	5/10	5	0	2
Ukraine	5/10 (4)	0/5/10	5/10	5	0	2
Uzbekistan	10	0/5/10	5/10	5	0	2

L

Latvia

Notes

1. No WHT from 1 January 2013.
2. No WHT from 1 January 2014, excluding companies in tax havens.
3. 15% applies to all payments to companies located in tax havens, with the following exceptions:
   - 10% for dividends paid by Latvian residents. Starting from 1 January 2013, dividend payments are exempt.
   - 5% for interest on deposits and current accounts paid by Latvian banks at their general rate.
   - Repayments of loan principal are exempt.
   - Goods originating in the tax haven are exempt.
4. A 25% minimum shareholding is required for the lower rate.
5. A 10% minimum shareholding is required for the lower rate.
6. A 25% and 75,000 United States dollars (USD) minimum shareholding is required for the lower rate.
7. A 20% minimum shareholding is required for the lower rate.
8. A 75% minimum shareholding is required for the 0% rate; a 25% minimum shareholding is required for the 5% rate.

Tax administration

Taxable period

The fiscal year may not exceed 12 months and is normally based on the calendar year. However, companies are permitted to choose alternative start and end dates for the tax year. The first year of trading may last up to 18 months.

Tax returns

Tax returns are filed annually, together with annual accounts, within one month after they have been approved but not later than four months after the end of financial year. Thus, if the financial year ends on 31 December, the CIT return and annual accounts must be filed not later than by 1 May of the following year. Larger companies may file the CIT return and annual accounts not later than seven months after the end of financial year.

Payment of tax

CIT usually is paid monthly on or before the 15th day of each month, with a final adjustment when the annual tax return is filed. Monthly tax instalments are based on the tax liability in the previous fiscal year and adjusted by the consumer price index. A company may choose quarterly instalments if its monthly advances in the previous period were less than LVL 500. For a new company, advance payments are voluntary.

Audit cycle

The tax audit commences with an audit note for open tax years (not more than three years since the tax payment was due). There are draft provisions suggesting that transfer pricing related issues can be audited for the prior five years. The duration of the audit may vary from a few weeks to a few months, in certain cases, not exceeding 90 days. In certain cases, it can be extended to 150 days.

Tax authorities should inform a taxpayer of a tax audit no later than ten working days prior to the commencement of the audit with notification about documents the tax authorities may like to receive.

During a tax audit, the auditor notifies the taxpayer about irregularities of calculation of tax payments and any possible fines that could be charged. Prior to issuing a decision of the audit, the auditor invites the taxpayer to final negotiations to discuss the tax audit results.

Following the audit and the notification of tax audit findings, the company may in turn:

- Negotiate with the tax authorities with a view to reducing the tax burden and achieve an 'out of court settlement'. The out-of court settlement offers the possibility to reduce fines and late payment penalties calculated (not the additional amount of tax calculated) by 50% to 85%. The conclusion of such a settlement presupposes that the company accepts the findings of the audit (e.g. of expenses) for the audited years.
- Appeal decision by requesting opinion of general director of Latvian State Revenue Service.
- Only after receiving decision of general director of Latvian State Revenue Service, taxpayer may take the case to court. An advance payment of additional tax calculated and late payment penalties are suggested. The first decision normally takes to two years and another two years until a decision by the Court of Appeal and Supreme Court is issued.

Statute of limitations
The right of the Latvian tax authorities to collect unpaid taxes is three years since the relevant tax payment was due.

Topics of focus for tax authorities
Topics of interest to Latvia tax authorities include:

- Transfer pricing.
- Non-business, marketing, and representation expenses.
- Payments to and from non-resident companies, including offshore companies.
- Obligation to register PE in Latvia.

L

Lebanon

PwC contact

Wadih AbouNasr
PricewaterhouseCoopers
Saba House bldg, Block B & C
Said Freiha Street
Hazmieh
Lebanon
Tel: +961 1 200577 ext. 1610
Email: wadih.abounasr@lb.pwc.com

Significant developments

The Ministry of Finance issued Decision No. 1291/1, dated 1 December 2011, and amended by Decision No.1363/1, dated 23 December 2011, to adjust some of the rates used to calculate the deemed profit with effect as of the fiscal year 2012. Among the major changes is the deemed profit rate for insurance activities, which is now fixed at 8% for all types of insurance activities (i.e. life, motor, accident, etc.). Prior to fiscal year 2012, it varied depending on the type of insurance activity.

The Ministry of Finance issued Memo No.1460/S2 stating that the double tax treaty (DTT) between Lebanon and Italy, signed on 22 November 2001, is enforced as of 21 November 2011.

Taxes on corporate income

Under the income tax law in Lebanon, tax is levied based on income type. Accordingly, the income tax law divides income into the following three categories:

- Chapter I - profits from industrial, commercial, and non-commercial professions.
- Chapter II - salaries and wages and pension salaries.
- Chapter III - revenues from moveable capital (chapter III mainly covers all types of dividend income, board member appropriations from profits, and interest income, including interest on bonds and treasury bills).

The income tax law does not provide for a single tax on income. Accordingly, where a taxpayer has income from different sources, each type of income is taxed according to the tax chapter it falls under. The applicable rates are as follows:

- Corporate income tax (CIT): 15%.
- Capital gains tax: 10%.
- Dividend distribution withholding tax (WHT): 10% (may be reduced to 5% in certain cases).
- Non-resident WHT: 7.5% for services and 2.25% for other than services.
- Payroll tax: from 2% to 20%.
- Moveable capital WHT: 5% or 10%.

Not all businesses are taxed in the same manner, and, depending on the relative size and structure of a business, the tax method applied is assessed depending on real (or actual) profits or deemed profits.

Lebanon

Real profit method

In Lebanon, tax is charged on the total income or profits derived in Lebanon. Based on the income tax law and the principle of territoriality, the main premise for considering a profit to have been realised in Lebanon is if it was generated through an effort or activity exerted in Lebanon.

The tax base (the determination of profits) and the tax rates differ between resident and non-resident tax payers.

For resident corporate entities, CIT is computed at 15% based on the taxpayer's accounting profits after adjustments resulting from tax rules through the schedule of accounting-to-tax calculation.

The use of the real profit method is mandatory for the following:

- Corporations (SAL).
- Limited liability companies (SARL).
- Companies of individuals.
- Branches of foreign companies.
- All entities employing more than four employees or importing goods.

Small entities may choose voluntarily to be subject to the real profit method; however, once they choose the real profit method, they cannot revert back to the deemed profit method.

Concerning tax non-residents, WHT applies at 2.25% on payments for goods and 7.5% on payments for services.

Deemed profit method

A deemed profit method is imposed on insurance and savings institutions, taxable transport companies, oil refineries, and public work contractors.

Taxation is based on deemed profits and is levied at a flat rate of 15%.

The rate of deemed profit for public work contractors, as approved by the Ministry of Finance, is currently set at either 10% or 15% of total amounts collected per year, based on the type of activity performed by the contractor.

For insurance companies, the deemed profit rate is 8% for all insurance activities. Prior to fiscal year 2012, the rate varied depending on the type of insurance activity (i.e. life, motor, accident, etc.).

In addition to the flat rate tax imposed on deemed profits, a distribution tax of 10% is levied on dividends.

Local income taxes

There are no local government taxes on income in Lebanon.

Corporate residence

Tax is levied on all corporeal/natural and incorporeal/artificial persons, resident in Lebanon or outside, on all profits that they generate in Lebanon. The main premise for considering profits to have been realised in Lebanon is when such profits have occurred

L

Lebanon

from an effort exerted in Lebanon, irrespective of the identity of the taxpayer or place of residency.

Tax is levied on profits generated by two categories of taxpayers: resident taxpayers and non-resident taxpayers.

Resident taxpayers
A person, establishment, or company is considered resident for tax purposes, even if not physically resident in Lebanon, when any of the following two terms are satisfied:

- Have an office or a fixed place of business in their name in Lebanon, even when they are not undertaking their business in a normal and repetitive manner.
- Practising a profession or business activity in a normal or repetitive manner in Lebanon, even if they do not have a known registered place of business in Lebanon. This is because they are considered to have practised their profession from the place in which they contact their customers, even if such place is a hotel or a café.

Non-resident taxpayers
Non-resident taxpayers can consist of persons residing in Lebanon and persons residing outside Lebanon. A corporeal person residing in Lebanon is subject to the non-resident WHT (*see the Withholding taxes section for more information*) if neither of the following two terms are satisfied:

- Practise a certain trade in a normal and repetitive manner in Lebanon, irrespective of whether or not they have a known registered place of business.
- Have a known registered place of business in Lebanon.

A person residing outside Lebanon is subject to the non-resident WHT on the amounts, revenues, profits, or proceeds obtained from Lebanon as a result of undertaking an activity in whole or in part on Lebanese territory or as a result of exploiting rights in Lebanon.

Permanent establishment (PE)
There are no clear provisions in the Lebanese income tax law to define PE.

Other taxes

Value-added tax (VAT)
The standard VAT rate in Lebanon is 10%. Unless specifically exempt, VAT is levied on all commercial transactions undertaken by business entities. Export of goods and services and export-related services, international transport, and some of the intermediate operations are zero-rated. Banking, financial services, and insurance operations are exempt from VAT.

Customs duties
Modern, simple, and efficient assessment means are adopted by the customs authorities (e.g. electronic declarations, declaration in advance, applying international procedures in clearing the goods, selective inspection, auditing the goods after their release, and adopting the unique declaration).

Customs rates are imposed and modified according to decisions from the Lebanese customs authorities. These decisions are adopted based on the need of the Lebanese markets of some goods and the will to protect national production sectors.

Lebanon

Safeguard measures are provided for in relation to imported goods. The purpose behind such measures is to protect the domestic production sectors when an increase of imports is witnessed when compared to the same period during the previous year.

The rates are determined based on a specific schedule created in conformity with the Harmonised System of Nomenclature. This conformity with the unified system allows Lebanon to represent an 'importer friendly' environment for importers.

The normal rates are applied where there is no preferential agreement. When the origin of the good or part of the good is from a country with which Lebanon has a preferential customs treatment, preferential rates apply.

Customs rates in Lebanon are either determined in percentage or paid as a lump sum per unit of imported products.

Excise taxes
Excise taxes are mainly applicable in Lebanon on certain beverages and spirits, tobacco products, gasoline, and vehicles.

Built property tax
The built property tax is an annual progressive tax, ranging between 4% and 14%, on built property.

Stamp duty
Two kinds of stamp duties are levied. A proportionate stamp duty of 0.3% is levied on all deeds and contracts (written or implied) that mention specific payments or other sums of money. A fixed stamp duty ranging between a minimum of 100 Lebanese pounds (LBP) and a maximum of LBP 2 million is applicable on documents in accordance with schedules appended to the stamp duty law.

Capital gains tax
Under local legislation, companies are permitted to revalue their fixed assets every five years. Capital gains recognised from such a revaluation, as well as any profits that may be realised from the disposal of fixed assets, are subject to a capital gains tax of 10%.

Income from disposal of shares realised by a company is subject to 10% capital gains tax when the shares are classified as financial assets in the company's balance sheet.

Income from disposal of shares realised by a company whose main activity is the acquisition of investments is subject to 15% CIT.

Registration taxes
The estimated cost of establishing a company in Lebanon is 7,500 United States dollars (USD). This includes lawyer's fees and registration fees. The registration fees will increase if the company is established with capital exceeding the minimum requirement. However, the registration fees should not normally exceed 1% of the value of capital.

For branch offices and representative offices, establishment costs are lower and may be estimated at USD 5,000.

When transferring ownership of real estate, registration fees of approximately 6% are applicable.

Lebanon

Payroll taxes

Employers are responsible for withholding and declaring payroll taxes on behalf of their employees. Payroll tax is levied at progressive rates of 2% to 20%.

Branch income

Net income derived from a branch's operations in Lebanon is subject to Lebanese CIT, levied under the real profit method at a rate of 15%. Taxable profits of foreign branch offices are deemed to be distributed and are subject to a dividend distribution tax at the rate of 10%.

Representative offices

Representative offices do not pay CIT as long as they do not carry out commercial activities. Representative offices are required to submit annual tax declarations along with detailed company information that includes employee information, a balance sheet, an income statement, a non-resident tax schedule, and a schedule of payments to professionals. The declaration, with all relevant documentation, should be submitted as one single set. All the information included should be based on accounting records. The deadline for submitting the declaration depends on the legal form of the parent company (i.e. before 1 June of the following year for SAL or SARL companies and before 1 May of the following year for others).

Income determination

Inventory valuation

For tax purposes, inventory is valued using the weighted average cost method.

Capital gains

Capital gains are not generally subject to CIT, but may be subject to capital gains tax. *See Capital gains tax in the Other taxes section for more information.*

Note that income from disposal of shares realised by a company whose main activity is the acquisition of investments is subject to 15% CIT.

Dividend income

Dividends received as a result of a taxable person's activity are deemed trading income and are subject to 15% CIT. Dividends received as passive income are subject to 10% tax in Lebanon. However, dividends received from Lebanese entities are exempt from CIT, as the dividend tax is withheld at source, but are not exempt from further tax upon distribution from the recipient entity.

Stock dividends

The Lebanese law is silent on the tax implications of stock dividends. However, when share capital is increased by reducing retained earnings, no tax is applicable.

Interest income

Interest earned by corporations is added to taxable income. Relief is given for the WHT suffered on bank accounts, treasury bills, and bonds issue to the extent of the CIT due.

Rental income

Rental income should be deducted from the accounting result to reach the taxable result. Moreover, expenses related to property that is rented out should be added back to the accounting result to reach the taxable result.

A built property tax is paid on rental income at progressive rates ranging between 4% and 14%.

Royalties income

Royalties received by a holding company from Lebanese companies for patents and the like are taxed at a rate of 10%. Royalties received by holding companies from abroad are exempt from tax.

Royalties received by other than holding companies are taxed as ordinary income at 15%.

Unrealised exchange gains/losses

Unrealised exchange gains and losses are not treated differently from any other gain or loss for tax purposes, i.e. unrealised exchange gains are subject to CIT at 15% and unrealised exchange losses are deductible for CIT purposes.

Foreign income

Resident corporations are not taxed on foreign-source income derived from activities carried out abroad through foreign branches.

L

Deductions

Depreciation

Depreciation of property, plant, and equipment (at rates fixed by ministerial decree) is deductible. The depreciation method to be used is the straight-line method. If a depreciation rate that is higher than the low rate is adopted, the Ministry of Finance should be notified. The allowable depreciation rates are as follows:

Assets	Low rate (%)	High rate (%)
Buildings (commercial, touristic, and services)	2	5
Buildings (industrial and artisanal)	3	10
Buildings and constructions (commercial or industrial)	6	20
Freehold improvements and decorations	6	25
Technical installations and industrial equipments	8	25
Computer hardware and software	20	50
Vehicles (cars)	10	25
Vehicles (transport of goods/buses)	6	20
Sea transport	5	10
Air transport	20	25
Office equipment and furniture	8	25
Glasswares and silverwares (hotels, restaurants, etc.)	Inventory at year-end	Inventory at year-end
Gas cylinders	8	20

Lebanon

Goodwill
Under Lebanese tax rules, goodwill cannot be amortised.

Organisation and start-up expenses
Organisation and start-up expenses are amortised over three to five years for tax purposes.

Interest expenses
Interest on business loans is deductible, under certain conditions. Interest paid on the taxpayer's capital is not deductible.

Bad debt
Bad debts are deductible if all means for collection of the debt have been exhausted.

Provisions for bad debts are deductible if a debtor has been declared bankrupt. Surplus provisions are added to profits.

Charitable contributions
Charitable contributions are deductible if made to approved charitable, social, cultural, or sporting institutions, within certain limits.

Gifts
Gifts given by the company in cash are non-deductible.

Gifts given by the company in-kind to customers when the amount of each gift exceeds LBP 1 million per person per year and when the total amount of gifts in-kind exceeds 1% of the turnover are non-deductible.

Fines and penalties
Fines and penalties are not deductible in Lebanon.

Taxes
Taxes and duties incurred in the course of business (except CIT) are deductible.

Taxes due to foreign governments on income earned in Lebanon are non-deductible.

Exceptional taxes and fines are non-deductible.

Other significant items
Other deductible expenses include:

* Cost of goods sold.
* Cost of services rendered.
* Rent of business premises or, if the premises are owned by the taxpayer, their depreciation.
* Salaries, wages, and other employee benefits, including end-of-service indemnities.
* General business expenses, including insurance premiums.
* Reserves for severance payments, pensions, and disability payments. Surplus provisions are added to profits.
* Advertising and publicity expenses, within certain limits.
* Travel, telephone, and vehicle expenses, within certain limits.
* Entertainment expenses that are properly supported.
* Board remuneration against services performed.
* Accrued expenses as long as their occurrence is certain.

- Employees' life insurance premiums are deductible as long as they are included in the employees' benefits subject to payroll tax.

Other non-deductible expenses include:

- With the exception of normal maintenance expenses, costs that increase the value of the property, plant, or equipment (such costs should be capitalised and depreciated in accordance with the fiscal depreciation rates).
- Losses or share-in-costs resulting from enterprises, offices, and branches situated outside Lebanon.
- Representation allowances in excess of 10% of an employee's basic salary, as well as unjustifiable and unreasonable salaries.
- Personal expenses, such as payments deducted by an employer or partner for the management of the business and for certain business expenses incurred by the employer or partner.
- Appropriations made to board members that do not comprise remuneration for work done.
- Provisions, other than those specifically allowed by law. Examples of non-deductible provisions include provisions for bad debts, provisions for slow moving items, and provisions for bonuses, contingencies, and charges.

Net operating and capital losses
Tax losses may be carried forward for up to three years after the year in which they were originally incurred. The carryback of losses is not available.

Capital losses may be used to offset taxable profits of the current year but may not be carried forward.

Payments to foreign affiliates
Payments to foreign affiliates are generally subject to WHT.

Based on guidance issued by the Ministry of Finance, recharges from the head office located abroad (including advertising) are deductible up to a certain limit, calculated as follows:

(Assets of the branch in Lebanon/Consolidated assets) x Central administrative expenses.

However, a ceiling of 3% of the branch's revenues is applied.

Group taxation

There is no group taxation in Lebanon.

Transfer pricing
In Lebanon, there are no clear and detailed transfer pricing or general anti-avoidance rules. However, even in the absence of clear transfer pricing rules, exchanges or transactions made between related parties should be done on an arm's-length basis.

The tax administration has the right to reassess related party transactions and adjust their value in order to reflect the taxable amount related to the period under study.

Lebanon

Thin capitalisation

In Lebanon, there are no clear or detailed thin capitalisation rules.

Tax credits and incentives

Holding companies

Lebanese holding companies are exempt from CIT and from WHT on dividends. However, they are subject to a tax on their paid-up capital and reserves. In any given tax year, total tax payments on paid-up capital and reserves are capped at LBP 5 million.

Interest, management fees, and royalties received by holding companies from abroad are exempt from CIT.

Holding companies are subject to a 10% tax on interest received from loans shorter than three years extended to companies operating in Lebanon. Management fees received by the holding company from companies operating in Lebanon are subject to a 5% tax. Capital gains on financial assets in Lebanese companies held for less than two years are subject to a 10% tax. Royalties received from Lebanese companies for patents and the like are taxed at a rate of 10%.

Offshore companies

Offshore companies are exempt from CIT and from the WHT on dividends, and are instead subject to a lump-sum annual tax of LBP 1 million. Contracts related to offshore activities outside Lebanon are exempt from Lebanese stamp duty.

Offshore companies are required to be registered as SAL companies and, with a few exceptions, are subject to the same regulations as a SAL company. The business objectives of an offshore company are limited.

Permanent exemptions from CIT

Companies and organisations that are granted an indefinite exemption from CIT include the following:

* Educational institutions.
* Hospitals, orphanages, asylums, and other shelters that admit patients free of charge.
* Shipping, sea, and air transport associations (subject to certain restrictions).
* Farmers, provided they do not display farm produce and cattle outlets or sell products and meat after conversion tax.
* Syndicates and other types of professional associations.
* Miscellaneous non-profit organisations and co-operatives.
* Holding companies and offshore companies.
* Public sector bodies that do not compete with private institutions.

Reinvestment incentives

Industrial companies using operating profit to finance certain capital investments are exempt from up to 50% of their CIT liabilities for a period of up to four years, provided that such exemptions do not exceed the original investments made. In areas designated 'development zones', 75% of a company's tax liabilities may be exempt.

In order to take advantage of this regulation, investments should consist of capital expenditures designed to increase a company's manufacturing capacity or of investments in housing facilities for the company's staff and other employees.

Withholding taxes

WHT on interest
The income, revenues, and interest earned from accounts opened at Lebanese banks and from treasury bonds are subject to a 5% WHT that is non-refundable and cannot be carried forward. This WHT is considered as an advance payment on the current CIT due to the extent of that amount and acts as a minimum tax in situations where the tax due is lower than the tax on interest paid.

Non-resident WHT
Revenues earned by non-residents in Lebanon are subject to an effective WHT of 2.25% on revenue from the sale of materials and equipment, and 7.5% on the revenue in the case of sale of services.

Movable capital WHT
A 10% WHT is levied on income derived from movable capital generated in Lebanon. Taxable income is comprised of the following:

• Distributed dividends, interest, and income from shares.
• Directors' and shareholders' fees.
• Distribution of reserves or profits.
• Interest from loans to corporations.

WHT on dividends
Tax is withheld from dividends paid to shareholders/partners at a rate of 10%. The dividend distribution tax rate may be reduced to 5% under specific conditions.

DTTs provide the following WHT benefits. Note that treaty rates do not override lower non-treaty rates. Treaty members may take advantage of the non-treaty rates.

Recipient	Dividends (%)	Interest (%)	Royalties (%)
Non-treaty	10	10	7.5
Treaty:			
Algeria	15	10	10
Armenia	5/10 (1)	8	5
Bahrain	0 (2)	0 (2)	0 (2)
Belarus	7.5	5	5
Bulgaria	5	7	5
Cyprus	5	5	0 (2)
Czech Republic	5	0 (2)	5/10 (3)
Egypt	10	10	5
France	0 (2)	0 (2)	0 (2)
Iran	5	5	5
Italy	5/15 (10)	0 (2)	0 (2)
Jordan	10	10	10
Kuwait	0 (2)	0 (2)	5
Malaysia	5	10	8
Malta	5 (4)	0 (2)	5
Morocco	5/10 (5)	10	5/10 (7)
Pakistan	10	10	7.5
Poland	5	5	5

Lebanon

Recipient	Dividends (%)	Interest (%)	Royalties (%)
Qatar	0 (2)	0 (2)	0 (2)
Romania	5	5	5
Russia	10	5	5
Senegal	10	10	10
Sultanate of Oman	5/10 (6)	10	10
Syria	5	10	18
Tunisia	5	5	5
Turkey	10/15 (8)	10	10
UAE	0 (2)	0 (2)	5
Ukraine	5/15 (9)	10	10
Yemen	10	5	7.5

Notes

1. Shall not exceed:
   - 5% of the gross amount of the dividends if the beneficial owner is a company (other than a partnership) which holds directly at least 25% of the equity capital of the company paying the dividends.
   - 10% of the gross amount of the dividends in all other cases.
2. Dividends, interest, or royalties arising in a Contracting State and paid to a resident of the other Contracting State shall be taxable only in that other State.
3. Shall not exceed:
   - 5% of the gross amount of royalties paid for the use of, or the right to use, any industrial, commercial or scientific equipment.
   - 10% of the gross amount of royalties paid for the use of or the right to use, any copyright of literary, artistic or scientific work, including cinematograph films and films or tapes for radio or television broadcasting any software, patent, trademark, design or model, plan, secret formula or process, or for information concerning industrial, commercial or scientific experience.
4. Where the dividends are paid by a company which is:
   - A resident of Lebanon to a resident of Malta who is the beneficial owner thereof, the Lebanese tax so charged shall not exceed 5% of the gross amount of the dividends.
   - A resident of Malta to a resident of Lebanon who is the beneficial owner thereof, the Malta tax on the gross amount of the dividends shall not exceed that chargeable on the profits out of which the dividends are paid.
5. Shall not exceed:
   - 5% of the gross amount of the dividends if the beneficial owner is a company (other than a partnership) which holds directly at least 10% of the equity capital of the company paying the dividends.
   - 10% of the gross amount of the dividends in all other cases.
6. Shall not exceed:
   - 5% of the gross amount of the dividends if the beneficial owner is a company (other than a partnership) which holds directly at least 20% of the equity capital of the company paying the dividends.
   - 10% of the gross amount of the dividends in all other cases.
7. Shall not exceed:
   - 10% of the gross amount of royalties paid for the use of or the right to use, any copyright of literary, artistic or scientific work, including cinematograph films and films or tapes for radio or television broadcasting.
   - 5% of the gross amount of royalties paid in other cases.
8. Shall not exceed:
   - 10% of the gross amount of the dividends if the beneficial owner is a company (other than a partnership) which holds directly at least 15% of the equity capital of the company paying the dividends.
   - 15% of the gross amount of the dividends in all other cases.
9. Shall not exceed:
   - 5% of the gross amount of the dividends if the beneficial owner is a company (other than a partnership) which holds directly at least 20% of the equity capital of the company paying the dividends.
   - 15% of the gross amount of the dividends in all other cases.
10. Shall not exceed:
    - 5% of the gross amount of the dividends if the beneficial owner is a company which has owned at least 10% of the capital of the company paying the dividends for a period of at least 12 months preceding the date the dividends were declared.

- 15% of the gross amount of the dividends in all other cases.

Tax administration

Taxable period
Lebanon's fiscal year runs from January to December and is based on the Gregorian calendar. With the special permission of the local tax authorities, companies may, however, use their own accounting year.

Tax returns
Taxes on business income in any given year are based on the profits of the previous financial year.

Tax returns by artificial persons (entities) must be filed by 31 March of the year following the year of income. Tax returns by capital companies must be filed by 31 May of the year following the year of income.

Submission deadlines of annual declarations for institutions that are exempt from income tax (other than companies) are as follows:

- Before 1 February for institutions adopting the cash basis accounting.
- Before 1 April for institutions adopting the accrual basis accounting and for representative offices that represent non-corporate entities.
- Before 1 June for representative offices that represent corporations.

If taxpayers fail to submit a tax return, realisation penalties will be due.

Payment of tax
The same deadlines for tax returns apply for tax payments.

If taxpayers fail to make payment, late payment penalties will be due.

Audit cycle
The most common ways for the tax authorities to select companies for tax audits are the size of the company, the type of business, and certain risk assessment measures.

Tax audits typically cover a single type of tax.

In a typical situation, a tax audit is likely to take less than one year from first information request to substantive resolution.

Statute of limitations
The tax administration has four years to collect its rights. The period is calculated from the end of year that follows the current business year.

The taxable person may request the refund of excess tax within four years starting from the end of the year where the refund right was created.

The tax administration can exceed the statute of limitations in cases where a profit or revenue has been proven by a court order, arbitration, or inheritance clearance. The extension is limited till the end of the calendar year following the end of the year in which the tax administration was notified of such event.

Lebanon

Under the statute of limitations, a company should keep its accounting books and documentation for ten years.

Topics of focus for tax authorities

Lately, several topics have been of interest to the tax authorities in Lebanon, including transfer pricing, payments of royalties, and management fees to non-resident parties, provisions, and employee compensation.

Other issues

Foreign ownership of real estate restrictions

- Up to 3,000 square metres does not require Council of Ministers approval.
- Exploitation and normal lease right extending for a period of more than ten years cannot be attained without obtaining approval.
- Real estate owned by foreigners, for which approval has been obtained, cannot exceed, over all of the Lebanese territory, 3% of the total area of Lebanon. In each province, the total area owned should not exceed 3% of its area. With respect to Beirut, the total area owned should not exceed 10% of its area.
- The approval is nullified if not acted upon during a period of one year.
- When approval is granted, the building on the real estate should be constructed within a period of five years (renewable once by the Council of Ministers).

Choice of business entity

Lebanon's commercial law provides for a range of business entities available to both local and foreign investors. These consist of the following:

- Sole proprietorships.
- General partnerships.
- Limited partnerships.
- Joint-stock companies (SAL).
- Limited liability companies (SARL).
- Holding companies.
- Offshore companies.
- Representative offices.

Legal structures commonly used by foreigners in conducting business in Lebanon are SALs, SARLs, and branch offices.

Joint-stock companies (Société anonyme libanaise or SAL)

Lebanese joint-stock companies are permitted to engage in all kinds of business activity. Shareholders of a SAL have no liability beyond their actual capital subscriptions.

With a small number of exceptions (such as real estate companies and banks), there are no limits on the amount of capital that can be held by foreign investors.

The management of a SAL is entrusted to a board of directors with a minimum of three and a maximum of 12 members. The majority of board members must be Lebanese, but the chairman may be a foreign national.

- Certain types of businesses such as banks and insurance companies are required to incorporate as joint-stock corporations. Minimum capital: LBP 30 million.
- Taxation: the applicable CIT rate is 15% in addition to a WHT on dividends of 10%, reduced to 5% in certain cases, mainly if the shares are listed.

Limited liability companies (Société à responsabilité limitée or SARL)

Members of a limited liability company are partners, and the company's capital is divided into parts rather than shares. Partners are liable only to the extent of their parts, and individual partners' claims on the company's capital are fixed in the partnership deed.

All partners may be foreigners, with the exception of companies seeking to engage in commercial representation.

Limited liability companies may not be active in certain sectors of the economy, such as in insurance, banking, fund management, or air transportation.

The transfer of parts in a limited liability company is subject to the consent of partners representing at least three-quarters of the capital. Existing partners enjoy priority in the purchase of parts offered for transfer.

- A limited liability company is managed by one or several directors (managers) who may or may not be selected from among the partners. Minimum capital: LBP 5 million.
- Taxation: the applicable CIT rate is 15% in addition to a WHT on dividends of 10%.

Intellectual property

The law in Lebanon does not contain a clear definition of author's rights. It protects all products of the human intellect whether written, pictorial, sculptural, scriptural, or oral regardless of its value, importance, destination, or form of expression.

The law provides patent protection for inventions and plant varieties and a sui generis protection for layout designs of integrated circuits. Furthermore, the law provides protection for undisclosed information. According to an assessment conducted by the World Intellectual Property Organization (WIPO) in July 2002, the Patent law is in complete conformity with the WTO's Agreement on Trade-Related Aspects of Intellectual Property Rights (TRIPS). It was also pointed out that the provisions of the Plant Varieties exceed the minimum requirements of the TRIPS Agreement.

The law does not explicitly protect notorious trademarks and geographical indications. However, those are provided protection via Lebanon's membership to the Paris Convention. Moreover, geographical indications are provided protection under the provisions of the new Law on Customs, the Law on Fraud Control, and the Criminal Law.

The copyright protection originally available to literary and artistic works is now extended to computer software, video films, and all kind of audio-visual works. The law provides stiffer penalties for offenders and better compensation to the persons whose rights have been infringed. The manner in which the copyright is breached has also been extended.

Libya

PwC contact

Husam Elnaili
PricewaterhouseCoopers/Al Motahedoon LLC
Aldool Street, Ben Ashour
Tripoli, Libya
Tel: +218 21 360 9830 ext. 110
Email: husam.elnaili@ly.pwc.com

Significant developments

There have been no significant corporate tax developments in Libya during the past year. Various suggestions for tax reforms are being considered but would not be implemented until the formation of the newly elected government, later in 2012.

Taxes on corporate income

For any Libyan registered entity, income arising both in Libya and abroad (i.e. worldwide) is assessable for corporate income tax (CIT) purposes in Libya.

CIT is imposed annually on the same basis for Libyan controlled corporate entities, foreign controlled corporate entities, and branches of foreign companies.

CIT is levied on taxable profits at a flat rate of 20%.

Jehad Tax
There is a flat rate of Jehad Tax assessed at 4% on taxable corporate profits.

Jehad Tax was established by Law 44 of 1970. The purpose of the tax is to further the Muslim cause, in a peaceful manner, throughout the world.

Local income taxes
Libya has no provincial income tax laws.

Corporate residence

Corporate residence is not specifically dealt with under the laws of Libya. The tax authorities will seek to assess any income derived from services provided in Libya.

Permanent establishment (PE)
Double tax treaties (DTTs) being signed introduce the concept of permanent establishment. However, general law requires that any foreign entity seeking to provide services in Libya should obtain a business licence, which necessitates it registering as a legal entity. Historically, unregistered foreign entities have provided services in Libya, but this is not in line with the law and it is becoming difficult to do so.

Other taxes

Value-added tax (VAT)
There is no VAT in Libya.

Custom duties

Customs duties were abolished in 2005, except for tobacco and tobacco products.

A service fee of 5% on the value on most imports also exists. There are various exemptions to this service fee, specifically under Investment Law and within the oil sector.

Other dues and taxes on importation are estimated at 0.5%. Initially, a temporary import licence is issued for six months that can be extended to a maximum of three years. A guarantee or a deposit can be provided by the importer to the Customs Department.

Excise taxes

Libya has no excise taxes.

Property taxes

Libya has no specific property taxes.

Transfer taxes

Libya has no transfer taxes.

Stamp duty

Stamp Duty Law levies a schedule of duties and rates on various documents and transactions. The most relevant to corporate entities is Schedule 28, which prescribes the rate of duties on contracts for the provision of services or supply. The duty on main contracts is 1% and on subcontracts is 0.1%. Note that there is a duty of 0.5% on all payments to the Tax Department as well.

L

Branch income

Tax rates on branch profits are the same as on corporate profits. However, the Income Tax Law allows the Tax Department to assess income tax on branches of foreign companies as a percentage of turnover via the 'deemed profit' basis of assessment. Tax is therefore payable even where tax losses are declared.

The level of deemed profit applied to turnover varies according to the branch's type of business activity. This ranges from 10% to 15% for civil works and contracting (turnkey projects), 15% to 25% for oil service, and between 25% and 40% in the case of design/consulting engineers. A deemed profit of between 5% and 7% is also assessed on supply. The deemed profit percentage applied to any year will be higher than the profit percentage declared in the annual tax return since the deemed profit basis is applied during the course of a tax audit and is effectively a revenue generating exercise for the tax authorities. Historically, tax audits have not resulted in credits or reimbursements.

Income determination

No specific rules apply on income determination for the following categories:

- Interest income.
- Partnership income.
- Rent/royalties income.
- Foreign income.

Libya

Income Tax Law allows entities to account on an accrual basis or on a cash basis.

Inventory valuation
The Commercial Code allows inventory to be valued at the lower of cost and net realisable value.

Capital gains
Any chargeable gains on the sale of capital assets are taxed as ordinary income. For entities assessed on a deemed profit basis, capital gains should be added to the deemed taxable income.

Dividend income
Historically, dividend income has not been subject to any additional taxes.

Inter-company dividends
Libyan taxation laws do not contain any special provisions regarding inter-company dividends.

Stock dividends
Stock dividends are not specifically dealt with in Libyan taxation laws. The current practice is for dividend distributions not to be taxed.

Deductions

Taxable income is determined after deducting all expenditure and costs incurred in the realisation of the gross income (*for more details on the deemed profit basis of assessment on branches of foreign companies, see the Branch income section*).

For any entity (not a foreign branch) seeking to be assessed on an add-back basis, it should ensure, in accordance with Stamp Duty Law, that the majority of its costs can be supported by tax registered documents, i.e. declared payrolls and registered contracts and invoices.

Depreciation
Depreciation should be calculated in accordance with the Executive Regulations of the law.

Assets	Depreciation rate (%)
Buildings	
Building in which machines are fixed	3
Building without fixed machines	2
Means of transport	
Passenger	20
Cargo and freight	10
Ships	4
Fishing boats	4
Aeroplanes	8
Furniture	
Office, ship, and domestic furniture	10
Hotel, restaurant, cafes, and hospital furniture	20
Work camps outside of cities	20

Assets	Depreciation rate (%)
Food utensils and furnishings for restaurants, hotels, and the like	25
Machines	
Office machines	10
Electric generators	20
Computers and accessories	10
Software	10
Other machines	15

Goodwill
Purchased goodwill can be amortised on a straight-line basis over five years.

Organisation and start-up expenditure
Organisational and start-up expenditure can be capitalised and amortised over five years on a straight-line basis.

Interest expenses
No specific rules apply for the deduction of interest expenses.

Bad debt
Bad debts are only recognised to the extent that they have been recognised as such legally.

Charitable contributions
Donations to charities recognised by the state are permitted, up to 2% of net income.

Fines and penalties
No specific rules apply for the deduction of fines and penalties.

Taxes
No specific rules apply for the deduction of taxes.

Net operating losses
Losses may be carried forward and deducted from future profits, for up to five years. The Income Tax Law has no provision for the carryback of losses.

Payments to foreign affiliates
No specific rules apply for the deduction of payments to foreign affiliates.

Group taxation

There is no recognition of a group for taxation purposes.

Transfer pricing
No transfer pricing rules exist in the general law.

Thin capitalisation
No thin capitalisation rules exist in the general law.

Libya

Tax credits and incentives

Foreign tax credit
Under general tax law, no provision exists for allowing the deduction of foreign tax credits.

CIT exemption
Exemptions to CIT exist, most notably, under the Investment Law. General projects registered under the Investment Law are permitted a five-year CIT holiday with a possibility to extend for a further three years.

Exemptions also exist for strategic infrastructure projects. Such exemptions must be awarded by the General People's Committee (GPC), which is the legislative body, either by ratifying the relevant contract, which includes a tax exemption clause, or by the issuance of a separate law.

Customs and stamp duties exemption
Investment law also provides exemptions for customs duties and stamp duty. The exemptions that exist are bestowed on subcontractors to the relevant projects.

Petroleum Law provides exemption to customs duties on oilfield specific equipment and materials, which is also provided to oil service companies.

Withholding taxes

Libyan law has no withholding taxes (WHTs). Generally, for unregistered foreign entities seeking to register a contract with the tax authorities, CIT will be assessed (and must be settled) on a deemed profit basis at the time of registration. It may be possible to negotiate a WHT in preference to the aforementioned general procedure for a significant contract where there is greater uncertainty as to the estimated contract value.

Tax administration

Taxable period
The tax year is generally a calendar year, although assessments can be made on the basis of a company's own year-end, provided permission is granted in advance from the Tax Department, and the company then adheres consistently to the same date.

Tax returns
All corporate entities must make an annual filing within four months of its year-end or within one month of its audit report, whichever is earlier.

Payment of tax
CIT is payable on a quarterly basis (10 March, 10 June, 10 September, and 10 December) normally commencing the first quarter date after an assessment has been issued.

Tax audit cycle
Tax audits typically occur every three or four years.

Statute of limitations
The statute of limitations for CIT purposes is seven years.

Late payment penalties
A late payment penalty is assessed on the tax due at the rate of 1% to a maximum of 12%. In addition, the remaining quarterly payments are due immediately for failing to make an instalment on time.

The law also imposes the following penalties:

- A fine of not less than three times the amount of unpaid tax due shall be applied to any person who fails to pay tax by the due date.
- Without prejudice to any harsher penalty, a fine of not less than four times the amount of tax due and unpaid will be applied to any person who, with intent to evade all or part of the tax, commits any of the following acts or abets, agrees, or aids a person who commits such an act:
  - The making of false statements in declarations submitted under this law.
  - The preparation of false accounts, books and records, reports, or budgets.
  - The use of fraudulent means to conceal or attempt to conceal taxable amounts due under this law.

Topics of focus for tax authorities
Various reforms are being considered, including the abolition of Jehad Tax; however, until a newly elected government is in place, such discussions are without substance.

Other issues

Statutory Books
Business entities operating in Libya are required by Libyan Law to maintain a General Ledger and a General Journal (i.e. the Statutory Books).

Before use, these must be stamped as registered with the Revenue Authorities and the Commercial Court. It should be noted that a Ledger or Journal will not be registered if it already contains accounting entries (i.e. one cannot register existing books of account).

Similarly, transactions pre-dating the date the books are registered will be disallowed. In theory, transactions should be entered daily, but in practice, most companies write up their statutory records on the basis of monthly transactions summaries.

The Tax Inspector will always request production of the Statutory Books at the commencement of a tax audit. If these are not available, a perfunctory audit of the English (or other language) books of account will be made, and it is likely that there will be a punitive increase in taxable income as a consequence.

The new Commercial Code allows approved computer based ledgers to be used instead of the traditional manual ledgers.

Liechtenstein

PwC contact

Peter Schmid
PricewaterhouseCoopers AG
Neumarkt 4/Kornhausstrasse 26
CH-9001 St Gallen
Switzerland
Tel: +41 58 792 7260
Email: peter.schmid@ch.pwc.com

Significant developments

Three new tax information exchange agreements (TIEAs), with Finland, Norway, and Iceland, recently entered into force. Liechtenstein is in negotiations for new TIEAs with Canada, China, Japan, Mexico, and South Africa.

Additionally, the double tax treaty (DTT) with Germany was signed in November 2011 and is now in parliament for ratification.

Taxes on corporate income

In principle, all corporations, foundations, and establishments are subject to a profit tax at a flat rate of 12.5%. Resident companies are subject to unlimited tax liability on worldwide income. Non-resident companies are subject to limited tax liability for income from properties or branches within Liechtenstein.

Minimum tax

All legal entities are subject to an annual minimum tax of 1,200 Swiss francs (CHF). This tax can be fully credited to the profit tax.

The full tax amount is due even if the corporation is not resident in Liechtenstein for the whole tax period.

Corporate residence

A company is considered to be resident in Liechtenstein if its registered seat (address) or place of effective management is within Liechtenstein.

Companies that have neither a domicile nor effective place of management in Liechtenstein, as well as special asset dedications without legal personality, are subject to limited tax liability for the following income:

- Corporate income from the cultivation of domestic real estate used for agriculture and forestry.
- Rental and lease income from real estate situated within Liechtenstein.
- Taxable net corporate income of permanent establishments (PEs) situated in Liechtenstein.

Permanent establishment (PE)

Please note that Liechtenstein has only a few DTTs (*see the Withholding taxes section*). However, Liechtenstein is in the process of negotiating various new DTTs and has included PE definitions according to the Organisation for Economic Co-operation and Development (OECD) model treaty.

Other taxes

Value-added tax (VAT)
Liechtenstein has adopted the VAT law of Switzerland, having its own administration in Vaduz.

The general VAT rate is 8%. A reduced rate of 2.5% is applicable to deliveries of food, drugs, newspapers, magazines, and books. Furthermore, lodging/accommodation is taxed at a reduced rate of 3.8%. Note that various services are VAT-exempt (e.g. health, social security, education, banking, insurance).

Any person who, irrespective of legal form, carries on a business is liable for VAT. Any person liable for VAT that is involved in domestic entrepreneurial activity with a taxable turnover that is less than CHF 100,000 within a financial year can be exempted from taxation. Special regulations apply for non-profit institutions as well as for non-profit sport or cultures clubs. Reverse charge is applicable for services and certain deliveries from an entity domiciled abroad.

Customs duties/import tariffs
According to the customs union treaty of 1923 between Liechtenstein and Switzerland, Switzerland customs duties and import tariffs are applicable for Liechtenstein as well. The tariffs and duties depend on various specifics attributes of the products and are listed on comprehensive tariffs and duties lists. Therefore, the specific tariffs and duties must be checked for every case individually.

L

Excise taxes
Several excise taxes apply in Liechtenstein (e.g. petroleum tax, tobacco tax, car tax, CO_2 tax, beer tax, salt tax, taxation of distilled spirits).

Property taxes
No property taxes are applicable in Liechtenstein.

Stamp duty
According to the customs union treaty of 1923 between Switzerland and Liechtenstein, the Swiss stamp duty tax law of 27 June 1927 is applicable in Liechtenstein. The stamp duty law includes the stamp duty tax and the security transfer tax.

Stamp duty tax
Upon the formation of legal entities whose capital is divided into shares (e.g. company limited by shares, limited liability company, establishment with capital divided into shares) the stamp duty amounts to 1% of the nominal value or the higher amount effectively paid (above par). The first CHF 1 million is tax exempt.

The same duty also becomes due when the capital is increased or when the shareholders make contributions without increasing the capital. Stamp duty is also due on bonds (0.6 per million to 1.2 per million) and money market certificates (0.6 per million).

Various exemptions should also be considered.

Liechtenstein

Security transfer tax
Security transfer tax is due on all transactions of qualifying securities, if a security dealer is involved. The tax amounts to 0.15% for domestic securities (Switzerland and Liechtenstein) and 0.3% for foreign securities.

In particular, banks and financial intermediaries are liable for settlement. Furthermore, legal entities with qualifying securities with a book value of more than CHF 10 million also qualify as security dealers.

Formation tax (Gründungsabgabe)
Unless Swiss stamp duty law applies, a formation tax in the amount of 1% of the statutory nominal capital is levied upon the formation or relocation of legal companies in Liechtenstein (e.g. foundations) as well as for capital increases.

The general tax rate of 1% is reduced to 0.5% for amounts greater than CHF 5 million and to 0.3% for amounts greater than CHF 10 million. The first CHF 1 million is tax exempt.

Foundations are subject to the formation tax at a tax rate of 0.2%.

Real estate profit tax
Capital gains from the sale of real estate, or equivalent actions with the same result, are subject to a separately assessed real estate profit tax. The taxable gain is generally the difference between proceeds of the sale and the original purchase price of the property plus any capital expenditure incurred. The basic tax rate is between approximately 2% and 14%, depending on the amount of taxable real estate gain. The transfer of the economic ownership of real estate (e.g. via the sale of the majority of the shares in a real estate company) triggers real estate tax as well.

Capital tax
As of 1 January 2011, annual capital tax has been abolished.

Tax on insurance premiums
Liechtenstein levies a tax on certain insurance premiums. The tax rate amounts to 5% of the cash premium (for life insurance 2.5%). Cash premiums in foreign currency have to be converted to Swiss francs at the time the tax claims arise.

Various exemptions should also be considered.

Branch income

The same principles applicable to corporations also apply for branch income, provided that transactions with the head office or other branches are at arm's length. Liechtenstein taxation is imposed on the profit attributable to branch and on the capital invested in the branch. The minimum tax of CHF 1,200 is also applicable.

There is no withholding tax (WHT) on profit transfer to the head office.

Liechtenstein

....

Income determination

The corporate profit tax is determined according to the taxable corporate net income, which is based on the financial statement under consideration of the following provisions.

Inventory valuation
Inventories must be stated at the lower of cost or market. Cost is generally determined by the first in first out (FIFO) or by the average cost method. The tax authorities permit a general reserve against stock contingencies of up to one-third of the inventory cost or market value at the balance sheet date without inquiry into its justification, provided a detailed record of inventory is available for review by the tax authorities. The need for a reserve in excess of this amount (e.g. for obsolescence, slow-moving-stocks) must be substantiated to the satisfaction of the tax authorities.

Capital gains
Capital gains derived from the sale of shares are tax-exempt. Capital gains from the sale of real estate are subject to a separately assessed real estate profit tax (*see the Other taxes section for more information*).

Dividend income
Dividend income and liquidation proceeds are tax-exempt.

Interest income
Interest income is taxable and must be at arm's length if it is in respect to related parties (*for safe harbour rates, see Interest expenses in the Deductions section*).

Foreign income
Resident corporations operating locally are generally taxed on their worldwide income. However, income from foreign real estate and PEs situated abroad is exempt from taxation in Liechtenstein.

....

Deductions

Depreciation and amortisation
Depreciation of tangible fixed assets and amortisation of intangible assets is allowed if it is 'commercially justified'. For tax purposes, either the straight-line (depreciation based on the acquisition value) or the declining-balance method (depreciation based on the book value) may be used. Depreciation and amortisation not recorded in statutory accounts are not deductible for tax purposes.

A special (higher) rate of depreciation may be allowed for assets used only for short periods or for assets for which a rapid decrease in value can be proved.

The depreciation/amortisation rate per annum of various property types are provided below. Note that these depreciation rates relate to write-downs on the book value. If the write-down is performed on the acquisition value, then the rates enumerated below should be reduced by half.

Liechtenstein

Property type	Rate per annum (%)
Immovable assets:	
Real estate (dwelling houses, offices, shops, restaurant and hotel buildings, industrial buildings, factories, warehouses, and parking spaces)	5
Movable assets:	
Mobile structures, technical installations (air conditioning plant, gas and electricity mains for industrial purposes), elevators, investments in foreign real estate, high rack warehouses, and airplanes	15
Office furniture and machines, workshop, and storeroom equipment	20
Furniture used for the hotel and restaurant trade	25
Machines and accessories for production purposes, vending machines, telephone installations, and operating applications	30
Machinery used in more than one shift or used under heavy conditions, motor vehicles	35
Information technology (hardware and software), office furniture and machines, workshop and storeroom equipment, hotel and restaurant cookery, cutlery, and linen	50
Officially approved installations and equipment against water pollution, energy-saving equipment, and installations using solar energy	50
Intangible assets:	
Goodwill, patent, licence, and other rights of use	40

Start-up expenses

Please see Formation tax (Gründungsabgabe) in the Other taxes section.

In general, the expenses for a start-up are tax deductable as long as they are economically justified.

Interest expenses

Interest paid by a corporation to a third party is a deductible business expense. Interest paid to related parties (affiliates or shareholder) has to reflect the fair market rate and has to be at arm's length.

With respect to related parties, the tax administration of Liechtenstein annually issues safe harbour interest rates to be used on loans denominated in Swiss francs on the one hand and in foreign currencies on the other hand. The corporation may deviate from these safe harbour rates as long as it can prove that the rates are at arm's length and more appropriate in the present case.

Safe harbour rates 2012

Loans in Swiss francs	Minimum interest rate (%)
For loans made to related parties	
Financed from equity and no interest-bearing debt capital	2.0
Financed from debt capital	
Cost price	+ 0.5
At least	2.0

	Maximum interest rate (%)
For loans received from related parties	2.0

Loans in euros (EUR) or United States dollars (USD)	Maximum interest rate (%)
For loans received from related parties	3.5

Equity interest deduction

The equity interest deduction is a standardised deduction for interest on equity based on the multiplication of the 'modified' equity by the interest rate (according to the annual finance law). For 2012, the equity interest rate is 4%.

To determine the modified equity, the following terms have to be considered:

- Paid-in capital and open reserves plus taxed hidden reserves:
  - Deduction of own shares.
  - Deduction of participations/shares.
  - Deduction of foreign real estate.
  - Deduction of assets belonging to foreign PEs.
  - Deduction of non-operating related assets.
- Equity increases and decreases, based on the capital at the beginning of the business year.

	Example 1	Example 2	Example 3	Example 4	Example 5	Example 6
Modified equity	1,000,000	500,000	500,000	1,000,000	1,000,000	1,000,000
Loans	0	500,000	500,000	0	0	0
Profit	100,000	100,000	200,000	1,000,000,000	30,000	60,000
Interest on loans (4%)	0	(20,000)	(20,000)	0	0	0
Profit	100,000	80,000	180,000	1,000,000,000	30,000	60,000
Interest on equity (4%)	(40,000)	(20,000)	(20,000)	(40,000)	(40,000)	(40,000)
Taxable profit	60,000	60,000	160,000	999,960,000	(10,000)	20,000
Profit tax rate	12.50%	12.50%	12.50%	12.50%	12.50%	12.50%
Tax burden	7,500	7,500	20,000	124,995,000	0	2,500
Effective tax rate	7.50%	9.38%	11.11%	12.50%	0.00%	4.17%

Provisions

Bad debt provision

It is admissible to set up an accounting provision for specific impaired debt; additionally, it is possible to account for a general bad debt provision of up to 10% on receivables from Liechtenstein and Switzerland and up to 15% on receivables from any other country, if no specific provision has been accounted for on the corresponding debt. These provisions are not accepted regarding receivables to corporations and institutions under public law, banks, or for intercompany receivables.

Inventory provision

See Inventory valuation in the Income determination section for a description of the inventory provision regime.

Provisions on financial investments

Provisions on financial investments are possible but must be proved by established corporate evaluation method or other suitable documents.

Liechtenstein

Other provisions
Provisions at the expense of the profit and loss statement are admissible for obligations during the business year whose amount is not yet determined or for other immediately imminent losses during the business year.

Charitable contributions
Charitable contributions to legal persons and special asset dedications with domicile in Liechtenstein, in another country member of the European Economic Area (EEA), or in Switzerland, which are exempt from tax liability in light of exclusively and irrevocably common-benefit purposes, are deductible, up to the amount of 10% of the taxable corporate net income.

Deduction for income from intellectual property (IP)
A deduction of 80% is allowed on the net IP income that was created or acquired after 1 January 2011. IP, in the sense of the tax law, consists of patents, trademarks, models, and utility models. According to a recent court decision, however, it is not clear at the moment which IP qualifies for the IP-deduction.

This tax rule was approved by the European Free Trade Association (EFTA) Supervising Authority on 1 June 2011.

Fines and penalties
Fines and penalties are generally not tax deductable.

Taxes
Taxes are not deductible in Liechtenstein.

Net operating losses
A loss can be carried forward and offset against the profits for future years. There is no limitation of loss carryforwards as well as loss offsetting. Losses cannot be carried back.

Payments to foreign affiliates
Interest, royalties and licences, and other fees to foreign affiliates are allowed as deductions to the extent that they meet the arm's-length test (i.e. equivalent to charges that would be made by an unrelated third party).

For interest payments between affiliated companies or between shareholders and companies, Liechtenstein tax authorities publish safe harbour rules annually (i.e. generally accepted interest).

Group taxation

Resident and non-resident corporations have the possibility to opt for group taxation if they meet the legal requirements (such as more than 50% of capital and 50% of voting rights). The ultimate group leader must either be a corporation domiciled in Liechtenstein or with the effective place of management in Liechtenstein.

In order to form multi-level group structures, sub-groups may also be built. The same rules are applicable for the group leader of the sup-group as for the primary group leader.

The group leader can decide, for each company that fulfils the conditions, which company will be included in the group or not.

Losses of group members can be offset against profits of the (sub) group leader within the same year. The offsetting is only possible under the following conditions:

- Only losses incurred after the option for group taxation can be considered.
- Losses need to be calculated according to Liechtenstein profit calculation rules.

The losses are allocated to the (sub) group leader according to the direct participation quota of the (sub) group leader to the group member whose losses should be offset. If the losses cannot be used at the level of the (sub) group leader, they can be allocated to other group members. However, the minimum tax is applicable for each group member.

Losses that have been attributed to the (sub) group leader must be adjusted in the following cases:

- Losses can be offset against profits on the level of the group member.
- Exit of group member from the group.
- Reduction of participation quota of a group member.
- Depreciation is made on a participation due to losses.

The (sub) group leader must provide evidence annually that no adjustment needs to be made.

Transfer pricing

Liechtenstein does not have specific transfer pricing rules apart from the rule that intra-group transactions are carried out at arm's-length terms.

Thin capitalisation

Liechtenstein does not have thin capitalisation rules.

Tax credits and incentives

As of 1 January 2011, tax privileges for certain legal structures, such as domiciliary and holding companies, have been abolished. Companies that benefited from such privileges will continue to be taxed accordingly through 2013, unless they opt for the ordinary taxation scheme. These companies also have to pay the minimum tax of CHF 1,200 annually.

The following tax incentives are applicable as of 1 January 2011:

- Profit tax exemption for corporations that have an irrevocable charitable, cultural, or ideal purpose without commercial activity.
- Profit tax exemption of dividend income and capital gains on shares/participations (especially interesting for holding companies).
- Notional interest deduction on equity.
- Private vehicle solution (PVS).

Private vehicle solution (Privatvermögensstrukturen or PVS)

Liechtenstein offers tax privileges for PVSs. A PVS has no economic activity. The purpose of a PVS is to acquire, hold, administrate, and sell financial instruments according to the assets management law as well as cash and bank accounts. Participations may only be held if it can be proved that the shareholders or beneficiaries have no influence on the administration of this company.

Liechtenstein

The articles of the PVS must contain a clause that the regulations for PVS are applicable. Exemptions of this rule are applicable for legal entities that existed before the introduction of the new tax law as of 1 January 2011.

The investors of a PVS must be individuals who administrate their own assets or structures acting in the interest of individuals.

The company or the audit company needs to confirm, upon formation or after major changes, that the conditions for the PVS structure are fulfilled. This is supervised by the tax authority or a neutral certified accountant.

A PVS only pays the minimum tax of CHF 1,200 annually.

This tax scheme was qualified as in conformity with the provisions on state aid set out in Article 61 of the Agreement on the European Economic Area by the EFTA Surveillance Authority (ESA).

Avoidance of double taxation
Foreign taxes shall be allowable against domestic taxes (credit method) under circumstances where (i) the income is derived or wealth is owned in a country that has concluded an agreement for the avoidance of double taxation with Liechtenstein and such agreement provides for a tax credit or (ii) reciprocity is granted. Income or wealth shall be exempted from taxation in Liechtenstein (exemption method) if the agreement for the avoidance of double taxation provides tax exemption or if reciprocity is granted.

Withholding taxes

Coupon (withholding) tax
Until the end of 2010, Liechtenstein had a coupon tax of 4% on dividend payments and certain interest payments. The coupon tax was abolished as of the beginning of 2011. This means that no coupon tax is due on new reserves incurred after the end of 2010 or on interest payments. However, the coupon tax still applies with regard to old reserves (reserves existing on 1 January 2011). The tax base for calculation of the coupon tax on old reserves is the taxable capital dated 31 December 2010 (i.e. equity according to commercial balance sheet, adjusted with taxed hidden reserves). With regards to future distributions, old reserves have priority.

Transitional rule
Distributions of old reserves in 2011 and 2012 will be taxed at a reduced rate of 2%. Companies can either distribute during this time frame or opt for the taxation of the old reserves without effective distribution.

Distributions of old reserves as of 2013 are taxed at the ordinary rate of 4%.

The transitional rule is not applicable for liquidations of ordinary taxed companies terminated before 30 June 2011.

Tax treaties
Currently, a comprehensive DTT on income is in effect with Austria, Hong Kong, Luxembourg, and San Marino, as well as a limited one with Switzerland.

The DDT with Germany was signed in November 2011 and is now in parliament for ratification.

Recently Liechtenstein initiated DTTs with Uruguay. Furthermore, various TIEAs have been concluded.

The governments of Liechtenstein and the United Kingdom (UK) signed a Memorandum of Understanding (MOU) relating to cooperation in tax matters, which includes the Liechtenstein disclosures facility (LDF). According to these regulations, financial intermediaries in Liechtenstein are required to show that their UK costumers have been declaring their Liechtenstein investments to Her Majesty's Revenue and Customs (HMRC). Disclosure can be made between 1 September 2009 and 31 March 2015 and benefiting from favourable rules. In certain circumstances, even accounts or assets outside of Liechtenstein can be transferred in order to take advantage of the terms of the LDF.

Tax administration

Taxable period
The tax year corresponds with the business year. Therefore, the applicable accounting period, which may end at any date within the calendar year, is the basis for corporate taxation.

Tax returns
Corporations resident in Liechtenstein or with PEs in Liechtenstein must file a tax return by 1 July of the calendar year following the fiscal year-end.

Due to a substantiated written request, the tax authority may extend the submission deadline by six months. The request must be made, at the latest, 30 days after the general due date (31 August). A deadline extension requires the payment of the provisional invoice. In especially justified cases, the submission deadline may be extended once again. Such a request must be made before expiry of the first deadline extension.

The tax assessment issued by the tax administration is based on the company's tax return, including the attachments and the financial statements filed.

Payment of tax
Companies must pay tax within 30 days of receipt of the assessment. The defaults charge rate is 5%.

Statute of limitations
The limitation of the right to assess a tax is five years, starting after the end of the tax year in terms of periodic tax and after the end of the year in which the taxable incidence had taken place in terms of non-periodic tax.

Other issues

Restructurings
Restructurings (e.g. change of corporate form, merger, spin-off) can be carried out tax neutrally, if certain conditions are met.

All reorganisations have in common that they can only be carried out tax neutrally if they are performed at tax book value and if the assets remain taxable within Liechtenstein. Furthermore, specific/additional conditions must be met for each kind of restructuring

Lithuania

PwC contact

Kristina Krisciunaite
PricewaterhouseCoopers UAB
J. Jasinskio 16B
LT-01112 Vilnius
Lithuania
Tel: +370 5 239 23 00
Email: kristina.krisciunaite@lt.pwc.com

Significant developments

The following recent amendments have been introduced into the Lithuanian tax legislation:

- Advanced pricing agreements (APAs) and binding rulings were introduced as of 1 January 2012.
- 0% withholding tax (WHT) on royalties paid to related parties meeting requirements of the European Commission (EC) Interest and Royalty Directive from 1 July 2011.
- As of 1 January 2012, the threshold of income for small companies (having not more than ten employees) that may apply the reduced corporate income tax (CIT) rate of 5% was increased to 1 million Lithuanian litas (LTL) (approximately 290,000 euros [EUR]). Previously, the threshold was LTL 500,000 (approximately EUR 145,000).

Taxes on corporate income

The standard CIT rate is 15%. However, small companies and agricultural companies can apply a reduced CIT rate of 5%, if certain conditions are met.

Generally, CIT is applied on taxable income received by a Lithuanian tax resident from its local and worldwide activities. Taxable income is calculated by reducing general income of a certain tax period with deductible expenses and non-taxable income.

Income of a tax resident company is not subject to taxation in Lithuania if it was received from activities through a permanent establishment (PE) in a foreign country which is in the European Economic Area (EEA) or which has a double tax treaty (DTT) with Lithuania and if the income was subject to taxation there.

Furthermore, CIT may be reduced or even not applied if foreign-sourced income received not through a PE is taxed with a WHT in a foreign country and this country has a DTT with Lithuania.

Non-resident companies are generally taxed on Lithuania-sourced income received through a local PE and reduced by deductible expenses or on income subject to WHT in Lithuania.

Reduced CIT rate for small companies

Entities with fewer than ten employees and less than LTL 1 million (approximately EUR 290,000) in gross annual revenues can benefit from a reduced CIT rate of 5%.

CIT regime for certain maritime activities

The rate of CIT on certain maritime activities is 15%, with the base set by reference to the functional capacity of the ship. This fixed CIT may be applied to maritime entities that fulfill certain conditions indicated in the law. An election must be made to the tax authorities to apply this regime.

Local income taxes

There is no local or municipal CIT.

Corporate residence

A company is resident in Lithuania if it incorporates there or its activities create a PE for tax purposes.

Permanent establishment (PE)

According to local legislation, a foreign company is deemed to have a PE in Lithuania when:

- it permanently carries out commercial activities in Lithuania in whole or in part
- it carries out its activities through a dependent representative (agent)
- it uses a building site or construction, assembly, or equipment objects, or
- it uses equipment, including drilling installations and ships, for exploration or extraction of natural resources.

DTTs may establish different rules of PE recognition. According to domestic law, where there is a DTT, the provisions of the treaty take precedence.

A PE must be registered as a taxpayer with the tax authorities in the territory where its activities are carried out. Its profits are subject to CIT at the rate of 15%.

Other taxes

Value-added tax (VAT)

The standard VAT rate is 21%.

A reduced rate of 9% applies to:

- Books and non-periodicals.
- Supply of heating of residential premises and the supply of hot water to residential premises as well as heating of cold water (applicable thru 31 December 2012).

A reduced rate of 5% applies to compensated pharmaceuticals and medical aid devices (applicable thru 31 December 2012).

The compensational rate for farmers is 6%.

In general, supplies of goods and services made by a taxable person performing its economic activity for a consideration within the territory of Lithuania, as well as imports of goods, are subject to VAT.

Lithuania

Exempt with credit (zero-rated)

Goods and services that are exempt with credit (zero-rated) include, but are not limited to, the following:

- Supply of goods exported outside of the European Union (EU).
- Goods acquired by non-EU resident passengers in Lithuania and carried out from the European Union.
- Goods and services for vessels and aircraft.
- Transportation and any directly linked ancillary services related to export of goods and any directly linked ancillary services related to the import of goods when the value of these services shall be included in the customs value of the goods.
- Transportation of imported goods carried to a VAT exemption warehouse or temporarily stored under customs' supervision, placed in a free economic zone or free warehouse, put under customs warehousing procedure, processed under customs' supervision, temporarily imported for processing without levying customs duties, temporarily imported without implicitly levying customs duties, or put under internal or external transit procedure.
- Issuance of International Road Transportation (TIR) and Admission Temporaire/ Temporary Admission (ATA) transportation documents.
- Insurance and certain financial services directly related to export of goods from the European Union.
- Supply of goods to sponsorship or charity recipients registered in Lithuania and listed in the Lithuanian law on charity and sponsorship, if the goods are exported by the recipients as sponsorship or charity to non-EU organisations which may be recipients of sponsorship or charity under the law.
- Supply of maintenance and processing services for movable property supplied to non-taxable persons established outside Lithuania that have no fixed establishment within the country, provided that the property was temporarily imported for maintenance, repair, processing, etc. in the European Union and will be carried out from the European Union after supply of these services.
- Services of disclosed agents participating in certain transactions of supply of goods or services to local taxable and non-taxable persons where zero-rated VAT is applied and transactions of supply of goods or services where the supply of goods or services is considered carried out outside the European Union.
- Supply of goods to VAT payers registered in another EU member state when these goods are carried out from Lithuania to another EU member state.
- Supply of new means of transport supplied to any person when new vehicles are carried out from Lithuania to another EU member state.
- Supply of goods subject to excise duty when they are supplied to a company not registered for VAT purposes and the goods are carried out from Lithuania to another EU member state.
- Supply of goods in certain cases related to international trade.

In order to apply zero-rated VAT on goods carried out from Lithuania, VAT payers must hold supporting documents as evidence that these goods were actually exported from the European Union or carried out from Lithuania to another EU member state.

Exempt without credit

Goods and services that are exempt without credit include, but are not limited to, the following:

- Personal or public health care services, under certain conditions.
- Supply of human organs, blood, human milk, and dental prostheses supplied by dentists or dental technicians.

- Transportation of ill, wounded, or other persons requiring medical care by special means of transport.
- Social services supplied by institutions for children and young people, nursing homes for the elderly, and/or by care or guardianship institutions for disabled or by other non-profit entities.
- Education and training services.
- Cultural and sports services rendered by non-profit entities.
- Services provided by political parties, trade unions, and other non-profit membership based legal entities to their members when these services correspond to that set out in the articles of association and are provided free-of-charge, except for membership fees.
- Services provided by religious communities, other communities, and centres to their members if these services correspond to the purposes of these communities set out in their canons, statutes, and other documents and are provided free-of-charge, except for donations.
- Postal services and directly related goods supplied by government-listed universal postal services providers, except for individually negotiated postal services.
- Radio and TV broadcasting services provided by non-profit legal entities.
- All types of insurance and re-insurance services and related services rendered by insurance and re-insurance agents.
- Financial services meeting certain requirements.
- Lotteries and gambling.
- Postage stamps and other government-listed special signs available for sale against their nominal value (this provision shall be applied only to the postage stamps which can be used as a confirmation of payment for postal services in Lithuania).
- Letting of residential premises (except for accommodation services provided by hotels, motels, camping, and other accommodation services or letting of residential premises not indicated above when the letting period does not exceed two months).
- Letting or sale of immovable property, other than residential premises (certain exceptions apply).
- Supply of goods where the VAT payer has not deducted any proportion of the VAT on purchases and/or importation thereof (certain conditions apply).

Intra-Community acquisitions (i.e. acquisitions of goods from other EU member states) are VAT-exempt provided that:

- the supply of such goods in Lithuania would be VAT-exempt or zero-rated or the import of such goods would be VAT-exempt
- the purchaser who is a foreign taxable person would be able to refund this VAT, and
- triangular transactions meet certain criteria.

Sale and contribution in kind of a business or part of a business is treated as being out of scope of VAT (under certain conditions).

Option to tax
Option to tax is applicable to:

- Lease of immovable property.
- Sale or other transfer of old immovable property (i.e. used for more than 24 months).
- Financial services meeting certain requirements.

Lithuania

Option to tax may be exercised only if the customer is a taxable person registered for VAT purposes. If a VAT payer decides to use the option to tax, it is valid for at least 24 months.

Customs duties

EU customs law is applicable in full.

EU customs law, also known as the Community Customs Code, compiles the rules, arrangements, and procedures applicable to goods traded between the European Community and non-member countries. The Community Customs Code indicates an obligation on a person to pay the amount of the import or export duties which apply to specific goods under the Community provisions in force. The application of the EU customs law means that:

- trade between Lithuania and other EU countries is customs-free
- imports from non-EU countries are subject to EU customs tariffs, and
- numerous free trade agreements concluded between EU and non-EU countries apply to Lithuania.

Excise taxes

Excise duty is imposed on the following goods produced in or imported into Lithuania: ethyl alcohol and alcoholic drinks, including beer and wine; processed tobacco, including cigarettes, cigars, cigarillos, and smoking tobacco; energy-related products, including petrol, kerosene, gasoline, fuel oil, natural gas, and their substitutes and additives; coal, coke, and lignite; and electricity. The tax rate depends on the type and quantity of goods.

Land tax

Lithuanian and foreign entities are subject to land tax collected by the municipalities for the land they own in Lithuania. Roads for general use and forestland are exempt. The annual tax rate is 1.5% of the taxable value, which is determined according to the rules established by the government. The assessment and payment terms are set forth by the municipalities, which are also entitled to grant land tax incentives.

As of 1 January 2013, the following amendments will come into force:

The main amendments	Currently in force	In force from 1 January 2013
Tax rate	1.5%	0.01% to 4%, defined by municipality
Taxable value	Value identified by the Centre of Registers multiplied by certain ratios.	The average market value determined in the map of values established according to the mass valuation.
		The mass valuation is performed not rarer than every five years.
		A possibility to apply the value determined during the individual valuation if it differs from the market value by more than 20% (principles are similar to real estate tax).
Declaration	Template of a tax return is completed and sent by the tax authorities until 1 October.	Template of a tax return is completed and sent by the tax authorities until 1 November.
Payments	One annual payment due 1 November.	One annual payment due 15 November.

The main amendments	Currently in force	In force from 1 January 2013
Additional comments		Transitional application: Gradual increase of the tax from 2013 to 2016.

Land lease tax
State-owned land that is leased for Lithuanian and foreign companies is subject to land lease tax at a rate established by the municipalities. The minimum tax rate set by the government is 0.1%, and the maximum rate is 4% of the value of the land.

Real estate tax
Real estate tax at a rate ranging from 0.3% up to 1% is levied on the value of real estate owned by individuals and used for commercial purposes or owned by legal entities (with certain exemptions). Municipal councils establish a specific tax rate for real estate situated in their territories annually.

State dues (stamp taxes)
State dues are payable on activities of state institutions, such as the issuance of documents having legal force and other deeds.

Environmental tax
Environmental tax is imposed on pollutants discharged into the environment, a few specified products (e.g. tyres, batteries), and certain types of packaging.

Tax on natural resources
A tax on natural resources is payable on the value of extracted natural resources.

Branch income

A branch of a foreign company is defined as a structural subunit of a foreign company, which has an establishment in Lithuania and is entitled to engage in commercial activities in Lithuania as well as conclude contracts and undertake obligations according to the power of attorney issued to the branch by its founder. A branch does not have the status of a legal person. It is taxed in the same manner as a PE (*see the Taxes on corporate income section*).

Income determination

Inventory valuation
Under domestic accounting legislation, stock used in the production and included in the cost of produced products is valued in the financial statements by the first in first out (FIFO) method. The last in first out (LIFO), weighted-average, progressive-average, actual-price, or another method that corresponds to the stocks' movement can also be used. However, the method used must be disclosed in the notes to the annual accounts, and, among other things, the note must report the profit that would have been calculated if the FIFO method of valuation had been used. For CIT purposes, usage of another method than FIFO should be approved by the tax authorities.

Capital gains
Capital gains are taxed as part of the corporate profit of the enterprise.

L

Lithuania

Capital gains are treated as non-taxable income when they are derived from the transfer of shares in a company incorporated in the European Economic Area or in a country with which Lithuania has a valid DTT and that pays CIT or an equivalent tax. This holds true if the Lithuanian holding company holds more than 25% of voting shares for a continuous period of (i) at least two years or (ii) at least three years when the shares were transferred in one of the established forms of reorganisation. Certain restrictions apply.

Dividend income
The receiving company does not include the dividends received from other entities in its taxable income.

Interest income
Interest income is treated as general taxable income and is subject to 15% CIT.

Exemptions from taxable income
The following types of income are exempt from CIT:

- Insurance indemnity not in excess of the value of lost property or other losses or damages, the refunded part of insurance premiums in excess of the premiums deducted from income in accordance with the procedure established, and the part of insurance indemnity in excess of the premiums deducted from income in accordance with the procedure established.
- Proceeds of a bankrupt company received from sale of its property.
- The balance of the formation fund of an insurance company as prescribed by the law on insurance.
- Investment income of investment companies with variable capital and closed-end investment companies acting in accordance with the law on collective investment undertakings, except for dividends and other distributable profits.
- Income derived by health care institutions for their services that are financed from the funds of the Compulsory Health Insurance fund.
- Income derived from revaluation of fixed assets and liabilities as established by laws and regulations, except for income derived from the revaluation of derivative financial instruments acquired for hedging purposes.
- Default interest except for that received from foreign companies registered or otherwise organised in blacklisted territories or residents of such territories (*see Blacklisted territories in the Deductions section*).
- All or part of the profit gained from legal entities of unlimited civil liability that are payers of CIT and with income that is subject to CIT under the law or to a similar tax under respective statutes of foreign countries, with certain exceptions.
- Fees collected by seaports and airports, charges for air traffic navigation services, and funds collected from the lease of seaport-owned land.
- Results arising from adjustments made for the previous tax periods as prescribed by the law on accounting.
- Indemnification for damages received by the company, with certain exceptions.
- Compensation received according to the Lithuanian programmes of the EU financial support relating to taking fishing ships for scrap.
- Life insurance payments received by insurance companies, provided the term of the life insurance policy is valid for not less than ten years or at the date of the receipt of the insurance benefit the recipient has reached the pension age in accordance with the additional law on pensions. Additionally, insurance investment income of insurance companies, except for dividends and other distributable profit, are exempt along with investment insurance income of insurance companies received according

to the contracts of life insurance occupational pensions concluded in accordance with the law on accumulation of occupational pensions.
- Direct and other compensational allowances, which are received by units performing agricultural activities to maintain their level of income, which meet the requirements established in the laws and other legal acts of Lithuania.

Foreign income

Income is not subject to taxation in Lithuania if it was received from activities through a PE in a foreign country which is in the European Economic Area or which has a DTT with Lithuania and if the income was subject to taxation there. Since such income is not subject to taxation in Lithuania, costs related to the income cannot be deducted from income that is subject to taxation in Lithuania.

....

Deductions

Allowable deductions include all the usual costs that an entity actually incurs for the purpose of earning income or receiving economic benefit unless the law on CIT provides otherwise.

Limited deductible expenses include the following:

- Depreciation or amortisation expenses of fixed assets: for tax purposes assets cannot be depreciated faster than indicated in the CIT law (*see below*).
- Maintenance, repair, and reconstruction expenses of tangible fixed assets: if the repair or reconstruction increase the service period and improve the qualities (useful characteristics of the fixed assets), the value of repair or reconstruction shall be added to the acquisition value of the tangible fixed assets.
- Business travel expenses: deductible with restrictions.
- Advertising and representation expenses: 75% of representation expenses are deductible.
- Natural losses: deduction limited to not more than 1% of turnover.
- Taxes: deductible with restrictions (*see below*).
- Bad debts (*see below*).
- Contributions and expenses for the benefit of employees: deductible with restrictions.
- Special provisions of credit institutions and insurance companies: calculated according to the methods established by the Bank of Lithuania and the Commission of Insurance Supervision.
- Sponsorship: the double amount deductible (i.e. 200% deduction is available) but only if provided to registered recipients and only up to 40% of taxable result before deduction of sponsorship and utilisation of tax losses carried forward.
- Membership fees, contributions, and premiums: deductible with restrictions.
- Losses of previous tax periods: losses can be carried forward for indefinite period if certain requirements are met (*see below*).

Non-deductible expenses include the following:

- VAT payable to the budget and CIT (*see below*).
- Default interest (forfeit), fines, and late interest paid to the state budget as well as other sanctions imposed for violations of laws and regulations of Lithuania.
- Interest or any other indemnity paid due to non-performance of contractual obligations by related parties.
- Amount of the limited deductible expenses in excess of the established limits.

Lithuania

- Expenses attributed to allowable deductions more than 18 months past, although the payments for goods or services supplied by the entities registered or otherwise organised in blacklisted territories (*see below*) have not been made.
- Sponsorship and gifts that do not correspond to the requirements of CIT law.
- Payments to blacklisted territories (*see below*) if they are not verified and payments are not subject to withholding tax (WHT).
- Indemnification for damages inflicted by the entity.
- Dividends or otherwise distributed profits.
- Other expenses not related to the deriving of income and not attributed to operating activities of the entity as well as the expenses that are not considered allowable deductions under the law.
- Amounts resulting from adjustments and corrections of errors of previous tax periods.
- Expenses related to revaluation of fixed assets and securities.
- Deductible or limited deductible expenses attributed to non-taxable income.
- Expenses related to income from certain international maritime activities, if a maritime entity chose to apply a fixed CIT.

Depreciation

Tangible and intangible assets may be depreciated using a directly proportional (straight-line) depreciation method, a production depreciation method, or a double-declining-balance depreciation method. Depreciation may not exceed maximum rates established by the law. For certain typical assets depreciation rates relevant for tax purposes are shown in the chart below:

Asset	Depreciation period (years)	Annual depreciation rate (%)
New buildings used for business activities	8	12.5
Residential buildings	20	5
Plant and machinery	5	20
Trucks (not older than 5 years)	4	25
Computer and communications equipment	3	33.3
Software	3	33.3

Goodwill

Goodwill can be amortised for tax purposes in a straight-line method over 15 years after a merger of a purchasing company and an acquired company, if certain conditions are met.

Start-up expenses

Generally, start-up expenses are deductible for tax purposes.

Interest expenses

Interest expenses are generally deductible for tax purposes. Interest expenses should be recognised as non-deductible for tax purposes if, after acquisition, a purchasing company and an acquired company are merged and a debt used for acquisition of shares is pushed down to the acquired company and certain conditions are not met.

Interest paid to related parties may be non-deductible for tax purposes if thin capitalisation rules are infringed and interest rate on a debt from related party does not correspond to a fair market interest rate (*see Transfer pricing and Thin capitalisation in the Group taxation section*).

Lithuania

Bad debts
Bad debts are deductible only if proved and specific criteria are met. Provisions are non-deductible.

Charitable contributions
Generally, double the amount of donation/sponsorship can be deducted for tax purposes (i.e. 200% deduction is available) but only if donation/sponsorship was provided to registered recipients and only up to a limit of 40% of taxable result before deduction of sponsorship and utilisation of tax losses carried forward.

Fines and penalties
Fines and penalties are generally non-deductible for tax purposes.

Taxes
All taxes, fees, and other compulsory payments to the state budget are deductible for CIT purposes, except VAT paid to the budget and CIT. Note that VAT can be treated as deductible for CIT purposes if it is input or paid import VAT which is non-refundable for VAT purposes and this input or paid import VAT is calculated on deductible expenses.

Net operating losses
Operating losses may be carried forward for an indefinite period, provided that certain requirements are met.

Current year operating losses incurred after 1 January 2010 can be transferred to another legal entity of the group if certain conditions are met.

Losses incurred due to the transfer of securities and/or derivative financial instruments may be carried forward for five years.

No carryback of losses is available in Lithuania.

Payments to foreign affiliates
Payments to foreign affiliates (e.g. interest, royalties, management fees, fees for other services) are deductible for tax purposes if the payment serves a business purpose, provides a benefit to the payer, is at arm's length, and is substantiated by sufficient documentation. Payments to foreign affiliates may also be subject to various WHTs. Certain payments to affiliates located in tax haven (blacklisted) countries are subject to 15% WHT rate.

Blacklisted territories
A blacklisted territory is a foreign country or territory that is included on a list of offshore territories established by the Minister of Finance that meets at least two of the following criteria:

- Similar tax rate in such territory is below 75% of that set in the Lithuanian CIT law.
- In such territory, different rules for levying a similar tax are applied, depending on the country where the parent company (controlling entity) is registered or otherwise organised.
- In such territory, different rules for levying a similar tax are applied, depending on the country where the business is conducted.
- The company (the controlled taxable entity) has entered into agreement with the tax administrator of that territory with regard to the application of a tax rate or tax base.
- There is no effective exchange of information in such territory.

Lithuania

- There is no financial and administrative transparency in such territory, the tax administration rules are not quite clear, and the application thereof is not communicated to tax administrators of other countries.

A list of 58 offshore territories has been published. With certain exceptions specified in the law, all payments to offshore companies or their branches for any work or services, commodities, interest on funding, insurance premiums, guarantees, etc. are non-deductible for CIT purposes unless the Lithuanian entity provides evidence to the state tax authorities that:

- the payments are related to usual activities of the paying and the receiving business entities
- the receiving foreign business entity manages the property necessary to carry out such usual activities, and
- there is a connection between the payment and the economically grounded business operation.

Group taxation

Group taxation legislation and regimes are not available in Lithuania. Each Lithuanian entity is regarded as a separate taxpayer and may not deduct tax losses accumulated from previous tax periods at the level of any other group entity.

However, recent amendments to CIT law allowed transfer of current year operating tax losses incurred as of 1 January 2010 to an entity of the same group of companies if certain requirements are met.

Transfer pricing
All transactions between associated parties must be performed at arm's length. The tax authorities have a right to adjust transaction prices if they do not conform to market prices.

The Lithuanian rules refer to the Transfer Pricing Guidelines for Multinational Enterprises and Tax Administrations established by Organisation for Economic Co-operation and Development (OECD) to the extent that they do not contradict with the domestic rules.

According to the Lithuanian transfer pricing regulations, companies may apply the following methods, although traditional methods should be given preference:

- Comparable uncontrolled price method.
- Resale price method.
- 'Cost plus' method.
- Profit split method.
- Transactional net margin method.

All entities with an annual revenue exceeding LTL 10 million (EUR 2.9 million), as well as all banks, insurance companies, and credit institutions are required to prepare transfer pricing documentation in a specifically prescribed form. The documentation may be in a foreign language, but upon request has to be translated to Lithuanian.

As of 1 January 2012, APAs and binding rulings were introduced in Lithuania. Taxpayers can apply for an APA or a binding ruling from the Lithuanian tax authority in respect of future transactions.

Decisions in the form of a binding ruling or APA will be issued by the Lithuanian tax authority regarding the application of tax legislation provisions and pricing principles. The above-mentioned decisions will be particularly relevant to companies planning to undertake new transactions where the taxation principles of such transactions are not clearly defined in the tax legislation and to international companies planning to perform significant transactions with associated parties.

Thin capitalisation

The Lithuanian thin capitalisation rules apply in respect to borrowings from related parties as well as borrowings from third parties guaranteed by related parties. The debt-to-equity ratio is 4:1. The above provisions do not apply if a Lithuanian company can prove that the same loan under the same conditions would have been granted by a non-related entity.

Tax credits and incentives

Foreign tax credit

A company may reduce tax payable on certain foreign-sourced income in Lithuania by taxes paid on that income in a foreign country if that Lithuanian company has received appropriate notice from that foreign country. The tax credit may not exceed CIT rate payable in Lithuania.

Investment project incentive

Entities involved in an investment project are able to reduce their taxable profits by up to 50% of the actually incurred acquisition costs of long-term assets meeting certain requirements. Please note that depreciation (amortisation) expenses of such assets shall be deducted in a common manner.

Taxable profits can be reduced by such costs incurred from 2009 to 2013.

The costs exceeding the above mentioned 50% limit can be carried forward for four years.

There are certain criteria defining what could be considered an investment project. The project should be precisely described to meet the criteria allowing it to use the tax relief, and the tax authorities should be properly notified about the project.

Tax relief for research and development (R&D)

Expenses, except for fixed assets' depreciation (amortisation) expenses, incurred for R&D purposes can be deducted three times in the tax period when they are incurred, provided that R&D works performed are related to ordinary business activities.

A company applying tax relief for R&D has to prepare R&D documentation. This documentation has to cover the performed project, substantiate conformity with certain tax requirements, and specify the amount of expenses for R&D activities.

Lithuania

Free economic zones

Entities that invest in Lithuanian free economic zones are entitled to partial or complete CIT relief (depending on the investment amount), relief of tax on real estate, and 50% relief of land lease tax.

Withholding taxes

Domestic legislation

Generally, income of a foreign entity in Lithuania not derived through a PE is deemed to be Lithuanian-source income and is subject to WHT at the following rates:

- Interest on any type of debt obligations, including securities: 10%.
- Proceeds from the sale, transfer (with title), or lease of immovable property located in Lithuania: 15%.
- Income derived from sports activities or performers' activities: 15%.
- Income from distributed profits: 15%.
- Royalties: 10%.
- Annual payments (*tantiems*) to the members of the board or supervisory board: 15%.
- Indemnities received for the infringement of copyrights or neighbouring rights: 10%.

As of 1 July 2011, the WHT rate on royalties paid to related parties meeting requirements of the EC Interest and Royalty Directive was reduced from 10% to 0%.

Lithuanian WHT on interest paid to EU entities or DTT tax residents is 0%.

WHT is not applied on government securities issued on international financial markets, interest accumulated and paid on deposits, and interest on subordinated loans which meet the criteria established by legal acts adopted by the Bank of Lithuania.

Dividends distributed by a resident company to another resident company are subject to a 15% CIT, which is withheld by a distributing company.

The dividends distributed by a resident company are exempt from WHT if the recipient company has held not less than 10% of the voting shares in the distributing company for at least a 12-month period and the distributing entity is subject to 5% or 15% Lithuanian CIT rate. However, this relief is not applied if the foreign entity (recipient) is registered or otherwise organised in blacklisted territories (*see Blacklisted territories in the Deductions section*), as specified by the Ministry of Finance. Please note that the requirement of the 12-month holding period does not necessarily have to be fulfilled on the day of dividend distribution.

The receiving company may reduce its payable CIT for that period when dividends were received by the amount of CIT withheld from the received dividends. Any excess credit may be offset with other taxes payable.

Dividends distributed by a foreign entity are subject to a 15% WHT which is to be paid by the receiving Lithuanian entity.

Dividends distributed by a foreign company to a Lithuanian company are exempt from WHT if the distributing foreign entity is established in the EEA and related profit is properly taxed in the domiciled country.

Lithuania

The dividends are also exempt from WHT if the recipient company has held not less than 10% of the voting shares in the distributing company for at least a 12-month period and the receiving entity is subject to 5% or 15% Lithuanian CIT rate. This participation exemption satisfies the requirements of the EC Parent-Subsidiary Directive. The exemption also applies to dividends paid by non-EU foreign companies, except those registered or organised in blacklisted territories.

Tax treaties

Where a treaty for the avoidance of double taxation and prevention of fiscal infringement with the country in question contradicts the local regulations, the treaty provisions prevail. Lithuania has now signed 49 DTTs with foreign countries; however, two of them (with Kirghizia and Mexico) are not yet enforced.

The following WHT rates apply to dividends, interest, and royalties paid to a recipient or beneficial owner resident in a tax treaty country. The lower of the domestic or the treaty rate is given.

Recipient	Dividends (%) (1)	Interest (%) (2)	Royalties (%) (3)
Non-treaty	0/15	0/10	10
Treaty:			
Armenia	0/15	0	10
Austria	0/15	0	0/5/10 (4)
Azerbaijan	0/10	0	10
Belarus	0/10	0	10
Belgium	0/15	0	0/5/10 (4)
Bulgaria	0/10	0	0/10
Canada	0/15	0	10
China, People's Rep. of	0/10	0	10
Croatia	0/15	0	10
Czech Republic	0/15	0	0/10
Denmark	0/15	0	0/5/10 (4)
Estonia	0/15	0	0/10
Finland	0/15	0	0/5/10 (4)
France	0/15	0	0/5/10 (4)
Georgia	0/15	0	10 (4)
Germany	0/15	0	0/5/10 (4)
Great Britain and Northern Ireland	0/15	0	0/5/10 (4)
Greece	0/15	0	0/5/10 (4)
Hungary	0/15	0	0/5/10 (4)
Iceland	0/15	0	5/10 (4)
Ireland, Republic of	0/15	0	0/5/10 (4)
Israel	0/15	0	5/10 (4)
Italy	0/15	0	0/5/10 (4)
Kazakhstan	0/15	0	10
Korea, Republic of	0/10	0	5/10 (4)
Latvia	0/15	0	0
Luxembourg	0/15	0	0/5/10 (4)
Macedonia	0/10	0	10
Malta	0/15	0	0/10

Lithuania

Recipient	Dividends (%) (1)	Interest (%) (2)	Royalties (%) (3)
Moldova	0/10	0	10
Netherlands	0/15	0	0/5/10 (4)
Norway	0/15	0	5/10 (4)
Poland	0/15	0	0/10
Portugal	0/10	0	0/10
Romania	0/10	0	0/10
Russian Federation	0/10	0	5/10 (4)
Serbia	0/10	0	5/10 (4)
Singapore	0/10	0	7.5
Slovakia	0/10	0	0/10
Slovenia	0/15	0	0/10
Spain	0/15	0	0/5/10 (4)
Sweden	0/15	0	0/5/10 (4)
Switzerland	0/15	0	5/10 (4)
Turkey	0/10	0	5/10 (4)
Ukraine	0/15	0	10
United States of America	0/15	0	5/10 (4)
Uzbekistan	0/10	0	10

Notes

1. Dividends are exempt from WHT if the recipient company has held not less than 10% of the voting shares in the distributing company for at least a 12-month period and the distributing entity is subject to a 5% or 15% Lithuanian CIT rate. However, this relief is not applied if the foreign entity (recipient) is registered or otherwise organised in blacklisted territories (see Blacklisted territories in the Deductions section), as specified by the Ministry of Finance. If participation exemption criteria are not met, the standard WHT rate of 15% should be applied. However, some of the DTTs allow applying WHT at a reduced rate of 10%.
2. Under the domestic law, the rate is nil if interest is paid to a company established in a country which has a DTT with Lithuania or is a member of a European Economic Area. In other cases, except for Latvia where 0% WHT is established in the DTT, 10% WHT rate should be applied.
3. Under the domestic law as of 1 July 2011, the WHT rate on royalties paid to related parties meeting requirements of the EC Interest and Royalty Directive was reduced from 10% to 0%.
4. Royalties for the use of industrial, commercial, or scientific equipment: 5%; other royalties: 10%.

Reduction of, or exemption from, WHT under a DTT may be obtained if a special residence certificate (Form DAS-1) is completed and approved by the tax authorities before a taxable payment is transferred. If a payment that would have been subject to a tax treaty has already been made and WHT at the local rate was withheld, it is possible to obtain an appropriate refund (reduction) by completing a special claim for a refund of the Lithuanian tax withheld at source (Form DAS-2) and obtaining the approval of the tax authorities.

In addition, the tax authorities may require completion of a special certificate giving information about income received and taxes paid in Lithuania (Form DAS-3).

Tax administration

Taxable period
The Lithuanian tax year runs from 1 January to 31 December. However, a corporation may apply to adopt a substitute year of reporting (e.g. 1 July to 30 June).

Lithuania

Tax returns

CIT
CIT returns must be submitted by the first day of the sixth month of the following tax period (1 June for companies using the calendar year).

If CIT is calculated based on activity results for the previous year, the advance CIT return for the first nine months of the tax period is to be submitted by the last day of the first month (usually January) of the tax period. The return for the remaining months of the tax period is to be submitted by the last day of the tenth month (usually October) of the tax period. If the taxpayer has chosen to pay the advance amount based on the projected amount of CIT for the current year, the return must be submitted not later than the last day of the first month of the tax period.

WHT on dividends
A tax-withholding entity must submit to the tax authorities a special form of a return reporting the dividends paid and tax withheld within ten calendar days after the end of the month of the dividend payment.

WHT on payments other than dividends
A tax-withholding entity must submit to the tax authorities a special form of a return reporting the amounts of payments paid and taxes withheld during the calendar month no later than 15 days after the end of the month in which the amounts were paid.

Payment of tax

CIT
Based on the activity results for the previous year, the advance amount of CIT for the first nine months of the tax period is calculated based on the actual CIT amount for the tax period before the previous tax period. For example, the CIT for the first nine months of 2012 would be calculated based on the appropriate portion of the actual amount of CIT for 2010. The advance amount for the remainder of the tax period is based on the actual amount of CIT for the previous period, for example, tax for the last three months of 2012 would be based on the appropriate portion of the actual amount of CIT for 2011. Thus, the advance CIT amount for each quarter would be equal to one-fourth of the actual tax amount calculated for the tax periods discussed.

The taxpayer may choose to pay the advance amount based on the projected amount of CIT calculated for the current year. The advance tax (one-fourth of the advance CIT) must be paid no later than the last day of the respective quarter, and for the last quarter by the 25th day of the last month of the quarter.

If the amount of tax indicated in the return exceeds the amount actually paid during the tax period, the taxpayer is obliged to transfer the additional amount no later than the return submission deadline. Overpaid tax can be offset with other tax dues or refunded in accordance with the law on tax administration.

WHT on dividends
WHT on dividends is to be calculated, withheld, and remitted by a Lithuanian company that pays dividends within ten calendar days after the end of the month of the payment.

Lithuania

WHT on payments other than dividends

WHT on payments other than dividends is to be calculated, withheld, and remitted by a Lithuanian company or a PE of a foreign company no later than the return submission deadline.

Audit cycle

The Lithuanian tax system for companies is based on self-assessment; however, the tax authorities undertake ongoing compliance activity to ensure corporations are meeting their tax obligations. The tax authorities take a risk-based and materiality approaches to compliance and audit activities, with efforts generally focused on taxpayers with a higher likelihood of non-compliance and/or material consequences of non-compliance. Compliance activities take various forms, including general risk reviews, questionnaires, reviews of specific issues, and tax audits.

Statute of limitations

Generally, the tax authorities may investigate current and five previous tax periods. However, the limit of ten previous tax periods applies where the tax authorities are of the opinion there has been fraud or tax evasion.

Luxembourg

PwC contact

Wim Piot
PricewaterhouseCoopers S.à r.l.
400, route d'Esch
B.P. 1443 L-1014 Luxembourg
Tel: +352 49 48 48 1
Email: wim.piot@lu.pwc.com

Significant developments

The Luxembourg tax environment proved once again its long-standing reputation of stability over the last 12 months.

Following the introduction over the past few years of a favourable tax regime for intellectual property (IP) rights, an increase of the rates applicable to investment tax credits, and the implementation of a transfer pricing framework for intra-group financing activities, no major changes have been introduced in the Luxembourg income tax law.

The government, nevertheless, continues its efforts in negotiating new tax treaties and also revisiting the existing ones in the view of introducing the internationally agreed tax standards in terms of exchange of information.

Taxes on corporate income

Luxembourg taxes its corporate residents on their worldwide income and non-residents only on Luxembourg-source income.

Businesses with taxable income lower than 15,000 euros (EUR) are subject to corporate income tax (CIT) at a rate of 20%. The CIT rate is currently 21% for companies with taxable income in excess of EUR 15,000.

The CIT does not apply to tax transparent entities (e.g. general or limited partnerships or European Economic Interest Grouping).

As of tax year 2011, EUR 1,500 minimal CIT (increased to EUR 1,575 by the 5% contribution to the employment fund) has been introduced for fully taxable resident entities which (i) do not require a business licence or the approval of a supervisory authority and (ii) own financial assets, transferable securities, and cash at bank (i.e. accounts no. 23, 50, or 51 of the Standard Chart of Accounts) exceeding 90% of their total balance sheet. For tax-consolidated entities, this measure will only apply once (at the level of the head of the tax consolidation).

Solidarity tax
A 5% solidarity tax is also imposed on the CIT amount.

Taking into account the solidarity tax, the aggregate CIT rate is 22.05% for companies with taxable income in excess of EUR 15,000.

Luxembourg

Municipal business tax on income

Municipal business tax is levied by the communes and varies from municipality to municipality. The municipal business tax for Luxembourg City is 6.75%.

The effective combined CIT rate (i.e. CIT, solidarity tax, and municipal business tax) for Luxembourg City is 28.80%.

Corporate residence

Based on domestic law, a company is considered to be resident in Luxembourg if either its registered office or place of central administration is located in Luxembourg. The registered office is designated as such in the company's articles of incorporation.

The place of central administration is generally understood to mean the place where the company is managed and controlled. While this term is not legally defined, the location of the company's major establishment is determined by facts and circumstances, including the following:

- The place where meetings of the board of directors are held.
- The place where shareholders meetings are held.
- The place where the company's officers make their decisions.
- The place where the company's books and records are kept.
- The place where other, similar factors evidencing management control occur.

Permanent establishment (PE)

The provisions on PEs included in the tax treaties concluded by Luxembourg generally follow the wording of the Organisation for Economic Co-operation and Development (OECD) model.

Under Luxembourg domestic tax law, a similar PE concept exists but is defined in a broader way and is to be understood as every fixed piece of equipment or place which serves for the operation of an established business.

Other taxes

Value-added tax (VAT)

Proceeds of sales and services, which are deemed to take place in Luxembourg, are subject to VAT at the standard rate of 15% (lowest standard VAT rate in the European Union (EU)) or, on certain transactions, at 12% (e.g. wine, advertising pamphlets), 6% (e.g. supply of gas or electricity), or 3% (e.g. food except alcohol beverages, pharmaceutical products, books [including e-books], radio and television broadcasting services [except adult entertainment]). Some transactions, such as export and related transport, are zero-rated.

Taxpayers whose activities are subject to VAT are entitled to offset against their VAT payable the amount of such tax charged to them by their suppliers or reverse charged (i.e. self-accounted) by them on import or acquisitions of goods or services from abroad.

Banking, financial, insurance, and reinsurance generally are exempt activities. The VAT paid on costs made for these transactions cannot be recovered except when related to services performed for persons established outside the European Union. VAT on

Luxembourg

expenses made in the context of 'passive' holding activities, which are considered as outside the scope of VAT, are not recoverable.

As of 2011, a Standard Audit File for Tax (SAF-T), which is a file containing reliable accounting data, has been implemented by the VAT authorities. This specific file is used by taxable persons to transfer information to Luxembourg VAT authorities during a VAT audit. Only specific taxable persons having a certain minimum number of transactions (+/- 500) and registered under a 'normal filing regime' with a turnover exceeding EUR 112,000 are firstly concerned. On the other hand, some entities, notably those subject to the supervision of the *Commission de Surveillance du Secteur Financier* (CSSF) and insurance/reinsurance companies, will not yet be subject to these SAF-T obligations.

A law regarding the creation of a VAT suspension regime was adopted in September 2011. This law, in force since 1 October 2011, introduced new VAT suspension regimes that can be operated either under a free zone or under VAT warehouses. These regimes complement the already existing customs warehousing regimes and are based on existing provisions in the European Union (EU) VAT Directive.

All operations (e.g. entry, transport, storage, packaging, evaluation, and realised sales) taking place under the suspension regime will be exempt from VAT until the goods are being removed from the regime.

The suspension of VAT liabilities is attractive for companies that are involved in the trading of goods and wishing to optimise VAT cash flows and compliance obligations in their supply chains.

As of January 2012, e-books benefit from a super-reduced VAT rate of 3%.

Customs duties/import tariffs
Based on a European Regulation, goods entering within the territory of the European Union could be subject to customs duties/import tariffs. Rates applying for determining customs duties/import tariffs are based on the nature and on the quantity of the products.

Excise duties
In addition to VAT, some products are subject to specific excise duties. In Luxembourg, these products are electricity, mineral oils, manufactured tobacco, and alcohol.

Excise duties are not based on the sale price of the products but on the quantity. Excise duty becomes chargeable at the time, and in the EU member state, of release for consumption. Release for consumption occurs in any of the following instances:

- The departure of excise goods from a duty suspension arrangement.
- The holding of excise goods outside a duty suspension arrangement where excise duty has not been levied pursuant to the applicable provisions of Community law and national legislation.
- The production of excise goods outside a duty suspension arrangement.
- The importation of excise goods, including irregular importation, unless the excise goods are placed, immediately upon importation, under a duty suspension arrangement.

Net wealth tax
Both Luxembourg resident companies and Luxembourg branches of non-resident companies are subject to net wealth tax levied at a rate of 0.5% on their net wealth,

Luxembourg

based on prescribed valuation methods. In general, assets are taken into account at market value (except for real estate, which is subject to a special regime). Shareholdings qualifying for the participation exemption (*see Dividend income in the Income determination section*) generally are exempt from net wealth tax.

Resident companies and Luxembourg branches of non-resident companies may claim a reduction of their net wealth tax liability by making an allocation to a special reserve before the closing of the tax year following the year for which the net wealth tax reduction is claimed. To this end, an amount corresponding to five times the net wealth tax that should have become payable must be kept in this special reserve for the five years following the year in which it was allocated. The reduction, however, may not be higher than the taxpayer's CIT liability, before tax credits, for that same year.

Subscription tax

Investment funds are subject to subscription tax (at various rates) on their total net assets evaluated at the last day of each quarter. Institutional funds and monetary funds are subject to an annual rate of 0.01% and the other funds to an annual rate of 0.05%. Funds of institutional funds and monetary institutional funds are exempt from subscription tax.

Exemptions from subscription tax are available for exchange traded funds, and an extension of exemption is available for funds dedicated to multi-employer pension vehicles or to several employers providing pension benefits to their employees.

Where a foreign Undertakings for Collective Investment (UCI) is managed by a Luxembourg-based management company (or where the UCI's place of effective management is located in Luxembourg), the UCI will not be deemed to be domiciled in Luxembourg and therefore not be subject to any tax in Luxembourg.

General registration taxes

General registration taxes (inclusive of the transcription tax described below) are levied at 7% on the market value of real estate purchased or transferred (10% in the commune of Luxembourg City for some categories of properties) and 1% on mortgages on real estate. The taxes are deductible for CIT purposes.

Note that a fixed registration duty of EUR 75 is levied on certain transactions involving Luxembourg entities (i.e. incorporation, amendment to the articles of association, and transfer of seat to Luxembourg).

For Luxembourg real estate assets, contribution made to a company remunerated by shares are subject to a proportional registration duty of 0.6% (0.9% for Luxembourg City for some categories of properties) and a transcription tax of 0.5%. Contribution remunerated by means other than shares remain subject to a proportional registration duty of 6% (9% for some categories of properties located in Luxembourg City) and a transcription tax of 1%. Transfers made within the framework of a corporate reorganisation may be exempt from any proportional registration duty under certain conditions.

Commune (municipalities) real estate tax

Communes (municipalities) levy an annual real estate tax, the basis of which is the unitary value of real estate, which represents its estimated value in 1941. The basic rate varies from 0.7% to 1% of the unitary value, according to the category of property, and is multiplied by a coefficient, which varies with communes and different types of property. For commercial properties, the coefficient in Luxembourg City is 750%,

Luxembourg

which should be applied to 1% of the unitary value. The real estate tax is deductible for CIT purposes.

Branch income

Branch income generally is taxed at CIT rates. However, the municipal business tax generally only applies if the branch is carrying on commercial activity within Luxembourg.

Income determination

Inventory valuation
Inventories generally are valued at the lower of actual or market cost. There is no statutory specified method. In general, the first in first out (FIFO), the last in first out (LIFO), and the weighted-average costs methods of inventory valuation are acceptable for income tax purposes, provided the method is in accordance with the facts.

Dividend income
Dividends received by a Luxembourg resident company (or by a domestic permanent establishment [PE] of a non-resident company in certain cases) should, in principle, be subject to CIT.

Participation exemption regime
Dividends received may be tax exempt in Luxembourg, according to the so-called 'participation exemption' regime, if the conditions described below are satisfied:

- The distributing company is:
  - a collective entity falling within the scope of article 2 of the amended version of the EU Council directive of 23 July 1990 (90/435/EEC), hereafter the 'Parent Subsidiary Directive'
  - a Luxembourg resident joint-stock company, which is fully taxable and does not take one of the forms listed in the appendix to paragraph 10 of article 166 of the Luxembourg Income Tax Law (LITL), or
  - a non-resident joint-stock company that is fully liable (in its state of residence) to a tax corresponding to the Luxembourg CIT (i.e. as a general rule, it is required that the foreign tax is compulsorily levied at an effective rate of at least 10.5%, on a basis similar to the Luxembourg one).
- The beneficiary company is:
  - a Luxembourg resident collective entity, which is fully taxable and takes one of the forms listed in the appendix to paragraph 10 of article 166 LITL
  - a Luxembourg resident joint-stock company, which is fully taxable and does not take one of the forms listed in the above-mentioned appendix
  - a domestic PE of a collective entity falling within the scope of article 2 of the amended version of the Parent-Subsidiary Directive
  - a domestic PE of a joint-stock company that is resident in a country with which Luxembourg has concluded a double tax treaty (DTT), or
  - a domestic PE of a joint-stock company or of a cooperative society, which is a resident of a European Economic Area (EEA) member state (other than an EU member state).

L

Luxembourg

- At the date on which the income is made available, the beneficiary has been holding or undertakes to hold, directly (or through a tax transparent entity - *see Transparent entities below*), for an uninterrupted period of at least 12 months, a participation in the share capital of the subsidiary of at least 10% or with an acquisition price of at least EUR 1.2 million.

Capital gains

Capital gains (and losses) generally are taxed as ordinary income (or losses). It is possible to defer the taxation of gains on certain fixed assets where the gain is used to acquire replacement items. Under certain conditions, exempted capital gains and hidden reserves may be unrealised in a merger or another form of reorganisation of resident companies or other EU companies.

In general, capital gains on the disposal of qualifying shareholdings held by entities eligible to the participation exemption regime are tax exempt, provided (i) the shareholding constitutes at least 10% of total ownership or an acquisition price of at least EUR 6 million and (ii) the disposing company has held or intends to hold the qualifying shareholding for at least 12 months.

A recapture system exists wherein the capital gain realised will become taxable up to the amount of the aggregate expenses and write-downs in relation to the participation deducted during the year of realisation of the exempt capital gain and in previous years.

The purpose of the system is to avoid a taxation vacuum, which could result if the deductibility of expenses and write-downs connected to the participation was allowed, while the income arising from the participation is tax exempt. This system should, in principle, remain tax neutral, as the company should have available carryforward losses for an equivalent amount (unless previously used to offset other taxable income).

Taxation of non-resident corporate investors on gains upon disposal of shares

In principle, should a non-resident corporate investor (non-treaty protected) derive income from the disposal of an important participation (i.e. representing at least 10% of the share capital) in a Luxembourg company within six months of its acquisition, said capital gain will be subject to CIT in Luxembourg unless a tax treaty provides otherwise.

Non-resident investors are not subject to the aforementioned capital gains tax upon disposal of shares in a Luxembourg *Société d'Investissement à Capital Variable* (SICAV), *Société d'Investissement en Capital à Risque* (SICAR), and *Société de gestion de Patrimoine Familial* (SPF).

Interest income

Under Luxembourg accounting and tax principles, interest income is recognised on an accrual basis and is fully subject to tax at the effective combined CIT rate of 28.80%.

Transparent entities

From a Luxembourg tax perspective, a transparent entity is seen as having no legal personality distinct from that of its partners (those transparent entities are commonly referred to as 'partnerships') for CIT and net wealth tax purposes, although it may be regarded as a separate legal entity from a civil/corporate law point of view. Provided that the partnership carries out a commercial activity, however, it will be liable to municipal business tax on its own.

Luxembourg

Foreign income

A Luxembourg tax resident company is liable for CIT on its worldwide income, whether derived from Luxembourg or from foreign sources. Luxembourg does not apply a territorial basis for taxation. Foreign-source income is therefore taxable in Luxembourg, unless a DTT provides for an exemption.

Dividends from foreign subsidiaries are taxed when received, except where exempt as mentioned above. Profits of a foreign branch which are not exempt by means of a DTT may, however, benefit from a foreign tax credit. Any foreign taxes paid in excess of the tax credit are deductible as expenses. Luxembourg is, however, using the exemption method in most of its DTTs.

Deferral of taxation for income earned abroad is not provided for under Luxembourg domestic tax law.

Deductions

Depreciation

Depreciation rates must be consistent with economic reality. The depreciation must be calculated on the total acquisition cost, bearing in mind the normal life of the asset and the estimated residual value.

Depreciation normally is calculated using the straight-line method. However, the declining-balance method is permitted for fixed assets, other than buildings and intangible assets. The depreciation rate may not, however, exceed three times the rate applicable according to the straight-line method, or 30% (four times the applicable rate in the case of assets used exclusively for scientific and technical research, or 40%).

It is permissible to change from the declining-balance method to the straight-line method, but the converse is not allowed. Tax depreciation must be reflected in the financial accounts prepared for commercial purposes.

In the event of a sale of a depreciated asset, the net book value at the moment of the disposal must be compared with the sale price of that asset. If this comparison indicates a profit, corresponding income tax may be due unless the sale price is reinvested in eligible assets. Capital losses are deductible.

Under certain conditions, fixed assets with a value of less than EUR 870 or an economic life that is not in excess of one year can be expensed fully in the year of acquisition. Special accelerated depreciation on 80% of the cost of fixed assets is available for assets that protect the national environment, save energy in Luxembourg, or permit the development of workplaces for handicapped workers, under certain conditions.

Goodwill

Goodwill is generally amortised over a five year maximum period. It can, however, be amortised for a period longer than five years provided that this period does not exceed the useful economic life of this asset. The Luxembourg tax treatment will follow the applicable accounting treatment.

Start-up expenses

Formation expenses can either be directly charged to the profit and loss account of the year in which they are incurred or depreciated on a straight-line basis over a five year maximum period. The accounting treatment is followed for Luxembourg tax purposes.

Luxembourg

Interest payments
Interest payments are, in principle, deductible to the extent they comply with the arm's-length principle (*see Transfer pricing in the Group taxation section*).

Non-deductibility of the interest payments may arise in case they depend on the profits realised by the company or are derived from loans structured in the form of bonds or similar securities. Also, the deductibility will be limited in case the company is considered as being thinly capitalised (*see Thin capitalisation in the Group taxation section*).

Bad debt
Provisions for bad debts are generally tax deductible.

Charitable contributions
Gifts for scientific, charitable, or public purposes and to institutions in the general interest are deductible, subject to a maximum of 20% of the net income or up to an amount of EUR 1 million (the minimum being EUR 120) with a possibility to spread the deduction over two years.

Shareholdings
Expenses linked to a shareholding qualifying for the participation exemption, including write-downs in the value of the shareholding booked as a consequence of a dividend distribution, are not deductible up to the amount of the exempt dividend. Recapture rules may apply in the event of disposal of the shareholding. Basically, the effect of this rule is that capital gains realised will become taxable up to the amount of the aggregate expenses and write-downs in relation to the participation, deducted during the year of disposal and the previous years. The qualifying shareholding is exempt from net wealth tax.

Severance payouts or 'golden handshakes'
Severance payouts or 'golden handshakes' are deductible for CIT and municipal business tax purposes, up to EUR 300,000.

Fines and penalties
Fines and penalties suffered by the taxpayer are not to be considered as operating expenses and are therefore non-tax deductible.

Taxes
Several taxes are deductible in determining income subject to CIT, including the registration duties and real estate tax. Also, certain taxes are credited against the computed amount of income tax owed, including taxes withheld from Luxembourg dividend income, tax withheld abroad from dividend and interest income received by a Luxembourg corporation (subject to limitations), and investment tax credits (*see the Tax credits and incentives section*).

The main non-deductible taxes are CIT, municipal business tax, net wealth tax as well as interest and penalties for late payment of said taxes.

Net operating losses
Net operating losses can be carried forward for an unlimited period but cannot be carried back.

Luxembourg

Payments to foreign affiliates

Royalties, management service fees, and interest charges paid to foreign affiliates by a Luxembourg company are deductible items, provided they are equal to what the company would pay an unrelated entity for comparable services.

Group taxation

Luxembourg permits tax unity. Generally, the conditions to qualify for tax unity include that:

- each company is a fully taxable company that is resident in Luxembourg (the top entity may be a Luxembourg PE of a fully taxable non-resident company)
- at least 95% of each subsidiary's capital is directly or indirectly held by the parent company
- each company's fiscal year starts and ends on the same date, and
- tax unity is requested jointly by the top company and each subsidiary that becomes member of the group.

Tax unity lasts for a five-year period, and taxable income/loss is computed on the consolidated result. Tax losses that occurred before the consolidation period may be offset only against tax profits of the company that incurred the loss. Tax losses that are sustained by a group member during the consolidation period are offset against the tax profits of the other group members. Tax losses arising during the consolidation period that exist after the consolidation period are attributed to the parent company.

Transfer pricing

Luxembourg largely follows the transfer pricing guidelines issued by the OECD in the absence of detailed transfer pricing regulations in Luxembourg. LITL has prescribed the general transfer pricing provisions in Article 56 LITL, which requires that transactions between related parties are carried out in line with the arm's-length principle. This article provides that where there is a transfer of profit possibly due to the fact that a Luxembourg taxpayer has a special economic relationship with a non-resident taxpayer, then the tax authorities may determine the financial result regardless of the reported profit. The concept of a special economic relationship can be described as any economic relationship that differs from a regular/commercial economic relationship between two parties. The special economic relationship goes beyond the related party definition as stated in article 9 of the OECD Model Convention.

Furthermore, Article 164(3) LITL characterises certain transactions as a hidden distribution of profits where a direct or indirect shareholder receives an advantage from a company that said shareholder would not have received if there had not been a shareholding relationship. The hidden distribution of profits in Luxembourg is included in the profit of the taxpayer and subject to tax at the prevailing statutory rate of corporation tax. In addition, it may be subject to 15% withholding tax (WHT) on the gross amount received, except in case a reduced rate applies under the provisions of the relevant DTT or the European Commission (EC) Parent-Subsidiary Directive.

Transfer pricing documentation is prepared based on OECD transfer pricing guidelines and EU transfer pricing documentation guidelines. Transfer pricing documentation is neither required at the time of the transaction nor at the filing of the tax return. During the course of a tax assessment, the tax authorities may request documentation from the taxpayer to evidence the reasonableness of an intra-group pricing arrangement. There are no transfer pricing methods prescribed for determining the arm's-length standard,

L

Luxembourg

and the taxpayers and the tax authorities largely follow the transfer pricing methods prescribed in the OECD transfer pricing guidelines.

In terms of the burden of proof, the tax authorities have to prove that there is an erosion of the taxable base in Luxembourg, whereas the taxpayer has to prove that the inter-company transactions did not result in a reduction or cancellation of taxes. The statute of limitations is generally five years from the end of the year in which the tax liability arises. This period may be extended if a deferred payment is granted. In case of tax evasion or fraud, the statute of limitations can be extended up to ten years. There are no specific penalties in relation to transfer pricing in Luxembourg, but the penalty regime under the corporate tax will be applicable.

Although Luxembourg has no formal procedure for applying advance pricing arrangements (APAs), the income tax authorities are quite flexible in this area. There have been a few cases in Luxembourg where bilateral APAs have been concluded, although in general, unilateral advanced tax agreements are obtained on an individual basis. Recently, the tax authorities have increased their focus on transfer pricing. As a result, two Circulars describing the tax treatment for intra-group financing transactions have been issued by the Luxembourg tax authorities.

According to the Circular of 28 January 2011 (L.I.R. n° 164/2), the internationally acceptable arm's-length principle should be applied for the determination of the compensation for Luxembourg companies which are principally engaged in on-lending transactions. The remuneration of the related entities should be determined based on the functions performed, assets utilised, and risks born by the Luxembourg company. A written confirmation from the tax authorities can be obtained if the Luxembourg company meets the substance and equity at risk requirements with regard to the on-lending activity. In respect of the equity at risk requirement, the Luxembourg company must be at risk for an amount equal to the lesser of 1% of the nominal value of the loan or EUR 2 million. In addition, the arm's-length price has to be determined by way of a transfer pricing analysis.

On 8 April 2011, the Luxembourg tax authorities issued a second Circular (L.I.R. n°164/2bis) clarifying the application of Circular L.I.R 164/2 of 28 January 2011. This Circular explains that, as of 1 January 2012, the income tax authorities are no longer bound by confirmation obtained before 28 January 2011 in relation to existing intra-group lending activities financed with borrowings falling within the scope of Circular L.I.R. 164/2.

Thin capitalisation
No thin capitalisation ratio is specifically provided by the Luxembourg tax law.

In practice, the tax authorities apply an 85:15 debt-to-equity ratio for the intra-group financing of participations. Should the 85:15 ratio not be complied with by the taxpayer, the surplus of interest could be re-qualified by the tax authorities as a hidden distribution of profits which would be non-deductible and potentially subject to a 15% WHT.

Tax credits and incentives

Foreign tax credit
See Foreign income in the Income determination section for a description of the foreign tax credit regime.

Luxembourg

Inbound and capital investment incentives

Luxembourg tax law provides for various incentives, with specific requirements, in the areas of risk-capital, audiovisual activities, and environmental protection as well as for research and development (R&D), professional training, and recruitment of unemployed persons.

The most commonly used incentives are the investment tax credits. Luxembourg tax law provides for two types of investment tax credits.

First, a tax credit is available which amounts to 13% of the increase in investment in tangible depreciable assets made during the tax year. The increase in investment over a given tax year is computed as the difference between the current value of all qualifying assets and the reference value allocated to the same type of assets.

Independently, the company may benefit from a 7% tax credit on the first EUR 150,000 of qualifying new investments, and a 3% tax credit on the amount of new investments exceeding EUR 150,000 in tangible depreciable assets as well as investments in sanitary and central heating installation in hotel buildings and investments in buildings used for social activities. The above 7% and 3% rates are increased to 8% and 4% for investments eligible for special depreciation (i.e. investments favouring the protection of the environment, the realisation of energy savings, or the creation of employment for handicapped workers). However, certain investments are excluded from the credit calculation, including investments in real property, intangible assets, and vehicles (unless specifically stated by the law).

Domestic law requires that investments be physically operated in Luxembourg in order to be eligible for the incentive, unless the investment consists in shipping vessels operating in international waters. In addition, the tax benefit of the tax credit is limited to investments that are made within a Luxembourg business establishment and that are intended to be used permanently in Luxembourg.

Further to the European Court of Justice's decision dated 22 December 2010 (Tankredeerei, C-287/10), the Luxembourg Tax Authorities issued a Circular letter dated 31 March 2011, confirming that the investment tax credit must be granted to any investment used within the EU and EEA member states. Although Luxembourg domestic tax law has not yet been amended accordingly, the application of investment tax credit may be requested for the current tax year, as well as for tax years already assessed but still subject to the introduction of a claim.

Intellectual property (IP) regime

An IP regime is applicable to qualifying IP rights acquired or developed after 31 December 2007. This regime provides for an 80% tax exemption of the net income deriving from the use and the right to use qualifying IP rights, under certain conditions. Qualifying IP rights include patents, trademarks, design, domain names, models, and software copyrights.

An 80% deduction of net deemed income is available also under certain conditions for self-developed patents, which are used internally by the taxpayer.

The net capital gain realised upon disposal of the qualifying IP rights also benefits from the 80% exemption.

Finally, qualifying IP rights may be fully tax exempt for net wealth tax purposes under certain conditions.

Luxembourg

R&D incentives

Luxembourg entities involved in innovative and R&D activities can benefit from financial support in addition to the specific IP tax regime and general tax incentives.

Innovation loans may be granted by the *Société Nationale de Crédit et d'Investissement* and may carry a fixed interest rate lower than the market rate. Financial support may also be granted in the form of cash grants or interest subsidies.

R&D projects or programmes receive financial support up to a maximum eligibility (percentage of costs eligible for the incentives) depending on the size of the beneficiary (private research companies or organisations) as follows:

* Large (25% to 100% depending on the investment).
* Mid-size (35% to 100%).
* Small (45% to 100%).

These incentives are available for:

* experimental development
* experimental development and cooperation
* industrial research
* industrial research and cooperation, or
* fundamental research.

Innovation in process and organisation and investment in innovation pools can benefit from financial support of between 15% and 35% (50% for public research companies).

Promotion and development of innovation pools can benefit from financial support of up to 50% for private organisations or 75% for public research companies.

Research regarding technical feasibility can benefit from financial support of up to 40% or 50% if prior to experimental development and up to 65% or 75% if prior to experimental research.

Other incentives by entity

Investment funds
Investment funds resident in Luxembourg generally are exempt from CIT, municipal business tax, and WHT on dividends. These investment funds are subject to the previously described subscription tax and to the general registration duty regime.

Financial participation company (Soparfi)
A Soparfi (*Société de Participation Financière*) is neither a specific type of company nor a special tax regime. It is rather used to refer to resident companies that hold and manage the shareholdings of subsidiaries. A Soparfi is subject to CIT, municipal business tax, and net wealth tax, but it does benefit from Luxembourg's DTTs, EU Directives (e.g. Parent-Subsidiary directive), the domestic participation exemption on dividends received, and capital gains on qualifying participations.

Private wealth management company (Société de gestion du Patrimoine Familial or SPF)
The SPF has been tailored to enter the private sphere of individuals for the purpose of wealth management. Its corporate objective is restricted to the acquisition, holding, management, and disposal of financial assets, to the exclusion of any commercial

activity. As a general rule, an SPF is exempt from Luxembourg taxation on income and wealth tax in Luxembourg. A yearly subscription tax of 0.25% is due on the basis of paid-up capital, share premium, and excessive debts. Subscription tax, however, is capped at EUR 125,000. No WHT applies on dividends distributed by an SPF. Non-resident investors are not taxed in Luxembourg on dividends paid by a SPF or on capital gains realised on shares in a SPF.

Securitisation companies (SC)
SCs are subject to normal corporate taxation. A securitisation company is a company which carries out securitisation activities or which participates in securitisation transactions. Securitisation companies are taxed based on their net accounting profit (i.e. gross accounting profits minus expenses). However, the commitment to remunerate the security holders (both capital and debt) issued by the securitisation company qualifies as interest on debt even if paid as return on equity. Securitisation companies are not subject to net wealth tax in Luxembourg.

Venture capital vehicle (Société d'Investissement en Capital à Risques or SICAR)
The SICAR benefits from an attractive tax regime. SICARs are notably exempt from net wealth tax. Incorporated under a corporate form, the SICAR is subject to income tax at the normal rate with the benefit of an exemption on income and gains (e.g. dividends, capital gains, liquidation proceeds, interest) from transferable securities qualifying as risk capital as well as income arising from investments in liquid assets pending their investment in risk capital for a maximum of 12 months. In addition, it can benefit from the European directives and DTTs. Under the form of a limited partnership, the SICAR is treated as a tax transparent entity, and investors are taxed according to the rules of their country of residence. SICARs treated as tax transparent entities do not benefit from the European directives and DTTs. The SICAR mainly targets qualified or informed investors (i.e. 'professional' investors).

Financial services companies
Banks, securities depositaries, insurance, and reinsurance companies as well as other financial service companies may benefit from preferential regulations when establishing their taxable basis for CIT (e.g. provision for the neutralisation of unrealised exchange gains, general banking risk provision, provision for guarantee of deposits, mathematical reserves, and/or catastrophe reserves).

Shipping companies
Luxembourg-resident shipping companies are not subject to municipal business tax and can benefit from investment tax credits and accelerated depreciation (even for used assets).

Withholding taxes

Dividends paid by a Luxembourg fully taxable company to its 'corporate' shareholders resident in a treaty country, which hold or commit themselves to hold a participation of at least 10% in the Luxembourg company (or shares with an acquisition price of at least EUR 1.2 million) for an uninterrupted period of at least 12 months, may be exempt from WHT (*see Note 1 below for more details*).

The following taxes are withheld on payments made. The WHT due on dividends paid to residents of a treaty country cannot exceed the non-treaty rate.

Luxembourg

	Dividends (%)			
Recipient	Portfolio	Substantial holdings (1)	Interest (%) (2)	Royalties (%) (3)
Resident corporations	15	0	0	0
Resident individuals	15	15	10 (4)	0
Non-resident corporations and individuals:				
Non-treaty	15	0/15	0	0
Treaty (1, 5):				
Armenia	15	0/5 (21)	0	0
Austria	15	0/5 (6)	0	0
Azerbaijan	10	0/5 (7)	0	0
Bahrain	10	0 (26)	0	0
Barbados	15	0 (27)	0	0
Belgium	15	0/10 (8)	0	0
Brazil	25	0/15 (9)	0	0
Bulgaria	15	0/5 (6)	0	0
Canada	15	0/5 (19)	0	0
China, P.R. (10)	10	0/5 (6)	0	0
Czech Republic	15	0/5 (6)	0	0
Denmark	15	0/5 (6)	0	0
Estonia	15	0/5 (6)	0	0
Finland	15	0/5 (12)	0	0
France	15	0/5 (12)	0	0
Georgia	10	0/5 (22)	0	0
Germany	15	0/10 (20)	0	0
Greece	7.5	0/7.5	0	0
Hungary	15	0/5 (6)	0	0
Hong Kong	10	0 (10)	0	0
Iceland	15	0/5 (6)	0	0
India	10	0	0	0
Indonesia	15	0/10 (6)	0	0
Ireland, Republic of	15	0/5 (20)	0	0
Israël	15	0/5 (21)	0	0
Italy	15	0	0	0
Japan	15	0/5 (15)	0	0
Korea, Republic of	15	0/10 (6)	0	0
Latvia	10	0/5 (6)	0	0
Liechtenstein	15	0/5 (25)	0	0
Lithuania	15	0/5 (6)	0	0
Malaysia	10	0/5 (16)	0	0
Malta	15	0/5 (6)	0	0
Mauritius	10	0/5 (9)	0	0
Mexico	15	0/5 (9)	0	0
Moldavia	10	0/5 (23)	0	0
Monaco	15	0/5 (21)	0	0
Mongolia	15	0/5 (16)	0	0
Morocco	15	0/10 (6)	0	0

Recipient	Dividends (%) Portfolio	Substantial holdings (1)	Interest (%) (2)	Royalties (%) (3)
Netherlands	15	0/2.5 (6)	0	0
Norway	15	0/5 (6)	0	0
Panama, Republic of	15	0/5 (9)	0	0
Poland	15	0/5 (6)	0	0
Portugal	15	0/15	0	0
Qatar	10	0/5 (24)	0	0
Romania	15	0/5 (6)	0	0
Russia	15	0/10 (17)	0	0
San Marino	15	0 (26)	0	0
Singapore	10	0/5 (18)	0	0
Slovak Republic	15	0/5 (6)	0	0
Slovenia	15	0/5 (6)	0	0
South Africa	15	0/5 (6)	0	0
Spain	15	0/5 (6)	0	0
Sweden	15	0 (26)	0	0
Switzerland	15	0/5 (28)	0	0
Thailand	15	0/5 (6)	0	0
Trinidad and Tobago	10	0/5 (9)	0	0
Tunisia	10	0/10	0	0
Turkey	20	0/5 (6)	0	0
United Arab Emirates	10	0/5 (9)	0	0
United Kingdom	15	0/5 (14)	0	0
United States	15	0/5 (13)	0	0
Uzbekistan	15	0/5 (6)	0	0
Vietnam	15	0/5/10 (11)	0	0

L

Notes

These notes are not extensive. The full text of the DTT should be checked for a comprehensive view on the conditions of application of reduced rates.

1. Under Luxembourg domestic law, no WHT is levied on dividends paid by a Luxembourg qualifying subsidiary to an entity which is:
   - a collective entity falling within the scope of article 2 of the amended version of the Parent - Subsidiary Directive
   - a Luxembourg resident joint-stock company, which is fully taxable and does not take one of the forms listed in the appendix to paragraph 10 of article 166 of the Luxembourg income tax law
   - a PE of a collective entity falling under the previous categories
   - a collective entity that is resident in a country with which Luxembourg has concluded a DTT and which is fully liable to a tax corresponding to the Luxembourg CIT, or a domestic PE of such an entity
   - a Swiss resident joint-stock company that is subject to Swiss CIT without benefiting from any exemption
   - a joint-stock company or a cooperative society which is resident in a EEA member state (other than a EU member state) and is fully liable to a tax corresponding to the Luxembourg CIT, or
   - a PE of a joint-stock company or of a cooperative society which is resident in a EEA member state (other than a EU member state), and
   - at the date on which the income is made available, the beneficiary has been holding or undertakes to hold, directly, for an uninterrupted period of at least 12 months, a participation of at least 10%, or with an acquisition price of at least EUR 1.2 million in the share capital of the income debtor.

   Qualifying shareholders need to be fully taxable collective entities subject in their country of residence to a tax similar to that imposed by Luxembourg. As a general rule, this requirement is met if the foreign tax is compulsorily levied at an effective rate of at least 10.5%, on a basis similar to the Luxembourg one.

Luxembourg

2. Interest paid to non-residents generally is not subject to WHT in Luxembourg. However, interest that represents a right to profit participation on a bond may be assimilated to a dividend and subject to WHT. Further analysis should be made to determine the applicable reduced rate on the basis of the treaty (i.e. pursuant to dividend or interest clause). The WHT that may be due as a consequence of the EU Savings Directive (Council Directive 2003/48/EC dated 3 June 2003) is not mentioned.
3. Royalties paid to non-residents are not subject to WHT in Luxembourg, whether the companies are associated or not.
4. A WHT of 10% is withheld on defined interest income paid by a Luxembourg paying agent to resident individuals. Interest indirectly cashed through investment funds are out of the scope of this WHT.
5. DTTs have been concluded with Albania, Cyprus, Kazakhstan, Kuwait, Kirghizstan, Lebanon, Macedonia, Oman, Pakistan, Seychelles, Serbia and Montenegro, Sri Lanka, Syria, Tajikistan, and Ukraine, but are not yet in force. A new DTT with Germany was signed on 23 April 2012, but domestic transposition procedures are still pending.
6. The recipient company holds at least 25% of the Luxembourg company's capital. In some rare cases, a holding period requirement may have to be met as well (e.g. Spain, Switzerland).
7. The recipient company owns at least 30% of the company's capital and the equivalent of an acquisition price of USD 300,000.
8. The recipient company owns a 25% investment or the equivalent of an acquisition price of EUR 6,197,338. The investments may be held by several Belgian companies, provided one owns at least 50% of the shares of each of the others. The investment must be held since the beginning of the financial year of the recipient of the dividends.
9. The recipient company holds at least 10% of the Luxembourg company's capital.
10. No WHT is levied if the recipient company holds at least 10% of the Luxembourg company's capital or a participation with an acquisition price of a least EUR 1.2 million.
11. The rate of 5% of WHT on the gross amount of the dividends applies where the effective recipient company owns directly or indirectly at least 50% of the share capital of the paying company or has contributed more than 10 million United States dollars (USD) or the equivalent in Luxembourg or in Vietnamese currency, in the capital of the company paying the dividends; the rate of 10% of WHT on the gross amount of the dividends applies where the beneficial owner is a company which holds directly or indirectly at least 25% but less than 50% of the capital of the company paying the dividends and has contributed not more than USD 10 million, or the equivalent in Luxembourg or Vietnamese currency, in the capital of the company paying the dividends.
12. The recipient company owns directly or indirectly 25% of the company's capital. Indirect participation includes the holding through several treaty resident companies located in the same country provided one owns more than 50% of the shares of each of the others.
13. A 5% WHT is levied on dividend distributions where the beneficial owner is a company which holds at least 10% of the voting rights of the paying company. No WHT is levied when the US company has held, during an uninterrupted period of two years, a direct shareholding of at least 25% of the voting power of the paying company and certain conditions regarding the nature of activities performed by the distributing company are met.
14. The recipient company owns directly or indirectly 25% of the company's voting rights. Indirect participation includes the holding through several treaty resident companies located in the same country provided one owns more than 50% of the voting rights of each of the others.
15. The recipient company holds at least 25% of the Luxembourg company's voting shares during the period of six months immediately before the end of the accounting period in which the distribution of profits takes place.
16. The dividends are taxable at a rate of 5% if the beneficial owner is a company that holds directly at least 10% of the capital of the company paying the dividends. No WHT is levied when the beneficiary company has held during the 12 preceding months a direct shareholding of at least 25% of the capital of the paying company. The holding period must be met before the date of distribution of the dividend. Furthermore, certain conditions regarding the nature of activities performed by the company must be met.
17. The recipient company holds at least 30% of the Luxembourg company's capital and the acquisition price reaches at least EUR 75,000 (or equivalent).
18. The recipient company holds at least 10% of the Luxembourg company's capital. Dividends paid to the government of Singapore are exempt.
19. The beneficial owner is a company (other than a partnership) which controls directly or indirectly at least 10% of the voting power in the company paying the dividends.
20. The recipient company holds at least 25% of the Luxembourg company's voting shares (Germany/ Luxembourg) or company's voting power (Ireland/Luxembourg).
21. The rate of 5% of WHT on the gross amount of dividends applies where the recipient company holds at least 10% of the Luxembourg company's capital.
22. The rate of WHT is 5% if the beneficial owner is a company that holds directly at least 10% of the capital of the company paying the dividends and made an investment in the capital of the paying company of more than EUR 100,000 or the equivalent in Georgian currency. No WHT is levied when the beneficiary company holds directly at least 50% of the capital of the company paying the dividends and made an investment in the capital of the paying company of more than EUR 2 million or the equivalent in Georgian currency.
23. The recipient company holds at least 20% of the Luxembourg company's capital.
24. No WHT is levied when the beneficiary company holds at least 10% of the company paying the dividends. The rate of 5% of WHT on the gross amount of dividends applies where the beneficial owner is an individual who holds directly at least 10% of the company paying the dividends and was

Luxembourg

a resident of the other contracting state for the 48-month period immediately preceding the year in which the dividends are paid.

25. No WHT is levied when the beneficiary of the dividend is a joint stock company, which has held directly a participation of at least 10% (or with an acquisition price of at least EUR 1.2 million) of the distributing company's share capital, for an uninterrupted period of at least 12 months. The rate of 5% of WHT applies if said participation has been held for less than 12 months.
26. No WHT is levied when the recipient company holds at least 10% of the Luxembourg company's capital. A holding period requirement has to be met for Sweden and San Marino.
27. No WHT is levied when the beneficiary of the dividends is a joint-stock company that has directly held a participation of at least 10% of the distributing company's capital for an uninterrupted period of at least 12 months preceding the decision to distribute the dividend.
28. A 5% WHT if the beneficial owner is a company (other than a partnership) that holds directly at least 25% of the capital of the company paying the dividends. No WHT is levied if the beneficial owner is a company (other than a partnership) that is a resident of the other contracting state and that holds, directly for an uninterrupted period of two years preceding the date of payment of such dividends, at least 25% of the capital of the company paying the dividends. The provision applies only to dividends from the fraction of the holding that has been the uninterrupted property of the company that is beneficial owner during said period of two years.

Tax administration

Tax returns
Companies must file their tax returns by 31 May of each year following the calendar year during which the income was earned.

Assessments are issued after the end of the tax year and normally can be finalised within five years, although the delay may extend to ten years if the declaration is found to be incomplete or inexact, with or without the intention of fraud. Once issued, the tax assessment notice is, in principle, final (unless new facts come to light).

A self-assessment procedure applies to Luxembourg resident companies. Tax assessments are issued by the tax authorities immediately upon receipt of the tax return, based on the taxable profit reported by the company. The tax authorities may then reassess or request more information on the return within the period of five years that follows the reception of the tax return.

Payment of tax
Quarterly tax advances must be paid. These payments are fixed by the tax administration on the basis of the tax assessed for the preceding year or on the basis of the estimate for the first year. This estimate is given by the company pursuant to the request of the Luxembourg tax authorities.

Final payment of CIT must be paid by the end of the month that follows the month of reception by the company of its tax assessment.

Macau

PwC contact

Pat Wong
PricewaterhouseCoopers (Macau) Ltd.
29/F, Bank of China Building
323 Avenida Doutor Mario Soares
Macau, SAR
Tel: +853 8799 5122
Email: pat.lk.wong@hk.pwc.com

Significant developments

Tax incentives for the tax year 2012

On 15 December 2011, the Legislative Assembly approved certain tax incentives proposed by the Chief Executive of Macau in the Budget for the financial year 2012. The key tax incentives include the following:

* The tax-free income threshold for complementary (corporate) tax will continue to be increased from 32,000 Macanese patacas (MOP) to MOP 200,000 for income derived in the tax year 2011. Taxable income between MOP 200,000 and MOP 300,000 is taxed at 9%, and taxable income over MOP 300,000 is taxed at 12%.
* The standard MOP 3,500 reduction in property tax liabilities will continue to be available in the tax year 2012 for both self-use and rental properties.
* Restaurants will continue to be exempt from tourism tax in the tax year 2012.
* Insurance policies written or renewed in the tax year 2012 and banking transactions in the tax year 2012 will continue to be exempt from stamp duty.
* Admission tickets for performances, exhibitions, and entertainment programs will continue to be exempt from stamp duty in the tax year 2012.
* Commercial and industrial operations will continue to be exempt from the annual industrial tax in the tax year 2012.

Revision of the Macau Property Tax Law

The Legislative Assembly approved certain amendments to the Macau Property Tax Law on 16 February 2011. The amendments became effective on 8 March 2011 and are applicable to benefits derived from properties for the tax year 2010 retrospectively.

Under the revised Law, the property tax rate for leased properties has been reduced from 16% to 10% on the actual rental income. For self-use properties, the property tax rate has been reduced from 10% to 6% on the official ratable value. The surcharge of 5% that was previously levied on the property tax payable on such properties has been abolished.

The annual deduction of 10% of the official ratable value to cover repair and maintenance expenses is automatically available for self-use properties under the revised Law. However, approval by the Macau Finance Bureau (MFB) is still required for a maximum deduction of 10% of the rental income derived for leased properties.

Revision of the Macau Stamp Duty Law

Effective as of 4 May 2011, the 0.5% stamp duty on intermediate transfer of immovable properties, so called 'confirmor sale', has been annulled.

The revision of the Macau Stamp Duty Law was intended to curb speculation activities in the real estate market. Under the revised Law, all property transfer, whether it be intermediate, final, or sale of uncompleted properties, will be subject to Macau Stamp Duty at a progressive rate scale ranging from 1% to 3%, thereby increasing the transactional costs of speculative property activities.

Law on Special Stamp Duty for transfer of residential properties approved

On 7 June 2011, the Legislative Assembly approved the Law on Special Stamp Duty for transfer of residential properties. The enactment of the Law was intended to further curb speculation activities in the residential real estate market. The Law was gazetted on 13 June 2011 and is effective from 14 June 2011.

Under the Law, the transferor of a residential property or property under construction acquired on or after 14 June 2011 will be subject to Special Stamp Duty of 20% on the value of the residential property if the property is resold within a year of its purchase. The Special Stamp Duty rate will be reduced to 10% if the resale takes place between one and two years after the purchase. The Special Stamp Duty is also applicable to transfer of 80% or more shareholding interest in a Macau company that has residential properties.

First Protocol to the People's Republic of China/Macau avoidance of double taxation arrangement (DTA)

The Central Government of the People's Republic of China (the PRC) and the Government of Macau signed the Protocol (Protocol) to the PRC/Macau DTA on 15 July 2009. The Protocol became effective on 15 September 2010 and is applicable to income arising as of 1 January 2011.

The PRC/Macau DTA was signed in 2003. Some of the provisions of the PRC/Macau DTA are less favourable than those of the PRC/Hong Kong DTA. Under the Protocol, the treaty-based rates for withholding tax (WHT) on dividends, interest, and royalty have been reduced. Further, the criteria for determination of a service permanent establishment (PE) and certain criteria for capital gains exemption under the PRC/ Macau DTA have been clarified. In summary, the Protocol has brought the PRC/Macau DTA broadly in line with the PRC/Hong Kong DTA. This has no doubt increased the competitiveness of Macau and provided added incentives for Macau companies to do business or invest in the People's Republic of China. Nevertheless, as Macau adopts a worldwide taxation system in its domestic tax regime, consideration should be given as to whether the use of a Macau company as a holding company for investments in the People's Republic of China is favourable from a tax perspective.

Second Protocol to the PRC/Macau DTA

The Central Government of the People's Republic of China and the Government of Macau signed the Second Protocol (Second Protocol) to the PRC/Macau DTA on 26 April 2011, and this Second Protocol became effective on 8 October 2011. The Second Protocol is aimed at amending Article 26 of the PRC/Macau DTA to implement the standards on transparency and exchange of information developed by the Organisation for Economic Co-operation and Development (OECD), which are endorsed by the Group of Twenty (G20) members.

Mozambique/Macau DTA

The ratification procedures for the DTA signed between the Government of Macau and the Government of Mozambique have been completed, and the DTA became effective on 11 January 2011.

Macau

Tax information exchange agreements (TIEAs)

On 29 April 2011, the Government of Macau signed TIEAs with the Nordic countries, which include Denmark, the Faroe Islands, Finland, Greenland, Iceland, Norway, and Sweden. The Government of Macau has further signed TIEAs with Australia and India on 12 July 2011 and 3 January 2012 respectively. Together with the five comprehensive tax arrangements/agreements that Macau has signed with the People's Republic of China, Portugal, Mozambique, Belgium, and Cape Verde, Macau has enlarged the network of agreements to implement the internationally agreed standards on transparency and exchange of information for tax purposes through the signing of a total of 14 DTAs or TIEAs to date.

The TIEAs will become effective upon completion of the necessary ratification procedures by the respective jurisdictions.

Taxes on corporate income

Complementary tax is imposed on the worldwide income earned by Macau registered entities, irrespective of where their residence or headquarters are situated and irrespective of the nature of the income. The exception to the foregoing is rental income from leasing of immovable properties located in Macau, which is taxed separately under the property tax regime.

Generally, if a foreign entity is engaged in commercial/industrial activities and/ or rendering services in Macau, the resultant gain from such commercial/industrial activities and/or services rendered will be subject to complementary tax.

According to the Macau Complementary Tax Law, complementary tax is imposed on a progressive rate scale ranging from 3% to 9% for taxable profits below or equal to MOP 300,000 and 12% for taxable profits over MOP 300,000. Taxable profits below MOP 32,000 are exempt from tax.

According to the Budget for the financial year 2012 approved by the Legislative Assembly (2012 Budget), the tax-free income threshold for complementary tax has been increased from MOP 32,000 to MOP 200,000 for income derived in the tax year 2011 (the next MOP 100,000 of taxable income is taxed at 9%, and taxable income in excess of MOP 300,000 is taxed at 12%). Such increase in the tax-free income threshold has been granted since the tax year 2007. While it is generally believed that the direction of the Macau government policy will remain stable at least for several years, the changes in tax-free income threshold and the tax brackets beyond the tax year 2011 are subject to approval by the Legislative Assembly on an annual basis, unless such amendments are written into the relevant tax laws.

Types of taxpayers and associated tax bases

Group A taxpayers

Taxpayer entities whose registered capital reached MOP 1 million, or whose average taxable profits reached MOP 500,000, per year in three consecutive years will automatically become Group A taxpayers in the tax year following the year in which the notification is issued by the Macau Finance Bureau. A taxpayer entity can also elect to become a Group A taxpayer by filing a Group A declaration form. Profits of Group A taxpayers are assessed based on the actual accounting income after making necessary tax adjustments.

Macau

Group B taxpayers

Group B taxpayers refer to any individual or any other form of companies not mentioned above and those taxpayers that do not keep detailed accounting records. Profits of Group B taxpayers are assessed on a deemed basis if the reported income is below the internal parameters set by the MFB for taxpayers in similar industries.

Corporate residence

Corporate residence is generally determined by reference to the place of establishment. The exception to the foregoing is a Macau offshore company or a Macau offshore financial institution that is established under Law 58/99/M. Such a Macau offshore company or financial institution is not considered as a Macau tax resident in the context of the comprehensive tax arrangement/agreements entered into between Macau and its treaty partners.

Permanent establishment (PE)

There is no specific definition of PE in the Macau Complementary Tax Law. Technically speaking, there are two major criteria for determining whether a foreign entity should be subject to complementary tax, and the key phrases are 'engaging in commercial/industrial activities' and/or 'rendering services in Macau'. These phrases are again not defined. Generally, if a foreign entity is engaged in commercial/industrial activities and/or rendering services in Macau, the resultant gain from such commercial/industrial activities and/or services rendered will be subject to complementary tax.

Other taxes

Value-added tax (VAT)

There is no VAT regime in Macau.

Customs duties/import tariffs

Apart from consumption tax imposed on tobacco and spirits entering into Macau, there are no customs duties/import tariffs in Macau.

Consumption tax (excise duty)

Consumption tax is imposed only on tobacco and spirits entering into Macau.

There are two methods for determining the amount of consumption tax payable, by quantity or by value. The former method of assessment is based on the weight or volume of goods and the latter is based on the price of the goods imported into Macau. The rate of consumption tax varies depending on the classification of the imported goods.

Property tax

Property tax is imposed annually on the owner of buildings situated in Macau. This is first payable after acquiring a property or upon the expiry of the property tax exemption period, if applicable. Different exemption periods are granted, depending on the location of the property. Additional exemption periods may apply in special cases.

For leased properties, property tax is charged at 10% on the actual rental income, and by application, a maximum deduction based on 10% of the rental income derived to cover repair and maintenance expenses incurred will be granted, if approved by the MFB.

M

Macau

For self-use properties, property tax is charged at 6% on the official ratable value as established by the appointed committee of the MFB. A deduction of 10% of the official ratable value to cover repair and maintenance expenses will be automatically granted for self-use property. If the property is not occupied, the owner can apply for an exemption from property tax, the approval of which is entirely at the discretion of the MFB.

According to the 2012 Budget, there is a standard MOP 3,500 reduction in the property tax liabilities assessed in the tax year 2012 for both self-used and rental properties.

Effective from 8 March 2011, the surcharge of 5% that was previously levied on property tax payable has been abolished.

Stamp duty

Stamp duty is payable on certain types of documents and stampable transactions at a small fixed amount or at rates ranging from 0.1% to 10% on the value represented by the documents and transactions.

The charge to stamp duty has been extended to property transfers and the irrevocable transfer of certain assets. Stamp duty at progressive rates ranging from 1% to 3% is payable on transfer of immovable property with a surcharge of 5% on the duty payable, resulting in effective stamp duty rates of 1.05% to 3.15%. The irrevocable transfer of certain assets without consideration is subject to a 5% stamp duty.

Insurance policies, written or renewed, and banking transactions have been exempt from stamp duty since 2005. This exemption has been approved by the Legislative Assembly and will continue to be available in the tax year 2012.

Admission tickets for performances, exhibitions, and any kind of entertainment programmes is exempt from stamp tax for the tax year 2012, as approved by the Legislative Assembly. This exemption, if extended, will be published by the Macau government on an annual basis.

Annual industrial tax

The annual industrial tax has been exempted for the tax year 2012 and has been exempted on an annual basis by the Macau government since 2002.

Under the Industrial Tax Code, all commercial or industrial operations carried out in Macau are subject to industrial tax at the beginning of each year. The amount of the tax is dependent upon the nature of the business. The table below is an illustration of the tax amounts applicable to certain types of businesses in Macau.

Type of business	Tax (MOP)
Commercial banks	80,000
Construction companies	500
Hotels	500
Insurance companies	500
Textile companies	500

Special gaming tax

Special gaming tax is levied at 35% on the gross gaming revenue derived by gaming concessionaires authorised to carry on the operation of games of chance in Macau under Law 16/2001.

Tourism tax

Tourism tax is imposed at the rate of 5% on bill of services, excluding telecommunication and laundry services, and service charges of up to 10%, rendered in Macau by establishments such as hotels, guest houses, dancing halls, night clubs, massage/sauna parlours, gymnasium, karaoke, and the like. Such tax is generally borne by consumers.

Restaurants are exempt from tourism tax in the tax year 2012 and have been exempt, via an exemption published on an annual basis by the Macau government, since 2002.

Motor vehicle tax

Motor vehicle tax is imposed on the sale of new motor vehicles to consumers and the importation of new motor vehicles for self-use. Exemptions are available to certain persons and organisations and for certain specific usages. Generally, motor vehicle tax is levied based on the listed selling prices as registered with the MFB. The rate of motor vehicle tax varies depending on the type of motor vehicle and its value.

Land rent

According to the 2012 Budget, land rent below MOP 100 shall not be collected by the MFB in the tax year 2012. However, any such amount already collected shall not be refunded.

M

Branch income

Branch income is subject to tax at the same rate as that for corporations. The taxable income is ascertained based on branch accounts.

Income determination

The paragraphs below describe the tax acceptable treatments under the prevailing Complementary Tax Law and are for reference only.

Inventory valuation

Inventory should be stated at actual cost, and conformity between book and tax reporting is required. Market selling price or replacement cost is allowed only in special circumstances, and prior approval of the Director of the MFB is required for adoption of such inventory valuation methods. The write-down of inventory values is not permitted.

Capital gains

Gains or losses from the realisation of capital assets of a corporate taxpayer are treated as current revenue or expense items for complementary tax purposes.

Dividend income

Dividends from all sources are subject to complementary tax in the hands of a recipient incorporated in Macau unless the dividends were paid out of profits that have been taxed at the corporate level in Macau. Where dividend to shareholders is paid out

Macau

of profits of a Macau entity that have not been taxed in Macau, complementary tax will technically be charged on the dividend distribution to the shareholders, except for distribution of tax exempt profits of approved offshore institutions, where complementary tax, in practice, has not been charged by the MFB to date.

Interest income
Interest income received by or accrued to a corporate taxpayer in Macau is subject to complementary tax.

Foreign income
Companies incorporated in Macau are subject to complementary tax on worldwide income, wherever received or credited. There are no provisions in the Macau Complementary Tax Law that allow foreign income to be deferred for tax purposes. Currently, double taxation relief is available under the respective avoidance of double taxation agreements/arrangement that Macau has with Portugal, the People's Republic of China, Mozambique, Belgium, and Cape Verde.

Deductions

Please note that the assessor is empowered to disallow any business expenses (e.g. entertainment, travelling) where the amount incurred is considered to be excessive.

Depreciation
An initial allowance of 20% is granted on buildings. The rates of tax depreciation are detailed in Decree-Law No.4/90/M, dated 5 March 1990. The Decree-Law prescribes the maximum annual tax depreciation rates and the number of years of asset life for different asset classes under the straight-line method. For illustration, the maximum depreciation rates and the maximum useful life currently applicable to the general types of assets are set out below:

Assets	Maximum annual percentage rate (%)	Maximum number of years
Industrial buildings	4	50
Office and residential buildings	2	100
Machinery and installations, air conditioning, elevators, equipment	10 to 20	20 to 10
Tools	20 to 33.3	10 to 6
Laboratory, telex and interior telephone equipment, furniture, filing systems, typewriters, and accounting machines	16.66 to 25	12 to 8
Computer hardware	25	8
Office installations	14.29	14
Trucks	14.29	14
Automobiles	20	10
Intangible assets, pre-operating expenses incurred prior to commencement of business	33.33	6
Deferred expenses arising in connection with increases in share capital, changes in form of business enterprises, issuance of debentures, marketing and other studies, and financial expenses incurred for the acquisition or own production of fixed assets prior to completion	33.33	6

Assets	Maximum annual percentage rate (%)	Maximum number of years
Patents	10	20
Manufacturing licences, concessionary agreements, and similar rights	*	*
Trademark	*	*

* At the discretion of the authorities.

In the case of commercial and industrial buildings, depreciation is not allowed for the value attributable to the cost of the freehold land. Where the value of the freehold land cannot be determined from the total cost of land and buildings, a portion equal to 20% is deemed to be attributable to the land value for the purpose of determining the value of buildings to be depreciated.

Depreciation can be claimed either on a prorated basis in accordance with the prescribed annual rates for assets that are not acquired at the beginning of the financial year or on an annual basis.

The cost of repairs and maintenance exceeding 10% of the acquisition cost of the asset in a given year is deemed to be an expense of a capital nature and should be capitalised and depreciated over the remaining life of the asset.

Goodwill
Cost of acquisition of goodwill/amortisation of goodwill is generally deductible to the extent it is incurred in the generation of assessable profits.

Interest expenses
There is no thin capitalisation rule in Macau. However, the MFB may assess the reasonableness of the interest rate charged for interest expense paid to related parties.

Bad debts
The amount provided against doubtful trade receivables is an allowable tax deduction, but the provision cannot exceed 2% of the total receivables, except in the case of banks, where the minimum provisions required under the local banking regulations are fully tax-deductible.

Debts considered uncollectible may be written off only when adequate proof can be shown, usually by way of bankruptcy court proceedings.

Charitable contributions
A deduction of up to 0.2% of the company's turnover is allowable for donations to charitable organisations recognised by the tax authority.

Pension expenses
The employer's contribution to the staff provident fund legally registered in Macau is fully tax-deductible up to 15% of the employees' basic salary.

Fine and penalties
Tax fines are not deductible.

Macau

Taxes paid
Taxes, except for complementary tax and taxes paid on corporate profits, are generally deductible to the extent they are incurred in the generation of assessable profits.

Other significant items
- An amount provided against stock obsolescence of up to 3% of the total stock value at year-end is allowed as a tax deduction.
- Losses arising from insurable risks are not allowable as a tax deduction.
- Staff social welfare expenses paid for the benefit of employees, for example canteens and libraries, are fully tax-deductible.

Net operating losses
Agreed tax losses can be carried forward for three consecutive years for Group A taxpayers. Group B taxpayers are not allowed to carry their tax losses forward to future years. Tax losses cannot be carried back in Macau.

Payments to foreign affiliates
The regulations make no specific mention of royalties and service fees paid to foreign affiliates. The MFB generally monitors the deductibility of such payments. Payments to foreign service providers for consulting services or construction-related services are not deductible if such consulting contracts are not properly registered in Macau.

Group taxation

There is no provision for group taxation in Macau.

Transfer pricing
There is no transfer pricing provision in the Macau tax regime.

Thin capitalisation
There is no thin capitalisation provision in the Macau tax regime.

Tax credits and incentives

Foreign tax credit
There is no foreign tax credit provision in the Macau Complementary Tax Law. Foreign tax credit is only available under the relevant provisions of the comprehensive tax arrangement/agreements that Macau has entered into with the People Republic of China, Portugal, Mozambique, Belgium, and Cape Verde respectively.

Capital investment incentives
A 50% reduction in complementary tax and stamp duty on certain transactions, as well as exemptions from annual industrial tax (currently exempt for all taxpayers) and property tax (up to periods prescribed by the MFB), are allowable for taxpayers in the manufacturing industry (as defined in the Decree Law) whose capital investment is aimed at the introduction of new products or high technology, improvement of productivity, and increase in exports of goods to new markets.

Where profits are retained in reserves and reinvested in installation of new equipment within the following three financial years, the reinvested reserves can be deducted from taxable profits, provided that the reinvested reserves are attributable to profits earned from normal business operations and the investment is considered to be beneficial for the economic development of Macau.

Offshore services business incentives

Profits derived by approved offshore institutions from prescribed offshore service-related activities are exempt from all forms of taxes, such as complementary tax, annual industrial tax (currently exempt for all taxpayers), and stamp duties.

Incentives for owners of touristic facilities

Additional incentives, such as an extended property tax exemption period, exemption from annual industrial tax (currently exempt for all taxpayers), reduction in stamp duty, as well as acceleration of depreciation for complementary tax purposes, are available to owners of facilities that qualify as touristic facilities.

Withholding taxes

Currently, there is no provision in the Macau Complementary Tax Law for the withholding of taxes from payments made by domestic corporations to overseas companies.

Tax administration

Taxable period

The Macau tax year is on a calendar-year basis.

Tax returns

Assessments are made by the MFB upon review of the tax returns, which must be lodged before 31 March or 30 June of each year for Group B or Group A taxpayers, respectively.

Payment of tax

A provisional tax payment calculated based on the declared taxable profit for a Group A taxpayer or final assessed profit for a Group B taxpayer is payable in two equal instalments, in September and November. However, if the amount is not greater than MOP 3,000, payment will be requested in one lump sum amount in September. For Group A taxpayers, a final tax assessment will be issued upon the completion of tax assessment by the MFB.

Statute of limitations

The statute of limitations period is five assessment years from the relevant year of assessment for both Group A and Group B taxpayers.

Exchange of information

Law 20/2009 is the legislation that governs the exchange of information by Macau with other tax jurisdictions within the scope of bilateral tax treaties or arrangements. Its objective is to promote the transparency of the Macau tax administration and to demonstrate Macau's willingness to cooperate with treaty partners in combating tax avoidance or tax evasion activities.

The information to be exchanged under Law 20/2009 is strictly confined to information collected for tax purposes only, and includes the following:

Macau

- Information collected within the jurisdiction of the MFB.
- Information collected by the MFB from financial institutions that are governed by the Macau Financial System Act and offshore institutions that are governed by the Macau Offshore Law (the Institutions).

So far, Macau has concluded TIEAS or DTAs that comply with the latest internationally agreed standards with 14 different tax jurisdictions. The following tables summarise the TIEAs and DTAs that Macau has signed, and the TIEAs and DTAs that are in negotiation:

TIEAs have been signed by Macau with the following countries:

- Australia
- Denmark
- Faroe Islands
- Finland
- Greenland
- Iceland
- India
- Norway
- Sweden

TIEAs are in negotiation with the following countries:

- Argentina
- Germany
- Ireland
- Jamaica
- Malta
- New Zealand

DTAs have been signed by Macau with the following countries:

Treaty partners	Effective date
The Mainland of China	1 January 2004 (Note: The first protocol and the second protocol became effective on 15 September 2010 and 8 October 2011 respectively)
Mozambique	11 January 2011
Portugal	1 January 1999
Belgium	Not yet effective
Cape Verde	Not yet effective

DTAs are in negotiation with the following countries:

- Hong Kong
- Vietnam

It is believed that more comprehensive DTAs or TIEAs will be signed between Macau and other tax jurisdictions in the near future to demonstrate Macau's willingness to continue to cooperate with the OECD countries in combating tax avoidance or evasion activities.

During the peer review meeting held from 19 September 2011 to 23 September 2011 by the OECD Global Forum on Transparency and Exchange of Information for Tax Purposes, the Phase I review report of Macau was adopted, and the peer review panel members unanimously agreed that Macau has the relevant legal and regulatory framework in place that could ensure the effective implementation of tax information exchange and that Macau complied with the internationally agreed standards.

As the information of a Macau taxpayer is becoming more transparent under comprehensive DTAs or TIEAs, it is important for Macau companies with cross-border transactions to perform periodic tax health checks to ensure that tax planning arrangements, if any, that have been put in place in the past, remain technically defensible. As Macau offshore companies continue to be a focus of investigations for many tax jurisdictions, it is important to ensure that such companies have adequate commercial substance in Macau and the companies' transfer pricing policies are supported by appropriate transfer pricing documentation and transfer pricing studies.

Other issues

Choice of business entity

A foreign company conducting business (except for a short term project) in Macau is obligated to set up a legal establishment, which could be in the form of a company or a branch.

There are two types of Macau companies: companies limited by shares and companies limited by quotas. The capital and corporate governance requirements for a company limited by shares are higher than a company limited by quotas, and, in general, a company limited by quotas is used by investors that are not in regulated industries.

M

Macedonia

PwC contact

Paul Tobin
PricewaterhouseCoopers
9-11 Maria Louisa Blvd., 8th Floor
1000 Sofia
Bulgaria
Tel: +359 2 9355 116
Email: paul.tobin@bg.pwc.com

Significant developments

New changes were introduced in the Corporate Income Tax (CIT) Law applicable as of 11 October 2011. The changes are in respect to the legal remedies available to the taxpayers should the tax authorities fail to respond to the request for decreasing the tax liability regarding introduced fiscal registers within the statutory deadline. The same changes are introduced regarding the request for tax refund.

Following the amendments to the CIT Law, a new Rulebook for the Manner of Calculation and Payment of CIT and Prevention of Double Exemption or Double Taxation ('the Rulebook') was enacted on 15 December 2011. The Rulebook generally explains in more details the CIT Law provisions and prescribes the forms of the annual tax returns and the withholding tax (WHT) exemption requests. It gives more detailed definitions for some items in the CIT Law, such as organised transport, organised food, individuals related to the legal entities, etc. These definitions will be applicable when determining the amount of non-deductible expenses deriving from the above-mentioned items. Further, it introduces the necessity of transfer pricing documentation supporting the prices used in transactions with related parties. The Rulebook gives more detailed information regarding the determination of the tax-deductible interest rate on loans between related parties as well as information on the applicability of the thin capitalisation rules. Additionally, it allows tax credit for all expenses, with deferred recognition for tax purposes for which the tax base has been increased in the previous periods. Finally, it introduces new forms for obtaining WHT exemption and the need of an existence of a double tax treaty (DTT) for using tax credit for the tax paid abroad.

The new changes in the Value-add Tax (VAT) Law applicable as of 11 October 2011 introduced additional supplies that will be subject to the preferential 5% VAT rate, as follows:

- Raw oil used in the food industry or for consumption.
- The first sale of residential premises within five years from the end of its construction.
- Accommodation services, bed and breakfast services, as well as half board and full board services provided by hotelkeepers in the country.

The changes in the Customs Law applicable as of 14 March 2012 introduce lower customs duty rate of 5% (previously 30%) on import of white sugar. Also, the importation of certain raw precious metals is exempt from customs duties.

Taxes on corporate income

Generally, all resident and non-resident legal entities operating through a permanent establishment (PE) are liable to pay CIT in Macedonia.

Macedonian resident entities are taxed on their worldwide income. Non-resident entities are taxed on their Macedonian-source income. Non-business organisations (including governmental bodies) are taxed on income from their business activities (if any).

The CIT rate is 10%.

There are two separate tax bases for CIT which are subject to filing of two separate tax returns.

The first tax base is the sum of taxable expenses and understated revenues decreased by any available tax credits and tax reliefs. In this case, tax is payable on an annual basis regardless of whether the corporate taxpayer incurs profit or loss.

The second tax base is the amount of dividends or other type of profit distributions by the taxpayer in monetary or non-monetary form. Under recent amendments, the definition of 'other type of profit distributions' was extended to cover also the increase of registered capital as a result of asset revaluation as well as payments from profit to shareholders, members of managing bodies, and employees, based on the taxpayer's decision.

Distribution of profit to resident legal entities is exempt from CIT. Therefore, only distributed profit to individuals (foreign or domestic residents) or to non-resident legal entities is taxable.

Taxpayers are obliged to cover the losses from previous years prior profit distribution. The distributed amount is taxed at the moment of payment. Upon each profit distribution, a corporate taxpayer is obliged to submit a tax return containing information for the dividend beneficiary and the year from which the profit to be distributed arises. If the profit arose prior to 2009, CIT is not payable.

Undistributed profit is tax exempt. Undistributed profit is determined in accordance with the accounting regulations and standards decreased by the amount of CIT paid on taxable expenses and understated revenue.

Simplified tax regime for companies

Under the amendments in the CIT Law effective as of 16 April 2011, more companies (except companies that provide banking, financial, and insurance services, as well as services in the field of games of chance and entertainment games) can choose to benefit from the simplified tax regime based on their overall annual income. Provided other criteria prescribed in the CIT Law are met, the companies will qualify for the simplified tax regime if their overall annual income from all sources is between 3 million Macedonian denari (MKD) and MKD 6 million. These companies will pay 1% CIT on their overall income from all sources as stated in their income statement and financial statements for the respective calendar year. Provided their overall annual income in the following three years is within the above range, the companies cannot request to be excluded from the simplified tax regime.

Macedonia

According to the amendments, exemption from tax is introduced for companies under the simplified tax regime with an overall annual income from all sources up to MKD 3 million.

Local income taxes
There are no local government taxes levied on corporate income.

Corporate residence

A company is resident in Macedonia for tax purposes if it is established or maintains its headquarters in the territory of Macedonia. Foreign legal entities with headquarters abroad are non-residents for tax purposes, but their Macedonian branches are liable for tax on any profit generated in the territory of Macedonia if they are considered as a PE for the foreign legal entity in Macedonia.

Permanent establishment (PE)
Generally, a PE is a fixed place of business through which the business of an enterprise is wholly or partly carried on, either directly or through a dependent agent.

More specifically, the domestic law provides that a PE may include a place of management, a branch office, an office, a factory, a workshop, mining activities, or any other place of extraction of natural resources.

A building site or construction or installation project, as well as related supervision activities, may constitute a PE if it lasts longer than six months.

Furthermore, the provision of services, including consulting services with regard to one or several related projects, is deemed to give rise to a PE if such activities last longer than 90 continuous days within any 12-month period. According to recent amendments effective as of April 2011, if one or several persons establish a PE as per above, any other non-related project on which they are working on becomes part of the PE irrespective of its duration.

The amendments also prescribe that the PE should be registered as a corporate taxpayer at the beginning of its activity in the country for the purposes of obtaining a tax number. However, this provision seems to contradict the Companies Law requirement, which states that if operating in Macedonia, the foreign companies are obliged to establish at least a branch in the country. Therefore, it should be further clarified whether tax registration of a PE shall be possible without establishment of a legal form as per the Macedonian Companies Law.

Other taxes

Value-added tax (VAT)
In general, the VAT regulations are in line with the provisions of the sixth European Union (EU) VAT directive.

The standard VAT rate is 18%. This rate applies to overall turnover and imports of goods and services. A lower rate of 5% applies to supplies of certain goods and services, such as supply of food for human consumption; drinking water from public supply systems; computers and software; agricultural material and equipment; pharmaceutics and medical equipment; publications such as books, pamphlets, newspapers, and other printed material, except for publications mainly used for advertising purposes; transport of passengers; and accommodation services, bed and breakfast services, as well as half board and full board services provided by hotelkeepers in the country.

As per recent amendments, all taxpayers whose total annual turnover exceeds MKD 2 million or whose total supplies, as projected at the beginning of the business activity, will exceed this amount, are liable to register for VAT purposes.

Residents that do not meet the criteria above may voluntarily register for VAT purposes at the beginning of each calendar year.

The standard VAT period is one calendar month. However, if the total turnover in the previous calendar year did not exceed MKD 25 million, the tax period is the calendar quarter. The tax period for voluntarily VAT registered taxpayers is the calendar year.

A taxpayer is obliged to submit a VAT return for each tax period within 25 days following the end of the relevant tax period.

Customs duties

Customs duties generally apply to most products imported into Macedonia. The customs rates under the most favoured nation treatment for agricultural products are up to 31%, whereas the customs rates for industrial products are below 23%.

Macedonia has signed trade agreements with Turkey, Ukraine, and European Free Trade Association (EFTA) member states. The country is a member state to the Central European Free Trade Agreement (CEFTA) and has signed a Stabilisation and Association Agreement with the European Community.

The import of industrial products with preferential origin is custom duty exempt as of 2011. In addition, the import of certain raw precious metals is also exempt as of 14 March 2012.

According to the Stabilisation and Association Agreement 2001 between Macedonia and the European Union, generally, products with Macedonian origin can be exported into EU countries free of customs duties.

Excise duties

Excise duties are levied with respect to a limited number of goods produced or imported in Macedonia. Petroleum products, alcohol and alcoholic beverages, tobacco products, and passenger motor vehicles are subject to an excise duty at a flat or percentage rate. The excise period is one calendar month, and excise duty is payable within 15 days as of the end of the calendar month. The excise duty for alcohol beverages and tobacco goods is levied by way of purchasing excise stamps.

The excise duty for petroleum products is payable per kilo/litre and ranges between MKD 0.1 and MKD 24.

Alcohol and alcoholic beverages are taxable per litre/percentage of alcohol. Some categories of alcoholic beverages (e.g. wine) are subject to no excise duty. Maximum excise duty payable is up to MKD 300 per litre on pure alcohol.

The excise duty for tobacco products is combined and is calculated both per peace/kilo and as a percentage from the retail price as follows:

Macedonia

- MKD 1.35 per cigar and 0% from its retail price.
- MKD 0.10 per cigarette and 35% of from its retail price.
- MKD 1,350 per kilo smoking tobacco and 0% from its retail price.

The excise duty for passenger motor vehicles is calculated as a percentage of the market value or the custom value of the vehicle. It ranges from 0% for vehicles valued up to 3,000 euro (EUR) to 18% for vehicles valued above EUR 30,000.

Property tax

Property tax is paid annually on the ownership of real estate, including land (agricultural, construction, forest, and pastures) and buildings (residential buildings or flats, business buildings and business premises, administrative buildings and administrative premises, buildings and flats for rest and recreation, and other construction facilities, as well as installations constructed on the buildings or below and permanently attached to the buildings).

The person liable for property tax is the legal entity or the individual owner of the property. If the owner is not known or cannot be reached, the person liable for property tax is the user of the property. A property taxpayer may also be the taxpayer who usufructs the property; and if the property is owned by several persons, each of them is a property taxpayer proportionately for the portion owned. A property taxpayer is also the legal entity who uses real estate owned by the state and the municipality.

The property tax base is the market value of the real estate. The market value of the real estate is determined by a special municipal commission in accordance with the methodology prescribed by the government.

Property tax rates are proportional and range from 0.10% to 0.20%. The rates may be determined on the basis of the type of the property. As an exception, property tax rates on agricultural land not used for agricultural production may be increased outside the above range (i.e. from three to five times in relation to the basic rates).

The amount of the rates is decided by the Municipal Councils.

Transfer tax

The transfer of the right to ownership of real estate for or without compensation, as well as other means of acquiring real estate for or without compensation, between legal entities is subject to transfer tax.

The person liable for transfer tax is the seller of the real estate. As an exception, a taxpayer may also be the buyer of the real estate, if agreed in the sale and purchase agreement. When replacing real estate, the taxpayer is the party that replaces the real estate of greater value.

When selling real estate in bankruptcy and executive procedure, as well as when realising agreements on mortgage, the taxpayer may be the buyer of the real estate.

In the case of transfer of ownership of an ideal share in real estate, taxpayers are each of the owners separately.

The tax base is the market value of the real estate at the moment the tax liability arises.

When replacing real estate, the tax base is the difference between the market values of the real estate being replaced.

Macedonia

When selling real estate in bankruptcy and executive procedure, the tax base is the attained selling price.

The market value is determined by a special municipal commission in accordance to the methodology prescribed by the government.

Tax rates are proportional and range from 2% to 4%. The tax rates are determined by the municipal councils by way of decision.

There are certain exemptions from transfer taxes available for specifically determined cases (i.e. transfer of shares, sale of securities, the first sale of residential premises for the first five years from the end of their construction, etc.).

Stamp taxes
Stamp taxes are not payable in Macedonia.

Garbage collection fee
A garbage collection fee is payable for immovable property depending on the type of property and on the surface area used. It is calculated on the basis of a tariff. It is collected together with the bills for water usage.

Companies and individuals are liable for paying communal taxes for usage of certain rights and services (mainly for usage of the urban space in the municipalities, posting commercials, etc.).

M

Branch income

Branch offices are registered in the Trade Registry. Branches are subject to CIT in accordance with the general statutory provisions. The foreign parent company is fully liable for the obligations of its established branch office in Macedonia.

A foreign company that is entitled to carry out commercial activities pursuant to its national legislation may establish a commercial representative office in Macedonia. Representative offices are not legal entities and may not carry out any commercial activities. Representative offices are not subject to CIT.

Income determination

Capital gains, as well as income from dividends, interest, rent, and royalties are treated as ordinary income of the taxpayer and are included in its general taxable base in accordance with accounting rules and standards. Since the accounting profits of a company are not taxable until distributed to individuals and non-resident legal entities, such income is not subject to CIT before that time.

Inventory valuation
As of 16 April 2011, the provisions in the tax legislation regarding inventory valuation were abolished. Prior to 16 April 2011, corporate taxpayers were restricted to value inventories for tax purposes in accordance to the weighted average price method.

Macedonia

Deductions

Tax base on taxable expenses and understated revenues
The CIT Law exhaustively lists the expenses which are not recognised for tax purposes and are part of the tax base on taxable expenses and understated revenues.

Hidden profit distribution
As of 16 April 2011, hidden profit distributions are taxable as part of the tax base on taxable expenses and understated revenues. The following transactions with shareholders or their related parties are considered as hidden profit distribution subject to CIT:

- Sales of goods/services on terms below the market price.
- Purchase of goods/services on terms above the market price.
- Providing loans with an interest lower than the market one.
- Arrangements under which gains are realised by the shareholders or their related parties.

Unjustified shortages are also taxed as hidden profit distribution if not reimbursed from the salary of the authorised person.

Some of the transactions as per above may be regulated under the transfer pricing provisions in the CIT Law as well. It seems that the purpose of this provision was to tax the non-fair transactions with shareholders and their related parties which do not fall under the 'related-party' definition as per the CIT Law.

Non-business-related expenses
Expenses which are not related to the business activity of the taxpayer are taxable.

Depreciation
As of April 2011, corporate taxpayers can apply depreciation methods and rates as well as perform impairment of their fixed assets under applicable accounting standards without any tax consequences.

Prior to the amendments, the depreciation of intangible and tangible assets was not taxable up to the amount calculated on the acquisition value of such assets, by applying depreciation rates within the limits set by the law. Once determined, the depreciation method was used until the final depreciation of the asset or group of assets.

Interest expenses
Interest paid on non-business related credits of the taxpayer as well as interest on credits for purchase of passenger vehicles, furniture, carpets, works of art, and decorative objects is a taxable expense. Interest on business-related credit is also taxable provided it falls under the thin capitalisation or transfer pricing rules (*see Thin capitalisation or Transfer pricing in the Group taxation section for more information*).

Impairment and write-off of receivables
Impairment of receivables is not taxable for banks, saving institutions, and insurance companies if impaired in accordance to the methods prescribed by law. As to other corporate taxpayers, impairment of receivables is a taxable expense if not based on an effective court decision or reported and confirmed as debts in liquidation or bankruptcy procedure. The taxpayers are entitled to a tax credit for the tax paid on collected impaired receivables in the year of collection.

Write-off of receivables is a taxable expense for all corporate taxpayers.

Charitable contributions
Donations and sponsorships expenses are taxable if not pursuant to the manner, the conditions, and the procedure set forth in the Law on Donations and Sponsorships in Public Activities. If compliant with the law requirements as per above, donations are taxable if the annual amount borne by the taxpayer exceeds 5% of its overall revenue, whereas sponsorship expenses are taxable if above 3% of the overall revenue of the taxpayer.

Compensation expenses
Employees' related expenditures (e.g. organised transportation to/from work, organised food (cantina), business trip allowance, field allowance, family separation allowance, one-off severance payment, retirement allowance, annual holiday allowance, anniversary awards) are taxable if paid over the amount prescribed by law and collective agreement.

Voluntary pension insurance contributions are taxable if their annual amount per employee exceeds four average monthly gross salaries paid out in the previous calendar year.

The monthly allowances and expenses to the managing board members are tax-deductible up to 50% of the average gross monthly salary paid out in the country in the previous year.

Insurance expenses
Personal insurance premiums paid for members of the management board and the employees (if not paid out of their salary) are taxable expenses. Only the collective insurance of the employees for work related injuries is a non-taxable expense for corporate taxpayers.

Entertainment expenses
Expenses for gifts, business dinners, recreation, and entertainment are taxable up to 90% of the annual amount borne by the taxpayer.

Scrapping
Expenses for scrapping exceeding the standards for the particular industry are taxable if not caused by *vis major* or an uncontrollable event.

Fines, penalties, and taxes
Fines and tax penalties, penalty interest on unpaid public duties, and expenses for enforced payments, as well as WHT borne by the taxpayer on behalf of third parties, are taxable.

Net operating losses
Loss carryforwards are not specifically regulated in the Macedonian tax legislation. However, due to the concept of corporate income taxation of distributed profit, in essence, accounting losses could be carried forward indefinitely. This is because of the fact that profit can be distributed only if losses from previous years are covered.

Loss carrybacks are not allowed under the Macedonian tax legislation.

Macedonia

Tax losses on taxable expenses and understated revenues

As of April 2011, tax losses arising from taxation of taxable expenses and understated revenues could be carried forward in the next consecutive five years. Such tax losses are recognised when the tax credit and reliefs exceed the amount of taxable expenses in the tax return on taxable expenses and understated revenues.

Payments to foreign affiliates

There are no specific provisions in the tax legislation with regard to payments towards foreign affiliates.

Group taxation

Tax consolidation provisions were abolished in Macedonia as of 1 January 2009.

Transfer pricing

As of 16 April 2011, the transfer pricing provisions are extended to cover not only the expenses but also the revenues resulting from related party transactions.

The difference between the market price and the transfer price is a taxable expense in the tax return on taxable expenses and understated revenues. As of April 2011, the cost plus method, in addition to the comparable uncontrolled price method, are applicable. No reference is made to other methods accepted by the Organisation for Economic Co-operation and Development (OECD).

The part of the interest paid on loans to related parties which exceeds or is below the interest payable between unrelated parties is considered taxable.

Penalty interest imposed between related parties shall be considered as a taxable expense.

Transfer pricing rules do not apply on expenses for interest under credits and penalty interest paid to related parties which are banks or financial institutions.

According to the changes in the CIT Rulebook applicable as of December 2011, upon request by the Macedonian tax authorities, companies should provide enough documentation as evidence that the transactions with related parties were in line with the 'arm's-length principle'.

Thin capitalisation

As of April 2011, part of the interest related to a loan received from a non-resident shareholder, who directly holds at least 25% of the capital in the company, that exceeds three times its share in the equity in the company will be taxable during a tax period. Thin capitalisation rules do not apply to loans received from banks or other financial organisations. Also, thin capitalisation rules do not apply for newly established companies within the first three years of operation.

Tax credits and incentives

Foreign tax credit

The taxpayer is allowed a tax credit for the tax paid on foreign income abroad up to the amount of tax payable for that income in Macedonia. The WHT on dividends and CIT paid abroad can be credited against the corporate tax liability on profit distribution. The foreign WHT paid on other types of income, except dividends, can be credited against the corporate tax liability on taxable expenses and understated revenues.

Technological industrial development zones

A taxpayer that is a registered user within a technological industrial development zone is exempt from profit tax payment for a period of ten years from the commencement of the performance of the activity in the zone under terms and conditions and according to a procedure determined with the Law on Technological Industrial Development Zones.

Withholding taxes

All domestic legal entities and domestic physical persons that are registered for carrying out an activity, as well as foreign legal entities or physical persons that are non-residents but have a PE in Macedonia, are obliged to withhold tax when paying certain types of income to a foreign legal person and to pay the tax withheld to a respective suspense account simultaneously with the payment of the income.

The WHT rate is 10% and is applied on the following forms of incomes payable abroad:

- Dividends.
- Interest.
- Royalties.
- Income from entertainment or sporting activities in Macedonia.
- Income from management, consulting, financial services, or services related to research and development.
- Income from insurance or reinsurance premiums.
- Income from telecommunications services between Macedonia and a foreign country.
- Income from the lease of immovable property in Macedonia.

As an exception, WHT is not applicable to the following forms of income:

- The after-tax profit of a PE transferred to its foreign headquarters.
- Interest from bonds issued or guaranteed by the government.
- Interest on deposits in banks located in Macedonia.
- Income from transactions in state securities on the international financial markets.

If a double taxation avoidance agreement is in place, WHT shall be payable in accordance with the provisions from the DTT. Taxpayers are obliged to obtain approval from the Macedonian tax authorities prior to applying the tax rates from the DTT.

Macedonia has signed DTTs with the 38 countries listed in the chart below:

Recipient	WHT (%)			
	Dividend	Interest	Royalties	Other income
Albania	10	10	10	0
Austria (1)	0/15	0	0	0
Belarus (2)	5/15	10	10	0
Belgium (2, 8)	10/15	15	10	0
Belgium (1)	5/15	10	10	0
Bulgaria (2)	5/15	10	10	0

Macedonia

Recipient	WHT (%)			
	Dividend	Interest	Royalties	Other income
China	10	10	10	0
Croatia (2)	5/15	10	10	0
Czech Republic (2)	5/15	0	10	0
Denmark (2, 3)	0/5/15	0	10	0
Egypt (4)	10	10	10	0
Estonia (2, 4)	0/5	5	5	0
Federal Republic of Yugoslavia (2, 5)	5/15	10	10	0
Finland (1)	0/15	10	0	0
France (1)	0/15	0	0	0
Germany (1, 4)	5/15	5	5	0
Hungary (2)	5/15	0	0	0
Iran (4)	10	10	10	0
Ireland (4, 6)	0/5/10	0	0	0
Italy (2)	5/15	10	0	0
Latvia (1, 7)	5/10	5	5/10	0
Lithuania (1)	0/10	10	10	0
Moldova (2)	5/10	5	10	0
Morocco (4)	10	10	10	0
Netherlands (1)	0/15	0	0	0
Norway (2)	10/15	5	5	0
Poland (2)	5/15	10	10	0
Qatar	0	0	5	0
Romania	5	10	10	0
Russia	10	10	10	0
Slovakia	5	10	10	0
Slovenia (2)	5/15	10	10	0
Spain (1)	5/15	5	5	0
Sweden (2)	0/15	10	0	0
Switzerland (2)	5/15	10	0	0
Taiwan	5	10	10	0
Turkey (2)	5/10	10	10	0
Ukraine (2)	5/15	10	10	0
United Kingdom (1, 9)	0/5/15	0	0	0

Notes

1. The lower rate applies to dividends paid out to a foreign company, which controls at least 10% of the share capital of the payer of the dividends.
2. The lower rate applies to dividends paid out to a foreign company, which controls at least 25% of the share capital of the payer of the dividends.
3. The zero rate applies to dividends paid out to pension funds.
4. These DTTs are still not in force.
5. The DTT with Federal Republic of Yugoslavia now applies both to Serbia and Montenegro.
6. The zero rate applies to dividends paid out to recognised pension funds and to foreign companies which continuously control at least 25% of the share capital of the payer of the dividends for 12 months before the dividends payment. The 5% rate applies to dividends paid out to foreign company which controls at least 10% of the share capital of the payer of the dividends. The 10% rate applies to dividends paid out in all other cases.

7. The tax rate of 10% for royalties payments applies only for utilisation or right to utilise cinematographic films and films or tapes for radio and television transmission. The 5% rate applies on all other cases.
8. The DTT concluded between the Socialist Federal Republic of Yugoslavia (SFRY) and Belgium is still applicable for Macedonia.
9. The zero rate applies to dividends paid out to pension schemes and to foreign companies which continuously control at least 25% of the share capital of the payer of the dividends for 12 months before the dividends payment. The 5% rate applies to dividends paid out to foreign company which controls at least 10% of the share capital of the payer of the dividends. The 15% rate applies to dividends paid out in all other cases.

Tax administration

Taxable period
The taxable period for which CIT is determined covers one calendar year.

Tax returns
Taxpayers are obligated to calculate and pay CIT on taxable expenses and understated revenues on the basis of a tax return on taxable expenses and understated revenues which must be submitted to the Public Revenue Office by the end of February the following year.

Taxpayers who distribute profit are obliged to calculate and pay CIT on the basis of a tax return on profit distribution, which should be submitted to the tax authorities up to the date of profit distribution.

Small taxpayers who fall under the simplified tax regime are obliged to calculate and pay the tax due on the basis of a tax return on overall income which should be submitted to the tax authorities by the end of February the following year.

Payment of tax
Corporate taxpayers are obliged to pay monthly CIT advance payments during the year within 15 days of the end of each month.

Monthly CIT advance payments are calculated as one-twelfth of the tax obligation on taxable expenses and understated revenues for the previous calendar year increased by the index of cumulative retail price growth as determined by the State Statistical Bureau.

The difference between the advance payments and the final CIT liability as determined in the tax return on taxable expenses and understated revenues should be paid within 30 days as of the dead-line for submission of the tax return on taxable expenses and understated revenues. Daily penalty interest of 0.03% is due on late tax payments.

In case the sum of monthly advance payments exceeds the final tax liability in the tax return on taxable expenses and understated revenues, the taxpayer may request for a refund of overpaid tax. The tax should be refunded within 60 days as of the date of submitting the request. If the taxpayer does not ask for a tax refund, the overpaid amounts will be considered as advance payment for the following period.

M

Macedonia

Other issues

Choice of business entity

The Macedonian Trade Companies Law provides for the following types of entities:

- General partnerships.
- Limited partnerships.
- Limited liability companies.
- Joint stock companies.
- Limited partnerships by shares.
- Foreign business entities may register a branch office or a representative office in Macedonia.

Madagascar

PwC contact

Andriamisa Ravelomanana
Rue Rajakoba Augustin,
Ankadivato,
Antananarivo,
Madagascar
Tel: +261 20 2221 763
Email: andriamisa.ravelomanana@mg.pwc.com

Significant developments

Reduction of income tax rate
Income tax rates, including corporate income tax (CIT), salary income tax, withholding tax on capital interest, and capital gain on real estate, decreased from 22% to 21% in 2012.

Financial year change
In 2012, the financial year may be spread over any period of 12 months.

Tax reduction for companies investing in the production and supply of renewable energy
In 2012, companies investing in the production and supply of renewable energy can benefit from a tax reduction equal to the tax corresponding to 50% of the amount of investment that they realised during the related tax year.

Value-added tax (VAT) developments
Transport companies are allowed to claim VAT input on gasoline used for land transportation. The objective is to reduce the impact of cost of oil and gas on transportation fees.

In 2012, all transactions made by a VAT vendor with a non-VAT vendor must be done via the banking system when the value of the transaction exceeds a threshold fixed by Decree.

Taxes on corporate income

Taxation of residents
Resident corporate entities are subject to CIT based on realised worldwide income.

A corporate entity having an annual turnover less than 20 million Malagasy ariary (MGA) is subject to CIT at a rate of 5% of 70% of turnover, with a minimum tax of MGA 16,000.

A corporate entity registered in Madagascar and having an annual turnover exceeding MGA 20 million is subject to CIT at a rate of 21%. Note that the CIT rate was 22% in 2011.

The tax payable cannot be less than 5/1,000 of turnover plus a fixed amount of MGA 100,000 for taxable persons carrying on agricultural, artisan, transportation, industrial, hotel, or mining activities. The minimum tax cannot be less than 5/1,000 of turnover plus MGA 320,000 for other activities.

M

Madagascar

Taxation of non-residents

Only Madagascar-source income is taxable for non-residents.

Revenue of foreign businesses that do not have a permanent establishment (PE) in Madagascar is subject to withholding income tax at a rate of 10% of any income realised in Madagascar.

Local income taxes

No other local income taxes are applicable in Madagascar.

Corporate residence

Companies are considered resident in Madagascar if they are registered in Madagascar or have a legal existence in Madagascar.

Permanent establishment (PE)

While there is no definition of PE in the Madagascar tax law, companies usually are required to have a legal existence when they carry out business in Madagascar or have revenue from ownership of assets in Madagascar.

Other taxes

Value-added tax (VAT)

The VAT rate is 20%, and the VAT rate on export is 0%. VAT input is recoverable under certain conditions.

VAT is applicable to all transactions realised in Madagascar by a VAT vendor. Services are considered to be performed in Madagascar if such services are used in Madagascar or invoiced to a taxpayer established in Madagascar.

Transport companies are allowed to claim VAT input on gasoline used for land transportation. The objective is to reduce the impact of cost of oil and gas on transportation fees.

Any corporate entity or individual person who realises an annual turnover exceeding MGA 200 million is a VAT vendor. For a business realising annual revenue less than MGA 200 million, VAT vendor registration is an option.

A foreign company that has no PE in Madagascar but renders services to a Madagascar taxpayer must appoint a tax representative to collect and pay VAT on its behalf. Otherwise, the beneficiary of the services must collect and pay VAT on behalf of the foreign supplier.

As of 2012, all transactions made by a VAT vendor with a non-VAT vendor must be done via the banking system when the value of the transaction exceeds a threshold fixed by Decree.

Custom and import tax

The importation of goods is subject to payment of custom and import tax payable to the custom office.

Madagascar

In addition, Gasynet fee corresponding to 0.5% of the cost, insurance, and freight (CIF) value of goods is applicable on importation of goods.

Excise taxes
Excise duty applies on a range of goods and services, such as tobacco, alcohol, lighters, and communication by mobile phones. Excise duty rate ranges from 7% to 200% or a fixed amount per litre or per unit.

Real estate ownership tax
Real estate ownership tax is imposed annually at the rate of 5% to 10% on the rental value of the property. Land ownership is also taxable at a rate depending on the nature of the land.

Registration fees
Registration fees are applicable to transfers of title ownership (e.g. sales, donations) of movable and immovable assets, to transfers of interests, to share capital increases, and to lease agreements.

Registration fee rates are 0.5% to 6%, depending on the nature of the transaction.

Payroll tax
Salary income taxes, called *Impôt sur les Revenus Salariaux et Assimilés* (IRSA), are levied at a rate of 21% on the total taxable remuneration of employees, including salaries, allowances, and benefits in kind. Employers are responsible for withholding and paying salary income taxes on behalf of employees.

Social security contributions
Employers must contribute to *Caisse Nationale de Prévoyance Sociale*, Madagascar's national social security fund, which includes pensions and accident insurance. The contribution is capped at 13% of eight times the legal minimum salary per employee.

Health contributions
Employers must contribute to the health system assessment at a rate of 5% of the total amount of taxable remuneration of its employees.

Tax on insurance contracts
All insurance or life annuity conventions concluded with a company, insurance firm, or with any other Madagascan or other insurer are subject to an annual tax on insurance contracts at a rate of 3% to 20% levied on the insurance premiums.

Branch income

The tax on branch income is the same as for corporate income. The branch income tax base is the income realised by the branch in Madagascar.

Income determination

Inventory valuation
There are no provisions for valuing inventories or determining inventory flows in Madagascar. The tax treatment will follow the accounting treatment.

Madagascar

Capital gains

There is no provision for capital gains in Madagascar, except for capital gains on the sale of real estate by an individual. Capital gains made by a company on the sale of assets and interests are considered as normal business income that is subject to CIT.

Dividend income

Dividends received by a company are considered as business income subject to CIT.

Stock dividends

Stock dividends are unusual, but they are considered as business income that is subject to CIT.

Interest income

Interest income received by a resident taxpayer from another entity established in Madagascar is subject to withholding tax (WHT) at a rate of 21%. Revenue already subject to WHT is no longer taxable to CIT.

Foreign income

Foreign income is considered as normal business income subject to CIT unless a tax treaty is established and indicates otherwise.

Deductions

Depreciation

The amount of deductible depreciation should not exceed the amount that is calculated according to the following rates of depreciation provided by the law:

Asset	Depreciation rate (%)
Industrial buildings	5
Plant and machinery	10
Mining exploration and development (licence)	33
Transportation (car)	20
Transportation (utility cars, vans, trucks)	25
Computers	25
Electricity generators	10

With the exception of buildings, it is also possible to practise a graduated depreciation. In this case, the annual depreciation corresponds to 30% of the net book value of the asset.

In case of loss, depreciation of assets can be deferred and carried forward to the next financial years until absorption.

Goodwill

There is no provision concerning deductibility of goodwill in the Madagascar tax code.

Start-up expenses

There is no specific tax provision on start-up expenses. Accounting rules are applicable for the profit and loss recognition.

Madagascar

Start-up and prospecting expenses for the installation of an overseas establishment, as well as the costs of running such a foreign establishment, for the first three years are tax deductible. However, the amounts deducted must be reported, in equal amounts, to the taxable income of the five consecutive years from the fifth year following the creation of the foreign establishment.

Interest expenses
Interest expenses are deductible. However, interests on inter-company loans are subject to thin capitalisation rule (*see Thin capitalisation in the Group taxation section for more information*).

Bad debt
To be tax-deductible, provisions for doubtful debt must be subject to justification of existence of amicable or judicial settlement.

Charitable contributions
Payments made for the benefit of educational, social, or cultural recognised public associations; accredited bodies for scientific research; or for the promotion and creation of businesses for achievement of planned economic and social development are deductible within the limits of 0.5% of annual turnover.

Gifts in kind or in cash granted in case of natural calamities and donations in cash granted to a corporation established by decree for the interest of the nation are also deductible.

Any other charitable contributions are not deductible.

Deductible wages
Salaries and wages that are not included in salary income taxes or not declared to *Caisse Nationale de Prévoyance Sociale* are not deductible.

Fines and penalties
Fines and penalties are not deductible for CIT purposes.

Taxes
Except for CIT, taxes in relation to business in Madagascar are deductible.

Third-party taxes borne by the company are not tax-deductible.

Net operating losses
Accumulated loss can be carried forward for the next five financial years following the period in which the loss occurs.

Payments to foreign affiliates
For branches, the deductible amount of overhead that the head office can charge to the branch is limited to 1% of the turnover of the branch.

For interest on inter-company loans, only interest calculated on twice the amount of the share capital, at a rate practised by the Central Bank plus two points, is deductible.

Group taxation

There is no provision regarding group taxation in Madagascar.

Madagascar

Transfer pricing

There is a provision in the tax law allowing the tax authority to claim a tax adjustment in cases where the transactions between a Madagascar entity and a foreign entity controlling or controlled by the Madagascar entity are not concluded on an arm's-length basis. However, there is no definition of arm's-length bases under the Malagasy law. In practice, deductibility of inter-company expenses is appreciated by the tax authority based on the following:

- The agreement must correspond to actual services.
- The amount invoiced must be reasonable compared to the market practice.
- The services rendered must be required for the exploitation.

Thin capitalisation

Under Malagasy tax law, deductible inter-company financial interest cannot exceed the interest calculated on twice the share capital at the rate of the Central Bank of Madagascar plus two points (the April 2012 rate of the Central Bank of Madagascar was 9.5%).

Tax credits and incentives

The following activities benefit from a special tax and/or customs regime:

Microfinance activity

Microfinance benefits are available for entities specialising in lending money on the basis of small or medium scale value. Entities duly licensed to practise microfinance activities are exempt from CIT during the first five years. After this period, the microfinance company is subject to CIT at a rate of 21%.

Free zone (free trade zone)

Free-zone law is available for industrial and other service providers that export all of their products. If eligible under the free-zone law, a CIT exemption is provided during the first two to five years and a reduced CIT of 10% is levied thereafter. Exemption from customs duties on importation is also provided.

Companies investing in the production and supply of renewable energy

Companies investing in the production and supply of renewable energy can benefit from a tax reduction equal to the tax corresponding to 50% of the amount of investment that they realised during the related tax year. The right to reduction that can be used under the tax year cannot exceed 50% of tax actually due. The balance is carried forward with the same limitation to subsequent years, until clearance.

Big investment mining

A mining company committing to invest more than USD 50 million is considered a big investment mining company. The big investment mining law provides a minimum income tax exemption, a reduced CIT rate for the transformation entity (i.e. the entity in charge of processing the extracted minerals), exemption from custom and importation duties, and VAT reimbursement on locally purchased equipment and investments.

Petroleum code

The petroleum code provides a custom and importation duties exemption for hydrocarbon research, exploration, and exploitation activities.

Madagascar

Leasing law
The leasing law provides that leasing activities can benefit from CIT exemption and reduction of tax rate during the first four years.

Foreign tax credit
Except under a tax treaty, there is no foreign tax credit rule under the Malagasy tax law.

Withholding taxes

WHTs are levied as follows:

- *Impôt sur les revenues des capitaux mobiliers* (IRCM): WHT on interest of 21% is applicable on financial loan interest. However, interest paid to banks, financial institution, and foreign financial organisation is exempt.
- WHT of 21% is applicable on remuneration of a member of a board of directors or a single director.
- Income tax for non-resident entity: Management fees, royalties, technical and assistance fees, licence fees, equipment rental fees, and any income realised by foreign suppliers is subject to withholding income tax at a rate of 10%.

Madagascar has signed two tax treaties.

Recipient	Dividends (%)	Loan interest (%)	Royalties, management fees, services fees (%)
No tax treaty	0	21	10
France	15 (max)	15	15 (max)
Mauritius	10 (max)	10	5 (max)

Tax administration

Taxable period
From 2012, the financial year may be spread over any period of 12 months. There is no need to obtain prior authorisation in order to close the financial year on a date other than 31 December or 30 June.

Tax returns
CIT returns are due before 15 May each year for companies whose financial year-ends at 31 December, before 15 November each year for companies whose financial year-ends at 30 June, and within four months from the date of closing of the financial year for all other year-ends.

Payment of tax
CIT is payable bi-monthly in provisional instalments. The balance is payable before 15 May each year for companies whose financial year ends at 31 December, before 15 November each year for companies whose financial year ends at 30 June, and within four months from the date of closing of the financial year for all other year-ends.

WHT on foreign services is payable to the tax authorities within one month of the date of payment.

Madagascar

WHT on interest and on payments to members of boards of directors are payable before 15 May each year for companies whose financial year ends at 31 December, before 15 November each year for companies whose financial year ends at 30 June, and within four months from the date of closing of the financial year for all other year-ends.

Audit cycle
According to the corporate law, an annual statutory audit is required. An auditor is appointed for six financial years for a corporation (*société anonyme* or SA) and for three years for a private limited liability company (*société à responsabilité limitée* or SARL).

Statute of limitations
The tax limitation period is three years.

Topics of focus for tax authorities
Areas where tax authorities usually claim adjustment are:

* VAT reverse on foreign services.
* Completeness of VAT output on revenue.
* Sales without invoices.
* Expenses without invoices.
* Employees remuneration not subject to salary tax.
* Payment to non-registered suppliers.

Malawi

PwC contact

Vyamala Moyo
PricewaterhouseCoopers
1st House
Blantyre, Malawi
Tel: +265 1 820 322
Email: vyamala.aggriel.moyo@mw.pwc.com

Significant developments

As of 1 July 2011, the following developments have entered into effect:

- Minimum tax based on turnover has been introduced on loss-making companies and companies with low profits, as follows: 1% of turnover for annual turnover of 50 million Malawian kwachas (MWK) or less; 2% of turnover for annual turnover of more than MWK 50 million.
- Investment allowances for manufacturers has been reduced from 100% to 40% of the cost for new and unused plant and machinery and industrial buildings and from 40% to 20% for used assets.
- Additional 50% training allowance has been abolished. Previously, the cost of training a Malawian employee to obtain a degree, diploma, or a certificate in the field relevant to the employee's job would attract a 50% additional training allowance.
- The rate of transport allowance for transportation of exports has been reduced from 25% of the cost to 15%.
- Corporate tax at 30% has been introduced on income of companies operating in Export Processing Zones. Previously, these companies would enjoy both income tax and import duty exemption.
- A levy of 0.2% has been introduced on the buyers of tobacco for every kilogram of tobacco bought.
- Withholding tax (WHT) threshold for casual labour has been increased from MWK 5,000 to MWK 12,000. Casual labour will be treated separately from services.
- WHT rate for rental income has been increased from 10% to 15%.
- WHT exemption has been re-introduced for compliant taxpayers (since 1 July 2010, issuance of WHT exemption certificates was abolished on supply of goods, including agricultural produce and food stuffs).

Taxes on corporate income

Malawi does not have separate legislation for the determination of taxable income of different types of legal persons. Taxation of all income is included in the Taxation Act.

Section 11 of the Taxation Act defines income as the total amount in cash or otherwise, including any capital gain, received by or accrued to in any year or period of assessment from a source within or deemed to be within Malawi. The taxpayer's assessable income excludes any amount exempt from tax under this act.

Income deemed to arise in Malawi

The liability for Malawi tax is based on the source of the income rather than residence of the person. Certain transactions may be deemed to be from a source within Malawi

Malawi

even if effected outside Malawi. Section 27 of the Taxation Act limits the income that may be deemed to have arisen in Malawi to the following:

- Remuneration for services rendered or work performed in Malawi.
- Remuneration for services rendered or work performed in or out of Malawi where the amount may be claimed as a tax-deductible expense by a permanent establishment (PE) in Malawi.
- Amounts incurred, claimed, or claimable in connection with a PE in Malawi.
- Realised exchange gains and losses arising in connection with a PE in Malawi or foreign exchange assets and liabilities held in Malawi.
- Capital gains and losses realised with respect to tangible property located in Malawi and interests in companies incorporated in Malawi.

Summary of tax rates

Entity	Income tax rate (%)
Locally incorporated companies (1)	30
Branches of companies not incorporated in Malawi	35
Companies in Export Processing Zones (2)	30
Companies in priority industries (3)	
For a period not exceeding ten years	0
In all other cases for companies incorporated in Malawi	15
In all other cases for Malawi branches of external companies	20

Notes

1. In the case of a mining company, an additional resource rent tax of 10% is levied on profits after tax if the company's rate of return exceeds 20%. The basis for calculating rate of return has not been defined.
2. Prior to 1 July 2011, these companies enjoyed an income tax exemption.
3. Priority industries have not been defined.

Minimum tax

As of 1 July 2011, companies are subject to minimum tax based on turnover, as follows: 1% of turnover for annual turnover of MWK 50 million or less; 2% of turnover for annual turnover of more than MWK 50 million.

Non-resident tax

Non-resident tax is payable on income due to a non-resident at the rate of 15% of the gross income.

Any income payable to a person who is not resident in Malawi (who has not been in Malawi for an aggregate period of 183 days) arising from a source within Malawi is liable to a final WHT of 15% of the gross of such income. Non-resident tax is applicable where the recipient of the income does not have a PE in Malawi from which the income emanated.

Non-resident tax should not be charged on income of residents of countries that have a standing double tax agreement (DTA) with Malawi. Currently, the following countries have a DTA with Malawi: Denmark, France, the Netherlands, Norway, South Africa, Sweden, Switzerland, and the United Kingdom.

Malawi

Corporate residence

A corporate entity is considered a resident for tax purposes in Malawi if it has a PE in Malawi.

Permanent establishment (PE)

The Taxation Act defines a PE as 'an office or other fixed place of business through which business activity is carried on'. This short definition is wide in scope. Care must be exercised when considering this definition in situations that may be affected by a DTA. Each DTA contains a specific and far more detailed definition of what constitutes a PE.

Other taxes

Value-added tax (VAT)

VAT is applicable on taxable goods and services. There are three classes of supplies for VAT: taxable supplies (at the rate of 16.5%), zero-rated supplies, and exempt supplies.

A taxable person can claim input VAT on inputs used in making taxable supplies.

A taxable person should complete VAT returns and make VAT payment, where applicable, on a monthly basis within 25 days after the end of the month.

Customs duties/Import tariffs

Customs duty is applicable on goods imported into Malawi. The basis for calculating duty is cost, insurance, and freight (CIF). There are three types of import duties: Customs duty, import excise, and import VAT. The rate of custom duty varies from product to product.

M

Excise duties

Domestic excise is chargeable on certain goods manufactured in Malawi and on certain services such as alcoholic drinks, tobacco, and cell phone airtime. The rate of excise varies depending on the goods and services.

Tobacco levy

Buyers of tobacco must pay a levy of 0.2% for every kilogram of tobacco bought.

Turnover tax

Turnover tax is applicable for businesses with a turnover between MWK 2 million and MWK 6 million. The turnover tax rate is 2% of turnover.

Resource rent tax for miners

Miners pay resource rent tax of 10% on after tax profits if the rate of return exceeds 20%. This kind of tax has been introduced recently and details of operation are not clear. For example, no formula has been provided for calculating the rate of return.

Fringe benefits tax (FBT)

A fringe benefit is defined as any asset, service, or other benefit in kind provided by or on behalf of an employer to an employee, if such benefit includes an element of personal benefit to the employee. And, the employer providing such benefits is liable for payment of FBT. FBT is charged at the rate of 30% of the taxable figure.

Malawi

Take note that a benefit need not be wholly for personal use in order to be considered for FBT.

Note as well that no benefit in cash, no matter what it is termed as, can be treated as a fringe benefit. All monies paid in cash (rather than in kind) should be considered for pay as you earn (PAYE) deduction.

However, subsistence allowances, given to employees working out of their duty station for instance, presumably to cater wholly, exclusively, and necessarily for the needs such as accommodation, meals, transport, etc. ought not be taxed. This applies also for reimbursement of expenses incurred in business.

Every employer shall register for FBT within the month in which one begins to provide fringe benefits.

The sums due as FBT shall be remitted to the Malawi Revenue Authority (MRA) in quarterly instalments not later than 14 days after the end of each quarter of a period of 12 months ending 30 June, and remittance should be accompanied with a duly completed FBT return in Form FBT 2.

Note that the value for FBT should not be included in the employee's certificate of gross emoluments.

Assessment of housing fringe benefits
The taxable value of a housing fringe benefit is the greatest of (i) 10% of salary where the house is unfurnished, (ii) 12% of salary if furnished, or (iii) the rental value.

Where the house occupied by the employee is owned by the employer, the taxable value is reduced by 50%.

Motor vehicles
FBT is applicable on motor vehicles allocated for use by members of staff and does not include pool cars or cars that are strictly commercial in nature.

The taxable value is 15% of the original cost of the vehicle.

School fees (for children/dependants)
50% of the cost to the employer for school fees is a taxable benefit, where payment is made directly to the educational institution. Education allowances payable to employees are not subject to FBT as the allowance is considered part of normal salary and taxable as such.

Utilities, household items, vacations, travel, and domestic services
The taxable value of utilities (e.g. electricity, water, and telephone expenses), household items, vacations, travel, and domestic services (e.g. gardener, cook, house boy, guard, nanny) is the entire cost to the employer. Except that for a house owned by the employer, the cost of gardener, security guard, and watchman shall not constitute a taxable benefit.

Interest free loans and loans given at interest lower than the commercial rate
Where an employer gives a loan to an employee that is interest free or bears interest that is lower than the predetermined commercial rate, the difference between the interest offered and the commercial rate is a taxable benefit.

Branch income

There is a 35% tax on taxable income of a branch of a foreign company. Locally incorporated companies pay tax at the rate of 30%.

No dividend WHT is applicable on repatriation of profits.

Income determination

Inventory valuation
Inventory is stated at cost for tax purposes.

Capital gains
The tax basis for capital gains is the cost of the asset adjusted by the applicable consumer price index (inflation index). Once determined, the taxable gain is subject to corporate tax at the rate applicable to the particular entity.

Capital gains arising from the disposal of personal and domestic assets not used in connection with trade are exempt from corporate tax.

As of 1 July 2011, capital gains arising from the sale of shares traded on the Malawi Stock Exchange are taxable.

Rollover relief
If a business asset is sold and the taxpayer acquires a qualifying replacement asset, the taxpayer may claim rollover relief. This means that the taxpayer does not immediately pay the tax on the gain. Instead, the cost of the replacement asset is reduced by the amount of the gain. The taxpayer must declare this in the tax return.

A qualifying replacement asset is an asset similar to, or related in service or use to, the asset disposed of. The replacement asset must be acquired within 18 months of the disposal giving rise to the gain.

Dividend income
Dividend income is exempt from corporate tax; however, dividends received from Malawi sources are subject to a 10% dividend WHT, which is a final tax. Note that although the word 'final' has not been defined, it is applied as meaning that dividend WHT suffered may not be offset against an income tax liability.

Foreign exchange gains and losses
Foreign exchange gains realised on foreign currency assets or liabilities are taxable.

Foreign exchange losses realised on foreign currency assets or liabilities are tax deductible.

Unrealised gains and losses are carried forward until realised and then included in income or allowable expenditures. The maintenance of records that accurately track unrealised exchange rate adjustments from year to year is necessary to ensure correct tax computations.

Tax-exempt income
The following are common examples of other tax-exempt income:

Malawi

- The income of agricultural, mining, and commercial institutions or societies not operating for private pecuniary profit or gain of the members.
- The income of clubs, societies, and associations formed, organised, and operated solely or principally for social welfare or civic improvement or other similar purpose provided that the income of such bodies may not be divided among or used for the benefit of the members or shareholders.
- The income of ecclesiastical, charitable, and educational institutions of a public character.

Foreign income
Generally, income whose source is not Malawi is not taxable in Malawi.

Deductions

Taxable income is calculated by deducting allowable items from assessable income. Section 28 of the Taxation Act defines tax-allowable deductions as any expenditures and losses (not being of a capital nature) wholly, exclusively, and necessarily incurred by the taxpayer for the purpose of trade or in the production of income.

Capital allowances
Capital allowances (i.e. depreciation allowances) are applicable as stipulated in the Taxation Act at various rates.

Capital allowances, which are available to companies and individuals in business, are allowed as follows:

Asset	Allowances (%)		
	Initial	Investment	Annual
Industrial and farm buildings, hotels, and docks (1, 2, 3)	10	20/40	5
Staff housing (3)	10	-	5
Plant, machinery, and equipment (1, 2, 3, 4)	20	20/40	10/20
Furniture and fittings (3)	20	-	10
Motor vehicles (3, 4, 5, 6)	20	-	20
Commercial buildings (7)	-	-	2.5
Computers	20	-	40

Notes

1. The 40% investment allowance is available only on new and unused qualifying assets as indicated above, belonging to and used by a manufacturer or farmer (prior to 1 July 2011, the investment allowance was 100%). The rate for used qualifying assets is 20% (40% prior to 1 July 2011). The investment allowance is claimable only in the first year of use.
2. Where an investment allowance is claimed, the initial allowance is not allowed to be claimed on the same asset. The initial allowance is claimable only in the first year of use.
3. Annual allowances at the above rates are based on cost less investment and initial and annual allowances previously granted.
4. Investment allowance on plant and machinery excludes motor vehicles intended or adapted for use on roads.
5. A 20% annual allowance is standard, but the Commissioner General may vary the amount.
6. No initial allowance is granted on private motor vehicles. These include saloons, sedans, station wagons, and double cabin pickups. However, the restriction does not apply where the motor vehicle is used for hiring purposes.
7. The building must be newly constructed at a cost of no less than MWK 100 million.

On disposal, assets are subject to balancing charges (capital gains) or balancing allowances.

If an asset is subject to extensive use, such as machinery working double shifts, so that its expected economic life is reduced, the commissioner general may agree to increase the rates of annual allowances.

Lease, patent, trademark, and copyright premium
The tax-deductible amount of a premium paid for the right of use or occupation of land or buildings, plant or machinery, patent design, trademark, copyright, or any other property of a similar nature is one of the following:

- The amount of premium or consideration divided by the number of years for which the right of occupation or use is granted.
- Where the period for which the right of occupation or use is granted exceeds 25 years, the deduction is one-twenty-fifth of the premium or consideration.

The premium is tax deductible only where the asset or right with respect to which the premium or consideration is paid is used for the generation of income. If a taxpayer acquires ownership of the asset or right, no further deduction of the premium or consideration is allowed from the date ownership is acquired.

Goodwill
The legislation does not prescribe treatment for goodwill. It has been the practice that goodwill is not deductible for tax purposes.

Pre-operating expenditures
A manufacturer may claim as a deduction any expenditure incurred in the course of establishing the business, provided that the following are true:

- The expenditure was incurred not more than 18 months before commencing business.
- The expenditure would have been allowed as a deduction if it had been incurred after commencing business.

Interest expenses
Interest that arises out of financing operations is allowable, while interest due to late payment of a debt is not allowable.

Bad debt
Specific bad debts are tax deductible and taxable in the following year. Bad debts written off are allowable and taxable upon eventual recovery.

Charitable contributions
Donations to approved charities and approved non-profit institutions formed for the purpose of social welfare, civic improvement, educational development, or other similar purposes are deductible. The minimum individual donation allowable is MWK 500. The minimum donation for other approved charities is MWK 250. In both cases, there is no maximum donation.

Research and development (R&D) expenditures
Research expenditures are fully allowable as a deduction if they are for 'experiments and research relating to trade'.

Malawi

Pension contributions
The tax-allowable amount of ordinary pension contributions made by an employer to an approved pension fund is subject to limitations. The limit with respect to each employee is the lowest of one of the following per annum:

- The actual contribution.
- 24% of the employee's compensation.
- MWK 9,000.

No allowance is available if an employee is entitled to a tax-free gratuity.

Fines and penalties
Fines and penalties are not tax deductible in any way.

Taxes
Taxes are not allowed as deductible expenses, except where they are local taxes.

Net operating losses
Current taxable income may be offset against net operating losses brought forward and current operating losses may be increased by net unexhausted trading losses brought forward. Manufacturers and taxpayers in the agricultural industry may carry losses forward indefinitely, while other taxpayers may carry losses forward for only six years. Net operating losses may not be carried back.

Payments to foreign affiliates
A deduction is allowed for payments to foreign affiliates if such payments are expended wholly, exclusively, and necessarily for the production of income or for the purposes of trade, and it can be demonstrated that the transaction is at arm's length.

....

Group taxation

Group taxation is not permitted in Malawi.

Transfer pricing
Transfer pricing regulations were introduced and effective as of 1 July 2009. There is also a tax anti-avoidance provision that is used to check transactions between related parties. If transactions between related parties result in profits that are lower than what would be expected if the company was trading with an independent party, then the tax authorities can challenge the transaction.

Thin capitalisation
There are no thin capitalisation rules in Malawi.

There are no restrictions on the level of external borrowings. If a Malawi company wants to borrow money from a foreign entity (whether or not a bank), it will require exchange control approval. In such instances, Reserve Bank does not consider the debt-to-equity ratio. It looks at the terms and conditions to see that they are what would be commonly available on the open market between unrelated parties. As you can see, this is an anti-transfer pricing measure.

If a new application is made for exchange control approval of foreign ownership (normally this is when there is a new business/investment into Malawi), Reserve Bank will look at the external debt to local equity ratio. There are no fixed rules, but Reserve

Bank does not normally like external debt to be more than twice equity (i.e. 1:2 equity to external debt). It does give approval for external ownership where the proportion of external debt is higher than this as it looks at each proposal on its own merit. The applicant would have to justify the higher level of external debt in such a case.

Controlled foreign companies (CFCs)
There is no CFC regime in Malawi.

Tax credits and incentives

Export allowances
Exporters, including those manufacturing in bond, are entitled to claim additional tax allowances for non-traditional exports:

- On the export of non-traditional products, there is a 15% tax allowance on taxable income derived from exports (prior to 1 July 2011, the allowance was 25%).
- There is a 15% transport tax allowance on international transport costs for non-traditional exports (prior to 1 July 2011, the allowance was 25%). Traditional exports are tea, coffee, cane sugar, and unmanufactured tobacco and tobacco refuse.

Export allowances may not be claimed in respect of exports from mining operations.

Investment allowance
There is a 40% investment allowance on plant and machinery and industrial buildings for taxpayers in the manufacturing industry (prior to 1 July 2011, the investment allowance was 100%).

Farming operations
Farming operations receive a 100% allowance with respect to expenditures incurred during any year of assessment on the following:

- Stumping, leveling, and clearing of land.
- Work in connection with the prevention of soil erosion.
- Boreholes.
- Wells.
- Aerial and geophysical surveys.
- Water control work, including any canal, channel, dyke, furrow, and any flood control structure, whether or not of a permanent nature.
- Water conservation work, meaning any reservoir, water dam, or embankment constructed for the impounding of water. In the case of water conservation work, the Taxation Act limits the amount deductible to amounts actually paid, where the farmer incurs a liability in terms of any law relating to natural resources.

Where a farmer derives taxable income from growing timber, the farmer may elect that the taxable income is determined in accordance with the following rules:

- Carryforward the cost of planting the timber until the timber reaches maturity.
- Add annually to the cost of planting the timber an amount calculated as 5% of the cost of planting the timber until the timber reaches maturity.
- When the timber is sold, a proportionate amount of the total of the carryforward cost and annual added cost is deducted from the proceeds.
- In each year of assessment, the annual added cost is treated as taxable income in the hands of the farmer.

Malawi

A farmer may not deduct any expenditures that have been recovered through a subsidy or claim a capital allowance on any assets where the expenditures have been recovered through a subsidy.

Mining operations

Mining operations receive a 100% allowance with respect to mining expenditures incurred during any year of assessment. Mining expenditures are defined as capital expenditures incurred in Malawi by a person carrying on or about to carry on mining operations in Malawi:

- In searching for or in discovering and testing or in winning access to deposits of minerals.
- In the acquisition of or of rights in or over such deposits, other than the acquisition from a person who has carried on mining operations in relation to such deposits.
- In the provision of plant and machinery and industrial buildings that would have little or no value to such person if the mine ceased to work.
- On the construction of any buildings or works that would have little or no value if the mine ceased to be worked.
- On development, general administration, and management prior to the commencement of mining operations.

Persons engaged in mining operations are not entitled to claim the export tax allowance on non-traditional exports or the 15% transport tax allowance on international transport costs for non-traditional exports.

Withholding taxes

WHT rates

Nature of payment	WHT rate (%)
Royalties	20
Rents	15
Payment of more than MWK 60,000 per annum for any supplies to traders and institutions	3
Commission	20
Payment for carriage and haulage	10
Payment to contractors and subcontractors in the building and construction industries	4
Payment for public entertainment	20
Payment of more than MWK 12,000 for casual labour	20
Services	20
Bank interest in excess of MWK 10,000	20
Fees	10

Dividend WHT

Dividend WHT is a final tax and is charged at 10%. The dividend is not included in the taxpayer's taxable income and the WHT is not deducted from the taxpayer's tax liability.

WHT exemption

As of 1 July 2011, WHT exemption has been re-introduced for compliant taxpayers (since 1 July 2010, issuance of WHT certificates was abolished on supply of goods, including agricultural produce and foodstuffs).

Malawi

Tax administration

Taxable period
The taxable period for income tax is a 12-month period ending on 30 June of each year. For businesses whose year end is 31 July and 31 August, the applicable tax year end is the preceding 30 June, while all the years ending in the subsequent months have the following 30 June as a year end.

Tax returns
Income tax returns are due within 180 days after the end of the financial year.

Payment of tax
Tax is payable in quarterly instalments within 25 days of the month following the end of the quarter, with the balance of the tax being paid upon submission of the return.

Penalties
A penalty for late submission of returns is MWK 200,000.

Audit cycle
The target for the tax authorities is to audit 30% of the taxpayers in any fiscal year. This translates to approximately three years per audit cycle.

Statute of limitations
There is no statute of limitations in Malawi.

Topics of focus for tax authorities
The tax authorities have recently focussed on transfer pricing and have consequently established a unit responsible for this. All multinationals are under scrutiny to check if they are dealing at arm's length with related entities.

Commissioner General's power to increase taxable income
The Commissioner General is empowered to increase the taxable income and liability of a taxpayer when of the opinion that the main purpose or one of the main purposes of a transaction was the avoidance or reduction of tax or where the main benefit that might have been expected to accrue from a transaction was the avoidance or reduction of tax.

M

Malaysia

PwC contact

Jagdev Singh
PricewaterhouseCoopers
Level 10, 1 Sentral
Jalan Travers
Kuala Lumpur Sentral
50470 Kuala Lumpur
Malaysia
Tel: +60 3 2173 1469
Email: jagdev.singh@my.pwc.com

Significant developments

To complement existing legislation, new rules in relation to transfer pricing and advance pricing arrangements were gazetted on 11 May 2012. These rules, which apply to controlled transactions and cross-border transactions respectively, are deemed to have come into operation on 1 January 2009 (*see Transfer pricing in the Group taxation section for more information*).

Taxes on corporate income

For both resident and non-resident companies, corporate income tax is (CIT) imposed on income accruing in or derived from Malaysia. The current CIT rates are provided in the following table:

Type of company	Chargeable income (MYR*)	CIT rate (%)
Resident company (other than company described below)		25
Resident company: • with paid-up capital of MYR 2.5 million or less • that does not control, directly or indirectly, another company that has paid-up capital of more than MYR 2.5 million, and	On the first 500,000	20
• is not controlled, directly or indirectly, by another company that has paid-up capital of more than MYR 2.5 million.	In excess of 500,000	25
Non-resident company		25

* Malaysian ringgit

Petroleum income tax

Petroleum income tax is imposed at the rate of 38% on profits from petroleum operations in Malaysia. No other taxes are imposed on income from petroleum operations.

Corporate residence

A company is tax resident in Malaysia in a basis year (normally the financial year) if, at any time during the basis year, the management and control of its affairs are exercised in Malaysia. Generally, a company is regarded as resident in Malaysia if at any time during the basis period for a year of assessment, at least one meeting of the Board of Directors is held in Malaysia concerning the management and control of the company.

Permanent establishment (PE)

Generally, a non-resident entity is regarded as having a PE in Malaysia if it has a fixed place of business in Malaysia, where the business of the entity is wholly or partly carried on. A non-resident company may also be deemed to have a PE in Malaysia under certain circumstances, such as the following:

- It is represented by a dependent agent in Malaysia, who has the authority to conclude contracts on its behalf and who has repeatedly exercised that authority.
- It carries on supervisory activities in Malaysia for six/nine months in connection with a construction, installation, or assembly project.

Other taxes

Sales tax

A single-stage *ad valorem* tax (sales tax), at rates ranging from 5% to 10%, is imposed on all goods imported into or manufactured in Malaysia, unless specifically exempted.

Service tax

Service tax is imposed at the rate of 6% on the value of taxable services sold or provided by taxable persons. A list of 'taxable services' and 'taxable persons' is found in the Service Tax Regulations 1975.

Goods and services tax (GST)

A GST of 4% was originally expected to be implemented in mid 2011, but its implementation is now delayed indefinitely. The reason reported for the delay is to allow the government more time to engage with the public in order to gather feedback on the implementation of the GST. When implemented, GST will replace the current sales tax and service tax.

Import duties

Import duties are levied on goods that are subject to import duties and imported into the country. Import duties are generally levied on an *ad valorem* basis but may also be imposed on a specific basis. The *ad valorem* rates of import duties range from 2% to 60%. Raw materials, machinery, essential foodstuffs, and pharmaceutical products are generally non-dutiable or subject to duties at lower rates.

Excise duties

Excise duties are imposed on a selected range of goods manufactured and imported into Malaysia. Goods that are subject to excise duty include beer/stout, cider and perry, rice wine, mead, un-denatured ethyl alcohol, brandy, whisky, rum and tafia, gin, cigarettes containing tobacco, motor vehicles, motorcycles, playing cards, and mahjong tiles.

The rate of excise duties vary from a composite rate of MYR 0.1 per litre and 15% of the value for certain types of spirituous beverages, to as much as 105% of the value of motorcars (depending on engine capacity).

Property tax

Property tax is levied on the gross annual value of property as determined by the local state authorities.

Malaysia

Real property gains tax (RPGT)

RPGT is charged upon gains from disposals of real property, which is defined as:

- any land situated in Malaysia, as well as any interest, option, or other right in or over such land, or
- shares in a real-property company (RPC), which is a controlled company holding real property or shares in another RPC or a combination of both, where the total defined value is not less than 75% of its total tangible assets.

RPGT is imposed as follows:

Holding period from date of acquisition	RPGT rate (%)
Up to two years	10
Exceeding two years and up to five years	5
Exceeding five years	0

Stamp duty

Malaysia imposes stamp duty, which is payable by the buyer/transferee, on chargeable instruments. Some examples are provided as follows:

Transaction type	Value chargeable	Stamp duty rate (%)
Sale/transfer of properties (excluding stock, shares, or marketable securities)	Market value	1 to 3
Sale/transfer of stock, shares, or marketable securities	Consideration paid or market value, whichever is higher	0.3
Service/loan agreements	Value of services/loans	0.5

Windfall profit levy

A levy is imposed on crude palm oil and crude palm kernel oil at a maximum of MYR 50 per ton where the price exceeds MYR 2,500 per ton in Peninsula Malaysia, and MYR 3,000 per ton in the states of Sabah and Sarawak.

Contract levy

A levy of 0.125% on contract works having a contract sum above MYR 500,000 is imposed on every registered contractor by the Construction Industry Development Board.

Human resource development levy

Employers engaged in the manufacturing and services sectors that employ more than a specified number of employees must contribute to the Human Resource Development Fund (HRDF). The levy required to be paid is at the rate of 1% of the employees' monthly wages on a monthly basis.

Branch income

Tax rates on branch profits of a company are the same as CIT rates. No tax is withheld on transfer of profits to a foreign head office.

Malaysia

Income determination

Inventory valuation

Inventories are generally stated at lower of cost or net realisable value. Cost may be determined using one of several methods (e.g. unit cost, average cost, or first in first out [FIFO]), as long as the basis used is consistent for each year.

Capital gains

Generally, gains on capital assets are not subject to tax, except for gains arising from the disposal of real property situated in Malaysia, which is subject to RPGT (*see the Other taxes section for more information*).

Dividend income

A single-tier system of taxation came into force on 1 January 2008, replacing the previous dividend imputation system. There is a six-year transitional period (until 31 December 2013) for all companies to migrate into the single-tier system.

Under the dividend imputation system, dividends received from Malaysian companies are taxed at gross value in the hands of shareholders, whether corporate or individuals. Companies distributing dividends are required to deduct tax at source at the prevailing corporate tax rate, from gross dividends payable, but the income tax deducted or deemed deducted is available as a credit against the income tax liability of the shareholder. If a dividend is paid by a company that is subjected to the reduced CIT rate of 20%, tax is deducted or deemed deducted from the dividend at the normal 25% CIT rate.

Under the single-tier tax system, dividends are exempt in the hands of shareholders. Companies are not required to deduct tax from dividends paid to shareholders, and no tax credits will be available for offset against the recipient's tax liability. Corporate shareholders receiving exempt single-tier dividends can, in turn, distribute such dividends to their own shareholders, who are also exempt on such receipts.

Stock dividends

A Malaysian corporation may distribute bonus shares tax-free to shareholders.

Interest income

Interest income accruing in or derived from Malaysia or received in Malaysia from outside Malaysia is subject to CIT. However, exemption is provided on interest income received in Malaysia from outside Malaysia. Other exemptions granted include interest income earned by a non-resident person from deposits placed in designated financial institutions in Malaysia.

Foreign income

Under the Income Tax Act 1967, a Malaysian tax-resident company and a unit trust are not taxed on their foreign-sourced income, regardless of whether such income is received in Malaysia. However, income of a resident company from the business of air/sea transport, banking, or insurance is assessable on a worldwide basis.

Taxation on a worldwide basis does not apply when income attributable to a Labuan business activity of a Labuan branch or subsidiary of a Malaysian bank is subject to tax under the Labuan Business Activity Tax Act 1990. This exception will not apply if the Labuan entity has made an irrevocable election to be taxed under the Income Tax Act 1967 in respect of its Labuan business activity.

Malaysia

In respect of Malaysian-owned banks, insurance companies, and takaful (Islamic insurance) companies, the profits of newly established branches abroad or remittances from new subsidiaries abroad are tax exempt for five years, provided that the applications to establish branches or subsidiaries abroad are received by the Central Bank of Malaysia no later than 31 December 2015.

Relief from double taxation is available by means of a bilateral credit if there is a governing tax treaty or unilateral relief where there is no treaty. The relief is restricted to the lower of Malaysian tax payable or foreign tax paid if there is a treaty, or one-half of the foreign tax paid if there is no treaty.

Undistributed income of foreign subsidiaries is not taxable.

Deductions

Capital allowance
Capital allowance (tax depreciation) on industrial buildings, plant, and machinery is available at prescribed rates for all types of businesses. Initial allowance is granted in the year the expenditure is incurred and the asset is in use for the purpose of the business. Annual allowance at the prescribed rates calculated on cost is given for every year during which the asset is in use at the end of the basis year for the purposes of the business. The following are examples of capital allowance rates currently available:

Qualifying asset	Initial allowance (%)	Annual allowance (%)
Industrial building, whether constructed or purchased	10	3
Heavy machinery	20	20
General plant and machinery	20	14
Furniture and fixtures	20	10
Office equipment	20	10
Motor vehicles*	20	20*
Small value assets of less than MYR 1,000 (subject to a maximum total cost of MYR 10,000)	-	100

* Restrictions apply on maximum qualifying capital expenditure.

Accelerated capital allowance is available for certain types of industrial building, plant, and machinery, some of which includes buildings used as a warehouse, buildings used as a school or an educational institution, computers, information technology equipment, environmental protection equipment, waste recycling equipment, and plant and machinery used in specific industries.

Goodwill
Cost of acquisition of goodwill/amortisation of goodwill is not deductible as these expenses are capital in nature.

Start-up expenses
In general, start-up expenses incurred before the commencement of a trade, profession, or business are capital in nature as they were expended to put the person in a position to earn income. However, there are specific deductions allowed, such as incorporation expenses and recruitment expenses (conditions apply).

Interest expenses

Interest expense is allowed as deduction if the expense was incurred on any money borrowed and employed in the production of gross income or laid out on assets used or held for the production of gross income. Where a borrowing is partly used to finance non-business operations, the proportion of interest expense will be allowed against the non-business income.

Bad debt

Debts must be specifically identified and reasonably estimated to be irrecoverable to qualify for a tax deduction.

Donations to charitable institutions

A deduction is allowed for cash donation to approved institutions (defined) made in the basis period for a year of assessment. The deduction is limited to 10% of the aggregate income of that company for a year of assessment.

Fines and penalties

Fines and penalties are generally not deductible.

Taxes

Taxes on income are generally not deductible, whereas indirect taxes, such as sales tax and service tax, are deductible.

Net operating losses

The carryforward of business losses and capital allowances is not available for deduction in subsequent years of assessment if the company does not meet the conditions of a shareholders' continuity test. However, per policy issued by the Ministry of Finance, these conditions currently apply only to dormant companies. Carryforward of business losses and capital allowances is unlimited in time for non-dormant companies.

Current-year business losses may be utilised against all sources of income. Utilisation of carried-forward losses is restricted to income from business sources only. Utilisation of capital allowance is also restricted to income from the same underlying business source.

Payments to foreign affiliates

A Malaysian company can claim a deduction for royalties, management service fees, and interest charges paid to foreign affiliates, provided that these are made at arm's length and the relevant withholding taxes (WHTs), where applicable, have been paid.

Group taxation

A company that qualifies for group relief may surrender a maximum of 70% of its adjusted loss for a year of assessment to one or more related companies if the following conditions are met by both the claimant and surrendering companies:

* Both must be resident and incorporated in Malaysia.
* Each has paid-up capital of ordinary shares exceeding MYR 2.5 million at the beginning of the basis period.
* Both have the same (12-month) accounting period.
* They are 'related' throughout the basis period for a particular year of assessment as well as the 12 months preceding that basis period.

Malaysia

- Both are not currently enjoying specific stipulated incentives, such as pioneer status, investment tax allowance, reinvestment allowance, etc.

'Related company' is defined by the Income Tax Act 1967 and involves the application of a two-tier test. The companies are regarded as 'related' if:

- either company owns at least 70% of the ordinary share capital of the other company or a third company owns at least 70% of each of the companies, and
- the holders of ordinary shares are entitled to at least 70% of the distributable profits and assets of the company on winding up.

Companies that wish to avail themselves of group relief must make an irrevocable election to surrender or claim the tax loss in the return to be filed with the Inland Revenue Board for that year of assessment.

Transfer pricing

The Director General of Inland Revenue (DGIR) is empowered to make adjustments on transactions of goods and services if the DGIR is of the opinion that the transactions were not entered into on an arm's-length basis.

To complement the above, two new rules were gazetted on 11 May 2012, and both are deemed to have come into operation on 1 January 2009. The transfer pricing rules that apply to controlled transactions (defined) (including financial assistance) specify the methods to determine the arm's-length price and the circumstances under which the DGIR may re-characterise transactions. The advance pricing arrangement rules that apply only to cross-border transactions outline the application procedures for unilateral, bilateral, or multilateral advance pricing arrangements.

Thin capitalisation

A new provision for thin capitalisation was introduced, effective as of 1 January 2009, under which the portion of the interest charge that relates to the amount of financial assistance that is excessive is disallowed as a deduction. However, the implementation of specific rules relating to this provision has been deferred to the end of December 2012.

Tax credits and incentives

Malaysia has a wide variety for incentives covering the major industry sectors. Tax incentives can be granted through income exemption or by way of allowances. Generally, when income is exempted, any dividends paid out of such exempt income are not taxable in the hands of the shareholders. Where incentives are given by way of allowances, any unutilised allowances generally may be carried forward indefinitely to be utilised against future statutory income. The following are the major types of incentives available in Malaysia.

Pioneer status (PS) and Investment tax allowance (ITA)

Companies in the manufacturing, agricultural, hotel, and tourism sectors, or any other industrial or commercial sector, that participate in a promoted activity or produce a promoted product may be eligible for either PS or ITA.

PS is given by way of exemption from CIT on 70% of the statutory income for five years and the remaining 30% is taxed at the prevailing CIT rate. ITA is granted on 60%

qualifying capital expenditure incurred for a period of five years to be utilised against 70% of the statutory income, while the balance 30% is taxed at the prevailing CIT rate.

A company which intends to undertake reinvestment before expiration of its PS or ITA status may opt for reinvestment allowance, provided it surrenders its PS or ITA status.

The PS and ITA incentives are enhanced for the following types of projects:

Qualifying industry	Pioneer status		Investment tax allowance	
	Incentive	TRP (1)	Incentive	TRP (1)
Projects of national and strategic importance involving heavy capital investment and high technology.	100% of SI (2)	5 + 5	100% QCE (3) against 100% SI	5
High-technology companies engaged in areas of new and emerging technologies.	100% of SI	5	60% QCE against 100% SI	5
Companies participating in an industrial linkage programme.	100% of SI	5	60% QCE against 100% SI	5
Companies manufacturing specialised machinery and equipment.	100% of SI	10	100% QCE against 100% SI	5
Existing locally owned companies reinvesting in production of heavy machinery, specialised machinery, and equipment.	70% of increased SI	5	60% new QCE against 70% SI	5
Companies providing technical and vocational training, and private higher education institution providing qualifying science courses.	-	-	100% QCE against 70% SI	10
New companies investing and existing companies reinvesting in utilising oil palm biomass to produce value-added products.	100% of SI	10	100% QCE against 100% SI	5
Small scale companies (defined) that meet with specified conditions.	100% of SI	5	60% QCE against 100% SI	5
Companies investing in new laboratories for testing medical devices (applications from 8 September 2007 to 31 December 2012).	100% of SI	5	60% QCE against 100% SI	5
Companies upgrading existing laboratories for testing medical devices (applications from 8 September 2007 to 31 December 2012).	-	-	60% QCE against 100% SI	5
Hotel operators undertaking new investments in 4 and 5 star hotels in Sabah/Sarawak (applications from 30 August 2008 to 31 December 2013).	100% of SI	5	100% QCE against 100% SI	5
Hotel operators undertaking new investments in 4 and 5 star hotels in Peninsular Malaysia (applications from 8 October 2011 to 31 December 2013).	70% of SI	5	60% QCE against 70% SI	5

M

Malaysia

Qualifying industry	Pioneer status		Investment tax allowance	
	Incentive	TRP (1)	Incentive	TRP (1)
Providers of industrial design services (applications received from 8 October 2011 until 31 December 2016).	70% of SI	5	-	-

Notes

1. Tax relief period (in terms of years).
2. Statutory income.
3. Qualifying capital expenditure.

Special incentive schemes

Reinvestment allowance

A resident company in operation for not less than 36 months that incurs capital expenditure to expand, modernise, automate, or diversify its existing manufacturing business or approved agricultural project is entitled to reinvestment allowance as follows:

- An allowance of 60% of QCE incurred to be utilised against 70% of statutory income. The remaining 30% is taxed as the prevailing CIT rate.
- The 70% restriction does not apply to projects located in the eastern corridor states of Peninsular Malaysia, Sabah, Sarawak, Labuan, the state of Perlis, and Mersing district in Johor (up to year of assessment 2011) or to projects that achieved the level of productivity as prescribed by the Minister of Finance.
- The allowance is given for 15 years from the first year of claim and will be withdrawn if the asset for which the allowance is granted is disposed of within five years.

Approved service projects

A resident company undertaking a project approved by the Minister of Finance in the transportation, communications, utilities, and services subsectors may enjoy the following incentives:

- Investment allowance of 60% of QCE incurred within five years to be utilised against 70% statutory income.
- Alternatively, income tax exemption of 70% of statutory income for a period of five years.
- Buildings used solely for the purposes of such projects qualify for an industrial building allowance.

Export incentives

A resident company engaged in manufacturing or agriculture that exports manufactured products, agricultural produce, or services is entitled for allowances between 10% to 100% of increased exports (subject to satisfying prescribed conditions), which is deductible up to 70% of statutory income.

Regional operations
Operational headquarters company (OHQ)

A Malaysian incorporated company that provides qualifying services to its offices and related companies, within or outside Malaysia, may enjoy CIT exemption for a period of ten years. Income exempted includes business income, interest, royalties, and income from services (not exceeding 20% of total income of qualifying services) provided to related companies in Malaysia.

Expatriates working in an OHQ are taxed only on the portion of chargeable income attributable to the number of days they are in Malaysia. An OHQ is also granted special facilities (subject to minimal conditions) including:

- Approvals for expatriate posts.
- Ability to obtain credit facilities in foreign currency from licensed banks in Malaysia, without approval of the Central Bank of Malaysia.
- Invest freely in foreign securities and lend to related companies outside Malaysia.
- Ability to open foreign currency accounts with licensed banks in Malaysia or banks in Labuan.

International procurement centre (IPC) and Regional distribution centre (RDC)

An IPC engaged in the procurement and sale of raw materials, components, and finished products to its related or unrelated companies within or outside Malaysia may, subject to conditions, enjoy income tax exemption for ten years on income from qualifying activities in respect of export sales.

An RDC operates similarly to an IPC, except an RDC is only allowed to deal with its own brand of goods. The RDC enjoys the same incentives as an IPC.

Other available non-fiscal incentives available to IPC/RDC include:

- Approval for expatriate posts.
- One or more foreign currency accounts for the retention of export proceeds with any licensed commercial bank, without any limit on account balances.
- Ability to enter into foreign exchange forward contracts with a licensed commercial bank to sell forward export proceeds based on projected export.
- Exemption from foreign equity ownership restrictions.

International trading company

International trading companies are exempt for five years on income equivalent to 20% of increased export value, up to a maximum of 70% of statutory income. To qualify for the incentive, the company must meet the following three conditions:

- Be incorporated in Malaysia, with 60% Malaysian ownership.
- Achieve minimum annual sales of MYR 10 million, not more than 20% of which may be derived from the trading of commodities.
- Use local services (banking, finance, and insurance) and infrastructure (local ports and airports) in its operations.

Financial services sector

Islamic securities

Tax deduction is allowed for expenses incurred in the issuance of Islamic securities, including Islamic Securities based on the Wakalah principle, approved by the Securities Commission or the Labuan Financial Services Authority, until year of assessment 2015 only.

M

Malaysia

Islamic banking and takaful business

Effective from year of assessment 2007 until year of assessment 2016, full income tax exemption for ten years is granted to:

- Islamic banks licensed under the Islamic Banking Act 1983, on income from Islamic banking business conducted in international currencies.
- Takaful (Islamic insurance) companies licensed under the Takaful Act 1984, on income from takaful business conducted in international currencies.

Islamic fund management

Full income tax exemption is available on statutory income on management fees received by resident fund management companies for managing funds of foreign and local investors established under Syariah principles (effective from year of assessment 2008 until year of assessment 2016). Such funds must be approved by the Securities Commission.

Special purpose vehicle (SPV) for Islamic financing

An SPV established solely for the purpose of issuance of Islamic securities under the Syariah principles (approved by the Securities Commission or established under the Labuan Companies Act 1990) is not subject to income tax and is not required to comply with administrative procedures under the income tax law. The company that establishes the approved SPV is deemed to be the recipient of the SPV's income and will be taxed accordingly, but that company will be allowed a deduction for the cost of issuance of Islamic securities.

Islamic stock broking company

Establishment expenditure incurred prior to the commencement of an Islamic stock-broking company is allowed as a deduction, provided the company commences business within two years from the date of approval. Applications must be received by the Securities Commission before 31 December 2015.

Treasury management centre (TMC)

It is proposed that locally incorporated companies establishing their TMC (a centre that provides financial and fund management services to a group of related companies within or outside the country) in Malaysia will enjoy the following incentives (applications to be received from 8 October 2011 until 31 December 2016):

- Income tax exemption of 70% of statutory income from qualifying treasury services rendered to related companies for five years.
- WHT exemption on interest payments on overseas borrowings from overseas used for qualifying activities.
- Stamp duty exemption on loan and service agreements for qualifying activities.
- Expatriates working in the TMC are taxed only on the portion of their chargeable income attributable to the number of days they are in Malaysia.

Kuala Lumpur International Financial District (KLIFD)

The KLIFD is a joint property development comprising office towers for finance and banking, residences, and retail spaces in Kuala Lumpur. To accelerate the development of the KLIFD, the following incentives are proposed:

- Full income tax exemption for ten years and stamp duty exemption on loan and service agreements for KLIFD status companies.
- Industrial building allowance and accelerated capital allowance for KLIFD Marquee Status Companies.

- Income tax exemption of 70% of statutory income for five years for property developers in KLIFD.

Real estate investment trusts (REIT)/Property trust fund (PTF)

REIT/PTFs are vehicles that mobilise funds from unit holders comprising individuals and companies for investments in the property sector and related assets. REIT/PTFs are exempted from tax on all income provided that at least 90% of their total income is distributed to unit holders. If the 90% distribution condition is not complied with, all income will be taxed at the prevailing income tax rate at the REIT/PTF level and tax credit will be claimed by the unit holders on distributions received from the REIT/PTF.

Unit holders are taxed as follows:

Unit holders	WHT rate
Individuals (whether resident or non-resident), body of persons, or other unincorporated persons	10% from 1 January 2009 to 31 December 2016
Non-resident company	25%
Resident company	None (income to be included in annual tax return)
Institutional investor (pension fund, collective investment scheme, or other person approved by the Minister of Finance)	10% from 1 January 2009 to 31 December 2016

Other incentives available are:

- Real property gains tax and stamp duty exemptions on disposal/transfer of real property to an REIT/PTF.
- Tax deduction given for consultancy, legal, and valuation service fees incurred on the establishment of an REIT.

Foreign fund management company

A foreign fund management company providing fund management services to foreign clients is taxed at a concessionary rate of 10% in respect of income derived from the management of foreign funds, while income arising from services rendered to clients in Malaysia is taxed at the prevailing CIT rate.

A foreign fund management company is a Malaysian incorporated company licensed under the Capital Markets and Services Act 2007. Its activities are regulated by the Securities Commission.

Export of financial services

Income tax exemption for a period of five years is granted to Malaysian banks, insurance companies, and takaful companies on profits of newly established branches overseas or income remitted by new overseas subsidiaries. Applications to establish new branches or subsidiaries overseas should be received by the Central Bank of Malaysia not later than 31 December 2015.

Venture capital company (VCC)

A VCC investing in a venture company (VC), which is not the VCC's related company at the point of first investment, will be given a deduction on the value of investment made in a VC. Where the deduction is not claimed, the VCC is eligible for the following income tax exemption on income from all sources, other than interest income from savings or fixed deposits, and profits from Syariah-based deposits:

Malaysia

Conditions	Exemption period
• At least 70% of invested funds is invested in VC, or • At least 50% of invested funds is invested in VC in the form of seed capital.	10 years
• At least 30% of invested funds is invested in VC in the form of seed capital, start-up, or early stage financing, and • Applications received by Securities Commission from 30 August 2008 to 31 December 2013	5 years

Special economic regions

The following special economic regions were launched as part of the Malaysian government's plan for regional growth and development:

Economic region	Location	Year of launch
Iskandar Malaysia (formerly known as Iskandar Development Region [IDR]) www.iskandarmalaysia.com.my	Southern Johor	2006
Northern Corridor Economic Region www.ncer.com.my	States of Perlis, Kedah, Penang, and northern Perak	2007
East Coast Economic Region www.ecerdc.com	States of Kelantan, Terengganu, Pahang, and district of Mersing in Johor	2007
Sabah Development Corridor www.sedia.my	Western, central, and eastern regions of Sabah	2008
Sarawak Corridor of Renewable Energy www.sarawakscore.com.my	Central Sarawak	2008

Special incentives, on top of the existing incentives given by the Malaysian government, will be customised for the purpose of each economic region. At present, special legislation has been enacted only in respect of Iskandar Malaysia (IM) to grant the following exemptions/incentives:

Entity	Incentive
IDR status company	10 years income tax exemption on statutory income from the provision of qualifying services to a person situated within designated nodes in the IDR or outside Malaysia. Operations to commence before 31 December 2015.
Developer	Income tax exemption on statutory income from the disposal of rights over land in designated nodes (until year of assessment 2015).
	Income tax exemption on rental or disposal of buildings in designated nodes (until year of assessment 2020).
Development manager	Income tax exemption on statutory income from the provision of management, supervisory, and marketing services to an approved developer (until year of assessment 2020).
Non-resident service provider	Income tax and WHT exemptions on income from technical fees, interest, or royalties received from approved developers in IDR designated nodes or IDR status companies.
Individuals working in IDR	A qualified knowledge worker is taxed at the rate of 15% on chargeable income from employment with a designated company engaged in a qualified activity (e.g. green technology, educational services, healthcare services, creative industries, financial advisory and consulting services, logistics services, tourism). Employment must commence between 24 October 2009 and 31 December 2015.

Information and communication technology

MSC Malaysia
MSC Malaysia is Malaysia's initiative for the global information technology (IT) industry and is designed to be the research and development (R&D) centre for industries based on IT. It is an information communication technology hub equipped with high-capacity global telecommunications and logistics networks. MSC Malaysia is also supported by secure cyber laws, strategic policies, and a range of financial and non-financial incentives for investors. It is managed by the Multimedia Development Corporation (MDeC), a 'one-stop shop' that acts as the approving authority for companies applying for MSC Malaysia status.

MSC Malaysia status is awarded to both local and foreign companies that develop or use multimedia technologies to produce or enhance their products and services as well as for process development. MSC Malaysia companies are eligible for incentives, which include the following:

- PS (five + extendable by five years) of 100% statutory income or ITA of 100% for five years for a new company or existing company on its additional income.
- Eligibility for R&D grants (for majority Malaysian-owned MSC Malaysia company).
- Exemption from indirect taxes on multimedia equipment.
- Unrestricted employment of local and foreign knowledge workers.
- Freedom to source funds globally for investments.
- Protection of intellectual property and cyber laws.
- No censorship of the internet.
- Globally competitive telecommunication tariffs and services guarantees, world-class physical and IT infrastructure, and excellent R&D facilities.

Offshore trading through websites in Malaysia
Income received by companies undertaking offshore trading (buying and selling of foreign goods to non-residents) via websites in Malaysia is taxed at a reduced rate of 10% for a period of five years. The approval of the Minister of Finance must be obtained.

Green incentives

Green Building Index (GBI) certification
A resident in Malaysia awarded a GBI certificate by the Board of Architects Malaysia from 24 October 2009 until 31 December 2014 is granted 100% allowance on qualifying expenditure incurred for the purpose of obtaining the GBI certificate, to be utilised against 100% of statutory income.

Renewable energy source
Companies engaged in generating energy from renewable sources (biomass, hydropower, or solar power) can enjoy the following incentives for applications received before 31 December 2015:

- Full income tax exemption on statutory income for ten years, or
- ITA of 100% QCE against 100% statutory income for five years.

Energy conservation
Companies undertaking contracting service activities to conserve usage of energy can enjoy the following incentives for applications received before 31 December 2015:

Malaysia

- Full income tax exemption on statutory income for ten years, or
- ITA of 100% QCE against 100% statutory income for five years.

Biotechnology industry

Biotechnology industry
Companies undertaking biotechnology activity with approved bionexus status from Malaysian Biotechnology Corporation Sdn Bhd will be eligible for the following incentives:

- Full income tax exemption for ten years from the first year in which the company derives statutory income or ITA of 100% on QCE incurred for a period of five years.
- Concessionary tax rate of 20% on statutory income from qualifying activities for ten years upon expiry of the tax exempt period.
- Accelerated industrial building allowance (over ten years) for buildings used solely purpose of its new business or expansion project.
- Exemption of import duty and sales tax on import of raw materials and machinery.

Research and development (R&D)

Contract R&D company
Companies that provide R&D services to third parties are eligible for:

- full exemption of their statutory income for a period of five years (extendable by five years), or
- ITA of 100% of QCE incurred within a period of ten (extendable by ten years) to be utilised against 70% of statutory income.

R&D company
The ITA incentive is also available to companies undertaking R&D services for their group and third parties.

In-house R&D
Companies undertaking in-house R&D projects are eligible for ITA at the rate of 50% of QCE incurred within a period of ten years.

Commercialisation of resource-based R&D findings
A company that invest for the sole purpose of financing a project on commercialisation of resource-based R&D findings (which is wholly owned by a public research institute or public institute of higher learning in Malaysia) is given a deduction equivalent to the value of that investment.

The subsidiary undertaking the commercialisation of R&D findings is granted 100% tax exemption on statutory income for ten years.

Other incentives

Shipping
A tax-resident person (including a partnership) carrying on shipping business using Malaysian ships is exempt from tax on income. Effective from year of assessment 2012, this exemption is reduced from 100% to 70% of statutory income and determined on a per ship basis. The balance of 30% of statutory income is deemed to be total income chargeable to tax.

Malaysia

Healthcare service providers

A healthcare service provider providing healthcare services to foreign clients (foreign companies, partnership, and citizens) are given income tax exemption equivalent to 100% of the value of increased services to be utilised against 70% of statutory income (year of assessment 2010 to 2014).

Healthcare facilities

Qualifying private healthcare facilities are eligible for 100% tax exemption on statutory income for five years in respect of the construction of hospitals and expansion and refurbishment of existing ones (applications to be made between 1 January 2010 to 31 December 2014).

Foreign tax credit

See Foreign income in the Income determination section for a discussion of the foreign tax credit regime.

Withholding taxes

Corporations making payments of the following types of income are required to withhold tax at the rates shown in the table below. *See Note 5 for other sources of income subject to WHT.*

Recipient	Dividends (1)	Interest (2)	Royalties (3a, 3b)	Special classes of income/ Rentals (4, 5)
Resident corporations	0	0	0	
Resident individuals	0	0/5	0	
Non-resident corporations and individuals:				
Non-treaty	0	0/15	10	10
Treaty:				
Albania	0	0/10	10	10
Australia	0	0/15	0/10	0
Austria	0	0/15	10	10
Bahrain	0	0/5	8 (3c)	10
Bangladesh	0	0/15	0/10	10
Belgium	0	0/10	10	10
Bosnia & Herzegovina *	0	0/10	8	10
Brunei	0	0/10	10	10
Canada	0	0/15	0/10 (3d)	10
China, P.R.	0	0/10	10	10
Chile	0	15	10	5
Croatia	0	0/10	10	10
Czech Republic	0	0/12	10	10
Denmark	0	0/15	0/10	10
Egypt	0	0/15	10	10
Fiji	0	0/15	10	10
Finland	0	0/15	0/10	10
France	0	0/15	0/10	10
Germany	0	0/10	7	7

Malaysia

	WHT (%)			
Recipient	Dividends (1)	Interest (2)	Royalties (3a, 3b)	Special classes of income/ Rentals (4, 5)
Hungary	0	0/15	10	10
India (new agreement)	0	0/10	10	10
Indonesia	0	0/10	10	10
Iran	0	0/15	10	10
Ireland, Republic of	0	0/10	8	10
Italy	0	0/15	0/10 (3d)	10
Japan	0	0/10	0/10	10
Jordan	0	0/15	10	10
Kazakhstan	0	0/10	10	10
Korea, Republic of	0	0/15	0/10	10
Kuwait	0	0/10	10	10
Kyrgyzstan	0	0/10	10	10
Laos	0	0/10	10	10
Lebanese Republic	0	0/10	8	10
Luxembourg	0	0/10	8	8
Malta	0	0/15	10	10
Mauritius	0	0/15	10	10
Mongolia	0	0/10	10	10
Morocco	0	0/10	10	10
Myanmar	0	0/10	10	10
Namibia	0	0/10	5	5
Netherlands	0	0/10	0/8	8
New Zealand	0	0/15	0/10 (3e)	10
Norway	0	0/15	0/10 (3f)	10
Pakistan	0	0/15	0/10	10
Papua New Guinea	0	0/15	10	10
Philippines	0	0/15	0/10	10
Poland	0	0/15	0/10	10
Qatar	0	0/5	8	8
Romania	0	0/15	0/10	10
Russian Federation	0	0/15	10	10
San Marino	0	0/10	10	10
Saudi Arabia	0	0/5	8	8
Senegal *	0	0/10	10	10
Seychelles Republic	0	0/10	10	10
Singapore	0	0/10	8	5
South Africa	0	0/10	5	5
Spain	0	0/10	7	5
Sri Lanka	0	0/10	10	10
Sudan	0	0/10	10	10
Sweden	0	0/10	8	8
Switzerland	0	0/10	0/10	10
Syria	0	0/10	10	10
Thailand	0	0/15	0/10 (3f)	10
Turkey	0	0/15	10	10
Turkmenistan	0	0/10	10	0
United Arab Emirates	0	0/5	10	10
United Kingdom	0	0/10	8	8
Uzbekistan	0	0/10	10	10
Venezuela	0	0/15	10	10

				WHT (%)	
Recipient	**Dividends (1)**	**Interest (2)**	**Royalties (3a, 3b)**	**Special classes of income/ Rentals (4, 5)**
Vietnam	0	0/10	10	10
Zimbabwe *	0	0/10	10	10

Notes

* Treaties pending ratification

Restricted tax treaties dealing with taxation of specific transport operations in international traffic have also been signed with Argentina and the United States.
1. Dividends:
   - A single-tier system of taxation came into force on 1 January 2008 that replaced the full imputation system (see the Income determination section for details).
   - Malaysia has no WHT on dividends in addition to tax on the profits out of which the dividends are declared. Some treaties provide for a maximum WHT on dividends should Malaysia impose such a WHT in the future.
2. Interest:
   - Interest on loans given to or guaranteed by the Malaysian government is exempt from tax.
   - Interest paid to a non-resident by a commercial or merchant bank operating in Malaysia is also exempt from tax.
3. Royalty:
   a. Approved royalty payments under certain treaty provisions are exempt from WHT.
   b. Royalty income received by non-resident franchisors under franchised education scheme programmes by the Ministry of Education is exempted from tax.
   c. Royalty does not include payments in respect of the operation of oil or gas wells, or the extraction of mineral deposits or other natural resources.
   d. Royalty does not include amount paid in respect of motion picture films or of tapes for radio or television broadcasting.
   e. Royalty does not include natural resource royalties.
   f. Royalty does not include royalty paid in respect of (literary or artistic copyrights - Norway only) or of motion picture films or of tapes for television (or radio - Thailand only) broadcasting, or of the operation of a mine, oil well, quarry, or any other place of extraction of natural resources or of timber or other forest produce.
4. Special classes of income:
   - Contract payments to non-resident contractors in respect of services under a contract project are subject to a 13% deduction of tax (10% on account of the contractors' tax liability and 3% on account of their employees' tax liability). This deduction of tax at source does not represent a final tax, which is determined upon the filing of the tax return.
   - Payments made to non-residents in respect of the provision of technical services performed in Malaysia and rental of movable properties are subject to a 10% WHT (unless exempted under statutory provisions for purpose of granting incentives).
5. Other income:
   - WHT is also applied in respect of income of a non-resident from sources other than the following:
     - Sources shown in the preceding table.
     - A business source.
     - An employment source.
   - The rate of WHT on such income is 10%. This is applicable on payments made to residents of all the treaty partners listed, except for certain countries (including Germany, Turkmenistan, Bosnia & Herzegovina, Senegal, and Jordan) where the respective tax treaties have provided for such type of income to be taxed only in the contracting state in which the recipient is resident.

Tax administration

Taxable period

Assessment of income is on a current-year basis. A company is taxed on income from all sources (whether business or non-business) arising in its financial year ending in the calendar year which coincides with that particular year of assessment. For example, a company that closes its accounts on 30 June of each year is taxed on income earned during the financial year ending on 30 June 2012 for year of assessment 2012.

Malaysia

Tax returns

Under the self-assessment system, companies are required to submit a return of income within seven months from the date of closing of accounts. Particulars required to be specified in the return include the amount of chargeable income and tax payable by the company. The tax return is deemed to be a notice of assessment and is deemed served on the company upon the date the tax return is submitted.

'E-filing' or online filing of tax returns via the Internet is available. E-filing is encouraged by the Inland Revenue Board.

Payment of tax

Tax payable under an assessment upon submission of a tax return is due and payable by the last day of the seventh month from the date of closing of accounts.

Companies are required to furnish estimates of their tax payable for a year of assessment no later than 30 days before the beginning of the basis period (normally the financial year). However, a newly established company with paid-up capital of MYR 2.5 million or less that meets with certain specified conditions is exempted from this requirement for two years, beginning from the year of assessment in which the company commences operation. A revised estimate can be submitted in the sixth and ninth months of the basis period for a year of assessment.

Companies are then required to pay tax by monthly instalments (based on the estimates submitted) commencing from the second month of the company's basis period.

From year of assessment 2011, a company commencing operations in a year of assessment is not required to furnish estimates of tax payable or to make instalment payments if the basis period for the year of assessment in which the company commences operations is less than six months.

Statute of limitations

Additional assessments can be made within six years after the expiration of the relevant year of assessment. This time limit is not applicable where fraud, wilful default, or negligence has been committed.

Audit cycle

The tax authorities have issued a Tax Audit Framework that outlines the rights and responsibilities of audit officers, taxpayers, and tax agents in respect of a tax audit. A tax audit may cover a period of one to three years of assessment determined in accordance with the audit focus. The years of assessment to be covered in a tax audit may, however, be extended depending on the issues identified during an audit.

Topics of focus for tax authorities

Some issues that the tax authorities have focused on recently include:

- Deductibility of certain expenses (e.g. entertainment, provisions, management service fees, allocated expenses from foreign related counterparts).
- The correctness of tax incentive claims.

Malta

PwC contact

Neville Gatt
PricewaterhouseCoopers
167 Merchants Street
Valletta VLT1174, Malta
Tel: +356 2564 6711
Email: neville.gatt@mt.pwc.com

Significant developments

A number of changes to Maltese tax legislation were published in 2011, including:

- The EU Directive 2011/96/EU of 30 November 2011 on the common system of taxation applicable in the case of parent companies and subsidiaries of different member states has been fully transposed into Maltese legislation.
- Rules establishing the taxation of securitisation of vehicles have been recently introduced into Maltese tax law. Such rules provide for tax neutrality in respect of a securitisation transaction. In terms of the rules, the income derived by a securitisation vehicle in respect of a securitisation transaction may effectively not be subject to any Maltese income tax.
- Among other double taxation treaties (DTTs) in force with Malta, a new treaty has recently entered into force between Malta and the People's Republic of China. The treaty applies with respect to income derived during taxable years starting on or after 1 January 2012. This new treaty replaces the DTT which was signed in 1993 and is expected to enhance Malta's attractiveness for the purposes of channelling investments in or from China.
- An income tax exemption has been introduced in respect of artistic royalties protected by copyrights. This extends the current exemption applicable on royalties derived from qualifying patents on inventions.
- Legislation providing for the taxation of private foundations that complements the Private Foundation Law embodied within Maltese Civil law.
- Incentives for businesses to regularise their value-added tax (VAT) position by means of the introduction of a scheme whereby businesses may settle VAT dues and pay a reduced amount of penalties and accumulated interest.
- A new scheme has been introduced whereby rental income derived from immovable property that has been restored will be subject to a final withholding tax (WHT) of 10% of the gross rental income received for residential purposes and 15% for commercial purposes.
- A reduced rate of WHT of 10% has been introduced with respect to a transfer of immovable property that has been restored, subject to the satisfaction of certain conditions.

M

Taxes on corporate income

Companies are subject to income tax at a flat rate of 35%. There is no corporation tax structure separate from income tax.

A company incorporated in Malta is considered as both domiciled and resident in Malta and is consequently taxable on a worldwide basis. A non-Maltese incorporated company which is resident in Malta through management and control is subject to Maltese tax on income arising in Malta and on income received in/remitted to Malta.

Malta

Petroleum profits tax
Petroleum profits tax is levied as income tax with similar deductions being allowed in respect of incurred expenditure. In the case of a Production Sharing Contract signed after 1 January 1996, any petroleum profits are taxed at the standard corporate tax rate of 35%. However, all other petroleum profits are subject to a 50% tax rate.

Insurance profits tax
Insurance profits tax is levied as income tax and subject to the normal standard tax rate of 35% as other corporate profits; however, the manner in which such profits are ascertained is subject to a number of detailed rules which take into account the special nature of the insurance industry. In the case of non-resident companies, the computation is applied with reference only to business carried on in or from Malta.

Shipping profits tax
A beneficial tonnage tax regime is applicable under Maltese law. Such regime covers profits from shipping activities as defined under the applicable regulations which are derived by qualifying Maltese-flagged and European Union (EU)/European Economic Area (EEA) vessels as well as non-EU/EEA vessels satisfying certain additional rules. Furthermore, qualifying ship management activities are also entitled to the benefits of the tonnage tax regime. Profits qualifying under the tonnage tax regime may also be distributed tax-free. The related company shares are exempt from the provisions of the Duty on Documents and Transfers Act (stamp duties).

Corporate residence

All companies incorporated in Malta are considered to be both domiciled and resident in Malta. Other bodies of persons (including companies incorporated overseas) are considered to be resident in Malta when the control and management of their business are exercised in the country.

Permanent establishment (PE)
Although Maltese tax legislation contains a number of references to the term 'permanent establishment', the term is not defined by Maltese legislation. Indeed, in terms of Maltese domestic tax law, a non-resident is, in principle, subject to Maltese tax on income arising in Malta, irrespective of the existence or otherwise of a PE in Malta (naturally subject to any DTT provisions, which would apply if in conflict with Maltese tax law).

In the event the Maltese Revenue is required to interpret such a term, reference would typically be made to the definition contained in the Organisation for Economic Co-operation and Development (OECD) Model Convention.

Other taxes

Value-added tax (VAT)
Supplies of goods and services in Malta are subject to VAT at the standard rate of 18% (7% on accommodation in hotels and licensed premises; 5% on supply of electricity, works of art, collector's items and antiques, certain confectionery, medical accessories, printed matter, and items for exclusive use by the disabled). Exports to countries outside the European Union, food, and certain other goods and services are exempt from VAT and provide a right to credit of VAT remitted.

Malta

A government initiative has been recently introduced that results in the reduction of administrative penalties incurred in terms of the Maltese Value Added Tax Act. This VAT amnesty is intended to encourage the submission of outstanding VAT returns, settle tax balances due, and assist businesses to regularise their VAT positions.

Customs duties
Goods imported from outside the European Union may be subject to customs duties. A Customs Code provides for customs procedures and concepts, which are based on European Community requirements.

Excise duties
Excise duties are chargeable on certain energy products, certain alcoholic drinks, certain manufactured tobacco products, and mobile telephony services at a 5% rate (although other rates may apply in different circumstances).

Property transfer taxes
Immovable property situated in Malta is generally subject to a final WHT of 12%, which is, in most cases, charged on the transfer value of the property. The term 'transfer' is attributed a very wide definition and encompasses any alienation of property under any title. There are, however, a number of instances where the transfer of immovable property is taxed under the normal taxing provisions, i.e. mainly the gain (not the transfer value) being chargeable at the corporate tax rate.

Stamp duty
Stamp duty is charged on, among other transactions, transfers of immovable property (5% for both residents and non-residents) and marketable securities (2%; 5% in the case of transfers of shares in property companies). Furthermore, in the event that the market value of shares held by a person is reduced following a change in the company's issued share capital or voting rights and the value shifts onto the other shareholders, the transferor would be deemed to have transferred the said value to the transferee(s) and such value shifting may be subject to a stamp duty liability (although certain exceptions/exemptions may apply).

Maltese legislation also provides for the possibility of a stamp duty exemption in a number of instances, subject to the satisfaction of certain conditions. Some of the more commonly availed of exemptions include the acquisition or disposal of marketable securities by or in the following: (i) licensed collective investment schemes; (ii) licensed persons providing management, administration, safekeeping or investment advice to collective investment schemes; (iii) companies being owned as to more than 50% by non-Maltese residents and satisfying certain other conditions; and (iv) a company that carries on or intends to carry on more than 90% of its business outside of Malta.

Employer's social security contributions
Employers are obliged to pay social security contributions at the rate of 10% of the individual employee's salary and at fixed rates of 37.85 euros (EUR) per week for annual salaries exceeding EUR 20,061, provided the employee is born on or after 1 January 1962 (note that the employee is also required to pay an equivalent weekly amount).

Branch income

The tax rate on branch income is the same as that for resident companies. Other than the tax charged on a branch's income, no tax is withheld on transfers of profits to the head office.

Malta

....

Income determination

Inventory valuation

Inventory valuations are generally made at the lower of cost or market value. In general, the book and tax methods of inventory valuation will conform. However, the last in first out (LIFO) method is not accepted for taxation purposes. Obsolescence is accepted where proven, but there are no provisions to take into account the effects of monetary inflation on the inventory valuation.

Capital gains

Tax is chargeable on capital gains realised on the transfer of immovable property (real estate), shares and other securities, business goodwill, business permits, copyrights, patents, trade names, trademarks, interests in a partnership, and beneficial interests in a trust. In the case of transfers of immovable property, a final WHT of 12% on the transfer value applies. Note that there are certain cases where the 12% final WHT on the transfer value may not apply, and the transfers would be subject to the normal tax on capital gains regime with the chargeable profit being taxed at the taxpayer's applicable rate(s).

No tax is levied on investments that yield a fixed rate of return. A tax exemption applies in certain instances and subject to the satisfaction of certain conditions on the capital gain arising on the transfer of shares in a company listed on a recognised stock exchange other than shares held in certain collective investment schemes. If the capital gain arising on the transfer of listed shares is subject to tax, then special rules apply with respect to the calculation of the gain and such gain would be subject to tax separately at the rate of 15%.

Subject to the satisfaction of certain conditions, if the asset is transferred between group companies, no loss or gain is deemed to arise from the transfer. Note that a provision has been enacted to bring to charge the transfer of shares in property companies (as specifically defined) that were originally subject to intra-group tax deferral when the transferor and the transferee cease to be members of the original group within six years from the date of such intra-group transfer.

Gains realised from the transfer of other assets fall outside the scope of the tax. Gains arising outside Malta and derived by a company that is either not domiciled or not ordinarily resident in Malta are not subject to tax. There are also a number of exemptions provided in the law. For example, capital gains realised by non-residents on transfers of units in Maltese collective investment schemes, similar investments relating to linked long-term insurance business and shares, or securities in Maltese companies (except for companies holding certain Maltese immovable property) are exempt from tax.

Rollover relief

Rollover relief is granted with respect to capital assets used in a business for a period of at least three years and which are transferred and replaced within one year by an asset used solely for similar business purposes (i.e. no tax is chargeable on the capital gain). In such instances, the cost of acquisition of the new asset is reduced by the gain on the transfer of the previous asset which would otherwise have been taxable.

Maltese tax law also provides for the surrendering and claiming of allowable losses between companies that form part of the same group (*see Group taxation for more information*) as well as for reorganisation relief, subject to certain specific conditions.

Dividend income

Dividends received by one resident company from another, whether or not a subsidiary, are taxable on the gross amount in the recipient's hands. If the distributed profits have been taxed, no further tax should be chargeable to the recipient company. However, for resident shareholders, if the corporate rate of tax in the year in which the profits are earned is lower than that in the year in which they are distributed, an amount equivalent to the difference in rates (topping up) is payable. If the distribution is made from untaxed income, the dividend would be tax-free in the hands of the recipient company.

Dividends and gains on disposal of shares received by a corporate investor from a non-resident company (or from a non-resident limited partnership) may qualify for a participation exemption in Malta, subject to the satisfaction of certain statutory conditions.

The participation exemption may also apply to gains upon the disposal of equity holdings in Maltese-resident entities. Distributions of taxed income by Maltese-resident companies are not subject to further tax under the full imputation system.

Stock dividends

A Maltese company may distribute bonus shares from profits, whether of an income or capital nature, and from share premium and capital redemption reserves. When bonus shares represent a capitalisation of profits, they are deemed to be dividends for tax purposes. Such bonus shares are subject to tax in the recipients' hands, gross of any tax paid at the corporate level on the relative profits, but tax credits equivalent to the gross-up of tax are available to stockholders.

Interest income

Interest is chargeable to tax under the provisions of Article 4(1)(c) of the Income Tax Act and subject to the standard corporate tax rate. Nevertheless, in the event the receipt of interest falls within the definition of 'investment income' as established by Maltese tax legislation, a WHT of 15% may be generally applicable. Furthermore, in the case of interest income payable to non-Maltese residents, such interest should be exempt from Maltese tax, subject to the satisfaction of certain statutory conditions.

Foreign income

A company is taxable on its worldwide income when it is ordinarily resident and domiciled in Malta. A company that is either not ordinarily resident or not domiciled in Malta is taxable on its foreign income only insofar as such income is remitted to/received in Malta. Foreign tax is relieved by way of tax credits. This may occur under the terms of a DTT. Where no treaty exists, the foreign tax can be relieved through a system of unilateral relief. Relief for underlying tax is also granted with respect to dividend income, either in terms of a DTT or as unilateral relief. Such relief may be available if, among other things, evidence of tax paid abroad is produced.

Profits of Malta resident companies are subdivided for Maltese tax purposes into five accounts: the Immovable Property Account, the Final Tax Account, the Maltese Taxed Account, the Untaxed Account, and the Foreign Income Account. The last of these includes, among other things, taxable profits of Maltese-resident companies resulting from foreign investments; profits of a foreign permanent establishment (PE); and profits resulting from foreign investments, assets, or liabilities of an onshore bank licensed in Malta. Income allocated to the Foreign Income Account for which no evidence of tax paid abroad is available can qualify for a flat-rate foreign tax credit of 25%.

M

Malta

The Immovable Property Account would include profits and income derived directly or indirectly from immovable property situated in Malta. The Final Tax Account would include, among other items, profits that have been subject to a final tax at source or were exempt from tax and such exemption is extended to shareholders upon a distribution of such profits. The Maltese Taxed Account would include any other taxed profits while the Untaxed Account would represent the difference between the distributable profits and the profits allocated to the other taxed accounts.

Under Malta's system of taxation of dividends, shareholders receiving distributions from the Maltese Taxed Account and/or the Foreign Income Account may be entitled to a tax refund of part or the full tax paid by the distributing Maltese company on such profits being distributed. The tax refund may be either a six-sevenths refund, a five-sevenths refund, a two-thirds refund, or a full refund of the tax suffered by the Maltese distributing company on the distributed profits. The type of the tax refund depends on the nature of the income to be distributed.

Deductions

The basic condition for deductibility of expenses is that deductions are allowable only with respect to expenditures which are wholly and exclusively incurred in the production of income. However, the Maltese Income Tax Act also provides a number of exceptions whereby specific expenses of a capital nature may also be tax deductible, subject to the satisfaction of the statutory conditions applicable thereto. The following are some further comments on specific items of expenditure.

Depreciation and depletion

Tax depreciation is computed on the straight-line method. The rate of depreciation on plant and machinery varies according to the category of the plant and machinery in question.

Maltese tax law prescribes the minimum number of years over which items of plant and machinery are to be depreciated as follows:

Category	Years
Computers and electronic equipment	4
Computer software	4
Motor vehicles	5
Furniture, fixtures, fittings, and soft furnishings	10
Equipment used for constructions of buildings and excavation	6
Catering equipment	6
Aircraft - aircraft airframe	6
Aircraft - engines	6
Aircraft - engine or airframe overhaul	6
Aircraft - interiors and other parts	4
Ships and vessels	10
Electrical and plumbing installations and sanitary fittings	15
Cable infrastructure	20
Pipeline infrastructure	20
Communications and broadcasting equipment	6

Category	Years
Medical equipment	6
Lifts and escalators	10
Air-conditioners	6
Equipment mainly designed or used for the production of water or electricity	6
Other machinery	5
Other plant	10

The wear and tear rate on industrial buildings and structures (including hotels) may not exceed 2% per annum. New acquisitions of industrial buildings and structures are entitled to a concurrent extra 10% allowance in the year of acquisition. Tax depreciation is not required to conform to book depreciation.

The total allowances over the asset's useful life may not exceed 100% of its cost. If a surplus arises on disposal of a tax-depreciated asset, it is either added to the year's income or utilised to reduce the cost of any replacement. If the asset has been under-depreciated, a balancing allowance is granted.

No deduction is available for the depletion of natural resources.

The rules on tax deductions for wear and tear of plant and machinery provide for certain specific treatment in particular situations, including, among other things, the following:

- To establish the cost of an asset when it is transferred between related companies, the lower of the actual cost of the asset or the tax written-down value adjusted by any balancing charge or allowance incurred by the transferring company should be applied.
- Deductions for wear and tear are allowed only where proper records and documentation have been kept that support the cost of the respective assets.
- A proportional deduction is allowed where an asset is used partly in the production of income and partly for other purposes.

Goodwill
In the event that goodwill were to fall within the purport of intellectual property (IP) for the purposes of the tax deductibility rules under Maltese tax law, then it may possibly be argued that an expenditure on goodwill may be tax deductible. However, this would need to be analysed on a case-by-case basis.

Start-up expenses
Certain pre-trading expenses are also allowed as a deduction, subject to the satisfaction of the following conditions:

a. The expenditure is incurred not more than 18 months before the commencement of the trade or business.
b. The expenditure is not deductible in ascertaining the trading or business income of the person carrying on such trade or business but would have been so deductible under (a) above had it been incurred after that time.

In the event the above conditions are satisfied, such expenditure is treated as incurred on the day on which the trade or business is first carried on by the person.

Malta

Interest expenses
Interest on any borrowed money is an allowable deduction if it is paid on capital employed in acquiring income. The expense is allowable even though the borrowing would have been made for a capital purpose, but it is deductible only against the income derived in the same year from the employment of that capital. This special rule is in addition to the deduction for interest paid on money due on revenue account (such interest should be deductible under the general rule of deductibility), such as interest on trade debts or charged on normal business overdraft facilities.

Bad debt
Bad debts incurred in any trade, business, profession, or vocation are allowed in the year they become bad if proved to the satisfaction of the tax authorities. No deduction is given for provisions for bad debts and for bad debts incurred in activities other than a trade, business, profession, or vocation. Any bad debt that is later recovered is deemed as income for the year in which it is received.

Charitable contributions
The general rule is that charitable contributions are not deductible for Maltese tax purposes unless expressly provided for by law.

Fines and penalties
The general rule is that fines and penalties are not deductible for Maltese tax purposes. Nevertheless, there is an exemption to this general rule which provides that interest paid or payable by any person in terms of the Maltese Value Added Tax Act will be treated as expenses incurred in the production of the income of that person for income tax purposes.

Taxes
The typical interpretation is that taxes suffered are not deductible for Maltese tax purposes, although certain exceptions may possibly apply.

Other significant items
Capital expenditures on scientific research, patents, and IP rights are written off over a number of years. In the case of scientific research, a deduction may be granted at 150% of the expenditure.

The Income Tax (Deductions) Rules of 2001 provide for specific conditions on deductions with respect to the use of cars and the payment of employee compensation. The cost on which capital allowances on certain motor vehicles may be claimed is restricted to EUR 14,000 as of year of assessment 2011. Deductions for lease payments on cars are restricted in a manner that corresponds with the stated restriction of EUR 14,000 (also as of year of assessment 2011) that applies to capital allowances on owned cars. With respect to payment of employee compensation, the Deduction Rules require that in order for employee compensation to be allowed as a deduction for tax purposes in the hands of the employing company, it must have been duly accounted for. In particular, the employee compensation must have been reported on the appropriate forms and within the statutory time limit to the Office of Inland Revenue. The rules also provide for restrictions on deductibility of emoluments with respect to the payment of certain fringe benefits to employees.

Net operating losses
Net operating losses may be carried forward indefinitely until absorbed. There is no carryback of losses, not even in terminal years. Unabsorbed capital allowances may be

carried forward only against the same underlying source of income. Where the source ceases to exist, any remaining balance of unabsorbed capital allowances is lost.

Payments to foreign affiliates

There are no restrictions on the deductibility of royalties, interest (except for interest, discount, or premium which are in any manner connected to Maltese immovable property and subject to the satisfaction of certain other statutory conditions, in which case, the interest/discount/premium should not be tax deductible in Malta), and service fees paid to foreign affiliates as long as the particular expenses are considered to be incurred in the production of the particular income and satisfy the applicable statutory conditions. Interest, discount, premium, or royalties derived by non-residents are exempt from tax, subject to the applicable statutory requirements.

Group taxation

Two companies that for tax purposes are resident exclusively in Malta, where one company is a 50% plus subsidiary of the other or both are 50% plus subsidiaries of a third Malta-resident company, qualify as members of a group of companies. Allowable losses may be surrendered by a company to another company within the group where both companies have concurrent accounting periods and form part of such group throughout the entire basis year for which this relief is claimed; however, such surrendering of losses may not occur where the surrendering or claimant company is carrying on the business of insurance. Each company must file a separate tax return, and no combined grouping or consolidated returns are permitted.

Transfer pricing

Malta does not operate a sophisticated transfer pricing regime. There are some general anti-avoidance provisions and brief references to transactions at arm's length. However, the Maltese tax authorities would typically still consider it desirable that transactions between residents and non-residents broadly adhere to the arm's-length principle, that is, prices that would have been concluded between independent enterprises. However, no specific rules are available on the manner in which an arm's-length price is to be established.

Thin capitalisation

The Maltese tax regime does not contain thin capitalisation rules.

Controlled foreign companies (CFCs)

No anti-CFC rules or legislation are applicable in Malta.

Tax credits and incentives

Foreign tax credit

A credit for foreign taxes may be applied against the Maltese tax charge (*see Foreign income in the Income determination section for more information*).

Inbound investment

Investments by foreigners may be readily repatriated together with profits.

The Malta Enterprise Act and other related legislation provide a comprehensive package of incentives for inbound investment. These incentives are reserved for enterprises carrying on certain activities in Malta, mainly manufacturing activities.

Malta

The focus is on high-value-added activities, and approval of a project's eligibility for benefits by the Malta Enterprise may be required. In general, eligibility does not depend on whether the company produces for the local or for export markets. The main tax incentives include the following:

- Enterprises carrying out qualifying activities, which mainly include manufacturing activities, qualify for investment tax credits whereby a percentage of up to 30% (50% in the case of small-sized enterprises and 40% in the case of medium-sized enterprises) of qualifying expenditures are off-set against the tax charge (not against taxable income). Any unused credits are carried forward and added to the credits for subsequent years. The amount carried forward is increased by a percentage rate which is based on EU parameters as updated from time to time.
- Certain tax credits and special incentives may be available, subject to certain conditions. These tax credits are calculated on the basis of specific expenditures incurred by a company while the special incentives grant tax exemptions on all or part of the chargeable income in specified circumstances.
- No further tax is charged on distributions from profits that had previously been taxed at a reduced rate. This benefit is also extended to amounts that were not subject to tax on account of the investment allowance, investment tax credits, and specific tax credits/special incentives.
- A 15.75% tax rate is applicable to profits reinvested in the enterprise, pursuant to a project approved by the Malta Enterprise.
- The combination of certain tax treaties and Maltese domestic law lowers the Maltese tax rate on certain companies receiving certain industrial assistance (i.e. mainly assistance in terms of the Malta Enterprise Act, Business Promotion Act, and Business Promotion Regulations) to 15%.

Capital investment

In the case of qualifying companies, an investment allowance of 50% on plant and machinery and of 20% on industrial buildings and structures may be available (subject to certain capping rules), bringing the total allowances granted during the lifetime of the assets up to 150% and 120%, respectively. Apart from the investment allowances, normal allowances for wear and tear are also available on such assets (*see Depreciation and depletion in the Deductions section for more information*).

International business profits

Tax benefits are available for shareholders with respect to distributions by such companies of specified types of income. A beneficial tax regime is also available in respect of collective investment schemes.

The Maltese fiscal implications relative to trusts vary, depending on a number of circumstances, including: (i) the particulars of the parties involved (e.g. domicile or residence of the trustees or beneficiaries), (ii) the act or event under review (e.g. the settlement of property, transfers of beneficial interests, distributions of trust assets), and (iii) the nature of the trust assets. Furthermore, in certain circumstances, tax transparency provisions are set out in the law, particularly so as to allow, among other things, the application of tax exemptions that would have applied to beneficiaries if there was no trust relationship.

An option exists for a step-up in the cost of acquisition of assets situated outside Malta (including companies) effecting a change in domicile or residence or becoming Maltese companies as a result of cross border mergers.

Any income derived from the ownership, use, or lease of aircraft when such aircraft is employed for international transport shall be deemed to arise outside Malta and hence outside the Maltese tax base, irrespective of the country of incorporation of the aircraft or whether the aircraft calls or operates from Malta.

Withholding taxes

Domestic corporations paying certain types of income are subject to deduction of tax-at-source obligations as follows:

Recipient	Dividends (%) (1)	Interest (%)	Royalties (%)
Resident corporations	35	35 (2)	0
Resident individuals	35	25 (2)	0
Non-resident corporations and individuals:			
Non-treaty	35	0 (3)	0 (3)
Treaty:	(4)	0 (3)	0 (3)
Albania	0		
Australia	0		
Austria	Possible imputation refund of 2.5% of the tax suffered at company level (4)		
Bahrain	0		
Barbados	0		
Belgium	0		
Bulgaria	Possible imputation refund of 5% of the tax suffered at company level (4)		
Canada	0		
China, P.R.	0		
Croatia	0		
Cyprus	0		
Czech Republic	0		
Denmark	0		
Egypt	0		
Estonia	0		
Finland	0		
France	0		
Georgia	0		
Germany	0		
Greece	0		
Hungary	0		
Iceland	0		
India	0		
Ireland	0		
Isle of Man	0		
Italy	0		
Jersey	0		

M

Malta

Recipient	Dividends (%) (1)	Interest (%)	Royalties (%)
Jordan	0		
Korea, Rep. of	0		
Kuwait	Possible imputation refund of 20% to 25% of the tax suffered at company level (4)		
Latvia	0		
Lebanon	0		
Libya	Possible imputation refund of 20% of the tax suffered at company level (4)		
Lithuania	0		
Luxembourg	0		
Malaysia	0		
Montenegro	0		
Morocco	0		
Netherlands	0		
Norway	0		
Pakistan	0		
Poland	0		
Portugal	0		
Qatar	0		
Romania	0		
San Marino	0		
Serbia	0		
Singapore	0		
Slovakia	0		
Slovenia	0		
South Africa	0		
Spain	0		
Sweden	0		
Syria	0		
Tunisia	0		
United Arab Emirates	0		
United Kingdom	0		
United States	0		

Notes

Treaties relating to international air and shipping traffic are in force with Switzerland and the United States.

The numbers in parentheses refer to the following notes:

1. Malta makes no distinction between portfolio and substantial holdings. No additional tax is imposed on distributions other than the tax charged on the company with respect to distributed profits. Under Malta's full-imputation system of taxation of dividends, the corporate tax is assimilated with the personal income tax of the shareholder with respect to the dividend. In the shareholder's hands, the dividend is taxed at the gross amount, and the relevant amount of corporate tax offsets the shareholder's tax liability on income from all taxable sources. Special provisions exist for taxation of distributions from income that would not have suffered tax at the corporate level.
2. Withholding of tax may be required only where the interest is debenture interest or interest on any other loan advanced to a corporation for capital purposes. The WHT is, in effect, a prepayment of the

recipient's final liability because a reassessment on income is made upon the submission of returns. Any resulting overpayment is refunded.

3. Interest and royalty income derived by non-residents is exempt from tax in Malta as long as certain conditions are complied with (e.g. they are not effectively connected to a PE of the recipient situated in Malta).

4. On the basis that Malta operates the full-imputation system of dividends, dividends are not subject to further tax when distributed by a company registered in Malta to a non-Maltese resident. Furthermore, if the rate provided under the Dividends Article in the respective treaty provides for a lower rate than the Maltese corporate tax rate incurred by the company on the respective profits (standard corporate tax rate of 35%), then this may result in a refund of Maltese tax in terms of Malta's full imputation system (such a refund situation may arise in the treaties with Austria, Bulgaria, Kuwait, Libya, and Romania). In a number of treaties, the rate of deduction and of tax is reduced to 15% in the case of companies enjoying certain tax incentives. *See also Note 1 with respect to Malta's full-imputation system of taxation of dividends.*

Tax administration

Taxable period

The year of assessment is a calendar year, but a company may obtain authorisation from the Maltese Revenue to have a different year end (i.e. other than 31 December).

Tax returns

An income tax return for income earned during the previous year must be filed for every year of assessment. The tax return for a company must be submitted by the later of nine months following the end of the financial year or by 31 March following the year of assessment (however, in recent years the Commissioner of Inland Revenue has provided concessionary extensions to such statutory deadlines in the case where the tax return is submitted electronically). Penalties are incurred on late filing of returns. The tax return submitted by the company is a self-assessment, and the Commissioner of Inland Revenue will not raise an assessment unless there is not agreement with the self-assessment.

Payment of tax

Companies pay tax in the currency in which their share capital is denominated.

During the basis tax year, a company is generally required to make provisional tax (PT) payments every four months. In general, the PT payments are based on the last self-assessment filed by the company, and payments are divided into three instalments of 20%, 30%, and 50%, respectively. Any tax liability that is still due at the tax return date after deducting all tax credits must be settled immediately with the submission of the return. Interest at 0.75% per month is charged on any unpaid tax.

In certain instances, especially for companies with mostly international operations, PT may not be payable, and the tax payment is normally paid on the earlier of the date profits are distributed or 18 months after the end of the relative accounting period.

The employer is required to withhold income tax and social security contributions from employees' salaries and pass on such tax/contributions to the Office of Inland Revenue. This system of WHT at source is referred to as the Final Settlement System (FSS), and the employer is legally required to operate such a system. The salary from which the withholding is to be effected should also include the value of any taxable fringe benefits. There are three main categories of fringe benefits: (i) use of motor vehicles, (ii) use of other assets including accommodation, and (iii) other benefits. The method of valuation in each case varies, and the employer is required to refer to the Fringe Benefits Regulations (and also to the fringe benefits guidelines) so as to calculate the

M

Malta

correct value of any fringe benefits being provided to the employees and to deduct the right amount of tax accordingly.

Audit cycle
A company's annual accounts need to be audited on a yearly basis, and certified auditors are required to report to the shareholders on every set of financial statements furnished at a company's annual general meeting.

Statute of limitations
An assessment (as from year of assessment 1999) may be issued by the Maltese Revenue by not later than six years from the end of the respective tax year. In the event of non-full disclosure or wilful incorrect/misleading information, the aforesaid prescription period would not apply.

In respect of the payment of tax, additional tax, interest, or any penalty, an action may be taken during any time from the date on which it becomes due and payable up to eight years from that date or, where an assessment in respect thereof has been made, from the date on which that assessment becomes final and conclusive.

Topics of focus for tax authorities
We are not aware of any particular topics of focus by the Maltese tax authorities. One might say that typically the Maltese Revenue is particularly wary with respect to activities and transactions concerning immovable property situated in Malta.

Mauritius

PwC contact

Anthony Leung Shing
PricewaterhouseCoopers
2rd floor
HSBC Centre
18 Cybercity, Ebène
Mauritius
Tel: +230 404 5071
Email: anthony.leung.shing@mu.pwc.com

Significant developments

New withholding tax (WHT) rates were enacted in the past year. *See the Withholding taxes section for a table of current rates.*

Taxes on corporate income

A corporation resident in Mauritius is subject to tax on its worldwide income. A non-resident corporation is liable to tax on any Mauritius-source income, subject to any applicable tax treaty provisions. Corporations are liable to income tax on their net income, currently at a flat rate of 15%.

Mauritius has a credit system of taxation whereby foreign tax credit is given on any foreign-source income declared in Mauritius on which foreign tax of similar character to Mauritian tax has been imposed. All corporate bodies incorporated in Mauritius (except companies holding a Category 2 Global Business Licence) are subject to income tax. This applies to all associations and other registered bodies. Income derived by local partnerships is shared and taxed in the hands of the partners. Foreign corporations carrying on business, or having a place of business, in Mauritius are also liable to income tax on income derived from Mauritius.

Income tax is payable on total net income before distribution at the following rates:

Entity	Rate (%)
Global Business Category 1 (GBC1) companies and offshore trusts (*see below*)	15
Freeport operators carrying on Freeport activities other than providing goods and services on local markets	Exempt
All other companies	15

* The normal tax rate will then apply after the exemption period.

Global Business Category 1 (GBC1) companies are liable to tax at the rate of 15%. However, they are entitled to a foreign tax credit equivalent to the higher of 80% of the Mauritius tax chargeable or the actual tax suffered abroad in respect of the foreign-source income.

Global Business Category 2 (GBC2) companies incorporated under the laws of Mauritius are exempt from income tax and are not tax residents for treaty purposes. *For more information, see the Tax credits and incentives section.*

Mauritius

Alternative minimum tax (AMT)

Companies paying or declaring dividends must pay tax either under the normal rules or an AMT, whichever is higher.

AMT is calculated where the normal tax payable for an income year by a company is less than 7.5% of its book profit. The AMT is the lesser of 7.5% of its book profit or 10% of dividends declared in respect of that year.

Book profit is the profit computed in accordance with internationally accepted accounting practices, excluding:

- dividends received from resident companies
- profits or loss on disposal of fixed assets, and
- profits or gains or loss from sale of securities.

AMT does not apply to the following:

- Companies which have not declared any dividend.
- Companies which are exempt from payment of tax.
- GBC1 companies.
- Where the amount representing 10% of dividends declared does not exceed the normal tax payable.

Special levies

Banks

All banks are required to pay a special levy calculated according to their book profit and their operating income derived during the preceding year. 'Operating income' means the sum of net interest income and other income before deducting non-interest expense.

The rates of the special levy on banks are as follows:

Year of assessment commencing	Rates
1 January 2011	3.4% on book profit; 1.0% on operating income
1 January 2012	3.4% on book profit; 1.0% on operating income
1 January 2013 and subsequent years	1.7% on book profit; 0.5% on operating income

One-off charge on banks

Every bank, except the Development Bank of Mauritius, has to create a one-off charge in the year immediately preceding the year of assessment 2012 for an amount equivalent to:

- 0.5% of the turnover and
- 1.25% of the book profit relating to the banking transactions with persons, other than non-residents and companies holding a Global Business Licence under the Financial Services Act.

The fund created is used to finance the new equity fund referred to in the Ministry's document entitled 'Facing The Euro Zone Crisis and Restructuring for Long Term Resilience' during the year immediately preceding the year of assessment 2012.

Where the amount used to finance the private equity fund is less than the one-off charge, the difference shall be remitted to the Mauritius Revenue Authority (MRA) on submission of the return for the year of assessment 2012.

Telephony service providers

Providers of public fixed or mobile telecommunication networks and services (including information and communication services such as value added services and mobile internet) are liable to a solidarity levy. The solidarity levy is calculated according to the book profit and turnover for the preceding income year of the operator. The applicable rates are as follows:

Years of assessment commencing on 1 July 2009, 1 January 2011, 1 January 2012, and 1 January 2013: 5% of the book profit and 1.5% of the turnover of the operator.

'Book profit' means the profit derived by an operator from all its activities and computed in accordance with International Financial Reporting Standards (IFRS).

Corporate Social Responsibility (CSR) Fund

Every year, a company has to set up a CSR Fund equivalent to 2% of its chargeable income of the preceding year to:

* implement an approved programme by the company
* implement an approved programme under the National Empowerment Foundation, or
* finance an approved non-governmental organisation (NGO).

Note that the following entities are not subject to the CSR regulations:

* A company holding a GBC1 Licence under the Financial Services Act;
* A bank holding a banking licence under the Banking Act, in respect of its income derived from its banking transactions with non-residents or with corporations holding a Global Business Licence under the Financial Services Act.
* An IRS company referred to in the Investment Promotion (Real Estate Development Scheme) Regulations 2007.
* A non-resident *société*, a trust, or a trustee of a unit trust scheme.

The CSR contribution is either disbursed by the company on approved projects/NGOs or remitted to the MRA if not expensed fully or paid into the CSR Fund. The CSR Fund is managed by government, and its specific objectives are to:

* encourage companies to manage their own programmes, impacting the intersection of economic with social and environmental development, and
* facilitate the contribution of companies to support existing Approved National Programmes implemented by companies, national agencies, or NGOs.

Local income taxes

Local income taxes levied by local administration, such as urban councils, do not exist in Mauritius.

Mauritius

Corporate residence

Under domestic law, a company is resident in Mauritius for tax purposes if it is incorporated in Mauritius or centrally managed or controlled in Mauritius.

A GBC2 company is not considered a resident in Mauritius for the purposes of double taxation treaties (DTTs).

Under a tax treaty, a company is considered a resident in Mauritius if it is incorporated in Mauritius or if its effective management is in Mauritius.

Permanent establishment (PE)

Generally, a PE is created under a tax treaty if one of the following criteria is met:

- Branch, office, factory, workshop, or installation used for extraction of natural resources.
- Building site, construction, installation, assembly, or supervisory services where the activity on the site lasts for a minimum of six months or 12 months, depending on the tax treaty.

Other taxes

Value-added tax (VAT)

VAT is charged by VAT-registered entities at the standard rate of 15% on all goods and services supplied by them in Mauritius (except those taxed at 0%), other than the following exempt supplies (not an exhaustive list):

- Rice, bread, butter.
- Medical, hospital, and dental services, including clinical laboratory services, services provided in a health institution, and veterinary services.
- Educational and training services provided by institutions approved by the Mauritius Qualification Authority.
- Construction of building for residential purpose, provided letter of intent relating to an Integrated Resort Scheme was issued prior to 1 October 2006.
- Sale or transfer of an immovable property, a building or part of a building, apartment, flat, or tenement.
- Banking services, except:
  - services provided to merchants accepting credit/debit card
  - services in respect of safe deposit locker, and issue and renewal of credit/debit cards
  - services for keeping and maintaining customer's accounts, and
  - services supplied by a bank holding a banking licence under Banking Act 2004 in respect of its banking transactions with non-residents and corporations holding a Global Business Licence.

An entity should register for VAT if turnover exceeds 2 million Mauritian rupees (MUR) a year. However, certain service providers (e.g. accountants and auditors, attorneys and solicitors, consultants, surveyors, valuers) should register for VAT irrespective of their turnover.

Customs duties

Customs duty is levied on commodities imported into Mauritius. The rate of duty applicable is the rate in force under the Customs Tariff Act at the time the bill of entry is validated at the Customs.

An excise duty is also levied at the time of importation on selected commodities, which includes spirits, vehicles, and petroleum products.

A number of exemptions and concessions are available to industries, organisations, and persons under the Customs Tariff Act.

Land transfer tax

Land transfer tax is levied on the transfer of land (excluding the value of any building thereon) and is payable by the transferor at the following rates.

- If the land was held by the transferor for a period of more than five years: 5% of the transfer value.
- If the land was held by the transferor for a period not exceeding five years: 10% of the transfer value.

Land transfer tax is also payable at the above rates by the transferor upon transfer of the shares of a company owning immovable properties based on the value of shares or property, whichever is the lower.

Leasehold tax

Leasehold tax is levied on the registration of a deed of transfer of leasehold rights in state land. Both the lessor and the lessee are liable to leasehold tax at the rate of 10% on the open market value of the leasehold right at the time of transfer.

M

Registration duty

The Registration Duty Act provides for a duty at an effective rate of 5% on the value of transfer of any immovable property. The duty is payable by the transferee at the time of the transfer.

The transfer of shares of a company other than those listed on the Stock Exchange of Mauritius or traded on the secondary market is subject to registration duty if the company holds immovable property.

The following transactions are not subject to registration duty:

- A transfer of immovable property from ascendant to descendent (or vice versa).
- A transfer of property made to a company holding a letter of approval for the implementation of a project under the Real Estate Development Scheme, provided that the transferor holds shares in the company equivalent to at least the value of the land transferred.
- A transfer of immovable property or shares between companies forming part of a group of companies, as defined in the Companies Act 2001.
- A transfer of immovable property where such transfer takes place between companies having the same shareholders for the sole purpose of merging.

Mauritius

Stamp duty

Stamp duty is levied and paid to the Registrar General on every document at the time of registration, transcription, inscription, or erasure of inscription. Stamp duty varies from MUR 25 to MUR 1,000.

Branch income

Tax rates on branch income are the same as on corporate profits. No tax is withheld on the remittance of profits by way of dividend to a head office.

Income determination

Inventory valuation
Inventories should be valued at the lower of historical cost or net realisable value. The last in first out (LIFO) basis of valuation is not allowed for tax purposes.

Conformity is required between book and tax reporting. Where the revenue authority is not satisfied that the basis of valuation is acceptable (e.g. where the LIFO basis has been applied) it will make such adjustment as it believes is appropriate to determine the profits arising from the business carried on.

Capital gains
There is no tax on capital gains in Mauritius. However, certain transactions are taxed as ordinary business profit instead of capital gains. Where a transaction is in the nature of trade, the revenue authority may take the view that it is an ordinary trading transaction and assess the gains derived as income.

Any gains derived from the sale of shares held for less than six months are classified as trading income and are therefore taxed as ordinary income.

Gains realised from the sale of any property or interest in property acquired in the course of a business, as part of a profit-making undertaking or scheme, are taxable as ordinary income.

Dividend income
Companies, whether resident or not, are exempt from tax on dividends received from resident companies.

Dividend income received from abroad by a company resident in Mauritius (non-GBC1 company) is subject to tax at the rate of 15%. Credit for any foreign tax withheld is given, subject to documentary evidence provided to the MRA.

Dividend income received from abroad by a GBC1 company is subject to tax at an effective rate of 3%.

Stock dividends
A resident company can distribute stock dividends (bonus shares) proportionately to all of its shareholders. Stock dividends per se or convertible into cash are not taxable in the hands of the recipient. Dividends in kind (i.e. other than cash or shares) are treated as taxable benefits.

Mauritius

Interest income

Interest income received by resident companies (non-GBC1 companies) is liable to tax at the rate of 15%.

A GBC1 company receiving interest income from abroad is liable to tax at the effective rate of 3%.

As of 1 March 2012, interest income received by non-residents is liable to WHT at the rate of 10% (final tax).

Interest paid by a GBC1 company to a non-resident is exempt from tax.

Foreign income

Resident corporations are taxed on their worldwide income, but tax credit and treaty relief is generally available in order to avoid double taxation (*see Foreign tax credits in the Tax credits and incentives section for more information*).

Undistributed income of foreign subsidiaries is not subject to any special taxation as long as the income of the foreign subsidiary before distribution is not included in the accounts of the local parent company. Dividends paid by the foreign subsidiary to the local parent company will, however, be taxable to the latter, whether or not such dividends are actually received in Mauritius.

Deductions

Depreciation

Annual allowance rates vary between 5% and 100% of base value (unless stated otherwise), as per the following table:

	Rate of annual allowance	
	Percentage of	
Capital expenditure incurred on	Base value	Cost
Industrial premises excluding hotels		5
Commercial premises		5
Hotels	30	
Plant or machinery		
Costing MUR 30,000 or less		100
Costing more than MUR 30,000		
Ships or aircrafts	20	
Aircrafts and aircraft simulators leased by a company engaged in aircraft leasing		100
Motor vehicles	25	
Electronic and high precision machinery or equipment, computer hardware and peripherals, and computer software	50	
Furniture and fittings	20	
Other	35	
Improvement on agricultural land for agricultural purposes	25	
Scientific research	25	
Golf courses	15	

M

Mauritius

	Rate of annual allowance	
	Percentage of	
Capital expenditure incurred on	Base value	Cost
Acquisition or improvement of any other item of a capital nature that is subject to depreciation under the normal accounting principles	5	

Tax depreciation need not conform to book depreciation. Depreciation is generally recaptured on disposal or sale when balancing charges or allowances are computed.

Leasing agreements
There has been a substantial increase in leasing activity over the last decade. Where an asset is transferred under a financial lease agreement, the lessee is entitled to capital allowances on the value of the asset, including finance charges, as if it was an outright sale by the lessor.

On the other hand, the lessor cannot capitalise the leased assets in its books, and no capital allowance is claimed on the assets leased. However, the lessor is taxable on the interest income derived from the assets leased.

There are no special rules for operating leases.

Set-up costs
Set-up costs are not allowed for tax purposes as they are considered as pre-operational expenses.

Interest expenses
Expenditure incurred on interest is deductible, provided it is incurred in respect of capital employed exclusively in the production of income.

Mauritius tax law does not provide for thin capitalisation rules, which require companies to maintain a prescribed ratio of share capital to loan capital.

Bad debts
A provision for bad or doubtful debts is generally not deductible unless a court ruling has been obtained against the debtor.

Contributions to charitable institutions
Donations/gifts, whether to charitable institutions or not, are not allowed for tax purposes.

Fines and penalties
Fines and penalties are not allowed for tax purposes as they are expenses not exclusively incurred for the production of gross income

Taxes
Income taxes and foreign taxes paid are not normally deductible; however, some taxes (e.g. municipal taxes relating to buildings, land transfer tax, irrecoverable input VAT) are deductible.

Other significant items
A bank or an approved financial institution may claim as deductions any irrecoverable loans due by a company in liquidation in respect of which winding-up procedures have started or by a company in receivership.

Net operating losses
Losses made in an accounting year are carried forward for a maximum of five years, provided the corporation can demonstrate a 50% continuity of shareholding between the year of loss and the year of claim. Losses resulting from capital allowances can be carried forward indefinitely. Loss carrybacks are not permitted.

Where a company takes over another company engaged in manufacturing activities, any unrelieved loss of the acquiree may be transferred to the acquirer in the income year in which the takeover takes place, on such conditions relating to safeguard of employment as may be approved by the Minister of Finance.

Payments to foreign affiliates
Royalties, interest, and service fees payable to foreign affiliates are allowed as expenses, provided they correspond to actual expenses incurred, are reasonable, and do not exceed what would be paid under an arm's-length agreement. There are certain limitations if the recipient of the interest is not liable to Mauritius tax. Royalties paid to non-residents by GBC1 companies, banks out of their foreign-source income as defined in the Income Tax Act, and trusts are tax-exempt.

Group taxation

M

There are no group taxation provisions in the Mauritius tax legislation other than the transfer of losses by tax incentive companies, sugar factory operators, subsidiaries located in the Island of Rodrigues, and manufacturing companies upon their take-over (*see Net operating losses in the Deductions section for more information*).

Transfer pricing
Mauritius does not have any specific transfer pricing legislation. However, it does contain an arm's-length provisions requiring transactions between related parties to reflect a commercially objective value which would be the amount charged for the services were the parties not connected.

Thin capitalisation
Mauritius does not have specific thin capitalisation legislation; however, it does have other anti-avoidance provisions.

Tax credits and incentives

Global Business Category 1 and 2 companies
Since January 2011, a GBC1 company can now trade with a Mauritian resident as well as non-residents. Transactions made with a Mauritian resident will be taxed at the rate of 15% whereas transactions with non-residents are taxed at an effective tax rate of 3%.

The registration and application of GBC1 companies should be submitted to the Financial Services Commission (FSC) through a duly licensed Management Company on a prescribed form accompanied by the following:

Mauritius

- The certified supporting documents.
- The applicable processing fees and relevant fees.

A GBC1 company is tax resident in Mauritius and may apply for a Tax Residence Certificate (TRC) from the Director General of the MRA should this be required by the tax authorities in the jurisdiction in which the company is conducting its business.

Investors may benefit from an extensive network of double taxation agreements (DTAs). Entities holding a GBC1 Licence wishing to avail to the benefits of a tax treaty must obtain a TRC issued by the MRA.

A GBC1 company is encouraged to have more substance in Mauritius by ascertaining the following:

- It has at least two directors, resident in Mauritius, of sufficient caliber to exercise independence of mind and judgment.
- It maintains at all times its principal bank account in Mauritius.
- It keeps and maintains, at all times, its accounting records at its registered office in Mauritius.
- It prepares, or proposes to prepare, its statutory financial statements and causes or proposes to have such financial statements to be audited in Mauritius.

A GBC1 company can apply for a TRC to show substance in Mauritius. The TRC is generally issued within a period of seven days from the date of application, provided that the person has submitted the return required under the Income Tax Act 1995.

A GBC2 company is required to have, at all times, a registered agent in Mauritius. Only a management company shall act as the registered agent of a company holding a GBC2 Licence. A GBC2 company is defined as a resident corporation conducting business outside Mauritius and can engage in activities other than the following:

- Banking.
- Financial services.
- Holding, managing, or otherwise dealing with a collective investment fund or scheme as a professional functionary.
- Providing registered office facilities, nominee services, directorship services, secretarial services, or other services for corporations.
- Providing trusteeship services by way of business.

An applicant for a GBC2 Licence must submit the following forms/documents to the FSC through a management company:

- The application form, duly filled in and signed.
- The certified supporting documents.
- The applicable processing fees and relevant fees.

The fees payable to the FSC for registering a GBC1 and a GBC2 company are as follows:

Fee	GBC1 (USD*)	GBC2 (USD)
Processing	500	100
Annual Licensing	1,750	235

* United States dollars

Mauritius

The TRC is renewable on an annual basis and issued in respect of a particular country.

A GBC2 company is a limited liability company incorporated in Mauritius. However, GBC2 companies are exempt from Mauritius tax and are not required to file tax returns. GBC2 companies are therefore not able to access the tax treaty network of Mauritius.

Companies in the Freeport zone
The income of a Freeport operator derived from Freeport activities is exempt from income tax, except income that is derived from goods or services provided on the local market.

Income tax exemption for vessel owners
Owners of foreign vessels registered in Mauritius are exempt from income tax on income derived from such vessels. Owners of local vessels registered in Mauritius are also exempt to the extent that the income is derived from deep-sea international trade.

Foreign tax credits
Generally, double taxation is avoided by means of a unilateral credit relief for foreign tax paid. The net amount of foreign income that has borne tax is grossed up at the foreign rate of tax, and the foreign tax paid is allowed as a credit against the Mauritius tax payable. However, the tax credit cannot exceed the Mauritius tax referable to the relevant foreign income. Unused credit is not refunded.

Regarding foreign income derived from countries with which Mauritius has treaties for the avoidance of double taxation, a tax credit is given for foreign tax in accordance with the treaties. There are clauses in the double taxation conventions which provide that income arising from certain specified foreign sources is to be exempt from Mauritius tax.

Mauritius has signed double taxation conventions with Bangladesh, Barbados, Belgium, Botswana, the People's Republic of China, Croatia, Cyprus, France, Germany, India, Italy, Kuwait, Lesotho, Luxembourg, Madagascar, Malaysia, Mozambique, Namibia, Nepal, Oman, Pakistan, Qatar, Rwanda, Senegal, Seychelles, Singapore, South Africa, Sri Lanka, Swaziland, Sweden, Thailand, Tunisia, Uganda, the United Kingdom, United Arab Emirates, and Zimbabwe.

Three treaties await ratification: Congo, Russia, and Zambia.

Five treaties await signature: Egypt, Ghana, Kenya, Malawi, and Nigeria.

13 treaties are being negotiated: Algeria, Burkina Faso, Canada, Czech Republic, Greece, Monaco, Portugal, Republic of Iran, Saudi Arabia, St. Kitts and Nevis, Tanzania, Vietnam, and Yemen.

A GBC1 company may, in the absence of evidence of payment of foreign tax, claim as tax credit (presumed tax credit) an amount equal to 80% of the Mauritius tax chargeable on the foreign-source income. The presumed tax credit may also be claimed by a bank against the tax payable on income derived from banking transactions with non-residents and with GBC1 and GBC2 companies.

In the case of foreign dividends, the general tax credit includes foreign tax imposed on the profits out of which the dividends are paid (underlying tax), provided that the shareholding in the foreign company is at least 5%.

Mauritius

Mauritius also allows a tax-sparing credit under its local tax legislation.

Withholding taxes

There is no WHT in Mauritius for payments made by GBC companies to non-residents not carrying out any business in Mauritius. There is no WHT on dividends received from resident companies. The table below shows the rates of WHT applicable for the following payments:

Payment	WHT (%)
Interest payable to a non-resident (other than interest paid by banks)	10
Royalties payable to:	
Resident	10
Non-resident	15
Rent	5
Payments to contractors and sub-contractors	0.75
Payments to providers of services (architect, attorney/solicitors, barrister, dentist, doctor, engineer, land surveyor, legal consultant, project manager in the construction industry, quantity surveyor)	3
Payment made by ministry, government department, local authority, statutory body, or the Rodrigues Regional Assembly on contracts, other than payments to contractors and subcontractors and payments to providers of services as specified at point above.	
For the procurement of goods and services under a single contract, where the payment exceeds MUR 300,000	1
For the procurement of goods under a contract, where the payment exceeds MUR 100,000	1
For the procurement of services under a contract, where the payment exceeds MUR 30,000 rupees	3
Payments made to the owner of an immovable property or agent	5
Payments made to a non-resident for any services rendered in Mauritius	10

Tax administration

Taxable period

Companies are assessed for a year beginning 1 January and ending 31 December on their income for the preceding year ending 31 December. Where a company closes its accounts at a date other than 31 December, it may elect to adopt as a basis year the accounting year ending in the 12-month period preceding the year of assessment.

Tax returns

Every company, both taxpayer and non-taxpayer, must file a return of its income on the basis of the income year preceding the year of assessment. The return must be filed within six months of the financial year-end.

Payment of tax

Any tax due should be paid when the return is filed and within the six months deadline.

Penalties

If timely payment is not made, a penalty representing 5% of the amount of tax due is payable. In addition, interest at the rate of 1% of the tax unpaid for each month or part of a month is payable until the tax is paid. A penalty of MUR 2,000 for each month or part of a month is also prescribed for failure to file a return, subject to a maximum of MUR 20,000.

Tax audits

Tax audits are carried out on a sample basis throughout the year. Generally, the audits are fairly detailed, but more protracted enquiries are carried out into cases where fraud is suspected.

Statute of limitations

While there is no statutory time limit for recovering tax already assessed, the Director General is barred from making an assessment for a period beyond four years preceding the current tax year.

M

Mexico

PwC contact

Mauricio Hurtado
PricewaterhouseCoopers
Mariano Escobedo No. 573
Col. Rincón del Bosque
CP 11580 México, DF
México
Tel: +52 55 5263 6045
Email: mauricio.hurtado@mx.pwc.com

Significant developments

On 10 October 2011, modifications to the Miscellaneous Foreign Trade rules were published in Mexico's Official Gazette and included a kind of clarification on the value-added tax (VAT) triggered on *Maquiladora* (IMMEX program) structures. The sale of a virtually exported good to a Mexican resident will be considered a domestic sale subject to VAT withholding, to be remitted by the Mexican resident purchaser of the good.

On 30 June 2011, the Mexican Tax Authorities (Hacienda) issued a comprehensive study on the performance of the flat tax and the possible repeal of certain chapters of the Income Tax Law to include them in the flat tax law with the purpose of having a unified tax law on net income. According to the study, the flat tax has achieved the government's goals and has become an important part of the tax structure in Mexico. However, the study recommended the continued application of the flat tax in coexistence with the income tax. Moreover, Mexico has negotiated the inclusion of the flat tax within its tax treaties.

The government believes that the current tax structure is adequate for the current circumstances. According to the study, the elimination of the corporate income tax (CIT) would produce several adverse consequences not only for taxpayers in Mexico but also to the Mexican economy.

On 30 March 2012, the Mexican government published in the Official Gazette a Decree intended to reduce the administrative tax burden for taxpayers. The Decree compiles several tax benefits that were spread out in different Decrees previously published. In addition, the Decree provides other measures to simplify the tax administration for certain qualified taxpayers.

As of 1 January 2012, the federal tax on the ownership of vehicles was abolished; however, the states may impose a similar tax.

In 2012, the tax authorities released criteria to determine whether a foreign tax can be claimed as a foreign tax credit.

Taxes on corporate income

Federal corporate income tax (CIT)
The CIT applies to Mexican resident taxpayers' income from worldwide sources, as well as to foreign residents on the income attributed to their permanent establishments (PEs) located in Mexico.

The federal CIT rate for 2012 is 30%. Beginning in 2013, the rate will drop to 29% and then back to 28% (as was in force until 2009) in 2014.

All corporate entities, including associations of a civil nature, branches, etc. are subject to the tax rules applicable to Mexican corporations (unless specifically ruled out, such as not-for-profit organisations).

The CIT rate applicable to taxpayers engaged exclusively in agriculture, livestock, fishing, and forestry activities is currently 21%.

Provisions to recognise the effects of inflation for tax purposes in the areas of monetary assets and liabilities (annual monetary adjustment) and depreciable assets are provided in the income tax law, even though recent inflation rates have been decreasing.

Once a corporation has paid its CIT, after-tax earnings (i.e. earnings arising from the after-tax earnings account, *Cuenta de Utilidad Fiscal Neta* or CUFIN) may be distributed to the shareholders with no tax charge at the corporate level and without income tax withholding, regardless of the tax residence of the recipient.

Nonetheless, if a corporation makes a distribution out of earnings that for any reason have not been subject to CIT, such as distributions of book earnings (i.e. not yet recognised for tax purposes in Mexico), the corporation will be subject to CIT on the grossed-up distributed earnings (gross-up factors are: 1.4286 in 2012, 1.4085 in 2013, and 1.3889 as from 2014).

Tax paid on dividends distributed in excess of CUFIN can be credited against the CIT of the year or in the two fiscal years following the year in which the tax on the non-CUFIN distributions was paid. The CUFIN of the tax years in which the credit is applied must be reduced by an amount equal to the grossed-up dividend distribution.

M

Federal flat tax

The flat tax applies to Mexican resident taxpayers' income from worldwide sources, as well as to foreign residents on the income attributed to their PEs located in Mexico. The current flat tax rate is 17.5% and is applied to the flat tax base.

In general, the flat tax base is the excess of income actually collected relating to: (i) the sale or disposal of property, (ii) the provision of independent services, and (iii) the granting of temporary use or enjoyment of assets (i.e. rental income and unrelated party royalty income) over amounts actually paid for: (i) the acquisition of assets, (ii) the receipt of independent services, and (iii) the temporary use or enjoyment of assets, as well as certain (iv) other cash expenses, with the exceptions noted below. Even though there are no tax losses for flat tax purposes, a tax credit (with similar results to the application of net operating losses) may be available where flat tax deductions exceed income in a fiscal year, provided certain conditions are met. This credit may be used against flat tax liabilities for the subsequent ten years.

Salaries and wages, employer contributions to the social security system, non-taxable employee benefits, most interest income, and royalties received from related parties for the temporary use or enjoyment of intangible assets are not included within taxable income under the flat tax legislation. Accordingly, payments in respect of these types of expenses are non-deductible items. Nevertheless, the employer can obtain a flat tax credit on 'taxable' wages paid and social security contributions made, which is generally equivalent to deducting these two items.

Mexico

Certain taxpayers are exempt from flat tax.

The flat tax operates as a supplemental tax to CIT, to the extent the flat tax due is higher than the income tax due for the fiscal year. Hence, the initial flat tax triggered is reduced by a 'credit' for an amount equal to CIT of the fiscal year plus any CIT on distributions exceeding the balance of the after-tax earnings account (i.e. non-CUFIN distributions).

Flat tax is computed on a cash-flow basis (with certain exceptions) and determined per calendar year. Nevertheless, advanced monthly flat tax payments are made based on the year-to-date flat tax gross income, minus the authorised deductions in that same period.

Depreciation and amortisation are not deductible for flat tax purposes since the purchase price paid on the acquisition of fixed assets is a deductible item.

Maquiladoras (factories importing duty free materials for processing and re-exporting) are subject to specific provisions that can significantly reduce their effective flat tax rates, to the extent certain conditions are satisfied.

Financial sector entities are subject to flat tax on their financing intermediation margin, less certain cash expenses paid, pursuant to specific rules applicable to these entities in the flat tax law.

Local income tax
There are no state taxes on corporate net income.

....

Corporate residence

The federal tax code provides that corporations are deemed residents in Mexico if the principal centre of administration or the effective place of management is located in Mexico. A specific definition of 'tax resident' in any tax treaty overrides domestic law definitions, if the taxpayer is eligible to apply the treaty.

When a company ceases to be a Mexican resident in terms of the Mexican federal tax code or any tax treaty, it is deemed to be liquidated for tax purposes. In such cases, a notification is required at least 15 days before the change, and the CIT return must be filed with the Mexican tax authorities within 15 working days following the date on which the change of tax residency takes place.

Permanent establishment (PE)
The income tax law considers a PE to be any place in Mexico where business activities or services are carried out or rendered by non-residents, such as agencies, offices, mining exploration sites, or any other place of exploration, extraction, or exploitation of natural resources, regardless of the length of time involved.

A foreign insurance company could also be considered as having a PE when it engages in activities consisting of insuring risk or collecting premiums (with the exception of reinsurance activities) in Mexico through a party other than an independent agent.

Sites used for display, storage, or purchasing facilities; inventories imported in-bond to be processed by a third party; short-term construction services; and offices to carry out auxiliary or preliminary activities and information gathering or scientific research are not considered to create a PE in Mexico. Non-residents may also keep merchandise in bonded warehouses (including merchandise delivered for importation into Mexico) without being considered as having a PE.

A non-resident is not considered to have a PE in Mexico as a result of the legal or economic relationships maintained with companies carrying out certain inventory processing activities (i.e. *Maquiladoras*) which normally process goods or merchandise maintained in Mexico by the non-resident by using assets provided by the non-resident or any related party, as long as certain requirements are met. The requirements include the conditions that the non-resident be resident in a tax treaty country and that the *Maquiladora* complies with the transfer pricing provisions provided in the law as well as the revised definition of *Maquiladora* operation that entered into force on 1 January 2011.

Maquila operations ('revised definition') are generally defined as those with the following characteristics:

- Raw materials are supplied by a foreign resident (with which a *Maquila* contract is in place) and are temporarily imported to be processed, transformed, or repaired and are subsequently exported, including for these purposes virtual import-export operations.
- The *Maquila* is also permitted to import goods in accordance with the permanent importation regime. Additionally, local purchases are allowed, as long as such goods are consumed in production and/or exported with the temporarily-imported inventory.
- The processing, transformation, or repair of goods must be performed with temporarily-imported machinery and equipment (M&E) which is the property of the foreign principal. In this regard, the foreign principal must own at least 30% of such M&E. It is important to mention that this M&E may not have been previously owned by the *Maquila* or by any other Mexican related party.

M

The limits for M&E will not apply to companies that were operating under an IMMEX program prior to 31 December 2009, if such companies have fulfilled all of their tax obligations, including those related to the transfer pricing safe harbour options under the Income Tax Law.

Maquiladoras under shelter programmes may not be considered as creating a PE in Mexico when assets of foreign residents are involved and certain information is provided to the Mexican Tax Administration in relation to the gross revenues earned and income taxes paid by its non-Mexican related party.

A definition of PE in any tax treaty overrides domestic law definitions where the taxpayer is eligible to apply the corresponding tax treaty.

Other taxes

Value-added tax (VAT)
VAT is payable at the general rate of 16% on sales of goods and services, as well as on lease payments and imports of goods and services, except in the border zones, where a 11% VAT rate generally applies (except on the sale of construction and developed real estate, which is subject to the general rate). The sale of medicines, as well as the sale of most food products, is zero-rated. The principal VAT-exempt transactions are the sale of land, credit instruments (including equity shares), residential construction, interest

Mexico

paid by banks, medical services, education, salaries and wages, rentals of residential property, and the sale of non-amortisable participation certificates on real estate investment trusts, provided specific requirements are satisfied.

The sale in Mexico of temporarily imported goods by non-residents to (i) other non-residents, (ii) *Maquiladoras*, or (iii) companies in the automotive industry is also VAT-exempt under certain circumstances.

The 0% VAT rate, which generally means that no VAT is payable, is applicable to a substantial number of transactions, including the sale of books, magazines, and newspapers published by the taxpayer, the exportation of goods and certain services (including some *Maquiladora* activities intended for exportation), the sale of certain basic foodstuffs, agricultural goods and services, sales and rentals of farm machinery and equipment, and other specified transactions.

Taxes paid by business enterprises on their purchases and expenses related to VAT taxable activities (including activities subject to the 0% VAT rate), may usually be credited against their liability for VAT they collect from customers on their own sales, services rendered, etc. The input VAT credit on goods or services of a general nature, or those not specially identified with either taxable or exempt activities for VAT purposes, is computed based on a VAT ratio proportional to the VAT taxable versus VAT activities (taxable and exempt) carried out by the taxpayer. Creditable VAT paid on purchases and expenses in excess of VAT collected from customers is recoverable via either a refund, offset against other Federal taxes, or a credit against subsequent VAT liabilities.

VAT is a 'cash basis' tax, with few exceptions (e.g. VAT on some types of interest must be paid on an accrued basis), therefore only the receipt of payment for goods or services triggers the output VAT liability, and an input VAT credit may be claimed only when the taxpayer pays VAT to its providers of goods and services. VAT is calculated for each calendar month as a final tax. In addition, VAT overpayments may be used to offset the tax liabilities arising from other federal taxes.

VAT must generally be withheld by Mexican residents acquiring or leasing tangible goods from non-residents if such foreign residents do not have a PE in the country to which income is attributed. Mexican business entities are required to withhold VAT on payments to individuals or entities for services consisting of ground transportation of goods. Mexican corporations must also withhold VAT on commissions paid to individuals, as well as on independent services rendered by Mexican individuals, and on tangible goods leased from individuals.

An information return related to the VAT taxable activities carried out by the taxpayer must be filed on a monthly basis. Definitive monthly VAT payments are required by the 17th day of the immediately following month.

Customs duties/import tariffs
Mexico's commercial conditions provide an excellent business and investment opportunity. Mexico is a member of the World Trade Organization (WTO), the Asia-Pacific Economic Cooperation Mechanism (APEC), and the Organisation for Economic Co-operation and Development (OECD).

Mexico lies in a strategic geographical location for international trade, sharing borders with the United States of America, while facing Europe and Asia, and representing an easy entry to the rest of Latin America.

Mexico

Mexico has signed 12 Free Trade Agreements (FTAs), which provide for preferential duty rates on foreign trade operations with 43 countries. FTAs signed by Mexico include NAFTA; Colombia; Costa Rica; Bolivia; Nicaragua; Chile; the European Union; Israel; Honduras, Guatemala and El Salvador (the Northern Triangle FTA), the European Free Trade Association, Uruguay, and Japan. Most FTAs provide 0% duty rates for almost 90% of the goods to be imported.

General Import Duty rates range from 0% to 35%, but most imports fall within the range of 3% to 20% (exceptionally, certain food products, shoes, and textiles pay higher duties).

Temporary imports are exempt from customs duties (except for fixed assets) and VAT payments.

Excise tax
The excise tax law (*Impuesto Especial Sobre Producción y Servicios* or IEPS) levies substantial federal excise rates on the importation and/or sale of certain taxable items, such as gasoline (% variable), beer (26.5%), wine (26.5% to 30%), spirits (53%), and cigarettes and other tobacco products (160% plus an additional quota), and on certain services related to these activities, such as commission, mediation, and distribution of excise taxable items as well as services for raffles and gambling (30%). Excise tax is also applicable to certain telecommunications services (3%).

In general terms, goods are exempt from IEPS when exported. Consequently, the input IEPS paid by exporters on their purchases is not creditable, and that tax becomes an additional cost.

M

IEPS is payable (output tax) and creditable (input tax) on a cash basis. It is payable on the date that the charge invoiced is collected from the client and can be credited when the respective payment is made to the supplier. On imports, IEPS is creditable when paid at the customs offices.

In certain cases, the IEPS legislation allows taxpayers that are not subject to this tax to credit IEPS paid on the acquisition and/or the importation of certain goods.

There is a specific procedure to calculate the tax for beer producers, bottlers, and importers; however, the tax can never be lower than 26.5%.

Among other obligations, IEPS taxpayers must file information regarding their 50 main clients and suppliers before the Mexican Tax Administration on a quarterly basis.

Property taxes
Annual taxes on real property are levied by the Federal District and all the states at widely varying rates applied to values shown in the property tax records. Assessed values have been increased substantially recently in the Federal District and some other areas.

Title transfer taxes
The transfer of real estate is almost without exception subject to a variable transfer tax at rates averaging 3% to 4%. The tax is levied by most states and the Federal District.

Stamp taxes
There are no stamp taxes in Mexico.

Mexico

Compulsory profit sharing

Although not a tax, every business unit with employees (irrespective of the type of organisation) is required to distribute a portion of its annual profits among all employees, except directors and the general manager. The amount distributable to the employees in most cases is 10% of taxable income, adjusted to eliminate income or deductions that relate to the recognition of inflation and include dividend income. Special rules apply to a limited number of specific businesses.

No profit sharing is paid during the first year of operations. Also, special rules apply for personal service entities and for entities deriving their income from rental activities, both of which can limit their profit sharing payment to the equivalent of one month of regular salary.

The profit sharing amount paid out is a deductible item for CIT purposes, provided certain requirements are met.

Vehicle taxes

As of 1 January 2012, the federal tax on the ownership of vehicles was abolished; however, the states may impose a similar tax.

Tax is still levied on the acquisition of new vehicles. This tax is payable in addition to the VAT on the purchase. Note that some vehicles considered as 'hybrid' (e.g. battery assisted vehicles) are not subject to the new vehicle acquisition tax.

Tax on cash deposits (IDE)

IDE is applicable at 3% on monthly cash bank deposits exceeding 15,000 Mexican pesos (MXN) or its equivalent in foreign currency. This tax can be credited against certain taxes, including CIT.

Branch income

Mexican branches of foreign corporations (i.e. PEs) are generally subject to the same tax rules as Mexican corporations, with some exceptions. Such exceptions include that branches may deduct pro rata allocations of home office expenses, provided certain requirements are complied with (such as the existence of an applicable tax treaty and a comprehensive agreement for the exchange of tax information between the relevant territory and Mexico), but may not deduct remittances to their home offices, even when such remittances are classified as royalties, fees, commissions, services, or interest.

In general terms, profit distributions to the head office (other than those regarded as a return to the head office of the capital invested into the branch) either in cash or in kind from branches or other PEs are subject to the statutory corporate tax rate on the grossed-up distribution, unless the remittance is made from the CUFIN account balance (i.e. the after-tax earnings account).

Income determination

Recognition of income

Income is generally recognised on an accrual basis. However, the service revenues of civil entities that render professional services (e.g. law and accounting firms) are reported on a cash basis.

Inventory valuation

The costing system to be used will be the incurred cost system, based on historic costs or pre-determined costs. If the requirements provided on the regulations of the income tax law are met, the direct cost system (based on historical costs) may be used.

Inventory may be determined by any of the following methods:

- First in first out (FIFO).
- Last in first out (LIFO).
- Identifiable costs.
- Average cost.
- Retail.

The FIFO and LIFO methods must be applied to each type of merchandise and each movement. The monetary FIFO and LIFO methods may not be used. Taxpayers selling goods that are identifiable by serial numbers, at a cost exceeding MXN 50,000, must determine their inventory by the identifiable cost method.

Once elected, a method is compulsory for five years and can be changed only if the requirements established in the regulations of the income tax law are fulfilled. The monetary results of the change in method are amortised over the following five years.

For accounting purposes, different methods and certain variations can be adopted. However, a record of the differences must be maintained, and such difference will not be taxable or deductible.

The cost of imported goods may be deducted (and included in the cost of goods sold) only if it can be supported that the goods were legally imported into the country.

Capital gains

Capital gains are taxed as follows.

Securities

Gains on securities are included in regular taxable income. There are two different procedures for computing the tax basis of a Mexican company's shares, depending on the period for which the shares are held (i.e. whether less or more than 12 months).

The tax basis of shares of Mexican corporations sold may be increased by the inflation adjustment applicable for the holding period.

In the case of shares with a holding period of more than 12 months, there are certain items to be considered when computing the tax basis, such as: (i) the movement in the after-tax earnings account (CUFIN) of the issuing company (including the possible negative CUFIN effects), as adjusted for inflation, (ii) the unamortised prior years' tax losses at the date of the sale, (iii) tax losses arising prior to the date on which the shares were acquired and amortised during the holding period, and (iv) any capital reductions of the issuing company.

When the sum of: (i) the CUFIN balance at the date of acquisition of the shares, (ii) the capital reductions paid, (iii) the unamortised prior years' tax losses at the date of the sale, and (iv) the negative CUFIN balance of the issuing corporation is higher than the sum of: (i) the CUFIN balance at the date of the sale and (ii) the tax losses arising prior to the date on which the shares were acquired, and amortised during the shares'

Mexico

holding period, the difference must be subtracted from the tax basis of the shares to be disposed (potentially resulting in the shares' tax basis being equal to zero).

When the aforementioned difference exceeds the tax basis of the shares disposed, this excess (restated by inflation) must be subtracted from the tax basis of the shares in any subsequent share sale by the same taxpayer, even if the shares are issued by a different company.

The aforementioned procedure allows the average cost (tax basis) of the shares to be determined, which is then updated and considered as the acquisition cost for future sales.

A different but simpler procedure applies for computing the tax basis of shares held during a period of 12 months or less.

Deduction of losses arising from the sale of shares is limited to the value of gains from similar transactions in the same or the following ten fiscal years. Losses may not be deducted by non-residents selling shares.

A gain from the sale of shares is considered Mexican-source income when the transferred shares are issued by a Mexican resident or when more than 50% of their book value arises directly or indirectly from immovable property located in Mexico, including cases where the shareholding is structured in different levels.

In general terms, the sale by non-residents of shares issued by a Mexican company is subject to a 25% withholding tax (WHT) applicable to the gross amount of the transaction (i.e. without deductions). However, there may be the option for gains realised by non-residents on the sale of shares issued by a Mexican company to be taxed by applying the statutory 30% rate to the net gain (i.e. the value of the transfer less the tax basis of the shares). The tax rate for these purposes is the same as that applicable to corporate taxpayers in each year, as mentioned above. Hence, in 2013 the rate will be reduced to 29% and to 28% in 2014.

This net income election is available only if the foreign shareholder is resident of a country that is not considered a 'preferred tax regime jurisdiction' (tax haven) or a country with a territorial tax system. The non-resident seller must have previously appointed a representative in Mexico and have a public accountant assigned to issue a statutory tax audit report on the transfer of shares. The public accountant issuing the respective report must specify the accounting value of the shares sold and explain the factors used in determining the sales price and the market value of the shares if shares are sold between related parties.

The representative is jointly liable for the tax on the sale of shares, even when the statutory report is issued by a public accountant.

The tax authorities may authorise the deferral of taxes that would otherwise be triggered by the transfer of shares in a group reorganisation (the authorisation must be obtained prior to the share transfer). The price used on the transaction must be at arm's length. The tax deferred, adjusted for inflation, is due upon the sale of the originally transferred shares outside the same interest group. An interest group consists of shareholders that have over 50% common voting stock of the companies.

In principle, authorisations for tax deferral are not granted if the party acquiring or selling the shares is resident in a tax haven or is a resident of a country that has not signed a comprehensive exchange of information agreement with Mexico. However, in the latter case, an authorisation may still be granted if the taxpayer provides documentation to the Mexican tax authorities stating that the taxpayer has authorised the foreign tax authorities to provide information to the Mexican authorities regarding the operation in question.

If the share sale qualifies as an exempt reorganisation under tax treaty rules, the non-resident must appoint a legal representative in Mexico prior to the sale and file a notice with the Mexican Tax Administration informing them of such appointment and the details of the reorganisation process intended to be carried out. Additionally, certain formal requirements are established in the regulations of the Mexican income tax law that must be satisfied when carrying out this type of transaction.

Tax treaty rules (optionally) override domestic law rules when the seller resides in a tax treaty country.

Shares sold through the stock market
In certain specific cases, the sale of shares is exempt from CIT when such shares are disposed of by individuals and residents abroad through authorised stock markets to the extent that certain requirements are met.

Real estate
In determining the taxable gain of real estate, the cost basis of land and buildings may be adjusted (i.e. increased) for tax purposes on the basis of the period of time for which the assets have been held. This adjustment is performed by applying inflation adjustment factors to the net undepreciated balance. Similar rules apply to non-residents electing to pay tax on net income by appointing a legal representative in Mexico. The rate of tax on the net gain is 30% (in 2013 the rate will be reduced to 29% and to 28% in 2014). Otherwise, the 25% final WHT on gross income applies to non-residents.

M

Machinery and equipment
Gains or losses from the disposal of machinery, equipment, and other fixed assets are also calculated after adjusting the basis in these assets, by applying inflation factors to the net undepreciated balance.

Inflationary gain or loss
Taxpayers are required to calculate an adjustment for inflation (resulting in additional taxable income or deductible expense) on an annual basis by applying the percentage increases in the National Consumer Price Index (NCPI) to the value of essentially all liabilities, reduced by monetary assets, including bank balances, investments (except in shares), and some debt and receivables.

Dividend income
Dividends received by Mexican corporations from other Mexican corporations need not be included in gross income. However, dividend income is subject to the 10% compulsory profit sharing and must be included within the recipient corporation's CUFIN.

No further taxes apply on dividends distributed out of the CUFIN. However, non-CUFIN distributions (i.e. distributions that for any reason have not been subject to CIT) are generally subject to tax at the level of the distributing company at the general income tax rate on the grossed-up distribution.

Mexico

Interest income

Interest received by Mexican corporations is generally subject to tax on an accrual basis and included in gross income (*see also inflationary gain or loss above*).

Foreign income

A Mexican corporation is taxed on foreign-source income when earned. Double taxation is reduced, or possibly avoided, by means of foreign tax credits. However, the undistributed profits of a foreign subsidiary are not subject to Mexican tax until dividends are paid, with the exception of companies with investments in entities located in a tax haven ('income subject to preferred tax regimes'), in which case income is generally taxable even if no distributions are received from those entities.

Investments in tax havens (income subject to preferred tax regime)

Investments in tax havens include those made directly or indirectly in entities, branches, real property, shares, bank accounts, or investment accounts, and any kind of participation in entities, trusts, joint ventures, or investment funds, as well as in any other similar legal entities created or incorporated in accordance with foreign law and located in a tax haven, and including those that are carried out through an intermediary.

A business, entity, trust, or joint venture is considered to be located in a tax haven when it has a physical presence, an address, a post office box, or effective management in a tax haven, or when its bank account is held in or through financing entities located in a tax haven.

Unless it can be demonstrated that the taxpayer does not have management control of the foreign investments, the taxpayer must include the income generated through such entities or foreign vehicles in the proportion that corresponds to their direct or indirect participation in the capital of the entity or vehicle.

Income and profits subject to preferred tax regimes (PTRs) are taxed separately. This income cannot be combined with other taxable income or losses and it is not considered for purposes of making advance income tax payments. Tax applicable to this type of income is payable together with the annual CIT return.

The classification of a PTR is not based on the location of the investment but on the tax effectively paid on the income generated abroad. An investment is considered subject to a PTR if the income tax paid abroad is less than 75% of the income tax that would have been incurred and paid in Mexico, if the income had been taxed under Mexican rules.

In general, interest income and the annual inflationary adjustment made to liabilities of the investment in the tax haven are included in taxable income without subtracting the annual inflationary adjustment on receivables.

However, the annual inflationary adjustment on receivables may be subtracted from interest income earned, provided an information return is filed.

Tax on investments in a PTR is determined by applying the general CIT rate to taxable income. Additionally, net operating loss carryforwards associated with an investment in a PTR may be amortised against the tax profit of the following tax years arising from investments in PTR, and tax deductions related to the investment may also be applied, as long as accounting records pertaining to those investments are available and the annual information return on the investments is filed on time.

Undistributed income from investments in entities located in a PTR need not be immediately included in taxable income (under the provisions discussed above) in certain particular cases (e.g. income arising from qualified active business activities in accordance with the applicable legislation and in the case of indirect investments in a tax haven when certain strict conditions are met).

Income earned in a PTR will be taxed until its distribution where the PTR income arises from a business activity. This treatment will not be applicable, however, if income such as interest, dividends, royalties, certain capital gains, and rents (i.e. passive income) represent more than 20% of the total income generated.

Other specific cases of income on which the tax may apply until distribution include the case of share transfers within the same group and for income derived from royalties and interest that do not represent a tax deduction for Mexican tax residents to the extent that certain specific requirements are fulfilled.

Maquiladoras

As discussed in the Corporate residence section, companies operating under an IMMEX programme (*Maquiladoras*/in-bond processing companies) are considered to not have a PE in Mexico. This is the case for the non-resident principal which owns the M&E and inventory, to the extent it is a resident of a country that has a tax treaty in force with Mexico, complies with all the terms and requirements of the treaty, satisfies any mutual agreements between Mexico and its treaty partner, and complies with the transfer pricing provisions provided in the law as well as the revised definition of *Maquiladora* that entered into force on 1 January 2011. This relief applies only if the *Maquiladora* complies with any of the following options stated under the domestic law:

- Maintenance of documentation on transfer pricing in accordance with the applicable legislation, adding to the *Maquila* fee 1% of the net book value of the M&E owned by the foreign related company and used by the *Maquiladora* in its activities.
- Reporting of a taxable income margin of a minimum of the higher of:
  - 6.9% of the value of assets used in the *Maquila* activity (including the inventories and fixed assets owned by the foreign related party) or
  - 6.5% of the value of the operating costs and expenses of the *Maquiladora*.
- Maintenance of documentation on transfer pricing using the transactional net margin method (TNMM) and considering a return on the net book value of M&E owned by the foreign related company used by the *Maquiladora* in its activities, adjusted by financing terms.

Maquiladoras that apply the first or third option may request an advanced pricing agreement (APA) from the Mexican tax authorities. However, this APA is not mandatory in order to obtain the PE exemption.

Maquiladoras that apply any of the three options above are not required to file an annual information return on transactions with foreign related parties. This exemption is only available in respect of the *Maquila* activity.

If the *Maquiladora* renders services other than exported *Maquila* services (including domestic sales), specific transfer pricing requirements apply and potential PE issues must be evaluated.

In general terms, the *Maquiladoras* receive a significant reduction on their effective income tax and flat tax rates to the extent certain conditions are satisfied.

M

Mexico

The Mexican Tax Administration has recently initiated a detailed review of the *Maquiladora* programme, hence it is expected that significant tax reforms will be approved in the coming years.

Deductions

The applicable deduction requirements must be complied with no later than the last day of the tax year to which the deduction applies, although the invoice supporting the expense may be provided up to the date on which the tax return for the period in question is filed (or comes due). An expense invoice must contain a date within the year for which the deduction is claimed.

Deductions for certain business expenses are limited in the case of business meals and use of company owned cars.

Depreciation, amortisation, and depletion
Straight-line depreciation is permitted at the rates specified in the law (i.e. estimated lives for assets are 20 years for buildings, 3.3 years for computers, 4 years for cars, 10 years for certain machinery and equipment, etc.), and the deduction may be increased by applying the percentage increases in the NCPI from the month in which the asset was originally acquired. When an asset is disposed of or becomes useless, the remaining undepreciated historical cost may also be deducted, after application of the appropriate inflation adjustment factor to the undepreciated historical cost.

Intangible assets for the exploitation of goods that are in the public domain, or for rendering public services under concession, are considered deferred assets (i.e. not deducted as incurred). Therefore, these assets are subject to amortisation for income tax purposes.

Specific annual depreciation rates are established for goods used in certain industries.

Goodwill
Goodwill is a non-deductible item for Mexican tax purposes, and the corresponding input VAT (if any) will not be creditable.

Start-up expenses
Start-up expenses incurred prior the commencement of operations may be amortised at the rate of 10% per year, after applying the adjustment factors. Taxpayers engaged in mining exploitation may also elect to deduct start-up expenses as incurred.

Interest expenses
In general terms, interest expenses are deductible items if, among others, the principal is invested in the main activity of the Mexican taxpayer, withholding obligations are complied with, informative returns disclosing information related to the loan and transactions carried out with related parties are filed, thin capitalisation rules (3:1 debt-to-equity ratio) are satisfied, the transaction is arm's length, and the interest does not fall into the deemed dividend criteria.

Bad debts
Bad debts may be deducted in the earlier of the date in which the debt prescribes or the date in which the taxpayer substantiates the practical impossibility of collection, as defined by the law, among other detailed rules.

Charitable contributions
The maximum amount for deductible donations is limited to 7% of the taxable income of the previous year.

Fines and penalties
In general terms, fines and penalties are non-deductible items for income tax purposes, except interest for underpayment of taxes.

Taxes
In general, all federal, state, and local taxes levied on a company (not including those required to be withheld from other parties) represent deductible expenses for CIT purposes, with the following exceptions:

- CIT.
- Flat tax.
- Federal VAT and excise tax when the company is entitled to credit the tax.
- Taxes on acquisitions of fixed assets and real estate, which must be capitalised and deducted as part of the total cost of such assets to be depreciated.

Net operating losses
Subject to certain limitations, losses incurred in prior years by a business may be carried forward and deducted from income earned over a subsequent ten-year period. Net operating loss carrybacks are not allowed.

Losses carried forward may be increased by the percentage increase in the NCPI between the seventh and 12th months of the fiscal year in which they are incurred and thereafter up to the sixth month of the fiscal year in which they are applied.

Tax loss carryforwards are non-transferable; however, they can be used by the surviving entity, in a merger with certain restrictions. In the case of a spin-off, tax loss carryforwards can be divided between the surviving entity and the spun-off entities in proportion to the following:

- Inventories and accounts receivable transferred in the case of commercial entities.
- Fixed assets transferred, in all other cases.

Current tax legislation limits the utilisation of tax losses in changes in ownership, with certain exceptions and limitations.

Payments to foreign affiliates
Taxable income and authorised deductions must be determined on the basis of prices that would be agreed with independent parties in comparable transactions (arm's-length values).

For this purpose, taxpayers must secure and maintain contemporaneous documentation supporting transactions with related parties residing abroad, demonstrating that income and deductions are based on market values. This documentation must be prepared per type of transaction and must include all operations carried out with related parties.

Domestic transactions must also be supported by the application of a recognised transfer pricing method selected in accordance with the preferred ordering methods determined in the legislation.

M

Mexico

Payments made to residents of tax havens (or PTRs) are considered non-deductible, unless it can be demonstrated that the price of the transaction is the same that would have been set between or among unrelated parties in comparable transactions. Unless the contrary is demonstrated, it is assumed that operations with companies, entities, or trusts resident in a PTR are carried out between or among related parties and that prices are not set as they would be in comparable operations between or among independent parties.

The sales price of shares (other than publicly traded shares) sold to a related party must be set at market value and the transaction must be supported by the corresponding contemporaneous transfer pricing documentation.

In order to be deductible, payments of technical assistance fees and for the transfer of technology or royalties must be made directly to companies with the required technical capabilities to provide the corresponding service and should correspond to services actually received.

Payments to non-residents of a prorated portion of expenses (i.e. allocations of expenses) are not deductible for Mexican corporations.

Group taxation

The income tax law contains a chapter that allows certain holding companies to file a consolidated income tax return with their majority-owned subsidiaries. Tax consolidation is applicable for CIT purposes but not for other taxes (e.g. flat tax and VAT) or compulsory employee profit sharing.

The principal requirements for a company to qualify as a holding company for fiscal consolidation are that it must be a Mexican tax resident with no more than 50% of its shares owned by other companies, regardless of their country of residence. Shares that qualify as placed among the general investing public and non-voting shares are not considered for this purpose.

Where more than 50% of the holding company's shares are held by a foreign corporation, the above qualifying rule precludes the possibility of filing a consolidated return for a Mexican group, for companies that would otherwise qualify. However, there is an exception in cases where the foreign corporation that owns the shares of the Mexican holding company is a resident in a country that has executed a comprehensive agreement for the exchange of tax information with Mexico.

As of 21 May 2012, Australia, Austria, Bahamas, Barbados, Bermudas, Brazil, Canada, Chile, China, the Czech Republic, Denmark, Ecuador, Finland, France, Germany, Greece, Iceland, India, Italy, Japan, New Zealand, the Republic of Korea, the Netherlands, the Netherlands Antilles, Norway, Panama, Poland, Portugal, Romania, Russia, Singapore, Slovak Republic, South Africa, Spain, Sweden, Switzerland, the United Kingdom, Uruguay, and the United States have agreements of this nature with Mexico, and other agreements or tax treaties that might contain such an agreement are awaiting ratification or being negotiated.

Likewise, Cayman Islands, Cook Islands, Guernsey, Hungary, Isle of Man, Jersey, and Luxembourg have a new comprehensive agreement for the exchange of tax information with Mexico, but they have not been officially included in the relevant list published in the Official Gazette by the Mexican tax authorities.

The Mexican Tax Administration must authorise the application of the consolidation regime, and financial statements and written consent of the legal representative must be filed before 15 August of the year prior to the first year of consolidation to request the proper authorisation. There is a minimum five-year period of fiscal consolidation, and special consolidated tax accounts should be prepared by the consolidated group.

There are some entities that are non-qualifying entities for inclusion in the consolidation regime, such as non-profit entities, credit institutions, insurance corporations, trusts, auxiliary credit institutions, stock exchange entities, foreign exchange houses and capital investment companies, non-resident companies, companies in liquidation, civil or social associations, and cooperatives.

In general terms, the consolidation regime allows certain benefits, such as:

- Individual company loss offset against profits of other companies in the same group during a deferral period.
- Deferral of tax on dividends in excess of the individual CUFIN, to the extent that the dividend flow remains within the consolidation group.
- Capital losses in the holding company from the sale of subsidiaries deducted as an ordinary loss in the year.

Prior to 2010, these deferral benefits were subject to recapture, and could generally be triggered if:

- A member leaves the consolidated group.
- The ownership percentage is reduced.
- The group is deconsolidated.
- Certain carryforward limitations expire (i.e. tax loss and capital loss recapture is required if any of the above three events occur during the ten-year period).

M

The significant 2010 tax reforms introduced important modifications to the consolidation regime, including a reduction of the recapture period from ten to five years in the case of tax losses and capital losses. Moreover, the introduction of new rules now trigger excess dividends over the CUFIN balance and other recapture items after five years while these deferrals were often considered indefinite before the reform, as long as the same group remained in the consolidation with the same ownership percentages.

As a result, most of the consolidated benefits will be reversed in five years, and the deferred income tax will be payable with the submission of the tax return starting from 'Year six', as follows:

- 25% in each of years six and seven.
- 20% in year eight.
- 15% in each of years nine and ten.

Similar transition rules have also been implemented for the recapture and repayment of certain consolidated benefits obtained in years prior to 2010.

Transfer pricing

Mexican transfer pricing legislation has significantly developed as a result of Mexico's admission to the Organisation for Economic Co-operation and Development (OECD) in 1994. This development has resulted in the implementation of transfer pricing guidelines that are in line with the global economy and market liberalisation.

Mexico

In general terms, from a Mexican transfer pricing perspective, all related party transactions (including certain Joint-Venture relationships) must be reported at arm's length.

Local legislation allows the selection of both traditional methods and profit-based methods consistent with the OECD guidelines. However the legislation requires a strict ordering for the application of a method.

Mexican legislation is generally 'form over substance' oriented; therefore contractual terms remain relevant when defining the economic substance of the transactions subject to the transfer pricing analysis.

Reliable financial information is not always publicly available for Mexican entities. Hence, reliance is often placed on foreign information, which is then adjusted to properly reflect local market conditions and render the transactions in question more comparable.

Thin capitalisation

Interest generated by excess debt lent by a related party is non-deductible for CIT purposes. Excess debt is defined as having an average level of liabilities amounting to more than three times the value of shareholders' equity (i.e. a 3:1 debt-to-equity ratio) as per the taxpayer's Mexican generally accepted accounting principles (GAAP) balance sheet.

In principle, all liabilities are considered in determining the annual average liabilities for purposes of calculating the ratio and thereby the disallowed interest expense amount. However, certain liabilities incurred for construction, operation, or maintenance of the productive infrastructure associated with the strategic areas of Mexico may be excluded from this computation.

Taxpayers may also be able to obtain a ruling from the Mexican Tax Administration in order to apply a higher financial leverage (i.e. not the 3:1 debt-to-equity ratio), owing to the characteristics of their activities. Also, the thin capitalisation rules do not apply to the financial sector.

In addition, taxpayers are entitled to use the sum of the average balances of the capital contributions account (CUCA) and the after-tax earnings account (CUFIN) to determine the 3:1 debt-to-equity ratio instead of shareholders' equity. Taxpayers that opt for this tax equity computation must continue to use it for at least five years. This alternative computation is mandatory for those taxpayers that do not account for capital following Mexican GAAP.

Specific provisions dealing with the disallowance of interest expenses for debt financing structured though back-to-back loans should also be closely observed.

Tax credits and incentives

Foreign tax credit

The income tax law allows Mexican corporations and individuals a foreign tax credit on income from foreign sources. The law provides that taxpayers may credit against their Mexican income tax liability the amount of income tax paid in foreign countries on their foreign-source income, as long as such income is subject to income tax in Mexico.

In general, credit is available in respect of foreign income taxes directly withheld from foreign-source income or paid with a tax return filed in the foreign country in the name of the Mexican resident or by a foreign branch of a Mexican corporation. However, in the case of dividends or distributions of profits received from corporations resident in a foreign country, when a Mexican corporation owns at least 10% of the capital of the foreign corporation for six months prior to the dividend, a deemed-paid credit can also be taken for the proportionate part of the underlying foreign corporate income tax paid by that corporation, corresponding to the dividend or distribution of profits received. In calculating the amount of income subject to Mexican tax in these cases, the dividend or distribution must be grossed up to include the proportionate amount of tax paid by the foreign corporation. This credit is allowed also on tax paid on a second holding tier, provided certain requirements are met.

The foreign tax credit will be allowed up to the effective Mexican rate of tax on the taxable income (tax result) shown by the annual return under an 'overall' type limitation. Taxpayers who are not in a position to take full credit for the taxes paid to a foreign country on foreign-source income are allowed a ten-year carryforward of such excess foreign taxes, provided certain compliance requirements are met and the credit is limited to the corporate tax rate of 30%.

In 2012, the Mexican tax authorities released the internal criteria that they will follow to determine whether or not a foreign tax is considered as an income tax for purposes of applying the tax credit.

Duty-deferral programmes

A deferral programme is an authorisation provided by the Mexican Ministry of Economy to those companies importing raw materials or fixed assets to manufacture finished products within Mexico.

In addition to the benefits described for CIT purposes in the Income determination section, *Maquiladoras* - i.e. entities with a Manufacturing, *Maquila*, and Export Service Program in force) are entitled to the following customs benefits:

- No payment of import duties and VAT for temporarily imported raw materials, as long as they are exported.
- Sales of temporarily imported goods to other *Maquila* companies at a 0% VAT rate, under certain circumstances.
- Temporary import of fixed assets without paying VAT.

Another programme allowing preferential duty rates is the Program of Sectoral Promotion (known as PROSEC), which allows manufacturers to apply lower duty rates on the permanent import of raw materials and machinery required for its productive processes, regardless of their country of origin and regardless of if they are for the Mexican market or for export. These programmes were created by the federal government in order to establish competitive tariff conditions for Mexican manufacturers needing to import raw materials and fixed assets from non-NAFTA countries due to the changes made in 2001, where non-originating merchandise exported to NAFTA countries must pay duties.

Companies in Mexico that had formerly performed import operations with values from MXN 200 million to MXN 400 million per semester can take advantage of significant customs and administrative benefits if registered into the 'Certified Company Registry' (authorised by the Ministry of Finance).

Mexico

In general terms, the main benefits provided by the Certified Company Registry allows simplified procedures to process imports and exports, including the reduction in time and number of reviews when clearing goods at customs facilities.

Accelerated depreciation
Investments in certain new fixed assets outside Mexico City, Guadalajara, and Monterrey are entitled to an accelerated depreciation deduction considering a present value discounted rate of the future stream of depreciation. Some taxpayers may benefit from this deduction in the aforementioned cities if they can show that their business operations do not contribute to pollution and do not require the intensive use of water.

Research and development (R&D) incentives
An income tax incentive for taxpayers involved in certain technological R&D projects carried out during the year allows a cash subsidy to be yearly determined by the tax authorities, based on a budget to be approved by the Mexican Congress.

Employment incentives
An incentive offers a credit equivalent to 100% of the income tax corresponding to the salary paid to workers/employees with certain types of disabilities.

An additional deduction is available for employers who hire first-job employees for newly-created positions, which is calculated using a specified method.

Incentives for investments in movie production
A limited credit is applicable for investments in movie production activities through an immediate tax credit which is capped at 10% of the total income tax of the prior year, provided certain requirements are met.

Incentives for investments in theatre production
A limited credit is applicable for investments in theatre production activities through an immediate tax credit which is capped at 10% of the total income tax of the prior year, provided certain requirements are met.

Marginal scarcely inhabited zones
Taxpayers investing in specific regions of Mexico considered to be 'marginal scarcely inhabited zones' (less than 50,000 inhabitants) can receive certain tax benefits, such as a 100% exemption on Social Security contributions to the extent certain requirements are met and financing benefits for the development of industrial facilities according to the guidelines and limitations provided by the Ministry of Economic Affairs in Mexico.

Real estate investment incentives
Several tax benefits exist for qualifying real estate investments (i.e. Mexican REITs such as FIBRAS, SIBRAS, etc.) in Mexico.

Capital investment
There are certain incentives to encourage risk capital investments in Mexico.

Other incentives
Certain other specific and limited tax incentives are available for taxpayers engaged in certain activities (e.g. those engaged in air or sea transportation of goods or passengers with respect to aircraft and ships with a federal government commercial concession or permit; in the agricultural and forestry sectors; and in-bond warehouses with respect to real property used for the storage, safeguarding, or conservation of goods or merchandise).

Withholding taxes

Payments to Mexican residents

Payments to resident corporations and PEs in Mexico are generally not subject to WHT.

Payments by resident corporations to resident individuals are subject to WHT as follows:

Payment	WHT (%)
Wages, salaries, and other remuneration	0 to 30
Fees:	
Members of boards of directors and advisory boards	30.0
Other professional fees	10.0
Lease payments on real property	10.0
Interest on securities (1)	0.6
Interest on nonqualified securities	20.0
Dividends	0.0
Miscellaneous types of income of individuals, usually sporadic payments	20.0

Note

1. WHT on interest paid by financial institutions to Mexican resident investors is generally set at 0.6% of the invested capital.

   To simplify the calculation of interest income from loans entered into with financial institutions, a new procedure has been proposed based on cash flow, which would enter into force on 1 January 2013.

   Through this procedure, financial services taxpayers would be relieved from the requirement to withhold the corresponding income tax on the principal of the loan. Income tax withheld would be considered as a final payment for individuals and an advance payment for corporations.

Payments to non-residents

Income tax must usually be withheld from payments to non-resident corporations and individuals. In the case of non-tax treaty countries, the statutory withholding rates are as noted below.

Income tax of 40%, with no deductions, must be withheld on most payments made to foreign related parties located in tax havens, in lieu of the tax provided in the domestic law for non-tax haven residents. This is not applicable in certain cases, such as on income not subject to Mexican taxation in accordance with the regular provisions for income earned by non-residents from a source of wealth located in Mexico, income from dividends, and certain types of interest, including interest payments made to foreign banks. In these cases, the regular provisions of the domestic law should be applied to determine the income tax withholding.

Additionally, revenues for intermediation services, including commissions for brokerage, agents, distribution, and assignment, and generally all income from the negotiation of third-party interests, are also subject to 40% WHT when paid to tax haven related residents. The 40% may be reduced if the beneficiary resides in a country with which Mexico has signed a comprehensive exchange of information agreement.

Non-residents' wages and salaries are taxed on the basis of a 12-month earnings period at the following income tax withholding rates:

M

Mexico

Taxable income (MXN)		WHT (%)
From	To	
0	125,900	0
125,901	1,000,000	15
1,000,001	and above	30

The above mentioned rates are also applicable to retirement fund payouts.

However, no tax arises on compensation (wages, salaries, or fees other than board fees) paid by a non-resident with no establishment in Mexico (even if not subject to tax) to which the services relate, provided the individual remains in Mexico for fewer than 183 days (consecutive or not) in any 12-month period.

The tax, when applicable, is withheld if the income is paid by a resident (or a non-resident with a PE in Mexico). Otherwise, the tax is generally payable within 15 working days of the associated payment, by the party earning the Mexican-sourced income.

Statutory withholding rates (not mentioned above) under local legislation are as follows:

Payment	WHT (%)
Professional fees for services rendered in Mexico	25
Lease payments:	
Lease of real property	25
Lease of containers, airplanes, and ships authorised by the Mexican Government to be commercially exploited in the transportation of goods or persons	5
Lease of personal property	25
Time-sharing services (1)	25
Charter agreements	10
Sales:	
Real property located in Mexico (1)	25
Shares of Mexican companies (1, 2)	25
Transfers of ownership of Mexican public debt by other than the original creditors (intended to cover debt-for-equity swaps) (1)	25
Derivative transactions:	
On capital (1)	25
On debt (3)	Same rates applicable to interest
Interest (4):	
Paid to foreign government financing entities, to duly registered foreign banks and other entities that provide financing with funds obtained by issuing publicly traded debt instruments abroad, registered with the Ministry of Finance (5)	10
Interest on debt instruments placed abroad (6)	4.9
Interest payments to specific foreign financial institutions (7)	4.9
Other interest payments (not otherwise included above) paid by Mexican financial institutions to residents abroad	21
Paid to foreign suppliers of M&E, to others to finance purchases of such assets or inventory or working capital loans, if the lender is duly registered	21

Mexico

Payment	WHT (%)
Paid to reinsurance entities	15
Other interest payments (11)	30
Financial leases (on the portion deemed to qualify as interest or finance charge)	15
Dividends	0
Royalties (8):	
For the use of railroad cars	5
For the use of copyrights on scientific, literary, or art works, including motion pictures and radio and television recordings, as well as software and payments for the transmission of video and audio signals via satellite, cable, optic fibre, and similar media	25
On patents, invention or improvement certificates, trademarks, brand names, and advertising (11)	30
For the use of drawings or models, plans, formulas, or procedures, and of scientific, commercial, and industrial equipment; on amounts paid for information regarding scientific, commercial, and industrial experience; and for technical assistance	25
Short-term construction and the respective installation, maintenance, technical direction, or supervision (9)	25
Reinsurance premiums	2
Income obtained by athletes and artists (1)	25
Income derived from prizes (e.g. lottery tickets or raffles) (10)	1/21
Other income (forgiven debts, indemnifications, rights to participate in business, investments, etc.) (11)	30

M

Notes

1. The non-resident may elect to pay tax at a rate of 30% in 2012 *(see Note 11 below for the rate applicable thereafter)* on the net taxable profit in the case of (i) time-sharing services, (ii) share sales, (iii) sales of real property, (iv) activities of sportsmen/artists, and (v) derivative stock and debt transactions provided that the non-resident recipient of the income has a legal representative resident in Mexico and to the extent that the following specific requirements are met:
   - For time-sharing services, the resident legal representative must keep the audited financial statements of the taxpayer available for inspection by the Mexican Tax Administration.
   - For share sales, a tax opinion issued by a registered public accountant is required.
   - For shares and debt-for-equity swap transactions, this election is available only where the foreign taxpayer is not a resident of a country classified as a tax haven or a country with a territorial tax system. It should be noted that there is an option to defer Mexican income tax arising from the sale of shares within the same group due to a corporate reorganisation provided certain conditions are met and that no legal representative is required for sales of real property by public deed.
2. The sale of shares through the Mexican Stock Exchange and government securities are exempt from income tax withholding provided certain rules are satisfied.
3. The applicable WHT rate (based on the WHT rates for interest) for debt-derivative transactions is applied on a net basis, that is, gross income less authorised deductions. However, if the transaction is liquidated in kind, the applicable WHT rate (on the same net basis) is 10%.
4. Interest payments to non-residents are exempt from Mexican income tax when they are paid on the following:
   - Loans to the federal government or to the Bank of Mexico (Central Bank) or bonds issued by the latter organisation to be acquired and paid abroad.
   - Loans for three or more years granted or guaranteed by duly registered financial entities that promote exports through special financing.
   - Preferential loans granted or guaranteed by foreign financial entities to institutions authorised to receive tax-deductible donations in Mexico, provided these institutions are properly registered and use the funds for purposes consistent with their status.
   - Loans derived from bonds issued by the federal government or the Bank of Mexico placed on a recognised national stock exchange, to the extent the beneficial owner is a foreign resident.
5. In 2012, a 4.9% WHT rate (the rate has been extended for another year) is applicable when the interest is paid to registered banks resident in countries with which Mexico has signed a tax treaty.
6. The 4.9% WHT rate applies, provided the placement is handled through banks or brokerage firms resident in a country with which Mexico has signed a tax treaty if there is compliance with the information requirements established in the general rules issued by the Ministry of Finance. If there is

Mexico

failure to comply with these requirements, the 10% WHT rate applies. The 4.9% and 10% WHT rates mentioned in the preceding paragraphs do not apply, and instead a 30% *(see Note 11 below for the rate applicable thereafter)* WHT rate is applicable to interest, when the direct or indirect beneficiaries of the interest, either individually or jointly with related parties, receive more than 5% of the interest arising from the instrument in question, and are either (i) holders of more than 10% of the voting shares of the issuing company, either directly or indirectly, either individually or jointly with related parties or (ii) business entities holding more than 20% of their shares, either directly or indirectly, either individually or jointly with parties related to the issuer.

7. The 4.9% WHT rate is applicable to interest payments made to foreign financial institutions in which the Mexican federal government or the Mexican Central Bank has an equity participation.
8. The WHT rate is applied to the gross amount of the payment.
9. The non-resident taxpayer may elect to pay 30% *(see Note 11 below for the rate applicable thereafter)* tax on the net profit in 2012 if the taxpayer has a resident legal representative and so advises the customer, who then makes no withholding. When business activities last for more than 183 days, the foreign taxpayer is deemed to have a PE in Mexico for tax purposes and is taxed in the same manner as a local resident corporation or branch.
10. The 21% federal rate is applied only in the case of non-qualifying prizes (i.e. income derived from prizes that is subject to a state tax that exceeds a rate of 6%).
11. A 30% WHT rate is applicable for 2012. Beginning in 2013, the rate will reduce to 29% and then back to 28% in 2014. The statutory WHT rates mentioned above may be reduced by applying tax treaty provisions. During the last decade, Mexico has embarked on a policy of negotiating a network of tax treaties with its principal trading and investment partners.

As of 21 May 2012, the treaties with the following countries are pending ratification while waiting for the completion of specific formalities by the respective governments in order to become effective, have not been published yet in the Official Gazette, or are under negotiation: Bahrain, Colombia, Estonia, Hong Kong, Kuwait, Latvia, Lebanon, Lithuania, Malaysia, Malta, Morocco, Nicaragua, Pakistan, Peru, Qatar, Saudi Arabia, Slovenia, Thailand, Turkey, Ukraine, United Arab Emirates, and Venezuela. Note that the tax treaties in force with Belgium and Italy are being renegotiated.

Tax treaties with Australia, Austria, Barbados, Belgium, Brazil, Canada, Chile, China, the Czech Republic, Denmark, Ecuador, Finland, France, Germany, Greece, Hungary, Iceland, India, Indonesia, Ireland, Israel, Italy, Japan, the Republic of Korea, Luxembourg, the Netherlands, New Zealand, Norway, Panama, Poland, Portugal, Romania, Russia, Singapore, the Slovak Republic, South Africa, Spain, Sweden, Switzerland, the United Kingdom, the United States, and Uruguay have been published in the Official Gazette and are in force.

The WHT rates negotiated under the tax treaties are as follows:

	Dividends (%)			
Recipient	Portfolio	Substantial holdings	Interest (%)	Royalties (%)
Australia	15	0 (1)	10/15 (25)	10
Austria	10	5 (4)	10	10
Barbados	10	5 (1)	10	10
Belgium	15	5 (2)	10/15 (16)	10
Brazil	15	10 (6)	15	10/15 (27, 29)
Canada	15	5 (4)	10	10
Chile	10	5 (6)	5/15 (26)	5/10 (29, 30)
China	5 (7)	5 (7)	10	10
Czech Republic	10 (7)	10 (7)	10	10
Denmark	15	0 (3)	5/15 (17)	10
Ecuador	5 (7)	5 (7)	10/15 (16)	10
Finland	0	0	10/15 (24)	10
France	0/5 (9)	0/5 (9)	5/10 (29, 17)	10 (29)

Recipient	Dividends (%)		Interest (%)	Royalties (%)
	Portfolio	Substantial holdings		
Germany	15	5 (1)	5/10 (18)	10
Greece	10 (7)	10 (7)	10	10
Hungary	15	5 (1)	10	10
Iceland	15	5 (1)	10	10
India	10 (7)	10 (7)	10	10 (31)
Indonesia	10 (7)	10 (7)	10	10
Ireland, Republic of	10	5 (4)	5/10 (17, 29)	10
Israel	10	5 (10)	10	10
Italy	15 (7)	15 (7)	10 (29)	15
Japan	15	5 (8)	10/15 (25)	10
Korea, Republic of	15	0 (1)	5/15 (17)	10
Luxembourg	15	8 (11)	10	10
Netherlands	15	0 (12)	5/10 (21)	10 (28)
New Zealand	15 (7, 13)	15 (7, 13)	10	10
Norway	15	0 (3)	10/15 (16)	10
Panama	7.5	5 (32)	5/10 (17)	10 (33)
Poland	15	5 (3)	10/15 (19)	10
Portugal	10 (7)	10 (7)	10	10
Romania	10 (7)	10 (7)	15	15
Russia	10 (7)	10 (7)	10	10
Singapore	0	0	5/15 (17)	10
Slovak Republic	0 (14)	0 (14)	10	10
South Africa	10	5 (1)	10	10
Spain	15	5 (3)	5/10/15 (21, 22, 29)	10
Sweden	15	5 (5)	10/15 (16)	10
Switzerland	15	0 (34)	5/10 (35)	10
United Kingdom	0	0	5/10/15 (21, 23)	10
United States	10	5 (4, 15)	4.9/10/15 (23, 20)	10
Uruguay	5 (7)	5 (7)	10	10

Notes

The applicable tax rates on dividends paid abroad in accordance with the tax treaties executed by Mexico are detailed below; however, no withholding is applied on dividend distributions under domestic law.

There are certain specific cases of interest paid to parties resident abroad that might be exempted by certain tax treaties (e.g. interest paid to a pension fund or paid by a bank, interest paid on certain loans granted or guaranteed by certain entities for exports under preferable conditions), which are not detailed in the information below.

1. This rate applies when the recipient corporation that is the beneficial owner of the dividend (except for civil partnerships) directly owns at least 10% of the capital of the distributing corporation. In the case of Barbados, Hungary, and South Africa, the specific exclusion of civil partnerships is not included.
2. This rate applies where the company that is the beneficial owner of the dividends directly or indirectly owns at least 25% of the capital of the distributing company.
3. This rate applies where the company that is the beneficial owner of the dividends (except for civil partnerships) directly owns at least 25% of the capital of the company distributing the dividends. In

Mexico

the case of Norway, taxation is limited to the country of residence of the party receiving the dividends, provided the aforementioned substantial holding rule is satisfied.

4. This rate applies where the recipient corporation that is the beneficial owner of the dividend owns at least 10% of the voting shares of the paying corporation. The Mexico-US tax treaty contains a most-favoured nation clause.
5. This rate applies where a company that is the beneficial owner of the dividends (except for civil partnerships, although limited liability partnerships are included) directly owns at least 10% of the voting shares of the company distributing the dividends.
6. This rate applies where a company that is the beneficial owner of the dividends owns at least 20% of the voting shares of the company paying the dividends.
7. This is the maximum WHT rate for dividends, with no distinction for substantial holdings. In the case of Ecuador and India, the tax payable on dividends paid to residents in Mexico must not exceed a limit established in the treaty.
8. The 5% rate applies when a company that is the beneficial owner of the dividends owns at least 25% of the voting shares of the company paying dividends during the six months prior to the end of the tax period in which dividends are paid. Under certain particular rules and provided this ownership requirement is complied with, dividend payments are only subject to tax in the country of residence of the recipient of the dividends.
9. No withholding applies when more than 50% of the shares of the recipient corporation are owned by residents of France or Mexico or when the beneficial owner of the dividend is a resident individual. Accordingly, the WHT applies to dividends when more than 50% of the recipient corporation's shares are owned by residents of other countries. However, the WHT must not exceed 5% when the party receiving the dividend is the effective beneficiary of said dividend. Dividends paid by a company resident in France to a resident of Mexico, other than a company which directly or indirectly holds at least 10% of the capital stock of the first-mentioned company, may also be taxed in France, in accordance with the law of France, but if the recipient of the dividends is the beneficial owner, the tax thus charged must not exceed 15% of the gross amount of the dividends.
10. The 5% rate applies where the company that is the beneficial owner of dividends directly or indirectly owns at least 10% of the capital of the company distributing the dividends. There is a 10% tax rate that applies when these same ownership requirements are complied with, but the company paying dividends is a resident of Israel (provided dividends are paid from earnings taxed in Israel at a tax rate lower than the regular corporate tax rate in Israel).
11. The applicable tax rate on the gross amount of the dividends when the recipient company (beneficial owner) (except for civil partnerships) directly holds at least 10% of the capital of the corporation paying the dividend must not exceed 5% in the case of Luxembourg and 8% in the case of Mexico. The protocol of the Mexico-Luxembourg tax treaty states that this rate might be reviewed in the future by the contracting states if the WHT is not fully creditable, and can be adjusted under the principle of avoiding double taxation, provided the adjusted WHT rate is not lower than 5%.
12. Dividends paid by a company resident in Mexico to a company resident in the Netherlands (which is the beneficiary of said dividends) are subject to a maximum tax of 5% on the gross amount of the dividends if the beneficial owner is a company that directly or indirectly owns at least 10% of the capital of the company paying said dividends. However, as long as a company resident in the Netherlands is not subject to Dutch income tax on dividends received from a company resident in Mexico under the terms of the Dutch income tax law and any future amendments thereto, the dividends mentioned in the preceding paragraph may only be taxed in the Netherlands (not in Mexico).
13. The Mexico-New Zealand tax treaty contains a most-favoured nation clause that may be applicable in the future.
14. The exemption on dividend WHT is not applicable in the case of deemed dividends.
15. To the extent certain requirements provided in the Protocol are met, the WHT may be reduced to 0%.
16. The 10% rate applies to loans from banks.
17. The 5% WHT rate is applicable to interest paid to banks.
18. The 5% rate applies to interest on loans from banks, insurance companies, and retirement and pension plans.
19. The 10% rate applies to interest on loans from banks, insurance companies, and securities regularly and substantially traded on a recognised national stock exchange.
20. The 4.9% rate applies to interest on loans from banks and insurance companies and to interest on securities regularly and substantially traded on a recognised national stock exchange.
21. In the case of the Netherlands, the 5% rate applies to interest on loans from banks and to interest on securities regularly and substantially traded on a recognised national stock exchange. In the case of Spain and the United Kingdom, the 5% rate extends to interest paid to insurance companies.
22. The 10% rate applies to interest paid by financial institutions and interest paid to the original seller of M&E.
23. The 10% rate on interest applies in the case of interest paid to the original seller of M&E and interest paid by banks.
24. The 10% rate applies to interest on loans from banks and to interest derived from bonds or securities that are regularly and substantially traded on a recognised securities market, as well as to interest paid by the purchaser of M&E to a beneficial owner that is the seller of the M&E.
25. The 10% rate applies to interest on loans from banks and insurance companies, to interest on securities regularly and substantially traded on a recognised national stock exchange, to interest paid to the original seller of M&E in a sale on credit and to interest paid by banks.

26. The 5% rate is applicable to interest on loans granted by banks and insurance companies, securities traded on a recognised securities market, and the sale on credit of M&E.
27. It is understood that the definition of royalties applies to any type of payment received for the provision of technical assistance services. The 15% rate applies to royalties arising from the use of, or the right to use, trademarks.
28. The original rate is 15% but has been reduced to 10% as long as the Netherlands does not impose a WHT.
29. Reduced WHT rate results from the application of the most-favoured nation clause.
30. The 5% rate applies to industrial, commercial, and scientific equipment.
31. The 10% rate also applies to fees for technical assistance which are payments of any kind, other than those mentioned in Articles 14 and 15 of the treaty as consideration for managerial or technical or consultancy services, including the provision of services of technical or other personnel.
32. This rate applies where the company that is the beneficial owner of the dividends directly owns at least 25% of the capital of the distributing company.
33. The treaty broadly defines royalties and includes payments related to certain software.
34. This rate applies where the company that is the beneficial owner of the dividends directly or indirectly owns at least 10% of the capital of the distributing company.
35. The 5% rate applies on the gross amount of the interest paid to, among others, banks and insurance institutions.

Tax administration

Taxable period
In general terms, the taxable period in Mexico is the calendar year.

Tax returns
Corporate taxpayers are required to file annual CIT and flat tax returns for the preceding calendar year by 31 March. Holding companies in the tax consolidation regime are required to file an annual consolidated tax return within four months of the end of the tax period (i.e. usually by 30 April).

Thereafter, the taxpayer is generally required to obtain a certification of tax compliance by an independent auditor and to file the related tax compliance opinion by the end of June. This certification process covers all federal taxes other than customs duties.

Business taxpayers meeting certain size criteria or belonging to a group that as a whole meets these criteria must also file a tax-compliance audit report on an annual basis with the Mexican Audit Administration. This report consists of audited financial statements and detailed schedules, together with a report by the auditor stating that no irregularities were observed in respect of the taxpayer's compliance with its federal tax liabilities. These reports must be filled electronically, and the auditor must be an independent certified public accountant (CPA) registered with the Mexican Audit Administration. The amount of detailed information required to be filed, and the auditor's responsibility in connection therewith, is significant. This obligation is now becoming elective for most companies and, for this, certain application rules will apply, provided also that certain additional information is submitted with their yearly tax return, in lieu of complying with the full certification process.

Employees' profit sharing payments are generally due by 31 May of the year following that in which the corresponding profit was obtained.

Information returns must also be filed no later than 15 February each year, reporting on, amongst others, the following activities performed in the immediately preceding year:

- Payments made to parties resident abroad.
- Loans received from or guaranteed by non-residents.

M

Mexico

- Transactions conducted through a business trust.
- Parties to which the taxpayer makes payments and withholds income tax.
- Parties to which the taxpayer has made donations.
- Parties to which the taxpayer has paid dividends, and the value of such payments.
- Transactions carried out with suppliers and clients, either local or overseas.

Taxpayers making salary payments are also required to file information returns reporting salaries paid and salary credit paid in the immediately preceding calendar year.

An annual information return must be filed on investments made or held in a tax haven. This must be filed in February of the immediately following year.

An information return on transactions carried out with non-resident related parties must be filed together with the annual CIT return (no later than March of the following year).

Annual information returns must also be filed disclosing items used in the flat tax computation.

Payment of tax
Corporate taxpayers are required to make estimated payments of CIT by the 17th day of each month based on their estimated taxable income at the end of the previous month and calculated principally by applying the profit factor to the cumulative monthly gross income. The profit factor is determined by dividing the taxable profit by gross income shown in the annual return for the preceding year, or, if no profit factor is to be found in that annual return, the factor appearing in the year preceding that and so on, up to five years, with certain adjustments. For this purpose, gross income includes nominal income, excluding inflationary adjustments. The balance of CIT for the year is due at the same time as the annual return.

Monthly flat tax advance payments are also required by the 17th day of the immediately following month. The balance of flat tax for the year is due at the same time as the annual return.

Special procedures are provided for computing advance CIT payments and for obtaining authorisation to reduce the amounts of monthly advances after the sixth month of the year. No advance payments or adjustments thereto are required in the first year of operations.

Audit cycle
In general terms, for taxpayers that are obligated or elected to file a tax-compliance audit report, the tax audit (tax inspection) may start with a review of the audit report prepared by the independent CPA. At this point, the tax authorities may finish the audit if they are satisfied with the information provided by the CPA; otherwise, tax authorities may initiate a direct review on the taxpayer either at the tax authority's offices or at the taxpayer's facilities. Tax authorities may request several documents from the taxpayer and third parties that carried out transactions with the audited taxpayer.

Tax audits should be concluded within the following 12 months after the audit was initiated. The period to conclude tax audits for taxpayers that are either part of the financial system or consolidated for tax purposes is 18 months. In cases where the Mexican tax authorities request information to tax authorities from foreign jurisdictions, the period to conclude the audit is two years. The above periods might be suspended under certain circumstances (e.g. a judicial recourse or appeal initiated by the taxpayer against the tax authorities). Upon conclusion of the audit, the tax authorities should issue either a notification explaining tax underpayments observed during the audit process or a notification of conclusion if no issues remain open at the end of the inspection.

Finally, tax authorities should issue a notification of assessment within the six months after the conclusion of the tax audit. At this point, all underpayments claimed by the tax authorities become due.

Statute of limitations

In general, the right of the tax authorities to collect taxes, review tax returns, or claim additional tax expires five years after the date the respective return is filed. However, in cases where the taxpayer has not secured a federal tax registration number, has no accounting records, has failed to keep accounting records for the required five-year period, or has not filed a tax return, the statute of limitations expires in ten years. Similarly, the period for claiming a refund of overpaid tax expires after five years.

Topics of focus for tax authorities

Although there are no formal written communications from the tax authorities dealing with this matter, in recent years the tax authorities have focused audits on transactions with non-residents, inter-company transactions, transfer pricing, social security contributions, and customs duties, among other areas.

Other issues

M

International Financial Reporting Standards (IFRS) adoption

All companies listed on the Mexican Stock Exchange are required to submit annual consolidated financial statements accompanied by the opinion of a Mexican independent CPA. Commencing in the year ending 31 December 2012, these financial statements must be prepared in conformity with IFRS and cover three years. Financial institutions and insurance companies must file audited financial statements with the appropriate regulatory agency.

The adoption of IFRS in Mexico presents companies with great challenges and opportunities. Changing from Mexican Financial Reporting Standards (MFRS) to IFRS requires companies to review their financial reporting procedures and criteria. Major changes in the requirements often have a ripple effect, impacting many aspects of a company's information reporting organisation.

Nevertheless, the benefits to Mexican companies in reporting under IFRS are numerous. Among the greatest of these is the opening up of the Mexican Stock Market to overseas investors. By adopting IFRS, investors are able to compare two companies on different sides of the world with greater ease, and thus it is hoped that the change will encourage investment in Mexican companies.

Adoption of IFRS is not a straightforward process, and it will require time and effort on the part of the adopting entities to be able to ensure a smooth transition from MFRS to IFRS and ensure that the changes and benefits from this transition are duly implemented.

Moldova

PwC contact

Ionut Simion
PricewaterhouseCoopers Advisory SRL
37 Maria Cibotari Street, MD 2012,
Chisinau, the Republic of Moldova
Tel: +40 21 225 3702 / +373 22 251 700
Email: ionut.simion@ro.pwc.com

Significant developments

Corporate income tax (CIT)

As of 2012, a 12% CIT rate is introduced, abolishing the 0% CIT rate that was applicable for the period 2008 through 2011.

As of 2012, small and medium companies that are not registered as value-added tax (VAT) payers (i.e. registered operational revenue up to 100,000 Moldovan lei [MDL] or approximately 6,600 euros [EUR] in the previous fiscal year) should apply a special CIT regime of 3% on their turnover. This special tax regime is optional for legal entities that are not VAT payers and that registered operational revenue between MDL 100,000 (approximately EUR 6,600) and MDL 600,000 (approximately EUR 39,500) during the previous year.

In the financial services sector, the transition from National Standards of Accounting to International Financial Reporting Standards (IFRS) is to be viewed as largely neutral from a CIT perspective. Therefore, income or expenses recorded within such transition should generally not be recognised for tax purposes.

Also starting in 2012, leasing companies are allowed to deduct provisions to cover claims related to non-recovery of lease rates and interest rates up to 5% from the weighted average balance from the account receivables, provided certain conditions are met.

The interest expenses incurred by legal entities, based on a loan contract, given to individuals and legal entities (except financial institutions, microfinance organisations, and leasing companies) can be deducted up to the weighted average interest rate applied for loans granted by the banking sector to legal entities for a period of up to 12 months and over 12 months (values are set by the National Bank of Moldova and published on its official website).

Tax incentives

Another important change for the 2012 year is the annulment of many tax incentives.

The following tax incentives are maintained:

- Residents of free entrepreneurial zones (FEZs) continue to receive preferential treatment (until the expiration of the period of activity of the FEZs).
- Interest income received by legal entities from bank deposits and corporate securities for a period not exceeding three years are tax exempt (until 1 January 2015).
- Certain tax incentives remain available for legal entities that made capital investments in the Free International Port 'Giurgiulesti' (within the investment agreement in this respect).

- There are some benefits available with respect to salary taxes on income of employees of companies whose main activity represents software development, under certain conditions (until 31 December 2016).

Withholding taxes (WHTs)

The WHTs applicable to certain types of income have been changed for residents and non-residents.

Starting in 2012, the WHT for dividends is 6% for both residents and non-residents. However, the distribution of dividends from profit earned during the period between 2008 and 2011 remain subject to the previously applicable final WHT rate of 15%.

The royalty and interest WHT for residents remains unchanged at 15%. For non-residents, however, it has been lowered to 12%.

As of 2012, the preliminary WHT on payments made for the benefit of resident individuals has been increased to 7%, unless such payments are tax exempted or are computed as employment salaries.

Value-added tax (VAT)

Legal entities registered as VAT payers will be liable to submit tax returns using automated methods of electronic reporting starting with:

- 1 January 2012: VAT payers which are administered by the Main State Tax Inspectorate and State Tax Inspectorates of the main cities (i.e. Chisinau, Balti, Comrat).
- 1 January 2013: All other VAT payers.

As of 1 July 2012, companies subject to VAT taxation from Chisinau and Balti will be required to register their VAT invoices that exceed the taxable value of MDL 100,000 (approximately EUR 6,600) in the new general electronic register. This liability will be gradually applicable to the rest of VAT payers.

Excise duties

The excise duty rates were amended for a series of excisable goods (e.g. wine from fresh grapes, denaturised ethyl alcohol and other fermented beverages, tobacco and cigarettes, gasoline and its derivatives, diesel, oils and cars). Also, some types of goods were excluded from the list of goods subject to excise duties (e.g. wines and fermented or partially fermented grape musts; crystal objects; video, web, and photo cameras).

Liquefied gas and inert gas (nitrogen and oxygen) became subject to excise duty.

Road taxes

The road tax rates for vehicles registered in Moldova have increased.

Taxes on corporate income

Resident companies generally must calculate their taxable base for CIT purposes on their worldwide income. Permanent establishments (PEs), unlike resident companies, are only required to calculate their taxable base for CIT purposes on income sourced in Moldova.

The CIT rate applicable in 2012 is 12%.

Moldova

In 2012, individual entrepreneurs are subject to progressive rates of 7% for annual income up to MDL 25,200 (approximately EUR 1,660) and 18% for annual income exceeding MDL 25,200 (approximately EUR 1,660).

Farming enterprises are subject to a 7% CIT rate in 2012.

Small and medium companies that are not registered as VAT payers (i.e. registered operational revenue up to MDL 100,000 or approximately EUR 6,600 in the previous fiscal year) should apply a special CIT regime of 3% on their turnover. This special tax regime is optional for legal entities that are not VAT payers and that registered operational revenue between MDL 100,000 (approximately EUR 6,600) and MDL 600,000 (approximately EUR 39,500) during the previous year.

If a Moldovan Tax Authorities (MTA) tax inspection, applying indirect methods, re-assesses the income amount compared to the declared gross income, a 15% CIT rate may be applied to the excess amount.

Corporate residence

According to Moldovan tax law, a tax resident is a legal entity organised or managed in Moldova or that has its main place of business in Moldova. In practice, tax residency is determined by the place of incorporation.

Permanent establishment (PE)

Based on the Moldovan tax law, a PE is a fixed place of business through which a non-resident carries out, wholly or partly, either directly or through a dependent agent, entrepreneurial activity in the territory of Moldova (e.g. other services and activities, if the period during which such services/activities are carried out exceeds three months).

Due to the regulatory environment in Moldova, foreign enterprises operating through a PE in Moldova are not common.

Other taxes

Value-added tax (VAT)

The standard VAT rate in Moldova is currently 20%. It is generally applied to local supplies of goods and services as well as to goods subject to import and services subject to the reverse charge mechanism.

The reverse charge refers to services rendered by a non-resident supplier to a Moldovan company, which have a place of supply deemed to be in Moldova (e.g. consulting services, supply of information, supply of staff) and which do not fall under any specific VAT exemption. Such reverse charge VAT is due and payable to the Moldovan budget at the date of external payment, including advance payments, duly confirmed under the correspondent documentation.

Apart from the above, certain types of supplies are subject to reduced VAT rates. For instance, local supplies of bread, bakery products, milk, and dairy products; the import and local supplies of sugar produced from sugar beet; and the import and local supply of drugs and certain pharmaceutical products are subject to the reduced 8% VAT rate.

A number of supplies are subject to the 0% VAT rate (i.e. VAT exempt with the right to exercise the input VAT deduction), including international transportation and exports of goods or services. Certain supplies are subject to VAT exemptions, including financial services and the sale or rental of dwellings and land.

Input VAT
It should be mentioned that input VAT incurred on acquisitions of goods and/or services may be deducted, provided it is incurred by a VAT registered payer to perform VAT-able supplies within its business activity.

A company is required to register for VAT purposes if the total turnover within the last 12 consecutive months reached the threshold of MDL 600,000 (approximately EUR 39,500).

If input VAT is incurred by a business not registered for VAT purposes, if input VAT relates to acquisitions used for supplying VAT exempt supplies, or if input VAT relates to purchases performed not for business purposes, such input VAT may not be deducted and shall be treated as a cost/expense.

If input VAT relates to acquisitions destined to perform mixed supplies (i.e. both VAT-able and VAT-exempt ones), the input VAT deduction right is exercised on a pro-rata basis.

Should a company register a deductible input VAT exceeding its output VAT, this balance can be partially refunded only if the company carries out a specific range of business activities (e.g. export supplies, international transportation services, production of bakery and dairy products, leasing activity). Otherwise, such VAT amount may be carried forward to the following months, offset against the company's future output VAT liabilities.

VAT refunds
Additionally, VAT payers performing capital investments in Moldova may be entitled to refund the recoverable VAT related to these kinds of capital investments. Prior to 2012, such refund was not available in Chisinau and Balti. Starting in 2012, however, the VAT refund has been extended for capital investments in these municipalities. Note that specific conditions must be met, and there are few exceptions to this rule (e.g. buildings and transport items).

The VAT refund for capital investments made until 31 December 2011 will still be performed only according to the law applicable to that date.

The possibility to refund the VAT against future obligations to the national public budget is also now available, at the request of taxpayers not having debts to the national public budget.

VAT administration
As of 1 July 2012, companies subject to VAT taxation from Chisinau and Balti will be required to register their VAT invoices that exceed the taxable value of MDL 100,000 (approximately EUR 6,600) in the new general electronic register. This liability will be gradually applicable to the rest of VAT payers.

The fiscal period for VAT purposes is considered the calendar month.

Moldova

Every VAT payer (sometimes also non-registered entities for VAT purposes) must submit VAT returns and must settle related payable VAT liabilities by the end of the month following the reporting one (except for VAT on services supplied by non-residents which are VAT-able in Moldova). VAT payers registered for VAT purposes in Balti, Chisinau, Comrat, and at the Main State Tax Inspectorate must submit electronic VAT returns.

Generally, VAT payers are required to issue VAT invoices for the VAT-able supplies performed, as well as to keep detailed records of their acquisitions and supplies in the correspondent VAT ledgers, according to a set of specific rules.

Customs duties

Moldova's current customs framework is regulated by the Customs Code, Law on Customs Tariff, International Agreements concluded by Moldova to date, and by other legal acts.

Customs duties include customs procedural taxes, customs taxes, VAT, and excise duties. In general, any kind of goods and means of transport may enter and leave the territory of Moldova without any restriction. However, certain limitations specifically provided by the legislation are in force, which cover goods and means of transport crossing the border by breaching state security, public order, environment, etc.

Customs regimes

Definitive and suspensive customs regimes are provided under Moldovan law.

Definitive customs regimes refer to import and export, while suspensive customs regimes comprise: transit, bonded warehouse, inward processing relief (with suspension), processing under customs control, temporary admission, and outward processing relief.

Of these customs regimes, the following are deemed to have economic impact: bonded warehouse, inward processing relief, processing under customs control, temporary admission, and outward processing relief.

The suspensive customs regimes allow for suspension of import duties payment, usually for a specific (limited) period and provided that certain conditions are fulfilled, whilst a customs regimes having economic impact triggers a specific economic advantage to the benefit of the company applying it (e.g. repayment of customs duties paid upon importation, application of lower customs duty rates or customs duties exemption).

Citizens of Moldova, as well as foreigners, are allowed to move any goods in or out of Moldova under a simplified customs regime, provided these goods are not intended for business or commercial purposes.

Note that there are also some environmental pollution taxes related to specific packaging and goods that importers should pay.

Customs tariff and duties

The Law on Customs Tariff establishes standard customs duty rates applicable upon import of goods into Moldova, depending on their specific customs tariff classification code. The Moldovan Customs Tariff is based on the Harmonised Commodity Description and Coding System.

Customs duty rates are generally indicated as percentages to be applied to the customs value (i.e. *ad valorem* duty rates) of goods imported into Moldova. The maximum *ad*

Moldova

valorem standard customs duty rate is 25%. There are also specific customs duty rates established, as well as combined rates.

Customs valuation
Under Moldovan customs legislation, the customs valuation is generally performed in accordance with the customs valuation principles in the General Agreement on Tariffs and Trade (GATT).

The customs value is determined based on one of the six provided valuation methods (i.e. transaction value, transaction value of identical goods, transaction value of similar goods, deductive value, computed value, and reserve method). If the first method is not applicable, then the second method should be applied and so forth.

Preferential tariff treatment
A preferential tariff treatment presumes a reduction of or exemption from customs duty, which may also be applied within a specific quota (settled either as value or quantity).

A preferential tariff treatment is granted for specific categories of goods depending on their origin and in accordance with the free trade arrangements (FTAs) to which Moldova is a party.

Moldova has concluded FTAs to date with most of the Commonwealth of Independent States (CIS) countries and is also a Central European Free Trade Agreement (CEFTA) contracting state.

From 1 March 2008 until 31 December 2012, Moldova benefits from Autonomous Trade Preferences (ATP) from the European Union (EU), which allows unlimited duty-free access to the EU market for all products originating in Moldova, except for certain agricultural products. Such agricultural products are accepted for import into the European Union either with exemptions from customs duties within the limits of specific tariff quotas (e.g. fresh, chilled, and frozen meat of bovine animals, dairy products, common wheat, barley, maize, white sugar) or with exemption of the *ad valorem* component of the import duty (e.g. tomatoes, grapes, apples).

To benefit from these preferential terms for imports of goods into the European Union, compliance with origin and certification requirements has to be observed.

Favourable tariff treatment
A favourable tariff treatment presumes a reduction or an exemption from customs duty upon import of specific goods into Moldova, depending on their type or final destination, according to domestic customs law or international agreements to which Moldova is a party.

Moldovan customs law provides the following exemptions, among others, from customs duty:

- Goods imported by individuals for personal use, not exceeding a specific threshold.
- Fixed assets aimed at being contributed in kind to a company's statutory capital.
- Goods released in Moldova under transit, bonded warehouse, or inward processing relief regimes.
- Moldovan goods previously exported and released back within a three-year term in the same status, as well as compensatory products obtained under outward processing relief.

Moldova

- Certain movable goods imported by legal entities carrying out leasing activities for the purpose of paying off their contractual liabilities derived from lease agreements concluded with Moldovan individuals or legal entities.
- Goods imported by legal entities for non-commercial purposes whose customs value does not exceed EUR 100.

Customs administration

Moldovan customs legislation provides for:

- the concepts and procedures of post clearance audit
- the obligation of individuals and companies to maintain the necessary documents for customs control for six years, and
- the obligation of individuals and companies that perform external trade transactions to maintain the related documents for the purposes of post clearance audit for five years.

We noticed a tendency of the customs authorities for intensifying the practical applicability of this concept. Moreover, the Moldova customs legislation provides for a number of fines for violation of these provisions. These fines vary between 40% and 100% of the customs value.

Excise duties

Excise duties apply to the production and import of cars, tobacco, alcohol, petrol and lubricants, and other goods. Special excise rates for each type of excisable goods are established in the tax code. The rates are widely variable and are based on multiple factors. The excise duty rates are generally indicated as a percentage applied to the value of goods (e.g. 30% for perfumes) or as a fixed amount for a certain quantity of excisable goods (e.g. MDL 1.85 [approximately EUR 0.12] applied to each litre of beer).

The following are liable for excise duties:

- Any individual or legal entity producing and/or processing excisable goods in the territory of Moldova.
- Any individual or legal entity importing excisable goods, unless there is no specific exemption provided.

Businesses or individuals that produce and/or process excisable goods in the territory of Moldova (or intend to do so) must possess excise duty certificates, which must be granted by the tax authorities before these operations are actually carried out. It is mandatory for individuals or businesses, upon submitting the relevant applications to the tax authorities, to attach the details of the excise premises.

Under certain circumstances, excise duty exemptions may apply. Some excise-liable goods are subject to mandatory excise stamp marking and labelling.

Recently, some major amendments were performed to the list of excisable goods as well as to the excise duty rates. For example, some types of goods were excluded from the list of goods subject to excise duties (e.g. wines and fermented or partially fermented grape musts; crystal objects; video, web, and photo cameras), while liquefied gas and inert gas (nitrogen and oxygen) became subject to excise duty.

Also, the excise duty rates have been increased for a series of excisable goods, for example:

- Wine from fresh grapes: increased from 10% of the goods' value (but not less than MDL 1.69 per litre) to MDL 15 per litre plus 15% of goods' value.
- Filter cigarettes: increased from MDL 10 for 1,000 units plus 18% of the goods' value to MDL 20 for 1,000 units plus 24% of the goods' value.

Tax on immovable property
Tax on immovable property is a local tax paid on real estate (i.e. land and/or construction on the land) by the proprietor or owner of material rights. Residents and non-residents owning real estate located in the territory of Moldova have similar obligations.

The 0.1% rate on immovable property used for entrepreneurial activity is applied either on the property's estimated value (if such exists) or on its book value, while the maximum tax rate on property used for agricultural activities is 0.1% of the property's book value.

Tax rates for real estate housing, including villages (communes) from Chisinau and Balti municipalities, have been increased.

As of 2012, separate rates have been introduced for agricultural land with construction buildings on it.

The actual tax rate on immovable property for a legal entity is established in monetary value (i.e. MDL), depending on its destination (e.g. land for agriculture usage) and location.

Tax on real estate housing, including villages (communes) from Chisinau and Balti municipalities, and agricultural land with constructions on them is paid in equal instalments on 15 August and 15 October for property owned before 1 July and is paid by 31 March for property acquired after 1 July. The respective tax shall be calculated based on the estimated value of the immovable property.

For the rest of immovable property, taxes have to be paid quarterly based on the book value.

Companies and individual entrepreneurs who own immovable property will be obliged to declare the immovable property tax by 1 July of the current fiscal period.

Local taxes
Local taxation in Moldova refers to the application of the following types of taxes and duties:

- Tax on the following natural resources:
  - Water.
  - Mineral exploration.
  - Geological exploration.
  - Mining operations.
  - Usage of underground areas for the construction of underground structures not related to mining operations.
  - Exploitation of underground structures within the performance of entrepreneurial activity, not related to mining operations.
  - Standing wood.
- Tax on immovable property.
- Duty for the right to perform local auctions and lotteries.

M

Moldova

- Tax on advertising placement.
- Fee for the right to use local symbols.
- Parking tax.
- Hotel room occupancy tax.
- Resort fee.

New amendments to the legislation provide that local authorities are now authorised to establish the list and the levels of tax rates for local taxes (i.e. previously it was the competence of the Moldovan Parliament to establish the maximum rates in this respect). Additionally,

- the publicity tax is no longer applied for placement of advertisements by means of broadcasting via TV, internet, radio, press, and printed media, and
- the terms of payment and submission of tax returns for some local taxes were amended (e.g. tax on organisation of auctions and lotteries in the territory of the administrative territorial unit, tax on passengers' transportation services within municipalities, cities, and villages).

Starting in 2012, the following local taxes have been introduced:

- Tax on transport unit owners, which is paid by legal entities or individuals that own transport units, depending on engine capacity, total weight, weight charge per axle, number of transport units owned.
- Parking fee, which is due by legal entities or individuals owning vehicles, depending on the parking space used for transport unit standing during a certain period of time. The specific conditions for fee assessment are to be provided by the local authorities.
- Tax for commercial and/or services providing units, which is to be paid by legal entities or individuals who have outdoor units selling products and/or services, depending on their surface.
- Tax on advertising devices, due by legal entities or individuals registered as entrepreneurs who own posters, banners, billboards, and other technical methods to place outdoor advertising, depending on the advertising device surface.

Road taxes

Road taxes are fees collected for the use of roads and/or protection zones of the roads outside the locality limits.

The system of road taxes includes the following:

- Tax for the use of roads by vehicles registered in Moldova.
- Tax for the use of roads of Moldova by vehicles not registered in Moldova.
- Tax for the use of roads by the vehicles with total mass, axle loads, or dimensions exceeding the admitted limits.
- Tax for the use of road protection zones outside the localities for carrying out construction or installation works.
- Tax for the use of road protection zones outside the locality limits for placing outdoor advertisements.
- Tax for the use of road protection zones outside the locality limits for placing roadside service objects.

Depending on the type of road tax, the tax law establishes the taxable person, deadlines for payment of the road tax, tax rates, exemptions (e.g. a legal entity or an individual shall pay road tax on vehicles registered in Moldova (i) on the date of state registration of vehicle, (ii) on the date of the vehicle inspection/annual technical testing of the vehicle).

Recently, road tax rates have been increased to the following:

Object of taxation	Tax (MDL)	Tax (EUR)
Motorcycles:		
Under 500 cm3 inclusive	100	6.5
Over 500 cm3	200	13
Cars, vehicles for special use on car or bus chassis, with engine (cylinder) capacity:		
Up to 1,500 cm3 inclusive	300	19
Over 6,000 cm3	3,600	235
Trailers with a lifting capacity indicated in the registration certificate in tonnes	120	8
Semitrailers with a lifting capacity indicated in the registration certificate:		
Up to 15 tonnes inclusive	100	6.5
Over 35 tonnes	1,000	6,500
Trucks, vehicles for special use on truck chassis, any other self-propelled vehicles, with total weight indicated in the registration certificate:		
Up to 1.6 tonnes	120	8
Minibuses and buses with a capacity: *		
Up to 11 seats	1,300	85
Over 40 seats	2,400	160

* For minibuses and buses, the number of seats was calculated without taking into account the driver's seat.

Branch income

Branches
Moldovan law does not distinguish between branches of non-resident companies and local companies established by a foreign investor. As such, a non-resident's branch is established and registered in Moldova as a legal enterprise fully owned by the foreign investor. As such, it is subject to the same tax regime as local incorporated companies.

On the other hand, the concept of a tax PE does exist in Moldova. Generally, the PE of a non-resident entity will be subject to CIT in Moldova on any profits attributable to that PE. While non-resident entities operating in Moldova without a locally established entity run the risk of creating a taxable PE, since there is no local concept of a legal branch that is not a legal entity, non-residents do not typically intentionally operate in Moldova through a taxable PE.

Representative offices
Representative offices are often established by non-resident entities as a first step to operating in Moldova. According to the tax law, a representative office can engage only in auxiliary or preparatory activities. A representative office can perform only a limited range of activities without being considered a PE of the non-resident.

M

Moldova

All representative offices must submit by 31 March of the year following the reporting year the required Tax Reporting Statement on the activity conducted during the year concerned.

Income determination

Resident legal entities are taxed on their worldwide income, while non-resident entities are taxed on their Moldovan-source income. Taxable income is computed as accounting income adjusted in accordance with tax legislation.

Inventory valuation
Moldovan law provides for the following inventory valuation methods: standard cost method, retail method, weighted average cost, first in first out (FIFO), and last in first out (LIFO).

Assets are generally valued at their acquisition cost, production cost, or market value.

Capital gains
The capital gains rule applies to Moldovan companies selling capital assets on an occasional basis and whose ordinary activity does not include transactions with land, buildings, and shares. Shares and other investment assets (e.g. land, property) are treated under the tax law as capital assets (i.e. property not used in the ordinary course of business).

The income earned from the sale, exchange, or disposal of capital assets is deemed to be a capital gain in the amount of 50% of the difference between the purchase price (i.e. all costs related to the acquisition of capital assets) and the sale price. This capital gain must be included in the total gross amount of income for the year in which the assets were sold. This amount is subject to CIT.

Capital gains may be decreased by capital losses registered in the current or previous year.

Dividend income
Starting with profits earned in 2012, dividends paid by Moldovan legal entities to other Moldovan legal entities are taxed with the applicable final 6% WHT, while the distribution of dividends from profit earned during the period between 2008 and 2011 remain subject to the previously applicable final WHT of 15%.

Dividends received by Moldovan legal entities from foreign legal entities are included in taxable income and taxed at the applicable 12% CIT rate. According to Moldovan legislation, the beneficiary of such dividends is entitled to a credit for the tax paid in the foreign country, within certain limits.

Exchange gains and losses
Revenues obtained from foreign exchange differences are to be included in taxable income. Foreign exchange losses are CIT deductible, in the period they are incurred.

In certain circumstances (e.g. high depreciation of the national currency), foreign exchange differences should be capitalised to the value of assets in relation to which the expenses were incurred.

Non-taxable revenues

Moldovan tax law provides for the following main types of non-taxable revenues:

- Contributions to the capital of an entity.
- Income earned while benefiting from an income tax exemption.
- Money received from special funds and which are used in accordance with fund destination.
- Interest derived by legal entities on bank deposits with a period exceeding three years, as well as the interest derived from corporate securities issued in the form of bonds for a period exceeding three years, is tax exempted until 1 January 2015.
- Interest derived from state bonds, until 1 January 2015.

The following elements have also been included in the list of non-taxable sources of income:

- Income arisen due to the transition from National Standards of Accounting to IFRS.
- Income resulting from revaluation of fixed assets and other assets.
- Dividends covering the fiscal periods up to 1 January 2008, payable to resident individuals.

Foreign income

Resident legal entities are taxed on their worldwide income, unless a double tax treaty (DTT) stipulates otherwise. The legal entities, under certain conditions, can benefit from tax credits provided under a DTT or can apply for unilateral tax credits against income tax paid in any foreign country, if this income is subject to taxation in the Republic of Moldova. Such tax credit shall not exceed the amount that would have been estimated at the CIT rate applicable in the given tax period. Otherwise, there is no specific tax deferral regime.

M

Deductions

As a general rule, expenses incurred by a company are deductible for CIT purposes only if they are deemed as ordinary and necessary, aimed at deriving taxable income, and justified with adequate supporting documentation.

Among others, the following expenses are generally CIT deductible:

- Depreciation of fixed assets calculated under the diminishing-balance method.
- Amortisation of intangible assets computed under the straight-line method.
- Research and development (R&D) expenses incurred during the fiscal year as current expenses, should certain conditions be met.
- Business trip expenses, protocol expenses, and expenses on insurance of business entities, within the limits approved by the government.
- Waste, spoilage, and perishability expenses, within the threshold approved by the company's manager.
- Bad debt, provided certain conditions are fulfilled and justifying documents are made available.
- Charity and sponsorship expenses borne for the benefit of public authorities and public institutions financed from the state budget, as well as non-profit organisations within certain conditions, at up to 10% of taxable income.

Moldova

As of 2012, the rate of deductible expenses for business purposes (ordinary and necessary) that are not adequately supported by necessary documentation has been increased from 0.1% to 0.2%.

Also starting in 2012, leasing companies are allowed to deduct provisions to cover claims related to non-recovery of lease rates and interest rates up to 5% from the weighted average balance from the account receivables, provided certain conditions are met.

Depreciation and amortisation
Fixed assets are subject to CIT depreciation under the diminishing-balance method if their useful economic life exceeds one year and acquisition costs exceed MDL 6,000 (approximately EUR 395).

According to the fiscal law, fixed assets are divided into five categories. These categories are set out according to specific rules, mainly on the assets' useful life (i.e. the number of years during which the assets' utilisation generates economic advantages; the useful life for each type of depreciating asset is regulated by governmental decision). The depreciation rates vary as follows:

- First category: 5%.
- Second category: 8%.
- Third category: 12.5%.
- Fourth category: 20%.
- Fifth category: 30%.

Intangible assets are subject to CIT amortisation according to the straight-line method.

Interest expenses
Different CIT deductibility rules apply for interest on loans used for carrying out operational activities and for loans used for investment activities performed on an occasional basis.

As a general rule, deductions for interest and foreign exchange losses are allowed for CIT purposes provided such expenses are deemed as ordinary and necessary for carrying out the activities of the business. Expenses should also be incurred for the purposes of obtaining taxable income and justified by adequate backup documentation.

If the interest paid by a Moldovan company relates to its operational or day-to-day activities, the related expenses are CIT-deductible. A few other provisions should also be considered, namely the following:

- Interest expenses incurred based on loan agreements, for the benefit of individuals and legal entities (except financial institutions and micro-financing organisations, and leasing companies), by businesses are CIT-deductible, limited to the average weighted interest rate on credit loans offered by banks to legal entities for the period of up to 12 months and over 12 months.
- If the loan is obtained to acquire/build fixed assets, the related interest expense should be capitalised to the initial fiscal value of assets until they are commissioned. The deductibility of this expense is capped at the above limit. The excess difference is treated as a CIT non-deductible expense for that fiscal year.
- If interest relates to an investment activity, the interest expense is CIT-deductible within the limit of the income derived from the investment.

Non-deductible expenses

Among others, the following expenses are generally not deductible for CIT purposes:

- Expenses not adequately supported by necessary documentation, except the 0.2% rate as mentioned above.
- Provisions, except for financial institutions and leasing companies as mentioned above.
- CIT as well as CIT related fines and penalties, or related to other taxes and due payments to the state budget, or for violations of legal acts.
- Losses incurred from transaction between affiliated parties.

Fiscal losses

Fiscal losses may only be carried forward in three equal instalments for three consecutive years following the year the losses were incurred, provided the company records taxable income. If the company recorded fiscal losses for more than one year, such losses are carried forward in the order in which they arose. Fiscal losses are recorded on off-balance-sheet accounts.

Losses may not be carried back.

Payments to foreign affiliates

A Moldovan legal entity generally may deduct payments to foreign affiliates to the extent that these amounts were actually paid and are not in excess of what it would have paid to an unrelated entity (i.e. arm's length). However, the payer is required to hold documentary evidence for the actually performed transactions. Still, certain types of expenses may follow general rules of deductibility that would limit their amount (e.g. interest expenses on loan agreements).

M

Group taxation

Moldovan tax law does not provide for group taxation.

Transfer pricing

Transfer pricing regulations are currently at the initial stage of development, as the law does not list any specific transfer pricing methods. Moreover, taking into account that Moldova is not currently an Organisation for Economic Co-operation and Development (OECD) member country, there is no possibility of enforcing the OECD Transfer Pricing Guidelines.

According to the law in force, transactions carried out between related parties should observe the arm's-length principle. Transactions that do not follow this rule are disregarded for tax purposes.

In accordance with Moldovan tax law, a company is considered the taxpayer's related party if it controls the taxpayer, is controlled by the taxpayer, or both the company and the taxpayer are under the common control of a third party.

From a tax perspective, control is the ownership (either directly or through one or more related parties) of 50% or more in value of the capital or voting power of one of the companies.

Losses incurred in dealings between related parties carried out directly or through intermediaries are treated as non-deductible for CIT purposes.

Moldova

According to current Moldovan tax law, there are no formal transfer pricing documentation requirements. However, at the time of writing, there is a proposal that formal transfer pricing documentation requirements will be introduced in the Moldovan tax law starting in 2014.

Thin capitalisation
Moldovan tax law does not provide for a specific thin capitalisation regime.

The deductibility of interest expenses follows the deductibility regime as described under Interest expenses in the Deductions section.

Tax credits and incentives

Foreign tax credit
Income tax paid in any foreign country, if this income is subject to taxation in the Republic of Moldova, is allowed for tax credit. The credit of the income tax may be made, provided that the taxpayer submits a document that justifies payment (withholding) of the income tax outside the Republic of Moldova, certified by the competent body of the respective foreign country, with its translation into the state language.

The amount of tax credit for any taxable year should not exceed the amount that would have been estimated at the rate applicable in the Republic of Moldova with regard to this income.

A tax paid in a foreign country should be creditable for the year in which the income is taxable in the Republic of Moldova.

Free entrepreneurial zones (FEZs)
FEZs are territories where domestic and foreign investors can carry out entrepreneurial activities on preferential terms (i.e. favourable tax, customs, visa, and other regimes). There are currently nine FEZs in Moldova.

The following types of activities may be carried out in a FEZ:

- Production of goods preferentially for export (i.e. supply of goods in the territory of Moldova does not exceed 30% of the total amount of goods and services supplied within one year).
- Sorting, packing, marking, and other similar operations of goods transiting the customs territory of Moldova.
- Other supportive activities.

FEZ incentives
For the 2012 year, the following CIT incentives for FEZ investors have been maintained:

- Entities that are established in the FEZ and export goods and services from the FEZ outside the customs territory of Moldova will be entitled to apply only 50% of the applicable CIT rate on such gains; for other cases, the CIT rate will be 75% of the established one.
- The income obtained from export of goods (services) originating from the FEZ outside the customs territory of Moldova is CIT exempted for a period of three years, provided that the FEZ residents invested in the fixed assets of their enterprises and/

or in development of the infrastructure of the FEZ capital equivalent to at least 1 million United States dollars (USD).

- The income obtained from export of goods (services) originating from the FEZ outside the customs territory of Moldova is CIT exempted for a period of five years, provided that the FEZ residents invested in the fixed assets of their enterprises and/or in development of the infrastructure of the FEZ capital equivalent to at least USD 5 million.

From a VAT standpoint, goods and services supplied in the FEZ from abroad, from the FEZ outside the customs territory of Moldova, in the FEZ from other areas of Moldova, and those supplied to residents of other FEZs are subject to 0% VAT.

According to the customs provisions, goods are introduced into the FEZ with no VAT or customs duty and are not subject to economic policy measures, according to specific criteria. However, certain taxes in specific situations might be incurred by residents of the FEZ. Investors in the FEZ are guaranteed and protected from changes in legislation for a general period of up to ten years, while under certain conditions this period may be extended to 20 years.

Withholding taxes

Residents
Resident legal entities making payments to individuals (other than salary payments) must withhold and pay WHT to the MTA at the following rates:

- 7% preliminary withholding of payments made for the benefit of resident individuals, unless such payments are tax exempt or are computed as employment salaries. The beneficiary deducts (i.e. recovers) the 7% WHT from annual income tax due.
- 10% final withholding of an individual's income derived from leasing, rent, usufruct of movable and immovable property, and advertising campaigns.
- 6% final withholding of dividends paid out to individuals, except for dividends for the profits received between 2008 and 2011, for which the WHT rate is 15%.
- 15% preliminary withholding from royalties and interests. The beneficiary deducts (i.e. recovers) the 15% WHT from annual income tax due.

Non-residents
Under the 2012 domestic tax provisions, the following WHT rates apply upon payments to non-residents:

- 6% for dividend payouts, except for dividends for the profits received between 2008 and 2011, for which the WHT rate is 15%.
- 12% for other revenues.

Double tax treaties (DTTs)
The DTTs in force between Moldova and other countries may provide for more favourable tax rates than those provided by the local provisions. For their application, the foreign beneficiary of such income should provide the paying entity with its fiscal residency certificate before the payments are actually made.

Operational DTTs to which Moldova is a party are outlined below:

Moldova

Recipient	Dividends (%) *	Interest (%)	Royalties (%)
Albania	5/10	5	10
Armenia	5/15	10	10
Austria	5/15	5	5
Azerbaijan	8/15	10	10
Belarus	15	10	15
Belgium	15	15	0
Bosnia & Herzegovina	5/10	10	10
Bulgaria	5/15	10	10
Canada	5/15	10	10
China	5/10	10	10
Croatia	5/10	5	10
Cyprus	5/10	5	5
Czech Republic	5/15	5	10
Estonia	10	10	10
Finland	5/15	5	3/7
Germany	15	5	0
Greece	5/15	10	8
Hungary	5/15	10	0
Ireland	5/10	5	5
Israel	5/10	5	5
Italy	5/15	5	5
Japan	15	10	0/10
Kazakhstan	10/15	10	10
Kyrgyzstan	5/15	10	10
Latvia	10	10	10
Lithuania	10	10	10
Luxembourg	5/10	5	5
Macedonia	5/10	5	10
Montenegro	5/15	10	10
The Netherlands	0/5/15	5	2
Oman	5	5	10
Poland	5/15	10	10
Portugal	5/10	10	8
Romania	10	10	10/15
Russian Federation	10	0	10
Serbia	5/15	10	10
Slovakia	5/15	10	10
Slovenia	5/10	5	5
Spain	0/5/10	5	8
Switzerland	5/15	10	0
Turkey	10/15	10	10
Tajikistan	5/10	5	10
Ukraine	5/15	10	10
Uzbekistan	5/15	10	15
United Kingdom	0/5/10	0/5	5

* If multiple rates are listed, then the WHT is limited if the beneficial owner is a company (other than a partnership) that holds directly at least 50%, 25%, 20%, or 10% of the capital of the company paying the dividends, depending on the treaty.

Tax administration

Taxable period

The tax year for CIT purposes is the calendar year. For new business entities, the fiscal year is considered the period beginning with the registration date until the end of the calendar year.

For WHT and VAT purposes, the fiscal period is the calendar month starting the first day of the month.

Tax returns

An annual CIT return must be submitted to the MTA by 31 March of the year following the reporting year.

WHT and VAT liabilities must be declared and settled monthly by the end of the month following the reporting month.

Farming enterprises with an annual average number of employees not exceeding three and not registered as VAT payers must submit a unified tax return, if certain conditions are met.

Adjusted tax returns

Starting in 2012, the specific procedure for taxpayers submitting adjusted tax returns (after the taxpayer identifies previous errors) has been changed. Taxpayers who discover that the tax return previously submitted contains an error are able to submit the revised tax return not being limited to certain tax periods, provided that no written decision was issued by the tax authority in order to initiate a tax audit.

Penalties will not be applicable in amounts higher than the tax liability resulting from the revised tax return submitted, and no fines will be applicable if the tax duties are paid before the announcement of a tax audit.

Under amendments to tax legislation, the penalty will not apply in certain circumstances of fiscal violations specified by law, and if already established, it will be entirely cancelled, if no additional tax liabilities arise.

Companies that have miscalculated the taxes, and this was not detected in the previous tax audit, are absolved from fines and penalties for violations identified within the repeated tax audit.

Companies keeping the accounting records and preparing financial reports under IFRS will be not fined for violation of accounting and record keeping for tax purposes for a period of up to two years from the date of implementation (transition) to those standards.

Payment of tax

Taxpayers must declare and pay the applicable CIT by 31 March of the year following the reporting year. Also, interim quarterly 2012 CIT payments were reintroduced. Therefore, in 2012, taxpayers that receive income from sources other than employment

Moldova

income, interest, or royalties (from which residents withhold an income tax at source) are required to pay, no later than 31 March, 30 June, 30 September, and 31 December, amounts equal to 25% of either the total estimated value of the CIT due for the 2012 fiscal period or the total value of the calculated CIT for the 2011 fiscal period.

Fines and penalties

The MTA is entitled to apply a fine of 15% to the amount by which a taxpayer under-reported its taxable income for the period between 2008 and 2011 for CIT purposes. For the period starting with 2012, a fine of 30% of the diminished tax liabilities (including CIT ones) will be applied.

Under the tax law, the MTA is entitled to apply a fine in the amount of the undeclared tax, if this is a result of tax evasion.

Taxpayers who settle amounts as assessed by the MTA within three business days and have no other outstanding liabilities qualify for certain tax incentives (i.e. 50% reduction of fines). As of 2012, the possibility to benefit from a 50% reduction for the fines applied by the customs authorities has also been introduced, provided the fines are paid within three business days from the date of handing the decision on their application.

In addition, certain special provisions regarding tax evasion apply. The term 'tax avoidance' is defined under Moldovan tax law as diminishing the tax liabilities by more than MDL 30,000 (approximately EUR 2,000) by means of including in accounting, tax, or financial documents deliberately distorted data on income or expenses or by hiding other objects of taxation. Should the amount of the tax due exceed MDL 30,000 (approximately EUR 2,000), the tax evasion is regarded as a criminal offence. According to the Moldovan Criminal Code, legal entities can be punished for tax evasion with a fine up to MDL 120,000 (approximately EUR 7, 905) and preclusion from performing certain activities or winding-up.

The fines for violations of tax legislation committed by taxpayers have been increased (some of which are capped), and new sanctions for non-compliance with applicable tax law have been introduced.

Among others fines that have been increased, the following are worthy of mention:

- The fine for the performance by the taxpayer of an economic activity with the issuance of a bill without using a cash register has been increased to MDL 10,000 or EUR 660, while such repeated action is sanctioned with a fine of MDL 50,000 or EUR 3,300.
- The fine for the failure to provide the VAT invoice in accordance with the tax law has been increased to MDL 3,600 or EUR 240 for each VAT invoice but capped to MDL 108,000 or EUR 7,200.
- The fine for hindering the execution of a tax audit by not providing access to production, storage, commercial, or other facilities has been increased from MDL 3,000 or (approximately EUR 200) to MDL 10,000 or (approximately EUR 650).
- The fine for submitting a tax return containing unauthentic information has increased from MDL 200 (approximately EUR 13) to MDL 1,000 (approximately EUR 65) for each tax return, but being capped to MDL 10,000 (approximately EUR 650).

Rulings

The law does not provide for the possibility of obtaining binding rulings. However, comfort letters can be obtained.

Taxpayers that inadequately computed tax liabilities due to incorrect written explanations issued by the MTA may not be subject to sanctions (i.e. fines and late-payment penalties). Tax liabilities may still be recomputed by the MTA. Written explanations are issued by the MTA free of charge and may remain valid for an indefinite period of time, unless cancelled by new legislation or other rulings. Such explanations are generally issued by the Moldovan competent authorities during a period of up to one month.

Other issues

The legislation and the approach of the state authorities in Moldova related to corporate taxation have been and are expected to be subject to significant changes.

Taxpayers should seek professional advice over specific issues, given that only limited interpretations have been issued by the MTA.

M

Mongolia

PwC contact

Abdulkhamid Muminov
PricewaterhouseCoopers Tax & Advisory LLP
Central Tower, 6th floor, Suite 601
Sukhbaatar Square, SBD-8
Ulaanbaatar 14200, Mongolia
Tel: +976 (11) 329089
Email: abdulkhamid.x.muminov@mn.pwc.com

Significant developments

The following important changes to the Corporate Income Tax Law came into effect as of 1 January 2012, impacting the requirements for Mongolian companies to withhold tax on amounts paid to non-residents:

- The word 'loan' was removed from the article requiring tax to be withheld on 'loan interest' paid to a non-resident, confirming that tax should be withheld on any interest paid to a non-resident.
- Mongolian companies are now required to withhold tax on all payments for services to non-residents. Previously, this was only required where the service was provided in the territory of Mongolia.

Taxes on corporate income

Mongolian resident economic entities are taxable on aggregate annual income earned worldwide. Non-resident economic entities carrying out business activities in Mongolia are taxable only on the income earned in the territory of Mongolia.

Mongolian corporate income tax (CIT) is levied at the following rates, using a progressive-rate scale that ranges from 10% to 25%, as follows:

- 10% applies to the first 3 billion Mongolian tugriks (MNT) of annual taxable income.
- 25% applies to any excess of MNT 3 billion of annual taxable income.

However, the income described in the chart below is excluded when determining the annual taxable income and is taxed at different tax rates on a gross basis:

Source of income	Applicable tax rate (%)
Dividends	10
Royalties	10
Interest	10
Gambling, betting games, and lotteries (net)	40
Sale of immovable property	2
Sale of rights (e.g. mining licenses, special activity licences, and other rights granted by the authorised organisations for conducting specific activities)	30

Local income taxes

The Mongolian tax system divides to state taxes or local taxes. Only individual income tax falls under local income tax, and other taxes that are concentrated in local budgets are not related to income.

Corporate residence

A resident legal entity is an economic entity formed under the laws of Mongolia or a foreign economic entity that has its headquarter office in Mongolia. There has not been further development of this concept, so it cannot be assumed that the standard place of effective management or control test will apply.

A non-resident company is a foreign economic entity that conducts its business for Mongolian clients.

Permanent establishment (PE)

The concept of a PE is not well developed. Therefore, non-resident companies will suffer a 20% withholding tax (WHT) on a range of payments unless treaty protection is available.

Other taxes

Value-added tax (VAT)

A VAT at the rate of 10% is imposed on the supply of taxable goods and services in the territory of Mongolia and on imports into Mongolia.

VAT is specifically levied on the following:

- Goods sold in Mongolia.
- Work performed and services rendered in Mongolia.
- All goods imported into Mongolia to be sold or used.
- Goods exported from Mongolia for use or consumption outside Mongolia.

Customs duty

A flat customs tariff of 5% applies with respect to most goods imported into Mongolia, except for information technology and medical equipment and pure-bred livestock, which are zero rated.

Equipment and spares imported by small and medium-size companies for the purposes of creating employment, replacing import goods, and supporting export goods are exempt from the customs tariff.

Export duties apply to certain exported goods, such as unprocessed camel wool, wood, and wooden materials.

Excise tax

Excise tax is levied on goods manufactured in or imported into Mongolia, such as tobacco, alcohol, gasoline and diesel fuel, and passenger vehicles. Excise tax is also levied on the physical units of special-purpose technical devices and equipment used for betting games and gambling and on the activities of individuals and legal entities that conduct such activities. The excise tax rate on the goods varies between 0.30 United States dollars (USD) and USD 10, according to the origin and type.

M

Mongolia

Excise tax imposed on imported gasoline and diesel varies depending on the port you import into and a decision of the Cabinet; but starting from the 11 November 2011 up until now there is no excise tax on imported gasoline and diesel.

If the gasoline and diesel is produced in Mongolia, the rates are:

- Gasoline:
  - USD 11 per tonne (up to 90 octane).
  - USD 12 per tonne (above 90 octane).
- Diesel: USD 15 per tonne.

Immovable property tax

Immovable property tax is an annual tax levied at 0.6% (this will vary from 0.6% to 1% depending on the decisions made by the local representatives' committee beginning 1 January 2013) of the value of the immovable property that is owned. For tax purposes, the value used is the value registered with the government registration authority. If the property is unregistered, the insured value is used. In the absence of either a registered or insured value, the accounting value is used.

This tax does not apply to property owned by persons and financed through the state budget, to any dwelling houses, or to any buildings and construction for public use.

Stamp duty

Under the Law of Mongolia on State Stamp Duties, there are 43 types of activities subject to stamp duties, including the following:

- Settlement of a legal dispute by a court.
- Court involvement in arbitration.
- Notary services.
- Consulate services.
- State registration services for legal entities.
- Registration services for foreign invested economic entities and representative offices of foreign organisations.
- Other specific activities that need permissions and rights from the state authorities.

The amount of duty varies depending on the types of services or activities involved.

Fees and taxes applicable to the extractive industry

A range of fees and other taxes are payable for activities in the extractive industry. The primary ones include the following:

- Mining License Fee, which is agreed up front and stated in the mining licence.
- Royalties, which are paid on the sale of mining products. The rate depends on the product being mined and the level of processing being performed in Mongolia.
- Air Pollution Fees.
- Land Use Fee.

Branch income

The repatriation of profits from branches of foreign legal entities is subject to branch profits tax at a rate of 20%.

Please note that it appears it is no longer possible for foreign legal entities to establish a branch in Mongolia. However, the above provision remains in place for branches that were previously established in Mongolia.

Income determination

Inventory valuation
There is no specific provision in the tax law for inventory valuation.

Capital gains
Capital and ordinary transactions are treated the same for tax purposes (i.e. included in annual taxable income). An exception is provided for income from sales of immovable property, which is subject to tax of 2% on gross sales proceeds.

Taxation of capital gains of non-residents is not clear. Conservative reading of corporate income law suggests that gross income (not net gain) from disposal of shares in a Mongolian company should be subject to 20% WHT. No mechanism currently exists if the transaction takes place between two non-residents.

Dividend income
Dividend income earned by a Mongolian resident entity is subject to WHT of 10%. Dividend income to be remitted out of the country to a foreign tax resident is subject to WHT at 20% but may be reduced by an applicable double taxation treaty (DTT).

Interest income
Interest income is subject to a special income tax of 10%. Interest income to be remitted out of the country to a foreign tax resident is subject to WHT at 20% but may be reduced by an applicable DTT.

M

Partnership income
Partnership income is treated as ordinary income to the partner.

Rental income
Rental income is included in taxable income for tax determination.

Royalty income
Royalty income is taxed at a special rate of 10%. Royalty income to be remitted out of the country to a foreign tax resident is subject to WHT at 20% but may be reduced by an applicable DTT.

Unrealised currency exchange gains/losses
Unrealised currency exchange gains are not considered as taxable income, and, at the same time, losses are not deductible from taxable income.

Foreign investment
Tax stability is available for foreign investments of a certain level.

Foreign income
Unremitted earnings are taxed the same as ordinary earnings.

Mongolia

Deductions

Expenses mostly associated with generating aggregate annual income are deductible for CIT purposes (provided proper documentation is in place), and a list of these is provided in the legislation. Expenses not on this list are not deductable.

Note that the CIT law stipulates that finance lease payments (except interest) are not deductible for tax purposes.

Accrued expenses
Accrued expenses are tax-deductible.

Contingent liabilities
Contingent liabilities are not tax-deductible.

Depreciation and amortisation
Depreciation of fixed assets and amortisation of intangibles are tax-deductible. A straight-line method is used and the years of usage are determined for tax purposes.

	Non-current asset class	Useful life (in years)
1	Building and construction	40
2	Machinery and equipment	10
3	Computer, computer parts, and software	3
4	Intangible asset with undefined useful life	10
5	Intangible asset with defined useful life (includes licence for mineral exploration and extraction)	Period in force
6	Other non-current asset	10
7	Building and facilities of manufacture, management of technology park, unit production, and buildings within technology park	20
8	Machineries, mechanism, equipment, technical parts of manufacturing within the management technology park, unit production, and technology park	3

Goodwill
There is no specific provision in the tax law regarding the deductibility of goodwill.

Organisational and start-up expenses
Organisational and start-up expenses are tax-deductible.

Interest expenses
Interest expenses are deductible. However, there are limits with respect to the deductibility of interest expense. *See Thin capitalisation in the Group taxation section for more information.*

Bad debt
Bad debt is not tax-deductible.

Charitable contributions
Charitable contributions are not tax-deductible, except for donations to the fund of vocational training.

Pension expenses

Compulsory pension insurance premiums paid to the Social Security Authority of Mongolia are deductible. Additional voluntary insurance premiums are tax-deductible but shall not exceed 15% of taxable income. Pension provisions or internal pension fund expenses are not deductible.

Payment for directors

If a payment for directors is a salary payment on which social insurance and personal income tax is levied, it is considered as deductible.

Bribes, kickbacks, and illegal payments

Bribes, kickbacks, and illegal payments are not in the list of permitted deductions. Per anti-corruption law, monetary amounts involved with respect to such payments will be confiscated and criminal proceedings will be instituted.

Fines and penalties

Fines and penalties are not deductible for tax purposes.

Net operating losses

Net operating losses generally may be carried forward for up to two years. However, the annual amount of carried forward losses deductible from taxable income may not exceed 50% of the taxable income in the tax year.

Legal entities involved in the infrastructure and mining industries may carry forward 100% of their losses for up to four to eight years, depending on their investment period and based on government regulations.

There is no provision for the carryback of losses.

Payments to foreign affiliates

Deductibility of payments to foreign affiliates depends on the nature of the payment, as follows:

- Interest payments are deductible but with restrictions (i.e. thin capitalisation rule may apply, interest paid on loan for construction of building and installation of equipments need to be capitalised during that period).
- Dividend payments are not deductible.
- Technical assistance service payments are deductible.
- Payments for other services are deductible.

Group taxation

There are no rules permitting grouping for tax purposes in Mongolia.

Transfer pricing

If the following relation is present with a taxpayer, it is considered as 'a related party':

- Holds 20% or more of the common stock.
- Has the right to receive 20% or more of the dividends or distributions.
- Has the right to appoint 20% or more of the management of the economic entity or is otherwise able to determine its policies.

M

Mongolia

If related parties have sold or transferred goods, performed work, or rendered services among themselves below or above fair market value, the tax authority shall determine gross taxable income of such goods, work, and services based on value involving transactions of similar goods, work, and services among non-related parties.

Thin capitalisation
A thin capitalisation rule (debt-to-equity ratio is 3:1) applies, and interest paid in excess of this ratio is not deductible and is treated as a dividend. This is applied on a shareholder-by-shareholder basis as opposed to the company as a whole; no restriction applies to interest that is not paid to a shareholder.

Tax credits and incentives

A 50% tax credit is available for an economic entity that produces or grows the following products:

- Cereal, potatoes, and vegetables.
- Milk.
- Fruits and berries.
- Fodder plants.

Foreign tax credit
Tax credit shall be granted to an economic entity that paid tax in a foreign country based on agreements for the avoidance of double taxation and tax evasion.

Withholding taxes

Dividends, interest, and royalties paid; goods sold; and work/services provided to non-residents are subject to WHT at a 20% rate.

Dividends, interest, and royalties paid to resident companies are all subject to WHT at 10%.

Dividends, interest, and royalties paid to resident individuals are subject to WHT at a 10% rate, but WHT on dividends and interest to individuals will only be effective as of 1 January 2013.

Current DTTs

Recipient	Beneficial WHT rates (%)			
	Dividends	Interest	Royalties	Technical fees
Austria	5/10 (1)	10	10	N/A
Belarus, Republic of	10	10	10	N/A
Belgium	5/15 (2)	10	5	N/A
Bulgaria	10	10	10	N/A
Canada	5/15 (3)	10	5/10	5
China	5	10	10	N/A
Czech	10	10	10	N/A
France	5/15 (3)	10	5	N/A
Germany	5/10 (1, 4)	10	10	N/A
Hungary	5/15 (5)	10	5	N/A

Recipient	Beneficial WHT rates (%)			
	Dividends	Interest	Royalties	Technical fees
India	15	15	15	15
Indonesia	10	10	10	N/A
Italy	5/15 (4)	10	5	5
Kazakhstan	10	10	10	N/A
Korea, Democratic People's Republic of	5	5	10	N/A
Korea, Republic of	5	5	10	N/A
Kuwait	5	5	10	N/A
Kyrgyzstan	10	10	10	N/A
Luxemburg	0/5/15 (4, 6)	10	5	5
Malaysia	10	10	10	10
Netherlands	0/15 (7)	10	5	5
Poland	10	10	5	N/A
Russia	10	10	In accordance with domestic legislation	N/A
Singapore	0/5/10 (5, 8)	5/10	5	N/A
Switzerland	5/15 (5)	10	5	N/A
Turkey	10	10	10	N/A
Ukraine	10	10	10	N/A
United Arab Emirates	0	0	10	N/A
United Kingdom	5/15 (3)	10	5	N/A
Vietnam	10	10	10	10

Notes

1. 5% if the recipient is a company (excluding partnerships) and directly owns at least 10% of the company.
2. 5% if the beneficial owner is a company (excluding partnerships) and directly or indirectly holds at least 10% of the company.
3. 5% if the beneficial owner is a company that controls, directly or indirectly, at least 10% of the voting power in the company.
4. 5% if the beneficial owner is a company (excluding partnerships) and directly owns at least 10% of the company.
5. 5% if the beneficial owner is a company (excluding partnerships) and directly owns at least 25% of the company.
6. No tax if the beneficial owner of the dividends is a company that has held, for 12 months before the date of dividend payment, a direct interest of at least 25%. Does not apply to dividend investments or management of investment acitivities, unless exercised by a banking or insurance company.
7. No tax if the beneficial owner of the dividends is a company holding at least 10% of the company.
8. No tax if dividends paid to the government/certian public bodies.

Pending DTTs
Mongolia has pending DTTS with Egypt and Thailand.

Tax administration

Taxable period
The tax year is the calendar year.

M

Mongolia

Tax returns
Companies must submit a quarterly return by the 20th day of the month following the end of each quarter.

A withholder must prepare and submit a quarterly return of the tax deducted by the 20th day of the first month of the following quarter and an annual return by 10 February after the end of the tax year.

Payment of tax
A taxpayer shall pay the taxes due in advance by the 25th day of each month in accordance with the payment schedule based on the previous year. Quarterly tax statements should be submitted to the corresponding tax authority by the 20th day of the first month of the following quarter, and an annual tax statement should be submitted by 10 February of the following year when the year-end settlement is made.

In practice, the Mongolian tax authorities allow concessions as follows:

Where total tax paid exceeds the tax liability, the excess may be credited against other taxes due or credited against future tax payments. The overpayment also may, theoretically, be refunded; however, the practice of refunding in Mongolia is not clear or consistent.

An economic entity or organisation that has withheld tax from a payment of dividends, royalties, sale of rights, or a payment of income to a taxpayer should transfer the WHT to the tax authorities within seven working days. Tax withheld relating to the sale of immovable property should be transferred to the tax authorities within ten working days.

Audit cycle
The tax audit cycle is not clearly stated in the tax laws. However, the regular cycle in Mongolia is three to five years in practice, and it is very common if the company requests a refund from tax authorities or liquidates its company. Moreover, a tax audit can come anytime if the tax authorities suspect some risk or misuse of the legislation or receive information from a trustworthy source about tax evasion.

Statute of limitations
The statute of limitations in Mongolia is five years for tax arrears, fines, and penalties. However, the dispute settlement timeframe shall not pertain to payment of tax, fine, and penalty debts.

Montenegro

PwC contact

Krzysztof Lipka
PricewaterhouseCoopers Consulting d.o.o.
Omladinskih brigada 88a
11070 Belgrade, Serbia
Tel: +381 11 3302100
E-mail: krzysztof.lipka@rs.pwc.com

Significant developments

The latest changes to the Corporate Profit Tax (CPT) Law became effective on 27 February 2012 and introduced amendments to a tax incentive for companies performing production activities in underdeveloped regions. The amendments stipulate CPT holiday for the first eight years from establishment of a company in an underdeveloped region. Also, the same incentive is applicable to companies whose business units involved in production are established in underdeveloped regions. In such cases, CPT holiday is proportional to the amount of profit generated by such unit over the total profit. However, amendments specify that taxpayers operating in the sector of primary production of agricultural products, transport, shipbuilding, fishery, and steel production cannot use this incentive.

Also, amendments to the CPT Law introduce official tax residency for the purpose of application of double tax treaties (DTTs).

Taxes on corporate income

Entities operating in Montenegro are subject to a 9% CPT.

Resident taxpayers are taxed on their worldwide profit. Non-resident taxpayers are taxed on their Montenegrin-sourced income or income attributed to their Montenegrin permanent establishment (PE). Non-residents are also subject to withholding tax (WHT) on income sourced in Montenegro. *See the Withholding taxes section for more information.*

Local income taxes
No local (i.e. municipality) corporate income taxes exist in Montenegro.

Corporate residence

A legal entity is considered to be a tax resident if it is incorporated in Montenegro. In addition, a foreign corporation may also be deemed a Montenegrin tax resident if the corporation has a place of effective management in Montenegro. No explicit rules exist for determination of effective management. In practice, it usually is the place where key managerial decisions are made or where the board of directors sits.

Permanent establishment (PE)
Montenegrin tax legislation contains very basic PE rules following, in main features, the guidelines set out in the Commentary to the Organisation for Economic Co-operation and Development (OECD) Model Tax Treaty. PE is defined as a fixed place of business through which a non-resident carries out business in Montenegro. PE is deemed to

Montenegro

exist in case of a non-resident having one of the following in Montenegro: place of management, branch office, office, factory, workshop, mine, gas or oil site, stone pit, or any other place of natural resources exploitation in Montenegro. A construction site constitutes a PE only if construction activities last longer than six months.

PE is not deemed to exist in case of a non-resident having storage of inventory in Montenegro only for the purpose of delivery of goods or having operations in Montenegro that are of a preparatory or auxiliary nature.

Other taxes

Value-added tax (VAT)

The main principles of the Montenegrin VAT are in line with the European Union (EU) Sixth Directive guidelines. Taxable supplies are subject to a general 17% VAT rate; however, certain supplies are taxed at a reduced 7% rate (e.g. bread, milk, books, medicines, computers) and 0% rate (e.g. export of goods, supply of gasoline for vessels in international traffic).

In principle, the VAT base is comprised of consideration (in cash, goods, or services) received for supplies, including taxes except VAT (e.g. customs, excise duty) and direct costs (e.g. commissions, cost of packing, transport). If the consideration is not paid in cash, or if an exchange of goods for services takes place, the tax base will be the market value of the goods or services received at the time of supply.

Registration for VAT in Montenegro may be either voluntary or mandatory. Voluntary VAT registration is possible for small taxpayers who have not realised turnover exceeding 18,000 euros (EUR) in the last 12-month period. Once registered, a company may not apply for deregistration for at least three years. VAT registration is mandatory for an entity that realises turnover exceeding the EUR 18,000 threshold in any 12-month period.

VAT is calculated and paid on a calendar-month basis (i.e. a VAT return must be submitted and VAT liability cleared monthly). VAT calculated on imports is paid along with custom duties.

Customs duty

Exports

There are no export duties in Montenegro, nor is it forbidden to export any goods. Exceptionally, the Montenegrin government can impose quantity limitation of exports only in case of critical shortage of certain goods or for the purpose of protection of non-renewable natural resources, under certain conditions.

Imports

Customs duties are paid on goods imported into the customs territory of Montenegro in accordance with the rates and tariffs set forth in the Customs Tariffs which is in line with the harmonised system of tariff codes prescribed by the World Trade Organization (WTO). Customs duties can be levied in two manners, as *ad valorem* or specific duty per unit of goods.

For agricultural - alimentary products, a combined duty has been determined, that is, both *ad valorem* and specific duty are charged simultaneously.

Ad valorem duties are prescribed within the scope from 0% to 30%. Specific duties range from EUR 0.04 per 1 kg to EUR 1 per 1kg.

Customs rates stipulated by international agreements are only applied to goods of preferential origin from countries covered by such agreements. The most important free trade agreements which Montenegro signed are with the European Union, the European Free Trade Association (EFTA), the Central European Free Trade Agreement (CEFTA) states, and, in the near future, with Ukraine.

Excise duty
Legal entities that are importers or producers of the following products are subject to the excise duty:

- Alcohol and alcohol beverages.
- Tobacco products.
- Mineral oils, their derivatives, and substitutes.
- Coffee and coffee products.
- Mineralised water with sugar or aroma.

Excise duty can be prescribed as a fixed amount and/or as a certain percentage (*ad valorem*).

Property tax
Property tax is payable by legal entities who own or have user rights over real estate located in Montenegro. The annual tax is levied at proportional rates, ranging from 0.1% to 1% on the market value of assets as of 1 January of the current year. In case of acquisition of new property, the taxpayer is obligated to submit a tax return to the tax authorities within 30 days from the acquisition date (i.e. registration return for property tax) and to declare annual property tax by the submission of annual returns. Tax is payable in two instalments, based on decisions issued by the tax authorities.

Property transfer tax
Transfer tax of 3% is payable on the acquisition of ownership rights over immovable property.

The taxable base is the market value of the immovable property at the time of the acquisition. A taxpayer (i.e. the acquirer of immovable property) is obliged to submit a tax return within 15 days from the contract date. The liability is payable within 15 days from the receipt of the tax administration decision.

Stamp taxes
No stamp taxes are in place in Montenegro.

Payroll tax
Employment income includes all receipts paid or provided to an individual based on employment (salaries, pensions, benefits in kind, insurance premiums, benefits, and awards above the non-taxable thresholds). Income generated through other types of personal engagements similar to employment (e.g. temporary jobs) is also considered employment income.

While employees are the taxpayers, the employer is responsible for calculating and withholding personal income tax on behalf of its employees.

Employment income is subject to WHT at a flat rate of 9%.

Montenegro

Social security contributions
Social security contributions for pension and disability insurance, health insurance, and unemployment insurance are calculated and withheld by an employer from the salary paid to an employee. Unlike the other two types of social security contributions, pension and disability insurance contributions are subject to a specific annual cap (EUR 50,000 for 2012).

Social security contributions are payable by the employer and employee at different rates. The amount borne by the employer is treated as an operating cost while the portion payable by the employee is taken from the gross salary.

The rates paid by the employer are as follows:

* Pension and disability insurance 5.5%.
* Health insurance 3.8%.
* Unemployment insurance 0.5%.

The rates paid by the employee are as follows:

* Pension and disability insurance 15%.
* Health insurance 8.5%.
* Unemployment insurance 0.5%.

Environmental charges
Legal entities are subject to environmental charges for the following:

* Use of firing or electrical feed equipment with power greater than 1MW.
* Import of substances harmful to the atmosphere.
* Production or deposit of dangerous waste.
* Tax for use of road vehicles (Vignettes).

Branch income

Non-residents carrying out business in Montenegro through a PE are taxed on their Montenegrin-source income at a rate of 9%. A branch is considered to be a PE.

Income determination

Taxable profit is calculated by adjusting the accounting profit (determined in accordance with International Financial Reporting Standards [IFRS] and accounting legislation) in accordance with the provisions of the CPT Law.

Inventory valuation
Inventory is valued by applying the average-weighted-cost method or the first in first out (FIFO) method. If another method is used for book purposes, an adjustment for tax purposes should be made.

Capital gains
Capital gains realised by the sale or transfer of real estate or other property rights, as well as shares and other securities, are subject to the 9% CPT rate.

Montenegro

Capital gains may be offset against capital losses occurring in the same period. A capital loss may be carried forward for five years.

Dividend income
Dividend income of the recipient is exempt from CPT in Montenegro if the distributor is a Montenegrin corporate taxpayer.

Interest income
Interest income is included in taxable profit and subject to 9% CPT.

Foreign income
A Montenegrin resident receiving foreign income is granted a tax credit in the amount of the tax paid abroad but limited to the amount that would be calculated using Montenegrin rates.

Deductions

The following expenditures are recognised for CPT purposes, up to the prescribed threshold:

* Depreciation computed in accordance with tax legislation.
* Expenses for health care, scientific, educational, humanitarian, religious, environmental protection, and sports-related purposes, up to 3.5% of total revenue.
* Entertaining expenses, up to 1% of total revenue.
* Membership fees paid to chambers of commerce and other associations (except political parties), up to 0.1% of gross revenue unless the amount of the fees has been determined by law.
* Provisions for redundancy payments and jubilee awards recognised as expenditures, up to the amount prescribed by the labour law.
* Provisions made by banks and insurance companies, in an amount not exceeding the amount prescribed by the legislation that regulates operation of these entities.
* Provisions for special risks of brokers and dealers, up to amount prescribed by the securities law.
* Provisions for renewable natural resources, warranties for the sale of goods and services (guarantee period), and the expected loss from court process (delicate agreements) if accounted for in accordance with the accounting legislation.
* Paid interest to non-residents, up to the amount of commercial interest.

Depreciation
Depreciable assets are tangible and intangible assets with a useful life of at least one year and an individual acquisition value of at least EUR 300.

Intangible and fixed assets are divided into five depreciation groups, with depreciation rates prescribed for each group (I - 5%, II - 15%, III - 20%, IV - 25%, and V - 30%). A straight-line depreciation method is prescribed for assets classified in the first group (real estate), while a declining-balance method is applicable for assets classified in the other groups.

Goodwill
Goodwill is determined according to IFRS and is subject to impairment. There are no other special provisions on goodwill.

Montenegro

Start-up expenses

There are no special provisions regarding treatment of start-up expenses. Therefore, they will be deductible if they are incurred for business purpose and properly documented under the general expense deductibility rule.

Interest expenses

Interest expenses are generally deductable if they are business related and properly documented. Also, interest and related cost of loans paid out to a creditor with the status of a related party are recognised as expenses only in the amount that does not exceed market interest rates between unrelated parties. The exceeding amount is not recognised as an expense, but it is included in the taxable profit and subject to 9% CPT.

Interest paid out to non-resident legal entities (unless it is revenue of a PE of a non-resident legal entity) is subject to WHT levied at 9%.

Bad debt

Write-offs and provisions for doubtful debts are considered deductible, provided that:

* written-off/provided receivables were previously included in taxpayer's revenues
* doubtful debts were written-off as uncollectible, and
* proof of unsuccessful collection of these debts exists.

Charitable contributions

Charitable contributions for healthcare, scientific, educational, humanitarian, religious, environmental protection, and sports-related purposes are recognised for CPT purposes, up to a threshold of 3.5% of total revenue.

Taxes

The basic deductibility rule is that business expenses incurred for business purposes are CPT deductible. Following that rule, CPT Law provides for full deductibility of taxes. However, penalty interest for late payment of taxes is not CPT deductible.

Net operating losses

The taxpayer is entitled to carry forward losses incurred in an accounting period over the following five years. Carryback of losses is not allowed.

Payments to foreign affiliates

Supplies of goods or services from a foreign group entity not established in Montenegro to a Montenegrin entity must be valued at arm's length. Excess expenses recorded over market value are treated as non-deductible expenses.

With respect to payment of charges of a PE, CPT Law provides that administrative costs charged by the non-resident head office are non-deductible for CPT at the level of PE.

Group taxation

Tax consolidation is permitted for a group of companies in which all of the members are Montenegrin residents and the parent company directly or indirectly controls at least 75% of the shares in the other companies. Each company files its own tax return, and the parent company files a consolidated tax return for the entire group.

Each company is taxed based on its contribution to the consolidated taxable profit (or loss) of the group.

Tax consolidation is binding for at least five years.

Transfer pricing

The difference between the transfer price and arm's-length price is included in the taxable profit and is taxed accordingly. Parties considered to be related are the parties between whom special relations exist, which could directly impact the conditions or economical results of the transaction between them.

Methods permitted in determining arm's-length price are: comparable uncontrolled price (CUP) method as the primary method, resale minus method, or cost plus method.

There are no other rules or guidelines introduced apart from the above rules in respect to transfer pricing.

Thin capitalisation

There are no thin capitalisation provisions in place in Montenegro.

Tax credits and incentives

The CPT Law provides only three tax incentives related to businesses: one for newly established businesses in non-developed municipalities, one for non-governmental organisations, and a foreign tax credit. The latest CPT amendments introduced the tax holiday for newly established business in underdeveloped municipalities.

Tax exemption for newly established business in underdeveloped municipalities

Newly established production companies located in underdeveloped municipalities are entitled to an eight year tax exemption.

The incentive is applicable to companies whose business units are established in underdeveloped regions. In that case, tax holiday is proportional to the amount of profit generated by such unit over the total profit for the period of eight years from establishment of the unit.

The tax incentive is not applicable to a taxpayers operating in the sector of primary production of agricultural products, transport, shipbuilding, fishery, and steel production.

Tax exemption for non-governmental organisations

Non-governmental organisations (NGOs) registered for business activity are permitted to decrease the corporate tax base by EUR 4,000 with the condition that this money is used for realisation of the main goals of an NGO.

Foreign tax credit

Resident taxpayers are entitled to a tax credit up to the amount of corporate tax paid in another country on income realised in that country. This tax credit is equal to the tax paid in another country but may not exceed the amount of the tax that would have been paid in Montenegro.

M

Montenegro

Withholding taxes

Montenegrin CPT Law imposes WHT on income realised from a Montenegrin source and distributed to a non-resident. The scope of the WHT applies to dividends and profit distribution, capital gains, interest, royalties, intellectual property rights fees, and rental income, as well as fees for consulting, market research, and audit services.

Distributions of dividends and share of profits are also subject to WHT if the recipient is a Montenegrin resident (either individual or legal entity).

The general WHT rate is 9%.

Application of a DTT may reduce or eliminate Montenegrin WHT. To qualify for the beneficial rates prescribed by the treaty, a non-resident must prove tax residency of a relevant treaty country and beneficial ownership over the income. In order to qualify for a preferential tax rate according to a DTT, a non-resident will need to provide the tax residency certificate filled out and stamped by the relevant authority of its country of residence.

Although Serbia is regarded as the legal successor of the Serbia and Montenegro State Union which ceased to exist in June 2006, the Republic of Montenegro, upon its Decision on Independence (dated 3 June 2006), continues to honour international treaties which were applicable in the State Union, including those executed by State Union's legal predecessors (Federal Republic of Yugoslavia and Socialist Federal Republic of Yugoslavia, i.e. former Yugoslavia). However, a quite low statutory WHT rate of 9%, which was enacted after the most of the treaties had been introduced, is usually more beneficial than treaty rates.

The list of the treaties is provided below:

Recipient	WHT (%)			Applicable from
	Dividends (1)	Interest	Royalties	
Non-treaty	9	9	9	
Albania	5/15	10	10	2006
Belgium	10/15	15	10	1982
Belorussia	5/15	8	10	1999
Bosnia and Herzegovina	5/10	10	10	2006
Bulgaria	5/15	10	10	2001
China	5	10	10	1998
Croatia	5/10	10	10	2005
Cyprus	10	10	10	1987
Czech Republic	10	10	5/10	2006
Denmark	5/15	0	10	1983
Egypt (2)	5/15	15	15	1989
Finland	5/15	0	10	1988
France	5/15	0	0	1976
Germany	15	0	10	1989
Ghana (3)	5/15	10	10	N/A
Hungary	5/15	10	10	2003

Recipient	WHT (%) Dividends (1)	Interest	Royalties	Applicable from
India (3)	5/15	10	10	N/A
Iran (3)	10	10	10	N/A
Ireland	5/10	10	5/10 (5)	2012
Italy	10	10	10	1986
Korea	10	10	10	2002
Kuwait	5/10	10	10	2004
Latvia	5/10	10	5/10 (5)	2006
Macedonia	5/15	10	10	1998
Malaysia	0 (6)	10	10	1991
Malta	5/10	10	5/10 (5)	N/A
Moldova (4)	5/15	10	10	N/A
Netherlands	5/15	0	10	1983
Norway	15	0	10	1986
Poland	5/15	10	10	1999
Romania	10	10	10	1998
Russia	5/15	10	10	1998
Serbia	10	10	5/10 (5)	2012
Slovak Republic	5/15	10	10	2002
Slovenia	5/10	10	5/10 (7)	2004
Sri Lanka	12.5	10	10	1987
Sweden	5/15	0	0	1982
Switzerland	5/15	10	10	2006
Turkey (4)	5/15	10	10	N/A
Ukraine	5/10	0/10 (8)	10	2002
United Kingdom	5/15	10	10	1983
Zimbabwe (3)	5/15	10	10	N/A

Notes

1. If the recipient company owns/controls at least 25% of the equity of the paying company, the lower of the two rates applies.
2. A new double taxation treaty was signed with Egypt in 2005, but it is not applicable yet. Meanwhile, the old treaty is still applicable.
3. Instruments of ratification have not been exchanged between the two countries.
4. The contract was signed, ratified, and should become applicable after the exchange of ratification instruments by the signatories.
5. A tax rate of 5% will be applicable to literary, scientific, and work of art, films and works created like films, or other sources of reproduction tone or picture. A tax rate of 10% will be applicable to patents, petty patents, brands, models and samples, technical innovations, secret formulas, or technical procedure.
6. Only in cases when dividends are to be paid to Montenegrin residents. If paid to Malaysian residents, they are taxable at 20% in Montenegro.
7. A 5% rate is applicable for intellectual property and 10% rate for industrial property.
8. A 0% rate is applicable in cases when the income recipient is the government or government owned banks.

M

Montenegro

Tax administration

Taxable period
The tax year in Montenegro is the calendar year.

Tax returns
Tax returns and supplementary documents (e.g. tax depreciation form) must be filed with the tax authorities by the end of March of the following year.

Payment of tax
CPT is paid by the end of March of the following year for the previous year. Alternatively, CPT may be paid in six annual instalments at the taxpayer's request.

Audit cycle
There are no particular provisions regarding the audit cycle in Montenegro.

Statute of limitations
The right to assess taxes expires within five years after the end of the year in which the tax should have been assessed.

The right to collect taxes expires within three years after the end of the year in which tax has been determined.

Topic on focus for tax authorities
According to our best knowledge, the focus of the tax authorities is proper documenting of expenses and VAT.

Apart from this, we are expecting that in the near future the focus of the tax authorities will be transfer pricing, following trends of the countries in the region.

Morocco

PwC contact

Mahat Chraibi
PricewaterhouseCoopers Maroc
35, Rue Aziz Bellal
Maârif - Casablanca
Maroc
Tel: +212 5 22 99 98 00
Email: mahat.chraibi@ma.landwellglobal.com

Significant developments

Sports companies
The provisions of Finance Law 2012 have set a reduced corporate income tax (CIT) rate of 17.5% for sports companies regularly established in accordance with the provisions of law n° 30-09 during the first five years following their incorporation.

Statement of tax losses or absence of tax benefits
Finance Law 2012 provides for a new provision that requires companies not generating positive income and subject to CIT or individual income tax to submit a statement explaining the origin of the tax loss or the absence of tax benefits.

This provision applies to taxable income returns submitted on or after 1 January 2013.

Social cohesion contribution
Finance Law 2012 introduced, solely for the year 2012, a contribution to support social cohesion. Such contributions are levied on companies liable for CIT. This contribution is not tax deductible.

The contribution for the year 2012 is calculated on the basis of the net profit for fiscal year 2012 according to the following rates:

Net profit (MAD*)	Contribution rate (%)
Between 50 million and 100 million	1.5
More than 100 million	2.5

* Moroccan dirhams

Exemption for companies established in export free zones
The Moroccan tax code states that companies that operate in the export free zones benefit:

- from the total exemption during the first five consecutive years starting from the first operation of exportation, and
- from a reduced tax rate of 17.5% for the following 20 years.

Finance Law 2012 provides that the exemption and the application of the reduced rate apply also to transactions between the companies established either in the same free zone or in different free zones.

Morocco

Taxes on corporate income

In general, the Moroccan tax code considers that all revenues and capital gains generated in Morocco are subject to Moroccan taxation.

Companies are taxed on the difference between their trading income and expenditure. Business expenses incurred in the operation of the business are generally deductible unless specifically excluded.

The standard CIT rate is 30%. A higher rate of 37% applies to leasing companies and credit institutions.

A reduced rate of 15% applies to small companies realising a turnover equal to or less than MAD 3 million.

Non-resident companies can, under certain conditions, opt for an alternative tax at the rate of 8% of the amount of their contract, whatever the taxable income is.

Minimum contribution

CIT cannot be lower than a minimum contribution of 0.5% (or 0.25% for specific products) levied on the turnover and other specific revenues. The minimum contribution is not due during the first 36 months following the beginning of activities.

The minimum contribution paid in case of loss or the portion of minimum contribution that exceeds the amount of CIT may be offset against the portion of CIT that exceeds the minimum contribution until the third year.

Local income taxes

There are no local taxes levied on income in Morocco.

Corporate residence

Companies, whether or not established in Morocco, will be subject to CIT on all profits or income relating to property which they own, activities which they carry on, and profit-making transactions which they carry out in Morocco, even when these are of an occasional nature.

Permanent establishment (PE)

The notion of PE is not explicitly defined under Moroccan tax law.

However, the Moroccan tax authorities apply this concept for non-resident companies according to some determined criteria that are inspired from the various tax treaties that Morocco has signed with other countries.

Indeed, the question of whether an entity will be deemed to have a PE in Morocco is a question of fact, in particular, subject to having, in Morocco, any fixed place of business through which a foreign entity conducts industrial or commercial activity for an indefinite or substantial period of time.

The term fixed place of business includes, for instance, a place of management or operations, a branch, an agency, a premises used as a sales outlet, a construction of assembly project, or a purchasing office. Also, in some specific cases, a non-resident company may be deemed as having a PE if it operates in Morocco through a dependant agent.

Other taxes

Valued-added tax (VAT)

VAT is levied under the Moroccan Tax Code and is due on all industrial, commercial, and handicraft transactions taking place in Morocco as well as on importation operations.

The standard rate of VAT is 20%. Lower rates of 7%, 10%, and 14% apply to specifically designated operations.

The sale of goods is considered as taking place in Morocco, and thus subject to VAT, if the goods sold are delivered in Morocco.

The sale of services is considered as taking place in Morocco, and thus subject to VAT, if the services sold are consumed or used in Morocco.

Two types of exemptions from VAT are provided. The first is an exemption with credit, equivalent to the zero tax concept. The second is an exemption without credit.

The zero-rated supplies include (but are not limited to) supplies of the following goods or services:

- Exported goods and services.
- Certain agricultural equipments supplied under prescribed circumstances.
- Investment goods recorded as fixed assets in the company accounting and acquired during the first 24 months following the beginning of activity.
- Offshore banks for certain specific operations, such as interest and commissions.
- Goods and services rendered to companies established in export free zones.
- Activities related to hydrocarbon exploration, etc.

Exempt supplies without deduction right include (but are not limited to) supplies of the following goods or services:

- Milk, sugar, bread, cereals.
- Fiscal stamps.
- Newspapers, books, documentaries.
- Interest on government loans.

Customs duties

Importation of goods in Morocco gives rise to payment of importation duties, the VAT on importation, and the special tax on importation called *Taxe Parafiscale à l'Importation* (TPI).

Customs duties are computed on the basis of the *ad valorem* value of the goods at the time of their entrance into Morocco.

Customs duties can be reduced if the imported products are covered by free trade agreements signed by Morocco or other specific regulatory dispositions.

Under Moroccan tax law, the importation operations are subject to VAT at the rate of 20%. Lower rates of 7%, 10% and 14% apply to specifically designated importations.

Morocco

The Moroccan tax law also offers some economical customs regimes that provide VAT exemptions with credit (equivalent to zero rate).

The TPI rate is 0.25% levied on the value of the imported goods.

Excise taxes
Excise taxes apply to specific products imported or produced in Morocco, such as tobacco, alcohol, and lubricants.

Registration duties
Registration duties are due on all written or verbal conventions, such as property transfer of real estate, shares, or rights; company set up; equity increase; and goodwill transfer.

The rates of registration duties range from 1% to 6%. A flat rate of MAD 200 is also applicable to specific operations and conventions.

For information purpose, the company set up and the capital increase are subject to registration duties at the rate of 1%.

The transfer of non-listed shares is subject to registration duties at the rate of 3%. However, a 6% rate is applicable to the transfer of shares of real estate companies.

The applicable rate for the transfer of goodwill is 6%.

Professional tax
A professional tax is levied on individuals and enterprises that carry out a professional activity in Morocco.

The tax consists of a tax on the rental value of business premises (rented or owned) and fixed assets. The tax rates range from 10% to 30% with exemption for the five first years of activity.

The rental value is exempted for the portion of cost exceeding MAD 50 million.

Branch income

Non-resident entities will be subject to income tax at normal corporate rates derived from all profits or income relating to property which they own, activities which they carry on, and profit-making transactions which they carry out in Morocco.

The taxation is levied to the portion of income allocable to the branch located in Morocco.

In addition, a 10% 'branch tax' applies to a non-resident's after-tax profits. The rate at which the branch tax is levied may be reduced to the withholding tax (WHT) rate on dividends prescribed in the relevant tax treaty.

For resident entities having branches in Morocco, the income is taxable in the hands of the head office at normal corporate rates.

Morocco

Income determination

Inventory valuation
Cost of inventory must be determined in accordance with the first in first out (FIFO) or the average cost method. The last in first out (LIFO) method is prohibited.

Capital gains
Capital gains are taxable as a part of ordinary business income.

Dividend income
Dividends received by corporate shareholders from Moroccan-resident entities subject to CIT must be included in business profits of the recipient company, but the dividends are 100% deductible in the computation of taxable income.

Participation exemption in Morocco is also applicable to dividends derived from foreign subsidiaries.

Interest income
Interest income is subject to a WHT at the rate of 20%. The WHT is deductible from CIT.

Rents/royalties income
Rents and royalties income are taxable as a part of ordinary business income.

Foreign income
The income derived from activities carried out in a foreign country is not subject to taxation in Morocco unless the taxation is granted by treaty dispositions.

Note that the participation exemption in Morocco is also applicable to dividends derived from foreign subsidiaries.

M

Deductions

Depreciation
Fixed assets are normally depreciated according to their economical life duration according to the provision of the accounting regulation.

Depreciation is computed according to two methods: the straight-line method and the declining-balance method.

The tax regulation (through administrative guidelines) has provided indicative depreciation rates applicable when the company activity or the asset to be depreciated is specific or particular.

Indicative depreciation rates are as follows:

Asset	Depreciation rate (%)
Business premises and buildings	4 to 5
Lights constructions (metal frame constructions)	10
Production equipments, tools, and constructions fitting	10 to 15
Huge computer facilities	10 to 20
Computers and related items (printers) and programs, as well as vehicles (cars, trucks, vans, lifters) and vehicules	20 to 25

Morocco

Asset	Depreciation rate (%)
Office furniture and software	20
Non-significant tools	30

Goodwill
Under Moroccan tax law, goodwill cannot be subject to amortisation. However, a decrease of the value of goodwill is allowed to be recorded through provisions.

Start-up expenses
The development as well as incorporation expenses shall be capitalised and be tax depreciated over a period of five years.

The carryforward of any loss due to the above expenses is limited to a period of four years.

Interest expenses
Interest on loans granted by direct shareholders is deductible if the capital is fully paid in. Also, (i) the deductible interest is limited to the portion of the loan that does not exceed the share capital equity and (ii) the interest rate exceeds a rate provided, annually, by the ministry of finance (3.44% in 2011).

Bad debt
Bad debts which are definitively non-recoverable (after all recovery procedures have been undertaken) are treated, from a tax point of view, as deductible losses.

Charitable contributions
Charitable contributions made by companies are deductible only if they are granted to foundations and societies explicitly provided by law.

The contributions made to the community enterprise are deductible up to 0.2% of the company turnover.

Fines and penalties
Fines and penalties are not tax deductible expenses if they relate to infringements to legal and regulatory dispositions.

Tax penalties provided under Moroccan law include penalties for late return submission as well as for late payment.

Taxes
Taxes constitute deductible expenses, except CIT itself and recoverable taxes.

Net operating losses
Tax losses may be carried forward for a period of four years from the end of the loss-making accounting period.

However, the portion of a loss that relates to depreciation may be carried forward indefinitely.

Carryback mechanism is not allowed under Moroccan law.

Payments to foreign affiliates
Payments to foreign affiliates are allowed under Moroccan law. However, such payments should respect the arm's-length principle and foreign exchange regulations.

Group taxation

Under Moroccan law, consolidation or group taxation is not allowed.

Transfer pricing
Morocco has a general provision within its tax legislation requiring transactions between related parties to be at arm's length.

Where a Moroccan company is directly or indirectly connected with enterprises situated inside or outside Morocco, profits transferred indirectly to such enterprises, by means of increases or decreases in buying or selling prices or by any other means, must be included among taxable profits on the tax return.

In order to determine the amount to be included among taxable profits, Moroccan tax authorities will make comparisons with other similar companies carrying on normal business activities or by mean of direct assessment based on information available to the tax authorities.

Thin capitalisation
No specific thin capitalisation rules exist in Morocco.

However, the tax law restricts the interest rate on debts issued by shareholders and the basis of calculating deductible interests.

Interest incurred is tax deductible if the shareholder's capital is fully paid. Additionally, the sum of the shareholder loans generating deductible interests should not exceed the equity capital subscribed, and the applicable interest rate should not exceed the official rate calculated annually on the basis of six months treasury bills.

Tax credits and incentives

The Moroccan tax law provides several tax incentives for specific sectors of activities.

Export companies
Export companies are exempt from CIT on their profits related to their export turnover during the first five years following their first export transaction. These companies benefit from a reduced rate of 17.5% in subsequent years.

Hotel companies
Hotel companies are fully exempt from tax on profits relating to foreign currency turnover for the first five years following their first accommodation operation in foreign currency. They also benefit from a reduced rate of 17.5% on such profits for subsequent years.

Mining companies
Exporting mining companies, including those that sell products to export companies, benefit from a reduced CIT rate of 17.5%.

Morocco

Agricultural enterprises
Agricultural enterprises are exempt from all taxes until the year 2013.

Capital risk companies
Capital risk companies are exempt from CIT on profits derived within the scope of their activities (these are profits related to purchases of companies' shares that support such companies' development and the sales of such shares thereafter).

Hydrocarbon companies
Companies holding hydrocarbon exploration and exploitation permits are exempt from CIT for ten years from the beginning of hydrocarbon regular production.

Banks and holding companies located in offshore zones
Banks and holding companies located in offshore zones benefit from a reduction in CIT for the first 15 years of operation.

Banks may opt for a minimum CIT of USD 25,000 or pay the tax at a reduced rate of 10%.

Holding companies pay a flat tax of USD 500 during the first 15 years.

Casablanca Finance City (CFC)
A law was enacted in 2010 for the setting up of a finance area in Casablanca, called, Casablanca Finance City.

The CFC statute may be granted to specific financial institutions as well as non-financial institutions that offer such services as auditing, fiscal, legal, financial, actuarial, and human resources management advisory.

The above statute may also be granted to regional and international headquarters.

Entities established in Casablanca Finance City are exempt, for their export turnover, from CIT during the first five years following the date they obtain CFC statute. These companies benefit, for the export turnover, from a reduced rate of 8.75% in subsequent years.

Free trade zones (FTZs)
The activities which must be necessarily performed by the companies established in the export free zones are mainly the followings (the activities may vary for each FTZ):

- Food processing industries.
- Textile and leather industries.
- Metallurgic, mechanic, electric, and electronic industries.
- Chemical and special chemical industries.
- Services connected with the aforementioned activities.

Entities established in FTZs are exempt, for their export turnover, from CIT during the first five years. These companies benefit, for the export turnover, from a reduced rate of 8.75% for the following 20 years.

Moreover, for entities established in FTZs, the dividends paid to non-residents relating to activities performed in the export free zone are totally exempted from the WHT on dividends.

Listed shares
Non-resident entities are exempted from capital gains derived from the sale of stocks listed on the Casablanca stock exchange, excluding the shares of real estate entities.

Withholding taxes

WHT on interests
The standard WHT on interest paid to non-resident entities is set at 10% as provided by the Moroccan law (unless reduced by treaty).

However, the Moroccan law provides that interests on loans granted in foreign currency with a maturity exceeding ten years are exempted from WHT.

WHT on dividends
The standard WHT rate on dividends is set at 10% according to the Moroccan law (unless reduced by treaty).

WHT does not apply to dividends paid to Moroccan companies subject to Moroccan corporate tax, subject to the delivery of a property attestation.

A branch tax of 10% applies to the net income transferred by the Moroccan branch to the foreign entities (maybe reduced by the tax treaty).

WHT on services paid to non-resident entities
According to the Moroccan tax code, all payments of all kind of services rendered by non-resident entities are subject to WHT at the rate of 10%.

However, it shall be noted that treaties dispositions limit the scope of application of WHT only to remunerations that constitute royalties. Such dispositions overrule the domestic tax law provided by the Moroccan law.

Treaty WHT rates
Payments to non-resident corporations and individuals are subject to WHT, as shown below.

	WHT (%)			
	Dividends			
Recipient	Individuals and non-qualified companies	Qualifying companies	Interest (1)	Royalties
Arab Maghreb Union (2)	(3)	(3)	(3)	(3)
Austria	10	5	10	10
Bahrain	10	5	10	10
Belgium	10	6.5	10	10
Bulgaria	10	7	10	10
Canada*	10	10	10	5/10 (4)
China (People's Rep.)	10	10	0/10	5/10
Czech Republic	10	10	10	10
Denmark*	10	10	10	10
Egypt*	10	10	10	10
Finland*	10	10	10	10
France*	10	10	10/10	5/10 (4)

Morocco

	WHT (%)			
	Dividends			
Recipient	**Individuals and non-qualified companies**	**Qualifying companies**	**Interest (1)**	**Royalties**
Germany*	10	5	10	10
Hungary*	10	10	10	10
India	10	10	10	10
Italy*	10	10	10	5/10 (4)
Jordan	10	10	10	10
Korea (Rep.)	10	5	10	10
Latvia	10	6	10	10
Lebanon	10	5	10	5/10 (4)
Luxembourg*	10	10	10	10
Malaysia	10	5	0/10	10
Malta	10	6.5	0/10	10
Netherlands*	10	10	10	10
Norway*	10	10	10	10
Oman	10	5	0/10	10
Pakistan	10	10	10	10
Poland*	10	7	10	10
Portugal*	10	10	10	10
Qatar	10	5	0/10	10
Romania	10	10	10	10
Russia	10	5	10	10
Spain*	10	10	10	5/10 (4)
Switzerland*	10	7	10	10
Syria*	10	7	10	10
Turkey	10	7	10	10
Ukraine	10	10	10	10
United Arab Emirates	10	5	10	10
United Kingdom*	10	10	10	10
United States*	10	10	10	10

Notes

* In case the rate provided by the double tax treaty (DTT) is higher than the one provided by the Moroccan Tax Code, the rate provided by the Moroccan Tax Code (10%) should apply.

1. Some treaties provide for an exemption for certain types of interest (e.g. interest paid to public bodies and institutions). Such exemptions are not dealt with in this treaty chart.
2. Arab Maghreb Union, the member states of which are Algeria, Libya, Mauritania, Morocco, and Tunisia.
3. There is no limitation on WHT under the treaty.
4. The lower rate (i.e. 5%) usually applies to copyright royalties and other similar payments in respect of the production or reproduction of any literary, artistic, or dramatic work (excluding cinematographic and television films), while the 10% rate applies to other types of royalties.

Tax administration

Taxable period

The taxable period corresponds to 12 months. The first taxable period can be less than one year but should never exceed it.

Tax returns
CIT returns must be filed within three months following the closing of the fiscal year.

Payment of tax
Payment of tax is made during the fiscal year by way of four instalments of 25% each based on the CIT of the previous year.

In case the CIT of the year exceeds the sum of the four instalments, the company should proceed to tax regularisation along with the submitting of the taxable income return after three months following the closing of the fiscal year (i.e. 31 March for fiscal year corresponding to the calendar year).

Otherwise, the exceeding tax amount can be imputed on the four following instalments. Any remaining excess is reimbursed by the tax authorities.

Statute of limitations
The statute of limitations runs until the end of the following fourth year. This period may be extended in case of deficits or credits.

Topics of focus of tax authorities
The topics of focus of tax authorities depend on each specific situation (sector of activity, company size, etc.). However, it is very common to find the following points:

* Transfer pricing.
* Tax treatment of provisions.
* Taxation of indemnities and benefits granted to employees.

.M

Other issues

Exchange controls
Foreign investors are allowed, following the accomplishment of some formalities, to freely transfer abroad the whole proceeds of their investments in Morocco (i.e. dividends, shares sale price, and liquidation income at the condition that the initial investment is realised in one of the foreign currencies listed by the Moroccan Central Bank).

However, some specific transfers of funds into and out of Morocco are subject to prior authorisations from the exchange control office.

Choice of business entity
The legal vehicles used by foreign companies for the purpose of setting up a business in Morocco are the branch and the subsidiary.

Under subsidiary form, the foreign entities generally opt for the corporation (SA) or the limited liability company (SARL).

The SARL is most adequate for companies with low investment capital while the SA is most appropriate for companies that are investing an important amount of capital. In general, the rules relating to the organisation and functioning of an SARL are more flexible than those required for an SA.

Mozambique

PwC contact

João Martins
PricewaterhouseCoopers, Lda
Pestana Rovuma Hotel
Centro de Escritòrios, 5th floor
Rua de Sé 114
Maputo
Mozambique
Tel: +258 21 350 400
Email: joao.l.martins@mz.pwc.com

Significant developments

There have been no significant corporate tax developments in Mozambique during the
past year.

Taxes on corporate income

Corporate income tax (CIT) is payable on general corporate income at a tax rate of
32%. For tax years ending prior to 1 January 2016, income arising from agricultural or
cattle breeding activities is subject to a reduced rate of 10%.

CIT is levied on taxable profits, defined as accounting profits adjusted to comply with
tax law rules.

Corporate entities and other entities with headquarters or permanent establishment
(PE) in Mozambique are subject to CIT based on their worldwide income. On the
other hand, corporate entities and other entities without headquarters or PE in
Mozambique (i.e. non-resident entities) are only subject to CIT on the income earned in
Mozambique.

Local income taxes
See Municipality taxes in the Other taxes section.

Corporate residence

Corporate residence is determined on the basis of a company's place of incorporation or
effective management. Thus, all companies with headquarters in Mozambique, as well
as any PE of non-resident entities, are considered tax residents and are liable for CIT on
their worldwide income.

Permanent establishment (PE)
Under the relevant internal legislation, a non-resident entity is deemed to have a PE in
Mozambique whenever any of the following circumstances exists:

- It has premises or other fixed places of business through which industrial, trading,
  agricultural, rendering of services, or similar activities are totally or partially
  carried out.
- It has an office, branch, plant, workshop, mines, quarries, oil or natural gas wells, or
  other places of extraction of natural resources.

- It has a construction, installation, or assembly site when the duration of works exceed six months, including the activities of coordination, inspection, and supervision connected to these sites.
- It has persons or hired personnel, acting and dealing in Mozambique, who are not independent agents in the terms of the law but rather acting on behalf of the company with legal capacity to conclude contracts on its behalf and its name within the scope of the company's activities.

Other taxes

Value-added tax (VAT)
VAT is chargeable on the sale of most goods and services as well as on imports. The standard rate is 17%. Usually, VAT is recoverable by corporate entities, except for those engaged in special business activities (e.g. financial and insurance operations, leasing [exemption with restrictions], sale of immovable property, some exempt activities).

Customs duties
Custom duties are charged on importation of goods into Mozambique, and the applicable rates vary from 0% to 20%. Mozambique is part of the Southern African Development Community (SADC) protocol on commercial trade that exempts from customs duties some goods produced within the SADC region. However, in order to benefit from the exemption, the importer should provide proof of the origin of the said goods through the presentation of the certificate of origin of goods.

Mozambique also has signed agreements with the European Union (EU) based on which preferential rates are applicable on certain goods imported from such region.

M

Excise taxes
Excise duties are levied on certain goods manufactured locally or imported, which are identified in a specific table that is an integrant part of the excise duty act that also indicates the applicable rates. Amongst others, the said table includes goods such as tobacco, beer and other alcoholic beverages, vehicles, cosmetics, cloths, airplanes, boats, etc.

Recently, the excise duty act was changed through Laws 2/2012 and 5/2012, both dated 23 January, and Decree 2/2012, dated 24 February, and some rates were increased as follows:

- Alcoholic beverages: Although the general rate is 40%, it was increased to 55% for wine of fresh grape.
- Tobacco: The general rate was increased by 10%, and the new rate is 75%.
- Air vehicle without engine: The applicable rate was reduced by 30%, and the new rate is 35%.
- Boats and other recreational or sportive crafts: The applicable rate was reduced by 5%, and the new rate is 35%.
- Cloths and respective accessories: The applicable rate was reduced by 10%, and the new rate is 30%.

Property transfer taxes (SISA)
In Mozambique, a property transfer tax is charged on transfers of real estate, excluding the land, which is owned by the state. The rate of tax is 2% of the selling price of the building.

Mozambique

Stamp taxes and service charges
Various documents require the payment of stamp duties. Service charges are payable for the performance of certain services for official purposes, such as those rendered by public notaries. These duties have been recently amended and vary generally from 0.03% to 50% on the amount of the transaction supported by the document to be stamped. In some other cases, the stamp tax comprises fixed amounts, ranging from 0.50 Mozambican meticals (MZN) to MZN 5,000.

Municipality taxes
Municipality taxes that should be considered for corporate purposes include the following:

Municipality tax on real estate
The municipality tax on real estate is levied annually on the value of immovable assets situated within the municipality and owned or possessed by corporate entities. Effective tax rates range from 0.2% to 1% of the building value, depending on the municipality.

Municipality tax on economic activities
The municipality tax on economic activities is levied on commercial or industrial activities carried out within a municipal territory. The tax depends on the activity being carried out, adjusted by coefficients, which are based on the zone and total area of the premises in square metres. In Maputo, this tax is calculated based on the following formula:

Maputo tax on economic activities = Basis rate x Index of category x Index of location x Index of area occupied

Where the basis rate is the applicable maximum amount of the national minimum salary (currently MZN 5,320, approximately 200 United States dollars [USD]).

Where the index of the location varies from 1.3 to 1.5 depending on the location of the premises within the municipality.

Where the index of the area occupied varies from 1.2 to 1.5 depending on the nature of the activities and the space occupied by the premises.

Municipal vehicles tax
This tax replaces the vehicles tax within the municipality and is levied on the use of specific vehicles (e.g. light and heavy vehicles less than 25 years old, motorcycles less than 15 years old, aeroplanes, and boats for private use). This tax is due by the owners who are residents of a municipality, regardless of the place of registration of the vehicle owned.

The rate varies, depending on specific criteria such as type of fuel, engine capacity, period of registration, and weight.

This tax must be paid between January and March or within 30 days after the acquisition of the vehicle.

Branch income

From a tax perspective, branches are liable for Mozambican CIT as a separate entity; therefore, the regime is the same that would apply to a Mozambican resident company. However, on the grounds that branches do not distribute dividends, the 20% withholding tax (WHT) does not apply to the after-tax profits arising in Mozambique.

Income determination

Inventory valuation
Special rules regarding valuation of inventories are still waiting for approval from the Minister of Finance. In the meantime, all inventory valuation methods generally accepted and according to international accounting principles are permitted for tax purposes, provided that the method is:

- used by the taxpayer consistently and
- based on arm's-length prices duly documented and effectively exercised.

Based on the above assumptions, last in first out (LIFO) and first in first out (FIFO) methods are allowed. Write-downs and depreciation of inventories are not allowed. Conformity between book and tax reporting is required.

In principle, large companies began adopting International Financial Reporting Standards (IFRS) in 2010.

Capital gains
Capital gains less any capital losses derived from the sale or disposal of tangible fixed assets, including insurance indemnities received in case of accident, are taxed as part of normal income. If a taxpayer reinvests the sale proceeds within three tax years following the year of sale, the gain may be deferred until the end of the third year. A four-year reinvestment period may be accepted provided a prior application is submitted to the Minister of Finance. However, if the taxpayer does not realise the reinvestment, the CIT that was not assessed during the three-year period will be assessed, along with compensatory interest.

Dividend income
In the case of resident companies, income arising from dividends is excluded from taxable income, provided that the shares that a resident company holds in another resident company represents at least 20% of the total capital and are held for at least two consecutive years (or with an undertaking to hold the shares for this period). The same applies to income arising from risk capital companies and holding companies (*Sociedade Gestora de Participações Sociais* or SGPSs) or from subsidiaries as a result of the application of technical reserves in insurance companies. However, in the case of holdings, the percentage of share capital decreases to 10% and shares should be held for at least one year.

If the shareholding falls outside the parameters indicated above, the tax withheld (20%) constitutes a payment on account. A tax credit corresponding to 62.5% of the CIT is attributable to the gross-up dividend.

Interest income
Interest is subject to 20% WHT. In the case of foreign entities, the WHT is considered as a definitive tax. In the case of resident entities, it is considered as an advance of the final tax.

M

Mozambique

Foreign income

Mozambican resident companies are taxed on the total income earned on a worldwide basis. Please note that there is no provision on tax deferral in Mozambique in relation to income earned abroad. Double taxation treaties (DTTs) allow tax paid abroad to offset Mozambican CIT. Mozambique has signed DTTs with Botswana, India, Italy, Macau, Mauritius, Portugal, South Africa, the United Arab Emirates, and Vietnam.

Deductions

Depreciation

Depreciation is a deductible cost for CIT purposes, according to the regulations of the Corporate Income Tax Code, subject to restrictive and specific rules.

The main legal principles regarding depreciation are as follows:

- The establishment of the applicable rates falls under the competence of the Ministry of Finance.
- The calculation is carried out on a straight-line basis in accordance with the rates applicable.

The main depreciation rates are:

Assets	Rate (%)
Tangible assets:	
Industrial buildings	4
Office and residential buildings	2
Machinery and installations, air conditioning, and telephone equipment	10
Lifts	8.33
Tools	25
Laboratory equipment	12.5
Telex and interior equipment	10
Furniture and filing systems	10
Typewriters and accounting machines	14.28
Computer hardware	16.66
Warehouse and filing installations:	
Of concrete	5
Of wood	6.66
Of steel	8.33
Trucks	20
Automobiles	25
Intangible assets:	
Pre-operating expenses incurred prior to the commencement of business	33.33
Deferred expenses arising in connection with increases in share capital, changes in form of business enterprises, issuance of debentures, marketing and other studies, and financial expenses incurred for the acquisition or own production of fixed assets prior to completion	33.33
Patents	10
Manufacturing licenses, concessionaire agreements, and similar rights	5 (1)
Trademark or premium of taking over leases of real estate (2)	

Notes

1. Subject to certain conditions set forth by the tax authorities.
2. Depreciation is only allowed in cases of effective reduction of value within the limits regarded as reasonable by the tax authorities.

Accelerated depreciation
New immovable assets, used for the furtherance of the business, may be depreciated by increasing to 50% the normal depreciation rates approved by law. This benefit is also granted to rehabilitated immovable assets, machinery, and equipment used in agro-industrial activities.

Bad debt
In Mozambique, companies are able to create all the provisions necessary and relevant for the normal course of business. However, for tax purposes, only the provisions listed below can be deducted as a cost:

- Bad debts.
- Depreciation of stock.
- Ongoing judicial procedures.
- Credit institutions/Insurance companies.
- Reconstruction of mines.
- Rehabilitation of land.

Any other provisions reflected in the company's accounts will not be accepted as tax deductible costs.

With regards to provisions for bad debts, companies are only allowed to deduct 1.5% per year (and 6% accumulated) of the provisions created for bad debts.

Charitable contributions
Donations can be deducted as cost for tax purposes, provided the beneficiaries thereof are:

- Social and cultural organisations that, acting without lucrative intent, carry out actions in art, education, science, health, preservation and restoration of cultural patrimony, or social activities: Donations can be deducted up to the limit of 5% of the previous year taxable income.
- The Mozambican state: Donations can be fully deducted.

Fines and penalties
Fines and other penalties paid due to any infringement, which do not have a contractual basis, including interest, are not accepted as tax deductible costs.

Taxes
Taxes paid in relation to the activities of a company are tax-deductible, excluding CIT itself.

Net operating losses
Carryback of losses is not allowed in Mozambique. On the other hand, losses may be carried forward for a period of five consecutive years.

Payments to foreign affiliates
Any payments to non-residents are allowed as deductible expenses provided that the amount does not exceed normal rates and that the taxpayer is able to prove

Mozambique

that a business transaction was carried out with the non-resident company. The tax authorities may redetermine taxable income if, due to a special relationship between the Mozambican and non-resident companies, certain conditions existed that allowed a calculation of profit that differed from the profit that would have been calculated without the existence of such relationship (i.e. the arm's-length principle).

Group taxation

There are no group taxation provisions available in Mozambique. Each member of a group of companies preparing consolidated accounts for accounting purposes must file separate tax returns in order to be taxed on its profits on a stand-alone basis.

Transfer pricing

The tax authorities may proceed with the necessary corrections for assessing the profits for tax purposes whenever:

- by virtue of special relations between the taxpayer and other entity, different conditions from those that should be normally agreed upon between independent entities have been established, and
- in consequence of those conditions, the profits for accounts purposes are different from those that would have resulted had such special relations not existed.

The corrections above shall be equally applicable whenever the profits for accounts purposes regarding non-resident entities are different from those that should have resulted if the non-resident entity were a separate entity carrying out similar activities in similar conditions and with total independence.

The corrections referred above will also be applicable to entities that carry out activities simultaneously subject and not subject to the CIT Code, provided that similar evasion regarding such activities is verified.

Whenever these corrections are applicable to one taxpayer of CIT (Taxpayer 1) by virtue of special relations with another taxpayer of CIT or of individual income tax (Taxpayer 2), the adjustments reflecting the corrections made in the calculation of the profits for tax purposes of Taxpayer 1 shall be applicable in the assessment of the profits for tax purposes of Taxpayer 2.

Thin capitalisation

Where loans from related foreign corporations exceed twice the corresponding equity in the borrowing Mozambican corporation, the interest on the excess borrowing is not tax-deductible. Thin capitalisation rules are in force.

According to the Mozambican thin capitalisation rules, subsidiaries are considered and treated as thinly capitalised companies if and to the extent that, as at any date of the tax period, any of their relevant debt to equity ratios exceeds a factor of two.

'Relevant debt to equity ratio', within the context of the law, means the ratio between, on one hand, the amount of direct and indirect indebtedness of a Mozambican company towards a specially related non-resident, and on the other, the amount of equity that this non-resident holds in the Mozambican company.

A 'specially related non-resident', for these purposes, is an entity with special links with another, which includes any entity that:

- holds, either directly or indirectly, at least 25% of the share capital of the Mozambican company
- though holding less than 25%, has a significant influence on its management, or
- both taxpayer and non-resident entity are under control of the same entity, which has participation in their share capital, either directly or indirectly.

Under any of these circumstances, interest paid to such specially related non-residents is not allowed as a tax deductible cost for the Mozambican company in the part that corresponds to the excessive indebtedness, unless the company can prove that it could have obtained the same level of indebtedness at comparable conditions from unrelated parties, taking into account the nature of its business, its sector of activity, dimension, and other relevant criteria.

Tax credits and incentives

Foreign tax credit
Resident companies are allowed to deduct a credit correspondent to a tax paid abroad. The tax credit to be deducted should be equal to the lower of the amount of Mozambican corporate tax imputed to income obtained abroad or the amount of foreign tax effectively paid.

Inbound investment incentives
In addition to the guarantees of ownership and remittance of funds abroad, the Mozambican government also guarantees the concession of tax and customs incentives. The incentives vary depending on whether a company is starting a new venture or rehabilitating one and also on the nature of the project to be developed. The incentives discussed in this section are the generic benefits applicable to standard projects. Certain specific benefits also may be applicable depending on the activities of the industry for the investment project (e.g. agriculture, tourism, science and technology).

Exemption from import duties
An exemption from customs duties and VAT applies upon the importation of capital equipment, listed in Section K of the Customs Tariff Schedule.

Tax credit for investment
Investments in new fixed tangible assets used in the operations of an enterprise within the Mozambican territory may benefit from an investment tax credit equal to 5% of the total investment realised, for a period of five years. This investment tax credit is offset against CIT, up to the total amount of the tax assessment. This incentive does not apply when the investment in tangible fixed assets is with respect to the construction, acquisition, restoration, or extension of buildings, passenger vehicles, furnishings, and articles of comfort and decoration, leisure equipment, advanced technology, or other assets not directly associated with the production activity carried out by the enterprise. When the project is located outside Maputo City, this tax credit is increased to up to 15% depending on the province.

Advanced technology incentive
The amount invested in specialised equipment classified as advanced technology, during the first five years from the date of commencement of activity, may be deducted from taxable income for purposes of calculating CIT, up to a maximum of 10% of taxable income.

M

Mozambique

Professional training incentive
Investment expenditures for professional training of Mozambican workers shall, up to a maximum amount of 5% of the taxable income (10% in case of professional training related to new/high technology equipment), be deductible from taxable income for the purposes of calculating CIT during the first five years from the date of the commencement of such activities.

Exploration incentives
During a period of five years counting from the date of exploration (i.e. the date the implementing company starts the activities approved under the investment project terms of authorisation), the following expenditure may be treated as deductible expenditures for purposes of calculating CIT:

- In the case of undertakings carried out in the City of Maputo, 110% of the value of expenditures for the construction and rehabilitation of roads, railways, airports, telecommunications, water supply, electric energy, and other works of public utility is deductible for tax purposes.
- In the case of undertakings carried out in the rest of the Provinces, an amount equal to 120% of the expenditures referred to in the paragraph above is deductible for tax purposes.
- In the case of expenditures for the acquisition for personal ownership of works of art and other objects that are representative of Mozambican culture, as well as activities that contribute to the development of such works, 50% of the expenditures are deductible for tax purposes.

Withholding taxes

Any non-resident entity carrying out economic activities in Mozambique, without being registered as a taxpayer, is liable to a final and definitive 20% WHT that is applied on all income earned. An exception exists for telecommunications and international transport as well as the respective installation and assembly of equipment made by those same entities, which are subject to a 10% WHT rate.

Both Mozambican resident and non-resident recipients are liable to tax on dividends at a tax rate of 20%.

Tax treaties
In accordance with Mozambique's DTTs, the following tax rates are applicable to dividends, interest, and royalties:

Recipient	WHT (%)			
	Dividends	Interest	Royalties	Capital gains on shares
Botswana	0/12 (4, 5)	10	10	0
India	7.5	10	10	0
Italy	15	10	10	0
Macau	10	10	10	0
Mauritius	8/10/15 (1, 2, 3)	8	5	0
Portugal	15	10	10	10
South Africa	8/15 (1, 3)	8	5	0
United Arab Emirates	0	0	5	0
Vietnam	10	10	10	0

Notes

1. The 8% rate applies if the recipient of the dividends is a company which has more than 25% of the share capital in the company that distributes the dividends.
2. The 10% rate applies if the recipient of the dividends is a company which has less than 25% of the share capital in the company that distributes the dividends.
3. The 15% rate applies in all other cases.
4. The 0% rate applies if the recipient of the dividends is a company which has more than 25% of the share capital in the company that distributes the dividends.
5. The 12% rate applies in all other cases.

Tax administration

Taxable period
The tax year is, as a general rule, the calendar year. A different tax year may be applied (if previously authorised by the Ministry of Finance) for companies that carry out activities that justify a different year or non-resident companies with a PE in Mozambique.

Tax returns
CIT assessment must be prepared by the companies on annual returns, based on the accounting records and on adjustments prescribed by the tax regulations.

The submission of the annual tax return is due by the last working day of May for companies using the calendar year as their tax year. For companies with a tax year that is not coincident with the calendar year, the presentation of the tax return is due by the last day of the fifth month subsequent to the respective year-end.

Payment of tax
Mozambican companies and non-resident companies with a PE in Mozambique must pay CIT in one of the two following ways:

- In three advance payments (based on 80% of the preceding tax year's CIT), due in May, July, and September of the respective tax year; or if the tax year chosen is not coincident with the calendar year, on the fifth, seventh, and ninth months of the respective tax year.
- In three special advance payments (based on 0.5% of the preceding year's turnover less the advance payments made in previous years, which cannot be less than MZN 30,000 or more than MZN 100,000) due in June, August, and October of the respective tax year; or if the tax year chosen is not coincident with the calendar year, on the sixth, eighth, and tenth months of the respective year.

Audit cycle
The tax authorities may carry out an inspection whenever necessary. Normally, the inspection occurs after the taxpayer files a refund application.

Statute of limitations
The statute of limitations period is five years.

M

Namibia, Republic of

PwC contact

Stéfan Hugo
PricewaterhouseCoopers
344 Independence Avenue
Windhoek, Namibia
Tel: +264 61 284 1000
Email: stefan.hugo@na.pwc.com

Significant developments

2012 National Budget
On 28 February 2012, the Honourable Minister of Finance, Ms. Saara Kuugongelwa-Amadhila again had the huge task to balance the 10th National Budget against a global economic background of a continued weak developed world (and the European Union [EU] in particular) while oil prices remain high. A rebound in Southern Africa Customs Union (SACU) transfers gave the Minister some extra resources to use to decrease the deficit while maintaining expenditures.

Some highlights of the Budget include the following:

- Measures to improve revenue collection were emphasised, including a voluntary disclosure programme and a planned simplified tax system for small and medium-sized enterprises (SMEs).
- Some tax measures were planned for 2012, including a revised corporate income tax for non-diamond mining companies, an environmental levy on a range of harmful products, a differentiated tax rate for the export of natural resources, an increase in non-resident shareholders tax, and a withholding tax (WHT) on fees paid to non-residents.
- The usual excise duty increases on liquor and tobacco products were announced.

Amendments to the value-added tax (VAT), stamp duty, and transfer duty are expected to be tabled during 2012.

Income Tax Third Amendment Act, Act 15 of 2011
The following amended legislation was promulgated as the Income Tax Third Amendment Act, Act 15 of 2011:

Mining licences/rights
Any sale/donation/expropriation cession, grant, or other alienation or transfer of ownership of a licence or right to mine minerals have been included in the definition of gross income. The definition also specifically includes a sale of shares in a company for a licence or right to mine minerals in Namibia.

The new legislation only covers mining licences/rights, whereas the original proposal referred to 'natural resources' that could impact other industries as well.

Section 15, as proposed, deems these profits to be from a Namibian source irrespective of:

- whether the transaction is concluded in or outside Namibia
- the place where the payment of such amount is made, or
- the place where the funds from which the payment is made are held.

Export allowance
Section 17C of the Act dealing with the export allowance for manufactured goods was amended to include only goods manufactured in Namibia.

WHT on interest
The reference to unit trust schemes was removed from the new definition of 'negotiable instrument'; consequently, WHT will be due from interest of any negotiable instrument issued by unit trust schemes.

Interest on negotiable instruments issued by a banking institution will not be subject to WHT on interest.

The treatment of undisclosed investors who are represented by an agent or any other person (excluding a stock broker) for WHT on interest purposes will apply to both financial institutions and unit trust schemes. This means that investments by undisclosed investors through their agents will be treated the same by financial institutions and unit trust schemes. Previously, the treatment of undisclosed investors was only applicable to financial institutions.

Section 34D was amended to include Subsection 7, which requires the WHT on interest from a deemed distribution (i.e. non distribution) to be paid within 60 days after the financial year end.

For the purposes of WHT on interest, 'gross interest' is defined as follows:

"gross interest means: interest excluding interest from stock or securities [which includes] ... Treasury Bills issued by the government of Namibia, a regional council, or local authority".

WHT on services
Section 35A introduces a 25% WHT on entertainment fees paid to a non-resident as well as consultancy, management, and directors fees paid to a non-resident for administrative, managerial, technical, consultative, or any similar services.

The resident person making the payment to the non-resident is liable to withhold and pay the tax within 20 days from the end of the month during which the amount was withheld.

Where the resident fails to pay over such tax, the resident will become liable for the amount of tax.

The WHT is applicable irrespective of where the services are performed. There is a presumption that where a payment is made to an address outside Namibia, the amount will be deemed to be made to a non-resident, and, accordingly, the WHT will apply.

Non-resident shareholders tax (NRST)
The NRST rate increased from 10% to 20%. The 10% rate will still be applicable to investors holding at least 25% of the share capital in the Namibian company.

Building allowance
The initial 20% building allowance will only be applicable on the cost of erection of a building used for purpose of trade and only in the year the building is brought into use. The 4% allowance is only claimable in the year following the year in which the building was brought into use.

Namibia, Republic of

The same applies with regards to the 20% and 8% building allowance in respect of buildings used solely for manufacturing.

Provisional tax payment penalties

Underestimation penalties (limited to 100% of the underpaid tax) and interest will be levied on both the first and second provisional tax payments where the estimate is less than 40% and 80% respectively of the actual taxable income for the year.

Late submission provisional returns will be is subject to a penalty of 100 Namibian dollars (NAD) per day that the form is late.

Late payment of provisional tax will further be subject to a penalty of 10% per month (limited to the tax payable). Previously, this was a once off 10% penalty.

Company-owned insurance policies

The 'gross income' definition will be extended to include the following company-owned insurance policies in taxable income:

"An amount received, including a loan or advance, by an insurer for any policy of insurance, on the life of an employee or director, if the premiums made to such a policy was allowed as a tax deduction".

A new Section 17(w) will allow a tax deduction for a taxpayer (employer) for any premiums paid under a long-term insurance policy, where the taxpayer (employer) is the policy holder. This deduction is allowed provided that all of the following requirements are met:

- The premium expended by the taxpayer (employer) is included in the taxable income of the employee for fringe benefit purposes.
- The taxpayer (employer) is insured against any loss due to death, disablement, or severe illness of an employee or director.
- The policy is a risk policy with no cash value prior to occurrence of payment.
- The policy is not the property of any other person (i.e. ceded to a creditor or financial institution as security for debt or loan).
- No transaction or arrangement exists where the taxpayer (employer) will pay any amount over to an employee or representative.

Pending legislation

Please note this information is current as of 1 June 2012. Typically, pending legislation is announced in June or July. Please visit the Worldwide Tax Summaries website at www.pwc.com/taxsummaries to see any significant corporate tax developments that occurred after 1 June 2012.

Taxes on corporate income

Namibia has a source-based tax system, which means that income from a source within Namibia or deemed to be within Namibia will be subject to tax in Namibia, unless a specific exemption is available.

Income earned by foreign companies from a source within or deemed to be within Namibia will be subject to tax in Namibia. In such cases, the foreign entity must determine whether it is obliged to register a local entity or branch. A company is required to register a branch if it has established a place of business in Namibia. A local subsidiary company may be registered as an alternative to a branch.

In the event that Namibia has entered into a double tax agreement (DTA) with the country where the foreign company resides, such entity will only be taxable in Namibia if it has established a permanent establishment (PE) in Namibia. If a PE exists, only the portion of income attributable to the PE will be subject to tax in Namibia.

Non-residents who do not have a place of business in Namibia may, however, be subject to WHT. *See the Withholding taxes section for more information.*

Calculation of taxable income

Gross income	The total amount, in cash or otherwise, received by or accrued to any person from a source within, or deemed to be within, Namibia, excluding receipts of a capital nature (provisions for specific inclusions in gross income and amounts deemed to be from a Namibian source exist).
Less: Exemptions	The Act provides for certain amounts to be specifically exempt from tax.
Equals: Income	
Less: Deductions	Expenditures and losses actually incurred to generate income may be deducted, provided that these expenses are not of a capital nature.
	The Act specifically provides for certain expenditures to be deductible and allows a deduction for capital allowances.
	Only expenses incurred to generate 'income' may be deducted. Expenses incurred to generate income exempt from tax are not deductible. Apportionment should be considered when expenses are incurred to generate both income and exempt income.
Equals: Taxable income	Taxable income is taxed at the corporate tax rate as set out under the tax rate section below.

Tax rates

The corporate tax rates are summarised below:

Entity	Current tax rate (%)
Domestic companies and close corporations (excluding entities mentioned below)	34
Branches of foreign companies	34
Registered manufacturers (only applicable for the first ten years of registration)	18
Diamond mining companies and companies that render services to such companies in connection with diamond mining	55
Mining companies (other than diamond mining companies) and companies that render services to such companies in connection with mining	37.5
Long-term insurers (the rate is applied to gross investment income)	13.6
Petroleum income tax rate	35

Corporate residence

The Namibian tax system is based on source and not on residency. Income derived or deemed to be derived from sources within Namibia are subject to tax.

Namibia, Republic of

The source is determined as the place where income originates or is earned, not the place of payment. If goods are sold pursuant to a contract entered into within Namibia, the source of income is deemed to arise in Namibia, regardless of the place of delivery or transfer of title.

Certain types of income arising outside Namibia may, in the hands of a domestic company, be deemed to arise in Namibia and be taxed as such. Examples are interest and certain copyright royalties arising outside Namibia.

Permanent establishment (PE)
A PE includes, in most cases, a fixed place of business. The establishment of a local entity or branch will usually create a PE, although the provisions of the related tax treaty should be considered.

Except for the PE concept embodied in the tax treaties, corporate residence is of little tax significance.

Other taxes

Value-added tax (VAT)
VAT is a transaction tax, and the implications will vary for different transactions. Some transactions are taxed at a rate of 15% or 0% while other transactions are exempt from VAT. Input tax deductions may be claimed, subject to certain provisions.

VAT is levied on every taxable supply by a registered person. A taxable supply means any supply of goods or services in the course or furtherance of a taxable activity. A taxable activity means any activity that is carried on continuously or regularly in Namibia which involves the supply of goods or services for consideration.

VAT is payable on all imports for home consumption in Namibia, subject to certain exemptions (e.g. in terms of a technical assistance agreement, donations to the state, goods of which the local supply is zero-rated).

Import VAT is payable on the greater of the free on board (FOB) value plus 10%, or the market value. The payment may be deferred in terms of an import VAT account registered with the Directorate of Inland Revenue to the 20th day of the month following the month of importation. Penalties of 10% per month or part of a month and 20% interest on outstanding import VAT, according to the Customs Asycuda reports on import VAT account numbers, are levied by the Directorate of Inland Revenue.

A company/branch is required to register for VAT if it supplies goods or services on a regular basis for consideration and if its taxable supplies (standard rated and zero-rated supplies) exceed NAD 200,000 in any 12-month period.

A registered VAT vendor is entitled to deduct input tax credits paid in the course of taxable supplies made to such person, provided that a tax invoice is available to support the input tax deduction. It is also important to take note of deemed input tax deductions and prohibited input deductions. Import VAT paid may be deducted only as input tax if the import was in furtherance of a taxable activity and the required documentation (e.g. stamped customs entries) is held by the importer.

VAT returns are due within 25 days following the month to which the VAT relates.

Customs and excise duties

Namibia is a member of the Southern African Customs Union (SACU), and customs duties are not levied on intra SACU trade (i.e. between Botswana, Lesotho, Namibia, South Africa, and Swaziland).

Customs duties are payable according to the Common Customs Tariff of SACU on imports from outside SACU. Preferential duty rates apply on imports from Southern African Development Community (SADC) countries, while goods may be imported free of customs duties from Zimbabwe in terms of the Namibia-Zimbabwe Free Trade Agreement.

Excise duties are levied on local production of excisable products (e.g. cigarettes, liquor, fuel) and are included on most excisable products imported from another SACU country in terms of the duty at source procedures. Identical excise duty rates are applied throughout the SACU. Importation of excisable products from outside the SACU is subject to customs duties and specific customs duties.

Current specific excise/customs duty rates for the above-mentioned products are as follows:

- Cigarettes: NAD 5.16/10 cigarettes.
- Beer: NAD 59.36/litre absolute alcohol (AA).
- Spirits (whisky, rum, brandy, gin, vodka, etc): NAD 111.64/litre AA.
- Petrol: NAD 39.09/litre.
- Diesel and biodiesel: NAD 38.17/litre.
- Illuminating kerosene (paraffin): NAD 38.14/litre.

Ad valorem excise/customs duties are levied on certain products (e.g. motor vehicles, perfumes) in addition to the normal customs duties.

Current *ad valorem* excise/customs duty rates are as follows for the above-mentioned goods:

- Motor vehicles: ([0.00003 x A] - 0.75)%, with a maximum of 25%, where 'A' is the recommended retail price, exclusive of VAT.
- Perfumes: 7%.

Fuel levies are payable on petrol, diesel, and illuminating kerosene and may be claimed back for certain non-road operations (e.g. mining, farming, and construction).

The current fuel levies are as follows:

- Petrol: NAD 0.12/litre.
- Diesel: NAD 0.10/litre.
- Illuminating kerosene (paraffin): NAD 0.47/litre.

Surety in the form of a provisional payment, bank, or insurance guarantee is required by Customs on all temporary importations to cover import VAT and customs duties (if applicable).

It is possible to import goods that are subject to customs duties into registered Customs' bonded warehouses, where goods are kept for later use. In this case, the payment of duties may be deferred until the goods are taken out of the bonded warehouse for home consumption or acquitted if the goods are subsequently exported.

Namibia, Republic of

Property taxes
Property taxes are levied by municipalities based on municipal valuations of properties.

Transfer duty
Transfer duty is payable at 12% of the acquisition value of real property acquired. While it is normally payable by the buyer, the agreement for the sale of the property may determine the person liable to pay these costs.

Amendments to the Transfer Duty Act that will levy transfer duty on the sales of shares/members interest in property-owning entities are expected to be tabled during 2012.

Stamp duty
Certain transactions may attract stamp duty. The amount of stamp duty payable differs and is based on the nature of every individual transaction.

The basic transactions can be summarised as follows:

Transaction	Stamp duty
Agreements or contracts (other than those where duty is specifically provided for in the Act)	NAD 5
Lease agreement or lease	The stamp duty will be based on lease payments, together with additional considerations specified in the lease agreement
Transfer or issue of marketable securities and other share transactions	NAD 2 for every NAD 1,000 or part thereof of the value/consideration, depending on the specific transaction
Transfer deed relating to immovable property purchased.	NAD 12 for every NAD 1,000 or part thereof of the value/consideration, depending on the specific transaction

Annual duty
Annual duty is levied in terms of the Companies Act at an amount of NAD 4.00 for every NAD 10,000 (or part thereof) of the issued share capital of a company, with a minimum duty of NAD 80.00 per annum. Issued share capital includes ordinary shares, share premium, and preference shares.

Since a branch does not issue share capital, the issued share capital of the head office will be used to calculate the annual duty payable in Namibia.

Branch income

Branch income that is received or accrued from a source within, or deemed to be within, Namibia is taxable in Namibia based on the normal corporate tax rules.

A branch is regarded as an extension of its foreign head office. A branch may, therefore, not deduct fees paid to its foreign head office (unless a tax treaty provides for such a deduction), as it is argued that a branch cannot transact with itself. Reimbursement of actual expenses may, however, be deducted, subject to the normal deduction rules.

Transfer pricing rules apply between a branch and its foreign head office or other cross-border related parties.

....

Income determination

Inventory valuation
Inventory is valued at cost for tax purposes in Namibia.

The last in first out (LIFO) basis of valuation is only accepted if:

* written consent was obtained from the Minister of Finance before such taxpayer renders one's income tax return for the first year of assessment for which the LIFO basis was adopted by the taxpayer, and
* various conditions are met by the taxpayer as determined by the Minister of Finance.

Capital gains
Other than profits on the sale of mining licences/rights, capital gains are not taxed in Namibia.

Mining licences/rights
Any sale/donation/expropriation cession, grant, or other alienation or transfer of ownership of a licence or right to mine minerals have been included in the definition of gross income. The definition also specifically includes a sale of shares in a company for a licence or right to mine minerals in Namibia.

The new legislation only covers mining licences/rights, whereas the original proposal referred to 'natural resources' that could impact other industries as well.

Section 15, as proposed, deems these profits to be from a Namibian source irrespective of:

* whether the transaction is concluded in or outside Namibia
* the place where the payment of such amount is made, or
* the place where the funds from which the payment is made are held.

N

Dividend income
Dividends received are exempt from tax. Non-resident shareholders tax (NRST) should be withheld on dividends declared to non-resident shareholders. *For more information on NRST, see the Withholding taxes section.*

Interest income
Namibian companies are taxed on interest received from a Namibian source. Persons other than Namibian companies are subject to a final WHT on interest from banks and unit trusts. *For more information, see the Withholding taxes section.*

Partnership income
The relevant partners of a partnership are regarded as the responsible taxpayers and not the partnership itself.

In practice, the assessment of a partnership is treated like that of a private business. The partnership is first treated as a business entity on its own in terms of income and expenditure. The profit or loss at the end of the year is then allocated to the individual partners. If they derived a profit from the partnership, it is added to their other non-partnership income; or if the partnership made a loss, the partners have the right to deduct it from their non-partnership income.

Namibia, Republic of

Rental income
Companies are taxed on rental income received from a Namibian source.

Royalty income
Companies are taxed on royalty income received from a Namibian source.

Foreign income
Corporate tax in Namibia is determined on the source basis, therefore, only income from a Namibian source or deemed Namibian source is subject to corporate tax.

....

Deductions

Capital allowances
The cost (including finance charges) of machinery, equipment, and other articles used by the taxpayer to generate income is deductible in three equal annual allowances. No apportionment is required where an asset is held for less than 12 months.

Buildings used by the taxpayer to generate income qualify for an initial allowance of 20% of erection costs in the year they are first brought into use. Thereafter, an annual allowance of 4% is deductible for each year following the year of erection. Additions to existing buildings (not alterations or repairs) qualify for the same 20% and 4% deductions. Note that the allowance is calculated on the cost of erection and not the cost of acquisition. The allowance is also only calculated for a period of 21 years from the date of erection.

Mining exploration expenditures incurred before commencement of production are deductible in full in the first year that income is generated from the mine. Subsequent developmental expenditures are written off in three equal annual allowances.

Capital allowances may also be deducted with respect to patents, trademarks, leasehold improvements, etc.

A recovery or recapture of allowances previously claimed should be included in the gross income of a taxpayer in the event that the allowance is recovered or recaptured by way of disposal, withdrawal from trade for non-trade purposes, or removal from Namibia. The recapture is calculated at the market value of the asset.

Goodwill
Goodwill does not constitute an intangible asset. Accordingly, the amortisation of goodwill is not deductible for tax purposes and should be excluded from calculating taxable income.

Start-up expenses

Mining
The Income Tax Act allows exploration expenditure to be deducted in full during the year in which the mine commences with production. All exploration expenses incurred before the commencement of mining is therefore deferred until such time that the mine commences production.

All other industries
The general deduction formula determines that only expenses incurred in the production of income that are not of a capital nature may be claimed for tax purposes. The Income Tax Act defines income as 'income in any year or period of assessment'.

Interest expenses
A deduction is allowed in respect of financing expenditure incurred in respect of any financing agreement (i.e. hire purchases) for the acquisition of fixed assets utilised in ordinary trade activities.

The general deduction formula determines that only expenses incurred in the production of taxable income that are not of a capital nature may be claimed for tax purposes. Therefore, where the interest can be argued to be incurred in the production of income, the interest expense will be deductible.

Thin capitalisation legislation may be applied to interest paid on related party loans (*see Thin capitalisation in the Group taxation section*).

Bad debt
The Income Tax Act allows a specific deduction for bad debts, provided that the amount written off was previously included in the taxpayer's income.

Charitable contributions/donations
A specific deduction for donations is allowed, provided that it is made to a registered welfare organisation or an approved educational institution. It is a further requirement under that a certificate should be issued by the welfare organisation/educational institution in respect of the donation in order for it to qualify as a deduction.

Fines and penalties
In terms of practise applied by Inland Revenue, penalties and fines are not deductible for tax purposes.

Taxes
Taxes levied on income are not allowed as a deduction.

Net operating losses
Assessed tax losses may be carried forward indefinitely, provided the company continues to trade. Tax laws do not allow losses to be transferred to other members of a group, and anti-avoidance provisions may be triggered by transactions designed to transfer or exploit assessed losses.

If a company ceases to trade for a full fiscal year, its assessed losses are forfeited, regardless of subsequent activities. Assessed losses are also reduced in the event of a compromise agreement with creditors.

Namibian tax legislation does not provide for carrying back tax losses.

Payments to foreign affiliates
For information on payments to foreign affiliates, please refer to the Branch income section, Group taxation section, and Withholding taxes section.

Namibia, Republic of

Group taxation

No taxation of combined operations is allowed in Namibia where operations are conducted by more than one company.

Transfer pricing

Namibia introduced transfer pricing legislation on 14 May 2005. The legislation was aimed at enforcing the arm's-length principle in cross-border transactions carried out between connected persons. On 5 September 2006, the Directorate of Inland Revenue issued Income Tax Practice Note 2 of 2006 that contains guidance on the application of the transfer pricing legislation. The Practice Note is based on guidance set out by the Organisation for Economic Co-operation and Development (OECD) Transfer Pricing Guidelines for multinational enterprises and tax administrations.

The objective of this Practice Note is to provide taxpayers with guidelines regarding the procedures to be followed in the determination of arm's-length prices, taking into account the Namibian business environment. It also sets out the Minister of Finance's views on documentation and other practical issues that are relevant in setting and reviewing transfer pricing in international agreements.

Transfer pricing legislation is essentially aimed at ensuring that cross-border transactions between companies operating in a multinational group are fairly priced and that profits are not stripped out of Namibia and taxed in lower tax jurisdictions. The legislation achieves this by giving the Minister of Finance (who essentially delegates to the Directorate of Inland Revenue) the power to adjust any non-market related prices charged or paid by Namibian entities in cross-border transactions with related parties to arm's-length prices and to tax the Namibian entity as if the transactions had been carried out at market-related prices.

In terms of the normal penalty provisions of the Income Tax Act, the Directorate of Inland Revenue may levy penalties of up to 200% on any amount of underpaid tax. Consequently, the Inland Revenue may invoke such provisions in the event that a taxpayer's taxable income is understated as a result of prices that were charged in affected transactions, which were not carried out at arm's length. Further, interest will be charged on the unpaid amounts at 20% per annum.

Thin capitalisation

The Minister may, if any amount of financial assistance provided by a foreign connected person is excessive in relation to a company's fixed capital (being share capital, share premium, accumulated profits, whether capital or not), disallow the deduction for income tax purposes of any interest or other charges payable by the Namibian person on the 'excessive portion' of the financial assistance provided by the foreigner.

There is no guidance that provides a definition for 'excessive'. Therefore, each case should be considered on the basis of the facts provided. The 3:1 ratio is applied by the Bank of Namibia for exchange control purposes, and this guideline is therefore deemed suitable until otherwise determined by Inland Revenue.

Tax credits and incentives

Manufacturing

The following is a high-level comparison of the different tax treatments for normal companies and registered manufacturing companies. This description does not consider the specific conditions that should be met in order for these incentives to be utilised.

Note that only the building allowance and preferential tax rate (*as set out below*) may create or increase a tax loss.

Building allowance

A building allowance is deductible with respect to buildings used for purposes of trade.

For normal companies, the allowance is calculated as 20% of the cost of construction in the year in which the building enters service and 4% during the 20 years that follow the year of construction.

For registered manufacturing companies, the allowance is calculated as 20% of the cost of construction in the year in which the building enters service and 8% during the ten years that follow the year of construction.

Employee allowances

For normal companies, expenditures for remuneration and training of employees are deductible for tax purposes.

For registered manufacturing companies, an additional allowance of 25% of remuneration and training of employees that are directly engaged in the manufacturing process are deductible.

Export expenditure allowance

For normal companies, export expenditures incurred are deductible for tax purposes.

For registered manufacturing companies, an additional allowance of 25% of costs incurred in an export country, in order to export Namibian manufactured goods to such country, may be deducted.

Export allowance

Any taxpayer that derives income from the export of manufactured goods, excluding meat or fish, may deduct an export allowance equal to 80% of the taxable income derived from the export of manufactured goods.

Gross profit derived from the export of manufactured goods as a percentage of total gross profit should be used to determine the percentage of taxable income that is used to calculate the export allowance.

Transport allowance

For normal companies, land-based transport costs (i.e. transport by road or rail) are deductible for tax purposes.

For registered manufacturing companies, an additional allowance of 25% of land-based transport cost in respect of material and components used in the manufacturing process or equipment imported for direct use in the manufacturing process may be deducted.

Namibia, Republic of

Preferential tax rate

For normal companies, the normal tax rate for companies other than mining companies or registered manufacturers is 34%.

The tax rate for a registered manufacturer for taxable income with respect to the manufacturing activity for which they are registered is 18%. This preferential rate is applicable for a period of ten years from registration as a manufacturer.

Export Processing Zones (EPZs)

In order to become an EPZ company, a particular entity must register with the EPZ governing body and obtain approval from Inland Revenue.

An EPZ company qualifies for the following benefits:

- The company is exempt from corporate tax.
- No VAT is payable on the sale of goods or services rendered in the zone.
- No VAT is payable on goods imported or manufactured in the zone.
- No customs or excise duty is payable on goods imported into the zone.
- No stamp duty or transfer duty is payable in relation to the transfer of movable or immovable property in the zone.
- A 75% refund of expenditures incurred in training Namibian citizens.
- Some of the provisions in the Labour Relations Act do not apply in the zone.

Enterprises must comply with the following requirements in order to qualify for EPZ status:

- Goods must be exported to countries other than countries in the SACU.
- Industrial employment must be created or increased.
- Namibia's export earnings must be increased as a result of manufactured goods exported.

EPZ companies may not be involved in retail business operations.

Withholding taxes

Withholding taxes (WHTs) are applicable where dividends and royalties, or similar payments, are declared or distributed to non-Namibian residents.

Dividends

Dividends declared by a Namibian company to a non-resident holding company are subject to non-resident shareholders tax (NRST), a WHT. NRST is payable at a rate of 10%, unless treaty relief is available. NRST is payable within 30 days after declaration of a dividend.

Royalties or similar payments

WHT on royalties are payable when a Namibian company pays a royalty to a non-resident. WHT is levied at a rate of 10.2% (30% of the corporate tax rate of 34%) and is payable within 14 days after the end of the month during which the liability for payment is incurred.

A royalty includes payment for the use or right to use any patent or design, trademark, copyright, model, pattern, plan, formula, or process, or any other property or right of a similar nature. A royalty also includes the imparting of any scientific, technical, industrial, or commercial knowledge or information for use in Namibia. The nature of fees payable should therefore be carefully considered in order to determine whether the relevant amount represents a royalty.

Interest

A WHT of 10%, calculated on the gross amount of interest, is payable on interest accruing to any person, other than a Namibian company, from a registered Namibian banking institution or unit trust scheme. The tax withheld is a final tax, and the financial institution is responsible to withhold the tax.

Namibian companies, however, are taxed on interest at the corporate tax rate.

It is the obligation of the financial institution to withhold the tax and pay such tax to the revenue authorities.

No WHT on interest applies to interest paid on loan accounts to foreign entities.

Services

Section 35A was recently introduced by the Ministry of Finance and applies to any Namibian resident (i.e. a company incorporated or managed and controlled in Namibia, and natural persons ordinarily resident in Namibia) paying a management, consultancy, or entertainment fee to a non-resident.

Management and consulting fees are specifically defined as: "any amount payable for administrative, managerial, technical, or consultative services or any similar services, whether such services are of a professional nature or not".

The legislation imposes the obligation on the Namibian resident to withhold a 25% WHT on such fees paid to the non-resident. It is important to note that the legislation also specifically includes any directors fees paid to a foreign director.

The official Directorate Inland Revenue effective date for Section 35A is 30 December 2011.

Summary of WHT payable

The WHT rates and treaty relief for Namibian DTAs can be summarised as follows. Note that the tax treaties contain certain requirements that should be met before the reduced tax rate may be applied.

The definitions of dividends, royalties, and interest in the various treaties should also be considered.

Recipient	WHT (%)				
	Dividends	Interest	Royalties	Technical fees	Directors fees
Non-treaty	10	10*	10.2	25	25
Botswana	10	10	10	15	25
France	5	10	10	0	25
Germany	10	0	10	0	25
India	10	10	10	10	25
Malaysia	5	10	5	5	25
Mauritius	5	10	5	0	25
Romania	N/A	10	5	0	25

Namibia, Republic of

Recipient	WHT (%)				
	Dividends	Interest	Royalties	Technical fees	Directors fees
Russian Federation	5	10	5	0	25
South Africa	5	10	10	0	25
Sweden	5	10	5	15	25
United Kingdom	5	N/A	5	0	25

* Namibian companies are taxed at the corporate tax rate on interest received.

'N/A' means that the provisions of the tax treaty limited the rate to a rate that is higher than the local Namibian rate. It should be noted that a treaty may only provide tax relief and cannot impose a higher tax rate.

Mining royalties

The Minerals (Prospecting and Mining) Act levies a royalty on minerals won or mined by a licence holder in Namibia, based on the table below:

Group of minerals	Percentage of market value of minerals leviable as a royalty (%)
Precious metals	3
Base and rare metals	3
Semi-precious stones	2
Nuclear fuel minerals	3*
Industrial minerals	2
Non-nuclear fuel minerals	2

* Applicable to all licence holders on nuclear fuel minerals, except Rössing Uranium Mine Ltd, where a 6% royalty is applicable.

Tax administration

Taxable period

The tax year for companies and close corporations is aligned with the financial year.

Tax returns

The income tax return is due within seven months after the financial year-end of the company and can be extended to five months after the seventh month due date, provided that no other prior year income tax returns are outstanding.

Payment of tax

The first provisional payment for income tax is due within six months from the commencement of the company's financial year (new tax amendments require that at least 40% of tax payable at year-end is paid on first submission). The second provisional payment is due on/before the last day of the respective tax year (new tax amendments require that at least 80% of tax payable at year-end is paid on second submission). The final provisional payment is due within seven months after the financial year-end of the company.

WHT on dividends are due within 30 days after declaration of the dividend.

WHT on royalties or similar payments are due within 14 days after the end of the month during which the liability for payment of the royalty was incurred.

WHT on services is payable to Inland Revenue within 20 days after the end of the month during which the amount was deducted or withheld.

It is advised that if relief is available under the DTA, a nil form should still be submitted when payment is made to non-residents. The amount of DTA relief claimed should be disclosed on the form submitted.

Penalties and interest
The penalties and interest due for late submissions and payments can be summarised as follows:

Tax area	Reason	Penalty	Interest (%)
1st provisional tax	Late submission	NAD 100 per day penalty for outstanding provisional tax returns	None
	Late payment	10%	20
2nd provisional tax	Late submission	NAD 100 per day penalty for outstanding provisional tax returns	20
	Late payment	10%	20
	Under-estimation	20%	20
Income tax return	Late submission	10%	20
	Late payment	None	20
	Omission/incorrect statement	Up to 200%	20
WHT	Late payment	10%	20

Anti-avoidance
Note that the Income Tax Act, Act 24 of 1981, contains an anti-avoidance section, Section 95, which enables the Receiver of Revenue to disregard the implications of a transaction or scheme if it can be proven that:

- such transaction or scheme had been entered into to avoid or postpone the payment of any duty or levy imposed by the Act
- such transaction or scheme was entered into or carried out by means or in a manner that would not normally be employed in the entering into or carrying out of a transaction, operation or scheme of the nature of the transaction, operation or scheme in question, or has created rights or obligations that would not normally be created between persons dealing at arm's length under a transaction, operation or scheme of nature of the transaction, operation or scheme in question, and
- such transaction or scheme was entered into or carried out solely or mainly for the purposes of the avoidance or the postponement of liability for the payment of any tax duty or levy.

The Receiver of Revenue can, at its sole discretion, impose Section 95 on any transaction or scheme, which will place the onus on the taxpayer to prove that any/all of the requirements noted above will not be applicable to the transaction or scheme.

The Netherlands

PwC contact

Sytso Boonstra
PricewaterhouseCoopers
Westgate, Thomas R. Malthusstraat 5
1066 JR Amsterdam
The Netherlands
Tel: +31 88 792 3470
Email: sytso.boonstra@nl.pwc.com

Significant developments

The corporate tax system of the Netherlands contains a number of well-known features providing for an attractive investment climate, such as: the fiscal unity regime with tax consolidation for group companies, a full participation exemption for capital gains and dividends from qualifying participations, and several favourable tax regimes (e.g. for patent income, investment vehicles, and income from ocean shipping activities).

The Dutch ministry of Finance recently published details of the Budget Agreement for 2013, which was agreed upon in the spring of 2012 by a coalition of five political parties. This agreement includes a number of fiscal measures aimed at reducing the Dutch European Monetary Union (EMU) gap to 3% in 2013. An accompanying legislative proposal with more detailed explanation of the measures is, however, not yet public. Among other measures, it has been agreed that the general value-added tax (VAT) rate will rise to 21% (currently 19%) in October 2012. For corporate taxpayers, the deduction of 'excessive' interest due on debt used to finance participations will be restricted.

As of 1 January 2012, a number of amendments in the corporate income tax (CIT) law from the 2012 Dutch Tax Package have taken effect. One of the most important aspects of the 2012 Dutch Tax Package was the introduction of a restriction on the deduction of interest (including costs and currency exchange results) on excess-acquisition debt. Further, foreign-sourced income (foreign-branch income, real estate income, and other income) is now 'excluded' from the Dutch taxable base.

In addition to the existing research and development (R&D) facilities, a new R&D deduction has been introduced as of 1 January 2012. The R&D deduction is calculated as 40% of the costs (other than wage costs) and expenses directly related to R&D activities performed by the taxpayer.

The announced possible reduction of the standard CIT rate to 24% has not (yet) been implemented.

The Netherlands pursue an active tax treaty policy in order to maintain and extend its wide tax treaty network. Most Dutch bilateral tax treaties are based on the Organisation for Economic Co-operation and Development (OECD) Model Tax Convention. In 2011, the Dutch Ministry of Finance published a Memorandum on the Dutch Tax Treaty Policy, expressing policy positions in regard of future treaty negotiations. With respect to the avoidance of double taxation on income and capital, the Netherlands has concluded bilateral tax treaties with about 90 other countries worldwide. In 2011, the new (or revised) tax treaties with the United Kingdom, the United Arab Emirates, Saudi Arabia, Barbados, and Slovakia have taken effect. New (or revised) treaties with Hong Kong, Japan, Oman, Panama, and Switzerland came into force in 2012.

Please note this information is current as of 1 June 2012. Typically, pending legislation is announced in June or July. Please visit the Worldwide Tax Summaries website at www.pwc.com/taxsummaries to see any significant corporate tax developments that occurred after 1 June 2012.

Taxes on corporate income

In general, a Dutch resident company is subject to CIT on its worldwide income. However, certain income can be exempted or excluded from the tax base. Non-resident entities only have a limited tax liability with regard to income from Dutch sources.

Standard corporate income tax (CIT) rate

The Dutch standard CIT rate has been reduced significantly over the past years. As of 1 January 2011, the standard CIT rate is 25%. There are two taxable income brackets. A lower rate of 20% applies to the first income bracket, for taxable income up to 200,000 euros (EUR).

Fiscal investment fund regime

In general terms, under the existing fiscal investment fund regime, the CIT rate for fiscal investment funds is 0%, provided that their profit is made available to the shareholders and holders of certificates of participation no later than eight months after year end.

Since 2007, fiscal investment funds may also invest in real estate development (or redevelopment) activities, provided that these activities take place through a subsidiary subject to Dutch CIT and the development (or redevelopment) activities are exercised for the benefit of real estate that is (or will be) forming part of the fund's own portfolio, an affiliated fiscal investment fund's portfolio, the portfolio of a company in which the fund or the affiliated fund has a substantial interest, or for the benefit of the subsidiary's own portfolio.

Exempt investment fund regime

The exempt investment fund regime exists next to the fiscal investment fund regime described above. In accordance with the exempt investment fund regime, investment funds as defined in the Dutch Financial Supervision Act ('Wet op het financieel toezicht') that meet certain conditions can request an exemption from CIT. Apart from the exempt status for CIT purposes, the exempt investment fund is not obliged to withhold dividend withholding tax (WHT) with regard to profit distributions to its shareholders.

Innovation box regime

A special regime applies with respect to profits, including royalties, derived from a self-developed intangible asset (developed after 31 December 2006). In this so-called innovation box, the taxpayer may opt, under certain conditions, for the application of a lower effective rate on taxable profits derived from these intangible assets. The effective tax rate of the innovation box is 5%.

The innovation box is applicable provided that at least 30% of the profits have been originated by the patent. Companies which have incurred certain qualified R&D costs for the development of intellectual property for which no patent was granted are also entitled to the favourable effective tax rate. This is subject to the condition that these qualified R&D assets became part of the company's assets after 31 December 2007.

The lower effective tax rate of 5% only applies to positive income, allowing innovation losses to be taken into account in full. As of 1 January 2011, it is also possible to include

N

profits from an intangible asset derived in the period between the patent application and the granting of the patent in the innovation box regime (not for R&D assets).

Tonnage tax regime

In order to stimulate entrepreneurs engaged in ocean shipping, a favourable regime (known as the Dutch tonnage tax regime) may be available to certain shipping companies. Under this regime, the taxable profit of a sea-going vessel is based on its registered net tonnage multiplied by a fixed amount of deemed profit per ton instead of the actual profits from the exploitation. The regime only applies to the calculation of the profit related to the qualifying shipping activities. These activities include operating vessels in international traffic (including transportation for the purpose of the exploitation of natural resources at sea), cable and pipe-laying activities at the bottom of the sea, and towing and dredging and connected activities. The profits from the qualifying activities are taxed at a deemed tonnage profit according to a five bracket regressive scale system. The tonnage tax regime applies upon request and for a fixed period of ten years or multiples of the ten-year period.

Local income taxes

There are no provincial or municipal corporate income taxes in the Netherlands.

Corporate residence

In the Netherlands, corporate residence is determined by each corporation's circumstances. Management and control are important factors in this respect. Companies incorporated under Dutch law are deemed to be residents of the Netherlands (although not with respect to certain provisions, such as the participation exemption and fiscal unity).

Permanent establishment (PE)

Non-resident companies that are neither incorporated nor effectively managed in the Netherlands are limited in their liability to tax in the Netherlands if they receive Dutch source income. This could be, for instance, business income derived from a Dutch permanent establishment (PE) or permanent representative. The definition of a PE for Dutch tax purposes is largely inspired by the OECD Model Convention definition and Commentary.

Other taxes

Value-added tax (VAT)

VAT, known in Dutch as the *Belasting over de Toegevoegde Waarde* or BTW, is payable on sales of goods and on services rendered in the Netherlands as well as on the importation of goods and on the 'intra-European' acquisition of goods. There are three VAT rates, which are 19%, 6%, and 0%.

The main VAT rate of 19% will be increased to 21% on 1 October 2012.

The reduced 6% VAT rate is applicable on certain prime necessities (and also on certain energy-saving insulation activities on houses).

The special 0% VAT rate is applicable mainly to intra-European Union (EU) supplies, exports, imports stored in bonded warehouses, services rendered in connection with the above, and certain other services.

The following are exempt from VAT:

- The supply of immovable property two years after putting it into use and lease. However, if the lessee's use of the immovable property is 90% or more for input VAT-deductible purposes, the lessor and lessee may opt to be subject to VAT on rent, in which case the lessor may deduct the VAT charged in respect of the property.
- Medical, cultural, social, and educational services.
- Services provided by banks and other financial institutions in connection with payment transactions and the granting of credit facilities.
- Insurance transactions.
- Transactions in shares.

Customs and excise tax

Many goods imported to the Netherlands from outside the European Union are subject to customs and excise duties. The tariffs and rates that apply to the different goods vary widely and change regularly.

An excise tax is levied on certain consumer goods (e.g. cigarettes, cigars, mineral oils, alcoholic products). If the goods are used solely as raw materials, no excise tax is levied. The excise tax is refundable if the article is exported.

Immovable property tax

Municipalities impose an annual immovable property tax on the owners of immovable property. The rates depend on the municipality. The taxable basis is the market value of the immovable property. Please note that the (assessment of the) value is also of importance for CIT, as depreciation might be limited based on this value (*see Limited depreciation of immovable property in the Deductions section*).

Transfer tax on immovable property

Acquisition of economic or legal ownership of immovable property in the Netherlands is subject to a 6% transfer tax on market value. Some exemptions are available. Real estate transfer tax on dwellings is reduced to 2% as of 1 July 2011, and will remain at 2% permanently.

Transfer tax on acquisition of shares in a real estate entity

The acquisition of shares in an entity that owns real estate may also be subject to transfer tax, if that entity is characterised as a so-called real estate entity. The threshold for qualifying as a real estate entity has been lowered as of 1 January 2011. In short, the threshold is met if more than 50% of the assets of the entity consist of real estate and at least 30% of Dutch immovable property. Prior to 2011, the threshold was met if more than 70% of the assets consisted of Dutch real estate.

Stamp duty

There are no stamp duties in the Netherlands.

Capital tax

The Netherlands do not levy capital tax on capital transactions (e.g. issue or increase capital).

Insurance tax

An insurance tax of 9.7% is payable on insurance premiums if the insured is a resident of the Netherlands or if the insured object is in the Netherlands. Several exemptions are available (e.g. insurances of ships and aircrafts operated in international traffic

The Netherlands

are exempt from insurance tax). In certain situations, an insurer outside the European Union may be required to take on a tax representative in the Netherlands.

Environmental charges on packaging
Producers or importers have to pay taxes on packaging. The tariff depends on the type and method of packaging. An exemption is granted to companies that bring less than 50,000 kilograms of packaging materials a year on the market. A refund of the packaging tax for indirect export also is available to foreign entrepreneurs.

Branch income

Rates for Dutch branch profits are the same as for other corporate profits, but no tax is withheld on transfers of profits to the head office. The tax base is, in principle, calculated on the same rules as for Dutch-resident companies.

Income determination

Inventory valuation
In general, stock/inventory is stated at the lower of cost or market value. Cost may be determined on the basis of first in first out (FIFO), last in first out (LIFO), base stock, or average cost. The LIFO system may be used for commercial/financial and tax purposes.

There is no requirement of conformity between commercial/financial and tax reporting.

Capital gains
Capital gains are taxed as ordinary income. However, capital gains realised on disposal of shares qualifying for the participation exemption are tax exempt (*see Dividend income below*).

The gain on disposal of depreciable assets may be carried over to a special tax deferral reinvestment reserve but must then be deducted from the acquisition cost of the later acquired assets. Except in special circumstances, the reserve cannot be maintained for more than three consecutive years. If the reserve has not been fully applied after three years, the remainder will be liable to taxation.

Capital losses are deductible, unless attributable to the disposal of a shareholding qualifying for the participation exemption.

Dividend income
Subject to meeting the conditions for the participation exemption, a Dutch company or branch of a foreign company is exempt from Dutch tax on all benefits connected with a qualifying shareholding, including cash dividends, dividends in kind, bonus shares, hidden profit distributions, capital gains, and currency exchange results.

Participation exemption
The participation exemption will apply to a shareholding in a Dutch company if the holding is at least 5% of the investee's capital, provided the conditions are met.

As a general rule, the participation exemption is applicable as long as the participation is not held as a portfolio investment. The intention of the parent company, which can be based on particular facts and circumstances, is decisive. Regardless of the company's intention, the participation exemption also is applicable if the sufficient tax test, which is if the income is subject to a real profit tax of at least 10%, or the asset test, if the subsidiary's assets do not usually consist of more than 50% of portfolio investments, is met.

For portfolio investment participations not qualifying for the participation exemption, double taxation will be avoided by applying the tax credit method, unless the portfolio investment shareholding effectively is not subject to tax at all. For EU shareholdings, it is optional to credit the actual underlying tax.

Dividends not qualifying under the participation exemption are taxable in full at the ordinary CIT rate.

Interests of 25% or more in a company of which the assets consist (nearly) exclusively of portfolio investments should be annually valued, as an asset, at the fair market value.

Costs related to the acquisition and disposal of a participation (e.g. legal fees, compensations, notary fees) are not deductible for corporate tax.

Losses arising from the liquidation of a (foreign) subsidiary are deductible for CIT, subject to certain conditions.

The recently published Budget Agreement for 2013 indicates that the deduction of 'excessive' interest due on debt used to finance participations will be restricted. An accompanying legislative proposal with more detailed explanation is, however, not yet available.

Profits derived from a company that was created by converting a foreign PE only qualify for the participation exemption after they exceed the losses from the PE during the previous years insofar as those losses reduced the taxable profits in the Netherlands before 1 January 2012. Under certain circumstances, such as the alienation of (part of) the shares of the company, all non-recaptured losses will be added to the profits of the Dutch parent company at once. Note that the scope of these anti-abuse provisions has been extended by including situations in which a foreign intermediate holding company is interposed.

Stock dividends
Stock dividends are taxed as dividend income to the extent that they are paid out of earned surplus. They are not taxable if paid out of share premium ('*agio*'), provided the share premium account was not created pursuant to a share-for-share merger, in which only Dutch companies were involved. In the case of a share-for-share merger, in which shares in foreign subsidiaries were contributed to a Dutch company, the Dutch company can distribute the difference between the fair market value and the paid-in capital of the subsidiaries being contributed as a stock dividend without triggering Dutch dividend WHT (step-up in basis), provided certain requirements are met.

Work in progress
Profits with regard to work in progress should be accounted before actual completion, to the extent that the work is completed. All project costs should be recognised in the year the costs occurred.

Foreign income
In general, a Dutch resident company is subject to CIT on its worldwide income. However, certain income can be exempted (e.g. due to the application of the participation exemption described above) or excluded from the tax base.

The Netherlands

As of 1 January 2012, certain foreign-sourced income (foreign branch income, real estate income, and other income) is 'excluded' from the Dutch taxable base. The so-called 'object exemption', a method to provide relief for international juridical double taxation in situations of Dutch companies with a PE abroad, is designed as a tax base adjustment instead of a real exemption. Consequently, losses of foreign PEs can no longer be offset against profits of the Dutch head office (except for final losses), but currency exchange results are still included in the tax base. Also, if the foreign activities cease, any losses upon 'liquidation' can, in principle, be deducted. For certain low-taxed passive PEs, the object exemption is replaced by a credit system.

Prior to 1 January 2012, double taxation of certain foreign-source income, including foreign branch income, was avoided by reducing Dutch tax by the ratio of foreign income (subject to a foreign income tax and/or covered by certain tax treaty provisions) to total income, the so-called exemption method. Currency exchange profits or losses on the head office's investment in its foreign branch were not considered 'foreign income' for the purposes of these relief provisions. Unilateral relief from double taxation for income from foreign financing branches was provided by means of a credit of 17.5% of the passive financing income for foreign taxes deemed paid or the foreign tax actually paid. However, the exemption method applied only if the taxpayer could demonstrate that the foreign branch was actively engaged in intra-group financing activities.

Double taxation of foreign dividends, interest, and royalties is relieved by a tax credit provided by Dutch tax treaties or unilaterally, if the payer of the income streams is a resident of a developing country, designated by Ministerial Order. If no treaty or unilateral relief applies, a deduction of the foreign tax paid is allowed in computing the net taxable income.

However, relief by exemption is given for dividends from foreign investments qualifying for the participation exemption, as discussed above. In that case, there is no Dutch tax to credit against taxes withheld in the subsidiary's country of residence.

In most circumstances, the foreign dividend is exempt for Dutch CIT under the participation exemption, as previously discussed. As a consequence, foreign WHT cannot be credited, and WHT constitute a real cost for the companies concerned. A credit of the foreign WHT is granted against Dutch dividend WHT due on the distribution to foreign parents of the Dutch company. The credit amounts to a maximum of 3% of the gross dividend paid, to the extent that it can be paid out of foreign-source dividends received that have been subject to at least a 5% WHT and the foreign company is liable for CIT. This tax credit does not result in taxable income for CIT purposes.

Deductions

Depreciation, amortisation, and depletion
Generally, depreciation may be computed by a straight-line or a reducing-balance method or, in accordance with any other sound business practice, on the basis of historical cost. Depreciation is applied from the date the asset comes into use. Dutch tax law includes specific rules (*see below*) that potentially limit the depreciation of assets (e.g. immovable property, goodwill, and other fixed assets).

To meet companies' urgent need for cash due to the worldwide credit crunch, a temporary provision was introduced, allowing accelerated depreciation (*see below*) of new investments in certain assets in 2009, 2010, and 2011. These measures are not extended for 2012.

A depletion allowance for natural resources may be granted for tax purposes, when it conforms to sound business practice and is appropriate for accounting purposes.

Limited depreciation of immovable property
There are special provisions for depreciation of immovable property. A distinction is made between immovable property held for investment purposes and buildings used in a trade or business.

Investment property cannot be depreciated to an amount lower than the official property's fair market value for tax purposes, which is known as *WOZ-waarde*. In other words, a property will not be subject to depreciation unless the carrying amount of the building and the land on which it is located is higher than its value for tax purposes. This value is determined by the municipal tax authorities annually. As this value is based on the assumption that the property is free of lease, the value for tax purposes of commercial real estate may be lower than fair market value.

Alternatively, the depreciation of buildings employed in a trade or business is limited to 50% of the property's value for tax purposes. It should still be possible to value immovable property at fair market value if this is demonstrably lower than the current book value. In addition, anti-abuse measures apply to prevent the division of land and buildings into separate legal entities or to related individuals.

Note that maintenance costs continue to qualify for tax relief and any maintenance-related value increase does not lead to a compulsory upward revaluation of the property. Moreover, a property is not required to be revaluated as its value increases due to market developments.

Depreciation of land is not permitted.

The sale of depreciated assets triggers tax on the difference between the sale price and the depreciated book value unless a reinvestment reserve is set up (*see Capital gains in the Income determination section*).

Limited amortisation of goodwill and depreciation of fixed assets
With regard to goodwill, the amortisation for tax purposes is limited to 10% of the purchase price per annum. Furthermore, the tax depreciation of other fixed assets (i.e. inventory, equipment) is limited to 20% of the purchase price or production costs per annum.

Accelerated depreciation
The law provides accelerated depreciation of several specific assets. Accelerated depreciation applies to investments in assets that are in the interest of the protection of the environment in the Netherlands and that appear on the so-called VAMIL ('*Vervroegde Afschrijving Milieu-investeringen*') list. In 2011, 2012, and 2013, the accelerated depreciation facility for investments in environment-improving assets is temporary limited to 75% of the total (investment) costs. As of 1 January 2014, this percentage will be 100%.

Accelerated depreciation also is available for certain other designated assets, for example, investments of starting entrepreneurs.

N

The Netherlands

Investment costs minus residual value of sea-vessels that are operated mainly from the Netherlands may be depreciated straight-line over five years. Instead of accelerated depreciation, these taxpayers may choose immediate taxation (*see Tonnage tax regime in the Taxes on corporate income section*).

As a temporary provision to stimulate the economy, companies may depreciate, under certain conditions, the value of assets bought and investments made in 2009, 2010, and 2011 in two years (or more), provided that the assets are not used formerly and the assets are not meant to be mainly put at the disposal of third parties, directly or indirectly. Further, the asset has to be brought into use before 1 January 2012, 1 January 2013, or 1 January 2014, respectively. This temporary provision is not extended to investments made in 2012.

The temporary possibility for accelerated depreciation, however, is prohibited for, among other things, buildings; ground, road, and hydraulic works; cars (except environmentally very clean and efficient cars); and intangible fixed assets. It is possible to depreciate up to 50% of the asset's value in the year of investment. The remainder may be depreciated, without the 50% limitation, in subsequent year(s). The annual amount to be depreciated before the asset has come into use is limited to the actual payments or investments made.

Anti-abuse rules regarding interest and loans
Due to existing anti-abuse rules, the deduction for interest paid on intra-group debts relating to certain transactions is disallowed. However, if the taxpayer provides credible evidence of overriding commercial reasons for the transaction as well as the loan, or of taxation of the interest in the hands of the recipient at an effective tax rate that is considered adequate by Dutch standards, the interest may be deductible.

Furthermore, interest paid on certain profit participating loans will be qualified as a dividend and will not be tax deductible. Interest received upon these loans may meet the definitions for the participation exemption if the creditor also holds a qualifying participation in the debtor. Intra-group conduits may be denied a credit of foreign WHT with respect to royalties or interest received if no economic risk is deployed.

If the interest payment to a group company relates to a loan that is directly or indirectly granted by a group company in order to finance an acquisition or capital contribution, the interest will be deductible only if the loan and the underlying transaction are based predominantly on sound business considerations or if the interest received is effectively and sufficiently taxed.

When the debt ultimately is financed externally (outside the group) and a direct relationship exists between the internal debt and the ultimate external financing, it can be substantiated that there are sound business reasons for the loan. Furthermore, the use of tax losses or similar relief claims by the recipient of the inter-company interest, may affect adversely the deductibility of the interest paid. Also the law states that the interest deduction related to indebted dividend distributions, paid back capital and capital contributions is not only possible in case of sound business reasons but also if the interest is taxed in the hands of the creditor at an effective tax rate that is considered adequate by Dutch standards. The latter requirement means that the interest needs to be subject to an effective tax rate of at least 10% over taxable profits determined according to Dutch standards. For the determination of 'a taxable base according to Dutch tax standards' the tax base limitation for the innovation box is not taken into account.

The Netherlands

If the taxpayer makes a reasonable case that the interest is taxable at an effective tax rate of at least 10%, the tax authorities, nevertheless, have the option to substantiate that either the liability or the corresponding transaction is not based on sound business reasons. The tax authorities also have the option to substantiate that the liability is incurred in order to compensate losses or other rights that were formed in that year or that will be formed shortly thereafter. This is also applicable to existing loans.

As of 15 November 2011, deduction of interest (including costs and currency exchange results) on excess acquisition debt is restricted if the acquired company subsequently joins a Dutch fiscal unity with the taxpayer. The acquisition debt is considered excessive in so far as it exceeds 60% of the acquisition price. The interest expenses may only be deducted from the acquiring company's 'own profits', meaning that the profits of the target company that was added to the fiscal unity are not taken into consideration. The restriction is not applicable if the interest on the debt does not exceed EUR 1 million. Contrary to the other existing interest deduction restrictions illustrated above, this new measure also relates to interest on loans obtained from third parties.

Provision for bad debt
It is possible to make a provision for future expenses with a cause existing on the balance sheet of the tax year in question. Therefore, a provision may be made for bad debts.

Charitable contributions
Charitable contributions are deductible if certain conditions are met. The gift must be documented in writing and contributed to a qualifying charity (ANBI or SBBI). The deductible amount may not exceed 50% of the taxable profits, with a maximum of EUR 100,000.

Limited deductibility of costs relating to remuneration by way of shares
Any remunerations by way of shares, profit-sharing certificates, option rights on shares, or similar rights are not deductible. However, grandfathering rules exist for situations where option rights have been granted to employees before 24 May 2006.

Costs related to so-called stock appreciation rights for employees that earn an income which exceeds EUR 500,000 are not deductible, as a result of tax legislation on 'excessive' remuneration.

Fines and penalties
Most criminal fines and tax penalties are not tax deductible. This applies, for instance, to fines imposed by a Dutch criminal judge, administrative fines, disciplinary fines, and penalties from a European institution.

Taxes
Certain taxes, such as the tax on insurance transactions, are deductible. Tax paid on the transfer of immovable property must be included in the cost price and taken into account in the course of normal depreciation. The corporate tax itself is not deductible.

Other significant items
Deduction of certain expenses (e.g. costs for food, drink, and entertainment) paid by employers for employees are not deductible, in part. These costs are often referred to as mixed costs. The non-deductable portion is 0.4% of the total taxable wages of all employees but never less than EUR 4,400 per year. Alternatively, the employer may choose to deduct only 73.5% of the actual expenses.

The Netherlands

Net operating losses

Tax losses can be carried back one year and carried forward to nine years. This also applies to start-up losses.

With regard to losses arising in the years 2009, 2010, and 2011, corporate taxpayers may opt for a temporary extension of the carryback period for losses from one to three years. This option, however, also means that the maximum period for loss carryforward will be limited to six years (instead of nine). Furthermore, the extended measure is limited to EUR 10 million loss carryback per extra year.

Complex rules may prohibit the utilisation of net operating losses after a change of 30% or more of the ultimate control in a company. Furthermore, limitations exist on loss utilisation for holding/finance companies. Based on these rules, losses incurred by a mere holding or group finance company can be offset only against holding or finance income in preceding and following years, provided that certain strict conditions are met. These conditions are meant to counter tax planning, whereby, the Dutch company concerned acquires (e.g. by way of equity contribution or exchange) other assets that enhance its income streams and its capacity to make use of the losses. Companies carrying out significant other activities (with 25 or more full-time employees) are, in principle, unaffected by these loss relief restrictions.

Payments to foreign affiliates

A Dutch corporation generally can claim a deduction for royalties, management service fees, and interest charges paid to foreign affiliates, to the extent that the amounts are not in excess of what it would pay an unrelated entity (i.e. arm's-length principle). Dutch companies are obliged to produce transfer pricing documentation describing the calculation of the transfer price and the comparability of the transfer price with third party prices.

Group taxation

Fiscal unity regime

A parent company and its Dutch-resident subsidiaries (if the parent owns at least 95% of the shares) may, under certain conditions, file a tax return as one entity (fiscal unity). Group taxation is available for companies having their place of effective management in the Netherlands, both for Dutch tax and treaty purposes.

The main feature of the fiscal unity is that profits of one company can be offset against losses of another company forming part of that fiscal unity. Furthermore, inter-company transactions are eliminated.

In February 2010, the European Court of Justice (ECJ) decided that the Dutch fiscal unity regime does not violate EU law (the freedom of establishment), insofar as it disallows a cross-border fiscal unity. However, the ECJ has not yet explicitly dealt with the effects of the fiscal unity regime, other than cross-border loss utilisation, such as the transfer of assets between group companies without immediate taxation and the use of 'final losses'. The Dutch Supreme Court will possibly deal with those issues at a later stage.

Transfer pricing rules

Based on a general transfer pricing provision in the corporation tax law, all transactions between related parties must be at arm's length. Furthermore, a specific transfer pricing provision exists with respect to the transactions of an interest and royalty conduit company. Dutch companies are obliged to produce transfer pricing documentation describing the calculation of the transfer price and the comparability of the transfer price with third party prices. If a transaction between related parties is not at arm's length, the taxable income may be corrected by the tax authorities. Moreover, transactions that do not meet the arm's-length test may constitute a contribution of informal capital or a hidden profit distribution.

On the basis of a decree of the State Secretary for Finance regarding transfer pricing, companies may request an advance tax ruling (ATR) and an advance pricing agreement (APA). An ATR may be requested on the classification of activities and an APA may be required on the classification of activities and the arm's-length character of the transfer price.

Thin capitalisation

Thin capitalisation rules limit the deductibility of interest paid on intra-group debts. These rules apply to all Dutch companies that are part of a domestic or international group of companies. The allowed debt-to-equity ratio is 3:1, based on the average of the tax equity at the beginning and at the end of the year. A higher ratio may apply at the request of the taxpayer if the group to which the Dutch company belongs has, according to the financial statements, a higher, worldwide debt-to-equity ratio. Interest paid on loans exceeding the 3:1 ratio is disallowed only to the extent it exceeds inter-company interest received. The deduction of interest paid on genuine third party loans is not limited by the thin capitalisation rules.

Tax credits and incentives

Foreign tax credit
See Foreign income in the Income determination section for a description of the foreign tax credit regime.

Small investments
There is a system of deductions for small investments, the so-called small scale investment deduction. To calculate this annual deduction, investments of more than EUR 450 each are totalled to determine the percentage of the deduction.

Total of investments (EUR)	Deduction
0 to 2,300	0
2,301 to 55,248	28% of the value of the total of small investments
55,249 to 102,311	EUR 15,470
102,312 to 306,931	EUR 15,470 minus 7.56% of the amount exceeding EUR 102,311
Above 306,931	No deduction

Investments in energy-efficient assets
For investments in energy-efficient assets, there is a deduction from corporate income of 41.5% of the value of the total annual amount of investments exceeding EUR 2,300, up to and including EUR 118 million.

Investments in environmental assets
For investments in certain new environmental improving assets exceeding EUR 2,300 per calendar year (with a maximum of EUR 25 million per taxpayer), a deduction from

The Netherlands

corporate income of 36%, 27%, or 13.5% exists (in 2011, 2012, and 2013), depending on the ministerial classification of the assets. Prior to 2011 and as of 2014, the deduction was/will be 40%, 30%, or 15%, depending on the type of investment.

New technology

Wage costs

Conducting certain R&D activities on applied new technology is subsidised by a reduction of wage tax to be paid on wages of employees engaged in R&D of technologically new products. The subsidy accrues to the employer when the employee is credited for the normal amount of wage tax. The amount of the reduction was substantially raised for the years 2009 (retroactively), 2010, and 2011 to stimulate the economy. For the year 2012, the reduction of the payroll tax and social security contributions amounts to 42% of the first EUR 110,000 in R&D wage costs (first bracket) and 14% of the excess costs. The benefit for each employer (or group of companies) may not exceed EUR 14 million per year.

To obtain the relief under the R&D incentive programme, taxpayers must file an electronic/online application with the so-called *Agentschap NL* (NL Agency), a department of the Ministry of Economic Affairs. The taxpayer will receive an R&D declaration. The budget for this subsidy is fixed, so the amount of the subsidy is dependent on budget availability. Note that self-developed and utilised software falls within the scope of the R&D incentive under certain conditions.

Other costs

In addition to the existing R&D facilities, a new R&D deduction is introduced as of 1 January 2012.

For 2012, the R&D deduction amounts to 40% of the costs (other than wage costs) and expenses directly related to R&D activities performed by the taxpayer. An expense of EUR 1 million will be taken into account over a period of five years, 20% each year.

Taxpayers must file an electronic/online application with the so-called *Agentschap NL*. The request must be filled together with the application for the R&D declaration. Application is first possible as of 1 May 2012.

Withholding taxes

Dividends from Dutch corporations are generally subject to a 15% Dutch dividend WHT. In general, this does not apply to the Dutch cooperative (i.e. 'co-op') in a business driven structure, a widely used vehicle for holding and financing activities.

The Netherlands does not levy a WHT on interest and royalty payments.

Domestic corporations are required to withhold taxes as follows:

Recipient	Dividends (%) (1)
Resident corporations	0/15
Resident individuals	15
Non-resident corporations and individuals:	
Non-treaty situations	15

Recipient	Dividends (%) (1)
Treaty:	
Albania	0/5/15 (30)
Argentina	10/15 (2)
Armenia	0/5/15 (3)
Aruba	5/7.5/8.3/15 (5, 21, 40)
Australia	15 (5)
Austria	0 (6) or 5/15 (3, 7)
Azerbaijan	5/10 (38)
Bahrain	0/10 (8)
Bangladesh	10/15 (8)
Barbados	0/15 (42)
Belarus	0/5/15 (2, 9)
Belgium	0 (6) or 5/15 (5, 8)
Bosnia Herzegovina	5/15 (2, 4)
Brazil	15 (5)
Bulgaria	0 (6)/5/15 (2)
Canada	5/15 (10)
Caribbean Netherlands (Bonaire, Saint Eustatius, and Saba)	0/15 (41)
China, P.R.	10 (5, 11)
Croatia	0/15(8)
Curaçao	15, 5, 7.5, or 8.3 (5, 21, 40)
Czech Republic	0 (6) or 0/10 (2, 5)
Denmark	0 (6) or 0/15 (8)
Egypt	0/15 (2)
Estonia	0 (6) or 5/15 (2)
Finland	0 (6) or 0/15 (37)
France	0 (6) or 5/15 (2, 5)
Georgia	0/5/15 (31)
Germany	0 (6) or 10/15 (5, 12)
Ghana	10 or 5 (8)
Greece	0 (6) or 5/15 (2)
Hong Kong	0/10 (42)
Hungary	0 (6) or 5/15 (2)
Iceland	0/15 (8)
India	10/15 (5, 32)
Indonesia	10 (2, 5)
Ireland, Republic of	0 (6) or 0/15 (13)
Israel	5/15 (2)
Italy	0 (6) or 5/10/15 (14)
Japan	0/5/10 (15)
Jordan	5/15 (8)
Kazakhstan	0/5/15 (17)
Korea, Republic of	10/15 (2)
Kuwait	0/10 (8)
Kyrgyzstan	15 (5, 24)
Latvia	0 (6) or 5/15 (2)

The Netherlands

Recipient	Dividends (%) (1)
Lithuania	0 (6) or 5/15 (2)
Luxembourg	0 (6, 18) or 2.5/15 (2, 18)
Macedonia	0/15 (8)
Malawi	15 (19)
Malaysia	0/15 (7)
Malta	0 (6) or 5/15 (2)
Mexico	5/15 (16)
Moldavia	0/5/15 (20)
Mongolia	0/15 (8)
Montenegro	5/15 (2, 4)
Morocco	10/15 (2)
New Zealand	15 (5)
Nigeria	12.5/15 (8)
Norway	0/15 (2)
Oman	0/10 (8)
Pakistan	10/15 (2)
Panama	0/15 (42)
Philippines	10/15 (8)
Poland	0 (6) or 5/15 (5, 8)
Portugal	0 (6)/10
Qatar	0/10 (39)
Romania	0 (6) or 0/5/15 (22)
Russian Federation	5/15 (23)
Saint Martin	5/7.5/8.3/15 (5, 21, 40)
Saudi Arabia	5/10 (8)
Serbia	5/15 (2, 4)
Singapore	0/15 (5, 7)
Slovak Republic	0 (6) or 0/10 (2, 5)
Slovenia	0 (6) or 5/15 (2)
South Africa	5/10 (16)
Spain	0 (6) or 5/15 (5, 25)
Sri Lanka	10/15 (2)
Surinam	7.5/15 (2)
Sweden	0 (6) or 0/15 (2)
Switzerland	0/15 (36,43)
Taiwan	10
Tajikistan	15 (24)
Thailand	5/15 (34)
Tunisia	0/15 (8)
Turkey	5/15 (2)
Turkmenistan	15 (5, 24)
Uganda	0/5/15 (35)
Ukraine	0/5/15 (26)
United Arab Emirates	5/10 (8)
United Kingdom	0 (6) or 0/10/15 (33)
United States	0/5/15 (27)
Uzbekistan	0/5/15 (28)

Recipient	Dividends (%) (1)
Venezuela	0/10 (2)
Vietnam	5/7/15 (29)
Zambia	5/15 (2)
Zimbabwe	10/15 (2)

Notes

1. A 0% WHT rate applies to payments to a resident corporation when its shareholding qualifies for the participation exemption and the shares form part of a company whose activities are carried on in the Netherlands. However, dividend WHT may be levied on certain profit participating loans.
2. The lower rate applies if the foreign company owns directly at least 25% of the capital of the Dutch company.
3. The 5% rate is applicable if the foreign company directly owns 10% of capital of the Dutch company. The 0% rate is applicable if the dividend originates from ordinary taxed profits and the dividend is tax exempt in the hands of the recipient.
4. Based upon the treaty concluded with former Yugoslavia.
5. Negotiations on (revisions of) tax treaties are currently pending with Angola, Aruba Australia, Belgium, Brazil, Chile, China, Colombia, Costa Rica, Curaçao, Czech Republic, Ethiopia, France, Germany, India, Indonesia, Kenya, New Zealand, Poland, Saint Martin, Singapore, Slovak Republic, and Spain.
6. Indicates that this country is a member state of the European Union. The EU Parent/Subsidiary Directive applies from 1 January 1992. According to the Directive, dividends paid by a Dutch company (BV or NV) to a qualifying parent company resident in another EU member state must be exempt from Dutch WHT, provided certain conditions are met. Among other things, the EU parent company must hold at least 15% (from 2009, the EU parent must hold 10%) of the Dutch dividend-paying company's capital (or, in certain cases, voting rights) for a continuous period of at least one year. A provisional exemption from dividend WHT will apply from the start of the one-year holding period. The exemption will be cancelled retroactively if, following the dividend distribution, the one-year holding requirement is not actually met. The Dutch dividend-distributing company must provide to the Dutch tax authorities a satisfactory guarantee for the payment of dividend WHT that, but for the provisional exemption, would be due. The exemption is also applicable if the parent company is a resident of a EU member state and owns at least 10% of the (voting) shares in the Dutch company but only on the basis of reciprocity (Finland, Germany, Greece, Luxembourg, Spain, and United Kingdom). Should the WHT exemption not be available under the EU Parent/Subsidiary Directive, the treaty rate(s) set out in the right-hand side of the same column (following 'or') will apply.
7. The lower rate applies if the foreign company owns, directly or indirectly, at least 25% of the capital of the Dutch company.
8. The lower rate applies if the foreign company directly owns at least 10% of the capital of the Dutch company.
9. The 0% rate applies if the foreign company directly owns at least 50% of the capital of the Dutch company, or invested more than EUR 250,000 in the Dutch company or owns directly 25% of the capital of the Dutch company and has a statement indicating that the investment in Dutch capital is, directly or indirectly, guaranteed by the government of Belarus.
10. The 5% rate applies if the foreign company owns, directly or indirectly, at least 25% of the capital or at least 10% of the voting rights in the Dutch company.
11. The treaty is not applicable for Hong Kong and Taiwan.
12. The lower rate applies if the foreign company owns at least 25% of the voting shares of the Dutch company.
13. The lower rate applies if the foreign company owns at least 25% of the voting rights in the Dutch company.
14. The 5% rate is applicable if the Italian company owns at least 50% of the voting shares in the Dutch company for a continuous period of at least 12 months prior to the date chosen for distribution of a dividend. The 10% rate is applicable if the Italian company owns at least 10% of the voting shares in the Dutch company for the continuous period mentioned above. In other cases, the dividend WHT rate is 15%.
15. The 5% rate applies if the foreign company owns at least 10% of the voting shares of the Dutch company for a continuous period of at least six months immediately before the end of the book year to which the dividend distribution relates. No WHT is levied if the foreign company owns directly or indirectly at least 50% of the voting power in the Dutch company distributing the dividends for a period of six months. Also, no WHT is levied if the foreign company is a pension fund.
16. The lower rate applies if the foreign company owns, directly or indirectly, at least 10% of the capital of the Dutch company.
17. The 0% rate is applicable if the foreign company owns, directly or indirectly, at least 50% of the capital of the Dutch company or if it has invested more than 1 million United States dollars (USD) in the Dutch company, insofar as the government of Kazakhstan has guaranteed the investment; the 5% rate applies if the recipient company owns at least 10% of the capital of the paying company.
18. These rates do not apply to dividend payments to Luxembourg '1929' holding companies.
19. The dividend article of the treaty is not applicable anymore. The national WHT rate is applicable.

N

The Netherlands

20. The 0% rate is applicable if the foreign company owns, directly or indirectly, at least 50% of the capital of the Dutch company and invested more than USD 300,000 in the Dutch company. The 5% rate is applicable if the foreign company owns directly 25% or more of the capital of the Dutch company. The 15% rate is applicable on portfolio investments.
21. The rate is 15% unless the dividend is paid to a company holding at least 25% of the paid-up capital in the Dutch company. In this latter case, the WHT rate will be reduced to: (i) 5% if the dividends received are subject to a profits tax in the other state of at least 5.5% on the dividend or (ii) 7.5% if the profits tax is less than 5.5%. The combined CIT of the other state and Dutch dividend WHT for participations of at least 25% must not exceed 8.3%. Depending on the tax percentage levied in the other state, the Dutch dividend WHT will be restituted accordingly.
22. The 5% rate is applicable if the recipient of the dividend is the beneficial owner and directly owns 10% of the capital of the Dutch company. The 0% rate is applicable if the recipient of the dividend is the beneficial owner and directly owns at least 25% of the capital of the Dutch company.
23. The 5% rate is applicable if the recipient of the dividend is the beneficial owner and directly owns at least 25% in the capital of the Dutch company with a minimum investment of at least EUR 75,000.
24. The Netherlands applies the treaty with the former Soviet Union unilaterally to Kyrgyzstan, Tajikistan, and Turkmenistan.
25. The lower treaty rate applies if the Spanish company owns 50% or more of the capital of the Dutch company or if the Spanish company owns 25% or more of the capital of the Dutch company and another Spanish company also owns 25% or more of that capital.
26. The 0% rate is applicable if the foreign company owns, directly or indirectly, at least 50% of the capital of the Dutch company or invested more than USD 300,000 in the Dutch company. The 5% rate is applicable if the foreign company owns directly 20% or more of the capital of the Dutch company.
27. The lower rate applies if the foreign company owns directly at least 10% of the voting rights in the Dutch company. On 8 March 2004, the Netherlands and the United States signed a protocol amending the applicable tax treaty. Based on this protocol, the WHT on dividends will be reduced to 0% if the receiving company owns 80% or more of the voting power of the distributing company, provided that certain other conditions are also met. This reduction of the dividend WHT has taken effect as of 1 January 2005.
28. The 5% rate is applicable if the foreign company owns directly 25% or more of the capital of the Dutch company. The 0% rate is applicable if the dividend for that company qualifies for the participation exemption in the Netherlands. The 15% rate is applicable to portfolio dividends.
29. The 5% rate is applicable if the foreign company owns, directly or indirectly, at least 50% of the capital of the Dutch company or invested more than USD 10 million in the Dutch company. The 7% rate applies to the foreign company owning, directly or indirectly, at least 25% of the capital of the Dutch company.
30. No dividend WHT is due provided the share in the participation is at least 50% and at least USD 250,000 capital is paid in, in the participation. A dividend WHT of 5% is due if the share in the participation is at least 25%.
31. A dividend WHT of 5% is due if the share in the participation is at least 10%. No dividend WHT is due provided the share in the participation is at least 50% and at least USD 2 million capital is paid in, in the participation.
32. Based upon most-favoured nation principle.
33. The 0% rate applies if a company controls at least 10% of the voting power of the Dutch company paying the dividends. The 15% rate applies to dividends arising from income from immovable property, distributed by certain tax exempt real estate investment vehicles (e.g. REITs or FBIs).
34. In case a Thai company holds at least a 25% share in a Thai company, the Dutch dividend WHT rate is 5%.
35. If a share of at least 50% is held by a company, no dividend WHT is due. If the share the company holds is less than 50%, 5% dividend WHT is due.
36. As of 29 December 2004, Switzerland and the European Union concluded a treaty in the light of the EU savings directive. The treaty, amongst others, contains a clause that no dividend tax is withheld if certain requirements are met. The main requirements are that a shareholding of at least 25% is held directly for a period of at least two years and both corporations are not subjected to a special tax regime. Please note that even though the treatment of dividend appears to be equal to the treatment on the basis of the EU-parent subsidiary directive, the directive is in fact not applicable to Switzerland.
37. The 0% rate applies if the foreign company owns directly at least 5% of the capital of the Dutch company.
38. The 5% rate applies if the foreign company owns directly at least 25% of the capital of the Dutch company with a minimum investment of at least EUR 200,000 in the Dutch company.
39. The 0% rate applies if the foreign company directly owns at least 7.5% of the capital of the Dutch company.
40. The WHT rates are based on the Dutch 'Belastingregeling voor het Koninkrijk'.
41. The WHT rates for the Caribbean Netherlands are based on the Dutch 'Belastingregeling voor het land Nederland'.
42. No WHT is levied if the foreign company (beneficial owner) receiving the dividends directly holds at least 10% (15% threshold for the Panama Treaty) of the shares of the Dutch company, provided that the shares of the foreign company are regularly traded on a recognised stock exchange or at least 50% of the shares of the foreign company is owned by residents of either contracting state or by companies the shares of which are regularly traded on a recognised stock exchange. Also, no WHT is levied if the foreign company is a bank or insurance company, a state or political subdivision, a headquarter owning at least 10% of the shares of the Dutch company, or a pension fund.

43. The 0% rate applies if the foreign company directly owns at least 10% of the capital of the Dutch company, is a pension fund, or, as far as Switzerland is concerned, the beneficial owner is a social security scheme.

Tax administration

Taxable period

Generally, the tax year is equal to the calendar year. However, corporate taxpayers may deviate from this by adopting a different financial year.

Tax returns

Tax returns must be filed either every calendar year or every financial year. The due date is generally five months after the end of the company's fiscal year. This filing due date may be extended upon request by the taxpayer. The Dutch tax authorities generally make a provisional assessment before issuing the final assessment after a full examination of the return.

Payment of tax

The CIT assessed must be paid within two months of the date of the assessment. In addition, provisional assessments are issued for the current tax year on the basis of the prior year's taxable income.

Audit cycle

Corporate taxpayers might be subject to regular audits by tax inspectors. This forms part of the so-called vertical monitoring tasks of the national tax authorities. In recent years, there has been a tendency towards a more enhanced co-operation between tax authorities and taxpayers in the Netherlands (*see Horizontal Monitoring in this section below*). Part of this trend is that there are to be less audits in retrospect.

N

Statute of limitations

Under certain conditions, the tax administration can impose an additional assessment within five years from the year in which the tax debt originated (if the filing due date was extended on request, this period is added). In case of income from abroad, the period for additional assessment is extended to 12 years.

Advance pricing agreement (APA)/Advance tax ruling (ATR)

Taxpayers are able to obtain (legal) certainty concerning their CIT positions. They may request the Dutch tax authorities to conclude an APA with respect to the transfer pricing of controlled transactions. Taxpayers may also request the Dutch tax authorities to a provide an ATR with respect to the CIT implications of a (contemplated) set of transactions.

Horizontal monitoring

If the taxpayer is willing, the Dutch tax authorities, in certain cases, shift their method from vertical monitoring to horizontal monitoring. Emphasis is placed on cooperation and on the responsibilities of the parties involved, instead of retrospectively control. Horizontal monitoring is based on mutual trust, understanding, and transparency between the taxpayers and the Dutch tax authorities. It aims at reducing administrative burdens and providing legal certainty in advance. Taxpayers need to have a solid Tax Control Framework.

New Zealand

PwC contact

Tony Gault
PricewaterhouseCoopers New Zealand
PricewaterhouseCoopers Tower
188 Quay Street
Auckland
New Zealand
Tel: +64 9 355 8000
Email: tony.gault@nz.pwc.com

Significant developments

Corporate tax rate reduced
The corporate tax rate has been reduced from 30% to 28% with effect from the beginning of the 2011/12 income year, which, for most companies, is 1 April 2011. The reduced rate applies to all resident and non-resident companies, including branches.

There will be a two year transition period to allow tax paid at 30% to be imputed to dividends at a rate of 30%.

Gift duty abolished
Gift duty was abolished with effect from 1 October 2011.

Changes to the thin capitalisation rules
The safe harbour threshold for the inbound thin capitalisation rules has been reduced from 75% to 60% effective from the beginning of the 2011/12 income year.

Broadly, New Zealand's inbound thin capitalisation rules limit the scope for non-residents to fund debt against their New Zealand operations and thereby reduce tax paid in New Zealand. Under the previous rules, New Zealand taxpayers controlled by non-residents were denied an interest deduction in New Zealand to the extent that their debt percentage (total group debt/total group assets) exceeded both 75% (now 60%) and 110% of the worldwide group's debt percentage.

The Taxation (International Investment and Remedial Matters) Act 2012 makes several additional changes to the thin capitalisation rules, including:

- Extending the thin capitalisation rules to New Zealand residents with foreign investment fund (FIF) interests that use the attributable FIF income method (i.e. the active income exemption) or the exemption for Australian resident FIFs. The changes apply to income years beginning on or after 1 July 2011.
- Introducing a new test to give certain New Zealand-based groups with high levels of arm's-length debt the option of using a ratio of interest expense to pre-tax cash flows, rather than a debt-to-asset ratio under the current test. The test applies retrospectively for income years beginning on or after 1 July 2009.
- Removing the application of the thin capitalisation rules for non-resident companies that do not carry on a business through a fixed establishment in New Zealand, if all their New Zealand-sourced income that is not relieved under a double tax agreement (DTA) is non-resident passive income (i.e. dividends, royalties, or interest). The changes apply for income years beginning on or after 1 July 2011.

The Taxation (Annual Rates, Returns Filing, and Remedial Matters) Bill also proposes to increase the minimum equity threshold of a foreign-held bank from 4% to 6% of the group's risk-weighted exposures.

Removal of depreciation on certain buildings
The depreciation rate for buildings with an estimated useful life of 50 years or more has been reduced to 0% from the 2011/12 income year.

Changes to the tax treatment of qualifying companies and new 'look-through companies'
New legislation took effect, from 1 April 2011, which does the following:

- Creates a new entity, the 'look-through company' (LTC), which is treated as a partnership for tax purposes. Income, expenses, tax credits, and losses of an LTC are able to be passed on to shareholders, subject to the application of a loss limitation rule.
- Allows existing qualifying companies (QC) and loss attributing qualifying companies (LAQCs) to continue to use the current QC rules but without the ability to attribute losses to shareholders until a review of the dividend rules for closely held companies has been completed.
- Allows existing QCs and LAQCs to elect to be subject to the new LTC rules, or to transition to a new structure such as a partnership, limited partnership, or sole trader, without incurring a tax cost.

Goods and services tax (GST)
Compulsory zero-rating (GST at 0%) applies to any supply involving land between two GST-registered parties from 1 April 2011, if:

- the purchaser acquires the land with the intention of using it to make taxable supplies, and
- the land is not intended to be used as a principal place of residence for either the purchaser or an associate.

Amendments have also been made to the change-in-use rules and the GST boundary between commercial and residential accommodation as well as the GST treatment of transactions involving nominee situations (e.g. where a named purchaser under a sale and purchase agreement directs a third party to take title). These rules apply from 1 April 2011.

The Taxation (Annual Rates, Returns Filing, and Remedial Matters) Bill introduced in September 2011 proposes an amendment to the GST rules to provide that late payment fees are subject to GST. This development will broaden the GST tax base to include fees that have never been subject to GST as they are not part of the price for the underlying goods and services.

Other proposed changes to GST rules include:

- A new rule precluding liquidators, receivers, and administrators from changing their GST accounting basis from payments to invoice basis to claim GST deductions (effective from the date of enactment).
- Confirmation that an assignment of a commercial lease can be zero-rated under the compulsory zero-rating (CZR) regime.

New Zealand

- Amendments to the nomination rules for non-land transactions to ensure a GST-registered contractual purchaser can claim a GST deduction even if the nominee is not GST-registered.

The government has not yet confirmed when these proposed changes will apply from if enacted.

International tax rules - changes to the FIF regime

The Taxation (International Investment and Remedial Matters) Act 2012 aligned the FIF rules with the controlled foreign company (CFC) rules where a New Zealand resident has an interest of 10% or more in a FIF. The changes apply to income years starting on or after 1 July 2011.

The Act also repeals the availability of the branch equivalent and accounting profits methods for calculating FIF income. Taxpayers that can access the information to prepare a branch equivalent calculation will be taxed on a notional income amount, even if the FIF is making losses.

Tax treatment of interests of 10% or more in a FIF

The Act repeals the current grey list exemption and replaces it with an Australian exemption.

The active business test that was previously only available for CFCs has been extended to apply to FIFs. This means that no income is taxable for FIFs that have passive income of less than 5% of their total gross income.

If a FIF fails the active business test, only its passive income is taxable.

The active business test may be applied to a group of foreign companies using consolidated accounting information where a FIF holds 50% or more of the voting interests in lower tier FIFs, regardless of jurisdiction. This differs from the CFC rules, which only allow CFCs in the same jurisdiction to be grouped and requires minority interests to be removed.

Investors who do not have enough information to perform the required calculations are able to use one of the attribution methods available for FIF interests of less than 10%, subject to certain restrictions.

Tax treatment of interests of less than 10% in a FIF

The active income exemption is not available. The default income attribution method will continue to be the fair dividend rate (FDR) method or the cost method if no market value is available for the FIF interest.

The comparative value (CV) method is also available for individuals and trustees. The CV method must be used for non-ordinary shares. If the CV method cannot be applied, the deemed rate of return method must be applied.

Revaluation of inherited FIF interests

The Act also revalues interests in grey list companies inherited before 1 April 2007 (i.e. when the grey list was abolished) to market value at the date the Act was enacted (i.e. 7 May 2012). The change is intended to prevent situations where a person has inherited investments in a FIF with a significant market value but is not required to attribute any FIF income as the investments fall under the *de minimis* threshold because the cost to the investor was nil or less than 50,000 New Zealand dollars (NZD).

Double tax agreements (DTAs)

Hong Kong - New Zealand DTA
A new DTA between Hong Kong and New Zealand came into force on 9 November 2011. The DTA brings withholding tax (WHT) rates into line with rates currently in operation with the United States (US) and Australia. The DTA applies in New Zealand for WHTs from 1 April 2012. In respect of all other taxes, the DTA applies in New Zealand for income years beginning on or after 1 April 2012.

Turkey - New Zealand DTA
A new DTA between Turkey and New Zealand came into force on 28 July 2011. The DTA is effective in New Zealand for WHTs from 1 January 2012. In respect of all other taxes, the DTA applies in New Zealand for income years beginning on or after 1 April 2012. In Turkey, the DTA is effective generally for taxable periods beginning on or after 1 January 2012.

Changes to Mexico and Chile DTAs
Lower non-resident WHT rates on dividends and royalty payments under New Zealand's DTAs with Chile and Mexico apply retrospectively from 1 May 2010. The reciprocal WHT rate on royalties arising in New Zealand and Chile has decreased from 10% to 5%. The WHT rate for dividend payments arising in New Zealand and Mexico has decreased from 15% to either 5% or zero, depending on the size of the investor's shareholding in the company paying the dividend and certain other criteria.

Canada - New Zealand DTA
New Zealand and Canada have signed a new DTA, which will replace the 1980 treaty. The updated agreement will come into force once both countries have given legal effect to it. In New Zealand, this will occur through an Order in Council.

The WHT rate on dividends will reduce from 15% to a maximum of 5% for an investor who holds at least 10% of the shares in the company that pays the dividend. The WHT rate on royalties will reduce from 15% to 10% generally, with a further reduced rate of 5% for royalties relating to copyright, computer software, and others.

DTAs under negotiation
New Zealand is currently negotiating DTAs with Papua New Guinea, the Netherlands, Luxembourg, the United Kingdom, and Vietnam.

Approved issuer levy and bonds
The Taxation (International Investment and Remedial Matters) Act 2012 also introduces an approved issuer levy (AIL) rate of zero (instead of the usual 2%) that applies to interest paid on qualifying bonds that meet certain requirements, including that the securities have been offered to the public, are not asset-backed securities, and are either listed on an exchange registered under the Securities Market Act 1988 or were issued to a group of at least 100 persons with no person (or group of associated persons) receiving 10% or more of the total securities.

The changes apply to interest payments made on or after 7 May 2012 (i.e. the date the Act was enacted).

Repeal of superannuation fund withdrawal tax
Superannuation fund withdrawal tax has been repealed as of 1 April 2011.

New Zealand

Broadly, the superannuation fund withdrawal tax provisions applied to make superannuation funds liable to income tax at the rate of 5% on amounts withdrawn from a superannuation fund prior to retirement to the extent they include employer contributions since 1 April 2000 (and earnings thereon).

KiwiSaver
The Taxation (Annual Rates, Returns Filing, and Remedial Matters) Bill raises the minimum employee and employer contribution rates for KiwiSaver from 2% to 3% of an employee's gross salary or wages. If enacted, the new rates apply from 1 April 2013.

Employer superannuation contribution tax (ESCT)
The exemption from ESCT for an employer's superannuation contributions (up to 2% of salary and wages) to an employee's KiwiSaver and complying superannuation fund accounts was removed from 1 April 2012.

From 1 April 2012, employers must calculate ESCT at a rate equivalent to an employee's marginal tax rate. The default deduction rate (a flat rate of 33%) is removed from 1 April 2012.

Unsuccessful software costs
The Taxation (Annual Rates, Returns Filing, and Remedial Matters) Bill introduces an upfront deduction for expenditure incurred on unsuccessful software development projects in the year that the development is abandoned. If enacted, this amendment will apply retrospectively from the 2007/08 and later income years.

Profit distribution plans (PDPs)
The Taxation (Annual Rates, Returns Filing, and Remedial Matters) Bill proposes to treat shares issued under PDPs as taxable dividends from 1 July 2012. The changes follow the government's announcement in April 2009 that it intended to tax bonus issues of shares distributed under PDPs in the same way as it taxes shares issued under other dividend reinvestment plans.

Taxes on corporate income

New Zealand resident companies are taxed on their worldwide income, and non-resident companies (including branches) are taxed on New Zealand-sourced income.

From the beginning of the 2011/12 income year, the tax rate is 28%. Prior to the 2011/12 income year, the income tax rate was 30%.

Local income taxes
There are no state and municipal income taxes in New Zealand.

Corporate residence

Residence is determined by place of incorporation, location of head office or centre of management, or by directors' exercising control of the company in New Zealand.

Permanent establishment (PE)
Generally, DTAs to which New Zealand is a party define a PE by reference to a fixed place of business through which the company's business is carried on. A PE can also

exist without a fixed place of business if the employees of the overseas company habitually exercise an authority to conclude contracts in New Zealand.

Other taxes

Goods and services tax (GST)

GST is a form of value-added tax (VAT) that applies to most supplies of goods and services. The narrow category of exempt supplies includes financial services. The rate applied to taxable supplies is currently 15% or 0%.

The 0% rate applies to a few supplies only, including exports and financial services supplied to other registered businesses. As of 1 April 2011, the 0% rate also applies to the sale of land between two registered parties if the purchaser acquires the land with the intention of using it to make taxable supplies and the land is not intended to be used as a principal place of residence for the purchaser or an associate.

There is also a 'reverse charge' mechanism that requires the self-assessment of GST on the value of certain services imported by GST registered persons.

Customs duties

Customs duty is levied on some imported goods at rates generally ranging from 1% to 10%.

Excise duty

Excise duty is levied, in addition to GST, on alcoholic beverages (e.g. wines, beers, spirits), tobacco products, and certain fuels (e.g. compressed natural gas, gasoline). The excise duties are levied item-by-item at rates that vary considerably.

Property taxes

Local authorities levy tax known as 'rates' on land within their territorial boundaries. Rates are levied on properties based on the properties' rateable value.

Stamp duty

Stamp duty has been abolished in respect of instruments executed after 20 May 1999.

Accident compensation levy

A statutory-based scheme of accident insurance is funded in part by premiums payable by employers and employees.

Premiums paid by employers (including the self-employed) fund insurance for work-related accidents. Employers are liable to pay a residual claims levy and an employer levy. The employer levy payable is determined according to the industry or risk classification of the employer and the level of earnings of employees.

Fringe benefit tax (FBT)

Employers are subject to a tax-deductible FBT on the value of non-cash fringe benefits provided to their employees. Employers can elect to pay FBT at flat rates (for the 2011/12 income year, 49.25% on attributed benefits and 42.86% on pool benefits, i.e. those benefits that cannot be attributed to a particular employee) applied against the value of the benefit or can attribute fringe benefits to individual employees and pay FBT based on each employee's marginal tax rate.

New Zealand

Under the attribution option, the applicable FBT rate depends on the net remuneration (including fringe benefits) (for the 2011/12 income year, 49.25% on attributed benefits and 42.86% on pool benefits, i.e. those benefits which cannot be attributed to a particular employee) applied against the value of the benefit or can attribute fringe benefits to individual employees and pay FBT based on each employee's marginal tax rate. Under the attribution option, the applicable FBT rate depends on the net remuneration (including fringe benefits) paid to the employee. The attribution calculation treats the fringe benefit as if it was paid in cash and calculates FBT as the notional increase in income that otherwise would have arisen.

The multi rates for the 2012/13 income tax year are:

Net remuneration (NZD)	FBT rate (%)
12,530 or less	11.73
12,531 to 40,580	21.21
40,581 to 55,980	42.86
Greater than 55,981	49.25

Fringe benefits include motor vehicles available for private use, loans at below prescribed interest rates, contributions to medical insurance schemes, and employer contributions to superannuation schemes.

In relation to motor vehicles, employers can value a vehicle on an annual basis either using 20% of the cost price or market value (GST inclusive) of the vehicle (depending on whether the vehicle is owned or leased by the employer) or 36% of the vehicle's tax written down value (GST inclusive). In each case, the FBT value must be reduced proportionately for whole days when the vehicle is not available for private use at any time.

FBT is also applicable to benefits received by an employee from a third party where there is an arrangement between the employer and the third party and where the benefit would be subject to FBT if it had been provided by the employer.

Gift duty
Previously, gift duty was payable by donors (including companies) on gifts which exceed NZD 27,000 in aggregate in any 12-month period. A gift statement had to be filed when the value of the gifts exceeded NZD 12,000 in aggregate in any 12-month period.

Gift duty has been repealed in respect of gifts made on or after 1 October 2011.

Employer superannuation contribution tax (ESCT)
Employers' contributions to an approved superannuation fund (excludes foreign schemes) are subject to ESCT, formally known as 'specified superannuation contribution withholding tax'.

From 1 April 2012, employer contributions to KiwiSaver (or other qualifying registered superannuation schemes) are subject to ESCT at an employee's marginal tax rate. From 1 April 2009 to 1 April 2012, there was an exemption from ESCT for employer contributions to KiwiSaver capped at 2% of the compulsory employer contribution (previously 4%).

Fund withdrawal tax (FWT)

FWT has been repealed as of 1 April 2011.

Prior to 1 April 2011, the FWT provisions made the superannuation fund liable to income tax at the rate of 5% on amounts withdrawn from a superannuation fund prior to retirement, to the extent they included employer contributions since 1 April 2000 (and earnings thereon). FWT applied where the superannuation fund member's income was above NZD 70,000.

Branch income

A non-resident company is taxed on income generated by business wholly or partially carried on in New Zealand. Branch profits are subject to ordinary corporate rates of taxation, and there is no WHT on repatriated profits.

Income determination

Inventory valuation

Inventory must be valued by a cost-valuation method or, where market-selling value is lower than cost, may be valued at market-selling value. If the inventory is shares, it must be valued at cost. Cost is determined under generally accepted accounting principles (GAAP). Acceptable cost flow methods are first in first out (FIFO) or weighted-average cost. Some valuation concessions are available to small taxpayers.

Capital gains

There is no separate capital gains tax. However, the income tax legislation specifically includes various forms of gain that would otherwise be considered a capital gain within the definition of 'income'. Taxable income includes gains on the sale of real estate in certain circumstances and on personal property where the taxpayer acquired the property for resale or deals in such property or where a profit-making purpose or scheme can be deemed or imputed.

N

Dividend income

Dividends derived from resident companies are exempt where there is 100% common ownership.

Dividends from a foreign company

A dividend derived by a company resident in New Zealand from a foreign company is treated as exempt income, unless it is:

- a dividend on a fixed rate share or a dividend for which the foreign company has received a tax deduction in its home jurisdiction, or
- a dividend from a portfolio FIF (i.e. interests under 10%) that is exempt from FIF rules (e.g. an interest in an Australian listed company).

Dividends from foreign companies derived by taxpayers other than companies are taxable (generally with a credit for any foreign withholding taxes).

Branch equivalent tax account (BETA)

Previously, taxpayers who were subject to tax on attributed foreign income under the CFC or FIF regimes and also taxed or liable to pay foreign dividend payments on dividends could elect to maintain a BETA. A BETA operates in a similar manner to an

New Zealand

Imputation Credit Account and helps avoid the double taxation of attributed foreign income and foreign dividend income.

As most foreign dividends received by New Zealand companies are exempt from tax, most companies therefore no longer need to maintain BETAs. The Taxation (International Investment and Remedial Matters) Act 2012 abolishes BETAs from the income year beginning on or after 1 July 2012.

Other

Previously, the foreign investor tax credit (FITC) regime ensured that foreign investors were not taxed at more than the New Zealand corporate tax rate by effectively rebating the New Zealand withholding tax to the extent that the dividend was fully imputed. As non-resident withholding tax (NRWT) rates have been reduced to nil on most fully imputed dividends, FITC is generally no longer required.

The FITC regime applies only to fully imputed dividends paid to shareholders holding less than 10% of the shares in the company on NRWT rates of at least 15%.

Broadly therefore:

- only portfolio investors (i.e. those with less than 10% holdings) with NRWT rates of at least 15% and supplementary dividend holding companies will qualify for relief under the supplementary dividend rules, and
- a zero rate of NRWT applies to dividends paid to non-portfolio shareholders (i.e. shareholders with more than 10% holdings) and to any other dividends subject to lower tax rates, to the extent they are fully imputed.

The changes affect provisional tax calculations for taxpayers who take into account their anticipated FITC in calculating their provisional tax. Taxpayers should also consider the need to impute dividends where a tax treaty applies to reduce the NRWT rate.

The supplementary dividend regime will cease to apply to holding companies from the 2013/14 income tax year.

Stock dividends

Bonus issues can be taxable or non-taxable. With a taxable bonus issue, the amount capitalised becomes available for tax-free distribution upon a subsequent share cancellation. With a non-taxable bonus issue, the amount capitalised is not available for tax-free distribution upon a subsequent share cancellation.

Draft legislation introduced in August 2011 introduces rules that ensure bonus issues of shares distributed under profit distribution plans (PDPs) are taxed in the same way as shares issued under other dividend reinvestment plans. These rules will apply from 1 July 2012.

Interest income

All interest derived by a company is income. The financial arrangement rules may require income for tax purposes to be recognised on an accrual basis. When this is not required (because the person is classified as a 'cash basis' person), interest income is recognised as and when it is received.

Other significant items

The taxation of debt and debt instruments is governed by the financial arrangements rules, a specific set of timing rules. Income or expenditure (including foreign exchange gains and losses) from financial arrangements must be recognised on an accrual basis (generally, yield to maturity or other commercially acceptable method). These rules do not apply to the income or expenditure of a non-resident if the financial arrangement does not relate to a business carried on in New Zealand.

Foreign income

A New Zealand corporation is taxed on foreign passive income as earned. Double taxation with respect to all types of taxable income, including interest, rents, and royalties, is avoided by the recognition of foreign tax credits. Foreign dividends received are exempt from income tax but are subject to the foreign dividend withholding payment. However, new rules exempt most foreign dividends received by New Zealand companies from domestic tax and repeals the foreign dividend payment (FDP) and underlying foreign tax credit rules.

New Zealand does not offer specific tax deferral rules.

Deductions

Depreciation and depletion

For tax purposes, depreciation of property can be computed under the diminishing value method, the straight-line method, or a pooling method. The rates of depreciation depend on the following factors:

- Type of asset.
- Whether the asset is acquired new or second-hand (i.e. used).

Taxpayers must use the economic depreciation rates prescribed by Inland Revenue, together with a 20% uplift in the case of new assets (other than buildings and imported motor vehicles) purchased on or before 20 May 2010 (the 20% uplift has been removed for assets purchased after this date). Fixed-life intangible property (including the right to use land and resource consents) is depreciable on a straight-line basis over its legal life. Any depreciation recovered on the sale of an asset (up to its original cost) is taxable in the year of sale.

The double-declining-balance (accelerated) method applies to most plant and equipment. Under the double-declining-balance method, equipment with an estimated useful life of ten years results in diminishing value depreciation deductions of 20% per annum (i.e. double the straight-line rate of 10% over the equipment's ten-year life). Buildings, certain motor vehicles, high-residual-value property, fixed-life intangible property, and property acquired prior to the introduction of the new rules cannot be depreciated under the double-declining-balance method.

The depreciation rate for buildings with an estimated useful life of 50 years or more is reduced to 0% as of the 2011/12 income year.

Goodwill

Goodwill is generally regarded as a capital asset, thus any payment for goodwill is non-deductible. There is a limited exception for payments made to preserve goodwill.

N

New Zealand

Start-up expenses
Expenses incurred by a company before the commencement of the business are generally regarded as outgoings of a capital nature and are therefore not deductible. However, certain expenditure on scientific research may be deductible, provided that it is incurred for the purpose of the company deriving assessable income.

Research and development (R&D)
R&D costs are tax deductible. Expenses written off as immaterial and not tested against certain asset-recognition criteria are not automatically deductible for tax purposes.

Interest expense
Generally, interest incurred by most companies is deductible, subject to thin capitalisation rules (*see the Group taxation section*).

Bad debt
A company is allowed a deduction for bad debt in the income year in which the debt is physically written off by the company.

Charitable contributions
A company is allowed a deduction for charitable contributions it makes to listed donee organisations. The list of approved donee organisations is available on Inland Revenue's website. The deduction available for charitable contributions is limited to the company's net income for that income year.

Entertainment expenditure
Entertainment expenditure is generally only 50% deductible. However, entertainment expenditure incurred overseas is 100% deductible.

Legal expenditure
Legal expenditure is deductible if the expenditure is:

* incurred in deriving assessable or excluded income or
* incurred in the course of carrying on a business for the purpose of deriving assessable or excluded income.

However, the expenditure is not deductible if it is of a capital, private, or domestic nature.

Taxpayers with business-related legal expenditure of NZD 10,000 or less are able to deduct the full amount of the expenditure in the year it is incurred, whether or not it is capital in nature.

Fines and penalties
Generally, no deduction is available where a company has incurred expenditure on fines or penalties paid in breach of statute or regulation. Expenditure on other fines and penalties requires further evaluation before its deductibility can be determined.

Taxes
FBT is deductible, as is GST payable on the value of a fringe benefit.

Net operating losses
Losses may be carried forward indefinitely for offset against future profits, subject to the company maintaining 49% continuity of ownership. There is no loss carryback. A legislative amendment in 2002 ensures that losses of a subsidiary are preserved on a

spinout (i.e. when shares in the subsidiary are transferred to shareholders of its parent company).

Payments to foreign affiliates

A New Zealand corporation can claim a deduction for royalties, management service fees, and interest charges paid to non-resident associates, provided the charges satisfy the 'arm's-length principle', which forms the basis of New Zealand's transfer pricing regime.

Group taxation

Companies that are 66% or more commonly owned constitute a 'group'. Group companies are able to offset losses by election as well as by subvention payment. A subvention payment is a payment made by the profit company to the loss company and is equal to the amount of loss to be offset. The payment is deductible to the profit company and assessable to the loss company. Certain companies subject to special bases of assessment (e.g. mining companies other than petroleum extraction companies) are excluded from the grouping provisions. Branches of non-resident companies may be included, provided they continue to carry on business in New Zealand through a fixed establishment.

Groups of resident companies that have 100% common ownership may elect to be subject to the consolidated group regime. The group is effectively treated as a single company and transfers of assets, dividends, interest, and management fees among members of the group are generally disregarded for tax purposes. The group files a single return and is issued a single assessment. Group members are jointly and severally liable for tax purposes.

Losses incurred by a dual-resident company are not available for offset by election or subvention payment.

Transfer pricing

The transfer pricing rules are based on Organisation for Economic Co-operation and Development (OECD) principles and require taxpayers to value for tax purposes all cross-border transactions with associates on an arm's-length basis.

The transfer pricing rules apply to arrangements for the acquisition or supply of goods, services, money, intangible property, and anything else (other than non-fixed rate shares), where the supplier and acquirer are associated persons. Similar rules apply to the apportionment of branch profits.

Various methods are available for determining the 'arm's-length consideration'. The taxpayer is required to use the method that produces the most reliable measure of the amount that independent parties would have paid or received in respect of the same or similar transactions. Inland Revenue has published guidelines that make it clear that documentation is required to support a taxpayer's transfer prices.

Thin capitalisation

'Inbound' thin capitalisation rules apply to New Zealand taxpayers controlled by non-residents, including branches of non-residents. The aim of the rules is to ensure that New Zealand entities or branches do not deduct a disproportionately high amount of the worldwide group's interest expense. This is achieved by deeming income in New

New Zealand

Zealand when, and to the extent that, the New Zealand entities in the group are thinly capitalised (i.e. excessively debt funded).

The 'outbound' thin capitalisation rules are intended to operate as a base protection measure to prevent New Zealand residents with CFC investments from allocating an excessive portion of their interest cost against the New Zealand tax base.

To reduce taxpayer compliance costs, the outbound thin capitalisation rules do not apply when the New Zealand taxpayer has:

* 90% or more of their assets in New Zealand or
* less than NZD 250,000 of interest deductions.

Further concessions are available to taxpayers who do not fall below the above thresholds. If the taxpayer's interest deduction and dividends paid for fixed rate shares (the finance cost) is below NZD 1 million, no apportionment of deductible interest is required. If the finance cost is above NZD 1 million, but below NZD 2 million, the apportionment is an adjustment.

An apportionment of deductible interest is required under the thin capitalisation rules when the debt percentage (calculated as the total group debt/total group assets of a New Zealand entity or group) exceeds both:

* 75% (for 'inbound' thin capitalisation, the 75% threshold is reduced to 60% from the beginning of the 2011/12 income year) and
* 110% of the worldwide group's debt percentage.

The use of the debt-to-asset ratio differs from most thin capitalisation models, which apply to an entity's debt-to-equity ratio. All interest (both related and unrelated party) is subject to apportionment.

Foreign-owned banks operating in New Zealand are subject to specific thin capitalisation rules that deem income if the bank does not hold a level of equity equivalent to 4% (draft legislation proposes that this threshold increase to 6%) of their New Zealand banking risk-weighted assets. In addition, banks are required to have sufficient equity to equity fund offshore investments that do not give rise to New Zealand taxable income in full.

Controlled foreign companies (CFCs)
The CFC regime imposes New Zealand tax on the notional share of income attributable to residents (companies, trusts, and individuals) with interests in certain CFCs.

Central to the regime is the definition of a CFC. When five or fewer New Zealand residents directly or indirectly control more than 50% of a foreign company, or when a single New Zealand resident directly or indirectly controls 40% or more of a foreign company (unless a non-associated non-resident has equal or greater control), that company is a CFC. For interests of less than 10%, the investment may be taxed under the FIF regime (*see below*).

For income years starting on or after 1 July 2009, new rules apply to the taxation of foreign companies controlled by New Zealand residents. Under the new rules, a person with an income interest of 10% or more in a CFC does not have attributed CFC income or losses if:

- the Australian exemption applies or
- the CFC passes an active business test.

If the exemptions do not apply, only the CFC's passive (attributable) income is subject to tax on attribution (on an accrual basis).

Active business test
A CFC passes the active business test if it has passive (attributable) income that is less than 5% of its total income. For the purposes of the test, taxpayers measure passive and total income using either financial accounting (audited International Financial Reporting Standards [IFRS] or New Zealand GAAP accounts) or tax measures of income.

CFCs in the same country may be consolidated for calculating the 5% ratio, subject to certain conditions.

The active exemption test may also be available to investors with less than 10% interest income in a CFC if certain criteria are satisfied.

Australian exemption
A person with an income interest of 10% or more in a CFC does not have attributed CFC income or a loss if the CFC is a resident in, and subject to income tax in, Australia and meets certain other criteria.

Passive (attributable) income
Attributable, or passive, income is income that is highly mobile and not location-specific (i.e. income where there is a risk that it could easily be shifted out of the New Zealand tax base).

The broad categories of attributable income are as follows:

- Certain types of dividend that would be taxable if received by a New Zealand resident company.
- Certain interest.
- Certain royalties.
- Certain rents.
- Certain amounts for financial arrangements.
- Income from services performed in New Zealand.
- Income from offshore insurance business and life insurance policies.
- Personal services income.
- Income from the disposal of revenue account property.
- Certain income related to telecommunications services.

Taxpayers must disclose interests in CFCs in their annual tax returns. Failure to disclose CFC interests can result in the imposition of penalties.

Foreign investment funds (FIFs)
The FIF regime is an extension of the CFC regime, which subjects persons with interests in certain foreign entities (which are not CFCs) to New Zealand tax. It also applies when the investor does not have a sufficient interest in a CFC to be taxed under that regime.

Common examples of investments classified as FIFs include foreign companies, unit trusts, foreign superannuation schemes, and life insurance policies issued by foreign entities not subject to New Zealand tax.

New Zealand

The FIF rules can be split into two regimes:

- The portfolio FIF rules, which apply to interests of less than 10% in a FIF.
- The non-portfolio FIF rules, which apply to interests of 10% or more that are outside the CFC rules.

Portfolio FIF rules

The portfolio FIF rules underwent significant reform in 2006. The new rules have applied from 1 April 2007. The portfolio FIF rules apply to interests of less than 10% in foreign companies, foreign superannuation schemes, and foreign life insurance policies issued by non-resident life insurers (if the CFC rules do not apply). However, a New Zealand resident does not generally have FIF income when:

- the total cost of FIF interests held by the individual does not exceed NZD 50,000
- the income interest is less than 10% in certain Australian Securities Exchange (ASX) listed companies or certain Australian unit trusts, or
- the CFC rules apply.

There are also exemptions for interests in certain foreign employment-related superannuation schemes. These include interests held by returning residents and new migrants acquired before the person became a New Zealand resident or within the first five years of New Zealand residence.

When an interest is exempt from the FIF rules, distributions are subject to tax on a receipts basis in accordance with normal principles.

The taxable income of a New Zealand resident with an interest in a FIF that does not qualify for one of the exemptions is calculated using one of the following methods:

- Fair dividend rate (FDR).
- Comparative value.
- Cost.
- Deemed rate of return.

The nature of the interest held and the availability of information restrict the choice of method.

Taxpayers must disclose interests in certain FIFs in their annual tax returns. Failure to disclose can result in the imposition of penalties.

Non-portfolio FIF rules

The Taxation (International Investment and Remedial Matters) Act 2012 reforms the non-portfolio FIF rules significantly. The new rules apply to income years starting on or after 1 July 2011. A key feature of the new rules is to extend the active income exemption (which applies for CFCs) to certain non-portfolio FIFs. If the FIF fails the active business test, passive income will be attributed to the New Zealand shareholders. The new rules also repeal the grey list exemption from the FIF rules and replaces it with an exemption for shareholders with a 10% or greater interest in a FIF that is resident and subject to tax in Australia.

When investors do not have sufficient information to perform the calculations required under the active business test (or choose not to apply the active business test), they will be able to use one of the attribution methods for portfolio FIF investments (*see above*). The accounting profits and branch equivalent methods, which were previously available to calculate FIF income, have also been repealed under the new rules for both non-portfolio and portfolio FIF interests.

Tax credits and incentives

Foreign tax credits
If a New Zealand resident company derives overseas income which is subject to New Zealand income tax, generally the company is allowed a credit for the foreign income tax paid in respect of that income. Generally, the credit is limited to the lesser of the actual overseas tax paid on the overseas income or the New Zealand tax applicable to the overseas income.

Inbound investment incentives
There are limited specific tax incentives designed to encourage the flow of investment funds into New Zealand.

Legislation enacted in 2004 encourages foreign venture capital investment into unlisted New Zealand companies. Gains derived by certain non-residents from the sale of shares (held on revenue account and owned for at least 12 months) in New Zealand unlisted companies that do not have certain prohibited activities as their main activity, are exempt from income tax. The rules apply to foreign investors who are resident in all of the countries with which New Zealand has a DTA (except Switzerland) and who invest into New Zealand venture capital opportunities.

Capital investment incentives
Investment allowances on fixed assets are not available.

Trans-Tasman imputation
Elective rules allow trans-Tasman groups of companies to attach both imputation credits (representing New Zealand tax paid) and franking credits (representing Australian tax paid) to dividends paid to shareholders.

Withholding taxes

Resident corporations paying certain types of income are required to withhold tax on gross income, as shown in the table below.

Recipient	Dividends (%)	Interest (%)	Royalties (%)
Resident corporations	33 (1)	28 (1)	0
Resident individuals	33	max 33	–
Non-resident corporations and individuals		(2)	
No treaty	30 (3)	15 (4)	15
Treaty:			
Australia	0/5/15 (9)	0/10 (9)	5
Austria	15	10	10
Belgium (12)	15	10	10
Canada (11)	15	15	15
Chile	15	10/15 (5)	5

New Zealand

Recipient	Dividends (%)	Interest (%)	Royalties (%)
China, P.R.	15	10	10
Czech Republic	15	10	10
Denmark	15	10	10
Fiji	15	10 (4)	15
Finland	15	10	10
France	15	10	10
Germany	15	10	10
Hong Kong	0/5/15	0/10	5
India	15	10	10
Indonesia	15	10	15
Ireland, Republic of	15	10	10
Italy	15	10	10
Japan	15	15 (4)	15
Korea, Republic of	15	10	10
Malaysia	15	15 (4)	15
Mexico	0/5/15 (13)	0/10 (14)	10
Netherlands	15	10	10
Norway	15	10	10
Philippines	15	10	15
Poland	15	10	10
Russian Federation	15	10	10
Singapore	5/15 (10)	10	5
South Africa	15	10	10
Spain	15	10	10
Sweden	15	10	10
Switzerland	15	10	10
Taiwan	15	10	10
Thailand	15	10	10/15 (6)
United Arab Emirates	15	10	10
United Kingdom (7)	15	10	10
United States (8)	0/5/15 (8)	10 (8)	5

Notes

1. Resident WHT applies to both interest and dividends. Unless the recipient corporation holds an exemption certificate, and if the recipient provides a tax file number, the default rate of the interest WHT is 28% (33% prior to 1 April 2011). Recipients can elect for the rate of interest withholding to be 30%. The rate of interest WHT is 30% where the recipient does not provide a tax file number. The rate of WHT on dividends paid is 33%, but the tax is reduced by the aggregate imputation and withholding payment credits attached to the dividend or taxable bonus share. Interest and dividends paid between group companies and in certain other limited circumstances are exempt from the WHT.
2. Resident corporations paying interest to non-associated, non-resident corporations and individuals need not withhold tax if they have approved-issuer status and the security under which interest is payable is registered with Inland Revenue. In this case, the resident corporation pays a 2% levy (tax deductible) on the interest payments instead of the WHT otherwise applicable.
3. Non-resident WHT is imposed on dividends at the following rates, regardless of the jurisdiction to which the dividends are paid:
   - 0% for fully imputed dividends paid to a shareholder holding 10% or more of the direct voting interests in the company and fully imputed non-cash dividends.
   - 15% for fully imputed cash dividends paid to a shareholder holding less than 10%.
   - 30% in most other cases, subject to any relief available under a DTA.
4. Net interest income is subject to reassessment at the company tax rate where the payer and the recipient are 'associated persons', but WHT is the minimum liability. Non-resident WHT is not imposed where the recipient of the interest has a fixed establishment in New Zealand.

5. 10% if the interest received is derived from loans granted by banks or insurance companies. In all other cases, 15%.
6. 10% or 15%, depending on the type of royalty.
7. The government has announced that it is re-negotiating New Zealand's DTA with the United Kingdom.
8. The WHT rate on dividends is reduced from 15% to a maximum of 5% for an investor who holds at least 10% of the shares in the company that pays the dividend and to 0% if the investor holds 80% or more of the shares in the company and meets other criteria.
   The rate on interest is generally 10%, although it will drop to 0% for interest paid to lending or finance businesses, provided that the 2% approved issuer levy is paid on New Zealand-sourced interest.
9. The WHT on dividends is reduced from 15% to 5% for an investing company that has at least a 10% shareholding in the company paying the dividend. The rate reduces to 0% if the investing company holds 80% or more of the shares in the other company and meets other criteria. The WHT rate on interest is 10% but is reduced to 0% if it is payable to eligible financial institutions.
10. The standard WHT rate on dividends reduces to 5% for an investing company that has at least a 10% shareholding in the company paying the dividend.
11. New Zealand and Canada have signed a new DTA, which will come into force once both countries have given legal effect to it. The WHT rate on dividends will reduce from 15% to a maximum of 5% for an investor who holds at least 10% of the shares in the company that pays the dividend. The WHT rate on royalties will reduce from 15% to 10% generally, with a further reduced rate of 5% for royalties relating to copyright, computer software, and others.
12. The government signed a Second Protocol in December 2009, which amends the 1981 DTA. Both sides are still working towards completing their procedures for entry into force. Negotiations for a Third Protocol to amend Article 25 (Exchange of Information) of the DTA are currently in progress.
13. The 0% WHT rate applies where the foreign company owns at least 80% of the voting rights in the paying company (directly or indirectly) for 12 months prior to the date the dividend is paid. The 5% rate applies if the foreign company has a direct interest of at least 10% of the voting rights in the paying company.
14. The 0% WHT rate applies to interest paid to or by government organisations or the central bank or is paid in respect of a loan (for a period of at least three years) granted, guaranteed, or insured by such entities.

Tax administration

Taxable period
Tax returns are based on the fiscal year ending 31 March, although other fiscal year-ends are possible if permission is obtained.

Tax returns
The system is one of self-assessment, under which the corporation files an income tax return each year. For those not linked to a tax agent, returns must be filed by 7 July for March balance dates, or by the seventh day of the fourth month following a substituted balance date. The terminal tax due date is extended by two months for taxpayers linked to a tax agent.

Payment of tax
The final assessed tax (terminal tax) is generally payable on the seventh day of the 11th month following the end of that income year or the 13th month following the end of that income year if the taxpayer has a tax agent with an 'extension of time' arrangement. For a standard (31 March) balance date, this means either 7 February or 7 April of the following year.

Provisional tax payments are generally due in three instalments: (1) 28th day of seventh month before balance date, (2) 28th day of third month before balance date, (3) 28th day of month following balance date.

Calculating provisional tax
For the 2012/13 income year (i.e. year ending 31 March 2013), provisional taxpayers have the following four options:

New Zealand

- Where the 2011/12 return of income has been filed, 2012/13 provisional tax can be based on 105% of the 2011/12 residual income tax.
- Where the 2011/12 return of income has not been filed, due to an extension of time for filing, 2012/13 provisional tax can be based on 105% (previously 110%) of the 2010/11 residual income tax, but only for the first two instalments. The final instalment must be calculated based on the first option above.
- Provisional tax can be based on a fair and reasonable estimate of 2012/13 residual income tax.
- The GST ratio option.

The GST ratio option has been introduced to enable smaller taxpayers to align their provisional tax payments with their cash flow and reduce their exposure to use of money interest. The option is intended to benefit those taxpayers with declining, seasonal, or fluctuating income. This option calculates provisional tax by reference to the taxpayer's GST taxable supplies in the relevant provisional tax instalment period.

Taxpayers can also make voluntary payments. Such payments can be made to minimise exposure to use of money interest. A taxpayer choosing to estimate residual income tax is required to take reasonable care when estimating.

When the taxpayer's return of income for the year is furnished, the provisional tax paid for that year is credited against the tax assessed. This results in either a refund or further tax to pay by way of terminal tax.

Where provisional tax paid is less than the amount of income tax deemed due on that instalment date, interest is imposed. If provisional tax is overpaid, interest is payable to the taxpayer. Interest is deductible for tax purposes by business taxpayers, and interest earned on overpaid provisional tax is gross income for tax purposes. The interest rate for unpaid tax is 8.40%, while the rate for overpaid tax is 1.75%.

Tax pooling
Taxpayers are able to pool their provisional tax payments with those of other taxpayers through an arrangement with a commercial intermediary. Tax pooling allows underpayments to be offset by overpayments within the same pool and vice versa.

Tax penalties
An initial late payment penalty of 1% applies if a tax payment is not made on the due date. A further 4% late payment penalty applies if the payment is not made within seven days of the due date. An incremental late payment penalty of 1% is then imposed monthly until payment is made.

Inland Revenue is required to notify a taxpayer the first time their payment is late rather than imposing an immediate late payment penalty. If payment is not made by a certain date, a late payment penalty will be imposed. Taxpayers will be entitled to one notification every two years. After receiving a first warning, the Inland Revenue will not send further notifications for two years, and an initial late payment penalty will be imposed in the normal manner.

Shortfall penalties
Shortfall penalties, calculated as a percentage of the tax shortfall resulting from the action or position taken by the taxpayer in a tax return, may also apply.

There is a 50% discount on certain penalties where the taxpayer has a past record of 'good behaviour' and, in certain circumstances, a cap of NZD 50,000 on shortfall penalties for not taking reasonable care or for taking an unacceptable tax position.

Audit cycle

Inland Revenue maintains an active audit programme across all tax types and taxpayer profiles and regularly publishes information about their compliance focus (*see 'Topics of focus of tax compliance' below*). Often, Inland Revenue audits are preceded by a risk review where Inland Revenue requests information in order to evaluate the risk of non-compliance. Where this review detects an issue that requires further inspection, Inland Revenue will then advise that an audit will be commenced.

Statute of limitations

The general rule is that Inland Revenue has four years from the end of the New Zealand income tax year (31 March) in which the return is filed to re-assess the return, unless the return is fraudulent, wilfully misleading, or omits income of a particular nature or source.

Topics of focus of tax compliance

Inland Revenue's compliance management programme

In July 2011, Inland Revenue announced its key areas of focus for 2011/12. These include complex financing arrangements, loss generation and usage, diverting personal income, and the 'hidden economy'.

Tax policy work programme

The focus of the government's tax policy work programme for 2012/13 is on increasing efficiency and fairness in the tax system. Specific areas of focus will include further simplification measures for small and medium businesses, deductibility of 'mixed-use assets', ensuring consistency in the tax treatment of employee benefits, reviewing the tax treatment of New Zealand residents' foreign superannuation, and ensuring deductibility of certain 'black hole' expenditure. Extending the active income exemption to branches and seeking mutual recognition of imputation and franking credits is also on the government's agenda for the next 18 months.

Other issues

International Financial Reporting Standards (IFRS)

The relationship between statutory accounting and taxable income is quasi-dependent. The year of final adoption for IFRS was 2007, and the impact on significant areas of tax law is as follows.

Comments on tax regime

New Zealand's determination of taxable income starts with the statutory accounts' accounting profit and then specific tax adjustments are made based on rules for revenue recognition and deductible expenditure in the tax legislation. Changes have been made to the tax treatment of 'financial arrangements' (a defined tax legislative term) to allow for the alignment to the accounting recognition of fair values on such arrangements in specific cases.

Year of adoption cash impact

Mandatory adoption of NZ IFRS accounting standards for most entities (except for small & medium enterprises) applied for balance dates beginning 1 January

New Zealand

2007. Depending on the specific IFRS adoption adjustment, the resulting income or expenditure is taken into taxable income based on the ordinary statutory tax provisions. The key areas, which were changed for tax under IFRS adoption, are the trading stock provisions (which align tax with accounting standards subject to some provisions) and the financial arrangement rules. These rules are very broad and deal with the tax treatment of accrual income or expenditure on debt instruments, debt type instruments, derivatives, etc.

Thin capitalisation
The thin capitalisation rules work on a debt over assets percentage. It relies mostly on the tax legislative definition for debt and the amount disclosed in the financial statements under generally accepted accounting practice as assets (although there are some other measurement alternatives).

Debt versus equity classifications
The classification of debt and equity instruments for tax is dependent on the tax legislative definitions for specific purposes (such as the spreading of any deductions or income where the financial arrangement rules apply, thin capitalisation, etc). Tax applies legal form and does not strictly rely upon the classification applied under IFRS.

Lease versus sale determinations
There are specific tax provisions dealing with finance leases.

Distributable reserves
The level of distributable reserves is based on the company law requirements of solvency and not specifically on the amounts shown as reserves in the financial statements.

Transfer pricing determination
There have been no specific comments released yet by the New Zealand Revenue Authority on the adoption of IFRS impact for transfer pricing.

Financial arrangements
Specific timing rules apply to the recognition for income tax purposes of income and expenditure in relation to financial arrangements, which apply to New Zealand residents or entities carrying on business in New Zealand.

A number of changes to the financial arrangements rules have been enacted to ensure that taxpayers who adopt IFRS can continue to use tax rules that rely on accounting practice. For other taxpayers, the existing tax spreading methodologies continue to apply but without the option of using the financial reporting method.

The new rules include a combination of compulsory methods and elective methods that are available subject to the taxpayer meeting certain qualification criteria. Two new methods (the expected value method and the equity-free fair value method) have been introduced to assist in reducing exposure to volatility that might otherwise arise under IFRS fair value accounting.

Nicaragua

PwC contact

Ramon Ortega
Scotiabank Building
3rd Floor
Santo Domingo, Dominican Republic
Tel: +809 567 7741
Email: ramon.ortega@do.pwc.com

Significant developments

There have been no significant corporate tax developments in Nicaragua during the past year.

Taxes on corporate income

Nicaragua has a territorial income tax system under which only income generated in, or that causes effects in, Nicaragua is generally subject to income tax. The corporate income tax (CIT) is imposed on a corporation's profits, which consist of business/ trading income, passive income, and capital gains. General business expenses are allowed as a deduction in computing taxable income.

Corporate income tax (CIT) rate

CIT is levied only on domestic-sourced income at a flat rate of the higher of:

* 30% of net taxable income (i.e. gross taxable income less allowed deductions) or
* a definitive minimum tax of 1% on gross income obtained during the fiscal year.

If the company does not have net income, 30% of net income will not be greater than 1% of gross income.

The law establishes the following exceptions to the 1% definitive minimum tax:

* First three fiscal periods of recently incorporated entities.
* Taxpayers whose sales prices are controlled by the government.
* Taxpayers that ceased operations on account of *force majeure*.

Local income taxes

See Municipal sales and services tax in the Other taxes section.

Corporate residence

In order to be considered as a tax resident, a legal entity must be registered first in the mercantile registry, then before the tax authorities. The legal forms permitted in Nicaragua to constitute a corporation are stock corporations or limited liability companies, either as subsidiaries or branches.

Permanent establishment (PE)

In principle, the Nicaraguan tax system does not recognise any rule for PE.

N

Nicaragua

....

Other taxes

Value-added tax (VAT)

VAT is imposed at a 15% rate on the sale of goods, rendering of services, grant of use of assets, and import of goods.

VAT exemptions are available for certain items, including medicine, real estate transfer, sale of used goods, basic food products, credit instruments, tuition, and textbooks and educational supplies.

Taxpayers may recover VAT paid for the purchase of goods and services used to generate other goods and services subject to VAT. This is known as VAT liquidation, which is determined by subtracting VAT credits paid on transactions needed to generate taxable income for VAT purposes from VAT collected on the sales of goods or the rendering of services. Note that VAT paid on transactions to generate non-taxable income for VAT purposes are not allowed as VAT credits.

VAT returns must be filed on a monthly basis, with payment due in full on the same day. Taxpayers registered as high-taxpayers (with annual income greater than 6 million Nicaraguan córdobas [NIO]) must present an advanced bi-weekly VAT return in the first five days after the 15th day of each month and a definite return in the first five days of the following month.

Selective consumption tax

A selective consumption tax is applied to goods that are considered to be non-essential. The tax base is the cost, insurance, and freight (CIF) price for imported items, and the tax is levied and paid only at that stage (based on the list of products published as an appendix to the Fiscal Equity Law and its reforms).

Customs duties

Customs duties relate to the importation of any good within the Nicaragua territory for commercial purposes. The following taxes apply to imports, depending on the product:

- Importation tax (DAI).
- Excise tax (ISC).
- VAT.

Excise taxes

A non-creditable excise tax on tobacco cigarettes applies on imports.

Transfer taxes

Nicaragua's tax system does not impose transfer taxes.

Stamp taxes

Stamp duty is levied on certain types of documents issued in Nicaragua.

Municipal sales and services tax

A monthly 1% tax is levied on all sales of goods and rendering of services in each of the municipalities of the country.

Municipal registration tax

An annual 2% tax is levied by each municipality on the average of income received in the months of October, November, and December of the previous year. In the case of the incorporation of a new establishment or enterprise, the municipal registration tax is 1% of the capital invested.

Real estate municipal tax
The real estate municipal tax is an annual tax that is levied at a rate of 1% on 80% of cadastral value, as recorded by the government. If the cadastral value is not available, the cost or fiscal appraisal value may be used.

Branch income

Branch income received is subject to the general CIT. The repatriation of income from the branch to the head office in the form of dividends, profits, capital gains, or any other form that suggest the income repatriated is an economic benefit in considered taxable.

Income determination

Taxable income is determined by the sum of all income or gains derived from Nicaraguan sources, less allowable deductions, which generally include all expenses necessary to generate taxable income. Taxable income is computed according to International Financial Reporting Standards (IFRS) and modified as required by Nicaraguan income tax law.

Inventory valuation
Last in first out (LIFO), first in first out (FIFO), and the average cost methods are accepted for inventory valuation purposes. Tax authorities shall authorise the change of a valuation method.

Capital gains and losses
Capital gains and losses are treated as ordinary taxable corporate income. Capital gain transactions that require any annotation in the public registry (e.g. real estate, vehicles) will be subject to a withholding tax (WHT) based on the amount of the transaction, as follows:

Good value (USD*)		WHT rate (%)
From	Through	
0.01	50,000.00	1
50,000.01	100,000.00	2
More than 100,000.01		3

* United States dollars

Dividend income
Stock dividends paid by Nicaraguan entities to resident or non-resident shareholders are subject to a 10% definitive WHT.

The Equity Tax Law Reform regulations define 'stock dividends' as stock dividends paid as well as the remittance of net income after income tax made by branches to headquarters and any payments considered as advance net income remittance abroad or locally.

Nicaragua

Interest income

Interest received from Nicaraguan source by residents or non-residents of Nicaragua, as well as the interest gained by resident from deposits placed in the national financial system, is subject to a 10% WHT.

Interest earned on government bonds and securities is considered taxable income subject to a 10% WHT.

Foreign income

Business enterprises are subject to CIT only on Nicaraguan-source income.

Deductions

Depreciation

Depreciation must be computed using the straight-line method. Depending on the type of construction and the estimated life of fixed assets, annual rates for depreciation are as follows:

Asset	Rate (%)
Buildings	3/5/10
Vehicles	12.5/20
Plant and equipment	10/15/20
Other assets	10/20

Alternative method of depreciation

Taxpayers under the Temporary Admission for Active Processing (TAP) regime may, at their convenience, request a different depreciation rate (i.e. accelerated depreciation) from tax authorities. Used fixed assets acquired abroad could also be subject to a different depreciation rate.

Goodwill

Goodwill, meaning the excess paid over book value in a transaction, can be deductible for CIT purposes if the capital gain is consider in the seller`s CIT return. However, the tax authorities must authorise the tax periods in which the goodwill will be amortised.

Start-up expenses

The Nicaraguan tax system does not recognise start-up expenses.

Interest expenses

A deduction is allowed for any interest paid on loans with national and foreign financial institutions.

In order for interest paid to a non-resident to be deductible, the corresponding 10% WHT must be withheld and paid.

Bad debt

Corporations are allowed a deduction for receivables as an allowance for doubtful accounts as long as there is supporting documentation of the credit, identification documents of the debtor and creditor, and administrative and judicial collection proof.

Charitable contributions
A deduction is allowed, up to 10% of the corporation's income, for charitable contributions made to the government and its institutions, Red Cross, and other organisations.

Compensation
A deduction is allowed for payments made to employees as bonuses or in addition to their salaries or wages.

Life insurance
A deduction is allowed for employee insurance payments made.

Fines and penalties
Penalties or charges made by tax, customs, Social Security, or municipal authorities are not deductible for CIT purposes.

Taxes
In principle, income tax expense is not deductible for CIT purposes. Municipal or local taxes (i.e. real estate tax, monthly sales and services tax, annual registration tax) are deductible from CIT.

Net operating losses
Losses may be carried forward and deducted from future profits, for up to three years. The carryback of losses is not allowed.

Payments to foreign affiliates
Payments made from affiliates to foreign related parties are deductible for CIT purposes, provided the following requirements are met:

* The expenses (i.e. royalties, interest, and services) are needed to generate taxable income.
* The expenses are duly supported (e.g. agreements, invoices, payment receipts).
* The expenses are incurred within the fiscal period.
* The WHT is applied and paid to the tax authorities.

Group taxation

Section 3 of the Equity Tax Law recognises 'economic units' as a taxpayer formed by many entities of one group. However, group taxation is permitted only when previously approved by the tax authorities. The economic group must submit a business case to the Tax Administration justifying the economic reason of their request.

Transfer pricing
The Nicaragua tax system recognises transfer pricing as a method of trading; however, it is not regulated yet.

Thin capitalisation
The Nicaragua tax system does not impose any form of thin capitalisation rules.

Nicaragua

Tax credits and incentives

Foreign tax credit
The Nicaragua tax system does not recognise any form of foreign tax credit.

Tourism incentives
Under present law, and on a case-by-case basis, new companies with tourist activities may request and the government may grant, during the facilities' construction phase, total exemption of customs duties and partial or total CIT exemption for a maximum period of ten years.

Renewable energy incentives
The renewable energy sector is covered by a special law with tax benefits or exemptions in CIT, VAT, customs duties, and municipal tax.

Free trade zones (FTZs)
FTZ industries have a special law with tax benefits or exemptions in CIT, VAT, customs duties, and municipal taxes.

An industrial export zone decree provides a 15-year exemption from CIT to those taxpayers located in certain FTZs. There is a 100% exemption for the first ten years and 60% exemption for the following five years. Additional requirements and provisions apply.

In accordance with the Agreement on Subsidies and Countervailing Measures issued by the World Trade Organization (WTO), by the end of year 2015 all tax exemptions granted to FTZs shall be eliminated. However, Nicaragua falls under the exception of section 27 of this agreement and qualifies as a country listed in Annex VII (for being a developing economy) as a country with per capita gross national product (GNP) of less than USD 1,000, based on World Bank estimates. Due to this exception, it is foreseen that the tax holiday will still apply to FTZ industries in Nicaragua past 2015.

Withholding taxes

Payments to residents
Dividend payments to resident shareholders (corporations or individuals) are subject to 10% WHT.

Payments of royalties to resident individuals or corporations are subject to 2% WHT.

Interest paid to a resident individual or legal entity is subject to 10% WHT.

Professional services provided by an individual are subject to 10% WHT.

Payments on the local acquisition of goods and services are subject to 1% WHT.

Payments to non-residents
Payments of royalties, interest, dividends, and service fees to non-resident corporations are subject to WHT, as follows:

Payment	WHT rate (%)
Royalties	21
Dividends	10
Services provided in general	10.5
Interest:	
Non-financial companies	10
Financial companies	10
TV and Radio programming or subscription	9

Payments of any kind of income to non-resident individuals are subject to WHT of 20%.

In principle, Nicaragua has not signed any agreement or treaty with any country to avoid double taxation.

Tax administration

Taxable period
The standard tax year in Nicaragua commonly ends on 30 June; however, companies can obtain authorisation from the tax authorities in order to change or have a different year-end: 31 March, 30 September, or 31 December.

Tax returns
Without exception, all corporations are required to file CIT returns for a fiscal year within the following three months after the fiscal year end.

Payment of tax
Corporations shall pay fiscal-year income tax in monthly advance payments. The monthly payable amount is calculated as 1% of gross income.

Final CIT payment is due with the final CIT return (i.e. within the following three months after the fiscal year end).

Audit cycle
The tax authority is entitled to conduct a tax audit of the taxpayer when considered necessary. The taxpayer has the obligation to submit before the tax auditor the corporate information and documents related to the generation of income.

Statute of limitations
The statute of limitation in Nicaragua is up to the last four fiscal ended periods.

PwC contact

Taiwo Oyedele
PricewaterhouseCoopers
Plot 252E Muri Okunola Street
Victoria Island
Lagos
Nigeria
Tel: +234 1 271 1700
Email: taiwo.oyedele@ng.pwc.com

Significant developments

A new National Tax Policy (NTP) developed in 2010 was re-launched in the first half of 2012 by the federal government of Nigeria. The NTP is now at the implementation stage, and, as a result, a number of changes have been made to existing tax laws and regulations. Notable changes include amendments to the Personal Income Tax Act; Companies Income Tax Act; and Tax Administration (Self Assessment) Regulations 2011. In addition, work is ongoing to further amend the Companies Income Tax Act to introduce transfer pricing regulations and thin capitalisation rules. The tax authorities are also intensifying efforts to implement a gradual move towards electronic tax filing and payments. It is expected that the new cash-less economy policy of the Central Bank of Nigeria will facilitate electronic tax payment. Also, there is an ongoing project to re-write the tax laws in plain English for ease of understanding, interpretation, and application.

Below are some of the recent developments in the tax environment and significant potential changes under consideration.

Amendment to the Companies Income Tax Act
The Fifth Schedule to the Companies Income Tax Act has been amended to cover more bodies to which tax deductible donations can be made. Generally, public institutions or funds established by a society or association for public interest related activities will qualify for tax deductible donations.

In addition, there is a proposed amendment to the Act to, among other things, provide tax incentives for economic growth and creation of employment opportunities.

The proposal, if passed into law, will grant a ten-year tax holiday to any new company established in an area with no electricity, water, or tarred road. Where such facilities provided by government are located at least 10 kms away, the company will be entitled to an investment allowance ranging from 20% to 100% of expenditure incurred in providing such facilities.

Also, the proposal seeks to increase the tax holiday of a new company going into mining of solid minerals or gas utilisation from the current three and five years to five and seven years, respectively.

Tax Administration (Self-Assessment) Regulations
New regulations dated 12 December 2011 have been issued to prescribe rules for self assessment tax filing. The regulations cover all major taxes, including corporate income tax (CIT), petroleum profits tax, personal income tax, value-added tax (VAT), and withholding tax (WHT). Based on the regulations, taxpayers are required to comply

strictly with tax filing and payment deadlines or face sanctions. The maximum number of tax instalments for CIT has been reduced from six to three, while the deadline for the final payment has been reduced from five to two months after the filing due date.

Revised Petroleum Industry Bill

The Petroleum Industry Bill seeks to combine 16 different petroleum laws. The bill, which has been undergoing legislative process for several years, is currently being redrafted. This became necessary due to the emergence of different versions of the bill and to address the major concerns of key stakeholders. The delay in passing the bill into law is estimated to be costing Nigeria billions of dollars annually in foreign direct investment into the oil and gas sector of the economy. The bill aims to ensure transparency, make industry participation more equitable, and maximise government revenue. Once enacted, a two-tier tax system consisting of a CIT and hydrocarbon tax will apply to exploration and production companies.

Industrial Training Fund Act

The Industrial Training Fund Act has been amended to make every employer with a minimum of five employees or annual turnover of 50 million Nigerian naira (NGN) liable to the Fund. Previously, the threshold was a minimum of 25 employees. The required contribution is 1% of payroll defined as the sum total of all basic pay allowances and other entitlements payable within and outside Nigeria to any employee in an establishment, public or private. 'Employees' mean all persons, whether or not they are Nigerians, employed in any establishment in return for salary, wages, or other consideration, and whether employed full-time or part-time and includes temporary employees who work for periods of not less than 30 days.

Where an employer provides verifiable training to its employees in line with guidelines issued by the Fund, a maximum refund of 50% of the amount contributed by an employer to the Fund may be granted.

Tax exemption for all bonds

The proposal to grant a tax waiver on interest on all bonds, including corporate and sub-national bonds, has been enacted into law. The enactment, which was made via the Personal Income Tax (Amendment) Act 2011, is, however, only applicable to individual investors. The waiver to cover corporate investors was included in the fiscal policy of the federal government for the 2012 fiscal year. The waiver is designed to encourage more activities in the bond market and ensure cheaper and stable long-term source of funds for project finance and economic development.

Transfer pricing regulations and thin capitalisation rules

The Federal Inland Revenue Service (FIRS) is set to issue transfer pricing regulations in the second half of 2012. When published, the regulations will be applicable to both local and multinational related party transactions for the financial period commencing after the publication. The regulations are in conformity with the Organisation for Economic Co-operation and Development (OECD) guidelines. Also, the FIRS is planning to introduce thin capitalisation rules to limit the ratio of related party debt-to-equity permissible for tax purposes. However, the rules are not likely to be published until early 2013, with an appropriate cut-off date or transition period for existing debts.

Taxes on corporate income

The CIT rate is 30%, assessed on a preceding year basis (i.e. tax is charged on profits for the accounting year ending in the year preceding assessment).

Nigeria

Resident companies are liable for CIT on their worldwide income while non-residents are subject to CIT on their Nigeria-source income. Investment income paid by a Nigerian resident to a non-resident is sourced in Nigeria and subject to WHT at source, which serves as the final tax.

In respect of business profits, a non-resident company which has a fixed base or a permanent establishment (PE) in Nigeria is taxable on the profits attributable to that fixed based. As such, it is required to register for CIT and file its tax returns. Any WHT deducted at source from its Nigeria-source income is available as offset against the CIT liability.

Small company rates
For small companies in the manufacturing industry and wholly export-oriented companies with turnover not exceeding NGN 1 million (about 6,300 United States dollars [USD]), the CIT rate is reduced to 20% in the first five calendar years of operation.

Petroleum profit tax (PPT)
PPT is a tax on the income of companies engaged in upstream petroleum operations in lieu of CIT.

The PPT rates vary as follows:

- 50% for petroleum operations under production sharing contracts (PSC) with the Nigerian National Petroleum Corporation (NNPC).
- 65.75% for non-PSC operations, including joint ventures (JVs), in the first five years during which the company has not fully amortised all pre-production capitalised expenditure.
- 85% for non-PSC operations after the first five years.

Education tax
An education tax is levied on every Nigerian resident company at the rate of 2% of the assessable profit for each year of assessment. The tax is payable within two months of an assessment notice from the Federal Inland Revenue Service (FIRS). In practice, many companies pay the tax on a self assessment basis along with their CIT.

For companies subject to PPT, education tax is to be treated as an allowable deduction. For other companies, income/profit taxes are not deductible in arriving at taxable income. Non-resident companies and unincorporated entities are exempt from education tax.

Minimum tax
Minimum tax is payable by companies having no taxable profits for the year or where the tax on profits is below the minimum tax. However, companies in the first four calendar years of business, companies engaged in the agriculture business, or companies that have foreign equity capital of at least 25% are exempt from minimum tax.

Minimum tax payable is calculated as follows:

- Where the turnover of the company is NGN 500,000 or below, minimum tax is the highest of:
  - 0.5% of gross profits
  - 0.5% of net assets

- 0.25% of paid up capital, or
- 0.25% of turnover of the company for the year.
- Where the turnover is higher than NGN 500,000, minimum tax is the highest of the calculations listed above plus 0.125% of turnover in excess of NGN 500,000.

Alternative tax on distribution
There is a tax on distribution where a company pays a dividend in excess of its taxable profit. Such a company will be charged tax on the dividend paid as if the dividend is the taxable profit of the company for that year of assessment.

Alternative tax on deemed income
Non-resident companies are subject to tax on the income or profit derived from Nigeria. The FIRS often assesses non-resident companies on a deemed income basis. This is done by applying 20% of turnover as deemed profit and then charging CIT at 30%, resulting in an effective tax rate of 6% on turnover.

Local income taxes
CIT is payable only to the federal government. State governments collect income taxes of individuals and unincorporated entities, while local governments are only allowed to collect levies and rates but not income tax.

Corporate residence

A company is considered resident in Nigeria if such a company is registered or incorporated under the Companies and Allied Matters Act. This means that a company formed outside Nigeria under the laws in force in the foreign territory will be considered as a non-resident company for tax purposes.

Permanent establishment (PE)
Fixed base is not defined but is generally considered to be a location with a degree of permanence. The following would generally not be considered to be a fixed base:

- The use of facilities solely for the purpose of storage or display of goods or merchandise.
- The use of facilities solely for the collection of information.

Other activities that could trigger a tax presence in Nigeria include a dependent agency arrangement, execution of a turnkey project, or artificial arrangements between related parties.

Other taxes

Value-added tax (VAT)
The standard VAT rate is 5%, but there is a plan to increase the rate to 10%. A bill is currently being drafted that includes the proposed increase in VAT rate. Once finalised, the draft bill will be presented to Parliament for enactment into law. Zero-rated items include non-oil exports, goods and services purchased by diplomats, and goods and services purchased for use in humanitarian donor funded projects. Exempt items include plants and machinery for use in export processing zones or free trade zones, basic food items, medical products and services, pharmaceutical products, books and educational materials, and exported services.

Nigeria

Government agencies and oil and gas companies are required to deduct at source VAT charged by their suppliers and remit to the tax authority. All other organisations are required to collect VAT charged on their invoices from their customers for filing and payment to the tax authority.

Customs duties
Customs duties in Nigeria are levied only on imports. Rates vary for different items, typically from 5% to 35%, and are assessed with reference to the prevailing Harmonized Commodity and Coding System (HS code).

Excise taxes
Excise duty is applicable on beer and stout, wines, spirits, cigarettes, and tobacco manufactured and sold in Nigeria at rates ranging from 5% to 20%.

Property taxes
Property taxes in Nigeria are usually levied annually by the state government with varying rates depending on the state and the location of the property within the state. The two major property taxes are governor's consent fee and land registration fee. In Lagos (which is the economic hub of Nigeria), governor's consent fee, land registration fees, and other levies payable to the state give rise to a total levy of 15% of the transfer value of the land. Also, Right of Occupancy fee and tenement rates are chargeable by state and local government authorities.

Stamp taxes
Under the Stamp Duty Act, stamp duty is payable on any agreement executed in Nigeria, or relating, whatsoever, to any property situated in or to any matter or thing done in Nigeria. Instruments which are required to be stamped under the Stamp Duties Act must be stamped within 40 days of first execution.

Stamp duty is chargeable either at fixed rates or *ad valorem* (i.e. in proportion to the value of the consideration) depending on the class of instrument. Stamp duty is imposed at the rate of 0.75% on the authorised share capital at incorporation of a company or on registration of new shares.

Capital gains tax (CGT)
Gains accruing to a chargeable person (individual or company) on the disposal of chargeable assets shall be subject to tax under the Capital Gains Tax Act at the rate of 10%. There is no distinction between long-term and short-term gains and no inflation adjustment to cost for CGT purposes.

All forms of assets, including options, debts, goodwill, and foreign currency, other than those specifically exempt, are liable for CGT. The gains on the disposal of shares are exempt from CGT.

CGT is applicable on the chargeable gains received or brought into Nigeria in respect of assets situated outside Nigeria.

Capital losses are not allowed as an offset against chargeable gains accruing to a person from the disposal of any assets.

Information technology levy
A company with an annual turnover of NGN 100 million or more is required to pay 1% of its profit before tax as information technology tax. This levy is tax deductible when

paid (typically in the year of assessment following that in which the payment was made).

This tax is applicable to:

- Banking and other financial activities, including capital and money market operators, mortgage institutions, and micro-finance banks.
- Insurance activities, including brokerage.
- Pension fund administration, pension management, and related services.
- GSM services providers and telecommunication companies.
- Cyber and internet services providers.

Levy on contracts awarded in the upstream oil and gas sector
The Nigerian Content Development Act was introduced to increase the level of Nigerian participation in the oil and gas industry. The Act introduces a levy of 1% on every contract awarded in the upstream oil and gas sector of the economy. Any violation of the Act is liable for a fine of 5% of the contract value and may result in outright cancellation of the contract.

Payroll contribution
Under the Employee Compensation Act, all employers are required to contribute 1% of their payroll cost in the first two years of commencement of the Act. Subsequently, assessments will be issued by the Nigeria Social Insurance Trust Fund, the body empowered to administer and implement the Act.

Branch income

Except in rare circumstances, it is illegal for a non-resident company to operate through a branch in Nigeria. The Nigeria-source income of a non-resident company is taxable at the CIT rate of 30% or via the alternative tax on deemed income (*see the Taxes on corporate income section for more information*).

Income determination

The following income is subject to CIT in Nigeria:

- Profits accruing in, derived from, brought into, or received in Nigeria in respect of any trade or business.
- Dividends, interest, royalties, discounts, charges, or annuities.
- Rent or any premium arising from the right granted to any person for the use or occupation of any property, where applicable.
- Any source of annual profits or gain not falling within the preceding categories.
- Fees, dues, and allowances (wherever paid) for services rendered.
- Any amount of profits or gains arising from the acquisition or disposal of short-term money instruments like federal government securities, treasury bills, treasury or savings certificates, debenture certificates, and treasury bonds.

Inventory valuation
The first in first out (FIFO) valuation method is commonly used. Average and standard cost methods are also allowed, but last in first out (LIFO) is not permitted. Other than the accounting requirement in the local generally accepted accounting principles (GAAP), there are no special statutory provisions for inventory valuation.

Nigeria

Capital gains

Capital gains are not subject to CIT, but may be subject to CGT. *See Capital gains tax in the Other taxes section for more information.*

Dividend income

Dividends received by a Nigerian resident company from another Nigerian resident company are taxable at source (*see Withholding taxes section for more information*) and not subject to further tax.

Dividends received from non-resident companies are taxable except if repatriated into Nigeria through government approved channels (i.e. any financial institution authorised by the Central Bank of Nigeria to deal in foreign currency transactions).

Stock dividends

Stock dividends (bonus shares) are not taxable at source or included in the taxable income of the recipient company.

Interest income

Interest payable to a non-resident investor is liable to WHT at 10%, which is the final tax. Recipients who are resident in a country with double taxation treaty (DTT) with Nigeria enjoy a reduced rate of 7.5%. Interest received by a Nigerian company is liable to tax at the CIT rate of 30% with tax withheld at 10% available as an offset against the final tax liability. Interest on government bonds is tax exempt.

Foreign income

A Nigerian resident company is taxable on its worldwide income. On the other hand, a non-resident company is subject to tax only on income derived from Nigeria.

Dividends, interest, rents, and royalties earned abroad and brought into Nigeria through government-approved channels are exempt from Nigerian tax; otherwise, the income is taxable at the CIT rate of 30% and education tax at 2%. Government-approved channels mean the Central Bank of Nigeria and any bank or financial institution authorised to carry out foreign exchange transactions.

Taxable foreign income earned by a Nigerian tax resident entity cannot be legally deferred.

Deductions

Expenses are deductible for tax purposes if they are wholly, reasonably, exclusively, and necessarily incurred for the business or trade.

Depreciation

Capital allowances are calculated on a straight-line basis. Capital allowances claimable in any year are restricted to two-third of assessable profits for all companies, except companies in the manufacturing and agricultural sectors which are excluded from this restriction.

The following are the capital allowance rates on fixed assets (qualifying expenditures):

Qualifying expenditure	Initial allowance (%)	Annual allowance (%)
Building (industrial and non-industrial)	15	10

Qualifying expenditure	Initial allowance (%)	Annual allowance (%)
Furniture and fittings	25	20
Plant expenditure (1)	50/95	0/25
Mining expenditure	95	0
Plantation equipment	95	0
Motor vehicle (2)	50/95	0/25
Ranching and plantation expenditure	30	50
Housing estate expenditure	50	25
Research and development	95	0

Notes

1. 95% initial allowance for plant used in agricultural production; others 50%.
2. 95% initial allowance is granted for motor vehicles used for public transportation if the company has a fleet of at least three buses; all other motor vehicles 50%.

The initial allowance is first deducted, and the balance is written off on a straight-line basis over a fixed period, depending on the rates of annual allowance. There is a requirement that assets not yet disposed of cannot be fully written off in the books. A nominal amount of NGN 10 per asset must be retained in the books till the assets are disposed of. However, where 95% has been claimed as an initial allowance, the 5% balance is the value that must be maintained in the books until the final disposal of the asset.

When assets are sold, the proceeds over the tax written-down value are taxed at 30% to the extent of the allowances already claimed.

Goodwill
There is no tax deduction for goodwill.

Start-up expenses
Start-up expenses are not specifically stated as non-deductible in the tax law, but, in practice, they are usually not allowed by the tax authority. This is based on the assumption that start-up expenses are not directly attributable to any taxable income of the company, which is a fundamental condition for tax deductibility of expenses.

Interest expense
Interest on money borrowed and employed in producing taxable income is a deductible expense. There is currently no thin capitalisation regulation in Nigeria, but general anti-avoidance rules are usually applied to limit deductible interest on related party loans.

Bad debt
Bad debt incurred in the course of trade is deductible.

Charitable contributions
Donations are deductible, subject to the provisions of the law.

Fines and penalties
Any punitive payments for default or violation of law are expressly not deductible for tax purposes. In practice, this is usually extended to include default surcharges and other avoidable fines.

Nigeria

Taxes

Any tax on income or profit is not deductible except where such tax was paid on profit earned outside Nigeria. In this case, if the source country has no DTT with Nigeria, the foreign tax paid is allowed as a deduction for CIT purposes. State and local taxes (business rates) and levies may be deducted from taxable income.

Other significant items

Other deductible expenses include the following:

- Sum payable by way of interest on capital borrowed.
- Rent for the period.
- Expenses incurred in respect of salary and wages.
- Expenses incurred for repair of assets.
- Liability incurred for purpose of trade.
- Research and development (R&D) costs.

Net operating losses

Losses can be carried forward indefinitely, except for insurance companies where losses can only be carried forward for four years. Losses made from one line of business cannot be relieved against another line of business. Losses cannot be carried back.

Payments to foreign affiliates

Payments considered to be artificial are not deductible for tax purposes. Royalties, management, and technical fees require the approval of the National Office for Technology Acquisition and Promotion (NOTAP) for exchange control purposes and for tax deduction. NOTAP approved royalties and technical fees are limited to a range of 1% to 5% of net sales, while management fees are limited to a range of 2% to 5% of profit before tax, and consultancy fees are limited to 5% of total project cost. Technical fees are limited to approved man-hour rates.

Trademark fees are disallowed where the trademark owner has more than 75% equity participation in the local company.

Group taxation

There are currently no provisions for group taxation, group relief, or group filing of tax returns in Nigeria. Each legal entity within a group is treated as distinct and separate for tax purposes.

Transfer pricing

There are no specific transfer pricing rules in Nigeria. However, the tax laws have a general anti-avoidance provision which requires transactions between related entities to be at arm's length.

The FIRS is currently working on the introduction of formal transfer pricing guidelines, which are expected to be published in the second half of 2012. The guidelines are expected to be in conformity with the OECD guidelines.

Thin capitalisation

Nigeria has no thin capitalisation rules. However, interest charged between related parties is expected to reflect arm's-length transactions. The tax authority may disallow any related party interest considered to be excessive.

Tax credits and incentives

Nigeria has various tax incentives intended to encourage investment in key sectors of the economy, as follows.

Tax holidays

Pioneer companies investing in specified industrial activities may, on application, be granted a tax holiday for a maximum period of five years. Examples of economic activities that may be granted a tax holiday include glass and glassware manufacturing, manufacturing of fertilisers, and steel manufacturing.

A new company that engages in the mining of solid minerals is exempt from tax for the first three years of its operation.

Rural location incentives

Certain incentives are available to companies located in rural areas. The incentives take the form of tax reductions at graduated rates for enterprises located at least 20 kilometres from available electricity, water, and tarred roads.

Export incentives

A company that is engaged in an approved manufacturing activity in an export processing zone (EPZ) and incurs expenditures in its qualifying building and plant equipment is entitled to 100% capital allowance in that year of assessment.

In addition, a company that is 100% export oriented but located outside an EPZ will enjoy a three year tax holiday, provided the company is not formed by splitting up or reconstruction of an already existing business and the export proceeds form at least 75% of its turnover.

Profits of companies whose supplies are exclusively inputs to the manufacture of products for export are exempt from tax. Such companies are expected to obtain a certificate of purchase of the input from the exporter in order to claim tax exemption.

Where plant and machinery are transferred to a new company, the tax written down value of the asset transferred must not exceed 25% of the total value of plant and machinery in the new company. The company should also repatriate at least 75% of the export earnings to Nigeria and place it in a Nigerian domiciliary account in order to qualify for a tax holiday.

Profits of any Nigerian company in respect of goods exported from Nigeria are exempt from tax, provided that the proceeds from such exports are repatriated to Nigeria and are used exclusively for the purchase of raw materials, plant, equipments, and spare parts.

Gas utilisation incentives

Companies engaged in gas utilisation are entitled to:

- A tax free period for up to five years.
- Accelerated capital allowance after the tax free period.
- Tax free dividends during the tax free period.

Nigeria

Tourism incentives
25% of the income derived from tourism by hotels in convertible currencies is exempt from tax if such income is put in a reserve fund to be utilised within five years for expansion or construction of new hotels and other facilities for tourism development.

Interest incentives
Interest accruing on deposit accounts of a non-resident company is tax-exempt, provided the deposits are made by transfer of funds to Nigeria on or after 1 January 1990 and the depositor does not become non-resident after making the deposit while in Nigeria.

Interest on foreign-currency domiciliary accounts is also tax-exempt.

Interest on any foreign loans, and interest on any loan granted by a bank for the purpose of manufacturing goods for export, is exempt from tax as follows:

Repayment period	Moratorium	Exemption (%)
Over 7 years	Not less than 2 years	100
5 to 7 years	Not less than 1.5 years	70
2 to 4 years	Not less than 1 year	40

Interest on any loan granted by a bank to a company engaged in agricultural trade, fabrication of local plant and machinery, or as working capital to any cottage industry is 100% tax free if the loan has a moratorium of not less than 18 months and the rate of interest is not more than the base lending rate.

Investment allowances
An investment allowance of 10% on the cost of qualifying expenditures in respect of plant and machinery is available as a deduction from assessable profits in the year of purchase. There is no restriction to the full claim of capital allowance in any year of assessment for companies in the mining, manufacturing, and agricultural sectors.

Foreign tax credit
Nigeria does not grant automatic tax credits to Nigerian companies for foreign tax on income derived from other countries. The Nigerian tax laws already provides for tax exemption for dividends, interest, and royalties.

Foreign tax credits are only granted based on the provisions of existing DTTs and partial credits as applicable to Commonwealth countries. In this regard, full tax credits are usually provided for in the DTTs. Tax credit for members of Commonwealth countries is granted up to half the Nigerian CIT rate.

Withholding taxes

WHT is applicable on specified transactions as indicated below. There is no distinction between the WHT rates for resident companies or individuals and non-resident companies or individuals.

Types of payment	WHT for companies (%)	WHT for individuals (%)
Dividends, interest, and rents	10	10
Directors fees	N/A	10

Types of payment	WHT for companies (%)	WHT for individuals (%)
Hire of equipment	10	10
Royalties	10	5
Commission, consultancy, technical, service fees	10	5
Management fees	10	5
Construction/building	5	5
Contracts other than sales in the ordinary course of business	5	5

The period for filing WHT is 21 days after the duty to deduct arose for deductions from companies.

The penalty for failure to deduct or remit tax is now 10% of the amount not deducted/remitted.

Note that companies are required to submit, in electronic form, a schedule of all their suppliers for the month showing the tax identification number (TIN), address of the suppliers, the nature of the transaction, WHT deducted, and invoice number.

Double tax treaties (DTTs)
Nigeria has DTTs with Belgium, Canada, China, Czech Republic, France, the Netherlands, Pakistan, Philippines, Romania, Slovak Republic, South Africa, and the United Kingdom.

The provisions of Nigeria's DTTs allow a reduced WHT rate of 7.5% on dividends, royalties, and interest payable to a beneficiary resident in a treaty country, compared to 10% for non-treaty residents.

Tax administration

Taxable period
The taxable period is the fiscal year, which runs from 1 January to 31 December.

Tax returns
Companies are required to register for tax and file their audited accounts and tax computations with the FIRS within six months of their financial year end on a self-assessment basis or 18 months after incorporation (whichever comes first). A company may file an application for extension of filing tax returns for up to two months at the discretion of the FIRS.

Upon registration, a company is issued a TIN which will serve as the company's file number for all federal taxes and future correspondence with the FIRS.

The company must file the following documents with the tax authority on an annual basis:

• Tax computation for the relevant year of assessment.
• The audited financial statements for the respective period; this should be in conformity with the local GAAP.
• A duly completed and signed self-assessment form for CIT.

Nigeria

- Evidence of remittance of the income tax liability (partly or in full).

PPT is payable on an actual year basis. Estimated tax returns must be filed within two months of the fiscal year. Actual tax returns should be filed within five months after the end of the accounting period, that is, not later than 31 May.

Assessment
Nigerian companies file their tax returns based on a self-assessment system where the taxpayer prepares its annual returns and determines its tax liability. However, the FIRS may apply a best of judgment (BOJ) assessment where it is of the opinion that the tax returns filed are deliberately misstated or where no returns are filed within the stipulated period.

Payment of tax

CIT
A company that files its self assessment within six months after the accounting year-end can apply to the FIRS in writing to pay its income tax in instalments. The maximum number of instalments the FIRS may approve has been reduced from six to three. Evidence of the first instalment has to accompany the tax returns filed in order to qualify for the instalmental payment. However, all payments have to be made not later than eight months after the financial year end.

Assessments are made on a preceding year basis. This means that the financial statements for a period ended in 2011 will form the basis for the 2012 year of assessment.

PPT
Payments with respect to PPT in any accounting period of 12 months are made in 12 instalments, with a final 13th instalment (if there is an underpayment). The first instalment for the year is due by the end of March.

Penalty for non-compliance
Late payment of taxes attracts a 10% penalty and interest at commercial rate.

A company that files its annual tax return late or fails to submit its accounts by the due date is liable for a nominal penalty.

Late submission of PPT returns attracts an initial penalty of NGN 10,000 and NGN 2,000 for each day such failure continues, while late payment of tax attracts a penalty of 5% of the tax not paid.

Audit cycle
Generally, the tax authority will commence a desk examination of a taxpayer's returns immediately after filing. This may be followed by a tax monitoring exercise whereby tax officers visit taxpayers to conduct interview and on-site high level review of their tax affairs.

Random or specific tax audit may be carried out usually within six years of filing tax returns. In unusual cases, a back-duty tax investigation may be conducted for more than six years, especially where a tax fraud or willful default is suspected.

Tax audits take a long time to conclude, usually between three to five years.

Statute of limitations

The tax authority may carry out tax audit and issue additional assessment within six years from the relevant tax year. However, the limitation does not apply in the event of a fraud, willful default, or neglect by the company.

Topics of focus for tax authorities

The tax authorities are focusing on possible ways to generate more tax revenue. As a result, certain areas of taxation that have previously received very little attention, such as capital gains tax, stamp duties, and excise duties are now key areas of focus by the tax authorities. In addition, related party transactions are increasingly being scrutinized, as well as non-resident entities doing business in Nigeria. This trend is expected to continue and possibly intensify in the coming years.

N

Norway

PwC contact

Bård Ivar Koppang
Advokatfirmaet PricewaterhouseCoopers AS
Kanalsletta 8,
Forus P.O.Box 150,
NO-4065 Stavanger
Norway
Tel: +47 952 61 172
Email: baard.koppang@no.pwc.com

Significant developments

Loss on receivables between group companies

As of 6 October 2011, loss on receivables between group companies (with more than 90% direct or indirect mutual ownership of shares) and partnerships is no longer tax deductible. However, trade receivables, already taxed receivables, and loss on receivables created in connection with mergers or demergers are still deductible for tax purposes.

Tax on correction income

Until 2012, Norwegian companies have been tax liable for so-called correction income ('No. korreksjonsinntekt') if a company has distributed untaxed profits or made appropriation for such distribution. These rules have been repealed as of income year 2012.

Alteration of the tax-exemption method

According to the tax-exemption method, income and capital gain derived from shares, etc. is exempt for certain entities, leaving 3% of the gain taxable at a 28% rate (0.84% effective tax rate). According to recent alterations, only 3% of dividend distributions will be taxed, leaving capital gain on realisation fully tax exempt. In addition, dividend distributions within a tax group (ultimate parent company owning, directly or indirectly, more than 90% of the shares and voting rights) will be fully tax exempt. The 3% rule will now also apply for certain distributions from partnerships and on certain conditions to foreign resident companies with a permanent establishment (PE) in Norway. The new regulations entered into force from the income year 2012.

Taxes on corporate income

A Norwegian resident company is, as a starting point, subject to CIT on its worldwide income. Non-resident companies are, as a starting point, liable for CIT in Norway when engaged in a business that is either conducted in or managed from Norway.

CIT is assessed at a rate of 28%.

As a general rule, income is taxable when the right to the benefit is earned and costs are deductible when the liability to cover the costs arises. The actual payment is generally not relevant.

Petroleum tax regime

All upstream petroleum activity on the Norwegian Continental Shelf (NCS) is taxable to Norway.

Taxation is based on net income at a marginal tax rate of 78%, which is composed of the ordinary 28% CIT rate and a 50% special tax. All income is subject to the 28% CIT, while only income from offshore production and pipeline transportation of petroleum from the NCS (offshore tax regime) is subject to the additional 50% special tax.

All upstream activity on the NCS must be consolidated within the company. There is no ring fence per oil field, and tax consolidation against other activity is limited. Crude oil sales from most of the fields are taxed at a predetermined market price set by an official board (i.e. the norm price). A norm price may be imposed on gas sales, but this has not been implemented. Investments in installations for exploitation and production of petroleum as well as investments in pipelines are depreciated linearly over six years.

An investment-based 'supplementary depreciation' (uplift) of 30% (7.5% per year for four years) is granted on investments in installations for exploitation and production of petroleum as well as investments in pipelines. The uplift is deducted against the special tax base. Loss and unused uplift may be carried forward indefinitely with an annual interest. Both depreciation and uplift may be claimed from the year of the investment, regardless of whether title has passed or the asset has been taken into use. If the upstream activity on the NCS ceases, the tax value of loss carryforward and unused uplift may either be sold or compensated by the Norwegian state. Exploration costs are tax deductible as incurred. If a loss is created due to exploration cost, the taxpayer may claim the tax value of such loss repaid in the year following the income year in which the loss was created.

Special rules apply as to the deductibility of net interest cost in the special tax basis (50%).

A special regime ensures that transfer of licenses on NCS are tax exempt, there is no step up in basis.

Note that income taxed under the special tax is not subject to dividend withholding tax (WHT).

Hydro power tax regime
The hydro power tax regime is applicable on taxation of income derived from production, sales, transfer, or distribution of hydro power.

Taxation is based on net income at a marginal tax rate of 58%, which is comprised of the ordinary 28% CIT rate and a 30% resource rent tax. All income is subject to the 28% CIT, while only income from hydro power production is subject to the additional 30% resource rent tax.

The resource rent is calculated per hydro power plant. The gross income is, with some exceptions, calculated based on spot market price per hour multiplied with actual production. In addition, actual income from green certificates is included in the gross income. Deductible costs will be the same as for the CIT; that is, expenses related to the power plant except for interest expenses, which are not deductible. Uplift is granted. Special rules apply to depreciations of investments in hydro power plants. Rent expenditure and depreciations related to waterfalls are not deductible, and waterfalls are not included in the basis for uplift. Tax consolidation is mandatory within the company and, provided the conditions for group taxation are fulfilled, available on a group level. Losses (negative resource rent) on a company (eventually on a group) level will be compensated by the Norwegian state.

Norway

Shipping tonnage tax regime

The tonnage tax rules are in line with the tonnage tax rules found in other European Union (EU)/European Economic Area (EEA) countries and imply that shipping income will be tax-exempt on a permanent basis.

Norwegian tonnage-taxed companies are allowed to keep only certain kinds of assets inside the model (legal assets) and are not allowed to have income from non-tonnage-taxed activities except financial income. If the requirements are not fulfilled, the company would fall outside the scope of the model and be taxed at ordinary rates (28%).

Qualifying assets

A tonnage-taxed company must own at least one qualifying asset (i.e. a vessel, for example bulk, tankers, container vessels, car carriers, tugboats, and entrepreneurial vessels and auxiliary vessels for use in the petroleum industry) new building contracts, a 3% share in another tonnage-taxed limited company, or a 3% ownership interest in a partnership or controlled foreign company (CFC).

Qualifying and legal business activities/income

Qualifying business income is income from operation of the company's own and chartered vessels. A tonnage-taxed company may, for example, charter vessels in and out on bareboat and time charter terms without limitations. Furthermore, gains upon disposal of vessels and new building contracts are exempt from taxation.

Income from related activities such as sales of goods and services onboard vessels, loading and discharging vessels or leasing out containers and operations of ticket offices is also exempt from taxation. The exemption also applies to income from the strategic and commercial management of the company's owned and chartered vessels, as well as vessels owned or operated by group companies (more than 50% joint ownership), and vessels operated according to a pool agreement. Pure management companies are not included (i.e. all companies must have at least one qualifying asset).

Financial income is permitted except for income from shares in unlisted companies and ownership interests in partnerships that are not taxed under the tonnage tax system. The condition is that financial activities do not constitute a separate business. Net financial income is subject to ordinary taxation (28%). Currency gains and losses are partly taxable/ deductible, and interest costs partly deductible corresponding to the proportion between the company's finance capital and total book capital.

Entrance into the tonnage tax system

Entry into the tonnage tax system is, as a starting point, optional and may take place with effect from 1 January every year, provided that the company has fulfilled the conditions for application of the tonnage tax system from the beginning of the year. Newly established companies will have direct entry and may enter into the tonnage tax system from the date of incorporation. All qualifying companies within the same group should be obliged to make the same election (tonnage taxation or ordinary taxation).

Companies that enter into the tonnage tax system are subject to a formal ten-year lock-in period. If a company exits the tonnage tax system before the lock-in period expires, it will be excluded from the tonnage tax system until after the initial lock-in period has ended.

Upon entry into the tonnage tax system, the difference between market value and tax value of the company's assets (including vessels, new building contracts, ownership interests in partnerships, and shares in CFCs/tax exempt assets) is taxed as a capital gain (28%) that can be offset to the gain and loss account and entered as income with 20% of the balance each year (balance method). There is continuity for financial assets and assets covered by the tax-exemption rules (qualifying shares and derivatives).

Exit from the tonnage tax system
A shipping company may exit the regime on a voluntary basis or may be obliged to do so after breaching specific requirements for companies within the tonnage tax system. As a starting point, there is no exit charge when leaving the regime, and the tax value on the company's assets will be adjusted to market value at the time of exit. However, a possible exit while the company has untaxed gain calculated upon entry into the tonnage tax system could result in tax liability upon exit.

Local income taxes
There is no county or municipal CIT in Norway.

Corporate residence

Companies incorporated in Norway in accordance with Norwegian company law and registered in Norway are, as a general rule, regarded as tax resident in Norway and taxable for their worldwide income. If management at the board/director level is carried out outside Norway, residency in Norway for tax purposes may cease, and the company may be subject to exit taxation. Note that several factors should be considered in order to determine whether tax residency has been moved (e.g. other management functions and the overall nexus to Norway).

Foreign corporations will be regarded as resident in Norway if the place of effective management is in Norway. The place of effective management will, for example, be deemed to be in Norway if the board of directors makes its decisions in Norway.

N

Permanent establishment (PE)
According to Norwegian domestic law, a foreign company is liable to tax in Norway when engaged in a business that is either conducted in or managed from Norway. The tax liability is limited to income that is derived from Norwegian sources. As a general rule, non-residents without a PE are not liable for tax on capital gains when selling Norwegian financial instruments. However, when the property has been used in a business that is conducted in or managed from Norway, the capital gain or loss has to be included.

The statute does not contain a reference to the treaty concepts of 'permanent establishment' or 'permanent representative'. The threshold for tax liability is normally lower under the statute than the taxing right afforded to source states under double tax treaties (DTTs).

With respect to DTT's, the Norwegian tax authorities will, to a large extent, follow the Organisation for Economic Co-operation and Development (OECD) Commentaries when interpreting the relevant DTT, if the wording is similar to the OECD Model Tax Convention.

Norway

....

Other taxes

Value-added tax (VAT)
The general VAT rate is 25% and applies to all supplies of goods and services not qualifying for another rate or an exemption. A reduced rate of 15% applies to supply of food and beverages, excluding tobacco, alcohol, medication, and water from waterworks. The reduced rate is not applicable to the supply of food and beverages consumed in restaurants and other food establishments.

A reduced rate of 8% applies to the television licence fee charged for broadcasting services provided by the Norwegian Broadcasting Company (NRK), domestic passenger transport services and procurement of such services, domestic ferry services related to transport of vehicles, accommodation services, and cinema tickets.

Exemptions with credit (zero-rated) include, but are not limited to, the following:

- Export of goods and services.
- Goods and services for Norwegian offshore and non-resident ships.
- Transfer of a going concern.
- Supply of newspapers and books to recipients.
- International transport services.
- Sale of vessels and aircrafts for use in taxable activity.

Exemptions without credit include, but are not limited to, the following:

- Supply of works of art owned by the artist.
- Health services.
- Social services.
- Financial services including banking, insurance, and the sale of shares.
- Educational services.
- Sale and lease of real estate (accommodation and lease of parking lots are taxable).
- Services supplied by cultural and entertainment institutions.

Exemptions, whereby an option to tax is available, include the letting of immovable property to VAT liable lessees following a specific VAT registration with the VAT authorities.

The registration threshold is met when VAT taxable supplies, as comprised by the Norwegian VAT legislation (including self-supplies), exceed 50,000 Norwegian kroner (NOK) during a 12-month period. For charitable and public utility institutions and organisations, the threshold is set at NOK 140,000.

Customs duties
There are quite extensive customs duties on agricultural products, which must be paid upon importation. However, it is often possible to avoid customs duties on these products partly or completely by applying for an exemption from the agricultural authorities in advance. Some of these exemptions are subject to tariff quotas.

Clothes are also subject to customs duties upon importation to Norway, but imports comprised by free trade agreements (such as the EEA with the European Union) and the General System of Preferences (for developing countries) are exempt. As a result, clothes will, as a general rule, not be subject to customs duties as long as the importer presents the necessary certificates of origin.

There are no customs duties on other products than agricultural products and clothes.

Excise taxes
Excise taxes are calculated on import and domestic production of the following:

- Petroleum products, including gas.
- Alcoholic beverages.
- Non-alcoholic beverages.
- Ethanol for technical purposes.
- Tobacco.
- Chocolate, candy, sugar etc.
- Maritime engines.
- Products containing the chemicals TRI/PER.
- Products containing the propellant gases HFK/PFK.

There are also excise taxes related to the following:

- Registration of vehicles.
- Use of vehicles (annual tax).
- Emissions of NOx.
- Waste treatment.
- Sale of electricity.

Property taxes
Real estate may, under certain conditions, be subject to property tax. It is up to the different municipalities to choose whether it wants to impose property tax or not on real estate. Not all municipalities impose property tax on real estate. The applicable rate varies between 0.2% and 0.7%, which is decided by the municipality. The tax base will normally be estimated market value with some adjustments.

Hydro power producers must pay property tax on the hydro power plant's capitalised value using a capital interest rate of 3.3% for the property tax year 2012 (4.5% for 2013). However, the basis for the calculation of the property tax for 2012 shall not exceed the range between NOK 0.95 and NOK 2.47 per kWh of the power plant average production the last seven years (NOK 0.95 and NOK 2.274 per kWh for 2013). For hydro power plants with nominal capacity less than 10,000 kVA, the property tax base will be the same as the tax value for income tax purposes.

Stamp taxes
A tax is levied on registration of change of ownership to real estate. The tax is calculated at 2.5% of the fair market value.

Net wealth taxes
There is no net wealth tax or other capital taxes for limited liability companies, investment funds, state-owned enterprises according to the State-owned Enterprise Act, inter-municipal companies, and companies in which somebody owns a part in or receives income from, when the responsibility for the companies' liabilities is limited to the companies' capital.

Some institutional holders (e.g. mutual insurance companies, savings banks, co-operatives, taxable pension funds, self-owned finance institutions, mortgage credit associations) pay 0.30% (state) net wealth tax. The maximum net wealth tax rate for a corporate body is 1.00% (state and municipal tax).

Norway

Shares in limited liability companies and equity funds are valued at 100% of quoted value for net wealth tax purposes as of 1 January of the year after the relevant income year. If quoted both on Norwegian and foreign stock exchange, the Norwegian stock exchange value will be applicable. If not quoted, the basis for taxation is the company's net taxable value for wealth tax purposes as per 1 January of the income year in question. The basis for taxation of not quoted shares in foreign companies is as a starting point the shares assumed market value as per 1 January of the assessment year.

Exit tax

The exit rules levy taxes upon the migration of assets or liabilities. The tax is calculated by reference to the accrued but unrealised gains at the time of migration at a rate of 28%. Exit tax is also levied if Norwegian CFC taxation lapses because the control requirement is no longer met or if a company:

- transfers its tax residency (effective management) to another country
- has assets or liabilities that are transferred to a PE that is tax exempt pursuant to a DTT, or
- has assets or liabilities that are transferred from a Norwegian PE of a foreign company to the head office or a foreign PE of the same company.

Transfer of assets or liabilities to a PE in a country where the DTT in question is based on the credit method is, however, not regarded as a taxable event.

According to the rules, the tax treatment is different depending on the type of assets being transferred. Business-related operational equipment and financial assets being transferred out of Norwegian taxing jurisdiction are considered as taxable events, but the tax charge may be deferred if certain conditions are met. In addition, the taxation may lapse if the assets are not sold within five years after they are transferred out of Norway. Transfer of intangible assets and inventory trigger immediate and unconditional exit taxation.

De minimis exception rules apply when determining whether the exit tax may be levied. Exit tax on the transfer of tangible assets is applicable only if the unrealised capital gains exceed NOK 5 million. Exit tax on the transfer of other assets and liabilities is only applicable if the unrealised capital gains exceed NOK 1 million.

Exit taxation at both the corporate and shareholder level will also be triggered when companies transfer tax residency (effective management) to another state.

If a company transfer's tax residency (effective management) to another jurisdiction within the EEA, the exit may be exempt. In the event the company is transferred to a low-tax jurisdiction within the EEA, the exemption is contingent on the company being actually established and conducting genuine economic activity in the new state of residence. To the extent any assets or liabilities are transferred out of Norwegian tax jurisdiction, these will be subject to a gain or loss recognition under the exit tax regime.

Carbon dioxide (CO2) tax

A CO2 tax is calculated on petroleum that is flared and natural gas emitted into the air, as well as on CO2 that is separated from petroleum and emitted into the air, on installations used for production or transportation of petroleum. The CO2 tax is regarded as a normal operating cost for CIT purposes and is a fully deductible cost both for corporate and special tax calculations.

Type of Petroleum	NOK per l/ Sm3/kg	NOK per tonne CO2
Petrol	0.89	384
Petroleum, high rate		
Aviation turbine kerosene	0.70	274
Petroleum		
Light oil, diesel oil	0.60	225
Residue	0.60	191
Petroleum reduced rate	0.31	
Light oil, diesel oil	0.31	116
Residue	0.31	99
Aviation turbine kerosene	0.42	165
Domestic used gas		
Natural gas	0.45	226
LPG	0.67	223
Reduced rate natural gas	0.05	25
Continental shelf	0.48	
Light oil, diesel oil	0.49	184
Residue	0.49	156
Natural gas	0.49	209

Natural resource tax

A NOK 0.013 per kWh natural resource tax applies to hydro power activities, based on 1/7 of the produced kWh for the income year in question and the six previous years. The natural resource tax is creditable against the standard CIT.

Branch income

Branch income is taxed at the corporate rate of 28% (the same as Norwegian companies). The basis for taxation is gross income less deductible costs. Both direct and indirect costs related to the activities carried out in Norway may be deductible.

There is no branch profit tax or other repatriation taxes. However, if assets and/or liabilities are transferred from a PE in Norway to the head office or another foreign PE of the same company, this may trigger exit taxation. The transfer of assets to another corporate entity is subject to regular taxation.

Income determination

Inventory valuation

Inventory is valued at cost. Cost is normally determined using the first in first out (FIFO) method. The last in first out (LIFO) method is not acceptable for tax purposes. Conformity between book and tax reporting is not required.

Capital gains

Capital gains realised in the course of a business activity are almost always regarded as taxable income. Gains resulting from real estate transactions are taxed, regardless of whether they are incurred in connection with business activity. Losses may be offset against the taxpayer's other income.

Norway

Capital gains realised on both business-related and non-business-related securities are, in principle, taxable. In general, any capital gains realised on bonds at maturity are regarded as taxable income. Correspondingly, realised losses will be eligible for deductions.

Tax-exemption rules for corporate shareholders

Under the tax-exemption rules, corporate shareholders are generally exempt from tax on dividends received and capital gains on qualifying shares and on derivatives where the underlying object is qualifying shares. Correspondingly, losses on shares are, in general, non-deductible. All operational expenses related to exempt income from shares are fully tax deductible. In order to limit the benefit of these deductions, the tax-exemption method is, with some exemptions, limited to 97% on received dividend, and the remaining 3% is taxable for Norwegian corporate shareholders (at a 0.84% effective tax rate). The 3% taxable income is calculated on dividends. Dividend distributions within a tax group (ultimate parent company is, directly or indirectly, owning more than 90% of the shares and voting rights) are fully tax exempt. In addition, the tax-exemption method also applies for certain distributions from partnerships and on certain conditions to foreign-resident companies with taxable activity in Norway (3% of the income taxable at 28%).

Note that an investment in a company resident in a low-tax country in the EEA has to fulfil certain substance requirements to qualify for the tax-exemption rules. These requirements are intended to be in line with the substance requirements of the European Court of Justice's (ECJ's) decision in the Cadbury Schweppes case. A country is considered a low-tax country if the level of effective taxation is less than two-thirds of the tax that would have been due had the foreign company been resident in Norway. This is the same test used for the CFC regime (*see the Group taxation section for more information*). The Directorate of Taxes has published a non-exhaustive list of low-tax jurisdictions (black list) and non low-tax jurisdictions (white list).

However, for investments outside the EEA, the exemption applies only if a shareholder owns 10% or more of the share capital and the voting rights of the foreign company for a consecutive period of two years or more. To be able to deduct losses on realisation of shareholdings outside the EEA, the shareholder and/or a related party may not own 10% or more of the share capital and the voting rights of the foreign company in a two-year period prior to the realisation. For dividends, the holding period of two years does not have to be met when dividends are distributed, but can also be met after the ex-dividend date.

Shareholdings in low-tax countries outside of the EEA do not qualify for the tax-exemption rules.

Acquisition and sales related costs (e.g. broker fees) must be activated (i.e. added to the cost price of the shares for tax purposes). Costs incurred to manage acquired tax-exempt shares are, however, tax deductible.

Norway's internal tax rules do not allow taxation of a non-resident's capital gain on disposal of financial instruments including, among others, shares in Norwegian companies, unless the non-resident has a PE to which the financial instrument may be allocated.

Stock dividends

Stock dividends (bonus shares) are not taxable on receipt, provided that the dividends have been distributed in accordance with the Limited Liability Company Acts and distributed in proportion with the ownership level of the shares.

Interest income

In general, interest income is taxable on an accrual basis.

Foreign income

A Norwegian resident company is subject to CIT on its worldwide income. Double taxation of foreign-source income, including foreign-branch income and CFC income, is mitigated either through tax treaties or domestic tax provisions. A deduction for foreign tax may either be claimed as an expense or as a credit against Norwegian tax payable on that income. In most circumstances, foreign dividends are exempt according to the tax-exemption rules. As a consequence, foreign WHTs may not be credited and constitute a real cost for the companies concerned.

Norway does not have any legislation for tax deferral of foreign income.

Deductions

Depreciation

For depreciation, the declining-balance method is mandatory. The depreciation rates given below are the maximum rates.

There is a duty to capitalise if the value of an asset subject to declining-balance method of depreciation is NOK 15,000 or higher and has an economic life of at least three years.

Asset	Depreciation rate (%)
Office machines, etc.	30
Acquired goodwill/business value	20
Trucks, lorries, buses, taxicabs, vehicles for persons with disabilities	20
Cars, tractors, other vehicular machinery, instruments, fixtures and furniture, etc.	20
Ships, vessels, offshore rigs, etc.	14
Aircraft, helicopters	12
Construction for transmission and distribution of electric power and electronic equipment in a power company	5*
Buildings and construction, hotels, hostels, inns, etc.	4 (10)**
Office buildings	2
Fixed technical installations in buildings, including heating plant, cooling and freezing plant, electrical installation, sanitary installation, elevator, etc.	10

* As of income year 2012, auxiliary and supplementary installations in industrial plants will be depreciated together with the building and constructions group (10% depreciation if expected operating time is less than 20 years). In addition, constructions for transfer and distribution of energy, and electronic equipment, used in other business activities than power generation will be depreciated at 5%.

** As of income year 2012, the applicable rate is 10% if, from the date of its erection, the structure has an economic life of 20 years or less. Prior to income year 2012, the depreciation rate was 8%.

Special depreciation rules apply to assets moved in and out of Norwegian jurisdiction to and from companies resident outside the EEA.

Norway

Goodwill
Acquired goodwill may be depreciated according to the declining-balance method at a maximum of 20% per annum. The tax authorities have, however, on several occasions recently questioned the allocation to goodwill and claimed that a part of the purchase price should be allocated to intellectual property, concessions, etc. (which may, as a rule, not be depreciated unless it is of a time-limited nature). Other intangibles are depreciable on condition that they are subject to an evident loss in value (impairment test) or if they are time-limited.

Start-up expenses
Start-up expenses are, in general, deductible, provided that the costs are borne by the company. Start-up costs could, for example, be costs related to registration in the Register of Business Enterprises, lawyers and accountants fees, drafting articles of association and shareholders agreement, etc.

Interest expenses
Interest expenses are, in general, deductible. Norway does not have rules distinguishing between different income categories (as in the United Kingdom). If income is exempt from taxation in Norway pursuant to a tax treaty, corresponding costs or losses would not be tax deductible.

Bad debt
In general, receivables are tax deductible, provided that the debt is clearly irrecoverable or realised and is sufficiently connected to the company's business (the business requirement). In case of accounts receivables, a calculated rate multiplied by the total account receivables at year-end may be deducted. The rate is calculated based on the two preceding years losses on such receivables multiplied by a fixed rate set by the Ministry of Finance.

As of 6 October 2011, loss on receivables between group companies (with more than 90% direct or indirect mutual ownership of shares) and partnerships is no longer tax deductible. However, trade receivables, already taxed receivables, and loss on receivables created in connection with mergers or demergers are still deductible for tax purposes.

Charitable contributions
Donations to certain charitable institutions are tax deductible. The upper limit for the tax deduction per year is NOK 12,000. The same limit applies to individuals and companies. The receiving entity must be preapproved by the Norwegian tax authorities.

Fines and penalties
Fines and penalties are normally not tax deductible. This also applies to some administrative charges that are penal in nature. Charges that have no statutory basis in Norwegian law may be tax deductible, provided that the general conditions are fulfilled.

Taxes
Real estate tax, as well as foreign income and capital taxes paid by the taxpayer, is deductible in determining corporate income. Foreign taxes derived from income that is taxable in Norway are deductible only if they have not been credited against Norwegian payable tax.

Net operating losses
Losses may be carried forward indefinitely. Losses incurred in the year of ceasing business may be carried back for a period of two years.

Payments to foreign affiliates
Royalties and service fees paid to related foreign companies are fully deductible, provided they meet the arm's-length standard. There are no formal thin capitalisation or income-stripping rules in Norway. In practice, the tax authorities require that the entity in question is able to service its debts. In addition, any loan terms should be comparable to those that would have been agreed upon by unrelated parties. Interest on financing, to the extent that these rules are not satisfied, may be regarded as dividends and thus non-deductible and, in addition, may be subject to Norwegian WHT.

Group taxation

Income taxes are assessed on companies individually, not on a consolidated basis. This may be avoided through group contributions between Norwegian companies, provided common direct or indirect (including foreign) ownership and voting rights is more than 90%. Furthermore, the Norwegian group contribution rules are, under certain conditions, also applicable to branches of foreign companies that are resident within the EEA. Note that group contributions are not deductible for companies engaged in oil and gas producing activities subject to the Petroleum Tax Act.

Assets may, pursuant to the Group Regulations, be transferred tax-free between group companies at tax book value for tax purposes and at market value for financial book purposes. Payment in this respect must equal market value of the assets transferred. The same applies to payment in shares. If the transferee loses the affiliation with the tax group while still owning the transferred assets, the transferor will be taxed for the difference between the tax book value and the market value of the assets.

Transfer pricing
In Norway, the arm's-length standard for related party transactions is incorporated into the Tax Act. The transfer pricing provision of the Tax Act makes reference to the OECD Guidelines; it is stated that the OECD Guidelines 'shall be taken into account' when addressing transfer pricing issues under Norwegian tax law.

A few years back, the resources of the Norwegian tax authorities were limited, and their interest tended to focus on intra-group services and the financing of operations. However, this has changed considerably as transfer pricing has increasingly become the focus of the tax authorities' attention, and the resource issues have been addressed. It is fairly common for the Norwegian tax authorities to pick test cases that are subject to substantial investment. During the most recent years, focus has been, *inter alia*, on business restructuring and commissionaire arrangements.

Norway does not yet have an advance pricing agreement regime. Nevertheless, it is becoming more common to discuss complex cases with the tax authorities in advance of implementation or before assessment. Furthermore, there are no safe harbour rules or any other official guidance of how to price specific transactions, etc.

Thin capitalisation
There is no fixed debt to equity ratio requirement in Norwegian tax law. However, if Norwegian income from a subsidiary is reduced due to the affiliation between the Norwegian company and a foreign company, adjustments may be made under the

Norway

arm's-length provisions. Generally, these provisions apply only if the company has obtained a larger loan from a group company than an independent credit institution would have granted, or if the agreed level of interest is higher than an independent credit institution would have required. As a rule of thumb, 25% to 30% equity is feasible. Naturally, this analysis will vary based on the actual company's credit worthiness, which would consist of several elements such as the nature of the business, financial status, future income possibilities, and group relationship. The company must also be able to service its debts.

If a Norwegian entity is regarded as being thinly capitalised, part of the entity's interest and debts may be reclassified to dividend and equity.

Controlled foreign companies (CFCs)

Norwegian residents are taxed directly for their allocable part of the profits from a CFC's income if the company is resident in a low-tax country, irrespective of whether income is distributed to the Norwegian investor. A low-tax country in this respect is a country where the effective foreign income taxation of the company's profits is less than two-thirds of the effective taxation which would have been due had the company been resident in Norway. A condition for such taxation is that 50% or more of the foreign company's shares or capital is held or controlled, directly or indirectly, by Norwegian taxpayers (alone or together), based on the status at the beginning and end of the income year in question.

Note that if Norwegian taxpayers own or control more than 60% of the shares or capital at the end of the income year, Norwegian control exists irrespective of the level of control at the beginning of the year. Norwegian control ceases to exist if Norwegian taxpayers own or control less than 50% of the shares or capital at both the beginning and end of the income year or less than 40% of the shares or capital at the end of the income year.

On condition that Norway has signed a tax treaty with the country involved and the company in question is covered by the treaty, the CFC rules will be applicable only if the income of the entity in question is mainly of a passive nature. Furthermore, CFC taxation may also be prohibited if the company in question is resident within the EEA and cannot be deemed as a wholly artificial arrangement as outlined in the ECJ's decision in the Cadbury Schweppes case. Hence, CFC taxation will be avoided for EEA companies that fulfil certain substance requirements.

Tax credits and incentives

Foreign tax credit

Norwegian limited liability companies that have paid taxes on foreign-source income may, under certain conditions, offset the Norwegian tax against the foreign tax paid. The tax credit is limited to the lowest of the Norwegian tax paid on the same type of foreign income and the foreign tax actually paid. It is possible to carry forward unused foreign taxes for five years. Credit claimed in accordance with the regulations stated above may not be used in addition to deductions pursuant to other rules and regulations. These rules are very technical, and it should be noted that there are three different 'baskets' of income.

Roll-over regulations

The Ministry of Finance has the authority to grant a tax relief in case of transfer of assets within a group upon application. The transfer may be carried out between group companies or partnerships with mainly the same owners. If a tax relief is granted, the transfer would not trigger any taxation at the time of the transfer, but all tax positions, including tax basis of the transferred assets, will be transferred to the acquiring company. A condition for the tax relief is normally that the companies remain within the group.

The Ministry of Finance also has the authority to grant a tax relief in case of reorganisation. The reorganisation must improve the efficiency of the business to qualify for tax relief; accordingly, administrative effects would not be sufficient. The tax relief must also ease the reorganisation. In addition, the tax relief must not erode the Norwegian tax base; the tax positions would be transferred to the new taxpayer.

Withholding taxes

Norway does not levy WHT on payments of royalties and interest except interest derived from primary capital certificates ('*No. Egenkapitalbevis*').

The internal WHT rate is 25%, which either may be reduced under the tax-exemption rules or an applicable tax treaty. To qualify for the tax-exemption rule, the recipient of the dividends has to be a corporate investor resident in an EEA country and also fulfil certain substance requirements.

Dividends

Recipient	Regular rate (%)	Parent/subsidiary rate (%)
Non-treaty	25	25
Treaty:		
Albania	15	5 (1)
Argentina	15	10 (1)
Australia	15	0 (11)/5 (4)
Austria	15	0 (1)
Azerbaijan	15	10 (2)
Bangladesh	15	10 (3)
Barbados	15	5 (3)
Belgium	15	5 (1)
Benin	20	20
Bosnia and Herzegovina	15	15
Brazil	25	25 (8)
Bulgaria	15	15
Canada	15	5 (4)
Chile	15	5 (5)
China, P.R.	15	15
Croatia	15	15
Cyprus	5	0 (6)
Czech Republic	15	0 (3)
Denmark	15	0 (3)
Egypt	15	15
Estonia	15	5 (1)
Faroe Islands	15	0 (3)
Finland	15	0 (3)

Norway

Recipient	Regular rate (%)	Parent/subsidiary rate (%)
France	15	5 (3)/0 (1)
Gambia	15	5 (1)
Germany	15	0 (1)
Greece	20	20
Greenland	15	5 (3)
Hungary	10	10
Iceland	15	0 (3)
India	10	10
Indonesia	15	15
Ireland, Republic of	15	5 (3)
Israel	15	5 (6)
Italy	15	15
Ivory Coast (Côte d'Ivoire)	15	15
Jamaica	15	15
Japan	15	5 (5)
Kazakhstan	15	5 (3)
Kenya	25	15 (5)
Korea, Republic of	15	15
Latvia	15	5 (1)
Lithuania	15	5 (1)
Luxembourg	15	5 (1)
Macedonia	15	10 (1)
Malawi	5	0 (6)
Malaysia	0	0
Malta	15	15
Mexico	15	0 (1)
Montenegro	15	15
Morocco	15	15
Nepal	15	5 (1)/10 (3)
Netherlands	15	0 (1)
Netherlands Antilles	15	5 (1)
New Zealand	15	15
Nordic Treaty	15	0 (3)
Pakistan	15	15
Philippines	25	15 (3)
Poland	15	0 (10)
Portugal	15	10 (1)
Qatar	15	5 (3)
Romania	10	10
Russia	10	10
Senegal	16	16
Serbia (not Montenegro)	15	15
Sierra Leone	5	0 (6)
Singapore	15	5 (1)
Slovak Republic	15	5 (1)
Slovenia	15	0 (9)

Recipient	Regular rate (%)	Parent/subsidiary rate (%)
South Africa	15	5 (1)
Spain	15	10 (1)
Sri Lanka	15	15
Sweden	15	0 (3)
Switzerland	15	0 (3)
Tanzania	20	20
Thailand	15	10 (3)
Trinidad and Tobago	20	10 (5)
Tunisia	20	20
Turkey	15	5 (12)
Uganda, Republic of	15	10 (1)
Ukraine	15	5 (1)
United Kingdom	15	5 (4)
United States	15	15
Venezuela	10	5 (3)
Vietnam	15	5/10 (7)
Zambia	15	15
Zimbabwe	20	15 (1)

Notes

1. 25% of the capital.
2. 30% of the capital and an investment of no less than 100,000 United States dollars (USD).
3. 10% of the capital.
4. 10% of the voting rights.
5. 25% of the voting rights.
6. 50% of the voting rights.
7. 5% for over 70% of the capital; 10% for 25% to 70% of the capital.
8. Internal Norwegian WHT rate (i.e. 25%).
9. 15% of the capital.
10. 10% of the capital for a uninterrupted 24-month period.
11. 80% of voting rights.
12. 20% of the capital provided that such dividends are exempt from tax in that other state.

Tax administration

Taxable period

The income tax year normally runs from 1 January to 31 December, with assessments being issued in early autumn of the following calendar year. Companies are liable for both advance payments and final settlements in the calendar year of assessment. Companies with a financial year other than the calendar year may use the financial year for tax purposes in certain instances (e.g. if they belong to a foreign group with a deviating accounting year, they may use the financial year of the group for tax purposes).

Tax returns

Companies are required to file their tax returns by the end of March in the year following their financial year. If filed electronically, the return must be filed by the end of May. Upon application, an extension of the time limit to file normally will be granted. The tax returns and the basic attachments are obligatory for all corporate taxpayers.

Norway

Additional requirements might apply for specific business sectors, such as hydro power production. Under the petroleum tax regime, the filing deadline is end of April, regardless of whether filed electronically or not.

The annual assessment is made by five regional departments of tax, which notify the taxpayer if taxable income is determined to deviate from what was submitted in the tax return.

Payment of tax

Companies are required to make advance payments of tax on 15 February and 15 April in the year following the income year. The two payments should together cover all of the expected CIT to be assessed. Any balance must be paid three weeks after the assessment has been made public (i.e. in early autumn of the year following the relevant accounting year).

The above applies to all corporate taxpayers, except for taxpayers under the petroleum tax regime, where tax shall be paid in six instalments.

Statute of limitations

The tax office has a ten-year limit for reassessing tax assessment (open years) from the year after the income year in question. However, a two-year limit applies for negative adjustment and a three-year limit for positive adjustment if the taxpayer has provided sufficient and correct information in the tax return.

The taxpayer may file an appeal on the tax assessment within six weeks after the taxpayer has received the tax assessment. The time limit for appealing other decisions is normally three weeks after the tax office's decision.

Topics of focus for tax authorities

The tax office's topics of focus vary from time to time and region. The tax office assessing most companies in the eastern region of Norway has stated that the topics of focus are, among others, tax loss on receivables, exit taxation, and taxation of shares and distributions from partnerships.

Oman

PwC contact

Russell Aycock
PricewaterhouseCoopers
Hatat House A
Suites 204-210
Wadi Adai, Muscat
Oman
Tel: +968 24 559 110
Email: russell.aycock@om.pwc.com

Significant developments

Executive Regulations relating to the 2010 Income Tax Law were published in early 2012, with effect from 1 January 2012.

Taxes on corporate income

The rate of income tax is uniform for all types of business entities, regardless of whether it is a corporate entity and/or whether it is registered or not.

The Income Tax Law seeks to tax worldwide income of entities formed in Oman and the Oman-source income of branches and other forms of permanent establishment (PE).

The income tax rate is as follows:

Taxable profits (OMR*)	Rate (%)
First 30,000	0
Over 30,000	12

* Omani rial

Petroleum income tax

Special provisions are applicable to the taxation of income derived from the sale of petroleum. The tax rate specified for such companies is 55%. However, the tax rates are applied on income as determined by the individual Exploration and Production Sharing Agreement entered into between the government of Oman and the company engaged in the sale of petroleum. Under these agreements, the government pays the company's share of income tax from amounts withheld from the government's share of production. Therefore, the income tax is not actually borne by the company.

Corporate residence

The term 'resident' is not defined in the tax law.

Permanent establishment (PE)

PE is defined in very broad terms and includes places of sale, places of management, branches, offices, factories, workshops, mines, quarries, and building sites for construction. However, the mere use of storage or display facilities does not constitute

Oman

a PE. The definition of PE references carrying on business in Oman, either directly or through a dependent agent.

Additionally, the definition stipulates that a total stay of 90 days during a 12-month period creates a PE in Oman. However, this 90 day period applies to rendering of consultancy services or other services only. Under this definition, while the sale of goods into Oman will not be deemed to be a taxable activity, a contract for the supply and installation of equipment is likely to attract tax. By the same criterion, services rendered by personnel visiting Oman will be treated as taxable activities, applying the 90 day rule.

Other taxes

Value-added tax (VAT)
There is no VAT or sales tax in Oman.

Customs duty
Customs duty of 5% of cost, insurance, and freight (CIF) value applies to most non-GCC source goods. Exemptions apply for certain food items, medical supplies, etc.

Excise taxes
There are no excise taxes in Oman.

Property taxes
There are no property taxes in Oman.

Stamp duty
Stamp duty is applicable on transfer of land and property at 3% of the value.

Municipal taxes
Municipal taxes apply to the following items:

- Property rents: 3%.
- Hotel occupancy: 5%.
- Leisure and cinema houses: 10%.

Branch income

Branches of foreign entities (regardless of country) are subject to tax at the rate of 12% on income over OMR 30,000.

Expenses incurred by the head office that can be identified as directly related to the branch's activity are deductible. The deduction for other head office expenses is limited to 3% of the branch's gross income for the year. This rate is 5% for banks and insurance companies, and 10% for high tech industrial activities.

Income determination

Inventory valuation
Inventory should be valued using a method that complies with International Accounting Standards.

Capital gains

Gains on sales of securities listed on the Muscat Securities Market are exempt from taxation. A recent Supreme Court ruling held that gains on transfers of other assets are taxable as ordinary income.

Dividend income

Dividends received from Omani entities are exempt from taxation. Foreign source dividends are taxable. Foreign source dividends are taxed as the same rates as corporate income.

Stock dividends

There are no provisions in the tax law that address stock dividends.

Interest income

Interest income is taxable as business income.

Rent/royalty income

Rental income and royalties are taxed as business income.

Unrealised exchange gains/losses

Unrealised exchange gains are not taxable. Similarly, any unrealised loss is not deductible from the total taxable income.

Foreign income

Worldwide income of an entity formed in Oman is taxed in Oman. Credit for foreign taxes paid is given under the law; however, this may not exceed the amount of Omani tax payable on such income.

The Oman tax law does not contain rules on deferral of foreign income.

O

Deductions

Depreciation

Depreciation is taken on a straight-line basis on the following classes of assets at the annual rates shown.

Asset	Rate (%)
Permanent buildings	4
Semi-permanent buildings	15
Docks, sea barriers in ports, pipelines, roads, and railway lines	10
Aircraft and ships	15
Hospital buildings, educational establishments, and equipment for scientific research	100

The rate of depreciation allowed is doubled in the case of buildings used for industrial purposes.

The tax law now provides for calculation of depreciation on a net book value basis for the following class of assets. A 'pooling' concept has been introduced, whereby assets subject to same rate of depreciation may be pooled together for purposes of depreciation.

Oman

Pool	Rate (%)
First pool is comprised of machinery and equipment, including computer software installations, furniture and fixtures, and vehicles	33.33
Second pool is comprised of drilling equipment	10
Third pool is comprised of 'other machinery and equipment' not included above	15

Goodwill
Goodwill is amortisable for tax purposes, generally over the life assigned for International Financial Reporting Standards (IFRS) accounting purposes.

Start-up expenses
Expenses incurred before the commencement of business are allowed as a deduction in the first taxable year (or period).

Interest expenses
Deduction of expenses incurred for the purpose of earning income is generally allowed. Interest expense is allowed for loans from unrelated parties or on loans from banks. Interest paid to related parties is allowed only to the extent the loan terms are at arm's length.

Charitable contributions
Charitable donations are limited to specified institutions and organisations and are subject to an overall limitation of 5% of total income.

Meals, entertainment, officers compensation, etc.
All expenses incurred for the generation of gross total income are allowed. There are no specific restrictions on deduction for expenses like meals and entertainment, compensation for officers, and life insurance payments for employees. There are limits on the deductibility of directors' fees.

Social security payments
Social security contributions paid by employers in respect of employees may also be deducted.

Pension payments
Contributions to pension funds, domestic and foreign, are deductible, provided the fund is licensed (in Oman or the country where it was established) and complies with certain other specified conditions.

Illegal payments
Payments of bribes or kickbacks, and other illegal payments, are not deductible.

Fines and penalties
Civil fines and penalties are not deductible.

Taxes
Taxes on income, whether incurred in Oman or elsewhere, are not deductible in arriving at taxable income. A credit may be available for taxes paid in a foreign jurisdiction.

Other significant items/restrictions on allowable expenses
The tax law has imposed restrictions on the deductibility of certain expenses. The principal items affected are the following:

- Sponsorship fees paid to Omani sponsors are restricted to 5% of net taxable income before sponsorship fees. Net taxable income is determined after offsetting any losses carried forward.
- Charges or expenses allocated from the head office or other group companies are limited to 3% of gross income (5% for banks and insurance companies, and 10% for high tech industrial activities).
- Commissions paid by insurance companies are restricted to 25% of net premiums collected.
- Amounts charged to the profit and loss account for creating provisions in respect of bad debts, stock obsolescence, warranties, and similar types of contingencies are not tax deductible. Deduction is allowed only at the time of write-off. However, provisions created by licensed banks in respect of bad debts are allowable within the limits approved/required by the Central Bank of Oman.
- Leasing companies are treated at par with banks as far as deduction for loan loss provision is concerned. Leasing companies are allowed deductions for loan loss provisions subject to the limits or recommendations of the Central Bank of Oman.
- Losses arising on sale of investments listed on the Muscat Security Market are not allowed as a deduction from taxable income.
- Any expense or costs which have been incurred to generate income exempted from tax are not allowed as a deduction from taxable income.
- Amounts paid as tax consultancy or advisory fees are disallowed.

Net operating losses
Carryforward of losses is limited to five years, except in the case of companies that incurred losses during a mandatory tax-exempt period, where the losses may be carried forward indefinitely for offset against future profits.

Carryback of losses is not allowed.

Payments to foreign affiliates
Payments to foreign affiliates normally receive in-depth scrutiny from the tax authorities. Accordingly, proper documentation should be obtained in order to establish that these transactions are made at an arm's-length basis.

Group taxation

Businesses are taxed as separate entities, and the tax law does not recognise group taxation.

Transfer pricing
Transactions between related parties must be valued at arm's length. There is no specific guidance on acceptable methods for determining an arm's-length price.

Inter-company payments
All inter-company payments are scrutinised in detail to ensure that the profits are not transferred to avoid payment of tax.

Thin capitalisation
If the debt-to-equity ratio exceeds 2:1 in the case of related party debt, interest on the excess debt is not deductible for tax purposes. This rule does not apply to banks and insurance companies, PEs of foreign companies, or proprietary (Omani owned) establishments.

Oman

Controlled foreign companies (CFCs)
There is no CFC regime in Oman.

Tax credits and incentives

Foreign tax credit
Foreign taxes paid to a country with whom Oman has a double tax treaty (DTT) are eligible for a credit to the maximum of the Oman tax that would have been payable on such income. The tax payer is required to submit an application to the Secretariat General for Taxation to claim such credit.

Exempt activities
Income from the principal activities listed below is exempt from tax, if an exemption is applied for and obtained.

- Industry and mining.
- Export of products manufactured or processed locally.
- Operation of hotels or tourist villages.
- Agriculture and animal husbandry and the processing of agricultural produce.
- Fishing and fish processing and aquaculture.
- University education, college or institutes of higher studies, private schools, nurseries, training colleges, and institutes.

The exemption is valid for a period of five years from the date of commencement of production or the practice of activities and may be made subject to such conditions as the Minister of Commerce and industry may specify. The exemption is renewable for a period not exceeding five years, subject to approval by the Financial Affairs and Energy Resources Council.

Exempt income
The following income is exempt from income tax in Oman:

- Dividends received from an Omani company.
- Profits or gains on disposal of securities listed on Muscat Security Market.
- Omani marine companies, whether wholly owned by Omanis or with foreign and Omani ownership and registered in Oman, are exempt from tax. Foreign marine companies conducting activities in Oman through an authorised agent are exempted from tax with effect from the date of commencement of activity, provided that reciprocal treatment is afforded by the country of the foreign company.
- Income realised by foreign airlines carrying on business through establishments in Oman is exempt from tax. This exemption is limited to the extent of the income from operating airplanes for international transport, provided reciprocal treatment is accorded in the airline's home country.
- Income realised by investment funds established in Oman under the Capital Market Authority Law or established overseas for dealing in shares and securities listed on Muscat Security Market is exempt.
- Foreign companies engaged in oil and gas exploration activities, while taxable under the law, normally have their tax obligations discharged by the government under the terms of the Exploration and Production Sharing Agreement.
- Foreign companies working for the government in projects deemed to be of national importance may be able to negotiate a tax protection clause whereby any tax paid by them is reimbursed by the government.

Withholding taxes

Foreign companies that do not have a PE in Oman for tax purposes and that derive income from Oman in the nature of the following are subject to withholding tax (WHT) at 10% of gross income from such sources:

- Royalty.
- Consideration for research and development (R&D).
- Consideration for use of or right to use computer software.
- Management fees.

Such WHT is required to be withheld by the Omani-based company and paid to the tax department within 14 days of the end of the month in which tax is deducted or payments are due or made to the foreign company.

There is no WHT on dividends and interest payments.

The term 'royalty' has been defined under the law to include consideration for the use of intellectual property, including computer software, cinematography films, tapes, discs, or any other media, patents, trademarks, drawings, etc. The term further includes consideration for using industrial, commercial, or scientific equipment and consideration for information concerning industrial, commercial, or scientific experience or consideration for granting rights to exploit mining or other natural resources.

Double tax treaties (DTTs)
The maximum WHT rates provided by the Oman DTTs are shown in the table below. There are also agreements with various countries which are not yet in force.

Recipient	Dividends (%)	Interest (%)	Royalties (%)
Algeria	5 (3)/10	5	10
Belarus	5	5	10
Brunei	-	-	-
Canada	5 (1)/15	10	10
China	5	10	10
Croatia	0	5	10
France	0	0	0
India	10 (1)/12.5	10	15
Iran	10	10	10
Italy	5 (3)/10	5	10
Korea	5 (1)/10	5	8
Lebanon	5 (4)/10	10	10
Mauritius	0	0	0
Moldova	5	5	10
Morocco	5 (1)/10	10	10
Pakistan	10 (1)/12.5	10	12.5
Seychelles	5	5	10
Singapore	5	7	8
South Africa	0	0	8
Sudan	-	-	-
Syria	-	-	-

Oman

Recipient	Dividends (%)	Interest (%)	Royalties (%)
Thailand	10	10 (5)/15	15
Tunisia	0	10	5
Turkey	10 (3)/15	10	10
United Kingdom	5 (1)/10	0	8
Uzbekistan	7	7	10
Vietnam	5 (6)/10 (7)/15	10	10
Yemen	5	10	10

Notes

1. 10% minimum shareholding required.
2. Distributions by real estate investment company/fund.
3. 15% minimum shareholding required.
4. 20% minimum shareholding required.
5. Interest received by financial institutions (including insurance companies) or loans/debt claims guaranteed by the government of the source state.
6. 60% minimum shareholding required.
7. 25% to 60% minimum shareholding required.

Tax administration

Taxable period
The tax year is the calendar year. Assessments can be made on the basis of a year-end other than 31 December, provided permission is granted in advance by the Omani tax authorities and the company then adheres to the year-end on a consistent basis.

Tax returns
A provisional declaration of tax must be submitted in the prescribed form within three months from the end of the accounting period to which it relates. The final annual return of income should be submitted in the prescribed format within six months from the end of the accounting period to which it relates. Reasonable time extensions can be sought and are normally provided for filing the provisional and annual returns of income, but these do not defer payment of tax, which will be subject to additional tax at 1% per month from the due date to the actual date of payment.

In the case of companies having a paid-up capital in excess of OMR 20,000, the annual return of income should be accompanied by audited accounts signed by an auditor registered in Oman. The law requires accounts to be drawn up in accordance with IFRS consistently applied. It specifically provides for accrual accounting unless prior permission of the Secretary General of Taxation (the Secretary General) has been obtained. The accounts must be submitted in local currency unless prior approval of the Secretary General has been obtained for submitting them in foreign currency.

Delay or failure in submitting the provisional or annual returns may attract a penalty of not less than OMR 100 and not more than OMR 1,000.

Failure to file the provisional or annual returns of income may result in an estimated profit assessment by the Secretary General.

Failure to submit audited accounts as required under the Law is deemed to result in an incomplete annual return of income and may attract an estimated profit assessment.

The law confers wide powers on the Secretary General for requesting information. Experience has shown that, notwithstanding the presentation of audited accounts, the tax department requests very detailed information and supporting documentation relating to revenue and expenses. Failure to provide such information or the provision of incorrect information can result in an additional assessment by the Secretary General and/or various penalties on the company and/or the officer responsible for providing the information.

Payment of tax

Any tax estimated to be payable in respect of an accounting period should be paid with the provisional assessment and 'topped up' for any additional amount computed as payable following submission of the annual return of income. Failure to pay taxes by the due date attracts interest at the rate of 1% per month from the date on which such tax was due to the date of payment.

The difference between the amount paid and the amount assessed, subject to filing of an objection, should be paid within one month from the date of the assessment. The additional amount assessed attracts interest at the rate of 1% per month from the date on which such tax was due to the date of payment.

Under the Law, the Secretary General has the authority, with the approval of the Minister and the Tax Committee, to sequester and sell the assets of a taxable entity to recover the taxes due.

If decisive proof is presented to the Secretary General that any person has paid tax for any year exceeding the tax due and payable for such tax year as finally settled, such person has the right to recover the tax. However, if any tax has become payable by such person in respect of another tax year, the excess amount will be adjusted against the future tax liability. Any request for recovery must be presented within five years from the end of the tax year to which it relates.

Where the taxpayer fails to declare correct income in the tax return for any tax year, the Secretary General may impose a fine not exceeding 25% of the difference between the amount on the basis of the correct taxable income and the amount of tax as per the return submitted.

Statute of limitation

The tax authorities have a period of up to five years from the end of the year in which a tax return is submitted to complete the assessment for that tax year. However where the entity has not submitted any tax return, the tax authorities have a period of ten years to complete the assessments.

Maintenance of records

The Law requires accounting records and supporting documentation to be maintained for ten years after the end of the accounting period to which these records relate.

Objections and appeals

A company has a right to object to any assessment issued by the Secretary General. The objection document should be prepared in writing (in English and in Arabic) and filed with the office of the Secretary General for Taxation within 45 days from the date of assessment. The Secretary General is required to give a judgment within five months, extendable up to another five months at the Secretary General's discretion, from the date of receiving the objection. The tax demanded may be kept in abeyance on request. No additional tax is payable until the Secretary General issues the judgment.

Pakistan

PwC contact

Syed Shabbar Zaidi
A.F. Ferguson & Co., Chartered Accountants (a member firm of pwc network)
State Life Building 1-A
I.I. Chundrigar Road
Karachi-74000
Pakistan
Tel: +92 21 32413849
Email: s.m.shabbar.zaidi@pk.pwc.com

Significant developments

The following significant developments in corporate taxation have recently occurred in Pakistan:

- The province of Sindh has introduced an Act to collect and levy sales tax on services.
- Minimum tax can now be carried forward for five years instead of three years.
- An advance ruling can now only be obtained by a non-resident not having a permanent establishment (PE) in Pakistan.
- Withholding tax (WHT) on cash withdrawals exceeding 25,000 Pakistani rupees (PKR) has been reduced from 0.3% to 0.2%.
- The general rate of sales tax has been reduced from 17% to 16%.
- Significant exemptions have been withdrawn from the levy of sales tax (i.e. computer software, certain special purpose vehicles, aircraft, specified ships, and certain specified machinery).

Taxes on corporate income

A resident company is taxed on its worldwide income. The federal corporate tax rates on taxable income are as follows:

Company type	Tax rate (%)
Banking company	35
Public company other than a banking company	35
Any other company	35
Small company (see the Tax credits and incentives section for more information)	25

The term 'public company' implies a company listed on any stock exchange in Pakistan or one in which not less than 50% of the shares are held by the federal government or a public trust.

In the case of a *modaraba* (*see the Income determination section for a definition*), income, except relating to trading activities, is exempt from tax, provided that 90% of its profit is distributed to the certificate holders as cash dividends.

The final tax regime (FTR) for resident taxpayers, a presumptive tax scheme where taxes are withheld at the source on the sale of goods and execution of contracts or collected at the time of import (for other than industrial raw materials), is considered a final tax liability in respect of income arising from the sale, contract, or import.

In the case of exports, tax collected at the time of realisation of foreign-exchange proceeds is treated as final tax for that income.

The FTR is also applicable to non-resident taxpayers, at their option. However, it is only applicable in cases of receipts on account of the execution of a contract for construction, assembly, or installation, including a contract for the supply of management activities in relation to such project as well as certain contracts for services and contract for advertisement services rendered by television satellite channels.

Taxation of a permanent establishment (PE) of a non-resident
The following principles shall apply in computing taxable income of a PE:

- It is a distinct and separate entity dealing independently with the non-resident of which it is a PE.
- In addition to business expenditure, executive and administrative expenditure, whether incurred in Pakistan or elsewhere, will be allowed as deductions.
- Head office expenditure, including rent, salaries, travelling, and any other expenditure which may be prescribed, shall be allowed as a deduction in proportion to the turnover of the PE in the same proportion as the non-resident's total head office expenditure bears to its worldwide turnover.
- Royalties, compensation for services (including management services), and interest on loans (except in banking business) payable or receivable to or from PE's head office shall be considered in computing taxable income of PE.
- No deduction will be allowed for any interest paid on loans acquired by a non-resident to finance the operations of a PE (or for the insurance premium in respect of such loans).

Minimum tax
Where the tax payable by a company is less than 1% of the turnover, except where the company is in loss before charging depreciation and other inadmissible expenses, the company is required to pay a minimum tax equivalent to 1% of the turnover. Tax paid in excess of normal tax liability, can be carried forward for adjustment against tax liability of a subsequent tax year. However, such tax can only be adjusted against tax liability of the five tax years immediately succeeding the tax year for which the amount was paid.

Local taxes on income
No local taxes are payable in respect of income of companies.

Corporate residence

A company is resident in Pakistan if it is incorporated or formed by or under the law of Pakistan or if the control and management of its affairs is situated wholly in Pakistan in that year.

The term 'company' includes a trust, a cooperative society, a finance society, or any other society established or constituted by or under any law; a corporate body incorporated outside Pakistan; and any foreign association, incorporated or unincorporated, which the Central Revenue authorities may declare to be a company.

Permanent establishment (PE)
PE is a place of business through which the business of a non-resident is wholly or partly carried out, including:

Pakistan

- A place of management, branch, office, factory or workshop, premises for soliciting orders, warehouse, permanent sales exhibition, or sales outlet, except a liaison office.
- An agriculture, pastoral, or forestry property.
- A mine, oil or gas well, quarry, or any other place of extraction of natural resources.
- A building site; a construction, assembly, or installation project; or supervisory activities connected with such site or project if such activity continued for more than 90 days within any 12-month period.
- The furnishing of services, including consultancy services, by any person through employees or other personnel engaged by the person for that purpose.
- A person acting in Pakistan on behalf of the person, other than an agent of independent status acting in the ordinary course of business.
- Any substantial equipment installed, or other asset or property capable of activity giving rise to income.

The definition of a PE provided in a double taxation treaty (DTT) will prevail in cases where a DTT is executed by Pakistan with the related country of origin of the PE.

Other taxes

Value-added tax (VAT)

VAT (locally termed as 'sales tax') is ordinarily levied at 16% on the value of goods, unless specifically exempt, after allowing related input credits.

Telecommunication services are levied VAT at the rate of 19.5%. VAT on other services is a provincial levy.

Significant zero-rated goods are as follows:

- Supplies and repair and maintenance of certain ships and aircrafts.
- Supplies to diplomatic missions and diplomats.
- Supplies against international tenders.
- Supplies of raw materials, components, and goods for export processing zones.
- Supplies of locally manufactured plant and machinery to export processing zones and supplies of certain specified machinery to exploration and production sector.
- Supplies to exporters.

Significant exemptions are as follows:

- Live animals and poultry.
- Live plants.
- Vegetables, pulses, fruits, certain spices, sugar cane, edible oils, etc.
- Milk preparations.
- Newsprints, newspapers, journals, periodicals, and books.
- Agricultural produce not subjected to any process.

Customs and import duties

Custom and certain other duties are collected at import stage at varying rates classified under Harmonized System (HS) Code.

Excise duty

Federal excise duty (FED) is levied at the rate of 16% on certain types of manufacturing, import of goods, and rendering of services, except telecommunications services, which are charged at the rate of 19.5%. FED, under the constitution, is to be levied and collected by the provinces. Sindh province has promulgated their statute, and others are expected to follow.

Property taxes
Property owners are required to pay property tax levied and collected by provincial governments through municipal governments at varying rates.

Stamp duty
In the case of sale or transfer of immovable property, stamp duty is payable (with varying rates on the basis of location of the property) on the value of the property.

Branch income

The rates of tax for a branch of a company incorporated outside Pakistan are the same as those applicable on resident companies, other than public and banking companies (i.e. 35%). Tax at the rate of 10% is levied on the transfer of profits to the head office, with an exception for companies engaged in oil and gas exploration and production business.

Payments to a branch in Pakistan of a non-resident are subject to deduction of tax at source, on the same basis as a resident in the case of sale of goods, rendering of professional services, and execution of contracts. In other circumstances, a reduced/0% WHT certificate can be obtained from the Commissioner of Income Tax.

Pakistan has signed agreements for avoidance of double taxation with over 60 countries.

Income determination

Inventory valuation
Inventories are to be stated at the lower of cost or market. The first in first out (FIFO) and average methods are accepted. Conformity of methods used for book and tax reporting is desirable, and the method used should be consistently applied.

Capital gains
Capital gain on the sale of immovable property, on which depreciation is not allowed, is not taxable.

Gain on the disposal of shares of a resident company or a non-resident company, whose assets wholly or principally consist of immovable property situated in Pakistan or rights to explore/exploit natural resources in Pakistan, shall be Pakistan-source income.

Capital gains on the sale of shares of public companies or *modaraba* (profit sharing) certificates are exempt from tax if held for a period of more than 12 months. Capital gains on shares and *modaraba,* if held for less than 12 months, are taxable under two categories, (i) held for less than six months and (ii) held for more than six months but less than 12 months at 7.5% and 10% to be gradually enhanced to 17.5% and 10% by 2015.

Pakistan

Capital gain, other than on statutory depreciable assets, realised within one year of acquisition is fully taxed; after one year, 75% of such gains are taxed and 25% are exempt.

Capital gains on statutory depreciable assets (other than immovable property) are chargeable to tax as normal business income in the year of sale. They are measured as the difference between the sale proceeds and the tax written-down value of the relevant asset sold.

In the case of an asset disposal transaction that is on a non-arm's-length basis, fair market value of the asset shall be taken to be the consideration received by the seller, as well as the cost for the buyer.

Where assets are transferred outside Pakistan, the original cost is treated as the sale price, which means that the entire depreciation is recaptured at the time of export, except if the assets are used in oil or gas exploration, in which case only the initial depreciation is recaptured.

No gain or loss shall be taken to arise on disposal of an asset by a resident company to another resident company, if certain conditions are met. The required conditions include, *inter alia*, that the transferor is 100% owned by the transferee or vice versa or both companies are 100% owned by a third company, and the transferee income is not exempt in the year of transfer. The scheme of arrangement is approved by the Securities and Exchange Commission of Pakistan or State Bank of Pakistan.

Any distribution to the shareholders of a company to the extent that it relates to undistributed profits is treated as a dividend.

Capital loss can be offset only against capital gains. Unabsorbed capital loss can be carried forward for adjustment against capital gains for six years.

Dividend income
Dividend income is subject to WHT of 10% or a lower tax treaty rate.

The deduction at source shall be the full and final discharge of tax liability on dividend income.

Stock dividends
Stock dividends declared by resident companies are exempt from tax.

Interest income
Interest earned by a company is taxed as its income from other sources. Interest earned by a non-resident company without a PE in Pakistan attracts WHT at the rate of 10%, except where a lower rate is provided in the related DTT, which is also the final tax on such income.

Income from royalties and fees for technical services (FTS)
Royalties received by non-residents are deemed to accrue or arise in Pakistan and are taxable if paid by a resident in Pakistan or borne by a PE of a non-resident in Pakistan.

Income from 'fees for technical services' (FTS) is deemed to accrue or arise in Pakistan if paid by a resident in Pakistan or borne by a PE of a non-resident in Pakistan. FTS means any consideration for the rendering of any managerial, technical, or consultancy services (including the provision of the services of technical or other personnel),

Pakistan

but does not include consideration for any construction, assembly, or like project undertaken by the recipient or consideration that would be income of the recipient chargeable under the head salary.

Other significant items
Liabilities allowed as a tax deduction in a tax year and remaining unpaid for three subsequent years are deemed to be income in the first tax year following the said three years. Such items are then allowed as a deduction in the year the liability is discharged.

Agricultural income is exempt from income tax.

Foreign income
A resident company is taxed on its worldwide income and on its foreign income as earned. Double taxation of foreign income is avoided by means of foreign tax credits; this relief is allowed to the resident company on the doubly taxed income at the lower of the Pakistan or foreign tax rate. Undistributed income of a non-resident subsidiary is not subject to tax.

Foreign loss can only be offset against foreign income and can be carried forward for six years.

Modaraba
Modaraba (profit sharing) is a financing vehicle that enables a management company to control and manage the business of a *modaraba* company with a minimum of 10% equity participation. The management company is entitled to remuneration based on an agreed percentage (but not exceeding 10%) of annual profits of the *modaraba* business. A *modaraba* can be for a specific purpose or many purposes and for a limited or unlimited period. The income of a *modaraba* not relating to trading activity is free from tax if 90% of its profits are distributed as cash dividend.

Deductions

Depreciation
Normal depreciation is allowed at the following prescribed rates by applying the reducing-balance method.

Assets	Depreciation rate (%)
Buildings	10
Furniture	15
Machinery and equipment, including motor vehicles and ships	15
Computer hardware, including monitors and printers	30
Aircraft and aero engines	30
Below-ground installations in mineral oil concerns	100
Offshore platform	20

All depreciable assets put into service for the first time in Pakistan during a tax year, other than road transport vehicles not plying for hire, furniture including fixtures, plant, and machinery used previously in Pakistan, or plant and machinery for which a deduction has been allowed under another section of this ordinance, for the entire cost of the asset, shall be entitled to an initial allowance at 50% of the cost of the asset.

Pakistan

Book depreciation need not conform to tax depreciation. Unabsorbed tax depreciation not set off against the income of the year is carried forward and added to depreciation of the assets of the same business in the following year. Tax depreciation can be carried forward without limit until fully absorbed.

Amortisation of intangibles
The cost incurred on acquisition of a patent, invention, design or model, secret formula or process, copyright, software, quota, licence, intellectual property or other like property or right and any expenditure that provides an advantage or benefit for a period of more than one year is allowed as a deduction on a straight-line basis over the useful life of the asset, but not exceeding a period of ten years.

Any payment made against acquisition of goodwill will also be amortised under these provisions.

Organisational and start-up expenses
Expenditure incurred before the commencement of a business wholly and exclusively to derive income chargeable to tax can be deducted over a period of five years.

Interest expense
Interest expense is allowed as an expense if required WHT is deducted and deposited in the government treasury.

Bad debt
The bad debts are allowed as deductible expenditure if the following conditions are satisfied:

• Debts are included previously in the income chargeable to tax.
• Debts are written off in the financial statements.
• There are reasonable grounds for believing that the debt is irrecoverable.

Charitable contributions
See Charitable donations credit in the Tax credits and incentives section.

Fines and penalties
Fines or penalties that are not paid or payable for the violation of any law, rule, or regulation are allowable as tax deductible expenses.

Taxes
Taxes on income are not deductible. Sales tax and excise tax are tax deductible where these are to be absorbed by the business; otherwise, these are passed on to the consumer.

Other significant items
The deductibility of a head office expenditure of a non-resident taxpayer is limited to the same proportion of total head office expenditure as the Pakistan turnover has with the total world turnover. However, such domestic rules are overridden if the branch is a tax resident of a country having an agreement for avoidance of double taxation (treaty) and that treaty provides a different basis.

Expenditure on scientific research incurred in Pakistan wholly and exclusively for the purpose of deriving income chargeable to tax is an allowable expenditure.

Exchange gains and loss on foreign currency loans specifically obtained for acquiring an asset are adjusted against the depreciable cost of the asset.

Any lease rental incurred by a person in the tax year to a scheduled bank, financial institution, approved *modaraba*, or approved leasing company shall be a deductible expense. However, financial charges paid for the above-mentioned leases are added back into the taxable income of the company.

Net operating losses
Operating loss may be carried forward and set off against the profits of the succeeding six years of the same business in which the loss was incurred. Unabsorbed depreciation can be carried forward indefinitely.

Carried forward loss of an entity in the case of group relief cannot be utilised if the ownership of the holding company is reduced to less than 55% and 75% if one of the companies is a listed company or none of the companies is a listed company, respectively.

Business loss can be carried forward up to a period of six years in the case of the amalgamation of two companies, with the condition that the same business is continued for a minimum period of five years.

Carryback of loss is not permitted.

Group taxation

A locally incorporated holding company and subsidiary of a 100% owned group may be taxed as one group by giving an irrevocable option for taxation as one fiscal unit. The relief is not available for losses prior to formation of the group. The group is available if the companies are designated as entitled to avail group relief by the Securities and Exchange Commission of Pakistan.

Any company that is the subsidiary of a holding company may surrender its loss for the year to its holding company or its subsidiary, or between another subsidiary of the holding company, provided that the holding company holds directly 55% or more capital of the subsidiary, if one of the companies is a listed company. However, if none of the companies is a listed company, the holding requirement is 75% or more. The loss can be surrendered for a maximum of three years, and the required holding is for at least five years.

Transfer pricing
The tax authorities have the power in respect of a transaction between associates to distribute, apportion, or allocate income, deductions, or tax credits between such associates to reflect the income that would have been realised in an arm's-length transaction.

Thin capitalisation
Where a foreign-controlled resident company (other than a financial institution or a banking company) or a branch of a foreign company operating in Pakistan has a foreign debt to foreign equity ratio in excess of 3:1 at any time during a year, a deduction shall be disallowed for the profit on debt (interest) paid by the company in that year on that part of the debt which exceeds the 3:1 ratio.

Pakistan

Tax credits and incentives

Any relief from Pakistani income tax that is provided in any other law and not provided for in the Income Tax Ordinance or a treaty is not valid.

Tax exemptions
Profits and gains derived from an electric power generation project set up in Pakistan are exempt from tax.

Profits and gains derived by a company from the export of computer software, information technology (IT) services, or IT enabled services are exempt from tax through 30 June 2016.

Small companies
Activities of small companies are encouraged with a reduced income tax rate of 25%.

A small company has been defined to mean a company that:

*   is registered on or after 1 July 2005 under the Companies Ordinance, 1984
*   has a paid up capital plus undistributed reserves not exceeding PKR 25 million (0.278 million United States dollars [USD])
*   has an annual turnover not exceeding PKR 250 million (USD 2.778 million), and
*   is not formed by splitting up or the reconstitution of business already in existence.

Charitable donations credit
Companies are allowed a tax credit equivalent to 20% of their taxable income in respect of donations to:

*   any board of education or university in Pakistan, established by or under federal or provincial law
*   any educational institution, hospital, or relief fund established or run in Pakistan by federal government, provincial government or local government, and
*   any non-profit organisation.

Foreign tax credit
Where a resident taxpayer derives foreign source income on which foreign income tax is paid within two years from the year in which it is derived, the taxpayer is allowed tax credit equal to the lower of (i) the foreign income tax paid or (ii) the Pakistan tax payable in respect of that income. However, foreign tax paid is not refundable.

Withholding taxes

WHT on payments of royalty and FTS, when royalty or FTS is not attributable to a PE in Pakistan, is 15% or a lower treaty rate, of royalty or gross fees. The tax withheld would be deemed to be the final tax liability of the non-resident. In the case of a non-resident where royalty or FTS is attributable to a PE in Pakistan, the amount of royalty/FTS shall be chargeable to tax as normal income, and withholding on payments can be avoided subject to approval of the commissioner. If a reduced rate is available in a tax treaty, such rate would be applicable.

Resident corporations making certain types of payments must withhold tax as follows:

Recipient (1, 2, 3)	Dividends (%)	Interest (%)	Royalties (%)
Resident individuals	10	10	N/A
Resident corporations	10	10	0
Non-resident individuals:			
Non-treaty	10 (10)	10	15
Treaty	10 (10)	(4)	(4)
Non-resident corporations:			
Non-treaty	10	(5)	15
Treaty:	(6)	(7)	
Austria	10/15 (11)	15	10
Azerbaijan	10	10	10
Bahrain	10	10	10
Bangladesh	10/15 (11)	15	15
Belarus	10/15 (11)	10	15
Belgium	10 (12)/15	15	15/20 (13)
Bosnia and Herzegovina	10	20	15
Canada	10/15 (12)/20 (11)	25	15/20 (13)
China	10	10	12.5
Denmark	10/15 (11)	15	12
Egypt	10/15 (14)/30 (11)	15	15
Finland	12/15 (14)/20 (11)	10 (15)/15	10
France	10/15 (11)	10	10
Germany	10/15 (11)	10 (15)/20	10
Hungary	10/15/20 (11)	15	15
Indonesia	10/15 (11)	15	15
Iran	5	10	10
Ireland, Republic of	10	(8)	(9)
Italy	15/25 (11)	30	30
Japan	5/7.5/10 (11)	10	10
Jordan	10	10	10
Kazakhstan	10/12.5/15 (11)	12.5	15
Korea, Republic of	10/12.5 (11)	12.5	10
Kuwait	10	0/10	10
Lebanon	10	10	7.5
Libya	(8)	(8)	(8)
Malaysia	10/15 (12)/20 (11)	15	15
Malta	10/15 (11)	10	10
Mauritius	10	10	12.5
Morocco	10	10	10
Netherlands	10/20 (11)	10 (15)/15/20 (11)	5/15
Nigeria	10/12.5/15 (11)	15	15
Norway	10/15 (11)	10	12
Oman	10/12.5 (11)	10	12.5
Philippines	10/15/25 (11)	15	15 (16)/25
Poland	15	(8)	15/20 (13)
Portugal	10/15 (11)	10	10
Qatar	5/10 (11)	10	10

Pakistan

Recipient (1, 2, 3)	Dividends (%)	Interest (%)	Royalties (%)
Romania	10	10	12.5
Saudi Arabia	5 (17)/10	10	10
Singapore	10 (12)/12.5 (14)/15	12.5	10
South Africa	10/15 (11)	10	10
Sri Lanka	10/15 (11)	10	20
Sweden	10/15 (11)	15	10
Switzerland	10/20 (11)	10	10
Syria	10	10	10/15/18
Tajikistan	5/10 (11)	10	10
Thailand	10/15/25 (11)	10 (15)/25	10/20
Tunisia	10	13	10
Turkey	10/15 (11)	10	10
Turkmenistan	10	10	10
United Arab Emirates	10/15 (11)	10	12
United Kingdom	10/15 (14)/20 (11)	15	12.5
United States	8.75	(8)	(9)
Uzbekistan	10	10	15
Vietnam	10/15 (11)	15	15
Yemen	10	10	10

Notes

1. This table is a summary only and does not reproduce all the provisions that may be relevant in determining the application of WHT in each tax treaty.
2. Resident and non-resident imply tax status.
3. Individuals and companies are required to render annual returns of income and pay tax at the applicable rates. Credit is given for WHT deducted.
4. WHT rates for interest and royalties given to non-resident corporations (treaty countries) also apply to non-resident individuals.
5. The general WHT rate for non-residents is 20%.
6. The following remarks for dividends should be noted:
    - The inter-corporate rate of tax on dividends received by a foreign corporation is 10%; corresponding treaty WHT rates in excess of 10% have been specified.
    - The rates given in the table for treaty countries relate to recipient corporations. The maximum rate, as stated above, in respect of inter-corporate dividends is 10%. The lower rates are expressly provided in respect of dividends paid to a parent/associated corporation that has a certain minimum holding in a Pakistan industrial undertaking. The level of holding are noted:
        - Japan: 25% and 50%
        - United States: 50%
7. Certain treaties provide for tax exemption of interest paid to the government or the central bank of the contracting state and on foreign loans specifically approved by the federal government.
8. No concession is provided under the treaty.
9. Royalties are exempt from tax, provided the recipient does not have a PE in Pakistan.
10. Inter-corporate dividend where companies are entitled to group relief is exempt.
11. WHT rate depends on percentage of holding in the company.
12. This rate applies if the paying company is engage in the industrial undertaking.
13. Consideration for technical know-how or information concerning industrial, commercial, or scientific experience.
14. This rate applies if the beneficial owner is a company.
15. This rate applies if the beneficial owner is a bank.
16. This rate applies if the paying company operates in preferred areas.
17. This rate applies if the company is owned by the government.

Tax administration

Taxable period
The tax year is 1 July through 30 June. However, tax authorities are empowered to approve a special year end.

Tax returns
All companies are required to file an income tax return each year by 31 December for the preceding financial year (1 July through 30 June) by accounting for business income on an accrual basis. If the special year granted by the tax authorities ends on 31 December, then the tax return is required to be filed by 30 September following the year-end.

An across-the-board self-assessment scheme is in place whereby assessment is taken to be finalised upon filing of the return. The Commissioner, however, has powers to amend the assessment if it is believed that the ordinance has been incorrectly applied or there is definite information that the assessment made is incorrect. These powers are to be exercised within a prescribed time frame. In the case of transactions between associates, the Commissioner can substitute the transaction value with the fair market consideration. The Commissioner is also empowered to determine tax liability according to the substance of the transaction, disregarding formal arrangements between the parties.

Payment of tax
Companies are required to pay advance tax on the basis of tax liability of the immediately preceding tax year in respect of their income (excluding capital gains and presumptive income). The advance tax is to be paid after adjusting the taxes withheld at source (other than the tax withheld relating to final tax regime).

Advance tax is required to be paid in four quarterly instalments on or before 25 September, 25 December, 25 March, and 15 June in each financial year. Credit for tax paid in a tax year shall be allowed against tax liability of that year.

The total tax liability is to be discharged at the time of filing the return of income.

Advance taxes and taxes withheld are adjustable against the tax payable with the return of income.

Statute of limitations
An audit of the tax return filed by a taxpayer can be conducted by the tax authorities within five years of the end of the financial year in which the return is filed.

Advance rulings
A non-resident not operating in Pakistan through a PE can apply to the Federal Board of Revenue to issue an advance ruling setting out the Board's position regarding application of the provisions of the Income Tax Ordinance to a transaction proposed or entered into by the taxpayer. The tax ruling, once issued, is binding on tax authorities.

Topics of focus of tax authorities
Tax authorities focus on the following issues:

- WHT.
- Transfer pricing.
- Relationship of expenditure with the business of the taxpayer.

Pakistan

- Advance tax.
- Payment of tax dues within the time prescribed.
- Audit of returns filed.
- Compliance by taxpayers.
- Collection of arrears.

Other issues

Special rules are applicable for computation of income from exploration and production of petroleum, mineral deposits, insurance business, and banking business.

Panama

PwC contact

Ramon Ortega
PricewaterhouseCoopers
Scotiabank Building
3rd floor
Santo Domingo
Dominican Republic
Tel: +1 809 567 7741
Email: ramon.ortega@do.pwc.com

Significant developments

Significant changes have been made on tax matters during fiscal year 2011 and 2012.

During fiscal year 2011, one of the most significant tax developments was the implementation of fiscal devices (printers and cashiers) to make sure that every transaction in the Republic of Panama is dully documented and that all taxes, withholdings, and deductions resulting from a commercial transaction are clearly printed on the invoice. These devices have to be authorised by the tax authorities for their use inside the territory of Panama. All commercial establishments had to purchase their fiscal device before 1 March 2012.

As a result of this purchase, the tax authorities will recognise a fiscal credit of 50% of the total value of the device, up to 700 United States dollars (USD). This fiscal credit recognition will be available one year after the date of purchase of the device and can be used on any tax except for value-added tax (VAT, known as ITBMS).

Another important change in tax law for 2011 was the implementation of the monthly advanced tax payment (AMIR), which replaced the yearly estimated tax payment for juridical persons. This new advanced tax calculation consists of the payment of 1% of the taxable income generated by the business in a monthly scale, which will constitute a fiscal credit to ensure the tax payment to the tax authorities.

As of May 2012, Panama has in force nine double taxation treaties (DTTs) to avoid double taxation: with Barbados, France, Luxembourg, Korea, Mexico, the Netherlands, Qatar, Singapore, and Spain. A treaty to exchange information with the United States (US) has also entered into force this year. There are two treaties to avoid double taxation that have been ratified by the National Deputies Assembly, with Portugal and Italy.

As of April 2011, loans to shareholders are deemed dividend distributions subject to a 10% withholding tax (WHT).

Taxes on corporate income

Panamanian income tax is levied based on the territoriality principle. Panamanian-source income is subject to taxation whether it is received by a resident or non-resident entity. Residency is only relevant to determine if the entity is subject to WHT or not.

As of 1 January 2011, corporations are subject to income tax at a fixed rate of 25%. Certain businesses and the related parties that render services to them were subject

Panama

to a 30% tax rate through 31 December 2011. As of 1 January 2012, this tax rate was reduced to 27.5%; and on 1 January 2014, it will be reduced even further to 25%.

The higher tax rate (i.e. the 27.5% rate) applies to either the generation or distribution of energy, telecommunication services in general, insurance, reinsurance, financial institutions regulated by Law No. 42 of 2001, cement industries, the operation and management of gambling games, mining in general, and entities dedicated to banking activities in Panama.

For companies in which the state owns more than 40% of the stock, the tax rate will remain at 30%.

The tax base (i.e. amount to which the tax rate will apply) for companies whose taxable income is greater than 1.5 million US dollars (USD) is the greater of:

- net taxable income calculated on the normal basis or
- 4.67% of the gross taxable income (excluding exempted and non-taxable income and foreign-source income); this is called the alternate calculation of income tax (*Calculo Alternativo del Impuesto sobre la Renta* or CAIR).

If the entity's tax year results in a loss due to the alternative calculation, the taxpayer may request to the Tax Administration (the General Directorate of Revenues, i.e. *Dirección General de Ingresos* or DGI) not to be subject to the CAIR.

The taxpayer may also request not to apply the CAIR if its effective income tax rate is higher than the applicable income tax rate (25% since January 2011). Here is an example of such an instance:

Net taxable income		USD
a	Total revenues	2,000.00
b	Deductible costs and expenses	1,950.00
c	Net taxable income	50.00

CAIR		USD
d	Presumptive net taxable income (4.67% x a)	93.40
e	Income tax (25% x d)	23.35

CAIR effective tax rate		
f	Presumptive income tax (e)	USD 23.35
g	Net taxable income (c)	USD 50.00
h	Effective tax rate (f/g)	46.70%

The DGI has a six-month period within which to reach a decision on such requests; otherwise, the petition will be considered as granted.

Corporate residence

A company is considered as a tax resident when it has been incorporated in Panama, regardless of where the main office is located or whether central management is exercised in Panama or abroad. Entities incorporated abroad may also be registered with the Tax Administration in order to avoid WHT.

Permanent establishment (PE)

Panama does not have formal PE rules. Under tax treaties signed, Organisation for Economic Co-operation and Development (OECD) rules will be applicable once treaties are in force.

Other taxes

Movable goods and services transfer tax (ITBMS)

The movable goods and services transfer tax (*Impuesto de Transferencia de Bienes Muebles y Prestación de Servicios* or ITBMS) is the Panamanian VAT.

The general tax rate is currently 7%.

Alcoholic beverages and hotel accommodation are taxed at 10%, and tobacco and tobacco-derived products are taxed at 15%.

ITBMS is calculated on the value-added through a method of tax credits (i.e. ITBMS paid on transactions to produce taxable transactions) and tax debits (i.e. ITBMS collected on transactions).

Exports are not taxed, and the ITBMS paid to generate the exports may be refunded. The sale of goods such as medicines, foods, and certain products for babies are not taxed and may allow the supplier to recover the ITBMS as an exporter if certain criteria is met.

Medical services and transportation among other services are not taxed but do not produce ITBMS credit for the supplier.

In April 2011, with Law 31, a new transferring of goods was excepted from the payment of ITBMS, this being the purchase of cement, additives, and derivates of such made by the contractors or subcontractors of the Panama Canal Authority for the construction of the third set of locks of the Panama Canal.

The statute of limitations is five years.

Customs duties

All goods introduced into the Panamanian territory from another country are subject to customs duties. The duty rates are provided by the Panamanian Customs and Tariffs Office.

Customs duties may only be assessed by authorised customs brokers.

Excise tax (selective consumption tax)

The selective consumption tax is applied to goods (e.g. jewellery, expensive automobiles, guns, tobacco, alcoholic beverages) and services (e.g. mobile, cable TV, satellite TV) that are considered as non-essential. The tax base is the cost, insurance, and freight (CIF) price plus import duties for imported items and sales price for all other activities. The tax is levied at only one stage: on the importation of the taxed products; the sale of taxed goods produced in Panama; and for services, when the service is invoiced, the service is completely rendered, or upon receipt of advance payments, whichever first occurs.

Panama

Different tax rates apply depending on the type of service or good, with a minimum of 5% on sodas and 100% on tobacco products.

Stamp duty

Stamp duty is charged at a rate of USD 0.10 per USD 100 (or fraction thereof) only on certain commercial contracts.

Capital gains tax

The transfer of real estate property and securities is subject to WHT on the gross transactions amount, but the taxpayer may make a special income tax assessment to pay the capital gain and may request a rebate of the difference between the WHT and the capital gain.

In the case of the transfer of real estate property, a 2% real estate transfer tax plus a 3% income tax advance payment must be remitted (done over the gross transaction amount or the cadastral value, whichever is greater). The 3% may be deemed definitive; contrariwise, the tax will be assessed at 10% of the gain and the 3% of the advance payment will be credited. Any amount in excess may be subject to rebate.

The rates as described in the table below will be applicable to the transfer of real estate if:

- the transferor´s core business is the sale of real estate with new constructions
- it is the first transfer of the real estate after the new construction is built, and
- the construction permit was issued after 1 January 2010.

New housing construction	Rate (%)
Up to USD 35,000	0.5
From USD 35,000 up to USD 80,000	1.5
Greater than USD 80,000	2.5
New commercial construction	4.5

When transferring new housing real estate, the real estate transfer tax (2%) does not apply.

If the first criterion is met but any of the other criteria needed to apply for the special tax rate table are not met, then the income tax will have to be assessed under the ordinary regime.

The transfer of securities is subject to a 5% WHT, and the tax rate on capital gain is 10%. The law establishes the application of a 5% WHT that will be applied by the buyer. The seller may accept the WHT as definitive or perform the calculation of the gain, apply the rate of 10%, and deduce the applied WHT. In case the WHT is superior, the taxpayer can choose to claim the return of payments made in excess.

Panama

Example:

Sales price (a)	1,000
Cost (b)	900
Benefit (c)	100
WHT at 5% of (a)	50
Tax at 10% of (c)	10
Payment in excess	40

The sale of fixed assets is subject to 10% on the capital gain, and there is no WHT.

Franchise tax

Franchise income tax must be paid by all corporations on an annual basis (USD 300 per year). The deadline for payment depends on the date of incorporation of the company. If the company was incorporated on any date during the first six months of the year, the due date for payment will be on 15 July of each year. If it was incorporated in the last six months, the due date will be 15 January of each year.

Non-profit organisations, cooperatives, and civil partnerships are not subject to franchise tax.

Operations notice tax

The notice of operations is an annual tax on equity at a rate of 2%, with a minimum tax amount of USD 100 and a maximum tax amount of USD 60,000. In the case of free zones or special trade areas, the tax will be calculated at a rate of 1% up to a maximum tax amount of USD 50,000.

The tax base is the outcome from total assets less total liabilities (excluding liabilities with related parties abroad).

Local municipal tax

Local municipal tax is charged based on the gross income generated by the business through the corresponding accounting period; it also depends on the type of activity being conducted by the corporation. In most cases, it cannot exceed USD 2,000 per month for each activity performed.

According to Municipal Agreement No. 40 of 2011, the monthly tax return was replaced by an Annual Municipal Tax Return for the District of Panama. This return must be filed before the Municipal Authorities in the first 90 calendar days after the ending of the fiscal year. In case the taxpayer does not file the return before the deadline, a USD 500 penalty will be applicable.

Branch income

For tax purposes, branches are considered separate entities from the head office and must therefore keep accounts separately and will have separate tax liability.

Branches located within the Panamanian territory must pay dividend tax through definitive WHT of 10% of net taxable income generated by the Panamanian branch, less all income taxes paid by the same corporation in Panama. This amount will be paid jointly on filing the corresponding income tax return.

Panama

....

Income determination

Under the territoriality principle, the following will not be considered as taxable income:

- All income produced outside Panama.
- All income generated from operations or services performed outside the Panamanian territory.

Inventory valuation

Inventory should be valued at the start of any business and, subsequently, at least once every accounting period. All assets must be put together, depending on their nature, and indicate different aspects (e.g. the unit of measurement, the name of the asset, the price of the unit, the total value of units). Reference to the accounting records should also be included.

Inventories are generally stated at cost and can be valued using the compound average cost method, first in first out (FIFO) method, retailer method, or specific identification method. Since all entities must keep legal records, any adjustment resulting from using different methods of inventory valuation for tax purposes and financial purposes should be recorded and must be reported to the proper authorities. Once a taxpayer adopts a method, they must maintain it for at least five years.

Capital gains

See Capital gains tax in the Other taxes section for a description of how capital gains are taxed in Panama.

Dividend income

Panamanian legislation establishes that distribution of dividends is subject to definitive WHT, applied at the moment of distribution. Generally, dividends are subject to income tax at a rate of 10% without taking into consideration the form of payment, types of stock, assets, or money.

Dividend tax applies at a 5% rate on dividends paid from foreign source income, from income derived from exports, as well as exempt income from banking account interests and interests and earnings derived from securities issued by the government.

Free zone users are taxed at a 5% rate as well for local source income.

Loans to shareholders are deemed as dividend distribution, subject to a 10% withholding even in the cases where the 5% tax rate applies.

Notwithstanding the aforementioned, if the entity's shares are issued to bearer, they will be subject to dividend tax at a rate of 20%.

Dividend tax is levied if the entity meets one of the following criteria: (i) requires an operation permit to operate in Panama, (ii) requires an operation key to operate at the Colon Free Zone; (iii) is established in a Fuel Free Zone; (iv) is established in a free zone or special zone; (v) produces Panamanian-source taxable income. Dividend tax also does not apply to dividends paid on income received as a dividend if the entity is not required to withhold dividend tax or if the entity withheld the tax.

A complementary tax applies each tax year that the entity distributes less than 40% of the net profits after income tax. The complementary tax is an advance payment of the dividend tax, calculated on the difference of the distributed dividends and 40% of the net profits after income tax and applies the corresponding tax rate. If complementary tax is paid, then the entity may offset the paid complementary tax with the dividend tax when the corresponding dividend is decreed.

Inter-company dividends
The distribution of dividends derived from income received as dividends from other entities is not subject to income tax or dividend tax as long as the entity that paid the dividend in the first instance was exempt from withholding any dividend tax, or if it was required to, made the corresponding withholding.

Foreign income
Panamanian resident companies are taxed on their income generated within the Panamanian territory. Any other income generated abroad will be exempt from income tax payment but may be subject to dividend tax (*see above*).

Deductions

Taxable income is determined by deducting from the Panamanian source income all costs, expenses, and non-taxable income applicable and permitted by law. The deductibility of costs and expenses depend on the relation of such costs and expenses with the generation or preservation of income source. Special restrictions apply to the following:

* Depreciation.
* Bad debt.
* Charitable contributions.

Costs and expenses related to non-taxable income are not considered as deductible. Thus, the taxpayer must split the expenses and costs related to taxable transactions from those related to non-taxable transactions. As of 1 July 2010, the expenses and costs allocated to taxed transactions may not exceed the amount from multiplying the portion of taxable income from the total income by the total costs and expenses.

Example:	Taxable	Non-taxable	Total
Income	100	50	150
	67%	34%	100%
Costs and expenses	83.75	41.25	125

The following deductions are subject to the deductions cap:

* Deductions on bad debts.
* Donations to the state, non-profit organisations, and education institutions (limited to 1% of the taxable income).

Depreciation and depletion
The straight-line and sum-of-the-years-digits methods of depreciation are allowed, as well as any other method.

Panama

Assets	Straight-line (%)
Buildings	3⅓ as maximum
Machinery and equipment	33 as maximum
Furniture and fixtures	33 as maximum
Vehicles	33 as maximum

In the case of mines, depletion will be deductible during the useful life or depending on the state contract methodology.

Goodwill
Goodwill expenses are deductible only when the transferring agent declares them as income.

Start-up expenses
Start-up expenses are deductible through the amortisation process, over a maximum term of five years.

Interest expenses
Interest expenses are deductible only in cases where the interest relates to the generation or conservation of taxable income from a Panamanian source. No thin capitalisation rules are in force.

Bad debt
A taxpayer may deduct bad debts by opting for one of the following options:

- Loading gains and losses annually to the value of such accounts in the fiscal year.
- Charging an annual profit and loss figure for the establishment of a reserve to meet contingencies of this nature.

Charitable contributions
Donations made in cash or in kind to the government, charitable or educational institutions, activities to promote HIV disease, or made for political parties are deductible, with certain restrictions.

Fines and penalties
Fines and penalties are not deductible.

Taxes
The national and municipal taxes that affect capital, sales, and other operations related to taxable income producing activity are deductible.

Net operating losses
Losses incurred by common taxpayers may be carried forward and deducted from the taxable profits for the following five years, at a rate of 20% each year, but limited to 50% of taxable income. Loss carrybacks are not allowed, and losses are not allowed for estimated income tax purposes.

Payments to foreign affiliates
A payment to a foreign entity (including affiliates) in a foreign country will be subject to WHT anytime it represents a deductible cost or expense for the payer. The tax base will be 50% of the remittance, and the income tax rate applicable is 25% as of 1 January 2011.

Group taxation

In Panama, there are no group taxation rules.

Transfer pricing

Transfer pricing rules are applicable only if a tax treaty to avoid double taxation is in use.

Thin capitalisation

There are currently no thin capitalisation rules in Panama.

Tax credits and incentives

Free zones

Entities established in free zones may enjoy exemption from import duties on goods, income tax, sales tax, export tax, and selective consumption tax derived from royalties on exportation and re-exportation activities. Aside from trading activities, the following businesses may also apply for the regime: higher education centres, scientific research centres, specialised centres for health services, high technology businesses, ensembling businesses, semi processed or finished products processing businesses, services businesses, environmental service businesses, general services, logistics services businesses, and manufacturing businesses.

Tourism, industry, and agriculture allowances

The Incentive Law for Tourism Development grants several tax benefits (e.g. exemption from import duties on certain tourism services and related goods, exemption from property tax for companies dedicated to tourism), but only for those corporations with a signed tourism agreement with the government. Income tax exemptions may apply in special cases.

In general, income from individuals or corporations that engage in agricultural production activities will be exempted from income tax if annual gross income is lower than USD 250,000.

Forestry plantations are totally exempted from income tax payment until 2018 if the lot planted has been duly registered at the Forestry Registry of the Environmental National Authority and resolution with approval from this authority has been issued.

Special laws

The Panamanian government has enacted special laws regarding tax exemptions for certain activities performed in Panama, such as call centres (Law No. 54 of 2001), and tax exemptions for certain appointed areas such as the Panama Pacific Economic Zone (Law No. 41 of 2004) and Law No. 41 of 2007, which creates a special regime for the establishment and operation of Regional Headquarters in Panama.

By means of Law No. 8 of 2010, Real Estate Investment Societies may deduct the profits distributed to their shareholders, provided that these Real Estate Investment Societies:

- raise long-term funds in a securities market
- are registered in the National Securities Commission
- distribute no less than 90% of their free cash flow
- register in the General Direction of Revenues, and

P

Panama

- withhold 20% of the profits distributed as an income tax advance payment on behalf of the shareholder, which may be deemed the definitive tax to be paid by the shareholder.

Withholding taxes

Royalties and commissions on services paid to foreign entities are taxed through the application of the corresponding tax rate (25% as of 1 January 2011) over 50% of remittance under the concept of WHT (effective tax rate is 12.5%). The taxpayer may decide not to withhold taxes and consequently not deduct the expense.

Payment of interest is also subject to income tax on 50% of the interest paid to a beneficiary abroad on loans invested in Panama, but the payer must proceed with the WHT even if one does not deduct the interest.

If the beneficiary is registered as a taxpayer in Panama before the Tax Administration, no WHT may be required.

Recipient	Dividends (%)	Interest (%)	Royalties (%)
Foreign corporations	5/10/20	12.5	12.5

In case of treaties, special rules are applicable in order to avoid double taxation.

Recipient	WHT (%)			
	Dividends	Interest	Royalties	Fees
Barbados	5/7.5	0/5/7.5	7.5	0/7.5
Korea	5/15	0/5	3/10	0
Luxembourg	5/15	0/5	5	5
Mexico	5/7.5	0/5/10	10	0/12.5
The Netherlands	0/15	0/5	5	0
Portugal	10/15	0/10	10	0/10
Qatar	6	0/6	6	0
Singapore	4/5	0/5	0/5	0
Spain	0/5/10	0/5	5	7.5

Tax administration

Taxable period

The accounting period is the period for which the company makes its accounts. Returns shall be made upon completion of the accounting period and may not exceed 12 months. For most companies, it is usually from 1 January to 31 December.

Tax returns

The due date for filing is three months after the end of the fiscal year, with the possibility for an extension of up to two additional months.

Payment of tax

Income tax payment shall be made depending on the income tax return and shall be made no longer than three months after closing of the corresponding accounting period.

Taxpayers must make income tax advance payments based on 1% of monthly gross income. The taxpayer will have to file monthly income tax returns assessing the advance payment within the next 15 days following the end of the month. VAT on purchases may be offset against this advance payment if the taxpayer is a seller in the local market of pharmaceutical products or food and meets certain criteria.

Statute of limitations

The Tax Administration may audit the income tax returns filed within the last three years from the last day of the year on which the tax return was filed.

P

Papua New Guinea

PwC contact

David Caradus
PricewaterhouseCoopers
Credit House
Cuthbertson Street
Port Moresby, NCD 121
Papua New Guinea
Tel: +675 321 1500
Email: david.caradus@pg.pwc.com

Significant developments

There were a number of amendments to existing tax law announced when the 2012 National Budget was handed down on 6 December 2011. The majority of these changes are effective as of 1 January 2012. In summary, the key taxation developments announced in the 2012 National Budget included:

- The general corporate income tax (CIT) rates remains at 30% for resident companies and at 48% for non-resident company.
- To support the 2015 Pacific Games being hosted by Papua New Guinea (PNG), income tax exemptions for athletes or participants were introduced as was a 150% income tax deduction for donations in excess of 500,000 Papua New Guinea kina (PGK) made to prescribed bodies in connection with the games.
- The current exemption from income tax for certain new manufactured products will be abolished from 1 January 2015.
- Income tax and stamp duty amendments have been made to encourage the use of property unit trusts.
- The period of application for the Banking Community Service Obligation tax credit scheme has been extended to 31 December 2017 to encourage the continued establishment of banking service in rural areas.
- The Highlands Highway tax credit scheme was re-introduced with limited application to emergency repair expenditure. Also of interest to resource projects are the new special deduction provisions dealing with the treatment of rehabilitation costs, including a mechanism to transfer tax losses arising from site rehabilitation costs to another resource project in which that taxpayer has an interest.
- The goods and services tax (GST) registration threshold increased from PGK 100,000 to PGK 250,000.

It continues to be reported that Papua New Guinea has negotiated double taxation treaties (DTTs) with Indonesia, Thailand, and New Zealand. Those DTTs have not yet been ratified in Papua New Guinea.

The Internal Revenue Commission (IRC) released guidance on transfer pricing matters in the form of Taxation Circular No. 2011/2 in late 2011.

The Internal Revenue Commission also released new tax return forms in March 2012 that are required to be used by all taxpayers for all tax returns from that time forward (including returns outstanding from prior years). These include additional disclosures pertaining to tax losses and transactions with international related parties.

Taxes on corporate income

Papua New Guinea resident companies are liable for income tax on their worldwide income. Companies that are not resident in Papua New Guinea are only required to remit tax on income sourced in Papua New Guinea. A non-resident's PNG-sourced passive income, including dividends, interest, and royalties, is generally only subject to withholding tax (WHT). It is ordinarily the case that the payer of the dividend, interest, or royalty must withhold the relevant amount of the tax and remit this to PNG's IRC.

Papua New Guinea levies CIT on companies on a flat rate basis. The operations of a company, rather than the company's taxable income level, will dictate the rate applied to the company's taxable income.

Generally, trading profits and other income (except income which is specifically exempt) of resident companies in Papua New Guinea are assessed tax at a rate of 30%, whereas non-resident companies operating in Papua New Guinea are assessed tax at a rate of 48%. There are, however, different tax rates for income derived from mining, petroleum, and gas operations.

Specifically, trading profits and other income from operations in Papua New Guinea are liable for CIT at the following rates:

Source of income	CIT rate (%)
Income other than income from mining, petroleum, or gas operations:	
Resident company	30
Non-resident company	48
Income from petroleum operations: *	
Existing projects	50
New projects	45
Incentive rate projects	30
Income from mining operations:	
Resident company	30
Non-resident company	40
Income from gas operations *	30

* The same rates of CIT apply to income from the petroleum operations listed above or gas operations derived by a resident or non-resident company.

Overseas shippers
Income derived by overseas shippers or charterers carrying passengers, livestock, mail, or goods out of Papua New Guinea is taxable in Papua New Guinea. The tax is calculated on a deemed taxable income equal to 5% of the gross income, which is taxable at the non-resident rate of 48% in the case of companies. The IRC may exempt the overseas shipper from tax if the shipper's home country exempts PNG shippers from a similar tax.

Local income taxes
There are no local income taxes in Papua New Guinea.

Papua New Guinea

Corporate residence

A company will be deemed a resident for CIT purposes if it meets either the (i) incorporation test or (ii) the management and control test.

Incorporation test
A company incorporated in Papua New Guinea is automatically regarded as a PNG tax resident. However, the operation of the law of another country and a relevant DTT may result in a company also being treated as resident in another country.

Management and control test
A company is a PNG tax resident if it is managed and controlled in Papua New Guinea, regardless of where it is incorporated. Generally, a company is managed and controlled in Papua New Guinea if key decisions affecting the company are made at directors' meetings held in Papua New Guinea. This also includes a company incorporated outside Papua New Guinea that trades in Papua New Guinea and has its voting power controlled by resident shareholders.

Dual residence
An entity may be a tax resident of both Papua New Guinea and another country by application of domestic legislation. A DTT entered into between Papua New Guinea and another country may contain a tiebreaker test to determine the country of residence for the purposes of the DTT.

Permanent establishment (PE)
The concept of 'permanent establishment' has limited significance in the domestic taxation law of Papua New Guinea and is defined to mean a place at or through which a person carries on any business. Under domestic taxation law, Papua New Guinea will seek to tax the PNG-sourced income of a non-resident irrespective of whether or not that income is derived at or through a PE in Papua New Guinea.

Where PNG has entered into a DTT, the concept of PE becomes more important as it will then be one of the factors determining Papua New Guinea's taxing rights over income sourced in Papua New Guinea, particularly with respect to the business profits of a non-resident company. In general terms, Papua New Guinea's DTTs:

- define a PE to be a fixed place at or through which the business of an enterprise is wholly or partly carried on, and
- deem a PE to exist in various circumstances, including those relating to the presence of substantial equipment in the contracting state and the time spent by personnel of an enterprise furnishing services in a contracting state.

Other taxes

Goods and services tax (GST)
The GST rate is 10% and applies to most goods and services supplied in Papua New Guinea. Exported goods and services attract a zero rate of GST. Goods and services, other than motor cars, supplied to mining, petroleum, or gas companies are also zero-rated. Some goods and services are exempt, including medical, educational, and financial services. Land is excluded from GST, but buildings and other improvements are subject to the tax.

Customs duties

The majority of manufacturing inputs (including plant and machinery) attract no custom duties, and other custom duty rates are being progressively reduced. The remaining rates for custom duties vary depending on the nature of the good being imported and are assessed on the total value of the goods imported, including cost, insurance, and freight (CIF). Customs bonds may be issued for the temporary importation of goods that are to be re-exported within 12 months.

Excise taxes

Although customs duties are now minimal in many cases, some goods, most notably motor vehicles, now attract excise tax. Private motor vehicles generally attract excise at the rate of 60%, whereas work vehicles attract excise tax of 10%. Excise taxes can also apply to some domestically produced goods, including refined fuel products, alcohol, and tobacco.

Land tax

Land tax is imposed by provincial governments on the unimproved value of the land, and the power to levy land tax is vested exclusively with the provincial governments. In Papua New Guinea, land tax is difficult to implement and faces major geographical and social problems.

Stamp duties

Stamp duty applies at varying rates on documents and certain transactions. Of particular note is duty charged on the conveyance of property, which rises to a maximum of 5% where the value of the property being transferred exceeds PGK 100,000. The duty is payable by the purchaser, and a 5% duty on the unencumbered value of land may also be payable where there is a transfer of shares in certain landholding companies.

Other dutiable transactions include share transfers (including some share buy-backs) which are subject to a rate of 1%. The Collector of Stamp Duties has the power to amend assessments and refund overpayments of stamp duty.

Stamp duty is payable on documents executed outside Papua New Guinea which relate to property or matters done or to be done in Papua New Guinea.

Export duties

Timber

Export duty on timber logs (not sawn timber or plantation logs) is calculated with reference to the FOB value per cubic meter of exported logs and rates that increase as the value of the exported logs increase.

Spices

Levies are imposed from time to time on the export of specified spices (e.g. vanilla).

Contributions to employee superannuation funds

Contributions to employee superannuation funds are compulsory for entities with 15 or more permanent employees. The employer's compulsory contribution is 8.4% of each employee's gross basic salary. The employee's minimum contribution is 6.0%.

Membership is generally compulsory for citizens. Non-citizens are currently exempt; however, this is under continuing review.

P

Papua New Guinea

Contributions must be paid to an authorised superannuation fund. Contributions paid to an authorised fund are tax-deductible to the extent that they do not exceed 15% of the relevant employee's gross taxable salary. Contributions to non-resident funds are not tax-deductible.

Training levy

All businesses whose annual payroll exceeds PGK 200,000 are subject to a 2% training levy, calculated on the sum of the taxable salaries, including benefits, of all personnel. Qualifying expenses incurred in training PNG citizen employees are creditable up to the actual amount of the levy. The training levy, if payable, is not tax-deductible.

Departure tax

A departure tax is collected by airlines issuing tickets for persons departing Papua New Guinea.

Gaming machine tax

Papua New Guinea imposes a 74% tax on gross revenue from gaming machines.

Resource project production levies

Production royalties of 2% are payable to the national government on the net smelter return from mining operations. These royalties are tax-deductible. A royalty, at the rate of 2% of the wellhead value, is also payable from the production of petroleum and gas operations. Holders of new petroleum development licences are entitled to treat royalties as income tax paid. However, new petroleum projects will also pay a tax-deductible development levy calculated at the same rate of 2% of the wellhead value.

Mining projects are also required to pay a production levy to the Mineral Resources Authority calculated at a rate between 0.25% and 0.5% of the assessable income from production.

Branch income

Income derived by a non-resident contractor for services in Papua New Guinea is usually subject to a WHT at the rate of 12% of gross income. This amount is calculated on deemed taxable income of 25% of the gross contract income, which is taxed at the foreign contractor tax rate of 48% (subject to tax treaties). The provisions extend to payments for the following:

- The installation, maintenance, and use in Papua New Guinea of substantial equipment or machinery.
- Construction projects.
- For the lease or charter of any industrial, commercial, or scientific equipment or any machinery or vehicle.
- Consultancy or management services.

Where the non-resident contractor rules do not apply, the non-resident company will be subject to income tax at the foreign contractor tax rate of 48% on its PNG sourced taxable income (*see the Income determination section for a definition of taxable income*).

PNG branch remittances are not liable for dividends WHT or any branch profits or similar tax.

Income determination

Taxable income is defined as the sum of assessable income minus the allowable deductions. In practice, profits are calculated for tax purposes by reference to the profits reported in the financial accounts. Accounts must be prepared in accordance with PNG accounting principles, which follow the International Financial Reporting Standards (IFRS).

Inventory valuation

There is no form of stock relief or trading stock valuation adjustment to recognise the effects of inflation in Papua New Guinea. There is a once-only option to adopt the lowest of the cost amount, the market selling value, or the replacement value (which, in practice, may mean that book and tax valuations for trading stock are not aligned). Where the option is not exercised, the value of the stock is deemed to be the cost price; however, neither the income tax law nor the associated regulations provide detailed guidance on what constitutes 'cost price' (the Commissioner General of Internal Revenue has not produced any related guidance to date). It will generally be the case that where a taxpayer has determined a cost price in accordance with IFRS than that cost price will also be accepted for income tax purposes.

In special circumstances, the Commissioner General of Internal Revenue may accept a lower valuation.

Capital gains

There is no general capital gains tax in Papua New Guinea. However, profits arising on the sale of property acquired for the purpose of resale at a profit, or from the carrying out of a profit-making scheme, are taxable as ordinary income.

Dividend income

Unless otherwise exempt from CIT, dividends are included in the assessable income of a shareholder.

Inter-company dividends

Dividends received by a resident company from other companies, whether resident or non-resident, while being assessable to tax, are generally subject to a full tax rebate and are effectively received tax-free. However, where a company has losses on other activities or losses carried over from earlier years, those losses are applied against dividend income before the calculation of the dividend rebate.

Stock dividends

In most cases, the payment of a dividend by way of the issue of shares is subject to the same taxation treatment as the payment of a dividend by way of cash or the distribution of other property. However, dividends paid by the issues of shares wholly and exclusively out of profits arising from the sale or revaluation of assets not acquired for the purpose of resale at a profit are exempt from income tax and dividends WHT.

Interest income

Unless exempt under specific provisions, interest paid or credited by a financial institution, the Central Bank, or a company to a person resident in Papua New Guinea, is includable in income, and the person making the payment of or crediting interest in the account is liable to withhold and pay tax upon the amount.

Papua New Guinea

Partnership income

A partner's share of the assessable income of the partnership less all allowable deductions to the partnership is includable in the partner's assessable income for the year of income. Likewise, the partner's individual interest in a partnership loss incurred in the year of income is an allowable deduction. Further, if income is exempt income to the partnership, this income will be exempt income to the individual partner relative to their individual interest.

Unrealised exchange gains/losses

Generally, foreign exchange gains realised and derived from debts made on or after 11 November 1986 or denominated in a currency other than the Papua New Guinea kina are included in assessable income.

Foreign income

PNG resident companies are liable for CIT on their income from all sources (i.e. including foreign sourced income). A foreign tax credit may be available to offset foreign tax paid against PNG tax payable (*see the Tax credits and incentives section for more information*).

There are no provisions in Papua New Guinea that permit the deferral of the taxation of income derived outside Papua New Guinea. Subject to the operation of a DTT, foreign-sourced income derived by a resident of Papua New Guinea is subject to tax in Papua New Guinea in the year in which it is derived irrespective of whether or not that income is repatriated to Papua New Guinea.

Deductions

General deduction provisions provide that all losses and expenditures, to the extent incurred in gaining or producing the assessable income or are necessarily incurred in carrying on a business for the purpose of gaining or producing that income, are allowable deductions. However, the general deduction provisions do not allow a deduction to the extent a loss or expenditure is an outgoing of capital, or of a capital, private, or domestic nature, or incurred in relation to the gaining or production of exempt income.

Depreciation

Depreciation is allowed for equipment and other assets at prescribed rates. A taxpayer must use the diminishing-value method unless an election is made to use the prime-cost method. The applicable diminishing-value rates are 150% of the prime-cost rates.

Plant, machinery, and equipment

Plant, machinery, and equipment (including buildings) are depreciable at rates according to their estimated lives. A taxpayer other than a taxpayer who derives income from mining, petroleum, or gas operations may elect to claim special accelerated depreciation rates for certain capital items. For example, flexible depreciation rates (up to 100%) may be claimed on new industrial plant with a life exceeding five years that is used for manufacturing purposes. Other new plant and articles used in manufacturing, construction, transport, storage, communication, and agricultural production are eligible for an accelerated deduction equal to 20% of cost in the year of purchase. New plant and articles used for tourism are eligible for an accelerated deduction equal to 55% of cost in the year of purchase.

Motor vehicles
Motor vehicles are generally depreciable at 20% of prime cost. There is no upper limit in value for depreciation purposes.

Buildings
Buildings forming an integral part of plant, machinery, and equipment are depreciable at a prime-cost rate of up to 7.5% depending on the construction materials. Buildings housing plants eligible for the one-year write-off deduction (*see comments on new industrial plant under Plant, machinery, and equipment above*) can be written off in the year of construction. Other income producing buildings may qualify for the accelerated deduction of 20% in the year of purchase.

Agricultural and fishing plants
Most items of new agricultural and commercial fishing plants qualify for 100% depreciation as do boats and ships, including ancillary equipment, used solely as dive boats or for scuba diving by accredited tour operators. Other new items having a life exceeding five years used by a person carrying on agricultural operations are eligible for accelerated depreciation in the initial year of use.

Goodwill
A deduction is not available for goodwill or the amortisation of goodwill in Papua New Guinea (this being an amount not deductible under ordinary concepts and an item for which there is no specific deduction provision).

Start-up expenses
It will generally be the case that start-up expenses will not be deductible in Papua New Guinea. Such expenses are generally either capital, or of a capital nature, or incurred prior to the derivation of assessable income. There is no specific deduction provision for the deductibility of start-up expenses.

Interest expenses
A deduction is generally available for interest incurred on an arm's-length basis, subject to meeting the general principles for deductibility. Where interest is incurred in connection with the construction or acquisition of an item of plant or capital asset, that interest is not immediately deductible. Rather, such interest is deemed to form part of the cost of that asset (and in the case of plant will then form part of the base from which future depreciation deductions may be claimed).

Where the interest is incurred in connection with a resource project, a 3:1 debt-to-equity ratio (with the concepts of debt and equity being based on IFRS and all debt being considered) must be maintained in respect of that resource project by the taxpayer seeking to deduct that interest in order for a full deduction to be available. Those thin capitalisation provisions have specific application to taxpayers engaged in resource operations only, and Papua New Guinea does not have thin capitalisation provisions for other taxpayers.

Bad debt
Bad debts are deductible if they have previously been included in assessable income and written off by year end or if the bad debt was in respect of money lent in the ordinary course of the taxpayer's business of money lending.

Papua New Guinea

Double deductions

An additional amount equal to the actual amount of expenditure incurred is deductible in respect of certain expenditures (e.g. export market development costs, some staff training costs, and certain donations). In other words, a 'double deduction' is available with respect to these items.

Donations

It is considered that donations made by a corporate taxpayer meet the general principles for deductibility and hence will generally be deductible (notwithstanding the specific provision dealing with gifts to charitable bodies has no current effect as there are no charitable bodies approved by the Commissioner General of Internal Revenue for this purpose).There are specific provisions in Papua New Guinea's taxation law dealing with the deductibility of certain donations, some of which provide a deduction for up to 200% of the value of the amount donated.

Pension expenses

Contributions paid to an authorised superannuation fund are tax-deductible to the extent that they do not exceed 15% of the relevant employee's gross taxable salary. Contributions to non-resident funds are not tax-deductible. *See the Other taxes section for more information.*

Fines and penalties

There are no specific provisions denying a deduction for fines or penalties in Papua New Guinea taxation law; however, arguably fines and penalties may not meet the general principles for deductibility, and their deductibility needs to be considered on a case-by-case basis.

Taxes

A deduction is not allowable in respect of payments of income tax or training levy. Other taxes may be deductible, subject to meeting the general principles for deductibility.

Net operating losses

Domestic

Trading losses may be offset against all income received in the same accounting period or carried forward and offset against future trading profits. The limitation period on the carryforward of losses is generally 20 years. Losses may not be carried back against prior years' profits. Primary production losses and resource project losses may be carried forward without a time limitation, although, again, they may not be carried back (*see the Tax credits and incentives section for more information*).

Note that the carryforward of losses is subject to a 50% or more continuity of shareholding and control test, or a continuity of business test where there is a breach of the ownership test.

Foreign

Losses incurred by a resident taxpayer from a source outside Papua New Guinea (other than in relation to export market development) are not deductible against assessable income derived within Papua New Guinea. In practice, overseas losses can be carried forward and offset against overseas income for up to 20 years.

Payments to foreign affiliates

The deduction available to a taxpayer for management fees paid to an associated person is limited to the greater of:

- 2% of assessable income derived from PNG sources by the taxpayer or
- 2% of the total allowable deductions, excluding management fees incurred by the taxpayer in Papua New Guinea.

The limitation applies to both resident and non-resident taxpayers. Special rules apply to mining, petroleum, and gas companies. These limits may not apply where the recipient of the management fee is resident in a country with which Papua New Guinea has a DTT or where it can be demonstrated that the management fee arrangements do not have the purposes or effect of avoiding or altering the income tax payable in Papua New Guinea.

Group taxation

Companies are assessed for CIT separately, regardless of whether they are part of a group of associated or related companies. Losses of one company within a group cannot be offset for tax purposes against the profits of another company within that group.

The Companies Act allows two or more companies to amalgamate and continue as one, and provisions are in place to allow this to occur without any adverse CIT consequences.

Transfer pricing
Papua New Guinea has transfer pricing provisions that require transactions with foreign affiliates to be conducted on an arm's-length basis.

Thin capitalisation
See Interest expenses in the Deductions section for a description of thin capitalisation rules in Papua New Guinea.

Tax credits and incentives

In this section, we comment on the more significant tax credits and incentives available in Papua New Guinea, followed by a summary of those with more limited application.

Foreign tax credit
A foreign tax credit may be available to offset foreign tax paid against PNG tax payable. The foreign tax credit is limited to either the foreign tax paid or the average PNG tax payable on that foreign income, whichever is less. There is no mechanism to carry forward excess foreign tax credits for utilisation in subsequent year.

Research & development (R&D) deduction
A 150% deduction is available for expenditures on R&D. The deduction is available to all sectors of the economy. Broadly, R&D expenditures are defined as systematic, investigative, and experimental activities that involve innovation or a high degree of technical risk carried out for the purpose of acquiring new knowledge, or creating new or improved materials, products, devices, processes, or services.

Primary production incentives
Key incentives that are available with specific application to primary production activities include:

Papua New Guinea

- Outright deductions for certain capital expenditures, including clearing, preparing, or conserving land for agriculture; eradicating pests; providing labourers' accommodation; and for the conservation and conveyance of water.
- A 100% deduction is available for a new plant used directly for the purposes of agricultural production, and an initial 20% accelerated depreciation deduction is allowed for a new plant with a life exceeding five years.
- Losses incurred in carrying on a primary production business can be carried forward indefinitely; they are not restricted to the 20-year limit that generally applies to company tax losses.
- Agricultural companies may transfer to their shareholders the benefit of the outright tax deduction available for many types of capital expenditures. The total deduction available to shareholders may not exceed the amounts paid on their shares.
- As part of promoting investment in primary production, a 20% tax rate is prescribed in respect of 'incentive rate primary production income' derived by a company (as opposed to the normal 30% tax rate for a resident company or 48% for a non-resident company) for up to 10 years.

Agricultural production extension services deduction
A 150% deduction is available for expenditures on services provided free of charge to smallholder growers, including the provision of advice, training, and technical assistance in relation to primary production to assist growers with production, processing, packaging, and marketing issues.

Incentive rate for large scale tourist accommodation facilities
A 20% tax rate applies to income derived by a taxpayer from the operation of a large scale tourist accommodation facility or a substantially improved large scale tourist accommodation facility. The rate applies for 14 years after the end of the year of income in which the taxpayer first derives income from the facility.

Double deduction for staff training costs
Certain staff training costs, including the cost of full-time training officers and tourism training, are eligible for a double deduction. The total tax saving is limited to 75% of the expenditure incurred.

Double deduction for export market development costs
Expenditures incurred in the promotion for sale outside Papua New Guinea of goods manufactured in Papua New Guinea or tourism promotion is eligible for double deduction. The total tax saving cannot exceed 75% of the expenditures incurred.

Export incentives
The net export income from the export sale of certain types of goods is exempt for the first four years of income, with a partial exemption in the following three years. This exemption will cease to apply from 1 January 2015 (except in respect of goods which qualified for the exemption prior to that date).

Tax credit for infrastructure development by agricultural, mining, petroleum, and gas companies
A tax credit is available to agricultural, mining, petroleum, gas, and certain tourism companies that incur expenditures on a prescribed infrastructure development. In the case of taxpayers engaged in mining, petroleum, and gas operations, the credit is limited to 0.75% of the assessable income or the amount of tax payable for the year (in respect of that mining, petroleum, or gas project), whichever is less. Excess expenditures over the 0.75% or tax payable may be included in the following year's rebate claim.

Unutilised credits or excess expenditures can generally only be carried forward for two years. In the case of taxpayers engaged in agricultural production, the credit is limited to 1.5% of the assessable income or the amount of tax payable for the year, whichever is less.

A prescribed infrastructure development includes a school, aid post, hospital road, and other capital assets that have been approved as such by the Department of National Planning and the IRC. It cannot be an expenditure required under the Mining Act or the Oil and Gas Act.

A 1.25% tax credit scheme also exists in respect of expenditure incurred in connection with the emergency repair of the Highlands Highway.

Other tax incentives in Papua New Guinea

Other tax incentives available in Papua New Guinea include:

- Manufacturers' wage subsidy.
- Immediate deduction for the costs of acquiring and installing solar heating plant.
- A ten year tax exemption for qualifying new business located in prescribed remote areas of Papua New Guinea.
- A specific deduction for environmental protection and clean-up costs.

Incentives for petroleum, mining, and gas operations

Special incentives and rules apply to mining, petroleum, and gas exploration, extraction, and production activities. The main aspects are as follows:

Project basis of assessment

A project basis of assessment (ring-fencing) is adopted for all resource projects. This means losses from other operations, regardless of whether or not they are resource related cannot generally be offset against resource project income from a particular ring-fenced project. However, there are some concessions to the ring-fencing principle in respect of exploration expenditures and expenditures in respect of discontinued projects and losses arising from site restoration costs.

In general, all costs incurred in the exploration and development phases of the project are accumulated and amortised over the life of the project. Once production starts, an immediate deduction is allowed for 'normal' operating and administration expenses. Capital expenditures incurred after the start of production are capitalised and amortised over the life of the project.

Rate of tax

The rates of tax in respect of income from a resource project are:

	CIT rate (%)	
Source of income	Non-resident companies	Resident companies
Mining	30	40
Petroleum:		
Existing projects	50	50
New projects	45	45
Incentive rate	30	30
Gas	30	30

Papua New Guinea

Interest deductions

Interest is not deductible prior to the commencement of a resource project. Following the issue of a resource development licence, a person carrying on a resource project or exploration in relation to a resource project may claim a deduction against resource income for interest on money borrowed for carrying on the relevant operations or exploration. This is subject to a number of conditions, including maintaining a debt-to-equity ratio of 3:1.

Capital allowances

Allowable exploration expenditures (AEE) are amortised over the life of the resource project. The deduction is calculated by dividing the unamortised balance by either the remaining life of the project or four, whichever is less. The amount of the deduction is limited to the amount of income remaining after deducting all other deductions, other than deductions for allowable capital expenditure. In other words, the deduction cannot create a tax loss.

Allowable capital expenditures (ACE) are amortised over the life of the resource project. The ACE is split into two categories: capital expenditures with an estimated effective life of more than ten years (long-life ACE) and capital expenditures with an estimated effective life of less than ten years (short-life ACE).

The annual deduction for long-life ACE is claimed on a straight-line basis over ten years.

Where the remaining life of the project is less than ten years, the rate at which the deduction is allowed is calculated by referring to the remaining life of the project. For short-life ACE, the annual deduction is calculated by dividing the unamortised balance by either the remaining life of the project or four, whichever is less. For new mining projects, the deductions for both long-life ACE and short-life ACE are calculated by dividing the unamortised balance by either the remaining life of the project or four, whichever is less.

The amount of the deduction for ACE is limited to the amount of income remaining after deducting all other deductions. In other words, the deduction cannot create a tax loss.

Off licence exploration expenditure

A major easing of the ring-fencing principle applies to taxpayers, which are involved in a producing project, where the taxpayer or a related party incurs exploration expenditures outside the area of the productive project. In this situation, the taxpayer can elect (whether or not it is currently involved in a producing project) to add such exploration expenditures to an exploration pool that can be amortised against income from the producing project.

The amount allowable as a deduction from this exploration pool in respect of resource operations carried on by the taxpayer or a related corporation is the lesser of:

- 25% of the total undeducted balance of expenditures in the exploration pool or
- such amount as reduces CIT (other than additional profits tax [see below]) which would, but for this deduction, be payable by the taxpayer and its related corporations in respect of those resource operations for that year of income, by 10% (or 25% for mining projects).

Management fees

Once a resource project derives assessable income, the deduction for management fees is restricted to 2% of operating expenses other than management fees. During the exploration phase of a project, the amount of management fees which can be treated as allowable exploration expenditure is limited to 2% of the exploration expenditure other than management fees. Furthermore, during the development phase, the amount of management fees that can be treated as allowable capital expenditure is limited to 2% of the allowable capital expenditure other than management fees.

Transfer of expenditures

When interests are transferred from one taxpayer to another, the vendor and purchaser can agree to transfer deduction entitlements for the unamortised balances of allowable exploration expenditure and allowable capital expenditure to the purchaser.

Liquefied natural gas (LNG) project

A number of provisions with specific application to the PNG LNG project have been included in the Income Tax Act, Stamp Duties Act, Goods and Services Tax Act, Customs Act, and Excise Act.

Other provisions were added or amended at the same time as the PNG LNG project-specific provisions, the most notable being the re-introduction of additional profits tax for all designated gas projects.

Additional profits tax

Designated gas projects are potentially subject to additional profits tax (this tax does not currently have application to mining or petroleum projects). This is essentially a tax on positive cash flows arising from a gas project in excess of a hurdle rate of return. There are two calculations required and, in summary, they operate as follows:

- Under Calculation X, once the cash flows become positive, after exceeding a 17.5% accumulation rate, the positive cash flow is subject to tax at a 7.5% rate.
- Under Calculation Y, once the cash flows become positive, after exceeding a 20.0% accumulation rate and any additional profits tax paid under Calculation X, the positive cash flow is subject to tax at a 10.0% rate.

P

Withholding taxes

Interest, dividend, royalties, and technical/management fees

The following WHT rates apply to interest, dividends, royalties, and technical fees under PNG domestic law and tax treaties. PNG domestic legislation provides an exemption from WHT for interest and dividends in certain circumstances. The higher rates quoted are the maximum rates allowable under the treaties.

Recipient	WHT rate (%)			
	Dividends (1)	Interest (2)	Royalties	Technical fees
Resident	17	15	0	0
Non-resident corporations and individuals	17	15	10/30 (3)	17
Treaty				
Australia	17	10	10	0
Canada	17	10	10	0

Papua New Guinea

	WHT rate (%)			
Recipient	Dividends (1)	Interest (2)	Royalties	Technical fees
China	15	10	10	0
Fiji	17	10	15	15
Germany (4)	15	10	10	10
Korea, Republic of	15	10	10	0
Malaysia	15	15	10	10
Singapore	15	10	10	0
United Kingdom	17	10	10	10

Notes

1. The rate of WHT on dividends paid by mining companies is 10%. Dividends paid to a resident or a non-resident out of income from petroleum or gas operations are exempt from income tax and are not subject to WHT. There are also some other specific exemptions from WHT on dividends.
2. There is no WHT on interest when:
   - interest is paid or credited to a licensed financial institution in Papua New Guinea, the Bank of Papua New Guinea, or the state
   - interest is paid or credited by a resource company to a non-resident lender, or
   - the interest income is otherwise exempt income in the hands of the recipient.
3. A royalty paid to a non-resident associate of the payee will suffer a 30% WHT. Where the non-resident is not an associate of the payee, the WHT rate will be 10% (or 48% of the taxable income derived from the royalty if the non-resident chooses to lodge an income tax return in Papua New Guinea).
4. The treaty with Germany has not yet been ratified by Germany.

Business income withholding tax

Income derived by local contractors in certain industries is covered by the business income WHT regime. The industries affected include:

- Building and construction
- Road transport
- Motor vehicle repairs
- Joinery and cabinet making
- Architecture
- Engineering
- Surveying
- Security
- Cleaning and maintenance
- Advertising
- Entertainment
- Consultancy
- Equipment hire

Businesses affected are required to have a certificate of compliance and to produce it when entering into contracts with their customers. Payers are required to file an annual income reporting statement where they make either an eligible payment of PGK 500 or more in relation to one contract or eligible payments for several contracts exceeding PGK 3,000 in the year of income in relation to a single payee. Payers are required to deduct a 10% WHT if payees do not produce a certificate of compliance.

Non-resident insurer withholding tax

Premiums paid to non-resident insurers in respect of insurance contracts on property situated in Papua New Guinea or insured events that can only occur in Papua New Guinea are subject to tax in Papua New Guinea. The tax is calculated on a deemed taxable income equal to 10% of the gross premium, which is taxed at the non-resident tax rates of 48% (companies) or 30% (unincorporated associations). Tax treaties may limit the rate of tax applied.

Tax administration

Taxable period

The tax year is generally the period 1 January to 31 December; however, application may be made for a substituted tax year-end. These will normally be granted where the substituted tax year-end coincides with the accounting year-end of an overseas holding company. A company's tax year does not need to be the same as its accounting period.

Tax returns

Papua New Guinea operates on a full assessment basis, and companies are required to lodge an annual CIT return showing the calculation of taxable income for the year. In addition, the return must provide detailed disclosures in relation to income derived and expenses incurred during the year of income.

A company must file a tax return by 28 February in the year following the year of income to which the return relates. However, the following automatic extensions apply where the company lodges its return through a registered tax agent:

- To 30 June for taxable returns and partnership returns.
- To 31 August for resource company returns.
- To 31 October for non-taxable returns.

Payment of tax

CIT is collected under a provisional tax system. Under this system, tax is paid in respect of a company's current year profits (i.e. payments made in the year of income are in respect of income derived in the same year as the payment is due).

Provisional tax is assessed by the IRC based on the last return lodged. In the event that no tax was payable on the previous year's return, the Commissioner General has the right to estimate the amount of tax based on any other information available.

Provisional tax is payable in three equal instalments by 30 April, 31 July, and 31 October.

Applications may be made to reduce provisional tax assessed if the tax due for the year in question is expected to be lower than the provisional tax assessed. Where estimated provisional tax is less than 75% of the income tax ultimately assessed, additional tax may be levied. Additional tax at a rate of 20% will be assessed, based on the difference between the estimate lodged and the provisional tax originally determined, or the actual tax payable, whichever is less. The Commissioner General has the discretion to require payment of additional tax.

Mining, petroleum, and gas companies are subject to advance payments tax, a system that broadly mirrors the provisional tax system in place for non-resource companies. The main difference for resource companies is they have the option to lodge an estimate of their taxable income for the year prior to 30 April, 31 July, and 31 October each year, which the IRC uses to assess each advance payments tax instalment.

Following the lodgement of the CIT return, the IRC will serve a notice of assessment on the company. The balance of tax payable for a year of income, after the application of

P

Papua New Guinea

provisional tax (or advance payments tax in the case of a resource company) and other tax credits or rebates, is due to be paid within 30 days of the date of service of the notice of assessment.

Audit cycle

There is no prescribed audit cycle in Papua New Guinea, and resource constraints have limited the IRC's audit activities.

Period for amendment of assessments

Where the IRC considers that a taxpayer made a full and true disclosure of all the material facts necessary for assessing their returns as originally assessed, the IRC may only amend an assessment that increases the tax liability of the taxpayer within three years from the date from the date that tax became due and payable under the original assessment.

Where the IRC considers that a taxpayer did not make a full and true disclosure of all the material facts necessary for the assessment of their returns, and there has been an avoidance of tax, then:

- the IRC may amend any assessments previously issued to the participants if the IRC is of the opinion that the avoidance of tax was due to fraud or evasion (i.e. no time limit applies), or
- in cases of tax avoidance due to reasons other than fraud or evasion, the IRC may amend an assessment within six years from the date from the date that tax became due and payable under the original assessment.

Topics of focus for the Internal Revenue Commission (IRC)

The IRC released guidance on transfer pricing matters in the form of Taxation Circular No. 2011/2 in late 2011. The IRC has indicated to tax agents that over time it will increase its focus on transfer pricing matters.

The IRC has not otherwise publicly announced areas of focus for tax compliance or audit programs.

Paraguay

PwC contact

Edgar Rubén Taboada
PricewaterhouseCoopers
General Díaz 521, 6th. floor
Edificio Internacional Faro
Asunción
Paraguay
Tel: +595 21 418 8000
Email: ruben.taboada@py.pwc.com

Significant developments

There have been no significant corporate tax developments in Paraguay during the past year.

Taxes on corporate income

Income is taxed in Paraguay according to the resource principle (i.e. the territorial system of taxation).

There are three tax systems in Paraguay, depending on the type of taxpayer, as follows:

- For income from commercial, industrial, and service activities, the general income tax rate of 10% applies. *See Capital gains and Dividend income in the Income determination section for a description of how such income is taxed.* Note that dividend distributions require an additional 5% tax that must be paid on the amount of dividend approved for distribution at the shareholder meeting.
- For income from agricultural and cattle activities, the rate ranges from 2.5% to 10% (determined by annual income).
- For those taxpayers with annual income of less than 100 million Paraguayan guaraníes (PYG), a single tax at a rate of 10% applies.

P

Corporate residence

Corporate legal residence is determined as the place where direction or central management takes place, unless the corporation's charter states otherwise.

Permanent establishment (PE)
The Paraguayan Tax Law establishes the definition of a PE.

The following activities may be considered as a PE in the country:

- Branches or agencies.
- A factory, industrial plant, or cattle ranch entity.
- Mine activities, or any other natural resources extraction activities.
- Civil construction or assemble activities that exceed 12 months.

If a person makes instructions related to the agreement of certain operations on behalf of a foreign entity, this operation may be considered as a PE in the country; except in cases where the mentioned instructions are related to goods purchasing.

Paraguay

Other taxes

Value-added tax (VAT)

VAT applies to all corporations and to individuals or associations of individuals rendering personal services.

The general VAT rate is 10%, but a special VAT rate of 5% applies for selling real estate, basic groceries, farming products, pharmaceutical products, and loan interest.

Custom taxes

As the products will be introduced into Paraguay directly by the local importer, the importer will be responsible for payment of the related taxes (VAT on imports) before clearing the goods from Paraguayan customs, apart from customs tariffs. The other expenses involved in the import of products are the following:

- Port rates (between 0.65% and 1.50% of customs valuation).
- Customs valuation service (0.5% of customs valuation).
- Consular fee (15 United States dollars [USD] for each commercial document receiving a visa from the Paraguayan consulate at the originating country and USD 30 for each document not subject to visa).
- Indian contribution fee (7% on consular fee).
- IT system utilisation fee (between USD 15 and USD 25 according to importation value).

Other expenses should be added to the above, such as photocopying, handling fees, customs agent fees, etc.

Excise taxes

The excise tax, called the selective tax on consumption, is assessed on local goods and imported products listed, either specifically or generically, in the legislation. The importation of goods listed and the first sale of goods produced in Paraguay are taxed. The selective tax on consumption is collected independently of custom duty.

Real estate tax

Real estate tax is levied annually at 1% of the fiscal value of the property, which is generally less than actual value. A tax rate of 0.5% applies if the area of rural property is smaller than five hectares and is used for agricultural or cattle ranching. In certain areas, an additional tax is levied on the fiscal value of vacant and semi-vacant land when the area of the built-up portion falls within certain determined percentage limits. Large tracts of land in rural areas are subject to an additional tax determined on a percentage basis and to a proportional tax of 0.5% to 1% on the fiscal value of tracts with areas ranging from 10,000 to 60,000 or more hectares.

The 1992 Paraguayan Constitution established that municipalities and departments are entitled to the tax revenues directly related to real estate. Collection of these taxes is the responsibility of municipal governments.

Stamp taxes

There are no taxes on acts and documents in Paraguay.

Paraguay

Branch income

Branches are taxed at the same rate as domestic corporations. Profits transferred or credited to the head office are subject to a 15% withholding tax (WHT) when remitted to the head office abroad.

Additionally, the payment of dividends (by the head office's instructions) is subject to a 5% WHT to be paid at the time of the remittance and charged to the local entity.

Income determination

Inventory valuation
Taxpayers may adopt any method of inventory valuation, provided it is technically acceptable according to Tax Administration criteria (e.g. first in first out [FIFO], average cost). The valuation must be applied consistently and may be changed only with the prior approval of the Treasury Ministry.

Damaged, deteriorated, and obsolete inventories may be written down to fixed values by the taxpayer. The tax administration can reject valuations that are not realistic.

Capital gains
Gains on all assets, tangible and intangible, are taxable as part of profits and subject to income tax at a rate of 10%.

Dividend income
Dividends are taxable income when the recipient (or shareholder) is a non-resident, in which case a 15% WHT applies. An additional 5% tax is charged to local entities when the income or dividend is distributed to a local or foreign (non-resident) shareholder.

Stock dividends
Stock dividends are not taxable income, except when dividends represent more than 30% of the taxable income of an investor. In the case when dividends represent more than 30% of an investor's taxable income, a tax rate of 15% and an additional tax rate of 5% apply.

Interest income
The income from interest for capital abroad of a Paraguayan resident is considering subject to income tax. This case is the only exception to the resource principle rules enacted under Paraguay Tax Law.

Foreign income
Foreign-source income is not taxable. Interest, commissions, and capital gains are considered Paraguayan-source income when the investor is resident in Paraguay.

Deductions

Depreciation and depletion
The maximum allowable depreciation rates range from 2.5% for urban buildings to 25% for computer equipment. Depreciation is calculated by the straight-line method based on the useful life of assets, as determined by the Treasurer. The Treasurer may also authorise the use of other depreciation or depletion methods that are deemed to be technically justified and generally accepted.

Paraguay

Fixed assets must be revalued annually based on the increase of the price index. Capital gains derived from the revaluation of fixed assets are not taxable income.

Goodwill
Amortisation of goodwill is not deductible.

Start-up expenses
Amortisation of start-up expenses may occur over three to five years, depending on the taxpayer's decision.

Interest expenses
The interest expenses on loans taken for Paraguayan residents or Paraguayan taxpayers may be considered as deductible expenses.

Additionally, it is important to mention that certain investment projects may be subject to a special exemption of the taxes on the interest, commission, and other expenses for loans taken for banking entities abroad (*see Investment incentives in the Tax credits and incentives section*).

Extraordinary losses/bad debts
The deduction of extraordinary losses and bad debts require the meeting of certain conditions (e.g. communication to Tax Authority, evaluation of the actual loss in monetary terms, audit review).

Charitable contributions
The deduction of a donation is subject to a formal registration of the beneficiary entity as a public benefactor before the Treasury Ministry.

Executive remuneration
The deduction of executive remuneration is limited to a percentage defined according to the enterprise's profits.

Fines and penalties
Fines and penalties are considered as non-deductible expenses for income tax purposes.

Taxes
In general, all taxes mentioned in the *Other taxes section* are deductible. Income tax and any fiscal surcharges or fines are not deductible.

Other significant items
General provisions for expenses or other potential losses are not deductible.

Other specific non-deductible items include:

- Interest on capital, loans, or any other investment by an owner, partner, or shareholder in a business.
- Personal expenses of an owner, partner, or shareholder.
- Money drawn on account of future earnings.
- Direct expenses incurred in earning non-taxable income.
- Earnings from any fiscal period that are retained in the business as capital increases or reserve accounts.

Paraguay

Net operating losses
Net operating losses are not permitted to be carried forward and applied against future years. However, Congress is considering amending the law to permit carrying forward of losses for three years.

Losses may not be carried back in Paraguay. However, a taxpayer may modify one's tax returns at a later date.

Payments to foreign affiliates
There are no limits on the deductibility of payments to foreign affiliates, including management fees, research and development (R&D), and general and administrative expenses, provided that the taxpayer maintains corresponding legal documentation that includes the country of origin and applies appropriate WHT. *See the Withholding taxes section for the applicable WHT rates.*

Group taxation

Group taxation is not permitted in Paraguay.

Transfer pricing
A significant fact is that there are no transfer pricing rules in current Paraguayan legislation requiring compliance with certain conditions or minimum prices for the purpose of fiscal deductions, etc., except for the following regulation applicable to importations and exportations:

"In the case of importers, it will be assumed that, in the absence of proof to the contrary, the cost of goods introduced to the country may not exceed the wholesalers price ruling in their place of origin plus freight and insurance costs and expenses to Paraguayan territory, and therefore, the excess of such value will constitute taxable income for the importers.

In the case of exporters, where a price has been fixed or the price declared is lower than the wholesalers price in Paraguay plus the freight and insurance costs and expenses to point of destination, this latter aggregate value shall be taken as the basis for determining the exporter's taxable income.

To this effect, the nature of the goods and the transaction mode adopted will be taken into account." (Section 16 of Law No. 2421/04).

Tax credits and incentives

Investment incentives
The framework of economic investment was established in the Law No. 60/90, which offers some special tax exemption benefits to foreign and local investors.

The benefits of the Law No. 60/90 may be available for the following investments:

* Cash, financing, provision of credit, or other financial instruments, under the conditions established by the administration of the President of Paraguay and the corresponding ministries.
* Capital goods, raw materials, and inputs for local industry for the fabrication of capital goods.
* Transfers of licensing rights with respect to trademarks, industrial processes and models, and other technologies.

Paraguay

- Technically specialised services.
- Capital leases.
- Other forms that the administration of the President of Paraguay and the corresponding ministries determined by law.

The investment incentives included in Law 60/90 that remain enacted after tax law modification (Law No. 2421/04) are the exemptions from certain fiscal, municipal, and customs duties taxes.

When the amount of financing for an investment is greater than USD 5 million, it will be exempt from WHTs on interest, commissions, and capital that have to be paid to financial or banking entities abroad. This benefit is for five years.

If the investment is at least USD 5 million and the project is approved for a term of at least ten years, the dividends and profits derived from the project are tax exempt. In this case, the taxes on those dividends and profits are not creditable in the country of origin.

Other incentives

Exports are exempt from certain customs duties and from VAT.

A Capital Market Law (No. 1284/98) established incentives for companies listed on the Asunción Stock Exchange.

In addition, Law 536/95 established incentives for forestry activities.

Withholding taxes

In accordance with the regulations in force, foreign entities may be subject to income tax withholdings in respect of services rendered to them deemed to be of Paraguayan source, including payments made by the branch of affiliate of a foreign home office.

Business income tax regulations consider that branches, agencies, or PEs of foreign entities are taxpayers, independently from the foreign home office status.

The withholdings are to be made from the payments made by local entities for such services.

WHT on payments made by a domestic corporation

	WHT (%)				
	Dividends (1)				
Recipient	Portfolio	Substantial holdings	Interest (2, 3)	Royalties (3, 4)	Fees (3, 5, 6)
Non-resident corporations	15	15	30	30	30
Non-resident individuals	10	10	30	10	10
Tax treaty with Chile					
Non-resident corporations	10	10	10/15 (7)		
Non-resident individuals	10	10			

Notes

1. Local entities are required to pay an additional 5% WHT when the income or dividend is distributed.
2. The WHT on interest is based on 100% of the amount paid when remitted to the head office abroad. In other cases, when the payment is not directly made to the head office or shareholders that have control

of the local subsidiary, the WHT is based on 50% of the amount paid. The tax rate is 30%. For financing loans, the WHT rate is 6%.

3. VAT is withheld on interest, royalties, and other services provided for non-resident corporations or individuals at a rate of 9.09%, except on fees for financing, which are withheld at a rate of 4.76%.
4. The WHT on royalties is based on 100% of the amount paid when remitted to the head office abroad. In other cases, when the payment is not directly made to the head office or shareholders that have control of the local subsidiary, the WHT is based on 50% of the amount paid. The tax rate is 30%.
5. The WHT on fees is based on 100% of the amount paid when remitted to the head office abroad. In other cases, it is based on 50% of the amount paid. The tax rate is 30%.
6. Fees for personal services rendered by non-resident corporations are subject to withholding income tax at a rate of 50% on the amount paid. The tax rate is 30% (effective tax rate of 15%).

   Fees for personal services rendered by non-resident individuals are subject to withholding of the personal income tax on 50% of the amount paid. The tax rate is 20% (effective tax rate of 10%). Congress is considering suspending this tax.
7. In case of a loan to Chile, the WHT on the interest is 15% if the loan is from a bank or insurance company. On the other hand, if the loan is from an associated company or head office, the tax rate is 10%. Regarding VAT WHT, see Note 3.

Tax administration

Taxable period
For the commercial income tax and the agriculture income tax, the taxable period is the calendar year.

Tax returns
Income tax returns are submitted on a fiscal-year basis as a self-assessment and must be filed by the fourth month following the end of the fiscal year.

Payment of tax
Income tax is due on varying days in the fourth month following the end of the fiscal year, depending on the taxpayer ID number, according to a calendar established by the treasury ministry. Four equal advance payments are made throughout the year, calculated based on 100% of the tax due in the previous year. Payments must be made in May, July, September, and November of each year after the due date for filing the income tax return, according to the calendar established by the tax authorities.

Penalties
Tax legislation provides the following penalties:

- Late payment of income tax is penalised by a fine varying from 4% to a maximum of 14%, plus interest at 0.116 per day.
- Tax fraud is punished by a charge of from one to three times the value of the tax in default.
- Tax law infringements are penalised through fines varying from the equivalent of USD 10 to USD 250.
- Omission of payment incurs a fine of 50% of the tax pending.

Audit cycle
The auditing process is performed by the tax authorities when there is a certainty or suspicion of tax evasion.

Additionally, the taxpayer may be audited according to a draw process that is made by the tax authority.

Statute of limitations
The tax authority may audit the last five fiscal years.

Peru

PwC contact

Miguel Mur
PricewaterhouseCoopers\Dongo-Soria, Gaveglio y Asociados Sociedad Civil
Av. Santo Toribio No. 143
Piso 8
Lima 27
Peru
Tel: +51 1 211 6500
Email: miguel.mur@pe.pwc.com

Significant developments

The following changes to the Peruvian tax legislation were incorporated during the past year.

Tax Obligatory Payment System (SPOT) amendment

On 28 March 2012, Superintendence Resolution N° 063-2012-SUNAT was published amending the list of services subject to the SPOT, which were included within Appendix 3 of the Superintendence Resolution N° 183-2004/SUNAT, which created the SPOT applicable to the sale of certain goods and the rendering of certain services subject to Peruvian VAT.

Per the amendments, the SPOT is extended to all services subject to VAT, unless expressly excluded, applying a withholding rate of 9%. This modification is effective as of 2 April 2012 and will be applied as long as the amount of the operation exceeds 700 Peruvian *nuevos soles* (PEN) (approximately 260 United States dollars [USD]).

Value-added tax (VAT) rate

As of 1 April 2011, the VAT rate is 18%.

Taxation of indirect disposal of shares in Peruvian entities

On 21 July 2011, Law N° 29757 was enacted, introducing amendments to Law N° 29663, which taxes the indirect disposal of shares of Peruvian entities and incorporates rules on issues that were not established in Law N° 29663. The main rules of this law are as follows:

De minimis indirect transfers of Peruvian shares

Law N° 29663 did not provide any thresholds, so even *de minimis* transfers of a foreign entity's shareholding (which in turn owned, directly or indirectly, shares of a Peruvian entity) triggered a taxable indirect transfer of Peruvian shares, provided certain conditions were met.

Under Law N° 29757, a taxable indirect transfer of Peruvian shares is deemed to occur when shares of a foreign entity, which in turn owns, directly or indirectly through other entities, shares of a Peruvian entity, are transferred and both of the following conditions are met:

- During the 12 months prior to the transfer, the fair market value (FMV) of the shares of the Peruvian entity owned by the foreign entity equals 50% or more of the FMV of the shares of the foreign entity.
- During any given 12-month period, shares representing 10% or more of the foreign entity's share capital are transferred.

If these two conditions are met, the taxpayer, when calculating the amount realised from the foreign entity's share transfer, should consider the transfers that occurred during the 12-month period mentioned in the second condition.

There will be a deemed indirect transfer whenever a foreign corporation who, directly or indirectly, owns shares of a local corporation issues new shares or stock through an increase in equity as a result of new capital contributions, credit capitalisation, or a reorganisation and places them under their market value.

Note that even when the provisions of Law N° 29757 are not clear in such connection, we consider that the condition related to the 10% of the foreign entity´s share capital is also applicable in the aforementioned scenario (i.e. when a foreign entity issues new shares as a consequence of a capital increase and such shares are issued below par value).

Calculation of gain from indirect share transfer

In connection with the calculation of gain arising from the indirect transfer of Peruvian shares, Law N° 29757 incorporates the following rules:

- The taxable income is determined by multiplying the FMV of the shares of the foreign entity that would be transferred by the proportion that the FMV of the Peruvian entity's shares bears to the FMV of the foreign entity's shares.
- The basis is determined by multiplying the basis of the foreign entity's shares being transferred by the proportion that the FMV of the Peruvian entity's shares bears to the FMV of the foreign entity's shares. This basis must be supported with documents issued in accordance with the laws of that foreign entity's jurisdiction or other documents listed by the Peruvian tax authorities (yet to be stipulated).

Note that the modifications to the Regulations to the Income Tax Law came in force through Supreme Decree N° 136-2011, since 10 July 2011, established that there is also no obligation to obtain a Certificate of Invested Capital in case of indirect transfer of Peruvian shares (which is a procedure that must be followed by foreign persons or entities to certify its tax cost of goods and/or shares prior to their disposal).

Basis of shares acquired prior to the effective date of Law N° 29663

For foreign entity shares acquired prior to the effective date of Law N° 29663, that is, 16 February 2011, Law N° 29757 provides that the basis is the greater of the FMV of these shares on 15 February 2011 or the basis itself. If the shares are traded in a centralised mechanism of negotiation (i.e. a stock exchange), then the FMV is deemed to be the closing price on 15 February 2011 or the last quote published. If they do not have a quote price or are not traded in a centralised mechanism of negotiation, then the FMV is determined based on the foreign entity's net equity based on a balance sheet audited by a firm with international prestige during the 12-month period prior to 15 February 2011.

Joint and several liability

Law N° 29663 provided that, in any event, the Peruvian entity whose shares are indirectly transferred has joint and several liability for the tax liability payment when, within any of the 12 months prior to the transfer, the foreign transferor qualified as a related party by reason of control, management, or equity.

However, Law N° 29757 narrows that joint and several liability because it includes a rule under which the Peruvian entity whose shares are transferred, directly or indirectly, would no longer be jointly and severally liable for the non-resident

P

Peru

transferor's capital gain tax liability, provided that the buyer is a Peruvian resident (since the buyer would have to withhold the corresponding capital gains tax).

Special taxation on mining industry

A new tax regime for the mining industry was recently introduced. The new mining royalty (NMR) regime, special mining tax (SMT), and special mining contribution (SMC) are economic considerations paid to the Peruvian government for the exploitation of mineral resources. The NMR applies to metallic and non-metallic mineral resources, while the SMT and SMC only apply to metallic mineral resources.

The SMC is only applicable to mining companies with projects with tax stability agreements in force. Such companies have voluntarily entered into agreements with the Peruvian government with the purpose of paying this contribution. This special contribution is determined for each stability agreement entered into.

In all three cases, the tax basis is the operating profit of the company and the special rates and considerations are explained below:

	New mining royalty (NMR)	Special mining tax (SMT)	Special mining contribution (SMC)
Concept	No tax stability	No tax stability	With tax stability
Regime	Previous mining royalty modified	New	New
Cumulative progressive scale based in operating margin	1% to 12%	2% to 8.4%	4% to 13.2%
Minimum payment	1% of the sales revenue	N/A	N/A

The amounts paid will be deductible for income tax purposes as long as they are actually paid during the fiscal year.

Taxes on corporate income

Companies incorporated in Peru are considered resident in Peru for tax purposes and thus subject to a corporate income tax rate of 30% on worldwide net income.

For purpose of determining taxable income, such entities are allowed to deduct expenses to the extent that they are necessary to generate or maintain the source of taxable income. Requirements, limitations and/or caps may apply to the deduction of certain expenses (thin capitalisation rules), bad debt provisions, salaries, travel expenses, gifts, donations, penalties, etc.

Peruvian Income Tax Law (PITL) allows crediting for various payments against income tax, including income taxes paid in advance, amounts paid for certain other taxes, and income taxes paid in foreign tax jurisdictions, provided that the foreign country's tax rate is not higher than the Peruvian corporate tax rate, and the taxable income qualifies as foreign-source income for Peruvian income tax purposes.

Dividends and any other type of profit distributions are taxed at a 4.1% rate, upon distribution, when the distribution is made to a non-resident entity (either individuals or legal entities) and, when the distribution is agreed to by the shareholders, if this happens first, to resident individuals (resident legal entities are not subject to 4.1%

withholding tax [WHT] over dividends received from other Peruvian corporations). The entity distributing dividends or profits is liable for WHT at a rate of 4.1%.

Nevertheless, enterprises are subject to an additional tax rate of 4.1% on every amount or payment in kind that, as result of a tax audit, is construed as taxable income to the extent that it is an indirect distribution of such income that escapes further control from the tax administration, including income that has not been declared.

On the other hand, companies incorporated abroad are considered as non-domiciled in Peru for tax purposes and thus subject, in most cases, to an income tax rate of 30% over the gross Peruvian-source income. As a general rule, foreign companies are not allowed to deduct expenses and are taxed on gross income.

Corporate residence

For income tax purposes, the following entities, among others, are considered as resident entities in Peru:

* Corporations duly incorporated in Peru.
* Branches, agencies, and permanent establishments (PE) in Peru of non-resident individuals or entities.
* Partnerships and limited liability companies.

Permanent establishment (PE)

According to PITL, a foreign company is considered to have a PE (i) if it has a fixed place of business through which it carries out business activities in whole or in part; (ii) if an individual has a power of attorney of a foreign entity and uses it on a regular base to sign agreements on behalf of the foreign entity; and (iii) if the person with powers of attorney of the foreign entity keeps in Peru inventory and/or goods to be negotiated in Peru on behalf of the foreign entity.

The consequence of a PE presence in Peru is that the PE would be obligated to comply with all the formal and substantial tax obligations of any domiciled taxpayer, meaning that it would have to be registered before with the tax administration (get a tax identification [RUC] number), keep full accounting books, file monthly and yearly tax returns, withhold taxes, allocate a reasonable income for its Peruvian source activities, etc. If a PE presence is determined, then the tax contingency will have to be quantified calculating the taxes, fines, and interest accrued as from the moment in which the PE presence can be deemed, except for the period barred by statute of limitations.

P

Other taxes

Value-added tax (VAT)

As of 1 April 2011, the general rate of VAT is 18% (19% prior to 1 April 2011) and is applicable to the following operations:

* Sale of goods within the country.
* Rendering or first use of services within the country.
* Construction contracts.
* The first sale of real estate made by construction firms.
* Import of goods.

Peru

For all transactions, the vendor is subject to VAT, except in the case of importation of goods or services rendered abroad, but economically used within Peru, for which VAT is self-assessed by the importers and users, respectively.

The VAT law follows a debit/credit system, and input VAT may be offset by output VAT. Should excess input VAT be obtained in a particular month, it shall offset output VAT obtained during the following months, until it is exhausted.

The export of movable goods (including the sale of goods in the international zone of ports and airports) is not subject to VAT, nor is the exportation of certain services. Thus, VAT paid upon the acquisition of goods, performance of services, construction agreements, and the importation of goods related to exported goods or services creates a positive VAT export balance.

The positive balance may offset output VAT, income tax, or any other outstanding tax debt in favour of the central government. If the positive balance is not completely offset, as the amount of the aforementioned tax obligations is insufficient, the taxpayer may apply for a refund.

Tax Obligatory Payment System (SPOT)

The SPOT was created by Superintendence Resolution N° 183-2004/SUNAT and is applicable to the sale of certain goods and the rendering of services subject to Peruvian VAT. The main purpose of the SPOT is to generate funds to enable the payment of tax obligations by the VAT-payer.

According to the SPOT, all the sales of goods and services listed in the appendices of the Resolution that are levied with VAT will be subject to withholding, applying the rates established for each kind of good and service.

Regarding services, Appendix 3 of the Resolution established that the services subject to the SPOT are:

1. Labour intermediation.
2. Lease of movable goods.
3. Maintenance and repair of movable goods.
4. Cargo movement.
5. Other entrepreneurial services.
6. Business commission.
7. Fabrication of goods by order.
8. People transport services.
9. Construction agreements.

As of 2 April 2012, item 10 has been included in the Appendix, so now any service subject to VAT, except expressly excluded, will be subject to the SPOT with a withholding rate of 9%. The exceptions mentioned in the law are the following:

- Services rendered by companies referred to in Article 16 of Law N° 26702, General Law of the Financial and Insurance System.
- Services rendered by the social system of health (EsSalud).
- Services rendered by the national pension fund (ONP).
- The sale of food and beverages in establishments open to the public, such as restaurants and bars.
- Non-permanent accommodation services, including its auxiliary services, rendered to the guest by the accommodation establishments referred to by the

Regulations of Accommodation Establishments, approved by Supreme Decree N° 029-2004-MINCETUR.
- Postal and fast courier services.
- Ground transport of goods mentioned on Superintendence Resolution N° 073-2006-SUNAT.
- Ground public passenger transport mentioned on Superintendence Resolution N° 057-2007-SUNAT.
- Services included in the exclusion envisage on numerals 6.a, 7.a, and 7.b of Appendix 3.

The purchaser or service recipient must withhold a percentage of the transaction price and deposit such amount within the seller's or service provider's State Bank (*Banco de la Nación*) account. It is important to note that the right of the purchaser or user of the service to offset input VAT related to such goods and services may be exercised only after the deposit with the State Bank has been executed.

The amount deposited is applied towards the payment of the seller or service provider's Peruvian tax obligations (not just VAT). If after four consecutive months such amount is not utilised, the seller or service provider may apply for a refund or use the amount to pay withholding applicable to purchasers or services recipients.

Customs duties
Customs duties applied to imports are linked to their classification under the Custom Tariff, given by NANDINA subheading that is determined by the information provided by the importer (through the invoice and other complementary information), as well as the physical recognition by the Customs Officer at the time of customs clearance.

As such, the taxes required are:

- *Ad valorem* custom duty (rates of 0%, 6%, and 11%, as the case may be).
- VAT (16%).
- Municipal promotion tax (2%).

Other taxes that may apply, depending on the equipment, include the following:

- Selective consumption tax.
- Specific duties.
- Antidumping and compensatory.
- VAT perception.

Excise tax
The sale of specific goods, including fuel, cigarettes, beer, liquor, and vehicles, is subject to excise tax.

Excise tax rates, and the manner on which the tax is applied, depend on the type of goods or services.

Real estate property tax
The real estate property tax is levied on the value of urban and rural real estate property. Individuals and legal entities owning the referred real estate properties are considered taxpayers for such purposes. The taxable base is calculated taking into account the value of all the properties owned in a specific local district, as reflected in the internal records of the corresponding local authorities.

Peru

The tax is calculated and paid on an annual basis applying the following progressive cumulative scale:

Real estate's value	Real estate property tax rate (%)
Up to 15 tax units	0.2
For the excess of 15 tax units and up to 60 tax units	0.6
Over 60 tax units	1.0

Real estate transfer tax (Alcabala)

The real estate transfer tax is levied on all transfers of urban and rural real estate property. The taxpayer is the purchaser of the property. The taxable base is equivalent to the consideration agreed upon by the parties to the transaction, provided it is higher than the property's value (in the relevant year for purposes of the real estate property tax) as reflected in the internal records of the corresponding local authorities.

The tax rate is 3% and must be borne exclusively by the buyer, regardless of whatever the parties agree. The first ten tax units (approximately USD 13,000) of the taxable base are exempt from this tax.

Financial transactions tax (FTT)

As of 1 April 2011, FTT is applied at a rate of 0.005% (0.05% prior to 1 April 2011) on all debits and/or credits on bank accounts held by the taxpayers.

The following operations, among others, are exempted from the FTT:

* Operations made between accounts of the same holder.
* Credits to bank accounts for payment of salaries.
* Credits and debits to bank accounts of diplomatic representations and international organisations recognised in Peru.

Payments of FTT are deductible as expenses for income tax purposes.

Temporary net assets tax (TNAT)

Companies subject to income tax are obliged to pay TNAT, except companies that are in preoperative stages or that commenced business on 1 January of the fiscal year in which TNAT must be paid.

The taxable basis is the value of the assets set forth in the taxpayer's balance sheet as of 31 December of the year prior to that of the tax payment, adjusted for deductions and amortisations accepted by the Peruvian law.

The amount of TNAT is determined by applying the following rates on the taxable basis:

* Up to PEN 1 million: 0%.
* Excess of PEN 1 million: 0.4%.

The amount paid for TNAT may be credited against the taxpayer's income tax.

Branch income

Branches, agencies, and PEs of non-resident companies or entities incorporated in Peru are subject to income tax at a 30% rate on their Peruvian-source income.

For tax purposes, branches or subsidiaries are subject to the same obligations applicable to all companies in Peru, including income tax, VAT, FTT, filing of the corresponding income tax and VAT returns, issuance of invoices, etc.

Nevertheless, the following important differences between subsidiaries and branches resident in Peru must be taken into account:

- Branches are subject to income tax only for their Peruvian-source income, while subsidiaries are subject to income tax on their global-source income (both Peruvian and foreign income).
- For branches, the 4.1% WHT on profit for distribution is applied on the date the annual income tax return is submitted. Subsidiaries are subject to the 4.1% WHT on the earlier of the date in which the corresponding shareholders agreement took place or the date when the beneficiary receives the dividends. For non-domiciled shareholders, the withholding will be applied whenever the dividend is actually paid, without taking into account the moment in which the shareholder agreement is executed.

Income determination

Inventory valuation
The first in first out (FIFO), average, specific-identification, retail, and normal or base-stock methods are allowed for inventory valuation. The last in first out (LIFO) method is not permitted.

Capital gains
Capital gains are taxed as ordinary income.

Dividend income
Cash dividends distributed to resident corporations are not subject to any taxes.

Interest income
PITL establishes that the WHT rate on interest arising from loans is 4.99%, provided the following requirements are met:

- In case of cash loans, the entrance into Peru of the foreign currency must be duly accredited.
- The credit must not accrue an effective interest that surpasses that of the LIBOR rate plus 7 points (for loans proceeding from Europe or the United States).
- The loan must be destined to finance business or taxable activities.
- The parties involved must not qualify as related parties for tax purposes.

If any of the above-mentioned conditions are not met, or to the extent they are not fulfilled, a withholding rate of 30% over the gross interest will be applied. A 30% WHT rate will also apply whenever the debtor and creditor are related parties or when the participation of the creditor only aims to conceal a transaction between related parties.

Peru

Foreign income

A Peruvian corporation is taxed on foreign-source income. Foreign-source income is recognised upon accrual. No tax deferral is allowed on this type of income. Double taxation may be avoided by means of foreign tax credits.

Deductions

Acceptable payment methods

Obligations that are fulfilled through cash payments exceeding PEN 3,500 must be made via bank account deposits, wire transfers, payment orders, credit cards, non-negotiable cheques, or other means of payment provided by entities of the Peruvian financial system. Failure to use one of these payment methods when such an obligation exists will result in the disallowance of deductions for any expenses or costs for income tax purposes and the disallowance of a credit for the corresponding VAT.

Expenses derived from transactions entered into with entities resident in tax havens

Certain expenses are not tax-deductible, including expenses incurred with respect to transactions with (i) entities resident in tax havens on the list attached to the PITL regulations, (ii) PEs located in tax havens, or (iii) entities that generate revenues or income through tax havens.

Nonetheless, expenses incurred from the following transactions are excluded from the above-mentioned limitations, provided the consideration paid falls within market value:

- Interest on loans.
- Insurance premiums.
- Leases of aircraft or ships.
- Maritime freight.
- Fees for passing through the Panama Canal.

Depreciation

Assets may be depreciated for tax purposes, via the straight-line method, capped at the following rates, but without exceeding the amount of the financial depreciation:

Assets	Depreciation rate (%)
Cattle (both labour and reproduction) and fishing nets	25
Vehicles (except trains) and any kind of ovens	20
Machines and equipment used for mining, oil and construction activities, excluding furniture, household, and office goods	20
Equipment for data processing	25
Machines and equipment acquired as of 1 January 1991	10
Other fixed assets	10

Buildings must be subject to a flat 5% depreciation rate, regardless of the financial depreciation.

Amortisation of intangibles assets

The amortisation of property rights, trademarks, patents, and manufacturing procedures, as well as other similar intangible assets, are not deductible for income tax purposes. However, the price paid for intangible assets of a limited duration, at the taxpayer's choice, may be considered as an expense and applied to the results in a single year or amortised proportionally in a ten-year term.

The Peruvian tax administration, prior to an opinion from the corresponding technical organisms, is permitted to determine the real value of those intangible assets for tax purposes, when the price does not reflects the real one.

Organisational and start-up expenses
Organisation expenses, pre-operating expenses (including initial operations and further expansion of operations), and interest accrued during the pre-operating period may be expensed in the first period of operation or amortised using the straight-line method over a maximum of ten years. However, once a company has elected to recover start-up costs via the straight-line method, it may revoke such election only upon receiving approval of the tax authorities.

Interest expenses
In general terms, interest on loans and related expenses are deductible, provided they are related to the acquisition of goods or services incurred, or to be incurred, in order to obtain or produce taxable income or to maintain the source of such income.

In the case of loans entered into between related parties, the amount of interest to be deducted is limited to interest from indebtedness not exceeding three times the net equity of the debtor as of the end of the previous fiscal year (*see Thin capitalisation in the Group taxation section*).

Bad debts
Write-offs of bad debts and equitable provisions are deductible, provided that the accounts to which they belong are determined. For the provisions of bad debts, it is necessary that:

- there is a debt due and the taxpayer can provide evidence of the financial difficulties of the debtor which could foresee a risk in the collection of the debt and
- the provision is registered separately in the inventory and balance book at the fiscal year closing. In this sense, generic bad debt provision will not be deductible in the assessment of the net taxable income, nor will bad debts whose terms have not yet elapsed.

Bear in mind that the following debts are not considered bad debts:

- Debts incurred between related parties.
- Debts guaranteed by banks or financial companies by means of rights over real property, money deposits, or purchase-sale agreements with reservation of right of legal ownership.
- Debts which have been subject to renewal or express extension.

Charitable contributions
Donations made to entities of the public sector, except companies, and to non-profit associations with certain purposes are deductible, provided that the receiver of the donation is duly qualified, through ministerial resolution, issued by the Ministry of Economy and Finance.

The deduction will be limited to 10% of the net income of the donor and only during the fiscal year in which it is granted (carryforward of the donation is disallowed). This

Peru

means that if the donor does not obtain taxable income in the fiscal year in which the donation is made, no deduction will be available.

Profit sharing
Entities with more than 20 employees, provided they obtain taxable income during the fiscal year, must distribute a percentage (5%, 8%, or 10% depending on the industry) of their profits (the basis is the tax profit of the fiscal year) among their employees. The amount of distribution for each employee depends on the effective working days during the year and annual remuneration.

Employee's retributions and health insurance premiums
Employee's retributions paid during a fiscal year may be deducted in such year, provided the payments are made by the employer before the term to file its annual income tax return expires. Likewise, health insurance premiums for employees, their spouses, and children are deductible.

Vehicle expenses deductions
Vehicle expenses may be deducted, provided the vehicles are essential to a company's business activities and are continually used for such purpose. There is a limitation on the tax deductibility of car expenses used for administrative of representation purposes, depending on the amount of income generated by the company. The number of company cars assigned to directors, managers, and representatives of a company may not exceed five under any circumstances.

Vehicles subject to these limitations are those classified in categories as A2, A3, and A4, pursuant to the provisions of the Ministry of Transportation and Communications.

Taxes
Other taxes assessable on properties and activities generating taxable income are deductible for income tax purposes.

Net operating losses
Tax losses may be offset according to either of the following systems:

* Against net income generated within the following four fiscal years after the year in which the loss is incurred. Any losses that are not offset within such period may not be carried forward to any future year.
* Against 50% of the net income generated in the following fiscal years after the year in which the loss was generated. Under this system, there is no time limitation for carrying forward the losses.

After choosing one of the aforementioned systems, the taxpayers may not change the system until the accumulated tax losses from prior fiscal years are exhausted. Losses may not be carried back to years prior to the year in which the loss is generated.

Payments to foreign affiliates
Payment of royalties to non-resident affiliates is permitted and deductible from gross income.

Group taxation

Group taxation is not permitted in Peru.

Transfer pricing

The rules related to market value and transfer pricing establish that in any kind of transaction, the value assigned to the goods and services must be market value for tax purposes. If such value differs from market value, either by overvaluation or sub-valuation, the tax administration will proceed to adjust it for both the purchaser and the seller. Should one of the parties be a non-domiciled company, such adjustment will be unilateral (only for the domiciled party). The adjustment will be imputed in the taxable period in which the operations with related parties were performed.

In case of transactions between related parties or those entered with tax havens, the market value will be equivalent to the value agreed with independent parties in similar transactions, being mandatory to support such value with a transfer pricing study.

Thin capitalisation

In the case of loans entered into between related parties, the amount of interest to be deducted is limited to interest from indebtedness not exceeding three times the entities net equity as of the end of the previous fiscal year. In this connection, even though Peruvian corporate law has no requirements as to a minimum amount of share capital to incorporate a legal entity, it should be noted that having a small share capital may jeopardise the deductibility of interest payable for loans granted by related entities since, in case of newly incorporated entities, the share capital (equity) to be considered for calculating the thin capitalisation limit is the original one (this is, the one with which the entity was incorporated). In any case, this will only trigger a deductibility problem for the fiscal year in which the entity is incorporated, since for the following fiscal year the thin capitalisation rule will be calculated on the basis of the net equity at the end of the prior fiscal year (which, at that moment, may have already been increased through new contributions or capitalisations).

Tax credits and incentives

Foreign tax credit

Pursuant to PITL, taxpayers will deduce the foreign income taxes paid due to their foreign-source income levied by PITL, provided that it doesn't exceed the amount that results from applying the average rate of the taxpayer to the incomes obtained abroad, or the tax paid abroad. The amount that, for any circumstance, is not used in the corresponding fiscal year cannot be set off (or compensated) in others fiscal years or be refunded.

Also, the following will be taken into account:

- Tax credit will be granted for the entire tax paid abroad that falls upon income taxed by PITL.
- Taxes paid abroad, whatever its denomination, shall bear the characteristics of income taxes.
- Tax credit will only be granted when the payment of the foreign income tax is supported by reliable documentation.

Early recovery of VAT

Companies in a preoperative stage with large projects in process may apply for early recovery of VAT prior to commencing operations. An investment agreement with the government (the Ministry of its sector) is required.

P

Peru

Stability agreement

Investors may enter into stability agreements with the government, either under the general regime or specific regimes (i.e. mining and petroleum).

Under the general regime, investors may enter into Juridical Stability Agreements that guarantee the following advantages for a ten-year period:

- Stability of the income tax regime in force at the time the agreement is entered into with respect to dividends and profit distribution.
- Stability of the Peruvian government monetary policy, according to which there is a complete absence of exchange controls, foreign currency can be freely acquired or sold at whatever exchange rate the market offers, and funds can be remitted abroad without any previous authorisation.
- Right of non-discrimination between foreign and local investors.

Under the mining regime, local mining companies may enter into stability agreements of guarantees and investment promotion measures that guarantee the following for ten or 15 years:

- Stability of the overall tax regime.
- Stability of the overall administrative regime.
- Free disposition of funds (foreign currency) arising from export operations.
- No exchange rate discrimination.
- Free trade of products.
- Stability of special regimes for tax refunds, temporary importation, etc.

Oil companies may enter into stability agreements that guarantee the following for the term of the contract:

- Stability of the overall tax regime.
- Free disposition of funds (foreign currency) arising from export operations.
- Free convertibility of its funds.
- Free trade of products.

Investment promotion in the Amazon

Certain tax benefits with regard to VAT and income tax have been established for taxpayers located in the area designated by the law as the 'Amazon' and that are engaged in the following activities:

- Agriculture and livestock enterprises.
- Aquaculture.
- Fishing.
- Tourism.
- Manufacturing activities linked to the processing, transformation, and commercialisation of primary products originating in the activities listed above and in forest transformation, provided these products are produced in the area.

Special zones - Centres of Export, Transformation, Industry, Commercialisation, and Services (CETICOS)

CETICOS are geographical areas duly delimited with custom primary zone status and special treatment, destined to generate development poles through industrial, maquila, assembling, or storage activities. CETICOS are located in Paita, Ilo, and Matarani cities.

Agribusiness and agro-exporting activities may be performed within a CETICOS. Agribusiness activity is primarily the transformation of agro-farming products produced in the country. Such transformation must be carried out at CETICOS.

Companies engaged in industrial, maquila, or assembling activities, established or set up in the CETICOS, until 31 December 2012, are exempt from income tax, VAT, excise tax, municipal promotion tax, as well as from any other taxes, fees, contributions levied by the Central Administration, and even taxes that require express exempt regulation.

Withholding taxes

Domestic corporations are required to withhold income tax with respect to income paid to non-resident entities at the following rates:

Type of payment	WHT (%)
Interest on non-related party loans, provided certain requirements are fulfilled	4.99
Interest on related party loans	30
Interest paid by Peruvian financial entities or banks to foreign beneficiaries for credit lines used in Peru	4.99
Royalties	30
Digital services	30
Technical assistance	15
Lease of vessels or aircraft	10
Dividends or profit distributions	4.1
Other income	30
Sale of securities within Peru	5
Sale of securities outside Peru	30

Note that resident taxpayers may not deduct the WHT of a third party, except in the case of loans provided by non-resident creditors, to the extent that the debtor has contractually assumed the obligation of bearing the WHT cost.

Capital gains derived from the sale of stocks issued by a Peruvian company through the stock exchange performed by a non-resident company are taxed at a 5% rate and are not subject to any withholding. In these cases, the income tax must be paid directly by the non-domiciled entity.

In the case of the services mentioned below that entail the execution of activities both in Peru and abroad, non-resident entities are subject to a 30% WHT on deemed Peru-source income determined by applying the following percentages to gross income:

Type of payment	Deemed Peruvian-source income (%)
Insurance	7
Lease of vessels	80
Lease of aircraft	60
Air transport	1
Maritime transport	2
Telecom services	5
International news services	10

P

Peru

Type of payment	Deemed Peruvian-source income (%)
Distribution of movies, records, and similar products	20
Rights for broadcasting live foreign TV shows within Peru	20

Tax treaties

Peru has entered into treaties with Brazil, Canada, and Chile regarding double taxation on income tax (the last three entered into in accordance with the Organisation for Economic Co-operation and Development [OECD] Model). Recently, Peru has entered into a double-taxation treaty (DTT) with Spain and Mexico (also entered into pursuant to the OECD Model), but the treaties have not yet entered into force, as the Peruvian Congress ratification required for such purpose is still pending. In addition, Peru is a member of the Andean Community of Nations (ACN), which also includes Bolivia, Colombia, and Ecuador.

Pursuant to the provisions of the tax treaties entered into in accordance with the OECD Model, income is taxable in the country of the service provider's residence, unless a PE is configured, in which case both countries are entitled to levy tax on income and the country of residence allows a credit for taxes paid in the other country.

On the other hand, according to the treaties with the ACN, income is taxable in the country in which its source is located, unless a PE is configured, in which case income tax is levied in the country where the PE is located. Thus, in transactions with entities resident from one of the member countries of the ACN, in certain cases income is taxable in Peru if the source of such income is located within Peru. For such purpose, the term 'source' is defined as the place where the activity, right, or goods that generates or will generate income is located.

Tax administration

Taxable period

According to law, the fiscal year is the calendar year.

Tax returns

The filing deadline for the income tax return is generally the first week of April. The system is one of self-assessment, but the tax return filed with the tax authorities is subject to review.

Payment of tax

Income tax is paid in advanced instalments calculated based on monthly revenue, either by applying a 2% rate or by a factor equivalent to the effective tax rate on net revenue of the prior year. Income tax is paid in 13 instalments (12 monthly payments and the annual income tax return). As noted, the first 12 payments must be made on a monthly basis and the last payment is due at the time that the annual tax return is filed. Late payment of interim or final instalments is subject to moratorium interest. Excess payments are subject to indexation up to the date of reimbursement or application to future taxes.

Tax authority

The tax authority in Peru is called 'Superintendencia Nacional de Administración Tributaria' (SUNAT). SUNAT is responsible for administering all of the aforementioned

Peru

taxes (income tax, VAT, etc.). Companies resident in Peru must be registered with the tax administration (Taxpayer's Registry).

The Tax Court (Tribunal Fiscal) is a specialised administrative tribunal, which depends on the Ministry of Economy and Finance, but is otherwise autonomous regarding its specific functions. Its mission is to rule over tax controversies that may arise between the tax administration and the taxpayers, by interpreting and applying the corresponding tax legislation, issuing mandatory observance jurisprudence, establishing homogenous criteria that continue to support the progress of the tax system.

Finally, taxpayers are entitled to file an appeal before the Judiciary (Superior Court) against resolutions issued by the Tax Court, but payment of the tax debt must be performed or guarantees must be provided.

P

Philippines

PwC contact

Alex Cabrera
PricewaterhouseCoopers\Isla Lipana & Co.
29th Floor Philamlife Tower
8767 Paseo de Roxas
Makati City 1226
Philippines
Tel: +63 2 459 2002
Email: alex.cabrera@ph.pwc.com

Significant developments

Threshold for value-added tax (VAT) exempt transactions

The threshold for entities required to register for VAT was increased by the Philippine Bureau of Internal Revenue (BIR) from annual sales or receipts of 1,500,000 Philippine pesos (PHP) to PHP 1,919,500, effective 1 January 2012.

Taxes on corporate income

A domestic corporation is subject to tax on its worldwide income. On the other hand, a foreign corporation is subject to tax only on income from Philippine sources (*see the subsections on Resident foreign corporations and Non-resident foreign corporations below*).

Domestic corporations

The following corporate income tax (CIT) rates apply to domestic corporations:

Income	CIT rate (%)
In general, on net income from all sources	30
Minimum corporate income tax (MCIT) on gross income, beginning in the fourth taxable year following the year in which business operations commence. MCIT is imposed where the CIT at 30% is less than 2% MCIT on gross income.	2
Proprietary educational institutions and non-profit hospitals:	
On net taxable income if gross income from unrelated trade, business, and other activities does not exceed 50% of the total gross income from all sources	10
On total net taxable income if gross income from unrelated activities exceeds 50% of income	30
Non-stock, non-profit educational institutions (all assets and revenues used actually, directly, and exclusively for educational purposes)	Exempt

Certain passive income from domestic sources is subject to final tax rather than ordinary income tax (*see the Income determination section*).

Improperly accumulated earnings tax

An improperly accumulated earnings tax of 10% is imposed on improperly accumulated income. The tax applies to every corporation formed or used for the purpose of avoiding income tax with respect to its shareholders, or the shareholders of any other corporation, by permitting earnings and profits to accumulate instead of being divided or distributed. Exceptions are made for publicly held corporations, banks and non-bank financial intermediaries, and insurance companies.

Local income taxes

Local government units impose local business taxes that are generally based on the prior year's gross sales or gross receipts. The local business tax shall not exceed 3%.

Resident foreign corporations

Resident foreign corporations are taxed in the same manner as domestic corporations (except on capital gains on the sale of buildings not used in business, which are taxable as ordinary income), but only on Philippine-source income. International carriers are subject to an income tax of 2.5% on their gross Philippine billings. Where there is a tax treaty, the preferential rate provided in it applies.

Income of offshore banking units (OBUs) and foreign currency deposit units (FCDUs) of depository banks from foreign currency transactions with non-residents, other OBUs, or FCDUs and local commercial banks (including branches of foreign banks) authorised by the Bangko Sentral ng Pilipinas (central bank) to transact business with OBUs and FCDUs are exempt from all taxes except net income specified by the Secretary of Finance upon recommendation of the Monetary Board. Interest income from foreign currency loans granted to residents other than OBUs or local commercial banks shall be subject to a 10% final income tax.

Non-resident foreign corporations

In general, non-resident foreign corporations are taxed on gross income received from sources within the Philippines at 30%, except for reinsurance premiums, which are exempt, and on interest on foreign loans, which is taxed at 20%. Dividends from domestic corporations are subject to a final withholding tax (WHT) at the rate of 15% if the country in which the corporation is domiciled does not impose income tax on such dividends or allows a tax deemed paid credit of 15%. If the recipient is a resident of a country with which the Philippines has a tax treaty, the treaty rate applies, if lower. Otherwise, the normal corporate rates apply.

Rentals and charter fees payable to non-resident owners of vessels chartered by Philippine nationals on leases or charters approved by the Maritime Industry Authority are subject to a final tax of 4.5%. Rentals, charter fees, and other fees payable to non-resident lessors of aircraft, machinery, and other equipment are subject to a final tax of 7.5%.

Regional or area headquarters of multinational corporations that do not earn or derive income from the Philippines, and that act as supervisory, communications, and coordinating centres for their affiliates, subsidiaries, or branches in the Asia-Pacific region and other foreign markets are not subject to CIT.

Corporate residence

A domestic corporation is a corporation that is created or organised under Philippine laws. A foreign corporation that is duly licensed to engage in trade or business within the Philippines is referred to as a 'resident foreign corporation'.

Permanent establishment (PE)

The business profits in most Philippine treaties permits the Philippines to tax only those profits attributable to a PE. While Philippine treaties adopt the United Nations (UN) Model Convention, Organisation for Economic Co-operation and Development (OECD) commentaries have often been cited by tax authorities to support their interpretation of treaty provisions. The main implication is that most Philippine treaties contain a rule

Philippines

deeming a PE to arise when services are performed in the Philippines for a specified period of time.

Other taxes

Value-added tax (VAT)

VAT applies to practically all sales of services and imports, as well as to sales, barter, exchange, or lease of goods or properties (tangible or intangible). The tax is equivalent to a uniform rate of 12%, based on the gross selling price of goods or properties sold, or gross receipts from the sale of services. On importation of goods, the basis of the tax is the value used by the Bureau of Customs in determining tariff and customs duties plus customs duties, excise taxes, if any, and other charges. Where the valuation used by the Bureau of Customs is by volume or quantity, the VAT basis is the landed cost plus excise taxes, if any.

Certain transactions are zero-rated or exempt from VAT. Export sales by VAT-registered persons are zero-rated.

Certain sales of services exempt from VAT, including services provided by financial intermediaries, are subject to percentage taxes based on gross sales, receipts, or income. A 3% percentage tax also applies to persons who are not VAT-registered because their annual sales or receipts do not exceed PHP 1,919,500.

Customs duties

Applicable customs duties are determined based on the tariff classification of the import product. As with the rest of the Association of South East Asian Nations (ASEAN) countries, tariff classification in the Philippines is based on the ASEAN Harmonised Tariff Nomenclature (AHTN), which is patterned after the Harmonised Commodity Classification and Coding System (HS) Convention and its 2002 revisions. The latest edition, HS 2007, was implemented in late 2007. HS 2007, in comparison with the 2004 edition, will impact 350 tariff classification numbers by mandating changes in both classification codes and customs duty rates. Recently, Executive Order No. 61 has been released to implement the Comprehensive Tariff Reform Program (CTRP) for 2012.

The Philippines adopts the World Trade Organization (WTO) Valuation Agreement, where the declared invoice price is used as the basis for determining customs duties.

As a protective measure, the Philippines retains higher tariff rates (20% to 50%) on sensitive agricultural products, such as grains, livestock and meat products, sugar, certain vegetables, and coffee. A few agricultural commodities are subject to minimum access volumes, but these represent less than 1% of all tariff lines.

In view of the existing free trade agreements in the region, such as the ASEAN Free Trade Area (AFTA), ASEAN-China Free Trade Area (ACFTA), ASEAN-Korea Free Trade Area (AKFTA), the ASEAN-Australia-New Zealand Free Trade Area (AANZFTA), the ASEAN-Japan Comprehensive Economic Partnership Agreement (AJCEPA), and the ASEAN-INDIA Free Trade Area, which has been implemented just recently, the Philippines has taken steps to progressively eliminate tariffs. Tariff reductions for the Philippines range from 10% to 35% for most products included in the Normal Track list.

Excise taxes

Excise tax is payable at varying rates on alcohol products, tobacco products, petroleum products, mineral products, and automobiles. Excise tax is also payable on all goods commonly or commercially known as jewelry, whether real or imitation; perfumes and toilet waters; and yachts and other vessels intended for pleasure or sport at 20% of the wholesale price or value of the importation used by the Bureau of Customs in determining tariff and custom duties.

Documentary stamp tax (DST)

DST is payable at varying rates on various documents and transactions. The following table contains selected examples:

Taxable document/transaction (tax base)	DTS rate
Original issue of shares	PHP 1.00 for every PHP 200 or fractional part of par value
Sale, barter or exchange of shares of stock listed and traded through the local stock exchange	Exempt
Other sales agreement, agreement to sell, memoranda of sales, delivery or transfer of shares or certificates of stock	PHP 0.75 for every PHP 200 or fractional part of par value
Certificate of profits, interest in property or accumulations	PHP 0.50 for every PHP 200 or fractional part of face value
Non-exempt debt instruments	PHP 1.00 for every PHP 200 or fractional value of the issue price.
Bank check, draft, certificate of deposit not bearing interest, other instruments	PHP 1.50 for each instrument
Life insurance policy	PHP 10 to PHP 100 depending upon the amount of insurance
Lease/hiring agreement	PHP 3.00 for the first PHP 2,000 or fractional part of amount stipulated in contract, and PHP 1.00 for every PHP 1,000 or fractional part in excess of PHP 2,000 for each year of contract term
Mortgage, pledge, deed of trust	PHP 20.00 for the first PHP 5,000 of amount secured, and P 10.00 for every PHP 5,000 or fractional part in excess of PHP 5,000
Deed of sale, conveyance of real property	PHP 15.00 for each PHP 1,000 of consideration/value or fractional part thereof

Capital gains tax

Capital gains arise from the sale or exchange of 'capital assets'. Capital assets are property held by the taxpayer (whether or not connected with its trade) other than the following:

- Inventories or property held primarily for sale to customers in the ordinary course of business.
- Real property or depreciable property used in trade or business.
- Property of a kind that would be included in the inventory of the taxpayer if on hand at the close of the taxable year.

Capital losses are deductible only to the extent of capital gains.

There are no holding period requirements for capital assets of corporations.

Philippines

A 6% final tax is imposed on the higher of the gross selling price or fair market value upon the sale, exchange, or disposition of land or buildings not actually used in the business of a corporation. The tax is withheld by the buyer at the time of sale.

Net capital gains derived from the sale, exchange, transfer, or similar transactions of shares of stock not traded through a local stock exchange are taxed at 5% of gains not over PHP 100,000, and 10% of gains in excess of PHP 100,000. Sales of shares of stock listed and traded on a local stock exchange, other than the sale by a dealer in securities, are subject to a stock transaction tax of 0.5%, based on the gross selling price.

Capital gains from the sale of bonds, debentures, or other certificates of indebtedness with a maturity of more than five years are exempt from tax.

A tax is levied on every sale, barter, exchange, or other disposition through an initial public offering (IPO) of shares of stock in closely held corporations. A 'close corporation' is any corporation of which at least 50% in value of the total outstanding capital stock, or at least 50% of the total combined voting power of all classes of stock entitled to vote, is owned directly or indirectly by, or for, not more than 20 individuals. The tax rates provided hereunder are based on the proportion of the gross selling price, or gross value in money, of the shares of stock sold, bartered, exchanged, or otherwise disposed of to the total outstanding shares of stock after listing on the local stock exchange.

Proportion of sale to total shares	Tax rate (%)
25% or less	4
Over 25% but not over 33.33%	2
Over 33.33%	1

Fringe benefits tax
A final tax of 32%, payable by the employer, is imposed on the grossed-up monetary value of fringe benefits (e.g. housing, expense accounts, vehicles of any kind, household personnel, interest on loans at lower than market rates (the current benchmark rate is 12%), membership dues for social and athletic clubs, foreign travel expenses, holiday and vacation expenses, educational assistance, insurance) furnished or granted to managerial or supervisory personnel by the employer. An exception is for fringe benefits required by the nature of or necessary to the trade, business, or profession of the employer, or when the fringe benefit is for the convenience or advantage of the employer.

The following fringe benefits are not subject to the tax:

*   Those authorised and exempted from tax under special laws.
*   Contributions of the employer for the benefit of the employee to retirement, insurance, and hospitalisation benefit plans.
*   Those granted to rank-and-file employees (however, the employees may be subject to WHT on compensation).
*   Those of relatively small value or *de minimis* benefits.

The fringe benefits tax is payable on the calendar quarter basis and is an additional deductible expense for the employer. Fringe benefits already subjected to fringe benefits tax will no longer be included in the employee's taxable income.

The grossed-up monetary value of the fringe benefit is generally computed by dividing the actual monetary value of the benefit by 68%.

Local government taxes
Local government units impose local (business) taxes and permit fees, which are generally based on the prior year's gross sales or gross receipts, and real property taxes, which are levied on the basis of a fixed proportion of the value of the real property (taxable value). Real property located in a province may be subject to real property tax of not more than 1% of its taxable value, while real property in a city (or municipality in Metro Manila) may be subject to real property tax of not more 2% of its taxable value.

Branch income

The income tax rate on branch profits is the same as on corporate profits. In general, profits remitted abroad by a branch office are subject to a 15% tax rate, based on the total profits applied or earmarked for remittance, without any deduction for the tax component thereof. A lower rate may apply under certain tax treaties. Profits from qualified activities remitted by a branch registered with the Philippine Economic Zone Authority (PEZA) are exempt.

Regional operating headquarters (ROHQ) pay a tax of 10% of their taxable income. A ROHQ is a branch established in the Philippines by a multinational company that is engaged in any of the following services: general administration and planning, business planning and coordination, sourcing and procurement of raw materials and components, corporate finance advisory services, marketing control and sales promotion, training and personnel management, logistic services, research and development services and product development, technical support and maintenance, data processing and communication, or business development.

Income determination

Inventory valuation
Inventories are generally stated at cost or at the lower of cost or market. Last in first out (LIFO) is not allowed for tax purposes. Generally, the inventory valuation method for tax purposes must conform to that used for book purposes.

Capital gains
Capital gains are not generally subject to CIT, but may be subject to capital gains tax. *See Capital gains tax in the Other taxes section for more information.*

Dividend income
Dividends received by a domestic or resident foreign corporation from another domestic corporation are not subject to tax. These dividends are excluded from the taxable income of the recipient.

Dividends received by a non-resident foreign corporation from a domestic corporation are subject to a final WHT at the rate of 15% if the country in which the corporation is domiciled either does not impose income tax on such dividends or allows tax deemed paid credit of 15%. If the recipient is a resident of a country with which the Philippines has a tax treaty, the treaty rate applies if lower. Otherwise, the normal CIT rate of 30% applies.

Philippines

Stock dividends
A Philippine corporation can distribute stock dividends tax-free, proportionately to all shareholders.

Interest income
Interest on bank savings, time deposits, and money market placements received by domestic or resident foreign corporations from a domestic corporation are subject to a final tax of 20%.

Interest income of domestic or resident foreign corporations from FCDU deposits is subject to a final tax of 7.5%. Such income is excluded from gross income reportable in CIT returns.

Interest income of OBUs and FCDUs from foreign currency loans granted to residents other than OBUs or local commercial banks shall be subject to 10% tax.

Royalty income
Royalties received by domestic or resident foreign corporations from a domestic corporation are subject to a final tax of 20%.

Other significant items
Other items exempt from CIT include the following:

- Proceeds of life insurance policies.
- Return of policy premium.
- Gifts, bequests, and devises.
- Interest on certain government securities.
- Income exempt under a treaty.
- Gains from sale, exchange, or retirement of bonds.
- Gains from redemption of shares of stock in mutual fund companies.

Foreign income
A Philippine (domestic) corporation is taxed on its worldwide income. A domestic corporation is taxed on income from foreign sources when earned or received, depending on the accounting method used by the taxpayer.

Income earned through foreign subsidiary is taxed only when paid to a Philippine resident shareholder as dividend. Meanwhile, income earned through a foreign branch is taxed as it accrues. The losses incurred by the foreign branch are deductible against other income earned by the Philippine corporation.

Double taxation is generally relieved through a credit for foreign taxes. However, a taxpayer can take a deduction for foreign taxes instead, if that leads to a more favourable outcome.

Deductions

Note that corporate taxpayers are given the option to avail themselves of the optional standard deduction computed at 40% of gross income. The optional standard deduction is in lieu of the itemised operating expenses.

Depreciation and depletion

Depreciation is generally computed on a straight-line basis, although any reasonable method may be elected if the aggregate amount of depreciation, plus salvage value at the end of the useful life of the property, will equal the cost of the property. Gain on the sale of depreciated property is taxable as ordinary income. Generally, tax depreciation should conform to book depreciation, unless the former includes incentives.

Properties used in petroleum operations may be depreciated over a period of ten years using the straight-line or declining-balance method, at the option of the service contractor. Properties used in mining operations with expected life of more than ten years may be depreciated over any number of years between five years and their expected life.

A cost depletion allowance is available as follows:

- For oil and gas wells, depletion is based on actual reduction in flow and production ascertained, not by flush flow, but by the settled production or regular flow.
- For mines, depletion is allowable up to an amount not to exceed the market value, as used for purposes of imposing the mining *ad valorem* taxes, of the products mined and sold during the year.

Goodwill
Goodwill is not deductible for tax purposes.

Start-up expenses
Start-up expenses are deductible when incurred.

Interest expenses
The allowable deduction for interest expense is reduced by an amount equal to 33% of interest income that is subject to final tax.

Bad debts
Bad debts are deductible expenses when written-off, subject to certain requirements.

Charitable contributions
The deduction for charitable contributions ordinarily may not exceed 5% of taxable income. However, contributions to certain institutions are 100% deductible, subject to certain conditions.

Entertainment expenses
Entertainment, amusement, and recreation expenses should not exceed 0.5% of net sales for taxpayers engaged in sale of goods or properties, or 1% of net revenue for taxpayers engaged in sale of services, including professionals and lessors of properties.

Special deductions
Special deductions are allowed for certain businesses (e.g. insurance, mining, petroleum, and real estate investment trust).

Fines and penalties
Fines and penalties are deductible as necessary and ordinary business expenses. Surcharge and compromise imposed for non-payment or late payment of taxes is not deductible for tax purposes.

Philippines

Taxes

Corporate taxpayers can claim a deduction for all taxes paid or accrued within the taxable year in connection with their trade or business, except for the following:

* Philippine CIT.
* Income taxes imposed by authority of any foreign country, unless the taxpayer elects to take a deduction in lieu of a foreign tax credit.
* Estate and donor's taxes.
* Taxes assessed against local benefits of a kind tending to increase the value of the property assessed.

In the case of a foreign corporation, deductions for taxes are allowed only if they are connected with income from sources within the Philippines.

Net operating losses

A net operating loss for any taxable year immediately preceding the current taxable year, which had not been previously offset as a deduction from gross income, may be carried over as a deduction from gross income for the next three consecutive taxable years immediately following the year of this loss (except losses during the period when the taxpayer was tax-exempt), provided there has been no substantial change in the ownership of the business or enterprise.

For mines, other than oil and gas wells, a net operating loss calculated without the benefit of incentives provided for under Executive Order (EO) No. 226, or the Omnibus Investments Code of 1987, as amended, incurred in any of the first ten years of operation may be carried over as a deduction from taxable income for the next five years immediately following the year of such loss.

Loss carrybacks are not allowed.

Payments to foreign affiliates

A Philippine corporation can claim a deduction for royalties, management service fees, and interest charges paid to foreign affiliates, provided such amounts are equal to what it would pay an unrelated entity, and the appropriate WHTs are withheld and remitted.

The registration of licensing and management agreements, now known as technology transfer arrangements (TTAs), has been liberalised. Only TTAs not conforming to certain provisions of the Intellectual Property Code require approval by, and registration with, the Documentation, Information, and Technology Transfer Bureau of the Intellectual Property Office (formerly Bureau of Patents, Trademarks, and Technology Transfer) to render the contracts enforceable.

Head office expense allocations

A resident foreign corporation is allowed to claim allocated head office expenses as a deduction, subject to compliance with certain requirements.

Group taxation

Group taxation is not permitted in the Philippines.

Philippines

Transfer pricing
There are no specific consolidated transfer pricing rules in the Philippines, but the OECD transfer pricing guidelines are being used until the tax authorities issue transfer pricing regulations.

Thin capitalisation
There are no thin capitalisation rules in the Philippines.

Controlled foreign companies (CFCs)
There are no CFC rules in the Philippines.

Tax credits and incentives

Foreign tax credit
Domestic corporations are allowed to claim a credit for any income taxes paid to a foreign country, provided that the taxes are not claimed as deductions. Foreign corporations are not allowed foreign tax credits.

Credits for foreign taxes are determined on a country by country basis. The amount of foreign tax credit in respect to the tax paid in a country shall not exceed the same proportion of the tax against which the tax credit is taken, which the taxpayer's income from the country bears to its entire taxable income. There is, however, a further limitation based on the total amount of foreign-sourced income that the taxpayer earns. The total amount of foreign tax credits shall not exceed the same proportion of the tax against which the tax credit is taken, which the taxpayer's foreign-sourced income bears to its entire taxable income.

Export incentives
Tax incentives available to export enterprises registered with the Board of Investments (BOI) are as follows:

- Income tax holiday (ITH) giving full exemption from CIT for six years for pioneer firms and those locating in less-developed areas and four years for non-pioneer firms from the date of commercial operation, or target date of operation, whichever is earlier. Expanding export-oriented firms are given three years. If prescribed conditions are met, an income tax holiday may be extended by up to three years. In no case, however, can an income tax holiday exceed eight years. Subject to certain exceptions, new and expansion projects located in the National Capital Region (NCR) or Metro Manila are no longer entitled to the income tax holiday.
- Tax and duty exemption on imported spare parts and supplies for export producers with a customs bonded manufacturing warehouse exporting at least 70% of annual production, if foreign-owned or 50%, if Filipino-owned.
- Full deduction of the cost of major infrastructure undertaken by enterprises in less-developed areas.
- Additional deduction of 50% of the incremental labour expense if the prescribed ratio of capital assets to annual labour is met and 100% of the incremental labour if located in less-developed areas within five years from date of registration (this incentive cannot be availed of simultaneously with the income tax holiday).
- Ten-year exemption from taxes and duties on importation of breeding stock and genetic materials.
- Tax credit on domestic breeding stocks and genetic materials (ten years).
- Exemption from wharfage, any export tax, duty, impost, or fees.

P

Philippines

- Tax credits equivalent to taxes and duties paid on purchases of raw materials, supplies, and semi-manufactured products forming part of the products for export.

Other incentives

Export and free-trade enterprises, information technology (IT) enterprises, and special economic zone developers/operators (including IT buildings located in Metro Manila and IT parks) registered with PEZA are entitled to an ITH of six years for pioneer firms and four years for non-pioneer firms. Foreign articles brought into the zones will be exempt from import duties and taxes. Local purchases of goods from VAT-registered suppliers outside the economic zones are zero-rated. After the lapse of the income tax holiday incentives, enterprises registered and operating within special economic zones/ export processing zones (EPZ) will pay only 5% final tax on gross income earned, in lieu of paying all local and national taxes.

A regional or area headquarters established in the country as a supervisory, communications, and coordination centre for a corporation's subsidiaries, affiliates, and branches in the Asia-Pacific region, and whose headquarters do not derive income from the Philippines, are not subject to any CIT nor VAT and are entitled to certain non-tax incentives.

ROHQ that are allowed to derive income in the Philippines by performing qualifying business services to its affiliates, subsidiaries, or branches in the Philippines, in the Asia-Pacific Region, and other foreign markets may avail itself of the following incentives:

- Income tax at the preferential rate of 10% of its taxable income.
- Exemption from all kinds of local taxes, fees, or charges imposed by a local government unit, except real property tax on land improvements and equipment.
- Tax and duty-free importation of equipment and materials for training and conferences which are needed and used solely for its functions as ROHQ and which are not locally available, subject to the prior approval of the BOI.
- Importation of new motor vehicles, subject to the payment of corresponding duties and taxes.
- Exemption from travel tax, specific immigration fees, and requirements, subject to certain conditions.

The following are the incentives granted to exporters under the Export Development Act (Republic Act No. 7844):

- Exemption from Presidential Decree No. 1853 (requiring 100% of Letter of Credit), provided that the importation shall be used for the production of goods and services of export.
- Tax credit for incremental export performance. The tax credit for increase in current export revenues shall be computed as a percentage to be applied on the incremental export revenue converted to pesos at the current rate. The percentages or rates are as follows:
  - For the first 5% increase in annual export revenues over the previous year: 2.5%.
  - For the next 5% increase: 5.0%.
  - For the next 5% increase: 7.5%.
  - In excess: 10.0%.

Note that this incentive is not available for exporters enjoying ITH or VAT exemption or whose local VAT is below 10%.

Philippines

In addition to the above incentive, all existing incentives being enjoyed by the enterprise if registered with the BOI, PEZA, Subic Bay Metropolitan Authority (SBMA), Clark Development Corporation (CDC), or other ecozone regulating agencies.

Withholding taxes

Corporations and individuals engaged in business and paying certain types of income to non-residents are required to withhold the appropriate tax, which generally is 30% in the case of payments to non-resident foreign corporations or 25% for non-resident aliens not engaged in trade or business. *For WHT on resident corporations, see the discussions in the Income determination section.*

Tax treaty rates
For countries with which the Philippines has concluded tax treaties, the taxes to be withheld are as follows:

As of April 2012:

Recipient	Dividends (%) (1)	Interest (%) (2)	Royalties (%)
Australia	15/25 (3, 4)	10/15 (5)	15/25 (6)
Austria	10/25 (37)	10/15 (5, 8)	10/15 (6, 9)
Bahrain	10/15 (7)	10	10/15 (10)
Bangladesh	10/15 (11)	15	15
Belgium	10/15 (7)	10	15
Brazil	15 /30	10/15 (5)	15/25 (12)
Canada	15/25 (3, 7)	10/15 (5)	25 (9)
China, P.R	10/15 (7)	10	10/15 (13)
Czech Republic	10/15 (7)	10	10/15 (14)
Denmark	10/15 (11)	10	15
Finland	15/30 (3, 7)	10/15 (5)	15/25 (15)
France	10/15 (3, 7)	10/15 (5)	15
Germany	10/15 (11)	10/15 (5, 16, 17)	10/15 (13)
Hungary	15/20 (3, 11)	15	15 (9)
India	15/20 (3, 7)	10/15 (5, 17)	15/30 (6)
Indonesia	15/20 (3, 11)	10/15 (5)	15/25 (6)
Israel	10/15 (7)	10	15 (9)
Italy	15	10/15 (5)	15/25 (6, 18)
Japan	10/15 (3, 7)	10	10/15 (20)
Korea, Republic of	10/25 (3, 11)	10/15 (5)	10/15 (6)
Malaysia	15/25	15	15/25 (6, 18)
Netherlands	10/15 (7)	10/15 (5, 16, 17)	10/15 (6)
New Zealand	15/25	10	15/25 (6)
Norway	15/25 (3, 7)	15	7.5/10/25 (9, 21)
Pakistan	15/25 (3, 11)	10/15 (5)	15/25 (6)
Poland	10/15 (11)	10	15
Romania	10/15 (11)	10/15 (5, 16, 17)	10/15/25 (22)
Russia	15	15	15
Singapore	15/25 (3, 23)	10/15 (5)	15/25 (6, 18)
Spain	10/15 (7)	10/15 (5, 16)	10/15/20 (24)

Philippines

Recipient	Dividends (%) (1)	Interest (%) (2)	Royalties (%)
Sweden	10/15 (11)	10	15
Switzerland	10/15 (7)	10	15
Thailand	15/30	10/15 (5)	15/25 (6, 18)
United Arab Emirates	10/15 (7)	10	10
United Kingdom	15/25 (3, 7)	10/15 (5)	15/25 (6, 20)
United States	20/25 (3, 7)	10/15 (5)	15/25 (6, 9)
Vietnam	10/15 (11)	15	15

Notes

1. The lower rate generally applies if the beneficial owner of the dividends is a company with a substantial ownership in the dividend paying company.
2. Interest derived by a foreign government or its agencies is typically exempt from Philippine tax. Many treaties also contain special rules for both Philippine and home country taxation of interest paid on instruments secured by a government agency of one of the countries. Such provisions have been excluded from the analysis.
3. A 15% rate applies under domestic law if the home country exempts the dividend from tax or permits a 15% or greater credit for corporate taxes paid by the company paying the dividend.
4. Entitlement to the lower rate depends on how the dividend will be taxed in Australia.
5. The 10% rate applies to interest paid in respect of the public issues of bonds, debentures, or similar obligations.
6. The lower rate applies to royalties paid by an enterprise registered with the Philippine BOI and engaged in preferred areas of activity.
7. The threshold for substantial ownership is 10%.
8. The 10% rate also applies to interest paid by a company registered with the BOI and engaged in preferred areas of investment in the Philippines.
9. The treaty also contains a most-favoured-nation rule, limiting the Philippine tax on royalties to the lowest rate of Philippine tax that may be imposed on royalties of the same kind paid in similar circumstances to a resident of a third state.
10. The 15% rate applies to royalties arising from the use of, or the right to use, any copyright of literary, artistic, or scientific work including cinematograph films or tapes for television or broadcasting.
11. The threshold for substantial ownership is 25%.
12. The 25% rate applies to royalties arising from the use or the right to use trademarks and cinematographic films, films or tapes for television or radio broadcasting. The 15% applies to any other royalties.
13. The 10% rate applies to the use of, or the right to use, any patent, trademark, design or model, plan, secret formula or process, or from the use of, or the right to use, industrial, commercial, or scientific equipment, or for information concerning industrial, commercial, or scientific experience. Strictly, application of the rate is generally at the discretion of the Philippine Competent Authorities, but the BIR has never raised this as an issue.
14. The 10% rate applies to royalties arising from the use of, or the right to use, any copyright of literary, artistic, or scientific work (other than copyright of cinematograph films), any patent, trademark, design or model, plan, secret formula or process, or from the use of, or the right to use, industrial, commercial, or scientific equipment, or for information concerning industrial, commercial, or scientific experience.
15. The 15% rate applies to royalties paid by an enterprise registered and engaged in preferred areas of activities, and to royalties in respect of cinematographic films or tapes for television or broadcasting, and for the use of, or the right to use, any copyright. The 25% rate applies to other royalties.
16. The 10% rate also applies to interest paid in connection with the sale on credit of any industrial, commercial, or scientific equipment.
17. The 10% rate also applies to interest paid on any loans granted by a bank.
18. The 15% rate also applies to royalties in respect of cinematographic films or tapes for television or broadcasting.
19. The 10% rate applies to interest paid on government securities, or bonds or debentures. The 15% rate applies to any other interest income.
20. The 15% rate applies to royalties paid for the use of, or the right to use, cinematographic films and films or tapes for radio or television broadcasting.
21. The 7.5% rate applies to the lease of containers. The 10% rate applies to royalties paid by an enterprise registered with the BOI. The 25% rate applies to other royalties.
22. The 10% rate applies to royalties paid by an enterprise registered with the BOI and engaged in preferred pioneer areas of activity. The 15% rate applies to rentals from cinematographic films and tapes for television or broadcasting. The 25% rate applies to all other royalties.
23. The threshold for substantial ownership is 15%.

24. The 10% rate applies to royalties paid by an enterprise registered with the BOI and engaged in preferred pioneer areas of activity. The 20% rate applies to rentals from cinematographic films and tapes for television or broadcasting. The 15% rate applies to all other royalties.

Tax administration

Taxable period
The accounting period may be either a calendar year or a fiscal year. With prior approval of the Commissioner of Internal Revenue, corporations may change their accounting period from calendar year to fiscal year, or vice versa.

Tax returns
Corporations should file their returns and compute their income on the basis of an accounting period of 12 months.

Corporate taxpayers file self-assessing returns. Electronic filing and payment of taxes are available under the Electronic Filing and Payment System (EFPS) of the BIR.

A domestic or resident foreign corporation is required to file income tax return on a quarterly basis. Within 60 days from the close of the first three quarters in its taxable year, the corporation must file in duplicate a return summarising its gross income and deductions for the year to date. A final annual income tax return must be filed on or before the 15th day of the fourth month following the close of the tax year.

Payment of tax
Every corporation files cumulative quarterly income tax returns for the first three quarters and pays the tax due thereon within 60 days after each quarter. A final adjustment return covering the total net taxable income of the preceding taxable year must be filed on the 15th day of the fourth month following the close of the taxable year. The balance of the tax due after deducting the quarterly payments must be paid, while the excess may be claimed as refund or tax credit. Excess estimated quarterly income taxes paid may be carried over and credited against estimated quarterly income tax liabilities for succeeding taxable years. Once the option to carry over has been made, such option is irrevocable for that taxable period, and no cash refund or tax credit certificate (TCC) is allowed.

Audit cycle
An annual statutory audit is required for all corporations with authorised capital stock or paid-up capital exceeding PHP 50,000, including branches of foreign corporations. It is also required for any corporation whose gross sales or earnings exceed PHP 150,000 in any quarter.

Statute of limitations
There is no statutory obligation on the Commissioner to make an assessment for internal revenue taxes, and most taxes are collected based on the taxpayer's self-calculation. If an assessment is to be issued, however, it must be done within three years from the deadline or the date of actual filing of the return, whichever comes later. The taxpayer and the Commissioner can, however, agree in writing to extend this period.

In the case of a false or fraudulent return or of failure to file a return, the tax may be assessed or a proceeding in court for collection may be commenced without assessment at any time within ten years from the discovery of the falsity, fraud, or omission.

Philippines

Any internal revenue tax that has been assessed within the period of limitation may be collected by distraint or levy or by a proceeding in court within five years following the assessment of the tax.

The prescription periods are suspended in certain circumstances, such as when the offender is absent from the Philippines, the Commissioner grants a taxpayer's request for a reinvestigation, or the taxpayer and the BIR agree to extend the prescriptive period for assessment through a written waiver.

In the case of overpayment of tax, a claim for refund or credit may be filed with the BIR within two years from the date of erroneous payment of the tax. If the claim is denied or no decision is received from the BIR, a petition for review may be filed with the Court of Tax Appeals (CTA). This must be filed before the two-year period expires, and in the case of a denied claim, within 30 days from the receipt of the denial.

Topics of focus for tax authorities
The BIR generally prepares an annual audit program that provides for mandatory cases subject to tax audit, as well as priority taxpayers.

Poland

PwC contact

Iwona Smith
PricewaterhouseCoopers
International Business Centre
Aleja Armii Ludowej 14
00-638 Warszawa, Poland
Tel: +48 22 523 4000
Email: iwona.smith@pl.pwc.com

Significant developments

Value-added tax (VAT) developments
As of 1 January 2012, the standard VAT rate will apply to supplies of children's clothing and footwear. Prior to 1 January 2012, the 8% reduced VAT rate is applicable for those goods.

New excise duty on coal
As of January 2012, there is an excise duty placed on coal. In practice, there are a wide range of excise duty exemptions; nevertheless, many new administrative obligations have been set for entities producing, distributing, and using coal. The fulfilment of those obligations is necessary in order to apply an excise duty exemption.

See Excise duties in the Other taxes section for more information.

Taxes on corporate income

The corporate income tax (CIT) is the only tax levied on corporate income. The CIT rate is 19%.

Polish residents are subject to tax on their worldwide income. Non-residents are taxed only on their Polish-sourced income. The tax authorities' right to tax a non-resident is further limited if the non-resident's home country concluded a double-tax treaty (DTT) with Poland. In this case, the Polish tax authorities are entitled to tax only the portion of the non-resident's income that is derived through a permanent establishment (PE) located in Poland. The exceptions relate to specific types of income such as royalties, interest, dividends, and capital gains that are taxed based on special DTT rules.

Further to these rules, the CIT applies to companies with foreign participation. Such companies may be set up as either limited liability companies or joint-stock companies. There is no limitation on the percentage of foreign participation. Both types are subject to the general CIT rules, including the 19% tax rate. The same rate applies to branches of foreign companies (*see the Branch income section for more information*).

Local income taxes
There are no provisions relating to local income taxes in the Polish Law.

Corporate residence

A company is considered to be a resident in Poland if its registered office or management is located in Poland.

Poland

From the group of taxpayers, certain entities are explicitly excluded in the CIT Law (e.g. Treasury, National Bank of Poland). As of 1 January 2011, European Union (EU)/ European Economic Area (EEA) based investment funds are also exempted on the grounds of such provision (before this date, only Polish investment funds enjoyed the exemption).

Permanent establishment (PE)

PE under Polish CIT Law
According to Polish CIT Law, a PE should be understood as:

- a permanent place of business through which a non-Polish tax resident conducts its business activities, in whole or in part, within the territory of Poland, in particular a branch, agency, office, factory, workshop, or place of extraction of natural resources
- a construction site, construction, assembly, or installation works carried on within the territory of Poland by non-Polish tax resident, or
- a person who, on behalf and for the benefit of non-Polish tax resident, operates in Poland, if such person holds and exercises a power of attorney to enter into agreements on one's behalf.

We note that Polish CIT Law:

- does not encompass any provisions concerning the period required for construction works to create a PE
- does not include provisions indicating that an independent agent does not create a PE, and
- does not include provisions indicating that actions of an auxiliary or preparatory character do not lead to creation of a PE in Poland.

PE from a DTT perspective
In general, the provisions of DTTs concluded by Poland are based on the Organisation for Economic Co-operation and Development (OECD) Model Tax Convention on Income and on Capital (OECD Model), except for provisions related to taxation of royalties, which are based on the United Nations (UN) Model Double Taxation Convention.

As a principle, treaties based on the OECD Model provide for the following concepts, which determine whether activities of a foreign entrepreneur constitute a PE (usually in Article 5):

- Fixed place of business concept.
- Dependant agent concept.
- Construction PE concept.

Note that some DTTs concluded by Poland also encompass other PE concepts (e.g. service PE concept or offshore PE concept).

....

Other taxes

Value-added tax (VAT)
Polish VAT applies to the following activities:

- Supplies of goods and services within the territory of Poland.

Poland

- Exports of goods outside the territory of the European Union.
- Imports of goods from countries that do not belong to the European Union.
- Intra-Community acquisitions of goods (imports from countries belonging to the European Union).
- Intra-Community supplies of goods (exports to the countries belonging to the European Union).

VAT rates
The VAT rates are 23% (standard rate), 8%, 5%, 0%, and exemption.

The standard 23% VAT rate generally applies to the supply of all goods and services, except for those that are covered by special VAT provisions that provide other rates or treatments.

Supplies covered by a reduced rate of 8% include, among others, supplies of pharmaceutical products and passenger transport services and also supply of goods for the Social Housing Programme (no greater than 150 square metres).

Supplies covered by a reduced rate of 5% include books and journals, unprocessed food, and basic food.

Zero-rated activities include, among others, exports of goods to countries outside the European Union.

VAT-exempt supplies include, among others, certain financial, insurance, and educational services.

As of 1 January 2012, the standard VAT rate applies to supplies of children's clothing and footwear. Prior to 1 January 2012, the 8% reduced VAT rate was applicable for those goods.

Basic calculation rules
In general, the VAT due equals the VAT on outputs decreased by the VAT on inputs (in other words, input VAT is deducted from output VAT). Input VAT may be deducted from output VAT when a business (with a VAT payer status) receives an invoice for goods or services purchased. Input VAT may not be deducted unless a purchased supply is linked to the VAT-able activities. Furthermore, the deductibility of input VAT is restricted by the VAT law with respect to the purchase of certain goods and services. In addition, subject to numerous conditions, output VAT may be reduced when receivables, resulting from VAT-able sales, become uncollectible.

VAT refunds
The Polish VAT law allows direct refunds when input VAT (available for deduction) exceeds output VAT.

A Polish business may also be entitled to the VAT refund owed by another country under certain circumstances. Likewise, a foreign business having seat or fixed place of business for VAT purposes in Poland may be, in most cases, entitled to the refund of Polish VAT. If the respective countries belong to the European Union, the procedure is substantially simplified due to the EU Directive which provides favourable rules for businesses based in EU countries that are seeking VAT refunds in other EU countries (i.e. electronic VAT refunds are possible).

Poland

Reporting rules

Generally, the VAT reporting period is one month. VAT returns should be submitted by the 25th day of the month following the VAT reporting period. All taxpayers may opt for a quarterly, instead of monthly, reporting period. Note that businesses involved in intra-community acquisitions or supplies of goods are obliged to submit additional VAT returns with respect to these particular transactions.

International services

The treatment of international services largely depends on the place of supply, since it is determinative of whether particular services are subject to the Polish VAT. The Polish VAT applies only to those services that are supplied within Poland.

Generally, the place of supply depends on the recipient of services. If the recipient is a business entity, the place of supply is determined to be the recipient's country; if the recipient is a private person, the place of supply is determined to be the service provider's country. Thus, according to general rules, if a Polish entity supplies services to a foreign business entity, the place of supply is outside Poland (these services are not subject to Polish VAT); if a foreign company supplies services to a Polish business entity, the place of supply (taxation) is in Poland. However, these general rules are subject to several exceptions.

If services are supplied by a taxpayer without seat or fixed place of business in Poland and the place of supply (taxation) is Poland, the purchaser who is the Polish VAT taxpayer has to apply the reverse-charge mechanism. Since 1 April 2011, the reverse charge is mandatory (i.e. the foreign supplier cannot voluntarily register and settle the Polish VAT).

As of 1 April 2011, an obligatory reverse-charge mechanism also applies to a domestic supply of goods performed by a taxpayer not having seat or fixed place of business in Poland to a purchaser who is a taxpayer and has seat or fixed place of business in Poland or is a legal entity (and is not taxpayer) and has a seat in Poland.

Customs duties

As a member of the European Union, Poland belongs to a customs union, thus only goods imported from non-EU countries or exported from Poland to the non-EU countries are subject to customs duties and formalities. Moreover, all the Community customs regulations are directly applicable in Poland. The most important act is the Community Customs Code and its implementing provisions, as well as the Community Customs Tariff.

These regulations are supplemented with certain Polish national rules, especially in respect to procedures and specific areas which are not defined in the Community customs law (e.g. strict regulations concerning the export of works of art and animals, limits on the amount of cash that may be brought from Poland to non-EU countries).

Excise duties

Excise duties are levied on the production, sale, import, and intra-community acquisition of 'excise goods', which are listed in the excise duty law and include (among others) alcohol, cigarettes, energy products (e.g. petrol, oils, gas), passenger cars, and electricity.

Depending on the excise goods in question, one of four methods of calculating excise tax may be applicable:

- A percentage of the taxable base.
- An amount per unit.
- A percentage of the maximum retail price.
- An amount per unit and a percentage of the maximum retail price.

The excise rate for car petrol is 1,565 Polish złoty (PLN) per 1,000 litres.

Passenger cars are subject to the following excise rates:

- 3.1% for cars with engine cubic capacity that does not exceed 2,000 cc.
- 18.6% for cars with engine cubic capacity that exceeds 2,000 cc.

Notwithstanding the above, Polish excise duty law provides for a wide system of excise duty exemptions as well as 0% taxation. Under specified circumstances, such preferential treatment may apply to specified goods that are otherwise taxed based on general rules. This concerns, for example, specific energy products used for other purposes than as a fuel or for heating.

As of January 2012, there is an excise duty placed on coal. Depending on the type of coal product, the excise rates are PLN 30.5 per 1,000 kg of coal, PLN 11 per 1,000 kg of lignite, and PLN 35.2 per 1,000 kg of coke. In practice, there are a wide range of excise duty exemptions (practically, Poland has used all the exemption options provided in the EU directive); nevertheless, many new administrative obligations have been set for entities producing, distributing, and using coal. The fulfilment of those obligations is necessary in order to apply an excise duty exemption.

Property taxes
Property tax rates are fixed by municipalities within limits set in the Law on Local Taxes and Fees. In 2012, land used for business purposes is subject to a rate limit of PLN 0.84 per square metre. Buildings used for business purposes are subject to a rate limit of PLN 21.94 per square metre.

Stamp duty
In Poland, there is no stamp tax, but some activities are charged by stamp duty. Method of payment are signs of stamp duty. Payment is required, for example, in connection with the submission of a power of attorney, after completion of an official act, or the issue of a certificate or permit.

Capital tax
A share capital increase (in case of corporations) and contribution/contribution increase (in case of partnerships) is subject to a 0.5% capital tax, payable by a company or partnership that receives a capital contribution. This tax applies equally to limited liability companies as well as joint-stock companies. A merger, division, or transformation of a corporation into another corporation is not subject to capital tax, even if the transaction results in a share capital increase. A similar exemption applies to a capital increase resulting from (i) an in-kind contribution of an enterprise or its organised part or (ii) contribution of shares of other corporation giving the majority of votes in this corporation or contribution of additional shares in case the corporation to which the shares are contributed already has the majority of votes.

Poland

Branch income

Foreign businesses are allowed, under certain conditions, to establish their branch offices (exclusively within the scope of their 'foreign' business activity) and representative offices (exclusively with regard to promotion and advertising) in Poland.

A branch office almost always has PE status in Poland. Once a branch is established, the foreign company pays CIT at the standard rate of 19%, based on the income attributable to the operations of the Polish branch. For this purpose, as well as for accounting purposes, a branch is obliged to keep accounting books that include all the data necessary to establish the taxable base. In this respect, general income determination rules relevant to Polish companies apply to branches as well. In the few cases in which a branch can demonstrate, based on a DTT, that its business presence in Poland does not amount to a PE, its profits are not subject to Polish CIT.

Income determination

The tax base is the overall income, which is the difference between aggregated taxable revenue and aggregated tax-deductible costs. A tax-deductible cost is defined as a 'cost incurred in order to generate revenue' as well as the cost incurred to 'protect a source of revenue'.

Subject to numerous exemptions, the tax base includes all sources of income. Consequently, there is no special treatment for income such as capital gains or interest.

In practice, taxable income is calculated by adjusting the profit reported for accounting purposes. The relevant adjustments are necessary due to differences between tax and accounting treatment of numerous revenue and cost items. As a result, the taxable base is usually higher than the accounting profit.

Inventory valuation

Generally, the value of inventory shortages may be included as a tax-deductible cost. Other write-offs in the value of inventory are not recognised for tax purposes until the inventory in question is sold.

When inventory is lost or sold, a tax deduction is allowed for the costs incurred when the inventory was purchased. The methods acceptable for inventory valuation for tax (and accounting) purposes are standard cost, average (weighted) cost, first in first out (FIFO), and last in first out (LIFO).

Capital gains

There is no separate capital gains tax. Capital gains or losses are aggregated with an entity's other taxable income or losses. Capital losses are tax-deductible.

Dividend income
Domestic dividend income

Dividends received from Polish residents (domestic dividends) are excluded from overall income. Instead, such dividends are subject to a 19% withholding tax (WHT), which is withheld and remitted to the tax office by the payer of dividends. Based on a participation exemption, however, domestic dividends are not subject to the 19% WHT if the Polish beneficiary holds at least a 10% share in the paying company for at least two years.

Poland

The revenue arising from voluntary redemption of shares is not treated as a dividend for tax purposes and does not enjoy the benefits of the participation exemption (i.e. the method of redemption, whether voluntary or automatic, will matter).

Dividend income from abroad

Generally, dividends collected by a Polish corporate tax resident, if paid by a non-resident, are treated as regular income and taxed at the standard CIT rate. CIT on such dividends paid in other countries may be credited proportionately against Polish CIT. The CIT law also provides for an 'underlying tax credit', which is related to the CIT paid by a foreign subsidiary under a foreign tax jurisdiction, subject to a number of conditions. Specifically, a DTT between Poland and the subsidiary's country of residence should be in place and the Polish recipient of the dividend should hold at least 75% of the shares in the foreign subsidiary.

Additionally, dividends received from entities seated in the European Union (including Poland), EEA member states, or Switzerland can benefit from CIT exemption, if the Polish company owns respectively at least 10% (in respect to companies seated in the EU/EEA member states) or 25% (in respect to companies seated in Switzerland) in the share capital of the payer for two consecutive years (and certain other conditions are met).

Dividends received from non-EU/non-EEA member states may benefit from underlying tax credit. If a Polish company or a PE of a company from an EU/EEA member state located in Poland receives a dividend from a company seated in a non-EU/non-EEA country, it may deduct the tax paid by the payer on profits out of which the dividend was paid. The deduction is only possible provided that the Polish company/company from EU/EEA, which PE is located in Poland, holds (for two consecutive works) at least 75% of shares of the dividend payer. The tax may be deducted in an appropriate proportion. Furthermore, the deduction is possible provided that there is a DTT. Based on the provisions of the relevant DTT or other agreement concluded by Poland, the Polish tax authority may exchange tax information with its counterparty.

Interest income

Interest income is aggregated with an entity's other taxable income.

Foreign income

Resident corporations are taxed on their worldwide income unless there is an applicable DTT in place between Poland and the relevant country that provides that the foreign income shall be exempt from taxation in Poland (*see Foreign tax credit in the Tax credits and incentives section*).

Deductions

Generally, a tax-deductible cost is defined as a cost incurred in order to generate taxable revenue or to 'protect a source of income'. The last element of the definition of a tax-deductible cost was added a few years ago to reduce uncertainties surrounding the deductibility of business expenses that do not directly generate revenue.

The CIT law provides a list of items that are not deductible for tax purposes, even if the items meet the general conditions described above. This list contains over 60 items including, among others, the following:

Poland

- Written-off, lapsed accounts receivable.
- Entertainment costs.
- Accrued but unpaid interest.
- Accounting and comparable provisions.
- Tax penalties and penalty interest.
- A portion of the insurance premium paid on a passenger car (i.e. the portion calculated on the excess of the car value over 20,000 euros [EUR]).
- A portion of the depreciation write-offs made on a passenger car (i.e. the portion calculated on the excess of the car value over EUR 20,000).

Furthermore, expenses incurred in connection with the acquisition of fixed and intangible assets (e.g. licences, trademarks, know-how) are not deductible directly. Instead, the acquired assets are subject to depreciation. If such assets are sold, a business is entitled to deduct the net value (cost of acquisition reduced by the overall value of the tax depreciation allowances made). Similar treatment relates to the acquisition of shares or land, except that these particular assets are not depreciable. Therefore, the full cost of an acquisition of shares or land may be deducted when such assets are sold.

Depreciation

Depreciation is treated as a tax-deductible cost. Generally, depreciation allowances are calculated based on the straight-line method and the maximum rates provided in the CIT law. If this is the case, a taxpayer deducts equal annual write-offs, calculated by multiplying the maximum rate of depreciation by the asset's initial value until the total value of write-offs equals the initial value (typically, the initial value equals the purchase price).

For certain categories of machinery and vehicles (but not passenger cars), the reducing-balance depreciation method may be applied. Under this method, the tax depreciation may be accelerated during the initial period of the asset's use by multiplying the statutory maximum rate by two. The rate is then applied to the net value of fixed assets (i.e. initial value reduced by earlier annual write-offs). The reducing-balance method is applied until the annual depreciation write-off equals the hypothetical write-off that would be made under the straight-line method. From this point, the depreciation allowance is taken based on the straight-line method for its remaining useful life.

The main categories of assets and the related statutory annual tax depreciation rate are as follows:

Assets	Depreciation rate (%)
Various buildings and constructions	1.5 to 10
Machinery and equipment (general)	7 to 20
Machinery for road building and construction	18 to 20
Machinery for paper industry	14
Office equipment	20
Computers	30

Apart from the above, the Polish CIT law includes provisions for accelerated depreciation (within specified limits) for assets used in deteriorated conditions and for second-hand assets.

Goodwill

Under the provisions of CIT Law, goodwill is subject to tax amortisation if it is created as a result of acquisition of an enterprise, or its organised part, made in one of the following ways: (i) purchase; (ii) payable use, provided that the user of such enterprise/organised part of an enterprise makes the depreciation write-offs; or (iii) contribution to a company based on commercialisation and privatisation regulations. The goodwill is amortised for tax purposes for a minimum period of five years.

Start-up expenses

There are no specific provisions in the Polish CIT Law relating to start-up expenses; the general rules of tax deductibility described above apply.

Interest expenses

Capitalised, accrued, and paid interest on loans and credit can be deductible from CIT. Polish CIT Law provides some exceptions, such as instances where costs are not associated with earning revenue.

In Poland, there are also some limitations of interest tax deductibility connected with thin capitalisation regulations. *See Thin Capitalisation in the Group Taxation section for more information.*

Bad debt

As a general rule, debts written off as uncollectable cannot be considered as tax deductible. However, in certain situations, the provisions of Polish CIT Law provide some exceptions. According to these provisions, only strictly defined uncollectable debts (which based on the CIT Law were booked as taxable revenues) may be considered by the taxpayer as a tax-deductible cost, provided that their uncollectability was properly documented (e.g. by a court decision). In some cases, uncollectability may be considered probable (e.g. debtor's death).

Also, a VAT-payer has a possibility to correct the output tax on the supply of goods or the provision of services, in addition to 'bad debts' whose uncollectability was made plausible. To do so, a few conditions must be met. They mainly concern the debtor's and creditor's VAT status, lapse of the time limit for payment (specified in an invoice), and proper notifications made by the taxpayer.

P

Charitable contributions

Companies are entitled to deduct donations for the purposes of public benefit and to volunteer activity organisations up to the total amount not exceeding 10% of income; however, deductions may not be made for donations to:

- natural persons or
- legal persons or organisational units having no legal personality who carry on economic activity consisting in the production of electronic goods; fuel; tobacco; spirits, wines, beers, and other alcohol beverages containing over 1.5% alcohol; products made of noble metals or containing such metals; or incomes received from trading in such goods.

Donations for religious practice purposes can be deducted up to the total amount not exceeding 10% of income.

Additionally, the donations of food products made for the purposes of so-called public benefit constitute tax deductible costs in the amount of production costs or purchase price.

Poland

Fines and penalties
Fines and penalties can be recognised as tax deductible items if they meet the general conditions. However, the Polish CIT Law provides some exceptions, which include contractual penalties and indemnities for defects in supplied goods, works, and services performed; delayed supply of non-defective goods; and delay in the elimination of defects in goods, works, and services performed.

Taxes
Income tax and, in most cases, VAT incurred on purchases are not deductible. However, as a rule, VAT is deductible for CIT purposes if it cannot be offset against the company's output VAT. Other taxes, if paid in the course of business activities, are generally deductible in full.

Net operating losses
A tax loss reported in a tax year may be carried forward over the next five consecutive tax years; however, in any particular tax year, the taxpayer may not deduct more than 50% of the loss incurred in the year in which it was reported. For example, a taxpayer that incurred PLN 100 annual loss in 2010 may carry it forward to 2011 through 2015. However, the maximum loss deduction in any of these years may not exceed PLN 50 (assuming that there are no other losses available for deduction).

Currently, there is no possibility to carry back tax losses in Poland.

Payments to foreign affiliates
Deductions may be claimed for royalties, management services, and interest charges paid to foreign affiliates. However, note that interest expenses are subject to the thin capitalisation restrictions (*see Thin capitalisation in the Group taxation section for more information*). Furthermore, note that transactions with related companies should be made according to the market conditions. Where a company shifts income to another entity (especially a foreign entity), the tax authorities may adjust the taxable base upward (*see Transfer pricing in the Group taxation section for more information*).

Group taxation

The CIT law includes provisions on group taxation (i.e. in theory, a group of companies) if it meets certain conditions and can be treated as a single taxpayer. However, the required conditions are extremely demanding and very few taxpayers of this type exist.

Transfer pricing
Transactions between related parties should be conducted in accordance with the arm's-length principle. The tax authorities may increase the taxable base if the pricing used between related parties differs from what would have been used between unrelated parties in a similar business transaction and the difference results in income being shifted from a Polish taxpayer to another entity (whether a Polish resident or not). Similar rules apply to transactions between Polish residents and the residents of tax haven countries. These transactions may be subject to the transfer pricing principles even if the parties thereto are not related. The CIT law also contains detailed requirements for transfer pricing documentation.

Taxpayers can reduce the transfer pricing risk by applying for an advance pricing arrangement (APA). An APA decision shall be issued by the Minister of Finance in response to a taxpayer's application. An APA will oblige a taxpayer to follow a specified methodology when calculating the transfer prices applicable to transactions between related entities. In exchange, the tax authorities may not challenge the agreed upon methodology.

Thin capitalisation

A portion of the interest paid by a Polish company on a loan granted by a qualified lender (a qualified shareholder or a qualified sister company) will not be considered a tax-deductible cost if the value of the Polish company's overall debt from the shareholders and other affiliates mentioned in the tax law exceeds three times the value of the Polish company's share capital (3:1 debt-to-equity ratio). A qualified shareholder is defined as a holder of 25% or more of the voting power of a Polish company. A qualified sister company is a company of which a shareholder holds at least 25% of the value of the shares.

Tax credits and incentives

Special Economic Zones (SEZs)

Polish legislation provides investment incentives related to business activities carried out in 14 zones defined as SEZs. A business entity can benefit from tax incentives, provided that the entity obtains a permit from the Ministry of the Economy to conduct business activities there and meets other legal requirements. Note that a CIT credit applies only to income earned on activity conducted within the territory of SEZs and covered by permit.

In general, the amount of the tax incentive depends on project location and size of the enterprise. For large enterprises, it can be 30%, 40%, or 50% of eligible expenditures (i.e. investment expenditures or two-year labour costs). In other words, the CIT credit allows the investor to avoid paying income tax up to the limit calculated on the basis of eligible expenditures and state aid intensity (percentage as above). In case of investment valued PLN 20 million and intensity aid of 40%, the investor would be entitled not to pay tax due up to PLN 8 million. If the available limit of the tax credit exceeds the annual tax due generated on SEZ activity, the excess may be utilised in the following tax years. Consequently, in the case of significant investments, it is possible for businesses that run activities in the SEZs to enjoy exemption from income tax for a considerable period. According to current regulations, the deadline for utilising available tax credit is the end of 2020.

Note that in the case of small enterprises, the limit of the tax credit may be increased by 20%. In the case of medium-sized enterprises, the limit of the tax credit may be increased by 10%.

Foreign tax credit

Resident corporations are taxed on their worldwide income unless there is an applicable DTT in place between Poland and the relevant country that provides that the foreign income shall be exempt from taxation in Poland. In all other cases (in particular, when the income is not covered by any treaty), Poland uses the ordinary credit method to avoid double taxation. Therefore, a Polish resident is liable for income tax imposed on its worldwide income, but the tax is proportionately reduced by the income tax paid abroad.

Poland

Withholding taxes

Domestic provisions: General rules
The general domestic WHT rate for dividends is 19%. Dividends encompass also income from liquidation of a company and the income from the redemption of shares (with the exception of gain from voluntary redemption, which is treated as a capital gain subject to 19% CIT rate in Poland if the gain is realised by a taxpayer from non-treaty country or the treaty includes a so-called real estate clause).

The general WHT rate on interest and royalties paid to non-residents is 20% (10% regarding services of sea or air transportation). These WHT rates may be reduced by DTTs.

There is also a 20% WHT on payments made to non-residents for intangible services (such as consulting services). However, if a payment is made to a country that has a DTT with Poland, this tax may be avoided with the completion of certain minimal administrative formalities. Few treaties treat payments for technical services as royalties (e.g. India).

Special treatment: EU directives
The CIT law provisions and certain EU directives provide special treatment for dividends, royalties, and interest paid to numerous European countries.

When joining the European Union, Poland was granted a transitional period to phase out the WHT on interest and royalty payments paid by Polish corporate residents to associated EU or EEA companies. As of 1 July 2009, the WHT rate on these payments is 5%. Starting on 1 July 2013, a full exemption will apply. In general, the transitional rules, as well as the full exemption after 1 July 2013, only apply to interest and royalty payments between associated companies (parent-subsidiary relationships or sister-sister relationships) in which capital involvements are significant.

Dividends paid to corporate residents of EU and EEA countries are exempt from WHT, subject to certain conditions specified in the CIT law. The basic requirement is that the foreign beneficiary holds at least 10% of the shares in the Polish company for a minimum of two years. This condition is also fulfilled if the required period passes after the day of payment of the dividend. If the period is interrupted afterwards, the company is obliged to pay the tax with standard rate with interest.

Note that several additional conditions have to be met for the reduced rate/exemption from the WHT based on the Directive to be applied (e.g. the company receiving the dividend/interest/royalty cannot be exempt from tax on all its income, regardless of its source; the recipient has to have ownership title to the shares in the Polish company).

Additionally, the amendments state that in order to enjoy the exemption from WHT on dividends and decreased WHT rate on interest and royalties, based on the Directives' provisions, the relevant DTT or other agreement concluded by Poland should allow exchange of tax information between the tax authorities of Poland and the country of the payment recipient.

Given the fact that Poland did not conclude a DTT with Liechtenstein, payments made to tax residents of Liechtenstein should not benefit from the Directive.

Treaty rates

If EU special rules do not apply, the domestic WHT rates can be decreased by a DTT concluded between Poland and the payment recipient's country of residence if certain administrative conditions are met (i.e. the payer obtains a valid certificate of a fiscal residence of the payment recipient/beneficial owner).

The following table lists the WHT rates as provided in the treaties concluded by Poland. Notably, the following table shows only rates that result from general treaty provisions; the treaties themselves occasionally include special provisions (applicable in special circumstances or to special entities) that provide lower WHT rates than the ones listed.

Furthermore, if a treaty rate is higher than a domestic one, the latter should apply.

Recipient	Dividends (%)	Interest (%)	Royalties (%)
Non-Treaty	19	20	20
Treaty:			
Albania	5 (1)/10	10	5
Armenia	10	5	10
Australia	15	10	10
Austria	5 (3)/15	0 (4)/5	5
Azerbaijan	10	0 (2)/10	10
Bangladesh	10 (5)/15	0 (6)/10	10
Belarus	10 (7)/15	10	0
Belgium	5 (8)/15	0 (9)/5	5
Bosnia & Herzegovina (Yugoslavian Treaty)	5 (1)/15	10	10
Bulgaria	10	0 (10)/10	5
Canada	15	0 (11)/15	0 (12)/10
Chile	5 (13)/15	15	5 (14)/15
China, P.R.	10	0 (15)/10	10 (16)/10 of 70 (14)
Croatia	5 (1)/15	0 (15)/10	10
Cyprus	10	0 (17)/10	5
Czech Republic	5 (18)/10	0 (10)/10	5
Denmark	0 (19)/5 (20)/15	0 (21)/5	5
Egypt	12	0 (22)/12	12
Estonia	5 (23)/15	0 (24)/10	10
Finland	5 (23)/15	5	5
France	5 (3)/15	0	0 (25)/10
Georgia	10	0 (26)/8	8
Germany	5 (3)/15	0 (27)/5	5
Greece	19 (74)	10	10
Hungary	10	0 (10)/10	10
Iceland	5 (23)/15	0 (10)/10 (75)	10
India	15	0 (28)/15	20
Indonesia	10 (13)/15	0 (10)/10	15
Iran	7	0 (29)/10	10
Ireland, Republic of	0 (30)/15	0 (31)/10	10
Israel	5 (32)/10	5	5 (14)/10
Italy	10	0 (33)/10	10
Japan	10	0 (34)/10	0 (35)/10

P

Poland

Recipient	Dividends (%)	Interest (%)	Royalties (%)
Jordan	10	0 (10)/10	10
Kazakhstan	10 (36)/15	0 (37)/10	10
Korea, Republic of	5 (3)/10	0 (38)/10	10
Kyrgyzstan	10	0 (39)/10	10
Kuwait	0 (40)/5	0 (41)/5	15
Latvia	5 (23)/15	0 (42)/10	10
Lebanon	5	0 (37)/5	5
Lithuania	5 (23)/15	0 (10)/10	10
Luxembourg	5 (23)/15	0 (43)/10	10
Macedonia	5 (23)/15	0 (10)/10	10
Malaysia	0 (44)/15	0 (45)/15	0 (46)/15
Malta	0 (79)/10 (78)	0 (2)/5	5 (80)
Mexico	5 (23)/15	0 (47)/5 (48)/15	10
Moldova	5 (23)/15	0 (37)/10	10
Mongolia	10	0 (10)/10	5
Montenegro (Yugoslavian Treaty)	5 (23)/15	10	10
Morocco	7 (18)/15	10	10
Netherlands	5 (3)/15	0 (76)/5	5
New Zealand	15	10	10
Norway	0 (49)/15	0 (4)/5	5
Pakistan	15	0 (50)/20	15 (51)/20 (52)
Philippines	10 (23)/15	0 (53)/10	15
Portugal	10 (54)/15	0 (55)/10	10
Romania	5 (23)/15	0 (42)/10	10
Russia	10	0 (56)/10	10
Serbia (Yugoslavian treaty)	5 (23)/15	10	10
Singapore	0 (57)/10	0 (58)/10	10
Slovak Republic	5 (18)/10	0 (42)/10	5
Slovenia	5 (23)/15	0 (59)/10	10
South Africa	5 (23)/15	0 (10)/10	10
Spain	5 (1)/15	0	0 (35)/10
Sri Lanka	0 (60)/15 (77)	0 (61)/10	0 (62)/10
Sweden	5 (23)/15	0	5
Switzerland	0 (20, 49)/15	10	0 (63)/10
Syria	10	0 (64)/10	18
Tajikistan	15	0 (39)/10	10
Thailand	19	0 (58)/10	0 (65)/5 (66)/15
Tunisia	5 (1)/10	12	12
Turkey	10 (23)/15	0 (10)/10	10
Ukraine	5 (23)/15	0 (37)/10	10
United Arab Emirates	0 (67)/5	0 (10)/5	5
United Kingdom	0 (68)/10	0 (69)/5	5
United States	5 (70)/15	0	10
Uzbekistan	5 (71)/15	0 (72)/10	10
Vietnam	10 (23)/15	10	10 (73)/15
Zimbabwe	10 (23)/15	10	10

Poland

Notes

1. When the beneficial owner is a company that holds directly at least 25% of the capital of the company paying the dividends.
2. When interest is paid to the government, the central bank of the state, including local authorities or other government bodies.
3. When the beneficial owner is a company (other than a partnership) that holds directly at least 10% of the capital of the company paying the dividends.
4. When interest is paid to the government, a political subdivision, or a local authority in connection with:
   - a loan granted, insured, or guaranteed by a governmental institution for the purposes of promoting exports
   - a sale on credit of any industrial, commercial, or scientific equipment, or
   - any loan granted by a bank.
5. When the beneficial owner is a company that holds directly at least 10% of the capital of the company paying the dividends.
6. When the interest is paid:
   - to the Central Bank of Poland
   - to the Central Bank of Bangladesh
   - to the government of the Republic of Poland or the government of the Republic of Bangladesh, or
   - in respect of a loan made or guaranteed or insured by the government of the other state, or any agency including a financial institution owned or controlled by the government.
7. When the beneficial owner is a company (other than a partnership) that holds directly at least 30% of the capital of the company paying the dividends.
8. When the beneficial owner is a company (other than a partnership):
   - that holds directly at least 25% of the capital of the company paying the dividends or
   - that holds directly at least 10% of the capital of the company paying the dividends, and the value of investments in the company is at least EUR 500,000 or is equal to the amount in the other currency.
9. When interest is paid:
   - on loan granted, guaranteed, or insured, or a credit granted, guaranteed, or insured, by a general system organised by the state, including political subdivisions or local authorities for purposes of promoting exports
   - on loan of whatever kind, except in the form of bearer securities, granted by a banking company, or
   - to other states, including political subdivisions and local authorities.
10. When interest is paid to the government, including local authorities, to the central bank or any financial institution controlled by that government, or on loans guaranteed by that government.
11. When interest is paid in respect of a loan made, guaranteed, or insured by the state or agreed public body.
12. Copyright royalties and other similar payments in respect of the production or reproduction of any literary, dramatic, musical, or artistic work (not including royalties in respect of motion picture films and works on film or videotape for use in connection with television).
13. When the beneficial owner is a company that controls directly 20% of the voting stock of the company paying the dividends.
14. For the use of, or the right to use any industrial, commercial, or scientific equipment.
15. When interest is paid:
   - to the government, a local authority, and the central bank or any financial institution wholly owned by that government or
   - to the other resident of the other state with respect to debt-claims indirectly financed by the government of the other state, a local authority, and the central bank or any financial institution wholly owned by the government.
16. For the use of, or the right to use, any copyright of literary, artistic, or scientific work, including cinematograph films, and films or tapes for radio or television broadcasting, or any patent, know-how, trademark, design or model, plan, secret formula, or process.
17. When interest is paid to the government, including political sub-divisions and local authorities, the central bank or any statutory body of the state with respect to loans or credits made or guaranteed by the government of the other state, including political sub-divisions and local authorities, the central Bank, or any statutory body of the other state.
18. When the beneficial owner is a company (other than a partnership) that holds directly at least 20% of the capital of the company paying the dividends.
19. When the beneficial owner is a company (other than a partnership) that holds directly at least 25% of the capital of the company paying the dividends, where such holding is being possessed for an uninterrupted period of no less than one year and the dividends are declared within that period.
20. When the beneficial owner is a pension fund or other similar institution providing pension schemes in which individuals may participate in order to secure retirement benefits, when such pension fund or other similar institution is established, recognised for tax purposes and controlled in accordance with the laws of the other state.
21. When interest is paid:
   - on loan whatever kind granted, insured, or guaranteed by a financial institution owned or controlled by the state
   - in connection with the sale on credit of any industrial, commercial, or scientific equipment

Poland

- in respect of a bond, debenture, or other similar obligations of the government of the state, or of a political subdivision or local authority, or
- to the other state, or to a political subdivision or local authority.
22. When interest is paid to the government of the other state, including local authorities and the central bank.
23. When the beneficial owner is a company (other than a partnership) that holds directly at least 25% of the capital of the company paying the dividends.
24. When interest is paid to the government of the other state, including political subdivisions and local authorities, the central bank, or any financial institution owned by the government or on loans guaranteed by the government.
25. From copyright of literary, artistic, or scientific work.
26. When the beneficial owner is the government of the other state or central bank.
27. When the interest, subject to certain exceptions related to silent shareholders, is paid:
    - to the government of Poland or Germany on a loan of whatever kind granted, insured, or guaranteed by a public institution for purposes of promoting exports
    - in connection with the sale on credit of any industrial, commercial, or scientific equipment
    - in connection with the sale on credit goods between companies, or
    - on any loan of whatever kind granted by a bank.
28. If the following conditions are met:
    - Interests paid to:
        - the government, a political sub-division, or a local authority of the other contracting state or
        - the central bank of other contracting state.
    - When the beneficial owner is a resident of the other contracting state and is derived in connection with a loan or credit extended or endorsed by:
        - Bank Handlowy (in scope of financing export and import) - for Poland
        - the Export-Import Bank of India (in scope of financing export and import) - for India
        - any institution in the other contracting state in charge of public financing of external trade, or
        - any other person, provided that the loan or credit is approved by the government of the first mentioned contracting state.
29. When the beneficial owner is the government, ministry, other governmental institution, municipality, central bank, or any other bank wholly owned by the government of the other contracting state.
30. When the beneficial owner is a resident of the other contracting state and holds directly at least 25% of the voting power of the company paying the dividends.
31. Interest paid in connection with:
    - the sale on credit of any industrial, commercial, or scientific equipment
    - the sale on credit of any merchandise by one enterprise to another, or
    - on any loan of whatever kind granted by the bank.
32. When the beneficial owner is a company that holds directly at least 15% of the capital of the company paying the dividends.
33. If the following conditions are met:
    - When the payer of interests is the government or contracting state or a local authority of thereof.
    - Interest is paid to the government of other contracting state or local authority thereof (including financing institutions) wholly owned by other contracting state or local authority thereof.
    - Interest is paid to any other entity, including financial institutions, in relation to loans made in application of an agreement concluded between governments of contracting states.
34. When beneficial owner is the government of other contracting state, including local authorities thereof, the central bank, any financial institutions controlled by that government or any resident of the other contracting state with respect to debt-claims, guaranteed or indirectly financed by institutions mentioned above.
35. For payments connected with copyrights, literary, artistic, and scientific activity, including payments connected with films for cinemas and films and tapes for TV.
36. When the beneficial owner is a company that holds directly or indirectly, at least 20% of the capital of the company paying the dividends.
37. When interest is paid to the government or local authorities.
38. When interest:
    - arising in contracting state and received by the government of the other contracting state, including political subdivision or a local authority thereof or the central bank of that other contracting state
    - arising in contracting state is paid in respect of loans and credits made or guaranteed:
        - by the Bank Handlowy - for Poland
        - by the Export-Import Bank of Korea and Korea Development Bank - for Korea
    - is paid in connection with the sale on credit of any industrial, commercial, or scientific equipment, or
    - is paid in connection with the sale on credit of any merchandise by one enterprise to another.
39. Interest paid to government or central bank.
40. When the beneficial owner is:
    - the government of the other contracting state, entity, or any governmental institution or
    - a company that is a resident of the other contracting state and at least 25% of its capital is owned directly or indirectly by the entities mentioned above.
41. If the following conditions are met:
    - When the beneficial owner is:
        - the government of the other contracting state, entity, or governmental institution or

- a company that is a resident of the other contracting state and at least 25% of its capital is owned directly or indirectly by the entities mentioned above
- When interest is paid in connection with loans guaranteed by the entities mentioned above.

42. When interest is paid:
- to the government, including the local authorities, to the central bank or any financial institution controlled by that government, or on loans guaranteed by that government or
- to the resident in the other contracting state.

43. If the following conditions are met:
- When the beneficial owner is other contracting state.
- When interest is paid in connection with loans and credits granted by bank.

44. Dividends paid by:
- a resident of Poland to a resident of Malaysia who is subject to Malaysian tax in respect thereof or
- a resident of Malaysia to a resident of Poland who is subject to Polish tax in respect thereof.

45. Interest paid to resident of Poland on an approved loan or a long-term loan.

46. Royalties paid to resident of Poland by resident of Malaysia and approved by the competent authority of Malaysia.

47. If the following conditions are met:
- When the beneficial owner is:
  - a contracting state, a political subdivision, or a local authority, or The National Bank of Poland or Banko de Mexico or
  - a recognised pension or retirement fund provided that its income is generally exempt from tax in this state.
- When interest:
  - is paid by any of entities mentioned above
  - arises in Poland and is paid in respect of a loan for a period not less than three years granted, guaranteed, or insured by Banco de Comercio Exterior, S.N.C., Nacional Financiera, S.N.C. or Banco National de Obras y Servicios Publicos S.N.C., or
  - arises in Mexico and is paid in respect of a loan for a period not less than three years granted, guaranteed, or insured by PKO S.A., Corporation of Credit Insurance, and Bank Handlowy in Warsaw.

48. If the following conditions are met:
- When the beneficial owner is a bank or insurance company.
- When interest is derived from bonds and securities that are regularly and substantially traded on a recognised securities market.

49. When dividends are paid to the company that holds directly at least 10% of the capital paying the dividends on the day they are paid and has done (or will do) so for an interrupted 24-month period from which that date falls.

50. When interests is paid:
- by a resident of Pakistan to a Polish company or enterprise on loans approved by the Ministry of Finance of the government of Pakistan
- to the State Bank of Pakistan from sources in Poland, or
- to Bank Handlowy in Poland from the sources in Pakistan.

51. For payments of any kind received in consideration for the use of, or the right to use:
- any copyright, patent, trademark, design or model, plan, secret formula, or process
- an industrial, commercial, or scientific equipment, or
- motion picture films, and works on films and videotapes for use in connection with television.

52. For payments received in consideration of technical know-how concerning industrial, commercial, or scientific experience.

53. Interests paid in respect of:
- a bond, debenture, or other similar obligations of the government, state, political subdivision, or local authority thereof or
- a loan or credit extended, guaranteed, insured, or refinanced by:
  - Central Bank of Philippines - for Philippines
  - Central Bank of Poland - for Poland, or
  - other lending institutions as specified and agreed in letters of exchange between competent authorities of the contracting states.

54. When dividends are paid to the company that holds directly at least 25% of the capital stock of the company paying the dividends for an uninterrupted 24-month period prior to the payment.

55. If the following conditions are met:
- When the debtor of such interests is the government, a political subdivision, or local authority.
- When the interest is paid to the government of other contracting state, a political subdivision, or local authority thereof, or an institution or body in connection with any financing granted by them under an agreement between the governments of the contracting states.
- Loans or credit made on central banks of contracting states and any other financial institution controlled by the state and financing external business that may be agreed upon between the competent authorities of the contracting states.

56. Interests paid to government, administrative, territorial, or the central bank.

57. Dividends paid by:
- the company that is a resident of Singapore to a resident of Poland (as long as Singapore does not impose a tax on dividends in addition to the tax chargeable on the profits or income of a company) or

P

Poland

- to government of either contracting state with respect to shares in joint stock companies of that other state.
58. Interest paid to government.
59. Interests paid to government, local authorities, or the central bank.
60. Exempt income tax in Sri Lanka, not exceeding 33 1/3% on the company that pays dividends and other than the additional tax not exceeding 6% on companies whose shares are not movable property situated in Sri Lanka for the purpose of the law of Sri Lanka relating to Estate duty.
61. Interests:
    - received by any banking institution that is a resident of contracting state
    - derived from contracting state of the other contracting state either directly or through any agency, or
    - accruing to any company, partnership, or other body of persons resident in the contracting state for any loans in money, goods, and services or in any other form, granted by them to the government of the other contracting state, or to a state corporation, or to any state institution, or to any other institution, to the capital of which, the other contracting state has made any contribution, or to a credit agency, or an undertaking in that other contracting state with the approval of the government of the same state.
62. For payment in consideration, for the use of, or the right to use, any copyrights or cinematograph films.
63. As long as Switzerland will not tax royalties paid to foreign recipients, the payments are taxed only in the country of residence of the recipient (currently there is no WHT in Switzerland).
64. If the following conditions are met:
    - When recipient is a contracting state, or one of its local authorities, or the statutory body of either, including the central bank; or when interests are paid by a contracting state, or one of its local authorities, or the statutory body of either.
    - Such interest is paid in respect of any debt-claim or loan guaranteed, insured, or supported by a contracting state or another person acting on state's behalf.
65. Payments payable to contracting state or a state owned company in respect of tape or films.
66. Royalties made as consideration, for the alienation, or the use of, or the right to use, any copyright of literary, artistic, or scientific work, excluding cinematographic films or tapes for television or broadcasting.
67. When the beneficial owner is the government or a government institution.
68. When dividends are paid to a company that is the resident of the other contracting state and that holds directly at least 10% of the capital, paying the dividends on the day they are paid and has done (or will do so) for an uninterrupted 24-month period from which that date falls.
69. When interests are paid to the government, a political subdivision, or a local authority in connection with:
    - a loan granted, insured, or guaranteed by a governmental institution for the purposes of promoting exports
    - the sale on credit of any industrial, commercial, or scientific equipment, or
    - any loan granted by a bank.
70. When the beneficial owner is a company that holds directly at least 10% of the outstanding shares of the voting stock of the company paying the dividends.
71. When the beneficial owner is a company that holds directly at least 20% of the capital of the company paying the dividends.
72. When the beneficial owner is:
    - the government or a local authority or
    - the National Bank of Poland or the Central Bank of Uzbekistan Republic.
73. For payment of any kind, received in consideration, for the use of, or the right to use:
    - any patent, design or model, plan, secret formula, or process or
    - any information concerning industrial or scientific experience.
74. Treaty allows application of the domestic tax rate.
75. As long as Iceland does not levy tax at source of income, interest is taxable only in the contracting state of which the beneficial owner of the interest is a resident.
76. When interest is paid to the government, a political subdivision, or a local authority in connection with:
    - a loan granted, insured, or guaranteed by a governmental institution for the purposes of promoting exports
    - a sale on credit of any industrial, commercial, or scientific equipment
    - any loan granted by a bank
    - in respect of a bond, debenture, or other similar obligations of the government of a contracting state, or of a political subdivision or local authority thereof, or
    - to the other contracting state, or to a political subdivision or local authority thereof.
77. Provided that any new contribution is made to the capital of a company resident in Sri Lanka by a company resident in Poland.
78. When the tax is charged by Poland.
79. When the dividends are paid by a company resident of Poland to a resident of Malta that holds directly at least 10% of the capital company paying the dividends on the date they are paid and has done so or will have done so for an uninterrupted 24-month period in which that date falls.
80. When the recipient is the beneficial owner.

Tax administration

Tax returns
The annual CIT return should be submitted to the tax office within three months following the end of the tax year.

Payment of tax
The same deadline as the CIT return applies to the settlement of the annual CIT liability. In financial terms, the final settlement is not significant since most of the annual liability is paid by CIT advances throughout the tax year.

The CIT advances should be paid for each month by the 20th day of the following month. Entities that started business activities (except for companies organised as a result of certain transformations) and entities whose gross sales revenue (including VAT) in the prior tax year did not exceed EUR 1.2 million are entitled to opt to make advance settlements on a quarterly basis (instead of a monthly basis).

Audit cycle
The tax authorities generally shall notify its intention to initiate a tax audit. The inspection shall be initiated not earlier than after seven days and not later than 30 days from the receipt of the notice.

The duration of all audits in one calendar year may not exceed the following:

- For micro entrepreneurs: 12 working days.
- For small entrepreneurs: 18 working days.
- For medium entrepreneurs: 24 working days.
- For large entrepreneurs: 48 working days.

Statute of limitations
Tax liability expires five years after the end of the calendar year in which the tax payment deadline passed. There are also situations when the statue of limitations can be suspended or interrupted (e.g. litigation).

Topics of focus for tax authorities
The Ministry of Finance publishes tasks for audit authorities every year. It is not an official document but rather an internal ordinance.

In 2012, the topics of focus for tax authorities include the following:

- Excise duty, especially connected with liquid fuels trade.
- VAT on intra-Community transactions.
- Tax frauds in VAT on domestic transactions.

In practice, the main fields of control held by audit authorities are as follows:

- Validity of the VAT refund.
- Possibility to correct excise duty resulting from post-transaction rebate.
- Correctness of VAT returns concerning scrap sales.
- Correctness of settlements concerning the use of a trademark.

Portugal

PwC contact

Jaime Esteves
PricewaterhouseCoopers & Associados - SROC, Lda.
Palácio Sottomayor
Rua Sousa Martins 1 - 4º
1069-316 Lisboa
Portugal
Tel: +351 225 433 212
Email: jaime.esteves@pt.pwc.com

Significant developments

May 2012: Amending 2012 State Budget

The 2012 State Budget Law, approved by Law No. 64-B/2011, dated 30 December, was amended following the publication of Law No. 20/2012, published in the Official Gazette of 14 May 2012. The following changes are relevant.

Property taxes

Rates
The aggravated rate of 7.5% of annual property tax (IMI) applicable in case of real estate owned by entities resident in blacklisted jurisdictions applies only to corporations; it is no longer applicable in case of ownership by individuals resident in blacklisted jurisdictions, which will now be subject to the standard rates (between 0.3% to 0.8%). The new rule applies to property tax due in 2012, assessed in 2011.

The aggravated rate of 10% of property transfer tax (IMT) applicable in case of real estate owned by entities resident in blacklisted jurisdictions applies only to corporations; it is no longer applicable in case of ownership by individuals resident in blacklisted jurisdictions, which will now be subject to the standard rates (5% for rural real estate and 6.5% for urban real estate and land for construction).

Tax benefits
The exemption from annual property tax (IMI) applicable to entities licensed to operate within the Madeira International Business Center does not apply in case of entities engaged in financial brokerage and insurance, including auxiliary entities related with such activities, as well as entities providing 'intra-group services' (coordination, treasury, and distribution centres).

Tax administration

It is mandatory that payments above 1,000 euros (EUR) (previously EUR 9,700) are made by a means that allows the identification of the recipient of the income (e.g. bank transfer, nominative cheque, or direct debit).

January 2012: 2012 State Budget Law

The 2012 State Budget Law was published in the Official Gazette of 30 December 2011. Law No. 64-B/2011 is effective as of 1 January 2012.

Corporate income tax (CIT)

Rates
CIT will now be levied at the single rate of 25%, as the 12.5% rate, previously applicable to taxable profits equal or below EUR 12,500, has been revoked.

The CIT applicable to entities with their head office in the Autonomous Region of Madeira (but not licensed to operate in the Madeira International Business Centre) is harmonised with the CIT rate levied in Portugal mainland, increasing from 20% to 25%. The reduced 10% CIT rate applicable in the Autonomous Region of Madeira to taxable profits equal to or below EUR 12,500 has also been revoked.

Withholding tax (WHT) rates
A new 30% WHT rate is applicable to capital income paid or made available to non-resident entities without a permanent establishment (PE) in Portugal that are resident in a country, territory, or region subject to a more favourable tax regime.

Information technology (IT) equipment
Impairment losses resulting from the write-off in 2012 of invoicing software and computer equipment, which is to be replaced as a result of new requirements for software certification, are fully deductible for tax purposes without the need of approval by the tax authorities.

In addition, the acquisition of this type of equipment and software in 2012 may be totally tax deducted in the period.

The use of invoicing software and equipment previously certified by the tax authorities is now mandatory.

Deduction of tax losses
There is an extension from four to five years for the tax-loss carryforward period, which applies to tax losses assessed in tax years starting on or after 1 January 2012.

It is no longer possible to fully offset the total amount of taxable profit with tax losses from prior years, as the deduction is capped at 75% of the taxable profit assessed in the relevant tax year. This limitation is applicable as of 2012 and applies to tax losses generated in tax years prior to 2012.

Payments to non-residents subject to a more favourable tax regime
Payments made or due, indirectly, to non-resident entities subject to a more favourable tax regime, when the taxable person has or should have had knowledge of the final purpose given to such payments, will be non-deductible for tax purposes, except if the taxpayer demonstrates that such charges relate to genuine transactions and are not of an abnormal or exaggerated amount. Such knowledge is presumed whenever there are special relations between the taxpayer and the entities subject to the more favourable tax regime or between the taxpayer and the legal representative, fiduciary, or intermediary.

Attribution of profits to non-residents entities subject to a more favourable tax regime (controlled foreign companies or CFCs)
CFC rules are also applicable whenever the profits or income resulting from an indirect holding is achieved through a legal representative, fiduciary, or intermediary. Nevertheless, the CFC regime shall no longer be applicable to entities resident in the European Union (EU) or in the European Economic Area (EEA) when the incorporation

Portugal

and functioning of such controlled entities has valid economic reasons and the entity develops agricultural, commercial, industrial, or services activities.

Additionally, the tax credit for international double taxation not used due to insufficient tax due may no longer be carried forward to subsequent tax periods.

Group taxation
The parent company will be responsible for demonstrating that the requirements for the application of the group taxation regime are fulfilled.

It has been clarified that in case the special tax regime for group taxation applies, the municipal surcharge should be individually computed by each of the companies included in the group, as it has been the opinion of the tax authorities, and not at the level of the group's taxable income.

Autonomous taxation rates
The application of the increased autonomous taxation rate on undocumented expenses (of 70%) is extended to entities with income subject to tax on gambling.

The rate of autonomous taxation on profits distributed to entities wholly or partially exempt from CIT, when the shareholding has not been held for a minimum period of one year has been increased from 20% to 25%.

State surcharge (Derrama Estadual)
The state surcharge is aggravated through the introduction of two taxation brackets: the first, with a 3% rate, applicable to taxable profits between EUR 1.5 million and EUR 10 million, and a second bracket, with a 5% rate, applicable to taxable profits exceeding EUR 10 million.

The rules for calculating the additional payments on account were revised accordingly. A rate of 2.5% is applicable to the taxable profits between EUR 1.5 million and EUR 10 million and a 4.5% rate is applicable to taxable profit above EUR 10 million, with reference to the previous tax year.

The new rules on the calculation of the state surcharge and additional payments on account are applicable to fiscal years 2012 and 2013.

Tax representation of non-resident entities
The appointment of a tax representative for non-resident entities without a PE in Portugal that obtain income derived from Portugal is not mandatory whenever the entity is resident in the EU or in the EEA.

Value-added tax (VAT)

Restructuring of reduced and intermediate rates
Several goods formerly subject to the reduced rate (6%) and intermediate rate (13%) are now subject to the standard VAT rate (23%).

VAT rates in Madeira
Effective as of 1 April 2012, the VAT rates in the Autonomous Region of Madeira have been increased to 22% (standard rate), 12% (intermediate rate), and 5% (reduced rate).

VAT-able amount of operations between related parties
A new anti-avoidance rule is introduced that ensures that, in respect of the supply of goods or services involving related parties, the taxable amount is the open market value.

The rule applies regardless of whether the purchasers or recipients are taxable persons or not.

The open market value may not be applied if the taxpayer proves that the price derives from circumstances other than the existence of special relations.

Sales of goods to national exporters
New conditions on the VAT exemption regime on sales to national exporters were introduced in order to simplify its application and increase the control of the application of the VAT exemption. Export certificates will be issued by electronic means.

Micro entities
Taxable persons that may benefit from the accounting standard for micro entities are relieved from filing the annual tax and accounting information declaration.

Excise duties

Excise duty on electricity
An excise duty on the consumption of electricity has been introduced, which is due at the time of:

- supply to the end-consumers
- self-consumption, or
- acquisition from end-consumers in organised markets.

Taxable persons (i.e. entities responsible for charging and paying the excise duty to the state) are retailers and producers who sell electricity directly to end-consumers, self-producers, and consumers who purchase electricity from organised markets.

The rate, set by Ruling No. 320-D/2011 of 30 December 2011, is EUR 1/MWh.

The supply of electricity is exempt if used:

- to produce or maintain the productive capacity for electricity
- for transport of passengers and goods by rail, metro or tram, and trolley bus, or
- by economically vulnerable end-consumers who benefit from the social tariff.

Other excise duties
The maximum tax rates of excise duties have been significantly increased, namely by 4.6% on spirit drinks, 17.9% on petrol, 16.9% on methane and petrol gases, and 53.8% on heating diesel.

Property taxes

Real estate acquired by entities resident in black-listed jurisdictions
There has been an increase of 2% (from 8% to 10%) in the property transfer tax (*Imposto Municipal sobre as Transmissões Onerosas de Imóveis* or IMT) rate for real estate acquired by entities resident in a black-listed jurisdiction.

Portugal

Forfeiture of benefits
Having been assigned benefits with a forfeiture term, the statute of limitations term for IMT is now counted only from the date on which the benefits expired.

Changes in the property tax (Imposto Municipal sobre Imóveis or IMI) rate
Both the minimum and maximum rates for urban real estate are increased by 0.1%, rising to 0.5% and 0.8% for real estate not yet valued according to the rules of the new code and 0.3% and 0.5% in case of urban real estate already valued according to the same rules.

Extension of the exemption from property taxes in Areas of Business Location (Áreas de Localização Empresarial or ALE)
The exemption from IMT and IMI on buildings acquired or completed in ALE has been extended until 31 December 2012.

The exemption from IMI is applicable for a period of ten years.

Vacant real estate
IMI rates are now increased three times when the urban real estate is vacant for a period of over one year.

Real estate owned by entities resident in black-listed jurisdictions
Real estate held by entities that have fiscal domicile in countries, territories, or regions subject to more favourable tax regime are subject to IMI at 7.5% (formerly 5%).

Real estate taxable value (VPT) regular updating
The taxable value of real estate used for commercial, industrial, and service purposes is now updated annually (previously on a triennial basis), based on the coefficients of currency devaluation.

Remaining urban real estate continues to be updated on a triennial basis, based on 75% of the coefficients of currency devaluation.

Tax benefits

Tax regime of holding companies (Sociedade Gestora de Participações Sociais or SGPS)
The tax regime of SGPS will remain unchanged and in force, including the exemption from taxation on capital gains.

Capital gains realised by non-residents
The exemption from CIT on capital gains realised on the transfer of shares, other securities, autonomous warrants, and derivatives does not apply in cases where the non-resident is domiciled in a black-listed jurisdiction.

Tax regime for investment support (Regime Fiscal de Apoio Ao Investimento or RFAI)
The RFAI has been extended until 31 December 2012.

Madeira International Business Centre (MIBC)
The tax benefits granted to shareholders of entities licensed in the MIBC, namely the exemption from CIT on dividends paid and interest on shareholders loans were revoked.

As of 1 January 2012, dividends and interest paid by MIBC entities to their shareholders are subject to a WHT rate of 25% (or 30% for black-listed entities).

For all MIBC entities with a licence issued between 1 January 2007 and 31 December 2013, the exemptions previously granted remain in force, namely exemptions from stamp duty and from WHT on interest (except interest on shareholders loans, as above); royalties; technical assistance; information provided and related with an experience in the industrial, commercial, and scientific sector; and services paid to non-resident entities, provided that these are related to the activity of the MIBC licensed entity.

Foreign pension funds - CIT exemption
As per the procedure set by the European Commission against Portugal (Case C-493/09, income obtained by pension funds established in another EU country or in an EEA member state (bound to administrative cooperation on tax matters) will be exempt from CIT. Foreign pension funds should cumulatively fulfil the following requirements:

- Exclusively assure the payment of retirement pensions granted from elderly, handicapped, surviving, pre-retired, health, and post-employment benefits, as well as death benefits when complementary and ancillary to the previously mentioned.
- Are managed by pension funds professional institutions to which Directive 2003/41/EC, of the European Parliament and Council, dated 3 June 2003, applies.
- Are the effective beneficiaries of the income.
- In the case of dividend distributions, the related shareholding should have been held for a consecutive one-year period.

Furthermore, proof should be made available to the entity responsible for the WHT, before the date on which income is made available, that all the necessary requirements are verified. These requirements should be certified by a statement to be issued, confirmed, and authenticated by the member state regulatory authorities.

Tax regime applicable to external loans
The CIT exemption applicable on interest derived from '*Schuldscheindarlehen*' loan agreements signed by the Public Treasury Institute (IGCP), on behalf of the Portuguese Republic, provided the creditor is not resident in Portugal and has no PE herein to which the loan can be allocated to, is extended to 2012. The tax exemption depends on the verification by IGCP of the established requirements.

Special tax regime applicable to debt securities issued by non-resident entities
A CIT exemption on income from debt securities representing public and non-public debt issued by non-residents is maintained.

The exemption applies provided the income is considered to be obtained in the Portuguese territory under Portuguese tax rules and paid by the Portuguese state as a guarantor of the obligations undertaken by the entities in which it owns participation together with other EU member states.

This exemption applies to effective beneficiaries that fulfil the requirements stated in the legal diploma of the debt securities regime.

Repo operations
The CIT exemption on gains obtained by non-resident financial institutions on securities' report operations, undertaken with resident credit institutions, is maintained. The exemption applies, provided such gains are not attributable to Portuguese PEs of non-resident financial institutions.

Portugal

Inland region investment
Inland region tax benefits have been revoked. These tax benefits established reduced CIT rates (10% and 15%), IMT exemption, additional deductions of costs, and extension of the period to carry forward tax losses, among others.

Tax administration

Increase of tax penalties
The general limits for tax penalties for companies have been increased by 50%, meaning new maximums of EUR 165,000 in the case of *dolus* and EUR 45,000 in the case of negligence.

There are new specific tax penalties regarding transfer pricing documentation and the CFC regime (between EUR 1,000 and EUR 20,000 for companies) and regarding omissions or inaccuracies regarding ruling requests (between EUR 750 and EUR 45,000 for companies in the case of urgent rulings or 25% of the previous amounts in the case of non-urgent rulings).

Fiscal crimes
Prison sentences for individual taxpayers have been increased in the case of qualified fraud above EUR 200,000 (from five to eight years), which may lead to serving effective jail time. Maximum fines for corporate taxpayers have been doubled, in case of qualified customs crimes. In addition, an (illegal) activity that leads to an economic tax gain above EUR 50,000 is considered as qualified fraud.

Late payment interest
The maximum three-year term for late payment interest is revoked, and such interest is due until the actual payment of the tax debt. The late interest payment rate is doubled (to around 14%) in cases where the taxpayer does not comply with a court decision.

Increase of statute of limitations
The statute of limitations, foreseen in the General Tax Law, has increased from four years to 12 years in the case of facts related to deposit and securities accounts in financial institutions outside the European Union, the existence and identification of which is not mentioned by taxpayers in the CIT return of the respective year.

The time limit for tax corrections involving black-listed jurisdictions has been raised to 12 years (the general term is four years) and the limit for tax collections to 15 years (the general term is eight years).

Anti-avoidance rules
The exceptional three-year term to initiate the procedure has been revoked, thereby applying the general term. The introduction of this procedure, now explicitly restricted to situations where it is applied to anti-avoidance rules, is more flexible in terms of proof by the tax authorities.

Anti-avoidance rules are not applicable in cases where a request for obtaining binding information is not answered by the tax authorities within 150 days.

Binding rulings
Regarding urgent binding rulings, the response terms by the tax authorities have been extended to 30 days (from 15 days) to accept an urgent binding ruling request and to 120 days (from 60 days) to provide the taxpayer with a binding position.

In addition, the underlying tax facts do not need to be previous to the request any longer. As to fees, the maximum amount is increased from EUR 10,200 to EUR 25,500. In the case of non-urgent rulings, the response term is extended from 90 days to 150 days.

Tax amnesty (RERT III)
The Budget foresees the introduction of a new tax amnesty, incentivising the declaration of assets that are located abroad, until 31 December 2010, and determining the payment of a flat rate of 7.5% on the corresponding values for which the actual repatriation is no longer necessary.

The term for the tax amnesty is 30 June 2012. This regime grants the exoneration of the responsibility for fiscal infractions and, within the relevant assets, includes shareholdings and other securities. In the absence of the declaration, as well as in case of omissions and inaccuracies, the tax due is subject to an increase of 60%, instead of 50%.

Tax arbitration
The Decree-Ruling, issued jointly by the Minister of Finance and the Minister of Justice, that binds the tax authorities to the tax arbitration will also establish both the type and maximum amount of the tax conflicts that can be analysed under a tax arbitration court.

These limits have already been established by Decree-Ruling No. 122-A/2011, dated 22 March.

Increase from eight days to 20 days of the deadline for the tax authorities to amend the act, before the settlement of the tax arbitration court.

The assessment of the tax is no longer suspended in case an issue related with the taxable income is being analysed by the tax arbitration court.

Taxes on corporate income

Resident companies in Portugal are taxed on their worldwide income. Tax is also applicable to Portugal-source income attributable to a PE of a non-resident company in Portugal. Special WHT rates apply to income generated in Portugal that is attributable to non-residents without a PE in Portugal (*see the Withholding taxes section for more information*).

From 1 January 2012 onwards, CIT income brackets were eliminated, and a flat rate of 25% applies on the global amount of taxable income realised by companies resident for tax purposes in Portugal mainland or in the Autonomous Region of Madeira (also applicable to Portuguese PEs of foreign entities).

Entities that do not carry out a commercial, industrial, or agricultural activity as their main activity are subject to a 21.5% CIT rate on the global amount of their taxable income.

A lower CIT rate of 17.5% applies to companies that are tax resident in the Autonomous Region of Azores, including PEs of foreign entities registered therein.

Portugal

Surtaxes

The following surtaxes may also apply:

- A local surtax (*Derrama*) of up to 1.5% of taxable income, prior to the deduction of any available carryforward tax losses, is levied in certain municipalities. The local surcharge is assessed and paid when filing the CIT return.
- A state surtax (*Derrama Estadual*) applies at the following rates:
  - 3% applicable to the taxable profit exceeding EUR 1.5 million up to EUR 10 million, prior to the deduction of any available carryforward tax losses.
  - 5% applicable to the taxable profit exceeding EUR 10 million.

The state surtax is levied on resident taxpayers carrying on commercial, industrial, or agricultural activity and by non-residents with a PE in Portugal, and it is expected to apply in the 2012 and 2013 tax years. The state surtax is paid in three instalments.

Autonomous taxation

The following autonomous taxation, self-assessed with CIT, applies at the rates provided:

- Representation and entertainment expenses: 10%.
- Company car expenses: 10%.
- Mileage allowance: 5%.
- *Per diem* allowance: 5%.
- Non-documented payments: 50% (70% for partially or fully exempted taxpayers).
- Company car expenses for which acquisition cost exceeds certain limits as established in the law: 20%.
- Dividends distributed to wholly or partially exempt taxpayers regarding participations held for less than one year: 25%.
- The total amount of the expenses incurred with any compensation paid as a result of the termination of functions of managers or board members, if not related to the productivity targets previously established under the existing labour relation; or the amount that exceeds the remuneration that would be received by the manager or the board member until the term of the labour agreement, in case of redundancy prior to that term; or in all cases, if the liability for the payment is shifted to another entity: 35%.
- The total amount of the expenses incurred with bonuses paid to managers or board members if the respective amount corresponds to more than 25% of the annual salary and exceeds EUR 27,500: 35%.

All the above-mentioned rates of autonomous taxation are increased by 10% if the taxpayer has tax losses in the same tax year.

Corporate residence

A resident company is one whose head office or effective management is located in Portugal.

Permanent establishment (PE)

Under Portuguese tax law, any fixed place of business in Portugal through which the business of an enterprise is wholly or partly carried on is deemed to constitute a PE in Portugal.

A fixed place of business comprises, among others, a place of management, a branch, an office, a factory, a workshop, a mine, an oil or gas well, a quarry, or any other place of extraction of natural resources, and also building site or a construction or installation project if it lasts more than six months (time period may differ considering the applicable tax treaty).

A PE may also be deemed to exist in case of a person (a dependent agent), which is not an independent agent, acting, in the Portuguese territory on behalf of a company, with powers to intermediate and conclude binding contracts for that company, within the scope of its business activity.

No PE should exist where a fixed place of business in Portugal is used solely for carrying out ancillary or preparatory activities, or, in case a company, carries out its activities in Portugal through a broker, general commission agent, or other agent of an independent status, acting in the normal course of its business, bearing all related business risks.

Additionally, the term PE shall be deemed not to include the following actions:

- Use of facilities solely for the purpose of storage, display, or delivery of goods or merchandise belonging to the enterprise.
- Maintenance of a stock of goods or merchandise belonging to the enterprise solely for the purpose of storage, display, or delivery.
- Maintenance of a stock of goods or merchandise belonging to the enterprise solely for the purpose of processing by another enterprise.
- Maintenance of a fixed place of business solely for the purpose of purchasing goods or merchandise or of collecting information, for the enterprise.
- Maintenance of a fixed place of business solely for the purpose of carrying on, for the enterprise, any other activity of a preparatory or auxiliary character.
- Maintenance of a fixed place of business solely for any combination of activities mentioned above, provided that the overall activity of the fixed place of business resulting from this combination is of a preparatory or auxiliary character.

Other taxes

Value-added tax (VAT)
Portuguese VAT is applicable at the standard rate of 23% (22% in the Autonomous Region of Madeira; 16% in the Autonomous Region of the Azores), at an intermediate rate of 13% (12% in Madeira; 9% in the Azores), and at a reduced rate of 6% (5% in Madeira; 4% in the Azores).

Following a revision of the respective reduced rates lists, several goods and services that in 2011 were subject to the reduced or intermediate VAT rates are now subject to the standard VAT rate, namely gyms, flowers and ornamental plants, as well as some legal services.

Restaurant services, basic canned foods, fruit jellies, fats, honey, coffee, natural water, fruit juices, decorative flowers, petroleum for heating and marked diesel fuel for agriculture and fishing activities, and certain ecological equipment are subject to the intermediate VAT rate of 13%. Basic food, some pharmaceutical products, milk products, and certain services are subject to the reduced VAT rate of 6%. Exports and intra-EU supplies of goods are zero-rated.

Portugal

There are two general rules for defining the deemed place of supply of services. The general rule for taxation of business-to-business (B2B) services is the place where the customer is established or has a PE, has a permanent address, or usually resides. For business-to-consumer (B2C) services, the general rule remains the place where the supplier is established. The place of supply of organisations of cultural, artistic, sporting, scientific, educational, entertainment, or similar events is determined according to the general rule; on 1 January 2013 and 1 January 2015, additional adjustments to the VAT rules will become effective.

The existing proceeding for obtaining a VAT refund in another EU member state other than the member state of establishment has been replaced by a new electronic proceeding, with a four month average payment term.

Customs duties

Custom duties are regulated by the Community Customs Code. Therefore, the rules foreseen for the import and export of goods in Portugal are similar to the rules applicable in other EU member states.

The custom duties' rates applied in Portugal vary according to the origin of the goods. There are several origin agreements which exempt from custom duties the importation of goods from certain countries or that determine reduced rates.

Excise duties

There are different types of excise duties, such as:

* petroleum and energy products tax
* alcohol and alcoholic beverages tax
* tobacco tax, and
* vehicle tax.

The tax applicable to petroleum and energetic products depends on the goods supplied, namely it varies between EUR 650 per 1,000 litres for leaded petrol and EUR 2.78 per gigajoule for natural gas used as fuel.

The tax applicable to alcohol and alcoholic beverages also depends on the type of good supplied, varying between EUR 7.11 per hectolitre for a certain type of beer and EUR 1,031.57 per hectolitre for spirits.

The tax applicable to tobacco also varies in accordance with the type of product supplied, namely it varies between 60% of the sale price for fine-cut tobacco for the rolling of cigarettes and 13% of the sale price for cigars and cigarillos.

The tax applicable to vehicles varies in accordance with the type of vehicle, the fuel used, and the cylinder of the vehicle. The higher taxation is applicable for cars used for the transport of passengers using petrol as fuel and the lower taxation is applicable for motorcycles.

An excise duty on consumption of electricity applies as of 1 January 2012, at a rate varying between 0 and EUR 1 per MWh due by producers, traders, self-producers, and consumers that buy electricity in organised markets.

Furthermore, the introduction in consumption of the products subject to excise duties is simplified, considering that the arrival of these goods from other EU member states is supported through an electronic document (e-DA).

The e-DA may also be issued by Portuguese entities to export the above goods and certify winery products. It is also possible to change or cancel an electronic document received.

Property tax (Imposto Municipal sobre Imóveis or IMI)

IMI is a municipal property tax upon which the taxable basis is calculated by reference to a formula based on objective criteria, such as the construction cost per square meter, area, age, construction quality, and comfort indexes.

Following the Memorandum of Understanding between the Portuguese Republic and the European Commission, the European Central Bank, and the IMF, which covers the financial assistance to be granted to Portugal by the European Fund for Financial Stability, reassessments of the tax value of real estate are expected in 2012 (increase to close the market value).

IMI is levied at the following rates, in addition to corporate or individual tax assessed on actual income generated by real estate:

Property type	IMI (%)
Urban real estate	0.5 to 0.8
Urban real estate (valued under the new rules)	0.3 to 0.5
Rural real estate	0.8

Note that the tax rate of IMI on properties owned by entities resident for tax purposes in a black-listed territory is 7.5% as of 2012 (previously 5%). This rule does not apply where the owner is an individual.

The list of countries, territories, and regions that provide a more favourable tax regime is presented below:

- Andorra (1)
- Anguilla (1)
- Antigua and Barbuda (1)
- Netherlands Antilles
- Aruba
- Ascension Island
- Bahamas
- Bahrain
- Barbados
- Belize (1)
- Bermuda (1)
- Bolívia
- Brunei
- Cayman Islands (1)
- Channel Islands (1, 2)
- Cocos (Keeling)
- Cook Islands
- Costa Rica
- Djibouti
- Dominica (1)
- Falkland Islands or Malvinas
- Fiji Islands
- Gambia
- Grenada
- Gibraltar (1)
- Guam
- Guyana
- Honduras
- Hong Kong
- Jamaica
- Jordan
- Queshm Island
- Kiribati
- Kuwait
- Labuan
- Lebanon
- Liberia (1)
- Liechtenstein
- The Maldives
- Isle of Man (1)
- Marianas
- Marshall Islands
- Mauritius
- Monaco
- Montserrat
- Nauru
- Christmas Island
- Niue Island
- Norfolk Island
- Sultanate of Oman
- Pacific Islands (3)
- Palau Islands
- Panama
- Pitcairn Island
- French Polynesia
- Porto Rico
- Qatar
- Solomon Islands
- American Samoa
- Western Samoa
- Saint Helena
- Saint Lucia (1)
- Saint Kitts and Nevis (1)
- San Marino
- Saint Pierre and Miquelon
- St Vicente and the Grenadines
- Seychelles
- Swaziland
- Svalbard (4)
- Tokelau
- Kingdom of Tonga
- Trinidad and Tobago

Portugal

- Tristan da Cunha
- Turks and Caicos (1)
- Tuvalu
- United Arab Emirates

- Uruguay
- Vanuatu
- British Virgin Islands (1)

- United States Virgin Islands
- Yemen Arab Republic

Notes

1. The Portuguese authorities have signed tax information exchange agreements (TIEAs) with these jurisdictions (in case of the Channel Islands, only with Guernsey and Jersey). The following TIEAs are in force: Andorra, Bermuda, Cayman Islands, Gibraltar, Jersey, Isle of Man, and Saint Lucia.
2. Alderney, Guernsey, Jersey, Great Stark, Herm, Little Sark, Brechou, Jethou, and Lihou.
3. Not included in the remaining numbers.

IMI rates are increased three times when the urban real estate is vacant for a period of over one year.

Property transfer tax (Imposto Municipal sobre as Transmissões Onerosas de Imóveis or IMT)

IMT is a municipal tax payable in Portugal on the onerous transfer of local real estate. The tax is levied on the purchaser, and the taxable basis is the same as for IMI or the price agreed upon by the contracting parties, whichever is higher.

The IMT rates are set at 5% for rural real estate and 6.5% for urban real estate and land for construction. For non-residents located in black-listed jurisdictions, the rate is 10%. This rule does not apply where the acquirer is an individual.

Stamp duty

Stamp duty is payable on a wide variety of transactions and documents, at rates that may be set in specific amounts or on a percentage basis. Important examples include the following:

Item	Stamp duty (%)
Loans (on the principal)	
With determined term, over one year	0.5 to 0.6
Current account/overdraft/credit with undetermined term or determined term under one year	0.04 per month or fraction
Credit to consumers	
With a term up to one year/current account, overdraft, or other form of credit with undetermined term	0.07 per month or fraction
With a term equal to or higher than one year	0.9
With a term equal to or higher than five years	1
Guarantees *	
Undetermined/five or more years	0.6
Over one year	0.5
Under one year or with undetermined term	0.04 per month or fraction
Bank interest and fees	4
Insurance premiums	3 to 9
Real estate purchases and sales	0.8
Donations and inheritances	10
Sale of business as a going concern	5

* Guarantees provided in favour of the state or social security institutions upon the payment of debt by instalments under enforcement procedures or relating to the recovery of tax and social security credits are exempt from stamp duty in 2012.

Branch income

Branch profits are taxed on the same basis as corporate profits. Income remitted by a branch to the head office is not subject to taxation.

Income determination

Taxable profit is based on accounting income adjusted according to specific provisions of the tax legislation, when applicable.

Inventory valuation

Inventories are valued at the lower of the following values: cost or net realisable value. The first in first out (FIFO) and average-cost methods of valuation are accepted. The last in first out (LIFO) method is not allowed.

Inventory adjustments are deductible for tax purposes on the amount accounted for in the tax year, capped at the difference between the acquisition or production value and, if lower, the net realisable value (duly documented) with reference to the balance sheet.

Capital gains

The positive net difference between capital gains and capital losses arising from the disposal of fixed assets or shares, held for more than one year, is taxed as part of normal income.

Capital gains and capital losses are determined by the difference between the sales proceeds, deducting any related cost, and the acquisition value, deducing impairment losses and tax deductible depreciation or amortisation, adjusted by the inflation index (in the case of at least two years of ownership).

Only half the amount of the negative difference between capital gains and capital losses arising from the disposal of shares or other negative net worth variations related to participations or other parts of the equity of a company, such as supplementary capital contributions, are considered for purposes of assessing the taxable income.

In certain circumstances, only 50% of the net gains on disposal of tangible fixed assets or shares are taxed, provided the sales proceeds are reinvested.

Capital losses regarding shares owned for less than three years when acquired from related companies, from black-listed entities, or from Portuguese companies subject to a special tax regime are not deductible. Capital losses are also not tax deductible if the shares are transferred to related parties to black-listed entities or to Portuguese resident entities subject to a more favourable tax regime.

Capital gains/losses realised by holding companies (*Sociedade Gestora de Participações Sociais* or SGPS) are not taxed/deductible, if the underlying shares have been held for more than one year (or three years if the shares were acquired from related parties, offshore companies, or Portuguese resident entities subject to a special tax regime).

P

Portugal

Dividend income

For Portuguese-resident companies holding shares in other Portuguese companies, or in companies resident in Portuguese African speaking countries, or in companies resident in the EU or the EEA (meeting the EU Parent/Subsidiary Directive 90/435/CEE), 100% of the dividends distributed are excluded from the taxable income. In case of Portuguese, EU, and EEA subsidiaries, the shares should represent at least 10% of total capital and have been held for at least one year (this minimum holding period should be met before or after distribution).

This also applies to regional development corporations (*Sociedades de desenvolvimento regional*), investment companies, securities dealers, and insurance companies (where technical reserves are concerned).

The deduction of the dividends when distributed by Portuguese, EU, or EEA subsidiaries only applies if the underlying income has been subject to 'effective taxation'. According to the Portuguese tax authorities, following Tax Circular 24/2011 released in November 2011, it is considered that profits have been subject to 'effective taxation' when they:

- have been subject to Portuguese CIT or to a comparable tax (no minimum amount of tax effectively paid is required)
- have been taxed at the level of the immediate subsidiary distributing the profits, or at any other lower tier of the corporate structure, or
- refer to profits distributed by a EU or EEA subsidiary, which are subject and not exempt from CIT.

The burden of proof lies with the Portuguese parent company (recipient of the dividends), which should be able to demonstrate that the profits received derive from income that has been effectively subject to taxation.

Foreign income

A Portuguese company is taxed on all its foreign income. Taxes paid abroad can be offset against corresponding Portuguese tax (*see Foreign tax credit in the Tax credits and incentives section for more information*).

There are no provisions concerning tax deferral of income earned abroad.

Deductions

Depreciation, amortisation, and depletion

The qualifying cost of an asset for tax purposes is the acquisition or production cost.

Depreciation must be computed by using the straight-line method or the declining-balance method. The latter cannot be applied to buildings, passenger vehicles, furniture, social welfare equipment, or second-hand assets. Straight-line rates of depreciation are normally consistent with rates privately used by business and industry and are increased, for the purposes of applying the declining-balance method, by coefficients of:

- 1.5 if assets have a useful life of less than five years.
- 2 if useful life is five or six years.
- 2.5 for useful lives in excess of six years.

Portugal

Different depreciation methods may be applied without previous approval from the tax authorities (annual depreciation cannot, however, exceed the depreciation resulting from using either the straight-line or declining-balance methods).

Some examples relating to the maximum straight-line depreciation rate are as follows:

Type of asset	Depreciation rate (%)
Office building	2
Industrial building	5
Electronic equipment	20
Computers	33.33
Ordinary tool and paintings	25
Engines and machine tools	12.5
Office equipment	20
Furniture	12.5
Software	33.33
Light passenger vehicles	25

Rates can be reduced by 50% in any one year at the taxpayer's option. If the reduction is more than 50%, the difference is allowed for tax purposes at a future date. Any depreciation in excess of the maximum allowed must be subsequently adjusted in the accounting records to be allowed for tax purposes in future years. A total of 60% of additional depreciation on revaluation of fixed assets, as permitted by law from time to time, is allowed for tax purposes.

Depreciation rates of tangible assets may be increased by 25% in the case of companies with a schedule of two shifts (for three shifts, 50%), given the faster deterioration of those assets.

Assets with an acquisition value lower than EUR 1,000 can be depreciated in the acquisition year, unless the assets are part of a set of elements that should be depreciated as a whole.

Depreciation of yachts and airplanes that are not essential for business activities is not allowed as a cost for tax purposes.

Depreciation of passenger cars and certain other vehicles on the part of their cost of acquisition that exceeds certain amounts (as defined by law), with reference to their acquisition value, is also disallowed as a cost for tax purposes. The following caps apply (i.e. disallowed cost above the values below):

- EUR 40,000 of acquisition cost, in the case of vehicles acquired until 31 December 2010.
- EUR 30,000 of acquisition cost, in the case of vehicles acquired from 1 January 2011 onwards.
- EUR 45,000 of acquisition cost, in the case of electric vehicles acquired from 1 January 2011 onwards.
- EUR 25,000 of acquisition cost, in the case of vehicles acquired from 1 January 2012 onwards.
- EUR 50,000 of acquisition cost, in the case of electric vehicles acquired from 1 January 2012 onwards.

Portugal

Development expenses, patents, trademarks, licenses, and similar rights may be amortised for tax purposes if acquired for a limited period of time.

Depreciation of non-consumable biological assets is tax deductible.

Expenses relating to assets generated internally are deductible for tax purposes in the tax year in which the cost is incurred.

Goodwill
Goodwill cannot be amortised for tax purposes (unless subject to an effective economic amortisation approved by the Portuguese tax authorities).

Organisational and start-up expenses
Start-up and research expenses are deductible for tax purposes in the respective tax year. Transitional adjustments of remaining start-up expenses incurred prior to the adoption of the new accounting system (*Sistema de Normalização Contabilística* or SNC) should be written off the balance sheet against equity and are deductible over a five-year period.

Interest on shareholder loans
If the rate applicable to interest and other compensation regarding loans provided by the shareholders to the company is higher than the Euro Interbank Offered Rate (EURIBOR) 12-month rate rounded up with a spread of 1.5% (at the date the loan was granted), the amount paid in excess is not tax deductible. This rule does not apply when the shareholder is a resident of a tax treaty country or when the interest rate is at arm's length under the transfer pricing provisions.

In the case of small and medium-sized companies, shareholders' loans with an interest rate of EURIBOR 12-month rate plus a spread up to 6% is tax deductible.

Bad debt
Impairment losses on doubtful debts are deductible for tax purposes when an insolvency or recovery has been requested or the credits have been claimed in court.

The annual amount of accumulated impairment losses on doubtful debts due for more than six months, with evidence that measures towards its perception were taken, is capped at the following percentages of the debts:

- More than 6 and less than 12 months: 25%.
- More than 12 and less than 18 months: 50%.
- More than 18 and less than 24 months: 75%.
- More than 24 months: 100%.

Amounts guaranteed by insurance or mortgage, or due or secured by the state, autonomous regions, or municipalities, or due by related parties (e.g. 10% shareholding) are not considered as doubtful debts, and the respective impairment loss is disallowed for tax purposes.

The ageing of bills of exchange is calculated from the date when the respective payment is due.

Uncollectable debts are allowed as tax deductible costs if supported under insolvency, recovery enforcement, or in an out-of-court conciliation procedure for the viability of insolvent companies or companies in difficult economic situation (mediated by the

Institute for the Support of Small and Medium-Sized Enterprises or IAPMEI). This rule applies to the amount of the uncollectable debts which were not deducted for tax purposes as impairment losses (or for which the amount was insufficient).

Charitable contributions

Donations to authorised charitable institutions are allowable up to 0.8% of turnover, with the possibility of the cost being raised up to 150%. Donations to authorised cultural institutions are allowable up to 0.6% of turnover, with the possibility of the cost being raised up to 130%.

Donations to the state, municipalities, and foundations where the state or municipalities participate in the initial capital are fully deductible, with the possibility of the cost being raised up to 140%. Special application may be made by certain entities in order to be included under the referred regime.

Donations of computers, software equipment, training, and consultancy in the area of computers granted to the state, municipalities, foundations, museums as well as to authorised charitable and cultural institutions are allowable up to 0.8% of turnover, with the possibility of the cost being raised up to 140%.

Vacation accrual

Vacation allowance is tax deductible in the year in which the benefit accrues, regardless of the year in which payment is made.

Pension expenses

Pension, invalidity, and health schemes are tax deductible up to a rate of 15% of annual staff expenses, provided they are available to all employees and the management and disposition of the benefits are outside the control of the taxpayer, such as under an insured scheme with vested benefits.

A specific regime applies for deduction of the additional (mandatory) contributions made to pension funds by insurance companies as a result of the adoption of the new accounting system (SNC). These contributions are not considered for purposes of computing the maximum annual amount accepted as a cost, but are considered as a cost in accordance with an annual instalment plan, during a term of five years that began in 2008.

Taxes

All taxes other than CIT, state surtax, and municipal surtax constitute a normal business expense.

Other significant items

The costs borne from the acquisition of social passes are regarded as tax-deductible costs to the extent the employer attributes them on a general basis.

Uninsured losses, including indemnities to third parties, are disallowed unless the risk could not be insured.

Non-documented expenses are not tax deductible and are subject to a 50% tax surcharge for fully taxable entities.

In the course of 2012, exceptional write-off arising from the replacement of invoicing programs or equipments, replaced due to software certification requirements, are

Portugal

considered as impairment losses, without the need of obtaining an approval by the tax authorities.

In the course of 2012, expenses on the acquisition of certified invoicing programs and hardware will be accepted as a cost for tax purposes in the relevant fiscal year.

Net operating losses

Tax losses generated prior to 2012 can be carried forward for four years (six years in the case of tax losses generated prior to 2010).

Tax losses generated from 2012 onwards can be carried forward for five years. As of the tax year of 2012, the deduction of tax losses carried forward (even in case of tax losses generated before 2012) will be limited to 75% of the taxable profit assessed in the relevant fiscal year. The unrelieved tax losses can be carried forward for the respective carryforward period (six years, four years, or five years, depending on whether the tax losses were generated respectively before 2010, in 2010 and 2011, or from 2012 onwards).

Carryback of losses is not allowed. The tax losses carried forward are lost if one of the following situations occurs:

- Change in direct ownership of the company of at least 50% shareholding or voting rights.
- Change in the scope of the business as stated in the articles of association or, regardless of any formal change, if the nature of the activity carried out by the company is substantially modified.

In special cases of economical merits, the Ministry of Finance may authorise the use of tax losses upon a request filed by the taxpayer before those changes occur.

Payments to foreign affiliates

A Portuguese corporation is allowed to deduct royalties, interest, and other costs paid to foreign affiliates, provided the amounts are at arm's length. Service fees paid are allowed if there is adequate proof that the service was effectively rendered, has economic substance, and qualifies as indispensable for the generation of taxable revenue, as well as if the amount is at arm's length.

Payments to non-residents subject to a more favourable tax regime

Payments made or due, indirectly, to non-resident entities subject to a more favourable tax regime, when the taxable person has or should have had knowledge of the final purpose given to such payments, will be non-deductible for tax purposes, except if the taxpayer demonstrates that such charges relate to genuine transactions and are not of an abnormal or exaggerated amount. Such knowledge is presumed whenever there are special relations between the taxpayer and the entities subject to the more favourable tax regime or between the taxpayer and the legal representative, fiduciary, or intermediary.

Group taxation

Special regime for group taxation

Taxation under the special tax regime for groups or companies is available, upon the filing of a special form with the tax authorities, to companies with head office and effective management in Portugal.

Portugal

The group taxation regime may apply, provided one of the companies, directly or indirectly, holds 90% or more of the statutory capital of the others and more than 50% of the voting rights. Tax grouping generally enables the group companies to offset losses incurred by one company against profits of another company.

Tax losses obtained prior to the beginning of the tax grouping can be carried forward only against the particular company's taxable income (*for the carryforward of tax losses regime, see Net operating losses in the Deductions section*).

To be taxed under this regime, the group companies must meet the following conditions:

- Must be tax resident in Portugal.
- Must be subject to the normal regime of taxation at the highest corporate tax rate.
- Must maintain a minimum holding participation of 90%.
- All companies must be held by the parent company for more than one year (excluding newly incorporated companies).
- Cannot be dormant for more than one year.
- Cannot be dissolved or insolvent.
- Cannot have tax losses in the three years prior to the regime application, unless the companies have been held by the parent company for more than two years.
- Cannot have a tax period different from that of the parent company.

Additionally, the parent company:

- should not be controlled by any other Portuguese-resident company that fulfils the requirements to be the parent company and
- should not have renounced to the application of this regime in the three previous years.

When the regime comes to an end or when one company ceases to qualify for this regime, the tax losses obtained during the regime cannot be carried forward and deducted against future individual taxable income of the companies.

The parent company is responsible for demonstrating that the requirements for the application of the group taxation regime are met.

Transfer pricing

The tax authorities are entitled to adjust taxable income if the taxpayer and another individual or entity, due to their special relationship, have established particular conditions which diverge from the conditions normally agreed upon between independent entities and distort the results that would arise if those relations were at arm's length. Portugal's transfer pricing legislation broadly follows the Organisation for Economic Cooperation and Development (OECD) guidelines.

Companies with sales and other profits higher than EUR 3 million are required to prepare transfer pricing documentation, which should be filed with the tax authorities if requested. Penalties arise from non-compliance with this obligation.

An advance pricing agreement (APA) mechanism has been introduced for taxpayers and Portuguese Tax Authorities (PTA) to establish agreements on a taxpayers' future transfer pricing policy. This aims to guarantee compliance with the arm's-length principle. This regime applies to transactions carried out with related parties and between a PE and the respective head office.

Portugal

The conclusion of an APA implies the payment of a charge calculated with reference to the taxpayers' turnover, capped at EUR 35,000. This charge is reduced by 50% in the case of a renewal or revision of an existing APA.

The assessment of an APA procedure takes 180 days for unilateral APAs, and 360 days for bilateral or multilateral APAs. This period is reduced to 100 business days for APAs concluded in connection with a relevant investment project in Portugal, as foreseen in the Tax Investment Code (*Código Fiscal do Investimento*).

For the PTA to confirm compliance of the transfer pricing method(s) with the terms and conditions set out in the APA, the taxpayer must prepare an annual report. The report must be made available to PTA before the last business day of May in the year following that in which the transactions took place (i.e. when the tax year corresponds to the calendar year). Failure to comply invalidates the APA.

Thin capitalisation
Where loans from non-EU-resident related parties exceed twice the parties' capital in the borrowing Portuguese entity, the interest on the excess borrowing is not tax deductible. This rule may not apply if the company (as long as it is not resident in a black-listed territory) proves under a safeguard clause, that takes into account the type of activity, the sector in which it operates, the dimensions, and other relevant criteria, that it would be possible to obtain the same loan on similar terms from an independent entity.

Controlled foreign companies (CFCs)
Profits derived by an affiliate resident in a black-listed offshore jurisdiction, or in a jurisdiction where it is subject to an effective tax rate equal to or lower than 60% of the Portuguese standard CIT rate, are imputed to the Portuguese shareholder, provided it holds, directly or indirectly, a minimum holding participation of 25% (10% if more than 50% of the capital is held by Portuguese shareholders). Upon distribution of the profits, a deduction is available for previously imputed income.

As of 2012, CFC rules also apply if the controlled company (*as defined above*) is held by a Portuguese entity through a legal representative, fiduciary, or intermediary.

CFC rules do not apply if the CFC is resident in another EU country or in an EEA member state (bound to administrative cooperation on tax matters), provided that there are valid economic reasons underlying the incorporation and running of such company and it carries out agricultural, commercial, industrial, or services activities.

Upon a dividend distribution by the CFC, the tax credit of the tax paid abroad, which is not used, cannot be carried forward to subsequent tax years.

Tax credits and incentives

Foreign tax credit
Taxes paid abroad can be offset against corresponding Portuguese tax capped at the lower of (i) the tax liability corresponding to the foreign income, net of costs directly or indirectly incurred, or (ii) the foreign tax paid. In both cases, it is limited to the foreign tax as foreseen in the applicable double-taxation treaty. No carryforward of foreign tax is allowed.

Portugal

General tax benefits and incentives
Following the enactment of the 2012 State Budget, several tax benefits ceased to exist as a result of the implementation of the measures foreseen in the Memorandum of Understanding between the Portuguese Republic and the European Commission, the European Central Bank, and the IMF, which covers the financial assistance to be granted to Portugal by the European Fund for Financial Stability.

Contractual tax incentives
Relevant investment projects up to 2020 (minimum investment of EUR 5 million) that qualify for strategic economic interest and promote the creation of jobs are eligible for tax incentives, as foreseen in the Tax Benefits Code and the Investment Tax Code.

These are granted on a case-by-case basis under a government contract for a period not exceeding ten years and include a tax credit of 10% to 20% of the investment and exemptions or reductions from property transfer tax, property tax, and stamp duty.

Investment funds
Portfolio investment funds are taxable at the following final rates:

Portfolio investment fund activity	CIT rate (%)
Capital gains (net of capital losses) on shares held less than 12 months, realised by closed or mixed investment funds	21.5
Capital gains (net of capital losses) on shares held greater than 12 months, realised by open investment funds	21.5
Other income:	
Earned in Portugal	20/25
Earned abroad	20/25

Real estate investment funds are subject to corporate tax at the following rates:

Real estate investment fund activity	CIT rate (%)
Rents (net of expenses)	20
Real estate capital gains (net of capital losses)	12.5
Capital gains (net of capital losses) on shares held less than 12 months, realised by closed or mixed real estate investment funds	20
Capital gains (net of capital losses) on shares held greater than 12 months, realised by open real estate investment funds	0
Other income:	
Earned in Portugal	20/25
Earned abroad	20/25

Income paid by portfolio and real estate investment funds to individuals is not subject to taxation. Income paid to companies is taxed as normal income, and taxes paid by the fund are considered as payment on account against the final CIT due.

Funds of funds
Income paid by investment funds of funds is exempt from CIT. Other income is subject to the same taxation as investment funds. Income received by individuals is not subject to further taxation. Income received by companies is taxed at the standard CIT rate on 40% of the respective amount as normal income.

Portugal

Pension funds

Pension funds are exempt from CIT and IMT.

The CIT exemption, which was only applicable to pension funds incorporated under the Portuguese law, is extended from 1 January 2012 onwards to pension funds established in another EU country or in an EEA member state (bound to administrative cooperation on tax matters) that cumulatively fulfil the following requirements:

* Exclusively assure the payment of retirement pensions granted from elderly, handicapped, surviving, pre-retired, health, and post-employment benefits, as well as death benefits when complementary and ancillary to the previously mentioned.
* Are managed by pension funds professional institutions to which Directive 2003/41/EC, of the European Parliament and Council, dated 3 June 2003, applies.
* Are the effective beneficiaries of the income.
* In the case of dividend distributions, the related shareholding should have been held for a consecutive one-year period.

Contractors for North Atlantic Treaty Organization (NATO) infrastructures

Contractors for NATO infrastructures are exempt from CIT.

Net young employment creation

150% of the costs related to net increase job creation, under labour contracts without term, for employees up to 35 years (including) of age and for long-term unemployed individuals may be deducted from taxable income. For this purpose, the fixed remunerations paid and the contributions made by the employer to social security should be considered. The maximum amount of annual increase on deductible costs for each eligible employee is 14 times the national minimum retribution (EUR 485 in 2012).

The increase in 50% of the expenses incurred with the same employer is applicable to more than one employee provided that there are no special relations.

This tax benefit is not cumulative with any tax benefits or other incentives (e.g. social security) concerning the same employee.

This deduction applies for a period of five years for each employee.

Research and development (R&D) *(Sistema de Incentivos Fiscais em Investigação e Desenvolvimento Empresarial or SIFIDE II)*

Portuguese tax resident companies carrying out commercial, industrial, or agricultural activities, and non-resident companies with a PE in the Portuguese territory, are allowed to deduct from the CIT due, up to the respective amount, the value of eligible expenses incurred with R&D, in a double percentage as follows:

* Base rate: 32.5% of the R&D expenses incurred; this rate is increased by 10% in case of small and medium-sized companies that do not benefit from the incremental rate of 50% (applicable to entities that had completed two years of activity).
* Incremental rate: 50% of the difference between the R&D expenses made in the tax year and the average amount of the R&D expenses made in the previous two years, up to the limit of EUR 1.5 million.
* The incremental rate is increased to 70% and the deduction limit is increased to EUR 1.8 million with respect to expenses incurred with the employment of people with a doctorate degree.

Expenses that, due to insufficient tax due, cannot be deducted in the tax year they were incurred can be carried forward for six years.

Eligible expenses related to allowances paid to personnel directly involved with R&D tasks are capped at 55% of the operational expenses incurred.

The deductibility of eligible expenses related to allowances paid to personnel directly involved with R&D tasks is capped at 90% of the respective value, in the case of entities that are not small and/or medium-sized enterprises.

Expenses related to demonstrations are eligible for the SIFIDE II regime, provided they are notified up front.

Expenses incurred with the execution of R&D projects, and related with mandatory public contractual obligations, are no longer eligible.

Expenses incurred with the acquisition, registration, and maintenance of patents, essential for the performance of R&D activities and audits, will be accepted only for micro, small, or medium-sized companies. The deduction of R&D expenses requires that the entity develops agricultural, industrial, or commercial activities or services as its main business activity.

The applications should be submitted by the end of July of the year following the year in which the investment was made, and applications referring to years previous to that fiscal year will not be accepted. This rule is only applicable to fiscal years beginning on or after 1 January 2012. Applications concerning fiscal years prior to 2012 should be submitted until the end of July 2012.

Tax regime aimed at fostering investment *(Regime Fiscal de Apoio Ao Investimento* or RFAI)

The tax regime aimed at fostering investment, which establishes several tax incentives to investment realised within specific business sectors, will remain in force during 2012.

Among other incentives, companies will still benefit from a deduction against CIT otherwise payable (capped at 25% of the CIT due) of 20% (for qualified investments lower than EUR 5 million) or 10% (for qualified investments higher than EUR 5 million) of the qualified investment; from being able to carry forward any unused credit for four years; and from an exemption from property transfer tax, property tax (IMI), and stamp duty on the acquisition of real estate for investment purposes. The property transfer tax exemptions are subject to the approval of the municipality where the real estate is located and where the investment is made.

Dividends from entities resident in the Portuguese Speaking African countries *(Países Africanos de Língua Oficial Portuguesa or PALOP)* and in East Timor

The payment of dividends from entities resident in Portuguese Speaking African countries (Angola, Cape Verde, Guinea-Bissau, Mozambique, and São Tomé e Príncipe) and in East Timor, are not subject to CIT at the level of the Portuguese parent, provided that:

- The entity in Portugal is subject and not exempt to CIT.
- The entities in the PALOP and in East-Timor are subject to and not exempt from a corporate tax.

Portugal

- The entity in Portugal holds a direct participation in the share capital of the subsidiary of not less than 25% for at least two years.
- Dividends distributed have been taxed at a rate of at least 10% and do not arise from a determined type of income expressly mentioned in the law.

Loan interest and lease rentals on imported equipment
When paid by the state, regional authorities, and public services, loan interest and lease rentals on imported equipment can qualify for partial or full exemption from tax upon an appropriate application.

Real Estate Investment Fund for Residential Lease (REIFRL)
A regime is applicable: (i) both to REIFRL and to Real Estate Investment Companies for Residential Lease (REICRL) incorporated in accordance with the Portuguese law within a term of five years following the entering into force of the State Budget for 2009; and (ii) to the real estate properties acquired by those entities during that same term, i.e. from 1 January 2009 until 31 December 2014.

The incorporation of the REIFRL will be done in accordance with the provisions applicable to the Real Estate Investment Funds (REIFs) laid down in the Portuguese law. The REIFRL portfolio is required to be comprised of at least 75% real estate properties located in Portugal destined for the lease of permanent residences.

The following benefits are established for this tax regime:

- CIT exemption on income obtained by REIFRLs.
- CIT exemption for the income obtained by participation unit holders, except for the capital gains arising from the sale of such participation units.
- Local property tax exemption established for the real estate properties destined for the lease of permanent residences that integrate the REIFRL.
- Municipal property transfer tax exemption on real estate property acquisition made within this regime by the REIFRL, as well as the acquisitions arising from the option for the acquisition by the lessees, until 2020, of the real estate properties that integrate the assets of the REIFRL.
- Stamp duty exemption is established for the acts arising from the transfer of the real estate properties by means of the conversion of holdings rights in real estate properties into a lease right with the option of acquisition in respect of the same real estate property by the lessee.

The above-referred tax regime and respective exemptions will not be applicable to entities resident in a country or jurisdiction with a more favourable taxable regime included in the Decree-Ruling published by the Ministry of Finance.

Incentives to urban rehabilitation
Incentives are applicable to real estate property covered by rehabilitation projects undertaken between 1 January 2008 and 2020.

Real estate investment funds incorporated between 2008 and 31 December 2012 may benefit from:

- CIT: the income obtained by real estate investment funds is tax exempt when the funds are incorporated in accordance with the Portuguese law, and respective assets are comprised of at least 75% real estate subject to rehabilitation projects in qualifying areas.

- Property transfer tax: urban property (buildings or autonomous units) destined for permanent residence and located in a rehabilitation area may benefit from an IMT exemption on the first transfer of such urban property upon undertaking of rehabilitation works. The granting of this exemption depends on a decision in this respect of the municipality of the area of the real estate property.
- Property tax: the IMI exemption granted in respect of urban properties subject to rehabilitation works is extended from eight to ten years (it is granted for a five years term and renewable for an additional five-year period). Again, the granting of this exemption depends on a decision in this respect of the municipality of the area of the real estate property.

Areas of Business Location
Buildings acquired or completed until 31 December 2012, located in Areas of Business Location (*Áreas de Localização Empresarial* or ALE) are exempt from IMT and IMI, for a period of ten years.

ALE are geographical areas in municipalities, and have a structuring nature. The exemption from IMT and IMI implies that municipalities renounce to the respective revenue in order to attract investment. The licensing regime of ALE is foreseen in Decree-Law no. 72/2009, dated 31 March 2009.

Public transportation vehicles
In 2012, the exemption from CIT on capital gains obtained on the sale of public passenger and goods transportation vehicles and taxis will be maintained if re-investment of the sales proceeds is made on the acquisition of new vehicles produced not before 2011. The re-investment should be undertaken in the same tax year or up to the end of the second tax year to which the sale relates to. The referred exemption is applicable to taxpayers licensed by the respective regulatory authority.

Tax benefits and incentives for non-resident corporate entities

Capital gains
Capital gains on the sale of shares and quotas held in a Portuguese company by a non-resident company may be tax exempt. However, there are some important exceptions, such as:

- Where the non-resident shareholder is owned more than 25%, directly or indirectly, by a Portuguese resident company.
- Where the non-resident shareholder is located in a country that is included in a black list from the Ministry of Finance.
- Where the assets of the company sold consist mainly of immovable property.

Government and corporate bonds
Interest and capital gains on government and corporate bonds are tax exempt (where held by entities not located in black-listed offshore jurisdictions) under certain conditions.

Interest paid by resident credit institutions
Interest paid by resident credit institutions to non-resident financial companies deriving from loans as well as gains arising from swap transactions are tax exempt.

Interest obtained by resident credit institutions
Interest obtained by non-resident credit institutions derived from term deposits held on resident entities authorised to receive such deposits are tax exempt.

Portugal

Madeira International Business Centre (MIBC)

Entities licensed to operate in the MIBC in the period between 2007 and 2013 benefit from a special tax regime, which is applicable until 31 December 2020. The MIBC is not available to entities pursuing financial and/or intra-group activities.

The 2007 MIBC special tax regime applies to companies licensed until 31 December 2013 and provides, besides full exemptions from taxation to non-resident shareholders (except for dividends and interest) and service providers, for the following reduced CIT rates for these entities, on their qualifying foreign source income, based on thresholds of income and subject to job creation requirements:

- 4% in 2012.
- 5% from 2013 to 2020.

MIBC based companies generally benefit from Portugal's network of double taxation treaties (DTTs). EU laws and regulations apply to Madeira.

MIBC based companies are, in general, exempt from annual property tax (IMI) regarding real estate used to pursue its business activity. This exemption does not apply in case of entities engaged in financial brokerage and insurance, including auxiliary entities related with such activities, as well as entities providing 'intra-group services' (coordination, treasury, and distribution centres).

Withholding taxes

General WHT rates

Recipient	Residents (%) (1)	Non-residents (%) (1)
Dividends	25 (2)	25 (3, 4)
Interest	25	25 (4)
Royalties	16.5	15
Interest & Royalties EU Directive	N/A	5 (5)
Banks deposits	25	25 (4)
Property income	16.5	15
Service charges	0	15 (6)
Other	25	25

Notes

1. For residents, tax withheld constitutes a payment on account of final corporate or individual income tax due. For non-residents, tax withheld is the final tax unless in case of property income, in which case it is a payment on account.
2. Not subject to WHT in the case of holdings of at least 10% owned for at least one year.
3. Not subject to WHT if the EU Parent/Subsidiary Directive 90/435/EC applies.
4. WHT rate is increased to 30% when the income is paid or due to entities resident in black-listed jurisdictions.
5. Until 30 June 2013, the applicable rate will be reduced to 5% and will be 0% from 1 July 2013 onwards.
6. Not subject to WHT if a tax treaty is applicable.

Tax treaty rates

Tax treaties reduce the above-mentioned rates as follows:

Recipient	Dividends (%)	Interest (%)	Royalties (%)
Algeria (3)	10/15	15	10
Angola (12)	-	-	-
Austria (1, 2)	15	10	10/15
Bahrain (12)	-	-	-
Barbados (3, 12)	5/15	10	5
Belgium (2)	15	15	10
Brazil (3)	10/15	15	15
Bulgaria (3)	10/15	10	10
Canada (3)	10/15	10	10
Cape Verde	10	10	10
Chile (3, 9, 10)	10/15	5/10/15	5/10
China, P.R.	10	10	10
Colombia (15)	10	10	10
Cuba (3)	5/10	10	5
Czech Republic (3)	10/15	10	10
Denmark (2)	10	10	10
East Timor (3, 15)	5/10	10	10
Estonia	10	10	10
Finland (2, 3)	10/15	15	10
France (2, 4, 5)	15	10/12	5
Gabon (12)	-	-	-
Germany (2, 6)	15	10/15	10
Greece (2)	15	15	10
Guinea Bissau (12)	10	10	10
Hong Kong (13)	5/10	10	5
Hungary (3)	10/15	10	10
Iceland (3)	10/15	10	10
India (3)	10/15	10	10
Indonesia	10	10	10
Ireland, Republic of (2)	15	15	10
Israel (11)	5/10/15	10	10
Italy (2)	15	15	12
Japan (6, 13, 15)	5/10	5/10	5
Korea, Republic of (3)	10/15	15	10
Kuwait (13)	5/10	10	10
Latvia	10	10	10
Lithuania	10	10	10
Luxembourg (2, 6)	15	10/15	10
Macau	10	10	10
Malawi (12)	-	-	-
Malta (3)	10/15	10	10
Mexico	10	10	10
Moldova	5/10	10	8
Morocco (3)	10/15	12	10
Mozambique	10	10	10
Netherlands (2)	10	10	10
Norway (3)	10/15	15	10

P

Portugal

Recipient	Dividends (%)	Interest (%)	Royalties (%)
Norway (14, 15)	5/15	10	10
Oman (12)	-	-	-
Pakistan	10/15	10	10
Panama (13, 15)	10/15	10	10
Poland (3)	10/15	10	10
Qatar (13, 15)	5/10	10	10
Romania (3)	10/15	10	10
Russia (3)	10/15	10	10
San Marino (12)	-	-	-
Saudi Arabia (12)	-	-	-
Senegal (12)	-	-	-
Singapore	10	10	10
Slovakia (3)	10/15	10	10
Slovenia (3)	5/15	10	5
South Africa (3)	10/15	10	10
Spain (2, 3)	10/15	15	5
Sweden	10	10	10
Switzerland (3)	10/15	10	5
Tunisia	15	15	10
Turkey (3, 8)	5/15	10/15	10
Ukraine (3)	10/15	10	10
United Arab Emirates (13)	5/15	10	5
United Kingdom (2, 3)	10/15	10	5
United States (3)	5/15	10	10
Uruguay (3)	5/10	10	10
Venezuela (7)	10	10	10/12
Vietnam (12)	-	-	-

Notes

1. The lower of the listed rates applies to royalties when the beneficiary holds 50% or less of the paying company's share capital.
2. There is no WHT on dividends if the EU Parent/Subsidiary Directive applies.
3. The lower of the listed rates applies to dividends when the beneficiary directly holds 25% or more of share capital. Depending on each DTT, a two year holding period may be required.
4. The lower of the listed rates applies to interest on debentures raised in France after 1 January 1965 or on significant loans or debentures raised in Portugal or abroad under major development projects listed in the treaty annex.
5. The lower of the listed rates applies to bank loans, but if interest is payable from Portugal, the bank loans must qualify as being of economic or social interest or fall under an approved development plan.
6. The lower of the listed rates applies to interest received by financial institutions.
7. The lower of the listed rates applies to technical assistance.
8. The lower of the listed rates applies on interest related to loans with a minimum maturity of two years.
9. The rate of 5% regarding interest applies to bonds interest or other securities transacted in the stock market. The rate of 10% applies to loans from banks or insurance companies or credit selling of equipment.
10. The rate of 5% regarding royalties applies to equipment lease.
11. The rate of 10% applies if the company which is paying the dividends is a resident of Israel and the dividends derive from profits which are subject to tax in Israel at a rate which is lower than the normal rate of Israel company tax. The rate of 5% applies if the beneficial owner is a company which holds directly at least 25% of the capital of the company paying the dividends.
12. Treaty signed, not yet in force; wording of the treaty not yet known.

13. The rate of 5% on dividends applies if the beneficial owner is a company (other than a partnership) which holds directly at least 10% of the capital of the company paying the dividends. Depending on each DTT, a one year holding period may be required.
14. Treaty signed in 2011 which will replace the treaty currently in force. The rate of 5% on dividends applies if the beneficial owner is a company (other than a partnership) that for an uninterrupted period of at least 12 months prior to the payment of the dividends or if the company paying the dividends has existed for less than 12 months, during the lifetime of the company, holds directly at least 10% of the capital of the company paying the dividends, or if the beneficial owner of the dividends is: (i) in the case of Portugal, the state, a political or administrative subdivision, or a local authority thereof, or the Bank of Portugal; and, (ii) in the case of Norway, the government of Norway, a political or administrative subdivision, or a local authority thereof, or the Central Bank of Norway.
15. Treaty signed, but not yet in force.

Tax administration

Taxable period
The tax year is, as a general rule, the calendar year. A different tax year is allowed in the case of companies obliged to the accounting consolidation and of PEs of non-resident entities, which can adopt the tax period of the non-resident company. If this option is taken, the new tax period must be maintained for a minimum of five years. The five year minimum period is not applicable if the taxpayer is transferred to a group of companies that are subject to consolidation of financial statements and the holding company has a fiscal year different from the one that was being adopted by the taxpayer.

Other entities may apply for a different tax period based on economic grounds.

Tax returns
The annual CIT return must be submitted by electronic data transmission by the last day of May of the year following the year of income.

Whenever the tax year ends on a date other than 31 December, the annual CIT return shall be submitted by electronic data transmission by the last day of the fifth month following the year end.

The system is one of self-assessment.

Payment of tax
Tax is paid in instalments. Three payments on account due on 15 July, 15 September, and 15 December of the year in which taxable income arises correspond to 90% of the previous year's corporate tax assessment (for taxpayers with a turnover above EUR 498,797; 70% if below this amount). A last instalment is paid (or received) through self-assessment upon filing the annual tax return in May of the following year.

If the tax year ends on a date other than 31 December, interim payments take place in the seventh, ninth, and 12th months of the tax year. Filing of the annual tax return together with the final payment is in the fifth month following the close of the tax year.

Given the introduction of a state surtax of 3% on the excess of taxable profit above EUR 1.5 million to EUR 10 million and 5% on the excess of taxable profit exceeding EUR 10 million, before the deduction of carryforward tax losses, three additional payments on account are due on the same dates as the interim payments mentioned above. The additional payments on account correspond to 2.5% of taxable profit above EUR 1.5 million and EUR 10 million and 4.5% of taxable profit above EUR 10 million assessed in the previous year.

Portugal

Payments on account are not required if the previous year's corporate tax assessment is less than EUR 199.52 and may be suspended upon declaring that no further tax is due in respect of the current year. However, interest is assessed at a rate of 4% if this results in postponing more than 20% of the tax that would otherwise have been paid.

In particular situations, a special payment on account is due of a minimum of EUR 1,000 up to EUR 70,000, paid in March, or in March and October (the third or the third and tenth month of the tax year if it ends on a date other than 31 December).

Interest and penalties

Late assessment interest is due in case of delay on the assessment of taxes due. Late assessment interest is computed on a daily basis, according to the following formula: tax due * interest rate * number of days outstanding / 365. The current rate of late assessment interest is 4% (year).

Late penalty interest is due in case of delay in the payment of the tax assessed. The current rate of approximately 7% has been established by Statement 24866-A/2011, dated 28 December 2011, issued by the Public Institute of Treasury Management and Public Credit.

Tax penalties for companies are capped at EUR 165,000 in the case of *dolus* and EUR 45,000 in the case of negligence.

In general, in case of failure or late payment of CIT, companies are liable to a penalty varying between 30% to 100% of the tax due, capped at EUR 45,000 (in case of negligence).

There are new specific tax penalties regarding transfer pricing documentation and the CFC regime (between EUR 1,000 and EUR 20,000 for companies) and regarding omissions or inaccuracies regarding ruling requests (between EUR 750 and EUR 45,000 for companies in the case of urgent rulings or 25% of the previous amounts in the case of non-urgent rulings).

There is the possibility of applying for penalty reduction, provided certain requirements are met (e.g. regularisation of the tax situation/payment of the tax due; situation where there was no damage to the Revenue).

Statute of limitations

The statute of limitation period is four years, but can be extended in case of tax losses. Regarding facts involving black-listed jurisdictions, the statute of limitation for the right to assess taxes is extended to 12 years while the time period allowed to collect taxes is extended to 15 years. The statute of limitation period is also increased from four to 12 years, in case of facts related to deposit and securities accounts in financial institutions outside the European Union.

Anti-avoidance

A general anti-avoidance provision is in force, pursuant to which contracts and other acts are ineffective whenever it is demonstrated that they were tax driven to reduce taxation that would be due under contracts bearing a similar economic effect, in which case taxation would be based on the latter.

The anti-avoidance procedure is initiated within the general term foreseen (statute of limitation) and is now more flexible in terms of proof by the tax authorities.

Anti-avoidance rules are not applicable in cases where a request for obtaining binding information is not answered by the tax authorities within 150 days.

Binding rulings

Binding rulings can be:

- Urgent: A decision should be taken in 120 days; these are subject to the payment of a fee ranging between EUR 2,500 and EUR 25,500, depending on the complexity of the matter; if no decision is taken within the deadline established, there is a tacit approval of the taxpayer's understanding of the tax matter.
- Non-urgent: A decision should be taken in 150 days; no fees are charged; a decision is required (no tacit approval, as in case of an urgent ruling).

Tax amnesty

The 2012 State Budget Law approved a tax amnesty regime (*Regime Excepcional de Regularização de Dívidas Tributárias* or RERT III).

RERT III is a special regime for tax regularisation, which is applicable to Portuguese tax residents (in 2010 and previous years) who held assets outside Portugal, as of 31 December 2010, which income was not declared to the tax authorities.

This regime allows that, until 30 June 2012, taxpayers regularise their tax situation, through the payment of a flat rate (7.5%) applicable to the value of the assets held outside Portugal.

The regime applies both to individuals and companies.

Under this regime, 'assets' includes deposits, deposit certificates, shareholdings, securities, and other financial instruments (including life insurance policies linked to investment funds).

The indirect ownership of the assets may also be subject to regularisation under RERT III, i.e. ownership via trusts, fund, fiduciary agent and nominee, beneficial ownership contract, etc.

The regularisation is made through the submission of a form, disclosing the assets to be regularised.

Payment of the rate associated with the regularisation (7.5% on the value of the assets held outside Portugal) is made at the moment of submission of the regularisation form, or within ten days of being filed with the Central Bank of Portugal or a bank established in Portugal.

It is not required to repatriate the regularised assets to Portugal.

The regime determines the extinction of any tax obligations and ruling out of liability for any tax fault in relation to the assets which income was not declared to the tax authorities for taxation periods that have ended by 31 December 2010.

It is a confidential process between the Central Bank of Portugal and the taxpayer.

As the regularisation is made with effects to 31 December 2010, any income obtained in 2011 is not covered by the regime.

P

Portugal

The non-submission of the tax regularisation declaration for the assets, as well as any omissions or inaccuracies in it, imply, in relation to them, an increase of 60% in the tax that would be due for the income corresponding to the referred assets.

If the taxpayer decides not to regularise its situation under RERT III, it will be liable for the taxes that were not paid to the Portuguese tax authorities, and also for the compensatory interest and penalties.

Not disclosing such income may also be considered tax fraud, and such income may be liable to tax penalties and/or legal penalties.

Fight against tax fraud and evasion
It is mandatory that payments above EUR 1,000 (previously EUR 9,700) are made by a means that allows the identification of the recipient of the income (e.g. bank transfer, nominative cheque, or direct debit).

Puerto Rico

PwC contact

Victor Rodríguez
PricewaterhouseCoopers
254 Munoz Rivera Avenue
BBVA Building
Suite 900
San Juan, Puerto Rico 00918
Puerto Rico
Tel: +1 787 772 7958
Email: victor.rodriguez@us.pwc.com

Significant developments

One of the most significant developments of 2011 was the enactment of Act 232, Technical Amendments to the 2011 Puerto Rico Internal Revenue Code (2011 Tax Code). This Act amended numerous provisions of the 2011 Tax Code, including corporate, individual, and partnership's provisions. Most relevant amendments have been included in the appropriate sections of this summary.

Act 218 was enacted on 7 November 2011, providing an amnesty covering various Puerto Rico taxes to alleviate and assist taxpayers with the payment of their debts. The amnesty was applicable to income tax, estate and gift tax, the special real property tax, withholding (WHT) tax, and payroll tax. This amnesty eliminated interests, surcharges, and penalties; therefore, taxpayers only had to pay the principal amount. This amnesty was effective until 29 February 2012.

On 19 April 2012, Act 64 was enacted to extend the previous tax amnesty. Act 64 is in effect from 1 March 2012 to 15 June 2012. In general, benefits of Act 64 are the same as of Act 218.

Taxes on corporate income

A domestic corporation is taxable in Puerto Rico on its worldwide income. A foreign corporation engaged in trade or business in Puerto Rico is taxed at the regular corporate tax rates on income from Puerto Rico sources that is effectively connected income and at a 29% WHT rate on its Puerto Rico-source gross income not effectively connected with that business.

The current corporate income tax (CIT) rate is comprised of a 20% normal tax and a graduated surtax (computed on the 'surtax net income') up to a maximum combined and effective tax rate of nearly 30%. The 'surtax net income' is basically the net taxable income subject to regular tax less a surtax deduction in the amount of 750,000 United States dollars (USD).

Surtax tax rates are as follows: (i) 5% for income up to USD 1,750,000 and (ii) USD 87,500 plus 10% of income in excess of USD 1,750,000 for a maximum nominal tax rate of nearly 30%. This latter 10% surtax might only be applicable up to 2013, leaving the maximum nominal tax rate at nearly 25% from 2014 thereafter, provided certain fiscal and economical conditions are met.

Puerto Rico

The determination of the applicable surtax rate is now made on a consolidated basis for controlled groups and related companies, whereas the net taxable income of all the entities subject to tax in Puerto Rico within said groups has to be combined for the determination of the 5% or 10% applicable surtax rate.

Alternative minimum tax (AMT)
The AMT tax rate is 20%. For certain companies purchasing personal property from related parties, the tentative AMT is the greatest of the above-mentioned 20% or 1% of said purchases of personal property. For AMT purposes, expenses paid or incurred for services performed by a related party outside Puerto Rico are considered a permanent adjustment in the determination of the alternative minimum net income (i.e. non-deductible for AMT purposes).

Tax on improper accumulation of income
A surtax of 50% is imposed on corporations that improperly accumulate earnings to prevent the imposition of tax on shareholders or partners, rather than paying the earnings out as dividends. The tax is not imposed on accumulated earnings and profits but is imposed on the net income for the year computed without taking capital loss carryover or net operating loss (NOL) carryover deductions, and reduced by the following items: Puerto Rico income taxes paid or accrued, disallowed net capital losses, and charitable contributions in excess of the deductible amount. The net income does not include industrial income exempted from income taxes under Industrial Incentives Acts. However, an exempt business can be subject to the penalty tax on non-exempt income.

Corporate residence

A corporation organised or created under the laws of Puerto Rico is a domestic corporation. A domestic corporation is a resident corporation even if it does not conduct business operations in Puerto Rico. A corporation created elsewhere is considered a foreign corporation.

Permanent establishment (PE)
The Puerto Rico Tax Code does not provide specific guidance on PE. Facts and circumstances need to be analysed in order to determine if a corporation has created a PE in Puerto Rico or not. However, having an office or fixed place of business in Puerto Rico may deem the corporation to be engaged in a trade or business in Puerto Rico (i.e. having a PE).

Sourcing rules pursuant to Act 154
Act 154's source rules are segregated into two parts. The first part treats a non-Puerto Rico resident manufacturing entity as having an office or fixed place of business in Puerto Rico merely as a result of engaging in transactions above a certain threshold with a related Puerto Rico entity. The second part treats a portion of the income earned by a non-Puerto Rico resident entity as Puerto Rico-source income.

Act 154's source rule applies where a non-Puerto Rico resident purchases goods and services from a related company that manufactures personal property or performs services in Puerto Rico that account for 10% or more of the total gross receipts of the seller from sales of such property or services in Puerto Rico, or at least 10% of the purchase cost of personal property and services acquired by the purchaser, for the taxable year or any of the three prior taxable years.

Where Act 154's source rule applies, a portion of the income of the non-Puerto Rico resident purchaser from the sale outside of Puerto Rico of personal property manufactured or produced in whole or part in Puerto Rico by the related Puerto Rico seller will be treated as Puerto Rico-source income that is effectively connected with the conduct of a Puerto Rico trade or business. The portion of the non-Puerto Rico resident's income that is treated as Puerto Rico source is determined under an equally weighted, four-factor (i.e. purchases, sales, property, and payroll) formulary apportionment method. Where the purchaser fails to provide adequate documentation regarding the formulary apportionment factors, 50% of the income of the non-Puerto Rico resident purchaser from the sale outside of Puerto Rico of personal property manufactured or produced in whole or part in Puerto Rico by the related Puerto Rico seller will be treated as sourced where the property is manufactured or produced (i.e. Puerto Rico). The source rule also will apply to agency and commissionaire arrangements, in addition to buy-sell transactions involving related parties. In addition, the source rule contains an anti-abuse provision that disregards a transaction, for purposes of the source rule, where one of the principal purposes of the transaction is avoidance of the source rule.

Other taxes

Sales and use tax (SUT)

As a general rule, the SUT shall be applied, collected, and paid on all transactions of taxable items in Puerto Rico. Taxable items consist of tangible personal property, taxable services, admissions, and what is known as bundled transactions. Excluded from this definition are professional associations and certain membership fees; stamps issued by professional associations, the Commonwealth of Puerto Rico, or the federal government; human blood, tissue, and organs; maintenance fees paid to resident associations; air and maritime tickets; real property; and bingos, raffles, and lottery. Other transactions that are exempt from SUT include export transactions; duty-free stores located at airport or maritime ports; prescription medicines; insulin; taxable items acquired for certain manufacturing operations (e.g. raw materials); and food and ingredients for food (except for prepared food, diet supplements, sweets, and carbonated beverages).

SUT is imposed at the state level at a 5.5% and an additional 1.5% at the municipal level, for an aggregate tax of 7%. The 7% tax should be remitted to the Puerto Rico government as follows: 6% to the Puerto Rico Treasury Department (PRTD) and the remaining 1% to the corresponding municipality. However, there are some municipalities that have entered into an administration agreement with the PRTD by which the PRTD will collect the entire 7% of the sales and use tax from merchants and remit the 1% to the municipality (collected on the municipality's behalf).

Every natural or juridical person who does or wishes to do business of any kind in Puerto Rico shall request registration in the Merchant's Registry of the PRTD at least 30 days before starting operations. Once the registration application is filled out and approved, the Secretary of Treasury will grant a Merchant's Registration Certificate. This certificate constitutes the merchant's authorisation to do business in Puerto Rico, and confirms the merchant's obligation as a withholding agent. The Merchant's Registration Certificate shall be displayed, at all times, in a visible place for the general public in the commercial establishment for which it was issued. Please note that if a merchant is doing business in one or more of the 78 municipalities in Puerto Rico, the merchant only needs to register with the PRTD.

Puerto Rico

Unless specifically exempted, all persons selling taxable items are required to file a monthly tax return. This return shall be delivered to the PRTD no later that the tenth day of the calendar month following the month during which the sales occurred. If the merchant wishes to claim any exemption corresponding to taxable items, the merchant needs to file the monthly return and claim the exemption in it.

Merchants whose SUT deposits exceeded USD 12,000 are required to file the monthly SUT return and remit the payment electronically. In addition, merchants with volume of business of USD 200,000 or more should remit the SUT withheld electronically.

There is a credit for purchases of products manufactured in Puerto Rico for purposes of SUT. In general, the credit will be 10% of the excess of the purchases of eligible products over the average of the purchases of eligible products for three out of ten prior taxable years. This credit can be carried forward until exhausted. It is important to note that the credit used will be considered taxable income for income tax purposes of the year the credit is taken.

Customs duties and import tariffs
Puerto Rico does not have customs duty and import tariff provisions. Since Puerto Rico is a Commonwealth of the United States, it follows the United States' customs duties and import tariffs.

Excise taxes
There are certain articles subject to a special excise tax, such as cigarettes, fuels, crude oils, vehicles, alcoholic beverages, cement, sugar, and plastic products, among others.

Act 154's excise tax
Companies with manufacturing operations in Puerto Rico may be subject to an excise tax on goods or services provided to offshore-related entities under Act 154 of 2010. This Act created an excise tax that works in tandem with Act 154's source rules. Where the excise tax applies, it is in lieu of the tax that otherwise would arise from the application of Act 154's source rules. Under this excise tax rule, offshore purchasers that acquire goods from Puerto Rico sellers with gross receipts in excess of USD 75 million for any of the three preceding taxable years and that otherwise meet the source-of-income rule thresholds (set forth above) are subject to this excise tax equal to the 'applicable percentage of the value' of such personal property or services, which is essentially a scaled-back percentage. The excise tax rate phases out over a six-year period as follows:

- 4.00% between 1 January 2011 and 31 December 2011.
- 3.75% between 1 January 2012 and 31 December 2012.
- 2.75% between 1 January 2013 and 31 December 2013.
- 2.50% between 1 January 2014 and 31 December 2014.
- 2.25% between 1 January 2015 and 31 December 2015.
- 1.00% between 1 January 2016 and 31 December 2016.

Regulations 7970, issued in December 2010, provide the following tax credits to offset the excise tax mentioned above:

1. General credit: up to USD 4 million for 2011 and a reduced amount going forward on the same proportion that the excise rate is reduced.

2. Alternative credit based on gross receipts: in lieu of the above-mentioned credit, and provided the gross receipts per average monthly number of employees in Puerto

Rico is less than USD 550,000, a credit of up to USD 7 million for 2011 and a reduced amount going forward on the same proportion that the excise rate is reduced.

3. Alternative credit when taxable acquisitions exceed certain thresholds: in lieu of the above-mentioned credits, if taxable acquisitions equals or exceed USD 4 billion, average monthly employees engaged in manufacturing or production in Puerto Rico is at least 400, and payroll equals or exceeds USD 20 million, then the credit for 2011 could be between USD 20 million and USD 80 million.

4. Additional credit for incremental increase in employees: for taxpayers meeting the requirements established in credit 3 above, an additional credit of USD 187,500 for each additional 25 employees over the employee baseline, up to a maximum of USD 3,750 million, will be available. A reduced credit will be available for years after 2011 on the same proportion that the excise rate is reduced.

5. Credit for controlled groups with facilities in multiple municipalities: in addition to credits 1 and 2 above but in lieu of credits 3 and 4 above, in the case of a controlled group that has one or more members that are engaged in manufacturing and production or manufacturing services in facilities located in three or more different municipalities in Puerto Rico as of 24 October 2010, a credit of USD 5 million per each municipality shall be allowed for each facility that has a monthly average of more than 30 employees, up to a maximum credit of USD 20 million. A reduced credit will be available for years after 2011 on the same proportion that the excise rate is reduced.

6. Credit for economically disadvantaged or critical industrial suppliers: additional credit of 100% or 150% of increase in purchases from economically disadvantaged or critical industrial suppliers over the average purchases for the last two years.

7. Knowledge corridor and research and development (R&D) investment credit: additional credit of 100% of direct contributions to the Puerto Rico Science, Technology, and Research Trust or Special Economic Development Fund and of the excess R&D invested in Puerto Rico over the average investment for the two last years, subject to certain limitations.

The excise tax is collected by the Puerto Rico seller on receipts from the sale of personal property or services rendered to a related offshore purchaser. The tax has to be deposited with the Secretary of the Treasury on or before the 15th day of the month following the sale. Each person required to collect the excise tax must file a quarterly excise tax return on 30 April, 31 July, 31 October, and 1 January and pay any remaining tax liability not deposited on a monthly basis, as outlined above.

Act 154 sets forth the process for which a credit may be claimed for (i) taxes paid to any of the states of the United States on the acquisition of personal property and services and (ii) taxes paid to Puerto Rico by another member of the taxpayer's controlled group on a series of purchases.

Personal property taxes
Every corporation engaged in a trade or business in Puerto Rico which on 1 January of each year owns personal property used in its trade or business within Puerto Rico, whether it is leased to another entity, is subject to tax on such property. The tax is self-assessed by the corporation and it is paid together with the filing of an annual return. The tax ranges between 5.08% and 8.23%, depending on the municipality. A 5%

Puerto Rico

statutory discount is available if payment is made in full on the return due date (15 May of each year).

In general, all personal property not specifically exempted, including cash, finished goods inventory, supplies, and depreciable property, is subject to the tax. The personal property tax is generally based on the book value of the asset as of 1 January. Finished goods inventory, however, is assessed on the average of the monthly balances for the 12-month period preceding 1 January of each year.

The valuation of the personal property subject to tax is determined by multiplying the book value of such property by the applicable tax rate determined by the municipality in which the property is located. If the book value of depreciable property is below its estimated residual value, the property should be assessed at its estimated residual value.

Real property taxes

The property tax system is administered by the Municipal Revenue Collection Center (MRCC). The tax on real property is directly assessed by the MRCC and may be paid in two instalments. The tax, (which varies from a minimum of 7.80% to a maximum of 10.23%, depending on the municipality) is applied to an amount based on the hypothetical fair market value (FMV) of the relevant property in the year 1957. In general terms, this hypothetical FMV normally ranges between 40% and 50% of the cost of the property.

Transfer taxes

Puerto Rico does not have transfer tax provisions.

Stamp taxes

Puerto Rico does not have stamp tax provisions. However, recordation fees are imposed at the time of officially recording a real estate transaction with the Puerto Rico Property Registry.

Municipal license tax

Every corporation is required to file an annual volume-of-business declaration with each of the municipalities in which it establishes or conducts business operations during the year. The declaration must indicate the actual volume of business (i.e. net sales, gross income from any service rendered, and other gross receipts) attributable to each municipality. When a business operates in more than one municipality but does not receive income in all of them, the license tax shall be computed based on a distribution of sales apportioned to each municipality by square feet of the building used in each municipality.

For a non-financial business, the license tax payment varies from a minimum of 0.20% to a maximum of 0.50%, depending on each municipality. The payment must be made in two equal instalments on or before 15 July and 15 January on the basis of the volume of business generated by the entity during its accounting year ended within the immediately preceding calendar year before the due date of the declaration. A 5% discount its available when the tax is fully paid on the declaration due date (on or before five working days after 15 April of each year).

For the first six months after a new business is established, the new company is generally exempt from the municipal license tax, provided that the business informs the municipality that it has established a new business in the municipality within the first 30 days of operations and request the provisional license tax as established in each municipality. A copy of the municipal licence is generally requested as a perquisite for obtaining other licences and permits in Puerto Rico.

Branch income

Corporations operating in Puerto Rico as a branch may be subject to a 10% tax on the dividend equivalent amount (commonly known as the branch profit tax or BPT). The BPT should be determined and paid along with the CIT return. There would not be an income tax withholding at source at the time cash transfers are made by the Puerto Rico branch to its home office outside of Puerto Rico.

Income determination

The gross income of a corporation generally includes business income, profits from the sale of property, interest, dividends, and income derived from any source unless specifically exempted by law.

A corporation's net income is generally calculated in accordance with the method used for financial statement purposes, except for various items of income and expenses, which are treated differently. For example, the cash method of accounting may not be used by a corporation with inventory or with an average annual gross income in excess of USD 1 million. Long-term contract methods and the installment method can be used for regular tax calculations.

Inventory valuation
In general, inventory is valued at the lower of cost or market. Retail merchants can use the retail method of accounting.

Capital gains
Tax-advantaged treatment is provided for net long-term gains (holding period of more than six months) from the sale of capital assets. For corporations, net long-term capital gains, reduced by any short-term capital losses, are subject to an alternative (preferential) tax of 15% in lieu of the regular CIT rates.

Dividend income
Dividends from a corporation that derives 20% or more of its profits from sources within Puerto Rico are taxable in Puerto Rico. However, a dividend-received deduction may apply.

Dividends-received deduction
All corporations engaged in trade or business in Puerto Rico are entitled to an 85% deduction on dividends received from a domestic corporation but not in excess of 85% of the net income of the corporation. A 100% dividend-received deduction applies for dividends received from taxable controlled domestic corporations (if ownership in a corporation is 80% or more).

Interest income
Interest income is generally taxable, except interest from obligations of the federal government or any state, or territory, or political subdivisions; the District of Columbia; and the Commonwealth of Puerto Rico or any of its instrumentalities or political subdivisions.

Puerto Rico

Royalty income

Royalties from property located in Puerto Rico or from any interest in such property are included in gross income.

Partnership income

The income (loss) of a partnership passes through to its partners so that the partnership itself is not subject to tax. Thus, each partner generally accounts for their distributive share of the partnership's taxable income (loss).

Other income

Service fees are generally taxable as ordinary income.

Foreign income

Generally, a Puerto Rico domestic corporation is taxed on its worldwide income, including foreign income earned and foreign dividends when received. Double taxation is avoided by means of foreign tax credit or deduction. In the case of resident foreign corporations, these are only taxed on their Puerto Rico-source income and on their effectively connected Puerto Rico income (i.e. foreign income won't be taxable for Puerto Rico purposes).

Deductions

All ordinary and necessary expenses paid or incurred during the taxable year in carrying on any trade or business are deductible by corporations operating in Puerto Rico.

Depreciation

A reasonable depreciation allowance is deductible for the exhaustion, wear and tear, and obsolescence of property used in business. The most common depreciation method used by corporations is the straight-line method. Nevertheless, any other consistent method may be used in lieu of the straight-line method as long as it is in accordance with the recognised trade practice. In addition, a corporation (other than one that is exempt under an Industrial Incentives Act) can elect an accelerated depreciation method for new or used tangible property acquired by purchase, on taxable years commencing after 30 June 1995.

For property acquired after 31 December 2009, when using the straight-line depreciation method, the useful life has to be determined based on the same rules of accelerated depreciation.

Assets	Useful life (years)
3 year property (e.g. computers, electronic equipment)	3
5 year property (e.g. automobiles, transportation equipment)	5
7 year property (e.g. certain furniture and fixtures, air transportation equipment)	7
10 year property (e.g. furniture and fixtures, printing equipment, other machinery and equipment)	10
15 year property (e.g. certain air transportation equipment, natural gas plants)	15
20 year property (e.g. vessels, land improvements)	20
Real property leased for residential purposes	30
Other real property	35

For intangibles (other than goodwill) acquired or created after 1 September 2010, the deduction is calculated using the straight-line method over the lower of a useful life of 15 years or the intangible useful life.

Goodwill
The cost of goodwill is generally capitalised and amortised ratably over 15 years.

Start-up expenses
Generally, start-up expenditures may be deducted in the tax year in which the trade or business begins or they may be ratably amortised over five years.

Interest expenses
In general, interest expense is deductible without limitation. However, interest expenses related to exempt income are not deductible. If interest is paid to a non-Puerto Rico resident related party, a 29% withholding at source would apply.

Bad debt
Bad debt resulting from a trade or business may be deducted in the year the debt becomes worthless (i.e. uncollectible). The reserve method is not admissible for Puerto Rico purposes.

Charitable contributions
Deductions for allowed charitable contributions are limited to 10% of net income, computed regardless of the contributions.

Rent expense
Corporations are entitled to a rent expense deduction if the rented property is used in the business.

Employee remuneration
Corporations may deduct payments of reasonable salaries or other compensation for services actually rendered.

Insurance premiums
Insurance premiums paid or accrued on risks related to a trade or business are deductible as well as premiums on group life policies covering employees, where the beneficiary is not the corporation. No deduction is allowed for premiums paid to an insurance company not authorised to provide insurance in Puerto Rico or through an agent or broker not authorised to operate in Puerto Rico.

Meals and entertainment
Meals and entertainment expenses are deductible, subject to a 50% limitation. Travelling expenses are fully deductible if the trip is for business purposes.

Automobiles expenses
A corporation is allowed to depreciate non-cargo automobiles used in trade or business over a five year useful life (three years in the case of sales persons) up to a maximum base of USD 30,000 for a maximum annual depreciation of USD 6,000.

On the other hand, for non-cargo automobile maintenance expenses (e.g. gas, repairs, insurance) a deduction based on USD 0.60 per mileage is allowed.

Puerto Rico

Taxes
A corporation is allowed a deduction for taxes paid (except for Puerto Rico CIT), including income tax paid to the United States, its other possessions, and any foreign country. The deduction is in lieu of claiming a foreign tax credit.

Other significant items
The cost of incidental repairs (not adding value to the property) is deductible as business expenses.

Subject to certain limitations, savings and retirement plans for the benefit of the employees are deductible, if qualified by the Secretary of the Treasury.

Net operating losses (NOLs)
All corporations are generally entitled to the NOL deduction in computing their tax. NOLs may be carried over for seven years (there are no carryback provisions). Also, losses from sales or exchanges of capital assets are allowed only to the extent of gains from such sales or exchanges. The carryforward period in this instance is, however, five years.

Act 171 increases the NOL carryforward period from seven taxable years to ten taxable years for NOLs generated from taxable years beginning after 31 December 2004 and before 31 December 2012.

Payments to foreign affiliates
Management fees paid to a foreign affiliate are deductible to the extent that they are reasonable compensation for the services rendered. However, the Secretary of the Treasury has the authority to reallocate items of income and expense to properly reflect the Puerto Rico taxable income.

Group taxation

Puerto Rico does not have group taxation rules. In other words, corporations can not file a consolidated return for Puerto Rico CIT purposes.

Transfer pricing
There are no specific transfer pricing rules in Puerto Rico.

Thin capitalisation
There are no specific thin capitalisation rules in Puerto Rico.

Tax credits and incentives

A corporation engaged in specific eligible activities may apply for a reduced CIT rate through the request of a Tax Exemption Grant to the Puerto Rico Office of Industrial Tax Exemption pursuant to Act 73 of 28 May 2008.

Tax rate incentives
Exempt entities may elect one of the following two scenarios:

- General scenario: 4% CIT rate with a WHT rate on royalty payments of 12%. Under this scenario, the amount of WHT on the royalty payments is creditable against the 4% CIT.

- Alternate scenario: 8% CIT rate with a WHT rate on royalty payments of 2%. Under this scenario, the WHT on royalty payments is creditable against the 8% CIT.

Companies may elect one of these scenarios at the time of applying for the benefits under the act. However, there are other possibilities:

- 4% fixed income tax rate on Incentive Development Income (IDI), excluding income from certain investments provided by Section 2(j).
- Existing exempt businesses currently taxed at a rate of 2% to 4% under the 1998 Act may continue to enjoy the same tax rate under the new act when it is determined by the Secretary of the Puerto Rico Economic Development (the Secretary) that said tax rate is in the best interest of Puerto Rico and the existing business complies with an employment commitment of at least 80% of its average employment during the three preceding years before the application of exemption under the new act. Note that the secretary could require a minimum income tax payment equal to the average income tax paid during said period.
- Pioneer industries are eligible for a 1% CIT rate.
- Activities for the development in Puerto Rico of intangible property are eligible for a 0% CIT rate.
- Any exempt business having operations at a municipality located in a 'low or intermediate development zone' may reduce its CIT rate by an additional 5%.
- Any exempt business having operations in Vieques and Culebra may be totally exempt from income taxes during the first ten years of operations as established in the new act. The remaining years covered by its tax decree may qualify for a 2% CIT rate.

Special deductions
Special deductions are eliminated, except for capital investment in buildings, structure, machinery and equipment, and the NOLs carryforward.

Credits

Credit for purchases of Puerto Rico manufactured product
Subject to certain limitations, the credit for purchases of products manufactured in Puerto Rico will remain at 25% (35% in the case of recycled products).

Job creation credit
There is a credit for every incremental job applicable to exempt business starting operations after 1 July 2008. The amount of the credit (maximum of USD 5,000 per each employment) depends upon the location of the industrial development zone.

R&D investment credit
A 50% credit is granted for the eligible investment in R&D activities, including operational expenditures, clinical trials, infrastructure, renewable energy, or intellectual property.

Energy investment credit
A 50% credit is granted for the eligible investment in the acquisition of machinery and equipment for the creation of energy.

Energy cost credit
There is also a 3% credit (which could be increased up to 10% if certain employment requirements are met) for payments made to the Puerto Rico Power Authority during the corresponding taxable year. This credit is available for a ten-year period starting as

Puerto Rico

of 1 July 2008. Additional credits (for the purpose of reducing the cost of energy) may be available to industrial units subject to certain limitations.

Technology transfer credit
A 12% credit (2% in the case of exempt businesses that opted for the alternate tax) is available for payments made to resident entities for the use or privilege of using intangible property in Puerto Rico.

Strategic projects investment credit
There is a 50% credit for eligible investment in strategic projects, including activities for the design, development, and construction of dams.

Industrial investment credit
There is a 50% credit, up to a maximum of USD 8 million, for cash invested in the purchase of 50% or more of the stock or operating assets of an exempt business that is in the process of shutting down operations, amount used to start-up small or medium-exempt business, or amounts used for a substantial expansion of an exempt business.

Several of the above-mentioned credits were also made available to entities operating under prior tax incentives acts.

On 3 January 2011, the PRTD issued Circular Letter 11-01 and Informative Bulletin 11-01 to introduce the new electronic system for integrated tax credits (CCI System, for its name in Spanish). Also, these communications introduced new processes to claim such credits against the income tax, notify of the sale of such credits, and to request the vouchers for the utilisation of these credits against the corporation's utilities, if applicable.

The CCI System will allow the PRTD to maintain an updated registry of the tax credits already granted.

Property tax incentives
Similar to the previous incentives laws, the current act allows for a 90% property tax exemption on personal and real property. However, the current act introduced a methodology for the classification and assessment of real property owned by the exempt businesses. Under the provisions of the current act, a taxpayer can self-assess one's real property tax responsibility (similar to the current personal property tax system) and remit the related tax liability due along with a real property tax return (to be issued by the MRCC) by 15 May of each year. The self-appraisal method is only applicable to real property that has not been appraised by the MRCC and is mainly limited to machinery and equipment classified as real property. Note that this method is not available for assets such as land, building, and building equipment.

Municipal license tax and other municipal tax incentives
The current act did not introduce many changes regarding treatment of exempted businesses for municipal license tax purposes. The tax exemption remains at the same 60% as it was under the 1998 Act. Exempt businesses operating in Vieques or Culebra are 90% exempt; small or medium-exempt businesses are 75% exempt; and central or regional corporate headquarters providing managerial services to affiliated companies are 100% exempt during the first five years after becoming eligible for the exemption.

Foreign tax credit
Generally, in any year, a taxpayer can choose whether to take as a credit (subject to limitation) or as a deduction foreign income and excess profit taxes paid or accrued

during the taxable year to any foreign country. A foreign tax credit reduces the Puerto Rico income tax liability dollar for dollar, while a deduction reduces the Puerto Rico income tax liability at the marginal rate of the taxpayer. There are no carryforward provisions for foreign tax credit purposes.

Withholding taxes

Corporations not engaged in a trade or business in Puerto Rico are subject to a 29% WHT at source on certain gross income items (considered fixed or determinable, annual or periodical [FDAP]) from Puerto Rico sources.

FDAP income may include interests received from a related person, rents, royalties, salaries, annuities, compensation, remuneration, and net capital gains. However, if the payment received is from dividends and partnership profits, a 10% WHT should apply.

The payer, as a withholding agent, is responsible for the deduction and remittance of the 29% (10% in the case of dividends) to the Puerto Rico Treasury Department. Such tax is due on or before the 15th day of the month following the receipt of the income by the non-resident corporation and it is reported in Form 480.31 'Deposit Slip of Non-residents Income Tax Withheld at Source'. An annual informative return is also required to be filed (Form 480.30 'Non-residents Annual Return of Income Tax Withheld at Source') no later than 15 April of the following year.

Tax treaties

There are no tax treaties between foreign countries and Puerto Rico. However, the Puerto Rico Supreme Court has recognised that, although Puerto Rico is generally not a signatory party to a treaty entered into by the United States, if an international treaty does not explicitly exclude Puerto Rico, the treaty would be applicable to Puerto Rico.

Tax administration

Taxable period

The annual accounting period may be on the basis of the calendar year, a fiscal year ending on the last day of a month, or a 52/53 week year.

Tax returns

The Puerto Rico tax system is based on the principle of self-assessment. A corporate taxpayer is required to file an annual income tax return (generally Form 480.20) by the 15th day of the fourth month following the close of its tax year. In general terms, a taxpayer can obtain an automatic extension of three months to file its income tax return. Failure to timely file can result in penalties. Any tax not covered with the estimated tax payments should be paid along with this return.

A corporate taxpayer may also be subject to file a personal property tax return by 15 May and/or a volume of business declaration by the 5th business day after 15 April.

Payment of tax

A corporation must substantially satisfy its annual income tax liability, if any, through estimated income tax payments. The amount of estimated income taxes should be paid on equal instalments on the 15th day of the fourth, sixth, ninth, and 12th month of the taxable year of the corporation. The estimated payments should equal or exceed 90% of the actual tax for the year or, in the case a CIT return was filed by the corporation in

Puerto Rico

the preceding year, 100% of such tax liability. Failure to pay the tax by the due dates indicated above may result in a penalty of 10% of the instalment due.

Annual report

Every corporation is required to file an annual corporation report with the Puerto Rico Department of State. This annual report must be filed by the 15th day of April along with a USD 150 annual fee and a balance sheet as of the close of operations of the prior year. The report should be filed through the Puerto Rico Department of State's website. In the case of for-profit corporations, if the volume of business exceeds USD 3 million, the annual report must be accompanied by a balance sheet certified by a certified public accountant (CPA) licensed in Puerto Rico. In the event that the volume of business does not exceed USD 3 million, a balance sheet prepared under generally accepted accounting principles (GAAP) by a person with a general knowledge in accounting has to be submitted along with the corporate annual report. An extension of 60 days, an additional 30 day period may be requested, for filing the annual report can be obtained if timely requested. The Secretary of State is authorised to impose penalty for failure to timely or accurately file the annual corporate report that would be between USD 75 and USD 2,000 if a non-profit corporation, and between USD 750 and USD 2,000 if a for-profit corporation.

Audited financial statements

Accounting records must be prepared in accordance with the general accepted accounting principles (GAAP) followed in the United States. Domestic corporations (i.e. incorporated in Puerto Rico) with volume of business of more than USD 3 million must include, with their CIT return, audited financial statements of the Puerto Rico operations for the accounting year ended on or before the preceding 31 December. The financial statements should be submitted with an audit report issued by a CPA licensed in Puerto Rico. Nevertheless, foreign corporations with volume of business of more than USD 3 million must include, with their CIT return, audited financial statements of the Puerto Rico operations.

Also, qualified and disclaimer opinions are now allowed to the extent that the qualification or disclaimer does not result from a restriction in scope. However, no adverse opinions are allowed. All groups of related entities engaged in a trade or business in Puerto Rico are required to file consolidated or combined financial statements (CFS), which should contain a consolidating schedule and general information of the related parties. The determination of the gross income threshold for purposes of the audited financial statement requirement should be made taking into consideration the volume of business of all the entities within a controlled group. In the case of foreign entities, these will be able to submit audited financial statements with their Puerto Rico operations on a stand-alone basis; in other words, the CFS will not be required. The requirement for audited financial statements will not apply to non-profit organisations. There was a waiver for the taxable year commencing after 31 December 2010 and before 1 January 2012. This waiver provided for the submission of stand-alone audited financial statements for all entities within a consolidated group with volume of business of more than USD 1 million, instead of the consolidated or combined audited financial statements.

With respect to the municipal license and personal property tax filings, the threshold amount for the audited financial statements requirement is gross revenues of more than USD 3 million, regardless the corporate residency (i.e. foreign or domestic).

Audit cycle
Many taxpayers are under audit by the PRTD. The audits may include income, payroll, withholding, and sales and use taxes.

Statute of limitations
The PRTD generally has four years after an original return is filed to assess income, payroll, and sales and use taxes. A return will be deemed to have been filed on the later of (i) its due date or (ii) the date the return was actually filed.

Topics of focus for tax authorities
Currently, the PRTD is focused on sales and use tax, intercompany loans, withholding at source, and payments to foreign affiliates, among others.

Qatar

PwC contact

Declan Mordaunt
PricewaterhouseCoopers
41st Floor Tornado Tower
West Bay
Doha, Qatar
Tel: +974 4419 2801
Email: declan.mordaunt@qa.pwc.com

Significant developments

Publication of final executive regulations

Following the introduction of a new tax law in 2010, the related executive regulations, which provide guidance on how the Qatar tax authorities will interpret and apply the provisions of the Qatar tax law in practice, were published in the official gazette on 1 June 2011. These regulations provide greater clarity in respect of matters that were previously uncertain. The regulations became effective as of 1 July 2011.

Circulars issued by Qatar tax authorities

The Qatar tax authorities have also issued a number of circulars to provide guidance on, amongst other things, the appeals process, the application of the retention rules and withholding tax (WHT), the requirement to notify the Qatar tax authorities of contracts with non-residents, and the policy in relation to the granting of tax exemptions.

Taxes on corporate income

An entity that is wholly or partially foreign owned and that derives income from sources in Qatar is taxable in Qatar. In the case of a joint venture, the tax liability of the joint venture is dependent upon the foreign partners' share of the joint venture's profit. Currently, no corporate income tax (CIT) is levied on a corporate entity that is wholly owned by Qatari nationals and Gulf Cooperation Council (GCC) nationals.

Unless specifically exempt from tax, an entity will be taxable in Qatar if it has generated Qatar-source income, regardless of the place of its incorporation.

Taxable income generally is subject to a flat (CIT) rate of 10%, with certain exceptions available.

The following tax rates apply in the specific circumstances noted:

- If a special agreement has been reached with the government of Qatar prior to 1 January 2010, the rate specified in the agreement continues to apply. If no rate is specified in the agreement, a rate of 35% will be used.
- The rate applied with respect to oil operations, as defined in Law No. 3 of 2007, may not be less than 35%.
- Payments made to non-residents with respect to certain service activities not connected with a permanent establishment (PE) in Qatar are subject to WHT (*see the Withholding taxes section*).

The amount of tax payable is reduced for companies that are partly foreign owned, depending on the extent of local ownership.

Qatar Financial Centre (QFC)

The QFC was established in 2005 to attract companies in the financial services sector. It should be noted that this summary is directed towards non-Qatar Financial Centre (QFC) entities with Qatar-source income. The QFC has its own tax regulations and rules, and the State of Qatar tax laws do not apply to the licensed activities of entities established in the QFC. QFC entities are subject to CIT in respect of activities undertaken pursuant to their QFC licence at the rate of 10%.

Corporate residence

It is important to recognise that residence is not the basis used to determine whether an entity is taxable for CIT purposes in Qatar. Accordingly, a CIT exposure in Qatar may arise even if a company is not resident in Qatar. Residence is, however, relevant when considering whether WHT will apply on payments received rather than CIT.

A company is resident in Qatar if it is incorporated in accordance with Qatari laws, its head office is situated in Qatar, or its place of effective management and control is in Qatar.

Permanent establishment (PE)

A PE has also been defined as a fixed place of business through which the business of a taxpayer is wholly or partly carried on. A PE is deemed to include a branch, office, factory, workshop, mine, oil or gas well, quarry, a building site, an assembly project or a place of exploration, extraction, or exploitation of natural resources. A PE also includes activity carried on by the taxpayer through a person acting on behalf of the taxpayer or in the taxpayer's interest, other than an agent of an independent status.

Other taxes

Value-added tax (VAT)

Qatar imposes no VAT or sales tax on operations in Qatar. However, the introduction of VAT in the GCC is currently under discussion.

Customs duties

Customs duties are applied to goods with an origin outside the GCC countries, normally at a rate of 5%. Higher rates sometimes apply for specific types of goods, such as tobacco products. Temporary import exemptions are sometimes available.

Excise taxes

There are no excise taxes in Qatar.

Property taxes

There are no property taxes in Qatar. However, fees may be payable to the government by the owner on the registration of property and by the landlord on the registration of leases.

Transfer taxes

There are no transfer taxes in Qatar.

Stamp taxes

There are no stamp taxes in Qatar.

Qatar

Branch income

The profits of a branch owned by a foreign parent entity are subject to the same tax rules as apply to other forms of taxable entities.

Income determination

CIT is levied on a company's Qatar-source income. Some examples of Qatar-source income include:

- Income derived from an activity carried on in Qatar.
- Income derived from contracts wholly or partially performed in Qatar.
- Income from real estate situated in Qatar, including income from the sale of shares of companies with assets consisting of mainly real estate situated in Qatar.
- Income from shares in companies resident in Qatar or listed on Qatar's stock market.

Inventory valuation
Inventory must be valued in accordance with International Financial Reporting Standards (IFRS).

Capital gains
Any chargeable gains on the sale of capital assets are taxed as ordinary income.

Dividend income
Dividends are not taxable in Qatar if received from profits that have been subject to Qatar tax or from companies that are exempt from Qatar tax.

Interest income
Interest arising in Qatar and bank interest realised outside Qatar, if it results from the taxpayer's activity in Qatar, are taxed as ordinary income.

Foreign income
Non-Qatar-sourced income is not subject to tax in Qatar.

Deductions

Taxable income is determined after deducting all expenditures, costs, and losses incurred to generate gross income. A deduction is usually available for expenses that are considered ordinary rather than 'capital' in nature and incurred in generating Qatar-source revenue.

Depreciation
Depreciation should be calculated in accordance with rates specified by the Qatar tax law and the related regulations.

For certain assets, depreciation is calculated on the cost on a straight-line basis. The rates of depreciation are as follows:

Assets	Depreciation rate (% per annum)
Buildings and constructions, including roads, bridges, pipelines, storage tanks, and port ducks inside the establishment and excluding ready-made light constructions	5
Ships and boats	10
Airplanes and helicopters	20
Drilling instruments	15
Intangible assets:	
Pre-establishment expenses	50
Trademarks, patents, and the like	Amortised on the expected lifetime of the asset, provided that the amortisation allowance shall not exceed 15% per annum.

Other assets will be divided into groups and depreciated on a reducing-balance basis. The rates of depreciation are as follows:

Group	Asset	Depreciation rate (% per annum)
I	Computer hardware and software accessories	10
II	Machinery, plant, equipment, electrical devices, means of transportation of goods and persons, including cars, vehicles, trucks, and cranes	20
III	Furniture, fixtures and fittings, and other fixed assets	15

Interest expenses
Interest on loans used in the activity is deductible.

Bad debt
Bad debts approved by the tax authorities in accordance with the criteria set out in the tax law are deductible.

Charitable contributions
Donations, gift aid, and subscriptions to charitable, humanitarian, scientific, cultural, or sporting activities paid in Qatar to government authorities or public bodies are deductible, provided the value does not exceed 5% of net profit in the year in which the deduction is claimed.

Taxes
Taxes and duties other than the income tax provided for in the law are deductible.

Other significant items
Other deductible expenditures include the following:

- Employee costs (including salaries, wages, gratuities, and other end of service benefits).
- Losses resulting from the sale of assets.
- Rents.
- Insurance premiums.

Qatar

Net operating losses
Losses may be deducted from net income during the year. Losses can be carried forward for three years after the year in which they were incurred. Losses cannot be carried back.

Allocations of overhead to branches
The branch's share of head office expenses (i.e. indirect or allocated overhead) generally is deductible only up to a certain limit. The deduction is capped at 3% (1% for banks) of the total revenue less certain other costs.

Group taxation

There is no definition of a 'group' for Qatar tax purposes; therefore, there is no concept of group taxation.

Anti-avoidance provision
The Qatar tax law contains an anti-avoidance provision which gives the Qatar tax authorities wide powers to counteract transactions that have been carried out with a tax avoidance purpose. These powers include substituting an arm's-length value or recharacterising transactions.

Transfer pricing
The executive regulations have made it clear that the anti-avoidance provision will be applied to related-party transactions. In determining the arm's-length value, the Unrelated Comparable Price Method should be used (i.e. the price of services or goods that would have been applied should the transaction be between unrelated parties). It is possible to make an application to the Qatar tax authorities to use another method approved by the Organisation for Economic Co-operation and Development (OECD).

Thin capitalisation
There are no specific thin capitalisation rules in Qatar.

Tax credits and incentives

Foreign tax credit
Unless double tax relief is available under a double tax treaty (DTT), there is no tax relief available under the Qatar tax law for tax suffered by Qatari companies overseas.

Qatar Science and Technology Park
Qatar has established the QSTP, which is aimed at entities with research and development (R&D) activities. QSTP entities can be fully exempt from Qatar tax; however, tax exempt entities are required to file tax returns.

Other tax exemptions
An application for a tax exemption may be made for certain projects that are considered to be strategically significant to the Qatar economy. The exemptions are generally granted for a period of three or six years. Applications for an exemption are assessed based on certain criteria set out in the Qatar tax law.

Notwithstanding the fact that an exemption is granted, an entity that is exempt is still required to file a tax return under the Qatar tax law.

Qatar

Withholding taxes

WHT is levied on certain payments made to non-residents in relation to royalties and technical services (the applicable rate is 5%) and on interest, commissions, brokerage fees, directors' fees, attendance fees, and any other payments for services carried out wholly or partly in Qatar (the applicable rate is 7%). WHT on interest was suspended until 1 July 2011, but is now applicable. The executive regulations have excluded certain payments from the scope of WHT.

The company that makes the payment to its foreign supplier is required to withhold the tax and remit to the tax department the funds that were withheld by the 16th day of the following month. In the event that the company does not make a payment to the tax department, the company will be liable for a penalty equal to the amount of unpaid tax due, in addition to the WHT.

Retention system

Pursuant to circulars issued by the tax department, a retention system is in place whereby certain final contract amounts are required to be retained from payments made by Qatari entities to foreign entities in connection with work performed in Qatar. All ministries; government departments; public, semi-public, and private establishments; and Qatar taxpayers are required to retain. Companies resident in Qatar and permanent branches can secure a release of the final payment by presenting a tax card. A retention equivalent to the higher of 3% of the contract value or the final contractual payment will apply to branches registered for activities of at least one year until they produce a tax clearance certificate from the Qatar tax authorities. All other non-residents are expected to be subject to WHT in respect of payments that fall within the scope of WHT.

Tax treaties

Qatar has a growing DTT network with around 50 DTTs currently in force. The WHT rates under these treaties in respect of dividends, interest, and royalties are as follows:

Recipient	WHT (%)			Effective date
	Dividends	Interest	Royalties	
Algeria	0	0	0/5 (12)	
Armenia	5/10 (1)	5	5	1 Jan 2008
Austria	0	0	5	1 Jan 2012
Azerbaijan	7	7	5	1 Jan 2009
Belarus	0/5/10 (2)	5	5	1 Jan 2008
Bulgaria (11)				1 Jan 2011
China (PRC)	10	10	10	1 Jan 2009
Croatia (11)				3 Mar 2009
Cuba	5/10 (3)	10	5	1 Jan 2009
Cyprus	0	0	5	1 Jan 2010
France	0	0	0	1 Jan 2007
Georgia	0	0	0	1 Jan 2012
Greece	5	5	5	1 Jan 2011
India	5/10 (4)	10	10	1 Jan 2001
Indonesia	10	10	5	1 Jan 2008
Iran (11)				21 Sep 2010
Italy	5/10 (3)	5	5	1 Jan 2010

Qatar

Recipient	WHT (%)			Effective date
	Dividends	Interest	Royalties	
Jordan (11)				21 Dec 2008
Korea, Republic of	10	0/10 (10)	5	1 Jan 2010
Lebanon	0	0	0	1 Jan 2010
Luxembourg	0/5/10 (2)	0	5	1 Jan 2011
Macedonia (11)				1 Jan 2009
Malaysia	5/10 (4)	5	8	1 Jan 2010
Malta	0	0	5	1 Jan 2010
Mauritius	0	0	5	1 Jan 2010
Monaco	0	0	5	1 Jan 2011
Morocco (11)				7 Apr 2009
Nepal	10	10	15	1 Jan 2010
Netherlands	0/10 (5)	0	5	1 Jan 2010
Norway	5/15 (6)	0	5	1 Jan 2010
Pakistan	5/10 (4)	10	10	1 Jan 2001
Panama	5	5	5	1 Jan 2012
Philippines	10/15 (13)	10	15	1 Jan 2012
Poland	5	0/5 (9)	5	1 Jan 2010
Romania	3	3	5	1 Jan 2004
Russia	5	5	0	1 Jan 2001
Senegal (11)				1 Jan 2010
Serbia	5/10 (4)	10	10	1 Jan 2011
Seychelles	0	0	5	1 Jan 2008
Singapore	0	5	10	1 Jan 2008
Slovenia	5	5	5	1 Jan 2011
Sri Lanka	10	10	10	1 Jan 2008
Switzerland	5/10/15 (7)	0	0	1 Jan 2011
Syria (11)				27 Apr 2009
Tunisia (11)				1 Jan 1999
Turkey	10/15 (8)	10	10	1 Jan 2009
United Kingdom	0/15	0	5	1 Jan 2011
Venezuela	5/10 (4)	5	5	1 Jan 2008
Vietnam (11)				1 Jan 2012
Yemen (11)				1 Jan 2008

Notes

1. 5% if capital exceeds USD 100,000, and 10% in all other cases.
2. 0% if the beneficial owner is a company that owns at least 10%, 5% if 10% direct participation is held by an individual who has resided in the relevant state for a period of at least 48 month, and 10% in all other cases.
3. 5% if the beneficial owner is a company that has owned directly or indirectly at least 25%, and 10% if participation is less than 25%.
4. 5% if the beneficial owner is a company that owns at least 10%, and 10% in all other cases (i.e. less than 10% shareholding).
5. 0% if the beneficial owner is a company that owns at least 7.5%, and 10% in all other cases (i.e. less than 7.5% shareholding).
6. 5% if the beneficial owner is a company that owns at least 10%, and 15% in all other cases (i.e. less than 10% shareholding).
7. 5% if the beneficial owner is a company that holds directly at least 10%, 10% if the beneficial owner is an individual that holds directly at least 10%, and 15% in all other cases.
8. 10% if the beneficial owner is a company that has owned at least 25%, and 15% in all other cases (i.e. less than 25% shareholding).

Qatar

9. 0% where the beneficial owner of the interest carries on business in the other contracting state where the interest arises (i.e. through a PE therein), and 5% if the contracting company does not have a PE.
10. 0% if interest arising in contracting state is derived from government debt, and 10% if the contracting company does not have a PE.
11. It should be noted that there is limited information available in respect of the treaty with this country, and the date provided above may be the date on which the treaty entered into force rather than its effective date.
12. Reduced to zero if the beneficial owner has a PE in the contracting state.
13. 10% if the beneficial owner is a company that has at least a 10% shareholding; 15% in all other cases.

Tax administration

Taxable period
The tax year is generally the same as the calendar year, although advance approval may be sought from the Qatar tax authorities to use a company's accounting year end.

Tax returns
The tax return is due within four months from the date of a company's tax filing period.

Payment of tax
The tax payable is based on the tax declaration and should be paid on the same day that the tax return is due.

Late filing penalties
The Qatar tax law contains a penalty regime, which imposes a penalty for the late filing of a tax return. In addition, a penalty applies where there is a late payment of tax.

Objection and appeals process
It is possible for a taxpayer to initially object directly to the tax department regarding a decision related to a tax position. If the objection is unsuccessful with respect to altering the tax department's decision, an appeal may be made by the taxpayer to the Tax Appeals Committee. Based on the Tax Appeals Committee's decision with respect to the appeal, a final appeal may be made by either the tax department or the taxpayer to the administrative chamber of the court. The law prescribes time limits for each stage of the appeal process.

Accounting and audit requirements
A company's CIT return is required to be accompanied by audited financial statements if the company's capital or profit exceeds 100,000 riyals (QAR) or the head office is situated outside Qatar. The audit report must be signed by a Qatar registered auditor.

Qatar tax law requires accounts to be prepared in accordance with IFRS.

Accounting record retention
All accounting books, registers, and documents relating to activity in Qatar are required to be retained in Qatar for a ten-year period.

Romania

PwC contact

Peter de Ruiter
PricewaterhouseCoopers
Lakeview Office
301-311 Barbu Vacarescu Street
RO-020276, Bucharest
Romania
Tel: +40 21 225 3500
Email: peter.deruiter@ro.pwc.com

Significant developments

Corporate taxation

- Specific fiscal rules have been introduced for financial institutions that apply the International Financial Reporting Standards (IFRS) as of 1 January 2012.
- If certain conditions are met, rescheduling of tax payment obligations may be granted upon request to taxpayers for a period of up to five years based on their financial situation and total tax burden.
- As of 1 October 2011, a new concept was introduced in the civil law regarding administration of patrimony fiduciary agreements. Specific tax treatment has also been provided for both profit and income tax purposes.
- As of 1 January 2013, taxpayers may opt to declare and pay the annual profit tax by making quarterly advanced payments, with some exceptions mentioned by the law (e.g. banks, non-profit organisations, taxpayers deriving income from agriculture).
- In cases where taxpayers have not submitted their tax returns, the tax authorities will assess by default the tax liabilities subject to self-assessment or withholding for every fiscal obligation in the taxpayer's fiscal liabilities records for each fiscal period for which tax returns were not submitted.
- Fuel expenses for vehicles, which meet certain characteristics, are now only 50% deductible for profit and income tax purposes. Starting 1 July 2012, this limitation will not apply for cars used exclusively for business purposes.
- For tax liabilities overdue as at 31 August 2011, late payment penalties can be reduced by 50% if the main fiscal obligations and the related interest are paid by 30 June 2012.

Value-added tax (VAT)

- Supplies of cereals and industrial crops performed in Romanian territory between companies registered for VAT purposes will be subject to the reverse charge mechanism. The measure applies until 31 May 2013.
- As of 1 February 2012, companies that are legally independent but are closely related in terms of financial, economic, and organisational purposes may choose to form a tax group, as long as they are administered by the same competent fiscal body.
- The VAT deduction right related to the acquisition of vehicles used exclusively for passenger transport, which meet certain characteristics, and also to the acquisition of fuel used for such vehicles is limited to 50%.
- The tax authorities may cancel *ex officio* a taxpayer's VAT registration if the taxpayer has not fulfilled certain compliance requirements.

Taxes on corporate income

The standard profit tax rate is 16% for Romanian companies and foreign companies operating through a permanent establishment (PE) in Romania. Resident companies are taxed on worldwide income, unless a double tax treaty (DTT) stipulates otherwise. Non-resident companies are taxed only on Romanian-source income.

The profit tax liability due from nightclubs and gambling operations cannot be less than 5% of the revenue obtained from such activities.

Micro-company tax regime

The 3% income tax for micro-companies was reintroduced as of 1 January 2011, with restrictive conditions for application. The tax is optional in the sense that qualifying taxpayers may apply for the micro-company tax regime or continue to be profit taxpayers.

Companies can opt for the micro-company regime if they the following criteria at the end of the previous year:

- Derive their turnover from activities other than banking, capital markets activity, insurance, gambling, consultancy, and management.
- Have between one and nine employees.
- Their annual turnover is lower than the Romanian leu (RON) equivalent of 100,000 euros (EUR).
- Their shares are not held by the state, local authorities, or a legal entity with more than 250 employees.

Payment of the tax and filing of the returns is made quarterly, by the 25th day of the month following the ending of the quarter for which the tax is computed.

The tax assessment base for micro companies' income is represented by income derived from any source.

The option to be transferred under this tax regime is communicated to the tax authorities by 31 January of the year for which tax on micro-company income is paid. The option is final for the respective fiscal year. If during the fiscal year one of the eligibility conditions is not met anymore, the micro-company is required to maintain for the respective fiscal year the same taxation system, without having the possibility to further benefit from these provisions for the next period, even if subsequently they return to being compliant.

Local income taxes

There are no local taxes on corporate income.

Corporate residence

A company is considered resident in Romania if it was set-up under Romanian law or has its place of effective management in Romania.

The tax code also introduced the concept of 'legal person set-up in accordance with European legislation'. Such legal persons become tax residents if they establish (or transfer) their registered office in Romania. As a result, such entities are subject to the same tax treatment as Romanian legal persons for taxation of profits and dividends.

Romania

Permanent establishment (PE)

PE is defined as being the place through which the activity of a non-resident is conducted, fully or partially, directly or through a dependent agent.

Once a PE is created, Romania has the right to tax the profits of the foreign enterprise derived from the activity performed on its territory.

The Romanian legislation explicitly states three conditions that should be met simultaneously in order to trigger a PE:

- A place of business must exist (e.g. premises, machinery, or equipment).
- The place of business must be fixed (i.e. must be established at a distinct place with a certain degree of permanence).
- The activity should be carried out through this fixed place of business (i.e. there are people dependent on the enterprise and conducting its business in the country where it is located).

The registration, filing, and payment requirements for a PE are similar to those for a Romanian company.

Other taxes

Value-added tax (VAT)

The standard rate of VAT is 24% and is applied to all supplies of goods and services (including imports) that do not qualify for an exemption (with or without credit) or for the VAT reduced rate.

The reduced VAT rate is 9% and is applicable to admission fees at museums, historical monuments, architecture and archaeological monuments, zoos and botanical gardens, fairs and exhibitions, cinema tickets, supply of school manuals, books, newspapers and periodicals, supply of prostheses and orthopaedic products (except for dentures), medicine for human and veterinary use, and accommodation in hotels or in areas with a similar function.

VAT exemption without credit applies to a range of activities, including banking, finance, and insurance.

However, some financial services are also subject to a 24% VAT (e.g. factoring, debt collection, managing, and depositing certain equity papers).

There are also operations that are exempt with credit (i.e. deduction right) for input VAT, such as the following:

- Export of goods, transport, and related services.
- Intra-community supply of goods.
- International transport of passengers.
- Goods placed in free trade zones and free warehouses.
- Supply of goods to a bonded warehouse, a VAT warehouse, and related services.
- Supply of goods, which are placed under suspensive customs regimes.
- Supply of services in connection with goods placed under suspensive customs regimes.
- Supply of goods and services to diplomatic missions, international organisations, and North Atlantic Treaty Organization (NATO) forces.

VAT on imported goods continues to be paid at customs, except for taxable persons registered for VAT purposes that obtain an import VAT deferment certificate from the customs authorities. For these taxpayers, the VAT is not paid at customs but is shown in the VAT return as both input and output VAT. The import VAT deferment is available only to companies for which the value of the imports performed in the previous year/previous 12 consecutive months has reached the threshold of minimum RON 100 million.

The rules for establishing the place of supply of goods and services (and therefore the place of VAT taxation) are fully aligned with the Recast of the European Union (EU) VAT Directive. Services provided by offshore entities to Romanian companies with deemed place of supply in Romania are subject to Romanian VAT.

Reduced VAT at the rate of 5% for sale of buildings
Companies selling buildings can apply for a reduced VAT, at the rate of 5%, in the following cases:

- The buildings are part of a social policy, such as homes for the elderly, retirement homes, orphanages, or rehabilitation centres for children with disabilities.
- The building is supplied as housing to an individual or family and has a maximum useful surface of 120 square metres and a value of less than RON 380,000 (exclusive of VAT).

Reverse charge mechanism
Under the VAT reverse charge mechanism, VAT is not actually paid, but only shown in the VAT return as both input and output tax, provided the beneficiary is registered for VAT purposes.

The reverse charge mechanism applies for services performed by offshore entities, and the place of supply is where the beneficiary is established or has a fixed establishment (e.g. consultancy, marketing services, telecommunications, and electronically supplied services). This is possible provided the suppliers are not established in Romania for VAT purposes.

Supplies of cereals and industrial crops performed on the Romanian territory between companies registered for VAT purposes will be subject to the reverse charge mechanism. The measure applies until 31 May 2013.

R

VAT compliance
As a general rule, the fiscal period is the calendar month. For taxable persons registered for VAT purposes whose previous year-end turnover did not exceed EUR 100,000, the fiscal period is the calendar quarter.

Taxable persons must keep complete and detailed records for calculation of VAT liabilities.

VAT returns should be submitted to the tax authorities by the 25th day of the month following the end of the fiscal period; the VAT is due by the same date. The VAT return should be submitted using an electronic carrier.

Taxable persons not registered for VAT purposes are required to pay VAT and to submit a special VAT return on services rendered by non-residents, which have a deemed place of supply in Romania. These obligations must be fulfilled by the 25th day of the month following that in which the services are performed.

Romania

Taxable persons are required to file twice yearly for acquisitions and supplies of goods and services performed on Romanian territory, based on the existence of invoices.

A taxable person who does not exceed the exemption threshold of EUR 35,000 during a calendar year may request, during the year, deregistration from the records of the persons registered for VAT purposes in order to apply the special exemption regime. As of 1 July 2012, the threshold was increased to RON 220,000 (approximately EUR 50,000).

Customs regulations
Customs values are determined and declared by importers in accordance with the provisions of the World Trade Organisation (WTO) Customs Valuation Agreement (i.e. the Agreement pertaining to the implementation of Article VII of the General Agreement on Trade and Tariffs [GATT]).

For chain transactions with goods intended for import, the customs value may be determined, under certain conditions, based on the price in any of the transactions in the chain (first sale principle). This way, the customs value can be determined based on a price lower than that paid or payable by the importer (e.g. based on the price of the first transaction in the chain).

The customs value can be modified within 12 months of the acceptance of the customs declaration for the release of the goods for free circulation, in specific cases (e.g. in the case of defective goods).

Under specific conditions, determining customs value upon import is possible, even if certain elements that need to be added to the customs value are not quantifiable on the importation date (e.g. licence fees, royalties) or are missing.

The customs authorities may inspect the customs value either during the customs clearance or during a post-import audit (the customs authorities are entitled to perform such an audit during a five-year period following the date of import).

It is also possible to amend or invalidate the customs declaration, as follows:

* Amendment of the customs declaration before the customs clearance is obtained.
* Invalidation of the customs declaration within 90 days of the customs clearance being obtained.
* Amendment after the customs clearance is obtained, which can be performed at the request of the traders within five years of the customs clearance date.

Customs duties
The customs duties are those specified in the EU Common Customs Tariff and are expressed as a percentage applied to the customs value (i.e. *ad valorem* taxes) or as a fixed amount applied to a specific quantity (i.e. specific taxes).

Agricultural products (i.e. products from chapters 1-24 of the EU Common Customs Tariff) are subject to specific taxation.

In certain cases (e.g. meat), the customs duty rate is established with regard to the cost, insurance, and freight (CIF) or the entry price of the products. In other cases, the customs duty rate is established by adding additional duties, such as agricultural components, to the *ad valorem* tax.

Customs representation

Legal entities established in non-EU states can declare goods by indirect representation. The indirect representation can be used for customs regimes such as transit or temporary importation.

Moreover, legal entities established in non-EU states can occasionally declare goods on their own or through direct representation, provided that the customs authorities consider this to be justified.

Customs brokers can be authorised to use the local customs clearance procedure or to submit simplified customs declarations for the companies they represent (either directly or indirectly). Any Romanian legal person can act as an indirect representative for a sole person using the simplified customs clearance procedures.

Authorised Economic Operator (AEO) status

Operators that obtain AEO status benefit from simplifications regarding customs inspection, obtaining customs authorisations, and performing customs formalities.

Moreover, through the AEO certificate, the holder is recognised by the customs authorities as a reliable person, giving comfort as regards observance of the safety and security standards.

Customs rulings

Companies can obtain rulings (binding tariff information or BTI) from Romanian customs authorities regarding the tariff classification of imported goods that are binding for the customs authorities for a six-year period, whenever goods identical to those described in the BTI are imported.

A similar type of ruling can also be obtained regarding the origin of goods (binding origin information or BOI). The BOI is valid for a three-year period.

Excise duties

Harmonised excisable products

The following products are subject to harmonised excise duties: ethyl alcohol and alcoholic beverages, tobacco products, energy products (e.g. unleaded petrol, diesel oil, gas, coal), and electricity.

Excise duties are due when excise goods are released for consumption (e.g. imported into Romania, taken out of an excise duty suspension regime).

Excisable products can be produced, transformed, held, and received under a duty suspension arrangement only in a tax warehouse, which should have prior approval from the tax authorities. Such excisable products can also be received from within the European Union under excise duty suspension arrangements by registered consignees.

Mandatory guarantees should be established for the production, processing, and storage, as well as for the movement, of excise goods under the excise duty suspension regime.

Ethyl alcohol and other alcoholic products are exempt from the payment of excise duties if they are denatured and used in the nutritional, pharmaceuticals, or cosmetics industry. There are also exemptions for ethyl alcohol and other alcoholic beverages when used in a manufacturing process, provided that the final product does not

R

Romania

contain alcohol, or as samples for analysis, for necessary production tests, or for scientific purposes.

Some energy products, subject to movement control, can be purchased to be used for purposes excepted from excise duty, provided that an end-user authorisation is obtained and the payment of excise duties is secured.

In some cases, traders can claim a refund of the excise duties paid (e.g. excise duty paid for goods released for consumption in Romania, but intended for consumption in other EU Member States; excise duties paid for goods released for consumption and then returned to the production tax warehouse for recycling, reprocessing, or destruction; excise duties paid for goods acquired from the European Union or imported and then returned to the suppliers).

Before being released for consumption in Romania, spirit-based beverages and tobacco products have to be marked with duty stamps. The responsibility for such marking lies with the tax warehouse keepers, registered consignees, and importers releasing such goods for consumption.

For cigarettes, the excise duty owed is equal to the sum of the specific excise duty and the *ad-valorem* excise duty. The specific excise duty expressed in EUR/1,000 cigarettes is annually determined based on the ponderate medium retail price, the legal percentage related to the *ad-valorem* excise duty and the total excise duty.

The level of the minimum excise duty for cigarettes is 96%.

The total level of excise duty on cigarettes is set at EUR 76.60/1,000 cigarettes. The minimum excise duty payable has been set at EUR 74/1000 cigarettes at 1 July 2011.

Excise duty rates for fermented still beverages, other than beer and wines, are set at EUR 100/hectolitre of product, and for intermediary products are set at EUR 165/hectolitre.

The current level of excise duties on gasoline and diesel are EUR 467/tonne and EUR 358/tonne, respectively.

Companies selling fuel in gas stations have to register with the tax authorities.

Other excisable products
Other excisable products are green coffee, roasted coffee (including coffee with substitutes), and soluble coffee (including blends with soluble coffee).

Companies performing exports or intra-community supplies of coffee may benefit from the refund of the excise duty paid for the coffee used as raw materials.

Traders purchasing coffee are entitled to a refund of the excise duties paid, if the products are exported, supplied to another EU member state, or returned unchanged to the supplier.

Property taxes

Building tax
For buildings owned by companies, the building tax rate is set by the Local Council at between 0.25% and 1.5% of the entry value of the building, adjusted by the value of

reconstruction, consolidation, modification and extension works, and the revaluation, if applicable. If a building has not been revalued in the last three years, the rate will be increased by between 10% and 20%, while if it has not been revalued in the last five years, the rate will be increased by between 30% and 40%. The taxable value of fully depreciated buildings is reduced by 15%.

Building tax is paid twice a year, by 31 March and 30 September, in equal instalments. As a general rule, if the building tax due for the entire year is paid in advance by 31 March, a reduction of up to 10% may be granted by the Local Council.

Land tax

Owners of land are subject to land tax established at a fixed amount per square metre, depending on the rank of the locality where the land is located and the area or category of land use, in accordance with the classification made by the Local Council.

Companies are not subject to land tax on land where buildings are sited.

Similar to building tax, land tax is paid twice a year, in equal instalments, by 31 March and 30 September. A 10% reduction is granted for full advance payment of this tax by 31 March.

Transfer taxes

There are no transfer taxes for companies for the transfer of property. The income derived from such a transfer will be included into the taxable profits of the company and subject to the flat tax rate.

Stamp duty

For judicial claims, issue of licences and certificates, and documentary transactions that require authentication, stamp duty has to be paid.

Environmental taxes

All producers of electric and electronic equipment (EEE) have to provide a guarantee to the Environmental Fund for the EEE placed on the market. The guarantee consists either in a bank guarantee letter or collateral, a waste recovery insurance policy, or adhering to one of the authorised collective organisations with attributions regarding EEE waste management, which acts on behalf of the producers.

In certain cases (e.g. packaging waste), the contribution to the Environmental Fund depends on the degree to which companies achieve the recovery/recycling targets stipulated by the relevant legislation on waste management. Thus, for packaging waste, the contribution to the Environmental Fund is currently RON 2 per kilogram of packaging introduced onto the market and is owed for the difference between the recovery target stipulated by law and the percentage actually achieved by companies.

A tax of RON 2/litre is levied on any shortfall of targeted waste recovery for industrial oils and lubricants placed on the market.

Companies conducting activities that result in the discharge of air-pollutant emissions from fixed sources (e.g. nitrogen oxides, sulphur oxides, persistent organic pollutants, heavy metal emissions, such as lead, cadmium, mercury) have to pay contributions to the Environmental Fund of between RON 0.02/kg (about EUR 0.0046) and RON 20/kg (about EUR 4.65).

Romania

Importers and producers of hazardous substances have to remit to the Environmental Fund a contribution of 2% of the value of the substances hazardous to the environment placed on the market. Companies selling ferrous and non-ferrous waste and administrators or owners of forests also have to make contributions to the Environmental Fund, currently set at 3% and 2%, respectively, of the resulted revenues.

Companies that store recoverable waste (i.e. waste resulting from extraction and processing of crude oil, waste resulting from primary processing of wood, waste resulting from alcohol manufacturing, carboniferous slurry, furnace slag, ashes from thermal power plants, pyrites ashes, phosphogypsum, metal slag) on new plots of land have to pay tax to the Environmental Fund. This tax ranges from RON 0.2 (about EUR 0.046) per square metre to RON 4 (about EUR 0.93) per square metre per year, depending on the type of waste stored on the new land.

The contribution for tyres placed on the market is RON 2/kg.

Producers/importers wishing to place batteries and chargeable cells on the market are required to register with the National Agency for Environmental Protection.

Placement on the market of portable batteries containing more than 0.002% cadmium by weight is prohibited. Distributors are also prohibited from selling batteries originating from unregistered producers.

Chemical substances and preparations traded on the market must be registered with the European Agency for Chemical Products. Registration is the only way for producers and importers of chemical substances to be allowed to continue production and import of chemical substances and preparations.

Social security contributions

Employers must pay social security contributions, calculated on the gross salary costs, as follows: 20.8%, 25.8%, or 30.8%, depending on working conditions. The monthly contribution is capped at five average gross salaries multiplied by the number of insured individuals.

Other contributions payable by employers for employees, calculated on gross salary costs, are as follows:

- Contribution for medical leaves: 0.85%
- Health fund: 5.2%
- Unemployment fund: 0.5%
- Guarantee fund: 0.25%
- Work accidents insurance fund: 0.15% to 0.85%

Branch income

Branch

A foreign company can set up a branch in Romania, as long as the branch only operates in the same field of activity as the parent company.

Profits derived by the branch are taxed at the standard profit tax rate of 16%.

Representative offices

Representative offices are often established as a first step to operating in Romania. A representative office can undertake only auxiliary or preparatory activities, cannot trade in its own name, and cannot engage in any contractual activity. A representative office can perform only a limited range of activities without being considered a PE for profit tax purposes.

Representative offices are subject to a yearly flat tax of EUR 4,000 (payable in local currency, i.e. Romanian leu). It has to be paid in two instalments, by 25 June and 25 December. If a representative office is set up or closed down during a year, the tax due for that year is prorated on the basis of the number of months the representative office operated in that fiscal year.

Income determination

The taxable profit of a company is calculated as the difference between the revenues derived from any source and the expenses incurred in obtaining taxable revenues throughout the tax year, adjusted for fiscal purposes by deducting non-taxable revenues and adding non-deductible expenses. Other elements similar to revenues and expenses are also to be taken into account when calculating the taxable profit.

For taxpayers that apply IFRS, there are specific rules in relation to fiscal value assessment, profit tax computation, adjustments for step-down in value, amortisation, and fiscal treatment of deferred profit tax.

Inventory valuation

The methods permitted for inventory valuation under Romanian law are standard cost, detailed sale price, average (weighted) cost, first in first out (FIFO), and last in first out (LIFO).

Assets are generally valuated at their acquisition cost, production cost, or market value. Fixed assets may be revaluated at certain points in time for various purposes.

Capital gains

Capital gains earned by a Romanian resident company are included in ordinary profits and are taxed at 16%. Capital losses related to sale of shares are, in general, tax-deductible. Capital gains obtained by non-residents from real estate property located in Romania or the sale of shares held in a Romanian company is also taxable in Romania. However, the income may be subject to treaty protection.

Dividend income

Dividends received by a Romanian company from another Romanian company are not subject to the profit tax, but are subject to a final withholding tax (WHT) of 16%.

Dividends received by a Romanian company from a foreign company are taxed at the normal profit tax rate in Romania. Credit is available for tax paid abroad.

Dividends received from a foreign or Romanian legal person from all member countries of the European Economic Area (EEA) are not taxable if the Romanian legal person has held a minimum of 10% of the shares in the foreign legal person for an uninterrupted period of at least two years on the date when the dividend is paid.

Romania

Interest and royalty income

Interest and royalty payments by Romanian companies to other Romanian companies are taxable income in the hands of the beneficiary.

As of 1 January 2011, Romania-sourced interest and royalty payments of an affiliated company, resident in a EU or European Free Trade Association (EFTA) member state, are exempt from WHT, provided certain conditions are met, e.g.:

* 25% minimum direct holding of the share capital (i.e. one company holds minimum 25% of the share capital in the other company or a third company holds more than 25% of the share capital in both companies involved in the payment of interest and royalties).
* The minimum holding period of two years until the date when the interest or royalty payments are made has lapsed.
* The company receiving the interest or royalties payment must be the beneficial owner of these payments.

Fiduciary contracts

Provisions regarding the fiscal treatment applicable to income realised from fiduciary contracts entered into force as of 1 October 2011. Therefore, if the constitutor is also the beneficiary,:

* the transfer of the patrimony mass from the constitutor to the fiduciary is not considered a taxable transfer, and
* the fiduciary will keep separate bookkeeping entry for the fiduciary patrimony mass and will communicate to the constitutor, on a quarterly basis, the income and expenses resulted from the administration of the patrimony.

If the beneficiary is the fiduciary or a third party, the expenses recorded from the transfer of the patrimony mass from the constitutor to the fiduciary is considered non-deductible.

Other significant items

The other most relevant types of non-taxable revenues stipulated by the Romanian Fiscal Code include the following:

* Favourable differences of participation titles, registered as a result of incorporating reserves, benefits, or issue premiums from companies in which participation titles are held.
* Revenues from reversal or cancellation of provisions/expenses that were previously non-deductible, recovery of expenses that were previously non-deductible, and revenues from reversal or cancellation of interest and late payment penalties that were previously non-deductible.
* Income from the annulment of a reserve registered as a result of a participation in nature to the capital of other legal entities.
* Income from deferred income tax and those representing a change in fair value of real estate investments, by taxpayers applying IFRS.
* Non-taxable income expressly provided for under agreements and memoranda.

Foreign income

Resident companies are taxed on worldwide income, unless a DTT stipulates otherwise. However, in case of foreign subsidiaries of Romanian companies, income is not taxed in Romania until remitted back. Otherwise, there is no specific tax deferral regime in place.

Deductions

From the deductibility standpoint, expenses fall into three categories: deductible expenses, limited deductibility expenses, and non-deductible expenses.

Deductible expenses
As a general rule, expenses are deductible only if incurred for the purpose of generating taxable income.

Some of the deductible expenses specifically mentioned by the Fiscal Code include the following:

* Marketing and advertising expenses.
* Research and development (R&D) expenses that do not meet the requirements to be recognised as intangible assets for accounting purposes.
* Expenses incurred for environmental protection and resource conservation.
* Expenses incurred for management improvement; updating information technology (IT) systems; introducing maintaining, and developing quality management systems; and obtaining quality compliance confirmation.
* Bad debt expenses are fully deductible in any of the following cases: the bankruptcy procedure of the debtor was closed based on a court decision; the debtor is deceased and the receivable cannot be recovered from the heirs; the debtor is dissolved or liquidated; the debtor has major financial difficulties affecting its entire patrimony.
* Expenses determined by unfavourable differences in value of long-term participation titles in legal persons, as well as unfavourable value differences related to long-term bonds.
* Travel and accommodation expenses related to business; this also includes personnel's transport to and from the workplace.
* Expenses incurred from professional training and development of employees.
* Expenses resulted from benefits granted to employees as equity instruments settled with cash, at the moment of the grant, if the benefits are subject to personal income tax (PIT).
* Expenses incurred in relation to work safety, prevention of work accidents and occupational diseases, the related insurance contributions, and professional risk insurance premiums.
* Expenses incurred with the acquisition of packaging materials, during the useful life set by the taxpayer.
* Fines, interest, penalties, and other increased payments due under commercial contracts.

R

Beneficiaries that acquire goods and/or services from inactive taxpayers (while they are inactive) cannot deduct the expenses related to such acquisitions, except for purchases made during enforcement proceedings.

Limited deductibility expenses
The deductibility of certain expenses is limited, as follows

* Interest and foreign exchange losses under thin capitalisation rules (*see the Group taxation section for more information*).
* Depreciation of assets under fiscal depreciation rules (*see details below*).
* Perishable goods capped as set by the relevant central administration bodies.
* Protocol expenses are deductible up to the limit of 2% of the difference between total taxable revenue and total expenses related to taxable revenue, except for protocol and profit tax expenses.

Romania

- Daily allowances for expenses from domestic and foreign travel by employees are deductible up to the level of 2.5 times the ceiling set for public institutions.
- Social expenses are deductible up to 2% of salary expenses. Among others, they can include maternity allowances, expenses for nursery tickets, funeral benefits, and allowances for serious or incurable diseases and prostheses, as well as expenses for the proper operation of certain activities or units under taxpayers' administration (i.e. kindergartens, nurseries, health services supplied for occupational diseases and work accidents prior to admission to health establishments, canteens, sports clubs, clubs, etc); expenses incurred for benefits granted under a collective labour agreement are also deductible within this limit.
- Health insurance premiums are deductible for employers up to the limit of EUR 250 per year, per person; private pension insurance premiums are deductible up to the limit of EUR 400 per year, per person.
- Taxes and contributions paid to non-government organisations and professional associations related to the taxpayer's activity are deductible up to the limit of EUR 4,000 per year.
- Expenses from operation, maintenance, and repair of vehicles used by individuals in company leadership and management positions for business purposes are deductible within the limits, but only for one vehicle per person.
- Fuel expenses for company vehicles weighing under 3,500 kg and with fewer than nine passenger seats (including driver's seat) that are not used exclusively for business purposes are deductible in a quantum of 50%. Exceptions to this rule are vehicles used in the following activities:
  - Intervention, repair, safety and security, courier services, cars used by sales and acquisitions agents.
  - Paid transportation services and taxi activities.
  - Rental.
  - Driving schools.
  - Vehicles used as commodities.

Non-deductible expenses
Expenses which are specifically non-deductible include, among others, the following:

- Domestic profit tax and profit tax paid in foreign countries.
- Expenses related to non-taxable revenues; note that revenues from dividends have no corresponding expenses.
- Expenses related to WHT supported by Romanian taxpayers on behalf of non-residents.
- Interest, fines, and penalties due to Romanian or foreign authorities.
- Expenses incurred from management, consultancy, assistance, or other supply of services if no contracts or any other lawful agreements are entered into and the beneficiary cannot justify the supply of such services for the activities performed and their necessity.
- Sponsorship and patronage expenses and expenses for private scholarships. Taxpayers are, however, granted a fiscal credit up to whichever is the lower of 0.3% of turnover and 20% of the profit tax due.
- Other salary and/or similar expenses (if not taxed at the level of the individual), except for those specifically exempted from individual income taxation.
- Expenses resulted from benefits granted to employees as equity instruments settled with shares. These are elements similar to expenses at the moment of the grant, if the benefits are subject to PIT.
- Expenses incurred from insurance premiums unrelated to company assets or business, save for those regarding goods which are bank collateral on loans used to

conduct the activity for which the taxpayer is authorised or those used under rental or leasing contracts.
- Bad debt expenses in excess of the deductible provision.
- Expenses recorded without justifying documents.
- Expenses in favour of shareholders, other than those related to goods or services provided by the shareholders at market value.
- Expenses incurred from fixed assets impairments as well as losses in value defined as provisory adjustments by the accounting regulations transposing European Accounting Directives.
- Expenses incurred from deferred profit tax and those representing a change in fair value of real estate investments by taxpayers applying IFRS.
- In the case of fiduciary contracts, expenses registered from the transfer of the patrimony mass from the constitutor to the fiduciary (if the beneficiary is the fiduciary or a third person).

Depreciation
Romanian law distinguishes between fiscal and accounting depreciation. Companies should maintain a separate record to reflect the separate computation of the fiscal and the accounting depreciation. Any accounting revaluations of fixed assets are not taken into account in computing the tax depreciation.

Assets are generally depreciated using the straight-line method. However, accelerated or digressive depreciation methods may be used to determine fiscal depreciation, while the accounting depreciation method may be different.

The useful lives to be used for tax purposes are the ones stated in the Official Fixed Assets Catalogue, published under government decision. Ranges are provided for classes of fixed assets, from which the taxpayers can choose the useful life (e.g. office and housing buildings: 40 to 60 years, commercial buildings: 32 to 48 years, commercial furnishings: 9 to 15 years, automobiles: 4 to 6 years).

Land cannot be depreciated.

Accelerated depreciation
Under the Fiscal Code, machinery and equipment, computers and their peripherals, as well as patents, may be depreciated by using the accelerated method, under which a maximum of 50% of the asset's fiscal value may be deducted during the first year of usage, while the rest of the asset's value can be depreciated using the linear method over the remaining useful life.

Goodwill
As a rule, goodwill is to be considered as a non-depreciable asset from a Romanian fiscal perspective.

Start-up expenses
Although according to accounting rules, start-up expenses may be capitalised and depreciated over a maximum five-year period, according to the fiscal rules, start up expenses should not be depreciated for tax purposes.

Fiscal losses
Profit tax is not deductible, nor are late payment interest and fines related to tax liabilities or social security obligations.

Romania

Provisions and reserves

Amounts used for setting up or increasing reserves or provisions are deductible as follows:

- Setting up or increasing the legal reserve fund to a limit of 5% of the yearly accounting profit before tax (with adjustments), until it reaches 20% of the share capital.
- Provisions for doubtful debts recorded after 1 January 2006, up to the limit of 30%, if the related receivables meet the following conditions simultaneously:
  - Booked after 1 January 2004.
  - Not collected for a period exceeding 270 days from the due date.
  - Not guaranteed by another person.
  - Due by a person not affiliated with the taxpayer.
  - Included in the taxable income of the taxpayer.
- Bad debt provisions, if all the following conditions are met:
  - Receivables are booked after 1 January 2007.
  - The debtor is a company declared bankrupt by a court ruling.
  - Receivables are not guaranteed by another person.
  - The debtor is not a related party.
  - Receivables were included in the taxable income of the taxpayer.
- Specific provisions established by credit institutions, non-banking financial institutions, and other similar entities.
- Technical reserves set up by insurance and reinsurance companies, in accordance with their regulatory legal framework, except for the equalisation reserve.
- Risk provisions for transactions carried out on financial markets, in accordance with the rules issued by the National Commission of Movable Assets.

The reduction or cancellation of any provision or reserve deducted from the taxable profit, due to changing the destination of the provision or reserve, distribution towards shareholders in any form, liquidation, spin-off, merger or any other reason, is included in the taxable revenues and taxed accordingly. The reconstruction of the legal reserve is also non-deductible.

Net operating losses

Companies are allowed to carry forward fiscal losses as declared in the yearly profit tax returns for a period of five years (for losses incurred prior to 2009) or seven years, based on a FIFO method. No related adjustment for inflation is allowed.

For foreign legal persons, this rule (i.e. carry forward of losses) applies only to revenues and expenses attributable to their PE in Romania.

Any loss incurred by a PE of a Romanian company located in a non-EU/EFTA member state or in a country which does not have a DTT in place with Romania is only deductible for tax purposes from the revenues derived by that PE, and losses can be carried forward only for a period of five years.

Carryback of losses is not available in Romania.

Group taxation

There is no tax consolidation or group taxation in Romania. Members of a group must file separate returns and are therefore taxed separately. No provision exists for offsetting the losses of group members against the profits of other group members.

Romania

Transfer pricing

Transfer pricing requirements are applicable to transactions between Romanian related parties as well as foreign related parties.

Transactions between related parties should observe the arm's-length principle. If transfer prices are not set at arm's length, the Romanian Tax Authorities have the right to adjust the taxpayer's revenues or expenses so as to reflect the market value.

Traditional transfer pricing methods (i.e. comparable uncontrolled prices, cost plus, and resale price methods), as well as any other methods that are in line with the Organisation for Economic Co-operation and Development (OECD) Transfer Pricing Guidelines (i.e. transactional net margin and profit split methods), may be used for setting transfer prices.

Transfer pricing documentation

Taxpayers engaged in related party transactions have to prepare and make their transfer pricing documentation file available upon the written request of the Romanian Tax Authorities.

Transfer pricing audit activity has significantly increased during the past year, and requests for presenting the transfer pricing documentation file have started to become common practice. We are aware of recent cases where the Romanian tax authorities adjusted the taxable result of a local taxpayer in accordance with the applicable regulations.

The content of the transfer pricing documentation file has been approved by order of the president of the National Agency for Tax Administration. The Order is supplemented by the Transfer Pricing Guidelines issued by the OECD Transfer Pricing Guidelines and the Code of Conduct on transfer pricing documentation for associated enterprises in the European Union Transfer Pricing Document (EUTPD).

The deadline for presenting the transfer pricing documentation file will not exceed three calendar months, with the possibility of a single extension equal to the period initially established.

Failure to present the transfer pricing documentation file or presenting an incomplete file following two consecutive requests may trigger estimation of transfer prices by the tax authorities, based on generally available information, as the arithmetic mean of three transactions considered similar.

Advance pricing agreement (APA)

Taxpayers engaged in transactions with related parties can request that the National Agency for Tax Administration issue an APA. These taxpayers can also schedule a pre-filing meeting to discuss the feasibility of the APA.

The request for an APA is filed together with the relevant documentation and payment evidence of the fee (ranging between EUR 10,000 and EUR 20,000). The required documentation is based on the EUTPD and suggests up-front the content of the APA.

The term provided by the Fiscal Procedural Code for issuance of an APA is 12 months for unilateral APAs and 18 months for bilateral and multilateral APAs. The APA is issued for a period of up to five years. In exceptional cases, such as long-term agreements, it may be issued for a longer period.

Romania

APAs are opposable and binding on the tax authorities as long as there are no material changes in the critical assumptions. In this view, the beneficiaries are obligated to submit an annual report on compliance with the terms and conditions of the agreement.

If taxpayers do not agree with the content of the APA, they can notify the National Agency for Tax Administration within 15 days. In this case, the agreement does not produce any legal effects.

Thin capitalisation
If the company's equity is negative or the debt-to-equity ratio is higher than 3:1, all the interest expenses and the net losses from foreign exchange differences related to credits or loans with a reimbursement period longer than 12 months are non-deductible in the year in which they are booked. These expenses are carried forward to the following fiscal years, and they will become deductible when the debt-to-equity ratio becomes lower than 3:1.

The interest expenses and the net losses from foreign exchange differences related to loans from Romanian or foreign banks, leasing companies, and other entities expressly mentioned by law are fully deductible, without being limited by the debt-to-equity ratio.

Loans contracted directly or indirectly from Romanian or foreign banks, leasing companies, mortgage companies, and other entities expressly mentioned by the law are no longer taken into account when computing the debt-to-equity ratio.

The tax deductibility threshold for interest on foreign currency loans from non-financial institutions is 6%.

Tax credits and incentives

Foreign tax credits
Tax credits may be obtained in Romania for foreign taxes only if the DTT concluded between Romania and the foreign state applies and proper documentation confirming the tax was paid is available.

Research and development (R&D) incentives
Companies can benefit from an additional deduction of 20% from the eligible expenses in respect of their R&D activities. Moreover, accelerated depreciation may be applied for devices and equipment used in the R&D activity.

Dividend tax exemption for reinvestments
Distributed dividends are exempted from taxation if they are invested in the same or in another Romanian company's share capital.

To benefit from this exemption, dividends must be reinvested to preserve and increase the number of employees and to boost existing lines of business.

Local tax exemptions for business located in industrial parks, and scientific and technological parks

Industrial parks
No property tax is due for buildings and constructions located in an industrial park. Also, land within industrial parks is exempt from land tax.

Scientific and technological parks
The incentives granted for the set-up and development of scientific and technological parks include:

- Lower taxes on tangible assets and land used by the park.
- Exemption of specific taxes on land.
- Development programmes for infrastructure, investments, and equipment endowments granted by the local and central public administration companies, and foreign financial assistance.
- Donations, concessions, and structural funds for development.

Employment incentives for special categories
For employment of recent graduates, employers can apply for a monthly grant of 1 to 1.5 (depending on the level of educational background) multiplied by the reference social indicator (currently set at RON 500) for each new graduate of a recognised institution for a period of 12 months. Employers benefiting from this incentive are obligated to keep this employment relationship for a time period of at least three years.

Moreover, employers may also be exempt for these 12 months from paying the unemployment contribution due for these graduates. In addition, grants amounting to the social security contributions for two years for recent graduates are available if they are still employed by the company for two additional years after the first three years pass.

The same incentives apply for the employment of recent graduates with disabilities, except that the period for which the exemption from contributions to the unemployment fund and the monthly grants apply is extended to 18 months.

Employers can also apply for exemption from unemployment fund contributions and for a monthly grant equal to the reference social indicator for each unemployed person with an age exceeding 45 years, or for each such person who is the sole family supporter. This monthly grant is available for a period of 12 months. Employers benefiting from this incentive have the obligation to keep this employment relationship for at least two years.

Employers running professional training programmes for their employees may apply for a refund of 50% of their expenses for up to 20% of their workforce, subject to certain conditions and limitations.

Other facilities granted to taxpayers
The tax authorities introduced, during 2011, the following series of measures aimed at supporting taxpayers who find themselves in difficulty due to temporary lack of funds as a consequence of the economic context:

- Rescheduling of tax payment obligations:
  - The rescheduling may be granted by the tax authorities to individuals and legal entities upon request. The time-frame for the rescheduling cannot be longer

Romania

than five years and is set after taking into consideration the taxpayer's financial situation and the total tax burden.
* In order to benefit from the rescheduling of the tax payment obligations, taxpayers must meet certain conditions and also constitute a guarantee which covers the rescheduled liabilities, interest, and also a supplementary percentage of the rescheduled liabilities, which will vary between 10% and 40% depending on the duration of the rescheduling time-frame.
* Possibility of reducing late-payment penalties:
    * Late payment penalties of fiscal obligations outstanding as at 31 August 2011 are reduced by 50% if the main fiscal obligations and related interest are paid or offset by 30 June 2012.
    * For late payment penalties calculated for local taxes outstanding at 31 August 2011, the annulment of 25% of the late payment penalties related to the main fiscal obligations is granted if the main fiscal obligations and 75% of the late payment penalties, calculated up to the date of payment, are paid or offset by 30 June 2012.

Withholding taxes

Domestic dividend tax
Dividend payments by a Romanian company to another Romanian company are subject to 16% dividend tax.

Dividends received by a Romanian company from another Romanian company are not taxed if the beneficiary has held at least 10% of the Romanian company's shares for a continuous period of at least two years by the date of dividends payment.

WHT for non-residents
Non-resident companies are subject to WHT at 16% on other revenues derived from Romania, such as interest, royalties, revenues from services performed in Romania, dividends, revenues obtained from management and consultancy, services (irrespective of where the services are performed), commissions, and revenues derived from liquidation of a Romanian legal entity.

A 25% WHT applies on gambling proceeds obtained by non-residents.

Certain specific provisions and exceptions apply to non-resident WHT, as follows:

* As Romania is an EU Member State, the provisions of the Parent-Subsidiary Directive are applied. Thus, dividends paid by Romanian companies to companies resident in one of the EU/EEA Member States are exempt from WHT if the dividend beneficiary has held a minimum of 10% of the shares of the Romanian company for a continuous period of at least two years by the date of dividends payment.
* Dividend and interest income obtained from Romania by EEA registered pension funds is exempt from WHT.
* Romania has implemented the Interest and Royalties Directive. As of 1 January 2011, payments of interest and royalties made by Romanian companies to companies resident in EU/EEA Member States and holding at least 25% of the share capital of the Romanian company for a continuous period of at least two years prior to the date of payment of interest or royalties are exempt from WHT .

To comply with European legislation, non-residents are required to present the certificate of tax residence and a declaration stating compliance with the necessary requirements, including that they are the beneficial owner of the income.

The following categories of income derived from Romania by non-residents are exempt from WHT:

- Bonds issued and/or guaranteed by the Romanian government.
- Revenues from consultancy services under free-financing agreements signed between the Romanian Government/public authorities and foreign Governments/ public authorities or international governmental/non-governmental organisations.
- Revenues from international transportation and accessory services.
- Prizes paid from public funds.
- Income obtained from a partnership constituted in Romania by a non-resident company. Such income is to be taxed under title II of the Fiscal Code, with corporate profit tax.

WHT rates for companies, and rates under some DTTs

Recipient	WHT (%)			
	Dividends	Interest	Royalties	Commissions
Non-Treaty	16	16	16	16
EU - Parent-Subsidiary Directive	0*	N/A	N/A	N/A
EU - Interest and Royalties Directive	N/A	0*	0*	N/A
Australia	5/15	10	10	N/A
Austria	0/5	0/3	3	N/A
Belgium	5/15	10	5	5
Bulgaria	10/15	15	15	N/A
Canada	5/15	10	5/10	N/A
Cyprus	10	10	5	5
Czech Republic	10	7	10	N/A
Denmark	10/15	10	10	4
Estonia	10	10	10	2
Finland	5	5	2.5/5	N/A
France	10	10	10	N/A
Germany	5/15	0/3	3	N/A
Greece	25/45	10	5/7	5
Hungary	5/15	15	10	5
Ireland	3	0/3	3	N/A
Israel	15	5/10	10	N/A
Italy	10	10	10	5
Japan	10	10	10/15	N/A
Luxembourg	5/15	0/10	10	5
Malta	5/30	5	5	10
Moldova	10	10	10/15	N/A
Netherlands	0/5/15	0	0	N/A
Norway	10	10	10	4
Poland	5/15	10	10	0/10
Portugal	10/15	10	10	N/A
Russia	15	15	10	N/A
Singapore	5	5	5	N/A

R

Romania

Recipient	WHT (%)			
	Dividends	Interest	Royalties	Commissions
Slovakia	10	10	10/15	N/A
South Africa	15	15	15	N/A
South Korea	7/10	0/10	7/10	10
Spain	10/15	10	10	5
Sweden	10	10	10	10
Switzerland	10	10	0	N/A
Turkey	15	10	10	N/A
Ukraine	10/15	10	10/15	N/A
United Kingdom	10/15	10	10/15	12.5
United States	10	10	10/15	N/A

* If certain conditions are met.

In case there are different taxation quotas in the domestic legislation or in the DTT, the more favourable of the taxation quotas shall apply. If a taxpayer is a resident of a member state of the European Union, the taxation quota that shall apply to the taxable income obtained by such taxpayer in Romania is the more favourable of the taxation quotas provided in the domestic legislation, in the legislation of the European Union, or in the DTT.

Tax administration

Taxable period
The fiscal year is considered to be the calendar year or the period during which the entity existed if it was set up or ceased to exist during that calendar year.

The accounting year is also usually the calendar year, but certain categories of entities (i.e. Romanian branches of foreign companies, Romanian consolidated subsidiaries and subsidiaries of the subsidiaries of foreign companies, except for credit institutions) are allowed to set an accounting year other than the calendar year, if the financial year of the parent company is different from the calendar year. However, establishing a financial reporting period different from the calendar year does not modify the period for which profit tax is calculated as defined by the Fiscal Code, namely the calendar year.

Tax returns
Taxpayers (except for banks, non-profit organisations, and taxpayers deriving most of their income from agriculture) must submit fiscal statements by the 25th day of the first month following the first, second, and third quarters. The annual income tax return is due by 25 March of the following year (25 April prior to 2013).

Banks and branches of foreign banks in Romania apply the system of anticipated quarterly profit tax payments.

Non-profit organisations and taxpayers that obtain income mainly from crop production have to declare annual profit tax by 25 February.

Large and medium size taxpayers have the obligation to submit fiscal forms online, using the www.e-guvernare.ro portal. The electronic signature of the tax returns can only be made using a qualified certificate issued by a legally accredited certification services provider. Other categories of taxpayers may use the electronic submitting method as an alternative way of compliance.

Taxpayers required to withhold tax, with the exception of salary payers, are obligated to submit a statement to the tax authorities regarding the tax withheld for each beneficiary by 30 June of the following year. This declarative obligation refers to tax withheld and paid by Romanian residents for income obtained in Romania by non-residents.

In cases where taxpayers have not submitted their tax returns, the tax authorities will assess by default the tax liabilities subject to self-assessment or withholding for every fiscal obligation in the taxpayer's fiscal liabilities records for each fiscal period for which tax returns were not submitted.

Payment of tax
Taxpayers (except for banks, non-profit organisations, taxpayers deriving most of their income from agriculture) must pay the quarterly profit tax by the 25th day of the first month following the first, second, and third quarters. The annual income tax has to be paid by 25 March of the following year (25 April prior to 2013).

Banks and branches of foreign banks in Romania apply the system of anticipated quarterly profit tax payments. The anticipated quarterly payments are calculated as a quarter of the previous year's profit tax increased by the consumer price index (CPI) inflation rate, and the payments are due by the 25th day of the month following the end of the quarter. The CPI inflation rate will be published by Order of the Ministry of Finance by 15 April of the year for which the anticipated payments are made. For 2011, the CPI inflation rate was 3.2%.

Non-profit organisations and taxpayers that obtain income mainly from crop production have to pay annual profit tax by 25 February.

Newly established companies (e.g. without a previous year history) or those which incurred fiscal losses in the previous year make quarterly advance payments at the level of the amount resulted from applying the profit tax rate on the accounting profit of the period for which the anticipated payment is made.

As of 1 January 2013, taxpayers (except those specifically mentioned by law) may opt to declare and pay the annual profit tax by making quarterly advanced payments. Such option has to be transmitted by 31 January of the fiscal year for which the taxpayer wants to apply it and has to be kept for at least two consecutive years.

Statute of limitations
The general statute of limitations period is five years, as of 1 January of the year following the one when the taxable events occurred, but is suspended during a tax inspection.

Non-resident companies
Non-resident companies deriving income from real estate property located in Romania or the sales of shares held in a Romanian company are obligated to declare and pay the related profit tax. Non-residents may appoint a tax agent to fulfil this requirement. However, if the payer of the income is a Romanian company or a PE, the non-resident companies have the obligation to pay and declare the profit tax.

Romania

For capital gains tax declaration and payment, the Romanian legislation requires the following tax returns to be submitted as follows:

* Quarterly statements, starting the 25th day of the month following the quarter in which the non-resident first earned capital gains taxable in Romania.
* An annual profit tax return.

The quarterly statements and annual return must be submitted during the entire period of time the non-resident is registered with the Romanian tax authorities, even if it no longer carries out transactions generating taxable revenues in Romania.

Late-payment penalty
The late-payment interest is 0.04% for each day of delay, and the following late-payment penalties are due:

* 5% of the fiscal liabilities, if the payment is made after 30 days but before the expiry of the 90 days from the due date.
* 15% of the remaining unpaid fiscal liabilities, if the payment is made after 90 days from the due date.

Late-payment penalties for the fiscal claims due to local budgets are owed in the amount of 2% of the fiscal claims, calculated for each month or part thereof.

Other issues

Mergers and acquisitions
Mergers, spin-offs, transfers of assets, and exchanges of shares between two Romanian companies should not trigger capital gains tax.

In the case of a relocation of the registered office of a European Company (SE) and European Cooperative Society (SCE) from Romania to another EU member state, there is no tax on the difference between the market value of the transferred assets and liabilities and their fiscal value, if certain conditions are met. There will also be no tax on such movements at the shareholder level. Therefore, a tax basis step-up may be achieved in the case of Romanian shareholders.

If a Romanian company has a PE in another EU member state, and the Romanian company is dissolved as a result of a cross-border reorganisation, the Romanian tax authorities will not have the right to tax the former PE.

Russian Federation

PwC contact

David John
PricewaterhouseCoopers
White Square Office Center
10 Butyrsky Val
Moscow, Russia 125047
Tel: +7 495 967 60 00
Email: david.c.john@ru.pwc.com

Significant developments

Recent significant changes in tax legislation

Transfer pricing legislation

The new transfer pricing legislation came into effect on 1 January 2012. Compared to the prior Russian transfer pricing rules, the new ones appear to be more technically elaborate and, to a certain extent, better aligned with the international transfer pricing principles developed by the Organisation for Economic Co-operation and Development (OECD).

The main changes are as follows:

- Change in the list of transactions where the Russian tax authorities may control prices for tax purposes.
- Expansion of the list of related parties.
- Burden of proof that prices of controlled transactions do not correspond to the market will rest with the Russian tax authorities.
- Introduction of the arm's-length principle as the fundamental principle of Russian transfer pricing rules.
- Abolishment of the 'safe harbor' provision (the 20% fluctuation of controlled transaction prices from market prices that was previously allowed).
- Expansion of the list of sources of information for determining market prices.
- Formally introducing a functional analysis as one of the comparability factors.
- Introduction of new methods for determining market prices, i.e. transactional net margin and profit split methods.
- Introduction of reporting and transfer pricing documentation requirements.
- Introduction of special transfer pricing audits to be performed by the Federal Tax Service.
- Introduction of penalties for non-compliance with reporting and transfer pricing documentation requirements. However, for the transitional period of 2012/13, no penalties can be assessed in case of transfer pricing adjustments.
- Introduction of unilateral and multilateral advance pricing agreements (APAs) for Russian companies registered as 'largest' taxpayers.

Consolidated taxpayer regime

The new consolidated taxpayer regime is available to large Russian groups starting from 1 January 2012.

A group can comprise two or more Russian organisations where the direct or indirect equity interest of one member in the charter/share capital of the other members equals at least 90%. To establish and apply the regime in 2013, all group members should meet the following requirements:

R

Russian Federation

- At least 10 billion Russian rubles (RUB) in total profits tax, value-added tax (VAT), excise tax, and mineral resources extraction tax (MRET) paid during 2011.
- At least RUB 100 billion in sales proceeds and other income in 2011.
- Total cost of assets of at least RUB 300 billion on 31 December 2011.

The advantages of application of the regime are the following. Firstly, transactions among members will not be controllable under the new transfer pricing legislation (with one exception - transactions with mineral resources subject to MRET with percentage rate will still be controlled). Secondly, for the purposes of calculating profits tax, it will become possible to consolidate members' profits and losses.

Social contributions
Social contributions of employers increased as of 1 January 2012. An additional 10% charge is imposed on salary that exceeds RUB 512,000 per annum per one employee (approximately 12,350 euros [EUR]). Contributions under RUB 512,000 are subject to contributions at a consolidated rate of 30% (previously, contributions under RUB 463,000 were subject to contributions at the rate of 34%).

Remuneration of foreign nationals temporarily staying in Russia is covered by pension insurance contributions at a rate of 22% within the threshold of RUB 512,000 and 10% top up charge on remuneration paid in excess of the threshold. The only exception is made for highly qualified specialists (with the respective work permit) and employees who have entered into a labour contract for a term of less than six months.

Significant changes expected in 2013 - 2015
The Russian government has approved the Key Directions in Russian tax policy for 2013 and the planning period 2014 and 2015. The document provides guidelines for taxpayers covering the next three years. It includes a range of measures to counter tax avoidance, including the introduction of international practices and concepts (e.g. controlled foreign company [CFC] rules). It also details measures to stimulate and support Russian taxpayers, as well as plans for the convergence of financial accounting with tax accounting. This, in turn, stands to reduce the administrative costs taxpayers incur when preparing their tax returns.

The following changes will have an impact on corporate taxpayers:

- Introduction of CFC rules.
- Introduction of the beneficial owner concept.
- Change of rules for establishing corporate tax residence based on several criteria.
- Changes in taxation for financing structures involving Eurobonds.
- Introduction of a cost sharing mechanism for a group of companies.
- Exemption of movable property from property tax.

Taxes on corporate income

Profits tax
The maximum profits tax rate for all taxpayers in the Russian Federation is established at 20% (2% is paid to the federal budget and 18% is paid to the budgets of constituent regions). The amount payable to the budgets of constituent regions may be reduced by such regions, so the total minimum tax rate may be 15.5% (e.g. the rate of 15.5% is established for certain categories of taxpayers located in the Smolensk region, the Arkhangelsk region, the Samara region, the Kaluga region, the Ulyanovsk region).

Russian legal entities pay tax on their worldwide income (credit relief is available for foreign tax paid up to the amount of the Russian tax liability that would have been due on the same amount under Russian rules).

Foreign legal entities pay tax on Russia-source income derived through a permanent establishment (PE) (at the rate of 20%) and are also subject to withholding tax (WHT) on income from Russian sources not related to a PE (at rates varying from 10% to 20%, depending on the type of income and the method used to calculate it).

Local income taxes
There are no local taxes on income.

Corporate residence

The effective Russian tax legislation does not contain terminology of corporate residence. The tax system in Russia distinguishes between Russian and foreign legal entities on the basis of their incorporation.

Permanent establishment (PE)
A PE is broadly defined as 'a branch, division, office, bureau, agency, or any other place through which a foreign legal entity regularly carries out its business activities in Russia'. Russia's various double tax treaties (DTTs) may define a PE differently. Conducting business through an agent also may create a taxable PE in Russia.

Other taxes

Value-added tax (VAT)
VAT is a federal tax in Russia, payable to the federal budget.

There is no separate VAT registration in Russia. The established general tax registration requirements are applicable to all taxes, including VAT.

Taxpayers follow a 'classical' input-output VAT system, whereby a VAT payer generally accounts for VAT on the full sales price of the transaction and is entitled to recover input VAT incurred on inventory costs and other related business expenses. The Russian VAT system, although not originally based on the European Union (EU) model has moved towards it. However, it still currently differentiates from the EU VAT system in multiple ways.

R

Output VAT
Generally, VAT applies to the value of goods, works, services, or property rights supplied in Russia. The standard VAT rate is 18% in Russia (with a lower rate of 10% applicable for certain basic foodstuff, children's clothing, medicines and medical products, certain printed publications, etc). The same VAT rates apply for imports of goods into Russia.

Exports of goods, international transportation and other services related to the export of goods from Russia, international passenger transportation, and certain other supplies are zero-rated with an input VAT recovery right. The application of the 0% VAT rate and recovery of the respective input VAT should be confirmed by submitting a number of documents to the tax authorities within certain time limits. Special rules are provided in

Russian Federation

respect of the documentary confirmation of the right to tax export supplies to Customs Union member countries with a 0% VAT rate, including an input VAT recovery right.

The list of VAT exempt goods and services includes basic banking and insurance services, educational services by certified establishments, sale of certain essential medical equipment, passenger transportation, and certain other socially important services. Most accredited offices of foreign legal entities (as well as the accredited employees of these offices) may be exempt from VAT on property rental payments. Performance of VAT exempt supplies gives no right for the recovery of the attributable input VAT; instead, costs associated with non-recoverable input VAT are, in most cases, deductible for profits tax purposes.

Withholding VAT
Russian VAT law contains rules for determining where services are supplied from a VAT perspective. These rules divide all services into different categories for determining where they are deemed to be supplied for VAT purposes. For example, certain services are deemed to be supplied where they are performed, some where the 'buyer' of the services carries out the activity, others where the immovable property is located, etc.

Under the reverse-charge mechanism, a Russian company must account for VAT on any payment it makes to a non-tax registered foreign company, if the payment is connected to a supply of goods or services regarded as supplied in Russia, based on the VAT place of supply rules and not falling under any VAT exemption based on the domestic VAT law. In such circumstances, according to the law, the Russian buyer shall act as a tax agent for Russian VAT purposes by withholding Russian VAT at the rate of 18/118 from payments to the foreign supplier and remit such withheld VAT to the Russian budget. The withheld VAT may be recovered by the Russian payers in accordance with the standard input VAT recovery rules provided by law.

Input VAT recovery
Generally, taxpayers are eligible to recover input VAT associated with the purchase of goods, works, services, or property rights, provided a set of rules established by the VAT legislation is met. Input VAT could potentially be recovered by the taxpayer in the following cases:

- VAT related to goods, services, or works acquired for the purpose of conducting VATable transactions.
- VAT related to the purchased goods, works, or services used in non-VATable transactions, if the portion of expenses related to non-VATable operations does not exceed 5% of total amount of expenses.
- Input VAT related to advance payments performed to Russian suppliers of goods (works, services) provided such acquired goods (works, services) are aimed at being used in VATable activities. Please note that application of this rule is the right of taxpayers (rather than an obligation), and taxpayers may choose whether to enjoy this right or not.

VAT compliance requirements
Each taxpayer performing supplies of goods, works, services, or property rights is liable to issue VAT invoices and provide them to customers. VAT invoices shall be issued within five days after the supply has occurred. The form of the VAT invoice is a standard one, established by the government. Compliance with invoicing requirements is critical to the buyer's ability to recover input VAT.

E-invoicing is also allowed under the Russian Tax Code. However, the e-invoice format and the necessary protocol are not yet established by the respective authorities. E-invoicing requires digital signature and data transfer via operators and is subject to mutual agreement of the transaction parties. Operators are companies who provide services for exchange of open and confidential information via telecommunication channels.

Generally, incoming and outgoing VAT invoices shall be registered by taxpayers in special purchases and sales VAT ledgers.

VAT returns shall be submitted to the tax authorities on a quarterly basis. VAT must be paid to the Russian budget after the end of each quarter in three instalments not later than the 20th day of each of the three consecutive months following the quarter, except for the remittal of VAT withheld by Russian buyers under the reverse charge mechanism, which is to be transferred to the Russian budget at the date of the external payment.

Import VAT
Import VAT is payable in customs upon importation of goods. The tax base for import VAT purposes is generally the customs value of the imported goods, including excise payments. Either the 18% or 10% VAT rate may apply upon import of goods in Russia, depending on the specifics of the goods.

A limited range of goods is eligible for exemption from import VAT. The list of such goods includes, for example, certain medical products and goods designated for diplomatic corps. Relief from import VAT is available on certain technological equipment (including their components and spare parts) analogues of which are not produced in Russia. The list of such equipment is established by the Russian government.

Import duties
In addition to VAT, customs duties are levied on assets imported into the Russian Federation. The rate varies according to the tariff code of the goods imported and the country of origin (generally the rate varies from 0% to 20% of the customs value of imported goods). There is special relief from customs duties for qualifying goods contributed to the charter capital of Russian companies with foreign investments.

R

The foundation of the Customs Union and deeper integration processes amongst Russia, Belarus, and Kazakhstan (hereinafter 'the CU') has resulted in unification of the customs legislation of the members of the CU and creation of a single customs territory, within which goods in mutual trade between the CU member states are moved without any customs clearance formalities. Members of the CU should apply unified customs tariffs and customs valuation methodology, general rules of non-tariff regulation, uniform technical regulations, etc.

Customs processing fee
Goods transported across the Russian Federation customs border are subject to a customs processing fee with a flat rate. The fee depends on a customs value of transported goods. Generally the fee is not significant.

Excise duty
Excise taxes apply to the production and import of cars, tobacco, alcohol, petrol, and lubricants. Special excise rates for each type of excisable goods are established in the Tax Code. The rates are widely variable and are based on multiple factors.

Russian Federation

Property tax

The maximum property tax rate is 2.2%, and regional legislative bodies have the right to reduce this rate. The property tax base includes only the annual book value of fixed assets recorded on the taxpayer's balance sheet (including property leased out). Intangible assets, inventories, work-in-progress, and financial assets are not subject to property tax in Russia.

Certain types of property are exempt from the tax. Relief is also available to a limited number of categories of taxpayers.

Transport tax

A transport tax is imposed on certain types of land, water, and air transport registered in Russia. Fixed rates apply (per unit of horsepower, gross tonnage, or unit of transport), which are differentiated based on engine capacity, gross tonnage, and type of transport. The actual rates in the regions may be subject to a maximum ten-fold increase/decrease by the legislative bodies of Russian Federation constituent subjects. Reporting and payment rules are established by regional legislative authorities.

Social contributions

Social contributions of employers increased as of 1 January 2012. An additional 10% charge will be imposed on salary that exceeds RUB 512,000 per annum per one employee (approximately EUR 12,350). Contributions under RUB 512,000 are subject to contributions at a consolidated rate of 30% (previously, contributions under RUB 463,000 were subject to contributions at the rate of 34%).

Remuneration of foreign nationals temporarily staying in Russia will be covered by pension insurance contributions at a rate of 22% within the threshold of RUB 512,000 and 10% top up charge on remuneration paid in excess of the threshold. The only exception is made for highly qualified specialists (with the respective work permit) and employees who have entered into a labour contract for a term of less than six months.

....

Branch income

Foreign legal entities pay tax on profits attributable to a PE. A PE's profits are computed on substantially the same basis as Russian legal entities, including the composition of tax-deductible expenses. The tax code does not provide specifically for the deductibility of expenses incurred abroad by a head office with respect to its PE in Russia (including a reasonable allocation of administration costs), although most DTTs provide for such an option.

A new provision regarding taxable income of a PE has been included in the Russian tax legislation (with effect from 1 January 2012). Taxable income of a PE in Russia should be determined taking into account the PE's functions, assets, and economic/commercial risks. The provision does not contain any guidance on specific transfer pricing methods that taxpayers should follow.

If a foreign legal entity conducts free-of-charge preparatory and/or auxiliary services for the benefit of third parties, a PE is considered to have been formed, and the tax base is calculated as 20% of its expenses relating to such activities.

Foreign legal entities operating in Russia through a PE are to follow the filing and payment schedules established for Russian legal entities, although they do not make monthly advance payments, but pay profits tax on a quarterly and annual basis only.

Income determination

The accounting period in Russia is a calendar year. Different periods are not permitted. The taxable base is calculated on an accrual basis (only small-scale taxpayers are still allowed to use the cash basis).

Taxable income is to be computed following the rules and principles established in the tax code. Taxpayers must maintain tax accounting registers. Statutory accounts may be used for computing tax items for which accounting methods are the same. In practice, most taxpayers use statutory accounts as a basis and apply adjustments to arrive at the taxable income.

Inventory valuation
Inventory can be valued using one of the following methods: first in first out (FIFO), last in first out (LIFO), average cost, and individual unit cost.

Capital gains
Capital gains are subject to the same 20% profits tax rate and are added to ordinary income to arrive at the taxable income.

Four separate tax baskets are calculated for tax purposes: (i) results from general operations, (ii) results from operations with listed securities, (iii) results from operations with non-listed securities, and (iv) results from operations with non-listed derivatives. A loss in one basket cannot be offset with income in another basket. Results from operations with listed derivatives are included into the general tax basket.

Gains from the sale of fixed assets and other property equal the difference between the sale price and their net book value for tax purposes. Losses resulting from the sale of fixed assets should be deducted in equal monthly instalments during the period, defined as the difference between their normative useful life and the actual time of use.

A significant exemption was introduced for capital gains from the sale or other disposal (including redemption) of shares in Russian entities (interests in Russian entities' charter capital), provided that, as of the date of sale, they have been continuously held by the taxpayer on the basis of a right of ownership or another proprietary right for more than five years. One of the following conditions must be met in order to apply a 0% tax:

- The shares have been non-listed securities over the entire period of the taxpayer's ownership of such shares.
- The shares are listed securities, and the company issuing shares has belonged to the technology/innovative sector of the economy over the entire period of the taxpayer's ownership of such shares.
- As of the date of acquisition by the taxpayer, the shares qualified as non-listed securities and, as of the date of their sale by this taxpayer or of another disposal (including redemption) by this taxpayer, they are listed securities of the high technology/innovative sector of the economy.

The beneficial tax treatment will only apply to shares and interests in charter capital acquired by taxpayers after 1 January 2011 (it means that the exemption may be first used in 2016).

R

Russian Federation

Dividend income

Dividends received by Russian legal entities from Russian or foreign legal entities are taxed in Russia at a 9% flat rate.

Dividends received from 'strategic investments' are exempt from Russian income tax. An investment is considered strategic when:

- the owner (recipient of dividends) owns at least 50% of the capital of the payer of dividends or owns depository receipts entitling it to receive at least 50% of the total amount of paid dividends and
- the share or depository receipts have been owned for at least 365 calendar days on the day dividends are declared.

Dividends from companies residing in 'offshore' zones with preferential tax regimes are not eligible for the tax exemption. The list of offshore zones is established by the Ministry of Finance.

Tax on dividends from abroad withheld in the source country may be credited against Russian tax.

The standard 15% tax rate is applicable to dividends paid by Russian legal entities to foreign legal entities. The tax should be withheld by the Russian legal entity paying dividends. The tax may be reduced based on a relevant DTT, typically to 10% or 5% (*please see the Withholding taxes section for more details*).

Interest income

Interest income is taxed on the accrual basis. A standard tax rate of 20% is applied to interest income, except for interest on state and municipal securities, which is taxed at 0%, 9%, or 15%, depending on the type of security. The rate may be reduced (typically to zero) based on a relevant tax treaty.

Exchange gains and losses

Foreign exchange gains and losses are recognised for tax purposes on the accrual basis. However, gains and losses from settlements in a local currency of amounts denominated in (tied to) a foreign currency are taxable (deductible) on payment.

Foreign income

Russian legal entities pay tax on their worldwide income. Credit relief is available for foreign taxes paid up to the amount of the Russian tax liability that would have been due on the same amount under Russian rules.

The effective tax legislation does not contain provisions that allow tax deferral in respect to foreign income.

Deductions

Expenses are deducted on the accrual basis. The main criteria for deductibility of expenses is that the expense is (i) incurred in the course of an income-generating activity, (ii) properly documented, and (iii) not mentioned in the tax code as non-deductible for tax purposes.

Depreciation and amortisation

Two methods of depreciation are allowed: the straight-line method and the declining-balance method. The ranges of useful life of assets for tax purposes are established in the Classification of Fixed Assets adopted by the Russian government, for example:

Fixed asset	Useful life (years)
Personal computer	2 to 3
Motor-car	3 to 5
Truck (capacity more than 5 tonnes)	7 to 10
Aircraft	10 to 15
Blast furnace	20 to 25

Accelerated depreciation is permitted for leased property, where a special ratio of up to three may be applied (with some exceptions).

An upfront premium is allowed, which means that a taxpayer has the right to deduct 10% (from 1 January 2009: 30% for certain categories of fixed assets) of the cost of fixed assets purchased (or constructed) in the month when the depreciation started. The balance is depreciated over the useful life of the asset. A premium must be recaptured if a relevant asset is sold within five years of its acquisition.

Intangible assets are amortised over their useful life (or over ten years if their useful life cannot be established).

Goodwill

According to the tax law, mark-up (difference between the acquisition value and net assets of the business [property complex] purchased) should be recognised as goodwill for tax purposes and may be amortised by a buyer over five years. The practice of implementation of such provision is not sufficient because the sellers hardly ever register the subject of a deal as a property complex.

Start-up expenses

Russian tax law does not contain specific provisions on deductibility of start-up expenses. In some cases, they may be lost for tax purposes.

Interest expenses

From 1 January 2011 till 31 December 2012, interest expenses are deductible within the following limits:

- The average interest rate on similar loans obtained within one quarter from Russian lenders multiplied by 1.2.
- If there are no similar loans, or at the taxpayer's discretion, the following limits are applied:
  - For loans denominated in a foreign currency: the refinancing rate of the Central Bank of Russia multiplied by 0.8 (the rate was established as 8% starting from 26 December 2011).
  - For loans denominated in rubles: the refinancing rate of the Central Bank of Russia multiplied by 1.8.

Bad debt

Generally, losses in the form of bad debts written off are deductible. Companies may create a bad debt reserve. The method of accrual for a bad debt reserve for tax purposes

R

Russian Federation

may differ from that in financial accounting because it is based only on the overdue payment period (i.e. if the delay exceeds 90 days, the full amount of the account receivable is included in the reserve).

Charitable contributions
Russian tax legislation does not provide any benefits in respect to charitable contributions. Such expenses are not deductible for tax purposes.

Research and development (R&D) expenses
Currently, R&D expenses (including R&D with a negative result) are deductible within one year after completion. Certain R&D expenses may be deducted using a coefficient of 1.5. The list of such types of R&D is established by the government.

The following amendments, with respect to R&D, were introduced on 7 June 2011 and came into effect on 1 January 2012:

- Expenses are recognised for tax purposes in the reporting (tax) period when the relevant R&D work (or work stage) is completed.
- Special reporting is introduced for taxpayers that deduct R&D expenses using a coefficient of 1.5.
- The amendments provide a right to set up a provision for future R&D expenses.

Insurance premiums
Expenses related to all types of obligatory insurance are deductible, subject to state tariff limitations, where established. Voluntary insurance expenses are deductible to the extent that they relate to the insurance of damage and losses related to certain classes of assets, and the insurance of construction activity risks. Contract liability insurance expenses are deductible to the extent that such insurance is required by an international treaty to which Russia is a party or a generally accepted international trade custom.

Long-term life and pension insurance is deductible within a limit of 12% of the payroll fund. Voluntary medical insurance is deductible within a limit of 6% of the payroll fund.

Fines and penalties
Fines and penalties paid to contractors for the violation of contractual terms may be deducted for tax purposes.

Fines and penalties paid to a budget are not deductible.

Taxes
Taxes paid by a taxpayer, as well as social contributions of employers, are deductible for tax purposes.

Net operating and capital losses
Tax losses may be carried forward for up to ten years without limitation (i.e. they can be used to offset the entire taxable profit before a loss carryforward deduction). Carryback of losses, however, is not allowed.

Losses from the sale of fixed assets are recognised evenly during the remaining useful life.

Losses and income from different tax baskets can't be offset (please see Capital gains in the Income determination section for more details).

Payments to foreign affiliates

There are no special tax provisions regarding deducibility of payments to foreign affiliates for services provided. They may be deducted in full if the general deductibility criteria are met. Charges with respect to administrative support provided by foreign affiliates may be deductible, but due care should be taken with regard to documentary support of the nature and actual receipt of the service.

Group taxation

Consolidated taxpayer regime

The new consolidated taxpayer regime is available to large Russian groups starting from 1 January 2012.

A group can comprise two or more Russian organisations where the direct or indirect equity interest of one member in the charter/share capital of the other members equals at least 90%. To establish and apply the regime in 2013, all group members should meet the following requirements:

*   At least RUB 10 billion in total profits tax, VAT, excise tax, and MRET paid during 2011.
*   At least RUB 100 billion in sales proceeds and other income in 2011.
*   Total cost of assets of at least RUB 300 billion on 31 December 2011.

The advantages of application of the regime are the following. Firstly, transactions among members will not be controllable under the new transfer pricing legislation (with one exception - transactions with mineral resources subject to MRET with percentage rate will still be controlled). Secondly, for the purposes of calculating profits tax, it will become possible to consolidate members' profits and losses.

Transfer pricing

The new transfer pricing legislation came into effect on 1 January 2012. Compared to the prior Russian transfer pricing rules, the new ones appear to be more technically elaborate and, to a certain extent, better aligned with the international transfer pricing principles developed by the OECD.

The main changes are as follows:

R

*   Change in the list of transactions where the Russian tax authorities may control prices for tax purposes.
*   Expansion of the list of related parties.
*   Burden of proof that prices of controlled transactions do not correspond to the market will rest with the Russian tax authorities.
*   Introduction of the arm's-length principle as the fundamental principle of Russian transfer pricing rules.
*   Abolishment of the 'safe harbor' provision (the 20% fluctuation of controlled transaction prices from market prices that was previously allowed).
*   Expansion of the list of sources of information for determining market prices.
*   Formally introducing a functional analysis as one of the comparability factors.
*   Introduction of new methods for determining market prices, i.e. transactional net margin and profit split methods.
*   Introduction of reporting and transfer pricing documentation requirements.
*   Introduction of special transfer pricing audits to be performed by the Federal Tax Service.

Russian Federation

- Introduction of penalties for non-compliance with reporting and transfer pricing documentation requirements. However, for the transitional period of 2012/13, no penalties can be assessed in case of transfer pricing adjustments.
- Introduction of unilateral and multilateral APAs for Russian companies registered as 'largest' taxpayers.

Thin capitalisation

Under the Russian Tax Code, interest on loans received from foreign shareholders (as well as their Russian affiliates, or loans guaranteed by foreign shareholders or their Russian affiliates) owning more than 20% of capital is deductible, provided the loans do not exceed by three times the amount of equity (12.5 times for banks and leasing companies). If the loans exceed this limit, the excess interest on the loans will be reclassified for taxation purposes as dividends paid to foreign shareholders. Such dividends are not deductible for profits tax purposes and are subject to WHT at the rate of 15% (treaty benefits may apply to reduce the rate).

Tax credits and incentives

At present, the following types of incentives exist in Russia:

- Regional incentives granted by regional or local authorities with respect to taxes paid to their budgets.
- Special tax regimes in special economic zones (SEZs).
- Incentives related to certain activities (e.g. activities related to R&D, information technology).
- Incentives related to particular projects (e.g. Skolkovo, Olympic Winter Games in Sochi).

The incentives are briefly described below.

It is also worth mentioning that the Russian tax legislation provides for special tax regimes to support small and medium-size businesses. Such regimes include a unified tax regime, simplified tax regime, and unified agricultural tax.

Regional incentives

Regional incentives in the form of reduced tax rates for taxes payable to regional budgets (primarily profits tax and property tax) are granted to certain classes of taxpayers (typically large investors or entities operating in specific industries). The extent of regional incentives and the willingness of regional authorities to grant them have been diminishing over time.

Special economic zones (SEZs)

The following types of SEZ are established in Russia:

- Technical research and implementation zones for scientific projects.
- Industrial production zones to develop industrial production.
- Tourism-recreation zones for the development and effective use of Russian tourist resources.
- Port zones.

SEZ residents may take advantage of different combinations of benefits, such as reduced profits tax, exemption from property tax and land tax, and, in some cases, exemption from customs duty and VAT.

Activities incentives

The following 'activities' incentives are available to taxpayers in Russia:

* Certain R&D services are exempt from VAT.
* Certain R&D service-related expenses, as listed by the government, are deductible using a coefficient of 1.5.
* Fixed assets used in the sphere of science and technology may be amortised with an accelerated coefficient up to 3.
* Reduced rates for contribution payments to social funds are established for information technology (IT) companies.

Special project incentives

The following 'special project' incentives are established in Russia:

* Participants in the Skolkovo innovation centre will enjoy a number of benefits, the primary of which are the following: exemption from profits and property taxes, exemption from VAT obligations, and reduced rates for mandatory contributions to social funds.
* Olympic Winter Games (Sochi 2014). The Russian tax legislation provides certain tax exemptions for foreign and Russian organisers of the Games, marketing partners of the International Olympic Committee, and official broadcasting companies in relation to their activity on the Games, as well as exemption from personal income tax for income received by sportsmen for participation in the Games.

Foreign tax credit

Credit relief is available for foreign taxes paid up to the amount of the Russian tax liability that would have been due on the same amount under Russian rules.

Withholding taxes

In accordance with the general provisions of the tax code, income received by a foreign legal entity and not attributed to a PE in Russia is subject to WHT in Russia (to be withheld at source). WHT rates are as follows:

* 15% on dividends and income from participation in Russian enterprises with foreign investments.
* 10% on freight income.
* 20% on certain other income from Russian sources, including royalties and interest.
* 20% of revenue or 20% of the margin on capital gains (from the sale of immovable property located in Russia or non-listed shares in Russian subsidiaries where the immovable property located in Russia represents more than 50% of assets).

Taxation of the margin (rather than the gross amount of income received from the above sales) may be applied only if proper documentary support of expenses is available.

As of 1 January 2011, income of foreign organisations (not performing activity in Russia through a PE) from the sale of certain listed securities of Russian entities (and their derivatives) is not regarded as income derived from sources in Russia subject to WHT.

Tax should be withheld by the tax agent and paid to the Russian budget. WHT rates may be reduced under a relevant DTT, whose provisions may be applied based on confirmation of tax residence, to be provided by a foreign company to the Russian

R

Russian Federation

tax agent prior to the date of payment (no advance permission from the Russian tax authorities is required) and also provided general conditions are fulfilled (proof of beneficial ownership, etc.).

The Russian tax authorities recognise the terms of former Union of Soviet Socialist Republics (USSR) treaties until they are renegotiated by the Russian Federation (RF) government, and the tax treaty network is continuously updated.

The list below is current as of 20 May 2012, and indicates the WHT rates stipulated in the treaties.

Recipient	Treaty benefits available from	WHT (%) Dividends	Interest (1)	Royalties	Construction site duration before creation of PE (months)
Albania/RF	1 January 1998	10	10	10	12
Algeria/RF	1 January 2009	5 (2)/15	0/15	15	6 months and an aggregated period of more than 3 months in any 12-month period for furnishing of services
Armenia/RF	1 January 1999	5 (3)/10	0	0	18
Australia/RF	1 January 2004	5 (4)/15	10	10	12
Austria/RF	1 January 2003	5 (5)/15	0	0	12
Azerbaijan/RF	1 January 1999	10	0/10	10	12
Belarus/RF	1 January 1998	15	0/10	10	No special provisions in the relevant DTT; local tax legislation provisions should apply
Belgium/RF	1 January 2001	10	0/10	0	12
Botswana	1 January 2010	5 (6)/10	0/10	10	6
Brazil	1 January 2010	10 (7)/15	0/15	15	9
Bulgaria/RF	1 January 1996	15	0/15	15	12
Canada/RF	1 January 1998	10 (8)/15	0/10	0 (9)/10	12
China/RF	1 January 1998	10	0/10	10	18
Croatia/RF	1 January 1998	5 (10)/10	10	10	12
Cuba/RF	1 January 2011	5 (11)/15	10	5	12
Cyprus/RF	1 January 2000 (12)	5 (13)/10	0	0	12
Czech/RF	1 January 1998	10	0	10	12 months and an aggregated period of more than 6 months in any 12-month period for furnishing of services

Russian Federation

Recipient	Treaty benefits available from	WHT (%)			Construction site duration before creation of PE (months)
		Dividends	Interest (1)	Royalties	
Denmark/RF	1 January 1998	10	0	0	12 months and an aggregated period of more than 365 days in any 18-month period for a drilling rig
Egypt	1 January 2001	10	0/15	15	6 months and an aggregated period of more than 6 months in any 12-month period for furnishing of services
Finland/RF	1 January 2003	5 (14)/12	0	0	12 months and an 18-month period for particular types of construction works
France/RF	1 January 2000	5 (15)/10 (16)/15	0	0	12
Germany/RF	1 January 1997	5 (17)/15	0	0	12
Greece/RF	1 January 2008	5 (18)/10	7	7	9
Hungary/RF	1 January 1998	10	0	0	12
Iceland/RF	1 January 2004	5 (19)/15	0	0	12
India/RF	1 January 1999	10	0/10	10	12 (may be extended on agreement with the competent authorities)
Indonesia/RF	1 January 2003	15	0/15	15	3
Iran/RF	1 January 2003	5 (20)/10	0/7.5	5	12
Ireland/RF	1 January 1996	10	0	0	12
Israel/RF	1 January 2001	10	0/10	10	12
Italy/RF	1 January 1999	5 (21)/10	10	0	12
Japan/USSR	1 January 1987	15	0/10	0 (22)/10	12
Kazakhstan/RF	1 January 1998	10	0/10	10	12
North Korea/RF	1 January 2001	10	0	0	12 months and an aggregated period of more than 6 months in any 12-month period for furnishing of services

Russian Federation

Recipient	Treaty benefits available from	WHT (%)			Construction site duration before creation of PE (months)
		Dividends	Interest (1)	Royalties	
South Korea/RF	1 January 1996	5 (23)/10	0	5	12 (may be extended up to 24 months upon agreement with the competent authorities)
Kuwait/RF	1 January 2004	0 (24)/5	0	10	6 months and an aggregated period of more than 3 months in any 12-month period for furnishing of services
Kyrgyzstan/RF	1 January 2001	10	0/10	10	12
Lebanon/RF	1 January 2001	10	0/5	5	12
Lithuania/RF	1 January 2006	5 (25)/10	0/10	5 (26)/10	9
Luxembourg/RF	1 January 1998	10 (27)/15	0	0	12
Macedonia/RF	1 January 2001	10	10	10	12
Malaysia/USSR	1 January 1989	0/15 (28)	0/15	10 (29)/15 (30)	12 months and more than a 6-month period for installation or assembly projects
Mali/RF	1 January 2000	10 (31)/15	0/15	0	No special provisions in the relevant DTT; local tax legislation provisions should apply
Mexico/RF	1 January 2009	10	0/10	10	6
Moldova/RF	1 January 1998	10	0	10	12
Mongolia/RF	1 January 1998	10	0/10	rates in accordance with local legislation	24
Montenegro/RF	1 January 1998	5 (32)/15	10	10	18
Morocco/RF	1 January 2000	5 (33)/10	0/10	10	8
Namibia/RF	1 January 2001	5 (34)/10	0/10	5	9 months and more than a 6-month period for furnishing of services and installation projects
Netherlands/RF	1 January 1999	5 (35)/15	0	0	12
New Zealand/RF	1 January 2004	15	10	10	12
Norway/RF	1 January 2003	10	0/10	0	12

Russian Federation

Recipient	Treaty benefits available from	WHT (%)			Construction site duration before creation of PE (months)
		Dividends	Interest (1)	Royalties	
Philippines/RF	1 January 1998	15	0/15	15	183 days and an aggregate period of more than 183 days in any 12-month period for furnishing of services)
Poland/RF	1 January 1994	10	0/10	10	12 (may be extended up to 24 months upon agreement with the competent authorities)
Portugal/RF	1 January 2003	10 (36)/15	0/10	10	12
Qatar/RF	1 January 2001	5	0/5	0	6
Romania/RF	1 January 1996	15	0/15	10	12
Saudi Arabia	1 January 2011	0 (37) or 5	0/5	10	6 months and an aggregated period of more than 6 months in any 12-month period for furnishing of services
Serbia/RF	1 January 1998	5 (38)/15	10	10	18
Singapore/RF	1 January 2010	5 (39)/10	0/7.5	7.5	6 months and an aggregated period of more than 3 months in any 12-month period for furnishing of services
Slovakia/RF	1 January 1998	10	0	10	12
Slovenia/RF	1 January 1998	10	10	10	12
South Africa/RF	1 January 2001	10 (40)/15	0/10	0	12
Spain/RF	1 January 2001	5 (41)/10 (42) /15	0/5	5	12
Sri Lanka/RF	1 January 2003	10 (43)/15	0/10	10	6 months and an aggregated period of more than 183 days in any 12-month period for furnishing of services
Sweden/RF	1 January 1996	5 (44)/15	0	0	12
Switzerland/RF	1 January 1998	5 (45)/15	0 (46)/5 (47)/10	0	12
Syria/RF	1 January 2004	15	0/10	4.5 (48)/13.5 (49)/18 (50)	6

R

Russian Federation

| Recipient | Treaty benefits available from | WHT (%) | | | Construction site duration before creation of PE (months) |
		Dividends	Interest (1)	Royalties	
Tajikistan/RF	1 January 2004	5 (51)/10	0/10	0	24 (may be extended on agreement with the competent authorities)
Thailand/RF	1 January 2010	15	0/10	15	6 months and an aggregated period of more than 3 months in any 12-month period for furnishing of services
Turkey/RF	1 January 2000	10	0/10	10	18
Turkmenistan/RF	1 January 2000	10	5	5	12
Ukraine/RF	1 January 2000	5 (52)/15	0/10	10	12
United Kingdom/RF	1 January 1998	10	0	0	12
United States/RF	1 January 1994	5 (53)/10	0	0	18
Uzbekistan/RF	1 January 1996	10	0/10	0	12
Venezuela	1 January 2010	10 (54)/15	0/5 (55)/10	10 (56)/15	9
Vietnam/RF	1 January 1997	10 (57)/15	10	15	6 months and more than a 12-month period for furnishing of services

Notes

1. In most cases, a 0% tax rate applies to interest payments to the governments of contracting states and to payments guaranteed by the government.
2. If the resident of the other contracting state directly holds at least 25% of the capital of the company paying the dividends.
3. If the resident of the other contracting state contributed at least 40,000 United States dollars (USD) (or an equivalent amount in the domestic currency of either of the contracting states) to the authorised capital of the enterprise paying the dividends.
4. If the following conditions are met:
   a. Dividends are paid to a company (other than a partnership) that directly holds at least 10% of the capital of the company paying the dividends.
   b. The resident of the other contracting state has invested a minimum of 700,000 Australian dollars (AUD), or an equivalent amount in Russian rubles, in the capital of that company.
   c. If the dividends are paid by a company that is resident in Russia, the dividends are exempt from Australian tax.
5. If the beneficial owner of the dividends is a company (other than a partnership) that directly holds at least 10% of the capital of the company paying the dividends and the participation exceeds USD 100,000 or an equivalent amount in any other currency.
6. If the resident of the other contracting state directly holds at least 25% of the capital of the company paying the dividends.
7. If the beneficial owner of the dividends directly holds at least 20% of the total capital of the company paying the dividends.
8. If the beneficial owner of the dividends is a company that owns at least 10% of the voting stock (or in the case of Russia, if there is no voting stock, at least 10% of the statutory capital) of the company paying the dividends.
9. 0% WHT is applied to the following types of Royalties:

- Royalties for the production or reproduction of any literary, dramatic, musical, or other artistic work (but not including royalties for motion picture films or works on film or videotape or other means of reproduction for use in connection with television broadcasting).
- Royalties for the use of, or the right to use, computer software.
- Royalties paid to an unrelated party for the use of, or the right to use, any patent or any information concerning industrial, commercial, or scientific experience.

10. If the beneficial owner of the dividends is a company that directly holds at least 25% of the capital of the company paying the dividends (this share should be at least USD 100,000 or its equivalent in another currency).
11. If the beneficial owner of the dividends is a company (excluding partnerships) that directly holds at least 25% of the capital of the company paying the dividends.
12. The Protocol to the Russia-Cyprus DTT introduces some new provisions that will come into effect from 2013.
13. If the beneficial owner of the dividends has directly invested in the capital of the company not less than USD 100,000 or its equivalent in another currency (according to the new version effective from 2013: EUR 100,000).
14. If the beneficial owner of the dividends is a company (other than a partnership) that directly holds at least 30% of the capital of the company paying the dividends, and the foreign capital invested exceeds USD 100,000 or its equivalent in the national currencies of the contracting states at the moment when the dividends become due and payable.
15. If the following conditions are met:
    a. Where the beneficial owner of the dividends has invested in the company paying the dividends, irrespective of the form or the nature of such investments, a total value of at least 500,000 French francs (FF) or the equivalent in another currency; as the value of each investment is appreciated as of the date it is made.
    b. Where that beneficial owner is a company that is liable to tax on profits under the general tax laws of the contracting state of which it is a resident and which is exempt from such tax in respect of such dividends.
16. If only one of the conditions of 15 (a) or 15 (b) are met.
17. If the beneficial owner of the dividends is a company that directly holds at least 10% of the basic or common stock of the company paying the dividends and such capital share amounts to at least EUR 80,000 or the equivalent value in rubles.
18. If the beneficial owner of the dividends is a company (other than partnership) that directly holds at least 25% of the capital of the company paying the dividends.
19. If the beneficial owner of the dividends is a company (other than a partnership) that directly holds at least 25% of the capital of the company paying the dividends and the foreign capital invested exceeds USD 100,000 or its equivalent in the national currency of the contracting state.
20. If the recipient of the dividends is a company (excluding partnership) that directly holds at least 25% of the capital of the company paying the dividends.
21. If the beneficial owner of the dividends is a company that directly holds at least 10% of the capital of the company paying the dividends (this share should be at least USD 100,000 or its equivalent in another currency).
22. Literary, artistic, or scientific work including cinematograph films and films or tapes for radio or television broadcasting.
23. If the beneficial owner of the dividends is a company (other than a partnership) that directly holds at least 30% of the capital of the company paying the dividends and invests not less than USD 100,000 or the equivalent in local currencies to the company paying the dividends.
24. The 0% rate applies to dividends paid to governmental agencies, financial institutions or companies controlled by the government, or companies where the government holds at least 25% of the capital of the company paying the dividends and the capital directly invested by this beneficial owner is not less than USD 100,000 or the equivalent in the national currency of the contracting state.
25. If the beneficial owner of the dividends is a company (other than a partnership) that directly holds at least 25% of the capital of the company paying the dividends and the capital directly invested by this beneficial owner is not less than USD 100,000 or the equivalent amount in the national currency of a contracting state.
26. For the use of industrial, commercial, or scientific equipment.
27. If the beneficial owner of the dividends directly holds at least 30% of the capital of the company paying the dividends and of an acquisition price of at least 75,000 European Currency Units (ECU) or its equivalent in national currency.
28. The 15% rate applies to profits received from a joint venture by a resident of Malaysia.
29. Any patent, trademark, design or model, plan, secret formula or process, or any copyright of scientific work, or for the use of, or the right to use, industrial, commercial, or scientific equipment, or for information concerning industrial, commercial, or scientific experience.
30. Cinematograph films, or tapes for radio or television broadcasting, any copyright of literary or artistic work.
31. If the invested amount equals or exceeds FF 1 million.
32. If the beneficial owner of the dividends is a company (other than a partnership) that directly holds at least 25% of the capital of the company paying the dividends and has invested in it at least USD 100,000 or the equivalent in the national currencies of the contracting states.
33. If the beneficial owner of the dividends has invested in the capital of the company paying dividends of more than USD 500,000.

Russian Federation

34. If the beneficial owner of the dividends is a company (other than a partnership) that directly holds at least 25% of the share capital of the company paying the dividends and has directly invested in the equity share capital of that company not less than USD 100,000 or its equivalent in another currency.
35. If the beneficial owner of the dividends is a company (other than a partnership) that directly holds at least 25% of the capital of the company paying the dividends and has invested in it at least ECU 75,000 or its equivalent in the national currencies.
36. If the beneficial owner of the dividends is a company that, for an uninterrupted period of two years prior to the payment of the dividends, directly owned at least 25% of the capital of the company paying the dividends.
37. The 0% rate applies to dividends paid to governmental agencies or financial institutions.
38. If the beneficial owner of the dividends is a company (other than a partnership) that directly holds at least 25% of the capital of the company paying the dividends and has invested in it at least USD 100,000 or its equivalent in the national currencies of the contracting states.
39. If the beneficial owner of the dividends is the government of the other contracting state or if the beneficial owner of the dividends is a company that directly holds at least 15% of the capital of the company paying the dividends and has invested in it at least USD 100,000 or its equivalent in other currencies.
40. If residents of the other contracting state hold at least 30% of the capital of the company paying the dividends and have directly invested in the equity share capital (authorised fund) of that company an amount of not less than USD 100,000 or its equivalent in the currency of the first state.
41. If the following conditions are met:
    a. The beneficial owner of the dividends is a company (other than a partnership) that has invested at least ECU 100,000 or its equivalent in any other currency in the capital of the company paying the dividends.
    b. Those dividends are exempt from tax in the other contracting state.
42. If only one of the conditions of 41 (a) or 41 (b) are met.
43. If the beneficial owner of the dividends is a company (other than a partnership) that directly holds at least 25% of the capital of the company paying the dividends.
44. If the beneficial owner of the dividends is a company (other than a partnership) that directly holds 100% of the capital of the company paying the dividends; or in the case of a joint venture not less than 30% of the capital of the joint venture; and in either case the foreign capital invested exceeds USD 100,000 or its equivalent in the national currencies of the contracting states at the moment of the actual distribution of the dividends.
45. If the beneficial owner of the dividends is a company (other than a partnership) that directly holds at least 20% of the capital of the company paying the dividends and the foreign capital invested exceeds 200,000 Swiss francs (CHF) or its equivalent in any other currency at the moment when the dividends become due.
46. A 0% tax rate may be applied provided such interest is paid:
    a. in connection with the sale on credit of any industrial, commercial, or scientific equipment or
    b. in connection with the sale on credit of any merchandise by one enterprise to another.
47. In the case of a loan of any kind granted by a bank.
48. Cinematography films, programmes, and recordings for radio or television broadcasting.
49. Any copyright of literary, artistic, or scientific work.
50. Any patent, trademark, design or model, plan, secret formula or process, any computer software program, or for information concerning industrial, commercial, or scientific experience.
51. If the beneficial owner of the dividends directly holds at least 25% of the capital of the company paying the dividends.
52. If a resident of the other contracting state has invested in its joint-stock capital (registered fund) at least USD 50,000 or its equivalent in the national currencies of the contracting states.
53. If the beneficial owner of the dividends is a company that owns at least 10% of the voting stock (or, in the case of Russia, if there is no voting stock, at least 10% of the statutory capital) of the company paying the dividends.
54. If the beneficial owner of the dividends is a company (other than a partnership) that directly holds at least 10% of the capital of the company paying the dividends and has invested in this company not less than the equivalent of USD 100,000.
55. In the case of banks.
56. In the case of fees for technical assistance.
57. If the residents of the other contracting state have directly invested in the equity share capital of that company not less than USD 10 million.

Tax administration

All taxpayers are required to obtain tax registration and be assigned a taxpayer identification number, irrespective of whether their activities are subject to Russian taxation.

Russian Federation

Taxable period
The taxable period runs from 1 January to 31 December.

Tax returns
An annual profits tax return must be filed by 28 March of the year following the end of the reporting year.

Payment of tax
Companies pay advance profits tax payments on a monthly basis. The final payment for the year is due by 28 March of the following year.

Statute of limitations
The statute of limitations is established as three years. For example, in 2012 the tax authorities may examine 2011, 2010, and 2009 profits tax returns through site tax audit.

Topics of focus for tax authorities
The recent court practice demonstrates that tax authorities concentrate on tax evasion schemes and relationships with one-day contractors.

R

Rwanda

PwC contact

Bernice Kimacia
PricewaterhouseCoopers Rwanda Limited
5th Floor,Blue Star House,Kacyiru
P O Box 1495
Kigali
Rwanda
Tel: +250 252 5882 03/04/05/06
Email: bernice.w.kimacia@rw.pwc.com

Significant developments

There have been no significant corporate tax developments in Rwanda during the past
year.

Taxes on corporate income

Rwanda principally operates a source-based system of taxation. This means that
any income that is deemed to be from sources within Rwanda will be liable to tax in
Rwanda unless it is specifically exempt from taxation under the law. The tax chargeable
may either be corporate income tax (CIT) at 30% levied on adjusted taxable profit (for
limited liability entities) or withholding tax (WHT) at 15%.

Resident entities are taxed on both domestic and foreign-sourced income, while non-
resident entities are taxed on income sourced through a permanent establishment (PE).

The standard CIT rate is 30%; however, small businesses and individuals (whose
business has a turnover of less than 20 million Rwanda francs [RWF] or 34,500 United
State dollars [USD] in a tax period) pay profit tax at the rate of 4% of turnover.

Special CIT regimes

There are special CIT rates for certain industries or sectors of the economy.

Newly listed companies on capital markets are taxed as follows for a period of five years:

- If a company sells at least 20% of their shares to the public, the CIT rate is 28%.
- If a company sells at least 30% of their shares to the public, the CIT rate is 25%.
- If a company sells at least 40% of their shares to the public, the CIT rate is 20%.

Venture capital companies registered with the Capital Markets Authority in Rwanda
enjoy a CIT rate of 0% for a period of five years. This is also the same rate applicable to
companies that carry out microfinance activities.

Investment entities that operate in a Free Trade Zone or foreign companies that have
their headquarters in Rwanda pay CIT at 0%.

Corporate residence

Rwanda incorporated companies or associations are treated as Rwanda resident
entities. In addition, companies incorporated overseas are also treated as Rwandan

resident companies if they have a place of effective management in Rwanda at any time during the tax period. The term 'effective management' is not defined in the tax law.

Rwandan government companies are also considered to be residents in Rwanda.

Permanent establishment (PE)

The definition of a PE for Rwanda is largely based on the Organisation for Economic Co-operation and Development (OECD) Model Tax Convention definition. According to Rwandan tax law, a PE means a fixed place of business through which the business of a person is wholly or partially carried on.

For non-resident companies, CIT liability will be arise if they have a PE in Rwanda through which a trade is carried on. The profits attributable to the PE will be taxed in Rwanda. However, there are no rules or guidance on how the PE's profit should be evaluated for Rwanda tax purposes. The general understanding is that entities are required to use transfer pricing methods to determine the level of profits that should be attributable to the PE based on the functions it performs.

In particular, the existence of the following triggers a PE: an administrative branch; a factory; a workshop; a mine, quarry, or any other place for the exploitation of natural resources; a building site; or a place where construction or assembly works are carried out.

There are a number of specific exceptions from the definition of a PE. A person is deemed not to have a PE if that person:

a. uses facilities solely for the purpose of storage or display of goods or merchandise
b. maintains a stock of goods or merchandise solely for the purpose storage or display
c. maintains a stock of goods or merchandise solely for the purpose of processing by another person
d. has a place of operation aimed purposely at purchasing goods or merchandise or of collecting information related to one's business, or
e. has a place of operation solely for the purpose of carrying on preparations of one's activities and performing any other activities that make them more effective.

Where an agent, except an independent person concerned with (e) above, acts on behalf of a company (or person) and the agent has capacity to conclude contracts in the name of that company, the company is considered as having a PE in respect of activities one's agent undertakes except if such activities of the agent are limited to those mentioned in (b) above.

However, a person is not considered as having a PE if it carries out activities through a broker, general commission agent, or any other private agent in accordance with procedures of the ordinary course of the activities of such an agent.

A company that controls or is controlled by another company does not of itself constitute either company to be a PE of the other.

Other taxes

Valued-added tax (VAT)

VAT is levied on the supply of taxable goods and services in Rwanda as well as on the importation of taxable goods and services into Rwanda.

Rwanda

The threshold for VAT registration is taxable turnover of RWF 20 million (approximately USD 34,000) in any relevant year or RWF 5 million in a calendar quarter.

The standard VAT rate is 18% and applies to goods and services which are neither exempt from VAT or zero rated.

Export of goods and services are subject to VAT at 0%. Supplies to privileged persons such as goods imported for official purposes of diplomatic missions, supplies made under special arrangements between the government of Rwanda and donors, and supplies or importation made under special technical aid agreements are subject to VAT at 0%. Persons entitled to zero rating of goods or supplies received by them are required to pay VAT at time of receiving the supply and then apply for a refund of the VAT paid.

Some supplies are exempt from VAT, the main categories being supply of water service, goods and services for health purposes, educational materials and services, transport services, books and newspapers, financial and insurance services, lending or leasing interests in land or building for residential purposes, funeral services, energy supplies, all unprocessed agricultural and livestock products, mobile handsets, and equipment for information, communication, and technology.

Suppliers who provide zero-rated services or goods are entitled to recover input VAT incurred in making the supply. This is unlike exempt supplies, where input VAT recovery is not allowed. Therefore, zero rating is preferable to exemption.

Goods and services are treated as taxable supplies where they are supplied by a taxable person (persons registered for VAT). Taxable persons include individuals, companies, partnerships, clubs, or associations who have satisfied VAT registration requirements and are registered for VAT and required by law to charge VAT on taxable supplies made by them.

For a transaction to fall within Rwandan scope of VAT, a supply of goods or services should take place and occur within Rwanda.

However, a person or business may not have a place of business in Rwanda but would be deemed to make a supply of services in Rwanda if the recipient of the service uses or obtains the benefit of the service in Rwanda.

Where a taxable supplier does not have a business establishment or usual place of residence in Rwanda, the Commissioner General may require the taxable supplier to appoint a 'tax agent' to act on one's behalf in matters relating to tax.

Where a local person imports services from a non-resident service provider, the law requires the local recipient to account for VAT reverse charge at 18% of the value of the services procured. The law further provides that the recipient may not reclaim the corresponding input VAT unless the services so procured are not available in the local market. The Rwanda Revenue Authority (RRA) may deem the services to be available in Rwanda even where the actual services procured are of a different specification/ quality standard to those available locally. However, consumers of transport services are allowed to recover the VAT reverse charge even if the services are available in Rwanda.

The VAT returns and relevant payment are due to the RRA on a monthly basis by the 15th day of the following month. However, VAT taxpayers with annual turnover of RWF 200 million (USD 340,000) or below may elect to file VAT returns or make payments on a quarterly or monthly basis.

Rwanda

Customs duties

Rwanda is a member of the East African Community, which uses the East African Community Customs Act (EACMA) for levying import duty. The EACMA prescribes Common External Tariffs (CET) for goods originating outside the Customs Union. Goods are generally subject to import duty of 0% for raw materials and capital goods, 10% for intermediate goods, and 25% for finished goods.

Goods will only enjoy the preferential community tariffs if they meet the EAC Customs Union Rules of Origin.

Certain industries and items are also entitled to exemptions under the customs law (e.g. assemblers of bicycles and motor cycle kits, importers of gas cylinders, certain hotel equipment, solar equipment, and energy saving bulbs).

Enterprises established in Free Trade Zones are exempt from customs duty on machinery and inputs for exported products. There also exists an import duty remission scheme, where import duty may be remitted for raw materials used to manufacture goods for export. This is subject to a requirement for proof of export and execution of the bond.

Excise taxes

Excise tax is imposed on the manufacturer or importation of certain commodities, mainly soft drinks, bottled water, cigarettes, alcohol, fuels, and lubricants.

The following rates apply in respect of products and services for which excise duty is applied:

- Juice from fruits: 5%.
- Soda and lemonade: 39%.
- Mineral water: 10%.
- Beer: 60%.
- Brandies, liquors, and whisky: 70%.
- Cigarettes: 150%.
- Telephone communication: 8%.
- Fuel (excluding benzene), gas oil, and lubricants: 76%.
- Powdered milk: 10%.
- Vehicles with an engine capacity of above 2500cc: 15%.
- Vehicles with an engine capacity of between 1500cc and 2500cc: 10%.
- Vehicles with an engine capacity of less than 1500cc: 5%.

Property taxes/fixed asset tax

Local government levies fixed asset tax on:

- the market value of parcels of land
- the market value of buildings and all improvements thereto registered with the land registration centre and for which the owner has obtained a title deed from the time the building is inhabited or used for other activities
- the value of land exploited for quarry purposes, and
- the market value of usufruct with a title deed.

The tax rate is fixed at a thousandth (1/1000) of the taxable value per year. The tax payment must be paid not later than 31 March of the year.

Rwanda

Transfer taxes
There is a fixed fee of RWF 20,000 on transfer of property. However, no transfer of ownership of a fixed asset can be effected without a tax clearance certificate issued by the concerned decentralised entity.

Stamp taxes
There are no stamp duties in Rwanda.

Trading licence fee
Districts charge a trading licence fee, which is paid by any person who commences a profit-oriented activity in Rwanda. The tax year starts on 1 January and the trading licence fee must be paid for a whole year. If such activity starts after January, the taxpayer must pay a trading licence fee equivalent to the remaining months, including the one in which the activities started.

The tax declaration is done not later than 31 March of the tax year. The trading licence fee is calculated on the basis of turnover, and the amount of the fee varies between RWF 60,000 (for turnover of RWF 40 million) to RWF 250,000 (for turnover of over RWF 150 million).

The turnover applied is as per the amount approved in the previous year by the RRA. Every year, not later than 31 January, the RRA submits the necessary data to the concerned decentralised entity.

There are also different rates for trading licence fee for other small traders, such as small scale technicians, transport activities by boat, traders, and technicians.

Branch income

The tax law does not prescribe special provisions for taxation of branches; consequently, tax rates on the profits of PEs are the same as for domestic corporations. PEs are subject to tax at a rate of 30% and treated as domestic companies.

A branch is considered a PE for the parent company; therefore, it is taxed on the income that is sourced from Rwanda only.

Non-resident entities are taxed in Rwanda through income generated from activities carried on by a PE based in Rwanda.

Income determination

Inventory valuation
Trading stock is valued at a lower of cost price or market price on the last day of the tax period. Work in progress is valued at cost.

Capital gains
There is a general capital gains tax law in Rwanda that provides that capital gains arising from the sale of commercial immovable property are subject to tax at the rate of 30%. However, capital gains arising from secondary market transactions on listed securities are exempt from taxation.

In addition, capital gains and losses arising on reorganisation are exempt from tax in respect of the transferring company. Reorganisation is defined to include the following:

- a merger of two or more resident companies
- the acquisition or a takeover of 50% or more of shares or voting rights by number or value in a resident company in exchange for shares of the purchasing company
- the acquisition of 50% or more of the assets and liabilities of a resident company by another resident company solely in exchange of shares in the purchasing company, or
- splitting of a resident company into two or more resident companies.

Dividend income
Dividend income includes income from shares and similar income distributed by companies, cooperative societies, public business enterprise, and partnerships. Dividend income is subject to WHT at flat rate of 15%.

If dividend distribution has been subjected to WHT, this becomes the final tax.

In determination of taxable business profit of a resident company or partnership, dividends and other profit-shares received from a resident entity are therefore excluded.

Interest income
Interest income includes income from loans, deposits, guarantees, and current accounts. It also includes income from government securities, income from bonds, and negotiable securities issued by public and private companies income from cash bonds.

Interest income is subject to WHT at flat rate of 15%.

Foreign income
Income from business carried out outside Rwanda by resident companies and enterprises is taxed on a worldwide basis. However, a foreign tax credit is granted in respect of taxes paid on the foreign income, subject to the limit of the tax that would have been paid in Rwanda on the same income.

Deductions

A trading company is generally permitted to deduct expenses that are incurred wholly and exclusively for purposes of the company's trade, provided these costs are not capital in nature and are charged to the profit and loss account.

The Rwandan tax law stipulates that deductible expenses should fulfill the following conditions:

- Used for direct purpose of and in normal course of business.
- Actual expenses substantiated by proper documents.
- Result in a decrease in net assets.
- Used for activities related to the tax period in which they are incurred.

Depreciation and amortisation
Accounting depreciation of fixed assets is not allowable as a deduction for tax purposes. The same applies in the case of amortisation of assets. However, businesses are allowed

Rwanda

specified deductions, referred to as tax depreciation in respect of specified classes of assets. This is deducted in arriving at taxable income.

Tax depreciation allowance is granted to persons who own depreciable assets at the end of the tax period and use such assets in the production of the income.

Land, fine arts, antiquities, jewellery, and any other assets that are not subject to wear and tear or obsolescence are not granted tax depreciation. Cost of refining or reconstruction of building, equipment, and heavy machinery fixed to the walls attract tax depreciation at the rate of 5%.

Intangible assets, including goodwill that is purchased from third party, enjoy tax depreciation at rate of 10%, while computers and accessories, information and communication systems, software products, and data equipment are granted tax depreciation at 50%.

Tax depreciation allowance is also available on all other classes at rate of 25%.

There is also an enhanced allowance in the form of an investment allowance that is granted to investors where they incur an investment of at least RWF 30 million (USD 50,000). The rate is 40% where the investment is within Kigali city or 50% where the investment is within priority sectors defined by the Rwandan Investment Code or registered business located outside Kigali. Businesses are required to hold the investment for at least three years in order to benefit from the investment allowance.

Goodwill

As already mentioned above, purchased goodwill will attract tax depreciation at the rate of 10%, which is an allowable deduction. However, amortisation of goodwill is not tax deductible.

Start-up expenses

There is no clear guidance on the tax treatment of start-up expenses. However, in practice, start-up expenses of a capital nature are not allowable for tax purposes. Where they relate to purchase of assets, respective tax depreciation is claimed. Start-up expenses of a revenue nature are tax deductible.

Interest expenses

Interest on borrowed money used for earning business profit or interest in respect of an amount payable for property acquired to earn income is deductible, provided the interest paid is pursuant to a legal obligation and is reasonable in the circumstances.

Thin capitalisation rules can limit interest deductions when debt owed to related entities exceeds four times the amount of the corporation's equity. Thin capitalisation does not apply to banks and insurance companies.

Bad debt

A bad debt provision will be deductible for tax purposes if it fulfils the following conditions:

- The amount was previously included in the income of the taxpayer.
- Debt is written off in the books of accounts.
- If all possible steps have been pursued by the taxpayer, and there is concrete proof that the debtor is insolvent.

It is the last condition that makes the criteria difficult to satisfy, and local taxpayers rarely obtain bad debt relief in practice.

However, licensed commercial banks and leasing entities duly licensed as such are allowed to deduct, in determining business profit, any increase of the mandatory reserve for non-performing loans as required by the directives related to management of bank loans and similar institutions of the National Bank of Rwanda. Similarly, the business profit is increased by the entire amount recovered from bad debts deducted from such reserves.

Charitable contributions
Donations and gifts to charitable organisations and other non-profit making organisations are tax deductible where the amounts are less than 1% of turnover. However, donations to profit making organisations are not allowed for tax, irrespective of the amount.

Fines and penalties
Fines and penalties imposed for breaking the law or for statutory offences, such as payment of taxes late, are not tax deductible.

The law does not specify which type of non-statutory fines or penalties are not allowed for tax. For example, there is no guidance on whether fines or penalties paid for breach of contract is deductible or not.

Taxes
Income tax paid on business profit and recoverable VAT are not-deductible for tax purposes. This includes any back taxes paid by the business.

Net operating losses
Tax losses can be carried forward for the next five tax periods, earlier losses being deducted before later losses.

If during a tax period, the direct or indirect ownership of the share capital or the voting rights of an unlisted company changes more than 25% by value or by number, such a company is restricted from carrying forward losses incurred during the tax period and previous tax periods.

Payments to foreign affiliates
Royalties, management fees, and similar payments to affiliated non-residents are deductible expenses to the extent that they are incurred to earn income of the Rwandan company and the payments adhere to the arm's-length principle and comply with transfer pricing requirements.

Group taxation

There is no provision for group taxation in Rwanda. Each individual corporate group member is required to submit their own tax return on a stand-alone basis.

Transfer pricing
Rwandan transfer pricing legislation and the prescribed transfer pricing methods are generally consistent with the OECD guidelines. The law requires that transactions between related parties be carried out under the arm's-length principle.

Rwanda

The tax law empowers the Commissioner General to adjust profits earned between related parties if he considers that the trading arrangements between related parties do not adhere to the arm's-length principle. The arm's-length principle requires that transfer prices charged between related parties are equivalent to those that would be charged between independent parties in the same circumstances.

Rwanda operates a self-assessment system; therefore, taxpayers are obliged to self assess their compliance to the tax legislation, which includes transfer pricing policy. However, there are no specific transfer pricing documentation requirements currently in place.

Rwanda's transfer pricing legislation provides an opportunity for advance pricing agreements (APAs) with the revenue authority, a progressive development giving businesses operating in Rwanda a greater degree of certainty. Taxpayers can discuss and negotiate their transfer pricing arrangements with the revenue authority and obtain an advance ruling confirming that their transfer pricing arrangement is appropriate. This is intended to minimise the potential for future disputes.

Thin capitalisation
The interest paid on loans and advances from related entities is not tax deductible to the extent that the total amount of loans/advances exceeds four times the amount of equity during the tax period. For purposes of determining the above, equity excludes provisions and reserves. This provision does not apply to commercial banks and insurance companies.

Tax credits and incentives

A variety of tax incentives are given in the form of enhanced tax depreciation allowances (known as capital allowances). The incentives are granted based on the type of assets purchased and used for business and the amount of investment made (*see Depreciation and amortisation in the Deductions section*).

There are also tax incentives in the form of lower CIT rates (*see Special CIT regimes in the Taxes on corporate income section*). These are provided for certain sectors, such as microfinance companies, venture capital companies registered with Capital Markets Authority, and newly listed companies.

Rwanda also grants tax incentives in the form of profit tax discounts. This is based on the number of Rwandans employed and maintained during a six-month period. The rate of profit tax discount ranges between 2% (for employees between 100 to 200 Rwandans) to 7% (where a company employs more than 900 Rwandans).

Companies that export commodities and services that bring into the country export revenue are also entitled to profit discount as follows: between USD 3 million to USD 5 million, the discount is 3%; over USD 5 million, the discount is 5%.

Foreign tax credit
Rwanda allows a foreign tax credit on income generated from business activities performed abroad by a tax resident. The income tax payable is offset by the foreign tax paid on that income. However, the foreign credit is limited to the amount of tax that would have been applicable on that income in Rwanda.

The credit is allowed where it is supported by appropriate evidence, such as a tax declaration, a WHT certificate, or any other similar acceptable document.

Withholding taxes

A resident individual or resident entity is required to deduct a WHT of 15% when making the following payments:

- Interest.
- Dividends.
- Royalties.
- Service fees, including management and technical service fees with the exclusion of international transport.
- Performance payments made to artists, a musician, or a sports person.
- Lottery and other gambling proceeds.
- Goods supplied by companies or physical persons not registered in tax administration.

There is also a WHT of 5% that is applicable on goods imported for commercial use. Public institutions are required to retain 3% on payments to winners of public tenders. However, businesses that posses a tax clearance certificate are exempted from deduction of the above WHT.

The WHT deducted should be remitted to the RRA within 15 days following the month of deduction.

Rwanda has double tax treaties (DTTs) with Belgium, Mauritius, and South Africa.

The DTT between Rwanda and Belgium provide for a lower rate of 10% on interest and royalties, but 15% on dividends.

The DTT between Rwanda and Mauritius provides for a 0% rate of WHT on management and professional fees, dividends, and interest income.

The DTT between Rwanda and South Africa provides for a lower WHT rate of 10%.

The DTT agreements contain conditions to be complied with for the preferential rates to apply; therefore, it is recommended that professional advice is sought before application.

Tax administration

Taxable period
The normal taxable period is between January and December. However, a different tax period can be allowed on approval by the Minister of Finance.

Tax returns
Companies are assessed with reference to accounting periods. This refers to the period for which a company prepares its accounts. However, an accounting period for CIT purposes cannot exceed 12 months, so companies preparing statutory accounts for longer than 12 months need to prepare more than one CIT return.

Rwanda

Rwanda operates a self-assessment regime. Quarterly tax returns are due on 30 June, 30 September, and 31 December (or by the sixth, ninth, and 12th month of the tax period). The annual tax return/declaration must be filed within three months after the tax period. The tax declaration must include audited financial statements as well as any other documents that may be requested by the tax administration.

Payment of tax

Advance CIT is payable in three instalments. Tax payments are due on 30 June, 30 September, and 31 December (or by the sixth, ninth, and 12th month of the tax period). Each instalment is 25% of the tax liability as calculated in the tax return/declaration of the previous tax period. This amount can be reduced by WHT paid during the tax period.

Audit cycle

Large taxpayers are selected for audit by the revenue authority on a regular basis. The revenue authority tends to audit two tax periods, but this can be extended on request by the taxpayer. Most audits are carried out onsite. From 26 March 2012, the RRA may conduct a desk audit of taxpayer's tax affairs where they note discrepancies on tax returns filed by the taxpayer or anomalies with turnover or any other situations that justify an audit.

Under normal in-depth audits, the RRA is required to issue a taxpayer with a draft notice of assessment following the completion of the field audit. The draft assessment is referred to as a rectification note. The taxpayer is granted 30 days within which to respond. In case the tax issues are not resolved, a final notice of assessment is issued. The taxpayer is allowed 30 days within which to appeal. Once an appeal is submitted to the Commissioner General, the RRA has 30 days within which to respond to the objection. This can be extended by another 30 days but not beyond this period. At this stage, the appeal is handled by the appeal committee, and the taxpayer and the taxpayer's agent are invited for a meeting to provide explanations.

Once the final assessment is issued, the tax due is payable, although the Commissioner has powers to suspend the payment pending the determination of the appeal.

A taxpayer that disagrees with response on the final assessment can appeal to the high court within 30 days.

Statute of limitations

Under the recent law, the revenue authority now has powers to audit a taxpayer for a period going back ten years. Taxpayers are now required to keep their records for a period of ten years.

Topics of focus for tax authorities

Topics of interest for the RRA include:

- Deduction of WHT on payments to non-resident persons and reverse VAT.
- Treatment of capital gains on disposal of assets.
- Recovery of reverse VAT on services that are regarded as being available on local market.
- Reconciliation of turnover per financial statements to receipts as per taxpayer bank statements.

Saint Kitts and Nevis

PwC contact

Jefferson Hunte
PricewaterhouseCoopers
PO Box 1038
Basseterre
St Kitts & Nevis
Tel: +1 869 466 8200
Email: jefferson.hunte@ag.pwc.com

Significant developments

There were no significant corporate tax developments during 2011; however, the government of Saint Kitts and Nevis (St. Kitts-Nevis) has indicated that it intends to introduce a new Corporate Income Tax Act in 2012.

Taxes on corporate income

Companies incorporated in St. Kitts-Nevis pay corporate income tax (CIT) on their worldwide income with relief available under existing double taxation agreements (DTAs). Non-resident companies deriving income from St. Kitts-Nevis are liable for CIT and should be registered if they have a physical presence in St. Kitts-Nevis.

St. Kitts-Nevis imposes CIT at a flat rate of 35%.

Taxable income or assessable income is ascertained by deducting from income all expenses that are wholly and exclusively incurred during the year in the production of the income. Assessable income is normally arrived at by adjusting the net profit per the financial statements for non-taxable income, non-deductible expenses, and prior period losses up to 50% of chargeable income.

Where a person resident in St. Kitts-Nevis makes to another person not resident in St. Kitts-Nevis a payment, *as noted in the Withholding taxes section*, then a withholding tax (WHT) at a rate of 10% must be deducted and remitted to the Inland Revenue within 15 days.

A company which carries on business exclusively with persons who are not resident in St. Kitts-Nevis is exempt from all income, capital gains, and WHTs.

Companies registered under the Condominium Act are governed by that act and are not required to pay CIT.

Corporate residence

A corporation is deemed to be resident if it is incorporated in St. Kitts-Nevis or if it is registered as an external company doing business in St. Kitts-Nevis under the Companies Act.

Permanent establishment (PE)
A PE is not defined in the Income Tax Act; however, any company which would meet the general definition of a PE must be registered.

Saint Kitts and Nevis

....

Other taxes

Value-added tax (VAT)
The standard VAT rate is 17%, while hotel accommodation, tour operators, and restaurants carry a reduced rate of 10%.

Persons who have made or are likely to make taxable supplies in excess of 96,000 East Caribbean dollars (XCD) for certain professional services and XCD 150,000 for other business activities in a continuous period of 12 calendar months are required to register for VAT.

Customs duties
All imports are subject to import duties, VAT, and customs service tax (CST). In all instances, certain exemptions will apply.

Customs duty is levied on a wide range of imported goods at rates from 0% to 70% as specified in the Custom Duties Act. VAT is applied at a rate of 17%, and CST at a rate of 6%. Customs duty is levied on goods based on the cost, insurance, and freight (CIF) values and rates determined by the Caribbean Community (CARICOM) Common External Tariff.

Excise tax
The excise tax applies to a small range of goods, such as alcoholic beverages, tobacco products, petroleum products, motor cycles, aerated beverages, and firearms. The excise tax rate ranges between 5% and 25%.

Property tax

Saint Kitts
Property tax in Saint Kitts is levied at varied rates on the basis of the market value of the real property (including land and building as assessed by the Chief Valuation Officer) and its class.

Property classes and rates of tax are as follows:

- Residential use property: 0.2%.
- Commercial use property: 0.3%.

Annual allowances and tax rebates are available as follows:

- Residential use property and condominium allowance of XCD 80,000 from the taxable value.
- No property tax will be assessed on any buildings, condominiums, etc. that are under construction.
- New residential use property and condominiums are exempt from tax for one year from the date certified by the valuation officer.

Note that residential use properties located in the South East Peninsula are assigned values based on fixed rates for land (XCD 20 per square foot) and building (XCD 300 per square foot). Property tax is then applied at a rate of 0.2%.

Where property situated in the South East Peninsula area is not developed within five years, a surcharge can be assessed at the rate of 1% of the assessed market value per annum, and increased annually at the rate of 1% thereafter until it reaches a maximum

Saint Kitts and Nevis

rate of 5% of the assessed market value while the property remains undeveloped. If property is less than one acre, undeveloped, and owned by a resident for the purpose of erecting a house, such property shall be exempt from the surcharge upon application in writing to the Comptroller of Inland Revenue.

Property tax is payable on or before 30 June of each year and is deemed to be in default if not paid within 30 days of becoming due. Interest is charged at a rate of 12% per annum on the unpaid taxes.

Nevis

Property tax in Nevis is levied at varied rates on the basis of the market value of the real property (including land and building as assessed by the Chief Valuation Officer) and its class.

Property class and rates are as follows:

Property class	Building tax rate (%)	Land tax rate (%)
Residential	0.156	0.075
Commercial	0.3	0.2
Accommodation	0.3	0.2
Certified farming	0	0.01
Institutional	0.2	0.15

Commercial use property is defined as property which does not include accommodation use property or property used for certified farming operations.

Accommodation use property is defined as property for short term accommodation and includes a guest house.

Annual allowances and tax rebates are available as follows:

- Residential use property and condominium allowance of XCD 80,000 from the taxable value.
- No property tax will be assessed on any buildings, condominiums, etc. that are under construction.

Property tax is payable on or before 30 June of each year and is deemed to be in default if not paid within 30 days of becoming due. Interest is charged at a rate of 12% per annum on the unpaid taxes.

Alien land holding licences

To hold land as an owner, a non-citizen must first obtain an alien land holding licence and pay 10% of the market value of property or XCD 750, whichever is greater.

A non-citizen is required to obtain a licence to hold shares in a company which owns land, to vote at shareholders meetings of the company, and to be a director of the company. Each licence costs XCD 250.

If a non-citizen purchases land in the Frigate Bay area, then there is no requirement to obtain a licence and only a minimal fee of XCD 50 is payable.

S

Saint Kitts and Nevis

If a non-citizen wishes to purchase land in the South East Peninsula, the non-citizen is required to obtain a licence prior to purchasing the property; however, the payment of the 10% license fee will be waived.

Stamp duty
Stamp duty applies to a very wide range of transactions (e.g. bill of sale, leases, mortgages, contract, bill of lading). Stamp duty on transfer of real property, transfer of shares, mortgages, and bank loans to aliens is specifically covered below.

Transfer of real property
Stamp duty is levied on the consideration for the sale or the value of property as assessed by the Chief Valuation Officer, whichever is higher.

The vendor is responsible for the payment of all stamp duty on property transfers on the following basis:

	Type of property transfer	Rate
a.	Transfer of property for consideration in money or value in kind of not less than the value of the property	12%
b.	Transfer of property for consideration in money or value in kind of less than the value of the property	12%
c.	Transfer of property without consideration in money or value in kind	6%
d.	Transfer of property in any Special Development Area other than the South East Peninsula	14%
e.	Transfer of property situated in the South East Peninsula	18.5%
f.	Transfer of property other than stock or debenture stock or funded debt or land	2%
g.	Transfer of property between husband and wife and between parents and children and vice versa	XCD 100
h.	Transfer of land by will or by similar instrument	XCD 100
i.	Transfer of registered condominium units	5%

Where a developer has obtained concessions in connection with a house or building constructed on the land being transferred, the developer is required to pay stamp duty on the same basis as noted in a, b, and c above.

Where a developer has obtained concessions in connection with a house or building to be constructed on the land being transferred, then the developer will be required to pay stamp duty initially on the land on the same basis as noted in a, b, and c above. However, when the house or building is subsequently constructed on the land with the aid of the concession, the owner of the building shall pay stamp duty on the house or building as provided in a, b, and c above as if the concessions or any part thereof had not been utilised.

Where a developer has not obtained concessions in connection with a house or building constructed on the land being transferred, the developer will be required to pay stamp duty on the same basis as noted in a, b, and c in respect of the land only.

Transfer of shares
Stamp duty is levied on the value of the consideration for the sale of shares or debentures issued by or on behalf of a company or at the value assessed by the Chief Valuation Officer, whichever is higher. The stamp duty is levied at a rate of 2%. If

the company owns property and its value exceeds 50% of the value of the company's assets, then the stamp duty is calculated using the applicable rate on the transfer of real property (*see above*).

Mortgages
Stamp duty is levied on the total amount secured and is applicable to both the registration and discharge of the mortgage. The standard rate is 1%. For amounts secured in relation to a Special Development Area, the rate is 2%.

Bank loans to aliens
Stamp duty is levied on the total amount of a bank loan to aliens. The standard rate is 2.5%. For loans to finance development in a Special Development Area, the rate is 5%.

Life insurance premium tax
A premium tax of 5% is levied on the premium income of all life insurance companies, whether resident or non-resident. In addition, a registration fee of XCD 2 per XCD 1,000 of income or XCD 30, whichever is less, must be paid to the Comptroller of Inland Revenue.

General insurance premium tax
A premium tax of 5% is levied on the premium income (net of agent's commission) of all general insurance companies, whether resident or non-resident.

Branch income

Branch income is taxed on the same basis and at the same rate as the income of a corporation. A resident branch of a foreign company shall be regarded as a separate company and shall be taxed on the same basis as that of a locally registered corporation.

Recharges of expenses from head office to the branch will be subject to WHT at a rate of 10%; however, the recharges have to be justified and cannot be based on a percentage allocation.

Income determination

Inventory valuation
Inventories are generally stated at the lower of cost or net realisable value. The first in first out (FIFO) and average cost methods of valuation are generally used for book and tax purposes. However, the Comptroller of Inland Revenue will normally accept a method of valuation that conforms to standard accounting practice in the trade concerned. The last in first out (LIFO) method is not permitted for tax or book purposes.

Capital gains
Capital gains tax will be imposed if an asset is sold within one year of the date of acquisition. The maximum rate of tax will be one half the CIT rate. Assets sold after one year will not attract capital gains tax.

Dividend income
Dividends received by a company resident in St. Kitts-Nevis from another company resident in St. Kitts-Nevis are taxed at source at the CIT rate of 35%. Credit is given to the recipient for the tax on the dividend in computing the tax liability.

Saint Kitts and Nevis

Interest income

Interest income received by a company registered in St. Kitts is taxed at the CIT rate of 35%. Interest earned on local and other CARICOM government securities are normally exempt from the payment of CIT.

Foreign income

A St. Kitts-Nevis corporation is taxed on foreign branch income when earned and on foreign dividends when received. Double taxation is avoided by means of foreign tax credits where active tax treaties exist and through deduction of foreign income taxes in other cases (the United Kingdom [UK] and CARICOM). There is also relief from British Commonwealth taxes. *See Foreign tax credit in the Tax credits and incentives section for more information.*

Deductions

Depreciation

Depreciation allowed for tax purposes is computed by the diminishing-balance method at prescribed rates. An initial allowance of 20% is granted on industrial buildings or structures and in respect of capital expenditure incurred on plant and machinery by a person carrying on a trade or undertaking, as defined. In addition, an annual allowance of between 2% and 5% is allowed on all buildings constructed after 1 March 1994. Concrete buildings are depreciated at a rate of 2%, while the rate varies for other buildings depending on the type of material used in construction. Conformity between book and tax depreciation is not required.

Any gain on the sale of depreciated assets is taxable as ordinary income up to the amount of tax depreciation recaptured.

Initial allowances and annual allowances cannot reduce the tax that would have been otherwise payable by more than 50%. Any initial allowance or annual allowance not utilised may be carried forward indefinitely.

Goodwill

Goodwill and trademarks are not depreciating assets, and amortisation is not allowed.

Start-up expense

There are no specific provisions in relation to deductions for start-up expenses. However, the policy is that certain start-up expenses, such as costs of incorporation and other initial start-up costs, may qualify for a three to five year straight-line write-off, depending on the total dollar value.

Interest expenses

No specific restrictions will apply to interest paid on loans owing to shareholders, directors, their spouses, children or relatives, or to any related parties. Interest is only deductible to the extent that it was incurred in producing chargeable income.

Restriction on bad debts

Specific bad or doubtful debts in excess of 5% of total trade receivables will not be allowed as a deduction.

Charitable donations

Charitable donations are not deductible for tax purposes.

Contributions to a pension fund

Contributions made by an employer to a pension fund (approved by the Comptroller) on behalf of its employees are deductible, up to a maximum of 5% of annual earnings of the employee or a maximum of XCD 2,000. Application should be made to the Ministry of Finance or to the Pension Fund Committee.

Restriction on compensation expenses

Salaries, wages, leave pay, fee, commission, bonus, gratuity, or any other perquisite or such other payment which an employee of a company receives in the course of one's employment or the value of any benefit to such employee or to any member of an employee's family in excess of XCD 60,000 per annum will not be allowed as a deduction from chargeable profit. However, if a person receives XCD 180,000 in annual income, a deduction can be claimed in three equal amounts of XCD 60,000 from three different branches, subsidiaries, or other related entities. Effective 1 January 2012, the XCD 60,000 deduction for personal income will now only be deductible from one related group entity.

Fines and penalties

Fines and penalties imposed under tax laws of St. Kitts are not deductible expenses.

Taxes

There are no provisions in the Income Tax Act in relation to the deductibility of taxes paid by a company. However, in general, VAT, VAT input tax, and adjustments under the VAT Act are disregarded for income tax purposes. Other taxes, including property tax, transfer taxes, payroll taxes, insurance, except income tax, and share transfer tax, are deductible to the extent they are incurred in producing chargeable income.

Net operating losses

Income tax losses may be carried forward for five years following the year in which the loss was incurred. However, the chargeable income of a company after deducting initial and annual capital allowances in any one income year may not be reduced by more than 50% by losses brought forward. No carryback of losses is permitted.

Payments to foreign affiliates

A company incorporated in St. Kitts-Nevis may claim a deduction for royalties, management fees, and interest charges paid to foreign affiliates, provided the payments are equal to or less than what the corporation would pay to an unrelated entity. The deductibility of any payments to a foreign affiliate will be subject to an arm's-length test, and WHT will be payable at a rate of 10%.

S

Group taxation

Group taxation is not permitted in St. Kitts-Nevis.

Transfer pricing

There are no provisions for transfer pricing in the tax laws of St. Kitts-Nevis.

Thin capitalisation

There are no provisions for thin capitalisation in the tax laws of St. Kitts-Nevis.

Saint Kitts and Nevis

Tax credits and incentives

Tax incentives are currently available under the following legislation.

Income Tax Act, No. 17 of 1966

The Income Tax Act provides that if a company is licensed under the Hotel Aids Ordinance and constructs a hotel with more than 30 rooms, the hotel will receive an exemption from CIT for a period of ten years beginning on the day it is first open for business. If the hotel has less than 30 rooms, then it will be entitled to a five year tax holiday. During the tax holiday period, no initial deductions or annual capital allowance deductions shall be allowed. Thereafter, only the annual allowance will be allowed and will be computed on the total capital expenditure incurred during the holiday period less any assets sold. The net losses arising during the tax holiday period (i.e. the excess of accumulated tax losses over total profits) may be carried forward and reduced against profits following the expiration of the tax holiday in accordance with the normal rules for set-off of losses.

The Income Tax Act also provides that if a licence is granted to a pioneer manufacturer under the Pioneer Industries Act, the manufacturer is entitled to a five year tax holiday (or up to ten years, at the discretion of the government) as provided in the licence.

Hotel Aids Act

The Hotel Aids Act provides that a licence may be granted to any person who desires to construct or extend an existing hotel to import building material and equipment free from import duties as specified in the licence for use in the construction of the hotel and to furnish and equip the hotel. The holder of a licence may not dispose of any hotel equipment within three years of being imported free of duties and taxes. Permission must be received from the Comptroller of Customs to dispose of any building material and hotel equipment within the three year period.

Fiscal Incentives Act

The Fiscal Incentives Act provides that if a company is declared to be an approved enterprise to manufacture certain 'approved products', then the manufacturer is entitled to a tax holiday period of between ten and 15 years depending on the classification of the approved enterprise. The net losses arising during the tax holiday period (i.e. excess of all losses over all profits) may be carried forward and set off against profits of the approved enterprise for the five year period following the tax holiday period.

Small Business Development Act, 2009

The Small Business Development Act provides the framework for the promotion of investment opportunities in St. Kitts-Nevis by introducing a system of registration of small businesses and a range of incentives which are available to locals. The available incentives and concessions to any small business that would be entitled for consideration are as follows:

* Concession on consumption tax applicable to professionals (e.g. engineers, doctors).
* Reduction on CIT for a minimum of three years to a maximum of five years.
* Relief on CIT by way of an allowable deduction on any monies borrowed from any financial institution including any bank, non-bank, or credit union.
* Export incentives.
* Rebate on CIT.
* Exemption from or reduction in customs duty on inputs imported for use in the small business.

Saint Kitts and Nevis

- Exemption from or reduction in customs duty on any plant, machinery, equipment, or motor vehicle imported for use in the small business.
- Reduction of property tax of up to 75%.

A small business to which this Act applies must meet all of the following criteria:

- No more than 25 employees.
- Net assets or paid up capital does not exceed XCD 1 million.
- Annual sales that do not exceed XCD 2 million.
- Owned by citizens of St. Kitts-Nevis.
- Not more than 25% owned or controlled by a company whose annual turnover or net assets exceed the limits noted above or by a subsidiary of a larger company.
- The composition of the board of directors is not controlled by a company whose annual turnover exceeds the criteria above.
- Has no agreement for managerial or other services to persons who are not citizens of St. Kitts-Nevis or other CARICOM territories.

The registration fee for an approved small business status is XCD 100. Each approved small business must, within six months after the end of its financial year, submit to the Registrar (person designated by the Minister to perform the functions of Registrar of Small Businesses) audited financial statements of its accounts audited by an auditor in accordance with generally accepted international auditing standards.

Other incentives
Approved manufacturing, agricultural, and tourist ventures are permitted to import building material and equipment free of customs duties.

A Memorandum of Understanding (MOU) between the government and small hotel operators provides for certain conditions under which small hotel operators will be eligible for duty free concessions on the refurbishment of their facilities every seven years, and on food and wine for their restaurant facilities where applicable. For the purposes of this new incentive package, a small hotel is defined as a hotel consisting of at least ten rooms and not exceeding 99 rooms.

Foreign tax credit
Double taxation is avoided by means of foreign tax credits where active tax treaties exist and through deduction of foreign income taxes in other cases (the United Kingdom and CARICOM). A foreign tax credit is also available to persons in St. Kitts-Nevis who have paid or are liable to pay British Commonwealth income tax.

Residents
The relief available from tax in St. Kitts-Nevis for a person resident in St. Kitts-Nevis from tax paid in St. Kitts-Nevis is the British Commonwealth income tax rate if that rate does not exceed one-half the tax rate in St. Kitts-Nevis. If the British Commonwealth income tax rate exceeds the St. Kitts-Nevis tax rate, then the relief will be limited to one-half the tax rate in St. Kitts-Nevis.

Non-residents
The relief available from tax in St. Kitts-Nevis for a person not resident in St. Kitts-Nevis from tax paid in St. Kitts-Nevis is one-half the British Commonwealth income tax rate if that rate does not exceed the tax rate in St. Kitts-Nevis. In any other case, the relief will be limited to the amount by which the St. Kitts-Nevis tax rate exceeded one-half the rate of British Commonwealth income tax.

Saint Kitts and Nevis

Withholding taxes

A WHT at the rate of 10% should be withheld from payments made to non-residents in respect of the following:

- Dividends.
- Interest, annuity, premium, and discount.
- Rent, lease, contract, and royalty payments.
- A natural resource payment.
- Commissions, remuneration, fees, and licences.
- Charges for the provision of personal services, commercial advice, and managerial skills.
- Administration, management, or head office expenses.
- Profit.
- Technical, professional, vocational, and any other service fees.
- Accounting, actuarial, legal, and audit expenses.
- Non-life insurance premiums.
- Any other annual or periodic payment or distribution.

Tax treaties
There is a tax treaty with the United Kingdom and a DTA between member states of CARICOM.

Tax administration

Taxable period
Taxes are assessed on a fiscal-year basis.

Tax returns
The taxpayer must file an information return on Form CIT-01 by the 15th day of the fourth month after the fiscal year end along with the financial statements. The authorities either accept the self-assessment or issue a revised assessment. If a return is not filed on a timely basis, the authorities have the power to issue estimated assessments. There is a 2.5% penalty for late filing (minimum of XCD 1).

The taxpayer can object to assessments raised within one month and ask the Comptroller of Inland Revenue to review and revise. In the event that the objection is unsuccessful, the taxpayer may appeal to the Commissioners of Income Tax.

Payment of tax
Advance tax is payable in quarterly instalments on 15 March, 15 June, 15 September, and 15 December of each year and is ordinarily based on the tax chargeable and assessed in the previous fiscal year. The standard amount of each instalment is determined as one-fourth of the tax chargeable in the previous fiscal year. If the assessment for the prior year has not been finalised, the Comptroller of Inland Revenue can raise an assessment based on best judgment.

The balance of tax due after the final assessment is issued, as notified in the assessment, is payable on or before the 15th day of the fourth month after the fiscal year end. If the Comptroller of Inland Revenue revises the assessment, then payment of the balance of taxes due is due one month after the date of issue of the revised assessment.

Tax is deemed to be in default if not paid by the 15th day of the fourth month after the fiscal year end or within one month of the date of the notice of assessment, whichever is later. Interest of 1% per month or 12% per annum is charged on unpaid taxes in default.

Statute of limitations

Assessments may be reviewed and revised by the Comptroller of Inland Revenue within the year of assessment or within six years of the expiration of the assessment year.

Saint Lucia

PwC contact

Richard Peterkin
PricewaterhouseCoopers
Pointe Seraphine
Castries, St. Lucia
Tel: +1 758 456 2600 Ext. 2626
Email: richard.n.peterkin@lc.pwc.com

Significant developments

The government of Saint Lucia will introduce the value-added tax (VAT) on
1 September 2012. In doing so, the government will fulfil undertakings given to
international institutions that VAT would be introduced during this financial year.

In the Budget Statement delivered by the Prime Minister and Minister of Finance on
8 May 2012, the overall rationale for the introduction of a VAT as a general tax on
consumption is to broaden the tax base and move towards a system that decreases the
tax burden on income in favour of consumption. This would allow for a removal of a
number of other duties and direct taxes; however, consistent with its manifesto, the
government promises it will:

* maintain a basket of goods that will be zero rated and
* delay the introduction of VAT on the payment of bills for electricity and water until
  the government is satisfied that the public is reasonably protected from arbitrary
  increases by the companies that provide these services.

In total, this should result in a simplification of the tax system.

Also, the following new tax measures were introduced:

* Reduce corporate tax after an impact assessment has been done following the
  introduction of VAT.
* Increase application fees for alien's landholding licences from 1,500 East Caribbean
  dollars (XCD) to XCD 4,050.
* Provide a 'short term' opportunity to the hotel sector by waiving 100% of both
  interest charges and penalties within the three-month period 1 June 2012 to 31
  August 2012 for amounts paid towards hotel accommodation tax on principal
  payments and for amounts paid during the six-month period 1 September 2012 to
  31 March 2013 by waiving 100% on penalties and 50% on interest charges.

Earlier this year, the government approved a tax amnesty on outstanding tax arrears
which offers a 100% waiver on interest and penalties on taxes due prior to 1 January
2012.

Taxes on corporate income

Resident companies are taxed on gains or profits accrued directly or indirectly from all
sources, whether in and out of Saint Lucia, and are subject to tax at a flat rate of 30%.
The 30% tax rate is only applicable to companies who prior to income year 2003 have
no tax arrears and have complied with the requirements of any enactment administered

by the Inland Revenue Department. The tax rate of 33.33% will still apply to those companies who have tax arrears and have not complied with the requirement.

Non-resident companies are taxed on Saint Lucia-source income. The gross amount of such income is liable to 25% withholding tax (WHT), while WHT of 15% applies to interest.

Associations of underwriters are taxed at 30% on 10% of the gross premium arising in Saint Lucia, and life insurance companies are taxed at 30% on 10% of the gross investment income arising in Saint Lucia.

Corporate residence

Companies are regarded as resident if they are incorporated in Saint Lucia or managed and controlled through a permanent establishment (PE) in Saint Lucia.

Permanent establishment (PE)
A PE is defined in Saint Lucia as a fixed place or premises through which the business is wholly or partly carried on.

Other taxes

Value-added tax (VAT)
VAT will be implemented in Saint Lucia on 1 September 2012. VAT is designed to streamline the tax system in Saint Lucia. Upon implementation, VAT will replace consumption tax, hotel accommodation tax, motor vehicle rental fee, mobile cellular telephone tax, and the environmental protection levy.

A standard VAT rate of 15% and a rate of 0% will be charged on certain goods and services; however, in respect of the hotel sector and related services, a reduced rate of 8% will apply until 31 March 2013. Between 1 September 2012 and 31 March 2013, the impact on the sector will be assessed and a final determination will be made on the rate to be applied beyond 31 March 2013.

A threshold for registered taxpayers of XCD 180,000 per annum will be established. This means that it is not mandatory for business earning less than XCD 180,000 per annum to register for VAT. The threshold is based on the annual sales turnover of the taxpayer.

A VAT rate of 0% will be legislated on certain supplies. Some of these supplies include, but are not limited to, the following:

- Goods to be exported.
- Goods for sale at duty-free shops.
- Fuel.
- Water.
- Electricity.

The following goods and services will be exempted from payment of VAT, but this list is not exhaustive:

- Domestic residential rental.
- Educational services.

Saint Lucia

- Financial services.
- Insurance services.
- Medical services.
- Local transportation services.
- Certain food items (e.g. chicken, rice, milk, flour, bread).

While the standard VAT rate of 15% will be charged on medical supplies, the government has secured the Caribbean Community and Common Market's (CARICOM's) approval to remove the import duty on medical supplies.

The government has also agreed to the establishment of a special VAT Refund Account in accordance with the provisions of the Financial Administration Act. This is to facilitate the timely processing and payment of refunds to taxpayers.

Consumption tax
Consumption tax is levied on goods manufactured in Saint Lucia and on a wide range of imported goods. Rates range between 5% and 35%. For manufactured goods, the tax is charged on their open market value. For imported articles, consumption tax is charged as a percentage of the cost, insurance, and freight (CIF) value plus customs duty.

With the implementation of VAT on 1 September 2012, consumption tax will be eliminated.

Custom duties
Customs duties are charged on a wide range of imported goods. Exemptions are granted for raw materials and plant and machinery used in manufacturing and for certain items imported by hotels under construction, extension, or refurbishing projects.

Excise tax
Excise taxes are imposed on home-produced goods, mainly liquor, beer, and cigarettes. XCD 1.44 per litre of liquid applies to beer in glass bottles and XCD 3.50 per liquid gallon applies to beers in metal cans.

There is also an excise tax on fuel when fuel is imported by a wholesaler. Tax is included on the price of fuel paid at the gas pump. The tax rate formula is based on the current price provided by the supplier and regulated price at the gas pump.

Commercial property tax
Commercial property tax is currently assessed annually at 0.4% of the open market value of the property. The owner is required to obtain a commercial valuation assessing the open market value of the property. All new commercial properties completed after 1 April 2001 can benefit from a three-year tax exemption from commercial property tax.

Residential property tax
The property tax rate for residential property is 0.25% of the open market value.

Stamp tax
Stamp tax is charged on any document that evidences a legal or contractual relationship between two or more parties. Additionally, many types of commercial and legal documents must be stamped, denoting the payment of taxes, which may be either at a fixed rate or at an *ad valorem* rate, depending, for example, on the value of the property transferred.

The current rate of stamp tax under the stamp duty regulations for the conveyance or transfer on sale of the debenture, stock, debt, or shares of a company and the release, renunciation, or reassignment of any shares or interest in any shares of a company or corporation is the greatest of the following:

- 0.5% of the net value of the assets of the company or corporation.
- XCD 10.
- Provided that at least 75% of the open market value of the assets of the company or corporation is comprised of immovable property, the stamp duty (including vendor's tax) based on the stamp duty on the sale of immovable property that would be payable on a conveyance or transfer on sale of such immovable property, as indicated below:
  - Conveyance or transfer on sale of any immovable property such duty to be paid by the purchaser: 2% *ad valorem*.
  - Conveyance or transfer on sale of any immovable property such duty to be paid by the vendor:
    - where the vendor is not a citizen of Saint Lucia or is a foreign company: 10% *ad valorem*.
    - where the vendor is a citizen of Saint Lucia or is a local company: 2.5% *ad valorem* from XCD 50,000 to XCD 75,000; 3.5% *ad valorem* from XCD 75,001 to XCD 150,000; 5% *ad valorem* from XCD 150,001 and over.

Branch income

The tax rate on branch income is the same as that on income earned by resident companies. No additional tax is withheld on transfers of profits to the head office.

Income determination

Inventory valuation
Stocks generally are valued at the lower of cost or market value. Obsolescence is permitted where it occurs, but there are no provisions to account for monetary inflation on inventory valuation.

Capital gains
There is no tax on capital gains except in instances where such gains comprise a portion of the income-earning activities of the business. In such instances, the corporate tax rate applies.

Dividend income
Dividends are tax exempt in Saint Lucia.

Inter-company dividends
Inter-company dividends are not subject to tax in Saint Lucia.

Interest income
The corporate tax rate applies to interest income. However, income earned on securities issued by member governments of the Eastern Caribbean Central Bank and income accruing from trading in securities under the Securities Act to any citizen or resident of any member state of the Organisation of Eastern Caribbean States or to any company incorporated in and registered in any member state of the Organisation of Eastern Caribbean States is tax exempt.

Saint Lucia

Any expenditure incurred for the purpose of producing exempt income is not deductible.

Royalty and rental income
The corporate tax rate applies to royalty and rental income. However, rental income from a residential accommodation shall be exempt from tax if certain requirements, as defined by regulations, are met.

Foreign exchange gains/losses
Foreign exchange gains or losses arising from foreign exchange transactions on trading items are assessable or deductible as realised gains or losses, if settled within normal credit terms. Gains or losses on other instruments, including inter-company loans, are recognised only when actually realised.

Unrealised exchange gains/losses are not taxable/deductible.

Bribes, kickbacks, illegal payments
Bribes, kickbacks, and illegal payments received by a company are includible in taxable income.

Foreign income
Resident companies are taxed in Saint Lucia on income earned outside Saint Lucia. Reciprocal understandings exist with some countries for the avoidance of double taxation, and foreign tax is allowed as a credit against tax charged in Saint Lucia. Saint Lucia has no tax treaties with other countries, except for the member states that make up CARICOM. There is an agreement among the governments of CARICOM for the avoidance of double taxation. Where no agreement exists, the foreign tax offset is the lesser of the foreign tax paid or the tax payable on that income in Saint Lucia.

Tax deferral is not permitted in Saint Lucia.

....

Deductions

Accrued expenses are deductible as long as they are business related. Contingent liabilities are deductible expenses once they are recognised in the book of accounts.

Depreciation
The following capital allowances are available in Saint Lucia:

- An initial allowance of 20% is granted on the acquisition of industrial, agricultural, and commercial buildings (except for hotels and rental properties); on plant and machinery, including motor vehicles and furniture; and on fixtures and equipment.
- Thereafter, annual allowances for wear and tear, ranging from 10% to 33.33%, are granted on the reducing-balance method, except for industrial and agricultural buildings, which are allowed an annual rate of 5% and commercial buildings (except for hotels and rental properties), which are allowed an annual rate of 2.5%.

The Comptroller of Inland Revenue may also grant, on application, a higher rate for annual allowance for assets that have higher or abnormal wear and tear.

Gains on disposal are taxable as ordinary income to the extent of depreciation recovered, and any proceeds in excess of the cost of the asset are treated as a capital gain, which is not subject to tax. Where the proceeds on disposal are lower than the tax written-down value of the asset, a balancing allowance is granted for the shortfall.

Goodwill
Neither the amortisation of impaired goodwill nor the related write-off of it is an allowable deduction.

Organisational and start-up expenses
All expenditures incurred in connection with incorporation costs for the establishment of a new small business enterprise are allowable deductions. A small business enterprise is an enterprise incorporated during the year of income and

- is wholly owned by citizens of Saint Lucia who have not been owners of previously incorporated businesses in Saint Lucia
- employs not more than 50 persons
- has gross income that does not exceed XCD 1 million
- engages in an activity on the listing of preferred business activities as approved by the Minister of Finance, and
- satisfies the provision of any law in force with respect to micro or small scale business.

Interest expenses
Interest on any loan, including interest payable on debentures, is an allowable deduction to the extent that the amount of such loan was used for the purpose of producing assessable income.

Bad debt
Bad debt expense is deductible provided it has been brought to account in generating the company's assessable income for any income year and that the company has taken all reasonable steps to establish that the collection of such debt is unlikely.

Charitable contributions
Charitable contributions are an allowable deduction when the contributions are made under a deed of covenant for a period of not less than three years to any religious, charitable, medical, or educational institution; sporting body; or fund of a public character, approved by Cabinet, if such contributions are made to the Saint Lucia National Trust. However, the deduction with respect to such contributions shall not exceed 25% of the assessable income of the company for that income year.

Pension expenses
Current annual contributions to an approved pension fund are deductible expenses. However, where a special payment is made to an approved pension fund, in relation to a period of service by an employee prior to the setting up of the approved pension fund, or to meet any actuarially ascertained insufficiency in the resources of the approved pension fund to meet its obligations to its employees, such amount shall be deductible as follows:

(i) Where the special payment does not exceed the current annual contribution, such amount is wholly deductible.
(ii) Where the special payment exceeds the current annual contribution, the special payment is an allowable deduction in such years of income, not exceeding five in number, as in the opinion of the Comptroller is reasonable in the circumstances.

Saint Lucia

(iii) Where under (ii) above, annual deductions are allowable over a number of years of income, the first such deduction is allowable for the income year for which the special payment is made.

Taxes

Consumption taxes paid on goods imported or purchased, and sold in the ordinary course of business, are deductible for tax purposes. Property taxes are deductible where the property is used in producing assessable income. Income taxes, penalties, and interest on tax in arrears are not deductible.

Other significant items

Meals and entertainment, officer's compensation/life insurance, and payment to directors are deductible expenses, provided they are wholly and exclusively incurred by a company during that year of income for the purpose of producing its assessable income.

Net operating losses

Net operating losses may be carried forward for up to six years if the losses have not been fully absorbed earlier. In carrying losses forward, the amount that can be claimed in any subsequent year is restricted to one-half of the assessable income of that year. Losses may not be carried back.

Payments to foreign affiliates

There are no restrictions on the deductibility of interest paid to foreign affiliates if the transaction is carried out at arm's length and at commercial rates. However, deductions for management charges, allocations of head office expenses, royalties, and other charges that are subject to 25% WHT are restricted to the lesser of the aggregate of those charges or 10% of all allowable business deductions, excluding cost of sales and capital allowances.

Group taxation

Group tax filing is not allowed in Saint Lucia; however, group tax relief is available under certain circumstances to allow the trading losses, excluding the current loss, of a resident company within a group to offset the profits of another resident company within the same group. A claim for group relief requires the consent of the Comptroller of the Inland Revenue Department and is only available to resident companies.

Transfer pricing

Related party transactions are accepted if they are made on an arm's-length basis. The Inland Revenue has the power under the Income Tax Act to make any adjustment deemed necessary to place such transactions at arm's length.

Thin capitalisation

No provision exists for thin capitalisation in Saint Lucia.

Tax credits and incentives

Foreign taxes credit

Where income has accrued to a resident and has been taxed in a foreign country with which there is no double tax agreement (DTA), or is income to which a DTA, if there is one, does not relate, credit for tax on such income is allowed for the lesser of the tax payable in the foreign country or the tax charged under Saint Lucia tax law.

Tax holidays

Tax holidays are available for manufacturing companies. The incentives are aimed at increasing the manufacturing base of Saint Lucia, the level of exports, and the use of local materials and labour in production. An approved manufacturing enterprise will be granted a tax holiday up to a maximum of 15 years. In determining the length of the tax holiday, the extent of the local value added to approved products is taken into account.

Investment incentives

Income tax incentives and other fiscal concessions are provided under the Fiscal Incentives Act, the Tourism Incentives Act, the Special Development Areas Act, and other concessions granted by the Cabinet of Ministers. The extent of the incentives and concessions granted are specific to the legislation or Cabinet conclusions and depend on the impact that the investment would have on local employment, exports, and the generation of foreign exchange earnings. The incentives granted include the following:

* Duty-free importation of raw materials, machinery, components, and spare parts and other inputs used in manufacturing, and the duty-free importation of construction materials, equipment, and other inputs used in the construction and operation of hotels and other hospitality products.
* Income tax waivers of up to 100% of the taxable income of companies engaged in manufacturing, tourism, and agriculture and other employment generating activities, for periods of up to 15 years.
* Whole or partial waivers of property tax, stamp duties, Alien Landholding Licence fees, WHT, and consumption taxes with respect to investments in specific areas, or in specific industries and activities.
* Guaranteed repatriation of capital and dividends. Remittance of profits and dividends are tax-free as they are not subject to WHT.
* Export allowances for goods manufactured in Saint Lucia and exported. Companies who engage in such activity are given tax exemption on the export of such goods up to a maximum of 10 to 15 years.

Employment incentives

Employment incentives are available in the Income Tax Act for the following:

* Hiring university graduates. An additional deduction of 25% of salaries is provided for a maximum period of three years.
* Hiring persons in the offshore financial services industry with skills not available in Saint Lucia. A special tax concession is given to such persons that allows a prescribed percentage of an employee's or contractor's salary or fees to be exempt from income tax.

Other incentives

Complete or partial waivers of income tax are available on the taxable profits of companies engaged in providing services to the offshore financial services industry.

Special tax concessions are also available for capital construction in the hotel industry. Capital expenditures on the construction of a hotel may offset profits for up to 15 years.

Saint Lucia

Withholding taxes

Resident corporations and persons that make certain payments of an income nature to residents or non-residents are required to withhold tax on these payments as follows:

Recipient	WHT (%)
Resident corporations:	
Payments to contractors	10
Equipment hire	10
Non-resident corporations:	
Interest	15/15 CARICOM
Royalties	25/15 CARICOM
Management fees	25/15 CARICOM
Commissions or fees (not by way of employment)	25
Income of a trust	25
Premiums, including insurance premiums	25
Any other payment of an income nature	25

Saint Lucia has only one DTA. This treaty, between the Caribbean territories, is referred to as the CARICOM Double Taxation Agreement. CARICOM is comprised of the following states:

- Antigua and Barbuda
- The Bahamas
- Barbados
- Belize
- Dominica
- Grenada
- Guyana
- Haiti
- Jamaica
- Montserrat
- St. Kitts and Nevis
- St. Vincent and the Grenadines
- Suriname
- Trinidad and Tobago

Tax administration

Taxable period

Returns must cover a 12-month period, which may be changed only with the Comptroller's permission.

Tax returns

Tax returns must be filed within three months of the company's fiscal year-end. An extension of the filing date may be obtained.

Financial statements must be submitted with the returns, together with a schedule reconciling taxable income with book income and various other schedules of additional information.

The system is one of self-assessment. Upon receipt of the returns, the Inland Revenue Department examines the information provided and issues a notice of assessment at any time, subject to the statute of limitations. The Revenue Department may also issue assessments in the absence of returns.

Payment of tax

Tax is payable in instalments on 25 March, 25 June, and 25 September in each year of income, based on the preceding year's income. Any remainder is payable within three months of the end of the financial year.

Appeals

Within 30 days after the date of service of a notice of assessment or reassessment, the taxpayer may submit a written objection to the Revenue Department on any matters in such assessment or reassessment. If the Revenue Department confirms its assessment, the taxpayer may file an appeal with the Appeal Commission, which comprises seven persons appointed by the Minister of Finance. A decision by that body may be further appealed to the Saint Lucia High Court within 30 days. An appeal against an order from this Court may be made to the Court of Appeal.

Audit cycle

The Inland Revenue Department carries out audits of a selection of tax returns, usually at the taxpayer's place of business. Audits may be carried out at any time prior to the expiration of the statute of limitations, whether or not notices of assessment have been issued. The Revenue Department has wide powers in determining the information it requires for these audits.

Statute of limitations

Assessments are not final until six years after the end of the income year, within which period assessments may be made at any time. In cases of misrepresentation or failure to disclose any material fact, a reassessment can be made at any time.

Penalties and interest

The following civil penalties and interest, which are non-deductible, are imposed:

- For late filing or for failure to file: 5% of the tax charge at filing date.
- For late payment: 10% of the unpaid tax at the due date.
- On tax and penalties unpaid: monthly interest at a rate of 1.04%.
- Tax knowingly evaded or sought to be evaded: 100% of the tax.

S

Saudi Arabia

PwC contact

Mohammed Yaghmour
PricewaterhouseCoopers
Jameel Square, Al Tahliah Street
PO Box 16415
Jeddah 21464
Kingdom of Saudi Arabia
Tel: +966 2 610 4400 Ext. 2228
Email: mohammed.yaghmour@sa.pwc.com

Significant developments

Withholding tax (WHT) on technical and consulting services provided by related parties

The High Appeal Committee (HAC) has ruled recently that 5% WHT is applicable on payments to non-resident related parties for technical and consulting services fees instead of 15%.

The appeal arguments were purely based on the local regulations and certain mismatches in the interpretation of the regulations between the Department of Zakat and Income Tax (DZIT) and the taxpayer. In general, the tax appeal rulings in Saudi Arabia do not necessarily constitute part of the regulations. However, taxpayers can still claim their rights based on such rulings when they become final.

The ruling is not yet final since the DZIT has filed an appeal against the HAC ruling with the Board of Grievance (BOG).

The BOG process may take longer than expected before concluding on this issue.

The expectation is that the DZIT may issue further clarification to make it clear once and for all that the rate should be 15% as per the current application or reduce it to 5%. Until that unknown time, the DZIT will most likely continue to apply and claim the 15%.

However, considering the significant impact on the taxpayers, it is expected that this issue will be one of the hot topics that the DZIT should address to put an end to the expected high pressure and follow up by taxpayers.

Taxes on corporate income

The rate of income tax is 20% of the net adjusted profits. Withholding tax (WHT) rates are between 5% and 20%. *Zakat*, an Islamic assessment, is charged on the company's *Zakat* base at 2.5%. *Zakat* base represents the net worth of the entity as calculated for *Zakat* purposes.

Only non-Saudi investors are liable for income tax in Saudi Arabia. In most cases, Saudi citizen investors (and citizens of the Gulf Cooperation Council [GCC] countries, who are considered to be Saudi citizens for Saudi tax purposes) are liable for *Zakat*. Where a company is owned by both Saudi and non-Saudi interests, the portion of taxable income attributable to the non-Saudi interest is subject to income tax, and the Saudi share goes into the basis on which *Zakat* is assessed.

According to the income tax law, the following persons are subject to income tax:

- A resident capital company to the extent of its non-Saudi shareholding.
- A resident non-Saudi natural person who carries on activities in Saudi Arabia.
- A non-resident person who carries out activities in Saudi Arabia through a permanent establishment (PE).
- A non-resident person who has other income subject to tax from sources within Saudi Arabia.
- A person engaged in natural gas investment fields.
- A person engaged in oil and other hydrocarbon production.

It should be noted that although the income tax rate is 20%, income from the following two activities is subject to different rates:

- Natural Gas Investment Tax (NGIT) shall be determined on the basis of the internal rate of return (IRR) on the cumulative annual cash flows of the taxpayer derived from natural gas investment activities. The rate applicable will be 30% if the IRR is 8% or less. The rate increases progressively up to 85% if the IRR equals or exceeds 20%.
- Income from oil and hydrocarbon production is subject to tax at the rate of 85%.

Corporate residence

A company is considered a resident company if it is formed under the Saudi Arabian Regulations for Companies or if its central management is located in Saudi Arabia.

Permanent establishment (PE)

According to the Saudi tax regulations, the following are the requirements for considering a non-resident party to have a PE:

- A PE of a non-resident in the Kingdom, unless otherwise provided below, consists of the permanent place of activity of the non-resident through which one carries out business, in full or in part, including business carried out through an agent.
- The following are considered a PE:
  - Construction sites, assembly facilities, and the exercise of its related supervisory activities.
  - Installations or sites used for surveying for natural resources, drilling equipment, or ships used for surveying for natural resources, and the exercise of its related supervisory activities.
  - A fixed location where a non-resident natural person carries out business.
  - A branch of a non-resident company which is licensed to carry out business in the Kingdom.
- A place is not considered a PE of a non-resident in the Kingdom if it is used in the Kingdom only to do the following:
  - Store, display, or deliver goods or products belonging to the non-resident.
  - Keep an inventory of goods or products belonging to the non-resident only for the purposes of processing by another person.
  - Purchase of goods or products only for the collection of information for the non-resident.
  - Perform any other activities that are preparatory or auxiliary in nature for the interests of the non-resident.
  - Prepare contracts relating to loans, supply of products or perform technical services for signature.

- Executing any group of the activities mentioned above.
- A non-resident partner in a resident personal company is considered an owner to a PE in the Kingdom in the form of a share in a personal company.

Furthermore, the agent mentioned in the above article is identified as a dependent agent who has any of the following authorities:

- Negotiate on behalf of a non-resident.
- Conclude contracts on behalf of a non-resident.
- Has a stock of goods, owned by a non-resident, on hand in the Kingdom to supply the clients' demands regularly on behalf of the non-resident.

A place from which a non-resident carries out insurance and/or reinsurance activity in the Kingdom through an agent is considered a PE of the non-resident even though the agent is not authorised to negotiate and conclude contracts on behalf of the non-resident.

Other taxes

Value-added tax (VAT)
There is currently no VAT system in Saudi Arabia.

Customs duties
Customs duties are imposed on imports according to tariffs rates that are effective on the payment date in accordance with the Saudi Customs regulations. Customs duties are imposed on the price of the imported goods. This price is assessed based on the actual cost paid or on the agreed upon cost denominated in the currency of the exporting country. The price consists of the price of the imported goods as packed for shipping from the port of export plus freight and insurance cost to the Saudi port which is converted to Saudi riyals at the exchange rates published by Saudi Arabian Monetary Agency (SAMA) on the date of the declaration. In case this procedure is not achievable, the imported goods will be priced based on the most proximate comparable value that could be ascertained. Imported goods that are subject to customs duties based on weight are assessed based on the gross weight or the net weight as shown in the tariff schedules. The gross weight of the goods includes the goods weight including all internal and external packing materials. Net weight of the goods excludes all internal and external packing materials including the items used for separating and arranging the goods.

To encourage joint ventures in manufacturing, the government grants tariff protection from competing imports to locally produced, quality goods. Rates can be as high as 20%.

Penalties on smuggling goods vary from confiscation, to collections of customs duties and penalties, to imprisonment.

Social insurance tax
Social insurance tax is paid monthly based on the monthly basic salary plus housing with an upper limit of 45,000 Saudi riyals (SAR), is computed at 2% for non-Saudi employees, and is paid by the employer. For Saudi employees, the rate is 20% and is paid by both the employee (9%) and the employer (11%).

Other taxes

There is no form of stamp duty, transfer, excise, sales, turnover, production, real estate, or property taxation except in so far as they may fall within the scope of *Zakat*, which is applicable only to Saudi nationals.

Branch income

Taxable income from a branch of a non-Saudi based corporation is taxed at 20%. Certain charges incurred by the headquarters are not deductible on the branch tax return.

Income determination

Inventory valuation
The weighted average-cost method is used for valuing inventory under Saudi tax law.

Capital gains
Capital gains are subject to income tax or *Zakat*, as appropriate, at the normal income tax or *Zakat* rate. However, capital gains realised from the disposal of shares in Saudi stock companies listed in the Saudi market are tax exempt, subject to certain conditions.

Dividend income
Dividend income that is received by a resident party is subject to income tax at the normal income tax rate. However, dividends paid to a non-resident party are subject to WHT at 5%.

Interest income
Interest income is subject to income tax at the normal income tax rate.

Imports and supply contracts
Saudi tax law provides that no profit will be considered to arise from a contract for the supply of goods to Saudi Arabia, provided delivery of the goods is either free on board (FOB) or cost, insurance, and freight (CIF) to a Saudi port. However, should the contract provide for the delivery and/or installation of materials at a point inside Saudi Arabia, the supplier may be considered to be carrying on business within Saudi Arabia, and, as a consequence, the contract may be subject to Saudi income taxation as follows:

- If the material cost was identified in the supply contract separately from the cost of work performed in Saudi Arabia, then, in the absence of a PE, a WHT on the work that will be performed in Saudi Arabia may be assessed, based on the type of services. However, if the contract qualifies the supplier to have a PE in Saudi, then income tax will be applied according to the Saudi tax regulations as for a normal taxpayer.
- If the supply contract indicates a total cost without segregation in the value of supply and the value of the other activities in Saudi Arabia, then the work performed in Saudi Arabia will be assigned a value equal to 10% of the contract value for each type of activity.

Foreign income
The gross income derived by a capital company resident in the Kingdom from its operations and of its branches inside and outside the kingdom is subject to tax in Saudi

Saudi Arabia

Arabia. However, in order to avoid double taxation on the same income, the following exceptions and clarifications are to be considered:

- With respect to the income realised from investments in other resident capital companies and in order to avoid double taxation, such income is to be excluded from being subject to tax under the following conditions:
  - That such income was subjected to tax in the Kingdom.
  - The percentage of ownership in the company invested in is not less than 10%.
  - The period of ownership of shares is not less than one year.
- With respect to the income realised from investments and operations outside the Kingdom, it will be subject to tax in the Kingdom unless an effective double tax treaty (DTT) between the Kingdom and the country invested in stipulates different provisions.

There are no restrictions on repatriation of profits, fees, capital, salaries, or other monies.

Deductions

All expenses that are necessary and normal to the business, paid or accrued, are allowable deductions, provided the expense meets the following conditions:

- It is an actual expense, supported by a verifiable document or other qualifying evidence.
- It is related to the generation of taxable income.
- It is related to the subject tax year.
- It is of a non-capital nature.

Depreciation

A depreciation deduction is allowed under the following limitations as stipulated by the law:

- The asset is not intended for resale and is to be used, in full or in part, for the entity's purposes.
- The asset is of a depreciable nature that loses value because of use or because of wear and tear and obsolescence and which has a value extending beyond the end of the taxable year.
- The asset is owned by the business, as per the ownership document for buildings and contracts and invoices for other assets.
- The asset depreciation is allowed even if the asset becomes inactive during the tax year.

Depreciation for tax purposes is calculated as follows, based on the following five categories of depreciable tangible or intangible assets, other than land:

Asset category	Depreciation rate (%)
Fixed buildings	5
Industrial and agricultural movable buildings	10
Factories, machines and equipment, computer application programs, passenger cars, and cargo vehicles	25
Expenditures for geological surveying, drilling, exploration, and other preliminary work to exploit and develop natural resources and their fields	20

Asset category	Depreciation rate (%)
All other tangible or intangible assets not included in previous categories, such as furniture, planes, ships and trains, and goodwill	10

The declining-balance method of depreciation, according to the above rates, should be followed for tax purposes.

There are also rules for depreciation relating to assets either acquired or disposed. Essentially, 50% of the allowable acquisition price or disposal proceeds is added to or subtracted from the asset pool in the first year, and the remaining 50% in the following year.

Assets under build, own, and transfer (BOT) and build, own, operate, and transfer (BOOT) are allowed to be depreciated over the contract period. This presumes, although it is not clear, that assets under the BOT and BOOT schemes actually will have a separate grouping in addition to the above prescribed groups.

Start-up expenses
Tax treatment of start-up expenses depend on how they were treated under Saudi generally accepted accounting principles (GAAP). Generally, they can be fully expensed at the first financial year or can be amortised.

Loan charges (interest expenses)
An interest deduction is limited to the lower of the loan charge incurred during the tax year, if related to income that is subject to tax, or the result of the following formula, whichever is less.

The taxpayer's total income from loan charges, plus 50% of (A minus B) as below:

A = income subject to tax other than income from loan charges.

B = expenses allowed under the law other than loan charge expenses.

Note that banks are not subject to this formula.

Bad debt
Bad debts are deductible, provided they meet all of the following conditions:

- The bad debt was previously declared in the appropriate year's income.
- The debt resulted from sale of goods or services.
- The company holds a certificate from the taxpayer's certified public accountant certifying that the debt has been written off in the taxpayer's books and records, based on a decision by the taxpayer at the appropriate management level.
- Serious efforts have been exerted by the taxpayer to collect the debt with no success and the inability of the debtor to pay has been proved based on a judicial ruling or bankruptcy.
- The debt is not from a related party.
- There is a commitment by the taxpayer to reinstate, as income, any written-off debt whenever collected.

Saudi Arabia

Charitable contributions
In determining the tax base of each taxpayer, a deduction is allowed for donations paid during the taxable year to public agencies or philanthropic societies licensed in the Kingdom which are non-profit organisations and are allowed to receive donations.

Allocations and reserves
Allocations and reserves formed during the year are deductible as follows:

* Bank allocations to a reserve fund for doubtful debts are allowable deductions. However, a bank must submit a certificate from the SAMA stating the amount of doubtful debts and the amount of doubtful debts collected during the year, which should be reinstated in the tax base of the year of collection.
* Insurance/reinsurance companies may deduct, based on industry standards, a reserve for unearned premiums and for unexpired risks, provided that it is reported in the tax base of the following year.

  A reserve for unearned premiums means a part of premium amounts collected or stated in books that covers risks related to the future tax year(s). A reserve for unexpired risks means the amount of compensation claimed or reported, but for which the payment process falls short of completion during the tax year.
* A taxpayer may reduce its book profit by the amount of reserves used during the year that had been readjusted when made, to increase income or decrease expenses in the year of formation. Examples of such reserves are end-of-service awards, doubtful debt, and drops in prices. Such amounts are deductible, provided the following conditions are met:
  * The used amount was paid or accrued during the year, and it is supported by documentation.
  * The reserve had been adjusted in the year of formation to increase the tax base.

School fees
School fees paid by taxpayers for their employees' children are deductible expenses, provided they meet the following conditions:

* They are paid to a local licensed school.
* This benefit is stated in the employment contract.

Pension fund
Employers' contributions to employees' pension funds or savings funds established under Saudi Arabia's rules and regulations are deductible, provided that such contribution, one payment or in aggregate, is not in excess of 25% of the employee's income before the employer's contributions and that the fund meets the following criteria:

* The fund is established according to special provisions that clearly stipulate conditions of subscription and rights of subscribers.
* Such obligation is stated in the employment contract or in the Articles of Association of the establishment.
* The fund has a character independent of the establishment and has separate accounts audited by an independent certified public accountant.

Research and development (R&D)
A deduction is allowed for R&D expenditure incurred during the tax year in connection with the generation of income that is subject to tax. Such expenditure relates to technical, scientific, and engineering experiments; computer systems; or similar

research. This provision does not apply to the acquisition of land and facilities, or to equipment used for research. Such facilities and equipment are subject to depreciation under the law.

Fines and penalties
Fines and penalties related to income tax, paid or payable in Saudi Arabia or to other countries, are not deductible.

Financial fines or penalties paid or payable to any party in Saudi Arabia, such as traffic fines or fines for causing damage to public utilities are also not deductible.

Fines or penalties paid for breach of contractual obligations, such as fines on delayed or defaulted completion of contracts, are deductible, provided they are documented by the contracting party and the income from such penalties is reported in the year of recovery.

Taxes
Income taxes are not deductible.

Non-deductible expenses
The following expenses are non-deductible:

- Wages, salaries, and whatever is so deemed, in cash or in kind, paid to an owner, partner, or shareholder or to a member of their families, being a parent, spouse, sons/daughters, and siblings (this provision does not apply to stockholders in a stock company).
- Compensation in cash or in kind paid to a partner, shareholder, or to a family member including a parent, spouse, sons/daughters, and siblings for a property or service to the extent that the compensation is higher than the fair market value of such property or service at time of transaction.
- Entertainment expenses incurred for events such as parties, sports competitions, entertainment trips and activities, etc.
- Expenses of a natural person for personal consumption, such as personal withdrawals, dependents' cost of living, or education.
- Any bribe or similar payment which is considered an illegal practice in Saudi Arabia, even if paid abroad.
- Insurance commission in excess of 3% of total premiums collected in Saudi Arabia through an agent or others and regardless of whether or not the agent is a partner.

Net operating losses
A taxpayer may carry forward operational losses as adjusted, to the years following the loss year until the cumulative loss is fully offset. The maximum profit percentage of any year that could be used to offset cumulative losses should not exceed 25% of the year's profit as reported in the taxpayer's return. Carryback of losses is not allowed.

Payments to foreign affiliates
Payments made to headquarter offices located abroad by wholly owned local subsidiaries or branches are not deductible. Such payments include:

- royalties or commissions
- loan charges (interest expense) or any other financial fees, and
- indirect administrative and general expenses allocated on an estimated basis.

Saudi Arabia

The value of goods or services delivered to the taxpayer by related parties is not deductible to the extent that it is in excess of an arm's-length value.

Group taxation

Double taxation on the income of foreign investors realised from their investments in other resident companies is eliminated under the following conditions:

- Such income was subjected to tax in Saudi Arabia.
- The percentage of ownership in the company invested in is not less than 10%.
- The period of ownership of shares is not less than one year.

With respect to the income realised by a resident capital company from its investments and operations outside Saudi Arabia, it will be subject to tax in Saudi Arabia (unless an effective DTT between Saudi Arabia and the country invested in stipulates different provisions).

However, for *Zakat* purposes, the concept of consolidation is acceptable and relief may be obtained for wholly owned subsidiaries by Saudi/GCC companies that are subject to *Zakat*.

Note that an entity operating in Saudi Arabia that has undertaken more than one project under the same commercial registration is required to consolidate the results of such projects into the financial statements of that entity and subject them to taxation as a single operation.

Transfer pricing

There are no specific transfer pricing rules in Saudi Arabia that impose or deem a charge to arise where the DZIT has reason to believe that a transaction has taken place at a value other than on an arm's-length basis. However, there is a generic provision that allows the DZIT to re-characterise or re-allocate income or expenses arising from a transaction if it is undertaken for the purposes of avoiding or reducing a tax liability in Saudi Arabia.

Thin capitalisation

There is no special legislation governing thin capitalisation for tax purposes. A Saudi company may deduct interest payments to affiliates, but not the head office, provided that the amount of debt and rate of interest are at arm's length and that interest deductibility formula is met. A Saudi company may be financed with minimum capital, and there is no limit to the amount of debt that may be used.

Tax credits and incentives

Incentives for investment in less-developed regions

The government of Saudi Arabia has granted tax concessions to the following six less-developed regions in Saudi Arabia, with the intention of attracting more investment:

- Ha'il.
- Jazan.
- Najran.
- Al-Baha.
- Al-Jouf.

- Northern territory.

These tax privileges are granted for a period of ten years from the start of any project.

The qualifying investing company's annual tax bill may be reduced by:

- Half the annual training expenditure on Saudis.
- Half the annual salaries paid to Saudis.
- 15% of the non-Saudi capital share, subject to certain conditions.

More deductions are granted if investment capital for any project exceeds SAR 1 million and if more than five employees of Saudi nationality have jobs of a technical or administrative nature with contracts of at least one year.

Customs incentives
An exemption from customs duties is available on machinery and raw materials that are required for approved projects, provided that they are not available in the local market. Such exemptions should be applied for prior to their importation and are subject to certain terms.

Withholding taxes

Payments made from a resident party or a PE to a non-resident party for services performed are subject to WHT. The rates vary between 5%, 15%, and 20% based on the type of service and whether the beneficiary is a related party.

The WHT should be paid within the first ten days of the month following the month during which the payment was made.

The domestic rate for WHT is 5% on dividends, 15% on royalties, and 5% on interest.

Tax treaties
Saudi Arabia has entered into tax treaties with several countries. Treaties currently or about to be in force are listed below. A number of other treaties are at various stages of negotiation.

DTTs have not yet been effectively tested in Saudi Arabia. However, they generally follow the Organisation for Economic Co-operation and Development (OECD) model treaty and may provide certain relief, including WHT on dividends, interest, and royalties.

The following are the treaty WHT rates for payments made from Saudi Arabia to treaty country recipients. Each tax treaty should be studied carefully because there could be exceptions to the general rules:

Recipient	Dividends (%)	Interest (%)	Royalties (%)
Non treaty country	5	5	15
Treaty country:			
Austria	5	5	10
Bangladesh	10	7.5	10

Saudi Arabia

Recipient	Dividends (%)	Interest (%)	Royalties (%)
Belarus	5	5	10
China (P.R.C.)	5	10	10
France	0	0	0
Greece	5	5	10
India	5	10	10
Italy	5/10 (1)	5	10
Japan	5/10 (9)	10	5/10 (10)
Malaysia	5	5	8
Netherlands	5/10 (2)	5	7
Pakistan	5/10 (3)	10	10
Russia	5	5	10
Singapore	5	5	8
South Africa	5/10 (2)	5	10
South Korea (R.O.K.)	5/10 (4)	5	5/10 (10)
Spain	0/5 (5)	5	8
Syria	0	7.5	15
Turkey	5/10 (6)	10	10
United Kingdom	5/15 (7)	0	5/8 (11)
Uzbekistan	7	7	10
Vietnam	5/12.5 (8)	10	7.5/10 (12)

Notes

1. Shall not exceed:
   * 5% of the gross amount of the dividends if the beneficial owner is a company (other than a partnership) that has owned directly or indirectly at least 25% of the capital of the company paying the dividends for a period of at least 12 months preceding the date the dividends were declared.
   * 10% of the gross amount of the dividends in all other cases.
2. Shall not exceed:
   * 5% of the gross amount of the dividends if the beneficial owner is a company (other than a partnership) that holds directly at least 10% of the capital of the company paying the dividends.
   * 10% of the gross amount of the dividends in all other cases.
3. Shall not exceed:
   * 5% of the gross amount of dividends if the beneficial owner is (i) a company or (ii) an entity wholly owned by the government.
   * 10% of the gross amount of the dividends in all other cases.
4. Shall not exceed:
   * 5% of the gross amount of the dividends if the beneficial owner is a company (other than a partnership) that holds directly at least 25% of the capital of the company paying the dividends.
   * 10% of the gross amount of the dividends in all other cases.
5. Shall not exceed:
   * 5% of the gross amount of the dividends.
   * The contracting state of which the company paying the dividends is a resident shall exempt from tax the dividends paid by that company to a company (other than a partnership) which is a resident of the other contracting state, as long as it holds directly at least 25% of the capital of the company paying the dividends.
6. Shall not exceed:
   * 5% of the gross amount of the dividends:
     * if the beneficial owner is a company (other than a partnership) that holds directly at least 20% of the capital of the company paying the dividends or
     * if the beneficial owner is central bank or an entity that is wholly owned by the government.
   * 10% of the gross amount of the dividends in all other cases.
7. Shall not exceed:
   * 15% of the gross amount of the dividends where qualifying dividends are paid by a property investment vehicle.
   * 5% of the gross amount of the dividends in all other cases.
8. Shall not exceed:

- 5% of the gross amount of the dividends if the beneficial owner is a company (other than a partnership) that holds directly at least 50% of the capital of the company paying the dividends, or has invested 20 million United States dollars (USD) or more, or any equivalent currency, in the capital of the company paying the dividends.
  - 12.5% of the gross amount of the dividends in all other cases.
9. Shall not exceed:
   - 5% of the gross amount of the dividends if the beneficial owner is a company that holds directly or indirectly, during the period of 183 days ending on the date on which entitlement to the dividends is determined, at least 10% of the voting shares or of the total issued shares of the company paying the dividends.
   - 10% of the gross amount of the dividends in all other cases.
10. Shall not exceed:
    - 5% of the gross amount of the royalties that are paid for the use of, or the right to use, industrial, commercial, or scientific equipment.
    - 10% of the gross amount of the royalties in all other cases.
11. Shall not exceed:
    - 5% of the gross amount of the royalties that are paid for the use of, or the right to use, industrial, commercial, or scientific equipment.
    - 8% of the gross amount of the royalties in all other cases.
12. Shall not exceed:
    - 7.5% of the gross amount of such royalties that are paid for rendering of any services or assistance of a technical or managerial nature.
    - 10% of the gross amount of such royalties in all other cases.

Tax administration

Taxable period
Tax filings are based on the company's fiscal year.

Tax returns
Returns are due to be filed with the DZIT within 120 days after the taxpayer's year-end. The system is one of self-assessment.

The tax authority has recently issued a circular requesting that companies that are owned by Saudis only, or by Saudis and non-Saudis, to file audited financial statements along with the tax return. However, this requirement is not applicable for companies that are 100% owned by non-Saudis.

Payment of tax
Final tax due must be paid with 120 days after taxpayer's year-end.

Three equal advance tax payments are required to be made on the last day of the sixth, ninth, and 12th months for a current tax year, provided that the taxpayer has earned income during the year. Each advance payment is equal to 25% of the amount resulting from the taxpayer's tax liability based on the previous year return minus the withheld tax on reported income, if any. The taxpayer is not required to make advance tax payments if the result of the said formula is less than SAR 500,000. Late payment of an advance payment is subject to a delay penalty of 1% of the amount due for every 30 days of delay.

Audit cycle
There is no specific audit cycle by the DZIT; however, the most common ways for the DZIT to select companies for tax audits are the size of the company, the companies' shareholders nationality (totally owned by foreigner and branches of foreign companies), and certain risk assessment measures.

Saudi Arabia

Statute of limitations

The DZIT may, with a reasoned notification, make or amend a tax assessment within five years from the end of the deadline specified for filing the tax declaration for the taxable year, or, at any time, upon a written consent of the taxpayer.

The DZIT may make or amend an assessment within ten years of the deadline specified for filing the tax declaration for the taxable year if a taxpayer does not file its tax declaration, or it is found that the declaration is incomplete or incorrect with the intent of tax evasion.

A taxpayer may request a refund of overpaid amounts at any time within five years from the end of the overpaid taxable year.

Topics of focus for tax authorities

It was noted recently that the DZIT is emphasising the submission of a certificate from General Organization for Social Insurance (GOSI) along with a reconciliation statement between salaries and wages subject to GOSI and salaries and wages charged to the taxpayer's accounts duly certified by a Saudi licensed CPA.

The DZIT started recently to focus on the payments made to non-resident parties to verify compliance with the WHT regulations by requesting a reconciliation statement for such payments with the annual WHT form.

The DZIT has also recently been requesting import value lists from the Customs Authority in order to confirm the value of goods imported and declared by taxpayers in their annual declarations during the financial period.

Senegal

PwC contact

Matthias Hubert
PricewaterhouseCoopers Tax & Legal
3 Place de l'Indépendance - BP 6454
Immeuble SDIH
Dakar
Senegal
Tel: +221 33 849 05 00
Email: matthias.hubert@sn.pwc.com

Significant developments

Through the Finance Bill for 2012, a 5% special contribution has been introduced by the Senegalese government. The contribution will apply to the cement industry as well as the fossil and mineral deposits industry.

The contribution shall apply on local sales, imports, and exports of the related products.

Phosphate, nitrates, salt, and mining products are exempt from the new contribution.

Taxes on corporate income

Branches and companies are liable for corporate income tax (CIT) at the rate of 25%.

Residents are taxed upon their worldwide income. Non-residents are generally taxed via the existence of a permanent establishment (PE) on Senegal-source income. Withholding taxes (WHTs) may also apply to non-residents, as per the services delivered to Senegalese taxpayers, subject to the application of a double tax treaty (DTT).

Minimum CIT
A minimum CIT is due in case of lack of profits, and the amount depends on the annual turnover, as follows:

Annual turnover (XOF*)	Minimum CIT (XOF)
Up to 250 million	500,000
250 million to 500 million	750,000
Over 500 million	1 million

* *Communauté financière d'Afrique* (Financial Community of Africa or CFA) francs (XOF)

Corporate residence

Companies are considered as Senegalese residents if they have a registered fixed establishment. Nonetheless, foreign companies that are not registered locally may be deemed to have a PE in Senegal in relation to their local activity, and will then be subject to tax liabilities.

Senegal

Permanent establishment (PE)

The criteria for a PE were derived from the General Tax Code and are close to the Organisation for Economic Co-operation and Development (OECD) standards. DTTs can be applicable and can provide specific definitions. These DTTs are based on the OECD model in most cases. *See the Withholding taxes section for a list of countries with which Senegal has concluded DTTs.*

Other taxes

Value-added tax (VAT)

Subject to certain exclusions, most commercial operations are subject to an 18% VAT.

As of 1 January 2011, VAT on tourism activities was reduced from 18% to 10%.

A 17% special tax on banking operations is applicable instead of the VAT.

VAT returns must be filed monthly.

Tax on built real estate

The tax on built real estate applies to owners of buildings, factories, industrial premises, or equipment fixed on the land. The tax rate is 5% for common buildings and 7.5% for factories and industrial premises. It is applied on the basis of the rental value of the lands, buildings, etc.

Taxes on real estate are due annually.

Tax on non-built real estate

The tax on non-built real estate applies to owners of land without buildings, factories, industrial premises, or equipment fixed on the land. The tax rate is fixed at 5%. It is applied on the basis of the rental value of the land.

Stamp/registration duties

There are many stamp and/or registration duties, depending on the operations, such as the following:

*   1% registration duty applicable to the incorporation of a company and the increase in cash of the share capital.
*   1% registration duty applicable to transfer of stocks.
*   1% registration duty applicable to transfer of debts.
*   15% registration duty applicable to sale of business.
*   15% registration duty applicable to transfer of real estate.
*   5% registration duty applicable to rent agreements.

Business license tax

Business license tax is an annual duty consisting of a fixed annual payment (fixed duty) and a proportional duty, calculated in most cases on the basis of the rental value of the premises used. The amounts and rates of these taxes are fixed according to the type and size of the activity carried out.

There is a table that includes several categories of business. For each category, a fixed tax is provided as well as the percentage that is applied on the assets at their fair value. In cases where the business does not fit any category, the closest business or the most similar one is considered by the tax administration in order to calculate the business license tax for the taxpayer.

As an example, the 'merchant' business license tax fixed duty classification rates are provided below. As per this classification, a 'merchant' will be liable for business license tax depending on its annual turnover. Indeed, it will have to pay a tax determined as follows:

Merchant turnover (XOF)	Fixed amount of tax (XOF)
Over 10,000,000,000	10,000,000
Between 5,000,000,000 and 10,000,000,000	5,000,000
Between 1,000,000,000 and 5,000,000,000	3,000,000
Between 500,000,000 and 1,000,000,000	1,500,000
Between 300,000,000 and 500,000,000	1,000,000
Between 200,000,000 and 300,000,000	700,000
Between 100,000,000 and 200,000,000	400,000
Between 50,000,000 and 100,000,000	300,000

The general rate of proportional tax is 19%, and it is levied on the annual rental value of the offices, stores, warehouses, yards, workshops, stations, wharfs, sites, other premises, and installations considered as constructions used for the activities of the company. In addition to that, the basis of the proportional tax includes also the assets or rented materials at their fair value.

Tax on telecommunication
The tax rate is 5% on telecommunication use and access. To offset the tax, the purchase of mobile telephones (and other types of telephones) remains exempt from VAT and customs duty.

Tax on vehicles
An owner of a motor vehicle (car, truck, or motorbike) must pay an annual registration tax ranging from XOF 18,000 to XOF 200,000 per vehicle, depending on its nature and horsepower.

Company tax on vehicles
In addition to the tax on vehicles, companies owning or renting vehicles (more than 15 days a year) must pay a specific annual tax on them. Rates range from XOF 50,000 to XOF 200,000, depending on the type and horsepower of the vehicle.

Branch income

In general, the tax on branch income is similar to that of corporate income. Nonetheless, a 10% duty is automatically applied to profits generated after CIT. It corresponds to an automatic application of the 10% tax on payment on dividends applicable to a company.

Headquarter expenses, which are a proration of the worldwide office expenses, may be allocated to the Senegal branch. This proration is based upon a ratio of the local turnover of the branch and the worldwide turnover of the parent company. It applies to the total amount of headquarters' expenses incurred by the company. In addition, the deductibility of headquarters expenses is limited to 20% of the accounting profits

Senegal

before the deduction. This limitation does not apply to other types of services provided by headquarters, such as technical assistance.

Income determination

Inventory valuation
Inventory is generally stated at the lower of cost or market value. Last in first out (LIFO) and first in first out (FIFO) are permitted. Book and tax conformity is required.

Capital gains
Capital gains derived from the transfer of assets are subject to the 25% CIT. There is no basket system. The taxable base will be reduced to one-third if the transfer of assets arises due to a cessation of activity. However, if the transfer of assets is made less than five years after the start of the business, a one-half reduction of the taxable base will be applicable.

Sales of stocks by a non-resident are liable to the 25% CIT, subject to the application of a DTT.

Dividend income
If a parent company domiciled in Senegal owns 20% of the subsidiary (main condition for the application of the parent-subsidiary corporation special taxation status), a 95% reduction on the dividends received is applicable for CIT purposes.

Stock dividends
Stock dividends are unusual in Senegal. However, this kind of distribution would be taxable at the general withholding tax (WHT) rate of 10% on the basis of its real value.

Foreign income
In general, profits generated in Senegal are taxed under Senegal's income tax law. Profits generated outside Senegal and constituting a PE in the relevant country are not taxed in Senegal. A DTT can provide different rules.

Deductions

Depreciation and depletion
The rates of depreciation are not provided by the law. The rate is determined on the normal and predictable duration of use of the asset by taking into account normal wear and tear. In practice, there are standard rates for common assets. Accelerated depreciation can be applicable, subject to conditions.

Goodwill
There are no provisions in Senegal for goodwill.

Start-up expenses
Start-up expenses are deductible if justified and approved by the shareholders.

Interest expenses
Interest paid to shareholders may be deducted when it relates to loans with an amount lower or equal to the amount of the share capital and whose rate is lower or equal to the base rate of the Central Bank of West African States plus two points.

Bad debt
There are no provisions in Senegal for bad debt.

Charitable contributions
Only payments made to specific chartered organisations are deductible, at a rate of up to 0.2/1,000 of turnover. On the contrary, payments made to non-chartered organisations are not deductible.

Fines and penalties
Fines and penalties are not deductible.

Taxes
CIT and the company tax on vehicles are deductible. Other local taxes are also deductible.

Other significant items
Provisions are deductible if they correspond to a risk or a probable cost that is more than possible and leads to a decrease in the assets. Provisions for paid holidays and retirement compensation are not deductible.

Net operating losses
Tax losses may be carried forward to the next three years. The carryback of losses does not exist. Losses corresponding to the depreciation of assets can be forwarded indefinitely.

Payments to foreign affiliates
Reasonable royalties, interest, and management service fees paid to foreign parent companies are tax-deductible. Supporting documents (e.g. invoices, contracts) will be necessary to prove that these expenses are justified.

Group taxation

Group taxation is not permitted in Senegal.

Transfer pricing
Transfer pricing regulations do not specifically exist in Senegal.

Thin capitalisation
There are no specific rules regarding thin capitalisation in Senegal. Nonetheless, the following tax and legal rules should be known:

- From a legal point of view (corporate law), the net assets must be equal at least half of the share capital of the company. In case the net assets are lower than this threshold, the situation should be regularised by any lawful means within a period of two years following the financial year it appears. Otherwise, any third party can request the closing of the entity before the courts.
- The deductibility of interest paid to a shareholder upon a loan or an advance in general is limited to a maximum rate calculated on the Central Bank base rate (currently fixed at 6.25%) plus 2 points, calculated on the amount of the share capital. Portions exceeding this limit are not deductible for CIT purpose.

Senegal

Tax credits and incentives

The Investment Code
The Investment Code applies to investments over XOF 100 million (mainly production, processing, industrial, tourism, agricultural, and complex trade). The benefits of the Investment Code include exemption from customs duties, suspension of VAT payment for three years, CIT limitation, etc.

Free export company status
Agriculture, industry, and telecommunications companies that have an exporting potential amounting to at least 80% of their turnover may qualify for the free export company status. There are several advantages for companies that qualify, including a CIT rate of 15%, exemption from dividend WHT, exemption from business license tax, exemption from taxes on real estate, and exemption from registration duty for incorporation or bylaws change purposes.

Miscellaneous incentives
There are a wide range of investment laws (i.e. negotiations with the government to set up a specific tax regime different from common rules) for investments greater than XOF 250 billion, including the mining code and the petroleum code, among others.

Withholding taxes

Senegal has various WHTs. The primary ones are as follows:

- 20% WHT on remuneration paid for services (including royalties) rendered by a foreign individual or foreign company.
- 10% WHT on dividends distributed.
- 13% WHT on bond interest.
- 8% WHT on deposits or guaranteed interest on accounts with a bank.
- 16% WHT on other revenues, notably interest on loans.

These WHTs may be limited by DTTs.

Double tax treaties (DTTs)
The DTTs concluded by Senegal are based on the OECD model in most cases.

Senegal has concluded such treaties with Belgium, Canada, France, Italy, Mauritania, Morocco, Norway, Qatar, Tunisia, and member states of the West African Economic and Monetary Union (WAEMU), including Benin, Burkina-Faso, Côte d'Ivoire, Guinea-Bissau, Mali, Niger, and Togo.

Treaty WHT rates are as follows:

Recipient	Dividends (%)	Interest (%)	Royalties (%)
Belgium	10	16	10
Canada	10	16	15
France	10	15	15
Italy	10	15	15
Mauritania	10	16	N/A
Morocco	10	10	10

Recipient	Dividends (%)	Interest (%)	Royalties (%)
Norway	10	16	16
Qatar	N/A	N/A	N/A
Tunisia	10	16	N/A
WAEMU	10	15	15

Tax administration

Taxable period
The tax year in Senegal is the calendar year.

Tax returns
Companies must file CIT returns by 30 April of the year following the tax year.

Payment of tax
CIT must be paid in two instalments (each equal to one-third of the previous year's tax) by 15 February and 30 April. The outstanding balance payment amount of the tax due must be paid by 15 June.

For the first financial year of a newly incorporated company, no instalment is due; the new company pays the whole CIT before 15 June of the following year.

Audit cycle
There is no specific tax audit cycle in Senegal.

Statute of limitations
The statute of limitations is, generally speaking, five years.

Serbia

PwC contact

Krzysztof Lipka
PricewaterhouseCoopers Consulting d.o.o.
Omladinskih brigada 88a
11070 Belgrade, Serbia
Tel: +381 11 3302100
Email: krzysztof.lipka@rs.pwc.com

Significant developments

The latest amendments of the Corporate Income Tax (CIT) Law, which came into effect in January 2012 (also applicable for 2011 CIT calculation), help create conditions for more tax efficient operations of free zones, create a more efficient process of financial restructuring of companies, and stimulate development of the market for government debt securities.

Taxes on corporate income

Residents are taxed on their income generated in Serbia, as well as on their worldwide income. Non-residents are taxed only on their income sourced through a permanent establishment (PE) in Serbian territory.

The CIT rate is 10%.

Corporate residence

A legal entity is considered to be a resident of Serbia if it is established or has its place of effective management and control in Serbia.

Permanent establishment (PE)
A PE is any permanent place of business through which a non-resident conducts its business.

Other taxes

Value-added tax (VAT)
The VAT was introduced on 1 January 2005 and generally follows the European Union's (EU's) Sixth Directive.

The standard VAT rate is 18% for most taxable supplies. A reduced VAT rate of 8% applies for basic food stuffs, daily newspapers, utilities, etc.

In addition to these tax rates, there is a 0% tax rate with the right of deduction of the input VAT which applies to the export of goods, transport and other services directly related to exports, international air transport, etc.

A 0% tax rate without the right of deduction of the input VAT applies to trading in shares and other securities, insurance and reinsurance, and the lease of apartments, business premises, etc.

A taxpayer for VAT purposes is a person who independently, and in the course of its business activities, undertakes the supply of goods and services or import of goods. Business activity is defined as the permanent activity of a manufacturer, salesperson, or service provider for the purpose of gaining income. A branch or other operating unit can be a taxpayer.

A non-resident without a head office or PE within Serbia cannot register for VAT purposes.

The VAT law requires taxpayers to file VAT returns and pay VAT within ten days of the end of each taxable period. The usual taxable period is a calendar month; however, if a taxpayer's total turnover (for the last 12 months) is less than 20 million Serbian dinars (RSD) or is forecast (for the next 12 months) to be so, the taxable period is three calendar months.

Customs duties

Goods imported into Serbia are subject to customs duty rates provided in the Law on Customs Tariff. These rates are *ad valorem* (the only exception is related to the importation of other cigarettes containing tobacco, where a combined *ad valorem* and specific customs duty rate is prescribed) and applies to goods originating in countries which have a most favoured nation (MFN) status in trading with Serbia. Goods originating in other countries are subject to MFN duty rates increased by 70%.

At the moment, the only trading partner with Serbia that does not have MFN status is Taiwan.

Customs duty rates in Serbia range from 0% to 57.6%, with most being under 30%. At the moment, the 57.6% rate only applies to cigarettes containing tobacco.

Excise duties

Excise duties are levied on producers and importers of the following goods:

* Oil derivatives.
* Tobacco products.
* Alcoholic beverages.
* Coffee (green, roasted, ground, and coffee extracts).

Excise duty in Serbia is specific (for oil derivatives, alcoholic beverages, cigars, and cigarillos), *ad valorem* (for coffee and pipe tobacco), and combined (specific + *ad valorem* on retail price for cigarettes).

Excise duties stated in Serbian currency are adjusted on a half-year basis according to variations of the consumer price index (CPI) declared by relevant government bodies in charge of statistics. For oil derivatives, the government can modify the specific excise duty amounts during the year according to changes in prices of crude oil on the market.

Property tax

Property tax is payable annually in Serbia by all legal entities and individuals who own or have rights over real estate located in Serbia, such as:

* Ownership rights.
* Right of occupancy.
* Tenancy rights over an apartment or a building for a period longer than one year or for an indefinite period.

Serbia

- Urban land usage right (municipal, public, and other state-owned land) larger than ten acres in area.

Where the taxpayer keeps books, the property tax on real estate is levied at a flat rate which cannot exceed 0.40%.

Transfer tax
Transfer tax is levied on the transfer for a consideration of rights over real estate (except first transfer of newly constructed buildings, which is subject to VAT), intellectual property rights, ownership over used vehicles, vessels, and aircrafts (unless owned by the state), right to use urban and/or public building land, as well as rights relating to expropriated real estate.

The contract price is used as a tax base; however, the tax authorities have the right to adjust the tax base in case they estimate that the price agreed to in the contract is lower than under market conditions. The tax is payable at a 2.5% rate.

Stamp taxes
There are no stamp taxes in Serbia.

Capital gains tax of non-residents
Capital gains realised by non-residents from both residents or other non-residents are subject to 20% capital gain tax. Non-residents should appoint a fiscal representative in Serbia who should submit a tax return within 15 days from the realisation of capital gain. Based on the tax return, tax authorities will issue a decision assessing tax liability (if any).

In order to benefit from application of a relevant double tax treaty (DTT), the same rules are applicable as for withholding tax (WHT). Non-residents (i.e. the income recipient) must provide a tax residency certificate on the form prescribed by the Serbian Ministry of Finance stamped by the relevant body from the non-resident's country of residence, and the income recipient must be the beneficial owner of income.

Branch income

Non-residents carrying on business in Serbia through a branch are taxed on their Serbian-sourced income at the CIT rate of 10%. A branch is considered to be a PE.

Income determination

Taxable profit is determined by adjusting the accounting profit as stated in the profit and loss statement (determined in accordance with International Financial Reporting Standards [IFRS] and local accounting and audit legislation) and in accordance with the provisions of the CIT Law.

For taxpayers who, according to local legislation, are not obliged to apply IFRS, taxable profit is determined according to the special guidelines prescribed by the Ministry of Finance.

Inventory valuation
Cost of materials and the purchase value of merchandise are tax-deductible up to an amount calculated by applying the average weighted cost method or the first in first

out (FIFO) method. If another method is used, an adjustment for tax purposes should be made.

Capital gains

Capital gains are generated by the sale or other transfer of real estate, rights related to industrial property, as well as shares, stocks, securities, certain bonds, and investment units. A capital gain is determined as the difference between the sale and purchase price of the asset concerned, determined in accordance with the provisions of the Law. If the amount is negative, a capital loss is realised.

Capital gains and operational profit are disclosed in the same tax return, but they are taxed separately. Consequently, capital gains/losses cannot be used to offset business losses/gains.

However, capital gains can be offset with capital losses occurring in the same period. A capital loss can be carried forward for five years.

The capital gains tax rate is 10%.

However, the rate applicable for capital gains incurred by non-residents is 20%, unless envisaged otherwise by a relevant DTT (*see the Other taxes section for more information*).

Dividend income

Dividends received by a Serbian company from another Serbian company are not subject to CIT.

Dividends received from a non-resident will be treated as taxable income of a Serbian company and subject to 10% CIT. However, a Serbian entity will have the right to decrease its tax liability by taking tax credit for the WHT and underlying CIT paid in a subsidiary's country (*see the Tax credits and incentives section for more information*).

Interest income

Interest income will be included in accounting profit determined in accordance with IFRS and will be taxable at the CIT rate of 10%. A Serbian resident has the right to decrease its CIT liability for WHT on interest paid abroad by its non-resident subsidiary.

Royalties

Royalty income will be treated as business income and subject to the general CIT rate.

A resident taxpayer also has the right to decrease its CIT liability for WHT on royalties paid abroad by its non-resident subsidiary.

Unrealised currency exchange gains

Unrealised currency exchange gains will be included in accounting profits under IFRS rules. Serbian legislation does not provide any exception of taxation of this income. CIT rate is 10%.

Foreign income

Companies resident in Serbia are taxed on their worldwide income.

When profit generated in another country is taxed in the foreign country, a company has the right to decrease its tax liability by claiming a tax credit from the tax authorities in Serbia (*see the Tax credits and incentives section for more information*).

Serbia

There are no provisions which provide for the possibility that taxation of income earned abroad may be deferred.

....

Deductions

Depreciation and amortisation

Fixed and intangible assets are divided into five groups, with depreciation and amortisation rates prescribed for each (Group I: 2.5%; II: 10%; III: 15%; IV: 20%; and V: 30%). A straight-line depreciation method is prescribed for the first group, which includes real estate, while a declining-balance method is applicable for assets in the other groups.

Assets subject to tax depreciation and amortisation are all tangible and intangible (except goodwill) assets with useful life longer than one year and acquisition value above the average monthly gross salary published in Serbia at the moment of acquisition.

Goodwill

Goodwill is not subject to tax amortisation.

Start-up expenses

Generally, start-up expenses are tax deductible for CIT purposes.

Interest expenses

Interest on related party loans exceeding thin capitalisation and transfer pricing thresholds are not deductible (*see the Group taxation section*).

Bad debts

Bad debt provisions are generally tax deductible if they are at least 60 days overdue.

Write-off of receivables is recognised as expense if all of the following conditions are met:

- The related revenue has already been accrued in accordance with IFRS (this condition does not apply in cases when IAS and IFRS do not envisage recognition of revenue in respect of the receivable in question).
- They were written off as uncollectable.
- The evidence of unsuccessful collection via court.

In case the above conditions are not fulfilled, the taxable base in the year in which the write-off is performed will be increased for the write-off expense in the current year, as well as for the total amount of bad debt provisions that were recognised in previous years.

Charitable contributions

Expenses for health care, scientific, educational, humanitarian, religious, ecological, cultural, and sport related purposes are deductible, up to 3.5% of total revenues.

Fines and penalties

Fines and penalties (both commercial and those charged by the authorities) are not deductible.

Taxes

All taxes, duties, and contributions that do not depend on the profitability of the company are deductible in the tax period that the liability in this respect was settled.

Other significant items

The following other expenses are not recognised for CIT purposes:

- Non-documented expenses.
- Provisions for receivables from entities that are creditors at the same time.
- Presents provided to political organisations.
- Presents provided to related parties.
- Penalty interest for late payment of taxes.
- Expenses related to forced collection of taxes and other liabilities.
- Non-business related expense.
- Share in the profit paid to employees or other individuals.
- Calculated but unpaid redundancy payments (deductible when paid).
- Impairment of assets (deductible in tax period in which asset is disposed of or used).
- Direct write-off of receivables (under certain conditions).
- Long-term provisions (except those for renewal of natural resources, expenses within warranty period, and other mandatory long-term provisions).

The following other expenses are recognised for CIT purposes only up to a certain limit:

- Advertising and promotional expenses, up to 5% of total revenues.
- Representation expenses, up to 0.5% of total revenues.
- Membership fees paid to chambers of commerce and other associations (except political parties), up to 0.1% of gross revenue.

Net operating losses

The taxpayer has the right to carry forward and utilise tax losses incurred over the following five years.

Carryback rules do not exist in Serbia.

Payments to foreign affiliates

Generally, there are no restrictions on the deductibility of royalties and service fees paid to foreign affiliates, provided they are at arm's length, appropriately documented (by agreements, contracts, calculation sheets, etc.), and incurred for business purpose only.

Payment of interest to foreign affiliates is restricted and regulated by thin capitalisation rules and transfer pricing rules (*see the Group taxation section*).

Group taxation

Tax grouping/consolidation is allowed to a group of companies where all members are Serbian residents and one company directly or indirectly controls at least 75% of the shares in another company. Each company files its own tax balance sheet, and the parent company files a consolidated tax balance sheet for the whole group.

In the consolidated tax balance sheet, losses of one or more companies are offset by the profits of other related companies. Each company is liable for the portion of tax attributable to its share of the group's taxable profit.

Serbia

Once approved by the Ministry of Finance, tax grouping/consolidation applies for at least five years.

Transfer pricing

A transfer price is the price of transactions between related parties. Related parties exist if there is a possibility of control or influence over business decisions between them. Ownership of 50% or more, or a majority of shares, is considered as potential control. Influence over business decisions exists when an associated party holds 50% or more, or individually holds the greatest portion, of votes in the taxpayer's management bodies. If the same persons participate in management or control of both companies, a connection between them will be deemed to exist.

A company should disclose transactions with related parties separately at transfer prices and at arm's-length prices in its CIT calculation. Positive difference between these prices (adjustments of expenses) and negative difference (adjustments of revenues) is included in taxable profit.

Transfer pricing rules for intra-group loans

Any interest incurred on related party loans exceeding the arm's-length interest rate is not tax deductible. Arm's-length interest is deemed to be the:

- weighted average key policy rate for the tax period, for loans denominated in dinars, and
- weighted average interest rate at which domestic banks borrowed from foreign lenders in related tax period, for foreign currency loans.

These indicators are determined by National Bank of Serbia and published by the Ministry of Finance.

Transfer pricing rules in this respect are applied up to the amount of tax deductible interest determined in accordance with the thin capitalisation threshold.

Thin capitalisation

The interest and related costs will be fully deductible provided that the loans from related parties do not exceed four times the taxpayer's net equity (ten times for banks). The amount of a taxpayer's net equity for this purpose is calculated as the average of the total assets less total liabilities on the beginning and the end of the year, while the amount of loan from related parties is calculated as a daily average for the year.

In cases where the loans from related parties exceed the prescribed threshold, the amount of non-deductible interest will be calculated as proportional to the amount of loans exceeding the 4:1 (10:1) threshold.

Tax credits and incentives

Profit earned on the basis of a concession is tax exempt for a period of five years.

Foreign tax credit

A Serbian entity is entitled to a tax credit for the WHT paid on distributed dividends and underlying CIT paid abroad (by its non-resident subsidiary). The tax credit cannot exceed the amount of CIT that would have been paid in Serbia. Non-utilised tax credit can be carried forward by the parent company for five years. The parent company is required to own not less than 25% of a non-resident subsidiary for at least one year before filing the tax return.

A resident taxpayer also has the right to decrease its tax liability for WHT paid abroad by its non-resident subsidiary on interest and authorship fees up to Serbian CIT due. Carryforward of unused tax credit is not allowed.

Tax holidays

A ten-year tax holiday is available for companies with a minimum investment in property, plant, and equipment (PPE) of RSD 800 million. To qualify for the credit, a taxpayer must employ at least 100 new workers for an indefinite period. The tax holiday is available for the ten-year period in proportion to the investment made. The number of employees employed in the tax period in which the taxpayer qualified for the tax holiday must be retained throughout the whole tax holiday period.

A five-year tax holiday is available for companies conducting business in undeveloped regions that invest at least RSD 8 million in fixed assets. In addition, the company is obliged to employ at least five new workers for an indefinite period. The tax holiday is available for the five year period in proportion to the investment made.

Other tax credits

A tax credit of 20% (40% for small enterprises) is available for qualifying investments in fixed assets. The credit is limited to 50% (70% for small enterprises) of the assessed CIT liability in the current tax period. Unused tax credits can be carried forward for ten years.

Taxpayers generating profit in a newly established operating unit in an underdeveloped region may claim tax credits for a period of two years in an amount proportional to the profit generated by that unit.

Taxpayers classified into one of the following industries: agriculture, fishing, production of textile yarn and fabrics, garments, leather, base metals, standard metal products, machines, office machines, electrical machines, radio, television and communication equipment, medical instruments, motor vehicles, recycling, and video production are entitled to receive a tax credit in the amount of 80% of investments made in fixed assets which were not previously in use in Serbia. Unused tax credits can be carried forward up to ten years.

Withholding taxes

WHT is calculated and paid at the rate of 20% on payments such as dividends/share in profit, royalties (including neighbouring authorship rights, intellectual property rights, and related rights), interest income, income from distributed surplus of company in bankruptcy, income derived from the liquidation surplus of the company in liquidation, and lease payments for real estate and other assets made to a non-resident, unless a DTT applies to provide a reduced rate.

WHT is also payable on a non-resident's income realised on the basis of performing entertaining, artistic, sports, and similar programs in Serbia, which is not taxed as income of an individual (performer, musician, sportsman etc.).

Serbia

As of 2012, WHT is no longer payable on interest incurred on the basis of securities issued by the Republic of Serbia, autonomous province, local government, or National Bank of Serbia.

In order to benefit from application of a relevant DTT, non-residents (i.e. the income recipient) must provide a tax residency certificate on the form prescribed by the Serbian Ministry of Finance stamped by the relevant body from the non-resident's country of residence.

WHT rates envisaged by applicable DTTs are provided in the following table.

Recipient	WHT (%)			
	Dividends (1)	Interest	Royalties (4)	Applicable from
Albania	5/15	10	10	2006
Austria	5/15	10	5/10	2011
Azerbaijan	10	10	10	2011
Belgium	10/15	15	10	1982
Belorussia	5/15	8	10	1999
Bosnia and Herzegovina	5/10	10	10	2006
Bulgaria	5/15	10	10	2001
China	5	10	10	1998
Croatia	5/10	10	10	2005
Cyprus	10	10	10	1987
Czech Republic	10	10	5/10	2006
Denmark (2)	5/15	0/10 (6)	10	2010
Egypt	5/15	15	15	2007
Estonia	5/10	0/10 (6)	5/10	2011
Finland	5/15	0	10	1988
France	5/15	0	0	1976
Germany	15	0	10	1989
Ghana (3)	5/15	10	10	N/A
Greece	5/15	10	10	2011
Hungary	5/15	10	10	2003
India	5/15	10	10	2009
Indonesia (3)	15	10	15	N/A
Iran (3)	10	10	10	2012
Ireland	5/10	10	5/10	2011
Italy	10	10	10	1986
Kuwait	5/10	10	10	2004
Latvia	5/10	10	5/10	2007
Libya	5/10	10	10	2011
Lithuania	5/10	10	10	2010
Macedonia	5/15	10	10	1998
Malaysia	0 (5)	10	10	1991
Malta	5/10 (7)	10	5/10	2011
Moldova	5/15	10	10	2007
Montenegro	10	10	5/10	2012
Netherlands	5/15	0	10	1983
North Korea	10	10	10	2002

Recipient	WHT (%) Dividends (1)	Interest	Royalties (4)	Applicable from
Norway	15	0	10	1986
Pakistan	10	10	10	2011
Poland	5/15	10	10	1999
Qatar	5/10	10	10	2011
Romania	10	10	10	1998
Russia	5/15	10	10	1998
Slovak Republic	5/15	10	10	2002
Slovenia	5/10	10	5/10	2004
Spain	5/10	10	5/10	2011
Sri Lanka	12.5	10	10	1987
Sweden	5/15	0	0	1982
Switzerland	5/15	10	10	2007
Turkey	5/15	10	10	2008
Ukraine	5/10	0/10 (6)	10	2002
United Kingdom	5/15	10	10	1983
Zimbabwe (3)	5/15	10	10	N/A

Notes

1. If the recipient company owns/controls at least 25% of the equity of the paying company, the lower of the two rates applies.
2. A new DTT was signed with Denmark in 2009 and is applicable from 2010.
3. The treaty has not been ratified by one of the parties.
4. A tax rate of 5% will be applicable to literary, scientific, and work of art; films and works created like films; or other source of reproduction tone or picture. A tax rate of 10% will be applicable to patents, petty patents, brands, models and samples, technical innovations, secret formulas, or technical procedures.
5. Only in cases when dividends are to be paid to Serbian residents. If paid to Malaysian residents, they are taxable at 20% in Serbia.
6. A 0% rate is applicable in cases when the income recipient is the government or government owned banks.
7. WHT rate refers solely to dividends distributed from Serbia. In Malta, WHT cannot be higher than CIT on profit before dividend distribution.

Tax administration

Taxable period
The tax period in Serbia is the calendar year. However, entities have a possibility to opt for a different tax period other than the calendar year (subject to the approval of the Ministry of Finance), but still 12 months long. Once approved, such tax period must be applied for at least five years.

Tax returns
CIT returns, together with all supporting documents (e.g. tax depreciation and tax credit forms), must be filed with the tax authorities by 10 March of the following year.

A newly established company needs to register with the tax authorities within 15 days of registration with the court.

Serbia

Payment of tax

CIT is payable monthly in advance instalments by the 15th day of the following month for the prior calendar month. The amount of payable advances is determined on the basis of a company's CIT calculation for the previous year.

The due date for final settlement of CIT liability for the previous year is 10 March of the current year.

Audit cycle

There are no specific rules regarding the audit cycle in Serbia.

Statute of limitations

The statute of limitations period for assessment of tax liabilities is five years from the year in which tax should have been assessed. The statute of limitations for collection of tax liabilities is five years from the year in which tax was due for payment. This is with the exception of pension insurance contributions, which do not become statute barred.

The statute of limitations commences from 1 January of the year following the year in which the tax return/liability was due.

A tax period is considered to be closed for further audits after the audit by the tax authorities has been finalised and final decision issued. A tax period can be reopened for audits in case of existence of new information that was not available at the time of the audit.

Topics of focus for tax authorities

Historically, audits by the tax authority have been focused primarily on VAT, personal income tax, and social security contributions assessment.

Singapore

PwC contact

Alan Ross
PricewaterhouseCoopers Services LLP
8 Cross Street, # 17-00
PWC Building
Singapore 048424
Tel: +65 6236 3388
Email: alan.ross@sg.pwc.com

Significant developments

The 2012 Budget was announced on 17 February 2012. Corporate tax changes include the following:

- Cash grant of 5% of the taxpayer's revenue (capped at 5,000 Singapore dollars [SGD]) for the year of assessment 2012 (i.e. income year 2011).
- Enhancements to the Productivity and Innovation Credit scheme.
- Enhancements to the Mergers and Acquisitions Allowance scheme.
- Introduction of guidelines to give certainty to investors when their gains from the disposal of equity investments will not be taxed.
- Introduction of enhanced writing down allowances for productive equipment placed overseas for approved projects.
- Changes to the incentives for the maritime, aviation, and financial sectors.
- Liberalisation of the double tax deduction for internationalisation activities.
- Changes to the filing and payment deadline for withholding tax (WHT).
- Liberalisation of writing down allowances for low-value assets and renovation costs.

Indirect tax changes include the following:

- Goods and services tax (GST) exemption on investment-grade gold and precious metals.
- Extension of the GST temporary import relief period.
- Extension of the GST Tourist Refund Scheme to certain international cruise tourists.
- Increase in the GST import relief for incoming travellers.
- Increase in excise duties for certain tobacco products.

For details of the 2012 Budget proposals, refer to our 2012 Budget Commentary at http://www.pwc.com/sg/en/budget-commentary/index.jhtml

Taxes on corporate income

Companies (resident and non-resident) which carry on a business in Singapore are taxed on their Singapore-sourced income when it arises and on foreign-sourced income when it is remitted or deemed remitted to Singapore. Non-residents are subject to WHT on certain types of income (e.g. interest, royalties, technical service fees, rental of movable property) where these are deemed to arise in Singapore (*for details, see the Withholding taxes section*).

Tax on corporate income is imposed at a flat rate of 17% for the year of assessment 2012 (i.e. income year 2011). There is an exemption of up to SGD 152,500 out of the first SGD 300,000 of taxable income.

Singapore

For qualifying start-up companies, a three-year tax exemption on the first SGD 100,000 and a further exemption of up to SGD 100,000 on the next SGD 200,000 of taxable income are available.

In addition, for the year of assessment 2012 (i.e. income year 2011), there is a one-off cash grant of 5% of the company's revenue (capped at SGD 5,000). The cash grant is available only to companies who have made contributions to the Central Provident Fund in 2011, which means they must have had at least one Singaporean or permanent resident employee in that year.

Singapore adopts a one-tier taxation system, under which all dividends are tax-exempt in the shareholder's hands.

Corporate residence

In Singapore, the tax residence of a corporation is determined by the place where the central management and control of its business is exercised. This is taken generally to mean the place where the directors meet to exercise *de facto* control, although the Inland Revenue Authority of Singapore (IRAS) has recently set out further qualifying criteria.

Permanent establishment (PE)

The presence of a PE is largely irrelevant, except for treaty purposes, as Singapore taxes with reference to the source of income rather than the presence of a PE.

However, a PE is a clear indication of source.

The definition of a PE in Singapore's double taxation agreements (DTAs) is largely based on the Organisation for Economic Co-operation and Development (OECD) Model Tax Convention definition.

It is generally taken to be a fixed place through which the business of an enterprise is wholly or partly carried on, and normally includes a place of management, a branch, an office, a factory, a workshop, and a place of extraction of natural resources, etc.

In addition, and subject to the terms of the relevant agreements, a non-resident may also have a PE in Singapore if one:

- has a building site or a construction, assembly, or installation project that lasts longer than a specified number of months, or supervisory activities connected with the building site or construction project
- furnishes services (including consultancy services) through employees in Singapore for more than a specified number of days or months, or
- has an agent in Singapore who has, and habitually exercises, a general authority to negotiate and conclude contracts on behalf of the enterprise.

The Singapore tax legislation defines a PE more broadly than most of the DTAs; however, as mentioned above, this is largely irrelevant where a treaty can take precedence.

Other taxes

Goods and services tax (GST)

GST is charged at 7% on the supply of goods and services made in Singapore by a taxable person in the course or furtherance of one's business.

The only exemptions from GST are prescribed financial services (including life insurance) and the sale or rental of residential properties. Zero-rating only applies to the export of goods and international services.

GST is also levied on imports of goods, at the time of importation. However, there are reliefs available to ease the cash-flow burden of import-export traders by suspending GST at the time of importation. GST is not currently charged on imports of services.

A taxable person is one who is, or is required to be, registered for GST. GST registration is required if one's taxable turnover exceeds SGD 1 million per year. Voluntary registration is permitted if the taxable turnover is below the registration limit, subject to conditions.

A supply of goods is made in Singapore if the goods are in Singapore at the time of supply, and a supply of services is made in Singapore if the supplier belongs in Singapore. Generally, a person belongs in Singapore if one's business (including carrying on a business through a branch or agency) or fixed establishment is in Singapore.

A taxable person is allowed to offset the input GST paid on taxable purchases against the output GST chargeable on supplies made. However, certain purchases are specifically denied an input GST deduction. These include supplies of goods and services such as non-business expenses, club subscription fees, family benefits, car rental expenses, motor vehicle expenses, medical expenses, and transactions involving betting, sweepstakes, lotteries, fruit machines, or games of chance.

A non-resident is not entitled to GST refunds except by appointing a resident tax agent to act on one's behalf. The resident tax agent can then recover import GST paid on behalf of the non-resident business but will be required to account for output GST on any subsequent supply of the non-resident's goods in Singapore.

Customs and excise duties

Singapore is essentially a free port with minimal import restrictions. Customs and excise duties are imposed on intoxicating liquors (SGD 48 to SGD 70 per litre of alcohol or SGD 90 per kilogram of non-liquid alcohol preparations), tobacco products (SGD 239 to SGD 352 per kilogram), motor vehicles (12% to 20% *ad valorem*), and petroleum products (SGD 3.70 to SGD 7.10 per dal).

Property tax

Property tax is levied annually at 10% on the annual value of houses, land, buildings, or tenements. The rates charged owner-occupied residential property, however, are graduated from 0% to 6% of the annual value of the property.

Stamp duties

Stamp duties are levied on written documents relating to stocks and shares at 0.2% and on those relating to immovable property in Singapore at graduated rates of up to 3%.

Leases with annual rents not exceeding SGD 1,000 are exempt from stamp duty.

Singapore

Seller's stamp duty is levied on the sale of residential property (this excludes sales by property developers) if the sale takes place within four years of the purchase date. Stamp duty rates of 4% to 16% apply, depending on the holding period.

Additional buyer's stamp duty (ABSD) is also levied on the purchase of residential property. A higher rate of 10% is applicable to purchases by foreigners and non-individuals, while 3% ABSD is levied on the second and subsequent property bought by permanent residents and on the third and subsequent property bought by Singaporeans.

Foreigners of certain nationalities who fall within the scope of the respective free trade agreements will be accorded the same treatment as Singaporeans.

Foreign Workers Levy (FWL)
The FWL is a monthly levy of up to SGD 470 that employers are liable to pay for each foreign employee (Work Permit or S Pass holders) hired. The levy rate depends on the employee's qualifications, the employer's industry, and the ratio of foreigners to Singaporeans and permanent residents employed in the company. The government has announced that the FWL will be gradually increased until July 2013.

Branch income

Tax rates on branch profits are the same as on corporate profits. There is no branch profits remittance tax on the repatriation of profits to the head office.

Income determination

Inventory valuation
There are no special rules as to which valuation basis should be adopted for inventories (stock-in-trade) in the case of a continuing business, as long as the basis is consistent from one year to another. However, a last in first out (LIFO) basis of valuation is not permitted for tax purposes. Generally, tax reporting conforms to book reporting.

Capital gains
There is no tax on capital gains. Where there is a series of transactions or where the holding period of an asset is relatively short, the tax authorities may take the view that a business is being carried on and attempt to assess the gains as trading profits of the corporation. The United Kingdom (UK) Badges of Trade, which are used in judicial decisions to distinguish capital and revenue transactions, are generally applied in determining this issue. They include the existence of a profit-seeking motive, the number of transactions, the nature of the asset, the existence of similar trading transactions or interests, changes to the asset, the way the sale was carried out, the source of finance, the interval of time between purchase and sale, and the method of acquisition.

During the 2012 Budget, it was announced that guidelines will be introduced to give certainty that gains from the disposal of equity investments that take place after 1 June 2012 will not be taxed if at least 20% of the shares in the investee company have been held for a continuous period of at least 24 months prior to the disposal. Further details will be released.

Singapore

Dividend income
Singapore dividends are exempt in the hands of the recipient.

Stock dividends
Stock dividends generally are not taxable. However, certain distributions could be treated as deemed dividends in certain circumstances.

Deemed dividends
Certain distributions to shareholders under a capital-reduction scheme, a share buy-back, or a share redemption exercise may be treated as dividends paid by the company. Under the one-tier taxation system, this is not a significant issue unless the transaction is not correspondingly treated as a dividend in the hands of the shareholder. In which case, the gain may be taxable if it is in respect of a trade or business.

Interest income
Singapore-sourced interest income is taxable when it arises, and foreign-sourced interest is taxable when it is remitted or deemed to be remitted to Singapore. *For further details on foreign-sourced interest income and the availability of foreign tax credit, refer to Foreign income below.*

Foreign income
A corporation, whether resident in Singapore or not, is taxed on foreign income when it is received in Singapore. Legislative provisions govern the basis of treating foreign income as received in Singapore. There are no special rules for taxing the undistributed income of foreign subsidiaries.

Where income is earned from treaty countries, double taxation is avoided by means of foreign tax credit granted under those treaties. For non-treaty countries, unilateral tax credit is given in respect of foreign tax on all foreign-sourced income. These foreign tax credits may be pooled with effect from the year of assessment 2012 (i.e. income year 2011), subject to certain conditions.

Foreign dividends, foreign branch profits, and foreign service fee income remitted to Singapore may be exempt from tax if they fulfil certain conditions.

Deductions

Depreciation
Tax depreciation is allowable at specified rates on buildings used in qualifying industry sectors, subject to conditions. However, in 2010, industrial building allowances were replaced by a Land Intensification Allowance. The latter provides for faster depreciation but is subject to approval as it is allowed as a tax incentive. Transitional provisions for industrial building allowances are available for taxpayers who committed to qualifying capital expenditure before 22 February 2010.

Tax depreciation is available on machinery and equipment on a straight-line basis over their specified working life for all types of business. In lieu of the straight-line basis, accelerated tax depreciation allowances can be claimed by all businesses on all machinery and equipment in equal instalments over three years.

A 100% depreciation allowance is available on capital expenditure incurred on computers, robots, standby generators, pollution control and energy-efficient equipment, certain diesel-driven vehicles, and prescribed automation equipment.

Singapore

Writing down allowances on a straight-line basis over five years are allowable on the cost of acquisition of intellectual property, subject to certain conditions.

In addition, enhanced allowances may be available for the acquisition of automation equipment and intellectual property (*see Productivity and Innovation Credit in the Tax credits and incentives section*).

Gains on tax depreciable property (i.e. the excess of proceeds over tax base) are taxed as ordinary income to the extent that tax depreciation has been allowed; that is, there is a clawback of tax depreciation on the disposal of the asset.

Goodwill
Payments for the acquisition of goodwill are generally capital in nature and not deductible.

Start-up expenses
Generally, expenses incurred prior to the commencement of business are not tax deductible. However, from the year of assessment 2012 (income year 2011), most businesses are allowed to deduct expenses incurred in the 12 months immediately preceding the accounting year in which the business earned its first dollar of trading income. Deductible expenses are those that would have been allowed a deduction had they been incurred after the business commenced operations.

In addition, deductions and writing down allowances are available for certain types of pre-commencement expenditure (acquisition of plant and machinery, R&D, etc.) that are deemed to be incurred on the first day on which the taxpayer carries on one's business.

Interest expenses
Interest incurred on capital employed in the production of income, and borrowing costs that are incurred as a substitute for interest or to reduce interest costs, will be allowed as a tax deduction.

R&D expenses
Expenses incurred in respect of R&D carried out in Singapore qualify for a tax deduction of 150% of the expenses incurred. If the R&D is carried out overseas, the expenses incurred can be deductible if they meet certain conditions.

From year of assessment 2012 (income year 2011), expenditure incurred in relation to R&D cost-sharing arrangements will qualify and be accorded the same tax treatment as R&D expenses. The 100% writing down allowance for expenditure on approved R&D cost-sharing arrangements that is available for arrangements entered into on or after 17 February 2006 will be phased out. Details have yet to be announced.

Enhanced deductions may also be available under the Productivity and Innovation Credit scheme (*see Productivity and Innovation Credit in the Tax credits and incentives section*).

Bad debts
Bad trade debts and provisions for trade debts are deductible to the extent that they are incurred in the business. Doubtful debts are deductible if they are properly estimated and specific. General provisions for bad debts are not deductible.

Singapore

Businesses that have elected to align their tax treatment of financial instruments with the accounting treatment prescribed by SFRS 39 (Financial Instruments: Recognition and Measurement) will be allowed a tax deduction for impairment losses on trade debts when they are incurred (regardless of whether they are general or specific provisions). Correspondingly, any reversal will be taxed.

Charitable contributions
Donations are deductible only if they are made in cash or another prescribed form and to an approved recipient. The deduction allowed for qualifying donations is generally 250% of the value of the donation.

Fines and penalties
Fines and penalties imposed for violations of the law are not deductible.

Taxes
Income taxes are generally not deductible in determining corporate income. However, irrecoverable GST is deductible under certain circumstances. The FWL and property taxes are deductible to the extent they are incurred wholly and exclusively in the production of income.

Other significant items
Private automobile expenses are not deductible.

The tax deduction for medical expenses is limited to 2% of total payroll if the employer implements certain portable medical insurance or benefit schemes. Otherwise, the amount deductible will be limited to 1% of total payroll. Where the company is exempt or taxed at a reduced rate, the expenses disallowed are effectively taxed at the prevailing corporate rate.

A tax deduction for employee share-based remuneration (stock awards or stock option schemes) is allowed only if treasury shares in the company or its holding company are purchased to fulfil such obligations. From year of assessment 2012, a company may also claim a tax deduction when the share-based remuneration scheme is administered by a special purpose vehicle (SPV). The deduction is restricted generally to the lowest of the actual outlay incurred by the company, its holding company, or the SPV.

Net operating losses
Loss carryover, including unutilised tax depreciation allowance, is unlimited, provided shareholdings in the loss-making corporation have not changed beyond 50% of the issued and paid-up capital. Additionally, for tax depreciation allowances to be carried forward, the same trade needs to be continued. The tax authorities may exercise discretion to allow carryover of tax losses and unutilised tax depreciation even when there has been a change in shareholding beyond 50%, absent any tax avoidance motives. Losses of up to SGD 100,000 incurred by the company in the current year can be carried back for one year.

Payments to foreign affiliates
Payments to non-residents, including foreign affiliates, are deductible, provided they are fair and reasonable, are revenue in nature, and can be seen to be relevant to earning the payer's income.

Singapore

Group taxation

A company is allowed to transfer excess current year trade losses, current year tax depreciation, and current year approved donations to another company within the same group if certain conditions are satisfied.

Broadly, to qualify for group relief, companies must be incorporated in Singapore, belong to the same '75%' group of companies such that there must be at least a 75% ownership relationship between claimant and transferor, and have the same accounting year-end. In addition, a group must comply with certain prescribed offset and apportionment rules.

Transfer pricing

The Income Tax Act contains provisions that may be used in a transfer pricing context to effectively allow IRAS to challenge and revise inter-company transactions. Additionally, specific transfer pricing provisions were introduced in 2009 that define the arm's-length principle and provide the IRAS with a right to make transfer pricing adjustments in cases where taxpayers do not comply with the arm's-length principle.

The IRAS has also issued transfer pricing guidelines to supplement the provisions in the Income Tax Act and the various treaties signed by Singapore. The guidelines cover the application of the arm's-length principle and documentation requirements relating to all related party transactions, including local related party transactions. The intention of the guidelines is to help taxpayers substantiate their transfer prices with their related entities by maintaining adequate documentation to mitigate the risk of tax adjustment by the IRAS and to safeguard them from potential double taxation. The IRAS has also provided guidance on matters relating to mutual agreement procedures (MAPs) and advance pricing arrangements (APAs).

In 2009, the IRAS also issued guidance on the application of the arm's-length principle to related party loans and services.

Although Singapore's income tax rates are traditionally lower than the majority of its trading partners, the IRAS is increasing its focus on transfer pricing issues.

Thin capitalisation

There are no formal thin capitalisation rules in Singapore. However, general anti-avoidance and transfer pricing provisions may operate in cases of blatant abuse.

Tax credits and incentives

There are various tax incentives available to taxpayers involved in specified activities or industries identified as being beneficial to Singapore's economic development.

Pioneer tax incentive

Corporations manufacturing approved products with high technological content, providing qualifying services, or engaging in countertrade activities may apply for tax exemption for five to 15 years under the pioneer tax incentive. Corporations may apply for their post-pioneer profits to be taxed at a reduced rate under the Development and Expansion Incentive, as discussed below.

Development and Expansion Incentive

Under the Development and Expansion Incentive, corporations engaging in new high-value-added projects, expanding or upgrading their operations, or undertaking incremental activities after their pioneer or post-pioneer period may apply for their profits to be taxed at a reduced rate of not less than 5% for an initial period of up to ten years. The total tax relief period is subject to a maximum of 20 years (inclusive of the post-pioneer relief period previously granted, if applicable).

Investment allowance

Under the investment allowance, a tax exemption is granted on an amount of profits based on a specified percentage (of up to 100%) of the capital expenditure incurred for qualifying projects or activities within a period of up to five years (up to eight years for assets acquired on hire-purchase). With effect from year of assessment 2013 (income year 2012), capital expenditure incurred for productive equipment placed overseas on approved projects may likewise be granted integrated investment allowances.

Productivity and Innovation Credit (PIC)

The PIC scheme provides for an enhanced 400% deduction for qualifying expenditure incurred in respect of six qualifying activities during the accounting periods that end between 2010 and 2014 (i.e. years of assessment 2011 to 2015). The six qualifying activities are:

- The acquisition or leasing of prescribed automation equipment.
- Staff training.
- The acquisition of intellectual property.
- The registration of intellectual property rights.
- R&D.
- Design.

The enhanced deduction is available only on the first SGD 400,000 of qualifying expenditure incurred each year on each of the qualifying activities although this cap may be combined for certain years of assessment. Certain activities are subject to approval or minimum ownership requirements.

Merger and acquisition allowance

The merger and acquisition allowance allows a write-off, over five years, of 5% of the value of qualifying merger or acquisition deals executed between 1 April 2010 and 31 March 2015, subject to a cap of SGD 5 million per year of assessment. This incentive is available only to companies that are incorporated, tax resident, and carrying on a business in Singapore. A 200% tax allowance will also be granted on transaction costs (capped at SGD 100,000 per year of assessment) incurred on qualifying deals from 17 February 2012 to 31 March 2015.

Financial services incentives

Financial sector incentive (FSI) scheme

The FSI scheme covers approved bond intermediaries, Asian currency units, approved derivative traders, approved fund managers, equity capital market intermediaries, operational headquarters, syndicated offshore credit and underwriting facilities, providers of high-value-added processing services supporting financial activities, futures members of the Singapore Exchange Limited, and members of the Singapore Commodity Exchange Limited.

S

Singapore

High growth, high-value-added activities such as services and transactions relating to the bond market, derivatives market, equity market (i.e. futures, securities trading, which includes sale of stocks, shares, bonds and other securities, and extends to brokerage, nominee, and custodian services in relation to securities trading), credit facilities syndication, and Islamic finance will be exempt from tax or taxed at 5%, whilst other broader range financial activities will only qualify for a 12% tax rate. The tax incentive period may last for five, seven, or ten years, subject to certain conditions being met.

Finance and treasury centre (FTC)

Income derived by an FTC from approved finance and treasury centre activities is taxed at a reduced rate of 10%. Approved activities include international treasury and fund management activities, corporate finance and advisory services, economic and investment research and analysis, and credit control and administration.

Interest payments to overseas banks and approved network companies are also exempt from WHT where the funds borrowed are used for approved activities.

Debt securities incentives

A package of tax exemptions and reduced tax rates is available to various players in the Singapore bond market, including those involved in certain Islamic financing arrangements.

Offshore insurance incentives

Approved insurance companies engaged in the business of insuring and reinsuring offshore risks are taxed at a rate of 10% on qualifying income arising from offshore risks business and at a rate of 5% on qualifying income arising from writing offshore Islamic insurance (*takaful*) and reinsurance (*retakaful*) business. Tax exemption is available for qualifying income from the writing of both onshore and offshore marine hull and liability risk insurance and offshore specialised risk insurance and for qualifying income of approved offshore captive insurance companies. In addition, a concessionary tax rate of 10% is available to qualifying insurance and reinsurance brokers on income derived from the provision of insurance broking and advisory services to non-Singapore based clients.

Real Estate Investment Trusts (REITs)

Distributions made to foreign non-individual investors by a listed REIT out of rental from Singapore real estate are subject to a reduced tax rate of 10%, subject to certain conditions. Listed REITs investing in foreign properties can apply for tax exemption for certain foreign income received in Singapore. Distributions out of this income similarly are exempt. Stamp duty relief is available upon the transfer of immovable Singapore property to a REIT, and GST concessions are available in respect of overseas non-residential properties and SPVs or sub-trusts.

Islamic financing arrangements

The income tax, stamp duty, and GST treatment of (a) Islamic financing arrangements based on (i) the cost-plus (*Murabaha*) concept, (ii) the investment-partnership (*Mudaraba*) concept, (iii) the leasing-with-option-to-purchase (*Ijara Wa Igtina*) concept for mortgage financing; and (b) Islamic debt securities (*Sukuk*) are aligned with conventional financing contracts that they are economically equivalent to, subject to certain conditions. In addition, concessionary tax rates are available for certain activities relating to Islamic financing (*see FSI scheme and Offshore insurance incentives above*).

Infrastructure project finance incentives

Tax exemption is available for interest income earned from qualifying investments in qualifying infrastructure projects/assets. FSI companies that provide project finance advisory services related to qualifying projects/assets pay tax at 5% on their qualifying income, and companies that provide management services to qualifying business trusts and funds pay tax at 10% on their qualifying income. Stamp duty relief is available also on the transfer of such projects/assets to listed companies.

Sovereign wealth funds

Tax exemption is available for income derived by a sovereign fund entity and an approved foreign government-owned entity from funds managed in Singapore.

Headquarters (HQ) schemes

Approved regional headquarters in Singapore are taxed at a concessionary rate of tax of 15% on qualifying overseas income. Approved international headquarters can negotiate for various tax incentives, including tax exemption or concessionary tax rates on qualifying income.

Maritime Sector Incentive (MSI) scheme

The MSI scheme consolidates all existing incentives for the maritime sector with effect from 1 June 2011. These include the tax exemption for shipping companies, the 10% concessionary tax rate for international freight and logistics operators, and the existing Maritime Finance Incentive (MFI) under which approved ship investment managers are taxed at 10% on their qualifying management-related income. It also includes approved ship investment vehicles, which are tax exempt on their qualifying vessel lease income; approved container investment enterprises, which are taxed at 5% or 10% on qualifying income from container-leasing; and approved container investment management companies, which are taxed at 10% on qualifying management fees.

During the 2012 Budget, it was announced that qualifying ship operators and lessors under the MSI scheme will be granted automatic tax exemption on gains from the disposal of vessels, vessels under construction, and new building contracts. This takes retrospective effect from 1 June 2011.

Other incentives

Incentives for not-for-profit organisations, international arbitration, investment holding companies, oil traders, international traders, general insurance companies, leasing companies, trust companies, cyber traders, and the provision of international legal services include tax exemptions or concessionary tax rates of 10% for qualifying income. The concessionary tax rate for liquefied natural gas (LNG) trading, aircraft leasing, qualifying oil traders, and international traders is further reduced to 5%.

Foreign tax credit

See Foreign income in the Income determination section for a description of the foreign tax credit regime.

Withholding taxes

Domestic corporations paying certain types of income to non-residents are required to withhold tax.

Unless a lower treaty rate applies, interest on loans and rentals from movable property are subject to WHT at the rate of 15%. Royalty payments are subject to WHT at the rate

Singapore

of 10%. The tax withheld represents a final tax, and applies only to non-residents who are not carrying on any business in Singapore or who have no permanent establishment in Singapore. Technical assistance and management fees for services rendered in Singapore are taxed at the prevailing corporate rate. However, this is not a final tax. Royalties, interest, rental of movable property, technical assistance, and management fees can be exempt from WHT in certain situations or subject to reduction in tax rates applicable, usually under fiscal incentives, or DTAs.

Payments made to public entertainers and non-resident professionals who perform services in Singapore are also subject to a final tax of 15% on the gross income. For public entertainers, this appears to be a final tax unless they qualify to be taxed as Singapore tax residents. However, non-resident professionals may elect to be taxed at the prevailing tax rate for non-resident individuals of 20% on net income if this results in a lower tax cost. The WHT rate on payments to non-resident entertainers has been reduced to 10% from 22 February 2010 to 31 March 2015.

With effect from 17 February 2012, ship charter fee payments are no longer subject to WHT.

The WHT rates are shown in the following table.

Recipient	Dividends (%) (1)	Interest (%) (2)	Royalties (%) (2)
Resident individuals	0	0	0
Resident corporations	0	0	0
Non-resident corporations and individuals:			
Non-treaty	0	15	10
Treaty:			
Albania	0	5 (3b)	5
Australia	0	10	10 (4a)
Austria	0	5 (3b, d)	5
Bahrain	0	5 (3b)	5
Bangladesh	0	10	10 (4a)
Belgium	0	5 (3b, d)	3/5 (4b)
Brunei	0	5/10 (3a, b)	10
Bulgaria	0	5 (3b)	5
Canada	0	15 (3e)	10
Chile (5a)	0	15	10
China, P.R.	0	7/10 (3a, b)	6/10 (4b)
Cyprus	0	7/10 (3a, b)	10
Czech Republic	0	0	10
Denmark	0	10 (3b)	10
Egypt	0	15 (3b)	10
Estonia	0	10 (3b)	7.5
Fiji Islands, Republic of	0	10 (3b)	10
Finland	0	5 (3b)	5
France	0	0/10 (3b, c)	0 (4a)

Singapore

Recipient	Dividends (%) (1)	Interest (%) (2)	Royalties (%) (2)
Georgia	0	0	0
Germany	0	8 (3b)	8
Hong Kong (5b)	0	15	10
Hungary	0	5 (3b, d)	5
India	0	10/15 (3a)	10
Indonesia	0	10 (3b, e)	10
Ireland	0	5 (3b)	5
Israel	0	7 (3b)	5
Italy	0	12.5 (3b)	10
Japan	0	10 (3b)	10
Kazakhstan	0	10 (3b)	10
Korea, Republic of	0	10 (3b)	10
Kuwait	0	7 (3b)	10
Latvia	0	10 (3b)	7.5
Libya	0	5 (3b)	5
Lithuania	0	10 (3b)	7.5
Luxembourg	0	10 (3b)	10
Malaysia	0	10 (3b, f)	8
Malta	0	7/10 (3a, b)	10
Mauritius	0	0	0
Mexico	0	5/15 (3a, b)	10
Mongolia	0	5/10 (3a, b)	5
Myanmar	0	8/10 (3a, b)	10
Netherlands	0	10 (3b)	0 (4a)
New Zealand	0	10 (3b)	5
Norway	0	7 (3b)	7
Oman	0	7 (3b)	8
Pakistan	0	12.5 (3b)	10 (4a)
Panama (5c)	0	5 (3b, d)	5
Papua New Guinea	0	10	10
Philippines	0	15 (3e)	10
Poland	0	10 (3b)	10
Portugal	0	10 (3b, f)	10
Qatar	0	5 (3b)	10
Romania	0	5 (3b)	5
Russian Federation	0	7.5 (3b)	7.5
Saudi Arabia (5c)	0	5	8
Slovak Republic	0	0	10
Slovenia	0	5 (3b)	5
South Africa	0	0	5
Spain (5d)	0	5 (3b, d, f, g)	5
Sri Lanka	0	10 (3a, b)	10 (4a)
Sweden	0	10/15 (3b, c)	0 (4a)
Switzerland	0	10 (3f)	5 (4a, d)
Taiwan	0	15	10
Thailand	0	10/15 (3a, b)	10
Turkey	0	7.5/10 (3a, b)	10

S

Singapore

Recipient	Dividends (%) (1)	Interest (%) (2)	Royalties (%) (2)
Ukraine	0	10 (3b)	7.5
United Arab Emirates	0	7 (3b)	5
United Kingdom	0	10 (3b)	10
United States (5b)	0	15	10
Uzbekistan	0	5	8
Vietnam	0	10 (3b)	5/10 (4c)

Notes

1. Singapore has no WHT on dividends over and above the tax on the profits out of which the dividends are declared. However, some treaties provide for a maximum WHT on dividends should Singapore impose such a WHT in the future.
2. The non-treaty rates (a final tax) apply only to non-residents who do not carry on business in Singapore or have a PE in Singapore. This rate may be further reduced by tax incentives.
3. Interest:
   a. Lower rate or exemption if received by a financial institution.
   b. Exempt if paid to the government.
   c. Lower rate or exemption if paid by an approved industrial undertaking.
   d. Exempt if paid by a bank and received by a bank.
   e. Exempt if paid to a bank but linked to a government loan agreement or paid to specific financial institutions/banks.
   f. Exempt if paid in respect of an approved loan or indebtedness.
   g. Exempt if paid to an approved pension fund.
4. Royalties:
   a. Royalties on literary or artistic copyrights, including film royalties, are taxed at the non-treaty rate.
   b. Lower rate for payments in connection with industrial, commercial, or scientific equipment.
   c. Lower rate for payments in connection with patents, designs, secret formulas/processes, or industrial, commercial, or scientific equipment/experience.
   d. Exempt for approved royalties.
5. Treaties:
   a. Treaty with Chile covers only international ship operations.
   b. Treaties with Hong Kong and the United States cover only shipping and air transport activities.
   c. Treaty applies from 1 January 2012.
   d. Treaty applies from 1 January 2013.

Tax administration

Taxable period
The tax basis period is the calendar year; however, for business profits, the accounting period will generally be adopted.

Tax returns
Tax is computed for each tax year based on the income earned in the preceding year (the tax basis period). The corporation files an estimate of its income within three months of the end of the accounting period followed by a return of income by 30 November of the tax year, and the tax is assessed by the Comptroller of Income Tax. There is no fixed date for the issue of assessments.

Payment of tax
Assessed tax is payable within one month after the service of the notice of assessment, whether or not a notice of objection to the assessment has been lodged with the tax authorities. Application may be made to the Comptroller to pay estimated tax liabilities on a monthly basis. However, the Comptroller is under no obligation to grant such an application.

Late payment of tax will attract penalties, up to a maximum of 17% of the outstanding tax.

Singapore

Audit cycle

The IRAS now adopts a risk-based approach to identifying compliance risk, with a focus on improving the behaviour of taxpayers who pose a higher risk of non-compliance. It also prioritises and tailors specific compliance programmes which aim to identify taxpayers who have made mistakes in their tax returns, create an audit presence in the community to deter non-compliance by other taxpayers, educate taxpayers on their tax obligations and how to comply with these, and identify areas of tax law, policies, and processes where the tax system can be simplified.

Statute of limitations

The statute of limitations is six years from the year of assessment (if the year of assessment is 2007 or a preceding year of assessment) or four years from the year of assessment (if the year of assessment is 2008 or a subsequent year of assessment). It does not apply where there has been fraud or wilful default by the taxpayer.

Topics of focus for tax authorities

In the past, the IRAS has focussed its compliance efforts on:

*   the timely filing of corporate tax returns
*   accurate filing of income and expenses, especially by family-owned and managed companies
*   abuse of the tax exemption scheme for new companies, and
*   claims for capital allowances.

The IRAS has announced that, in addition to the above, it will also be focussing on:

*   the classification of income and expenses by companies enjoying tax incentives
*   related-party transactions and the allocation of development costs by real estate developers, and
*   income declarations by companies whose principal activities are that of tutoring services or tuition agencies.

Other issues

Adoption of International Financial Reporting Standards (IFRS)

Companies incorporated in Singapore and Singapore branches of foreign companies are required by the Companies Act to prepare and present financial statements that comply with the Singapore Financial Reporting Standards (SFRS). In Singapore, the Accounting Standards Council (ASC) has the statutory authority to issue SFRS for adoption.

The SFRS is principally based on and substantially similar to the International Financial Reporting Standards (IFRS) that are issued by the International Accounting Standards Board (IASB). The ASC's strategic direction was the convergence of SFRS with IFRS by 2012 for use by listed companies. However, a few key outstanding issues remain to be resolved before full convergence can be implemented. These depend on the progress of certain IASB projects that are not expected to take effect before 1 January 2015. For unlisted companies, the development of IFRS for small and medium-sized entities is being observed and evaluated.

Companies are required to submit financial statements as part of their tax return filing. The IRAS generally accepts financial statements prepared for statutory filing, although companies that have been allowed to prepare their financial statements using standards

Singapore

other than SFRS, such as IFRS or the Generally Accepted Accounting Principles (GAAP) adopted by the United States, may be required to explain and/or account for any differences and make the necessary tax adjustments, if any.

In relation to financial instruments, the Income Tax Act was amended to align the tax treatment with the accounting treatment prescribed by SFRS 39 (Financial Instruments: Recognition and Measurement). As a concession, the IRAS allows taxpayers to elect to align their tax reporting of lease income to the accounting treatment prescribed by SFRS 17 (Leases), which requires operating lease income to be recognised using the 'effective rent method'.

Sample corporate tax calculation
Accounting period ended 31 December 2011 (year of assessment 2012).

	SGD	SGD
Net profit before tax per accounts		5,857,500
Less:		
Singapore dividend (exempt)	1,500	
Foreign-sourced dividend (exempt)	2,200	
Foreign-sourced interest (exempt)	1,600	
Profit on sale of fixed assets	34,000	
Capital exchange gain	6,750	(46,050)
		5,811,450
Add:		
Depreciation	650,485	
Foreign pension contribution	100,000	
Medical expenses (non-deductible)	500	
Legal fees (capital in nature)	15,500	
Automobile expenses	33,500	
Donations	9,000	
Penalties and fines	2,000	810,985
Adjusted profit before capital allowances		6,622,435
Less:		
Unutilised capital allowances brought forward	1,152,000	
Capital allowances (current year)	3,000,000	
Balancing charge	(7,700)	(4,144,300)
Adjusted profit after capital allowances		2,478,135
Less: Unutilised losses brought forward		(67,500)
Adjusted profit after capital allowances and unutilised losses brought forward		2,410,635

Singapore

	SGD	SGD
Less: Approved donations (250% deduction)		(22,500)
Chargeable income before partial exemption		2,388,135
Less: Partial exemption		
75% of first SGD 10,000	7,500	
50% of the next SGD 290,000	145,000	(152,500)
Chargeable income after partial exemption		2,235,635
Tax thereon at 17%		380,057.95
YA 2012 cash grant (lower of 5% of revenue or SGD 5,000)		(5,000.00)
Tax payable after set off of cash grant		375,057.95

Sint Maarten

PwC contact

Steve Vanenburg
PricewaterhouseCoopers
Julianaplein 38
Willemstad, Curaçao
Tel: +599 9 4300 000
Email: steve.r.vanenburg@an.pwc.com

Significant developments

At this moment there are no proposed changes, nor have changes been implemented recently. However, the Minister of Finance has installed a committee to review the existing tax regulations and propose changes to improve the fiscal competitiveness of Sint Maarten (St. Maarten). The committee will be seeking ways to implement a significant reduction of the personal and corporate income tax rate in exchange for a major simplification by reducing or abolishing deductions, accelerated depreciation of assets, investment allowances, and tax holidays, as well as a broadening of the tax base in general. The government's aim is to introduce these changes by 2013.

Transitional legislation

While the offshore tax regime was abolished in 2001, qualifying offshore companies incorporated before 1 January 2002 may continue to apply the old regime until 2019, provided that certain conditions are met under transitional legislation.

Taxes on corporate income

Resident corporations are taxed on worldwide income. Non-resident companies are taxed on the following St. Maarten-source income:

- Income attributable to a permanent establishment (PE).
- Income from real property situated in St. Maarten.
- Interest on loans secured by a mortgage on property situated in St. Maarten.

Capital gains are not differentiated from operating income and are subject to the same applicable rates. Corporations are taxed on their income as reflected in their profit and loss account, less certain deductible items.

Companies are generally taxed at a flat rate of 34.5%. Special minimum rates apply to the taxable income of certain companies:

Type of company	Rate (%)
New industries and hotels	2
Land development companies	2

Shipping business

Shipping companies are subject to the general profit tax rate of 34.5% but may apply for the tonnage regime. If applicable, their profit is calculated based on the rates in the table below. If a shipping company applies the tonnage regime, the actual profits or losses are not taken into account, regardless of whether they are regular profits or capital gains.

The calculated profit based on the table below is subject to the general tax rate of 34.5%.

Over (tons)	Not over (tons)	Profit per net ton (ANG*)
0	10,000	2.00
10,000	25,000	1.35
25,000		0.60

* Antilles guilders

Exempt companies
Please see the Tax credits and incentives section for more information on tax exempt companies.

Companies under transitional offshore rules
Transitional rules distinguish three types of offshore companies.

- Offshore companies which, on the last day of the financial year that ended before 1 January 2002, had all (or almost all) investments in or revenues from portfolio investments, royalties, holding companies, finance companies, or technical support subject to tax rates of 2.4% to 3% (while capital gains and losses were not taken into account) will be grandfathered through the last day of the financial year of the company that starts before 1 July 2019.
- Offshore companies which, on the last day of the financial year that ended before 1 January 2002, had all (or almost all) their profit subject to tax rates of 4.8% to 6% or, under certain circumstances, 2.4% to 3% and which had a valid ruling with the tax inspector (e.g. trading companies, banks, captives commissions, and fee-earning companies) on the aforementioned date or for which a request for (extension of) such a ruling had been filed on that date will be grandfathered through the last day of the financial year of the company that starts before 1 July 2019.
- Offshore companies that, on the last day of the financial year that ended before 1 January 2002, had invested all (or almost all) investments in or revenues from real estate property or rights connected thereto, located outside the Netherlands Antilles. These revenues were, under the old offshore regime, exempt from tax. For profit tax purposes, these companies will be grandfathered through the last day of the financial year of the company that starts before 1 July 2019.

Specific rules are applicable to companies that were incorporated after 30 June 1999 but before 31 December 2001. These companies may also qualify for the aforementioned transitional rules provided that these companies have been active in a meaningful way. In principle, a company will not be considered to have been active in a meaningful way if the assets of the companies consist predominantly of deposits or receivables on shareholders or affiliated parties.

The grandfathering period continues until 2019.

Corporate residence

Corporate residence is, in principle, determined by the place of incorporation. However, other factors may also determine residence. For example, a foreign company with effective management in St. Maarten is considered to be a resident. A company that has been established in St. Maarten will always be considered a resident of St. Maarten.

Sint Maarten

Offshore entities in St. Maarten must have a local managing director. This function is easily provided by one of the many trust companies established in St. Maarten.

Permanent establishment (PE)
The definition of a PE in St. Maarten is generally in line with the Organisation for Economic Co-operation and Development (OECD) model.

Transfer of legal seat
Legislation has been enacted under which a St. Maarten company is allowed to transfer its legal seat to another jurisdiction (if permitted under the laws of the outside jurisdiction) and a foreign company is allowed to migrate to St. Maarten.

Other taxes

Turnover tax
A 5% turnover/sales tax is levied on the revenue derived from services and deliveries rendered by an entrepreneur or company in St. Maarten. Note that non-resident service providers are also subject to this tax as of 11 February 2011.

A limited number of services and deliveries are exempt, such as:

* Exports.
* Certain basic food and other products.
* Electricity and water.
* Medical services.
* Services at the airport or in the harbour regarding imported or exported goods or goods in transit.
* Advisory and management services provided to or by offshore companies and offshore banks.

An entrepreneur liable to turnover/sales tax must file a declaration, with the Tax Inspectorate before the 16th day of the month following the month concerned, at the Tax Collector's office.

Customs duties/import tariffs
In general, there are no customs duties or import tariffs on St. Maarten, except for a special import tariff on gasoline. The rate is ANG 29 per hectolitre.

Excise duties
There are no excise duties in St. Maarten.

Property taxes
There is no property tax in St. Maarten.

Transfer tax
The transfer of immovable property located in St. Maarten is subject to a 4% transfer duty.

Stamp taxes
A stamp tax is levied in two ways, in the form of stamps and as stamped paper.

Stamp tax applies to documents such as government licences, leases, agreements, and court documents. The rate depends on the type of document. As an example, the stamp tax for bank checks is ANG 0.25. The general rate for each page of a legal document is ANG 5.

Branch income

Tax rates on the profits of PEs are the same as for resident corporations.

There are specific rules for the PE of an insurance company. In that case, the company may elect to declare profit based on a percentage of premiums received by the PE, as well as premiums the company has received from insured residents and from insured risks in St. Maarten. The insurance company may also elect to declare a profit that is in the same proportion to total profit of the company as the aforementioned premiums to total premiums.

No tax is withheld on transfers of profits to the head office.

Income determination

Inventory valuation
Both the last in first out (LIFO) and first in first out (FIFO) methods of inventory valuation are permitted, provided the chosen method conforms to sound commercial practice. Conformity of book and tax reporting is not required. However, occasions or situations for differences are very rare.

Capital gains
Capital gains or losses are, in principle, considered ordinary income and subject to standard corporate rates. An exemption from profit tax is granted for advantages (dividends and capital gains) from a qualifying participation (*see Dividend income below*).

The gain on disposal of depreciable assets may be carried over to a special tax deferral reinvestment reserve but must then be deducted from the acquisition cost of the later acquired asset. The reserve may be maintained for a maximum of four years. If the reserve has not been fully applied, the remainder will be liable to taxation in the fourth year.

Under the transitional regime for offshore companies (investment, holding, finance, and patent holding companies), capital gains and losses are tax exempt.

Dividend income
In general, a full participation exemption applies to all local as well as foreign participations for dividends as well as for capital gains. However, it is now required that dividends be derived from an active participation (non-portfolio investment) or a participation that is subject to tax.

Expenses incurred in connection with a qualifying participation (including capital losses) are not deductible, unless it can be demonstrated that these are indirectly incurred to realise profits that are subject to tax in St. Maarten.

Non-portfolio investment clause
A participation is deemed to be active if the gross income of that participation consists of not more than 50% of dividends, interest, or royalties received other than from an enterprise of that participation.

Subject-to-tax clause
A participation is deemed to be subject to tax if it is subject to a tax rate of at least 10%.

Sint Maarten

If at least one of these clauses has been met, the 100% participation exemption will apply. If none of these clauses are met, the participation exemption is limited to 70% of dividends. Consequently, the dividends would be subject to an effective tax rate of 10.35% (30% x 34.5% regular tax rate).

The 100% exemption also applies to income other than dividends, such as capital gains derived from qualifying participations.

Immovable property
The aforementioned clauses do not apply to dividends from a participation that (almost) exclusively (directly or indirectly) holds immovable property. The 100% participation exemption applies to these dividends.

Definition of dividend
A dividend is defined as a distribution of profits on shares or profit-sharing notes, paid from statutory profits or profit reserves. Dividends shall not be considered payments for the purchase of own shares or profit-sharing notes, distributions on shares upon liquidation, repayment of paid-up capital, or the distribution of bonus shares.

Minimum cost-price threshold for participations
The minimum cost-price threshold for shareholdings, profit-sharing notes, or voting rights of less than 5% is ANG 890,000.

Interest income
There is no specific regime for interest received. Interest income is therefore taxed at the same rate as other income.

Foreign income
A St. Maarten corporation is taxed on foreign interest and other income as earned, and on foreign dividends when received. Undistributed income of foreign subsidiaries is not taxable.

St. Maarten has adopted a definition of a branch (permanent establishment/permanent representatives) that is in line with the definition in the OECD Model Double Taxation Convention on Income and Capital.

The profits of a PE on Aruba, Curaçao, or the Netherlands, including the Caribbean Netherlands, are tax exempt in St. Maarten based on the tax arrangement with the Kingdom of the Netherlands. In the case of a PE outside the Kingdom of the Netherlands (i.e. the Netherlands, Aruba, Curaçao, and St. Maarten), the income realised through the PE, after deduction of foreign taxes, is tax exempt. In the case of a foreign loss, this is not deductible.

Foreign real estate is always deemed to be part of a PE and, as such, is fully tax exempt.

Deductions

Depreciation and amortisation
Depreciation of tangible fixed assets, excluding land, is taken over the estimated useful life of the asset. The depreciable base includes purchase price, customs duties, shipping costs, and installation costs, less residual value, if any. The straight-line method is customary, but the declining-balance method is also acceptable. In addition, an accelerated deduction of one-third of the assets' depreciable basis may

be taken. The assets' remaining cost basis (two-thirds) is depreciated using one of the acceptable methods.

The cost basis of certain intangible assets, such as patents, trademarks, and copyrights, can be amortised over their expected useful lives. Goodwill and other intangibles resulting from the excess of purchase price over the cost basis of assets purchased are amortised over three to five years.

The tax department has issued the following estimated depreciation table:

Asset	Rate (%)	Residual value (%)
Buildings	2/2.5	10
Renovation	10	0
Inventory	10/20	10
Computer		
Hardware	33/50	0
Mainframe	10/12.5	0
Machinery and installations	10	10
Transportation		
Cars	20	10
Rental cars	33	15
Trucks and buses	10	15
Start-up costs	20	0
Goodwill	20	0

Start-up expenses

Start-up expenses should be capitalised and may be depreciated, comparable to goodwill, over five years.

Anti-abuse rules regarding interest and loans

Due to existing anti-abuse rules, the deduction for interest paid on intra-group debts relating to certain transactions is disallowed. However, if the taxpayer provides credible evidence of overriding commercial reasons for the transaction, or in case the interest in the hands of the recipient is taxed at an effective tax rate that is considered adequate by St. Maarten standards, the interest may be deductible.

In case of intra-group financing, for profit tax purposes the amount of interest paid or received should be based on arm's-length principles.

In case of profit participating loans, the interest will be qualified as dividend and will not be deductible. Interest received on such loans may meet the definitions of the participation exemption if the creditor also holds a qualifying participation in the debtor.

A write-down of an intra-group loan may be denied in case of a profit-participating loan, or if at the time of issuance it was foreseeable that the loan would never be repaid fully.

Charitable donations

Charitable donations to qualifying entities within the Kingdom of the Netherlands may be deducted to the extent that they exceed 1% of net income and ANG 100 after utilisation of tax loss carryforwards. The maximum deduction is 3% of net income.

Sint Maarten

Fines and penalties
Fines and penalties are not deductible in cases where they have been imposed by a criminal court in St. Maarten, or have been paid to avoid prosecution, and in cases of administrative fines imposed by a government agency in St. Maarten.

Taxes
Taxes, other than the corporate tax itself, incurred in the course of doing business are deductible.

Bribes, kickbacks, and illegal payments
Expenses that are connected to a criminal offence for which a taxpayer has been convicted are not deductible. Bribes paid to public servants and politicians are not deductible.

Net operating losses
Losses may be carried forward for a period of ten years. Start-up losses during the first four years for companies having tax holidays may be carried forward indefinitely. Carrybacks are not permitted.

Payments to foreign affiliates
The Corporate Tax Act provides for specific limitations for deduction of interest in certain cases of restructuring and refinancing involving the creation of artificial flows of interest payments to persons who are tax exempt or subject to lower taxes in their jurisdiction.

Group taxation

Fiscal unity
The Corporate Tax Act provides for fiscal unity treatment for corporate profit tax purposes. Resident companies with wholly owned resident subsidiaries could qualify for this regime. The parent company is entitled to submit one consolidated income tax return on behalf of the entire fiscal unity group. As a result, only the parent company is assessed.

Within certain limitations, losses of one company can be offset against the profits made by another company in the fiscal unity group. No profits need to be recognised on inter-company transactions, as these are disregarded for tax purposes. The fiscal unity applies for profit tax purposes only; the participating entities remain separate and identifiable under civil law.

Fiscal unity relief is confined to companies organised under the laws of St. Maarten, the Netherlands, Aruba, or Curaçao. The companies that invoke this relief must have their place of management in St. Maarten.

On the basis of the non-discrimination provision of a relevant tax treaty, entities established under the laws of a tax treaty party may also be admitted to the fiscal unity regime provided that they are resident in St. Maarten.

Transfer pricing
There are no specific regulations with regard to transfer pricing. However, based on case law, businesses can be required to show that in case of intra-company transactions, these transactions have been made at arm's length.

Thin capitalisation

In cases where a company receives a loan from an associated exempt private limited liability company (*Besloten Vennootschap* or BV), and the amount of the loan is more than three times the net equity of the company, the interest on the loan is not deductible for the part that is more than three times the net equity.

Tax credits and incentives

Foreign tax credit

A tax credit applies to income from abroad that has been subject to tax at source or to another tax on income. The tax credit is allowed for the income tax levied abroad, but shall not exceed the St. Maarten profit tax that is attributable to that foreign income.

Inward investment and capital investment

There are tax incentives or holidays for the establishment of new economic enterprises and hotels with a predetermined minimum employment and capital investment. Special provisions relate to the taxation of shipping and insurance companies.

Investment allowance

For a minimum investment of ANG 5,000, an 8% investment allowance on acquisitions and improvements (for new buildings, 12%) is permitted as a deduction from taxable profit in the year of investment and in the subsequent year, for businesses operating in St. Maarten.

Accelerated depreciation and tax rollover reserve

An accelerated deduction of one-third of the assets' depreciable basis may be taken. If a profit results at the time of sale of capital assets with the intention to replace that asset, the profit may be placed in a tax rollover account.

Tax exempt company

It is possible to elect tax-exempt status for a BV. To qualify for the exemption, a number of conditions must be met, including (but not limited to) the disclosure of beneficiaries, management, financials, and the activities (only investment and financing activities) of the company. Recently, the licensing of intellectual and industrial property rights, and other comparable property and usage rights, have been added to the list of allowed activities.

Another condition has been added that requires that no more than 5% of the revenues of the exempt company consist of dividends from subsidiaries that are not subject to a tax regime comparable to that of St. Maarten. A profit tax regime is comparable to that of St. Maarten if the foreign tax regime provides for a profit tax rate of at least 15% (50% of the old Netherlands Antillean rate, excluding island surcharges).

The subject-to-tax requirement is also met if the foreign tax regime appears on a list of comparable tax regimes. The list that has been issued includes all European Union (EU) and OECD member states and all jurisdictions with which St. Maarten has a tax treaty. According to the list, the subject-to-tax requirement is also met in the case of a jurisdiction that is included in the white list issued by the OECD, provided that no special tax regime is applicable.

Independent expert

Currently, an independent expert is required to certify that the exempt company meets the requirements for exempt status. If more than 5% of the revenues of the exempt

Sint Maarten

company consist of dividends from subsidiaries that are not subject to a tax comparable to that of St. Maarten, the independent expert must inform the Inspectorate of Taxes. The inspector notifies the company that it no longer meets the requirements for exempt status. The exempt status is then terminated starting the first day of the year following the year in which the notification becomes final.

Ocean shipping companies
Ocean shipping companies are taxed on a fixed profit per net ton of ANG 0.60 up to ANG 2.00 (or per 10 net ton in case of management and control). International aviation companies may apply a reduced tax rate against 80% of their profit, as their profits are deemed to be gained outside of St. Maarten. As a result, the overall effective tax rate is 9.66%.

New industries and hotels
New industries and hotels are granted partial exemption from profit tax and a minimum 2% tax rate for a period of five to 11 years. A minimum investment is required. Losses incurred during the first four years of operations may be used to offset taxable income for an indefinite period of time.

Land development companies
Land development companies are granted a tax holiday. They are exempt from tax on profits realised on the sale of the developed land. A minimum investment of ANG 1 million is required. Activities should be expected to enhance the economic development of St. Maarten.

Private foundations
Private foundations are exempt from St. Maarten profit tax, and their distributions are exempt from St. Maarten gift tax, as are contributions of assets to the foundation by a non-resident. Gift tax in the contributor's country may be applicable.

The 'private' foundation is a variant of the long-existing 'common' foundation. The most important difference is that the purposes of a common foundation may not include making distributions (other than distributions of an idealistic or social nature). This restriction does not apply to private foundations, whose purpose may include making distributions to the founders and others. A private foundation may not run a business or enterprise for profit. Acting as a holding company or investment company is not considered running a business. The private foundation is intended to be an alternative to the Anglo-Saxon trust, especially in civil law jurisdictions.

Withholding taxes

Although a dividend withholding tax (WHT) was approved in 1999, it has been decided that for the foreseeable future this tax will not enter into force. If it is decided that the tax will enter into force, there is a mandatory transitional period during which the tax will not be applicable to legal entities resident at that time in St. Maarten.

Tax treaties
St. Maarten currently has tax treaties in effect with the Netherlands, Aruba, Curaçao, and Norway. A double tax agreement (DTA) has been negotiated with Jamaica, but this has not entered into force yet. Furthermore, tax information exchange agreements (TIEAs) have been signed with several countries, including Australia, Canada, Denmark, Mexico, Spain, Sweden, New Zealand, and the United States. As a result, St. Maarten, as part of the former Netherlands Antilles, has been moved to the white list of the OECD Global Forum.

Tax arrangement for the Kingdom of the Netherlands (TAK)

As part of the Kingdom of the Netherlands (TAK), St. Maarten is party to a federal tax agreement with the Netherlands, Aruba, and St. Maarten. Subject to this treaty, dividends, interest, and royalties paid out to a St. Maarten company may qualify for reduced rates of WHT in the subject countries.

Dutch dividend WHT is 15% if the St. Maarten company owns less than 25% of the Dutch company. In St. Maarten, only 5% of these dividends are taxed, at a rate of 34.5%, which results in an effective profit tax rate of 1.725%.

If the St. Maarten company's interest is 25% or more, Dutch WHT can be reduced to 8.3%. This tax is then paid, under a special procedure, to the St. Maarten tax authorities. These dividends are fully exempt from profit tax in St. Maarten.

Capital gains derived from shareholdings in Netherlands' corporations are fully exempt from profit tax in St. Maarten, provided that the shareholding amounts to at least 25% interest in the corporation. If the shareholding amounts to less than 25%, the capital gain is tax exempt for 95%.

The WHT regime in the TAK also applies to the old St. Maarten offshore companies.

The TAK is to be revised. Negotiations have already started between Aruba and Curaçao each with the Netherlands. In the end, the existing TAK will then be replaced by separate tax agreements between two countries (e.g. between Aruba, Curaçao, and St. Maarten each with the Netherlands), as well as separate agreements between the three islands Aruba, Curaçao, and St. Maarten. The aim is to have the new agreements in place in 2013.

Tax administration

Taxable period

Profit tax is levied by way of a self-assessment system. Returns are to be filed on a calendar-year basis. Non-resident corporations may file their returns based on a calendar year basis or on a different book-year. On request, this may also apply, for example, when a resident company is the subsidiary of a foreign parent company (i.e. only a local company must request for a different tax year-end).

Tax returns

A provisional return must be filed within three months after the end of the book-year. A final return must be filed within six months after the end of the book-year.

For the provisional return, no extensions are granted. For the final return, an extension may be requested. In general, no extensions will be granted for more than 12 months after the book-year.

Payment of tax

Payment is to be made at the time of filing and in a lump sum on the basis of the self-assessment. This means that if the book-year equals the calendar year, the provisional return is due before 1 April of the following year, and the final return before 1 July of the following year.

Sint Maarten

In general, at the time of filing the provisional return, an amount equal to the profit tax of the previous year must be paid; the remaining balance due for the year for which the return is filed must be paid at the time of filing the final return.

For example, if the tax due for the year 2011 was 100, then at the time of filing the provisional return for 2012, which is due before 1 April 2013, that same amount must be declared and paid. If there is reason to believe that the amount for the year 2012 will be lower than for 2011, the estimated lower amount may be paid at the time of filing the provisional return, upon request.

At the time of filing the final return for the year 2012, which is due before 1 July 2013, the balance due must be paid; or if the total amount is less than the amount already paid up, a repayment will follow.

Audit cycle
As the profit tax is levied based on self-assessment, the tax department does not issue a final tax assessment. There is no specific cycle for audits. Depending on a desk review of the tax returns of the last couple of years, an audit may follow.

Statute of limitations
A reassessment can be imposed until five years after the tax year. In cases where the tax payer is considered to be in bad faith, a reassessment can be imposed until ten years after the tax year.

Topics of focus for tax authorities
There are no specific topics of focus. In case an audit is started, each aspect may be investigated. Often the audit will not only focus on the profit tax, but also the other tax obligations, such as sales tax, wage tax, and social security premiums.

Other issues

Exchange controls
In general, exchange control regulations are very liberal for offshore companies. Offshore companies established in St. Maarten can obtain non-resident status for exchange control purposes, which basically provides for total exemption from exchange controls. Onshore companies are subject to slightly stricter rules. These companies are subject to a licence fee of 1%.

Business combinations
The Corporate Tax Act provides for a tax facility for business mergers. In a business merger, a company acquires all or a substantial part of the trade or business of another company with a view towards combining the business operations of the two companies into a permanent financial and economic organisation. If the business is transferred as part of a business merger, the gains realised by the transferor are not subject to profit tax if certain conditions are met.

Although there is no specific provision in the Corporate Tax Act with regard to legal mergers, legal split-ups, and re-incorporations, the Tax Inspectorate has announced that when certain conditions are met, a tax facility also applies in these cases.

Slovak Republic

PwC contact

Todd Bradshaw
PricewaterhouseCoopers Tax, k.s.
Námestie 1. mája 18
815 32 Bratislava
Slovak Republic
Tel: +421 2 59 350 600
Email: todd.bradshaw@sk.pwc.com

Significant developments

The tax legislation in the Slovak Republic (Slovakia) has not been significantly amended recently. Nevertheless, the legislation is subject to frequent amendments and new official interpretations. Therefore, it is advisable to contact PwC Bratislava for up-to-date information.

The information included in this summary reflects the tax law as of 31 December 2011, unless otherwise stated.

Taxes on corporate income

As a member state of the Organisation for Economic Co-operation and Development (OECD), the Slovak Republic's system of corporate taxation generally follows OECD guidelines and principles.

Corporate income tax (CIT) applies to the profits generated by all companies, including branches of foreign companies.

Slovak tax residents are taxed on their worldwide income. Slovak tax residents may utilise a method of elimination of double taxation, if their income is taxed abroad. The exemption or credit method can be used to eliminate the double taxation depending on relevant double tax treaty (DTT) and the type of income.

Slovak tax non-residents are taxable in Slovakia on their Slovak-source income only. Slovak-source income is defined by local tax law and includes, inter alia, the business income of permanent establishments (PEs) and passive types of income, such as royalties, interest, and income from disposal of assets.

Slovakia has a flat CIT rate of 19%.

Local income taxes
Slovakia does not have local, state, or provincial CIT.

Corporate residence

A company is a tax resident in the Slovak Republic if it has its registered seat or effective place of management in the Slovak Republic.

Slovak Republic

Permanent establishment (PE)

A foreign company may create a PE if (i) its employees (or persons working for it) are present and providing services in the Slovak Republic on behalf of the foreign company where this activity is carried out through a permanent place of business, (ii) the employees conclude and negotiate agreements on the foreign entity's behalf, or (iii) the foreign entity establishes a building site within the territory of the Slovak Republic.

Other taxes

Value-added tax (VAT)

A basic VAT rate of 20% applies to all taxable supplies, with certain exceptions. Medical products and printed materials have a VAT rate of 10%. Exempt supplies without credit entitlement include postal services, financial and insurance services, education, public radio and TV broadcasting services, health and social services, the transfer and leasing of real estate (with exceptions), and lottery services. There are also other VAT-exempt transactions without credit entitlement, as well as exempt taxable supplies with credit entitlement.

VAT grouping is possible if certain conditions are met.

Customs duties

- Goods imported from non-European Union (EU) countries are subject to import customs clearance.
- Goods exported from the EU customs territory have to be declared for export customs clearance.
- The person responsible for paying the customs debt is the declarant.
- The declarant is the person making the customs declaration in one's own name, or the person in whose name the customs declaration is made.
- The custom declaration should be made in the prescribed form and manner (in writing or by another action).
- Import or export duties are customs duties and other charges payable on the import or export of goods (import VAT, excise duties, and charges under the common agricultural policy).
- The customs authorities require declarants to provide a deposit to cover the customs debt in the event that a customs debt arises. Such a deposit may be in cash, or may be provided by a guarantor.

To communicate with the customs offices, each person must have an Economic Operator Registration and Identification Number (EORI), which is registered by the customs authorities on request. EORI registration is mandatory for customs clearance.

The European customs rate, customs nomenclature, and customs tariffs are set by EU legislation.

Excise taxes

Excise tax is charged on the release to free tax circulation or import of tobacco products, wine, spirits, beer, mineral oil, electric energy, coal, and natural gas.

Immovable property tax

Immovable property tax, which is divided into land tax, building tax, and tax on apartments, is governed by the Act on Local Taxes. Immovable property tax is calculated based on the area of the real estate, its location, and its type, as well as the tax rate of each self-governing region.

Slovak Republic

The immovable property tax rate may vary significantly. Please find below the spread of the tax charges per square metre.

Tax rates in EUR	Four floor office building in centre of city of Bratislava	One floor hall rural area
Immovable property tax per square metre	8.30 *	0.73 - 1.012

* For each another floor, add an additional tax of EUR 0.33.

Transfer taxes
There are no transfer taxes in the Slovak Republic. Real estate transfer tax was abolished as of 1 January 2005.

Stamp taxes
There are no stamp duties or similar taxes on share or other property transfers in the Slovak Republic, although small administrative fees are payable to register such transactions.

Turnover taxes
There are no turnover taxes in the Slovak Republic.

Registration taxes
There are no registration taxes in the Slovak Republic.

Motor vehicle tax
Vehicle tax applies to vehicles that are used for business purposes in the Slovak Republic, regardless of where they may be registered. The taxpayer is the entity that uses the vehicle for business purposes. The tax rate depends on engine capacity, vehicle size, and the decision of each self-governing region.

Vehicle	Tons	Motor vehicle tax (EUR) Bratislava region	Presov region
Personal vehicles (1)		67 - 235	56 - 195
Commercial motor vehicles and buses (2)			
Vehicles with one or two axletrees	0 to 12	75 - 667	63 - 554
	12 to 30	835 - 2,456	693 - 2,038
	above 30	2,678	2,224
Vehicles with three axletrees	0 to 15	613	507
	15 to 40	726 - 2,792	604 - 2,317
	above 40	3,015	2,503
Vehicles with four and more axletrees	0 to 23	781	647
	23 to 40	949 - 2,347	787 - 1,948
	above 40	2,570	2,134

Notes

1. Tax rate is raised proportionally to number of cubic centimetres of swept volume of cylinder.
2. Tax rate is raised proportionally to weight and number of axletrees of the vehicle.

Slovak Republic

Branch income

A foreign company may trade through a Slovak branch, which must be registered in the Slovak Commercial Register. The taxable income of the branch must not be lower than that which an independent entity (e.g. a Slovak company) would achieve from carrying out similar activities under similar conditions. If the branch's taxable income cannot be assessed based on its income less costs, as adjusted for tax purposes, certain other methods may be used. A taxpayer may ask the tax authorities in writing to approve such a method.

Income determination

The tax base is generally the accounting result as determined under Slovak statutory accounting rules, adjusted for tax purposes. Under the transfer pricing rules, the tax base should be increased by the difference in prices charged between a Slovak entity and its foreign related parties compared with those that would be charged between independent parties. Slovak tax law generally reflects OECD rules with respect to transfer-pricing methods (*see Transfer pricing in the Group taxation section for more information*).

Inventory valuation
Stock (i.e. inventory) is valued at cost. Slovak legislation specifically provides for the use of the arithmetical average cost and first in first out (FIFO) methods to value stock. Last in first out (LIFO) may not be used. The tax treatment follows the accounting treatment.

Capital gains
Capital gains from the disposal of assets are included in the CIT base. The tax treatment of capital losses depends on the type of asset on which they arose.

Dividend income
Dividends paid out of profits earned on or after 1 January 2004, and liquidation surpluses and settlement amounts to which shareholders became entitled on or after 1 January 2004, are not subject to tax. Income from acquiring new shares due to an increase in share capital from retained profits or mergers and demergers within the Slovak Republic or the European Union is also not subject to tax.

Interest and royalty income
Slovak-source interest income earned by taxpayers with limited, as well as unlimited, tax liability is subject to withholding at a flat tax rate of 19%, except where the recipient of the deposit interest or the yield is a Slovak investment fund, Slovak supplementary pension fund, Slovak bank or the branch of a foreign bank, or the Slovak Export-Import Bank.

Royalty income is subject to the 19% corporate flat tax rate.

Interest and royalty income is exempt if it is paid by a Slovak payer to a recipient who is a tax resident in the European Union and is a beneficial owner of this income, provided that for 24 months before the payment:

* the payer owns at least 25% direct shareholding of the recipient of the income
* the recipient owns at least 25% direct shareholding of the payer of the income, or

- a third entity resident in European Union owns at least 25% direct shareholding on both the payer and the recipient of the income.

Unrealised foreign exchange gains/losses
The taxpayer may decide whether to include unrealised foreign exchange differences relating to unsettled payables and receivables in the tax base in the tax period when they are accounted for or in the tax period when they are realised. However, the decision to include these differences when they are realised must be made in writing to the Tax Office before the start of the tax period. Any subsequent decision to revert back to including these differences must be made before the end of the tax period concerned.

Foreign income
Companies resident in the Slovak Republic are taxed on their worldwide income, including income of its foreign branches. A Slovak tax resident entity is able to deduct from its tax base a tax loss made by its taxable PE (e.g. branch) outside the Slovak Republic, adjusted for Slovak tax purposes.

Credit relief is available for foreign tax paid under most of Slovakia's DTTs. Alternatively, exemption of foreign income taxed abroad from taxation in Slovakia may apply.

Slovakia does not have provisions related to deferral.

Deductions

Depreciation and amortisation
Tax depreciation is calculated on an asset-by-asset basis using a straight-line or reducing-balance method at statutory rates, and is generally available for expenditure incurred on tangible fixed assets. Some types of assets are excluded from depreciation (i.e. land, artwork, and national monuments).

Tangible fixed assets are classified into tax depreciation groups to which different depreciation periods apply, as follows:

Depreciation group	Assets	Depreciation (years)
1	Motor vehicles, office machines and computers, and tools and implements	4
2	Engines, most production line equipment, furniture	6
3	Buildings made of metal, turbines, air-conditioning systems, and ships	12
4	Buildings of a permanent nature	20

Taxpayers do not have to depreciate an asset every year. Tax depreciation may be interrupted in any year and continued in a later year without a loss of the total tax depreciation available.

A lessee can depreciate a tangible fixed asset held under a financial lease. For tax purposes, the depreciation period equals the leasing period, and the tax depreciation base equals the acquisition value of the leased asset without VAT and financing costs, plus expenses related to acquisition of the leased asset that the lessee incurred before the asset was put into use.

Slovak Republic

The value to be used as the basis for tax depreciation depends on how the asset is acquired and is usually based on one of the following:

- Acquisition costs (i.e. the price for which the asset was acquired).
- The taxpayer's own costs incurred, if the asset is acquired or produced internally.

Intangibles are amortised for tax purposes in line with their accounting amortisation (i.e. over the useful life of the intangible asset).

Goodwill
Amortisation of purchase goodwill, including the goodwill on purchase of a business as a going concern, if it represents an identifiable intangible asset, is tax deductible.

For goodwill created at the contribution of business as a going concern or goodwill created at a merger, the tax deductibility of the goodwill depends on the method of tax treatment of this reorganisation. If the reorganisation is performed for tax purposes in fair market values, the goodwill created will be tax effective. On the other hand, if the reorganisations are made in original values, the goodwill created is not tax effective.

Start-up expenses
Start-up expenses are tax deductible in the period when incurred.

Interest expenses
Interest expenses incurred in order to generate taxable income can be treated as tax deductible.

However, since dividends are tax exempt, the costs of interest on loan incurred to acquire the shares should be treated for tax purposes as costs incurred to generate non-taxable income, i.e. as not tax deductible.

Bad debt provisions
Provisions for unsecured receivables from loans created by banks, and bad debts of regular commercial companies, are fully tax deductible (subject to certain conditions) once the debt has been overdue for more than 1,080 days (20% of the bad debt is tax deductible when it has been overdue for more than 360 days, and 50% after 720 days), provided certain conditions are met.

Charitable contributions
Charitable contributions are treated as gifts, which are not tax deductible.

Pension expenses
Contributions to supplementary pension savings made by the Slovak employer on behalf of the employee, up to 6% of the gross salary of the employee participating in these plans, are tax deductible.

Fines and penalties
Statutory penalties and fines are not tax deductible. Contractual penalties and late payment interests are generally tax deductible on a cash basis.

Taxes
Road tax, real estate tax, and most of other taxes are tax deductible. Social security contributions paid by an employer with respect to employees are also tax deductible.

Income tax is not tax deductible.

Other non-deductible expenses
Expenses are generally tax deductible if incurred to generate, secure, and maintain the entity's taxable income. However, certain other costs are specifically not tax deductible. These include entertainment costs, various provisions (e.g. provisions to tangible and intangible assets, certain bad debt provisions), and certain expenses in excess of statutory limits (e.g. employee travel expenses and meal allowances).

Net operating losses
A company or branch may carry forward and utilise a tax loss for a period of up to five years following the year in which the loss arose, and for up to seven years for tax losses reported after 31 December 2009. Each year's tax loss should be considered separately, and can be utilised over its own five or seven-year period.

Carryback of losses is not available in the Slovak Republic.

Payments to foreign affiliates
Generally, deductions may be claimed for royalties, management service fees, and interest charges paid to foreign affiliates, provided such amounts are at arm's length.

Group taxation

There is no concept of group CIT in the Slovak Republic. Each company in a group is taxed individually.

Transfer pricing
Under the transfer pricing rules, prices in transactions between a Slovak company and its foreign-related parties should be at arm's length, which means the prices should be at rates similar to those that would be charged between unrelated parties for the same or similar transactions under comparable conditions. Although the OECD Transfer Pricing Guidelines were formally not implemented, these are usually followed for determination of arm's-length prices.

If transactions between the related parties are not made at arm's length, and this results in a reduction in the Slovak entity's corporate tax base, then the tax authorities can adjust the corporate tax base to that which it would have been achieved if arm's-length prices had been used.

Transfer pricing documentation
All Slovak taxpayers must keep sufficient transfer pricing documentation to justify prices charged by or to their foreign related parties. The Slovak Ministry of Finance has issued a guideline setting out detailed requirements for transfer pricing documentation (the Guideline) for entities which are obliged to prepare their financial statements under International Financial Reporting Standards (IFRS).

The EU code of conduct was formally not implemented. However, the Guideline requires maintaining transfer pricing documentation in a form generally in line with the EU standards.

Slovak tax inspectors may require transfer pricing documentation during a tax inspection. Without such documentation, transfer pricing adjustments (increased tax base) are much more likely to be imposed. In addition, entities reporting under IFRS may be specifically penalised for not keeping transfer pricing documentation or for non-compliance of their documentation within the Guideline requirements.

Slovak Republic

Thin capitalisation

There are no thin capitalisation rules in the Slovak Republic.

Controlled foreign companies (CFCs)

There is no CFC regime in place in the Slovak Republic.

Treatment of inter-company items

Dividends are not treated as taxable costs if they are paid out of the profit after tax earned since 2004.

Royalties, commissions, and other payments paid to foreign related parties are tax-deductible, provided they would be taxable if paid to a third party and if the charges are in line with transfer pricing rules.

Tax credits and incentives

There are several types of investment incentives potentially available, including corporate tax credits, discounts on the price of publicly owned real estate, and financial support for creating jobs or for training employees. All of these are treated as state aid.

Various conditions must be met in order for a company to qualify for state aid. These include a minimum amount of investment in fixed assets, where the amount depends mainly on the type of project and where it is located.

Investment incentives

Investment incentives (including tax credits) are potentially available for projects in the following areas:

- Industry.
- Technology centres.
- Shared services centres.
- Tourism.

The granting of a tax relief is subject to approval of the Slovak authorities. If certain conditions are met, a taxpayer may apply tax relief in the five subsequent years following the tax period in which the relief was granted.

Research and development (R&D) incentives

R&D incentives currently available under Slovak law include the following:

- Subsidies for R&D projects from the state budget.
- Income tax relief at the amount incurred for R&D.

Types of projects which can be granted investment incentives include:

- Fundamental research projects.
- Experimental development projects.
- Applied research projects.
- Feasibility studies.
- Protection of intellectual and industrial property.
- Staffing of R&D functions.

Withholding taxes

Mainly, the following payments are subject to withholding tax (WHT) when made by Slovak companies to foreign parties. However, a DTT may reduce or eliminate the rate:

Payments	WHT (%)
Management fees for services provided in the Slovak Republic	19
Royalties *	19
Interest on loans and deposits *	19

* Royalties and interest paid to related EU-resident companies are not subject to WHT if certain conditions are met.

Dividends paid out of profits arising in 2004 and later years are not subject to Slovak WHT.

WHT should be paid to the Tax Office no later than 15 days from the end of the calendar month following that in which the payment was made. The withholding obligation lies with the Slovak resident taxpayer. The taxpayer must also notify the tax administrator of the tax withheld and transferred. If the tax is not properly withheld, the unpaid tax becomes the Slovak tax resident's tax liability, and a penalty may be assessed.

Double tax treaties (DTTs)
This table highlights countries with which Slovakia has entered into a DTT.

Recipient	Interest (%)	Royalties (%)
Australia	10	10
Austria	0	0/5 (1)
Belarus	0/10 (3)	5/10 (1)
Belgium	0/10 (2a)	5
Bosnia and Herzegovina	0	10
Brazil	0/10/15 (2, 3)	15/25 (1b)
Bulgaria	0/10 (3)	10 (6)
Canada	0/10 (14)	0/10 (1)
China, P.R.	0/10 (4)	10
Croatia	10	10
Cyprus	0/10 (3)	0/5 (1)
Czech Republic	0	0/10 (1)
Denmark	0	0/5 (1)
Egypt (17)	N/A	N/A
Estonia	0/10 (15)	10
Finland	0	0/1/5/10 (8)
France	0	0/5 (1)
Germany	0	5
Georgia (17)	N/A	N/A
Greece	0/10 (3)	0/10 (1)
Hungary	0	10
Iceland	0	10
India	0/15 (4)	30
Indonesia	0/10 (3)	10/15 (5)

S

Slovak Republic

Recipient	Interest (%)	Royalties (%)
Ireland	0	0/10 (1)
Israel	2/5/10 (9)	5
Italy	0	0/5 (1)
Japan	0/10 (4)	0/10 (1)
Kazakhstan	0/10 (3)	10
Korea	0/10 (4, 11)	0/10 (1)
Latvia	0/10 (4)	10
Libya (18)	0/10 (3)	0/5
Lithuania	0/10 (4)	10
Luxembourg	0	0/10 (1)
Macedonia	10	10
Malta	0	5
Mexico	0/10 (3)	10
Moldavia	10	10
Mongolia	0	0
Montenegro	10	10
Netherlands	0	5
Nigeria	0/15 (3)	10
Norway	0	0/5 (1)
Poland	0/10 (4)	5
Portugal	10	10
Romania	0/10 (4)	10/15 (1a)
Russia	0	10
Serbia	10	10
Singapore	0	10
Slovenia	10	10
South Africa	0	10
Spain	0	0/5 (13)
Sri Lanka	0/10 (12)	0/10 (1)
Sweden	0	0/5 (13)
Switzerland (19)	0/10 (7, 11)	0/5/10 (1, 10)
Syria	0/10 (3)	12
Tunisia	0/12 (3)	5/15 (1)
Turkey	0/10 (3)	10
Turkmenistan	0/10 (3)	10
Ukraine	10	10
United Kingdom & North Ireland	0	0/10 (1)
United States	0	0/10 (1)
Uzbekistan	10	10
Vietnam	0/10 (3)	5/10/15 (16)

Notes

1. The lower rate applies to cultural royalties.
   a. In the case of Romania, the rate of 10% applies to royalties in respect of the use of trademarks, patents, or know-how. The higher rate applies in any other cases.
   b. In the case of Brazil, the rate of 25% applies to royalties for the use of trademarks. The lower applies in other cases.

2. The lower rate applies to interest on loans and credits granted by a bank for at least ten years in connection with the sale of industrial equipment; with the study, installation, or furnishing of industrial or scientific units; or with public works.
   a. The zero rate applies to interest on certain commercial debt-claims, loans guaranteed by public entities for export promotion, accounts/loans between banks/public institutions of the two states, and interest paid to another state or political subdivision of a local authority.
3. The zero rate applies if the interest is received by the government/the central bank/other state institutions (see the respective treaty for exact wording).
4. The zero rate applies if the interest is received by the government or the central bank or other state institutions, or if the receivables on which the interest is paid are guaranteed/financed/indirectly financed by the government/governmental institutions (see treaty for exact wording).
5. The rate of 10% applies to royalties for cinematography, TV broadcasting, and radio broadcasting, and to giving up rights related to royalties. The higher rate applies in other cases.
6. This rate also applies to payment for services.
7. WHT is 0% on bank loans.
8. The rate applies to copyrights; 1% applies to finance lease of equipment; 5% applies to equipment rental and royalties for software, cinematography, and TV and radio broadcasting; and 10% applies to payments for the use of trademarks and know-how.
9. The rate of 2% applies to state bonds, obligations, and loans insured or guaranteed by the National Bank of Slovakia/Israel, Slovak Society for Insurance of Foreign Credits and Loans, or Israel Society for Insurance of Foreign Trade; 5% applies if interest is received by a financial institution; and 10% applies in all other cases.
10. Slovakia can apply the rate of 5% to royalties for the use of trademarks, patents, or know-how paid from Switzerland to Slovakia, if Switzerland does not apply the 10% rate.
11. The zero-rate applies to interest on loans and credits in connection with the sale of industrial, business, or scientific equipment, or the sale of goods.
12. The zero-rate applies if the interest received is related to loans (monetary or non-monetary) provided to the government of the other contracting state corporation or any other institution with state shareholding or to loans provided to a bank institution under a governmental approval.
13. The zero-rate applies to copyrights.
14. The zero-rate applies to interest received by a resident of one state in respect of indebtedness of the other state government or political subdivision/local authority, or in respect of a loan made/guaranteed by the other state government in respect of imports/exports.
15. The zero-rate applies if the interest is received by the government, the central bank, or other state institutions, or if the receivables on which the interest is paid are guaranteed/financed/indirectly financed by the government/governmental institutions (see treaty for exact wording).
16. The rate of 5% applies to royalties for the use or the right to use of patent, draft or model, plan, confidential formula or procedure, for information related to industrial or scientific experience and for the use or the right to use of an industrial, business, or scientific device. The rate of 10% applies to royalties for the use or the right to use of trademark or for information related to business experience. The rate of 15% applies to royalties, other than those stated above.
17. Slovakia is waiting for Egypt and Georgia to announce their approval of DTTs.
18. DTT between Slovakia and Libya is effective as of 21 June 2010.
19. Slovakia and Switzerland signed the Protocol to a DTT on 8 February 2011, which is not ratified yet. Based on this Protocol, the interest rate will be maximum 5%. Industrial royalties are subject to 10%, but the potential reduction of the rate is in case the royalties are paid within European Union, and entities are considered to be related companies with direct share exceeding 25% for more than 24 months, which is in accordance with the EU Directive on interest and royalty payments made between associated companies.

Tax administration

Taxable period
The standard fiscal year is a calendar year, but a Slovak entity may opt to change this to a different 12-month period.

Tax returns
A corporate tax return must be filed together with the entity's financial statements within three months following the fiscal year-end. A three-month extension to the filing deadline may be used. Also, if part of the income to be reported in the tax return is from sources abroad, the taxpayer may extend the filing deadline by up to six months. To extend the filing deadline, the taxpayer must notify the Tax Office before the normal filing deadline. After notification, the deadline is automatically extended.

Slovak Republic

Payment of tax

The balance of tax due for a fiscal year is payable by the filing deadline.

Advance payments of corporate tax must be paid monthly or quarterly during the current tax period. Instalments are usually based on the last known tax liability of the entity. It is not necessary to pay tax advances if the last tax liability did not exceed 1,659.70 euros (EUR).

Statute of limitations

A tax may not normally be assessed or additionally assessed more than five years (ten years when DTT treaty was applied, including transactions with foreign related parties) after the end of the year during which the obligation to file a tax return arose, or during which the taxpayer was obliged to pay the tax. If a tax inspection is undertaken within this five-year period, another five-year period commences from the end of the year in which the taxpayer was notified of this action.

If a taxpayer utilises a tax loss, a tax or additional tax cannot be assessed more than seven years after the end of the year in which the obligation to file a tax return in which a taxpayer reported the tax loss arose.

However, tax may be assessed, or additionally assessed, no later than ten years after the end of the year during which the obligation to file a tax return arose, or during which the taxpayer was obliged to pay the tax.

Audit cycle

Generally the tax authority selects the taxpayers subject to tax audit based on certain criteria, which are not communicated to the public.

The taxpayers that utilise state aid in form of tax relief are subject to specific tax audit in the year of utilisation of the tax relief.

The tax audit has to be finalised within one year.

Topics of focus for tax authorities

The tax authorities, within a tax inspection, generally focus on transfer pricing, VAT, limited tax deductibility of special types of costs (e.g. entertainment, promotion costs), and tax incentives.

....

Other issues

Reserve fund

When a joint-stock company is incorporated, it must create a reserve fund of at least 10% of its share capital. The statutory reserve fund must be increased annually by an amount set out in the company's Articles of Association, but not less than 10% of its net profit, up to a total of 20% of the share capital.

A limited liability company must create a reserve fund following the first year in which it reports a profit, at the latest. The minimum contribution is then 5% of the net profit each year (or more if specified in the company's Articles of Association) up to a total of at least 10% of the company's share capital.

A branch of a foreign company is not required to set up a reserve fund.

A reserve fund may be used to cover prior year losses of the company, and in certain other limited situations, but it is not distributable.

Business combinations

Two alternative tax treatments may be used for business combinations, including in-kind contributions to a company's share capital, mergers, and demergers.

Under the first alternative, the taxpayer should value assets for tax purposes using their current market values, and the revaluation difference must be reflected in the appropriate company's tax returns within seven years of the transaction.

Under the second alternative, the taxpayer should continue to use the original tax book values of the assets, and revaluation difference is not taxable/tax deductible.

When selling a business, the purchaser must include goodwill or negative goodwill, acquired as part of the purchase, in its tax base within seven tax periods.

Adoption of International Financial Reporting Standards (IFRS)

Slovakia has adopted most of the principles of IFRS in its accounting law. However, there are still some differences between IFRS and Slovak accounting standards.

Obligation to prepare statutory financial statements according to IFRS

Financial institutions (banks, insurance companies, etc.) must prepare their statutory financial statements according to IFRS. In addition, a company which fulfils two or more of the following conditions, in two consecutive accounting periods, must prepare its statutory financial statements according to IFRS:

- The total value of assets is more than EUR 165,969,594.
- Net turnover exceeds EUR 165,969,594.
- The average number of employees in the individual accounting period exceeds 2,000.

If the Slovak taxpayer is obliged to prepare its financial statements under IFRS, the tax base is derived from either:

- the profit before tax under IFRS, adjusted for tax purposes using the 'IFRS Tax Bridge' issued by the Slovak Ministry of Finance or
- the profit before tax under Slovak statutory accounting standards.

S

Slovenia

PwC contact

Ákos Burján
PricewaterhouseCoopers
Cesta v Klece 15
SI-1000 Ljubljana, Slovenia
Tel: +386 1 58 36 058
Email: akos.burjan@si.pwc.com

Significant developments

Amendments to corporate taxation

The Slovene Corporate Income Tax (CIT) Act was amended in 2012. The changes became effective retroactively as of 1 January 2012.

The amendments, which are summarised below, aim to reduce the tax burden on business during the global economic downturn and to facilitate investments in equipment, intangible assets, and research and development (R&D).

Progressive reduction of CIT to 15%

Changes to the CIT law aim to decrease the CIT rate by 2% in 2012 and by a further 3% in the coming three years (1% per year), lowering the CIT rate to 15% by 2015.

Increase in investment allowance

The tax allowance for investments into equipment and intangible assets increased from 30% to 40%, whereas the threshold of 30,000 euros (EUR) per period was abolished.

Increase in R&D allowance

The general tax relief for investments in R&D increased from 40% to 100%, regardless of the regional location of the company.

Amendments to value-added tax (VAT)

Input VAT deduction should no longer depend on the payment of the invoice

Up to 2012, in accordance with the Slovene VAT legislation, VAT was only deductible provided that the invoice was actually paid or reported to the debt collection offset payment system.

Pursuant to the decision of European Commission No. 2011/4182, such a rule is not in line with European VAT legislation.

Consequently, in 2012, the amendment of the Slovene VAT Law abolished this condition and allowed VAT-able persons to deduct input VAT regardless of the payment of the invoice.

Changes to double tax treaties (DTTs)

Slovenia has recently ratified four new DTTs that will come into force after both contracting countries finalise all their internal procedures. These treaties are between Slovenia and:

- Armenia
- Egypt
- Germany (amendments as to Article 26 of the DTT), and

- Kuwait.

A DTT with Belarus came into force in 2011.

Taxes on corporate income

Slovenian tax residents are liable to pay corporate income tax (CIT) on their worldwide income. Slovenian tax non-residents are taxed only on income from sources in Slovenia, including income earned through permanent establishments (PEs) in Slovenia.

In 2012, the CIT rate is a flat rate of 18% (previously 20%).

A special tax regime is granted for certain economic zones where additional tax allowances for investment and employment may be available (*see the Tax credits and incentives section*).

Taxpayers, such as non-profit or charitable organisations, associations, foundations, etc., are exempt from CIT on their non-profit-making activities.

Investment funds, as well as pension funds, pension insurance companies, and venture capital companies, may be taxed at a rate of 0% if certain conditions are met.

Tonnage tax
A company may request to be subject to tonnage tax instead of CIT if it meets certain conditions (i.e. it operates in maritime transport in international shipping) and notifies the tax authorities in advance.

The tax base for tonnage tax is the sum of the tax bases for each of an entity's ships that are included in the tonnage tax regime. The tax base for a particular ship is calculated by multiplying the number of ship operating days by the daily tax base shown in the following table:

Net tonnage (NT)	EUR/day for 100 net tonnes
For the first 1,000 tonnes	0.90
For the next 1,001 to 10,000 tonnes	0.67
For the next 10,001 to 25,000 tonnes	0.40
Above 25,001 tonnes	0.20

Local income taxes
There are no state or local taxes on income.

Corporate residence

A legal entity is considered to be a Slovenian tax resident if the entity has its statutory (registered) seat or place of effective management located in Slovenia. These conditions, however, do not exclude a society or any association of persons, including an association under civil or foreign law that does not have legal identity, from also being considered to be a Slovene tax resident.

Slovenia

Permanent establishment (PE)

The Slovene definition of a PE is generally in line with the definition set out in the Organisation for Economic Co-operation and Development (OECD) model tax treaty. Thus, it is a place of business in Slovenia in or through which the non-resident's activities are conducted in whole or in part. The following, in particular, are considered to constitute a PE:

- An office, branch, factory, workshop, mine, quarry, or other place where natural resources are obtained or exploited.
- A building site; construction, assembly, or installation site; or the supervision thereof, if the duration of the activities concerned exceeds 12 months.

A place of business is not considered a non-resident's PE if the non-resident:

- only uses the premises in question for storage, display, or delivery of goods belonging to oneself
- only maintains inventories of goods belonging to oneself for the purpose of storage, display, or delivery
- only maintains inventories of goods belonging to oneself for the purpose of processing by third parties
- only maintains the place of business in question for the purpose of purchasing goods or collecting information for oneself
- only maintains the place of business for the purpose of engaging in any other preparatory or auxiliary activity for oneself, or
- only maintains the place of business in question for the purpose of any combination of activities referred to above, provided that the overall activity of the fixed place of business resulting from this combination is of a preparatory or auxiliary character.

Other taxes

Value-added tax (VAT)

A basic VAT rate of 20% applies to all taxable supplies.

A lower VAT rate of 8.5% generally applies to foodstuffs, live animals, seeds, plants, water supplies, medicines, medical equipment, transport of passengers, books, admission fees, royalties for writers and performers, certain works of art, certain residential properties, hotel accommodation, use of sport facilities, burial and cremation services, public hygiene services, minor repairs of bicycles, shoes and clothing, domestic care services, and hairdressing services.

Exempt supplies without credit entitlement include financial and insurance/ reinsurance services, rent and lease of immovable goods (with exceptions), tax and court stamps, lottery services, trade of land, health and social services, etc. There are also other VAT-exempt transactions without a credit entitlement as well as exempt taxable supplies with a credit entitlement.

VAT grouping is not possible within Slovenia.

Customs duties

Goods imported from non-European Union (EU) countries are subject to import customs clearance, and goods being exported from the EU customs territory must be declared for export customs clearance. The person responsible for paying the customs debt is the declarant. The declarant is the person making the customs declaration in its own name, or the person in whose name the customs declaration is made. The customs declaration should be made in the prescribed form and manner (in writing or by another action specified by law). Import or export duties are customs duties and other charges payable on the import or export of goods (import VAT, excise duties, environmental tax, and motor vehicle tax).

For purposes of communication with the customs offices, each person has to be identified by an EORI number (Economic Operator Registration and Identification Number), which is registered by the customs authorities on request. EORI registration is mandatory for customs clearance.

Excise tax
Excise tax is charged on the release into free tax circulation or import of tobacco products, alcohol and alcoholic drinks, fuel and mineral oils, and electricity.

Types of product	Excise tax rate
Cigarettes	45.63% from retail price
Beer	EUR 11 per 1 vol.% alcohol in 1 hl
Alcohol drinks (except wine)	EUR 120 per 1 hl
Ethyl alcohol	EUR 1,200 per 100 vol.% alcohol in 1 hl
Unleaded petrol	EUR 490.67 per 1,000 l
Natural gas	EUR 0.0180 per m3
Heating oil	EUR 15.02 per 1,000 kg
Electricity	EUR 3.05 per 1 MWh

Property tax
Slovenia has not yet introduced property tax.

Real estate tax
Real estate tax of 2% is charged on real estate transfers and leases, unless VAT has been charged on the transaction.

Stamp tax
There is no stamp duty in Slovenia.

Environmental tax
Environmental tax is charged on carbon dioxide (CO_2) emissions, waste disposal, lubricating oils and fluids, and used motor vehicles.

Motor vehicle tax
Motor vehicle tax applies to all vehicles that are registered for the first time in Slovenia. The taxpayer is the entity that imports the vehicle from EU or non-EU countries. The tax rate depends on fuel range and emission of CO_2 and ranges from 0.5% to 31%.

Insurance premium tax
Insurance premium tax is levied on insurance premiums at the rate of 6.5% and paid by insurance companies.

Slovenia

Branch income

If a branch meets the conditions, as set out in the tax legislation and relevant DTT, to be treated as a PE, then it will be liable to pay tax in Slovenia on profits that are attributable to the PE.

The profit that is attributed to a PE is determined broadly in line with OECD principles. Generally, the attributable profit is the profit that would be expected to be earned by the PE if it were an independent taxpayer performing the same or similar activities and/ or business.

A branch whose activities do not create a PE is not subject to CIT in Slovenia.

Income determination

Taxable profits are assessed in accordance with Slovenian Accounting Standards 2006 or International Financial Reporting Standards (IFRS) and modified for certain revenues and certain expenses, which are partly or wholly tax non-deductible.

Inventory valuation

Slovenian law allows the application of all the most commonly used inventory valuation methods, including the first in first out (FIFO), weighted average cost, and floating average prices methods.

Capital gains

Under certain circumstances, the gains made by a Slovenian taxpayer on the disposal of an equity shareholding are effectively 47.5% exempt from taxation. Similarly, 50% of a loss arising on the disposal of such a shareholding would not be deductible for CIT. This treatment applies to the disposal of shareholdings of at least 8% that have been held for at least six months and where the taxpayer disposing of the holding employed at least one person during the six-month holding period.

The above treatment is not available for the disposal of a shareholding of a company which is resident in a country that:

- is outside the EU
- has a corporate tax rate less than 12.5%, and
- is included in a list published by the Ministry of Finance.

Dividend income

Dividends and similar income received by a Slovenian taxpayer are generally 95% exempt from taxation as long as the distributor was subject to Slovenian CIT or to a comparable profits tax. The exceptions to this are where dividends represent untaxed reserves of the distributor or where the distributor is tax resident in a country that:

- is outside the EU
- has a corporate tax rate less than 12.5%, and
- is included in a list published by the Ministry of Finance.

Interest income

Interest and similar income received by a Slovenian taxpayer is included in the taxable base and can be reduced in the amount of a tax liability paid abroad. Interest between related parties needs to be calculated in accordance with the arm's-length principle.

Slovenia

Foreign income

Foreign income, except dividends, received by a Slovenian entity from foreign sources is included in taxable income for CIT purposes in the same tax year as it arises unless the applicable DTT provides for an exemption.

Deductions

In general, business expenses which are necessary to generate taxable revenues are fully tax-deductible. The following expenses are considered unnecessary for the generation of taxable revenues and are not deductible for tax purposes:

- Expenses which are not directly necessary for performing business activities or are not incurred as a consequence of a business activity.
- Expenses of a private character.
- Expenses which do not correspond to standard business practice.

Some of the most common non-deductible expenses include:

- Penalties and the cost of bribes.
- Input VAT that could have been reclaimed in accordance with the VAT act.
- Entertainment costs, which are only 50% tax-deductible.
- Costs relating to the supervisory board, which are only 50% tax-deductible.
- Legal and other costs of incorporation, which may be deductible for the parent company but not for the entity being incorporated.

Depreciation and amortisation

Depreciation of tangible fixed assets, amortisation of intangible assets, and depreciation of investment property are recognised as expenditures in line with the accounting treatment, up to a maximum of the amount calculated using the straight-line depreciation method and the maximum tax depreciation rates listed below. Any accounting depreciation in excess of these rates is not tax-deductible in the period concerned, but may be deductible in subsequent tax periods, until the asset is fully depreciated or disposed of.

The maximum annual depreciation rates are as follows:

Depreciation category	Types of assets	Annual depreciation rate (%)
1	Buildings, including investment property	3
2	Parts of buildings, including investment property	6
3	Equipment, vehicles, and machinery	20
4	Parts of equipment, and equipment for research activities	33.3
5	Computer equipment, hardware, and software	50
6	Crops lasting several years	10
7	Breeding animals	20
8	Other fixed assets	10

Slovenia

Goodwill

In general, if goodwill is impaired for accounting purposes, then the impairment cost may be treated as tax-deductible. The amount that may be treated as tax-deductible in any one tax period is limited to 20% of the initial value of the goodwill.

Start-up expenses

In accordance with Slovene legislation, costs which occur prior to the entry of a legal entity into court register may not be treated as tax deductible. Such a principle arises from a common legal principle whereby an entity may be subject to rights and obligations only after its establishment date. The date of entry into the court register is deemed to be the date of the establishment.

Provisions

Certain provisions are only 50% tax-deductible when accrued, with the remaining 50% being treated as tax-deductible when the provision is utilised. The provisions which are subject to this treatment are provisions for warranties granted when selling products or providing services, reorganisations/redundancies, anticipated losses from onerous contracts, pensions, long-service bonuses, and severance payments on retirement.

Bad debt

Bad debt provisions are only tax-deductible if the amount does not exceed the lower of:

- the arithmetic mean of the bad debts written-off in the past three tax periods, under certain conditions specified in the tax law, and
- the amount corresponding to 1% of taxable revenues of the tax period.

In order to take advantage of this deduction, a company must be able to calculate amounts for both tests and then take the lower of the two amounts so calculated. If the company is not able to determine the amount for either, the cost of the bad debt provision is not tax-deductible until the provision is utilised.

Costs of bad debts are tax-deductible when the debt is finally written-off, provided there is a finalised court procedure, the creditor can demonstrate that it would cost more to pursue the debtor than the debt is worth, or the creditor can demonstrate that it has done everything required by good business practice to try to recover the debt.

Related-party interest

Companies may deduct interest expense on loans from their owners or other associated parties up to a maximum of the amount calculated by using the prescribed interest rate published by the Ministry of Finance. Taxpayers must increase taxable profits by the amount of any excess interest expense, unless they can prove that they could have received the loan on comparable terms from an unrelated party.

Charitable contributions

A taxpayer may claim a reduction of its taxable profits for donations made for humanitarian, disabled, charitable, scientific, educational, medical, sports, cultural, ecological, and religious purposes to residents of Slovenia or of EU or European Economic Area (EEA) member states, up to 0.3% of the taxable person's taxable revenues. An additional allowance of 0.2% of the taxpayers' taxable revenues is available for payments made for cultural purposes and to voluntary organisations that work for the public interest to protect the public from natural and other disasters.

A taxpayer may decrease its taxable base for payments made to political parties and representative trade unions, up to an amount equal to three times the average monthly salary per employee of the taxpayer.

Compensation

Salaries and other payments relating to employment (e.g. wage compensation, holiday allowances, employer's social security contributions, long-service awards, severance benefits paid upon retirement, solidarity assistance, and reimbursement of business related expenses) are generally fully tax-deductible.

The costs of benefits in kind are also tax-deductible if such benefits are taxed for the individual under the Personal Income Tax Act.

Pension allowances

Under certain conditions, a tax-deductible allowance for voluntary supplementary pension insurance may apply, of up to 24% of compulsory contributions for pension and disability insurance for insured employees, but may not exceed EUR 2,755.71 annually per employee.

Fines and penalties

Costs relating to compulsory collection of taxes and other levies are, in accordance with Slovene legislation, not tax deductible.

Taxes

Taxes paid by a shareholder as a natural person and VAT that was not deducted as an input VAT, even though there was a right to deduct, are not tax deductible. In addition, interests on late payment of taxes are not tax deductible.

Net operating losses

Tax losses may be carried forward to reduce taxable profits indefinitely, but loss carrybacks are not permitted. Loss relief may not exceed the amount of current taxable income. Generally, losses that are generated in multiple tax years are absorbed chronologically. The right to carry losses forward may be forfeited if the ownership of the capital or voting power of the taxpayer claiming the loss carry forward changes by more than 50% within the tax period and the taxpayer either has not performed business activities for two years prior to the change of ownership or substantially changes its business activity two years prior to or after the change in ownership.

Treatment of tax losses mentioned in the preceding paragraph does not apply for those losses that are generated in the year of the change of ownership or prior tax periods.

Payment to foreign affiliates

Payments to foreign affiliates are normally subject to withholding tax (WHT) if there is no right to apply exemptions in accordance with Slovenian legislation or DTT. Payments similar to dividends, including disguised distribution of profit, are not tax deductible. Any other payments to foreign affiliates are tax deductible if they are made in accordance with the arm's-length principle.

Group taxation

Group tax returns were abolished with the introduction of the CIT Act on 1 January 2007. However, special transitional provisions allow a group of taxable persons to

Slovenia

continue to file a group tax return, until the period for which approval was granted to file a group tax return expires.

Transfer pricing
Prices between a Slovenian entity and its related parties must be set, for tax purposes, at fair market value using the arm's-length principle. Broadly speaking, taxpayers are related by direct, indirect, or common shareholdings of over 25%; through a participation in management; or by control through other means, including through contractual terms.

For transactions between two related Slovenian tax residents, provided neither is in an 'advantaged' position (advantaged usually means having unutilised tax losses), there is no actual requirement for the companies to adjust their tax returns to reflect an arm's-length price.

Taxable persons must prepare transfer pricing documentation. The Slovenian rules regarding such documentation follow the EU Code of Conduct on transfer pricing documentation for associated enterprises in the EU (EU TPD).

Thin capitalisation
Interest payments on loans granted, or guaranteed, by a related party (a party which directly or indirectly owns at least 25% of the shares or voting rights in the taxpayer) are not tax-deductible to the extent that the loan amount exceeds the thin capitalisation threshold specified in law. This does not apply to loan recipients who are banks or insurance companies.

Generally speaking, the thin capitalisation threshold is exceeded if the debt-to-equity ratio exceeds 4:1.

Tax credits and incentives

Foreign tax credit
Tax paid abroad can be credited against tax liability in Slovenia. The amount of tax that can be credited is the amount of final and actually paid tax. If there is DTT made between countries in question, the amount of tax that can be credited is the amount calculated at the rate determined in the DTT. A taxpayer needs to provide proof of the amount of foreign tax, the basis for calculation of the tax, and the amount of the tax paid.

Investment allowances
A tax allowance for investment in equipment and intangible assets is available for investments made after 1 January 2008. The tax allowance is limited to 40% of the value of the assets acquired.

Research and development (R&D) allowances
A 100% investment allowance is granted for investments in R&D within the tax period, regardless of the location of establishment of the company within Slovenia. Such an investment tax allowance may be obtained for expenditures on:

- internal R&D activities within the company and
- the purchase of R&D equipment from related or unrelated parties or from a private research institution.

Allowances for employing certain individuals

A taxpayer that employs trainees or students to undertake practical work may reduce its taxable profits by an additional 20% of the average monthly payment paid to such persons, for every month the person carries out the work.

A taxpayer that employs disabled persons may decrease its taxable profits by an additional 50% of the salary paid to such persons (in addition to the deduction for their actual salary cost). A taxpayer that employs a severely disabled person or a person with a combination of total hearing loss and speech impairment may reduce its taxable base by an additional 70% of the salary paid to such a person (in addition to the deduction for their actual salary cost).

Tax relief for investments in the Pomurje region

Entities based in the Pomurje region of Slovenia may claim additional employment incentives and additional tax relief for investments. These extra benefits are available from 2010 to 2015. As a result, provided certain conditions are met, entities with their seat in Pomurje are entitled to a 70% tax allowance for investments in equipment and intangible assets as well as to certain employment allowances.

Tax relief for employment of hard-to-place workers

A taxpayer who employs a hard-to-place worker may be able to benefit from a tax allowance for both CIT and tax on activity. A hard-to-place worker is a person younger than 26 or older than 55 who has been registered as unemployed for at least six months and who has not been employed by the taxpayer or a related party in the past 24 months. The tax allowance equates to 45% of the salary paid to the person during the first 24 months of their employment, up to the amount of the tax base.

Withholding taxes

In Slovenia, tax must be calculated and withheld on the payments made by residents and non-residents on Slovenian-sourced income to recipients outside Slovenia.

Payments to which the WHT rules apply include payments for dividends, interest, copyrights, patents, licences, leases on real estate situated in Slovenia, services of performing artists, and services charged from low-tax jurisdictions.

The WHT rate is 15%.

If a DTT exists, the WHT rate may be reduced in line with the provisions of the treaty. Similarly for payments of interest, royalties, and dividends within Europe, the Interest and Royalties directive and the Parent Subsidiary directive, respectively, may also reduce this WHT rate to zero.

Furthermore, WHT is not deducted on dividends paid to a parent company in another EU member state if those dividends are subject to an exemption from tax in the hands of the recipient, provided certain conditions are met.

Subject to certain conditions, tax is not required to be withheld on interest on non-exchangeable debt securities issued outside Slovenia by a Slovenian tax resident corporation through a public placement on an international clearing system (i.e. Euroclear).

Slovenia

Treaties in force

Recipient	Dividends (%) (1)	Interest (%) (2)	Royalties (%)
Albania	5/10	7	7
Austria	5/15	5	5
Belarus	5	5	5
Belgium	5/15	10	5
Bosnia and Herzegovina	5/10	7	5
Bulgaria	5/10	5	5/10 (6)
Canada	5/15	10	10
China, People's Republic of	5	10	10
Croatia	5	5	5
Cyprus	10	10	10
Czech Republic	5/15	5	10
Denmark	5/15	5	5
Estonia	5/15	10	10
Finland	5/15	5	5
France	0/15	5	5
Germany	5/15	5	5
Greece	10	10	10
Hungary	5/15	5	5
India	5/15	10	10
Ireland	5/15	5	5
Israel	5/10/15 (5)	5	5
Italy (3)	5/15	10	5
Korea	5/15	5	5
Latvia	5/15	10	10
Lithuania	5/15	10	10
Luxembourg	5/15	5	5
Macedonia	5/15	10	10
Malta	5/15	5	5
Moldova	5/10	5	5
Netherlands	5/15	5	5
Norway	0/15	5	5
Poland	5/15	10	10
Portugal	5/15	10	5
Qatar	5	5	5
Romania	5	5	5
Russian Federation	10	10	10
Serbia/Montenegro	5/10	10	5/10 (7)
Singapore	5	5	5
Slovakia	5/15	10	10
Spain	5/15	5	5
Sweden	5/15	0	0
Switzerland	5/15	5	5
Thailand	10	10/15	10/15 (8)
Turkey	10	10	10
Ukraine	5/15	5	5/10 (7)

Recipient	Dividends (%) (1)	Interest (%) (2)	Royalties (%)
United Kingdom and Northern Ireland	0/15	5	5
United States	5/15	5	5

Treaties not yet in force (4)

Recipient	Dividends (%) (1)	Interest (%) (2)	Royalties (%)
Armenia	5/10	10	5
Egypt	8/13	13	15
Germany *			
Kuwait	5	5	10

Notes

1. Under certain treaties, the WHT rate depends on whether, and to what extent, the recipient participates in the capital of the distributor. Generally, if the recipient holds a participation of more than 25% in the distributing company, the dividends are subject to a lower 5% WHT rate. The higher WHT rate is, however, normally due when the participation is less than 25%.
2. Some DTTs include specific provisions whereby interest payments are subject to a 0% WHT rate, if certain conditions are met.
3. The rates shown apply from 1 January 2011, when the new treaty with Italy came into effect.
4. These treaties have yet to be ratified by both parties.
5. 5% rate if the beneficial owner is a company (other than a partnership) which holds directly at least 10% of the capital of the company paying the dividend; 10% rate if the beneficial owner is a company which holds directly at least 10% of the capital of the company paying the dividends and the dividends are paid out of profits which by virtue of the law of the state in which the payer is a resident, are exempt from company tax or subject to company tax at a rate that is lower than the normal rate in that state; 15% rate applicable in all other cases.
6. 5% rate applicable to the gross amount of: (i) royalties paid for the use of, or the right to use, any copyright of literary, artistic, or scientific work (but not including cinematograph films) and (ii) royalties paid for the use of, or the right to use, industrial, commercial, or scientific equipment, 10% rate applicable in all other cases.
7. 5% rate applicable to royalties for the use of, or the right to use, any copyright of literary, artistic, or scientific work, including cinematograph films or films or tapes used for radio or television broadcasting; 10% rate applicable to royalties for the use of, or the right to use, any patent, trade mark, design or model, plan, secret formula or process, or for the use of, or the right to use, industrial, commercial, or scientific equipment, or for information concerning industrial, commercial, or scientific experience.
8. 10% rate applicable to royalties for the use of, or the right to use, any copyright of literary or artistic work including motion pictures, live broadcasting, film, tape, or other means of the use or reproduction in connection with radio and television broadcasting, and for the use of, or the right to use industrial, commercial, or scientific equipment; 15% rate applicable to royalties in all other cases.

* Protocol amending Article 26 of the DTT otherwise in force.

Tax administration

Taxable period
The tax period should be the calendar year. However, a tax period may differ from the calendar year, but may not exceed a period of 12 months. In this case, the tax authorities must be informed about the chosen tax period, and the taxable entity will not be allowed to change its tax period for the following three years.

Tax returns
A tax return must be submitted to the tax authorities by the end of the third month following the end of the tax year.

Slovenia

Payment of tax

CIT is paid in advance in monthly instalments (if the amount of prepayment exceeds EUR 400 per month) or in quarterly instalments (if the amount of prepayment is less than EUR 400 per month) determined on the basis of the previous year's assessment.

The final CIT payment must be made within 30 days of the tax return submission.

Audit cycle

Slovene legislation does not define an audit cycle. However, we understand that the Slovene tax administration has its own criteria for how to determine audit targets, which is in accordance with their annual tax plan.

Statute of limitations

Under Slovene legislation, a tax inspection may be initiated within five years from the date when a tax return was due for submission to the tax authorities. However, the five year period runs following each interrupting act (generally, certain actions by the Tax Office or the taxpayer within the tax period may be considered as interrupting act), but may not surpass a maximum of ten years counting from the date when the tax return is due. A concluded tax inspection will foreclose any further tax authorities' inspection only for the period and the items that were subject of the concluded tax inspection. Any issue not examined remains open for a future tax inspection. The right of the tax authorities to assess and collect tax permanently expires after ten years counted from the date when the tax return is due.

Topics of focus for tax authorities

Recently, we have noticed that tax authorities focus on appropriateness of transfer pricing for multinational companies.

South Africa

PwC contact

Paul De Chalain
PricewaterhouseCoopers Inc
2 Eglin Road
Sunninghill 2157
South Africa
Tel: +27 11 797 4260
Email: paul.de.chalain@za.pwc.com

Significant developments

After the switch from the source-based taxation to the worldwide taxation of South African (SA) residents in 2000, and the introduction of capital gains tax in 2001, the SA tax system has not undergone fundamental changes. Smaller reforms, however, are ongoing. The most significant recent changes were:

* The introduction of new anti-avoidance provisions on corporate reorganisation transactions.
* Refinement of the headquarter company regime.
* New transfer pricing legislation from 1 April 2012.
* New statutory source rules from 1 January 2012.
* Additional anti-avoidance provisions for hybrid equity instruments and third-party backed shares.
* New anti-avoidance provisions for dividend cessions and borrowed shares.
* New incentive regimes for research and development (R&D) and film production.
* Reform of the controlled foreign company (CFC) provisions.
* The extension of corporate reorganisation relief to CFCs.
* Introduction of dividends tax from 1 April 2012 at a rate of 15%.
* Withholding tax (WHT) on interest (January 2013).
* Employer's contribution to retirement funds on behalf of an employee will be treated as a taxable fringe benefit in the hands of an employee (March 2014).
* Further tax relief for small and micro businesses.
* Increase in the capital gains tax effective rate from 14% to 18.67%.

Introduction of a dividend tax

The Secondary Tax on Companies (STC) was replaced on 1 April 2012 by dividends WHT imposed at a rate of 15%, which is an attempt to align the SA system of taxing corporate profits with worldwide practice. The tax is withheld by the company declaring the dividend but is ultimately borne by the beneficial owner of the dividend.

Administrative developments

The Tax Administration Bill 11 of 2011 has been introduced in Parliament. Its objective is to consolidate the administrative provisions of many of the 19 Tax Act's administered by the South African Revenue Service (SARS). It also introduces more powers to SARS (e.g. enhanced information gathering and collection powers) and introduces a Tax Ombud.

The submission of certain annual returns has been increased to a bi-annual basis. This includes reconciliation returns for employment taxes by employers as well returns by reporting institutions on investment returns (e.g. banks, certain financing organs of state, listed companies in respect of certain debt instruments).

South Africa

SARS has also increased its reporting and reconciling requirements on companies who now have to submit a new IT14SD form, which requires the taxpayer to reconcile its financial information and various taxes, including corporate income tax (CIT), employment taxes, value-added tax (VAT), and customs and excise duties.

Taxes on corporate income

An SA-resident company is subject to normal CIT on its worldwide income, irrespective of source. Non-residents are taxable on SA actual or deemed source income.

In South Africa, the normal CIT rate applicable for corporate income of companies for tax years ending between 1 April 2012 and 31 March 2013 is a flat 28%.

Close corporations, which are essentially a simplified form of company, are taxed at the same rate as companies and are subject to the same taxation rules.

Small business corporations (i.e. companies with only natural persons as members/ owners and with gross income of not more than 14 million South African rand [ZAR]) are taxed at 0% on the first ZAR 63,556 of taxable income earned, 7% on the amount above ZAR 63,556 but not exceeding ZAR 350,000, and ZAR 20,051 and 28% on the amount exceeding ZAR 350,000.

A personal service provider company (i.e. a company that provides certain services that are performed by persons who have an interest in the company) is taxed at 28% of its taxable income. Similarly, a non-resident company is taxed at 28%.

Special CIT rates apply in certain industries, such as mining and insurance (see below).

Alternative turnover-based tax for very small companies
To reduce the compliance costs for very small companies, a turnover-based presumptive tax is available. Companies with a turnover of less than ZAR 1 million per year can elect to pay this tax instead of normal CIT, at a rate ranging from 0% to 6%, depending on the turnover. This election for the tax year commencing on or after 1 March 2012 must be made before 29 June 2012.

Dividends tax
Dividends tax is imposed at 15% from 1 April 2012 on dividends declared and paid by resident companies and by non-resident companies in respect of shares listed on the Johannesburg Stock Exchange (JSE) paid to SA residents.

Dividends are tax exempt if the beneficial owner of the dividend is an SA resident company, retirement fund, or other prescribed exempt person.

The tax is to be withheld by companies paying the taxable dividends or by regulated intermediaries in the case of dividends paid through a regulated intermediary. In the case of *in specie* dividends, the company declaring the *in specie* dividend is liable for the dividends tax and not the beneficial owner of the dividends.

Exemptions from dividends tax and treaty imposed reduced rates only apply if the beneficial owner of the dividend has made the required declaration to the declaring company or regulated intermediary.

The balance of STC credits as on 31 March 2012 that a resident company had prior to dividends tax remains available to that company to be set-off against dividends declared to reduce the amount subject to dividends tax. All STC credits must, however, be utilised before 31 March 2015, or they will be forfeited.

CIT for mining companies

Previously, there were two formulae for determining CIT for mining companies: one for gold-mining companies that were subject to STC and the other for such companies that had elected to be exempt from STC. However, with the implementation of the dividends tax, STC was repealed and all gold mining companies must now use the standard formula to calculate the tax rate from years of assessment ending during the 12-month period before 31 March 2013.

The maximum tax rate that applies to companies' income from oil and gas activities is capped at 28%.

CIT for long-term insurance companies

Life insurance companies are obliged to follow the 'four-fund approach', with policies divided into four funds, depending on the nature of the beneficiary. Each fund is then allocated assets according to the risk carried by the fund. Funds are treated as separate taxpayers and taxed at four separate rates. These rates are 30% for individual policyholder funds, 0% for untaxed policyholder funds, 28% for company policyholder funds, and 28% for corporate funds.

Local income taxes

No local government taxes on income apply to either SA-resident or non-resident companies.

Corporate residence

A company is resident in South Africa if it is incorporated, established, or formed in South Africa or has its place of effective management in South Africa. However, a company that is deemed to be exclusively resident in another country by the terms of a double taxation agreement (DTA) is excluded from SA residency.

The place of effective management is, in terms of an Interpretation Note issued by SARS, interpreted as the place where the strategic decisions of the directors are implemented. However, this approach has not yet been tested by the South African courts. Where international precedent applies a different meaning to the term, it is expected that the South African courts would interpret the term in accordance with international precedent for both domestic law and treaty purposes. SARS has indicated that it intends to amend the Interpretation Note in the near future to align it with internationally accepted principles.

Permanent establishment (PE)

South Africa does not, as a general rule, tax non-residents on the basis of having a PE in South Africa. Rather, non-residents are subject to income tax in South Africa on income derived or deemed to have been derived from a South African source. The primary exception to this rule is in relation to capital gains where non-residents are subject to tax on assets attributable to a PE in South Africa. A PE is defined by reference to the definition thereof in the Organisation for Economic Co-operation and Development (OECD) Model Tax Convention.

South Africa

Other taxes

Value-added tax (VAT)
VAT is an indirect tax, which is largely directed at the domestic consumption of goods and services and at goods imported into South Africa. The tax is designed to be paid mainly by the ultimate consumer or purchaser in South Africa. It is levied at two rates, namely a standard 14% rate and a zero rate (0%).

Very few business transactions carried out in South Africa are not subject to VAT. The tax is collected by businesses which are registered as vendors with SARS on all taxable supplies throughout the production and distribution chain. Sales or supplies by non-vendors are not subject to VAT.

VAT registration and administration
All suppliers of goods and services having an annual turnover currently exceeding ZAR 1 million are obliged to register as VAT vendors and to charge output VAT. Other vendors may elect to register as VAT vendors, provided their annual turnover exceeds ZAR 50,000. If they do not register, they are prohibited from charging VAT on goods or services they supply and claiming an input tax (rebate of VAT paid) on goods and services which they acquire.

Under the VAT system, vendors normally pay VAT on expenses (input tax) and charge VAT on supplies made (output tax). This mechanism, therefore, ensures that only the so-called 'added-value' is taxed. Due to VAT being a self-assessment system, the output tax collected may be reduced by input tax paid. Thereafter, the net amount is payable to, or refundable by, the SARS. The self-assessment returns are due regularly within prescribed periods (tax periods).

Taxable supplies
Standard rated and zero-rated supplies are known as taxable supplies. Other supplies are known as exempt and non-supplies.

Goods and services
For a liability for VAT to exist, there must be a supply or importation of goods or services. Goods are corporeal movable things, fixed property, and real rights in such things and property. The meaning of 'services' is very broad and includes the granting, assignment, cession, or surrender of any right or the making available of any facility or advantage.

Imports
Services imported by a vendor and utilised or consumed by the vendor for the making of taxable supplies are not subject to VAT. In addition, the VAT Act has a schedule that lists goods that are exempt from VAT on importation, whether by a vendor or an unregistered person.

Zero-rated supplies
The VAT Act contains a list of the supplies of goods or services that are taxed at the zero rate. Most of the items refer to exports and international transport, but other specified goods utilised for farming purposes, the sale of an enterprise as a going concern, fuel subject to the fuel levy, and deemed supplies by welfare organisations are also zero-rated.

A zero-rated supply made by a vendor is subject to VAT but at a rate of 0%. Under a zero-rated supply, a vendor does not charge VAT on the consideration for the supply and obtains a refund or credit for the VAT paid on taxable supplies utilised in the making of the zero-rated supplies.

Exempt supplies

In addition to zero-rated supplies, the VAT Act contains a list of the supplies of goods or services that are exempt from VAT. While all fee-based financial services are subject to VAT, the charging of interest is exempt. Other exempt supplies include residential rentals, basic foodstuffs, non-international passenger transport by road or rail, and educational services.

Under exempt supplies by vendors, the vendors do not charge VAT on the supply, and they are not entitled to a deduction or credit for the VAT paid by them on goods and services supplied to them for the making of the exempt supply. Accordingly, vendors treat the VAT paid by them, and for which they do not obtain a deduction or credit, as another cost and recover it in the consideration they charge for the making of the exempt supply.

Customs duties

Customs duties are charged on importation of goods into South Africa which range between 3% and 20%, excluding clothing and apparel which may be as high as 45%. The import duties may also include anti-dumping and countervailing duties of up to 150%. No customs duties are charged on trade between South Africa and Botswana, Lesotho, Namibia, and Swaziland, as these five countries constitute a Southern African Customs Union.

Excise duties

Excise duty is levied on certain locally manufactured goods as well as their imported equivalents. A specific duty at a pre-determined amount is levied on tobacco (52% including excise and VAT) and liquor (23% to 43%), and an *ad valorem* duty (calculated as a percentage of price) on monitors (7%) cosmetics, televisions, audio equipment, and luxury automobiles (marginal rate of 25%). Relief from excise duty is available for exported products and for certain products produced in the course of specified farming, forestry, and (limited) manufacturing activities.

Property taxes

Local municipalities levy rates on land. These rates are based on a percentage of the municipal valuation of land and improvements and vary from municipality to municipality. Generally, a higher rate is levied on properties zoned for business use.

Transfer duty

Transfer duty levied on the sale of immovable property has been revised. The revised rate structure applies to properties acquired under purchase agreements concluded on or after 23 February 2011. The duty is payable by the person acquiring the property within six months from the date of acquisition at the following rates:

Purchase price (ZAR)	Transfer duty rate (%)
Not exceeding 600,000	0
600,000 to 1 million	3
1 million to 1.5 million	5
Exceeding 1.5 million	8

South Africa

Prior to 23 February 2011, the rate applicable to companies was 8% calculated on the higher of the purchase price or market value. Transfers of immovable property subject to VAT are exempt from transfer duty.

Securities transfer tax (STT)
STT is levied at a rate of 0.25% of the taxable amount in respect of the transfer of a security. The taxable amount is usually the consideration for which the security is purchased or the market value of the security, if the consideration declared is less than the market value or if no consideration was paid. STT is payable by the company that issued the securities in question. However, the company can recover the tax from the person acquiring the shares. Slightly different rules apply in the case of listed securities.

Skills Development Levy (SDL)
SDL is a compulsory levy to fund the education and training as envisaged by the Skills Development Act. It is payable by an employer and cannot be deducted from the remuneration payable to an employee. Small employers with an annual payroll of less than ZAR 500,000 are exempt from the levy. SDL is levied at the rate of 1% of payroll. It is payable monthly, together with income tax that the employer has withheld on its employees' salaries.

Unemployment Insurance Fund (UIF) contributions
Employers are required to contribute on behalf of their employees on a personalised basis to the UIF. The rate of contributions is 1% of gross remuneration payable to an employee; however, the monthly cap of ZAR 124.78 applies. Another 1%, subject to the same cap, is payable by the employee and withheld by the employer.

Compensation for Occupational Injuries and Diseases Act (COIDA) fund
Employers are liable for making annual contributions to the COIDA fund. COIDA contributions are a payroll cost that cannot be deducted from the employee's salary with a maximum salary cap of ZAR 292,032 per annum applying from 1 April 2012. The rates vary depending on the employer's industry (e.g. a rate of 1.62% is applied to the salaries of employees involved in the manufacture of pottery up to a maximum salary band of ZAR 292,032 per annum).

Donations tax
Disposals of assets below their market value are a deemed donation and, at least theoretically, subject to donations tax. Donations tax is payable by resident companies at a flat rate of 20% on donations made. An annual exemption of ZAR 10,000 is available.

Public companies, comprised of mostly listed companies, are exempt from donations tax. An exemption is also available for donations made to certain charities and other non-profit organisations.

Vehicle emissions tax
An environmental levy is levied on new motor vehicles based on gram per kilometre of CO_2 emissions of the vehicle over a stated level. The levy is currently ZAR 75 to ZAR 100 per gram per kilometre over the CO_2 threshhold level.

Fuel levy
A fuel levy is charged on petroleum fuel sold. The general fuel levy for 2012/13 is 197.5 cents per litre of petrol and 182.5 cents per litre of diesel.

Electricity levy

To support energy efficiency, the government has implemented a levy on electricity generated from non-renewable sources at 3.5 cents/kWh (2.5 cents/kWh prior to 1 July 2012). The levy is collected at source by the electricity producer.

Air passenger tax

As of 1 October 2011, passengers departing on international flights must pay air passenger tax at the rate of ZAR 100 on flights to Botswana, Lesotho, Namibia, and Swaziland, and ZAR 190 on other flights. The tax is added to the price of the ticket. Departure prior to 1 October 2011 was subject to air passenger tax at the rate of ZAR 80 and ZAR 150 respectively.

Branch income

SA branches of foreign companies are not considered to be separate legal entities for tax purposes, and no tax is withheld on transfers of profits to the head office. Branches of foreign companies are taxed at a rate of 28% and are not liable for dividends tax or any branch profits repatriation tax.

Note that a branch must register as a taxpayer and submit tax returns. Separate financial statements must be drawn up for the SA-trading operations. For all practical purposes, the SARS will treat the branch as a separate entity. For example, inter-branch cost recoveries levied by the head office incurred in the production of SA income normally will be allowed as a deduction by the branch.

In terms of DTAs, the taxation of branches is limited to cases where the branch constitutes a PE.

Income determination

Inventory valuation

Inventories generally are stated at the lower of cost or net realisable value. Write-downs of inventory for slow-moving and obsolete items must be justified, and a general policy on a percentage basis is not permitted. Last in first out (LIFO) is not accepted for tax purposes.

Capital gains

Although the capital gains tax forms part of income tax, the two taxes are not fully integrated. Gains realised by companies are taxed at the normal CIT rate; however, only 66.66% of gains are included in taxable income.

Dividend income

As of 1 April 2012, dividends are taxed in the hands of the shareholder at a rate of 15%. The amount is withheld by the company declaring the dividend on behalf of the shareholder receiving it. *In specie* dividends are not subject to tax in the hands of the shareholders.

Foreign dividends received by or accrued to an SA resident taxpayer are included in income based on a formula and taxed at the normal CIT rate, which results in an effective tax rate of 15%. Qualifying foreign dividends are also generally not subject to tax where they are received by resident shareholders holding in excess of 10% of the equity shares and voting rights of the company declaring the dividend. Dividends

South Africa

received by residents holding less than 10% of such shares will generally be taxable in South Africa, subject to a tax credit for foreign taxes payable by the recipient shareholder.

Stock dividends
Stock dividends (capitalisation issues of shares) are not subject to CIT or dividends tax.

Interest income
Interest income for resident companies is taxed at the normal CIT rate. Interest received by non-resident companies is only subject to CIT if it is from a source in South Africa. As of 1 January 2012, statutory source rules apply to interest.

As of 1 January 2013, a 10% WHT on interest will apply to interest paid on certain debt instruments to non-resident companies.

Foreign income
Foreign income of an SA-resident company is subject to tax in South Africa on an earliest of receipt or accrual basis. However, income that may not be remitted to South Africa in terms of the laws of the country where the amount arose is deferred until the income can be remitted. Double taxation may be avoided under certain DTAs or by way of unilateral credit or deduction for foreign tax payable on foreign income (*see Foreign tax credit in the Tax credits and incentives section*).

Deductions

Depreciation and depletion
A depreciation (wear and tear) allowance may be deducted on movable assets used for the purpose of trade. There are no statutory provisions relating to rates of wear and tear, but SARS has published a table of periods over which the assets may be written off. The rates of wear and tear, based on the cash cost, are calculated either according to the straight-line or diminishing-balance method.

New and unused machinery used in the process of manufacture or in a similar process is depreciable at the rate of 40% in the first year of use and 20% in the three following years. If the machinery is not new and unused, an allowance of 20% per year over five years is available.

An accelerated depreciation allowance (50% in the first year of use, 30% in the second, and 20% in the third year) applies to the machinery and articles used in farming, production of biodiesel or bio-ethanol, and production of energy from certain renewable sources.

Specific allowances are also provided for pipelines, transmission lines, railway lines, airport property, ships, mining operations, and other qualifying industrial assets.

Buildings and other permanent structures may not be depreciated, apart from an annual allowance for each of the following:

- Buildings used in a process of manufacture or a process similar to a process of manufacture: For buildings erected before 1 January 1989, a 2% rate applies per year. For buildings erected after 1 January 1989, a 5% rate applies.
- Hotel buildings: For buildings built prior to 4 June 1988, a 2% rate applies per year. For hotel buildings erected after 4 June 1988, a 5% rate applies. Improvements

within the existing building framework that commenced on or after 17 March 1993 are depreciated at the rate of 20%.

- Agricultural cooperative storage buildings: For buildings built prior to 1 January 1989, a 2% rate applies per year. For buildings erected on or after 1 January 1989, a 5% rate applies.
- Housing projects of not less than five units: Housing projects of not less than five units of residential accommodation, which consist of more than one room and the erection of which commenced on or after 1 April 1982 and before 21 October 2008, are subject to a 2% rate of depreciation. After 21 October 2008, an allowance of 5% is available on this type of property. The 5% depreciation rate is available to the taxpayer provided that the unit is used by the taxpayer solely for trade purposes, the unit is situated in South Africa, and the taxpayer owns at least five units in South Africa used for the purposes of trade. An additional allowance is available for a low-cost residential unit. Additionally, from 21 October 2008, taxpayers are granted relief for the transfer of ownership on a contract for deed basis of employer provided low cost residential units to employees.
- Buildings in urban development zones: Improvements to an existing building in an urban development zone, where the existing structural or exterior framework is preserved and brought into before 31 March 2014, qualify for an accelerated allowance of 20% per year. Buildings that are erected, extended, or added to in an urban development zone on or after 21 October 2008 and which are not covered by the first mentioned allowance qualify for a 20% allowance in the first year and a 8% allowance in the following ten years. As of 21 October 2008, new and unused low-income residential units located in urban development zone demarcations are subject to an additional annual depreciation allowance. The rate is 25% in the first year, 13% in the succeeding five years, and 10% in the year following the last year. Improvements are subject to a depreciation allowance of 25% over a period of four years.
- Commercial buildings: The cost to the taxpayer of any new and unused building owned by the taxpayer, or any new and unused improvement to any building owned by the taxpayer, if that building or improvement wholly or mainly is used by the taxpayer for trade purposes, other than the provision of residential accommodation, is subject to a 5% rate of depreciation. This allowance is applicable to any building or improvement contracted for on or after 1 April 2007 and the construction of which commenced on or after 1 April 2007.

An allowance for assets disposed of or scrapped during a year of assessment is determined by reference to the cost less allowances already granted and the proceeds on disposal (if any). Recoupments of allowances granted are taxable where disposal proceeds exceed the tax basis at the time of sale. Such recoupments cannot exceed the cost of the asset. Proceeds above cost will be taxed as a capital gain.

Book depreciation does not need to be consistent with tax depreciation.

No cost or percentage depletion is available for natural resources.

Cost of inventory
The cost of inventory is, in principle, deductible as soon as the inventory is acquired. However, at the end of each year, the cost of the inventory still on hand has to be added to the company's income. Then in the next year, it can be deducted again. This has the effect of timing the deduction of the cost of inventory to match the time of its realisation.

South Africa

Assets acquired for shares issued

When assets are acquired by a company in return for the shares or debt instruments issued to the seller, the purchaser of the assets is deemed to have incurred expenditure of the lesser of the market value of the assets immediately after acquisition or the market value of the shares immediately after acquisition.

Taxes

Payroll taxes are deductible from taxable income for the corporation.

Net operating losses

Losses may be carried forward indefinitely, provided an active trade or business of a similar nature is carried on without interruption. There is no loss carryback in South Africa.

Payments to foreign affiliates

Deductions may be claimed for royalties, managerial service fees, and interest charges paid to foreign affiliates, provided such amounts approximate those that would be paid to an unrelated entity in an arm's-length transaction.

Interest deductions may be limited where the paying company is thinly capitalised (*see Thin capitalisation in the Group taxation section*).

Specific provisions apply for 'bullet interest' (i.e. a one-off, upfront lump sum payment of interest). Any interest expenditure must be spread over the life of the interest-bearing arrangement on the compounding accrual basis.

Group taxation

Group taxation generally is not permitted in South Africa. However, relief is given for transactions between group companies to allow for reorganisations, provided certain requirements are met.

In general, the relief will only apply to transactions between companies within the same group. A group of companies is defined as a controlling company and one or more controlled companies in relation to that controlling company. A controlling company means a company holding directly or indirectly at least 70% of the equity of any other company. Foreign-incorporated companies do not form part of a group of companies for the purposes of this relief, although relief is extended to CFCs in certain circumstances.

Corporate rollover relief is available for asset-for-share transactions, amalgamation transactions, intra-group transactions, unbundling transactions, and transactions relating to liquidation, winding-up, and deregistration.

The relief may cover the capital gains tax arising from the disposal of capital assets, income tax arising from the disposal of a depreciable asset, income tax arising from the disposal of trading stock, donations tax arising from the disposal of an asset, dividends tax, and transaction taxes.

As of 3 June 2011, companies that finance intra-group transactions and liquidation transactions with debt have to apply for approval to be able to claim the interest on the debt as a tax deduction.

Transfer pricing and thin capitalisation

Section 31 has been substantially amended with effect from years of assessment commencing after 1 April 2012. The amendments serve to modernise the transfer pricing and thin capitalisation rules in line with the OECD and international tax principles; to remove structural problems caused by a literal translation which focuses on isolated transactions rather than the overall arrangements; and to narrow focus which leads to the application of artificial arguments supporting certain arrangements, rather than focusing on the true economic substance.

Section 31 will no longer separately address transfer pricing and thin capitalisation. Rather, thin capitalisation will be treated as simply a breach of the general arm's-length standard.

The previous Section 31 departure points of resident and non-resident, and who are 'connected', are retained.

The most critical difference from the previous rules is the broadening and generalisation of the application concepts. Specifically, the combination of:

- the rules apply if any of the parties derive a 'tax benefit'
- the transactional concepts of 'goods and services' in Section 31(2) are removed and replaced with a much broader 'transaction, operation, scheme, agreement, or understanding'
- the use of 'directly or indirectly' in referring to the transactions entered into between the taxpayer and any connected person
- the general 'arm's-length' standard, and
- the introduction of secondary adjustments in the form of transfer pricing adjustments being deemed to be loans to which the transfer pricing provisions apply, thereby giving rise to further transfer pricing adjustments on the deemed loan.

Regarding 'financial assistance', the generalisation of the concepts discussed above make them broad enough to catch both excessive debt amounts as well as excessive interest rates. The previous concept of 'financial assistance' will be retained, i.e. including the provision of any loan, advance or debt, or any security or guarantee.

Importantly, the discretion given to SARS to adjust the price is removed, as the taxpayer is obligated in terms of the Income Tax Act to apply the arm's-length standard, i.e. "... the taxable income must be calculated as if the transaction (etc.) ... had been entered into ... had those persons been independent persons dealing at arm's length". This therefore removes uncertainty that taxpayers had in respect of performing self adjustments on the tax return.

The much broader concept of 'connected persons' in the previous provisions in respect of intellectual property will be retained in a new Section 31(3) but is extended to also apply in respect of financial assistance.

Controlled foreign companies (CFCs)

If one or more residents together, directly or indirectly, hold more than 50% of the voting or participation rights in a foreign company, then it is a CFC in relation to those residents. The income of a CFC is imputed to the residents in proportion to their holdings, subject to certain exclusions and tax credits, where applicable.

South Africa

Tax credits and incentives

Foreign tax credit
The South African Income Tax Act makes provision for a rebate against normal CIT tax in respect of foreign taxes paid on foreign sourced income or a deduction against income of foreign taxes paid on SA-sourced income. In both instances, the taxpayer must be an SA resident, the income must be included in taxable income and is not exempt, and that income was subject to a foreign tax which is not recoverable. The rebate is limited to the total normal tax payable calculated by applying the ratio of the total taxable income attributable to the foreign tax to the total taxable income. The deduction, however, may not exceed the income on which the foreign tax was levied.

A new foreign tax rebate applies from 1 January 2012 to grant relief to amounts relating to services rendered in South Africa that are subject to tax in a foreign jurisdiction where the general foreign tax rebate does not apply.

Tax exempt grants
Cash grants received within the terms of a Government Incentive Scheme by taxpayers with manufacturing operations or similar processes are exempt from CIT on such grants.

Research and development (R&D)
To encourage innovation, the current costs related to certain R&D activities carried on in South Africa are 150% deductible. However, the incentive has been revised from 1 April 2012 whereby the incentive has been split into two parts with 100% R&D expenses being automatically deductible and the other 50% being subject to pre-approval by a government appointed approval committee. The cost of machinery and other capital assets acquired for the purposes of R&D may be depreciated 50% in the first year of use, 30% in the second, and 20% in the third year. As of 1 April 2012, this changed to 40%/20%/20%/20% for machinery and other capital assets and to a 20-year write off for buildings used in the process of R&D.

Headquarter company regime
For years of assessment commencing on or after 1 January 2011, a 'headquarter company' regime is introduced to encourage the use of South Africa as a location for intermediate holding companies.

The benefits on offer to a headquarter company are:

- Exemption from South Africa's CFC rules.
- Exemptions on the headquarter company's dividend distributions.
- Exemption from South Africa's transfer pricing rules on back-to-back loans.
- Capital gains tax exemption upon the disposal of shares by the headquarter company.

The requirements for a headquarter company are as follows:

- The headquarter company must be SA resident.
- Each shareholder in the headquarter company must hold at least 10% of the headquarter company's equity shares and voting rights. This means that a headquarter company can never have more than ten shareholders.
- At least 80% of the headquarter company's assets (measured on a 'cost' basis and excluding cash and certain bank deposits) must be comprised of certain assets

South Africa

related to the foreign companies in which the headquarter company holds at least 10% of the equity shares and voting rights. Specifically, these assets must be:
- the equity shares in those companies
- loans to those companies, and
- intellectual property licensed to those companies.
- At least 50% of the headquarter company's gross income must be comprised of dividends, interest, royalties, rentals, or fees from its 10%-plus holdings, where the gross income exceeds ZAR 5 million.

The requirements regarding the headquarter company's shareholders must be fulfilled from the incorporation of the headquarter company. The requirements regarding the headquarter company's assets and its receipts accruals are tested only at year-end but must, in the case of assets, be fulfilled every year over the lifetime of the headquarter company. If a company does not meet the gross income requirements in any year, it will not be a headquarter company for that year, but will not be permanently excluded on this ground.

Industrial policy projects
In 2008, a ZAR 20 billion incentive package for investors in energy efficient projects was announced. The incentive is available for industrial projects participating in the manufacturing sector (other than alcohol or alcohol related products, tobacco or tobacco related products, arms and ammunition, and bio-fuels, which have a negative impact on food security). Companies are divided into those with a qualifying status and those with a preferred status. The status is determined in terms of a point system.

The proposed project must either be a 'brownfield project' (expansion or upgrade of an existing industrial project) or a 'greenfield project' (a wholly new industrial project, which uses new and unused manufacturing assets). Approved projects may be granted a tax allowance known as an additional investment allowance equal to 55% (100% if located in an industrial development zone) of the cost of any manufacturing asset used in an industrial policy project with preferred status or 35% (75% if located in an industrial development zone) of the cost of any manufacturing asset used in any other approved industrial policy project.

Note that the additional investment allowance may not exceed ZAR 900 million in the case of any greenfield project with a preferred status, ZAR 550 million in the case of any other greenfield project, ZAR 550 million in the case of any brownfield project with a preferred status, or ZAR 350 million in the case of any other brownfield project.

In addition to the above, a company may also claim a deduction known as an additional training allowance.

Venture capital companies
In order to assist small and medium-sized businesses to raise capital to finance businesses, a tax incentive for investors in small and medium-sized enterprises through venture capital companies has been introduced.

A deduction is allowed from the income of a taxpayer in respect of expenditures actually incurred by that person in respect of shares issued to that person by a venture capital company.

South Africa

Withholding taxes

Payments to residents
No WHT, other than payroll taxes, are currently levied on payments to resident corporations.

Royalties payable to non-residents
Royalties and know-how payments made to non-residents for the use of or right to use intellectual property rights in South Africa are deemed to be from an SA source. The payer of the royalty or know-how payment is obliged to deduct a WHT of 12% of this payment, which is a final tax payable by the recipient of such income. The treaty rate is only the maximum allowable rate to be charged by the treaty countries; where this rate is higher than the domestic tax rate, the latter will apply.

Dividends payable to non-residents
A dividend WHT of 15% applies from 1 April 2012 to any dividend paid by a resident company or non-resident company in respect of shares listed on an SA exchange to SA residents. The tax is imposed on the beneficial owner of the dividend and not on the company, with the exception of *in specie* dividends. The payer of the dividend or regulated intermediary is obliged to deduct the 15% WHT from the payment. The treaty rate is only the maximum allowable rate to be charged by the treaty countries; where this rate is higher than the domestic tax rate, the latter will apply.

Interest payable to non-residents (as of 1 January 2013)
A 10% WHT on interest will apply to interest payable to non-residents that are not a CFC on certain debt instruments from 1 January 2013 on interest from an SA source. The resident payer of the interest is obliged to deduct the 10% WHT from the payment. The treaty rate is only the maximum allowable rate to be charged by the treaty countries; where this rate is higher than the domestic tax rate, the latter will apply.

Treaty rates for dividends, interest, and royalties
The WHT may be reduced by the terms of the relevant tax treaty, as follows:

Recipient	WHT (%)		
	Dividends	Interest	Royalties
Non-treaty	15	10	12
Treaty:			
Algeria (1, 11)	10/15	10	10
Australia (1, 2, 12D)	5/15	10	5
Austria (11D)	5/15	0	0
Belarus (1, 2, 6, 11D, 27)	5/15	5/10	5/10
Belgium (1, 11)	5/15	10	0
Botswana (1, 2, 11)	10/15	10	10
Brazil (1, 2, 7, 11)	10/15	15	10/15
Bulgaria (1, 2, 6, 8, 11D)	5/15	5	5/10
Canada (1, 4, 12D)	5/15 (33)	10	6/10
China, People's Republic of (5)	5	10	10
Croatia (11, 26)	5/10	0	5
Cyprus (1, 10, 26)	0	0	0
Czech Republic (1, 11D, 26)	5/15	0	10

Recipient	WHT (%)		
	Dividends	Interest	Royalties
Denmark (1, 11, 26)	5/15	0	0
Egypt (1)	15	12	15
Ethiopia (1, 2)	10	8	20
Finland (1, 12, 26)	5/15	0	0
France (1, 2, 12D, 28)	5/15	0	0
Germany (2, 13D)	7.5/15	10	0
Ghana (1, 2, 12, 32)	5/10	5/10	10
Greece (1, 2, 9, 11D)	5/15	8	5/7
Hungary (1, 11D, 26)	5/15	0	0
India (1)	10	10	10
Indonesia (1, 12)	10/15	10	10
Iran (1)	10	5	10
Ireland (1, 12D, 26)	5/10	0	0
Israel (2, 3)	25	25	0/15
Italy (1, 14)	5/15	10	6
Japan (1, 15)	5/15	10	10
Korea, Republic of (1, 11D)	5/15	10	10
Kuwait (1, 2, 10, 26)	0	0	10
Lesotho (1)	15	10	10
Luxembourg (1, 11D, 26)	5/15	0	0
Malawi (2, 22, 29)	15	10	0
Malaysia (1, 2, 11)	5/10	10	5
Malta (1, 16)	5	10	10
Mauritius (1, 12, 26)	5/15	0	0
Mexico (1, 2, 12)	5/10	10	10
Mozambique (1, 2, 11)	8/15	8	5
Namibia (1, 11)	5/15	10	10
The Netherlands (1, 2, 12, 25, 26)	5/10	0	0
New Zealand (1, 11)	5/15 (34)	10	10
Nigeria (1, 2, 12)	7.5/10	7.5	7.5
Norway (1, 2, 11D, 26)	5/15	0	0
Oman (1, 10, 26)	0	0	8
Pakistan (1, 12)	10/15	10	10
Poland (1, 11D)	5/15	10	10
Portugal (1, 2, 17D)	10/15	10	10
Romania (1)	15	15	15
Russia (2, 18)	10/15	10	0
Rwanda (1, 11)	10/20	10	10
Saudi Arabia (1, 2, 12D)	5/10	5	10
Seychelles (1, 2, 10, 26)	0	0	0
Singapore (1, 12, 26)	5/15	0	5
Slovak Republic (1, 11D, 26)	5/15	0	10
Spain (1, 2, 11D)	5/15	5	5
Swaziland (1, 11)	10/15	10	0
Sweden (1, 2, 19, 28)	0	0	0
Switzerland (1, 2, 20D)	5/15	5	0

S

South Africa

Recipient	WHT (%)		
	Dividends	Interest	Royalties
Taiwan (1, 12D)	5/15	10	10
Tanzania (1, 21)	10/20	10	10
Thailand (1, 11, 30)	10/15	10/15	15
Tunisia (1, 31)	10	5/12	10
Turkey (1, 11D)	10/15	10	10
Uganda (1, 11)	10/15	10	10
Ukraine (1, 20)	5/15	10	10
United Kingdom (2, 22, 26)	5/10/15	0	0
United States (1, 2, 23)	5/15	0	0
Zambia (2, 24, 26)	15	0	0
Zimbabwe (2, 24, 29)	15	10	0

Notes

'D' refers to direct capital holding.

1. Recipient is the beneficial owner of the royalty.
2. Royalty is subject to tax in recipient country.
3. 15% is levied on royalties for cinematographic or television films.
4. The maximum rate for copyright royalties, royalties for use of computer software, and patents concerning industrial, commercial, and scientific experience is 6% of the royalties paid, otherwise 10%.
5. Maximum rate of 10% of the adjusted amount (being 70% of the gross royalties) for use of industrial, commercial, or scientific equipment.
6. The 5% rate applies to royalties for the use of a copyright. A 7% rate applies to royalties for the use of patents, trademarks, designs, models, etc.
7. In respect of right to use industrial, commercial, or scientific equipment and transport vehicles, a 10% rate applies.
8. The lower rate of 5% applies to any cultural, dramatic, musical, or other artistic work (but not including royalties in respect of motion picture films) as well as industrial, commercial, or scientific works. The lower rate of 10% applies in all other cases.
9. The 5% lower rate applies to use of literary, artistic, and scientific works. The 7% lower rate applies to right of use of patents, trademarks, designs, and models.
10. No right to tax interest in payor state if the beneficial owner of the interest is resident in the payee state.
11. Lower rate applies to a beneficial owner that is a company and has a minimum holding of 25% of capital, and the higher rate applies in other cases.
12. Lower rate applies to a beneficial owner that is a company and has a minimum holding of 10% of capital, and the higher rate applies in other cases.
13. Lower rate applies to a beneficial owner that is a company and has a minimum holding of 25% of voting shares, and the higher rate applies in other cases.
14. Lower rate applies to a beneficial owner that is a company and has a minimum holding of 25% of capital and a minimum 12-month holding period prior to the end of the accounting period prior to the dividend payment, and the higher rate applies in other cases.
15. Lower rate applies to a beneficial owner that is a company and has a minimum holding of 25% of voting shares and a minimum six-month holding period prior to the end of the accounting period prior to the dividend payment, and the higher rate applies in other cases.
16. SA resident payor to Maltese resident beneficial owner (Maltese resident payor to SA resident beneficial owner is limited to tax on profits).
17. Lower rate applies to a beneficial owner that is a company and has a minimum holding of 25% of capital and a minimum two-year uninterrupted holding period prior to the dividend payment, and the higher rate applies in other cases.
18. Lower rate applies to a beneficial owner who has a minimum holding of 30% of capital and a minimum direct investment of 100,000 United States dollars (USD) in the company declaring the dividend, and the higher rate applies in other cases.
19. Lower rate applies to a beneficial owner that is a company and has a minimum holding of 10% of capital, and the higher rate applies in other cases. However, a 'most favoured nations' clause applies, which will limit the above rates to the lowest treaty rate in terms of any other treaty.
20. Lower rate applies to a beneficial owner that is a company and has a minimum holding of 20% of capital, and the higher rate applies in other cases.
21. Lower rate applies to a beneficial owner that is a company and has a minimum holding of 15% of capital, and the higher rate applies in other cases.

22. Lower rate of 5% applies to a beneficial owner that is a company and has a minimum holding of 10% of capital. Lower rate of 10% applies in all other cases. 15% rate applies to all dividends from property investment companies.
23. Lower rate applies to a beneficial owner that is a company and has a minimum holding of 10% of voting power (directly), and the higher rate applies in other cases.
24. The treaty contains no provisions regarding dividends WHT, thus the domestic rate will apply
25. The Netherlands Protocol has a 'most favoured nations' provision whereby the rate most favourable in any other treaty will apply over the default treaty rate. This, however, only applies to treaties concluded after this treaty.
26. No right to tax interest in payor state if the beneficial owner of the interest is resident in the payee state.
27. The 5% rate applies to interest derived by a bank or any other financial institution, and the 10% rate applies in other cases.
28. No right to tax interest in payor state if the beneficial owner of the interest is resident in the payee state and provided interest is taxable in that other state.
29. No provision is made for interest taxing in the DTA. Source state may therefore charge at its domestic rate.
30. The 10% rate applies to interest received by a financial institution (including an insurance company), and the 15% rate applies in other cases.
31. The 5% rate applies to interest on loans made by banks, and the 12% rate applies in other cases.
32. The 5% rate applies if the interest is paid to a bank; the 10% rate applies in other cases.
33. In Canada, a beneficial owner that is a company controls a minimum of 10% of the voting power (directly/indirectly), but excludes non-resident owned investment corporation resident in Canada.
34. In New Zealand, dividends are taxed at a flat rate of 15%.

Non-resident entertainers and sportspersons
A WHT at the rate of 15% applies to all payments made to non-resident entertainers and sports persons in respect of their activities exercised in South Africa.

Disposal of immovable property by non-residents
Any person who pays an amount to a non-resident in respect of the sale of immovable property in South Africa must withhold from the amount payable an amount equal to:

- 5% if the non-resident seller is an individual
- 7.5% if the non-resident seller is a company, or
- 10% if the non-resident seller is a trust.

The amount so withheld is not a final tax for the non-resident seller. Instead, this amount is regarded as an advance payment of the non-resident seller's normal tax liability for the year of assessment during which the property is disposed of. The non-resident seller is still obliged to submit an income tax return for that year.

Tax administration

Taxable period
The corporate fiscal year is the same as the company's financial year. It may be changed upon application showing reasonable cause.

Tax returns
Annual income tax returns must be submitted within one year from the end of the company's fiscal year.

Payments
Payments are made with provisional returns filed at six-month intervals from the fiscal year-end based on an estimate of taxable income for the year. Interest is charged on any underpayment outstanding for more than six months after the fiscal year-end except in the case of February year-ends, in which case it is seven months. Any balance (together with interest) is then paid following assessment.

South Africa

Audit cycle

There is no prescribed audit process, and an audit can be initiated by any factor as determined by SARS. The audit or inspection will commence with a request from SARS for the taxpayer to make available any such records or information as may be required.

Statute of limitations

Tax debts to the state prescribe after a period of 30 years. Tax returns submitted that have been assessed may not be reopened after a period of three years from date of assessment unless there has been fraud, misrepresentation, or non-disclosure by the taxpayer.

Topics of focus for tax authorities

SARS, in their 2012-2016 Compliance Program, stated that they will focus on the following areas:

- Large multinational business will be focused on in respect of transfer pricing, international tax compliance, and under declaration of provisional tax.
- The construction industry has been identified as having very low tax compliance, and this will be a focus, especially in relation to companies who receive government tenders.
- SARS envisages a clamp down on illicit cigarette trade whereby cigarette as smuggled via warehouses or cigarettes destined for export are diverted for local consumption.
- Undervaluation of imports in the clothing and textile industry is another focus area. The practice will be confronted by inter-governmental department cooperation and establishing a frequent revision of a reference pricing database and more cooperative border management.
- Small business registrations will be encouraged, with SARS conducting registration drives. Abuse of the VAT system by small business will also be focused on.

Spain

PwC contact

Santiago Barrenechea
PwC Tax & Legal services
Torre PwC, Pº de la Castellana, 259 B
28046 Madrid
Spain
Tel: +34 915 684 400
Email: santiago.barrenechea@es.pwc.com

Significant developments

Over the past year, the following significant amendments have been made to Spanish law on the taxation of companies.

Royal Decree-Law 18/2012, on the write-down and sale of real estate assets by the financial sector, was published in the Official State Gazette on 12 May 2012. The main tax measures included in this reform that affect companies' taxation are as follows:

- Capital gains obtained on any type of transfer of urban real estate assets that are non-current assets or non-current assets held for sale purposes (not stock) and that were previously acquired for valuable consideration between 31 May 2012 and 31 December 2012 are exempt for 50% of the gains.

Royal Decree-Law 12/2012, published in the Official State Gazette on 31 March 2012, introduces several tax and administrative measures aimed at reducing the public deficit. The main tax measures are summarised below:

- Until 30 November 2012, personal income tax (PIT), corporate income tax (CIT) and non-resident income tax (NRIT) taxpayers owning assets or rights at 31 December 2010 that do not conform to the income declared for such taxes may file a return and pay in 10% of the amount involved or acquisition value of such assets or rights. Submission and payment of the return will not trigger penalties, interest, or surcharges. The regularisation will also release the taxpayer from criminal liability.

  The above will not be applicable to taxes and tax periods where submission of the return and payment take place following the notification of the commencement of inspection or audit proceedings.

- For companies with turnover in the previous 12 months of 20 million euros (EUR) or more, advance payments will amount to at least 8% of the accounting profit for the first 3, 9, or 11 months of each calendar year, less any offsettable tax losses in accordance with the applicable limits.

  The minimum advance payment for April 2012 will amount to 4%.

  For companies whose turnover relates at least 85% to income to which the international double tax exemption or the internal 100% double tax deduction for dividends applies, the rate will be 4% (2% for the advance payment for April 2012).

  This will apply to the tax periods commencing in 2012 and 2013.

Spain

- The rule concerning unrestricted depreciation of investments in new tangible fixed assets and investment property has been repealed effective 31 March 2012.

  A transitional regime is provided for investments made prior to that date. Under this transitional regime, unrestricted depreciation tax relief may be applied to these investments although with certain limits during the tax periods commencing in 2012 and 2013.

- The amount of net deductible financial expenses in the tax period is generally reduced to 30% of operating profit (applying certain adjustments) for the year, financial expenses of less than EUR 1 million being in any event deductible. The limit will not apply to companies that do not form part of a group within the meaning of Article 42 of the Code of Commerce, with exceptions.

  For such purposes, net financial expenses will be considered to be the excess of financial expenses (excluding the non-deductible expenses mentioned below) with respect to income deriving from the assignment of capital to third parties accrued in the tax period.

  For companies taxed under the tax consolidation regime, the deduction limit will refer to the tax group. Nonetheless, the entity's net financial expenses available for deduction at the time of its inclusion in the group will be deducted up to the limit of 30% of operating profit. When an entity stops forming part of the group or the group is extinguished and there are net financial expenses available for deduction, the rule will be similar to that for assigning tax losses to the entities that formed part of the group.

  These limits will apply to tax periods commencing on and after 1 January 2012.

- The financial expenses deriving from debts with group companies aimed at the acquisition of interests in other group companies or the contribution to capital or equity of other group companies will not be deductible unless it is evidenced that there are valid economic reasons, as has been required by the tax authorities in the last few years.

  These limits will apply to the tax periods commencing on and after 1 January 2012.

- For the tax periods commencing in 2012 and 2013, the limits for the application of tax credits to promote the performance of certain activities are reduced from 35% to 25% of gross tax payable, less the tax credits for internal and international double taxation.

  When the research and development (R&D) and technological innovation tax credits for expenses and investments in the year exceed 10% of the tax payable mentioned above, the limit is reduced from 60% to 50%. In parallel with the foregoing, the period for applying tax credits not applied owing to insufficient tax payable is extended to 15 years (18 years for R&D and technological innovation tax credits).

  The limits will also apply to the tax credit for the reinvestment of extraordinary profits.

- Effective for tax periods commencing in 2012 and 2013, the deduction of goodwill is limited to 1%. This limit affects both goodwill on direct business acquisitions and resulting from corporate restructuring operations.

For dividends and capital gains on the transfer of interests in non-resident companies that do not fulfil the requirement envisaged in Article 21.1.b) of the CIT Law (i.e. that the investee has been subject to a foreign tax identical or analogous in nature to Spanish CIT) but which meet the other requirements set forth in the above mentioned Article 21.1. and which accrue before 1 December 2012, the taxpayer may opt not to include them in the tax base, in which case they will be subject to a special tax of 8%.

A Royal Decree-Law, passed on 30 December 2011 (RDL 20/2011), introduced urgent budgetary, tax, and financial measures to be taken to correct Spain's public deficit. The tax measures laid down in this legislation included, most notably, the following:

- The general rate of withholding has increased from 19% to 21%, applicable from 1 January 2012 to 31 December 2013.
- The reduced CIT rate for job maintenance or creation applicable for micro companies has been maintained for 2012.
- The tax treatment established for CIT for investments made and expenses incurred to train staff in the use of new communication and computing technologies has been maintained.
- The regulations regarding advance CIT payments have been updated.
- For 2012 and 2013, the tax rate for real estate tax has increased for urban real estate, depending on the year in which the corresponding official tables of values approved by local municipalities to assess the rateable values of properties came into force.
- Various rules laid down in the Spanish general tax law have been amended to ensure that the Council Directive 2010/24/EU, of 16 March 2010, concerning mutual assistance for the recovery of claims relating to taxes, duties, and other measures, is correctly transposed in Spanish law.

A Royal Decree-Law, passed on 19 August 2011 (RDL 9/2011), approved certain measures to improve the quality and cohesion of the Spanish national health system, contribute to fiscal consolidation, and increase the maximum amount of state guarantees for 2011. The tax measures laid down in this legislation included, most notably, the following:

- Advance payments of CIT made by companies whose turnover (in accordance with VAT law) exceeded EUR 6,010,121.04 during the 12 months prior to the beginning of the tax period (large companies) have been increased for tax periods beginning in 2011 (only for advance payments made in October and December), 2012, and 2013. *See Payment of tax in the Tax administration section for more information.*
- The amount of tax-loss carryforwards which may be offset in tax periods beginning in 2011, 2012, and 2013 is also limited for large companies. *See Net operating losses in the Deductions section for more information.*
- The maximum period to offset tax-loss carryforwards is extended from 15 to 18 years. This amendment takes effect for tax-loss carryforwards existing in tax periods beginning as of 1 January 2012, regardless of when the losses were or are incurred.
- Maximum 5% annual amortisation of financial goodwill arising from the acquisition of an interest in a non-resident entity has been temporally reduced to 1% for tax periods beginning in 2011, 2012, and 2013.

Taxes on corporate income

The general CIT rate in Spain is currently 30%. Other tax rates (ranging from 25% to 35%) may apply depending on the type of company that is taxed and the type of business carried out.

Spain

Resident companies are taxed on their worldwide income.

For permanent establishments (PEs) in Spain of foreign companies, non-residents' income tax is chargeable on their Spain-source taxable income at a 30% tax rate.

Non-residents' income tax is also chargeable on non-established foreign companies/individuals that obtain income in Spain (*see the Withholding taxes section*).

Small companies

Companies with a turnover under EUR 10 million in the preceding tax year are considered small companies for CIT purposes and are taxed at the following rates:

- Taxable income up to EUR 300,000 is taxed at a 25% tax rate.
- The part of the taxable income which exceeds this threshold is taxed at the general tax rate of 30%.

The tax rate levied on companies forming part of a group depends on the total amount of the group companies' turnovers. The general 30% tax rate is levied when the sum of the group companies' turnovers exceeds EUR 10 million.

Micro companies

Lower tax rates are established for companies that maintain or increase their staff levels in the tax years 2009 through 2012:

The rates for tax years 2011 and 2012 are as follows:

- Taxable income up to EUR 300,000 is taxed at a 20% tax rate.
- The part of the taxable income which exceeds this threshold is taxed at the general tax rate of 25%.

These lower rates of 20% and 25% are applicable subject to compliance with, amongst others, the following requirements:

- The income generated by all of the company's business activities does not exceed EUR 5 million.
- The company's total staff does not exceed 25 employees.
- The company's average number of employees during the 12-month period following the commencement of the tax year in question is not less than one employee and not less than the company's average number of employees during the 12-month period prior to the first tax year commencing as of 1 January 2009.

Business and professional activities tax

The business and professional activities tax is a local direct tax levied annually on the performance in Spain of business, professional, or artistic activities, regardless of whether or not they are carried out in a particular premises. The tax payable depends on different factors, such as the type of activity carried out and the location and size of the premises where the activity is carried out. As regards limits, it may not exceed 15% of the presumed average profits of the professional/economical activity.

CIT payers and non-resident companies carrying on an activity in Spain through a PE are exempt from this tax if their net turnover for the tax year of the last corporate/non-residents' income tax return filed prior to the date of accrual of the local tax (1 January) was less than EUR 1 million.

Corporate residence

A company is resident in Spain and subject to CIT on its worldwide income when:

- it has been incorporated in accordance with Spanish law
- its registered office is in Spain, and/or
- its 'effective' head office is in Spain.

Under Spanish law, a company's 'effective', head office is in Spain when its business activities are managed and controlled from Spain.

Companies established in a country or territory where no tax is levied or which is a tax haven are deemed to be tax resident in Spain in the following cases:

- When the company's main assets consist, directly or indirectly, of property located or rights fulfilled or exercised in Spain.
- When the company's core business activity is carried on in Spain.

This presumption may be refuted by the company if it can prove that it is effectively administered and managed in the country or territory in which it is established and that it was incorporated and operates for valid economic and business reasons and not merely for the purpose of managing securities or other assets.

Permanent establishment (PE)
Taxpayers operating in Spain through a PE are subject to non-residents' income tax.

Most Spanish tax conventions for the avoidance of double taxation contain a definition of PE in line with Organisation for Economic Co-operation and Development (OECD) criteria.

In the absence of a tax convention, internal law states that an individual or company is considered to operate through a PE when, by any legal means, one has continuous or habitual work facilities in Spain or a place to do any kind of work where one performs all or part of one's activity, or when one acts in Spain through an agent with powers to enter into an agreement in the name and on behalf of the non-resident individual or company, provided said powers are exercised on a regular basis.

In particular, management offices, branches, offices, factories, workshops, warehouses, shops or other establishments; mines, oil or gas wells, quarries, farms, forestry facilities, livestock farms, or any other site where natural resources are collected; and construction, installation, or assembly sites whose duration lasts more than six months will be considered PEs.

Other taxes

Value-added tax (VAT)
Spanish VAT is payable on supplies of goods and services carried out in Spanish VAT territory and on imports/intra-European Union (EU) acquisitions of goods and services. There are three rates for the different types of goods and services, which are as follows:

- Ordinary rate of 18%, applied on regular supplies of goods and services.

Spain

- Reduced rate of 8%, applied on basic necessities (e.g. food and agricultural products not included in the 'super reduced' 4% rate, dwellings, and other qualifying services).
- Super reduced rate of 4%, applied on basic necessities other than those classified under the reduced rate (e.g. bread, milk, books, medicine).

In the Canary Islands, a specific tax is applied in lieu of VAT, called the Canary Island General Indirect Tax (IGIC). The ordinary IGIC rate is 5%, and the other IGIC rates are 0%, 2%, 9%, and 13% (20% for tobacco). IGIC is similar to VAT but it has some significant differences, such as the exemption established for telecommunications services. Imports of tangible goods into the Canary Islands are subject to this tax.

In Ceuta and Melilla, sales tax is applied instead of VAT.

Customs duties
Many goods imported into Spain from outside the European Union are subject to customs duties. The rates of duty are provided by the EU's Common Customs Tariff and vary widely.

Excise duties
Excise duties are chargeable on most hydrocarbon oil products, alcoholic drinks, and tobacco products imported into or produced in Spain. Purely as examples, most road fuels carry a duty of about EUR 0.31 per litre, cigarettes carry a duty of about EUR 12.7 per thousand (plus 57% of the maximum retail sale price), tobacco of about EUR 8 per thousand (plus 41.5% of the maximum retail sale price), most wines of EUR 0 per litre, and spirits of about EUR 8.3 per litre of pure alcohol included.

Tax on non-resident companies owning real estate in Spain
Non-resident companies which own real estate or hold real property rights in Spain are subject to a special levy accrued on 31 December and declared and paid in January of the following year in the place and manner established by law. The tax is equal to 3% of the assessed value of the real estate. This special levy is not applicable to companies resident in a country which has signed a convention for the avoidance of double taxation with Spain, including an exchange-of-information provision, if the ultimate shareholders of such companies are individuals resident in Spain or individuals that may benefit from the application of a convention for the avoidance of double taxation.

In addition, some other exceptions are established for this levy.

Transfer tax
A transfer tax of 6% to 10%, depending upon the region, is generally levied on *inter vivos* transfers, including real estate transfers and real estate leases that are exempt from VAT.

Second and ulterior transfers of buildings are exempt from VAT and thus, they are in principle, subject to transfer tax.

Residential leases are exempt from VAT and therefore subject to transfer tax.

Transfers of quoted or unquoted (listed or unlisted) securities are, in principle, exempt from both transfer tax and VAT, except in the following cases:

- Transfers of securities of a company whose real estate assets in Spain represent more than 50% of its total assets or whose assets include securities in another company

whose real estate assets in Spain represent at least 50% of its total assets are subject to and not exempt from transfer tax if the acquirer gains control of the real estate company as a result of the transfer.
- Transfers of securities received in exchange for real estate contributions carried out on the incorporation of a company or on the execution of a subsequent capital increase are also subject to and not exempt from transfer tax provided that not more than three years have elapsed between the date on which the contribution was made and the date on which the securities are transferred.

From 12 May 2012, these exceptions will not apply to transfers of securities received as a result of the incorporation by banks of asset management companies and to transfers of securities of banks affected by the integration plans regulated by Royal Decree-Law 9/2009, which will therefore be exempt from transfer tax. In addition, acquisitions of assets by new businesses in the Canary Islands are exempt from transfer tax, subject to compliance with certain requirements.

Restructuring transactions are exempt from transfer tax. For these purposes, mergers, spin-offs, exchanges of shares, and certain in-kind contributions are considered to be restructuring transactions.

Stamp duty
A stamp duty is mostly levied on notarial instruments and records documenting transactions which have an economic value and need to be registered in public registries (e.g. company, land, and industrial property registries). Stamp duty is incompatible with transfer tax and capital duty, but compatible with VAT. The general rate is between 0.75% and 1.2% depending on the region of Spain and the taxable event.

Stamp duty is also levied on certain commercial documents (e.g. bills of exchange, promissory notes), court, and administrative documents.

Capital duty
Incorporations of companies, capital increases, contributions by shareholders, and the transfer to Spain of the place of effective management or the registered office of a company where neither one nor the other were previously located in a member state of the European Union are exempt from capital duty.

Restructuring transactions are not subject to capital duty. For these purposes, mergers, spin-offs, exchanges of shares, and certain in-kind contributions are considered to be restructuring transactions.

The transfer of the place of effective management or the registered office between EU member states is not subject to capital duty. 1% capital duty is levied on capital reductions and company dissolution, to be paid by the shareholders.

Capital duty is incompatible with transfer tax and stamp duty in certain cases, but it is compatible with VAT.

Other local taxes
In addition to the taxes stated above, the following other local taxes may be charged on companies:

- Real estate tax, levied annually by local authorities on the ownership of real estate.

Spain

- Local tax levied on the increase in the value of urban land, chargeable when urban real estate is sold.
- Motor vehicle tax, charged on the ownership of vehicles.
- Tax on constructions, installations, and building works, charged on the cost of certain works which require town planning licences.
- Waste collection fees.

Branch income

Income obtained by a branch in Spain of a non-resident company is taxed at the standard CIT rate of 30% and, in most cases, the regulations established by tax law for resident companies are applicable.

Payments made by a branch to its head office or a PE of its head office for royalties, interest, commissions, or technical assistance fees are not tax deductible. Management and general administrative expenses incurred by the foreign head office that can be allocated to the branch are tax deductible if the payments for these expenses are made following a criteria of continuity and rationality and provided that certain documentary requirements and other formalities are fulfilled.

Under Spanish law, income obtained by a branch that is repatriated to its head office is taxed at source at the general withholding tax (WHT) rate of 21% (applicable rate from 1 January 2011 to 31 December 2013). This tax is not chargeable in the case of a PE of a company resident in the European Union (unless the company is resident in a tax haven). Most tax treaties signed by Spain do not establish any provisions on this matter, and, in such cases, no tax is chargeable on income repatriated by branches. Some tax treaties, such as the treaties with Canada, Indonesia, the United States (US), expressly establish a tax on income repatriated by branches. For example, US head offices are taxed at a 10% rate on the repatriated profits of a Spanish branch under the US/Spanish tax treaty.

Income determination

The general rule for determining income for CIT purposes is that accounting rules must be followed unless tax law establishes otherwise. In order to maintain this consistency, CIT/PE non-residents' income tax returns include pages in which the company's accounting/commercial balance sheet and profit and loss account figures must be entered.

In Spain, the tax authorities are authorised to modify accounting results exclusively for the purpose of determining tax results if they observe that a company's accounting results have not been calculated in accordance with Spanish Generally Accepted Accounting Principles (GAAP).

Inventory valuation
Inventory is valued at acquisition price or production cost under the average and first in first out (FIFO) valuation methods (the replacement and base stock valuation methods may only be used in exceptional cases). Again, since there are no specific tax rules for determining taxable income, accounting rules are also applicable for calculating valuation and obsolescence provisions for inventory.

Capital gains

Capital gains are taxable in the tax year in which they arise. They are treated as normal income and taxed at the standard CIT rate of 30% (in the case of gains from real estate after taking into consideration an increase in the cost base for tax indexation purposes). *Please see the Tax credits and incentives section for a description of a tax credit for reinvestment of capital gains.*

Dividend income

The amount of dividends included in the calculation of taxable income must be the gross amount.

Upon meeting certain requirements, companies may be eligible for a tax credit for dividends equal to the tax rate applied by the company on the dividends received. This tax credit is generally allowed for the total dividends received from taxable domestic companies when the interest of the company receiving the dividend in the other company is 5% or more and such interest has been held for at least one year. This one-year holding period is deemed to be complied with if it is completed after the dividend is distributed.

This tax regime is to some extent the same as a tax exemption regime. When an interest in a company is less than 5% or is held for less than one year, the tax credit is 30% of half of the amount of the dividends received.

In addition, taxation on capital gains arising from the sale of shares in domestic companies by a company with at least a 5% interest in the subsidiary held for at least one year prior to the sale can be reduced by means of a tax credit at the tax rate applicable on the undistributed part of the subsidiary's profits generated during the company's holding period. The reason for this tax relief is that this capital gain is understood to be an underlying dividend.

Internal tax credits for the avoidance of double taxation may be carried forward for up to seven years.

Stock dividends

CIT is not levied on bonus shares (i.e. shares partially or totally given to shareholders in a capital increase charged against distributable reserves), although they must be taken into account when calculating the average cost of shares held for the levying of tax when the shares are sold.

Interest income

Interest income is treated as normal income and taxed at the standard CIT rate of 30%.

Other significant items

The following items, amongst others, are excluded or deferred from taxable income:

- Distributed dividends corresponding to profits obtained by companies in tax years in which the flow-through tax regime (internal and international) has been applied.
- Assets written up in accordance with revaluation laws and tax-protected restructuring transactions involving accounting capital gains.

Foreign income

Resident companies are taxed on their worldwide income. For foreign-source income, total or partial tax relief in the form of tax credits or exemptions is given if tax is

Spain

levied on the income in both Spain and the foreign country where the income has been generated.

This tax relief may be available for the following:

- Economic double taxation, which is when the same income is taxed in the hands of two different taxpayers. For example, another government taxes a foreign company on the income earned in that country and a Spanish resident shareholder is taxed on the dividends that it receives from the foreign company or the capital gains from transfers of its shares.
- Juridical double taxation, which is when the same income is taxed in two countries in the hands of the same taxpayer. For example, the income is taxed (via a WHT) in the country where the income is generated and again in the other country where the recipient is resident.

The main characteristics of double tax relief are discussed below.

Dividends or profit-sharing income received by a Spanish company from a foreign company are tax exempt, subject to compliance with the following requirements:

- The Spanish company has at least a 5% interest in the foreign company during the entire tax year prior to the tax year in which the dividend is paid. This one-year holding period is deemed to be complied with if it is completed after the dividend is distributed.
- The foreign company is subject to a similar tax to Spanish CIT and is not resident in a tax haven. The foreign tax is deemed to be similar to Spanish CIT if the foreign company is resident in a country with which Spain has signed a tax treaty containing an exchange-of-information provision.
- The income out of which the dividend is paid is generated from the business activities of the foreign company carried out abroad stipulated in CIT law.

Capital gains arising from the sale of shares in foreign companies also qualify for a tax exemption provided that the requirements stated above are complied with during the holding period and the acquiring company is not resident in a tax haven. Tax exemption is limited in certain cases.

As an alternative to this 'tax exemption' regime and applicable to dividend distributions only, a tax credit based on imputation is established. This tax credit allows the crediting of the foreign tax paid abroad on the income from which the dividends are paid and the foreign WHT paid on the profit distribution, up to the limit of the tax that would have been paid on the gross amount in Spain. The only requirement for the application of this 'tax imputation' regime is that the Spanish company has at least a 5% interest in the foreign company during the 12 months prior to the date on which the dividend is due and payable. This one-year holding period is deemed to be complied with if it is completed after the dividend is distributed. This tax relief may be carried forward for up to ten years.

Spanish international legislation provides for CIT relief on 'juridical' double taxation by applying the 'tax imputation' regime. Under this regime, gross foreign income (including foreign WHT paid) is included for Spanish tax calculation purposes, and a tax credit for the foreign WHT paid is applicable up to the amount of the CIT that the company would have paid if such gross income had been obtained in Spain. The tax credit can be carried forward for up to ten years, but the rate will be the rate applicable at the moment when the tax credit is applied.

Under Spanish tax treaties and implemented EU tax directives, several methods have been established to avoid double taxation. The main one is the traditional deduction of a tax credit from tax effectively paid. However, some treaties establish a tax exemption or the exclusive right to tax. Also, a tax-sparing clause is included in some treaties which allows for the deduction of not only the tax actually paid but a higher amount of tax.

Deductions

Depreciation, amortisation, and depletion

All assets, except land, are depreciable for tax purposes. Guideline tables of tax depreciation rates are established which state maximum per annum rates and maximum years of useful life for each asset type, classified by business sector. Please see the table below as an example of the maximum per annum rates and maximum years of useful life of some assets that are typically depreciated:

Asset	Maximum per annum depreciation rate (%)	Maximum useful life (years)
Industrial buildings and warehouses	3	68
Administrative and commercial buildings	2	100
Passenger cars	16	14
Furniture and office equipment (excluded computers)	10	20
Computers	25	8
Software	33	6
Tools	30	8

The straight-line depreciation method is normally used, calculated over the asset's useful life and applied on the asset's cost or written-up value (if such a write-up is acceptable for tax purposes). Off-book adjustments must be included in tax assessments if accounting depreciation exceeds tax depreciation.

Qualifying assets with a useful life of more than one year can also be depreciated using one of the following declining-balance methods:

- By applying a constant percentage on the carrying amount of the asset multiplied by 1.5, 2, or 2.5 depending on the useful life of the asset (below five years, between five and eight years, and over eight years, respectively).
- By using the sum-of-digits method, whereby the asset's acquisition price is multiplied by the ratio between the number of the years in which it is depreciated in a descending order (e.g. in a three-year useful life, three for the first year, two for the second, and one for the third) and the total numbers for the years of the asset's useful life (1 + 2 + 3 = 6 for 3 years of useful life).

Buildings, furniture, and fittings cannot be depreciated using the declining-balance methods.

Special depreciation plans for new assets can be approved by the tax authorities upon request, when they are subject to wear-and-tear at a higher rate than the normal rate applicable.

S

Spain

Recorded depreciation is fully tax deductible, even when it is higher than the depreciation which would arise by applying any of the tax depreciation methods stated above, if the taxpayer is able to justify that the depreciation is real.

Mining assets and assets used for R&D, amongst others, but not including buildings, can be freely depreciated/amortised for tax purposes.

Free depreciation

Unrestricted depreciation of investments in new tangible fixed assets and real estate used in business activities was regulated for investments made by taxpayers in tax periods commencing in 2011, 2012, 2013, 2014, and 2015. This tax relief was also available for tax periods commencing in 2009 and 2010, but it could only be availed of if the requirement that the taxpayer's staff levels were maintained or increased was met.

Due to the tax reform carried out by Royal Decree-Law 12/2012, this tax incentive has been repealed effective 31 March 2012.

A transitional regime is provided for investments made prior to that date. Under this transitional regime, unrestricted depreciation tax relief may be applied to these investments although with certain limits during the tax periods commencing in 2012 and 2013.

Amortisation of intangibles

A 50% reduction may be applied for income obtained from licensing certain intangible assets, subject to compliance with certain requirements (the effective tax on this income would be 15%).

Goodwill cannot be amortised under Spanish GAAP. However, it can be amortised for tax purposes at a maximum annual rate of 5% (1% for tax periods commencing in 2012 and 2013), subject to compliance with certain requirements (e.g. it is acquired for consideration from an unrelated party in accordance with the provisions of Section 42 of the Spanish Commercial Code and an obligatory non-distributable reserve is established).

Intangible assets with a specific useful life may be amortised and such amortisation is tax deductible even if it is not recorded in the company's profit and loss account, when the company complies with the following requirements:

* The assets are acquired for consideration.
* The company does not form part of a group as defined in Section 42 of the Spanish Commercial Code. The tax deduction of the amortisation is up to 10% per annum, unless a lower useful life can be evidenced.

If the two requirements stated above are complied with, amortisation on intangible assets which do not have a specific useful life is also tax deductible up to the 10% annual limit, regardless of whether they are amortised under Spanish GAAP or not.

Depletion

Depletion is allowed for mining companies and companies involved in exploring/investigating natural oil resources as established in applicable legislation.

Spain

Financial goodwill

To promote the internationalisation of Spanish companies, in 2002 a rule was introduced that financial goodwill arising from the acquisition of an interest in a non-resident company (financial goodwill being, in this case, the excess price paid for the acquisition of the business over its net book value at the date of the acquisition that cannot be allocated to the non-resident company's assets in Spain) could be amortised up to a maximum of 5% per year.

To apply this tax relief, the following requirements had to be met:

- A minimum 5% interest had to be held in the non-resident company.
- The non-resident company had to be subject to a similar tax to Spanish CIT.
- The income obtained by the non-resident company had to be generated from business activities carried out abroad in accordance with Spanish CIT law.

Decisions of the European Commission dated 28 October 2009 (regarding interest in non-resident EU companies) and 12 January 2011 (regarding interest in non-resident non-EU companies) considered that this tax relief was unlawful state aid.

According to the Commission's decisions, only acquisitions of interests in non-resident companies carried out before 21 December 2007 (or before 21 May 2011 for majority interests in non-resident companies established in countries with explicit obstacles to cross-border business combination transactions) can continue applying this tax relief until the financial goodwill is wholly amortised.

For companies that, in accordance with the above, can continue applying financial goodwill tax relief, the maximum 5% annual amortisation is temporally reduced to 1% for tax periods commencing in 2011, 2012, and 2013.

Start-up expenses

According to Spanish GAAP, start-up expenses are considered to be expenses in the financial year in which they are incurred. As no special rule is provided for tax purposes, they are deductible for CIT purposes in the year in which they are incurred.

Financial expenses

With effect for tax periods commencing on or after 1 January 2012, Royal Decree-Law 12/2012 has introduced the following rules for the deduction of financial expenses.

General limits on the deduction of financial expenses

The amount of net deductible financial expenses in the tax period is generally reduced to 30% of operating profit (similar to EBITDA, applying certain adjustments) for the year, financial expenses of less than EUR 1 million being in any event deductible. The limit will not apply to companies that do not form part of a group within the meaning of Article 42 of the Spanish Code of Commerce, with exceptions.

This limit will not be applicable to advance CIT payments for April 2012.

For such purposes, net financial expenses will be considered to be the excess of financial expenses (excluding the non-deductible expenses mentioned below) with respect to income deriving from the assignment of capital to third parties accrued in the tax period.

For companies taxed under the tax consolidation regime, the deduction limit will refer to the tax group. Nonetheless, the company's net financial expenses available for

Spain

deduction at the time of its inclusion in the group will be deducted, up to the limit of 30% of its operating profit. When a company stops forming part of the group or the group is extinguished and there are net financial expenses available for deduction, the rule will be similar to that for assigning tax losses to the companies that formed part of the group.

Specific limit on the deduction of financial expenses on acquisitions of intra-group ownership interests
Over the past few years, a large number of tax inspections have adjusted the tax effects of acquisitions of shares from group companies with intra-group debt. Many of these operations were acquisitions of shares in non-resident companies, so that the dividends and capital gains arising from the acquisition of the shares were covered by the exemption for the avoidance of double taxation established in Article 21 of the Spanish CIT Act. In addition, the lenders of these operations were usually located in low tax territories.

In the absence of specific limitation rules on financial expenses tax deductibility in previous years, the reaction of the tax authorities to these kinds of operations has been to apply general anti-abuse rules.

With this scenario, Royal Decree-Law 12/2012 has introduced a limitation rule for the deduction of intra-group financial expenses that is applicable for tax periods commencing on or after 1 January 2012. In accordance with this rule, financial expenses arising from debts with group companies generated from acquisitions of interests in other group companies or contributions to capital or equity of other group companies will not be deductible unless there is evidence that there are valid economic reasons for such expenses.

Bad debt provisions
Provisions for covering the risk derived from possible bad debts are tax deductible when, at the time the tax accrues, any of the following circumstances exists:

* Six months have elapsed since the obligation became due.
* The debtor is declared bankrupt.
* The debtor is prosecuted for an offence of embezzlement.
* The obligations have been claimed judicially or are the subject of a legal dispute or arbitration proceedings, and collection depends on the solution thereof.

Provisions for the credits listed below are not tax deductible unless they are the subject of arbitration or legal proceedings concerning their existence or the amount thereof:

* Credits owed or guaranteed by Public Law entities.
* Credits guaranteed by credit entities or mutual guarantee societies.
* Credits guaranteed by pledges (real property rights), ownership reservation agreements, or liens, except in the event of loss or degradation of the guarantee.
* Credits guaranteed by a credit or guarantee insurance contract.
* Credits that have been expressly extended or renewed.

Provisions to cover the risk derived from possible bad debts of persons or companies related to the creditor will not be deductible, except in the case of legally declared insolvency, and neither will provisions made on the basis of overall estimates of the risk of bad debts of clients and debtors.

Special rules apply to bank entities.

Charitable donations

Donations are considered to be non-deductible expenses for CIT purposes.

This notwithstanding, a tax credit may be availed for donations to non-profit organisations that comply with certain requirements. The tax credit in this case is 35% of the donation.

In addition, the tax credit is not limited to 35% of the donating company's gross tax payable less the tax credits for internal and international double taxation and tax relief for income obtained in Ceuta and Melilla, for export activities, and for local public services that is applicable for other tax credits (25% in 2012 and 2013).

The tax credit base cannot exceed 10% of the taxable income of the financial year. Any excess may be carried forward for a period of ten years.

For donations to listed priority sponsorship activities, the tax credit may be increased by 5% (up to 40%) and the tax credit base 10% limit can be increased to 15%.

Fines and penalties

Penalties imposed due to the failure to pay taxes and surcharges for late filing/payment or for other tax infringements are not tax deductible.

Late-payment interest recorded as an expense is, in principle, tax deductible.

Taxes

Taxes, other than CIT, that are recorded as an expense due to their nature (e.g. business and professional activities tax, but not withholdings) are tax deductible expenses. In some cases, indirect taxes such as non-deductible VAT or transfer tax could be added to the value of assets for depreciation purposes.

Net operating losses

Tax losses may be carried forward for 18 years, but they cannot be carried back. There are no tax loss 'baskets' (operating/capital) under Spanish law.

The amount of tax-loss carryforwards that may be offset in tax periods beginning in 2011, 2012, and 2013 is limited for large companies as follows:

- For companies whose turnover in the 12 months preceding the beginning of the tax period was between EUR 20 million and EUR 60 million, the amount of tax-loss carryforwards which may be offset is limited to 75% of their previous taxable income.
- For companies whose turnover in the 12 months preceding the beginning of the tax period was EUR 60 million or more, the amount of tax-loss carryforwards which may be offset is limited to 50% of their previous taxable income.

Complex rules may limit the use of tax losses of a company dissolved as a result of a restructuring operation and, in certain circumstances, when it has a change of shareholders.

Payments to foreign affiliates

Supplies of goods or services by a company not established in Spain to a Spanish group company must be valued at arm's length. If recorded expenses for such goods/services exceed arm's-length price, the tax deductibility of the excess amounts could be challenged in a tax inspection. The tax deductibility of expense charges received

S

Spain

from tax havens is fully disallowed unless proper evidence of an actual service valued at arm's length can be provided.

Management services received from outside Spain and recorded as distributions of costs of a group centre do not have to be documented in a written agreement entered into before the commencement of the services to ensure the tax deductibility of the expenses (as previously was the case), although it would be recommendable to have such an agreement. For any other types of services, an agreement recorded before a notary public is not obligatory under Spanish law, but it is advisable.

As regards the taxation in Spain of the foreign company which supplies the services, the WHT rate to be applied on the gross income obtained by the company is 24.75%. Dividends, interest, and capital gains generated as a result of a transfer of assets are taxed at a 21% WHT rate. If management services, technical assistance, or the performance of studies are solely used outside Spain and are linked to business carried on abroad, then no WHT is applicable. In addition, under most tax treaties signed by Spain, 'business profits' obtained in Spain by non-residents are exempt from WHT. However, 'business profits' is a miscellaneous residual category. For instance, if the amount obtained qualifies as a royalty payment, WHT is applicable at the reduced tax treaty rates if the foreign company can obtain a document from the tax authorities of its country of residence certifying its tax residence. If no tax treaty applies, then the above 24.75% WHT rate is applicable (*see the Withholding taxes section for more information*).

Group taxation

Tax groupings for CIT purposes

Under Spanish tax law, companies can form a group and apply a special tax consolidation regime for CIT purposes. Companies forming a tax group must formally pass a resolution agreeing to do so before the beginning of the first tax year in which the tax consolidation regime will be applied.

To apply the tax consolidation regime, the controlling company of the tax group must hold a 75% or higher interest, either directly or indirectly, in the companies forming the tax group at the beginning of the first tax year in which the tax consolidation regime is applied, and this interest must be maintained during the year unless the dependent company is dissolved. The interest requirement is 70% for companies listed on a stock exchange.

The main characteristics of the tax consolidation regime are as follows:

- The taxable income of the tax group is the sum of the taxable incomes of each of the companies forming the group.
- The tax losses of any of the companies forming the group can be offset against the tax profits of any of the other group companies.
- For the calculation of consolidated taxable income, the tax profits (losses) generated from transactions carried out between group companies are eliminated and only included in consolidated taxable income when:
  - they are carried out with third parties
  - a group company participating in the internal operation ceases to form part of the tax group, and
  - the tax consolidation regime is no longer applied by the group for whatever reason.

- Specific limitations apply regarding the offsetting of tax losses or the application of tax credits generated by the group companies before they formed part of the tax group. Such tax losses/credits may be offset (applied) by the tax group up to the limit of the tax profits/tax liability of the company which generated the losses/credits.
- No WHT is chargeable on payments made between companies of the tax group (e.g. interest, dividends).

Tax groupings for VAT purposes

Groups of companies may also choose to be taxed under a special tax consolidation regime for VAT purposes. This special regime is optional, but once it has been opted for, it must be applied for a minimum of three years which is extendible unless it is expressly waived by the companies.

The VAT consolidation regime may only be applied by groups resident in Spanish VAT territory which do not form part of any other VAT grouping.

The controlling company of the group must be a legal entity or PE which is not dependent on any other entity established in Spanish VAT territory, and it must hold at least a 50% interest in the subsidiary companies of the group for the entire calendar year.

With the application of the VAT consolidation regime, there are two different options for taxation:

- The aggregation system, where the balances of the VAT returns of the individual companies of the group are totalled. The right to a tax deduction is exercised by the individual companies.
- The consolidation system, where an individual company can opt to reduce VAT taxable income for inter-company operations which is limited to the 'external' cost.

Transfer pricing

All related-party transactions must be valued at market price, following the arm's-length standard (e.g. the value which in normal market conditions would have been established between unrelated parties).

For this purposes, related persons or entities shall be:

- A company and its shareholders or members.
- A company and its board members or directors.
- A company and the spouses of or persons related to its shareholders or members, board members, or directors, either in a direct line or collaterally, by consanguinity or affinity up to the third degree.
- Two companies of a group.
- A company and the shareholders or members of another company, when both companies form part of a group.
- A company and the board members or directors of another company, when both companies form part of a group.
- A company and the spouses of or persons related to the shareholders or members of another company, either in a direct line or collaterally, by consanguinity or affinity up to the third degree, when both companies form part of a group.
- A company and another company in which the former company has at least a 25% holding, held indirectly, in its share capital or shareholders' equity.

Spain

- Two companies in which the same shareholders or members or their spouses, or persons related to them either in a direct line or collaterally, by consanguinity or affinity up to the third degree, have at least a 25% holding, whether directly or indirectly, in their share capital or shareholders' equity.
- A company resident in Spanish territory and its PEs abroad.
- A company not resident in Spanish territory and its PEs in Spanish territory.
- Two companies forming part of a group taxed under the tax regime for groups of cooperative companies.

For cases where association exists as a result of a shareholder/member-company relationship, the shareholding must be 5% or more, or 1% if the shares are quoted on a regulated stock exchange. The reference to directors shall include *de facto* and *de jure* directors.

The determination of the market value by taxpayers must be done through the application of one of the following transfer pricing methodologies, in order of preference as follows: Comparable Uncontrolled Price (CUP) method, Cost Plus (CP) method, or Resale Price Method (RPM), usually referred to as traditional transaction methods.

If the application of any of the above methods is not possible, the Profit Split Method (PSM) or Transactional Net Margin Method (TNMM) could be applied, usually referred to as transactional profit methods.

Documentation is also a requirement, with taxpayers required to produce group-level and taxpayer-specific documentation for each tax year. Related persons or entities must keep such documentation available for the tax authorities as from the end of the voluntary return or assessment period in question. Exceptionally, no documentation requirements will be applied in the following cases, among others:

- With some exceptions, transactions carried out within a tax period with one related person or entity will not be subject to documentation requirements when the sum of the considerations of all these transactions does not exceed EUR 250,000.
- Transactions carried out within a group of companies taxed under the Spanish special tax consolidation regime.
- Transactions carried out by economic interest groups and temporary business associations.
- Transactions involving the purchase or sale of publicly traded shares.

Documentation is always required for transactions with entities, whether related parties or otherwise, which are resident in tax havens.

Please note that specific penalties may be imposed in the event of the absence of documentation or where data are omitted, inaccurate, or false.

Thin capitalisation
Thin capitalisation rules have been repealed effective for tax periods starting on or after 1 January 2012.

Controlled foreign companies (CFCs)
Spanish CFC rules seek to avoid the effects produced when Spanish tax resident entities or individuals place their capital in low-taxed foreign entities to avoid including passive income generated by such capital in their taxable bases.

Under this regime, Spanish tax resident entities are subject to Spanish CIT on certain kinds of positive passive income obtained by entities which are not resident in the European Union for tax purposes in which they own, individually or together with tax related entities or persons, more than 50% of the share capital, equity, profits, or voting rights, provided that the CIT due by the non-resident entity is below 75% of the tax that would have been due in Spain.

The types of passive income to which CFC rules apply are as follows: (i) income from immovable property not used for business activities; (ii) income derived from equity in other entities or from capital assigned to third parties (interest and dividends); (iii) transfer of the above mentioned immovable property and financial assets; and (iv) income arising from credit, financial, insurance, and service activities carried out directly or indirectly with related Spanish tax resident entities in which a tax deductible expense is generated.

Passive income mentioned in numbers (i) to (iii) above obtained by the non-resident entity will not be considered taxable income of the Spanish tax resident entity when it arises from entities in which the latter holds a direct or indirect interest of over 5%, provided that the non-resident entity controls and manages the interest using the relevant human and material resources and provided at least 85% of the income obtained from such participated entities comes from business activities.

Moreover, the passive income mentioned in numbers (i) to (iii) above will not be included in the Spanish entity's taxable base when it amounts in total to less than 15% of the total profits obtained by the CFC or less than 4% of its total turnover.

Tax credits and incentives

Foreign tax credit
See Foreign income in the Income determination section for a description of double tax relief.

CIT relief
No specific tax relief is established in Spanish law for foreign investors. Relief may be availed of by Spanish and foreign-owned companies alike. The tax relief available under CIT law in Spain is as follows.

Most of the tax credits that have been established to promote certain investments have been or must be reduced and eliminated. However, the largest tax credits are maintained (tax credit to prevent internal and international double taxation, tax credit for the reinvestment of extraordinary profits, and tax credit for R&D).

Tax relief for business activity/place of business activity
- 50% tax credit on CIT levied on income obtained in Ceuta and Melilla through companies established and carrying on activities during a full business cycle in these enclaves.
- 99% tax credit on the CIT levied on income obtained from the supply of local public services, except when the state company in question is owned, partially or wholly, by a quoted/non-quoted company or individual.
- 25% tax credit on the CIT levied on income obtained from exports of films, books, and similar cultural items if profits are reinvested in the acquisition of assets used for such activities. This tax credit will be gradually reduced over the coming years and eliminated in 2014.

Spain

R&D credits
A 25% tax credit can be availed of for expenses incurred from R&D activities. If the expenses are higher than the average R&D expenses incurred by the company during the previous two years, the tax credit is 42% for the excess amount.

An additional tax credit of 17% can be availed of for staff expenses incurred for staff exclusively carrying out and qualified to carry out R&D activities.

An 8% tax credit can be availed of for investments made in tangible fixed assets (excluding buildings) and intangible assets which are exclusively assigned to R&D activities.

Technological innovation credits
A 12% tax credit can be availed of for technological innovation activities.

Tax credit for environmental investments
The tax credit for environmental investments in installations is 8%

The tax credit for environmental investments in vehicles and the tax credit for environmental investments in assets to promote the exploitation of renewable energies have been eliminated.

Reinvestment of extraordinary income
A 12% tax credit can be availed of for sales of assets which are used for the company's business activities when the amount obtained from the sale is reinvested in similar types of assets during a four-year period (as from one year prior to the sale up to three years after the sale). This tax credit therefore reduces the effective tax levied on sales of certain assets to 18%.

In the case of a sale of company shares, to be eligible for this tax credit, the interest in the company must be a minimum of 5% and must have been held for more than one year prior to the sale.

The asset in which the reinvestment is made must be maintained for five years (three in the case of moveable assets) unless its useful life is shorter.

Other CIT relief
The tax credit for film productions will be eliminated for tax periods commencing on or after 1 January 2013.

The tax credit for investments in heritage assets (4% in 2012 and 2% in 2013) and book publishing (2% in 2012 and 1% in 2013) will be eliminated for tax periods commencing on or after 1 January 2014.

A tax credit of 1% to 2% may be obtained on expenses incurred in, or related to, financing ongoing staff education programmes. This tax credit can also be availed of for expenses incurred by companies to familiarise staff in the use of new technologies. These expenses are not a benefit in kind for the staff. The tax credit related to education programmes was eliminated in 2011, but the tax credit related to expenses incurred to familiarise staff in the use of new technologies will not be eliminated until 2013.

A tax credit can be applied for increases in the number of disabled workers contracted per year on a permanent and full-time basis (EUR 6,000 per worker contracted). This increase is calculated by taking the average number of company workers meeting these requirements in the tax year in question and comparing it with the company's average number of staff in the previous tax year.

Limits on the amount of tax credit applied

The combined sum of all investment tax credits may not exceed 35% of the company's gross tax payable less any tax credits for internal and international double taxation and tax relief for income obtained in Ceuta and Melilla, for export activities, and for local public services. This percentage is reduced to 25% for tax periods commencing in 2012 and 2013.

When R&D and technological innovation tax credits for expenses and investments in the year exceed 10% of the company's gross tax payable, less tax credits and relief mentioned above, the limit will be 50% (60% for tax periods commencing on or after 1 January 2014).

For tax periods commencing in 2012 and 2013, these limits will also apply for the tax credit for reinvestments of extraordinary profits.

Time limits for the application of tax credits

Tax credits that are not applied in the tax period owing to insufficient tax payable may be applied in tax periods ending in the 15 years immediately thereafter (ten years for the tax periods commencing before 1 January 2012). However, R&D and technological innovation tax credits may be applied in tax periods ending in the 18 years immediately thereafter (15 years for tax periods commencing before 1 January 2012).

Special tax regimes

Special tax regimes are applicable, among others, in the following cases:

Spanish and European Economic Interest Groupings and Temporary Consortia of Entities

- Spanish Economic Interest Groupings (SEIGs) that meet certain requirements will not be subject to Spanish CIT on the part of the taxable income which corresponds to members resident in Spain for tax purposes. Such part of the positive or negative taxable income shall be deemed to be the profits/losses of the SEIG members. The proportional part of tax credits and payments in advance will also be assigned to the Spanish tax resident members of the SEIG where they are subject to CIT or PIT. Dividends distributed to SEIG members that have been subject to imputation will not be taxed under CIT or PIT on distributions. Dividends distributed to Spanish non-resident SEIG members will be taxed in accordance with the Spanish Non-Resident Income Tax Act and Conventions for the Avoidance of Double Taxation.
- European Economic Interest Groupings (EEIGs) will be taxed under the above-mentioned regime with the following exception: EEIG will not be subject to Spanish CIT.

If the EEIG is not resident in Spain for tax purposes, Spanish tax resident members will include the corresponding part of the profits or losses determined for the grouping, corrected by applying the rules for determining taxable income for CIT or PIT purposes, as applicable. When the activity carried out by the members through the grouping determines the existence of a PE abroad, the rules provided for in this Law or in the respective treaty for the avoidance of double international taxation will be applicable.

Spain

Non-Spanish tax resident members will only be subject to Spanish Non-Resident Income Tax when the activity they perform through the grouping determines the existence of a PE in Spanish territory.

Dividends distributed to non-Spanish tax resident members that have been subject to imputation will not be taxed in Spain on the distribution.

- Temporary Consortia of Entities (TCEs) are taxed under the SEIG regime. As an exception, members of a TCE that operates abroad may benefit from exemptions for income obtained abroad.

Restructuring transactions

For restructuring transactions, the special tax regime is a tax neutrality regime implemented under EU Directive 90/434. As a general rule, under this regime, asset transfers carried out through such transactions do not have any tax implications (either from a direct, indirect, or other Spanish tax perspective) for the parties involved (transferor, beneficiary, and shareholder), until a subsequent transfer takes place which is not protected by this regime.

The transactions which can be taxed under this regime are mergers, global transfers, spin-offs of business units/majority interests, splits, share-to-share transactions, contributions of business units, and contributions of assets (this last transaction is not fully tax-protected). Each of them must comply with a series of requirements for the application of the regime.

The tax credit position of a company dissolved as a result of a tax-protected restructuring transaction is 'acquired' in full by the beneficiary company in the case of universal succession.

The 'acquired' tax credits only include tax credits which are obtained in relation to assets transferred in transactions where the transferor is not dissolved or the succession is not a full succession for Spanish commercial purposes.

Regarding tax losses, the Spanish tax authorities hold the view that tax losses may not be transferred when the transferring company is not dissolved. When the transferring company is dissolved, the tax losses may be applied by the beneficiary company up to certain limits and subject to certain restrictions.

Financial goodwill arising in a merger transaction is amortised for tax purposes at a maximum annual rate of 5% at the level of the Spanish beneficiary company of the merger (1% for tax periods commencing in 2012 and 2013), if the seller of the shares giving rise to the 'merger' goodwill has been actually taxed for the equivalent capital gain in Spain or in any other EU country (excluding tax havens), and provided that certain requirements are met. Amortisation of financial goodwill does not have to be recorded in the profit and loss account for it to be tax deductible, although an annual amount must be charged to a non-distributable reserve (either from annual profits or from freely-distributable reserves), which must be at least the tax deductible amount.

This tax regime cannot be applied if the transaction is carried out for the purpose of tax fraud or evasion (anti-abuse clause). An additional anti-abuse clause in line with the clause established by the EU directive is established in Spanish law to ensure that the tax regime cannot be applied if the transaction is not carried out for valid economic reasons, such as the streamlining of activities or group restructuring to gain efficiency, but to obtain a tax benefit.

Spain

The tax authorities must be notified of the application of this tax regime.

Tax transparency
Tax transparency (under international CFC rules) is not applicable for companies resident in the European Union. *See CFCs in the Group taxation section for more information.*

Venture capital companies and funds
Venture capital companies (VCCs) and funds (VCFs) may benefit from the following tax regime if certain requirements are met:

*   Dividends from target companies may benefit from a 100% tax credit for the avoidance of double taxation or tax exemption.
*   Capital gains arising from the transfer of shares in target companies may be 99% exempted from CIT, provided that such shares have been held for a period between 2 and 15 years.
*   Profit distributions to VCC and VCF shareholders may benefit from a 100% tax credit for the avoidance of double taxation if the shareholders are Spanish tax residents or have a PE in Spain. Income from profit distributions to non-Spanish tax resident shareholders without a PE in Spain is not subject to taxation in Spain unless it is obtained through a tax haven. The same regime applies to the transfer of shares in VCCs and VCFs.

Collective Investment Institutions (CIIs)
CIIs are subject to CIT at a reduced rate of 1%. They are not entitled to apply any tax credits. Dividends distributed by these institutions are subject to the general WHT regime. Shareholders are taxed on dividends received from the CII and on capital gains obtained for the transfer of the CII without being entitled to the application of a tax credit for the avoidance of double taxation.

Lease transactions
Financial leasing contracts with a purchase option that may be exercised at the end of the lease period may benefit from a special tax regime if they meet certain requirements. According to this regime, the lessee may deduct the following expenses from its taxable income:

*   The part of the lease instalments corresponding to the financial charge (interest) paid to the lessor.
*   The part of the lease instalments paid which corresponds to the recovery of the cost of the good. Tax deductibility for this amount may not exceed the result of applying twice the straight-line depreciation rate which corresponds to the good in question in accordance with the officially-approved depreciation tables.

Spanish holding companies of foreign companies (Entidad de Tenencia de Valores Extranjeros or ETVE) regime
Spanish resident companies whose corporate purpose includes the holding and management of foreign companies' shares are granted some tax benefits subject to compliance with certain requirements.

The tax authorities must be notified of the application of this tax regime.

Companies taxed under this tax regime are granted a tax exemption on dividends and capital gains when they have a 5% direct interest or, if their interest is less than 5%, when the acquisition value of their interest is at least EUR 6 million.

Spain

In addition, the distribution of profits by the holding company to non-resident companies or individual shareholders is not taxable in Spain (unless the profits are distributed to a tax haven). Resident company shareholders are now entitled to an internal tax credit on dividends under Spanish law.

Small and medium-sized companies
Small and medium-sized companies are eligible for tax relief such as accelerated depreciation/amortisation, or more favourable bad debt provision treatment. Accelerated depreciation/amortisation can be applied for assets acquired using amounts obtained from sales of trading assets. To be eligible for this relief, turnover in the previous tax year must not exceed EUR 10 million. In the case of a group, the turnover of all the companies must be considered for this purpose.

A reduced CIT rate of 25% is levied on the first EUR 300,000 of annual tax profits.

Special economic and tax regime of the Canary Islands
Due to the distance to and isolation of the Canary Islands, they have traditionally enjoyed a special economic and tax regime with specific economic and tax measures different to those established for the rest of Spain.

Regarding direct taxes, the Canary Island economic and tax regime establishes the following tax benefits for companies and businesses domiciled in the Canary Islands or with a PE in the Canary Islands:

- Up to 90% of annual undistributed accounting profits can be allocated to a special investment reserve and not taxed providing that they are invested within a four-year period (including the period during which the profits are obtained) in qualifying assets in the Canary Islands, or in certain public debt securities or shares in other companies operating in the Canary Islands which invest in qualifying assets.
- Most Spanish CIT relief is 80% higher for companies and businesses located in the Canary Islands.
- A 25% tax credit can be availed of for investments in new tangible fixed assets and, subject to compliance with certain requirements, second-hand assets.
- A tax credit of 50% of the CIT liability is granted for taxable income generated from the production of tangible goods while carrying on agricultural, farming, industrial, and fishing activities.
- A tax credit of 90% of the CIT liability is granted for profits of shipping companies generated from ships registered in the Canary Islands Special Ships and Shipping Companies Register. For sailors of such ships, a 50% tax exemption can be applied to PIT levied on their employment income and a 90% reduction to the part of their Social Security contributions paid by their employers.

Regarding indirect taxes, in addition to lower taxation through the Canary Island general indirect tax (IGIC at the general rate of 5%) compared to VAT and specific IGIC exemptions, the following should be noted:

- Companies domiciled in the Canary Islands which are CIT-payers and which are newly incorporated, start new activities or improve their existing activities may benefit from the following tax relief:
  - Exemption from IGIC on supplies and imports of capital goods if the company has a deduction percentage that is not 100%.
  - Shipping companies qualify for an exemption from transfer tax for any contracts related to ships registered in the Canary Islands Special Ships and Shipping Companies Register.

Spain

- Custom Free areas are available. Upon EU demand, there are restrictions on the application of certain tax relief (special investment reserve, tax credits for production, and new business indirect tax relief) for the following industrial sectors: shipbuilding, synthetic fibres, automobile, iron and steel, and coal.

Canary Islands Special Zone tax regime

In January 2000, a special Canary Island Special Zone tax regime was approved by the European Union. The main regulations of this regime, established by the Spanish government, are as follows:

- New companies may qualify for the application of this tax regime and, on the approval of the tax authorities, may be registered up to 31 December 2013 (applying the tax regime up to 31 December 2019). This may be extended by the European Union.
- To qualify for this tax regime, the company must:
  - covenant to make an investment in fixed assets of at least EUR 100,000 in Gran Canaria or Tenerife, or EUR 50,000 in Fuerteventura, Lanzarote, La Palma, El Hierro, or La Gomera, within the first two years of their business activity
  - covenant to create at least five new jobs in Gran Canaria or Tenerife, or three in the other islands
  - provide a description of the business activities to be carried out which support the company's solvency, viability, international competitiveness, and contribution to the economic and social development of the Canary Islands
  - establish its registered office and place of effective management in the Special Area
  - have at least one company director who resides in the Canary Islands, and
  - carry out one of the qualifying business activities.

- The territory where this tax regime can be applied includes all the Canary Islands, except for companies which intend to carry out industrial or commercial activities involving tangible goods, which must be located in specific controlled areas.
- Companies applying the tax regime may operate outside the Canary Islands through branches if separate accounting books are kept, but the tax regime will not be applicable to such branches' activities.
- Activities for which the tax regime can be applied include a wide range of industrial and commercial activities, most services and holdings. Credit and insurance entities are excluded, and no stock exchanges are allowed.
- Companies applying the tax regime are subject to CIT in Spain at a 4% rate for companies authorised from 1 January 2007 onwards and at a variable rate of between 1% and 5% for companies authorised before this date. The special 4% rate shall be levied on a maximum amount of the taxable income, which will depend on the number of jobs created and the type of activity carried out by the company. The general CIT regime establishes a 30% tax rate for Spanish companies. For small companies, the tax rate is 25% for the first EUR 300,000 of profits and 30% for remaining profits.
- Under this tax regime, companies can avail themselves of large tax exemptions for IGIC, transfer tax, and stamp duty, and large reductions and simplified regulations for local taxes.
- Interest and some other returns from moveable goods paid by companies under this tax regime are exempt from Spanish non-residents' income tax, except when paid to residents in tax havens.
- Benefits established in the EU Parent-Subsidiary Directive are extended to non-EU residents. These benefits are not applicable when the income is paid to residents in tax havens.

Spain

- A fee of EUR 732.51 is payable to be registered as a company which applies this tax regime, and an annual fee of EUR 1,098.76 is payable to continue to be registered as qualifying for the tax regime.

Finally, the Spanish Parliament has recently proposed some amendments to the law regulating the Canary Island Special Zone tax regime, including, among other tax benefits, a reduction in the special CIT rate for companies which apply the regime to 1% for the first tax base segment.

Withholding taxes

Ordinarily, WHT is the mechanism by which the Spanish tax authorities collect the final tax levied on non-residents. In the case of resident beneficiaries, however, it is simply an advance payment of a tax that is then normally self-assessed by the resident taxpayer in the final annual tax return.

The advance payment system of WHT for resident beneficiaries referred to above also applies if non-resident companies/individuals not established in Spain sell their title to Spanish real estate. In this case, the acquirer of the real estate must levy a 3% WHT on the selling price on account of the 21% tax chargeable to the seller on its capital gain. Other capital gains (for instance, from a sale by a non-resident of a substantial interest in a Spanish company where neither a tax treaty nor internal rules establish a tax exemption) are taxed in the hands of the non-resident transferor, but the mechanics of levying the tax are not those of a WHT. In this case, the non-resident's tax is paid directly, through its representative or by the depositor or manager of the assets in question, if any.

The following table states the general WHT rates on income obtained by resident/non-resident companies. The most significant peculiarities regarding the rates for each type of income are stated in footnotes to the table.

Withholding rates

Recipient	Dividends (%)	Interest (%)	Royalties (%)
Resident corporations and individuals	21 (1)	21 (2a)	21 (2b)
Non-resident corporations and individuals:			
Non-treaty	21 (3)	21 (4)	24.75 (5)
Treaty (*):			
Albania	10 (6)	6 (10, 22)	0
Algeria	5 (17)	5 (8, 9, 10, 11)	7 (12)
Argentina	10 (14)	12.5 (8, 9, 10, 14)	15 (15)
Armenia	10 (104)	5	10 (105)
Australia	15	10	10
Austria	10 (3, 16)	5 (4)	5 (5)
Barbados	0 (98)	0	0
Belgium	15 (3, 18)	10 (4, 18, 19)	5 (5, 18)
Bolivia	10 (13, 18)	15 (8, 9, 10, 14, 18)	15 (18, 20)
Bosnia	5 (21)	7 (22)	7
Brazil	10 (23)	15 (9, 24, 25)	12.5 (26)
Bulgaria	5 (3, 27)	0 (4)	0 (5)

Spain

Recipient	Dividends (%)	Interest (%)	Royalties (%)
Canada	15	15 (28)	10 (20, 28)
Chile	5 (29)	15 (30)	10 (31)
China	10	10	10 (32)
Columbia	5 (33)	10 (34)	10
Costa Rica	12 (35)	10 (34, 36a)	10
Croatia	0 (13, 18)	8 (9, 18, 36b)	8 (18)
Cuba	5 (13 ,18)	10 (18, 37)	5 (18, 20)
Czech Republic	5 (3, 27)	0 (4)	5 (5, 38)
Ecuador	15	10 (39)	10 (40)
Egypt	12 (41)	10 (42)	12
El Salvador	12 (43)	10 (22)	10
Estonia	5 (3, 13, 18)	10 (4, 9, 10, 11, 18)	10 (5, 18, 31)
Finland	10 (3, 13)	10 (4)	5 (5)
France	15 (3, 45)	10 (4, 46)	5 (5, 47)
Georgia	0 (99)	0	0
Germany	10 (3, 13)	10 (4, 48)	5 (5)
Greece	5 (3, 49)	8 (4, 50)	6 (5)
Hong Kong	10 (106)	5 (59)	5
Hungary	5 (3, 13)	0	0
Iceland	5 (13, 18)	5 (18)	5 (18)
India	15	15 (9, 51, 52)	20 (53)
Indonesia / Timor Oriental	10 (13)	10 (9, 54, 55)	10
Iran	5 (56)	7.5 (9, 10, 11)	5
Ireland	15 (3, 18)	10 (4, 18, 55)	10 (5, 18, 57)
Israel	10 (18)	10 (18, 58)	7 (18, 40)
Italy	15 (3)	12 (4, 9)	8 (5, 60)
Jamaica	5 (49, 61)	10 (22, 61)	10 (61)
Japan	10 (23)	10	10
Kazakhstan	5 (90)	10 (8, 9, 97)	10
Latvia	5 (3, 18, 49)	10 (4, 9, 10, 18)	10 (5, 18, 31)
Lithuania	5 (3, 18, 49)	10 (4, 9, 10, 18)	10 (5, 18, 31)
Luxembourg	10 (3, 62)	10 (4, 9, 63)	10 (5, 64)
Macedonia	5 (7)	5 (65)	5
Malaysia	5 (18, 66)	10 (8, 18)	7 (18, 67)
Malta	5 (3, 68)	0	0
Mexico	5 (13)	15 (69)	10 (20, 38)
Moldova	0 (70)	5 (22)	8
Morocco	10 (13)	10	10 (40)
Netherlands	15 (3, 71)	10 (4)	6 (5, 72)
New Zealand	15	10	10
Norway	10 (13)	10 (9, 10, 36a, 55)	5 (64, 73a)
Panama	5 (100, 101)	5 (10,44)	5
Pakistan	10 (73b)	10 (8, 9, 97)	7.5
Philippines	10 (74)	15 (75)	15 (76)
Poland	5 (3, 23)	0 (4)	10 (5, 20)
Portugal	10 (3, 13, 18)	15 (4, 18)	5 (5, 18)
Romania	10 (3, 13)	10 (4, 77)	10 (5)

Spain

Recipient	Dividends (%)	Interest (%)	Royalties (%)
Russian Federation	15 (18, 78)	5 (9, 18, 79)	5 (18)
Saudi Arabia	5 (68)	5 (8, 9)	8
Serbia	5 (13)	10 (9)	10 (80)
Singapore	0 (102)	5 (103)	5
Slovakia	5 (3, 27)	0 (4)	5 (5, 38)
Slovenia	5 (3, 13, 18)	5 (4, 8, 9, 18)	5 (5, 18)
South Africa	5 (13, 18)	5 (18, 81)	5 (18)
South Korea	10 (13)	10 (9, 82)	10
States of the former USSR (except Russia)	18	0	5
Sweden	10 (3, 16)	15 (4)	10 (5)
Switzerland	15 (83)	10 (84)	5 (85)
Thailand	10	15 (86a)	15 (86b)
Trinidad and Tobago	0 (70, 87a)	8 (8, 9, 63, 82, 87a)	5 (87a)
Tunisia	5 (87b)	10 (88)	10
Turkey	5 (13)	15 (89)	10
United Arab Emirates	5 (9, 90)	0	0
United Kingdom	10 (3, 7)	12 (4)	10 (5)
United States	10 (13)	10 (9, 65)	10 (57, 91a)
Uruguay	5 (91b)	10 (8, 9, 92)	10 (93)
Venezuela	0 (49)	10 (94, 95)	5
Vietnam	7 (18, 96)	10 (9, 18, 63)	10 (18)

Notes

The general rates in the table above are for guidance only and should not be treated as tax advice.

The rates above are for income obtained by non-residents which is not related to any PEs they may have in Spain.

(*) Aside from these tax treaties, the following tax treaties are not yet in force as they are currently being negotiated or are not yet approved or published: Azerbaijan, Belarus, Dominican Republic, Kuwait, Namibia, Nigeria, Oman, Peru, Senegal, Singapore, and Syria.

1. If a corporate taxpayer, as a shareholder, is entitled to full tax relief on the dividend received, no WHT is levied. As a general rule, corporate shareholders with at least a 5% interest held for at least one year are granted full tax relief.
2.
   a. The 21% WHT rate does not apply if, amongst other cases, the recipient is a resident bank or savings or other financial institution subject to CIT, provided that this income is not portfolio income. In addition, no WHT is levied on interest arising between companies taxed under the tax consolidation regime.
   b. A 21% WHT rate is levied on income generated under royalty and technical assistance agreements, from leases or from the granting of rights when ownership is not transferred. A 24.75% rate is levied on fees received by a company for the transfer of rights to an image or consent or authorisation to its use.
3. Implementation of the EU Parent-Subsidiary Directive in Spanish law gives EU shareholders a WHT exemption on dividends from Spanish companies, subject to compliance with certain requirements. Luxembourg recipients of income which are companies under paragraph 1 of the protocol to the Tax Treaty with Spain (holding companies) are not allowed this exemption.
4. The EU Interest and Royalties Directive WHT exemption for interest obtained by EU lenders is applicable when appropriate.
5. Taxable income from supplies of services, technical assistance, or assembly/installation work under engineering contracts provided or carried out by non-resident companies with no PE in Spain does not follow the general rule for gross income. In such cases, total income can be reduced by related staff costs, certain supplies (water, electricity, telephone) and materials used for the services/work, provided that, in the case of staff costs, evidence can be furnished that they were actually taxed in Spain. According to the EU Interest and Royalties Directive, royalties paid to other EU member state associate companies are exempt from WHT as of 1 July 2011.

6. A 5% WHT is levied if the recipient is a company which holds at least 10% of the capital of the company paying the dividends; no WHT is levied if the recipient company holds at least 75% of the capital of the company paying the dividends.
7. Levied if the recipient is a company holding at least a 10% interest in the paying company; otherwise, a 15% rate is levied.
8. Interest paid by certain public institutions is tax exempt.
9. Interest paid to certain public institutions is tax exempt.
10. Interest arising from the acquisition of commercial, industrial or scientific equipment is tax exempt.
11. Interest paid on loans granted by a bank or other financial institution is tax exempt.
12. For royalties for any copyright of artistic, scientific, or literary work (including cinematograph films and films or tapes for radio or television broadcasting), the rate levied is 14%.
13. Levied if the recipient is a company holding at least a 25% interest in the paying company; otherwise, a 15% rate is levied.
14. No WHT is levied on interest when both contracting states agree this and the loan is for no less than five years.
15. A 3% WHT rate is levied on royalties for the use of or right to use news. A 5% WHT rate is levied on royalties for any copyright of artistic, theatrical, musical, or literary work. A 10% WHT rate is levied on royalties for the use of or right to use copyright of industrial property, know-how, or scientific, commercial, or industrial equipment.
16. Levied if the recipient is a company holding a direct interest of at least 50% in the paying company for at least one year; otherwise, a 15% rate is levied.
17. No WHT is levied if the recipient is a company holding at least a 25% interest in the paying company.
18. Reduced WHT rates or exemptions are not levied/applied if the income is paid to a company resident in a contracting state more than 50% of whose shares are directly or indirectly held by non-residents. This clause will not apply if the company can prove that it carries out important industrial or commercial activities and does not merely manage or hold shares.
19. A tax exemption can be applied to interest on commercial loans, loans guaranteed by public bodies for the promotion of exports, and on current accounts in banks or nominative advances between banks of both contracting states.
20. Royalties for any copyright of literary, theatrical, musical, or artistic work (with some exceptions, such as films and TV programs) are exempt from WHT.
21. 5% WHT is levied if the recipient (beneficial owner) is the shareholder of the paying company with at least a 20% interest; otherwise, 10% WHT is levied.
22. No WHT is levied on interest if: (i) the recipient is the other contracting state, its central bank, or its political divisions; (ii) the payer is a contracting state or its political divisions; (iii) the interest arises from a loan or credit granted or guaranteed by a contracting state or its political divisions; (iv) the recipient is a financial institution; or (v) the recipient is a pension fund qualifying for tax purposes in a contracting state and the income from such fund is tax exempt in the contracting state paying the dividend.
23. Levied if the recipient is a company with at least a 25% interest in the paying company with voting rights; otherwise, a 15% rate is levied.
24. The maximum WHT is 10% for interest paid to financial institutions for loans and credits granted for a minimum term of ten years for the purchase of capital equipment.
25. Interest arising from securities issued by a contracting state is exempt from WHT.
26. A 10% WHT rate is levied on royalties for copyrights of any literary, scientific, or artistic work (including films and TV programs).
27. Levied if the beneficial owner is a company (excluding partnerships) with at least a 25% interest in the paying company held directly or indirectly; otherwise, a 15% rate is levied.
28. A reduced WHT rate is only levied if the income is taxed in Canada; otherwise the general rate is levied.
29. Levied if the recipient is a company with at least a 20% interest in the paying company held directly or indirectly; otherwise, a 10% rate is levied.
30. Interest arising from bank or insurance company loans, bonds, some securities that are regularly negotiated on stock markets, and credit sales of industrial equipment are taxed at a 5% tax rate.
31. A 5% WHT rate is levied on royalties for the use of industrial, commercial or scientific equipment.
32. WHT is levied on 60% of gross royalties for the use of industrial, commercial or scientific equipment.
33. A 0% WHT rate is levied if the recipient is a company with at least a 20% interest in the paying company held directly or indirectly.
34. No WHT is levied if: (i) the beneficiary is a contracting state, one of its political subdivisions or one of its local entities; (ii) interest is paid in connection with the sale on credit of merchandise or equipment to a company of a contracting state; or (iii) interest is paid on a loan granted by a bank or financial institution resident in a contracting state.
35. A 5% WHT is levied if the beneficial owner is a company which directly holds at least 20% of the capital of the company paying the dividends.
36.
    a. 5% WHT is levied if the interest is paid on a long-term loan (more than five years).
    b. No WHT is levied: (i) if interest is paid to a Croatian bank, (ii) on interest arising from the acquisition of commercial, industrial, or scientific equipment, (iii) on interest arising from a credit sale.
37. No WHT is levied if: (i) the beneficiary is a contracting state, one of its political subdivisions or one of its local entities; (ii) interest is paid in connection with the sale on credit of merchandise or equipment

Spain

to a company of a contracting state; or (iii) interest is paid on a long-term loan (five or more years) granted by a bank or financial institution resident in a contracting state.
38. Royalties for copyrights of any literary, theatrical, musical, or artistic work, excluding films and TV programs, are tax exempt if the recipient is resident in the other contracting state and taxed on such income in such state.
39. A 5% WHT rate is levied on interest arising from the sale of industrial, commercial or scientific equipment, the sale of merchandise from one business to another business, or the financing of construction, installation or assembly works. No WHT is levied if the interest is paid on a long term loan (more than five years) or if the interest is paid to the other contracting state or one of its political subdivisions or a financial institution totally owned by the other contracting state or one of its political subdivisions.
40. A 5% WHT rate is levied on royalties for copyrights of any literary, theatrical, musical, or artistic work (excluding films and TV programs).
41. A 9% WHT rate is levied on the gross amount of the dividends if the beneficiary owner is a company (other than a partnership) which has at least a 25% direct interest in the company paying the dividends.
42. WHT is not levied on interest if the recipient is a contracting state, one of its political subdivisions, or one of its public bodies or local authorities, or if the interest is paid to the Central Bank of the other contracting state.
43. No WHT is levied if the recipient is a company with at least a 50% direct interest in the company paying the dividends, provided that the dividends are distributed from profits taxed in Spain.
44. No WHT is levied on interest if: (i) the recipient is the other contracting state, its central bank or its political divisions; (ii) the payer is a contracting state or its political divisions, (iii) the interest arises from a loan or credit granted by a contracting state or its political divisions, (iv) the recipient is a qualifying financial institution; or (v) the recipient is a pension fund qualifying for tax purposes in a contracting state and the income from such fund is tax exempt in the contracting state paying the dividend.
45. No WHT is levied if the French company has at least a 10% direct interest in the company distributing the dividend.
46. No WHT is levied if the French company receives interest (i) from the other contracting state or any of its political divisions, (ii) from a resident in the other contracting state from an underlying commercial or industrial activity, (iii) in connection with a credit sale of industrial, commercial or scientific equipment, or (iv) for a loan granted by a financial institution.
47. No WHT is levied on royalties on copyright of any literary or artistic work (excluding films and TV programs) if the recipient is the beneficiary owner or royalties paid for the use or licensing of containers and bare hull vessels or aircraft used in international trade.
48. No WHT is levied on interest paid to 'Deutsche Bundesbank' or 'Kreditanstalt für Wiederaufbau'.
49. Levied if the recipient is a company with at least a 25% direct interest in the paying company; otherwise, a 10% rate is levied.
50. No WHT is levied on interest if: (i) the interest is paid by a contracting state, one of its political subdivisions, or one of its local entities; (ii) the interest is paid to the other contracting state, one of its political subdivisions, or one of its local entities or to a body (including financial institutions) of such contracting state; or (iii) the interest is paid to another body (including financial institutions) in relation to loans granted by virtue of an agreement between both contracting states.
51. No WHT is levied on interest paid to the Central Bank of the other contracting state.
52. No WHT is levied on interest paid to companies in the other contracting state if the operation that generates the debt has been authorised by the government of the state where the company paying the interest is resident.
53. A 10% WHT rate is levied on royalties for the use or cession of use of industrial, commercial, or scientific equipment. The general 20% WHT rate is levied on technical services and other royalties.
54. No WHT is levied on interest if the recipient is a contracting state, one of its political subdivisions, or one of its local entities or if the interest is paid to the Central Bank or a financial institution controlled by the other contracting state, its political subdivisions, or its local entities.
55. No WHT is levied on interest arising from the credit sale of industrial, commercial, or scientific equipment.
56. Levied if the recipient is a company with at least a 20% interest in the paying company; otherwise, a 10% rate is levied.
57. Royalties for copyright on literary, theatrical, musical, or artistic work are taxed at a 5% WHT rate. Royalties on films or other means of audio or video transmission, for the use or right to use industrial, commercial, or scientific equipment, or on scientific works or under agreements between both states are taxed at an 8% rate.
58. A 5% WHT rate is levied on interest arising from the sale of industrial, commercial, or scientific equipment, the sale of merchandise from one business to another business or loans granted by a financial institution.
59. No WHT is levied on interest if the beneficial owner of the interest is a resident of the other contracting state and: (i) the beneficial owner of the interest is that contracting state, its central bank, a political subdivision, or a local authority; (ii) the interest is paid by the contracting state in which the interest arises or by a political subdivision, a local authority, or non profit-making statutory body thereof; (iii) the interest is paid in respect of a loan, debt-claim, or credit that is owed to, or made, provided, guaranteed, or insured by that contracting state or a political subdivision, a local authority, or an export facilitating agency thereof; (iv) the beneficial owner of the interest is a financial

institution; or (v) the beneficial owner of the interest is a qualifying pension fund and the income of that fund is generally exempt from tax in that other contracting state.

60. A 4% WHT rate is levied on royalties for copyright on literary, theatrical, musical, or artistic work (excluding films and TV programs).

61. Reduced WHT rates are not levied when more than 75% of the shares of the recipient company resident in a contracting state are owned directly or indirectly by non-residents and the income generated by the paying company is not taxed in its country of residence.

62. Levied if the recipient is a company with at least a 25% interest in the paying company; otherwise, a 15% rate is levied.

63. No WHT is levied on interest arising from a loan guaranteed by a contracting state.

64. Consideration received for waiving, either totally or partially, the use or right to use goods or rights is considered to be a royalty.

65. No WHT is levied on interest paid in connection with the sale on credit of merchandise or equipment to a company of a contracting state or on interest paid on a long-term loan (five or more years) granted by a bank or credit institution resident in a contracting state.

66. No WHT is levied if the recipient is a company with at least a 5% direct interest in the paying company.

67. A 5% WHT rate is levied on royalties for technical services.

68. No WHT is levied on dividends paid to a shareholder resident in the other contracting state of the company distributing the dividend with at least a 25% interest.

69. A 10% WHT rate is levied on interest received by a bank (beneficial owner).

70. Levied if the recipient is a company with at least a 50% direct interest in the paying company. A 5% WHT rate is levied if the recipient is a shareholder with at least a 25% direct interest; otherwise, a 10% rate is levied. WHT is reduced to 5% if the recipient company is not taxed in the Netherlands for this dividend.

71. WHT is reduced to 10% if the recipient is a Dutch company with at least a 50% direct interest in the paying company or if the recipient holds 25% of its capital and another Dutch company holds at least the other 25%.

72. No WHT is levied on capital gains from sales of assets/rights when they are considered to be a royalty.

73.
    a. No WHT is levied on fees paid for the use or licensing of containers and bare hull vessels or aircraft used in international trade.
    b. A 5% WHT is levied if the beneficial owner is a company that has owned directly, during a period of six months, at least 50% of voting shares of the company paying the dividends; a 7.5% WHT is levied if the beneficial owner is a company that has owned directly, during a period of six months, at least 25% of voting shares of the company paying the dividends.

74. Levied if the recipient is a shareholder of the paying company holding voting rights with at least a 10% direct interest; otherwise, a 15% rate is levied.

75. A 10% WHT rate is levied on interest paid for bonds or similar securities generally offered to investors and related to transfers of industrial, commercial, or scientific equipment. No WHT is levied on interest from bonds or similar securities issued by the state or a local entity or from loans given or guaranteed by either of the two contracting states, Central Banks, or financial institutions as agreed between the contracting states.

76. A 20% WHT rate is levied on royalties for films or audio or TV tapes.

77. No WHT is levied on interest from loans granted or guaranteed by a contracting state.

78. If the recipient has invested more than EUR 100,000 in the company that pays the dividend or the dividend is tax exempt in its country of residence, the WHT rate levied is 10%. If both of these requirements are fulfilled, the rate applicable is 5%.

79. Interest on loans with a maturity period of over seven years is tax exempt.

80. A 10% WHT rate is levied on any patents, trademarks, designs or models, plans, secret formulae, or processes and computer software, or for the use of, or the right to use, industrial, commercial, or scientific equipment, or for information concerning industrial, commercial, or scientific experiences. A 5% WHT rate is levied on any copyright of literary, artistic, or scientific work, excluding computer software and including cinematographic films or tapes used for radio or television broadcasting.

81. No WHT is levied on interest paid to a contracting state, one of its political subdivisions, or one of its local entities or interest paid in connection with the sale on credit of merchandise or equipment to a company of a contracting state or interest paid on any long-term loan (seven years minimum) granted by a bank resident in a contracting state.

82. No WHT is levied on interest arising from the credit sale of industrial, commercial, or scientific equipment or merchandise.

83. No WHT is levied on dividends when they are paid to a shareholder with at least a 25% interest held for at least two years, provided that the company distributing the dividends is effectively taxed.

84. No WHT is levied on interest paid to a bank resident in Switzerland on a long-term loan (over five years).

85. No WHT is levied if the royalties are paid between associated companies, affiliated by at least a 25% direct interest held for at least two years or both held by a third company with at least a 25% interest in both companies, and CIT is levied on all of the companies.

86.
    a. A 10% WHT rate is levied on interest received by financial and insurance entities. No WHT is levied on interest from loans granted by the government, Central Bank, or certain institutions.

S

Spain

    b. A 5% WHT rate is levied on royalties for any copyright of literary, artistic, theatrical, musical, or scientific work (excluding cinematograph films and films or tapes for radio or television broadcasting); an 8% WHT is levied on financial leasing related with the use or the right to use industrial, commercial, or scientific equipment.

87.

    a. Reduced WHT rates or exemptions are not levied/applied if the income is paid to a company resident in a contracting state more than 75% of whose shares are directly or indirectly held by non residents and such income is not subject to taxation in such contracting state.

    b. Levied if the recipient is a shareholder of the paying company with at least a 50% interest; otherwise, a 15% rate is levied.

88. A 5% WHT rate is levied for long-term loans (more than seven years).

89. The WHT rate is 10% if the interest arises from a loan granted by a bank or is related to a credit acquisition of merchandise or equipment.

90. Levied if the recipient is a shareholder of the paying company with at least a 10% interest; otherwise, a 15% rate is levied.

91.

    a. No WHT is levied on royalties paid for the use or licensing of containers used in international trade.

    b. No WHT is levied on dividends when they are paid to a company holding at least a 75% direct interest in the paying company.

92. No WHT is levied if the interest is paid on a long-term loan (more than three years) to finance investment projects, if the interest is paid to a pension fund that meets certain requirements, or if the interest is paid in relation to a credit acquisition of merchandise, equipment, or services.

93. A 5% WHT is levied on royalties for any copyright of literary, artistic, or scientific work.

94. A 4.95% WHT rate is levied on interest received by financial institutions.

95. No WHT is levied on interest if: (i) the recipient is the other contracting state, its central bank, or its political divisions; (ii) the interest is paid by one contracting state or its political divisions, (iii) the interest arises from a loan or credit granted or guaranteed by a contracting state to promote exports and development, (iv) the recipient is a pension fund qualifying for tax purposes in a contracting state and the income generated from the fund is tax exempt in the contracting state paying the dividend, or (v) the interest is paid in relation to the credit acquisition of industrial, commercial or scientific equipment.

96. Levied if the recipient is a shareholder of the paying company with at least a 50% interest. A 10% WHT rate is levied if the recipient is a company with at least a 25% direct interest; otherwise, a 15% rate is levied.

97. No WHT is levied on interest arising from loans granted or guaranteed by qualifying public institution or interest paid to public financial institutions.

98. No WHT is levied if the recipient is a company (other than a partnership) with at least a 25% direct interest in the paying company; otherwise, a 5% rate is levied.

99. No WHT is levied if the recipient is a company with at least a 10% direct interest in the paying company; otherwise, a 10% rate is levied.

100. 5% WHT rate is levied if the recipient (excluding partnerships) is a shareholder with at least a 40% direct interest in the paying company; otherwise a 10% rate is levied. No WHT is levied if the recipient is a shareholder with at least a 80% direct interest in the paying company, and (i) its shares are listed on a stock exchange, (ii) the recipient is at least 50% owned by residents from either of the two countries, (iii) the recipient is owned by shareholders resident for tax purposes in third countries by a proportion of less than 25%, and (iv) the recipient is owned (an interest of more than 25%) by residents in third countries provided that a tax treaty for the avoidance of double taxation has been signed with the country of the company paying the dividends and that this tax treaty establishes the same or more favourable conditions. No WHT is levied for dividends paid to pension funds.

101. Reduced rates/exemptions are not applicable when a Panama tax-resident company pays dividends, interest, or royalties to a Spanish tax resident and such income has been obtained either in Spain or in a country that has not signed a tax treaty for the avoidance of double taxation with Spain.

102. Levied if the recipient is a company (excluding partnerships) with at least a 10% direct interest in the paying company; otherwise, a 5% rate is levied. In the case of distributions made out of a real estate investment trust, 5% is levied if the beneficial owner holds, directly or indirectly, less than 10% of the value of the capital in such trust.

103. No WHT is levied on interest if: (i) the recipient is a contracting state of the treaty, its central bank, or its political divisions; (ii) the payer is a contracting state or its political divisions; (iii) the payer is a financial institution of a contracting state and interest is paid to a financial institution of the other contracting state (iv) the recipient is a pension fund qualifying for tax purposes in a contracting state and the income from such fund is tax exempt in the contracting state paying the dividend;(v) the interest is paid in respect of a loan, debt-claim or credit that is owed to, made, provided, guaranteed or insured by an export financing agency of a contracting state or political division, or guaranteed or insured by that state or political division; (vi) the recipient is an institution wholly or mainly owned by a contracting state as may be agreed from time to time between the competent authorities; (vii) the recipient is the government of Singapore Investment Corporation Pte Ltd.

104. No WHT is levied on dividends if the beneficial owner is a company resident in the other contracting state whose capital is wholly or partly divided into shares and it has held at least 25% of the capital of the company paying the dividends for at least two years before the date of such payment and such dividends are not subject to profit tax in the other contracting state.

105. 5% WHT rate is levied on royalties paid for the use of, or the right to use, any copyright of literary, artistic, or scientific work, including cinematographic films or films and tapes used for radio or television broadcasting.
106. No WHT is levied on dividends if the beneficial owner is a company (other than a partnership) that holds at least 25% of the capital of the company paying the dividends.

Tax administration

Taxable period
The tax year for CIT purposes is the company's accounting year. The tax year cannot exceed 12 months, and the commencement, termination, or change of a tax year can give rise to a period of less than one year.

Tax returns
The tax system in Spain is a self-assessment system, and tax returns may be inspected by the tax authorities.

Annual CIT returns must be filed within 25 calendar days following the six months subsequent to the end of the tax year (i.e. if the tax year coincides with the calendar year, the return must be filed between 1 July and 25 July of the following calendar year).

Payment of tax
For CIT, three advance payments of the annual tax payment must be made during the first 20 calendar days of April, October, and December. The final CIT payment must be made with the annual CIT return.

For companies whose turnover, in accordance with Spanish VAT law, for the 12 months prior to the beginning of a tax period exceeds EUR 6,010,121.04, the advance payments are calculated by applying the following percentages to the taxable income (reduced by any applicable tax-loss carryforwards) for each advance-payment period, i.e. at 31 March, 30 September, and 30 November:

- Generally, 21%.
- For tax periods commencing in 2011, 2012, and 2013, this percentage is increased to:
  - 24% for companies whose turnover, in accordance with Spanish CIT law, for the 12 months prior to the beginning of the tax period was between EUR 20 million and EUR 60 million.
  - 27% for companies whose turnover, in accordance with Spanish CIT law, for the 12 months prior to the beginning of the tax period was EUR 60 million or more.

Some allowances and the previous advance payments of the year can be credited against this percentage of taxable income.

Small and medium-sized companies can opt to calculate their advance payments in the same way as large companies (applying a percentage of 21%) or to apply a rate (currently 18%) on the tax liability of their last advance CIT return filed on 1 April, 1 October, or 1 December.

Minimum advance payment for 2012 and 2013
For companies whose turnover, in accordance with Spanish CIT law, for the prior 12 months is EUR 20 million or more, the advance payments should be at least 8% of the

Spain

company's accounting profits for the first 3, 9, or 11 months of the calendar year less any tax-loss carryforwards that may be applied in accordance with the applicable limits.

The minimum advance payment for April 2012 is 4%.

For companies whose turnover, in accordance with Spanish CIT law, is income for which the international double tax exemption or the internal 100% double tax deduction for dividends applies (to at least 85% of the income), the tax rate is 4% (2% for the advance payment for April 2012).

This will apply to tax periods commencing in 2012 and 2013.

Tax inspections

The Spanish tax authorities have a tax inspection department that is responsible, amongst other things, for verifying that taxpayers' obligations are correctly complied with and, if necessary, for making adjustments to their tax affairs by issuing one or more tax assessments.

As part of its responsibilities, the tax inspection department may investigate a taxpayer's tax affairs to ensure that they are correct and verify the accuracy of filed tax returns.

Taxpayers' tax returns to be examined by the tax inspection department are chosen on the basis of different criteria, such as: (i) by random sample, (ii) if debt push down restructuring transactions have been carried out that involve Spanish companies with material debt levels, (iii) if companies have recurring tax-loss carryforwards, or (iv) if companies are related to a family group and lack a production or commercial structure and where their personal and business assets are not clear.

If taxpayers disagree with a tax assessment issued by the tax inspection department as a result of a tax inspection, they may file an appeal firstly with the Spanish economic-administrative tribunal for tax appeals, and if the appeal is not upheld by the tribunal, with the ordinary courts.

If taxpayers have paid incorrect amounts of tax to the tax authorities, they may claim a refund of any excess tax paid from the authorities within the statute of limitation period (four years) by means of a special procedure that commences with the filing of a request with the tax authorities.

Statute of limitations

The statute of limitations for taxes in Spain is four years commencing from the day following the date of termination of the voluntary tax filing period.

This four-year period may re-start for a tax if the tax authorities carry out any actions or procedures, with the formal acknowledgement of the taxpayer, to acknowledge, adjust, review, inspect, guarantee, or collect all, or any part of, a tax obligation, or due to actions by the taxpayer such as the filing of a new or late tax return that alters or rectifies a previous tax return or the filing of an appeal or claim by the taxpayers regarding the tax.

Topics of focus for the tax authorities

Every year, the Spanish tax authorities issue general guidelines on the authorities' annual tax and customs control plan. These guidelines identify areas where the tax authorities intend to adopt a greater role of verification, inspection, and monitoring during a certain tax year.

Other issues

Special tax regime applicable in the Basque Country
The three provinces that make up the region of the Basque Country (Alava, Guipúzcoa, and Vizcaya) have an 'economic agreement' with Spain's central government (laid down and regulated by Law 12 of 23 May 2002) in accordance with which these regions are granted the right to regulate their own tax regimes.

There are certain provisions in this law regarding CIT which make this area of Spain more attractive for companies.

General tax rate
The general tax rate is 28%.

Lower tax rates
A reduced rate of 24% is levied on small companies. A small company is considered to be a company that meets the following requirements in the year prior to the application of the special tax regime:

* Carries on an economic business activity.
* Net turnover or assets under EUR 10 million.
* Average number of staff under 50.

An interest of 25% or more in the company is not held, directly or indirectly, by a company that does not meet the above requirements.

For real estate companies that comply with the following requirements, a 20% tax rate is levied on taxable income up to EUR 10,000 and 22% on any excess for companies in Alava and Vizcaya, and a 20% tax rate is levied on taxable income up to EUR 4,000 and 23% on any excess for companies in Guipúzcoa:

* Their share capital is wholly owned by individuals during the whole tax year.
* More than half of their assets are securities or more than half of their assets are not used for economic business activities during at least 90 days of the tax year.
* At least 90% of their profits are generated from investment income and capital gains.

A 21% rate is levied on companies that are floated on the Bilbao Stock Exchange and on brokerages and cooperatives. Companies that are floated on the Bilbao Stock Exchange are taxed at this rate for three years, as long as they are in compliance with certain requirements.

Tax-loss carryforwards
Tax losses may be carried forward for the following 15 years in Guipúzcoa. In Vizcaya and Alava, there is no time limit for the offsetting of tax losses.

For tax years commencing from 1 January 2012, companies that do not comply with the requirements to be considered a small company can offset tax-loss carryforwards of prior years up to a maximum of 70% of their prior taxable income. There is no limit for small companies. Before 1 January 2012, no limit was applicable for any companies.

Tax deductibility of amortisation of goodwill and intangible assets
Amortisation recorded for intangible assets (irrespective of whether they have a specific useful life or not), including goodwill, is tax deductible up to a maximum annual limit of 20%, subject to compliance with the following requirements:

Spain

- The assets have been acquired for consideration.
- The acquiring and transferring companies are not associated parties.

Financial goodwill

Financial goodwill is tax deductible over a period of five years when at least a 5% interest is acquired in the company and these shares are not quoted on a stock exchange or, if they are quoted on a stock exchange, they are shares of group or associated companies.

If the company from which the shares have been acquired has an interest in another company, the equity, assets and rights recorded in the group's consolidated annual accounts must be taken into consideration for the purpose of calculating the amount of the financial goodwill.

If the company from which the shares have been acquired is a non-resident company, in addition to the requirements stated above, the following requirements must be fulfilled:

- The company is subject in its country of residence to a tax which is identical or similar to Spanish CIT.
- The company carries on business activities abroad.

If the shares are not acquired on a stock market, the company which acquires the shares must not be in any of the situations provided for in Article 42 of the Spanish Commercial Code in relation to the transferring company.

Depreciation periods

The depreciation periods for assets are shorter than those under state CIT law.

Reinvestment of extraordinary income

Income obtained from the sale of tangible fixed assets or intangible assets can be deducted from taxable income, subject to compliance with the following requirements:

- The amount obtained from the sale is reinvested in similar types of assets within a four-year period (as from one year prior to the sale up to three years after the sale).
- The asset in which the reinvestment is made is maintained for five years (three in the case of movable assets), unless its useful life is shorter.
- For sales of shares in other companies when the interest held is at least 5% and has been held for a period of one year prior to the date of sale, 60% of the income obtained from the sale can be deducted from taxable income.

Income generated from intellectual or industrial property

30% of the income obtained from the transfer of intellectual or industrial property rights can be deducted from taxable income, subject to compliance with certain requirements, and 60% if the company has created the intellectual or industrial property itself. There are no quantity limits to be complied with for the application of this deduction.

Investments in new tangible fixed assets

A 10% tax credit can be applied to investments in new tangible fixed assets, subject to compliance with certain requirements. The minimum depreciation period for the assets, excluding computer equipment, is five years.

The total amount of the investment must be over EUR 60,100 and the investment must comply with at least one of the following requirements:

- Exceeds 10% of the carrying amounts (minus depreciation/amortisation) of the company's tangible fixed assets, buildings and software during the previous year.
- Exceeds 15% of the carrying amount of the same type of tangible fixed assets of the company during the previous year.

Special reserve for investments in production
A tax credit can be applied for the distribution of profits to a special reserve for investments in production, subject to compliance with the following requirements:

- The company invests the amount distributed to the reserve in new tangible fixed assets during the following two years.
- These assets are maintained by the company during a five-year period or during their useful life if it is less than five years.
- The company's shareholder's equity is increased by the amount distributed to the reserve, and this increase is maintained for a five-year period as from the date on which the investment was made.

The tax credit is 10% of the profits distributed to the reserve.

Research and development (R&D)
A 30% tax credit can be availed of for expenses incurred from R&D activities. If the expenses are higher than the average expenses incurred by the company during the previous two years, the tax credit is 50% on the excess amount.

An additional tax credit of 20% can be availed of for the following expenses:

- Staff expenses incurred for staff exclusively carrying out and qualified to carry out R&D activities.
- Expenses incurred for projects contracted from certain universities and public organisations.

A 10% tax credit can be availed of for investments made in tangible fixed assets (excluding buildings) and intangible assets which are exclusively assigned to R&D activities.

Technological innovation
A 20% or 15% tax credit can be availed of for certain expenses incurred for technological innovation.

Expenses incurred for environmental conservation and improvement and for conservation of energy
Companies are eligible for a 30% tax credit for investments made in the equipment listed in the Basque List of Environmental Technologies, subject to compliance with certain requirements.

Companies may also qualify for a 15% tax credit for investments made and expenses incurred in respect of tangible fixed assets, subject to compliance with certain requirements.

Export investments (e.g. foreign advertising, formation of companies, and branches abroad)
As in state CIT law, for periods commencing from 1 January 2011, there is no tax credit for export investments.

Spain

Staff training
A 10% tax credit can be applied for expenses incurred in staff training. If the expenses are higher than the average training expenses incurred by the company during the previous two years, there is an additional tax credit of 15% for the excess amount.

A tax credit can also be applied for expenses incurred to obtain the Occupational Health and Safety Assessment Sequence (OHSAS) 18001 certificate and to train staff in new technologies.

Job creation
For tax years commencing on or after 1 January 2012, the following tax credits can be availed of for job creation, subject to compliance with the requirements stated:

*   EUR 4,900 for each job created provided that a permanent employment contract is signed with the employee (for tax years commencing before 1 January 2012, the amount was EUR 4,600 per employee).
*   EUR 9,200 for each job created provided that a permanent employment contract is signed with the employee and a person who has special difficulties in finding employment is contracted (for tax years commencing before 1 January 2012, the amount was EUR 8,600 per employee).

The company's average number of staff with permanent employment contracts must be increased by at least the same number of contracts that generated the tax credit and this increase must be maintained by the company for two years.

Corporate contribution to an EPSV
For tax years commencing on or after 1 January 2012, a tax credit of 10% applies to corporate contributions to certain pension schemes in favour of the staff of the company, up to the limit of EUR 6,000 per employee each year (for tax years commencing before 1 January 2012, the amount was EUR 8,000 per employee.)

For tax years commencing before 31 December 2011, an additional tax credit of 50%, up to the limit of EUR 200 per employee, could be applied on the excess amount contributed in comparison with the previous year's contribution.

Time limits for the application of tax credits
In Guipúzcoa, tax credits can be carried forward for a period of 15 years as from the date on which the company qualifies for them. In Vizcaya and Alava, there is no time limit for the application of tax credits.

Limits on the amount of tax credit applied
For tax years commencing on or after 1 January 2012, the combined sum of all investment tax credits, excluding tax credits for R&D and technological innovation, may not exceed 35% of the company's CIT liability (45% for small companies). For tax years commencing before 1 January 2012, the rate was 45% for all companies.

Advanced CIT tax
There is no obligation to make advanced payments on account of CIT.

Special regime for small and medium-sized companies
A small company is considered to be a company which meets the following requirements during the year prior to the application of the special tax regime:

- Carries on an economic business activity.
- Net turnover or assets under EUR 10 million.
- Average number of staff under 50.
- An interest of 25% or more in the company is not held, directly or indirectly, by a company that does not meet the above requirements.

A medium company is considered to be a company which meets the following requirements during the year prior to the application of the special tax regime:

- Carries on an economic business activity.
- Net turnover under EUR 50 million or assets under EUR 43 million.
- Average number of staff under 250.
- An interest of 25% or more in the company is not held, directly or indirectly, by a company that does not meet the above requirements.

The benefits derived from this special tax regime are as follows:

- Free depreciation for new tangible assets (except buildings) for small-sized companies (general free depreciation relief set forth for tax years 2009 to 2015 is not applicable in the Basque Country).
- Accelerated depreciation for new tangible assets (except buildings) for medium-sized companies.
- Global bad debt provisions up to 1% of credit sales and services of small and medium-sized companies are tax deductible for CIT purposes. Provisions for possible insolvency of credit sales and services are tax deductible up to a limit of 1% of the amount of credit sales and services at the end of the tax period.

Sri Lanka

PwC contact

Yudhishtran (Yudy) Kanagasabai
PricewaterhouseCoopers
No. 100, Braybrooke Place
Colombo 00200
Sri Lanka
Tel: +94 11 7 719838 ext. 502
Email: yudhishtran.kanagasabai@lk.pwc.com

Significant developments

In the determination of business profits, a deduction will now be allowed for the following:

* 50% of the cost of acquisition (as depreciation allowance) on high tech plant, machinery, or equipment for energy efficiency purposes acquired on or after 1 April 2012.
* Local and foreign travel expenses incurred by companies exclusively providing the service of design development or product innovation.

Businesses that are liable to corporate income tax (CIT) will not be liable for Economic Service Charge (ESC) from 1 April 2012. Accordingly, ESC will be applicable only if the business is enjoying a CIT exemption or is incurring a loss during the tax year immediately prior to the tax year to which each quarter belongs. The prior threshold for ESC of 25 million Sri Lankan rupees (LKR) per quarter has been increased to LKR 50 million per quarter, effective from the tax year commencing from 1 April 2012.

Taxes on corporate income

Resident companies and public corporations are liable for CIT on their worldwide taxable income. Non-resident companies are liable for CIT of their Sri Lanka-source taxable income.

CIT rates are based on the nature of the income and the institution earning the income, as follows:

Income/Institution	CIT rate (%)	
	2011/12	2012/13
Undertaking for manufacture of any product for export or for supply to an exporter for export, being a product having domestic value addition over 65% and a Sri Lanka brand name with patent rights received in Sri Lanka	10	10
Undertaking for operation and maintenance of facilities for storage, local development of software, or supply of labour	10	10
Agricultural undertakings referred to in Section 16 of the Act for any tax year commencing from 1 April 2011	10	10
Educational services	10	10
Undertaking (not being a holding company, subsidiary company, or any associate company of a group of companies) with an annual turnover not exceeding LKR 300 million, other than buying and selling activities	10	10

Income/Institution	CIT rate (%)	
	2011/12	2012/13
Unit trusts and mutual funds *	10	10
Shipping agents approved by the Director of Merchant Shipping in respect of profits attributable to agency fees connected to transshipment activity and received in foreign currency	15	15
Companies engaged in non-traditional export (other than exempt), including deemed exporters and suppliers of specified services to garment exporters; performance of any service of ship repair, ship breaking, and refurbishment of marine cargo containers; and provision of computer software, programmes, systems, or recording of computer data paid for in foreign currency	12	12
Undertakings engaged in agriculture, manufacture of animal feed, promotion of tourism, or construction work carried on by a resident person	12	12
Venture capital companies	12	12
Any company of which the taxable income does not exceed LKR 5 million (not applicable to a company of a group of companies)	12	12
Petroleum exploration	12	12
Local manufacture of handloom products	28	12
Healthcare services	28	12
Joint venture between a grower cum manufacturer or a manufacturer of tea with a tea exporter for exporting Sri Lanka tea in value added form, on the manufacturing income attributable to the quantum of tea purchased	28	12
Research and development (R&D) activities	28	20
Branch of commercial bank dedicated to development banking	28	24
Any company with taxable income of LKR 5 million or more; banks, including profits from offshore banking activities; public corporations and government owned business undertakings; and holding companies, subsidiary companies, or associated companies of a group of companies	28	28
Manufacture and sale, or import and sale, of liquor or tobacco products	40	40
Business of lottery, betting, or gaming activity	40	40

* Unit trusts and mutual funds are treated like resident companies for CIT purposes. Units of investment are treated like company shares, and returns to investors are treated like company dividends. The tax rate is 10% on the profits derived by any unit trust or mutual fund.

Marginal relief

Where the taxable income of any company (other than a group company) for any year of assessment exceeds LKR 5 million but does not exceed LKR 6,111,111, then such part of the CIT computed for such year of assessment as is attributable to such excess shall not be more than such excess (i.e. the maximum CIT on LKR 6 million taxable income is LKR 1.6 million, *see below*).

	LKR
Taxable income	6,000,000
CIT for LKR 5 million at 12%	600,000
Excess LKR 1 million	1,000,000
Total CIT	1,600,000

Sri Lanka

Dividend tax
A dividend tax is payable at 10% on the gross dividends distributed by a resident company, other than such dividends distributed out of any dividend received from another resident company (and few other exceptions).

Deemed dividend tax
A deemed dividend tax of 15% is payable by any resident company in any tax year if the said company has, in the preceding tax year, distributed dividends of less than 10% of the distributable profits (duly defined) for that preceding tax year.

The tax base for the 15% deemed dividend tax is the book profits of the company reduced by the aggregate of the CIT payable by that company for that tax year, the cost incurred by the company in that tax year in the acquisition of any land or any capital asset, and any notional profit computed on the basis of a revaluation of any capital asset included in such book profit and increased by the aggregate of the allowance for depreciation deducted in respect of any capital asset and any notional loss computed on the basis of a revaluation of any capital asset included in such book profit.

Special tax on public corporations
In the case of a public corporation, where not less than 75% of the capital is provided by the government (other than via a loan), a tax of 25% of the balance profits, after deducting CIT payable, will be charged. However, where the total gross dividends distributed are not less than 25% of such balance, no special tax will be charged in the relevant years. Where the total gross dividends distributed are less than 25% of such balance, the tax chargeable will be the difference between such balance and the dividends distributed.

Remittance tax
Where profits of a non-resident company are remitted in a tax year, a remittance tax of 10% of the remittances is payable.

Corporate residence

A company is treated as resident for tax purposes in Sri Lanka if its registered or principal office is in Sri Lanka or if the control and management of its business is exercised in Sri Lanka.

Permanent establishment (PE)
PE is only a treaty concept in Sri Lanka. If a non-resident company creates a PE in Sri Lanka in terms of a double tax treaty (DTT), then such company is liable to Sri Lanka CIT. In this absence of a DTT, the domestic tax laws will apply.

Other taxes

Value-added tax (VAT)
VAT is payable on imported goods and on the supply of goods (excluding, in particular, the supply to merchants who purchase goods locally) and services in Sri Lanka. Provisions are made for filing returns monthly or quarterly, based on specified criteria. Even where returns can be filed quarterly, the tax payments are required to be made on a monthly basis. Certain specified imports and domestically supplied goods and/or services are exempt.

Sri Lanka

VAT is payable on the prescribed valuations of imports and domestic supplies at a standard rate of 12%. Exports and certain specified international services are zero-rated.

No registration for VAT is necessary if the total value of taxable supplies is LKR 650,000 or less in a quarter, or LKR 2.5 million or less in a year.

The input tax paid on the imports and supplies of goods (including capital goods) and services in a month, and used in the business of making taxable supplies in that month, can be deducted from the tax payable (output tax) on such supplies, subject to a limitation of the lesser of 100% of output tax or the actual input tax paid.

Refunds of excess VAT paid are available to zero-rated supplies, to suppliers who are qualified to issue suspended tax invoices, and to new businesses registered under Section 22 (7) of the VAT Act.

Customs duties
Customs duty is levied on the value for customs duty (i.e. transaction value). World Trade Organization (WTO) rules on customs valuations are implemented. Sri Lanka has a simplified four tier tariff structure. The rates are published in the government gazettes. The current rates are 5%, 15%, 30%, and 0% (applies to few goods).

Excise duties
Excise duties and special excise levies are charged on tobacco, cigarettes, liquor, motor vehicles, selected petroleum products, paints, air conditioners, dishwashers, household washing machines, and other products at various rates and at unit rates.

Stamp duty
Stamp duty is payable on specified instruments and documents at rates prescribed in the Gazette.

Economic Service Charge (ESC)
Effective from 1 April 2012, ESC is payable quarterly by businesses that are enjoying a tax holiday or incurring a loss in the previous tax year at 0.25% of the aggregate turnover of the trade, business, profession, or vocation if the total turnover exceeds LKR 50 million for that quarter. ESC so paid is deductible from the CIT payable for that tax year. ESC is not refundable but can be carried forward for four immediately succeeding tax years to be set off against CIT payable. Maximum ESC payable for any quarter is LKR 30 million.

Prior to 1 April 2012, every person was liable to pay ESC in respect of the aggregate turnover at rates varying from 0.1% to 1%, depending on the business activity, if the total turnover exceeded LKR 25 million for that quarter.

Nation Building Tax (NBT)
NBT is chargeable at 2% from every person (a person includes a company) who imports any article on the 'liable turnover' from such importation and who carries on the business of manufacture of any article, providing a service of any description, or wholesale or retail sale of any article (other than such sale by the manufacturer of that article) on the liable turnover of the relevant quarter. Certain specified articles or services are exempt from NBT.

Liable turnover means:

Sri Lanka

- In the case of importer, the value of any article ascertained under Section 6 of the VAT Act for the purpose of importation.
- In the case of manufacturer, the proceeds receivable, whether received or not, from the manufacture and sale of goods in Sri Lanka.
- In the case of service provider, the proceeds receivable, whether received or not.
- In the case of wholesale or retail traders, the proceeds receivable, whether received or not, other than pharmaceuticals, gems and jewellery sold for payment in foreign currency, and any article subject to the Special Commodity Levy sold by an importer.

In case of wholesale and retail traders, 50% of the liable turnover will be taxed at a zero rate and the remaining 50% will be taxed at 2%. In the case of a distributor as defined in the ESC Act, 75% of the liable turnover will be taxed at a zero rate and the remaining 25% will be taxed at 2%.

Bad debts, VAT, excise duty rebate under export development, or services in relation to an international event should not be included in the liable turnover.

Construction industry guarantee fund levy
Construction industry guarantee fund levy is payable by each construction contractor or subcontractor on the contract value arising from any contract entered into, calculated at rates varying from 0.25% to 1%, depending on the value of the construction contract. As of 1 April 2009, any person or partnership that makes any payment, which is subject to such levy, to a contractor or subcontractor should deduct such levy as a withholding tax (WHT) and remit the amount withheld to the Commissioner General of Inland Revenue.

Tourism development levy
Tourism development levy is payable by tourist hotels and institutions licensed under the Tourist Development Act on the turnover of such institution at the rate of 1%.

Employees Provident Fund (EPF)
Employers and employees are required to contribute specified percentages (employer 12%; employee 8%) of each employee's monthly emoluments/salary to the EPF established by the government. Alternatively, employers and employees can contribute to certain private provident funds approved by the labour authority.

Employees Trust Fund
Employers are also required to contribute a specified percentage (currently 3%) of each employee's monthly emoluments/salary to the Employees Trust Fund established by the Government.

Share transaction levy
Share transaction levy at the rate of 0.3% is chargeable from both the buyer and the seller on the sale value of listed shares transacted through the Colombo Stock Exchange.

Local taxes
Taxes (more usually called rates) are currently assessed and collected annually from the owners of land and premises by the local authorities of the areas in which the properties are located. These authorities also charge and collect annual licence fees from certain businesses as well.

Sri Lanka

Branch income

Foreign companies are permitted to register a place of business in Sri Lanka or to be registered as an overseas company under local company law, where the business carried on conforms to the stipulations made under the Exchange Control Law.

An overseas company registered under the Companies Act may also carry on in Sri Lanka any non-commercial, non-trading, or non-industrial activities, such as the activities undertaken or carried on by a liaison office, representative office, regional office, or other similar office, provided such activities do not provide any income directly or indirectly to the company.

In addition to paying the standard CIT, a trading branch is also subject to the 10% remittance tax on remittance to its foreign head office.

The Sri Lanka-source income of foreign companies from a local 'place of business' is taxed at the CIT rate. However, under most DTTs that Sri Lanka has entered into, the income of a turnkey or service project will not be liable for CIT if its duration is less than the period specified in the treaty concerned.

Where branch or project income is liable for CIT but the income is not readily ascertainable, the tax authority may prescribe that the income be computed on a fair percentage (not less than 6%) of the branch or project turnover in Sri Lanka.

Income determination

Business accounting for CIT purposes should, unless otherwise specified by the tax statute, conform to Sri Lanka Accounting Standards.

Inventory valuation
Inventories should be measured at the lower of cost and net realisable value.

Capital gains
There is no capital gains tax. Capital gains from transfer of property are exempt from CIT.

Dividend income
Resident company dividends paid on shares held by resident or non-resident persons are not assessable to the recipients if income tax is withheld on such dividends (*see the Withholding taxes section*), the dividends are exempt from income tax, or the dividends are paid out of dividends received from resident companies.

Stock dividends
Stock dividends (bonus shares) are not taxable in the hands of a shareholder at the time of issue; however, where such shares are capitalised out of company profits and there is a return of this capital to the shareholder within six years from the date of issue, the amount of capital returned to the extent of the paid-up value of the bonus shares is treated by definition as a dividend and is taxable in the hands of the shareholder. However, if the shareholder is a company, this dividend may not be assessable, as explained above.

Sri Lanka

Interest income
Interest income forms part of the total statutory income, if not exempt under the tax statute.

Foreign income
Foreign income of a resident person forms part of the total statutory income, if not exempt under the tax statute.

....

Deductions

In ascertaining the total income liable to CIT from the financial accounts filed by a company, deductions from revenue are permitted for outgoing and matching expenses incurred in producing the income, including special deductions.

Depreciation
An annual allowance for depreciation for wear and tear is calculated at:

- 50% for high tech plant, machinery, or equipment for energy efficiency purposes acquired on or after 1 April 2012.
- 33 $\frac{1}{3}$% for plant, machinery, or equipment for a period of three years.
- 25% of the cost of any information technology for a period of four years.
- 20% of the cost of acquisition of any motor vehicle or furniture for a period of five years.
- 10% of the cost of any qualified building for a period of ten years.

The cost of renewal of any capital asset, if no allowance exists, is deductible for the purpose of ascertaining profits and income.

Goodwill
Amortisation is not allowed on the acquisition of goodwill.

Formation or liquidation expenses of a company
In the case of a company, expenses incurred in the formation or liquidation of that company are allowed in computing the taxable income.

Interest expenses
Interest paid or payable on borrowings for purposes of business are deductible, subject to the thin capitalisation rules (*see the Group taxation section*).

Bad debts and doubtful debts
A sum equal to the bad debts incurred in any trade, business, profession, or vocation that have become bad debts during the period for which the profits are being ascertained is allowed for tax purposes.

In the case of a bank or financial institution, deductibility of a specific bad debt provision is restricted to the lesser of the actual amount of the provision or 1% of the aggregate debts as of the end of the period for which profits are ascertained.

Charitable contributions
Relief is available as a deduction from assessable income for contributions in money to an approved charity, if the charity is established for the provision of institutionalised care for sick or the needy, and contributions in money or in kind to the Government of Sri Lanka. The deduction for the former is subject to a ceiling of one-fifth of the

assessable income of the company. In the case of the latter, there is no limit to the deduction, and any un-recouped excess of such contributions over the assessable income can be carried forward and deducted from the following year's assessable income and so on.

Terminal gratuities

Termination gratuities paid to employees on cessation of business and annual payments made to an approved fund, held for payment under compulsory legislation of gratuities to employees upon termination of their services, are deductible.

Fine and penalties

Fine and penalties, paid or payable, are not allowed for tax purposes.

Taxes

Sri Lanka income tax payable or any income tax or other similar tax payable in any country with which Sri Lanka has a DTA is not deductible, other than the excess of the foreign-country tax on doubly taxed income over the maximum amount of the credit allowed in the foreign country for the Sri Lanka income tax on that income.

Taxes paid in a foreign country that does not have a tax treaty with Sri Lanka may be deducted.

NBT paid/payable is fully deductible.

Input VAT is not deductible from CIT if creditable against output VAT.

Any other prescribed tax or levy is not deductible.

Non-deductible expenses

Deductions not permitted for certain expenses or allowances, in the determination of total income, are itemised below:

- Business entertainment expenses incurred or entertainment allowances paid to executive officers.
- Any expenditure of a capital nature or any loss of capital, including book depreciation of capital assets.
- Depreciation allowances or rentals or annual payments or renewals in respect of vehicles used for purposes of business travel, or capital assets provided for the use of employees at their places of residence, other than motorcycles or bicycles used by non-executive staff and motor coaches used to transport employees to and from their places of work.
- The excess of management fee paid over LKR 2 million or 1% of turnover, whichever is lower, or such amount as may be determined by the tax authorities. This restriction does not apply to a venture capital company, unit trust, or mutual fund.
- Royalties paid to a person outside Sri Lanka to another person outside Sri Lanka.

Other significant items

Expenses incurred solely in connection with the promotion of the export trade or the provision of any services for payment in foreign currency or in carrying out an approved programme for the promotion of tourism are fully allowed.

As of 1 April 2011, any foreign travel or foreign training expense incurred in the production of income of any trade, business profession, or vocation is also deductible,

Sri Lanka

subject to a maximum limit of 2% of the previous year's statutory income from the respective trade or business.

Deductions from the total income from all sources of a company are allowed for any interest payable on loans used for the construction or purchase of any building or the purchase of any site for construction of a building; for any annuity, ground rent, or royalty payable; or for a business loss.

Net operating losses

No deduction from total income is allowed in a tax year for a business loss if, at any time in that year, more than one-third of the issued share capital of the loss-making company is held by persons who did not hold such share capital at any time in the year in which the loss was incurred. In such circumstances, the loss is deferred for deduction only from profits of the particular business in which the loss was incurred.

Any loss incurred in any business of life insurance can be deducted to the extent of any profits from such business included in such total statutory income. Similarly, any loss incurred in any business of finance leasing can be deducted to the extent of any profits from such leasing business included in such total statutory income.

Losses incurred in the conduct of a trade or business may be carried forward indefinitely but only up to 35% of statutory income of a given tax year.

Carryback of losses is not permitted.

Payments to foreign affiliates

Any payment made to an affiliate is allowed for tax purposes, if such payment is in the nature of revenue and is incurred in the production of income.

Group taxation

There are no special provisions for taxation of companies in a group in Sri Lanka. Each company is taxed independently of others in the group.

Transfer pricing

Any profits and income arising, derived, or accruing from, or any loss incurred in, any transaction entered into between two associated undertakings shall be ascertained with regard to the arm's-length price.

Thin capitalisation

Deductible interest payments made between members of a group of companies, including holding companies, are restricted to the debt-to-equity ratio of 3:1 for manufacturing companies and 4:1 for other companies.

Tax credits and incentives

Foreign tax credit

Where any DTT is entered into between the government of Sri Lanka and the government of any other territory outside Sri Lanka, a credit is to be granted in respect of any tax paid or payable outside Sri Lanka in respect of profit or income arising outside Sri Lanka. Such credit should not exceed the amount of the Sri Lanka tax payable in respect of such profits or income.

Where any non-resident person or any partnership registered outside Sri Lanka providing certain services is liable to pay income tax in Sri Lanka and income tax in any other country, then such person or partnership shall be entitled to relief from income tax payable in Sri Lanka of an amount equal to the excess, if any, of the income tax in respect of such income payable in Sri Lanka over the income tax in respect of such income payable in such other country.

Tax holidays

Exemptions for new enterprises

Qualifying enterprises	Qualifying criteria		Tax holiday (years)
	Specified activities	Investment criteria	
Small scale enterprises	Agriculture and/or agro processing, animal husbandry and/or processing, fisheries and/or fish processing, and creative work including art work	Minimum investment of LKR 25 million	4
Medium scale enterprises	Any specified activity	LKR 50 million to LKR 100 million	4
		LKR 100 million to LKR 200 million	5
		More than LKR 200 million	6
Large scale enterprises	Agriculture or forestry, animal husbandry, specified manufacture, specified services, processing and solid waste management, and any other activity approved by the Minister of Finance	LKR 300 million to LKR 500 million	6
		LKR 500 million to LKR 700 million	7
		LKR 700 million to LKR 1,000 million	8
		LKR 1,000 million to LKR 1,500 million	9
		LKR 1,500 million to LKR 2,500 million	10
		More than LKR 2,500 million	12
New enterprises in specified activities	Cement	USD* 50 million	5 and a 12% concessionary tax rate thereafter
	Steel	USD 30 million	
	Pharmaceuticals	USD 10 million	
	Fabric	USD 5 million	
	Milk powder	USD 30 million	

* United States dollars

- A five-year tax holiday is available to a new venture capital company satisfying specified criteria.
- A five-year tax holiday is granted for the profits from the new undertaking of a company that is engaged solely in R&D in the field of science or technology with the object of using the results thereof for the production or improvement of products with a minimum investment of LKR 2 million.
- Tax holidays outside the purview of the tax statute are also available in specified areas of investment to companies that enter into agreements with the BOI and to any strategic development projects indentified in accordance with the provisions of the

Sri Lanka

Strategic Development Projects Act No 14 of 2008. The specified areas include non-traditional export-oriented manufacturing and thrust industries, export-oriented services, large-scale projects of which the project cost exceed LKR 500 million. Generous waiver of import duties on specified imports and other concessions are also available for these companies.
* Profits and income derived from the sectors of fishing, cultivation, and primary processing of agricultural seeds or planting materials will be exempt from CIT for a period of five years reckoned from the tax year commencing from 1 April 2011.

Inbound investment incentives
* Exemption from CIT is granted on the profits and income earned in foreign currency by any resident company in Sri Lanka from any services, excluding commissions, discounts, or similar type of receipt, rendered in or outside Sri Lanka, if such profits and income (less such amount expended outside Sri Lanka as is considered by the Commissioner General to be reasonable expenses) are remitted to Sri Lanka through a bank.
* Exemption from CIT is granted in respect of dividends or interest received on investments made outside Sri Lanka, provided that dividends and interest are remitted to Sri Lanka through a bank.

Other incentives
* New or existing companies that export non-traditional goods are entitled to be taxed on the profits from these exports or services at a concessionary rate of 12% for a period of 20 years, ending on 31 March 2014 and 2015, respectively. Dividends paid by such companies out of profits earned from the exports of non-traditional goods, which are taxed at 15%, are in turn liable to tax of 10% in the hands of corporate shareholders where the income tax is already withheld from the dividends (*see the Withholding taxes section*).
* Exemption from CIT is granted on the profits arising from trading in shares, rights to any share, bonus, or share warrants in respect of which the share transaction levy has been charged.
* Exemption from CIT is granted on an amount equal to the interest or the discount paid or allowed to any non-resident person or to any licensed commercial bank in Sri Lanka by the issuer of any sovereign bond denominated in foreign currency, issued on or after 21 October 2008, by or on behalf of the government of Sri Lanka and on the profits and income from the sale of such sovereign bond.
* Exemption from CIT is granted on an amount equal to the interest or the discount paid or allowed to any person on or after 1 April 2009, on any Sri Lanka Development Bond denominated in United States dollars, issued by the Central Bank of Sri Lanka and on the profits and income from the sale of such Sri Lanka Development Bond.
* Exemption from CIT is granted on the profits and income derived by or accruing to any person or partnership from investment in Economic Resurgence Certificates, utilising money lying to credit of any account opened in any commercial bank or in any specialised bank with the approval of the Central Bank of Sri Lanka from and out of monies deposited in such account on or after 1 February 2009.

Withholding taxes

Resident companies are entitled to withhold income tax at 10% of gross dividends payable to any shareholder that is chargeable with CIT, excluding any dividend received from another resident company and any dividend that is exempt from CIT.

Any person in Sri Lanka who pays or credits to a person or partnership outside Sri Lanka any sum due as interest, rent, ground rent, royalty, or annuity is required to withhold income tax at a rate of 20% of the sum, but the requirement to withhold income tax does not apply to (i) interest not sourced in Sri Lanka, (ii) interest on any loan or advance made by a banker, (iii) interest paid in foreign currency held in an account with a foreign currency banking unit, (iv) interest on any corporate debt security, or (v) any interest that is exempt from income tax under any provisions of the Income Tax Act.

In particular instances, the tax authority may prescribe that CIT be withheld at a rate other than 20%, or the rate may be reduced for sums falling due as interest or royalties in respect of persons resident in countries with which Sri Lanka has DTAs in force. Sri Lanka-source income from loan interest or royalties accruing to a non-resident company is taxed at a flat 15%, in the absence of a lower rate in the tax treaty with the home country of the non-resident.

However, interest accruing to any overseas lender from a loan granted by that overseas lender to the Sri Lanka government or institution, public corporation, any commercial bank, or to any other undertaking if such loan is granted on or after 1 April 2012, is exempt from income tax.

Every bank and financial institution is required to withhold income tax at 10% on the amount of any interest paid to a company on any sum of money deposited with it. The depositor is entitled to receive a certificate setting out the gross amount of interest, the amount of tax withheld, and the net amount of interest paid. With respect to Treasury bills and Treasury bonds issued by the Central Bank, the WHT rate of 10% applies to an investor from any country. This WHT is deducted at the time of the sale of the Treasury bills and Treasury bonds by the Central Bank in the primary market.

Recipient	Dividends (%)	Interest (%)	Royalties (%)
Australia	15	10	10
Bangladesh	15	15	15
Belgium	15	10	10
Canada	15	15	10
China	10	10	10
Denmark	15	10	10
Finland	15	10	10
France	15	10	0/10 (1)
Germany	15	10	10
Hong Kong (4)	-	-	-
India	15	10	10
Indonesia	15	15	15
Iran	10	10	8
Italy	15	10	10
Japan	10	15 (2)	(3), 0 (1)
Korea, Republic of	10/15 (5)	10	10
Kuwait (4)	-	-	-
Malaysia	15	10	10
Mauritius	10/15 (6)	10/15	10
Nepal	15	10/15	15
Netherlands	10/15 (5)	10/15	10

Sri Lanka

Recipient	Dividends (%)	Interest (%)	Royalties (%)
Norway	15	10	0/10 (1)
Oman (4)	-	-	-
Pakistan	15	10	20
Philippines	10	10	10
Poland	15	10	10
Qatar	10	10	10
Romania	12.5	10	10
Russia	10/15 (5)	10	10
Saudi Arabia	-	-	-
Singapore	15	10	15
Sweden	15	10	10
Switzerland	10/15 (5)	10	10
Thailand	15	10	15
United Arab Emirates	10	10	10
United Kingdom	15	10	10
United States	15	10	10
Vietnam	10	10	15

Notes

1. 0% for copyright royalties.
2. 0% in certain circumstances.
3. 50% of normal tax, which is 7.5%.
4. These treaties are limited to the avoidance of double taxation of income from international transport by air.
5. 10% applies if the beneficial owner is a company that holds directly at least 25% of the capital of the company paying the dividends. In all other cases, the rate is 15%.
6. 10% applies if the beneficial owner is a company that holds directly at least 10% of the capital of the company paying the dividends. In all other cases, the rate is 15%.

Tax administration

Taxable period
A tax year is any period of 12 consecutive months reckoned from 1 April in any calendar year to 31 March of the following year.

Tax returns
CIT returns are due on 30 November, immediately following the end of the tax year.

Statement of accounts
Where any trade, business, profession, or vocation is being carried on or exercised by any quoted public company or any other company having a turnover of not less than LKR 250 million or net profit of not less than LKR 100 million, such quoted company or such other company should furnish a statement of accounts in support of a return of income. Such statement of accounts is to be prepared by an approved accountant on the basis of an audit carried out by such approved accountant.

Payment of tax
Sri Lanka has a pay-and-file system under which the CIT payable for each tax year is required to be paid in four instalments, on or before 15 August, 15 November, and 15 February of the tax year and 15 May immediately following the end of the tax year. If each instalment is not less than one-quarter of the CIT payable for the tax year

immediately preceding, the balance of any CIT payable may be paid on or before 30 September immediately following the end of the tax year without incurring penalties.

Statute of limitations

No assessment of the income tax payable by any person:

a. who has made a return of one's income on or before the 30th day of November of the tax year immediately succeeding that tax year shall be made after the expiry of a period of two years from the 30th day of November of the immediately succeeding tax year or
b. who has failed to make a return on or before such date as referred to in paragraph (a) shall be made after the expiry of a period of four years from the 30th day of November of the immediately succeeding tax year.

However, such limitation shall not apply where any fraud, evasion, or wilful default has been committed.

Swaziland

PwC contact

Theo Mason
PricewaterhouseCoopers
MTN Office Park
Old Tavern Hotel Site
Karl Grant Street
Mbabane
Swaziland
Tel: +268 2 404 2861
Email: theo.mason@sz.pwc.com

Significant developments

As of 1 January 2011, the Swaziland Revenue Authority was established. This Authority amalgamated the Department of Customs and the Department of Taxes. Although no amendments were made to their corresponding governing legislation, the letter of the law is being applied with a policy of zero tolerance for non-compliance.

Taxes on corporate income

Income tax is levied on all income derived from sources generated within or deemed to be generated within the country, irrespective of whether the recipient of the income is actually resident in Swaziland.

All companies generating income within Swaziland are taxed on that income at a flat rate of 30%.

Corporate residence

Permanent establishment (PE)
PE in Swaziland is determined according to physical presence.

Other taxes

Value-added tax (VAT)
As of 1 April 2012, VAT replaced the sales tax as the standard rate of 14%.

Prior to 1 April 2012, sales tax was levied at a rate of 14% (25% for liquor and cigarettes) on goods imported into Swaziland and on the first sale of goods manufactured for sale in Swaziland. Customs and excise duties were also imposed on such goods. The 14% sales tax was also applicable to most professional services.

Customs duties
Swaziland has a provision for customs duties for various goods imported into the country. Details are available in the Harmonized Tariff Schedule (HTS).

Swaziland

Excise duties
Swaziland has an excise duty provision for various goods manufactured in the country.

Goods	Excise duty rate (%)
Cigarettes	6.34
Cigarette tobacco	8.00
Cigars	6.19
Other tobacco products	16.10
Spirits	8.90
Beer	8.20
Alcoholic fruit beverage	8.30
Wine	8.10

Property taxes
There are no property taxes in Swaziland.

Transfer taxes
Transfer taxes are applied on a variable rate basis to property transfers based on the fair market value of the property being transferred.

Stamp taxes
Swaziland has a provision for stamp taxes on various documents. The tax is determined either by way of a set fee or on a sliding scale percentage basis.

Branch income

Income tax on registered branch profits is calculated as for a resident company, and a branch profits tax of 15% is assessed for deemed repatriated income. In practice, however, branches are rare since most foreign companies incorporate local subsidiary companies.

	SZL*
Net profit before tax	100
Tax @ 30%	(30)
Repatriated income	70

* Swaziland lilangeni

Income determination

Inventory valuation
Inventory valuation is not specific but is effectively at the lower of cost (i.e. first in first out [FIFO] or average cost) and net realisable value.

Capital gains
Capital gains are not subject to income tax, provided it can be demonstrated that the gains are of a capital and not an income nature (i.e. not recurring transactions).

Swaziland

Dividend income
Dividend income is taxable via withholding tax (WHT) for non-residents (*see the Withholding taxes section*). No tax is due if received from another local company.

Inter-company dividends
Inter-company dividends are not subject to income tax.

Stock dividends
Stock dividends are paid out of taxed profits. Such dividends are not subject to income tax when received by a local company, but they are subject to taxation in the hands of local individual taxpayers at the rate of 10%.

Interest income
Interest income sourced in Swaziland is taxable.

Foreign income
Foreign income is not subject to income tax unless it is deemed to be from a Swaziland source.

Deductions

Depreciation
Depreciation (wear-and-tear) allowances calculated by the net-reducing-balance method are available as follows:

Asset	Depreciation rate (%)
Aircraft	25
Casino equipment	15
Construction equipment	25
Computer hardware	33.33
Computer software	33.33
Furniture and fittings	10
Hotel soft furnishings, including carpets	10
Legal and professional libraries	5
Lifts and elevators	25
Motor vehicles:	
Buses	33.33
Cars	20
Light delivery vehicles	25
Lorries	33.33
Office equipment	10
Plant and machinery	10
Sound and projection equipment	20
Television sets	20
Tractors	25
Trailers	20
Video recorders	33.33
Videotapes	25

For the first year after the addition of an asset, the wear-and-tear allowance is calculated on a monthly basis. With respect to leased assets, the lessor's claim for wear-and-tear allowance is usually spread over the lease period.

An initial allowance of 50% is granted for plant and machinery used in a manufacturing process, including hotel equipment. An initial allowance of 50% is granted for industrial buildings used for manufacturing purposes and hotels, together with a 4% annual allowance.

Interest expenses
Interest is deductible as long as it is incurred in the production of income.

Bad debt
Swaziland does allow a deduction for bad debts, subject to the Commissioner's approval and provided that the debts were included in the taxpayer's income in the year of assessment or in years past.

Charitable contributions
Subject to the Commissioner's approval in regard to the amount allowable as a deduction in the year of grant and subsequent years, Swaziland allows a deduction for, among other things, grants made to the government for the building of schools and hospitals.

Fines and penalties
Fines and penalties resulting from late payment of any tax or levied as payable under any Act administered by the Commissioner will be a non-deductible expense.

Taxes
Taxes are not deductible.

Net operating losses
Losses may not be carried back but may be carried forward for as long as trading continues (i.e. indefinitely). If any break in trading occurs, however, the losses are forfeited.

Payments to foreign affiliates
Deductions may be claimed for payments of management service fees, interest, and royalties to foreign affiliates, provided the payments are made under a written agreement, are reasonable, and receive exchange control approval for transfers outside the rand monetary area. Note that this approval is routinely given without any significant delay for bona fide transactions.

Group taxation

Swaziland does not have group taxation legislation. All companies are assessed on their individual profits and losses.

Transfer pricing
Swaziland does not have transfer pricing legislation; however, under the anti-avoidance provision, the Revenue Authority will look for arm's-length transactions.

Thin capitalisation
Swaziland does not have thin capitalisation rules.

Swaziland

Tax credits and incentives

Development Approval Order
The Minister of Finance, along set guidelines and with prior consent of the Cabinet, may nominate a business as a developmental enterprise (i.e. a business the Minister deems to be beneficial to the development of the economy) for a grant of a Development Approval Order. If approved, the business generally will be granted tax concessions, such as a lower corporate tax rate.

Withholding taxes

Non-resident WHTs are levied as follows.

Dividends
WHT for dividends is payable at the rate of 15% (12.5% for companies registered in Botswana, Lesotho, and the Republic of South Africa).The rate drops to 10% under the double taxation agreement (DTA) with South Africa where the holding company owns more than 25% of the shares. Non-resident shareholders' WHT is payable within 30 days of the date on which the dividend is payable.

Interest
WHT for interest is payable at the rate of 10%. Non-resident WHT on interest is payable within 14 days of the date of the accrual of the interest.

Royalties
WHT for royalties is payable at the rate of 15%. The rate drops to 10% if there is a DTA in place.

Entertainers and sportsmen
WHT is payable at the rate of 15% on income earned in Swaziland by entertainers and sportsmen. This tax relates only to public entertainers and sportsmen not ordinarily resident in Swaziland. The payer is required to deduct the tax and pay it within 15 days.

Contractors or professionals
WHT is payable at the rate of 15% on services provided by contractors or professionals in Swaziland (materials are not taxed to the extent that materials are incidental to the overall charge). The Commissioner of Taxes must be notified of any agreement relating to construction operations or professional services under which payments are made to non-resident persons within 30 days after entering into the agreement. It is required that the tax be paid within 15 days from the date of payment.

Tax administration

Taxable period
The tax year runs from 1 July to 30 June. Companies are required to have a 30 June year end unless another year end date is approved by the Commissioner of Taxes; such approval is routinely given.

Tax returns

Income tax returns should be submitted within 90 days of 30 June, unless an extension of time for submission is granted, which also is routinely given.

Payment of tax

Notice of the date of payment is usually given on the tax assessment.

Provisional tax payments

With respect to companies, provisional tax is payable in two instalments: one payment is due within six months of the company's financial year-end, and the other payment is due no later than the last day of the company's financial year.

The estimate of taxable income for provisional tax purposes should not be less than the taxable income assessed for the latest preceding year of assessment, for which an assessment has been issued not less than 21 days before the date the estimate is made. This rule does not apply if the taxpayer can convince the Commissioner of Taxes that the taxable income for the current year will be less than the taxable income for the preceding year.

A provisional taxpayer becomes liable to pay a penalty if the estimate for taxable income for the second payment of provisional tax is found to be both less than 90% of the taxable income as finally determined and less than the taxable income as assessed for the immediately preceding tax year.

S

Sweden

PwC contact

Gunnar Andersson
PwC Sweden, International Tax Services
Torsgatan 21
SE-113 21 Stockholm
Sweden
Tel: +46 8 555 338 60
Email: gunnar.andersson@se.pwc.com

Significant developments

There have been just a few significant corporate tax developments in Sweden during the past year.

In March 2012, the Ministry of Finance issued a proposal for new Swedish interest stripping restrictions, to become applicable for interest expenses accruing after 31 December 2012. The current restrictions from 2009 disallow a tax deduction for interest payments on intra-group loans related to an acquisition of shares from an affiliate unless either the creditor is taxed for the interest at least at 10% or it is shown that both the share transfer and the debt are based on commercial reasons. The new proposal extends the scope of the current restrictions to apply in respect of interest expenses on any loans within a group, whatever its purpose. The minimum 10% tax test at the creditor level (the person entitled to the interest) will still allow interest deduction according to the proposal, but the tax agency is given powers (with hindsight) to still refuse a deduction if it is shown that mainly tax reasons were behind the loan. Commercial reasons for the loan are still an alternative test for deduction; however, according to the proposal, only if the creditor is resident within the European Economic Area (EEA) or in a jurisdiction with which Sweden has a full tax treaty. As the proposed new restrictions apply for interest accruing in 2013, they might also naturally affect many existing, old loans. Usual legislative and parliamentary procedures still remain to be completed in respect of this proposal, but there is little doubt from a political standpoint that the current restrictions actually will be extended (in some way).

A governmental committee has, for some time, been appointed for a major review of the corporate tax system with the aim of broadening the tax base and, *inter alia*, creating neutrality between equity and debt, with reports scheduled in 2013.

New tax administration rules apply, including, *inter alia*, a split of the current single tax filing date in May into four different dates and new tax payment dates, as from 2013 year-endings.

Taxes on corporate income

State (national) income tax

Resident legal entities are liable for tax on their worldwide income unless tax treaties or special exemptions apply. Non-resident entities are taxed on income that is deemed to have its source within Sweden.

Taxable income is subject to tax at the rate of 26.3%. All income of corporate entities is treated as business income.

Local income taxes
No local income taxes apply to Swedish corporations.

Corporate residence

A company is considered to be a tax resident of Sweden if it is incorporated in Sweden.

Permanent establishment (PE)
The term 'permanent establishment' is defined in Sweden as a fixed place of business through which the business is carried on from a specific establishment, such as a place of management, branch, office, factory, or workshop. Places where construction work is carried on are also regarded as PEs, as well as if an agent who is dependent upon the foreign company habitually exercises authority in Sweden.

Other taxes

Value-added tax (VAT)
The Swedish VAT system is harmonised with the European Union (EU) rules. The general VAT rate of 25% is chargeable on most goods and services. Reduced rates apply to a few goods and services, such as foodstuffs, restaurant meals, and non or low alcoholic drinks (12%), as well as to transport of passengers (6%). Certain financial and insurance services are exempt from VAT.

VAT returns are filed and tax is paid monthly or quarterly. However, for companies with a turnover of less than 1 million Swedish kronor (SEK), VAT may be reported in the income tax return.

Customs duties
As a member of the European Union, Sweden is also part of the Customs union enforcing the community Customs code. Most EU Customs duties are calculated as a percentage of the value of the goods being imported. All imported goods must be classified according to the EU Customs tariff (TARIC), and the duty rates applied depend on the economic sensitivity of the goods. The actual duty rate to be applied also depends on other factors, such as the country of origin of the product and any free trade agreements that may be applicable.

Excise duties
The three main Swedish excise duties are harmonised with EU rules. These are alcohol tax, tobacco tax, and tax on fuels and electricity.

Fuels are subject to energy tax, carbon dioxide tax, and sulphur tax. Depending on the use of fuels, taxes may be partly or fully reduced. For bio-fuels, certain exemptions may also apply.

Other Swedish excise duties are waste tax, tax on advertisement, and the on traffic insurance premiums.

The Swedish parliament has decided on changes in the Energy Tax Act, meaning that the reductions for industrial manufacturing activities will be changed. The reductions are applicable on taxable fuels, and the changes will be introduced gradually by 2015. For an industrial company that does not participate in emissions trading systems (EU

Sweden

ETS), the tax cost will increase significantly. For participants in the EU ETS, the tax cost will be slightly lower.

Real estate tax
The annual real estate tax rate on business premises is 1% of the tax assessed value. For industrial property, the tax rate is 0.5%. Other rates exist for special property.

Stamp tax
Stamp tax at 4.25% is payable on a transfer of real estate. The tax base consists of the highest of the purchase consideration or the tax assessed value of the real estate. Stamp tax on an intra-group transfer of real estate may be deferred as long as the real estate remains within the group.

Social fees
Mandatory social security charges payable by employers on remuneration to employees (or by the self-employed) are levied at approximately 31%. Reduced rates apply for very young or old people. Social security charges are deductible for corporate tax purposes.

Pension benefits beyond the mandatory system are customary amongst most Swedish employers. A special salary tax is levied at approximately 24% on these additional pension premiums/commitments and is deductible for corporate tax purposes.

Branch income

Branch income (i.e. PE income) is taxed at the corporate tax rate of 26.3%, and general corporate tax rules apply for branch offices in Sweden. No withholding tax (WHT) is levied on the outbound repatriation of taxed profits.

The receipt of Swedish source royalties or fees for use of tangible or intangible assets by a foreign resident is also (subject to treaty restrictions) regarded as a special form of PE income.

Income determination

Inventory valuation
Inventories (stock-in-trade) are valued at acquisition cost or market value, whichever is lower. As an alternative, inventories may be valued at 97% of the total acquisition cost, which is determined on a first in first out (FIFO) basis. The last in first out (LIFO) method is not permitted. Generally, inventories should be stated at the same amount for tax and accounting purposes.

Capital gains
There is a capital gains tax exemption for Swedish corporate entities on gains related to the disposal of shares held for business reasons. This abolishment of capital gains taxation for corporations, under the participation exemption provisions, has made Sweden a favourable holding company location.

Note that non-tax-exempt capital gains are included in business income and taxed at the corporate tax rate.

Shares in Swedish corporations as well as in foreign companies can qualify as shares held for business reasons. Unquoted/unlisted shares will always be considered as held for business reasons. Quoted/listed shares are considered held for business reasons provided that the company has a holding corresponding to at least 10% of the voting rights or the shares are held in the course of the business. An additional condition regarding quoted/listed shares is that the shares must be held for a period of at least one year.

Shares in partnerships (tax transparent entities) and indirect holdings via partnerships are also included in the participation exemption regime.

An exception from the capital gains tax exemption applies for the sale of shares in a 'shell company', which is a company or partnership where the market value of cash, shares and other marketable instruments (other than shares held for business reasons), and similar assets exceeds 50% of the consideration paid for the shares. The sale of a shell company results in harsh taxation of the gross consideration. Provided certain formalities are fulfilled, however, it is possible to avoid such taxation.

A consequence of the participation exemption is that capital losses on shares or participations held for business reasons are not deductible.

Capital losses on portfolio holdings of shares, share options, convertible debentures, and similar financial instruments are allowed only as an offset to capital gains on the same group of financial instruments.

Certain special rules apply to computation of capital gains and losses on real estate.

Dividend income
A participation exemption applies for dividends received on shares held for business reasons (*see above*) and on qualifying holdings via partnerships.

Interest income
Interest received by a corporation is included in the corporate tax basis.

Foreign income
Companies resident in Sweden are taxed on their worldwide income. Non-resident entities are taxed on income that is deemed to have its source within Sweden.

A Swedish corporation is taxed on foreign branch income. Double taxation normally is avoided by means of either a deduction for foreign tax, or a foreign tax credit.

Dividends and capital gains from foreign subsidiaries are generally exempt from taxation according to the participation exemption provisions applicable to shares held for business reasons (*see above*).

Deductions

Depreciation, amortisation, and depletion
Depreciation on fixed assets
Land improvements may be depreciated at the rate of 5% per year of the acquisition cost. The maximum allowance is 100% of the tax basis of the improvement.

Buildings may be depreciated at rates between 2% and 5% per year of the taxable basis, depending on type and usage of the building. The maximum allowance is 100% of the tax basis of the building.

Sweden

For machinery and equipment, the depreciation for tax purposes should correspond to the depreciation charged in the books and accounts, as long as the total net value of the assets is not less than the 70% of net value in previous accounts plus additions less proceeds of sales (i.e. 30% declining-balance depreciation) or cost less 20% per year (i.e. 20% straight-line depreciation on remaining assets). An alternative 25% declining-balance method without correspondence to the books also exists.

Immediate deduction of certain assets
The cost of assets having an expected life of not more than three years and the cost of assets not exceeding certain limits, depending on size of operations, may be deducted immediately. Certain costs for repairs, maintenance, and modifications of buildings may also be deducted immediately.

Amortisation of intangibles and goodwill
The amortisation of patents, leaseholds, and goodwill follows the same rules as depreciation for machinery and equipment (*see above*).

Depletion of mines and quarries
The entire cost of mines and quarries may be depleted over their expected exploitation period. These depletion amounts may be deducted annually but are limited to 100% of the acquisition cost of the mine or quarry.

Start-up expenses
General start-up expenses for generating and maintaining business income are, as a rule, deductible for Swedish tax purposes.

Interest expenses
Interest expenses are, as a general rule, fully deductible, provided that the arm's-length principle is complied with in outbound accruals to a foreign affiliate. Sweden has enacted anti-debt push down provisions (i.e. interest stripping restrictions) under which a deduction is not allowed for interest accruing on any intra-group loan for the acquisition of shares from an affiliate, unless the creditor (i.e. the person entitled to the interest) is taxed on the interest income at a rate of at least 10% or it is shown that the share transfer and the debt is based on commercial reasons.

Bad debt
Business bad debts are deductible if they are proven wholly or partially worthless.

Charitable contributions
Purely charitable contributions are generally non-deductible.

Fines and penalties
Fines and penalties are non-deductible for Swedish tax purposes.

Taxes
Generally, Swedish taxes are not deductible for tax purposes. However, specific taxes, fees, and foreign taxes may be deductible. Recoverable VAT is not treated as an expense or cost.

Net operating losses
Tax losses may be carried forward indefinitely, subject to restrictions or forfeiture upon ownership changes, mergers and demergers, dispositions with creditors, and certain other reorganisations. No carryback of losses is possible.

Payments to foreign affiliates

Transactions with an affiliate not liable for tax in Sweden must be at arm's length. Formal transfer pricing documentation requirements apply.

Group taxation

Swedish companies are not taxed on a consolidated basis. However, it is possible for qualifying groups (i.e. a holding of greater than 90% of the capital which must have been owned during the whole fiscal year) to effectively offset operating losses of one Swedish company against operating profits of another Swedish company by way of group contributions, which are tax deductible for the contributor and taxable for the recipient. EEA companies are regarded as Swedish companies for these purposes, if the recipient is taxable in Sweden.

A similar Swedish deductibility is, under certain circumstances, also available for cross-border consolidation within the EEA for final subsidiary losses.

Transfer pricing

The Swedish transfer pricing regime is generally an Organisation of Economic Co-operation and Development (OECD) type of regime. Sweden has formal transfer pricing documentation requirements in place.

Thin capitalisation

There are no thin capitalisation rules for tax purposes in Sweden; however, interest stripping restrictions exist.

Controlled foreign companies (CFCs)

Sweden's CFC provisions aim at taxing a Swedish resident shareholder for shareholdings in low-taxed foreign entities. A Swedish resident shareholder with a holding in a CFC-entity will annually be taxed for its ownership portion of the CFC's income, according to provisions applicable to a Swedish corporation. For a corporation, the portion will be taxed at the Swedish corporate tax rate. Only holdings, direct or indirect through other foreign entities, corresponding to at least 25% (capital or voting rights) in the foreign entity could lead to CFC taxation. A foreign company is considered lowly taxed if the income in the company, calculated in accordance with Swedish provisions, is taxed at a rate below 14.47%. However, if the foreign entity is resident in an 'approved country', CFC taxation should not arise. Approved countries appear in an official 'black/white' list. Active EEA entities are, under certain circumstances, excluded from CFC taxation.

Tax credits and incentives

There are no specific tax incentives in Sweden for corporations. However, some generally applicable regimes exist.

For example, Sweden has an accruals reserve regime. The accruals reserve regime allows for a tax-deductible appropriation for corporations of 25% of the taxable profit before appropriation to a reserve. Each year's appropriation forms a separate reserve that must be reversed to income no later than the sixth year following the appropriation. However, a standardised interest income is imposed on former years' appropriations at 72% of the interest rate on governmental debt notes.

Sweden

Foreign tax credit

A foreign tax credit is generally available, provided certain conditions are fulfilled, and the tax credit allowed is limited to an amount corresponding to the Swedish tax on the foreign income. Unutilised foreign taxes may be carried forward for five years. Tax treaty implications may exist.

Withholding taxes

There are no Swedish taxes on interest and service fees paid to non-resident corporations or individuals. Such payments to resident corporations and individuals are taxed as ordinary income.

WHT on dividends, royalties, and certain rentals vary according to domestic law and tax treaties, as shown below.

Apart from the highlighted treaties, Sweden has concluded agreements on exchange of information in tax matters and partial tax treaties with many tax haven jurisdictions.

Recipient	Cash dividends (%) (1, 2)	Royalties, certain rentals (%) (3)
Resident corporations	0 (4)	0 (5)
Resident individuals	30 (4)	0 (5)
Non-resident corporations and individuals:		
Non-treaty	30	26.3 (5)
Treaty:	(6)	
Albania	5/15	5
Argentina	10/15 (7)	3/5/10/15 (7)
Australia	15	10
Austria	5/10 (6)	0/10 (8)
Bangladesh	10/15	10
Barbados	5/15	0/5 (9)
Belarus	0/5/10	3/5/10 (10)
Belgium	5/15 (6)	0
Bolivia	0/15	15
Botswana	15	15
Brazil	15/25	15/25
Bulgaria	10	5
Canada	5/10/15	0/10 (11)
Chile (12)	5/10	5/10
China, P.R (13)	5/10	6/10
Cyprus	5/15 (6)	0
Czech Republic (14)	0/10 (6)	0/5 (9)
Denmark (15, 16)	0/15 (6, 16)	0 (16)
Egypt	5/20	14
Estonia	5/15 (6)	5/10 (17)
Faroe Islands (15, 16)	0/15 (16)	0 (16)
Finland (15, 16)	0/15 (6)	0
France	0/15 (6)	0

Recipient	Cash dividends (%) (1, 2)	Royalties, certain rentals (%) (3)
Gambia	0/5/15	5/12.5 (18)
Germany	0/15 (6)	0
Greece	0 (6)	5
Hungary	5/15(6)	0
Iceland (15, 16)	0/15 (16)	0 (16)
India	10	0/10
Indonesia	10/15	10/15 (19)
Ireland, Republic of	5/15 (6)	0
Israel	5/15	0
Italy	10/15 (6)	5
Jamaica	10/22.5	10
Japan	0/5/15	10
Kazakhstan	5/15	10
Kenya	15/25	20
Korea, Republic of	10/15	10/15 (20)
Latvia	5/15 (6)	5/10 (17)
Lithuania	5/15 (6)	5/10 (17)
Luxembourg	0/15 (6)	0
Macedonia	0/15	0
Malaysia (12)	0/15	8
Malta	0/15 (6)	0
Mauritius	5/15	15
Mexico	5/15	10
Namibia	0/5/15	5/15 (21)
Netherlands	0/15 (6)	0
New Zealand	15	10
Norway (15, 16)	0/15 (16)	0 (16)
Pakistan	15/30	10
Philippines	10/15	15
Poland (12)	5/15 (6)	5
Portugal	0/10 (6)	10
Romania	10	10
Russia	5/15	0
Singapore	10/15	0
Slovak Republic (14)	0/10 (6)	0/5 (9)
South Africa	0/7.5/15	0
Spain	10/15 (6)	10
Sri Lanka	15	10
Switzerland	0/15	0
Taiwan	10	10
Tanzania	15/25	20
Thailand	15/20/30	15
Trinidad and Tobago	10/20	0/20 (22)
Tunisia	15/20	5/15 (23)
Turkey	15/20	10
Ukraine	0/5/10	0/10
United Kingdom	0/5 (6)	0

Sweden

Recipient	Cash dividends (%) (1, 2)	Royalties, certain rentals (%) (3)
United States	0/5/15	0
Venezuela	5/10	7/10 (24)
Vietnam	5/10/15	5/15 (25)
Yugoslavia (former) (26)	5/15	0
Zambia	5/15	10
Zimbabwe	15/20	10

Notes

1. According to domestic law there is no WHT on dividends to a foreign company on shares held for business reasons *(for the definition of shares held for business reasons, see Capital gains in the Income determination section),* provided that the foreign company is similar to a Swedish limited liability company (and some other legal entities) and is subject to income tax at similar level to that imposed on a Swedish company. Further, there is no tax liability for a legal entity of a member state of the European Union if the entity owns 10% or more of the share capital in the distributing company and fulfils the conditions of the Directive (90/435) regarding parent company and subsidiaries.
2. The reduced rate shown before a stroke (/) refers to payments to corporations having requisite control. Where appropriate, the particular treaty should be consulted to see whether the reduced rate is applicable.
3. Swedish source royalties and certain rental fees are treated as a special form of PE, taxable at the corporate tax rate, subject to treaty reduction or waiver. Royalties paid from Sweden to a company within the European Union should not be taxed in Sweden if one of the companies holds at least 25% (capital) of the other, or where there are two companies concerned, at least 25% are held by another company within the European Union. Indirect participation does not benefit from the legislation. Both the payer and the recipient must be legal entities under the EU directive.
4. Payments to resident corporations and individuals are taxed as ordinary income. Only resident banks and similar entities are required to withhold tax on payments of cash dividends to resident individuals.
5. Royalties and certain rentals paid by Swedish licensees are treated as business income taxable in Sweden and do not incur WHT *(see Note 3).*
6. Note also the domestic provision stating a 0% WHT on dividends distributed on shares held for business reasons to qualifying entities *(see Note 1).*
7. Dividends: 10% of the gross amount if the company receiving the dividends owns at least 25% of the foreign company's capital. Royalties: of the gross amount paid for the use of, or the right to use:
   - News: 3%.
   - Copyright of literary, dramatic, musical, or other artistic work: 5%.
   - Any patent, trademark, design or model, plan, or secret formula or process; industrial or scientific equipment or information concerning industrial, commercial or scientific experience; payments for the rendering of technical assistance: 10%.
   - All other cases: 15%.
8. Royalties are normally taxable only in the recipient's home country. However, where the royalty is paid by a Swedish legal entity that is more than 50% owned by one Austrian recipient, entity or individual, the tax in Sweden is a maximum of 10%.
9. Literary, artistic, or scientific royalties: 0%; other royalties: 5%.
10. Royalties for use of industrial, commercial, or scientific equipment: 5%; with respect to patents, secret formulas or processes, or for information concerning industrial, commercial, or scientific experience: 3%; other royalties: 10%.
11. Royalties for use of copyright and literary, dramatic, musical, and artistic royalties: 0%. Other royalties: 10%. (Treaty should be consulted).
12. The treaty has effect on income derived on or after 1 January 2006.
13. The double taxation treaty does not include Hong Kong.
14. The same treaty is applicable to the Czech Republic and the Slovak Republic.
15. According to the Nordic multilateral tax treaty.
16. Dividends are exempt from tax if the recipient of the dividends is a company directly owning at least 10% of the capital of the company paying out the dividends. Certain rentals are subject to tax if there is a PE in a country other than the home country and the claim is connected with the business carried on from the PE. Concerning Iceland, dividends are normally exempt from tax for companies, but the tax rate is 15% if the dividends have been deducted from the income of the distributing company.
17. Royalties for the use of industrial, commercial, or scientific equipment: 5%; other royalties: 10%.
18. Royalties with respect to patents, secret formulas or processes, or for information concerning industrial, commercial, or scientific experience: 5%; other royalties: 12.5%.
19. Royalties for the use of industrial, commercial, or scientific equipment or for information concerning industrial, commercial, or scientific experience: 10%; other royalties: 15%. (Treaty should be consulted.)
20. Literary, artistic, or scientific royalties including films: 15%; other royalties: 10%. (Treaty should be consulted.)

21. Royalties with respect to patents, secret formulas or processes, or for information concerning industrial or scientific experience: 5%; other royalties: 15%.
22. Commercial royalties, including films: 20%; copyright, literary, dramatic, musical, or artistic royalties: 0%.
23. Commercial royalties, including films: 15%; literary, dramatic, musical, or artistic royalties: 5%.
24. Literary, artistic, scientific, or film royalties: 10%; other royalties: 7%.
25. Royalties with respect to patents, designs or models, secret formulas or processes, or for information concerning industrial or scientific experience or for the use of industrial, commercial, or scientific equipment involving a transfer of know-how: 5%; other royalties: 15%.
26. The treaty is applicable to all republics and autonomous provinces of the former Yugoslavia with the exception of Macedonia, with which Sweden has concluded a bilateral treaty.

Tax administration

Taxable period

If the income is derived from business, the basis for tax assessment is the financial year. The year-end for a company may be fixed at any calendar month ending. Swedish subsidiaries of foreign parents are generally permitted to adopt the same year-end as the parent company, provided it ends on the last day of the month.

Tax returns

Every corporate entity or registered branch must file an annual corporate income tax return, which generally should be filed by 2 May each year, covering the financial year ending during the preceding calendar year. An extension may be available. The annual assessments are made by the local tax offices during the calendar year following the income year and should be completed by the end of November. Employer returns (employee Pay As You Earn [PAYE] and employer withholding) are normally due on a monthly basis.

For financial year endings in 2012, these rules still apply. For financial years ending in 2013, however, the tax administration system will be revised and the due dates will depend on the month in which the financial year ends.

Payment of tax

Income taxes are collected during the year in which the income is earned, under a preliminary tax system. A corporate entity's preliminary tax liability is determined by a preliminary tax assessment based either on the latest available final tax assessment or on a preliminary tax return filed by the company. The preliminary taxes are payable in monthly instalments. Interest surcharges on underpayment of preliminary taxes, however, generally apply from 12 February the year after the financial year (the assessment year). Any balance owed by the taxpayer is payable in 90 days after the assessment has been made. Normally, any balance owed to the taxpayer is refunded in December of the assessment year.

For financial year endings in 2012, these rules still apply. For financial years ending in 2013, however, the tax administration system will be revised and the due dates will depend on the month in which the financial year ends.

Tax penalty

A taxpayer that submits incorrect or insufficient information in a tax return is charged a penalty amounting to up to 40% of the tax which, if the incorrect information had been accepted, would have been imposed or credited. The penalty and the rate may vary depending on the type of the incorrect information given.

Sweden

Appeals

Taxes are assessed by the tax agency. Depending on the circumstances, reassessments and/or appeals generally can be initiated within one and five years after the assessment year. Appeals can be made to the administrative court, and onwards to the administrative court of appeal, and in case of granted trial dispensation, onwards to the supreme administrative court.

Switzerland

PwC contact

Andreas Staubli
PricewaterhouseCoopers AG
Birchstrasse 160
8050 Zurich
Switzerland
Tel: +41 58 792 4400
Email: andreas.staubli@ch.pwc.com

Significant developments

Abolition of issuance stamp tax on the issuance of Swiss bonds and money market instruments

On 1 March 2012, the amendment of the Swiss banking act (so called 'too big to fail rules') was enacted. These rules include the abolition of Swiss issuance stamp tax on the issuance of Swiss bonds and money market instruments. Accordingly, the issuance of Swiss bonds and money market instruments will no longer be subject to Swiss issuance stamp tax.

In addition, the conversion of contingent convertible bonds (CoCos) into equity will also not trigger Swiss issuance stamp tax on the newly created equity. This relief applies to CoCos according to the Swiss banking law only; other convertible bonds will still trigger Swiss issuance stamp tax if converted into equity. The abolition of issuance stamp tax on debt instruments is to be seen as a starting point in the promotion of issuing debt instruments in Switzerland.

Taxes on corporate income

Resident companies are subject to Swiss corporate income tax (CIT) on their taxable profits generated in Switzerland. CIT is levied at the federal, cantonal, and communal level. Foreign-source income attributable to foreign permanent establishments (PEs) or real estate property located abroad is excluded from the Swiss tax base and only taken into account for rate progression purposes in the cantons that apply progressive tax rates.

Non-resident companies may be subject to Swiss CIT if they are (alternatively) partners of a Swiss business, have a PE in Switzerland, own real estate property in Switzerland, have loan receivables secured by a mortgage on Swiss real estate property, or deal with or act as a broker of Swiss real estate property. Non-resident companies are taxed on their income generated in Switzerland only (*see the Branch income section*).

Federal level

Switzerland levies a direct federal CIT at a flat rate of 8.5% on profit after tax. Accordingly, CIT is deductible for tax purposes and reduces the applicable tax base (i.e. taxable income). Consequently, the direct federal CIT rate on profit before tax amounts to approximately 7.83%. At the federal level, no corporate capital tax is levied.

Cantonal/communal level

In addition to the direct federal CIT, each canton has its own tax law and levies cantonal and communal income and capital taxes at different rates. Therefore, the tax burden of

S

Switzerland

income (and capital) varies from canton to canton. Some cantonal and communal taxes are imposed at progressive rates.

Overall tax rates

As a general rule, the overall approximate range of the maximum CIT rate on profit before tax for federal, cantonal, and communal taxes is between 11.5% and 24.2%, depending on the company's location of corporate residence.

Corporate residence

A company is considered resident in Switzerland if its domicile is in Switzerland. Residency is also linked to the place of effective management, which may be the centre from which day-to-day activities are directed or the place from which managerial decisions are made.

Permanent establishment (PE)

For Swiss tax law purposes the term 'permanent establishment' means a fixed place of business through which the business activity of an enterprise is wholly or partly carried on. In particular, PEs are branches, factories, workshops, sales agencies, permanent representations, mines and other places of extraction of natural resources, as well as building or construction sites that last at least 12 months. This definition is generally in line with the criteria according to Article 5 paragraph 2 of the Organisation for Economic Co-operation and Development (OECD) Model Tax Convention on Income and Capital.

Other taxes

Value-added tax (VAT)

As a matter of principle, proceeds of sales and services conducted in Switzerland are subject to VAT at the standard rate of 8%. Goods for basic needs are subject to VAT at the rate of 2.5%. These rates include a temporary increase that went into effect on 1 January 2011 and will remain applicable until 31 December 2017. On 1 January 2018, if no extension or change is enacted, the rates should decrease from 8% to 7.6%, and from 2.5% to 2.4%. Services in connection with the provision of lodging are subject to VAT at the rate of 3.8% (limited until 31 December 2013).

Any person, regardless of legal form, objects, and intention to make a profit is liable to VAT if that person carries on a business and is not exempt from the tax liability. A person carries on a business if one independently performs a professional or commercial activity with the aim of sustainably earning income from supplies and acts externally under one's own name. Persons, who are taxable, must register with the Swiss Federal Tax Administration of their own accord in writing within certain deadlines. Anyone, who in Switzerland generates less than 100,000 Swiss francs (CHF) turnover within a year from taxable supplies is exempt from the aforementioned liability. A registered taxpayer generally is entitled to offset the amount of VAT charged by suppliers or paid on imports against the VAT payable.

The VAT rates are dependent on the goods sold or the services provided. Some supplies are just exempt from the tax without credit (e.g. hospital treatment, cultural services, insurance and reinsurance turnovers, specific turnovers in the field of money and capital transactions) and some supplies are fully exempt from the tax (e.g. supply of goods that are transported or dispatched directly abroad). The difference relates to the fact that the input VAT related to supplies exempt from the tax without credit cannot be deducted, whereas supplies exempt from the tax are fully eligible for input VAT deduction.

Customs duties

All goods arriving in Switzerland from abroad are generally subject to customs duty and import VAT. The customs duty is calculated on the gross weight of imported goods, where category-specific weight rates apply. Products like alcoholic drinks, tobacco products, food, and textiles are typical categories of higher duty rates. Furthermore, imported goods are subject to import VAT of generally 8%. A reduced rate of 2.5% applies on certain goods, like food, non-alcoholic beverages, books, magazines, pharmaceutical products, etc.

Excise taxes

In Switzerland, various excises taxes are levied. To name a few, the following excise taxes are levied at the federal level:

- VAT (*see above*).
- Petroleum tax.
- Performance-related Heavy Vehicle Fee.
- National road tax (motorway tax sticker).
- Beer excise tax/Tax on alcohol.
- Tobacco excise tax.

Property taxes

With regard to the ownership and the transfer of real estate property in Switzerland, property taxes may apply. Dependant on the location of the real estate property, ownership related property taxes are levied at the cantonal and/or communal level or do not exist at all.

In case of the sale of real estate property, real estate transfer tax and taxes on the capital gain may apply.

At the federal level, the capital gain realised on the sale of real estate property is subject to ordinary income tax. At the cantonal and communal level, the capital gain realised is either subject to the ordinary income tax (dualistic method) or subject to the real estate capital gain tax (monistic method).

It is in the authority of the cantons to decide how real estate capital gains shall be taxed within their territory.

Securities transfer tax

Swiss securities transfer tax (often called 'securities turnover tax' or 'transfer stamp tax') is levied on the transfer of Swiss or foreign securities in which Swiss security dealers participate as contracting parties or as intermediaries. The ordinary tax rate of Swiss securities transfer tax is 0.15% for securities issued by a tax resident of Switzerland and 0.3% for securities issued by a tax resident of a foreign country.

Swiss security dealers are defined as any person professionally engaged in the buying or selling of securities for one's own account or for another person, including Swiss banks and other Swiss bank-like institutions. The definition also includes companies holding taxable securities whose book value exceeds CHF 10 million and remote members of a Swiss stock exchange.

Switzerland

Taxable securities include, but are not limited to, shares and bonds. Options and many other derivative instruments are not subject to Swiss securities transfer tax. However, the exercise of such financial instruments or derivatives may result in a taxable transfer of a security.

Various transactions are exempt from the Swiss securities transfer tax. Generally, no Swiss securities transfer tax is levied in the case of a merger or a reorganisation in which a Swiss security dealer is involved and taxable securities (including participations) are transferred. Furthermore, the like-kind exchange of a participation by a Swiss security dealer is also exempt from the Swiss securities transfer tax. This is particularly important for holding companies, which may qualify as Swiss security dealers.

Issuance stamp tax

Issuance stamp tax (often known as capital duty) on the issuance and the increase of the equity of Swiss corporations is levied at the rate of 1% on the fair market value of the assets contributed, with an exemption on the first CHF 1 million of capital paid in, whether it is made in an initial or subsequent contribution.

A tax ruling may be obtained to apply for and confirm exemption of a multitude of transactions from issuance stamp tax. In particular, special tax provisions allow for most reorganisations to take place on a tax neutral basis. In addition, an existing non-resident company may generally transfer assets to Switzerland without incurring Swiss issuance stamp tax. However, if the company was formed abroad and re-domiciled to Switzerland exclusively or mainly in order to avoid Swiss stamp taxes, the issuance stamp tax may apply.

On 1 March 2012, the amendment of the Swiss banking act (so called 'too big to fail rules') was enacted. These rules include the abolition of Swiss issuance stamp tax on the issuance of Swiss bonds and money market instruments. Accordingly, the issuance of Swiss bonds and money market instruments will no longer be subject to Swiss issuance stamp tax.

In addition, the conversion of contingent convertible bonds (CoCos) into equity will also not trigger Swiss issuance stamp tax on the newly created equity. This relief applies to CoCos according to the Swiss banking law only; other convertible bonds will still trigger Swiss issuance stamp tax if converted into equity. The abolition of issuance stamp tax on debt instruments is to be seen as a starting point in the promotion of issuing debt instruments in Switzerland.

Capital tax

Corporate capital tax is only levied at the cantonal and the communal level (not at the federal level). It is based on a corporation's equity (i.e. the taxable equity corresponds to the sum of nominal capital, paid in surplus, retained earnings, other equity reserves, and - according to Swiss thin capitalisation rules - potential deemed equity). The ordinary capital tax rates vary between 0.001% and 0.525%, depending on the company's location of corporate residence. Reduced capital tax rates are applicable for companies subject to a special cantonal tax regime (e.g. holding companies, mixed trading companies).

Since 1 January 2009, the cantons are allowed to credit CIT against a corporation's capital tax. As of 10 May 2012, the following cantons have implemented such credit system: Argovie, Appenzell Innerrhoden, Berne, Basel-Land, Geneva, Glarus, Neuchâtel, St. Gallen, Solothurn, Schwyz, Thurgau, and Vaud.

Branch income

Foreign legal entities having a branch in Switzerland become subject to limited taxation in Switzerland. Such branches generally qualify as PEs in line with the OECD Model Tax Convention. The branch's income is, in general, subject to the same CIT rules that apply for Swiss corporations. It is worth noting that there is no Swiss withholding tax (WHT) on profit transfers from the Swiss branch to its foreign head office.

Income determination

The statutory accounts of a Swiss company (or in the case of a non-resident company, the branch accounts) serve as the basis for determining taxable income. There are generally very few differences between statutory profit and taxable profit apart from the participation relief for dividend and capital gains income (*see below*), adjustments required by tax law, and the usage of existing tax loss carryforwards (*see Net operating losses in the Deductions section*).

Inventory valuation

Swiss CIT treatment does, in principle, follow underlying Swiss statutory accounting treatment. Inventory valuation is therefore determined according to the accounting rules of the Swiss code of obligations.

Accordingly, the maximum inventory value represents the inventory's acquisition costs or its production costs. In case these costs exceed the inventory's market value at the balance sheet date, the latter lower market value must be applied. In order to determine the inventory's acquisition or production cost, various methods exist.

It is at the corporate taxpayer's discretion to determine which method shall apply (e.g. weighted average method, first in first out [FIFO], last in first out [LIFO], highest in first out) (*see Obsolete inventory provision in the Deductions section*).

Participation relief

Participation relief is the name generally attributed to the tax relief on qualifying dividend income and capital gains from the disposal of a subsidiary. Participation relief is not an outright tax exemption, but rather a tax abatement mechanism. It is therefore also commonly referred to as 'participation deduction'.

Participation relief is a percentage deduction from CIT that is equal to net participation income divided by taxable income. Net participation income consists of the gross participation income from qualifying dividends and (usually) qualifying capital gains less related administration and financing costs and any depreciation of the participation that is linked to the dividend distribution. In most cases, participation relief results in a full exemption of participation income from federal CIT, or one close thereto. Note that participation relief may be diluted in certain cases (e.g. if loss carryforwards are offset).

The participation relief on dividend income is mandatory at the federal CIT as well as at the cantonal/communal level. The participation relief on capital gains is voluntary for cantonal/communal tax purposes, but nevertheless implemented by all cantonal tax acts. Specific privileged cantonal/communal tax regimes may foresee more favourable rules for dividend income and capital gains than the participation relief (*see Privileged cantonal tax regimes in the Tax credits and incentives section*).

S

Switzerland

Dividend income

Dividends qualifying for participation relief are those from participations representing at least 10% of the share capital or 10% of profits and reserves of another company or those having a market value of at least CHF 1 million. Note that there is neither a minimum holding period nor a requirement that the dividend paying subsidiary is liable to income tax in its jurisdiction of residence.

Capital gains

Capital gains derived from the disposal of a qualifying participation are entitled to participation relief if the following conditions are cumulatively met:

- The participation sold was owned by the company for a period of at least one year.
- The amount sold constitutes at least 10% of the share capital or 10% of profits and reserves of the underlying subsidiary. Partial sales of residual holdings of less than 10% are possible, provided their market value at the beginning of the year still amounted to at least CHF 1 million.

It is noteworthy that capital gains are only entitled to participation relief to the extent the sales price exceeds the original investment costs of the participation, whereas the so-called 'recaptured depreciation' (i.e. the amount of former depreciations) is taxable.

Interest income

Interest income earned is taxable income. It is of no relevance whether the payment of the interest was made by a related party (affiliated company or shareholder) or by a third party (*see Interest expense in the Deductions section*).

Foreign exchange gains

Realised foreign exchange gains (transaction gains) are included in the tax basis of a corporation as taxable. Based on a federal court decision in 2009, unrealised gains (or losses) resulting from the translation of financial statements in a foreign (functional) currency to CHF (presentation currency) may not be taxable (respectively tax deductible).

Foreign income

Swiss tax resident corporations are basically taxed on their worldwide income. However, income attributable to a foreign PE (i.e. outside Switzerland) is not taxed in Switzerland. It may only be taken into account to determine the applicable tax rate, in case progressive tax rates apply. The same rule applies for income from real estate property situated abroad.

Dividends, interest, and royalties from Swiss or foreign sources are included in taxable income. However, in certain cantons, special methods of assessment may apply for dividend and other income originating outside Switzerland. For dividend income, a relief generally is available at the federal income tax level as well as at the cantonal/communal level (*see Participation relief above*). The irrecoverable portion of foreign WHT of most treaty countries can be credited against the related Swiss income taxes on the same income. Foreign WHT of all non-treaty countries generally are not creditable, but they are deductible for income tax purposes.

There are no controlled foreign company (CFC) rules in Switzerland. Consequently, undistributed income of foreign subsidiaries is usually not taxed in Switzerland (*see Controlled foreign companies [CFCs] in the Group taxation section*).

Deductions

The statutory accounts of a Swiss company are the basis for determining taxable income. To be tax deductible, an expense has to be booked in the statutory accounts accordingly.

Generally, all business expenses that are booked in the statutory accounts are tax deductible assuming they are economically justified from a tax perspective. If an expense is not a justifiable business expense in the sense of the tax law, it will be added back to taxable income. Examples typically include excessive depreciation, non-justified payments to related parties (e.g. hidden profit distributions), etc.

Depreciation and amortisation

Maximum depreciation/amortisation rates allowed for tax purposes are issued by the Federal Tax Administration. Higher depreciation/amortisation is allowed for tax purposes if the taxpayer can prove that such higher depreciation/amortisation is required (not only allowed) from a statutory accounting perspective. Some cantons follow the federal guidelines, whereas some cantons apply their own (more liberal) applicable depreciation/amortisation rates.

The following summary of the rates specified by the Federal Tax Administration provides the general range of tax accepted depreciation:

Assets	Declining-balance (%)	Straight-line (%)
Commercial buildings		
Buildings alone	4	2
Buildings and land combined	3	1.5
Equipment		
Office furniture and equipment	25	12.5
Computer hardware and software	40	20
Other assets		
Motor vehicles	40	20
Intangible assets	40	20

Some cantons (e.g. Basel-City, Berne, Grison, Zurich) take a more liberal approach and even permit a write-down of certain assets (including fixed assets) to 20% or nil of the purchase price in the first year, provided that such write-downs do not, in the aggregate, result in a drastic decline in taxable income or even a tax loss. For tax purposes, such write-downs must be booked in the statutory accounts and generally disclosed in the tax return. As the cantonal tax authorities are responsible for assessing not only cantonal/communal CIT but also federal CIT, the accelerated depreciation will typically be accepted for federal CIT purposes as well.

S

Goodwill

Only acquired goodwill (derivative goodwill) may be capitalised in the statutory accounts and be amortised. Amortisation is generally allowed straight-line over five years. Special limitations apply to acquired shares, whereas the purchase price for these shares partly represents inherent goodwill.

Switzerland

Interest expense

Interest paid by a corporation to a third party is a deductible business expense. Interest paid to related parties (affiliated company or shareholder) has to reflect the fair market rate and is subject to limitations (*see Thin capitalisation in the Group taxation section*).

With respect to related parties, the Federal Tax Administration annually issues safe harbour interest rates to be used on loans denominated in CHF on the one hand and in foreign currencies on the other hand. The corporation may deviate from these safe harbour rates as long as it can prove that the rates used are at arm's length and more appropriate in the present case. The cantons usually follow these federal guidelines.

The safe harbour rules for loans denominated in CHF applicable as of 1 January 2012 are as follows:

For loans made to related parties	Minimum interest rate (%)
Financed from equity	1½
Financed from debt (actual costs plus at least):	
On amount up to CHF 10 million	½
On amounts of more than CHF 10 million	¼
But in all cases at least	1½

For loans from related parties	Maximum interest rate (%)	
Type of loan	Home construction/ agriculture	Industry and business
Real estate loans	1½	2
A loan up to the amount generally acceptable for mortgages (i.e. 2/3 of the market value of the real estate)		
Rest, whereby the following maximum interest rates for debt are applicable:	2¼	2¾
Land, villas, residences, vacation houses, business premises up to 70% of the market value		
Other real estate up to 80% of the market value		
Operational loans		
Made to trading and production companies	-	3¾*
Made to holding and asset administration companies	-	3¼*

* In calculating the amount of the maximum interest permissible from a tax perspective, any potentially existing hidden equity (under Swiss thin capitalisation rules) has to be considered.

Bad debt provision

Based on a longstanding but not published practice in Switzerland, it is admissible to set up an accounting provision for specific impaired debts, which will be accepted for income tax purposes. Unlike most other countries, it is also possible in Switzerland to account for an additional ('lump sum') bad debt provision of 5% on all domestic and 10% on all foreign receivables (i.e. after deduction of specific impaired debts), except for intercompany receivables and receivables to the public, enabling the taxpayer to defer the related tax liability until this provision has been released. Some cantons, such as Zurich, accept an even higher reserve (i.e. 10% on domestic and 20% on foreign receivables). This additional bad debt provision may have the character of a 'hidden' (i.e. undisclosed) reserve and is appropriate because the Swiss accounting standards favour prudence over true and fair view accounting principles.

Obsolete inventory provision

Similarly to the bad debt provision, it is also possible to account for a 'hidden' (i.e. undisclosed) reserve on a company's inventory. This provision, which must also be booked in the statutory accounts, is accepted for tax purposes (similar to the bad debt provision). Specifically, a company may book a provision for obsolete inventory as well as a hidden reserve on 33.3% of the inventory value after deduction of the obsolete inventory.

Charitable contributions

At the federal level, charitable contributions up to 20% of the net profit (after tax) of a company are tax deductible, if certain criteria are met. In particular, the charitable contribution has to be remitted to (i) Swiss legal entities which are exempt from taxation based on their public welfare or exclusively charitable objective or to (ii) the Swiss Federation, a Swiss canton or municipality, or their agencies (*Anstalten*). The cantons usually apply the same rules and similar thresholds.

Sponsoring contributions are only tax deductible if commercially justified (without specific thresholds).

Royalties

Royalty payments are generally deductible for tax purposes as long as the royalty rate is at arm's length.

Costs of employee share plans and stock option plans

The cost of employee share plans and stock option plans are generally deductible, assuming the employees eligible for the plan are employed by the Swiss company. The same holds true for the recharge of costs for plans covering local employees.

Fines and penalties

Under Swiss tax law, tax fines are not tax deductible. The potential tax deductibility of other fines or penalties has to be analysed with respect to the specific case.

Tax expenses

Corporate income and capital taxes paid to the federal government as well as to the cantons and the municipalities are tax deductible.

Net operating losses

Tax losses can be carried forward for, at maximum, seven years and can be offset against the taxable income of the following seven years. There is no carryback of tax losses in Switzerland.

Payments to foreign affiliates

Management and services fees paid by a Swiss company to a related party are generally tax deductible as long as the fees are at arm's length.

Group taxation

Tax is levied on each corporation as a separate entity. A parent company and its Swiss subsidiaries are taxed separately, and only the dividends from the subsidiaries (but not their profits) are taxable in the parent company's hands. However, usually for dividend

Switzerland

income, the participation relief is applicable (*see Participation relief in the Income determination section*). For income and capital taxes, no rules on group taxation exist.

Transfer pricing

Switzerland is of the opinion that transfer pricing matters cannot be addressed by legislation and therefore has no plans to issue any domestic provisions on transfer pricing in the near future. There is, however, an increasing awareness of the issue and concern on the part of the Swiss tax authorities that taxpayers may transfer profits without economic justification to countries with strict transfer pricing rules and documentation requirements in order to avoid challenges by the respective local tax authorities. In this context, Swiss tax authorities take an increasing interest in a company's transfer pricing position in order to defend their own position. Some cantonal tax authorities started to particularly focus on low risk/low profit entities located in Switzerland.

Switzerland follows the OECD Guidelines as closely as possible and recognises the arm's-length principle based on interpretation of actual legislation. To clarify transfer pricing issues, Switzerland offers an informal procedure for agreeing to pricing policies in advance.

Thin capitalisation

Swiss thin capitalisation rules are, in general, only applicable for related parties. In case of a thin capitalisation, the related party debts can be treated as taxable equity. The respective circular letter issued by the Federal Tax Administration provides for debt/equity ratios as safe harbour rules. As an example, the debt/equity ratio is generally fixed at 6:1 for finance companies (safe harbour). Interest paid on loans that exceed the relevant ratios are not deductible; further, these interest may be deemed as a hidden distribution and hence subject to Swiss WHT. There are no limitations on the financing of Swiss corporations by independent third parties (e.g. banks).

Interest rates paid to affiliated companies are also subject to periodically fixed ceilings (*see Interest expense in the Deductions section*). The deduction of interest in excess of the permitted rate may be disallowed and treated as a hidden distribution subject to Swiss WHT.

Controlled foreign companies (CFCs)

In Switzerland, no CFC or 'subject to tax' rules exist. Foreign companies are therefore recognised for Swiss tax purposes if they are managed and controlled offshore and are not set-up purely for the reason of avoiding Swiss taxes.

Tax credits and incentives

Generally, cantons offer competitive tax rates for cantonal and communal tax purposes. Depending on the specific cantonal and communal tax location in Switzerland, the ordinary overall (federal, cantonal, and communal) effective CIT rates may vary between 11.5% and 24.2% (*see the Taxes on corporate income section*). The cantons continually try to improve their attractiveness as business locations. As a result of the corporate tax reform II, the cantons may now choose to credit CIT against the capital tax to reduce the overall tax burden (*see Capital tax in the Other taxes section*). As a further example, the canton of Nidwalden introduced a tax relief for certain licensing income (so-called license-box), whereupon net licence income from the use of intangible assets is taxed separately at a reduced corporate tax rate of $^1/_5$ of the regular rate.

In addition, many cantons offer tax incentives for newly established companies or for expansion investments, such as tax holidays or significant tax relief for cantonal and communal tax purposes for up to ten years. In some cantons or for specific regions, a tax holiday may even be granted for federal CIT purposes if certain conditions are met.

Privileged cantonal tax regimes
Many cantons offer privileged corporate tax regimes. Usually, an up-front confirmation for such privileged tax regimes can be obtained by way of an advance tax ruling with the respective cantonal tax authorities. Such ruling process usually takes at least four to six weeks.

The privileged tax regimes, as described below, are usually granted for an unlimited period of time and can be relied upon unless the Swiss company's circumstances change materially.

Holding company tax regime
A qualifying holding company is exempt from all cantonal/communal CIT (with the exception of income from Swiss real estate, which is subject to tax after deduction of typical mortgage expenditures on such real estate).

Consequently, a holding company is in principle only subject to an effective income tax rate of 7.83% (i.e. federal CIT rate) prior to participation relief for qualifying dividends and capital gains. Further, usually a reduced capital tax rate at the cantonal/communal level applies.

Companies which meet the following conditions are eligible for the holding company tax status:

- The primary purpose of the company must be to hold and to manage long term equity investments in subsidiaries, and this purpose must be stated in the by-laws.
- The company must not be engaged in a commercial activity in Switzerland.
- The company must pass an alternative asset or income test, whereby either two-thirds of the company's assets must consist of substantial shareholdings or participations or two-thirds of total income of the company must consist of participation income (dividend income or capital gains) from such shareholdings and participations.

A tax ruling may be obtained from the cantonal tax authorities in the proposed canton of residence in order to confirm eligibility for the holding company status prior to forming the holding company.

Domicile company tax regime
Companies which only carry out administrative functions in Switzerland but have no commercial activities are eligible for the domicile company tax status.

Insofar as a company fulfils the above mentioned criteria, it may apply with the cantonal tax authorities in the proposed canton of residence for a tax ruling entitling it to the following taxation:

- A modest portion of foreign source income (i.e. from 0% to 15%) is subject to tax in accordance with the importance of the administrative function in Switzerland.
- Income from qualifying participations (including dividends, capital gains, and re-evaluation gains) is usually tax exempt (whereas losses deriving from qualifying participations usually are not tax deductible).

Switzerland

- All income from Swiss sources is taxed at ordinary rates.
- Expenditures which are justified for business purposes are deductible from the income to which they have a business correlation.
- Reduced capital tax rates usually are applicable.

The conditions to qualify as a domicile company vary from canton to canton. This is particularly the case with regard to determining the percentage of income from foreign sources subject to tax in Switzerland and to the definition of exactly what type of income is considered foreign source income.

A domicile company can be expected to be subject to an effective tax rate of 7.83% to 11% on foreign-source income.

Mixed trading company tax regime

This tax status, which is very similar to the domicile company tax status, was given different names by the cantons. Internationally, it is most often referred to as the 'mixed trading company' tax status.

In contrast to the pure domicile company tax status, a mixed trading company is allowed to undertake limited commercial activities in Switzerland. As a general rule, at least 80% of the income from commercial activities of a mixed trading company must derive from non-Swiss sources (i.e. a maximum of 20% of income may be linked to Swiss sources). Many cantons additionally require that at least 80% of the costs must be related to activities undertaken abroad.

Insofar as a company fulfils the above mentioned criteria, it may apply with the appropriate cantonal tax authorities for a tax ruling entitling it to a tax treatment analogous to the rules set forth above for domicile companies. Depending on the concrete Swiss activity and infrastructure, the portion subject to cantonal and communal income taxes generally varies between 5% and 25% of the foreign source income and is generally higher than is the case for domicile companies. The exact portion needs to be clarified with the responsible cantonal tax authorities in the tax ruling.

Foreign tax credit

Swiss tax resident corporations may suffer foreign non-recoverable WHTs on dividend, interest, and royalty income derived from foreign sources. As such foreign-source income is generally subject to income taxation in Switzerland, a double taxation occurs. In case a double tax treaty (DTT) exists and in order to mitigate or to avoid double taxation, Switzerland usually applies the credit method. Specific conditions and formalities will need to be met to benefit from foreign tax credits.

Withholding taxes

The statutory rate of Swiss WHT is 35%. Relief, if any, is generally granted by refund. With respect to related companies, a mere notification/reporting procedure may be requested for the fraction of the Swiss WHT exceeding the residual WHT. The table further below shows the residual/remaining tax for the recipient. Credit for the unrelieved portion of Swiss WHT may (in case the notification/reporting procedure does not apply) be available in the country of the recipient.

Capital contribution principle

Since 1 January 2011, the capital contribution principle allows the repayment of qualifying shareholders' capital contributions without deduction of Swiss WHT at the level of the distributing company and without income tax implications at the level of Swiss individual shareholders (holding the shares as private assets). Based on the applicable legal provisions, capital contributions that were accumulated after 31 December 1996 and meet some further requirements (e.g. special and timely recordings in the statutory books and vis-à-vis the tax authority) are deemed 'qualifying capital contributions'. In general, the capital contribution principle applies for premiums, additionally paid-in capital, and contributions into the reserves of a company without increasing the nominal share capital.

Treaties in force (as of 1 May 2012)

Recipient	Portfolio (%)	Dividends Substantial holdings (%)	Minimum Shareholding (%)	Interest (%) (1)	Royalties (%) (2)
Resident corporations and individuals	0 (3)	0	(4)	0 (1)	0
Non-resident corporations and individuals:					
Non-treaty	35	35	-	0/35 (1)	0
Treaty:					
Albania	15	5	25	5	0
Algeria	15	5	20	10 (5)	0
Armenia	15	5	25	10 (5)	0
Australia	15	15	N/A	10	0
Austria*	15	0	20	0	0
Azerbaijan	15	5 (17)	20 (17)	10 (5, 8)	0
Bangladesh	15	10	20	10 (5)	0
Belarus	15	5	25	8 (5, 8)	0
Belgium*	15	10	25	10 (5)	0
Bulgaria*	15	5	25	10 (5)	0
Canada	15	5	10	10 (5)	0
Chile	15	15	N/A	5/15 (23)	0
China	10	10	N/A	10 (5)	0
Columbia	15	0	20	10	0
Croatia	15	5	25	5	0
Czech Republic*	15	5	25	0	0
Denmark*	15	0	10	0	0
Ecuador	15	15	N/A	10 (5)	0
Egypt	15	5	25	15 (5)	0
Estonia*	15	5	20	10 (5, 15)	0
Finland*	10	0	10	0	0
France*	15	0/15 (6)	10	0	0
Georgia	10	0	10	0	0
Germany*	15	0/5 (20)	10 (26)	0/30 (19)	0
Ghana	15	5	10	10 (5)	0
Greece*	15	5	25	7	0

Switzerland

Recipient	Dividends Portfolio (%)	Substantial holdings (%)	Minimum Shareholding (%)	Interest (%) (1)	Royalties (%) (2)
Hungary*	10	10	N/A	10	0
Iceland	15	5	25	0	0
India	10	10	N/A	10 (5)	0
Indonesia	15	10	25	10	0
Iran	15	5	15	10 (5, 13)	0
Ireland*	15	10	25	0	0
Israel	15	5	10	10 (5, 7, 8)	0
Italy*	15	15	N/A	12.5	0
Ivory Coast	15	15	N/A	15	0
Jamaica	15	10	10	10 (5)	0
Japan	10	5	10 (27)	10 (5)	0
Kazakhstan	15	5 (9)	10	10 (5)	0
Korea (South)	15	10	25	10 (5)	0
Kuwait	15	15	N/A	10	0
Kyrgyzstan	15	5	25	5	0
Latvia*	15	5	20	10 (5)	0
Lithuania*	15	5	20	10 (5)	0
Luxembourg*	15	0/5 (24)	10	10	0
Macedonia	15	5	25	10 (5)	0
Malaysia	15	5	25	10	0
Mexico	15	0	10	5/10 (5, 25)	0
Moldova	15	5	25	10 (5, 13)	0
Mongolia	15	5	25	10 (5, 13)	0
Montenegro	15	5	20	10	0
Morocco	15	7	25	10	0
Netherlands*	15	0	10	0	0
New Zealand	15	15	N/A	10	0
Norway	15	0	10	0	0
Pakistan	20	10	20	10	0
Philippines	15	10	10	10	0
Poland*	15	0	10 (28)	10 (29)	0
Portugal*	15	10	25	10	0
Qatar	15	5	10	0	0
Romania*	10	10	N/A	10 (5)	0
Russia	15	5 (18)	20 (18)	10 (5, 8, 12)	0
Serbia	15	5	20	10	0
Singapore	15	10	25	10	0
Slovakia*	15	5	25	10 (5, 13)	0
Slovenia*	15	5	25	5	0
South Africa	15	5	20	5/10 (22)	0
Spain*	15	0 (16)	25 (16)	0	0
Sri Lanka	15	10	25	10 (8)	0
Sweden*	15	0	25	5	0
Taiwan (Chinese Taipei)	15	10	20	10	0

Recipient	Dividends			Interest (%) (1)	Royalties (%) (2)
		Substantial holdings			
	Portfolio (%)	(%)	Minimum Shareholding (%)		
Tajikistan	15	5	20	10	0
Thailand	15	10	10	15 (5, 10)	0
Trinidad and Tobago	20	10	10	10	0
Tunisia	10	10	N/A	10	0
Turkey (30)	15	5	20	5/10 (31)	0
Ukraine	15	5	20	10 (5, 13)	0
United Kingdom*	15	0	10	0	0
United States	15	0/5 (11)	10	0	0
Uruguay	15	5	25	10	0
Uzbekistan	15	5	20	5 (5, 13)	0
Venezuela	10	0	25	5 (5, 14)	0
Vietnam	15	7/10 (21)	20/50 (21)	10 (5)	0

* Bilateral Agreements (in particular Article 15 of the Savings Agreement) between Switzerland and the European Union (EU) apply as of 1 July 2005 and provide the following benefits:

Upon request, Swiss WHT on dividends paid by a Swiss subsidiary company to its EU parent company may be reduced to 0% (reduction at source) and is only subject to a notification/reporting procedure, if the following conditions are cumulatively met:

- Direct minimum holding of 25% of the subsidiary's capital for at least two years.
- Both companies are subject to CIT.

Upon request, WHT on interest and royalty payments made between associated companies or their PE resident respectively situated in Switzerland and the European Union may be reduced to 0% (reduction at source) in the source state, if the following conditions are cumulatively met:

- Direct minimum holding of 25% for at least two years (parent/subsidiary) or direct holding by a third company of minimum 25% in the capital of both companies for at least two years (sister companies).
- Both companies are subject to CIT.

Transition periods/rules:

- Greece, Latvia, Poland, and Portugal: WHT rate on interest is at maximum 5% as of 1 July 2009 to 30 June 2013, afterwards 0%.
- The above mentioned transition rules only cover the Swiss outbound perspective. Further transition rules may apply for Swiss inbound payments (e.g. for royalties paid to a Swiss company), e.g. with respect to Czech Republic and Spain.

In general, the Bilateral Agreements between Switzerland and the European Union are applicable with all EU countries. Consequently, the 35% Swiss WHT can also be reduced in connection with the EU countries, if the requirements above are met. In lack of a DTT, this is in particular to be mentioned with respect to Malta and Cyprus. The application of the Bilateral Agreements is subject to foreign and Swiss misuse conditions.

DTTs between Switzerland and EU countries with more favourable tax treatment of dividend, interest, and royalty payments remain unaffected.

Notes

1. In Switzerland, there is no WHT on interest deriving from regular loan agreements. The Swiss WHT of 35% is only levied on interest paid by banking institutions (or paid by entities tax-wise qualified as 'banking institutions') to non-banks, interest on bonds, and interest on bond-like loans. Further, the Swiss WHT of 35% may be levied on interest paid on mortgage loans with respect to Swiss located real estate; however, this is not covered in the table above.

2. There is no Swiss WHT on royalties, licences, and similar fees payable by Swiss individuals or corporations (provided that the dealing at arm's-length principle is met).
3. The statutory Swiss WHT rate of 35% is levied but refunded, provided that the respective earnings are declared as income for tax purposes.
4. Between Swiss group companies, the Swiss WHT of 35% is usually fully refundable; in many cases, the tax liability can be met by the notification/reporting procedure. For this purpose, a substantial holding is a participation of at least 10% in the share capital or profits and reserves or otherwise a market value of at least CHF 1 million.
5. Certain types of interest payments income deriving from several countries are exempt from WHT.
6. 15% residual tax for companies with more than 10% shareholding if the company receiving the dividend is directly or indirectly controlled by a shareholder not resident in the European Union or Switzerland and cannot prove that the company is not set up only to profit from the 0% WHT on dividends.
7. Full relief of the WHT on interest paid for a loan granted by the Israel Government (including political subdivisions and local corporate bodies) or granted by the Israel Central Bank.
8. Interest on bank loans is 5%.
9. Full relief if certain requirements are met.
10. Interest on bank loans is 10%.
11. Full relief for certain dividend payments to certain United States (US) pension funds.
12. Full relief on certain categories of interest.
13. Interest on bank loans is 0%.
14. According to the territorial principle of Venezuela, only certain persons can benefit from the tax relief.
15. Interest on bank loans to corporations is 0%.
16. 0% WHT rate on dividends of participations of at least 25% if participation was held for at least two years.
17. 20% minimal shareholding plus foreign investment of minimal 200,000 United States dollars (USD).
18. 20% minimal shareholding plus foreign investment of minimal CHF 200,000.
19. 30% only on income bonds ('*Gewinnobligationen*') and on profit participating loans ('*partiarische Darlehen*').
20. 5% for specific power houses ('*Grenzkraftwerke*').
21. 10% WHT for shareholdings between 20% and 50%; 7% WHT for shareholdings of more than 50%.
22. 5% WHT for shareholdings of more than 20%; 10% WHT for others.
23. 5% WHT on loans from banks and insurance institutions, bonds or other securities traded on a stock market and on certain credit buying; 15% on any other interest.
24. 5% WHT if the shareholding of 10% was held less than two years, 0% WHT if the shareholding of 10% was held longer than two years.
25. 5% WHT if interest is paid to a bank or a securities dealer or an insurance/reinsurance institution; 10% Swiss WHT in all other cases.
26. Only applicable if holding period is at least 12 months.
27. Only applicable if holding period is at least six months.
28. Only applicable if holding period is at least 24 months.
29. As of 1 July 2013, WHT on interest will be reduced to 0%.
30. New DTT between Switzerland and Turkey, in force since 8 February 2012, applicable from 1 January 2013.
31. 5% WHT on interest in connection with export promotion; 10% on any other interest.

Tax administration

Taxable period

The tax year is the business year. Thus, the basis for corporate taxation is the applicable accounting period, which may end at any date within a calendar year.

Tax returns

The tax system is based on taxpayers' declarations, with subsequent assessments being issued by the tax authorities on the basis of the tax returns filed. The tax return filing deadlines vary from canton to canton. Companies are initially assessed on a provisional basis, with the final assessments being issued after the tax base was either subject of a tax audit or declared final by the authorities.

Payment of tax

Unless instalment payments are specifically requested, federal, cantonal, and communal taxes on income and capital are, in most cantons and for federal tax purposes, payable only upon receipt of a demand based on a provisional or final assessment.

Note that cantonal exemptions apply. As an example, based on the date of maturity of the respective tax year (30 September), the canton of Zurich levies late payment interest to the extent that the full (final) tax amount had not been paid in time (independent from any earlier provisional tax invoices). About one month before the due date, a (provisional) tax bill based on the latest tax return filed or the assessment of the preceding period is sent to the taxpayer. Payment is usually made in two or three instalments. If the entire amount is paid up front, a discount may be granted.

The provisional federal CIT is usually due by 31 March of the year following the tax period at question. The due date of the final federal CIT and the provisional and definitive cantonal CIT varies.

Other issues

Reorganisations

Most corporate reorganisations (e.g. mergers, de-mergers, transfer of business assets within a group of companies, vertical and horizontal spin-off of business or part of business, share-for-share transactions and cross-border reorganisation where the Swiss tax residence is maintained, and replacement of participations) are typically possible without triggering adverse tax consequences (tax neutrality). In addition, special rules provide for a legal framework to tax neutrally substitute assets and qualifying shareholdings.

Syria

PwC contact

Wadih AbouNasr
PricewaterhouseCoopers
Saba House bldg, Block B & C
Said Freiha Street
Hazmieh
Lebanon
Tel: +961 1 200577 ext. 1610
Email: wadih.abounasr@lb.pwc.com

Significant developments

Decree 23, dated 8 December 2011, has reduced the consumption tax imposed on a
number of food items and on the hospitality sector. In addition, the decree now levies a
fixed price measured in Syrian pounds (SYP) per kilogram (kg) (instead of a percentage
on the value of the invoice) on a number of food items, from SYP 1 per kg to SYP 10 per
kg, depending on the food item.

Due to the political instability in Syria, there have been no other significant corporate
tax developments during the past year.

Taxes on corporate income

Except for the special cases listed below, common corporate income tax (CIT) rates
(including branches of a non-resident entity) vary between 10% and 28% of profits, as
follows:

Taxable profit (SYP)	CIT rate (%)
Up to 200,000	10
From 200,001 to 500,000	15
From 500,001 to 1,000,000	20
From 1,000,001 to 3,000,000	24
Over 3,000,000	28

CIT is levied on all corporeal and incorporeal persons, residents and non-residents,
on all profits generated in Syria. Profits are considered to be realised in Syria if they
occurred from efforts exerted in Syria, irrespective of the taxpayer's identity or place of
residency.

Syria does not tax residents on a worldwide basis. Syria's tax is based on territoriality.

Surtaxes
Depending on the location of the taxpayer, an additional local administration surtax of
4% to 10% (of the CIT amount) will apply.

Joint stock companies (JSCs) with more than 50% shares offered to the public
JSCs offering more than 50% of their shares to the public are subject to a flat CIT rate of
14% on profits. In this case, the 4% to 10% administration surtax does not apply.

Other JSCs, limited liability companies (LLCs), and projects included under investment encouragement laws

JSCs offering less than 50% of their shares to the public, LLCs, and projects signed with Syrian companies included under the investment encouragement laws are subject to a flat CIT rate of 22% on profits. In this case, the 4% to 10% local administration surtax applies.

Hotels, restaurants, and recreational establishments

International standard, first and second-class hotels, restaurants, lodging houses, related services, and all recreational establishments are subject to tax based on their turnover. The tax rate is 3%, and it covers both CIT and salary tax.

Contracts with public sector, oil companies, and non-residents

A Syrian company contracting with the public sector and/or with an oil company or with a non-resident entity will be subject to a withholding tax (WHT) based on the contract value (on that specific contract only) rather than CIT on real profits.

The same tax rate applies to non-residents operating directly from abroad; they are subject to a 1%, 2%, 4%, 7%, or 10% WHT on the value of the contract. The applicable rates vary according to the nature of the contract and the customer. The non-resident tax covers both income tax and salary tax of the foreign and local employees working on the contract.

Corporate residence

The following entities are considered Syrian residents for tax purposes:

- An entity whose principal activities are administered in Syria.
- An entity that adopts the Syrian Arab Republic as its headquarters.
- Branches or offices of foreign companies in Syria.

Permanent establishment (PE)

In Syria, the law does not discuss PE.

Other taxes

Value-added tax (VAT)

There is no VAT in Syria.

Customs duties

In setting the rules for valuation of merchandise, Syrian customs take into consideration the related explanatory notes issued by the World Trade Organization (WTO).

Customs duties classified in the Harmonized Tariff Schedule apply to goods introduced into Syria. Import operations are subject to prior licenses granted to all importers after they present their documents to the commercial registration and chambers of commerce or industry in Syria.

The value of the goods imported to Syria that should be declared is based on the transaction value. It includes the price which is actually paid or payable for the goods when purchased for the purpose of being exported to Syria and any and all other subsequent expenses incurred by the buyer that were not covered by the price

Syria

(including but not limited to, shipment, insurance, unloading, etc.) until the arrival of goods to Syria.

In practice, customs duty is levied on the higher of the value of the transaction to which are added subsequent expenses or the price specified by the General Foreign Trade Organization (GFTO).

Ordinary tariffs and preferential tariffs

Ordinary tariffs apply to goods which are not qualified for preferential tariffs. Preferential tariffs apply to all goods or part thereof originating from a country or a group of countries with which Syria is bound by special customs agreements that qualify these goods for preferential status within limits specified in the said agreements.

Merchandise that has been put into use in a country other than its country of origin, and that is imported from that country, is subject to the higher customs tariff between country of origin and country of import. Merchandise that has been manufactured in a country other than its country of origin is subject to customs tariff related to country of origin or country of manufacture depending on the degree of manufacture in each country and according to the rules set by the Minister.

Consumption tax/Excise tax

Consumption tax is imposed on certain services and luxury goods, with rates ranging from 1.5% to 40%. Taxpayers are required to register for consumption tax purposes, and tax is withheld by the party provided the service or goods or by customs (at import) and paid on a monthly basis to the Ministry of Finance.

Decree 23, dated 8 December 2011, has reduced the consumption tax imposed on a number of food items and on the hospitality sector. In addition, the decree now levies a fixed price measured in Syrian pounds per kg (instead of a percentage on the value of the invoice) on a number of food items, from SYP 1 per kg to SYP 10 per kg, depending on the food item.

Property taxes

Tax on real estate ranges from 14% to 60% annually, based on the type of property. Property tax is also paid on rental income at progressive rates ranging from between 14% and 60%.

Stamp duty

Stamp duty generally is imposed on transactions (e.g. the formation of corporations, the execution of documents, licences, contracts) at a rate ranging from 0.4% to 0.7%.

The surtax is applicable on the stamp duty tax.

Registration taxes

The estimated cost of establishing a company ranges from 4,000 United States dollars (USD) to USD 8,300 plus 0.5% of the capital stamp duty plus local administration tax of 5% of the stamp duty.

For branch offices, establishment costs are lower and may be estimated at USD 3,000.

Branch income

The taxes on branch income are the same as taxes on corporate income (i.e. tax rate varies between 10% and 28%). *See the Taxes on corporate income section for more information.*

Income determination

Inventory valuation

Inventory is typically valued at the specific cost. Otherwise, inventory may be valued via the first in first out (FIFO) or weighted average cost method.

Capital gains

Capital gains are considered taxable income and are taxed at the normal CIT rates (10% to 28%).

Capital gains include dividends, interest, revenue, premiums, and other cash income sources.

Dividend income

Dividends paid by Syrian corporations on previously taxed income are not subsequently subject to tax upon distribution.

Dividends received from a non-resident entity are subject to tax upon distribution in Syria of 7.5%.

Interest income

Interest income is taxed at the normal CIT rates (10% to 28%).

Rental income

Rental income should be deducted from the accounting result to reach the taxable result.

Property tax is paid on rental income at progressive rates ranging between 14% and 60%.

Royalty income

Royalties received are taxed as ordinary income.

Partnership income

Profits of partnerships are deemed to be distributed and are taxed at progressive rates of 10% to 28%.

Foreign income

Resident corporations are not taxed on foreign-source income derived from activities carried out abroad through foreign branches. However, all income considered to be managed from Syria is considered to be sourced in Syria and will be taxed in Syria.

Syria

Deductions

Depreciation
Depreciation of property, plant, and equipment (at rates fixed by ministerial decree) is deductible. The depreciation method to be used is the straight-line method.

Goodwill
Goodwill is not amortised over a specific period of time. An annual impairment test is performed, and the result is recorded as a gain or loss that is included in the CIT calculation.

Start-up expenses
There are no specific regulations concerning the deductibility of start-up expenses.

Interest expenses
There are no specific regulations concerning the deductibility of interest expenses.

Bad debt
There are no specific regulations concerning the deductibility of bad debt.

Charitable contributions
Grants paid by taxable persons against official receipts for known public or private entities are deductible on condition that the grants do not exceed 3% of net profits.

Fines and penalties
Fines and penalties are not deductible in Syria.

Taxes
Taxes and duties levied during the year, except CIT, are deductible.

Other significant items
The following expenses are also deductible:

- Cost of goods sold.
- Cost of services rendered.
- Rent paid for the business premises (or rent value if the taxable entity owns the property).
- Salaries and incentives paid to employees/workers.
- Payments representing employer's portion of social security contributions.
- Indemnities and allowances (end of service) paid according to the labour law.

The following expenses are not deductible:

- Expenses leading to the increase of the value of fixed assets (capital expenditures).
- Personal expenses considered by the business owner (or/and his partner) as personal compensation.
- Compensations for partners in some business entities.

Net operating losses
Losses may be carried forward for five years. The carryback of losses is not available.

Payments to foreign affiliates
Payments to foreign affiliates are considered normal payments because Syria has no transfer pricing rules. However, the payments may be subject to WHT.

Group taxation

There is no group taxation in Syria.

Transfer pricing
No transfer pricing rules exist in Syria.

Thin capitalisation
No thin capitalisation rules exist in Syria.

Tax credits and incentives

Investment incentives
Investment encouragement regulations allow foreign investors to benefit from customs exemptions for the imports used in the investment.

Permanent CIT exemptions
Physical and moral persons and associations exempted from CIT, either through the real profit or lump-sum profit method, are the following:

* Types of consumers and investors' cooperative associations.
* Farmers harvesting and selling crops; this exemption includes animals and livestock bred on their farming lands.
* Facilities in which stocks are bred or where poultry farming is exercised; subject to CIT according to the real-profit tax.
* Day-care centres.
* Institutes and associations taking care of people with special needs.
* 75% of the yearly net profits for air and maritime transportation.
* 50% of net profits of stock breeding and poultry farming facilities.

Withholding taxes

Interest
The income, revenue, and interest earned from accounts opened at Syrian banks and from treasury bonds are subject to an 8.25% total WHT (i.e. 7.5% WHT and 10% surtax).

Royalties
Royalties paid to non-residents are subject to a 7% total WHT (i.e. 5% CIT as well as a 2% salary tax).

Resident contractors
When a Syrian company performs contracts with the public sector, with an oil company, or with a non-resident entity, it will be subject to a WHT based on the contract value (on that specific contract) rather than CIT on real profits.

Non-resident contractors
Revenue earned by non-resident contractors in Syria is subject to a WHT based on the contract value (of that specific contract) rather than CIT on real profits.

S

Syria

Double taxation treaties (DTTs)

The table below shows the treaty and non-treaty WHT rates. If the treaty rates are higher, the recipient may choose the non-treaty rates.

Recipient	Dividends (%)	Interest (%)	Royalties (%)
Non-treaty	0	7.5	7
Treaty:			
Algeria	10	10	18
Armenia	10	10	12
Bahrain	(1)	10	18
Bulgaria	10	10	18
Croatia	(10)	10	12
Cyprus	15	10	(8)
Czech Republic	10	10	12
Egypt	15	15	20
France	15	10	N/A
Germany	(2)	10	12
India	(2)	10	10
Indonesia	10	10	(9)
Iran	7	10	17
Italy	(3)	10	18
Jordan	10	10	18
Korea, DPR	10	10	18
Kuwait	(1)	10	20
Lebanon	5	10	18
Malaysia	(3)	10	12
Malta	(4)	10	18
Pakistan	10	10	(5)
Poland	10	10	18
Romania	(1)	10	(6)
Russia	15	10	(7)
Slovak Republic	5	10	12
Tunisia	0	10	18
Turkey	10	10	(8)
Ukraine	(1)	10	18
United Arab Emirates	(1)	10	18

Notes

1. Taxed only in the dividend beneficiary's jurisdiction (when the beneficiary is owner of the shares).
2. Tax should not exceed:
   * 5% of the gross amount of the dividends if the beneficial owner is a company (other than a partnership) that owns at least 10% of the shares of the company paying the dividends or
   * 10% of the gross amount of the dividends in all other cases.
3. Tax should not exceed:
   * 5% of the gross amount of the dividends if the beneficial owner is a company that has owned at least 25% of the capital of the company paying the dividends or
   * 10% of the gross amount of the dividends in all other cases.
4. Total Malta or Syrian tax on the profits of a company and the dividends distributed by such company, as the case may be, shall not exceed the maximum tax chargeable on the company's profits out of which the dividends are paid.
5. Tax should not exceed:

- 18% of the gross amount for any patent, trademark, design or model, plan, secret formula or process, industrial or scientific equipment, or for information concerning industrial or scientific experience
- 15% of the gross amount paid for any copyright of literary, artistic, or scientific work, or
- 10% of the gross amount paid for any copyright of cinematographic films, or tapes for television, or radio broadcasting.

6. Tax should not exceed:
   - 10% of gross amount paid for cinematographic films, magnetic films, and tapes for television and radio or
   - 5% of the sum paid for any copyright of a literary, artistic, or scientific work, including cinematographic films and films and recordings for other forms of radio transmission or television transmission; any patent, trademark, design or model, plan, secret formula, or secret process, as well as for the use or right to use industrial, commercial, or scientific equipment, and for information related to experience in the industrial, commercial, or scientific area.

7. Tax should not exceed:
   - 18% of the gross amount of royalties paid for any patent, trademark, design or model, plan, secret formula or process, any computer software program, or for information concerning industrial, commercial, or scientific experience
   - 13.5% of the gross amount of royalties paid for any copyright of literary, artistic, or scientific work, or
   - 4.5% of the gross amount of royalties paid for cinematographic films, programmes, and recordings for radio or television broadcasting.

8. Tax should not exceed:
   - 15% of the gross amount of royalties paid for any patent, trademark, design or model, plan, secret formula or process, or for information concerning industrial, commercial, or scientific experience or
   - 10% of the gross amount of the royalties for the use of or the right to use any copyright of literary, artistic, or scientific work including cinematographic films and recordings for radio and television.

9. Tax should not exceed:
   - 20% of the gross amount of royalties paid for any patent, trademark, design or model, plan, or any industrial or scientific equipment, or for information concerning industrial or scientific experience or
   - 15% of the gross amount of the royalties for any copyright of literary, artistic, or scientific work including cinematographic films, or tapes for television or radio broadcasting.

10. Tax should not exceed:
    - 5% of the gross amount of the dividends if the beneficial owner is a company (other than a partnership) which holds directly at least 10% of the capital of the company paying the dividends or
    - 10% of the gross amount of the dividends in all other cases.

Tax administration

Taxable period
The tax year in Syria is the calendar year.

Tax returns
Taxpayers in Syria shall comply with the following requirements:

- Tax returns must be filed by 31 May for JSCs and LLCs and 31 March for other types of companies.
- Salary WHT should be submitted by the employer on a semi-annual basis.

Payment of tax
Payment is due at the time of filing.

Penalties
A penalty is assessed for late payments 30 days after the filing date at a rate of 10%, up to the amount of the tax liability.

Statute of limitations
In Syria, the statute of limitations with respect to tax is five years.

Syria

Other issues

Choice of business entity

In 2011, a bill was issued (Law No. 13/2011) to encourage Syrian companies to transfer to limited liability and shareholding forms. This law extends the facilities provided by Law No. 61/2007 and grants additional ones to companies. The law provides for companies to pay between 1% and 2% of the difference in the value of their assets as taxes after their revaluation, instead of a rate of between 14% and 28%, and exempts them from any additional taxes or fees that would fall on them because of the revaluation.

In 2011, Syria also approved a law regulating the establishment and operations of companies, less than three years after a similar bill was passed. The new text, Law No. 29/2011, brings a number of additions and improvements to the rules regulating the establishment of companies in Syria, such as:

* the establishment of one-person limited liabilities
* the transformation of state-owned entities into companies (currently state-owned institutions operate under specific regulations)
* the establishment of holding firms as limited liabilities, and
* the establishment of non-public shareholding companies.

The minimum face value of shares to be sold by JSCs is SYP 100.

In order to ease the establishment of LLCs, investors are able to apply to set their company up through the regional offices of the Syrian Investment Agency, the Industrial Cities located across the country, or the Domestic Trade Directorate of the Governorates.

Holding companies are now able to assume the form of a limited liability, while previously constrained to JSC form. Also, state owned entities can now opt to become public JSCs, post-approval from the Prime Minister, and abide by the Company Law.

In addition, one person LLCs are a new type of company allowed by Law No. 29/2011 that may be established by either Syrian or foreign persons or entities. However, foreign shareholders may establish one person LLCs only in the case where they have projects licensed by specified Syrian authorities.

The minimum capital for such LLCs has been set at SYP 5 million, which is well above the capital set for a standard LLC of SYP 400,000.

These one person LLCs may be transformed into standard LLCs or JSCs at a later stage.

Taiwan

PwC contact

Rosamund Fan
PricewaterhouseCoopers
International Trade Building,
27F, 333 Keelung Road, Section 1
Taipei 110
Taiwan
Tel: +886 2 2729 6077
Email: rosamund.fan@tw.pwc.com

Significant developments

The Taiwan-Switzerland tax treaty came into effect on 13 December 2011. Under this tax treaty, the withholding tax (WHT) rate imposed on dividends has been reduced from 20% to 15%, and may be further reduced to 10% under specified circumstances. WHT rates on royalties and interest have been reduced from 20% to 10%. Taiwan currently has effective double taxation agreements (DTAs) with 23 countries.

Taxes on corporate income

The current corporate income tax (CIT) rate is 17%.

Resident companies in Taiwan are taxed on their worldwide income as follows:

Taxable income (TWD*)	Tax thereon
Up to 120,000	Exempt
120,001 and over	17% of total taxable income

* New Taiwan dollars

A non-resident company is taxed on income derived from Taiwan sources. A non-resident company with a fixed place of business (FPOB) or business agent in Taiwan will be taxed similarly to a resident company (i.e. subject to filing of an annual CIT return based on the same CIT rate provided above). A non-resident company having no FPOB or business agent in Taiwan is subject to WHT at source on its Taiwan-sourced income. WHT rates on dividends, interest, and royalties may be reduced if the recipient is a tax resident of a tax treaty country and the relevant treaty provides for a reduced rate. *See the Withholding taxes section for more information.*

Tonnage tax system
A qualifying enterprise having its head office in Taiwan engaged in maritime transportation may elect to be taxed under the tonnage tax system, where a lump sum tax is calculated on the net tonnage of their fleet. Once the application is approved, the enterprise must remain under the tonnage tax system and cannot switch to the regular tax system at its discretion for ten consecutive years. Furthermore, loss carryforwards and tax incentives are not eligible under the tonnage tax system.

Profit retention tax
An additional 10% profit retention tax is imposed on any current earnings that remain undistributed by the end of the following year.

T

Taiwan

Imputation tax system

Taiwan operates an imputation tax system to eliminate double taxation on earnings of a corporation. The 17% CIT and 10% profit retention tax already paid by the corporation can be distributed to the resident individual shareholders as tax credits to offset against their individual income tax. However, the tax credits distributable to shareholders are subject to certain limitations.

Non-resident shareholders may credit the 10% profit retention tax previously paid by the investee company against the dividend WHT where the dividends are distributed from retained earnings that have already been subject to the 10% profit retention tax. Please note that credit for profit retention tax from dividend WHT is calculated based on a prescribed formula.

Income basic tax (IBT)

All Taiwan resident companies, as well as non-resident companies with a FPOB or business agent in Taiwan, should calculate IBT if they earn certain income that is tax-exempt. The basic income of a company is the amount calculated in accordance with a formulae stipulated by the government, with a deduction of TWD 2 million. Currently, the IBT rate is 10%. If the IBT amount is greater than the regular CIT amount, taxpayers must pay income tax based on the regular CIT amount plus the difference between the IBT amount and the regular CIT amount. On the other hand, if the regular CIT amount is greater than the IBT amount, no special action is required.

Corporate residence

A company is a resident of Taiwan for CIT purposes if it is incorporated in Taiwan. A non-resident company which has a FPOB or business agent in Taiwan is obligated to file a CIT return in Taiwan on its Taiwan-sourced income.

Permanent establishment (PE)

The term 'permanent establishment' only exists under the underlying DTAs with Taiwan. Taiwan domestic tax regulations only refer to FPOB and business agent, which generally follows the definitions of FPOB and agency PE in the Organisation for Economic Co-operation and Development (OECD) model tax convention.

Other taxes

Business tax

All sales of goods and services in Taiwan, as well as the importation of goods into Taiwan, are subject to business tax. There are two types of business tax systems: value-added tax (VAT) and gross business receipts tax (GBRT).

The sellers and service providers are generally obligated to pay business tax for the sales of goods or services within Taiwan unless the law provides otherwise. For importation of goods, the business tax will be paid by the goods receivers or buyers via customs. For importation of services sold by foreign companies to Taiwanese buyers, business tax shall be paid by the service buyers. However, if the foreign service purchased is under TWD 3,000 per transaction, the business tax shall not apply. Furthermore, the service buyer (corporate entity) will not be required to pay business tax if it adopts the VAT system and is exclusively engaged in taxable transactions.

Value-added tax (VAT)
VAT is applicable to general industries, and the VAT rate is 5%. Under the VAT system, each seller collects output VAT from the buyer at the time of sale, deducts input VAT paid on purchases from output VAT, and remits the balance to the tax authority.

Gross business receipts tax (GBRT)
GBRT is applicable to specified industries (e.g. financial institutions, small businesses). For banks, insurance companies, investment trust companies, securities and futures firms, short-term commercial paper enterprises, and pawnshops, the rate is 2%. For re-insurance enterprises, the rate is 1%.

Customs duties
Taiwan uses the Customs Cooperation Council Nomenclature (CCCN) to classify goods and set duty rates. The customs duty is payable by the consignee or the holder of the bill of lading for imported goods and is based on the dutiable value or the volume of goods imported.

Commodity tax
Commodity tax (excise duty) is levied on certain commodities, as specified in the Commodity Tax Act (including rubber tyres, beverages, cement, plate glass, oil and gas, electrical appliances, and vehicles), at the time when such goods are dispatched from a factory or when imported. Tax rates vary from 8% to 30% and are applicable to different types of commodities based on the value of the goods or the volume in specific circumstances.

Type of commodity	Tax rates/Amount
Rubber tyres	10% or 15%
Beverages	8% or 15%
Cement	TWD 280 to TWD 600 per ton
Plate glass	10%
Oil and gas	TWD 110 to TWD 6,830 per kiloliter or TWD 690 per ton
Electrical appliances	10% to 20%
Vehicles	15% to 30%

Property tax
A tax is levied on land and buildings annually. The land tax rate ranges from 1% to 5.5% of the assessed land value. The building tax rate for business properties is 3% of the assessed value and the rate for non-business properties is 1.2% or 2% of the assessed value.

T

Stamp tax
Stamp taxes are imposed on each copy of the following documents executed within the territory of Taiwan (with the following respective tax rates):

- Monetary receipts must have a revenue stamp of 0.4% of the amount received per piece. However, a receipt for the money deposited by the bidder requires a revenue stamp of 0.1% of the amount received per piece.
- Contract or deed for the sale or purchase of movable property must have revenue stamp of TWD 12 per piece.
- Contractual agreement under which one party agrees to complete a specific piece of work for the other party for consideration must have a revenue stamp of 0.1% of the contract price.

Taiwan

- Contract for the sale, transfer, and partition of real estate must have a revenue stamp of 0.1% of the contract price.

Securities transaction tax

Tax is levied on securities transactions at the rate of 0.3% on gross proceeds from the sale of domestic shares. Trading in corporate bonds and financial bonds issued by Taiwan companies is temporarily exempt from securities transaction tax assessment.

Luxury tax

With an aim to curb real estate speculation, Selective Goods and Services Tax (also known as luxury tax) of 10% applies on real estate properties purchased not for self use and sold within two years, as well as various luxury products, such as upscale automobiles, yachts, private jets, helicopters, fur, ivory, high-end furniture, and membership rights. However, the rate is increased to 15% where real estate properties purchased not for self use are sold within one year.

Branch income

A non-resident company whose head office is located outside of Taiwan must keep separate books for its branch in Taiwan. A head office or regional headquarters' general and administrative expenses may be allocated to the branch under certain conditions. CIT is assessed only on the branch's profits. A Taiwan branch should complete an annual CIT return.

A Taiwan branch of a foreign company may remit after-tax profits to its foreign head office without further tax due.

Motion picture leasing

A foreign motion picture's branch in Taiwan can deem 45% of its revenue from leasing of motion pictures as cost. However, if a foreign enterprise with no branch office in Taiwan leases motion pictures through agents, 50% of the revenues can be deemed as taxable income.

Deemed profit method

A non-resident company which is engaged in international transportation, construction contracting, provision of technical services, or machinery and equipment leasing within Taiwan, and where the cost and expenses are proven to be difficult to calculate, may apply for an advance approval from the National Tax Administration (NTA) to adopt the deemed profit method to determine the taxable income as 10% or 15% of the gross revenues. This will effectively reduce the WHT rate to 2% to 3% on gross revenues once the approval is obtained from the NTA.

Income determination

A Taiwan resident company is taxed on its net income, which is defined as gross annual income after deduction of costs, expenses, losses, and taxes. Except for certain exempt items, income from all sources, including offshore and onshore, is subject to CIT.

A non-resident company is only taxed on its Taiwan-sourced income. Article 8 of the Income Tax Act and the related Guideline defines the types of income that should be regarded as sourced from Taiwan. For example, fees received by a non-resident company for service performed entirely outside of Taiwan are exempt from income tax assessment, subject to supporting evidentiary documents.

Inventory valuation

Inventory must be valued at cost. If cost exceeds the net realisable value, the latter may be used as the valuation basis. Cost may be determined by the first in first out (FIFO), moving-average, weighted-average, specific identification, or any other method approved by the tax authorities. Conformity between financial and tax reporting is not required.

Capital gains

Gains on the disposal of fixed assets are taxable as current-year income of the company, with the exception of gains on the sales of land. The capital gains tax on marketable securities is currently exempt. Instead, securities transaction tax is levied on the sales proceeds (*see the Other taxes section*). However, if a non-resident company has a FPOB or business agent in Taiwan, capital gains on the sale of marketable securities may trigger IBT.

Dividend income

Dividends received from resident investee companies by a resident corporate shareholder are not included in taxable income. In addition, the imputation tax credit derived from the dividend income of the investee corporation can be distributed to the domestic corporate shareholders, but this tax credit cannot be used to offset the domestic corporation's income tax liability; rather, the tax credits must be recorded in a separate book until they are further distributed to the resident individual shareholders of the resident corporate shareholders.

Dividends received from foreign subsidiaries are taxable, but credits are given for the WHT paid offshore, limited to the incremental tax liability that would result if the dividends were added to the Taiwan corporate shareholder's taxable income and taxed at the Taiwan CIT rate.

Interest income

Interest received on commercial paper and certain other interest-bearing financial instruments are subject to WHT of 10% and 15% for resident and non-resident taxpayers, respectively (*see the Withholding taxes section*). This income should be reported as current-year income, and the WHT paid can be deducted against the income tax payable.

Foreign income

Taiwan adopts a worldwide tax system to tax its resident company (including the Taiwan subsidiaries of foreign companies). In theory, taxation on foreign investment income of a Taiwanese company is deferred until cash is repatriated to Taiwan and then subject to CIT. However, given Taiwan also taxes undistributed profits based on net income shown on the income statement (*see Profit retention tax in the Taxes on corporate income section*), foreign investment income may still be taxed in Taiwan before cash is repatriated back to Taiwan.

Deductions

Depreciation

Depreciation on all fixed assets other than land, including premises, plants (buildings), and equipment, used to generate income is allowed as a deduction. The straight-line,

Taiwan

fixed percentage on diminishing book value, sum-of-years-digit, unit-of-production, and working-hour methods are acceptable depreciation methods to the tax office. The useful lives of typical assets are shown below:

Asset category	Useful life
Computer equipment	3
Furniture and fixtures	5
Automobile	5
Building	50

With the approval of the tax authority, a company may revalue its fixed assets each time the government's wholesale price index increases by 25% over the base period. A company's base period is established at the time of purchase of fixed assets or at such time when a company revalues its fixed assets. Any increase in fixed assets may then be depreciated for tax purposes.

Goodwill
Goodwill is commonly realised from merger and acquisition, which should follow the purchase method as defined under Taiwan Generally Accepted Accounting Principles (GAAP). Goodwill should be amortised for 15 years if a valuation report is issued by a creditable professional valuation firm and the net identifiable assets are valued separately. However, in practice, the amortisation of goodwill is frequently challenged by the Taiwan tax authority.

Start-up expenses
Start-up expenses during the start-up period can be deducted in the year incurred. The start-up period is from the preparatory stage to the date the business starts to generate significant revenue from its primary business operation.

Interest expenses
Interests on loans that are used for business purposes are deductible in the year incurred. However, for a loan from a non-financial institution, the interest rate shall not exceed 15.6% per annum. As for interest on inter-company loans, the deductible amount is subject to the thin capitalisation rule and transfer pricing regulations (*see the Group taxation section*).

Bad debt
Actual losses on bad debts are allowed for deduction when certain legal proceedings or time requirements have been satisfied. The loss should first be charged against the bad debt provision, which should not exceed either 1% of accounts receivable and notes receivable outstanding or actual average bad debt ratio for the past three years.

Charitable contributions
Charitable contributions to support national defence construction, troop morale, contribution to government of any level, and donation made with special approval of the Ministry of Finance (MOF) are not subject to any tax limit. Donations to other parties are subject to prescribed limits under the relevant regulations.

Fines and penalties
Fines and penalties arising from violation of various tax laws are generally not deductible.

Taxes

All taxes other than income tax are generally deductible, unless where such taxes are related to tax-exempt income. However, tax penalties are not deductible. The tax associated with the acquisition of real estate should be included in the cost of the land or building.

Other significant items

If a company invests in a foreign entity and holds at least 20% equity ownership (this limitation does not apply if special approval is obtained from the Executive Yuan), the company can attribute 20% of the investment amount to a 'reserve for foreign investment loss'.

Net operating losses

A company's net operating losses can be carried forward for ten years. Losses cannot be carried back.

Payments to foreign affiliates

Royalties, interest, and service fees paid to a foreign affiliate are subject to WHT. Royalties or service fees paid to a foreign entity may be tax-exempt if certain requirements are met and prior approval is obtained.

Group taxation

Group enterprises meeting certain criteria under the Financial Holding Company Act and Business Mergers & Acquisitions Act may file consolidated tax returns for the Taiwan parent and its first tier Taiwan subsidiaries. For other enterprises, group taxation is not permitted. The Taiwan parent is eligible to file consolidated tax returns if it continuously holds over 90% of the shares of the subsidiaries for 12 months in a tax year.

Transfer pricing

Transfer pricing regulations were established to constrain multinational corporations from leaving their profits in countries with lower tax rates. For applicable companies, the disclosure of related party transactions in the CIT return and the preparation of a transfer pricing report is required. Upon request, the transfer pricing report will have to be submitted to the Taiwan tax authority within one-month of notice. The transfer pricing report must demonstrate the company's good faith effort to comply with the assessment rules. Without proper reason, failure to comply with such rules will result in additional tax payable and financial penalties. The types of transactions governed by these regulations include the following: transfer of tangible assets, use of tangible assets, transfer of intangible assets, use of intangible assets, rendering of services, use of funds, and other types of transactions prescribed by the MOF.

Thin capitalisation

In January 2011, Taiwan introduced a thin capitalisation rule in the amended Income Tax Act. From 2011 onwards, deductible interest expense on inter-company loans is capped at a prescribed debt-to-equity ratio of 3:1. The thin capitalisation rule generally applies to profit-seeking enterprises, except banks, credit cooperatives, financial holding companies, bills finance companies, insurance companies, and securities companies.

Taiwan

Tax credits and incentives

Certain tax incentives are provided to investors if they are located in prescribed areas, such as science parks, economic processing zones, free-trade-zones, etc. Other tax credits are granted to qualifying companies that invest in specific businesses or industries promoted by the government, such as biotech.

Research and development (R&D) tax incentive

Under the Statute for Innovating Industries (SII), R&D credits are available for up to 15% of qualified R&D expenses incurred, with the maximum amount of tax credit capped at 30% of the tax payable for the year in which the expenses were incurred, including the 10% profit retention tax. Unutilised R&D credits will be forfeited and cannot be carried back or carried forward.

According to Regulation Governing R&D Investment Tax Credit (ITC) Available to Profit-seeking Enterprises, a single annual application for R&D ITC should be made with the central competent authorities within four months prior to the CIT return filing due date. Information relating to R&D ITC should be provided with the CIT return.

Tax concessions on merger

Under the Business Mergers and Acquisitions Act, a merger or consolidation of companies can be exempt from stamp tax, deed tax, securities transaction tax, and business tax if certain conditions are met. After the merger or consolidation, any tax concession previously enjoyed by the merged entities will continue to be applicable to the surviving company (or new company) after the merger or consolidation. However, the surviving company is required to manufacture the same products or provide the same services which were approved for tax concessions by the merged entities in order to continue the concessions obtained previously.

The unexpired and unutilised NOLs of the participating entities prior to the merger or consolidation may be carried over to the surviving or newly-created entity according to the percentage of shareholding in the surviving or newly-created entity held by all shareholders of the participating entities.

Free-trade-zones

According to the Statute for the Establishment and Management of Free-trade-zones, foreign companies or their branch offices in Taiwan that apply for establishment in the free-trade-zone or delegate companies already established in the free-trade-zone to store and/or perform simple processing in the free-trade-zone and selling the goods to customers within and outside of Taiwan shall be exempted from CIT. However, in the event that the annual domestic sales exceed 10% of the total annual domestic and foreign sales, the portion in excess shall not be exempted from CIT.

Foreign tax credit

Taiwan uses the credit method to avoid double taxation of income. Foreign taxes paid on foreign-sourced income may be credited against a company's total Taiwan income tax liability. However, the credit is limited to the incremental taxes derived from foreign-sourced income.

Withholding taxes

Resident corporations paying certain types of income are required to withhold tax as follows:

Taiwan

Recipient	Dividends (%)	Interest (%)	Royalties (%)
Resident corporations and individuals	N/A	10	10
Non-treaty	20	15/20 (1)	0/20 (2)
Treaty:			
Australia	10/15 (3)	10	12.5
Belgium	10	10	10
Denmark	10	10	10
France	10	10	10
Gambia	10	10	10
Hungary	10	10	10
India (8)	12.5	10	10
Indonesia	10	10	10
Israel	10	7/10 (4)	10
Macedonia	10	10	10
Malaysia (5)	12.5	10	10
Netherlands	10	10	10
New Zealand	15	10	10
Paraguay	5	10	10
Senegal	10	15	12.5
Singapore	(6)	Not prescribed	15
Slovakia (9)	10	10	5/10 (10)
South Africa	5/15 (7)	10	10
Swaziland	10	10	10
Sweden	10	10	10
Switzerland	10/15 (11)	10	10
United Kingdom	10	10	10
Vietnam	15	10	15

Notes

1. For non-resident enterprises, a 15% WHT applies to interest income derived from short-term bills, securitised certificates, corporate bonds, government bonds, or financial debentures, as well as interest derived from repurchase transactions involving these bonds or certificates. The rate in all other cases is 20%, unless reduced under a tax treaty.
2. Royalties received by foreign enterprises that are specially approved in advance by the government are exempt from income tax.
3. A rate of 10% for shareholders that are companies (other than partnerships) with at least a 25% shareholding.
4. 7% of the gross amount of the interest arising in a territory and paid on any loan of whatever kind granted by a bank of the other territory.
5. The WHT rate on technical service fee is reduced to 7.5%.
6. The total tax burden of CIT and dividends tax is not to exceed 40% of the total profits of the company.
7. A rate of 5% for shareholders with at least a 10% shareholding.
8. Reduced WHT rates on dividends, royalties, and interests are effective from 1 January 2012 onward for those derived from Taiwan and are effective from 1 April 2012 onward for those derived from India.
9. Reduced WHT rates on dividends, royalties, and interests are effective from 1 January 2012 onward.
10. A rate of 5% for the use of (or the right to use) industrial, commercial, or scientific equipment.
11. A rate of 10% for shareholders with at least a 20% shareholding.

Tax treaties

Tax treaties entered into with Australia, Belgium, Denmark, France, Gambia, Hungary, India, Indonesia, Israel, Macedonia, Malaysia, Netherlands, New Zealand, Paraguay,

Taiwan

Senegal, Singapore, Slovakia, South Africa, Swaziland, Sweden, Switzerland, the United Kingdom, and Vietnam relate to corporate and individual income tax.

Treaties with Canada, the European Union, Germany, Israel, Japan, Korea, Luxembourg, Macau, Netherlands, Norway, Sweden, Thailand, and the United States relate to certain earnings from the operation of ships and/or aircraft.

Tax administration

Taxable period
The tax year in Taiwan runs from 1 January to 31 December. Businesses may request approval from the local collection authority to file CIT returns using a fiscal year-end other than 31 December.

Tax returns
Tax returns are filed on a self-assessment basis. CIT returns are due no later than five months after the end of the tax year.

Payment of tax
Tax is paid on a self-assessment basis in two instalments. The first payment is based on 50% of the tax liability of the prior year's tax return and is made in the ninth month of the enterprise's fiscal year. However, if the taxpayer meets certain requirements, it may self-assess the provisional tax based on the taxable income of the first half of the current fiscal year. The second payment is made at the time of filing the annual tax return. The returns are subsequently reviewed by the tax authorities, and a final assessment is issued.

Any overpaid tax as a result of the tax collection authority's mistake shall be refunded to the taxpayer within two years of acknowledgement of such mistake and shall not be subject to the original five-year period for applying for refund where the taxpayer is responsible for the mistake.

Audit cycle
Taiwan does not have a fixed audit cycle. Tax audit can be carried out any time prior to the expiration of the statute of limitations. Companies may be selected for audit if certain criteria are met.

Statute of limitations
The statute of limitations in Taiwan is five years from the tax return filing date if the return is filed on time. Where a taxpayer fails to file annual tax return within the statutory deadline or evades tax by fraud or any other unrighteous means, the statute of limitations is extended to seven years.

Recent focus of Taiwan tax authorities
The tax authorities have developed sophisticated and comprehensive tax audit techniques and approaches over the years. The following sets out some of the common items frequently challenged or audited by the tax authorities:

- Management fees allocated from the foreign parent company or affiliates: The tax authorities frequently question the economic substance of the services rendered, the allocation method, and the availability of sufficient documents to support the tax deduction claim.

- Amortisation of goodwill: The tax authorities frequently challenge the valuation report supporting the calculation of goodwill and whether the transaction itself should give rise to goodwill.
- Amortisation of business rights: The tax authorities have taken a more conservative view which limits 'business rights' to those explicitly authorised by laws (e.g. those regulated under certain public utilities act).
- Eligibility for R&D tax credits.
- WHT compliance.
- Transfer pricing compliance.
- Business tax audit.

T

Tajikistan

PwC contact

Richard Bregonje
PricewaterhouseCoopers Tax & Advisory LLP
34 Al-Farabi Avenue
Building A, 4th Floor
050059 Almaty, Kazakhstan
Tel: +7 727 330 32 01
Email: richard.bregonje@kz.pwc.com

Significant developments

On 7 June 2011, Tajikistan and Austria signed a double tax treaty (DTT) that will provide support and development in economic and trade procedures between the countries. The DTT is not yet ratified.

On 2 November 2011, the government introduced the Concept of Tax Policy until 2015, which should develop tax legislation, as well as cooperation of Tajik entrepreneurs and individuals with tax authorities, for improving the economic situation in the country and provide more understandable tax services to taxpayers.

Taxes on corporate income

All Tajik legal entities are subject to corporate income tax (CIT) in Tajikistan. CIT is computed by applying the statutory 15% rate to taxable income (25% for enterprises operating in transport, communication, banking, and service sectors), which is calculated based on gross income decreased by allowed deductions and losses carried forward from previous periods.

Tajik residents are taxed on their worldwide income. Non-residents are subject to CIT in Tajikistan only on Tajikistan-source income. Non-residents operating through a permanent establishment (PE) are generally subject to the same CIT provisions.

Minimum income tax
In Tajikistan, there is a minimum income tax on company income at the rate of 1% of aggregate annual income. The minimum income tax should always be paid in full. If CIT is less than the minimum income tax, then CIT should not be paid. If CIT is greater than the minimum income tax, then only the positive difference between CIT and the minimum income tax should be paid.

Local income taxes
There are no local income taxes in Tajikistan.

Corporate residence

Legal entities formed under Tajik law, as well as legal entities whose effective control (management) is in Tajikistan, are recognised as residents for CIT purposes.

Permanent establishment (PE)
Under general provisions of the Tax Code, any place of activity associated with production, assembling, packaging, supply, construction, and exploration activity on

the territory of Tajikistan, regardless of duration of such activities, will be deemed as PE of a non-resident.

Non-residents providing services in the territory of Tajikistan continuously during 90 days in any consecutive 12-month period also create PE in Tajikistan.

Other taxes

Value-added tax (VAT)
VAT is generally assessed on taxable turnover, which includes goods and services. The current VAT rate is 18%. Individuals and businesses are required to register as VAT payers if the taxpayer's taxable turnover exceeds a threshold of 200,000 Tajikistan somoni (TJS) (approximately 42,000 United States dollars [USD]) for the preceding 12-month period.

Generally, the Tax Code exempts the following from VAT: goods and services that are not provided in Tajikistan under the place of supply rules; sale, transfer, or rent of real property; financial services; medical services; publishing; and certain other goods and services.

For goods, the place of supply is determined as the initial point of transportation. Services are generally considered to be provided at the place of business of the service provider or the actual place where services are rendered. However, for certain types of services, such as consulting and accounting, the services are considered to be provided at the location of the buyer.

A VAT refund is generally available for qualified exporters if input VAT exceeds assessed VAT.

VAT returns, together with issued and received invoices, are filed monthly, not later than the 15th day of the month following the reporting month. Payments are due by the same date.

Customs duties
The tariff rates established by the government, ranging from 0% to 15%, are applied on an *ad valorem* basis, at a specific rate, or via a combination of the two. The tax rate of 0% is granted to certain types of goods (e.g. some types of printed publication, unwrought wool, gaseous hydrocarbons, electricity).

Note that Tajikistan is signatory to several free trade agreements, primarily among the following Commonwealth of Independent States (CIS) countries: Russia, Belarus, Kazakhstan, and Kyrgyzstan.

Customs fees
Customs clearance could not be performed without certification of goods, for which importer should pay based on time spent by certification specialist. Fees for customs clearance range from approximately USD 10 to USD 450, depending on customs value.

Excise taxes
Excise tax is assessed on beverages, tobacco products, fuel, tyres, and passenger automobiles. Excise tax rates are established by the government.

T

Tajikistan

Land tax

Land tax is paid annually based on the area of the land plot and varies depending on the location. The land tax rate ranges from TJS 180 to TJS 500 (approximately USD 39 to 108) per hectare, depending on the location of the land plot.

Real estate tax

Real estate tax is paid annually and applies to immovable real property such as buildings, houses, and flats. The real estate tax rate is calculated by multiplying the land tax rates by relevant coefficients (from 15 to 60), which depend on the purpose of real property and may be adjusted by the state authorities in each specific case.

Transfer taxes

There are no transfer taxes in Tajikistan.

Stamp taxes

There are no stamp taxes in Tajikistan.

Social tax

An employer is obliged to make social tax payments at the rate of 25% of salary.

Road tax

The formula for calculating road tax is total deductions of the reporting year multiplied by the 2% tax rate (0.5% for trade companies). If actual deductions do not exceed 70% of gross income, the tax base for road tax would be 70% of gross income.

Vehicle tax

Vehicle tax is computed as a percentage of the calculation index applied for horsepower of the vehicle engine. The percentage ranges from 2.5% to 13.75%.

Branch income

In addition to CIT, PEs are subject to branch profit tax at the rate of 8% of net profit after CIT, unless a lower rate is prescribed by an applicable DTT.

Income determination

Income tax is assessed on taxable income, which is the difference between gross income and allowed exemptions and deductions.

Inventory valuation

Inventory accounting for tax purposes follows inventory accounting for financial reporting purposes. Starting from 2011, legal entities should apply International Financial Reporting Standards (IFRS).

Capital gains

In general, capital gains on securities are taxed as business profits.

Dividend income

Under the Tax Code, dividends are defined as any distribution of income or property of legal entity between its shareholders. Dividends should be included into annual aggregate income.

Inter-company dividends

Inter-company dividends received by a resident parent company from a resident subsidiary are exempt from annual aggregate income.

Interest income

The Tax Code defines interest income as income received from any fees associated with a debt obligation, including the tax liability, payments for any loans, and contributions on deposit (accounts). Interest income is subject to CIT in Tajikistan and should be included into the annual aggregate income.

Foreign income

Tajik residents are taxed on their worldwide income. Non-residents are subject to CIT in Tajikistan only on Tajikistan-source income. There are no provisions in the Tax Code for tax deferral.

For information about Controlled foreign company provisions, see the Group taxation section.

Deductions

In general, all business expenses (e.g. materials, payroll) are allowed as a deduction if the expenses are connected with the earning of income, not of a capital nature, and supported by proper documentation.

Depreciation

The deduction for costs related to fixed assets generally is made through depreciation at rates ranging from 7% to 20%, using the declining-balance method.

Goodwill

There are no special provisions for goodwill deduction in the Tax Code; however, goodwill is not deductible in accordance with the general rules on intangible assets amortisation.

Interest expenses

Interest deductibility is generally limited to three times the refinancing rate of the National Bank of Tajikistan (currently 9%). For certain entities, additional limitations may apply.

Bad debts

A taxpayer is allowed a bad debts deduction in cases where the income associated with such bad debts is already recognised for CIT purposes. Bad debts are deductible when they are written-off in the accounting books. Special provisions apply for banks and other financial institutions.

Charitable contributions

Charitable contributions are limited to 10% of taxable income.

Fines and penalties

Fines and penalties paid to the budget of Tajikistan and other states are not deductible.

Taxes

Taxes paid to the budget of Tajikistan and other states are deductible, except for CIT and minimum income tax.

Tajikistan

Other significant items
Among other deductions specifically mentioned in the Tax Code are research and development (R&D), repair expenses, and geological and geophysical expenses.

Non-deductible expenses
Non-deductible expenses specifically mentioned by the Tax Code include meals and entertainment, personal expenses, passenger vehicles, and non-business expenses.

Net operating losses
Net operating losses may be carried forward for three years but may not be carried back.

Payment to foreign affiliates
No special provisions for deduction of payments to foreign affiliates exist in the Tax Code; therefore, general rules for deductibility of expenses should apply.

Group taxation

There are no rules permitting grouping for tax purposes in Tajikistan.

Transfer pricing
The tax authorities have the right to review prices applied in the following transactions for their compliance with market-level pricing:

- Transactions between related parties.
- Barter transactions.
- Cross-border transactions.
- All transactions with deviation of more than 30% from market level.

Thin capitalisation
There are no thin capitalisation rules in Tajikistan; however, interest deductibility is limited *as described in the Deductions section*.

Controlled foreign companies (CFCs)
The Tax Code contains controlled foreign company (CFC) provisions, according to which, income received by the resident's subsidiary (more than 10% ownership) registered in countries with privileged taxation should be included in the income of the resident.

Tax credits and incentives

Foreign tax credit
Taxes paid outside Tajikistan may be credited against the same types of taxes in Tajikistan, if appropriate supporting documents are provided. The amount of credit may not exceed the amount of tax assessed in respect of such income at the rates applicable in Tajikistan.

Special economic zones
Tax incentives include the special economic zones of Sogd, Panj, Ishkoshim, and Dangara. Sodj and Pyandj are actively functioning economic zones.

Free Economic Zone (FEZ) 'Sogd' was formed in October 2008 and has 14 operating business units. The main activities of businesses should be connected with industrial production and attracting international technologies in production of local goods. To date, this FEZ has attracted international investments of USD 1.7 million out of USD 48 million planned.

FEZ 'Panj' has two operating units and is a manufacturing and trade free zone for agricultural products, specifically vegetables, fruit, meat, leather, and cotton.

Both FEZs has created over 110 workplaces for local people and produced goods in amount of USD 5 million. The businesses that work in the FEZs pay only social tax and some portion of import duties. Foreigners who wish to work there have a 50% discount on visa application duties. These two FEZs will be working for 50 years.

In addition, there are two FEZs, 'Ishkoshim' and 'Dangara', that are currently at the developing stage and will mainly provide industrial products. The tax incentives and regimes will be the same as for the active FEZs.

CIT exemptions

An exemption from CIT is available for taxpayers that have made a certain amount of investments into chartered capital of a production company, as follows:

- Two years exemption if volume of investments is up to USD 500,000.
- Three years exemption if volume of investment is from USD 500,000 up to USD 2 million.
- Four years exemption if volume of investment is from USD 2 million up to USD 5 million.
- Five years exemption if volume of investment exceeds USD 5 million.

Withholding taxes

Tajikistan-source income of non-residents is subject to withholding tax (WHT) at its source at the rates shown in the following table:

Types of income at source of payment	Tax rate (%)
Dividends and interest	12
Insurance and reinsurance premiums	4
International transport and telecommunications	4 to 6
Royalties, rent, lease income, management fees, and other income	15

In accordance with the DTTs as of 1 January 2012, the rate of WHT may be reduced as follows:

Recipient	Dividends (%)	Interest (%)	Royalties (%)
No treaty	12	12	15
Armenia	10	10	10
Azerbaijan	10	10	10
China	5/10 (1)	8	8
Czech Republic	5	7	10
Germany	5/15 (2)	0	5

Tajikistan

Recipient	Dividends (%)	Interest (%)	Royalties (%)
India	10	10	10
Kazakhstan	10/15 (3)	10	10
Kyrgyzstan	5/15 (4)	10	10
Latvia	0/5/10 (5)	7	5/10 (6)
Moldova	5/10 (7)	5	10
Pakistan	5/10 (7)	10	10
Poland	5/15 (8)	10	10
Russia	5/10 (9)	10	15
Switzerland	5/15 (11)	10	5
Turkey	10	10 (10)	10
Turkmenistan	10	10	10
Ukraine	10	10	10

Notes

1. A rate of 5% of the gross amount of the dividends if the recipient is an enterprise (except a partnership) that directly holds at least 25% of the capital of the company paying the dividends; 10% of the gross amount of the dividends in all other cases.
2. A rate of 5% of the gross amount of the dividends if the beneficial owner is a company (other than a partnership) that holds directly at least 10% of the capital of the company paying the dividends; 15% of the gross amount of the dividends in all other cases.
3. A rate of 10% of the gross amount of the dividends if the beneficial owner is a legal entity and directly holds no less than a 30% stake in the company paying the dividends; 15% of the gross amount of the dividends in all other cases.
4. A rate of 5% of the gross amount of the dividends if the beneficial owner is a company that holds at least 50% of the share capital of the company paying the dividends; 15% of the gross amount of the dividends in all other cases.
5. A rate of 0% of the gross amount of the dividends if the beneficial owner is a company (other than a partnership) that holds directly at least 75% of the capital of the company paying the dividends; 5% of the gross amount of the dividends if the beneficial owner is a company (other than a partnership) that holds directly at least 25% of the capital of the company paying the dividends; 10% of the gross amount of the dividends in all other cases.
6. A rate of 5% of the gross amount of the royalties paid for the use of or the right to use software, or industrial, commercial, or scientific equipment; 10% of the gross amount of the royalties in all other cases.
7. A rate of 5% of the gross amount of the dividends if the beneficial owner is a company (other than a partnership) that holds directly at least 25% of the share capital of the company paying the dividends; 10% of the gross amount of the dividends in all other cases.
8. A rate of 5% of the gross amount of the dividends if the beneficial owner is a company (other than a partnership) that holds directly at least 25% of the share capital of the company paying the dividends; 15% of the gross amount of the dividends in all other cases.
9. A rate of 5% of the gross amount of the dividends if the beneficial owner is a person who holds directly at least 25% of the share capital of the company paying the dividends; 10% of the gross amount of the dividends in all other cases.
10. Interest arising in Tajikistan and paid to the government of Turkey or to the Central Bank of Turkey shall be exempt from Tajikistan tax; interest arising in Turkey and paid to the government of Tajikistan or to the National Bank of Tajikistan shall be exempt from Turkish tax.
11. A rate of 5% of the gross amount of the dividends if the beneficial owner is a company (other than a partnership) that holds directly at least 20% of the capital of the company paying the dividends; 15% of the gross amount of the dividends in all other cases.

Tax administration

Taxable period
The Tax Code prescribes a calendar year as the tax year.

Tax returns
Annual CIT declarations are due by 1 April in the year following the tax year-end.

Taxpayers are required to submit their estimated calculation of monthly advance payments of CIT.

Payment of tax
With respect to CIT, advance payments are due every 15th day of the month. Payment of any outstanding CIT liabilities is required not later than 10 April following the reporting tax period.

The settlement of minimum income tax should be done by 10 April following the reporting tax period in cases where it exceeds CIT liability.

Fines and interest penalties
The fine for failure to file a tax return ranges from a minimum amount of 1 calculation index (CI), which is currently TJS 40 (approximately USD 8.4), to a maximum fine of 100 CI, or TJS 4,000 (approximately USD 840). The amount of the fine depends on the taxpayer's category and should be assessed based on each ten days of delay. In the absence of tax returns, the tax authorities are entitled to assess taxes based on any information available.

Fines may be assessed in the amount of 10% to 20% of the understated tax liabilities. In severe cases, a violation may be considered a criminal offence.

A fine for failure to withhold and remit tax may be assessed in the amount of 3 to 200 CI (approximately TJS 120 to 8,000 [approximately USD 25 to 1,680]) of the tax not withheld.

Interest penalties may apply to late tax payments in the amount of 0.08% of the underpaid tax amount, for each day of tax underpayment.

Statute of limitations
Taxpayers are allowed to make changes to prior period tax returns within the statute of limitations (three years). No fines should apply to corrections in this case.

Other issues

Accounting system
In accordance with the governmental Resolution of the Republic of Tajikistan concerning International Standards of Financial Statements, the Ministry of Finance of the Republic of Tajikistan shall adopt IFRS through a step-by-step approach. Starting from 2011, juridical legal entities should apply IFRS.

Accounting policies and practices are being revised in light of the legal requirement that companies adopt IFRS and International Accounting Standards. Such revised accounting policies should be adopted by companies' boards of directors and disseminated to all the accounting units with clear instructions on how to introduce and follow the new policies and procedures.

Tanzania

PwC contact

David Tarimo
PricewaterhouseCoopers
Pemba House
369 Toure Drive, Oyster Bay
Dar es Salaam, Tanzania
Tel: +255 22 2192600
Email: david.tarimo@tz.pwc.com

Significant developments

No significant changes were announced in 2011. However, for most entities, 2011 is the first year of income to be affected by the thin capitalisation rule introduced in the 2010 Finance Act. This thin capitalisation rule replaced the predecessor interest cover provision (*see Thin capitalisation in the Group taxation section*).

Taxes on corporate income

A Tanzanian resident is taxed on worldwide income, irrespective of source. Non-residents are taxable on income with a source in Tanzania.

Income tax is charged at a rate of 30% on income of a resident corporation and of a permanent establishment (PE) of a non-resident corporation. Certain payments to non-residents are subject to tax at the relevant non-resident withholding tax (WHT) rates (*see the Withholding taxes section for the relevant rates*).

Income from the disposal of investments in Tanzania is subject to income tax where such investments fall within the source rules, and, in such a case, the income will be taxed at a rate of 30%.

Reduced rate for newly listed companies
A reduced corporate tax rate of 25% applies for three consecutive years for companies newly listed on the Dar es Salaam Stock Exchange (DSE). To qualify, at least 30% of the company's shares must be issued to the public.

Alternative minimum tax
Alternative minimum tax applies at a rate of 0.3% of the gross turnover of a company that is in 'perpetual loss status' for a period of at least three consecutive years as a result of tax incentives. The practical application of this tax is unclear.

Local income taxes
There are no local income taxes levied by local authorities.

Corporate residence

A company is tax resident if it is incorporated or formed under the laws of Tanzania or if the management and control of its affairs is exercised in Tanzania.

Permanent establishment (PE)

A non-resident entity has a PE in Tanzania if it carries on business in Tanzania. This includes a place where a person (i) is carrying on business through a dependent agent; (ii) has used or installed, or is using or installing, substantial equipment or machinery; and (iii) is engaged in a construction, assembly, or installation project for six months or more, including a place where a person is conducting supervisory activities in relation to such a project.

Other taxes

Value-added tax (VAT)

VAT is chargeable on all taxable goods and services supplied in, or imported into, mainland Tanzania. For imported goods, VAT is payable at the time of importation together with any customs and excise duties. For imported services, VAT is accounted for by registered businesses through a 'reverse charge' mechanism. The standard rate of VAT is currently at 18%, but the export of goods and certain services is eligible for zero rating. Businesses with an annual taxable turnover of more than 40 million Tanzanian shillings (TZS) must register for VAT.

The Commissioner for VAT has the discretion to register as intending traders those investors whose projects have not commenced production but who wish to be VAT-registered in order to reclaim the tax they incur on start-up costs. VAT payable with respect to capital goods (as defined), which are imported or purchased in Tanzania, may be permanently deferred, subject to certain procedures being followed.

Exempt supplies include supplies of unprocessed food, crops and livestock supplies, health supplies, transport services, financial and insurance services, and certain petroleum products. This list is not exhaustive. A business that only makes exempt supplies is unable to register for VAT and consequently unable to recover the VAT incurred on inputs. However, businesses in this category that import taxable services with a value over the registration threshold must register for VAT to account for the VAT on such services.

Certain goods and services supplied to specified entities are eligible for 'special relief' from VAT. The 'special relief' provisions enable supplies, which would otherwise be chargeable with VAT, to be made VAT free, provided certain administrative requirements are followed.

Registered businesses must submit VAT returns, and pay any tax due, on a monthly basis.

Businesses entitled to VAT refunds can claim any remaining credit six months after a refund first became due, subject to all intervening returns being rendered. Any claim for a VAT refund must be supported by an auditor's certificate. Businesses in a consistent refund position (e.g. exporters) can apply for approval to lodge their refund claims on a monthly basis.

Zanzibar has its own VAT Act, but it is similar to the Mainland Tanzania Act.

Customs duties

Tanzania is a member of the East African Community, which became a Customs Union on 1 January 2005 on the implementation of the East African Customs Union Protocol. This protocol provides for a common external tariff (CET), elimination of internal

Tanzania

tariffs, rules of origin, anti-dumping measures, a common customs law, and common export promotion schemes.

The customs duty rates applicable under the CET are as follows:

Category	Rate (%)
Raw materials, capital goods, agricultural inputs, pure-bred animals, medicines	0
Semi-finished goods	10
Finished final consumer goods	25

Tanzania is also a member of the Southern African Development Community (SADC). Where goods are subject to a lower rate of duty from another trade bloc, such as SADC, the lower duty rate applies until such a time as the trading arrangements between the trading blocs are harmonised.

Excise duties

Excise duty rates apply as follows:

Item	Rate for FY 2011/12 (TZS)
Sugared mineral water, sugared carbonated drinks, and sugared aerated water	69 per litre
Other not containing sugar, including club soda	54 per litre
Malt beer	420 per litre
Clear beer (with 100% local unmalted barley)	249 per litre
Wine with more than 25% imported grapes	1,345 per litre
Wine with domestic grapes content exceeding 75%	420 per litre
Spirits	1,993 per litre
Cigarettes without filter containing more than 75% domestic tobacco	6,830 per 1,000
Cigarettes with filter containing more than 75% domestic tobacco	16,114 per 1,000
Other cigarettes not mentioned above	29,264 per 1,000
Cut rag/filler	14,780 per kg
Motor spirit (gasoline) premium	339 per litre
Motor spirit (gasoline) regular	339 per litre
Gas oil (diesel)	215 per litre
Jet fuel	0 per litre
Illuminated kerosene	400 per litre
Other medium oil and preparation	9.32 per litre
Industrial diesel oil	392 per litre
Heavy furnace oil	40 per litre
Lubrication oil	500 per m3
Lubrication greases	0.75 per kg

Item	Rate for FY 2011/12 (%)
Satellite and cable television broadcasting	5
Airtime for mobile phones	10
Disposable plastic bags	50
Liquefied petroleum gas (LPG)	0
Motor car with cylinder capacity exceeding 1000cc but not exceeding 2000cc	5

Item	Rate for FY 2011/12 (%)
Motor vehicle with engine size greater than 2000cc	10
Old motor vehicles (ten years or more)	20

Fuel levy
Fuel levy is charged on petroleum products at a rate of TZS 200 per litre.

Stamp duty
Examples of instruments giving rise to stamp duty obligations include conveyances, leases, share transfers, and issue and transfer of debentures.

The current rate is 1% of the transaction value.

Payroll taxes
Payroll taxes include a skills and development levy at 6% of payroll cash costs and a 20% social security contribution. The social security contribution is normally split equally between employer and employee (i.e. 10% each).

Local taxes

Property taxes
The local government levies a property tax based on the value of a premise. The rates vary depending on the value and location of the property.

Service levy
The local government is entitled to charge a 0.3% service levy based on turnover generated in the relevant district.

Cess levy
For agricultural produce and livestock, there is a cess levy, currently capped at 5% of the producer price.

Branch income

The income tax liability of a person with a PE in Tanzania is calculated as if the person and the PE are independent but as if the PE is resident in Tanzania. The income of the PE is taxed at the normal income tax rate for entities, namely 30%.

The PE is also subject to a tax on 'repatriated income', which applies at a rate of 10% (the same rate as a company would withhold on dividends).

In certain circumstances, business activities of the head office may be attributed to the branch. Arrangements between a PE and head office generally are not recognised, other than the transfer of an asset or liability between the two. Amounts derived (or payments received) and expenditures incurred (or payments made) that relate to assets held by, or liabilities owed by, the business of the PE are attributed to the PE.

Tanzania

Income determination

Subject to any provision to the contrary in the Income Tax Act, income is to be calculated in accordance with generally accepted accounting principles (GAAP). Corporations must apply an accrual basis of accounting.

Inventory valuation
Trading stock is valued at the end of the year at the lower of cost and market value. Special rules apply for the valuation of long term work in progress.

Capital gains
There is no separate capital gains tax in Tanzania. Instead, income tax is charged on the taxable profit arising on a gain arising from the realisation of an 'investment asset' (a term that [subject to certain exceptions] includes shares, interests in land and buildings, and a beneficial interest in a non-resident trust). The gain is determined as the difference between costs incurred and sale proceeds.

Dividend income
Dividend payments are taxed by way of WHT, and this is a final tax.

No WHT applies to a dividend paid by a resident corporation to another resident corporation holding 25% or more of shares and voting rights in the corporation paying the dividend.

Interest income
Interest income is treated as income from investment. The term 'interest' is defined as payment for the use of money and includes payment made or accrued under a debt obligation that is not a repayment of capital, any gain realised by way of a discount, premium, swap payment, or similar payment.

Interest income is taxed by way of WHT.

Foreign income
A resident person's foreign-source income or loss (from employment, business, and investment) is calculated as that person's worldwide income or loss less any income sourced in Tanzania and plus any loss sourced in Tanzania.

A resident person may claim a foreign tax credit on any foreign tax paid by the person on foreign income. However, such credit should not exceed the Tanzanian tax rate applicable to that income. Any unrelieved amount of foreign tax credit may be carried forward (subject to the 'change in control' provisions). An election may be made to relinquish foreign tax credit and claim a deduction for the amount of foreign income tax.

Deductions

In calculating taxable profit, deductions are allowed for revenue expenditures incurred wholly and exclusively in the production of income, with some statutory exceptions. For capital expenditures, there are specific tax depreciation allowances.

There are special rules with regard to the valuation of trading stock and long-term contracts and in relation to the treatment of instalment sales and finance leases.

Tanzania

There is ring-fencing of mining operations per licence area.

Depreciation
The categories of depreciable assets and their tax depreciation rates are set out in the table below.

Expenditures on plant and machinery are generally written off on a reducing-balance basis at rates of 37.5%, 25%, or 12.5%, depending on the category of the asset. Certain plant and machinery for manufacturing, fish farming, and tourist hotels benefit from a 50% allowance in the first year, with the normal rates applying to the remaining balance in subsequent years. There is an immediate write-off of expenditures on plant and machinery used in agriculture.

Expenditures on buildings qualify for a depreciation allowance of 5% per year on a straight-line basis. For intangible assets, the write-off is over the useful life of the asset.

Apart from the immediate write-off of plant and machinery, agricultural businesses also benefit from the immediate write-off of agricultural improvement expenditures (including the costs of clearing land, excavating irrigation channels, and planting perennial crops or tree bearing crops). Buildings, structures, dams, water reservoirs, fences, and similar works of a permanent nature used in agriculture, livestock, or fish farming are written off on a straight-line basis over five years.

Mining companies are entitled to a 100% capital deduction with respect to capital expenditures on exploration and development.

Depreciation allowances rates

Class	Depreciable assets	Rate (%)
1	Computers and data handling equipment, together with peripheral devices; automobiles, buses, and minibuses with a seating capacity of less than 30 passengers; goods vehicles with a load capacity of less than seven tonnes; construction and earth-moving equipment.	37.5
2	Buses with a seating capacity of 30 or more passengers, heavy general purpose or specialised trucks, trailers, and trailer-mounted containers; railroad cars, locomotives, and equipment; vessels, barges, tugs, and similar water transportation equipment; aircraft, other self-propelling vehicles; plant and machinery (including windmills, electric generators, and distribution equipment) used in manufacturing or mining operations; specialised public utility plant and equipment; and machinery or other irrigation installations and equipment.	25
3	Office furniture, fixtures, and equipment; any asset not included in another class.	12.5
4	Natural resource exploration and production rights and assets in respect of natural resource prospecting, exploration, and development expenditure. (However, note that the Income Tax Act 2004 does provide for predecessor capital deduction provisions in the Income Tax Act 1973 to continue for the holders of mining rights.)	20
5	Buildings, structures, dams, water reservoirs, fences, and similar works of a permanent nature used in agriculture, livestock farming, or fishing farming.	20
6	Buildings, structures, and similar works of permanent nature other than those mentioned in Class 5.	5

Tanzania

Class	Depreciable assets	Rate (%)
7	Intangible assets other than those in Class 4.	1 divided by the useful life of the asset in the pool and rounded down to the nearest half year
8	Plant and machinery (including windmills, electric generators, and distribution equipment) used in agriculture.	100

Goodwill
Goodwill does not qualify for depreciation allowance as it is excluded from the definition of 'depreciable asset'.

Start-up expenses
Start-up expenses are deductible to the extent that they meet the general deduction criteria (i.e. they are revenue in nature and were incurred wholly and exclusive in the production of income). The definition of 'business' includes a prospective business.

Interest expenses
Interest expenses are deductible on an accrual basis, subject to thin capitalisation rules (*see Thin capitalisation in the Group taxation section*).

Bad debt
In order to claim relief for bad debt, it is necessary to demonstrate that all reasonable steps have been taken to pursue payment and that there is a reasonable belief that the debt claim will not be satisfied.

Charitable contributions
The Income Tax Act allows deduction for contributions made:

1. to charitable institutions (approved by the Commissioner to operate as such) and social development projects
2. under Section 12 of the Education Fund Act 2001, or
3. to local government authorities under statutory obligations to support community developments projects.

The deduction available under item (1) above is restricted to 2% of the company's taxable income before such deduction.

Fines and penalties
Fines and similar penalties payable to a government or a political subdivision of any country for the breach of any law or subsidiary legislation are not deductible.

Taxes
Taxes payable under the Income Tax Act 2004 are not deductible.

Net operating losses
There is no limit on the carryforward period for tax losses. However, there is ring-fencing of tax losses as follows:

- Losses from agricultural business can only be offset against profits derived from agricultural business.
- Foreign source losses can only be offset against foreign source profits.

- Losses on investments can only be offset against investment income.
- Foreign source losses on investments can only be offset against foreign source investment income.

In certain circumstances, tax losses may be forfeited on a change in the underlying control of an entity.

Tax losses can be carried back only in long-term contracts in a case where a contract is completed and a person has unrelieved losses for that period or a previous period that is attributable to the long-term contract These losses can then be carried back to a previous year of income and treated as unrelieved loss for that year.

Payments to foreign affiliates
Payments to foreign affiliates are deductible to the extent they are wholly and exclusively incurred in the production of the company's income. The deduction is subject to transfer pricing provisions *as detailed in the Group taxation section.*

Group taxation

There are no provisions for tax consolidation or group relief in Tanzania.

Transfer pricing
With respect to transactions between related parties, there is an obligation to 'quantify, apportion, and allocate amounts' for income tax purposes on an arm's-length basis. If the Commissioner considers that a person has failed to comply with this requirement, the Commissioner may make such adjustments as the Commissioner thinks appropriate.

The Commissioner has the power to make counteractive adjustments to a person's tax liability where the Commissioner considers that an arrangement is a tax-avoidance arrangement.

Thin capitalisation
There is a thin capitalisation restriction on the amount of deductible interest for what are termed 'exempt-controlled resident entities', where the debt-to-equity ratio exceeds 70:30.

Controlled foreign trusts and corporations
There are provisions that relate to the treatment of unallocated income of controlled foreign trusts and corporations; however, in practice, this is more of academic interest as there is limited outward investment from Tanzania.

Other anti-avoidance provisions
Other anti-avoidance provisions exist to address the following:

- A change in the underlying control of an entity, accompanied by some change in the conduct of the business.
- Income or dividend stripping arrangements.
- Income splitting.

Tanzania

Tax credits and incentives

Foreign tax credit

See *Foreign income* in the Income determination section for a description of the foreign tax credit.

Agriculture, manufacturing, mining, and tourism incentives

Tax incentives by way of generous capital deduction provisions are given for specific sectors, namely agriculture, manufacturing, mining, and tourism. *See the Deductions section for more information.*

Export processing zones (EPZs) and special economic zones (SEZs)

There are special benefits for EPZs and SEZs. Included in the benefits available to a person licensed to carry on business in an EPZ, as well as to SEZ investors selling in export markets, are a ten-year income tax holiday and WHT holiday, subject to a requirement to export at least 80% of production.

Withholding taxes

WHT rates

Payment	Resident (%)	Non-resident (%)
Dividend		
To a company controlling 25% or more of the voting power and holding 25% or more of the shares	0	10
From a DSE listed company	5	5
Otherwise	10	10
Interest	10	10
Rent		
Land and buildings	10	15
Aircraft lease	0	0
Other	0	15
Royalty	15	15
Natural resource payment	15	15
Service fees		
Technical services provided to mining companies	5	15
Other	0	15
Insurance premium	0	5
Payments to residents without a tax identification number certificate	2	N/A

Double tax treaty (DTT) rates

Recipient	WHT (%)			
	Dividend	Interest	Royalties	Management / technical fees
Domestic rate *	10	10	15	15
Canada	20/25	15	20	20
Denmark	15	12.5	20	20
Finland	20	15	20	20

Tanzania

	WHT (%)			
Recipient	Dividend	Interest	Royalties	Management / technical fees
India	10/15	12.5	20	20
Italy	10	15	15	15
Norway	20	15	20	20
South Africa	10/20	10	10	0
Sweden	15/25	15	20	20
Zambia	0	0	0	0
East African Community **	5	10	10	10

* The domestic WHT rates apply where the DTT rates are higher than the domestic WHT rates.
** Signed but awaiting ratification.

Tax administration

Taxable period
While the year of income for tax purposes is the calendar year, an entity may apply to use its own accounting period rather than the calendar year.

Tax returns
A statement of estimated tax payable, which contains an estimate of the chargeable income and the tax payable thereon, is due for submission within three months from the beginning of the accounting period. A final tax return must be furnished within six months from the end of the accounting period.

WHT returns must be submitted every half year.

A late filing penalty applies monthly at an amount equal to the higher of (i) TZS 100,000 or (ii) 2.5% applied to unpaid tax. If estimated tax is significantly underestimated, a penalty may also apply.

Payment of tax
Instalment tax is payable in four equal instalments not later than three months, six months, nine months, and 12 months from the beginning of the accounting period. Final tax is payable on the date on which the final return is due for submission, namely six months after the end of the accounting period.

WHT is due seven days after the month of deduction.

Interest on late payment is charged at the Bank of Tanzania discount rate plus 5%.

Audit cycle
The normal practice is for the Revenue Authority to carry out a review every two or three years.

Statute of limitations
There is a three year time limit for the Revenue Authority to adjust an income tax return filed by a taxpayer. The three years runs from the due date of filing the final tax return.

Tanzania

Topics of focus for tax authorities

The current topics of focus for the Revenue Authority are transfer pricing, WHT on payments to non-residents, and compliance on payroll taxes.

Functional currency

Taxable income and deductible expenditure is quantified in Tanzanian shillings. The Commissioner has the power, by notice in writing, to permit quantification in a foreign currency convertible to Tanzanian shillings.

Thailand

PwC contact

Thavorn Rujivanarom
PricewaterhouseCoopers Legal & Tax Consultants Ltd.
15th Floor, Bangkok City Tower
179/74-80 South Sathorn Road
Bangkok 10120
Thailand
Tel: +66 2 344 1000
Email: thavorn.rujivanarom@th.pwc.com

Significant developments

Reduction of corporate income tax (CIT) rate
The general 30% flat rate of CIT has been temporarily reduced to 23% for the accounting period which begins on or after 1 January 2012 and to 20% for the following two accounting periods that begin on or after 1 January 2013.

The above reduced rates also apply to companies listed on the Stock Exchange of Thailand (SET) and the Market for Alternative Investment (MAI) for the same periods.

The reduced rates and qualifications for companies with low paid-in capital have also been changed.

Taxes on corporate income

Thailand incorporated companies are taxed on worldwide income. A foreign incorporated company is taxed on profits arising from or in consequence of the business carried on in Thailand. A foreign company not carrying on business in Thailand is subject to a withholding tax (WHT) on certain types of assessable income (e.g. interest, dividends, royalties, rentals, and service fees) paid from or in Thailand. The rate of WHT is generally 15%, except for dividends which is 10%, while other rates may apply under the provisions of double tax treaties (DTTs).

The general 30% flat rate of CIT has been temporarily reduced to 23% for the accounting period which begins on or after 1 January 2012 and to 20% for the following two accounting periods that begin on or after 1 January 2013.

Reduced rates for companies with low paid-in capital and income
Companies and juristic partnerships with a paid-in capital not exceeding 5 million Thai baht (THB) at the end of any accounting period and income from the sale of goods and/ or the provision of service not exceeding THB 30 million in any accounting period will be subject to CIT at the following rates:

For the accounting period beginning on or after 1 January 2012:

Net profit (THB)	CIT rate (%)
0 to 150,000	0
150,001 to 1,000,000	15
Over 1,000,000	23

Thailand

For accounting periods beginning on or after 1 January 2013:

Net profit (THB)	CIT rate (%)
0 to 150,000	0
150,001 to 1,000,000	15
Over 1,000,000	20

Reduced rates for banks
Banks are subject to CIT at the rate of 10% with respect to profits derived from lending to non-Thai residents from foreign currency funds obtained from non-Thai sources (so-called 'out-out' business).

Petroleum income tax
Taxation on income from petroleum operations is imposed on petroleum concessionaire companies by the Petroleum Income Tax Acts (PITA). Companies taxed under the PITA are exempt from taxes and duties on income imposed under the Revenue Code and under any other laws. The exemption applies so long as the company pays taxes and duties on income subject to the PITA or on dividends paid out of income subject to the PITA.

Petroleum companies are taxed at the rate of 50% of their annual net profit from petroleum operations, including profit from the transfer of their concession interests and other activities incidental to petroleum operations. Deductions are allowed for 'ordinary and necessary' business expenses, as well as depreciation on capital expenditure, petroleum royalties, and other charges. Certain types of expenses are specifically disallowed for deduction, including interest.

Local income taxes
There are no local government taxes on income in Thailand.

Corporate residence

Corporate residence is determined by the place of incorporation. A company incorporated under the laws of Thailand is a resident company.

A company incorporated abroad is subject to CIT in Thailand if it is considered to be carrying on business in Thailand. The term 'carrying on business in Thailand' is broad and, subject to the provisions of DTTs, includes the presence of an employee, representative, or go-between that results in a foreign corporation deriving income or gains in Thailand.

Other taxes

Value-added tax (VAT)
VAT, at the current rate of 7%, is levied on the sale of goods and provision of services. However, exports are zero rated while a number of goods and services are exempt (e.g. basic groceries, education, healthcare, interest, leasing of immovable property, and sale of real estate).

Thailand

Customs duties

Basis of taxation
Customs duties are imposed under the Customs Act and the Customs Tariff Decree. Customs duties are collected on both imports and a very limited number of exports. Classification of imports is based on the Harmonized Commodity Description and Coding System (the so-called 'Harmonized System'). Thailand has adopted the ASEAN Harmonized Tariff Nomenclature ('AHTN') 2012, which is based on the Harmonized System 2012, as its latest import tariff nomenclature.

Duties are levied on a specific or an *ad valorem* basis, whichever is the higher, and the applied *ad valorem* duties range between 0% and 80%. Exemptions from import duties are available on particular items of goods as prescribed in the Customs Tariff Decree. Preferential duty rates are available on imported goods from countries that have a preferential free trade agreement (FTA) with Thailand.

Currently, Thailand has FTAs with the following countries:

* ASEAN member states (i.e. Singapore, Vietnam, Malaysia, Indonesia, Philippines, Cambodia, Laos, Myanmar, and Brunei).
* Peru.
* New Zealand.
* Australia.
* India.
* Japan.

Also, as part of ASEAN, Thailand has preferential trade agreements with the following countries:

* China.
* Korea.
* Japan.
* Australia and New Zealand.
* India.

Generally, the value of imports is based on their CIF (cost, insurance, and freight), whereas exported goods are based on their FOB (free on board).

Thailand has implemented the World Trade Organization (WTO) Valuation Agreement. The primary basis for the customs value is transaction value (i.e. the price actually paid or payable for the goods when sold for export). This is subject to adjustments for certain elements which are considered to form a part of the value for customs purposes, but are not yet included in the selling price. The elements that may need to be added include: royalties and license fees that are related to the goods and paid as a condition of sale; proceeds from subsequent resale in the importing country; value of goods or services supplied by the buyer, such as design or development fee related to imported goods; etc. If the declared price is evidently low or is unlikely to be the true value of such goods, Thai Customs will dispute the declared price.

Customs controls and procedures
Customs procedures for goods arriving in Thailand in any manner are similar to those existing in most other countries.

T

Thailand

An importer is required to file an entry form together with other requisite documents, including a bill of lading, invoice, and packing list via the e-Customs system.

Customs duties are due upon the arrival of the vessel carrying the imported goods, and goods may be stored in a bonded warehouse. Landing and storage charges must be paid before the goods are released.

Customs incentives schemes
Various customs incentives schemes, each with its own specific conditions and duty privileges, are available in Thailand, including the following:

- Duty and tax compensation ('Tax Coupons').
- Duty drawback under Section 19 bis for imported raw materials used in export production.
- Duty drawback for re-export in the same state under Section 19.
- Free zones (Customs or Industrial Estate Authority of Thailand Free Zones).
- Manufacturing bonded warehouses.
- General bonded warehouses.
- Board of Investment (BOI) promotion.

Excise tax

Basis of taxation
Excise tax is imposed on the sale of a selected range of commodities, whether manufactured locally or imported. Tax rates are based on *ad valorem* or a specific rate, whichever is higher. Tax liabilities arise on locally manufactured goods when leaving the factory and at the time of importation for imported goods.

Taxable goods and services

Commodities	Excise tax rate (%)
Fuel oil and petroleum products	0 to 36
Certain non-alcoholic beverages	0 to 25
Certain electrical appliances	0 to 30
Crystal glassware	0 to 15
Motor vehicles	0 to 50
Boats	0
Perfume products and cosmetics	0 to 15
Entertaining services, turf courses, and golf courses	0 to 10
Alcoholic beverages	0.1 to 60
Cigarettes containing tobacco	0.1 to 79
Woollen carpets	20
Motorcycles	3 to 5
Batteries	5 to 10
Playing cards	THB 30/100 card board
Ozone depleting substances	30

The manufacturer of the products must file a return and remit the tax due prior to taking the goods from the factory or bonded warehouse. If a VAT liability arises before the goods are taken out of such locations, the manufacturer must file a return and remit the excise tax to the Excise Department within 15 days from the end of the month.

Thailand

Stamp duty

Stamp duty is levied on 28 different types of documents and instruments, including contracts for hire of work, loans, share transfers, leases of land or buildings, and insurance policies. The rate of stamp duty varies depending on the type on agreement, but ranges from THB 1 per THB 1,000 of value on most contracts and agreements to a fixed amount per instrument on most commercial and other documents. Unstamped documents are not admissible as evidence in a civil lawsuit, and the surcharge can be as high as 600% of the duties for failure to pay the stamp duty on a timely basis.

Specific business tax (SBT)

SBT is collected on the gross revenue of certain businesses, not subject to VAT, at fixed rates. Commercial banking, similar financial businesses, and the sale of immovable property are taxed at 3% and life insurance at 2.5%.

The rate of SBT has been reduced to 0.01% for certain revenue derived by commercial banks and finance, securities, and credit foncier businesses as well as businesses with regular transactions similar to commercial banking.

An additional 10% of SBT is levied as municipality tax.

Capital taxes

There are no capital taxes in Thailand.

Local taxes

There are three major local taxes:

Household and land tax

Household and land tax is levied at 12.5% of assessable economic rental income.

Signboard tax

Signboard tax is levied at varying rates according to size. The minimum tax is THB 200 per annum.

Local development tax

Local development tax is levied at rates ranging between 0.25% and 0.95% of the value of land assessed by local authorities. This tax does not apply if the property is subject to household and land tax.

Branch income

Branches of foreign corporations pay income tax at the CIT rate on locally earned profits only. Branch profits remitted to the foreign head office are subject to additional tax at the rate of 10%. However, this is a tax on disposition of profits abroad and is not limited to remittances. For example, a credit of profits to the head office account in the books is held to be a disposition of profits abroad even though no remittance of funds takes place.

Income determination

Inventory valuation

Inventory is valued at the lower of cost or market price. Any recognised method of ascertaining the cost price may be used, but a change in the method may be made only

www.pwc.com/taxsummaries

Thailand **1895**

Thailand

with the prior approval of the director-general of the Revenue Department. Conformity between book and tax reporting is required.

Capital gains

There is no specific legislation governing capital gains. All capital gains earned by a Thai company are treated as ordinary revenue for tax purposes. Capital gains on the sale of investments derived from or in Thailand by a foreign company not carrying on business in Thailand are subject to a tax of 15%, withheld at source by the purchaser, unless otherwise exempt under a DTT.

The following income earned by a foreign company not carrying on business in Thailand is subject to 15% WHT:

- Interest on bonds/debentures issued by state enterprises.
- Difference between the redemption price and the initial sale price of bonds issued by the government, state enterprises, and specified institutions.
- Gains on the transfer of bonds issued by the government, state enterprises, and specified institutions.

Dividend income

Dividends received from a Thai company by a company listed on the SET are exempt from tax. Dividends received by a non-listed company from other Thai companies are also exempt from tax, provided that the company receiving the dividends holds at least 25% of the total voting shares without any cross-shareholding. The tax exemption applies on the condition that the shares must be held for at least three months before and three months after the dividends are received.

In other cases, where one Thai company receives dividends from another Thai company, one half thereof is exempt from tax.

Dividends received from outbound investment are exempt from tax provided that the Thai company receiving the dividends holds at least 25% of the shares with voting rights of the company paying the dividends for a period of not less than six months before the date on which the dividends are received and the dividends must be derived from net profit in the foreign country taxed at a rate of not less than 15%. In the event that a 'special law' in a particular foreign country provides a reduced tax rate or exemption for the net profit, the limited company which receives the dividends is still eligible for tax exemption.

Share of profits received by a Thai company or a foreign company carrying on business in Thailand from an unincorporated joint venture carrying on business in Thailand are exempt from CIT.

Stock dividends

Stock dividends are taxable to the recipient as ordinary income.

Interest income

Interest is taxable as income on the accrual basis.

Foreign income

Thailand incorporated companies are taxed on worldwide income. The Revenue Code does not describe how foreign income received by a Thailand-incorporated company is taxed, but the Revenue Department regards foreign branch income as taxable when earned and foreign dividend income as taxable when received. Double taxation is relieved by way of a credit against the tax chargeable in Thailand (*see Foreign tax credit in the Tax credits and incentives section*).

Deductions

Depreciation, amortisation, and depletion

Deductions for wear and tear and depreciation are allowed as a percentage of cost. If the rate of deduction adopted by a company under its own accounting method is lower than the maximum percentage of cost permitted, a deduction will be allowed only at the rate adopted by the company. The straight-line basis is the method most commonly used by companies, but any generally accepted basis, such as sum-of-the-years-digits method or double declining method, is permitted. The maximum permitted rates are as shown:

Asset	Maximum permitted rate (%)
Buildings:	
Durable buildings	5
Temporary buildings	100
Cost of acquisition of depletable natural resources	5
Cost of acquisition of lease rights:	
If there is no written lease agreement or if there is a written lease agreement containing a renewal clause whereby continual renewals are permitted	10
If there is a written lease agreement containing no renewal clause or containing a renewal clause but restricting renewable periods to a definitely limited duration	Percentage rate equals 100 divided by the sum of years of the original and renewable lease periods
Cost of acquisition of the right in a process, formula, goodwill, trademark, business license, patent, copyright, or any other right:	
If the period of use is unlimited	10
If the period of use is limited	Percentage rate equals 100 divided by the number of years of use
Other assets not mentioned above, excluding land and inventory	20

Special depreciation methods for certain assets

- Machinery and equipment for research and development (R&D) may initially be depreciated at 40% of cost with the remaining balance being depreciated at the above maximum rate of 20% per annum.
- Computer hardware and software may be depreciated within three accounting periods.
- Machinery acquired by companies located in officially-declared flooded areas and which have suffered from floods during the period from 25 July 2011 to 31 December 2012 may initially be depreciated at 40% of cost with the remaining balance being depreciated at the maximum rate of 20% per annum. The machines can be used for manufacturing own products or provision of manufacturing services and must be acquired and be ready for use between 25 July 2011 and 31 December 2012.

Thailand

Special depreciation method for small companies
Companies and juristic partnerships with fixed assets, excluding land, at a value of no more than THB 200 million and with no more than 200 employees are entitled to the following special depreciation methods in addition to those noted above:

* Machinery and equipment may initially be depreciated at 40% of cost, and the remaining balance will then be depreciated at a maximum rate of 20%.
* Computer hardware and software may initially be depreciated at 40% of cost, and the remaining balance can then be depreciated within three accounting periods.
* Factory buildings may initially be depreciated at 25% of cost, and the remaining balance will then be depreciated at a maximum rate of 5%.

Start-up expenses
Start-up expenses, such as incorporation expenses and registration fees, are deductible when the expenses are incurred.

Interest expenses
Interest on money borrowed for the purpose of acquiring profits or for the purpose of business is deductible. Interest incurred in respect of the construction or installation of fixed assets that require a period of time to get them ready for their intended use is considered to be capital expenditure.

Bad debts
Bad debts written off are deductible, provided that they are consistent with the rules, procedures, and conditions prescribed by the Ministerial Regulations.

Charitable contributions
Deductions for allowable charitable contributions and certain other donations may not exceed 2% of net taxable profit. Deductions for educational support as approved by the Ministry of Education may be allowed at the rate of 200% of the actual expense, but not exceeding 10% of net profit before deductions of the allowable charitable contributions and certain other donations. Furthermore, deductions for the support of public recreational facilities may also be allowed at the rate 200% of the actual expense, but not exceeding 10% of net profit before deductions of the allowable charitable contributions and certain other donations after including the educational support expense.

Fines and penalties
Fines, penalties, and surcharges charged under the Revenue Code are not deductible.

Taxes
In general, all taxes are deductible except CIT and VAT.

Other significant items
Other non-deductible expenses include, but are not limited to, the following:

* Expenses in the nature of provisions or reserves.
* Contributions to any fund (except an approved provident fund).

Net operating losses
Losses may be carried forward for the following five accounting periods. Carryback of losses is not permitted. A change in control of a loss company does not impact its loss carryforward.

Payments to foreign affiliates

A Thailand incorporated company may claim a deduction for royalties, management service fees, and interest charges, provided they are expended exclusively for the purpose of generating profits or for purposes of business in Thailand and are determined on an arm's-length basis.

Group taxation

Group taxation is not permitted in Thailand.

Transfer pricing

Thailand has no detailed transfer pricing legislation. However, transfer pricing guidelines issued by the Revenue Department define the term 'market price', detail the permitted transfer pricing methods, describe the transfer pricing documentation requirements, and allow taxpayers to apply for advance pricing agreements (APAs) in respect of any intended related party transaction.

The transfer pricing guidelines do not have the status of legislation but are internal directives that the Revenue officials must adhere to when conducting tax audits, reviews, or investigations. The guidelines are also intended to inform taxpayers about transfer pricing practices.

The guidelines authorise the use of both transactional transfer pricing methods (e.g. the comparable uncontrolled price, the resale price, and the cost plus methods) as well as profit based methods, in order to determine the market price of a transaction. No one method is preferred over another, and there is no hierarchy of acceptable methods. Although the Revenue Department would generally accept a taxpayer's chosen method, it retains the right to select an alternative method if it deems it to be more appropriate.

Thin capitalisation

There are no thin capitalisation rules. However, for certain businesses or as part of tax incentive conditions, a minimum capital requirement is needed.

Tax credits and incentives

The Board of Investment (BOI), by virtue of the Investment Promotion Act, provides tax incentives to certain activities within the following categories:

- Agriculture and agricultural products.
- Mining, ceramics, and basis metals.
- Light industry.
- Metal products, machinery, and transport equipment.
- Electronic industry and electrical appliance.
- Chemicals, paper, and plastics.
- Service and public utilities.

The tax incentives available include the following:

- Exemption from or reduction of import duties on imported machinery.
- Exemption from import duties on raw materials and components imported for manufacturing for export.

Thailand

* A reduction of up to 90% of import duties on raw or essential materials imported for manufacturing for domestic sale.
* Exemption from CIT equal to the amount of the investment, excluding the cost of land and working capital, for up to eight years depending on the promoted activity and location.
* Exclusion of dividends derived from promoted enterprises from taxable income during the period of exemption from CIT.

Additional incentives for enterprises located in an industrial estate or promotion zone include the following:

* Reduction of 50% of CIT for five years after the end of the tax holiday.
* Double deduction from taxable income of the cost of transportation, electricity, and water supply.
* Deduction from net profit of the project's infrastructure installation or construction costs in addition to normal depreciation; such deduction can be made from the net profit of one or several years within ten years from the date when revenue was first derived from the promoted activity.
* 75% import duty reduction of the normal rate on raw or essential materials used in manufacturing for domestic sales for five years.

Privileges for sustainable investment

Under a BOI policy in regard to sustainable investment, all areas of the country, except Bangkok, are designated as Investment Promotion Zones until December 2012. The BOI also provides special privileges to target industries, which have been classified in three categories as follows:

* Activities related to energy conservation and alternative energy.
* Activities related to eco-friendly materials and products.
* High-technology businesses.

Any activity which is classified under the above categories will obtain special privileges as a priority activity, e.g. CIT exemption for a period of eight years with no limit on the amount, import duty exemption for the import of machinery, 50% reduction in the rate of CIT on net profit for five years after the end of the tax holiday, etc.

Applications for the above measures must be submitted before 31 December 2012.

Special development zone

A special development zone has been established in five provinces in the far south of Thailand in which a company or juristic partnership located therein will be subject to CIT at the rate of 3% of the net profit derived from the revenue earned from the manufacture or sale of goods or provision of services from the accounting period that begins on or after 1 January 2010, until the accounting period that ends on or after 31 December 2012.

Regional operating headquarters (ROH)

ROH means a company organised under the Thai law providing administrative, technical assistance, or supporting services to its domestic or overseas affiliated enterprises or branches in at least three countries other than Thailand with a paid-in capital of at least THB 10 million on the last day of any accounting period.

Tax incentives available to ROH are under two packages, known as the old and the new package, either of which taxpayers may elect to follow. However, the applications to obtain the privilege under the new package have to be made before 14 November 2015.

The following corporate tax incentives are available under the old package:

- 10% CIT on service income derived from foreign branches or affiliated enterprises.
- 10% CIT on interest income received as a result of re-lending to foreign branches or affiliated enterprises funds borrowed by the ROH.
- 10% CIT on royalty income derived from foreign branches or affiliated enterprises and which is generated from R&D work performed in Thailand.
- CIT exemption on dividends received from domestic or overseas affiliated enterprises.
- WHT exemption on dividends received by foreign corporate shareholders not carrying on business in Thailand from the qualified ROH profit.

The corporate tax incentives available under the new package are as follows:

- In the case where service fees and royalties received by the ROH from affiliated enterprises in foreign countries amount to at least 50% of the total income of the ROH (ROH income plus non-ROH income):
  - CIT exemption for ten years on service income derived from foreign branches or affiliated enterprises (*see Note below*).
  - 10% CIT for ten years on service income derived from domestic branches or affiliated enterprises and on qualified royalties and qualified interest income (*see Note below*).
  - CIT exemption for ten years on dividends received by ROH from domestic or overseas affiliated enterprises (*see Note below*).
  - WHT exemption on dividends received by foreign corporate shareholders not carrying on business in Thailand from the qualified ROH profit.
- In the case where service fees and royalties received by the ROH from affiliated enterprises in foreign countries amount to less than 50% of the total income of the ROH (ROH income plus non-ROH income):
  - CIT exemption for ten years on service income derived from foreign branches or affiliated enterprises (*see Note below*).
  - 10% CIT for ten years on service income derived from domestic branches or affiliated enterprises (*see Note below*).

Note: The corporate tax benefits will be extended to 15 years provided that as at the end of the tenth fiscal year, the accumulated business spending paid to recipients in Thailand for ten fiscal periods has exceeded THB 150 million.

International procurement center (IPC)
The IPC will be subject to CIT on its net profit from qualified income at the rate of 15% for five consecutive accounting periods. IPC refers to a company established under Thai law carrying on the business of procuring and selling goods, raw materials, and parts to affiliated companies.

Qualified income includes:

- Income from procuring and selling goods outside Thailand to affiliated companies situated abroad whereby the goods must not be brought into Thailand.
- Income from procuring parts and raw materials either in Thailand or abroad for sale to affiliated companies situated abroad for manufacturing goods outside Thailand by the affiliated companies.

T

Thailand

Applications to obtain the privilege must be submitted within two years from 9 May 2011.

Foreign tax credit

A Thai company can use foreign tax paid on business income or dividends as a credit against its CIT liability. However, the credit cannot exceed the amount of Thai tax on the income.

Withholding taxes

WHT rate schedule

Recipient	Dividends (%)	Interest (%)	Royalties (%)
Resident corporations	0/10 (1)	0/1 (2)	3
Resident individuals	10	15	Progressive rate (3)
Non-resident corporations and individuals:			
Non-treaty	10	15	15
Treaty:			
Armenia	10	10/15 (4)	15
Australia	10	10/15 (4)	15
Austria	10	10/15 (4)	15
Bahrain	10	10/15 (4)	15
Bangladesh	10	10/15 (4)	15
Belgium	10	10/15 (4)	5/15 (9)
Bulgaria	10	10/15 (4)	5/15 (5)
Canada	10	10/15 (4)	5/15 (6)
Chile	10	10/15 (4)	10/15 (26)
China	10	10/15 (4)	15
Cyprus	10	10/15 (23)	5/10/15 (7)
Czech Republic	10	10/15 (4)	5/10/15 (8)
Denmark	10	10/15 (4)	5/15 (9)
Finland	10	10/15 (4)	15
France	10	3/10/15 (10)	0/5/15 (11)
Germany	10	10/15 (4)	5/15 (9)
Hong Kong	10	10/15 (12)	5/10/15 (13)
Hungary	10	10/15 (4)	15
India	10	10/15 (4)	15
Indonesia	10	10/15 (4)	15
Israel	10	10/15 (4)	5/15 (14)
Italy	10	10/15 (4)	5/15 (9)
Japan	10	10/15 (4)	15
Korea, Republic of	10	10/15 (12)	5/10/15 (28)
Kuwait	10	10/15 (4)	15
Laos	10	10/15 (4)	15
Luxembourg	10	10/15 (4)	15
Malaysia	10	10/15 (4)	15

Recipient	Dividends (%)	Interest (%)	Royalties (%)
Mauritius	10	10/15 (4)	5/15 (5)
Myanmar	10	10	5/10/15 (24)
Nepal	10	10/15 (4)	15
Netherlands	10	10/15 (4)	5/15 (9)
New Zealand	10	10/15 (12)	10/15 (15)
Norway	10	10/15 (4)	5/10/15 (16)
Oman	10	10/15 (17)	15
Pakistan	10	10/15 (4)	0/10/15 (18)
Philippines	10	10/15 (27)	15
Poland	10	10/15 (4)	0/5/15 (19)
Romania	10	10/15 (4)	15
Russia	10	10/15 (25)	15
Seychelles	10	10/15 (4)	15
Singapore	10	10/15 (4)	15
Slovenia	10	10/15 (4)	10/15 (20)
South Africa	10	10/15 (4)	15
Spain	10	10/15 (4)	5/8/15 (21)
Sri Lanka	10	10/15 (4)	15
Sweden	10	10/15 (4)	15
Switzerland	10	10/15 (4)	5/10/15 (8)
Turkey	10	10/15 (4)	15
Ukraine	10	10/15 (4)	15
United Arab Emirates	10	10/15 (4)	15
United Kingdom	10	10/15 (4)	5/15 (9)
United States	10	10/15 (12)	5/8/15 (22)
Uzbekistan	10	10/15 (4)	15
Vietnam	10	10/15 (4)	15

Notes

1. The zero rate applies to a recipient company listed on the SET.
2. The 1% rate applies to interest paid to all resident corporations other than banks or finance companies, except where interest arises from bonds or debentures.
3. The progressive rate is in accordance with the personal income tax schedule.
4. The 10% rate applies to interest paid to a recipient that is a bank or financial institution (including an insurance company).
5. The 5% rate applies to royalties paid for the use of, or the right to use, any copyright of literary, artistic, or scientific work excluding cinematograph films and films, tapes or discs for radio, or television broadcasting.
6. The 5% rate applies to royalties paid for the production or reproduction of any literary, dramatic, musical, or artistic work excluding royalties with respect to motion picture films and works on film or videotape for use in connection with television.
7. The 5% rate applies to royalties paid for the use of, or the right to use, any copyright of literary, dramatic, musical, artistic, or scientific work including software, cinematograph films or films or tapes used for radio or television broadcasting; and the 10% rate applies to royalties paid for the use of, or the right to use, industrial, commercial, or scientific equipment or for information concerning industrial, commercial, or scientific experience.
8. The 5% rate applies to royalties paid for the alienation or the use of, or the right to use, any copyright of literary, artistic, or scientific work excluding cinematograph films or films or tapes used for radio or television broadcasting, and the 10% rate for the alienation of any patent, trademark, design, or model, plan, secret formula, or process.
9. The 5% rate applies to royalties paid for the use of, or the right to use, any copyright of literary, artistic, or scientific work.
10. The 3% rate applies to interest paid on loans or credits granted for four years or more with the participation of a financing public institution to a statutory body or to an enterprise in relation to the sale of any equipment or to the survey, the installation, or the supply of industrial, commercial,

T

Thailand

or scientific premises and of public works. The 10% rate applies to interest paid to any financial institution.

11. The zero rate applies to royalties paid to a contracting state or state-owned company with respect to films or tapes, and the 5% rate to royalties for the alienation or the use of, or the right to use, any copyright of literary, artistic, or scientific work.

12. The 10% rate applies to (i) interest paid to a bank or financial institution (including an insurance company) and (ii) interest paid with respect to indebtedness arising as a consequence of a sale on credit of any equipment, merchandise, or services, except where the sale was between persons not dealing with each other at arm's length.

13. The 5% rate applies to royalties paid for the use of, or the right to use, any copyright of literary, artistic, or scientific work and the 10% rate for the use of, or the right to use, any patent, trademark, design, or model, plan, secret formula, or process.

14. The 5% rate applies to royalties paid for the use of, or the right to use, any copyright of literary, artistic, or scientific work excluding cinematograph films or films, or tapes used for radio, or television broadcasting.

15. The 10% rate applies to royalties paid for the use of, or the right to use, any copyright; or the use of, or the right to use, any industrial, scientific, or commercial equipment; or the use of, or the right to use, any motion picture film, or film or videotape or any other recording for use in connection with television, or tape or any other recording for use in connection with radio broadcasting; or the reception of, or the right to receive, visual images or sounds, or both, transmitted to the public by satellite or, cable, optic fibre, or similar technology; or the use in connection with television or radio broadcasting, or the right to use in connection with television or radio broadcasting, visual images, or sounds, or both, transmitted by satellite or cable, optic fibre, or similar technology.

16. The 5% rate applies to royalties paid for the use of, or the right to use, any copyright of literary, artistic, or scientific work, and the 10% rate applies to royalties paid for the use of, or the right to use, industrial, commercial, or scientific equipment.

17. The 10% rate applies to (i) interest paid to a bank or financial institution (including an insurance company) and (ii) interest from a loan or debt claim that is guaranteed by the government.

18. The zero rate applies to royalties paid to a contracting state or a state-owned company with respect to films or tapes, and the 10% rate applies to royalties paid for the alienation or the use of, or the right to use, any copyright of literary, artistic, or scientific work.

19. The zero rate applies to royalties paid to a contracting state or a state owned company with respect to films or tapes. The 5% rate applies to royalties paid for the alienation or the use of, or the right to use, any copyright of literary, artistic, or scientific work excluding cinematograph films or tapes used for television or broadcasting.

20. The 10% rate applies to royalties paid for the use of, or the right to use, any copyright of literary or artistic work including motion pictures, live broadcasting, film, tape, or other means of the use or reproduction in connection with radio and television broadcasting, and for the use of, or the right to use industrial, commercial, or scientific equipment.

21. The 5% rate applies to royalties paid for the use of, or the right to use, any copyright of literary, dramatic, musical, artistic, or scientific work excluding cinematograph films or films or tapes used for radio or television broadcasting. The 8% rate applies to royalties in consideration of financial leasing for the use of, or the right to use, industrial, commercial, or scientific equipment.

22. The 5% rate applies to royalties paid for the use of any copyright of literary, artistic, or scientific work including software, motion pictures, and works on film, tape, or other means of reproduction for use in connection with radio or television broadcasting. The 8% rate applies to royalties paid for the use of, or the right to use, industrial, commercial, or scientific equipment.

23. The 10% rate applies to interest paid (i) to a recipient that is a bank or financial institution (including an insurance company); (ii) in connection with the sale on credit of any industrial, commercial, or scientific equipment; or (iii) in connection with the sale on credit of any merchandise by one enterprise to another enterprise.

24. The 5% rate applies to royalties paid for the use of, or the right to use, any copyright of literary, artistic, or scientific work. The 10% rate applies to royalties for the consideration for any services of a managerial or consultancy nature or for information concerning industrial, commercial, or scientific experience.

25. The 10% rate applies to interest paid to the following recipients (i) in the case of a resident of Russia, any institution having a license to carry on banking operations; and (ii) in the case of a resident of Thailand, any financial institution (including an insurance company).

26. The 10% rate applies to royalties paid for the use of, or the right to use, any copyright of literary, artistic, or scientific work, or for the use of, or the right to use, industrial, commercial, or scientific equipment.

27. In case of interest arising in Thailand, the 10% rate applies to interest paid to a Philippines financial institution (including an insurance company). In the case of interest arising in the Philippines, the 10% rate applies in respect of public issues of bonds, debentures, or similar obligations.

28. The 5% rate applies to royalties paid for the use of, or the right to use, any copyright of literary, artistic, or scientific work including software and motion pictures and works on film, tape, or other means of reproduction for use in connection with radio or television broadcasting. The 10% rate applies to the use of, or the right to use, any patent, trademark, design, or model, plan, secret formula, or process.

Tax administration

Taxable period

The tax year for a company is its accounting period, which must be of 12 months' duration. However, it may be less than 12 months in the case of the first accounting period after incorporation, the accounting period of dissolution, or after approval for a change in the accounting period has been received from the Revenue Department and the Business Development Department.

Tax returns

The Thai system is one of self-assessment. A company prepares and files its tax returns by the due dates and at the same time pays the taxes calculated to be due. The annual CIT return is due 150 days from the closing date of the accounting period.

Payment of tax

CIT is paid twice in each year. A half-year return must be filed within two months after the end of the first six months of an accounting period. The tax to be paid is computed on one-half of the estimated profit for the full accounting period, except for listed companies, banks, certain other financial institutions, and other companies under prescribed conditions where the tax is based on the actual net profit for the first six months. The balance of the tax due is payable within 150 days from the closing date of the accounting period, along with the annual tax return. Credit is given for the amount of tax paid at the half-year.

Audit cycle

If, within a period of two years from the date of filing a tax return, the assessment officer has reason to believe that false or inadequate information has been declared in a return, the assessment officer has the power to issue a summons requesting the presence of the person responsible, or a witness, for examination, and to order either of them to produce accounts or other relevant evidence, provided that advance notice of seven days is given. The subsequent examination of the books and records is normally carried out at the company›s offices if it is inconvenient to transfer all the documents to the tax office. After completion of the examination, the assessment officer has the power to adjust the amounts previously assessed or included in a return on the basis of the evidence, and issue a further assessment for tax together with penalties and surcharges, or adjust the amount of losses available for carryforward.

Tax audits may cover the previous five accounting periods from the date of filing a tax return with the approval of the Director-General if the assessment officer has evidence of an intention to evade tax or in the case of a claim for a refund of tax.

However, under the Civil and Commercial Code, the Revenue Department can assess tax for up to ten years.

Statute of limitations

The statute of limitations for tax is ten years.

Topics of focus for tax authorities

Topics of focus for tax authorities include the following:

- Deductibility of management service fees or expenses allocated to Thailand by foreign affiliates.
- International inter-company transactions and transfer pricing.

T

Timor-Leste

PwC contact

Tim Watson
PT Prima Wahana Caraka - PricewaterhouseCoopers
Plaza 89, Jl. H.R. Rasuna Said Kav. X-7 No.6
Jakarta 12940 - Indonesia
Tel: +62 21 5212901
Email: tim.robert.watson@id.pwc.com

Significant developments

Timor-Leste initially adopted the Indonesian tax laws in place in 1999 with appropriate modifications. In 2008, however, Timor-Leste embarked upon a policy of taxation reform. The cornerstone of this reform was the introduction of the Tax and Duties Act (TDA). The TDA provided for the consolidation of the taxation regimes previously applicable to Timor-Leste. This consolidation extended to the taxation of petroleum operations with the general exception of petroleum operations in the Joint Petroleum Development Area (JPDA). As a result, considerable tax variation continues to exist in relation to petroleum activities according to the oil and gas concession in question.

Taxes on corporate income

Timor-Leste residents are subject to income tax on taxable income that is essentially the difference between gross income and allowable deductions. The income of companies is generally subject to corporate income tax (CIT) at a flat rate of 10%.

Companies, etc. are taxable on a stand-alone basis (i.e. there is no grouping or ability to transfer tax losses). Timor-Leste has also not entered into any double tax treaties (DTTs).

Industry-specific CIT rates
The rate of CIT for oil and gas contractors is, however, 30%, while sub-contractors are subject to CIT at the flat rate of (generally) 6%.

Supplemental Petroleum Tax (SPT) also applies for oil and gas contractors and is imposed on 'accumulated net receipts' using a specific formula. SPT is deductible for CIT calculation purposes.

Separate tax arrangements apply for petroleum activities in the JPDA (*see the Other issues section*).

Corporate residence

The definition of a corporate resident (resident legal person) covers a wide range of entities, such as companies, partnerships, trusts, governmental institutions, and unincorporated associations incorporated, formed, organised, or established in Timor-Leste.

Permanent establishment (PE)
A PE is defined as a fixed place of business through which the business of a person is wholly or partly carried on, including:

- A place of management.
- A branch.
- A representative office.
- An office.
- A factory.
- A workshop.
- A mine, an oil or gas well, a quarry, or any other place of extraction of natural resources, including any place of drilling for mineral exploration.
- A fishery, place where animal husbandry is conducted, farm, plantation, or forest.
- A construction, installation, or assembly project.
- The furnishing of a service through employees or other personnel, if conducted for more than 60 days in any 12-month period.
- A natural or legal person acting as dependent agent.
- An agent or employee of a non-resident insurance company, if the agent or employee collects premiums or insures risks in Timor-Leste.

Other taxes

Sales tax
Sales tax is imposed on the sales tax value of:

- taxable goods imported into Timor-Leste and
- taxable goods sold or taxable services provided in Timor-Leste on or after the date specified by Parliament.

Taxpayers liable for sales tax are as follows:

- A taxpayer who imports taxable goods into Timor-Leste.
- A taxpayer who sells taxable goods in Timor-Leste.
- A taxpayer who provides taxable services in Timor-Leste.

The rates of sales tax are 2.5% for taxable goods imported into Timor-Leste and 0% for the sale of taxable goods and provision of taxable services in Timor-Leste.

Services tax
Services tax is imposed at 5% on any gross consideration of more than 500 United States dollars (USD) received by a taxpayer for the provision of hotel, restaurant and bar, or telecommunication services.

Import duties
Import duty applies to imported goods (except for specifically exempted goods) at 2.5% of the 'customs value' of the goods. Customs value is the fair market value including cost, insurance, and freight (CIF), as stated in the General Agreement on Tariffs and Trade (GATT) rules.

The following goods are exempted from import duty:

- Goods accompany a person arriving in Timor-Leste from another territory (limitations apply).
- Imports of the type exempted under specific international conventions.
- Goods re-imported in the same condition as when they were exported.
- Goods, other than alcohol or tobacco, imported by registered charitable organisations, registered under any law of Timor-Leste, provided the goods are to

T

Timor-Leste

be used for charitable purposes of humanitarian assistance and relief, education, or health care.
- Other goods for temporary admission, if the importer has provided security for the import duty in the prescribed manner.
- Goods for consumption by international staff of the United Nations Integrated Mission in East Timor or members of peace keeping forces from contingent countries, if the goods are sold in conformity with prescribed rules of sale.
- Certain infant and female hygiene products.
- Other goods imported into Timor-Leste other than as personal goods accompanying a traveller and where the import duty that would be imposed on the import would be USD 10 or less.

Excise tax

Excise tax is imposed on excisable goods where removed from a warehouse by a registered manufacturer for consumption in Timor-Leste or imported into Timor-Leste.

Below is the list of excisable goods and the respective rates of excise tax:

Goods	Excise tax rate
Beer	USD 1.90/litre
Wine, vermouth, fermented beverages (such as cider)	USD 2.50/litre
Ethyl alcohol (other than denatured) and other alcoholic beverages	USD 8.90/litre
Gasoline, diesel fuel products, and other petroleum products	USD 0.06/litre
Tobacco and tobacco products	USD 19.00/kg
Cigarette lighters	12% of the excise value
Smoking pipes	12% of the excise value
Arms and ammunition	200% of the excise value
Motor cars and small passenger vehicles (with an excise value exceeding USD 70,000)	35% of the excise value
Private boats and aircrafts	20% of the excise value

Note that the excise value of excisable goods imported into Timor-Leste is the total of the customs value and any import duty imposed. The excise value of excisable goods manufactured in Timor-Leste is their fair market value at the time of removal from the manufacturer's warehouse.

Goods on the above list are excisable goods, other than:

- goods imported into Timor-Leste that are exempt from import duty, or
- goods exported from Timor-Leste within 28 days after their production or import, as long as the taxpayer liable to excise tax submits to the Banking and Payments Authority documentary proof of the export of goods.

Branch income

The taxable income of a non-resident carrying out business activities through a PE is calculated by reference to:

- the income attributable to the PE

- any sales of goods or merchandise of the same or similar kind as those sold through the PE, and
- any other business activities carried on in Timor-Leste of the same or similar kind as those effected through the PE.

Other principles for determining the taxable income of a PE in Timor-Leste are:

- Profit is calculated as if the PE was a Timor-Leste entity engaged in the same or similar activities under the same or similar conditions and dealt with wholly independently from the non-resident person of which it is a PE.
- Subject to this, deductions may be claimed for expenses incurred for the purposes of the business activities of the PE, including head office expenditures, whether incurred in Timor-Leste or elsewhere.
- No deductions may be claimed for amounts paid or payable by the PE to its head office or to another PE of the non-resident person, other than towards the reimbursement of actual expenses incurred by the non-resident person to third parties, by way of:
  - royalties, fees, or other similar payments
  - compensation for any services (including management services) provided to the PE, and
  - interest on money lent to the PE (except for banking businesses).

Income determination

Taxable business profits are determined on the basis of net profit for financial accounting purposes in accordance with International Financial Reporting Standards (IFRS), subject to certain modifications in the TDA. In general, income is assessable when 'receivable', while expenses are deductible when 'payable'. A taxpayer with turnover of less than USD 100,000 may, however, elect to pay tax on a cash basis.

Gross income is defined widely to mean "any realised increase in economic capacity in whatever name or form which can be used for consumption or to increase the wealth of the taxpayer other than wages that are subject to Wages Income Tax (WIT)".

The gross income for a tax year is the total amount earned by the taxpayer, including but not limited to, business income, property income, lottery prizes or awards, and refunds of tax payments previously deducted as an expense.

Exempted income
The following income is tax exempt:

- Any aid or donations, provided that the donor and recipient do not have any business or control relationship.
- Gifts received by relatives within one degree of direct lineage, or by a religious, educational, or charitable organisation, provided that the donor and recipient do not have any business or control relationship.
- Inheritance.
- Assets (including cash) received by a resident in exchange for shares or a capital contribution.
- Any amount paid by an insurance company to a resident in connection with health, accident, life, or education.
- Dividends.
- Any contribution paid by an employer or employee to an approved pension fund.

Timor-Leste

- Income derived by an approved pension fund.
- Remuneration received for services provided by a natural person (individual) if the remuneration is financed out of the Trust Fund for East Timor.

Foreign income

Under the worldwide income principle, a resident taxpayer is required to calculate income that is not only Timor-Leste sourced but also foreign sourced. In the case that the foreign-sourced income is taxed at source, Timor-Leste allows a foreign tax credit for the particular tax year (*see Foreign tax credit in the Tax credits and incentives section*).

Deductions

The taxable income of residents and non-residents who have a PE in Timor-Leste shall be determined on the basis of gross income reduced by:

- expenditure and losses incurred from the alienation of assets or the discharge of debt in the conduct of a taxable business activity
- expenditure incurred in deriving any other amounts included in gross income
- any loss on disposal of an asset other than assets held on personal account
- contributions to an approved pension fund, and
- bad and doubtful debts (subject to various tests).

Depreciation and amortisation

'Depreciable assets' include any tangible movable property with a useful life exceeding one year that is wholly or partly used for taxable business activities. 'Intangible assets' include property, other than tangible movable property or immovable property, with a useful life exceeding one year that is used for taxable business activities.

There are provisions for election of either straight-line or double-declining methods, the pooling of assets and *de minimis* exceptions.

The rate of tax depreciation/amortisation (for non-petroleum operations) is, however, set at 100%, meaning that taxpayers are, in effect, entitled to a full and up-front deduction. In circumstances where the asset is only partly used for the conduct of taxable business activities, the deduction is reduced by the proportion of its non-taxable business use.

Deductions not allowed or conditional deductions

The following are not deductible to a resident or non-resident with a PE in Timor-Leste:

- The distribution of profits in whatever name or form.
- Expenses incurred for the personal benefit of a taxpayer, a taxpayer's dependents, shareholders, partners, or members.
- Reserves, other than as provided for under the TDA.
- Insurance premiums for health, accident, life, or education insurance paid by a natural person, except where paid by an employer and treated as part of the income of the employee.
- Excessive compensation paid by a legal person to a member of the legal person, or paid between associates.
- Gifts, aid, donations, or inheritances if exempt from income tax in the hands of the recipient.
- Timor-Leste or foreign income tax.
- Salaries paid to a partner in a partnership.

- Tax and other penalties for violation of law and regulation.
- Interest expenses, unless the expense is incurred by a financial institution.
- A bribe, or any similar payment.
- Expenditure or losses incurred to the extent recoverable under an insurance policy or a contract of indemnities.
- Bad debts.

Losses
Losses from previous years may be carried forward indefinitely. However, the carried forward loss from the disposal of assets may only be utilised against gains arising the disposal of assets. Foreign-sourced losses may be offset only against foreign-sourced income of a particular country.

Group taxation

Companies, etc. are taxable on a stand-alone basis (i.e. there is no grouping or ability to transfer tax losses).

Tax credits and incentives

Foreign tax credit
A resident taxpayer is entitled to a credit for any foreign income tax paid in respect of foreign-source income. The foreign tax credit is calculated separately for each foreign country from which income is derived by a taxpayer. The value of such tax credits is limited to the value of the Timor-Leste income tax payable on that income. There is no deduction or carryforward of any excess foreign tax credit.

Withholding taxes

Withholding tax (WHT) is imposed on the following payments by residents to a resident:

Type of payment	WHT rate (%)	Final/non-final tax
Royalties	10	Not final, except where paid to an individual
Rent (land and building)	10	Not final, except where paid to an individual
Prize and winnings	10	Final
Construction/building activities	2	Final *
Construction consulting services	4	Final *
Air and sea transportation	2.64	Final *
Mining and mining support services	4.5	Final *

* The default position is that such amounts will be final taxed. The income recipient can elect to have these payments for services not subjected to final tax by submitting a notification letter to the Timor-Leste Revenue Service.

Payments of Timor-Leste source income made by a resident to a non-resident are subject to WHT at 10%. Timor-Leste has also not entered into any DTTs.

Timor-Leste

Where WHT is applied as a final tax, the taxed income is not included in the recipients' taxable income for income tax purposes. Accordingly, expenses incurred in deriving income that is subject to final tax are not deductible for income tax purposes.

Tax administration

Taxable period

The standard tax year is the calendar year, although different accounting year-ends can be granted upon application.

Tax returns

CIT returns are to be filed annually by the 15th day of the third month following the year end.

Service tax, excise tax, sales tax, and WHT are to be filed monthly by the 15th day of the following month.

Payment of tax

CIT due shall be settled to the Banking and Payments Authority or another entity nominated by the Tax Administration by the date of filing (*see above*).

Service tax, excise tax, sales tax, and WHT should be settled to the Banking and Payments Authority or another entity nominated by the Tax Administration by the 15th day after the end of the following month.

Penalties

If a taxpayer fails to deliver the tax form on time, it shall be liable to an additional tax of USD 100. If a taxpayer failed to deliver all or part of any tax due by the due date, that taxpayer shall be liable to an additional tax of 5% of the amount due plus an additional 1% of the tax due on the 15th day of each month following the due date and:

- if the failure was due to gross carelessness on the part of the person, further additional tax of 25% of the tax that remains unpaid, or
- if the failure was due to a deliberate attempt to avoid payment of tax, further additional tax of 100% of the tax that remains unpaid.

If a taxpayer has understated the tax due in the tax form, that taxpayer shall be liable to an additional tax of 15% and:

- if the understatement was due to gross carelessness on the part of the taxpayer, further additional tax of 25% of the tax understated, or
- if the understatement was due to a deliberate attempt to avoid payment of tax, further additional tax of 100% of the tax understated.

Statute of limitations

The Timor-Leste tax authority may issue an assessment notice or amend an assessment notice only within five years from the date of filing of the return. In the event of a deliberate tax evasion or fraud, there is no time limit for the issuance of an assessment notice.

Assessments may occur upon the following:

- The delivery of a tax return form and payment.

- After receipt of a return where the Commissioner believes a return is incorrect.
- Where a taxpayer fails to file a return.

Assessments may be amended according to the following events:

- By the taxpayer upon delivery to the Commissioner of an amended assessment.
- Via a taxpayer request to the Commissioner.
- Via specific amendment by the Commissioner.

Other issues

Taxation of petroleum operations

The taxation of petroleum operations in Timor-Leste is partly covered by the TDA. However, the TDA operates only to modify the taxation of petroleum activities pursuant to a number of legacy tax regimes. These modifications apply to contractors, sub-contractors, and any other parties receiving income from the supply of goods or services to a contractor or sub-contractor.

A contractor is defined as a person who has an interest in a petroleum agreement (being a Production Sharing Contract or PSC) with the designated authority in Timor-Leste. A sub-contractor includes any person supplying goods or services directly or indirectly to a contractor in respect of petroleum operations.

Specific provisions for the taxation of petroleum operations include:

- A CIT rate for contractors of 30% on taxable income, while sub-contractors will generally be taxed on a final WHT basis at rate 6% (although see JPDA below).
- No tax on branch profit remittances (although see JPDA below).
- Where 'net receipts' exceed specified levels, a SPT can apply.
- The 'ring fencing' of income and expenditure within the contract area.
- Modified deductibility rules, including around the deductibility of interest for contractors and a modified depreciation regime.
- A specific WHT regime.

Special tax regime for the JPDA

The JPDA is a geographical area in the Timor Sea known to be rich in hydrocarbon deposits. The JPDA covers the 'Annex F' PSCs (see below) known as Bayu-Undan (including the Elang Kakatua and Kakatua North fields) PSCs, and Greater Sunrise. The JPDA also covers a number of non-Annex F PSCs.

Pursuant to the Timor Sea Treaty (TST), the JPDA is technically within the taxation jurisdiction of both in Timor-Leste and Australia and therefore falls under the joint control and management of Timor-Leste and Australia. Annex F of the TST refers to the PSCs with commercial discoveries at the time of the TST signing and so imbeds a number of historical tax principles.

Control of the JPDA is exercised by a 'Joint Authority' containing representation from Australia and Timor-Leste. The petroleum activities covering the exploration, development, processing, transportation, and marketing of hydrocarbons are carried out pursuant to PSCs entered into between the designated authority and the oil company in question.

T

Timor-Leste

Under the TST, revenue from the JPDA PSCs is split 90% for Timor-Leste and 10% for Australia. Accordingly, for tax calculation purposes, business profits or losses of an entity carrying on business in the JPDA are reduced by the 'reduction percentage' of 90% for Timor-Leste and 10% for Australia. This effectively means that the tax rates applied by Timor-Leste and Australia are at 90% and 10% of their respective national level.

For Timor-Leste, these tax rates are generally 30% for all participants with PEs and an 8% or 20% final WHT for non-residents (according to the PSC). A 10% VAT also applies.

The tax regime as outlined under 'Taxation of petroleum operations' above also applies in the JPDA (except for Annex F PSCs) .This is, however, with a number of important modifications, including the exclusion of the service tax, excise tax, sales tax , import duty, and WIT.

Trinidad and Tobago

PwC contact

Allyson West
PricewaterhouseCoopers
11 - 13 Victoria Avenue, Port of Spain, Trinidad & Tobago
Tel: +1 868 299 0700
Email: allyson.west@tt.pwc.com

Significant developments

The following developments occurred in the last year:

- The VAT registration threshold for companies making commercial supplies increased from 200,000 Trinidad and Tobago dollars (TTD) to TTD 360,000 for a 12-month period.
- Furniture and fittings previously allocated to Class A and subject to wear and tear allowance (tax depreciation) at the rate of 10% under the declining-balance method have been re-allocated to Class B and now attract wear and tear at the rate of 25%.
- 130% wear and tear allowance is now available for expenditure incurred in compressed natural gas (CNG) related initiatives.
- An allowance of 50% of the expenditure incurred on the purchase of equipment for the retail dispensing of CNG and liquefied natural gas (LNG) is now available, up to a maximum of TTD 2 million per station.
- 150% wear and tear allowance is now available on the expense incurred in relation to solar heaters, wind turbines, and photovoltaic systems.

Taxes on corporate income

A Trinidad and Tobago resident corporation is taxed on worldwide income. A non-resident company engaged in business in Trinidad and Tobago is taxed only on income directly or indirectly accruing in or derived from Trinidad and Tobago.

The standard corporation tax rate is 25%, but this varies in the case of certain classes of companies. The current corporation tax rates are as follows:

Type of company	Corporation tax rate (%)
Ordinary companies	25
Petroleum related companies	35
Life insurance companies	15
Petroleum production companies (petroleum profits tax)	50

Business levy

Corporations are subject to a business levy at the rate of 0.2% of gross revenue or receipts where the levy exceeds the corporation tax liability. Exemption is available for certain companies, including petroleum companies and companies whose annual turnover is less than TTD 200,000. The levy is a non-deductible expense for corporation tax purposes.

T

Trinidad and Tobago

Green fund levy
A green fund levy of 0.1% is applicable to companies and partnerships doing business in Trinidad and Tobago. This levy is payable quarterly and is neither a deduction in computing chargeable income nor a credit against corporation tax due.

Unemployment levy
Only petroleum companies remain liable to the unemployment levy, at the rate of 5% of taxable profits. No set-off for prior year losses is permitted in computing the liability.

Supplementary petroleum tax (SPT)
SPT is chargeable on the gross income (derived from the sale of crude oil) less royalties and overriding royalties paid on the crude oil sold. The tax is computed separately in respect of land and marine operations and is a quarterly tax based on the actual gross income for each quarter.

The SPT is deductible in arriving at profits subject to petroleum profits tax.

Corporate residence

Corporate residence is determined by reference to the location of the central management and control of the business of a company.

Other taxes

Value-added tax (VAT)
VAT is applicable to a wide range of goods and services. The standard rate applicable to commercial supplies is 15%.

Certain basic unprocessed foods and agricultural supplies are zero-rated, as are crude oil, natural gas, and all exported goods and services. Hotel accommodations and yachting services to non-residents are zero-rated.

A number of services, including financial services, real estate brokerage, residential rentals, and educational services, are exempt. However, certain financial services are subject to a transaction tax at a rate of 15%. Imported inputs of highly capital-intensive manufacturers are exempt from VAT.

The VAT registration threshold for companies making commercial supplies is TTD 360,000 for a 12-month period.

Hotel accommodation tax
Hotels are subject to a hotel accommodation tax at a rate of 10% of the value of the accommodation.

Insurance premium tax
A tax at the rate of 6% has been imposed on insurance premiums in respect of general insurance contracts. Life insurance and reinsurance premiums are exempt.

Branch income

A branch is subject to Trinidad and Tobago taxation on all income directly or indirectly accruing in or derived from Trinidad and Tobago. The tax rates applicable on branch profits are the same as on corporate profits. In addition, branch profits, after deduction of corporation tax and reinvestments, are subject to withholding tax (WHT) at the rate of 5%. This may be varied by the provisions of any applicable double tax treaties (DTTs).

Income determination

Inventory valuation
Inventories are generally stated at the lower of cost or market value. Cost may be determined by the first in first out (FIFO) or the average-cost method. The last in first out (LIFO) and base-stock methods are not generally accepted for tax purposes.

Capital gains
Gains on the disposal of chargeable assets within 12 months of acquisition are subject to tax at standard corporation tax rates. *See Depreciation in the Deductions section for capital gains information on the sale of tax-depreciable assets.*

Dividend income
Dividends received by a Trinidad and Tobago company from both domestic subsidiaries and other domestic corporations are fully exempt from tax.

Stock dividends
A Trinidad and Tobago corporation can distribute tax-free a dividend of common stock (bonus issue) proportionately to all resident common stockholders.

Deductions

Depreciation
Tax depreciation rates (wear-and-tear allowances) have been standardised by statute. Fixed assets are to be classified into one of four classes:

Asset class	Depreciation rate (%)
Class A: Buildings and improvements	10
Class B: Motor vehicles, furniture and fittings, plant and machinery	25
Class C: Heavy equipment, motor lorries, trucks, and computer equipment	33.3
Class D: Extra heavy equipment, airplanes	40

The allowance will be calculated at the rate applying to aggregate expenditure incurred on assets within the class on a declining-balance basis.

Accelerated tax depreciation is allowed to manufacturers in the form of an initial allowance at the rate of 90% on capital expenditure on plant and machinery. The allowance is to be claimed in the year that the asset is first brought into use. For those companies engaged in the production of sugar, petroleum, or petrochemicals, or enjoying concessions under the Fiscal Incentives Act, the rate is 20%.

Trinidad and Tobago

Gains on the sale of tax-depreciable assets are taxable as ordinary income (i.e. a balancing charge) but only when the written-down value of the assets of a class goes into credit. Prior to this, the proceeds of sale are credited to the particular class thereby reducing the written down value of the class. Tax depreciation is not required to conform to book depreciation.

Petroleum operations

A company engaged in petroleum production business is entitled to capital allowances on tangible costs and intangible drilling and development costs as follows:

- Tangible costs: Initial allowance at 20% and annual allowance at 20% under the straight-line method.
- Intangible costs: Initial allowance at 10% and annual allowance at 20% under the reducing-balance method.

Allowances in respect of petroleum operations are granted from the earlier of (i) the year following the year in which the expenditure was incurred or (ii) the year in which commercial production commences (save that in the case of exploration activity the allowances are to commence from the year incurred).

Charitable contributions

Charitable contributions under deeds of covenant to approved charities are deductible, up to a maximum of 15% of total income.

Taxes

Other than SPT, taxes or levies are not generally deductible in arriving at taxable profit.

Other significant items

Contributions by local insurance companies to 'catastrophe reserve funds' are deductible for tax purposes, up to the value of 20% of net premium income from property insurance business.

Net operating losses

A trading loss may be carried forward indefinitely to be set-off against future profits. Loss carrybacks are not permitted.

A limited form of group loss relief has been introduced, whereby current year losses may be surrendered to a claimant company within a group, except that the claimant's tax liability cannot be reduced by more than 25%. Such companies must be resident in Trinidad and Tobago.

Payments to foreign affiliates

A corporation engaged in business in Trinidad and Tobago may claim a deduction for royalties and interest charges paid to foreign affiliates, provided the appropriate WHT is deducted and properly accounted. For interest to be deductible for tax purposes, the funds borrowed must have been utilised in the production of income and the recipient must be subject to tax in Trinidad and Tobago or otherwise specifically exempt from local tax.

Deduction for management charges (as this term is defined) paid to a non-resident is restricted to the lower of the management charges or 2% of outgoings and expenses exclusive of the charges. Tax depreciation allowances may not be treated as an expense for this purpose. WHT may also be applicable to management charges paid to non-resident persons.

Group taxation

There is no provision for group taxation in Trinidad and Tobago; however, a limited form of group loss relief is available (*see Net operating losses in the Deductions section*).

Tax credits and incentives

Foreign tax credit
Double taxation is avoided or mitigated by means of foreign tax credits.

Tax holidays

Fiscal Incentives Act, 1979
An approved enterprise, which must be a locally incorporated resident corporation, may be granted an exemption from corporation tax for a period of up to ten years, depending on the category under which it is approved. Exemption may be total or partial. Subject to approval, profits may be distributed tax free to shareholders, except in the case of certain non-resident shareholders, where the relief is restricted to so much of the tax as exceeds their liability in their country of residence. Net losses during the tax holiday period (i.e. the excess of total losses over total profits) may be carried forward for set-off without limitation for five years from the end of the tax holiday period, after which the normal set-off provisions for losses apply. As of 1 January 2007, the tax holiday in respect of corporation tax is no longer granted.

Approved tourism projects
Under the Tourism Development Act 2000, approved tourism development projects, including hotels, are granted a tax holiday for periods of up to seven years. In addition, a carryover from a tax exemption period is permitted of any loss arising out of the operation or renting of an approved tourism project to be written off against profits in accordance with normal income tax loss provisions, subsequent to the tax holiday period. An approved tourism project means a project declared to be so by the government.

Approved mortgage and other companies
The profits of an approved company are exempt from corporation tax. The exempt profits, when distributed to shareholders, are exempt from corporation tax and income tax. Expenses incurred in the course of the approved mortgage business remain fully deductible.

Business expansion scheme
The business expansion scheme was introduced in 1988 to allow approved small companies carrying on business in a regional development area and companies carrying out certain approved activities a tax credit of 15% of their chargeable profit. This scheme is to be restructured to encourage both individual and corporate investors to invest in venture capital companies by allowing a 'tax rebate' on their investment. As of 2006, the tax credit has been removed and replaced by a five year tax holiday.

Free Zone
The profits of an approved company operating in a designated Free Zone are free from corporation tax. In addition, payments to non-residents are free of WHT. Approved activities include manufacturing.

Trinidad and Tobago

Other allowances/incentives

Promotional expenses

Promotional expenses incurred by local firms to promote the expansion of existing markets and/or the creation of new ones for the export of specified services or locally produced goods are tax deductible as an expense at 150% of the actual outlay. Tax-deductible promotional expenses are defined as those expenses incurred in respect of specified services or goods produced in Trinidad and Tobago. This includes such items as advertising in foreign markets and participation in trade fairs and missions.

Scholarship allowance

Companies can deduct the actual expenses incurred in granting scholarships to nationals who are not employees, directors, or associates of directors of the company for tertiary education.

Market development grants

An Export Development Corporation was established to manage government export-development programs and also to do all things necessary and appropriate for the encouragement, promotion, and expansion of export-oriented business. The Corporation was empowered to give financial assistance to exporters by way of market development grants. In 1994, the Tourism and Industrial Development Corporation was formed to incorporate in a single entity the functions of the Export Development Corporation, the Tourism Development Authority and the Industrial Development Corporation. This is now the authority responsible for administering the grants.

These grants are not exempt from taxation unless (i) they have been made in respect of expenses incurred by an exporter prior to the export of the first commercial shipment of goods produced in Trinidad and Tobago and (ii) the foreign market is not in a country specified as an 'excluded country'.

Market development grants will be awarded to exporters that meet the criteria set out by the Corporation. Qualifying expenses include costs incurred in research in foreign markets, product design, and testing abroad.

Production company allowance

An allowance equal to 150% of actual expenses incurred in respect of the company's own audio, visual, or video productions for educational or local entertainment, or local culture, is available.

Allowances are granted in respect of each of the following activities, based on the actual expenditure incurred but not exceeding TTD 2 million in aggregate:

- Art and culture allowance.
- Sportsman/sporting activity allowance.
- Audio, visual, or video production allowance.

Child care/Home work facility

A deduction is allowed for the actual cost incurred in setting up a facility for dependents of employees who are minors, up to a maximum of TTD 500,000 for each facility, subject to an aggregate sum of TTD 3 million in any year.

Withholding taxes

WHT is imposed at varying rates up to 15%, depending on the nature of the payment, the status of the payee, and the applicability of DTTs. The tax treaty rate in some instances is now higher than the statutory rate. In such cases, the lower statutory rate applies. The rates below have been adjusted to reflect these reductions:

Recipient		Dividends (%) Portfolio	Substantial holdings	Interest (%)
Resident corporations and individuals		0	0	0
Non-resident corporations and individuals:				
Non-treaty	(1)	10	10	15
	(2)	5/10	5/10	15
Treaty:				
Canada (3)	(1)	10	10	10
	(2)	10	5	15
CARICOM countries	(1)	0	0	15
	(2)	0	0	15
China	(1)	10	10	10
	(2)	10	5	10
Denmark	(1)	10	10	15
	(2)	10	5	15
France	(1)	10	10	10
	(2)	10	5	0/10 (4)
Germany	(1)	10	10	0/10/15 (5)
	(2)	10	5	0/10/15 (5)
India	(1)	10	10	10
	(2)	10	5	10
Italy	(1)	10	10	10
	(2)	10	5	10
Luxembourg	(1)	10	10	10
	(2)	10	5	7.5/10
Norway	(1)	10	10	15
	(2)	10	5	15
Spain	(1)	10	10	8
	(2)	10	0/5/10	8
Sweden	(1)	10	10	15
	(2)	10	5	0/10/15 (6)
Switzerland	(1)	10	10	10
	(2)	10	10	10
United Kingdom	(1)	10	10	10
	(2)	10	5	10
United States	(1)	10	10	15
	(2)	10	5	0/15/20 (7)
Venezuela	(1)	10	10	15
	(2)	10	5	15

T

Trinidad and Tobago

Recipient	Royalties (%)		
	(8)	(9)	(10)
Resident corporations, individuals	0	0	0
Non-resident corporations, individuals:			
Non-treaty	15	15	15
Treaty:			
Canada	10	0	15
CARICOM countries	15	15	15
China	10	10	15
Denmark	15	0	15
France	10	0	15
Germany	10	0	15
India	10	10	15
Italy	5	0	15
Luxembourg	10	10	15
Norway	15	0	15
Spain	5	5	15
Sweden	15	0	15
Switzerland	10	0	15
United Kingdom	10	0	15
United States	15	0	15
Venezuela	10	10	15

Notes

1. Individuals.
2. Corporations. The lesser rate applies to parent companies.
3. The lesser rate applies to companies, other than investment companies, that control at least 10% of the voting power.
4. The rate is 10% of the gross amount if interest is paid to a resident of France; it is 0% if the interest is paid to the French government or to any agency or instrumentality of the French government.
5. The rate is 10% of the gross amount if the interest is paid to a bank that is a resident of Germany, 0% where interest is paid to certain stated governmental institutions, and 15% of the gross amount in all other cases.
6. The rate is 10% of the gross amount if the interest is paid to a bank that is a resident of Sweden, 0% where interest is paid to certain specified governmental institutions, and 15% of the gross amount in all other cases.
7. The rate is 15% of the gross amount if the interest is paid to a bank or financial institution in the United States (US) that does not have a permanent establishment (PE) in Trinidad and Tobago, 0% where the interest is paid to the US government or to any agency or instrumentality wholly owned by the US government, and 20% of the gross amount in all other cases.
8. The rate applies to patent royalties.
9. The rate applies to copyright royalties and similar payments.
10. The rate applies to royalties paid in respect of the operations of mines or quarries or of the extraction or removal of natural resources.

Tax administration

Tax returns
The taxpayer is required to file a tax return with the Board of Inland Revenue (BIR) by 30 April following the end of the fiscal period. An automatic six-month grace period is allowed, following which a penalty is imposed of TTD 1,000 for every six months or part thereof that the return remains unfiled.

Payment of tax

Corporation tax, business levy, and green fund levy are payable quarterly in advance on 31 March, 30 June, 30 September, and 31 December. Any balance of tax due is payable on or before 30 April of the following year. Instalments of corporation tax are based on an estimate of the current year's liability or on the actual chargeable profits for the previous year, whichever is greater. If the current year's estimate is lower, the company may apply to the BIR to reduce its quarterly instalment. The levy liabilities are based on the actual receipts for the quarter.

Tunisia

PwC contact

Mabrouk Maalaoui Immeuble
PricewaterhouseCoopers
Rue du Lac d'Annecy,
Les Berges du Lac Tunis,
1053 Tunisia
Tel: +00 216 71 160 105
Email: mabrouk.maalaoui@tn.pwc.com

Significant developments

The following significant corporate tax developments occurred during the past year.

Wholly exporting companies

Wholly exporting companies are allowed to continue to benefit from the total deduction from their taxable results of the benefits derived from their activity until 31 December 2012.

Capital gains

Prior to 1 January 2011, capital gains derived from the sale by non-Tunisian tax resident persons of shares held in the capital of Tunisian resident corporations were exempt from corporate tax and any related withholding tax (WHT).

As of 1 January 2011, capital gains derived by non-Tunisian tax resident persons from the disposal of shares held in the capital of Tunisian resident corporations are subject to the following tax regime:

- With regard to shares listed in the Tunisian Stock Exchange:
  - In cases where the shares were purchased prior to 1 January 2011, then capital gains will not be subject to tax in Tunisia.
  - In cases where the shares are purchased after 1 January 2011 and will be sold before the end of the year following the one during which they were acquired, then capital gains will be subject to tax. Otherwise (i.e. in case the shares will be sold after the expiry of the year following the one during which they were acquired), capital gains will not be subject to tax.
- With regard to shares not listed in the Tunisian Stock Exchange:
  - Capital gains derived from the disposal by non-Tunisian resident persons of non-listed shares are subject to tax in Tunisia.
- The due tax will be levied through WHTs due at the rate of:
  - 10% on the basis of the realised capital gains, with a ceiling of 2.5% of the selling price in cases where the seller is an individual.
  - 30% on the basis of the realised capital gains, with a ceiling of 5% of the selling price in cases where the seller is a company.

However, in cases where the seller realises, during the same fiscal year, capital gains and capital losses derived from the disposal of shares, then the seller may opt for filing an annual tax return with the Tunisian tax authorities and the payment of the tax due at the rate of:

- 10% for individuals, on the basis of the balance between the realised capital gains and realised capital losses, minus 10,000 Tunisian dinars (TND).
- 30% for corporations, on the basis of the balance between the realised capital gains and realised capital losses.

Exploitation losses

Exploitation losses (other than deferred amortisation) are to be carried forward for five years, starting from the year following the one during which they are booked.

....

Taxes on corporate income

Benefits subject to corporate tax in Tunisia are those realised by all Tunisian-resident companies as well as any other revenue realised by non-Tunisian-resident companies in case the taxation is attributable to Tunisia by virtue of a double taxation treaty (DTT).

Permanent establishments (PEs) of non-Tunisian-resident companies are subject to corporate tax in the same way and under the same conditions as Tunisian-resident companies. However, certain particularities, related mainly to deductions, exist.

Corporate tax is also due by non-resident not established companies on Tunisian-sourced income, and this through WHTs.

Corporate tax is broadly levied on the total net income resulting from the statutory financial statements of the company, duly adjusted according to the specific tax rules.

Positive/negative items of income are taxed/deducted based on the accrual basis. Income items accruing in a tax period where the above principle is not met are not allowed for tax deduction nor taxed in that tax period. Tax deduction/taxation is correspondingly deferred to the future tax periods where the principle will be met.

Income items have to be certain in their occurrence and objectively determined or determinable in their amount.

Corporate tax rates

The general corporate tax rate is 30%.

However, specific rates are foreseen for specific sectors of activity. Indeed, corporate tax is due at the rate of:

- 10% for:
  - companies carrying out craft activities, agricultural and fishing activities, and fitting out fishing boats
  - trading groups of retail businesses organised as service cooperatives, governed by the general cooperation legislation
  - service cooperatives formed between producers for the wholesale of their production
  - consumer cooperatives governed by the general cooperation legislation, and
  - exporting companies that realise their first exportation operation as of 1 January 2013. Corporate tax is also due at the rate of 10% for exporting companies during the first decade of activity ending, at the latest, on 31 December 2012.
- 35% for:
  - financial institutions governed by the law n° 2001-65, as modified and completed by the law n° 2006-19
  - offshore financial institutions governed by the code related to financial services destined to non residents, and this only for the benefits derived from services provided to non-resident persons
  - investment companies governed by the law n° 88-92, as modified and completed by the subsequent laws, mainly by the law n° 2005-104

Tunisia

- insurance and reinsurance companies governed by the assurance code promulgated by the law n° 92-24, as completed and modified by the subsequent laws, mainly the law n° 2005-86
- debt collection companies governed by the law n° 98-4, as modified and completed by the subsequent laws, mainly the law n° 2003-42
- telecommunication companies governed by the telecommunications code promulgated by the law n° 2001-1, as modified and completed by the law n° 2002-46
- companies operating in the oil and gas service field and governed by the Hydrocarbons code promulgated by the law n° 99-93, as modified and completed by the subsequent laws, mainly the law n° 2004-61
- companies operating in the production and the transport of hydrocarbons and governed by particular conventions, as well as companies operating in the transfer of hydrocarbons via pipeline, and
- companies operating in the oil refining sector and the wholesale of hydrocarbon products, foreseen by the law n° 91-45.

Minimum corporate tax

A minimum corporate tax is due at the rate of 0.1% of the local turnover, including value-added tax (VAT), in case:

- the company realises losses or
- the corporate tax due at the rate of 10%, 30%, or 35% is less than the minimum corporate tax of 0.1% of the local turnover, including VAT.

The minimum corporate tax is not due by companies established in the regional development zones during the period of tax holidays. These latter are fixed by decree.

Corporate residence

A company is tax resident in Tunisia if it is registered or has its effective place of management therein.

Permanent establishment (PE)

No definition of PE is given by the Tunisian domestic law. In practice, the Tunisian tax authorities refer to the definitions given by DTTs.

Other taxes

Valued-added tax (VAT)

VAT scope and rates

VAT is levied under the Tunisian VAT Code and is due on all transactions taking place in Tunisia. The sale of goods is considered as taking place in Tunisia and thus subject to VAT if the goods sold are delivered in Tunisia. The sale of services is considered as taking place in Tunisia and thus subject to VAT if the services sold are exploited or used in Tunisia.

The standard rate of VAT is 18%. Lower rates of 6% and 12% apply to specifically designated operations.

Tunisia

Some operations, products, or services are out of the scope of VAT in Tunisia, and some others are expressly exempt from VAT.

Some goods and services may be acquired VAT free, based on a certificate delivered for the purpose by the relevant tax authorities. This exemption is granted mainly to wholly exporting companies, oil and gas companies, their contracts, and their subcontractors.

Registration for VAT purposes may be either obligatory or optional.

Voluntary registration is allowed where persons:

* carry out activities that are outside the scope of the Tunisian VAT, in which case the option has to be a full option, which means that all the activities carried out by these persons will be subject to VAT, and
* carry out operations that are exempt from VAT and that are destined for export, or supply products and services that are exempt from VAT to persons liable to VAT, in which case the option may be a partial or a full option.

Output VAT
Output VAT is calculated on the basis of the amount of the invoice excluding VAT.

Input VAT
Individuals and companies that are subject to VAT may deduct the input VAT incurred on the purchase of goods and services necessary to carry out activities subject to VAT.

VAT incurred on the following expenses may not be deducted as input VAT:

* Purchases of passenger cars, other than those that constitute the main activity of the business.
* Expenses related to the functioning or maintenance of passenger cars.
* VAT unduly charged (charged by mistake by a supplier who is not liable for VAT).
* VAT mentioned on invoices that do not comply with the VAT requirements, i.e. invoices that do not mention the compulsory information, such as the amount excluding VAT, rate and amount of the VAT, amount including VAT, and the name and address of the client.

In order to allow the deduction of the input VAT, invoices have to be properly issued and have to include:

* the name and address of the supplier
* the name and address of the client
* the VAT identification of the supplier
* the designation of the goods or services
* the transaction date
* the amount excluding VAT
* the VAT rate, and
* the VAT amount.

Partial exemption
Partial exemption applies if the company is carrying on two or more activities and one or several activities are not subject to VAT. In this case, the input VAT to be deducted is a portion of the whole input VAT incurred. This portion is calculated by multiplying the total amount of the input VAT by a quotient where:

Tunisia

- the numerator is the total amount of the turnover subject to VAT plus the turnover realised from exportations increased by the hypothetical VAT (due on the turnover derived from exportation), plus the turnover realised from sales made to persons allowed to acquire goods and services necessary for their activities VAT-free, based on a certificate issued by the tax authorities, and
- the denominator is the total amount of the numerator increased by the turnover realised from sales exempt from VAT and sales outside the scope of VAT.

Adjustments
During the course of the year, the company deducts the input VAT on a *pro rata* basis (*as described above*). The quotient applied is calculated by using the data of the previous year. At the end of the current year, the company must calculate the quotient to be applied and corresponding to that year. If the difference exceeds 5%, the company must adjust the input VAT.

VAT declaration
The VAT is declared and paid on a monthly basis.

Refunds
If the input VAT exceeds the output VAT, the VAT credit resulting from the difference between the input VAT and the output VAT may be reimbursed on the basis of a written request made to the tax authorities.

The VAT credit is refundable if it arises from:

- exportation operations of goods and services, sales made to clients allowed to acquire goods and services VAT-free, and WHT made on the remunerations paid to companies that are neither resident nor established in Tunisia (such VAT credit is refundable if it is shown at least on one monthly tax return)
- investments destined for the carrying out of new projects as provided for in the Tunisian Incentives Investment Code (such VAT credit is refundable if it is shown on at least three successive monthly tax returns)
- suspension of activity (such VAT credit is refundable after a tax audit), or
- other operations (such VAT credit is refundable if it is shown on at least six successive monthly tax returns).

In order to benefit from the refund of VAT credits, the taxpayer has to file supporting documents, such as declarations relating to exportation of goods, documents proving that the service rendered by the Tunisian taxpayer was used or consumed outside Tunisia, authorisations to sell VAT-free, and WHT certificates.

To benefit from the refund of VAT credits, the taxpayer must already have submitted all tax returns and paid all taxes due at the time of submission of the request for the refund.

An advance payment of 15% of the VAT credit is to be paid to the taxpayer as soon as the taxpayer presents the request for refund if the VAT credit arises from operations other than export, suspension of activity, and operations of companies that are neither resident nor established in Tunisia. This rate is to be increased to 50% if the taxpayer is a company of which the financial statements are subject to legal audit, and to 100% if the VAT credit is originated from exports.

Time limits
The taxpayer may claim for the VAT credit within three years starting from the date from which the VAT credit becomes refundable.

Tunisia

Customs duties/Import tariffs

Import VAT
Importation of goods and services are subject to import VAT unless:

- the imported good is expressly exempt, e.g.:
  - Fresh milk, uncondensed and unsweetened, whether skimmed or full-fat.
  - Milk flour.
  - Devices intended for use by physically disabled persons.
  - Pure-bred breeding animals.
  - Equipment with no similar manufactured locally, expressly designated.
  - Boats destined to maritime navigation and fishing, other pleasure boats.
- the importer benefits from the acquisition of goods necessary to its activity VAT free (e.g. oil and gas companies).

Customs duties
Customs duties are due on importations other than those made from the European Union (EU).

Some equipment expressly designated by the Tunisian domestic law is exempt from customs duties, whether imported from EU countries or not.

Customs duties are not due in cases where the importer is expressly exempt, even if the goods are imported from outside the European Union.

For temporary importation of equipment, the due customs duties are to be calculated in proportion to the period spent in Tunisia. 1/60 of the total customs duties are due per month spent in Tunisia.

Property taxes
A real estate tax (RET) is calculated by the relevant municipalities and is notified annually to the taxpayers at the beginning of the civil year.

For companies subject to the payment of the local authority tax (LAT) (*see below*) and in case the LAT paid over the year is less than the RET notified by the municipalities, then the differential is due and is payable as complementary LAT. In other words, the RET constitutes a minimum of due LAT per year.

Transfer taxes
The registration of some operations is compulsory. In these cases, the registration fees are expressly determined by the Registration and Stamp Fees Code.

The registration remains optional for certain operations. In case of optional registration, the registration fees due to be paid are equal to TND 20 per page and per copy.

In case of compulsory registration, the fees due depend on the nature of the transaction and the goods involved.

Some transactions are subject to proportional registration fees, for example:

- 5% on the transfer of immovable properties.
- 2.5% for the transfer of goodwill (*fonds de commerce*).

T

Tunisia

Transactions that are not subject to proportional registration fees, as well as transactions the registration of which is optional, are subject to insignificant fixed registration fees (TND 20 per page, TND 100 per contract, etc.)

Stamp taxes
Stamp duties are due in general on certain contracts expressly designated as well as invoices, unless the customer is expressly exempt.

In general, stamp duties range from TND 0.4 for invoices, to TND 2 per page for contracts, to TND 60 for passports.

Certain documents are expressly exempt from stamp duties, mainly judgments, checks, etc.

Social logging tax
Employers established in Tunisia, regardless of being liable or not to income tax, are subject to a social logging tax, calculated at 1% of the gross amount of salaries paid to its employees, including benefits in kind.

The social logging tax is filed on the monthly tax return through which VAT and other direct taxes, except corporate tax, are filed.

This tax is payable monthly before the 28th day of the following month.

Vocational training tax
Entities subject to corporate tax are subject to vocational training tax, calculated at 2% of the gross amount of salaries paid to its employees, including benefits in kind. The rate of this tax is 1% for industrial companies.

This tax is payable monthly before the 28th day of the following month.

Local authority tax (LAT)
LAT is payable by entities subject to corporate tax, except entities operating in the tourism sector. The tourism sector is defined as accommodation, entertainment, tourist transportation, thermals, congressional tourism, companies managing hotels and entertainment centres, and travel agencies.

If a company is engaged in several activities, some of which are subject to LAT and the remaining are not subject to LAT, the taxable base to be considered is constituted only by the turnover of the activities which are subject to LAT.

The LAT paid to the local authority is of 0.2% of the total turnover of the entity, with a minimum calculated on the basis of the number of square metres of construction used by the entity.

LAT is payable monthly before the 28th day of each month.

Hotels tax
The hotels tax is due by entities operating in the tourism sector under the law decree n° 73-3, which defines the activities covered as any entity that works with tourists, providing accommodation, food and beverages, or organises leisure activities for these clients. The tax is calculated at 2% of the gross turnover generated from the tourism and relating activities.

This tax is payable monthly before the 28th day of the following month.

Tourism Sector Development Fund (FDCST)
The FDCST tax is a tax that is paid by entities operating in the tourism sector. The tax is calculated at 1% of the turnover, excluding VAT, generated from tourism and relating activities.

Branch income

The income attributable to a PE corresponds to:

- the revenues generated directly by the PE further to the exercise of its activity
- the revenues corresponding to works carried out by it, even if invoiced by the head office, and
- the revenues that would have been realised by an independent company carrying out the same business, in case the activity of the PE is provided for free.

The following charges are deductible for the purpose of the determination of the taxable results of a PE:

- All the charges incurred directly by this PE and necessary for its proper functioning. These charges have to be supported by proper documentation.
- Direct charges incurred by the head office exclusively for the PE and supported by proper documentation.
- A proportion of the indirect charges (real central administration costs) incurred by the head office. The proportion tax admitted for deduction is most often calculated on the basis of the turnover of the Tunisian branch against the global turnover of the head office. The deduction is limited to 10% of the Tunisian turnover in case this latter is resident of state which did not conclude a DTT with Tunisia.

Income determination

Inventory valuation
Inventory is valued at cost.

Capital gains
According to the provisions of article 11 of the Income and Corporate Tax Code, "the net income of a company is determined as the result of all the operations undertaken by the company, including mainly the transfer of assets…"

Consequently, capital gains, if any, arising from the transfer of assets will be considered as taxable income and will be subject to corporate tax.

However, capital gains are not to be subject to tax separately, in the meaning that they are to be added to the global taxable income and as such, they will increase or reduce the company's tax liability.

Capital gains are calculated as the difference between the sale price, which is supposed to be equal to the fair market value, and the net book value.

Tunisia

In the particular case of goodwill (*fonds de commerce*) generated internally, capital gains will be equal to the total sale price, as goodwill, other than derived from acquisitions, has no value on the books of the company.

All tangible and intangible transaction assets have to be valued at their fair market value.

The goodwill (*fonds de commerce*) generated internally, even if not booked as an asset of the company, also has to be valued at fair market value.

Particular case of capital gains resulting from mergers
Capital gains arising from the transfer of assets, other than inventories, on the occasion of a merger operation are deductible from the taxable income of the merged company and are to be added back to the taxable income of the absorbing company at up to 50% of their amount, spread out over five years.

Dividend income
Dividends distributed by Tunisian resident companies are exempt from corporate tax.

Dividends distributed by non-resident companies are subject to tax in Tunisia, unless otherwise provided for by the DTTs concluded by Tunisia.

Interest income
Interest arising from Tunisia or outside is part of the taxable results of the company, unless expressly exempt by the law (e.g. interests on deposits in foreign currencies).

Royalty income
Royalty income is part of the taxable results of the company, except those derived from exports.

Deductions

Depreciation
Depreciation expenses of fixed assets that are the ownership of the company and within the limit of the depreciation expense calculated according to the straight-line method are deductible for the purpose of determination of taxable income at a maximum depreciation rate fixed by decree.

Buildings may be depreciated according to the accounting legislation. However, the tax deductible depreciation expense must not exceed the depreciation expense calculated at a maximum depreciation rate of 5%, according to the straight-line method. Extra depreciation expenses are to be added back to the taxable base subject to corporate tax.

Equipment and machinery may be depreciated according to the accounting legislation. However, the tax deductible depreciation expense must not exceed the depreciation expense calculated at a maximum depreciation rate of 15%, according to the straight-line method. Extra depreciation expenses are to be added back to the taxable base subject to corporate tax.

The equipment and machinery depreciation rate may be increased by 50% if the equipment is used at least 16 hours a day, or doubled if used 24 hours a day, but the tax deductible depreciation expense must not exceed the depreciation expense calculated at a maximum depreciation rate of 15% according to the straight-line method, multiplied by 1.5 or by 2 depending on whether the equipment will be used 16 or 24 hours.

Depreciation expenses of assets exploited under leasing contracts are also deductible for the purpose of determination of taxable income. In fact, even if assets exploited under leasing contracts are not the ownership of the company, they are booked as assets in the balance sheet and depreciated accordingly over a minimum period fixed by decree, as follows:

Asset exploited under leasing contracts	Minimum period (years)
Constructions	7 years
Machinery and equipment	4 years
Transportation equipment	3 years

Goodwill
Goodwill (*fonds de commerce*) amortisation expenses are not tax deductible for the purpose of the determination of the taxable results.

Start-up expenses
Star-up expenses, as per the Tunisian accounting legislation, are to be capitalised and amortised over a three-year period.

Tax wise, the maximum amortisation expense allowed for deduction is equal to 100% of the start-up expenses.

Bad debt
Provisions for bad debts are tax deductible within the limit of 50% of the taxable result (after adjustments: deduction of non-taxable revenues and add back of non-deductible charges).

For this purpose, provision for bad debts have to be first of all, added back totally to the accounting result, among the other non-deductible charges to be added back.

Then, once the taxable result is determined, the company may deduct provisions for bad debts only up to 50% of this latter. Consequently, the deduction of provisions for bad debts never results in creating or increasing losses.

The deduction of bad debts is subject to the presentation of a detailed statement of the concerned creditors, while filing the annual corporate tax return, as well as court cases against these latter in order to claim payment.

Reversal on bad debts provisions are deductible within the limit of the correspondent provisions that were subject to tax during the tax year of their built-up (provisions that were added back but not limited within the authorised deduction limit).

Charitable contributions
Charitable contributions are either:

- deductible totally in cases where they are granted to proprietary organisms, the list of which is fixed by decree, or
- within 0.2% of the revenue, in the other cases.

The deduction of charitable contributions is subject to the presentation of a detailed statement of the beneficiaries, while filing the annual corporate tax return of the year during which these charitable contributions were granted.

T

Tunisia

Fines and penalties

Transactions, fines, and any other penalties for violating legal provisions are not tax deductible.

However, contractual penalties (for late payment for example) remain tax deductible.

Taxes

All taxes due by the company are considered as tax deductible charges, except corporate income tax.

Note that when the tax due by non-resident not established persons on royalties is borne by a Tunisian established company (the debtor), then the correspondent charge is not tax deductible.

Net operating losses

Under the Tunisian tax legislation, tax losses are divided into two categories:

* operating losses, and
* deferred depreciation.

Operating losses are to be carried forward for five years starting from the year following the one during which they were booked.

Deferred depreciation is to be carried forward indefinitely starting from the year following the one during which they were booked.

To benefit from the previous regime, the amount of the deferred depreciation has to be mentioned separately in the Notes to the Financial Statements.

Payments to foreign affiliates

See Transfer pricing in the Group taxation section.

Group taxation

According to article 49 of the Income and Corporate Tax Code, companies belonging to the same group have the possibility, if certain requirements are met, to opt for the tax consolidation regime.

The tax consolidation regime allows the determination of one taxable basis given by the algebraic sum of the taxable profits/losses determined by each of the companies participating in the scheme, with apportionment in relation to the corporate tax rate applicable to each company in comparison with the corporate tax rate applicable to the consolidating entity.

The tax consolidation regime is applicable for a minimum period of five years, renewable by tacit agreement for a five-year period each time.

The election to the tax consolidation scheme is subject to the prior authorisation of the Ministry of Finance if certain conditions are met:

* The mother company has to be listed in the Tunisian Stock Exchange. In case the mother company is not listed in the Tunisian Stock Exchange, it has to undertake to be listed by no later than the end of the year following the first year during which the

tax consolidation regime comes into effect; this deadline may be extended by one additional year.
- Participations held by the mother company in the capital of the other group-companies electing to the tax consolidation regime, whether directly or indirectly, have to be equal to at least 75% of the capital of each company during the whole period of the tax consolidation scheme.
- Companies electing to the tax consolidation regime have to be resident in Tunisia.
- Companies electing to the tax consolidation regime have to be subject to corporate tax.

According to the tax law into force, companies benefitting from tax holidays during a certain period of time may elect to the tax consolidation scheme even if no minimum tax is due.
- Companies electing to the tax consolidation scheme have to consider the same opening and closing dates for the fiscal years covered by the scheme.

The taxable result of each group-company participating in the tax consolidation scheme is determined according to the common law.

However, and unlike the general rules applicable to the determination of the taxable result, interests generated by sums of money deposited in inter-company current accounts are not taken into consideration for the purpose of determination of the taxable base subject to corporate tax.

Differed depreciation as well as operating losses generated by a group-company prior to the tax consolidation scheme enters into effect are to be carried forward at the level of the same company.

Taxable results of companies subject to the same corporate tax rate as the mother company are to be considered for their whole amount whereas taxable results of companies subject to corporate tax rates different from the one applicable to the mother company are to be reprocessed.

In fact, in this latter case, only a proportion of the taxable result is to be considered for the sake of computation of the consolidated tax.

This portion is determined according to the following formula:

Taxable base * (corporate tax rate applicable to the company / corporate tax rate applicable to the mother company)

Once the taxable results of the group-companies are added together, they are to be reprocessed by the mother company as follows:

- Add back provisions for bad debts booked and deducted by a group-company, before the tax consolidation scheme enters into effect, for doubtful receivables from the other group-companies.
- Add back benefits reinvested by a group-company in the capital of another group-company after tax consolidation scheme enters into effect, unless they are reinvested lately within the receiving entity itself.
- Deduct remission of debts by a group-company to the benefit of another group-company, both of them participating in the tax consolidation scheme.

Tunisia

Corporate tax is calculated at the rate applicable to the consolidating entity on the basis of the consolidated taxable result calculated as outlined previously.

However, a minimum corporate tax equal to 0.1% of the total gross turnover of the group-companies participating to the tax consolidation scheme remains due in case the taxable results shows a deficit or in case the minimum corporate tax is greater than the one calculated by applying the corporate tax rate applicable to the consolidating company to the consolidated taxable profit.

All pre-payments, WHTs, instalments, and tax surpluses generated by a group-company before the election to the tax consolidation scheme are creditable against the corporate tax to be paid by the consolidation entity.

The surplus, if any, remains deductible from corporate tax due on the subsequent years.

Transfer pricing

According to the Tunisian tax legislation, where there is evidence for the tax authorities of the existence of commercial or financial business transactions between a company and other dependent companies, which, for the determination of their value, are based on rules that differ from those governing relations between independent companies and which result in the reduction of taxable benefits, the tax department is allowed to add back to the taxable result of the invoicing company the differential between the benefits that would have been realised if the practiced prices were in line with the arm's-length principle and those actually accounted for by the company.

The burden of proof is on the tax department.

Thin capitalisation

Projects may be financed by shareholder's equity, shareholder's loans, or external debts.

Interest due on shareholder's loans is tax deductible within the limit of an interest rate of 8%, provided that the following conditions are met:

- the capital is fully paid-up and
- the amount of the sums put at the disposal of the company must not exceed 50% of the capital.

In case shareholders loans exceed 50% of the share capital, then interests due in the part exceeding 50% are not tax deductible.

Tax credits and incentives

In order to harmonise investment legislation with general economic objectives , the Incentives Investment Code (IIC) has been promulgated.

The IIC provides a number of incentives applicable to all projects covered by the code and approved by the competent government institutions and specifically developed in the following sectors:

- Agriculture and fisheries.
- Manufacturing industries.
- Public works.
- Tourism.

- Handicrafts.
- Transport.
- Education and learning.
- Professional training.
- Cultural production and industries.
- Promotion of young people and children's education.
- Healthcare.
- Environmental protection.
- Property promotion.
- Other non-financial activities and services.

The IIC foresees common and specific incentives.

The considered common incentives are detailed as follow:

- Deduction by an entity from the taxable base of profits reinvested by subscribing to initial capital or to capital increases in companies operating under the IIC, within the limit of 35% of its net taxable profits, and within the limit of the minimum corporate tax rate, which means that the corporate tax cannot be less than 20% of what it would have been without deducting the considered profits.

The main conditions for benefiting from the aforementioned incentives are that the:

- subscribing company keeps its accounts in accordance with Tunisian accounting standards
- new shares must be issued for the subscribed amount
- registered subscribed capital may not be reduced during the five years following 1 January of the year following the reinvestment, except for the purpose of absorbing losses
- subscribing company must join to its corporate tax return a certificate proving that the capital in which they subscribed is entirely paid.
- subscribed shares must not be sold before the end of the two years following the payment of the capital, and
- reinvested profits have to be posted in a 'special investment reserve account' under the liabilities in the balance sheet before the final date for filing the corporate tax return relating to the year during which the benefits were reinvested and deducted.
- Deduction from the taxable base of profits reinvested in the company itself (activities extension) providing the respect of the minimum tax rate condition of 20% and the following other conditions:
  - The reinvested profits have to be posted in a 'special investment reserve account' under the liabilities in the balance sheet before the final date for filing the corporate tax return relating to the year during which the benefits were reinvested and deducted.
  - The benefits posted in the 'special investment reserve account' have to be incorporated/included in the capital of the company before the end of the year during which the reserve was posted/booked.
  - An investment plan is to be joined to the income tax return.
  - The investment must be realised before the end of the year during which the reserve was posted/booked.
  - The assets acquired must not be transferred during at least two years after the date of the start of production.

Tunisia

- The registered capital must not be reduced during the five years following the date of the incorporation of the reinvested benefits in the capital, except for the purpose for absorbing losses.

The IIC foresees specific advantages which apply to:

- Exportation activities.
- Investments in regional development zones.
- Agricultural development.
- Environmental protection.
- Research and development (R&D) and technological development.
- Small enterprise and trade development.
- Investments of support (learning, training, etc.).

Wholly exporting activities

The following are considered as wholly exporting companies:

- Companies the production of which is totally destined to be sold outside Tunisia.
- Companies the services they provide are totally utilised/exploited outside Tunisia.
- Companies working exclusively with wholly exporting companies as defined above.
- Companies working exclusively with financial and banking institutions working mainly with non-Tunisian resident persons.
- Companies set up in the Economical Free Zones in Tunisia.

Note that wholly exporting companies may commercialise locally, during a given year, up to 30% of the turnover of the previous year, and this without losing the status of a wholly exporting company.

Profits derived from exportation by companies that have already obtained an investment certificate from the relevant authorities (the Agency of Promotion of the Investment in the particular case of industrial companies) before 1 January 2013 and that will enter into production during 2013 may benefit from the deduction of the benefits derived from exportation operations during the first decade of activity, and this starting from the first exportation operation.

In addition to the above mentioned deduction, the company may also benefit from the deduction of other profits in connection with exportation during the first decade of activity.

The concerned profits are detailed as follows:

- Investment allowances granted under the legislation of investment incentives, allowances of upgrading granted under an approved upgrade program, and allowances granted within the frame of support to the export operations.
- Capital gains derived from the sale outside Tunisia or to other wholly exporting companies of tangible assets used to carry out the exportation activity, excluding constructions, lands, and goodwill (*fonds de commerce*).
- Realised exchange profits in connection with the exportation activity.
- Remission of debt for the benefit of the wholly exporting companies.

However, all the other profits (financial interests, rentals, etc.) remain subject to corporate tax at the rate of 30%.

After the expiry of this period, profits derived from the main activity are to be subject to corporate tax at the rate of 10% and all other revenues will be subject to corporate tax at the rate of 30%.

According to article 12 of the IIC, wholly exporting companies created as of 1 January 2013 will be subject to corporate tax at the rate of:

- 10% of the basis of the benefits derived from exportation and
- 30% on the basis of the benefits derived from local sales as well as the other profits.

To note that companies are subject to a minimum corporate tax calculated at the rate of 0.1% on the basis of the local turnover.

According to the same article, wholly exporting companies, benefit from:

- the exemption from VAT on purchases based on a certificate delivered for the purpose by the relevant tax authorities, to be presented by the Tunisian entity to its suppliers and the exemption from VAT at sales based on a certificate delivered for the purpose by the relevant tax authorities to be presented by the client to the Tunisian entity
- the exemption from other indirect taxes, including customs duties
- the exemption from LAT due at the rate of 0.2% of the gross turnover
- the exemption from professional training tax due at the rate of 1% of the gross salaries
- the exemption from registration fees and stamp duties, and
- the exemption from social logging tax due at the rate of 1% of the gross salaries.

However, they remain subject to the payment of the following insignificant taxes and duties only:

- Taxes and duties to passenger cars.
- The single compensation tax on road transport.
- Taxes on real estate: calculated on the number of square metres of construction used by the entity.
- Taxes and duties by virtue of services rendered directly in compliance with the current legislation.

Regional development zones activities
The IIC provides that investments in certain activities (industry, tourism, handicraft, and certain other services) carried out by entities established in regional development zones benefit from a number of tax advantages, detailed as follows:

- Deduction from the taxable profits of the entity of the profits derived from the investments in the regional development zones during a period of:
  - Five years, in case the investments are realised in the development zones enumerated in category one.
  - Ten years, in case the investments are realised in the development zones enumerated in category two.
  - Ten years, in case the investments are realised in the development zones of priority. During the second decade of activity, the deduction is reduced to 50% of the profits generated on the investments.

In addition to the above mentioned deduction, companies carrying out investment in regional development zones may also benefit from the deduction of other profits in connection with the main activity.

Tunisia

The concerned profits are detailed as follows:

- Investment allowances granted under the legislation of investment incentives, allowances of upgrading granted under an approved upgrade program, and allowances granted within the frame of support to the export operations.
- Capital gains derived from the sale of tangible assets used to carry out the exportation activity, excluding constructions, lands, and goodwill (*fonds de commerce*).
- Realised exchange profits in connection with the exportation activity.
- Remission of debt for the benefit of the wholly exporting companies.

Other benefits include:

- Deduction from the taxable profits of the revenues reinvested in the subscription to initial capital or to capital increases in these companies, up to 100% of the taxable result and without any minimum tax. However, the deduction is subject to the remaining conditions listed under the common incentives section.
- Exemption from social logging tax (1% of the gross salaries).
- Exemption from vocational training tax (2% of the gross salaries).

Support activities
The supporting investments activities are defined as being the following:

- Training of children.
- Education.
- Teaching.
- Scientific research.
- Professional training.
- Cultural production and co-ordination of young people.
- Healthcare services.

The investments made by institutions for these considered activities give entitlement to the following tax incentives:

- Exemption from customs duties and taxes with a similar effect.
- Suspension of VAT and consumption duty for imported equipment with no locally manufactured equivalent that is necessary for the realisation of the investments, as well as suspension of VAT on equipment manufactured locally.

Foreign tax credit
In the absence of DTTs, corporate tax (or any WHT in connection with) paid outside Tunisia is not deductible from the tax due in Tunisia.

However, in the presence of DTTs, in cases where profits derived from outside Tunisia were subject to corporate tax in Tunisia, the foreign tax, if any, is deductible, but only up to the correspondent Tunisian tax on these profits.

Withholding taxes

The payments of certain remunerations are subject to corporate WHT in Tunisia.

The WHT is an advance payment of corporate tax and is thus deductible from the corporate tax due by the invoicing entity. To this end, the paying entity shall withhold the tax at the appropriate rate. It shall then issue a WHT certificate to the invoicing company to enable the latter to use the certificate as proof of the payment at the moment of filing its corporate tax return. The paying entity subsequently pays the withheld amount to the tax authorities.

The withheld tax is to be declared and repaid by the paying entity each month before the 28th day of the following month.

The rates of the WHT differ according to the nature of the goods/services, and the rates applicable within the framework of the DTTs.

Applicable WHT rates in Tunisia are as follows:

- 15% of the gross amount of the invoices related to fees, commissions, brokerage fees, rentals, payment of non-commercial activities (non-commercial activities include especially independent scientific, literary, artistic, educational, or teaching activities, such as independent activities of physicians, dentists, lawyers, consultants, architects, engineers, accountants, etc.).

  This rate is reduced to 5% for fees (including those paid for non-commercial activities) and hotel rentals when these amounts are paid to entities subject to corporate tax and individuals who keep proper accounts in accordance with the Tunisian accounting principles.
- 20% on interest and director's attendance allowance. This does not include interest on deposits and bonds in foreign currency or convertible dinars.
- 5% on bank loans extended by non-Tunisian resident banks.
- 2.5% on the sales price indicated in a real estate sale, in case the seller is an individual.
- 1.5% on payments, the amount of which exceeds TND 2,000 (including VAT), made for the acquisition of goods and services necessary to the activity and which are not subject to specific WHT rate.
- 15% on payments made to non-Tunisian tax resident persons.

DTT rates
Note that the following interest WHT rates are applicable to interest payable to non-resident, not established companies and financial institutions according to DTTs concluded by Tunisia.

Recipient	WHT (%)		Royalties
	Interest		
	Banks (45)	Other companies	
Austria	10	10	10/15 (1)
Belgium	5/10 (46)	10	11 (2)
Cameroon	15	15	15 (3)
Canada	15	15	15/20 (4)
China	0/10 (47)	10	5/10 (5)
Czech Republic	12	12	5/15 (6)
Denmark	12	12	15 (7)
Egypt	10	10	15 (8)
Ethiopia	0/11 (48)	11	5 (9)
France	12	12	5/15/20 (10)
Germany	0/10 (49)	10	10/15 (11)
Greece	15	15	10 (12)

Tunisia

Recipient	WHT (%)		
	Interest		
	Banks (45)	Other companies	Royalties
Hungary	12	12	12 (13)
Indonesia	12	12	15 (14)
Iran	0/10 (50)	10	8 (15)
Italy	0/12 (51)	12	5/12/16 (16)
Jordan	15	15	(17)
Kuwait	0/2.5 (52)	10	5 (18)
Lebanon	0/5 (53)	0/5 (54)	5 (19)
Luxemburg	7.5/10 (55)	10	12 (20)
Mali	5	5	(21)
Malta	12	12	12 (22)
Mauritius Islands	2.5	2.5	2.5 (23)
Netherlands	7.5/10 (56)	7.5/10 (56)	7.5/11 (24)
Norway	12	12	5/15/20 (25)
Pakistan	13	13	10 (26)
Poland	12	12	12 (27)
Portugal	15	15	10 (28)
Qatar	5	20	5 (29)
Romania	10	10	12 (22)
Senegal	5	20	(30)
South Africa	5	12	10/12 (31)
South Korea	0/12 (57)	12	15 (32)
Spain	5/10 (58)	5/10 (58)	10 (33)
Sudan	10	10	5 (34)
Sultanate of Oman	10	10	5 (35)
Sweden	12	12	5/15 (36)
Switzerland	10	10	10 (37)
Syria	10	10	18 (38)
Turkey	10	10	10 (39)
United Arab Emirates	2.5/5 (59)	10	7.5 (40)
United Kingdom	10	12	15 (41)
United Maghreb Arab	5	20	(42)
United States of America	0/15 (60)	15	10/15 (43)
Yemen	10	10	7.5 (44)

Notes

1. 10% of the gross amount of the royalties for the use of, or the right to use, any copyright of literary, artistic, or scientific work.

    15% of the gross amount of the royalties for:
    *   cinematographic films and TV films, patents, trademarks, designs or models, plans, secret formulae, or processes
    *   technical and economical studies
    *   information concerning industrial, agricultural, commercial, or scientific experience, and
    *   the use of or the right to use agricultural, industrial, commercial, or scientific equipment.
2. 11% of the gross amount of the royalties for the use of:
    *   the use of, or the right to use, any copyright of literary, artistic, or scientific work, including cinematographic films and films for TV broadcasting, patents, trademarks, designs or models, plans, secret formulae, or processes
    *   information concerning industrial, commercial, or scientific experience

Tunisia

- the use of, or the right to use, industrial, commercial, scientific equipment, or port facilities, and
- economical and technical studies, and technical assistance realised in the state of source.
3. 15% of the gross amount of royalties for:
   - the use of, or the right to use, any copyright of literary, artistic, or scientific work, including cinematographic films, patents, trademarks, designs or models, plans, secret formulae, or processes
   - information concerning industrial, commercial, or scientific experience
   - the use of, or the right to use, industrial, commercial, or scientific equipment, and
   - technical assistance and studies in all fields.
4. 20% of the gross amount of the royalties for:
   - the use of, or the right to use, licences, trademarks, cinematographic films, and films and discs for radio or television broadcasting, and
   - the use of, or the right to use, industrial, commercial, scientific equipment, or port facilities.

15% of the gross amount of the royalties for all the other cases, mainly:
- technical and economical studies
- the use of, or the right to use, copyrights, patents, trademarks, designs or models, plans, secret formulae, or processes, and
- information concerning industrial, commercial, or scientific experience.
However, royalties paid for the use of, or the right to use, copyrights of literary, dramatic, musical, or artistic work, except royalties in respect of cinematographic films and films and discs for TV broadcasting, are taxable in the state of residency and thus cannot be subject to tax nor to any WHT in connection with the state in which they arise.
5. 10% of the gross amount of the royalties for:
   - the use of, or the right to use, any copyright of literary, artistic, or scientific work, including cinematographic films and films, tapes, or discs for radio or television broadcasting, patents, trademarks, designs or models, plans, secret formulae, or processes, and
   - information in respect of industrial, commercial, or scientific experience.

5% of the gross amount of the royalties for technical and economical studies and technical assistance.
6. 5% of the amount of the royalties for the use of, or the right to use, any copyright of literary, artistic, or scientific work, including cinematographic and films for TV and radio broadcasting.

15% of the amount of the royalties for:
- the use of, or the right to use, patents, trademarks, designs or models, plans, secret formulae, or processes
- information in respect of industrial, commercial, or scientific experience
- the use of, or the right to use, industrial, commercial, or scientific equipment, and
- technical and economical studies and technical assistance rendered in the state in which they arise.
7. 15% of the gross amount of royalties for:
   - the use of, or the right to use, any copyright of literary, artistic, or scientific work, including cinematographic films and films, tapes, or discs for radio or television broadcasting, patents, trademarks, designs or models, plans, secret formulae, or processes
   - information in respect of industrial, commercial, or scientific experience
   - the use of, or the right to use, industrial, commercial, or scientific equipment, and
   - technical and economical studies.
8. 15% of the gross amount of royalties for:
   - the right to publish any literary, artistic, or scientific work, patents, trademarks, designs or models, plans, secret formulae, or processes
   - information in respect of industrial, commercial, or scientific experience
   - the use of, or the right to use, industrial, commercial, or scientific equipment, and
   - cartoons, films, and videos for TV broadcasting.
9. 5% of the gross amount of royalties for:
   - the use of, or the right to use, any copyright of literary, artistic, or scientific work, including cinematographic films and films, tapes, or discs for radio or television broadcasting, patents, trademarks, designs or models, plans, secret formulae, or processes
   - information in respect of industrial, commercial, or scientific experience, and
   - the use of, or the right to use, industrial, commercial, or scientific equipment.
10. 5% of the gross amount of the royalties for the use of, or the right to use, any copyright of literary, artistic, or scientific work.

15% of the gross amount of the royalties for:
- the use of, or the right to use, patents, trademarks, designs or models, plans, secret formulae, or processes
- information in respect of industrial, commercial, or scientific experience, and
- economical and technical studies.

20% of the gross amount of the royalties for:
- the use of, or the right to use, agricultural, industrial, commercial, scientific equipment, or port facilities, and

T

Tunisia

- licences, trademarks, cinematographic films, and films for TV broadcasting.
However, payments made to public entities for the use of cinematographic films or broadcasting on radio and TV are exempt from WHT.
11. 10% of the gross amount of the royalties for:
    - the use of, or the right to use, any copyright of literary, artistic, or scientific work
    - information concerning agricultural, industrial, commercial, or scientific experience, and
    - technical and economical studies.

    15% of the gross amount of the royalties for:
    - patents, trademarks, designs or models, plans, secret formulae, or processes, and
    - cinematographic films or films for television.
12. 10% of the gross amount of the royalties for:
    - the use of, or the right to use, any copyright of literary, artistic, or scientific work, including cinematographic films and films, tapes, or discs for radio or television broadcasting, patents, trademarks, designs or models, plans, secret formulae, or processes
    - information concerning industrial, commercial, or scientific experience
    - the use of, or the right to use, industrial, agricultural, commercial, scientific equipment, or port facilities, except remunerations for chartering of vessels and aircrafts, and
    - technical and economical studies.
13. Royalties may be subject to tax in the contracting state in which they arise in cases where the legislation of that state allows such taxation, at a maximum rate of 12%.
14. 15% of the gross amount of royalties for:
    - the use of, or the right to use, any copyright of literary, artistic, or scientific work, including cinematographic films and films, tapes, or discs for radio or television broadcasting, patents, trademarks, designs or models, plans, secret formulae, or processes
    - information in respect of industrial, commercial, or scientific experience
    - the use of, or the right to use, industrial, commercial, or scientific equipment, and
    - technical services such as technical and economical studies and technical assistance.
15. 8% of the gross amount of royalties for:
    - the use of, or the right to use, any copyright of literary, artistic, or scientific work, including cinematographic films and films, tapes, or discs for radio or television broadcasting, patents, trademarks, designs or models, plans, secret formulae, or processes
    - information in respect of industrial, commercial, or scientific experience, and
    - the use of, or the right to use, agricultural, industrial, commercial, scientific equipment, or port facilities, except remunerations for the chartering of vessels and aircrafts used for international transport.
16. 5% of the gross amount of the royalties for the use of, or the right to use, any copyright of literary, artistic, or scientific work.

    12% of the gross amount of the royalties for:
    - the use of, or the right to use, patents, trademarks, designs or models, plans, secret formulae, or processes
    - information in respect of industrial, commercial, or scientific experience, and
    - economical and technical studies.

    16% of the gross amount of the royalties for:
    - the use of, or the right to use, industrial, commercial, or scientific equipment
    - licences, trademarks, cinematographic films, and films for TV broadcasting.
17. Royalties may be subject to tax in the contracting state in which they arise in case the legislation of that state allows such taxation and according to the legislation of that state for:
    - the use of, or the right to use, any copyright of literary, artistic or scientific work, patents, trademarks, designs or models, plans, secret formulae, or processes
    - information in respect of industrial, commercial, or scientific experience, and
    - the use of, or the right to use, industrial, commercial, or scientific equipment.
18. 5% of the gross amount of royalties for:
    - the use of, or the right to use, any copyright of literary, artistic, or scientific work, including cinematographic films and films, tapes, or discs for radio or television broadcasting, patents, trademarks, designs or models, plans, secret formulae, or processes, and
    - information in respect of industrial, commercial, or scientific experience.
19. 5% of the gross amount of royalties for:
    - the use of, or the right to publish, any literary, artistic, or scientific work, including cinematographic films and films, tapes, or discs for radio or television broadcasting, a transmission by satellite or optical fibre transmission or similar means of transmission, patents, trademarks, designs or models, plans, secret formulae, or processes
    - information in respect of industrial, commercial, or scientific experience, and
    - the use of, or the right to use, industrial, commercial, or scientific equipment.
20. 12% of the gross amount of royalties for:
    - the use of, or the right to use, any copyright of literary, artistic, or scientific work, including cinematographic films, patents, trademarks, designs or models, plans, secret formulae, or processes

- information in respect of industrial, commercial, or scientific experience, except remuneration for vessels and aircrafts chartering in respect of international transport
- the use of, or the right to use, industrial, agricultural, commercial, or scientific equipment, and
- technical services, such as technical and economical studies, and technical assistance carried out in the debtor state of the correspondent remuneration.

21. Royalties may be subject to tax in the contracting state in which they arise in cases where the legislation of that state allows such taxation and according to its legislation for:
    - the use of, or the right to use, any copyright of literary, artistic, or scientific work, including cinematographic films recording for radio or television broadcasting, patents, trademarks, designs or models, plans, secret formulae, or processes
    - information in respect of industrial, commercial, or scientific experience, and
    - the use of, or the right to use, industrial, commercial, or scientific equipment.

22. 12% of the gross amount of royalties for:
    - the use of, or the right to use, any copyright of literary, artistic, or scientific work, including cinematographic films and films, tapes, or discs for radio or television broadcasting, patents, trademarks, designs or models, plans, secret formulae, or processes
    - information in respect of industrial, commercial, or scientific experience
    - the use of, or the right to use, industrial, agricultural, commercial, or scientific equipment, and
    - technical and economical studies and technical assistance.

23. 2.5% of the gross amount of royalties for:
    - the use of, or the right to use, any copyright of literary, artistic, or scientific work, including cinematographic films, patents, trademarks, designs or models, plans, secret formulae, or processes
    - information in respect of industrial, commercial, or scientific experience, and
    - the use of, or the right to use, industrial, agricultural, commercial, or scientific equipment, except remunerations for the chartering of vessels and aircrafts used for international transport.

24. Royalties may be subject to tax in the contracting state in which they arise in case the legislation of that state allows such taxation; but if the recipient is the beneficial owner of the royalties, the tax so charged shall not exceed 11% of their amount.

However, this rate is reduced to 7.5% in case royalties received by a resident of Tunisia are not subject to WHT in the Netherlands and as long as the Netherlands does not proceed to the modification of its tax legislation.

Remunerations paid for the following are considered royalties:
- the use of, or the right to use, any copyright of literary, artistic, or scientific work, including cinematographic films and films, tapes, or discs for radio or television broadcasting, patents, trademarks, designs or models, plans, secret formulae, or processes
- information in respect of industrial, commercial, or scientific experience
- the use of, or the right to use, industrial, commercial, or scientific equipment, except remunerations paid for the exploitation of vessels and aircrafts in respect of international transport, and
- technical and economical studies and technical assistance rendered in the state from which royalties are paid.

25. 5% of the gross amount of the royalties for the use of, or the right to use, any copyright of literary, artistic, or scientific work, except cinematographic films and films for TV broadcasting.

15% of the gross amount of the royalties for:
- the use of, or the right to use, patents, trademarks, designs or models, plans, secret formulae, or processes
- information in respect of industrial, commercial, or scientific experience, and
- economical and technical studies.

20% of the gross amount of the royalties for:
- the use of, or the right to use, agricultural, industrial, commercial, scientific equipment, or port facilities, and
- the use of, or the right to use, trademarks and cinematographic films and films for TV broadcasting.

26. 10% of the gross amount of royalties for:
    - the use of, or the right to use, any copyright of literary, artistic, or scientific work, including cinematographic films, patents, trademarks, designs or models, plans, secret formulae, or processes
    - the use of, or the right to use, industrial, agricultural, commercial, scientific equipment, or port facilities, except remuneration for vessels and aircrafts chartering in respect of international transport, and
    - technical and economical studies and technical assistance.

27. 12% of the gross amount of royalties for:
    - the use of, or the right to use, any copyright of literary, artistic, or scientific work, including cinematographic films, patents, trademarks, designs or models, plans, secret formulae, or processes
    - information in respect of industrial, commercial, or scientific experience

Tunisia

- the use of, or the right to use, industrial, agricultural, commercial, scientific equipment, or port facilities, and
- technical and economical studies and technical assistance.
28. 10% of the gross amount of royalties for:
- the use of, or the right to use, any copyright of literary, artistic, or scientific work, including cinematographic films and films, tapes, or discs for radio or television broadcasting, patents, trademarks, designs or models, plans, secret formulae, or processes
- information in respect of industrial, commercial, or scientific experience
- the use of, or the right to use, industrial, commercial, or scientific equipment, and
- technical and economical studies and technical assistance in respect of the use of, or the right to use, the equipments, rights, and information mentioned above.
29. 5% of the gross amount of royalties for:
- the use of, or the right to use, any copyright of literary, artistic, or scientific work, patents, trademarks, designs or models, plans, secret formulae, or processes
- information in respect of industrial, commercial, or scientific experience, and
- the use of, or the right to use, industrial, commercial, or scientific equipment.
30. Royalties are subject to tax in the state of residency of the beneficiary.

However, the non-exclusive taxation right attributable to the state of residency does not prohibit the taxation of such royalties in the state in which they arise in cases where the legislation of that state allows such taxation and according to its legislation.

Remunerations paid for the following are considered royalties and thus are subject to tax in the state in which they arise:
- the use of, or the right to use, any copyright of literary, artistic, or scientific work, including cinematographic films, patents, trademarks, designs or models, plans, secret formulae, or processes
- information in respect of industrial, commercial, or scientific experience, and
- the use of, or the right to use, industrial, commercial, or scientific equipment that is not considered as an asset in the meaning of article 6 of the present treaty.
31. 10% of the gross amount of the royalties for:
- the use of, or the right to use, any copyright of literary, artistic, or scientific work, including cinematographic films and films, tapes, or discs for radio or television broadcasting, patents, trademarks, designs or models, plans, secret formulae, or processes, and
- information in respect of industrial, commercial, or scientific experience.

12% of the gross amount of the royalties for technical services, such as technical and economical studies and technical assistance.
32. 15% of the gross amount of royalties for:
- the use of, or the right to use, any copyright of literary, artistic, or scientific work, including cinematographic films and films, tapes, or discs for radio or television broadcasting, patents, trademarks, designs or models, plans, secret formulae, or processes
- the use of, or the right to use, industrial, agricultural, commercial, or scientific equipment, and
- economical and technical studies and technical assistance.
33. 10% of the gross amount of royalties for:
- copyrights, patents, trademarks, designs or models, plans, secret formulae, or processes
- studies and information in respect of industrial, commercial, or scientific experience
- the use of, or the right to use, industrial, commercial, or scientific equipment, and
- cinematographic films and video tapes for TV broadcasting.
34. 5% of the gross amount of royalties for:
- the use of, or the right to use, any copyright of literary, artistic, or scientific work, including cinematographic films and films, tapes, or discs for radio or television broadcasting, patents, trademarks, designs or models, plans, secret formulae, or processes
- information in respect of industrial, commercial, or scientific experience, and
- the use of, or the right to use, industrial, agricultural, commercial, or scientific equipment, except chartering of ships and aircrafts used for the international transport.
35. 5% of the gross amount of royalties for remunerations paid for the use of, or the right to use, any copyright of literary, artistic, or scientific work, including cinematographic films and films, tapes, or discs for radio or television broadcasting, patents, trademarks, software, designs or models, plans, secret formulae, or processes.
36. 5% of the amount of the royalties for the use of, or the right to use, any copyright of literary, artistic, or scientific work, excluding cinematographic and films for TV and radio broadcasting.

15% of the amount of the royalties for:
- the use of, or the right to use, cinematographic films, films for TV and radio broadcasting, patents, trademarks, designs or models, plans, secret formulae, or processes
- information in respect of industrial, commercial, or scientific experience
- the use of, or the right to use, industrial, commercial, or scientific equipment, and
- technical and economical studies.
37. 10% of the gross amount of royalties for:

- the use of, or the right to use, any copyright of literary, artistic, or scientific work, including cinematographic films, patents, trademarks, designs or models, plans, secret formulae, or processes
- information in respect of industrial, commercial, or scientific experience, and technical and economical studies and technical assistance related to these information, and
- the use of, or the right to use, industrial, commercial, or scientific equipment.

38. 18% of the gross amount of royalties for:
- the use of, or the right to use, any copyright of literary, artistic, or scientific work, including cinematographic films and films, tapes or discs for radio or television broadcasting, patents, trademarks, designs or models, plans, secret formulae, or processes
- information in respect of industrial, commercial, or scientific experience, and
- the use of, or the right to use, industrial, commercial, or scientific equipment.

39. 10% of the gross amount of royalties for:
- the use of, or the right to use, any copyright of literary, artistic, or scientific work, including cinematographic films and films, tapes, or discs for radio or television broadcasting, patents, trademarks, designs or models, plans, secret formulae, or processes
- information in respect of industrial, commercial, or scientific experience, and
- the use of, or the right to use, industrial, commercial, or scientific equipment.

40. 7.5% of the gross amount of royalties for:
- the use of, or the right to use, any copyright of literary, artistic, or scientific work, including cinematographic films and films, tapes, or discs for radio or television broadcasting, patents, trademarks, designs or models, plans, secret formulae, or processes
- information in respect of industrial, commercial, or scientific experience, and
- the use of, or the right to use, industrial, commercial, or scientific equipment.

41. 15% of the gross amount of royalties for:
- the use of, or the right to use, any copyright of literary, artistic, or scientific work, including cinematographic films and films, tapes, or discs for radio or television broadcasting, patents, trademarks, designs or models, plans, secret formulae, or processes
- information in respect of industrial, commercial, or scientific experience
- the use of, or the right to use, industrial, agricultural, commercial, or scientific equipment, and
- technical and economical studies.

42. Royalties are only taxable in the contracting state in which they arise in cases where the legislation of that state allows such taxation and according to its legislation for:
- the use of, or the right to use, any copyright of literary, artistic, or scientific work, including cinematographic films and films for TV broadcasting, patents, trademarks, designs or models, plans, secret formulae, or processes
- information in respect of industrial, commercial, or scientific experience
- the use of or the right to use industrial, commercial, scientific equipment or port facilities, and
- economical and technical studies and technical assistance.

43. 15% of the gross amount of the royalties for:
- copyright of literary, artistic, or scientific work, including cinematographic films and films, tapes, or discs for radio or television broadcasting, patents, trademarks, designs or models, plans, secret formulae, or processes
- information in respect of industrial, commercial, or scientific experience, and
- profits from any ownership, depending from the productivity, the use, or the alienation of that ownership.

10% of the gross amount of the royalties for:
- the use of, or the right to use, industrial, commercial, or scientific equipment, other than vessels and aircrafts used for international transport, and
- technical studies paid from public funds or political subdivisions or local authorities or technical assistance for the use of the ownership of the rights above mentioned, in case the service is realised in the state of source.

44. 7.5% of the gross amount of royalties for:
- the use of, or the right to use, any copyright of literary, artistic, or scientific work, including cinematographic films and films, tapes, or discs for radio or television broadcasting, patents, trademarks, designs or models, plans, secret formulae, or processes, and
- the use of, or the right to use, industrial, commercial, or scientific equipment and port facilities, except remunerations paid for vessels and aircrafts used in international transport.

45. These rates are applicable, in certain cases, to the loans extended by the Central Bank.
46. 5% for loans extended by banks and not represented by bonds or other debt securities.
47. 0% for loans granted by financial institutions, the capital of which is held up to 100% by the Chinese state.
48. 0% for loans granted by financial institutions, the capital of which is held at least up to 50% by the Ethiopian state, its political subdivisions, or local authorities.
49. 0% for loans granted by the Deutsche Bundesbank, Kreditanstalt für Wiederaufbau, and the Deutsche Gesellschaft für wirtschaftliche zusammenarbeite Gmbh. (Entwicklumgsgesells).
50. 0% for loans granted by financial institutions, the capital of which is held up to 100% by the state of Iran.
51. 0% for loans granted by financial institutions, the capital of which is totally held by the Italian state or its local authorities.

Tunisia

52. 0% for loans granted by financial institutions, the capital of which is held up to 100% by the state of Kuwait.
53. 0% for loans granted by financial institutions, the capital of which is totally held by the state of Lebanon, its political subdivisions, or local authorities.
54. 0% for loans granted by companies, the capital of which is totally held by the state of Lebanon, its political subdivisions, or local authorities.
55. 7.5% for loans guaranteed or granted by financial institutions and the reimbursement period of which exceeds five years.
56. 7.5% as long as the tax legislation of the Netherlands provides that interest paid by a company resident in the Netherlands to a company resident in Tunisia is exempt from any WHT.
57. 0% for loans, the reimbursement period of which exceeds seven years.
58. 5% for loans, the reimbursement period of which exceeds seven years, and 10% in the other cases.
59. 2.5% for bank loans, as long as the Tunisian domestic tax legislation provides that interest on bank loans extended by non-established banks is subject to a 2.5% WHT rate, and 5% for the above-mentioned bank loans in cases where an increase of the WHT rate is applicable to interest paid to non-established banks.
60. 0% for loans granted by financial institutions, provided that the reimbursement period exceeds seven years.

Tax administration

Taxable period
Under Tunisian law, both the accounting year and tax year follow the calendar year. However, derogation is possible if prior authorisation is obtained from the Ministry of Finance.

Tax returns
Tunisian established companies have the obligation to file monthly tax returns, an annual corporate tax return, and an annual Employer's Declaration.

Monthly tax returns include WHTs, VAT, LAT, social logging tax, and professional training tax, and must be filed each month before the 28th day of the following month. Filing and payment take place simultaneously.

The annual tax return is the corporate tax return, which must be filed before 25 March of the following year. The deadline for filing the corporate tax return is moved to 25 June for public liability companies and private liability companies subject to statutory audit. Filing and payment take place simultaneously.

The Employer's Declaration has to be filed each year before 28/29 February of the following year. This declaration must list all fees and salaries paid or incurred, even if not yet paid, to service suppliers and employees during the concerned year. No payment is due in connection with this filing, but fees not listed on this declaration are not recognised as deductible costs.

Payment of tax
Corporate tax is paid through:

- WHTs applied on certain payments and operated by the debtor on behalf of the taxpaying entity.
- Beginning from the second year of activity, three provisional instalments, each calculated at 30% of the total corporate tax due for the previous year. The instalments fall due on 28 June, 28 September, and 28 December.
- An annual tax return.

Both WHTs and provisional payments of income tax are creditable against the annual/final tax due.

Filing and payment take place simultaneously.

The most common process is the filing in person at the tax office. In this case, payment is made cash or by check.

However, companies, the turnover of which exceeds TND 1 million, are constrained to file their tax returns electronically. Electronic filing remains optional for other companies. In this case, payment is made through bank transfer.

Audit cycle
Tax controllers may proceed either with preliminary tax audit or an in-depth tax audit.

Preliminary tax audit
In case of a preliminary tax audit, the taxpayer under control is not notified prior to starting the audit.

The tax audit is conducted in the offices of the tax administration and deals with the documents made available to them (tax returns, registered contracts, etc.). However, preliminary tax audits can never deal with the taxpayer's accounts.

The results of the tax control are notified in writing to the taxpayer within a tax audit report, whereby the outcome of the audit activity must be detailed and the findings, if any, must be illustrated and motivated.

It is worth pointing out that the tax audit report is not an executive act against the taxpayer and does not bear any request for payment of taxes or penalties.

Indeed, the taxpayer has the possibility to answer to the tax audit report within 30 days starting from the date of the receipt of this report. Failing that, the taxpayer will receive a tax assessment notice which brings forth requests for payment of taxes and penalties to the tax payer.

However, in case the taxpayer answers to the notification of the results of the tax audit and brings additional explanations, clarifications, and documents to the tax auditors, then these will be constrained to examine the evidence provided by the taxpayer and answer to the taxpayer's opposition, but no deadline is fixed.

Once the taxpayer receives the answer of the tax authorities to the taxpayer's opposition, the taxpayer will have the possibility to file a second opposition, in case the taxpayer still disagrees with some or all the points raised by the tax controllers.

Once the second answer is filed by the tax payer, there will be no other written correspondences with the tax auditors.

In cases where the tax administration agrees to the clarifications, explanations, arguments, and documents provided by the taxpayer, then the tax audit will be closed.

However, in cases where the tax administration still disagrees with some or all the evidence provided by the taxpayer, then the taxpayer will receive a tax assessment notice and will have to pay the notified taxes.

The tax assessment notice has to take into consideration the taxpayer's observations enclosed in the first and the second opposition filed by the taxpayer.

T

Tunisia

Further to the receipt of the tax assessment notice, the taxpayer may make an appeal to the relevant court.

A preliminary tax audit does not prevent an in-depth tax audit of the same period and the same taxes.

In-depth tax audit
In case of an in-depth tax audit, the taxpayer under control is notified 15 days prior to starting the audit. This period may be extended to a maximum period of 60 days.

In-depth tax audits deal with the accounts of the taxpayer under control (in cases where the taxpayer has the obligation to maintain accounts according to the accounting legislation into force) as well as any other evidence (presumptions, registered contracts, etc.)

In-depth tax audits take place, as a general rule, in the business premises of the taxpayer.

However, and upon the request of the taxpayer or the tax controllers, the tax audit can be conducted in the tax authorities' office. In this case, books, records, and any other documentation deemed necessary to the tax auditors to complete the audit have to be moved to the tax auditors' office

In-depth tax audits last for:

* six months, in case the taxpayer under control is constrained by the law to maintain accounts, and
* one year, in the other cases.

At the end of this period, the tax audit must come to an end and the tax auditors must draw up a tax audit report to be sent to the taxpayer, whereby the outcome of the audit activity must be detailed and the findings, if any, must be illustrated and motivated.

Once the tax audit report is sent to the taxpayer, the procedure will be the same as for preliminary tax audits.

Statute of limitations
The period open for tax audit, unless it was subject to a previous in-depth tax audit, is:

* Four years, in case of partial omission; an omission is considered as partial in case the tax return is filed but the taxable base is not determined properly or in case the WHT rates applied to payments made to third parties are lower than the rates provided for by the law.
* Ten years, in case of total omission; an omission is considered as total in case the tax return is not filed at the date when the company becomes under tax control.

The four-year period and the ten-year period begin to run from 1 January (in case the fiscal year coincides with the calendar year) of the year following the completion of sales, earnings, receipt, or disbursement of any sum to be taxed.

Turkey

PwC contact

Zeki Gündüz
PricewaterhouseCoopers
Suleyman Seba Cad. No:48
BJK Plaza B Blok K.9
Istanbul, Besiktas 34357
Turkey
Tel: +90 212 326 6060
Email: zeki.gunduz@tr.pwc.com

Significant developments

Accounting rules
Please note that the new Commercial Code has now been approved. According to this new legislation, the International Financial Reporting Standards (IFRS) based accounting and reporting rules will apply starting from 2013.

For the current and previous periods, unless a company operates as a financial institution or is listed in a stock exchange, it is not compulsory for them to consider IFRS in their books. Accordingly, such companies are required to keep their books in accordance with the requirements of tax legislation and Turkish Generally Accepted Accounting Principles (GAAP), which is tax driven.

New tax law
Law No. 6322, which makes amendments to various tax laws, was promulgated in the Official Gazette dated 15 June 2012. The Law comprises 44 articles together with enforcement and effectiveness articles. The Law amends some articles of Corporate Income Tax (CIT) Law, which are summarised below.

Incentives for overseas services
50% of the earnings derived from architecture, engineering, design, software, medical reporting, bookkeeping, call centre, and data storage services, as well as training and health services, rendered to parties located outside of Turkey can be deducted from the CIT base on condition that such services are rendered in Turkey and benefitted from abroad. Please note that such earnings must be shown separately on the CIT return.

Deductable activities can be divided into two groups. The first group includes services of architecture, engineering, design, software, medical reporting, bookkeeping, call centre, and data storage rendered in Turkey and benefitted from abroad. Education and health services fall into the second group. To benefit from the deduction, the companies involved in these activities:

- should perform their activities by obtaining the necessary permits, and
- should provide the service to parties not resident in Turkey.

The requirement that the service should be exclusively benefitted from abroad does not apply to education and health services.

Restriction on financial expenses
A portion (yet to be determined by the Council of Ministers) of interest and similar expenses incurred on foreign resources will not qualify as a deduction for CIT purposes. According to the arrangement:

Turkey

- credit institutions, financial institutions, financial leasing, factoring, and financing companies shall not be subject to finance cost restrictions
- cost restrictions shall apply exclusively to the portion of liabilities that exceed a company's shareholder's equity
- restrictions shall not exceed 10% of financial expenses and the rate may be amended per industry by the Council of Ministers, and
- restrictions shall not apply to interest and similar payments added to investment costs.

The arrangement shall be effective as of 1 January 2013.

Taxes on corporate income

Corporations are liable for CIT at a rate of 20% on net profits generated, as adjusted for exemptions and deductions and including prior-year losses carried forward, to a limited extent.

According to Turkish tax legislation, income taxation differs significantly based on the taxpayer's place of residence. Resident entities are subject to tax on their worldwide income, whereas non-resident entities are taxed solely on the income derived from activities in Turkey.

Corporate residence

If both the legal and the business headquarters of a company are located outside Turkey, the company is regarded as a non-resident entity for Turkish tax purposes. If one of these headquarters is located within Turkey, the company is regarded as a resident entity for Turkish tax purposes.

Note that there is no distinction between CIT and value-added tax (VAT) registration in Turkey. Therefore, corporations or PEs are liable for all taxes (e.g. CIT, VAT, withholding tax [WHT], stamp tax) once they are registered for tax purposes in Turkey.

Permanent establishment (PE)

Unlike the provisions of the Organisation for Economic Co-operation and Development (OECD) Model Tax Convention on Income and on Capital, there is no minimum period of presence in Turkey before a presence is regarded under the Turkish tax legislation as a PE. In this regard, we believe that the PE evaluation should be made for each case depending on the merit of the cases both from a local legislation perspective and from a treaty (if applicable) perspective.

Other taxes

Value-added tax (VAT)

Deliveries of goods and services are subject to VAT at rates varying from 1% to 18%. The general rate is 18%. VAT payable on local purchases and on imports is regarded as 'input VAT', and VAT calculated and collected on sales is considered 'output VAT'. Input VAT is offset against output VAT in the VAT return filed at the related tax office. If output VAT is in excess of input VAT, the excess amount is paid to the related tax office. Conversely, if input VAT exceeds output VAT, the balance is carried forward to the following months to be offset against future output VAT. With the exception of a few situations such as exportation and sales to an investment incentive holder, there is no cash refund to recover excess input VAT.

Turkish VAT principles contain a 'reverse-charge VAT mechanism', which requires the calculation of VAT by resident entities on payments to persons in foreign countries. Under this mechanism, VAT is calculated and paid to the related tax office by the resident entity. The resident entity treats this VAT as input VAT and offsets it in the same month. This VAT does not create a tax burden for the resident or non-resident entity, except for its cash flow effect on the former if there is insufficient output VAT to offset the input VAT.

Banking and insurance transactions tax (BITT)
The transactions being performed by licensed banks and insurance companies are generally exempt from VAT but are subject to BITT at a rate of 5%, which is due on the gains of such corporations from their transactions.

The purchase of goods and services by banks and insurance companies are subject to VAT, but this is considered an expense or cost item. Therefore, it is not recoverable (i.e. for VAT purposes by offsetting against the output VAT) in the hands of these corporations.

Special consumption tax
There are four main product groups that are subject to special consumption tax:

- Petroleum products, natural gas, lubricating oil, solvents, and derivatives of solvents.
- Automobiles and other vehicles, motorcycles, planes, helicopters, yachts.
- Tobacco and tobacco products, alcoholic beverages.
- Luxury products.

Unlike VAT, which is applied on each delivery, special consumption tax is charged only once (except for some activities such as production).

Customs and foreign trade
PwC Turkey's customs and foreign trade specialist team would be pleased to assist in determination of customs duties and in providing extensive information regarding the local excise regime.

Property taxes
Buildings and land owned in Turkey are subject to real estate tax at different rates.

Stamp tax
Stamp tax applies to a wide range of documents, including but not limited to agreements, financial statements, and payrolls. Stamp tax is levied as a percentage of the value stated on the agreements at rates varying between 0.165% and 0.825%.

Salary payments are subject to stamp tax at a rate of 0.66% over the gross amounts, whereas a lump-sum stamp tax is calculated for certain types of documents such as the printed copies of the financial statements.

Resource utilisation support fund (RUSF)
Foreign loans (including trade payables) obtained by Turkish resident individuals or legal entities (except for banks or financial institutions) are subject to RUSF at the following rates:

Turkey

- 6% at the customs stage on purchases on credit.
- 3% over the principal or the interest amount (note that this depends on the currency denomination and on the average maturity).
- 0% in case of locally obtained loans.

Note that special exemptions may apply in cases where one is investing in certain industries.

Branch income

Branches are taxed solely on the income derived from activities in Turkey since they are regarded as non-resident entities for Turkish tax purposes. Branch profits are subject to Turkish CIT at the rate of 20%.

The branch profit transferred to headquarters (i.e. upstream income repatriation) is subject to dividend WHT at a rate of 15%, which might be reduced if there is a bilateral tax treaty between Turkey and the country of which the principal is a resident for income tax purposes. *See the Withholding taxes section for a list of countries with which Turkey has an applicable tax treaty.*

Income determination

Inventory valuation
The weighted average and first in first out (FIFO) methods are allowed for calculating the value of year-end stock or goods sold. Last in first out (LIFO) is not permitted. Stock-count deficits are recorded as disallowable expenses, whereas stock-count surpluses are treated as income at year-end for CIT purposes. Necessary VAT adjustments should also be made accordingly.

Capital gains
No separate rules exist with respect to capital gains taxation in Turkey. Capital gains and losses are included in the determination of taxable corporate income.

See Capital gains exemption in the Tax credits and incentives section for information about an incentive that can reduce the effective CIT rate on capital gains in certain instances.

Dividend income
In dividend distribution's between Turkish resident companies, the dividend payer is exempt from WHT and the recipient is exempt from CIT.

Interest income
In principle, all interest income is subject to tax. Interest income on bank deposits denominated in both Turkish lira and foreign currency is subject to WHT. Interest income is recorded at gross, and any WHT incurred on this income is offset against CIT calculated.

Foreign income
In principle, foreign-sourced income is taxable in Turkey. However, foreign-sourced dividend income may also be subject to a participation exemption, if certain conditions are fulfilled. A participation exemption for capital gains generated from a foreign subsidiary may also be available in Turkey, under certain conditions.

Turkey

Other foreign-sourced income, such as royalties and interest, is fully taxable in Turkey. Partial relief from taxation is granted insofar as the foreign tax paid does not exceed the rate of tax payable for the same income in Turkey.

Although undistributed income of foreign subsidiaries should not be taxable in Turkey, controlled foreign company (CFC) rules should also be taken into consideration in this respect. *See Controlled foreign companies (CFCs) in the Group taxation section for more information.*

Deductions

Turkish CIT legislation allows a deduction for all the "ordinary and necessary expenses paid or incurred for the generation and sustenance of income during the taxable year in carrying on any trade or business".

The general principle for tax deductibility is that the payment should be a necessary business expense and it should be properly documented in accordance with the relevant provisions of the Turkish transfer pricing regulations and those in the local tax procedural law.

Depreciation and amortisation
Fixed assets are subject to depreciation at rates determined by the Turkish Ministry of Finance (MoF), based on their useful life.

Intangible assets (i.e. licence, franchise, copyright, etc.) and goodwill are depreciated over 15 years and five years, respectively. Additionally, leasehold improvement is depreciated based on lease period.

Depreciation can be calculated by applying either the straight-line or declining-balance method, at the taxpayer's discretion. The taxpayer may also change the option from declining-balance to straight-line (but not vice versa) at any time during the life of the asset. The applicable rate for the declining-balance method is twice the rate of the straight-line method, subject to certain limitations. Furthermore, in special cases, the tax authorities may determine higher depreciation rates.

Intangible assets are amortised by the straight-line method over their estimated useful lives, if objectively determinable.

Profits or losses on disposal of fixed assets (i.e. the difference between the proceeds and the written-down values) are included in taxable income in the year of disposal. If the renewal of disposed-of assets is considered necessary by the owners of the business concern, the profit accrued may be retained for a certain amount of time. After the purchase of new fixed assets, the profits may be offset against the depreciation of the new assets.

Start-up expenses
Start-up expenses are considered as deductible expenses as incurred. Also, the taxpayer has the option to capitalise such expenses and to depreciate them over five years.

Bad debt
Bad and doubtful accounts receivable are deductible under certain conditions. Amounts of the receivables collected afterwards are added to the profits of the year in which they are collected.

Turkey

Pensions and employee termination benefits
Payments for pensions and employee termination benefits are deductible for CIT purposes under certain conditions and are not subject to WHT beyond a certain limit.

Fines and penalties
In principle, fines and penalties incurred due to the wrong-doings of the taxpayer or its employees are not tax deductible.

Taxes
Essentially, the CIT itself and VAT are, subject to certain exceptions, not deductible for CIT purposes.

Fees and duties paid in relation to assets of the company are, in principle, deductible in determining taxable corporate income.

Net operating losses
Corporate losses may be carried forward for five years. Losses cannot be carried back.

Payments to foreign affiliates
Charges for royalties and interest by foreign affiliates may be deductible for CIT purposes, provided that transfer pricing and thin capitalisation rules are followed (*see the Group taxation section for more information*).

Group taxation

Consolidation of the accounts of group companies for tax purposes is not allowed in Turkey since each company is regarded as a separate taxpayer.

Transfer pricing
The new corporate income tax law includes considerable amendments to transfer pricing regulations, using the OECD's guidelines as a basis. If a taxpayer enters into transactions regarding the sale or purchase of goods and services with related parties in which prices are not set in accordance with the arm's-length principle, the related profits are considered to have been distributed in a disguised manner through transfer pricing. Such disguised profit distribution through transfer pricing is not accepted as deductible for CIT purposes. The methods prescribed in the law are the traditional transaction methods described in the OECD's transfer pricing guidelines.

Thin capitalisation
According to local thin capitalisation regulation, if the ratio of the borrowings from shareholders or from persons related to the shareholders exceeds triple the shareholders' equity of the borrower company at any time within the relevant year, the exceeding portion of the borrowing will be considered thin capital and the corresponding interest will not be deductible. Accordingly, the ratio of loans received from related parties to shareholders' equity must be no more than 3:1 in order to eliminate Turkish thin capitalisation issues.

Controlled foreign companies (CFCs)
A CFC is a company established abroad with at least 50% of the organisation controlled directly or indirectly by tax-resident companies and real persons by means of separate or joint participation in the capital or dividends voting rights. A CFC also must meet certain conditions (e.g. 25% or more of its gross revenue must be comprised of passive

income), and it must be subject to an effective income tax rate lower than 10% for its commercial profit in its home country.

The CFC's profit is included in the CIT base of the controlling resident corporation at the rate of the shares controlled, irrespective of whether it is distributed.

Tax credits and incentives

Foreign tax credit
A partial relief from income taxation is granted for the foreign tax paid that does not exceed the rate of tax payable for the same income in Turkey.

Participation exemption for dividends
There is an unconditional CIT and dividend WHT exemption for dividend income between Turkish companies. If a Turkish company has a shareholding in a foreign company, this dividend income is exempt from CIT, under certain conditions.

Exemption for income from foreign construction and repair activities
The profit from construction and repair activities carried out by Turkish corporations in foreign countries may be exempt from CIT in Turkey under the Turkish CIT law. It should be noted that if loss occurs from these activities, it is not possible to deduct this loss amount from the income generated through domestic activities since deduction of a loss relating to foreign activities that are exempt from CIT in Turkey is not allowed for deduction.

Capital gains exemption
For capital gains generated from the sale of shares in a company, a 75% CIT exemption is applicable under certain conditions. This partial exemption may also be applicable for the capital gains derived from the alienation of real estate investments under certain conditions.

In the event a foreign subsidiary is sold by a Turkish company, a CIT exemption at the rate of 100% is applicable under certain conditions.

Investment incentives
The Turkish government provides investment incentives (state aids) to eliminate inter-regional economic imbalance, facilitate a larger capital contribution by public and foreign investors to the capital build-up of the country, and support activities that have a positive effect on employment. Generally speaking, state aid can be classified as either a tax or a non-tax incentive.

The principal prerequisite for benefiting from state aid, except investment allowance, is to obtain an Investment Incentive Certificate (IIC). The IIC is a document granted to investors for their investments by the Undersecretariat for the Treasury. It allows utilisation of the said benefits. The import of machinery and equipment (excluding raw materials, intermediate, and operating products) is exempt from customs duty and RUSF payments. In addition, a VAT exemption is also applicable on the importation of eligible machinery and equipment.

According to investment incentive legislation, in order to obtain an IIC, the minimum amount of total investment should be at least 1 million Turkish lira (TRY), except for certain geographical locations with lower requirements.

Turkey

The advantages of an IIC can be summarised as exemption from customs duty, RUSF, and VAT.

From an income tax perspective, the legislation related to investment incentives has changed substantially. There are six main components of the new investment regulation:

- Reduced CIT rate.
- VAT exemption.
- Exemption for social security premium (employer's portion).
- Customs duty exemption.
- Interest support.
- Allocation of land for investments.

Free trade zone
Free trade zones are special sites that lie geographically within the country but are deemed to be outside the customs territory. In these regions, the normal regulations related to foreign trade and other financial and economic areas are either inapplicable, partly applicable, or superseded by new regulations.

In general, activities such as manufacturing, storage, packing, general trading, banking, insurance, and trade may be performed in Turkish free trade zones. Goods moving between Turkey and the zones are treated, for all purposes, as exports or imports. However, operations within the zones are subject to the supervision of the zone management (and customs authorities), to whom regular activity reports must be submitted. Consequently, there is a requirement for zone users to maintain full accounting records (in Turkish) with respect to their activities. These accounting requirements extend to inventory records. Customs duty is levied on any unexplained inventory losses as though the goods had been imported into the country.

The right to operate in a free zone is conferred by an operating licence obtained from the Undersecretariat for Foreign Trade, which reviews the application for conformity with the objectives and types of activity specified by the Economic Affairs Coordination Council.

Portfolio investment income
In line with the amendments in the Turkish income tax law certain investment income (e.g. capital gains on listed equities acquired after 1 January 2006 and interest and capital gains from domestic government bonds or treasury bills issued after 1 January 2006), derived by non-resident corporations without having a PE in Turkey and by non-resident individuals, is currently subject to WHT at source.

The following investors will qualify for WHT at a rate of 0%:

- Turkish resident capital corporations (limited liability companies, joint stock companies, and comandite companies whose capital is divided into shares).
- Non-resident corporations which have the same characteristics as Turkish capital corporations.
- Turkish investment funds (regulated in accordance with the Capital Markets Board or CMB).
- Non-resident investment funds similar to Turkish investment funds.
- Those non-residents similar to Turkish investment funds and trusts which engage in investment in securities and other capital markets instruments as their only business

in Turkey, to derive income and capital gains from these instruments, and to exert the rights attached to these instruments.

WHT is applied at a rate of 10% for both resident and non-resident individuals and for all other entities which are not qualified for 0% WHT (i.e. those who are not listed above).

The withholding will be applied by local intermediary banks, brokerage houses, or local custodian banks, instead of the conventional self-declaration mechanism, and this withholding would be the final taxation in Turkey both for non-residents and Turkish individuals.

Research and development (R&D) activities
In the last decade, the Turkish Parliament has enacted several regulations to provide incentives for R&D activities in Turkey. The three primary R&D incentives include significant advantages granted to investors planning R&D activities in science, software, and technology in special zones known as 'techno-parks', cash subsidies from the Scientific and Technological Research Council of Turkey (TUBITAK), and corporate tax deductions.

One of the objectives of the special R&D law is to attract foreign investors with significant R&D activities abroad to invest in Turkey, by enabling non-resident companies with a subsidiary or branch in Turkey to benefit from R&D tax incentives. The main incentives introduced by this R&D law are listed as follows:

R&D deduction
All eligible innovation and R&D expenditures made in technology centres or R&D centres, which must employ at least 50 full-time equivalent R&D personnel, or R&D and innovation projects supported by foundations established by law or international funds can be deducted from the CIT base at a rate of 100%.The same expenditures can also be capitalised and expensed through amortisation over five years in the case of successful projects, whereas the R&D expenditure on failed projects can be expensed immediately.

Companies with separate R&D centres employing more than 500 R&D personnel can, in addition to the aforementioned deduction, deduct half of any increase in R&D expenditures over similar money spent in the previous period.

Any unutilised R&D deduction can be carried forward for an unlimited period of time, indexed to the revaluation rate, which is an approximation of the inflation rate.

Income WHT exemption on salaries
80% of the salary income of eligible R&D and support personnel is exempt from income WHT. However, this rate is increased to 90% for personnel with a doctorate degree.

Support for the contributions to the Turkish social security institution
The MoF will pay half the employer portion of social security premiums for R&D and support personnel for five years.

Stamp tax exemption
Documents prepared in relation to R&D activities are exempt from stamp tax.

Turkey

Withholding taxes

There is no WHT on payments to resident corporations by other resident corporations, except for a 3% WHT on progress payments to contractors, both domestic and foreign, within the scope of construction work spanning more than one calendar year.

The local WHT rates are as follows:

Income derived by non-resident individual or corporation not constituting PE in Turkey	WHT (%)
Rental from immovable assets	20
Leasing of goods (within the scope of the conditions regulated under Turkish Financial Leasing Law No. 3226)	1
Royalties (e.g. on patents, copyrights, licence)	20
Professional services	20
Petroleum services	5
Wages & salaries (progressive rates are applied for employees' income taxes)	15 to 35
Interest on loan arrangements	
Interest payments made to foreign banks and corporations that are authorised in their own jurisdictions and customarily lend not only to related parties but also to third parties	0
Interest payments made in relation to securitisation loans	1
Other loans	10
Interest on time deposits	15
Reverse-repo income derived from bonds	15
Income derived by resident eligible entities *	**WHT (%)**
Capital gains on Treasury bills and domestic government bonds issued after 1 January 2006	0
Interest income on Treasury bills and domestic government bonds issued after 1 January 2006	0
Capital gains from listed equities purchased after 1 January 2006	0
Income derived by other entities and individuals	**WHT (%)**
Capital gains on Treasury bills and domestic government bonds issued after 1 January 2006	10
Interest income on Treasury bills and domestic government bonds issued after 1 January 2006	10
Capital gains from listed equities purchased after 1 January 2006 (excluding those purchased by securities investment trusts after 1 January 2006)	0
Capital gains from equities of securities investment trusts purchased after 1 January 2006	10
Turkish investment funds	**WHT (%)**
Eligible entities * (both residents and non-residents)	0
Other entities and individuals ** (both residents and non-residents)	10

* Under the *Communiqué* No. 277 of Income Tax Law, the eligible entities refer to the following:

* Turkish resident capital corporations (limited liability companies, joint stock companies, and commandite companies whose capital is divided into shares).
* Non-resident corporations which have the same characteristics as Turkish capital corporations.
* Turkish investment funds (regulated in accordance with the Capital Markets Board).
* Non-resident investment funds similar to Turkish investment funds.
* Those non-residents similar to Turkish investment funds and trusts which engage in investment in securities and other capital markets instruments as their only business in Turkey, to derive income and capital gains from these instruments and to exert the rights attached to these instruments.

Turkey

Under the aforementioned *Communiqué*, the investor should be an institutional portfolio investor. However, what is meant by 'institutional' is not crystal clear. It seems to us that the intention of the MoF is to treat all non-resident portfolio investors (other than the individuals) as institutional portfolio investors. The *Communiqué* does not have a principle based approach, rather it enlists a number of 'institutional investor' examples, such as limited liability partnerships (LLPs), sovereign funds, investment funds, investment institutions, and investment companies.

** Income derived from the redemption of participation certificates which continuously invest at least 51% of their assets in equities that are registered on the Istanbul Stock Exchange are not subject to WHT if they are held at least for one year.

Please refer to the following tables for local WHT on interest, royalties, and dividends, respectively:

Turkish WHT on interest and royalties

Recipient	Interest (%)	Royalties (%)
Albania	10	10
Algeria	10	10
Austria	5/10/15 (1, 2, 15)	10 (2)
Azerbaijan	10	10
Bahrain	10	10
Bangladesh	10	10
Belarus	10	10
Belgium	15 (1)	10
Bosnia Herzegovina	10	10
Bulgaria	10	10
Canada	15 (1, 19)	10
China (People's Republic of)	10	10
Croatia	10	10
Czech Republic	10	10
Denmark	15 (1)	10
Egypt	10	10
Estonia	10	5/10 (12)
Ethiopia	10	10
Finland	15 (1)	10
France	15 (1)	10
Georgia	10	10
Germany	15 (1, 14)	10 (14)
Greece	12 (1)	10
Hungary	10	10
India	10/15 (1, 6)	15
Indonesia	10	10
Iran	10	10
Ireland	10/15 (1, 17)	10
Israel	10	10
Italy	15 (1)	10
Japan	10/15 (1, 5)	10
Jordan	10	12
Kazakhstan	10	10
Korea, Republic of	10/15 (1, 3)	10
Kuwait	10	10
Kyrgyzstan	10	10

Turkey

Recipient	Interest (%)	Royalties (%)
Latvia	10	5/10 (12)
Lebanon	10	10
Lithuania	10	5/10 (12)
Luxembourg	10/15 (1, 4)	10
Macedonia	10	10
Malaysia	15 (1)	10
Moldova	10	10
Mongolia	10	10
Morocco	10	10
Netherlands, The	10/15 (1, 4)	10
New Zealand	15 (1, 21)	10
Northern Cyprus, Turkish Republic of	10	10
Norway	15 (1, 20)	10
Oman	10 (18)	10
Pakistan	10	10
Poland	10	10
Portugal	10/15 (1, 4)	10
Qatar	10	10
Romania	10	10
Russia	10	10
Saudi Arabia	10 (16)	10
Serbia-Montenegro	10	10
Singapore	7.5/10 (8)	10
Slovakia	10	10
Slovenia	10	10
South Africa	10	10
Spain	10/15 (1, 9)	10
Sudan	10	10
Sweden	15 (1)	10
Syria	10	10/15 (13)
Tajikistan	10	10
Thailand	10/15 (1, 10)	15
Tunisia	10	10
Turkmenistan	10	10
Ukraine	10	10
United Arab Emirates (UAE)	10	10
United Kingdom	15 (1)	10
United States (US)	10/15 (1, 7)	5/10 (11)
Uzbekistan	10	10
Yemen	10 (18)	10

Notes

1. The local rate of 10% will be applied in the event a higher rate is stipulated in the agreement.
2. Provisions for WHT at source are effective for amounts paid or credited on or after 1 January 2010.
3. A rate of 10% if the loan or other debt claim is for a period exceeding two years; 15% in all other cases (1).
4. A rate of 10% if the loan is taken for a period exceeding two years; 15% in all other cases (1).
5. A rate of 10% if the loan/credit is taken from a financial institution; 15% in all other cases (1).
6. A rate of 10% if the loan is taken from a bank or a financial institution; 15% in all other cases (1).

7. A rate of 10% if the credit/loan is taken from a bank, financial or savings institution, insurance company; 15% in all other cases (1).
8. A rate of 7.5% if the loan is taken from a financial institution; 10% in all other cases.
9. A rate of 10% if the interest is the result of a loan provided/given by a bank or if the interest is paid in return for an article of merchandise, or equipment given to the contracting state on credit; 15% in all other cases (1).
10. A rate of 10% if the loan is taken from a financial institution, including insurance companies; 15% in all other cases (1).
11. A rate of 10% for the use of, the right to use, or the sale (contingent on the productivity, use, or disposition) of any copyright of literary, artistic, or scientific work, including royalties in respect of motion pictures and works on film, tape, or other means of reproduction for use in connection with radio or television broadcasting, any patent, trademark, design or model, plan, secret formula, or process, or for information concerning, industrial, commercial, or scientific experience; 5% for the use of or the right to use industrial, commercial, or scientific equipment.
12. A rate of 5% for the use of industrial, commercial, or scientific equipment; 10% in all other cases.
13. A rate of 15% for patent, trademark, design or model, plan, secret formula or process, or for information concerning industrial, commercial, or scientific experience; 10% for the use of or the right to use any copyright of literary, artistic, or scientific work including cinematographic films and recordings for radio and television.
14. The treaty has been terminated by Germany. The termination is applied for the periods following 1 January 2011.
15. A rate of 5% in respect of a loan or credit made, guaranteed, or insured for the purposes of promoting export by the *Oesterreichische Kontrollbank AG* or a similar Turkish public entity the objective of which is to promote the export; 10% if the interest is derived by a bank; 15% in all other cases (1).
16. If the beneficial owner of the 'income from debt claims' is a resident of Saudi Arabia, the tax so charged shall not exceed 10% of the gross amount of income.
17. A rate of 10% in respect of a loan or other debt claim for a period exceeding two years or if the interest is received by a financial institution; 15% in all other cases (1).
18. Interest arising in one of the contracting states and paid to the government of Turkey or the Central Bank of Turkey shall be exempt from income taxes in the contracting state. Similarly, interest arising in the Republic of Turkey and paid to the government or the Central Bank of the other contracting state shall be exempt from income taxes in Turkey.
19. Interest arising in Turkey and paid to the government of Canada or to the Bank of Canada shall be exempt from Turkish tax. Similarly, interest arising in Canada and paid to the government of Turkey or to the Central Bank of Turkey *(Türkiye Cumhuriyet Merkez Bankasi)* shall be exempt from Canadian Tax.
20. The rate of the income tax shall not exceed (i) 10% if the interest is paid to a bank (also note that in the case of Turkey, a lower rate of 0% may apply for eligible financial institutions' and banks' loans under the domestic regulation) or (ii) 5% if the interest is paid to the Norwegian Government Pension Fund *(Statens Pensjonsfond)*, the Norwegian Guarantee Institute for Export Credits *(Garantiinstituttet for Eksportkreditt)*, the Turkish Social Security Fund *(Sosyal Guvenlik Fonu)* and the Eximbank of Turkey *(Turkiye Ihracat Kredi Bankasi)*.
21. The rate of the income tax (i) shall not exceed 10% if the interest is paid to a bank (also note that in the case of Turkey, under the domestic regulation, a lower rate of 0% may apply for the loans provided by eligible financial institutions and banks). The interest shall be exempt from income taxes in the contracting state where it arises, if the payment is made to the government of Turkey, to the Central Bank of Turkey *(Turkiye Cumhuriyeti Merkez Bankasi)*, to the government of New Zealand, or to the Reserve Bank of New Zealand.

Turkish WHT on dividends

Dividend distributions to individuals and to non-resident persons who are shareholders are subject to WHT at a local rate of 15%. This rate might be reduced for non-resident shareholders in the presence of a tax treaty. Please note that dividend distributions to resident entities and branches of non-resident entities are not subject to WHT.

Recipient	Shareholding interest	WHT rate (%)
Albania	If greater than or equal to 25%	5
	In all other cases	15
Algeria		12
Austria	If greater than or equal to 25%	5 (2, 7)
	In all other cases	15 (2, 7)
Azerbaijan		12
Bahrain	If greater than or equal to 25%	10

Turkey

Recipient	Shareholding interest	WHT rate (%)
	In all other cases	15
Bangladesh		10
Belarus	If greater than or equal to 25%	10
	In all other cases	15
Belgium	If greater than or equal to 10%	15 (2)
	In all other cases	20 (1, 2)
Bosnia Herzegovina	If greater than or equal to 25%	5
	In all other cases	15
Bulgaria	If greater than or equal to 25%	10
	In all other cases	15
Canada	If greater than or equal to 10%	15
	In all other cases	20 (1)
China (People's Republic of)		10
Croatia		10
Czech Republic		10
Denmark	If greater than or equal to 25%	15
	In all other cases	20 (1)
Egypt	If greater than or equal to 25%	5
	In all other cases	15
Estonia		10
Ethiopia		10
Finland	If greater than or equal to 25%	15
	In all other cases	20 (1)
France	If greater than or equal to 10%	15
	In all other cases	20 (1)
Georgia		10
Germany	If greater than or equal to 10%	15 (6)
	In all other cases	20 (1, 6)
Greece		15
Hungary	If greater than or equal to 25%	10
	In all other cases	15
India		15
Indonesia	If greater than or equal to 25%	10
	In all other cases	15
Iran	If greater than or equal to 25%	15
	In all other cases	20 (1)
Ireland	If greater than or equal to 25%	5/10 (2, 9)
	In all other cases	15 (2)
Israel		10
Italy		15
Japan	If greater than or equal to 25%	10 (4)
	In all other cases	15
Jordan	If greater than or equal to 25%	10
	In all other cases	15
Kazakhstan		10
Korea, Republic of	If greater than or equal to 25%	15
	In all other cases	20 (1)

Recipient	Shareholding interest	WHT rate (%)
Kuwait		10
Kyrgyzstan		10
Latvia		10
Lebanon	If greater than or equal to 15%	10
	In all other cases	15
Lithuania		10
Luxembourg	If greater than or equal to 25%	10
	In all other cases	20 (1)
Macedonia	If greater than or equal to 25%	5
	In all other cases	10
Malaysia	If greater than or equal to 25%	10
	In all other cases	15
Moldova	If greater than or equal to 25%	10
	In all other cases	15
Mongolia		10
Morocco	If greater than or equal to 25%	7
	In all other cases	10
Netherlands, The	If greater than or equal to 25%	15 (2)
	In all other cases	20 (1, 2)
New Zealand	If greater than or equal to 25%	5 (11)
	In all other cases	15
Northern Cyprus, Turkish Republic of	If greater than or equal to 25%	15
	In all other cases	20 (1)
Norway	If greater than or equal to 20%	5
	In all other cases	15 (10)
Oman	If greater than or equal to 15%	10
	In all other cases	15
Pakistan	If greater than or equal to 25%	10
	In all other cases	15
Poland	If greater than or equal to 25%	10
	In all other cases	15
Portugal	If greater than or equal to 25%	5
	In all other cases	15
Qatar	If greater than or equal to 25%	10
	In all other cases	15
Romania		15
Russia		10
Saudi Arabia	If greater than or equal to 20%	5 (8)
	In all other cases	10
Serbia-Montenegro	If greater than or equal to 25%	5
	In all other cases	15
Singapore	If greater than or equal to 25%	10
	In all other cases	15
Slovakia	If greater than or equal to 25%	5
	In all other cases	10
Slovenia		10
South Africa	If greater than or equal to 25%	10

Turkey

Recipient	Shareholding interest	WHT rate (%)
	In all other cases	15
Spain	If greater than or equal to 25%	5 (5)
	In all other cases	15
Sudan		10
Sweden	If greater than or equal to 25%	15
	In all other cases	20 (1)
Syria		10
Tajikistan		10
Thailand	If greater than or equal to 25%	10
	In all other cases	15
Tunisia	If greater than or equal to 25%	12
	In all other cases	15
Turkmenistan		10
Ukraine	If greater than or equal to 25%	10
	In all other cases	15
United Arab Emirates (UAE)	If greater than or equal to 25%	10 (3)
	In all other cases	12
United Kingdom	If greater than or equal to 25%	15
	In all other cases	20 (1)
United States (US)	If greater than or equal to 10%	15
	In all other cases	20 (1)
Uzbekistan		10
Yemen		10

Notes

1. The local rate is 15% for dividends. Unless a lower rate is stated in the Agreement, the local rate is applied.
2. As per the provisions of the protocol amending the agreement, the rate may be (partially or wholly) reduced;
   - For the Netherlands: to 10%, as long as, under the provisions of the Netherlands Company Tax Act and to the future amendments thereto, a company which is a resident of the Netherlands is not charged tax with respect to dividends the company receives from a company which is a resident of Turkey.
   - For Belgium: to 10%, as long as, under the provisions of the Belgian laws and of the future amendments thereto, a company which is a resident of Belgium is not charged tax with respect to dividends the company receives from a company which is a resident of Turkey.
   - For Austria: to 5%, if the beneficial owner is a company (other than a partnership) which holds directly at least 25% of the capital of the company paying the dividends, provided that such dividends are exempt from tax in Austria.
   - For Ireland: to 5%, where the beneficial owner is a company (other than a partnership) which holds directly at least 25% of the voting power of the company paying the dividends. 15% in all other cases.
3. Subject to 5% of the gross amount of the dividends if the recipient is the government, or a public institution which is wholly owned by the government or its political subdivisions, or local authorities of the UAE.
4. The tax rate shall be 15% where the amount of the Turkish tax imposed on the income of the company paying dividends is less than 40% of such income derived in the accounting period ending immediately before the date when such dividends become payable.
5. The income should be subject to full corporate taxation in the hands of the Turkish tax-resident subsidiary.
6. The treaty has been terminated by Germany. The termination is applied for the periods following 1 January 2011.
7. The provisions for WHT at source are effective for amounts paid or credited on or after 1 January 2010.
8. If the beneficial owner of the dividends is a resident of Saudi Arabia, the tax so charged shall not exceed 5% of the gross amount of the dividends provided: (i) the beneficial owner is a company (other than a partnership) which holds directly at least 20% of the capital of the Turkish company

paying the dividends or (ii) the beneficial owner is a central bank or an entity which is wholly owned by the government.
9. In case of Turkey, the tax rate shall not exceed 5%, to the extent that they are paid out of profits that have been subject to full rate of CIT in Turkey (i.e. without benefiting from tax exemption).
10. The rate of the income tax shall not exceed 5% if it is derived by the Government Pension Fund *(Statens Pensjonsfond)* or by the Government Social Security Fund *(Sosyal Guvenlik Fonu)*, provided that such dividends are exempt from tax in the contracting state where the beneficial owner is a resident.
11. The treaty-reduced rate of 5% shall apply if such dividends are exempt from tax in the contracting state of which the beneficial owner is a resident.

Anti-tax haven provisions

According to the law, all sorts of payments made to corporations (including branches of resident corporations) that are established or operational in countries that are regarded by the Turkish Council of Ministers to undermine fair tax competition (through taxation or other practices) may be subject to taxation in Turkey through withholding at a rate of 30%.

In the meantime, the Turkish Council of Ministers has not yet determined which countries receiving payments are considered 'tax havens'.

Tax administration

All Turkish taxes are imposed under laws drafted by or with the involvement of the Turkish MoF and are promulgated by the Turkish Parliament. The central government, acting through the MoF, imposes most of them, although local authorities have certain rights over some minor transaction charges. Tax procedures are governed by the Turkish tax procedural law.

Taxable period

The taxable period is the calendar year. Note that a different fiscal year is also allowed.

Tax returns

A self-assessment system is used in Turkey.

In principle, residents and non-resident entities having a PE in Turkey are obligated to be registered for all taxes in Turkey (e.g. CIT, VAT, WHT, stamp tax) and file annual CIT returns.

The last date of submission of the CIT return is the 25th day of the fourth month following the fiscal year-end. This date will be 25 April if CIT returns are filed on a calendar-year basis.

Payment of tax

Taxable income is declared on a quarterly-basis as advance tax on the 14th day of the second month following each quarter, and corresponding tax is payable on the 17th day of the same period. Advance CIT paid is offset against the final (i.e. fiscal year-end) CIT calculated in the annual CIT return.

The last date of payment of CIT is the 30th day of the fourth month following the fiscal year-end.

Turkey

Audit cycle
The tax authorities in Turkey do not have a regular audit cycle for every taxpayer. Tax audits are usually performed based on selection through risk assessment software, where they can conduct either sector-specific or issue-specific audits.

Statute of limitations
The Turkish tax system is based on self-assessment, and there is no procedure to agree the filed tax returns with the tax authorities that can prevent further inspections. Tax returns filed by companies remain open to tax inspection until the end of the five-year statute of limitations according to the provisions of Turkish Tax Procedural Law.

Corporate income tax certification
In Turkey, a special kind of tax control mechanism is established called 'corporate income tax certification'. Under this mechanism, the tax authority accepts accounts and tax returns of taxpayers whose accounts are audited and certified by Sworn Fiscal Advisors (SFAs) to be true and correct unless proved to be incorrect. On the other hand, the MoF has announced that those companies that do not have their tax returns certified as such will be on the priority list for tax inspection. The Ministry sets standards of work to be done for any taxpayer wanting to use an SFA. At the end of each year, SFAs have to prepare a comprehensive report to be submitted to the MoF and to certify the accuracy of the CIT return.

The work is carried out over the statutory financials that are subject to tax calculations. Note that this service is not of a 'statutory audit' nature, technically it is a 'non-audit assurance' work.

The tax certification process helps to identify and take corrective measures against erroneous applications that may otherwise be detected only upon a tax investigation by the Turkish MoF.

Other issues

For up-to-date information
For up-to-date information on the most recent and significant developments in Turkish tax regulations, please refer to the tax bulletins added to our tax portal, *Vergi Portali*, which can be accessed at Vergiportali.com.

Turkmenistan

PwC contact

Abdulkhamid Muminov
PricewaterhouseCoopers
52/1 Garashsyzlyk Street
Kopetdag Arap
Ashgabat 744000, Turkmenistan
Tel: +993 12 48 6015
Email: abdulkhamid.muminov@uz.pwc.com

Significant developments

A new law on currency regulations allows branches of foreign legal entities to execute transactions in foreign currencies within Turkmenistan.

A new law on state pension insurance, effective 1 January 2013, introduces obligatory pension insurance contributions payable by employers at the rate of 20% of total remuneration of the employees (Turkmen citizens and foreign individuals permanently residing in Turkmenistan). At this time, it is unclear whether the new pension insurance contribution is to replace the existing Social Security Contribution, which is currently paid by employers on payroll related to Turkmen citizens at the rate of 20%.

Taxes on corporate income

Residents of Turkmenistan are subject to corporate income tax (CIT) on worldwide income; non-residents are subject to CIT only in respect of their Turkmenistan-sourced income. The CIT base is determined as gross income less allowable deductions.

Branches of foreign legal entities are subject to a 20% CIT, whereas Turkmen legal entities are subject to an 8% CIT.

Companies involved in oil and gas operations are subject to a 20% CIT, irrespective of the legal status/ownership structure.

Special purpose duty for improvement of urban and rural territories
A special duty aimed at improving urban and rural territories is imposed on registered entities (e.g. legal entities and branches). The duty applies at 1% of the taxable base for CIT purposes. Generally, contractors and subcontractors operating under the umbrella of the petroleum law may be exempt from this duty.

Local income taxes

Contributions to Agriculture Development and Ashgabat City Development Funds
The contributions to the Agriculture Development Fund and Ashgabat City Development Fund are outside of the general tax legislation (tax code) and are provided for by specific decrees. Permanent establishments (PEs)/branches of foreign legal entities are subject to these contributions on the same terms as local legal entities.

Contribution to the Ashgabat City Development Fund only applies to entities located in Ashgabat City.

T

Turkmenistan

The base for the contributions is comprised of the accounting income. The contribution rate for the Agriculture Development Fund is 3%, and the contribution rate for the Ashgabat City Development Fund is 0.5%.

Generally, contractors and subcontractors operating under the umbrella of the petroleum law may be exempt from these contributions.

Corporate residence

Legal entities are treated as residents for CIT purposes if they are established in accordance with Turkmenistan law or their place of effective management is located in Turkmenistan.

Permanent establishment (PE)

The general definition of a PE under domestic legislation is similar to the one per the Organisation for Economic Co-operation and Development (OECD) model convention. A PE is a permanent place of the foreign legal entity in Turkmenistan, through which it, fully or partially, conducts entrepreneurial (commercial) activity, including that through an authorised person.

Other taxes

Value-added tax (VAT)

VAT is generally payable at the rate of 15%. A zero-rate applies to exports of goods (except for oil and gas) and international transport services. Generally, contractors operating under the umbrella of the petroleum law may be exempt from this tax.

The tax base is sales turnover including excise tax. If a sale is made by state-fixed prices, then the tax base is the respective sales turnover including VAT and excise tax. The amount of input VAT incurred may be offset against the amount of output VAT. The amount of input VAT related to capital expenditures should be capitalised.

Customs duties

The import of certain goods into Turkmenistan is subject to customs duties. The taxable base is determined as the customs value of imported goods. Although the list of items that are subject to customs duty is relatively limited (i.e. around 50 items) the rates of customs duties may vary from 5% (e.g. products from cement) to 100% (e.g. carbonic acid) depending on the type of imported goods. In most cases, the customs duty is set on an *ad valorem* basis. There is also a customs clearance fee of 0.2% from the customs value of imported goods.

Excise taxes

Excise tax is paid on goods or products that are considered in the list of excised goods or products. Normally, excised goods consist of alcoholic beverages, tobacco products, and automobiles. Excise rates vary based on the type of goods as well as by domestic production or import.

Property tax

Property tax in Turkmenistan generally applies at the rate of 1% on the average annual net book value of fixed assets and average annual value of tangible assets used for business purposes and located in Turkmenistan. Generally, contractors and subcontractors operating under the umbrella of the petroleum law may be exempt from this tax.

Transfer taxes
There are no transfer taxes in Turkmenistan.

Stamp taxes
Although state duties of various amounts set forth by the government may apply to certain actions (e.g. branch registration), there is no unified stamp tax/duty mechanism as normally practiced in other countries.

Subsurface-use tax
Subsurface-use taxpayers are legal entities and individual entrepreneurs extracting natural resources and using land or subsoil waters for the extraction of chemical products. This tax does not normally apply to contractors and subcontractors operating under the umbrella of the petroleum law.

Taxable operations include the sale of natural resources extracted by taxpayers and utilisation of natural resources for consumption. Tax rates vary depending on the goods being extracted. Natural or associated gas extraction is taxed at 22%, and crude oil extraction is taxed at 10%. Tax rates for other mineral resources vary depending on profitability (internal rate of return) from 0% to 50%.

Social security payments
Social security is payable by employers at 20% of the total remuneration provided to local employees. Income paid to expatriate employees should not be subject to the social security contribution.

Advertising levy
An advertising levy is imposed on the amount of expenses on commercial advertising and is to be paid quarterly at the rate of 3% to 5% depending on the location of the payer within Turkmenistan. Generally, contractors operating under the umbrella of the petroleum law may be exempt from this levy.

Branch income

Branches pay CIT at the rate of 20%.

Branches are taxed on profits received from activities in Turkmenistan. The gross income is reduced for expenses incurred (both inside and outside of Turkmenistan) in relation to the activities in Turkmenistan. The procedure for determining the taxable base for branches is generally similar to the one for Turkmen legal entities.

Branches subject to the standard tax regime also pay and file returns with respect to the other taxes described in this summary.

Income determination

Inventory valuation
Inventory is valued at cost, including costs relating to its acquisition. The law permits the use of the weighted average, first in first out (FIFO), and last in first out (LIFO) methods for tax purposes.

Turkmenistan

Capital gains
Capital gains are taxable as normal business income in Turkmenistan.

Dividend income
Generally, dividend income paid by Turkmen taxpayers is subject to taxation at the source of payment at the rate of 15%, irrespective of whether paid to residents of Turkmenistan or to non-residents.

Inter-company dividends
The tax code provides for relief from economic double taxation of inter-company dividends.

The withholding tax (WHT) rate on dividends payable by Turkmen legal entities to their foreign shareholders may be reduced under applicable double tax treaties (DTTs).

Technically, Turkmen branches of foreign legal entities may also be subject to 15% WHT on repatriation of income to their head offices. However, if the head office collects the income from its clients directly to its bank account abroad, the mechanism of collecting the dividend tax is unclear.

Interest income
Turkmenistan sourced interest income paid to non-residents that do not have PEs in Turkmenistan is subject to WHT of 15%. The above rate may be reduced under the applicable DTTs.

Foreign income
A resident company is subject to tax on its worldwide income (including capital gains). There are no provisions for tax deferrals in Turkmenistan tax legislation.

Deductions

In general, taxpayers may deduct expenses paid or accrued during the year in connection with their business and aimed at income generation. All expenses must be substantiated by documentary proof.

The deduction of certain expenses is subject to specific ceilings. Such expenses include representation expenses, which are deductible at up to 1% of gross income. Furthermore, deductible norms for business travel expenses are established periodically by the government.

Depreciation
Tax depreciation is based on accounting depreciation. Depreciation is accrued based on the straight-line method. Accelerated depreciation is also allowed based on specific consent of the Ministry of Finance. A new Presidential Decree establishes the maximum depreciation rates ranging from 5% to 25% for five different groups of assets.

Generally, for the purposes of CIT, depreciation accrued is deductible. Fixed assets acquired free of charge as well as assets of non-commercial legal entities, budget organisations, and public associations should be excluded from depreciable assets for CIT purposes, even if they are used for generating income.

Fixed assets provided under operational lease shall be depreciated by the lessor. Fixed assets provided under financial lease shall be depreciated by the lessee.

Goodwill
There are no provisions for goodwill in Turkmenistan tax legislation.

Start-up expenses
Pre-incorporation costs are generally non-deductible.

Interest expenses
Interest expense occurring from debt instruments of any kind should be deductible for CIT purposes provided that the purpose of the underlying debt relates to the entrepreneurial activity of the taxpayer.

Interest expense incurred by a foreign legal entity abroad and recharged to its branch in Turkmenistan is generally not deductible, unless specifically addressed by applicable DTTs.

Bad debts
The Tax Code permits a taxpayer to include provisions for uncollectable debts as well as losses incurred as a result of expiration of the collection period for accounts receivable.

Charitable contributions
There are no specific restrictions on deductibility of charitable contributions. However, they may be disallowed under the general restriction of non-business related deductions.

Repair and maintenance expenses
Deductible expenditures for the repair of fixed assets shall be comprised of the cost of spare parts and consumable materials used for repair, remuneration of employees carrying out the repairs, and other expenditures associated with such repairs, including payments to third parties for the purpose of such repairs.

Research and development (R&D) expenses
R&D costs (including those that produced no positive result) shall be subject to deduction from gross revenue, except for costs associated with the purchase of fixed assets, their installation, and other costs of a capital nature.

Fines and penalties
Fines, penalties, and other financial sanctions (except for tax-related ones) are deductible for CIT purposes.

Taxes
For CIT purposes, the following taxes are deductible: property tax; subsurface-use tax; levies established by the tax code (except the special-purpose duty for the improvement of urban and rural territories); accrued amounts of VAT in selling goods, performing work, and rendering of services; and amounts of excise tax included in the price of sold excisable goods by manufacturers of such goods.

Net operating losses
Loss is defined as excess of allowable deductions over gross revenue. Losses shall be carried forward and deducted in subsequent tax (reporting) periods, but not for more than three years. Losses cannot be carried back.

Payments to foreign affiliates
Administrative and management expenses incurred by the head office of a branch in Turkmenistan are not deductible at the branch level.

Turkmenistan

Group taxation

There is no group taxation in Turkmenistan.

Transfer pricing
The Turkmenistan Tax Code contains provisions concerning state supervision of transfer pricing. According to these rules, the tax authorities monitor and control transfer pricing of certain types of transactions, including transactions between related parties, foreign trade operations, and transactions where the tax authorities during tax audits perceive considerable deviation from the market price (i.e. more than 20%).

Thin capitalisation
There are no provisions for thin capitalisation in Turkmenistan tax legislation.

Tax credits and incentives

Tax and investment incentives may be negotiated on a case-by-case basis. The President has often issued special decrees granting taxation exemptions and other privileges to specific investors. However, since adopting a new edition of the tax code in 2004, such practice has been significantly reduced.

Foreign tax credit
Foreign tax credits are available to tax residents of Turkmenistan based on the provisions of the respective tax treaties. The tax credited shall not exceed the tax liability computed in accordance with Turkmenistan regulations.

Withholding taxes

Turkmenistan-source income generated by a foreign legal entity that has no PE in Turkmenistan generally is subject to WHT at the source of payment at 15% (6% for income from the lease of sea vessels and aircrafts).

Relief may be available for WHT if a foreign entity is a resident of a country that has a valid DTT with Turkmenistan and if the foreign entity complies with certain administrative procedures.

Currently, Turkmenistan has only a few DTTs in force. Turkmenistan is a successor to a number of DTTs concluded by the USSR, while some treaties were concluded and ratified by the government of Turkmenistan. The countries listed below are considered to have valid tax treaties with Turkmenistan:

Recipient	Dividends (%)	Interest (%)	Royalties (%)
Armenia	5/15 (1)	10	10
Austria *	0	0	0
Belarus	15	10	15
Belgium *	15	0/15 (2)	0
China	5/10 (3)	0/10 (4)	10
France *	15	0/10 (5)	0
Georgia	10	0/10 (6)	10
Germany *	15	0/5 (6, 7)	0

Turkmenistan

Recipient	Dividends (%)	Interest (%)	Royalties (%)
Great Britain *	0	0	0
India	10	0/10 (6, 8)	10
Iran	10	0/10 (9)	5
Japan *	10	0/15 (9)	10
Kazakhstan	10	0/10 (6)	10
Malaysia	10	0/10 (6)	10
Pakistan	10	10	10
Romania	10	10	15
Russia	10	5	5
Slovakia	10	0/10 (6)	10
Tajikistan	10	0/10 (6)	10
Turkey	10	0/10 (6)	10
Ukraine	10	0/10 (6)	10
United Arab Emirates	0	0	10
United States *	0	15	0
Uzbekistan	10	0/10 (10)	10

* USSR treaties honoured by Turkmenistan.

Notes

1. 5% where beneficial owner holds at least 25% of the authorised capital of the company paying the dividends.
2. 0% where one of the following conditions is met: (i) interest paid to the government of the other contracting state or interest paid in respect of a loan guaranteed by that other state or by an institution authorised by that state; (ii) interest from commercial debt-claims relating to installment payments for supplying merchandise, goods, or services; (iii) interest on loans, not represented by bearer instruments, from banks; or (iv) interest on cash deposits, not represented by bearer instruments, with banks, including public credit institutions.
3. 5% where beneficial owner is a company (other than a partnership) that holds directly at least 25% of the capital of the company paying the dividends.
4. Interest arising in a contracting state and paid to, or on loans guaranteed or insured by, the government or a local authority thereof, the Central Bank, or any financial institution wholly owned by the government of the other contracting state, shall be exempt from tax in the first-mentioned state.
5. Interest on bank credits and loans and interest on commercial credits arising from sources located in one of the states and received by a resident of the other state shall not be taxable in the first state.
6. 0% where interest is paid by the governments, Central Bank, or National Bank of the contracting states.
7. 0% where the loan has been guaranteed by the state or by an organisation authorised by it for that purpose.
8. 0% where interest is paid by government, a political sub-division, or a local authority of the other contracting state.
9. Interest paid by government, ministries, other governmental institutions, municipalities, Central Bank, and other banks wholly owned by the government of the other contracting state shall be exempt from tax.
10. 0% where the recipients of the interest are governments of contracting states or any governmental body, as well as the Central Banks ('the bank of banks' of a contracting state), a state export or import credit underwriting organisation, or another similar organisation to which, in accordance with the law of a contracting state, the relevant rights were delegated.

T

Tax administration

Taxable period

The taxable period comprises a calendar year (i.e. 1 January to 31 December).

Turkmenistan

Tax returns
Reports are generally filed quarterly within the month following the reporting quarter. Annual income tax declaration and financial statements of branches of foreign legal entities are due by 20 March of the year following the reporting one.

Tax agents must file WHT reports not later than the 20th day of the month following the one when the respective tax liability occurred.

Payment of tax
Advance CIT payments under the standard tax regime are made before the 13th and 28th days of each month (unless agreed otherwise with tax authorities). Final payments upon results of the first quarter, first half-year, nine months, and tax year are made within five days from the reporting deadlines.

Under the Petroleum Law tax regime, CIT is reported and paid once annually based on dates indicated in the respective Product Share Agreement (PSA).

Audit cycle
Statutory financial audit is required on an annual basis. Auditor's opinion is submitted along with annual financial statement to tax authorities.

Statute of limitations
Statute of limitations for tax purposes is five years.

Topics of focus for tax authorities
The tax administration environment in Turkmenistan is form-driven. Therefore, the quality of documentation supporting the deductions should be of particular importance.

Cross-border transactions are normally scrutinised by tax authorities during statutory tax audits in view of WHT and reverse charge VAT implications.

Another area of focus for tax authorities is the deductions taken by Turkmenistan branches of foreign legal entities in respect of expenses incurred by their head offices abroad.

Uganda

PwC contact

Francis Kamulegeya
PricewaterhouseCoopers
Communications House
10th Floor
1 Colville Street
Kampala
Uganda
Tel: +256 41 4 236 018
Email: francis.kamulegeya@ug.pwc.com

....

Significant developments

Following the reading of the national budget in June 2011, a few amendments were made to the Income Tax Act, the Value-added Tax (VAT) Act, and the Finance Act. The key notable amendments include the following.

Income tax
- Definition of a branch has been widened to include a place where a person is installing substantial equipment or substantial machinery for 90 days or more.
- Income derived from agro-processing is exempt from income tax based on the following criteria:
  - The tax exemption cannot be claimed by a company that has an associate or sister company that is already engaged in the business of agro-processing of a similar or related agricultural product in Uganda.
  - For a person to qualify for the tax exemption, they must invest in new plant and machinery that has not been previously used in Uganda by any person in agro-processing to process agricultural products for final consumption.
  - An application has to be made to the Commissioner for a certificate of exemption, and the certificate, if issued, will last for one year; it is renewable annually.
- Transfer pricing regulations (i.e. 'The Income Tax Transfer Pricing Regulations 2011') were introduced effective July 2011.

Value-added tax (VAT)
- Exemption of the following items from VAT:
  - The supply of ambulances.
  - The supply of power generated by solar.
- Thermal and electric energy, heating, gas, refrigeration, air conditioning, and water were deleted from the definition of goods, meaning that the supply of any of these is now a service.
- VAT paid on imported services cannot be claimed back as input tax.
- Zero rating the supply of water, excluding mineral water.
- Importation of VAT exempt services will no longer be subject to reverse VAT.
- Place of supply of goods is now amended to apply to all goods delivered, made available, or whose transportation commences in Uganda.
- Supply of services is now amended to imply that a supply of services takes place in Uganda if the business of the supplier from which the services are made is in Uganda.
- The investment trader incentive was scrapped; consequently, a person can no longer claim input VAT before making taxable supplies.

U

Uganda

....

Taxes on corporate income

The income tax rate applicable to the chargeable income of companies is 30%, with the exception of:

- Mining companies.
- Non-resident air transport, shipping, and some telecommunication services.
- Resident companies whose turnover is less than 50 million Ugandan shillings (UGX).

Chargeable income is gross income for the year less the total deductions allowed under the Income Tax Act (ITA). A resident company is taxed on its income from all geographical sources. A non-resident company is only subject to Uganda income tax on income derived from sources in Uganda.

Mining companies
The income tax rate applicable to mining companies is calculated according to the following specified formula:

Annual tax rate = 70 minus (1500/x), where x is the ratio of the company's chargeable income to the gross revenue for the year.

Note that the derived tax rate is subject to a minimum tax rate of 25% and a maximum tax rate of 45%.

Non-resident air transport, shipping, and some telecommunications services
Non-resident ship operators, charterers, and air transport operators who derive income from carriage of passengers who embark, or cargo or mail which is embarked, in Uganda, as well as road transport operators who derive income from carriage of cargo or mail which is embarked in Uganda, are taxed at the rate of 2%.

A non-resident person who carries on the business of transmitting messages by cable, radio, optical fibre, or satellite communication and derives income through transmission of such messages by apparatus established in Uganda, whether or not such messages originated from Uganda, is taxed on one's gross income at a rate of 5%. Similarly, a non-resident person who derives income from providing direct-to-home pay television services to subscribers in Uganda is taxed on one's gross income at a rate of 5%.

Resident companies with turnover of less than UGX 50 million
A rate of 1% of turnover is used to determine income tax payable by a resident company whose turnover is between UGX 20 million and UGX 50 million (approximately between 10,000 United States dollars [USD] and USD 25,000), subject to certain thresholds.

However, on application to the Commissioner, a resident company with a turnover of less than UGX 50 million may be taxed at 30%.

This category excludes professionals, public entertainment services, public utility services, or construction services.

Uganda

Corporate residence

A company is resident in Uganda for a year of income if it meets one of the following criteria:

- Is incorporated or formed under the laws of Uganda.
- Has its management and control exercised in Uganda at any time during the year of income.
- Undertakes the majority of its operations in Uganda during a year of income.

Permanent establishment (PE)

A PE (branch) means a place where a person carries on business, and includes:

- A place where a person is carrying on business through an agent, other than a general agent of independent status acting in the ordinary course of business as such.
- A place where a person has, is using, or is installing substantial equipment or substantial machinery.
- A place where a person is engaged in a construction, assembly, or installation project for 90 days or more, including a place where a person is conducting supervisory activities in relation to such a project.

Other taxes

Value-added tax (VAT)

VAT is governed by the VAT Act and administered by the Uganda Revenue Authority (URA). VAT is charged at the rate of 18% on the supply of most goods and services in the course of business in Uganda. Specified goods and services, as well as exports outside of Uganda, attract a zero rate of tax.

Some supplies are exempt from VAT, the main categories being government subsidies, the supply of unprocessed foodstuffs, agricultural products and livestock, financial services, insurance services, unimproved land, leases and sale of certain residential properties, betting and gaming, education, medical and health services, social welfare services, pesticides, petroleum products subject to excise duty, machinery for processing agricultural or dairy products, accommodation in hotels outside specified areas, computers, computer accessories, software, and biodegradable packaging materials. The supply of power generated by solar is also now exempt from VAT.

The supply of specialised vehicles, plants, and machinery; engineering designs; feasibility studies; consultancy services; and civil works related to hydro-power, road and bridge construction, public water works, agriculture, education, and health sectors is also exempt.

Zero rating is preferable to exemption because the VAT on costs incurred in making a zero-rated supply can be recovered while that incurred in making an exempt supply cannot be recovered.

The zero rated supplies include the supply of goods and services exported from Uganda; the supply of drugs and medicines; the supply of seeds, fertilisers, pesticides and hoes; the supply of machinery, tools, and implements suitable for use only in agriculture; the supply of milk, including milk treated in any way to preserve it; and the supply of

Uganda

leased aircraft, aircraft engines, spare engines, spare parts for aircraft, and aircraft maintenance equipment.

The annual threshold for VAT registration is UGX 50 million (approximately USD 25,000). Persons who make supplies that are VAT-able and whose turnover exceeds UGX 50 million are required to register for VAT with the URA. VAT registered persons are required to:

- Charge VAT whenever they make supplies that are VAT-able.
- File monthly returns before the 15th day of the month following the reporting month.

Credit for input tax
A person making exempt, zero-rated, and standard supplies can recover all the input VAT if the exempt supplies are less than 5% of the total supplies. However, if the exempt supplies are more than 5% but less than 95%, the person is required to recover only a portion of the VAT input tax corresponding to the percentage of the taxable supplies. If the exempt supplies exceed 95%, the person cannot recover any input VAT.

Imported services
The VAT Act defines a supply of service to mean any supply which is not a supply of goods or money, including the performance of services for another person.

An imported service is one provided by a person normally resident outside Uganda who is not required to register for VAT in Uganda. According to regulation 14 of the VAT Regulations 1996, any person who imports a service into the country must account for VAT on such a service. The Regulations require the person importing the service to account for the VAT at the time when performance of the service is completed, when payment for the service is made, or when the invoice is received from the foreign supplier, whichever is earliest.

The tax on such imported services is computed at the rate of 18% of the cost of the service. VAT registered companies are no longer required to prepare self-billed tax invoices, thus they are unable to claim the VAT paid as input tax. Further, if the importer of the services is not registered for VAT, the importer is required to calculate and pay the VAT to URA.

The VAT on imported services is now a cost to the importer whereas prior to 1 July 2011 there was no effect on the cash flow position due to the requirement for the preparation of a self-billed tax invoice, which has now been abolished. Failure to pay VAT on non-exempt imported services is tantamount to lack of compliance with the law, and a penalty of 2% per month compounded may apply.

VAT representative for non-resident persons
The VAT Act provides for the appointment of a VAT representative by a non-resident person who may be required by the Commissioner to register for VAT in Uganda but has no fixed place of business. If the non-resident person does not appoint the VAT representative within 30 days after being required to register for VAT, the Commissioner may appoint the representative for the non-resident person. The VAT representative of the non-resident person shall be a person who is ordinarily residing in Uganda, may be an agent for more than one non-resident person, and will have the responsibility for doing all things required of the non-resident person under the VAT Act.

Customs duties

Many goods imported into Uganda are subject to customs duties. However, exemptions are available to various classes of plant and machinery imported into Uganda. The rates of duty are provided by the East African Community common external tariff code. Certain products imported from the East African Community and the Common Market for Eastern and Southern Africa (COMESA) region enjoys special custom duty rates. Imported items are classified according to the nomenclature established under the international convention on the harmonised commodity description and coding system. Duty's range from 0% to 60% depending on the item imported.

Excise taxes

Excise duties are imposed on goods considered luxuriant. Examples include locally manufactured soft drinks, cigarettes, alcoholic drinks, and spirits. A schedule of some of the rates is provided below:

Goods	Excise tax
Cigarettes	Between UGX 20,000 and UGX 50,000 per 1,000 sticks subject to the type of cigarette
Cigars and other smoking tobacco	150%
Beer made from malt	60%
Beer made from local raw material	20%
Beer produced from barley grown and malted in Uganda	40%
Spirits	60%
Wine produced from local raw materials	20%
Other wine	70%
Air time	12%
Fuel and oils	Between UGX 200 and UGX 720 per litre depending on the type of fuel/oil

Property taxes

Property taxes are administered by the local authorities annually. They are based on the value of the property as assessed by the local authorities.

Stamp taxes

Stamp duty is charged on a number of transactions at varying rates. Stamp duty is charged at 1% of the total value for a number of instruments, including hire purchase agreements, composition deeds, leases, exchange of property, conveyance, transfers, share warrants, gifts, and agreement relating to deposit of title deeds.

Stamp duty of 0.5% is incurred on formation of a company, capital-raising activities such as increase of share capital, debentures, equitable mortgages, and mortgage deeds.

Stamp duty of 1% applies on transfer of shares.

No stamp duty is charged on the increase of share capital where it is in fulfilment of a condition precedent for acquiring loan funds for a development project or where it is made on becoming public through the stock exchange.

Stamp duty of UGX 5,000 is also charged in a number of various other instruments.

U

Uganda

Turnover taxes

Every promoter of gaming and pools promoted within Uganda and every principal agent of a promoter of gaming and pools promoted outside Uganda is liable to tax at 15% of the total amount of money received or the total amount of bets.

A tax of 5% is charged on gross income earned by non-resident persons carrying on the business of transmitting messages by cable, radio, optical fibre, satellite, or provision of direct to home pay television services to subscribers in Uganda.

Environmental taxes

Environmental levies are charged on every person who imports motor vehicles that are eight years old or older. Levies are also imposed on the importation of used household appliances. The levy on motor vehicles is 20% of the value of the vehicle as determined for customs duty purposes. Levies on electrical appliances range from UGX 20,000 to UGX 50,000 per item depending on the nature of the item.

Branch income

Tax is imposed on the income of a non-resident company derived from running a branch in Uganda. The chargeable income of a branch in Uganda is taxed at the corporation tax rate of 30% after deduction of allowable expenses.

In addition to corporation tax, branches are subject to extra tax at a rate of 15% on any repatriated income for a year of income. The repatriated income is calculated using the A + (B - C) - D approach. Where A is the net assets at the beginning of the year, B is the net profit for the year, C is the tax charge for the year, and D is the net assets at the end of the year.

Income determination

In arriving at chargeable income (taxable income) one has to go through the process of adjusting profits by taking into account deductions allowed and deductions not allowed.

Inventory valuation

A taxpayer is allowed a deduction for the cost of trading stock disposed of during the year, which is determined by adding to the opening value of the trading stock the cost of trading stock acquired during the year and subtracting the closing value of stock. The opening value of the stock is the closing value for the previous year or, where the taxpayer commenced business during the year, the market value at the time of commencement of the business of the trading stock acquired prior to commencement. The closing stock valuation method is the lower of cost or market value. Trading stock is allowed to be valued using either the absorption costing or prime cost method. The stock valuation method chosen may not be changed, except with written permission of the Commissioner.

Capital gains

Capital gains are included in and taxed together with the business income at a rate of 30%. There is no separate capital gains tax. Capital gains arise on disposal of non-depreciable business assets as well as sale of shares.

Dividend income

The general rule is that dividend income is taxable as part of business income at a rate of 30%. Dividend income is also subject to withholding tax (WHT) at the rate of 15%. The WHT paid in respect of the dividend income is creditable where the income is subject to the corporation tax rate of 30%. The WHT rate for dividend payments to resident persons is 15%. For dividends paid out by companies listed on the stock exchange to individuals, the rate is 10%.

Dividend income is exempt from tax if the recipient company directly or indirectly controls the paying company through ownership of 25% or more of the voting power of the paying company.

Interest income

The general rule is that interest income is taxable as part of business income at a rate of 30%. Interest income is also subject to WHT at the rate of 15%. The WHT paid in respect of the interest income is creditable where the income is subject to the corporation tax rate of 30%. However, interest income earned by financial institutions with respect to agricultural loans is not subject to tax. Also, interest income earned by financial institutions with respect to government securities is subject to tax at 15% as a final tax.

Rental income

Rental income for companies is included in gross income and taxed at the 30% corporate tax rate.

Foreign income

Foreign income is taxable on resident recipients, and tax suffered in the country where it is sourced (if any) is creditable subject to the provisions of any double taxation agreements (DTAs). This credit is limited to the amount of Ugandan tax payable on that income.

Deductions

The ITA sets out the following conditions for deductibility of an expense:

- There must be an expenditure or loss.
- The expenditure or loss must be incurred by a person during the year of income.
- The expenditure must be incurred in the production of income included in gross income.

A taxpayer who is accounting for tax purposes on an accrual basis derives income when it is receivable by the taxpayer and incurs expenditure when it is payable by the taxpayer.

An amount is treated as payable by the taxpayer when all the events that determine liability have occurred and the amount of the liability can be determined with reasonable accuracy, but not before economic performance with respect to the amount occurs. Economic performance occurs:

- with respect to the acquisition of services or property, at the time the services or property are provided
- with respect to the use of property, at the time the property is used, or

Uganda

- in any other case, at the time the taxpayer makes payment in full satisfaction of the liability.

Contingent liabilities are not tax-deductible in Uganda.

Depreciation

A deduction is allowed for the depreciation of the person's depreciable assets, other than minor assets, in accordance with the appropriate applicable rates. The ITA allows a taxpayer a deduction for the depreciation of their depreciable assets on a reducing balance basis. Depreciable assets are classified in four classes as follows:

Class	Assets included	Rate of tax depreciation (%)
1	Computers and data handling equipment.	40
2	Automobiles, buses, and mini-buses with a seating capacity of less than 30 passengers; goods vehicles with a load capacity of less than 7 tonnes; construction and earth moving equipment (cost of motor vehicle sealed at approximately USD 24,000).	35
3	Buses with a seating capacity of 30 or more passengers; goods vehicles designed to carry or pull loads of 7 tonnes or more; specialised trucks, tractors; trailer-mounted containers; plant and machinery used in farming, manufacturing, or mining operations.	30
4	Rail cars, locomotives, and equipment; vessels, barges, tugs, and similar water transportation equipment; aircraft, specialised public utility plant, equipment, and machinery; office furniture, fixtures, and equipment, and any depreciable asset not included in another class.	20

Initial allowance

Where a taxpayer places an item of eligible property into service for the first time during the year of income, they qualify for a tax deduction for that year of income which is equal to 75% of the cost of the asset if the property is put into use outside Kampala, Entebbe, Namanve, Jinja, and Njeru. However, if the property is put into use in the above named areas, the tax deduction is equal to 50%.

Eligible property is defined to mean plant and machinery wholly used in the production of income included in gross income but does not include goods or passenger vehicles; appliances of a kind ordinarily used for household purposes; or office or household furniture, fixtures, and fittings.

Industrial building allowance

A company is eligible for an industrial building allowance on its industrial and commercial buildings at a tax rate of 5% per annum on a straight-line basis. The industrial building allowance will be granted on the actual cost incurred in constructing the buildings.

In addition to the above, a company is entitled to an initial allowance at the rate of 20% on an industrial building in the first year the building is put to use. The industrial building allowance is computed on the residual value after the initial allowance of 20%.

An industrial building is defined to mean any building which is wholly or partly used, or held ready for use, by a person in manufacturing operations, research and development into improved or new methods of manufacture, mining operations, an approved hotel business, an approved hospital, or approved commercial buildings.

Goodwill
Goodwill is treated as an intangible asset and is amortisable over its useful life.

Start-up expenses
A company setting up business for the first time or engaged in the initial public offer at the stock market will be entitled to a tax deduction for all its start-up costs that are of capital nature that would otherwise not be tax-deductible under the ordinary tax rules. The start-up costs will be allowed as tax-deductible costs over a period of four years at a straight-line basis at the rate of 25% per annum.

Interest expenses
Interest is deductible if the interest is incurred in respect of a debt obligation by the company in the production of income included in the company's gross income. Interest arising from non-trade-related debt obligation is not deductible.

Interest charged before capital investment is put to use has to be capitalised. Interest incurred after capital investment is put to use is allowed as a deduction.

If the company is foreign controlled, then the interest arising from the loan in excess of two times the company's equity will not be allowed (*see Thin capitalisation rules in the Group taxation section for more information*).

Bad debt
A deduction is allowed for bad debt only if:

- the amount was included in the person's income in the year of income
- it is in respect of money that was lent in the ordinary course of business by a financial institution in the production of income, or
- the amount of the debt claim was in respect of a loan granted to any person by a financial institution for the purpose of farming, forestry, fish farming, beekeeping, animal and poultry husbandry, or similar operations.

For the bad debt to be deductible, the taxpayer must demonstrate to the URA that reasonable steps to collect the debt were taken and that the taxpayer failed to recover the debt. In relation to a financial institution, it should be a debt in respect of which a loss reserve held against presently identified losses or potential losses, and which is therefore not available to meet losses which subsequently materialise, has been made.

Charitable contributions
Charitable donations are deductible if made to amateur sporting associations; religious, charitable, or educational institutions of public character; trade unions; and other similar associations which have been issued with a written ruling by the Commissioner currently in force stating that it is an exempt organisation. The donations should not exceed 5% of the person's chargeable income.

Meals, refreshments, and entertainment
Expenses for meals, refreshments, and entertainment are deductible only where the value is included in the employment income of the employees or is excluded from employment income owing to the fact that it is provided on equal terms to all workers.

Pension expenses
Employers are allowed a deduction for the contributions made to pension schemes on behalf of their employees. Employees, on the other hand, do not get a deduction for the contributions they make to pension funds.

U

Uganda

Payment for directors
Directors are treated as employees, so expenses incurred in respect of directors are deductible expenses.

Bribes, kickbacks, illegal payments
Non-business expenses are not tax-deductible, including those of a private nature.

Fines and penalties
No deduction is allowed for any fine or similar penalty paid to a government or its subdivision for breach of any law.

Taxes
No deduction is allowed for income tax payable in Uganda or in a foreign country.

Other significant items
No deduction is allowed for the following other expenditures:

- Any expenditure or loss of a domestic or private nature.
- Any expenditure or loss of a capital nature.
- Any expenditure or loss recoverable under insurance contract or indemnity.
- Any contribution or similar payment made to a retirement fund by the employee or for the benefit of any other person (e.g. National Social Security Fund (NSSF) contributions).
- Any premium or similar payment made in respect of a life insurance policy for the life of the person paying the premium or on the life of some other person.
- Any income appropriated to a reserve fund or capitalised in any way.
- The amount of pension paid to any person.

Net operating losses
A deduction is allowed for any assessed tax losses carried forward from previous years of income. Such tax losses are carried forward and deducted against future taxable profit of the business in the subsequent years of income. The losses can be carried forward indefinitely. There is no ring-fencing of losses except in the following circumstances:

- Where, during a year of income, there has been a change of 50% or more in the underlying ownership of a company, as compared with its ownership one year previously, the company is not permitted to deduct an assessed loss in the year of income or in subsequent years, unless the company, for a period of two years after the change or until the assessed loss has been exhausted if that occurs within two years after the change:
  - continues to carry on the same business after the change as it carried on before the change and
  - does not engage in any new business or investment after the change where the primary purpose of the company or the beneficial owners of the company is to utilise the assessed loss so as to reduce the tax payable on the income arising from the new business or investment.
- In cases where losses relate to farming, the assessed farming loss can only be deducted from farming income of the taxpayer in the following year and not from any other income.

There is no provision for carryback of losses in Uganda.

Payments to foreign affiliates
Payments to foreign affiliates are deductible as long as they are charged at an arm's length and incurred in the production of income.

Group taxation

There are no specific provisions in the law covering groups, so companies in a group do not get any special treatment for tax purposes in Uganda.

Transfer pricing
Uganda introduced transfer pricing regulations that came into force on 1 July 2011. The regulations apply to controlled transactions if a person who is a party to the transactions is located in and is subject to tax in Uganda and the other person who is a party to the transaction is located in or outside Uganda.

The URA Practice Note issued on 14 May 2012 gives details on the transfer pricing documentation to be maintained by the taxpayer. These include company details and transaction details, including agreements and the pricing methodology used in determining the arm's-length price.

In addition, the anti-avoidance provisions contained in Sections 90 and 91 of the ITA require transactions between associates to be at arm's-length basis. These are the provisions that are often applied by the URA in instances where they are of the view that a non-resident person may be transferring profits from Uganda. The Commissioner has yet to issue guidelines in respect of records expected to be maintained by a taxpayer as evidence that related party transactions are consistent with the arm's-length principle.

Thin capitalisation
Where a company intends to finance some of its Uganda operations by use of foreign debt, the ITA provides for thin capitalisation rules in Uganda, and the safe harbour debt: equity ratio is 2:1.

The thin capitalisation rules are provided for in Section 89 (1) of the ITA. According to this Section, where a foreign controlled resident company which is not a financial institution has a foreign debt to foreign equity ratio in excess of 2:1 at any time during that year of income, a deduction is disallowed for the interest paid by the company during that year on that part of the debt which exceeds the 2:1 ratio.

Controlled foreign companies (CFCs)
Uganda does not have a CFC regime.

U

Tax credits and incentives

Foreign tax credit
A resident taxpayer is entitled to a foreign tax credit for any foreign income tax paid by the taxpayer in respect of foreign-source income included in the gross income of the taxpayer. The foreign tax credit allowed is subject to the income tax rate (i.e. 30%) in Uganda.

Uganda

Tax holidays for exporters
A tax holiday of ten years is available to exporters who export at least 80% of their produce of finished goods, subject to certain conditions.

Scientific research expenditure, training expenditure, and mineral exploration expenditure
A 100% allowance is available for scientific research expenditures, training expenditures, and mineral exploration expenditures in the year of expenditure.

Incentives for the importation of plant and machinery
Plant and machinery is exempt from customs duty and WHT on importation. Also a VAT deferral facility is available where VAT is deferred on importation of plant and machinery and subsequently waived upon approval by the relevant authorities.

Employment incentives
A deduction of 2% of income tax payable is granted to any employer who can prove to the URA that at least 5% of their employees on full time basis are people with disabilities.

Other incentives
* Income derived from agro processing is exempt from income tax, subject to certain conditions.
* Business income derived by a person managing or running an educational institution is exempt from income tax.

Withholding taxes

According to Section 83(1) of the ITA, a tax is imposed on every non-resident person who derives any dividend, interest, royalty, rent, natural resource payment, or management charge from sources in Uganda. WHT at a rate 15% therefore applies on gross dividend payments, interest, management fees, and royalty payments in respect of non-treaty countries.

However, Section 83(5) exempts interest paid by a resident company in respect of debentures, which:

* were issued by the company outside Uganda for the purpose of raising a loan outside Uganda
* were widely issued for the purpose of raising funds for use by the company in a business carried on in Uganda or the interest is paid to a bank or a financial institution of a public character, and
* the interest is paid outside Uganda.

A debenture is defined in the ITA as any form of debt, including debenture stock, mortgage stock, loan, loan stock, or any similar instrument acknowledging indebtedness, whether secured or unsecured. The term widely issued is also specifically defined.

Double taxation agreements (DTAs)
A taxpayer may benefit from the provisions of a DTA that Uganda has with another country. Please find below a table showing the countries with which Uganda has DTAs and the applicable WHT rates on various categories of income.

According to Section 88 (2) of the ITA, the terms of the international agreement to which Uganda is a party prevails over the provisions of ITA in case the terms of the international agreement are inconsistent with the provisions of the Act.

Recipient	Dividend	Royalty	WHT (%) Management fees	Taxation of branch profits	Repatriation of branch profits
Denmark	15	10	10	30	15
India	10	10	10	30	15
Mauritius	10	10	10	30	15
Netherlands	15 (1)	10	15	30	15
Norway	10	10	10	30	15
South Africa	10	10	10	30	15
United Kingdom	15	15	15	30	15

Note

1. With respect to the Uganda/Netherland DTA, the rate applicable on dividends is 15%, except where the investment is new or is an expansion of the current investment made after the DTA entered into (10 September 2006).

   For new investments and expansions of current investment, the rates are:
   • 0% if the beneficiary holds at least 50% of the shares in the company paying the dividends.
   • 5% if the beneficiary holds less than 50% of the shares in the company making the payment.

Tax administration

Tax returns
The ITA provides for two provisional returns within a 12-month period (financial year). The first provisional return is due within the first six months of the accounting year while the second is due by the end of the twelfth month of the accounting year.

The Self Assessment Return (SAR) is due by the sixth month after the end of the accounting year.

Electronic filing has been introduced for all tax returns.

Payment of tax
For all companies, a system of provisional payments on account, based on estimated profits, is in place. The first payment of 50% is due in the sixth month of the accounting period and the second payment is due in the 12th month. The balance is expected to be paid together with the SAR.

Statute of limitations
The ITA requires a taxpayer to maintain records for at least five years after the end of the year to which the records relate.

The VAT Act provides for records to be maintained for six years after the end of the tax period to which they relate.

Topics of focus for tax authorities
The focus of the URA keeps shifting but is generally based on the risk analysis of the information availed to them. Currently, the focus is on transfer pricing.

U

Ukraine

PwC contact

Ron Barden
PricewaterhouseCoopers
75 Zhylyanska Street
Kyiv 01032
Ukraine
Tel: +380 44 490 67 77
Email: ron.j.barden@ua.pwc.com

Significant developments

Ukraine continues to develop its tax system. Specifically, the Tax Code has been modified and now includes the following:

Corporate income tax (CIT)

The CIT rate has been reduced from 23% to 21% for the year 2012.

Taxes on corporate income

CIT applies to taxable profits earned by resident entities in Ukraine and abroad and non-residents with a permanent establishment (PE) in Ukraine. Resident entities are taxed on their worldwide income. Non-resident entities are taxed on their Ukrainian-source income.

As of 1 January 2012, Ukraine's CIT has a uniform rate of 21% (standard CIT rate). The rate will be reduced to 19% from 1 January 2013 and to 16% from 1 January 2014.

Withholding tax (WHT) at a rate of 15% applies for the majority of income payments for non-residents, unless relief is given under a double taxation treaty (DTT). Ukraine has 68 effective DTTs in place. *See the Withholding taxes section for more information.*

Favourable tax regime for agricultural producers

Agricultural producers are entitled to use a very favourable tax regime, provided certain requirements are met. The main criterion requires that income from the sale of their own agricultural products constitutes not less than 75% of their total gross revenue.

Reduced rates for insurance companies

Reduced CIT rates of 0% and 3% are applicable for income of insurance companies in 2012. Long-term life insurance premiums and pension insurance premiums are subject to 0% rate. Otherwise, the 3% rate applies for gross insurance premiums regarding other insurance. Profits earned by insurance companies from non-insurance activities are taxed at the standard CIT rate.

Simplified (unified) tax regime

Starting from 1 January 2012, entities and individuals (i.e. private entrepreneurs) are entitled to use a simplified tax regime if certain requirements concerning the level of income (up to 3 million Ukrainian hryvni [UAH] for private entrepreneurs and UAH 5 million for entities) and number of employees (up to 20 and 50 individuals accordingly) are met. This regime foresees a lower effective tax rate (from 1% of minimal salary per month up to 5% of turnover, depending of the type of taxpayer) and easier reporting for small businesses. However, specific types of business activities are prohibited under such tax regime (*inter alia*, transactions with certain excise products, exploration/ production/sale of precious metals and stones, company management, communication services).

Local income taxes
No CIT is levied at the regional or local level.

Corporate residence

Corporate residence is determined by the place of incorporation.

Permanent establishment (PE)
The Ukrainian definition of a PE generally follows the PE definition from the Organisation for Economic Co-operation and Development (OECD) Model Tax Convention, but with stronger agency tests.

In particular, a non-resident PE is defined as a fixed place of business through which the business activity of a non-resident entity is wholly or partly carried out in Ukraine. A PE includes, among other things, a place of management, affiliate, office, etc.

The Tax Code has introduced the concept of a service PE whereby the provision of services (apart from the provision of personnel), including consultancy services, by a non-resident through its employees or other personnel in Ukraine, shall constitute a Ukrainian PE of this non-resident, provided such activities (within the frame of one project) last more than six months in any 12-month period.

Moreover, a construction site in Ukraine may also give rise to a taxable presence of a non-resident in Ukraine in the form of PE, if the length of the construction activities exceeds six months.

Recent amendments to the Tax Code introduced the concept of a non-depended agent. Specifically, a Ukrainian agent acting on behalf of more than one non-resident in the ordinary course of its business should not constitute a PE in Ukraine.

The Tax Code has also contributed a list of exclusions from the PE definition. In particular, auxiliary and preparatory services of a non-resident should not result in the creation of a PE.

In practice, the Ukrainian tax authorities usually interpret the term 'business activity' in a very broad sense, and, without DTT protection, may consider any type of activity as giving rise to a taxable presence (i.e. a PE) of a foreign entity in Ukraine.

U

Other taxes

Value-added tax (VAT)
There are two VAT rates: 20% and 0%. The rate of 20% applies to almost all transactions subject to VAT except the export of goods and related services, which is taxable at 0%. The zero rate also applies to the supply of international transport services (confirmed by a single international shipping document) and toll manufacturing services.

Ukraine

Provision of services to a non-resident is not considered to be zero rated. Such services are subject to 20% VAT or considered to be outside the scope of VAT (effectively exempt with no right to claim input VAT), depending on the place of supply.

Transactions that are subject to VAT include the following:

- The supply of goods and services when the place of supply is in Ukraine, including when the supply is made free of charge without consideration.
- The importation of goods and ancillary services (i.e. services costs which are included in goods customs value) into Ukraine.
- Exportation of goods.

Transactions that are not subject to VAT include the following (among others):

- The issue, sale, and exchange of securities.
- The transfer of property from a lesser to a lessee under an operating lease and the return of property upon expiration of the operating lease (other than in the course of import operations).
- Interest/commission element of lease payments under financial lease agreements.
- Provision of financial loans and bank guarantees.
- Insurance and reinsurance services supplied by licensed insurers and services of insurance/reinsurance agents and brokers.
- Payment of royalties.
- Reorganisation of a legal entity (merge, spin-off, accession, division).
- Transit of cargo and passengers through Ukrainian territory.

VAT registration
Tax registration as a VAT payer is compulsory if the volume of an entity's taxable transactions exceeds the compulsory registration threshold. The current registration threshold is UAH 300,000 for the previous 12 months. An entity qualifying as a taxable entity should register with the tax authorities at the place of its location and obtain a VAT registration number. In addition, voluntarily VAT registration is available if a person makes taxable supplies within 12 previous months and at least 50% of supplies are to VAT payers, or the amount of its statutory share capital or the book value of its assets exceeds UAH 300,000. There is no mechanism for a non-resident to register without a PE in Ukraine. Accordingly, any Ukrainian VAT incurred by a non-resident is non-recoverable.

VAT recovery and refunds
Generally, VAT incurred by a registered entity on the purchase and/or importation of goods and services used for the purpose of its own business (except for VAT incurred in relation to exempt supply) may be recovered by way of a credit against output VAT. In case VAT credit exceeds VAT output for two months consecutively, a VAT refund is available in the form of a cash payment or an offset against future VAT liabilities (subject to certain rules and limitations).

As of 2011, an automatic VAT refund procedure has been introduced for eligible exporters. In practice, obtaining a VAT refund by other taxpayers is difficult.

VAT returns
VAT returns must be filed by the taxpayer on a monthly basis. Monthly tax returns are due within 20 calendar days following the end of the reporting month. Taxes payable assessed on the basis of tax returns are due within ten calendar days following the deadline for filing the relevant tax returns.

Customs duties

Customs duties are payable by the importer upon import of the goods into Ukraine and applicable in accordance with the Customs Tariff. Currently there are two duty rates: relieved and full rates. Relieved rates of duty apply to goods originating from World Trade Organization (WTO) countries and countries which have granted Ukraine 'most favoured nation' trade status. Full rates of duty apply to goods originating from all other countries or where the country of origin cannot determined.

Ukraine has concluded free-trade agreements with Georgia, the Commonwealth of Independent States (CIS) countries, and Macedonia. Ukraine has also ratified a free-trade agreement with the European Free Trade Association (EFTA) countries, which is expected to come into force starting from 1 June 2012. These agreements allow many goods to be imported into Ukraine duty-free, subject to compliance with preferential rules of origin. The 2009 CIS Preferential Rules of Origin are used to determine whether goods originate from a particular CIS country to qualify for these duty exemptions.

The Ukrainian government is now negotiating a free-trade agreement with the European Union.

Ukraine has no export duties except on natural gas, scrap metal, livestock, rawhide, barley, and certain oil seeds.

Special kinds of import duties (i.e. seasonal, special, anti-dumping, countervailing) may be applicable on the import of certain goods.

Excise taxes

Excise tax applies to certain goods imported to or produced in Ukraine. Excisable goods include alcoholic beverages, tobacco and tobacco products, cars and car bodies, as well as liquefied gas, petrol, and diesel fuel. Ukraine is currently experiencing a gradual augmentation of excise tax on tobacco goods, ethyl alcohol, and alcoholic beverages.

Rates of excise tax can be *ad valorem* (a percentage of the value of the goods), specific (in monetary units per unit of goods), or combined.

Property taxes

There is no tax on commercial property in Ukraine (apart from the land tax). A local tax on residential property owned by entities and individuals (a real estate tax) will be introduced from 1 July 2012.

Land tax

Land tax is assessed annually for the following year and is paid monthly in equal instalments by the owners or users of the land. The rate of land tax depends on the category, location, and the existence of a state valuation for each particular land plot.

Stamp taxes

Stamp duty is imposed on certain actions, including the notarisation of contracts and the filing of documents with the courts. In most cases, the amounts involved are nominal. Operations carried out at commodity exchanges and the sale of real property attract a stamp duty of 1%.

Special Pension Fund charges

The following special charges are payable to the State Pension Fund:

Ukraine

- 3% charge based on the transfer value of a car.
- 1% charge on the acquisition of real estate payable by individuals and legal entities that purchase real estate.
- 7.5% charge on mobile communication services.
- 5% charge on sales of jewellery.

Charges on environmental pollution

Environmental pollution charges (ecological taxes) are imposed on any legal entity that discharges contaminants into the environment (air or water) or disposes of waste. The actual rate depends on the type and toxicity of each contaminant.

Charge for subsoil usage

Companies engaged in extracting mineral resource in Ukraine, regardless of the form of their ownership, are liable to a charge for use of subsoil. For gas and gas condensate, the specific tax rates are applied to the volume of the extracted mineral resources. The payments to be made are calculated as follows:

volume of extracted mineral resources X specific tax rate X a coefficient

Separate charge rates for the use of subsoil apply to the storage of oil and gas products (the amounts are immaterial).

Charges for the use of subsoil are deductible for CIT purposes.

Rental payments (oil and gas industry)

Rental payments are to be made by companies that have the appropriate licences authorising the extraction of oil, gas, and gas condensate.

The tax base is calculated as the volume of extracted mineral resources multiplied by the tax rate. The adjusting coefficients apply to tax rates on rental payments for oil, gas condensate, and for natural gas other than that sold to a buyer authorised by the Cabinet of Ministers. Such coefficient is calculated by the Ministry of Economy (for oil and gas condensate) and the Ministry of Finance (for natural gas) for each reporting period.

Rental payments are deductible for CIT purposes. Product Sharing Agreements (PSA) covered by the Tax Code provide an exemption from these rental payments.

Other local taxes

According to the Tax Code, there are four local taxes that may be levied at the discretion of the local authorities: tax on real estate other than land plots (will come into force starting from 1 July 2012), vehicle parking place duties, duties for the exercise of some entrepreneurial activities, and tourism duty.

Branch income

Domestic incorporated branches or other separate units are treated as separate taxpayers for CIT purposes. However, their head offices may pay consolidated CIT.

In Ukraine, it is not currently possible to register a branch of a foreign legal entity. A foreign company may set up a representative office in Ukraine, which is similar to an unincorporated branch. A non-resident company conducting business activities via a representative office is deemed to carry out business in Ukraine through a PE and may

Ukraine

be subject to CIT at 21% in 2012 (19% starting from 1 January 2013) unless protected by a DTT. When a foreign company conducts business in Ukraine through a PE, taxable income should be determined on the same basis as for domestic entities. If the PE has no separate accounts, the taxable income may be determined as 30% of sales proceeds attributed to the PE.

Distributions made by a PE (out of after-tax income) to its head office should not trigger any further taxation in Ukraine, provided that the head office is in a jurisdiction which has an effective DTT with Ukraine.

Income determination

The Tax Code determines taxable profits as taxable income (items of income defined by the Tax Code) less deductible expenses (expenses allowed for deduction by the Tax Code), including depreciation charges. Taxable income includes any operational (business) income received or accrued within a reporting period (e.g. quarter) and other income, which includes generally passive and irregular receivables. Items of income are recorded when a legal title on goods is transferred or when a document confirming the rendering of services is signed by the parties.

Inventory valuation
A taxpayer is entitled to adopt any of the methods of inventory valuation prescribed by the accounting standards, namely: the first in first out (FIFO) method, weighted average methods, identified cost of unit of goods, normative cost, or sale price. The last in first out (LIFO) method does not apply.

Capital gains on the sale of property
Capital gains realised by the local entity on the sale of buildings are calculated as the difference between the sales price of the fixed asset and its net book value. Capital gains on the sale of land are computed as the difference between the sale price of the land and adjusted purchase price of the land.

Income from securities
Income from securities is calculated separately from other income and is based on the so called 'pooling method'. Taxable income is determined by deducting the aggregate cost of acquiring each class of securities from the aggregate proceeds from selling such securities. If aggregate acquisition costs for the year exceed aggregate sales proceeds, the excess is carried forward and applied against sales of securities in subsequent years.

Recent amendments to the Tax Code introduced separate tax accounting rules for transactions with derivatives and repurchase agreements.

Dividend income
Dividends received by a Ukrainian entity from another Ukrainian entity are exempt from CIT. Dividends received by Ukrainian companies from foreign companies controlled (at last 20% shareholding) by these Ukrainian companies (except for those having 'offshore status') are exempt from CIT.

Companies paying dividends are required to pay advance CIT at the standard rate, unless the dividends are paid to individuals or out of received dividends (with some other exceptions). The advance payment is used to meet subsequent CIT liabilities (other than for insurance companies). If the advance tax is not able to be used in the year the dividend is paid, it is carried over to future years, but cannot be refunded.

U

Ukraine

Interest income
Interest received by taxpayers is included in their taxable income on a general basis.

Rent/royalties income
Income from rent/royalties received by taxpayers is included in their taxable income on a general basis.

Foreign exchange gains/losses
Taxable income in foreign currency is revaluated in Ukrainian hryvni at the National Bank of Ukraine's (NBU's) official exchange rate at the date when the respective taxable income should be recognised under the general rules of the Tax Code, and, in terms of previously received payments, at the exchange rate on the receipt date.

Expenses incurred (and not paid) by the taxpayer in a foreign currency on the purchase of goods, works, and services are recognised at the NBU's official exchange rate on the date of such purchase, and, in case of a previous payment, at the exchange rate on the payment date.

Realised and non-realised foreign exchange gains/losses are generally treated as taxable/deductible. Foreign currency differences arising from unsettled debt balances and foreign currency account balances are computed according to accounting standards.

Other significant items
Ukrainian tax legislation does not provide special tax treatment for bribes, kickbacks, or illegal payments. However, all income should be included in taxable income unless a specific provision in the law says otherwise.

Funds or property returned to the holder of corporate rights issued by a legal entity after that entity's liquidation, but not in excess of the shares' par value, are not taxable.

Interest-free loans from non-residents are taxable (and deductible upon repayment), unless they are received from shareholders for a period not exceeding 365 calendar days.

Foreign income
Foreign income is taxed under the general rules, and there are no special rules regarding anti-deferral or unremitted earnings.

Deductions

Deductible expenses include any operational (related to the cost of goods/services sold) or other expenses actually incurred or accrued in respect of the taxpayer's business, excluding non-allowable expenses specified by the Tax Code.

Generally, operational expenses are recognised at the date of income recognition from the goods/services sold; other expenses are recognised when they are actually incurred.

Depreciation and amortisation
Assets costing more than UAH 2,500 for the year 2012 that have a useful life exceeding one year are required to be depreciated. Depreciation is determined on a monthly basis and is computed using the following methods:

- Straight-line.
- Reducing balance.
- Method of accelerated reduction of a residual value.
- Cumulative.
- Production-based.

Fixed assets are divided into 16 groups according to their statutory minimal useful life. The useful life of fixed assets may be extended by a taxpayer.

Land value may not be depreciated unless the land plot is purchased together with a building (object of Group 1).

Intangibles may be amortised according to the standard depreciation methods over the assets' useful economic lives as defined in the documents certifying the rights to the intangibles. If such term is not set by these documents, the intangible is amortised over ten years of usage.

Goodwill
Payments in respect of goodwill and amortisation of goodwill are not deductible.

Organisational and start-up expenses
Deduction of organisational and start-up expenses incurred prior to the entity's registration is not explicitly allowed by the law.

Research and development (R&D) expenses
R&D expenses other than those subject to amortisation are deductible when incurred, provided they are business-related.

Interest expenses
Interest paid is generally deductible for CIT purposes if incurred for business needs. However, a limitation for deducting interest expense applies if at least 50% of the borrower's capital belongs to non-residents and the interest is payable to non-residents (and related entities) that have a holding on the borrower's capital. The deductible interest paid to those persons and their related parties cannot exceed the amount of interest income derived plus 50% of the company's taxable profit (excluding interest income and before the deduction of interest). Any interest paid to affiliates in excess of this limit is carried forward to future tax periods.

Bad debt
The decrease of taxable income for bad and doubtful debt is allowed if (i) the creditor applies to the court with a claim for debt collection or for initiating bankruptcy proceedings or (ii) the creditor has a note of execution for collection executed by a notary. At the same time, the cost of goods/services sold should be adjusted as well.

When a creditor pursues action to recover the debt, the debtor is required to adjust its deductions at the moment of (i) taking effect of the court's decision or (ii) delivery of the note on debt collection by the notary.

Charitable contributions
Charitable donations made by a CIT taxpayer in monetary or non-monetary form to certain types of non-profit organisations are deductible, up to a limit of 4% of the prior year's taxable profit.

Ukraine

Pension expenses

The obligatory Ukrainian social security insurance contributions, including state pension contributions charged on payroll expenses, are deductible for employers.

If an employer pays non-state pension contributions at its own expense, such contributions may be deducted. Based on the Transition Provisions of the Tax Code, such deduction is limited to 15% of the annual salary of each employee insured (cumulatively for the year), but shall not exceed the respective limit (the amount of social tax allowance - UAH 1,500 per employee per month in 2012).

Payment for directors

Payments (including bonuses) of a business nature are normally deductible payments, if properly structured.

Fines and penalties

Fines and penalties are not deductible.

Taxes

CIT, personal income taxes, WHT/remittance taxes, and VAT incurred on purchases are disallowed for deductions. Fines and penalties paid to the budget are not deductible.

VAT is deductible if it cannot be offset against output VAT. Other taxes, if paid in the course of business activities, are generally deductible in full.

Other significant items

Examples of other non-deductible items include the following:

- Expenses that are not supported by relevant documents (e.g. contracts, vouchers, receipts, cheques).
- Service fees paid to related entities, unless there is documentation to prove that the fees are paid in relation to services actually performed.
- Expenses related to receptions, presentations, entertainment, sampling, and the free of charge provisions of goods and services. However, advertising expenses are deductible according to the general rule.
- Fees for consultancy, marketing, and advertising services, as well as royalties, paid to non-residents, are limited for deduction (up to 4% of net revenue separately for royalties and the services for the year preceding the reporting one, excluding VAT and excise). They are not deductible entirely if their recipient is not a beneficial owner (for royalty payments) or residents in an offshore jurisdiction. In addition, royalties paid to a person who shall not be taxed with regard to such royalty in the country of its residence or for intellectual property rights generated in Ukraine are also not fully deductible.
- Engineering fees payable to a non-resident are deductible only up to 5% of the customs value of the equipment imported under a related contract. The engineering fees are not deductible entirely if their recipient is not a beneficial owner or a resident in an offshore jurisdiction.
- Business trip expenses for individuals that are not employees or members of the taxpayer`s management/supervising bodies. Business trip expenses for employees are deductible within the limits set by the Cabinet of Ministers of Ukraine.
- Expenses relating to providing employees with uniforms, safety clothes, shoes, and food, if the amount exceeds the norms established by the Cabinet of Ministers of Ukraine.
- Banks will be entitled to a tax deduction of 20% of loan-loss provisions, excluding off-balance (including interest and commissions accrued, the amount of guarantees

issued, and in respect of all securities purchased, etc.). There will be a deduction limit of 30% on such provisions in 2012. Other financial institutions are entitled to a deduction of up to 10% of all loan-loss provisions.

Net operating losses
Ukrainian tax legislation does not provide refunds for deductions. However, tax losses may be carried forward indefinitely. In the past, Parliament regulated specific losses that could be carried forward. For example, taxpayers were able to use only 20% of their losses on 1 January 2010 when paying tax under a return for 2010. No such restriction has been adopted for 2012. At the same time, the current position of the Ukrainian tax authorities regarding tax losses that arose in periods before 1 January 2011 is restrictive.

Ukrainian tax legislation does not provide for refunds for losses carried back.

Payments to foreign affiliates
Payments of a business nature are normally deductible payments. When such payments are made to related parties, however, the payer is required to hold documentary evidence that the payments are for services actually rendered. The amount of the payment may also not exceed the 'usual' (market) price. Reimbursement of costs incurred by holding companies is directly prohibited for deduction.

Payments for goods or services, as well as interest, to foreign entities registered in listed jurisdictions operating offshore tax regimes (36 tax haven jurisdictions are listed by Ukraine's Cabinet of Ministers) are deductible at 85% of payments, unless evidence is held that the foreign entity is subject to the ordinary tax rules of the respective foreign jurisdiction (i.e. it does not benefit from the offshore tax regime).

Group taxation

In Ukraine, each company is taxed individually. However, companies that have domestic unincorporated branches may pay consolidated CIT or as separate branches.

Transfer pricing
Ukraine's transfer pricing rules are based on the arm's-length principle for transactions between related parties. Parties are 'related' if, among other things, one party controls, directly or indirectly, a shareholding interest representing more than 20% of the charter capital of the other party.

The law places strong emphasis on the comparable uncontrolled price (CUP) method. If it is not possible to determine the usual price because information on comparable transactions is absent or not publicly available, the law deems the contractual price to be the usual price. The Tax Code introduced a 'safe harbour' threshold whereby no adjustments to the tax records are required, provided the contractual price in the transactions with related parties and non-CIT payers is within a 20% deviation from the market (usual) price.

Starting from 2013, new transfer pricing methods similar to those of the OECD will be introduced.

Thin capitalisation
Ukraine does not have thin capitalisation rules as such. Instead, there are restrictions on related parties' interest deductibility rules. The interest paid to a related party (as

Ukraine

defined in the Tax Code) is deductible within the amount of interest income plus 50% of the company's taxable profit (excluding interest income and before the deduction of interest). Any interest paid to affiliates in excess of this limit is carried forward to future tax periods.

Controlled foreign companies (CFCs)
There are no specific CFC rules in Ukraine.

Treatment of intercompany items
Ukrainian tax legislation provides the following treatment for intercompany items:

- Dividends paid by Ukrainian companies are not tax deductible. Dividends received are not generally taxable.
- The payer of royalties is required to hold documentary evidence that the royalty payments are made for services actually rendered. The amount of the payment also may not exceed the 'usual' (market) price. Royalties paid to a non-resident are deductible only up to 4% of net revenue of the previous year. Royalties are completely non-deductible in respect of intangibles originated in Ukraine and paid to residents of the offshore jurisdictions, paid to persons who are not beneficial owners, or paid to persons that will not be taxed with regard to such royalty in the country of residence.
- Expenses in relation to the financing of management bodies, including holding companies, are not tax deductible.
- Cost-sharing and similar intra-group payments, other than remuneration for services actually rendered, may not be deductible.
- Transactions for the receipt (provision) of financial aid between a taxpayer and its branches and other separate units without the legal entity status located in Ukraine shall not affect their taxable income or deductible expenses.
- Interest on loans is limited (*see Interest expenses in the Deductions section*).

Tax credits and incentives

Ukraine currently has very few tax incentives, although some are available. The following businesses are entitled to benefit from them:

- Income of publishing and agricultural entities may be tax exempt.
- Income received by investment funds is tax exempt.
- For enterprises selling domestically produced energy saving goods in Ukraine, up to 80% of profits may be tax exempt; and for enterprises adopting energy saving projects, up to 50% of profits may be exempt.
- A tax exemption is available for producers of electric and heat energy generated from bio-energy fuel, as well as for producers of bio-energy powered domestic equipment. Tax incentives are also available for producers of gas (methane).
- Certain tax incentives are granted to the Union of European Football Associations (UEFA) and its companies during the hosting stage of 2012 UEFA European Football Championship in Ukraine and to specific segments of the tourism industry (including ten years of CIT exemption for 3, 4, and 5-star hotels).
- The light industry is tax exempt until 2021.

Tax holidays
The Tax Code introduced tax holidays for small businesses, which are unlikely to impact international businesses. In particular, till the end of the year 2015, a zero income tax rate is applicable for those taxpayers who met certain criteria (including

maximum amount of total income for reporting period, minimal amount of salary paid to employees, date of incorporation, etc.)

Foreign tax credit

Tax residents are allowed a credit for foreign taxes paid on income received abroad, provided there is a DTT between Ukraine and the relevant foreign state. The amount of foreign tax credit is limited to the amount of Ukrainian tax that would arise from the equivalent income in Ukraine (i.e. maximum 21%, 19% as of 1 January 2013). To claim a tax credit, the taxpayer requires an official confirmation of payment issued by the relevant foreign tax authority.

Withholding taxes

WHT must be remitted to the authorities no later than the date when the payment is made to the income recipient.

Passive income (dividends, interest, royalties) from Ukrainian sources that is paid to non-resident entities is generally subject to 15% WHT. Other payments, including payments for engineering services, lease payments, and agency and brokerage fees, are also subject to 15% WHT, but payments for most other services are not subject to withholding.

A 15% WHT rate applies to income on the sale of real estate and on profits from the sale of securities.

Payments for freight services (including sea freight) are subject to 6% WHT.

WHT rates may be reduced under a relevant tax treaty.

The non-resident recipient of income sourced in Ukraine must also be considered the beneficial owner of such income in order to benefit from reduced tax rates under relevant tax treaties. According to the Tax Code, agents, nominee holders, and other intermediaries in respect of received income cannot be beneficial owners of income sourced in Ukraine, and, therefore, are not entitled to favourable treaty provisions.

Payments to non-resident persons for advertising services are not subject to withholding. However, the resident payer is required to pay, from its own funds, a 20% remittance tax based on the value of such services.

A resident payer is similarly required to pay, from its own funds, a 12% remittance tax if a payment is made to a foreign insurer or reinsurer whose rating of financial reliability does not meet requirements set by the authorised state agency. Otherwise, 0% or 4% rates apply.

As taxes on advertising and insurance are levied on a resident party, they cannot be relieved using a tax treaty.

Recipient	Dividends (%) Non-portfolio (1)	Portfolio	Interest (%) (2)	Royalties (%) (3)
Domestic rates:				
Non-resident individuals	5/15 (16)	5/15 (16)	0/5 (4)	15
Non-resident corporations	15	15	15	15

Ukraine

Recipient	Dividends (%) Non-portfolio (1)	Portfolio	Interest (%) (2)	Royalties (%) (3)
Treaty rates:				
Algeria	5	15	10	10
Armenia	5	15	10	0
Austria	5	10	2/5 (5)	0/5
Azerbaijan	10	10	10	10
Belarus	15	15	10	15
Belgium	5	15	2/10 (5)	0/10
Brazil	10	15	15	15
Bulgaria	5	15	10	10
Canada	5	15	10	0/10
China (PRC)	5	10	10	10
Croatia	5	10	10	10
Cyprus (6)	0	0	0	0
Czech Republic	5	15	5	10
Denmark	5	15	0/10 (7)	0/10
Egypt	12	12	12	12
Estonia	5	15	10	10
Finland	0/5 (8)	15	5/10 (7)	0/5/10
France	0/5 (9)	15	2/10 (5)	0/5/10
Georgia	5	10	10	10
Germany	5	10	2/5 (5)	0/5
Greece	5	10	10	10
Hungary	5	15	10	5
Iceland	5	15	10	10
India	10	15	10	10
Indonesia	10	15	10	10
Iran	10	10	10	10
Israel	5/10	15	5/10 (10)	10
Italy	5	15	10	7
Japan (6)	15	15	10	0/10
Jordan	10	15	10	10
Kazakhstan	5	15	10	10
Korea (ROK)	5	15	5	5
Kuwait	5	5	0	10
Kyrgyzstan	5	15	10	10
Latvia	5	15	10	10
Lebanon	5	15	10	10
Libya	5	15	10	10
Lithuania	5	15	10	10
Macedonia	5	15	10	10
Malaysia (6)	15	15	15	10/15
Moldova	5	15	10	10
Mongolia	10	10	10	10
Morocco	10	10	10	10
Netherlands	0/5 (11)	15	2/10 (5)	0/10

Ukraine

Recipient	Dividends (%)		Interest (%) (2)	Royalties (%) (3)
	Non-portfolio (1)	Portfolio		
Norway	5	15	10	5/10
Pakistan	10 (17)	15	10	10
Poland	5	15	10	10
Portugal	10/15 (12)	15	10	10
Romania	10	15	10	10/15
Russian Federation	5 (13)	15	10	10
Serbia and Montenegro	5	10	10	10
Singapore	5	15	10	7.5
Slovakia	10	10	10	10
Slovenia	5	15	5	5/10
South Africa	5	15	10	10
Spain (6)	15	15	0	0/5
Sweden	0/5 (14)	10	0/10 (5)	0/10
Switzerland	5	15	0/10 (5)	0/10
Syria	10	10	10	15
Tajikistan	10	10	10	10
Thailand	10	15	10/15 (10)	15
Turkey	10	15	10	10
Turkmenistan	10	10	10	10
United Arab Emirates	5	15	3	0/10
United Kingdom	5	10	0	0 (15)
United States	5	15	0	10
Uzbekistan	10	10	10	10
Vietnam	10	10	10	10

Notes

1. The ownership threshold for the non-portfolio rate is 10%, 20%, 25%, or 50%, depending on the specific provisions in the treaty.
2. Several treaties contain a rate of 0% on interest paid to or guaranteed by a government or one of its agencies.
3. If more than one rate is shown, this means that the rate will depend on the type of royalties paid.
4. The lower rate applies to interest on current or deposit bank accounts and certificates of deposit until 1 January 2015.
5. The lower rate applies to interest paid on certain credit sales and on loans granted by a financial institution.
6. The treaties with Cyprus, Japan, Malaysia, and Spain were entered into by the USSR before it dissolved. Ukraine will continue to honour these treaties, unless they are superseded.
7. The lower rate applies to interest paid in connection with the sale on credit of any industrial, commercial, or scientific equipment, unless the indebtedness is between associated enterprises.
8. The 0% rate applies if the investor holds at least 50% of the capital of the company paying the dividends and the capital invested is at least 1 million United States dollars (USD); the payer of dividends should not operate in the field of gambling, show business or an intermediation business, or in auctions.
9. The 0% rate will apply if a French company or companies hold, directly or indirectly, at least 50% of the capital of the Ukrainian company, and the aggregate investments exceed 5 million French francs.
10. The lower rate applies to interest paid on any loan granted by a bank.
11. The 0% rate applies if the investor directly holds at least 50% of the capital of the company paying the dividends, and the capital invested is at least USD 300,000.
12. The 10% rate applies if the company receiving the dividend has, for an uninterrupted period of two years before the dividend is paid, owned at least 25% of the capital stock of the company paying the dividends.
13. The 5% rate applies if the capital invested is at least USD 50,000.
14. The 0% rate applies if the Swedish company directly holds at least 25% of the voting power of the company paying the dividends and at least 50% of the Swedish company is held by Swedish residents.

U

Ukraine

15. The 0% rate applies only if the royalties are taxable in the United Kingdom.
16. The 15% rate applies to dividends from privileged shares or other fixed payments on shares, as well as to disguised employment income.
17. The 10% rate applies if the company receiving the dividend directly owns at least 25% of the capital stock of the company paying the dividends.

Tax administration

Taxable period
The reporting year for companies generally follows the calendar year. The exception is for agricultural manufacturers, whose reporting period starts from 1 July of the current reporting year and ends on 30 June of the next reporting year. Returns are submitted and payments of tax are made on a quarterly basis, generally reflecting the accumulated taxable profit for the year to date.

Tax returns
Quarterly returns are due within 40 calendar days following the last day of the reporting quarter. Resident companies and non-resident entities with a PE in Ukraine must keep records that comply with the tax rules.

Payment of tax
Taxes payable assessed on the basis of tax returns are due within ten calendar days following the deadline for filing of the relevant tax returns.

Audit cycle
The tax authorities may carry out scheduled audits once a year. Taxpayers must be notified of the audit in writing at least ten days in advance. In addition, the tax authorities may perform out-of-schedule audits in certain circumstances (e.g. if a taxpayer does not file tax returns on a timely basis or is reorganised or liquidated).

Statute of limitations
Under Ukrainian tax legislation, a three year statute of limitations applies on any outstanding Ukrainian tax liability, starting from the date a tax return is due to be filed and/or tax, if assessed by the tax authorities, is due to be paid. There is no limit on the period in which an assessment may be made if a taxpayer has deliberately evaded tax (if proven in court) or when a taxpayer fails to file a return.

Penalties
The tax authorities will charge significant penalties for late filing or understatement of tax liabilities. If a taxpayer fails to withhold tax when required, a penalty of up to 75% of the deficient tax is imposed.

Tax advice
Tax advice may be sought from the tax authorities, who are required to issue such clarifications. Tax advices are not legally binding and may be challenged in court. A taxpayer may use the tax advice as guidance on the methodology to be applied by the taxpayer. In practice, the tax advice often does not provide solid protection against assessment of tax, but protects from penalties.

Other issues

Exchange controls

The key issues regarding Ukraine's current exchange control regulations are as follows:

- Trade related settlements between residents and non-residents can be made in foreign currency and Ukranian hryvni.
- Payments in foreign currencies between residents in the territory of Ukraine are generally prohibited.
- Salaries to Ukrainian staff must be paid in Ukrainian currency (but expatriate employees can be paid in hard currency).
- Foreign loans must be registered with the NBU before funds are remitted to Ukraine. The NBU has reinstated a maximum interest rate and other charges that may be applied to foreign currency loans obtained from non-residents.
- The maximum allowable interest rates for foreign fixed rate loans in hard currency (inclusive of any fees and charges due under the loan agreement) are 9.8% per annum for loans up to one year; 10% per annum for loans for one to three years; and 11% per annum for loans over three years. For loans with floating interest rates, the maximum allowable interest rate is three months of USD LIBOR plus 7.5%.
- Proceeds from exports must be credited to the exporter's Ukrainian bank account within 180 days from the date of customs clearance (for goods) or the date of service delivery. Similarly, prepaid goods must be imported and cleared through customs within 180 days of payment. Failure to do so results in a fine of 0.3% of the amount due or paid for each day of delay.

Payments by Ukrainian business entities for services rendered by non-residents for amounts exceeding 100,000 euros (EUR) (annually) require confirmation from the Foreign Markets Monitoring Centre (FMMC) that the fee for the services does not exceed market prices. Provided the relevant documentation is in place, this should not delay payment. However, the process cannot be taken lightly. If the FMMC rejects an application, no payment will be permitted.

A number of foreign currency transactions may be undertaken only if an individual licence has been obtained from the NBU.

Choice of business entity

Generally, a limited liability company is the most widely used corporate vehicle in Ukraine for both residents and non-residents. A limited liability company has a simple registration procedure, is inexpensive, and is easy to maintain. It also provides more flexibility in terms of repatriating dividends from Ukraine.

Business and tax treatment of intellectual property

Ukrainian laws concerning intellectual property rights provide for a rather developed background for intellectual property usage. Economic rights of authors and neighboring rights owners may be assigned or licensed. Moral rights are not transferable. However, in the fields of enforcement, tax, and court practice, there is an enormous lack of practical experience.

Tax treatment for intellectual property transactions is subject to separate analysis on case-by-case basis, as the Ukrainian tax legislation provides different approaches depending on the nature of the concluded agreement. For instance, the transfer of intellectual property may be treated as its sale, as the provision of services, or as a royalty agreement.

U

Ukraine

Mergers and acquisitions (M&A) from a business and tax perspective
There are no specific laws regulating public takeovers or mergers in Ukraine.

M&A activity in the Ukrainian market continues to recover after the global financial crisis, and it is expected that the market will increase further in 2012, provided there is stability at the local and international economic level.

The Ukrainian Tax Code provides some guidance on the tax regime for corporate mergers and acquisitions that is generally favourable for M&A transactions. However, no VAT refund in cash will be available for 12 months after the transaction. Also, no deduction of tax losses is available if the acquired entity was a related party to its acquirer for less than 18 months.

United Arab Emirates

PwC contact

Dean Kern
PricewaterhouseCoopers UAE
Emaar Square,
Building 4, Level 8
PO Box 11987
Dubai
United Arab Emirates
Tel: +971 4 3043575
Email: dean.kern@ae.pwc.com

Significant developments

There is a growing trend of tax reforms in the Middle East region, and this may result in changes to the tax laws in the United Arab Emirates (UAE).

In particular, the United Arab Emirates (along with the other Gulf Cooperation Council or GCC states) has committed to introduce a value-added tax (VAT) system. The UAE government has made significant progress towards the introduction of VAT; however, there is no formal legislative announcement yet on its introduction.

Advice should therefore be sought to confirm the current status of the UAE tax laws and reforms.

Taxes on corporate income

The United Arab Emirates is a federation of seven emirates: Abu Dhabi, Dubai, Sharjah, Ajman, Umm Al-Qaiwain, Ras Al-Khaimah, and Fujairah. Currently, the UAE federation does not impose a federal corporate income tax (CIT) in the emirates. However, most of the emirates introduced income tax decrees in the late 1960s, and taxation is therefore determined on an emirate-by-emirate basis.

Under the emirate-based tax decrees, CIT may be imposed on all companies (including branches and permanent establishments [PEs]) at rates of up to 55%. However, in practice, CIT is currently imposed only on branches of foreign banks and companies that produce, trade in, or trade in rights over oil, gas, or other hydrocarbon products (i.e. oil & gas companies) having operations in the emirate.

In addition, some of the emirates have introduced their own specific banking tax decrees, which impose tax on branches of foreign banks at the rate of 20%.

Corporate residence

Tax residence under the tax decrees of the various emirates is based upon the French concept of territoriality. Basically, the French territoriality concept taxes profits based on territorial nexus, rather than taxing profits earned outside the country.

Permanent establishment (PE)
For non-resident companies, the CIT liability will also depend on the existence of any kind of PE. Most of the emirate tax decrees include a definition of a PE that generally

United Arab Emirates

includes a branch, management or other fixed place of business, and presence through an agent that has and habitually exercises authority to conclude contracts on behalf of such corporation. The definitions need to be considered individually under the applicable tax decree.

Other taxes

Value-added tax (VAT)
The United Arab Emirates does not currently operate a VAT regime. However, the United Arab Emirates has made significant progress towards its introduction, and it is known that the introduction of a VAT is expected in the near future.

Customs duties
Generally, a customs duty of 5% is imposed on the cost, insurance, freight (CIF) value of imports. Other rates may apply to certain goods, such as alcohol and tobacco, and certain exemptions may also be available.

Excise taxes
Currently, there are no separate excise taxes levied in the United Arab Emirates.

Municipal or property tax
Most emirates impose a municipality tax on properties, mostly by reference to the annual rental value. It is generally the tenants' obligation to pay the tax; however, the tenants' employer will typically pay the tax on behalf of the employee. In some cases, separate fees are payable by both tenants and property owners. For example, in Emirate of Dubai, it is currently imposed at 5% of the annual rental value for tenants or for property owners at 5% of the specified rental index.

Further, a land registration fee may also be levied on transfer of ownership of land or property. For example, a land registration fee is levied in the Emirate of Dubai at a rate of 2% of the sale value of the property (shared between the buyer and seller), payable to the Dubai Land Department.

These levies are imposed and administered differently by each emirate.

Stamp taxes
Currently, there are no separate stamp taxes levied in the United Arab Emirates.

Hotel tax and tourism levies
Most emirates impose a hotel tax of 5% to 10% on the value of hotel services and entertainment. In addition, there may be tourist fees/charges of up to 10% levied for practice of certain tourist/entertainment activities (e.g. events and shows).

These levies are imposed and administered differently by each emirate.

Branch income

As each emirate has a different CIT decree, the decree of each emirate must be consulted to determine the treatment of branches of foreign corporations.

In certain emirates, branches of foreign banks are governed by special banking tax decrees where they are taxed at 20% of their adjusted taxable income.

Income determination

The tax decrees of the various emirates levy taxation on financial accounting profits. The tax decrees may provide for additional adjustments in specific situations. Currently, these adjustments may not be too relevant given that CIT is not imposed for most companies (except for oil & gas companies and branches of foreign banks having operations in the emirate) in the United Arab Emirates.

Deductions

Deductions are determined based on accounting principles and the tax decrees of the various emirates. Currently, these deductions may not be too relevant given that CIT is not imposed for most companies (except for oil & gas companies and branches of foreign banks having operations in the emirate) in the United Arab Emirates.

Group taxation

The United Arab Emirates does not currently permit group taxation.

Tax credits and incentives

The United Arab Emirates offers numerous incentives in the form of tax holidays/ exemptions, including offering a range of free trade zones.

Free trade zones (FTZs)
Currently, there are over 30 FTZs (and business parks) in the United Arab Emirates, each having its own regulations. Businesses (and their employees) established in FTZs are generally eligible for guaranteed tax holidays for ten to 50 year (renewable) periods. The FTZs also offer exemption from customs duties. The laws granting these holidays and exemptions are not consistent among the various FTZs, and each FTZ therefore needs to be considered separately.

Withholding taxes

There are currently no withholding taxes (WHTs) in the United Arab Emirates.

Tax treaty network
Taxpayers resident in the United Arab Emirates have access to an extensive tax treaty network. These treaties may not be immediately relevant for UAE WHTs (which are not imposed under the UAE tax decrees); however, they may continue to allow for other beneficial tax provisions (e.g. right to tax in the other treaty country). For completeness, the treaties currently in force are listed below. A number of other treaties are at various stages of negotiation.

Recipient	Dividends (%)	Interest (%)	Royalties (%)	In force
Algeria	0	0	10	25-Jun-04
Armenia	0/3	0	5	19-Dec-04
Austria	0	0	0	1-Sep-04
Azerbaijan	5/10	0/7	5/10	In force

United Arab Emirates

Recipient	Dividends (%)	Interest (%)	Royalties (%)	In force
Belarus	5/10	5	5/10	1-Jan-01
Belgium	0/5/10	0/5	0/5	6-Jan-04
Bosnia & Herzegovina	0/5/10	0	5	30-Apr-07
Bulgaria	0/5	0/2	0/5	16-Nov-08
Canada	5/10/15	0/10	10	25-May-04
China	7	7	10	28-Aug-94
Cyprus	0	0	0	Pending
Czech Republic	0/5	0	10	2-Aug-97
Egypt	0	0/10	10	16-Jul-95
Estonia	0	0	0	29-Mar-12
Finland	0	0	0	26-Dec-97
France	0	0	0	1-Jul-90
Georgia	0	0	0	28-Apr-11
Germany (new treaty)	5/10/15	0	10	14-Jul-11
Greece	0/5	0/5	0/5	Pending
Hong Kong	N/A	N/A	N/A	Pending
India	10	0/5/12.5	10	22-Sep-93
Indonesia	10	0/5	5	8-Nov-96
Ireland	0	0	0	6-Feb-11
Italy	5/15	0	10	5-Nov-97
Jordan	N/A	N/A	N/A	Pending
Kazakhstan	5	10	10	In force
Korea, Republic of	5/10	0/10	0	2-Mar-05
Lebanon	0	0	5	21-May-99
Libya	N/A	N/A	N/A	Pending
Luxembourg	5/10	0	0	1-Jan-10
Malaysia	10	0/5	10	10-Feb-00
Malta	0	0	0	18-May-07
Mauritius	0	0	0	31-Jul-07
Mongolia	0	0	10	In force
Morocco	0/5/10	0/10	0/10	2-Jul-00
Mozambique	0	0	0/5	15-Apr-04
Netherlands	5/10	0	0	2-Jun-10
New Zealand	15	0/10	10	29-Jul-04
Pakistan	10/15	0/10	12	30-Nov-94
Philippines	0/10/15	0/10	10	2-Oct-08
Poland	0/5	0/5	5	21-Apr-94
Portugal	5/15	0/10	5	In force
Romania	0/3	0/3	3	23-Jan-96
Seychelles	0	0	5	23-Apr-07
Singapore	5	0/7	5	30-Aug-96
Spain	5/15	0	0	2-Apr-07
Sri Lanka	0/10	0/10	10	1-Apr-04
Sudan	0	0	5	In force
Switzerland	5/15	0	0	Pending
Syria	0	0/10	18	In force
Tajikistan	0	0	10	27-Mar-00

Recipient	Dividends (%)	Interest (%)	Royalties (%)	In force
Thailand	10	10/15	15	28-Dec-00
Tunisia	0	2.5/5/10	7.5	27-May-97
Turkey	5/10/12	0/10	10	26-Dec-94
Turkmenistan	0	0	10	In force
Ukraine	0/5	0/3	0/10	9-Mar-04
Uzbekistan	0/5/15	0/10	10	In force
Venezuela	5/10	10	10	1-Jan-12
Vietnam	0/5/15	0/10	10	In force
Yemen	0	0	10	In force

Tax administration

Most companies operating in the United Arab Emirates (except oil & gas companies and branches of foreign banks) are currently not required to file CIT returns in the United Arab Emirates.

United Kingdom

PwC contact

Kevin Nicholson
PricewaterhouseCoopers LLP
1 Embankment Place
London WC2N 6RH
United Kingdom
Tel: + 44 1509 604232
Email: kevin.nicholson@uk.pwc.com

Significant developments

Several notable changes to the United Kingdom's (UK's) corporate tax system have been made in the past year. The government has also announced a number of reform measures for corporation tax, together with a programme of future changes and consultations, including a roadmap of how reform will develop in the years to 2015. The overall aim is to improve the international tax competitiveness of the UK economy by reforming four main areas:

- Rate of corporation tax.
- The corporate tax base.
- Policy making.
- Administration and collection.

Because the UK legislative process can lag behind the announcement of proposals, certain changes are already law, others are very likely, or practically certain, to become law, whilst others are issues announced for wider consultation and future enactment into law.

The Finance Act 2011 became substantively enacted on 5 July 2011 and fully enacted on 19 July 2011, with implications for financial reporting under UK and US Generally Accepted Accounting Principles (GAAP) and International Financial Reporting Standards (IFRS).

Significant measures introduced and fully enacted in law, which have full impact in 2011 and 2012, include a reduction in the rates of corporation tax, together with reductions in capital allowances (tax depreciation). These changes and other areas of future reform and consultation are discussed below.

Changes that have taken effect in the past year

The recent introduction of complex and far reaching reforms of the taxation of foreign profits impacts UK inbound, outbound, and purely domestic businesses through 2012 and beyond. The elements of the reform package which took effect in 2011, or after, include:

- The main rate of corporation tax was reduced to 24% as of 1 April 2012. There are proposals for reductions after that (*see below*).
- Profits of foreign branches of UK companies can be elected out of UK corporation tax with effect for accounting periods commencing after the election.
- The introduction of a principles-based rule to neutralise any UK tax advantage that arises as a result of financial 'group mismatches', i.e. where intra-group financial transactions are treated differently for tax purposes in the individual group members concerned.

- Simplification of certain elements of the corporate capital gains regime, effective as of July 2011. These elements include reducing the impact of degrouping charges (by election, a group can take advantage of these changes from 1 April 2011), and facilitating group reorganisations and other corporate transactions.
- With effect from 1 April 2012, the main rates of capital allowances (in effect, statutory tax depreciation rates) were reduced; the general rate for plant and machinery was reduced from 20% to 18% per annum, and the rate for long-life and special plant from 10% to 8% per annum.

The rate of the bank levy will increase on 1 January 2013. *See Bank levy in the Other taxes section for more information.*

Changes enacted but not yet in force
There are no significant changes enacted but not in force, but a number of important proposed reforms for 2012 and beyond are described elsewhere.

Consultations and proposals - ongoing
There are a number of announced proposals for future reform, on which consultations are currently in progress or proposed, most significantly:

- Further reductions in the main rate of corporation tax to 23% as of April 2013 and 22% as of April 2014.
- The simplification of reliefs and allowances, including reform of capital allowances on fixtures within buildings.
- Measures to tackle tax avoidance, including use of high-risk tax avoidance schemes and consultation on the introduction of a moderate and narrowly focussed general anti-avoidance rule (GAAR). Legislation will be introduced in 2013, although commencement is uncertain and could be earlier.
- Major reform of the complex controlled foreign company (CFC) regime, with effect as of 1 January 2013, so that most genuine overseas businesses will be exempt from the CFC charge. The proposals include a gateway test to exempt smaller businesses entirely, together with safe harbours which will exclude many others. A partial participation exemption is proposed for the finance income of UK-based businesses. In effect, this will tax such income at no more than 5.50% by 2014 and permits UK businesses to lend to associated companies in a tax advantaged manner.
- A review of the practical application of the recent debt cap rules which restrict, for tax purposes only, the UK deduction of financing costs by reference to the worldwide position of the group.
- Abolition of the 2% 'entry charge' for property businesses wishing to convert to the tax advantaged regime for real estate investment trusts (REITs) as of April 2012 together with measures making them a more likely prospect for residential investment.
- A refocusing of research and development (R&D) tax credits on hi-tech companies, small firms, and start-ups, and a proposal for an 'above the line' R&D credit from 2013.
- An increase in the rate of R&D credit for small and medium companies to 225% from 1 April 2012.
- The introduction of a reduced 10% rate of corporation tax on UK patent income as of April 2013, otherwise to be known as the UK 'patent box'.
- The introduction in 2012 of a tax advantaged scheme to encourage investment in small start-up businesses.
- The introduction of a remote gambling tax regime based on the place of consumption.

U

United Kingdom

- Establishing the future relationship between the tax agent community and Her Majesty's Revenue and Customs (HMRC).

The overall impact of the reduced rates of corporation tax and income tax, together with the improved CFC regime, the existing dividend exemption, substantial shareholdings exemption, 0% rate dividend withholding tax (WHT), and greater certainty over interest deductibility, are designed to make the United Kingdom a more attractive holding company and business hub location.

Most of the above reforms, together with other measures which have also been the subject of new or additional consultation documents and draft legislation published during 2011 and 2012, are included in the Finance Bill in March 2012. This is expected to become law in Finance Act 2012 in July 2012, although the effective date for many of the provisions will be earlier or later.

The European Union (EU) is presently working towards a common consolidated corporate tax base (CCCTB) (and/or a common corporate tax base [CCTB]) to harmonise the corporate tax base (but generally not corporate tax rates, although Germany and France intend to adopt a common rate) across the European Union. It is not clear whether the United Kingdom will adopt any final proposal, nor when it will take effect.

Taxes on corporate income

Resident companies are taxable in the United Kingdom on their worldwide profits (subject to an opt out for non-UK branches), while non-resident companies are subject to UK corporate tax only on the trading profits attributable to a UK permanent establishment (PE) plus UK income tax (generally by way of withholding, though this is not the case with UK-source rental profits) on certain UK-source income. *See the Corporate residence section for more information.*

General corporation tax rates
The normal rate of corporation tax is 24% for the year ending 31 March 2013. The rate for the year ending 31 March 2012 was 26% and for 31 March 2011 was 28%. The rate from 2008 to 2011 was 30%. This main rate applies to companies with profits in excess of 1.5 million pound sterling (GBP). It is proposed that this rate will fall to 23% from 1 April 2013 and to 22% from 1 April 2014.

For UK resident companies with tax-adjusted profits below GBP 300,000, a lower rate is generally applicable. This small profits rate is 20% from 1 April 2011 (21% to 31 March 2011). For companies with tax-adjusted profits between GBP 300,000 and GBP 1.5 million, there is a sliding scale of tax rates. For corporate entities with associated companies, both profit limits are divided by the number of active companies worldwide. There are no proposals for future changes to this small profits rate.

Special corporation tax regimes
With two specific exceptions, there are no special regimes for specific types of business activity; in general, all companies in all sectors are subject to the same corporate tax rates.

Profits which arise from oil or gas extraction, or oil or gas rights, in the United Kingdom and the UK Continental Shelf ('ring-fence profits') are subject to tax in the United Kingdom in accordance with rates applicable in 2006, i.e. a full rate of 30% and a small profits rate of 19%. Such activities also attract 100% capital allowances on most capital expenditure. A supplementary tax charge of 32% (increased from 20% from 24 March 2011) applies to 'adjusted' ring fence profits in addition to normal corporation tax.

Life insurance businesses are also taxed under a special regime, which effectively includes different corporate tax rates as well as special rules for quantifying profits.

Petroleum revenue tax (PRT)
A tax of 50% is levied on profits accruing from oil and gas extracted in the United Kingdom and in the UK territorial sea and continental shelf in respect of fields given development consent before 16 March 1993. PRT has effectively been abolished, together with associated relief and allowances, for fields that received development consent after 15 March 1993. PRT paid is deductible in computing corporation tax on the company's total profits.

Income tax for non-resident companies
A non-resident company is subject to UK corporation tax only on the trading profits of a UK PE. Any other UK-source income received by a non-resident company is subject to UK income tax at the basic rate, currently 20%, without any allowances (subject to any relief offered by a double tax treaty [DTT] if applicable). This charge most commonly arises in relation to UK rental income earned by a non-resident landlord (NRL). The United Kingdom therefore operates an NRL scheme which requires the NRL's letting agent or tenants to withhold the appropriate tax at source unless they have been notified that the NRL has applied for and been given permission to receive gross rents.

Local income taxes
There are no local or provincial taxes on income.

Corporate residence

UK incorporated companies are generally treated as UK resident. However, companies resident in the United Kingdom under domestic law, but treated as solely resident in a different country under that country's DTT with the United Kingdom, are not treated as UK resident for the purposes of UK domestic tax law.

Additionally, subject to the above exception, companies incorporated overseas are also treated as UK resident if their central management and control is situated in the United Kingdom. That is, if the place of the highest form of control and direction over a company's affairs, as opposed to decisions on the day-to-day running of the business, is in the United Kingdom.

Permanent establishment (PE)
For non-resident companies, the liability to corporation tax depends on the existence of any kind of PE through which a trade is carried on. The meaning of PE for UK tax purposes is set out in statute; it is largely based on the Organisation for Economic Co-operation and Development (OECD) Model Tax Convention definition, but is not identical in all respects. Subject to the terms of the relevant double taxation agreement, a non-resident company will have a PE in the United Kingdom if it either:

- has a fixed place of business in the United Kingdom through which the business of the company is wholly or partly carried on, or
- an agent acting on behalf of the company has and habitually exercises authority to do business on behalf of the company in the United Kingdom.

United Kingdom

A fixed place of business includes (but is not limited to) a place of management; a branch; an office; a factory; a workshop; an installation or structure for the exploration of natural resources; a mine, oil or gas well, quarry, or other place of extraction of natural resources; or a building, construction, or installation project. However, a company is not regarded as having a UK PE if the activities for which the fixed place of business is maintained or which the agent carries on are only of a preparatory or auxiliary nature (also defined in the statute).

Special rules exist to explain how the PE's profits should be evaluated for UK tax purposes (*see the Branch income section for more information*).

Other taxes

Value-added tax (VAT)
The standard VAT rate of 20% applies to most goods and services, apart from domestic fuel and power and certain other reduced-rate supplies, which are subject to VAT at 5% (note that the standard rate was increased from 17.5% with effect from 4 January 2011).

Most exports, most food, most public transport, books and publications, and certain other essential goods and services are zero-rated. Some supplies are exempt, the main categories being the grant of certain interests in land, insurance, financial services, betting and gaming, education, certain sports services, cultural services, and health and welfare. Zero-rating is preferable to exemption because the VAT on costs incurred in making a zero-rated supply can be recovered while that incurred in making an exempt supply cannot.

VAT is chargeable on the supply of most goods and services made in the United Kingdom by 'taxable persons' in the course of business, when their taxable turnover exceeds the registration thresholds. Taxable persons include individuals, companies, partnerships, clubs, associations, or charities.

Taxable persons who are not normally resident in the United Kingdom, do not have a business establishment in the United Kingdom, and, in the case of companies, are not incorporated in the United Kingdom, but who make taxable supplies, sales to unregistered persons in the United Kingdom, or acquisitions of goods in the United Kingdom above the relevant limits, may be required to register and account for VAT in the United Kingdom.

If the value of taxable supplies is over a specified limit, registration for VAT is compulsory unless the taxable supplies made are wholly or mainly zero-rated, in which case it is possible to apply for exemption from registration. The government confirmed in Budget 2012 that with effect from 1 December 2012, a zero VAT registration threshold will apply for businesses not established in the United Kingdom.

The rules applying to VAT and territoriality are different to those applying to direct tax in that they derive from the principles of the place of supply in EU law, as enshrined in European Commission (EC) VAT Directives. Having determined that a supply of goods or services has taken place, the second condition to be determined, if the transaction is to fall within the scope of UK VAT, is whether the supply takes place within the United Kingdom. The place of supply rules are different for goods and for services. A person or business belonging outside the United Kingdom, with no place of business in the United

Kingdom, may nevertheless be liable to UK VAT registration where the place of supply of those goods or services is in the United Kingdom.

For goods, the basic rule is that a supply of goods is taxable in the territory where those goods are physically located at the time of supply. Hence, if goods are supplied in the United Kingdom by a non-established taxable person, there will still be a liability for VAT purposes, and the person must register for VAT in the United Kingdom if the taxable supplies exceed the current UK VAT registration thresholds.

For services, the basic rule is that services are treated as made where the customer 'belongs' or is established for VAT purposes, and the customer is responsible for accounting for the VAT due via the reverse charge procedure. However, this is subject to a number of special rules and exceptions. Determining where a business is established for VAT purposes is based on EU law criteria.

For business to consumer (B2C) supplies, the basic rule is that services are treated as made where the supplier 'belongs' or is established for VAT purposes.

VAT returns and payments
VAT returns must be completed at preset intervals (usually every three months). Larger companies may be required to file monthly returns or make monthly payments on account. As of 1 April 2012, all businesses are required to file VAT returns online and make electronic payments. Smaller enterprises can apply for annual returns. VAT returns are usually required to be filed 30 days after the end of the period.

Annual accounting is available for taxable persons with annual turnover (taxable supplies, excluding VAT) not exceeding GBP 1,350,000.

Cash accounting is available for taxable persons with annual turnover (taxable supplies, excluding VAT) not exceeding GBP 1,350,000.

In addition, a flat rate scheme operates for small businesses and is intended to simplify VAT accounting procedures.

Customs and excise duties
Many goods imported into the United Kingdom from outside the European Union are subject to customs duties. The rates of duty are provided by the EU's Common Customs Tariff and vary widely.

Excise duties are chargeable on most hydrocarbon oil products, alcoholic drinks, and tobacco products imported into or produced in the United Kingdom. Examples include the following:

Products	Excise duty (GBP)
Road fuels	0.5795 per litre
Cigarettes	167 per thousand (plus 16.5% of the retail price)
Tobacco	164 per kg
Wines	2.53 per litre
Spirits	26.81 per litre of pure alcohol included

U

United Kingdom

Stamp taxes

Stamp duty is charged at 0.5% on instruments effecting sales of shares. Agreements to sell shares usually attract stamp duty reserve tax (SDRT) at 0.5%. The liability to SDRT may be cancelled by paying the stamp duty due on a stock transfer form (or other transfer instrument) executed in pursuance of the agreement. Stamp duty is not usually charged on an issue of shares, but is charged at a higher rate of 1.5% on an issue of shares in bearer form. Issues or transfers of shares to clearance services or depositary receipt systems may attract SDRT at 1.5% (stamp duty at 1.5% may be payable on instruments effecting transfers of shares to such services or systems).

Transfers of non-residential or mixed land and buildings are charged stamp duty land tax at graduated rates up to 4%. Acquisitions of residential property by companies are charged at graduated rates of up to 15% (whereas acquisitions by individuals are capped at 7%). Grants of new leases are charged stamp duty land tax at 1% of the net present value of the rents payable in excess of GBP 150,000 (or GBP 125,000 for residential property) plus up to 4% (or 15% for grants of new leases of residential property to companies) on any premium paid.

Bank levy

A bank levy was introduced as of 1 January 2011 and takes the form of an annual tax on certain liabilities of most UK-based banks and building societies. The tax is levied at the following annualised rates:

- January and February 2011: 0.05% of a bank's short-term relevant liabilities and 0.025% of long-term equity and liabilities.
- March and April 2011: 0.1% of a bank's short-term relevant liabilities and 0.05% of long-term equity and liabilities.
- 1 May 2011 to 31 December 2011: 0.075% of a bank's short-term relevant liabilities and 0.0375% of long-term equity and liabilities.
- From 1 January 2012: 0.088% of a bank's short-term relevant liabilities and 0.044% of long-term equity and liabilities.
- From 1 January 2013: 0.105% of a bank's short-term relevant liabilities and 0.0525% of long-term equity and liabilities.

The levy is not charged on the first GBP 20 billion of chargeable liabilities and is not deductible for corporation tax purposes.

Insurance premium tax (IPT)

IPT at the standard rate of 6% applies to premiums for most general insurance, such as for buildings and contents and motor insurance, where the insured risk is in the United Kingdom (note that the standard rate was increased from 5% from 4 January 2011). Life assurance and other long term insurance remain exempt, though there are anti-avoidance rules surrounding long-term medical care policies.

As an anti-avoidance measure, a higher rate of 20% applies to insurance sold by suppliers of specified goods or services, e.g. mechanical breakdown insurance, travel insurance (irrespective of supplier), insurance sold with TV and car hire, and 'non-financial' guaranteed asset protection (GAP) insurance sold through suppliers of motor vehicles or persons connected with them. Further anti-avoidance rules affect administration or similar fees connected with contracts of insurance, charged under separate contracts by brokers and other intermediaries (note that the higher rate was increased from 17.5% from 4 January 2011).

Airport passenger duty

Individuals leaving the United Kingdom by air are obliged to pay a duty, which in practice is invariably included in the cost of the air ticket. Rates of duty are based on a system of geographical banding and class of travel, ranging from a reduced rate of GBP 13 for short haul destinations in the lowest class of travel to GBP 184 for long haul destinations in higher classes of travel. Certain exemptions and lower rates apply for some geographically outlying areas of the United Kingdom.

Environmental taxes

There are several environmental taxes, including the following.

Landfill tax

The landfill tax is a tax on waste disposal in landfill sites. The standard rate from 1 April 2012 is GBP 64 per tonne, increasing to GBP 72 per tonne from 1 April 2013 and GBP 80 from 1 April 2014. The reduced rate for inert waste is GBP 2.50 per tonne.

Climate change levy

The climate change levy is a tax on energy used in the United Kingdom, such as electricity, gas, coal, etc., and is charged at rates that depend on the nature of the fuel used. There are reduced rates and exclusions from the charge, e.g. supplies to domestic or charitable users and to those who carry out specific energy-saving measures.

Aggregates levy

The aggregates levy is a tax on the extraction or importation of sand, gravel, and crushed rock for commercial exploitation in the United Kingdom. The rate of tax is GBP 2.00 per tonne increasing to GBP 2.10 per tonne from 1 April 2013.

Employers' national insurance contributions (NICs)

Employers are obliged to pay NICs based on a percentage of each employee's earnings. For the year ending 5 April 2012, the rate is 13.8% on all earnings above GBP 140 per week. There is some reduction for employees 'contracted out' of the state pension scheme into a private scheme.

Pension protection fund levy

All defined benefit pension schemes pay a levy, based on pension fund liabilities and the financial risk of the employing company. This levy funds a compensation fund for pensioners and employees of failed schemes.

Local municipal taxes

Local taxes are not based on income, but rather are levied on the occupiers of business property by reference to a deemed annual rental (or 'rateable') value for the property concerned. These taxes (known as 'rates') are administered by regional local government authorities rather than central government. The amounts paid are deductible for corporation tax purposes, provided they meet all the usual requirements for deductibility.

U

Branch income

Tax rates on the profits of PEs are the same as for domestic corporations, except that the small profits rate is not available to non-UK resident corporations unless under the terms of a DTT.

United Kingdom

There are specific rules setting out how the PE's profits should be evaluated for UK tax purposes, which broadly seek to treat the business as if it were a standalone company. Financing arrangements between the branch and head office must be disregarded, and there are special rules for banks to stop under-performing loans being allocated to the UK branch in a way that is considered unacceptable and similar potential manipulations. However, a deduction is given for a proportion of head office costs.

No tax is withheld on transfers of profits to the head office.

Taxable income determination

A UK resident company is taxed on its worldwide total profits.

The UK tax system requires those total profits to be calculated by finding the aggregate of (i) the company's net income from each source and (ii) the company's net chargeable gains arising from the sale of capital assets.

The main sources of income recognised by the legislation are (i) profits of a trade, (ii) profits of a property business, (iii) non-trading profits (or losses) from loan relationships, mainly interest receivable or payable, (iv) non-trading gains (or losses) on intangible fixed assets, and (v) non-exempt dividends or other company distributions. Determining income for sources (i) to (iv) relies heavily on the company's accounts. Taxable income from non-exempt dividends and calculating chargeable gains or income from other sources is based on actual amounts.

The rules for determining the gross income in each category differ in certain respects according to the source concerned and are different again when calculating gains. Likewise, there are also subtle differences in the rules concerning the deductions that are permissible in respect of different sources of income and in respect of gains. Because of this continuing reliance on taxing companies on a 'source-by-source' basis, the UK system is not well suited to being analysed in terms of income determination and deductions as two wholly separate topics.

Basic rules for accounts-based sources

A company's trading profits are based on its worldwide profit before tax in its accounts. Adjustments are made for non-trading receipts (such as dividends from other companies and income from property) and non-deductible expenditure (such as capital expenditure or expenditure which is not incurred for the purposes of the trade). Depreciation for tax purposes (known as capital allowances) is calculated and substituted for the depreciation charged in the accounts. There are also a number of other statutory adjustments to be made; three important ones are that pension contributions and deferred pay are broadly deductible only when paid, that a deduction is available for the notional cost of certain share awards to employees, and that where acquired intangibles are not depreciated in the accounts a 4% flat-rate deduction can usually be claimed. There are, however, many other adjustments.

Similar principles apply in relation to the calculation of profits of a property business.

The profits from a company's trading and non-trading loan relationships and related matters are based on the accounts. For this source of income, the distinction between 'capital' and 'revenue' receipts and deductions is not relevant. All credits and debits in the accounts are aggregated in order to find the net profit or deficit. Certain statutory adjustments have to be made, which include an interest capping limitation ('debt cap'). Broadly, the same regime applies to income and expenses relating to intangibles, including goodwill. For a trader, these are therefore specific areas where capital amounts can be taxed or allowed.

For traders, any profit or loss on loan relationships, and/or on intangibles, is generally included within the trading profits; they become a single source of profits. For loan relationships and intangibles not connected with a trade, the company has a separate source of profits or a separate class of loss.

Income losses
Where a loss arises in respect of a particular source of income, there are detailed rules regarding the possible offset of the loss. Carryback and sideways reliefs are often allowed within limits; carryforward is generally allowed and carried forward losses do not time expire. Losses can also be utilised by other group companies (*see the Group taxation section*).

More specifically, dealing with the main sorts of income losses,

* trading losses may be set off against any other source of profit (or gains) in the same year, may be carried back one year (three years on the cessation of the trade) against any other source of profit (or gain), or may be carried forward without time limit against profits of the same trade only
* property losses may also be set off against any other source of profit (or gains) in the same year, or may be carried forward without time limit against profits of any sort; they cannot, however, be carried back, and
* non-trading deficits (i.e. interest and financing losses) can again be set off against any other source of profit (or gains) in the same year, may be carried back one year against non-trading credits (i.e. interest and financing profits), or may be carried forward without time limit against non-trading profits.

Non-trading companies may deduct non-capital management expenses incurred in managing their investments from their total profits. Any excess management expenses can be carried forward without limit to set against profits in future years.

While income losses can generally be offset against capital gains of the same accounting period, capital losses are never available for offset against any type of income.

Inventory valuation
In general, the book and tax methods of inventory valuation will conform. In practice, inventories are normally valued for tax purposes at the lower of cost or net realisable value. A first in first out (FIFO) basis of determining cost where items cannot be identified is acceptable, but not the base-stock or the last in first out (LIFO) method.

Capital gains
Gains on capital assets are taxed at the normal corporation tax rates. The chargeable gain (or allowable loss) arising on the disposal of a capital asset is calculated by deducting from gross proceeds the costs of acquisition and subsequent improvements, plus the incidental costs of sale and indexation allowance. Indexation allowance compensates for the increase in costs based on the percentage rise (if any) in the UK retail prices index to the date of disposal. Indexation allowance is, however, limited; it cannot create or increase a capital loss, it can only reduce or eliminate a chargeable gain. These calculations must be done in sterling, so any foreign exchange gains and losses will be taxed (or relieved) on disposal.

United Kingdom

Special rules apply to assets held since 31 March 1982.

Most acquisitions and disposals between UK group companies are treated as made on a no gain no loss basis (i.e. at base cost plus indexation). Otherwise, acquisitions from, or disposals to, affiliates are treated as made at fair market value, as are other acquisitions or disposals not at arm's length.

Capital losses are allowed only as an offset to capital gains. An excess of capital losses over capital gains in a company's accounting period may be carried forward without limitation but may not be carried back.

There is a good deal of anti-avoidance legislation concerning the computation of chargeable gains, notably to stop losses being created or gains avoided where assets are depreciated by intra-group transactions, or where losses are 'bought in' from third parties.

Gains realised on certain types of assets can be deferred where all or most of the proceeds are reinvested in other assets of those types within a specified period (generally three years). The 'rolled-over' gain then crystallises as and when the latter assets are sold. At present, the main asset categories qualifying for roll-over are land and buildings used for a trade.

Most disposals by trading groups of shareholdings of 10% or more are exempt from tax. The main exceptions will be those of non-trading subsidiaries or subgroups, or of companies acquired within the previous year. Note that gains on goodwill and other intangibles acquired after March 2002 are taxed as income, not as capital gains.

Dividend income
Most foreign and UK dividends received by UK companies have been exempt from corporation tax since July 2009; one of several criteria has to be met, but these are widely drawn (one test, for example, is that the recipient controls the payer). For non-exempt foreign source dividends, double tax relief (DTR) will be available on a dividend by dividend basis. It is unusual for companies to be taxed on UK dividends because of the breadth of the exemption; however, where they are taxed, there is no concept of DTR for UK dividends.

Realised and unrealised exchange gains/losses
Unrealised exchange gains and losses tend to arise on debts and derivatives; they are then taxed or allowed, together with realised amounts, on an accounts basis in the same way as other debits and credits arising out of loan relationships. Where gains or losses arise on other payables or receivables, to a trader or property investor, they will again generally be taxed or allowed on an accounts basis. For a trader, the taxable or allowable amount will become simply part of the trading profit or loss; for other companies, it will become a separate source of taxable profit (a 'non-trading credit') or loss (a 'non-trading deficit').

Where unrealised differences arise on other capital assets, they will not generally be taxable or allowable at that stage; instead, the exchange difference becomes part of the computation and is effectively taxed or allowed when the asset is disposed of and any difference is realised.

Partnership income
In broad terms, if companies participate in UK partnerships (whether general partnerships, limited partnerships, or limited liability partnerships) they will be taxed

on a flow through basis. This will, in very broad terms, mean that UK corporate partners will be taxed on trading, property, or financing income as it arises in the partnership accounts, and on non-exempt dividends on a receipts basis.

When considering overseas entities, the UK authorities will not be bound by how the entity is classified in its country of origin. Case law has determined a number of matters that should be considered when establishing whether a non-UK entity should be taxed in the UK as if it were a company or a partnership. HMRC also maintains a public list of non-UK entities and the decisions it has previously made regarding their classification. However, if the parties have flexibility regarding the constitution of such entities, then their classification may be viewed differently, either by HMRC or the courts. This area is complex and therefore specialist advice should be sought.

Foreign income
In principle, the United Kingdom taxes on a worldwide basis, although non-UK branch profits can be exempted from UK taxation by election. The election can be made at any date on or after 19 July 2011 and applies to all accounting periods starting after the election is made and to all the branches of the company (so it cannot be made on a PE by PE basis). The election is irrevocable and has the effect of exempting all profits of the branch, including gains (other than for close companies). Equally, relief for branch losses will be denied. Profits will be measured by reference to double taxation treaties, or, in absence, OECD principles. Certain businesses may not elect to exempt profits (e.g. life insurance, shipping and aircraft operations, and most investment activity).

Where no election is made, profits from non-UK branches are computed and taxed in the normal way for UK tax resident companies. However, UK tax will generally be reduced by credit for local direct taxes paid, either under a treaty or via the UK's unilateral relief rules (*see Foreign tax credit in the Tax credits and incentives section for more information*).

General rules for deductions
As noted in the income section, the UK tax system requires taxable profits to be calculated by aggregating (i) the company's net income from each source and (ii) the company's net chargeable gains arising from the sale of capital assets. This approach gives rise to a particularly complicated regime so far as deductions are concerned. Expenses are usually allocated to the source of income (or occasionally by reference to income generally) or to the particular gain to which they relate. The rules governing their deductibility differ according to whether the expense relates to a capital gain or to income, and indeed according to the particular source of income concerned. For example, there is a considerable difference in the manner in which tax relief is given for expenses incurred by companies trading in property as compared to those that invest in property. The regime also has a large number of specific rules dealing with particular types of deductions which take priority over the more general rules for each type of income.

We have therefore set out the general rule for trading expenses, being the most common category and, following that analysis, considered some specific common exceptions.

General rules for trading expenses
A trading company is generally permitted to deduct expenses that are incurred wholly and exclusively for the purposes of the company's trade, provided those costs are not capital in nature and are charged to the profit and loss account. There is a significant

U

United Kingdom

amount of case law surrounding whether expenses have been incurred wholly and exclusively for the purposes of a company's trade and whether they are capital or not.

Relief is generally given in the period the expenses are accrued in the accounts, subject to some specific exceptions. In particular, contributions to a registered pension scheme are only allowed on a 'paid' basis, with some further provisions under which some contributions may be spread over a number of years; and if bonuses and other staff costs are paid out more than nine months after the end of the accounting period in which they are accrued, they are only allowed on a paid basis.

The general rule is made subject to a raft of specific statutory provisions, some of which allow deductions and others of which limit them; some of the more important of these are discussed below, but there are many others. There is, as one example, a bar to deducting the costs of business entertainment, except within quite strict limits.

Depreciation and amortisation
Depreciation of fixed assets (other than of goodwill and other assets within the intangible fixed asset regime, *see below*) is not allowable as a deduction from any source of income. However, traders, and most non-traders, are instead allowed specified rates of annual deduction in respect of specified classes of assets, together referred to as 'capital allowances', which are deducted in calculating trading income for traders, and (broadly) against income derived from the use of the fixed assets for non-traders.

In the period of expenditure, capital allowances are available, generally at 18% (post April 2012) of the cost of machinery and equipment acquired for use in a trade or property rental business; thereafter, capital allowances are taken generally at 18% per annum on the reducing-balance basis. With some exceptions (notably cars, ships, and machinery and equipment in offices and other non-industrial buildings), the rate of capital allowances for machinery and equipment with an expected useful life when new of at least 25 years, and purchased after 25 November 1996, is 8%. Since 1 April 2008, this 8% rate also applies to certain integral features in buildings and thermal insulation.

Capital allowances are given on cars at rates dependent on emission levels.

All businesses, regardless of size, can claim an annual investment allowance of 100% on the first GBP 25,000 per year of most qualifying expenditure (from April 2012, previously GBP 100,000 since 2010). This is restricted to a single allowance for groups of companies or associated businesses.

Enhanced allowances, typically at a rate of 100%, are available for expenditure on certain energy saving plant and other specific categories. The products and technologies supported by this regime are reviewed and updated regularly.

The rate of capital allowance of most plant or machinery leased to non-residents is restricted, generally to 8% but in some cases to nil. However, HMRC now accept that in some circumstances these rules may be contrary to EU law, and for leases finalised on or after 1 April 2006 where the lessee is resident in an European Economic Area (EEA) country which does not give the lessee relief broadly equivalent to the UK's capital allowances, HMRC will accept that the lessor is entitled to allowances at the normal 18% rate; in addition, the 0% rate will not be enforced in the case of other EEA lessees.

No capital allowance is normally allowed on buildings, apart from certain machinery and equipment embodied in the fabric of the buildings. Prior to April 2011, limited

United Kingdom

capital allowance was given for new industrial buildings, agricultural buildings, and certain hotels. This allowance is now withdrawn.

Capital allowance of machinery and equipment, and of industrial buildings, can be disclaimed in whole or in part, thereby deferring allowances.

Capital allowances may also be available in respect of the cost of the acquisition of mineral assets and other qualifying expenditures relating to mineral extraction, generally at the rates of 10% and 25% respectively on the reducing-balance basis, and in respect of various other types of capital expenditure, including the cost of ships, construction of public roads, and dredging.

Excess capital allowances are generally recaptured on disposal. The recapture is calculated on a 'pool' basis for most machinery and equipment, in which case there is no recapture unless the sale proceeds exceeds the total tax written down value of the pooled assets. The rules concerning which pool an asset goes into can be complex; a large company will generally have several pools ranging from single asset pools to a single large pool for most of its plant and machinery. There is no recapture for sales of industrial buildings.

Where assets are leased, capital allowances are generally available to the lessor rather than the lessee. However, this is an area of complexity, and in some situations (generally relating to finance leases), the allowances are only available to the lessee.

Intangible fixed assets

A special regime applies to intangible assets, such as patent rights, know-how and trademarks, and including goodwill. Royalties are generally deductible on an accounts basis, and, except in relation to 'grandfathered' assets owned by the group on 31 March 2002, the accounts' amortisation of intangible assets is also deductible (with an option to take a flat 4% deduction even if not amortised in the accounts). Traders will take the deductions in computing trading income; non-traders will create a 'non-trading loss on intangible fixed assets' which can be relieved as a loss against any profits of the year, carried back one year, or carried forward indefinitely.

Income costs relating to R&D are normally deductible in any event, but there is a special incentive connected with R&D which generally allows an additional deduction (*see the Tax credits and incentives section for more information*).

Management expenses

Holding companies are permitted a deduction for expenses to the extent that they are expenses of managing the company's investment business and are not capital in nature. Such costs would typically include audit fees, directors' costs, rent, local rates, and office costs. These costs can be set against any sources of profit the company may have (such as financing income). For the top company of a listed group, such expenses can be very substantial.

If the company has inadequate income (given that most dividend income will not be taxable), the excess can be surrendered as group relief. Alternatively, it can be carried forward to set against future income, with no time limit.

Many of the specific prohibitions on the deduction of trading expenses (though not all) are extended to create a similar bar on the deduction of such costs as management expenses for non-traders; conversely, many rules giving traders a specific deduction for certain costs are extended to allow non-traders similar relief. But this is not invariably

United Kingdom

the case. For example, traders can only deduct costs 'wholly and exclusively' incurred for the purposes of the trade; there is no similar rule for management expenses. However, the two specific limitations on trading deductions referred to above (pension contributions and late-paid remuneration) are extended to management expenses.

Employee share schemes
A deduction is often available to an employing company for the deemed cost of providing shares to employees, on a formula basis rather than the accounts charge (if any); this depends on the nature of the share plan and of the shares provided. This regime will generally allow a deduction to a subsidiary company whose employees receive shares (or options over shares) in the parent company.

Funding costs
Funding costs (primarily fees and interest) are broadly deductible on an accounts basis, even if capital in nature, but subject to thin capitalisation constraints (with no explicit safe harbours) and an interest cap based on the group's external debt levels. This extends to foreign exchange deductions relating to debts owed and receivable.

Traders will generally take the deductions in computing trading income (which is also accounts based). Deductions relating to loans not used for trading purposes will give rise to 'non-trading deficits' which, if not group relieved, can be offset against profits of that year generally, carried back one year (against that year's funding profits), or carried forward indefinitely against non-trading profits.

Bad debts, provisions, and reserves
A provision will be deductible for tax purposes if (or to the extent that) it:

- is in respect of allowable revenue expenditure
- is made in accordance with acceptable accounting practice
- does not conflict with any statutory rule governing the timing of relief (e.g. in relation to payment of staff costs), and
- is estimated with sufficient accuracy.

This rule extends to bad debts on trading account. Generally, however, bad debts are dealt with under the 'loan relationships' rules for financing costs and financing income. The rules there, however, are broadly the same; if the bad debt can be identified specifically enough to allow a bad debt provision which satisfies UK accounting standards, it should be deductible.

Charitable donations
Most donations to charities by companies are deductible.

Fines, penalties, and bribes
Any payments that would constitute a criminal offence (e.g. a bribe), or would do so if paid inside the United Kingdom, are expressly not deductible as trading expenses or management expenses. Likewise, fines and penalties imposed for breaking the law are also not deductible, although a deduction is usually available for legal costs incurred in defending such an action. Civil penalties, interest, and default surcharges (e.g. relating to certain VAT defaults) are also generally non-deductible, except for damages which are compensatory rather than punitive (e.g. damages for defamation payable by a newspaper company).

The rule that any amount paid by way of a penalty for breach of the criminal law is not deductible derives largely from case law and was explicitly said to be a policy rule. It is applied strictly; parking fines and fines for breaches of regulations, or for price-fixing, are not deductible.

The rule does not, however, extend to compensatory payments which are not punitive. So settlements in relation to negligence which harms customers or patients, or for breach of contract, or with employees for wrongful dismissal, ought to remain deductible.

Taxes

Local municipal taxes (business rates) may be deducted from taxable income.

Net operating and capital losses

Income losses may be carried forward indefinitely, and, in general, set against any type of non-trading profits; in contrast, losses of a particular trade can be carried forward only against profits of the same trade. Unlimited loss carryback is available for trading losses against total profits of (normally) the previous 12 months (provided the same trade was being carried on in that period). There is a more limited facility to carry back certain non-trading losses, also normally for 12 months. Losses can also generally be surrendered to other group companies to set against their taxable profits for the same period.

Capital losses may also be carried forward indefinitely but may not be carried back. There is no ability to surrender capital losses to fellow group members, but gains or losses arising on a particular asset can be allocated to another group member (by means of a joint election on an asset-by-asset basis). Therefore, there is a limited ability for the capital losses of one company to be offset against the gains of a fellow group member in the same or subsequent period.

Note that there are complex anti-avoidance rules which restrict the utilisation of losses where there is a change in ownership of the company.

Payments to foreign affiliates

There are no special rules for payments to foreign affiliates, so their tax treatment follows the basic rules for deductions set out above. The transfer pricing rules will impose an arm's-length price.

Group taxation

Each individual corporate group member is required to submit their own tax return on a stand-alone basis, with the exception of the election available with respect to VAT (*discussed below*). However, there are a variety of ways in which one's relationship with fellow group members is recognised in the UK tax system for the purposes of corporation tax, VAT, and stamp duty.

Corporation tax

The corporation tax system includes a number of measures that advantage UK members of qualifying groups, all of which are subject to anti-avoidance measures.

Operating taxable profits and losses arising in the same period can usually be offset between UK resident 75% affiliates within a worldwide group. This extends to offsetting the UK profits attributed to a UK PE of a non-UK resident group member. There are some restrictions, primarily where one of the two companies is not an economic 75%

United Kingdom

subsidiary of the group or is subject to arrangements under which it might leave the group.

Intra-group transfers of capital assets between UK companies, including UK PEs, are normally tax-free, though the definition of group for these purposes is slightly different than the definition of group relief for losses. This treatment is also extended to intra-group transfers of loan relationships, derivatives, and intangibles. There is generally a 'degrouping' charge if the transferee company leaves the group within six years.

There is no automatic offset of capital gains and losses where these arise in different group companies, but it is normally possible for offset to be arranged by the appropriate tax-free transfer of the asset being disposed of to the third party. Such a tax-free transfer can either be actually done (prior to the third party disposal) or notionally only (by election between the companies concerned).

A UK resident parent company is able to claim group relief for income losses of a non-UK subsidiary which is resident in the EEA or which has incurred the relevant losses in a PE within the EEA, provided that all possibilities of non-UK relief for the losses have been exhausted and future relief is unavailable. The EC has referred the United Kingdom to the European Court of Justice (ECJ) over this 'all possibilities' test and the fact that it must be met immediately after the end of the accounting period in which the loss arises, together with the fact that this extension of loss relief only applies to losses incurred after 1 April 2006.

In addition, the corporation tax system also has a number of measures that seek to prohibit groups unfairly manipulating the tax system by shifting profits between group members (either internationally or within the United Kingdom) in a way that is considered unacceptable.

A debt cap applicable to accounting periods beginning on or after 1 January 2010 limits the aggregated UK tax deductions group members may claim for finance costs to the level of a group's external finance expense.

VAT

Group companies can, subject to certain requirements, elect to account for VAT as if they were one taxable person; where this is done, no VAT is charged on intra-group supplies of goods or services. The registration is made in the name of the representative member, who is responsible for completing and rendering the single return on behalf of the group. All the companies are jointly and severally liable for any VAT debts. VAT grouping is subject to detailed anti-avoidance provisions.

Stamp duty and stamp duty land tax

Transfers of assets within worldwide 75% groups are generally exempt from stamp duty and stamp duty land tax. For stamp duty land tax, the relief can be retrospectively withdrawn in certain circumstances, primarily where the transferee leaves the group within three years of the transfer.

Transfer pricing and thin capitalisation

The United Kingdom has widely drafted transfer pricing rules that are intended to apply to almost any kind of transaction made or imposed between related parties that gives rise to:

- a provision that differs from one that would have been made between third parties and

- a UK tax advantage (potential or actual) to one or more of the parties.

These rules apply to UK-to-UK transactions as well as cross-border transactions.

The regime therefore applies not only to the provision of products and services but also to finance arrangements, including both the rate of return charged and the amount of loan principle (or equivalent) made available. It is therefore the mechanism by which the UK's revenue authorities address the issue of thin capitalisation. Unlike many other territories, the United Kingdom does not operate any 'safe harbours' of any kind in relation to the amount of debt or interest (or equivalents) it considers demonstrates that a UK company or group is not thinly capitalised. Note that the United Kingdom also has a debt cap regime which limits the amount of finance expense for which a UK tax deduction will be available by reference to the worldwide group's external finance expense.

Parties are considered related for this purpose where either one controls the other or both are under common control. Control here is not confined to situations in which one party is the majority shareholder in the other. Effectively, control exists where one party has the power to ensure that the affairs of another party are conducted in accordance with the first party's wishes. The concept is also subject to two important extensions:

- The rules apply to many joint venture companies where two parties each have an interest of at least 40%.
- There are attribution rules to trace control relationships through a number of levels in determining whether parties are controlled for the purposes of the transfer pricing rules.

In addition, the regime restricts interest deductions to an arm's-length basis where a financier and persons who collectively control a company or a partnership have 'acted together' in relation to the financing arrangements of that company or partnership. The financier (usually a bank) can then be taken as controlling the company or partnership, and the loan becomes subject to transfer pricing limitations.

There are a number of exemptions which essentially exclude small or medium-sized enterprises (SMEs) and dormant companies from the regime.

The effect of the rules is to require an arm's-length provision to be substituted for the actual one, thereby increasing the party's UK tax liability and cancelling out the UK tax advantage that would otherwise have arisen.

Where both parties to the transaction are UK taxpayers, the disadvantaged party will generally be entitled to claim a compensating adjustment (except where the transaction falls within the transfer pricing regime because of the 'acting together' provisions), but only after the UK adjustment has been made. The legislation also provides that parties may make balancing payments to each other in such circumstances, of any amount up to the transfer pricing adjustment, which will neither be taxable for the recipient nor tax deductible for the payer.

U

Where the disadvantaged party is outside the UK tax net, they can pursue a claim for relief under the relevant double tax agreement, if that provides a mechanism for such relief; where the adjustment in the United Kingdom is to reduce a deduction for an amount paid under deduction of UK tax, the compensating adjustment rules should allow the overseas party to reclaim any WHT paid on the disallowed amount.

United Kingdom

UK taxpayers are required to self assess their compliance with this arm's-length principle. Companies and partnerships must therefore identify and make transfer pricing adjustments when submitting their tax returns. This is the case even where the disadvantaged party would be entitled to claim a compensating adjustment equal to the transfer pricing adjustment. An important implication of this approach is the potential for interest and penalties if the adjustment made is subsequently held to be wrong.

Controlled foreign companies (CFCs)
Under the CFC regime, a UK resident company may be taxed on a proportion of the undistributed profits of certain UK-controlled non-resident companies in which the resident company has an interest.

No liability arises where one of a number of tests (e.g. the 'exempt activities' test) can be satisfied. An 'acceptable distribution' exemption was withdrawn in 2009 when the rules regarding the taxation of dividends were changed.

As a result of a ECJ decision that the EC Treaty allows intra-EU CFC charges only where the arrangements are 'wholly artificial', an additional exemption (not written into the statute) is available to those CFCs that are actually established in an EEA state and carry on genuine economic activity there.

The government is currently consulting on a radical overhaul of the CFC regime. Some interim changes were made in Finance Act 2011, with more major reform under consultation for 2012, *as noted in the Significant developments section*.

Tax credits and incentives

Foreign tax credit
The United Kingdom has an extensive network of DTTs. Unilateral relief is generally available, in any event, to credit overseas tax paid on non-UK source profits against the UK tax on the same profits; while the relevant treaty might sometimes extend that relief, their main function for UK companies is to limit overseas WHTs that would otherwise be payable on passive income.

The United Kingdom has a complex regime allowing 'underlying' tax relief in respect of foreign dividends, so that tax suffered at lower levels can be relieved (at least in part) where dividends flow to the United Kingdom via a chain of companies. This exemption is of limited application since 2009 because most foreign dividends are now exempt from tax.

Enhanced capital allowances
A variety of tax incentives are given in the form of enhanced tax depreciation allowances (known as capital allowances, *see Depreciation and amortisation in the Taxable income determination section*). Some of these incentives are given by reference to the expenditure concerned and others by reference to the size of the company incurring that expenditure.

For example, a full write-off can be claimed in the year of expenditure on a range of 'green' products and technologies. The list of items supported in this way is reviewed annually. It currently consists of the following: designated energy saving equipment; designated environmentally beneficial plant and machinery; cars with low emissions; plant or machinery relating to gas stations for refuelling vehicles with natural gas or hydrogen fuel incurred prior to 31 March 2013; and conversion or renovation of business premises in designated disadvantaged areas of the UK for expenditure incurred up to 11 April 2012.

Annual investment allowance
All businesses, regardless of size, can claim an annual investment allowance of 100% on the first GBP 100,000 per year of most qualifying expenditure but reducing to GBP 25,000 from April 2012. This is restricted to a single allowance for groups of companies or associated businesses.

R&D incentives
A deduction currently equal to 130% of the qualifying expenditure on R&D can also be claimed by large companies. For small and medium companies, as defined, a deduction equal to 225% (from April 2012, previously 200%) of the qualifying expenditure on R&D is given in the year in which it is incurred, which can be surrendered for a cash payment (at a rate of GBP 24.75 for each GBP 100 of qualifying R&D spend) by companies that are trading at a loss or have not yet started to trade.

Other incentives
A deduction equal to 150% of the qualifying expenditure on the remediation of contaminated or derelict land is given in the year incurred, which can be surrendered for a cash payment (at a rate of GBP 16 for each GBP 100 of qualifying land remediation spend) by companies that are trading at a loss. This relief is likely to be abolished during 2012.

There are special tax reliefs available for certain expenditure on UK film production.

There are no tax holidays and no foreign investment incentives in the United Kingdom.

Withholding taxes

Under UK domestic law, a company may have a duty to withhold tax in relation to the payment of either interest or royalties (or other sums paid for the use of a patent). The circumstances in which such a liability arises are discussed below.

There is no requirement to deduct WHT from dividends. Therefore, dividends may always be paid gross, regardless of the terms of the applicable DTT.

Please note, however, that this is not an exhaustive list of all the deductions that might be required to be made in respect of UK tax from payments made to or by companies. In particular, non-resident companies that are subject to UK income tax on UK-source rental profits (*see the Taxes on corporate income section for more information*) will find their letting agent or tenants are obliged to withhold the appropriate tax at source (currently 20% without any allowances) from their rental payments unless the recipient has first applied and been given permission to receive gross rents under the Non-Resident Landlord Scheme. Two other important examples are the UK's deduction at source regime for entertainers and sportsmen, and the scheme under which payments to unregistered subcontractors working on big building projects may need to have tax deducted at source.

Interest WHT
As a general rule, UK domestic law requires companies making payments of interest to withhold tax at 20%. However, there are a number of exceptions to this general rule. The key exclusions are:

United Kingdom

- Payments of interest by UK resident companies if the beneficial owner of the interest is also a UK resident company, or a UK PE, provided the interest concerned will be taxed in the United Kingdom as part of the PE's trading profits.
- Payments of interest on a quoted Eurobond.
- Payments of interest that qualify for exemption under the EU Interest and Royalties Directive.
- Payments of interest paid to or by a UK bank (or a UK branch of a foreign bank).
- Payments of 'short' interest. This is, broadly speaking, interest on loans that will not be in place for more than a year. However, the definition can be contentious, and detailed advice should be taken on this if intending to utilise this exemption.
- Payments of interest that do not 'arise' in the United Kingdom. Whether a payment constitutes UK-source interest is a complex issue, and specialist advice needs to be taken if seeking to use this exception.

If none of these exceptions apply, a payment of interest must be made after the deduction of WHT unless (or until) HMRC has given authorisation that the payment may be made gross (or with a reduced rate of WHT) because of the applicability of treaty relief for the recipient.

Royalties WHT
UK domestic law requires companies making payments of patent, copyright, and design royalties that arise in the United Kingdom to deduct WHT at 20%. In addition, there is also the possibility that other royalties that arise in the United Kingdom may also be subject to the same rate of WHT if they constitute 'qualifying annual payments', so specialist advice will be needed to clarify this. However, certain types of royalties, such as film royalties and equipment royalties, will generally not be subject to UK WHT.

Unlike the rule regarding interest, a company may make a royalty payment gross of WHT (or subject to a reduced rate of WHT under a treaty) without prior clearance having been given by HMRC if they reasonably believe at the time the payment is made that the payee is entitled to relief under the treaty. However, if that belief is later found to be incorrect, HMRC may direct that the payment must be made net of WHT, with the WHT paid to HMRC, and the payer may be subject to interest and penalties in respect of the WHT that should have been withheld (even if their belief was reasonable).

Double taxation treaties (DTTs)
The table below sets out the rates of WHT applicable to payments of dividends, interest, and royalties under UK domestic law where such a liability arises and the reduced rates that may be available under an applicable DTT.

Recipient	Dividends (%) (1)	Interest (%) (2)	Royalties (%) (3)
Resident corporations		0/20 (4)	0/20 (4)
Resident individuals		20	20
Non-resident corporations and individuals:			
Non-treaty		20	20
Treaty (5):			
Antigua and Barbuda		20	0
Argentina		12 (6, 7)	15 (8)
Armenia (48)		5	5
Australia (41)		10 (6)	5
Austria	*	0	0 (36)
Azerbaijan (12)		10 (6)	10 (10)

United Kingdom

Recipient	Dividends (%) (1)	Interest (%) (2)	Royalties (%) (3)
Bangladesh		10 (6, 11)	10
Barbados	*	15 (50)	0 (37)
Belarus (12)		0	0
Belgium (13)	*	15	0
Belize	*	20	0
Bolivia		15 (7)	15
Bosnia-Herzegovina (14)		10	10
Botswana	*	10 (6, 34)	10 (34)
British Virgin Islands		20	20
Brunei	*	20	0
Bulgaria		0	0
Burma (Myanmar)		20	0
Canada		10 (6, 7)	10 (33)
Cayman Islands		20	20
Channel Islands:			
Guernsey		20	20
Jersey		20	20
Chile		10	10
Croatia (16, 41)	*	10	10
Cyprus	*	10	0 (38)
Czech Republic (15)		0	10 (16)
Denmark		0	0
Egypt		15 (6)	15
Estonia (12)		10 (6)	10 (20)
Falkland Islands		0	0
Faroes (44)		0	0
Fiji	*	10 (7)	15 (13)
Finland		0 (7)	0
France		0	0
Gambia	*	15 (6)	12.5
Georgia (12)		0	0
Germany		0	0
Ghana		12.5 (6)	12.5
Greece		0	0
Grenada		20	0
Guyana		15 (6, 7)	10
Hong Kong (47)		0 (48)	3
Hungary (49)		0	0
Iceland	*	0	0
India	* (9)	15 (6, 7, 17)	15 (18)
Indonesia	*	10 (31)	15 (30)
Ireland, Rep. of		0	0
Isle of Man		20	20
Israel (41)		15	0/15 (19)
Italy	*	10 (6, 7)	8
Ivory Coast (Côte d'Ivoire)		15 (6)	10
Jamaica	*	12.5 (7)	10

U

United Kingdom

Recipient	Dividends (%) (1)	Interest (%) (2)	Royalties (%) (3)
Japan		10 (6)	0
Jordan		10 (6)	10
Kazakhstan (12)		10 (6, 7)	10
Kenya	*	15 (31)	15
Kiribati	*	20	0
South Korea (Rep. of Korea)		10 (6, 7)	10 (32)
Kuwait		0	10
Latvia (12)		10 (31)	10 (20)
Lesotho		10 (7, 31)	10
Libya (45)		0	0
Lithuania (12)		10 (6)	10 (23)
Luxembourg	*	0	5
Macedonia (14)	*	10	0
Malawi	*	0 (20)	0 (20)
Malaysia		10 (31)	8
Malta	*	10 (6)	10
Mauritius	*	20 (6)	15
Mexico		15 (7, 21)	10
Moldova (12)	*	5 (6)	5
Mongolia		10 (7, 22)	5
Montenegro (14)		10	10
Montserrat		20	0
Morocco		10 (6)	10
Namibia (13)		20	0 (13)
Netherlands		0	0
New Zealand (41)		10 (6)	10
Nigeria		12.5 (31)	12.5
Norway		0	0
Oman		0	8
Pakistan		15 (6)	12.5
Papua New Guinea		10 (6)	10
Philippines	*	15 (6, 23)	15/25 (24)
Poland (40)		5 (6)	5
Portugal		10	5
Qatar		0	5
Romania	*	10	15 (25)
Russian Federation (12)		0	0
St. Kitts and Nevis (aka St Christopher and Nevis)		20	0
Saudi Arabia		0	8 (20)
Serbia (14)		10	10
Sierra Leone		20	0
Singapore		10 (6)	10
Slovak Republic (15)		0	10 (16)
Slovenia (14)	*	5 (6)	5
Solomon Islands	*	20	0
South Africa		0	0

Recipient	Dividends (%) (1)	Interest (%) (2)	Royalties (%) (3)
Spain (41)	*	12 (7)	10
Sri Lanka		10 (6)	10 (28)
Sudan	*	15	10
Swaziland		20	0
Sweden	*	0	0
Switzerland	*	0	0
Taiwan		10 (6)	10
Tajikistan (12)		0	0
Thailand (41)	*	20 (6, 26)	15 (27)
Trinidad and Tobago	*	10 (6)	10 (39)
Tunisia		12 (30)	15
Turkey		15 (6)	10
Turkmenistan (12)		0	0
Tuvalu	*	20	0
Uganda		15 (31)	15
Ukraine (12)		0	0
United States		0 (42)	0
Uzbekistan (12)		5 (6, 7, 29)	5 (29)
USSR (former) (12)		N/A	N/A
Venezuela		5 (6)	7 (35)
Vietnam		10 (6)	10
Yugoslavia (former) (14)		N/A	N/A
Zambia	*	10	10
Zimbabwe	*	10 (6)	10
Significant treaties which have been signed but are not yet in force (43):			
Bahrain		0	0
China		10	10
Ethiopia		5	7.5

Notes

1. A tax credit is available to UK resident individual shareholders on dividends received, as described above. Some DTTs allow a half or full tax credit (less, normally, a 5% to 15% notional WHT) also to non-resident individuals and usually to corporate portfolio investors. Treaties that allow a payable credit are indicated by an asterisk (*). However, since 6 April 1999, the credit has been reduced from one quarter to one ninth, which has the result that, unless note 14 below applies, the tax credit indicated by the asterisk is now in effect useless, since it is wholly eliminated by the (usually 15%) WHT allowed by the treaty.
2. WHT applies only to 'annual interest' (i.e. excluding interest on certain short-term loans). Banks and similar financial institutions are also normally able to pay annual interest to non-UK residents free of WHT. In addition, most of the UK treaties provide for a zero-rate of withholding on interest paid to governmental and quasi-governmental lenders. Such exemptions are not separately indicated in the table below.
3. Some types of royalties are not subject to UK WHT, including film royalties and equipment royalties. Treaty provisions specifically relating to these are therefore not mentioned here.
4. From 6 April 2001, payments to any UK resident company (not just banks, as before) can be made free of WHT if the recipient is chargeable to tax on the interest or royalty. Discussions continue as to whether this provision will be extended to recipients who are exempt from UK tax on the interest or royalty.
5. Where a reduced rate of withholding is allowed by any treaty, whether on interest or royalties, it is usual for this reduced rate to be stated not to apply to amounts which are in excess of a normal commercial rate of interest/royalty, or where the interest/royalty is effectively connected to a PE in the United Kingdom of the recipient or where the debt/license was created primarily to obtain the advantage of the treaty; such general limitations are not specifically indicated in the table below.
6. Zero-rate on certain loans.

U

United Kingdom

7. Treaty rate not applicable to certain loans held by tax-exempt holders and resold within three months of acquisition.
8. Lower rates, primarily of 3% on use of news, 5% on copyright royalties other than films and TV, and 10% on certain intellectual property, will in practice apply in almost all cases.
9. No repayable tax credit for companies.
10. A 5% rate on literary/artistic copyright royalties.
11. A 7.5% rate on interest paid to banks and other financial institutions.
12. The United Kingdom announced that the old UK/USSR treaty ceased to apply to certain former Soviet Republics on 5 April 2002 (such that from that date there was no treaty in force with any of those countries), whilst it continued to apply to others until new treaties were concluded. Treaties have subsequently been signed with a number of these states such that the old UK/USSR treaty currently only continues to apply to Tajikistan, Turkmenistan, and Belarus (the last of which concluded a new treaty with the United Kingdom in 1995 which is not yet in force). The only remaining states without a treaty in force with the United Kingdom post 5 April 2002 are Armenia and Kyrgyzstan. Moldova signed a new treaty with the United Kingdom on 8 November 2007 which took effect in the United Kingdom from 6 April 2009.
13. Zero-rate on literary/artistic or scientific copyright royalties, excluding payments in respect of cinematograph films and films or tapes for radio or TV broadcasting.
14. The United Kingdom's treaty with the former Yugoslavia is regarded as still in force between the United Kingdom and Croatia, Montenegro, Serbia, and Bosnia-Herzegovina. Macedonia signed a new treaty with the United Kingdom on 8 November 2006, which took effect for UK WHT purposes on 1 January 2008. A new treaty with Slovenia was signed on 13 November 2007 and came into effect in the United Kingdom in April 2009.
15. The independent states of the Czech Republic and the Slovak Republic have confirmed that they will honour the treaty between the United Kingdom and the former Czechoslovakia.
16. The 10% rate applies to royalties for use of industrial, commercial, or scientific equipment or experience as well as royalties in respect of patent, trademarks, and know-how. Zero-rate on all other royalties.
17. A rate of 10% on certain bank loans.
18. A rate of 10% in certain cases.
19. A rate of 15% on film and TV royalties.
20. A rate of 5% on royalties for use of industrial, commercial, or scientific equipment.
21. Zero-rate on government and local authority loans. The rate is 5% where the beneficial owner is a bank or insurance company or the interest is derived from bonds and securities that are regularly and substantially traded on a recognised securities market. The rate is 10% where the beneficial owner is not a bank or insurance company but the interest is paid by a bank or by the purchaser of machinery and equipment to a person who sold that equipment on credit.
22. A rate of 7% on interest paid to banks.
23. A rate of 10% on interest on bonds issued to the public.
24. A rate of 15% on royalties on films, TV, and radio broadcasting.
25. A rate of 10% on copyright royalties.
26. A rate of 10% on interest paid to banks and other financial institutions.
27. A rate of 5% on literary/artistic/scientific copyright royalties.
28. Full relief for copyright royalties.
29. Lower rate may be substituted to match any lower rate agreed in a treaty between Uzbekistan and a third OECD country.
30. A rate of 10% for royalties on industrial, commercial, or scientific equipment.
31. Zero-rate on certain government loans.
32. A rate of 2% for royalties on industrial, commercial, or scientific equipment.
33. Zero-rate on literary/artistic copyright royalties, patent royalties, and royalties for use of industrial, commercial, or scientific know-how and computer software.
34. The new treaty effective for UK income tax (and therefore WHT) from 6 April 2007 reduced WHT on both interest and royalties to the rates shown in the table. Prior to this, the rate of WHT on interest and royalties was 15% in both cases (subject, in the case of interest, to note 7).
35. A rate of 5% on royalties for the use of a patent, etc. concerning industrial, commercial, or scientific experience.
36. A rate of 10% can be withheld if the recipient of the royalties controls more than 50% of the voting power of the payer.
37. A rate of 15% can be withheld on royalties in respect of cinematograph or television films.
38. A rate of 5% can be withheld on royalties in respect of cinematograph or television films.
39. Full relief is available for literary, artistic, or scientific copyright (excluding royalties on cinematograph films and films or tapes for TV or radio broadcasting). No relief is available for amounts paid in respect of the extraction or removal of natural resources.
40. A new treaty with Poland was signed on 20 July 2006 and entered into force on 27 December 2006. It took effect in respect of UK withholding taxes from 1 January 2007, changing the rates to those shown in the table above. The rates were previously zero in respect of interest and 10% in respect of royalties.
41. HMRC continues discussions on new or revised treaties with Australia, Croatia, Israel, New Zealand, Spain, and Thailand.
42. Relief may be restricted to 15% in certain circumstances.

43. New tax treaties/protocols have been signed but have not yet entered into force. These agreements will enter into force once both countries have completed the required Parliamentary procedures and exchange of diplomatic notes and will take effect on the dates set out therein.
44. Treaty effective in the United Kingdom for WHT purposes from 6 April 2009.
45. The first tax treaty between the United Kingdom and Libya entered into force on 8 March 2010 and has effect in the United Kingdom for WHT purposes from 6 April 2010.
46. The first tax treaty between the United Kingdom and Hong Kong entered into force on 8 March 2010 and has effect in the United Kingdom for WHT purposes from 6 April 2011.
47. Provided one of several conditions is specified, one of which is that the recipient is quoted, another being that HMRC accepts that the interest is not paid in connection with tax avoidance (broadly).
48. In force February 2012, with varying implementation dates.
49. Effective January 2012.
50. Reduces to 0% under treaty of May 2012 when it is fully in force on completion of Parliamentary procedures.

....

Tax administration

Taxable period
Companies are assessed by reference to accounting periods. Normally, the accounting period is the period for which the company makes up its accounts. However, an accounting period for corporation tax purposes cannot exceed 12 months, so companies preparing statutory accounts for longer than 12 months need to prepare more than one corporation tax return.

Tax returns
Companies must file their statutory accounts and tax return within one year from the end of the accounting period; the return must include a self-assessment of the tax payable, eliminating the need for assessment by HMRC (though HMRC retains assessing powers for certain cases where it is not satisfied with the return, or where the company fails to make a return).

Payment of tax
For smaller companies, corporation tax is payable nine months after the end of the accounting period to which it relates (i.e. before the return must be filed). For larger companies and groups, a system of quarterly payments on account (based on estimated profits) is in place, with the first payment being due in the seventh month of the accounting period concerned. A company will generally be considered large for this purpose in any accounting period in which it has taxable profits in excess of GBP 1.5 million (that limit being reduced by reference to the number of companies under common control, where relevant).

Electronic filing requirements
Requirements to file online and pay electronically are being phased in for corporation tax from 2011. As of 1 April 2011, returns for accounting periods ending after 31 March 2010 must be filed online, and such returns must be filed in a specified format which is machine readable by the tax authorities.

Other filing requirements
Large companies (those with turnover greater than GBP 200 million or balance sheet assets over GBP 2 billion) are required to notify HMRC of the identity of their senior accounting officer, who must certify annually that the accounting systems are adequate for the purposes of accurate tax reporting. Penalties are chargeable on the officer and the company for careless or deliberate failure to meet these obligations.

Certain tax planning and structuring transactions and arrangements must be disclosed to HMRC either before or on implementation of the transaction under the Disclosure

U

United Kingdom

of Tax Avoidance Schemes (DOTAS) regime. This scheme covers most taxes and is a reporting system only, with responsibility placed on taxpayers and advisors to report. HMRC are not required to respond to the reporting, and this is not an advance clearance or approval process. It is a reporting mechanism only, and, on occasions, new legislation has been introduced to block specific arrangements reported.

Statute of limitations

For companies which are members of medium or large groups, there is generally a period of one year after the statutory filing dates for the tax authorities to start an enquiry into any aspect of the return. For other companies, enquiries can be started up to 12 months after the date of actual filing. These periods are extended for returns submitted after the filing deadline, that are amended by the taxpayer, or where an issue is subsequently discovered that was not sufficiently disclosed within the standard period.

Penalties

The UK tax system can impose numerous penalties for failing to adhere to the self-assessment system. These include penalties for late filing of returns, failing to maintain appropriate records, submitting an incorrect return, making errors in certain documents sent to HMRC, unreasonably failing to report errors in assessments by HMRC, and failing to respond to a notice of enquiry from the tax authorities within the specified time limit.

Other issues

Adoption of IFRS

IFRS is mandatory for the consolidated financial statements of listed UK companies.

All companies continue to have the choice of adopting IFRS or remaining on UK GAAP for their non-consolidated (solus) accounts. Many groups therefore continue to apply UK GAAP in their solus accounts.

The UK Accounting Standards Board (ASB) is proposing a new three-tier system of reporting. It is proposed that all publicly accountable UK registered companies will have to report under IFRS (as endorsed by the EU) in accounting periods beginning on or after 1 January 2014. In addition, UK registered SMEs (broadly entities that do not have public accountability and publish general purpose financial statements for external users) must apply the Financial Reporting Standard for Medium-Sized Entities (the 'FRSME' based on a simplified IFRS) from the same date. Finally, the Financial Reporting Standard for Smaller Entities (FRSSE) will still be an option for small companies or small groups as defined by the Companies Act 2006. However, the options available to a company are subject to the requirements of the UK Company Law framework for consistency of GAAP within a group.

In our experience, many large groups are considering early adoption of EU-endorsed IFRS. However, under current UK law, early adoption of the FRSME or FRSSE is not possible.

UK tax legislation

Announcements of proposed new legislation generally occur at least once a year. The main announcement is made on Budget Day (generally in March), when tax rates are set for the coming year. Other announcements can be made at other times and, subject to becoming approved and adopted law, can apply from a specified date. The new legislation is then included in an annual Finance Act, which is normally finalised in July. Much of the legislation introduced in recent years has been due to challenges under the EC treaty, or as a result of the tax planning being notified under the UK's tax avoidance disclosure regulations. In years of a general election (such as 2010), there may be additional Budget Days and Finance Acts.

UK tax law is periodically consolidated. Until recently, the latest consolidation Act dated from 1988, which covered both income tax and corporation tax. Over the last few years, income tax and corporation tax legislation has been consolidated separately, and currently the latter is to be found in the Corporation Tax Acts 2009 and 2010, and the Taxation (International and Other Provisions) Act 2010.

U

United States

PwC contact

Mark Mendola
PricewaterhouseCoopers LLP
300 Madison Avenue
24th floor
New York, New York 10017
United States of America
Tel: +1 646 471 4000
Email: mark.j.mendola@us.pwc.com

Significant developments

Numerous temporary tax provisions expired at the end of 2011. The fate of these provisions is unclear. The general business incentives that have expired include the following provisions:

* 100% bonus depreciation.
* Increased Section 179 expensing limit of 500,000 United States dollars (USD) with USD 2 million phaseout threshold and expanded definition of Section 179 property (*see the Deductions section for a description of the Section 179 deduction*).
* Research credit.
* Subpart F exception for active financing income (*see the Income determination section for a description of Subpart F income*).
* Look-through treatment of payments between related controlled foreign companies (CFCs) under the foreign personal holding company rules.
* 15-year straight-line cost recovery for qualified leasehold improvements, restaurant buildings and improvements, and retail improvements.
* Seven-year recovery period for motor sports entertainment complexes.
* Work opportunity tax credit.
* Wage credit for employers of active-duty military members.
* Railroad track maintenance credit.
* Special expensing rules for qualified film and television productions.
* Expensing of qualified brownfield decontamination costs.
* Mine rescue team training credit.
* Expensing of advanced mine safety equipment.
* Treatment of some dividends of regulated investment companies.
* Special rule for regulated investment company (RIC) stock held in estates of non-resident noncitizens.
* RICs considered qualified investment entities under the 1980 Foreign Investment in Real Property Tax Act.
* Special rules for qualified small business stock.
* Reduction in S corporation recognition period for built-in gains tax (*see the Taxes on corporate income section for a description of S corporations*).

Taxes on corporate income

In the United States (US), resident corporations are taxed based on worldwide income. Generally, a foreign corporation engaged in a US trade or business is taxed at regular US corporate tax rates on income from US sources that is effectively connected with that business and at 30% on US-source income not effectively connected with that business.

The US corporate income tax (CIT) rate is based on a progressive rate schedule; however, an alternative minimum tax (AMT) provides for a flat rate with fewer deductions.

2012 taxable income		CIT		
OVER (USD)	But not over (USD)	Pay + (USD)	% on excess	of the amount over (USD)
0	50,000	0	15	0
50,000	75,000	7,500	25	50,000
75,000	100,000	13,750	34	75,000
100,000	335,000	22,250	39	100,000
335,000	10,000,000	113,900	34	335,000
10,000,000	15,000,000	3,400,000	35	10,000,000
15,000,000	18,333,333	5,150,000	38	15,000,000
18,333,333			35	0

The 39% tax rate applies to taxable income between USD 100,000 and USD 335,000 to eliminate the benefit of the 15% and 25% rates, and the 38% tax rate applies to taxable income between USD 15,000,000 and USD 18,333,333 to eliminate the benefit of the 34% rate. Special rules apply to personal service corporations and personal holding companies.

Alternative minimum tax (AMT)
An AMT is imposed on corporations other than S corporations (*see below*) and small C corporations (generally those with no three year average annual gross receipts exceeding USD 7.5 million). The tax is 20% of alternative minimum taxable income (AMTI) in excess of a USD 40,000 exemption amount (subject to a phase out). AMTI is computed by adjusting the corporation's regular taxable income by specified adjustments and 'tax preference' items. Tax preference or adjustment items could arise, for example, if a corporation has substantial accelerated depreciation, percentage depletion, intangible drilling costs, or non-taxable income.

S corporations
Corporations with 100 or fewer shareholders, none of whom may be corporations, that meet certain other requirements may elect to be taxed under Subchapter S of the Internal Revenue Code (IRC or 'the Code') and are thus known as S corporations. S corporations are taxed in a manner similar, but not identical, to partnerships (i.e. all tax items [e.g. income, deductions] flow through to the owners of the entity). Thus, S corporations generally are not subject to US federal income tax.

Gross transportation income taxes
Foreign corporations and non-resident alien individuals are subject to a yearly 4% tax on their US-source gross transportation income (USSGTI) that is not effectively connected with a US trade or business. Transportation income is any income derived from, or in connection with, (i) the use (or hiring or leasing) of any vessel or aircraft, or (ii) the performance of services directly related to the use of any vessel or aircraft.

U

Local income taxes
CIT rates vary from state to state and generally range from 1% to 12% (although some states impose no income tax). The most common taxable base is federal taxable income, which is modified by state provisions and generally is allocated to a state on the basis of a three factor formula: tangible assets and rental expense, sales and other receipts,

United States

and payroll. State and municipal taxes are deductible expenses for federal income tax purposes.

Corporate residence

A corporation organised or created in the United States under the law of the United States or of any state is a domestic corporation. A domestic corporation is a resident corporation even though it does no business or owns no property in the United States.

Permanent establishment (PE)
A PE generally is defined as a fixed place of business.

Other taxes

Sales taxes
No provisions exist for a sales tax or value-added tax (VAT) at the federal level. However, sales and use taxes constitute a major revenue source for the 45 states that impose such taxes and the District of Columbia. Sales and use tax rates vary from state to state and generally range from 2.9% to 7.25% at the state level. Most states also allow a 'local option' that permits local jurisdictions such as cities and counties to impose an additional percentage on top of the state-level tax and to keep the related revenues.

In general, a sales tax is a tax applied to the retail sale of tangible personal property and certain services. Although the form of the tax may vary, it is usually imposed either directly upon the retail sale of the taxable item, on the gross receipts from the sales of taxable items, or on the person engaged in the business of making retail sales of taxable items. The use tax compliments the sales tax and is usually assessed on purchases made out of state and brought into the jurisdiction for use, storage, or consumption. Typically, either a sales tax or a use tax can be assessed on a transaction, but not both.

Customs duties and import tariffs
All goods imported into the United States are subject to entry and are dutiable or duty-free in accordance with their classification under the applicable items in the Harmonized Tariff Schedule of the United States. The classification also identifies eligibility for special programs and free trade agreement preferential duty rates.

When goods are dutiable, *ad valorem*, specific, or compound duty rates may be assessed. An *ad valorem* rate, which is the type of rate most often applied, is a percentage of the value of the merchandise, such as 7% *ad valorem*. A specific rate is a specified amount per unit of weight or other quantity, such as 6.8 cents per dozen. A compound rate is a combination of both an *ad valorem* rate and a specific rate, such as 0.8 cents per kilo plus 8% *ad valorem*. Customs requires that the value of the goods be properly declared regardless of the dutiable status of the merchandise.

Liability for the payment of duty becomes fixed at the time an entry is filed with US Customs and Border Protection (CBP). The obligation for payment is upon the person or firm in whose name the entry is filed, the importer of record.

Excise taxes
Excise taxes are generally imposed by the federal and state governments on a wide range of goods and activities, including gasoline and diesel fuel used for transportation, air travel, manufacturing of specified goods, and indoor tanning services.

The excise tax rates are as varied as the goods and activities upon which they are levied. For example, the excise imposed on indoor tanning services is 10% of the amount paid for the services while the excise imposed on the sale of coal mined in the United States is the lower of USD 1.10 per ton or 4.4% of the sale price.

Property taxes
Most states, and some cities, impose a variety of property taxes on both real and personal property.

Stamp taxes
No provisions exist for a stamp tax at the federal level. However, state and local governments frequently impose stamp taxes at the time of officially recording a transaction based upon the value of real estate. The sales tax on real estate may be a stamp tax on the documents recording the transfer of the real estate.

Capital gain taxes
On current transactions, the long-term capital gains tax rate is the same as the tax rates applicable to ordinary income. Thus, the maximum rate is 35%, excluding the additional phase out rates. However, differences may arise where AMT is imposed.

Accumulated earnings tax
Corporations (other than S corporations, domestic and foreign personal holding companies, corporations exempt from tax under Subchapter F of the Code, and passive foreign investment companies) accumulating earnings and profits for the purpose of avoiding shareholder personal income tax are subject to a penalty tax in addition to any other tax that may be applicable. The accumulated earnings tax is equal to 15% of 'accumulated taxable income'. Generally, accumulated taxable income is the excess of taxable income with certain adjustments, including a deduction for regular income taxes, over the dividends paid deduction and the accumulated earnings credit. Note that a corporation can justify the accumulation of income, and avoid tax, based on its reasonable business needs.

Personal holding company tax
US corporations and certain foreign corporations that receive substantial 'passive income' and are 'closely held' may be subject to personal holding company tax. The personal holding company tax is 15% of undistributed personal holding company income and is levied in addition to the regular tax.

Payroll taxes
Employers are subject to federal unemployment insurance tax (FUTA) of 6.2% on the first USD 7,000 of wages paid to employees meeting certain criteria. In addition, states impose workers' compensation insurance tax at varying rates depending on state law and the nature of employees' activities. For 2012, employers also are subject to social security contributions tax of 7.65% (including 1.45% Medicare tax) on the first USD 110,100 (up from USD 106,800 for 2011) of wages paid to employees and 1.45% of Medicare tax on any wages in excess of USD 110,100 (up from USD 106,800 for 2011).

Environmental tax
Importers, manufacturers, and sellers of petroleum or other ozone-depleting chemicals (ODC) are subject to an environmental tax calculated per weight of the ODC used in the manufacture of the product. The tax is determined under an exact or table method provided in the instructions to Form 6667. If the weight cannot be determined, the tax is 1% of the entry value of the product.

United States

Other state and municipal taxes

Other taxes that states may impose, in lieu of or in addition to taxes based on income, include franchise taxes and taxes on the capital of a corporation. State and municipal taxes are deductible expenses for federal income tax purposes.

Branch income

Tax rates on branch profits are the same as on corporate profits. The law also imposes a 30% branch profits tax in addition to US corporate level income taxes on a foreign corporation's US branch earnings and profits for the year that are effectively connected with a US business. The taxable base for the branch profits tax is increased (decreased) by any decrease (increase) in the US net equity of the branch. The branch profits tax on profits may be reduced or eliminated entirely if a relevant treaty so provides (subject to strict 'treaty shopping' rules). The purpose of the branch profits tax is to treat US operations of foreign corporations in much the same manner as US corporations owned by foreign persons.

With certain exceptions, a 30% (or lower treaty rate) branch profits tax also will be imposed on interest payments by the US branch to foreign lenders. In addition, the tax will apply if the amount of interest deducted by the branch on its US tax return exceeds the amount of interest actually paid during the year.

Income determination

Inventory valuation

Inventories generally are stated at the lower of cost or market on a first in first out (FIFO) basis. Last in first out (LIFO) may be elected for tax purposes on a cost basis only and generally requires book and tax conformity.

The tax law requires capitalisation for tax purposes of several costs allocable to the manufacturing process that frequently are expensed as current operating costs for financial reporting (e.g. the excess of tax depreciation over financial statement depreciation).

Capital gains

Gains or losses on the sale or exchange of capital assets held for more than 12 months are treated as long-term capital gains or losses. Gains or losses on the sale or exchange of capital assets held for 12 months or less are treated as short-term capital gains or losses. The excess of net long-term capital gain over net short-term capital loss is considered net capital gain. Capital losses are allowed only as an offset to capital gains. An excess of capital losses over capital gains in a taxable year may be carried back three years and carried forward five years to be used against (offset) capital gains.

For dispositions of personal property and certain non-residential real property used in a trade or business, net gains are first taxable as ordinary income to the extent of the depreciation/cost recovery, with any remainder generally treated as capital gain. For other trade or business real property, net gains generally are taxed as ordinary income to the extent that the depreciation or cost recovery claimed exceeds the straight-line amount, with any remainder treated as capital gain.

An exception to capital gain treatment exists to the extent that losses on business assets were recognised in prior years. A net loss from the sale of business assets is treated as an ordinary loss. Future gains, however, will be treated as ordinary income to the extent of such losses recognised in the five immediately preceding years.

Dividend income

A US corporation generally may deduct 70% of dividends received from other US corporations in determining taxable income. The dividends received deduction is increased from 70% to 80% if the recipient of the dividend distribution owns at least 20% but less than 80% of the distributing corporation. Generally, dividend payments between US corporations that are members of the same affiliated group (*see the Group taxation section*) are deferred or eliminated until a transaction with a third party occurs. With minor exceptions, a US corporation may not deduct dividends it receives from a foreign corporation.

Stock dividends

A US corporation can distribute a tax-free dividend of common stock proportionately to all common stock shareholders. If the right to elect cash is given, all distributions to all shareholders are taxable as dividend income whether cash or stock is taken. There are exceptions to these rules, and extreme caution must be observed before making such distributions.

Interest income

Interest income is generally includible in the determination of taxable income.

Rental income

Rental income is generally includible in the determination of taxable income.

Royalty income

Royalty income is generally includible in the determination of taxable income.

Partnership income

The income (loss) of a partnership passes through to its partners so that the partnership itself is not subject to tax. Thus, each partner generally accounts for their distributive share of the partnership's taxable income.

Foreign income (Subpart F income) of US taxpayers

Generally, a US corporation is taxed on its worldwide income, including foreign branch income earned and foreign dividends when received. Double taxation is avoided by means of foreign tax credits. Alternatively, a deduction may be claimed for actual foreign taxes that are paid. In the case of foreign subsidiaries that are more than 50% owned (by vote or value) by US shareholders (commonly known as controlled foreign companies or CFCs), certain types of undistributed income will be taxed currently to the US shareholders (Subpart F income). Generally, Subpart F income includes income that is easily transferred to a low-tax jurisdiction.

Income from certain passive foreign investment companies (where 75% or more of the income is passive or at least 50% of the assets held produce passive income) also is subject to current taxation. Current taxation occurs if the corporation elects to be a qualified electing fund (QEF) or there are actual distributions. If a QEF election is not made and the corporation makes an actual distribution, the distribution will be treated as an excess distribution to the extent it exceeds 125% of the average of the distributions made with respect to the stock over the three immediately preceding years. The excess distribution is spread over the taxpayer's holding period, and the amount allocated to each year in the holding period is subject to tax at the highest marginal tax rate in effect for that year. This deferred tax amount also is subject to an interest charge. The interest

United States

charge is designed to pay the benefit of the tax deferral that arises out of having an overseas investment that pays no US income taxes.

....

Deductions

Depreciation and amortisation

Depreciation deductions are allowances that may be taken for capital outlays for tangible property. For property placed in service after 1986, capital costs must be recovered by using the modified accelerated cost recovery system (MACRS) method. Depending on the type of tangible property, the general cost recovery periods are three, five, seven, ten, 15, 20, 27.5, and 39 years (31.5 years for property placed in service before 13 May 1993). The cost recovery methods and periods are the same for both new and used property. Most tangible personal property is in the three, five, or seven year class. Property placed in the three, five, seven, or ten year class is depreciated by first applying the 200% declining-balance method and then switching to the straight-line method at such a time as when use of the straight-line method maximises the depreciation deduction. Property in the 15 or 20 year class is depreciated by using the 150% declining-balance method and later switching to the straight-line method. An election may be made to use the alternative depreciation system (basically, the straight-line method over prescribed lives). Residential rental property generally is depreciated by the straight-line method over 27.5 years. Non-residential real property is depreciated by the straight-line method over 39 years (31.5 years for property placed in service before 13 May 1993).

An election to use the straight-line method over the regular recovery period or a longer recovery period also is available. Alternatively, taxpayers may elect to use the 150% declining-balance method over the regular recovery period for all property other than real property. This method is required for AMT purposes.

For most tangible personal and real property placed in service in the United States after 1980 but before 1 January 1987, capital costs were recovered using the accelerated cost recovery system (ACRS), which applied accelerated methods of cost recovery over periods specified by statute. The general ACRS recovery periods were three, five, ten, 15, 18, and 19 years.

Special rules apply to automobiles and certain other 'listed' property. Accelerated depreciation deductions can be claimed only if the automobile is used 50% or more for qualified business use as defined in related regulations. Further, for automobiles placed in service after 1986, the allowable yearly depreciation deduction cannot exceed specific dollar limitations.

Separate methods and periods of cost recovery are specified by statute for certain tangible personal and real property used outside the United States.

Rapid amortisation may be allowable for certain pollution control facilities.

Tax depreciation is not required to conform to book depreciation. Tax depreciation generally is subject to recapture on the sale or disposition of certain property, to the extent of gain, which is subject to tax as ordinary income.

The cost of most intangibles assets is generally capitalised and amortisable rateably over 15 years.

United States

Section 179 deduction

Corporations can elect to expense, up to a statutory amount per year, the cost of certain eligible property used in the active conduct of a trade or business. This is commonly referred to as the Section 179 deduction. As of 2011, the maximum annual expensing amount is USD 25,000. The maximum deduction amount is reduced dollar for dollar where the corporation places in service during the tax year qualified tangible personal property in excess of USD 200,000 for tax years that begin in 2011.

In addition, the deduction under this election is limited to the taxable income of the business. The annual expensing limit is increased by an additional USD 35,000 for qualifying assets placed in service in certain distressed communities. The annual expensing limit also is increased for certain property placed in service in the Gulf Opportunity Zone or Kansas disaster area.

Bonus depreciation

A 50% special first year depreciation allowance (i.e. bonus depreciation) applies (unless an election out is made) for new MACRS property with a recovery period of 20 years or less, certain computer software, water utility property, and certain leasehold improvements acquired after 31 December 2007 and before 1 January 2010. The special allowance applies for regular income tax and AMT purposes. No AMT adjustment is made if the special allowance is used. The property must be placed in service before 2010 (before 2011 for certain longer lived property). The special allowance does not apply to property that must be depreciated using the alternative depreciation system or to 'listed property' not used predominantly for business. The special allowance reduces basis before regular depreciation is figured. Additionally, claiming bonus depreciation on automobiles may affect the first year depreciation limits on such automobiles.

The 'Tax Relief, Unemployment Insurance Reauthorization, and Job Creation Act of 2010', signed into law on 17 December 2010, extends bonus depreciation and temporarily increases the available deduction. Bonus depreciation, which provides an additional first-year depreciation deduction equal to 50% of the cost of qualifying property, is extended through 31 December 2012 (31 December 2013 for long-production period property [LPPP] and certain aircraft). This provision was set to expire on 31 December 2010 (31 December 2011 for LPPP and certain aircraft) as extended by the Small Business Jobs Act of 2010.

- The legislation provides a temporary 100% bonus depreciation deduction for qualifying property acquired and placed in service after 8 September 2010, through 31 December 2011 (31 December 2012 for LPPP and certain aircraft). Under this provision, property acquired pursuant to a written binding contract entered into before 1 January 2008 is not qualified property for purposes of the 100% bonus depreciation deduction.
- The legislation does not change the definition of eligible property under the current bonus depreciation rules. Current-law rules generally provide that property with a recovery period of 20 years or less, water utility property, certain computer software, and qualified leasehold improvements are eligible.
- The 100% bonus depreciation provision in the legislation operates by substituting '100' for '50' in the applicable 100% period. Thus, property that meets the 100% bonus depreciation requirements will not be eligible property for purposes of the 50% bonus depreciation requirement. For such property, a taxpayer could claim 100% bonus depreciation or elect to forego the bonus depreciation deduction altogether.
- The bonus depreciation provisions, including 100% bonus depreciation, are mandatory. However, as indicated above, a taxpayer may make an election out of

U

United States

bonus depreciation for any particular tax year. This election is made on a class-by-class and entity-by-entity basis.

- The legislation re-enacts the provision allowing a corporation to elect to accelerate AMT credits in lieu of bonus depreciation. This election is available for property placed in service after 31 December 2010, and before 1 January 2013 (1 January 2014 for LPPP and certain aircraft).

Depletion

For natural resource properties other than timber and certain oil and gas properties, depletion may be computed on a cost or a percentage basis.

Cost depletion is a method of depletion applied to exhaustible natural resources, including timber, which is based on the adjusted basis of the property. Each year, the adjusted basis of the property is reduced, but not below zero, by the amount of depletion calculated for that year. The current year cost depletion deduction is based on an estimate of the number of units that make up the deposit and the number of units extracted and sold during the year.

Percentage depletion is a method of depletion applied to most minerals and geothermal deposits, and, to a more limited extent, oil and gas. Percentage depletion is deductible at rates varying from 5% to 25% of gross income, depending on the mineral and certain other conditions. Percentage depletion may be deducted even after the total depletion deductions have exceeded the cost basis. However, percentage depletion is limited to 50% (100% for oil and gas properties) of taxable income from the property (computed without allowance for depletion). Generally, percentage depletion is not available for oil or gas wells. However, exceptions exist for natural gas from geopressurised brine and for independent producers of oil and gas.

Goodwill

The cost of goodwill is generally capitalised and amortisable rateably over 15 years.

Start-up expenses

Generally, start-up expenditures must be amortised over a 15 year period; however, certain taxpayers may elect to deduct some expenses in the tax year in which the trade or business begins.

US manufacturing deduction

Over the last several decades, various tax incentive systems have been enacted in the United States to encourage exports and were later repealed, including the extraterritorial income (ETI) regime, which was repealed as a result of a World Trade Organization (WTO) ruling that the ETI regime favoured US goods and violated the national treatment provisions of the General Agreement on Tariffs and Trade. In response, the United States enacted the American Jobs Creation Act of 2004, which introduced a phase-out repeal of ETI and introduced the domestic production activities deduction under Section 199, seeking to compensate US manufacturers for the loss of ETI benefits.

Under Section 199, taxpayers are allowed a 9% deduction for qualified production activities (QPA) income (subject to a taxable income limitation). The deduction is available to all taxpayers actively engaged in QPA. For corporate taxpayers, the deduction generally will mean a federal income tax rate of 31.85% on QPA income. Importantly, the deduction also applies in calculating the AMT. There is a limit on the amount of the deduction equal to 50% of W-2 wages allocable to QPA (subject to a specific effective date), and the deduction is not allowed for taxpayers that incur a loss from their production activities or have an overall loss (including a carryover loss) from all activities.

A taxpayer's QPA income is calculated using the following formula: domestic production gross receipts less the sum of cost of goods sold allocable to such receipts and other expenses, losses, or deduction which are properly allocable to such receipts.

Bad debt
Bad debt resulting from a trade or business may be deducted in the year the debt becomes worthless. Determining the date the debt becomes worthless may present difficulty.

Charitable contributions
Deductions for allowable charitable contributions may not exceed 10% of taxable income computed without regard to certain deductions, including charitable contributions themselves. Deductions for contributions so limited may be carried over to the five succeeding years, subject to the 10% limitation annually.

Employee benefit plans (pension plans and expenses)
Through the Code, the government provides incentives for employers to provide retirement benefits to workers, including employee benefit, qualifying profit-sharing, or stock bonus plans. Usually, the employer will be allowed a current deduction for any contributions made to the fund, and the employee's tax liability will be deferred until the benefit is paid. For profit, non-government employers generally have two types of available plans, which generally are subject to the reporting and disclosure requirements set forth under the Employee Retirement Income Security Act of 1974 (ERISA).

The first category of employee benefit plans is the defined benefit plan, or more commonly known as a pension plan, to which an employer contributes money, on an ongoing basis, to cover the amount of retirement income owed to retired employees under the plan (which will vary based on years of service, average salary, and/or other factors). Any investment gains or losses will not affect the amount of benefits paid to participants but will affect the amount an employer needs to contribute in order to cover its obligation.

The second category of employee benefit plans is the defined contribution plan, or more commonly known in the United States as a '401(k) plan', to which an employer's contributions (if any) are allocated amongst the separate accounts of participating employees, who also may contribute to their respective accounts. Investment gains or losses and the history of contributions will affect the value of a participant's account at retirement but would not affect an employer's contributions since the employer is not obligated to ensure any specified level of benefit in the plan.

Non profits, including churches and government entities, have similar employee benefit plans, except different requirements apply. Small employers and self-employed individuals also have similar options available but are subject to different requirements.

Fines and penalties
No deduction generally is allowed for fines or penalties paid to the government for violation of any law.

Bribes, kickbacks, and illegal payments
An amount paid, directly or indirectly, to any person that is a bribe, kickback, or other illegal payment is not deductible.

United States

Taxes
State and municipal taxes are deductible expenses for federal income tax purposes.

Other significant items
- No deduction generally is allowed for a contingent liability until such liability is fixed and determinable.
- Costs incurred for entertainment must meet strict tests in order to be deductible. The deduction for business meal and entertainment expenses is 50% of the expenses incurred. There are also limitations on the deductibility of international and domestic business travel expenses.
- Royalty payments, circulation costs, mine exploration, and development costs, and other miscellaneous costs of carrying on a business are deductible, subject to certain conditions and limits.
- Depending on the taxpayer's tax accounting method, research and experimental expenditures may be deducted as incurred or treated as deferred expenses and amortised over a period of not less than 60 months; however, in general, the method used must be consistently applied.

Net operating losses (NOLs)
An NOL is generated when business deductions exceed gross income in a particular tax year. Depending on current tax law, an NOL may be carried back to offset past income and possibly obtain a refund or carried forward to offset future income. Generally, a loss may be carried back two years and, if not fully used, carried forward 20 years. For tax years beginning before 6 August 1997, a loss may be carried back three years and, if not fully used, carried forward 15 years. For state tax purposes, carryback and carryforward provisions are often similar to the federal provisions, except that several states do not permit any carrybacks or carryforwards.

Special rules surrounding NOLs may apply if a taxpayer is located in a qualified disaster area.

Special rules also apply relating to specified liability losses.

Complex rules may limit the use of NOLs after a reorganisation or other change in corporate ownership. Generally, if the ownership of more than 50% in value of the stock of a loss corporation changes, a limit is placed on the amount of future income that may be offset by losses carried forward.

Payments to foreign affiliates
A US corporation generally may claim a deduction for royalties, management service fees, and interest charges paid to foreign affiliates, to the extent the amounts are actually paid and are not in excess of what it would pay an unrelated entity, (i.e. are at arm's length). In addition, US withholding on these payments may be required.

....

Group taxation

An affiliated group of US 'includible' corporations, consisting of a parent and subsidiaries directly or indirectly 80% owned, generally may offset the profits of one affiliate against the losses of another affiliate within the group by electing to file a consolidated federal income tax return. A foreign incorporated subsidiary may not be consolidated into the US group, except for certain Mexican and Canadian incorporated entities. A partnership may not be included in a consolidated return, even if it is 100% owned by members of an affiliated group, since a partnership is not a corporation. However, a member's earnings that flow through from a partnership are included as part of the consolidated group's taxable income or loss. Filing on a consolidated (combined) basis is also allowed (or may be required or prohibited) in certain states.

Sales, dividends, and other transactions between corporations that are members of the same group generally are deferred or eliminated until such time as a transaction occurs with a non-member of the group. Losses incurred on the sale of members of the group are disallowed under certain circumstances.

Transfer pricing

Transfer pricing regulations govern how related entities set internal prices for the transfers of goods, intangible assets, services, and loans in both domestic and international contexts. The regulations are designed to prevent tax avoidance among related entities and place a controlled party on par with an uncontrolled taxpayer by requiring an arm's-length standard. The arm's-length standard generally is met if the results of a controlled transaction are consistent with results that would have been realised if uncontrolled taxpayers had engaged in a similar transaction under similar circumstances. If a company is not in compliance with the arm's-length standard, the Internal Revenue Service (IRS) may raise taxable income and tax payable in the United States. After a transfer pricing adjustment, a multinational company may face double tax, paying tax twice on the same income in two countries. Multinational companies may request competent authority relief from double taxation through a tax treaty.

In order to avoid potential transfer pricing penalties, one avenue available to companies may be to obtain an advance pricing agreement (APA) with the IRS, unilaterally, or with the IRS and another tax authority, bilaterally, covering inter-company pricing.

Thin capitalisation

Thin capitalisation rules may apply to disallow interest payments related to excess debt and to re-characterise such payments as dividends. The interest expense deduction can be limited and suspended if more than 50% of the adjusted taxable income of a thinly-capitalised corporation (with similar rules for a corporate partner in a partnership) is sheltered by interest paid to a related party (or paid to a third-party but guaranteed by the related party) who is not subject to US tax on the income.

Controlled foreign companies (CFCs)

Under the Subpart F regime, a CFC is any foreign corporation with respect to which more than 50% of either the voting power of all classes of stock entitled to vote or the total value of all classes of the corporation's stock is owned by US shareholders on any day during the foreign corporation's taxable year.

Tax credits and incentives

Foreign tax credit (FTC)

Generally, in any year, a taxpayer can choose whether to take as a credit (subject to limitation) or as a deduction foreign income, war profits, and excess profit taxes paid or accrued during the taxable year to any foreign country or US possession. An FTC reduces US income tax liability dollar for dollar, while a deduction reduces the US income tax liability at the marginal rate of the taxpayer. For taxpayers with NOLs, the FTC is of no value in such year. However, a benefit might be received either in an earlier year (through a refund of previously paid taxes) or a later year (through a reduction of future taxes). It also should be noted that a taxpayer has an ability to switch from credit to deduction (or from deduction to credit) at any time in a ten-year period commencing

United States

when the foreign taxes were paid or accrued. Generally, an FTC may be carried back one year and, if not fully used, carried forward ten years.

In addition, the FTC goes beyond direct taxes to include foreign taxes paid 'in lieu of' a tax upon income, war profits, or excess profits, which would otherwise generally be imposed. It also includes deemed-paid (indirect) taxes paid for certain US corporate shareholders of non-portfolio foreign corporations when actual or deemed dividends are received. Furthermore, the FTC system has numerous limitations to mitigate the potential abuses of the credit by the taxpayer.

General business credit

Various business credits are available to provide special incentives for the achievement of certain economic objectives. In general, these credits are combined into one 'general business credit' for purposes of determining each credit's allowance limitation for the tax year. The general business credit that may be used for a tax year is limited to a tax based amount. In general, the current year's credit that cannot be used in a given year because of the credit's allowance limitation may be carried back to the tax year preceding the current year and carried forward to each of the 20 years following the current year.

In general, the current year business credit is a combination of the following credits:

- Investment credit.
- Work opportunity credit (currently expired).
- Alcohol fuels credit.
- Research credit (currently expired).
- Low-income housing credit.
- Enhanced oil recovery credit.
- Disabled access credit for certain eligible small businesses.
- Renewable electricity production credit.
- Empowerment zone employment credit.
- Indian employment credit.
- Employer social security credit.
- Orphan drug credit.
- New markets tax credit (currently expired).
- Small employer pension plan startup cost credit for eligible employers.
- Employer-provided child care credit.
- Railroad track maintenance credit (currently expired).
- Biodiesel fuels credit (currently expired).
- Low sulfur diesel fuel production credit.
- Marginal oil and gas well production credit.
- Distilled spirits credit.
- Advanced nuclear power facility production credit.
- Non-conventional source production credit.
- New energy efficient home credit (currently expired).
- Energy efficient appliance credit (currently expired).
- A portion of the alternative motor vehicle credit.
- A portion of the alternative fuel vehicle refueling property credit.
- Hurricane Katrina housing credit.
- Hurricane Katrina employee retention credit.
- Hurricane Rita employee retention credit.
- Hurricane Wilma employee retention credit.
- Mine rescue team training credit (currently expired).
- Agricultural chemicals security credit for eligible businesses.
- Differential wage payment credit.

United States

- Carbon dioxide sequestration credit.
- A portion of the new qualified plug-in electric drive motor vehicle credit for vehicles that will vary based on the date of purchase.

Employment credits
A 'work opportunity tax credit' is available for employment of certain types of workers who began work for an employer after 30 September 1996 and before 1 September 2011. 'Creditable' wages generally are the first USD 6,000 of wages paid to each qualified employee for the year. The credit is 40% of creditable wages, for a maximum credit of USD 2,400.

Research and development (R&D) credit
The credit for qualified research expenses, as noted above, expired at the end of 2011 and has not yet been renewed or extended. It therefore is not currently available with respect to qualified research expenses (QREs) incurred after 31 December 2011. For QREs incurred on or before that date, a credit against the federal income tax equal to 20% of the sum of QREs in excess of the 'base amount' and basic research payments (*as discussed below*) to a qualified organisation may be obtained for certain periods.

The base amount cannot be less than 50% of current-year QREs. In tax years ending after 8 August 2005, the research expense credit also includes 20% of the taxpayer's expenditures on qualified energy research undertaken by an energy research consortium.

In addition, for tax years ending after 2006, taxpayers may be able to use the new alternative simplified credit (ASC), which does not use a gross receipts factor. The ASC generally equals 12% for tax years ending after 2006 and beginning before 2008 for QREs that exceed 50% of the average QREs for the three tax years preceding the credit determination year. For other tax years, the applicable ASC percentage is 14%.

The deduction for R&D expenditures must be reduced by the entire amount of the credit unless an election is made to reduce the amount of the credit.

Inbound investment incentives
There generally are no specific incentives related to inbound investment at the federal level, other than certain portfolio debt and bank deposit exceptions. The portfolio debt exception enables non-residents and foreign corporations to invest in certain obligations (which must meet certain statutory requirements to qualify as 'portfolio debt') in the United States without being subject to US income (or withholding) tax on the interest income. Certain state and local benefits may also be available.

Qualified private activity bonds
Interest income received on certain qualified private activity bonds generally is exempt from federal income tax. This enables a business enterprise to issue the bonds at a lower interest rate.

Other tax incentives
State and local governments provide numerous incentives to encourage business and, thus, employment in their jurisdictions.

United States

Withholding taxes

Under US domestic tax laws, a foreign person generally is subject to 30% US tax on its US-source income. US persons making payments ('withholding agents') to foreign persons generally must withhold 30% of the payment amount as tax withheld at source on payments, such as dividends and royalties, made to foreign persons. In other situations, withholding agents may apply reduced rates or be exempted from withholding tax (WHT) at source when there is a tax treaty between the foreign person's country of residence and the United States.

The United States has entered into various income tax treaties with countries in order to avoid double taxation of the same income and to prevent tax evasion. The table below, from IRS Publication 901 (April 2011), summarises the benefits resulting from these treaties.

Recipient	Interest paid by US obligors in general (%)	Dividends paid by US corporations in general (%) (1)	Dividends qualifying for direct dividend rate (%) (1, 2)	Royalties* (%)
Non-treaty	30	30	30	30/30/30
Treaty rates:				
Australia (3)	10 (6, 23)	15 (24)	5 (24, 26)	5/5/5
Austria (3)	0 (21)	15 (11)	5 (11)	0/10/0
Bangladesh (3)	10 (13, 21)	15 (24)	15 (24)	10/10/10
Barbados (3)	5	15 (11)	5 (11)	5/5/5
Belgium (3)	15 (21)	15 (29, 30)	5 (26, 29, 30)	0/0/0
Bulgaria (3)	5 (21, 23, 29)	10 (29, 30)	5 (29, 30)	5/5/5
Canada (3)	0 (21)	15 (24)	5 (24)	0/10/0
China, People's Republic of (3)	10	10	10	10 (10)/10/10
Commonwealth of Independent States (CIS)	0 (8)	30	30	0/0/0
Cyprus (3)	10	15	5	0/0/0
Czech Republic (3)	0	15 (11)	5 (11)	10/0/0
Denmark (3)	0 (22)	15 (29, 30)	5 (26, 29, 30)	0/0/0
Egypt	15 (4)	15 (4)	5 (4)	30/30/15 (3)
Estonia (3)	10 (22)	15 (11)	5 (11)	10/10/10
Finland (3)	0 (22)	15 (29, 30)	5 (26, 29, 30)	0/0/0
France (3)	0	15 (24)	5 (24, 26)	0/0/0
Germany (3)	0 (21)	15 (29, 30)	5 (26, 29, 30)	0/0 (16)/0
Greece (4)	0	30	30	0/30/0
Hungary (3)	0	15	5	0/0/0
Iceland (3)	0 (22)	15 (17, 24)	5 (17, 24)	0 (5)/5/0
India (3)	15 (14)	25 (11)	15 (11)	15/15/15
Indonesia (3)	10	15	10	10 (15)/10/10
Ireland (3)	0	15 (24)	5 (24)	0/0/0
Israel (3)	17.5 (14, 19)	25 (11)	12.5 (11)	30/10/10
Italy (3)	10 (25)	15 (24)	5 (24)	8/8/0
Jamaica (3)	12.5	15	10	10/10/10
Japan (3, 27)	10 (28, 29)	10 (29, 30)	5 (29, 30)	0/0/0

United States

Recipient	Interest paid by US obligors in general (%)	Dividends paid by US corporations in general (%) (1)	Dividends qualifying for direct dividend rate (%) (1, 2)	Royalties* (%)
Kazakhstan (3)	10	15 (18)	5 (18)	10/10/10
Korea, South (3)	12	15	10	15/10/10
Latvia (3)	10 (22)	15 (11)	5 (11)	10/10/10
Lithuania (3)	10 (22)	15 (11)	5 (11)	10/10/10
Luxembourg (3)	0 (4)	15 (31)	5 (11)	0/0/0
Malta (3)	10 (21)	15 (29, 30)	5 (29, 30)	10/10/10
Mexico (3)	15 (20)	10 (24, 15)	5 (10, 24, 26)	10/10/10
Morocco	15 (3)	15 (3)	10 (3)	10 (4)/10 (3)/10 (3)
Netherlands (3)	0	15	5	0/30/0
New Zealand (3)	10	15	5 (24, 26)	5/5/5
Norway (3)	0	15	15	0/30/0
Pakistan (4)	30	30	15	30/30/0
Philippines (3)	15	25	20	15/15/15
Poland (3)	0	15	5	10/10/10
Portugal (3)	10	15 (11)	5 (11)	10/10/10
Romania (3)	10	10	10	15/10/10
Russia (3)	0	10 (18)	5 (18)	0/0/0
Slovak Republic (3)	0	15 (11)	5 (11)	10/0/0
Slovenia (3)	5	15 (24)	5 (24)	5/5/5
South Africa (3)	0 (21)	15 (11)	5 (11)	0/0/0
Spain (3)	10	15 (11)	10 (11)	10/8/5 (12)
Sri Lanka (3)	10 (21)	15 (32)	15 (32)	10/10/10
Sweden (3)	0	15 (29, 30)	5 (26, 29, 30)	0/0/0
Switzerland (3)	0 (21)	15 (11)	5 (11)	0/0/0
Thailand (3)	15 (14)	15 (11)	10 (11)	15/5/5
Trinidad & Tobago (3)	30	30	30	15/30/0 (16)
Tunisia (3)	15	20 (11)	14 (11)	10 (15)/15/15
Turkey (3)	15 (7, 14)	20 (11)	15 (11)	10/10/10
Ukraine (3)	0	15 (18)	5 (18)	10/10/10
United Kingdom (3, 27)	0 (22)	15 (24)	5 (24, 26)	0/0/0
Venezuela (3)	10 (22, 23)	15 (24)	5 (24)	10/10/10

Notes

* Please note the tax rates and associated footnotes appearing in the 'Royalties' column in the table address three types of royalties, as denoted in the most recent IRS publication. These three are industrial royalties, motion picture and television copyright royalties, and 'other' copyright royalties. The slashes '/' between each figure and associated footnote(s) are meant to demarcate these three types of royalties, respectively.

1. No US tax is imposed on a dividend paid by a US corporation that received at least 80% of its gross income from an active foreign business for the three-year period before the dividend is declared.
2. The reduced rate applies to dividends paid by a subsidiary to a foreign parent corporation that has the required percentage of stock ownership. In some cases, the income of the subsidiary must meet certain requirements (e.g. a certain percentage of its total income must consist of income other than dividends and interest). For Italy, the reduced rate is 10% if the foreign corporation owns 10% to 50% of the voting stock (for a 12-month period) of the company paying the dividends. For Japan, dividends received from a more than 50% owned corporate subsidiary are exempt if certain conditions are met.
3. The exemption or reduction in rate does not apply if the recipient has a PE in the United States and the property giving rise to the income is effectively connected with this PE. Under certain treaties, the

United States

exemption or reduction in rate also does not apply if the property producing the income is effectively connected with a fixed base in the United States from which the recipient performs independent personal services. Even with the treaty, if the income is not effectively connected with a trade or business in the United States by the recipient, the recipient will be considered as not having a PE in the United States under IRC Section 894(b).

4. The exemption or reduction in rate does not apply if the recipient is engaged in a trade or business in the United States through a PE that is in the United States. However, if the income is not effectively connected with a trade or business in the United States by the recipient, the recipient will be considered as not having a PE in the United States to apply the reduced treaty rate to that item of income.

5. The rate is 5% for royalties for the use of, or the right to use, a trademark and any information concerning industrial, commercial, or scientific experience provided in connection with a rental or franchise agreement that includes rights to use a trademark.

6. Interest determined with reference to the profits of the issuer or one of its associated enterprises is taxed at 15%.

7. Contingent interest that does not qualify as portfolio interest is treated as a dividend and is subject to the rates under those columns, as appropriate.

8. The exemption applies only to interest on credits, loans, and other indebtedness connected with the financing of trade between the United States and the CIS member. It does not include interest from the conduct of a general banking business.

9. The rate for royalties with respect to tangible personal property is 7%.

10. Tax imposed on 70% of gross royalties for rentals of industrial, commercial, or scientific equipment.

11. The rate in column 3 applies to dividends paid by a RIC or a real estate investment trust (REIT). However, that rate applies to dividends paid by a REIT only if the beneficial owner of the dividends is an individual holding less than a 10% interest (25% in the case of Portugal, Spain, and Tunisia) in the REIT.

12. The rate is 8% for copyrights of scientific work.

13. The rate is 5% for interest (i) beneficially owned by a bank or other financial institution (including an insurance company) or (ii) paid due to a sale on credit of any industrial, commercial, or scientific equipment, or of any merchandise to an enterprise.

14. The rate is 10% if the interest is paid on a loan granted by a bank or similar financial institution. For Thailand, the 10% rate also applies to interest from an arm's-length sale on credit of equipment, merchandise, or services.

15. This is the rate for royalties for the use of, or the right to use, industrial, commercial, and scientific equipment. The rate for royalties for information concerning industrial, commercial, and scientific know-how is subject to the rate in column 5 ('other royalties').

16. The rate is 15% for copyrights of scientific work.

17. Amounts paid to a pension fund or employee benefit organisation that are not derived from the carrying on of a business, directly or indirectly, by the fund or organisation are exempt.

18. The rate in column 3 applies to dividends paid by a RIC. Dividends paid by a REIT are subject to a 30% rate.

19. An election can be made to treat this interest income as if it were industrial and commercial profits taxable under article 8 of this treaty.

20. The rate is 4.9% for interest derived from (i) loans granted by banks and insurance companies and (ii) bonds or securities that are regularly and substantially traded on a recognised securities market. The rate is 10% for interest not described in the preceding sentence and paid (i) by banks or (ii) by the buyer of machinery and equipment to the seller due to a sale on credit.

21. The rate is 15% (10% for Bulgaria; 30% for Germany and Switzerland) for contingent interest that does not qualify as portfolio interest.

22. The rate is 15% for interest determined with reference to (i) receipts, sales, income, profits, or other cash flow of the debtor or a related person, (ii) any change in the value of any property of the debtor or a related person, or (iii) any dividend, partnership distribution, or similar payment made by the debtor to a related person.

23. Interest received by a financial institution is tax exempt. For Venezuela, the rate is 4.95% if the interest is beneficially owned by a financial institution (including an insurance company).

24. The rate in column 3 applies to dividends paid by a RIC or REIT. However, that rate applies to dividends paid by a REIT only if the beneficial owner of the dividends is (i) an individual (or pension fund, in the case of France or New Zealand) holding not more than a 10% interest in the REIT, (ii) a person holding not more than 5% of any class of the REIT's stock and the dividends are paid on stock that is publicly traded, or (iii) a person holding not more than a 10% interest in the REIT and the REIT is diversified.

25. Interest paid or accrued on the sale of goods, merchandise, or services between enterprises is exempt. Interest paid or accrued on the sale on credit of industrial, commercial, or scientific equipment is exempt.

26. Dividends received from an 80%-owned corporate subsidiary are exempt if certain conditions are met.

27. Exemption does not apply to amount paid under, or as part of, a conduit arrangement.

28. Interest is exempt if (i) paid to certain financial institutions, or (ii) paid on indebtedness from the sale on credit of equipment or merchandise.

29. Amounts paid to a pension fund that are not derived from the carrying on of a business, directly or indirectly, by the fund are exempt. This includes amounts paid by a REIT only if the conditions in footnote 31 are met. For Sweden, to be entitled to the exemption, the pension fund must not sell or make a contract to sell the holding from which the dividend is derived within two months of the date the pension fund acquired the holding.

30. The rate in column 3 applies to dividends paid by a RIC or REIT. However, that rate applies to dividends paid by a REIT only if the beneficial owner of the dividends is (i) an individual or a pension fund holding not more than a 10% interest in the REIT, (ii) a person holding not more than 5% of any class of the REIT's stock and the dividends are paid on stock that is publicly traded, or (iii) a person holding not more than a 10% interest in the REIT and the REIT is diversified. Dividends paid to a pension fund from a RIC, or a REIT that meets the above conditions, are exempt. For Sweden, the pension fund must also satisfy the requirements in footnote 30.
31. The exemption does not apply if the recipient of the gain is an individual who is present in the United States for more than 119 days during the year.
32. The rate applies to dividends paid by a REIT only if the beneficial owner of the dividends is (i) an individual holding less than a 10% interest in the REIT, (ii) a person holding not more than 5% of any class of the REIT's stock and the dividends are paid on stock that is publicly traded, or (iii) a person holding not more than a 10% interest in the REIT and the REIT is diversified.

Tax administration

Taxable period

US corporate taxpayers are taxed on an annual basis. Corporate taxpayers may choose a tax year that is different from the calendar year. New corporations may use a short tax year for their first tax period, and corporations may also use a short tax year when changing tax years.

Tax returns

The US tax system is based on the principle of self assessment. A corporate taxpayer is required to file an annual tax return (generally Form 1120) by the 15th day of the third month following the close of its tax year. A taxpayer can obtain an additional six month extension of time to file its tax return. Failure to timely file may result in penalties.

Important tax return due dates

Form No.	Title	Purpose	Due date
W-2	Wage and Tax Statement	Employers must provide employees with statements regarding total compensation and amounts withheld during year.	Must be sent to employees on or before 31 January.
1099 series	Various	Information returns to be provided to recipients of dividends and distributions, interest income, miscellaneous income, etc.	Must be sent on or before 31 January.
1120 series, including 1120S (for S Corps)	US Corporation Income Tax Return	Income tax returns for domestic corporations or foreign corporations with US offices.	15 March (Form 7004 may be filed to obtain an automatic six-month extension)
Schedule K-1	Partner's Share of Income (Loss) from an Electing Large Partnership	Information returns to be provided to partners by large partnerships.	15 March
1065	US Return of Partnership Income	Information returns to be filed by large partnerships.	15 April (Form 7004 may be filed to obtain an automatic six-month extension)
State tax returns	Various	Income tax returns for states where corporation carries on trade/business.	Varies, often 15 April

United States

Payment of tax

A taxpayer's tax liability generally is required to be prepaid throughout the year in four equal estimated payments and fully paid by the date the tax return is initially due for that year. However, because a corporation that expects its tax liability for the tax year to exceed the small sum of $500 (based on its tax liability for the preceding year), almost all corporations are required to pay their full estimated tax liability for the year in their four estimated tax payments. For calendar year corporations, the four estimated payments are due by the 15th day of April, June, September, and December. For fiscal year corporations, the four estimated payments are due by the 15th day of the fourth, sixth, ninth, and 12th month of the tax year. Generally, no extensions to pay are allowed. Failure to pay the tax by the due dates as indicated above can result in estimated tax and late payment penalties and interest charges.

The instalment payments must include estimates of regular CIT, AMT, environmental tax, and, for foreign corporations, the tax on gross transportation income. To avoid a penalty, corporations must calculate the instalment payments based on at least 25% of the lesser of (i) the tax shown on the current tax return or (ii) the prior year's tax liability, provided that the tax liability was a positive amount in the prior year and that such year consisted of 12 months. However, corporations with taxable income of at least USD 1 million (before use of NOLs or capital loss carryforwards) in any of the three preceding years are not permitted to calculate the instalment based payment on the prior year's tax liability, except in determining the first instalment payment. Instead, such corporations must calculate the instalment payments based on the tax shown on the current tax return.

Corporations with more than USD 1 billion in assets will be required to make estimated tax payments that are 100.25% of the amount otherwise due in July, August, or September of 2014. Such overpayments will be balanced out in October, November, or December of 2014 when payments of 99.75% of the amount otherwise due will be paid by corporations with more than USD 1 billion in assets.

Audit cycle

Generally, the US tax system is based on self-assessment; however, many large and mid-size businesses are under continuous audit by the IRS and state tax authorities. The audits may include the entire list of taxes for which the business is liable. Smaller business and persons with lower incomes are generally subject to audit on a random basis.

Statute of limitations

The IRS generally has three years after an original return is filed to assess income taxes. A return will be deemed to have been filed on its due date, even if the return is actually filed on an earlier date.

Topics of focus for tax authorities

Currently, the IRS is focused on abusive payments related to contribution to capital of a corporation, domestic manufacturing deduction, foreign earnings repatriation, FTC generators, repairs vs. capitalisation change in accounting method, research credit claims, transfer of intangibles/offshore cost sharing, WHTs, and employee classification.

Tax shelter

Treasury regulations require taxpayers to disclose transactions determined to be abusive or possibly abusive. Current information on these transactions, known as listed and reportable transactions, is available from the IRS website (*www.irs.gov*).

United States

Accounting for income taxes

For US federal tax purposes, the two most important characteristics of a tax method of accounting are (i) timing and (ii) consistency. If the method does not affect the timing for including items of income or claiming deductions, it is not an accounting method and generally IRS approval is not needed to change it. In order to affect timing, the accounting method must determine the year in which an income or expense item is to be reported.

In general, in order to establish an accounting method, the method must be consistently applied. Once an accounting method has been adopted for federal tax purposes, any change must be requested by the taxpayer and approved by the IRS. Changes in accounting methods cannot be made through amending returns. The two most common methods of accounting are the accrual basis and cash basis methods.

Penalties

Civil and criminal penalties may be imposed for failing to follow the Code when paying US taxes. The civil penalty provisions may be divided into four categories: delinquency penalties, accuracy-related penalties, information reporting penalties, and preparer, promoter, and protester penalties. Many, but not all, have exception provisions to cover reasonable cause. In addition, many have provisions directing how the penalties interact with the other penalties.

These four main civil penalty categories may further be divided. First, the delinquency penalties may be divided into failure to file, failure to pay, and failure to make timely deposits of tax. Failure to make timely deposits of tax applies to taxpayers required to make instalment payments and WHT payments.

Second, the penalties relating to the accuracy of tax returns are divided into the negligence penalty, the substantial understatement penalty, substantial overstatement of pension liabilities, substantial estate or gift tax valuation underestimate, and the valuation penalties. These penalties are also coordinated with the fraud penalty to eliminate any stacking of the penalties. Again, like other provisions, the fraud penalty is not intended to be imposed as a stacked penalty.

The third category of penalties is the information reporting penalties. These penalties may be imposed upon those who only have a duty to report information to the IRS.

The fourth and final major categories of civil penalties are the preparer, promoter, and protester penalties. Currently, the most notable of these is the return preparer penalty for which there is a penalty for a position on a return for which the preparer did not have substantial authority. Also included in this provision is a penalty for wilful or reckless attempt to understate the tax liability of another person. Additionally, return preparer penalties may be imposed for failure to furnish a copy of a return or claim for refund to the taxpayer, sign the return or claim for refund, furnish his or her identifying number, or file a correct information return.

Other promoter and protestor penalties include a penalty for promoting abusive tax shelters, aiding and abetting the understatement of tax liability, and filing frivolous income tax returns. Additionally, a court may award sanctions and costs if a person institutes or maintains a proceeding primarily for delay, takes a position that is frivolous, or unreasonably fails to pursue available administrative remedies.

In addition to these major civil penalties, international tax related penalties for failures other than timely and accurate filing (e.g. wilful failure to report international boycott

United States

activity, failure of an agent to furnish a notice of a false affidavit relating to the WHT on dispositions of US real property interests, failure of a US person to furnish information relating to CFCs and controlled foreign partnerships, failure of a US person to report foreign bank accounts, etc.) exist. Pension and employee benefit related tax penalties exist that protect the policy reasons for the tax incentives including, most notably, early withdrawal of pension funds. Another group of specialised penalties apply to exempt organisations.

Criminal penalties exist for situations when the failures to stay within the tax system are more egregious. Although applicable to corporate taxpayers, they are applied more frequently to individuals.

In addition to the penalty provisions, interest at statutory rates generally applies to underpayments of tax.

Other issues

Tax accounting and internal controls

Accounting Standards Codification (ASC) 740, Income Taxes (formerly known as Financial Accounting Standards Board [FASB] Statement No. 109, Accounting for Income Taxes) addresses how companies should account for and report the effects of taxes based on income. ASC 740's principles and requirements apply to domestic and foreign entities in preparing financial statements in accordance with US generally accepted accounting principles (GAAP), including not-for-profit entities with activities that are subject to income taxes. This scope includes: (i) domestic federal (national) income taxes (US federal income taxes for US enterprises) and foreign, state, and local (including franchise) taxes based on income; and (ii) an enterprise's domestic and foreign operations that are consolidated, combined, or accounted for by the equity method.

In recent years, controls around the accounting for income taxes have been a critical source of material weaknesses in companies' internal controls over financial reporting. Accounting for income taxes also has been a primary reason for restating financial statements. Management should ensure that its judgments and estimates are reasonable (e.g. assessing the need for a valuation allowance on deferred taxes) and that the underlying internal control processes are reliable.

The adoption of International Financial Reporting Standards (IFRS) in the United States is set by the Securities and Exchange Commission (SEC). The timeline included in the SEC's roadmap provides for adoption of IFRS in the United States between 2014 and 2016. The SEC has stated that it will reassess the transition to IFRS in 2011.

Corporate reorganisations

In general, a corporate reorganisation involving a merger, acquisition, or consolidation is a taxable event under the general recognition provisions of the Code. However, a corporate reorganisation that meets certain statutory and judicial requirements may qualify as a tax-free transaction, with gain or loss generally not recognised or deferred to a later date.

US possessions

Puerto Rico, American Samoa, Guam, the Commonwealth of the Northern Mariana Islands, and the US Virgin Islands have their own independent tax departments. Accordingly, they have their own rules. *See the Puerto Rico summary for more information about Puerto Rico taxation.*

Uruguay

PwC contact

Sergio Franco
PricewaterhouseCoopers
Cerrito 461
1st floor
Montevideo 11000
Uruguay
Tel: +598 2 916 0463
Email: sergio.franco@uy.pwc.com

Significant developments

Uruguay has signed double tax treaties (DTTs) following, in general, the model
of the Organisation for Economic Co-operation and Development (OECD) with
Germany (renegotiation in force since December 1991), Hungary (in force since
1994), Mexico (in force as of December 2010), Spain (in force as of April 2011), and
Switzerland (in force as of December 2011), as well as a memorandum to cooperate
in the exchange of information with France (in force as of December 2010). DTTs with
Portugal, Liechtenstein, Ecuador, Malta, India, and Finland are currently undergoing
the approval processes in the national Parliament. DTTs with South Korea, Norway,
Sweden, Denmark, Faroe Islands, Greenland, and Argentina have reached the stage of a
'technical agreement' (most of them being a memorandum to cooperate in the exchange
of information). Finally, DTTs with Belgium, Canada, Romania, Australia, Malaysia,
Luxembourg, Holland, the United Kingdom, Italy, and Brazil are under negotiation.

The government is implementing an electronic invoicing plan, which consists of
replacing the paper-based system. This new development will help to achieve an
important improvement in the business negotiation process, will reduce costs, and make
e-commerce easier. Those who request to be approved or those who are notified by the
authorities are going to be implementing this system.

During this year, nearly 250 companies will be included in this program, and it will
be mandatory for the rest of the national companies in 2014. In September 2011, the
Senate issued a decree giving tax benefits to those companies that invest in the necessary
hardware and software for the implementation of the electronic billing system.

On 29 December 2011, the Executive Power approved a Law that creates the Rural Real
Estate Concentration Tax (ICIR, for its Spanish abbreviation). This tax will be imposed on
the ownership of rural real estate.

Taxes on corporate income

Net income derived from business activities conducted in Uruguay, obtained by
legal entities resident in Uruguay and non-residents operating through a permanent
establishment (PE) in Uruguay, is taxed at a corporate income tax (CIT) rate of 25%
under the source principle (i.e. the territorial system of taxation). Accordingly, Uruguay
taxes only income that is derived from activities conducted within its borders, income
generated from property located in Uruguayan territory, or income derived from the
economic use of rights within its territory (*see Foreign income in the Income determination
section for an exception to this principle*).

U

Uruguay

In order to determine the net taxable income, all accrued expenses that are necessary for the generation of Uruguayan-source income and that are duly documented are allowed as deductions. Additionally, a taxpayer will be able to deduct expenses from its gross income if such expenses are subject to taxation (either foreign or local taxation) in the hands of the other party. A compulsory proportional deduction must be calculated if the tax is at a rate that is lower than 25%.

A 12% withholding tax (WHT) is imposed on Uruguayan-sourced income obtained by non-residents, except in cases where the income is obtained through the operations of a PE in Uruguay (*see the Withholding taxes section for more information*).

Trading companies

Uruguayan corporations that sell and buy foreign goods or services from Uruguay (which are not physically introduced to the country, in the case of goods, or which are not economically used in Uruguay, in the case of services) may determine the net Uruguayan-source income on a notional basis of 3% of the gross margin (difference between the selling price and the purchase price). This gross margin has to be compliant with transfer pricing rules (in line with OECD guidelines). The applicable effective CIT rate is 0.75% (25% x 3%).

Local income taxes

No taxes on corporate income may be levied by municipal authorities or other local governments.

Corporate residence

Legal entities are deemed to be resident in Uruguay when they are incorporated according to the local legislation.

Permanent establishment (PE)

The concept of PE in the Uruguayan tax legislation follows, in general terms, the definition provided in the OECD Model Tax Convention, although it has some special clauses that may be found in the United Nations (UN) Model Tax Convention. From a Uruguayan law perspective, the term PE means a fixed place of business through which the business of an enterprise is wholly or partly carried on in Uruguay. The term PE especially includes: (i) places of management; (ii) branches; (iii) offices; (iv) factories; (v) workshops; (vi) mines; oil or gas wells; quarries or any other place of extraction of natural resources; (vii) buildings, constructions, installation projects, or the management activities associated to them, when they last more than three months; and (viii) services rendered (in particular consultancy) by a non-resident through employees or hired personnel in Uruguay during a period or periods exceeding six months on an annual basis. Please note that item (viii) constitutes an exception to the OECD model and is based on the provisions of the UN model.

Other taxes

Value-added tax (VAT)

Uruguayan VAT is levied at a general rate of 22% on the provision of services and on the circulation of goods within the limits of the Uruguayan territory. The import of goods and value-added in regard to the construction of immovable assets are also within the scope of this tax.

The following items are either subject to a reduced 10% VAT rate or exempt from VAT entirely.

Items subject to the 10% VAT rate:

- Food and medicines.
- Hotel services.
- Health services.
- The first sale of immovable assets.

Items exempt from VAT:

- Milk.
- Books.
- Magazines.
- Agricultural machinery.
- Certain bank services.
- Accessories.

Exports are VAT zero rated. VAT on purchases of the exporters can be recovered in the form of credit certificates that can be (i) used to pay other taxes, (ii) used to pay social security contributions, or (iii) endorsed to suppliers who can pay their own national taxes or their own social security contributions.

This tax requires monthly payments and may require monthly or annual tax returns, depending on the qualification of the taxpayer.

Customs duties
- Consular duty: 2%.
- Customs computer services duty: a scale flat duty, with a limit of 50 United States dollars (USD).
- Customs extraordinary duty: a scale flat duty, with a limit of USD 600.
- Global customs duty (TGA): depends on the origin of goods. If they come from Mercosur, the TGA is generally zero (some goods still apply the payment of the TGA). If not, it varies depending on the type of product, with a maximum rate of 20%, with exceptional levels that range from 23% to 55% (corresponding mainly to certain types of shoes, sugar, automotives, and peaches). For goods classified as capital goods or information and telecommunication goods, there is a special regime.

All imports and exports duties are applied on the 'customs value' (in general, in imports it is considered as cost, insurance, and freight [CIF], and in exports as freight on board [FOB]).

On imports, VAT is also applicable according to the following detail:

- Goods subject to the general VAT rate (22%):
  - 'Import VAT' at the rate of 22%.
  - 'Advanced payment import VAT' at a rate of 10%.
- Goods subject to the reduced VAT rate (10%):
  - 'Import VAT' at the rate of 10%.
  - 'Advanced payment import VAT' at a rate of 3%.

The tax base of VAT on imports is the customs value plus the customs duties.

U

Uruguay

Additionally, some goods are also subject to an 'advanced payment import on account of CIT' at a rate of 10%, which can be deducted from the amount of CIT for the fiscal year.

Export duties

Exports are not subject to any taxes, and there are almost no prohibitions regarding the type of goods to be exported. On the contrary, several instruments are offered to promote exports, such as the reimbursement of taxes. *For VAT on exports, please see VAT above.*

For the reimbursement of indirect taxes, the exporter may recover internal taxes that are added to the cost of the products exported. The amount to be reimbursed is a percentage of the FOB value set by the Executive Power for each product.

Additionally, temporary admission consists of the import of raw materials, pieces, motors, package material, and other industrial input without import duties or taxes. To be subject to this customs duties exemption, the company has to export the finished goods within 18 months from the introduction of the exempt goods or materials. The subsequent local sale of such finished goods is not entitled to this benefit.

Excise tax

In general, excise tax applies on the first transaction effected in the domestic market by manufacturers or importers of goods. Exports are not taxable.

Excise tax rates vary for each item, and they are generally fixed by the government within maximum parameters established by law.

Goods subject to the highest rates are alcoholic beverages (from 20.20% to 80%, depending on the alcohol degree), tobacco (from 28% to 70%), lubricants (from 5% to 35%) gasoline, fuel, and other petroleum products (from 5% to 133%).

This tax requires monthly payments and/or tax returns.

Net wealth tax (NWT)

All types of legal entities and business enterprise owners are subject to an annual NWT at a rate of 1.5% on the value of net assets. This tax also follows the source principle, whereby only assets located or economically used in Uruguay are taxable. Taxpayers may reduce their capital tax liability in determining the NWT basis, up to their total amount of CIT for the fiscal year. In practice, taxpayers deduct 1%, which was established prior to the tax reform law.

The deduction of liabilities from the amount of taxable assets to determine the NWT basis is limited to: (i) the average of debts with financial institutions, (ii) debts with suppliers of goods and services, (iii) taxes not yet due, (iv) debts with governments, international credit offices of which Uruguay is a member and with foreign state financial institutions that lend funds for long-term productive projects, and (v) debts documented in debentures and obligations, if their emission is done in a public offering and such papers are quoted in a stock exchange.

Property taxes

Regarding taxes of relevance for those doing business in Uruguay, *please see Net Wealth Tax above*. There are additional property taxes of less significance, levied by Municipal authorities (e.g. *Contribución Inmobiliaria*) and by National authorities (e.g. *Impuesto de Primaria*).

Uruguay

Tax on real estate transfer

A tax on real estate transfer applies to the transfer of immovable assets. Transfer is defined in an ample sense, as a sale, a cession of the right to use, a transfer of inheritance rights, etc.

Both parties to the transfer contract are subject to this tax at a rate of 2% on the property's tax value (according to a National Register, a value generally lower than market value). When the property is transferred without payment, the beneficiary pays tax at a rate of 4% on the property tax valuation, except in instances where the property is transferred to direct heirs or legatees, who pay this tax at a rate of 3%.

Stamp taxes

Stamp taxes are not applicable in Uruguay.

Tax of control of corporations

Upon the set up of a corporation, a tax is payable at a 1.5% rate on a notional basis amount, which is determined annually by the authorities. For fiscal year 2012, the estimated amount of this tax (lump sum) is approximately USD 1,026.

This tax is also due annually at the end of each fiscal year, at a rate of 0.75% on said notional amount, and can be deducted from the NWT. For fiscal year 2012, the estimated amount of this tax (lump sum) is approximately USD 512.

Rural Real Estate Concentration Tax (ICIR)

ICIR taxes the rural real estate ownership that, as a whole, exceeds 2,000 hectares with a CONEAT index of 100 (C100) or equivalent (the CONEAT index is established by the government and represents the productivity of the soil).

The tax is levied as a fixed amount (expressed in 'indexed units') and may vary from approximately USD 0 to USD 16 per hectare, depending on the amount of hectares (not progressive).

The ICIR will be determined taking into account the situation of the taxpayers as of 31 December 31 every year. Furthermore, the law empowers the tax authorities to settle advanced payments for this tax, although they have not executed that power yet.

Social Security Contributions (SSC)

The Uruguayan Social Security regime states that hiring personnel under a dependency relationship implicates the obligation (both for employer and employee) of making contributions over the compensations that constitute the taxable basis.

Taxable basis consists of all earning that in a regular and permanent basis, in cash or kind, susceptible to pecuniary appreciation, is perceived by the dependant personnel, in concept of remuneration and product of its personal activity in the frame of the working relationship. As a general rule, any compensation originated in activities carried out in Uruguay are subject to SSC.

The SSC rates are applicable on gross remunerations, according to the following percentages:

Concept	Employer contributions (%)	Employee contributions (%)
Retirement contributions *	7.5	15
Health insurance	5	3/4.5/6/8 **

U

Uruguay

Concept	Employer contributions (%)	Employee contributions (%)
Labor restructuring fund	0.125	0.125
Total SSC	12.625	18.125 to 23.125

* Both employer and employee retirement contributions rates are applicable, up to the monthly amount of 84,202 Uruguayan pesos (UYU) (approximately USD 4,200); the exceeding amount will be exempt.

** May vary depending on whether the employee is married and whether they have children.

Branch income

CIT is imposed at a rate of 25% on net income derived from business activities carried out in Uruguay. A 7% WHT is imposed on profits remitted or credited to a home office. Dividends and/or profits paid or credited to non-resident shareholders will not be subject to WHT when they are paid out of non-taxable income for CIT purposes.

Income determination

Inventory valuation
Replacement cost is permitted for tax purposes, as well as the first in first out (FIFO), last in first out (LIFO), or average cost methods, irrespective of the inventory valuation method used for accounting purposes.

Capital gains
Capital gains are treated as ordinary income for CIT purposes.

As a general rule, capital gains are calculated as the selling price minus the fiscal cost (usually acquisition cost updated by certain inflationary indexes) of goods being sold. In certain cases, not all the fiscal cost may be deductible depending on the application or not of the compulsory proportional deduction *mentioned previously in the Taxes on corporate income section*.

Furthermore, for certain capital gains, there are special ways of determining the taxable income (e.g. based on notional income).

Dividend income
Dividends received from local subsidiaries are exempt. Dividends received from foreign subsidiaries are out of the scope of this tax since they are considered foreign-sourced, thus non-taxable, income.

Interest income
Uruguayan-sourced interest income, derived by companies resident in the country, is subject to CIT under the general regime (i.e. taxed at 25%).

Foreign income
Uruguayan legal entities (CIT taxpayers) and non-residents operating through a PE in Uruguay are only subject to tax on income from Uruguayan sources under the territorial system of taxation. Hence, foreign-source income is not subject to tax.

However, there is an exception to this principle, as follows. When a CIT taxpayer obtains income as a consequence of rendering technical services outside the limits of Uruguayan territory to another CIT taxpayer and such technical services are used by the recipient to obtain its income subject to CIT, the income obtained by the company rendering the services will be subject to CIT, even when foreign sourced. Technical services are those rendered in the fields of management, technical administration, or advice of any kind.

Income derived from activities performed, assets located, or rights utilised outside Uruguay, regardless of the nationality, domicile, or residence of the parties participating in the transactions and the place where the transaction agreements are subscribed, is not subject to CIT.

Income adjustment for inflation
An income adjustment for inflation has been in force since 1 January 1981 and is calculated by multiplying the variation in the wholesalers' price index for the financial year by the difference between:

1. total assets at the beginning of the year (excluding fixed assets) and
2. total liabilities at the beginning of the year.

If (1) is higher than (2), then an inflation loss adjustment is deducted from gross income. However, if (2) is higher than (1), then an inflation gain adjustment is added.

Deductions

As a general rule, duly documented expenses that are necessary to obtain and preserve gross taxable income are tax deductible. On the contrary, those expenses associated with deriving or preserving income not subject to CIT are not deductible from the taxable basis. Furthermore, for CIT purposes, all costs and expenses will be subject to the compulsory proportional deduction *mentioned in the Taxes on corporate income section (with some exceptions)*.

Depreciation and depletion
Straight-line depreciation over useful life is mandatory. Specific rates exist for the following cases: (i) 2% per year for urban buildings, (ii) 3% per year for rural buildings, and (iii) no less than 10% per year for new vehicles. Other rates are accepted if economically justified. No conformity between book and tax depreciation is required.

Percentages for depletion computed on the cost of natural resource properties are allowed in accordance with generally accepted criteria.

Depreciation and depletion percentages are computed on the historical cost of fixed assets revaluated at year-end, based on the variation of the wholesalers' price index. Capital gains derived from the revaluation of fixed assets are not taxable income.

Goodwill
When transferring a business or a business unit, the difference between selling price and fiscal costs of the assets being transferred constitutes 'goodwill'. This goodwill constitutes an asset for the buyer and must not be depreciated neither for CIT nor NWT purposes.

Start-up expenses
Start-up expenses should be depreciated within a period of three to five years. The taxpayer may elect the number of years to depreciate those expenses within those period limits.

Uruguay

Interests expenses

Interests expenses, as well as other costs and expenses, are subject to the compulsory proportional deduction *mentioned in the Taxes on corporate income section.*

When companies derive both income subject to CIT and either income exempt or not included in CIT (e.g. from a foreign source), interest expenses associated to the former (i.e. deductible interest) will be determined by applying a proportion based on assets.

Bad debt

As a general rule, only those debts that are at least 18 months old will be deductible as 'bad debts'. However, national rules allow deductions under some other special situations.

Charitable contributions

Deductibility of charitable contributions will depend on the organisations receiving them.

Furthermore, there is a special regime to certain charitable contributions under which the contributor may deduct 25% of the contribution and the other 75% will be recovered through credit certificates that may be used to pay taxes (with certain limitations).

Fines and penalties

Fines and penalties generated in unduly paid taxes are not deductible for CIT purposes.

Taxes

CIT and NWT are not deductible.

Net operating losses

Losses may be carried forward and deducted from the net taxable income of the following five years, once adjusted for inflation. There are no loss carrybacks.

Payments to foreign affiliates

All accrued expenses that are necessary for the generation of Uruguayan-source income and that are duly documented are allowed as deductions. Additionally, a taxpayer may deduct expenses from its gross income provided such expenses are subject to taxation (either via foreign or local taxation) in the hands of the other party. A compulsory proportional deduction must be calculated if the tax is at a rate that is lower than the CIT rate of 25%.

Group taxation

Group taxation is not permitted in Uruguay.

Transfer pricing

As a general principle, transfer pricing rules are applicable to international transactions between related parties. However, Uruguayan legislation has extended the scope of these regulations to transactions carried out with low-tax or no-tax jurisdictions or regimes (either international or domestic) and to certain operations through third intermediaries. Domestic transactions with Uruguayan Free Zone users fall under this category.

The definition adopted by the law for related parties is quite broad. Such a relationship is configured when both parties are subject (directly or indirectly) to the management or control of the same individuals or legal entities, or when they have power of decision to direct or define the taxpayer´s activities due either to their participation in capital interest, the level of their credit rights, or their functional or any other type of influence (whether contractual or not).

Thin capitalisation
Thin capitalisation rules do not apply in Uruguay.

Tax credits and incentives

CIT reduction for income reinvested in fixed assets
40% of income reinvested in the purchase of (i) industrial and agricultural machinery, (ii) vehicles and installations, (iii) computers, (iv) telecommunications equipment, and (v) some assets for the tourism industry is exempt from CIT.

20% of income reinvested in the construction and expansion of industrial, agricultural, and tourism buildings is exempt from CIT (limited to 40% of net taxable income in the year of expenditure).

The joint amount of said investments can be deducted from the taxable basis, with a limit of 40% of the annual net profit, once the amount of other exemptions has been deducted. The excess can be deducted (with the same limitations) in the following two tax periods. It is important to mention that income exempt by these provisions cannot be distributed and must be retained as a reserve account, which ultimately can only be capitalised.

NWT exemption
Movable fixed assets directly connected to the industrial cycle and equipment for data processing are exempt from NWT.

All assets directly associated to the development of agricultural and/or farming activities will be exempt from NWT as long as the owners are individuals or companies with nominatives shares also owned by individuals.

Investments law (IL)
Uruguay has modified the IL, achieving a better framework for local and foreign investments carried out in the country. To obtain tax benefits, the IL requires that enterprises obtain a government statement in this regard. The Bureau of Investor Assistance is in charge of monitoring the correct compliance of these projects.

The IL grants two types of benefits:

Automatic benefits
This kind of benefit is only for manufacturing, extractive, or farming/ranching activities, and includes:

- Exemption from NWT for chattel property directly engaged in the production cycle and data-processing equipment.
- Exemption from VAT and CIT paid on the importation of such goods, and reimbursement of VAT in the case of locally purchased items.

Discretionary benefits
Benefits that may be obtained at the discretion of the Executive Power for any type of business activity (not cumulative with automatic benefits) include:

U

Uruguay

- VAT and CIT exemptions (among other taxes) on importation of fixed assets items.
- NWT exemptions: permanent for chattel property items, for a period of eight years for construction work in Montevideo (capital city), and for a period of ten years in the rest of the country.
- VAT reimbursement on local purchase of goods and services for civil construction work.
- Increased deductions for CIT in respect of fees and remunerations related to technological developments.
- Exemption from CIT, depending on the nature and size of the project to be carried out. The Executive Power takes into account the following criteria to grant this benefit:
  - Addition of technology to improve competitiveness.
  - Contribution to export growth and diversification.
  - Contribution to geographic decentralisation.
  - Improvement of technological investigation, innovation, and development.
  - Generation of employment.

Auto-saving 'direction' benefit

The auto-saving 'direction' benefit allows a company to deduct from the CIT basis the amount of the capital increase that occurred as a consequence of the reserves capitalisation or of the in-kind distribution of shares, for an amount equivalent to the investment carried out with the investor's own funds. The amount of the CIT deduction and the period/s to which said exemption will apply is granted by the government through a statement issued by the Executive Power.

Free zones (FZs)

Following the approval of the FZ law in 1987, this system has become an important tool for attracting investments to Uruguay.

It has been utilised for carrying out traditional activities in the FZs (warehousing, logistics, and distribution), for the provision of services (software, finance, call centres, etc.) and for manufacturing activities such as cellulose pulp and leather production. In a clear sign of stability, none of the administrations in office over the last three decades has modified the basics of the FZ system.

The law defines FZs as privately or publicly owned isolated and fenced off areas of Uruguayan territory determined by the Executive Branch with the purpose of carrying out all types of manufacturing, commercial, and service activities within the zone, while enjoying tax exemptions and other benefits envisaged in the law.

Companies in these areas cannot carry out industrial, trading, or service activities in the non-FZ Uruguayan territory, except for services expressly authorised by the government (listed below) but are allowed to render all types of services within the FZs or to third countries.

FZ users are allowed to render the following services to the non-FZ Uruguayan territory (the provision of these services is subject to the general tax system, not to the tax holidays):

- International call centres, except for those whose main destination is the non-FZ Uruguayan territory.
- E-mail, distance learning, electronic signature certificate issuance.
- Software production, technology consulting, and related training services.

- Accounting, administration, and management services rendered to related companies who carry out port and shipping logistics activities, if said services are lower than 20% of the total income obtained during the fiscal year.
- Processing of film material and data.

FZ users are exempt from all current and future national taxes, including those taxes for which a specific legal exemption is required, in connection with the activities performed within the FZs. The Uruguayan government guarantees all the exemptions and benefits granted by the law for the term of their contracts. FZs can be located outside or inside the cities; it depends on the kind of FZ.

Social security taxes, as well as certain WHTs, are excluded from the exemption. WHT on payments of dividends made by these companies to their non-resident shareholders are exempt.

Industrial park incentives
Individuals or legal entities that establish industrial parks within Uruguayan territory, as well as companies located within such industrial parks, are entitled to CIT exemption for their industrial equipment, excise tax and VAT exemption on the acquisitions of such goods, and other benefits.

Holding companies
Uruguayan legal entities holding shares in non-resident entities or investing in assets not located in Uruguay are not subject to tax (due to the application of the source principle).

Industry-specific incentives

Printing industry incentives
Companies that print books and educational material are exempt from the NWT and VAT.

Electric power industry incentives
Companies which generate electric power from non-traditional energy sources have special benefits regarding CIT (from 40% to 90% exemption).

Machinery industry incentives
Companies that build and/or assemble (under certain conditions) machinery with agricultural purposes have special benefits regarding CIT (from 50% to 90% exemption).

Shipping industry incentives
Imports of material, supplies, and equipment required for the construction, maintenance, and repair of shipyards or vessels are exempt from VAT. The shipbuilding industry has special benefits regarding CIT (from 50% to 100% exemption).

Water and air transportation incentives
The income of water and air transportation companies is tax exempt. In the case of foreign companies, the exemption is subject to reciprocal treatment. The Government may exempt from CIT companies engaged in transportation by land, subject also to the conditions of reciprocal treatment.

Forestry plantation incentives
Income derived from forestry plantations up to July 2007 is tax exempt. Income derived from new forestry plantations is also tax exempt, but under strict conditions, such as wood quality.

Uruguay

Software industry incentives
Software production and related services are exempt from CIT as long as either the final product or the related services are entirely used in a foreign country.

Electronic industry incentives
The production of electronic devices has special benefits regarding CIT (from 50% to 100% exemption).

Tourism industry incentives
Investments in the tourism industry have tax benefits related to CIT, VAT, and NWT, as follows:

- Deduction of up to 40% of CIT in investments made in the fiscal year in hotel equipment and equipment for improving entertainment and information services to tourists and deduction of up to 20% of CIT in investments made in construction and expansion of hotel buildings, with the limits mentioned in previous sections (40% of the annual net profit, once the amount of other exemptions has been deducted).
- VAT refund included in local acquisitions of goods and services for construction, improvement, or expansion of tourist complexes.
- VAT exemption on import of goods for construction, improvement, or expansion of tourist complexes.
- The list of operations included in the concept of exports of services for VAT purposes (thus zero-rated) was broadened to include, among others, services related to accommodation that hotels, apartments, and rural tourism establishments provide to tourists.
- NWT exemption for ten years on investments in infrastructure and civil work for construction, improvement, or expansion of tourist complexes.
- NWT exemption for four years on fixed assets investment for tourist complexes.
- 50% exemption of import duties on materials and goods for construction, improvement, or expansion as well as fixed assets of tourist complexes.

Withholding taxes

All Uruguayan-sourced income obtained by non-residents (other than those obtained through a PE in Uruguay) is taxed at flat rates of up to 12% on gross income, with some exceptions. This tax is basically collected by way of WHT.

The exceptions are as follows:

- Interest on deposits in local currency for terms exceeding one year is taxed at 3%.
- Interest on public bonds is not taxed.
- Dividends paid or credited by CIT taxpayers are taxed at 7%, provided they are derived from taxable income.

Profits originated in the alienation of stock of CIT taxpayer companies obtained by non-residents are exempt only if the capital of the local company is expressed in bearer shares. The alienation of registered stock is taxed at a rate of 12%.

Although the Uruguayan tax law follows the source principle, technical services (defined as services rendered in the fields of management, technical administration, or advice of any kind) rendered in another country by non-residents but associated with taxable income obtained by the local user in Uruguay are considered to be Uruguayan sourced for tax purposes and subject to WHT. However, when the taxable income obtained by the local user of the service does not exceed 10% of its total income, then only 5% of the service fee paid or credited abroad will be subject to non-resident WHT. Therefore, in these cases, the effective WHT rate is only 0.6% (5% x 12%).

This WHT should be declared and paid to the Tax Office on the month following the one in which the tax is withheld.

For those countries with which Uruguay has entered DTTs, the WHT rates are the following:

Country	Dividends (%)	Interest (%)	Royalties (%)
Internal law	0/7	0/12	0/12
Germany	5/15 (4)	10	10
Hungary	15	15	15
Mexico	5	10	10
Spain	0/5 (1)	10	5/10 (2)
Switzerland	5/15 (3)	10	10

Notes

1. Source country may tax at a rate not higher than 5%. However, if the beneficial owner is a company resident in the other contracting state and holds at least 75% of the capital of the company distributing dividends, then the WHT will be 0%.
2. Will depend on the kind of royalty paid.
3. Source country may tax at a rate not higher than 15%. However, if the beneficial owner is a company resident in the other contracting state and holds at least 25% of the capital of the company distributing dividends, then the WHT will be 5%.
4. Source country may tax at a rate not higher than 15%. However, if the beneficial owner is a company resident in the other contracting state and holds at least 10% of the capital of the company distributing dividends, then the WHT will be 5%.

Tax administration

Taxable period
The taxable period may be chosen by the company. However, certain sectors or industries have mandatory fiscal year closing dates.

Tax returns
CIT and NWT are self assessed and their tax returns are filed on the fourth month following the date of the year-end.

Payment of tax
Income and capital taxes are paid monthly by way of advanced payments, which are calculated on the basis of the previous year's tax. The difference between the advanced tax payments and the total annual tax calculated at fiscal year-end is paid four months after the fiscal year-end.

U

Uzbekistan, Republic of

PwC contact

Abdulkhamid Muminov
PricewaterhouseCoopers
5, 1st proezd Kichik Mirobod Street
Yakkasaray District
Tashkent 100070
Uzbekistan
Tel: +998 71 1206 101
Email: abdulkhamid.muminov@uz.pwc.com

Significant developments

There have been no significant corporate tax developments in Uzbekistan during the past year.

Taxes on corporate income

Resident corporations pay corporate income tax (CIT) on their worldwide income, whereas non-residents (i.e. foreign legal entities that have a permanent establishment [PE] in Uzbekistan or have income from sources in Uzbekistan not associated with a PE) pay CIT on income resulting from activities/sources in Uzbekistan.

Non-resident corporations are taxed directly at the level of their Uzbek PE, if there is one, or via withholding tax (WHT) at the source of payment of the Uzbek-source income.

CIT is charged on taxable profit calculated as a difference between gross income and deductible expenses reduced by applicable incentives granted by the Tax Code, other laws, or presidential decrees.

The CIT rate is set annually by presidential decree. By virtue of the government's annual initiatives for rate reduction, the CIT rate has been reduced over time as follows:

2012: 9%	2007: 10%	2002: 24%
2011: 9%	2006: 12%	2001: 26%
2010: 9%	2005: 15%	2000: 31%
2009: 10%	2004: 18%	1999: 33%
2008: 10%	2003: 20%	1998: 35%

In 2012, enterprises (i.e. legal entities) are generally subject to CIT at the rate of 9%. Commercial banks are subject to CIT at the rate of 15%.

Local income taxes

There is a local tax on accounting profit (less CIT), an infrastructure development tax, which is charged at a maximum rate of 8%.

Corporate residence

For Uzbek tax purposes, corporations are classified as resident or non-resident. A resident corporation is a legal entity that passed state registration in Uzbekistan (i.e. Uzbek legal entity). Other legal entities would be regarded as non-resident corporations for tax purposes.

Permanent establishment (PE)

PE is defined by the Tax Code as "any place through which non-resident carries out entrepreneurial activity in the Republic of Uzbekistan, including activity carried out through an authorised person. PE would also be existent where non-resident carries on entrepreneurial activity for 183 days (or more) in any consequent 12-month period ending in the current tax period".

Other taxes

Value-added tax (VAT)

Legal entities are subject to VAT, which is applied to taxable turnover and taxable imports. The rate for taxable turnover is 20%. This rate also applies to taxable imports, for which the tax base is determined as the customs value plus import duties and excise tax (on excise-liable goods). Export of goods for hard currency is generally zero-rated. Insurance and most types of financial services are exempt.

Customs duties

Import of certain goods to Uzbekistan is subject to customs duties. The taxable base is determined as the customs value of imported goods. Rates of customs duties vary from 5% to 40% depending on the type of imported goods. There is also a customs clearance fee of 0.2% from the customs value of imported goods.

Excise taxes

Legal entities producing or importing excise-able goods (e.g. cigarettes, jewellery, petrol, alcohol drinks) are subject to excise tax. Rates vary from 5% to 200% depending on the type of goods produced/imported. The taxable base is determined as the value of produced/imported goods excluding VAT.

Property taxes

The property tax rate in 2012 is 3.5% for legal entities. The tax is computed quarterly, based on the net book value of the fixed assets, adjusted for the effect of revaluation, which should be performed annually on 1 January, the residual value of intangibles, and the value of overdue construction-in-progress. The rate is doubled for equipment not installed in due time.

As of 1 January 2011, a charge of 0.25% of the historic value of outdated equipment is collected from legal entities (except for micro-firms and small enterprises) for exploitation of fully depreciated equipment.

Newly opened enterprises are exempt from property tax for a period of two years from their date of registration, unless such enterprises have been created on the basis of production facilities or assets of existing enterprises. There is also a rate reduction benefit available to companies engaged in production and export of goods (work, services). Property tax exemption is also available in respect to leased property, for a period of the lease, and new technological equipment, for a period of up to five years.

U

Uzbekistan, Republic of

Land tax

Enterprises, including foreign legal entities operating in Uzbekistan via a PE, owning land plots or rights of their use are subject to land tax or land lease payment annually. Land tax is charged at fixed fees that vary depending on the quality, location, and level of water supply of each land plot. Land lease payment is charged at negotiable rates; however, the minimum amount cannot be less that the land tax rate for the respective land plot. Land tax and land lease payment are computed based on the area of the land being in use.

Stamp duties

According to Uzbek legislation, stamp duty is an obligatory payment charged for performance of legal actions and/or issuance of legal documents. The following actions, among others, are subject to stamp duties: filing claims, performing notary actions, civil registration, state registration of a legal entity, obtaining licences/ permits to carry out certain activities, etc.

The rates of stamp duties generally vary from 0.5 to 20 times minimum monthly wage (MMW, approximately 35 United States dollars [USD]), depending on the type of action executed. For instance, duty for filing a claim depends on the amount of claim. If the amount is less than 20 MMW, the duty comprises 5% of this amount; if the amount exceeds 80 MMW, the duty is 20% of this amount. Duty for notarisation of copies of documents for legal entities is 2% of the MMW per each page of the document. Duty for registration of legal entities with foreign investment comprises five times the MMW plus USD 500.

Turnover taxes

There are three mandatory contributions that are charged on the enterprise's gross annual turnover (less VAT and excise tax):

- Road fund to be imposed at a rate of 1.4%.
- Pension fund at a rate of 1.6%.
- Educational and medical institutions fund (for reconstruction, capital repair, and equipment) at a rate of 0.5%.

The taxable base (and tax rate in exceptional cases) for these mandatory contributions may differ depending on the type of activity of a company.

Water-use tax

Enterprises (including PEs) using water in their production are subject to water-use tax. The tax rate is set by the Cabinet of Ministers and depends on the source of water consumption (i.e. surface or underground). Water-use tax is calculated based on the volume of the water consumed.

Unified social payment (USP)

Employers are subject to USP assessed on total payroll cost related to local and expatriate staff. This payment is collected by the tax authorities. The rate of USP is 25%.

As of 1 January 2012, income of foreign personnel paid to non-resident legal entities as part of secondment fees under personnel provision agreements is subject to USP. The taxable base for calculation of USP on such income shall be the income of foreign personnel provided, but not less than 90% of the secondment fee payable under the personnel provision agreement.

Taxes of subsurface users

In addition to standard taxes, subsurface users (i.e. legal entities and individuals exploring and extracting natural resource) are subject to subsurface users' specific taxes, as listed below:

Subsurface use tax (royalty)

Subsurface use tax is charged on volume of produced (extracted) natural resources that are ready for sale or transfer (including free of charge) and consumption for internal purposes. Taxable base is determined as average weighted sales price.

Business activity	Tax rate examples
Extraction of natural resources	natural gas 30%, precious stones 24%, oil 20%, gold 5%, silver 8%
Utilisation of by-products received during the extraction of natural resources	30% of tax rate applicable to main natural resources extracted

Excess profits tax

Excess profits tax is assessed on the difference between the selling price of the extracted natural resources (as per the list) and the statutory price set by the legislation. Excess profits tax is not payable by entities operating under production sharing agreements.

The list of natural resources and goods subject to excess profits tax includes copper, cement, natural gas, polyethylene granules, and clinker. Excess profits tax is paid at 50% of the taxable base.

Signing and commercial discovery bonuses

Signing and commercial discover bonuses are one-off payments to the state budget. The signing bonus is payable for the right to engage in exploration and extraction of natural resources and range from 100 to 10,000 times the MMW, depending on the type of minerals. The commercial discovery bonus is paid for each field where a subsurface user discovers the natural resources and comprises 0.1% from the cost of the proved reserve volume.

Branch income

There is no concept of a 'branch' of a foreign legal entity in the Uzbek legislation. Instead, such entities use a PE registration to perform business activities without establishing an Uzbek company.

In addition to CIT, non-residents operating in Uzbekistan via PE pay net profit tax assessed at 10% on accounting profit less CIT.

U

Income determination

Inventory valuation

Uzbek legislation permits the application of the weighted average cost method (AVECO) and the first in first out (FIFO) method for the valuation of inventory for tax purposes.

Uzbekistan, Republic of

Capital gains

Capital gains arising from the disposal of tangible and intangible assets are calculated as the difference between the selling price and the net book value of an asset. The capital gain is included in taxable profits (unless specifically exempt), and the capital losses are deductible (only if the disposed asset had been used for business purposes for three or more years). This is applicable to Uzbek legal entities and PEs of foreign legal entities. Capital gains on non-resident companies may be subject to WHT at 20% as 'other' income.

Dividend income

Dividends paid by a domestic subsidiary are subject to 10% WHT at the source. The net dividends received by its domestic parent company are then excluded from its CIT base. Such net dividends received by a foreign parent company are taxed in accordance with the respective country's internal legislation or DTT provisions (if Uzbekistan has a DTT with this country). *See the Withholding taxes section for a list of countries with which Uzbekistan has an applicable tax treaty.*

Interest income

Interest income is subject to 10% WHT at the source. The net interest income received by companies is then excluded from its CIT base. Such net interest income received by foreign companies is taxed in accordance with the respective country's internal legislation or DTT provisions (if Uzbekistan has a DTT with this country). *See the Withholding taxes section for a list of countries with which Uzbekistan has an applicable tax treaty.*

Foreign income

Gross foreign income of a resident corporation (e.g. income from its foreign branch) should be included in its aggregate income on an accrual basis, regardless of remittance date. Expenses incurred abroad in relation to such foreign income would be deducted subject to provisions of the Uzbek Tax Code. Foreign income tax paid on such income should be credited against the Uzbek CIT only if this branch is registered in a country with which Uzbekistan has a DTT. There are no deferrals for foreign income to be recognised for Uzbek tax purposes.

Deductions

The tax base for CIT purposes varies significantly from the computation of taxable profits in most Western jurisdictions. Expenditures such as entertaining, benefits in-kind, and business trip allowances exceeding the statutory norms (that are generally low) are non-deductible.

There are additional costs that cannot be deducted by PEs of foreign legal entities, such as interest on head office loans; commission fees charged by the head office; and royalty, administrative, and management expenses of the head office incurred outside Uzbekistan. However, PEs are eligible to deduct expenses incurred outside of Uzbekistan if they directly relate to their business in Uzbekistan.

Depreciation and amortisation

For tax purposes, depreciation/amortisation is calculated with application of rates defined by the Tax Code. If depreciation for accounting purposes is charged at higher rates (compared with the Tax Code rates), the difference would be treated as a temporary difference for CIT purposes (i.e. deducted in future periods).

Depreciation is calculated from a month following the month when the asset was put into use until it is fully depreciated, disposed, or written off. The maximum annual depreciation rates applicable to different types of fixed assets are outlined in the table below.

Depreciable item	Rate (%)
Buildings and other structures	5
Cars, tractors, special equipment, computers and related hardware	20
Lorries, buses, special cars and trucks, industrial machinery and equipment, agricultural machinery and equipment, oil extraction and mining equipment, office furniture	15
Railway, river and air transport vehicles, thermo-technical equipment, turbines, electric and diesel drives, power supply and communication lines, pipelines	8
Depreciable assets not mentioned above	10

For statutory accounting purposes, fixed assets can be depreciated using one of the following methods:

- Straight-line method.
- Production method.
- Double-declining-balance method.
- Sum-of-the-years' (cumulative) method.

Intangible assets, including leases and other property rights, are amortised over the shorter of an asset's useful life or the period of activity of the enterprise. Where an asset's useful life cannot be determined, the asset would be amortised over five years.

Expenses related to geological exploration and developmental works necessary for the extraction of natural resources are deductible for CIT purposes through depreciation at the rate of 15% per annum.

Goodwill
For tax purposes, expenses incurred for acquisition of goodwill should be deductible through monthly amortisation charges at norms calculated by the taxpayers based on historical cost of goodwill and its useful life.

Start-up expenses
Current legislation does not provide specific guidance on tax treatment of start-up expenses. However, as per Uzbek accounting legislation, certain types of start-up expenses (e.g. expenses for acquisition of right for production, right for rendering services and carrying out works, right to use economic or other privileges) can be considered as expenses for procurement of intangible assets and, respectively, can be deducted through monthly depreciation charges.

Interest on short-term loans
Interest is deductible, except for interest on overdue/delayed loans (i.e. 'penalty interest') and interest capitalised in the value of fixed assets (i.e. in cases where a loan was obtained to purchase fixed assets).

Bad debt
Bad debts are deductible for tax purposes in cases where they are recognised in accordance with Uzbek accounting legislation. Otherwise, such expenses should be

U

Uzbekistan, Republic of

considered as non-deductible. According to the current Uzbek legislation, arrears are recognised as bad debts upon expiration of three-years from their due date.

Charitable contributions

Charitable contributions are generally treated as non-deductible expense and added-back to the taxable base.

However, taxable income can be reduced for the amount of charitable contributions to ecological and charitable foundations and cultural, medical, educational, and municipal institutions, not exceeding 2% of the taxable income.

Fines and penalties

Fines and penalties are considered as non-deductible expenses.

Taxes

Generally, taxes are deductible for CIT purposes. The exceptions are the infrastructure development tax based on after-tax profits and the net profit tax for PEs.

Other tax losses

In cases where goods or services are sold below cost (or given for free), the revenue should be adjusted for tax purposes to the cost or purchase price of the goods or services.

Production wastes and defects within statutory norms, and losses resulting in *force-majeure* circumstances, are generally deductible.

Losses from the disposal of fixed assets also may be deducted, if the fixed asset has been used for three or more years.

Net operating losses

Tax losses may be carried forward for a period of five years, allowing a reduction of taxable income of the respective year by up to 50%. Loss carrybacks are not permitted.

Payments to foreign affiliates

There are no special tax provisions regarding deductibility of payments to foreign affiliates for services provided. They may be deducted in full if the general deductibility criteria are met (*see Transfer pricing in the Group taxation section*).

Group taxation

There is no provision for consolidation of income or losses by related companies for tax purposes in Uzbekistan. A foreign legal entity that has several PEs in Uzbekistan may not consolidate those for tax purposes.

Transfer pricing

As of 1 January 2010, the transfer pricing concept was reintroduced in the Uzbek Tax Code. However, it is limited to a couple of paragraphs stating that tax authorities may adjust prices used by interrelated parties if these prices differ from the prices which would have been used in transactions with independent parties. There is no further guidance for application of this rule, which gives rise to different interpretation by tax authorities and taxpayers.

Thin capitalisation

Effective legislation does not provide for thin capitalisation rules, except for debt-to-equity ratios set up by the Central bank of Uzbekistan (CBU) for commercial banks.

Tax credits and incentives

The current tax legislation offers tax incentives for enterprises in oil and gas exploration/development projects, enterprises engaged in the production and export of goods for foreign currency (when export share exceeds 15%), and companies rendering certain services.

Incentives for oil and gas exploration and extraction companies

Foreign companies carrying out oil and gas exploration works, as well as their foreign contractors/subcontracts engaged in such works, are exempt from payment of all forms of taxes and contributions to non-budget funds during the exploration period. Additionally, import by these companies of equipment, material, and technical resources and services necessary for the exploration and related works is exempt from customs duties.

Resident corporations supplying materials and rendering services to foreign companies carrying out oil and gas exploration are exempt from VAT.

Furthermore, if foreign companies carrying out oil and gas exploration form joint venture companies for extraction of oil and gas at respective fields, such companies are granted a seven-year CIT holiday starting from the date of commencement of extraction.

Incentives for carrying out export activities

Enterprises exporting goods (works, services) of their own production for freely convertible currency may apply reduced rates of CIT as follows:

- If export share of total sales ranges from 15% to 30%, the effective rate shall be reduced by 30%.
- If export share of total sales is 30% or more, the effective tax rate shall be reduced by 50%.

This incentive is applied likewise in regards to property tax as follows:

- If export share ranges from 15% to 30%, the property tax rate is reduced by 30%.
- If export share is 30% or more, the property tax rate is reduced by 50%.

The incentive in both cases is subject to a restriction that it does not apply to wholesale/retail sale or intermediary companies, nor to revenues from the export of specific items such as cotton fibre, oil, gas, precious metals, etc.

Producers can also defer payment of their import VAT in respect of material and technical resources used for production of goods to be exported. The deferral is granted for up to 90 days without application of any interest.

Incentives for service companies

Micro-firms and small enterprises engaged in certain types of activity are exempt from CIT and unified tax payment until 1 January 2014. These types include, without

U

Uzbekistan, Republic of

limitation, leasing, insurance, auditing/bookkeeping services, and repair of footwear and leather goods.

Exemptions from customs payments

There are certain customs exemptions offered by the legislation for the following:

- Technological equipment imported by foreign investors as their charter fund contribution.
- Technological equipment imported under projects for creation of new or the modernisation of existing production facilities (with appropriate certificates issued by an authorised bank).
- Property imported for production needs by foreign investors and enterprises with foreign investment with foreign participation in the equity of not less than 33%.

Foreign tax credit

In accordance with international tax treaties of the Republic of Uzbekistan, legal entities/residents of Uzbekistan can obtain a tax credit in respect of CIT paid outside of Uzbekistan. In order to claim tax credit, legal entities should provide a copy of tax payment order, confirmation from a competent tax authority, or any other document confirming payment of the tax outside of Uzbekistan.

Withholding taxes

WHT is to be withheld and remitted to the state budget by entities paying income to non-residents if these entities qualify under a tax agent definition (i.e. by (i) Uzbek legal entities and (ii) non-residents operating in Uzbekistan via PE).

The domestic WHT rates are as follows:

Payment	WHT (%)
Dividends and interest	10
Insurance and reinsurance payments	10
Freight	6
Royalties, services (including management, consulting services), rents, other income	20

Double taxation treaty (DTT) relief

Foreign legal entities that do not carry on activities in Uzbekistan through a PE are subject to WHT on income from sources in Uzbekistan, subject to the terms of a relevant DTT. Uzbekistan has signed DTTs with 50 countries; 48 of them are in force.

DTTs in force establish WHT rates as follows:

Recipient	Dividends (%)	Interest (%)	Royalties (%)
Austria	5 (2)/15	10	5
Azerbaijan	10	10	10
Bahrain	8	8	8
Belarus	15	10	15
Belgium	5 (2)/15	10	5
Bulgaria	10	10	10
Canada	5 (1)/15	10	5 (3, 4)/10

Recipient	Dividends (%)	Interest (%)	Royalties (%)
China	10	10	10
Czech Republic	10	5	10
Finland	5 (1)/15	5	5 (5)/10 (4)
France	5 (2)/10	0 (7, 9, 12)/5	0
Georgia	5 (8)/15	10	10
Germany	5 (8)/15	0 (9)/5	3 (3, 10)/5 (4)
Greece	8	0 (7)/10	8
Hungary	10	0 (15)/10	10
India	15	0 (7)/15	15
Indonesia	10	10	10
Iran	8	10	5
Israel	10	10	5 (4)/10
Italy	10	0 (9)/5	5
Japan	15	0 (7, 9)/10	0 (4)/10 (3, 5, 6, 10)
Jordan	7 (8)/10	10	20
Kazakhstan	10	0 (7, 9)/10	10
Kuwait	5 (8)/10	0 (7, 9)/8	20
Kyrgyzstan	5	5	15
Latvia	10	0 (7, 9)/10	10
Lithuania	10	0 (7, 9)/10	10
Luxembourg	5 (8)/15	0 (7)/10	5
Malaysia	10	0 (9)/10	10
Moldova	5 (1)/15	0 (7, 9)/10	15
(The) Netherlands	5 (8)/15	10	10
Oman	7	7	10
Pakistan	10	0 (7, 14)/10	15
Poland	5 (11)/15	0 (7, 9)/10	10
Romania	10	0 (14)/10	10
Russia	10	0 (7, 14)/10	0
Saudi Arabia	7	7	10
Singapore	5	5	8
Slovak Republic	10	10	10
South Korea	5 (8)/15	5	2 (10)/5
Switzerland	5 (11)/15	0 (12)/5	5
Thailand	10	0 (9)/10 (13)/15	15
Turkey	10	0 (7, 9)/10	10
Turkmenistan	10	0 (7, 9)/10	10
UAE	0 (7a)/5 (8)/15	0 (7a)/10	10
Ukraine	10	10	10
United Kingdom	5 (11)/10	5	5
Vietnam	15	0 (9, 12)/10	15

Notes

1. Where the beneficial shareholder owns no less than 10% of the voting shares.
2. Where the beneficial owner holds at least 10% of the capital of the paying entity.
3. Where royalties are paid for patents, trademarks, know-how, etc.
4. Where royalties are paid for copyrights on literature, cinema, musical works, etc.
5. Where royalties are paid for secret formulas, processes, or know-how.

Uzbekistan, Republic of

6. Where royalties are paid for computer software, patents, designs, models, or plans.
7. Where one of the following conditions is met: (a) recipient is a local authority or corporate body constituted under public law, including the central bank of the state, or interest is paid by the local authorities or corporate bodies; (b) interest is paid in respect to debt claims or loans, guaranteed, insured, or aided by the state or on behalf of the state; (c) interest is paid in respect to credit sales of industrial, commercial, scientific equipment of goods and merchandise or provision of services by an enterprise to another enterprise; or (d) interest is paid in respect to a loan of any kind granted by a bank.
8. Where the beneficial shareholder owns no less than 25% of the capital of the paying entity.
9. Where the recipients of the interest are governments of contracting states or any governmental body (such interest is exempt from WHT).
10. Where royalties are paid in respect to uses or the rights to use industrial, commercial, or scientific equipment.
11. Where the beneficial shareholder owns no less than 20% of the voting shares.
12. Where interest is paid in respect to: (a) a loan made, guaranteed, or insured by the government of the other state; (b) the sale on credit of industrial, commercial, or scientific equipment; (c) the sale of merchandise by an enterprise to another enterprise; or (d) a loan of any kind granted by a bank.
13. Where the interest is received by any financial institution (including insurance companies).
14. Where interest is beneficially owned by the other contracting state or local authority or an instrumentality of such other state authority and is not subject to tax by that other state.
15. Where the recipients of the interest are governments of contracting states, National Bank of Hungary, Eximbank Hungary Pte. Ltd., Central Bank of Uzbekistan, or the National Bank of Uzbekistan for foreign economic activity (such interest is exempt from WHT).

Note that there may be other WHT rates offered by protocols to the individual treaties.

Tax administration

Taxable period
The taxable period for CIT is a calendar year.

Tax returns
CIT is reported quarterly before the 25th day of the month following the reporting quarter, with an annual return due by 25 March following the reporting year for enterprises with foreign investment and 15 February following the reporting year for other categories of CIT payers. PEs report on CIT once a year prior to 25 March following the reporting year.

Payment of tax
Uzbek enterprises, including enterprises with foreign investment, are required to make advance instalments of CIT in each quarter based on estimated profits in the quarter. The instalments are payable by the tenth day of each month. Final quarterly payments based on actual profit figures are payable no later than the filing deadline for the quarterly tax returns (which is the 25th day of the month following the period of assessment). In case the final quarterly payment is more than 10% higher than advance instalments made in this quarter, tax authorities have the right to recalculate the advance instalments based on the actual quarterly profit figures and charge late payment interest accordingly.

Final CIT payment should be made no later than the date set as the deadline for annual return submission.

Payment of CIT by PE is made annually within a month after the filing deadline.

Audit cycle
Scheduled statutory tax audits are to be carried out once in three years (once in four years for micro-firms, small enterprises) by the tax authority of the district where the

enterprise is registered, i.e. district tax inspectorates. However, in certain cases, the tax audit is undertaken by the State Tax Committee, which is the highest tax authority.

The tax audits are aimed at verification of the tax returns submitted by the taxpayer. Normally, the tax authorities will review the accounting records, copies of tax returns, and source documents as required.

There can also be un-scheduled tax audits (e.g. in case of liquidation of the enterprise) and counter tax audits (e.g. to review transactions with the enterprise's supplier/customer who is under the scheduled tax audit).

In case of tax breaches revealed during tax audits, taxpayers should remove tax violations and pay respective taxes/obligatory payments and late payment interest within 30 days after the tax authority's decision is released. If accomplished within the deadline, the tax authority's decision on applying penalty may be cancelled. If not accomplished, the unpaid taxes/obligatory payments and late payment interest are to be withdrawn from (i) the taxpayer's bank accounts (by issuing tax liability claim without acceptance), (ii) the taxpayer's debtors (by issuing tax liability claim on the debts payable to taxpayer), (iii) the taxpayer's property (by issuing tax liability claim upon decision of the court).

Another form of monitoring accuracy and completeness of fulfilment of tax liabilities imposed by the tax authorities is 'cameral control', which is performed at the time of tax returns submission. The tax authorities may require the taxpayer to amend the tax return(s) if they have revealed mistakes or inconsistencies therein. The amended tax returns should be filed within ten days.

Statute of limitations
The statute of limitations for tax purposes in Uzbekistan is set to five years.

Topics of focus for tax authorities
There are no officially announced areas of focus during tax audits. In practice, the tax authorities usually focus on currency control, cash discipline, deductibility of expenses for CIT purposes, and taxes on resources (e.g. excess profits tax, subsurface use tax).

U

Venezuela

PwC contact

Pedro Pacheco
Espiñeira, Pacheco y Asociados
Avenida Principal de Chuao
Edificio Del Río, Apartado 1789
Caracas 1010-A, Estado Miranda
Venezuela
Tel: +58 212 7006 112
Email: pedro.pacheco@ve.pwc.com

Significant developments

Tax reforms and new taxes taking place in year 2011 mainly correspond to those elaborated in the Other taxes section (*see the Other taxes section for more information*).

Taxes on corporate income

Corporations resident in Venezuela are subject to corporate income tax (CIT) on their Venezuelan and foreign-source income, whereas corporations resident abroad with a permanent establishment (PE) in Venezuela are levied CIT on only their Venezuelan and foreign-source income attributable to said PE. Corporations are able to claim any similar taxes paid abroad on foreign source income as a tax credit. Non-resident corporations without a PE are subject to CIT only on Venezuela-source income.

Corporate income is taxed at the following progressive rates based on tax units (TU) (*see below*) (i.e. Tariff 2):

Taxable income		Rate (%)	Subtract (TU)
Over (TU)	Not over (TU)		
0	2,000	15	0
2,000	3,000	22	140
3,000	-	34	500

Tax units (TU)
The 1994 Income Tax Law reform established the concept of a taxable unit as an element that reduces the negative effects created by inflation on the determination of the tax rates. The tax code established the initial TU at 1 *bolívar fuerte* (VEF), with annual basis adjustments according to the variation on the consumer price index (CPI) from the previous year. For 2011, TU was VEF 76. For 2012, TU is VEF 90.

Additional rates and considerations
Income for oil exploitation and certain related activities is taxed at a flat rate of 50%. Related activities are comprised of those such as refinery, transportation, and purchases for the exports of hydrocarbons and by-products for the exploitation. Joint venture corporations are also subject to a 50% CIT rate.

The above indicated regime does not apply to corporations engaged in the exploration and exploitation of non-associated gas (and the processing, refining, transportation, distribution, commercialisation, and exportation of the gas and its components) or companies exclusively engaged in the refining of hydrocarbons or improvement of extra heavy oil, which are subject to Tariff 2.

Local income taxes

See Municipal business licence tax in the Other taxes for a description of local taxes on income.

Corporate residence

According to the Venezuelan tax code, the following companies are regarded as resident:

- Companies incorporated in Venezuela and registered with the Mercantile Registry as established by commercial law.
- Foreign companies registered with the Superintendence of Foreign Investments (SIEX) to be resident in Venezuela as branches duly registered with the Mercantile Registry.

The following companies are non-residents but subject to Venezuelan taxes:

- Foreign companies registered with SIEX to provide technical assistance, technological services, royalty items, and professional services from abroad.
- Foreign banks granting loans to local companies.
- Foreign companies leasing goods to local companies.
- Foreign companies deriving income from economic activities carried out in Venezuela or from assets in Venezuela.

Permanent establishment (PE)

According to the Venezuela Income Tax Law (VITL), generally, a passive party is deemed to be carrying out operations in Venezuela through a PE when:

- The passive party owns, directly or through an agent, employee, or representative in the Venezuelan territory,:
  - an office, fixed place of business, or an activity centre where its activities are totally or partially carried on
  - management head quarters, branches, offices, factories, shops, facilities, warehouses, stores, construction, installations, or assembling works, when the duration thereof exceeds six months, or
  - agencies or representatives authorised (according to the VITL) to contract in the name of or on behalf of the passive party.
- The passive party performs, directly or through an agent, employee, or representative in the Venezuelan territory, professional, artistic activities.
- The passive party possesses, directly or through an agent, employee, representative, or other contracted personnel in the Venezuelan territory, other work places where the operations are wholly or partially performed.

Any agent acting independently shall be excluded from this definition, except if such representative has the power to conclude contracts in the name of the principal.

V

Venezuela

....

Other taxes

Value-added tax (VAT)

Federal VAT (*Impuesto al Valor Agregado* or IVA), is a one-time tax payable by the ultimate consumer of all types of products and services. However, each business entity involved in the process from the sale of raw materials to the production and distribution of finished products to the ultimate consumer is required to include the tax on its products to customers (output tax) and to pay the tax on its purchases or imports of goods and services (input tax), crediting the amounts paid against the amounts due on its own activities. The net amount payable by each entity is considered to represent a tax on the value added.

In general, VAT does not represent an additional cost to business enterprises because even though all types of business enterprises, including government departments and agencies (with some exceptions), are required to accept charges of the tax by suppliers on their purchases of goods and services, such amounts are normally deductible from the liability of the business enterprises for the tax on their bills to customers.

There are exceptions, principally when the sales of an enterprise are exempt from VAT, in which case the enterprise is treated as the final consumer and must absorb any VAT charges on its purchases except insofar as its activities are subject to the zero rate (*see below*). However, input tax paid on goods or services used to produce items that are exempt from VAT may be deducted for CIT purposes.

Taxable transactions

In general, VAT is payable on all sales, rental, and importation of goods, and rendering of services executed or used in the country, although a number of significant exceptions are provided by law.

Sales of goods

The law defines a sale as any transmission of tangible goods, including those made on a conditional basis or through an irrevocable trust. The taxable amount of a sale includes the sale price as well as other amounts charged to the purchaser for other taxes, duties, interest, or surcharges of whatever nature. VAT becomes payable when the goods are invoiced or shipped to the customers or when the price is paid in full or in part.

Exempt sales include the following:

- Certain foods and other products for human consumption.
- Fertilisers as well as any natural gas used in the manufacturing thereof.
- Some products for animal consumption.
- Medicine.
- Products derived from hydrocarbons and some raw materials intended to improve the quality of gasoline.
- Wheelchairs.
- Books, magazines, newspapers, and the paper used in producing these products.
- Vehicles, aircraft, and trains for passenger transport.
- Machinery and equipment for agribusiness.
- Scientific equipment purchased by the government.

Services

Taxable services are those rendered within Venezuela by one person to another on an independent basis, transportation of passengers or goods, agency activities, technical assistance, and transfer of technology. VAT is payable to service providers at the time the invoice is issued, the service is rendered, or the fee becomes demandable, whichever comes first. The taxable amount includes not only the price of services, but also charges to the customers for other taxes, interest, etc.

Exempt services include the following:

- Domestic land and maritime transportation of passengers.
- Educational services.
- Accommodations for students and persons with disabilities.
- Healthcare and dental services, surgery, and hospitalisation.
- Theatres, sports, and cultural events.
- Food services for employees and students.
- Certain utilities (e.g. electricity, water).
- Housecleaning.
- Transport services for hydrocarbon-derived fuels.
- Services involving livestock, poultry, and other minor species including breeding and production.

Exports

Exports are zero rated. Consequently, VAT is not payable on exports, including exports of in-bond processing companies, technical fees to foreign residents, and sales to in-bond processing companies and companies that export their entire production. Sale of natural hydrocarbon by joint ventures regulated by the Hydrocarbon Law to Petroleos de Venezuela S.A. (PDVSA) and affiliated companies are also taxable at 0%. Though exporters do not collect VAT on export sales, they may recover VAT charges on their purchases of goods and services by means of a refund certificate. This certificate may be used to pay other tax obligations. If such exporters carry out sales in the country, they will be entitled to recover only input VAT related to foreign sales.

Additionally, a zero rate applies to independent personal services provided by residents in Venezuela that are used solely by and for the benefit of persons abroad without a PE or fixed base in Venezuela.

Tax rates

The rate may change every year, within the range of 8% to 16.5%. Currently the general VAT rate is 12%.

An additional tax rate of 10% is applicable to the sale and imports of luxury products (e.g. vehicles valued at more than 30,000 United States dollars [USD], motorcycles with a cylinder capacity of 500 cc, nickel or token game machines, aircraft used for recreational or sport purposes, fighting bulls, trained horses, caviar, jewellery with precious stones valued at a price exceeding USD 500).

An 8% VAT applies to the following transactions:

- Goats, sheep, and minor species for slaughter or breeding.
- Meats in their natural state, or refrigerated, frozen, or salted meats, or meats in brine of goats, sheep, and poultry.
- Shortening.
- Rendering of professional services to any government entity, in any level or branch of government, provided such services do not involve any commercial transactions but rather predominantly intellectual work or efforts.
- Domestic air passenger transportation.

V

Venezuela

Payment and collection

Excess VAT charged or chargeable to customers over VAT paid to vendors or customs authorities (*Servicio Nacional Integrado de Administración, Aduanera y Tributaria* or SENIAT) including the correspondent payment, must be remitted to SENIAT within the first 15 days of the following month.

VAT exoneration

Among the fiscal policy measures applicable pursuant to the conjuncture, sector, and regional situation of the country's economy, the National Executive is entitled to exonerate the import and sales of goods and the rendering of services set forth in the respective decree from the payment of VAT.

Refunds/special regime for industrial projects

The VAT law stipulates a special regime for taxpayers engaged in the execution of industrial projects, whose duration exceeds six taxable periods. Pursuant to this regime, taxpayers will be able to suspend the use of input VAT generated during their operating stage, until such time as they begin generating fiscal output VAT.

Taxpayers engaged in the execution of industrial projects aimed at exporting or generating foreign currency may (with prior consent of the tax authorities), choose to recover the tax supported in construction operations involving the project, provided that they are carried out during the pre-operating stage of such project.

Input VAT subject to recovery must be determined after computing output VAT. In other words, input VAT originated from purchases of goods and reception of services is not subject to recovery if output VAT was not subtracted.

VAT withholding regimes

Taxpayers qualified by the tax administration as special taxpayers and public entities are designated as liable parties in their capacity as withholding agents in regard to payment of the VAT generated in their purchase of tangible goods or services received by providers that are regular taxpayers for VAT purposes.

The amount to be withheld on the part of the agents will be equal to multiplying the invoiced price of the taxed goods or services by 75% of the tax rate, except for those cases in which the VAT does not appear separately from the price, when the respective invoice does not comply with the formalities or requirements set forth in the tax law, or when the supplier is not registered for tax purposes. In these latter cases, 100% of the generated tax is to be withheld.

Suppliers may discount the VAT withheld from the tax liability determined for the period in which the VAT was withheld, provided that they have the receipt issued by the withholding agent. In those cases in which the tax withheld from the taxpayer exceeds the taxpayer's VAT liability corresponding to the relevant tax period, such taxpayer may discount the tax withheld from VAT liability corresponding to the following tax periods until their total exhaustion.

Customs duties

As a general rule, the importation of goods into Venezuela is subject to customs duties. These duties are generally levied on the cost, insurance, and freight (CIF) value of the product being imported, excluding VAT.

Custom duty rates generally range from 5% to 35%. The duty rates vary depending on the product involved. In general, import tariffs are 5% for capital goods, 10% to 15%

for raw materials and intermediate goods, and 15% to 35% for finished products. In addition, all imports are subject to customs handling charge, a duty import, and VAT.

Excise taxes

Tax on alcohol and alcoholic beverages
In general terms, the manufacture, commercialisation, and importation of alcohol and alcoholic beverages are subject to excise taxes. The Law of Tax on Alcohol and Alcoholic Beverages provides for three main types of excise taxes:

* Tax on the national production and importation of alcohol and alcoholic beverages, which is established on the basis of TU per litre and varies depending on the type of product.
* Additional excise tax per litre for national and imported beer and for other alcoholic beverages is levied on the sale of those products to the public, which is also provided on the basis of TU per litre, depending on the type of product.
* In addition to the above, another excise tax is imposed on the importation or local sale of national and imported alcoholic beverages to the public, which is levied on the sales price, which is provided on the basis of a percentage on the price of sale to the public and varies depending on the type of product.

Tax on cigarettes and manufacturing of tobacco
The importation and national production of cigarettes and tobacco to be consumed in Venezuela is subject to an excise tax. This proportional tax is levied at a rate of 70% on the retail price of cigarettes, tobacco, and its derivates.

Urban Property Tax
The Urban Property Tax is a local or municipal tax payable by any person who owns property rights or any other real rights on urban real estates. The taxable basis is the value of the urban real estate. For these purposes, the fair market value of the real estate is provided as a point of reference. The applicable rate varies according to each municipality.

Public registry tax
Commercial companies are registered with the Mercantile Registry Office and are subject to a tax levied upon incorporation of a company and registration of capital increases. The tax is 1% of the amounts of subscribed or increased capital.

The sale of a going concern is also registered in the Mercantile Registry Office and is subject to a tax levied upon the total amount of the sell. The tax is 2% of the amount.

Stamp duties
The Stamp Duties Law establishes a number of stamp duties on the issuance of official documents (e.g. certificates, permits, authorisation, registrations). Stamp duties may be levied at fixed amounts (ranging from TU 0.01 to TU 10,000) or at a rate based on the value of the transaction or work in question.

District Capital stamp tax
Until May 2012, under their own interpretation of the District Capital Stamp Law, Mercantile Registries of the District Capital were charging 10% of the amount of subscribed or increased capital of companies and 20% for the sale of a going concern. An amendment on this Law enacted on 2 May 2012 reduced the applicable stamp tax to subscribed or increased capital of companies to 2%.

Venezuela

Gift tax

Overall, the Inheritance and Donations Tax Law, published on 1999, stipulates the taxes attributable to inheritances left by individuals. Nonetheless, this Law provides regulation about donations, which are significant to corporations. Subject to payment of the gift tax are the beneficiaries of gifts in the form of movable or real property, rights, or shares located in the country.

For tax calculation purposes, the progressive tax rate (up to 55%) set forth in the Law will be applied to the donated good. Both donors and donees are jointly liable for the tax generated from the gift.

The gift tax is applicable from the time in which the donors manifest before the National Treasury their will to donate and must be paid before the registration of any document formalising or evidencing the authenticity of the gift. Should the donation not be perfected due to express will of the donor or rejection on the part of the donee, the obligation to pay the tax will be eliminated and reimbursement may be requested of the amounts paid in this connection.

Under the transfer pricing rules contained in the Venezuelan Income Tax Law, the tax authorities are empowered to impute income in inter-company transactions at a price reflecting the fair market value of the property being transferred.

Before the introduction of transfer pricing rules, under the Inheritance and Donations Tax Law, the tax authorities could and still can presume in transactions involving a sale, assignment, barter, or transfer, the existence of a donation if, for instance, the price stipulated in such transaction does not reflect the real value of the property being transacted. In such a case, a gift tax may be imposed on the difference between the fair market value of the property being transacted and the consideration received in return.

Also, a cancellation of a debt gives rise to gift tax issues. In this regard, the Inheritance and Donations Tax Law provides that the total or partial forgiveness or cancellation of a loan must be viewed as a gift and, as such, subject to gift tax.

Increase of the windfall tax on oil production

Decree N° 8.163, dated 18 April 2011, provides for the increase of the windfall tax on oil companies. The aforesaid Decree abrogates the regulations on the tax published on April 2008. According to the enacted Decree, the tax is provided in the following terms:

- The contribution on extraordinary oil prices is a 20% tax on the difference in price when the internationally quoted price per barrel exceeds the budgeted price per barrel (for purposes of the Venezuelan Annual Budget Law), provided that the quoted price per barrel is equivalent or lower than USD 70 per barrel (i.e. the maximum basis is the difference between USD 70 per barrel and the current budgeted price of USD 50).
- The contribution on exorbitant oil prices is comprised of the following:
  - 80% tax on income generated by quoted oil prices between USD 70 and USD 90 per barrel (i.e. 80% on the range from USD 70 to USD 90 quoted price per barrel).
  - 90% tax on the difference in the quoted oil prices between USD 90 and USD 100 per barrel.
  - 95% tax on the difference over the threshold of USD 100 per barrel.

The tax is payable by oil companies exporting with sale purposes. Also, the Decree provided that the mixed companies (*empresas mixtas*) created in accordance with the

Master Hydrocarbons Law that sell oil and by-products to the state-owned company (PDVSA), or any of its affiliates, are also obliged to pay the above described tax.

On the other hand, tax exemption is provided for the following cases:

- For mixed companies working on the execution of projects on the development of new oil fields and those projects aimed at boosting oil production as declared by the Ministry of the Popular Power for Oil and Energy, until they have recovered their total investment. Parameters to determine the recovery of investment are to be separately established by the aforesaid Ministry by Resolution.
- Exports executed in connection with cooperation or financing international agreements.
- Exonerations may be granted by the National Executive Power for exports executed under economic or international cooperation measures.

The tax is payable on a monthly basis in foreign currency. Other terms of payments are to be regulated by Resolution.

The Decree also establishes USD 70 per barrel as the maximum price to be used as calculation basis for the payment of royalties, extraction tax, and export registration tax provided for in the Master Hydrocarbons Law.

The Decree was partially amended on 27 February 2012 to establish that PDVSA will act as perception agent.

Hydrocarbons Organic Law
The state is entitled to 30% of the volume of hydrocarbons extracted from any deposit, by way of royalties. The National Executive can reduce this within certain limits, when it is shown that certain types of deposits are not economically exploitable.

Persons conducting activities related to hydrocarbons must pay the following taxes:

Surface tax
For the portion of the surface area granted that is not under development, the equivalent of 100 TU for each square kilometre or portion of a square kilometre for every elapsed year is due as a surface tax. This tax will increase annually by 2% during the first five years and 5% during the following years.

Tax on own consumption
10% of the value of each cubic metre of hydrocarbon byproducts produced and consumed as fuel in wholly-owned operations, based on the price of the end consumer, is due as a tax. In the case that said product fails to be sold in a domestic market, the Ministry of Energy and Mines shall provide the price.

General consumption tax
For every litre of hydrocarbon byproducts sold in the domestic market, a tax is due at the rate of between 30% and 50% of the price paid by the end consumer, whose aliquot should be implemented annually between the two extremes under the Budget Law. This levy to be paid by the end consumer should be withheld at the supply source, to be handed over to the National Treasury on a monthly basis.

The National Executive may waive, in whole or in part, by the time specified, the general consumption tax, in order to encourage certain activities of public or general

V

Venezuela

interest. The National Executive can also reinstate this levy to its original level when the causes for the waiver cease to exist.

Gaseous Hydrocarbons Organic Law

The Gaseous Hydrocarbons Organic Law establishes a system of royalties, determinable by the volumes of gaseous hydrocarbons extracted from any deposit and not re-injected. The state is also entitled to a 20% share for this item.

The exploitation companies of gaseous hydrocarbons shall pay for the gaseous hydrocarbons consumed like fuel, the taxes settle down on the matter by applicable laws.

Contribution to support Organic Law on Sports, Physical Activity, and Physical Education

The Organic Law on Sports, Physical Activity, and Physical Education (Sports Law) was published on 23 August 2011. The purpose of the Law is to establish the public service nature of physical education and the promotion, organisation, and administration of sports and physical activity, as well as their organisation as an economic activity with social aims.

The provision of the Sports Law are of a public nature and are applicable to the public national, state, and municipal administration and organisations, and also to individuals and legal entities that conduct any activity related to the practice, promotion, organisation, sponsorship, administration, or any economic activity associated with sports or physical activities and education.

The Sports Law creates the National Fund for the Development of Sports, Physical Activity, and Physical Education, which will be constituted with the contributions made by companies or other public or private organisations that perform economic activities for profit in the country; by donations, gifts, or any other special contribution made by the Republic, the states, the municipalities, or any other public or private entity; and by the revenue produced by such funds.

The contribution will be 1% of the annual net of accounting profit and will be payable by all companies or other public or private organisations that perform economic activities within the country and obtain an annual net or accounting profit of more than TU 20,000. Up to 50% of the contribution can be for the implementation of the taxpayer´s own projects, provided the respective project follows the guidelines to be issued by the National Sports Institute, which will be updated every two years.

Anti-drugs contribution

The Organic Drug Law published on 15 September 2010 stipulates that any company employing 50 or more employees must make an annual contribution from their operating profit equivalent to 1%. On the other hand, corporations with the specifications mentioned before but that are dedicated to the manufacture or import of alcohol beverages, tobacco, or their mixtures are required to make a contribution equivalent of 2% from their operating profit. Under the definitions established by this Law, operating profit can be understood as the result from subtracting the operating expenses from the income profit in accordance with the accepted Venezuelan general accounting principles.

This contribution will be collected by the National Anti-Drug Fund (FONA), within 60 continuous days counted from the end of the fiscal year.

Note that this contribution can be retrieved if the company performs:

- prevention programs and projects intended for the company employees and their family environment
- prevention programs for children and adolescents, or
- programs to fight drug trafficking.

Payroll taxes and other contributions

Contributions applicable to resident companies in Venezuela:

Contributions	Basis	Contribution basis (cap)	Employer contributions (%)	Employee contributions (%)	Notes
Mandatory social security regime contribution	Wages (normal or regular wages)	Up to five minimum salaries for urban workers	9/10/11	4	(1, 2, 5)
Employment benefit regime contribution	Wages (normal or regular wages)	Up to ten minimum salaries for urban workers	2	0.5	(1)
Housing regime contribution	Total monthly (or integral) salary	No cap (5, 6)	2	1	(5, 6)
Employee training contribution (INCES)	Total salaries paid by the employer for purposes of the employer's contribution.	No cap	2	0.5 (4)	(3, 4)
Workplace prevention, conditions, and environment contribution (LOPCYMAT)	Total salaries paid to employees	No cap is established	From 0.75 to 10	N/A	(7, 8)

Notes

1. As of 1 May 2012, the minimum monthly metropolitan salary amount was increased to VEF 1,780.45, and it will increase to VEF 2,047.52 as of 1 September 2012.
2. According to the current system, the employer's contribution to social security will depend on the company's risk qualification (minimum risk, middle risk, or maximum risk).
3. Regarding Instituto Nacional de Capacitación y Educación Socialista (INCES) contribution, the employer must contribute 2% of the total wages and salaries paid to employees.
4. Employers are also required to withhold 0.5% of the annual profit-sharing bonus paid to employees.
5. According to the Ley Orgánica del Sistema de Seguridad Social (LOSSS), the general rule for contribution basis for the new systems may not exceed ten minimum salaries. The transition rules establish a contribution basis of five metropolitan minimum salaries for urban workers for social security purposes. No cap is expressly established in the transition rules for the housing system and work, security, and health regime.
6. The basis of calculation of the housing contributions is the 'Integral Salary'. The Integral Salary is a concept established in the Organic Labour Law, and it comprises the following payments: commissions, gratifications, profit sharing bonuses, vacation bonus as well as surcharges for holidays, overtime, night shifts, among others, all of which are made to the employee and correspond to the services rendered by the individual.
7. Contributions to be made to this regime are exclusively for the employer and vary depending on the risk associated to the company. A company's risk is to be determined by the Instituto Nacional de Prevención, Salud y Seguridad Laborales (INPSASEL). To date, INPSASEL has not been created and employers will continue making their contributions to the Venezuela Social Security Institute.
8. Ley Orgánica de Prevención, Condiciones y Medio Ambiente de Trabajo (LOPCYMAT) regulations do not establish a cap for the contribution. However, as mentioned, the LOSSS establishes a maximum of the minimum urban salaries. For this reason, there are several contrary interpretations on whether a cap should be applied in this case.

V

Venezuela

Other contributions	Basis	Contribution basis (cap)	Employer contributions (%)	Employee contributions (%)
Science, technology, and innovation contribution (LOCTI) (1)	Total annual income	N/A	0.50/1/2	N/A
Anti-drug contribution (LOD) (2)	Operating profit	N/A	1/2 (3)	N/A

Notes

1. *Ley Orgánica de Ciencia, Tecnología e Innovación* (LOCTI) *(see below)*.
2. *Ley Orgánica de Drogas* (LOD).
3. 2% in the case of companies that manufacture or import alcohol beverages or tobacco. 1% for companies that employed 50 or more employees.

Science, technology, and innovation contribution

The Law on Science, Technology, and Innovation (LOCTI, by its Spanish acronym), dated 16 December 2010, establishes a mandatory contribution to be paid by companies that obtained, in the previous fiscal year, over TU 100,000 in gross income.

The kind of companies that are required to pay this contribution are stock companies, limited liability companies, partnerships, communities, irregular associations, associations, foundations, and permanent establishments or fixed bases located inside or outside the national territory with current activities in Venezuela.

Contributions established in the LOCTI are as follows:

- Contributions made from companies related to bingos and casinos activities, alcoholic drinks, or tobacco: the companies engaged in activities related to bingos and casinos, alcoholic drinks, or tobacco must contribute annually the equivalent of 2% of gross income.
- Contributions made by private companies engaged in hydrocarbon or mining activities: the companies that are engaged in hydrocarbon activities, including gaseous hydrocarbons, or mining activities, must contribute the equivalent amount of 1% of gross income.
- Contributions made by companies engaged in other economic activities: these companies must contribute annually the equivalent of 0.5% of gross income.
- The company that performs activities with two different percentages will apply the highest one.

The National Fund for Science, Technology, and Innovation (FONACIT) is the entity responsible for the administration, collection, control, verification, and qualitative and quantitative determination of the contributions.

Although the contribution to FONACIT is mandatory, companies can retrieve these resources, providing in the third quarter of each year an annual investment in science, technology, and innovation containing the projects planned for the next year, in line with priority areas and guidelines established by the national authority.

At present, the National Government has given informally the following areas as a priority to which projects should focus on the annual plan:

- Housing and habitat.
- Dynamics, trends, and challenges for urban development.
- Impact of climate change.
- Energy efficiency.

Municipal business licence tax

Companies and business entities, as well as individuals and unincorporated companies, are subject to municipal tax on gross income from industrial or trade activities carried on in the municipality during the fiscal year. The rates range from 0.1% to 10.0%, depending on the activity and the municipality.

Other municipal taxes

Municipalities also tax vehicles, public entertainment, legal bets, and commercial advertisements. There also are various municipal tariffs and fees.

Branch income

Branches of foreign corporations are subject to the same tax rules as Venezuelan corporations. Inter-branch income and deductions must be eliminated. The positive difference between a branch's annual book and taxable income is deemed to be remitted to the branch's head office (branch profits tax). Such remittances are subject to the 34% flat dividend tax (*see Dividend tax in the Income determination section for more information*) regardless of whether there is an actual payment unless the branch can provide proof of reinvestment of its profits for a five-year period. If such proof is established, no deemed remittance is assumed.

A Venezuelan taxpayer has to recognise, annually on an accrual basis, income generated in a company or other legal entity it controls which is located in a jurisdiction with low fiscal taxation (JLFT). Further, investments in JLFT must be declared to the SENIAT.

Income determination

Inventory valuation

Inventories may be valued at cost or the lower of cost or market value. Any method generally accepted for accounting purposes can be accepted for tax purposes.

Capital gains

Capital gains are taxable as ordinary income, and capital losses are deductible from ordinary income. Note that capital losses resulting from the sale of stock, capital reduction, or liquidation of a company are only deductible if they meet one of the following conditions:

- The cost of the capital stock was not in excess of the price quoted on a stock exchange or an amount with a reasonable relationship to the book value of the capital stock.
- The holding period of the investment was for at least two years immediately preceding the date of the sale.
- The stockholder proves that the company selling the shares carried on economic activities for at least two years, preceding the date of sale.

At present, the tax law contains two different rulings relevant to the deductibility of losses incurred through operations on the Venezuelan Stock Market, one of which has

Venezuela

been described above. The second ruling pertains to income obtained from operations on the local market. This income is subject to a final 1% tax that is withheld at the source. Losses in this kind of operation are not deductible against other income. Corporate shareholders not domiciled in Venezuela may not deduct such losses from other taxable income other than dividends arising from Venezuelan sources.

Gains upon liquidation or reduction of capital are taxable to the liquidating entity.

Dividend income

A dividend tax is levied at a flat rate of 34% on the positive difference between book income and tax income generated after 2000. Book income is understood to be that approved at a shareholders' meeting and based on the financial statements prepared pursuant to generally accepted accounting principles (GAAP). To determine the applicable difference, a last in first out (LIFO) method applies. The tax is triggered when dividend is paid and shall be remitted via withholding. Withholding is to be made at the moment a dividend is declared or credited to the account a recipient. The 34% (domestic) rate can be mitigated under tax treaties.

Dividends obtained from companies incorporated or resident abroad or incorporated abroad and resident in Venezuela are taxed at a flat 34% rate.

Stock dividends

Dividends of stock are subject to payment of the aforementioned dividend tax. Moreover, stock dividends are subject to an advanced payment of dividend tax equivalent to 1% of the dividend distributed. Stock dividends have no cost for tax purposes.

Interest income

Unless the debtor can prove otherwise, any sum paid by a debtor in excess of the principal is deemed to be interest. As a general rule, interest is sourced in Venezuela if it is derived from activities carried out in Venezuela or from property located in Venezuela. Specifically, interest is deemed to be derived from activities carried out in Venezuela if the loan principal is used or enjoyed in the country. Interest received by non-resident corporations is therefore subject to Venezuelan income tax if the loan is granted or invested in Venezuela.

Interest paid on loans granted by non-resident financial institutions is subject to a final withholding tax (WHT) at source at a rate of 4.95% on gross income. Interest paid to other non-resident legal entities is subject to tax at a rate of 34% applied to 95% of the gross income.

Foreign income

Extraterritorial income is subject to Venezuelan CIT based on the concept of worldwide income taxation, according to which:

- Resident companies must pay a tax on total income whether from national or foreign source.
- Non-resident companies with PE in Venezuela will pay tax on their income, whether of national or foreign source, attributable to the Venezuelan PE.
- Non-resident companies will pay taxes on their income originated or caused in Venezuela.
- Resident companies as well as non-resident companies with PE in Venezuela may credit the tax paid abroad for earnings of an extraterritorial source against the income tax payable in Venezuela, subject to limitations.

Venezuela

- In general terms, taxation of foreign-source income is ruled by domestic provisions on taxation of territorial-source income. Foreign source dividends are taxable when dividends are received. However, in case of investments located in JLFT, anti-deferral rules in the international fiscal transparency regime apply (*see below*).

Foreign technical assistance and services
Taxable income of foreign taxpayers providing technical assistance or technological services from abroad to individuals or entities that use them in Venezuela or assign them to third parties is presumed to be 30% of gross income for technical assistance fees and 50% of gross income for technological service fees. If the contract does not specify the proportion in which the services are rendered, the law provides that 60% of the technical assistance and technological service fees are deemed to be rendered abroad (i.e. foreign-source), with the other 40% deemed to rendered in Venezuela. The law also provides that 75% of the entire income related to technological services and 25% of that related to technological assistance is rendered abroad if not otherwise specified in the contract. *See the Withholding taxes section for more information.*

International fiscal transparency regime
A regime of international fiscal transparency is created for the purpose of establishing special standards of fiscal control, governing capital investments in countries classified as JLFT, or tax havens. Under certain conditions, a Venezuelan taxpayer may be required to recognise income generated in its JLFT subsidiary on an accrual basis in its tax return.

Inflation adjustment
A system for the adjustment of non-monetary assets, non-monetary liabilities, and shareholder's equity has been established. 'Non-monetary assets' include land, construction, machinery, vehicles, installations, inventories, and investments other than in securities (e.g. bonds and stocks).

There are two phases to the adjustments: (i) initial adjustments and (ii) annual adjustments. Both phases are mandatory adjustments for taxpayers engaged in commercial, industrial, financial, and insurance operations, and in the exploitation of mines and hydrocarbons. The annual adjustment is optional for taxpayers performing non-business activities.

Initial adjustment
The initial adjustment on depreciable fixed assets requires a registration tax of 3% on the amount of the adjustment.

The initial adjustment must be filed at the closing date of any fiscal year ending after 1 January 1993. This adjustment is applicable to all non-monetary assets and non-monetary liabilities.

The initial adjustment is calculated by applying the variations between the CPI of the Caracas Metropolitan Area prevailing in the month in which the non-monetary assets were acquired and the month corresponding to the initial adjustment. Assets acquired before 1950 are deemed to have been acquired in January 1950.

A registry tax of 3% is applied exclusively to the initial revaluation adjustment of depreciable fixed assets. For payment, taxpayers must be registered with the Asset Revaluation Registry, maintained by the tax administration. The resulting tax may be paid in three consecutive annual instalments, beginning on the date of registration.

V

Venezuela

Companies in the pre-operating stage, deemed to end with the first invoice, must determine and pay a 3% tax once the pre-operating period has ended.

Depreciation or amortisation on the revaluation adjustment is allowed, based on the original estimated life of the asset.

Annual adjustment

The annual adjustment is applied each year in determining taxable income. The adjustment factor must be applied to the following balance sheet items at the closing date of the fiscal year. The resulting adjustment will increase or decrease taxable income.

Balance sheet items	Adjustment factor	Tax effect
Non-monetary assets:		
Inventories (including inventories in transit) (2)	Annual variation of the CPI	Increase taxable income
Fixed assets (3)	Annual variation of the CPI	Increase taxable income
Other assets, trademarks, patents, production licenses, other rights, and investments in stock not registered in the *Superintendencia Nacional de Valores* (SNV) and deferred charges (except interest).	Annual variation of the CPI	Increase taxable income
Investments in shares registered in the SNV	Adjusted to the share market value at the end of the year	Increase taxable income
Non-monetary liabilities:		
Deferred credits (except interest)	Annual variation of the CPI	Decrease taxable income
Equity:		
Tax initial equity (1)	Annual variation of the CPI	Decrease taxable income

Notes

1. Tax initial equity is defined as the difference between assets and liabilities at the beginning of the tax year, less accounts receivable from administrators, affiliated, and related companies. In order to determine the initial tax equity, assets not located in the country as well as goods, debts, and liabilities entirely applied to the production of deemed, exempt, or exonerated income are excluded.
2. Inventories are to be valued at historical cost for purposes of applying the CPI. The provisions of the income tax law detail the procedures for applying the CPI. The revaluation of inventories in the tax year is included as part of the initial inventories of the following year.
3. The annual revaluation adjustment of fixed assets is considered part of the cost when the assets are sold.

Net losses arising from the annual adjustment that have not been offset may be carried forward only to the next tax period (one year).

Gains or losses originating from the adjustment of accounts receivable or investments, as well as debts and liabilities in foreign currency or with a re-adjustability clause, are deemed to be carried out during the fiscal year in which they become demandable, collected, or paid, whichever comes first.

Deductions

Depreciation and amortisation
Companies may deduct depreciation of tangible fixed assets and amortisation of intangible fixed assets that are used in the production of income. Depreciation is generally computed on a straight-line basis although any other generally accepted method for accounting purposes is also accepted. Depreciation is not allowed on real estate used as rental property. Depreciation on the stepped-up portion of assets revalued by any method other than the inflation adjustments (*see the Income determination section*) is not permitted. In principle, useful lives of assets shall be consistent with the parameters used in accordance with accounting principles. Although domestic standards provide that tables with depreciation and amortisation rates to be applied by taxpayers may be provided via the Income Tax Rules, such a table has not been provided to date.

Organisational and pre-operating expenses
Domestic income tax regulations do not provide for specific guidance as to the treatment of organisational and pre-operating expenses. The accepted practice is to follow GAAP.

Interest expenses
Interest paid on a loan, the principal of which is invested to generate income, is deductible.

Bad debt
Losses arising from bad debts are deductible provided:

- the loan concerned was granted as part of the taxpayer's business
- the amount of the debt was previously included in the taxpayer's gross revenue (except in the case of loans granted by financial institutions or by employers to their employees), and
- either the debtor and his guarantors are insolvent or the amount of the loan does not justify collection expenses.

Charitable contributions
Deductions for allowable charitable contributions are limited to 10% of taxable income (before deducting contributions) when taxable income does not exceed TU 10,000. When taxable income exceeds TU 10,000, charitable contributions are limited to 8% of taxable income. For oil extraction companies, the deduction is limited to 1% of the pre-contribution tax amount.

Taxes
Municipal, state, and local taxes are deductible in determining taxable income. Corporate taxes are not deductible.

Other significant items
Payments required by the labour law, such as profit sharing (generally between 15 days and four months' salary) and severance indemnity accruals are also deductible. In cases of unjustified dismissals, double severance indemnities must be paid. However, accruals for such additional indemnities are generally not deductible until paid.

Venezuela

Net operating losses

Losses may be carried forward for three years. Losses may not be carried back. Note that losses from inflation adjustments may be carried forward only one year.

Foreign losses may be offset only against foreign profits.

Payments to foreign affiliates

A Venezuelan corporation may claim a deduction for royalties and technical assistance and for technical service fees paid to foreign affiliates, subject to the following conditions:

- The contract is registered within 60 days of execution with the SIEX.
- Income tax payable by the recipient is withheld at the source.
- Transfer pricing requirements are met.
- In the case of technical assistance and technological services fees, the expenses may be deducted if such services cannot be otherwise provided in Venezuela.

Foreign companies domiciled in Venezuela are allowed to deduct royalties paid to parent companies or foreign affiliates. Companies must notify the SIEX of payments made within 60 days (*see the Withholding taxes section for more information*). Branches of foreign companies, however, may not deduct such payments to head offices or related parties.

Group taxation

Group taxation is no longer possible in Venezuela.

Transfer pricing

Taxpayers that carry out operations with related parties abroad must calculate their income, costs, and deductions by applying a defined methodology of transfer pricing. This regime is applicable to imports, exports, and interest paid to recipients abroad as well as technical assistance, technological services, and royalty fees.

Thin capitalisation

Thin capitalisation rules limit the deduction of interest from debt with related parties in excess of a 1:1 debt-to-equity ratio. Under these rules, if the average of a taxpayer's debt (with related and unrelated parties) exceeds the average amount of its equity for the respective fiscal year, the excess debt is treated as equity for income tax purposes. Consequently, the ability to deduct interest on related-party loans may be affected.

Tax credits and incentives

Foreign tax credit

Foreign income tax paid on taxable foreign income may be offset by the payable Venezuelan tax, up to the proportion of Venezuelan payable tax related to foreign-source income. Taxpayers must keep documentation of foreign tax. No carryforward rules are provided for in domestic regulations.

Capital investment

A special 10% investment tax credit is granted on the value of new investments in fixed assets (excluding land) made by those legal entities obtaining income from industrial and agro-industrial activities, construction, electricity, telecommunications, science, technology, and generally any industrial activity that represents an investment in advanced technology. This tax credit may be taken if such new investments are dedicated to effectively improving the productive capacity or creating a new enterprise.

The tourist sector is entitled to a 75% investment tax credit on the amount of new investments. The agricultural sector enjoys an 80% investment tax credit.

An additional 10% tax credit is granted on the amount of investments in assets, programmes, and activities aimed at the preservation and protection of the natural environment.

Investment tax reductions may be carried forward up to three years.

Other incentives

Customs duty incentives are also available, such as drawbacks on the import of materials used for exporting products. This may take the form of a tax refund certificate issued by the Ministry of Finance. The certificate is a negotiable bond and will be accepted by the Treasury Funds Office for payment of national taxes. Determination of the amount of the refund will take into account the import duties effectively paid at the time the materials used in the manufacture of the exported product were received in Venezuela.

Withholding taxes

Resident corporations making certain types of payments must withhold taxes. T2 refers to Tariff 2. These include the following:

	Resident (%) (1)		Non-resident (%)	
	Corporation	Individual	Corporation	Individual
Commissions (2)	5	3	5	34
Dividends (5)	34	34	34	34
Royalties (3)	5	3	T2 on 90	34 on 90
Interest to foreign financial institutions	N/A	N/A	4.95	N/A
Other interest	5	3	T2 on 95	34 on 95
Professional fees	5	3	T2 on 90	34 on 90
Technical assistance fees (3)	5	3	T2 on 30	34 on 30
Technological service fees (3)	5	3	T2 on 50	34 on 50
Real estate rentals	5	3	5	34
Tangible personal property rentals	5	3	5	34
Contractor and subcontractor services	2	1	T2	34
Film and television exhibition rights	5	3	T2 on 25	34 on 25
Insurance and reinsurance premiums	N/A	N/A	10 on 30	N/A
Payments to international media organisations	5	3	T2 on 15	N/A
Acquisition of Venezuela commercial funds	5	3	5	34
Payments to non-domiciled international transportation companies (4)	N/A	N/A	T2 on 5	N/A

V

Venezuela

Notes

1. WHTs constitute prepayments against final tax liabilities as determined by the income tax return when filed.
2. Includes commissions earned in instances other than through a dependent relationship (e.g. employer/employee). Commissions are subject to withholdings in the same manner as salaries and wages.
3. The rates for non-residents are similar to those rates applicable for payments to a non-domiciled corporation not resident in a treaty country and rendering services from abroad with no PE in Venezuela.
4. Excludes payments exempted under international shipping agreements.
5. Withholding applicable only on the excess on profits taxed at the corporate level (*see Dividend income in the Income determination section*).

Tax treaties

There are currently comprehensive treaties for the avoidance of double taxation with the following countries:

Recipient	WHT (%)		
	Dividend	Interest	Royalties
Non-treaty (1)	34	4.95/T2 on 95 (2)	T2 on 90
Austria	5/15 (3)	4.95/10 (4)	5
Barbados	5/10 (5)	5/15 (6)	10
Belarus	5/15 (7)	5	5/10 (8)
Belgium	5/15 (9)	10	5
Brazil (not in force)	10/15 (10)	15	15
Canada	10/15 (11)	10	5/10 (12)
China	5/10 (13)	5/10 (14)	10
Cuba	10/15 (15)	10	5
Czech Republic	5/10 (16)	10	12
Denmark	5/15 (17)	5	5/10 (18)
France	0/5/15 (19)	5	5
Germany	5/15 (20)	5	5
Indonesia	10/15 (21)	10	10/20 (22)
Iran	5/10 (23)	5	5
Italy	10	10	7/10 (24)
Korea	5/10 (25)	5/10 (26)	5/10 (27)
Kuwait	5/10 (28)	5	20
Malaysia	5/10 (29)	15	10
Mexico (not in force)	5	4.95/10/15 (30)	10
Netherlands	0/10 (31)	5	5/7/10 (32)
Norway	5/10 (33)	5/15 (34)	9/12 (35)
Portugal	10	10	10/12 (36)
Qatar	5/15 (37)	5	5
Russia	10/15 (38)	5/10 (39)	10/15 (40)
Spain	0/10 (41)	4.95/10 (42)	5
Sweden	5/10 (43)	10	7/10 (44)
Switzerland	0/10 (45)	5	5
Trinidad and Tobago	5/10 (46)	15	10
United Kingdom	0/10 (47)	5	5/7 (48)
United States	5/15 (49)	4.95/10 (50)	5/10 (51)
Vietnam	5/10 (52)	10	10

Venezuela

Notes

1. Domestic rate applicable to payments to non-resident corporations.
2. The 4.95% rate applies to non-resident financial institutions, and the Tariff 2 on 90% on the gross income in all other cases of non-resident entities.
3. The 5% rate applies when the beneficial owner is a company that holds at least 15% of the capital of the company paying the dividends, and the 15% rate applies in all other cases.
4. The 4.95% rate applies to interest paid to banks, and the 10% rate applies in other cases.
5. The 5% rate applies when the beneficial owner is a company that holds at least 5% of the capital of the company paying the dividends, and the 10% rate applies in all other cases.
6. The 5% rate applies to interest paid to banks, and the 15% rate applies in other cases.
7. The 5% rate applies when the beneficial owner is a company that holds at least 25% of the capital of the company paying the dividends, and the 15% rate applies in all other cases.
8. The 5% rate applies to payments for the use or the right to use copyrights on scientific work, software, trademarks or for the use or the right to use any type of equipment or transportation vehicles. The 10% rate applies in all other cases.
9. The 5% rate applies when the beneficial owner is a company that holds at least 25% of the capital of the company paying the dividends, and the 15% rate applies in all other cases.
10. The 5% rate applies when the beneficial owner is a company that holds at least 20% of the capital of the company paying the dividends, and the 15% rate applies in all other cases.
11. The 10% rate applies when the beneficial owner is a company that holds at least 25% of the capital of the company paying the dividends, and the 15% rate applies in all other cases
12. The 5% rate applies to artistic copyright, computer software, patent, and industrial, commercial, and scientific royalties.
13. The 5% rate applies when the beneficial owner is a company that holds at least 10% of the capital of the company paying the dividends, and the 10% rate applies in all other cases.
14. The 5% rate applies to interest paid to banks, and the 10% rate applies in other cases
15. The 10% rate applies when the beneficial owner is a company that holds at least 25% of the capital of the company paying the dividends, and the 15% rate applies in all other cases
16. The 5% rate applies when the beneficial owner is a company that holds at least 15% of the capital of the company paying the dividends, and the 10% rate applies in all other cases
17. The 5% rate applies when the beneficial owner is a company that holds at least 25% of the capital of the company paying the dividends, and the 15% rate applies in all other cases.
18. The 10% rate applies to royalties, and the 5% rate applies to technical assistance.
19. No withholding applies when the beneficial owner is a company that holds at least 10% of the capital of the company paying the dividends. The 5% rate applies in all other cases. The 15% rate applies to a resident of Venezuela who receives from a company that is a resident of France dividends that would give the right to a tax credit (avoir fiscal) if they were received by a resident of France and shall have the right to a payment from the French Treasury of an amount equal to this tax credit (avoir fiscal), subject to deduction of the tax.
20. The 5% rate applies when the beneficial owner is a company that holds at least 15% of the capital of the company paying the dividends, and the 15% rate applies in all other cases.
21. The 10% rate applies when the beneficial owner is a company that holds at least 10% of the capital of the company paying the dividends, and the 15% rate applies in all other cases.
22. The 20% rate applies to royalties, and the 10% rate applies to technical assistance.
23. The 5% rate applies when the beneficial owner is a company that holds at least 10% of the capital of the company paying the dividends, and the 15% rate applies in all other cases.
24. The 7% rate applies to literary, artistic, and scientific work copyright royalties, and the 10% rate applies in other cases.
25. The 5% rate applies when the beneficial owner is a company that holds at least 10% of the capital of the company paying the dividends, and the 10% rate applies in all other cases.
26. The 5% rate applies to interest in case of banks, and the 10% rate in other cases.
27. The 5% rate applies to royalties paid for the use of industrial, commercial, or scientific equipment. The 10% rate applies in other cases.
28. The 5% rate applies when the beneficial owner is a company that holds at least 10% of the capital of the company paying the dividends, and the 10% rate applies in all other cases.
29. The 5% rate applies when the beneficial owner is a company that holds at least 10% of the capital of the company paying the dividends, and the 10% rate applies in all other cases.
30. The 4.95% rate applies to interest in case of banks and insurance companies. The 10% rate applies to the aforesaid entities when the payment is carried out by banks. The 15% applies in other cases.
31. No withholding applies when the beneficial owner is a company whose capital is totally or partially divided into shares and controls at least 25% of the capital of the company paying the dividends. The 10% rate applies in other cases.
32. The 7% rate applies to patent royalties and to industrial, commercial, and scientific equipment royalties, the 7% rate applies to trademark royalties, and the 10% rate applies to literary, artistic, and scientific work copyright royalties.
33. The 5% rate applies if the beneficial owner is a company that directly controls at least 10% of the company paying the dividends.
34. The 5% rate applies to interest paid to banks, and the 15% rate applies in other cases.
35. The 12% rate applies in case of royalties, and the 9% rate applies to technical assistance.
36. The 12% rate applies in case of royalties, and the 10% rate applies to technical assistance.

Venezuela

37. The 5% rate applies when the beneficial owner is a company that holds at least 10% of the capital of the company paying the dividends, and the 15% rate applies in all other cases.
38. The 10% rate applies when the beneficial owner is a company that holds at least 10% of the capital of the company paying the dividends and has invested in this company not less than the equivalent to USD 100,000. The 10% rate applies in all other cases.
39. The 5% rate applies to interest in case of banks, and the 10% rate in other cases.
40. The 15% rate applies to royalties, and the 10% rate applies to technical assistance.
41. No withholding applies when the beneficial owner is a company whose capital is totally or partially divided into shares and controls at least 25% of the capital of the company paying the dividends. The 10% rate applies in other cases.
42. The 4.95% rate applies to interest in case of banks. The 10% rate applies in other cases.
43. The 5% rate applies when the beneficial owner is a company that holds at least 25% of the capital of the company paying the dividends. The 10% rate applies in all other cases.
44. The 10% rate applies to literary, artistic, and scientific work copyright royalties, and the 7% rate applies in other cases.
45. No withholding applies when the beneficial owner is a company that controls at least 25% of the capital of the company paying the dividends. The 10% rate applies in other cases.
46. No withholding applies when the beneficial owner is a company that holds at least 25% of the capital of the company paying the dividends. The 10% rate applies in other cases.
47. No withholding applies when the beneficial owner is a company that controls at least 10% of the capital of the company paying the dividends. The 10% rate applies in other cases.
48. The 5% rate applies to patent and trademark literary, artistic, or scientific work copyrights, including films, and the 7% rate applies in other cases.
49. The 5% rate applies if the beneficial owner is a company that owns at least 10% of the voting stock of the company paving the dividends. The 15% rate applies in other cases.
50. The 4.95% rate applies to interest to financial institutions (including insurance companies), and the 10% applies in other cases.
51. The 5% rate applies to industrial, commercial, and scientific equipment royalties, and the 10% rate applies in other cases.
52. The 5% rate applies if the beneficial owner is a company that controls at least 10% of the capital of the company paying the dividends. The 10% rate applies in other cases.

The treaties with Brazil and Mexico have been published in the Official Gazette and signed by the contracting parties but have not entered into force since diplomatic notes have not been exchanged.

Treaties with other countries outside the countries listed above are being negotiated.

Tax administration

Tax returns
Final tax returns must be filed within three months following the end of the tax year. The system is one of self-assessment.

Payment of tax
The total amount of tax due must be paid at the time of filing the annual return. Estimated tax payments must be paid consecutively in six monthly instalments. Companies engaged in mining, hydrocarbon exploitation, and related activities must make 12 equal monthly estimated tax payments.

Other issues

Corporate tax calculation

Taxable income (manufacturing company)	VEF	290,000.00
Divided by the value of the TU (VEF 76/1 TU)	VEF	90
Taxable income in TU	TU	3,222.22
Tax thereon:		
Tariff 2: 34%	TU	1,095.56

Venezuela

Subtract (per tax table)	TU	(500)
Total tax	TU	595.56
Less: Withholding taxes	TU	(100)
Less: Advance payments	TU	(100)
Net income tax payable in TU	TU	395.56
Net Income tax payable in VEF *	VEF	35,600.00

* Multiplied by the TU value, (i.e. VEF 90/1TU)

Exchange control

In January 2003, the Venezuelan government and the Venezuelan Central Bank (VCB) restricted the free trade of foreign currency and established an Exchange Control Regime, which is characterised by the following aspects:

- VCB centralises the purchase and sales of foreign currency.
- All foreign currency derived from the export of goods, services, and technology must be sold to the VCB, through the financial system and at the official exchange rate. Exporters are to be registered with the Users Registry and are to consign certain documentation certifying good fiscal status. Likewise, the sale of every foreign currency, introduced in the country for various concepts, including direct foreign investment, to the VCB is mandatory. In such case, said foreign currency is to be registered with the SIEX for re-exportation and remittance purposes. The acquisition of foreign currency for imports is also subject to application for 'Foreign Currency Authorisation', which is subject to certain conditions.
- As of 14 June 2010, a mechanism was put in place that regulates the purchase of securities denominated in foreign currency through the System of Transactions with Securities stated in Foreign Currency (SITME by its Spanish acronym), which is regulated and controlled by the VCB. The aforesaid mechanism is limited to certain transactions, and companies are allowed to purchase up to USD 350,000 per month (i.e. USD 4.2 million per year).

The Law on Foreign Exchange Crimes is in effect, thereby establishing the actions that constitute exchange crimes and their respective penalties. Said penalties may be both criminal and pecuniary.

V

Vietnam

PwC contact

David Fitzgerald
PricewaterhouseCoopers (Vietnam) Limited
Saigon Tower, 4th Floor
29 Le Duan Boulevard
District 1
Ho Chi Minh City
Vietnam
Tel: +84 8 3823 0796
Email: david.fitzgerald@vn.pwc.com

Significant developments

The government has released amended Decrees on special sales tax (SST), value-added tax (VAT), and corporate income tax (CIT) respectively. Subsequently, Circulars providing guidance to these new Decrees on SST and VAT have also been issued by the Ministry of Finance. Their effective dates are as follows:

• Decree 113 and guiding Circular 05 on SST took effect from 1 February 2012.
• Decree 121 and guiding Circular 06 on VAT took effect from 1 March 2012.
• Decree 122 on CIT took effect from 1 March 2012 but applies from the 2012 tax year.

The notable amendments are described below.

CIT amendments

Amounts treated as 'other' taxable income
Other taxable income is treated separately and generally does not qualify for tax incentives.

To be treated as other income	To be treated as operating income
Income from the transfer of (i) projects or (ii) rights to exploit, explore, and process minerals.	Reversal of provisions for inventory devaluation, financial investment loss, bad debts, warranties, and salary.
Income from selling scrap that is not directly related to tax incentivised activities.	
Exchange gains on revaluation of payables dominated in foreign currencies at the end of the fiscal year.	
Gains on revaluation of fixed assets on conversion of a state owned enterprise to a joint stock company	

Determination of taxable income
Income from leasing assets can now be either allocated over the lease term or recognised in full in one tax year. However, in order to determine taxable income during a period eligible for tax incentives, the rental must be allocated over the lease term.

Taxable income includes profits from share swaps upon restructuring or the transfer of securities for non-cash consideration.

Gains on revaluation of land use rights used for capital contribution are spread over a maximum of ten years.

Profits from the transfer of projects or rights to exploit, explore, and process minerals must be separately recorded and profits/losses of these activities are not allowed to be offset against the results of other business activities (but may be set off amongst themselves or against transfers of property).

Non-taxable income
- Income from transferring Certified Emission Reductions (CERs) within one year from the date of issuance.
- Share premiums on the issue of shares.

Deductible expenses
- Foreign exchange losses on revaluation of payables denominated in foreign currency.
- Bonuses and life insurance premiums for employees, subject to documentation requirements.
- Commissions for multi-level marketing will not be subject to the advertising and promotion cap (which normally limits the deduction of advertising and promotion costs to 10% of total other deductible expenditure).

Provisions for severance allowance are not deductible, except for enterprises that are not subject to mandatory unemployment insurance contributions (e.g. those with less than ten employees).

Tax incentives
Taxpayers with tax incentives based on export criteria that have been removed from the end of 2011 may select and notify the tax authorities of alternative CIT incentives and apply them for the remaining period in accordance with either:

- the regulations effective during the period from when the enterprise was incorporated until Decree 24/2007 came into effect (i.e. 21 March 2007) or
- the regulations effective at the time the CIT incentives are revised due to World Trade Organization (WTO) commitments (i.e. 31 December 2011).

Generally, the former will provide more generous incentives.

Foreign contractor withholding tax (FCWT)
Certain FCWT CIT rates are amended as follows:

	Old tax rate (%)	New tax rate (%)
Casino/hotel/restaurant management services	5	10
Interest	10	5
Re-insurance	2	0.1
Drilling rig rental	5	5 *
Financial derivatives	2	2 *

* No change. Previous official letter position elevated to Decree status.

FCWT will not apply to foreign companies brokering sales of services overseas (previously this only applied to brokering sales of goods overseas).

V

Vietnam

VAT amendments

0% VAT on exported services

A number of conditions must be met in order for exported services to enjoy VAT zero-rating. In particular, the foreign customer must not have a permanent establishment (PE) and not be a 'VAT payer' (widely defined) in Vietnam.

Circular 06 now adds a further requirement for a written confirmation by the foreign customer that it does not have a PE and is not a VAT payer in Vietnam in order for exported services to enjoy 0% VAT. No guidance on what form this confirmation should take is given, but, clearly, companies that export services will need to address this issue as soon as possible given that this Circular is now in force.

The Circular also sets out various services provided in Vietnam to foreign customers that are not entitled to 0% VAT, including online payments, digitised services, sports competitions, arts and cultural performance, entertainment, conferences, hotels, training, advertising, and tourism.

New activities not subject to output VAT

A new category was introduced that includes supplies not subject to output VAT, but related input VAT can, nevertheless, be claimed. This category includes the following:

* Goods and services provided outside Vietnam.
* Other financial income, except interest income of non-bank lenders. This exception appears to indicate that interest charged on loans made by onshore non-bank lenders is VAT-able, and interest on loans from overseas non-bank lenders is subject to VAT withholding.
* Fixed assets that are transferred between a parent company and its subsidiaries, or between subsidiaries of the same parent company, and which are used for producing/providing VAT-able goods/services; capital contributions in the form of assets; transfers of assets between dependent units of the same company, or in the case of split/merger/restructuring.
* Collections of compensation/indemnities by insurance companies from third parties.
* Collections on behalf of other parties that are not related to the provision of goods/services (e.g. if company A purchases goods/services from company B, but pays to company C and subsequently company C pays to company B, then the payment from company C to company B is not subject to VAT).
* Commissions earned by (i) agents selling services, including postal, telecommunications, lottery, airlines/bus/ship/train tickets, at prices determined by principals; and (ii) agents for international transportation, airlines and shipping services entitled to 0% VAT; or (iii) insurance agents.
* Commissions from the selling of goods/services not subject to VAT.

New provisions on input VAT

* Input VAT on goods (either purchased or produced by the company itself) that are used as gifts to promote the sale of VAT-able goods/services is creditable.
* Where an invoice supplementing/revising an original invoice is issued, the six month timeframe to claim input VAT now counts from the date on which the amending invoice is issued.
* Input VAT on goods/services purchased by authorised parties is creditable (including pre-operating expenses paid by parent companies).
  This is a welcome development, and will help in a number of scenarios. For example, a company can now claim input VAT on expenses arising during its pre-operating

period, which are paid for by the foreign parent company to local suppliers, as long as a payment authorisation is in place.
* Companies using goods for internal consumption are allowed to claim input VAT credits on these goods if the internal consumption relates to the making of VAT-able supplies.
* Various cases of what constitute payments via the banking system mentioned in official letters are formalised in the Circular.
* Input VAT incurred during a pre-operating period is not creditable if the project terminates before generating revenue from its registered main business activities.

VAT-able value
* For sales of real estate, expenses such as payments to the state budget for land use rights, land rental fee, and site clearance expense can be deducted from the sales price in calculating the VAT-able value.
* For services provided both inside and outside Vietnam, where there is no separation of the revenue relating to the onshore and offshore portions, the VAT-able value of each is calculated based on the ratio of the expenses incurred in Vietnam over the total expenses.

VAT taxable supplies
The definition of VAT taxable supplies is expanded to include sales of assets held as collateral where the borrower is a VAT payer or the ownership of the assets has been transferred to the lender.

VAT-exempt supplies
The definition of VAT-exempt supplies is expanded to include:

* Rediscount of negotiable instruments and other valuable papers.
* Credit card issuance.
* Debt factoring (including selling of debts).
* Management of securities investment companies, services related to securities registered or deposited with the Vietnam Securities Depository, loans granted for margin trading, and advances to sellers of securities.
* Foreign exchange trading.
* Certain public utility services.

Application of VAT 'direct' method
Where there is negative value added from the trading of gold, silver, or precious stones in a period, it can be offset against the positive value added of those activities. Any remaining negative balance can be carried forward to a subsequent period in the same calendar year.

Taxpayers having both gold/silver/precious stone trading and processing activities should declare VAT for both activities under the direct method.

The use of the direct method is no longer permitted for foreign entities or individuals providing goods or services for carrying out prospecting, exploration, development, or exploitation of oil and gas fields. Instead, the Vietnamese customer is required to withhold VAT on their behalf, at a rate to be determined by the Ministry of Finance. Such withheld VAT may be offset against the foreign party's VAT liability where they are VAT registered and file normal VAT returns.

_V_

Vietnam

SST amendments

Out of scope of SST:
Circular 05 supplements conditions for certain goods not subject to SST, including:

- Cars designed by manufacturers to use as ambulances, vehicles transporting prisoners, cars operating in entertainment and sporting areas, etc.
- Air conditioners less than 90,000 BTU installed in transportation vehicles.
- Some specific chemicals (e.g. naphtha, condensate) used as input material for production (excluding fuel production).

In case these specific goods are used for other purposes, they will be subject to SST.

Taxable price
In respect of goods, price for SST calculation is exclusive of SST, VAT, and environment protection tax (EPT) (if any).

Where a manufacturer produces goods subject to SST and sells such goods through an agent, the minimum price for calculation of SST shall be 90% of the average selling price of the agent. However, for automobiles, the agent's average selling price used for this purpose shall exclude the cost of additional equipment and accessories installed at the customer's request.

Where a manufacturer produces goods under a licensing agreement and delivers goods to a branch or representative of an overseas company in Vietnam, the SST price shall be the selling price set by the branch or representative.

Tax credit
Taxpayers producing SST liable goods from SST liable raw materials shall be entitled to claim a credit for the SST amount already paid on raw materials imported or directly purchased from domestic manufacturers.

Taxes on corporate income

Standard rates
All taxes are imposed at the national level. The standard CIT rate is 25%. Enterprises operating in the oil and gas industry will be subject to CIT rates ranging from 32% to 50%, depending on each project.

There is no concept of tax residency for CIT. Business organisations established under the laws of Vietnam are subject to CIT and taxed on worldwide income. 25% CIT shall be applicable to foreign income. There are no provisions for tax incentives for such income.

Foreign organisations/individuals carrying out business in Vietnam without setting up a legal entity in Vietnam and/or having Vietnam-sourced income are considered foreign contractors, irrespective of whether the services are performed inside or outside Vietnam. Payments to foreign contractors are subject to FCWT, which consists of VAT and CIT elements. *See the Withholding taxes section for more information.*

Preferential rates
Preferential CIT rates of 10% and 20% are available where certain criteria are met. *See the Tax credits and incentives section for more information.*

Calculation of taxable profits

Taxable profit is the difference between total revenue, whether domestic or foreign sourced, and deductible expenses (*see the Deductions section*), plus other assessable income.

Taxpayers are required to prepare an annual CIT return that includes a section for making adjustments between accounting profits and taxable profits.

Local income taxes

There are no local, state, or provincial income taxes in Vietnam.

Corporate residence

There is no concept of tax residency for CIT. Enterprises established under the law of Vietnam are subject to CIT in Vietnam. In addition, Vietnam has a broadly worded PE definition.

Permanent establishment (PE)

In Vietnam, a PE is defined as "a fixed place of business through which a foreign enterprise carries out part or the whole of its business or production activities in Vietnam and earns income. The permanent establishment of a foreign enterprise shall include:

- A branch, an operating office, a factory, a workshop, means of transportation, a mine, an oil and gas field, any place relating to the exploitation of natural resources in Vietnam.
- A building site; a construction, installation, or assembly project.
- An establishment providing services including consultancy services through its employees or other persons.
- An agent for a foreign enterprise.
- A representative in Vietnam where [one] has authority to sign contracts under the name of the foreign enterprise, or where [one] does not have authority to sign contracts under the name of the foreign enterprise but regularly delivers goods or provides services in Vietnam."

Foreign enterprises with their PEs in Vietnam shall pay tax on the taxable income earned in Vietnam (irrespective of whether it relates to the PE) and on the taxable income generated out of Vietnam and related to operations of the PEs.

Where a treaty on avoidance of double taxation to which Vietnam is a signatory contains different provisions relating to PE, such treaty shall apply (*see the Withholding taxes section for a list of countries with which such treaties exist*).

Other taxes

Value-added tax (VAT)

VAT is applied to goods and services used for production, trading, and consumption in Vietnam (including goods and services purchased from abroad), with certain exemptions. Depending on the category of goods or services, the VAT rates are as follows:

Vietnam

- A 0% rate applies to exported goods, including goods sold to enterprises without PEs in Vietnam (including companies in non-tariff zones), goods processed for export or in-country export, goods sold to duty free shops, exported services, construction and installation carried out abroad or for export processing enterprises, aviation, marine, and international transportation services.
- A 5% rate applies generally to areas of the economy concerned with the provision of essential goods and services. This includes clean water, fertiliser production, teaching aids, books, foodstuffs, medicine and medical equipment, husbandry feed, various agricultural products and services, technical/scientific services, rubber latex, sugar and its by-products.
- The 10% 'standard' rate applies to activities not specified as exempt or subject to the 0% or 5% rate.

Activities not subject to output VAT
A new category was introduced that includes supplies not subject to output VAT, but related input VAT can, nevertheless, be claimed. This category includes the following:

- Goods and services provided outside Vietnam.
- Other financial income, except interest income of non-bank lenders.
- Fixed assets that are transferred between a parent company and its subsidiaries, or between subsidiaries of the same parent company, and which are used for producing/providing VAT-able goods/services; capital contributions in the form of assets; transfers of assets between dependent units of the same company, or in the case of split/merger/restructuring.
- Collections of compensation/indemnities by insurance companies from third parties.
- Collections on behalf of other parties that are not related to the provision of goods/services (e.g. if company A purchases goods/services from company B, but pays to company C and subsequently company C pays to company B, then the payment from company C to company B is not subject to VAT).
- Commissions earned by (i) agents selling services, including postal, telecommunications, lottery, airlines/bus/ship/train tickets, at prices determined by principals; and (ii) agents for international transportation, airlines and shipping services entitled to 0% VAT; or (iii) insurance agents.
- Commissions from the selling of goods/services not subject to VAT.

Exempt goods and services
There are stipulated categories of VAT exemptions, including transfer of land use rights, various financial services, capital assignments, certain types of insurance, medical services, education, printing/publishing, public transportation, export of unprocessed natural resources, etc.

When a supply cannot be readily classified based on the tax tariff, VAT must be calculated based on the highest rate applicable for the particular range of goods which the business supplies.

Taxpayers must file monthly VAT returns and remit the VAT payable no later than the 20th day of the following month.

Customs duties
Import duty rates are classified into three categories: ordinary rates, preferential rates, and special preferential rates.

Preferential rates are applicable to imported goods from countries that have most-favoured-nation (MFN, also known as normal trade relations) status with Vietnam. The

Vietnam

MFN rates are in accordance with Vietnam's WTO commitments and are applicable to goods imported from other member countries of the WTO.

Special preferential rates are applicable to imported goods from countries that have a special preferential trade agreement with Vietnam.

Import duty exemptions are provided for encouraged projects and goods imported in certain circumstances.

Export duties are charged only on a few items, basically certain natural resources. Rates range from 0% to 30%.

Special sales tax (SST)

SST is a form of excise tax that applies to selected goods and services, such as alcohol, imported automobiles having less than 24 seats, motorcycles, airplanes, boats, petroleum, air-conditioners up to 90,000 British thermal units (BTU), cigarettes, playing cards, discotheques, massages, karaoke, casinos, gambling, golf clubs, and entertainment with betting and lotteries. For goods, SST is charged at the production or importation stage.

The SST rates are as follows:

Products/services	SST rate (%)
Cigar/cigarette	65
Spirit/wine	25 to 45
Beer	45
Automobiles having less than 24 seats	10 to 60
Motorcycle of cylinder capacity above 125cm^3	20
Airplane	30
Boat	30
Petrol	10
Air-conditioners (not more than 90,000 BTU)	10
Playing cards	40
Votive paper	70
Discotheques	40
Massage, karaoke	30
Casinos, jackpot games	30
Entertainment with betting	30
Golf	20
Lottery	15

Property taxes

The rental of land use rights by foreign investors (if not contributed as capital) is, in effect, a form of property tax. It is usually known as land rental, and the range of rates is wide depending upon the location, infrastructure, and the industrial sector in which the business is operating.

Stamp taxes

Certain assets, including houses, land, automobiles and motorcycles, etc., that are subject to registration of ownership are subject to stamp duty. The stamp duty rates vary depending on the asset transferred.

V

Vietnam

Production royalties

Production royalties in the form of a natural resource tax (NRT) are payable in industries exploiting natural resources such as oil and gas, other minerals, forests, fisheries, and natural water. The tax rates vary depending on the natural resource being exploited, ranging from 1% to 40%, and are applied to the production output at a specified taxable value per unit. Various methods are available for the calculation of the taxable value of the resources, including cases where the commercial value of the resources cannot be determined.

Environment protection tax (EPT)

EPT took effect from 1 January 2012. It is an indirect tax applicable to the production and importation of certain goods, including petroleum products. The tax is calculated as an absolute amount on the quantity of the goods.

The tax rates are as follows:

Goods	Unit	Tax range (VND*)
Petrol, oil, grease	Litre/kg	300 to 4,000
Coal	Tone	10,000 to 50,000
HCFC	Kg	1,000 to 5,000
Nylon bags	Kg	30,000 to 50,000
Limited usage chemicals	Kg	500 to 3,000

* Vietnamese dong

The previously stipulated regulations on petrol, oil fee are superseded. Organisations/individuals engaged in petrol/oil trading activities are not required to declare and pay EPT for the petrol/oil volume of which fee was already declared and paid before 1 January 2012.

Branch income

Branches of foreign entities are subject to the same CIT regime as entities incorporated in Vietnam.

Income determination

Inventory valuation

At present, there are no provisions for valuing inventories or determining inventory flows. The tax treatment follows the accounting treatment.

Asset revaluation

Gains from the revaluation of assets for the purposes of capital contribution or transfer upon division, demerger, consolidation, merger, or conversion of business are subject to 25% CIT.

Capital gains

Gains made by a foreign investor on the transfer of an interest (as opposed to shares) in a limited liability company are subject to 25% CIT. The assignee is required to withhold the tax due from the payment to the assignor, and account for this to the tax authorities.

Gains earned by a foreign investor from selling securities (i.e. bonds, shares of public joint-stock companies, irrespective of whether they are listed or non-listed) are subject to CIT at a deemed rate of 0.1% of the sales proceeds. 25% CIT will apply to any gains earned by a foreign company (not incorporated in Vietnam) upon a sale of shares in a non-public joint-stock company.

Dividend income
Dividends received from investments in other companies in Vietnam are from after tax profits and are not subject to CIT.

Interest income
Interest income is subject to 25% CIT and is not entitled to tax incentives (including preferential tax rate and exemption/reduction).

Other significant items
The following other income items are subject to 25% CIT and are not entitled to tax incentives (including preferential tax rate and exemption/reduction):

- Income from transfer of real estate.
- Income from royalty, leasing of assets.
- Income from transfer of assets.
- Income from trading of foreign currency.
- Reversal of provisions, except for reversal of provisions for inventory devaluation, financial investment loss, bad debts, warranties, and salary.
- Collected written off debts.
- Unidentified payables.
- Difference between penalties and compensation for breaching economic contracts.
- Gain from the revaluation of assets.
- Income from the transfer of projects and the rights to exploit, explore, and process minerals.
- Income from selling scrap, which is not directly related to tax incentivised activities.
- Exchange gains on revaluation of payables denominated in foreign currencies at the end of the fiscal year.

Foreign income
Foreign income, under the domestic tax law, is subject to 25% CIT with tax credits available (*see Foreign tax credit in the Tax credits and incentives section*).

Foreign income shall be taxed when earned. There are no provisions for tax deferral or preferential tax rates for foreign income.

....

Deductions

Depreciation and amortisation
Tax depreciation may differ from accounting depreciation. Depreciation in excess of the rates specified in the regulations on tax depreciation is not deductible. These regulations specify maximum and minimum permissible effective lives for various classes of assets, including intangibles. Current straight-line tax depreciation rates are as follows:

Vietnam

Asset	Rates (%)
Buildings	2 to 16.67
Office equipment	10 to 20
Automobiles	3.33 to 16.66
Machinery and equipment	5 to 33.33
Intangible assets	Not more than 5
Goodwill	33.33

Start-up expenses

Pre-establishment expenses (i.e. expenses for setting up a company) and certain expenses (i.e. training, advertising before establishment, costs for the research stage, relocation cost) can be amortised over a period of up to three years from the commencement of operations. In order for pre-establishment and pre-operating expenses to be deductible for CIT purposes, supporting documents to substantiate the fact that these pre-operating expenses were necessarily and legitimately incurred for the establishment of the company should be available.

Interest expenses

Interest on loans corresponding to the portion of charter capital not yet contributed is not deductible.

Interest on loans from non-economic and non-credit organisations exceeding 1.5 times the interest rate set by the State Bank of Vietnam is not deductible.

Bad debt

Provisions for bad debts are deductible if the provision is made in accordance with the guidance by the Ministry of Finance. Certain conditions must be satisfied in order to set up a provision for bad debts (e.g. the debts must be supported by original documentation, confirmation from clients of the overdue amounts, and that the debt is overdue under the terms of an economic contract). In the absence of satisfying the necessary conditions, the provision for bad debts will generally not be deductible until incurred and supported by invoices.

Charitable contributions

Donations are generally non-deductible, except certain donations for education, health care, natural disasters, or building charitable homes for the poor.

Fines and penalties

Administrative penalties and fines are specifically considered non-deductible.

Taxes

Creditable input VAT, CIT, and other fees/charges are not deductible for CIT purposes.

Other significant items

The following other expenditures are specifically stated to be non-deductible:

- Depreciation of fixed assets, which is not in accordance with the prevailing regulations.
- Employee remuneration expenses that are not actually paid or are not stated in a labour contract, collective labour agreement, or the financial regulations of the company.

Vietnam

- Life insurance premiums for employees that are not stated in a labour contract, collective labour agreement, or the financial regulations of the company.
- The portion of costs of raw materials, materials, fuel or goods that are used in excess of the reasonable consumption levels.
- Reserves for research and development (R&D) not in accordance with the prevailing regulations.
- Provisions for stock devaluation, bad debts, financial investment losses, product warranties, or construction work, which are not in accordance with the prevailing regulations.
- Advertising, promotion (except certain items), conferences/parties, commissions, and prompt payment discounts exceeding 10% of total other deductible expenses (this cap is increased to 15% for newly-established enterprises for the first three operating years).
- Unrealised foreign exchange gain/losses due to the revaluation of foreign currency items other than account payables at the end of a financial year.
- Management expenses allocated to PEs in Vietnam by the foreign company's head office, which are not in accordance with the regulations.

For certain businesses (e.g. insurance companies, securities trading, lotteries), the Ministry of Finance provides specific guidance on deductible expenses for CIT purposes.

Net operating losses
Losses may be carried forward fully and consecutively for a maximum of five years. Carryback of losses is not permitted.

Payments to foreign affiliates
There are no special restrictions on the deductibility of royalties, loan interest, and service fees paid to foreign affiliates (except for those paid by branches). However, the payment must be defendable on an arm's-length basis as required by transfer pricing regulations (*see Transfer pricing in the Group taxation section*). Certain contracts for the transfer of technology and foreign loans must be registered with the competent authorities.

Group taxation

There is no provision for any form of consolidated filing or group loss relief in Vietnam.

Transfer pricing
Vietnam has transfer pricing regulations that outline various situations where transactions will be considered as being between related parties and the mechanisms for determining the market 'arm's length' transaction value (e.g. comparable uncontrolled price, cost plus, resale price, comparable profits, and profit split).

Under the wide ranging definition of associated parties, the control threshold is lower than in many other countries (20%), and the definition also extends to certain significant supplier, customer, and funding relationships between otherwise unrelated parties.

Compliance requirements include an annual declaration of related party transactions and transfer pricing methodologies used, which is required to be filed together with the annual CIT return.

Vietnam

Companies that have related party transactions must prepare and maintain contemporaneous transfer pricing documentation.

Thin capitalisation

There are no thin capitalisation requirements in the tax legislation. However, the level of permitted debt funding will be limited by virtue of licensing requirements. The maximum amount of debt funding is the difference between the licensed investment capital and charter capital.

Tax credits and incentives

Foreign tax credit

In respect of Vietnamese enterprises earning income from overseas investment, CIT (or a kind of tax with a nature similar to CIT) paid in a foreign country or paid on behalf by its partner in the country receiving the investment (including tax levied on the dividend) is allowed to be creditable. The credit shall not exceed the CIT amount payable in Vietnam.

The foreign income tax that is entitled to exemption or reduction in accordance with the foreign law shall also be credited.

Inbound investment incentives

Tax incentives are granted based on regulated encouraged sectors and difficult socio-economic locations. The sectors that are encouraged by the Vietnamese government include education, health care, sport/culture, high technology, environmental protection, scientific research, infrastructural development, and computer software manufacture.

The two preferential rates of 10% and 20% are available starting from the commencement of operating activities. When the preferential rate expires, the CIT rate reverts to the standard rate.

Criteria for preferential tax rates are as follows:

- 10% tax rate for 15 years shall be applied to the newly-established enterprises which:
  - operate in regions with specially difficult socio-economic conditions, in economic zones, and high technology zones
  - invest in high technology, science research and technology development, development of water plants, power plants, water supply, and drainage systems; bridges, roads, railways; airports, sea ports, river ports; airfields, stations, and other especially important infrastructure facilities decided by the Prime Minister, or
  - invest in production of computer software.
- 10% tax rate for the duration of operations is available for the income earned from activities in the fields of education/training, vocational training, public health, culture, sport, and environment (socialised fields).
- 20% tax rate shall be applied for 10 years to new enterprises established from investment projects in regions with difficult socio-economic conditions.
- 20% tax rate for the duration of operations is available for the income earned from agricultural service cooperatives and people's credit fund.

Tax holidays

Investors may be considered for tax holidays and reductions. The holidays take the form of a complete exemption from CIT for a certain period beginning immediately after the enterprise first makes profits, followed by a further period where tax is charged at 50% of the applicable rate. However, where the enterprise has not derived profits within three years of the commencement of operations, the tax holidays/tax reduction will start from the fourth year of operation. Criteria for eligibility to these holidays and reductions are set out in the CIT regulations as follows:

- Four years of tax exemption and nine subsequent years of 50% reduction shall be applied to the newly-established enterprises which:
  - operate in regions with specially difficult socio-economic conditions, in economic zones, and high technology zones
  - invest in high technology, science research and technology development, development of water plants, power plants, water supply, and drainage systems; bridges, roads, railways; airports, sea ports, river ports; airfields, stations, and other especially important infrastructure facilities decided by the Prime Minister
  - invest in production of computer software, or
  - operate in the socialised fields and in regions with difficult or especially difficult socio-economic conditions.
- Four years of tax exemption and 50% tax reduction for five subsequent years shall be given to new enterprises operating in the socialised fields and in regions not included in the list of regions with difficult or especially difficult socio-economic conditions.
- Two years of tax exemption and four subsequent years of 50% reduction shall be applied to newly-established enterprises operating in regions with difficult socio-economic conditions.

From 1 January 2012, tax incentives based on export criteria and domestic material usage ratios have been removed. Taxpayers with previously awarded tax incentives based on export criteria may select and notify the tax authorities of alternative CIT incentives and apply them for the remaining period.

Employment incentives

Additional tax reductions may be available for engaging in manufacturing, construction, and transportation activities that employ several female staff and/or ethnic minorities. CIT reduction must correspond with the actual payment for those employees.

Research and Development Fund

Business entities in Vietnam are allowed to set up a tax deductible Research and Development Fund. Enterprises can appropriate up to 10% of annual profits before tax to the fund. Various conditions apply.

CIT reduction and deferral

Eligible small and medium size enterprises (SMEs, as regulated) and labour intensive enterprises engaged in (i) production and processing of agriculture products, forestry and aquatic products, textiles and garments, footwear and electronic components; and (ii) construction/installation of certain infrastructure projects (e.g. water, power, roads, railroads, airports, hospitals, schools) can be entitled to 30% CIT reduction and enjoy a one year deferral of 2011 CIT payments.

However, the incentives are not provided for enterprises earning profits from lotteries, property trading, securities business, finance, banking, insurance or goods/services

Vietnam

subject to special sales tax; SMEs belonging to State Economic Groups and classified as first or special rank; and SMEs which are majority owned by a holding company which is not a SME. In addition, 30% CIT reduction is not allowed to profits from the exploitation and processing of minerals.

The Prime Minster has recently approved a further three month deferral of CIT payments for Quarter I and Quarter II of 2011.

Withholding taxes

Interest
The interest withholding tax (WHT) applied to payments to an overseas lender was reduced from 10% to 5% from 1 March 2012. Interest on pre-1999 loans may be exempt from WHT. Offshore loans provided by certain government or semi-governmental institutions may obtain an exemption from the interest WHT where a relevant double taxation agreement (DTA) or Inter-Government Agreement applies.

Interest earned from bonds (except for tax-exempt bonds) and certificates of deposit are subject to 5% WHT (10% prior to 1 March 2012). The sale of bonds and certificates of deposits are subject to deemed tax of 0.1% of the gross sales proceeds.

Royalties, licence fees, etc.
A 10% royalty WHT applies in the case of payments made to a foreign party for transfers of technology, unless the transfers are contributed as part of legal capital (akin to equity). Transfers of technology are defined very broadly. Certain contracts for the transfer of technology must be registered with the competent authorities.

Management fees and head office charges
WHT applies on management fees and head office charges at the rates applicable to services (*see below*).

Payments to foreign contractors
FCWT on payments to foreign contractors applies where a Vietnamese contracting party (including a foreign-invested enterprise incorporated in Vietnam) contracts with a foreign party that does not have a licensed presence in Vietnam, irrespective of whether the services are provided in Vietnam or overseas.

Foreign contractors can apply to be deduction-method VAT payers if they adopt the Vietnamese accounting system. If accounting records are adequate, the foreign contractor will pay CIT on actual profits, but otherwise on a deemed-profit basis.

For direct (non-deduction-method) foreign contractors, VAT and CIT will be withheld by the contracting party at a deemed percentage of taxable turnover. Various rates are specified according to the nature of the contract performed. For CIT, the WHT rate varies from 0.1% to 10%. For VAT, the effective WHT rate can also range from 3% to 5%. The VAT withheld by the contracting party is an allowable input credit in its VAT return.

A summary of VAT and CIT WHT rates follow:

Types of payment	Effective VAT rate (%)	Deemed CIT rate (%)
Trading: distribution, supply of goods, materials, machinery, and equipment in Vietnam.	Exempt (1)	1
Casino, hotel, and restaurant management services	5	10
Other services	5	5
Services together with supply of machinery and equipment	3	2
Construction, installation (2) without supply of materials or machinery, equipment.	5	2
Construction, installation (2) with supply of materials or machinery, equipment.	3	2
Leasing of machinery and equipment	5	5
Leasing of aircraft, vessels (including components)	Not specified	2
Transportation	3	2
Interest	Exempt	5
Royalties	Exempt	10
Insurance	Exempt	0.1
Transfer of securities	Exempt	0.1
Manufacturing, other business activities	3	2
Financial derivatives	Exempt	2

Notes

1. On the basis that import VAT is paid.
2. Relates to VAT only.

Cross-border leases

A Vietnam-based lessee is required to withhold tax from payments to an offshore lessor. 5% VAT and 5% CIT is applicable to the rental charge if it is an operating lease. If it is a finance lease, the interest portion will be exempt from VAT and subject to 10% CIT.

Tax treaties

The above WHT rates may be affected by a relevant DTA.

Recipient	Interest (%)	Royalties (%)
Algeria (1)	-	-
Australia	10	10
Austria (2, 4)	10	7.5/10
Bangladesh (2, 3)	15	15
Belarus (2, 3)	10	15
Belgium (2, 3, 4)	10	5/10/15
Brunei Darussalam (3)	10	10
Bulgaria (2, 3)	10	15
Canada (4)	10	7.5/10
China (3)	10	10
Cuba	10	10
Czech Republic (3)	10	10
Denmark (2, 3, 4)	10	5/15
Egypt (1)	-	-

V

Vietnam

Recipient	Interest (%)	Royalties (%)
France	0	10
Finland	10	10
Germany (3, 4)	10	7.5/10
Hong Kong (3, 4)	10	7/10
Hungary	10	10
Iceland (3)	10	10
India (3)	10	10
Indonesia (2, 3)	15	15
Israel (2, 3, 4)	10	5/7.5/15
Italy (3, 4)	10	7.5/10
Ireland (2, 3, 4)	10	5/10/15
Japan (3)	10	10
Kazakhstan (1)	-	-
Korea (North) (3)	10	10
Korea (South) (2, 4)	10	5/15
Kuwait (1)	-	-
Laos	10	10
Luxembourg (3)	10	10
Malaysia (3)	10	10
Mongolia (3)	10	10
Morocco (1)	-	-
Mozambique (1)	-	-
Myanmar (3)	10	10
Netherlands (2, 3, 4)	10	5/10/15
Norway (3)	10	10
Oman (3)	10	10
Pakistan (2)	15	15
Philippines (2)	15	15
Poland (2, 3, 4)	10	10/15
Qatar (1)	-	
Romania (2)	10	15
Russia (2)	10	15
Saudi Arabia (1)	-	-
Seychelles (2,3)	10	10
Singapore (2, 3, 4)	10	5/15
Slovakia	-	-
Spain (3)	10	10
Sri Lanka (2, 3)	10	15
Sweden (3, 4)	10	5/15
Switzerland	10	10
Taiwan (2, 3)	10	15
Thailand (2, 3)	10/15	15
Tunisia (1)	-	-
UAE (1)	-	-
Ukraine (3)	10	10
United Kingdom (3)	10	10
Uzbekistan (2)	10	15

Recipient	Interest (%)	Royalties (%)
Venezuela	-	-

Notes

1. The treaty is not yet in force
2. In some cases, the limits set by the treaty are not lower than the present withholding rate under domestic law. Therefore, the domestic rates will apply.
3. Interest derived by certain government bodies is exempt from WHT.
4. Royalty WHT rates vary for certain types of royalties.

Tax administration

Taxable period
The standard tax year is the calendar year. However, different accounting year-ends can be used if approval is obtained from the authorities.

Tax returns
The annual final CIT return and the audited financial statements must be filed within 90 days from the end of the financial year.

Payment of tax
CIT shall be declared and paid provisionally on a quarterly basis (based on actual revenues and expenses of each quarter). Quarterly CIT returns and payment must be made no later than the 30th day of the next quarter.

Final payment of CIT is due with the final CIT return (i.e. the 90th day of the following financial year).

Audit cycle
Tax audits are carried out regularly and often cover a number of tax years. Prior to an audit, the tax authorities send the taxpayer a written notice of time and scope of the audit inspection.

Statute of limitations
The general statute of limitations for imposing tax administration penalties is two years. The tax authorities can collect under declared and unpaid tax at any time.

Penalties
There are detailed regulations setting out penalties for various tax offences. These range from relatively minor administrative penalties through to tax penalties amounting to various multiples of the additional tax assessed.

In practice, imposition of penalties has been arbitrary and inconsistent. However, in recent periods there has been a much tougher stance adopted by the tax authorities. Hence, where tax is paid late (e.g. as a result for of a tax audit investigation), there is a significant likelihood of penalties being imposed. Notably, where tax adjustments are made at a tax audit, any resulting additional taxable profits are not eligible for any CIT incentives to which a company may be entitled.

V

Vietnam

....

Other issues

Foreign investment restrictions

In several fields, foreign investment will not be licensed or will only be licensed under special conditions. The List of Conditional Investment Sectors include television, production and publishing cultural products, telecommunication, transportation by all means, cigarette production, exploring and processing natural resources, real-estate business, education, and medical services and distribution.

Exchange controls

All buying, selling, lending, and transfer of foreign currency need to be made through credit institutions and other financial institutions authorised by the State Bank of Vietnam (SBV).

Outflow of foreign currency by transfer is authorised for certain transactions such as payments for imports and services abroad, refund of loans contracted abroad and payment of interest accrued thereon, transfer of profits and dividends, and revenues from transfer of technology.

All monetary transactions in Vietnam must be undertaken in Vietnamese dong. Exceptions are applicable to payments for exports made between principals and their agents, and payments for goods and services purchased from institutions authorised to receive foreign currency payments such as for air tickets, shipping and air freight, insurance, and international communications.

Forms of doing business

According to the Law on Enterprises, a foreign-invested enterprise may be established as either a single member limited liability or a limited liability with more than one member, a joint-stock company, or a partnership.

Intellectual property

Intellectual property rights are protected by the Civil Code (1995 and 2005), the Law on Intellectual Property (2005), and a host of subordinate legislation.

Vietnam is signatory to the Paris Convention, the Madrid Agreement on International Trademark Registration, and the Patent Cooperation Treaty and is a member of the World Intellectual Property Organisation. Vietnam has entered into an agreement on copyrights with the United States. According to the Vietnam-United States (US) Bilateral Trade Agreement, Vietnam is further under the obligation to adhere to the Berne Convention.

Zimbabwe

PwC contact

Manuel Lopes
PricewaterhouseCoopers
Arundel Office Park, Building 4
Norfolk Road
Mount Pleasant
Harare
Zimbabwe
Tel: +263 4 33 8362-8
Email: manuel.lopes@zw.pwc.com

Significant developments

Zimbabwe's annual budget presentation was held on 24 November 2011 by the Minister of Finance, the Honorable Tendai Biti, and the proposed changes have been promulgated into law.

The announcements relating to corporate tax can be summarised as follows.

Value-added tax (VAT)

Beginning 1 January 2012, it is mandatory for all registered operators with an annual turnover exceeding 240,000 United States dollars (USD) to use electronic fiscal registers (EFRs) that can be linked to the Zimbabwe Revenue Authority (ZIMRA). Penalties of up to USD 25 per day per point of sale may be imposed.

Customs duties

25% surtaxes have been imposed on a number of imported goods (including footwear, clothing, and foodstuffs) in order to protect the local manufacturing sector.

Corporate income tax (CIT)

There have been no significant CIT developments in Zimbabwe during the past year.

Taxes on corporate income

The corporate tax rate for companies (other than mining companies with special mining leases, but including branches) continues at 25.75%. This rate includes a base rate of 25% plus a 3% AIDS levy.

Zimbabwe presently operates on a source-based tax system. This means that income from a source within, or deemed to be within, Zimbabwe will be subject to tax in Zimbabwe unless a specific exemption is available. The specific circumstances of a transaction should always be considered to determine whether the transaction gives rise to taxation in Zimbabwe.

Income earned by foreign companies from a source within, or deemed to be within, Zimbabwe will be subject to tax in Zimbabwe. In such a case, one should determine whether the foreign entity is obliged to register a local entity. A company is required to register a branch if it has established a place of business or is otherwise considered to be trading in Zimbabwe. A local subsidiary company may be registered as an alternative to a branch operation.

Z

Zimbabwe

Non-residents who do not have a place of business in Zimbabwe may, however, be subject to withholding tax (WHT). *See the Withholding taxes section for additional details.*

Note that Zimbabwe is currently considering a move to a residence-based tax system.

Local income taxes
There are no local income taxes payable in Zimbabwe.

Corporate residence

Currently, the Zimbabwean tax system is based on source and not on residency. Zimbabwe is moving towards a residence-based taxation system, but the details are still to be announced. Income derived, or deemed to be derived, from sources within Zimbabwe is subject to tax.

Source is the place where income originates or is earned, not the place of payment. If goods are sold pursuant to a contract entered into within Zimbabwe, the source of income is deemed to arise in Zimbabwe, regardless of the place of delivery or transfer of title.

Certain types of income arising outside Zimbabwe may, in the hands of a domestic company, be deemed to arise in Zimbabwe and be taxed as such. Examples include interest and certain copyright royalties arising outside Zimbabwe. Where the income is deemed to be from Zimbabwe, relief of the foreign tax suffered, up to a maximum of the Zimbabwe tax, may be allowed as a tax credit.

Permanent establishment (PE)
In the event that Zimbabwe has entered into a double taxation agreement with the country where the foreign company resides, the entity will only be taxable in Zimbabwe if it operates through a PE, which, in most cases, includes a fixed place of business. The establishment of a local entity or branch will usually create a PE, although the provisions of the related tax treaty should be considered. If a PE exists, only the portion of the income attributable to the PE will be subject to tax in Zimbabwe.

Otherwise, and except for the PE concept embodied in the tax treaties, corporate residence is of little tax significance.

Other taxes

Value-added tax (VAT)
VAT is a transaction tax, and the implications will vary for different transactions. Some transactions are taxed at a rate of 15% or 0% while other transactions are exempt from VAT. Input tax deductions may be claimed, subject to certain provisions. Advice on VAT implications of specific transactions related to corporate operations should be obtained prior to execution of transactions.

VAT shall be levied on every taxable supply by a registered person. A taxable supply means any supply of goods or services in the course or furtherance of a taxable activity. A taxable activity means any activity that is carried on continuously or regularly in Zimbabwe which involves the supply of goods or services for consideration.

VAT is payable on all imports for home consumption into Zimbabwe, subject to certain exemptions (e.g. in terms of a technical assistance agreement, donations to the state, goods of which the local supply is zero-rated). Import VAT is payable on the import value plus the applicable customs duty.

A company/branch is required to register for VAT if it supplies goods or services on a regular basis for consideration and if its taxable supplies (standard-rated and zero-rated supplies) exceed USD 60,000 in any 12-month period.

A registered VAT vendor is entitled to deduct input tax credits paid in the course of taxable supplies made to such person, provided that a tax invoice is available to support the input tax deduction. It is also important to take note of deemed input tax deductions and prohibited input deductions. Import VAT paid may only be deducted as input tax if the import was in furtherance of a taxable activity and the required documentation (e.g. stamped customs entries) is held by the importer.

VAT returns are due by the 25th day following the month to which the VAT relates.

Beginning 1 January 2012, it is mandatory for all registered operators with an annual turnover exceeding USD 240,000 to use EFRs that can be linked to ZIMRA. Penalties of up to USD 25 per day per point of sale may be imposed.

Customs duties

Zimbabwe is a member of the Southern African Development Community (SADC) as well as the Common Market for Eastern and Southern Africa (COMESA). Customs duties are payable according to the general customs tariffs that are legislated for in Zimbabwe. Preferential duty rates apply on imports from SADC or COMESA countries, while goods may be imported free of customs duties from Namibia in terms of the Zimbabwe-Namibia Free Trade Agreement.

25% surtaxes have been imposed on a number of imported goods (including footwear, clothing, and foodstuffs) in order to protect the local manufacturing sector.

A security deposit is required by Customs on all temporary importations to cover import VAT and customs duties (if applicable).

It is possible to import goods that are subject to customs duties into registered Customs' bonded warehouses, where goods are kept for later use. In this case, the payment of duties may be deferred until the goods are taken out of the bonded warehouse for home consumption or acquitted if the goods are subsequently exported.

Excise duties

Excise duties are levied on local production of excisable products and are included on most excisable products imported from other countries. Examples of the excise products and applicable rates include the following:

- Cigarettes: 40% + USD 5 per 100.
- Spirits: USD 2 per litre.
- Wine: USD 0.50 per litre.

Excise and fuel levies are also levied on petrol, diesel, and illuminating kerosene.

Z

Zimbabwe

Property taxes

Property taxes are levied by cities, towns, and rural councils. Each of these bodies conducts periodic valuations of the properties in their area and annually set out a 'rates schedule' based on a percentage of the valuations. These may alter each year depending upon the entities budgetary requirements for funds. Valuations of the properties are usually based on estimates as there are very few qualified property valuators operating in Zimbabwe at present.

Transfer duty

Transfer duty is payable on the acquisition value of property acquired at the following rates:

Value of the property (USD)	Rate of transfer duty
0 to 5,000	1%
5,001 to 20,000	2% of the value above 5,000
20,001 to 100,000	3% on the value above 20,000
100,001 and above	4% of the value above 100,000

Transfer duty is normally payable by the buyer, but the agreement for the sale of the property will determine the person liable to pay these costs. In addition, conveyance costs of up to 3% (plus 15% VAT) must be added on.

Stamp duty

Certain transactions may attract stamp duty. The amount of stamp duty payable will differ and will be based on the nature of every individual transaction.

The basic transactions can be summarised as follows:

Transaction	Stamp duty
Bonds	0.4% (USD 0.40 for every USD 100 or part thereof)
Brokers notes - purchase of securities	0.25% (USD 0.25 per every USD 100 or part thereof)
Brokers notes - purchase/sale of any movable property other than a security	0.10% (USD 0.10 per every USD 100 or part thereof)
Brokers notes - purchase/sale of any immovable property	1% (USD 1.00 per every USD 100 or part thereof)
Off market share transfer instruments	2% or USD 2
Cheques	0.05% (USD 0.05)

Tax advice should be obtained for major transactions in respect of the transactions mentioned above in order to ensure that the correct stamp duty implications are considered.

Capital gains tax

It should be noted that capital gains tax is payable in Zimbabwe on the disposal of immovable property or shares that are held in listed (on the Zimbabwean Stock Exchange) or unlisted companies at the following rates:

Acquired pre-February 2009

- Listed securities: 1% of proceeds.

- Property: 5% of proceeds.
- Unlisted securities: 5% of proceeds.

Acquired post-February 2009
- Listed securities: 1% of proceeds.
- Property: 20% of capital gain.
- Unlisted securities: 20% of capital gain.

Branch income

Branch income that is received or has accrued from a source within, or deemed to be within, Zimbabwe is taxable in Zimbabwe in terms of the normal corporate tax rules.

A branch is regarded as an extension of its foreign head office. A branch may therefore not deduct fees paid to its foreign head office (unless a tax treaty makes provision for such deduction) as it is argued that a branch cannot transact with itself. Reimbursement of actual expenses may, however, be deducted, subject to the normal deduction rules.

A 15% WHT is imposed on any payments made in respect of head office charges.

The amount of fees charged by the head office to the Zimbabwe branch is also subject to a limitation, usually based on a maximum of 1% of total expenditure (excluding the charge itself and any capital allowances). Exchange control regulations also limit the remittability of administration and management fees to 2% of turnover.

Income determination

The Zimbabwe Income Tax Act (Act) tax base for CIT is taxable income rather than profits. The source and nature of the income determines whether the amount is taxable or not. In addition to amounts received or accrued from actual Zimbabwean sources, there are deeming provisions that bring income from foreign sources into Zimbabwean taxable income.

In general, all receipts from a Zimbabwe source are taxed, excluding amounts that are proven by the taxpayer as being capital receipts. Most expenditure items and some specified exemptions are deductible against income. Capital expenditure is generally not deductible, with amounts on specific items being deductible by way of annual allowances spread over a period.

Inventory valuation
The legislation permits three methods of inventory valuation: historic cost, cost of replacement, or net realisable value. Standard cost based on first in first out (FIFO) is normally used for accounts valuations and is an accepted basis for tax purposes. Last in first out (LIFO) is not permitted for tax or for accounting purposes. The tax valuation may differ from the accounting valuation; this is a rare occurrence in Zimbabwe but is acceptable.

Capital gains
See Capital gains tax in the Other taxes section.

Z

Zimbabwe

Dividend income
Dividends received from Zimbabwe incorporated companies are tax exempt. When received from non-Zimbabwe companies, they are taxed at a flat rate of 20%; however, relief is granted by allowing any foreign tax suffered as a tax credit.

Interest income
Interest accruing from 'financial institutions' is subject to a 15% WHT and thereafter is exempt from CIT (the WHT becomes a final tax). Interest from other local or foreign sources is included in gross income and is taxed at the normal CIT rate. Relief will be granted for any foreign tax paid, up to the maximum Zimbabwe tax rate.

Partnership income
The partnership itself is not taxed directly; however, the taxable income of the partnership is calculated in the same way as corporate income and is then allocated amongst the partners in accordance to their agreed profit sharing ratios. This income is taxed in their hands at the basic CIT rate.

Rent/royalties income
Rents and royalties are generally treated as normal taxable income and are taxed at the basic CIT rate. Rent arising in respect of land and buildings situated outside of Zimbabwe, however, is exempt from local tax.

Foreign income
Where income (including business profits) is deemed to be from a Zimbabwe source, it will form a part of the local company's taxable income and will be subject to tax at the basic CIT rate. Relief in respect of foreign taxes suffered will be granted unless it is clear that the true source of the income is, in fact, Zimbabwe.

Deductions

The Act makes provisions for specific deductions. Some of the deductions, such as the deduction of foreign exchange losses, development and exploration costs, hire purchase allowances, and manufacturing allowances can be more complex.

Capital allowances
The cost (including finance charges) of machinery, implements, and other articles used by the taxpayer in the production of income is deductible in four equal annual allowances. No apportionment is required where the asset was held for less than 12 months.

Industrial buildings (including hotels) constructed and used by the taxpayer in the production of income qualify for an initial allowance of 25% of construction cost in the year they enter service. Thereafter, an annual allowance of 25% is deductible for each year following the year of construction. Additions to existing buildings (not alterations or repairs) qualify for the same deductions. It is important to note that the allowance is calculated on the cost of construction and not the cost of acquisition. In the latter case, the allowances are set at 5% of the cost.

A mining exploration expenditure incurred before commencement of production is deductible in full in the first year of production against income derived from the mine. Subsequent development expenditure is presently written off in the year expended. Note that this aspect of Zimbabwe's mining legislation is currently under review.

Capital allowances may also be deducted with respect to patents, trademarks, and leasehold improvements.

A recovery or recoupment of allowances previously claimed should be included in the gross income of a taxpayer in the event that the allowance is recovered or recouped by way of disposal. The recoupment is presently calculated on the capital allowances previously granted.

Goodwill
Goodwill is not deductible for tax purposes in Zimbabwe.

Start-up expenses
Start-up expenses may be deducted if incurred within 18 months of commencement of business and not considered to be capital in nature.

Interest expenses
Zimbabwe has thin capitalisation rules based on a 3:1 debt-to-equity ratio. A portion of the overall interest may be disallowed if this ratio is exceeded.

Bad debt
Bad debts written off may be claimed, but not a provision for bad debts.

Charitable contributions
Donations (with varying maximum limits) made to specified charities and educational bodies may be claimed.

Entertainment expenses
Entertainment expenses are not deductible for tax purposes.

Fines and penalties
Fines and penalties are not deductible for tax purposes.

Net operating losses
Assessed tax losses may be carried forward (but not backwards) for up to six years, provided the company continues to trade. This restriction does not apply to mining companies. Tax laws do not allow for losses to be transferred to other group companies, and anti-avoidance provisions may be triggered by transactions designed to transfer or exploit assessed losses.

Assessed losses are reduced in the event of a compromise agreement with creditors.

Payments to foreign affiliates
The law prohibits the deduction of amounts incurred in excess of specified limits in respect of management and general administration expenses, as well as interest. This applies to branches or subsidiaries of both local and foreign companies.

The limit on management and general administration expenses is based on such expenses exceeding 1% and 0.75% respectively for a company already in production and prior to production of total tax-deductible expenses.

Zimbabwe

Group taxation

No taxation of combined operations is allowed in Zimbabwe, including where operations are conducted by more than one company.

Transfer pricing
No detailed transfer pricing legislation is currently in place in Zimbabwe. The law does, however, allow the Commissioner General to substitute a new sales price for a transaction in which the Commissioner General considers the declared sales price to be too high or low.

Thin capitalisation
The limit on the deductibility of interest is based on a company incurring interest charged by a subsidiary, a fellow subsidiary, or a holding company when the debt-to-equity ratio exceeds 3:1.

Tax credits and incentives

It has been announced by the Minister of Finance that Zimbabwe is moving away from taxation incentives; however, the following are still available.

Note that this is a high-level summary, and certain conditions should be met in order to utilise these incentives.

Person for whom incentive is available and duration of incentive	Tax incentive	Tax treatment for normal taxpayers
Taxpayers operating at designated growth point areas.	The capital allowance is calculated as 25% of the cost of construction of a commercial or industrial building in growth point areas in the year when the building enters service and 25% during the three years that follow the year of construction.	Capital allowances are calculated as 25% of the cost of construction of industrial building in the year when the building enters service and 25% during the three years that follow the year of construction.
Taxpayers operating at designated growth point areas.	Deduction of an investment allowance at 15% on cost of specified assets.	No investment allowance granted.
For all taxpayers in build, own, operate, and transfer (BOOT) or build, operate, and transfer (BOT) arrangements.	First five years: Taxed at 0%. Second five years: Taxed at 15%. Thereafter: Taxed at normal rate.	Taxed at 25%.
Exporting taxpayers.	An additional allowance of 100% of cost incurred in an export country in order to export Zimbabwean goods to such country may be deducted.	Export expenditure incurred is deductible for tax purposes.
For all manufacturing taxpayers exporting 50% or more of output (by volume).	Taxed at a reduced rate of 20%.	Taxed at 25%.
Mining company holding a special mining lease.	Taxed at a reduced rate of 15%.	Taxed at 25%.

Person for whom incentive is available and duration of incentive	Tax incentive	Tax treatment for normal taxpayers
Operator of a tourist facility in a tourist development zone.	First five years: Taxed at 0%. Thereafter: Taxed at normal rate.	Taxed at 25%.
Industrial park developer.	First five years: Taxed at 0%. Thereafter: Taxed at normal rate.	Taxed at 25%.

Withholding taxes

WHTs are applicable where dividends and royalties or similar payments are declared or distributed to non-Zimbabwean residents (and Zimbabwean residents in some instances).

Dividends
Dividends declared by a Zimbabwean company to a non-resident holding company will be subject to non-resident shareholders tax (NRST), a WHT. NRST is payable at a rate of 15% unless treaty relief is available. Dividends from companies listed on the Zimbabwe Stock Exchange have a rate of 10%. NRST is payable within ten days after declaration of the dividend.

Royalties or similar payments
WHT on royalties are payable once a Zimbabwean company pays a royalty to a non-Zimbabwean resident. WHT is levied at a rate of 15% and is payable within ten days of the date of payment.

A royalty includes payment for the use or right to use any patent or design, trademark, copyright, model, pattern, plan, formula or process, or any other property or right of a similar nature. It also includes the imparting of any scientific, technical, industrial, or commercial knowledge or information for use in Zimbabwe. The nature of the amount payable should therefore be carefully considered in order to determine whether the relevant amount represents a royalty.

Fees
Fees are defined to include amounts that are technical, managerial, administrative, or consultative in nature; costs are paid externally. There are some exceptions, but the definition is broad and brings in most costs that may be charged to a Zimbabwean person.

WHT is levied at a rate of 15% and is payable within ten days of the date of payment.

Interest
WHT of 15%, calculated on the gross amount of interest, is payable on interest accruing to any person resident in Zimbabwe. This applies to interest arising from a registered banking institution or unit trust scheme. The tax withheld is a final tax, and the financial institution is responsible to withhold the tax.

Non-resident investors, however, are exempt from any WHT on interest.

Z

Zimbabwe

Summary of WHT payable

The non-residents WHT rates and treaty relief for Zimbabwean double tax agreements can be summarised as follows. It should be noted that the tax treaties contain certain requirements that should be met before the reduced tax rate may be applied.

The definitions of dividends, royalties, and interest in the various treaties should also be considered.

Recipient	Dividends (%)	Interest (%)	Royalties (%)	Fees (%)
Zimbabwe tax legislation	15*	15**	15	15
Bulgaria	10	N/A	10	10
Canada	10	N/A	10	10
France	10	N/A	10	10
Germany	10	N/A	7.5	7.5
Malaysia	10	N/A	10	10
Mauritius	10	N/A	15	15
Netherlands	10	N/A	10	10
Norway	15	N/A	10	10
Poland	10	N/A	10	15
South Africa	15	N/A	15	15
Sweden	15	N/A	10	10
United Kingdom	5	N/A	10	10

* Applies to unlisted companies. The rate for companies listed on the Zimbabwe Stock Exchange is reduced to 10%.

** Resident persons have a 15% WHT on interest arising from financial institutions. Interest from other sources is taxed at the corporate tax rate.

'N/A' means that the provisions of the tax treaty limited the rate to a rate that is higher than the local Zimbabwean rate. It should be noted that a treaty can only provide tax relief and cannot impose a higher tax rate.

These are payable within ten days of the date of distribution or accrual.

Zimbabwe has either negotiated, or is currently negotiating, tax treaties with the following countries:

- Botswana
- Democratic Republic of the Congo
- Indonesia
- Iran
- Jamaica
- Namibia
- Serbia and Montenegro
- Seychelles
- Tanzania
- Tunisia
- Zambia

Tax administration

Taxable period

The tax year end is 31 December each year. Applications may be made for a different year-end if good reasons are given (e.g. to comply with the international group year-end). In the first year of trade, a longer or shorter period than 12 months may be accepted to tie in with a future year end.

Tax returns

The CIT return is due by 30 April in the following tax year.

Payment of tax

Zimbabwe regulates the payment of CIT on four dates during the course of the current tax year; these are referred to as Quarterly Payment Dates (QPDs). The first payment of 10% is due by 25 March of the respective tax year. The second payment of 25% is due by 25 June of the respective tax year. The third payment of 30% is due by 25 September of the respective tax year. The fourth payment of 35% is due by 20 December of the respective tax year.

All taxes are expected to have been paid by the 25th day of December. If there is an adjustment after the year end accounts have been finalised, a top-up payment must be made. There is no set date for this. However, in practice, this payment should not be more than 10% of the annual tax liability. ZIMRA often imposes a 10% per annum interest charge on any underpayments of QPDs.

WHT payments are due within ten days from the date of distribution or accrual.

Audit cycle

Tax audits do not, at present, have a set cycle; however, the aim is to establish a three year cycle in the future.

Statute of limitations

The statute of limitations is generally three years unless ZIMRA considers that there is fraud or misrepresentation involved. In those circumstances, there is no set limit on how far back ZIMRA can go, but they usually do not go beyond six years in practice.

Topics of focus for tax authorities

ZIMRA is focused on ensuring that all compliance issues are in order and that VAT and payroll taxes have been correctly calculated.

Anti-avoidance

Please note that Zimbabwe legislation contains basic anti-avoidance sections that empower the Commissioner General to disregard the implications of a transaction or scheme if it can be proven that:

- such a transaction or scheme had been entered into to avoid or postpone the payment of any duty or levy imposed by the Zimbabwe Income Tax Act
- it was entered into or carried out by means or in a manner that would not normally be employed in the entering into or carrying out of a transaction, operation, or scheme of the nature of the transaction, operation, or scheme in question, or
- it has created rights or obligations that would not normally be created between persons dealing at arm's length under a transaction, operation, or scheme of the nature of the transaction, operation, or scheme in question.

The Commissioner General may, at the Commissioner General's sole discretion, impose this legislation on any transaction or scheme, which will place the burden of proof on the taxpayer to prove that any/all of the requirements noted above will not be applicable to the transaction or scheme.

Z

Zimbabwe

Other issues

Exchange control

Zimbabwe has been operating a multi-currency system since February 2009. The Zimbabwe dollar (ZWD) was demonetarised effective April 2009. This has had a significant impact on the country's exchange control regulations.

The Exchange Control Handbook in Zimbabwe is not available to the public; only banking institutions have access to these regulations.

Transactions that involve the transfer of funds to countries outside Zimbabwe are generally subject to bank approval.

The issue of shares in a Zimbabwe company to persons residing outside of Zimbabwe requires specific exchange control approvals. Under recent legislation, a limit of 49% is available for non-residents. A 51% local shareholding by indigenous persons is a requirement. Applications may be made for increased levels; each case will be decided on its own merits.

Global Tax
Contacts

Global Tax

PwC is the leading
provider of tax services
worldwide

J. Richard Stamm
Global Vice Chairman, Tax
+1 646 471 1035
rick.stamm@us.pwc.com

John M. Kelly
Global Tax Chief Operating Officer
+353 1 792 6307
john.m.kelly@ie.pwc.com

Frits Litjens
Global Tax Service Networks
and Markets Leader
+31 88 792 15 04
frits.litjens@nl.pwc.com

John Preston
Global Leader, Tax Policy and
Administration
+44 20 7804 2645
john.preston@uk.pwc.com

The increasing Tax burden is one of the most important concerns of
CEOs[1], driving the adoption of proper internal controls and robust
financial reporting processes to satisfy tax authorities, regulators and
other stakeholders. At the same time, tax authorities worldwide are
concerned with ensuring both increased compliance amongst taxpayers,
and that their fiscal policies are not overtaken by global business and
economic developments.

[1] CEO Survey 2012 - http://www.pwc.com/gx/en/ceo-survey/key-findings/business-risk.jhtm.

PwC is the leading provider of tax services worldwide both in terms of the size and scope of our tax practice and our reputation[2]. Clients engage us because we combine a strong understanding of their business and economic environments with specialist tax knowledge in hundreds of national and local jurisdictions across the globe. As tax codes become increasingly complex and tax planning more controversial, we help companies to:

- identify and manage tax risks,
- understand and meet their compliance obligations,
- implement tax strategies that complement their business and operational objectives,
- resolve disagreements with tax authorities when they arise, and
- manage tax accounting and reporting issues and design of best in class tax functions.

The advice we provide to clients is based on our Global Tax Code of Conduct, which guides the way as we help organizations think through the legal basis for their planning and the reputational issues that may result. In difficult economic times when companies are focused on paying their fair share of taxes as efficiently as possible and governments need to collect the maximum amount of tax revenue, we look forward to being a productive participant in these discussions.

We take pride in our role as an essential and productive part of global tax administration and compliance. Our policy specialists advise regulators, governments, corporations, and supra-national bodies worldwide on the technical and practical aspects of developing and implementing tax policy initiatives. We lead the debate with tax authorities and governments around the world, changing the way we all think about tax.

[2] The Global Tax Monitor recognises PwC as the leading tax adviser globally, by reputation, with a very strong lead over the competition. These results are based on the year-ending Q1 2012 figures, with a sample size of 3,297 primary buyers of tax services globally.

Launched in 2000, the Global Tax Monitor (GTM) is an independent survey conducted by research agency TNS, that examines the competitive position of the top firms in the tax advisory market — globally, regionally, nationally and on an industry basis. It provides a comprehensive measure of firm reputation, client service and brand health, gained currently from just over 3,000 telephone interviews annually with key decision makers (CFOs and Tax Directors) in 33 key markets.

Human Resource Services

One of the world's largest human resource advisory networks

Global Leader, Human Resource Services
Michael Rendell
+44 20 7212 4945
michael.g.rendell@uk.pwc.com

Global Leader, International Assignment Services
Peter Clarke
+1 203 539 3826
peter.clarke@us.pwc.com

Employees are probably your organisation's greatest asset and your biggest challenge. The PwC Human Resource Services (HRS) network helps you create value by helping you actively manage your people. We have one of the world's largest human resource (HR) advisory networks with solid grounding in areas such as HR transformation, compensation, benefits, pensions, HR transactions, labour law, HR data metrics and deploying talent around the world. We can put together the team that is right for you to give you all the support you need. And our 6,000 professionals in over 100 countries follow the same multi-disciplinary approach to people management to give you the consistency that is so important when working across borders.

Human Resource Services

Albania	Loreta Peci	+355 4 2245 254	loreta.peci@al.pwc.com
Algeria	Karine Lasne	+33 6 08 33 1657	karine.lasne@fr.landwellglobal.com
Angola	Pedro Calixto	+244 222 395 004	pedro.calixto@ao.pwc.com
Antigua and Barbuda	Robert Wilkinson	+1 268 462 3000 ext. 103	robert.j.wilkinson@ag.pwc.com
Argentina	Lilian Falcon	+54 11 4850 6763	lilian.falcon@ar.pwc.com
Armenia	Robin McCone	+995 32 250 8063	robin.mccone@ge.pwc.com
Australia	Jim Lijeski	+61 2 8266 8298	jim.lijeski@au.pwc.com
Austria	Aline Kapp	+43 1 501 880	aline.kapp@de.pwc.com
Azerbaijan	Movlan Pashayev	+994 12 497 7405	movlan.pashayev@az.pwc.com
Bahrain	Ebrahim Karolia	+973 175 40554	ebrahim.b.karolia@bh.pwc.com
Barbados	Christopher Sambrano	+1 246 467 6701	christopher.sambrano@bb.pwc.com
Belarus	Oleg Gvozd	+375 17 335 4000	oleg.gvozd@by.pwc.com
Belgium	Nicolas de Limbourg	+32 2 710 7418	nicolas.de.limbourg@be.pwc.com
Bermuda	Alistair McNeish	+1 441 298 9708	alistair.s.mcneish@bm.pwc.com
Bolivia	Boris Mercado	+591 2 408 181	boris.mercado@bo.pwc.com
Bosnia and Herzegovina	Krzysztof Lipka	+381 11 330 2100	krzysztof.lipka@rs.pwc.com
Botswana	Butler Phirie	+267 395 2011	butler.phirie@bw.pwc.com
Brazil	Edmar Perfetto	+55 11 3674 3722	edmar.perfetto@br.pwc.com
Bulgaria	Mina Kapsazova	+359 2 93 55 163	mina.kapsazova@bg.pwc.com
Burkina Faso	Dominique Taty	+225 20 31 5467	d.taty@ci.pwc.com
Cameroon	Nadine Tinen	+237 99 96 2202	nadine.tinen@cm.pwc.com
Canada	Dave Peters	+1 403 509 7481	dave.peters@ca.pwc.com
Cape Verde	Leendert Verschoor	+351 212 599 642	leendert.verschoor@pt.pwc.com
Chad	Nadine Tinen	+237 33 43 2443	nadine.tinen@cm.pwc.com
Chile	Roberto Carlos Rivas	+56 2 9400 000	roberto.carlos.rivas@cl.pwc.com
China, People's Republic of	Mandy Kwok	+852 2289 3900	mandy.kwok@hk.pwc.com
Colombia	Maria Helena Diaz	+57 1 635 1125	maria_helena.diaz@co.pwc.com
Congo, Republic of	Emmanuel Le Bras	+242 534 0907	emmanuel.lebras@cg.pwc.com
Costa Rica	Carlos Barrantes	+506 2224 1555	carlos.barrantes@cr.pwc.com
Croatia	Cherie Ford	+385 1 6328 880	cherie.ford@hr.pwc.com
Cyprus	Philippos Soseilos	+57 22 555 606	philippos.soseilos@cy.pwc.com
Czech Republic	Steve Couch	+420 251 15 1111	steve.couch@cz.pwc.com
Denmark	Mona Lorentsen	+45 3945 3398	mona.lorentsen@dk.pwc.com
Dominican Republic	Jeffrey Johnson	+1 809 567 7741	jeffrey.johnson@do.pwc.com
Ecuador	Pablo Aguirre	+593 2 256 4142 ext. 361	pablo.aguirre@ec.pwc-ag.com
Egypt	Amr El Monayer	+202 2 2759 7879	amr.elmonayer@eg.pwc.com
El Salvador	Edgar Mendoza	+502 2420 7800	edgar.mendoza@gt.pwc.com
Equatorial Guinea	Sebastien Lechene	+240 333 09 1434 / +240 222 27 3841	sebastien.lechene@ga.pwc.com
Estonia	Erkki Paulus	+372 614 1814	erkki.paulus@ee.pwc.com
Fiji Islands	Jenny Seeto	+679 331 3955	jenny.seeto@fj.pwc.com
Finland	Risto Lof	+358 9 2280 1811	risto.lof@fi.pwc.com
France	Pascale Jouble	+33 1 56 57 4005	pascale.jouble@fr.landwellglobal.com
Gabon	Laurent Pommera	+241 76 2371/618	laurent.pommera@ga.pwc.com
Gambia	George Kwatia	+233 302 761 500	george.kwatia@gh.pwc.com
Georgia	Robin McCone	+995 32 250 8063	robin.mccone@ge.pwc.com
Germany	Petra Raspels	+49 21 1981 7680	petra.raspels@de.pwc.com
Ghana	George Kwatia	+233 302 761 500	george.kwatia@gh.pwc.com
Greece	Lina Foka	+30 210 6874 546	lina.foka@gr.pwc.com
Guatemala	Edgar Mendoza	+502 2420 7800	edgar.mendoza@gt.pwc.com
Guinea (Conakry)	Mohamed Lahlou	+224 30 45 14 43	mohamed.lahlou@gn.pwc.com
Honduras	Ramon Morales	+504 552 3060	ramon.morales@hn.pwc.com
Hong Kong	Mandy Kwok	+852 2289 3900	mandy.kwok@hk.pwc.com
Hungary	Beáta Horváthné Szabó	+36 1 461 9283	beata.horvathne@hu.pwc.com
Iceland	Friðgeir Sigurðsson	+354 550 5366	fridgeir.sigurdsson@is.pwc.com
India	Kaushik Mukerjee	+91 80 4079 6002	kaushik.mukerjee@in.pwc.com

Human Resource Services

Indonesia	Paul Raman	+62 21 5289 1027	paul.raman@id.pwc.com
Iran	Dennis Allen	+974 4419 2830	dennis.allen@qa.pwc.com
Iraq	Stephan Stephan	+962 6 500 1300	stephan.stephan@jo.pwc.com
Ireland	Mark Carter	+353 1 792 6548	mark.p.carter@ie.pwc.com
Israel	Dennis Allen	+974 4419 2830	dennis.allen@qa.pwc.com
Italy	Luca Barbera	+390 2 9160 5300	luca.barbera@it.pwc.com
Ivory Coast (Côte d'Ivoire)	Dominique Taty	+225 20 31 5467	d.taty@ci.pwc.com
Jamaica	Tony Lewars	+1 876 932 8383	tony.lewars@jm.pwc.com
Japan	Kojiro Endo	+81 3 5251 2443	kojiro.endo@jp.pwc.com
Jordan	Stephan Stephan	+962 6 500 1300	stephan.stephan@jo.pwc.com
Kazakhstan	Anar Khassenova	+7 727 330 3200	anar.khassenova@kz.pwc.com
Kenya	Judy Muigai	+254 20 285 5575	judy.x.muigai@ke.pwc.com
Korea, Republic of	Younsung Chung	+82 2 709 0538	younsung.chung@kr.pwc.com
Kosovo	Loreta Peci	+355 4 2245 254	loreta.peci@al.pwc.com
Kyrgystan	Anar Khassenova	+7 727 330 3200	anar.khassenova@kz.pwc.com
Kuwait	Dennis Allen	+974 4419 2830	dennis.allen@qa.pwc.com
Latvia	Zlata Elksnina	+371 6 709 5414	zlata.elksnina@lv.pwc.com
Lebanon	Wadih AbouNasr	+961 1 200 577 ext. 1610	wadih.abounasr@lb.pwc.com
Lesotho	Hennie Smit (PwC Bloemfontein)	+27 51 503 4100	hennie.smit@za.pwc.com
Liberia	George Kwatia	+233 302 761 500	george.kwatia@gh.pwc.com
Libya	Dennis Allen	+974 4419 2830	dennis.allen@qa.pwc.com
Lithuania	Jurate Krikstopaitiene	+370 5 239 2381	jurate.krikstopaitiene@lt.pwc.com
Luxembourg	Michiel Roumieux	+352 49 4848 3055	michiel.roumieux@lu.pwc.com
Macau	Christina Lam	+853 8799 5133	christina.wc.lam@hk.pwc.com
Macedonia	Miroslav Marchev	+389 23 111 012	miroslav.marchev@mk.pwc.com
Madagascar	Andriamisa Ravelomanana	+261 20 22 217 63	andriamisa.ravelomanana@mg.pwc.com
Malawi	Vyamala Moyo	+265 1 820 322	vyamala.moyo@mw.pwc.com
Malaysia	Sakaya Johns Rani	+60 3 2173 1553	sakaya.johns.rani@my.pwc.com
Mali	Dominique Taty	+225 20 31 5467	d.taty@ci.pwc.com
Malta	David Ferry	+356 2564 6712	david.ferry@mt.pwc.com
Mauritius	Anthony Leung Shing	+230 404 5000	anthony.leung.shing@mu.pwc.com
Mexico	Claudia Campos	+52 55 5263 5774	claudia.campos@mx.pwc.com
Middle East	Dennis Allen	+974 4419 2830	dennis.allen@qa.pwc.com
Moldova	Svetlana Ceban	+373 22 238 122	svetlana.ceban@ro.pwc.com
Montenegro	Krzysztof Lipka	+381 11 3302 100	krzysztof.lipka@rs.pwc.com
Morocco	Mahat Chraibi	+212 5 22 99 98 98	mahat.chraibi@ma.pwc.com
Mozambique	Joao Martins	+258 21 307 620	joao.l.martins@mz.pwc.com
Namibia, Republic of	Stefan Hugo	+264 61 284 1102	stefan.hugo@na.pwc.com
Netherlands	Henk van Cappelle	+31 10 407 5517	henk.van.cappelle@nl.pwc.com
New Zealand	Steve Camage	+64 9 355 8116	steve.c.camage@nz.pwc.com
Nicaragua	Francisco Castro	+505 2270 9950	francisco.castro@ni.pwc.com
Niger	Dominique Taty	+225 20 31 5467	d.taty@ci.pwc.com
Nigeria	Ken Aitken	+234 805 802 1530	ken.aitken@ng.pwc.com
Norway	Erland Norstebo	+47 95 26 0669	erland.norstebo@no.pwc.com
Oman	Dennis Allen	+974 4419 2830	dennis.allen@qa.pwc.com
Pakistan	Naeem Akhtar	+92 21 3241 1628	naeem.akhtar@pk.pwc.com
Palestine	Dennis Allen	+974 4419 2830	dennis.allen@qa.pwc.com
Panama	Francisco Barrios	+507 206 9217	francisco.barrios@pa.pwc.com
Paraguay	Ruben Taboada	+595 21 445 003	ruben.taboada@py.pwc.com
Peru	Monica Nieva	+51 1 211 6500	monica.nieva@pe.pwc.com
Philippines	Myrna Fernando	+63 2 459 2003	myrna.fernando@ph.pwc.com
Poland	Camiel van der Meij	+22 523 4959	camiel.van.der.meij@pl.pwc.com
Portugal	Ana Duarte	+351 213 599 604	ana.duarte@pt.pwc.com
Puerto Rico	Jose Osorio	+1 787 772 8057	jose.osorio@us.pwc.com
Qatar	Dennis Allen	+974 4419 2830	dennis.allen@qa.pwc.com
Romania	Mihaela Mitroi	+40 21 202 8717	mihaela.mitroi@ro.pwc.com
Russian Federation	Karina Khudenko	+7 495 967 5418	karina.khudenko@ru.pwc.com

Human Resource Services

Rwanda	Nelson Ogara	+254 202 855 297	nelson.o.ogara@rw.pwc.com
Saudi Arabia	Dennis Allen	+974 4419 2830	dennis.allen@qa.pwc.com
Senegal	Matthias Hubert	+221 33 849 0500	matthias.hubert@sn.pwc.com
Serbia	Krzysztof Lipka	+381 11 330 2100	krzysztof.lipka@rs.pwc.com
Sierra Leone	George Kwatia	+233 302 761 500	george.kwatia@gh.pwc.com
Singapore	James Clemence	+65 6236 3948	james.clemence@sg.pwc.com
Slovakia	Marc-Tell Madl	+421 259 350 470	m.madl@sk.pwc.com
Slovenia	Sonja Omerza	+386 1 5836 023	sonja.omerza@si.pwc.com
South Africa	Alan Seccombe	+27 11 797 4110	alan.seccombe@za.pwc.com
Spain	Borja Montesino	+34 915 685 767	borja.montesino@es.pwc.com
St Lucia	Anthony Atkinson	+758 456 2600	anthony.d.atkinson@lc.pwc.com
Sri Lanka	Lasanga Abeysuriya	+93 11 471 9838	lasanga.abeysuriya@lk.pwc.com
Swaziland	Theo Mason	+268 2404 2861	theo.mason@sz.pwc.com
Switzerland	Andrew Chapman	+41 58 792 5021	chapman.andrew@ch.pwc.com
Syria	Dennis Allen	+974 4419 2830	dennis.allen@qa.pwc.com
Taiwan	Lucy Ho	+886 2 2729 5518	lucy.ho@tw.pwc.com
Tajikistan	Abdulkhamid Muminov	+998 711 206 101	abdulkhamid.muminov@uz.pwc.com
Tanzania	Rishit Shah	+255 22 219 2601	rishit.shah@tz.pwc.com
Thailand	Prapasiri Kositthanakorn	+66 2 344 1228	prapasiri.kositthanakorn@th.pwc.com
Togo	Dominique Taty	+225 20 31 5467	d.taty@ci.pwc.com
Trinidad and Tobago	Bert Jones	+1 868 623 0281	bert.jones@tt.pwc.com
Tunisia	Mabrouk Maalaoui	+216 719 6900	mabrouk.maalaoui@tn.pwc.com
Turkey	Bilgutay Yasar	+90 212 326 6414	bilgutay.yasar@tr.pwc.com
Turkmenistan	Abdulkhamid Muminov	+998 711 206 101	abdulkhamid.muminov@uz.pwc.com
Uganda	Francis Kamulegeya	+256 412 36018 / +256 312 354400	francis.kamulegeya@ug.pwc.com
Ukraine	Ron Barden	+380 44 490 6777	ron.j.barden@ua.pwc.com
United Arab Emirates	Dennis Allen	+974 4419 2830	dennis.allen@qa.pwc.com
United Kingdom	Jon Andrews	+44 20 7804 9000	jon.andrews@uk.pwc.com
United States	Peter Clarke	+1 203 539 3826	peter.clarke@us.pwc.com
Uzbekistan, Republic of	Abdulkhamid Muminov	+998 711 206 101	abdulkhamid.muminov@uz.pwc.com
Venezuela	Jose Javier Garcia	+58 281 267 0845	jose.j.garcia@ve.pwc.com
Vietnam	David Fitzgerald	+66 2 344 1500	david.fitzgerald@vn.pwc.com
Zambia	Jyoti Mistry	+260 122 8809 / +260 211 256471/2	jyoti.mistry@zm.pwc.com
Zimbabwe	Manuel Lopes	+263 4 33 8362/8	manuel.lopes@zw.pwc.com

Indirect Taxes

We customise the support we give you, and use the latest technology

Global Leader, Indirect Taxes
Stephen Coleclough
+44 20 7212 4911
stephen.coleclough@uk.pwc.com

To give the best advice on indirect taxation, we believe you need to work closely with the people devising it. At PwC we do this. And we have a thorough understanding of indirect taxes from every perspective - we appreciate that indirect taxes can be very different depending on which industry sector you work in. Across the world, our indirect tax and customs specialists work closely with PwC industry specialists to really understand the specific issues in your sector, and give you advice with genuine insight. And because the implications of indirect taxes can be so important to your business, we customise the support we give you, and use the latest technology, to provide you with what you need, wherever you are and whenever you need us. We can assist you with strategy, risk, process and margin improvement.

Country	Contact	Phone	Email
Afghanistan	Syed Shabbar Zaidi	+92 21 24 13 849	s.m.shabbar.zaidi@pk.pwc.com
Albania	Loreta Peci	+355 4 2242 254	loreta.peci@al.pwc.com
Algeria	Stéphane Henrion	+33 1 56 57 4139	stephane.henrion@fr.landwellglobal.com
Angola	Pedro Calixto	+244 222 311 166	pedro.calixto@ao.pwc.com
Antigua and Barbuda	Neil Coates	+268 462 3000 ext. 134	neil.m.coates@ag.pwc.com
Argentina	Ricardo Tavieres	+54 11 4850 6722	ricardo.d.tavieres@ar.pwc.com
Armenia	Paul Cooper	+374 10 59 2150	paul.cooper@am.pwc.com
Australia	Peter Konidaris	+61 3 8603 1168	peter.konidaris@au.pwc.com
Austria	Christine Weinzierl	+43 1 501 88 3630	christine.weinzierl@at.pwc.com
Azerbaijan	Movlan Pashayev	+994 12 497 7405	movlan.pashayev@az.pwc.com
Bahamas	Kevin D. Seymour	+242 352 8471	kevin.d.seymour@bs.pwc.com
Bahrain	Jeanine Daou	+961 1 200 577 ext. 1691	jeanine.daou@lb.pwc.com
Barbados	Louisa Lewis-Ward	+246 467 6756	louisa.ward@bb.pwc.com
Belgium	Wouter Villette	+32 2 710 7302	wouter.villette@pwc.be
Bolivia	Cesar Lora	+591 721 47 235	cesar.lora@bo.pwc.com
Bosnia and Herzegovina	Mubera Brkovic	+387 33 295 721	mubera.brkovic@ba.pwc.com
Botswana	Seema Ramdas	+26 7 395 2011	seema.ramdas@bw.pwc.com
Brazil	Celso Grazioli	+55 11 3674 3701	celso.grazioli@br.pwc.com
Bulgaria	Nevena Haygarova	+359 895 449 560	nevena.haygarova@bg.pwc.com
Cambodia	Thy Heng	+855 23 218 086 ext. 1502	heng.thy@kh.pwc.com
Cameroon, Republic of	Nadine Tinen	+237 33 43 2443	nadine.tinen@cm.pwc.com
Canada	Michael P. Firth	+1 416 869 8718	michael.p.firth@ca.pwc.com
Cape Verde	Susana Caetano	+351 213 599 648	susana.caetano@pt.pwc.com
Central and Eastern Europe	Hubert Jadrzyk	+48 225 234 837	hubert.jadrzyk@pl.pwc.com
Chad	Nadine Tinen	+237 33 43 2443	nadine.tinen@cm.pwc.com
Chile	Sandra Benedetto	+56 2 940 0546	sandra.benedetto@cl.pwc.com
China, People's Republic of	Alan Wu	+86 10 6533 2889	alan.wu@cn.pwc.com
Colombia	Carlos M. Chaparro	+57 163 405 55 ext. 216	carlos.chaparro@co.pwc.com
Congo, Democratic Republic of the	David Guarnieri	+243 810 336 801	guarnieri.david@cd.pwc.com
Congo, Republic of	Moïse Kokolo	+242 533 20 57	moise.kokolo@cg.pwc.com
Costa Rica	Carlos Barrantes	+506 2224 1555 ext. 163	carlos.barrantes@cr.pwc.com
Croatia	Ivo Bijelic	+385 1 632 8802	ivo.bijelic@hr.pwc.com
Cyprus	Chrysilios Pelekanos	+357 22 555 280	chrysilios.pelekanos@cy.pwc.com
Czech Republic	Peter Skelhorn	+420 251 152 811	peter.skelhorn@cz.pwc.com
Denmark	Jan Huusmann Christensen	+45 3945 9452	jan.huusmann.christensen@dk.pwc.com
Dominican Republic	Ramon Ortega	+1 809 567 7741	ramon.ortega@do.pwc.com
Ecuador	Pablo Aguirre	+593 2 256 4142 ext. 361	pablo.aguirre@ec.pwc-ag.com
Egypt	Abdallah Eladly	+20 2 2759 7887	abdallah.eladly@eg.pwc.com
El Salvador	Carmen Elena Pineda	+503 2243 8619	carmen.e.pineda@sv.pwc.com
Equatorial Guinea	Sébastien Lechêne	+240 333 09 1434 / +240 222 27 3841	sebastien.lechene@ga.pwc.com
Estonia	Ain Veide	+372 614 1978	ain.veide@ee.pwc.com
Fiji Islands	Jerome S. Kado	+679 331 5199	jerome.kado@fj.pwc.com
Finland	Juha Laitinen	+358 9 2280 1409	juha.laitinen@fi.pwc.com
France	Patricia More	+33 1 56 57 43 07	patricia.more@fr.landwellglobal.com
Gabon	Laurent Pommera	+241 76 2371	laurent.pommera@ga.pwc.com
Germany	Götz Neuhahn	+49 30 2636 5445	goetz.neuhahn@de.pwc.com
Georgia	Sergi Kobakhidze	+995 32 508 066	sergi.kobakhidze@ge.pwc.com
Ghana	George Kwatia	+233 302 761 459	george.kwatia@gh.pwc.com

Indirect Taxes

Greece	Panagiotis Tsouramanis	+30 210 6874 547	panagiotis.tsouramanis@gr.pwc.com
Guatemala	Edgar Mendoza	+502 2420 7800 ext. 844	edgar.mendoza@gt.pwc.com
Guernsey (Channel Islands)	Mark Watson	+44 1481 752029	m.watson@gg.pwc.com
Honduras	Ramon Morales	+504 553 3060	ramon.morales@hn.pwc.com
Hungary	Laszlo Deak	+36 1 461 9590	laszlo.deak@hu.pwc.com
Iceland	Elin Arnadottir	+354 550 5322	elin.arnadottir@is.pwc.com
India	Vivek Mishra	+91 124 330 6518	vivek.mishra@in.pwc.com
Indonesia	Abdullah Azis	+62 21 528 90601	abdullah.azis@id.pwc.com
Iraq	Jeanine Daou	+961 1 200 577 ext. 1691	jeanine.daou@lb.pwc.com
Ireland	John Fay	+353 1 792 8701	john.fay@ie.pwc.com
Isle of Man	George Sharpe	+44 1624 689689	george.sharpe@iom.pwc.com
Israel	Liat Neuwirth	+972 3519 2531	liat.neuwirth@il.pwc.com
Italy	Luca Lavazza	+ 39 02 9160 5701	luca.lavazza@it.pwc.com
Ivory Coast (Côte d'Ivoire)	Dominique Taty	+225 20 31 5467	d.taty@ci.pwc.com
Jamaica	Paul A. Cobourne	+1 876 932 8350	paul.cobourne@jm.pwc.com
Japan	Masanori Kato	+81 3 5251 2536	masanori.kato@jp.pwc.com
Jersey (Channel Islands)	Wendy Dorman	+44 1534 838233	wendy.dorman@je.pwc.com
Jordan	Jeanine Daou	+961 1 200 577 ext. 1691	jeanine.daou@lb.pwc.com
Kazakhstan	Andrey Kudyarov	+7 727 330 3001 ext. 4023	andrey.x.kudyarov@kz.pwc.com
Kenya	Phillip Korir	+254 20 285 5472	phillip.korir@ke.pwc.com
Korea, Republic of	Dong-Keon Lee	+82 2 709 0561	dong-keon.lee@kr.pwc.com
Kosovo	Loreta Peci	+355 4 242 254	loreta.peci@al.pwc.com
Kuwait	Jeanine Daou	+961 1 200 577 ext. 1691	jeanine.daou@lb.pwc.com
Kyrgyzstan	Saken Shayakhmetov	+7 727 330 3201	saken.shayakhmetov@kz.pwc.com
Lao PDR	Thavorn Rujivanarom	+66 2 286 9999	thavorn.rujivanarom@th.pwc.com
Latvia	Ilze Rauza	+371 6709 4512	ilze.rauza@lv.pwc.com
Lebanon	Jeanine Daou	+961 1 200 577 ext. 1691	jeanine.daou@lb.pwc.com
Liechtenstein	Niklaus Honauer	+41 61 270 5942	niklaus.honauer@ch.pwc.com
Lithuania	Kristina Krisciunaite	+370 5 2392 365	kristina.krisciunaite@lt.pwc.com
Luxembourg	Laurent Grençon	+352 49 4848 2060	laurent.grencon@lu.pwc.com
Macedonia	Miroslav Marchev	+389 23 111 012	miroslav.marchev@mk.pwc.com
Malawi	Vyamala Aggriel Moyo	+265 1 82 0322	vyamala.aggriel.moyo@mw.pwc.com
Malaysia	Wan Heng Choon	+60 3 2173 1488	heng.choon.wan@my.pwc.com
Malta	David Ferry	+356 2564 6712	david.ferry@mt.pwc.com
Mauritius	Dheerend Puholoo	+230 207 5079	d.puholoo@mu.pwc.com
Mexico	Ivan Jaso	+52 55 5263 8535	ivan.jaso@mx.pwc.com
Moldova	Ionut Simion	+40 21 225 3702	ionut.simion@ro.pwc.com
Monaco	Stephen Dale	+33 1 5657 4161	stephen.dale@fr.landwellglobal.com
Mongolia	Abdulkhamid Muminov	+998 71 1204 870	abdulkhamid.muminov@uz.pwc.com
Montenegro	Jovana Stojanovic	+381 11 3302 116	jovana.stojanovic@yu.pwc.com
Morocco	Stéphane Henrion	+33 1 56 57 4139	stephane.henrion@fr.landwellglobal.com
Mozambique	Joao Martins	+258 21 307 620	joäo.l.martins@mz.pwc.com
Namibia, Republic of	Chantell Husselmann	+264 61 284 1327	chantell.husselmann@na.pwc.com
Netherlands	Bertjan Janzen	+31 88 792 5171	bertjan.janzen@nl.pwc.com
New Zealand	Eugen Trombitas	+64 9 355 8686	eugen.x.trombitas@nz.pwc.com
Nicaragua	Francisco Castro	+505 2270 9950	francisco.castro@ni.pwc.com
Nigeria	Yemi Idowu	+234 1 271 1700 ext. 3105	yemi.idowu@ng.pwc.com
Norway	Trond Ingebrigtsen	+47 95 26 0810	trond.ingebrigtsen@no.pwc.com
Oman	Jeanine Daou	+961 1 200 577 ext. 1691	jeanine.daou@lb.pwc.com

Pakistan	Syed Shabbar Zaidi	+92 21 3241 3849	s.m.shabbar.zaidi@pk.pwc.com
Panama	Francisco Barrios	+507 206 9217	francisco.barrios@pa.pwc.com
Papua New Guinea	David Caradus	+675 321 1500	david.caradus@pg.pwc.com
Paraguay	Ruben Taboada	+595 21 445 003	ruben.taboada@py.pwc.com
Peru	Rudolf Röder	+51 1 211 6500	rudolf.roeder@pe.pwc.com
Philippines	Carlos Carada	+63 2 845 2728	carlos.t.carado@ph.pwc.com
Poland	Hubert Jadrzyk	+48 22 523 4837	hubert.jadrzyk@pl.pwc.com
Portugal	Susana Caetano	+351 213 599 648	susana.caetano@pt.pwc.com
Qatar	Jeanine Daou	+961 1 200 577 ext. 1691	jeanine.daou@lb.pwc.com
Romania	Daniel Anghel	+40 21 202 8688	daniel.anghel@ro.pwc.com
Russian Federation	Vladimir Konstantinov	+7 495 967 6236	vladimir.konstantinov@ru.pwc.com
San Marino	Nicola Broggi	+39 02 9160 5100	nicola.broggi@it.pwc.com
Saudi Arabia	Jeanine Daou	+961 1 200 577 ext. 1691	jeanine.daou@lb.pwc.com
Serbia	Jovana Stojanovic	+381 11 3302 116	jovana.stojanovic@yu.pwc.com
Singapore	Soo How Koh	+65 6236 3600	soo.how.koh@sg.pwc.com
Slovak Republic	Eva Fricova	+421 259 350 613	eva.fricova@sk.pwc.com
Slovenia	Marijana Ristevski	+386 1 5836 019	marijana.ristevski@si.pwc.com
South Africa	Charles De Wet	+27 21 529 2377	charles.de.wet@za.pwc.com
Spain	Alberto Monreal	+34 915 685 570 ext. 15570	alberto.monreal@es.pwc.com
Sweden	Lars Henckel	+46 8 555 333 26	lars.henckel@se.pwc.com
Switzerland	Michaela Merz	+41 58 792 4429	michaela.merz@ch.pwc.com
Syria	Jeanine Daou	+961 1 200 577 ext. 1691	jeanine.daou@lb.pwc.com
Taiwan	Lily Hsu	+886 2 2729 6207	lily.hsu@tw.pwc.com
Tajikistan	Elena Kaeva	+7 727 298 0620	elena.kaeva@kz.pwc.com
Tanzania	Rishit Shah	+255 22 219 2601	rishit.shah@tz.pwc.com
Thailand	Darika Soponawat	+66 2 344 1015	darika.kriengsuntikul@th.pwc.com
Trinidad and Tobago	Allyson West	+1 868 623 1361	allyson.west@tt.pwc.com
Tunisia	Mabrouk Maalaoui	+216 71 963 900	mabrouk.maalaoui@tn.pwc.com
Turkey	Cenk Ulu	+90 212 355 5852	cenk.ulu@tr.pwc.com
Turkmenistan	Jamshid Juraev	+998 71 120 6101	jamshid.juraev@uz.pwc.com
Uganda	Francis Kamulegeya	+256 414 236 018	francis.kamulegeya@ug.pwc.com
Ukraine	Viktoria Tymoshenko	+380 44 490 6777	viktoria.tymoshenko@ua.pwc.com
United Arab Emirates	Jeanine Daou	+961 1 200 577 ext. 1691	jeanine.daou@lb.pwc.com
United Kingdom	Michael Bailey	+44 20 7804 3254	michael.bailey@uk.pwc.com
United States	Tom Boniface (VAT partner)	+1 646 471 4579	thomas.a.boniface@us.pwc.com
	John M. Cooney (Sales & Use Tax partner)	+ 1 713 356 8080	john.m.cooney@us.pwc.com
Uruguay	Patricia Marques	+598 2 916 0463 ext. 1348	patricia.marques@uy.pwc.com
Uzbekistan, Republic of	Abdulkhamid Muminov	+998 71 1204 870	abdulkhamid.muminov@uz.pwc.com
Venezuela	Elys Aray	+58 241 825 6434	elys.aray@ve.pwc.com
Vietnam	Huong Giang Nguyen	+84 4 9462 246 ext. 3020	n.huong.giang@vn.pwc.com
West Bank and Gaza	Wael H. Sa'adi	+ 972 2 532 6660 ext. 21	wael.h.saadi@ps.pwc.com
Yemen	Jeanine Daou	+961 1 200 577 ext. 1691	jeanine.daou@lb.pwc.com
Zambia	Jyoti Mistry	+260 211 256471 ext. 4023	jyoti.mistry@zm.pwc.com
Zimbabwe	Edmore Mandizha	+263 4 338 3628	edmore.mandizha@zw.pwc.com

International Tax Services

> *It's this combination of local and global expertise that gives you real insight*

Global Leader,
International Tax Services
Tony Clemens
+61 2 8266 2953
tony.e.clemens@au.pwc.com

The pressures on business to manage tax across borders, along with growing regulation and the need to stay competitive in a global market, means that a local perspective on international tax is not enough. With specialists experienced in complex international tax matters across the world, our network is well positioned to give you top quality advice. It's this combination of local and global expertise that gives you real insight into managing tax across borders.

Albania	Paul Tobin	+359 2 91 003	paul.tobin@bg.pwc.com
Angola	Fernando Barros	+244 222 395 004	fernando.barros@ao.pwc.com
Argentina	Andres M. Edelstein	+54 11 4850 6722	andres.m.edelstein@ar.pwc.com
Armenia	Robin McCone	+995 32 250 8050	robin.mccone@ge.pwc
Aruba	Hans Ruiter	+297 522 1630	hans.ruiter@an.pwc.com
Antigua and Barbuda	Charles Walwyn	+1 268 462 3000	charles.walwyn@ag.pwc.com
Australia	Peter Collins	+61 3 8603 6247	peter.collins@au.pwc.com
Austria	Friedrich Roedler	+43 1 501 88 3600	friedrich.roedler@at.pwc.com
Azerbaijan	Movlan Pashayev	+994 12 497 7405	movlan.pashayev@az.pwc.com
Barbados	Russ Jones	+1 246 626 6754	russ.jones@bb.pwc.com
Belarus	Oleg Gvozd	+375 17 335 4000	oleg.gvozd@by.pwc.com
Belgium	Axel Smits	+32 2 259 3120	axel.smits@be.pwc.com
Bolivia	Cesar Lora	+591 721 47 235	cesar.lora@bo.pwc.com
Bosnia and Herzegovina	Krzysztof Lipka	+381 11 330 2133	krzysztof.lipka@rs.pwc.com
Botswana	Butler Phirie	+267 395 2011	butler.phirie@bw.pwc.com
Brazil	Nélio Weiss	+55 11 3674 3557	nelio.weiss@br.pwc.com
Bulgaria	Orlin Hadjiiski	+359 2 91 003	orlin.hadjiiski@bg.pwc.com
Cameroon, Republic of	Pierre Roger Ngangwou	+237 33 43 2443	pierre.roger.ngangwou@cm.pwc.com
Canada	Bill Holms	+1 604 806 7052	william.holms@ca.pwc.com
Caribbean Netherlands	Lennart Huijsen	+599 9 430 0000	lennart.f.huijsen@an.pwc.com
Cayman Islands	Paul Anderton	+1 345 914 8602	paul.anderton@ky.pwc.com
Central and Eastern Europe	Gabriella Erdos	+36 1 461 9130	gabriella.erdos@hu.pwc.com
Chad	Oscar Deffosso	+235 52 38 96	oscar.deffosso@cm.pwc.com
Chile	Francisco Selame	+56 2 940 0462	francisco.selame@cl.pwc.com
China, People's Republic of	Edwin Wong	+86 10 6533 2100	edwin.wong@cn.pwc.com
Colombia	Carlos Chaparro	+57 163 405 55 ext. 216	carlos.chaparro@co.pwc.com
Congo, Democratic Republic of the	David Guarnieri	+243 810 336 801	guarnieri.david@cd.pwc.com
Congo, Republic of	Emmanuel Le Bras	+242 534 0907	emmanuel.lebras@cg.pwc.com
Costa Rica	Carlos Barrantes	+506 224 1555	carlos.barrantes@cr.pwc.com
Croatia	Ivo Bijelic	+385 1 632 8802	ivo.bijelic@hr.pwc.com
Curacao	Lennart Huijsen	+599 9 430 0000	lennart.f.huijsen@an.pwc.com
Cyprus	Panikos N. Tsiailis	+357 22 555 255	panikos.n.tsiailis@cy.pwc.com
Czech Republic	David Borkovec	+420 251 152 561	david.borkovec@cz.pwc.com
Denmark	Søren Jesper Hansen	+45 3945 3320	soren.jesper.hansen@dk.pwc.com
Dominican Republic	Andrea Paniagua	+1 809 567 7741	andrea.paniagua@do.pwc.com
Ecuador	Pablo Aguirre	+593 2 256 4142 ext. 361	pablo.aguirre@ec.pwc-ag.com
Egypt	Sherif Mansour	+20 2 2759 7700 ext. 7888	sherif.mansour@eg.pwc.com
El Salvador	Carlos Morales Recinos	+503 2243 6344	carlos.morales.recinos@sv.pwc.com
Equatorial Guinea	Sébastien Lechene	+240 333 09 1434 / +240 222 27 3841	sebastien.lechene@ga.pwc.com
Estonia	Erki Uustalu	+372 614 1890	erki.uustalu@ee.pwc.com
Finland	Martti Virolainen	+358 9 2280 1396	martti.virolainen@fi.pwc.com
Fiji	Jerome Kado	+679 331 3955	jerome.kado@fj.pwc.com
France	Renaud Jouffroy	+33 1 56 57 4229	renaud.jouffroy@fr.landwellglobal.com
Gabon	Christophe Relongoue	+241 76 25 08	christophe.relongoue@ga.pwc.com
Georgia	Robin McCone	+995 32 250 8050	robin.mccone@ge.pwc
Germany	Claus Jochimsen	+49 89 5790 5420	claus.jochimsen@de.pwc.com
Ghana	Darcy White	+233 21 761 576	darcy.white@gh.pwc.com
Gibraltar	Robert G. Guest	+350 200 78777	robert.g.guest@gi.pwc.com
Greece	Vassilios Vizas	+30 210 6874 019	vassilios.vizas@gr.pwc.com
Guatemala	Rolando Díaz	+502 2420 7840	rolando.diaz@gt.pwc.com

International Tax Services

Guernsey (Channel Islands)	Mark Watson	+44 1481 752029	m.watson@gg.pwc.com
Honduras	Ramon Morales	+504 553 3060	ramon.morales@hn.pwc.com
Hong Kong	Nick Dignan	+852 2289 3702	nick.dignan@hk.pwc.com
Hungary	Gabriella Erdos	+36 1 461 9130	gabriella.erdos@hu.pwc.com
Iceland	Elin Arnadottir	+354 550 5322	elin.arnadottir@is.pwc.com
India	Nitin Karve	+91 22 6689 1477	nitin.karve@in.pwc.com
Indonesia	Ray Headifen	+62 21 528 90800	ray.headifen@id.pwc.com
Ireland	Denis Harrington	+353 1 792 8629	denis.harrington@ie.pwc.com
Isle of Man	Kevin Cowley	+44 1624 689689	kevin.cowley@iom.pwc.com
Israel	Gerry Seligman	+972 3 795 4476	gerry.seligman@il.pwc.com
Italy	Franco Boga	+390 2 9160 5400	franco.boga@it.pwc.com
Ivory Coast (Côte d'Ivoire)	Dominique Taty	+225 20 31 5467	d.taty@ci.pwc.com
Jamaica	Eric Crawford	+1 876 932 8323	eric.crawford@jm.pwc.com
Japan	Jun J. Takashima	+81 3 5251 2574	jun.takashima@jp.pwc.com
Jersey (Channel Islands)	Wendy Dorman	+44 1534 838233	wendy.dorman@je.pwc.com
Jordan	Stephan Stephan	+962 6 569 7431	stephan.stephan@jo.pwc.com
Kazakhstan	Richard Bregonje	+7 727 298 0866	richard.bregonje@kz.pwc.com
Kenya	Simeon Cheruiyot	+254 20 285 5000	simeon.cheruiyot@ke.pwc.com
Korea, Republic of	Alex Joong-Hyun Lee	+82 2 709 0598	alex.joong-hyun.lee@kr.pwc.com
Kuwait	Fouad Douglas	+965 2299 7894	fouad.douglas@kw.pwc.com
Latvia	Zlata Elksniņa	+371 6709 4400	zlata.elksnina@lv.pwc.com
Lebanon	Wadih AbouNasr	+961 1 200 577	wadih.abounasr@lb.pwc.com
Lichtenstein	Stefan Schmid	+41 58 792 4482	stefan.schmid@ch.pwc.com
Lithuania	Kristina Krisciunaite	+370 5 2392 365	kristina.krisciunaite@lt.pwc.com
Luxembourg	Sami Douénias	+352 49 4848 3060	sami.douenias@lu.pwc.com
Macedonia	Miroslav Marchev	+389 23 111 012	miroslav.marchev@mk.pwc.com
Madagascar	Andriamisa Ravelomanana	+261 20 22 217 63	andriamisa.ravelomanana@mg.pwc.com
Malaysia	Chuan Keat Khoo	+60 3 2694 6368	chuan.keat.khoo@my.pwc.com
Malta	Neville Gatt	+356 2564 6711	neville.gatt@mt.pwc.com
Mauritius	Anthony Leung Shing	+230 404 5071	anthony.leung.shing@mu.pwc.com
Mexico	Carlos Montemayor	+52 55 5263 6066	carlos.montemayor@mx.pwc.com
Middle East Region	Dean Rolfe	+971 4304 3351	dean.rolfe@ae.pwc.com
Moldova	Brian Arnold	+40 21 225 3660	brian.arnold@ro.pwc.com
Monaco	Renaud Jouffroy	+33 1 5657 4229	renaud.juffroy@fr.landwellglobal.com
Mongolia	Abdulkhamid Muminov	+998 71 1204 870	abdulkhamid.muminov@uz.pwc.com
Montenegro	Krzysztof Lipka	+381 11 330 2133	krzysztof.lipka@rs.pwc.com
Morocco	Mahat Chraibi	+212 22 99 9800	mahat.chraibi@ma.landwellglobal.com
Mozambique	João Martins	+258 21 307 620	joao.l.martins@mz.pwc.com
Namibia, Republic of	Albé Botha	+264 61 284 1000	albe.botha@na.pwc.com
Netherlands	Jeroen Schmitz	+31 20 568 7018	jeroen.schmitz@nl.pwc.com
New Zealand	Stewart McCulloch	+64 9 355 8751	stewart.j.mcculloch@nz.pwc.com
Nicaragua	Francisco Castro	+505 2270 4346 ext. 102	francisco.castro@ni.pwc.com
Nigeria	Ken Aitken	+234 1 271 1700	ken.aitken@ng.pwc.com
Norway	Steinar Hareide	+47 95 26 0429	steinar.hareide@no.pwc.com
Pakistan	Soli R. Parakh	+92 21 3241 6434	soli.r.parakh@pk.pwc.com
Panama	Francisco Barrios	+507 206 9217	francisco.barrios@pa.pwc.com
Paraguay	Ruben Taboada	+595 21 445 003	ruben.taboada@py.pwc.com
Peru	Rudolf Röder	+51 1 211 6500	rudolf.roeder@pe.pwc.com
Philippines	Alex Cabrera	+63 2 845 2728	alex.cabrera@ph.pwc.com
Poland	Camiel van der Meij	+48 22 523 4959	camiel.van.der.meij@pl.pwc.com
Portugal	Jorge Figueiredo	+351 213 599 636	jorge.figueiredo@pt.pwc.com
Qatar	Ian Clay	+974 467 5581	ian.clay@qa.pwc.com
Oman	Dean Rolfe	+971 4304 3351	dean.rolfe@ae.pwc.com
Papua New Guinea	David Caradus	+675 321 1421	david.caradus@pg.pwc.com
Romania	Mihaela Mitroi	+40 21 202 8717	mihaela.mitroi@ro.pwc.com
Russian Federation	Natalia Kuznetsova	+7 495 967 6271	natalia.kuznetsova@ru.pwc.com

International Tax Services

Senegal	Matthias Hubert	+221 33 849 05 00	matthias.hubert@sn.pwc.com
Serbia	Krzysztof Lipka	+381 11 330 2133	krzysztof.lipka@rs.pwc.com
Singapore	Paul Cornelius	+65 6236 3718	paul.cornelius@sg.pwc.com
Sint Maarten	Lennart Huijsen	+599 9 430 0000	lennart.f.huijsen@an.pwc.com
Slovak Republic	Christiana Serugova	+421 2 59 350 614	christiana.serugova@sk.pwc.com
South Africa	David Lermer	+27 21 529 2364	david.lermer@za.pwc.com
Spain	Ramon Mullerat	+34 915 685 534	ramon.mullerat@es.pwc.com
Sri Lanka	Charmaine Tillekeratne	+94 1147 19838	charmaine.tillekeratne@lk.pwc.com
St. Kitts & Nevis	Charles Walwyn ext. 121	+1 268 462 3000	charles.walwyn@ag.pwc.com
Swaziland	Theo Mason	+268 404 2861	theo.mason@sz.pwc.com
Sweden	Jörgen Haglund	+46 8 555 331 51	jorgen.haglund@se.pwc.com
Switzerland	Stefan Schmid	+41 58 792 4482	stefan.schmid@ch.pwc.com
Taiwan	Steven Go	+886 2 2729 5229	steven.go@tw.pwc.com
Tanzania	David Tarimo	+255 22 219 2201	david.tarimo@tz.pwc.com
Thailand	Paul Stitt	+66 2 344 1119	paul.stitt@th.pwc.com
Trinidad and Tobago	Allyson West	+1 868 299 0700	allyson.west@tt.pwc.com
Tunisia	Mabrouk Maalaoui	+216 71 963 900	mabrouk.maalaoui@tn.pwc.com
Turkey	Kadir Bas	+90 212 326 6408	kadir.bas@tr.pwc.com
Uganda	Francis Kamulegeya	+256 414 236 018	francis.kamulegeya@ug.pwc.com
Ukraine	Ron Barden	+380 44 490 6777	ron.j.barden@ua.pwc.com
United Arab Emirates	Dean Rolfe	+971 4304 3351	dean.rolfe@ae.pwc.com
United Kingdom	David J. Burn	+44 161 247 4046	david.j.burn@uk.pwc.com
United States	Tim Anson	+1 202 414 1664	tim.anson@us.pwc.com
	Michael Urse	+1 216 875 3358	michael.urse@us.pwc.com
Uruguay	Daniel Garcia	+598 2 916 0463	garcia.daniel@uy.pwc.com
Uzbekistan, Republic of	Abdulkhamid Muminov	+998 71 1204 870	abdulkhamid.muminov@uz.pwc.com
Venezuela	José Javier García	+58 212 700 6283	jose.j.garcia@ve.pwc.com
Vietnam	Richard Irwin	+84 8 3824 0117	r.j.irwin@vn.pwc.com
Zambia	Jyoti Mistry	+260 2112 56471/2	jyoti.mistry@zm.pwc.com
Zimbabwe	Manuel Lopes	+263 4 338 3628	manuel.lopes@zw.pwc.com

Legal Services

Over 2,000 corporate lawyers in more than 80 countries

Global Leader, Legal Services
Leon Flavell
+44 20 7212 1945
leon.flavell@pwclegal.co.uk

We understand that one size doesn't fit all when it comes to legal services.

With over 2,000 corporate lawyers in more than 80 countries, we're able to tackle problems in a way that is genuinely specific to your business. As well as specialist legal advice, we also offer day-to-day general counsel support. We support businesses with teams drawn from the range of skills within the PwC global network. Depending on your legal issues, we might include tax advisers, human capital consultants, corporate finance specialists, actuaries, management consultants, or accountants. We'll put together whatever it takes to give you a creative solution in the least possible time.

Albania	Loreta Peci	+355 4 2242 254	loreta.peci@al.pwc.com
Algeria	Samir Hamouda	+213 21 48 4183	samir.hamouda@fr.pwc.com
Argentina	Eduardo Gil Roca	+54 11 4850 6740	eduardo.gil.roca@ar.pwc.com
Australia	Andrew Wheeler	+61 2 8266 6401	andrew.wheeler@au.pwc.com
Azerbaijan	Farhad Hajizade	+994 12 497 7391	farhad.hajizade@az.pwc.com
Barbados	Ronaele Dathorne	+1 246 467 6652	ronaele.dathorne@bb.pwc.com
Belarus	Oleg Gvozd	+375 17 335 4000	oleg.gvozd@by.pwc.com
Belgium	Karin Winters	+32 2 710 7404	karin.winters@be.pwc.com
Bolivia	Fidel Navarro	+591 2 240 8181 ext. 113	fidel.navarro@bo.pwc.com
Brazil	Fernando Loeser	+55 11 3879 2802	fernando.loeser@lpadv.com.br
Bulgaria	Irina B. Tsvetkova	+359 2 9355 100	irina.tsvetkova@bg.pwc.com
Cameroon, Republic of	Nadine Tinen	+237 33 43 2443	nadine.tinen@cm.pwc.com
Chad	Nadine Tinen	+237 33 43 2443	nadine.tinen@cm.pwc.com
Chile	Francisco Selame	+56 2 940 0150	francisco.selame@cl.pwc.com
China, People's Republic of	Anthea Wong	+852 2289 3352	anthea.wong@hk.pwc.com
Colombia	Eliana Bernal	+57 1 634 0527	eliana.bernal@co.pwc.com
Congo, Republic of	Prosper Bizitou	+242 557 9198	prosper.bizitou@cg.pwc.com
Costa Rica	Carlos Barrantes	+506 2224 1555 ext. 107	carlos.barrantes@cr.pwc.com
Croatia	Dzenet Garibovic	+385 1 632 8803	dzenet.garibovic@hr.pwc.com
Cyprus	Spyros A. Evangelou	+357 22 559 999	spyros.evangelou@cy.pwc.com
Czech Republic	Daniel Cekal	+420 251 152 900	daniel.cekal@pwclegal.cz
Dominican Republic	Edgar Orlando Mendoza	+1 502 2420 7800 ext. 844	edgar.mendoza@gt.pwc.com
El Salvador	Edgar Orlando Mendoza	+1 502 2420 7800 ext. 844	edgar.mendoza@gt.pwc.com
Equatorial Guinea	Dominique Taty	+225 20 31 5467	d.taty@ci.pwc.com
Finland	Jukka-Pekka Joensuu	+358 9 2280 1335	jukka-pekka.joensuu@fi.pwc.com
France	Bruno Thomas	+33 1 56 57 8375	bruno.thomas@fr.landwellglobal.com
Gabon	Christophe Relongue	+241 76 2508	christophe.relongue@ga.pwc.com
Georgia	Gia Tskhovrebadze	+995 322 508 050	gia.tskhovrebadze@ge.pwc.com
Germany	Thomas Fischer	+49 69 9585 5561	t.fischer@de.pwc.com
Gibraltar	Edgar C. Lavarello	+350 200 73520	edgar.c.lavarello@gi.pwc.com
Greece	Mary Psylla	+30 210 6874 543	mary.psylla@gr.pwc.com
Guatemala	Edgar Orlando Mendoza	+1 502 2420 7800 ext. 844	edgar.mendoza@gt.pwc.com
Honduras	Edgar Orlando Mendoza	+1 502 2420 7800 ext. 844	edgar.mendoza@gt.pwc.com
Hungary	László Réti	+36 1 461 9890	laszlo.reti@hu.landwellglobal.com
Iceland	Elín Árnadóttir	+354 550 5300	elin.arnadottir@is.pwc.com
India	Deepak Gupta	+91 11 4115 0307	deepak.gupta@in.pwc.com
Italy	Gaetano Arnò	+390 2 9160 5210	gaetano.arno@it.pwc.com
Ivory Coast (Côte d'Ivoire)	Dominique Taty	+225 20 31 5467	d.taty@ci.pwc.com
Jordan	Emad M. Majid	+962 6 567 8707	emad.majid@jo.pwc.com
Kazakhstan	Liza Zhumakhmetova	+7 7272 980 948	liza.zhumakhmetova@kz.pwc.com
Lao PDR	Varavudh Meesaiyati	+856 21 222 718	varavudh.meesaiyati@th.pwc.com
Latvia	Vita Sakne	+371 6709 4425	vita.sakne@lv.pwc.com
Luxembourg	Christophe Loly	+352 49 4848 5114	christophe.loly@lu.pwc.com
Lithuania	Rokas Bukauskas	+370 5 239 2341	rokas.bukauskas@lt.pwc.com
Macedonia	Miroslav Marchev	+389 23 111 012	miroslav.marchev@mk.pwc.com
Madagascar	Dominique Taty	+225 20 31 5467	d.taty@ci.pwc.com
Malta	Neville Gatt	+356 2564 6791	neville.gatt@mt.pwc.com
Mexico	Carlos Manuel Martinez	+52 81 8152 2043	carlos.manuel.martinez@mx.pwc.com
Moldova	Alexandru Munteanu	+373 22 23 8122	alexandru.munteanu@ro.pwc.com
Morocco	Nicolas Granier	+33 1 5657 8669	nicolas.granier@fr.landwellglobal.com
Mozambique	Joao Martins	+258 21 307 620	joao.l.martins@mz.pwc.com
Netherlands	Frank Erftemeijer	+31 20 568 5930	frank.erftemeijer@nl.pwc.com

Legal Services

Nicaragua	Edgar Orlando Mendoza	+1 502 2420 7800 ext. 844	edgar.mendoza@gt.pwc.com
Nigeria	Dafe Akpeneye	+234 1 271 3114	dafe.akpeneye@ng.pwc.com
Norway	Kjell Richard Manskow	+47 95 26 1176	kjell.richard.manskow@no.pwc.com
Panama	Amanda de Wong	+507 206 9219	amanda.de.wong@pa.pwc.com
Paraguay	Patricia Marques	+598 2 916 0463 ext. 1348	patricia.marques@uy.pwc.com
Peru	Miguel Mur	+51 1 211 6500 ext. 8044	miguel.mur@pe.pwc.com
Philippines	Alex Cabrera	+63 2 459 2002	alex.cabrera@ph.pwc.com
Poland	Ewa Szurmińska-Jaworska	+48 22 746 7352	ewa.szurminska-jaworska@pl.pwc.com
Romania	Sorin David	+40 21 202 8770	sorin.david@david-baias.ro
Russian Federation	Yana Zoloeva	+7 495 232 5761	yana.zoloeva@ru.pwc.com
Senegal	Pierre Michaux	+221 33 849 0500	pierre.michaux@ga.pwc.com
Serbia & Montenegro	Predrag Milovanovic	+381 11 3302 100	predrag.milovanovic@rs.pwc.com
Slovak Republic	Marc-Tell Madl	+421 2 59 350 470	m.madl@sk.pwc.com
Slovenia	Nana Sumrada	+386 1 583 6031	nana.sumrada@si.pwc.com
Spain	José Luis Beotas	+34 915 684 522	jose.luis.beotas@es.pwc.com
Switzerland	Gema Olivar Pascual	+41 58 792 4377	gema.olivar.pascual@ch.pwc.com
Taiwan	Eric Tsai	+886 2 2729 6687	eric.tsai@tw.pwc.com
Thailand	Siripong Supakijjanusorn	+66 2 344 1124	siripong.supakijjanusorn@th.pwc.com
Tunisia	Rachid Tmar	+216 71 862 156	rachid.tmar@tn.pwc.com
Trinidad and Tobago	Allyson West	+1 868 623 1361	allyson.west@tt.pwc.com
Turkey	Nilgun Serdar	+90 212 326 6368	nilgun.serdar@tr.pwc.com
Ukraine	Rob Shantz	+380 44 490 6777	rob.shantz@ua.pwc.com
United Arab Emirates	Waseem Khokhar	+971 4 304 3181	waseem.khokhar@pwclegal.co.ae
United Kingdom	Leon Flavell	+44 20 7212 1945	leon.flavell@pwclegal.co.uk
Uruguay	Patricia Marques	+598 2 916 0463 ext. 1348	patricia.marques@uy.pwc.com
Venezuela	Elys Aray	+58 241 825 6434	elys.aray@ve.pwc.com
Vietnam	Richard J. Irwin	+66 2286 9999 ext. 4880	r.j.irwin@vn.pwc.com

Mergers and Acquisitions

An international
network of almost 1,000
Mergers and Acquisitions
specialists, experienced in
every type of transaction

Global Leader,
Mergers and Acquisitions
Hans-Martin Eckstein
+49 69 9585 6382
hm.eckstein@de.pwc.com

Whether you're buying, selling or merging, it's vital to
extract as much value as possible from a transaction.
With an international network of almost 1,000 Mergers
and Acquisitions (M&A) specialists, experienced in every
type of transaction, we know how to help you structure
and finance the transaction to your best advantage.
Our M&A Tax specialists support you through every
stage of the transaction. They work closely with our
transactions services, corporate finance and legal teams,
so that all aspects of the transaction are covered by
experienced specialists.

Mergers and Acquisitions

Algeria	Alain Chedal	+33 1 56 57 4019	alain.chedal@fr.landwellglobal.com
Angola	Pedro Calixto	+244 222 311 166	pedro.calixto@ao.pwc.com
Antigua and Barbuda	Charles Walwyn	+1 268 462 3000 ext. 121	charles.walwyn@ag.pwc.com
Argentina	Daniel Santiago	+54 11 4850 6707	daniel.santiago@ar.pwc.com
Aruba	Hans Ruiter	+297 522 1630	hans.ruiter@an.pwc.com
Australia	Mark O'Reilly	+61 2 8266 2979	mark.oreilly@au.pwc.com
Austria	Bernd Hofmann	+43 1 501 88 3332	bernd.hofmann@at.pwc.com
Bahrain	Phil Robinson	+973 17 540 554 ext. 317	p.robinson@bh.pwc.com
Barbados	Russ Jones	+1 246 626 6754	russ.jones@bb.pwc.com
Belgium	Jan Muyldermans	+32 2 710 7423	jan.muyldermans@be.pwc.com
Bermuda	Richard Irwin	+1 441 299 7136	richard.e.irvine@bm.pwc.com
Bolivia	Cesar Lora	+591 721 47 235	cesar.lora@bo.pwc.com
Botswana	Mike Benetello	+27 11 797 4299	mike.benetello@za.pwc.com
Brazil	Rodrigo Bastos	+55 11 3674 3543	rodrigo.bastos@br.pwc.com
British Virgin Islands	Russ Jones	+1 246 626 6754	russ.jones@bb.pwc.com
Canada	Doug Frost	+1 416 365 8852	doug.l.frost@ca.pwc.com
Caribbean Netherlands	Lennart Huijsen	+599 9 430 0000	lennart.f.huijsen@an.pwc.com
Cayman Islands	Frazer Lindsay	+1 345 914 8606	frazer.lindsay@ky.pwc.com
Central African (East)	Simeon Cheruiyot	+254 20 285 5000	simeon.cheruiyot@ke.pwc.com
Central America	Ramon Ortega	+1 809 567 7741	ramon.ortega@do.pwc.com
Central and Eastern Europe	Cherie Ford	+385 1 6328 880	cherie.ford@hr.pwc.com
Chad	Nadine Tinen	+ 237 99 96 2202	nadine.tinen@cm.pwc.com
Chile	German Campos	+56 2 940 0098	german.campos@cl.pwc.com
China, People's Republic of	Edwin Wong	+86 10 6533 2100	edwin.wong@cn.pwc.com
Colombia	Eliana Bernal	+57 1 634 0527	eliana.bernal@co.pwc.com
Croatia	Cherie Ford	+385 1 6328 880	cherie.ford@hr.pwc.com
Curacao	Lennart Huijsen	+599 9 430 0000	lennart.f.huijsen@an.pwc.com
Cyprus	Nicos Chimarides	+357 22 555 270	nicos.chimarides@cy.pwc.com
Czech Republic	Viera Kucerova	+420 251 151 255	viera.kucerova@cz.pwc.com
Denmark	Daniel Noe Harboe	+45 3945 9582	daniel.noe.harboe@dk.pwc.com
Dominican Republic	Ramon Ortega	+1 809 567 7741	ramon.ortega@do.pwc.com
Ecuador	Pablo Aguirre	+593 2 256 4142 ext. 361	pablo.aguirre@ec.pwc-ag.com
Egypt	Yehia Zakaria	+20 2 2759 7886	yehia.zakaria@eg.pwc.com
El Salvador	Carlos Morales	+503 2248 8600	carlos.morales.recinos@sv.pwc.com
Fiji	Jerome Kado	+679 331 3955	jerome.kado@fj.pwc.com
Finland	Markku Hakkarainen	+358 9 2280 1801	markku.hakkarainen@fi.pwc.com
France	Anne-Valérie Attias-Assouline	+33 1 56 57 6909	anne-valerie.attias-assouline@fr.landwellglobal.com
Gabon	Laurent Pommera	+241 76 2371	laurent.pommera@ga.pwc.com
Germany	Hans-Martin Eckstein	+49 69 9585 6382	hm.eckstein@de.pwc.com
Ghana	Darcy White	+233 21 761 576	darcy.white@gh.pwc.com
Gibraltar	Edgar Lavarello	+350 200 73520	edgar.c.lavarello@gi.pwc.com
Greece	Mariza Sakellaridou	+30 210 6874 557	mariza.sakellaridou@gr.pwc.com
Guatemala	Edgar Mendoza	+502 2420 7800	edgar.mendoza@gt.pwc.com
Guernsey (Channel Islands)	Mark Watson	+44 1481 752029	m.watson@gg.pwc.com
Honduras	Ramon Morales	+504 553 3060	ramon.morales@hn.pwc.com
Hong Kong	Nick Dignan	+852 2289 3702	nick.dignan@hk.pwc.com
Hungary	Janos Kelemen	+36 1 461 9310	janos.kelemen@hu.pwc.com
Iceland	Fridgeir Sigurdsson	+354 550 5315	fridgeir.sigurdsson@is.pwc.com
India	Vivek Mehra	+91 11 2321 0542	vivek.mehra@in.pwc.com
Indonesia	Ali Mardi	+62 21 528 90622	ali.mardi@id.pwc.com
Iraq	Stephan Stephan	+962 6 500 1300	stephan.stephan@jo.pwc.com
Ireland	Ronan MacNioclais	+353 1 792 6000	ronan.mancnioclais@ie.pwc.com
Isle of Man	Kevin Cowley	+44 1624 689689	kevin.cowley@iom.pwc.com
Israel	Doron Sadan	+972 3 7954 460	doron.sadan@il.pwc.com
Italy	Nicola Broggi	+390 2 9160 5700	nicola.broggi@it.pwc.com
Jamaica	Eric Crawford	+1 876 932 8323	eric.crawford@jm.pwc.com
Japan	Jun J. Takashima	+81 3 5251 2574	jun.takashima@jp.pwc.com

Jersey (Channel Islands)	Wendy Dorman	+44 1534 838233	wendy.dorman@je.pwc.com
Jordan	Stephan Stephan	+962 6 500 1300	stephan.stephan@jo.pwc.com
Kenya	Simeon Cheruiyot	+254 20 285 5000	simeon.cheruiyot@ke.pwc.com
Korea	Alex Lee	+82 2 709 0598	alex.joong-hyun.lee@kr.pwc.com
Lebanon	Wadih AbouNasr	+961 1 200 577 ext. 609	wadih.abounasr@lb.pwc.com
Luxembourg	Vincent Lebrun	+352 49 4848 2584	vincent.lebrun@lu.pwc.com
Madagascar	Andriamisa Ravelomanana	+261 20 22 21 763	andriamisa.ravelomanana@mg.pwc.com
Malawi	Vyamala Aggriel Moyo	+265 1 82 0322	vyamala.aggriel.moyo@mw.pwc.com
Malaysia	Frances Po	+60 3 2173 1618	frances.po@my.pwc.com
Malta	Neville Gatt	+356 2564 6711	neville.gatt@mt.pwc.com
Mauritius	Anthony Leung Shing	+230 4040 5071	anthony.leung.shing@mu.pwc.com
Mexico	Jesus Chan	+52 55 5263 6000	jesus.chan@mx.pwc.com
Morocco	Mahat Chraibi	+212 22 99 9800	mahat.chraibi@fr.landwellglobal.com
Mozambique	Joao Martins	+258 21 350 400	joao.l.martins@mz.pwc.com
Namibia, Republic of	Stefan Hugo	+264 61 284 1102	stefan.hugo@na.pwc.com
Netherlands	Oscar Kinders	+31 10 407 5348	oscar.kinders@nl.pwc.com
New Caledonia	Daniel Teyssier	+687 28 6100	daniel.teyssier@nc.pwc.com
New Zealand	Peter Boyce	+64 9 355 8547	peter.boyce@nz.pwc.com
Nicarágua	Juan Carlos Cortés	+505 2270 9950 ext. 136	juan.c.cortes@ni.pwc.com
Nigeria	Taiwo Oyedele	+234 1 271 1700 ext. 3100	taiwo-oyedele@ng.pwc.com
Norway	Steinar Hareide	+47 95 26 04 29	steinar.hareide@no.pwc.com
Oman	Russel Aycock	+968 2455 9122	russell.aycock@om.pwc.com
Pakistan	Soli R. Parakh	+92 21 3241 6434	soli.r.parakh@pk.pwc.com
Panama	Ramon Ortega	+1 809 567 7741	ramon.ortega@do.pwc.com
Papua New Guinea	David Caradus	+675 321 1500	david.caradus@pg.pwc.com
Paraguay	Ruben Taboada	+595 21 445 003	ruben.taboada@py.pwc.com
Peru	Orlando Marchesi	+51 1 211 6500	orlando.marchesi@pe.pwc.com
Philippines	Malou Lim	+63 2 845 2728	malou.p.lim@ph.pwc.com
Poland	Mike Ahern	+48 22 523 4985	mike.ahern@pl.pwc.com
Portugal	Maria Torres	+351 225 433 113	maria.torres@pt.pwc.com
Russian Federation	Galina Naumenko	+7 495 232 5753	galina.naumenko@ru.pwc.com
Saudi Arabia	Phil Robinson	+973 17 540 554 ext. 317	p.robinson @bh.pwc.com
Seychelles	Anthony Leung Shing	+230 404 5071	anthony.leung.shing@mu.pwc.com
Singapore	Chris Woo	+65 6236 3688	chris.woo@sg.pwc.com
Sint Maarten	Lennart Huijsen	+599 9 430 0000	lennart.f.huijsen@an.pwc.com
Slovenia	Cherie Ford	+385 1 6328 880	cherie.ford@hr.pwc.com
South Africa	Mike Benetello	+27 11 797 4299	mike.benetello@za.pwc.com
Spain	David Ramirez	+34 932 532 722	david.ramirez.garcia@es.pwc.com
Sri Lanka	Charmaine Tillekeratne	+94 11 471 9838	charmaine.tillekeratne@lk.pwc.com
St. Kitts and Nevis	Charles Walwyn	+1 268 462 3000	charles.walwyn@ag.pwc.com
Swaziland	Theo Mason	+268 2404 2861	theo.mason@sz.pwc.com
Sweden	Johan Sjöqvist	+ 46 8 555 335 99	johan.sjoqvist@se.pwc.com
Switzerland	Markus Prinzen	+41 58 792 5310	markus.prinzen@ch.pwc.com
Syria	Wadih AbouNasr	+961 1 200 577 ext. 609	wadih.abounasr@lb.pwc.com
Taiwan	Elaine Hsieh	+886 2 2729 6666	elaine.hsieh@tw.pwc.com
Tanzania	David Tarimo	+255 22 219 2000	david.tarimo@tz.pwc.com
Thailand	Paul Stitt	+66 2 344 1119	paul.stitt@th.pwc.com
Trinidad and Tobago	Allyson West	+1 868 299 0700	allyson.west@tt.pw.com
Tunisia	Mabrouk Maalaoui	+216 71 862 156	mabrouk.maalaoui@tn.pwc.com
Turkey	Kadir Bas	+90 212 326 6408	kadir.bas@tr.pwc.com
Uganda	Francis Kamulegeya	+ 256 41 236 018	francis.kamulegeya@ug.pwc.com
United Kingdom	Sanjay Shah	+44 20 7213 2611	sanjay.r.shah@uk.pwc.com
United States	Mark Boyer	+1 202 414 1629	mark.boyer@us.pwc.com
Uruguay	Patricia Marques	+598 2 916 0463 ext. 1348	patricia.marques@uy.pwc.com
Venezuela	Josè Manuel Cobos	+58 212 700 6142	jose.manuel.cobos@ve.pwc.com
Vietnam	Richard Irwin	+84 8 3824 0117	r.j.irwin@vn.pwc.com
Zimbabwe	Manuel Lopes	+2634 338 362/8	manuel.lopes@zw.pwc.com

Sustainability and Climate Change Tax

Advice that anticipates
what legislative and
policy changes are likely
to happen

*Global Leaders, Sustainability
and Climate Change Tax*

Stephen Coleclough
(Global Indirect Taxes)
+44 20 7212 4911
stephen.coleclough@uk.pwc.com

James Koch
(Global Energy, Utilities & Mining Tax)
+1 713 356 4626
james.koch@us.pwc.com

John Preston
(Global Tax Policy)
+44 20 7804 2645
john.preston@uk.pwc.com

Sustainability and climate change continues to evolve as
a business issue.

Momentum is building. As such, you need more than
advice on the current state – you need advice that
anticipates what legislative and policy changes are likely
to happen. You need that advice to help you to predict
how these developments will impact your business.
You also need to understand how your organisation is
changing to address sustainability and climate change
as a business issue and how existing taxes impact on
those changes. Our Sustainability and Climate Change
Tax network helps businesses and investors in two
ways: it helps them stay on top of global trends and
developments in climate change related policy; and it
helps businesses address the tax implications of climate
change related policy and their own organisation's
response to the business issue.

Sustainability and Climate Change Tax

Argentina	Jorge San Martin	+54 11 4850 6722	jorge.a.san.martin@ar.pwc.com
Australia	Suzi Russell	+61 2 8266 1057	suzi.russell@au.pwc.com
Belgium	Maarten Tas	+32 2 710 7402	maarten.tas@be.pwc.com
Brazil	Carlos Iacia	+ 55 11 3674 3544	carlos.iacia@br.pwc.com
Canada	Ian Heine	+1 604 806 7706	ian.d.heine@ca.pwc.com
Central and Eastern Europe	Martin A Scott	+420 251 152 544	martin.a.scott@cz.pwc.com
China, People's Republic of	Alan Wu	+ 86 10 6533 2889	alan.wu@cn.pwc.com
Denmark	Søren Jesper Hansen	+45 3945 3320	soren.jesper.hansen@dk.pwc.com
France	Xavier Etienne	+ 33 1 5657 8395	xavier.etienne@fr.landwellglobal.com
Germany	Frank Schmidt	+49 69 9585 6711	frank.r.schmidt@de.pwc.com
India	Ajay Kumar	+91 12 4330 6509	ajay.kumar@in.pwc.com
Indonesia	Anthony Anderson	+62 21 528 90642	anthony.j.anderson@id.pwc.com
Ireland	Ronan MacNioclais	+353 1 792 6006	ronan.macnioclais@ie.pwc.com
Italy	Valentino Guarini	+39 02 9160 5807	valentino.guarini@it.pwc.com
Japan	Jun Takashima	+81 3 5251 2574	jun.takashima@jp.pwc.com
Korea, Republic of	Sang-Keun Song	+82 2 709 0559	sang-keun.song@kr.pwc.com
Luxembourg	Catherine Dupont	+352 49 48 48 3125	catherine.dupont@lu.pwc.com
Malta	David Ferry	+356 2564 6712	david.ferry@mt.pwc.com
Mexico	Arturo Mendez	+52 33 3648 1013	arturo.mendez@mx.pwc.com
Middle East	Dean Rolfe	+971 4 304 3100	dean.rolfe@ae.pwc.com
Netherlands	Christianne Noordermeer Van Loo	+31 8879 26821	christianne.noordermeer.van.loo@nl.pwc.com
Romania	Daniel Anghel	+40 21 225 3688	daniel.anghel@ro.pwc.com
South Africa	Kyle Mandy	+27 11 797 4977	kyle.mandy@za.pwc.com
Spain	Araceli Zatarain	+34 963 032 048	araceli.zatarain@es.landwellglobal.com
Sweden	Lars Henckel	+46 8 555 333 26	lars.henckel@se.pwc.com
Switzerland	Markus Hertel	+41 58 792 83 88	markus.hertel@ch.pwc.com
Turkey	Tolga Tasdelen	+90 212 326 6484	tolga.tasdelen@tr.pwc.com
United Kingdom	Andrew Norris	+44 20 7212 6545	andrew.norris@uk.pwc.com
United States	Matthew Haskins	+1 202 414 1570	matthew.haskins@us.pwc.com

Tax Controversy and Dispute Resolution

> *We think being effective is about more than just knowledge; it's about having an insight into what could happen next*

Global Leader,
Tax Controversy and Dispute Resolution
David Swenson
+1 202 414 4650
david.swenson@us.pwc.com

By giving you insight into your company's risks and exposures across different territories and disciplines, we can be the effective option to help you deal with tax disputes, audits, and examinations, from prevention through to management and resolution. Our specialists also use their experience to help businesses put in place consistent and defensible practices and policies, so they know what to expect in the future. The Tax Controversy and Dispute Resolution network brings together former revenue authorities and government officials, accountants, economists, international tax litigators, and industry sector specialists, in all areas of direct and indirect tax, as well as customs duties, employment taxes, and tax fraud. We think being effective is about more than just knowledge; it's about having an insight into what could happen next, so we build strong relationships with governments and policy makers worldwide. That way, we're close to the people who are setting the dispute agenda, and know how to work with them to get the right results.

Tax Controversy and Dispute Resolution

Argentina	Eduardo Gil Roca	+54 11 4850 6728	eduardo.gil.roca@ar.pwc.com
Australia	Peter Le Huray	+61 3 8603 6192	peter.le.huray@au.pwc.com
Belgium	Xavier Van Vlem	+32 9 268 8311	xavier.van.vlem@be.pwc.com
Brazil	Durval Portela	+55 11 3879 2800	durval.portela@br.pwc.com
Bulgaria	Orlin Hadjiiski	+359 2 93 55 142	orlin.hadjiiski@bg.pwc.com
Canada	Nick Pantaleo	+1 416 365 2701	nick.pantaleo@ca.pwc.com
Chile	Francisco Selame	+56 2 940 0462	francisco.selame@cl.pwc.com
China, People's Republic of	Matthew Mui	+86 10 6533 3028	matthew.mui@cn.pwc.com
Ecuador	Pablo Aguirre	+593 2 382 9351	pablo.aguirre@ec.pwc.com
Finland	Veli-Matti Tala	+358 9 2280 1329	veli.matti.tala@fi.pwc.com
France	Michel Combe	+33 1 5657 4586	michel.combe@fr.landwellglobal.com
Germany	Andreas Kempf	+49 201 438 1970	andreas.kempf@de.pwc.com
Hungary	Geza Reczei	+36 1 461 9737	geza.reczei@hu.pwc.com
India	Pawan Kumar	+91 12 4330 6517	pawan.kumar@in.pwc.com
Indonesia	Ay Tjhing Phan	+62 21 521 2909	ay.tjhing.phan@id.pwc.com
Italy	Paolo Comuzzi	+39 02 9160 5804	paolo.comuzzi@it.pwc.com
Japan	Daisuke Miyajima	+81 3 5251 2552	daisuke.miyajima@jp.pwc.com
Korea, Republic of	Henry An	+82 2 3781 2594	henry.an@kr.pwc.com
Mexico	Karina Perez Delgadillo	+52 55 5263 5734	karina.perez.delgadillo@mx.pwc.com
Netherlands	Stef van Weeghel	+31 88 792 6763	stef.van.weeghel@nl.pwc.com
Norway	Morten Beck	+47 95 26 0650	morten.beck@no.pwc.com
Poland	Hubert Jadrzyk	+48 22 523 4837	hubert.jadrzyk@pl.pwc.com
Romania	Dan Dascalu	+40 21 202 8683	dan.dascalu@david-baias.ro
Russian Federation	Yana Proskurina	+7 495 232 5757	yana.proskurina@ru.pwc.com
Slovak Republic	Christiana Serugova	+421 259 350 614	christiana.serugova@sk.pwc.com
South Africa	Paul de Chalain	+27 11 797 4260	paul.de.chalain@za.pwc.com
Spain	Miguel Cruz	+34 915 684 609	miguel.cruz@es.pwc.com
Sweden	Marcus Hammarstrand	+46 31 793 1434	marcus.hammarstrand@se.pwc.com
Switzerland	Benjamin Koch	+41 58 792 4334	benjamin.koch@ch.pwc.com
Ukraine	Andrey Pronchenko	+380 44 490 6777	andrey.pronchenko@ua.pwc.com
United Kingdom	Simon Wilks	+44 20 7804 1938	simon.wilks@uk.pwc.com
United States	Kevin Brown	+1 202 346 5051	kevin.brown@us.pwc.com
Uruguay	Patricia Marques	+598 2 916 0463 ext. 1348	patricia.marques@uy.pwc.com

Tax Management and Accounting Services

*Insight and credentials
that help teams navigate
today's business changes*

Global Leader,
Tax Management and Accounting Services
Buddy Tinley
+1 678 419 8838
buddy.tinley@us.pwc.com

Today, when it comes to managing taxes, many businesses find
that the approaches they've taken in the past are no longer
optimal nor sustainable to manage risks and the dynamics of
today's operating environment. This could be due to changes in
their industry or organization, changing legislation, structural
transformations, pressure from shareholders and regulators, or
budget pressures. Our global Tax Management and Accounting
Services (TMAS) network has the experience to help you define
and implement an operating model that works for your business,
so that you retain effective control over your global taxes. PwC's
TMAS network can provide insight and credentials that help teams
navigate today's business changes and build efficient, effective
and adaptable tax functions to support global tax management
responsibilities. In addition to assisting you in building internal
capabilities, we can also coordinate the outsourcing of your
compliance – enabled by software that gives you central control
and visibility to the status of your compliance across borders – for
direct and indirect taxes, statutory financial statement production
and tax reporting.

Tax Management and Accounting Services

Africa Central	Rajesh Shah	+254 20 285 5326	rajesh.k.shah@ke.pwc.com
Albania	Loreta Peci	+355 4 2242 254	loreta.peci@al.pwc.com
Antigua and Barbuda	Charles Walwyn	+1 268 462 3000	charles.walwyn@ag.pwc.com
Argentina	Daniel Cravino	+54 11 4850 6000	daniel.h.cravino@ar.pwc.com
Armenia	Robin McCone	+995 32 250 8050	robin.mccone@ge.pwc.com
Australia	Tim Cox	+61 3 8603 6181	tim.cox@au.pwc.com
Austria	Christine Weinzierl	+43 1 501 88 3630	christine.weinzierl@at.pwc.com
Azerbaijan	Movlan Pashayev	+994 12 497 7405	movlan.pashayev@at.pwc.com
Bahrain	Ebrahim B Karolia	+973 17540 554 ext. 250	ebrahim.karolia@bh.pwc.com
Belarus	Oleg Gvozd	+375 17 335 4000	oleg.gvozd@by.pwc.com
Belgium	Dirk Vermussche	+32 2 710 7100	dirk.vermussche@be.pwc.com
Bolivia	Cesar Lora	+591 721 47235	cesar.Lora@bo.pwc.com
Bosnia & Herzegovina	Krzysztof Lipka	+381 11 3302 100	krzysztof.lipka@rs.pwc.com
Brazil	Manuel Marinho	+55 19 3794 5435	manuel.marinho@br.pwc.com
Bulgaria	Paul Tobin	+359 2 935 5116	paul.tobin@bg.pwc.com
Cambodia	Richard J. Irwin	+66 2 286 9999	r.j.irwin@vn.pwc.com
Canada	John Gotts	+1 905 972 4125	john.gotts@ca.pwc.com
Channel Islands	Mark Watson	+44 1481 752029	m.watson@gg.pwc.com
Chile	Germán Campos Kennett	+56 2 940 0150	german.campos@cl.pwc.com
China, People's Republic of	Matthew Wong	+86 21 2323 3052	matthew.mf.wong@cn.pwc.com
Colombia	Maria Helena Diaz	+57 1 635 1125	maria_helena.diaz@co.pwc.com
Costa Rica	Carlos Barrantes	+506 2224 1555	carlos.barrantes@cr.pwc.com
Croatia	Cherie Ford	+385 1 6328 880	cherie.ford@hr.pwc.com
Cyprus	Theo Parperis	+357 22 555 477	theo.parperis@cy.pwc.com
Czech Republic	Zuzana Vaneckova	+420 25 115 2800	Zuzana.vaneckova@cz.pwc.com
Denmark	Charlotte Dohm	+45 3945 9428	charlotte.dohm@dk.pwc.com
Dominican Republic	Ramon Ortega	+1 809 567 7741 ext. 2348	ramon.ortega@do.pwc.com
Ecuador	Pablo Aguirre	+593 2 256 4142 ext. 361	pablo.aguirre@ec.pwc-ag.com
Egypt	Abdallah ElAdly	+20 2 2759 7887	abdallah.eladly@eg.pwc.com
El Salvador	Edgar Mendoza	+502 2420 7800 ext. 844	edgar.mendoza@gt.pwc.com
Estonia	Villi Tontson	+372 614 1816	villi.tontson@ee.pwc.com
Fiji Islands	Jerome Kado	+679 331 3955	jerome.kado@fj.pwc.com
Finland	Kaj Wasenius	+358 9 2280 1302	kaj.wasenius@fi.pwc.com
France	Thierry Morgant	+33 1 56 57 49 88	thierry.morgant@fr.landwellglobal.com
Georgia	Robin McCone	+995 32 250 8050	robin.mccone@ge.pwc.com
Germany	Heiko Schafer	+49 69 9585 6227	heiko.schaefer@de.pwc.com
Gibraltar	Edgar C Lavarello	+350 200 73520	edgar.c.lavarello@gi.pwc.com
Greece	Constantine Karydis	+30 210 6874 050	constantine.karydis@gr.pwc.com
Guatemala	Edgar Mendoza	+502 2420 7800 ext. 844	edgar.mendoza@gt.pwc.com
Honduras	Ramon Morales	+504 553 3060	ramon.morales@hn.pwc.com
Hong Kong	Suzanne Wat	+852 2289 3002	suzanne.wat@hk.pwc.com
Hungary	David Williams	+36 1 461 9354	david.williams@hu.pwc.com
Iceland	Elin Arnadottir	+354 550 5322	elin.arnadottir@is.pwc.com
India	Vikram Bapat	+91 80 4079 6003	vikram.bapat@in.pwc.com
Indonesia	Ray Headifen	+62 21 528 90800	ray.headifen@id.pwc.com
Iraq	Stephan Stephan	+962 6 500 1300	stephan.stephan@jo.com
Ireland	Susan Kilty	+353 1 792 6740	susan.kilty@ie.pwc.com
Israel	Gerry Seligman	+972 3 795 4476	gerry.seligman@il.pwc.com
Italy	Domenico Coldani	+390 2 9160 5800	domenico.coldani@it.pwc.com
Ivory Coast (Côte d'Ivoire)	Dominique Taty	+225 20 31 5460	d.taty@ci.pwc.com
Jamaica	Eric Crawford	+876 932 8323	eric.crawford@jm.pwc.com
Japan	Masanori Kato	+81 3 5251 2536	masanori.kato@jp.pwc.com
Jordan	Stephan Stephan	+962 6 500 1300	stephan.stephan@jo.com
Kazakhstan	Elena Kaeva	+7 727 298 0620	elena.kaeva@kz.pwc.com
Korea, Republic of	Alex Joong-Hyun Lee	+82 2 709 0598	alex.joong-hyun.lee@kr.pwc.com

Tax Management and Accounting Services

Kuwait	Sherif Abd Fattah	+965 2222 5777	sherif.abdel-fattah@kwt.pwc.com
Lao PDR	Thavorn Rujivanarom	+66 2 344 1444	thavorn.rujivanarom@th.pwc.com
Latvia	Zlata Elksnina	+371 6709 4400	zlata.elksnina@lv.pwc.com
Lebanon	Wadih AbouNasr	+961 1 200577 ext. 1610	wadih.abounasr@lb.pwc.com
Libya	Husam Elnaili	+218 21 360 9830-32 ext. 110	husam.elnaili@ly.pwc.com
Lithuania	Giedre Cater	+370 5 254 6934	giedre.cater@lt.pwc.com
Luxembourg	Luc Trivaudey	+352 49 4848 5055	luc.trivaudey@lu.pwc.com
Macedonia	Paul Tobin	+359 2 9355 116	paul.tobin@bg.pwc.com
Malaysia	Wee Hong Teh	+60 3 2173 1595	wee.hong.teh@my.pwc.com
Malta	Chris Galea	+356 2564 6911	chris.galea@mt.pwc.com
Mexico	Jesus Chan	+52 55 5263 5766	jesus.chan@mx.pwc.com
Moldova	Ionut Simion	+40 21 225 3702	ionut.simion@ro.pwc.com
Mongolia	Abdulkhamid Muminov	+998 71 1206 101	abdulkhamid.muminov@uz.pwc.com
Montenegro	Aleksandra Cekic	+381 11 3302 143	aleksandra.cekic@yu.pwc.com
Morocco	Mahat Chraibi	+212 5 2299 9898	mahat.chraibi@ma.pwc.com
Mozambique	Joao Martins	+258 21 307 620	joao.l.martins@mz.pwc.com
Namibia, Republic of	Patty Karuaihe-Martin	+264 61 284 1258	patty.karuaihe-martin@na.pwc.com
Netherlands	Lars Wagemans	+31 88 792 3826	lars.wagemans@nl.pwc.com
New Zealand	Ian Rowe	+64 4 462 7274	ian.rowe@nz.pwc.com
Nicaragua	Francisco Castro	+505 2270 9950	francisco.castro@ni.pwc.com
Norway	Pål Hasner	+47 95 26 0550	paal.hasner@no.pwc.com
Oman	Russell Aycock	+968 2455 9122	russell.aycock@om.pwc.com
Panama	Francisco Barrios	+507 206 9217	francisco.barrios@pa.pwc.com
Paraguay	Gabriel Gonzalez	+598 2 916 0463	gonzalez.gabriel@py.pwc.com
Peru	John Casas Aguilar	+511 211 6500 ext. 8048	john.casas@pe.pwc.com
Philippines	Fedna Parallag	+63 2 459 3109	fedna.parallag@ph.pwc.com
Poland	Keith Sinclair	+48 22 523 4781	keith.c.sinclair@pl.pwc.com
Portugal	Paulo Fernando Ribeiro	+351 213 599 513	paulo.fernando.ribeiro@pt.pwc.com
Puerto Rico	Victor R. Rodriguez	+1 787 772 7958	victor.r.rodrigues@us.pwc.com
Qatar	Declan Mordaunt	+974 4419 2801	declan.mordaunt@qa.pwc.com
Romania	Peter deRuiter	+40 21 225 3670	peter.deruiter@ro.pwc.com
Russian Federation	Kirill Nikitin	+7 495 967 6442	kirill.nikitin@ru.pwc.com
Saint Kitts and Nevis	Jefferson Hunte	+1 869 466 8200	jefferson.hunte@ag.pwc.com
Saint Lucia	Richard N. Peterkin	+758 456 2626	richard.n.peterkin@lc.pwc.com
Saudi Arabia	Mohammed Yaghmour	+966 2 610 4400	mohammed.yaghmour@sa.pwc.com
Serbia	Krzysztof Lipka	+381 11 330 2100	krzysztof.lipka@rs.pwc.com
Singapore	Paul Cornelius	+65 6236 3718	paul.cornelius@sg.pwc.com
Slovak Republic	Todd Bradshaw	+421 2 59350 600	todd.bradshaw@sk.pwc.com
Slovenia	Akos Burjan	+386 1 583 6058	akos.burjan@si.pwc.com
South Africa	Ine-Lize Terblanche	+27 11 797 5498	ine-lize.terblanche@za.pwc.com
Spain	Rafael Rebate	+34 915 684 408	rafael.rebate@es.pwc.com
Sri Lanka	Hiranthi C. Ratnayake	+94 11 771 9838	hiranthi.c.ratnayake@lk.pwc.com
Swaziland	Theo Mason	+268 2404 2861	theo.mason@sz.pwc.com
Sweden	Lennart Svantesson	+46 8 555 331 44	lennart.svantesson@se.pwc.com
Switzerland	Christoph Schaerer	+41 58 792 4282	christoph.schaerer@ch.pwc.com
Taiwan	Rosamund Fan	+886 2 2729 6077	rosamund.fan@tw.pwc.com
Thailand	Thavorn Rujivanarom	+66 2 344 1444	thavorn.rujivanarom@th.pwc.com
Turkey	Ayse B. Isim	+90 212 355 5812	ayse.b.isim@tr.pwc.com
Turkmenistan	Abdulkhamid Muminov	+998 71 1206 101	abdulkhamid.muminov@uz.pwc.com
Ukraine	Magdalena Patrzyk	+380 44 490 6777	magdalena.patrzyk@ua.pwc.co
United Arab Emirates	Damian de Backer	+20 2 2759 7705	damian.de.backer@eg.pwc.co
United Kingdom	Kenneth Moore	+44 20 7804 1073	kenneth.moore@uk.pwc.com
United States	Buddy Tinley	+1 678 419 8838	buddy.tinley@us.pwc.com
Uruguay	Gabriel Gonzalez	+598 2 916 0463	gonzalez.gabriel@uy.pwc.com
Uzbekistan, Republic of	Abdulkhamid Muminov	+998 71 1206 101	abdulkhamid.muminov@uz.pwc.com
Venezuela	Elys Aray	+58 241 8252 361	elys.aray@ve.pwc.com
Vietnam	Richard J. Irwin	+66 2 286 9999	r.j.irwin@vn.pwc.com
Zimbabwe	Manuel Lopes	+263 4 33 8362-8	manuel.lopes@zw.pwc.com

Tax Policy & Administration

Insight into today's
critical legislative and
tax policy issues

Global Leader, Tax Policy and Administration
John Preston
+44 20 7804 2645
Email: john.preston@uk.pwc.com

Richard Stuart Collier
Partner, Policy and Administration
+44 20 7212 3395
Email: richard.collier@uk.pwc.com

Our Tax Policy and Administration network provides insight into today's policy trends and issues worldwide. There are a number of elements to this which include:

- helping our clients to understand and comply with their fiscal and regulatory obligations in relation to tax,
- helping our clients maximise value for all stakeholders over time on the basis of full disclosure and in compliance with our Global Code of Conduct,
- using our knowledge and experience to assist policy makers in both developed and developing countries improve the efficiency and effectiveness of their tax systems, and
- being seen as acting fairly, openly and consistently with all stakeholders such that we are trusted by all parties.

For this purpose, 'stakeholders' include, as well as our clients, revenue authorities, governments, legislators, governmental departments and their officials, non-governmental organisations, supra-national bodies, regulators, the media, professional bodies and trade associations.

Our specialist knowledge and expertise in these areas sits mainly with the members of our network and tax country leaders. For assistance in tax policy and administration matters please do not hesitate to contact us.

Tax Policy & Administration

Australia	Ian Farmer	+61 2 8266 2802	ian.farmer@au.pwc.com
Belgium	Ine Lejeune	+32 9 268 8300	ine.lejeune@pwc.be
Brazil	Nelio Weiss	+55 11 3674 3557	nelio.weiss@br.pwc.com
Canada	Nick Pantaleo	+1 416 365 2701	nick.pantaleo@ca.pwc.com
China, Peoples Republic of	Matthew Mui	+86 10 6533 3028	matthew.mui@cn.pwc.com
Czech Republic	Peter Chrenko	+420 251 152 600	peter.chrenko@cz.pwc.com
Egypt	Amr El Monayer	+20 2 759 7700	amr.elmonayer@eg.pwc.com
France	Michel Combe	+33 1 56 57 4586	michel.combe@fr.landwellglobal.com
Germany	Jürgen Lüdicke	+49 40 6378 8423	juergen.luedicke@de.pwc.com
Greece	Mary Psylla	+30 210 687 4543	mary.psylla@gr.pwc.com
Hungary	Tamás Lőcsei	+36 1 461 9358	tamas.locsei@hu.pwc.com
India	Vijay Mathur	+91 124 330 6511	vijay.mathur@in.pwc.com
Ireland	Feargal O'Rourke	+353 1 792 6480	feargal.orourke@ie.pwc.com
Italy	Fabrizio Acerbis	+39 2 9160 5001	fabrizio.acerbis@it.pwc.com
Japan	Sachihiko Fujimoto	+81 3 5251 2423	sachihiko.fujimoto@jp.pwc.com
Kazakhstan	Peter Burnie	+7 727 330 3200	peter.burnie@kz.pwc.com
Korea, Republic of	Soo-Hwan Park	+82 2 709 0705	soo-hwan.park@kr.pwc.com
Luxembourg	Wim Piot	+352 49 4848 3052	wim.piot@lu.pwc.com
Mexico	Karina Perez Delgadillo	+52 55 5263 5734	karina.perez.delgadillo@mx.pwc.com
	Patricia Gonzalez	+52 55 5263 6057	patricia.gonzalez@mx.pwc.com
Netherlands	Sytso Boonstra	+31 8879 23470	sytso.boonstra@nl.pwc.com
Poland	Katarzyna Czarnecka-Zochowska	+48 22 523 4843	katarzyna.czarnecka-zochowska@pl.pwc.com
Romania	Ionut Simion	+40 21 225 3702	ionut.simion@ro.pwc.com
Russian Federation	Andrey Kolchin	+7 495 967 6197	andrey.kolchin@ru.pwc.com
Singapore	Alan Ross	+65 6236 7578	alan.ross@sg.pwc.com
South Africa	Paul de Chalain	+27 11 797 4260	paul.do.chalain@za.pwc.com
Spain	José Félix Gálvez	+34 915 684 530	jose.felix.galvez@es.pwc.com
Sweden	Ingrid Melbi	+46 10 213 3788	ingrid.melbi@se.pwc.com
Switzerland	Andreas Staubli	+41 58 792 4472	andreas.staubli@ch.pwc.com
Ukraine	Slava Vlasov	+380 44 490 6782	slava.vlasov@ua.pwc.com
United Kingdom	Mary Monfries	+44 20 7212 7927	mary.c.monfries@uk.pwc.com
	Richard Collier	+44 20 7212 3395	richard.collier@uk.pwc.com
	Phil Greenfield	+44 20 7212 6047	philip.greenfield@uk.pwc.com
United States	Pam Olson	+1 202 414 1401	pam.olson@us.pwc.com
	George Forster	+1 646 471 5002	george.forster@us.pwc.com
	Peter Merrill	+1 202 414 1666	peter.merrill@us.pwc.com

Transfer Pricing

Extensive experience in dealing with revenue authorities around the world

Global Leader, Transfer Pricing
Garry Stone
+1 312 298 2464
garry.stone@us.pwc.com

The scrutiny of transfer pricing by tax authorities worldwide has intensified and our network of 2,000 transfer pricing specialists in over 75 countries has extensive experience in dealing with revenue authorities around the world. Using their expertise in accounting, economics, dispute resolution and your industry, they can help you prepare for the challenges this scrutiny will present. As a network of specialists, we help companies develop sustainable arm's length pricing, tax efficient structures, help make them more compliant with legal requirements and help them respond quickly to an audit and resolve transfer pricing disputes. More importantly, we work to ensure they're less exposed to transfer pricing risks in the future.

Transfer Pricing

Country	Contact	Phone	Email
Argentina	Juan Carlos Ferreiro	+54 11 4850 6720	juan.carlos.ferreiro@ar.pwc.com
Australia	Lyndon James	+61 2 8266 3278	lyndon.james@au.pwc.com
Austria	Herbert Greinecker	+43 1 501 88 3301	herbert.greinecker@at.pwc.com
Belgium	Isabel Verlinden	+32 2 710 7295	isabel.verlinden@be.pwc.com
Brazil	Cristina Medeiros	+55 11 3674 2582	cristina.medeiros@br.pwc.com
Bulgaria	Irina Tsvetkova	+359 2 9355 100	irina.tsvetkova@bg.landwellglobal.com
Canada	Charles Theriault	+1 514 205 5144	charles.theriault@ca.pwc.com
Chile	Roberto Carlos Rivas	+56 2 940 0151	roberto.carlos.rivas@cl.pwc.com
China, People's Republic of	Spencer Chong	+86 21 2323 1135	spencer.chong@cn.pwc.com
Colombia	Carlos Mario Lafaurie	+57 1 634 0492	carlos_mario.lafaurie@co.pwc.com
Croatia	Ivo Bijelic	+385 1 6328 802	ivo.bijelic@hr.pwc.com
Czech Republic	David Borkovec	+420 251 152 549	david.borkovec@cz.pwc.com
Denmark	Jørgen Juul Andersen	+45 3945 9434	jju@pwc.dk
Ecuador	Pablo Aguirre	+593 2 382 9350	pablo.aguirre@ec.pwc.com
Finland	Sari Takalo	+358 9 2280 1262	sari.takalo@fi.pwc.com
France	Pierre Escaut	+33 1 5657 4295	pierre.escaut@fr.landwellglobal.com
Germany	Lorenz Bernhardt	+49 30 2636 5204	lorenz.bernhardt@de.pwc.com
Greece	Antonis Desipris	+30 210 6874 016	antonis.desipris@gr.pwc.com
Hong Kong	Cecilia SK Lee	+85 22 289 5690	cecilia.sk.lee@hk.pwc.com
Hungary	Zaid Sethi	+36 1 461 9512	zaid.sethi@hu.pwc.com
Iceland	Elin Arnadottir	+354 550 5322	elin.arnadottir@is.pwc.com
India	Rahul K. Mitra	+91 124 330 6501	rahul.k.mitra@in.pwc.com
Indonesia	Ay Tjhing Phan	+62 21 5289 0658	ay.tjhing.phan@id.pwc.com
Ireland	Gavan Ryle	+353 1 792 8704	gavan.ryle@ie.pwc.com
Israel	Vered Kirshner	+972 3 795 4849	vered.kirshner@il.pwc.com
Italy	Gianni Colucci	+390 2 9160 5500	gianni.colucci@it.pwc.com
Japan	Akio Miyamoto	+81 3 5251 2337	akio.miyamoto@jp.pwc.com
Kazakhstan	Peter Burnie	+7 727 330 3200	peter.burnie@kz.pwc.com
Korea, Republic of	Henry An	+82 2 3781 2594	henryan@samil.com
Latvia	Ilze Berga	+371 6709 4432	Ilze.berga@lv.pwc.com
Lithuania	Nerijus Nedzinskas	+370 5 239 2352	nerijus.nedzinskas@lt.pwc.com
Luxembourg	Begga Sigurdardottir	+352 49 4848 3194	begga.sigurdardottir@lu.pwc.com
Malaysia	Thanneermalai Somasundaram	+60 3 2173 1482	thanneermalai.somasundaram@my.pwc.com
Malta	Neville Gatt	+356 2564 6711	neville.gatt@mt.pwc.com
Mexico	Fred Barrett	+52 55 5263 6069	fred.barrett@mx.pwc.com
Namibia, Republic of	Chantell Husselman	+264 61 284 1327	chantell.husselmann@na.pwc.com
Netherlands	Arnout van der Rest	+31 88 792 3971	arnout.van.der.rest@nl.pwc.com
New Zealand	Erin Venter	+64 9 355 8862	erin.l.venter@nz.pwc.com
Norway	Morten Beck	+47 95 26 0650	morten.beck@no.pwc.com
Philippines	Carlos Carado	+63 2 459 2020	carlos.carado@ph.pwc.com
Poland	Mike Ahern	+48 22 523 4985	mike.ahern@pl.pwc.com
Portugal	Jaime Esteves	+351 225 433 212	jaime.esteves@pt.pwc.com
Romania	Ionut Simion	+40 21 202 8708	ionut.simion@ro.pwc.com
Russian Federation	Svetlana Stroykova	+7 495 967 6024	svetlana.stroykova@ru.pwc.com
Singapore	Nicole Fung	+65 6236 3618	nicole.fung@sg.pwc.com
Slovak Republic	Christiana Serugová	+421 2 59 350 614	christiana.serugova@sk.pwc.com
South Africa	David Lermer	+27 21 529 2364	david.lermer@za.pwc.com
Spain	Javier González Carcedo	+34 915 684 542	javier.gonzalez.carcedo@es.pwc.com
Sweden	Mika Myllynen	+46 8 555 338 76	mika.myllynen@se.pwc.com
Switzerland	Norbert Raschle	+41 58 792 4306	norbert.raschle@ch.pwc.com
Taiwan	Lily Hsu	+886 2 2729 6207	lily.hsu@tw.pwc.com
Thailand	Peerapat Poshyanonda	+66 2 344 1220	peerapat.poshyanonda@th.pwc.com
Turkey	Zeki Gunduz	+90 212 326 6080	zeki.gunduz@tr.pwc.com
United Arab Emirates	Dan Axelsen	+971 4 304 3396	dan.axelsen@ae.pwc.com
United Kingdom	Ian Dykes	+44 121 265 5968	ian.dykes@uk.pwc.com
United States	Horacio Pena	+1 646 471 1957	horacio.pena@us.pwc.com
Venezuela	Jose G. Garcia	+58 212 7006 802	jose.g.garcia@ve.pwc.com
Vietnam	Van Dinh Thi Quynh	+84 4 3946 2246 ext. 4202	dinh.quynh.van@vn.pwc.com

Value Chain Transformation

*Creating sustainable
business change*

Global Leader, Value Chain Transformation - Tax
Steven Tseng
+86 21 2323 2766
steven.tseng@cn.pwc.com

Global Leader, Value Chain Transformation - Advisory
Joel Segal
+44 20 7804 1161
joel.segal@uk.pwc.com

Business transformation invariably leads to complex operational, tax and legal implications. PwC's Value Chain Transformation (VCT) can help. VCT is defined as the integrated and cross-border portfolio of capabilities to support organizations to align their tax, legal and operating models to achieve sustainable financial and operational benefits during business transformation. VCT helps you to align and optimizing key elements to improve profitability, efficiency, controls and visibility throughout the value chain. Our deep industry experience in key sectors and our international network of 600 cross-disciplinary VCT specialists allows us to manage the complexity involved in business transformation and help clients build the foundation for sustainable growth.

Value Chain Transformation

Australia	Helen Fazzino	+61 3 8603 3673	helen.fazzino@au.pwc.com
Belgium	Sabine Wahl	+32 2 710 4554	sabine.wahl@be.pwc.com
Brazil	Cristina Medeiros	+55 11 3674 2249	cristina.medeiros@br.pwc.com
Canada	Howard Quon	+1 416 869 2396	howard.quon@ca.pwc.com
China, Peoples Republic of	Steven Tseng	+86 21 2323 2766	steven.tseng@cn.pwc.com
Denmark	Jørgen Juul Andersen	+45 3945 9434	jorgen.juul.andersen@dk.pwc.com
Finland	Martti Virolainen	+358 9 2280 1396	martti.virolainen@fi.pwc.com
France	Michel Combe	+33 1 5657 4586	michel.combe@fr.landwellglobal.com
Germany	Volker Booten	+49 30 2636 5217	volker.booten@de.pwc.com
Hong Kong	Joyce Law	+852 2289 5621	joyce.cy.law@hk.pwc.com
Hungary	Gabriella Erdos	+36 1 461 9130	gabriella.erdos@hu.pwc.com
India	Rakesh Mishra	+91 80 4079 6250	rakesh.mishra@in.pwc.com
Indonesia	Ay Tjhing Phan	+62 21 5289 0658	ay.tjhing.phan@id.pwc.com
Ireland	Ronan Finn	+353 1 792 6105	ronan.finn@ie.pwc.com
Italy	Alessandro Caridi	+390 2 9160 5003	alessandro.caridi@it.pwc.com
Japan	Akio Miyamoto	+81 3 5251 2337	akio.miyamoto@jp.pwc.com
Korea, Republic of	Henry An	+82 2 3781 2594	henry.an@kr.pwc.com
Macau	Steven Tseng	+86 21 2323 2766	steven.tseng@cn.pwc.com
Malaysia	Jagdev Singh	+60 3 2173 1469	jagdev.singh@my.pwc.com
Mexico	Adriana Rodriguez	+52 55 5263 8527	adriana.rodriguez@mx.pwc.com
Netherlands	Marc Diepstraten	+31 8879 26358	marc.diepstraten@nl.pwc.com
Russian Federation	Mikhail Filinov	+7 495 967 6041	mikhail.filinov@ru.pwc.com
Singapore	Alan Ross	+65 6236 7578	alan.ross@sg.pwc.com
South Africa	Mark Badenhorst	+27 11 797 4641	mark.badenhorst@za.pwc.com
Spain	Javier Gonzalez Carcedo	+34 915 684 542	javier.gonzalez.carcedo@es.pwc.com
Sweden	Mika Myllynen	+46 10 213 3876	mika.myllynen@se.pwc.com
Switzerland	Carl Bellingham	+41 58 792 8129	carl.bellingham@ch.pwc.com
Taiwan	Elliot Liao	+886 2 2729 6217	elliot.liao@tw.pwc.com
Thailand	Peerapat Poshyanonda	+66 2 344 1220	peerapat.poshyanonda@th.pwc.com
United Kingdom	Adrian Yeeles	+44 20 7213 5453	adrian.t.yeeles@uk.pwc.com
United States	John M. Ranke	+1 312 298 3508	john.m.ranke@us.pwc.com
	Thomas F. Quinn	+1 312 298 2733	thomas.f.quinn@us.pwc.com

Global Tax Industry Leaders

Consumer, Industrial Products and Services
Jay Oyer
+1 973 236 4177
jay.oyer@us.pwc.com

Automotive
Horst Raettig
+49 30 2636 5301
horst.raettig@de.pwc.com

Energy, Utilities and Mining
James Koch
+1 713 356 4626
james.koch@us.pwc.com

Industrial Products
Michael Burak
+1 973 236 4459
michael.burak@us.pwc.com

Pharma and Life Sciences
Michael Swanick
+1 267 330 6060
michael.f.swanick@us.pwc.com

Retail and Consumer
Rich Klein
+1 646 471 0690
richard.a.klein@us.pwc.com

Financial Services
David Newton
+44 20 7804 2039
david.newton@uk.pwc.com

Asset Management
William Taggart
+1 646 471 2780
william.taggart@us.pwc.com

Banking and Capital Markets
Hans-Ulrich Lauermann
+49 69 9585 6174
hansulrich.lauermann@de.pwc.com

Insurance
Peter Barrow
+44 20 7804 2062
peter.barrow@uk.pwc.com

Real Estate
Uwe Stoschek
+49 30 26 36 5286
uwe.stoschek@de.pwc.com

Sovereign Wealth Funds
Oscar Teunissen
+1 646 471 3223
oscar.teunissen@us.pwc.com

Technology, Information, Communications and Entertainment
Diane Baylor
+1 408 817 5005
diane.baylor@us.pwc.com

Entertainment
Christ Economos
+1 646 471 0612
christ.h.economos@us.pwc.com

Technology
Brad Silver
+1 646 471 0696
brad.silver@us.pwc.com

The Worldwide Tax Summaries – Corporate Taxes 2012/13 guide represents the combined efforts of more than 500 local PwC tax specialists in over 150 countries and territories. While too numerous to name individually, we thank them for their efforts in preparing this guide.

To obtain regularly updated information on the corporate and individual tax rules in operation in over 150 countries, please visit the Worldwide Tax Summaries online at www.pwc.com/taxsummaries.

To download an ebook version of the Worldwide Tax Summaries - Corporate Taxes 2012/13, please visit www.pwc.com/taxsummaries/ebook.

Worldwide Tax Summaries editorial team

Liana Gravers
Christopher Wooley
James Calderon
Penny Vaughn

To contact the editorial team, please email us at worldwide.tax.summaries@us.pwc.com.